CAB Thesaurus

CAB Thesaurus

Volume 1 (A–I)

1990 Edition
C·A·B INTERNATIONAL

C·A·B International
Wallingford
Oxon OX10 8DE
UK

Tel: Wallingford (0491) 32111
Telex: 847964 (COMAGG G)
Telecom Gold/Dialcom: 84: CAU001
Fax: (0491) 33508

British Library Cataloguing in Publication Data
CAB thesaurus.
1990 ed.
1. Agriculture – Thesauri
I. CAB International
025.4963

ISBN 0–85198–687–0
ISBN 0–85198–685–4 v. 1
ISBN 0–85198–686–2 v. 2 pbk

Printed and bound in the UK by BPCC Wheatons, Exeter

Preface

In the preface to the second edition of the CAB Thesaurus, I wrote that developing a thesaurus is one of those tasks that is never finished. But there has to come a point at which the need to publish what has been done exceeds the need to incorporate further changes and improvements. In August 1988, at a meeting in Beltsville (Maryland) of the thesaurus experts of CABI and the National Agricultural Library (NAL), it was agreed that a new edition should be published in 1990, incorporating all changes up to February 1990.

As set out in the greatly augmented Introduction, the third edition not only includes new terms to cover expanding fields such as biotechnology, but also has innovations in the shape of history notes, a simple clear distinction between British and American spelling, and the adoption of a standard classification scheme for plant viruses. All these developments have had the strong support of myself and Joseph Howard, Director of NAL.

In working together on a unified search vocabulary, CAB International and NAL are steadily making retrieval from our databases both easier and more effective. But, as before, we still need your input. Please contact the editor if you experience any difficulties when using the CAB Thesaurus in online searches or when indexing your own document collections. We will be grateful for all suggested improvements to either the content or the format of the thesaurus.

J. R. Metcalfe
Director, Information Services
March 1990

Introduction and Guidelines

This thesaurus is designed primarily for use by (a) staff of CAB International (CABI) and of the National Agricultural Library (NAL) of the United States Department of Agriculture to index bibliographic records for the CAB ABSTRACTS and AGRICOLA databases, respectively, and (b) users of these databases to formulate searches. It will also be useful to researchers, information scientists and librarians indexing their own document collections or other information resources.

Development

When the first edition of the CAB Thesaurus was published in the autumn of 1983, it contained some 48000 terms and was the world's largest English language thesaurus for agriculture and related subjects. The second edition saw extensive revisions to the hierarchies for plants, fungi, bacteria, helminths, insects and chemicals. New descriptors were added, synonymy was reduced and redundant terms were weeded out. This work has been continued for the third edition with particular attention to plant viruses and the descriptors required to index new or expanding subjects such as biotechnology.

Approximately 3000 new terms were added during the preparation of this edition. The thesaurus now contains 18% more terms than the first edition.

New Features

New features added for this edition are History Notes, a simple and clear distinction between American and British spelling variants, and cross-references to indicate concepts indexed by post-coordination.

Another important change has been the adoption, under PLANT VIRUSES, of the group names approved by the the International Committee on Taxonomy of Viruses (ICTV). Standards for nomenclature of individual plant viruses have not been established, and names included here are those used recently by ICTV and in *AAB Descriptions of Plant Viruses*. Other names published in the second edition of the CAB Thesaurus and indexed more than once in AGRICOLA or CAB ABSTRACTS will be retained under MISCELLANEOUS PLANT VIRUSES until approved or synonymized.

AGRICOLA and the CAB Thesaurus

In 1985 NAL adopted the CAB Thesaurus for indexing AGRICOLA and staff at NAL have made a very large contribution to the revision of the thesaurus. There are some subjects covered by AGRICOLA which are not within the scope of CAB ABSTRACTS. Approximately 1160 descriptors for these subjects, which mainly cover human ecology (home economics) and aspects of food service and food technology, have been incorporated into the thesaurus. To avoid confusing CABI users who might otherwise try to use these descriptors as search terms with CAB ABSTRACTS, they have been labelled by adding the suffix "(AGRICOLA)". This suffix is only a label and is not part of the descriptor itself. It should be omitted when using the descriptor as an indexing term or as a search term.

Typical examples of (AGRICOLA) terms are:

LATCHKEY CHILDREN (AGRICOLA)
SCHOOL FOOD SERVICE (AGRICOLA)

Subject Scope

The subject scope of the thesaurus is determined by the combined coverage of the CAB ABSTRACTS and AGRICOLA databases. This scope is agriculture in the widest possible sense and includes many related fields. The main areas are : crop production, protection and breeding; forestry and forest products; soil science; animal husbandry, health, breeding, nutrition and parasitology; dairy science and technology; agricultural engineering; economics; rural development, sociology and education. Other fields include: human nutrition; human ecology; medical mycology, entomology and parasitology; and leisure, recreation and tourism.

For full details of the subject coverage users should consult the CAB ABSTRACTS Online Manual and the AGRICOLA guides. Individual CABI abstract journals, derived from CAB ABSTRACTS, also provide details of coverage for specific subjects.

Selection of Terms

The thesaurus contains the current, core vocabulary used to index the two databases and the CABI abstract journals. It reflects actual usage and cannot anticipate usage.

The thesaurus does not include every single term that has been used to index the CAB ABSTRACTS database since its inception in 1973. The scientific names of plants, animals and microorganisms are too numerous to list exhaustively in any reasonably sized thesaurus. All valid taxonomic names and also the names of chemicals and soil types may be used in the subject indexes but if their occurrence in the indexes is very infrequent they are not entered in the thesaurus.

AGRICOLA, in contrast, uses only preferred terms from the thesaurus in the descriptor field. Uncontrolled terms are entered in an identifier field.

Spelling and Usage Variants

For approximately 530 descriptors, the British and American spellings or usage differ. Both versions are shown in the thesaurus and are labelled BF (British Form) and AF (American Form), respectively. The British Form, which is always preferred in CAB ABSTRACTS, is shown with its full hierarchy as in the example below. Entries for the American Form, which is preferred in AGRICOLA, show only the corresponding British Form and any RTs, NTs or BTs which contain the same variant. To examine the full hierarchy for an American Form the user should turn to the entry for its British equivalent.

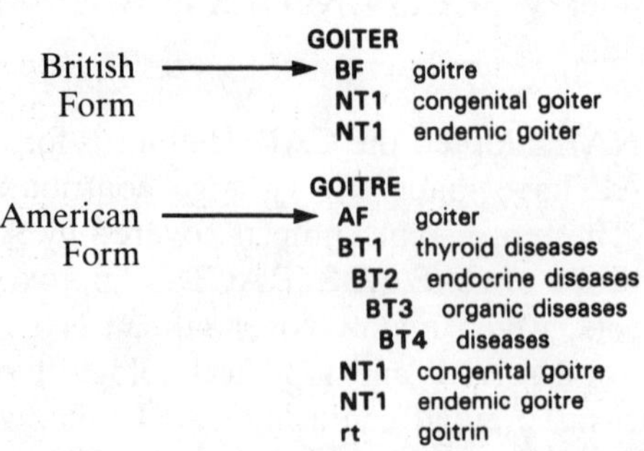

The variations in spelling are found in descriptors which contain the following words or stems:

BRITISH	AMERICAN
aeolian	eolian
aestivation	estivation
aetiology	etiology
aluminium	aluminum
amenorrhoea	amenorrhea
amoebicides	amebicides
anaemia	anemia
anaesthesia	anesthesia
analogues	analogs
behaviour	behavior
biocoenosis	biocenosis
cadastres	cadasters
caecotrophy	cecotrophy
caecum	cecum
caesium	cesium
catalogues	catalogs
centres	centers
chimaeras	chimeras
coeliac	celiac
colour	color
defence	defense
diarrhoea	diarrhea
draught	draft
driers	dryers
dykes	dikes
dyspnoea	dyspnea
encyclopaedias	encyclopedias
faeces	feces
felspar	feldspar
fibre(s)	fiber(s)
flavour	flavor
formulae	formulas
goitre	goiter
haem-	hem-
harbours	harbors
labelling	labeling
labour	labor
laevulinic acid	levulinic acid
less favoured areas	less favored areas
licences	licenses
liquorice	licorice
manoeuverability	maneuverability
milking parlours	milking parlors
moult	molt
moulds	molds
multistorey cropping	multistory cropping
neighbourhoods	neighborhoods
odour	odor
oedema	edema
oesophagus	esophagus
oestrus	estrus
orthopaedics	orthopedics
paediatric(s)	pediatric(s)
palaeo-	paleo-
plateaux	plateaus
plough	plow

programmes	programs
seborrhoea	seborrhea
soya-	soy-
steatorrhoea	steatorrhea
theatre	theater
tumour(s)	tumor(s)
tyres	tires
vapour	vapor
vigour	vigor

Construction

The ISO Standard for the establishment and development of mono-lingual thesauri (ISO 2788:1986 = BS 5723:1987) has been followed during the compilation of this thesaurus except for the guidelines on the syntactical factoring of compound terms. Rigid adherence to these guidelines would lead to an unacceptable loss of precise expression and consequent problems during database searches. Therefore, a pragmatic approach to the selection of compound descriptors has been adopted, based on their perceived usefulness for retrieval.

Abbreviations

The abbreviations used in the text are:

BT = Broader term
NT = Narrower term
RT = Related term
HN = History note
AF = American form
BF = British form
UF = Used for
UFA = reciprocal of a cross-reference of the use/and type (*see* non-preferred terms below)

Scope Notes

Scope notes appear in parentheses in the lines immediately following some descriptors. They are there to help the user by explaining coverage, specialized usage, or guidelines for assigning a descriptor. The number of scope notes has been increased in this edition but they are still included for only a minority of descriptors. Comprehensive definitions should be unnecessary as the context in which a descriptor is used is indicated by its hierarchy or related terms and it should always be used in that context.

Scope notes are also used to give the International Union of Biochemistry Enzyme Commission (EC) notation for enzymes.

History Notes

History Notes (HN) are now included to indicate when terms have been added to or deleted from the thesaurus, or changed in some other way such as spelling. The History Notes only show changes which have occurred since 1988.

goals
HN was used until 1990 in agricola
USE **objectives**

GOBRA
HN from 1990; previously "senegal fulani"
uf *senegal fulani*
BT1 cattle breeds
BT2 breeds

Non-preferred Terms

Non-preferred terms are terms not currently used in indexing. They may have been used as indexing terms in the past or they may be included because they are synonyms or quasi-synonyms. They are italicised and the entries are of three types. There are one-to-one relationships such as *glasshouses* use GREENHOUSES; there are cases where a choice has to be made between two preferred terms as with the term *buffel grass* use CENCHRUS CILIARIS or UROCHLOA MOSAMBICENSIS; and finally there are entries which instruct the user to combine two preferred terms in order to express a specific concept (post-coordination). This last type of non-preferred term entry is a new feature in the thesaurus. It has not been used very often but an example is

goat colostrum
USE **colostrum**
AND **goats**

When constructing search profiles, users should remember that non-preferred terms may have been used as indexing terms in the past and should be included in retrospective searches.

Hierarchies and Related Terms

Hierarchies (cascades) are displayed in full and may contain up to seven levels. Hierarchical relationships (Broader term/Narrower term), related terms and cross-references are always in alphabetical order and are always displayed both ways.

For an illustration of these features one can examine the entries for the plant species BROMUS CARINATUS. This has the name of the genus, BROMUS, as a broader term (BT) and it also belongs to a hierarchy labelled PASTURE PLANTS. The descriptor BROMUS has the broader term GRAMINEAE, the name of the botanical family to which the genus belongs. Under the main entry for GRAMINEAE the terms BROMUS and BROMUS CARINATUS are displayed as narrower terms (NT) at different levels. Similarly, if the main entry for PASTURE PLANTS is examined the descriptor BROMUS CARINATUS will be found as a narrower term.

Logic might suggest that the terms GRAMINEAE and PASTURE PLANTS should have the broader term PLANTS, which is also to be found in the thesaurus, but if this were to be done the result would be a massive hierarchy of doubtful value occupying a large amount of space. In this case and the parallel cases of other plant and animal names the addition of broader terms has been stopped at a suitable level to avoid such long hierarchies. The user is guided to the logical continuation of the hierarchies either by a scope note or by the presence of the logical broader or narrower term as a related term. The names of the top terms for plants are the names of the botanical families and the names given as related terms under the descriptor PLANTS. The names of the top terms for animals can be found by starting at the terms INVERTEBRATES and VERTEBRATES.

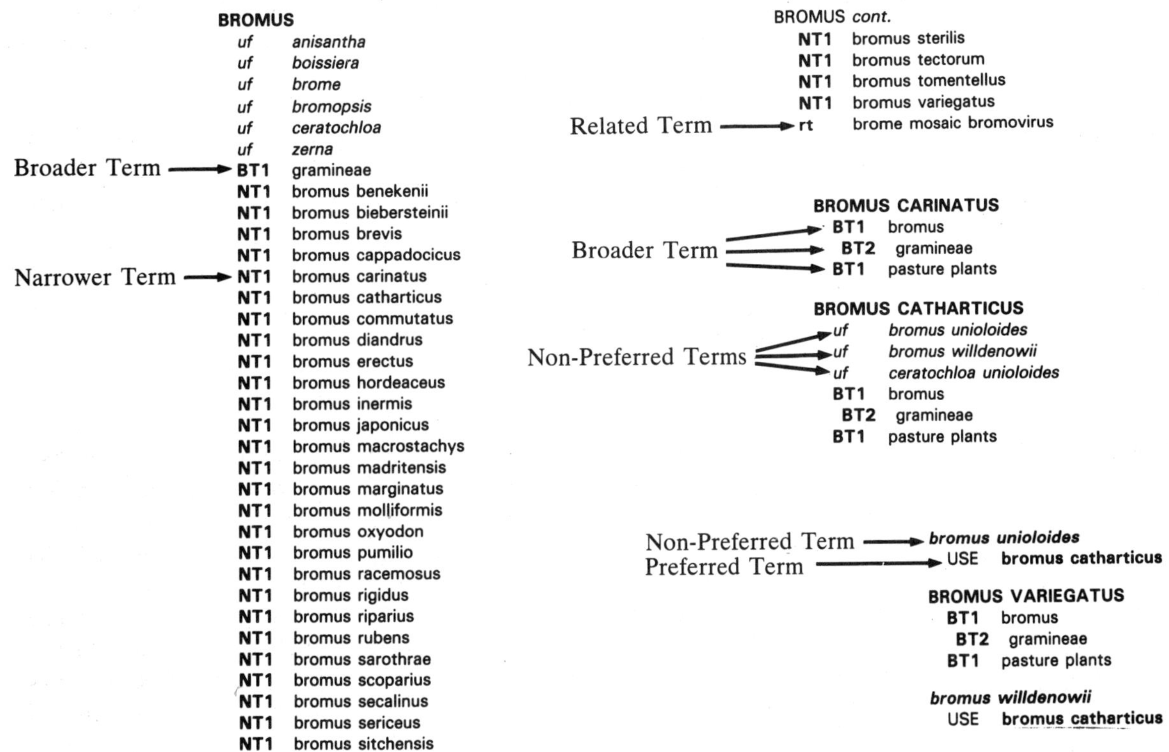

Related terms (RT) have a close connection with the entry term but do not belong to the logical hierarchy. Users are advised always to check the main entries for the related terms of the descriptor(s) in which they are interested. The related terms may have narrower terms that are of interest or they may provide the continuation of a hierarchy.

Singular or Plural?

Terms now given in the plural may have been indexed in the singular in the past and terms given in the singular may have been used in the plural; therefore, searchers should include both alternatives in their retrospective searches.

Format

In addition to this printed version the thesaurus is also available on magnetic tapes. For further details contact: Marketing and Sales Division, CAB International, Wallingford, Oxon OX10 8DE, UK or CAB International North American Office, 845 North Park Avenue, Tucson, Arizona 85719, USA.

Authorities Used

A complete checklist of the birds of the world. Howard,R.; Moore,A. (1980) Oxford University Press, UK.

A dictionary of flowering plants and ferns. Willis, J. C. (eighth edition, 1973) Cambridge University Press, UK.

A world list of mammalian species. Corbet, G. B.; Hill, J. E. (second edition, 1986) British Museum (Natural History), London, U K.

AAB Descriptions of Plant Viruses (1970-1989). Association of Applied Biologists, Wellesbourne, Warwick, UK.

Agricultural economics and rural sociology multilingual thesaurus. (1979) Commission of the European Communities, Luxembourg.

Approved lists of bacterial names. Edited by Sherman, V. B. D.; McGowan, V.; Sneath, P. H. A. on behalf of the International Committee on Systematic Bacteriology (1980) American Society for Microbiology, Washington, D. C., USA.

Classification and nomenclature of viruses. Fourth report and draft fifth report of the International Committee on Taxonomy of Viruses. Matthews, R. E. F. (1982) *Intervirology* 17, 1-200; Franki, R. (1990) personal communication.

Enzyme Nomenclature. Recommendations of the Nomenclature Committee of the International Union of Biochemistry (1984) Academic Press, New York, USA.

Fishes of the world. Nelson, J. S. (second edition, 1984) John Wiley & Sons, Chichester, U K.

Guide to plant pathogenic bacteria. Bradbury, J. F. (1986) CAB International Mycological Institute, Kew, UK.

International nonproprietary names (INN) for pharmaceutical sub-stances. World Health Organization, Geneva.

ISTA list of stabilized plant names. International Seed Testing Association. (1984)

Medical subject headings of the National Library of Medicine. Bethesda, Maryland, USA.

The pesticide manual. Worthing, C. R. (editor) (eighth edition, 1987). British Crop Protection Council. UK.

Acknowledgements

Many members of CABI's staff have contributed to the preparation of this edition and their contributions are gratefully acknowledged. Special tribute must be paid to Mr. Alan Wood who has carefully and methodically implemented the amendments to the thesaurus file. Thanks are also due to Martha Hood and other indexing staff of the National Agricultural Library in the USA for their cooperation in the preparation of this edition.

Peter Wightman
Editor

A HORIZONS
BT1 horizons
BT2 soil morphological features
rt topsoil

aardvark
USE **orycteropus afer**

aba
USE **abscisic acid**

abaca
USE **musa textilis**

ABACARUS
BT1 eriophyidae
BT2 prostigmata
BT3 acari
NT1 abacarus hystrix

ABACARUS HYSTRIX
BT1 abacarus
BT2 eriophyidae
BT3 prostigmata
BT4 acari

ABALONES
BT1 shellfish
BT2 aquatic invertebrates
BT3 aquatic animals
BT4 animals
BT4 aquatic organisms
rt haliotis

ABAMECTIN
uf *avermectin b1*
BT1 anthelmintics
BT2 antiparasitic agents
BT3 drugs
BT1 antibiotic insecticides
BT2 antibiotics
BT2 insecticides
BT3 pesticides
BT1 antibiotic nematicides
BT2 antibiotics
BT2 nematicides
BT3 pesticides
BT1 avermectins
BT2 antibiotics

ABANDONED LAND
BT1 land types
rt fallow
rt farm closures
rt shifting cultivation

ABATTOIRS
uf *slaughterhouses*
BT1 buildings
rt meat byproducts
rt meat hygiene
rt meat inspection
rt meat production
rt meatworks effluent
rt slaughter
rt slaughterhouse waste
rt slaughtering equipment

ABBREVIATA
BT1 physalopteridae
BT2 nematoda

ABDOMEN
BT1 body regions
NT1 umbilicus
rt abdominal cavity
rt belly
rt body cavities
rt laparotomy
rt peritoneum

ABDOMINAL CAVITY
BT1 body cavities
BT2 body parts
rt abdomen

ABDOMINAL FAT
BT1 body fat
BT2 fat

ABELIA
BT1 caprifoliaceae
NT1 abelia grandiflora

ABELIA GRANDIFLORA
BT1 abelia
BT2 caprifoliaceae
BT1 ornamental woody plants

ABELIOPHYLLUM
BT1 oleaceae
NT1 abeliophyllum distichum
rt ornamental plants

ABELIOPHYLLUM DISTICHUM
BT1 abeliophyllum
BT2 oleaceae
BT1 ornamental woody plants

ABELMOSCHUS
BT1 malvaceae
NT1 abelmoschus esculentus
NT1 abelmoschus ficulneus
NT1 abelmoschus manihot
NT1 abelmoschus moschatus
NT1 abelmoschus sativa
rt hibiscus

ABELMOSCHUS ESCULENTUS
uf *hibiscus esculentus*
BT1 abelmoschus
BT2 malvaceae
rt okra mosaic tymovirus
rt okras

ABELMOSCHUS FICULNEUS
BT1 abelmoschus
BT2 malvaceae

ABELMOSCHUS MANIHOT
BT1 abelmoschus
BT2 malvaceae

ABELMOSCHUS MOSCHATUS
uf *hibiscus abelmoschus*
BT1 abelmoschus
BT2 malvaceae
BT1 essential oil plants
BT2 oil plants
BT1 fibre plants

ABELMOSCHUS SATIVA
BT1 abelmoschus
BT2 malvaceae
BT1 fibre plants

ABERDEEN-ANGUS
BT1 cattle breeds
BT2 breeds

ABERRANT SPIKELETS
uf *spikelets, aberrant*
rt spikelets

ABETALIPOPROTEINAEMIA
AF abetalipoproteinemia
BT1 hypolipoproteinaemia
BT2 hypolipaemia
BT3 lipid metabolism disorders
BT4 metabolic disorders
BT5 animal disorders
BT6 disorders
BT2 hypoproteinaemia
BT3 blood protein disorders
BT4 blood disorders
BT5 animal disorders
BT6 disorders
rt lipoproteins

ABETALIPOPROTEINEMIA
BF abetalipoproteinaemia
BT1 hypolipoproteinemia
BT2 hypolipemia
BT2 hypoproteinemia

ABGRALLASPIS
BT1 diaspididae
BT2 coccoidea
BT3 sternorrhyncha
BT4 homoptera
NT1 abgrallaspis cyanophylli
rt aspidiotus

ABGRALLASPIS CYANOPHYLLI
uf *aspidiotus cyanophylli*
BT1 abgrallaspis
BT2 diaspididae
BT3 coccoidea
BT4 sternorrhyncha

ABGRALLASPIS CYANOPHYLLI *cont.*
BT5 homoptera

ABIES
uf *firs*
BT1 pinaceae
NT1 abies alba
NT1 abies amabilis
NT1 abies balsamea
NT1 abies borisii-regis
NT1 abies bornmuelleriana
NT1 abies cephalonica
NT1 abies cilicica
NT1 abies concolor
NT1 abies equi-trojani
NT1 abies firma
NT1 abies fraseri
NT1 abies grandis
NT1 abies holophylla
NT1 abies homolepis
NT1 abies lasiocarpa
NT1 abies magnifica
NT1 abies maracana
NT1 abies mariesii
NT1 abies mayriana
NT1 abies nebrodensis
NT1 abies nephrolepis
NT1 abies nordmanniana
NT1 abies numidica
NT1 abies pardei
NT1 abies pindrow
NT1 abies pinsapo
NT1 abies procera
NT1 abies religiosa
NT1 abies sachalinensis
NT1 abies sibirica
NT1 abies tazaotana
NT1 abies veitchii

ABIES ALBA
BT1 abies
BT2 pinaceae
BT1 essential oil plants
BT2 oil plants
BT1 forest trees
BT1 ornamental conifers
BT2 conifers
BT2 ornamental woody plants

ABIES AMABILIS
BT1 abies
BT2 pinaceae
BT1 forest trees

ABIES BALSAMEA
BT1 abies
BT2 pinaceae
BT1 forest trees
BT1 ornamental conifers
BT2 conifers
BT2 ornamental woody plants
rt oleoresins

ABIES BORISII-REGIS
BT1 abies
BT2 pinaceae

ABIES BORNMUELLERIANA
BT1 abies
BT2 pinaceae

ABIES CEPHALONICA
BT1 abies
BT2 pinaceae
BT1 forest trees

ABIES CILICICA
BT1 abies
BT2 pinaceae

ABIES CONCOLOR
BT1 abies
BT2 pinaceae
BT1 forest trees
BT1 ornamental conifers
BT2 conifers
BT2 ornamental woody plants

ABIES EQUI-TROJANI
BT1 abies
BT2 pinaceae

ABIES FIRMA
BT1 abies

ABIES FIRMA *cont.*
BT2 pinaceae
BT1 forest trees

ABIES FRASERI
BT1 abies
BT2 pinaceae
BT1 forest trees

ABIES GRANDIS
BT1 abies
BT2 pinaceae
BT1 forest trees
BT1 ornamental conifers
BT2 conifers
BT2 ornamental woody plants

ABIES HOLOPHYLLA
BT1 abies
BT2 pinaceae
BT1 forest trees

ABIES HOMOLEPIS
BT1 abies
BT2 pinaceae

ABIES LASIOCARPA
BT1 abies
BT2 pinaceae
BT1 forest trees

ABIES MAGNIFICA
BT1 abies
BT2 pinaceae
BT1 forest trees

ABIES MARACANA
BT1 abies
BT2 pinaceae

ABIES MARIESII
BT1 abies
BT2 pinaceae
BT1 forest trees

ABIES MAYRIANA
BT1 abies
BT2 pinaceae

ABIES NEBRODENSIS
BT1 abies
BT2 pinaceae

ABIES NEPHROLEPIS
BT1 abies
BT2 pinaceae

ABIES NORDMANNIANA
BT1 abies
BT2 pinaceae
BT1 forest trees

ABIES NUMIDICA
BT1 abies
BT2 pinaceae

ABIES PARDEI
BT1 abies
BT2 pinaceae

ABIES PINDROW
BT1 abies
BT2 pinaceae
BT1 forest trees

ABIES PINSAPO
BT1 abies
BT2 pinaceae

ABIES PROCERA
BT1 abies
BT2 pinaceae
BT1 forest trees
BT1 ornamental conifers
BT2 conifers
BT2 ornamental woody plants

ABIES RELIGIOSA
BT1 abies
BT2 pinaceae

ABIES SACHALINENSIS
BT1 abies
BT2 pinaceae
BT1 forest trees

ABIES SIBIRICA
BT1 abies
BT2 pinaceae
BT1 forest trees
BT1 medicinal plants

ABIES TAZAOTANA
BT1 abies
BT2 pinaceae

ABIES VEITCHII
BT1 abies
BT2 pinaceae
BT1 forest trees

ABIETIC ACID
BT1 diterpenoids
BT2 terpenoids
BT3 isoprenoids
BT4 lipids
BT1 resin acids
BT2 carboxylic acids
BT3 organic acids
BT4 acids

ABIOTIC INJURIES
BT1 injuries
rt damage
rt mechanical damage

ABLATION
HN from 1990
BT1 surgical operations

ABLERUS
BT1 aphelinidae
BT2 hymenoptera
NT1 ablerus clisiocampae

ABLERUS CLISIOCAMPAE
BT1 ablerus
BT2 aphelinidae
BT3 hymenoptera

ABNORMAL BEHAVIOR
BF abnormal behaviour
BT1 behavior
NT1 compulsions (agricola)
NT2 compulsive eating (agricola)

ABNORMAL BEHAVIOUR
AF abnormal behavior
uf deviant behaviour
BT1 behaviour
NT1 cannibalism
NT1 feather pecking
NT1 hyperactivity
NT1 tail biting
NT1 vices
rt neuroses

ABNORMAL DEVELOPMENT
(in plants)
uf development, abnormal
NT1 cavities in trees
NT1 fasciation
rt abnormal heartwood
rt abnormalities
rt adaptation
rt development

ABNORMAL HEARTWOOD
BT1 heartwood
BT2 wood
BT1 wood defects
BT2 defects
rt abnormal development

ABNORMALITIES
(in animals and man)
NT1 congenital abnormalities
NT2 anorectal atresia
NT2 aplasia
NT3 anencephaly
NT3 segmental aplasia
NT3 taillessness
NT3 wolffian duct aplasia
NT2 arthrogryposis
NT2 brachygnathia
NT2 cleft palate
NT2 coloboma
NT2 congenital functional anomalies

ABNORMALITIES *cont.*
NT3 strabismus
NT2 congenital goitre
NT2 congenital hernia
NT3 spina bifida
NT2 congenital metabolic anomalies
NT3 retinal atrophy
NT2 congenital neoplasms
NT2 congenital tremor
NT2 down's syndrome
NT2 ectopia
NT2 epitheliogenesis imperfecta
NT2 genetic disorders
NT2 hepatolenticular degeneration
NT2 hip dysplasia
NT2 hyperplasia
NT3 interdigital hyperplasia
NT3 mammary hyperplasia
NT3 megacolon
NT2 hypoplasia
NT3 hypotrichosis
NT3 microphthalmia
NT2 musculoskeletal anomalies
NT2 organ duplication
NT2 phimosis
NT2 prader-willi syndrome
NT2 schizosoma reflexum
NT2 sex differentiation disorders
NT3 dysgenesis
NT3 intersexuality
NT4 freemartinism
NT4 pseudohermaphroditism
NT3 sex reversal
NT3 testicular feminization
NT2 sickle cell anaemia
NT2 supernumerary organs
NT3 polydactylia
NT2 syndactyly
NT2 teratogenesis
NT1 crooked neck
NT1 cryptorchidism
NT1 dysplasia
NT1 eccentricities
NT1 fistula
NT1 genetic defects
NT2 genetic disorders
NT2 phenylketonuria
NT1 hypertrophy
NT2 hyperkeratosis
NT2 muscular hypertrophy
NT1 leg weakness
NT1 malformations
NT2 atresia
NT1 malpositions
NT2 embryo malpositions
NT1 nephropathy
NT2 balkan endemic nephropathy
rt abnormal development
rt animal disorders
rt defects
rt deformities
rt hypotrophy
rt variation

ABOMASUM
BT1 stomach
BT2 digestive system
BT3 body parts

ABONDANCE
HN from 1990
BT1 cattle breeds
BT2 breeds

ABORTION
BT1 reproductive disorders
BT2 functional disorders
BT3 animal disorders
BT4 disorders
NT1 mycotic abortion
NT1 spontaneous abortion (agricola)
rt abortion law (agricola)
rt birth
rt brucellosis
rt fetal death
rt induced abortion
rt infertility

ABORTION *cont.*
rt reproduction

ABORTION LAW (AGRICOLA)
BT1 law
BT2 legal systems
rt abortion

ABRAMIS
BT1 cyprinidae
BT2 cypriniformes
BT3 osteichthyes
BT4 fishes
NT1 abramis brama

ABRAMIS BRAMA
uf bream (freshwater)
BT1 abramis
BT2 cyprinidae
BT3 cypriniformes
BT4 osteichthyes
BT5 fishes

ABRASION
rt abrasion resistance
rt abrasive wear
rt injuries
rt wear

ABRASION RESISTANCE
BT1 resistance
rt abrasion
rt abrasive wear
rt sanding
rt woodworking

ABRASION RESISTANT FINISHES (AGRICOLA)
BT1 textile finishes (agricola)
BT2 finishes

ABRASIVE WEAR
uf wear, abrasive
BT1 wear
rt abrasion
rt abrasion resistance

ABRAXAS
BT1 geometridae
BT2 lepidoptera
NT1 abraxas grossulariata

ABRAXAS GROSSULARIATA
BT1 abraxas
BT2 geometridae
BT3 lepidoptera

abrothrix
USE **akodon**

abrothrix longipilis
USE **akodon longipilis**

ABRUS
BT1 leguminosae
NT1 abrus cantoniensis
NT1 abrus precatorius

ABRUS CANTONIENSIS
BT1 abrus
BT2 leguminosae

ABRUS PRECATORIUS
BT1 abrus
BT2 leguminosae
BT1 medicinal plants
BT1 poisonous plants

ABRUZZI
BT1 italy
BT2 western europe
BT3 europe

ABSCESSES
rt bacterial diseases
rt inflammation
rt lesions
rt pus

ABSCISIC ACID
uf aba
BT1 growth inhibitors
BT2 inhibitors
BT2 plant growth regulators
BT3 growth regulators

ABSCISIC ACID *cont.*
BT1 sesquiterpenoids
BT2 terpenoids
BT3 isoprenoids
BT4 lipids
rt dihydrophaseic acid
rt phaseic acid

ABSCISSION
uf leaf abscission
NT1 leaf fall
rt deblossoming
rt defoliants
rt drop
rt glyoxime
rt leaf duration
rt litter (plant)
rt loosening
rt meristems
rt shedding

ABSCONDING
BT1 swarming
BT2 animal behaviour
BT3 behaviour
rt honeybee colonies
rt swarms

absentee landlords
USE **absentee landowners**

ABSENTEE LANDOWNERS
uf absentee landlords
BT1 landowners

ABSIDIA
BT1 mucorales
NT1 absidia blakesleeana
NT1 absidia corymbifera
NT1 absidia cylindrospora

ABSIDIA BLAKESLEEANA
BT1 absidia
BT2 mucorales

ABSIDIA CORYMBIFERA
uf absidia ramosa
BT1 absidia
BT2 mucorales

ABSIDIA CYLINDROSPORA
HN from 1989
BT1 absidia
BT2 mucorales

absidia ramosa
USE **absidia corymbifera**

ABSORBANCE
HN from 1990
(ability of a layer of a substance to absorb radiation)
uf density, optical
uf optical density
BT1 optical properties
BT2 physical properties
BT3 properties
rt densitometers
rt densitometry
rt transmittance

ABSORBENTS
NT1 antidiarrhoea agents
NT2 calcium carbonate
NT2 kaolin
NT2 pectins
NT1 hygroscopic materials
NT1 starch
NT2 amylopectin
NT2 amylose
NT2 cassava starch
NT2 maize starch
NT2 potato starch
rt absorption
rt absorptivity
rt adsorbents
rt hygroscopicity
rt uptake

ABSORPTION
BT1 sorption
NT1 endocytosis
NT1 fat absorption
NT1 lipid absorption

ABSORPTION *cont.*
NT1 mineral absorption
NT2 calcium absorption
NT2 iron absorption
NT1 protein absorption
NT2 protein intake
NT2 protein uptake
rt absorbents
rt absorptivity
rt adsorption
rt desorption
rt digestive absorption
rt hygroscopicity
rt imbibition
rt intestinal absorption
rt nutrient uptake
rt osmosis
rt reabsorption
rt resorption
rt root pressure
rt uptake
rt water uptake

ABSORPTION FLAME PHOTOMETRY
BT1 flame photometry
BT2 photometry
BT3 analytical methods
BT4 methodology

ABSORPTIVITY
BT1 physicochemical properties
BT2 properties
rt absorbents
rt absorption
rt hygroscopicity
rt nutrient uptake
rt osmosis
rt root hairs
rt uptake
rt water uptake

ABSTRACTING
BT1 information processing
BT2 information

ABU DHABI
BT1 united arab emirates
BT2 persian gulf states
BT3 west asia
BT4 asia

ABUSE (AGRICOLA)
NT1 child abuse
NT1 elder abuse (agricola)
NT1 spouse abuse (agricola)
NT1 substance abuse (agricola)

ABUTA
BT1 menispermaceae
NT1 abuta rufescens

ABUTA RUFESCENS
BT1 abuta
BT2 menispermaceae

ABUTILON
BT1 malvaceae
NT1 abutilon asiaticum
NT1 abutilon bidentatum
NT1 abutilon indicum
NT1 abutilon megapotamicum
NT1 abutilon pictum
NT1 abutilon polyandrum
NT1 abutilon sellowianum
NT1 abutilon theophrasti

ABUTILON ASIATICUM
BT1 abutilon
BT2 malvaceae
BT1 fibre plants

abutilon avicennae
USE **abutilon theophrasti**

ABUTILON BIDENTATUM
BT1 abutilon
BT2 malvaceae

ABUTILON INDICUM
BT1 abutilon
BT2 malvaceae
BT1 medicinal plants

ABUTILON MEGAPOTAMICUM
BT1 abutilon
BT2 malvaceae
BT1 ornamental woody plants

ABUTILON MOSAIC VIRUS
BT1 miscellaneous plant viruses
BT2 plant viruses
BT3 plant pathogens
BT4 pathogens

ABUTILON PICTUM
uf *abutilon striatum*
BT1 abutilon
BT2 malvaceae
BT1 ornamental woody plants

ABUTILON POLYANDRUM
BT1 abutilon
BT2 malvaceae
BT1 fibre plants

ABUTILON SELLOWIANUM
BT1 abutilon
BT2 malvaceae
BT1 ornamental woody plants

abutilon striatum
USE **abutilon pictum**

ABUTILON THEOPHRASTI
uf *abutilon avicennae*
BT1 abutilon
BT2 malvaceae

abyssinia
USE **ethiopia**

ABYSSINIAN
BT1 sheep breeds
BT2 breeds

ACACIA
uf *faidherbia*
uf *wattle (plant)*
BT1 leguminosae
NT1 acacia acuminata
NT1 acacia albida
NT1 acacia aneura
NT1 acacia aroma
NT1 acacia aulacocarpa
NT1 acacia auriculiformis
NT1 acacia baileyana
NT1 acacia berlandieri
NT1 acacia campylacantha
NT1 acacia catechu
NT1 acacia caven
NT1 acacia concinna
NT1 acacia confusa
NT1 acacia coolgardiensis
NT1 acacia crassicarpa
NT1 acacia cunninghamii
NT1 acacia cyanophylla
NT1 acacia cyclops
NT1 acacia dealbata
NT1 acacia decurrens
NT1 acacia drepanolobium
NT1 acacia ehrenbergiana
NT1 acacia farnesiana
NT1 acacia ferruginea
NT1 acacia flavescens
NT1 acacia georginae
NT1 acacia gerrardii
NT1 acacia greggii
NT1 acacia harpophylla
NT1 acacia hebeclada
NT1 acacia hockii
NT1 acacia holosericea
NT1 acacia homalophylla
NT1 acacia howittii
NT1 acacia jacquemontii
NT1 acacia karroo
NT1 acacia koa
NT1 acacia koaia
NT1 acacia laeta
NT1 acacia leucophloea
NT1 acacia longifolia
NT1 acacia mangium
NT1 acacia mearnsii
NT1 acacia melanoxylon
NT1 acacia mellifera
NT1 acacia modesta
NT1 acacia moniliformis

ACACIA *cont.*
NT1 acacia nilotica
NT1 acacia nubica
NT1 acacia pendula
NT1 acacia pulchella
NT1 acacia pycnantha
NT1 acacia raddiana
NT1 acacia reficiens
NT1 acacia rigidula
NT1 acacia salicina
NT1 acacia saligna
NT1 acacia schweinfurthii
NT1 acacia senegal
NT1 acacia seyal
NT1 acacia sieberiana
NT1 acacia sophorae
NT1 acacia sowdenii
NT1 acacia tetragonophylla
NT1 acacia tortilis
NT1 acacia tortuosa
NT1 acacia verticilliata
NT1 acacia victoriae
NT1 acacia villosa
NT1 acacia zanzibarica
rt robinia

ACACIA ACUMINATA
BT1 acacia
BT2 leguminosae

ACACIA ALBIDA
uf *faidherbia albida*
BT1 acacia
BT2 leguminosae
BT1 forest trees

ACACIA ANEURA
uf *mulga*
BT1 acacia
BT2 leguminosae
BT1 forest trees

acacia arabica
USE **acacia nilotica**

ACACIA AROMA
BT1 acacia
BT2 leguminosae

ACACIA AULACOCARPA
BT1 acacia
BT2 leguminosae
BT1 forest trees

ACACIA AURICULIFORMIS
BT1 acacia
BT2 leguminosae
BT1 forest trees

ACACIA BAILEYANA
BT1 acacia
BT2 leguminosae
BT1 ornamental woody plants

ACACIA BERLANDIERI
BT1 acacia
BT2 leguminosae

ACACIA CAMPYLACANTHA
BT1 acacia
BT2 leguminosae

ACACIA CATECHU
BT1 acacia
BT2 leguminosae
BT1 algicidal plants
BT1 dye plants
BT1 forest trees
BT1 medicinal plants
BT1 molluscicidal plants
BT2 pesticidal plants
BT1 tan plants
rt catechin

ACACIA CAVEN
BT1 acacia
BT2 leguminosae

ACACIA CONCINNA
BT1 acacia
BT2 leguminosae
rt detergents

ACACIA CONFUSA
BT1 acacia

ACACIA CONFUSA *cont.*
BT2 leguminosae
BT1 forest trees

ACACIA COOLGARDIENSIS
BT1 acacia
BT2 leguminosae

ACACIA CRASSICARPA
HN from 1990
BT1 acacia
BT2 leguminosae
BT1 forest trees

ACACIA CUNNINGHAMII
BT1 acacia
BT2 leguminosae

ACACIA CYANOPHYLLA
BT1 acacia
BT2 leguminosae

ACACIA CYCLOPS
HN from 1990
BT1 acacia
BT2 leguminosae
BT1 forest trees

ACACIA DEALBATA
BT1 acacia
BT2 leguminosae
BT1 forest trees
BT1 ornamental woody plants

ACACIA DECURRENS
BT1 acacia
BT2 leguminosae
BT1 forest trees
BT1 medicinal plants
BT1 ornamental woody plants
BT1 tan plants

ACACIA DREPANOLOBIUM
BT1 acacia
BT2 leguminosae

ACACIA EHRENBERGIANA
BT1 acacia
BT2 leguminosae
BT1 medicinal plants

acacia, false
USE **robinia**

ACACIA FARNESIANA
BT1 acacia
BT2 leguminosae
BT1 essential oil plants
BT2 oil plants
BT1 forest trees
BT1 medicinal plants
BT1 ornamental woody plants
BT1 tan plants

ACACIA FERRUGINEA
BT1 acacia
BT2 leguminosae

ACACIA FLAVESCENS
BT1 acacia
BT2 leguminosae

ACACIA GEORGINAE
BT1 acacia
BT2 leguminosae

ACACIA GERRARDII
BT1 acacia
BT2 leguminosae

ACACIA GREGGII
BT1 acacia
BT2 leguminosae

ACACIA HARPOPHYLLA
BT1 acacia
BT2 leguminosae
BT1 dye plants

ACACIA HEBECLADA
BT1 acacia
BT2 leguminosae

ACACIA HOCKII
BT1 acacia
BT2 leguminosae

ACACIA HOLOSERICEA
BT1 acacia
BT2 leguminosae
BT1 forest trees

ACACIA HOMALOPHYLLA
BT1 acacia
BT2 leguminosae
BT1 browse plants

ACACIA HOWITTII
BT1 acacia
BT2 leguminosae

ACACIA JACQUEMONTII
BT1 acacia
BT2 leguminosae

ACACIA KARROO
BT1 acacia
BT2 leguminosae
BT1 forest trees
BT1 tan plants

ACACIA KOA
BT1 acacia
BT2 leguminosae
BT1 forest trees

ACACIA KOAIA
BT1 acacia
BT2 leguminosae

ACACIA LAETA
BT1 acacia
BT2 leguminosae

ACACIA LEUCOPHLOEA
BT1 acacia
BT2 leguminosae
BT1 forest trees

ACACIA LONGIFOLIA
BT1 acacia
BT2 leguminosae
BT1 forest trees
BT1 ornamental woody plants

ACACIA MANGIUM
BT1 acacia
BT2 leguminosae
BT1 forest trees

ACACIA MEARNSII
uf acacia mollissima
BT1 acacia
BT2 leguminosae
BT1 forest trees

ACACIA MELANOXYLON
BT1 acacia
BT2 leguminosae
BT1 forest trees

ACACIA MELLIFERA
BT1 acacia
BT2 leguminosae
BT1 antibacterial plants

ACACIA MODESTA
BT1 acacia
BT2 leguminosae
BT1 forest trees

acacia mollissima
USE **acacia mearnsii**

ACACIA MONILIFORMIS
BT1 acacia
BT2 leguminosae

ACACIA NILOTICA
uf acacia arabica
BT1 acacia
BT2 leguminosae
BT1 algicidal plants
BT1 forest trees
BT1 medicinal plants
BT1 molluscicidal plants
BT2 pesticidal plants
BT1 tan plants

ACACIA NUBICA
BT1 acacia
BT2 leguminosae

ACACIA PENDULA
BT1 acacia
BT2 leguminosae

ACACIA PULCHELLA
BT1 acacia
BT2 leguminosae
BT1 forest trees

ACACIA PYCNANTHA
BT1 acacia
BT2 leguminosae
BT1 tan plants

ACACIA RADDIANA
BT1 acacia
BT2 leguminosae
BT1 medicinal plants

ACACIA REFICIENS
BT1 acacia
BT2 leguminosae

ACACIA RIGIDULA
BT1 acacia
BT2 leguminosae

ACACIA SALICINA
BT1 acacia
BT2 leguminosae

ACACIA SALIGNA
BT1 acacia
BT2 leguminosae
BT1 forest trees

ACACIA SCHWEINFURTHII
BT1 acacia
BT2 leguminosae

ACACIA SENEGAL
BT1 acacia
BT2 leguminosae
BT1 forest trees
BT1 gum plants
rt gum arabic

ACACIA SEYAL
BT1 acacia
BT2 leguminosae

ACACIA SIEBERIANA
BT1 acacia
BT2 leguminosae

ACACIA SOPHORAE
BT1 acacia
BT2 leguminosae
BT1 browse plants

ACACIA SOWDENII
BT1 acacia
BT2 leguminosae
BT1 browse plants

ACACIA TETRAGONOPHYLLA
BT1 acacia
BT2 leguminosae
BT1 browse plants

ACACIA TORTILIS
BT1 acacia
BT2 leguminosae
BT1 forest trees

ACACIA TORTUOSA
BT1 acacia
BT2 leguminosae

ACACIA VERTICILLIATA
BT1 acacia
BT2 leguminosae
BT1 ornamental woody plants

ACACIA VICTORIAE
HN from 1990
BT1 acacia
BT2 leguminosae
BT1 forest trees

ACACIA VILLOSA
BT1 acacia
BT2 leguminosae

ACACIA ZANZIBARICA
BT1 acacia

ACACIA ZANZIBARICA *cont.*
BT2 leguminosae

ACADEMIC ACHIEVEMENT (AGRICOLA)
BT1 achievement (agricola)
NT1 knowledge level (agricola)
rt academic standards (agricola)
rt achievement tests (agricola)
rt education
rt learning ability
rt mastery learning (agricola)
rt mental ability

ACADEMIC STANDARDS (AGRICOLA)
rt academic achievement (agricola)
rt competency based education (agricola)
rt mastery learning (agricola)

ACAENA
BT1 rosaceae
NT1 acaena integerrima

ACAENA INTEGERRIMA
BT1 acaena
BT2 rosaceae

ACALITUS
BT1 eriophyidae
BT2 prostigmata
BT3 acari
NT1 acalitus essigi
NT1 acalitus phloeocoptes
rt aceria
rt eriophyes

ACALITUS ESSIGI
uf aceria essigi
uf eriophyes essigi
BT1 acalitus
BT2 eriophyidae
BT3 prostigmata
BT4 acari

ACALITUS PHLOEOCOPTES
uf aceria phloeocoptes
uf eriophyes phloeocoptes
BT1 acalitus
BT2 eriophyidae
BT3 prostigmata
BT4 acari

ACALYMMA
BT1 chrysomelidae
BT2 coleoptera
NT1 acalymma vittatum

ACALYMMA VITTATUM
BT1 acalymma
BT2 chrysomelidae
BT3 coleoptera

ACALYPHA
BT1 euphorbiaceae
NT1 acalypha australis
NT1 acalypha macrophylla
NT1 acalypha wilkesiana

ACALYPHA AUSTRALIS
BT1 acalypha
BT2 euphorbiaceae
BT1 ornamental woody plants

ACALYPHA MACROPHYLLA
BT1 acalypha
BT2 euphorbiaceae
BT1 ornamental woody plants

ACALYPHA WILKESIANA
BT1 acalypha
BT2 euphorbiaceae
BT1 ornamental woody plants

ACANTHACEAE
NT1 acanthus
NT2 acanthus hungaricus
NT2 acanthus ilicifolius
NT2 acanthus mollis
NT2 acanthus spinosus
NT1 adhatoda
NT2 adhatoda vasica

ACANTHACEAE *cont.*
NT1 andrographis
NT2 andrographis paniculata
NT1 aphelandra
NT2 aphelandra squarrosa
NT1 arrhostoxylum
NT2 arrhostoxylum elegans
NT1 asystasia
NT2 asystasia gangetica
NT2 asystasia macrocarpa
NT1 barleria
NT2 barleria cristata
NT2 barleria prionitis
NT1 beloperone
NT2 beloperone guttata
NT1 cardanthera
NT2 cardanthera triflora
NT1 crossandra
NT2 crossandra infundibuliformis
NT1 daedalacanthus
NT1 eranthemum
NT2 eranthemum pulchellum
NT2 eranthemum tricolor
NT1 fittonia
NT2 fittonia verschaffeltii
NT1 hygrophila
NT2 hygrophila spinosa
NT1 hypoestes
NT2 hypoestes aristata
NT2 hypoestes phyllostachya
NT2 hypoestes sanguinolenta
NT1 isoglossa
NT1 jacobinia
NT2 jacobinia carnea
NT1 justicia
NT2 justicia americana
NT2 justicia gendarussa
NT2 justicia pectoralis
NT2 justicia procumbens
NT2 justicia prostrata
NT2 justicia simplex
NT2 justicia trinerva
NT1 pachystachys
NT2 pachystachys lutea
NT1 perilepta
NT2 perilepta dyeriana
NT1 peristrophe
NT2 peristrophe bicalyculata
NT1 ruellia
NT2 ruellia simplex
NT2 ruellia tuberosa
NT1 rungia
NT2 rungia klossii
NT1 strobilanthes
NT2 strobilanthes callosus
NT2 strobilanthes cusia

ACANTHAMOEBA
BT1 sarcomastigophora
BT2 protozoa
NT1 acanthamoeba astronyxis
NT1 acanthamoeba castellanii
NT1 acanthamoeba comandoni
NT1 acanthamoeba culbertsoni
NT1 acanthamoeba griffini
NT1 acanthamoeba lenticulata
NT1 acanthamoeba palestinensis
NT1 acanthamoeba polyphaga
NT1 acanthamoeba rhysodes
NT1 acanthamoeba royreba

ACANTHAMOEBA ASTRONYXIS
BT1 acanthamoeba
BT2 sarcomastigophora
BT3 protozoa

ACANTHAMOEBA CASTELLANII
BT1 acanthamoeba
BT2 sarcomastigophora
BT3 protozoa

ACANTHAMOEBA COMANDONI
BT1 acanthamoeba
BT2 sarcomastigophora
BT3 protozoa

ACANTHAMOEBA CULBERTSONI
BT1 acanthamoeba
BT2 sarcomastigophora
BT3 protozoa

ACANTHAMOEBA GRIFFINI
BT1 acanthamoeba
BT2 sarcomastigophora
BT3 protozoa

ACANTHAMOEBA LENTICULATA
BT1 acanthamoeba
BT2 sarcomastigophora
BT3 protozoa

ACANTHAMOEBA PALESTINENSIS
BT1 acanthamoeba
BT2 sarcomastigophora
BT3 protozoa

ACANTHAMOEBA POLYPHAGA
BT1 acanthamoeba
BT2 sarcomastigophora
BT3 protozoa

ACANTHAMOEBA RHYSODES
BT1 acanthamoeba
BT2 sarcomastigophora
BT3 protozoa

ACANTHAMOEBA ROYREBA
BT1 acanthamoeba
BT2 sarcomastigophora
BT3 protozoa

ACANTHELLAE
BT1 acanthocephalan larvae
BT2 helminth larvae
BT3 helminths
BT4 parasites
BT3 larvae
BT4 developmental stages

ACANTHIOPHILUS
BT1 tephritidae
BT2 diptera
NT1 acanthiophilus helianthi

ACANTHIOPHILUS HELIANTHI
BT1 acanthiophilus
BT2 tephritidae
BT3 diptera

ACANTHOBOTHRIUM
BT1 onchobothriidae
BT2 eucestoda
BT3 cestoda

ACANTHOCEPHALA
uf *acanthocephalans*
NT1 centrorhynchidae
NT2 centrorhynchus
NT1 echinorhynchidae
NT2 acanthocephalus
NT2 echinorhynchus
NT3 echinorhynchus truttae
NT1 fessisentidae
NT2 fessisentis
NT1 filicollidae
NT2 filicollis
NT3 filicollis anatis
NT1 gigantorhynchidae
NT2 mediorhynchus
NT1 moniliformidae
NT2 moniliformis
NT3 moniliformis dubius
NT3 moniliformis moniliformis
NT1 neoechinorhynchidae
NT2 neoechinorhynchus
NT3 neoechinorhynchus rutili
NT1 oligacanthorhynchidae
NT2 macracanthorhynchus
NT3 macracanthorhynchus hirudinaceus
NT2 oncicola
NT3 oncicola canis
NT1 polymorphidae
NT2 bolbosoma
NT2 polymorphus
NT3 polymorphus minutus
NT1 pomphorhynchidae
NT2 pomphorhynchus
NT3 pomphorhynchus laevis
NT1 quadrigyridae
NT2 pallisentis
rt acanthocephalan larvae
rt helminths
rt invertebrates

ACANTHOCEPHALAN LARVAE
BT1 helminth larvae
BT2 helminths
BT3 parasites
BT2 larvae
BT3 developmental stages
NT1 acanthellae
NT1 acanthors
NT1 cystacanths
rt acanthocephala

acanthocephalans
USE **acanthocephala**

ACANTHOCEPHALUS
BT1 echinorhynchidae
BT2 acanthocephala

ACANTHOCYCLOPS
BT1 cyclopoida
BT2 copepoda
BT3 crustacea
BT4 arthropods
NT1 acanthocyclops bicuspidatus
NT2 acanthocyclops bicuspidatus thomasi
NT1 acanthocyclops robustus
NT1 acanthocyclops vernalis
NT1 acanthocyclops viridis
rt cyclops

ACANTHOCYCLOPS BICUSPIDATUS
uf *cyclops bicuspidatus*
BT1 acanthocyclops
BT2 cyclopoida
BT3 copepoda
BT4 crustacea
BT5 arthropods
NT1 acanthocyclops bicuspidatus thomasi

ACANTHOCYCLOPS BICUSPIDATUS THOMASI
BT1 acanthocyclops bicuspidatus
BT2 acanthocyclops
BT3 cyclopoida
BT4 copepoda
BT5 crustacea
BT6 arthropods

ACANTHOCYCLOPS ROBUSTUS
BT1 acanthocyclops
BT2 cyclopoida
BT3 copepoda
BT4 crustacea
BT5 arthropods

ACANTHOCYCLOPS VERNALIS
BT1 acanthocyclops
BT2 cyclopoida
BT3 copepoda
BT4 crustacea
BT5 arthropods

ACANTHOCYCLOPS VIRIDIS
BT1 acanthocyclops
BT2 cyclopoida
BT3 copepoda
BT4 crustacea
BT5 arthropods

ACANTHOLYDA
BT1 pamphiliidae
BT2 hymenoptera
NT1 acantholyda posticalis

acantholyda pinivora
USE **acantholyda posticalis**

ACANTHOLYDA POSTICALIS
uf *acantholyda pinivora*
BT1 acantholyda
BT2 pamphiliidae
BT3 hymenoptera

acanthomia
USE **clavigralla**

acanthomia horrida
USE **clavigralla horrida**

acanthomia tomentosicollis
USE **clavigralla tomentosicollis**

ACANTHOPANAX
BT1 araliaceae
NT1 acanthopanax sessiliflorus
rt eleutherococcus

acanthopanax senticosus
USE **eleutherococcus senticosus**

ACANTHOPANAX SESSILIFLORUS
BT1 acanthopanax
BT2 araliaceae

acanthopanax sieboldianus
USE **eleutherococcus sieboldianus**

ACANTHOPHIPPIUM
BT1 orchidaceae
NT1 acanthophippium bicolor

ACANTHOPHIPPIUM BICOLOR
BT1 acanthophippium
BT2 orchidaceae
BT1 ornamental orchids

ACANTHOPHYLLUM
BT1 caryophyllaceae
NT1 acanthophyllum glandulosum
NT1 acanthophyllum gypsophiloides
NT1 acanthophyllum microcephalum
NT1 acanthophyllum paniculatum
NT1 acanthophyllum sordidum

ACANTHOPHYLLUM GLANDULOSUM
BT1 acanthophyllum
BT2 caryophyllaceae

ACANTHOPHYLLUM GYPSOPHILOIDES
BT1 acanthophyllum
BT2 caryophyllaceae

ACANTHOPHYLLUM MICROCEPHALUM
BT1 acanthophyllum
BT2 caryophyllaceae

ACANTHOPHYLLUM PANICULATUM
BT1 acanthophyllum
BT2 caryophyllaceae

ACANTHOPHYLLUM SORDIDUM
BT1 acanthophyllum
BT2 caryophyllaceae

acanthoplusia
USE **ctenoplusia**

acanthoplusia agnata
USE **chrysodeixis agnata**

ACANTHORS
BT1 acanthocephalan larvae
BT2 helminth larvae
BT3 helminths
BT4 parasites
BT3 larvae
BT4 developmental stages

ACANTHOSCELIDES
BT1 bruchidae
BT2 coleoptera
NT1 acanthoscelides obtectus

ACANTHOSCELIDES OBTECTUS
BT1 acanthoscelides
BT2 bruchidae
BT3 coleoptera

ACANTHOSICYOS
BT1 cucurbitaceae
NT1 acanthosicyos horridus

ACANTHOSICYOS HORRIDUS
BT1 acanthosicyos
BT2 cucurbitaceae

ACANTHOSIS
BT1 skin diseases
BT2 organic diseases

ACANTHOSIS *cont.*
BT3 diseases

ACANTHOSPERMUM
BT1 compositae
NT1 acanthospermum australe
NT1 acanthospermum glabratum
NT1 acanthospermum hispidum

ACANTHOSPERMUM AUSTRALE
BT1 acanthospermum
BT2 compositae

ACANTHOSPERMUM GLABRATUM
BT1 acanthospermum
BT2 compositae

ACANTHOSPERMUM HISPIDUM
BT1 acanthospermum
BT2 compositae
BT1 weeds

ACANTHOSTOMIDAE
BT1 digenea
BT2 trematoda
NT1 acanthostomum

ACANTHOSTOMUM
BT1 acanthostomidae
BT2 digenea
BT3 trematoda

ACANTHUS
BT1 acanthaceae
NT1 acanthus hungaricus
NT1 acanthus ilicifolius
NT1 acanthus mollis
NT1 acanthus spinosus

acanthus balcanicus
USE **acanthus hungaricus**

ACANTHUS HUNGARICUS
uf *acanthus balcanicus*
BT1 acanthus
BT2 acanthaceae
BT1 ornamental herbaceous plants

ACANTHUS ILICIFOLIUS
BT1 acanthus
BT2 acanthaceae

ACANTHUS MOLLIS
BT1 acanthus
BT2 acanthaceae
BT1 medicinal plants
BT1 ornamental herbaceous plants

acanthus spinosissimus
USE **acanthus spinosus**

ACANTHUS SPINOSUS
uf *acanthus spinosissimus*
BT1 acanthus
BT2 acanthaceae
BT1 ornamental herbaceous plants

ACAPHYLLA
BT1 eriophyidae
BT2 prostigmata
BT3 acari
NT1 acaphylla theae

ACAPHYLLA THEAE
BT1 acaphylla
BT2 eriophyidae
BT3 prostigmata
BT4 acari

ACARAPIDAE
BT1 prostigmata
BT2 acari
NT1 acarapis
NT2 acarapis vagans
NT2 acarapis woodi

ACARAPIS
BT1 acarapidae
BT2 prostigmata
BT3 acari
NT1 acarapis vagans

ACARAPIS *cont.*
NT1 acarapis woodi

ACARAPIS VAGANS
BT1 acarapis
BT2 acarapidae
BT3 prostigmata
BT4 acari

ACARAPIS WOODI
BT1 acarapis
BT2 acarapidae
BT3 prostigmata
BT4 acari
rt acarine disease

ACARI
uf *acarina*
NT1 astigmata
NT2 acaridae
NT3 acarus
NT4 acarus farris
NT4 acarus siro
NT3 aleuroglyphus
NT4 aleuroglyphus ovatus
NT3 caloglyphus
NT4 caloglyphus berlesei
NT3 rhizoglyphus
NT4 rhizoglyphus callae
NT4 rhizoglyphus echinopus
NT4 rhizoglyphus robini
NT3 tyrophagus
NT4 tyrophagus longior
NT4 tyrophagus perniciosus
NT4 tyrophagus putrescentiae
NT2 analgidae
NT3 megninia
NT4 megninia cubitalis
NT4 megninia ginglymura
NT2 atopomelidae
NT3 chirodiscoides
NT4 chirodiscoides caviae
NT2 carpoglyphidae
NT3 carpoglyphus
NT4 carpoglyphus lactis
NT2 chortoglyphidae
NT3 chortoglyphus
NT4 chortoglyphus arcuatus
NT2 falculiferidae
NT3 pterophagus
NT4 pterophagus strictus
NT2 glycyphagidae
NT3 blomia
NT4 blomia tjibodas
NT4 blomia tropicalis
NT3 glycyphagus
NT4 glycyphagus domesticus
NT3 gohieria
NT4 gohieria fusca
NT3 lepidoglyphus
NT4 lepidoglyphus destructor
NT2 histiostomatidae
NT3 histiostoma
NT2 knemidokoptidae
NT3 knemidokoptes
NT4 knemidokoptes mutans
NT4 knemidokoptes pilae
NT2 lardoglyphidae
NT3 lardoglyphus
NT4 lardoglyphus konoi
NT2 listrophoridae
NT3 leporacarus
NT4 leporacarus gibbus
NT3 listrophorus
NT2 myocoptidae
NT3 myocoptes
NT4 myocoptes musculinus
NT2 psoroptidae
NT3 chorioptes
NT4 chorioptes bovis
NT3 otodectes
NT4 otodectes cynotis
NT3 psoroptes
NT4 psoroptes cuniculi
NT4 psoroptes equi
NT4 psoroptes ovis
NT2 pyroglyphidae
NT3 dermatophagoides
NT4 dermatophagoides farinae

ACARI *cont.*
NT4 dermatophagoides microceras
NT4 dermatophagoides pteronyssinus
NT4 dermatophagoides scheremetewskyi
NT3 euroglyphus
NT4 euroglyphus maynei
NT3 hirstia
NT3 sturnophagoides
NT2 sarcoptidae
NT3 notoedres
NT4 notoedres cati
NT3 sarcoptes
NT4 sarcoptes scabiei
NT3 trixacarus
NT4 trixacarus caviae
NT2 winterschmidtiidae
NT3 suidasia
NT4 suidasia pontifica
NT1 cryptostigmata
NT2 camisiidae
NT3 camisia
NT2 cepheidae
NT3 eupterotegaeus
NT4 eupterotegaeus rostratus
NT2 damaeidae
NT3 epidamaeus
NT2 phthiracaridae
NT3 steganacarus
NT4 steganacarus magnus
NT2 scheloribatidae
NT3 scheloribates
NT4 scheloribates latipes
NT1 mesostigmata
NT2 ameroseiidae
NT2 ascidae
NT3 blattisocius
NT4 blattisocius keegani
NT4 blattisocius tarsalis
NT3 melichares
NT3 proctolaelaps
NT4 proctolaelaps pygmaeus
NT2 dermanyssidae
NT3 dermanyssus
NT4 dermanyssus gallinae
NT4 dermanyssus hirundinis
NT3 liponyssoides
NT2 laelapidae
NT3 androlaelaps
NT4 androlaelaps casalis
NT4 androlaelaps fahrenholzi
NT3 echinonyssus
NT3 eulaelaps
NT4 eulaelaps stabularis
NT3 haemogamasus
NT4 haemogamasus nidi
NT3 hirstionyssus
NT4 hirstionyssus isabellinus
NT3 hypoaspis
NT4 hypoaspis aculeifer
NT3 laelaps
NT4 laelaps agilis
NT4 laelaps algericus
NT4 laelaps echidnina
NT4 laelaps hilaris
NT4 laelaps muris
NT3 raillietia
NT4 raillietia auris
NT4 raillietia caprae
NT3 tropilaelaps
NT4 tropilaelaps clareae
NT2 macrochelidae
NT3 macrocheles
NT4 macrocheles glaber
NT4 macrocheles muscaedomesticae
NT4 macrocheles peregrinus
NT4 macrocheles perglaber
NT2 macronyssidae
NT3 ornithonyssus
NT4 ornithonyssus bacoti
NT4 ornithonyssus bursa
NT4 ornithonyssus sylviarum
NT2 parasitidae
NT3 parasitus
NT3 pergamasus
NT4 pergamasus longicornis
NT3 poecilochirus

ACARI *cont.*
NT2 phytoseiidae
NT3 amblyseius
NT4 amblyseius herbicolus
NT4 amblyseius largoensis
NT4 amblyseius potentillae
NT4 amblyseius swirskii
NT3 anthoseius
NT4 anthoseius caudiglans
NT3 euseius
NT4 euseius finlandicus
NT4 euseius gossipi
NT4 euseius hibisci
NT3 iphiseius
NT3 kampimodromus
NT4 kampimodromus aberrans
NT3 metaseiulus
NT4 metaseiulus occidentalis
NT3 neoseiulus
NT4 neoseiulus anonymus
NT4 neoseiulus californicus
NT4 neoseiulus chilenensis
NT4 neoseiulus cucumeris
NT4 neoseiulus fallacis
NT4 neoseiulus idaeus
NT4 neoseiulus longispinosus
NT3 phytoseiulus
NT4 phytoseiulus longipes
NT4 phytoseiulus macropilis
NT4 phytoseiulus persimilis
NT3 phytoseius
NT4 phytoseius finitimus
NT4 phytoseius macropilis
NT4 phytoseius plumifer
NT3 seiulus
NT4 seiulus tiliarum
NT3 typhlodromus
NT4 typhlodromus exhilaratus
NT4 typhlodromus pyri
NT3 typhloseiopsis
NT2 polyaspididae
NT3 trachytes
NT2 rhinonyssidae
NT3 sternostoma
NT4 sternostoma tracheacolum
NT2 rhodacaridae
NT3 gamasellus
NT4 gamasellus racovitzai
NT2 varroidae
NT3 varroa
NT4 varroa jacobsoni
NT2 veigaiidae
NT3 veigaia
NT4 veigaia nemorensis
NT1 metastigmata
NT2 argasidae
NT3 argas
NT4 argas arboreus
NT4 argas japonicus
NT4 argas persicus
NT4 argas radiatus
NT4 argas reflexus
NT4 argas robertsi
NT4 argas vespertilionis
NT4 argas walkerae
NT3 ornithodoros
NT4 ornithodoros capensis
NT4 ornithodoros concanensis
NT4 ornithodoros coriaceus
NT4 ornithodoros erraticus
NT4 ornithodoros lahorensis
NT4 ornithodoros maritimus
NT4 ornithodoros moubata
NT5 ornithodoros moubata porcinus
NT4 ornithodoros muesebecki
NT4 ornithodoros parkeri
NT4 ornithodoros puertoricensis
NT4 ornithodoros savignyi
NT4 ornithodoros tartakovskyi
NT4 ornithodoros tholozani
NT4 ornithodoros turicata
NT4 ornithodoros verrucosus
NT3 otobius

ACARI *cont.*
NT4 otobius megnini
NT2 ixodidae
NT3 amblyomma
NT4 amblyomma americanum
NT4 amblyomma brasiliense
NT4 amblyomma cajennense
NT4 amblyomma cohaerens
NT4 amblyomma cooperi
NT4 amblyomma cyprium
NT4 amblyomma dissimile
NT4 amblyomma gemma
NT4 amblyomma hebraeum
NT4 amblyomma inornatum
NT4 amblyomma integrum
NT4 amblyomma lepidum
NT4 amblyomma maculatum
NT4 amblyomma marmoreum
NT4 amblyomma neumanni
NT4 amblyomma oblongoguttatum
NT4 amblyomma ovale
NT4 amblyomma pomposum
NT4 amblyomma testudinarium
NT4 amblyomma triguttatum
NT4 amblyomma variegatum
NT3 anocentor
NT4 anocentor nitens
NT3 boophilus
NT4 boophilus annulatus
NT4 boophilus decoloratus
NT4 boophilus geigyi
NT4 boophilus kohlsi
NT4 boophilus microplus
NT3 dermacentor
NT4 dermacentor albipictus
NT4 dermacentor andersoni
NT4 dermacentor auratus
NT4 dermacentor daghestanicus
NT4 dermacentor marginatus
NT4 dermacentor nuttalli
NT4 dermacentor occidentalis
NT4 dermacentor parumapertus
NT4 dermacentor pictus
NT4 dermacentor reticulatus
NT4 dermacentor silvarum
NT4 dermacentor variabilis
NT3 haemaphysalis
NT4 haemaphysalis aciculifer
NT4 haemaphysalis bancrofti
NT4 haemaphysalis bispinosa
NT4 haemaphysalis concinna
NT4 haemaphysalis flava
NT4 haemaphysalis inermis
NT4 haemaphysalis intermedia
NT4 haemaphysalis japonica
NT4 haemaphysalis kinneari
NT4 haemaphysalis kyasanurensis
NT4 haemaphysalis leachii
NT4 haemaphysalis leporispalustris
NT4 haemaphysalis longicornis
NT4 haemaphysalis parva
NT4 haemaphysalis pospelovashtromae
NT4 haemaphysalis punctata
NT4 haemaphysalis silacea
NT4 haemaphysalis spinigera
NT4 haemaphysalis sulcata
NT4 haemaphysalis turturis
NT4 haemaphysalis verticalis
NT3 hyalomma
NT4 hyalomma aegyptium
NT4 hyalomma anatolicum
NT5 hyalomma anatolicum anatolicum
NT5 hyalomma anatolicum excavatum
NT4 hyalomma arabica
NT4 hyalomma asiaticum
NT4 hyalomma brevipunctata
NT4 hyalomma detritum

ACARI *cont.*
NT4 hyalomma dromedarii
NT4 hyalomma hussaini
NT4 hyalomma impeltatum
NT4 hyalomma impressum
NT4 hyalomma lusitanicum
NT4 hyalomma marginatum
NT5 hyalomma marginatum isaaci
NT5 hyalomma marginatum marginatum
NT5 hyalomma marginatum rufipes
NT5 hyalomma marginatum turanicum
NT4 hyalomma nitidum
NT4 hyalomma truncatum
NT3 ixodes
NT4 ixodes apronophorus
NT4 ixodes arboricola
NT4 ixodes canisuga
NT4 ixodes cookei
NT4 ixodes crenulatus
NT4 ixodes dammini
NT4 ixodes dentatus
NT4 ixodes granulatus
NT4 ixodes hexagonus
NT4 ixodes holocyclus
NT4 ixodes kingi
NT4 ixodes lividus
NT4 ixodes nipponensis
NT4 ixodes ovatus
NT4 ixodes pacificus
NT4 ixodes pavlovskyi
NT4 ixodes persulcatus
NT4 ixodes redikorzevi
NT4 ixodes ricinus
NT4 ixodes rubicundus
NT4 ixodes scapularis
NT4 ixodes texanus
NT4 ixodes trianguliceps
NT4 ixodes uriae
NT4 ixodes ventalloi
NT3 margaropus
NT4 margaropus winthemi
NT3 nosomma
NT4 nosomma monstrosum
NT3 rhipicephalus
NT4 rhipicephalus appendiculatus
NT4 rhipicephalus bursa
NT4 rhipicephalus evertsi
NT5 rhipicephalus evertsi evertsi
NT5 rhipicephalus evertsi mimeticus
NT4 rhipicephalus glabroscutatum
NT4 rhipicephalus guilhoni
NT4 rhipicephalus haemaphysaloides
NT4 rhipicephalus longus
NT4 rhipicephalus lunulatus
NT4 rhipicephalus muhsamae
NT4 rhipicephalus pravus
NT4 rhipicephalus pulchellus
NT4 rhipicephalus pumilio
NT4 rhipicephalus pusillus
NT4 rhipicephalus rossicus
NT4 rhipicephalus sanguineus
NT4 rhipicephalus simus
NT4 rhipicephalus sulcatus
NT4 rhipicephalus turanicus
NT4 rhipicephalus zambeziensis
NT1 prostigmata
NT2 acarapidae
NT3 acarapis
NT4 acarapis vagans
NT4 acarapis woodi
NT2 acarophenacidae
NT3 acarophenax
NT4 acarophenax tribolii
NT2 anystidae
NT3 anystis
NT4 anystis baccarum
NT2 arrenuridae
NT3 arrenurus
NT2 bdellidae
NT3 bdellodes
NT4 bdellodes lapidaria

ACARI *cont.*
NT3 biscirus
NT2 cheyletidae
NT3 acaropsellina
NT4 acaropsellina docta
NT3 acaropsis
NT4 acaropsis aegyptiaca
NT3 cheletogenes
NT4 cheletogenes ornatus
NT3 cheyletia
NT3 cheyletus
NT4 cheyletus aversor
NT4 cheyletus eruditus
NT4 cheyletus malaccensis
NT3 hemicheyletia
NT2 cheyletiellidae
NT3 cheyletiella
NT4 cheyletiella blakei
NT4 cheyletiella parasitivorax
NT4 cheyletiella yasguri
NT2 cunaxidae
NT3 cunaxa
NT3 rubroscirus
NT2 demodicidae
NT3 demodex
NT4 demodex bovis
NT4 demodex brevis
NT4 demodex canis
NT4 demodex caprae
NT4 demodex cati
NT4 demodex criceti
NT4 demodex folliculorum
NT4 demodex kutzeri
NT4 demodex ovis
NT4 demodex phylloides
NT2 eriophyidae
NT3 abacarus
NT4 abacarus hystrix
NT3 acalitus
NT4 acalitus essigi
NT4 acalitus phloeocoptes
NT3 acaphylla
NT4 acaphylla theae
NT3 aceria
NT4 aceria chondrillae
NT4 aceria eriobotryae
NT4 aceria guerreronis
NT4 aceria litchii
NT4 aceria mangiferae
NT4 aceria oleae
NT4 aceria sheldoni
NT4 aceria tritici
NT4 aceria tulipae
NT3 aculops
NT4 aculops lycopersici
NT4 aculops pelekassi
NT3 aculus
NT4 aculus fockeui
NT4 aculus schlechtendali
NT3 calacarus
NT4 calacarus carinatus
NT3 calepitrimerus
NT4 calepitrimerus vitis
NT3 cecidophyes
NT3 cecidophyopsis
NT4 cecidophyopsis ribis
NT3 colomerus
NT4 colomerus vitis
NT3 epitrimerus
NT4 epitrimerus pyri
NT3 eriophyes
NT4 eriophyes pyri
NT3 metaculus
NT4 metaculus mangiferae
NT3 oxycenus
NT4 oxycenus maxwelli
NT3 phyllocoptes
NT4 phyllocoptes gracilis
NT3 phyllocoptruta
NT4 phyllocoptruta oleivora
NT3 tegonotus
NT3 vasates
NT2 eupodidae
NT3 halotydeus
NT4 halotydeus destructor
NT2 halarachnidae
NT3 pneumonyssoides
NT4 pneumonyssoides caninum
NT3 pneumonyssus
NT4 pneumonyssus simicola

ACARI *cont.*
NT2 myobiidae
NT3 myobia
NT4 myobia musculi
NT2 nalepellidae
NT3 phytoptus
NT4 phytoptus avellanae
NT3 trisetacus
NT2 psorergatidae
NT3 psorergates
NT3 psorobia
NT4 psorobia bos
NT4 psorobia ovis
NT2 pyemotidae
NT3 pyemotes
NT4 pyemotes tritici
NT4 pyemotes ventricosus
NT2 pygmephoridae
NT3 siteroptes
NT4 siteroptes cerealium
NT4 siteroptes graminum
NT2 scutacaridae
NT3 scutacarus
NT2 stigmaeidae
NT3 agistemus
NT4 agistemus exsertus
NT4 agistemus fleschneri
NT4 agistemus floridanus
NT4 agistemus terminalis
NT3 zetzellia
NT4 zetzellia mali
NT2 syringophilidae
NT3 syringophilus
NT4 syringophilus bipectinatus
NT2 tarsonemidae
NT3 hemitarsonemus
NT3 phytonemus
NT4 phytonemus pallidus
NT3 polyphagotarsonemus
NT4 polyphagotarsonemus latus
NT3 steneotarsonemus
NT4 steneotarsonemus laticeps
NT4 steneotarsonemus panshini
NT3 tarsonemus
NT2 tenuipalpidae
NT3 brevipalpus
NT4 brevipalpus californicus
NT4 brevipalpus lewisi
NT4 brevipalpus obovatus
NT4 brevipalpus phoenicis
NT3 cenopalpus
NT4 cenopalpus pulcher
NT3 raoiella
NT4 raoiella indica
NT3 tenuipalpus
NT4 tenuipalpus granati
NT4 tenuipalpus punicae
NT2 tetranychidae
NT3 bryobia
NT4 bryobia praetiosa
NT4 bryobia ribis
NT4 bryobia rubrioculus
NT3 eotetranychus
NT4 eotetranychus carpini
NT4 eotetranychus hicoriae
NT4 eotetranychus pruni
NT4 eotetranychus sexmaculatus
NT4 eotetranychus willamettei
NT3 eutetranychus
NT4 eutetranychus banksi
NT4 eutetranychus orientalis
NT3 mononychellus
NT4 mononychellus progresivus
NT4 mononychellus tanajoa
NT3 oligonychus
NT4 oligonychus coffeae
NT4 oligonychus gossypii
NT4 oligonychus indicus
NT4 oligonychus mangiferus
NT4 oligonychus peruvianus
NT4 oligonychus pratensis
NT4 oligonychus punicae
NT4 oligonychus ununguis
NT3 panonychus

ACARI *cont.*
NT4 panonychus citri
NT4 panonychus ulmi
NT3 petrobia
NT4 petrobia latens
NT3 schizotetranychus
NT4 schizotetranychus celarius
NT3 tetranychus
NT4 tetranychus arabicus
NT4 tetranychus cinnabarinus
NT4 tetranychus cucurbitacearum
NT4 tetranychus desertorum
NT4 tetranychus evansi
NT4 tetranychus fijiensis
NT4 tetranychus kanzawai
NT4 tetranychus lambi
NT4 tetranychus lombardinii
NT4 tetranychus ludeni
NT4 tetranychus mcdanieli
NT4 tetranychus neocaledonicus
NT4 tetranychus pacificus
NT4 tetranychus tumidus
NT4 tetranychus turkestani
NT4 tetranychus urticae
NT4 tetranychus viennensis
NT2 trombiculidae
NT3 ascoschoengastia
NT3 euschoengastia
NT3 eutrombicula
NT4 eutrombicula alfreddugesi
NT4 eutrombicula splendens
NT3 hirsutiella
NT4 hirsutiella zachvatkini
NT3 leptotrombidium
NT4 leptotrombidium akamushi
NT4 leptotrombidium arenicola
NT4 leptotrombidium deliense
NT4 leptotrombidium pallidum
NT4 leptotrombidium scutellare
NT3 neoschoengastia
NT4 neoschoengastia americana
NT3 neotrombicula
NT4 neotrombicula autumnalis
NT4 neotrombicula japonica
NT3 trombicula
NT2 trombidiidae
NT3 allothrombium
NT4 allothrombium fuliginosum
NT3 podothrombium
NT2 tydeidae
NT3 homeopronematus
NT4 homeopronematus anconai
NT3 lorryia
NT3 orthotydeus
NT4 orthotydeus californicus
NT3 pronematus
NT4 pronematus ubiquitus
NT3 tydeus
rt acaricides
rt arachnida
rt mites
rt pest control
rt plant pests

ACARICIDAL PLANTS
BT1 pesticidal plants
NT1 ailanthus altissima
NT1 amorpha fruticosa
NT1 azadirachta indica
NT1 breynia disticha
NT1 cyrtomium falcatum
NT1 kalanchoe daigremontiana
NT1 mentha piperita
rt acaricidal properties
rt acaricides
rt plants

ACARICIDAL PROPERTIES
BT1 pesticidal properties

ACARICIDAL PROPERTIES *cont.*
BT2 properties
rt acaricidal plants
rt acaricides

ACARICIDE RESISTANCE
BT1 pesticide resistance
BT2 resistance
rt acaricides

ACARICIDES
BT1 pesticides
NT1 antibiotic acaricides
NT2 ivermectin
NT2 nikkomycins
NT2 tetranactin
NT2 thuringiensin
NT1 bridged diphenyl acaricides
NT2 benzyl benzoate
NT2 bromopropylate
NT2 chlorfenethol
NT2 chlorfenson
NT2 chlorfensulphide
NT2 chlorobenzilate
NT2 chloropropylate
NT2 dicofol
NT2 tetradifon
NT2 tetrasul
NT1 carbamate acaricides
NT2 benomyl
NT2 carbaryl
NT2 metolcarb
NT2 oxime carbamate acaricides
NT3 aldicarb
NT3 butocarboxim
NT2 propoxur
NT1 dinitrophenol acaricides
NT2 binapacryl
NT2 dinobuton
NT2 dinocap
NT1 formamidine acaricides
NT2 amitraz
NT2 chlordimeform
NT2 formetanate
NT1 fungal acaricides
NT2 hirsutella thompsonii
NT1 mite growth regulators
NT2 clofentezine
NT2 flubenzimine
NT2 flufenoxuron
NT2 hexythiazox
NT1 organochlorine acaricides
NT2 bromocyclen
NT2 ddt
NT2 dienochlor
NT2 endosulfan
NT2 lindane
NT1 organophosphorus acaricides
NT2 organophosphate acaricides
NT3 crotoxyphos
NT3 tetrachlorvinphos
NT2 organothiophosphate acaricides
NT3 amidithion
NT3 azinphos-ethyl
NT3 azinphos-methyl
NT3 carbophenothion
NT3 coumaphos
NT3 demeton-s-methyl
NT3 demeton-s-methylsulphon
NT3 dialifos
NT3 diazinon
NT3 dioxathion
NT3 ethion
NT3 formothion
NT3 malathion
NT3 parathion
NT3 phenkapton
NT3 phosalone
NT3 phosmet
NT3 phoxim
NT3 quintiofos
NT3 triazophos
NT2 phosphonate acaricides
NT3 trichlorfon
NT2 phosphoramidothioate acaricides
NT3 propetamphos
NT1 organotin acaricides

ACARICIDES *cont.*
NT2 azocyclotin
NT2 cyhexatin
NT2 fenbutatin oxide
NT1 pyrethroid acaricides
NT2 bifenthrin
NT2 cypermethrin
NT2 fenpropathrin
NT2 flucythrinate
NT2 flumethrin
NT2 fluvalinate
NT2 permethrin
NT1 quinoxaline acaricides
NT2 chinomethionat
NT2 thioquinox
NT1 sulfite ester acaricides
NT2 propargite
NT1 unclassified acaricides
NT2 benzoximate
NT2 chloromethiuron
NT2 closantel
NT2 crotamiton
NT2 nifluridide
NT2 sulfur
rt acari
rt acaricidal plants
rt acaricidal properties
rt acaricide resistance
rt ectoparasiticides
rt mite control

ACARIDAE
BT1 astigmata
BT2 acari
NT1 acarus
NT2 acarus farris
NT2 acarus siro
NT1 aleuroglyphus
NT2 aleuroglyphus ovatus
NT1 caloglyphus
NT2 caloglyphus berlesei
NT1 rhizoglyphus
NT2 rhizoglyphus callae
NT2 rhizoglyphus echinopus
NT2 rhizoglyphus robini
NT1 tyrophagus
NT2 tyrophagus longior
NT2 tyrophagus perniciosus
NT2 tyrophagus putrescentiae

acaridida
USE **astigmata**

acarina
USE **acari**

ACARINE DISEASE
BT1 bee diseases
BT2 animal diseases
BT3 diseases
rt acarapis woodi

ACAROLOGY
BT1 zoology
BT2 biology

ACAROPHENACIDAE
BT1 prostigmata
BT2 acari
NT1 acarophenax
NT2 acarophenax tribolii

ACAROPHENAX
BT1 acarophenacidae
BT2 prostigmata
BT3 acari
NT1 acarophenax tribolii

ACAROPHENAX TRIBOLII
BT1 acarophenax
BT2 acarophenacidae
BT3 prostigmata
BT4 acari

ACAROPSELLINA
BT1 cheyletidae
BT2 prostigmata
BT3 acari
NT1 acaropsellina docta
rt acaropsis

ACAROPSELLINA DOCTA
uf *acaropsis docta*
BT1 acaropsellina

ACAROPSELLINA DOCTA *cont.*
BT2 cheyletidae
BT3 prostigmata
BT4 acari

ACAROPSIS
BT1 cheyletidae
BT2 prostigmata
BT3 acari
NT1 acaropsis aegyptiaca
rt acaropsellina

ACAROPSIS AEGYPTIACA
BT1 acaropsis
BT2 cheyletidae
BT3 prostigmata
BT4 acari

acaropsis docta
USE **acaropsellina docta**

ACARTIA
BT1 calanoida
BT2 copepoda
BT3 crustacea
BT4 arthropods
NT1 acartia clausi
NT1 acartia tonsa

ACARTIA CLAUSI
BT1 acartia
BT2 calanoida
BT3 copepoda
BT4 crustacea
BT5 arthropods

ACARTIA TONSA
BT1 acartia
BT2 calanoida
BT3 copepoda
BT4 crustacea
BT5 arthropods

ACARUS
uf *tyroglyphus*
BT1 acaridae
BT2 astigmata
BT3 acari
NT1 acarus farris
NT1 acarus siro

ACARUS FARRIS
BT1 acarus
BT2 acaridae
BT3 astigmata
BT4 acari

ACARUS SIRO
BT1 acarus
BT2 acaridae
BT3 astigmata
BT4 acari

ACAULOSPORA
BT1 endogonales
BT1 mycorrhizal fungi
BT2 fungi
NT1 acaulospora elegans
NT1 acaulospora laevis
NT1 acaulospora spinosa
NT1 acaulospora trappei

ACAULOSPORA ELEGANS
BT1 acaulospora
BT2 endogonales
BT2 mycorrhizal fungi
BT3 fungi

ACAULOSPORA LAEVIS
BT1 acaulospora
BT2 endogonales
BT2 mycorrhizal fungi
BT3 fungi

ACAULOSPORA SPINOSA
BT1 acaulospora
BT2 endogonales
BT2 mycorrhizal fungi
BT3 fungi

ACAULOSPORA TRAPPEI
BT1 acaulospora
BT2 endogonales
BT2 mycorrhizal fungi
BT3 fungi

ACC
uf *1-aminocyclopropanecarboxylic acid*
BT1 ethylene releasers
BT2 plant growth regulators
BT3 growth regulators

ACCA
BT1 myrtaceae
NT1 acca sellowiana
rt feijoa

ACCA SELLOWIANA
uf *feijoa sellowiana*
BT1 acca
BT2 myrtaceae
rt feijoas

ACCELERATED AGING
BT1 aging
BT2 physiological functions

ACCELERATED RIPENING
HN from 1990
BT1 cheese ripening
BT2 cheesemaking

ACCELERATED TESTING
uf *testing, accelerated*
BT1 testing
rt rapid methods

ACCELERATION
rt accelerators
rt accelerometers
rt movement

ACCELERATORS
BT1 controls
rt acceleration
rt accelerometers

ACCELEROMETERS
BT1 instruments
rt acceleration
rt accelerators

ACCEPTABILITY
NT1 food acceptability (agricola)
rt compatibility
rt reception

ACCESS
rt right of access

accession
USE **land transfers**
OR **succession**

accessories
USE **ancillary equipment**

ACCESSORY CHROMOSOMES
uf *chromosomes, accessory*
uf *supernumerary chromosomes*
BT1 chromosomes
BT2 nuclei
BT3 organelles
BT4 cell structure
NT1 b chromosomes

ACCESSORY GLANDS
uf *accessory sex glands*
BT1 glands (animal)
BT2 body parts
BT2 glands
BT1 male genitalia
BT2 genitalia
BT3 urogenital system
BT4 body parts
NT1 bulbo-urethral gland
NT1 prostate
NT1 vesicular gland
rt semen

accessory sex glands
USE **accessory glands**

ACCESSORY SPERMATOZOA
HN from 1990
BT1 spermatozoa
BT2 gametes
BT2 germ cells
BT3 cells

ACCIDENT BENEFITS
uf *benefits, accident*
BT1 social insurance
BT2 insurance
BT2 social security

ACCIDENT PREVENTION
BT1 prevention
BT1 safety at work
BT2 safety
BT2 working conditions
rt accidents
rt guards
rt safety devices

ACCIDENTAL INFECTION
HN from 1990
BT1 infection
BT2 disease transmission
BT3 transmission
rt iatrogenic diseases

ACCIDENTS
NT1 falls (agricola)
NT1 home accidents (agricola)
NT1 industrial accidents (agricola)
NT1 traffic accidents
NT1 water accidents (agricola)
rt accident prevention
rt electrocution
rt ergonomics
rt first aid
rt protective clothing
rt safety
rt safety at work
rt safety devices

ACCIPITER
BT1 accipitridae
BT2 falconiformes
BT3 birds
NT1 accipiter cooperii
NT1 accipiter gentilis
NT1 accipiter striatus

ACCIPITER COOPERII
BT1 accipiter
BT2 accipitridae
BT3 falconiformes
BT4 birds

ACCIPITER GENTILIS
BT1 accipiter
BT2 accipitridae
BT3 falconiformes
BT4 birds

ACCIPITER STRIATUS
BT1 accipiter
BT2 accipitridae
BT3 falconiformes
BT4 birds

ACCIPITRIDAE
BT1 falconiformes
BT2 birds
NT1 accipiter
NT2 accipiter cooperii
NT2 accipiter gentilis
NT2 accipiter striatus
NT1 aquila
NT2 aquila chrysaetos
NT1 circus
NT2 circus cyaneus
rt eagles
rt hawks
rt kites

ACCLIMATIZATION
rt adaptability
rt adaptation
rt climate
rt modification
rt resistance
rt species trials

ACCOMMODATION
NT1 holiday accommodation
NT2 bed and breakfast accommodation
NT2 camp sites
NT2 caravan sites
NT2 farmhouse accommodation

ACCOMMODATION *cont.*
NT2 guest houses
NT2 holiday camps
NT2 holiday chalets
NT2 holiday villages
NT2 hotels
NT3 budget hotels
NT3 economy hotels
NT3 luxury hotels
NT3 middle market hotels
NT3 reception
NT2 second homes
NT2 self catering accommodation
NT2 timesharing
NT1 occupancy rates
rt homes
rt reservations

ACCOUNTABILITY (AGRICOLA)
HN from 1989

accountancy
USE **accountants**

ACCOUNTANTS
uf *accountancy*
BT1 occupations
rt accounts

ACCOUNTING
NT1 balance sheets
NT2 cash flow
NT1 book-keeping
NT2 single entry book-keeping
NT2 stock accounting
NT1 cash flow analysis
NT1 cost analysis
NT2 cash flow analysis
NT2 returns
NT3 marginal returns
NT1 farm accounting
NT1 national accounting
NT2 multipliers
NT3 tourism multipliers
NT1 regional accounting
rt accounts
rt auditing
rt depreciation
rt professional services

ACCOUNTS
NT1 aggregate accounts
NT1 annual accounts
NT1 capital accounts
NT1 economic accounts
NT1 farm accounts
NT2 farm results
NT3 farm comparisons
NT3 farm indebtedness
NT3 gross margins
rt accountants
rt accounting
rt assets
rt liabilities
rt losses
rt profits

ACCULTURATION
BT1 cultural environment
BT2 environment
rt culture

accumulated temperature
USE **heat sums**

accumulation funds
USE **reserve funds**
OR **savings**

ACCURACY
rt correction factors
rt measurement
rt recording
rt repeatability
rt variance

ACEPHATE
BT1 phosphoramidothioate insecticides
BT2 organophosphorus insecticides
BT3 insecticides
BT4 pesticides

ACEPHATE *cont.*
BT3 organophosphorus pesticides
BT4 organophosphorus compounds

ACER
BT1 aceraceae
NT1 acer buergeranum
NT1 acer campestre
NT1 acer circinatum
NT1 acer erianthum
NT1 acer ginnala
NT1 acer grandidentatum
NT1 acer griseum
NT1 acer japonicum
NT1 acer komarovii
NT1 acer lancifolia
NT1 acer macrophyllum
NT1 acer miyabei
NT1 acer mono
NT1 acer negundo
NT1 acer nigrum
NT1 acer nikoense
NT1 acer opalus
NT1 acer palmatum
NT1 acer pensylvanicum
NT1 acer platanoides
NT1 acer pseudoplatanus
NT1 acer rubrum
NT1 acer saccharinum
NT1 acer saccharum
NT1 acer spicatum
NT1 acer tataricum
NT1 acer tschonoskii
rt maples

ACER BUERGERANUM
BT1 acer
BT2 aceraceae
BT1 ornamental woody plants

ACER CAMPESTRE
BT1 acer
BT2 aceraceae
BT1 forest trees
BT1 ornamental woody plants

ACER CIRCINATUM
BT1 acer
BT2 aceraceae
BT1 ornamental woody plants

acer dasycarpum
USE **acer saccharinum**

ACER ERIANTHUM
BT1 acer
BT2 aceraceae
BT1 ornamental woody plants

ACER GINNALA
BT1 acer
BT2 aceraceae
BT1 ornamental woody plants

ACER GRANDIDENTATUM
BT1 acer
BT2 aceraceae
BT1 ornamental woody plants

ACER GRISEUM
BT1 acer
BT2 aceraceae
BT1 ornamental woody plants

ACER JAPONICUM
BT1 acer
BT2 aceraceae
BT1 ornamental woody plants

ACER KOMAROVII
BT1 acer
BT2 aceraceae

ACER LANCIFOLIA
BT1 acer
BT2 aceraceae

ACER MACROPHYLLUM
BT1 acer
BT2 aceraceae
BT1 forest trees

ACER MIYABEI
BT1 acer
BT2 aceraceae
BT1 ornamental woody plants

ACER MONO
uf *acer pictum*
BT1 acer
BT2 aceraceae
BT1 forest trees

ACER NEGUNDO
BT1 acer
BT2 aceraceae
BT1 forest trees
BT1 ornamental woody plants

ACER NIGRUM
BT1 acer
BT2 aceraceae

ACER NIKOENSE
BT1 acer
BT2 aceraceae
BT1 ornamental woody plants

ACER OPALUS
BT1 acer
BT2 aceraceae

ACER PALMATUM
BT1 acer
BT2 aceraceae
BT1 ornamental woody plants

ACER PENSYLVANICUM
BT1 acer
BT2 aceraceae
BT1 forest trees

acer pictum
USE **acer mono**

ACER PLATANOIDES
BT1 acer
BT2 aceraceae
BT1 forest trees
BT1 ornamental woody plants

ACER PSEUDOPLATANUS
BT1 acer
BT2 aceraceae
BT1 forest trees
BT1 ornamental woody plants
rt sycamores

ACER RUBRUM
BT1 acer
BT2 aceraceae
BT1 forest trees
BT1 ornamental woody plants

ACER SACCHARINUM
uf *acer dasycarpum*
BT1 acer
BT2 aceraceae
BT1 forest trees
BT1 ornamental woody plants

ACER SACCHARUM
BT1 acer
BT2 aceraceae
BT1 forest trees
BT1 ornamental woody plants
BT1 sugar crops
rt maple syrup

ACER SPICATUM
BT1 acer
BT2 aceraceae
BT1 forest trees
BT1 ornamental woody plants

ACER TATARICUM
BT1 acer
BT2 aceraceae
BT1 ornamental woody plants

ACER TSCHONOSKII
BT1 acer
BT2 aceraceae

ACERACEAE
NT1 acer
NT2 acer buergeranum

ACERACEAE *cont.*
NT2 acer campestre
NT2 acer circinatum
NT2 acer erianthum
NT2 acer ginnala
NT2 acer grandidentatum
NT2 acer griseum
NT2 acer japonicum
NT2 acer komarovii
NT2 acer lancifolia
NT2 acer macrophyllum
NT2 acer miyabei
NT2 acer mono
NT2 acer negundo
NT2 acer nigrum
NT2 acer nikoense
NT2 acer opalus
NT2 acer palmatum
NT2 acer pensylvanicum
NT2 acer platanoides
NT2 acer pseudoplatanus
NT2 acer rubrum
NT2 acer saccharinum
NT2 acer saccharum
NT2 acer spicatum
NT2 acer tataricum
NT2 acer tschonoskii

ACERATONEUROMYIA
BT1 eulophidae
BT2 hymenoptera
NT1 aceratoneuromyia indica

ACERATONEUROMYIA INDICA
uf *syntomosphyrum indicum*
BT1 aceratoneuromyia
BT2 eulophidae
BT3 hymenoptera
BT1 biological control agents
BT2 beneficial organisms

ACERENTOMIDAE
BT1 protura
NT1 acerentomon
NT1 berberentulus
NT1 gracilentulus

ACERENTOMON
BT1 acerentomidae
BT2 protura

ACERIA
BT1 eriophyidae
BT2 prostigmata
BT3 acari
NT1 aceria chondrillae
NT1 aceria eriobotryae
NT1 aceria guerreronis
NT1 aceria litchii
NT1 aceria mangiferae
NT1 aceria oleae
NT1 aceria sheldoni
NT1 aceria tritici
NT1 aceria tulipae
rt acalitus
rt eriophyes
rt phytoptus

ACERIA CHONDRILLAE
uf *phytoptus chondrillae*
BT1 aceria
BT2 eriophyidae
BT3 prostigmata
BT4 acari

ACERIA ERIOBOTRYAE
BT1 aceria
BT2 eriophyidae
BT3 prostigmata
BT4 acari

aceria essigi
USE **acalitus essigi**

ACERIA GUERRERONIS
uf *eriophyes guerreronis*
BT1 aceria
BT2 eriophyidae
BT3 prostigmata
BT4 acari

ACERIA LITCHII
uf *eriophyes litchii*
BT1 aceria

ACERIA LITCHII *cont.*
BT2 eriophyidae
BT3 prostigmata
BT4 acari

ACERIA MANGIFERAE
uf *eriophyes mangiferae*
BT1 aceria
BT2 eriophyidae
BT3 prostigmata
BT4 acari

ACERIA OLEAE
uf *eriophyes oleae*
BT1 aceria
BT2 eriophyidae
BT3 prostigmata
BT4 acari

aceria phloeocoptes
USE **acalitus phloeocoptes**

ACERIA SHELDONI
uf *eriophyes sheldoni*
BT1 aceria
BT2 eriophyidae
BT3 prostigmata
BT4 acari

ACERIA TRITICI
BT1 aceria
BT2 eriophyidae
BT3 prostigmata
BT4 acari

ACERIA TULIPAE
uf *eriophyes tulipae*
BT1 aceria
BT2 eriophyidae
BT3 prostigmata
BT4 acari

ACETALDEHYDE
BT1 aldehydes
BT1 fumigant insecticides
BT2 fumigants
BT3 pesticides
BT2 insecticides
BT3 pesticides
rt metaldehyde

ACETAMIDE
BT1 amides
BT2 organic nitrogen compounds

ACETAMINOPHEN
uf *paracetamol*
BT1 analgesics
BT2 neurotropic drugs
BT3 drugs
BT1 antipyretics
BT2 drugs

ACETARSOL
uf *acetarsone*
BT1 anthelmintics
BT2 antiparasitic agents
BT3 drugs
BT1 antiprotozoal agents
BT2 antiparasitic agents
BT3 drugs

acetarsone
USE **acetarsol**

ACETATE-COA LIGASE
(ec 6.2.1.1)
uf *acetyl-coa synthetase*
BT1 acid-thiol ligases
BT2 ligases
BT3 enzymes

ACETATE (FIBER) (AGRICOLA)
BT1 cellulosic fibers (agricola)
BT2 textile fibers
BT3 fibers
BT1 manmade fibers (agricola)
BT2 textile fibers
BT3 fibers
rt triacetate (agricola)

ACETATES
NT1 acetates (esters)
NT2 bornyl acetate

ACETATES *cont.*
NT2 cellulose acetate
NT2 isopentyl acetate
NT2 retinyl acetate
NT2 sucrose octaacetate
NT2 triacetin
NT1 acetates (salts)
NT2 lead acetate
NT2 sodium acetate
rt acetic acid

ACETATES (ESTERS)
BT1 acetates
BT1 fatty acid esters
BT2 esters
NT1 bornyl acetate
NT1 cellulose acetate
NT1 isopentyl acetate
NT1 retinyl acetate
NT1 sucrose octaacetate
NT1 triacetin

ACETATES (SALTS)
BT1 acetates
BT1 organic salts
BT2 salts
NT1 lead acetate
NT1 sodium acetate

ACETAZOLAMIDE
BT1 diuretics
BT2 drugs
BT1 enzyme inhibitors
BT2 metabolic inhibitors
BT3 inhibitors
rt glaucoma

ACETIC ACID
BT1 food preservatives
BT2 preservatives
BT1 monocarboxylic acids
BT2 carboxylic acids
BT3 organic acids
BT4 acids
BT1 silage additives
BT2 additives
rt acetates
rt vinegar

acetoacetate
USE **acetoacetic acid**

ACETOACETIC ACID
uf *acetoacetate*
BT1 keto acids
BT2 carboxylic acids
BT3 organic acids
BT4 acids
BT2 ketones
BT1 ketone bodies

acetoacetyl-coa thiolase
USE **acetyl-coa acetyltransferase**

ACETOBACTER
BT1 acetobacteraceae
BT2 gracilicutes
BT3 bacteria
BT4 prokaryotes
NT1 acetobacter aceti

ACETOBACTER ACETI
BT1 acetobacter
BT2 acetobacteraceae
BT3 gracilicutes
BT4 bacteria
BT5 prokaryotes

ACETOBACTERACEAE
BT1 gracilicutes
BT2 bacteria
BT3 prokaryotes
NT1 acetobacter
NT2 acetobacter aceti

ACETOCHLOR
BT1 chloroacetanilide herbicides
BT2 anilide herbicides
BT3 amide herbicides
BT4 herbicides
BT5 pesticides

ACETOIN
BT1 ketones

acetonaemia
USE **ketosis**

ACETONE
uf *2-propanone*
BT1 ketone bodies
BT1 ketones
BT1 solvents

acetonuria
USE **ketonuria**

ACETYL-COA ACETYLTRANSFERASE
(ec 2.3.1.9)
uf *acetoacetyl-coa thiolase*
BT1 acyltransferases
BT2 transferases
BT3 enzymes

ACETYL-COA CARBOXYLASE
(ec 6.4.1.2)
BT1 ligases
BT2 enzymes

acetyl-coa synthetase
USE **acetate-coa ligase**

ACETYL COENZYME A
BT1 esters
rt coenzyme a

ACETYLACETONE
BT1 ketones

ACETYLAMINOFLUORENE
BT1 amides
BT2 organic nitrogen compounds
BT1 carcinogens
BT2 toxic substances

ACETYLATION
BT1 chemical modification of wood
BT2 chemical treatment

ACETYLCHOLINE
BT1 biogenic amines
BT2 amines
BT3 amino compounds
BT4 organic nitrogen compounds
BT1 neurotransmitters
BT1 parasympathomimetics
BT2 neurotropic drugs
BT3 drugs
BT1 quaternary ammonium compounds
BT2 ammonium compounds
BT2 organic nitrogen compounds
rt acetylcholinesterase
rt choline
rt cholinergic mechanisms
rt nervous system

ACETYLCHOLINESTERASE
(ec 3.1.1.7)
BT1 carboxylic ester hydrolases
BT2 esterases
BT3 hydrolases
BT4 enzymes
rt acetylcholine

ACETYLDEOXYNIVALENOLS
HN from 1989
BT1 trichothecenes
BT2 mycotoxins
BT3 toxins

ACETYLENE
uf *ethyne*
BT1 alkynes
BT2 hydrocarbons
rt acetylene reduction
rt calcium carbide
rt welding

ACETYLENE REDUCTION
BT1 biochemical techniques
BT2 techniques

ACETYLENE REDUCTION *cont.*
BT1 reduction
BT2 chemical reactions
rt acetylene
rt nitrogen fixation

acetylenes
USE **alkynes**

N-ACETYLGLUCOSAMINE
BT1 hexosamines
BT2 amino sugars
BT3 amino compounds
BT4 organic nitrogen compounds
BT3 sugars
BT4 carbohydrates

N-ACETYL-β-GLUCOSAMINIDASE
(ec 3.2.1.30)
(for retrieval spell out "beta")
uf *β-n-acetylglucosaminidase*
BT1 n-glycoside hydrolases
BT2 glycosidases
BT3 hydrolases
BT4 enzymes

β-n-acetylglucosaminidase
USE **n-acetyl-β-glucosaminidase**

ACETYLGLUTAMIC ACID
BT1 amino acid derivatives
BT2 amino compounds
BT3 organic nitrogen compounds

β-N-ACETYLHEXOSAMINIDASE
(ec 3.2.1.52)
(for retrieval spell out "beta")
uf *hexosaminidase*
BT1 n-glycoside hydrolases
BT2 glycosidases
BT3 hydrolases
BT4 enzymes

ACETYLMETHIONINE
BT1 amino acid derivatives
BT2 amino compounds
BT3 organic nitrogen compounds

acetylsalicylic acid
USE **aspirin**

ACETYLUREA
BT1 ureides
BT2 amides
BT3 organic nitrogen compounds

ACEVALTRATE
BT1 valepotriates
BT2 iridoids
BT3 isoprenoids
BT4 lipids

ACHAEA
BT1 noctuidae
BT2 lepidoptera
NT1 achaea janata

ACHAEA JANATA
BT1 achaea
BT2 noctuidae
BT3 lepidoptera

ACHAEARANEA
BT1 theridiidae
BT2 araneae
BT3 arachnida
BT4 arthropods
NT1 achaearanea tepidariorum

ACHAEARANEA TEPIDARIORUM
HN from 1989
BT1 achaearanea
BT2 theridiidae
BT3 araneae
BT4 arachnida
BT5 arthropods

ACHATINA
BT1 achatinidae
BT2 gastropoda

ACHATINA *cont.*
BT3 mollusca
NT1 achatina fulica

ACHATINA FULICA
BT1 achatina
BT2 achatinidae
BT3 gastropoda
BT4 mollusca

ACHATINIDAE
BT1 gastropoda
BT2 mollusca
NT1 achatina
NT2 achatina fulica
NT1 rumina
NT2 rumina decollata

ACHELIDONIUM
BT1 papaveraceae

ACHERONTIA
BT1 sphingidae
BT2 lepidoptera
NT1 acherontia atropos
NT1 acherontia lachesis
NT1 acherontia styx

ACHERONTIA ATROPOS
BT1 acherontia
BT2 sphingidae
BT3 lepidoptera

ACHERONTIA LACHESIS
BT1 acherontia
BT2 sphingidae
BT3 lepidoptera

ACHERONTIA STYX
BT1 acherontia
BT2 sphingidae
BT3 lepidoptera

ACHETA
BT1 gryllidae
BT2 orthoptera
NT1 acheta domesticus
rt gryllus

acheta assimilis
USE **gryllus assimilis**

ACHETA DOMESTICUS
uf *gryllus domesticus*
BT1 acheta
BT2 gryllidae
BT3 orthoptera

acheta pennsylvanicus
USE **gryllus pennsylvanicus**

ACHIEVEMENT (AGRICOLA)
NT1 academic achievement (agricola)
NT2 knowledge level (agricola)
rt achievement tests (agricola)

ACHIEVEMENT TESTS (AGRICOLA)
BT1 tests
rt academic achievement (agricola)
rt achievement (agricola)

ACHILLEA
BT1 compositae
NT1 achillea ageratum
NT1 achillea asiatica
NT1 achillea biebersteinii
NT1 achillea cartilaginea
NT1 achillea eriophora
NT1 achillea filipendulina
NT1 achillea kitaibeliana
NT1 achillea millefolium
NT1 achillea ptarmica
NT1 achillea santolina
NT1 achillea setacea
NT1 achillea vermicularis

ACHILLEA AGERATUM
BT1 achillea
BT2 compositae

ACHILLEA ASIATICA
BT1 achillea

ACHILLEA ASIATICA *cont.*
BT2 compositae
BT1 medicinal plants

ACHILLEA BIEBERSTEINII
BT1 achillea
BT2 compositae

ACHILLEA CARTILAGINEA
BT1 achillea
BT2 compositae

ACHILLEA ERIOPHORA
BT1 achillea
BT2 compositae

achillea eupatorium
USE **achillea filipendulina**

ACHILLEA FILIPENDULINA
uf *achillea eupatorium*
BT1 achillea
BT2 compositae
BT1 ornamental herbaceous plants

ACHILLEA KITAIBELIANA
BT1 achillea
BT2 compositae

ACHILLEA MILLEFOLIUM
BT1 achillea
BT2 compositae
BT1 antiviral plants
BT1 essential oil plants
BT2 oil plants
BT1 insecticidal plants
BT2 pesticidal plants
BT1 medicinal plants
BT1 ornamental herbaceous plants

ACHILLEA PTARMICA
BT1 achillea
BT2 compositae
BT1 ornamental herbaceous plants

ACHILLEA SANTOLINA
BT1 achillea
BT2 compositae
BT1 medicinal plants

ACHILLEA SETACEA
BT1 achillea
BT2 compositae

ACHILLEA VERMICULARIS
BT1 achillea
BT2 compositae

ACHIMENES
BT1 gesneriaceae
rt ornamental bulbs

ACHLORHYDRIA
BT1 stomach diseases
BT2 gastrointestinal diseases
BT3 digestive system diseases
BT4 organic diseases
BT5 diseases
rt pernicious anaemia

ACHLYA
BT1 saprolegniales

ACHOLEPLASMA
BT1 acholeplasmataceae
BT2 acholeplasmatales
BT3 mollicutes
BT4 tenericutes
BT5 bacteria
BT6 prokaryotes
NT1 acholeplasma laidlawii

ACHOLEPLASMA LAIDLAWII
BT1 acholeplasma
BT2 acholeplasmataceae
BT3 acholeplasmatales
BT4 mollicutes
BT5 tenericutes
BT6 bacteria
BT7 prokaryotes

ACHOLEPLASMATACEAE
BT1 acholeplasmatales
BT2 mollicutes
BT3 tenericutes
BT4 bacteria
BT5 prokaryotes
NT1 acholeplasma
NT2 acholeplasma laidlawii

ACHOLEPLASMATALES
BT1 mollicutes
BT2 tenericutes
BT3 bacteria
BT4 prokaryotes
NT1 acholeplasmataceae
NT2 acholeplasma
NT3 acholeplasma laidlawii

achorion
USE **trichophyton**

achorion quinckeanum
USE **trichophyton quinckeanum**

achorion schoenleinii
USE **trichophyton schoenleinii**

achras zapota
USE **manilkara zapota**

ACHROIA
BT1 pyralidae
BT2 lepidoptera
NT1 achroia grisella

ACHROIA GRISELLA
uf *wax moths*
BT1 achroia
BT2 pyralidae
BT3 lepidoptera

achromycin
USE **tetracycline**

achrysocharella
USE **chrysonotomyia**

achrysocharella formosa
USE **chrysonotomyia formosa**

achrysocharis
USE **chrysonotomyia**

ACHRYSOCHAROIDES
BT1 eulophidae
BT2 hymenoptera

ACHYRANTHES
BT1 amaranthaceae
NT1 achyranthes aspera

ACHYRANTHES ASPERA
BT1 achyranthes
BT2 amaranthaceae
BT1 antifungal plants
BT1 medicinal plants

ACID AMENDMENTS
BT1 soil amendments
BT2 amendments

ACID ANHYDRIDE HYDROLASES
(ec 3.6)
BT1 hydrolases
BT2 enzymes
NT1 adenosinetriphosphatase
NT1 pyrophosphatases
NT2 atp pyrophosphatase
NT2 inorganic pyrophosphatase

ACID BASE DISORDERS
BT1 metabolic disorders
BT2 animal disorders
BT3 disorders
NT1 acidosis
NT2 diabetic acidosis
NT2 ketoacidosis
NT2 ketosis
NT2 lactic acidosis
NT1 alkalosis
rt acid base imbalance (agricola)
rt antacids
rt digestion

ACID BASE EQUILIBRIUM
BT1 equilibrium
rt acid base imbalance (agricola)
rt acidity
rt acidosis
rt alkali reserve
rt alkali treatment
rt alkalosis
rt antacids
rt buffering capacity
rt buffers
rt digestion
rt electrolytes
rt ph

ACID BASE IMBALANCE (AGRICOLA)
BT1 imbalance
rt acid base disorders
rt acid base equilibrium

ACID BROWN SOILS
BT1 cambisols
BT2 soil types (genetic)

ACID DEGREE VALUE
rt lipolysis

ACID DEPOSITION
HN from 1989
BT1 pollution
NT1 acid rain

ACID MUCOPOLYSACCHARIDES
uf *mucopolysaccharides, acid*
BT1 mucopolysaccharides
BT2 polysaccharides
BT3 carbohydrates
NT1 chondroitin sulfate
NT1 heparin
NT1 hyaluronic acid

ACID PHOSPHATASE
(ec 3.1.3.2)
uf *acid phosphomonoesterase*
uf *phosphatase, acid*
BT1 phosphoric monoester hydrolases
BT2 esterases
BT3 hydrolases
BT4 enzymes

acid phosphomonoesterase
USE **acid phosphatase**

ACID RAIN
BT1 acid deposition
BT2 pollution
rt rain

ACID SOILS
BT1 soil types (chemical)
rt soil acidity

ACID SULFATE SOILS
uf *acid sulphate soils*
BT1 fluvisols
BT2 soil types (genetic)

acid sulphate soils
USE **acid sulfate soils**

ACID-THIOL LIGASES
(ec 6.2.1)
BT1 ligases
BT2 enzymes
NT1 acetate-coa ligase
NT1 long-chain-fatty-acid-coa ligase

ACID TREATMENT
rt acids
rt treatment

ACIDAEMIA
AF acidemia
BT1 blood disorders
BT2 animal disorders
BT3 disorders
NT1 butyryl acidaemia
NT1 citrullinaemia
NT1 histidinaemia
NT1 methylmalonic acidaemia
NT1 propionic acidaemia

ACIDANTHERA
BT1 iridaceae
NT1 acidanthera bicolor

ACIDANTHERA BICOLOR
BT1 acidanthera
BT2 iridaceae
BT1 ornamental bulbs
rt corms

ACIDEMIA
BF acidaemia
NT1 butyryl acidemia
NT1 citrullinemia
NT1 methylmalonic acidemia
NT1 propionic acidemia

ACIDIFICATION
rt acidity
rt acids
rt ph
rt processing
rt soil formation

ACIDIFIED MILK
uf *milk, acidified*
BT1 cultured milks
BT2 milk products
BT3 products

ACIDITY
BT1 chemical properties
BT2 properties
NT1 saponification number
NT1 soil acidity
NT2 exchange acidity
NT2 titratable acidity
rt acid base equilibrium
rt acidification
rt acidosis
rt acids
rt aciduria
rt antacids
rt flavour
rt hyperacidity (agricola)
rt ph

ACIDOPHILIN
BT1 cultured milks
BT2 milk products
BT3 products

ACIDOPHILUS MILK
BT1 cultured milks
BT2 milk products
BT3 products

ACIDOSIS
uf *metabolic acidosis*
BT1 acid base disorders
BT2 metabolic disorders
BT3 animal disorders
BT4 disorders
NT1 diabetic acidosis
NT1 ketoacidosis
NT1 ketosis
NT1 lactic acidosis
rt acid base equilibrium
rt acidity
rt alkali treatment
rt antacids
rt digestion

ACIDS
NT1 inorganic acids
NT2 boric acid
NT2 gastric acid
NT2 hydrochloric acid
NT2 hydrofluoric acid
NT2 molybdic acid
NT2 nitric acid
NT2 phosphoric acid
NT2 polyphosphoric acid
NT3 superphosphoric acid
NT2 silicic acid
NT2 sulfuric acid
NT2 sulfurous acid
NT1 organic acids
NT2 aromatic acids
NT3 4-pyridoxic acid
NT3 6-chloropicolinic acid
NT3 benzoic acids
NT4 aminobenzoic acids

ACIDS *cont.*
NT5 p-aminobenzoic acid
NT5 aminosalicylic acid
NT5 hydroxyanthranilic acid
NT4 benzoic acid
NT4 phenolic acids
NT5 4-hydroxybenzoic acid
NT5 dihydroxybenzoic acid
NT5 gallic acid
NT5 hydroxyanthranilic acid
NT5 protocatechuic acid
NT5 salicylic acids
NT6 3,5-dimethoxysalicylic acid
NT6 aminosalicylic acid
NT6 aspirin
NT6 salicylic acid
NT5 syringic acid
NT5 tannins
NT5 vanillic acid
NT4 phthalic acid
NT4 tibric acid
NT3 nicotinic acid
NT3 picolinic acid
NT3 xanthurenic acid
NT2 carboxylic acids
NT3 amino acids
NT4 branched chain amino acids
NT5 aminoisobutyric acid
NT5 valine
NT4 cyclic amino acids
NT5 cycloleucine
NT5 desmosine
NT5 hypoglycine a
NT5 methylhistidine
NT4 diamino amino acids
NT5 diaminopimelic acid
NT4 essential amino acids
NT5 arginine
NT5 histidine
NT5 isoleucine
NT5 leucine
NT5 lysine
NT5 methionine
NT5 phenylalanine
NT5 threonine
NT5 tryptophan
NT5 valine
NT4 iodo amino acids
NT5 diiodothyronine
NT5 iodothyronine
NT5 thyroxine
NT6 d-thyroxine
NT6 l-thyroxine
NT5 triiodothyronine
NT4 limiting amino acids
NT4 nitrosoamino acids
NT4 nonessential amino acids
NT5 γ-carboxyglutamic acid
NT5 alanine
NT5 asparagine
NT5 aspartic acid
NT5 cystine
NT5 glutamic acid
NT5 glutamine
NT5 glycine
NT5 hydroxylysine
NT5 hydroxyproline
NT5 proline
NT5 serine
NT5 tyrosine
NT4 nonprotein amino acids
NT5 α-aminobutyric acid
NT5 γ-aminobutyric acid
NT5 aminoadipic acid
NT5 aminolaevulinic acid
NT5 canavanine
NT5 citrulline
NT5 dopa
NT6 levodopa
NT5 hippuric acid
NT5 homoserine
NT5 kynurenine
NT5 mimosine
NT5 ornithine
NT5 pipecolic acid
NT5 taurine
NT5 thyronine
NT4 seleno amino acids

ACIDS *cont.*
NT5 selenomethionine
NT4 sulfur amino acids
NT5 cystathionine
NT5 cysteic acid
NT5 cysteine
NT5 cystine
NT5 ethionine
NT5 homocysteine
NT5 methionine
NT5 penicillamine
NT5 taurine
NT3 benzenealkanoic acids
NT4 homovanillic acid
NT4 mandelic acid
NT4 phenylacetic acid
NT4 phenyllactic acid
NT4 vanillomandelic acid
NT3 benzenealkenoic acids
NT4 cinnamic acid
NT4 coumaric acids
NT5 p-coumaric acid
NT5 caffeic acid
NT5 ferulic acid
NT5 sinapic acid
NT3 cyclohexanecarboxylic acids
NT4 chlorogenic acid
NT4 cyclohexanecarboxylic acid
NT4 quinic acid
NT4 shikimic acid
NT3 dicarboxylic acids
NT4 α-ketoglutaric acid
NT4 adipic acid
NT4 diferulic acid
NT4 diglycine
NT4 fumaric acid
NT4 glutaric acid
NT4 guanidinosuccinic acid
NT4 malic acid
NT4 malonic acid
NT4 methylmalonic acid
NT4 oxalic acid
NT4 oxaloacetic acid
NT4 phthalic acid
NT4 porphobilinogen
NT4 succinic acid
NT4 tartaric acid
NT3 fatty acids
NT4 branched chain fatty acids
NT5 phytanic acid
NT4 cyclopropenoid fatty acids
NT5 cyclopropenoic acid
NT5 sterculic acid
NT4 essential fatty acids
NT5 arachidonic acid
NT5 linoleic acid
NT5 linolenic acid
NT4 hydroxy fatty acids
NT5 3-hydroxybutyric acid
NT5 ricinoleic acid
NT5 trihydroxyoctadecenoic acid
NT4 long chain fatty acids
NT5 arachidonic acid
NT5 docosenoic acids
NT6 brassidic acid
NT6 erucic acid
NT5 elaidic acid
NT5 gadoleic acid
NT5 linoleic acid
NT5 oleic acid
NT5 palmitic acid
NT5 palmitoleic acid
NT5 pentadecanoic acid
NT5 stearic acid
NT5 tetracosadienoic acid
NT4 medium chain fatty acids
NT5 3,5-tetradecadienoic acid
NT5 decanoic acid
NT5 dodecanoic acid
NT5 myristic acid
NT5 nonanoic acid
NT5 octanoic acid
NT5 tridecanoic acid
NT4 odd chain fatty acids

ACIDS *cont.*
NT5 nonanoic acid
NT5 pentadecanoic acid
NT5 tridecanoic acid
NT4 saturated fatty acids
NT5 decanoic acid
NT5 dodecanoic acid
NT5 hexanoic acid
NT5 myristic acid
NT5 nonanoic acid
NT5 octanoic acid
NT5 palmitic acid
NT5 pentadecanoic acid
NT5 phytanic acid
NT5 stearic acid
NT5 tridecanoic acid
NT4 short chain fatty acids
NT5 hexanoic acid
NT5 maleic acid
NT5 sorbic acid
NT4 trans fatty acids
NT5 brassidic acid
NT5 elaidic acid
NT4 unsaturated fatty acids
NT5 dienoic fatty acids
NT6 3,5-tetradecadienoic acid
NT6 linoleic acid
NT6 sorbic acid
NT6 tetracosadienoic acid
NT5 monoenoic fatty acids
NT6 docosenoic acids
NT7 brassidic acid
NT7 erucic acid
NT6 elaidic acid
NT6 gadoleic acid
NT6 maleic acid
NT6 oleic acid
NT6 palmitoleic acid
NT5 polyenoic fatty acids
NT4 volatile fatty acids
NT5 butyric acid
NT5 isobutyric acid
NT5 valeric acid
NT3 keto acids
NT4 α-ketoglutaric acid
NT4 acetoacetic acid
NT4 aminolaevulinic acid
NT4 branched chain keto acids
NT4 laevulinic acid
NT4 oxaloacetic acid
NT4 phenylpyruvic acid
NT4 pyruvic acid
NT3 lichenic acids
NT3 monocarboxylic acids
NT4 3-nitropropionic acid
NT4 4-pyridoxic acid
NT4 6-aminohexanoic acid
NT4 6-chloropicolinic acid
NT4 acetic acid
NT4 acrylic acid
NT4 allantoic acid
NT4 chlorophenoxyisobutyric acid
NT4 chrysanthemic acid
NT4 fluoroacetic acid
NT4 formic acid
NT4 glycolic acid
NT4 glyoxylic acid
NT4 iodoacetic acid
NT4 jasmonic acid
NT4 kaurenoic acid
NT4 lactic acid
NT4 mevalonic acid
NT4 orotic acid
NT4 peracetic acid
NT4 propionic acid
NT4 retinoic acid
NT4 steviol
NT4 triterpene acids
NT5 oleanolic acid
NT5 ursolic acid
NT4 valproic acid
NT4 xanthurenic acid
NT3 resin acids
NT4 abietic acid
NT4 palustric acid
NT4 pimaric acid
NT3 sugar acids
NT4 aldaric acids

ACIDS *cont.*
NT5 glucaric acid
NT5 tartaric acid
NT4 aldonic acids
NT5 ascorbic acids
NT6 ascorbic acid
NT6 dehydroascorbic acid
NT6 diketogulonic acid
NT6 isoascorbic acid
NT5 gluconic acid
NT5 neuraminic acid
NT5 sialic acids
NT4 uronic acids
NT5 galacturonic acid
NT5 glucuronic acid
NT3 tricarboxylic acids
NT4 aconitic acid
NT4 citric acid
NT4 isocitric acid
NT2 chrysophanic acid
NT2 eicosanoids
NT3 leukotrienes
NT3 prostaglandins
NT4 prostacyclin
NT3 thromboxanes
NT2 ellagic acid
NT2 fulvic acids
NT2 humic acids
NT2 nucleic acids
NT3 dna
NT4 antisense dna
NT4 mitochondrial dna
NT4 recombinant dna
NT4 repetitive dna
NT4 ribosomal dna
NT4 satellite dna
NT5 minisatellites
NT4 z dna
NT3 rna
NT4 antisense rna
NT4 messenger rna
NT4 ribosomal rna
NT4 small nuclear rna
NT4 transfer rna
rt acid treatment
rt acidification
rt acidity
rt neutralization
rt saponification number

acids, aromatic
USE **aromatic acids**

acids, inorganic
USE **inorganic acids**

acids, organic
USE **organic acids**

ACIDULANTS
(for food; for acidulants for soil, use "soil acidulants")
BT1 food additives
BT2 additives
NT1 citric acid
NT1 fumaric acid
NT1 gluconolactone
NT1 tartaric acid
rt acidulation

acidulants, soil
USE **soil acidulants**

ACIDULATED PHOSPHATES
BT1 phosphorus fertilizers
BT2 fertilizers

ACIDULATION
BT1 fertilizer technology
BT2 technology
rt acidulants

ACIDURIA
BT1 metabolic disorders
BT2 animal disorders
BT3 disorders
NT1 aminoaciduria
NT2 cystinuria
NT2 homocystinuria
NT1 argininosuccinic aciduria
NT1 glutaric aciduria
NT1 methylglutaconic aciduria
NT1 methylmalonic aciduria

ACIDURIA *cont.*
NT1 orotic aciduria
NT1 oxaluria
rt acidity
rt urine

ACIFLUORFEN
BT1 nitrophenyl ether herbicides
BT2 herbicides
BT3 pesticides

ACIGONA
BT1 noctuidae
BT2 lepidoptera
rt bissetia
rt coniesta
rt haimbachia

acigona ignefusalis
USE **coniesta ignefusalis**

acigona infusellus
USE **haimbachia infusella**

acigona steniellus
USE **bissetia steniella**

ACINETOBACTER
BT1 neisseriaceae
BT2 gracilicutes
BT3 bacteria
BT4 prokaryotes
NT1 acinetobacter calcoaceticus

ACINETOBACTER CALCOACETICUS
BT1 acinetobacter
BT2 neisseriaceae
BT3 gracilicutes
BT4 bacteria
BT5 prokaryotes

ACINONYX
BT1 felidae
BT2 fissipeda
BT3 carnivores
BT4 mammals
NT1 acinonyx jubatus

ACINONYX JUBATUS
uf *cheetahs*
BT1 acinonyx
BT2 felidae
BT3 fissipeda
BT4 carnivores
BT5 mammals

ACINOS
BT1 labiatae
NT1 acinos alpinus
NT1 acinos suaveolens

ACINOS ALPINUS
uf *calamintha alpina*
uf *satureja alpina*
BT1 acinos
BT2 labiatae
BT1 essential oil plants
BT2 oil plants

ACINOS SUAVEOLENS
uf *calamintha suaveolens*
BT1 acinos
BT2 labiatae
BT1 essential oil plants
BT2 oil plants

ACIPENSER
BT1 acipenseridae
BT2 acipenseriformes
BT3 osteichthyes
BT4 fishes
NT1 acipenser gueldenstaedti
NT1 acipenser ruthenus
NT1 acipenser stellatus
NT1 acipenser transmontanus
rt caviar
rt sturgeons

ACIPENSER GUELDENSTAEDTI
uf *russian sturgeon*
BT1 acipenser
BT2 acipenseridae
BT3 acipenseriformes
BT4 osteichthyes

ACIPENSER GUELDENSTAEDTI *cont.*
BT5 fishes

ACIPENSER RUTHENUS
BT1 acipenser
BT2 acipenseridae
BT3 acipenseriformes
BT4 osteichthyes
BT5 fishes

ACIPENSER STELLATUS
BT1 acipenser
BT2 acipenseridae
BT3 acipenseriformes
BT4 osteichthyes
BT5 fishes

ACIPENSER TRANSMONTANUS
uf *white sturgeon*
BT1 acipenser
BT2 acipenseridae
BT3 acipenseriformes
BT4 osteichthyes
BT5 fishes

ACIPENSERIDAE
BT1 acipenseriformes
BT2 osteichthyes
BT3 fishes
NT1 acipenser
NT2 acipenser gueldenstaedti
NT2 acipenser ruthenus
NT2 acipenser stellatus
NT2 acipenser transmontanus
NT1 huso
NT2 huso huso
rt sturgeons

ACIPENSERIFORMES
BT1 osteichthyes
BT2 fishes
NT1 acipenseridae
NT2 acipenser
NT3 acipenser gueldenstaedti
NT3 acipenser ruthenus
NT3 acipenser stellatus
NT3 acipenser transmontanus
NT2 huso
NT3 huso huso
NT1 polyodontidae
NT2 polyodon

ACLERDA
BT1 aclerdidae
BT2 coccoidea
BT3 sternorrhyncha
BT4 homoptera
NT1 aclerda campinensis

ACLERDA CAMPINENSIS
BT1 aclerda
BT2 aclerdidae
BT3 coccoidea
BT4 sternorrhyncha
BT5 homoptera

ACLERDIDAE
BT1 coccoidea
BT2 sternorrhyncha
BT3 homoptera
NT1 aclerda
NT2 aclerda campinensis

ACLERIS
BT1 tortricidae
BT2 lepidoptera
NT1 acleris comariana
NT1 acleris gloverana
NT1 acleris notana
NT1 acleris sparsana
NT1 acleris variana

ACLERIS COMARIANA
BT1 acleris
BT2 tortricidae
BT3 lepidoptera

ACLERIS GLOVERANA
BT1 acleris
BT2 tortricidae
BT3 lepidoptera

ACLERIS NOTANA
uf *acleris tripunctana*

ACLERIS NOTANA *cont.*
BT1 acleris
BT2 tortricidae
BT3 lepidoptera

ACLERIS SPARSANA
BT1 acleris
BT2 tortricidae
BT3 lepidoptera

acleris tripunctana
USE **acleris notana**

ACLERIS VARIANA
BT1 acleris
BT2 tortricidae
BT3 lepidoptera

ACLONIFEN
BT1 nitrophenyl ether herbicides
BT2 herbicides
BT3 pesticides

ACLYPEA
BT1 silphidae
BT2 coleoptera
NT1 aclypea opaca
rt silpha

ACLYPEA OPACA
uf *silpha opaca*
BT1 aclypea
BT2 silphidae
BT3 coleoptera

ACMOPOLYNEMA
BT1 mymaridae
BT2 hymenoptera
NT1 acmopolynema hervali

ACMOPOLYNEMA HERVALI
BT1 acmopolynema
BT2 mymaridae
BT3 hymenoptera

ACNE
BT1 skin diseases
BT2 organic diseases
BT3 diseases

ACOKANTHERA
BT1 apocynaceae
NT1 acokanthera longiflora
NT1 acokanthera oblongifolia
NT1 acokanthera ouabaio

ACOKANTHERA LONGIFLORA
BT1 acokanthera
BT2 apocynaceae

ACOKANTHERA OBLONGIFOLIA
uf *acokanthera spectabilis*
BT1 acokanthera
BT2 apocynaceae

ACOKANTHERA OUABAIO
uf *acokanthera schimperi*
BT1 acokanthera
BT2 apocynaceae
BT1 medicinal plants

acokanthera schimperi
USE **acokanthera ouabaio**

acokanthera spectabilis
USE **acokanthera oblongifolia**

ACOMYS
BT1 murinae
BT2 muridae
BT3 rodents
BT4 mammals
NT1 acomys cahirinus

ACOMYS CAHIRINUS
BT1 acomys
BT2 murinae
BT3 muridae
BT4 rodents
BT5 mammals

ACONITIC ACID
BT1 tricarboxylic acids
BT2 carboxylic acids
BT3 organic acids
BT4 acids

ACONITIC ACID *cont.*
rt aconitum

ACONITUM
BT1 ranunculaceae
NT1 aconitum ajanense
NT1 aconitum albo-violaceum
NT1 aconitum carmichaelii
NT1 aconitum chasmanthum
NT1 aconitum chinense
NT1 aconitum delphinifolium
NT1 aconitum falconeri
NT1 aconitum ferox
NT1 aconitum heterophyllum
NT1 aconitum japonicum
NT1 aconitum karakolicum
NT1 aconitum kirinense
NT1 aconitum koreanum
NT1 aconitum krylovii
NT1 aconitum mitakense
NT1 aconitum napellus
NT1 aconitum nasutum
NT1 aconitum paniculatum
NT1 aconitum pentheri
NT1 aconitum raddeanum
NT1 aconitum sczukinii
NT1 aconitum septentrionale
NT1 aconitum variegatum
NT1 aconitum yezoense
rt aconitic acid

ACONITUM AJANENSE
BT1 aconitum
BT2 ranunculaceae

ACONITUM ALBO-VIOLACEUM
BT1 aconitum
BT2 ranunculaceae

ACONITUM CARMICHAELII
BT1 aconitum
BT2 ranunculaceae
BT1 medicinal plants
BT1 ornamental herbaceous plants

ACONITUM CHASMANTHUM
BT1 aconitum
BT2 ranunculaceae

ACONITUM CHINENSE
BT1 aconitum
BT2 ranunculaceae

ACONITUM DELPHINIFOLIUM
BT1 aconitum
BT2 ranunculaceae
BT1 ornamental herbaceous plants

ACONITUM FALCONERI
BT1 aconitum
BT2 ranunculaceae

ACONITUM FEROX
BT1 aconitum
BT2 ranunculaceae

ACONITUM HETEROPHYLLUM
BT1 aconitum
BT2 ranunculaceae
BT1 medicinal plants

ACONITUM JAPONICUM
BT1 aconitum
BT2 ranunculaceae

ACONITUM KARAKOLICUM
BT1 aconitum
BT2 ranunculaceae

ACONITUM KIRINENSE
BT1 aconitum
BT2 ranunculaceae

ACONITUM KOREANUM
BT1 aconitum
BT2 ranunculaceae

ACONITUM KRYLOVII
BT1 aconitum
BT2 ranunculaceae

ACONITUM MITAKENSE
BT1 aconitum

ACONITUM MITAKENSE *cont.*
BT2 ranunculaceae

ACONITUM NAPELLUS
BT1 aconitum
BT2 ranunculaceae
BT1 ornamental herbaceous plants

ACONITUM NASUTUM
BT1 aconitum
BT2 ranunculaceae
BT1 antifungal plants

ACONITUM PANICULATUM
BT1 aconitum
BT2 ranunculaceae

ACONITUM PENTHERI
BT1 aconitum
BT2 ranunculaceae

ACONITUM RADDEANUM
BT1 aconitum
BT2 ranunculaceae

ACONITUM SCZUKINII
BT1 aconitum
BT2 ranunculaceae

ACONITUM SEPTENTRIONALE
BT1 aconitum
BT2 ranunculaceae

ACONITUM VARIEGATUM
BT1 aconitum
BT2 ranunculaceae

ACONITUM YEZOENSE
BT1 aconitum
BT2 ranunculaceae

ACONTYLUS
BT1 hoplolaimidae
BT2 nematoda
NT1 acontylus vipriensis

ACONTYLUS VIPRIENSIS
BT1 acontylus
BT2 hoplolaimidae
BT3 nematoda

ACORNS
rt quercus

ACORUS
BT1 araceae
NT1 acorus calamus
NT1 acorus gramineus

ACORUS CALAMUS
BT1 acorus
BT2 araceae
BT1 insecticidal plants
BT2 pesticidal plants
BT1 medicinal plants

ACORUS GRAMINEUS
BT1 acorus
BT2 araceae

ACOUSTIC PROPERTIES
BT1 physical properties
BT2 properties
NT1 compressional wave velocity
NT1 dilational wave velocity
NT1 impedance
NT1 shear wave velocity
rt acoustics
rt resonance wood
rt sound pressure
rt sounds

ACOUSTIC TRACKING
uf *tracking, acoustic*
BT1 tracking
rt acoustics
rt sounds
rt ultrasonic tracking

ACOUSTICS
BT1 physics
rt acoustic properties
rt acoustic tracking
rt hearing

ACOUSTICS *cont.*
rt noise
rt sounds
rt ultrasonics

ACP
(african, caribbean and pacific partners to the lome convention with the european communities)
BT1 international organizations
BT2 organizations
rt africa
rt africa south of sahara
rt bahamas
rt barbados
rt belize
rt benin
rt botswana
rt burkina faso
rt burundi
rt cameroon
rt cape verde
rt caribbean
rt central african republic
rt chad
rt comoros
rt congo
rt developing countries
rt djibouti
rt dominica
rt economic regions
rt economic unions
rt equatorial guinea
rt ethiopia
rt european communities
rt fiji
rt gabon
rt gambia
rt ghana
rt grenada
rt guinea
rt guinea-bissau
rt guyana
rt ivory coast
rt jamaica
rt kenya
rt kiribati
rt lesotho
rt liberia
rt lome convention
rt madagascar
rt malawi
rt mali
rt mauritania
rt mauritius
rt niger
rt nigeria
rt oceania
rt papua new guinea
rt rwanda
rt sao tome and principe
rt senegal
rt seychelles
rt sierra leone
rt solomon islands
rt somalia
rt st. lucia
rt st. vincent and grenadines
rt sudan
rt surinam
rt swaziland
rt tanzania
rt togo
rt tonga
rt trinidad and tobago
rt tuvalu
rt uganda
rt vanuatu
rt western samoa
rt zaire
rt zambia
rt zimbabwe

ACQUIRED CHARACTERS
BT1 characteristics
rt genetics
rt genotrophs
rt lamarckism

ACQUIRED IMMUNE DEFICIENCY SYNDROME
uf *aids*

ACQUIRED IMMUNE DEFICIENCY SYNDROME *cont.*
BT1 human diseases
BT2 diseases
BT1 viral diseases
BT2 infectious diseases
BT3 diseases
BT1 viral immunosuppression
BT2 immunological deficiency
BT3 deficiency
BT3 immunological diseases
BT4 diseases
rt homosexuals
rt human immunodeficiency virus
rt immunocompromised hosts
rt intravenous drug users

acquired immunity
USE **immunity**

ACQUIRED IMMUNOTOLERANCE
HN from 1990 (antigen-specific immunological unresponsiveness induced artificially; for immunotolerance arising naturally use "natural immunotolerance")
uf *immunotolerance, acquired*
uf *immunotolerance, artificial*
BT1 specific immunosuppression
BT2 immunosuppression
BT3 immunotherapy
BT4 therapy
NT1 adoptive immunotolerance

ACQUISITION
NT1 acquisition of ownership
NT2 purchasing
NT3 compulsory purchase
NT3 food purchasing (agricola)
NT3 rent then buy (agricola)
NT2 succession

ACQUISITION OF OWNERSHIP
BT1 acquisition
NT1 purchasing
NT2 compulsory purchase
NT2 food purchasing (agricola)
NT2 rent then buy (agricola)
NT1 succession

ACRADENIA
BT1 rutaceae
rt ornamental plants

ACRANTUS
uf *chaetoptelius*
BT1 scolytidae
BT2 coleoptera
NT1 acrantus vestitus
rt hylesinus

ACRANTUS VESTITUS
uf *chaetoptelius vestitus*
uf *hylesinus vestitus*
BT1 acrantus
BT2 scolytidae
BT3 coleoptera

ACREAGE
rt farm area

ACREMONIUM
BT1 deuteromycotina
NT1 acremonium coenophialum
NT1 acremonium diospyri
NT1 acremonium falciforme
NT1 acremonium kiliense
NT1 acremonium recifei
NT1 acremonium strictum
rt cephalosporium
rt epichloe

ACREMONIUM COENOPHIALUM
uf *epichloe typhina*
BT1 acremonium
BT2 deuteromycotina

ACREMONIUM DIOSPYRI
BT1 acremonium
BT2 deuteromycotina

ACREMONIUM FALCIFORME
uf *cephalosporium falciforme*
BT1 acremonium
BT2 deuteromycotina

ACREMONIUM KILIENSE
uf *cephalosporium kiliense*
BT1 acremonium
BT2 deuteromycotina

ACREMONIUM RECIFEI
uf *cephalosporium recifei*
BT1 acremonium
BT2 deuteromycotina

ACREMONIUM STRICTUM
uf *cephalosporium acremonium*
BT1 acremonium
BT2 deuteromycotina

ACRIDIDAE
BT1 orthoptera
NT1 ageneotettix
NT2 ageneotettix deorum
NT1 aiolopus
NT2 aiolopus thalassinus
NT1 anacridium
NT2 anacridium aegyptium
NT1 calliptamus
NT2 calliptamus italicus
NT1 camnula
NT2 camnula pellucida
NT1 chorthippus
NT2 chorthippus brunneus
NT1 chortoicetes
NT2 chortoicetes terminifera
NT1 chrotogonus
NT2 chrotogonus trachypterus
NT1 cyrtacanthacris
NT1 dociostaurus
NT2 dociostaurus maroccanus
NT1 eyprepocnemis
NT2 eyprepocnemis plorans
NT1 hieroglyphus
NT2 hieroglyphus banian
NT2 hieroglyphus nigrorepletus
NT1 locusta
NT2 locusta migratoria
NT3 locusta migratoria migratorioides
NT1 locustana
NT2 locustana pardalina
NT1 melanoplus
NT2 melanoplus bivittatus
NT2 melanoplus differentialis
NT2 melanoplus femurrubrum
NT2 melanoplus infantilis
NT2 melanoplus packardii
NT2 melanoplus sanguinipes
NT1 oedaleus
NT2 oedaleus senegalensis
NT1 oxya
NT2 oxya velox
NT1 patanga
NT2 patanga septemfasciata
NT1 phaulacridium
NT2 phaulacridium vittatum
NT1 poekilocerus
NT2 poekilocerus pictus
NT1 pyrgomorpha
NT2 pyrgomorpha conica
NT1 schistocerca
NT2 schistocerca americana
NT2 schistocerca cancellata
NT2 schistocerca gregaria
NT2 schistocerca nitens
NT1 valanga
NT2 valanga nigricornis
NT1 zonocerus
NT2 zonocerus elegans
NT2 zonocerus variegatus

ACRIDINE ORANGE
BT1 acridines
BT2 heterocyclic nitrogen compounds
BT3 organic nitrogen compounds
BT1 mutagens

ACRIDINES
BT1 heterocyclic nitrogen compounds

ACRIDINES *cont.*
BT2 organic nitrogen compounds
NT1 acridine orange
NT1 ethacridine
NT1 quinacrine mustard
rt dyes

ACRIDIOPHAGA
BT1 sarcophagidae
BT2 diptera

ACRIDOTHERES
BT1 sturnidae
BT2 passeriformes
BT3 birds
NT1 acridotheres ginginianus
NT1 acridotheres tristis

ACRIDOTHERES GINGINIANUS
BT1 acridotheres
BT2 sturnidae
BT3 passeriformes
BT4 birds

ACRIDOTHERES TRISTIS
uf *mynah, common*
BT1 acridotheres
BT2 sturnidae
BT3 passeriformes
BT4 birds

ACRIFLAVINE
BT1 antiprotozoal agents
BT2 antiparasitic agents
BT3 drugs
BT1 antiseptics
BT2 antiinfective agents
BT3 drugs

ACRILAN (AGRICOLA)
BT1 acrylics (agricola)
BT2 noncellulosic fibers (agricola)
BT3 manmade fibers (agricola)
BT4 textile fibers
BT5 fibers

ACRISOLS
BT1 soil types (genetic)
NT1 hapludults
NT1 red yellow podzolic soils
NT1 udults
NT2 paleudults
NT1 ultisols
rt red soils

ACROBASIS
BT1 pyralidae
BT2 lepidoptera
NT1 acrobasis caryae
NT1 acrobasis indigenella
NT1 acrobasis nuxvorella

ACROBASIS CARYAE
BT1 acrobasis
BT2 pyralidae
BT3 lepidoptera

ACROBASIS INDIGENELLA
BT1 acrobasis
BT2 pyralidae
BT3 lepidoptera

ACROBASIS NUXVORELLA
BT1 acrobasis
BT2 pyralidae
BT3 lepidoptera

ACROBATES
BT1 burramyidae
BT2 marsupials
BT3 mammals

ACROBELOIDES
BT1 cephalobidae
BT2 nematoda

ACROBELUS
HN from 1990
BT1 belondiridae
BT2 nematoda

ACROCARPUS
BT1 leguminosae

ACROCENTRIC CHROMOSOMES
BT1 chromosomes
BT2 nuclei
BT3 organelles
BT4 cell structure

ACROCERAS
BT1 gramineae
NT1 acroceras macrum

ACROCERAS MACRUM
BT1 acroceras
BT2 gramineae
BT1 pasture plants

ACROCERCOPS
BT1 gracillariidae
BT2 lepidoptera
NT1 acrocercops syngramma
NT1 acrocercops zygonoma
rt conopomorpha

acrocercops cramerella
USE **conopomorpha cramerella**

ACROCERCOPS SYNGRAMMA
BT1 acrocercops
BT2 gracillariidae
BT3 lepidoptera

ACROCERCOPS ZYGONOMA
BT1 acrocercops
BT2 gracillariidae
BT3 lepidoptera

ACROCOMIA
BT1 palmae
NT1 acrocomia intumescens
NT1 acrocomia lasiopatha
NT1 acrocomia sclerocarpa
NT1 acrocomia totai

ACROCOMIA INTUMESCENS
BT1 acrocomia
BT2 palmae

ACROCOMIA LASIOPATHA
BT1 acrocomia
BT2 palmae
BT1 fibre plants

ACROCOMIA SCLEROCARPA
BT1 acrocomia
BT2 palmae
BT1 fibre plants
BT1 oilseed plants
BT2 fatty oil plants
BT3 oil plants

ACROCOMIA TOTAI
BT1 acrocomia
BT2 palmae

ACROCYLINDRIUM
BT1 deuteromycotina
rt sarocladium

acrocylindrium oryzae
USE **sarocladium oryzae**

ACRODERMATITIS
BT1 dermatitis
BT2 skin diseases
BT3 organic diseases
BT4 diseases
NT1 acrodermatitis enteropathica

ACRODERMATITIS ENTEROPATHICA
BT1 acrodermatitis
BT2 dermatitis
BT3 skin diseases
BT4 organic diseases
BT5 diseases

ACROLEIN
BT1 aldehydes
BT1 unclassified herbicides
BT2 herbicides
BT3 pesticides
rt perfumery

ACROLEPIOPSIS
BT1 yponomeutidae
BT2 lepidoptera

ACROLEPIOPSIS *cont.*
NT1 acrolepiopsis assectella

ACROLEPIOPSIS ASSECTELLA
BT1 acrolepiopsis
BT2 yponomeutidae
BT3 lepidoptera

ACROMEGALY
BT1 pituitary diseases
BT2 endocrine diseases
BT3 organic diseases
BT4 diseases

ACROMYRMEX
BT1 formicidae
BT2 hymenoptera
NT1 acromyrmex octospinosus

ACROMYRMEX OCTOSPINOSUS
BT1 acromyrmex
BT2 formicidae
BT3 hymenoptera

ACRONICTA
uf *apatele*
BT1 noctuidae
BT2 lepidoptera
NT1 acronicta euphorbiae
NT1 acronicta leporina
NT1 acronicta psi
NT1 acronicta rumicis

ACRONICTA EUPHORBIAE
uf *apatele euphorbiae*
BT1 acronicta
BT2 noctuidae
BT3 lepidoptera

ACRONICTA LEPORINA
BT1 acronicta
BT2 noctuidae
BT3 lepidoptera

ACRONICTA PSI
BT1 acronicta
BT2 noctuidae
BT3 lepidoptera

ACRONICTA RUMICIS
uf *apatele rumicis*
BT1 acronicta
BT2 noctuidae
BT3 lepidoptera

ACRONYCHIA
BT1 rutaceae
NT1 acronychia baueri
NT1 acronychia pedunculata

ACRONYCHIA BAUERI
BT1 acronychia
BT2 rutaceae

ACRONYCHIA PEDUNCULATA
BT1 acronychia
BT2 rutaceae

ACROPTILON
BT1 compositae
NT1 acroptilon repens

ACROPTILON REPENS
BT1 acroptilon
BT2 compositae

ACROSIN
(ec 3.4.21.10)
BT1 proteinases
BT2 peptide hydrolases
BT3 hydrolases
BT4 enzymes
rt acrosome

ACROSOME
BT1 spermatozoa
BT2 gametes
BT2 germ cells
BT3 cells
rt acrosin
rt acrosome reaction

ACROSOME REACTION
rt acrosome

ACROSPORIUM
BT1 deuteromycotina
rt oidium

acrosporium mangiferae
USE **oidium mangiferae**

ACROSTERNUM
BT1 pentatomidae
BT2 heteroptera
NT1 acrosternum hilare

ACROSTERNUM HILARE
BT1 acrosternum
BT2 pentatomidae
BT3 heteroptera

ACRYLAMIDES
BT1 amides
BT2 organic nitrogen compounds
BT1 soil conditioners
BT2 soil amendments
BT3 amendments
rt polyacrylamide

ACRYLIC ACID
BT1 monocarboxylic acids
BT2 carboxylic acids
BT3 organic acids
BT4 acids
rt polyacrylic acid

ACRYLICS (AGRICOLA)
uf *orlon*
BT1 noncellulosic fibers (agricola)
BT2 manmade fibers (agricola)
BT3 textile fibers
BT4 fibers
NT1 acrilan (agricola)

acth
USE **corticotropin**

ACTIA
BT1 tachinidae
BT2 diptera
NT1 actia nudibasis

ACTIA NUDIBASIS
BT1 actia
BT2 tachinidae
BT3 diptera

ACTIAS
BT1 saturniidae
BT2 lepidoptera
NT1 actias selene

ACTIAS SELENE
BT1 actias
BT2 saturniidae
BT3 lepidoptera

ACTIN
BT1 contractile proteins
BT2 proteins
BT3 peptides
BT1 globulins
BT2 proteins
BT3 peptides
rt muscle fibres
rt myofibrils

actinedida
USE **prostigmata**

ACTING
BT1 drama
BT2 performing arts
BT3 arts
rt actors

ACTINIDES
BT1 transition elements
BT2 metallic elements
BT3 elements
BT3 metals
NT1 americium
NT1 curium
NT1 neptunium
NT1 plutonium
NT1 protactinium
NT1 thorium

ACTINIDES *cont.*
NT1 uranium

ACTINIDIA
BT1 actinidiaceae
NT1 actinidia arguta
NT1 actinidia chinensis
NT2 actinidia chinensis var. chinensis
NT1 actinidia deliciosa
NT1 actinidia kolomikta
NT1 actinidia polygama

ACTINIDIA ARGUTA
BT1 actinidia
BT2 actinidiaceae

ACTINIDIA CHINENSIS
(for cultivated kiwifruits use "actinidia deliciosa" or "kiwifruits")
BT1 actinidia
BT2 actinidiaceae
NT1 actinidia chinensis var. chinensis

ACTINIDIA CHINENSIS VAR. CHINENSIS
HN from 1990
BT1 actinidia chinensis
BT2 actinidia
BT3 actinidiaceae

actinidia chinensis var. deliciosa
USE **actinidia deliciosa**
OR **kiwifruits**

actinidia chinensis var. hispida
USE **actinidia deliciosa**
OR **kiwifruits**

ACTINIDIA DELICIOSA
uf *actinidia chinensis var. deliciosa*
uf *actinidia chinensis var. hispida*
uf *chinese gooseberries*
BT1 actinidia
BT2 actinidiaceae
rt kiwifruits

ACTINIDIA KOLOMIKTA
BT1 actinidia
BT2 actinidiaceae
BT1 ornamental woody plants

ACTINIDIA POLYGAMA
BT1 actinidia
BT2 actinidiaceae

ACTINIDIACEAE
NT1 actinidia
NT2 actinidia arguta
NT2 actinidia chinensis
NT3 actinidia chinensis var. chinensis
NT2 actinidia deliciosa
NT2 actinidia kolomikta
NT2 actinidia polygama

ACTINOBACILLUS
BT1 firmicutes
BT2 bacteria
BT3 prokaryotes
NT1 actinobacillus equuli
NT1 actinobacillus lignieresii
NT1 actinobacillus pleuropneumoniae

ACTINOBACILLUS EQUULI
BT1 actinobacillus
BT2 firmicutes
BT3 bacteria
BT4 prokaryotes

ACTINOBACILLUS LIGNIERESII
BT1 actinobacillus
BT2 firmicutes
BT3 bacteria
BT4 prokaryotes

ACTINOBACILLUS PLEUROPNEUMONIAE
uf *haemophilus pleuropneumoniae*
BT1 actinobacillus

ACTINOBACILLUS PLEUROPNEUMONIAE *cont.*
BT2 firmicutes
BT3 bacteria
BT4 prokaryotes

ACTINOCEPHALUS
BT1 apicomplexa
BT2 protozoa

ACTINODAPHNE
BT1 lauraceae
NT1 actinodaphne hookeri
NT1 actinodaphne maderaspatana
NT1 actinodaphne obovata

ACTINODAPHNE HOOKERI
BT1 actinodaphne
BT2 lauraceae

ACTINODAPHNE MADERASPATANA
BT1 actinodaphne
BT2 lauraceae

ACTINODAPHNE OBOVATA
BT1 actinodaphne
BT2 lauraceae

ACTINOMADURA
BT1 nocardiaceae
BT2 actinomycetales
BT3 firmicutes
BT4 bacteria
BT5 prokaryotes
NT1 actinomadura madurae
NT1 actinomadura pelletieri
rt nocardia

ACTINOMADURA MADURAE
uf *nocardia madurae*
uf *streptomyces madurae*
BT1 actinomadura
BT2 nocardiaceae
BT3 actinomycetales
BT4 firmicutes
BT5 bacteria
BT6 prokaryotes

ACTINOMADURA PELLETIERI
uf *nocardia pelletieri*
uf *streptomyces pelletieri*
BT1 actinomadura
BT2 nocardiaceae
BT3 actinomycetales
BT4 firmicutes
BT5 bacteria
BT6 prokaryotes

ACTINOMYCES
BT1 actinomycetaceae
BT2 actinomycetales
BT3 firmicutes
BT4 bacteria
BT5 prokaryotes
NT1 actinomyces bovis
NT1 actinomyces israelii
NT1 actinomyces naeslundii
NT1 actinomyces odontolyticus
NT1 actinomyces pyogenes
NT1 actinomyces viscosus
rt actinomycosis
rt antibiotics

ACTINOMYCES BOVIS
BT1 actinomyces
BT2 actinomycetaceae
BT3 actinomycetales
BT4 firmicutes
BT5 bacteria
BT6 prokaryotes

ACTINOMYCES ISRAELII
BT1 actinomyces
BT2 actinomycetaceae
BT3 actinomycetales
BT4 firmicutes
BT5 bacteria
BT6 prokaryotes

ACTINOMYCES NAESLUNDII
BT1 actinomyces
BT2 actinomycetaceae

ACTINOMYCES NAESLUNDII *cont.*
BT3 actinomycetales
BT4 firmicutes
BT5 bacteria
BT6 prokaryotes

ACTINOMYCES ODONTOLYTICUS
BT1 actinomyces
BT2 actinomycetaceae
BT3 actinomycetales
BT4 firmicutes
BT5 bacteria
BT6 prokaryotes

ACTINOMYCES PYOGENES
uf corynebacterium pyogenes
BT1 actinomyces
BT2 actinomycetaceae
BT3 actinomycetales
BT4 firmicutes
BT5 bacteria
BT6 prokaryotes

ACTINOMYCES VISCOSUS
BT1 actinomyces
BT2 actinomycetaceae
BT3 actinomycetales
BT4 firmicutes
BT5 bacteria
BT6 prokaryotes

ACTINOMYCETACEAE
BT1 actinomycetales
BT2 firmicutes
BT3 bacteria
BT4 prokaryotes
NT1 actinomyces
NT2 actinomyces bovis
NT2 actinomyces israelii
NT2 actinomyces naeslundii
NT2 actinomyces odontolyticus
NT2 actinomyces pyogenes
NT2 actinomyces viscosus
NT1 bifidobacterium
NT2 bifidobacterium adolescentis
NT2 bifidobacterium bifidum
NT2 bifidobacterium breve
NT2 bifidobacterium infantum
NT2 bifidobacterium longum
NT1 kineosporia
NT2 kineosporia aurantiaca

ACTINOMYCETALES
uf actinomycetes
BT1 firmicutes
BT2 bacteria
BT3 prokaryotes
NT1 actinomycetaceae
NT2 actinomyces
NT3 actinomyces bovis
NT3 actinomyces israelii
NT3 actinomyces naeslundii
NT3 actinomyces odontolyticus
NT3 actinomyces pyogenes
NT3 actinomyces viscosus
NT2 bifidobacterium
NT3 bifidobacterium adolescentis
NT3 bifidobacterium bifidum
NT3 bifidobacterium breve
NT3 bifidobacterium infantum
NT3 bifidobacterium longum
NT2 kineosporia
NT3 kineosporia aurantiaca
NT1 dermatophilaceae
NT2 dermatophilus
NT3 dermatophilus congolensis
NT1 faenia
NT2 faenia rectivirgula
NT1 frankiaceae
NT2 frankia
NT3 frankia ceanothi
NT1 micromonosporaceae
NT2 micropolyspora
NT2 thermoactinomyces
NT3 thermoactinomyces candida
NT3 thermoactinomyces sacchari

ACTINOMYCETALES *cont.*
NT3 thermoactinomyces vulgaris
NT2 thermopolyspora
NT1 nocardiaceae
NT2 actinomadura
NT3 actinomadura madurae
NT3 actinomadura pelletieri
NT2 nocardia
NT3 nocardia asteroides
NT3 nocardia brasiliensis
NT3 nocardia caviae
NT3 nocardia farcinica
NT2 nocardiopsis
NT2 rhodococcus (bacteria)
NT3 rhodococcus equi
NT3 rhodococcus fascians
NT1 renibacterium
NT2 renibacterium salmoninarum
NT1 streptomycetaceae
NT2 streptomyces
NT3 streptomyces albus
NT3 streptomyces collinus
NT3 streptomyces galbus
NT3 streptomyces griseus
NT3 streptomyces ipomoea
NT3 streptomyces olivocinereus
NT3 streptomyces scabies
NT3 streptomyces somaliensis
NT3 streptomyces viridosporus
rt thermophilic actinomycetes

actinomycetes
USE **actinomycetales**

actinomycin d
USE **dactinomycin**

ACTINOMYCOSIS
BT1 bacterial diseases
BT2 infectious diseases
BT3 diseases
NT1 cervicofacial actinomycosis
rt actinomyces

ACTINOPLANACEAE
NT1 actinoplanes
NT2 actinoplanes tsinanensis
NT1 ampullariella

ACTINOPLANES
BT1 actinoplanaceae
NT1 actinoplanes tsinanensis

ACTINOPLANES TSINANENSIS
BT1 actinoplanes
BT2 actinoplanaceae

ACTION RESEARCH
BT1 research

ACTIVATED CARBON
BT1 adsorbents
BT1 soil amendments
BT2 amendments
rt carbon
rt charcoal
rt filters

ACTIVATED SLUDGE
BT1 sewage sludge
BT2 growing media
BT2 sewage
BT3 wastes
BT2 sludges

activation, complement
USE **complement activation**

activation, lymphocyte
USE **lymphocyte transformation**

active immunity
USE **immunity**

active immunization
USE **immunization**

ACTIVE RECREATION
uf physical recreation
BT1 recreation

ACTIVE RECREATION *cont.*
NT1 climbing

ACTIVE TRANSPORT
BT1 transport processes
rt ion transport
rt transport

activities, cultural
USE **cultural activities**

ACTIVITY
NT1 catalytic activity
rt activity ratios
rt activity sampling
rt diurnal activity
rt nocturnal activity
rt physical activity

ACTIVITY BOOKS (AGRICOLA)
BT1 books
BT2 publications
rt children's literature (agricola)

ACTIVITY HOLIDAYS
BT1 holidays
BT2 tourism

ACTIVITY RATIOS
BT1 indexes of nutrient availability
BT2 indexes
BT1 ratios
rt activity
rt soil fertility

ACTIVITY SAMPLING
uf sampling, activity
BT1 sampling
BT2 techniques
BT1 work study
rt activity

ACTORS
rt acting

ACTUATORS
BT1 controllers
rt servomotors
rt transducers

ACUARIA
BT1 acuariidae
BT2 nematoda
NT1 acuaria anthuris

ACUARIA ANTHURIS
BT1 acuaria
BT2 acuariidae
BT3 nematoda

ACUARIIDAE
BT1 nematoda
NT1 acuaria
NT2 acuaria anthuris
NT1 echinuria
NT2 echinuria uncinata
NT1 streptocara
NT2 streptocara crassicauda
NT1 synhimantus
NT2 synhimantus nasuta
rt animal parasitic nematodes

ACULOPS
BT1 eriophyidae
BT2 prostigmata
BT3 acari
NT1 aculops lycopersici
NT1 aculops pelekassi
rt aculus
rt vasates

ACULOPS LYCOPERSICI
uf vasates destructor
BT1 aculops
BT2 eriophyidae
BT3 prostigmata
BT4 acari

ACULOPS PELEKASSI
uf aculus pelekassi
BT1 aculops
BT2 eriophyidae
BT3 prostigmata

ACULOPS PELEKASSI *cont.*
BT4 acari

ACULUS
BT1 eriophyidae
BT2 prostigmata
BT3 acari
NT1 aculus fockeui
NT1 aculus schlechtendali
rt aculops
rt vasates

aculus cornutus
USE **aculus fockeui**

ACULUS FOCKEUI
uf aculus cornutus
uf vasates cornutus
BT1 aculus
BT2 eriophyidae
BT3 prostigmata
BT4 acari

aculus pelekassi
USE **aculops pelekassi**

ACULUS SCHLECHTENDALI
BT1 aculus
BT2 eriophyidae
BT3 prostigmata
BT4 acari

ACUPUNCTURE
rt anaesthesia
rt therapy

ACUTE COURSE
HN from 1990
BT1 disease course

ACYL-COA DEHYDROGENASE
(ec 1.3.99.3)
BT1 oxidoreductases
BT2 enzymes

ACYL-COA DESATURASE
(ec 1.14.99.5)
uf fatty acid desaturase
uf stearyl-coa desaturase
BT1 oxygenases
BT2 oxidoreductases
BT3 enzymes

acyl-coa synthetase
USE **long-chain-fatty-acid-coa ligase**

acylalanine fungicides
USE **xylylalanine fungicides**

ACYLGLYCEROLS
uf glycerides
uf glycerol esters
BT1 fatty acid esters
BT2 esters
BT1 neutral fats
BT2 fats
BT3 lipids
NT1 diacylglycerols
NT1 monoacylglycerols
NT2 monoolein
NT1 olein
NT1 stearin
NT1 sucroglycerides
NT1 triacylglycerols
NT2 long chain triacylglycerols
NT3 triolein
NT2 medium chain triacylglycerols
NT3 trilaurin
NT3 trioctanoin
NT2 short chain triacylglycerols
NT3 triacetin
NT3 tributyrin

ACYLTRANSFERASES
(ec 2.3.1)
BT1 transferases
BT2 enzymes
NT1 5-aminolevulinate synthase
NT1 acetyl-coa acetyltransferase
NT1 aminoacyltransferases
NT2 d-glutamyltransferase
NT2 γ-glutamylcyclotransferase

ACYLTRANSFERASES *cont.*
NT2 γ-glutamyltransferase
NT2 peptidyltransferase
NT1 carnitine acetyltransferase
NT1 carnitine palmitoyltransferase
NT1 chloramphenicol acetyltransferase
NT1 cholesterol acyltransferase
NT1 choline acetyltransferase
NT1 fatty-acid synthase
NT1 glycerol-3-phosphate acyltransferase
NT1 naringenin-chalcone synthase
NT1 phosphatidylcholine-sterol acyltransferase

ACYRTHOSIPHON
BT1 aphididae
BT2 aphidoidea
BT3 sternorrhyncha
BT4 homoptera
NT1 acyrthosiphon assiniboinensis
NT1 acyrthosiphon caraganae
NT1 acyrthosiphon gossypii
NT1 acyrthosiphon kondoi
NT1 acyrthosiphon pisum
rt aulacorthum
rt macrosiphum
rt metopolophium
rt rhodobium

ACYRTHOSIPHON ASSINIBOINENSIS
BT1 acyrthosiphon
BT2 aphididae
BT3 aphidoidea
BT4 sternorrhyncha
BT5 homoptera

ACYRTHOSIPHON CARAGANAE
BT1 acyrthosiphon
BT2 aphididae
BT3 aphidoidea
BT4 sternorrhyncha
BT5 homoptera

acyrthosiphon dirhodum
USE **metopolophium dirhodum**

acyrthosiphon festucae
USE **metopolophium festucae**

ACYRTHOSIPHON GOSSYPII
uf *acyrthosiphon sesbaniae*
BT1 acyrthosiphon
BT2 aphididae
BT3 aphidoidea
BT4 sternorrhyncha
BT5 homoptera

ACYRTHOSIPHON KONDOI
BT1 acyrthosiphon
BT2 aphididae
BT3 aphidoidea
BT4 sternorrhyncha
BT5 homoptera

acyrthosiphon onobrychis
USE **acyrthosiphon pisum**

ACYRTHOSIPHON PISUM
uf *acyrthosiphon onobrychis*
uf *macrosiphum pisum*
BT1 acyrthosiphon
BT2 aphididae
BT3 aphidoidea
BT4 sternorrhyncha
BT5 homoptera

acyrthosiphon porosum
USE **rhodobium porosum**

acyrthosiphon sesbaniae
USE **acyrthosiphon gossypii**

acyrthosiphon solani
USE **aulacorthum solani**

ad libitum feeding
USE **unrestricted feeding**

ADALIA
BT1 coccinellidae
BT2 coleoptera
NT1 adalia bipunctata
NT1 adalia decempunctata
rt coccinella
rt lioadalia

ADALIA BIPUNCTATA
uf *coccinella bipunctata*
BT1 adalia
BT2 coccinellidae
BT3 coleoptera

ADALIA DECEMPUNCTATA
uf *coccinella decempunctata*
BT1 adalia
BT2 coccinellidae
BT3 coleoptera

adalia flavomaculata
USE **lioadalia flavomaculata**

ADAMAWA
HN from 1990
BT1 cattle breeds
BT2 breeds

ADANSONIA
BT1 bombacaceae
NT1 adansonia digitata

ADANSONIA DIGITATA
BT1 adansonia
BT2 bombacaceae
BT1 antibacterial plants
BT1 forest trees
BT1 medicinal plants

ADAPTABILITY
rt acclimatization
rt adaptation
rt modification
rt stability

ADAPTATION
NT1 dark adaptation
NT1 heat adaptation
NT1 modulation
rt abnormal development
rt acclimatization
rt adaptability
rt adjustment
rt aestivation
rt altitude
rt climate
rt climatic factors
rt environmental factors
rt evolution
rt modification
rt mutations
rt temperature resistance
rt thermoregulation

ADDICTION
BT1 delinquent behaviour
BT2 social behaviour
BT3 behaviour
NT1 drug addiction
rt alcoholism
rt gambling

ADDING
BT1 manipulations
BT2 beekeeping

ADDITION LINES
BT1 lines
rt chromosome addition
rt substitution lines

ADDITIVES
uf *adjuncts*
NT1 adjuvants
NT1 ammonia additives
NT1 antioxidants
NT2 α-tocopherol
NT2 ascorbic acid
NT2 benomyl
NT2 butylated hydroxyanisole
NT2 butylated hydroxytoluene
NT2 citric acid
NT2 diludin
NT2 ethoxyquin

ADDITIVES *cont.*
NT2 ethylene diurea
NT2 fumaric acid
NT2 hydroquinone
NT2 isoascorbic acid
NT2 nordihydroguaiaretic acid
NT2 propyl gallate
NT2 sodium metabisulfite
NT1 feed additives
NT2 bambermycin
NT2 biuret
NT2 diammonium phosphate
NT2 ethoxyquin
NT2 methionine hydroxy analogue
NT2 monensin
NT2 probiotics
NT2 thiopeptin
NT2 tiamulin
NT1 food additives
NT2 acidulants
NT3 citric acid
NT3 fumaric acid
NT3 gluconolactone
NT3 tartaric acid
NT2 bulking agents
NT3 methylcellulose
NT2 dextran
NT2 enzyme preparations
NT2 flavour enhancers
NT3 monosodium glutamate
NT2 flavourings
NT3 caramel
NT2 food colourants
NT3 p-dimethylaminoazobenzene
NT3 annatto
NT3 canthaxanthin
NT3 caramel
NT3 erythrosine
NT3 tartrazine
NT2 leavening agents (agricola)
NT2 modified starches
NT2 sweeteners
NT3 sugar substitutes
NT4 artificial sweeteners
NT5 aspartame
NT5 saccharin
NT5 sodium cyclamate
NT4 high fructose corn syrup
NT2 tenderizers (agricola)
NT2 thickeners
NT1 semen diluent additives
NT1 silage additives
NT2 acetic acid
NT2 butyric acid
NT2 formaldehyde
NT2 formic acid
NT2 hydrochloric acid
NT2 lactic acid
NT2 natamycin
NT2 propionic acid
NT1 wetters
rt binding
rt protectants
rt soil amendments
rt supplements
rt whiteners (agricola)

ADELEA
BT1 apicomplexa
BT2 protozoa

ADELGES
uf *chermes*
BT1 adelgidae
BT2 aphidoidea
BT3 sternorrhyncha
BT4 homoptera
NT1 adelges laricis
NT1 adelges tardus
rt cholodkovskya
rt dreyfusia
rt gilletteella
rt sacchiphantes

adelges abietis
USE **sacchiphantes abietis**

adelges cooleyi
USE **gilletteella cooleyi**

ADELGES LARICIS
BT1 adelges
BT2 adelgidae
BT3 aphidoidea
BT4 sternorrhyncha
BT5 homoptera

adelges nordmannianae
USE **dreyfusia nordmannianae**

adelges piceae
USE **dreyfusia piceae**

ADELGES TARDUS
BT1 adelges
BT2 adelgidae
BT3 aphidoidea
BT4 sternorrhyncha
BT5 homoptera

adelges viridanus
USE **cholodkovskya viridana**

adelges viridis
USE **sacchiphantes viridis**

ADELGIDAE
BT1 aphidoidea
BT2 sternorrhyncha
BT3 homoptera
NT1 adelges
NT2 adelges laricis
NT2 adelges tardus
NT1 cholodkovskya
NT2 cholodkovskya viridana
NT1 dreyfusia
NT2 dreyfusia nordmannianae
NT2 dreyfusia piceae
NT1 gilletteella
NT2 gilletteella cooleyi
NT1 pineus
NT2 pineus pini
NT1 sacchiphantes
NT2 sacchiphantes abietis
NT2 sacchiphantes viridis

ADELINA
BT1 apicomplexa
BT2 protozoa
NT1 adelina mesnili
NT1 adelina tribolii

ADELINA MESNILI
BT1 adelina
BT2 apicomplexa
BT3 protozoa

ADELINA TRIBOLII
BT1 adelina
BT2 apicomplexa
BT3 protozoa
BT1 entomopathogenic protozoa
BT2 entomopathogens
BT3 pathogens

ADELOCERA
BT1 elateridae
BT2 coleoptera
NT1 adelocera subcostata

ADELOCERA SUBCOSTATA
BT1 adelocera
BT2 elateridae
BT3 coleoptera

ADELPHOCORIS
BT1 miridae
BT2 heteroptera
NT1 adelphocoris lineolatus

ADELPHOCORIS LINEOLATUS
BT1 adelphocoris
BT2 miridae
BT3 heteroptera

aden
USE **yemen democratic republic**

ADENANTHERA
BT1 leguminosae
NT1 adenanthera pavonina

ADENANTHERA PAVONINA
BT1 adenanthera

ADENANTHERA PAVONINA *cont.*
BT2 leguminosae
BT1 dye plants
BT1 forest trees
BT1 ornamental woody plants

ADENANTHOS
BT1 proteaceae
rt ornamental plants

ADENIA
BT1 passifloraceae
NT1 adenia digitata

ADENIA DIGITATA
BT1 adenia
BT2 passifloraceae
BT1 medicinal plants

ADENINE
BT1 adenines
BT2 purines
BT3 heterocyclic nitrogen compounds
BT4 organic nitrogen compounds

ADENINE PHOSPHORIBOSYLTRANSFERASE
(ec 2.4.2.7)
BT1 pentosyltransferases
BT2 glycosyltransferases
BT3 transferases
BT4 enzymes

ADENINES
BT1 purines
BT2 heterocyclic nitrogen compounds
BT3 organic nitrogen compounds
NT1 adenine
NT1 benzyladenine
NT1 isopentenyladenine
NT1 kinetin
NT1 zeatin

ADENIUM
BT1 apocynaceae
NT1 adenium obesum
NT1 adenium swazicum

ADENIUM OBESUM
BT1 adenium
BT2 apocynaceae
BT1 ornamental succulent plants
BT2 succulent plants
BT1 poisonous plants

ADENIUM SWAZICUM
BT1 adenium
BT2 apocynaceae
BT1 ornamental succulent plants
BT2 succulent plants

ADENO-ASSOCIATED VIRUS
BT1 parvoviridae
BT2 viruses
NT1 avian adeno-associated virus

ADENOCALYMMA
BT1 bignoniaceae

adenocalymma alliaceae
USE **pseudocalymma alliaceum**

ADENOCAULON
BT1 compositae
NT1 adenocaulon himalaicum

ADENOCAULON HIMALAICUM
BT1 adenocaulon
BT2 compositae

adenohypophysis
USE **anterior pituitary**

ADENOHYPOPHYSIS HORMONES
BT1 pituitary hormones
BT2 hormones
rt anterior pituitary

ADENOMA
BT1 neoplasms

ADENOMA *cont.*
BT2 diseases
rt pulmonary adenomatosis

ADENOPHORA
BT1 campanulaceae
NT1 adenophora latifolia
NT1 adenophora tetraphylla

ADENOPHORA LATIFOLIA
BT1 adenophora
BT2 campanulaceae

ADENOPHORA TETRAPHYLLA
BT1 adenophora
BT2 campanulaceae

ADENOSINE
BT1 ribonucleosides
BT2 nucleosides
BT3 glycosides
BT4 carbohydrates
rt adenosine deaminase
rt adenosine phosphates

ADENOSINE DEAMINASE
(ec 3.5.4.4)
BT1 amidine hydrolases
BT2 hydrolases
BT3 enzymes
rt adenosine
rt nucleosides

adenosine diphosphate
USE **adp**

adenosine monophosphate
USE **amp**

adenosine monophosphate, cyclic
USE **c-amp**

ADENOSINE PHOSPHATES
BT1 phosphates (esters)
BT2 esters
BT2 phosphates
BT1 purine nucleotides
BT2 nucleotides
BT3 glycosides
BT4 carbohydrates
NT1 adp
NT1 amp
NT1 atp
NT1 c-amp
rt adenosine

adenosine triphosphate
USE **atp**

ADENOSINE TRIPHOSPHATE CYCLE
BT1 biochemical pathways
rt atp

ADENOSINETRIPHOSPHATASE
(ec 3.6.1.3)
uf *atpase*
BT1 acid anhydride hydrolases
BT2 hydrolases
BT3 enzymes
rt atp

ADENOSTEMMA
BT1 compositae
NT1 adenostemma lavenia

ADENOSTEMMA LAVENIA
BT1 adenostemma
BT2 compositae

ADENOSTOMA
BT1 rosaceae
NT1 adenostoma fasciculatum
NT1 adenostoma sparsifolium

ADENOSTOMA FASCICULATUM
BT1 adenostoma
BT2 rosaceae

ADENOSTOMA SPARSIFOLIUM
BT1 adenostoma
BT2 rosaceae

ADENOSYLHOMOCYSTEINE
BT1 amino acid derivatives
BT2 amino compounds

ADENOSYLHOMOCYSTEINE *cont.*
BT3 organic nitrogen compounds
BT1 ribonucleosides
BT2 nucleosides
BT3 glycosides
BT4 carbohydrates
rt homocysteine

ADENOSYLMETHIONINE
BT1 amino acid derivatives
BT2 amino compounds
BT3 organic nitrogen compounds
BT1 ribonucleosides
BT2 nucleosides
BT3 glycosides
BT4 carbohydrates
rt methionine

ADENOSYLMETHIONINE DECARBOXYLASE
(ec 4.1.1.50)
BT1 carboxy-lyases
BT2 lyases
BT3 enzymes

ADENOVIRIDAE
BT1 viruses
NT1 aviadenovirus
NT2 haemorrhagic enteritis virus
NT1 mastadenovirus
NT2 bovine adenovirus
NT2 canine adenovirus
NT3 canine hepatitis virus
NT2 equine adenovirus
NT2 ovine adenovirus
NT2 porcine adenovirus
rt oncogenic viruses

ADENYLATE CYCLASE
(ec 4.6.1.1)
BT1 phosphorus-oxygen lyases
BT2 lyases
BT3 enzymes

ADENYLATE KINASE
(ec 2.7.4.3)
BT1 kinases
BT2 transferases
BT3 enzymes

ADHATODA
BT1 acanthaceae
NT1 adhatoda vasica

ADHATODA VASICA
BT1 adhatoda
BT2 acanthaceae
BT1 medicinal plants
BT1 nematicidal plants
BT2 pesticidal plants

ADHESION
BT1 mechanical properties
BT2 properties
rt adhesives
rt bond strength
rt cohesion
rt friction
rt slip
rt stickiness

ADHESIONS
rt postoperative complications

ADHESIVES
uf *glues*
NT1 sucrose octaacetate
rt adhesion
rt gluing
rt gums
rt mucilages
rt resins

ADIANTACEAE
NT1 adiantum
NT2 adiantum capillus-veneris
NT2 adiantum hispidulum
NT2 adiantum monochlamys
NT2 adiantum pedatum
NT2 adiantum raddianum
NT2 adiantum scutum

ADIANTACEAE *cont.*
NT2 adiantum tenerum
NT2 adiantum tracyi

ADIANTUM
BT1 adiantaceae
NT1 adiantum capillus-veneris
NT1 adiantum hispidulum
NT1 adiantum monochlamys
NT1 adiantum pedatum
NT1 adiantum raddianum
NT1 adiantum scutum
NT1 adiantum tenerum
NT1 adiantum tracyi

ADIANTUM CAPILLUS-VENERIS
BT1 adiantum
BT2 adiantaceae
BT1 ornamental ferns
BT2 ferns
BT2 ornamental foliage plants
BT3 foliage plants

adiantum cuneatum
USE **adiantum raddianum**

ADIANTUM HISPIDULUM
uf *adiantum pubescens*
BT1 adiantum
BT2 adiantaceae
BT1 ornamental ferns
BT2 ferns
BT2 ornamental foliage plants
BT3 foliage plants

ADIANTUM MONOCHLAMYS
BT1 adiantum
BT2 adiantaceae

ADIANTUM PEDATUM
BT1 adiantum
BT2 adiantaceae
BT1 ornamental ferns
BT2 ferns
BT2 ornamental foliage plants
BT3 foliage plants

adiantum pubescens
USE **adiantum hispidulum**

ADIANTUM RADDIANUM
uf *adiantum cuneatum*
BT1 adiantum
BT2 adiantaceae

ADIANTUM SCUTUM
BT1 adiantum
BT2 adiantaceae

ADIANTUM TENERUM
BT1 adiantum
BT2 adiantaceae
BT1 ornamental ferns
BT2 ferns
BT2 ornamental foliage plants
BT3 foliage plants

ADIANTUM TRACYI
BT1 adiantum
BT2 adiantaceae

ADIASPIROMYCOSIS
BT1 mycoses
BT2 infectious diseases
BT3 diseases
rt emmonsia

ADINA
BT1 rubiaceae
NT1 adina cordifolia

ADINA CORDIFOLIA
BT1 adina
BT2 rubiaceae

ADIPIC ACID
BT1 dicarboxylic acids
BT2 carboxylic acids
BT3 organic acids
BT4 acids

ADIPOCYTES
uf *fat cells*
BT1 cells
rt adipose tissue

ADIPOCYTES *cont.*
rt body fat
rt fat cell theory (agricola)

ADIPOKINETIC HORMONES
BT1 arthropod hormones
BT2 hormones
rt lipotropin

ADIPOSE TISSUE
BT1 animal tissues
BT2 tissues
rt adipocytes
rt body fat
rt obesity
rt subcutaneous fat

adipose tissue, brown
USE **brown fat**

ADISURA
BT1 noctuidae
BT2 lepidoptera
NT1 adisura atkinsoni

ADISURA ATKINSONI
BT1 adisura
BT2 noctuidae
BT3 lepidoptera

adjuncts
USE **additives**

ADJUSTABLE LIFE INSURANCE (AGRICOLA)
BT1 life insurance
BT2 insurance

ADJUSTMENT
NT1 modulation
rt adaptation
rt modulation
rt regulation

ADJUSTMENT OF PRODUCTION
BT1 production policy
BT2 economic policy
NT1 agricultural adjustment
rt agricultural structure
rt production structure
rt setting up grants
rt structural policy

ADJUVANTS
BT1 additives
rt immunostimulants
rt nonspecific immunostimulation
rt pesticides
rt spraying

adlay
USE **coix lacryma-jobi**

ADMINISTRATION
uf *public administration*
NT1 forest administration
NT1 local government
rt administrative areas
rt government
rt institution building
rt management
rt planning
rt policy
rt public authorities

ADMINISTRATIVE AREAS
BT1 areas
NT1 local authority areas
rt administration
rt regions

adolescence
USE **adolescents**

ADOLESCENT DEVELOPMENT (AGRICOLA)
rt adolescents
rt development

ADOLESCENTS
uf *adolescence*
uf *teenagers*
BT1 age groups
BT2 groups

ADOLESCENTS *cont.*
BT1 people
NT1 pregnant adolescents (agricola)
rt adolescent development (agricola)
rt adults
rt children
rt school children
rt young adults (agricola)

adonia
USE **hippodamia**

adonia undecimnotata
USE **hippodamia oculata**

adonia variegata
USE **hippodamia variegata**

ADONIS
BT1 ranunculaceae
NT1 adonis aestivalis
NT1 adonis amurensis
NT1 adonis annua
NT1 adonis apennina
NT1 adonis chrysocyatha
NT1 adonis leiosepala
NT1 adonis mongolica
NT1 adonis tianschanica
NT1 adonis turkestanica
NT1 adonis vernalis
NT1 adonis wolgensis

ADONIS AESTIVALIS
BT1 adonis
BT2 ranunculaceae
BT1 medicinal plants
BT1 ornamental herbaceous plants

ADONIS AMURENSIS
BT1 adonis
BT2 ranunculaceae
BT1 ornamental herbaceous plants

ADONIS ANNUA
uf *adonis autumnalis*
BT1 adonis
BT2 ranunculaceae

ADONIS APENNINA
uf *adonis sibirica*
BT1 adonis
BT2 ranunculaceae

adonis autumnalis
USE **adonis annua**

ADONIS CHRYSOCYATHA
BT1 adonis
BT2 ranunculaceae

ADONIS LEIOSEPALA
BT1 adonis
BT2 ranunculaceae

ADONIS MONGOLICA
BT1 adonis
BT2 ranunculaceae

adonis sibirica
USE **adonis apennina**

ADONIS TIANSCHANICA
BT1 adonis
BT2 ranunculaceae

ADONIS TURKESTANICA
BT1 adonis
BT2 ranunculaceae

ADONIS VERNALIS
BT1 adonis
BT2 ranunculaceae
BT1 ornamental herbaceous plants

ADONIS WOLGENSIS
BT1 adonis
BT2 ranunculaceae

ADOPTED CHILDREN (AGRICOLA)
BT1 children
BT2 people

ADOPTED CHILDREN (AGRICOLA) *cont.*
rt adoption (agricola)
rt foster children (agricola)

ADOPTION (AGRICOLA)
rt adopted children (agricola)

adoption of innovations
USE **innovation adoption**

ADOPTIVE IMMUNITY
HN from 1990
BT1 passive immunity
BT2 immunity

ADOPTIVE IMMUNOTOLERANCE
HN from 1990
uf *immunotolerance, adoptive*
BT1 acquired immunotolerance
BT2 specific immunosuppression
BT3 immunosuppression
BT4 immunotherapy
BT5 therapy

ADORETUS
BT1 scarabaeidae
BT2 coleoptera

ADOXA
BT1 adoxaceae
NT1 adoxa moschatellina

ADOXA MOSCHATELLINA
BT1 adoxa
BT2 adoxaceae
BT1 medicinal plants

ADOXACEAE
NT1 adoxa
NT2 adoxa moschatellina

ADOXOPHYES
BT1 tortricidae
BT2 lepidoptera
NT1 adoxophyes orana

ADOXOPHYES ORANA
uf *adoxophyes reticulana*
BT1 adoxophyes
BT2 tortricidae
BT3 lepidoptera

adoxophyes reticulana
USE **adoxophyes orana**

ADP
uf *adenosine diphosphate*
BT1 adenosine phosphates
BT2 phosphates (esters)
BT3 esters
BT3 phosphates
BT2 purine nucleotides
BT3 nucleotides
BT4 glycosides
BT5 carbohydrates

ADRENAL CORTEX
BT1 adrenal glands
BT2 endocrine glands
BT3 glands (animal)
BT4 body parts
BT4 glands

ADRENAL CORTEX HORMONES
BT1 corticoids
BT1 hormones
NT1 glucocorticoids
NT2 corticosterone
NT2 cortisone
NT2 hydrocortisone
NT1 mineralocorticoids
NT2 aldosterone
NT2 corticosterone
NT2 cortisone
NT2 desoxycortone
NT2 hydrocortisone
rt adrenal glands
rt pituitary hormones
rt steroid hormones

adrenal diseases
USE **adrenal gland diseases**

ADRENAL GLAND DISEASES
uf *adrenal diseases*
BT1 endocrine diseases
BT2 organic diseases
BT3 diseases
NT1 cushing's syndrome
rt adrenal glands

ADRENAL GLANDS
uf *adrenals*
BT1 endocrine glands
BT2 glands (animal)
BT3 body parts
BT3 glands
NT1 adrenal cortex
NT1 adrenal medulla
rt adrenal cortex hormones
rt adrenal gland diseases
rt adrenal medulla hormones
rt adrenalectomy

ADRENAL MEDULLA
BT1 adrenal glands
BT2 endocrine glands
BT3 glands (animal)
BT4 body parts
BT4 glands

ADRENAL MEDULLA HORMONES
BT1 hormones
NT1 epinephrine
NT1 norepinephrine
rt adrenal glands

ADRENALECTOMY
BT1 surgical operations
rt adrenal glands

adrenaline
USE **epinephrine**

adrenals
USE **adrenal glands**

β-ADRENERGIC AGONISTS
HN from 1989
(for retrieval spell out "beta")
BT1 agonists

adrenergic beta receptor blockaders
USE **β-blockers**

ADRENERGIC INNERVATION
HN from 1990
BT1 innervation
BT2 neurons
BT3 nerve tissue
BT4 animal tissues
BT5 tissues

ADRENERGIC RECEPTORS
BT1 receptors
NT1 α-adrenergic receptors
NT1 β-adrenergic receptors

α-ADRENERGIC RECEPTORS
(for retrieval spell out "alpha")
BT1 adrenergic receptors
BT2 receptors

β-ADRENERGIC RECEPTORS
(for retrieval spell out "beta")
BT1 adrenergic receptors
BT2 receptors
rt β-blockers

adrenocorticotropic hormone
USE **corticotropin**

adrenocorticotropin
USE **corticotropin**

adriamycin
USE **doxorubicin**

ADRIATIC SEA
BT1 mediterranean sea
BT2 atlantic ocean
BT3 marine areas

ADRIS
BT1 noctuidae
BT2 lepidoptera
NT1 adris tyrannus

ADRIS TYRANNUS
BT1 adris
BT2 noctuidae
BT3 lepidoptera

ADSORBENTS
NT1 activated carbon
NT1 aluminium hydroxide
NT1 bone char
NT1 charcoal
NT1 lactose
NT1 montmorillonite
NT1 mucins
rt absorbents
rt adsorption

ADSORPTION
BT1 sorption
rt absorption
rt adsorbents
rt desorption
rt haemadsorption reaction
rt phosphatation
rt resorption

ADULT DAY CARE (AGRICOLA)
HN from 1989
BT1 day care (agricola)
rt adults

ADULT DEVELOPMENT (AGRICOLA)
rt adult education
rt adults
rt development
rt midlife transitions (agricola)

ADULT EDUCATION
uf *education, adult*
BT1 education
NT1 continuing education
NT2 professional continuing education (agricola)
NT1 non-formal education
NT1 parent education (agricola)
NT1 practical education
rt adult development (agricola)
rt adult learning (agricola)
rt adults
rt extension education (agricola)
rt lifelong learning (agricola)
rt postsecondary education (agricola)
rt professional education (agricola)

ADULT LEARNING (AGRICOLA)
BT1 learning
rt adult education
rt adults

ADULTERANTS
NT1 herbicide impurities
rt adulteration
rt contaminants
rt foreign bodies

ADULTERATION
rt adulterants
rt contamination
rt herbicide impurities

ADULTS
NT1 men
NT1 middle-aged adults (agricola)
NT1 women
NT2 employed women (agricola)
NT2 housewives
NT2 lactating women (agricola)
NT2 rural women
NT2 widows
NT1 young adults (agricola)
rt adolescents
rt adult day care (agricola)
rt adult development (agricola)
rt adult education
rt adult learning (agricola)
rt age groups

ADVANCE GROWTH
BT1 growth

ADVANCE GROWTH *cont.*
rt natural regeneration
rt regeneration
rt regeneration surveys
rt volunteer plants

ADVANCING CIRCUIT
HN from 1990
rt monitoring
rt sugar boiling
rt supersaturation

ADVENTITIOUS ROOTS
BT1 roots
BT2 plant

ADVERSE EFFECTS
uf *adverse reactions*
uf *side effects*
BT1 damage
BT1 effects
rt iatrogenic diseases
rt nontarget effects
rt toxicity

adverse reactions
USE **adverse effects**

ADVERTISING
BT1 marketing techniques
BT2 techniques
NT1 food advertising (agricola)
NT1 television commercials (agricola)
rt publicity
rt sales promotion

ADVISORY CENTERS
BF advisory centres

ADVISORY CENTRES
AF advisory centers
BT1 information centres
BT2 information services
BT3 services
NT1 demonstration farms
rt advisory officers
rt educational institutions
rt extension
rt professional services

ADVISORY COMMITTEES (AGRICOLA)
BT1 committees (agricola)
rt consultants

ADVISORY OFFICERS
BT1 occupations
NT1 socioeconomic advisers
rt advisory centres
rt extension
rt professional services

advisory services
USE **extension**

adzuki beans
USE **vigna angularis**

AECHMEA
BT1 bromeliaceae
NT1 aechmea arenosa
NT1 aechmea bracteata
NT1 aechmea fasciata
NT1 aechmea magdalenae

AECHMEA ARENOSA
BT1 aechmea
BT2 bromeliaceae
BT1 ornamental bromeliads

AECHMEA BRACTEATA
BT1 aechmea
BT2 bromeliaceae
BT1 ornamental bromeliads

AECHMEA FASCIATA
BT1 aechmea
BT2 bromeliaceae
BT1 ornamental bromeliads

AECHMEA MAGDALENAE
BT1 aechmea
BT2 bromeliaceae

AECIOSPORES
BT1 fungal spores
BT2 spores
BT3 cells
rt uredinales

AEDEOMYIA
BT1 culicidae
BT2 diptera
NT1 aedeomyia squamipennis

AEDEOMYIA SQUAMIPENNIS
HN from 1989
BT1 aedeomyia
BT2 culicidae
BT3 diptera

AEDES
BT1 culicidae
BT2 diptera
NT1 aedes abserratus
NT1 aedes aegypti
NT1 aedes africanus
NT1 aedes albifasciatus
NT1 aedes albopictus
NT1 aedes alcasidi
NT1 aedes ambreensis
NT1 aedes angustivittatus
NT1 aedes annulipes
NT1 aedes apicoargenteus
NT1 aedes atlanticus
NT1 aedes atropalpus
NT1 aedes campestris
NT1 aedes canadensis
NT1 aedes cantans
NT1 aedes cantator
NT1 aedes caspius
NT1 aedes cataphylla
NT1 aedes cinereus
NT1 aedes circumluteolus
NT1 aedes communis
NT1 aedes cooki
NT1 aedes cumminsii
NT1 aedes cyprius
NT1 aedes dentatus
NT1 aedes detritus
NT1 aedes diantaeus
NT1 aedes dorsalis
NT1 aedes durbanensis
NT1 aedes echinus
NT1 aedes epactius
NT1 aedes esoensis
NT1 aedes euedes
NT1 aedes excrucians
NT1 aedes fitchii
NT1 aedes flavescens
NT1 aedes flavopictus
NT1 aedes fluviatilis
NT1 aedes fryeri
NT1 aedes fulvus
NT1 aedes furcifer
NT1 aedes galloisi
NT1 aedes geniculatus
NT1 aedes guamensis
NT1 aedes hebrideus
NT1 aedes hendersoni
NT1 aedes hexodontus
NT1 aedes impiger
NT1 aedes implicatus
NT1 aedes increpitus
NT1 aedes infirmatus
NT1 aedes ingrami
NT1 aedes intrudens
NT1 aedes japonicus
NT1 aedes juppi
NT1 aedes kochi
NT1 aedes koreicoides
NT1 aedes koreicus
NT1 aedes leucomelas
NT1 aedes lineatopennis
NT1 aedes luridus
NT1 aedes luteocephalus
NT1 aedes mariae
NT1 aedes mascarensis
NT1 aedes mediovittatus
NT1 aedes melanimon
NT1 aedes metallicus
NT1 aedes montchadskyi
NT1 aedes monticola
NT1 aedes nevadensis
NT1 aedes nigripes
NT1 aedes nigromaculis

AEDES *cont.*
NT1 aedes nipponicus
NT1 aedes notoscriptus
NT1 aedes novalbopictus
NT1 aedes opok
NT1 aedes pembaensis
NT1 aedes phoeniciae
NT1 aedes pionips
NT1 aedes poicilia
NT1 aedes polynesiensis
NT1 aedes pseudalbopictus
NT1 aedes pseudoscutellaris
NT1 aedes pulchritarsis
NT1 aedes pullatus
NT1 aedes punctodes
NT1 aedes punctor
NT1 aedes refiki
NT1 aedes riparius
NT1 aedes rusticus
NT1 aedes samoanus
NT1 aedes scapularis
NT1 aedes scutellaris
NT2 aedes scutellaris katherinensis
NT2 aedes scutellaris malayensis
NT1 aedes seatoi
NT1 aedes serratus
NT1 aedes sierrensis
NT1 aedes simpsoni
NT1 aedes sollicitans
NT1 aedes spencerii
NT1 aedes squamiger
NT1 aedes sticticus
NT1 aedes stimulans
NT1 aedes stokesi
NT1 aedes subdiversus
NT1 aedes taeniorhynchus
NT1 aedes tarsalis
NT1 aedes taylori
NT1 aedes terrens
NT1 aedes thelcter
NT1 aedes thibaulti
NT1 aedes togoi
NT1 aedes tormentor
NT1 aedes triseriatus
NT1 aedes trivittatus
NT1 aedes unidentatus
NT1 aedes varipalpus
NT1 aedes vexans
NT1 aedes vigilax
NT1 aedes vittatus
NT1 aedes w-albus
NT1 aedes watteni
NT1 aedes zoosophus
rt haemagogus

AEDES ABSERRATUS
BT1 aedes
BT2 culicidae
BT3 diptera

AEDES AEGYPTI
BT1 aedes
BT2 culicidae
BT3 diptera

AEDES AFRICANUS
BT1 aedes
BT2 culicidae
BT3 diptera

AEDES ALBIFASCIATUS
BT1 aedes
BT2 culicidae
BT3 diptera

AEDES ALBOPICTUS
BT1 aedes
BT2 culicidae
BT3 diptera

AEDES ALCASIDI
BT1 aedes
BT2 culicidae
BT3 diptera

AEDES AMBREENSIS
HN from 1989
BT1 aedes
BT2 culicidae
BT3 diptera

AEDES ANGUSTIVITTATUS
BT1 aedes
BT2 culicidae
BT3 diptera

AEDES ANNULIPES
BT1 aedes
BT2 culicidae
BT3 diptera

AEDES APICOARGENTEUS
BT1 aedes
BT2 culicidae
BT3 diptera

AEDES ATLANTICUS
BT1 aedes
BT2 culicidae
BT3 diptera

AEDES ATROPALPUS
BT1 aedes
BT2 culicidae
BT3 diptera

AEDES CAMPESTRIS
BT1 aedes
BT2 culicidae
BT3 diptera

AEDES CANADENSIS
BT1 aedes
BT2 culicidae
BT3 diptera

AEDES CANTANS
BT1 aedes
BT2 culicidae
BT3 diptera

AEDES CANTATOR
BT1 aedes
BT2 culicidae
BT3 diptera

AEDES CASPIUS
BT1 aedes
BT2 culicidae
BT3 diptera

AEDES CATAPHYLLA
BT1 aedes
BT2 culicidae
BT3 diptera

AEDES CINEREUS
BT1 aedes
BT2 culicidae
BT3 diptera

AEDES CIRCUMLUTEOLUS
BT1 aedes
BT2 culicidae
BT3 diptera

AEDES COMMUNIS
BT1 aedes
BT2 culicidae
BT3 diptera

AEDES COOKI
BT1 aedes
BT2 culicidae
BT3 diptera

AEDES CUMMINSII
HN from 1989
BT1 aedes
BT2 culicidae
BT3 diptera

AEDES CYPRIUS
BT1 aedes
BT2 culicidae
BT3 diptera

AEDES DENTATUS
BT1 aedes
BT2 culicidae
BT3 diptera

AEDES DETRITUS
BT1 aedes
BT2 culicidae
BT3 diptera

AEDES DIANTAEUS
BT1 aedes
BT2 culicidae
BT3 diptera

AEDES DORSALIS
BT1 aedes
BT2 culicidae
BT3 diptera

AEDES DURBANENSIS
BT1 aedes
BT2 culicidae
BT3 diptera

AEDES ECHINUS
BT1 aedes
BT2 culicidae
BT3 diptera

AEDES EPACTIUS
BT1 aedes
BT2 culicidae
BT3 diptera

AEDES ESOENSIS
BT1 aedes
BT2 culicidae
BT3 diptera

AEDES EUEDES
BT1 aedes
BT2 culicidae
BT3 diptera

AEDES EXCRUCIANS
BT1 aedes
BT2 culicidae
BT3 diptera

AEDES FITCHII
BT1 aedes
BT2 culicidae
BT3 diptera

AEDES FLAVESCENS
BT1 aedes
BT2 culicidae
BT3 diptera

AEDES FLAVOPICTUS
BT1 aedes
BT2 culicidae
BT3 diptera

AEDES FLUVIATILIS
HN from 1989
BT1 aedes
BT2 culicidae
BT3 diptera

AEDES FRYERI
BT1 aedes
BT2 culicidae
BT3 diptera

AEDES FULVUS
BT1 aedes
BT2 culicidae
BT3 diptera

AEDES FURCIFER
BT1 aedes
BT2 culicidae
BT3 diptera

AEDES GALLOISI
BT1 aedes
BT2 culicidae
BT3 diptera

AEDES GENICULATUS
BT1 aedes
BT2 culicidae
BT3 diptera

AEDES GUAMENSIS
BT1 aedes
BT2 culicidae
BT3 diptera

AEDES HEBRIDEUS
BT1 aedes
BT2 culicidae
BT3 diptera

AEDES HENDERSONI
BT1 aedes
BT2 culicidae
BT3 diptera

AEDES HEXODONTUS
BT1 aedes
BT2 culicidae
BT3 diptera

AEDES IMPIGER
BT1 aedes
BT2 culicidae
BT3 diptera

AEDES IMPLICATUS
BT1 aedes
BT2 culicidae
BT3 diptera

AEDES INCREPITUS
BT1 aedes
BT2 culicidae
BT3 diptera

AEDES INFIRMATUS
BT1 aedes
BT2 culicidae
BT3 diptera

AEDES INGRAMI
BT1 aedes
BT2 culicidae
BT3 diptera

AEDES INTRUDENS
BT1 aedes
BT2 culicidae
BT3 diptera

AEDES JAPONICUS
BT1 aedes
BT2 culicidae
BT3 diptera

AEDES JUPPI
HN from 1990
BT1 aedes
BT2 culicidae
BT3 diptera

AEDES KOCHI
HN from 1989
BT1 aedes
BT2 culicidae
BT3 diptera

AEDES KOREICOIDES
BT1 aedes
BT2 culicidae
BT3 diptera

AEDES KOREICUS
BT1 aedes
BT2 culicidae
BT3 diptera

aedes leucocelaenus
USE **haemagogus leucocelaenus**

AEDES LEUCOMELAS
BT1 aedes
BT2 culicidae
BT3 diptera

AEDES LINEATOPENNIS
BT1 aedes
BT2 culicidae
BT3 diptera

AEDES LURIDUS
BT1 aedes
BT2 culicidae
BT3 diptera

AEDES LUTEOCEPHALUS
BT1 aedes
BT2 culicidae
BT3 diptera

aedes malayensis
USE **aedes scutellaris malayensis**

AEDES MARIAE
BT1 aedes
BT2 culicidae
BT3 diptera

AEDES MASCARENSIS
BT1 aedes
BT2 culicidae
BT3 diptera

AEDES MEDIOVITTATUS
BT1 aedes
BT2 culicidae
BT3 diptera

AEDES MELANIMON
BT1 aedes
BT2 culicidae
BT3 diptera

AEDES METALLICUS
BT1 aedes
BT2 culicidae
BT3 diptera

AEDES MONTCHADSKYI
BT1 aedes
BT2 culicidae
BT3 diptera

AEDES MONTICOLA
BT1 aedes
BT2 culicidae
BT3 diptera

AEDES NEVADENSIS
BT1 aedes
BT2 culicidae
BT3 diptera

AEDES NIGRIPES
BT1 aedes
BT2 culicidae
BT3 diptera

AEDES NIGROMACULIS
BT1 aedes
BT2 culicidae
BT3 diptera

AEDES NIPPONICUS
BT1 aedes
BT2 culicidae
BT3 diptera

aedes niveus
USE **aedes watteni**

AEDES NOTOSCRIPTUS
BT1 aedes
BT2 culicidae
BT3 diptera

AEDES NOVALBOPICTUS
BT1 aedes
BT2 culicidae
BT3 diptera

AEDES OPOK
BT1 aedes
BT2 culicidae
BT3 diptera

AEDES PEMBAENSIS
BT1 aedes
BT2 culicidae
BT3 diptera

AEDES PHOENICIAE
BT1 aedes
BT2 culicidae
BT3 diptera

AEDES PIONIPS
BT1 aedes
BT2 culicidae
BT3 diptera

AEDES POICILIA
BT1 aedes
BT2 culicidae
BT3 diptera

AEDES POLYNESIENSIS
BT1 aedes
BT2 culicidae

AEDES POLYNESIENSIS *cont.*
BT3 diptera

AEDES PSEUDALBOPICTUS
HN from 1990
BT1 aedes
BT2 culicidae
BT3 diptera

AEDES PSEUDOSCUTELLARIS
BT1 aedes
BT2 culicidae
BT3 diptera

AEDES PULCHRITARSIS
BT1 aedes
BT2 culicidae
BT3 diptera

AEDES PULLATUS
BT1 aedes
BT2 culicidae
BT3 diptera

AEDES PUNCTODES
BT1 aedes
BT2 culicidae
BT3 diptera

AEDES PUNCTOR
BT1 aedes
BT2 culicidae
BT3 diptera

AEDES REFIKI
BT1 aedes
BT2 culicidae
BT3 diptera

AEDES RIPARIUS
BT1 aedes
BT2 culicidae
BT3 diptera

AEDES RUSTICUS
BT1 aedes
BT2 culicidae
BT3 diptera

AEDES SAMOANUS
HN from 1989
BT1 aedes
BT2 culicidae
BT3 diptera

AEDES SCAPULARIS
BT1 aedes
BT2 culicidae
BT3 diptera

AEDES SCUTELLARIS
BT1 aedes
BT2 culicidae
BT3 diptera
NT1 aedes scutellaris katherinensis
NT1 aedes scutellaris malayensis

AEDES SCUTELLARIS KATHERINENSIS
HN from 1990
BT1 aedes scutellaris
BT2 aedes
BT3 culicidae
BT4 diptera

AEDES SCUTELLARIS MALAYENSIS
HN from 1990
uf aedes malayensis
BT1 aedes scutellaris
BT2 aedes
BT3 culicidae
BT4 diptera

AEDES SEATOI
BT1 aedes
BT2 culicidae
BT3 diptera

AEDES SERRATUS
BT1 aedes
BT2 culicidae
BT3 diptera

AEDES SIERRENSIS
BT1 aedes
BT2 culicidae
BT3 diptera

AEDES SIMPSONI
BT1 aedes
BT2 culicidae
BT3 diptera

AEDES SOLLICITANS
BT1 aedes
BT2 culicidae
BT3 diptera

AEDES SPENCERII
BT1 aedes
BT2 culicidae
BT3 diptera

AEDES SQUAMIGER
BT1 aedes
BT2 culicidae
BT3 diptera

AEDES STICTICUS
BT1 aedes
BT2 culicidae
BT3 diptera

AEDES STIMULANS
BT1 aedes
BT2 culicidae
BT3 diptera

AEDES STOKESI
BT1 aedes
BT2 culicidae
BT3 diptera

AEDES SUBDIVERSUS
BT1 aedes
BT2 culicidae
BT3 diptera

AEDES TAENIORHYNCHUS
BT1 aedes
BT2 culicidae
BT3 diptera

AEDES TARSALIS
BT1 aedes
BT2 culicidae
BT3 diptera

AEDES TAYLORI
BT1 aedes
BT2 culicidae
BT3 diptera

AEDES TERRENS
BT1 aedes
BT2 culicidae
BT3 diptera

AEDES THELCTER
BT1 aedes
BT2 culicidae
BT3 diptera

AEDES THIBAULTI
BT1 aedes
BT2 culicidae
BT3 diptera

AEDES TOGOI
BT1 aedes
BT2 culicidae
BT3 diptera

AEDES TORMENTOR
BT1 aedes
BT2 culicidae
BT3 diptera

AEDES TRISERIATUS
BT1 aedes
BT2 culicidae
BT3 diptera

AEDES TRIVITTATUS
BT1 aedes
BT2 culicidae
BT3 diptera

AEDES UNIDENTATUS
BT1 aedes
BT2 culicidae
BT3 diptera

AEDES VARIPALPUS
BT1 aedes
BT2 culicidae
BT3 diptera

AEDES VEXANS
BT1 aedes
BT2 culicidae
BT3 diptera

AEDES VIGILAX
HN from 1989
BT1 aedes
BT2 culicidae
BT3 diptera

AEDES VITTATUS
BT1 aedes
BT2 culicidae
BT3 diptera

AEDES W-ALBUS
BT1 aedes
BT2 culicidae
BT3 diptera

AEDES WATTENI
uf aedes niveus
BT1 aedes
BT2 culicidae
BT3 diptera

AEDES ZOOSOPHUS
BT1 aedes
BT2 culicidae
BT3 diptera

aegeria
USE **sesia**

aegeria exitiosa
USE **synanthedon exitiosa**

aegeria myopaeformis
USE **synanthedon myopaeformis**

aegeria pictipes
USE **synanthedon pictipes**

aegeria scitula
USE **synanthedon scitula**

AEGICERAS
BT1 myrsinaceae
NT1 aegiceras corniculatum

AEGICERAS CORNICULATUM
BT1 aegiceras
BT2 myrsinaceae

AEGILOPS
BT1 gramineae
NT1 aegilops bicornis
NT1 aegilops caudata
NT1 aegilops columnaris
NT1 aegilops comosa
NT1 aegilops crassa
NT1 aegilops cylindrica
NT1 aegilops juvenalis
NT1 aegilops longissima
NT1 aegilops lorentii
NT1 aegilops mutica
NT1 aegilops ovata
NT1 aegilops speltoides
NT1 aegilops squarrosa
NT1 aegilops triaristata
NT1 aegilops triuncialis
NT1 aegilops umbellulata
NT1 aegilops uniaristata
NT1 aegilops variabilis
NT1 aegilops vavilovii
NT1 aegilops ventricosa
rt wheat

AEGILOPS BICORNIS
BT1 aegilops
BT2 gramineae

AEGILOPS CAUDATA
BT1 aegilops
BT2 gramineae

AEGILOPS COLUMNARIS
BT1 aegilops
BT2 gramineae

AEGILOPS COMOSA
BT1 aegilops
BT2 gramineae

AEGILOPS CRASSA
BT1 aegilops
BT2 gramineae

AEGILOPS CYLINDRICA
BT1 aegilops
BT2 gramineae

AEGILOPS JUVENALIS
BT1 aegilops
BT2 gramineae

AEGILOPS LONGISSIMA
BT1 aegilops
BT2 gramineae

AEGILOPS LORENTII
BT1 aegilops
BT2 gramineae

AEGILOPS MUTICA
BT1 aegilops
BT2 gramineae

AEGILOPS OVATA
BT1 aegilops
BT2 gramineae

AEGILOPS SPELTOIDES
BT1 aegilops
BT2 gramineae

AEGILOPS SQUARROSA
BT1 aegilops
BT2 gramineae

AEGILOPS TRIARISTATA
BT1 aegilops
BT2 gramineae

AEGILOPS TRIUNCIALIS
BT1 aegilops
BT2 gramineae

AEGILOPS UMBELLULATA
BT1 aegilops
BT2 gramineae

AEGILOPS UNIARISTATA
BT1 aegilops
BT2 gramineae

AEGILOPS VARIABILIS
BT1 aegilops
BT2 gramineae

AEGILOPS VAVILOVII
BT1 aegilops
BT2 gramineae

AEGILOPS VENTRICOSA
BT1 aegilops
BT2 gramineae

AEGINETIA
BT1 orobanchaceae
NT1 aeginetia indica

AEGINETIA INDICA
BT1 aeginetia
BT2 orobanchaceae
BT1 medicinal plants

AEGIPHILA
BT1 verbenaceae
NT1 aegiphila sellowiana

AEGIPHILA SELLOWIANA
BT1 aegiphila
BT2 verbenaceae

AEGLE
BT1 rutaceae
NT1 aegle marmelos

AEGLE MARMELOS
uf *bael*
BT1 aegle
BT2 rutaceae
BT1 antibacterial plants
BT1 antifungal plants
BT1 dye plants
BT1 medicinal plants
BT1 subtropical tree fruits
BT2 subtropical fruits
BT3 fruit crops
BT2 tree fruits

AEGOLIUS
BT1 strigidae
BT2 strigiformes
BT3 birds
NT1 aegolius funereus

AEGOLIUS FUNEREUS
BT1 aegolius
BT2 strigidae
BT3 strigiformes
BT4 birds

AEGOPODIUM
BT1 umbelliferae
NT1 aegopodium podagraria

AEGOPODIUM PODAGRARIA
BT1 aegopodium
BT2 umbelliferae

AEGYPTIANELLA
BT1 anaplasmataceae
BT2 rickettsiales
BT3 bacteria
BT4 prokaryotes
NT1 aegyptianella pullorum

AEGYPTIANELLA PULLORUM
BT1 aegyptianella
BT2 anaplasmataceae
BT3 rickettsiales
BT4 bacteria
BT5 prokaryotes

AELIA
BT1 pentatomidae
BT2 heteroptera
NT1 aelia acuminata
NT1 aelia cognata
NT1 aelia germari
NT1 aelia rostrata

AELIA ACUMINATA
BT1 aelia
BT2 pentatomidae
BT3 heteroptera

AELIA COGNATA
BT1 aelia
BT2 pentatomidae
BT3 heteroptera

AELIA GERMARI
BT1 aelia
BT2 pentatomidae
BT3 heteroptera

AELIA ROSTRATA
BT1 aelia
BT2 pentatomidae
BT3 heteroptera

AELUROPUS
BT1 gramineae
NT1 aeluropus lagopoides
NT1 aeluropus littoralis
rt halophytes

AELUROPUS LAGOPOIDES
BT1 aeluropus
BT2 gramineae

AELUROPUS LITTORALIS
BT1 aeluropus
BT2 gramineae

AELUROSTRONGYLUS
BT1 angiostrongylidae
BT2 nematoda
NT1 aelurostrongylus abstrusus
rt lungworms

AELUROSTRONGYLUS ABSTRUSUS
BT1 aelurostrongylus
BT2 angiostrongylidae
BT3 nematoda

AENEOLAMIA
BT1 cercopidae
BT2 cercopoidea
BT3 auchenorrhyncha
BT4 homoptera
NT1 aeneolamia contigua
NT1 aeneolamia selecta
NT1 aeneolamia varia

AENEOLAMIA CONTIGUA
BT1 aeneolamia
BT2 cercopidae
BT3 cercopoidea
BT4 auchenorrhyncha
BT5 homoptera

AENEOLAMIA SELECTA
BT1 aeneolamia
BT2 cercopidae
BT3 cercopoidea
BT4 auchenorrhyncha
BT5 homoptera

AENEOLAMIA VARIA
BT1 aeneolamia
BT2 cercopidae
BT3 cercopoidea
BT4 auchenorrhyncha
BT5 homoptera

AEOLANTHUS
BT1 labiatae
NT1 aeolanthus gamwelliae

AEOLANTHUS GAMWELLIAE
BT1 aeolanthus
BT2 labiatae

AEOLIAN DEPOSITS
AF eolian deposits
BT1 soil parent materials
NT1 aeolian sands

AEOLIAN SANDS
AF eolian sands
BT1 aeolian deposits
BT2 soil parent materials
rt sand

AEOLIAN SOILS
AF eolian soils
BT1 soil types (lithological)

AEOLOTHRIPIDAE
BT1 thysanoptera
NT1 aeolothrips
NT2 aeolothrips fasciatus
NT2 aeolothrips intermedius

AEOLOTHRIPS
BT1 aeolothripidae
BT2 thysanoptera
NT1 aeolothrips fasciatus
NT1 aeolothrips intermedius

AEOLOTHRIPS FASCIATUS
BT1 aeolothrips
BT2 aeolothripidae
BT3 thysanoptera

AEOLOTHRIPS INTERMEDIUS
BT1 aeolothrips
BT2 aeolothripidae
BT3 thysanoptera

AEPYCEROS
BT1 bovidae
BT2 ruminantia
BT3 artiodactyla
BT4 mammals
BT4 ungulates
NT1 aepyceros melampus

AEPYCEROS MELAMPUS
uf *impalas*
BT1 aepyceros
BT2 bovidae
BT3 ruminantia
BT4 artiodactyla

AEPYCEROS MELAMPUS *cont.*
BT5 mammals
BT5 ungulates

AERANGIS
BT1 orchidaceae
rt ornamental plants

AERANTHES
BT1 orchidaceae
NT1 aeranthes africana

AERANTHES AFRICANA
BT1 aeranthes
BT2 orchidaceae

AERATED STEAM
uf *air, saturated*
uf *saturated air*
BT1 steam
BT2 water vapour
BT3 vapour
BT4 gases
rt soil sterilization
rt sterilizers
rt sterilizing

AERATION
rt agitation
rt agitators
rt carbonation
rt oxidation ditches
rt pneumatophores
rt processing
rt swath aerators
rt ventilation

AERIAL APPLICATION
BT1 application methods
BT2 methodology
rt aerial sowing
rt aerial sprayers
rt aerial spraying
rt agricultural aviation
rt spraying

AERIAL COLLECTION
BT1 collection
rt agricultural aviation

aerial colour photography
USE **aerial photography**
OR **colour photography**

AERIAL INSECTS
BT1 insects
BT2 arthropods

AERIAL METHODS
BT1 methodology
rt agricultural aviation
rt air transport
rt remote sensing

aerial multispectral photography
USE **aerial photography**

aerial panchromatic photography
USE **aerial photography**
OR **panchromatic photography**

AERIAL PHOTOGRAPHY
uf *aerial colour photography*
uf *aerial multispectral photography*
uf *aerial panchromatic photography*
BT1 photography
BT2 techniques
rt aerial surveys
rt agricultural aviation
rt mapping
rt photointerpretation
rt remote sensing
rt remote sensors
rt surveying

AERIAL ROOTS
rt roots

AERIAL SOWING
BT1 sowing methods
BT2 sowing
BT3 planting

AERIAL SOWING *cont.*
rt aerial application
rt aircraft

AERIAL SPRAYERS
uf *sprayers, aerial*
BT1 sprayers
BT2 spraying equipment
BT3 application equipment
BT4 equipment
rt aerial application
rt aerial spraying
rt agricultural aviation
rt spraying

AERIAL SPRAYING
uf *spraying, aerial*
BT1 spraying
BT2 application methods
BT3 methodology
rt aerial application
rt aerial sprayers
rt agricultural aviation
rt spraying equipment

AERIAL SURVEYS
uf *surveys, aerial*
BT1 surveys
NT1 satellite surveys
rt aerial photography
rt agricultural aviation
rt aircraft
rt helicopters
rt mapping
rt photointerpretation
rt remote sensing
rt surveying
rt surveying instruments

AERIDES
BT1 orchidaceae
NT1 aerides multiflorum

AERIDES MULTIFLORUM
BT1 aerides
BT2 orchidaceae

aerobacter
USE **enterobacter**

aerobacter aerogenes
USE **enterobacter aerogenes**

AEROBES
BT1 microorganisms
rt aerobiosis
rt anaerobes
rt oxygen

aerobic stabilization
USE **aerobic treatment**

AEROBIC TREATMENT
uf *aerobic stabilization*
rt anaerobic treatment
rt slurries
rt treatment
rt waste treatment

AEROBICS (AGRICOLA)
BT1 physical fitness
BT2 health

AEROBIOSIS
rt aerobes
rt oxygen

AERODYNAMIC PROPERTIES
rt aerodynamics
rt air flow
rt aircraft

AERODYNAMICS
BT1 dynamics
BT2 mechanics
BT3 physics
rt aerodynamic properties
rt aircraft
rt wind effects

AEROMONAS
BT1 vibrionaceae
BT2 gracilicutes
BT3 bacteria
BT4 prokaryotes

AEROMONAS *cont.*
NT1 aeromonas hydrophila
NT1 aeromonas salmonicida

AEROMONAS HYDROPHILA
BT1 aeromonas
BT2 vibrionaceae
BT3 gracilicutes
BT4 bacteria
BT5 prokaryotes

AEROMONAS SALMONICIDA
BT1 aeromonas
BT2 vibrionaceae
BT3 gracilicutes
BT4 bacteria
BT5 prokaryotes

AEROSOL SPRAYERS
uf *sprayers, aerosol*
BT1 sprayers
BT2 spraying equipment
BT3 application equipment
BT4 equipment
rt aerosols
rt dispersion
rt fogs
rt mists
rt spraying

AEROSOLS
BT1 colloids
rt aerosol sprayers
rt fogs
rt freons
rt mists
rt nebulization
rt smoke
rt sprays

AEROSPORTS
BT1 outdoor recreation
BT2 recreation
BT1 sport
NT1 gliding
NT2 hang gliding

AERVA
BT1 amaranthaceae
NT1 aerva javanica
NT1 aerva lanata
NT1 aerva persica

AERVA JAVANICA
BT1 aerva
BT2 amaranthaceae

AERVA LANATA
BT1 aerva
BT2 amaranthaceae

AERVA PERSICA
BT1 aerva
BT2 amaranthaceae

AESCHYNANTHUS
BT1 gesneriaceae
NT1 aeschynanthus hildebrandii
NT1 aeschynanthus radicans
NT1 aeschynanthus speciosus

AESCHYNANTHUS HILDEBRANDII
BT1 aeschynanthus
BT2 gesneriaceae
BT1 ornamental woody plants

aeschynanthus lobbianus
USE **aeschynanthus radicans**

AESCHYNANTHUS RADICANS
uf *aeschynanthus lobbianus*
BT1 aeschynanthus
BT2 gesneriaceae
BT1 ornamental woody plants

AESCHYNANTHUS SPECIOSUS
BT1 aeschynanthus
BT2 gesneriaceae
BT1 ornamental woody plants

AESCHYNOMENE
BT1 leguminosae
NT1 aeschynomene americana
NT1 aeschynomene elaphroxylon
NT1 aeschynomene indica

AESCHYNOMENE *cont.*
NT1 aeschynomene scabra
NT1 aeschynomene sensitiva
NT1 aeschynomene virginica

AESCHYNOMENE AMERICANA
BT1 aeschynomene
BT2 leguminosae
BT1 pasture legumes
BT2 legumes
BT2 pasture plants

AESCHYNOMENE ELAPHROXYLON
BT1 aeschynomene
BT2 leguminosae
BT1 pasture legumes
BT2 legumes
BT2 pasture plants

AESCHYNOMENE INDICA
BT1 aeschynomene
BT2 leguminosae
BT1 pasture legumes
BT2 legumes
BT2 pasture plants

AESCHYNOMENE SCABRA
BT1 aeschynomene
BT2 leguminosae
BT1 pasture legumes
BT2 legumes
BT2 pasture plants

AESCHYNOMENE SENSITIVA
BT1 aeschynomene
BT2 leguminosae
BT1 pasture legumes
BT2 legumes
BT2 pasture plants

AESCHYNOMENE VIRGINICA
BT1 aeschynomene
BT2 leguminosae
BT1 pasture legumes
BT2 legumes
BT2 pasture plants

AESCULIN
AF esculin
uf *esculoside*
BT1 glucosides
BT2 glycosides
BT3 carbohydrates
BT1 radiation protection agents
BT2 protectants
rt aesculus
rt sunburn

AESCULUS
BT1 hippocastanaceae
NT1 aesculus californica
NT1 aesculus carnea
NT1 aesculus glabra
NT1 aesculus hippocastanum
NT1 aesculus indica
NT1 aesculus parviflora
NT1 aesculus rubra
rt aesculin

AESCULUS CALIFORNICA
BT1 aesculus
BT2 hippocastanaceae

AESCULUS CARNEA
BT1 aesculus
BT2 hippocastanaceae
BT1 medicinal plants
BT1 ornamental woody plants

AESCULUS GLABRA
BT1 aesculus
BT2 hippocastanaceae
BT1 ornamental woody plants

AESCULUS HIPPOCASTANUM
uf *horse chestnut*
BT1 aesculus
BT2 hippocastanaceae
BT1 antibacterial plants
BT1 forest trees
BT1 ornamental woody plants

AESCULUS INDICA
BT1 aesculus
BT2 hippocastanaceae
BT1 forest trees
BT1 ornamental woody plants

AESCULUS PARVIFLORA
BT1 aesculus
BT2 hippocastanaceae
BT1 ornamental woody plants

AESCULUS RUBRA
BT1 aesculus
BT2 hippocastanaceae

AESHNA
BT1 aeshnidae
BT2 odonata
NT1 aeshna cyanea

AESHNA CYANEA
BT1 aeshna
BT2 aeshnidae
BT3 odonata

AESHNIDAE
BT1 odonata
NT1 aeshna
NT2 aeshna cyanea
NT1 anax
NT2 anax guttatus

AESTHETIC VALUE
rt areas of outstanding natural beauty
rt beautification (agricola)
rt ornamental value
rt quality

AESTIVATION
AF estivation
BT1 dormancy
rt adaptation
rt flowers

AETHIA
BT1 alcidae
BT2 charadriiformes
BT3 birds

AETHOMYS
BT1 murinae
BT2 muridae
BT3 rodents
BT4 mammals

AETHUSA
BT1 umbelliferae
NT1 aethusa cynapium

AETHUSA CYNAPIUM
BT1 aethusa
BT2 umbelliferae

AETIOLOGY
AF etiology
rt disease distribution
rt disease transmission
rt diseases
rt epidemiology
rt mixed infections
rt pathogenicity
rt plant diseases
rt spread

AEXTOXICON
BT1 euphorbiaceae
NT1 aextoxicon punctatum

AEXTOXICON PUNCTATUM
BT1 aextoxicon
BT2 euphorbiaceae

afars and issas territory
USE **djibouti**

affective behaviour
USE **emotions (agricola)**

AFFINATION
HN from 1990
BT1 sugar refining
BT2 processing
rt affination syrup

AFFINATION SYRUP
HN from 1990
BT1 sugar industry intermediates
BT1 syrups
BT2 liquids
rt affination

AFFORESTATION
uf *reafforestation*
uf *reforestation*
BT1 forestry development
rt choice of species
rt forestry practices
rt group planting
rt regeneration
rt soil conservation
rt species trials

AFGHAN ARABI
HN from 1990
BT1 sheep breeds
BT2 breeds

AFGHANISTAN
BT1 west asia
BT2 asia
rt developing countries
rt least developed countries

AFLATOXICOSIS
BT1 mycotoxicoses
BT2 poisoning
rt aflatoxins

AFLATOXINS
BT1 carcinogens
BT2 toxic substances
BT1 mycotoxins
BT2 toxins
rt aflatoxicosis
rt hepatotoxins

AFRAEGLE
BT1 rutaceae
NT1 afraegle paniculata

AFRAEGLE PANICULATA
BT1 afraegle
BT2 rutaceae
BT1 medicinal plants

AFRAMOMUM
BT1 zingiberaceae
NT1 aframomum melegueta

AFRAMOMUM MELEGUETA
BT1 aframomum
BT2 zingiberaceae
BT1 spice plants

AFRICA
NT1 africa south of sahara
NT2 central africa
NT3 burundi
NT3 cameroon
NT3 central african republic
NT3 chad
NT3 congo
NT3 equatorial guinea
NT3 gabon
NT3 sao tome and principe
NT3 zaire
NT2 east africa
NT3 chagos archipelago
NT3 djibouti
NT3 ethiopia
NT3 kenya
NT3 malawi
NT3 rwanda
NT3 seychelles
NT3 somalia
NT3 sudan
NT3 tanzania
NT4 zanzibar
NT3 uganda
NT2 southern africa
NT3 angola
NT3 botswana
NT3 comoros
NT3 lesotho
NT3 madagascar
NT3 mauritius
NT3 mayotte
NT3 mozambique

AFRICA *cont.*
NT3 namibia
NT3 reunion
NT3 south africa
NT4 south african homelands
NT5 bophuthatswana
NT5 ciskei
NT5 kwazulu
NT5 transkei
NT5 venda
NT3 st. helena
NT4 ascension
NT4 tristan da cunha
NT3 swaziland
NT3 zambia
NT3 zimbabwe
NT2 west africa
NT3 benin
NT3 burkina faso
NT3 cape verde
NT3 gambia
NT3 ghana
NT3 guinea
NT3 guinea-bissau
NT3 ivory coast
NT3 liberia
NT3 mali
NT3 mauritania
NT3 niger
NT3 nigeria
NT3 senegal
NT3 sierra leone
NT3 togo
NT3 western sahara
NT1 north africa
NT2 algeria
NT2 egypt
NT2 libya
NT2 morocco
NT2 tunisia
NT1 sahel
rt acp
rt anglophone africa
rt developing countries
rt francophone africa
rt tropical africa

africa, central
USE **central africa**

africa, east
USE **east africa**

africa, english speaking
USE **anglophone africa**

africa, french speaking
USE **francophone africa**

africa, maghreb
USE **maghreb**

africa, north
USE **north africa**

africa (sahelian zone)
USE **sahel**

AFRICA SOUTH OF SAHARA
BT1 africa
NT1 central africa
NT2 burundi
NT2 cameroon
NT2 central african republic
NT2 chad
NT2 congo
NT2 equatorial guinea
NT2 gabon
NT2 sao tome and principe
NT2 zaire
NT1 east africa
NT2 chagos archipelago
NT2 djibouti
NT2 ethiopia
NT2 kenya
NT2 malawi
NT2 rwanda
NT2 seychelles
NT2 somalia
NT2 sudan
NT2 tanzania
NT3 zanzibar
NT2 uganda

AFRICA SOUTH OF SAHARA *cont.*
NT1 southern africa
NT2 angola
NT2 botswana
NT2 comoros
NT2 lesotho
NT2 madagascar
NT2 mauritius
NT2 mayotte
NT2 mozambique
NT2 namibia
NT2 reunion
NT2 south africa
NT3 south african homelands
NT4 bophuthatswana
NT4 ciskei
NT4 kwazulu
NT4 transkei
NT4 venda
NT2 st. helena
NT3 ascension
NT3 tristan da cunha
NT2 swaziland
NT2 zambia
NT2 zimbabwe
NT1 west africa
NT2 benin
NT2 burkina faso
NT2 cape verde
NT2 gambia
NT2 ghana
NT2 guinea
NT2 guinea-bissau
NT2 ivory coast
NT2 liberia
NT2 mali
NT2 mauritania
NT2 niger
NT2 nigeria
NT2 senegal
NT2 sierra leone
NT2 togo
NT2 western sahara
rt acp
rt anglophone africa
rt francophone africa
rt sadcc countries
rt sahel
rt tropical africa

africa, south-west
USE **namibia**

africa, southern
USE **southern africa**

africa, west
USE **west africa**

african buffalo
USE **synceros caffer**

AFRICAN CASSAVA MOSAIC GEMINIVIRUS
HN from 1990; previously "african cassava mosaic virus"
uf african cassava mosaic virus
uf cassava latent geminivirus
uf cassava latent virus
BT1 geminivirus group
BT2 plant viruses
BT3 plant pathogens
BT4 pathogens
rt cassava
rt manihot esculenta

african cassava mosaic virus
USE **african cassava mosaic geminivirus**

african coast fever
USE **theileria parva**

african elephants
USE **loxodonta africana**

AFRICAN HISTOPLASMOSIS
BT1 histoplasmosis
BT2 mycoses
BT3 infectious diseases
BT4 diseases

AFRICAN HISTOPLASMOSIS *cont.*
rt histoplasma duboisii

AFRICAN HORSE SICKNESS
BT1 horse diseases
BT2 animal diseases
BT3 diseases
BT1 vector-borne diseases
BT2 diseases
BT1 viral diseases
BT2 infectious diseases
BT3 diseases
rt african horse sickness virus

AFRICAN HORSE SICKNESS VIRUS
BT1 orbivirus
BT2 arboviruses
BT3 pathogens
BT2 reoviridae
BT3 viruses
rt african horse sickness

AFRICAN SWINE FEVER
BT1 swine diseases
BT2 animal diseases
BT3 diseases
BT1 viral diseases
BT2 infectious diseases
BT3 diseases
rt african swine fever virus

AFRICAN SWINE FEVER VIRUS
BT1 arboviruses
BT2 pathogens
BT1 iridoviridae
BT2 viruses
rt african swine fever

AFRICANDER
HN from 1990; previously "afrikander"
uf afrikander
BT1 cattle breeds
BT2 breeds

afrikander
USE **africander**

afrormosia
USE **pericopsis**

AFROTROPICAL REGION
uf ethiopian region
BT1 zoogeographical regions

AFTER-RIPENING
HN from 1990
BT1 plant physiology
BT2 physiology
rt dormancy breaking
rt germination
rt seed dormancy
rt seeds

AFZELIA
BT1 leguminosae
NT1 afzelia africana
NT1 afzelia bella

AFZELIA AFRICANA
BT1 afzelia
BT2 leguminosae

AFZELIA BELLA
BT1 afzelia
BT2 leguminosae

AGALACTIA
uf lactation failure
BT1 lactation disorders
BT2 puerperal disorders
BT3 reproductive disorders
BT4 functional disorders
BT5 animal disorders
BT6 disorders

AGALINIS
BT1 scrophulariaceae
NT1 agalinis purpurea

AGALINIS PURPUREA
BT1 agalinis
BT2 scrophulariaceae

AGALLIA
BT1 cicadellidae
BT2 cicadelloidea
BT3 auchenorrhyncha
BT4 homoptera
NT1 agallia constricta
NT1 agallia laevis
rt anaceratagallia

AGALLIA CONSTRICTA
BT1 agallia
BT2 cicadellidae
BT3 cicadelloidea
BT4 auchenorrhyncha
BT5 homoptera

AGALLIA LAEVIS
uf anaceratagallia laevis
BT1 agallia
BT2 cicadellidae
BT3 cicadelloidea
BT4 auchenorrhyncha
BT5 homoptera

AGAMA
BT1 agamidae
BT2 sauria
BT3 reptiles
NT1 agama caudospinum

AGAMA CAUDOSPINUM
BT1 agama
BT2 agamidae
BT3 sauria
BT4 reptiles

AGAMIDAE
BT1 sauria
BT2 reptiles
NT1 agama
NT2 agama caudospinum

AGAMOMERMIS
BT1 mermithidae
BT2 nematoda

AGAPANTHUS
BT1 alliaceae
NT1 agapanthus africanus
NT1 agapanthus praecox

AGAPANTHUS AFRICANUS
uf agapanthus umbellatus
BT1 agapanthus
BT2 alliaceae
BT1 ornamental herbaceous plants

agapanthus orientalis
USE **agapanthus praecox**

AGAPANTHUS PRAECOX
uf agapanthus orientalis
BT1 agapanthus
BT2 alliaceae
BT1 ornamental herbaceous plants

agapanthus umbellatus
USE **agapanthus africanus**

AGAPETA
uf euxanthis
BT1 tortricidae
BT2 lepidoptera
NT1 agapeta zoegana

AGAPETA ZOEGANA
HN from 1989
BT1 agapeta
BT2 tortricidae
BT3 lepidoptera

AGAPORNIS
BT1 psittacidae
BT2 psittaciformes
BT3 birds

AGAPOSTEMON
BT1 apidae
BT2 hymenoptera

AGAR
BT1 culture media
BT1 galactans

AGAR *cont.*
BT2 polysaccharides
BT3 carbohydrates
BT1 laxatives
BT2 gastrointestinal agents
BT3 drugs
BT1 mucilages
BT2 polysaccharides
BT3 carbohydrates
rt agarose
rt algae
rt alginates
rt colloids
rt gelatin
rt seaweeds

AGARICALES
NT1 agaricus
NT2 agaricus arvensis
NT2 agaricus bisporus
NT2 agaricus bitorquis
NT2 agaricus chionodermus
NT2 agaricus macrocarpus
NT2 agaricus macrosporoides
NT2 agaricus purpurescens
NT2 agaricus silvicola
NT2 agaricus subedulis
NT1 agrocybe
NT2 agrocybe aegerita
NT1 amanita
NT2 amanita caesarea
NT2 amanita muscaria
NT2 amanita pantherina
NT2 amanita phalloides
NT2 amanita virosa
NT1 armillaria
NT2 armillaria elegans
NT2 armillaria luteobubalina
NT2 armillaria mellea
NT2 armillaria obscura
NT2 armillaria ostoyae
NT2 armillaria tabescens
NT1 calocybe
NT2 calocybe indica
NT1 clitocybe
NT2 clitocybe geotropa
NT2 clitocybe illudens
NT2 clitocybe nebularis
NT1 collybia
NT2 collybia velutipes
NT1 conocybe
NT2 conocybe smithii
NT1 coprinus
NT2 coprinus aratus
NT2 coprinus atramentarius
NT2 coprinus comatus
NT2 coprinus micaceus
NT1 cortinarius
NT2 cortinarius armillatus
NT1 crinipellis
NT2 crinipellis perniciosa
NT1 flammulina
NT2 flammulina velutipes
NT1 hebeloma
NT2 hebeloma crustuliniforme
NT2 hebeloma cylindrosporum
NT1 kuehneromyces
NT2 kuehneromyces mutabilis
NT1 laccaria
NT2 laccaria laccata
NT1 lactarius
NT2 lactarius chrysorrus
NT2 lactarius rufus
NT2 lactarius sanguifluus
NT2 lactarius torminosus
NT1 lepiota
NT2 lepiota naucina
NT1 lyophyllum
NT2 lyophyllum decastes
NT1 macrolepiota
NT2 macrolepiota zeyheri
NT1 marasmiellus
NT2 marasmiellus cocophilus
NT1 pholiota
NT2 pholiota mutabilis
NT2 pholiota squarrosa
NT1 pleurotus
NT2 pleurotus cornucopiae
NT2 pleurotus eous
NT2 pleurotus eryngii
NT2 pleurotus flabellatus

AGARICALES *cont.*
NT2 pleurotus florida
NT2 pleurotus ostreatus
NT2 pleurotus sajor-caju
NT2 pleurotus salignus
NT2 pleurotus sapidus
NT2 pleurotus tuber-regium
NT1 psilocybe
NT2 psilocybe caerulescens
NT2 psilocybe pelliculosa
NT2 psilocybe semilanceata
NT2 psilocybe stuntzii
NT1 russula
NT2 russula versicolor
NT1 termitomyces
NT1 tricholoma
NT2 tricholoma matsutake
NT2 tricholoma nudum
NT1 volvariella
NT2 volvariella diplasia
NT2 volvariella esculenta
NT2 volvariella speciosa
NT2 volvariella volvacea
rt fungi

AGARICUS
BT1 agaricales
NT1 agaricus arvensis
NT1 agaricus bisporus
NT1 agaricus bitorquis
NT1 agaricus chionodermus
NT1 agaricus macrocarpus
NT1 agaricus macrosporoides
NT1 agaricus purpurescens
NT1 agaricus silvicola
NT1 agaricus subedulis

AGARICUS ARVENSIS
BT1 agaricus
BT2 agaricales
BT1 edible fungi
BT2 fungi
BT2 vegetables

AGARICUS BISPORUS
uf *agaricus brunnescens*
BT1 agaricus
BT2 agaricales
rt mushrooms

AGARICUS BITORQUIS
BT1 agaricus
BT2 agaricales
BT1 edible fungi
BT2 fungi
BT2 vegetables

agaricus brunnescens
USE **agaricus bisporus**

AGARICUS CHIONODERMUS
BT1 agaricus
BT2 agaricales
BT1 edible fungi
BT2 fungi
BT2 vegetables

AGARICUS MACROCARPUS
BT1 agaricus
BT2 agaricales
BT1 edible fungi
BT2 fungi
BT2 vegetables

AGARICUS MACROSPOROIDES
BT1 agaricus
BT2 agaricales
BT1 edible fungi
BT2 fungi
BT2 vegetables

AGARICUS PURPURESCENS
BT1 agaricus
BT2 agaricales
BT1 edible fungi
BT2 fungi
BT2 vegetables

AGARICUS SILVICOLA
BT1 agaricus
BT2 agaricales
BT1 edible fungi
BT2 fungi
BT2 vegetables

AGARICUS SUBEDULIS
BT1 agaricus
BT2 agaricales
BT1 edible fungi
BT2 fungi
BT2 vegetables

AGAROSE
BT1 galactans
BT2 polysaccharides
BT3 carbohydrates
rt agar

AGASICLES
BT1 chrysomelidae
BT2 coleoptera
NT1 agasicles hygrophila

AGASICLES HYGROPHILA
BT1 agasicles
BT2 chrysomelidae
BT3 coleoptera
BT1 biological control agents
BT2 beneficial organisms

AGASTACHE
BT1 labiatae
NT1 agastache foeniculum

AGASTACHE FOENICULUM
BT1 agastache
BT2 labiatae

AGASTACHYS
BT1 proteaceae
NT1 agastachys odorata

AGASTACHYS ODORATA
BT1 agastachys
BT2 proteaceae
BT1 ornamental woody plants

agathis
USE **agathis (araucariaceae)**
OR **agathis (hymenoptera)**

AGATHIS (ARAUCARIACEAE)
uf *agathis*
BT1 araucariaceae
NT1 agathis australis
NT1 agathis beccarii
NT1 agathis borneensis
NT1 agathis dammara
NT1 agathis labillardieri
NT1 agathis lanceolata
NT1 agathis macrophylla
NT1 agathis microstachya
NT1 agathis moorei
NT1 agathis palmerstonii
NT1 agathis philippinen
NT1 agathis robusta
NT1 agathis vitiensis

AGATHIS AUSTRALIS
BT1 agathis (araucariaceae)
BT2 araucariaceae
BT1 forest trees

AGATHIS BECCARII
BT1 agathis (araucariaceae)
BT2 araucariaceae

AGATHIS BORNEENSIS
BT1 agathis (araucariaceae)
BT2 araucariaceae

AGATHIS CINCTA
BT1 agathis (hymenoptera)
BT2 braconidae
BT3 hymenoptera

AGATHIS DAMMARA
uf *agathis loranthifolia*
BT1 agathis (araucariaceae)
BT2 araucariaceae
BT1 forest trees

AGATHIS GIBBOSA
BT1 agathis (hymenoptera)
BT2 braconidae
BT3 hymenoptera

AGATHIS (HYMENOPTERA)
uf *agathis*
BT1 braconidae

AGATHIS (HYMENOPTERA) *cont.*
BT2 hymenoptera
NT1 agathis cincta
NT1 agathis gibbosa
NT1 agathis pumila

AGATHIS LABILLARDIERI
BT1 agathis (araucariaceae)
BT2 araucariaceae

AGATHIS LANCEOLATA
BT1 agathis (araucariaceae)
BT2 araucariaceae

agathis loranthifolia
USE **agathis dammara**

AGATHIS MACROPHYLLA
BT1 agathis (araucariaceae)
BT2 araucariaceae
BT1 forest trees

AGATHIS MICROSTACHYA
BT1 agathis (araucariaceae)
BT2 araucariaceae

AGATHIS MOOREI
BT1 agathis (araucariaceae)
BT2 araucariaceae

AGATHIS PALMERSTONII
BT1 agathis (araucariaceae)
BT2 araucariaceae

AGATHIS PHILIPPINEN
BT1 agathis (araucariaceae)
BT2 araucariaceae

AGATHIS PUMILA
BT1 agathis (hymenoptera)
BT2 braconidae
BT3 hymenoptera
BT1 biological control agents
BT2 beneficial organisms

AGATHIS ROBUSTA
BT1 agathis (araucariaceae)
BT2 araucariaceae

agathis rufipes
USE **microdus rufipes**

AGATHIS VITIENSIS
BT1 agathis (araucariaceae)
BT2 araucariaceae

AGATHOSMA
BT1 rutaceae
NT1 agathosma serratifolia

agathosma betulina
USE **barosma betulina**

agathosma crenulata
USE **barosma crenulata**

AGATHOSMA SERRATIFOLIA
BT1 agathosma
BT2 rutaceae

AGAVACEAE
NT1 agave
NT2 agave amaniensis
NT2 agave americana
NT2 agave angustifolia
NT2 agave attenuata
NT2 agave aurea
NT2 agave avellanidens
NT2 agave brachystachys
NT2 agave cantala
NT2 agave cocui
NT2 agave deserti
NT2 agave ellemeetiana
NT2 agave falcata
NT2 agave fourcroydes
NT2 agave funkiana
NT2 agave ghiesbreghtii
NT2 agave goldmaniana
NT2 agave haynaldii
NT2 agave lechuguilla
NT2 agave letonae
NT2 agave maculosa
NT2 agave parrasana
NT2 agave parryi
NT2 agave rigida

AGAVACEAE *cont.*
NT2 agave rigidissima
NT2 agave salmiana
NT2 agave shawii
NT2 agave sisalana
NT2 agave tequilana
NT2 agave univittata
NT2 agave utahensis
NT2 agave vera-cruz
NT2 agave virginica
NT2 agave wrightii
NT1 beschorneria
NT1 cordyline
NT2 cordyline australis
NT2 cordyline cannifolia
NT2 cordyline fruticosa
NT2 cordyline indivisa
NT1 dasylirion
NT1 dracaena
NT2 dracaena angustifolia
NT2 dracaena deremensis
NT2 dracaena fragrans
NT2 dracaena marginata
NT2 dracaena sanderiana
NT1 furcraea
NT2 furcraea cabuya
NT2 furcraea foetida
NT2 furcraea macrophylla
NT2 furcraea marginata
NT1 hesperaloe
NT1 nolina
NT1 phormium
NT2 phormium cookianum
NT2 phormium tenax
NT1 polianthes
NT2 polianthes tuberosa
NT1 prochnyanthes
NT1 sansevieria
NT2 sansevieria roxburghiana
NT2 sansevieria trifasciata
NT2 sansevieria zeylanica
NT1 yucca
NT2 yucca aloifolia
NT2 yucca australis
NT2 yucca brevifolia
NT2 yucca elata
NT2 yucca elegantissima
NT2 yucca filamentosa
NT2 yucca flaccida
NT2 yucca glauca
NT2 yucca gloriosa
NT2 yucca recurvifolia
NT2 yucca schidigera
NT2 yucca torreyi
rt liliaceae

AGAVE
uf *manfreda*
BT1 agavaceae
NT1 agave amaniensis
NT1 agave americana
NT1 agave angustifolia
NT1 agave attenuata
NT1 agave aurea
NT1 agave avellanidens
NT1 agave brachystachys
NT1 agave cantala
NT1 agave cocui
NT1 agave deserti
NT1 agave ellemeetiana
NT1 agave falcata
NT1 agave fourcroydes
NT1 agave funkiana
NT1 agave ghiesbreghtii
NT1 agave goldmaniana
NT1 agave haynaldii
NT1 agave lechuguilla
NT1 agave letonae
NT1 agave maculosa
NT1 agave parrasana
NT1 agave parryi
NT1 agave rigida
NT1 agave rigidissima
NT1 agave salmiana
NT1 agave shawii
NT1 agave sisalana
NT1 agave tequilana
NT1 agave univittata
NT1 agave utahensis
NT1 agave vera-cruz
NT1 agave virginica

AGAVE *cont.*
NT1 agave wrightii

AGAVE AMANIENSIS
uf *blue sisal*
BT1 agave
BT2 agavaceae
BT1 fibre plants

AGAVE AMERICANA
BT1 agave
BT2 agavaceae
BT1 ornamental succulent plants
BT2 succulent plants

AGAVE ANGUSTIFOLIA
BT1 agave
BT2 agavaceae

agave atrovirens
USE **agave salmiana**

AGAVE ATTENUATA
BT1 agave
BT2 agavaceae

AGAVE AUREA
BT1 agave
BT2 agavaceae

AGAVE AVELLANIDENS
BT1 agave
BT2 agavaceae

AGAVE BRACHYSTACHYS
BT1 agave
BT2 agavaceae

AGAVE CANTALA
BT1 agave
BT2 agavaceae
BT1 fibre plants
BT1 medicinal plants
BT1 molluscicidal plants
BT2 pesticidal plants

AGAVE COCUI
BT1 agave
BT2 agavaceae

AGAVE DESERTI
BT1 agave
BT2 agavaceae

AGAVE ELLEMEETIANA
BT1 agave
BT2 agavaceae

AGAVE FALCATA
BT1 agave
BT2 agavaceae
BT1 fibre plants

AGAVE FOURCROYDES
BT1 agave
BT2 agavaceae
BT1 fibre plants
rt henequen

AGAVE FUNKIANA
BT1 agave
BT2 agavaceae
BT1 fibre plants

AGAVE GHIESBREGHTII
BT1 agave
BT2 agavaceae

AGAVE GOLDMANIANA
BT1 agave
BT2 agavaceae

AGAVE HAYNALDII
BT1 agave
BT2 agavaceae

AGAVE LECHUGUILLA
BT1 agave
BT2 agavaceae
BT1 fibre plants

AGAVE LETONAE
BT1 agave
BT2 agavaceae

agave lophantha
USE **agave univittata**

AGAVE MACULOSA
BT1 agave
BT2 agavaceae
BT1 ornamental succulent plants
BT2 succulent plants

AGAVE PARRASANA
BT1 agave
BT2 agavaceae

AGAVE PARRYI
BT1 agave
BT2 agavaceae
BT1 ornamental succulent plants
BT2 succulent plants

AGAVE RIGIDA
BT1 agave
BT2 agavaceae
BT1 fibre plants

AGAVE RIGIDISSIMA
BT1 agave
BT2 agavaceae

AGAVE SALMIANA
uf *agave atrovirens*
BT1 agave
BT2 agavaceae
BT1 antibacterial plants
BT1 industrial crops

AGAVE SHAWII
BT1 agave
BT2 agavaceae

AGAVE SISALANA
BT1 agave
BT2 agavaceae
BT1 fibre plants
rt sisal

AGAVE TEQUILANA
BT1 agave
BT2 agavaceae
BT1 industrial crops

AGAVE UNIVITTATA
uf *agave lophantha*
BT1 agave
BT2 agavaceae
BT1 medicinal plants

AGAVE UTAHENSIS
BT1 agave
BT2 agavaceae

AGAVE VERA-CRUZ
BT1 agave
BT2 agavaceae

AGAVE VIRGINICA
BT1 agave
BT2 agavaceae

AGAVE WRIGHTII
BT1 agave
BT2 agavaceae
BT1 medicinal plants

AGE
NT1 age at first calving
NT1 age at first egg
NT1 age at first insemination
NT1 age at first kidding
NT1 age at first lambing
NT1 age at first mating
NT1 age at weaning
NT1 age composition
NT1 age differences
NT1 age of soil
NT1 age of trees
NT1 leaf age
NT2 leaf duration
NT1 marriage age
NT1 middle age
NT1 physiological age
NT1 seed age
NT1 seedling age
NT1 skeletal age
rt age determination
rt age groups

AGE *cont.*
rt age structure
rt aging
rt dendrochronology
rt duration
rt exploitable age or size
rt longevity
rt maturity
rt menopause
rt old and fossil wood
rt puberty
rt seed aging
rt time

AGE AT FIRST CALVING
BT1 age
rt calving

AGE AT FIRST EGG
BT1 age
rt egg production
rt eggs
rt sexual maturity

AGE AT FIRST INSEMINATION
BT1 age
rt artificial insemination

AGE AT FIRST KIDDING
BT1 age
rt kidding

AGE AT FIRST LAMBING
BT1 age
rt lambing

AGE AT FIRST MATING
HN from 1989
BT1 age
rt mating

AGE AT WEANING
HN from 1989
BT1 age
rt weaning

AGE COMPOSITION
BT1 age

AGE DETERMINATION
BT1 determination
BT2 techniques
NT1 dendrochronology
NT1 radiocarbon dating
rt age
rt growth rings

AGE DIFFERENCES
BT1 age
rt aging
rt gonoration conflict
rt population structure

AGE GROUPS
BT1 groups
NT1 adolescents
NT2 pregnant adolescents (agricola)
NT1 old age
NT1 youth
NT2 disadvantaged youth (agricola)
NT2 rural youth
rt adults
rt age
rt age structure
rt retired people

AGE OF SOIL
BT1 age
rt soil

AGE OF TREES
BT1 age
rt growth rings
rt veteran or remarkable trees

AGE STRUCTURE
BT1 population dynamics
rt age
rt age groups

aged
USE **elderly (agricola)**

AGELAEA
BT1 connaraceae
NT1 agelaea obliqua

AGELAEA OBLIQUA
BT1 agelaea
BT2 connaraceae

AGELASTICA
BT1 chrysomelidae
BT2 coleoptera
NT1 agelastica alni

AGELASTICA ALNI
BT1 agelastica
BT2 chrysomelidae
BT3 coleoptera

AGELENIDAE
HN from 1989
BT1 araneae
BT2 arachnida
BT3 arthropods
NT1 tegenaria
NT2 tegenaria agrestis

AGENEOTETTIX
BT1 acrididae
BT2 orthoptera
NT1 ageneotettix deorum

AGENEOTETTIX DEORUM
BT1 ageneotettix
BT2 acrididae
BT3 orthoptera

AGENIASPIS
BT1 encyrtidae
BT2 hymenoptera
NT1 ageniaspis fuscicollis

AGENIASPIS FUSCICOLLIS
BT1 ageniaspis
BT2 encyrtidae
BT3 hymenoptera

AGERATINA
BT1 compositae
NT1 ageratina riparia

AGERATINA RIPARIA
BT1 ageratina
BT2 compositae

AGERATUM
BT1 compositae
NT1 ageratum conyzoides
NT1 ageratum houstonianum

AGERATUM CONYZOIDES
BT1 ageratum
BT2 compositae
BT1 essential oil plants
BT2 oil plants
BT1 insecticidal plants
BT2 pesticidal plants
BT1 medicinal plants
BT1 ornamental herbaceous plants

AGERATUM HOUSTONIANUM
uf *ageratum mexicanum*
BT1 ageratum
BT2 compositae
BT1 ornamental herbaceous plants

ageratum mexicanum
USE **ageratum houstonianum**

agevillea
USE **paradiplosis**

agevillea abietis
USE **paradiplosis abietis**

agglutinating factor
USE **agglutinins**

AGGLUTINATION
NT1 autoagglutination
NT1 bacterial agglutination
NT1 haemagglutination
NT2 passive haemagglutination
rt agglutination tests
rt agglutinins

AGGLUTINATION *cont.*
rt antigen antibody reactions
rt combination
rt immune response

AGGLUTINATION TESTS
uf *milk ring test*
BT1 immunological techniques
BT2 techniques
BT1 tests
NT1 haemagglutination tests
NT2 antiglobulin test
NT2 coombs test
NT2 haemagglutination inhibition test
NT1 immunosorbent agglutination assay
NT1 latex agglutination test
rt agglutination

AGGLUTININS
uf *agglutinating factor*
BT1 antibodies
BT2 immunoglobulins
BT3 glycoproteins
BT4 proteins
BT5 peptides
BT3 immunological factors
NT1 haemagglutinins
NT2 viral haemagglutinins
NT1 lectins
NT2 phytohaemagglutinins
NT3 concanavalin a
NT3 limulins
NT3 ricin
rt agglutination
rt antigens

AGGREGATE ACCOUNTS
BT1 accounts
rt aggregate data
rt economic accounts
rt national accounting
rt regional accounting

AGGREGATE DATA
NT1 consumer expenditure
NT2 household expenditure
NT2 tourist expenditure
NT3 souvenirs
NT1 final consumption
NT1 final production
NT1 gross national product
NT2 national income
NT1 value added
rt aggregate accounts
rt aggregate statistics
rt national expenditure

AGGREGATE DENSITY
BT1 soil density
BT2 density
BT2 soil physical properties
BT3 soil properties
BT4 properties
rt aggregates

AGGREGATE STATISTICS
HN from 1990
uf *aggregation, statistical*
BT1 statistics
rt aggregate data

AGGREGATES
BT1 soil structural units
BT2 soil structure
BT3 soil physical properties
BT4 soil properties
BT5 properties
NT1 microaggregates
rt aggregate density
rt micelles

AGGREGATION
BT1 animal behaviour
BT2 behaviour
rt aggregation disrupters
rt aggregation disruption
rt aggregation pheromones

AGGREGATION DISRUPTERS
BT1 inhibitors
rt aggregation

AGGREGATION DISRUPTERS *cont.*
rt aggregation disruption
rt aggregation pheromones

AGGREGATION DISRUPTION
BT1 disruption
BT1 insect control
BT2 pest control
BT3 control
rt aggregation
rt aggregation disrupters

AGGREGATION PHEROMONES
BT1 pheromones
BT2 semiochemicals
NT1 brevicomin
NT1 frontalin
NT1 ipsdienol
NT1 ipsenol
NT1 multistriatin
rt aggregation
rt aggregation disrupters
rt antiaggregation pheromones
rt pheromone traps

aggregation, statistical
USE **aggregate statistics**

AGGRESSION
rt aggressive behaviour

AGGRESSIVE BEHAVIOR
BF aggressive behaviour
BT1 behavior

AGGRESSIVE BEHAVIOUR
AF aggressive behavior
uf *violence*
BT1 behaviour
NT1 balling
NT1 colony defence
NT1 fighting
NT1 robbing
NT1 stinging
rt aggression
rt agonistic behaviour
rt bites
rt stings
rt terrorism

AGING
BT1 physiological functions
NT1 accelerated aging
NT1 seed aging
rt age
rt age differences
rt death
rt geriatrics
rt longevity
rt maturity
rt old age
rt ripening
rt senescence
rt senility

aging of seeds
USE **seed aging**

AGISTEMUS
BT1 stigmaeidae
BT2 prostigmata
BT3 acari
NT1 agistemus exsertus
NT1 agistemus fleschneri
NT1 agistemus floridanus
NT1 agistemus terminalis

AGISTEMUS EXSERTUS
BT1 agistemus
BT2 stigmaeidae
BT3 prostigmata
BT4 acari

AGISTEMUS FLESCHNERI
BT1 agistemus
BT2 stigmaeidae
BT3 prostigmata
BT4 acari

AGISTEMUS FLORIDANUS
BT1 agistemus
BT2 stigmaeidae
BT3 prostigmata
BT4 acari

AGISTEMUS TERMINALIS
BT1 agistemus
BT2 stigmaeidae
BT3 prostigmata
BT4 acari

AGITATION
BT1 processing
rt aeration
rt agitators
rt mixing
rt movement
rt spraying
rt stirrers

AGITATORS
BT1 equipment
rt aeration
rt agitation
rt mixing
rt stirrers

AGLAIS
BT1 nymphalidae
BT2 lepidoptera
NT1 aglais urticae

AGLAIS URTICAE
BT1 aglais
BT2 nymphalidae
BT3 lepidoptera

AGLAONEMA
BT1 araceae
NT1 aglaonema commutatum
NT1 aglaonema crispum

AGLAONEMA COMMUTATUM
uf *aglaonema treubii*
BT1 aglaonema
BT2 araceae
rt ornamental foliage plants

AGLAONEMA CRISPUM
uf *aglaonema roebelinii*
BT1 aglaonema
BT2 araceae
rt ornamental foliage plants

aglaonema roebelinii
USE **aglaonema crispum**

aglaonema treubii
USE **aglaonema commutatum**

AGLAOPE
BT1 zygaenidae
BT2 lepidoptera
NT1 aglaope infausta

AGLAOPE INFAUSTA
BT1 aglaope
BT2 zygaenidae
BT3 lepidoptera

AGLAOSPORA
BT1 pyrenulales
rt tunstallia

aglaospora aculeata
USE **tunstallia aculeata**

AGLENCHUS
BT1 tylenchidae
BT2 nematoda
NT1 aglenchus agricola
rt coslenchus

AGLENCHUS AGRICOLA
BT1 aglenchus
BT2 tylenchidae
BT3 nematoda

aglenchus costatus
USE **coslenchus costatus**

AGLINET
uf *agricultural library network*
BT1 information services
BT2 services
BT1 international organizations
BT2 organizations
rt libraries

AGMATINE
BT1 guanidines

AGMATINE *cont.*
BT2 organic nitrogen compounds

AGONIS
BT1 myrtaceae
NT1 agonis flexuosa

AGONIS FLEXUOSA
BT1 agonis
BT2 myrtaceae
BT1 ornamental woody plants

AGONISTIC BEHAVIOR
BF agonistic behaviour
BT1 behavior

AGONISTIC BEHAVIOUR
AF agonistic behavior
BT1 behaviour
rt aggressive behaviour
rt athletics
rt vices

AGONISTS
NT1 β-adrenergic agonists
rt antagonists

AGONOMYCETALES
NT1 rhizoctonia
NT2 rhizoctonia cerealis
NT2 rhizoctonia fragariae
NT2 rhizoctonia solani
NT2 rhizoctonia tuliparum
NT1 sclerotium
NT2 sclerotium cepivorum
rt fungi

AGONOSCENA
BT1 aphalaridae
BT2 psylloidea
BT3 sternorrhyncha
BT4 homoptera
NT1 agonoscena targionii

AGONOSCENA TARGIONII
BT1 agonoscena
BT2 aphalaridae
BT3 psylloidea
BT4 sternorrhyncha
BT5 homoptera

AGONUM
BT1 carabidae
BT2 coleoptera
NT1 agonum dorsale

AGONUM DORSALE
BT1 agonum
BT2 carabidae
BT3 coleoptera

AGOUTI
uf *cuniculus*
BT1 dasyproctidae
BT2 rodents
BT3 mammals

AGRARIAN COUNTRIES
BT1 countries
rt agricultural society
rt developing countries
rt pastoral society

AGRARIAN REFORM
NT1 land reform
rt agricultural structure
rt collectivization
rt structural policy
rt tenure systems

AGRAULIS
BT1 nymphalidae
BT2 lepidoptera
NT1 agraulis vanillae

AGRAULIS VANILLAE
BT1 agraulis
BT2 nymphalidae
BT3 lepidoptera

AGREP
(inventory of research projects in the ec)
BT1 international organizations

AGREP *cont.*
BT2 organizations
rt diffusion of research

AGRIA
BT1 sarcophagidae
BT2 diptera
NT1 agria housei

AGRIA HOUSEI
BT1 agria
BT2 sarcophagidae
BT3 diptera

AGRIBUSINESS
BT1 agroindustrial sector
rt agroindustrial complexes
rt contract farming
rt postagricultural sector
rt vertical integration

AGRICOLA
HN from 1990
BT1 information services
BT2 services

AGRICULTURAL ADJUSTMENT
BT1 adjustment of production
BT2 production policy
BT3 economic policy
rt agricultural structure

AGRICULTURAL AVIATION
uf *aviation, agricultural*
rt aerial application
rt aerial collection
rt aerial methods
rt aerial photography
rt aerial sprayers
rt aerial spraying
rt aerial surveys
rt air transport
rt aircraft

AGRICULTURAL BANKS
uf *banks, agricultural*
BT1 banks
BT2 financial institutions
BT3 organizations

AGRICULTURAL BUDGETS
BT1 budgets
rt financial planning

agricultural buildings
USE **farm buildings**

AGRICULTURAL BYPRODUCTS
BT1 byproducts
NT1 cereal byproducts
NT2 bran
NT3 maize bran
NT3 oat bran (agricola)
NT3 rice bran
NT3 wheat bran
NT2 brewers' grains
NT2 chaff
NT2 maize byproducts
NT3 maize bran
NT3 maize cobs
NT3 maize stover
NT3 maize straw
NT2 rice byproducts
NT3 rice bran
NT3 rice polishings
NT3 rice straw
NT2 rye middlings
NT1 cocoa byproducts
NT1 meat byproducts
NT2 meat and bone meal
NT2 meat meal
NT3 tendon meal
NT3 whale meal
NT2 offal
NT3 brain as food
NT3 heart as food
NT3 kidneys as food
NT3 livers as food
NT4 foie gras
NT4 goose liver
NT3 sweetbreads
NT1 milk byproducts
NT1 peel
NT2 cassava peel

AGRICULTURAL BYPRODUCTS *cont.*
NT2 orange peel
NT1 straw
NT2 barley straw
NT2 bean straw
NT2 groundnut haulm
NT2 maize straw
NT2 oat straw
NT2 rape straw
NT2 rice straw
NT2 rye straw
NT2 ryegrass straw
NT2 sorghum stalks
NT2 soya straw
NT2 stover
NT3 maize stover
NT2 wheat straw
NT1 sugarcane byproducts
NT2 sugarcane bagasse
NT2 sugarcane pith
NT2 sugarcane tops
rt plant residues

AGRICULTURAL CENSUSES
BT1 censuses
BT2 surveys
NT1 livestock censuses
NT1 world census of agriculture
rt descriptive statistics
rt european farm accounting network
rt farm numbers
rt farm surveys

AGRICULTURAL CHEMICALS
(see also under attractants, chemosterilants, fertilizers, growth regulators, pesticides, repellents)
uf *agrochemicals*
rt agrochemical centres
rt chemical industry
rt chemicals
rt chemoprophylaxis
rt farm inputs
rt formulations

AGRICULTURAL COLLEGES
BT1 educational institutions
rt agricultural education
rt colleges (agricola)
rt higher education

AGRICULTURAL CREDIT
uf *credit, agricultural*
BT1 credit
BT2 finance
rt agricultural financial policy
rt cooperative credit
rt preferential interest rates
rt support measures

AGRICULTURAL CRISES
BT1 agricultural disasters
BT2 disasters
BT1 agricultural situation
BT1 crises (agricola)
rt economic depression

AGRICULTURAL DEVELOPMENT
uf *development, agricultural*
BT1 agricultural situation
NT1 green revolution
rt development
rt development policy
rt economic development
rt modernization
rt rural development
rt sectoral development

AGRICULTURAL DISASTERS
uf *disasters, agricultural*
BT1 disasters
NT1 agricultural crises
rt agricultural insurance
rt climatic factors
rt compensation
rt crop insurance
rt damage
rt natural disasters
rt subsidies

AGRICULTURAL ECONOMICS
uf *economics, agricultural*

AGRICULTURAL ECONOMICS *cont.*
BT1 economics
rt agricultural economists
rt agricultural sciences

AGRICULTURAL ECONOMISTS
BT1 occupations
rt agricultural economics
rt american agricultural economics association

AGRICULTURAL EDUCATION
uf *education, agricultural*
BT1 education
NT1 dairy education
rt agricultural colleges
rt science education

AGRICULTURAL ENGINEERING
BT1 agricultural sciences
BT1 engineering
rt agricultural machinery industry
rt agriculture
rt farm machinery
rt mechanical methods
rt mechanization
rt technical progress

AGRICULTURAL ENTOMOLOGY
BT1 entomology
BT2 zoology
BT3 biology

AGRICULTURAL FINANCIAL POLICY
uf *financial policy*
uf *policy, agricultural financial*
BT1 agricultural policy
rt agricultural credit
rt financial planning
rt fiscal policy
rt policy
rt subsidies
rt support measures

AGRICULTURAL GEOGRAPHY
BT1 geography
rt agricultural regions
rt rural areas
rt rural environment

AGRICULTURAL HOUSEHOLDS
BT1 households
rt farm dwellings
rt farm families
rt rural housing

AGRICULTURAL INSURANCE
BT1 insurance
NT1 animal insurance
NT1 crop insurance
NT1 hail insurance
rt agricultural disasters
rt cooperative insurance
rt social insurance

AGRICULTURAL LAND
BT1 land resources
BT2 non-renewable resources
BT3 natural resources
BT4 resources
BT1 land types
NT1 arable land
NT1 farmland
rt deforestation
rt farmland
rt land classification
rt land clearance
rt land use

AGRICULTURAL LAW
BT1 law
BT2 legal systems
rt contract legislation
rt rural law

agricultural library network
USE **aglinet**

AGRICULTURAL MACHINERY INDUSTRY
BT1 input industries
BT2 industry

AGRICULTURAL MACHINERY INDUSTRY *cont.*
rt agricultural engineering
rt farm machinery
rt machinery

AGRICULTURAL MANPOWER
uf agricultural workers
BT1 labour
NT1 farm workers
NT2 milkers
NT1 peasant workers

AGRICULTURAL METEOROLOGY
uf agrometeorology
BT1 meteorology
rt agroclimatology
rt climate
rt climatic factors
rt meteorological factors
rt weather data

AGRICULTURAL PLANNING
uf planning, agricultural
BT1 sectoral planning
BT2 planning
rt agricultural policy
rt farm planning
rt socialist agriculture

AGRICULTURAL POLICY
uf policy, agricultural
NT1 agricultural financial policy
NT1 cap
NT1 regional agricultural policy
NT1 structural policy
rt agricultural planning
rt agricultural situation
rt economic policy
rt food policy
rt forest policy
rt marketing policy
rt policy
rt price policy
rt support measures
rt trade policy

AGRICULTURAL POPULATION
uf population, agricultural
BT1 rural population
rt human population

AGRICULTURAL PRICES
uf prices, agricultural
BT1 prices
NT1 milk payments
NT1 reference prices
NT1 sluicegate prices
NT1 target prices
NT1 threshold prices
NT1 withdrawal prices
rt price policy
rt producer prices

AGRICULTURAL PRODUCTION
BT1 production
NT1 animal production
NT2 calf production
NT2 chick production
NT2 egg production
NT3 turkey egg production
NT2 foal production
NT2 kid production
NT2 kit production
NT2 meat production
NT3 beef production
NT3 broiler production
NT3 lamb production
NT2 milk production
NT2 piglet production
NT2 progeny production
NT1 crop production
NT1 extensive production
NT2 extensive farming
NT3 extensive husbandry
NT3 extensive livestock farming
NT4 ranching
NT1 intensive production
NT1 wool production
rt agricultural situation
rt farming
rt horticulture

AGRICULTURAL PRODUCTION *cont.*
rt production possibilities

AGRICULTURAL PRODUCTS
uf products, agricultural
BT1 products
rt animal products
rt commodities
rt non-food products
rt plant products
rt primary products

AGRICULTURAL REGIONS
BT1 regions
rt agricultural geography

AGRICULTURAL RESEARCH
uf research, agricultural
BT1 research
NT1 dairy research
NT1 farming systems research
rt agricultural sciences
rt agriculture

AGRICULTURAL SCIENCES
NT1 agricultural engineering
NT1 agronomy
NT1 dairy science
NT1 horticulture
NT2 floriculture
NT2 fruit growing
NT2 vegetable growing
NT2 viticulture
NT1 soil science
rt agricultural economics
rt agricultural research
rt agriculture
rt biology
rt botany
rt entomology
rt genetics
rt helminthology
rt mycology
rt pedology
rt veterinary science
rt zoology

AGRICULTURAL SECTOR
BT1 agroindustrial sector
NT1 farm sector

AGRICULTURAL SHOWS
BT1 trade fairs
BT2 marketing techniques
BT3 techniques
rt agriculture
rt extension
rt publicity

AGRICULTURAL SITUATION
NT1 agricultural crises
NT1 agricultural development
NT2 green revolution
rt agricultural policy
rt agricultural production
rt agricultural structure
rt capital allocation
rt economic situation
rt farm indebtedness

agricultural societies
USE **farmers' associations**

AGRICULTURAL SOCIETY
BT1 society
NT1 pastoral society
rt agrarian countries
rt agriculture
rt rural society
rt traditional society

AGRICULTURAL SOILS
BT1 soil types (cultural)

AGRICULTURAL STATISTICS
BT1 statistics
NT1 dairy statistics
rt agriculture
rt descriptive statistics

AGRICULTURAL STRUCTURE
NT1 farm closures
NT1 farm numbers
NT1 farming systems

AGRICULTURAL STRUCTURE *cont.*
NT1 production structure
rt adjustment of production
rt agrarian reform
rt agricultural adjustment
rt agricultural situation
rt agriculture
rt concentration of production
rt farm amalgamations
rt farm entrants
rt land reform
rt structural change
rt structural policy
rt structure

agricultural systems
USE **farming systems**

agricultural tenure
USE **tenure systems**

AGRICULTURAL TRADE
BT1 trade
rt commodities

AGRICULTURAL TRADE UNIONS
BT1 trade unions
BT2 interest groups
BT3 groups
BT3 organizations
rt farm workers
rt farmers' associations

AGRICULTURAL UNEMPLOYMENT
uf unemployment, agricultural
BT1 rural unemployment
BT2 unemployment
BT3 employment

AGRICULTURAL WASTES
uf farm wastes
BT1 wastes
NT1 bagasse
NT2 sisal bagasse
NT2 sugarcane bagasse
NT1 banana waste
NT1 cotton waste
NT1 dairy wastes
NT1 hatchery waste
NT1 potato waste
NT1 tomato waste
rt animal wastes
rt crop residues
rt organic wastes
rt wastage

agricultural workers
USE **agricultural manpower**
OR **farm workers**

AGRICULTURE
NT1 capitalist agriculture
NT1 prehistoric agriculture
NT1 suburban agriculture
rt agricultural engineering
rt agricultural research
rt agricultural sciences
rt agricultural shows
rt agricultural society
rt agricultural statistics
rt agricultural structure
rt agroindustrial complexes
rt agroindustrial relations
rt agronomy
rt farming
rt forestry
rt horticulture
rt husbandry
rt ministries of agriculture

agriforestry
USE **agroforestry**

AGRILUS
BT1 buprestidae
BT2 coleoptera
NT1 agrilus anxius

AGRILUS ANXIUS
BT1 agrilus
BT2 buprestidae
BT3 coleoptera

AGRIMONIA
BT1 rosaceae
NT1 agrimonia eupatoria
NT1 agrimonia pilosa

AGRIMONIA EUPATORIA
BT1 agrimonia
BT2 rosaceae
BT1 dye plants

AGRIMONIA PILOSA
BT1 agrimonia
BT2 rosaceae
BT1 medicinal plants

agriolimax
USE **deroceras**

agriolimax reticulatus
USE **deroceras reticulatum**

AGRION
BT1 calopterygidae
BT2 odonata

AGRIOSTOMUM
BT1 chabertiidae
BT2 nematoda
NT1 agriostomum vryburgi

AGRIOSTOMUM VRYBURGI
BT1 agriostomum
BT2 chabertiidae
BT3 nematoda

AGRIOTES
BT1 elateridae
BT2 coleoptera
NT1 agriotes brevis
NT1 agriotes gurgistanus
NT1 agriotes lineatus
NT1 agriotes obscurus
NT1 agriotes sordidus
NT1 agriotes sputator
NT1 agriotes squalidus
NT1 agriotes ustulatus

AGRIOTES BREVIS
BT1 agriotes
BT2 elateridae
BT3 coleoptera

AGRIOTES GURGISTANUS
BT1 agriotes
BT2 elateridae
BT3 coleoptera

AGRIOTES LINEATUS
BT1 agriotes
BT2 elateridae
BT3 coleoptera

AGRIOTES OBSCURUS
BT1 agriotes
BT2 elateridae
BT3 coleoptera

AGRIOTES SORDIDUS
BT1 agriotes
BT2 elateridae
BT3 coleoptera

AGRIOTES SPUTATOR
BT1 agriotes
BT2 elateridae
BT3 coleoptera

AGRIOTES SQUALIDUS
BT1 agriotes
BT2 elateridae
BT3 coleoptera

AGRIOTES USTULATUS
BT1 agriotes
BT2 elateridae
BT3 coleoptera

AGRIS
BT1 information services
BT2 services
rt food and agriculture organization

agrisilvicultural systems
USE **agrosilvicultural systems**

agrisilviculture
USE **agrosilvicultural systems**

AGRIUS
BT1 sphingidae
BT2 lepidoptera
NT1 agrius cingulatus
NT1 agrius convolvuli

AGRIUS CINGULATUS
BT1 agrius
BT2 sphingidae
BT3 lepidoptera

AGRIUS CONVOLVULI
BT1 agrius
BT2 sphingidae
BT3 lepidoptera

agro-forestry
USE **agroforestry**

AGROBACTERIUM
BT1 plant pathogenic bacteria
BT2 plant pathogens
BT3 pathogens
BT1 rhizobiaceae
BT2 gracilicutes
BT3 bacteria
BT4 prokaryotes
NT1 agrobacterium radiobacter
NT1 agrobacterium rhizogenes
NT1 agrobacterium rubi
NT1 agrobacterium tumefaciens

AGROBACTERIUM RADIOBACTER
BT1 agrobacterium
BT2 plant pathogenic bacteria
BT3 plant pathogens
BT4 pathogens
BT2 rhizobiaceae
BT3 gracilicutes
BT4 bacteria
BT5 prokaryotes
BT1 fungal antagonists
BT2 fungicides
BT3 pesticides
BT2 microbial pesticides
BT3 pesticides

AGROBACTERIUM RHIZOGENES
BT1 agrobacterium
BT2 plant pathogenic bacteria
BT3 plant pathogens
BT4 pathogens
BT2 rhizobiaceae
BT3 gracilicutes
BT4 bacteria
BT5 prokaryotes

AGROBACTERIUM RUBI
BT1 agrobacterium
BT2 plant pathogenic bacteria
BT3 plant pathogens
BT4 pathogens
BT2 rhizobiaceae
BT3 gracilicutes
BT4 bacteria
BT5 prokaryotes

AGROBACTERIUM TUMEFACIENS
BT1 agrobacterium
BT2 plant pathogenic bacteria
BT3 plant pathogens
BT4 pathogens
BT2 rhizobiaceae
BT3 gracilicutes
BT4 bacteria
BT5 prokaryotes
rt crown gall

AGROCHEMICAL CENTERS
BF agrochemical centres

AGROCHEMICAL CENTRES
AF agrochemical centers
BT1 services
rt agricultural chemicals

agrochemicals
USE **agricultural chemicals**

AGROCLIMATOLOGY
BT1 climatology

AGROCLIMATOLOGY *cont.*
rt agricultural meteorology

AGROCYBE
BT1 agaricales
NT1 agrocybe aegerita

AGROCYBE AEGERITA
BT1 agrocybe
BT2 agaricales
BT1 edible fungi
BT2 fungi
BT2 vegetables

AGROFORESTRY
(land use system in which woody perennials are deliberately grown with agricultural crops, with or without animals)
uf *agriforestry*
uf *agro-forestry*
BT1 forestry
rt agroforestry systems
rt community forestry
rt farm forestry
rt farm woodlands
rt intercropping
rt land use
rt multiple land use
rt multipurpose trees
rt shifting cultivation
rt social forestry
rt sustainability

AGROFORESTRY SYSTEMS
(land use systems in which woody perennials are deliberately grown with agricultural crops, with or without animals)
NT1 agrosilviaquacultural systems
NT1 agrosilvicultural systems
NT2 alley cropping
NT2 forest gardens
NT2 mixed gardens
NT2 multistorey cropping
NT2 taungya
NT2 tree gardens
NT1 agrosilvopastoral systems
NT2 home gardens
NT1 aquasilvicultural systems
NT1 silvopastoral systems
NT2 live fences
NT2 protein banks
NT1 village forest gardens
rt agroforestry
rt corridor systems
rt hedges
rt multipurpose trees
rt shifting cultivation

AGROHORDEUM
BT1 gramineae
NT1 agrohordeum macounii

AGROHORDEUM MACOUNII
BT1 agrohordeum
BT2 gramineae
BT1 pasture plants

AGROINDUSTRIAL BYPRODUCTS
BT1 byproducts
NT1 brewery byproducts
NT2 brewers' grains
NT1 hydrol
NT1 milling byproducts
rt agroindustrial sector

AGROINDUSTRIAL COMPLEXES
BT1 socialist agriculture
rt agribusiness
rt agriculture
rt agroindustrial relations
rt vertical integration

AGROINDUSTRIAL RELATIONS
uf *industry and agriculture*
rt agriculture
rt agroindustrial complexes
rt production controls
rt relationships

AGROINDUSTRIAL SECTOR
uf *food and agricultural sector*

AGROINDUSTRIAL SECTOR *cont.*
NT1 agribusiness
NT1 agricultural sector
NT2 farm sector
NT1 postagricultural sector
NT1 preagricultural sector
rt agroindustrial byproducts
rt economic sectors
rt food industry

agroindustry
USE **industry**

agrometeorology
USE **agricultural meteorology**

AGROMYCES
BT1 firmicutes
BT2 bacteria
BT3 prokaryotes
NT1 agromyces ramosus

AGROMYCES RAMOSUS
BT1 agromyces
BT2 firmicutes
BT3 bacteria
BT4 prokaryotes

AGROMYZA
BT1 agromyzidae
BT2 diptera
NT1 agromyza frontella
NT1 agromyza oryzae
rt chromatomyia
rt melanagromyza
rt ophiomyia

agromyza atricornis
USE **chromatomyia horticola**
OR **chromatomyia syngenesiae**

AGROMYZA FRONTELLA
BT1 agromyza
BT2 agromyzidae
BT3 diptera

agromyza obtusa
USE **melanagromyza obtusa**

AGROMYZA ORYZAE
BT1 agromyza
BT2 agromyzidae
BT3 diptera

agromyza phaseoli
USE **ophiomyia phaseoli**

AGROMYZIDAE
BT1 diptera
NT1 agromyza
NT2 agromyza frontella
NT2 agromyza oryzae
NT1 calycomyza
NT1 chromatomyia
NT2 chromatomyia horticola
NT2 chromatomyia nigra
NT2 chromatomyia syngenesiae
NT1 liriomyza
NT2 liriomyza bryoniae
NT2 liriomyza cepae
NT2 liriomyza cicerina
NT2 liriomyza huidobrensis
NT2 liriomyza sativae
NT2 liriomyza trifoliearum
NT2 liriomyza trifolii
NT1 melanagromyza
NT2 melanagromyza obtusa
NT2 melanagromyza sojae
NT1 napomyza
NT2 napomyza carotae
NT1 ophiomyia
NT2 ophiomyia centrosematis
NT2 ophiomyia lantanae
NT2 ophiomyia phaseoli
NT2 ophiomyia shibatsujii
NT2 ophiomyia simplex
NT1 phytobia
NT1 phytomyza
NT2 phytomyza ilicicola
NT2 phytomyza orobanchia
NT2 phytomyza ranunculi
NT1 tropicomyia
NT2 tropicomyia theae

AGRONOMIC CHARACTERISTICS
BT1 characteristics
NT1 plant height
NT1 resistance to penetration
NT1 resistivity
NT1 wind resistance
rt genotypes

AGRONOMY
BT1 agricultural sciences
rt agriculture
rt crop husbandry

AGROPASTORAL SYSTEMS
(land use systems with agricultural crops and livestock but no trees)
rt multiple land use
rt pastoral society
rt pastoralism

agropisciculture
USE **aquaculture**
OR **fish farming**

AGROPYRON
uf *eremopyrum*
uf *roegneria*
uf *wheatgrass*
BT1 gramineae
NT1 agropyron cristatum
NT1 agropyron desertorum
NT1 agropyron fragile
NT1 agropyron imbricatum
NT1 agropyron scabrum

agropyron caninum
USE **elymus caninus**

AGROPYRON CRISTATUM
uf *agropyron pectinatum*
uf *agropyron pectiniforme*
BT1 agropyron
BT2 gramineae
BT1 pasture plants

agropyron dasystachyum
USE **elymus lanceolatus**

agropyron dentatum
USE **elymus dentatus**

AGROPYRON DESERTORUM
BT1 agropyron
BT2 gramineae
BT1 pasture plants

agropyron elongatum
USE **elymus elongatus**

agropyron fibrosum
USE **elymus fibrosus**

AGROPYRON FRAGILE
uf *agropyron sibiricum*
BT1 agropyron
BT2 gramineae
BT1 pasture plants

agropyron glaucum
USE **elymus hispidus**

AGROPYRON IMBRICATUM
BT1 agropyron
BT2 gramineae
BT1 pasture plants

agropyron intermedium
USE **elymus hispidus**

agropyron junceiforme
USE **elymus farctus**

agropyron latiglume
USE **elymus kronokensis**

agropyron pectinatum
USE **agropyron cristatum**

agropyron pectiniforme
USE **agropyron cristatum**

agropyron pungens
USE **elymus pungens**

agropyron repens
USE **elymus repens**

agropyron riparium
USE **elymus lanceolatus**

AGROPYRON SCABRUM
BT1 agropyron
BT2 gramineae
BT1 pasture plants

agropyron sibiricum
USE **agropyron fragile**

agropyron smithii
USE **elymus smithii**

agropyron spicatum
USE **elymus spicatus**

agropyron tenerum
USE **elymus trachycaulus**

agropyron trachycaulum
USE **elymus trachycaulus**

agropyron trichophorum
USE **elymus hispidus subsp. barbulatus**

AGROSIL
BT1 soil conditioners
BT2 soil amendments
BT3 amendments
rt sodium silicate

AGROSILVIAQUACULTURAL SYSTEMS
(agroforestry systems combining woody perennials, agricultural crops and raising freshwater aquatic animals)
uf *agrosilvofishery*
BT1 agroforestry systems

AGROSILVICULTURAL SYSTEMS
(agroforestry systems with woody perennials and agricultural crops)
uf *agrisilvicultural systems*
uf *agrisilviculture*
BT1 agroforestry systems
NT1 alley cropping
NT1 forest gardens
NT1 mixed gardens
NT1 multistorey cropping
NT1 taungya
NT1 tree gardens
rt farm forestry
rt home gardens
rt shelterbelts
rt shifting cultivation
rt windbreaks

agrosilvipastoral systems
USE **agrosilvopastoral systems**

agrosilvofishery
USE **agrosilviaquacultural systems**

AGROSILVOPASTORAL SYSTEMS
(agroforestry systems with woody perennials, food crops, pastures and livestock)
uf *agrosilvipastoral systems*
BT1 agroforestry systems
NT1 home gardens

AGROSTEMMA
BT1 caryophyllaceae
NT1 agrostemma githago

AGROSTEMMA GITHAGO
uf *lychnis githago*
BT1 agrostemma
BT2 caryophyllaceae
BT1 antiviral plants

AGROSTIS
uf *bent*
BT1 gramineae
NT1 agrostis alba
NT1 agrostis avenacea
NT1 agrostis borealis
NT1 agrostis canina
NT1 agrostis capillaris
NT1 agrostis castellana
NT1 agrostis exarata

AGROSTIS *cont.*
NT1 agrostis gigantea
NT1 agrostis hiemalis
NT1 agrostis lazica
NT1 agrostis planifolia
NT1 agrostis setacea
NT1 agrostis stolonifera
NT1 agrostis stolonifera var. palustris

AGROSTIS ALBA
BT1 agrostis
BT2 gramineae

agrostis alba subsp. gigantea
USE **agrostis gigantea**

agrostis alba subsp. stolonifera
USE **agrostis stolonifera**

AGROSTIS AVENACEA
BT1 agrostis
BT2 gramineae
BT1 pasture plants

AGROSTIS BOREALIS
BT1 agrostis
BT2 gramineae
BT1 pasture plants

AGROSTIS CANINA
BT1 agrostis
BT2 gramineae
BT1 lawns and turf
BT1 pasture plants

AGROSTIS CAPILLARIS
uf *agrostis tenuis*
uf *agrostis vulgaris*
BT1 agrostis
BT2 gramineae
BT1 lawns and turf
BT1 pasture plants

AGROSTIS CASTELLANA
BT1 agrostis
BT2 gramineae
BT1 lawns and turf

AGROSTIS EXARATA
BT1 agrostis
BT2 gramineae
BT1 pasture plants

AGROSTIS GIGANTEA
uf *agrostis alba subsp. gigantea*
uf *agrostis nigra*
BT1 agrostis
BT2 gramineae
BT1 lawns and turf
BT1 pasture plants

AGROSTIS HIEMALIS
BT1 agrostis
BT2 gramineae
BT1 pasture plants

AGROSTIS LAZICA
BT1 agrostis
BT2 gramineae
BT1 pasture plants

agrostis nigra
USE **agrostis gigantea**

agrostis palustris
USE **agrostis stolonifera var. palustris**

AGROSTIS PLANIFOLIA
BT1 agrostis
BT2 gramineae
BT1 pasture plants

AGROSTIS SETACEA
BT1 agrostis
BT2 gramineae

AGROSTIS STOLONIFERA
uf *agrostis alba subsp. stolonifera*
BT1 agrostis
BT2 gramineae
BT1 lawns and turf

AGROSTIS STOLONIFERA *cont.*
BT1 pasture plants

AGROSTIS STOLONIFERA VAR. PALUSTRIS
uf *agrostis palustris*
BT1 agrostis
BT2 gramineae
BT1 pasture plants

agrostis tenuis
USE **agrostis capillaris**

agrostis vulgaris
USE **agrostis capillaris**

AGROTHEREUTES
BT1 ichneumonidae
BT2 hymenoptera
NT1 agrothereutes tunetanus

AGROTHEREUTES TUNETANUS
BT1 agrothereutes
BT2 ichneumonidae
BT3 hymenoptera

AGROTIS
uf *scotia*
BT1 noctuidae
BT2 lepidoptera
NT1 agrotis biconica
NT1 agrotis crassa
NT1 agrotis exclamationis
NT1 agrotis fucosa
NT1 agrotis gladiaria
NT1 agrotis ipsilon
NT1 agrotis malefida
NT1 agrotis orthogonia
NT1 agrotis segetum
rt euxoa
rt ochropleura
rt peridroma
rt xestia

AGROTIS BICONICA
uf *agrotis spinifera*
uf *euxoa spinifera*
BT1 agrotis
BT2 noctuidae
BT3 lepidoptera

agrotis c-nigrum
USE **xestia c-nigrum**

AGROTIS CRASSA
uf *scotia crassa*
BT1 agrotis
BT2 noctuidae
BT3 lepidoptera

AGROTIS EXCLAMATIONIS
uf *scotia exclamationis*
BT1 agrotis
BT2 noctuidae
BT3 lepidoptera

agrotis flammatra
USE **ochropleura flammatra**

AGROTIS FUCOSA
BT1 agrotis
BT2 noctuidae
BT3 lepidoptera

AGROTIS GLADIARIA
BT1 agrotis
BT2 noctuidae
BT3 lepidoptera

AGROTIS IPSILON
uf *agrotis ypsilon*
uf *scotia ipsilon*
BT1 agrotis
BT2 noctuidae
BT3 lepidoptera

AGROTIS MALEFIDA
BT1 agrotis
BT2 noctuidae
BT3 lepidoptera

AGROTIS ORTHOGONIA
BT1 agrotis
BT2 noctuidae
BT3 lepidoptera

agrotis saucia
USE **peridroma saucia**

AGROTIS SEGETUM
uf *euxoa segetum*
uf *scotia segetum*
BT1 agrotis
BT2 noctuidae
BT3 lepidoptera

agrotis spinifera
USE **agrotis biconica**

agrotis ypsilon
USE **agrotis ipsilon**

AGRYPON
BT1 ichneumonidae
BT2 hymenoptera
NT1 agrypon flaveolatum

AGRYPON FLAVEOLATUM
BT1 agrypon
BT2 ichneumonidae
BT3 hymenoptera
BT1 biological control agents
BT2 beneficial organisms

AHASVERUS
BT1 silvanidae
BT2 coleoptera
NT1 ahasverus advena

AHASVERUS ADVENA
BT1 ahasverus
BT2 silvanidae
BT3 coleoptera

AHEMERAL REGIME
HN from 1990
BT1 light regime
BT2 lighting

ai
USE **artificial insemination**

AI BULLS
BT1 bulls
BT2 male animals
BT3 animals
rt artificial insemination
rt semen
rt semen characters
rt semen production

aid
USE **development aid**

aids
USE **acquired immune deficiency syndrome**

aids htlv-iii
USE **human immunodeficiency virus**

AIKINETOCYSTIS
BT1 apicomplexa
BT2 protozoa
NT1 aikinetocystis singularis

AIKINETOCYSTIS SINGULARIS
BT1 aikinetocystis
BT2 apicomplexa
BT3 protozoa

AILANTHUS
BT1 simaroubaceae
NT1 ailanthus altissima
NT1 ailanthus excelsa
NT1 ailanthus grandis
NT1 ailanthus integrifolia
NT1 ailanthus malabricum
NT1 ailanthus triphysa

AILANTHUS ALTISSIMA
uf *ailanthus glandulosa*
BT1 acaricidal plants
BT2 pesticidal plants
BT1 ailanthus
BT2 simaroubaceae
BT1 antibacterial plants
BT1 forest trees
BT1 medicinal plants
BT1 ornamental woody plants

AILANTHUS EXCELSA
BT1 ailanthus
BT2 simaroubaceae

ailanthus glandulosa
USE **ailanthus altissima**

AILANTHUS GRANDIS
BT1 ailanthus
BT2 simaroubaceae
BT1 medicinal plants

AILANTHUS INTEGRIFOLIA
BT1 ailanthus
BT2 simaroubaceae
BT1 medicinal plants

AILANTHUS MALABRICUM
BT1 ailanthus
BT2 simaroubaceae

AILANTHUS TRIPHYSA
HN from 1990
BT1 ailanthus
BT2 simaroubaceae
BT1 forest trees

AILUROPODA
BT1 ailuropodidae
BT2 fissipeda
BT3 carnivores
BT4 mammals
NT1 ailuropoda melanoleuca

AILUROPODA MELANOLEUCA
BT1 ailuropoda
BT2 ailuropodidae
BT3 fissipeda
BT4 carnivores
BT5 mammals

AILUROPODIDAE
BT1 fissipeda
BT2 carnivores
BT3 mammals
NT1 ailuropoda
NT2 ailuropoda melanoleuca
NT1 ailurus
NT2 ailurus fulgens

AILURUS
BT1 ailuropodidae
BT2 fissipeda
BT3 carnivores
BT4 mammals
NT1 ailurus fulgens

AILURUS FULGENS
BT1 ailurus
BT2 ailuropodidae
BT3 fissipeda
BT4 carnivores
BT5 mammals

AIOLOPUS
BT1 acrididae
BT2 orthoptera
NT1 aiolopus thalassinus

AIOLOPUS THALASSINUS
BT1 aiolopus
BT2 acrididae
BT3 orthoptera

AIR
BT1 gases
NT1 drying air
rt air conditioners
rt air conditioning
rt air filters
rt air flow
rt air ionization
rt air microbiology
rt air pollutants
rt air pollution
rt air quality
rt air sacs
rt air spora
rt air temperature
rt air transport
rt aircraft
rt atmosphere
rt entrapped air

AIR ASSISTED SPRAYERS
BT1 sprayers
BT2 spraying equipment
BT3 application equipment
BT4 equipment

AIR BAGS (AGRICOLA)
BT1 safety devices

AIR BRAKES
uf *brakes, air*
uf *brakes, pneumatic*
uf *pneumatic brakes*
BT1 brakes
BT2 components
rt pneumatic power

AIR CLEANERS
BT1 cleaners
BT2 machinery
rt air conditioners
rt air conditioning
rt air filters
rt air quality
rt dust extractors

AIR CONDITIONERS
BT1 equipment
rt air
rt air cleaners
rt air conditioning
rt air filters
rt dust extractors
rt humidifiers

AIR CONDITIONING
rt air
rt air cleaners
rt air conditioners
rt air quality
rt artificial ventilation
rt environmental control
rt ventilation

AIR COOLED ENGINES
uf *engines, air cooled*
BT1 engines
BT2 machinery

AIR DRYING
BT1 drying
BT2 dehydration
BT3 processing
rt driers
rt drying air
rt sample processing

AIR FILTERS
uf *filters, air*
BT1 filters
rt air
rt air cleaners
rt air conditioners
rt air quality

AIR FLOW
BT1 flow
BT2 movement
rt aerodynamic properties
rt air
rt aspirators
rt drag
rt drift
rt fans
rt flow constants
rt flow meters
rt flow resistance
rt turbulent flow
rt ventilation
rt wind effects

air freight
USE **air transport**

AIR HEATERS
uf *heaters, air*
BT1 heaters
BT2 equipment

AIR IONIZATION
BT1 ionization
BT1 techniques
rt air

AIR LAYERING
uf *marcotting*
BT1 layering
BT2 vegetative propagation
BT3 propagation

AIR LIFT PUMPS
BT1 pumps
BT2 machinery

AIR MICROBIOLOGY
uf *microbiology, air*
BT1 microbiology
BT2 biology
NT1 air spora
rt air
rt microbial flora

AIR POLLUTANTS
BT1 pollutants
NT1 exhaust gases
NT1 factory fumes
rt air
rt air pollution
rt pollution

AIR POLLUTION
uf *atmospheric pollution*
BT1 pollution
rt air
rt air pollutants
rt air quality
rt factory fumes
rt fallout
rt nitrogen oxides
rt scrubbers

AIR QUALITY
BT1 quality
rt air
rt air cleaners
rt air conditioning
rt air filters
rt air pollution

air resistance
USE **drag**

AIR SACS
BT1 respiratory system
BT2 body parts
NT1 pneumatophores
rt air
rt respiratory gases

air, saturated
USE **aerated steam**

AIR SPORA
BT1 air microbiology
BT2 microbiology
BT3 biology
rt air

AIR TEMPERATURE
BT1 temperature
rt air
rt convection
rt environmental temperature
rt solar radiation
rt terrestrial radiation

AIR TRANSPORT
uf *air freight*
uf *aviation*
uf *transport, air*
BT1 transport
rt aerial methods
rt agricultural aviation
rt air
rt aircraft
rt airports

AIRA
BT1 gramineae
NT1 aira caryophyllea
NT1 aira multiculmis
NT1 aira praecox

AIRA CARYOPHYLLEA
BT1 aira
BT2 gramineae
BT1 pasture plants

AIRA MULTICULMIS
BT1 aira
BT2 gramineae
BT1 pasture plants

AIRA PRAECOX
BT1 aira
BT2 gramineae

AIRBORNE INFECTION
BT1 infection
BT2 disease transmission
BT3 transmission

AIRCRAFT
NT1 balloons
NT1 helicopters
NT1 microlight aircraft
rt aerial sowing
rt aerial surveys
rt aerodynamic properties
rt aerodynamics
rt agricultural aviation
rt air
rt air transport
rt airports
rt bird strikes
rt hovercraft
rt propellers
rt vehicles

airfields
USE **airports**

AIRPORT MALARIA
BT1 malaria
BT2 human diseases
BT3 diseases
BT2 mosquito-borne diseases
BT3 vector-borne diseases
BT4 diseases
BT2 protozoal infections
BT3 parasitoses
BT4 diseases

AIRPORTS
uf *airfields*
rt air transport
rt aircraft

AIRTIGHT STORAGE
uf *storage, airtight*
BT1 storage
rt leakage

AIZOACEAE
uf *mesembryaceae*
NT1 carpobrotus
NT2 carpobrotus edulis
NT1 cephalophyllum
NT2 cephalophyllum loreum
NT1 conophytum
NT1 delosperma
NT2 delosperma alba
NT1 dorotheanthus
NT2 dorotheanthus bellidiformis
NT1 drosanthemum
NT2 drosanthemum hispidum
NT1 faucaria
NT2 faucaria bosscheana
NT1 fenestraria
NT1 galenia
NT2 galenia pubescens
NT1 gisekia
NT2 gisekia pharmacoides
NT1 lampranthus
NT2 lampranthus productus
NT1 lithops
NT2 lithops bromfieldii
NT2 lithops divergens
NT2 lithops fulviceps
NT2 lithops marmorata
NT1 malephora
NT2 malephora croceus
NT2 malephora luteolus
NT1 mesembryanthemum
NT2 mesembryanthemum crystallinum
NT1 nelia
NT2 nelia meyeri
NT1 pleiospilos
NT2 pleiospilos nobilis
NT1 sesuvium

AIZOACEAE *cont.*
NT2 sesuvium portulacastrum
NT1 trianthema
NT2 trianthema decandra
NT2 trianthema portulacastrum
NT2 trianthema triquetra

AJELLOMYCES
uf *emmonsiella*
BT1 gymnoascales
NT1 ajellomyces capsulatus
NT1 ajellomyces dermatitidis
rt blastomyces

AJELLOMYCES CAPSULATUS
uf *emmonsiella capsulata*
BT1 ajellomyces
BT2 gymnoascales
rt histoplasma capsulatum

AJELLOMYCES DERMATITIDIS
BT1 ajellomyces
BT2 gymnoascales
rt blastomyces dermatitidis

AJMAN
BT1 united arab emirates
BT2 persian gulf states
BT3 west asia
BT4 asia

AJUGA
BT1 labiatae
NT1 ajuga chamaepitys
NT1 ajuga iva
NT1 ajuga reptans

AJUGA CHAMAEPITYS
BT1 ajuga
BT2 labiatae
BT1 antibacterial plants
BT1 antifungal plants
BT1 insecticidal plants
BT2 pesticidal plants
BT1 medicinal plants

AJUGA IVA
BT1 ajuga
BT2 labiatae
BT1 insecticidal plants
BT2 pesticidal plants

ajuga repens
USE **ajuga reptans**

AJUGA REPTANS
uf *ajuga repens*
BT1 ajuga
BT2 labiatae

AKABANE VIRUS
BT1 bunyavirus
BT2 arboviruses
BT3 pathogens
BT2 bunyaviridae
BT3 viruses

AKAGANEITE
BT1 nonclay minerals
BT2 minerals

AKEBIA
BT1 lardizabalaceae
NT1 akebia lobata

AKEBIA LOBATA
BT1 akebia
BT2 lardizabalaceae
BT1 temperate small fruits
BT2 small fruits
BT2 temperate fruits
BT3 fruit crops

AKHAL-TEKE
BT1 horse breeds
BT2 breeds

AKIBA
BT1 apicomplexa
BT2 protozoa
NT1 akiba caulleryi

AKIBA CAULLERYI
BT1 akiba
BT2 apicomplexa

AKIBA CAULLERYI *cont.*
BT3 protozoa

AKODON
uf *abrothrix*
BT1 hesperomyinae
BT2 muridae
BT3 rodents
BT4 mammals
NT1 akodon longipilis
rt bolomys

akodon arviculoides
USE **bolomys lasiurus**

AKODON LONGIPILIS
uf *abrothrix longipilis*
BT1 akodon
BT2 hesperomyinae
BT3 muridae
BT4 rodents
BT5 mammals

ALA-TAU
BT1 cattle breeds
BT2 breeds

ALABAMA
BT1 southeastern states of usa
BT2 southern states of usa
BT3 usa
BT4 north america
BT5 america

ALABAMA ARGILLACEA
BT1 alabama (lepidoptera)
BT2 noctuidae
BT3 lepidoptera

ALABAMA (LEPIDOPTERA)
BT1 noctuidae
BT2 lepidoptera
NT1 alabama argillacea

ALACHLOR
BT1 antitranspirants
BT1 chloroacetanilide herbicides
BT2 anilide herbicides
BT3 amide herbicides
BT4 herbicides
BT5 pesticides

ALAFIA
BT1 apocynaceae
NT1 alafia multiflora

ALAFIA MULTIFLORA
BT1 alafia
BT2 apocynaceae
BT1 antibacterial plants

ALAI
HN from 1990
BT1 sheep breeds
BT2 breeds

ALAMBADI
BT1 cattle breeds
BT2 breeds

ALAMELLA
BT1 encyrtidae
BT2 hymenoptera
NT1 alamella kerrichi

ALAMELLA KERRICHI
BT1 alamella
BT2 encyrtidae
BT3 hymenoptera

ALANGIACEAE
NT1 alangium
NT2 alangium lamarckii

ALANGIUM
BT1 alangiaceae
NT1 alangium lamarckii

ALANGIUM LAMARCKII
uf *alangium salvifolium*
BT1 alangium
BT2 alangiaceae

alangium salvifolium
USE **alangium lamarckii**

ALANINE
BT1 nonessential amino acids
BT2 amino acids
BT3 carboxylic acids
BT4 organic acids
BT5 acids
BT3 organic nitrogen compounds
rt alanine aminotransferase
rt alanine dehydrogenase

alanine aminopeptidase
USE **microsomal aminopeptidase**

ALANINE AMINOTRANSFERASE
(ec 2.6.1.2)
uf *alanine transaminase*
uf *glutamate pyruvate transaminase*
uf *glutamic pyruvic transaminase*
uf *gpt*
BT1 aminotransferases
BT2 transferases
BT3 enzymes
rt alanine

ALANINE DEHYDROGENASE
(ec 1.4.1.1)
BT1 amine oxidoreductases
BT2 oxidoreductases
BT3 enzymes
rt alanine

alanine transaminase
USE **alanine aminotransferase**

ALARIA
BT1 diplostomidae
BT2 digenea
BT3 trematoda
NT1 alaria alata

ALARIA ALATA
BT1 alaria
BT2 diplostomidae
BT3 digenea
BT4 trematoda

ALARM PHEROMONES
BT1 pheromones
BT2 semiochemicals
NT1 2-heptanone

alarm systems
USE **alarms**

ALARMS
uf *alarm systems*
uf *burglar alarms*
NT1 smoke alarms (agricola)
rt environmental control
rt ergonomics
rt fire prevention
rt monitoring
rt safety devices

ALASKA
BT1 pacific states of usa
BT2 western states of usa
BT3 usa
BT4 north america
BT5 america

ALATASPORA
BT1 myxozoa
BT2 protozoa

ALAUDIDAE
BT1 passeriformes
BT2 birds

ALBANIA
BT1 eastern europe
BT2 europe
rt balkans
rt mediterranean countries

ALBANIAN
BT1 cattle breeds
BT2 breeds
BT1 horse breeds
BT2 breeds

ALBEDO
rt insolation
rt reflectance
rt solar radiation

albedo, citrus
USE **mesocarp**

ALBENDAZOLE
BT1 anthelmintics
BT2 antiparasitic agents
BT3 drugs
BT1 benzimidazoles
BT2 heterocyclic nitrogen compounds
BT3 organic nitrogen compounds

ALBERTA
BT1 canada
BT2 north america
BT3 america

ALBINISM
BT1 pigmentation disorders
BT2 animal disorders
BT3 disorders
rt albinos
rt pigmentation

ALBINOS
rt albinism
rt pigmentation disorders

ALBIZIA
BT1 leguminosae
NT1 albizia acle
NT1 albizia arunachalensis
NT1 albizia chinensis
NT1 albizia falcataria
NT1 albizia julibrissin
NT1 albizia lebbek
NT1 albizia lophantha
NT1 albizia lucida
NT1 albizia odoratissima
NT1 albizia procera

ALBIZIA ACLE
BT1 albizia
BT2 leguminosae

ALBIZIA ARUNACHALENSIS
BT1 albizia
BT2 leguminosae

ALBIZIA CHINENSIS
BT1 albizia
BT2 leguminosae
BT1 browse plants

albizia distachya
USE **albizia lophantha**

albizia falcata
USE **albizia falcataria**

ALBIZIA FALCATARIA
uf *albizia falcata*
uf *albizia moluccana*
BT1 albizia
BT2 leguminosae
BT1 forest trees

ALBIZIA JULIBRISSIN
BT1 albizia
BT2 leguminosae
BT1 forest trees
BT1 ornamental woody plants

ALBIZIA LEBBEK
BT1 albizia
BT2 leguminosae
BT1 forest trees
BT1 medicinal plants
BT1 molluscicidal plants
BT2 pesticidal plants

ALBIZIA LOPHANTHA
uf *albizia distachya*
BT1 albizia
BT2 leguminosae

ALBIZIA LUCIDA
BT1 albizia
BT2 leguminosae

albizia moluccana
USE **albizia falcataria**

ALBIZIA ODORATISSIMA
BT1 albizia
BT2 leguminosae
BT1 forest trees

ALBIZIA PROCERA
BT1 albizia
BT2 leguminosae
BT1 forest trees
BT1 medicinal plants

ALBUGO
BT1 peronosporales
NT1 albugo bliti
NT1 albugo candida
NT1 albugo ipomoeae-panduratae
NT1 albugo tragopogonis

ALBUGO BLITI
BT1 albugo
BT2 peronosporales

ALBUGO CANDIDA
uf *albugo cruciferarum*
BT1 albugo
BT2 peronosporales

albugo cruciferarum
USE **albugo candida**

ALBUGO IPOMOEAE-PANDURATAE
BT1 albugo
BT2 peronosporales

ALBUGO TRAGOPOGONIS
BT1 albugo
BT2 peronosporales

albumen
USE **egg albumen**

albuminoids
USE **scleroproteins**

ALBUMINS
BT1 proteins
BT2 peptides
NT1 egg albumen
NT1 lactalbumin
NT2 α-lactalbumin
NT1 ovalbumin
NT1 ricin
NT1 serum albumin
NT2 bovine serum albumin
rt endosperm
rt hypoalbuminaemia

ALCA
BT1 alcidae
BT2 charadriiformes
BT3 birds
NT1 alca torda

ALCA TORDA
uf *razorbill*
BT1 alca
BT2 alcidae
BT3 charadriiformes
BT4 birds

ALCALIGENES
BT1 gracilicutes
BT2 bacteria
BT3 prokaryotes
NT1 alcaligenes faecalis
NT1 alcaligenes latus
NT1 alcaligenes paradoxus

ALCALIGENES FAECALIS
BT1 alcaligenes
BT2 gracilicutes
BT3 bacteria
BT4 prokaryotes

ALCALIGENES LATUS
BT1 alcaligenes
BT2 gracilicutes
BT3 bacteria
BT4 prokaryotes

ALCALIGENES PARADOXUS
BT1 alcaligenes
BT2 gracilicutes
BT3 bacteria
BT4 prokaryotes

ALCARRENA
HN from 1990
BT1 sheep breeds
BT2 breeds

ALCEA
BT1 malvaceae
NT1 alcea flavovirens
NT1 alcea rosea

ALCEA FLAVOVIRENS
BT1 alcea
BT2 malvaceae
BT1 medicinal plants

ALCEA ROSEA
uf *althaea rosea*
uf *hollyhocks*
BT1 alcea
BT2 malvaceae
BT1 medicinal plants
BT1 ornamental herbaceous plants

ALCEDINIDAE
uf *kingfishers*
BT1 coraciiformes
BT2 birds
NT1 alcedo
NT2 alcedo atthis
NT1 halcyon
NT2 halcyon chloris
NT2 halcyon smyrnensis
NT1 pelargopsis
NT2 pelargopsis capensis

ALCEDO
BT1 alcedinidae
BT2 coraciiformes
BT3 birds
NT1 alcedo atthis

ALCEDO ATTHIS
BT1 alcedo
BT2 alcedinidae
BT3 coraciiformes
BT4 birds

ALCELAPHUS
BT1 bovidae
BT2 ruminantia
BT3 artiodactyla
BT4 mammals
BT4 ungulates
NT1 alcelaphus buselaphus

ALCELAPHUS BUSELAPHUS
uf *hartebeest*
BT1 alcelaphus
BT2 bovidae
BT3 ruminantia
BT4 artiodactyla
BT5 mammals
BT5 ungulates

ALCES
BT1 cervidae
BT2 ruminantia
BT3 artiodactyla
BT4 mammals
BT4 ungulates
NT1 alces alces

ALCES ALCES
uf *elks, european*
uf *moose*
BT1 alces
BT2 cervidae
BT3 ruminantia
BT4 artiodactyla
BT5 mammals
BT5 ungulates

ALCHEMILLA
BT1 rosaceae
NT1 alchemilla microcarpa
NT1 alchemilla mollis

ALCHEMILLA MICROCARPA
BT1 alchemilla
BT2 rosaceae

ALCHEMILLA MOLLIS
BT1 alchemilla
BT2 rosaceae

ALCHORNEA
BT1 euphorbiaceae
NT1 alchornea cordifolia

ALCHORNEA CORDIFOLIA
BT1 alchornea
BT2 euphorbiaceae
BT1 antibacterial plants
BT1 medicinal plants

ALCIDAE
uf *puffins*
BT1 charadriiformes
BT2 birds
NT1 aethia
NT1 alca
NT2 alca torda
NT1 cepphus
NT1 fratercula
NT2 fratercula arctica
NT2 fratercula corniculata
NT1 lunda
NT2 lunda cirrhata
NT1 uria
NT2 uria aalge
NT2 uria lomvia

ALCIDODES
BT1 curculionidae
BT2 coleoptera
NT1 alcidodes haemopterus

ALCIDODES HAEMOPTERUS
BT1 alcidodes
BT2 curculionidae
BT3 coleoptera

ALCOHOL DEHYDROGENASE
(ec 1.1.1.1)
BT1 alcohol oxidoreductases
BT2 oxidoreductases
BT3 enzymes

alcohol, ethyl
USE **ethanol**

ALCOHOL OXIDOREDUCTASES
(ec 1.1)
BT1 oxidoreductases
BT2 enzymes
NT1 (s)-2-hydroxy-acid oxidase
NT1 l-gulonolactone oxidase
NT1 l-iditol dehydrogenase
NT1 alcohol dehydrogenase
NT1 glucose oxidase
NT1 glucose-6-phosphate dehydrogenase
NT1 glycerol dehydrogenase
NT1 glycerol-3-phosphate dehydrogenase
NT1 hydroxymethylglutaryl-coa reductase
NT1 hydroxysteroid dehydrogenase
NT1 isocitrate dehydrogenase
NT1 lactate dehydrogenase
NT1 malate dehydrogenase
NT1 malate oxidase
NT1 malic enzyme
NT1 methylenetetrahydrofolate reductase
NT1 phosphogluconate dehydrogenase
NT1 xanthine dehydrogenase
NT1 xanthine oxidase

ALCOHOL TEST
BT1 tests
rt ethanol
rt milk quality

ALCOHOLIC BEVERAGES
uf *beverages, alcoholic*
BT1 beverages
NT1 beers
NT2 light beer (agricola)

ALCOHOLIC BEVERAGES *cont.*
NT1 cider
NT1 distilled spirits
NT2 brandy
NT2 gin
NT2 liqueurs
NT3 amaretto (agricola)
NT2 rum
NT2 vodka
NT2 whisky
NT1 mead
NT1 sake
NT1 wines
NT2 champagne and sparkling wines
NT2 quality wine
NT2 table wine
rt alcoholism
rt beverage industry
rt brewing
rt distilling industry
rt ethanol
rt molasses
rt public houses

ALCOHOLICS ANONYMOUS (AGRICOLA)
BT1 organizations
rt alcoholism

ALCOHOLISM
BT1 human diseases
BT2 diseases
rt addiction
rt alcoholic beverages
rt alcoholics anonymous (agricola)
rt fetal alcohol syndrome (agricola)

ALCOHOLS
NT1 1-decanol
NT1 1-hexanol
NT1 1-propanol
NT1 allyl alcohol
NT1 amino alcohols
NT2 atenolol
NT2 cysteamine
NT2 ephedrine
NT2 ethanolamine
NT2 isoprenaline
NT2 methoxamine
NT2 metoprolol
NT2 oxprenolol
NT2 propranolol
NT2 sphingosine
NT2 tyramine
NT1 amyl alcohol
NT1 benzyl alcohol
NT1 butanol
NT1 ethanol
NT1 fatty alcohols
NT2 1-dodecanol
NT2 1-dotriacontanol
NT2 1-hexadecanol
NT2 farnesol
NT2 triacontanol
NT1 flavanols
NT2 catechin
NT2 epicatechin
NT1 flavonols
NT2 isorhamnetin
NT2 kaempferol
NT2 quercetin
NT1 geraniol
NT1 glycols
NT2 bronopol
NT2 butanediol
NT2 ethylene glycol
NT2 polyethylene glycol
NT2 propanediols
NT3 propylene glycol
NT2 sphingosine
NT2 styrene glycol
NT1 isopropyl alcohol
NT1 linalool
NT1 methanol
NT1 phenols
NT2 2,4,5-trichlorophenol
NT2 2,4-dichlorophenol
NT2 2,4-dinitrophenol
NT2 2-iodophenol

ALCOHOLS *cont.*
NT2 2-phenylphenol
NT2 creosote
NT2 cresols
NT3 o-cresol
NT3 p-cresol
NT2 dichlorophen
NT2 disophenol
NT2 gossypol
NT2 guaiacol
NT2 hydroquinone
NT2 naphthols
NT3 1-naphthol
NT2 nitrophenols
NT3 o-nitrophenol
NT3 p-nitrophenol
NT2 phenol
NT2 polyphenols
NT2 probucol
NT2 pyrocatechol
NT2 pyrogallol
NT2 resorcinols
NT3 alkylresorcinols
NT3 pinosylvin
NT3 resorcinol
NT3 resorcylic acid lactones
NT4 zearalenol
NT4 zearalenone
NT4 zeranol
NT2 thymol
NT2 vanillin
NT1 polyols
NT2 sugar alcohols
NT3 alditols
NT4 arabinitol
NT4 erythritol
NT4 galactitol
NT4 glycerol
NT4 lactitol
NT4 maltitol
NT4 mannitol
NT4 palatinit
NT4 sorbitol
NT4 xylitol
NT3 cyclitols
NT4 myo-inositol
NT4 pinitol
NT1 polyprenols
NT2 dolichols
NT1 resinols
NT1 sterols
NT2 25-hydroxyergocalciferol
NT2 cholecalciferol derivatives
NT3 hydroxycholecalciferols
NT4 1α-hydroxycholecalciferol
NT4 24,25-dihydroxycholecalciferol
NT4 25,26-dihydroxycholecalciferol
NT4 calcitriol
NT2 cholesterol
NT2 coprostanol
NT2 dihydrotachysterol
NT2 ergosterol
NT2 lanosterol
NT2 phytosterols
NT3 betulafolienetriol
NT3 brassinosteroids
NT4 brassinolide
NT3 campesterol
NT3 cucurbitacins
NT3 solanidine
NT3 stigmasterol
NT2 tachysterol
NT1 zeaxanthin
rt non-food products
rt organic compounds
rt thiols

ALDARIC ACIDS
BT1 sugar acids
BT2 carboxylic acids
BT3 organic acids
BT4 acids
BT2 monosaccharides
BT3 carbohydrates
NT1 glucaric acid
NT1 tartaric acid

ALDEHYDE DEHYDROGENASE
(ec 1.2.1.3)

ALDEHYDE DEHYDROGENASE *cont.*
BT1 aldehyde oxidoreductases
BT2 oxidoreductases
BT3 enzymes
rt aldehydes

ALDEHYDE-LYASES
(ec 4.1.2)
uf *aldolases*
BT1 lyases
BT2 enzymes
NT1 fructose-bisphosphate aldolase

ALDEHYDE OXIDOREDUCTASES
(ec 1.2)
BT1 oxidoreductases
BT2 enzymes
NT1 2-oxoisovalerate dehydrogenase (lipoamide)
NT1 aldehyde dehydrogenase
NT1 glyceraldehyde-3-phosphate dehydrogenase
NT1 pyruvate dehydrogenase (lipoamide)
NT1 pyruvate oxidase

ALDEHYDES
NT1 acetaldehyde
NT1 acrolein
NT1 benzaldehyde
NT1 citral
NT2 geranial
NT2 neral
NT1 formaldehyde
NT1 furfural
NT1 hmf
NT1 iridodial
NT1 malonaldehyde
NT1 pyridoxal
NT1 retinal
NT1 vanillin
rt aldehyde dehydrogenase
rt aldoses
rt carbonyl compounds
rt organic compounds

alders
USE **alnus**

ALDICARB
BT1 oxime carbamate acaricides
BT2 carbamate acaricides
BT3 acaricides
BT4 pesticides
BT3 carbamate pesticides
BT1 oxime carbamate insecticides
BT2 carbamate insecticides
BT3 carbamate pesticides
BT3 insecticides
BT4 pesticides
BT1 oxime carbamate nematicides
BT2 carbamate nematicides
BT3 carbamate pesticides
BT3 nematicides
BT4 pesticides

ALDITOLS
BT1 sugar alcohols
BT2 carbohydrates
BT2 polyols
BT3 alcohols
NT1 arabinitol
NT1 erythritol
NT1 galactitol
NT1 glycerol
NT1 lactitol
NT1 maltitol
NT1 mannitol
NT1 palatinit
NT1 sorbitol
NT1 xylitol

aldolases
USE **aldehyde-lyases**

aldomet
USE **methyldopa**

ALDONIC ACIDS
BT1 sugar acids

ALDONIC ACIDS *cont.*
BT2 carboxylic acids
BT3 organic acids
BT4 acids
BT2 monosaccharides
BT3 carbohydrates
NT1 ascorbic acids
NT2 ascorbic acid
NT2 dehydroascorbic acid
NT2 diketogulonic acid
NT2 isoascorbic acid
NT1 gluconic acid
NT1 neuraminic acid
NT1 sialic acids

ALDOSE 1-EPIMERASE
HN from 1990
(ec 5.1.3.3)
uf *mutarose*
BT1 isomerases
BT2 enzymes
rt mutarotation

ALDOSES
BT1 monosaccharides
BT2 carbohydrates
BT1 reducing sugars
BT2 sugars
BT3 carbohydrates
NT1 hexoses
NT2 2-deoxy-d-glucose
NT2 fucose
NT2 galactose
NT2 glucose
NT2 mannose
NT2 rhamnose
NT1 pentoses
NT2 arabinose
NT2 ribose
NT2 xylose
NT1 tetroses
NT2 erythrose
NT1 trioses
NT2 glyceraldehyde
rt aldehydes

ALDOSTERONE
BT1 mineralocorticoids
BT2 adrenal cortex hormones
BT3 corticoids
BT3 hormones
BT1 pregnanes
BT2 steroids
BT3 isoprenoids
BT4 lipids

ALDOXYCARB
BT1 oxime carbamate insecticides
BT2 carbamate insecticides
BT3 carbamate pesticides
BT3 insecticides
BT4 pesticides
BT1 oxime carbamate nematicides
BT2 carbamate nematicides
BT3 carbamate pesticides
BT3 nematicides
BT4 pesticides

ALDRICHINA
BT1 calliphoridae
BT2 diptera
NT1 aldrichina grahami
rt calliphora

ALDRICHINA GRAHAMI
uf *calliphora grahami*
BT1 aldrichina
BT2 calliphoridae
BT3 diptera

ALDRIN
BT1 cyclodiene insecticides
BT2 organochlorine insecticides
BT3 insecticides
BT4 pesticides
BT3 organochlorine pesticides
BT4 organochlorine compounds
BT5 organic halogen compounds

ALECTORIS
BT1 phasianidae
BT2 galliformes
BT3 birds
NT1 alectoris chukar
NT1 alectoris graeca
NT1 alectoris rufa

ALECTORIS CHUKAR
BT1 alectoris
BT2 phasianidae
BT3 galliformes
BT4 birds

ALECTORIS GRAECA
BT1 alectoris
BT2 phasianidae
BT3 galliformes
BT4 birds

ALECTORIS RUFA
BT1 alectoris
BT2 phasianidae
BT3 galliformes
BT4 birds

alectorobius
USE **ornithodoros**

alectorobius tartakovskyi
USE **ornithodoros tartakovskyi**

alectorobius tholozani
USE **ornithodoros tholozani**

alectorolophus
USE **rhinanthus**

alectorolophus major
USE **rhinanthus angustifolius**

ALECTRA
BT1 scrophulariaceae
NT1 alectra orobanchoides
NT1 alectra vogelii

ALECTRA OROBANCHOIDES
BT1 alectra
BT2 scrophulariaceae
BT1 parasitic plants
BT2 parasites

ALECTRA VOGELII
BT1 alectra
BT2 scrophulariaceae
BT1 parasitic plants
BT2 parasites

ALEIODES
HN from 1989
BT1 braconidae
BT2 hymenoptera

ALENTEJANA
HN from 1990; previously "alentejo"
uf *alentejo*
BT1 pig breeds
BT2 breeds

alentejo
USE **alentejana**

ALEOCHARA
BT1 staphylinidae
BT2 coleoptera
NT1 aleochara bilineata
NT1 aleochara bimaculata
NT1 aleochara bipustulata

ALEOCHARA BILINEATA
BT1 aleochara
BT2 staphylinidae
BT3 coleoptera

ALEOCHARA BIMACULATA
BT1 aleochara
BT2 staphylinidae
BT3 coleoptera

ALEOCHARA BIPUSTULATA
BT1 aleochara
BT2 staphylinidae
BT3 coleoptera

ALEURITES
BT1 euphorbiaceae
NT1 aleurites fordii
NT1 aleurites moluccana
NT1 aleurites montana
rt insecticidal plants

ALEURITES FORDII
BT1 aleurites
BT2 euphorbiaceae
BT1 forest trees
rt tung

ALEURITES MOLUCCANA
uf *aleurites triloba*
BT1 aleurites
BT2 euphorbiaceae

ALEURITES MONTANA
BT1 aleurites
BT2 euphorbiaceae
BT1 forest trees
rt tung

aleurites triloba
USE **aleurites moluccana**

ALEUROCANTHUS
BT1 aleyrodidae
BT2 aleyrodoidea
BT3 sternorrhyncha
BT4 homoptera
NT1 aleurocanthus citriperdus
NT1 aleurocanthus spiniferus
NT1 aleurocanthus woglumi

ALEUROCANTHUS CITRIPERDUS
BT1 aleurocanthus
BT2 aleyrodidae
BT3 aleyrodoidea
BT4 sternorrhyncha
BT5 homoptera

ALEUROCANTHUS SPINIFERUS
BT1 aleurocanthus
BT2 aleyrodidae
BT3 aleyrodoidea
BT4 sternorrhyncha
BT5 homoptera

ALEUROCANTHUS WOGLUMI
BT1 aleurocanthus
BT2 aleyrodidae
BT3 aleyrodoidea
BT4 sternorrhyncha
BT5 homoptera

ALEUROCYBOTUS
BT1 aleyrodidae
BT2 aleyrodoidea
BT3 sternorrhyncha
BT4 homoptera
NT1 aleurocybotus indicus

ALEUROCYBOTUS INDICUS
BT1 aleurocybotus
BT2 aleyrodidae
BT3 aleyrodoidea
BT4 sternorrhyncha
BT5 homoptera

ALEURODICUS
BT1 aleyrodidae
BT2 aleyrodoidea
BT3 sternorrhyncha
BT4 homoptera
NT1 aleurodicus cocois
NT1 aleurodicus dispersus

ALEURODICUS COCOIS
BT1 aleurodicus
BT2 aleyrodidae
BT3 aleyrodoidea
BT4 sternorrhyncha
BT5 homoptera

ALEURODICUS DISPERSUS
BT1 aleurodicus
BT2 aleyrodidae
BT3 aleyrodoidea
BT4 sternorrhyncha
BT5 homoptera

ALEUROGLYPHUS
BT1 acaridae

ALEUROGLYPHUS *cont.*
BT2 astigmata
BT3 acari
NT1 aleuroglyphus ovatus

ALEUROGLYPHUS OVATUS
BT1 aleuroglyphus
BT2 acaridae
BT3 astigmata
BT4 acari

ALEUROLOBUS
BT1 aleyrodidae
BT2 aleyrodoidea
BT3 sternorrhyncha
BT4 homoptera
NT1 aleurolobus barodensis

ALEUROLOBUS BARODENSIS
BT1 aleurolobus
BT2 aleyrodidae
BT3 aleyrodoidea
BT4 sternorrhyncha
BT5 homoptera

ALEURONE CELLS
BT1 cells
rt aleurone layer
rt endosperm
rt proteins

ALEURONE LAYER
BT1 plant tissues
BT2 plant
BT2 tissues
rt aleurone cells
rt bran
rt proteins

ALEUROTHRIXUS
BT1 aleyrodidae
BT2 aleyrodoidea
BT3 sternorrhyncha
BT4 homoptera
NT1 aleurothrixus floccosus

ALEUROTHRIXUS FLOCCOSUS
BT1 aleurothrixus
BT2 aleyrodidae
BT3 aleyrodoidea
BT4 sternorrhyncha
BT5 homoptera

ALEUTIAN DISEASE
BT1 mink diseases
BT2 animal diseases
BT3 diseases
BT1 viral diseases
BT2 infectious diseases
BT3 diseases
rt aleutian disease virus

ALEUTIAN DISEASE VIRUS
BT1 parvovirus
BT2 parvoviridae
BT3 viruses
rt aleutian disease

alewife
USE **alosa pseudoharengus**

ALEXA
BT1 leguminosae
NT1 alexa imperatricis

ALEXA IMPERATRICIS
BT1 alexa
BT2 leguminosae

alexin
USE **complement**

ALEYRODES
BT1 aleyrodidae
BT2 aleyrodoidea
BT3 sternorrhyncha
BT4 homoptera
NT1 aleyrodes brassicae
NT1 aleyrodes proletella

ALEYRODES BRASSICAE
BT1 aleyrodes
BT2 aleyrodidae
BT3 aleyrodoidea
BT4 sternorrhyncha

ALEYRODES BRASSICAE *cont.*
BT5 homoptera

ALEYRODES PROLETELLA
BT1 aleyrodes
BT2 aleyrodidae
BT3 aleyrodoidea
BT4 sternorrhyncha
BT5 homoptera

ALEYRODIDAE
uf *whiteflies*
BT1 aleyrodoidea
BT2 sternorrhyncha
BT3 homoptera
NT1 aleurocanthus
NT2 aleurocanthus citriperdus
NT2 aleurocanthus spiniferus
NT2 aleurocanthus woglumi
NT1 aleurocybotus
NT2 aleurocybotus indicus
NT1 aleurodicus
NT2 aleurodicus cocois
NT2 aleurodicus dispersus
NT1 aleurolobus
NT2 aleurolobus barodensis
NT1 aleurothrixus
NT2 aleurothrixus floccosus
NT1 aleyrodes
NT2 aleyrodes brassicae
NT2 aleyrodes proletella
NT1 bemisia
NT2 bemisia giffardi
NT2 bemisia tabaci
NT1 dialeurodes
NT2 dialeurodes citri
NT2 dialeurodes citrifolii
NT1 parabemisia
NT2 parabemisia myricae
NT1 siphoninus
NT2 siphoninus phillyreae
NT1 trialeurodes
NT2 trialeurodes abutiloneus
NT2 trialeurodes vaporariorum

ALEYRODOIDEA
BT1 sternorrhyncha
BT2 homoptera
NT1 aleyrodidae
NT2 aleurocanthus
NT3 aleurocanthus citriperdus
NT3 aleurocanthus spiniferus
NT3 aleurocanthus woglumi
NT2 aleurocybotus
NT3 aleurocybotus indicus
NT2 aleurodicus
NT3 aleurodicus cocois
NT3 aleurodicus dispersus
NT2 aleurolobus
NT3 aleurolobus barodensis
NT2 aleurothrixus
NT3 aleurothrixus floccosus
NT2 aleyrodes
NT3 aleyrodes brassicae
NT3 aleyrodes proletella
NT2 bemisia
NT3 bemisia giffardi
NT3 bemisia tabaci
NT2 dialeurodes
NT3 dialeurodes citri
NT3 dialeurodes citrifolii
NT2 parabemisia
NT3 parabemisia myricae
NT2 siphoninus
NT3 siphoninus phillyreae
NT2 trialeurodes
NT3 trialeurodes abutiloneus
NT3 trialeurodes vaporariorum

ALFALFA
BF lucerne
rt alfalfa hay
rt alfalfa haylage
rt alfalfa juice
rt alfalfa meal
rt alfalfa pellets
rt alfalfa protein
rt alfalfa protein concentrate
rt alfalfa silage
rt alfalfa transient streak virus
rt dried alfalfa
rt medicago sativa

ALFALFA HAY
BF lucerne hay
rt alfalfa

ALFALFA HAYLAGE
BF lucerne haylage
rt alfalfa

ALFALFA JUICE
BF lucerne juice
rt alfalfa

alfalfa latent carlavirus
USE **pea streak carlavirus**

ALFALFA MEAL
BF lucerne meal
rt alfalfa

ALFALFA MOSAIC VIRUS
BT1 alfalfa mosaic virus group
BT2 plant viruses
BT3 plant pathogens
BT4 pathogens
rt lucerne
rt medicago sativa

ALFALFA MOSAIC VIRUS GROUP
HN from 1990
BT1 plant viruses
BT2 plant pathogens
BT3 pathogens
NT1 alfalfa mosaic virus

ALFALFA PELLETS
BF lucerne pellets
rt alfalfa

ALFALFA PROTEIN
BF lucerne protein
rt alfalfa
rt alfalfa protein concentrate

ALFALFA PROTEIN CONCENTRATE
BF lucerne protein concentrate
rt alfalfa
rt alfalfa protein

ALFALFA SILAGE
BF lucerne silage
rt alfalfa

ALFALFA TRANSIENT STREAK VIRUS
BF lucerne transient streak virus
rt alfalfa

ALFISOLS
BT1 argilluvic soils
BT2 soil types (genetic)
NT1 aqualfs

ALGAE
(for blue-green algae see cyanobacteria)
NT1 bacillariophyta
NT2 asterionella
NT3 asterionella formosa
NT2 cyclotella
NT3 cyclotella meneghiniana
NT2 fragilaria
NT3 fragilaria crotonensis
NT2 melosira
NT3 melosira italica
NT2 navicula
NT3 navicula atomus
NT2 nitzschia
NT3 nitzschia dissipata
NT1 charophyta
NT2 chara
NT3 chara globularis
NT3 chara vulgaris
NT3 chara zeylanica
NT2 nitella
NT3 nitella hookeri
NT1 chlorophyta
NT2 ankistrodesmus
NT3 ankistrodesmus falcatus
NT2 cephaleuros
NT3 cephaleuros virescens
NT2 chlamydomonas

ALGAE *cont.*
NT3 chlamydomonas eugametos
NT3 chlamydomonas reinhardtii
NT2 chlorella
NT3 chlorella ellipsoidea
NT3 chlorella pyrenoidosa
NT3 chlorella sorokiniana
NT3 chlorella vulgaris
NT2 chlorococcum
NT3 chlorococcum hypnosporum
NT2 cladophora
NT3 cladophora glomerata
NT2 cystobia
NT2 diplodina
NT2 dunaliella
NT3 dunaliella tertiolecta
NT2 eudorina
NT3 eudorina elegans
NT2 gonospora
NT2 hydrodictyon
NT3 hydrodictyon reticulatum
NT2 pithophora
NT3 pithophora oedogonia
NT2 prototheca
NT3 prototheca wickerhamii
NT3 prototheca zopfii
NT2 pterospora
NT2 rhizoclonium
NT3 rhizoclonium hieroglyphicum
NT2 scenedesmus
NT3 scenedesmus bijugatus
NT3 scenedesmus quadricauda
NT2 stigeoclonium
NT3 stigeoclonium tenue
NT1 chrysophyta
NT2 prymnesium
NT3 prymnesium parvum
NT1 dinophyta
NT2 amphidinium
NT2 gymnodinium
NT2 peridinium
NT3 peridinium cinctum
NT3 peridinium cinctum f. westii
NT1 euglenophyta
NT2 euglena
NT3 euglena gracilis
NT1 phaeophyta
NT2 laminaria
NT2 sargassum
NT3 sargassum muticum
NT1 rhodophyta
NT2 chondrus
NT3 chondrus crispus
NT1 xanthophyta
NT2 vaucheria
NT3 vaucheria dichotoma
NT3 vaucheria geminata
rt agar
rt algae culture
rt algae meal
rt algal cultures
rt algal diseases
rt algal protein
rt algicidal plants
rt algicidal properties
rt algicides
rt alginates
rt alginic acid
rt hydrobiology
rt lichens
rt plants
rt seaweeds

ALGAE CULTURE
BT1 aquaculture
BT2 enterprises
rt algae
rt algal cultures

ALGAE MEAL
BT1 meal
NT1 scenedesmus meal
NT1 seaweed meal
rt algae

ALGAL CULTURES
(properties of cultures; for culture techniques use "algae culture")
BT1 cultures
rt algae
rt algae culture
rt algal protein
rt cultured products

ALGAL DISEASES
BT1 infectious diseases
BT2 diseases
NT1 protothecosis
rt algae

ALGAL PROTEIN
BT1 single cell protein
BT2 protein products
BT3 products
rt algae
rt algal cultures
rt plant protein
rt seaweeds

ALGARVE CHURRO
BT1 sheep breeds
BT2 breeds

ALGERIA
BT1 north africa
BT2 africa
rt arab countries
rt developing countries
rt francophone africa
rt maghreb
rt mediterranean countries
rt opec
rt threshold countries

ALGERIAN ARAB
BT1 sheep breeds
BT2 breeds

ALGICIDAL PLANTS
NT1 acacia catechu
NT1 acacia nilotica
NT1 allemanda cathartica
NT1 arctostaphylos uva-ursi
NT1 caesalpinia coriaria
NT1 hamamelis virginiana
NT1 plumeria rubra
NT1 terminalia chebula
rt algae
rt algicidal properties
rt algicides
rt herbicides
rt horticultural crops
rt industrial crops
rt krameria
rt plants

ALGICIDAL PROPERTIES
BT1 herbicidal properties
BT2 pesticidal properties
BT3 properties
rt algae
rt algicidal plants
rt algicides

ALGICIDES
BT1 herbicides
BT2 pesticides
NT1 fentin hydroxide
NT1 tannins
NT1 tributyltin oxide
rt algae
rt algicidal plants
rt algicidal properties

ALGINATES
BT1 emulsifiers
BT2 surfactants
BT1 polyuronides
BT2 polysaccharides
BT3 carbohydrates
BT1 seaweed products
BT2 products
BT1 stabilizers
rt agar
rt algae
rt alginic acid
rt seaweeds

ALGINIC ACID
BT1 mucilages
BT2 polysaccharides
BT3 carbohydrates
BT1 polyuronides
BT2 polysaccharides
BT3 carbohydrates
rt algae
rt alginates
rt colloids
rt seaweeds

ALGORITHMS
BT1 mathematics
rt computer analysis

ALHAGI
BT1 leguminosae
NT1 alhagi maurorum
NT1 alhagi pseudalhagi
rt desert plants

ALHAGI MAURORUM
BT1 alhagi
BT2 leguminosae

ALHAGI PSEUDALHAGI
BT1 alhagi
BT2 leguminosae

aliesterase
USE **carboxylesterase**

ALIMENTARY PASTES
BT1 cereal products
BT2 plant products
BT3 products

alimentary tract
USE **digestive system**

ALIPHATIC NITROGEN FUNGICIDES
BT1 fungicides
BT2 pesticides
NT1 butylamine
NT1 cymoxanil
NT1 dodicin
NT1 dodine
NT1 guazatine
NT1 propamocarb
NT1 prothiocarb

ALISMA
BT1 alismataceae
NT1 alisma canaliculatum
NT1 alisma plantago-aquatica
NT1 alisma subcordatum

ALISMA CANALICULATUM
BT1 alisma
BT2 alismataceae

ALISMA PLANTAGO-AQUATICA
BT1 alisma
BT2 alismataceae

ALISMA SUBCORDATUM
BT1 alisma
BT2 alismataceae

ALISMATACEAE
NT1 alisma
NT2 alisma canaliculatum
NT2 alisma plantago-aquatica
NT2 alisma subcordatum
NT1 echinodorus
NT2 echinodorus rostratus
NT1 lophotocarpus
NT2 lophotocarpus calycinus
NT2 lophotocarpus guyanensis
NT1 sagittaria
NT2 sagittaria graminea
NT2 sagittaria trifolia

ALKALI METALS
BT1 metallic elements
BT2 elements
BT2 metals
NT1 caesium
NT1 lithium
NT1 potassium
NT1 rubidium
NT1 sodium

ALKALI RESERVE
BT1 blood chemistry
BT2 blood composition
BT3 composition
rt acid base equilibrium
rt bicarbonates

alkali soils
USE **alkaline soils**
OR **sodic soils**

ALKALI TREATMENT
rt acid base equilibrium
rt acidosis
rt antacids
rt digestion
rt treatment

ALKALINE EARTH METALS
BT1 metallic elements
BT2 elements
BT2 metals
NT1 barium
NT1 beryllium
NT1 calcium
NT1 magnesium
NT1 radium
NT1 strontium

ALKALINE PHOSPHATASE
(ec 3.1.3.1)
uf *alkaline phosphomonoesterase*
uf *phosphatase, alkaline*
BT1 phosphoric monoester hydrolases
BT2 esterases
BT3 hydrolases
BT4 enzymes
rt phosphatase test

alkaline phosphomonoesterase
USE **alkaline phosphatase**

ALKALINE PULPING
BT1 pulping
BT2 processing

ALKALINE SOILS
uf *alkali soils*
BT1 soil types (chemical)
rt saline sodic soils
rt saline soils
rt soil alkalinity
rt solonchaks

ALKALINE VENOM GLAND
BT1 venom glands
BT2 glands (animal)
BT3 body parts
BT3 glands
rt venoms

ALKALINE WATER
BT1 irrigation water
BT2 water

ALKALINITY
BT1 chemical properties
BT2 properties
NT1 soil alkalinity
NT2 titratable basicity
rt alkalis

ALKALINIZATION
BT1 soil formation

ALKALIS
BT1 bases
NT1 sodium bicarbonate
NT1 sodium carbonate
NT1 sodium hydroxide
rt alkalinity
rt neutralization
rt titratable basicity

ALKALOIDS
NT1 imidazole alkaloids
NT2 pilocarpine
NT1 indole alkaloids
NT2 ergot alkaloids
NT3 dihydroergocryptine
NT3 ergometrine
NT2 gramine

ALKALOIDS *cont.*
NT2 physostigmine
NT2 psilocin
NT2 psilocybine
NT2 reserpine
NT2 strychnine
NT2 vinblastine
NT2 yohimbine
NT1 isoquinoline alkaloids
NT2 colchicine
NT2 dehydroemetine
NT2 demecolcine
NT2 emetine
NT1 lycorine
NT1 opium alkaloids
NT2 codeine
NT2 morphine
NT2 papaverine
NT2 thebaine
NT1 perloline
NT1 pyridine alkaloids
NT2 anabasine
NT2 arecoline
NT2 cathidine
NT2 mimosine
NT2 nicotine
NT2 nornicotine
NT2 trigonelline
NT1 pyrrolidine alkaloids
NT1 pyrrolizidine alkaloids
NT2 lasiocarpine
NT1 quinoline alkaloids
NT2 quinine
NT1 quinolizidine alkaloids
NT2 sparteine
NT1 steroid alkaloids
NT2 glycoalkaloids
NT3 α-tomatine
NT3 lanatosides
NT3 solanine
NT2 solanidine
NT1 tropane alkaloids
NT2 atropine
NT2 cocaine
NT1 xanthine alkaloids
NT2 caffeine
NT2 theobromine
NT2 theophylline
rt heterocyclic nitrogen compounds
rt secondary metabolites
rt toxic substances

ALKALOSIS
BT1 acid base disorders
BT2 metabolic disorders
BT3 animal disorders
BT4 disorders
rt acid base equilibrium

ALKANES
uf *paraffins*
BT1 hydrocarbons
NT1 biogas
NT1 decane
NT1 ethane
NT1 heptane
NT1 hexane
NT1 methane
NT1 nonane
NT1 octane
NT1 paraffin wax
NT1 pentane
NT1 petrolatum
NT1 propane
NT1 tricosane

ALKANNA
BT1 boraginaceae
NT1 alkanna tuberculata

alkanna tinctoria
USE **alkanna tuberculata**

ALKANNA TUBERCULATA
uf *alkanna tinctoria*
BT1 alkanna
BT2 boraginaceae
BT1 antibacterial plants
BT1 dye plants

ALKAPTONURIA
BT1 amino acid disorders

ALKAPTONURIA *cont.*
BT2 metabolic disorders
BT3 animal disorders
BT4 disorders
NT1 ochronosis
rt urine

ALKENES
BT1 hydrocarbons
NT1 2-methyl-1-propene
NT1 allene
NT1 ethylene
NT1 propylene
NT1 squalene

ALKYL (ARYL) TRANSFERASES
(ec 2.5)
BT1 transferases
BT2 enzymes
NT1 glutathione transferase
NT1 methionine adenosyltransferase

alkylammonium compounds
USE **quaternary ammonium compounds**

ALKYLATING AGENTS
NT1 busulfan
NT1 dimethyl sulfate
NT1 ethyl methanesulfonate
NT1 ethyleneimine
NT1 isopropyl methanesulfonate
NT1 maleic hydrazide
NT1 methyl methanesulfonate
NT1 tepa

ALKYLRESORCINOLS
BT1 resorcinols
BT2 phenols
BT3 alcohols
BT3 phenolic compounds
BT4 aromatic compounds

ALKYNES
uf *acetylenes*
BT1 hydrocarbons
NT1 acetylene
NT1 polyacetylenes

ALLACTAGA
BT1 dipodidae
BT2 rodents
BT3 mammals
NT1 allactaga sibirica

ALLACTAGA SIBIRICA
BT1 allactaga
BT2 dipodidae
BT3 rodents
BT4 mammals

ALLAGOPTERA
uf *diplothemium*
BT1 palmae
NT1 allagoptera arenaria

ALLAGOPTERA ARENARIA
BT1 allagoptera
BT2 palmae

ALLANTOCYSTIS
BT1 apicomplexa
BT2 protozoa
NT1 allantocystis dasyhelei

ALLANTOCYSTIS DASYHELEI
BT1 allantocystis
BT2 apicomplexa
BT3 protozoa

ALLANTOIC ACID
BT1 monocarboxylic acids
BT2 carboxylic acids
BT3 organic acids
BT4 acids
rt allantoin
rt allantois

ALLANTOIC FLUID
HN from 1989
BT1 body fluids
BT2 fluids
rt allantois

ALLANTOIN
BT1 dermatological agents
BT2 drugs
BT1 imidazoles
BT2 azoles
BT3 heterocyclic nitrogen compounds
BT4 organic nitrogen compounds
rt allantoic acid
rt allantois
rt purines
rt uric acid
rt urine

ALLANTOIS
BT1 fetal membranes
BT2 membranes
rt allantoic acid
rt allantoic fluid
rt allantoin
rt placenta
rt urachus

ALLANTONEMATIDAE
BT1 nematoda
NT1 contortylenchus
NT1 heterotylenchus
NT2 heterotylenchus autumnalis
NT1 howardula
NT1 neoparasitylenchus
NT1 parasitylenchus
rt entomophilic nematodes

ALLANTOSOMA
BT1 ciliophora
BT2 protozoa

ALLELES
BT1 genes
NT1 multiple alleles
NT1 neutral alleles
NT1 rare alleles
rt allelic exclusion
rt allelism
rt dominance
rt heterozygosity
rt heterozygotes
rt segregation

alleles, multiple
USE **multiple alleles**

ALLELIC EXCLUSION
rt alleles
rt inheritance

ALLELISM
rt alleles
rt relationships

ALLELOCHEMICALS
uf *allelochemics*
BT1 semiochemicals
NT1 allomones
NT2 2-tridecanone
NT2 α-terthienyl
NT2 α-tomatine
NT2 allelopathins
NT2 azadirachtin
NT2 canavanine
NT2 chlorogenic acid
NT2 defensive secretions
NT2 dimboa
NT2 gossypol
NT2 phytoalexins
NT3 p-coumaric acid
NT3 capsidiol
NT3 casbene
NT3 dimethoxyisoflavone
NT3 ferulic acid
NT3 lubimin
NT3 medicarpin
NT3 phaseollin
NT3 phytoncides
NT3 phytuberin
NT3 phytuberol
NT3 pisatin
NT3 rishitin
NT3 solavetivone
NT3 wyerone
NT2 rutoside
NT2 sinigrin

ALLELOCHEMICALS *cont.*
NT1 kairomones

allelochemics
USE **allelochemicals**

ALLELOPATHINS
BT1 allomones
BT2 allelochemicals
BT3 semiochemicals
rt allelopathy
rt plant interaction

ALLELOPATHY
BT1 plant interaction
rt allelopathins
rt competitive ability
rt herbicidal properties
rt plant competition
rt toxicity

ALLEMANDA
BT1 apocynaceae
NT1 allemanda cathartica

ALLEMANDA CATHARTICA
uf *allemanda grandiflora*
BT1 algicidal plants
BT1 allemanda
BT2 apocynaceae
BT1 ornamental woody plants

allemanda grandiflora
USE **allemanda cathartica**

ALLENE
BT1 alkenes
BT2 hydrocarbons

ALLENROLFEA
BT1 chenopodiaceae
NT1 allenrolfea occidentalis

ALLENROLFEA OCCIDENTALIS
BT1 allenrolfea
BT2 chenopodiaceae

ALLERGENS
BT1 antigens
BT2 immunological factors
NT1 brucellin
rt allergies
rt immediate hypersensitivity
rt immune desensitization
rt skin tests

ALLERGIC BRONCHOPULMONARY ASPERGILLOSIS
BT1 aspergillosis
BT2 mycoses
BT3 infectious diseases
BT4 diseases
BT2 respiratory diseases
BT3 organic diseases
BT4 diseases
rt aspergillus

ALLERGIC ENCEPHALOMYELITIS
BT1 encephalitis
BT2 brain disorders
BT3 nervous system diseases
BT4 organic diseases
BT5 diseases
BT1 immunological diseases
BT2 diseases

ALLERGIC REACTIONS
BT1 immediate hypersensitivity
BT2 hypersensitivity
BT3 immune response
BT4 immunity

allergic responses
USE **hypersensitivity**

ALLERGIES
BT1 immunological diseases
BT2 diseases
NT1 arthropod allergies
NT1 drug allergies
NT1 farmer's lung
NT1 food allergies
NT2 milk allergy
NT1 humidifier disease
rt allergens

ALLERGIES *cont.*
rt anaphylaxis
rt antihistaminics
rt hypersensitivity
rt immune response
rt immunity

allergy, arthropod
USE **arthropod allergies**

allergy, drug
USE **drug allergies**

allergy, food
USE **food allergies**

allergy, insect
USE **arthropod allergies**

allergy, milk
USE **milk allergy**

allescheria
USE **pseudallescheria**

allescheria boydii
USE **pseudallescheria boydii**

ALLETHRIN
BT1 pyrethroid insecticides
BT2 insecticides
BT3 pesticides
BT2 pyrethroids

ALLEY CROPPING
uf *hedgerow intercropping*
uf *zonal cropping*
BT1 agrosilvicultural systems
BT2 agroforestry systems
BT1 intercropping
BT2 cropping systems

ALLIACEAE
NT1 agapanthus
NT2 agapanthus africanus
NT2 agapanthus praecox
NT1 allium
NT2 allium aflatunense
NT2 allium albanum
NT2 allium altaicum
NT2 allium ampeloprasum
NT2 allium ascalonicum
NT2 allium atropurpureum
NT2 allium bouddhae
NT2 allium caeruleum
NT2 allium carinatum
NT2 allium cepa
NT2 allium chinense
NT2 allium christophii
NT2 allium decipiens
NT2 allium elatum
NT2 allium fistulosum
NT2 allium flavum
NT2 allium karataviense
NT2 allium kurrat
NT2 allium ledebourianum
NT2 allium lusitanicum
NT2 allium macrostemon
NT2 allium moly
NT2 allium neapolitanum
NT2 allium nutans
NT2 allium oreophilum
NT2 allium porrum
NT2 allium ramosum
NT2 allium rosenbachianum
NT2 allium roseum
NT2 allium rubellum
NT2 allium sativum
NT2 allium schoenoprasum
NT2 allium schubertii
NT2 allium scorodoprasum
NT2 allium suvorovii
NT2 allium textile
NT2 allium tricoccum
NT2 allium triquetrum
NT2 allium tuberosum
NT2 allium unifolium
NT2 allium ursinum
NT2 allium vineale
NT2 allium zebdanense
NT1 brodiaea
NT1 tulbaghia

ALLIARIA
BT1 cruciferae
NT1 alliaria petiolata

alliaria officinalis
USE **alliaria petiolata**

ALLIARIA PETIOLATA
uf *alliaria officinalis*
BT1 alliaria
BT2 cruciferae

ALLIDOCHLOR
uf *cdaa*
BT1 amide herbicides
BT2 herbicides
BT3 pesticides

ALLIED HEALTH OCCUPATIONS (AGRICOLA)
BT1 occupations
NT1 home health aides (agricola)
rt health services

ALLIGATOR
BT1 alligatoridae
BT2 crocodylia
BT3 reptiles

ALLIGATORIDAE
BT1 crocodylia
BT2 reptiles
NT1 alligator
NT1 caiman

ALLIUM
BT1 alliaceae
NT1 allium aflatunense
NT1 allium albanum
NT1 allium altaicum
NT1 allium ampeloprasum
NT1 allium ascalonicum
NT1 allium atropurpureum
NT1 allium bouddhae
NT1 allium caeruleum
NT1 allium carinatum
NT1 allium cepa
NT1 allium chinense
NT1 allium christophii
NT1 allium decipiens
NT1 allium elatum
NT1 allium fistulosum
NT1 allium flavum
NT1 allium karataviense
NT1 allium kurrat
NT1 allium ledebourianum
NT1 allium lusitanicum
NT1 allium macrostemon
NT1 allium moly
NT1 allium neapolitanum
NT1 allium nutans
NT1 allium oreophilum
NT1 allium porrum
NT1 allium ramosum
NT1 allium rosenbachianum
NT1 allium roseum
NT1 allium rubellum
NT1 allium sativum
NT1 allium schoenoprasum
NT1 allium schubertii
NT1 allium scorodoprasum
NT1 allium suvorovii
NT1 allium textile
NT1 allium tricoccum
NT1 allium triquetrum
NT1 allium tuberosum
NT1 allium unifolium
NT1 allium ursinum
NT1 allium vineale
NT1 allium zebdanense

ALLIUM AFLATUNENSE
BT1 allium
BT2 alliaceae
BT1 ornamental bulbs

ALLIUM ALBANUM
BT1 allium
BT2 alliaceae

ALLIUM ALTAICUM
BT1 allium
BT2 alliaceae

ALLIUM AMPELOPRASUM
BT1 allium
BT2 alliaceae

ALLIUM ASCALONICUM
BT1 allium
BT2 alliaceae
rt shallot latent carlavirus
rt shallots

ALLIUM ATROPURPUREUM
BT1 allium
BT2 alliaceae
BT1 ornamental bulbs

allium bakeri
USE **allium chinense**

ALLIUM BOUDDHAE
BT1 allium
BT2 alliaceae

ALLIUM CAERULEUM
BT1 allium
BT2 alliaceae
BT1 ornamental bulbs

ALLIUM CARINATUM
uf *allium pulchellum*
BT1 allium
BT2 alliaceae

ALLIUM CEPA
BT1 allium
BT2 alliaceae
rt onion yellow dwarf potyvirus
rt onions

ALLIUM CHINENSE
uf *allium bakeri*
BT1 allium
BT2 alliaceae
BT1 bulbous vegetables
BT2 vegetables
BT1 medicinal plants

ALLIUM CHRISTOPHII
BT1 allium
BT2 alliaceae
BT1 ornamental bulbs

allium cowanii
USE **allium neapolitanum**

ALLIUM DECIPIENS
BT1 allium
BT2 alliaceae

ALLIUM ELATUM
BT1 allium
BT2 alliaceae
BT1 ornamental bulbs

ALLIUM FISTULOSUM
BT1 allium
BT2 alliaceae
rt welsh onions

ALLIUM FLAVUM
BT1 allium
BT2 alliaceae
BT1 ornamental bulbs

ALLIUM KARATAVIENSE
BT1 allium
BT2 alliaceae

ALLIUM KURRAT
BT1 allium
BT2 alliaceae

ALLIUM LEDBOURIANUM
BT1 bulbous vegetables
BT2 vegetables

ALLIUM LEDEBOURIANUM
BT1 allium
BT2 alliaceae

ALLIUM LUSITANICUM
BT1 allium
BT2 alliaceae

ALLIUM MACROSTEMON
BT1 allium

ALLIUM MACROSTEMON *cont.*
BT2 alliaceae

ALLIUM MOLY
BT1 allium
BT2 alliaceae
BT1 ornamental bulbs

ALLIUM NEAPOLITANUM
uf *allium cowanii*
BT1 allium
BT2 alliaceae
BT1 ornamental bulbs

ALLIUM NUTANS
BT1 allium
BT2 alliaceae

allium odoratum
USE **allium tuberosum**

allium odorum
USE **allium ramosum**

ALLIUM OREOPHILUM
uf *allium ostrowskianum*
BT1 allium
BT2 alliaceae
BT1 ornamental bulbs

allium ostrowskianum
USE **allium oreophilum**

ALLIUM PORRUM
BT1 allium
BT2 alliaceae
rt leek yellow stripe potyvirus
rt leeks

allium pulchellum
USE **allium carinatum**

ALLIUM RAMOSUM
uf *allium odorum*
BT1 allium
BT2 alliaceae
BT1 bulbous vegetables
BT2 vegetables

ALLIUM ROSENBACHIANUM
BT1 allium
BT2 alliaceae
BT1 ornamental bulbs

ALLIUM ROSEUM
BT1 allium
BT2 alliaceae
BT1 ornamental bulbs

ALLIUM RUBELLUM
BT1 allium
BT2 alliaceae

ALLIUM SATIVUM
BT1 allium
BT2 alliaceae
rt garlic

ALLIUM SCHOENOPRASUM
BT1 allium
BT2 alliaceae
rt chives

ALLIUM SCHUBERTII
BT1 allium
BT2 alliaceae
BT1 ornamental bulbs

ALLIUM SCORODOPRASUM
BT1 allium
BT2 alliaceae
BT1 bulbous vegetables
BT2 vegetables

ALLIUM SUVOROVII
BT1 allium
BT2 alliaceae

ALLIUM TEXTILE
BT1 allium
BT2 alliaceae

ALLIUM TRICOCCUM
BT1 allium
BT2 alliaceae

ALLIUM TRIQUETRUM
BT1 allium
BT2 alliaceae
BT1 ornamental bulbs

ALLIUM TUBEROSUM
uf *allium odoratum*
uf *allium uliginosum*
BT1 allium
BT2 alliaceae
BT1 medicinal plants

allium uliginosum
USE **allium tuberosum**

ALLIUM UNIFOLIUM
BT1 allium
BT2 alliaceae
BT1 ornamental bulbs

ALLIUM URSINUM
BT1 allium
BT2 alliaceae

ALLIUM VINEALE
BT1 allium
BT2 alliaceae

ALLIUM ZEBDANENSE
BT1 allium
BT2 alliaceae
BT1 ornamental bulbs

ALLMANIA
BT1 amaranthaceae
NT1 allmania nodiflora

ALLMANIA NODIFLORA
BT1 allmania
BT2 amaranthaceae

alloceraea
USE **haemaphysalis**

alloceraea inermis
USE **haemaphysalis inermis**

ALLOCHRUSA
BT1 caryophyllaceae
NT1 allochrusa gypsophiloides

ALLOCHRUSA GYPSOPHILOIDES
BT1 allochrusa
BT2 caryophyllaceae

ALLOCREADIIDAE
BT1 digenea
BT2 trematoda
NT1 allocreadium
NT1 crepidostomum
NT2 crepidostomum farionis
NT2 crepidostomum metoecus

ALLOCREADIUM
BT1 allocreadiidae
BT2 digenea
BT3 trematoda

ALLODAPE
BT1 apidae
BT2 hymenoptera

ALLODONTERMES
BT1 termitidae
BT2 isoptera

ALLOGRAFTS
BT1 grafts
rt histocompatibility

ALLOGRAPTA
BT1 syrphidae
BT2 diptera
NT1 allograpta obliqua
NT1 allograpta pulchra

ALLOGRAPTA OBLIQUA
BT1 allograpta
BT2 syrphidae
BT3 diptera

ALLOGRAPTA PULCHRA
BT1 allograpta
BT2 syrphidae
BT3 diptera

ALLOLOBOPHORA
BT1 lumbricidae
BT2 oligochaeta
BT3 annelida
NT1 allolobophora chlorotica
rt aporrectodea

allolobophora caliginosa
USE **aporrectodea caliginosa**

ALLOLOBOPHORA CHLOROTICA
BT1 allolobophora
BT2 lumbricidae
BT3 oligochaeta
BT4 annelida

allolobophora longa
USE **aporrectodea longa**

allolobophora trapezoides
USE **aporrectodea caliginosa**

allolobophora tuberculata
USE **aporrectodea caliginosa**

ALLOMETRY

ALLOMONES
BT1 allelochemicals
BT2 semiochemicals
NT1 2-tridecanone
NT1 α-terthienyl
NT1 α-tomatine
NT1 allelopathins
NT1 azadirachtin
NT1 canavanine
NT1 chlorogenic acid
NT1 defensive secretions
NT1 dimboa
NT1 gossypol
NT1 phytoalexins
NT2 p-coumaric acid
NT2 capsidiol
NT2 casbene
NT2 dimethoxyisoflavone
NT2 ferulic acid
NT2 lubimin
NT2 medicarpin
NT2 phaseollin
NT2 phytoncides
NT2 phytuberin
NT2 phytuberol
NT2 pisatin
NT2 rishitin
NT2 solavetivone
NT2 wyerone
NT1 rutoside
NT1 sinigrin
rt pest resistance
rt phototoxins

ALLOPHANE
BT1 clay minerals
BT2 minerals
rt allophanic soils

ALLOPHANIC SOILS
BT1 soil types (mineralogical)
rt allophane

ALLOPLECTUS
BT1 gesneriaceae
NT1 alloplectus schlimii

ALLOPLECTUS SCHLIMII
BT1 alloplectus
BT2 gesneriaceae
BT1 ornamental bulbs
rt tubers

ALLOPURINOL
BT1 antineoplastic agents
BT2 drugs
BT1 antiprotozoal agents
BT2 antiparasitic agents
BT3 drugs
BT1 enzyme inhibitors
BT2 metabolic inhibitors
BT3 inhibitors
BT1 pyrimidines
BT2 heterocyclic nitrogen compounds
BT3 organic nitrogen compounds

ALLOPURINOL *cont.*
rt gout
rt uric acid

ALLORHOGAS
BT1 braconidae
BT2 hymenoptera

ALLOTEUTHIS
BT1 loliginidae
BT2 cephalopoda
BT3 mollusca
rt squids

allotheobaldia
USE **culiseta**

allotheobaldia longiareolata
USE **culiseta longiareolata**

ALLOTHROMBIUM
BT1 trombidiidae
BT2 prostigmata
BT3 acari
NT1 allothrombium fuliginosum

ALLOTHROMBIUM FULIGINOSUM
BT1 allothrombium
BT2 trombidiidae
BT3 prostigmata
BT4 acari

ALLOTMENTS
BT1 domestic gardens
BT2 gardens

ALLOTYPES
rt genetic polymorphism
rt genotypes
rt immunoglobulins
rt species

ALLOWANCES
NT1 family allowances
rt income

ALLOXAN
BT1 antineoplastic agents
BT2 drugs
BT1 pyrimidines
BT2 heterocyclic nitrogen compounds
BT3 organic nitrogen compounds
rt diabetes

ALLOXYDIM
BT1 cyclohexene oxime herbicides
BT2 herbicides
BT3 pesticides

ALLOXYSTA
BT1 charipidae
BT2 hymenoptera
NT1 alloxysta victrix

alloxysta brassicae
USE **alloxysta victrix**

ALLOXYSTA VICTRIX
uf *alloxysta brassicae*
BT1 alloxysta
BT2 charipidae
BT3 hymenoptera

ALLOYS
BT1 metals
BT1 mixtures
NT1 ferrous alloys
NT2 cast iron
NT2 steel
NT3 stainless steel
NT3 structural steel
NT1 non-ferrous alloys
NT2 brass
rt case hardening
rt metallurgy

alloys, ferrous
USE **ferrous alloys**

alloys, nonferrous
USE **non-ferrous alloys**

ALLSPICE
BT1 spices
BT2 plant products
BT3 products
rt pimenta dioica

ALLUAUDIA
BT1 didiereaceae
NT1 alluaudia dumosa
NT1 alluaudia procera

ALLUAUDIA DUMOSA
BT1 alluaudia
BT2 didiereaceae

ALLUAUDIA PROCERA
BT1 alluaudia
BT2 didiereaceae
BT1 ornamental succulent plants
BT2 succulent plants

ALLUAUDIOPSIS
BT1 didiereaceae
NT1 alluaudiopsis marnierana

ALLUAUDIOPSIS MARNIERANA
BT1 alluaudiopsis
BT2 didiereaceae
BT1 ornamental succulent plants
BT2 succulent plants

alluvial deposits
USE **alluvium**

ALLUVIAL LAND
BT1 land types
rt alluvial soils
rt alluvium
rt bottomlands
rt deltas
rt floodplains
rt fluvisols

alluvial materials
USE **alluvium**

ALLUVIAL SOILS
BT1 fluvisols
BT2 soil types (genetic)
BT1 soil types (lithological)
rt alluvial land

ALLUVIUM
uf *alluvial deposits*
uf *alluvial materials*
BT1 soil parent materials
rt alluvial land
rt dredgings
rt mud
rt sediment

ALLYL ALCOHOL
BT1 alcohols

ALLYL ISOTHIOCYANATE
BT1 isothiocyanates
BT2 esters
BT2 organic sulfur compounds
BT1 volatile compounds
rt mustard oil

ALLYXYCARB
BT1 carbamate insecticides
BT2 carbamate pesticides
BT2 insecticides
BT3 pesticides

ALMOND OIL
BT1 seed oils
BT2 plant oils
BT3 oils
BT3 plant products
BT4 products
rt almonds

ALMONDS
BT1 temperate tree nuts
BT2 nut crops
rt almond oil
rt prunus dulcis

ALNETOIDIA
BT1 cicadellidae
BT2 cicadelloidea
BT3 auchenorrhyncha

ALNETOIDIA *cont.*
BT4 homoptera
NT1 alnetoidia alneti

ALNETOIDIA ALNETI
BT1 alnetoidia
BT2 cicadellidae
BT3 cicadelloidea
BT4 auchenorrhyncha
BT5 homoptera

ALNUS
uf *alders*
BT1 betulaceae
NT1 alnus acuminata
NT1 alnus cordata
NT1 alnus crispa
NT1 alnus fauriei
NT1 alnus firmifolia
NT1 alnus formosana
NT1 alnus glutinosa
NT1 alnus hirsuta
NT1 alnus incana
NT1 alnus inokumae
NT1 alnus japonica
NT1 alnus jorullensis
NT1 alnus kamtschatica
NT1 alnus koehnei
NT1 alnus nepalensis
NT1 alnus nitida
NT1 alnus rhombifolia
NT1 alnus rubra
NT1 alnus rugosa
NT1 alnus sinuata
NT1 alnus spaethii
NT1 alnus subcordata
NT1 alnus viridis

ALNUS ACUMINATA
HN from 1990
BT1 alnus
BT2 betulaceae
BT1 forest trees

ALNUS CORDATA
BT1 alnus
BT2 betulaceae
BT1 forest trees

ALNUS CRISPA
BT1 alnus
BT2 betulaceae
BT1 forest trees
BT1 ornamental woody plants

ALNUS FAURIEI
BT1 alnus
BT2 betulaceae

ALNUS FIRMIFOLIA
BT1 alnus
BT2 betulaceae

ALNUS FORMOSANA
BT1 alnus
BT2 betulaceae
BT1 forest trees

ALNUS GLUTINOSA
BT1 alnus
BT2 betulaceae
BT1 forest trees
BT1 ornamental woody plants
BT1 tan plants

ALNUS HIRSUTA
BT1 alnus
BT2 betulaceae
BT1 forest trees

ALNUS INCANA
BT1 alnus
BT2 betulaceae
BT1 forest trees
BT1 ornamental woody plants

ALNUS INOKUMAE
BT1 alnus
BT2 betulaceae

ALNUS JAPONICA
BT1 alnus
BT2 betulaceae
BT1 forest trees

ALNUS JORULLENSIS
BT1 alnus
BT2 betulaceae

ALNUS KAMTSCHATICA
BT1 alnus
BT2 betulaceae

ALNUS KOEHNEI
BT1 alnus
BT2 betulaceae

ALNUS NEPALENSIS
BT1 alnus
BT2 betulaceae
BT1 forest trees

ALNUS NITIDA
BT1 alnus
BT2 betulaceae

ALNUS RHOMBIFOLIA
BT1 alnus
BT2 betulaceae
BT1 ornamental woody plants

ALNUS RUBRA
BT1 alnus
BT2 betulaceae
BT1 forest trees

ALNUS RUGOSA
BT1 alnus
BT2 betulaceae
BT1 forest trees

ALNUS SINUATA
BT1 alnus
BT2 betulaceae
BT1 ornamental woody plants

ALNUS SPAETHII
BT1 alnus
BT2 betulaceae
BT1 ornamental woody plants

ALNUS SUBCORDATA
BT1 alnus
BT2 betulaceae

ALNUS VIRIDIS
BT1 alnus
BT2 betulaceae
BT1 ornamental woody plants

ALOCASIA
BT1 araceae
NT1 alocasia cucullata
NT1 alocasia macrorrhiza

ALOCASIA CUCULLATA
BT1 alocasia
BT2 araceae
rt ornamental foliage plants

alocasia lindenii
USE **homalomena lindenii**

ALOCASIA MACRORRHIZA
BT1 alocasia
BT2 araceae
BT1 root vegetables
BT2 root crops
BT2 vegetables

ALOE
BT1 liliaceae
NT1 aloe arborescens
NT1 aloe barbadensis
NT1 aloe candelabrum
NT1 aloe cheranganiensis
NT1 aloe chrysostachys
NT1 aloe ferox
NT1 aloe fibrosa
NT1 aloe fleurentinorum
NT1 aloe korijensis
NT1 aloe lensaytiensis
NT1 aloe meruana
NT1 aloe polyphylla
NT1 aloe pretoriensis
NT1 aloe rivierei
NT1 aloe saponaria
NT1 aloe schliebenii
NT1 aloe schweinfurthii

ALOE ARBORESCENS
BT1 aloe
BT2 liliaceae
BT1 medicinal plants
BT1 ornamental succulent plants
BT2 succulent plants

ALOE BARBADENSIS
uf *aloe vera*
BT1 aloe
BT2 liliaceae
BT1 medicinal plants
BT1 nematicidal plants
BT2 pesticidal plants
BT1 ornamental succulent plants
BT2 succulent plants
rt ornamental foliage plants

ALOE CANDELABRUM
BT1 aloe
BT2 liliaceae

ALOE CHERANGANIENSIS
BT1 aloe
BT2 liliaceae

ALOE CHRYSOSTACHYS
BT1 aloe
BT2 liliaceae

ALOE FEROX
BT1 aloe
BT2 liliaceae

ALOE FIBROSA
BT1 aloe
BT2 liliaceae

ALOE FLEURENTINORUM
BT1 aloe
BT2 liliaceae

ALOE KORIJENSIS
BT1 aloe
BT2 liliaceae

ALOE LENSAYTIENSIS
BT1 aloe
BT2 liliaceae

ALOE MERUANA
BT1 aloe
BT2 liliaceae

ALOE POLYPHYLLA
BT1 aloe
BT2 liliaceae
BT1 ornamental succulent plants
BT2 succulent plants

ALOE PRETORIENSIS
BT1 aloe
BT2 liliaceae

ALOE RIVIEREI
BT1 aloe
BT2 liliaceae

ALOE SAPONARIA
BT1 aloe
BT2 liliaceae
BT1 medicinal plants

ALOE SCHLIEBENII
BT1 aloe
BT2 liliaceae

ALOE SCHWEINFURTHII
BT1 aloe
BT2 liliaceae

aloe vera
USE **aloe barbadensis**

ALOPECIA
BT1 skin diseases
BT2 organic diseases
BT3 diseases
rt hair
rt hypotrichosis

ALOPECURUS
BT1 gramineae
NT1 alopecurus aequalis
NT1 alopecurus aequalis var. amurensis

ALOPECURUS *cont.*
NT1 alopecurus brevifolius
NT1 alopecurus bulbosus
NT1 alopecurus geniculatus
NT1 alopecurus myosuroides
NT1 alopecurus pratensis
rt gastridium

ALOPECURUS AEQUALIS
BT1 alopecurus
BT2 gramineae
BT1 pasture plants

ALOPECURUS AEQUALIS VAR. AMURENSIS
BT1 alopecurus
BT2 gramineae

ALOPECURUS BREVIFOLIUS
BT1 alopecurus
BT2 gramineae
BT1 pasture plants

ALOPECURUS BULBOSUS
BT1 alopecurus
BT2 gramineae
BT1 pasture plants

ALOPECURUS GENICULATUS
BT1 alopecurus
BT2 gramineae
BT1 weeds

ALOPECURUS MYOSUROIDES
BT1 alopecurus
BT2 gramineae
BT1 weeds

ALOPECURUS PRATENSIS
uf *meadow foxtail*
BT1 alopecurus
BT2 gramineae
BT1 pasture plants

alopecurus ventricosus
USE **gastridium ventricosum**

ALOPEX
BT1 canidae
BT2 fissipeda
BT3 carnivores
BT4 mammals
NT1 alopex lagopus

ALOPEX LAGOPUS
uf *arctic fox*
uf *foxes, arctic*
BT1 alopex
BT2 canidae
BT3 fissipeda
BT4 carnivores
BT5 mammals
BT1 furbearing animals
BT2 animals

ALOPHORA
BT1 tachinidae
BT2 diptera
NT1 alophora subcoleoptrata
rt phasia

ALOPHORA SUBCOLEOPTRATA
uf *phasia subcoleoptrata*
BT1 alophora
BT2 tachinidae
BT3 diptera

ALOPIAS
BT1 lamnidae
BT2 lamniformes
BT3 chondrichthyes
BT4 fishes

ALOSA
BT1 clupeidae
BT2 clupeiformes
BT3 osteichthyes
BT4 fishes
NT1 alosa pseudoharengus
NT1 alosa sapidissima

ALOSA PSEUDOHARENGUS
uf *alewife*
BT1 alosa
BT2 clupeidae

ALOSA PSEUDOHARENGUS *cont.*
BT3 clupeiformes
BT4 osteichthyes
BT5 fishes

ALOSA SAPIDISSIMA
uf *shad*
BT1 alosa
BT2 clupeidae
BT3 clupeiformes
BT4 osteichthyes
BT5 fishes

ALOUATTA
BT1 cebidae
BT2 primates
BT3 mammals

ALOYSIA
BT1 verbenaceae
NT1 aloysia lycioides
NT1 aloysia triphylla

ALOYSIA LYCIOIDES
BT1 aloysia
BT2 verbenaceae

ALOYSIA TRIPHYLLA
uf *lippia citriodora*
BT1 aloysia
BT2 verbenaceae
BT1 antibacterial plants
BT1 essential oil plants
BT2 oil plants
BT1 ornamental woody plants

ALPACAS
uf *lama pacos*
BT1 wool-producing animals
BT2 animals
rt camelidae

ALPHA-ADRENERGIC RECEPTORS
(sorted under adrenergic receptors)

ALPHA-AMANITIN
(sorted under amanitin)

ALPHA-AMINOBUTYRIC ACID
(sorted under aminobutyric acid)

ALPHA-AMYLASE
(sorted under amylase)

ALPHA-BISABOLOL
(sorted under bisabolol)

ALPHA-CAROTENE
(sorted under carotene)

ALPHA-CASEIN
(sorted under casein)

ALPHA-CHLOROHYDRIN
(sorted under chlorohydrin)

ALPHA-CUBEBENE
(sorted under cubebene)

ALPHA-CYPERMETHRIN
(sorted under cypermethrin)

ALPHA-ECDYSONE
(sorted under ecdysone)

ALPHA-FETOPROTEIN
(sorted under fetoprotein)

ALPHA-GALACTOSIDASE
(sorted under galactosidase)

ALPHA-GLUCAN
(sorted under glucan)

ALPHA-GLUCOSIDASE
(sorted under glucosidase)

ALPHA-IONONE
(sorted under ionone)

ALPHA-KETOGLUTARIC ACID
(sorted under ketoglutaric acid)

ALPHA-LACTALBUMIN
(sorted under lactalbumin)

ALPHA-MANNOSIDASE
(sorted under mannosidase)

ALPHA-PINENE
(sorted under pinene)

ALPHA RADIATION
BT1 radiation
rt polonium

ALPHA-TERTHIENYL
(sorted under terthienyl)

ALPHA-TOCOPHEROL
(sorted under tocopherol)

ALPHA-TOMATINE
(sorted under tomatine)

ALPHAVIRUS
BT1 arboviruses
BT2 pathogens
BT1 togaviridae
BT2 viruses
NT1 chikungunya virus
NT1 equine encephalomyelitis virus
NT2 eastern equine encephalitis virus
NT2 venezuelan equine encephalitis virus
NT2 western equine encephalitis virus
NT1 getah virus
NT1 ross river virus
NT1 semliki forest virus
NT1 sindbis virus
NT1 una virus

ALPHITOBIUS
BT1 tenebrionidae
BT2 coleoptera
NT1 alphitobius diaperinus
NT1 alphitobius laevigatus

ALPHITOBIUS DIAPERINUS
BT1 alphitobius
BT2 tenebrionidae
BT3 coleoptera

ALPHITOBIUS LAEVIGATUS
uf *alphitobius piceus*
BT1 alphitobius
BT2 tenebrionidae
BT3 coleoptera

alphitobius piceus
USE **alphitobius laevigatus**

ALPHITONIA
BT1 rhamnaceae
NT1 alphitonia excelsa

ALPHITONIA EXCELSA
BT1 alphitonia
BT2 rhamnaceae

ALPHONSEA
BT1 annonaceae
NT1 alphonsea arborea

ALPHONSEA ARBOREA
BT1 alphonsea
BT2 annonaceae
BT1 antibacterial plants

ALPINE GRASSLANDS
uf *grasslands, alpine*
BT1 grasslands
BT2 vegetation types
rt alpine vegetation
rt hill grasslands
rt mountain areas
rt mountain grasslands

ALPINE MEADOW SOILS
BT1 soil types (ecological)

ALPINE PLANTS
uf *rock garden plants*
rt alpine vegetation
rt ornamental plants
rt plants
rt rock gardens

alpine soils
USE **mountain soils**

ALPINE VEGETATION
BT1 vegetation
rt alpine grasslands
rt alpine plants
rt arctic tundra

ALPINIA
BT1 zingiberaceae
NT1 alpinia galanga
NT1 alpinia katsumadai
NT1 alpinia officinarum
NT1 alpinia purpurata
NT1 alpinia zerumbet

ALPINIA GALANGA
BT1 alpinia
BT2 zingiberaceae
BT1 antibacterial plants
BT1 antifungal plants
BT1 essential oil plants
BT2 oil plants
BT1 medicinal plants
BT1 spice plants

ALPINIA KATSUMADAI
BT1 alpinia
BT2 zingiberaceae

alpinia nutans
USE **alpinia zerumbet**

ALPINIA OFFICINARUM
BT1 alpinia
BT2 zingiberaceae
BT1 antifungal plants
BT1 essential oil plants
BT2 oil plants
BT1 spice plants

ALPINIA PURPURATA
BT1 alpinia
BT2 zingiberaceae

alpinia speciosa
USE **alpinia zerumbet**

ALPINIA ZERUMBET
uf *alpinia nutans*
uf *alpinia speciosa*
BT1 alpinia
BT2 zingiberaceae
BT1 essential oil plants
BT2 oil plants

ALSACE
BT1 france
BT2 western europe
BT3 europe

alsike clover
USE **trifolium hybridum**

ALSOBIA
BT1 gesneriaceae
NT1 alsobia punctata

ALSOBIA PUNCTATA
uf *episcia punctata*
BT1 alsobia
BT2 gesneriaceae
BT1 ornamental herbaceous plants

ALSOPHILA
BT1 geometridae
BT2 lepidoptera
NT1 alsophila pometaria

ALSOPHILA POMETARIA
BT1 alsophila
BT2 geometridae
BT3 lepidoptera

ALSTONIA
BT1 apocynaceae
NT1 alstonia boonei
NT1 alstonia congensis
NT1 alstonia deplanchei
NT1 alstonia macrophylla
NT1 alstonia muelleriana
NT1 alstonia odontophora
NT1 alstonia scholaris

ALSTONIA *cont.*
NT1 alstonia spectabilis
NT1 alstonia venenata

ALSTONIA BOONEI
BT1 alstonia
BT2 apocynaceae
BT1 medicinal plants

ALSTONIA CONGENSIS
BT1 alstonia
BT2 apocynaceae

ALSTONIA DEPLANCHEI
BT1 alstonia
BT2 apocynaceae

ALSTONIA MACROPHYLLA
BT1 alstonia
BT2 apocynaceae

ALSTONIA MUELLERIANA
BT1 alstonia
BT2 apocynaceae

ALSTONIA ODONTOPHORA
BT1 alstonia
BT2 apocynaceae

ALSTONIA SCHOLARIS
BT1 alstonia
BT2 apocynaceae
BT1 antibacterial plants
BT1 medicinal plants

ALSTONIA SPECTABILIS
BT1 alstonia
BT2 apocynaceae

ALSTONIA VENENATA
BT1 alstonia
BT2 apocynaceae

ALSTROEMERIA
BT1 alstroemeriaceae

ALSTROEMERIACEAE
NT1 alstroemeria
NT1 bomarea
NT2 bomarea cantabrigiensis

ALTAI
BT1 horse breeds
BT2 breeds
BT1 sheep breeds
BT2 breeds

ALTAI MOUNTAIN
HN from 1990
BT1 goat breeds
BT2 breeds

altamura
USE **altamurana**

ALTAMURANA
HN from 1990; previously "altamura"
uf *altamura*
BT1 sheep breeds
BT2 breeds

ALTERNANTHERA
BT1 amaranthaceae
NT1 alternanthera brasiliana
NT1 alternanthera ficoidea
NT1 alternanthera hassleriana
NT1 alternanthera philoxeroides
NT1 alternanthera polygonoides
NT1 alternanthera pungens
NT1 alternanthera sessilis

alternanthera amoena
USE **alternanthera ficoidea**

ALTERNANTHERA BRASILIANA
BT1 alternanthera
BT2 amaranthaceae

ALTERNANTHERA FICOIDEA
uf *alternanthera amoena*
BT1 alternanthera
BT2 amaranthaceae

ALTERNANTHERA HASSLERIANA
BT1 alternanthera

ALTERNANTHERA HASSLERIANA
cont.
BT2 amaranthaceae

ALTERNANTHERA PHILOXEROIDES
BT1 alternanthera
BT2 amaranthaceae

ALTERNANTHERA POLYGONOIDES
BT1 alternanthera
BT2 amaranthaceae

ALTERNANTHERA PUNGENS
BT1 alternanthera
BT2 amaranthaceae

ALTERNANTHERA SESSILIS
BT1 alternanthera
BT2 amaranthaceae

ALTERNARIA
BT1 deuteromycotina
NT1 alternaria alternata
NT1 alternaria brassicae
NT1 alternaria brassicicola
NT1 alternaria burnsii
NT1 alternaria carthami
NT1 alternaria cheiranthi
NT1 alternaria cichorii
NT1 alternaria citri
NT1 alternaria crassa
NT1 alternaria dauci
NT1 alternaria helianthi
NT1 alternaria kikuchiana
NT1 alternaria longipes
NT1 alternaria longissima
NT1 alternaria macrospora
NT1 alternaria mali
NT1 alternaria padwickii
NT1 alternaria panax
NT1 alternaria porri
NT1 alternaria radicina
NT1 alternaria raphani
NT1 alternaria solani
NT1 alternaria tagetica
NT1 alternaria tenuissima
NT1 alternaria triticina
NT1 alternaria zinniae
rt trichoconis

ALTERNARIA ALTERNATA
uf *alternaria tenuis*
BT1 alternaria
BT2 deuteromycotina

ALTERNARIA BRASSICAE
BT1 alternaria
BT2 deuteromycotina

ALTERNARIA BRASSICICOLA
uf *alternaria circinans*
uf *alternaria oleracea*
BT1 alternaria
BT2 deuteromycotina

ALTERNARIA BURNSII
BT1 alternaria
BT2 deuteromycotina

ALTERNARIA CARTHAMI
BT1 alternaria
BT2 deuteromycotina

ALTERNARIA CHEIRANTHI
BT1 alternaria
BT2 deuteromycotina

ALTERNARIA CICHORII
BT1 alternaria
BT2 deuteromycotina

alternaria circinans
USE **alternaria brassicicola**

ALTERNARIA CITRI
BT1 alternaria
BT2 deuteromycotina

ALTERNARIA CRASSA
BT1 alternaria
BT2 deuteromycotina

ALTERNARIA DAUCI
BT1 alternaria
BT2 deuteromycotina

ALTERNARIA HELIANTHI
BT1 alternaria
BT2 deuteromycotina

ALTERNARIA KIKUCHIANA
BT1 alternaria
BT2 deuteromycotina

ALTERNARIA LONGIPES
BT1 alternaria
BT2 deuteromycotina

ALTERNARIA LONGISSIMA
BT1 alternaria
BT2 deuteromycotina

ALTERNARIA MACROSPORA
BT1 alternaria
BT2 deuteromycotina
BT1 mycoherbicides
BT2 herbicides
BT3 pesticides
BT2 microbial pesticides
BT3 pesticides

ALTERNARIA MALI
BT1 alternaria
BT2 deuteromycotina

alternaria oleracea
USE **alternaria brassicicola**

ALTERNARIA PADWICKII
uf *trichoconis padwickii*
BT1 alternaria
BT2 deuteromycotina

ALTERNARIA PANAX
BT1 alternaria
BT2 deuteromycotina

ALTERNARIA PORRI
BT1 alternaria
BT2 deuteromycotina

alternaria porri f.sp. solani
USE **alternaria solani**

ALTERNARIA RADICINA
uf *stemphylium radicinum*
BT1 alternaria
BT2 deuteromycotina

ALTERNARIA RAPHANI
BT1 alternaria
BT2 deuteromycotina

ALTERNARIA SOLANI
uf *alternaria porri f.sp. solani*
BT1 alternaria
BT2 deuteromycotina

ALTERNARIA TAGETICA
BT1 alternaria
BT2 deuteromycotina

alternaria tenuis
USE **alternaria alternata**

ALTERNARIA TENUISSIMA
BT1 alternaria
BT2 deuteromycotina

ALTERNARIA TRITICINA
BT1 alternaria
BT2 deuteromycotina

ALTERNARIA ZINNIAE
BT1 alternaria
BT2 deuteromycotina

ALTERNARIOL
BT1 mycotoxins
BT2 toxins

alternative complement pathway
USE **complement activation**

ALTERNATIVE FARMING
BT1 farming
NT1 organic farming
rt sustainability

ALTERNATIVE HOSTS
BT1 hosts

ALTERNATIVE SPLICING
HN from 1990
rt dna
rt transcription

ALTERNATIVE TOURISM
BT1 tourism

alternatives to animal testing
USE **animal testing alternatives**

ALTHAEA
BT1 malvaceae
NT1 althaea armeniaca
NT1 althaea lenkoranica
NT1 althaea nudiflora
NT1 althaea officinalis
NT1 althaea rhyticarpa

ALTHAEA ARMENIACA
BT1 althaea
BT2 malvaceae

ALTHAEA LENKORANICA
BT1 althaea
BT2 malvaceae

ALTHAEA NUDIFLORA
BT1 althaea
BT2 malvaceae

ALTHAEA OFFICINALIS
BT1 althaea
BT2 malvaceae

ALTHAEA RHYTICARPA
BT1 althaea
BT2 malvaceae

althaea rosea
USE **alcea rosea**

ALTICA
uf *haltica*
BT1 chrysomelidae
BT2 coleoptera
NT1 altica carduorum

ALTICA CARDUORUM
BT1 altica
BT2 chrysomelidae
BT3 coleoptera

ALTICOLA
BT1 microtinae
BT2 muridae
BT3 rodents
BT4 mammals
rt voles

ALTINGIA
HN from 1990
BT1 altingiaceae
NT1 altingia excelsa

ALTINGIA EXCELSA
HN from 1990
BT1 altingia
BT2 altingiaceae
BT1 forest trees

ALTINGIACEAE
NT1 altingia
NT2 altingia excelsa
NT1 liquidambar
NT2 liquidambar formosana
NT2 liquidambar macrophylla
NT2 liquidambar styraciflua

ALTITUDE
uf *elevation*
NT1 high altitude
rt adaptation
rt anoxia
rt atmospheric pressure
rt height
rt mountains
rt position
rt site factors
rt topography

ALTRUISM
HN from 1990
BT1 behaviour

ALUMINIUM
AF aluminum
BT1 metallic elements
BT2 elements
BT2 metals
rt aluminium foil
rt aluminium hydroxide
rt aluminium oxide
rt aluminium phosphate
rt aluminium sulfate
rt bauxite
rt cryolite
rt gibbsite

aluminium ethyl phosphite
USE **fosetyl**

ALUMINIUM FOIL
AF aluminum foil
uf *foil, aluminium*
BT1 foil
BT2 mulches
BT2 packaging materials
BT3 materials
rt aluminium

ALUMINIUM HYDROXIDE
AF aluminum hydroxide
BT1 adsorbents
BT1 antacids
BT2 bases
BT2 gastrointestinal agents
BT3 drugs
BT1 hydroxides
BT2 inorganic compounds
BT1 nonclay minerals
BT2 minerals
rt aluminium

ALUMINIUM OXIDE
AF aluminum oxide
BT1 nonclay minerals
BT2 minerals
BT1 oxides
BT2 inorganic compounds
rt aluminium

ALUMINIUM PHOSPHATE
AF aluminum phosphate
BT1 antacids
BT2 bases
BT2 gastrointestinal agents
BT3 drugs
BT1 nonclay minerals
BT2 minerals
BT1 phosphates (salts)
BT2 inorganic salts
BT3 inorganic compounds
BT3 salts
BT2 phosphates
BT1 phosphorus fertilizers
BT2 fertilizers
rt aluminium

ALUMINIUM SULFATE
AF aluminum sulfate
uf *aluminium sulphate*
BT1 antiseptics
BT2 antiinfective agents
BT3 drugs
BT1 soil amendments
BT2 amendments
BT1 sulfates (inorganic salts)
BT2 inorganic salts
BT3 inorganic compounds
BT3 salts
BT2 sulfates
BT1 tanstuffs
rt aluminium

aluminium sulphate
USE **aluminium sulfate**

ALUMINUM
BF aluminium
rt aluminum foil
rt aluminum hydroxide
rt aluminum oxide
rt aluminum phosphate

ALUMINUM *cont.*
rt aluminum sulfate

ALUMINUM FOIL
BF aluminium foil
rt aluminum

ALUMINUM HYDROXIDE
BF aluminium hydroxide
rt aluminum

ALUMINUM OXIDE
BF aluminium oxide
rt aluminum

ALUMINUM PHOSPHATE
BF aluminium phosphate
rt aluminum

ALUMINUM SULFATE
BF aluminium sulfate
rt aluminum

ALUTERA
BT1 balistidae
BT2 tetraodontiformes
BT3 osteichthyes
BT4 fishes

ALVEOLAR HYDATIDS
uf hydatids, alveolar
uf multilocular hydatids
BT1 hydatids
BT2 metacestodes
BT3 developmental stages
rt echinococcus multilocularis

alveonasus
USE **ornithodoros**

alveonasus lahorensis
USE **ornithodoros lahorensis**

ALVESIA
BT1 labiatae
NT1 alvesia rosmarinifolia

ALVESIA ROSMARINIFOLIA
BT1 alvesia
BT2 labiatae

ALYSICARPUS
BT1 leguminosae
NT1 alysicarpus rugosus
NT1 alysicarpus vaginalis

ALYSICARPUS RUGOSUS
BT1 alysicarpus
BT2 leguminosae
BT1 fodder legumes
BT2 fodder plants
BT2 legumes
BT1 pasture legumes
BT2 legumes
BT2 pasture plants

ALYSICARPUS VAGINALIS
BT1 alysicarpus
BT2 leguminosae
BT1 fodder legumes
BT2 fodder plants
BT2 legumes
BT1 pasture legumes
BT2 legumes
BT2 pasture plants

ALYSSUM
BT1 cruciferae
NT1 alyssum argentum

ALYSSUM ARGENTUM
BT1 alyssum
BT2 cruciferae
BT1 ornamental herbaceous plants

alyssum maritimum
USE **lobularia maritima**

ALYXIA
BT1 apocynaceae
NT1 alyxia lucida
NT1 alyxia oliviformis
NT1 alyxia rubricaulis

ALYXIA LUCIDA
BT1 alyxia
BT2 apocynaceae
BT1 medicinal plants

ALYXIA OLIVIFORMIS
BT1 alyxia
BT2 apocynaceae
BT1 ornamental woody plants

ALYXIA RUBRICAULIS
BT1 alyxia
BT2 apocynaceae

ALZHEIMER'S DISEASE
BT1 human diseases
BT2 diseases
BT1 nervous system diseases
BT2 organic diseases
BT3 diseases
BT1 psychoses
BT2 mental disorders
BT3 functional disorders
BT4 animal disorders
BT5 disorders

AMABILIIDAE
BT1 eucestoda
BT2 cestoda
NT1 tatria

amalgamations
USE **farm amalgamations**

AMANITA
BT1 agaricales
NT1 amanita caesarea
NT1 amanita muscaria
NT1 amanita pantherina
NT1 amanita phalloides
NT1 amanita virosa
rt amatoxins

AMANITA CAESAREA
BT1 amanita
BT2 agaricales

AMANITA MUSCARIA
BT1 amanita
BT2 agaricales
BT1 hallucinogenic fungi
BT2 fungi
BT1 poisonous fungi
BT2 fungi
BT2 poisonous plants

AMANITA PANTHERINA
BT1 amanita
BT2 agaricales
BT1 poisonous fungi
BT2 fungi
BT2 poisonous plants

AMANITA PHALLOIDES
BT1 amanita
BT2 agaricales
BT1 poisonous fungi
BT2 fungi
BT2 poisonous plants

AMANITA VIROSA
BT1 amanita
BT2 agaricales
BT1 poisonous fungi
BT2 fungi
BT2 poisonous plants

α-AMANITIN
HN from 1989; previously amanitin
(for retrieval spell out "alpha")
BT1 amatoxins
BT2 mycotoxins
BT3 toxins

AMANTADINE
BT1 antiviral agents
BT2 antiinfective agents
BT3 drugs

AMARANTH DYE
BT1 dyes
rt amaranthus

AMARANTHACEAE
NT1 achyranthes
NT2 achyranthes aspera
NT1 aerva
NT2 aerva javanica
NT2 aerva lanata
NT2 aerva persica
NT1 allmania
NT2 allmania nodiflora
NT1 alternanthera
NT2 alternanthera brasiliana
NT2 alternanthera ficoidea
NT2 alternanthera hassleriana
NT2 alternanthera philoxeroides
NT2 alternanthera polygonoides
NT2 alternanthera pungens
NT2 alternanthera sessilis
NT1 amaranthus
NT2 amaranthus albus
NT2 amaranthus ascendens
NT2 amaranthus bispinosus
NT2 amaranthus blitoides
NT2 amaranthus blitum
NT2 amaranthus caudatus
NT2 amaranthus cruentus
NT2 amaranthus dubius
NT2 amaranthus flavus
NT2 amaranthus graecizans
NT2 amaranthus hybridus
NT2 amaranthus hypochondriacus
NT2 amaranthus leucocarpus
NT2 amaranthus lividus
NT2 amaranthus palmeri
NT2 amaranthus patulus
NT2 amaranthus powellii
NT2 amaranthus quitensis
NT2 amaranthus retroflexus
NT2 amaranthus sanguineus
NT2 amaranthus spinosus
NT2 amaranthus tricolor
NT2 amaranthus tuberculatus
NT2 amaranthus viridis
NT1 brayulinea
NT2 brayulinea densa
NT1 celosia
NT2 celosia argentea
NT2 celosia argentea var. cristata
NT2 celosia argentea var. plumosa
NT2 celosia crenata
NT1 digera
NT2 digera alternifolia
NT2 digera arvensis
NT1 gomphrena
NT2 gomphrena celosioides
NT2 gomphrena globosa
NT1 iresine
NT1 philoxerus
NT2 philoxerus vermicularis

AMARANTHUS
uf grain amaranths
BT1 amaranthaceae
NT1 amaranthus albus
NT1 amaranthus ascendens
NT1 amaranthus bispinosus
NT1 amaranthus blitoides
NT1 amaranthus blitum
NT1 amaranthus caudatus
NT1 amaranthus cruentus
NT1 amaranthus dubius
NT1 amaranthus flavus
NT1 amaranthus graecizans
NT1 amaranthus hybridus
NT1 amaranthus hypochondriacus
NT1 amaranthus leucocarpus
NT1 amaranthus lividus
NT1 amaranthus palmeri
NT1 amaranthus patulus
NT1 amaranthus powellii
NT1 amaranthus quitensis
NT1 amaranthus retroflexus
NT1 amaranthus sanguineus
NT1 amaranthus spinosus
NT1 amaranthus tricolor
NT1 amaranthus tuberculatus
NT1 amaranthus viridis
rt amaranth dye

AMARANTHUS *cont.*
rt amaranthus leaf mottle potyvirus

AMARANTHUS ALBUS
BT1 amaranthus
BT2 amaranthaceae

AMARANTHUS ASCENDENS
BT1 amaranthus
BT2 amaranthaceae

AMARANTHUS BISPINOSUS
BT1 amaranthus
BT2 amaranthaceae
BT1 leafy vegetables
BT2 vegetables

AMARANTHUS BLITOIDES
BT1 amaranthus
BT2 amaranthaceae

AMARANTHUS BLITUM
BT1 amaranthus
BT2 amaranthaceae
BT1 leafy vegetables
BT2 vegetables

AMARANTHUS CAUDATUS
BT1 amaranthus
BT2 amaranthaceae
BT1 leafy vegetables
BT2 vegetables
BT1 ornamental herbaceous plants
BT1 pseudocereals
BT2 grain crops

amaranthus chlorostachys
USE **amaranthus cruentus**

AMARANTHUS CRUENTUS
uf amaranthus chlorostachys
uf amaranthus paniculatus
BT1 amaranthus
BT2 amaranthaceae
BT1 leafy vegetables
BT2 vegetables
BT1 pseudocereals
BT2 grain crops

AMARANTHUS DUBIUS
BT1 amaranthus
BT2 amaranthaceae
BT1 leafy vegetables
BT2 vegetables

AMARANTHUS FLAVUS
BT1 amaranthus
BT2 amaranthaceae
BT1 leafy vegetables
BT2 vegetables

amaranthus gangeticus
USE **amaranthus tricolor**

AMARANTHUS GRAECIZANS
BT1 amaranthus
BT2 amaranthaceae
BT1 leafy vegetables
BT2 vegetables

AMARANTHUS HYBRIDUS
BT1 amaranthus
BT2 amaranthaceae
BT1 leafy vegetables
BT2 vegetables
BT1 ornamental herbaceous plants
BT1 weeds

AMARANTHUS HYPOCHONDRIACUS
BT1 amaranthus
BT2 amaranthaceae

AMARANTHUS LEAF MOTTLE POTYVIRUS
HN from 1990
BT1 potyvirus group
BT2 plant viruses
BT3 plant pathogens
BT4 pathogens
rt amaranthus

AMARANTHUS LEUCOCARPUS
BT1 amaranthus
BT2 amaranthaceae
BT1 leafy vegetables
BT2 vegetables
BT1 pseudocereals
BT2 grain crops

AMARANTHUS LIVIDUS
BT1 amaranthus
BT2 amaranthaceae
BT1 leafy vegetables
BT2 vegetables

AMARANTHUS PALMERI
BT1 amaranthus
BT2 amaranthaceae

amaranthus paniculatus
USE **amaranthus cruentus**

AMARANTHUS PATULUS
BT1 amaranthus
BT2 amaranthaceae

AMARANTHUS POWELLII
BT1 amaranthus
BT2 amaranthaceae
BT1 weeds

AMARANTHUS QUITENSIS
BT1 amaranthus
BT2 amaranthaceae

AMARANTHUS RETROFLEXUS
BT1 amaranthus
BT2 amaranthaceae
BT1 leafy vegetables
BT2 vegetables
BT1 weeds

AMARANTHUS SANGUINEUS
BT1 amaranthus
BT2 amaranthaceae

AMARANTHUS SPINOSUS
BT1 amaranthus
BT2 amaranthaceae

AMARANTHUS TRICOLOR
uf *amaranthus gangeticus*
BT1 amaranthus
BT2 amaranthaceae
BT1 leafy vegetables
BT2 vegetables
BT1 ornamental herbaceous plants

AMARANTHUS TUBERCULATUS
BT1 amaranthus
BT2 amaranthaceae

AMARANTHUS VIRIDIS
BT1 amaranthus
BT2 amaranthaceae
BT1 leafy vegetables
BT2 vegetables

AMARETTO (AGRICOLA)
BT1 liqueurs
BT2 distilled spirits
BT3 alcoholic beverages
BT4 beverages

AMARINE
BT1 amaryllidaceae
NT1 amarine tubergenii

AMARINE TUBERGENII
BT1 amarine
BT2 amaryllidaceae
BT1 ornamental bulbs

AMARYLLIDACEAE
NT1 amarine
NT2 amarine tubergenii
NT1 amaryllis
NT2 amaryllis belladonna
NT1 brunsvigia
NT2 brunsvigia radulosa
NT1 clivia
NT2 clivia miniata
NT2 clivia nobilis
NT1 crinum
NT2 crinum asiaticum

AMARYLLIDACEAE *cont.*
NT2 crinum bulbispermum
NT2 crinum moorei
NT1 cyrtanthus
NT2 cyrtanthus elatus
NT1 doryanthes
NT1 eucharis
NT1 galanthus
NT2 galanthus nivalis
NT1 habranthus
NT2 habranthus tubispathus
NT1 haemanthus
NT2 haemanthus albiflos
NT2 haemanthus katherinae
NT2 haemanthus multiflorus
NT1 hippeastrum
NT2 hippeastrum puniceum
NT2 hippeastrum vittatum
NT1 hymenocallis
NT2 hymenocallis festalis
NT2 hymenocallis littoralis
NT2 hymenocallis speciosa
NT1 ixiolirion
NT2 ixiolirion tataricum
NT1 leucojum
NT2 leucojum aestivum
NT2 leucojum vernum
NT1 lycoris
NT2 lycoris radiata
NT1 narcissus
NT2 narcissus minor
NT2 narcissus pseudonarcissus
NT2 narcissus tazetta
NT1 nerine
NT1 pancratium
NT1 paramongaia
NT2 paramongaia weberbaueri
NT1 sprekelia
NT2 sprekelia formosissima
NT1 sternbergia
NT2 sternbergia candida
NT2 sternbergia lutea
NT1 ungernia
NT2 ungernia spiralis
NT2 ungernia victoris
NT1 urceolina
NT2 urceolina amazonica
NT2 urceolina grandiflora
NT2 urceolina longipetala
NT1 vallota
NT1 zephyranthes
NT2 zephyranthes sulphurea

AMARYLLIS
BT1 amaryllidaceae
NT1 amaryllis belladonna

AMARYLLIS BELLADONNA
BT1 amaryllis
BT2 amaryllidaceae
BT1 antifungal plants
BT1 medicinal plants
BT1 ornamental bulbs

amaryllis vittata
USE **hippeastrum vittatum**

AMATEURS
BT1 performers
rt artists
rt musicians

amathes
USE **xestia**

amathes c-nigrum
USE **xestia c-nigrum**

AMATOXINS
HN from 1989
BT1 mycotoxins
BT2 toxins
NT1 α-amanitin
rt amanita

AMAZONA
BT1 psittacidae
BT2 psittaciformes
BT3 birds

AMBELANIA
BT1 apocynaceae
NT1 ambelania acida

AMBELANIA ACIDA
BT1 ambelania
BT2 apocynaceae

AMBER
BT1 minor forest products
BT2 forest products
BT3 products
BT1 resins

AMBERBOA
BT1 compositae
NT1 amberboa moschata

AMBERBOA MOSCHATA
uf *centaurea moschata*
BT1 amberboa
BT2 compositae
BT1 ornamental herbaceous plants

AMBLYCERA
BT1 mallophaga
BT2 phthiraptera
NT1 boopiidae
NT2 heterodoxus
NT3 heterodoxus longitarsus
NT3 heterodoxus spiniger
NT1 gyropidae
NT2 gliricola
NT3 gliricola porcelli
NT2 gyropus
NT1 menoponidae
NT2 colpocephalum
NT3 colpocephalum turbinatum
NT2 gallacanthus
NT3 gallacanthus cornutus
NT2 menacanthus
NT3 menacanthus stramineus
NT2 menopon
NT3 menopon gallinae

amblymerus
USE **mesopolobus**

amblymerus verditer
USE **mesopolobus verditer**

AMBLYOMMA
BT1 ixodidae
BT2 metastigmata
BT3 acari
NT1 amblyomma americanum
NT1 amblyomma brasiliense
NT1 amblyomma cajennense
NT1 amblyomma cohaerens
NT1 amblyomma cooperi
NT1 amblyomma cyprium
NT1 amblyomma dissimile
NT1 amblyomma gemma
NT1 amblyomma hebraeum
NT1 amblyomma inornatum
NT1 amblyomma integrum
NT1 amblyomma lepidum
NT1 amblyomma maculatum
NT1 amblyomma marmoreum
NT1 amblyomma neumanni
NT1 amblyomma oblongoguttatum
NT1 amblyomma ovale
NT1 amblyomma pomposum
NT1 amblyomma testudinarium
NT1 amblyomma triguttatum
NT1 amblyomma variegatum

AMBLYOMMA AMERICANUM
BT1 amblyomma
BT2 ixodidae
BT3 metastigmata
BT4 acari

AMBLYOMMA BRASILIENSE
BT1 amblyomma
BT2 ixodidae
BT3 metastigmata
BT4 acari

AMBLYOMMA CAJENNENSE
BT1 amblyomma
BT2 ixodidae
BT3 metastigmata
BT4 acari

AMBLYOMMA COHAERENS
BT1 amblyomma
BT2 ixodidae
BT3 metastigmata
BT4 acari

AMBLYOMMA COOPERI
BT1 amblyomma
BT2 ixodidae
BT3 metastigmata
BT4 acari

AMBLYOMMA CYPRIUM
BT1 amblyomma
BT2 ixodidae
BT3 metastigmata
BT4 acari

AMBLYOMMA DISSIMILE
BT1 amblyomma
BT2 ixodidae
BT3 metastigmata
BT4 acari

amblyomma fossum
USE **amblyomma ovale**

AMBLYOMMA GEMMA
BT1 amblyomma
BT2 ixodidae
BT3 metastigmata
BT4 acari

AMBLYOMMA HEBRAEUM
uf *amblyomma theileri*
BT1 amblyomma
BT2 ixodidae
BT3 metastigmata
BT4 acari

AMBLYOMMA INORNATUM
HN from 1990
BT1 amblyomma
BT2 ixodidae
BT3 metastigmata
BT4 acari

AMBLYOMMA INTEGRUM
BT1 amblyomma
BT2 ixodidae
BT3 metastigmata
BT4 acari

AMBLYOMMA LEPIDUM
BT1 amblyomma
BT2 ixodidae
BT3 metastigmata
BT4 acari

AMBLYOMMA MACULATUM
BT1 amblyomma
BT2 ixodidae
BT3 metastigmata
BT4 acari

AMBLYOMMA MARMOREUM
HN from 1989
BT1 amblyomma
BT2 ixodidae
BT3 metastigmata
BT4 acari

AMBLYOMMA NEUMANNI
HN from 1990
BT1 amblyomma
BT2 ixodidae
BT3 metastigmata
BT4 acari

AMBLYOMMA OBLONGOGUTTATUM
BT1 amblyomma
BT2 ixodidae
BT3 metastigmata
BT4 acari

AMBLYOMMA OVALE
uf *amblyomma fossum*
BT1 amblyomma
BT2 ixodidae
BT3 metastigmata
BT4 acari

AMBLYOMMA POMPOSUM
BT1 amblyomma

AMBLYOMMA POMPOSUM *cont.*
BT2 ixodidae
BT3 metastigmata
BT4 acari

AMBLYOMMA TESTUDINARIUM
BT1 amblyomma
BT2 ixodidae
BT3 metastigmata
BT4 acari

amblyomma theileri
USE **amblyomma hebraeum**

AMBLYOMMA TRIGUTTATUM
HN from 1989
BT1 amblyomma
BT2 ixodidae
BT3 metastigmata
BT4 acari

AMBLYOMMA VARIEGATUM
BT1 amblyomma
BT2 ixodidae
BT3 metastigmata
BT4 acari

AMBLYOSPORA
BT1 microspora
BT2 protozoa
NT1 amblyospora opacita

AMBLYOSPORA OPACITA
BT1 amblyospora
BT2 microspora
BT3 protozoa

AMBLYPELTA
BT1 coreidae
BT2 heteroptera
NT1 amblypelta cocophaga
NT1 amblypelta lutescens
NT1 amblypelta nitida
NT1 amblypelta theobromae

AMBLYPELTA COCOPHAGA
BT1 amblypelta
BT2 coreidae
BT3 heteroptera

AMBLYPELTA LUTESCENS
BT1 amblypelta
BT2 coreidae
BT3 heteroptera

AMBLYPELTA NITIDA
BT1 amblypelta
BT2 coreidae
BT3 heteroptera

AMBLYPELTA THEOBROMAE
BT1 amblypelta
BT2 coreidae
BT3 heteroptera

AMBLYSEIUS
uf *typhlodromips*
BT1 phytoseiidae
BT2 mesostigmata
BT3 acari
NT1 amblyseius herbicolus
NT1 amblyseius largoensis
NT1 amblyseius potentillae
NT1 amblyseius swirskii
rt euseius
rt kampimodromus
rt neoseiulus
rt typhlodromus

amblyseius aberrans
USE **kampimodromus aberrans**

amblyseius anonymus
USE **neoseiulus anonymus**

amblyseius californicus
USE **neoseiulus californicus**

amblyseius chilenensis
USE **neoseiulus chilenensis**

amblyseius cucumeris
USE **neoseiulus cucumeris**

amblyseius fallacis
USE **neoseiulus fallacis**

amblyseius finlandicus
USE **euseius finlandicus**

amblyseius gossipi
USE **euseius gossipi**

AMBLYSEIUS HERBICOLUS
BT1 amblyseius
BT2 phytoseiidae
BT3 mesostigmata
BT4 acari

amblyseius hibisci
USE **euseius hibisci**

amblyseius idaeus
USE **neoseiulus idaeus**

AMBLYSEIUS LARGOENSIS
BT1 amblyseius
BT2 phytoseiidae
BT3 mesostigmata
BT4 acari

amblyseius longipes
USE **phytoseiulus longipes**

amblyseius longispinosus
USE **neoseiulus longispinosus**

AMBLYSEIUS POTENTILLAE
uf *typhlodromus potentillae*
BT1 amblyseius
BT2 phytoseiidae
BT3 mesostigmata
BT4 acari

AMBLYSEIUS SWIRSKII
BT1 amblyseius
BT2 phytoseiidae
BT3 mesostigmata
BT4 acari

AMBLYTELES
BT1 ichneumonidae
BT2 hymenoptera
NT1 amblyteles castigator
NT1 amblyteles inspector
rt ctenichneumon

AMBLYTELES CASTIGATOR
BT1 amblyteles
BT2 ichneumonidae
BT3 hymenoptera

AMBLYTELES INSPECTOR
BT1 amblyteles
BT2 ichneumonidae
BT3 hymenoptera

amblyteles panzeri
USE **ctenichneumon panzeri**

AMBROSIA
BT1 compositae
NT1 ambrosia ambrosioides
NT1 ambrosia artemisiifolia
NT1 ambrosia bidentata
NT1 ambrosia chenopodiifolia
NT1 ambrosia coronopifolia
NT1 ambrosia deltoidea
NT1 ambrosia dumosa
NT1 ambrosia eriocentra
NT1 ambrosia ilicifolia
NT1 ambrosia psilostachya
NT1 ambrosia pumila
NT1 ambrosia trifida

AMBROSIA AMBROSIOIDES
BT1 ambrosia
BT2 compositae

AMBROSIA ARTEMISIIFOLIA
uf *ambrosia elatior*
BT1 ambrosia
BT2 compositae
BT1 weeds

AMBROSIA BIDENTATA
BT1 ambrosia
BT2 compositae

AMBROSIA CHENOPODIIFOLIA
BT1 ambrosia
BT2 compositae

AMBROSIA CORONOPIFOLIA
BT1 ambrosia
BT2 compositae

AMBROSIA DELTOIDEA
BT1 ambrosia
BT2 compositae

AMBROSIA DUMOSA
BT1 ambrosia
BT2 compositae

ambrosia elatior
USE **ambrosia artemisiifolia**

AMBROSIA ERIOCENTRA
BT1 ambrosia
BT2 compositae

AMBROSIA ILICIFOLIA
BT1 ambrosia
BT2 compositae

AMBROSIA PSILOSTACHYA
BT1 ambrosia
BT2 compositae

AMBROSIA PUMILA
BT1 ambrosia
BT2 compositae

AMBROSIA TRIFIDA
BT1 ambrosia
BT2 compositae

AMBYSTOMA
BT1 ambystomatidae
BT2 caudata
BT3 amphibia

AMBYSTOMATIDAE
BT1 caudata
BT2 amphibia
NT1 ambystoma

AMEBICIDES
BF amoebicides

amegilla
USE **anthophora**

AMELANCHIER
BT1 rosaceae
NT1 amelanchier alnifolia
NT1 amelanchier asiatica
NT1 amelanchier canadensis
NT1 amelanchier florida
NT1 amelanchier laevis
NT1 amelanchier oligocarpa
NT1 amelanchier ovalis
NT1 amelanchier sanguinea
NT1 amelanchier spicata
NT1 amelanchier utahensis
rt aronia

AMELANCHIER ALNIFOLIA
BT1 amelanchier
BT2 rosaceae

AMELANCHIER ASIATICA
BT1 amelanchier
BT2 rosaceae

AMELANCHIER CANADENSIS
BT1 amelanchier
BT2 rosaceae
BT1 ornamental woody plants

AMELANCHIER FLORIDA
BT1 amelanchier
BT2 rosaceae

AMELANCHIER LAEVIS
BT1 amelanchier
BT2 rosaceae
BT1 ornamental woody plants

amelanchier melanocarpa
USE **aronia melanocarpa**

AMELANCHIER OLIGOCARPA
BT1 amelanchier
BT2 rosaceae

AMELANCHIER OVALIS
uf *amelanchier vulgaris*

AMELANCHIER OVALIS *cont.*
BT1 amelanchier
BT2 rosaceae
BT1 ornamental woody plants

AMELANCHIER SANGUINEA
BT1 amelanchier
BT2 rosaceae

AMELANCHIER SPICATA
BT1 amelanchier
BT2 rosaceae

AMELANCHIER UTAHENSIS
BT1 amelanchier
BT2 rosaceae
BT1 browse plants

amelanchier vulgaris
USE **amelanchier ovalis**

AMELIORATION OF FOREST SITES
BT1 land improvement
rt rehabilitation

amendment application
USE **application methods**

AMENDMENTS
NT1 soil amendments
NT2 acid amendments
NT2 activated carbon
NT2 aluminium sulfate
NT2 commercial soil additives
NT2 evaporation suppressants
NT3 atrazine
NT2 ferrous sulfate
NT2 leonardite
NT2 liming materials
NT3 calcium carbonate
NT3 calcium chloride
NT3 calcium hydroxide
NT3 calcium oxide
NT3 calcium silicate
NT3 calcium sulfate
NT3 cement dust
NT3 chalk
NT3 crab waste
NT3 dolomite
NT3 fluidized bed wastes
NT3 fly ash
NT3 lime
NT3 limestone
NT4 magnesian limestone
NT3 magnesium carbonate
NT3 marl
NT3 oyster shells
NT3 scrubber sludge
NT3 sepiolite
NT3 slags
NT3 slaked lime
NT2 organic amendments
NT3 manures
NT4 animal manures
NT5 cattle manure
NT5 farmyard manure
NT5 fish manure
NT5 horse manure
NT5 night soil
NT5 pig manure
NT5 poultry manure
NT5 sheep manure
NT4 coal
NT5 brown coal
NT4 composts
NT5 bark compost
NT5 leaf mould
NT5 mushroom compost
NT5 refuse compost
NT4 feedlot effluent
NT4 feedlot wastes
NT4 filter cake
NT4 green manures
NT5 azolla pinnata
NT5 buckwheat
NT5 calopogonium mucunoides
NT5 canavalia campylocarpa
NT5 canavalia ensiformis
NT5 canavalia gladiata
NT5 cassia leschenaulthiana

AMENDMENTS *cont.*
NT5 centrosema plumieri
NT5 centrosema pubescens
NT5 crotalaria anagyroides
NT5 crotalaria juncea
NT5 desmodium tortuosum
NT5 lablab purpureus
NT5 leucaena leucocephala
NT5 lupinus albus
NT5 lupinus angustifolius
NT5 lupinus luteus
NT5 lupinus mutabilis
NT5 medicago lupulina
NT5 medicago orbicularis
NT5 medicago polymorpha
NT5 mucuna aterrima
NT5 mucuna deeringiana
NT5 najas flexilis
NT5 ornithopus sativus
NT5 phacelia tanacetifolia
NT5 secale cereale
NT5 tephrosia purpurea
NT5 trifolium alexandrinum
NT5 trifolium incarnatum
NT5 tripsacum laxum
NT5 vicia articulata
NT5 vicia benghalensis
NT5 vicia cracca
NT5 vicia narbonensis
NT5 vicia pannonica
NT5 vicia sativa
NT5 vicia villosa
NT5 vigna hosei
NT5 vigna unguiculata
NT5 vigna vexillata
NT4 guano
NT4 hoof and horn meal
NT4 liquid manures
NT4 sewage products
NT4 tannery sludge
NT3 peat
NT2 pumice
NT2 sapropel
NT2 soil acidulants
NT2 soil conditioners
NT3 acrylamides
NT3 agrosil
NT3 bark
NT4 pine bark
NT3 bentonite
NT3 butadiene-styrene copolymer
NT3 cellulose xanthate
NT3 cement
NT4 wood cement
NT3 cotton waste
NT3 ferric sulfate
NT3 hygromull
NT3 iron oxides
NT4 maghaemite
NT4 magnetite
NT3 lignosulfonates
NT4 ammonium lignosulfonate
NT3 nonionic surfactants
NT3 poly(vinyl acetate)
NT3 poly(vinyl alcohol)
NT3 polyacrylamide
NT3 polyacrylonitrile
NT3 polystyrenes
NT3 polyurethanes
NT3 sand
NT3 separan
NT3 sodium silicate
NT3 spent hops
NT3 zeolites

AMENITY AND RECREATION AREAS
uf *recreation areas*
BT1 areas
NT1 camp sites
NT1 caravan sites
NT1 open spaces
NT2 green belts
NT1 show grounds
rt amenity forests
rt amenity value of forests
rt parks
rt playgrounds
rt recreational facilities

AMENITY AND RECREATION AREAS *cont.*
rt tourist attractions

AMENITY FORESTS
BT1 forests
BT2 vegetation types
rt amenity and recreation areas
rt amenity value of forests
rt forest recreation
rt national parks

AMENITY VALUE OF FORESTS
NT1 forest recreation
rt amenity and recreation areas
rt amenity forests
rt forest policy
rt forest recreation

AMENORRHEA
BF amenorrhoea

AMENORRHOEA
AF amenorrhea
BT1 menstruation
BT2 oestrous cycle
BT3 biological rhythms
BT3 sexual reproduction
BT4 reproduction
rt menopause
rt pregnancy
rt reproductive disorders
rt sexual rest

AMERICA
NT1 caribbean
NT2 anguilla island
NT2 antigua
NT2 bahamas
NT2 barbados
NT2 british virgin islands
NT2 cayman islands
NT2 cuba
NT2 dominica
NT2 dominican republic
NT2 grenada
NT2 guadeloupe
NT2 haiti
NT2 jamaica
NT2 martinique
NT2 montserrat
NT2 netherlands antilles
NT3 aruba
NT3 bonaire
NT3 curacao
NT3 saba
NT3 st. eustatius
NT3 st. maarten
NT2 puerto rico
NT2 st. kitts-nevis
NT2 st. lucia
NT2 st. vincent and grenadines
NT2 trinidad and tobago
NT2 turks and caicos islands
NT2 united states virgin islands
NT1 central america
NT2 belize
NT2 costa rica
NT2 el salvador
NT2 guatemala
NT2 honduras
NT2 nicaragua
NT2 panama
NT2 panama canal zone
NT1 north america
NT2 bermuda
NT2 canada
NT3 alberta
NT3 british columbia
NT3 canadian northwest territories
NT3 manitoba
NT3 new brunswick
NT3 newfoundland
NT3 nova scotia
NT3 ontario
NT3 prince edward island
NT3 quebec
NT3 saskatchewan
NT3 yukon

AMERICA *cont.*
NT2 greenland
NT2 mexico
NT2 st. pierre and miquelon
NT2 usa
NT3 north central states of usa
NT4 corn belt of usa
NT5 illinois
NT5 indiana
NT5 iowa
NT5 missouri
NT5 ohio
NT4 lake states of usa
NT5 michigan
NT5 minnesota
NT5 wisconsin
NT4 northern plains states of usa
NT5 kansas
NT5 nebraska
NT5 north dakota
NT5 south dakota
NT3 northeastern states of usa
NT4 middle atlantic states of usa
NT5 new jersey
NT5 new york
NT5 pennsylvania
NT4 new england
NT5 connecticut
NT5 maine
NT5 massachusetts
NT5 new hampshire
NT5 rhode island
NT5 vermont
NT3 southern states of usa
NT4 appalachian states of usa
NT5 delaware
NT5 district of columbia
NT5 kentucky
NT5 maryland
NT5 north carolina
NT5 tennessee
NT5 virginia
NT5 west virginia
NT4 delta states of usa
NT5 arkansas
NT5 louisiana
NT5 mississippi
NT4 southeastern states of usa
NT5 alabama
NT5 florida
NT5 georgia
NT5 south carolina
NT4 southern plains states of usa
NT5 oklahoma
NT5 texas
NT3 western states of usa
NT4 mountain states of usa
NT5 arizona
NT5 colorado
NT5 idaho
NT5 montana
NT5 nevada
NT5 new mexico
NT5 utah
NT5 wyoming
NT4 pacific states of usa
NT5 alaska
NT5 california
NT5 hawaii
NT5 oregon
NT5 washington
NT1 south america
NT2 argentina
NT3 argentina andina
NT3 argentina centro
NT3 argentina littoral
NT3 argentina norte
NT3 patagonia
NT2 bolivia
NT2 brazil
NT3 central west brazil
NT3 east brazil
NT3 north brazil
NT3 north east brazil

AMERICA *cont.*
NT3 south brazil
NT2 chile
NT2 colombia
NT2 ecuador
NT3 galapagos islands
NT2 falkland islands
NT2 french guiana
NT2 guyana
NT2 paraguay
NT2 peru
NT2 surinam
NT2 uruguay
NT2 venezuela
rt latin america
rt tropical america

america, central
USE **central america**

america, latin
USE **latin america**

america, north
USE **north america**

america, south
USE **south america**

AMERICAN AGRICULTURAL ECONOMICS ASSOCIATION
BT1 organizations
rt agricultural economists

AMERICAN ANGUS
HN from 1990
BT1 cattle breeds
BT2 breeds

american bison
USE **bison**

AMERICAN BROWN SWISS
HN from 1990; previously "brown swiss"
uf *brown swiss*
BT1 cattle breeds
BT2 breeds

american buffaloes
USE **bison**

AMERICAN FOOTBALL
HN from 1989
BT1 football
BT2 ball games
BT3 games
BT3 sport

AMERICAN FOUL BROOD
BT1 foul brood
BT2 bee diseases
BT3 animal diseases
BT4 diseases
rt bacillus larvae
rt honeybee brood

AMERICAN HOP LATENT VIRUS
BT1 miscellaneous plant viruses
BT2 plant viruses
BT3 plant pathogens
BT4 pathogens

AMERICAN INDIANS
BT1 ethnic groups
BT2 groups
rt tribal society

AMERICAN LANDRACE
BT1 pig breeds
BT2 breeds

AMERICAN MERINO
BT1 sheep breeds
BT2 breeds

AMERICAN OCEANIA
uf *pacific islands (us)*
uf *trust territory of pacific islands*
uf *us pacific island trust territory*
BT1 oceania
NT1 american samoa
NT1 guam

AMERICAN OCEANIA *cont.*
NT1 johnston island
NT1 mariana islands
NT1 midway islands
NT1 pacific islands trust territory
NT2 belau
NT2 federated states of micronesia
NT2 marshall islands
NT1 wake island
rt pacific islands
rt south pacific commission
rt usa

american oceania (mariana islands)
USE **mariana islands**

american oceania (marshall islands)
USE **marshall islands**

american oceania (wake island)
USE **wake island**

american oil palm
USE **elaeis oleifera**

american quarter horse
USE **quarter horse**

AMERICAN RAMBOUILLET
BT1 sheep breeds
BT2 breeds

AMERICAN SADDLE HORSE
BT1 horse breeds
BT2 breeds

AMERICAN SAMOA
uf *samoa, american*
BT1 american oceania
BT2 oceania

AMERICAN TROTTER
BT1 horse breeds
BT2 breeds

AMERICAN TUNIS
BT1 sheep breeds
BT2 breeds

AMERICAN YORKSHIRE
HN from 1990
BT1 pig breeds
BT2 breeds

AMERICIUM
BT1 actinides
BT2 transition elements
BT3 metallic elements
BT4 elements
BT4 metals

AMEROSEIIDAE
BT1 mesostigmata
BT2 acari

AMETASTEGIA
BT1 tenthredinidae
BT2 hymenoptera
NT1 ametastegia glabrata

AMETASTEGIA GLABRATA
BT1 ametastegia
BT2 tenthredinidae
BT3 hymenoptera

amethopterin
USE **methotrexate**

AMETRIDIONE
BT1 triazinone herbicides
BT2 herbicides
BT3 pesticides
BT2 triazines
BT3 heterocyclic nitrogen compounds
BT4 organic nitrogen compounds

AMETRYN
uf *ametryne*
BT1 triazine herbicides
BT2 herbicides
BT3 pesticides
BT2 triazines

AMETRYN *cont.*
BT3 heterocyclic nitrogen compounds
BT4 organic nitrogen compounds

ametryne
USE **ametryn**

AMFETAMINE
uf *amphetamine*
BT1 amphetamines
BT2 phenethylamines
BT3 amines
BT4 amino compounds
BT5 organic nitrogen compounds
BT1 analeptics
BT2 neurotropic drugs
BT3 drugs

AMHERSTIA
BT1 leguminosae
NT1 amherstia nobilis

AMHERSTIA NOBILIS
BT1 amherstia
BT2 leguminosae
BT1 ornamental woody plants

AMICARBALIDE
BT1 antiprotozoal agents
BT2 antiparasitic agents
BT3 drugs

AMIDASE
HN from 1989
(ec 3.5.1.4)
BT1 amide hydrolases
BT2 hydrolases
BT3 enzymes

AMIDE HERBICIDES
BT1 herbicides
BT2 pesticides
NT1 allidochlor
NT1 anilide herbicides
NT2 arylalanine herbicides
NT3 benzoylprop-ethyl
NT3 flamprop
NT2 chloranocryl
NT2 chloroacetanilide herbicides
NT3 acetochlor
NT3 alachlor
NT3 butachlor
NT3 delachlor
NT3 diethatyl
NT3 dimethachlor
NT3 metazachlor
NT3 metolachlor
NT3 pretilachlor
NT3 propachlor
NT3 prynachlor
NT3 terbuchlor
NT2 clomeprop
NT2 cypromid
NT2 diflufenican
NT2 mefenacet
NT2 monalide
NT2 pentanochlor
NT2 perfluidone
NT2 propanil
NT1 benzadox
NT1 benzipram
NT1 bromobutide
NT1 cdea
NT1 chlorthiamid
NT1 cyprazole
NT1 diphenamid
NT1 fomesafen
NT1 isoxaben
NT1 napropamide
NT1 naptalam
NT1 propyzamide
NT1 tebutam
rt amides

AMIDE HYDROLASES
(ec 3.5.1-2)
BT1 hydrolases
BT2 enzymes
NT1 β-lactamase
NT1 amidase

AMIDE HYDROLASES *cont.*
NT1 asparaginase
NT1 glutaminase
NT1 urease

AMIDE SYNTHASES
(ec 6.3.1)
BT1 ligases
BT2 enzymes
NT1 aspartate-ammonia ligase
NT1 glutamate-ammonia ligase

AMIDES
(not including peptides)
BT1 organic nitrogen compounds
NT1 acetamide
NT1 acetylaminofluorene
NT1 acrylamides
NT1 benzoylphenylureas
NT2 chlorfluazuron
NT2 diflubenzuron
NT2 penfluron
NT2 teflubenzuron
NT2 triflumuron
NT1 biguanides
NT2 buformin
NT2 metformin
NT1 bisazir
NT1 capsaicin
NT1 diethyltoluamide
NT1 dimethylformamide
NT1 hippuric acid
NT1 hydroxycarbamide
NT1 imidocarb
NT1 niclosamide
NT1 nicotinamide
NT1 oxamide
NT1 phosphoric triamides
NT2 hempa
NT2 metepa
NT2 tepa
NT2 thiotepa
NT1 phosphorodiamides
NT2 phenyl phosphorodiamidate
NT1 salicylamide
NT1 sulfonamides
NT2 chlorpropamide
NT2 dapsone
NT2 sulfanilamides
NT3 furosemide
NT3 sulfachlorpyridazine
NT3 sulfadiazine
NT3 sulfadimethoxine
NT3 sulfadimidine
NT3 sulfadoxine
NT3 sulfafurazole
NT3 sulfamerazine
NT3 sulfamethoxazole
NT3 sulfamethoxypyridazine
NT3 sulfamonomethoxine
NT3 sulfanilamide
NT3 sulfapyrazole
NT3 sulfapyridine
NT3 sulfaquinoxaline
NT3 sulfathiazole
NT2 sulfonylureas
NT3 glibenclamide
NT3 gliclazide
NT3 glipizide
NT3 sulfonylurea herbicides
NT4 bensulfuron
NT4 chlorimuron
NT4 chlorsulfuron
NT4 metsulfuron
NT4 pyrazosulfuron
NT4 sulfometuron
NT4 triasulfuron
NT3 tolbutamide
NT2 toluenesulfonamide
NT1 thioamides
NT2 methallibure
NT2 phenylthiourea
NT2 thiourea
NT1 tribromsalan
NT1 urea
NT1 ureides
NT2 acetylurea
NT2 biuret
rt amide herbicides

AMIDINE HYDROLASES
(ec 3.5.3-4)
BT1 hydrolases
BT2 enzymes
NT1 adenosine deaminase
NT1 amp deaminase
NT1 arginase
NT1 formiminoglutamase
NT1 guanine deaminase

AMIDINE-LYASES
(ec 4.3.2)
BT1 lyases
BT2 enzymes
NT1 argininosuccinate lyase

AMIDINES
BT1 organic nitrogen compounds
NT1 bunamidine
NT1 diminazene

AMIDITHION
BT1 organothiophosphate acaricides
BT2 organophosphorus acaricides
BT3 acaricides
BT4 pesticides
BT3 organophosphorus pesticides
BT4 organophosphorus compounds

AMIDO BLACK METHOD
BT1 dye binding
BT2 analytical methods
BT3 methodology
rt milk protein

AMIDOPHOSPHORIBOSYLTRANSFERASE
(ec 2.4.2.14)
BT1 pentosyltransferases
BT2 glycosyltransferases
BT3 transferases
BT4 enzymes

AMIDOSTOMATIDAE
BT1 nematoda
NT1 amidostomum
NT2 amidostomum anseris
rt animal parasitic nematodes

AMIDOSTOMUM
BT1 amidostomatidae
BT2 nematoda
NT1 amidostomum anseris

AMIDOSTOMUM ANSERIS
BT1 amidostomum
BT2 amidostomatidae
BT3 nematoda

aminazine
USE **chlorpromazine**

amine oxidase
USE **amine oxidase (flavin-containing)**

AMINE OXIDASE (COPPER-CONTAINING)
(ec 1.4.3.6)
uf *diamine oxidase*
BT1 amine oxidoreductases
BT2 oxidoreductases
BT3 enzymes

AMINE OXIDASE (FLAVIN-CONTAINING)
(ec 1.4.3.4)
uf *amine oxidase*
uf *monoamine oxidase*
BT1 amine oxidoreductases
BT2 oxidoreductases
BT3 enzymes

AMINE OXIDOREDUCTASES
(ec 1.4-5)
BT1 oxidoreductases
BT2 enzymes
NT1 l-amino-acid oxidase
NT1 alanine dehydrogenase

AMINE OXIDOREDUCTASES *cont.*
NT1 amine oxidase (copper-containing)
NT1 amine oxidase (flavin-containing)
NT1 dihydrofolate reductase
NT1 glutamate dehydrogenase
NT1 glutamate synthase
NT1 pyridoxamine-phosphate oxidase
NT1 saccharopine dehydrogenase

AMINES
(not including amino acids, ammonium compounds)
BT1 amino compounds
BT2 organic nitrogen compounds
NT1 biogenic amines
NT2 acetylcholine
NT2 cadaverine
NT2 carnitine
NT2 catecholamines
NT3 dopamine
NT3 epinephrine
NT3 norepinephrine
NT2 choline
NT2 histamine
NT2 hordenine
NT2 octopamine
NT2 phenethylamine
NT2 putrescine
NT2 serotonin
NT2 spermine
NT2 tryptamine
NT2 tyramine
NT1 diamines
NT2 cadaverine
NT2 putrescine
NT1 monoamines
NT2 1-decanamine
NT2 1-dodecanamine
NT2 1-tetradecanamine
NT2 4-aminopyridine
NT2 5-aminouracil
NT2 methylamine
NT2 phenoxybenzamine
NT1 phenethylamines
NT2 amphetamines
NT3 amfetamine
NT3 benfluorex
NT3 fenfluramine
NT2 methoxamine
NT2 phenethylamine
NT1 polyamines
NT2 colestipol
NT2 melamine
NT2 spermidine
NT2 spermine
NT1 primary amines
NT2 1-decanamine
NT2 1-dodecanamine
NT2 1-tetradecanamine
NT2 methylamine
NT1 secondary amines
NT2 diethylamine
NT2 dimethylamine
NT2 diphenylamine
NT1 tertiary amines
NT2 triethylamine
NT2 trimethylamine
NT1 tryptamines
NT2 melatonin
NT2 serotonin
NT2 tryptamine
rt amino acids
rt amino alcohols

AMINITROZOLE
BT1 coccidiostats
BT2 antiprotozoal agents
BT3 antiparasitic agents
BT4 drugs

amino acid analogues
USE **amino acid derivatives**

AMINO ACID ANTAGONISTS
BT1 antagonists
BT2 metabolic inhibitors
BT3 inhibitors

AMINO ACID ANTAGONISTS *cont.*
NT1 p-fluorophenylalanine
NT1 arginine antagonists
NT1 cycloleucine
NT1 methylmethionine
rt amino acid metabolism
rt amino acids

AMINO ACID DERIVATIVES
uf amino acid analogues
BT1 amino compounds
BT2 organic nitrogen compounds
NT1 s-methylcysteine sulfoxide
NT1 γ-hydroxyornithine
NT1 acetylglutamic acid
NT1 acetylmethionine
NT1 adenosylhomocysteine
NT1 adenosylmethionine
NT1 cysteinesulfinic acid
NT1 folcysteine
NT1 formiminoglutamic acid
NT1 mecysteine
NT1 methyldopa
NT1 nopaline
NT1 octopine
NT1 saccharopine
NT1 theanine
rt amino acids

AMINO ACID DISORDERS
BT1 metabolic disorders
BT2 animal disorders
BT3 disorders
NT1 alkaptonuria
NT2 ochronosis
NT1 hyperaminoacidaemia
NT2 hyperargininaemia
NT2 hyperglycinaemia
NT2 hypermethioninaemia
NT2 hyperphenylalaninaemia
NT1 hyperaminoaciduria
NT1 ketonuria
NT2 phenylketonuria
NT1 maple syrup urine disease
rt amino acids

AMINO ACID METABOLISM
HN from 1990
BT1 metabolism
rt amino acid antagonists
rt amino acids

L-AMINO-ACID OXIDASE
(ec 1.4.3.2)
BT1 amine oxidoreductases
BT2 oxidoreductases
BT3 enzymes

AMINO ACIDS
BT1 carboxylic acids
BT2 organic acids
BT3 acids
BT1 organic nitrogen compounds
NT1 branched chain amino acids
NT2 aminoisobutyric acid
NT2 valine
NT1 cyclic amino acids
NT2 cycloleucine
NT2 desmosine
NT2 hypoglycine a
NT2 methylhistidine
NT1 diamino amino acids
NT2 diaminopimelic acid
NT1 essential amino acids
NT2 arginine
NT2 histidine
NT2 isoleucine
NT2 leucine
NT2 lysine
NT2 methionine
NT2 phenylalanine
NT2 threonine
NT2 tryptophan
NT2 valine
NT1 iodo amino acids
NT2 diiodothyronine
NT2 iodothyronine
NT2 thyroxine
NT3 d-thyroxine
NT3 l-thyroxine
NT2 triiodothyronine

AMINO ACIDS *cont.*
NT1 limiting amino acids
NT1 nitrosoamino acids
NT1 nonessential amino acids
NT2 γ-carboxyglutamic acid
NT2 alanine
NT2 asparagine
NT2 aspartic acid
NT2 cystine
NT2 glutamic acid
NT2 glutamine
NT2 glycine
NT2 hydroxylysine
NT2 hydroxyproline
NT2 proline
NT2 serine
NT2 tyrosine
NT1 nonprotein amino acids
NT2 α-aminobutyric acid
NT2 γ-aminobutyric acid
NT2 aminoadipic acid
NT2 aminolaevulinic acid
NT2 canavanine
NT2 citrulline
NT2 dopa
NT3 levodopa
NT2 hippuric acid
NT2 homoserine
NT2 kynurenine
NT2 mimosine
NT2 ornithine
NT2 pipecolic acid
NT2 taurine
NT2 thyronine
NT1 seleno amino acids
NT2 selenomethionine
NT1 sulfur amino acids
NT2 cystathionine
NT2 cysteic acid
NT2 cysteine
NT2 cystine
NT2 ethionine
NT2 homocysteine
NT2 methionine
NT2 penicillamine
NT2 taurine
rt amines
rt amino acid antagonists
rt amino acid derivatives
rt amino acid disorders
rt amino acid metabolism
rt aminoaciduria
rt free amino acids
rt gluconeogenesis
rt hyperaminoacidaemia
rt hyperaminoaciduria
rt protein hydrolysates
rt proteins

amino acids, branched chain
USE **branched chain amino acids**

amino acids, essential
USE **essential amino acids**

amino acids, free
USE **free amino acids**

amino acids, iodo
USE **iodo amino acids**

amino acids, limiting
USE **limiting amino acids**

amino acids, non-essential
USE **nonessential amino acids**

amino acids, nonprotein
USE **nonprotein amino acids**

AMINO ALCOHOLS
uf hydroxyamines
BT1 alcohols
BT1 amino compounds
BT2 organic nitrogen compounds
NT1 atenolol
NT1 cysteamine
NT1 ephedrine
NT1 ethanolamine
NT1 isoprenaline
NT1 methoxamine

AMINO ALCOHOLS *cont.*
NT1 metoprolol
NT1 oxprenolol
NT1 propranolol
NT1 sphingosine
NT1 tyramine
rt amines

AMINO COMPOUNDS
(not including amides, amino acids)
BT1 organic nitrogen compounds
NT1 amines
NT2 biogenic amines
NT3 acetylcholine
NT3 cadaverine
NT3 carnitine
NT3 catecholamines
NT4 dopamine
NT4 epinephrine
NT4 norepinephrine
NT3 choline
NT3 histamine
NT3 hordenine
NT3 octopamine
NT3 phenethylamine
NT3 putrescine
NT3 serotonin
NT3 spermine
NT3 tryptamine
NT3 tyramine
NT2 diamines
NT3 cadaverine
NT3 putrescine
NT2 monoamines
NT3 1-decanamine
NT3 1-dodecanamine
NT3 1-tetradecanamine
NT3 4-aminopyridine
NT3 5-aminouracil
NT3 methylamine
NT3 phenoxybenzamine
NT2 phenethylamines
NT3 amphetamines
NT4 amfetamine
NT4 benfluorex
NT4 fenfluramine
NT3 methoxamine
NT3 phenethylamine
NT2 polyamines
NT3 colestipol
NT3 melamine
NT3 spermidine
NT3 spermine
NT2 primary amines
NT3 1-decanamine
NT3 1-dodecanamine
NT3 1-tetradecanamine
NT3 methylamine
NT2 secondary amines
NT3 diethylamine
NT3 dimethylamine
NT3 diphenylamine
NT2 tertiary amines
NT3 triethylamine
NT3 trimethylamine
NT2 tryptamines
NT3 melatonin
NT3 serotonin
NT3 tryptamine
NT1 amino acid derivatives
NT2 s-methylcysteine sulfoxide
NT2 γ-hydroxyornithine
NT2 acetylglutamic acid
NT2 acetylmethionine
NT2 adenosylhomocysteine
NT2 adenosylmethionine
NT2 cysteinesulfinic acid
NT2 folcysteine
NT2 formiminoglutamic acid
NT2 mecysteine
NT2 methyldopa
NT2 nopaline
NT2 octopine
NT2 saccharopine
NT2 theanine
NT1 amino alcohols
NT2 atenolol
NT2 cysteamine
NT2 ephedrine
NT2 ethanolamine
NT2 isoprenaline

AMINO COMPOUNDS *cont.*
NT2 methoxamine
NT2 metoprolol
NT2 oxprenolol
NT2 propranolol
NT2 sphingosine
NT2 tyramine
NT1 amino sugars
NT2 hexosamines
NT3 n-acetylglucosamine
NT3 galactosamine
NT3 glucosamine
NT2 neuraminic acid
NT2 sialic acids
NT1 aminobenzoic acids
NT2 p-aminobenzoic acid
NT2 aminosalicylic acid
NT2 hydroxyanthranilic acid
rt deamination
rt transamination

AMINO NITROGEN
uf nitrogen, amino
BT1 chemical composition
BT2 composition
rt nitrogen

AMINO SUGARS
BT1 amino compounds
BT2 organic nitrogen compounds
BT1 sugars
BT2 carbohydrates
NT1 hexosamines
NT2 n-acetylglucosamine
NT2 galactosamine
NT2 glucosamine
NT1 neuraminic acid
NT1 sialic acids

AMINOACIDURIA
BT1 aciduria
BT2 metabolic disorders
BT3 animal disorders
BT4 disorders
NT1 cystinuria
NT1 homocystinuria
rt amino acids
rt urine

AMINOACYL-HISTIDINE DIPEPTIDASE
(ec 3.4.13.3)
BT1 peptidases
BT2 peptide hydrolases
BT3 hydrolases
BT4 enzymes

AMINOACYLTRANSFERASES
(ec 2.3.2)
BT1 acyltransferases
BT2 transferases
BT3 enzymes
NT1 d-glutamyltransferase
NT1 γ-glutamylcyclotransferase
NT1 γ-glutamyltransferase
NT1 peptidyltransferase

AMINOADIPIC ACID
BT1 nonprotein amino acids
BT2 amino acids
BT3 carboxylic acids
BT4 organic acids
BT5 acids
BT3 organic nitrogen compounds

P-AMINOBENZOIC ACID
uf paba
BT1 aminobenzoic acids
BT2 amino compounds
BT3 organic nitrogen compounds
BT2 benzoic acids
BT3 aromatic acids
BT4 aromatic compounds
BT4 organic acids
BT5 acids
BT1 vitamin b complex
BT2 water-soluble vitamins
BT3 vitamins

AMINOBENZOIC ACIDS
BT1 amino compounds
BT2 organic nitrogen compounds
BT1 benzoic acids
BT2 aromatic acids
BT3 aromatic compounds
BT3 organic acids
BT4 acids
NT1 p-aminobenzoic acid
NT1 aminosalicylic acid
NT1 hydroxyanthranilic acid

2-aminobutane
USE **butylamine**

α-AMINOBUTYRIC ACID
(for retrieval spell out "alpha")
BT1 nonprotein amino acids
BT2 amino acids
BT3 carboxylic acids
BT4 organic acids
BT5 acids
BT3 organic nitrogen compounds

γ-AMINOBUTYRIC ACID
(for retrieval spell out "gamma")
uf gaba
BT1 neurotransmitters
BT1 nonprotein amino acids
BT2 amino acids
BT3 carboxylic acids
BT4 organic acids
BT5 acids
BT3 organic nitrogen compounds

ε-aminocaproic acid
USE **6-aminohexanoic acid**

AMINOCARB
BT1 carbamate insecticides
BT2 carbamate pesticides
BT2 insecticides
BT3 pesticides

1-aminocyclopropanecarboxylic acid
USE **acc**

AMINOGLYCOSIDE ANTIBIOTICS
BT1 antibiotics
BT1 glycosides
BT2 carbohydrates
NT1 framycetin
NT1 gentamicin
NT1 kanamycin
NT1 paromomycin
NT1 spiramycin
NT1 streptomycin

6-AMINOHEXANOIC ACID
uf ε-aminocaproic acid
BT1 monocarboxylic acids
BT2 carboxylic acids
BT3 organic acids
BT4 acids
rt fertility

AMINOISOBUTYRIC ACID
BT1 branched chain amino acids
BT2 amino acids
BT3 carboxylic acids
BT4 organic acids
BT5 acids
BT3 organic nitrogen compounds

aminolaevulinate dehydratase
USE **porphobilinogen synthase**

AMINOLAEVULINIC ACID
AF aminolevulinic acid
BT1 keto acids
BT2 carboxylic acids
BT3 organic acids
BT4 acids
BT2 ketones
BT1 nonprotein amino acids
BT2 amino acids
BT3 carboxylic acids
BT4 organic acids
BT5 acids

AMINOLAEVULINIC ACID *cont.*
BT3 organic nitrogen compounds

5-AMINOLEVULINATE SYNTHASE
(ec 2.3.1.37)
BT1 acyltransferases
BT2 transferases
BT3 enzymes

AMINOLEVULINIC ACID
BF aminolaevulinic acid

AMINOPEPTIDASE
(ec 3.4.11.11)
BT1 aminopeptidases
BT2 peptidases
BT3 peptide hydrolases
BT4 hydrolases
BT5 enzymes

aminopeptidase (cytosol)
USE **cytosol aminopeptidase**

AMINOPEPTIDASES
BT1 peptidases
BT2 peptide hydrolases
BT3 hydrolases
BT4 enzymes
NT1 aminopeptidase
NT1 cytosol aminopeptidase
NT1 microsomal aminopeptidase

AMINOPHYLLINE
BT1 diuretics
BT2 drugs
rt theophylline

AMINOPTERIN
BT1 antineoplastic agents
BT2 drugs
BT1 enzyme inhibitors
BT2 metabolic inhibitors
BT3 inhibitors
BT1 folate antagonists
BT2 vitamin b antagonists
BT3 vitamin antagonists
BT4 antagonists
BT5 metabolic inhibitors
BT6 inhibitors
BT1 pteridines
BT2 heterocyclic nitrogen compounds
BT3 organic nitrogen compounds

2-AMINOPURINE
BT1 mutagens
BT1 purines
BT2 heterocyclic nitrogen compounds
BT3 organic nitrogen compounds

4-AMINOPYRIDINE
BT1 avicides
BT2 pesticides
BT1 detoxicants
BT2 drugs
BT1 monoamines
BT2 amines
BT3 amino compounds
BT4 organic nitrogen compounds
BT1 pyridines
BT2 heterocyclic nitrogen compounds
BT3 organic nitrogen compounds

AMINOQUINOLINES
BT1 quinolines
BT2 heterocyclic nitrogen compounds
BT3 organic nitrogen compounds
NT1 amodiaquine
NT1 chloroquine
NT1 primaquine
rt antimalarials

AMINOSALICYLIC ACID
BT1 aminobenzoic acids
BT2 amino compounds

AMINOSALICYLIC ACID *cont.*
BT3 organic nitrogen compounds
BT2 benzoic acids
BT3 aromatic acids
BT4 aromatic compounds
BT4 organic acids
BT5 acids
BT1 antibacterial agents
BT2 antiinfective agents
BT3 drugs
BT1 salicylic acids
BT2 phenolic acids
BT3 benzoic acids
BT4 aromatic acids
BT5 aromatic compounds
BT5 organic acids
BT6 acids
BT3 phenolic compounds
BT4 aromatic compounds

aminosidine
USE **paromomycin**

AMINOTRANSFERASES
(ec 2.6.1)
uf transaminases
BT1 transferases
BT2 enzymes
NT1 alanine aminotransferase
NT1 asparagine-oxo-acid aminotransferase
NT1 aspartate aminotransferase
NT1 branched-chain-amino-acid aminotransferase
NT1 leucine aminotransferase
NT1 ornithine-oxo-acid aminotransferase
NT1 tyrosine aminotransferase

aminotriazole
USE **amitrole**

5-AMINOURACIL
BT1 monoamines
BT2 amines
BT3 amino compounds
BT4 organic nitrogen compounds
BT1 mutagens
BT1 uracil derivatives
BT2 pyrimidines
BT3 heterocyclic nitrogen compounds
BT4 organic nitrogen compounds

AMIPROFOS-METHYL
BT1 organophosphorus herbicides
BT2 herbicides
BT3 pesticides
BT2 organophosphorus pesticides
BT3 organophosphorus compounds

AMITERMES
BT1 termitidae
BT2 isoptera
NT1 amitermes evuncifer
NT1 amitermes meridionalis

AMITERMES EVUNCIFER
BT1 amitermes
BT2 termitidae
BT3 isoptera

AMITERMES MERIDIONALIS
BT1 amitermes
BT2 termitidae
BT3 isoptera

AMITOSIS
BT1 cell division
rt mitosis

AMITRAZ
BT1 ectoparasiticides
BT2 antiparasitic agents
BT3 drugs
BT1 formamidine acaricides
BT2 acaricides
BT3 pesticides

AMITRAZ *cont.*
BT1 formamidine insecticides
BT2 insecticides
BT3 pesticides

AMITROLE
uf *aminotriazole*
BT1 triazole herbicides
BT2 herbicides
BT3 pesticides
BT2 triazoles
BT3 azoles
BT4 heterocyclic nitrogen compounds
BT5 organic nitrogen compounds

AMITUS
BT1 platygasteridae
BT2 hymenoptera
NT1 amitus hesperidum

AMITUS HESPERIDUM
BT1 amitus
BT2 platygasteridae
BT3 hymenoptera

AMMALO
BT1 arctiidae
BT2 lepidoptera
rt pareuchaetes

ammalo insulata
USE **pareuchaetes insulata**

AMMANNIA
BT1 lythraceae
NT1 ammannia auriculata
NT1 ammannia coccinea
NT1 ammannia latifolia
NT1 ammannia teres

AMMANNIA AURICULATA
BT1 ammannia
BT2 lythraceae

AMMANNIA COCCINEA
BT1 ammannia
BT2 lythraceae

AMMANNIA LATIFOLIA
BT1 ammannia
BT2 lythraceae

AMMANNIA TERES
BT1 ammannia
BT2 lythraceae

AMMI
BT1 umbelliferae
NT1 ammi majus
NT1 ammi visnaga
rt coumarins

AMMI MAJUS
BT1 ammi
BT2 umbelliferae
BT1 medicinal plants

AMMI VISNAGA
BT1 ammi
BT2 umbelliferae

ammo-phos
USE **ammonium phosphates**

AMMODAUCUS
BT1 umbelliferae
NT1 ammodaucus leucotrichus

AMMODAUCUS LEUCOTHRICHUS
BT1 medicinal plants

AMMODAUCUS LEUCOTRICHUS
BT1 ammodaucus
BT2 umbelliferae

AMMODENDRON
BT1 leguminosae
NT1 ammodendron argenteum
NT1 ammodendron conollyi
NT1 ammodendron eichwaldii

AMMODENDRON ARGENTEUM
BT1 ammodendron
BT2 leguminosae

AMMODENDRON CONOLLYI
BT1 ammodendron
BT2 leguminosae

AMMODENDRON EICHWALDII
BT1 ammodendron
BT2 leguminosae

AMMODYTES
BT1 ammodytidae
BT2 perciformes
BT3 osteichthyes
BT4 fishes

AMMODYTIDAE
BT1 perciformes
BT2 osteichthyes
BT3 fishes
NT1 ammodytes
NT1 hyperoplus

AMMONIA
BT1 gases
BT1 inorganic compounds
rt ammonia additives
rt ammonia synthesis gas
rt ammonia treatment
rt ammoniated feeds
rt ammonification
rt ammonium compounds
rt ammonium fertilizers
rt ammonium nitrogen
rt anhydrous ammonia
rt aqueous ammonia
rt hyperammonaemia
rt nitriding
rt nitrification
rt nitrogen

AMMONIA ADDITIVES
BT1 additives
rt ammonia

ammonia, anhydrous
USE **anhydrous ammonia**

ammonia, liquid
USE **anhydrous ammonia**

AMMONIA-LYASES
(ec 4.3.1)
BT1 lyases
BT2 enzymes
NT1 histidine ammonia-lyase
NT1 phenylalanine ammonia-lyase

ammonia nitrogen
USE **ammonium nitrogen**

AMMONIA SYNTHESIS GAS
BT1 gases
rt ammonia
rt fertilizer technology

AMMONIA TREATMENT
BT1 processing
rt ammonia

AMMONIATED FEEDS
BT1 feeds
rt ammonia

AMMONIATED SUPERPHOSPHATE
BT1 ammonium fertilizers
BT2 nitrogen fertilizers
BT3 fertilizers
BT1 superphosphates
BT2 phosphorus fertilizers
BT3 fertilizers

AMMONIATED TRIPLE SUPERPHOSPHATE
BT1 ammonium fertilizers
BT2 nitrogen fertilizers
BT3 fertilizers
BT1 superphosphates
BT2 phosphorus fertilizers
BT3 fertilizers

AMMONIATED VERMICULITE
BT1 ammonium fertilizers
BT2 nitrogen fertilizers
BT3 fertilizers

AMMONIATED VERMICULITE *cont.*
BT1 silicon fertilizers
BT2 trace element fertilizers
BT3 fertilizers

AMMONIFICATION
BT1 mineralization
rt ammonia
rt nitrogen
rt soil biology

AMMONIUM
BT1 cations
BT2 ions
rt fixed ammonium

AMMONIUM BICARBONATE
BT1 ammonium fertilizers
BT2 nitrogen fertilizers
BT3 fertilizers
BT1 ammonium salts
BT2 ammonium compounds
BT1 bicarbonates
BT2 inorganic salts
BT3 inorganic compounds
BT3 salts
BT1 expectorants
BT2 antitussive agents
BT3 respiratory system agents
BT4 drugs

ammonium calcium trimetaphosphate
USE **calcium ammonium trimetaphosphate**

AMMONIUM CHLORIDE
uf *ammonium hydrochloride*
BT1 ammonium fertilizers
BT2 nitrogen fertilizers
BT3 fertilizers
BT1 ammonium salts
BT2 ammonium compounds
BT1 chlorides
BT2 halides
BT3 inorganic salts
BT4 inorganic compounds
BT4 salts
BT1 chlorine fertilizers
BT2 trace element fertilizers
BT3 fertilizers
BT1 diuretics
BT2 drugs
BT1 expectorants
BT2 antitussive agents
BT3 respiratory system agents
BT4 drugs

AMMONIUM COMPOUNDS
NT1 ammonium salts
NT2 ammonium bicarbonate
NT2 ammonium chloride
NT2 ammonium fluoride
NT2 ammonium formate
NT2 ammonium humate
NT2 ammonium hydroxide
NT2 ammonium lactate
NT2 ammonium lignosulfonate
NT2 ammonium nitrate
NT2 ammonium oxalate
NT2 ammonium perchlorate
NT2 ammonium phosphates
NT3 ammonium metaphosphates
NT3 ammonium polyphosphates
NT4 ammonium polyphosphate sulfate
NT4 ammonium pyrophosphate
NT4 ammonium tripolyphosphate
NT4 diammonium pyrophosphate
NT4 tetraammonium pyrophosphate
NT4 triammonium pyrophosphate
NT4 urea ammonium polyphosphate
NT3 diammonium phosphate
NT3 magnesium ammonium phosphate

AMMONIUM COMPOUNDS *cont.*
NT3 monoammonium phosphate
NT3 triammonium phosphate
NT3 urea ammonium phosphate
NT3 urea ammonium pyrophosphate
NT2 ammonium sulfamate
NT2 ammonium sulfate
NT2 ammonium thiocyanate
NT2 ammonium thiosulfate
NT2 mama
NT1 quaternary ammonium compounds
NT2 acetylcholine
NT2 benzalkonium chloride
NT2 bephenium
NT2 betaine
NT2 bethanechol
NT2 carnitine
NT2 cetrimonium
NT2 chlormequat
NT2 chlorphonium
NT2 choline
NT2 clidinium
NT2 decamethonium
NT2 gallamine triethiodide
NT2 homidium
NT2 isometamidium
NT2 neostigmine
NT2 quaternary ammonium herbicides
NT3 cyperquat
NT3 diethamquat
NT3 difenzoquat
NT3 diquat
NT3 morfamquat
NT3 paraquat
NT2 sultroponium
NT2 suxamethonium
rt ammonia
rt ammonium nitrogen

ammonium dihydrogen phosphate
USE **monoammonium phosphate**

AMMONIUM FERTILIZERS
BT1 nitrogen fertilizers
BT2 fertilizers
NT1 ammoniated superphosphate
NT1 ammoniated triple superphosphate
NT1 ammoniated vermiculite
NT1 ammonium bicarbonate
NT1 ammonium chloride
NT1 ammonium lignosulfonate
NT1 ammonium nitrate
NT1 ammonium phosphates
NT2 ammonium metaphosphates
NT2 ammonium polyphosphates
NT3 ammonium polyphosphate sulfate
NT3 ammonium pyrophosphate
NT3 ammonium tripolyphosphate
NT3 diammonium pyrophosphate
NT3 tetraammonium pyrophosphate
NT3 triammonium pyrophosphate
NT3 urea ammonium polyphosphate
NT2 diammonium phosphate
NT2 magnesium ammonium phosphate
NT2 monoammonium phosphate
NT2 triammonium phosphate
NT2 urea ammonium phosphate
NT2 urea ammonium pyrophosphate
NT1 ammonium sulfate
NT1 anhydrous ammonia
NT1 aqueous ammonia
NT1 calcium ammonium nitrate
NT1 urea ammonium nitrate

AMMONIUM FERTILIZERS *cont.*
NT1 urea ammonium sulfate
rt ammonia

AMMONIUM FIXATION
BT1 fixation
rt fixed ammonium
rt nitrogen

AMMONIUM FLUORIDE
BT1 ammonium salts
BT2 ammonium compounds
BT1 fluorides
BT2 halides
BT3 inorganic salts
BT4 inorganic compounds
BT4 salts

AMMONIUM FORMATE
BT1 ammonium salts
BT2 ammonium compounds
BT1 formates (salts)
BT2 formates
BT2 organic salts
BT3 salts

AMMONIUM HUMATE
BT1 ammonium salts
BT2 ammonium compounds
BT1 humates
BT2 organic fertilizers
BT3 fertilizers
BT2 organic salts
BT3 salts

ammonium hydrochloride
USE **ammonium chloride**

AMMONIUM HYDROXIDE
BT1 ammonium salts
BT2 ammonium compounds
BT1 hydroxides
BT2 inorganic compounds
rt aqueous ammonia

AMMONIUM LACTATE
BT1 ammonium salts
BT2 ammonium compounds
BT1 lactates
BT2 organic salts
BT3 salts

AMMONIUM LIGNOSULFONATE
uf *ammonium lignosulphonate*
BT1 ammonium fertilizers
BT2 nitrogen fertilizers
BT3 fertilizers
BT1 ammonium salts
BT2 ammonium compounds
BT1 lignosulfonates
BT2 soil conditioners
BT3 soil amendments
BT4 amendments

ammonium lignosulphonate
USE **ammonium lignosulfonate**

AMMONIUM METAPHOSPHATES
BT1 ammonium phosphates
BT2 ammonium fertilizers
BT3 nitrogen fertilizers
BT4 fertilizers
BT2 ammonium salts
BT3 ammonium compounds
BT2 nitrogen-phosphorus fertilizers
BT3 compound fertilizers
BT4 fertilizers
BT2 phosphates (salts)
BT3 inorganic salts
BT4 inorganic compounds
BT4 salts
BT3 phosphates
BT2 phosphorus fertilizers
BT3 fertilizers
BT1 metaphosphates
BT2 condensed phosphates
BT3 phosphorus fertilizers
BT4 fertilizers
BT2 phosphates (salts)
BT3 inorganic salts
BT4 inorganic compounds
BT4 salts
BT3 phosphates

AMMONIUM NITRATE
BT1 ammonium fertilizers
BT2 nitrogen fertilizers
BT3 fertilizers
BT1 ammonium salts
BT2 ammonium compounds
BT1 nitrate fertilizers
BT2 nitrogen fertilizers
BT3 fertilizers
BT1 nitrates (inorganic salts)
BT2 inorganic salts
BT3 inorganic compounds
BT3 salts
BT2 nitrates

ammonium nitrate/calcium carbonate
USE **calcium ammonium nitrate**

AMMONIUM NITROGEN
uf *ammonia nitrogen*
uf *nitrogen, ammonia*
uf *nitrogen, ammonium*
BT1 chemical composition
BT2 composition
rt ammonia
rt ammonium compounds
rt nitrogen
rt nitrogen fertilizers

AMMONIUM OXALATE
BT1 ammonium salts
BT2 ammonium compounds
BT1 oxalates
BT2 organic salts
BT3 salts

AMMONIUM PERCHLORATE
BT1 ammonium salts
BT2 ammonium compounds
BT1 perchlorates
BT2 inorganic salts
BT3 inorganic compounds
BT3 salts

AMMONIUM PHOSPHATES
uf *ammo-phos*
BT1 ammonium fertilizers
BT2 nitrogen fertilizers
BT3 fertilizers
BT1 ammonium salts
BT2 ammonium compounds
BT1 nitrogen-phosphorus fertilizers
BT2 compound fertilizers
BT3 fertilizers
BT1 phosphates (salts)
BT2 inorganic salts
BT3 inorganic compounds
BT3 salts
BT2 phosphates
BT1 phosphorus fertilizers
BT2 fertilizers
NT1 ammonium metaphosphates
NT1 ammonium polyphosphates
NT2 ammonium polyphosphate sulfate
NT2 ammonium pyrophosphate
NT2 ammonium tripolyphosphate
NT2 diammonium pyrophosphate
NT2 tetraammonium pyrophosphate
NT2 triammonium pyrophosphate
NT2 urea ammonium polyphosphate
NT1 diammonium phosphate
NT1 magnesium ammonium phosphate
NT1 monoammonium phosphate
NT1 triammonium phosphate
NT1 urea ammonium phosphate
NT1 urea ammonium pyrophosphate

AMMONIUM POLYPHOSPHATE SULFATE
uf *ammonium polyphosphate sulphate*
BT1 ammonium polyphosphates

AMMONIUM POLYPHOSPHATE SULFATE *cont.*
BT2 ammonium phosphates
BT3 ammonium fertilizers
BT4 nitrogen fertilizers
BT5 fertilizers
BT3 ammonium salts
BT4 ammonium compounds
BT3 nitrogen-phosphorus fertilizers
BT4 compound fertilizers
BT5 fertilizers
BT3 phosphates (salts)
BT4 inorganic salts
BT5 inorganic compounds
BT5 salts
BT4 phosphates
BT3 phosphorus fertilizers
BT4 fertilizers
BT1 polyphosphates
BT2 condensed phosphates
BT3 phosphorus fertilizers
BT4 fertilizers
BT1 sulfur fertilizers
BT2 fertilizers

ammonium polyphosphate sulphate
USE **ammonium polyphosphate sulfate**

AMMONIUM POLYPHOSPHATES
BT1 ammonium phosphates
BT2 ammonium fertilizers
BT3 nitrogen fertilizers
BT4 fertilizers
BT2 ammonium salts
BT3 ammonium compounds
BT2 nitrogen-phosphorus fertilizers
BT3 compound fertilizers
BT4 fertilizers
BT2 phosphates (salts)
BT3 inorganic salts
BT4 inorganic compounds
BT4 salts
BT3 phosphates
BT2 phosphorus fertilizers
BT3 fertilizers
NT1 ammonium polyphosphate sulfate
NT1 ammonium pyrophosphate
NT1 ammonium tripolyphosphate
NT1 diammonium pyrophosphate
NT1 tetraammonium pyrophosphate
NT1 triammonium pyrophosphate
NT1 urea ammonium polyphosphate

AMMONIUM PYROPHOSPHATE
BT1 ammonium polyphosphates
BT2 ammonium phosphates
BT3 ammonium fertilizers
BT4 nitrogen fertilizers
BT5 fertilizers
BT3 ammonium salts
BT4 ammonium compounds
BT3 nitrogen-phosphorus fertilizers
BT4 compound fertilizers
BT5 fertilizers
BT3 phosphates (salts)
BT4 inorganic salts
BT5 inorganic compounds
BT5 salts
BT4 phosphates
BT3 phosphorus fertilizers
BT4 fertilizers
BT1 pyrophosphates
BT2 phosphates (salts)
BT3 inorganic salts
BT4 inorganic compounds
BT4 salts
BT3 phosphates
BT2 polyphosphates
BT3 condensed phosphates
BT4 phosphorus fertilizers
BT5 fertilizers

ammonium quaternary compounds
USE **quaternary ammonium compounds**

AMMONIUM SALTS
BT1 ammonium compounds
NT1 ammonium bicarbonate
NT1 ammonium chloride
NT1 ammonium fluoride
NT1 ammonium formate
NT1 ammonium humate
NT1 ammonium hydroxide
NT1 ammonium lactate
NT1 ammonium lignosulfonate
NT1 ammonium nitrate
NT1 ammonium oxalate
NT1 ammonium perchlorate
NT1 ammonium phosphates
NT2 ammonium metaphosphates
NT2 ammonium polyphosphates
NT3 ammonium polyphosphate sulfate
NT3 ammonium pyrophosphate
NT3 ammonium tripolyphosphate
NT3 diammonium pyrophosphate
NT3 tetraammonium pyrophosphate
NT3 triammonium pyrophosphate
NT3 urea ammonium polyphosphate
NT2 diammonium phosphate
NT2 magnesium ammonium phosphate
NT2 monoammonium phosphate
NT2 triammonium phosphate
NT2 urea ammonium phosphate
NT2 urea ammonium pyrophosphate
NT1 ammonium sulfamate
NT1 ammonium sulfate
NT1 ammonium thiocyanate
NT1 ammonium thiosulfate
NT1 mama

AMMONIUM SULFAMATE
uf *ammonium sulphamate*
uf *ams*
BT1 ammonium salts
BT2 ammonium compounds
BT1 inorganic herbicides
BT2 herbicides
BT3 pesticides
BT1 sulfamates
BT2 inorganic salts
BT3 inorganic compounds
BT3 salts

AMMONIUM SULFATE
uf *ammonium sulphate*
BT1 ammonium fertilizers
BT2 nitrogen fertilizers
BT3 fertilizers
BT1 ammonium salts
BT2 ammonium compounds
BT1 sulfates (inorganic salts)
BT2 inorganic salts
BT3 inorganic compounds
BT3 salts
BT2 sulfates
BT1 sulfur fertilizers
BT2 fertilizers

ammonium sulphamate
USE **ammonium sulfamate**

ammonium sulphate
USE **ammonium sulfate**

AMMONIUM THIOCYANATE
BT1 ammonium salts
BT2 ammonium compounds
BT1 thiocyanates
BT2 inorganic salts
BT3 inorganic compounds
BT3 salts

AMMONIUM THIOSULFATE
uf *ammonium thiosulphate*
BT1 ammonium salts
BT2 ammonium compounds
BT1 nitrification inhibitors
BT2 metabolic inhibitors
BT3 inhibitors
BT1 thiosulfates
BT2 inorganic salts
BT3 inorganic compounds
BT3 salts
BT1 urease inhibitors
BT2 enzyme inhibitors
BT3 metabolic inhibitors
BT4 inhibitors

ammonium thiosulphate
USE **ammonium thiosulfate**

AMMONIUM TRIPOLYPHOSPHATE
BT1 ammonium polyphosphates
BT2 ammonium phosphates
BT3 ammonium fertilizers
BT4 nitrogen fertilizers
BT5 fertilizers
BT3 ammonium salts
BT4 ammonium compounds
BT3 nitrogen-phosphorus fertilizers
BT4 compound fertilizers
BT5 fertilizers
BT3 phosphates (salts)
BT4 inorganic salts
BT5 inorganic compounds
BT5 salts
BT4 phosphates
BT3 phosphorus fertilizers
BT4 fertilizers

AMMOPHILA
BT1 gramineae
NT1 ammophila arenaria
NT1 ammophila breviligulata

AMMOPHILA ARENARIA
BT1 ammophila
BT2 gramineae
rt sand stabilization

AMMOPHILA BREVILIGULATA
BT1 ammophila
BT2 gramineae
rt sand stabilization

AMMOTRAGUS
BT1 bovidae
BT2 ruminantia
BT3 artiodactyla
BT4 mammals
BT4 ungulates
NT1 ammotragus lervia

AMMOTRAGUS LERVIA
BT1 ammotragus
BT2 bovidae
BT3 ruminantia
BT4 artiodactyla
BT5 mammals
BT5 ungulates

AMNIOCENTESIS
BT1 diagnostic techniques
BT2 techniques

AMNION
BT1 fetal membranes
BT2 membranes
rt amniotic fluid

AMNIOTIC FLUID
BT1 body fluids
BT2 fluids
rt amnion
rt fetus

AMODIAQUINE
BT1 aminoquinolines
BT2 quinolines
BT3 heterocyclic nitrogen compounds
BT4 organic nitrogen compounds
BT1 antimalarials
BT2 antiprotozoal agents

AMODIAQUINE *cont.*
BT3 antiparasitic agents
BT4 drugs

AMOEBA
BT1 sarcomastigophora
BT2 protozoa

AMOEBA DISEASE
BT1 bee diseases
BT2 animal diseases
BT3 diseases
rt malpighamoeba mellificae

AMOEBAE
rt sarcomastigophora

amoebic dysentry
USE **entamoeba histolytica**

AMOEBICIDES
AF amebicides
BT1 antiprotozoal agents
BT2 antiparasitic agents
BT3 drugs
NT1 clioquinol
NT1 dehydroemetine
NT1 diloxanide
NT1 emetine
NT1 metronidazole
NT1 ornidazole
NT1 paromomycin
NT1 secnidazole
NT1 tetracycline
NT1 tinidazole

AMOEBOAPHELIDIUM
rt fungi
rt protozoa

AMOEBOTAENIA
BT1 dilepididae
BT2 eucestoda
BT3 cestoda
NT1 amoebotaenia sphenoides

AMOEBOTAENIA SPHENOIDES
BT1 amoebotaenia
BT2 dilepididae
BT3 eucestoda
BT4 cestoda

AMOMUM
BT1 zingiberaceae
NT1 amomum medium
NT1 amomum subulatum

amomum cardamomum
USE **elettaria cardamomum**

AMOMUM MEDIUM
BT1 amomum
BT2 zingiberaceae

AMOMUM SUBULATUM
BT1 amomum
BT2 zingiberaceae
BT1 spice plants

AMOORA
BT1 meliaceae
NT1 amoora cucullata
NT1 amoora rohituka

AMOORA CUCULLATA
BT1 amoora
BT2 meliaceae

AMOORA ROHITUKA
BT1 amoora
BT2 meliaceae
BT1 medicinal plants

AMORPHA
BT1 leguminosae
NT1 amorpha canescens
NT1 amorpha fruticosa

AMORPHA CANESCENS
BT1 amorpha
BT2 leguminosae

AMORPHA FRUTICOSA
BT1 acaricidal plants
BT2 pesticidal plants
BT1 amorpha

AMORPHA FRUTICOSA *cont.*
BT2 leguminosae
BT1 antibacterial plants
BT1 medicinal plants
BT1 ornamental woody plants

AMORPHOPHALLUS
BT1 araceae
NT1 amorphophallus campanulatus
NT1 amorphophallus konjac

AMORPHOPHALLUS CAMPANULATUS
uf *arum campanulatum*
BT1 amorphophallus
BT2 araceae
BT1 root vegetables
BT2 root crops
BT2 vegetables
BT1 starch crops

AMORPHOPHALLUS KONJAC
BT1 amorphophallus
BT2 araceae
BT1 root vegetables
BT2 root crops
BT2 vegetables
BT1 starch crops

AMORPHOTHECA
BT1 helotiales
NT1 amorphotheca resinae
rt hormoconis

AMORPHOTHECA RESINAE
uf *cladosporium resinae*
uf *hormoconis resinae*
BT1 amorphotheca
BT2 helotiales

AMORPHOUS SUGAR
HN from 1990
BT1 sugar
BT2 plant products
BT3 products
rt instant sugar

AMORTIZATION
(gradually liquidating a debt by making regular payments of both principal and interest)
rt book-keeping
rt investment
rt productive life

AMOSCANATE
BT1 anthelmintics
BT2 antiparasitic agents
BT3 drugs

AMOXICILLIN
BT1 penicillins
BT2 antibacterial agents
BT3 antiinfective agents
BT4 drugs
BT2 heterocyclic nitrogen compounds
BT3 organic nitrogen compounds

AMP
uf *adenosine monophosphate*
BT1 adenosine phosphates
BT2 phosphates (esters)
BT3 esters
BT3 phosphates
BT2 purine nucleotides
BT3 nucleotides
BT4 glycosides
BT5 carbohydrates
rt c-amp

AMP DEAMINASE
(ec 3.5.4.6)
BT1 amidine hydrolases
BT2 hydrolases
BT3 enzymes

AMPELAMUS
BT1 asclepiadaceae
NT1 ampelamus albidus

AMPELAMUS ALBIDUS
BT1 ampelamus
BT2 asclepiadaceae

AMPELODESMOS
BT1 gramineae
NT1 ampelodesmos mauritanica

AMPELODESMOS MAURITANICA
BT1 ampelodesmos
BT2 gramineae
BT1 pasture plants

AMPELOMYCES
BT1 deuteromycotina
NT1 ampelomyces quisqualis
rt cicinnobolus

AMPELOMYCES QUISQUALIS
uf *cicinnobolus cesati*
BT1 ampelomyces
BT2 deuteromycotina

amphetamine
USE **amfetamine**

AMPHETAMINES
BT1 phenethylamines
BT2 amines
BT3 amino compounds
BT4 organic nitrogen compounds
NT1 amfetamine
NT1 benfluorex
NT1 fenfluramine
rt analeptics
rt anorexiants
rt sympathomimetics

AMPHIBDELLA
BT1 dactylogyridae
BT2 monogenea

AMPHIBIA
uf *amphibians*
NT1 anura
NT2 bufonidae
NT3 bufo
NT4 bufo bufo
NT4 bufo marinus
NT4 bufo melanostictus
NT4 bufo paracnemis
NT4 bufo regularis
NT4 bufo typhonius
NT4 bufo viridis
NT2 hylidae
NT3 hyla
NT4 hyla arborea
NT4 hyla fuscovaria
NT2 pipidae
NT3 xenopus
NT4 xenopus fraseri
NT4 xenopus laevis
NT2 ranidae
NT3 rana
NT4 rana catesbeiana
NT4 rana cyanophlyctis
NT4 rana hexadactyla
NT4 rana limnocharis
NT4 rana nigromaculata
NT4 rana perezi
NT4 rana pipiens
NT4 rana ridibunda
NT4 rana temporaria
NT4 rana tigrina
NT1 caudata
NT2 ambystomatidae
NT3 ambystoma
rt aquatic animals
rt frogs
rt toads
rt vertebrates

amphibians
USE **amphibia**

AMPHIBIOUS VEHICLES
HN from 1990
BT1 vehicles

AMPHICOTYLIDAE
BT1 eucestoda
BT2 cestoda
NT1 eubothrium

AMPHIDINIUM
BT1 dinophyta
BT2 algae

AMPHILINA
HN from 1990
BT1 cestodaria
BT2 cestoda

AMPHIMALLON
BT1 scarabaeidae
BT2 coleoptera
NT1 amphimallon majalis
NT1 amphimallon solstitiale

AMPHIMALLON MAJALIS
BT1 amphimallon
BT2 scarabaeidae
BT3 coleoptera

AMPHIMALLON SOLSTITIALE
BT1 amphimallon
BT2 scarabaeidae
BT3 coleoptera

AMPHIPODA
BT1 malacostraca
BT2 crustacea
BT3 arthropods
NT1 corophium
NT1 gammarus
NT2 gammarus fossarum
NT2 gammarus oceanicus
NT2 gammarus pulex
rt aquatic animals

AMPHIPSYLLA
BT1 leptopsyllidae
BT2 siphonaptera
NT1 amphipsylla kuznetzovi
NT1 amphipsylla rossica

AMPHIPSYLLA KUZNETZOVI
BT1 amphipsylla
BT2 leptopsyllidae
BT3 siphonaptera

AMPHIPSYLLA ROSSICA
BT1 amphipsylla
BT2 leptopsyllidae
BT3 siphonaptera

AMPHOROPHORA
BT1 aphididae
BT2 aphidoidea
BT3 sternorrhyncha
BT4 homoptera
NT1 amphorophora agathonica
NT1 amphorophora rubi
rt hyperomyzus

AMPHOROPHORA AGATHONICA
BT1 amphorophora
BT2 aphididae
BT3 aphidoidea
BT4 sternorrhyncha
BT5 homoptera

amphorophora lactucae
USE **hyperomyzus lactucae**

AMPHOROPHORA RUBI
BT1 amphorophora
BT2 aphididae
BT3 aphidoidea
BT4 sternorrhyncha
BT5 homoptera

AMPHOTERICIN B
BT1 antifungal agents
BT2 antiinfective agents
BT3 drugs
BT1 antiprotozoal agents
BT2 antiparasitic agents
BT3 drugs

AMPICILLIN
BT1 penicillins
BT2 antibacterial agents
BT3 antiinfective agents
BT4 drugs
BT2 heterocyclic nitrogen compounds
BT3 organic nitrogen compounds

AMPLICEPHALUS
BT1 cicadellidae
BT2 cicadelloidea
BT3 auchenorrhyncha
BT4 homoptera

AMPLIFICATION
HN from 1990
ufa *gene amplification*
NT1 dna amplification
NT1 rna amplification

amplification, dna
USE **dna amplification**

amplification, rna
USE **rna amplification**

AMPLIMERLINIUS
HN from 1990
BT1 dolichodoridae
BT2 nematoda

AMPROLIUM
BT1 coccidiostats
BT2 antiprotozoal agents
BT3 antiparasitic agents
BT4 drugs

AMPULLA
BT1 ductus deferens
BT2 male genitalia
BT3 genitalia
BT4 urogenital system
BT5 body parts

AMPULLARIELLA
BT1 actinoplanaceae

AMPULLARIIDAE
BT1 gastropoda
BT2 mollusca
NT1 marisa
NT2 marisa cornuarietis
NT1 pila
NT2 pila globosa
NT1 pomacea

AMPUTATION
BT1 surgical operations
rt debeaking
rt resection

AMPUTEES (AGRICOLA)
BT1 handicapped persons
BT2 people

AMRASCA
uf *sundapteryx*
BT1 cicadellidae
BT2 cicadelloidea
BT3 auchenorrhyncha
BT4 homoptera
NT1 amrasca biguttula
NT1 amrasca devastans
rt empoasca

AMRASCA BIGUTTULA
uf *empoasca biguttula*
uf *sundapteryx biguttula*
BT1 amrasca
BT2 cicadellidae
BT3 cicadelloidea
BT4 auchenorrhyncha
BT5 homoptera

AMRASCA DEVASTANS
uf *empoasca devastans*
BT1 amrasca
BT2 cicadellidae
BT3 cicadelloidea
BT4 auchenorrhyncha
BT5 homoptera

AMRITMAHAL
BT1 cattle breeds
BT2 breeds

ams
USE **ammonium sulfamate**

AMSACTA
BT1 arctiidae
BT2 lepidoptera
NT1 amsacta albistriga

AMSACTA *cont.*
NT1 amsacta moorei

AMSACTA ALBISTRIGA
BT1 amsacta
BT2 arctiidae
BT3 lepidoptera

AMSACTA MOOREI
BT1 amsacta
BT2 arctiidae
BT3 lepidoptera

AMSINCKIA
BT1 boraginaceae
NT1 amsinckia hispida
NT1 amsinckia intermedia

AMSINCKIA HISPIDA
BT1 amsinckia
BT2 boraginaceae

AMSINCKIA INTERMEDIA
BT1 amsinckia
BT2 boraginaceae

AMSONIA
BT1 apocynaceae
NT1 amsonia angustifolia
NT1 amsonia elliptica
NT1 amsonia tabernaemontana

AMSONIA ANGUSTIFOLIA
BT1 amsonia
BT2 apocynaceae
BT1 medicinal plants

AMSONIA ELLIPTICA
BT1 amsonia
BT2 apocynaceae

AMSONIA TABERNAEMONTANA
BT1 amsonia
BT2 apocynaceae

AMUSEMENT MACHINES
uf *gambling machines*
BT1 entertainment
BT2 leisure activities
BT1 mechanized recreation
BT2 recreation
BT2 sport
rt gambling

amusements
USE **entertainment**

AMYELOIS
uf *paramyelois*
BT1 pyralidae
BT2 lepidoptera
NT1 amyelois transitella

AMYELOIS TRANSITELLA
uf *paramyelois transitella*
BT1 amyelois
BT2 pyralidae
BT3 lepidoptera

AMYEMA
BT1 loranthaceae
NT1 amyema miquelii

AMYEMA MIQUELII
HN from 1990
BT1 amyema
BT2 loranthaceae

AMYGDALA
BT1 cerebellum
BT2 brain
BT3 central nervous system
BT4 nervous system
BT5 body parts

AMYGDALIN
uf *laetrile*
BT1 cyanogenic glycosides
BT2 cyanogens
BT3 toxic substances
BT2 glycosides
BT3 carbohydrates
BT1 glucosides
BT2 glycosides
BT3 carbohydrates

amygdalus
USE **prunus**

amygdalus communis
USE **prunus dulcis**

amygdalus persica
USE **prunus persica**

AMYL ALCOHOL
BT1 alcohols
rt gerber method

α-AMYLASE
(ec 3.2.1.1)
(for retrieval spell out "alpha")
BT1 amylases
BT2 o-glycoside hydrolases
BT3 glycosidases
BT4 hydrolases
BT5 enzymes

β-AMYLASE
(ec 3.2.1.2)
(for retrieval spell out "beta")
BT1 amylases
BT2 o-glycoside hydrolases
BT3 glycosidases
BT4 hydrolases
BT5 enzymes

AMYLASES
BT1 o-glycoside hydrolases
BT2 glycosidases
BT3 hydrolases
BT4 enzymes
NT1 α-amylase
NT1 β-amylase
rt starch

amyloglucosidase
USE **glucan 1,4-α-glucosidase**

AMYLOID
BT1 glycoproteins
BT2 proteins
BT3 peptides
rt amyloidosis
rt starch

AMYLOIDOSIS
BT1 skin diseases
BT2 organic diseases
BT3 diseases
rt amyloid

AMYLOODINIUM
BT1 sarcomastigophora
BT2 protozoa
NT1 amyloodinium ocellatum

AMYLOODINIUM OCELLATUM
BT1 amyloodinium
BT2 sarcomastigophora
BT3 protozoa

AMYLOPECTIN
BT1 starch
BT2 absorbents
BT2 glucans
BT3 polysaccharides
BT4 carbohydrates

AMYLOSE
BT1 starch
BT2 absorbents
BT2 glucans
BT3 polysaccharides
BT4 carbohydrates

AMYLOSTEREUM
BT1 aphyllophorales
NT1 amylostereum areolatum
rt stereum

AMYLOSTEREUM AREOLATUM
uf *stereum areolatum*
BT1 amylostereum
BT2 aphyllophorales

AMYNA
uf *ilattia*
BT1 noctuidae
BT2 lepidoptera
NT1 amyna octo

AMYNA OCTO
BT1 amyna
BT2 noctuidae
BT3 lepidoptera

AMYNOTHRIPS
BT1 phlaeothripidae
BT2 thysanoptera
NT1 amynothrips andersoni

AMYNOTHRIPS ANDERSONI
BT1 amynothrips
BT2 phlaeothripidae
BT3 thysanoptera

AMYOTEA
BT1 pentatomidae
BT2 heteroptera
NT1 amyotea malabarica

AMYOTEA MALABARICA
BT1 amyotea
BT2 pentatomidae
BT3 heteroptera

β-AMYRIN
(for retrieval spell out "beta")
BT1 triterpenoids
BT2 terpenoids
BT3 isoprenoids
BT4 lipids

AMYRIS
BT1 rutaceae
NT1 amyris balsamifera
NT1 amyris madrensis
NT1 amyris plumieri

AMYRIS BALSAMIFERA
BT1 amyris
BT2 rutaceae
BT1 incense plants

AMYRIS MADRENSIS
BT1 amyris
BT2 rutaceae
BT1 ornamental woody plants

AMYRIS PLUMIERI
BT1 amyris
BT2 rutaceae

ANABAENA
BT1 cyanobacteria
BT2 prokaryotes
NT1 anabaena azollae
NT1 anabaena circinalis
NT1 anabaena cylindrica
NT1 anabaena doliolum
NT1 anabaena flos-aquae
NT1 anabaena hassalii
NT1 anabaena scheremetievi
NT1 anabaena variabilis

ANABAENA AZOLLAE
BT1 anabaena
BT2 cyanobacteria
BT3 prokaryotes

ANABAENA CIRCINALIS
BT1 anabaena
BT2 cyanobacteria
BT3 prokaryotes

ANABAENA CYLINDRICA
BT1 anabaena
BT2 cyanobacteria
BT3 prokaryotes

ANABAENA DOLIOLUM
BT1 anabaena
BT2 cyanobacteria
BT3 prokaryotes

ANABAENA FLOS-AQUAE
BT1 anabaena
BT2 cyanobacteria
BT3 prokaryotes

ANABAENA HASSALII
BT1 anabaena
BT2 cyanobacteria
BT3 prokaryotes

ANABAENA SCHEREMETIEVI
BT1 anabaena
BT2 cyanobacteria
BT3 prokaryotes

ANABAENA VARIABILIS
BT1 anabaena
BT2 cyanobacteria
BT3 prokaryotes

ANABANTIDAE
HN from 1990
BT1 perciformes
BT2 osteichthyes
BT3 fishes
NT1 anabas
NT2 anabas testudineus

ANABAS
HN from 1990
BT1 anabantidae
BT2 perciformes
BT3 osteichthyes
BT4 fishes
NT1 anabas testudineus

ANABAS TESTUDINEUS
HN from 1990
BT1 anabas
BT2 anabantidae
BT3 perciformes
BT4 osteichthyes
BT5 fishes

ANABASINE
BT1 botanical insecticides
BT2 insecticides
BT3 pesticides
BT1 pyridine alkaloids
BT2 alkaloids
BT2 pyridines
BT3 heterocyclic nitrogen compounds
BT4 organic nitrogen compounds

ANABASIS
BT1 chenopodiaceae
NT1 anabasis aphylla
NT1 anabasis salsa

ANABASIS APHYLLA
BT1 anabasis
BT2 chenopodiaceae
BT1 insecticidal plants
BT2 pesticidal plants
BT1 medicinal plants

ANABASIS SALSA
BT1 anabasis
BT2 chenopodiaceae

ANABOLIC STEROIDS
uf steroids, anabolic
BT1 anabolics
BT1 growth promoters
BT2 growth regulators
BT2 promoters
BT1 synthetic androgens
BT2 synthetic hormones
NT1 metandienone
NT1 methandriol
NT1 mibolerone
NT1 nandrolone
NT1 oxymesterone
NT1 trenbolone
rt steroids

ANABOLICS
NT1 anabolic steroids
NT2 metandienone
NT2 methandriol
NT2 mibolerone
NT2 nandrolone
NT2 oxymesterone
NT2 trenbolone
NT1 zearalenone

ANABOLISM
BT1 metabolism
rt catabolism

ANABROLEPIS
BT1 encyrtidae

ANABROLEPIS *cont.*
BT2 hymenoptera
NT1 anabrolepis zetterstedtii

ANABROLEPIS ZETTERSTEDTII
BT1 anabrolepis
BT2 encyrtidae
BT3 hymenoptera

ANABRUS
BT1 tettigoniidae
BT2 orthoptera
NT1 anabrus simplex

ANABRUS SIMPLEX
BT1 anabrus
BT2 tettigoniidae
BT3 orthoptera

ANACAMPTODES
BT1 geometridae
BT2 lepidoptera
NT1 anacamptodes clivinaria

ANACAMPTODES CLIVINARIA
BT1 anacamptodes
BT2 geometridae
BT3 lepidoptera

ANACANTHOTERMES
BT1 hodotermitidae
BT2 isoptera
NT1 anacanthotermes ahngerianus
NT1 anacanthotermes ochraceus

ANACANTHOTERMES AHNGERIANUS
BT1 anacanthotermes
BT2 hodotermitidae
BT3 isoptera

ANACANTHOTERMES OCHRACEUS
BT1 anacanthotermes
BT2 hodotermitidae
BT3 isoptera

ANACARDIACEAE
NT1 anacardium
NT2 anacardium curatellifolium
NT2 anacardium occidentale
NT1 buchanania
NT2 buchanania lanzan
NT1 campnosperma
NT2 campnosperma panamensis
NT1 cotinus
NT2 cotinus coggygria
NT2 cotinus obovatus
NT1 cyrtocarpa
NT1 lannea
NT2 lannea coromandelica
NT1 lithraea
NT2 lithraea caustica
NT1 loxopterygium
NT2 loxopterygium huasango
NT1 mangifera
NT2 mangifera altissima
NT2 mangifera indica
NT2 mangifera minor
NT1 ozoroa
NT2 ozoroa mucronata
NT1 poupartia
NT2 poupartia birrea
NT2 poupartia caffra
NT1 rhus
NT2 rhus aromatica
NT2 rhus copallina
NT2 rhus coriaria
NT2 rhus glabra
NT2 rhus microphylla
NT2 rhus parviflora
NT2 rhus succedanea
NT2 rhus trilobata
NT2 rhus typhina
NT2 rhus verniciflua
NT1 schinus
NT2 schinus lentiscifolius
NT2 schinus molle
NT2 schinus terebinthifolius
NT1 semecarpus
NT2 semecarpus anacardium

ANACARDIACEAE *cont.*
NT2 semecarpus gardneri
NT2 semecarpus obscura
NT2 semecarpus subpeltata
NT2 semecarpus walkeri
NT1 spondias
NT2 spondias dulcis
NT2 spondias mombin
NT2 spondias pinnata
NT2 spondias purpurea
NT1 swintonia
NT2 swintonia floribunda
NT1 toxicodendron
NT2 toxicodendron diversilobum
NT2 toxicodendron quercifolium
NT2 toxicodendron radicans

ANACARDIUM
BT1 anacardiaceae
NT1 anacardium curatellifolium
NT1 anacardium occidentale

ANACARDIUM CURATELLIFOLIUM
BT1 anacardium
BT2 anacardiaceae

ANACARDIUM OCCIDENTALE
BT1 anacardium
BT2 anacardiaceae
BT1 forest trees
rt cashews

ANACERATAGALLIA
BT1 cicadellidae
BT2 cicadelloidea
BT3 auchenorrhyncha
BT4 homoptera
rt agallia

anaceratagallia laevis
USE **agallia laevis**

ANACRIDIUM
BT1 acrididae
BT2 orthoptera
NT1 anacridium aegyptium

ANACRIDIUM AEGYPTIUM
BT1 anacridium
BT2 acrididae
BT3 orthoptera

ANACYSTIS
BT1 cyanobacteria
BT2 prokaryotes
NT1 anacystis cyanea
NT1 anacystis incerta
NT1 anacystis nidulans

ANACYSTIS CYANEA
BT1 anacystis
BT2 cyanobacteria
BT3 prokaryotes

ANACYSTIS INCERTA
BT1 anacystis
BT2 cyanobacteria
BT3 prokaryotes

ANACYSTIS NIDULANS
BT1 anacystis
BT2 cyanobacteria
BT3 prokaryotes

ANADARA
BT1 arcidae
BT2 bivalvia
BT3 mollusca

ANADASMUS
BT1 stenomidae
BT2 lepidoptera
NT1 anadasmus porinodes

ANADASMUS PORINODES
BT1 anadasmus
BT2 stenomidae
BT3 lepidoptera

ANADENANTHERA
BT1 leguminosae
NT1 anadenanthera macrocarpa
NT1 anadenanthera peregrina

ANADENANTHERA MACROCARPA
HN from 1990
BT1 anadenanthera
BT2 leguminosae
BT1 forest trees

ANADENANTHERA PEREGRINA
BT1 anadenanthera
BT2 leguminosae

ANAEMIA
AF anemia
BT1 blood disorders
BT2 animal disorders
BT3 disorders
NT1 aplastic anaemia
NT1 equine infectious anaemia
NT1 haemoglobinuria
NT1 haemolytic anaemia
NT1 hypochromic anaemia
NT1 iron deficiency anaemia
NT1 macrocytic anaemia
NT1 megaloblastic anaemia
NT1 microcytic anaemia
NT1 nutritional anaemia
NT1 pernicious anaemia
NT1 sickle cell anaemia
NT1 sideroblastic anaemia
NT1 thalassaemia
rt cachexia
rt chicken anaemia agent
rt erythrocytes
rt gaucher's disease
rt haemoglobin
rt haemoglobin value
rt haemolysis

ANAEROBES
uf *microorganisms, anaerobic*
BT1 microorganisms
rt aerobes
rt anaerobic conditions
rt anaerobiosis
rt anoxia
rt oxygen
rt oxygen requirement

ANAEROBIC CONDITIONS
BT1 atmosphere
rt anaerobes
rt anaerobic digesters
rt anaerobiosis
rt anoxia
rt oxygen
rt soil air

ANAEROBIC DIGESTERS
BT1 digesters
BT2 equipment
rt anaerobic conditions
rt anaerobic digestion
rt anaerobic treatment

ANAEROBIC DIGESTION
BT1 anaerobic treatment
rt anaerobic digesters
rt biogas
rt methane production
rt wastes

anaerobic stabilization
USE **anaerobic treatment**

ANAEROBIC TREATMENT
uf *anaerobic stabilization*
NT1 anaerobic digestion
rt aerobic treatment
rt anaerobic digesters
rt anoxia
rt methane production
rt odour abatement
rt slurries
rt treatment
rt waste treatment

ANAEROBIOSIS
rt anaerobes
rt anaerobic conditions
rt anoxia
rt oxygen
rt oxygen requirement
rt soil air

ANAESTHESIA
AF anesthesia
NT1 conduction anaesthesia
NT1 electronarcosis
NT1 local anaesthesia
rt acupuncture
rt anaesthetics
rt dissociation
rt narcosis
rt preanaesthetic medication
rt surgical operations

ANAESTHETICS
AF anesthetics
uf *narcotics*
BT1 neurotropic drugs
BT2 drugs
NT1 inhaled anaesthetics
NT2 ethyl ether
NT2 halothane
NT2 methoxyflurane
NT2 nitrous oxide
NT1 injectable anaesthetics
NT2 chloral hydrate
NT2 etomidate
NT2 etorphine
NT2 fentanyl
NT2 ketamine
NT2 methadone
NT2 methitural
NT2 metomidate
NT2 pentobarbital
NT2 phencyclidine
NT2 phenobarbital
NT2 thiopental
NT2 urethane
NT1 local anaesthetics
NT2 benzocaine
NT2 lidocaine
NT2 procaine
rt anaesthesia
rt narcotic antagonists

ANAGALLIS
BT1 primulaceae
NT1 anagallis arvensis

ANAGALLIS ARVENSIS
BT1 anagallis
BT2 primulaceae
BT1 antiviral plants
BT1 nematicidal plants
BT2 pesticidal plants
BT1 ornamental herbaceous plants

anagasta
USE **ephestia**

anagasta kuehniella
USE **ephestia kuehniella**

ANAGONIA
BT1 tachinidae
BT2 diptera
NT1 anagonia anguliventris

ANAGONIA ANGULIVENTRIS
BT1 anagonia
BT2 tachinidae
BT3 diptera

anagrapha
USE **syngrapha**

ANAGRUS
BT1 mymaridae
BT2 hymenoptera
NT1 anagrus atomus
NT1 anagrus epos

ANAGRUS ATOMUS
BT1 anagrus
BT2 mymaridae
BT3 hymenoptera

ANAGRUS EPOS
BT1 anagrus
BT2 mymaridae
BT3 hymenoptera

ANAGYRUS
BT1 encyrtidae
BT2 hymenoptera

ANAGYRUS *cont.*
NT1 anagyrus fusciventris
NT1 anagyrus pseudococci

ANAGYRUS FUSCIVENTRIS
BT1 anagyrus
BT2 encyrtidae
BT3 hymenoptera

ANAGYRUS PSEUDOCOCCI
BT1 anagyrus
BT2 encyrtidae
BT3 hymenoptera

ANAL GLANDS
BT1 glands (animal)
BT2 body parts
BT2 glands
rt anus

ANALEPTICS
BT1 neurotropic drugs
BT2 drugs
NT1 amfetamine
NT1 caffeine
NT1 diprenorphine
NT1 doxapram
NT1 strychnine
rt amphetamines
rt stimulants

ANALGESICS
uf *pain killers*
BT1 neurotropic drugs
BT2 drugs
NT1 acetaminophen
NT1 aspirin
NT1 codeine
NT1 etorphine
NT1 eugenol
NT1 fentanyl
NT1 indometacin
NT1 metergoline
NT1 methadone
NT1 morphine
NT1 opium
NT1 oxyphenbutazone
NT1 pethidine
NT1 phenacetin
NT1 phenazone
NT1 phenylbutazone
NT1 quinine
NT1 salicin
NT1 salicylamide
NT1 sodium salicylate
NT1 xylazine
rt pain

ANALGIDAE
BT1 astigmata
BT2 acari
NT1 megninia
NT2 megninia cubitalis
NT2 megninia ginglymura

ANALOGS
BF analogues
rt juvenile hormone analogs
rt meat analogs
rt methionine hydroxy analog

ANALOGUES
AF analogs
rt chemicals
rt computers
rt juvenile hormone analogues
rt meat analogues
rt methionine hydroxy analogue
rt models

ANALYSIS
rt analytical methods
rt assays
rt blood analysis (agricola)
rt chemical analysis
rt chromosome analysis
rt computer analysis
rt detection
rt determination
rt dimensional analysis
rt economic analysis
rt factor analysis

ANALYSIS *cont.*
rt fertilizer analysis
rt food analysis (agricola)
rt genetic analysis
rt genome analysis
rt growth analysis
rt normal values
rt particle size analysis
rt plant analysis
rt pollen analysis
rt problem analysis
rt quantitative analysis
rt resolution
rt simultaneous equation analysis
rt single equation analysis
rt sociological analysis
rt soil analysis
rt spatial equilibrium analysis
rt statistical analysis
rt stress analysis
rt task analysis (agricola)
rt tests

ANALYSIS OF COVARIANCE
uf *covariance analysis*
BT1 statistical analysis
BT2 data analysis
BT2 statistics
rt analysis of variance
rt covariance
rt variance
rt variance components
rt variance covariance matrix

ANALYSIS OF VARIANCE
uf *variance analysis*
BT1 statistical analysis
BT2 data analysis
BT2 statistics
rt analysis of covariance
rt variance
rt variance components
rt variance covariance matrix

ANALYTICAL METHODS
uf *analytical techniques*
BT1 methodology
NT1 anodic stripping voltammetry
NT1 babcock method
NT1 chromatography
NT2 gas chromatography
NT3 pyrolysis gas chromatography
NT2 gas liquid chromatography
NT2 gel filtration chromatography
NT2 ion exchange chromatography
NT2 liquid chromatography
NT3 hplc
NT2 lysimetric chromatography
NT2 paper chromatography
NT3 northern blotting
NT3 southern blotting
NT2 spot test chromatography
NT2 thin layer chromatography
NT1 colorimetry
NT1 coprecipitation
NT1 densitometry
NT1 direct microscopic count
NT1 dye binding
NT2 amido black method
NT1 electrometric methods
NT1 electronic separation
NT1 electrophoresis
NT2 immunoelectrophoresis
NT3 counterimmunoelectro-phoresis
NT2 isoelectric focusing
NT2 northern blotting
NT2 page
NT3 sds-page
NT2 pulsed field electrophoresis
NT2 southern blotting
NT1 electrostatic separation
NT1 electroultrafiltration
NT1 flocculation
NT1 fractionation
NT1 gamma attenuation
NT1 gerber method

ANALYTICAL METHODS *cont.*
NT1 interferometry
NT1 kjeldahl method
NT1 kofranyi method
NT1 liquid scintillation counting
NT1 mojonnier method
NT1 nephelometry
NT1 neutron activation analysis
NT1 neutron moderation
NT1 photometry
NT2 flame photometry
NT3 absorption flame photometry
NT1 polarography
NT1 qualitative techniques
NT1 radiometry
NT1 rapid methods
NT1 reflectometry
NT2 time domain reflectometry
NT1 refractometry
NT1 ring test
NT1 rose-gottlieb method
NT1 sediment test
NT1 selective dissolution
NT1 specific ion electrodes
NT1 spectrophotometry
NT2 atomic absorption spectrophotometry
NT2 infrared spectrophotometry
NT1 spectroscopy
NT2 atomic absorption spectroscopy
NT2 atomic fluorescence spectroscopy
NT2 electron paramagnetic resonance spectroscopy
NT2 fluorescence emission spectroscopy
NT2 infrared spectroscopy
NT2 laser fluorescence spectroscopy
NT2 mossbauer spectroscopy
NT2 nuclear magnetic resonance spectroscopy
NT2 photoelectron spectroscopy
NT2 plasma emission spectroscopy
NT2 spectral analysis
NT2 ultraviolet spectroscopy
NT1 thermal analysis
NT1 thermogravimetry
NT1 titration
NT2 formol titration method
NT1 titrimetry
NT2 thermometric titrimetry
NT1 turbidimetry
NT1 ultracentrifugation
NT1 van gulik method
NT1 weibull-stoldt method
NT1 wet digestion
NT1 x ray diffraction
rt analysis
rt extraction
rt laboratory methods
rt oxidation
rt techniques
rt tests

analytical techniques
USE **analytical methods**

ANAMET PROCESS
HN from 1990
BT1 processing
BT1 waste water treatment
BT2 waste treatment
rt sugar refining

ANAMIRTA
BT1 menispermaceae
NT1 anamirta cocculus

ANAMIRTA COCCULUS
uf menispermum cocculus
BT1 anamirta
BT2 menispermaceae
BT1 medicinal plants

ANANAS
BT1 bromeliaceae
NT1 ananas comosus

ANANAS COMOSUS
BT1 ananas
BT2 bromeliaceae
rt pineapples

ANAPHALIS
BT1 compositae
NT1 anaphalis contorta
NT1 anaphalis morrisonicola

ANAPHALIS CONTORTA
BT1 anaphalis
BT2 compositae
BT1 antifungal plants
BT1 medicinal plants

ANAPHALIS MORRISONICOLA
BT1 anaphalis
BT2 compositae

ANAPHES
uf patasson
BT1 mymaridae
BT2 hymenoptera
NT1 anaphes flavipes
NT1 anaphes fuscipennis

ANAPHES FLAVIPES
BT1 anaphes
BT2 mymaridae
BT3 hymenoptera

ANAPHES FUSCIPENNIS
BT1 anaphes
BT2 mymaridae
BT3 hymenoptera

ANAPHOTHRIPS
BT1 thripidae
BT2 thysanoptera
NT1 anaphothrips obscurus

ANAPHOTHRIPS OBSCURUS
BT1 anaphothrips
BT2 thripidae
BT3 thysanoptera

anaphylactic reactions
USE **anaphylaxis**

anaphylactic shock
USE **anaphylaxis**

ANAPHYLAXIS
(acute immediate hypersensitivity, generalized or localized)
uf anaphylactic reactions
uf anaphylactic shock
BT1 immediate hypersensitivity
BT2 hypersensitivity
BT3 immune response
BT4 immunity
rt allergies

anaphylaxis, food
USE **food allergies**

anaphylaxis, passive cutaneous
USE **passive cutaneous anaphylaxis test**

ANAPLASMA
BT1 anaplasmataceae
BT2 rickettsiales
BT3 bacteria
BT4 prokaryotes
NT1 anaplasma centrale
NT1 anaplasma marginale
NT1 anaplasma ovis
rt anaplasmosis

ANAPLASMA CENTRALE
BT1 anaplasma
BT2 anaplasmataceae
BT3 rickettsiales
BT4 bacteria
BT5 prokaryotes

ANAPLASMA MARGINALE
BT1 anaplasma
BT2 anaplasmataceae
BT3 rickettsiales
BT4 bacteria
BT5 prokaryotes

ANAPLASMA OVIS
BT1 anaplasma
BT2 anaplasmataceae
BT3 rickettsiales
BT4 bacteria
BT5 prokaryotes

ANAPLASMATACEAE
BT1 rickettsiales
BT2 bacteria
BT3 prokaryotes
NT1 aegyptianella
NT2 aegyptianella pullorum
NT1 anaplasma
NT2 anaplasma centrale
NT2 anaplasma marginale
NT2 anaplasma ovis
NT1 eperythrozoon
NT2 eperythrozoon coccoides
NT2 eperythrozoon felis
NT2 eperythrozoon ovis
NT2 eperythrozoon suis
NT2 eperythrozoon wenyoni
NT1 haemobartonella
NT2 haemobartonella bovis
NT2 haemobartonella canis
NT2 haemobartonella felis
NT2 haemobartonella muris
NT1 paranaplasma
NT2 paranaplasma caudata

ANAPLASMOSIS
BT1 bacterial diseases
BT2 infectious diseases
BT3 diseases
BT1 cattle diseases
BT2 animal diseases
BT3 diseases
BT1 tickborne diseases
BT2 vector-borne diseases
BT3 diseases
rt anaplasma

ANAPULVINARIA
BT1 coccidae
BT2 coccoidea
BT3 sternorrhyncha
BT4 homoptera
NT1 anapulvinaria pistaciae

ANAPULVINARIA PISTACIAE
BT1 anapulvinaria
BT2 coccidae
BT3 coccoidea
BT4 sternorrhyncha
BT5 homoptera

ANARHICHADIDAE
BT1 perciformes
BT2 osteichthyes
BT3 fishes
NT1 anarhichas

ANARHICHAS
BT1 anarhichadidae
BT2 perciformes
BT3 osteichthyes
BT4 fishes

ANARSIA
BT1 gelechiidae
BT2 lepidoptera
NT1 anarsia ephippias
NT1 anarsia lineatella

ANARSIA EPHIPPIAS
BT1 anarsia
BT2 gelechiidae
BT3 lepidoptera

ANARSIA LINEATELLA
BT1 anarsia
BT2 gelechiidae
BT3 lepidoptera

ANAS
BT1 anatidae
BT2 anseriformes
BT3 birds
NT1 anas crecca
NT1 anas discors
NT1 anas gibberifrons
NT1 anas platyrhynchos
NT1 anas querquedula

ANAS CRECCA
BT1 anas
BT2 anatidae
BT3 anseriformes
BT4 birds

ANAS DISCORS
BT1 anas
BT2 anatidae
BT3 anseriformes
BT4 birds

ANAS GIBBERIFRONS
BT1 anas
BT2 anatidae
BT3 anseriformes
BT4 birds

ANAS PLATYRHYNCHOS
uf mallard
BT1 anas
BT2 anatidae
BT3 anseriformes
BT4 birds

ANAS QUERQUEDULA
BT1 anas
BT2 anatidae
BT3 anseriformes
BT4 birds

ANASTATUS
BT1 eupelmidae
BT2 hymenoptera
NT1 anastatus bifasciatus
NT1 anastatus gastropachae
NT1 anastatus japonicus

ANASTATUS BIFASCIATUS
BT1 anastatus
BT2 eupelmidae
BT3 hymenoptera

anastatus disparis
USE **anastatus japonicus**

ANASTATUS GASTROPACHAE
BT1 anastatus
BT2 eupelmidae
BT3 hymenoptera

ANASTATUS JAPONICUS
uf anastatus disparis
BT1 anastatus
BT2 eupelmidae
BT3 hymenoptera

ANASTOMOSIS
BT1 surgical operations

ANASTOMOSIS GROUPS
HN from 1990
rt fungi

ANASTREPHA
BT1 tephritidae
BT2 diptera
NT1 anastrepha fraterculus
NT1 anastrepha ludens
NT1 anastrepha obliqua
NT1 anastrepha pickeli
NT1 anastrepha suspensa

ANASTREPHA FRATERCULUS
BT1 anastrepha
BT2 tephritidae
BT3 diptera

ANASTREPHA LUDENS
BT1 anastrepha
BT2 tephritidae
BT3 diptera

anastrepha mombinpraeoptans
USE **anastrepha obliqua**

ANASTREPHA OBLIQUA
uf anastrepha mombinpraeoptans
BT1 anastrepha
BT2 tephritidae
BT3 diptera

ANASTREPHA PICKELI
BT1 anastrepha

ANASTREPHA PICKELI *cont.*
BT2 tephritidae
BT3 diptera

ANASTREPHA SUSPENSA
BT1 anastrepha
BT2 tephritidae
BT3 diptera

ANATASE
BT1 nonclay minerals
BT2 minerals
BT1 pigments
BT1 titanium dioxide
BT2 oxides
BT3 inorganic compounds
rt paints

ANATIDAE
BT1 anseriformes
BT2 birds
NT1 anas
NT2 anas crecca
NT2 anas discors
NT2 anas gibberifrons
NT2 anas platyrhynchos
NT2 anas querquedula
NT1 anser
NT2 anser caerulescens
NT1 cairina
NT1 cygnus
NT2 cygnus columbianus
NT2 cygnus cygnus
NT3 cygnus cygnus buccinator
NT2 cygnus olor
rt ducks
rt geese
rt muscovy ducks
rt swans

ANATOLIAN
HN from 1990
BT1 buffalo breeds
BT2 breeds

ANATOLIAN BLACK
BT1 cattle breeds
BT2 breeds
BT1 goat breeds
BT2 breeds

ANATOLIAN NATIVE
BT1 horse breeds
BT2 breeds

ANATOMY
BT1 biology
NT1 animal anatomy
NT1 plant anatomy
NT2 seed anatomy
NT2 wood anatomy
NT3 growth rings
NT4 earlywood
NT4 latewood
NT3 latex tubes
NT3 rays
NT3 trabeculae
rt body composition
rt histology
rt morphology

ANATONCHUS
HN from 1990
BT1 mononchidae
BT2 nematoda

ANAUTOGENY
BT1 reproduction
rt autogeny
rt blood-meals

ANAUXITE
BT1 clay minerals
BT2 minerals

ANAX
BT1 aeshnidae
BT2 odonata
NT1 anax guttatus

ANAX GUTTATUS
BT1 anax
BT2 aeshnidae
BT3 odonata

ANCESTORS
rt ancestry

ANCESTRY
NT1 coancestry
NT1 grandparents
NT1 parentage
NT1 parents
NT2 dams (mothers)
NT3 bull dams
NT2 employed parents (agricola)
NT2 fathers
NT2 mothers
NT2 sires
NT3 sire of fetus
rt ancestors
rt breeds
rt inheritance
rt pedigree
rt provenance
rt relationships

ANCHOA
BT1 engraulidae
BT2 clupeiformes
BT3 osteichthyes
BT4 fishes

ANCHOMANES
BT1 araceae
NT1 anchomanes difformis

ANCHOMANES DIFFORMIS
BT1 anchomanes
BT2 araceae
BT1 medicinal plants

ANCHOVIES
BT1 marine fishes
BT2 aquatic animals
BT3 animals
BT3 aquatic organisms
rt anchovy meal
rt anchovy oil
rt coilia
rt engraulidae
rt engraulis

ANCHOVY MEAL
BT1 fish meal
BT2 feeds
BT2 fish products
BT3 animal products
BT4 products
BT2 meal
rt anchovies
rt anchovy oil

ANCHOVY OIL
BT1 fish liver oils
BT2 fish oils
BT3 animal oils
BT4 fatty oils
BT5 oils
BT3 fish products
BT4 animal products
BT5 products
rt anchovies
rt anchovy meal

ANCHUSA
BT1 boraginaceae
NT1 anchusa arvensis
NT1 anchusa officinalis

ANCHUSA ARVENSIS
BT1 anchusa
BT2 boraginaceae

ANCHUSA OFFICINALIS
BT1 anchusa
BT2 boraginaceae
BT1 medicinal plants

ANCIENT MONUMENTS
BT1 monuments
rt archaeological material
rt cultural heritage
rt historic buildings
rt historic sites

ANCILLARY ENTERPRISES
(non-farm activities carried out on farm)
uf *enterprises, ancillary*
BT1 farm enterprises
BT2 enterprises
NT1 farm holidays
NT1 on-farm processing
rt aquaculture
rt camping
rt caravan sites
rt diversification
rt farmhouse accommodation
rt handicrafts
rt non-farm income
rt part time farming

ANCILLARY EQUIPMENT
uf *accessories*
BT1 equipment
rt tools

ANCISTROCACTUS
BT1 cactaceae

ANCISTROCOMA
BT1 ciliophora
BT2 protozoa

ANCISTRUM
BT1 ciliophora
BT2 protozoa
NT1 ancistrum mytili

ANCISTRUM MYTILI
BT1 ancistrum
BT2 ciliophora
BT3 protozoa

ANCORA
BT1 apicomplexa
BT2 protozoa

ANCYLIDAE
BT1 gastropoda
BT2 mollusca
NT1 ancylus
NT2 ancylus fluviatilis

ANCYLIS
BT1 tortricidae
BT2 lepidoptera
NT1 ancylis achatana
NT1 ancylis comptana

ANCYLIS ACHATANA
BT1 ancylis
BT2 tortricidae
BT3 lepidoptera

ANCYLIS COMPTANA
BT1 ancylis
BT2 tortricidae
BT3 lepidoptera

ANCYLOSCELIS
BT1 apidae
BT2 hymenoptera

ANCYLOSTOMA
BT1 ancylostomatidae
BT2 nematoda
NT1 ancylostoma braziliense
NT1 ancylostoma caninum
NT1 ancylostoma ceylanicum
NT1 ancylostoma duodenale
NT1 ancylostoma tubaeforme

ANCYLOSTOMA BRAZILIENSE
BT1 ancylostoma
BT2 ancylostomatidae
BT3 nematoda
rt hookworms

ANCYLOSTOMA CANINUM
BT1 ancylostoma
BT2 ancylostomatidae
BT3 nematoda
rt hookworms

ANCYLOSTOMA CEYLANICUM
BT1 ancylostoma
BT2 ancylostomatidae
BT3 nematoda
rt hookworms

ANCYLOSTOMA DUODENALE
BT1 ancylostoma
BT2 ancylostomatidae
BT3 nematoda
rt hookworms

ANCYLOSTOMA TUBAEFORME
BT1 ancylostoma
BT2 ancylostomatidae
BT3 nematoda
rt hookworms

ANCYLOSTOMATIDAE
BT1 nematoda
NT1 ancylostoma
NT2 ancylostoma braziliense
NT2 ancylostoma caninum
NT2 ancylostoma ceylanicum
NT2 ancylostoma duodenale
NT2 ancylostoma tubaeforme
NT1 bunostomum
NT2 bunostomum phlebotomum
NT2 bunostomum trigonocephalum
NT1 gaigeria
NT2 gaigeria pachyscelis
NT1 globocephalus
NT2 globocephalus urosubulatus
NT1 necator
NT2 necator americanus
NT1 uncinaria
NT2 uncinaria stenocephala
rt animal parasitic nematodes

ANCYLUS
BT1 ancylidae
BT2 gastropoda
BT3 mollusca
NT1 ancylus fluviatilis

ANCYLUS FLUVIATILIS
BT1 ancylus
BT2 ancylidae
BT3 gastropoda
BT4 mollusca

ANCYMIDOL
BT1 growth inhibitors
BT2 inhibitors
BT2 plant growth regulators
BT3 growth regulators

ANCYROCEPHALUS
BT1 dactylogyridae
BT2 monogenea

ANDALUSIAN
BT1 cattle breeds
BT2 breeds
BT1 horse breeds
BT2 breeds

ANDALUSIAN BLACK
BT1 cattle breeds
BT2 breeds

ANDALUSIAN BLACK EARTHS
BT1 vertisols
BT2 soil types (genetic)

ANDALUSIAN BLOND
BT1 cattle breeds
BT2 breeds
BT1 pig breeds
BT2 breeds

ANDALUSIAN SPOTTED
BT1 pig breeds
BT2 breeds

ANDAMAN AND NICOBAR ISLANDS
BT1 india
BT2 south asia
BT3 asia

ANDEAN GROUP
rt bolivia
rt colombia
rt economic regions
rt economic unions
rt ecuador

ANDEAN GROUP *cont.*
rt peru
rt venezuela

ANDEAN POTATO MOTTLE COMOVIRUS
HN from 1990; previously "potato andean mottle virus"
uf *potato andean mottle virus*
BT1 comovirus group
BT2 plant viruses
BT3 plant pathogens
BT4 pathogens
rt potatoes
rt solanum tuberosum

ANDEPTS
BT1 andosols
BT2 soil types (genetic)
NT1 dystrandepts
NT1 vitrandepts

ANDESITE
BT1 soil parent materials

ANDESITE SOILS
BT1 soil types (lithological)

ANDHRA PRADESH
BT1 india
BT2 south asia
BT3 asia

ANDISOLS
BT1 andosols
BT2 soil types (genetic)

ANDORRA
BT1 western europe
BT2 europe
rt france
rt spain

ANDOSOLS
BT1 soil types (genetic)
NT1 andepts
NT2 dystrandepts
NT2 vitrandepts
NT1 andisols
NT1 kuroboku soils
NT1 trumao soils
NT1 vitric andosols
NT1 yellow brown pumice soils
rt volcanic ash soils

ANDRENA
uf *callandrena*
uf *melandrena*
uf *tylandrena*
BT1 apidae
BT2 hymenoptera

ANDRICUS
BT1 cynipidae
BT2 hymenoptera

ANDROCTONUS
BT1 buthidae
BT2 scorpiones
BT3 arachnida
BT4 arthropods
NT1 androctonus aeneas
NT1 androctonus amoreuxi
NT1 androctonus australis
NT2 androctonus australis hector
NT1 androctonus mauretanicus

ANDROCTONUS AENEAS
BT1 androctonus
BT2 buthidae
BT3 scorpiones
BT4 arachnida
BT5 arthropods

ANDROCTONUS AMOREUXI
BT1 androctonus
BT2 buthidae
BT3 scorpiones
BT4 arachnida
BT5 arthropods

ANDROCTONUS AUSTRALIS
BT1 androctonus

ANDROCTONUS AUSTRALIS *cont.*
BT2 buthidae
BT3 scorpiones
BT4 arachnida
BT5 arthropods
NT1 androctonus australis hector

ANDROCTONUS AUSTRALIS HECTOR
HN from 1990
BT1 androctonus australis
BT2 androctonus
BT3 buthidae
BT4 scorpiones
BT5 arachnida
BT6 arthropods

ANDROCTONUS MAURETANICUS
BT1 androctonus
BT2 buthidae
BT3 scorpiones
BT4 arachnida
BT5 arthropods

ANDROECIUM
BT1 flowers
BT2 inflorescences
BT3 plant
NT1 stamens
NT2 anthers
NT3 pollen
rt plant organs

ANDROGENESIS
BT1 parthenogenesis
BT2 reproduction
rt anther culture
rt haploidy
rt sex differentiation

ANDROGENS
BT1 sex hormones
BT2 hormones
NT1 androstenedione
NT1 androsterone
NT1 prasterone
NT1 testosterone
rt steroid hormones
rt steroidogenesis
rt synthetic androgens

androgens, synthetic
USE **synthetic androgens**

ANDROGRAPHIS
BT1 acanthaceae
NT1 andrographis paniculata

ANDROGRAPHIS PANICULATA
BT1 andrographis
BT2 acanthaceae
BT1 medicinal plants

ANDROLAELAPS
uf *haemolaelaps*
BT1 laelapidae
BT2 mesostigmata
BT3 acari
NT1 androlaelaps casalis
NT1 androlaelaps fahrenholzi

ANDROLAELAPS CASALIS
BT1 androlaelaps
BT2 laelapidae
BT3 mesostigmata
BT4 acari

ANDROLAELAPS FAHRENHOLZI
uf *haemolaelaps glasgowi*
BT1 androlaelaps
BT2 laelapidae
BT3 mesostigmata
BT4 acari

ANDROMEDA
BT1 ericaceae
NT1 andromeda polifolia

andromeda japonica
USE **pieris japonica**

ANDROMEDA POLIFOLIA
BT1 andromeda
BT2 ericaceae

ANDROPOGON
BT1 gramineae
NT1 andropogon annulatus
NT1 andropogon bicornis
NT1 andropogon distachyos
NT1 andropogon divergens
NT1 andropogon filifolius
NT1 andropogon gayanus
NT1 andropogon gerardii
NT1 andropogon hallii
NT1 andropogon lateralis
NT1 andropogon paniculatus
NT1 andropogon perligulatus
NT1 andropogon schirensis
NT1 andropogon tectorum
NT1 andropogon virginicus
rt bothriochloa
rt chrysopogon
rt schizachyrium

ANDROPOGON ANNULATUS
BT1 andropogon
BT2 gramineae
BT1 pasture plants

andropogon barbinodis
USE **bothriochloa barbinodis**

ANDROPOGON BICORNIS
BT1 andropogon
BT2 gramineae
BT1 pasture plants

andropogon contortus
USE **heteropogon contortus**

ANDROPOGON DISTACHYOS
BT1 andropogon
BT2 gramineae
BT1 pasture plants

ANDROPOGON DIVERGENS
BT1 andropogon
BT2 gramineae
BT1 pasture plants

ANDROPOGON FILIFOLIUS
BT1 andropogon
BT2 gramineae
BT1 pasture plants

ANDROPOGON GAYANUS
BT1 andropogon
BT2 gramineae
BT1 pasture plants

ANDROPOGON GERARDII
uf *big bluestem*
BT1 andropogon
BT2 gramineae
BT1 pasture plants

andropogon gryllus
USE **chrysopogon gryllus**

ANDROPOGON HALLII
BT1 andropogon
BT2 gramineae
BT1 pasture plants

andropogon ischaemum
USE **bothriochloa ischaemum**

ANDROPOGON LATERALIS
BT1 andropogon
BT2 gramineae
BT1 pasture plants

ANDROPOGON PANICULATUS
BT1 andropogon
BT2 gramineae
BT1 pasture plants

ANDROPOGON PERLIGULATUS
BT1 andropogon
BT2 gramineae
BT1 pasture plants

ANDROPOGON SCHIRENSIS
BT1 andropogon
BT2 gramineae
BT1 pasture plants

andropogon scoparius
USE **schizachyrium scoparium**

andropogon stolonifer
USE **schizachyrium stoloniferum**

ANDROPOGON TECTORUM
BT1 andropogon
BT2 gramineae

ANDROPOGON VIRGINICUS
BT1 andropogon
BT2 gramineae
BT1 pasture plants

ANDROSACE
BT1 primulaceae
NT1 androsace rotundifolia
NT1 androsace septentrionalis

ANDROSACE ROTUNDIFOLIA
BT1 androsace
BT2 primulaceae

ANDROSACE SEPTENTRIONALIS
BT1 androsace
BT2 primulaceae
BT1 medicinal plants

ANDROSTANES
BT1 steroids
BT2 isoprenoids
BT3 lipids
NT1 androstenedione
NT1 androsterone
NT1 metandienone
NT1 methandriol
NT1 methyltestosterone
NT1 oxymesterone
NT1 prasterone
NT1 testosterone

ANDROSTENEDIONE
BT1 androgens
BT2 sex hormones
BT3 hormones
BT1 androstanes
BT2 steroids
BT3 isoprenoids
BT4 lipids
BT1 ketosteroids
BT2 steroids
BT3 isoprenoids
BT4 lipids

ANDROSTERONE
BT1 androgens
BT2 sex hormones
BT3 hormones
BT1 androstanes
BT2 steroids
BT3 isoprenoids
BT4 lipids
BT1 ketosteroids
BT2 steroids
BT3 isoprenoids
BT4 lipids

ANDRYA
BT1 anoplocephalidae
BT2 eucestoda
BT3 cestoda

ANEILEMA
BT1 commelinaceae
NT1 aneilema japonicum
NT1 aneilema keisak

ANEILEMA JAPONICUM
BT1 aneilema
BT2 commelinaceae

ANEILEMA KEISAK
BT1 aneilema
BT2 commelinaceae

ANEMIA
BF anaemia
NT1 aplastic anemia
NT1 equine infectious anemia
NT1 hemolytic anemia
NT1 hypochromic anemia
NT1 iron deficiency anemia
NT1 macrocytic anemia
NT1 megaloblastic anemia
NT1 microcytic anemia

ANEMIA *cont.*
NT1 nutritional anemia
NT1 pernicious anemia
NT1 sickle cell anemia
NT1 sideroblastic anemia
NT1 thalassemia
rt chicken anemia agent

ANEMOMETERS
BT1 meteorological instruments
BT2 instruments
rt wind
rt wind speed

ANEMONE
BT1 ranunculaceae
NT1 anemone canadensis
NT1 anemone coronaria
NT1 anemone hupehensis
NT1 anemone obtusiloba
NT1 anemone palmata
NT1 anemone pavonina
NT1 anemone ranunculoides
NT1 anemone rivularis
rt antifungal plants

ANEMONE CANADENSIS
uf *anemone dichotoma*
BT1 anemone
BT2 ranunculaceae
BT1 ornamental herbaceous plants

ANEMONE CORONARIA
BT1 anemone
BT2 ranunculaceae
BT1 ornamental bulbs
rt tubers

anemone dichotoma
USE **anemone canadensis**

anemone elegans
USE **anemone hupehensis**

anemone hortensis
USE **anemone pavonina**

ANEMONE HUPEHENSIS
uf *anemone elegans*
BT1 anemone
BT2 ranunculaceae
BT1 antibacterial plants
BT1 ornamental herbaceous plants

ANEMONE OBTUSILOBA
BT1 anemone
BT2 ranunculaceae

ANEMONE PALMATA
BT1 anemone
BT2 ranunculaceae
BT1 ornamental bulbs
rt tubers

ANEMONE PAVONINA
uf *anemone hortensis*
BT1 anemone
BT2 ranunculaceae
BT1 ornamental bulbs
rt tubers

ANEMONE RANUNCULOIDES
BT1 anemone
BT2 ranunculaceae

ANEMONE RIVULARIS
BT1 anemone
BT2 ranunculaceae
BT1 ornamental herbaceous plants

ANEMOPSIS
BT1 saururaceae
NT1 anemopsis californica

ANEMOPSIS CALIFORNICA
BT1 anemopsis
BT2 saururaceae

ANENCEPHALY
BT1 aplasia
BT2 congenital abnormalities
BT3 abnormalities

ANENCEPHALY *cont.*
rt teratogenesis

ANESTHESIA
BF anaesthesia
NT1 conduction anesthesia
NT1 local anesthesia
rt anesthetics
rt preanesthetic medication

ANESTHETICS
BF anaesthetics
NT1 inhaled anesthetics
NT1 injectable anesthetics
NT1 local anesthetics
rt anesthesia

ANESTRUS
BF anoestrus
BT1 estrous cycle

ANETHUM
BT1 umbelliferae
NT1 anethum ghoda
NT1 anethum graveolens
NT1 anethum sesquipedale
NT1 anethum sowa
NT1 anethum vareli

ANETHUM GHODA
BT1 anethum
BT2 umbelliferae

ANETHUM GRAVEOLENS
BT1 anethum
BT2 umbelliferae
BT1 antibacterial plants
BT1 antifungal plants
BT1 culinary herbs
BT1 essential oil plants
BT2 oil plants
BT1 medicinal plants
BT1 nematicidal plants
BT2 pesticidal plants
BT1 spice plants
rt dill

ANETHUM SESQUIPEDALE
BT1 anethum
BT2 umbelliferae

ANETHUM SOWA
BT1 anethum
BT2 umbelliferae
BT1 antifungal plants
BT1 essential oil plants
BT2 oil plants

ANETHUM VARELI
BT1 anethum
BT2 umbelliferae

ANEUPLOIDY
uf *monosomics*
uf *polysomics*
BT1 heteroploidy
NT1 monosomy
NT1 trisomy
rt chromosome number
rt somatic reduction

aneurin
USE **thiamin**

ANEURYSM
BT1 vascular diseases
BT2 cardiovascular diseases
BT3 organic diseases
BT4 diseases
rt arteries

ANGELICA
BT1 umbelliferae
NT1 angelica acutiloba
NT1 angelica apaensis
NT1 angelica archangelica
NT1 angelica dahurica
NT1 angelica decursiva
NT1 angelica gigas
NT1 angelica glauca
NT1 angelica keiskei
NT1 angelica koreana
NT1 angelica pachycarpa
NT1 angelica pubescens

ANGELICA *cont.*
NT1 angelica sylvestris
NT1 angelica tschimganica

ANGELICA ACUTILOBA
BT1 angelica
BT2 umbelliferae
BT1 medicinal plants

ANGELICA APAENSIS
BT1 angelica
BT2 umbelliferae

ANGELICA ARCHANGELICA
uf *angelica officinalis*
uf *archangelica officinalis*
BT1 angelica
BT2 umbelliferae
BT1 culinary herbs
BT1 essential oil plants
BT2 oil plants
BT1 insecticidal plants
BT2 pesticidal plants
BT1 medicinal plants

ANGELICA DAHURICA
BT1 angelica
BT2 umbelliferae
BT1 medicinal plants

ANGELICA DECURSIVA
BT1 angelica
BT2 umbelliferae

ANGELICA GIGAS
BT1 angelica
BT2 umbelliferae
BT1 medicinal plants

ANGELICA GLAUCA
BT1 angelica
BT2 umbelliferae

ANGELICA KEISKEI
BT1 angelica
BT2 umbelliferae

ANGELICA KOREANA
BT1 angelica
BT2 umbelliferae
BT1 medicinal plants

angelica officinalis
USE **angelica archangelica**

ANGELICA PACHYCARPA
BT1 angelica
BT2 umbelliferae

ANGELICA PUBESCENS
BT1 angelica
BT2 umbelliferae
BT1 medicinal plants

ANGELICA SYLVESTRIS
BT1 angelica
BT2 umbelliferae
BT1 insecticidal plants
BT2 pesticidal plants

ANGELICA TSCHIMGANICA
BT1 angelica
BT2 umbelliferae

ANGELN
BT1 cattle breeds
BT2 breeds

ANGELN SADDLEBACK
BT1 pig breeds
BT2 breeds

ANGELONIA
BT1 scrophulariaceae
NT1 angelonia salicariifolia

angelonia grandiflora
USE **angelonia salicariifolia**

ANGELONIA SALICARIIFOLIA
uf *angelonia grandiflora*
BT1 angelonia
BT2 scrophulariaceae
BT1 ornamental herbaceous plants

angiography
USE **radiography**

ANGIOMA
BT1 neoplasms
BT2 diseases

angiopathy
USE **vascular diseases**

ANGIOSPERMS
rt plants

ANGIOSTRONGYLIDAE
BT1 nematoda
NT1 aelurostrongylus
NT2 aelurostrongylus abstrusus
NT1 angiostrongylus
NT2 angiostrongylus cantonensis
NT2 angiostrongylus costaricensis
NT2 angiostrongylus malaysiensis
NT2 angiostrongylus vasorum
rt animal parasitic nematodes

ANGIOSTRONGYLUS
BT1 angiostrongylidae
BT2 nematoda
NT1 angiostrongylus cantonensis
NT1 angiostrongylus costaricensis
NT1 angiostrongylus malaysiensis
NT1 angiostrongylus vasorum

ANGIOSTRONGYLUS CANTONENSIS
BT1 angiostrongylus
BT2 angiostrongylidae
BT3 nematoda

ANGIOSTRONGYLUS COSTARICENSIS
BT1 angiostrongylus
BT2 angiostrongylidae
BT3 nematoda

ANGIOSTRONGYLUS MALAYSIENSIS
BT1 angiostrongylus
BT2 angiostrongylidae
BT3 nematoda

ANGIOSTRONGYLUS VASORUM
BT1 angiostrongylus
BT2 angiostrongylidae
BT3 nematoda

ANGIOTENSIN
BT1 neuropeptides
BT2 peptides
BT1 oligopeptides
BT2 peptides
BT1 renal hormones
BT2 hormones
BT1 slow reacting substances
rt saralasin

ANGLE COUNT
BT1 forest inventories
BT2 inventories
rt mensuration
rt relascopes
rt sampling

ANGLE OF INCIDENCE
rt light
rt reflection

ANGLE OF REPOSE
rt friction
rt sliding
rt sliding friction

angle of wetting
USE **contact angle**
OR **wetting**

ANGLERFISHES
BT1 marine fishes
BT2 aquatic animals
BT3 animals
BT3 aquatic organisms

ANGLERFISHES *cont.*
rt lophius

ANGLING
(recreational fishing)
uf *fishing, recreational*
uf *sport fishing*
BT1 water recreation
BT2 recreation
NT1 sea fishing
rt animal sports
rt game fishes

ANGLO-NUBIAN
BT1 goat breeds
BT2 breeds

ANGLOPHONE AFRICA
uf *africa, english speaking*
uf *english speaking africa*
rt africa
rt africa south of sahara
rt botswana
rt francophone africa
rt gambia
rt ghana
rt kenya
rt lesotho
rt liberia
rt malawi
rt mauritius
rt namibia
rt nigeria
rt seychelles
rt sierra leone
rt south africa
rt st. helena
rt sudan
rt swaziland
rt tanzania
rt uganda
rt zambia
rt zimbabwe

ANGOLA
BT1 sadcc countries
BT1 southern africa
BT2 africa south of sahara
BT3 africa
rt developing countries
rt portugal

ANGONI
BT1 cattle breeds
BT2 breeds

ANGOPHORA
BT1 myrtaceae
NT1 angophora floribunda
rt forest trees

ANGOPHORA FLORIBUNDA
BT1 angophora
BT2 myrtaceae

ANGORA
BT1 goat breeds
BT2 breeds

angouan
USE **comoros**

ANGRAECOPSIS
BT1 orchidaceae
NT1 angraecopsis gracillima

ANGRAECOPSIS GRACILLIMA
BT1 angraecopsis
BT2 orchidaceae
BT1 ornamental orchids

ANGRAECUM
BT1 orchidaceae
NT1 angraecum eburneum

ANGRAECUM EBURNEUM
BT1 angraecum
BT2 orchidaceae

angraecum sesquipedale
USE **macroplectrum sesquipedale**

ANGUILLA
BT1 anguillidae

ANGUILLA *cont.*
BT2 anguilliformes
BT3 osteichthyes
BT4 fishes
NT1 anguilla japonica
NT1 anguilla reinhardtii
NT1 anguilla rostrata
rt eels

anguilla anguilla
USE **european eels**

ANGUILLA ISLAND
uf *st. kitts-nevis-anguilla*
BT1 caribbean
BT2 america

ANGUILLA JAPONICA
BT1 anguilla
BT2 anguillidae
BT3 anguilliformes
BT4 osteichthyes
BT5 fishes

ANGUILLA REINHARDTII
BT1 anguilla
BT2 anguillidae
BT3 anguilliformes
BT4 osteichthyes
BT5 fishes

ANGUILLA ROSTRATA
BT1 anguilla
BT2 anguillidae
BT3 anguilliformes
BT4 osteichthyes
BT5 fishes

ANGUILLIDAE
BT1 anguilliformes
BT2 osteichthyes
BT3 fishes
NT1 anguilla
NT2 anguilla japonica
NT2 anguilla reinhardtii
NT2 anguilla rostrata
rt eels

ANGUILLIFORMES
BT1 osteichthyes
BT2 fishes
NT1 anguillidae
NT2 anguilla
NT3 anguilla japonica
NT3 anguilla reinhardtii
NT3 anguilla rostrata
NT1 muraenidae
NT2 gymnothorax
NT2 muraena
NT3 muraena helena

ANGUILLOSPORA
BT1 deuteromycotina

ANGUINA
BT1 anguinidae
BT2 nematoda
NT1 anguina agrostis
NT1 anguina graminis
NT1 anguina tritici

ANGUINA AGROSTIS
BT1 anguina
BT2 anguinidae
BT3 nematoda

ANGUINA GRAMINIS
BT1 anguina
BT2 anguinidae
BT3 nematoda

ANGUINA TRITICI
BT1 anguina
BT2 anguinidae
BT3 nematoda

ANGUINIDAE
BT1 nematoda
NT1 anguina
NT2 anguina agrostis
NT2 anguina graminis
NT2 anguina tritici
NT1 ditylenchus
NT2 ditylenchus angustus

ANGUINIDAE *cont.*
NT2 ditylenchus destructor
NT2 ditylenchus dipsaci
NT2 ditylenchus myceliophagus
NT1 neoditylenchus
NT1 nothotylenchus
NT1 subanguina
rt plant parasitic nematodes

angular velocity
USE **rotational speed**

ANGYLOCALYX
BT1 leguminosae
NT1 angylocalyx oligophyllus

ANGYLOCALYX OLIGOPHYLLUS
BT1 angylocalyx
BT2 leguminosae

ANHUI
uf *anhwei*
uf *china (anhwei)*
BT1 china
BT2 east asia
BT3 asia

anhwei
USE **anhui**

ANHYDRITE
BT1 nonclay minerals
BT2 minerals

ANHYDROBIOSIS
HN from 1990
BT1 dormancy

ANHYDROUS AMMONIA
uf *ammonia, anhydrous*
uf *ammonia, liquid*
uf *liquid ammonia*
BT1 ammonium fertilizers
BT2 nitrogen fertilizers
BT3 fertilizers
rt ammonia

ANIBA
BT1 lauraceae
NT1 aniba canelilla
NT1 aniba duckei
NT1 aniba hostmanniana
NT1 aniba rosaeodora
NT1 aniba terminalis

ANIBA CANELILLA
BT1 aniba
BT2 lauraceae

ANIBA DUCKEI
BT1 aniba
BT2 lauraceae

ANIBA HOSTMANNIANA
BT1 aniba
BT2 lauraceae

ANIBA ROSAEODORA
BT1 aniba
BT2 lauraceae

ANIBA TERMINALIS
BT1 aniba
BT2 lauraceae

ANIGOZANTHOS
uf *macropidia*
BT1 haemodoraceae
NT1 anigozanthos flavidus
NT1 anigozanthos fuliginosus
NT1 anigozanthos manglesii

ANIGOZANTHOS FLAVIDUS
BT1 anigozanthos
BT2 haemodoraceae
BT1 ornamental herbaceous plants

ANIGOZANTHOS FULIGINOSUS
BT1 anigozanthos
BT2 haemodoraceae
BT1 ornamental herbaceous plants

ANIGOZANTHOS MANGLESII
BT1 anigozanthos

ANIGOZANTHOS MANGLESII *cont.*
BT2 haemodoraceae
BT1 ornamental herbaceous plants

anilastus
USE **campoletis**

ANILAZINE
BT1 unclassified fungicides
BT2 fungicides
BT3 pesticides

ANILIDE FUNGICIDES
BT1 fungicides
BT2 pesticides
NT1 benzanilide fungicides
NT2 benodanil
NT2 flutolanil
NT2 mebenil
NT1 cyprofuram
NT1 furanilide fungicides
NT2 cyclafuramid
NT2 fenfuram
NT2 furcarbanil
NT2 furmecyclox
NT1 ofurace
NT1 oxadixyl
NT1 oxathiin fungicides
NT2 carboxin
NT2 oxycarboxin
NT1 pyracarbolid

ANILIDE HERBICIDES
BT1 amide herbicides
BT2 herbicides
BT3 pesticides
NT1 arylalanine herbicides
NT2 benzoylprop-ethyl
NT2 flamprop
NT1 chloranocryl
NT1 chloroacetanilide herbicides
NT2 acetochlor
NT2 alachlor
NT2 butachlor
NT2 delachlor
NT2 diethatyl
NT2 dimethachlor
NT2 metazachlor
NT2 metolachlor
NT2 pretilachlor
NT2 propachlor
NT2 prynachlor
NT2 terbuchlor
NT1 clomeprop
NT1 cypromid
NT1 diflufenican
NT1 mefenacet
NT1 monalide
NT1 pentanochlor
NT1 perfluidone
NT1 propanil

ANILOFOS
BT1 organophosphorus herbicides
BT2 herbicides
BT3 pesticides
BT2 organophosphorus pesticides
BT3 organophosphorus compounds

ANIMAL ANATOMY
uf *body*
uf *body components*
BT1 anatomy
BT2 biology
rt body fluids
rt body parts
rt body regions
rt integument
rt nervous system
rt organs
rt serosa

ANIMAL BEHAVIOR
BF animal behaviour
BT1 behavior

ANIMAL BEHAVIOUR
AF animal behavior
BT1 behaviour

ANIMAL BEHAVIOUR *cont.*
NT1 aggregation
NT1 broodiness
NT1 burrowing
NT1 clustering
NT1 communication between animals
NT2 dances
NT2 piping
NT1 drifting
NT1 dust bathing
NT1 eviction
NT1 fanning
NT1 fearfulness
NT2 gunshyness
NT1 fright
NT1 grooming
NT1 group effect
NT1 imprinting
NT1 mimicry
NT1 nesting
NT1 social dominance
NT1 soil ingestion
NT1 supersedure
NT1 swarming
NT2 absconding
NT2 swarming impulse
NT2 swarming preparations
NT1 tameness
NT1 territoriality
rt animal burrows
rt animal experiments
rt animal housing
rt animal welfare
rt conditioned reflexes
rt group size
rt heat regulation
rt milkability
rt movement in soil
rt orientation
rt psychology
rt training of animals

ANIMAL BREEDING
uf *breeding, animal*
BT1 breeding
NT1 horse breeding
rt animal breeding methods
rt animal husbandry
rt breeders' rights
rt breeding efficiency
rt breeding life
rt breeding season
rt breeding value
rt breeds
rt broiler lines
rt embryo transfer
rt herd improvement
rt inheritance

ANIMAL BREEDING METHODS
BT1 breeding methods
BT2 methodology
NT1 artificial insemination
NT2 intrauterine insemination
NT1 crossbreeding
NT1 mating combinations
NT2 polygamy
NT2 polygyny
NT1 outbreeding
NT1 progeny testing
NT2 boar progeny testing
NT2 contemporary comparisons
NT3 improved contemporary comparisons
NT1 sire evaluation
NT2 direct sire comparisons
rt animal breeding
rt provenance trials

ANIMAL BURROWS
BT1 soil morphological features
rt animal behaviour
rt burrowing

ANIMAL CLINICS
uf *clinics, animal*

ANIMAL COMPETITION
HN from 1990
BT1 biological competition

ANIMAL DISEASES
uf *livestock disorders*
BT1 diseases
NT1 bee diseases
NT2 acarine disease
NT2 amoeba disease
NT2 apimyiasis
NT2 chalk brood
NT2 foul brood
NT3 american foul brood
NT3 european foul brood
NT2 nosema disease
NT2 rickettsial disease
NT2 stone brood
NT1 cat diseases
NT1 cattle diseases
NT2 anaplasmosis
NT2 anthrax
NT2 bovine spongiform encephalopathy
NT2 foot and mouth disease
NT2 rinderpest
NT1 dog diseases
NT1 fish diseases
NT1 goat diseases
NT1 horse diseases
NT2 african horse sickness
NT2 contagious equine metritis
NT2 dourine
NT2 equine infectious anaemia
NT2 glanders
NT2 sweet itch
NT1 mink diseases
NT2 aleutian disease
NT2 wet belly disease
NT1 poultry diseases
NT2 avian infectious bursitis
NT2 avian leukosis
NT2 duck diseases
NT2 egg drop syndrome
NT2 fowl diseases
NT2 marek's disease
NT2 newcastle disease
NT1 rabbit diseases
NT1 sheep diseases
NT2 border disease
NT2 foot rot
NT2 scrapie
NT2 sheep pox
NT1 swine diseases
NT2 african swine fever
NT2 foot and mouth disease
NT2 porcine stress syndrome
NT2 swine dysentery
NT2 swine fever
NT1 young animal diseases
NT2 calf diseases
NT2 foal diseases
NT2 lamb diseases
NT2 omphalitis
NT2 piglet diseases
rt animal pathology
rt disease statistics
rt organic diseases
rt systemic diseases
rt zoonoses

ANIMAL DISORDERS
(including human disorders)
BT1 disorders
NT1 blood disorders
NT2 acidaemia
NT3 butyryl acidaemia
NT3 citrullinaemia
NT3 histidinaemia
NT3 methylmalonic acidaemia
NT3 propionic acidaemia
NT2 anaemia
NT3 aplastic anaemia
NT3 equine infectious anaemia
NT3 haemoglobinuria
NT3 haemolytic anaemia
NT3 hypochromic anaemia
NT3 iron deficiency anaemia
NT3 macrocytic anaemia
NT3 megaloblastic anaemia
NT3 microcytic anaemia
NT3 nutritional anaemia
NT3 pernicious anaemia
NT3 sickle cell anaemia
NT3 sideroblastic anaemia

ANIMAL DISORDERS *cont.*
NT3 thalassaemia
NT2 avian erythroblastosis
NT2 blood coagulation disorders
NT3 disseminated intravascular coagulation
NT3 haemophilia
NT3 thrombocythaemia
NT3 thrombocytopenia
NT3 thrombocytopenic purpura
NT3 thrombosis
NT2 blood protein disorders
NT3 hyperproteinaemia
NT4 hyperlipoproteinaemia
NT5 hyperchylomicronaemia
NT4 hyperprolactinaemia
NT3 hypoproteinaemia
NT4 hypoalbuminaemia
NT4 hypogammaglobulinaemia
NT4 hypolipoproteinaemia
NT5 abetalipoproteinaemia
NT4 hypoprothrombinaemia
NT3 methaemoglobinaemia
NT3 myohaemoglobinaemia
NT2 bone marrow disorders
NT3 aplastic anaemia
NT2 haemolysis
NT2 histiocytosis
NT2 hypovolaemia
NT2 leukocyte disorders
NT3 avian myeloblastosis
NT3 chediak-higashi syndrome
NT3 eosinophilia
NT4 tropical eosinophilia
NT3 leukaemia
NT3 leukopenia
NT3 leukosis
NT4 avian leukosis
NT4 bovine leukosis
NT3 monocytosis
NT2 lipaemia
NT2 pancytopenia
NT2 polycythaemia
NT2 polycythaemia vera
NT1 fetal development disorders
NT1 functional disorders
NT2 behavior disorders (agricola)
NT2 circulatory disorders
NT3 vasoconstriction
NT2 collapse
NT2 digestive disorders
NT3 appetite disorders
NT4 anorexia
NT5 anorexia nervosa
NT4 bulimia
NT4 bulimia nervosa (agricola)
NT4 compulsive eating (agricola)
NT4 geophagia
NT4 pica
NT3 bloat
NT3 chinese restaurant syndrome
NT3 colic
NT3 constipation
NT3 diarrhoea
NT4 giardiasis
NT3 dyspepsia
NT3 flatus
NT3 gizzard erosion
NT3 grass sickness
NT3 hyperacidity (agricola)
NT3 malabsorption
NT3 milk intolerance
NT3 obstruction
NT4 cholestasis
NT4 intestinal obstruction
NT5 duodenal obstruction
NT5 intussusception
NT3 phytobezoariasis
NT3 sialuria
NT3 vomiting
NT4 hyperemesis gravidarum
NT4 nausea
NT2 dysregulation
NT3 coma
NT4 diabetic coma

ANIMAL DISORDERS *cont.*
NT3 convulsions
NT3 spasms
NT3 spastic paresis
NT3 tremor
NT4 congenital tremor
NT2 equilibrium disorders
NT2 fever
NT2 mental disorders
NT3 depression
NT3 down's syndrome
NT3 emotional disturbances (agricola)
NT3 mental retardation
NT3 neuroses
NT3 psychoses
NT4 alzheimer's disease
NT4 delusory parasitoses
NT4 schizophrenia
NT2 movement disorders
NT3 ataxia
NT4 cerebellar ataxia
NT3 lameness
NT4 navicular disease
NT3 staggers
NT4 phalaris staggers
NT4 ryegrass staggers
NT3 swayback
NT2 polydipsia
NT2 reproductive disorders
NT3 abortion
NT4 mycotic abortion
NT4 spontaneous abortion (agricola)
NT3 cryptorchidism
NT3 eclampsia
NT3 embryo malpositions
NT3 endometritis
NT3 female infertility
NT4 pseudopregnancy
NT3 male infertility
NT4 impotence
NT4 spermiostasis
NT3 nymphomania
NT3 parturition complications
NT4 dystocia
NT4 uterine torsion
NT3 pregnancy complications
NT4 extrauterine pregnancy
NT4 hydramnios
NT4 preeclampsia
NT3 puerperal disorders
NT4 lactation disorders
NT5 agalactia
NT5 galactorrhoea
NT5 lactation persistency
NT4 parturient paresis
NT4 placental retention
NT4 pregnancy toxaemia
NT3 sex differentiation disorders
NT4 dysgenesis
NT4 intersexuality
NT5 freemartinism
NT5 pseudohermaphroditism
NT4 sex reversal
NT4 testicular feminization
NT2 respiratory disorders
NT3 asphyxia
NT3 asthma
NT3 atelectasis
NT3 cough
NT3 dyspnoea
NT3 hypercapnia
NT3 hypoxia
NT2 sensory disorders
NT3 anosmia
NT3 hearing impairment
NT4 deafness
NT3 vision disorders
NT4 blindness
NT4 night blindness
NT2 urination disorders
NT3 polyuria
NT3 urinary incontinence
NT1 growth disorders
NT2 dwarfism
NT2 gigantism
NT2 hypotrophy
NT2 metaplasia

ANIMAL DISORDERS *cont.*
NT2 runting
NT1 metabolic disorders
NT2 acid base disorders
NT3 acidosis
NT4 diabetic acidosis
NT4 ketoacidosis
NT4 ketosis
NT4 lactic acidosis
NT3 alkalosis
NT2 aciduria
NT3 aminoaciduria
NT4 cystinuria
NT4 homocystinuria
NT3 argininosuccinic aciduria
NT3 glutaric aciduria
NT3 methylglutaconic aciduria
NT3 methylmalonic aciduria
NT3 orotic aciduria
NT3 oxaluria
NT2 amino acid disorders
NT3 alkaptonuria
NT4 ochronosis
NT3 hyperaminoacidaemia
NT4 hyperargininaemia
NT4 hyperglycinaemia
NT4 hypermethioninaemia
NT4 hyperphenylalaninaemia
NT3 hyperaminoaciduria
NT3 ketonuria
NT4 phenylketonuria
NT3 maple syrup urine disease
NT2 carbohydrate metabolism disorders
NT3 disaccharidosis
NT3 fructose intolerance
NT3 galactosaemia
NT3 glycogenosis
NT3 glycosuria
NT3 hyperglycaemia
NT3 hypoglycaemia
NT3 lactose intolerance
NT3 mannosidosis
NT3 mucopolysaccharidosis
NT3 sucrose intolerance
NT2 diabetes
NT3 diabetes insipidus
NT3 diabetes mellitus
NT3 diabetic acidosis
NT3 diabetic neuropathy
NT3 experimental diabetes
NT2 food-related disorders (agricola)
NT2 gout
NT2 hepatolenticular degeneration
NT2 hyperammonaemia
NT2 hyperbilirubinaemia
NT2 hyperinsulinaemia
NT2 hyperketonaemia
NT2 hyperoxaluria
NT2 hyperoxia
NT2 hyperuricaemia
NT2 ketonaemia
NT2 lesch-nyhan syndrome
NT2 lipid metabolism disorders
NT3 cholesterol metabolism disorders
NT4 hypercholesterolaemia
NT4 hypocholesterolaemia
NT3 fatty degeneration
NT3 fatty kidney
NT3 gaucher's disease
NT3 hyperlipaemia
NT4 hypercarotenaemia
NT4 hypercholesterolaemia
NT4 hyperlipoproteinaemia
NT5 hyperchylomicronaemia
NT4 hypertriglyceridaemia
NT3 hypolipaemia
NT4 hypocholesterolaemia
NT4 hypolipoproteinaemia
NT5 abetalipoproteinaemia
NT3 lipidosis
NT4 sphingolipidosis
NT5 gangliosidosis
NT3 triglyceride storage disease
NT2 menkes' disease
NT2 milk alkali syndrome

ANIMAL DISORDERS *cont.*
NT2 mineral metabolism disorders
NT3 calcinosis
NT3 haemochromatosis
NT3 hypercalciuria
NT3 hypermagnesaemia
NT3 hyperphosphataemia
NT3 hyperphosphaturia
NT3 hypocalciuria
NT3 hypocupraemia
NT3 hypomagnesaemia
NT4 grass tetany
NT3 hypophosphataemia
NT3 pseudohypoparathyroidism
NT3 rickets
NT4 experimental rickets
NT4 hypophosphataemic rickets
NT4 scurvy rickets
NT4 vitamin resistant rickets
NT2 obesity hyperglycaemia syndrome
NT2 protein metabolism disorders
NT3 protein intolerance
NT2 proteinuria
NT3 haemoglobinuria
NT3 myoglobinuria
NT2 rheumatism
NT2 water metabolism disorders
NT3 dehydration (physiological)
NT3 hydrops
NT3 oedema
NT4 congenital oedema
NT5 hydrocephalus
NT4 nutritional oedema
NT2 water-electrolyte imbalance
NT3 hypercalcaemia
NT3 hyperkaliaemia
NT3 hypernatraemia
NT3 hypocalcaemia
NT4 tetany
NT3 hypokaliaemia
NT3 hyponatraemia
NT2 xanthomatosis
NT1 nutritional disorders
NT2 deficiency diseases
NT3 beriberi
NT3 black tongue
NT3 cheilosis
NT3 iron deficiency anaemia
NT3 kwashiorkor
NT3 mulberry heart disease
NT3 night blindness
NT3 pellagra
NT3 perosis
NT3 phrynoderma
NT3 scurvy
NT3 xerophthalmia
NT2 emaciation
NT2 nutritional anaemia
NT2 obesity
NT3 prader-willi syndrome
NT2 osteodystrophy
NT2 protein energy malnutrition
NT3 marasmus
NT1 occupational disorders
NT1 pigmentation disorders
NT2 albinism
NT2 haemochromatosis
NT2 melanosis
NT2 porphyria
NT2 vitiligo
rt abnormalities

ANIMAL EXPERIMENTS
uf *animal research*
BT1 experiments
rt animal behaviour
rt animal testing alternatives
rt experimental infection
rt laboratory animals
rt laboratory rearing

ANIMAL FAT
BT1 fat
NT1 milk fat
NT2 buffalo milk fat

ANIMAL FAT *cont.*
NT2 human milk fat
NT1 mutton fat
NT1 myelin
NT1 pig fat
NT2 lard
NT1 poultry fat
NT2 chicken fat
NT1 suet
NT1 tallow
rt carcasses
rt fat products
rt livestock products

ANIMAL FEEDING
BT1 feeding
NT1 dog feeding
NT1 fattening
NT2 cattle fattening
NT3 bull fattening
NT2 dry lot feeding
NT2 flushing
NT2 pig fattening
NT3 boar fattening
NT3 piglet fattening
NT2 poultry fattening
NT3 duck fattening
NT3 fowl fattening
NT3 goose fattening
NT3 guineafowl fattening
NT3 turkey fattening
NT2 rabbit fattening
NT2 sheep fattening
NT3 lamb fattening
NT1 livestock feeding
NT2 horse feeding
NT3 mare feeding
NT2 pig feeding
NT3 boar feeding
NT3 piglet feeding
NT3 sow feeding
NT2 poultry feeding
NT3 duck feeding
NT3 fowl feeding
NT3 goose feeding
NT3 guineafowl feeding
NT3 hen feeding
NT3 turkey feeding
NT4 turkey hen feeding
NT4 turkey poult feeding
NT2 ruminant feeding
NT3 buffalo feeding
NT3 cattle feeding
NT4 bull feeding
NT4 calf feeding
NT3 deer feeding
NT3 goat feeding
NT4 kid feeding
NT3 sheep feeding
NT4 ewe feeding
NT4 lamb feeding
NT1 rabbit feeding
NT1 rat feeding
NT1 suckling
rt animal husbandry
rt feeds

ANIMAL FIBERS
BF animal fibres
BT1 fibers
rt natural fibers (agricola)

ANIMAL FIBRES
AF animal fibers
BT1 animal products
BT2 products
BT1 fibres
NT1 bristles
NT1 camel's hair (agricola)
NT1 cashmere
NT1 mohair
NT1 silk
NT1 wool
NT2 finewool
NT2 reprocessed wool (agricola)
NT2 reused wool (agricola)
NT2 semifine wool
NT2 virgin wool (agricola)
rt fleece

animal geography
USE **zoogeography**

ANIMAL HEALTH
BT1 health
rt animal husbandry
rt animal welfare

animal health products
USE **veterinary products**

ANIMAL HOSPITALS
uf *hospitals, animal*
BT1 buildings

ANIMAL HOUSING
uf *livestock buildings*
uf *livestock housing*
NT1 aquaria
NT1 aviaries
NT1 cages
NT2 battery cages
NT2 flat deck cages
NT2 flight cages
NT2 metabolism cages
NT2 perches
NT1 cattle housing
NT2 calf housing
NT2 cow housing
NT3 cubicles
NT1 creeps
NT1 deep litter housing
NT1 goat housing
NT1 kennels
NT1 loose housing
NT1 milking parlours
NT1 pens
NT2 farrowing pens
NT2 floor pens
NT1 pig housing
NT2 farrowing houses
NT2 sties
NT1 poultry housing
NT2 brooders
NT2 chicken housing
NT2 incubators
NT1 rabbit housing
NT1 service crates
NT1 sheep housing
NT1 shelters
NT1 stables
NT1 stalls
NT1 tethered housing
rt animal behaviour
rt animal husbandry
rt barns
rt farm buildings
rt floor space
rt hives
rt housing
rt laboratory rearing
rt mats
rt paddocks
rt slatted floors
rt stocking density

ANIMAL HUSBANDRY
uf *livestock husbandry*
uf *livestock management*
BT1 husbandry
BT1 zootechny
NT1 artificial rearing
NT1 barrier husbandry
NT1 battery husbandry
NT1 cattle husbandry
NT1 floor husbandry
NT1 free range husbandry
NT1 goat keeping
NT1 poultry farming
NT1 small animal rearing
rt animal breeding
rt animal feeding
rt animal health
rt animal housing
rt animal production
rt animal welfare
rt beekeeping
rt extensive husbandry
rt grazing systems
rt herd improvement
rt intensive husbandry
rt intensive livestock farming

ANIMAL HUSBANDRY *cont.*
rt livestock
rt livestock farming
rt ranching

ANIMAL INSURANCE
uf *livestock insurance*
BT1 agricultural insurance
BT2 insurance

animal litter
USE **litter**

ANIMAL MANURES
uf *manures, animal*
BT1 manures
BT2 organic amendments
BT3 soil amendments
BT4 amendments
NT1 cattle manure
NT1 farmyard manure
NT1 fish manure
NT1 horse manure
NT1 night soil
NT1 pig manure
NT1 poultry manure
NT1 sheep manure
rt animal wastes

ANIMAL MODELS
HN from 1989
BT1 models
rt disease models

ANIMAL NUTRITION
BT1 nutrition
NT1 embryo nutrition
NT1 nutrient balance
NT2 nutritive ratio
NT2 protein balance
NT1 protein turnover
rt feeding
rt feeds
rt flushing
rt fodder plants
rt mineral nutrition
rt n s ratio
rt refeeding
rt underfeeding

ANIMAL OILS
BT1 fatty oils
BT2 oils
NT1 butter oil
NT1 fish oils
NT2 fish liver oils
NT3 anchovy oil
NT3 cod liver oil
NT3 menhaden oil
NT2 herring oil
rt cooking oils
rt fatty acid esters

ANIMAL PARASITIC NEMATODES
uf *nematodes, animal parasitic*
BT1 parasites
rt acuariidae
rt amidostomatidae
rt ancylostomatidae
rt angiostrongylidae
rt anisakidae
rt anthelmintics
rt ascarididae
rt ascaridiidae
rt atractidae
rt camallanidae
rt chabertiidae
rt cosmocercidae
rt crenosomatidae
rt dictyocaulidae
rt dioctophymatidae
rt dracunculidae
rt filariidae
rt filaroididae
rt gnathostomatidae
rt gongylonematidae
rt habronematidae
rt hartertiidae
rt heligmonellidae
rt heligmosomidae
rt helminths
rt heteroxynematidae
rt kathlaniidae

ANIMAL PARASITIC NEMATODES *cont.*
rt metastrongylidae
rt nematoda
rt onchocercidae
rt ornithostrongylidae
rt oxyuridae
rt pharyngodonidae
rt philometridae
rt physalopteridae
rt protostrongylidae
rt rhabdochonidae
rt rictulariidae
rt spirocercidae
rt spiruridae
rt strongylidae
rt strongyloididae
rt subuluridae
rt syngamidae
rt tetrameridae
rt thelaziidae
rt trichinellidae
rt trichostrongylidae
rt trichuridae

ANIMAL PATHOLOGY
BT1 pathology
rt animal diseases
rt parasitoses
rt veterinary medicine

ANIMAL PHYSIOLOGY
BT1 physiology
NT1 blood physiology
NT2 blood coagulation
NT2 haematopoiesis
NT3 erythropoiesis
NT3 thrombocytopoiesis
NT2 haemostasis
NT1 endocrinology
NT1 muscle physiology
NT2 muscle contraction
NT2 muscle fatigue
NT1 neurophysiology
NT1 reproductive physiology
rt physiological functions

ANIMAL POWER
uf *power, animal*
BT1 power
rt draught animals
rt human power
rt working animals

ANIMAL PRODUCTION
uf *production, animal*
BT1 agricultural production
BT2 production
NT1 calf production
NT1 chick production
NT1 egg production
NT2 turkey egg production
NT1 foal production
NT1 kid production
NT1 kit production
NT1 meat production
NT2 beef production
NT2 broiler production
NT2 lamb production
NT1 milk production
NT1 piglet production
NT1 progeny production
rt animal husbandry
rt laboratory rearing
rt litter performance
rt liveweight gain

ANIMAL PRODUCTS
BT1 products
NT1 animal fibres
NT2 bristles
NT2 camel's hair (agricola)
NT2 cashmere
NT2 mohair
NT2 silk
NT2 wool
NT3 finewool
NT3 reprocessed wool (agricola)
NT3 reused wool (agricola)
NT3 semifine wool
NT3 virgin wool (agricola)

ANIMAL PRODUCTS *cont.*
NT1 fish products
NT2 canned fish
NT2 dried fish
NT2 fermented fish
NT2 fish
NT2 fish livers
NT2 fish meal
NT3 anchovy meal
NT2 fish oils
NT3 fish liver oils
NT4 anchovy oil
NT4 cod liver oil
NT4 menhaden oil
NT3 herring oil
NT2 fish pastes
NT2 fish protein concentrate
NT2 fish protein hydrolysate
NT2 fish roe
NT3 caviar
NT2 fish sticks (agricola)
NT2 frozen fish
NT2 salted fish
NT2 smoked fish
NT1 furs
NT1 hides and skins
NT1 hive products
NT2 bee-collected pollen
NT2 beeswax
NT2 honey
NT3 artificial honey
NT3 chunk honey
NT3 comb honey
NT3 creamed honey
NT3 dried honey
NT3 extracted honey
NT3 granulated honey
NT3 section honey
NT3 strained honey
NT3 stringy honey
NT2 honeybee venom
NT2 propolis
NT2 royal jelly
NT1 leather
NT2 suede (agricola)
NT1 livestock products
NT1 meat
NT2 beef
NT3 ground beef (agricola)
NT2 buffalo meat
NT2 camel meat
NT2 crab meat
NT2 dark cutting meat
NT2 game meat
NT2 goat meat
NT2 horse meat
NT2 pigmeat
NT3 bacon
NT3 ham
NT2 poultry meat
NT3 chicken meat
NT3 duck meat
NT3 goose meat
NT3 turkey meat
NT2 rabbit meat
NT2 seal meat
NT2 sheepmeat
NT3 lamb (meat)
NT3 mutton
NT2 turtle meat
NT2 variety meats (agricola)
NT2 veal
NT2 venison
NT2 whale meat
NT1 meat products
NT2 bacon
NT2 canned meat
NT2 cured meats (agricola)
NT3 corned beef (agricola)
NT2 dried meat
NT2 frozen meat
NT2 hamburgers (agricola)
NT2 luncheon meats (agricola)
NT2 meat pastes
NT2 mechanically deboned meat (agricola)
NT2 preformed meats (agricola)
NT2 salami (agricola)
NT2 sausages
NT3 hot dogs (agricola)
NT2 smoked meats

ANIMAL PRODUCTS *cont.*
NT1 milk
NT2 bulk milk
NT2 cheese milk
NT2 homogenized milk
NT2 liquid milk
NT2 market milk
NT2 pasteurized milk
NT2 raw milk
NT2 residual milk
NT3 strippings
NT2 sterilized milk
NT2 uht milk
NT1 parchment
NT1 poultry products
NT2 egg products
NT3 dried egg
NT2 eggs
NT3 duck eggs
NT3 goose eggs
NT3 turkey eggs
NT1 whale solubles
rt agricultural products
rt fat products
rt livestock products
rt protein concentrates
rt tallow

ANIMAL PROTEIN
(feeds and body protein; for names of specific compounds or groups of compounds see "animal proteins")
uf *protein, animal*
BT1 protein
NT1 blood protein
NT1 egg protein
NT1 liver protein
NT1 milk protein
NT2 whey protein
rt animal protein concentrates
rt animal proteins

ANIMAL PROTEIN CONCENTRATES
BT1 protein concentrates
BT2 concentrates
BT3 feeds
BT3 foods
BT2 feed supplements
BT3 supplements
rt animal protein
rt livestock products

ANIMAL PROTEINS
(specific compounds or groups of compounds; for feeds and body protein see "animal protein")
uf *proteins, animal*
BT1 proteins
BT2 peptides
NT1 blood proteins
NT2 α-fetoprotein
NT2 blood coagulation factors
NT2 ceruloplasmin
NT2 erythropoietin
NT2 fibrin
NT2 fibrinogen
NT2 haemoglobin
NT3 haemoglobin a1
NT3 haemoglobin a2
NT3 methaemoglobin
NT2 haptoglobins
NT2 myoglobin
NT2 opsonins
NT2 postalbumin
NT2 prealbumin
NT2 properdin
NT2 prothrombin
NT2 seromucoid
NT2 serum albumin
NT3 bovine serum albumin
NT2 sex-limited protein
NT2 thrombin
NT2 thromboplastin
NT2 transcobalamins
NT2 transferrin
NT2 transthyretin
NT2 x-protein
NT1 circumsporozoite proteins
NT1 early pregnancy factor
NT1 egg proteins

ANIMAL PROTEINS *cont.*
NT2 conalbumin
NT2 egg albumen
NT2 lysozyme
NT2 ovalbumin
NT2 ovoglobulin
NT2 vitellins
NT1 milk proteins
NT2 casein
NT3 αs-casein
NT4 αs1-casein
NT4 αs2-casein
NT3 α-casein
NT3 β-casein
NT3 γ-casein
NT3 κ-casein
NT3 λ-casein
NT2 lactalbumin
NT3 α-lactalbumin
NT2 lactoferrin
NT2 lactoglobulins
NT3 β-lactoglobulin
NT2 proteose peptones
NT1 neural cell adhesion molecule
rt animal protein
rt livestock products
rt meat

animal research
USE **animal experiments**

animal rights
USE **animal welfare**

animal science
USE **zoology**

ANIMAL SPORTS
BT1 outdoor recreation
BT2 recreation
BT1 sport
NT1 horse racing
NT1 horse riding
NT2 pony trekking
NT2 show jumping
NT1 hunting
rt angling

ANIMAL TESTING ALTERNATIVES
HN from 1990
uf *alternatives to animal testing*
BT1 bioethics
rt animal experiments
rt animal welfare
rt computer techniques
rt culture techniques
rt laboratory tests
rt mathematical models
rt research
rt tissue culture

ANIMAL TISSUES
BT1 tissues
NT1 adipose tissue
NT1 bone tissue
NT1 connective tissue
NT1 endothelium
NT2 reticuloendothelial system
NT1 epidermis
NT2 cuticle
NT1 epithelium
NT2 rumen epithelium
NT3 rumen mucosa
NT2 spermatogenic epithelium
NT1 glycogen body
NT1 mammary tissue
NT1 muscle tissue
NT2 muscle fibres
NT2 myofibrils
NT2 sarcomeres
NT2 sarcosomes
NT2 smooth muscle
NT1 nerve tissue
NT2 gap junctions
NT2 internodes
NT2 myelin
NT2 nerve endings
NT3 carotid body
NT2 neuroglia
NT2 neurons
NT3 innervation

ANIMAL TISSUES *cont.*
NT4 adrenergic innervation
NT1 periodontal tissue
NT1 uterine tissue
rt histocompatibility

animal viruses
USE **viruses**

ANIMAL WASTES
uf *livestock wastes*
BT1 wastes
NT1 cattle slurry
NT1 crab waste
NT1 excreta
NT2 faeces
NT3 buffalo dung
NT3 cat faeces
NT3 cattle dung
NT3 dog faeces
NT3 horse dung
NT3 human faeces
NT3 poultry droppings
NT3 rabbit droppings
NT3 sheep dung
NT2 urine
NT1 feedlot wastes
NT1 fish scrap
NT1 oyster shells
NT1 pig slurry
NT1 slaughterhouse waste
NT2 carcass waste
NT2 scrapings
NT2 tankage
rt agricultural wastes
rt animal manures
rt slurries

ANIMAL WELFARE
uf *animal rights*
rt animal behaviour
rt animal health
rt animal husbandry
rt animal testing alternatives
rt pet care (agricola)

ANIMALS
NT1 aquatic animals
NT2 aquarium fishes
NT2 aquatic invertebrates
NT3 aquatic arthropods
NT4 aquatic insects
NT4 water mites
NT3 freshwater molluscs
NT3 marine nematodes
NT3 shellfish
NT4 abalones
NT4 clams
NT5 hard clams
NT5 surf clams
NT4 crabs
NT4 crayfish
NT4 lobsters
NT4 mussels
NT4 oysters
NT4 prawns
NT4 scallops
NT4 shrimps
NT2 brackish water fishes
NT2 crocodiles
NT2 diadromous fishes
NT3 atlantic salmon
NT3 european eels
NT3 lampreys
NT3 sturgeons
NT2 freshwater fishes
NT3 ayu
NT3 brown trout
NT3 carp
NT3 freshwater catfishes
NT3 goldfish
NT3 perch
NT3 pike
NT3 pike perch
NT3 rainbow trout
NT2 frogs
NT2 game fishes
NT3 trout
NT2 manatees
NT2 marine fishes
NT3 anchovies
NT3 anglerfishes

ANIMALS *cont.*
NT3 bass
NT3 bonitos
NT3 cod
NT3 dogfishes
NT3 eels
NT3 flatfishes
NT4 dover soles
NT4 flounder
NT4 halibut
NT4 plaice
NT4 turbot
NT3 groupers
NT3 haddock
NT3 hake
NT3 herrings
NT3 mackerels
NT3 marlins
NT3 menhaden
NT3 mullets
NT3 pompanos
NT3 sardines
NT3 sea bass
NT3 sea bream
NT3 sea catfish
NT3 sharks
NT3 smelts
NT3 sprats
NT3 sunfishes
NT3 tuna
NT3 whitefish
NT3 whiting
NT3 yellowtails
NT2 marine mammals
NT3 dolphins
NT3 whales
NT2 ornamental fishes
NT2 otters
NT2 sealions
NT2 seals
NT2 toads
NT2 waterfowl
NT1 aviary birds
NT2 budgerigars
NT2 parakeets
NT1 desert animals
NT2 desert rodents
NT1 domestic animals
NT2 cats
NT2 dogs
NT1 female animals
NT2 bitches
NT2 cows
NT3 beef cows
NT3 dairy cows
NT3 heifers
NT4 bred heifers
NT3 nurse cows
NT2 daughters
NT2 ewes
NT2 gilts
NT2 hens
NT2 lactating females
NT2 mares
NT2 ovariectomized females
NT2 prepubertal females
NT2 queens
NT3 queen honeybees
NT4 mated queen honeybees
NT4 virgin queen honeybees
NT2 sows
NT2 superovulated females
NT2 synchronized females
NT1 furbearing animals
NT2 alopex lagopus
NT2 castor canadensis
NT2 chinchillas
NT2 foxes
NT2 mink
NT2 nutria
NT2 ocelots
NT2 polecats
NT2 rabbits
NT2 sables
NT2 skunks
NT1 game animals
NT2 game birds
NT3 grouse
NT3 partridges
NT3 pheasants
NT1 laboratory animals

ANIMALS *cont.*
NT2 germfree animals
NT2 gnotobiotic animals
NT2 laboratory mammals
NT3 gerbils
NT3 guineapigs
NT3 hamsters
NT4 golden hamsters
NT3 macaca mulatta
NT3 marmosets
NT3 mice
NT3 monkeys
NT3 rabbits
NT3 rats
NT1 livestock
NT2 cattle
NT3 beef cattle
NT4 beef bulls
NT4 beef cows
NT3 dairy cattle
NT4 dairy bulls
NT4 dairy cows
NT2 goats
NT2 horses
NT2 native livestock
NT2 pigs
NT2 poultry
NT3 ducks
NT4 muscovy ducks
NT3 fowls
NT4 bantams
NT4 broilers
NT4 capons
NT3 geese
NT3 guineafowls
NT3 japanese quails
NT3 pigeons
NT3 quails
NT3 turkeys
NT2 sheep
NT1 male animals
NT2 boars
NT2 bucks
NT2 bulls
NT3 ai bulls
NT3 beef bulls
NT3 dairy bulls
NT3 steers
NT2 cocks
NT2 rams
NT3 wethers
NT2 sons
NT2 stallions
NT1 meat animals
NT2 beef cattle
NT3 beef bulls
NT3 beef cows
NT2 bison
NT2 buffaloes
NT2 capybaras
NT2 deer
NT3 fallow deer
NT3 red deer
NT3 reindeer
NT2 goats
NT2 guineapigs
NT2 hares
NT2 horses
NT2 lizards
NT2 pigs
NT2 rabbits
NT2 sheep
NT2 snakes
NT2 turtles
NT2 veal calves
NT2 whales
NT2 yaks
NT1 milk-yielding animals
NT2 dairy cows
NT2 mares
NT1 nonruminants
NT1 ornamental birds
NT2 canaries
NT2 parrots
NT2 peafowls
NT2 swans
NT1 pets
NT2 gerbils
NT2 goldfish
NT2 guineapigs
NT2 hamsters

ANIMALS *cont.*
NT3 golden hamsters
NT2 mice
NT2 rabbits
NT1 plumage birds
NT2 emus
NT2 ostriches
NT1 ruminants
NT2 antelopes
NT3 chamois
NT2 banteng
NT2 bison
NT2 cattle
NT3 beef cattle
NT4 beef bulls
NT4 beef cows
NT3 dairy cattle
NT4 dairy bulls
NT4 dairy cows
NT2 deer
NT3 fallow deer
NT3 red deer
NT3 reindeer
NT2 gayals
NT2 goats
NT2 mouflon
NT2 sheep
NT2 yaks
NT2 zebu
NT1 skin producing animals
NT2 bison
NT2 cattle
NT3 beef cattle
NT4 beef bulls
NT4 beef cows
NT3 dairy cattle
NT4 dairy bulls
NT4 dairy cows
NT2 chamois
NT2 crocodiles
NT2 goats
NT2 kids
NT2 lizards
NT2 pigs
NT2 reindeer
NT2 snakes
NT2 tortoises
NT2 turtles
NT1 small mammals
NT2 hares
NT2 lemmings
NT2 lemurs
NT2 mice
NT2 rabbits
NT2 rats
NT2 shrews
NT2 squirrels
NT2 viscacha
NT2 voles
NT1 stray animals
NT1 wild animals
NT2 badgers
NT2 chimpanzees
NT2 coyotes
NT2 elephants
NT2 gaur
NT2 gorillas
NT2 jackals
NT2 jaguars
NT2 kangaroos
NT2 leopards
NT2 lions
NT2 mongooses
NT2 opossums
NT2 porcupines
NT2 przewalski's horse
NT2 raccoon dogs
NT2 sloths
NT2 tigers
NT2 wallabies
NT2 wild birds
NT3 jungle fowls
NT3 penguins
NT3 woodpeckers
NT2 wild goats
NT2 wild pigs
NT2 wild sheep
NT2 wolves
NT2 zebras
NT1 wool-producing animals
NT2 alpacas

ANIMALS *cont.*
NT2 goats
NT2 llamas
NT2 sheep
NT2 vicunas
NT1 working animals
NT2 buffaloes
NT2 camels
NT2 circus animals
NT2 donkeys
NT2 draught animals
NT2 dromedaries
NT2 ferrets
NT2 guard dogs
NT2 guide dogs
NT2 hinnies
NT2 horses
NT2 hunting dogs
NT2 llamas
NT2 mules
NT2 racing animals
NT3 greyhounds
NT3 racehorses
NT3 racing pigeons
NT2 riding animals
NT2 sheep dogs
NT2 yaks
NT2 zebu
NT1 young animals
NT2 buffalo calves
NT2 calves
NT3 veal calves
NT2 chicks
NT2 colts
NT2 ducklings
NT2 foals
NT2 fry
NT2 goslings
NT2 heifers
NT3 bred heifers
NT2 infants
NT3 low birth weight infants (agricola)
NT3 neonates
NT3 premature infants
NT2 kids
NT2 kittens
NT2 lambs
NT2 newborn animals
NT2 piglets
NT2 poults
NT2 pullets
NT2 puppies
NT2 pups
NT1 zoo animals
rt invertebrates
rt vertebrates
rt zoology

ANIMATION
BT1 extension
NT1 rural animation
rt community development
rt cultural activities
rt education
rt leadership
rt non-formal education
rt visitor interpretation

ANION EXCHANGE
BT1 ion exchange
rt anion exchange capacity
rt anion exchange resins
rt anions
rt cation exchange

ANION EXCHANGE CAPACITY
BT1 ion exchange capacity
rt anion exchange
rt anion exchange resins

ANION EXCHANGE RESINS
BT1 ion exchange resins
BT2 resins
NT1 colestipol
rt anion exchange
rt anion exchange capacity
rt anions

ANIONS
BT1 ions
NT1 bromide

ANIONS *cont.*
NT1 carbonate
NT1 chloride
NT1 dithionite
NT1 fluoride
NT1 iodide
NT1 nitrate
NT1 organic anions
NT1 sulfate
NT1 tungstate
rt anion exchange
rt anion exchange resins
rt cations

ANISAKIDAE
BT1 nematoda
NT1 anisakis
NT1 contracaecum
NT1 pseudoterranova
NT2 pseudoterranova decipiens
NT1 terranova
NT1 thynnascaris
rt animal parasitic nematodes

ANISAKIS
BT1 anisakidae
BT2 nematoda

anisandrus
USE **xyleborus**

anisandrus dispar
USE **xyleborus dispar**

anisantha
USE **bromus**

anise
USE **pimpinella anisum**

aniseed
USE **pimpinella anisum**

ANISOCHRYSA
BT1 chrysopidae
BT2 neuroptera
rt chrysoperla
rt mallada

anisochrysa boninensis
USE **mallada boninensis**

anisochrysa carnea
USE **chrysoperla carnea**

ANISODUS
BT1 solanaceae
NT1 anisodus tanguticus

ANISODUS TANGUTICUS
BT1 anisodus
BT2 solanaceae
BT1 medicinal plants

ANISOLABIIDAE
BT1 dermaptera
NT1 anisolabis
NT1 euborellia
NT2 euborellia annulipes

ANISOLABIS
BT1 anisolabiidae
BT2 dermaptera
rt euborellia

anisolabis annulipes
USE **euborellia annulipes**

ANISOPHYLLEA
BT1 anisophylleaceae
NT1 anisophyllea boehmii
NT1 anisophyllea pomifera

ANISOPHYLLEA BOEHMII
BT1 anisophyllea
BT2 anisophylleaceae

ANISOPHYLLEA POMIFERA
BT1 anisophyllea
BT2 anisophylleaceae

ANISOPHYLLEACEAE
NT1 anisophyllea
NT2 anisophyllea boehmii
NT2 anisophyllea pomifera

ANISOPLIA
BT1 scarabaeidae
BT2 coleoptera
NT1 anisoplia segetum

ANISOPLIA SEGETUM
BT1 anisoplia
BT2 scarabaeidae
BT3 coleoptera

ANISOPTERA
BT1 dipterocarpaceae
NT1 anisoptera thurifera
rt forest trees

ANISOPTERA THURIFERA
BT1 anisoptera
BT2 dipterocarpaceae

ANISOPTEROMALUS
uf *aplastomorpha*
BT1 pteromalidae
BT2 hymenoptera
NT1 anisopteromalus calandrae

ANISOPTEROMALUS CALANDRAE
uf *aplastomorpha calandrae*
BT1 anisopteromalus
BT2 pteromalidae
BT3 hymenoptera

ANISOTOME
BT1 umbelliferae
NT1 anisotome haastii
NT1 anisotome latifolia

ANISOTOME HAASTII
BT1 anisotome
BT2 umbelliferae

ANISOTOME LATIFOLIA
BT1 anisotome
BT2 umbelliferae

ANISOTREMUS
BT1 haemulidae
BT2 perciformes
BT3 osteichthyes
BT4 fishes

ANISUM
BT1 umbelliferae
rt pimpinella

anisum vulgare
USE **pimpinella anisum**

ANKISTRODESMUS
BT1 chlorophyta
BT2 algae
NT1 ankistrodesmus falcatus

ANKISTRODESMUS FALCATUS
BT1 ankistrodesmus
BT2 chlorophyta
BT3 algae

ANKOLE
BT1 cattle breeds
BT2 breeds

ANKYLOSIS
BT1 joint diseases
BT2 organic diseases
BT3 diseases

ANNATTO
BT1 food colourants
BT2 food additives
BT3 additives
rt bixa orellana

ANNELIDA
NT1 hirudinea
NT2 erpobdellidae
NT3 dina
NT4 dina anoculata
NT3 erpobdella
NT4 erpobdella octoculata
NT2 glossiphoniidae
NT3 glossiphonia
NT4 glossiphonia complanata
NT3 haementeria
NT3 helobdella
NT4 helobdella stagnalis

ANNELIDA *cont.*
NT3 placobdella
NT3 theromyzon
NT4 theromyzon rude
NT2 haemadipsidae
NT3 haemadipsa
NT2 hirudidae
NT3 hirudo
NT4 hirudo medicinalis
NT2 piscicolidae
NT3 piscicola
NT4 piscicola geometra
NT1 oligochaeta
NT2 enchytraeidae
NT3 enchytraeus
NT4 enchytraeus albidus
NT3 fridericia
NT4 fridericia galba
NT2 glossoscolecidae
NT3 pontoscolex
NT4 pontoscolex corethrurus
NT2 lumbricidae
NT3 allolobophora
NT4 allolobophora chlorotica
NT3 aporrectodea
NT4 aporrectodea caliginosa
NT4 aporrectodea longa
NT3 dendrobaena
NT3 dendrodrilus
NT4 dendrodrilus rubidus
NT3 eisenia
NT4 eisenia fetida
NT4 eisenia nordenskioldi
NT3 lumbricus
NT4 lumbricus rubellus
NT4 lumbricus terrestris
NT3 octolasion
NT4 octolasion cyaneum
NT2 megascolecidae
NT3 lampito
NT4 lampito mauritii
NT3 metapheretima
NT3 perionyx
NT4 perionyx excavatus
NT3 pheretima
NT2 moniligastridae
NT3 drawida
NT2 octochaetidae
NT3 millsonia
NT4 millsonia anomala
NT3 octochaetus
NT2 tubificidae
NT3 branchiura (annelida)
NT4 branchiura sowerbyi
NT3 tubifex
NT4 tubifex tubifex
NT1 polychaeta
rt invertebrates
rt sipunculoidea

ANNONA
BT1 annonaceae
NT1 annona cherimola
NT1 annona diversifolia
NT1 annona montana
NT1 annona muricata
NT1 annona purpurea
NT1 annona reticulata
NT1 annona senegalensis
NT1 annona squamosa
rt atemoyas

ANNONA CHERIMOLA
BT1 annona
BT2 annonaceae
rt cherimoyas

ANNONA DIVERSIFOLIA
BT1 annona
BT2 annonaceae
BT1 tropical tree fruits
BT2 tree fruits
BT2 tropical fruits
BT3 fruit crops

ANNONA MONTANA
BT1 annona
BT2 annonaceae
BT1 medicinal plants
BT1 tropical tree fruits
BT2 tree fruits
BT2 tropical fruits

ANNONA MONTANA *cont.*
BT3 fruit crops

ANNONA MURICATA
BT1 annona
BT2 annonaceae
BT1 tropical tree fruits
BT2 tree fruits
BT2 tropical fruits
BT3 fruit crops

ANNONA PURPUREA
BT1 annona
BT2 annonaceae
BT1 tropical tree fruits
BT2 tree fruits
BT2 tropical fruits
BT3 fruit crops

ANNONA RETICULATA
uf *bullock's heart*
uf *custard apples*
BT1 annona
BT2 annonaceae
BT1 insecticidal plants
BT2 pesticidal plants
BT1 tropical tree fruits
BT2 tree fruits
BT2 tropical fruits
BT3 fruit crops

ANNONA SENEGALENSIS
BT1 annona
BT2 annonaceae
BT1 medicinal plants

ANNONA SQUAMOSA
uf *sugar apples*
uf *sweetsops*
BT1 annona
BT2 annonaceae
BT1 insecticidal plants
BT2 pesticidal plants
BT1 medicinal plants
BT1 nematicidal plants
BT2 pesticidal plants
BT1 tropical tree fruits
BT2 tree fruits
BT2 tropical fruits
BT3 fruit crops

ANNONACEAE
NT1 alphonsea
NT2 alphonsea arborea
NT1 annona
NT2 annona cherimola
NT2 annona diversifolia
NT2 annona montana
NT2 annona muricata
NT2 annona purpurea
NT2 annona reticulata
NT2 annona senegalensis
NT2 annona squamosa
NT1 artabotrys
NT2 artabotrys hexapetalus
NT1 asimina
NT2 asimina parviflora
NT2 asimina triloba
NT1 cananga
NT2 cananga odorata
NT1 cymbopetalum
NT2 cymbopetalum baillonii
NT1 dennettia
NT2 dennettia tripetala
NT1 duguetia
NT2 duguetia calycina
NT1 enantia
NT2 enantia polycarpa
NT1 fusaea
NT2 fusaea longifolia
NT1 goniothalamus
NT2 goniothalamus andersonii
NT2 goniothalamus macrophyllus
NT2 goniothalamus malayanus
NT2 goniothalamus velutinus
NT1 guatteria
NT2 guatteria elata
NT2 guatteria modesta
NT1 hexalobus
NT2 hexalobus monopetalus
NT1 isolona
NT2 isolona campanulata

ANNONACEAE *cont.*
NT1 miliusa
NT2 miliusa tomentosa
NT1 monanthotaxis
NT2 monanthotaxis cauliflora
NT1 monodora
NT2 monodora angolensis
NT2 monodora myristica
NT1 pachypodanthium
NT2 pachypodanthium staudtii
NT1 polyalthia
NT2 polyalthia emarginata
NT2 polyalthia longifolia
NT2 polyalthia oligosperma
NT2 polyalthia suaveolens
NT1 rollinia
NT2 rollinia emarginata
NT1 uvaria
NT2 uvaria angolensis
NT2 uvaria chamae
NT2 uvaria elliotiana
NT2 uvaria kirkii
NT1 uvariopsis
NT2 uvariopsis congolana
NT1 xylopia
NT2 xylopia aethiopica
NT2 xylopia quintasii

ANNUAL ACCOUNTS
BT1 accounts

ANNUAL DRESSINGS
BT1 application methods
BT2 methodology
rt dressings

ANNUAL GRASSLANDS
HN from 1990
BT1 grasslands
BT2 vegetation types

ANNUAL HABIT
BT1 habit
rt life cycle
rt lifespan

annual reports
USE **reports**

annual reviews
USE **reviews**

annual rings
USE **growth rings**

ANNUAL WATER BALANCE
BT1 soil water balance
BT2 water balance

ANNUALS
rt bedding plants
rt ornamental herbaceous plants
rt plants

ANNUITIES
BT1 income
rt old age benefits
rt pensions

ANNULMENT (AGRICOLA)
rt divorce (agricola)

ANOBIIDAE
BT1 coleoptera
NT1 anobium
NT2 anobium punctatum
NT1 hadrobregmus
NT2 hadrobregmus pertinax
NT1 lasioderma
NT2 lasioderma serricorne
NT1 stegobium
NT2 stegobium paniceum

ANOBIUM
BT1 anobiidae
BT2 coleoptera
NT1 anobium punctatum

ANOBIUM PUNCTATUM
BT1 anobium
BT2 anobiidae
BT3 coleoptera

ANOCENTOR
BT1 ixodidae
BT2 metastigmata
BT3 acari
NT1 anocentor nitens
rt dermacentor

ANOCENTOR NITENS
uf *dermacentor nitens*
BT1 anocentor
BT2 ixodidae
BT3 metastigmata
BT4 acari

ANODA
BT1 malvaceae
NT1 anoda cristata

ANODA CRISTATA
BT1 anoda
BT2 malvaceae
BT1 weeds

ANODENDRON
BT1 apocynaceae
NT1 anodendron affine

ANODENDRON AFFINE
BT1 anodendron
BT2 apocynaceae

ANODIC STRIPPING VOLTAMMETRY
BT1 analytical methods
BT2 methodology

ANOECIA
BT1 aphididae
BT2 aphidoidea
BT3 sternorrhyncha
BT4 homoptera
NT1 anoecia corni

ANOECIA CORNI
BT1 anoecia
BT2 aphididae
BT3 aphidoidea
BT4 sternorrhyncha
BT5 homoptera

ANOECTOCHILUS
BT1 orchidaceae
rt ornamental orchids

ANOESTRUS
AF anestrus
BT1 oestrous cycle
BT2 biological rhythms
BT2 sexual reproduction
BT3 reproduction
rt breeding season
rt libido

anoetidae
USE **histiostomatidae**

ANOGEISSUS
BT1 combretaceae
NT1 anogeissus acuminata
NT1 anogeissus latifolia
NT1 anogeissus leiocarpus
NT1 anogeissus pendula

ANOGEISSUS ACUMINATA
BT1 anogeissus
BT2 combretaceae

ANOGEISSUS LATIFOLIA
BT1 anogeissus
BT2 combretaceae
BT1 forest trees

ANOGEISSUS LEIOCARPUS
BT1 anogeissus
BT2 combretaceae

ANOGEISSUS PENDULA
BT1 anogeissus
BT2 combretaceae

ANOGMUS
BT1 pteromalidae
BT2 hymenoptera
NT1 anogmus laricis

ANOGMUS LARICIS
BT1 anogmus
BT2 pteromalidae
BT3 hymenoptera

ANOMALA
BT1 scarabaeidae
BT2 coleoptera
NT1 anomala cuprea
NT1 anomala cupripes
rt blitopertha
rt mimela
rt phyllopertha

ANOMALA CUPREA
BT1 anomala
BT2 scarabaeidae
BT3 coleoptera

ANOMALA CUPRIPES
BT1 anomala
BT2 scarabaeidae
BT3 coleoptera

anomala horticola
USE **phyllopertha horticola**

anomala orientalis
USE **blitopertha orientalis**

anomala testaceipes
USE **mimela testaceipes**

ANOMIS
uf *cosmophila*
BT1 noctuidae
BT2 lepidoptera
NT1 anomis flava
NT1 anomis sabulifera

ANOMIS FLAVA
uf *cosmophila flava*
BT1 anomis
BT2 noctuidae
BT3 lepidoptera

ANOMIS SABULIFERA
BT1 anomis
BT2 noctuidae
BT3 lepidoptera

ANOMOTAENIA
BT1 dilepididae
BT2 eucestoda
BT3 cestoda

ANOPHELES
BT1 culicidae
BT2 diptera
NT1 anopheles aconitus
NT1 anopheles albimanus
NT1 anopheles albitarsis
NT1 anopheles algeriensis
NT1 anopheles amictus
NT1 anopheles annularis
NT1 anopheles annulipes
NT1 anopheles aquasalis
NT1 anopheles arabiensis
NT1 anopheles atroparvus
NT1 anopheles atropos
NT1 anopheles balabacensis
NT1 anopheles bancroftii
NT1 anopheles barberi
NT1 anopheles barbirostris
NT1 anopheles beklemishevi
NT1 anopheles bellator
NT1 anopheles bradleyi
NT1 anopheles campestris
NT1 anopheles claviger
NT1 anopheles coustani
NT1 anopheles crucians
NT1 anopheles cruzii
NT1 anopheles culicifacies
NT1 anopheles darlingi
NT1 anopheles demeilloni
NT1 anopheles dirus
NT1 anopheles dthali
NT1 anopheles earlei
NT1 anopheles farauti
NT1 anopheles flavirostris
NT1 anopheles fluviatilis
NT1 anopheles freeborni
NT1 anopheles funestus
NT1 anopheles gambiae

ANOPHELES *cont.*
NT1 anopheles hancocki
NT1 anopheles hargreavesi
NT1 anopheles hilli
NT1 anopheles hispaniola
NT1 anopheles hyrcanus
NT1 anopheles jamesii
NT1 anopheles koliensis
NT1 anopheles labranchiae
NT1 anopheles lesteri
NT2 anopheles lesteri anthropophagus
NT1 anopheles leucosphyrus
NT1 anopheles lindesayi
NT1 anopheles litoralis
NT1 anopheles maculatus
NT1 anopheles maculipennis
NT1 anopheles marshallii
NT1 anopheles mascarensis
NT1 anopheles melanoon
NT1 anopheles melas
NT1 anopheles merus
NT1 anopheles messeae
NT1 anopheles minimus
NT1 anopheles multicolor
NT1 anopheles neivai
NT1 anopheles nigerrimus
NT1 anopheles nili
NT1 anopheles nivipes
NT1 anopheles nuneztovari
NT1 anopheles occidentalis
NT1 anopheles oswaldoi
NT1 anopheles pharoensis
NT1 anopheles philippinensis
NT1 anopheles plumbeus
NT1 anopheles pretoriensis
NT1 anopheles pseudopunctipennis
NT2 anopheles pseudopunctipennis franciscanus
NT1 anopheles pulcherrimus
NT1 anopheles punctimacula
NT1 anopheles punctipennis
NT1 anopheles punctulatus
NT1 anopheles quadriannulatus
NT1 anopheles quadrimaculatus
NT1 anopheles rivulorum
NT1 anopheles rufipes
NT1 anopheles sacharovi
NT1 anopheles sergentii
NT1 anopheles sinensis
NT1 anopheles splendidus
NT1 anopheles squamosus
NT1 anopheles stephensi
NT1 anopheles subalpinus
NT1 anopheles subpictus
NT1 anopheles sundaicus
NT1 anopheles superpictus
NT1 anopheles tenebrosus
NT1 anopheles tessellatus
NT1 anopheles theobaldi
NT1 anopheles triannulatus
NT1 anopheles turkhudi
NT1 anopheles vagus
NT1 anopheles wellcomei
NT1 anopheles ziemanni

ANOPHELES ACONITUS
BT1 anopheles
BT2 culicidae
BT3 diptera

ANOPHELES ALBIMANUS
BT1 anopheles
BT2 culicidae
BT3 diptera

ANOPHELES ALBITARSIS
HN from 1989
BT1 anopheles
BT2 culicidae
BT3 diptera

ANOPHELES ALGERIENSIS
BT1 anopheles
BT2 culicidae
BT3 diptera

ANOPHELES AMICTUS
BT1 anopheles
BT2 culicidae

ANOPHELES AMICTUS *cont.*
BT3 diptera

ANOPHELES ANNULARIS
BT1 anopheles
BT2 culicidae
BT3 diptera

ANOPHELES ANNULIPES
BT1 anopheles
BT2 culicidae
BT3 diptera

ANOPHELES AQUASALIS
BT1 anopheles
BT2 culicidae
BT3 diptera

ANOPHELES ARABIENSIS
BT1 anopheles
BT2 culicidae
BT3 diptera

ANOPHELES ATROPARVUS
BT1 anopheles
BT2 culicidae
BT3 diptera

ANOPHELES ATROPOS
BT1 anopheles
BT2 culicidae
BT3 diptera

ANOPHELES BALABACENSIS
BT1 anopheles
BT2 culicidae
BT3 diptera

ANOPHELES BANCROFTII
HN from 1989
BT1 anopheles
BT2 culicidae
BT3 diptera

ANOPHELES BARBERI
HN from 1989
BT1 anopheles
BT2 culicidae
BT3 diptera

ANOPHELES BARBIROSTRIS
BT1 anopheles
BT2 culicidae
BT3 diptera

ANOPHELES BEKLEMISHEVI
BT1 anopheles
BT2 culicidae
BT3 diptera

ANOPHELES BELLATOR
BT1 anopheles
BT2 culicidae
BT3 diptera

ANOPHELES BRADLEYI
BT1 anopheles
BT2 culicidae
BT3 diptera

ANOPHELES CAMPESTRIS
BT1 anopheles
BT2 culicidae
BT3 diptera

ANOPHELES CLAVIGER
BT1 anopheles
BT2 culicidae
BT3 diptera

ANOPHELES COUSTANI
BT1 anopheles
BT2 culicidae
BT3 diptera

ANOPHELES CRUCIANS
BT1 anopheles
BT2 culicidae
BT3 diptera

ANOPHELES CRUZII
BT1 anopheles
BT2 culicidae
BT3 diptera

ANOPHELES CULICIFACIES
BT1 anopheles
BT2 culicidae
BT3 diptera

ANOPHELES DARLINGI
BT1 anopheles
BT2 culicidae
BT3 diptera

ANOPHELES DEMEILLONI
BT1 anopheles
BT2 culicidae
BT3 diptera

ANOPHELES DIRUS
HN from 1989
BT1 anopheles
BT2 culicidae
BT3 diptera

ANOPHELES DTHALI
BT1 anopheles
BT2 culicidae
BT3 diptera

ANOPHELES EARLEI
BT1 anopheles
BT2 culicidae
BT3 diptera

ANOPHELES FARAUTI
BT1 anopheles
BT2 culicidae
BT3 diptera

ANOPHELES FLAVIROSTRIS
HN from 1989
BT1 anopheles
BT2 culicidae
BT3 diptera

ANOPHELES FLUVIATILIS
BT1 anopheles
BT2 culicidae
BT3 diptera

anopheles franciscanus
USE **anopheles pseudopunctipennis franciscanus**

ANOPHELES FREEBORNI
BT1 anopheles
BT2 culicidae
BT3 diptera

ANOPHELES FUNESTUS
BT1 anopheles
BT2 culicidae
BT3 diptera

ANOPHELES GAMBIAE
BT1 anopheles
BT2 culicidae
BT3 diptera

ANOPHELES HANCOCKI
BT1 anopheles
BT2 culicidae
BT3 diptera

ANOPHELES HARGREAVESI
BT1 anopheles
BT2 culicidae
BT3 diptera

ANOPHELES HILLI
BT1 anopheles
BT2 culicidae
BT3 diptera

ANOPHELES HISPANIOLA
BT1 anopheles
BT2 culicidae
BT3 diptera

ANOPHELES HYRCANUS
BT1 anopheles
BT2 culicidae
BT3 diptera

ANOPHELES JAMESII
BT1 anopheles
BT2 culicidae
BT3 diptera

ANOPHELES KOLIENSIS
BT1 anopheles
BT2 culicidae
BT3 diptera

ANOPHELES LABRANCHIAE
BT1 anopheles
BT2 culicidae
BT3 diptera

ANOPHELES LESTERI
BT1 anopheles
BT2 culicidae
BT3 diptera
NT1 anopheles lesteri anthropophagus

ANOPHELES LESTERI ANTHROPOPHAGUS
HN from 1990
BT1 anopheles lesteri
BT2 anopheles
BT3 culicidae
BT4 diptera

ANOPHELES LEUCOSPHYRUS
BT1 anopheles
BT2 culicidae
BT3 diptera

ANOPHELES LINDESAYI
BT1 anopheles
BT2 culicidae
BT3 diptera

ANOPHELES LITORALIS
BT1 anopheles
BT2 culicidae
BT3 diptera

ANOPHELES MACULATUS
BT1 anopheles
BT2 culicidae
BT3 diptera

ANOPHELES MACULIPENNIS
BT1 anopheles
BT2 culicidae
BT3 diptera

ANOPHELES MARSHALLII
BT1 anopheles
BT2 culicidae
BT3 diptera

ANOPHELES MASCARENSIS
BT1 anopheles
BT2 culicidae
BT3 diptera

ANOPHELES MELANOON
BT1 anopheles
BT2 culicidae
BT3 diptera

ANOPHELES MELAS
BT1 anopheles
BT2 culicidae
BT3 diptera

ANOPHELES MERUS
BT1 anopheles
BT2 culicidae
BT3 diptera

ANOPHELES MESSEAE
BT1 anopheles
BT2 culicidae
BT3 diptera

ANOPHELES MINIMUS
BT1 anopheles
BT2 culicidae
BT3 diptera

ANOPHELES MULTICOLOR
BT1 anopheles
BT2 culicidae
BT3 diptera

ANOPHELES NEIVAI
BT1 anopheles
BT2 culicidae
BT3 diptera

ANOPHELES NIGERRIMUS
BT1 anopheles
BT2 culicidae
BT3 diptera

ANOPHELES NILI
BT1 anopheles
BT2 culicidae
BT3 diptera

ANOPHELES NIVIPES
HN from 1989
BT1 anopheles
BT2 culicidae
BT3 diptera

ANOPHELES NUNEZTOVARI
BT1 anopheles
BT2 culicidae
BT3 diptera

ANOPHELES OCCIDENTALIS
HN from 1989
BT1 anopheles
BT2 culicidae
BT3 diptera

ANOPHELES OSWALDOI
BT1 anopheles
BT2 culicidae
BT3 diptera

ANOPHELES PHAROENSIS
BT1 anopheles
BT2 culicidae
BT3 diptera

ANOPHELES PHILIPPINENSIS
HN from 1989
BT1 anopheles
BT2 culicidae
BT3 diptera

ANOPHELES PLUMBEUS
BT1 anopheles
BT2 culicidae
BT3 diptera

ANOPHELES PRETORIENSIS
BT1 anopheles
BT2 culicidae
BT3 diptera

ANOPHELES PSEUDOPUNCTIPENNIS
BT1 anopheles
BT2 culicidae
BT3 diptera
NT1 anopheles pseudopunctipennis franciscanus

ANOPHELES PSEUDOPUNCTIPENNIS FRANCISCANUS
uf *anopheles franciscanus*
BT1 anopheles pseudopunctipennis
BT2 anopheles
BT3 culicidae
BT4 diptera

ANOPHELES PULCHERRIMUS
BT1 anopheles
BT2 culicidae
BT3 diptera

ANOPHELES PUNCTIMACULA
BT1 anopheles
BT2 culicidae
BT3 diptera

ANOPHELES PUNCTIPENNIS
BT1 anopheles
BT2 culicidae
BT3 diptera

ANOPHELES PUNCTULATUS
BT1 anopheles
BT2 culicidae
BT3 diptera

ANOPHELES QUADRIANNULATUS
BT1 anopheles
BT2 culicidae

ANOPHELES QUADRIANNULATUS *cont.*
BT3 diptera

ANOPHELES QUADRIMACULATUS
BT1 anopheles
BT2 culicidae
BT3 diptera

ANOPHELES RIVULORUM
BT1 anopheles
BT2 culicidae
BT3 diptera

ANOPHELES RUFIPES
BT1 anopheles
BT2 culicidae
BT3 diptera

ANOPHELES SACHAROVI
BT1 anopheles
BT2 culicidae
BT3 diptera

ANOPHELES SERGENTII
BT1 anopheles
BT2 culicidae
BT3 diptera

ANOPHELES SINENSIS
BT1 anopheles
BT2 culicidae
BT3 diptera

ANOPHELES SPLENDIDUS
BT1 anopheles
BT2 culicidae
BT3 diptera

ANOPHELES SQUAMOSUS
BT1 anopheles
BT2 culicidae
BT3 diptera

ANOPHELES STEPHENSI
BT1 anopheles
BT2 culicidae
BT3 diptera

ANOPHELES SUBALPINUS
BT1 anopheles
BT2 culicidae
BT3 diptera

ANOPHELES SUBPICTUS
BT1 anopheles
BT2 culicidae
BT3 diptera

ANOPHELES SUNDAICUS
BT1 anopheles
BT2 culicidae
BT3 diptera

ANOPHELES SUPERPICTUS
BT1 anopheles
BT2 culicidae
BT3 diptera

ANOPHELES TENEBROSUS
BT1 anopheles
BT2 culicidae
BT3 diptera

ANOPHELES TESSELLATUS
BT1 anopheles
BT2 culicidae
BT3 diptera

ANOPHELES THEOBALDI
BT1 anopheles
BT2 culicidae
BT3 diptera

ANOPHELES TRIANNULATUS
BT1 anopheles
BT2 culicidae
BT3 diptera

ANOPHELES TURKHUDI
BT1 anopheles
BT2 culicidae
BT3 diptera

ANOPHELES VAGUS
BT1 anopheles

ANOPHELES VAGUS *cont.*
BT2 culicidae
BT3 diptera

ANOPHELES WELLCOMEI
BT1 anopheles
BT2 culicidae
BT3 diptera

ANOPHELES ZIEMANNI
BT1 anopheles
BT2 culicidae
BT3 diptera

ANOPHRYS
BT1 ciliophora
BT2 protozoa

ANOPLOCEPHALA
BT1 anoplocephalidae
BT2 eucestoda
BT3 cestoda
NT1 anoplocephala magna
NT1 anoplocephala perfoliata

ANOPLOCEPHALA MAGNA
BT1 anoplocephala
BT2 anoplocephalidae
BT3 eucestoda
BT4 cestoda

ANOPLOCEPHALA PERFOLIATA
BT1 anoplocephala
BT2 anoplocephalidae
BT3 eucestoda
BT4 cestoda

ANOPLOCEPHALIDAE
uf *anoplocephalids*
BT1 eucestoda
BT2 cestoda
NT1 andrya
NT1 anoplocephala
NT2 anoplocephala magna
NT2 anoplocephala perfoliata
NT1 avitellina
NT2 avitellina centripunctata
NT1 bertiella
NT2 bertiella studeri
NT1 moniezia
NT2 moniezia autumnalia
NT2 moniezia benedeni
NT2 moniezia expansa
NT1 paranoplocephala
NT2 paranoplocephala mamillana
NT1 stilesia
NT2 stilesia globipunctata
NT2 stilesia hepatica
NT1 thysaniezia
NT2 thysaniezia giardi
NT1 thysanosoma
NT2 thysanosoma actinioides

anoplocephalids
USE **anoplocephalidae**

ANOPLOCNEMIS
BT1 coreidae
BT2 heteroptera
NT1 anoplocnemis curvipes

ANOPLOCNEMIS CURVIPES
BT1 anoplocnemis
BT2 coreidae
BT3 heteroptera

ANOPLOLEPIS
BT1 formicidae
BT2 hymenoptera
NT1 anoplolepis custodiens
NT1 anoplolepis longipes

ANOPLOLEPIS CUSTODIENS
BT1 anoplolepis
BT2 formicidae
BT3 hymenoptera

ANOPLOLEPIS LONGIPES
BT1 anoplolepis
BT2 formicidae
BT3 hymenoptera

ANOPLON
BT1 orobanchaceae

ANOPLOPHRYA
BT1 ciliophora
BT2 protozoa

ANOPLOPOMA
BT1 anoplopomatidae
BT2 scorpaeniformes
BT3 osteichthyes
BT4 fishes
NT1 anoplopoma fimbria

ANOPLOPOMA FIMBRIA
uf sablefish
BT1 anoplopoma
BT2 anoplopomatidae
BT3 scorpaeniformes
BT4 osteichthyes
BT5 fishes

ANOPLOPOMATIDAE
BT1 scorpaeniformes
BT2 osteichthyes
BT3 fishes
NT1 anoplopoma
NT2 anoplopoma fimbria

ANOPLURA
BT1 phthiraptera
NT1 haematopinidae
NT2 haematopinus
NT3 haematopinus asini
NT3 haematopinus eurysternus
NT3 haematopinus quadripertusus
NT3 haematopinus suis
NT3 haematopinus tuberculatus
NT1 hoplopleuridae
NT2 hoplopleura
NT3 hoplopleura acanthopus
NT1 linognathidae
NT2 linognathus
NT3 linognathus africanus
NT3 linognathus ovillus
NT3 linognathus pedalis
NT3 linognathus setosus
NT3 linognathus stenopsis
NT3 linognathus vituli
NT2 solenopotes
NT3 solenopotes capillatus
NT1 pediculidae
NT2 pediculus
NT3 pediculus capitis
NT3 pediculus humanus
NT1 polyplacidae
NT2 polyplax
NT3 polyplax spinulosa
NT1 pthiridae
NT2 pthirus
NT3 pthirus pubis

ANOPTERUS
BT1 saxifragaceae
NT1 anopterus glandulosa
NT1 anopterus macleayanus

ANOPTERUS GLANDULOSA
BT1 anopterus
BT2 saxifragaceae

ANOPTERUS MACLEAYANUS
BT1 anopterus
BT2 saxifragaceae

ANORECTAL ATRESIA
BT1 congenital abnormalities
BT2 abnormalities
rt rectum

anorectics
USE **anorexiants**

ANOREXIA
uf inappetence
BT1 appetite disorders
BT2 digestive disorders
BT3 functional disorders
BT4 animal disorders
BT5 disorders
NT1 anorexia nervosa
rt anorexiants
rt appetite
rt weight reduction

ANOREXIA NERVOSA
BT1 anorexia
BT2 appetite disorders
BT3 digestive disorders
BT4 functional disorders
BT5 animal disorders
BT6 disorders

ANOREXIANTS
uf anorectics
uf appetite depressants
uf appetite suppressors
BT1 drugs
NT1 benfluorex
NT1 fenfluramine
NT1 satietin
rt amphetamines
rt anorexia
rt antifeedants
rt appetite
rt appetite control

ANOSMIA
HN from 1989
BT1 sensory disorders
BT2 functional disorders
BT3 animal disorders
BT4 disorders
BT2 nervous system diseases
BT3 organic diseases
BT4 diseases
rt smell

ANOSTRACA
BT1 branchiopoda
BT2 crustacea
BT3 arthropods
NT1 artemia
NT2 artemia salina

ANOUROSOREX
BT1 soricidae
BT2 insectivores
BT3 mammals
NT1 anourosorex squamipes

ANOUROSOREX SQUAMIPES
BT1 anourosorex
BT2 soricidae
BT3 insectivores
BT4 mammals

ANOXIA
rt altitude
rt anaerobes
rt anaerobic conditions
rt anaerobic treatment
rt anaerobiosis
rt hypoxia
rt oxygen requirement

ANREDERA
BT1 basellaceae

ANSER
BT1 anatidae
BT2 anseriformes
BT3 birds
NT1 anser caerulescens

ANSER CAERULESCENS
BT1 anser
BT2 anatidae
BT3 anseriformes
BT4 birds

anser domesticus
USE **geese**

ANSERIFORMES
BT1 birds
NT1 anatidae
NT2 anas
NT3 anas crecca
NT3 anas discors
NT3 anas gibberifrons
NT3 anas platyrhynchos
NT3 anas querquedula
NT2 anser
NT3 anser caerulescens
NT2 cairina
NT2 cygnus
NT3 cygnus columbianus
NT3 cygnus cygnus

ANSERIFORMES *cont.*
NT4 cygnus cygnus buccinator
NT3 cygnus olor

ANT HILLS
BT1 soil morphological features

ant lions
USE **myrmeleonidae**

ANTACIDS
BT1 bases
BT1 gastrointestinal agents
BT2 drugs
NT1 aluminium hydroxide
NT1 aluminium phosphate
NT1 calcium carbonate
NT1 sodium bicarbonate
rt acid base disorders
rt acid base equilibrium
rt acidity
rt acidosis
rt alkali treatment
rt digestive disorders

ANTAGONISM
BT1 incompatibility
NT1 drug antagonism
rt behaviour
rt compatibility
rt synergism

ANTAGONISTS
BT1 metabolic inhibitors
BT2 inhibitors
NT1 amino acid antagonists
NT2 p-fluorophenylalanine
NT2 arginine antagonists
NT2 cycloleucine
NT2 methylmethionine
NT1 hormone antagonists
NT2 bromocriptine
NT2 juvenile hormone antagonists
NT3 precocenes
NT4 precocene i
NT4 precocene ii
NT4 precocene iii
NT2 saralasin
NT2 spironolactone
NT2 thyroid antagonists
NT3 goitrin
NT3 propylthiouracil
NT2 urogastrone
NT1 vitamin antagonists
NT2 vitamin a antagonists
NT2 vitamin b antagonists
NT3 4-deoxypyridoxine
NT3 benzimidazole
NT3 biotin antagonists
NT4 avidin
NT3 folate antagonists
NT4 aminopterin
NT4 methotrexate
NT3 picolinic acid
NT3 riboflavin antagonists
NT3 thiamin antagonists
NT4 pyrithiamine
NT2 vitamin c antagonists
NT3 dehydroascorbic acid
NT2 vitamin k antagonists
NT3 dicoumarol
NT3 warfarin
rt agonists
rt fungal antagonists

ANTARCTIC OCEAN
BT1 marine areas

ANTARCTICA
(all antarctic territories)
uf south polar region
rt cold zones

anteaters
USE **myrmecophagidae**

ANTECHINUS
BT1 dasyuridae
BT2 marsupials
BT3 mammals
NT1 antechinus swainsonii

ANTECHINUS SWAINSONII
BT1 antechinus
BT2 dasyuridae
BT3 marsupials
BT4 mammals

ANTELOPES
BT1 ruminants
BT2 animals
NT1 chamois
rt game animals
rt meat animals

ANTEMORTEM EXAMINATIONS (AGRICOLA)
BT1 meat inspection
BT2 food inspection
BT3 inspection
BT4 quality controls
BT5 consumer protection
BT6 protection
BT5 controls

ANTENNAE
BT1 sense organs
BT2 body parts
rt electroantennograms

ANTENNARIA
BT1 compositae
NT1 antennaria dioica
NT1 antennaria microphylla

ANTENNARIA DIOICA
uf gnaphalium dioicum
BT1 antennaria
BT2 compositae
BT1 ornamental herbaceous plants

ANTENNARIA MICROPHYLLA
BT1 antennaria
BT2 compositae

ANTERIOR PITUITARY
uf adenohypophysis
uf pituitary, anterior
BT1 pituitary
BT2 endocrine glands
BT3 glands (animal)
BT4 body parts
BT4 glands
rt adenohypophysis hormones

ANTESTIOPSIS
BT1 pentatomidae
BT2 heteroptera
NT1 antestiopsis intricata
NT1 antestiopsis orbitalis

ANTESTIOPSIS INTRICATA
BT1 antestiopsis
BT2 pentatomidae
BT3 heteroptera

ANTESTIOPSIS ORBITALIS
BT1 antestiopsis
BT2 pentatomidae
BT3 heteroptera

ANTHELMINTICS
BT1 antiparasitic agents
BT2 drugs
NT1 abamectin
NT1 acetarsol
NT1 albendazole
NT1 amoscanate
NT1 anthiolimine
NT1 antimony potassium tartrate
NT1 arecoline
NT1 artemether
NT1 benacil
NT1 bephenium
NT1 bithionol
NT1 bitoscanate
NT1 bromofenofos
NT1 bromophos
NT1 brotianide
NT1 bunamidine
NT1 calcium cyanamide
NT1 cambendazole
NT1 carbaryl
NT1 carbon tetrachloride
NT1 ciclobendazole

ANTHELMINTICS *cont.*
NT1 cinnamic acid
NT1 clioxanide
NT1 clorsulon
NT1 copper sulfate
NT1 coumaphos
NT1 creosote
NT1 crufomate
NT1 cyacetacide
NT1 diamfenetide
NT1 dichlorophen
NT1 dichlorvos
NT1 diethylcarbamazine
NT1 disophenol
NT1 dithiazanine iodide
NT1 emetine
NT1 febantel
NT1 fenbendazole
NT1 flubendazole
NT1 furapyrimidone
NT1 gentian violet
NT1 halofuginone
NT1 haloxon
NT1 hexachloroethane
NT1 hexachloroparaxylene
NT1 hexachlorophene
NT1 hexylresorcinol
NT1 hycanthone
NT1 hygromycin b
NT1 ivermectin
NT1 kamala
NT1 lucanthone
NT1 luxabendazole
NT1 mebendazole
NT1 medamine
NT1 melarsonyl
NT1 metronidazole
NT1 metyridine
NT1 milbemycin d
NT1 mitomycin
NT1 morantel
NT1 naftalofos
NT1 niclofolan
NT1 niclosamide
NT1 nicotine
NT1 niridazole
NT1 nitroscanate
NT1 nitroxinil
NT1 novel anthelmintics
NT1 oxamniquine
NT1 oxantel
NT1 oxfendazole
NT1 oxyclozanide
NT1 parbendazole
NT1 phenothiazine
NT1 piperazine
NT1 praziquantel
NT1 pyrantel
NT1 pyrvinium chloride
NT1 rafoxanide
NT1 sodium stibocaptate
NT1 stibophen
NT1 suramin
NT1 tetramisole
NT2 levamisole
NT1 thiabendazole
NT1 thiacetarsamide sodium
NT1 thiofuradene
NT1 tribromsalan
NT1 trichlorfon
NT1 triclabendazole
rt animal parasitic nematodes
rt benzimidazoles
rt ovicides and larvicides
rt veterinary helminthology

ANTHEMIS
BT1 compositae
NT1 anthemis arvensis
NT1 anthemis austriaca
NT1 anthemis cotula
NT1 anthemis jailensis
NT1 anthemis pseudocotula
NT1 anthemis tinctoria

ANTHEMIS ARVENSIS
BT1 anthemis
BT2 compositae

ANTHEMIS AUSTRIACA
BT1 anthemis
BT2 compositae

ANTHEMIS COTULA
uf mayweed
BT1 anthemis
BT2 compositae
BT1 weeds

ANTHEMIS JAILENSIS
BT1 anthemis
BT2 compositae

anthemis nobilis
USE **chamaemelum nobile**

ANTHEMIS PSEUDOCOTULA
BT1 anthemis
BT2 compositae

ANTHEMIS TINCTORIA
BT1 anthemis
BT2 compositae
BT1 dye plants

ANTHEMOSOMA
BT1 apicomplexa
BT2 protozoa
NT1 anthemosoma garnhami

ANTHEMOSOMA GARNHAMI
BT1 anthemosoma
BT2 apicomplexa
BT3 protozoa

ANTHEPHORA
BT1 gramineae
NT1 anthephora pubescens

ANTHEPHORA PUBESCENS
BT1 anthephora
BT2 gramineae
BT1 pasture plants

ANTHER CULTURE
uf pollen culture
BT1 tissue culture
BT2 in vitro culture
BT3 culture techniques
BT4 biological techniques
BT5 techniques
rt androgenesis
rt haploidy

ANTHERAEA
uf telea
BT1 saturniidae
BT2 lepidoptera
NT1 antheraea mylitta
NT1 antheraea pernyi
NT1 antheraea polyphemus

ANTHERAEA MYLITTA
BT1 antheraea
BT2 saturniidae
BT3 lepidoptera

ANTHERAEA PERNYI
BT1 antheraea
BT2 saturniidae
BT3 lepidoptera
BT1 silkworms
BT2 beneficial insects
BT3 beneficial arthropods
BT4 beneficial organisms
BT3 insects
BT4 arthropods

ANTHERAEA POLYPHEMUS
uf telea polyphemus
BT1 antheraea
BT2 saturniidae
BT3 lepidoptera

ANTHERICUM
BT1 liliaceae
NT1 anthericum liliago

ANTHERICUM LILIAGO
BT1 anthericum
BT2 liliaceae
BT1 ornamental herbaceous plants

ANTHERS
BT1 stamens
BT2 androecium
BT3 flowers

ANTHERS *cont.*
BT4 inflorescences
BT5 plant
NT1 pollen

anthesis
USE **flowering**

ANTHIDIELLUM
BT1 apidae
BT2 hymenoptera

ANTHIDIUM
BT1 apidae
BT2 hymenoptera

ANTHIOLIMINE
uf antimony lithium thiomalate
BT1 anthelmintics
BT2 antiparasitic agents
BT3 drugs

ANTHOCEPHALUS
BT1 rubiaceae
NT1 anthocephalus chinensis
rt nauclea

anthocephalus cadamba
USE **anthocephalus chinensis**

ANTHOCEPHALUS CHINENSIS
uf anthocephalus cadamba
uf nauclea cadamba
BT1 anthocephalus
BT2 rubiaceae
BT1 forest trees
BT1 nematicidal plants
BT2 pesticidal plants

ANTHOCLEISTA
BT1 loganiaceae
NT1 anthocleista grandiflora
NT1 anthocleista zambesiaca

ANTHOCLEISTA GRANDIFLORA
BT1 anthocleista
BT2 loganiaceae

ANTHOCLEISTA ZAMBESIACA
BT1 anthocleista
BT2 loganiaceae

ANTHOCORIDAE
BT1 heteroptera
NT1 anthocoris
NT2 anthocoris nemoralis
NT2 anthocoris nemorum
NT1 orius
NT2 orius albidipennis
NT2 orius insidiosus
NT2 orius minutus
NT2 orius niger
NT2 orius tristicolor
NT2 orius vicinus
NT1 xylocoris
NT2 xylocoris flavipes

ANTHOCORIS
BT1 anthocoridae
BT2 heteroptera
NT1 anthocoris nemoralis
NT1 anthocoris nemorum

ANTHOCORIS NEMORALIS
BT1 anthocoris
BT2 anthocoridae
BT3 heteroptera

ANTHOCORIS NEMORUM
BT1 anthocoris
BT2 anthocoridae
BT3 heteroptera

ANTHOCYANIDINS
BT1 flavonoids
BT2 aromatic compounds
BT2 plant pigments
BT3 pigments
NT1 cyanidin
NT1 delphinidin
NT1 pelargonidin
rt anthocyanins

ANTHOCYANINS
BT1 glycoflavones

ANTHOCYANINS *cont.*
BT2 flavonoids
BT3 aromatic compounds
BT3 plant pigments
BT4 pigments
BT2 glycosides
BT3 carbohydrates
NT1 cyanin
NT1 delphinin
NT1 rubrobrassicin
rt anthocyanidins

ANTHOLYZA
BT1 iridaceae
rt ornamental bulbs

ANTHOMYIIDAE
BT1 diptera
NT1 botanophila
NT1 delia
NT2 delia antiqua
NT2 delia coarctata
NT2 delia floralis
NT2 delia florilega
NT2 delia platura
NT2 delia radicum
NT1 hylemya
NT1 lasiomma
NT1 pegomya
NT2 pegomya betae
NT2 pegomya hyoscyami
NT1 phorbia
NT2 phorbia haberlandti
NT2 phorbia securis
NT1 strobilomyia
NT2 strobilomyia anthracina
NT2 strobilomyia laricicola
NT2 strobilomyia melania

ANTHONOMUS
BT1 curculionidae
BT2 coleoptera
NT1 anthonomus grandis
NT1 anthonomus pomorum
NT1 anthonomus rubi

ANTHONOMUS GRANDIS
BT1 anthonomus
BT2 curculionidae
BT3 coleoptera
rt grandlure

ANTHONOMUS POMORUM
BT1 anthonomus
BT2 curculionidae
BT3 coleoptera

ANTHONOMUS RUBI
BT1 anthonomus
BT2 curculionidae
BT3 coleoptera

ANTHOPHILA
uf simaethis
BT1 choreutidae
BT2 lepidoptera
rt choreutis

anthophila pariana
USE **choreutis pariana**

ANTHOPHORA
uf amegilla
uf paramegilla
BT1 apidae
BT2 hymenoptera

ANTHOSEIUS
BT1 phytoseiidae
BT2 mesostigmata
BT3 acari
NT1 anthoseius caudiglans
rt neoseiulus
rt typhlodromus

ANTHOSEIUS CAUDIGLANS
uf neoseiulus caudiglans
uf typhlodromus caudiglans
BT1 anthoseius
BT2 phytoseiidae
BT3 mesostigmata
BT4 acari

ANTHOXANTHUM
BT1 gramineae
NT1 anthoxanthum alpinum
NT1 anthoxanthum odoratum
NT1 anthoxanthum puelii

ANTHOXANTHUM ALPINUM
BT1 anthoxanthum
BT2 gramineae
BT1 pasture plants

ANTHOXANTHUM ODORATUM
uf *sweet vernal grass*
uf *vernal grass*
BT1 anthoxanthum
BT2 gramineae
BT1 pasture plants

ANTHOXANTHUM PUELII
BT1 anthoxanthum
BT2 gramineae
BT1 pasture plants

ANTHRACITE WASTE
BT1 growing media
BT1 industrial wastes
BT2 wastes
rt coal

ANTHRACOIDEA
HN from 1990
BT1 ustilaginales
NT1 anthracoidea caricis
NT1 anthracoidea subinclusa
rt cintractia

ANTHRACOIDEA CARICIS
HN from 1990
uf *cintractia caricis*
BT1 anthracoidea
BT2 ustilaginales

ANTHRACOIDEA SUBINCLUSA
HN from 1990
uf *cintractia subinclusa*
BT1 anthracoidea
BT2 ustilaginales

ANTHRAQUINONES
BT1 quinones
BT2 aromatic compounds
NT1 emodin

ANTHRAX
BT1 bacterial diseases
BT2 infectious diseases
BT3 diseases
BT1 cattle diseases
BT2 animal diseases
BT3 diseases
rt bacillus anthracis

ANTHRENUS
BT1 dermestidae
BT2 coleoptera
NT1 anthrenus flavipes
NT1 anthrenus fuscus
NT1 anthrenus verbasci

ANTHRENUS FLAVIPES
uf *anthrenus vorax*
BT1 anthrenus
BT2 dermestidae
BT3 coleoptera

ANTHRENUS FUSCUS
BT1 anthrenus
BT2 dermestidae
BT3 coleoptera

ANTHRENUS VERBASCI
BT1 anthrenus
BT2 dermestidae
BT3 coleoptera

anthrenus vorax
USE **anthrenus flavipes**

ANTHRIBIDAE
BT1 coleoptera
NT1 araecerus
NT2 araecerus fasciculatus

ANTHRISCUS
BT1 umbelliferae

ANTHRISCUS *cont.*
NT1 anthriscus cerefolium
NT1 anthriscus sylvestris

ANTHRISCUS CEREFOLIUM
uf *chervil*
BT1 anthriscus
BT2 umbelliferae
BT1 culinary herbs

ANTHRISCUS SYLVESTRIS
BT1 anthriscus
BT2 umbelliferae

ANTHROPOGENIC HORIZONS
BT1 horizons
BT2 soil morphological features

anthropogenic soil types
USE **soil types (anthropogenic)**

ANTHROPOLOGY
BT1 social sciences
NT1 ethnobotany
NT1 social anthropology
rt man

ANTHROPOMETRIC DIMENSIONS
uf *anthropometric measurements*
BT1 dimensions
NT1 arm circumference (agricola)
rt biometry
rt body measurements
rt ergonomics

ANTHROPOMETRIC DUMMIES
BT1 dummies
rt ergonomics
rt models

anthropometric measurements
USE **anthropometric dimensions**

ANTHURIUM
BT1 araceae
NT1 anthurium polyschistum
NT1 anthurium scherzerianum
NT1 anthurium warocqueanum

ANTHURIUM POLYSCHISTUM
BT1 anthurium
BT2 araceae
BT1 ornamental herbaceous plants

ANTHURIUM SCHERZERIANUM
BT1 anthurium
BT2 araceae
BT1 ornamental herbaceous plants

ANTHURIUM WAROCQUEANUM
BT1 anthurium
BT2 araceae
BT1 ornamental herbaceous plants

ANTHYLLIS
BT1 leguminosae
NT1 anthyllis montana
NT1 anthyllis vulneraria

ANTHYLLIS MONTANA
BT1 anthyllis
BT2 leguminosae
BT1 pasture legumes
BT2 legumes
BT2 pasture plants

ANTHYLLIS VULNERARIA
uf *kidney vetch*
BT1 anthyllis
BT2 leguminosae
BT1 medicinal plants
BT1 pasture legumes
BT2 legumes
BT2 pasture plants

ANTIAGGREGATION PHEROMONES
BT1 pheromones
BT2 semiochemicals
rt aggregation pheromones

ANTIARIS
BT1 moraceae
NT1 antiaris africana
NT1 antiaris toxicaria

ANTIARIS AFRICANA
BT1 antiaris
BT2 moraceae

antiaris saccidora
USE **antiaris toxicaria**

ANTIARIS TOXICARIA
uf *antiaris saccidora*
BT1 antiaris
BT2 moraceae
BT1 poisonous plants

antiarrhythmic agents
USE **myocardial depressants**

ANTIAUXINS
BT1 plant growth regulators
BT2 growth regulators
NT1 2,4,6-t
NT1 chlorophenoxyisobutyric acid
NT1 tiba

ANTIBACTERIAL AGENTS
BT1 antiinfective agents
BT2 drugs
NT1 aminosalicylic acid
NT1 antimycobacterial agents
NT1 apramycin
NT1 arsanilic acid
NT1 aspergillic acid
NT1 avoparcin
NT1 bacitracin
NT1 bambermycin
NT1 benzalkonium chloride
NT1 carbadox
NT1 cefamandole
NT1 cefazolin
NT1 cefoxitin
NT1 cephalosporins
NT1 chloramphenicol
NT1 chlortetracycline
NT1 clindamycin
NT1 cycloserine
NT1 dapsone
NT1 dihydrostreptomycin
NT1 erythromycin
NT1 framycetin
NT1 furaltadone
NT1 gentamicin
NT1 gentian violet
NT1 gloxazone
NT1 gougerotin
NT1 gramicidin
NT1 gramicidin s
NT1 isoniazid
NT1 kanamycin
NT1 kasugamycin
NT1 lincomycin
NT1 nalidixic acid
NT1 neomycin
NT1 nifuroxazide
NT1 nitrofurantoin
NT1 nitrovin
NT1 novobiocin
NT1 oleandomycin
NT1 oxytetracycline
NT1 penicillins
NT2 amoxicillin
NT2 ampicillin
NT2 carbenicillin
NT2 cloxacillin
NT2 oxacillin
NT1 polymyxin b
NT1 rifampicin
NT1 rifamycin
NT1 roxarsone
NT1 spectinomycin
NT1 spiramycin
NT1 streptomycin
NT1 sulfachlorpyridazine
NT1 sulfadiazine
NT1 sulfadimethoxine
NT1 sulfadimidine
NT1 sulfadoxine
NT1 sulfafurazole
NT1 sulfamerazine

ANTIBACTERIAL AGENTS *cont.*
NT1 sulfamethoxazole
NT1 sulfamethoxypyridazine
NT1 sulfamonomethoxine
NT1 sulfanilamide
NT1 sulfapyrazole
NT1 sulfapyridine
NT1 sulfathiazole
NT1 tetracycline
NT1 thiopeptin
NT1 tiamulin
NT1 trimethoprim
NT1 turimycins
NT1 tylosin
NT1 virginiamycin
NT1 xantocillin
NT1 zinc bacitracin
rt antibacterial properties
rt sulfonamides

antibacterial finishes
USE **antiseptic finishes (agricola)**

ANTIBACTERIAL PLANTS
uf *bactericidal plants*
NT1 acacia mellifera
NT1 adansonia digitata
NT1 aegle marmelos
NT1 aesculus hippocastanum
NT1 agave salmiana
NT1 ailanthus altissima
NT1 ajuga chamaepitys
NT1 alafia multiflora
NT1 alchornea cordifolia
NT1 alkanna tuberculata
NT1 aloysia triphylla
NT1 alphonsea arborea
NT1 alpinia galanga
NT1 alstonia scholaris
NT1 amorpha fruticosa
NT1 anemone hupehensis
NT1 anethum graveolens
NT1 argyreia nervosa
NT1 aristolochia acuminata
NT1 aristolochia multiflora
NT1 arnica montana
NT1 artemisia herba-alba
NT1 artocarpus blancoi
NT1 athyrium filix-femina
NT1 atylosia trinervia
NT1 azadirachta indica
NT1 baccharis crispa
NT1 bletilla striata
NT1 blumea malcolmii
NT1 boswellia serrata
NT1 caesalpinia crista
NT1 calendula officinalis
NT1 callicarpa candicans
NT1 callicarpa formosana
NT1 callitris columellaris
NT1 cardaria draba
NT1 carrots
NT1 carum carvi
NT1 cashews
NT1 cassia obtusifolia
NT1 ceiba pentandra
NT1 celery
NT1 ceratostigma plumbaginoides
NT1 chrysanthemums
NT1 cinnamomum tamala
NT1 cinnamomum zeylanicum
NT1 cneorum tricoccon
NT1 coriandrum sativum
NT1 croton sonderianus
NT1 curcuma longa
NT1 cymbopogon citratus
NT1 cymbopogon nervatus
NT1 cynoglossum officinale
NT1 cystopteris fragilis
NT1 diplodiscus paniculatus
NT1 dryopteris carthusiana
NT1 dryopteris filix-mas
NT1 elettaria cardamomum
NT1 entada africana
NT1 eremophila mitchellii
NT1 eucalyptus citriodora
NT1 eucalyptus dives
NT1 eucalyptus polybractea
NT1 eucalyptus radiata
NT1 eupatorium ayapana

ANTIBACTERIAL PLANTS *cont.*
NT1 eupatorium capillifolium
NT1 eupatorium odoratum
NT1 fagara zanthoxyloides
NT1 forsythia suspensa
NT1 garcinia kola
NT1 garlic
NT1 ginkgo biloba
NT1 glossocardia bosvallia
NT1 glycosmis pentaphylla
NT1 glycyrrhiza glabra
NT1 glycyrrhiza lepidota
NT1 guavas
NT1 guiera senegalensis
NT1 gymnophyton isatidicarpum
NT1 gypsophila perfoliata
NT1 haplophyllum tuberculatum
NT1 hedera helix
NT1 heliotropium europaeum
NT1 hemidesmus indicus
NT1 hibiscus sabdariffa
NT1 hunnemannia fumariifolia
NT1 hyacinthoides non-scripta
NT1 hypericum perforatum
NT1 iboza riparia
NT1 jatropha podagrica
NT1 knowltonia capensis
NT1 laggera aurita
NT1 lamium album
NT1 lawsonia inermis
NT1 limonia acidissima
NT1 lonchocarpus violaceus
NT1 loxopterygium huasango
NT1 lychnis flos-cuculi
NT1 lycium chinense
NT1 lysimachia vulgaris
NT1 maclura pomifera
NT1 magnolia grandiflora
NT1 mahonia aquifolium
NT1 mammea longifolia
NT1 mangoes
NT1 mangosteens
NT1 manotes longiflora
NT1 melaleuca alternifolia
NT1 melaleuca quinquenervia
NT1 melaleuca viridiflora
NT1 melia azedarach
NT1 mentha piperita
NT1 mimosa hamata
NT1 monarda fistulosa
NT1 moringa oleifera
NT1 myristica fragrans
NT1 myrtus communis
NT1 nardostachys jatamansi
NT1 nigella sativa
NT1 ocimum basilicum
NT1 ocimum sanctum
NT1 oil palms
NT1 onions
NT1 ononis natrix
NT1 osmunda regalis
NT1 ozoroa mucronata
NT1 paeonia lactiflora
NT1 paris quadrifolia
NT1 parthenium hysterophorus
NT1 pawpaws
NT1 peganum harmala
NT1 pelargonium graveolens
NT1 peltophorum pterocarpum
NT1 pentadiplandra brazzeana
NT1 peucedanum hystrix
NT1 phytolacca americana
NT1 piper methysticum
NT1 piper nigrum
NT1 pisonia umbellifera
NT1 plumbago zeylanica
NT1 polyalthia longifolia
NT1 polygonatum intermedium
NT1 polygonum hydropiper
NT1 pongamia pinnata
NT1 primula veris
NT1 prosopis ruscifolia
NT1 quassia amara
NT1 rehmannia glutinosa
NT1 rhododendron canadense
NT1 rollinia emarginata
NT1 rosmarinus officinalis
NT1 ruta graveolens
NT1 salvia officinalis
NT1 salvia sclarea
NT1 sambucus nigra

ANTIBACTERIAL PLANTS *cont.*
NT1 santalum lanceolatum
NT1 satureja montana
NT1 selinum tenuifolium
NT1 senecio bicolor
NT1 silene vulgaris
NT1 sisymbrium irio
NT1 solanum pseudocapsicum
NT1 sophora japonica
NT1 spondias mombin
NT1 strawberries
NT1 strychnos afzelii
NT1 strychnos floribunda
NT1 syzygium aromaticum
NT1 tagetes erecta
NT1 talauma villariana
NT1 tamarinds
NT1 taxus canadensis
NT1 thalictrum minus
NT1 thalictrum rugosum
NT1 thymus karamarianicus
NT1 thymus marschallianus
NT1 thymus pulegioides
NT1 thymus vulgaris
NT1 tilia tomentosa
NT1 trachyspermum ammi
NT1 trianthema portulacastrum
NT1 tribulus alatus
NT1 tulips
NT1 urtica dioica
NT1 uvaria chamae
NT1 viburnum lantana
NT1 vigna luteola
NT1 vitex agnus-castus
NT1 wedelia glauca
NT1 xylopia aethiopica
NT1 zingiber officinale
rt antibacterial properties
rt dryopteris
rt dysoxylum
rt horticultural crops
rt industrial crops
rt medicinal plants
rt pesticidal plants
rt plants
rt senecio
rt sideritis
rt tabernaemontana

ANTIBACTERIAL PROPERTIES
uf bactericidal properties
BT1 antimicrobial properties
BT2 properties
rt antibacterial agents
rt antibacterial plants
rt bacteria
rt bacterial diseases
rt bactericides
rt bacteriophages
rt phytoncides

ANTIBIOSIS
BT1 varietal resistance
BT2 pest resistance
BT3 resistance
BT2 varietal reactions

ANTIBIOTIC ACARICIDES
BT1 acaricides
BT2 pesticides
BT1 antibiotics
NT1 ivermectin
NT1 nikkomycins
NT1 tetranactin
NT1 thuringiensin

ANTIBIOTIC FUNGICIDES
BT1 antibiotics
BT1 fungicides
BT2 pesticides
NT1 aureofungin
NT1 blasticidin-s
NT1 cycloheximide
NT1 griseofulvin
NT1 kasugamycin
NT1 natamycin
NT1 polyoxins
NT1 validamycin

ANTIBIOTIC HERBICIDES
BT1 antibiotics
BT1 herbicides

ANTIBIOTIC HERBICIDES *cont.*
BT2 pesticides
NT1 bilanafos
NT1 glufosinate

ANTIBIOTIC INSECTICIDES
BT1 antibiotics
BT1 insecticides
BT2 pesticides
NT1 abamectin
NT1 ivermectin
NT1 thuringiensin
rt destruxins

ANTIBIOTIC NEMATICIDES
BT1 antibiotics
BT1 nematicides
BT2 pesticides
NT1 abamectin

ANTIBIOTIC RESIDUES
BT1 drug residues
BT2 residues
rt antibiotics

antibiotic supplements
USE **feed supplements**

ANTIBIOTICS
NT1 aminoglycoside antibiotics
NT2 framycetin
NT2 gentamicin
NT2 kanamycin
NT2 paromomycin
NT2 spiramycin
NT2 streptomycin
NT1 antibiotic acaricides
NT2 ivermectin
NT2 nikkomycins
NT2 tetranactin
NT2 thuringiensin
NT1 antibiotic fungicides
NT2 aureofungin
NT2 blasticidin-s
NT2 cycloheximide
NT2 griseofulvin
NT2 kasugamycin
NT2 natamycin
NT2 polyoxins
NT2 validamycin
NT1 antibiotic herbicides
NT2 bilanafos
NT2 glufosinate
NT1 antibiotic insecticides
NT2 abamectin
NT2 ivermectin
NT2 thuringiensin
NT1 antibiotic nematicides
NT2 abamectin
NT1 antimycin a
NT1 apramycin
NT1 aspergillic acid
NT1 avermectins
NT2 abamectin
NT2 ivermectin
NT1 avoparcin
NT1 azaserine
NT1 bacitracin
NT1 bacteriocins
NT2 colicins
NT1 bambermycin
NT1 candicidin
NT1 cefamandole
NT1 cefazolin
NT1 cefoxitin
NT1 cephalosporins
NT1 chartreusin
NT1 chloramphenicol
NT1 chlortetracycline
NT1 citrinin
NT1 cycloserine
NT1 cyclosporins
NT1 dactinomycin
NT1 dihydrostreptomycin
NT1 doxorubicin
NT1 fumagillin
NT1 fusaric acid
NT1 gramicidin
NT1 gramicidin s
NT1 grisein
NT1 heliomycin
NT1 hygromycin b

ANTIBIOTICS *cont.*
NT1 imanin
NT1 kojic acid
NT1 lasalocid
NT1 macrolide antibiotics
NT2 clindamycin
NT2 erythromycin
NT2 lincomycin
NT2 oleandomycin
NT2 spiramycin
NT1 milbemycins
NT2 milbemycin d
NT1 mitomycin
NT1 narasin
NT1 neomycin
NT1 nigericin
NT1 nisin
NT1 nosiheptide
NT1 novobiocin
NT1 nucleoside antibiotics
NT2 blasticidin-s
NT2 cordycepin
NT2 gougerotin
NT2 nikkomycins
NT2 polyoxins
NT2 puromycin
NT2 toyocamycin
NT1 oligomycin
NT1 oxytetracycline
NT1 penicillic acid
NT1 polymyxin b
NT1 rifamycin
NT1 roridins
NT1 salinomycin
NT1 spectinomycin
NT1 subtilin
NT1 tetracycline
NT1 thiopeptin
NT1 tiamulin
NT1 trichodermin
NT1 trichothecin
NT1 turimycins
NT1 tylosin
NT1 valinomycin
NT1 verrucarins
NT1 virginiamycin
NT1 xantocillin
rt actinomyces
rt antibiotic residues
rt antiinfective agents
rt bacterial products
rt feed additives
rt growth promoters
rt mycotoxins
rt penicillins
rt phytoalexins
rt secondary metabolites
rt tetracyclines

ANTIBLOAT AGENTS
BT1 gastrointestinal agents
BT2 drugs
NT1 simethicone
rt bloat
rt digesta
rt digestive disorders

ANTIBODIES
BT1 immunoglobulins
BT2 glycoproteins
BT3 proteins
BT4 peptides
BT2 immunological factors
NT1 agglutinins
NT2 haemagglutinins
NT3 viral haemagglutinins
NT2 lectins
NT3 phytohaemagglutinins
NT4 concanavalin a
NT4 limulins
NT4 ricin
NT1 antitoxins
NT1 autoantibodies
NT1 gliadin antibodies
NT1 haemolysins
NT2 melittin
NT1 local antibodies
NT1 maternal antibodies
NT1 natural antibodies
NT1 opsonins
NT1 precipitins
rt antibody formation

ANTIBODIES *cont.*
rt antigen antibody reactions
rt antigens
rt humoral immunity
rt immune response
rt immune serum
rt immunity
rt immunochemistry
rt immunological diseases
rt reticuloendothelial system
rt serum
rt vaccines

ANTIBODY FORMATION
BT1 immune response
BT2 immunity
rt antibodies
rt antigens
rt plasma cells

ANTICAKING AGENTS
rt anticaking treatment
rt caking
rt fertilizers

ANTICAKING TREATMENT
rt anticaking agents
rt caking
rt treatment

ANTICARSIA
BT1 noctuidae
BT2 lepidoptera
NT1 anticarsia gemmatalis

ANTICARSIA GEMMATALIS
BT1 anticarsia
BT2 noctuidae
BT3 lepidoptera

ANTICHOLESTEREMIC AGENTS (AGRICOLA)
BT1 antilipemics
rt cholesterol
rt hypercholesterolemia
rt lipotropic factors

ANTICOAGULANTS
BT1 haematologic agents
BT2 drugs
NT1 dicoumarol
NT1 edta
NT1 heparin
NT1 sodium citrate
NT1 warfarin
rt blood
rt blood coagulation
rt coagulation
rt coumarins

anticoccidials
USE **coccidiostats**

ANTICONVULSANTS
BT1 neurotropic drugs
BT2 drugs
NT1 magnesium sulfate
NT2 epsom salts
NT1 phenobarbital
NT1 phenytoin
NT1 sultroponium
NT1 valproic acid
rt barbiturates
rt convulsions
rt epilepsy

ANTIDEPRESSANTS
BT1 psychotropic drugs
BT2 neurotropic drugs
BT3 drugs
BT1 stimulants
BT2 drugs
NT1 desipramine
rt depression

ANTIDESMA
BT1 euphorbiaceae
NT1 antidesma bunius
NT1 antidesma dallachryanum
NT1 antidesma frutescens
NT1 antidesma menasu

ANTIDESMA BUNIAS
BT1 tropical small fruits

ANTIDESMA BUNIAS *cont.*
BT2 small fruits
BT2 tropical fruits
BT3 fruit crops

ANTIDESMA BUNIUS
BT1 antidesma
BT2 euphorbiaceae

ANTIDESMA DALLACHRYANUM
BT1 antidesma
BT2 euphorbiaceae
BT1 tropical small fruits
BT2 small fruits
BT2 tropical fruits
BT3 fruit crops

ANTIDESMA FRUTESCENS
BT1 antidesma
BT2 euphorbiaceae

ANTIDESMA MENASU
BT1 antidesma
BT2 euphorbiaceae
BT1 medicinal plants

antidiabetics
USE **hypoglycaemic agents**

ANTIDIARRHEA AGENTS
BF antidiarrhoea agents
rt diarrhea

ANTIDIARRHOEA AGENTS
AF antidiarrhea agents
BT1 absorbents
BT1 gastrointestinal agents
BT2 drugs
NT1 calcium carbonate
NT1 kaolin
NT1 pectins
rt diarrhoea

antidiuretic hormone
USE **vasopressin**

ANTIDORCAS
BT1 bovidae
BT2 ruminantia
BT3 artiodactyla
BT4 mammals
BT4 ungulates
NT1 antidorcas marsupialis

ANTIDORCAS MARSUPIALIS
BT1 antidorcas
BT2 bovidae
BT3 ruminantia
BT4 artiodactyla
BT5 mammals
BT5 ungulates

ANTIDOTES
BT1 detoxicants
BT2 drugs
NT1 dimercaprol
NT1 glutathione
NT1 methylene blue
NT1 pralidoxime
rt starch

antidotes, herbicide
USE **herbicide safeners**

ANTIEMETICS
BT1 gastrointestinal agents
BT2 drugs
NT1 chlorpromazine
rt emetics
rt vomiting

ANTIFEEDANTS
uf *feeding deterrents*
uf *feeding inhibitors*
uf *phagodeterrents*
BT1 inhibitors
NT1 fentin acetate
NT1 fentin chloride
NT1 fentin hydroxide
NT1 guazatine
rt anorexiants
rt feeding
rt insect control

antiflatulents
USE **carminatives**

ANTIFOULING AGENTS
BT1 biocides
rt biofouling

ANTIFUNGAL AGENTS
(therapeutic, not including agricultural and industrial fungicides)
BT1 antiinfective agents
BT2 drugs
NT1 amphotericin b
NT1 benzalkonium chloride
NT1 candicidin
NT1 clotrimazole
NT1 cycloheximide
NT1 dehydroacetic acid
NT1 econazole
NT1 fenticonazole
NT1 fluconazole
NT1 flucytosine
NT1 gentian violet
NT1 griseofulvin
NT1 itraconazole
NT1 ketoconazole
NT1 miconazole
NT1 monensin
NT1 natamycin
NT1 nystatin
NT1 oligomycin
NT1 partricin
NT1 phenylmercury nitrate
NT1 propionic acid
NT1 terbinafine
NT1 thiomersal
NT1 tolnaftate
NT1 trichodermin
rt antifungal plants
rt antifungal properties
rt fungicides
rt plant disease control

ANTIFUNGAL PLANTS
uf *fungicidal plants*
NT1 achyranthes aspera
NT1 aconitum nasutum
NT1 aegle marmelos
NT1 ajuga chamaepitys
NT1 alpinia galanga
NT1 alpinia officinarum
NT1 amaryllis belladonna
NT1 anaphalis contorta
NT1 anethum graveolens
NT1 anethum sowa
NT1 argyreia nervosa
NT1 artabotrys hexapetalus
NT1 artemisia maritima
NT1 asparagus racemosus
NT1 aster alpinus
NT1 avocados
NT1 azadirachta indica
NT1 bauhinia candicans
NT1 black currants
NT1 boehmeria cylindrica
NT1 callistemon citrinus
NT1 calotropis procera
NT1 canna indica
NT1 cannabis sativa
NT1 carnations
NT1 carrots
NT1 cashews
NT1 catharanthus roseus
NT1 celery
NT1 cestrum diurnum
NT1 chelidonium majus
NT1 chenopodium amaranticolor
NT1 chloranthus japonicus
NT1 chrysanthemum alpinum
NT1 chrysanthemums
NT1 cistus laurifolius
NT1 clematis gouriana
NT1 coconuts
NT1 coffee
NT1 commiphora mukul
NT1 coriandrum sativum
NT1 crinum moorei
NT1 crotalaria madurensis
NT1 cupressus torulosa
NT1 curcuma amada
NT1 curcuma angustifolia

ANTIFUNGAL PLANTS *cont.*
NT1 curcuma aromatica
NT1 curcuma longa
NT1 cymbopogon flexuosus
NT1 cymbopogon martinii
NT1 cymbopogon winterianus
NT1 cyperus scariosus
NT1 daemonorops draco
NT1 datura metel
NT1 datura stramonium
NT1 digitalis grandiflora
NT1 elettaria cardamomum
NT1 enkianthus perulatus
NT1 eucalyptus citriodora
NT1 eupatorium odoratum
NT1 garcinia kola
NT1 garlic
NT1 ginkgo biloba
NT1 glossocardia bosvallia
NT1 glycyrrhiza glabra
NT1 grevillea robusta
NT1 hedera helix
NT1 hedychium coronarium
NT1 heterophragma quadriloculare
NT1 hibiscus sabdariffa
NT1 hops
NT1 hymenocallis festalis
NT1 hymenocallis littoralis
NT1 hyptis suaveolens
NT1 inula racemosa
NT1 irvingia gabonensis
NT1 jatropha podagrica
NT1 justicia pectoralis
NT1 kaempferia galanga
NT1 kigelia pinnata
NT1 lantana camara
NT1 lawsonia inermis
NT1 lentinula edodes
NT1 lepidium ruderale
NT1 limes
NT1 limonia acidissima
NT1 luvunga scandens
NT1 lychnis flos-cuculi
NT1 mangoes
NT1 mangosteens
NT1 melissa officinalis
NT1 mentha arvensis
NT1 mentha piperita
NT1 mesua ferrea
NT1 miliusa tomentosa
NT1 myristica fragrans
NT1 myrtus communis
NT1 nardostachys jatamansi
NT1 ocimum gratissimum
NT1 ocimum kilimandscharicum
NT1 ocimum sanctum
NT1 onions
NT1 origanum vulgare
NT1 paris quadrifolia
NT1 pawpaws
NT1 peganum harmala
NT1 peucedanum hystrix
NT1 peucedanum oreoselinum
NT1 pharbitis nil
NT1 phytolacca americana
NT1 phytolacca octandra
NT1 piper betle
NT1 piper nigrum
NT1 plumbago zeylanica
NT1 polyalthia longifolia
NT1 polygonatum intermedium
NT1 polygonatum verticillatum
NT1 pongamia pinnata
NT1 portulaca indica
NT1 prosopis cineraria
NT1 pterocarpus soyauxii
NT1 ranunculus sceleratus
NT1 rosmarinus officinalis
NT1 ruta graveolens
NT1 salvia officinalis
NT1 santalum album
NT1 saponaria ocymoides
NT1 solanum aviculare
NT1 solanum khasianum
NT1 solanum xanthocarpum
NT1 sophora angustifolia
NT1 strobilanthes cusia
NT1 syzygium aromaticum
NT1 tamarinds
NT1 thymus capitatus

ANTIFUNGAL PLANTS *cont.*
NT1 thymus karamarianicus
NT1 thymus serpyllum
NT1 thymus vulgaris
NT1 tomatoes
NT1 trachyspermum ammi
NT1 urceolina longipetala
NT1 veronica fruticulosa
NT1 vetiveria zizanioides
NT1 vincetoxicum hirundinaria
NT1 walnuts
NT1 zingiber officinale
NT1 ziziphus mauritiana
rt anemone
rt antifungal agents
rt antifungal properties
rt cymbidium
rt diospyros
rt fungicidal properties
rt fungicides
rt horticultural crops
rt industrial crops
rt medicinal plants
rt pesticidal plants
rt plants
rt tabernaemontana

ANTIFUNGAL PROPERTIES
rt antifungal agents
rt antifungal plants
rt antimicrobial properties
rt fungal diseases
rt fungi
rt fungicidal properties
rt fungicides
rt mycoses

ANTIGASTRA
BT1 pyralidae
BT2 lepidoptera
NT1 antigastra catalaunalis

ANTIGASTRA CATALAUNALIS
BT1 antigastra
BT2 pyralidae
BT3 lepidoptera

antigen antibody complexes
USE **immune complexes**

ANTIGEN ANTIBODY REACTIONS
uf *antigenic reactions*
BT1 immune response
BT2 immunity
NT1 cross reaction
NT1 rosette formation
NT1 virus neutralization
rt agglutination
rt antibodies
rt antigens
rt conglutination
rt haemolysis
rt immunological techniques
rt immunoprecipitation tests

ANTIGENIC DETERMINANTS
rt antigens

antigenic reactions
USE **antigen antibody reactions**

ANTIGENS
uf *immunogens*
BT1 immunological factors
NT1 allergens
NT2 brucellin
NT1 autoantigens
NT1 bacterial antigens
NT2 tuberculin
NT1 blood group antigens
NT1 circulating antigens
NT1 exoantigens
NT1 fungal antigens
NT2 coccidioidin
NT2 histoplasmin
NT2 spherulin
NT1 group specific antigens
NT1 h-y antigen
NT1 haptens
NT1 histocompatibility antigens
NT1 lipopolysaccharides
NT1 lymphocyte antigens

ANTIGENS *cont.*
NT1 neoplasm antigens
NT1 somatic antigens
NT1 surface antigens
NT1 toxoids
NT1 viral antigens
rt agglutinins
rt antibodies
rt antibody formation
rt antigen antibody reactions
rt antigenic determinants
rt immune response
rt immunization
rt immunology

ANTIGLOBULIN TEST
HN from 1990
BT1 haemagglutination tests
BT2 agglutination tests
BT3 immunological techniques
BT4 techniques
BT3 tests

ANTIGONON
BT1 polygonaceae
NT1 antigonon leptopus

ANTIGONON LEPTOPUS
BT1 antigonon
BT2 polygonaceae

ANTIGUA
uf *barbuda*
uf *redonda*
BT1 caribbean
BT2 america
rt caribbean community
rt commonwealth of nations

antihistamines
USE **antihistaminics**

ANTIHISTAMINICS
uf *antihistamines*
BT1 drugs
NT1 cimetidine
NT1 cyproheptadine
NT1 doxylamine
NT1 promethazine
rt allergies
rt capillaries
rt histamine

ANTIHYPERTENSIVE AGENTS
BT1 cardiovascular agents
BT2 drugs
NT1 chlorothiazide
NT1 diazoxide
NT1 furosemide
NT1 methyldopa
NT1 phenoxybenzamine
rt diuretics
rt hypertension

ANTIINFECTIVE AGENTS
uf *antimicrobials*
BT1 drugs
NT1 antibacterial agents
NT2 aminosalicylic acid
NT2 antimycobacterial agents
NT2 apramycin
NT2 arsanilic acid
NT2 aspergillic acid
NT2 avoparcin
NT2 bacitracin
NT2 bambermycin
NT2 benzalkonium chloride
NT2 carbadox
NT2 cefamandole
NT2 cefazolin
NT2 cefoxitin
NT2 cephalosporins
NT2 chloramphenicol
NT2 chlortetracycline
NT2 clindamycin
NT2 cycloserine
NT2 dapsone
NT2 dihydrostreptomycin
NT2 erythromycin
NT2 framycetin
NT2 furaltadone
NT2 gentamicin
NT2 gentian violet

ANTIINFECTIVE AGENTS *cont.*
NT2 gloxazone
NT2 gougerotin
NT2 gramicidin
NT2 gramicidin s
NT2 isoniazid
NT2 kanamycin
NT2 kasugamycin
NT2 lincomycin
NT2 nalidixic acid
NT2 neomycin
NT2 nifuroxazide
NT2 nitrofurantoin
NT2 nitrovin
NT2 novobiocin
NT2 oleandomycin
NT2 oxytetracycline
NT2 penicillins
NT3 amoxicillin
NT3 ampicillin
NT3 carbenicillin
NT3 cloxacillin
NT3 oxacillin
NT2 polymyxin b
NT2 rifampicin
NT2 rifamycin
NT2 roxarsone
NT2 spectinomycin
NT2 spiramycin
NT2 streptomycin
NT2 sulfachlorpyridazine
NT2 sulfadiazine
NT2 sulfadimethoxine
NT2 sulfadimidine
NT2 sulfadoxine
NT2 sulfafurazole
NT2 sulfamerazine
NT2 sulfamethoxazole
NT2 sulfamethoxypyridazine
NT2 sulfamonomethoxine
NT2 sulfanilamide
NT2 sulfapyrazole
NT2 sulfapyridine
NT2 sulfathiazole
NT2 tetracycline
NT2 thiopeptin
NT2 tiamulin
NT2 trimethoprim
NT2 turimycins
NT2 tylosin
NT2 virginiamycin
NT2 xantocillin
NT2 zinc bacitracin
NT1 antifungal agents
NT2 amphotericin b
NT2 benzalkonium chloride
NT2 candicidin
NT2 clotrimazole
NT2 cycloheximide
NT2 dehydroacetic acid
NT2 econazole
NT2 fenticonazole
NT2 fluconazole
NT2 flucytosine
NT2 gentian violet
NT2 griseofulvin
NT2 itraconazole
NT2 ketoconazole
NT2 miconazole
NT2 monensin
NT2 natamycin
NT2 nystatin
NT2 oligomycin
NT2 partricin
NT2 phenylmercury nitrate
NT2 propionic acid
NT2 terbinafine
NT2 thiomersal
NT2 tolnaftate
NT2 trichodermin
NT1 antiseptics
NT2 acriflavine
NT2 aluminium sulfate
NT2 benzalkonium chloride
NT2 borax
NT2 cetrimonium
NT2 dodicin
NT2 formaldehyde
NT2 iodine
NT2 malachite green
NT2 mandelic acid

ANTIINFECTIVE AGENTS *cont.*
NT2 mercuric chloride
NT2 mercuric oxide
NT2 methylene blue
NT2 naphthalene
NT2 potassium permanganate
NT2 safrole
NT2 thiram
NT1 antiviral agents
NT2 amantadine
NT2 floxuridine
NT2 hygromycin b
NT2 idoxuridine
NT2 imanin
NT2 interferon
NT2 lysozyme
rt antibiotics
rt antiparasitic agents
rt biocides
rt dermatological agents
rt disinfection
rt infections
rt infectious diseases
rt nitrofurans
rt plant disease control

ANTIINFLAMMATORY AGENTS
BT1 drugs
NT1 betamethasone
NT1 dexamethasone
NT1 fludrocortisone
NT1 flumetasone
NT1 flunixin
NT1 hydrocortisone
NT1 indometacin
NT1 oxyphenbutazone
NT1 prednisolone
NT1 prednisone
NT1 triamcinolone
rt dermatological agents
rt inflammation
rt synthetic glucocorticoids

ANTILIPAEMICS
AF antilipemics
BT1 haematologic agents
BT2 drugs
NT1 d-thyroxine
NT1 3-hydroxy-3-methylglutaric acid
NT1 bezafibrate
NT1 clofibrate
NT1 colestipol
NT1 colestyramine
NT1 halofenate
NT1 niceritrol
NT1 ornithine
NT1 probucol
NT1 sucrose polyester

ANTILIPEMICS
BF antilipaemics
NT1 anticholesteremic agents (agricola)
rt hyperlipemia

antilles
USE **caribbean**

antilles, netherlands
USE **netherlands antilles**

ANTILOCAPRA
BT1 antilocapridae
BT2 ruminantia
BT3 artiodactyla
BT4 mammals
BT4 ungulates
NT1 antilocapra americana

ANTILOCAPRA AMERICANA
uf *pronghorns*
BT1 antilocapra
BT2 antilocapridae
BT3 ruminantia
BT4 artiodactyla
BT5 mammals
BT5 ungulates

ANTILOCAPRIDAE
BT1 ruminantia
BT2 artiodactyla
BT3 mammals

ANTILOCAPRIDAE *cont.*
BT3 ungulates
NT1 antilocapra
NT2 antilocapra americana

ANTILOPE
BT1 bovidae
BT2 ruminantia
BT3 artiodactyla
BT4 mammals
BT4 ungulates
NT1 antilope cervicapra

ANTILOPE CERVICAPRA
BT1 antilope
BT2 bovidae
BT3 ruminantia
BT4 artiodactyla
BT5 mammals
BT5 ungulates

ANTIMALARIALS
BT1 antiprotozoal agents
BT2 antiparasitic agents
BT3 drugs
NT1 amodiaquine
NT1 artemether
NT1 artesunate
NT1 chloroquine
NT1 chlorproguanil
NT1 cycloguanil embonate
NT1 dapsone
NT1 doxycycline
NT1 floxacrine
NT1 halofantrine
NT1 mefloquine
NT1 menoctone
NT1 mepacrine
NT1 piperaquine
NT1 primaquine
NT1 proguanil
NT1 pyrimethamine
NT1 pyronaridine
NT1 qinghaosu
NT1 quinine
NT1 sulfadoxine
NT1 sulfalene
rt aminoquinolines
rt malaria
rt plasmodium

antimetabolites
USE **metabolic inhibitors**

ANTIMICROBIAL PROPERTIES
BT1 properties
NT1 antibacterial properties
NT1 antiviral properties
rt antifungal properties

antimicrobials
USE **antiinfective agents**

ANTIMONY
BT1 metallic elements
BT2 elements
BT2 metals

antimony dimercaptosuccinate
USE **sodium stibocaptate**

antimony lithium thiomalate
USE **anthiolimine**

ANTIMONY POTASSIUM TARTRATE
BT1 anthelmintics
BT2 antiparasitic agents
BT3 drugs

ANTIMYCIN A
BT1 antibiotics
BT1 metabolic inhibitors
BT2 inhibitors
rt streptomyces

ANTIMYCOBACTERIAL AGENTS
BT1 antibacterial agents
BT2 antiinfective agents
BT3 drugs

ANTINEOPLASTIC AGENTS
uf *cytotoxic agents*
BT1 drugs

ANTINEOPLASTIC AGENTS *cont.*
NT1 allopurinol
NT1 alloxan
NT1 aminopterin
NT1 azaserine
NT1 busulfan
NT1 cyclophosphamide
NT1 dactinomycin
NT1 demecolcine
NT1 doxorubicin
NT1 floxuridine
NT1 fluorouracil
NT1 hydroxycarbamide
NT1 melengestrol
NT1 methotrexate
NT1 mitomycin
NT1 puromycin
NT1 spectinomycin
NT1 tenuazonic acid
NT1 tretamine
NT1 trichodermin
NT1 urethane
NT1 vinblastine
rt cytotoxic compounds
rt neoplasms

ANTINUTRITIONAL FACTORS
HN from 1990
rt nutrition
rt toxic substances

ANTIOXIDANTS
BT1 additives
NT1 α-tocopherol
NT1 ascorbic acid
NT1 benomyl
NT1 butylated hydroxyanisole
NT1 butylated hydroxytoluene
NT1 citric acid
NT1 diludin
NT1 ethoxyquin
NT1 ethylene diurea
NT1 fumaric acid
NT1 hydroquinone
NT1 isoascorbic acid
NT1 nordihydroguaiaretic acid
NT1 propyl gallate
NT1 sodium metabisulfite
rt feed additives
rt food preservatives
rt oxidants
rt oxidation
rt oxygen

ANTIPARASITIC AGENTS
uf *parasiticides*
BT1 drugs
NT1 anthelmintics
NT2 abamectin
NT2 acetarsol
NT2 albendazole
NT2 amoscanate
NT2 anthiolimine
NT2 antimony potassium tartrate
NT2 arecoline
NT2 artemether
NT2 benacil
NT2 bephenium
NT2 bithionol
NT2 bitoscanate
NT2 bromofenofos
NT2 bromophos
NT2 brotianide
NT2 bunamidine
NT2 calcium cyanamide
NT2 cambendazole
NT2 carbaryl
NT2 carbon tetrachloride
NT2 ciclobendazole
NT2 cinnamic acid
NT2 clioxanide
NT2 clorsulon
NT2 copper sulfate
NT2 coumaphos
NT2 creosote
NT2 crufomate
NT2 cyacetacide
NT2 diamfenetide
NT2 dichlorophen
NT2 dichlorvos
NT2 diethylcarbamazine

ANTIPARASITIC AGENTS *cont.*
NT2 disophenol
NT2 dithiazanine iodide
NT2 emetine
NT2 febantel
NT2 fenbendazole
NT2 flubendazole
NT2 furapyrimidone
NT2 gentian violet
NT2 halofuginone
NT2 haloxon
NT2 hexachloroethane
NT2 hexachloroparaxylene
NT2 hexachlorophene
NT2 hexylresorcinol
NT2 hycanthone
NT2 hygromycin b
NT2 ivermectin
NT2 kamala
NT2 lucanthone
NT2 luxabendazole
NT2 mebendazole
NT2 medamine
NT2 melarsonyl
NT2 metronidazole
NT2 metyridine
NT2 milbemycin d
NT2 mitomycin
NT2 morantel
NT2 naftalofos
NT2 niclofolan
NT2 niclosamide
NT2 nicotine
NT2 niridazole
NT2 nitroscanate
NT2 nitroxinil
NT2 novel anthelmintics
NT2 oxamniquine
NT2 oxantel
NT2 oxfendazole
NT2 oxyclozanide
NT2 parbendazole
NT2 phenothiazine
NT2 piperazine
NT2 praziquantel
NT2 pyrantel
NT2 pyrvinium chloride
NT2 rafoxanide
NT2 sodium stibocaptate
NT2 stibophen
NT2 suramin
NT2 tetramisole
NT3 levamisole
NT2 thiabendazole
NT2 thiacetarsamide sodium
NT2 thiofuradene
NT2 tribromsalan
NT2 trichlorfon
NT2 triclabendazole
NT1 antiprotozoal agents
NT2 acetarsol
NT2 acriflavine
NT2 allopurinol
NT2 amicarbalide
NT2 amoebicides
NT3 clioquinol
NT3 dehydroemetine
NT3 diloxanide
NT3 emetine
NT3 metronidazole
NT3 ornidazole
NT3 paromomycin
NT3 secnidazole
NT3 tetracycline
NT3 tinidazole
NT2 amphotericin b
NT2 antimalarials
NT3 amodiaquine
NT3 artemether
NT3 artesunate
NT3 chloroquine
NT3 chlorproguanil
NT3 cycloguanil embonate
NT3 dapsone
NT3 doxycycline
NT3 floxacrine
NT3 halofantrine
NT3 mefloquine
NT3 menoctone
NT3 mepacrine
NT3 piperaquine

ANTIPARASITIC AGENTS *cont.*
NT3 primaquine
NT3 proguanil
NT3 pyrimethamine
NT3 pyronaridine
NT3 qinghaosu
NT3 quinine
NT3 sulfadoxine
NT3 sulfalene
NT2 buparvaquone
NT2 chloramphenicol
NT2 chlortetracycline
NT2 clindamycin
NT2 clotrimazole
NT2 coccidiostats
NT3 aminitrozole
NT3 amprolium
NT3 arprinocid
NT3 buquinolate
NT3 clopidol
NT3 decoquinate
NT3 diaveridine
NT3 dinitolmide
NT3 ethopabate
NT3 halofuginone
NT3 lasalocid
NT3 monensin
NT3 narasin
NT3 nequinate
NT3 nicarbazin
NT3 nitrofural
NT3 ormetoprim
NT3 parvaquone
NT3 robenidine
NT3 salinomycin
NT3 sulfadimethoxine
NT3 sulfadimidine
NT3 sulfanitran
NT3 sulfaquinoxaline
NT3 toltrazuril
NT2 dichlorophen
NT2 diiodohydroxyquinoline
NT2 dimetridazole
NT2 fumagillin
NT2 furazolidone
NT2 imidocarb
NT2 ipronidazole
NT2 meglumine antimonate
NT2 miconazole
NT2 mitomycin
NT2 neoarsphenamine
NT2 nimorazole
NT2 novel antiprotozoal agents
NT2 oxytetracycline
NT2 partricin
NT2 pentamidine
NT2 quinuronium sulfate
NT2 ronidazole
NT2 secnidazole
NT2 sodium stibogluconate
NT2 spiramycin
NT2 sulfadiazine
NT2 sulfamethoxazole
NT2 sulfamonomethoxine
NT2 tinidazole
NT2 trimethoprim
NT2 trypanocides
NT3 benznidazole
NT3 diminazene
NT3 gossypol
NT3 homidium
NT3 isometamidium
NT3 melarsonyl
NT3 melarsoprol
NT3 nifurtimox
NT3 nitrofural
NT3 pentamidine
NT3 puromycin
NT3 pyritidium
NT3 quinapyramine
NT3 suramin
NT3 tryparsamide
NT1 ectoparasiticides
NT2 amitraz
NT2 benzyl benzoate
NT2 bromocyclen
NT2 carbaryl
NT2 chloromethiuron
NT2 chlorpyrifos
NT2 closantel
NT2 coumaphos

ANTIPARASITIC AGENTS *cont.*
NT2 crotamiton
NT2 crotoxyphos
NT2 crufomate
NT2 cyhalothrin
NT2 cypermethrin
NT2 cyromazine
NT2 cythioate
NT2 ddt
NT2 deltamethrin
NT2 diazinon
NT2 dichlorvos
NT2 dioxathion
NT2 ethion
NT2 famphur
NT2 fenchlorphos
NT2 fenthion
NT2 fenvalerate
NT2 flucythrinate
NT2 flumethrin
NT2 ivermectin
NT2 lindane
NT2 malathion
NT2 metolcarb
NT2 nifluridide
NT2 permethrin
NT2 phosalone
NT2 phosmet
NT2 phoxim
NT2 propetamphos
NT2 propoxur
NT2 quintiofos
NT2 rafoxanide
NT2 tetrachlorvinphos
NT2 trichlorfon
NT1 ovicides and larvicides
NT2 calcium cyanamide
NT2 calcium hydroxide
NT2 copper sulfate
NT2 disophenol
rt antiinfective agents
rt parasites

ANTIPROTOZOAL AGENTS
BT1 antiparasitic agents
BT2 drugs
NT1 acetarsol
NT1 acriflavine
NT1 allopurinol
NT1 amicarbalide
NT1 amoebicides
NT2 clioquinol
NT2 dehydroemetine
NT2 diloxanide
NT2 emetine
NT2 metronidazole
NT2 ornidazole
NT2 paromomycin
NT2 secnidazole
NT2 tetracycline
NT2 tinidazole
NT1 amphotericin b
NT1 antimalarials
NT2 amodiaquine
NT2 artemether
NT2 artesunate
NT2 chloroquine
NT2 chlorproguanil
NT2 cycloguanil embonate
NT2 dapsone
NT2 doxycycline
NT2 floxacrine
NT2 halofantrine
NT2 mefloquine
NT2 menoctone
NT2 mepacrine
NT2 piperaquine
NT2 primaquine
NT2 proguanil
NT2 pyrimethamine
NT2 pyronaridine
NT2 qinghaosu
NT2 quinine
NT2 sulfadoxine
NT2 sulfalene
NT1 buparvaquone
NT1 chloramphenicol
NT1 chlortetracycline
NT1 clindamycin
NT1 clotrimazole
NT1 coccidiostats

ANTIPROTOZOAL AGENTS *cont.*
NT2 aminitrozole
NT2 amprolium
NT2 arprinocid
NT2 buquinolate
NT2 clopidol
NT2 decoquinate
NT2 diaveridine
NT2 dinitolmide
NT2 ethopabate
NT2 halofuginone
NT2 lasalocid
NT2 monensin
NT2 narasin
NT2 nequinate
NT2 nicarbazin
NT2 nitrofural
NT2 ormetoprim
NT2 parvaquone
NT2 robenidine
NT2 salinomycin
NT2 sulfadimethoxine
NT2 sulfadimidine
NT2 sulfanitran
NT2 sulfaquinoxaline
NT2 toltrazuril
NT1 dichlorophen
NT1 diiodohydroxyquinoline
NT1 dimetridazole
NT1 fumagillin
NT1 furazolidone
NT1 imidocarb
NT1 ipronidazole
NT1 meglumine antimonate
NT1 miconazole
NT1 mitomycin
NT1 neoarsphenamine
NT1 nimorazole
NT1 novel antiprotozoal agents
NT1 oxytetracycline
NT1 partricin
NT1 pentamidine
NT1 quinuronium sulfate
NT1 ronidazole
NT1 secnidazole
NT1 sodium stibogluconate
NT1 spiramycin
NT1 sulfadiazine
NT1 sulfamethoxazole
NT1 sulfamonomethoxine
NT1 tinidazole
NT1 trimethoprim
NT1 trypanocides
NT2 benznidazole
NT2 diminazene
NT2 gossypol
NT2 homidium
NT2 isometamidium
NT2 melarsonyl
NT2 melarsoprol
NT2 nifurtimox
NT2 nitrofural
NT2 pentamidine
NT2 puromycin
NT2 pyritidium
NT2 quinapyramine
NT2 suramin
NT2 tryparsamide
rt nitroimidazoles
rt protozoa
rt protozoal infections

ANTIPYRETICS
BT1 drugs
NT1 acetaminophen
rt fever

antipyrine
USE **phenazone**

antiroll structures
USE **roll over protection structures**

ANTIRRHINUM
BT1 scrophulariaceae
NT1 antirrhinum majus
NT1 antirrhinum molle
NT1 antirrhinum mollissimum
NT1 antirrhinum orontium

ANTIRRHINUM MAJUS
BT1 antirrhinum
BT2 scrophulariaceae
BT1 ornamental herbaceous plants

ANTIRRHINUM MOLLE
BT1 antirrhinum
BT2 scrophulariaceae

ANTIRRHINUM MOLLISSIMUM
BT1 antirrhinum
BT2 scrophulariaceae

ANTIRRHINUM ORONTIUM
BT1 antirrhinum
BT2 scrophulariaceae

ANTISENSE DNA
HN from 1989
BT1 dna
BT2 nucleic acids
BT3 organic acids
BT4 acids

ANTISENSE RNA
BT1 rna
BT2 nucleic acids
BT3 organic acids
BT4 acids

ANTISEPTIC FINISHES (AGRICOLA)
uf antibacterial finishes
BT1 textile finishes (agricola)
BT2 finishes

ANTISEPTICS
BT1 antiinfective agents
BT2 drugs
NT1 acriflavine
NT1 aluminium sulfate
NT1 benzalkonium chloride
NT1 borax
NT1 cetrimonium
NT1 dodicin
NT1 formaldehyde
NT1 iodine
NT1 malachite green
NT1 mandelic acid
NT1 mercuric chloride
NT1 mercuric oxide
NT1 methylene blue
NT1 naphthalene
NT1 potassium permanganate
NT1 safrole
NT1 thiram
rt disinfectants

antiserum
USE **immune serum**

ANTISOCIAL BEHAVIOR (AGRICOLA)
BT1 human behavior
BT2 behavior
NT1 child abuse
NT1 child neglect (agricola)
NT1 delinquent behavior
NT1 discipline problems (agricola)
NT1 elder abuse (agricola)
NT1 incest (agricola)
NT1 sexual harassment (agricola)
NT1 spouse abuse (agricola)
NT1 theft (agricola)
NT2 employee theft (agricola)
rt behavior disorders (agricola)
rt behavior problems (agricola)
rt substance abuse (agricola)

ANTISTATIC FINISH (AGRICOLA)
BT1 textile finishes (agricola)
BT2 finishes

antithiamin
USE **thiamin antagonists**

antithyroid substances
USE **thyroid antagonists**

ANTITOXINS
BT1 antibodies
BT2 immunoglobulins

ANTITOXINS *cont.*
BT3 glycoproteins
BT4 proteins
BT5 peptides
BT3 immunological factors
rt bacteria
rt immune serum
rt immunity
rt passive immunization
rt serum
rt toxins

ANTITRANSPIRANTS
NT1 1-hexadecanol
NT1 alachlor
NT1 aspirin
NT1 atrazine
NT1 chlormequat
NT1 farnesol
NT1 hydroxyquinoline
NT1 kaolin
NT1 phenylmercury acetate
NT1 pinolene
NT1 poly(vinyl alcohol)
NT1 poly(vinyl chloride)
NT1 polyethylene
NT1 wax coatings
rt evaporation suppressants
rt stomata
rt transpiration

ANTITROGUS
BT1 scarabaeidae
BT2 coleoptera
NT1 antitrogus mussoni
rt rhopaea

ANTITROGUS MUSSONI
uf rhopaea mussoni
BT1 antitrogus
BT2 scarabaeidae
BT3 coleoptera

ANTITRUST LAW (AGRICOLA)
BT1 law
BT2 legal systems

ANTITRYPSIN
BT1 trypsin inhibitors
BT2 proteinase inhibitors
BT3 enzyme inhibitors
BT4 metabolic inhibitors
BT5 inhibitors

ANTITUSSIVE AGENTS
uf cough suppressants
BT1 respiratory system agents
BT2 drugs
NT1 expectorants
NT2 ammonium bicarbonate
NT2 ammonium chloride
NT2 creosote
NT2 eucalyptol
NT2 guaiacol
NT2 guaifenesin
NT2 potassium iodide
NT2 turpentine

ANTIVIRAL AGENTS
BT1 antiinfective agents
BT2 drugs
NT1 amantadine
NT1 floxuridine
NT1 hygromycin b
NT1 idoxuridine
NT1 imanin
NT1 interferon
NT1 lysozyme
rt antiviral properties
rt phytoalexins
rt viruses

ANTIVIRAL PLANTS
NT1 achillea millefolium
NT1 agrostemma githago
NT1 anagallis arvensis
NT1 aubergines
NT1 avena sterilis
NT1 boerhavia diffusa
NT1 bursera penicillata
NT1 capparis spinosa
NT1 capsicum annuum
NT1 carnations

ANTIVIRAL PLANTS *cont.*
NT1 cassia occidentalis
NT1 cassia siamea
NT1 cestrum nocturnum
NT1 chamomilla recutita
NT1 cherries
NT1 clivia miniata
NT1 cuscuta reflexa
NT1 cycas revoluta
NT1 datura fastuosa
NT1 datura metel
NT1 datura stramonium
NT1 dianthus caryophyllus
NT1 dioscorea floribunda
NT1 eclipta alba
NT1 embelia ribes
NT1 euphorbia hirta
NT1 fumaria officinalis
NT1 glycyrrhiza glabra
NT1 grapes
NT1 hymenocallis littoralis
NT1 hypericum erectum
NT1 matricaria perforata
NT1 melia azedarach
NT1 mushrooms
NT1 paeonia lactiflora
NT1 paeonia suffruticosa
NT1 peaches
NT1 phyllanthus emblica
NT1 phyllanthus niruri
NT1 physalis minima
NT1 physalis peruviana
NT1 phytolacca americana
NT1 pittosporum tobira
NT1 plumbago zeylanica
NT1 plumeria rubra
NT1 podophyllum peltatum
NT1 saponaria officinalis
NT1 solanum khasianum
NT1 solanum nigrum
NT1 solanum xanthocarpum
NT1 syzygium aromaticum
NT1 tamarix gallica
NT1 terminalia arjuna
NT1 terminalia chebula
NT1 tinospora cordifolia
NT1 tomatoes
rt antiviral properties
rt eriophyllum
rt horticultural crops
rt industrial crops
rt medicinal plants
rt medicinal properties
rt narcissus
rt pelargonium
rt pesticidal plants
rt plants

ANTIVIRAL PROPERTIES
BT1 antimicrobial properties
BT2 properties
rt antiviral agents
rt antiviral plants
rt viruses

antivitamins
USE **vitamin antagonists**

ANTLERS
BT1 horns
BT2 integument
BT3 body parts
NT1 velvet

ANTONINA
BT1 pseudococcidae
BT2 coccoidea
BT3 sternorrhyncha
BT4 homoptera
NT1 antonina graminis

ANTONINA GRAMINIS
BT1 antonina
BT2 pseudococcidae
BT3 coccoidea
BT4 sternorrhyncha
BT5 homoptera

ants
USE **formicidae**

ANTWERP
uf *belgium (antwerp)*

ANTWERP *cont.*
BT1 belgium
BT2 western europe
BT3 europe

ANURA
uf *salientia*
BT1 amphibia
NT1 bufonidae
NT2 bufo
NT3 bufo bufo
NT3 bufo marinus
NT3 bufo melanostictus
NT3 bufo paracnemis
NT3 bufo regularis
NT3 bufo typhonius
NT3 bufo viridis
NT1 hylidae
NT2 hyla
NT3 hyla arborea
NT3 hyla fuscovaria
NT1 pipidae
NT2 xenopus
NT3 xenopus fraseri
NT3 xenopus laevis
NT1 ranidae
NT2 rana
NT3 rana catesbeiana
NT3 rana cyanophlyctis
NT3 rana hexadactyla
NT3 rana limnocharis
NT3 rana nigromaculata
NT3 rana perezi
NT3 rana pipiens
NT3 rana ridibunda
NT3 rana temporaria
NT3 rana tigrina
rt frogs
rt toads

ANURAPHIS
BT1 aphididae
BT2 aphidoidea
BT3 sternorrhyncha
BT4 homoptera
NT1 anuraphis farfarae
rt dysaphis
rt nearctaphis

anuraphis bakeri
USE **nearctaphis bakeri**

anuraphis devecta
USE **dysaphis devecta**

ANURAPHIS FARFARAE
BT1 anuraphis
BT2 aphididae
BT3 aphidoidea
BT4 sternorrhyncha
BT5 homoptera

ANURIDA
BT1 hypogastruridae
BT2 collembola
NT1 anurida granulata

ANURIDA GRANULATA
BT1 anurida
BT2 hypogastruridae
BT3 collembola

ANUS
BT1 digestive system
BT2 body parts
NT1 cloaca
rt anal glands
rt colostomy
rt haemorrhoids
rt perineum

ANVILLEA
BT1 compositae
NT1 anvillea garcini

ANVILLEA GARCINI
BT1 anvillea
BT2 compositae
BT1 medicinal plants

ANXIETY (AGRICOLA)
rt mental stress

anysis
USE **cephaleta**

anysis alcocki
USE **cephaleta brunniventris**

ANYSTIDAE
BT1 prostigmata
BT2 acari
NT1 anystis
NT2 anystis baccarum

ANYSTIS
BT1 anystidae
BT2 prostigmata
BT3 acari
NT1 anystis baccarum

ANYSTIS BACCARUM
BT1 anystis
BT2 anystidae
BT3 prostigmata
BT4 acari

AOLPECURUS AEQUALIS
BT1 pasture plants

AONIDIELLA
BT1 diaspididae
BT2 coccoidea
BT3 sternorrhyncha
BT4 homoptera
NT1 aonidiella aurantii
NT1 aonidiella citrina
NT1 aonidiella orientalis

AONIDIELLA AURANTII
BT1 aonidiella
BT2 diaspididae
BT3 coccoidea
BT4 sternorrhyncha
BT5 homoptera

AONIDIELLA CITRINA
BT1 aonidiella
BT2 diaspididae
BT3 coccoidea
BT4 sternorrhyncha
BT5 homoptera

AONIDIELLA ORIENTALIS
BT1 aonidiella
BT2 diaspididae
BT3 coccoidea
BT4 sternorrhyncha
BT5 homoptera

AONIDOMYTILUS
BT1 diaspididae
BT2 coccoidea
BT3 sternorrhyncha
BT4 homoptera
NT1 aonidomytilus albus

AONIDOMYTILUS ALBUS
BT1 aonidomytilus
BT2 diaspididae
BT3 coccoidea
BT4 sternorrhyncha
BT5 homoptera

AORTA
BT1 arteries
BT2 blood vessels
BT3 cardiovascular system
BT4 body parts
rt aortic rupture

AORTIC RUPTURE
BT1 vascular diseases
BT2 cardiovascular diseases
BT3 organic diseases
BT4 diseases
rt aorta

AOSTA
BT1 cattle breeds
BT2 breeds

AOTUS
BT1 cebidae
BT2 primates
BT3 mammals
NT1 aotus trivirgatus

AOTUS TRIVIRGATUS
BT1 aotus
BT2 cebidae
BT3 primates
BT4 mammals

APAMEA
uf *crymodes*
BT1 noctuidae
BT2 lepidoptera
NT1 apamea anceps
NT1 apamea arctica
NT1 apamea devastatrix
NT1 apamea sordens

apamea amputatrix
USE **apamea arctica**

APAMEA ANCEPS
BT1 apamea
BT2 noctuidae
BT3 lepidoptera

APAMEA ARCTICA
uf *apamea amputatrix*
BT1 apamea
BT2 noctuidae
BT3 lepidoptera

APAMEA DEVASTATRIX
uf *crymodes devastator*
BT1 apamea
BT2 noctuidae
BT3 lepidoptera

APAMEA SORDENS
BT1 apamea
BT2 noctuidae
BT3 lepidoptera

APAMIN
BT1 neurotoxins
BT2 toxins
rt honeybee venom

APANTELES
BT1 braconidae
BT2 hymenoptera
NT1 apanteles diatraeae
NT1 apanteles fumiferanae
NT1 apanteles subandinus
rt cotesia
rt dolichogenidea
rt glyptapanteles
rt illidops
rt pholetesor
rt xanthomicrogaster

apanteles africanus
USE **glyptapanteles africanus**

apanteles albipennis
USE **dolichogenidea albipennis**

apanteles bicolor
USE **pholetesor bicolor**

apanteles circumscriptus
USE **pholetesor circumscriptus**

apanteles congestus
USE **cotesia tibialis**

APANTELES DIATRAEAE
BT1 apanteles
BT2 braconidae
BT3 hymenoptera

apanteles dignus
USE **xanthomicrogaster dignus**

apanteles flavipes
USE **cotesia flavipes**

APANTELES FUMIFERANAE
BT1 apanteles
BT2 braconidae
BT3 hymenoptera

apanteles glomeratus
USE **cotesia glomerata**

apanteles hyphantriae
USE **cotesia hyphantriae**

apanteles kurdjumovi
USE **cotesia kurdjumovi**

apanteles marginiventris
USE **cotesia marginiventris**

apanteles melanoscelus
USE **cotesia melanoscelus**

apanteles militaris
USE **glyptapanteles militaris**

apanteles ornigis
USE **pholetesor ornigis**

apanteles pallipes
USE **glyptapanteles pallipes**

apanteles plutellae
USE **cotesia plutellae**

apanteles porthetriae
USE **glyptapanteles porthetriae**

apanteles rubecula
USE **cotesia rubecula**

apanteles ruficrus
USE **cotesia ruficrus**

apanteles scutellaris
USE **illidops scutellaris**

APANTELES SUBANDINUS
BT1 apanteles
BT2 braconidae
BT3 hymenoptera
BT1 biological control agents
BT2 beneficial organisms

apanteles telengai
USE **cotesia telengai**

apanteles tibialis
USE **cotesia tibialis**

apanteles turionellae
USE **dolichogenidea turionellae**

APARTMENTS (AGRICOLA)
BT1 homes
BT2 housing

apatele
USE **acronicta**

apatele euphorbiae
USE **acronicta euphorbiae**

apatele rumicis
USE **acronicta rumicis**

APATEMON
BT1 strigeidae
BT2 digenea
BT3 trematoda
NT1 apatemon gracilis

APATEMON GRACILIS
BT1 apatemon
BT2 strigeidae
BT3 digenea
BT4 trematoda

APATITE
BT1 calcium phosphates
BT2 phosphates (salts)
BT3 inorganic salts
BT4 inorganic compounds
BT4 salts
BT3 phosphates
BT2 phosphorus fertilizers
BT3 fertilizers
BT1 nonclay minerals
BT2 minerals
NT1 phosphorite
rt rock phosphate

APECHTHIS
BT1 ichneumonidae
BT2 hymenoptera
NT1 apechthis quadridentatus
NT1 apechthis resinator
NT1 apechthis rufatus
rt ephialtes

apechthis ontario
USE **ephialtes ontario**

APECHTHIS QUADRIDENTATUS
BT1 apechthis
BT2 ichneumonidae
BT3 hymenoptera

APECHTHIS RESINATOR
BT1 apechthis
BT2 ichneumonidae
BT3 hymenoptera

APECHTHIS RUFATUS
BT1 apechthis
BT2 ichneumonidae
BT3 hymenoptera

APERA
BT1 gramineae
NT1 apera interrupta
NT1 apera spica-venti

APERA INTERRUPTA
BT1 apera
BT2 gramineae
BT1 pasture plants

APERA SPICA-VENTI
BT1 apera
BT2 gramineae
BT1 weeds

apes
USE **pongidae**

APHAERETA
BT1 braconidae
BT2 hymenoptera
NT1 aphaereta minuta
NT1 aphaereta pallipes

APHAERETA MINUTA
BT1 aphaereta
BT2 braconidae
BT3 hymenoptera

APHAERETA PALLIPES
BT1 aphaereta
BT2 braconidae
BT3 hymenoptera

APHALARIDAE
BT1 psylloidea
BT2 sternorrhyncha
BT3 homoptera
NT1 agonoscena
NT2 agonoscena targionii
NT1 diaphorina
NT2 diaphorina citri

APHANAMIXIS
BT1 meliaceae

aphanamixis polystachya
USE **ricinocarpodendron polystachyum**

APHANES
BT1 rosaceae
NT1 aphanes arvensis
NT1 aphanes microcarpa

APHANES ARVENSIS
BT1 aphanes
BT2 rosaceae

APHANES MICROCARPA
BT1 aphanes
BT2 rosaceae

aphaniptera
USE **siphonaptera**

APHANIZOMENON
BT1 cyanobacteria
BT2 prokaryotes
NT1 aphanizomenon flos-aquae
NT1 aphanizomenon hoisatica

APHANIZOMENON FLOS-AQUAE
BT1 aphanizomenon
BT2 cyanobacteria
BT3 prokaryotes

APHANIZOMENON HOISATICA
BT1 aphanizomenon
BT2 cyanobacteria
BT3 prokaryotes

APHANOCAPSA
BT1 cyanobacteria
BT2 prokaryotes

APHANOGMUS
BT1 ceraphronidae
BT2 hymenoptera

APHANOMYCES
BT1 saprolegniales
NT1 aphanomyces astaci
NT1 aphanomyces cochlioides
NT1 aphanomyces euteiches

APHANOMYCES ASTACI
uf crayfish plague fungus
BT1 aphanomyces
BT2 saprolegniales

APHANOMYCES COCHLIOIDES
BT1 aphanomyces
BT2 saprolegniales

APHANOMYCES EUTEICHES
BT1 aphanomyces
BT2 saprolegniales

APHANUS
BT1 lygaeidae
BT2 heteroptera
rt elasmolomus

aphanus sordidus
USE **elasmolomus sordidus**

APHASMATYLENCHUS
BT1 hoplolaimidae
BT2 nematoda
NT1 aphasmatylenchus straturatus

APHASMATYLENCHUS STRATURATUS
BT1 aphasmatylenchus
BT2 hoplolaimidae
BT3 nematoda

APHELANDRA
BT1 acanthaceae
NT1 aphelandra squarrosa

APHELANDRA SQUARROSA
BT1 aphelandra
BT2 acanthaceae
BT1 ornamental woody plants

APHELENCHIDAE
BT1 nematoda
NT1 aphelenchus
NT2 aphelenchus avenae
NT1 paraphelenchus
NT2 paraphelenchus myceliophthorus
rt entomophilic nematodes
rt free living nematodes
rt plant parasitic nematodes

APHELENCHOIDES
BT1 aphelenchoididae
BT2 nematoda
NT1 aphelenchoides arachidis
NT1 aphelenchoides besseyi
NT1 aphelenchoides bicaudatus
NT1 aphelenchoides blastophthorus
NT1 aphelenchoides composticola
NT1 aphelenchoides fragariae
NT1 aphelenchoides ritzemabosi

APHELENCHOIDES ARACHIDIS
HN from 1990
BT1 aphelenchoides
BT2 aphelenchoididae
BT3 nematoda

APHELENCHOIDES BESSEYI
BT1 aphelenchoides
BT2 aphelenchoididae
BT3 nematoda

APHELENCHOIDES BICAUDATUS
BT1 aphelenchoides
BT2 aphelenchoididae
BT3 nematoda

APHELENCHOIDES BLASTOPHTHORUS
BT1 aphelenchoides
BT2 aphelenchoididae
BT3 nematoda

APHELENCHOIDES COMPOSTICOLA
BT1 aphelenchoides
BT2 aphelenchoididae
BT3 nematoda

APHELENCHOIDES FRAGARIAE
BT1 aphelenchoides
BT2 aphelenchoididae
BT3 nematoda

APHELENCHOIDES RITZEMABOSI
BT1 aphelenchoides
BT2 aphelenchoididae
BT3 nematoda

APHELENCHOIDIDAE
BT1 nematoda
NT1 aphelenchoides
NT2 aphelenchoides arachidis
NT2 aphelenchoides besseyi
NT2 aphelenchoides bicaudatus
NT2 aphelenchoides blastophthorus
NT2 aphelenchoides composticola
NT2 aphelenchoides fragariae
NT2 aphelenchoides ritzemabosi
NT1 bursaphelenchus
NT2 bursaphelenchus mucronatus
NT2 bursaphelenchus xylophilus
NT1 cryptaphelenchus
NT1 ektaphelenchus
NT1 parasitaphelenchus
NT1 rhadinaphelenchus
NT2 rhadinaphelenchus cocophilus
rt entomophilic nematodes
rt free living nematodes
rt plant parasitic nematodes

APHELENCHUS
BT1 aphelenchidae
BT2 nematoda
NT1 aphelenchus avenae

APHELENCHUS AVENAE
BT1 aphelenchus
BT2 aphelenchidae
BT3 nematoda

APHELINIDAE
BT1 hymenoptera
NT1 ablerus
NT2 ablerus clisiocampae
NT1 aphelinus
NT2 aphelinus abdominalis
NT2 aphelinus asychis
NT2 aphelinus mali
NT2 aphelinus semiflavus
NT2 aphelinus thomsoni
NT1 aphytis
NT2 aphytis africanus
NT2 aphytis chrysomphali
NT2 aphytis diaspidis
NT2 aphytis hispanicus
NT2 aphytis holoxanthus
NT2 aphytis lepidosaphes
NT2 aphytis lingnanensis
NT2 aphytis melinus
NT2 aphytis mytilaspidis
NT2 aphytis proclia
NT2 aphytis yanonensis
NT1 cales
NT2 cales noacki
NT1 coccobius
NT2 coccobius fulvus
NT1 coccophagus
NT2 coccophagus cowperi
NT2 coccophagus lycimnia
NT1 encarsia

APHELINIDAE *cont.*
NT2 encarsia berlesei
NT2 encarsia citrina
NT2 encarsia formosa
NT2 encarsia lahorensis
NT2 encarsia lutea
NT2 encarsia perniciosi
NT1 eretmocerus
NT2 eretmocerus haldemani
NT2 eretmocerus mundus
NT1 marietta
NT2 marietta javensis
NT1 protaphelinus

APHELINUS
BT1 aphelinidae
BT2 hymenoptera
NT1 aphelinus abdominalis
NT1 aphelinus asychis
NT1 aphelinus mali
NT1 aphelinus semiflavus
NT1 aphelinus thomsoni
rt aphytis
rt protaphelinus

APHELINUS ABDOMINALIS
uf aphelinus flavipes
BT1 aphelinus
BT2 aphelinidae
BT3 hymenoptera

APHELINUS ASYCHIS
BT1 aphelinus
BT2 aphelinidae
BT3 hymenoptera

aphelinus diaspidis
USE **aphytis diaspidis**

aphelinus flavipes
USE **aphelinus abdominalis**

APHELINUS MALI
BT1 aphelinus
BT2 aphelinidae
BT3 hymenoptera
BT1 biological control agents
BT2 beneficial organisms

APHELINUS SEMIFLAVUS
BT1 aphelinus
BT2 aphelinidae
BT3 hymenoptera

APHELINUS THOMSONI
BT1 aphelinus
BT2 aphelinidae
BT3 hymenoptera
BT1 biological control agents
BT2 beneficial organisms

APHIDENCYRTUS
BT1 encyrtidae
BT2 hymenoptera
NT1 aphidencyrtus africanus
NT1 aphidencyrtus aphidivorus

APHIDENCYRTUS AFRICANUS
BT1 aphidencyrtus
BT2 encyrtidae
BT3 hymenoptera

APHIDENCYRTUS APHIDIVORUS
BT1 aphidencyrtus
BT2 encyrtidae
BT3 hymenoptera

APHIDIDAE
BT1 aphidoidea
BT2 sternorrhyncha
BT3 homoptera
NT1 acyrthosiphon
NT2 acyrthosiphon assiniboinensis
NT2 acyrthosiphon caraganae
NT2 acyrthosiphon gossypii
NT2 acyrthosiphon kondoi
NT2 acyrthosiphon pisum
NT1 amphorophora
NT2 amphorophora agathonica
NT2 amphorophora rubi
NT1 anoecia
NT2 anoecia corni
NT1 anuraphis

APHIDIDAE *cont.*
NT2 anuraphis farfarae
NT1 aphis
NT2 aphis craccae
NT2 aphis craccivora
NT2 aphis euonymi
NT2 aphis fabae
NT3 aphis fabae solanella
NT2 aphis forbesi
NT2 aphis frangulae
NT2 aphis gossypii
NT2 aphis medicaginis
NT2 aphis middletonii
NT2 aphis nasturtii
NT2 aphis nerii
NT2 aphis pomi
NT2 aphis punicae
NT2 aphis spiraecola
NT1 aulacorthum
NT2 aulacorthum circumflexum
NT2 aulacorthum solani
NT1 brachycaudus
NT2 brachycaudus cardui
NT2 brachycaudus helichrysi
NT2 brachycaudus persicae
NT2 brachycaudus schwartzi
NT1 brachycolus
NT1 brachycorynella
NT2 brachycorynella asparagi
NT1 brevicoryne
NT2 brevicoryne brassicae
NT1 capitophorus
NT2 capitophorus elaeagni
NT2 capitophorus hippophaes
NT2 capitophorus horni
NT1 cavariella
NT2 cavariella aegopodii
NT1 cedrobium
NT2 cedrobium laportei
NT1 chaetosiphon
NT2 chaetosiphon fragaefolii
NT1 chromaphis
NT2 chromaphis juglandicola
NT1 cinara
NT2 cinara pinea
NT2 cinara pini
NT1 corylobium
NT2 corylobium avellanae
NT1 diuraphis
NT2 diuraphis noxia
NT1 drepanosiphum
NT2 drepanosiphum dixoni
NT2 drepanosiphum platanoidis
NT1 dysaphis
NT2 dysaphis crataegi
NT2 dysaphis devecta
NT2 dysaphis plantaginea
NT2 dysaphis pyri
NT2 dysaphis reaumuri
NT1 elatobium
NT2 elatobium abietinum
NT1 eriosoma
NT2 eriosoma lanigerum
NT2 eriosoma ulmi
NT1 eucallipterus
NT2 eucallipterus tiliae
NT1 eulachnus
NT2 eulachnus rileyi
NT1 eutrichosiphum
NT1 hyadaphis
NT2 hyadaphis coriandri
NT1 hyalopterus
NT2 hyalopterus amygdali
NT2 hyalopterus pruni
NT1 hyperomyzus
NT2 hyperomyzus lactucae
NT1 hysteroneura
NT2 hysteroneura setariae
NT1 illinoia
NT1 lachnus
NT1 lipaphis
NT2 lipaphis erysimi
NT1 macrosiphoniella
NT2 macrosiphoniella sanborni
NT1 macrosiphum
NT2 macrosiphum euphorbiae
NT2 macrosiphum rosae
NT1 megoura
NT2 megoura viciae
NT1 melanaphis
NT2 melanaphis sacchari

APHIDIDAE *cont.*
NT1 melanocallis
NT2 melanocallis caryaefoliae
NT1 metopolophium
NT2 metopolophium dirhodum
NT2 metopolophium festucae
NT1 microlophium
NT2 microlophium carnosum
NT1 monellia
NT2 monellia caryella
NT2 monellia nigropunctata
NT1 monelliopsis
NT2 monelliopsis pecanis
NT1 myzocallis
NT2 myzocallis castanicola
NT2 myzocallis coryli
NT1 myzus
NT2 myzus ascalonicus
NT2 myzus cerasi
NT2 myzus persicae
NT2 myzus varians
NT1 nasonovia
NT2 nasonovia ribisnigri
NT1 nearctaphis
NT2 nearctaphis bakeri
NT1 pachypappa
NT2 pachypappa tremulae
NT1 pemphigus
NT2 pemphigus bursarius
NT2 pemphigus fuscicornis
NT1 pentalonia
NT2 pentalonia nigronervosa
NT1 periphyllus
NT2 periphyllus acericola
NT1 phloeomyzus
NT2 phloeomyzus passerinii
NT1 phorodon
NT2 phorodon cannabis
NT2 phorodon humuli
NT1 rhodobium
NT2 rhodobium porosum
NT1 rhopalosiphoninus
NT2 rhopalosiphoninus latysiphon
NT1 rhopalosiphum
NT2 rhopalosiphum insertum
NT2 rhopalosiphum maidis
NT2 rhopalosiphum padi
NT2 rhopalosiphum rufiabdominalis
NT1 schizaphis
NT2 schizaphis graminum
NT1 schizolachnus
NT2 schizolachnus pineti
NT1 semiaphis
NT2 semiaphis heraclei
NT1 sipha
NT2 sipha elegans
NT2 sipha flava
NT2 sipha maydis
NT1 sitobion
NT2 sitobion avenae
NT2 sitobion fragariae
NT1 tetraneura
NT2 tetraneura nigriabdominalis
NT2 tetraneura ulmi
NT1 therioaphis
NT2 therioaphis riehmi
NT2 therioaphis trifolii
NT3 therioaphis trifolii form maculata
NT1 toxoptera
NT2 toxoptera aurantii
NT2 toxoptera citricidus
NT2 toxoptera odinae
NT1 uroleucon
NT2 uroleucon ambrosiae
NT2 uroleucon carthami
NT2 uroleucon compositae
NT2 uroleucon sonchi

aphidiidae
USE **braconidae**

APHIDIUS
BT1 braconidae
BT2 hymenoptera
NT1 aphidius colemani
NT1 aphidius ervi
NT1 aphidius gifuensis
NT1 aphidius matricariae
NT1 aphidius nigripes

APHIDIUS *cont.*
NT1 aphidius picipes
NT1 aphidius rhopalosiphi
NT1 aphidius rosae
NT1 aphidius smithi
NT1 aphidius uzbekistanicus
rt diaeretiella
rt lysiphlebus

aphidius brassicae
USE **diaeretiella rapae**

APHIDIUS COLEMANI
BT1 aphidius
BT2 braconidae
BT3 hymenoptera

APHIDIUS ERVI
BT1 aphidius
BT2 braconidae
BT3 hymenoptera

APHIDIUS GIFUENSIS
BT1 aphidius
BT2 braconidae
BT3 hymenoptera

APHIDIUS MATRICARIAE
BT1 aphidius
BT2 braconidae
BT3 hymenoptera

APHIDIUS NIGRIPES
uf aphidius pulcher
BT1 aphidius
BT2 braconidae
BT3 hymenoptera

APHIDIUS PICIPES
BT1 aphidius
BT2 braconidae
BT3 hymenoptera

aphidius pulcher
USE **aphidius nigripes**

APHIDIUS RHOPALOSIPHI
BT1 aphidius
BT2 braconidae
BT3 hymenoptera

APHIDIUS ROSAE
BT1 aphidius
BT2 braconidae
BT3 hymenoptera

APHIDIUS SMITHI
BT1 aphidius
BT2 braconidae
BT3 hymenoptera
BT1 biological control agents
BT2 beneficial organisms

aphidius testaceipes
USE **lysiphlebus testaceipes**

APHIDIUS UZBEKISTANICUS
BT1 aphidius
BT2 braconidae
BT3 hymenoptera

APHIDOIDEA
uf aphids
BT1 sternorrhyncha
BT2 homoptera
NT1 adelgidae
NT2 adelges
NT3 adelges laricis
NT3 adelges tardus
NT2 cholodkovskya
NT3 cholodkovskya viridana
NT2 dreyfusia
NT3 dreyfusia nordmannianae
NT3 dreyfusia piceae
NT2 gilletteella
NT3 gilletteella cooleyi
NT2 pineus
NT3 pineus pini
NT2 sacchiphantes
NT3 sacchiphantes abietis
NT3 sacchiphantes viridis
NT1 aphididae
NT2 acyrthosiphon
NT3 acyrthosiphon assiniboinensis

APHIDOIDEA *cont.*
NT3 acyrthosiphon caraganae
NT3 acyrthosiphon gossypii
NT3 acyrthosiphon kondoi
NT3 acyrthosiphon pisum
NT2 amphorophora
NT3 amphorophora agathonica
NT3 amphorophora rubi
NT2 anoecia
NT3 anoecia corni
NT2 anuraphis
NT3 anuraphis farfarae
NT2 aphis
NT3 aphis craccae
NT3 aphis craccivora
NT3 aphis euonymi
NT3 aphis fabae
NT4 aphis fabae solanella
NT3 aphis forbesi
NT3 aphis frangulae
NT3 aphis gossypii
NT3 aphis medicaginis
NT3 aphis middletonii
NT3 aphis nasturtii
NT3 aphis nerii
NT3 aphis pomi
NT3 aphis punicae
NT3 aphis spiraecola
NT2 aulacorthum
NT3 aulacorthum circumflexum
NT3 aulacorthum solani
NT2 brachycaudus
NT3 brachycaudus cardui
NT3 brachycaudus helichrysi
NT3 brachycaudus persicae
NT3 brachycaudus schwartzi
NT2 brachycolus
NT2 brachycorynella
NT3 brachycorynella asparagi
NT2 brevicoryne
NT3 brevicoryne brassicae
NT2 capitophorus
NT3 capitophorus elaeagni
NT3 capitophorus hippophaes
NT3 capitophorus horni
NT2 cavariella
NT3 cavariella aegopodii
NT2 cedrobium
NT3 cedrobium laportei
NT2 chaetosiphon
NT3 chaetosiphon fragaefolii
NT2 chromaphis
NT3 chromaphis juglandicola
NT2 cinara
NT3 cinara pinea
NT3 cinara pini
NT2 corylobium
NT3 corylobium avellanae
NT2 diuraphis
NT3 diuraphis noxia
NT2 drepanosiphum
NT3 drepanosiphum dixoni
NT3 drepanosiphum platanoidis
NT2 dysaphis
NT3 dysaphis crataegi
NT3 dysaphis devecta
NT3 dysaphis plantaginea
NT3 dysaphis pyri
NT3 dysaphis reaumuri
NT2 elatobium
NT3 elatobium abietinum
NT2 eriosoma
NT3 eriosoma lanigerum
NT3 eriosoma ulmi
NT2 eucallipterus
NT3 eucallipterus tiliae
NT2 eulachnus
NT3 eulachnus rileyi
NT2 eutrichosiphum
NT2 hyadaphis
NT3 hyadaphis coriandri
NT2 hyalopterus
NT3 hyalopterus amygdali
NT3 hyalopterus pruni
NT2 hyperomyzus
NT3 hyperomyzus lactucae
NT2 hysteroneura
NT3 hysteroneura setariae
NT2 illinoia

APHIDOIDEA *cont.*
NT2 lachnus
NT2 lipaphis
NT3 lipaphis erysimi
NT2 macrosiphoniella
NT3 macrosiphoniella sanborni
NT2 macrosiphum
NT3 macrosiphum euphorbiae
NT3 macrosiphum rosae
NT2 megoura
NT3 megoura viciae
NT2 melanaphis
NT3 melanaphis sacchari
NT2 melanocallis
NT3 melanocallis caryaefoliae
NT2 metopolophium
NT3 metopolophium dirhodum
NT3 metopolophium festucae
NT2 microlophium
NT3 microlophium carnosum
NT2 monellia
NT3 monellia caryella
NT3 monellia nigropunctata
NT2 monelliopsis
NT3 monelliopsis pecanis
NT2 myzocallis
NT3 myzocallis castanicola
NT3 myzocallis coryli
NT2 myzus
NT3 myzus ascalonicus
NT3 myzus cerasi
NT3 myzus persicae
NT3 myzus varians
NT2 nasonovia
NT3 nasonovia ribisnigri
NT2 nearctaphis
NT3 nearctaphis bakeri
NT2 pachypappa
NT3 pachypappa tremulae
NT2 pemphigus
NT3 pemphigus bursarius
NT3 pemphigus fuscicornis
NT2 pentalonia
NT3 pentalonia nigronervosa
NT2 periphyllus
NT3 periphyllus acericola
NT2 phloeomyzus
NT3 phloeomyzus passerinii
NT2 phorodon
NT3 phorodon cannabis
NT3 phorodon humuli
NT2 rhodobium
NT3 rhodobium porosum
NT2 rhopalosiphoninus
NT3 rhopalosiphoninus latysiphon
NT2 rhopalosiphum
NT3 rhopalosiphum insertum
NT3 rhopalosiphum maidis
NT3 rhopalosiphum padi
NT3 rhopalosiphum rufiabdominalis
NT2 schizaphis
NT3 schizaphis graminum
NT2 schizolachnus
NT3 schizolachnus pineti
NT2 semiaphis
NT3 semiaphis heraclei
NT2 sipha
NT3 sipha elegans
NT3 sipha flava
NT3 sipha maydis
NT2 sitobion
NT3 sitobion avenae
NT3 sitobion fragariae
NT2 tetraneura
NT3 tetraneura nigriabdominalis
NT3 tetraneura ulmi
NT2 therioaphis
NT3 therioaphis riehmi
NT3 therioaphis trifolii
NT4 therioaphis trifolii form maculata
NT2 toxoptera
NT3 toxoptera aurantii
NT3 toxoptera citricidus
NT3 toxoptera odinae
NT2 uroleucon
NT3 uroleucon ambrosiae
NT3 uroleucon carthami

APHIDOIDEA *cont.*
NT3 uroleucon compositae
NT3 uroleucon sonchi
NT1 mindaridae
NT2 mindarus
NT3 mindarus abietinus
NT1 phylloxeridae
NT2 phylloxera
NT2 viteus
NT3 viteus vitifoliae
NT1 thelaxidae
NT2 thelaxes

APHIDOLETES
BT1 cecidomyiidae
BT2 diptera
NT1 aphidoletes abietis
NT1 aphidoletes aphidimyza

APHIDOLETES ABIETIS
BT1 aphidoletes
BT2 cecidomyiidae
BT3 diptera

APHIDOLETES APHIDIMYZA
uf *aphidoletes cucumeris*
BT1 aphidoletes
BT2 cecidomyiidae
BT3 diptera

aphidoletes cucumeris
USE **aphidoletes aphidimyza**

aphids
USE **aphidoidea**

APHIS
uf *doralis*
BT1 aphididae
BT2 aphidoidea
BT3 sternorrhyncha
BT4 homoptera
NT1 aphis craccae
NT1 aphis craccivora
NT1 aphis euonymi
NT1 aphis fabae
NT2 aphis fabae solanella
NT1 aphis forbesi
NT1 aphis frangulae
NT1 aphis gossypii
NT1 aphis medicaginis
NT1 aphis middletonii
NT1 aphis nasturtii
NT1 aphis nerii
NT1 aphis pomi
NT1 aphis punicae
NT1 aphis spiraecola
rt brachycaudus
rt rhopalosiphum
rt toxoptera

aphis citricidus
USE **toxoptera citricidus**

aphis citricola
USE **aphis spiraecola**

APHIS CRACCAE
BT1 aphis
BT2 aphididae
BT3 aphidoidea
BT4 sternorrhyncha
BT5 homoptera

APHIS CRACCIVORA
BT1 aphis
BT2 aphididae
BT3 aphidoidea
BT4 sternorrhyncha
BT5 homoptera

APHIS EUONYMI
BT1 aphis
BT2 aphididae
BT3 aphidoidea
BT4 sternorrhyncha
BT5 homoptera

APHIS FABAE
uf *doralis fabae*
BT1 aphis
BT2 aphididae
BT3 aphidoidea
BT4 sternorrhyncha

APHIS FABAE *cont.*
BT5 homoptera
NT1 aphis fabae solanella

APHIS FABAE SOLANELLA
uf *aphis solanella*
BT1 aphis fabae
BT2 aphis
BT3 aphididae
BT4 aphidoidea
BT5 sternorrhyncha
BT6 homoptera

APHIS FORBESI
BT1 aphis
BT2 aphididae
BT3 aphidoidea
BT4 sternorrhyncha
BT5 homoptera

APHIS FRANGULAE
BT1 aphis
BT2 aphididae
BT3 aphidoidea
BT4 sternorrhyncha
BT5 homoptera

APHIS GOSSYPII
BT1 aphis
BT2 aphididae
BT3 aphidoidea
BT4 sternorrhyncha
BT5 homoptera

aphis helichrysi
USE **brachycaudus helichrysi**

aphis maidiradicis
USE **aphis middletonii**

aphis maidis
USE **rhopalosiphum maidis**

APHIS MEDICAGINIS
BT1 aphis
BT2 aphididae
BT3 aphidoidea
BT4 sternorrhyncha
BT5 homoptera

APHIS MIDDLETONII
uf *aphis maidiradicis*
uf *brachycaudus maidiradicis*
BT1 aphis
BT2 aphididae
BT3 aphidoidea
BT4 sternorrhyncha
BT5 homoptera

APHIS NASTURTII
BT1 aphis
BT2 aphididae
BT3 aphidoidea
BT4 sternorrhyncha
BT5 homoptera

APHIS NERII
BT1 aphis
BT2 aphididae
BT3 aphidoidea
BT4 sternorrhyncha
BT5 homoptera

APHIS POMI
BT1 aphis
BT2 aphididae
BT3 aphidoidea
BT4 sternorrhyncha
BT5 homoptera

APHIS PUNICAE
BT1 aphis
BT2 aphididae
BT3 aphidoidea
BT4 sternorrhyncha
BT5 homoptera

aphis solanella
USE **aphis fabae solanella**

APHIS SPIRAECOLA
uf *aphis citricola*
BT1 aphis
BT2 aphididae
BT3 aphidoidea

APHIS SPIRAECOLA *cont.*
BT4 sternorrhyncha
BT5 homoptera

APHODIUS
BT1 scarabaeidae
BT2 coleoptera
NT1 aphodius fimetarius
NT1 aphodius rufipes
NT1 aphodius tasmaniae

APHODIUS FIMETARIUS
BT1 aphodius
BT2 scarabaeidae
BT3 coleoptera

APHODIUS RUFIPES
BT1 aphodius
BT2 scarabaeidae
BT3 coleoptera

APHODIUS TASMANIAE
BT1 aphodius
BT2 scarabaeidae
BT3 coleoptera

APHOLATE
BT1 chemosterilants
BT2 sterilants

APHOMIA
uf *wax moths*
BT1 pyralidae
BT2 lepidoptera

APHONOPELMA
HN from 1989
BT1 theraphosidae
BT2 araneae
BT3 arachnida
BT4 arthropods
NT1 aphonopelma seemanni

APHONOPELMA SEEMANNI
HN from 1989
BT1 aphonopelma
BT2 theraphosidae
BT3 araneae
BT4 arachnida
BT5 arthropods

APHROPHORA
BT1 aphrophoridae
BT2 cercopoidea
BT3 auchenorrhyncha
BT4 homoptera
NT1 aphrophora alni

APHROPHORA ALNI
BT1 aphrophora
BT2 aphrophoridae
BT3 cercopoidea
BT4 auchenorrhyncha
BT5 homoptera

APHROPHORIDAE
BT1 cercopoidea
BT2 auchenorrhyncha
BT3 homoptera
NT1 aphrophora
NT2 aphrophora alni
NT1 philaenus
NT2 philaenus spumarius

APHTHONA
BT1 chrysomelidae
BT2 coleoptera
NT1 aphthona abdominalis
NT1 aphthona euphorbiae

APHTHONA ABDOMINALIS
BT1 aphthona
BT2 chrysomelidae
BT3 coleoptera

APHTHONA EUPHORBIAE
BT1 aphthona
BT2 chrysomelidae
BT3 coleoptera

APHTHOVIRUS
uf *fmd virus*
uf *foot and mouth disease virus*
BT1 picornaviridae

APHTHOVIRUS *cont.*
BT2 viruses
rt foot and mouth disease

APHYCUS
BT1 encyrtidae
BT2 hymenoptera
rt metaphycus

aphycus helvolus
USE **metaphycus helvolus**

aphycus punctipes
USE **metaphycus punctipes**

APHYLLOPHORALES
NT1 amylostereum
NT2 amylostereum areolatum
NT1 athelia
NT2 athelia epiphylla
NT1 bjerkandera
NT2 bjerkandera adusta
NT1 chaetoporus
NT2 chaetoporus radula
NT1 chondrostereum
NT2 chondrostereum purpureum
NT1 coltricia
NT2 coltricia tomentosa
NT1 coniophora
NT2 coniophora puteana
NT1 coriolus
NT2 coriolus hirsutus
NT2 coriolus versicolor
NT1 corticium
NT2 corticium fuciforme
NT2 corticium galactinum
NT2 corticium invisum
NT2 corticium rolfsii
NT2 corticium salmonicolor
NT2 corticium theae
NT1 daedalea
NT2 daedalea quercina
NT1 fomes
NT2 fomes fomentarius
NT2 fomes hartigii
NT2 fomes tremulae
NT1 fomitopsis
NT2 fomitopsis pinicola
NT2 fomitopsis rosea
NT1 ganoderma
NT2 ganoderma applanatum
NT2 ganoderma lucidum
NT2 ganoderma philippii
NT1 gloeophyllum
NT2 gloeophyllum sepiarium
NT2 gloeophyllum trabeum
NT1 grandinia
NT2 grandinia maxima
NT1 heterobasidion
NT2 heterobasidion annosum
NT1 hirschioporus
NT1 inonotus
NT2 inonotus hispidus
NT2 inonotus nidus-pici
NT2 inonotus radiatus
NT1 irpex
NT2 irpex lacteus
NT1 laetiporus
NT2 laetiporus sulphureus
NT1 lentinula
NT2 lentinula edodes
NT1 lentinus
NT2 lentinus cornucopiae
NT2 lentinus lepideus
NT1 lenzites
NT1 moniliophthora
NT2 moniliophthora roreri
NT1 oligoporus
NT2 oligoporus placenta
NT1 pellicularia
NT1 peniophora
NT1 phaeolus
NT2 phaeolus schweinitzii
NT1 phanerochaete
NT2 phanerochaete chrysosporium
NT1 phellinus
NT2 phellinus igniarius
NT2 phellinus noxius
NT2 phellinus pini
NT2 phellinus pomaceus

APHYLLOPHORALES *cont.*
NT2 phellinus robustus
NT2 phellinus weirii
NT1 phlebia
NT2 phlebia gigantea
NT1 polyporus
NT2 polyporus baudonii
NT1 polystictus
NT1 poria
NT2 poria hypolateritia
NT2 poria monticola
NT2 poria vincta
NT1 pycnoporus
NT2 pycnoporus sanguineus
NT1 rigidoporus
NT2 rigidoporus lignosus
NT2 rigidoporus ulmarius
NT2 rigidoporus zonalis
NT1 schizophyllum
NT2 schizophyllum commune
NT1 serpula
NT2 serpula lacrimans
NT1 spongipellis
NT2 spongipellis borealis
NT1 stereum
NT2 stereum sanguinolentum
NT1 thanatephorus
NT2 thanatephorus cucumeris
NT2 thanatephorus praticola
NT2 thanatephorus sasakii
NT1 thelephora
NT2 thelephora terrestris
NT1 trametes
NT2 trametes pruni-spinosae
NT1 trichaptum
NT2 trichaptum abietinum
NT1 typhula
NT2 typhula idahoensis
NT2 typhula incarnata
NT2 typhula ishikariensis
rt fungi

APHYTIS
BT1 aphelinidae
BT2 hymenoptera
NT1 aphytis africanus
NT1 aphytis chrysomphali
NT1 aphytis diaspidis
NT1 aphytis hispanicus
NT1 aphytis holoxanthus
NT1 aphytis lepidosaphes
NT1 aphytis lingnanensis
NT1 aphytis melinus
NT1 aphytis mytilaspidis
NT1 aphytis proclia
NT1 aphytis yanonensis
rt aphelinus

APHYTIS AFRICANUS
BT1 aphytis
BT2 aphelinidae
BT3 hymenoptera

APHYTIS CHRYSOMPHALI
BT1 aphytis
BT2 aphelinidae
BT3 hymenoptera
BT1 biological control agents
BT2 beneficial organisms

APHYTIS DIASPIDIS
uf *aphelinus diaspidis*
BT1 aphytis
BT2 aphelinidae
BT3 hymenoptera

APHYTIS HISPANICUS
BT1 aphytis
BT2 aphelinidae
BT3 hymenoptera

APHYTIS HOLOXANTHUS
BT1 aphytis
BT2 aphelinidae
BT3 hymenoptera
BT1 biological control agents
BT2 beneficial organisms

APHYTIS LEPIDOSAPHES
BT1 aphytis
BT2 aphelinidae
BT3 hymenoptera
BT1 biological control agents

APHYTIS LEPIDOSAPHES *cont.*
BT2 beneficial organisms

APHYTIS LINGNANENSIS
BT1 aphytis
BT2 aphelinidae
BT3 hymenoptera
BT1 biological control agents
BT2 beneficial organisms

APHYTIS MELINUS
BT1 aphytis
BT2 aphelinidae
BT3 hymenoptera
BT1 biological control agents
BT2 beneficial organisms

APHYTIS MYTILASPIDIS
BT1 aphytis
BT2 aphelinidae
BT3 hymenoptera
BT1 biological control agents
BT2 beneficial organisms

APHYTIS PROCLIA
BT1 aphytis
BT2 aphelinidae
BT3 hymenoptera

APHYTIS YANONENSIS
BT1 aphytis
BT2 aphelinidae
BT3 hymenoptera

apiaceae
USE **umbelliferae**

APIARIES
BT1 beekeeping
NT1 apiary layout
NT1 apiary sites
NT1 apiary size
NT1 out apiaries
NT1 wall apiaries
rt bee houses

APIARY LAYOUT
BT1 apiaries
BT2 beekeeping
rt apiary sites
rt apiary size

APIARY SITES
BT1 apiaries
BT2 beekeeping
rt apiary layout
rt apiary size

APIARY SIZE
BT1 apiaries
BT2 beekeeping
rt apiary layout
rt apiary sites
rt size

APICAL DOMINANCE
rt branching
rt determinate and indeterminate habit
rt plant growth regulators

APICAL MERISTEMS
uf *meristems, apical*
BT1 meristems
BT2 plant tissues
BT3 plant
BT3 tissues
rt branching
rt buds
rt shoot tip culture

APICOMPLEXA
uf *sporozoa*
BT1 protozoa
NT1 actinocephalus
NT1 adelea
NT1 adelina
NT2 adelina mesnili
NT2 adelina tribolii
NT1 aikinetocystis
NT2 aikinetocystis singularis
NT1 akiba
NT2 akiba caulleryi
NT1 allantocystis

APICOMPLEXA *cont.*
NT2 allantocystis dasyhelei
NT1 ancora
NT1 anthemosoma
NT2 anthemosoma garnhami
NT1 apolocystis
NT1 ascogregarina
NT2 ascogregarina barretti
NT1 babesia
NT2 babesia argentina
NT2 babesia beliceri
NT2 babesia bigemina
NT2 babesia bovis
NT2 babesia caballi
NT2 babesia calcaratus
NT2 babesia canis
NT2 babesia capreoli
NT2 babesia caucasica
NT2 babesia colchica
NT2 babesia divergens
NT2 babesia equi
NT2 babesia galagolata
NT2 babesia gibsoni
NT2 babesia herpailuri
NT2 babesia hylomysci
NT2 babesia jakimovi
NT2 babesia major
NT2 babesia microti
NT2 babesia motasi
NT2 babesia musculi
NT2 babesia ovata
NT2 babesia ovis
NT2 babesia rodhaini
NT2 babesia trautmanni
NT2 babesia vesperuginis
NT2 babesia vitalii
NT1 babesiosoma
NT1 besnoitia
NT2 besnoitia besnoiti
NT2 besnoitia darlingi
NT2 besnoitia jellisoni
NT2 besnoitia wallacei
NT1 caryospora
NT2 caryospora simplex
NT1 cephaloidophora
NT2 cephaloidophora conformis
NT1 chagasella
NT1 coelotropha
NT1 cometoides
NT1 conchophthirius
NT1 cryptosporidium
NT1 cystobia
NT1 cystoisospora
NT1 cytauxzoon
NT2 cytauxzoon felis
NT1 dactylophorus
NT1 dactylosoma
NT2 dactylosoma ranarum
NT1 dermocystidium
NT2 dermocystidium anguillae
NT1 didymophyes
NT2 didymophyes gigantea
NT1 diplocystis
NT2 diplocystis clerci
NT2 diplocystis johnsoni
NT2 diplocystis major
NT2 diplocystis metselaari
NT2 diplocystis minor
NT2 diplocystis oxyxani
NT2 diplocystis schneideri
NT2 diplocystis zootermopsidis
NT1 diplodina
NT1 doliocystis
NT1 echinomera
NT1 eimeria
NT2 eimeria acervulina
NT2 eimeria adenoeides
NT2 eimeria ahsata
NT2 eimeria alabamensis
NT2 eimeria andreusi
NT2 eimeria anguillae
NT2 eimeria anseris
NT2 eimeria arabiana
NT2 eimeria arloingi
NT2 eimeria auburnensis
NT2 eimeria bareillyi
NT2 eimeria bateri
NT2 eimeria bistratum
NT2 eimeria bovis
NT2 eimeria brasiliensis
NT2 eimeria brunetti

APICOMPLEXA *cont.*
NT2 eimeria bukidnonensis
NT2 eimeria cameli
NT2 eimeria canadensis
NT2 eimeria canis
NT2 eimeria capreoli
NT2 eimeria carpelli
NT2 eimeria caviae
NT2 eimeria cerdonis
NT2 eimeria citelli
NT2 eimeria clupearum
NT2 eimeria coecicola
NT2 eimeria colchici
NT2 eimeria columbarum
NT2 eimeria confusa
NT2 eimeria contorta
NT2 eimeria debliecki
NT2 eimeria dericksoni
NT2 eimeria dispersa
NT2 eimeria dukei
NT2 eimeria dunsingi
NT2 eimeria duodenalis
NT2 eimeria ellipsoidalis
NT2 eimeria environ
NT2 eimeria europaea
NT2 eimeria falciformis
NT2 eimeria faurei
NT2 eimeria ferrisi
NT2 eimeria funduli
NT2 eimeria gadi
NT2 eimeria gallopavonis
NT2 eimeria granulosa
NT2 eimeria grenieri
NT2 eimeria gruis
NT2 eimeria hagani
NT2 eimeria hungarica
NT2 eimeria indentata
NT2 eimeria intestinalis
NT2 eimeria iroquoina
NT2 eimeria irresidua
NT2 eimeria keilini
NT2 eimeria kotlani
NT2 eimeria kriygsmanni
NT2 eimeria labbeana
NT2 eimeria lancasterensis
NT2 eimeria leporis
NT2 eimeria leuckarti
NT2 eimeria magna
NT2 eimeria marsica
NT2 eimeria mascoutini
NT2 eimeria matsubayashii
NT2 eimeria maxima
NT2 eimeria media
NT2 eimeria meleagrimitis
NT2 eimeria minima
NT2 eimeria mitis
NT2 eimeria mivati
NT2 eimeria myopotami
NT2 eimeria necatrix
NT2 eimeria neodebliecki
NT2 eimeria nieschulzi
NT2 eimeria ninakohlyakimovae
NT2 eimeria ontarioensis
NT2 eimeria os
NT2 eimeria ovina
NT2 eimeria pacifica
NT2 eimeria panda
NT2 eimeria papillata
NT2 eimeria parva
NT2 eimeria pellerdyi
NT2 eimeria pellita
NT2 eimeria pellucida
NT2 eimeria perforans
NT2 eimeria perminuta
NT2 eimeria phasiani
NT2 eimeria pintoensis
NT2 eimeria poljanskyi
NT2 eimeria ponderosa
NT2 eimeria praecox
NT2 eimeria pragensis
NT2 eimeria procyonis
NT2 eimeria reichenowi
NT2 eimeria robertsoni
NT2 eimeria ruficaudati
NT2 eimeria sardinae
NT2 eimeria sciurorum
NT2 eimeria semisculpta
NT2 eimeria separata
NT2 eimeria septentrionalis
NT2 eimeria sigmodontis
NT2 eimeria smithi

APICOMPLEXA *cont.*
NT2 eimeria solipedum
NT2 eimeria somateriae
NT2 eimeria spinosa
NT2 eimeria stiedai
NT2 eimeria subspherica
NT2 eimeria suis
NT2 eimeria superba
NT2 eimeria tenella
NT2 eimeria tetartooimia
NT2 eimeria tetricis
NT2 eimeria townsendi
NT2 eimeria truncata
NT2 eimeria uniungulati
NT2 eimeria utahensis
NT2 eimeria variabilis
NT2 eimeria vermiformis
NT2 eimeria vison
NT2 eimeria wenrichi
NT2 eimeria weybridgensis
NT2 eimeria wyomingensis
NT2 eimeria zapi
NT2 eimeria zuernii
NT1 endorimospora
NT1 enterocystis
NT2 enterocystis ensis
NT2 enterocystis ephemerae
NT2 enterocystis fungoides
NT2 enterocystis grassei
NT2 enterocystis hydrophili
NT2 enterocystis palmata
NT2 enterocystis racovitza
NT2 enterocystis rhithrogenae
NT1 entopolypoides
NT1 erhardorina
NT1 farinocystis
NT2 farinocystis tribolii
NT1 ferraria
NT1 filopodium
NT1 frenkelia
NT2 frenkelia clethrionomyobuteonis
NT2 frenkelia glareoli
NT1 ganymedes
NT2 ganymedes anaspidis
NT1 gigaductus
NT1 gonospora
NT1 goussia
NT1 grebneckiella
NT2 grebneckiella gracilis
NT2 grebneckiella pixellae
NT1 gregarina
NT2 gregarina blaberae
NT2 gregarina coccinellae
NT2 gregarina cuneata
NT2 gregarina dimorpha
NT2 gregarina garnhami
NT2 gregarina hylobii
NT2 gregarina munieri
NT2 gregarina nigra
NT2 gregarina ovata
NT2 gregarina polymorpha
NT2 gregarina saenuridis
NT1 haematoxenus
NT2 haematoxenus separatus
NT2 haematoxenus veliferus
NT1 haematractidium
NT1 haemogregarina
NT2 haemogregarina aegyptia
NT2 haemogregarina bigemina
NT2 haemogregarina boueti
NT2 haemogregarina crocodilinorum
NT2 haemogregarina cyprini
NT2 haemogregarina eremiae
NT2 haemogregarina gracilis
NT2 haemogregarina sachai
NT2 haemogregarina serpentinum
NT2 haemogregarina stepanowi
NT1 haemoproteus
NT2 haemoproteus borgesi
NT2 haemoproteus brodkorbi
NT2 haemoproteus canachites
NT2 haemoproteus columbae
NT2 haemoproteus crumenium
NT2 haemoproteus danilewskyi
NT2 haemoproteus fallisi
NT2 haemoproteus fringillae
NT2 haemoproteus handai
NT2 haemoproteus maccallumi

APICOMPLEXA *cont.*
NT2 haemoproteus meleagridis
NT2 haemoproteus meleagris
NT2 haemoproteus multiparasitans
NT2 haemoproteus nettionis
NT2 haemoproteus orizivorae
NT2 haemoproteus passeris
NT2 haemoproteus pelouroi
NT2 haemoproteus plataleae
NT2 haemoproteus sacharovi
NT2 haemoproteus velans
NT2 haemoproteus wenyoni
NT1 hammondia
NT2 hammondia hammondi
NT2 hammondia heydorni
NT1 hepatocystis
NT2 hepatocystis brayi
NT2 hepatocystis kochi
NT2 hepatocystis malayensis
NT2 hepatocystis oriheli
NT1 hepatozoon
NT2 hepatozoon canis
NT2 hepatozoon domerguei
NT2 hepatozoon erhardovae
NT2 hepatozoon griseisciuri
NT2 hepatozoon sylvatici
NT2 hepatozoon triatomae
NT2 hepatozoon tupinambis
NT1 hirmocystis
NT1 hoplorhynchus
NT1 isospora
NT2 isospora arctopitheci
NT2 isospora belli
NT2 isospora bigemina
NT2 isospora buteonis
NT2 isospora canaria
NT2 isospora canis
NT2 isospora endocallimici
NT2 isospora felis
NT2 isospora heydorni
NT2 isospora hominis
NT2 isospora lacazei
NT2 isospora laidlawi
NT2 isospora lieberkuehni
NT2 isospora ohioensis
NT2 isospora rivolta
NT2 isospora schwetzi
NT2 isospora serini
NT2 isospora suis
NT2 isospora turdi
NT2 isospora vulpina
NT2 isospora wallacei
NT1 karyolysus
NT1 klossia
NT2 klossia helicina
NT1 klossiella
NT2 klossiella equi
NT2 klossiella muris
NT1 koellikerella
NT1 lankesterella
NT2 lankesterella garnhami
NT1 lankesteria
NT2 lankesteria ascidiae
NT2 lankesteria culicis
NT1 lecudina
NT1 leidyana
NT1 leucocytozoon
NT2 leucocytozoon bonasae
NT2 leucocytozoon caulleryi
NT2 leucocytozoon dubreuili
NT2 leucocytozoon fringillinarum
NT2 leucocytozoon majoris
NT2 leucocytozoon marchouxi
NT2 leucocytozoon mathisi
NT2 leucocytozoon sabrazesi
NT2 leucocytozoon simondi
NT2 leucocytozoon smithi
NT2 leucocytozoon tawaki
NT2 leucocytozoon toddi
NT2 leucocytozoon ziemanni
NT1 lithocystis
NT1 mantonella
NT1 mattesia
NT2 mattesia bombi
NT2 mattesia dispora
NT2 mattesia trogodermae
NT1 monocystella
NT1 monocystis
NT2 monocystis agilis

APICOMPLEXA *cont.*
NT1 nematocystis
NT1 nematopsis
NT1 nycteria
NT1 odonaticola
NT1 oligochaetocystis
NT1 ophioidina
NT1 ophryocystis
NT1 pachyporospora
NT1 parahaemoproteus
NT1 paraophioidina
NT1 perkinsus
NT2 perkinsus marinus
NT1 plasmodium
NT2 plasmodium agamae
NT2 plasmodium azurophilum
NT2 plasmodium balli
NT2 plasmodium berghei
NT2 plasmodium brasilianum
NT2 plasmodium cathemerium
NT2 plasmodium chabaudi
NT2 plasmodium circumflexum
NT2 plasmodium coatneyi
NT2 plasmodium columbae
NT2 plasmodium coturnicis
NT2 plasmodium cynomolgi
NT2 plasmodium durae
NT2 plasmodium falciparum
NT2 plasmodium fallax
NT2 plasmodium fieldi
NT2 plasmodium floridense
NT2 plasmodium foleyi
NT2 plasmodium fragile
NT2 plasmodium gallinaceum
NT2 plasmodium girardi
NT2 plasmodium hermani
NT2 plasmodium hexamerium
NT2 plasmodium inui
NT2 plasmodium juxtanucleare
NT2 plasmodium knowlesi
NT2 plasmodium lemuris
NT2 plasmodium lophurae
NT2 plasmodium lutzi
NT2 plasmodium malariae
NT2 plasmodium mexicanum
NT2 plasmodium ovale
NT2 plasmodium pedioecetii
NT2 plasmodium pinottii
NT2 plasmodium pitheci
NT2 plasmodium polare
NT2 plasmodium praecox
NT2 plasmodium relictum
NT2 plasmodium silvaticum
NT2 plasmodium simiovale
NT2 plasmodium simium
NT2 plasmodium tenue
NT2 plasmodium tropiduri
NT2 plasmodium vaughani
NT2 plasmodium vinckei
NT2 plasmodium vivax
NT2 plasmodium yoelii
NT1 pleurocystis
NT1 polychromophilus
NT1 polyrhabdina
NT1 porospora
NT2 porospora pisae
NT2 porospora portunidarum
NT1 pseudolankesteria
NT1 pseudomonocystis
NT1 pterospora
NT1 pyxinia
NT1 quadruspinospora
NT1 rasajeyna
NT2 rasajeyna nannyla
NT1 retractocephalus
NT1 rhabdocystis
NT1 rhynchocystis
NT1 rotundula
NT2 rotundula gammari
NT1 sarcocystis
NT2 sarcocystis asinus
NT2 sarcocystis bertrami
NT2 sarcocystis booliati
NT2 sarcocystis bovicanis
NT2 sarcocystis bovifelis
NT2 sarcocystis bovihominis
NT2 sarcocystis cameli
NT2 sarcocystis capracanis
NT2 sarcocystis cervi
NT2 sarcocystis cruzi
NT2 sarcocystis cuniculi

APICOMPLEXA *cont.*
NT2 sarcocystis dispersa
NT2 sarcocystis equicanis
NT2 sarcocystis fayeri
NT2 sarcocystis fusiformis
NT2 sarcocystis gigantea
NT2 sarcocystis gracilis
NT2 sarcocystis grueneri
NT2 sarcocystis hemionilatrantis
NT2 sarcocystis hirsuta
NT2 sarcocystis kortei
NT2 sarcocystis leporum
NT2 sarcocystis levinei
NT2 sarcocystis lindemanni
NT2 sarcocystis miescheriana
NT2 sarcocystis moulei
NT2 sarcocystis muris
NT2 sarcocystis nesbitti
NT2 sarcocystis orientalis
NT2 sarcocystis ovicanis
NT2 sarcocystis ovifelis
NT2 sarcocystis rileyi
NT2 sarcocystis singaporensis
NT2 sarcocystis suicanis
NT2 sarcocystis suihominis
NT2 sarcocystis tenella
NT2 sarcocystis villivillosi
NT2 sarcocystis wapiti
NT1 saurocytozoon
NT1 schellackia
NT1 schneideria
NT2 schneideria schneiderae
NT1 spiriopsis
NT1 steinina
NT1 stenoductus
NT1 stenophora
NT2 stenophora ozakii
NT1 stylocephalus
NT1 theileria
NT2 theileria annulata
NT2 theileria cervi
NT2 theileria hirci
NT2 theileria lawrencei
NT2 theileria mutans
NT2 theileria orientalis
NT2 theileria ovis
NT2 theileria parva
NT2 theileria recondita
NT2 theileria sergenti
NT2 theileria taurotragi
NT2 theileria velifera
NT1 toxoplasma
NT2 toxoplasma gondii
NT1 trichorhynchus
NT1 tyzzeria
NT2 tyzzeria perniciosa
NT1 urospora
NT1 wenyonella
NT1 zeylanocystis
NT1 zygocystis
rt coccidia
rt gregarines
rt oocysts
rt piroplasms
rt schizonts
rt sporozoites

apiculture
USE **beekeeping**

APIDAE
uf *bees*
BT1 hymenoptera
NT1 agapostemon
NT1 allodape
NT1 ancyloscelis
NT1 andrena
NT1 anthidiellum
NT1 anthidium
NT1 anthophora
NT1 apis
NT2 apis cerana
NT3 apis cerana indica
NT2 apis dorsata
NT2 apis florea
NT2 apis mellifera
NT3 apis mellifera adansonii
NT3 apis mellifera capensis
NT3 apis mellifera carnica
NT3 apis mellifera caucasica
NT3 apis mellifera cypria

APIDAE *cont.*
NT3 apis mellifera lamarckii
NT3 apis mellifera ligustica
NT3 apis mellifera mellifera
NT3 apis mellifera scutellata
NT3 apis mellifera unicolor
NT1 ashmeadiella
NT1 augochlora
NT1 augochlorella
NT1 augochloropsis
NT1 bombus
NT1 braunsapis
NT1 callanthidium
NT1 calliopsis
NT1 centris
NT1 ceratina
NT1 chalicodoma
NT1 chelostoma
NT1 coelioxys
NT1 colletes
NT1 ctenoplectra
NT1 dasypoda
NT1 diadasia
NT1 dialictus
NT1 dianthidium
NT1 dufourea
NT1 emphoropsis
NT1 epeolus
NT1 epicharis
NT1 euaspis
NT1 eucera
NT1 euglossa
NT1 eulaema
NT1 eulonchopria
NT1 eupetersia
NT1 euryglossa
NT1 exaerete
NT1 exomalopsis
NT1 exoneura
NT1 gaesischia
NT1 habropoda
NT1 halictus
NT1 heteranthidium
NT1 holcopasites
NT1 homalictus
NT1 hoplitis
NT1 hylaeus
NT1 hypotrigona
NT1 inquilina
NT1 lasioglossum
NT1 leioproctus
NT1 lestrimelitta
NT1 lithurge
NT1 megachile
NT2 megachile rotundata
NT1 melecta
NT1 melipona
NT1 melissodes
NT1 melitoma
NT1 melitta
NT1 melitturga
NT1 mesoplia
NT1 nomada
NT1 nomadopsis
NT1 nomia
NT2 nomia melanderi
NT1 nomioides
NT1 osmia
NT1 oxaea
NT1 palaeorhiza
NT1 panurginus
NT1 panurgus
NT1 paratetrapedia
NT1 perdita
NT1 pithitis
NT1 protandrena
NT1 proteriades
NT1 pseudagapostemon
NT1 psithyrus
NT1 ptiloglossa
NT1 rhathymus
NT1 rhophites
NT1 sphecodes
NT1 stelis
NT1 stenotritus
NT1 svastra
NT1 synhalonia
NT1 systropha
NT1 tetragonisca
NT1 tetralonia
NT1 tetrapedia

APIDAE *cont.*
NT1 triepeolus
NT1 trigona
NT1 xenoglossa
NT1 xylocopa
rt honeybees

APIMYIASIS
BT1 bee diseases
BT2 animal diseases
BT3 diseases
BT1 myiasis
BT2 ectoparasitoses
BT3 parasitoses
BT4 diseases
rt senotainia

APIOCARPELLA
HN from 1990
BT1 deuteromycotina
rt ascochyta

apiocarpella agropyri
USE **ascochyta agropyri-repentis**

APIOCREA
HN from 1990
BT1 clavicipitales
NT1 apiocrea chrysosperma
rt sepedonium

APIOCREA CHRYSOSPERMA
HN from 1990
uf *sepedonium chrysospermum*
BT1 apiocrea
BT2 clavicipitales

APIOGNOMONIA
BT1 diaporthales
NT1 apiognomonia errabunda
NT1 apiognomonia veneta
rt gnomonia

APIOGNOMONIA ERRABUNDA
uf *gnomonia tiliae*
BT1 apiognomonia
BT2 diaporthales

APIOGNOMONIA VENETA
HN from 1990
uf *gnomonia veneta*
BT1 apiognomonia
BT2 diaporthales

APION
BT1 apionidae
BT2 coleoptera
NT1 apion antiquum
NT1 apion apricans
NT1 apion assimile
NT1 apion corchori
NT1 apion fulvipes
NT1 apion seniculus
NT1 apion trifolii
NT1 apion ulicis
NT1 apion virens
NT1 apion vorax

APION ANTIQUUM
BT1 apion
BT2 apionidae
BT3 coleoptera
BT1 biological control agents
BT2 beneficial organisms

APION APRICANS
BT1 apion
BT2 apionidae
BT3 coleoptera

APION ASSIMILE
BT1 apion
BT2 apionidae
BT3 coleoptera

APION CORCHORI
BT1 apion
BT2 apionidae
BT3 coleoptera

apion dichroum
USE **apion fulvipes**

apion flavipes
USE **apion fulvipes**

APION FULVIPES
HN from 1990
uf *apion dichroum*
uf *apion flavipes*
BT1 apion
BT2 apionidae
BT3 coleoptera

APION SENICULUS
BT1 apion
BT2 apionidae
BT3 coleoptera

APION TRIFOLII
BT1 apion
BT2 apionidae
BT3 coleoptera

APION ULICIS
BT1 apion
BT2 apionidae
BT3 coleoptera
BT1 biological control agents
BT2 beneficial organisms

APION VIRENS
BT1 apion
BT2 apionidae
BT3 coleoptera

APION VORAX
BT1 apion
BT2 apionidae
BT3 coleoptera

APIONIDAE
BT1 coleoptera
NT1 apion
NT2 apion antiquum
NT2 apion apricans
NT2 apion assimile
NT2 apion corchori
NT2 apion fulvipes
NT2 apion seniculus
NT2 apion trifolii
NT2 apion ulicis
NT2 apion virens
NT2 apion vorax
NT1 cylas
NT2 cylas formicarius
NT3 cylas formicarius elegantulus
NT2 cylas puncticollis

APIOS
BT1 leguminosae
NT1 apios americana

APIOS AMERICANA
uf *apios tuberosa*
BT1 apios
BT2 leguminosae
BT1 root vegetables
BT2 root crops
BT2 vegetables

apios tuberosa
USE **apios americana**

APIOSOMA
BT1 ciliophora
BT2 protozoa
NT1 apiosoma piscicola

APIOSOMA PISCICOLA
BT1 apiosoma
BT2 ciliophora
BT3 protozoa

APIOSPORA
uf *papularia*
BT1 sphaeriales
NT1 apiospora montagnei

APIOSPORA MONTAGNEI
uf *papularia arundinis*
BT1 apiospora
BT2 sphaeriales

APIOSPORINA
HN from 1990
BT1 dothideales

APIOSPORINA *cont.*
NT1 apiosporina morbosa
rt dibotryon

APIOSPORINA MORBOSA
HN from 1990
uf *dibotryon morbosum*
BT1 apiosporina
BT2 dothideales

APIS
uf *synapis*
BT1 apidae
BT2 hymenoptera
NT1 apis cerana
NT2 apis cerana indica
NT1 apis dorsata
NT1 apis florea
NT1 apis mellifera
NT2 apis mellifera adansonii
NT2 apis mellifera capensis
NT2 apis mellifera carnica
NT2 apis mellifera caucasica
NT2 apis mellifera cypria
NT2 apis mellifera lamarckii
NT2 apis mellifera ligustica
NT2 apis mellifera mellifera
NT2 apis mellifera scutellata
NT2 apis mellifera unicolor
rt honeybees
rt social insects

APIS CERANA
BT1 apis
BT2 apidae
BT3 hymenoptera
NT1 apis cerana indica
rt honeybees

APIS CERANA INDICA
uf *apis indica*
BT1 apis cerana
BT2 apis
BT3 apidae
BT4 hymenoptera

APIS DORSATA
BT1 apis
BT2 apidae
BT3 hymenoptera
rt honeybees

APIS FLOREA
BT1 apis
BT2 apidae
BT3 hymenoptera
rt honeybees

apis indica
USE **apis cerana indica**

APIS MELLIFERA
uf *apis mellifica*
BT1 apis
BT2 apidae
BT3 hymenoptera
NT1 apis mellifera adansonii
NT1 apis mellifera capensis
NT1 apis mellifera carnica
NT1 apis mellifera caucasica
NT1 apis mellifera cypria
NT1 apis mellifera lamarckii
NT1 apis mellifera ligustica
NT1 apis mellifera mellifera
NT1 apis mellifera scutellata
NT1 apis mellifera unicolor
rt honeybees

APIS MELLIFERA ADANSONII
BT1 apis mellifera
BT2 apis
BT3 apidae
BT4 hymenoptera

APIS MELLIFERA CAPENSIS
uf *cape honeybee*
BT1 apis mellifera
BT2 apis
BT3 apidae
BT4 hymenoptera

APIS MELLIFERA CARNICA
uf *carniolan honeybee*
BT1 apis mellifera

APIS MELLIFERA CARNICA *cont.*
BT2 apis
BT3 apidae
BT4 hymenoptera

APIS MELLIFERA CAUCASICA
uf *caucasian honeybee*
BT1 apis mellifera
BT2 apis
BT3 apidae
BT4 hymenoptera

APIS MELLIFERA CYPRIA
uf *cyprian honeybee*
BT1 apis mellifera
BT2 apis
BT3 apidae
BT4 hymenoptera

APIS MELLIFERA LAMARCKII
uf *egyptian honeybees*
BT1 apis mellifera
BT2 apis
BT3 apidae
BT4 hymenoptera

APIS MELLIFERA LIGUSTICA
uf *italian honeybees*
BT1 apis mellifera
BT2 apis
BT3 apidae
BT4 hymenoptera

APIS MELLIFERA MELLIFERA
BT1 apis mellifera
BT2 apis
BT3 apidae
BT4 hymenoptera

APIS MELLIFERA SCUTELLATA
BT1 apis mellifera
BT2 apis
BT3 apidae
BT4 hymenoptera

APIS MELLIFERA UNICOLOR
BT1 apis mellifera
BT2 apis
BT3 apidae
BT4 hymenoptera

apis mellifica
USE **apis mellifera**

APIUM
BT1 umbelliferae
NT1 apium graveolens
NT1 apium graveolens var. rapaceum
NT1 apium leptophyllum
NT1 apium nodiflorum

APIUM GRAVEOLENS
BT1 apium
BT2 umbelliferae
rt celery
rt celery mosaic potyvirus

APIUM GRAVEOLENS VAR. RAPACEUM
BT1 apium
BT2 umbelliferae
rt celeriac

APIUM LEPTOPHYLLUM
BT1 apium
BT2 umbelliferae

APIUM NODIFLORUM
BT1 apium
BT2 umbelliferae

aplanobacter populi
USE **xanthomonas populi**

APLASIA
BT1 congenital abnormalities
BT2 abnormalities
NT1 anencephaly
NT1 segmental aplasia
NT1 taillessness
NT1 wolffian duct aplasia

APLASTIC ANAEMIA
AF aplastic anemia

APLASTIC ANAEMIA *cont.*
BT1 anaemia
BT2 blood disorders
BT3 animal disorders
BT4 disorders
BT1 bone marrow disorders
BT2 blood disorders
BT3 animal disorders
BT4 disorders

APLASTIC ANEMIA
BF aplastic anaemia
BT1 anemia

aplastomorpha
USE **anisopteromalus**

aplastomorpha calandrae
USE **anisopteromalus calandrae**

APLOCHEILIDAE
BT1 cyprinodontiformes
BT2 osteichthyes
BT3 fishes
NT1 aplocheilus
NT2 aplocheilus latipes

APLOCHEILUS
BT1 aplocheilidae
BT2 cyprinodontiformes
BT3 osteichthyes
BT4 fishes
NT1 aplocheilus latipes

APLOCHEILUS LATIPES
BT1 aplocheilus
BT2 aplocheilidae
BT3 cyprinodontiformes
BT4 osteichthyes
BT5 fishes

APLODINOTUS
BT1 sciaenidae
BT2 perciformes
BT3 osteichthyes
BT4 fishes

APLODONTIA
BT1 aplodontidae
BT2 rodents
BT3 mammals
NT1 aplodontia rufa

APLODONTIA RUFA
BT1 aplodontia
BT2 aplodontidae
BT3 rodents
BT4 mammals

APLODONTIDAE
BT1 rodents
BT2 mammals
NT1 aplodontia
NT2 aplodontia rufa

APLOPARAKSIS
BT1 hymenolepididae
BT2 eucestoda
BT3 cestoda

APLUDA
BT1 gramineae
NT1 apluda mutica

APLUDA MUTICA
uf *apluda varia*
BT1 apluda
BT2 gramineae

apluda varia
USE **apluda mutica**

apoanagyrus
USE **epidinocarsis**

apoanagyrus lopezi
USE **epidinocarsis lopezi**

APOCYNACEAE
NT1 acokanthera
NT2 acokanthera longiflora
NT2 acokanthera oblongifolia
NT2 acokanthera ouabaio
NT1 adenium

APOCYNACEAE *cont.*
NT2 adenium obesum
NT2 adenium swazicum
NT1 alafia
NT2 alafia multiflora
NT1 allemanda
NT2 allemanda cathartica
NT1 alstonia
NT2 alstonia boonei
NT2 alstonia congensis
NT2 alstonia deplanchei
NT2 alstonia macrophylla
NT2 alstonia muelleriana
NT2 alstonia odontophora
NT2 alstonia scholaris
NT2 alstonia spectabilis
NT2 alstonia venenata
NT1 alyxia
NT2 alyxia lucida
NT2 alyxia oliviformis
NT2 alyxia rubricaulis
NT1 ambelania
NT2 ambelania acida
NT1 amsonia
NT2 amsonia angustifolia
NT2 amsonia elliptica
NT2 amsonia tabernaemontana
NT1 anodendron
NT2 anodendron affine
NT1 apocynum
NT2 apocynum cannabinum
NT2 apocynum lancifolium
NT2 apocynum pictum
NT2 apocynum venetum
NT1 aspidosperma
NT2 aspidosperma cuspa
NT2 aspidosperma exalatum
NT2 aspidosperma nitidum
NT2 aspidosperma polyneuron
NT2 aspidosperma quebrachoblanco
NT2 aspidosperma rhombeosignatum
NT1 baissea
NT1 beaumontia
NT2 beaumontia grandiflora
NT1 bleekeria
NT2 bleekeria vitiensis
NT1 carissa
NT2 carissa bispinosa
NT2 carissa carandas
NT2 carissa macrocarpa
NT2 carissa opaea
NT2 carissa ovata
NT2 carissa spinarum
NT1 catharanthus
NT2 catharanthus lanceus
NT2 catharanthus longifolius
NT2 catharanthus ovalis
NT2 catharanthus phyllanthoides
NT2 catharanthus roseus
NT2 catharanthus trichophyllus
NT1 cerbera
NT2 cerbera manghas
NT2 cerbera odollam
NT1 couma
NT2 couma macrocarpa
NT1 coutinia
NT2 coutinia succuba
NT1 crioceras
NT2 crioceras dipladeniiflorus
NT1 dipladenia
NT2 dipladenia sanderi
NT1 dyera
NT2 dyera costulata
NT1 echites
NT2 echites hirsuta
NT1 ervatamia
NT2 ervatamia heyneana
NT2 ervatamia lifnana
NT2 ervatamia orientalis
NT1 funtumia
NT2 funtumia elastica
NT1 hazunta
NT2 hazunta modesta
NT1 holarrhena
NT2 holarrhena congolensis
NT2 holarrhena floribunda
NT2 holarrhena pubescens
NT2 holarrhena wulfsbergii

APOCYNACEAE *cont.*
NT1 hunteria
NT2 hunteria congolana
NT2 hunteria elliottii
NT1 landolphia
NT1 malouetia
NT2 malouetia glandulifera
NT1 melochia
NT2 melochia corchorifolia
NT2 melochia cordifolia
NT2 melochia tomentosa
NT1 motandra
NT2 motandra guineensis
NT1 neobracea
NT2 neobracea valenzuelana
NT1 neopracea
NT1 nerium
NT2 nerium oleander
NT1 ochrosia
NT2 ochrosia borbonica
NT2 ochrosia elliptica
NT2 ochrosia lifuana
NT2 ochrosia oppositifolia
NT2 ochrosia vieillardii
NT1 pachypodium
NT2 pachypodium lamerei
NT1 parsonsia
NT2 parsonsia heterophylla
NT1 peschiera
NT2 peschiera affinis
NT2 peschiera fuchsiaefolia
NT1 plumeria
NT2 plumeria alba
NT2 plumeria obtusifolia
NT2 plumeria rubra
NT1 rauvolfia
NT2 rauvolfia caffra
NT2 rauvolfia cambodiana
NT2 rauvolfia capuroni
NT2 rauvolfia cumminsii
NT2 rauvolfia macrophylla
NT2 rauvolfia mombasiana
NT2 rauvolfia obscura
NT2 rauvolfia oreogiton
NT2 rauvolfia perakensis
NT2 rauvolfia psychotrioides
NT2 rauvolfia reflexa
NT2 rauvolfia serpentina
NT2 rauvolfia suaveolens
NT2 rauvolfia tetraphylla
NT2 rauvolfia verticillata
NT2 rauvolfia volkensii
NT2 rauvolfia vomitoria
NT2 rauvolfia yunnanensis
NT1 rhazya
NT2 rhazya stricta
NT1 stenosolen
NT2 stenosolen heterophyllus
NT1 strophanthus
NT2 strophanthus gratus
NT2 strophanthus hispidus
NT2 strophanthus kombe
NT2 strophanthus speciosus
NT2 strophanthus splendens
NT2 strophanthus wightianus
NT1 tabernaemontana
NT2 tabernaemontana accedens
NT2 tabernaemontana albiflora
NT2 tabernaemontana arborea
NT2 tabernaemontana boiteaui
NT2 tabernaemontana coronaria
NT2 tabernaemontana crassa
NT2 tabernaemontana divaricata
NT2 tabernaemontana fuchsiaefolia
NT2 tabernaemontana glandulosa
NT2 tabernaemontana heyneana
NT2 tabernaemontana holstii
NT2 tabernaemontana johnstonii
NT2 tabernaemontana pandacaqui
NT1 tabernanthe
NT2 tabernanthe iboga
NT1 thevetia
NT2 thevetia peruviana
NT1 trachelospermum
NT2 trachelospermum asiaticum

APOCYNACEAE *cont.*
NT2 trachelospermum fragrans
NT2 trachelospermum jasminoides
NT1 trachomitum
NT2 trachomitum sarmatiense
NT1 vallesia
NT2 vallesia glabra
NT1 vinca
NT2 vinca elegantissima
NT2 vinca erecta
NT2 vinca herbacea
NT2 vinca libanotica
NT2 vinca major
NT2 vinca minor
NT2 vinca perenne
NT2 vinca pusilla
NT2 vinca sardoa
NT1 voacanga
NT2 voacanga africana
NT2 voacanga chalotiana
NT2 voacanga globosa
NT1 wrightia
NT2 wrightia calycina
NT2 wrightia tinctoria
NT2 wrightia tomentosa

APOCYNUM
BT1 apocynaceae
NT1 apocynum cannabinum
NT1 apocynum lancifolium
NT1 apocynum pictum
NT1 apocynum venetum

APOCYNUM CANNABINUM
BT1 apocynum
BT2 apocynaceae

APOCYNUM LANCIFOLIUM
BT1 apocynum
BT2 apocynaceae

APOCYNUM PICTUM
BT1 apocynum
BT2 apocynaceae

APOCYNUM VENETUM
BT1 apocynum
BT2 apocynaceae

APODANTHERA
BT1 cucurbitaceae
NT1 apodanthera undulata

APODANTHERA UNDULATA
BT1 apodanthera
BT2 cucurbitaceae

APODEMUS
uf *field mice*
BT1 murinae
BT2 muridae
BT3 rodents
BT4 mammals
NT1 apodemus agrarius
NT1 apodemus argenteus
NT1 apodemus flavicollis
NT1 apodemus speciosus
NT1 apodemus sylvaticus

APODEMUS AGRARIUS
BT1 apodemus
BT2 murinae
BT3 muridae
BT4 rodents
BT5 mammals

APODEMUS ARGENTEUS
BT1 apodemus
BT2 murinae
BT3 muridae
BT4 rodents
BT5 mammals

APODEMUS FLAVICOLLIS
BT1 apodemus
BT2 murinae
BT3 muridae
BT4 rodents
BT5 mammals

APODEMUS SPECIOSUS
BT1 apodemus
BT2 murinae

APODEMUS SPECIOSUS *cont.*
BT3 muridae
BT4 rodents
BT5 mammals

APODEMUS SYLVATICUS
BT1 apodemus
BT2 murinae
BT3 muridae
BT4 rodents
BT5 mammals

APODIDAE
uf *swifts*
BT1 apodiformes
BT2 birds
NT1 apus
NT2 apus affinis
NT2 apus apus

APODIFORMES
BT1 birds
NT1 apodidae
NT2 apus
NT3 apus affinis
NT3 apus apus
NT1 trochilidae

APOGONIA
BT1 scarabaeidae
BT2 coleoptera

APOLIPOPROTEINS
BT1 apoproteins
BT2 proteins
BT3 peptides

APOLOCYSTIS
BT1 apicomplexa
BT2 protozoa

APOLYSIS
BT1 moulting
BT2 biological rhythms
BT2 shedding

APOMIXIS
BT1 asexual reproduction
BT2 reproduction
rt parthenogenesis

APOMORPHINE
BT1 emetics
BT2 gastrointestinal agents
BT3 drugs
rt morphine
rt opium alkaloids
rt vomiting

APONOGETON
BT1 aponogetonaceae
rt ornamental aquatic plants

APONOGETONACEAE
NT1 aponogeton

APOPHALLUS
BT1 heterophyidae
BT2 digenea
BT3 trematoda

APOPHYLLUM
BT1 capparidaceae
NT1 apophyllum anomalum

APOPHYLLUM ANOMALUM
BT1 apophyllum
BT2 capparidaceae

APOPLEXY
BT1 cerebrovascular disorders
BT2 brain disorders
BT3 nervous system diseases
BT4 organic diseases
BT5 diseases
BT2 vascular diseases
BT3 cardiovascular diseases
BT4 organic diseases
BT5 diseases

APOPROTEINS
BT1 proteins
BT2 peptides
NT1 apolipoproteins

APORIA
BT1 pieridae
BT2 lepidoptera
NT1 aporia crataegi

APORIA CRATAEGI
BT1 aporia
BT2 pieridae
BT3 lepidoptera

APORRECTODEA
uf *nicodrilus*
BT1 lumbricidae
BT2 oligochaeta
BT3 annelida
NT1 aporrectodea caliginosa
NT1 aporrectodea longa
rt allolobophora

APORRECTODEA CALIGINOSA
uf *allolobophora caliginosa*
uf *allolobophora trapezoides*
uf *allolobophora tuberculata*
uf *aporrectodea trapezoides*
uf *aporrectodea tuberculata*
uf *nicodrilus caliginosus*
BT1 aporrectodea
BT2 lumbricidae
BT3 oligochaeta
BT4 annelida

APORRECTODEA LONGA
uf *allolobophora longa*
BT1 aporrectodea
BT2 lumbricidae
BT3 oligochaeta
BT4 annelida

aporrectodea trapezoides
USE **aporrectodea caliginosa**

aporrectodea tuberculata
USE **aporrectodea caliginosa**

APPALACHIAN STATES OF USA
BT1 southern states of usa
BT2 usa
BT3 north america
BT4 america
NT1 delaware
NT1 district of columbia
NT1 kentucky
NT1 maryland
NT1 north carolina
NT1 tennessee
NT1 virginia
NT1 west virginia

APPALOOSA
BT1 horse breeds
BT2 breeds

APPARATUS
BT1 equipment

apparel
USE **clothing**

appelia
USE **brachycaudus**

appelia schwartzi
USE **brachycaudus schwartzi**

APPENDICITIS (AGRICOLA)
BT1 human diseases
BT2 diseases
BT1 intestinal diseases
BT2 gastrointestinal diseases
BT3 digestive system diseases
BT4 organic diseases
BT5 diseases

APPENNINE
HN from 1990
BT1 sheep breeds
BT2 breeds

APPENZELL
BT1 goat breeds
BT2 breeds

APPENZELL CHEESE
HN from 1989
BT1 cheeses

APPENZELL CHEESE *cont.*
BT2 milk products
BT3 products

APPETITE
BT1 nutrition physiology
BT2 physiology
NT1 appetite control
rt anorexia
rt anorexiants
rt appetite disorders
rt food intake
rt hunger
rt overeating
rt satiety

APPETITE CONTROL
BT1 appetite
BT2 nutrition physiology
BT3 physiology
rt anorexiants
rt food intake

appetite depressants
USE **anorexiants**

APPETITE DISORDERS
uf *eating disorders*
BT1 digestive disorders
BT2 functional disorders
BT3 animal disorders
BT4 disorders
NT1 anorexia
NT2 anorexia nervosa
NT1 bulimia
NT1 bulimia nervosa (agricola)
NT1 compulsive eating (agricola)
NT1 geophagia
NT1 pica
rt appetite
rt cannibalism
rt overeating

APPETITE STIMULANTS
BT1 stimulants
BT2 drugs
NT1 brotizolam
NT1 elfazepam
rt phagostimulants

appetite suppressors
USE **anorexiants**

APPETIZERS (AGRICOLA)
rt meals

APPLE CHLOROTIC LEAF SPOT VIRUS
BT1 miscellaneous plant viruses
BT2 plant viruses
BT3 plant pathogens
BT4 pathogens
rt malus pumila

APPLE FLAT LIMB VIRUS
BT1 miscellaneous plant viruses
BT2 plant viruses
BT3 plant pathogens
BT4 pathogens
rt malus pumila

APPLE JUICE
BT1 fruit juices
BT2 fruit products
BT3 plant products
BT4 products
BT2 juices
BT3 liquids
rt apple pomace
rt cider

APPLE MALUS PLATYCARPA DWARF VIRUS
BT1 miscellaneous plant viruses
BT2 plant viruses
BT3 plant pathogens
BT4 pathogens
rt malus pumila

APPLE MALUS PLATYCARPA SCALY BARK VIRUS
BT1 miscellaneous plant viruses
BT2 plant viruses
BT3 plant pathogens

APPLE MALUS PLATYCARPA SCALY BARK VIRUS *cont.*
BT4 pathogens
rt malus pumila

APPLE MOSAIC ILARVIRUS
HN from 1990; previously "apple mosaic virus"
uf *apple mosaic virus*
BT1 ilarvirus group
BT2 plant viruses
BT3 plant pathogens
BT4 pathogens
rt apples
rt malus pumila

apple mosaic virus
USE **apple mosaic ilarvirus**

APPLE POMACE
BT1 pomace
BT2 fruit products
BT3 plant products
BT4 products
BT2 plant residues
BT3 residues
rt apple juice
rt apples
rt cider
rt malus pumila

APPLE RUBBERY WOOD VIRUS
BT1 miscellaneous plant viruses
BT2 plant viruses
BT3 plant pathogens
BT4 pathogens
rt malus pumila

APPLE SPY 227 EPINASTY AND DECLINE VIRUS
BT1 miscellaneous plant viruses
BT2 plant viruses
BT3 plant pathogens
BT4 pathogens
rt malus pumila

APPLE STEM GROOVING CAPILLOVIRUS
HN from 1990; previously "apple stem grooving virus"
uf *apple stem grooving virus*
BT1 capillovirus group
BT2 plant viruses
BT3 plant pathogens
BT4 pathogens
rt apples
rt malus pumila

apple stem grooving virus
USE **apple stem grooving capillovirus**

APPLE STEM PITTING VIRUS
BT1 miscellaneous plant viruses
BT2 plant viruses
BT3 plant pathogens
BT4 pathogens

APPLES
BT1 pome fruits
BT2 temperate tree fruits
BT3 temperate fruits
BT4 fruit crops
BT3 tree fruits
rt apple mosaic ilarvirus
rt apple pomace
rt apple stem grooving capillovirus
rt applesauce (agricola)
rt bitter pit
rt brown core
rt brown heart
rt cider
rt core flush
rt cork spot
rt corking
rt cox disease
rt cox spot
rt flesh browning
rt internal bark necrosis
rt malus pumila
rt scald
rt scarfskin

APPLES *cont.*
rt water core

APPLESAUCE (AGRICOLA)
BT1 sauces
rt apples

APPLIANCES (AGRICOLA)
NT1 coffeemakers (agricola)
NT1 dishwashers (agricola)
NT1 home appliances (agricola)
NT1 irons (agricola)
NT1 large appliances (agricola)
NT1 refrigerators (agricola)
NT1 small appliances (agricola)
NT1 washing machines (agricola)
rt blenders (agricola)
rt household equipment (agricola)

APPLICATION
NT1 application to land
rt application date
rt application depth
rt application equipment
rt application methods
rt application rates

APPLICATION DATE
rt application
rt application methods
rt date

APPLICATION DEPTH
rt application
rt application methods
rt depth

APPLICATION EQUIPMENT
BT1 equipment
NT1 applicators
NT2 wiper applicators
NT1 fertilizer distributors
NT2 liquid fertilizer distributors
NT1 fumigation equipment
NT1 injectors
NT2 soil injectors
NT2 tree injectors
NT1 spraying equipment
NT2 lances
NT2 nozzles
NT3 cone nozzles
NT3 fan nozzles
NT3 spinning disc nozzles
NT2 spray guns
NT2 spray races
NT2 sprayers
NT3 aerial sprayers
NT3 aerosol sprayers
NT3 air assisted sprayers
NT3 band sprayers
NT3 electrostatic sprayers
NT3 field sprayers
NT3 high volume sprayers
NT3 logarithmic sprayers
NT3 low volume sprayers
NT4 ultralow volume sprayers
NT3 mist blowers
NT3 mist sprayers
NT3 orchard sprayers
NT3 overhead sprayers
NT3 plot sprayers
NT4 small plot sprayers
NT3 portable sprayers
NT4 knapsack sprayers
NT3 recirculatory sprayers
NT3 tower sprayers
NT2 spraylines
NT1 spreaders
NT2 bait spreaders
NT2 lime spreaders
NT2 manure spreaders
NT2 slurry spreaders
rt application
rt application methods
rt incorporators

APPLICATION METHODS
uf *amendment application*
BT1 methodology
NT1 aerial application
NT1 annual dressings

APPLICATION METHODS *cont.*
NT1 basal dressings
NT1 boluses
NT1 broadcasting
NT1 controlled release
NT1 cutaneous application
NT1 dipping
NT1 dressings
NT1 drilling
NT2 direct sowing
NT2 precision drilling
NT1 drug delivery systems
NT1 dusting
NT1 ear tags
NT1 flea collars
NT1 fogging
NT1 foliar application
NT1 fumigation
NT2 soil fumigation
NT1 inhalation
NT1 injection
NT2 intramuscular injection
NT2 intraperitoneal injection
NT2 intravenous injection
NT2 soil injection
NT2 subcutaneous injection
NT2 tree injection
NT1 inoculation methods
NT2 seed inoculation
NT2 soil inoculation
NT1 instillation
NT1 mist application
NT1 oral administration
NT1 parenteral administration
NT2 transfusion
NT1 periodic dressings
NT1 placement
NT2 band placement
NT2 deep placement
NT1 release techniques
NT1 root treatment
NT1 rope wick
NT1 seed dressings
NT1 sidedressing
NT1 soil treatment
NT1 split dressings
NT1 spraying
NT2 aerial spraying
NT2 band spraying
NT2 basal stem spraying
NT2 controlled droplet application
NT2 drift spraying
NT2 electrostatic spraying
NT2 foliar spraying
NT2 ground surface spraying
NT2 high volume spraying
NT2 intermittent spraying
NT2 low volume spraying
NT3 ultralow volume spraying
NT2 spot spraying
NT1 starter dressings
NT1 subsurface application
NT1 top dressings
NT1 topical application
NT1 unimolecular films
rt application
rt application date
rt application depth
rt application equipment
rt bed nets
rt fertilizer carriers

APPLICATION RATES
rt application
rt dosage effects
rt fertilizer requirement determination

APPLICATION TO LAND
uf land application
uf land disposal
BT1 application

APPLICATIONS
NT1 industrial applications

APPLICATORS
BT1 application equipment
BT2 equipment
NT1 wiper applicators

APPLIED NUTRITION (AGRICOLA)
BT1 nutrition

APPLIED RESEARCH
uf research, applied
BT1 research

APPRENTICESHIP
BT1 inservice training
BT2 vocational training
BT3 training
rt continuing education
rt on-the-job training (agricola)
rt school leavers

APPRESSORIA
BT1 fungal morphology
BT2 morphology

APPROPRIATE TECHNOLOGY
uf intermediate technology
uf low cost technology
BT1 technology
rt human power
rt low energy cultivation
rt mechanization
rt technical aid
rt technical progress
rt technology transfer

APPROVAL SCHEMES
BT1 marketing techniques
BT2 techniques
rt sales promotion

APRAMYCIN
BT1 antibacterial agents
BT2 antiinfective agents
BT3 drugs
BT1 antibiotics

APRICOT KERNELS
rt apricots
rt seeds

APRICOTS
BT1 stone fruits
BT2 temperate tree fruits
BT3 temperate fruits
BT4 fruit crops
BT3 tree fruits
rt apricot kernels
rt prunus armeniaca
rt prunus mume

APROAEREMA
BT1 gelechiidae
BT2 lepidoptera
NT1 aproaerema modicella
rt biloba
rt stomopteryx

APROAEREMA MODICELLA
uf aproaerema subsecivella
uf biloba subsecivella
uf stomopteryx subsecivella
BT1 aproaerema
BT2 gelechiidae
BT3 lepidoptera

aproaerema subsecivella
USE **aproaerema modicella**

APROSTOCETUS
BT1 eulophidae
BT2 hymenoptera
NT1 aprostocetus diplosidis
NT1 aprostocetus galactopus
NT1 aprostocetus hagenowii
NT1 aprostocetus purpureus
NT1 aprostocetus venustus
rt tetrastichus

APROSTOCETUS DIPLOSIDIS
uf tetrastichus diplosidis
BT1 aprostocetus
BT2 eulophidae
BT3 hymenoptera

APROSTOCETUS GALACTOPUS
HN from 1989; previously tetrastichus galactopus
uf tetrastichus galactopus
BT1 aprostocetus
BT2 eulophidae

APROSTOCETUS GALACTOPUS *cont.*
BT3 hymenoptera

APROSTOCETUS HAGENOWII
HN from 1990
uf tetrastichus hagenowii
BT1 aprostocetus
BT2 eulophidae
BT3 hymenoptera

APROSTOCETUS PURPUREUS
uf tetrastichus purpureus
BT1 aprostocetus
BT2 eulophidae
BT3 hymenoptera

APROSTOCETUS VENUSTUS
uf tetrastichus venustus
BT1 aprostocetus
BT2 eulophidae
BT3 hymenoptera

APSILUS
BT1 lutjanidae
BT2 perciformes
BT3 osteichthyes
BT4 fishes

APTENODYTES
BT1 spheniscidae
BT2 sphenisciformes
BT3 birds

APTERYGIDAE
BT1 apterygiformes
BT2 birds
NT1 apteryx

APTERYGIFORMES
BT1 birds
NT1 apterygidae
NT2 apteryx

APTERYX
BT1 apterygidae
BT2 apterygiformes
BT3 birds

APTINOTHRIPS
BT1 thripidae
BT2 thysanoptera
NT1 aptinothrips rufus
NT1 aptinothrips stylifer

APTINOTHRIPS RUFUS
BT1 aptinothrips
BT2 thripidae
BT3 thysanoptera

APTINOTHRIPS STYLIFER
BT1 aptinothrips
BT2 thripidae
BT3 thysanoptera

APULIA
uf puglia
BT1 italy
BT2 western europe
BT3 europe

APULIAN
BT1 goat breeds
BT2 breeds

apulian (cattle breed)
USE **apulian podolian**

apulian merino
USE **gentile di puglia**

APULIAN PODOLIAN
HN from 1990; previously "apulian"
uf apulian (cattle breed)
BT1 cattle breeds
BT2 breeds

APUS
BT1 apodidae
BT2 apodiformes
BT3 birds
NT1 apus affinis
NT1 apus apus

APUS AFFINIS
BT1 apus
BT2 apodidae
BT3 apodiformes
BT4 birds

APUS APUS
BT1 apus
BT2 apodidae
BT3 apodiformes
BT4 birds

AQUACULTURE
uf agropisciculture
BT1 enterprises
NT1 algae culture
NT1 fish culture
NT2 eel culture
NT2 salmon culture
NT1 frog culture
NT1 seaweed culture
NT1 shellfish culture
NT2 lobster culture
NT2 mollusc culture
NT3 mussel culture
NT3 oyster culture
NT2 shrimp culture
NT1 turtle culture
rt ancillary enterprises
rt aquarium fishes
rt fish farming
rt fish farms
rt fisheries
rt water

aquaforestry
USE **aquasilvicultural systems**

AQUALFS
BT1 alfisols
BT2 argilluvic soils
BT3 soil types (genetic)
rt argilluvic soils
rt luvisols
rt podzoluvisols

AQUARIA
BT1 animal housing
rt aquarium fishes

AQUARIUM FISHES
BT1 aquatic animals
BT2 animals
BT2 aquatic organisms
rt aquaculture
rt aquaria
rt fish culture
rt fishes

AQUASILVICULTURAL SYSTEMS
(agroforestry systems combining woody perennials with raising aquatic animals)
uf aquaforestry
BT1 agroforestry systems

AQUATIC ANIMALS
BT1 animals
BT1 aquatic organisms
NT1 aquarium fishes
NT1 aquatic invertebrates
NT2 aquatic arthropods
NT3 aquatic insects
NT3 water mites
NT2 freshwater molluscs
NT2 marine nematodes
NT2 shellfish
NT3 abalones
NT3 clams
NT4 hard clams
NT4 surf clams
NT3 crabs
NT3 crayfish
NT3 lobsters
NT3 mussels
NT3 oysters
NT3 prawns
NT3 scallops
NT3 shrimps
NT1 brackish water fishes
NT1 crocodiles
NT1 diadromous fishes
NT2 atlantic salmon

AQUATIC ANIMALS *cont.*
NT2 european eels
NT2 lampreys
NT2 sturgeons
NT1 freshwater fishes
NT2 ayu
NT2 brown trout
NT2 carp
NT2 freshwater catfishes
NT2 goldfish
NT2 perch
NT2 pike
NT2 pike perch
NT2 rainbow trout
NT1 frogs
NT1 game fishes
NT2 trout
NT1 manatees
NT1 marine fishes
NT2 anchovies
NT2 anglerfishes
NT2 bass
NT2 bonitos
NT2 cod
NT2 dogfishes
NT2 eels
NT2 flatfishes
NT3 dover soles
NT3 flounder
NT3 halibut
NT3 plaice
NT3 turbot
NT2 groupers
NT2 haddock
NT2 hake
NT2 herrings
NT2 mackerels
NT2 marlins
NT2 menhaden
NT2 mullets
NT2 pompanos
NT2 sardines
NT2 sea bass
NT2 sea bream
NT2 sea catfish
NT2 sharks
NT2 smelts
NT2 sprats
NT2 sunfishes
NT2 tuna
NT2 whitefish
NT2 whiting
NT2 yellowtails
NT1 marine mammals
NT2 dolphins
NT2 whales
NT1 ornamental fishes
NT1 otters
NT1 sealions
NT1 seals
NT1 toads
NT1 waterfowl
rt amphibia
rt amphipoda
rt aquatic communities
rt branchiopoda
rt echinodermata
rt freshwater ecology
rt hydrobiology
rt marine ecology
rt rotifera
rt sirenia
rt water

AQUATIC ARTHROPODS
BT1 aquatic invertebrates
BT2 aquatic animals
BT3 animals
BT3 aquatic organisms
NT1 aquatic insects
NT1 water mites
rt arthropods

AQUATIC COMMUNITIES
BT1 communities
NT1 plankton
NT2 krill
NT2 phytoplankton
NT2 zooplankton
NT1 pleuston
NT1 seston
rt aquatic animals

AQUATIC COMMUNITIES *cont.*
rt aquatic environment
rt aquatic fungi
rt aquatic organisms
rt aquatic plants
rt freshwater ecology
rt marine ecology
rt water

AQUATIC ENVIRONMENT
BT1 ecosystems
BT1 environment
rt aquatic communities
rt aquatic organisms
rt water

AQUATIC FUNGI
BT1 aquatic organisms
BT1 fungi
rt aquatic communities
rt water

AQUATIC INSECTS
BT1 aquatic arthropods
BT2 aquatic invertebrates
BT3 aquatic animals
BT4 animals
BT4 aquatic organisms
BT1 insects
BT2 arthropods

AQUATIC INVERTEBRATES
BT1 aquatic animals
BT2 animals
BT2 aquatic organisms
NT1 aquatic arthropods
NT2 aquatic insects
NT2 water mites
NT1 freshwater molluscs
NT1 marine nematodes
NT1 shellfish
NT2 abalones
NT2 clams
NT3 hard clams
NT3 surf clams
NT2 crabs
NT2 crayfish
NT2 lobsters
NT2 mussels
NT2 oysters
NT2 prawns
NT2 scallops
NT2 shrimps

AQUATIC ORGANISMS
NT1 aquatic animals
NT2 aquarium fishes
NT2 aquatic invertebrates
NT3 aquatic arthropods
NT4 aquatic insects
NT4 water mites
NT3 freshwater molluscs
NT3 marine nematodes
NT3 shellfish
NT4 abalones
NT4 clams
NT5 hard clams
NT5 surf clams
NT4 crabs
NT4 crayfish
NT4 lobsters
NT4 mussels
NT4 oysters
NT4 prawns
NT4 scallops
NT4 shrimps
NT2 brackish water fishes
NT2 crocodiles
NT2 diadromous fishes
NT3 atlantic salmon
NT3 european eels
NT3 lampreys
NT3 sturgeons
NT2 freshwater fishes
NT3 ayu
NT3 brown trout
NT3 carp
NT3 freshwater catfishes
NT3 goldfish
NT3 perch
NT3 pike
NT3 pike perch

AQUATIC ORGANISMS *cont.*
NT3 rainbow trout
NT2 frogs
NT2 game fishes
NT3 trout
NT2 manatees
NT2 marine fishes
NT3 anchovies
NT3 anglerfishes
NT3 bass
NT3 bonitos
NT3 cod
NT3 dogfishes
NT3 eels
NT3 flatfishes
NT4 dover soles
NT4 flounder
NT4 halibut
NT4 plaice
NT4 turbot
NT3 groupers
NT3 haddock
NT3 hake
NT3 herrings
NT3 mackerels
NT3 marlins
NT3 menhaden
NT3 mullets
NT3 pompanos
NT3 sardines
NT3 sea bass
NT3 sea bream
NT3 sea catfish
NT3 sharks
NT3 smelts
NT3 sprats
NT3 sunfishes
NT3 tuna
NT3 whitefish
NT3 whiting
NT3 yellowtails
NT2 marine mammals
NT3 dolphins
NT3 whales
NT2 ornamental fishes
NT2 otters
NT2 sealions
NT2 seals
NT2 toads
NT2 waterfowl
NT1 aquatic fungi
NT1 aquatic plants
NT2 aquatic weeds
NT2 ornamental aquatic plants
NT3 nelumbo lutea
NT3 nelumbo nucifera
NT3 nuphar advena
NT3 nuphar lutea
NT3 nuphar variegata
NT3 nymphaea alba
NT3 nymphaea caerulea
NT3 nymphaea lotus
NT3 nymphaea odorata
NT3 nymphaea tuberosa
NT3 nymphoides aquatica
NT3 nymphoides peltata
NT3 typha latifolia
NT3 victoria amazonica
rt aquatic communities
rt aquatic environment
rt benthos
rt freshwater biology (agricola)
rt freshwater ecology
rt hydrobiology
rt marine ecology
rt water

AQUATIC PLANT HARVESTERS
uf *harvesters, aquatic plant*
BT1 harvesters
BT2 farm machinery
BT3 machinery
rt aquatic plants
rt water

AQUATIC PLANTS
BT1 aquatic organisms
NT1 aquatic weeds
NT1 ornamental aquatic plants
NT2 nelumbo lutea
NT2 nelumbo nucifera
NT2 nuphar advena

AQUATIC PLANTS *cont.*
NT2 nuphar lutea
NT2 nuphar variegata
NT2 nymphaea alba
NT2 nymphaea caerulea
NT2 nymphaea lotus
NT2 nymphaea odorata
NT2 nymphaea tuberosa
NT2 nymphoides aquatica
NT2 nymphoides peltata
NT2 typha latifolia
NT2 victoria amazonica
rt aquatic communities
rt aquatic plant harvesters
rt freshwater ecology
rt hydrobiology
rt marine ecology
rt plants
rt water

AQUATIC WEEDS
BT1 aquatic plants
BT2 aquatic organisms
rt plants
rt weed control
rt weed cutting launches
rt weeds

AQUEOUS AMMONIA
BT1 ammonium fertilizers
BT2 nitrogen fertilizers
BT3 fertilizers
rt ammonia
rt ammonium hydroxide

AQUEOUS CONCENTRATES
BT1 formulations
rt water

AQUIC REGIMES
BT1 soil water regimes

AQUIFERS
rt geology
rt hydrology
rt springs (water)
rt wells

AQUIFOLIACEAE
NT1 ilex
NT2 ilex aquifolium
NT2 ilex attenuata
NT2 ilex cassine
NT2 ilex ciliospinosa
NT2 ilex colchica
NT2 ilex cornuta
NT2 ilex crenata
NT2 ilex decidua
NT2 ilex glabra
NT2 ilex integra
NT2 ilex latifolia
NT2 ilex opaca
NT2 ilex paraguariensis
NT2 ilex perado
NT2 ilex rotunda
NT2 ilex serrata
NT2 ilex spinigera
NT2 ilex verticillata
NT2 ilex vomitoria

AQUILA
BT1 accipitridae
BT2 falconiformes
BT3 birds
NT1 aquila chrysaetos

AQUILA CHRYSAETOS
BT1 aquila
BT2 accipitridae
BT3 falconiformes
BT4 birds

AQUILARIA
BT1 thymelaeaceae
NT1 aquilaria agallocha

AQUILARIA AGALLOCHA
BT1 aquilaria
BT2 thymelaeaceae

AQUILEGIA
BT1 ranunculaceae
NT1 aquilegia canadensis
NT1 aquilegia flabellata

AQUILEGIA CANADENSIS
BT1 aquilegia
BT2 ranunculaceae
BT1 ornamental herbaceous plants

AQUILEGIA FLABELLATA
BT1 aquilegia
BT2 ranunculaceae
BT1 ornamental herbaceous plants

AQUITAINE
BT1 france
BT2 western europe
BT3 europe

aquitaine blond
USE **blonde d'aquitaine**

aquocobalamin
USE **hydroxocobalamin**

ARAB
BT1 horse breeds
BT2 breeds

ARAB COUNTRIES
BT1 islamic countries
rt algeria
rt bahrain
rt djibouti
rt egypt
rt iraq
rt jordan
rt kuwait
rt lebanon
rt libya
rt mauritania
rt middle east
rt morocco
rt north africa
rt oman
rt qatar
rt saudi arabia
rt somalia
rt sudan
rt syria
rt tunisia
rt united arab emirates
rt west asia
rt yemen arab republic
rt yemen democratic republic

arab republic of egypt
USE **egypt**

ARABI
BT1 sheep breeds
BT2 breeds

ARABIAN SEA
BT1 western indian ocean
BT2 indian ocean
BT3 marine areas

ARABIDOPSIS
BT1 cruciferae
NT1 arabidopsis thaliana

ARABIDOPSIS THALIANA
BT1 arabidopsis
BT2 cruciferae

ARABINITOL
BT1 alditols
BT2 sugar alcohols
BT3 carbohydrates
BT3 polyols
BT4 alcohols
rt arabinose

ARABINOSE
BT1 pentoses
BT2 aldoses
BT3 monosaccharides
BT4 carbohydrates
BT3 reducing sugars
BT4 sugars
BT5 carbohydrates
rt arabinitol

ARABIS
BT1 cruciferae
NT1 arabis alpina

ARABIS *cont.*
NT1 arabis caucasica
rt arabis mosaic nepovirus

arabis albida
USE **arabis caucasica**

ARABIS ALPINA
BT1 arabis
BT2 cruciferae
BT1 ornamental herbaceous plants

ARABIS CAUCASICA
uf *arabis albida*
BT1 arabis
BT2 cruciferae
BT1 ornamental herbaceous plants

ARABIS MOSAIC NEPOVIRUS
HN from 1990; previously "arabis mosaic virus"
uf *arabis mosaic virus*
BT1 nepovirus group
BT2 plant viruses
BT3 plant pathogens
BT4 pathogens
rt arabis

arabis mosaic virus
USE **arabis mosaic nepovirus**

ARABLE FARMING
BT1 farming
rt arable land
rt arable soils
rt cropping systems

ARABLE LAND
BT1 agricultural land
BT2 land resources
BT3 non-renewable resources
BT4 natural resources
BT5 resources
BT2 land types
rt arable farming
rt arable soils

ARABLE SOILS
BT1 soil types (cultural)
rt arable farming
rt arable land

ARACEAE
NT1 acorus
NT2 acorus calamus
NT2 acorus gramineus
NT1 aglaonema
NT2 aglaonema commutatum
NT2 aglaonema crispum
NT1 alocasia
NT2 alocasia cucullata
NT2 alocasia macrorrhiza
NT1 amorphophallus
NT2 amorphophallus campanulatus
NT2 amorphophallus konjac
NT1 anchomanes
NT2 anchomanes difformis
NT1 anthurium
NT2 anthurium polyschistum
NT2 anthurium scherzerianum
NT2 anthurium warocqueanum
NT1 arisaema
NT2 arisaema tortuosum
NT2 arisaema triphyllum
NT1 arisarum
NT1 arum
NT2 arum italicum
NT2 arum maculatum
NT2 arum orientale
NT1 caladium
NT2 caladium hortulanum
NT2 caladium humboldtii
NT1 calla
NT1 colocasia
NT2 colocasia antiquorum
NT2 colocasia esculenta
NT1 cyrtosperma
NT2 cyrtosperma chamissonis
NT1 dieffenbachia
NT2 dieffenbachia amoena

ARACEAE *cont.*
NT2 dieffenbachia bausei
NT2 dieffenbachia exotica
NT2 dieffenbachia maculata
NT1 epipremnum
NT2 epipremnum pinnatum
NT1 homalomena
NT2 homalomena lindenii
NT1 monstera
NT2 monstera deliciosa
NT2 monstera gigantea
NT1 nephthytis
NT1 orontium
NT1 peltandra
NT2 peltandra virginica
NT1 philodendron
NT2 philodendron bipinnatifidum
NT2 philodendron scandens
NT2 philodendron selloum
NT2 philodendron tuxtlanum
NT1 pinellia
NT2 pinellia ternata
NT1 pistia
NT2 pistia stratiotes
NT1 remusatia
NT2 remusatia vivipara
NT1 rhaphidophora
NT1 scindapsus
NT2 scindapsus pictus
NT1 spathiphyllum
NT2 spathiphyllum floribundum
NT1 symplocarpus
NT1 syngonium
NT2 syngonium podophyllum
NT1 typhonium
NT2 typhonium giganteum
NT1 xanthosoma
NT2 xanthosoma atrovirens
NT2 xanthosoma brasiliense
NT2 xanthosoma sagittifolium
NT2 xanthosoma violaceum
NT1 zantedeschia
NT2 zantedeschia aethiopica

ARACHIDONIC ACID
uf *eicosatetraenoic acid*
BT1 essential fatty acids
BT2 fatty acids
BT3 carboxylic acids
BT4 organic acids
BT5 acids
BT3 lipids
BT1 long chain fatty acids
BT2 fatty acids
BT3 carboxylic acids
BT4 organic acids
BT5 acids
BT3 lipids
BT1 polyenoic fatty acids
BT2 unsaturated fatty acids
BT3 fatty acids
BT4 carboxylic acids
BT5 organic acids
BT6 acids
BT4 lipids

ARACHINS
BT1 globulins
BT2 proteins
BT3 peptides
BT1 plant proteins
BT2 proteins
BT3 peptides
rt arachis hypogaea

ARACHIS
BT1 leguminosae
NT1 arachis glabrata
NT1 arachis hypogaea
NT1 arachis pintoi

ARACHIS GLABRATA
HN from 1990
BT1 arachis
BT2 leguminosae
BT1 fodder legumes
BT2 fodder plants
BT2 legumes

ARACHIS HYPOGAEA
BT1 arachis

ARACHIS HYPOGAEA *cont.*
BT2 leguminosae
BT1 fodder legumes
BT2 fodder plants
BT2 legumes
rt arachins
rt groundnut chlorotic spot virus
rt groundnut rosette virus
rt groundnuts
rt peanut clump furovirus
rt peanut mottle potyvirus
rt peanut stripe potyvirus
rt peanut stunt cucumovirus
rt peanuts

arachis oil
USE **groundnut oil**

ARACHIS PINTOI
HN from 1990
BT1 arachis
BT2 leguminosae
BT1 fodder legumes
BT2 fodder plants
BT2 legumes

ARACHNIDA
(acarine suborders, families, genera and species are listed at acari)
BT1 arthropods
NT1 araneae
NT2 agelenidae
NT3 tegenaria
NT4 tegenaria agrestis
NT2 araneidae
NT3 araneus
NT4 araneus diadematus
NT3 argiope
NT4 argiope argentata
NT3 nephila
NT4 nephila clavata
NT2 clubionidae
NT3 cheiracanthium
NT4 cheiracanthium mildei
NT2 ctenidae
NT3 phoneutria
NT2 dipluridae
NT2 heteropodidae
NT3 heteropoda
NT2 hexathelidae
NT3 atrax
NT4 atrax robustus
NT2 linyphiidae
NT3 erigonidium
NT4 erigonidium graminicolum
NT3 oedothorax
NT4 oedothorax insecticeps
NT2 loxoscelidae
NT3 loxosceles
NT4 loxosceles laeta
NT4 loxosceles reclusa
NT4 loxosceles rufescens
NT2 lycosidae
NT3 lycosa
NT4 lycosa pseudoannulata
NT3 trochosa
NT2 oxyopidae
NT3 oxyopes
NT4 oxyopes salticus
NT2 pholcidae
NT3 pholcus
NT4 pholcus phalangioides
NT2 tetragnathidae
NT3 tetragnatha
NT4 tetragnatha laboriosa
NT2 theraphosidae
NT3 aphonopelma
NT4 aphonopelma seemanni
NT2 theridiidae
NT3 achaearanea
NT4 achaearanea tepidariorum
NT3 latrodectus
NT4 latrodectus geometricus
NT4 latrodectus hasseltii
NT4 latrodectus hesperus
NT4 latrodectus katipo
NT4 latrodectus mactans
NT4 latrodectus tredecimguttatus

ARACHNIDA *cont.*
NT3 theridion
NT1 opiliones
NT1 pseudoscorpiones
NT1 scorpiones
NT2 buthidae
NT3 androctonus
NT4 androctonus aeneas
NT4 androctonus amoreuxi
NT4 androctonus australis
NT5 androctonus australis hector
NT4 androctonus mauretanicus
NT3 buthotus
NT4 buthotus minax
NT4 buthotus tamulus
NT3 buthus
NT4 buthus martensi
NT4 buthus occitanus
NT3 centruroides
NT4 centruroides gracilis
NT4 centruroides limpidus
NT5 centruroides limpidus limpidus
NT5 centruroides limpidus tecomanus
NT4 centruroides noxius
NT4 centruroides sculpturatus
NT3 leiurus
NT4 leiurus quinquestriatus
NT3 mesobuthus
NT3 tityus
NT4 tityus serrulatus
NT2 scorpionidae
NT3 heterometrus
NT4 heterometrus bengalensis
NT4 heterometrus fulvipes
NT4 heterometrus scaber
NT3 pandinus
NT1 solifugae
rt acari

ARACHNIDISM
HN from 1990
rt araneae
rt bites
rt envenomation

ARACHNIODES
BT1 aspidiaceae
NT1 arachniodes adiantiformis
rt rumohra

ARACHNIODES ADIANTIFORMIS
uf polystichum adiantiformis
uf rumohra adiantiformis
BT1 arachniodes
BT2 aspidiaceae
BT1 ornamental ferns
BT2 ferns
BT2 ornamental foliage plants
BT3 foliage plants

ARACHNIS
BT1 orchidaceae
rt aranda
rt ornamental orchids

ARADIDAE
BT1 heteroptera
NT1 aradus
NT2 aradus cinnamomeus

ARADO
HN from 1990
BT1 cattle breeds
BT2 breeds

ARADUS
BT1 aradidae
BT2 heteroptera
NT1 aradus cinnamomeus

ARADUS CINNAMOMEUS
BT1 aradus
BT2 aradidae
BT3 heteroptera

ARAECERUS
BT1 anthribidae

ARAECERUS *cont.*
BT2 coleoptera
NT1 araecerus fasciculatus

ARAECERUS FASCICULATUS
BT1 araecerus
BT2 anthribidae
BT3 coleoptera

ARAEOLAIMIDAE
BT1 nematoda
NT1 araeolaimus
rt free living nematodes
rt marine nematodes

ARAEOLAIMUS
BT1 araeolaimidae
BT2 nematoda

aragon
USE **aragonese**

ARAGONESE
HN from 1990; previously "aragon"
uf aragon
BT1 sheep breeds
BT2 breeds

ARALIA
BT1 araliaceae
NT1 aralia cordata
NT1 aralia elata
NT1 aralia racemosa
NT1 aralia schmidtii
NT1 aralia spinosa

ARALIA CORDATA
BT1 aralia
BT2 araliaceae

ARALIA ELATA
uf aralia mandshurica
BT1 aralia
BT2 araliaceae
BT1 medicinal plants

aralia elegantissima
USE **dizygotheca elegantissima**

aralia filicifolia
USE **polyscias filicifolia**

aralia fruticosa
USE **polyscias fruticosa**

aralia japonica
USE **fatsia japonica**

aralia mandshurica
USE **aralia elata**

ARALIA RACEMOSA
BT1 aralia
BT2 araliaceae

ARALIA SCHMIDTII
BT1 aralia
BT2 araliaceae
BT1 medicinal plants

aralia sieboldii
USE **fatsia japonica**

ARALIA SPINOSA
BT1 aralia
BT2 araliaceae

ARALIACEAE
NT1 acanthopanax
NT2 acanthopanax sessiliflorus
NT1 aralia
NT2 aralia cordata
NT2 aralia elata
NT2 aralia racemosa
NT2 aralia schmidtii
NT2 aralia spinosa
NT1 cussonia
NT2 cussonia barteri
NT1 didymopanax
NT2 didymopanax morototoni
NT1 dizygotheca
NT2 dizygotheca elegantissima
NT1 echinopanax
NT1 eleutherococcus
NT2 eleutherococcus senticosus

ARALIACEAE *cont.*
NT2 eleutherococcus sieboldianus
NT1 fatshedera
NT2 fatshedera lizei
NT1 fatsia
NT2 fatsia japonica
NT1 hedera
NT2 hedera colchica
NT2 hedera helix
NT2 hedera helix subsp. canariensis
NT2 hedera rhombea
NT2 hedera taurica
NT1 kalopanax
NT2 kalopanax pictus
NT1 oplopanax
NT2 oplopanax elatus
NT2 oplopanax horridus
NT1 panax
NT2 panax japonicus
NT2 panax pseudoginseng
NT2 panax quinquefolius
NT2 panax trifolius
NT1 polyscias
NT2 polyscias balfouriana
NT2 polyscias filicifolia
NT2 polyscias fruticosa
NT2 polyscias grandifolia
NT1 pseudopanax
NT1 schefflera
NT2 schefflera actinophylla
NT2 schefflera arboricola

ARANDA
BT1 orchidaceae
rt arachnis
rt ornamental orchids
rt vanda

ARANEAE
uf spiders
BT1 arachnida
BT2 arthropods
NT1 agelenidae
NT2 tegenaria
NT3 tegenaria agrestis
NT1 araneidae
NT2 araneus
NT3 araneus diadematus
NT2 argiope
NT3 argiope argentata
NT2 nephila
NT3 nephila clavata
NT1 clubionidae
NT2 cheiracanthium
NT3 cheiracanthium mildei
NT1 ctenidae
NT2 phoneutria
NT1 dipluridae
NT1 heteropodidae
NT2 heteropoda
NT1 hexathelidae
NT2 atrax
NT3 atrax robustus
NT1 linyphiidae
NT2 erigonidium
NT3 erigonidium graminicolum
NT2 oedothorax
NT3 oedothorax insecticeps
NT1 loxoscelidae
NT2 loxosceles
NT3 loxosceles laeta
NT3 loxosceles reclusa
NT3 loxosceles rufescens
NT1 lycosidae
NT2 lycosa
NT3 lycosa pseudoannulata
NT2 trochosa
NT1 oxyopidae
NT2 oxyopes
NT3 oxyopes salticus
NT1 pholcidae
NT2 pholcus
NT3 pholcus phalangioides
NT1 tetragnathidae
NT2 tetragnatha
NT3 tetragnatha laboriosa
NT1 theraphosidae
NT2 aphonopelma
NT3 aphonopelma seemanni
NT1 theridiidae

ARANEAE *cont.*
NT2 achaearanea
NT3 achaearanea tepidariorum
NT2 latrodectus
NT3 latrodectus geometricus
NT3 latrodectus hasseltii
NT3 latrodectus hesperus
NT3 latrodectus katipo
NT3 latrodectus mactans
NT3 latrodectus tredecimguttatus
NT2 theridion
rt arachnidism
rt webs

ARANEIDAE
HN from 1990
uf argiopidae
BT1 araneae
BT2 arachnida
BT3 arthropods
NT1 araneus
NT2 araneus diadematus
NT1 argiope
NT2 argiope argentata
NT1 nephila
NT2 nephila clavata

ARANEUS
HN from 1990
BT1 araneidae
BT2 araneae
BT3 arachnida
BT4 arthropods
NT1 araneus diadematus

ARANEUS DIADEMATUS
HN from 1990
BT1 araneus
BT2 araneidae
BT3 araneae
BT4 arachnida
BT5 arthropods

ARANTHERA
BT1 orchidaceae
rt ornamental plants

ARAUCARIA
BT1 araucariaceae
NT1 araucaria angustifolia
NT1 araucaria araucana
NT1 araucaria bidwillii
NT1 araucaria columnaris
NT1 araucaria cunninghamii
NT1 araucaria heterophylla
NT1 araucaria hunsteinii

ARAUCARIA ANGUSTIFOLIA
BT1 araucaria
BT2 araucariaceae
BT1 forest trees
BT1 ornamental conifers
BT2 conifers
BT2 ornamental woody plants

ARAUCARIA ARAUCANA
uf araucaria imbricata
BT1 araucaria
BT2 araucariaceae
BT1 forest trees
BT1 ornamental conifers
BT2 conifers
BT2 ornamental woody plants

ARAUCARIA BIDWILLII
BT1 araucaria
BT2 araucariaceae

ARAUCARIA COLUMNARIS
BT1 araucaria
BT2 araucariaceae

ARAUCARIA CUNNINGHAMII
BT1 araucaria
BT2 araucariaceae
BT1 forest trees

araucaria excelsa
USE **araucaria heterophylla**

ARAUCARIA HETEROPHYLLA
uf araucaria excelsa
BT1 araucaria

ARAUCARIA HETEROPHYLLA *cont.*
BT2 araucariaceae
BT1 ornamental conifers
BT2 conifers
BT2 ornamental woody plants

ARAUCARIA HUNSTEINII
uf *araucaria klinkii*
BT1 araucaria
BT2 araucariaceae
BT1 forest trees

araucaria imbricata
USE **araucaria araucana**

araucaria klinkii
USE **araucaria hunsteinii**

ARAUCARIACEAE
NT1 agathis (araucariaceae)
NT2 agathis australis
NT2 agathis beccarii
NT2 agathis borneensis
NT2 agathis dammara
NT2 agathis labillardieri
NT2 agathis lanceolata
NT2 agathis macrophylla
NT2 agathis microstachya
NT2 agathis moorei
NT2 agathis palmerstonii
NT2 agathis philippinen
NT2 agathis robusta
NT2 agathis vitiensis
NT1 araucaria
NT2 araucaria angustifolia
NT2 araucaria araucana
NT2 araucaria bidwillii
NT2 araucaria columnaris
NT2 araucaria cunninghamii
NT2 araucaria heterophylla
NT2 araucaria hunsteinii
rt coniferae

ARAUJIA
BT1 asclepiadaceae
NT1 araujia hortorum
NT1 araujia sericofera

ARAUJIA HORTORUM
BT1 araujia
BT2 asclepiadaceae

ARAUJIA SERICOFERA
BT1 araujia
BT2 asclepiadaceae

ARBITRATION
BT1 legal systems
rt collective agreements
rt contracts

ARBORETA
BT1 plant collections
BT2 collections
rt arboriculture
rt botanical gardens

ARBORICIDES
BT1 herbicides
BT2 pesticides
NT1 cacodylic acid

ARBORICULTURE
BT1 forestry
rt arboreta
rt silviculture

ARBOVIRUSES
BT1 pathogens
NT1 african swine fever virus
NT1 alphavirus
NT2 chikungunya virus
NT2 equine encephalomyelitis virus
NT3 eastern equine encephalitis virus
NT3 venezuelan equine encephalitis virus
NT3 western equine encephalitis virus
NT2 getah virus
NT2 ross river virus
NT2 semliki forest virus
NT2 sindbis virus

ARBOVIRUSES *cont.*
NT2 una virus
NT1 borna disease virus
NT1 bunyavirus
NT2 akabane virus
NT2 barranqueras virus
NT2 cache valley virus
NT2 california encephalitis virus
NT2 calovo virus
NT2 jamestown canyon virus
NT2 la crosse virus
NT2 oropouche virus
NT2 snowshoe hare virus
NT2 tahyna virus
NT2 trivittatus virus
NT1 flavivirus
NT2 dengue virus
NT2 japanese encephalitis virus
NT2 kumlinge virus
NT2 kyasanur forest disease virus
NT2 louping ill virus
NT2 murray valley encephalitis virus
NT2 powassan virus
NT2 rocio virus
NT2 st. louis encephalitis virus
NT2 tickborne encephalitis virus
NT2 tyuleniy virus
NT2 wesselsbron virus
NT2 west nile virus
NT2 yellow fever virus
NT1 nairovirus
NT2 crimean-congo haemorrhagic fever virus
NT2 dugbe virus
NT2 hughes virus
NT2 nairobi sheep disease virus
NT1 orbivirus
NT2 african horse sickness virus
NT2 bluetongue virus
NT2 chuzan virus
NT2 colorado tick fever virus
NT2 epizootic haemorrhagic disease of deer virus
NT2 ibaraki virus
NT2 kemerovo virus
NT1 phlebovirus
NT2 rift valley fever virus
NT2 sandfly fever viruses
NT3 sandfly fever (naples) virus
NT3 sandfly fever (sicily) virus
NT2 toscana virus
NT1 uukuvirus
NT2 uukuniemi virus
NT2 zaliv terpeniya virus
rt disease vectors
rt vector-borne diseases
rt viruses

ARBUTUS
BT1 ericaceae
NT1 arbutus andrachne
NT1 arbutus menziesii
NT1 arbutus unedo

ARBUTUS ANDRACHNE
BT1 arbutus
BT2 ericaceae
BT1 ornamental woody plants

ARBUTUS MENZIESII
BT1 arbutus
BT2 ericaceae
BT1 forest trees
BT1 ornamental woody plants

ARBUTUS UNEDO
BT1 arbutus
BT2 ericaceae
BT1 tan plants
rt ornamental plants

ARCA
BT1 arcidae
BT2 bivalvia
BT3 mollusca

ARCANGELISIA
BT1 menispermaceae
NT1 arcangelisia flava

ARCANGELISIA FLAVA
BT1 arcangelisia
BT2 menispermaceae
BT1 dye plants

ARCEUTHOBIUM
BT1 viscaceae
NT1 arceuthobium abietinum
NT1 arceuthobium abietis-religiosae
NT1 arceuthobium americanum
NT1 arceuthobium aureum
NT1 arceuthobium azoricum
NT1 arceuthobium campylopodum
NT1 arceuthobium cyanocarpum
NT1 arceuthobium divaricatum
NT1 arceuthobium douglasii
NT1 arceuthobium globosum
NT1 arceuthobium juniperi-procerae
NT1 arceuthobium laricis
NT1 arceuthobium microcarpum
NT1 arceuthobium minutissimum
NT1 arceuthobium occidentale
NT1 arceuthobium oxycedri
NT1 arceuthobium pusillum
NT1 arceuthobium rubrum
NT1 arceuthobium tsugense
NT1 arceuthobium vaginatum
rt mistletoes

ARCEUTHOBIUM ABIETINUM
BT1 arceuthobium
BT2 viscaceae
BT1 parasitic plants
BT2 parasites

ARCEUTHOBIUM ABIETIS-RELIGIOSAE
BT1 arceuthobium
BT2 viscaceae

ARCEUTHOBIUM AMERICANUM
BT1 arceuthobium
BT2 viscaceae
BT1 parasitic plants
BT2 parasites

ARCEUTHOBIUM AUREUM
BT1 arceuthobium
BT2 viscaceae

ARCEUTHOBIUM AZORICUM
BT1 arceuthobium
BT2 viscaceae

ARCEUTHOBIUM CAMPYLOPODUM
BT1 arceuthobium
BT2 viscaceae

ARCEUTHOBIUM CYANOCARPUM
BT1 arceuthobium
BT2 viscaceae

ARCEUTHOBIUM DIVARICATUM
BT1 arceuthobium
BT2 viscaceae

ARCEUTHOBIUM DOUGLASII
BT1 arceuthobium
BT2 viscaceae
BT1 parasitic plants
BT2 parasites

ARCEUTHOBIUM GLOBOSUM
BT1 arceuthobium
BT2 viscaceae

ARCEUTHOBIUM JUNIPERI-PROCERAE
BT1 arceuthobium
BT2 viscaceae

ARCEUTHOBIUM LARICIS
BT1 arceuthobium
BT2 viscaceae
BT1 parasitic plants
BT2 parasites

ARCEUTHOBIUM MICROCARPUM
BT1 arceuthobium
BT2 viscaceae
BT1 parasitic plants

ARCEUTHOBIUM MICROCARPUM *cont.*
BT2 parasites

ARCEUTHOBIUM MINUTISSIMUM
BT1 arceuthobium
BT2 viscaceae
BT1 parasitic plants
BT2 parasites

ARCEUTHOBIUM OCCIDENTALE
BT1 arceuthobium
BT2 viscaceae
BT1 parasitic plants
BT2 parasites

ARCEUTHOBIUM OXYCEDRI
BT1 arceuthobium
BT2 viscaceae
BT1 parasitic plants
BT2 parasites

ARCEUTHOBIUM PUSILLUM
BT1 arceuthobium
BT2 viscaceae
BT1 parasitic plants
BT2 parasites

ARCEUTHOBIUM RUBRUM
BT1 arceuthobium
BT2 viscaceae

ARCEUTHOBIUM TSUGENSE
BT1 arceuthobium
BT2 viscaceae
BT1 parasitic plants
BT2 parasites

ARCEUTHOBIUM VAGINATUM
BT1 arceuthobium
BT2 viscaceae

ARCHAEOLOGICAL MATERIAL
rt ancient monuments
rt archaeology
rt history

ARCHAEOLOGY
rt archaeological material
rt history
rt pollen analysis
rt prehistoric agriculture

ARCHANGELICA
BT1 umbelliferae

archangelica officinalis
USE **angelica archangelica**

ARCHERY
BT1 outdoor recreation
BT2 recreation

ARCHIBOREOIULUS
BT1 blaniulidae
BT2 diplopoda
BT3 myriapoda
BT4 arthropods
NT1 archiboreoiulus pallidus

ARCHIBOREOIULUS PALLIDUS
BT1 archiboreoiulus
BT2 blaniulidae
BT3 diplopoda
BT4 myriapoda
BT5 arthropods

ARCHIDENDRON
BT1 leguminosae
NT1 archidendron oblongum

ARCHIDENDRON OBLONGUM
BT1 archidendron
BT2 leguminosae

archin
USE **emodin**

archippus
USE **archips**

archippus breviplicanus
USE **archips breviplicanus**

ARCHIPS
uf *archippus*

ARCHIPS *cont.*
uf *cacoecia*
BT1 tortricidae
BT2 lepidoptera
NT1 archips argyrospilus
NT1 archips breviplicanus
NT1 archips cerasivoranus
NT1 archips crataeganus
NT1 archips fuscocupreanus
NT1 archips podanus
NT1 archips rosanus
NT1 archips semiferanus
NT1 archips xylosteanus
rt ptycholoma

ARCHIPS ARGYROSPILUS
BT1 archips
BT2 tortricidae
BT3 lepidoptera

ARCHIPS BREVIPLICANUS
uf *archippus breviplicanus*
BT1 archips
BT2 tortricidae
BT3 lepidoptera

ARCHIPS CERASIVORANUS
BT1 archips
BT2 tortricidae
BT3 lepidoptera

ARCHIPS CRATAEGANUS
uf *cacoecia crataegana*
BT1 archips
BT2 tortricidae
BT3 lepidoptera

ARCHIPS FUSCOCUPREANUS
uf *ptycholoma fuscocupreana*
BT1 archips
BT2 tortricidae
BT3 lepidoptera

ARCHIPS PODANUS
uf *cacoecia podana*
BT1 archips
BT2 tortricidae
BT3 lepidoptera

ARCHIPS ROSANUS
uf *cacoecia rosana*
BT1 archips
BT2 tortricidae
BT3 lepidoptera

ARCHIPS SEMIFERANUS
BT1 archips
BT2 tortricidae
BT3 lepidoptera

ARCHIPS XYLOSTEANUS
BT1 archips
BT2 tortricidae
BT3 lepidoptera

ARCHITECTURE
rt building construction
rt buildings
rt design
rt visual arts

ARCHONTOPHOENIX
BT1 palmae
NT1 archontophoenix alexandrae
NT1 archontophoenix cunninghamiana

ARCHONTOPHOENIX ALEXANDRAE
BT1 archontophoenix
BT2 palmae
BT1 ornamental palms

ARCHONTOPHOENIX CUNNINGHAMIANA
uf *seaforthia elegans*
BT1 archontophoenix
BT2 palmae
BT1 ornamental palms

ARCHOSARGUS
BT1 sparidae
BT2 perciformes
BT3 osteichthyes
BT4 fishes

ARCHOSARGUS *cont.*
rt sea bream

ARCHYTAS
BT1 tachinidae
BT2 diptera
NT1 archytas marmoratus

ARCHYTAS MARMORATUS
BT1 archytas
BT2 tachinidae
BT3 diptera

ARCIDAE
BT1 bivalvia
BT2 mollusca
NT1 anadara
NT1 arca

ARCTAGROSTIS
BT1 gramineae
NT1 arctagrostis latifolia

ARCTAGROSTIS LATIFOLIA
BT1 arctagrostis
BT2 gramineae
BT1 pasture plants

ARCTE
BT1 noctuidae
BT2 lepidoptera
NT1 arcte coerula

ARCTE COERULA
BT1 arcte
BT2 noctuidae
BT3 lepidoptera

ARCTIA
BT1 arctiidae
BT2 lepidoptera
NT1 arctia caja

ARCTIA CAJA
BT1 arctia
BT2 arctiidae
BT3 lepidoptera

arctic fox
USE **alopex lagopus**

ARCTIC OCEAN
BT1 marine areas
NT1 barents sea
NT1 beaufort sea
NT1 kara sea
NT1 norwegian sea

ARCTIC REGIONS
uf *north polar regions*
rt cold zones

arctic soils
USE **frigid soils**

ARCTIC TUNDRA
BT1 tundra
BT2 cold zones
BT3 climatic zones
BT2 vegetation types
rt alpine vegetation

arctic zones
USE **cold zones**

ARCTICA
BT1 arcticidae
BT2 bivalvia
BT3 mollusca
NT1 arctica islandica

ARCTICA ISLANDICA
BT1 arctica
BT2 arcticidae
BT3 bivalvia
BT4 mollusca

ARCTICIDAE
BT1 bivalvia
BT2 mollusca
NT1 arctica
NT2 arctica islandica

ARCTIIDAE
BT1 lepidoptera
NT1 ammalo

ARCTIIDAE *cont.*
NT1 amsacta
NT2 amsacta albistriga
NT2 amsacta moorei
NT1 arctia
NT2 arctia caja
NT1 diacrisia
NT1 estigmene
NT2 estigmene acraea
NT1 hyphantria
NT2 hyphantria cunea
NT1 pareuchaetes
NT2 pareuchaetes insulata
NT1 pericallia
NT2 pericallia ricini
NT1 spilosoma
NT2 spilosoma casigneta
NT2 spilosoma imparilis
NT2 spilosoma lubricipeda
NT2 spilosoma obliqua
NT2 spilosoma virginica
NT1 tyria
NT2 tyria jacobaeae
NT1 utetheisa
NT2 utetheisa ornatrix
NT2 utetheisa pulchella

ARCTIUM
BT1 compositae
NT1 arctium lappa

ARCTIUM LAPPA
BT1 arctium
BT2 compositae
BT1 medicinal plants

ARCTOCEPHALUS
BT1 otariidae
BT2 pinnipedia
BT3 carnivores
BT4 mammals
NT1 arctocephalus pusillus

ARCTOCEPHALUS PUSILLUS
BT1 arctocephalus
BT2 otariidae
BT3 pinnipedia
BT4 carnivores
BT5 mammals

ARCTOPHILA
BT1 gramineae
NT1 arctophila fulva

ARCTOPHILA FULVA
BT1 arctophila
BT2 gramineae

ARCTOSTAPHYLOS
BT1 ericaceae
NT1 arctostaphylos alpinus
NT1 arctostaphylos columbiana
NT1 arctostaphylos crustacea
NT1 arctostaphylos glandulosa
NT1 arctostaphylos nummularia
NT1 arctostaphylos patula
NT1 arctostaphylos pungens
NT1 arctostaphylos uva-ursi

ARCTOSTAPHYLOS ALPINUS
BT1 arctostaphylos
BT2 ericaceae

ARCTOSTAPHYLOS COLUMBIANA
BT1 arctostaphylos
BT2 ericaceae

ARCTOSTAPHYLOS CRUSTACEA
BT1 arctostaphylos
BT2 ericaceae

ARCTOSTAPHYLOS GLANDULOSA
BT1 arctostaphylos
BT2 ericaceae

ARCTOSTAPHYLOS NUMMULARIA
BT1 arctostaphylos
BT2 ericaceae

ARCTOSTAPHYLOS PATULA
BT1 arctostaphylos

ARCTOSTAPHYLOS PATULA *cont.*
BT2 ericaceae

ARCTOSTAPHYLOS PUNGENS
BT1 arctostaphylos
BT2 ericaceae

ARCTOSTAPHYLOS UVA-URSI
BT1 algicidal plants
BT1 arctostaphylos
BT2 ericaceae
BT1 medicinal plants
BT1 molluscicidal plants
BT2 pesticidal plants
BT1 tan plants
BT1 temperate small fruits
BT2 small fruits
BT2 temperate fruits
BT3 fruit crops

ARCTOTHECA
BT1 compositae
NT1 arctotheca calendula

ARCTOTHECA CALENDULA
BT1 arctotheca
BT2 compositae

ARCTOTIS
BT1 compositae
NT1 arctotis stoechadifolia

arctotis grandis
USE **arctotis stoechadifolia**

ARCTOTIS STOECHADIFOLIA
uf *arctotis grandis*
BT1 arctotis
BT2 compositae
BT1 medicinal plants
BT1 ornamental herbaceous plants

ARCYOPHORA
BT1 noctuidae
BT2 lepidoptera
NT1 arcyophora patricula
NT1 arcyophora zanderi

ARCYOPHORA PATRICULA
BT1 arcyophora
BT2 noctuidae
BT3 lepidoptera

ARCYOPHORA ZANDERI
BT1 arcyophora
BT2 noctuidae
BT3 lepidoptera

ARDEA
BT1 ardeidae
BT2 ciconiiformes
BT3 birds
NT1 ardea cinerea
NT1 ardea herodias
NT1 ardea purpurea

ARDEA CINEREA
BT1 ardea
BT2 ardeidae
BT3 ciconiiformes
BT4 birds

ARDEA HERODIAS
BT1 ardea
BT2 ardeidae
BT3 ciconiiformes
BT4 birds

ARDEA PURPUREA
BT1 ardea
BT2 ardeidae
BT3 ciconiiformes
BT4 birds

ARDEIDAE
uf *herons*
BT1 ciconiiformes
BT2 birds
NT1 ardea
NT2 ardea cinerea
NT2 ardea herodias
NT2 ardea purpurea
NT1 ardeola
NT1 bubulcus

ARDEIDAE *cont.*
NT2 bubulcus ibis
NT3 bubulcus ibis coromandus
NT1 butorides
NT2 butorides striatus
NT1 egretta
NT2 egretta alba
NT2 egretta garzetta
NT1 nycticorax
NT2 nycticorax caledonicus
NT2 nycticorax nycticorax

ardeiformes
USE **ciconiiformes**

ARDEOLA
BT1 ardeidae
BT2 ciconiiformes
BT3 birds
rt bubulcus

ardeola ibis
USE **bubulcus ibis**

ARDIS
BT1 tenthredinidae
BT2 hymenoptera
NT1 ardis brunniventris

ARDIS BRUNNIVENTRIS
BT1 ardis
BT2 tenthredinidae
BT3 hymenoptera

ARDISIA
BT1 myrsinaceae
NT1 ardisia crenata
NT1 ardisia solanacea

ARDISIA CRENATA
uf *ardisia crenulata*
BT1 ardisia
BT2 myrsinaceae
BT1 ornamental woody plants

ardisia crenulata
USE **ardisia crenata**

ARDISIA SOLANACEA
BT1 ardisia
BT2 myrsinaceae

AREA
NT1 basal area
NT1 farm area
NT1 foliage area
NT1 leaf area
NT1 surface area
NT2 body surface area
rt floor area

AREAS
NT1 administrative areas
NT2 local authority areas
NT1 amenity and recreation areas
NT2 camp sites
NT2 caravan sites
NT2 open spaces
NT3 green belts
NT2 show grounds
NT1 coastal areas
NT2 heritage coasts
NT1 conservation areas
NT2 areas of outstanding natural beauty
NT1 frontier areas
NT1 heritage areas
NT2 heritage coasts
NT1 less favoured areas
NT1 lowland areas
NT1 military areas
NT1 reserved areas
NT2 reserved forests
NT1 rural areas
NT1 urban areas
NT2 residential areas
NT2 suburban areas
NT2 urban hinterland
rt marine areas
rt regions

AREAS OF OUTSTANDING NATURAL BEAUTY

AREAS OF OUTSTANDING NATURAL BEAUTY *cont.*
BT1 conservation areas
BT2 areas
rt aesthetic value
rt national parks

ARECA
BT1 palmae
NT1 areca catechu
rt tropical tree nuts

ARECA CATECHU
BT1 areca
BT2 palmae
BT1 medicinal plants
BT1 stimulant plants
rt arecanuts
rt piper betle

ARECANUTS
rt areca catechu

ARECASTRUM
BT1 palmae
NT1 arecastrum romanzoffianum

ARECASTRUM ROMANZOFFIANUM
uf *syagrus romanzoffianumn*
BT1 arecastrum
BT2 palmae

ARECOLINE
BT1 anthelmintics
BT2 antiparasitic agents
BT3 drugs
BT1 parasympathomimetics
BT2 neurotropic drugs
BT3 drugs
BT1 pyridine alkaloids
BT2 alkaloids
BT2 pyridines
BT3 heterocyclic nitrogen compounds
BT4 organic nitrogen compounds
rt nicotinic acid

arenaria
USE **arenaria (birds)**
OR **arenaria (caryophyllaceae)**

ARENARIA (BIRDS)
uf *arenaria*
BT1 scolopacidae
BT2 charadriiformes
BT3 birds

ARENARIA (CARYOPHYLLACEAE)
uf *arenaria*
BT1 caryophyllaceae

ARENAVIRIDAE
BT1 viruses
NT1 arenavirus
NT2 junin virus
NT2 lassa virus
NT2 lymphocytic choriomeningitis virus
NT2 machupo virus
NT2 pichinde virus

ARENAVIRUS
BT1 arenaviridae
BT2 viruses
NT1 junin virus
NT1 lassa virus
NT1 lymphocytic choriomeningitis virus
NT1 machupo virus
NT1 pichinde virus

ARENGA
BT1 palmae
NT1 arenga engleri
NT1 arenga pinnata

ARENGA ENGLERI
BT1 arenga
BT2 palmae

ARENGA PINNATA
uf *arenga saccharifera*
BT1 arenga

ARENGA PINNATA *cont.*
BT2 palmae

arenga saccharifera
USE **arenga pinnata**

ARENOSOLS
BT1 soil types (genetic)
rt sandy soils

ARGANIA
BT1 sapotaceae
NT1 argania spinosa

ARGANIA SPINOSA
BT1 argania
BT2 sapotaceae
BT1 oilseed plants
BT2 fatty oil plants
BT3 oil plants

ARGAS
BT1 argasidae
BT2 metastigmata
BT3 acari
NT1 argas arboreus
NT1 argas japonicus
NT1 argas persicus
NT1 argas radiatus
NT1 argas reflexus
NT1 argas robertsi
NT1 argas vespertilionis
NT1 argas walkerae

ARGAS ARBOREUS
BT1 argas
BT2 argasidae
BT3 metastigmata
BT4 acari

ARGAS JAPONICUS
HN from 1990
BT1 argas
BT2 argasidae
BT3 metastigmata
BT4 acari

ARGAS PERSICUS
BT1 argas
BT2 argasidae
BT3 metastigmata
BT4 acari

ARGAS RADIATUS
BT1 argas
BT2 argasidae
BT3 metastigmata
BT4 acari

ARGAS REFLEXUS
BT1 argas
BT2 argasidae
BT3 metastigmata
BT4 acari

ARGAS ROBERTSI
BT1 argas
BT2 argasidae
BT3 metastigmata
BT4 acari

ARGAS VESPERTILIONIS
BT1 argas
BT2 argasidae
BT3 metastigmata
BT4 acari

ARGAS WALKERAE
BT1 argas
BT2 argasidae
BT3 metastigmata
BT4 acari

ARGASIDAE
BT1 metastigmata
BT2 acari
NT1 argas
NT2 argas arboreus
NT2 argas japonicus
NT2 argas persicus
NT2 argas radiatus
NT2 argas reflexus
NT2 argas robertsi
NT2 argas vespertilionis
NT2 argas walkerae

ARGASIDAE *cont.*
NT1 ornithodoros
NT2 ornithodoros capensis
NT2 ornithodoros concanensis
NT2 ornithodoros coriaceus
NT2 ornithodoros erraticus
NT2 ornithodoros lahorensis
NT2 ornithodoros maritimus
NT2 ornithodoros moubata
NT3 ornithodoros moubata porcinus
NT2 ornithodoros muesebecki
NT2 ornithodoros parkeri
NT2 ornithodoros puertoricensis
NT2 ornithodoros savignyi
NT2 ornithodoros tartakovskyi
NT2 ornithodoros tholozani
NT2 ornithodoros turicata
NT2 ornithodoros verrucosus
NT1 otobius
NT2 otobius megnini

ARGE
BT1 argidae
BT2 hymenoptera
NT1 arge ochropus
NT1 arge pectoralis
NT1 arge pullata

ARGE OCHROPUS
BT1 arge
BT2 argidae
BT3 hymenoptera

ARGE PECTORALIS
BT1 arge
BT2 argidae
BT3 hymenoptera

ARGE PULLATA
HN from 1990
BT1 arge
BT2 argidae
BT3 hymenoptera

ARGEMONE
BT1 papaveraceae
NT1 argemone mexicana
NT1 argemone ochroleuca
NT1 argemone polyanthemos
NT1 argemone subfusiformis

ARGEMONE MEXICANA
BT1 argemone
BT2 papaveraceae
BT1 medicinal plants
BT1 nematicidal plants
BT2 pesticidal plants
BT1 oilseed plants
BT2 fatty oil plants
BT3 oil plants

ARGEMONE OCHROLEUCA
BT1 argemone
BT2 papaveraceae

ARGEMONE POLYANTHEMOS
BT1 argemone
BT2 papaveraceae

ARGEMONE SUBFUSIFORMIS
BT1 argemone
BT2 papaveraceae
BT1 medicinal plants

ARGENTINA
BT1 south america
BT2 america
NT1 argentina andina
NT1 argentina centro
NT1 argentina littoral
NT1 argentina norte
NT1 patagonia
rt developing countries
rt threshold countries

argentina (andina)
USE **argentina andina**

ARGENTINA ANDINA
uf *argentina (andina)*
BT1 argentina
BT2 south america
BT3 america

argentina (centro)
USE **argentina centro**

ARGENTINA CENTRO
uf *argentina (centro)*
BT1 argentina
BT2 south america
BT3 america

ARGENTINA (FISHES)
uf *argentines*
BT1 argentinidae
BT2 salmoniformes
BT3 osteichthyes
BT4 fishes

ARGENTINA LITTORAL
uf *argentina (littoral)*
BT1 argentina
BT2 south america
BT3 america

argentina (littoral)
USE **argentina littoral**

ARGENTINA NORTE
uf *argentina (norte)*
BT1 argentina
BT2 south america
BT3 america

argentina (norte)
USE **argentina norte**

argentina (patagonia)
USE **patagonia**

ARGENTINE CRIOLLO
BT1 horse breeds
BT2 breeds

ARGENTINE FRIESIAN
HN from 1990; previously "holando-argentino"
uf *holando-argentino*
BT1 cattle breeds
BT2 breeds

ARGENTINE MERINO
BT1 sheep breeds
BT2 breeds

argentines
USE **argentina (fishes)**

ARGENTINIDAE
BT1 salmoniformes
BT2 osteichthyes
BT3 fishes
NT1 argentina (fishes)

ARGIDAE
BT1 hymenoptera
NT1 arge
NT2 arge ochropus
NT2 arge pectoralis
NT2 arge pullata

ARGILLACEOUS ROCKS
BT1 rocks

ARGILLANS
BT1 cutans
BT2 soil micromorphological features
BT3 soil morphological features
rt clay translocation

ARGILLIC HORIZONS
BT1 horizons
BT2 soil morphological features
rt argilluviation

ARGILLUVIATION
uf *clay illuviation*
BT1 soil formation
rt argillic horizons
rt clay translocation

ARGILLUVIC SOILS
BT1 soil types (genetic)
NT1 alfisols
NT2 aqualfs
NT1 duplex soils
NT1 podzolic soils

ARGILLUVIC SOILS *cont.*
NT1 red yellow soils
NT1 secondary podzolic soils
NT1 ultisols
NT1 yellow brown soils
NT1 yellow grey soils
NT1 yellow podzolic soils
rt aqualfs

ARGINASE
(ec 3.5.3.1)
BT1 amidine hydrolases
BT2 hydrolases
BT3 enzymes
BT1 urea cycle enzymes
BT2 enzymes

ARGININE
BT1 essential amino acids
BT2 amino acids
BT3 carboxylic acids
BT4 organic acids
BT5 acids
BT3 organic nitrogen compounds
rt arginine antagonists
rt argininosuccinic aciduria

ARGININE ANTAGONISTS
BT1 amino acid antagonists
BT2 antagonists
BT3 metabolic inhibitors
BT4 inhibitors
rt arginine

ARGININE VASOTOCIN
HN from 1989
BT1 vasotocin
BT2 neuropeptides
BT3 peptides
BT2 oligopeptides
BT3 peptides
BT2 pituitary hormones
BT3 hormones

ARGININOSUCCINATE LYASE
(ec 4.3.2.1)
BT1 amidine-lyases
BT2 lyases
BT3 enzymes
BT1 urea cycle enzymes
BT2 enzymes

ARGININOSUCCINATE SYNTHASE
(ec 6.3.4.5)
BT1 ligases
BT2 enzymes
BT1 urea cycle enzymes
BT2 enzymes

ARGININOSUCCINIC ACIDURIA
BT1 aciduria
BT2 metabolic disorders
BT3 animal disorders
BT4 disorders
rt arginine

ARGIOPE
HN from 1990
uf *argyope*
BT1 araneidae
BT2 araneae
BT3 arachnida
BT4 arthropods
NT1 argiope argentata

ARGIOPE ARGENTATA
HN from 1990
BT1 argiope
BT2 araneidae
BT3 araneae
BT4 arachnida
BT5 arthropods

argiopidae
USE **araneidae**

ARGON
BT1 noble gases
BT2 inert gases
BT3 gases
BT2 nonmetallic elements
BT3 elements

ARGOPECTEN
BT1 pectinidae
BT2 bivalvia
BT3 mollusca
NT1 argopecten irradians

ARGOPECTEN IRRADIANS
BT1 argopecten
BT2 pectinidae
BT3 bivalvia
BT4 mollusca

ARGULUS
BT1 branchiura (arthropods)
BT2 crustacea
BT3 arthropods

argyope
USE **argiope**

ARGYREIA
BT1 convolvulaceae
NT1 argyreia nervosa
NT1 argyreia splendens

ARGYREIA NERVOSA
uf *argyreia speciosa*
uf *convolvulus nervosus*
BT1 antibacterial plants
BT1 antifungal plants
BT1 argyreia
BT2 convolvulaceae
BT1 medicinal plants

argyreia speciosa
USE **argyreia nervosa**

ARGYREIA SPLENDENS
uf *convolvulus splendens*
BT1 argyreia
BT2 convolvulaceae
BT1 ornamental woody plants

ARGYRESTHIA
BT1 yponomeutidae
BT2 lepidoptera
NT1 argyresthia conjugella
NT1 argyresthia pruniella

ARGYRESTHIA CONJUGELLA
BT1 argyresthia
BT2 yponomeutidae
BT3 lepidoptera

argyresthia ephippella
USE **argyresthia pruniella**

ARGYRESTHIA PRUNIELLA
uf *argyresthia ephippella*
BT1 argyresthia
BT2 yponomeutidae
BT3 lepidoptera

argyropile
USE **megachile**

argyroploce
USE **olethreutes**

argyroploce lacunana
USE **olethreutes lacunana**

argyroploce schistaceana
USE **tetramoera schistaceana**

ARGYROSOMUS
BT1 sciaenidae
BT2 perciformes
BT3 osteichthyes
BT4 fishes
NT1 argyrosomus argentatus
NT1 argyrosomus hololepidotus

ARGYROSOMUS ARGENTATUS
BT1 argyrosomus
BT2 sciaenidae
BT3 perciformes
BT4 osteichthyes
BT5 fishes

ARGYROSOMUS HOLOLEPIDOTUS
HN from 1990
BT1 argyrosomus
BT2 sciaenidae
BT3 perciformes
BT4 osteichthyes

ARGYROSOMUS HOLOLEPIDOTUS *cont.*
BT5 fishes

ARGYROTAENIA
BT1 tortricidae
BT2 lepidoptera
NT1 argyrotaenia ljungiana
NT1 argyrotaenia velutinana

ARGYROTAENIA LJUNGIANA
uf *argyrotaenia pulchellana*
BT1 argyrotaenia
BT2 tortricidae
BT3 lepidoptera

argyrotaenia pulchellana
USE **argyrotaenia ljungiana**

ARGYROTAENIA VELUTINANA
BT1 argyrotaenia
BT2 tortricidae
BT3 lepidoptera

ARGYROXIPHIUM
BT1 compositae
NT1 argyroxiphium kauense
NT1 argyroxiphium sandwicence

ARGYROXIPHIUM KAUENSE
BT1 argyroxiphium
BT2 compositae

ARGYROXIPHIUM SANDWICENCE
BT1 argyroxiphium
BT2 compositae

ARHOPALUS
uf *criocephalus*
BT1 cerambycidae
BT2 coleoptera
NT1 arhopalus rusticus
NT1 arhopalus syriacus

ARHOPALUS RUSTICUS
uf *criocephalus rusticus*
BT1 arhopalus
BT2 cerambycidae
BT3 coleoptera

ARHOPALUS SYRIACUS
uf *criocephalus syriacus*
BT1 arhopalus
BT2 cerambycidae
BT3 coleoptera

ariboflavinosis
USE **riboflavin deficiency**

ARID CLIMATE
uf *desert climate*
BT1 climate
rt arid lands
rt arid regions
rt arid zones
rt deserts
rt drought
rt dry conditions

ARID LANDS
BT1 land types
rt arid climate

ARID REGIONS
BT1 arid zones
BT2 climatic zones
NT1 deserts
NT2 gobi desert
NT2 kalahari desert
NT2 mojave desert
NT2 sahara desert
NT1 sahel
rt arid climate
rt arid soils
rt desertification
rt dry conditions
rt dry farming
rt semi-desert scrub
rt semiarid climate
rt semiarid zones
rt succulent plants
rt xerophytes

ARID SOILS
BT1 soil types (climatic)

ARID SOILS *cont.*
rt arid regions
rt desert soils
rt desertification
rt semiarid soils
rt yermosols

ARID ZONES
BT1 climatic zones
NT1 arid regions
NT2 deserts
NT3 gobi desert
NT3 kalahari desert
NT3 mojave desert
NT3 sahara desert
NT2 sahel
rt arid climate

ARIDIC SOILS
BT1 soil types (genetic)
NT1 sedosols

ARIIDAE
BT1 siluriformes
BT2 osteichthyes
BT3 fishes
NT1 arius
NT1 bagre
rt sea catfish

ARIKURYROBA
BT1 palmae
NT1 arikuryroba schizophylla

ARIKURYROBA SCHIZOPHYLLA
BT1 arikuryroba
BT2 palmae
BT1 ornamental palms

ARIMA
uf autoregressive integrated moving average
BT1 regression analysis
BT2 statistical analysis
BT3 data analysis
BT3 statistics

ARIOCARPUS
BT1 cactaceae
rt ornamental succulent plants

ARIOLIMAX
BT1 limacidae
BT2 gastropoda
BT3 mollusca
NT1 ariolimax columbianus

ARIOLIMAX COLUMBIANUS
BT1 ariolimax
BT2 limacidae
BT3 gastropoda
BT4 mollusca

ARION
BT1 arionidae
BT2 gastropoda
BT3 mollusca
NT1 arion ater
NT1 arion circumscriptus
NT1 arion distinctus
NT1 arion fasciatus
NT1 arion hortensis
NT1 arion intermedius
NT1 arion silvaticus
NT1 arion subfuscus

ARION ATER
HN from 1990
BT1 arion
BT2 arionidae
BT3 gastropoda
BT4 mollusca

ARION CIRCUMSCRIPTUS
HN from 1990
BT1 arion
BT2 arionidae
BT3 gastropoda
BT4 mollusca

ARION DISTINCTUS
HN from 1990
BT1 arion
BT2 arionidae

ARION DISTINCTUS *cont.*
BT3 gastropoda
BT4 mollusca

ARION FASCIATUS
BT1 arion
BT2 arionidae
BT3 gastropoda
BT4 mollusca

ARION HORTENSIS
HN from 1990
BT1 arion
BT2 arionidae
BT3 gastropoda
BT4 mollusca

ARION INTERMEDIUS
HN from 1990
BT1 arion
BT2 arionidae
BT3 gastropoda
BT4 mollusca

ARION SILVATICUS
HN from 1990
BT1 arion
BT2 arionidae
BT3 gastropoda
BT4 mollusca

ARION SUBFUSCUS
HN from 1990
BT1 arion
BT2 arionidae
BT3 gastropoda
BT4 mollusca

ARIONIDAE
BT1 gastropoda
BT2 mollusca
NT1 arion
NT2 arion ater
NT2 arion circumscriptus
NT2 arion distinctus
NT2 arion fasciatus
NT2 arion hortensis
NT2 arion intermedius
NT2 arion silvaticus
NT2 arion subfuscus

ARISAEMA
BT1 araceae
NT1 arisaema tortuosum
NT1 arisaema triphyllum

ARISAEMA TORTUOSUM
BT1 arisaema
BT2 araceae
BT1 ornamental bulbs
rt tubers

ARISAEMA TRIPHYLLUM
BT1 arisaema
BT2 araceae
BT1 ornamental bulbs
rt tubers

ARISARUM
BT1 araceae
rt ornamental bulbs

aristavena setacea
USE **deschampsia setacea**

ARISTIDA
BT1 gramineae
NT1 aristida acutiflora
NT1 aristida adscensionis
NT1 aristida browniana
NT1 aristida caerulescens
NT1 aristida congesta
NT1 aristida contorta
NT1 aristida cyanantha
NT1 aristida dichotoma
NT1 aristida divaricata
NT1 aristida funiculata
NT1 aristida hamulosa
NT1 aristida jubata
NT1 aristida junciformis
NT1 aristida karelinii
NT1 aristida latifolia
NT1 aristida leptopoda
NT1 aristida longiflora

ARISTIDA *cont.*
NT1 aristida longiseta
NT1 aristida meccana
NT1 aristida murina
NT1 aristida mutabilis
NT1 aristida oligantha
NT1 aristida pallens
NT1 aristida pungens
NT1 aristida purpurea
NT1 aristida ramosa
NT1 aristida rhiniochloa
NT1 aristida rufescens
NT1 aristida setifolia
NT1 aristida stipitata
NT1 aristida stricta
NT1 aristida transvaalensis
rt stipagrostis

ARISTIDA ACUTIFLORA
BT1 aristida
BT2 gramineae
BT1 pasture plants

ARISTIDA ADSCENSIONIS
BT1 aristida
BT2 gramineae
BT1 pasture plants

ARISTIDA BROWNIANA
BT1 aristida
BT2 gramineae
BT1 pasture plants

ARISTIDA CAERULESCENS
BT1 aristida
BT2 gramineae
BT1 pasture plants

ARISTIDA CONGESTA
BT1 aristida
BT2 gramineae
BT1 pasture plants

ARISTIDA CONTORTA
BT1 aristida
BT2 gramineae
BT1 pasture plants

ARISTIDA CYANANTHA
BT1 aristida
BT2 gramineae
BT1 pasture plants

ARISTIDA DICHOTOMA
BT1 aristida
BT2 gramineae

ARISTIDA DIVARICATA
BT1 aristida
BT2 gramineae

ARISTIDA FUNICULATA
BT1 aristida
BT2 gramineae
BT1 pasture plants

ARISTIDA HAMULOSA
BT1 aristida
BT2 gramineae

ARISTIDA JUBATA
BT1 aristida
BT2 gramineae
BT1 pasture plants

ARISTIDA JUNCIFORMIS
BT1 aristida
BT2 gramineae
BT1 pasture plants

ARISTIDA KARELINII
BT1 aristida
BT2 gramineae

ARISTIDA LATIFOLIA
BT1 aristida
BT2 gramineae
BT1 pasture plants

ARISTIDA LEPTOPODA
BT1 aristida
BT2 gramineae
BT1 pasture plants

ARISTIDA LONGIFLORA
BT1 aristida
BT2 gramineae
BT1 pasture plants

ARISTIDA LONGISETA
BT1 aristida
BT2 gramineae
BT1 pasture plants

ARISTIDA MECCANA
BT1 aristida
BT2 gramineae
BT1 pasture plants

ARISTIDA MURINA
BT1 aristida
BT2 gramineae
BT1 pasture plants

ARISTIDA MUTABILIS
BT1 aristida
BT2 gramineae
BT1 pasture plants

ARISTIDA OLIGANTHA
BT1 aristida
BT2 gramineae
BT1 pasture plants

ARISTIDA PALLENS
BT1 aristida
BT2 gramineae
BT1 pasture plants

aristida pennata
USE **stipagrostis pennata**

aristida plumosa
USE **stipagrostis plumosa**

ARISTIDA PUNGENS
BT1 aristida
BT2 gramineae
BT1 pasture plants

ARISTIDA PURPUREA
BT1 aristida
BT2 gramineae
BT1 pasture plants

ARISTIDA RAMOSA
BT1 aristida
BT2 gramineae
BT1 pasture plants

ARISTIDA RHINIOCHLOA
BT1 aristida
BT2 gramineae
BT1 pasture plants

ARISTIDA RUFESCENS
BT1 aristida
BT2 gramineae

ARISTIDA SETIFOLIA
BT1 aristida
BT2 gramineae
BT1 pasture plants

ARISTIDA STIPITATA
BT1 aristida
BT2 gramineae

ARISTIDA STRICTA
BT1 aristida
BT2 gramineae
BT1 pasture plants

ARISTIDA TRANSVAALENSIS
BT1 aristida
BT2 gramineae
BT1 pasture plants

ARISTOLOCHIA
BT1 aristolochiaceae
NT1 aristolochia acuminata
NT1 aristolochia argentina
NT1 aristolochia bracteata
NT1 aristolochia clematitis
NT1 aristolochia indica
NT1 aristolochia macrophylla
NT1 aristolochia multiflora
NT1 aristolochia tagala
NT1 aristolochia taliscana

ARISTOLOCHIA ACUMINATA
BT1 antibacterial plants
BT1 aristolochia
BT2 aristolochiaceae

ARISTOLOCHIA ARGENTINA
BT1 aristolochia
BT2 aristolochiaceae

ARISTOLOCHIA BRACTEATA
BT1 aristolochia
BT2 aristolochiaceae
BT1 insecticidal plants
BT2 pesticidal plants

ARISTOLOCHIA CLEMATITIS
BT1 aristolochia
BT2 aristolochiaceae

aristolochia durior
USE **aristolochia macrophylla**

ARISTOLOCHIA INDICA
BT1 aristolochia
BT2 aristolochiaceae
BT1 medicinal plants

ARISTOLOCHIA MACROPHYLLA
uf aristolochia durior
BT1 aristolochia
BT2 aristolochiaceae
BT1 ornamental herbaceous plants

ARISTOLOCHIA MULTIFLORA
BT1 antibacterial plants
BT1 aristolochia
BT2 aristolochiaceae

ARISTOLOCHIA TAGALA
BT1 aristolochia
BT2 aristolochiaceae

ARISTOLOCHIA TALISCANA
BT1 aristolochia
BT2 aristolochiaceae
BT1 medicinal plants

ARISTOLOCHIACEAE
NT1 aristolochia
NT2 aristolochia acuminata
NT2 aristolochia argentina
NT2 aristolochia bracteata
NT2 aristolochia clematitis
NT2 aristolochia indica
NT2 aristolochia macrophylla
NT2 aristolochia multiflora
NT2 aristolochia tagala
NT2 aristolochia taliscana
NT1 asarum
NT2 asarum caudatum
NT2 asarum caulescens
NT2 asarum europaeum

ARISTOTELIA
BT1 elaeocarpaceae
NT1 aristotelia chilensis
NT1 aristotelia serrata

ARISTOTELIA CHILENSIS
BT1 aristotelia
BT2 elaeocarpaceae
BT1 ornamental woody plants

ARISTOTELIA SERRATA
BT1 aristotelia
BT2 elaeocarpaceae
BT1 ornamental woody plants

ARIUS
uf galeichthys
BT1 ariidae
BT2 siluriformes
BT3 osteichthyes
BT4 fishes

ARIZONA
BT1 mountain states of usa
BT2 western states of usa
BT3 usa
BT4 north america
BT5 america

ARKANSAS
BT1 delta states of usa
BT2 southern states of usa
BT3 usa
BT4 north america
BT5 america

ARKANSAS BEE VIRUS
BT1 bee viruses
BT2 insect viruses
BT3 entomopathogens
BT4 pathogens

ARLES MERINO
BT1 sheep breeds
BT2 breeds

ARM CIRCUMFERENCE (AGRICOLA)
BT1 anthropometric dimensions
BT2 dimensions

ARMA
BT1 pentatomidae
BT2 heteroptera
NT1 arma custos

ARMA CUSTOS
BT1 arma
BT2 pentatomidae
BT3 heteroptera

ARMADILLIDIIDAE
BT1 isopoda
BT2 malacostraca
BT3 crustacea
BT4 arthropods
NT1 armadillidium
NT2 armadillidium vulgare

ARMADILLIDIUM
BT1 armadillidiidae
BT2 isopoda
BT3 malacostraca
BT4 crustacea
BT5 arthropods
NT1 armadillidium vulgare

ARMADILLIDIUM VULGARE
BT1 armadillidium
BT2 armadillidiidae
BT3 isopoda
BT4 malacostraca
BT5 crustacea
BT6 arthropods

armadillos
USE **dasypodidae**

ARMED FORCES
rt military entomology
rt war

armeniaca
USE **prunus**

armeniaca sibirica
USE **prunus sibirica**

armeniaca vulgaris
USE **prunus armeniaca**

ARMENIAN SEMICOURSEWOOL
HN from 1990
BT1 sheep breeds
BT2 breeds

ARMENIAN SSR
uf ussr in asia
BT1 ussr
rt ussr in europe

ARMERIA
BT1 plumbaginaceae
NT1 armeria maritima
NT1 armeria plantaginea

ARMERIA MARITIMA
BT1 armeria
BT2 plumbaginaceae

ARMERIA PLANTAGINEA
BT1 armeria
BT2 plumbaginaceae

ARMIGERES
BT1 culicidae
BT2 diptera
NT1 armigeres subalbatus

ARMIGERES SUBALBATUS
BT1 armigeres
BT2 culicidae
BT3 diptera

ARMILLARIA
uf armillariella
BT1 agaricales
NT1 armillaria elegans
NT1 armillaria luteobubalina
NT1 armillaria mellea
NT1 armillaria obscura
NT1 armillaria ostoyae
NT1 armillaria tabescens
rt clitocybe
rt tricholoma

ARMILLARIA ELEGANS
uf armillariella elegans
BT1 armillaria
BT2 agaricales

ARMILLARIA LUTEOBUBALINA
BT1 armillaria
BT2 agaricales

armillaria matsutake
USE **tricholoma matsutake**

ARMILLARIA MELLEA
uf armillariella mellea
BT1 armillaria
BT2 agaricales

ARMILLARIA OBSCURA
HN from 1990
BT1 armillaria
BT2 agaricales

ARMILLARIA OSTOYAE
BT1 armillaria
BT2 agaricales

ARMILLARIA TABESCENS
uf armillariella tabescens
uf clitocybe tabescens
BT1 armillaria
BT2 agaricales

armillariella
USE **armillaria**

armillariella elegans
USE **armillaria elegans**

armillariella matsutake
USE **tricholoma matsutake**

armillariella mellea
USE **armillaria mellea**

armillariella tabescens
USE **armillaria tabescens**

ARMILLIFER
BT1 porocephalida
BT2 pentastomida
BT3 arthropods
NT1 armillifer armillatus

ARMILLIFER ARMILLATUS
BT1 armillifer
BT2 porocephalida
BT3 pentastomida
BT4 arthropods

ARMORACIA
BT1 cruciferae
NT1 armoracia rusticana

ARMORACIA RUSTICANA
uf cochlearia armoracia
uf cochlearia rusticana
BT1 armoracia
BT2 cruciferae
BT1 culinary herbs
BT1 insecticidal plants
BT2 pesticidal plants
BT1 root vegetables
BT2 root crops
BT2 vegetables
rt horseradish

ARNEBIA
BT1 boraginaceae
NT1 arnebia nobilis
NT1 arnebia pulchra

ARNEBIA NOBILIS
BT1 arnebia
BT2 boraginaceae

ARNEBIA PULCHRA
uf macrotomia echioides
BT1 arnebia
BT2 boraginaceae

arnel
USE **triacetate (agricola)**

ARNICA
BT1 compositae
NT1 arnica amplexicaulis
NT1 arnica chamissonis
NT1 arnica foliosa
NT1 arnica lanceolata
NT1 arnica longifolia
NT1 arnica montana
NT1 arnica parryi
NT1 arnica sachalinensis

ARNICA AMPLEXICAULIS
BT1 arnica
BT2 compositae

ARNICA CHAMISSONIS
BT1 arnica
BT2 compositae

ARNICA FOLIOSA
BT1 arnica
BT2 compositae

ARNICA LANCEOLATA
uf arnica mollis
BT1 arnica
BT2 compositae
BT1 medicinal plants
BT1 ornamental herbaceous plants

ARNICA LONGIFOLIA
BT1 arnica
BT2 compositae

arnica mollis
USE **arnica lanceolata**

ARNICA MONTANA
BT1 antibacterial plants
BT1 arnica
BT2 compositae
BT1 medicinal plants

ARNICA PARRYI
BT1 arnica
BT2 compositae

ARNICA SACHALINENSIS
BT1 arnica
BT2 compositae

AROMA
BT1 odours
BT2 organoleptic traits
BT3 physicochemical properties
BT4 properties
BT3 traits
rt aromatic compounds
rt boar taint
rt diacetyl
rt flavour
rt fragrance
rt olfactory stimulation

AROMATIC ACID HERBICIDES
BT1 herbicides
BT2 pesticides
NT1 benzoic acid herbicides
NT2 2,3,6-tba
NT2 chloramben
NT2 dicamba
NT1 picolinic acid herbicides
NT2 clopyralid
NT2 picloram
NT1 quinolinecarboxylic acid herbicides

AROMATIC ACID HERBICIDES *cont.*
NT2 quinclorac
NT2 quinmerac

AROMATIC ACIDS
uf *acids, aromatic*
BT1 aromatic compounds
BT1 organic acids
BT2 acids
NT1 4-pyridoxic acid
NT1 6-chloropicolinic acid
NT1 benzoic acids
NT2 aminobenzoic acids
NT3 p-aminobenzoic acid
NT3 aminosalicylic acid
NT3 hydroxyanthranilic acid
NT2 benzoic acid
NT2 phenolic acids
NT3 4-hydroxybenzoic acid
NT3 dihydroxybenzoic acid
NT3 gallic acid
NT3 hydroxyanthranilic acid
NT3 protocatechuic acid
NT3 salicylic acids
NT4 3,5-dimethoxysalicylic acid
NT4 aminosalicylic acid
NT4 aspirin
NT4 salicylic acid
NT3 syringic acid
NT3 tannins
NT3 vanillic acid
NT2 phthalic acid
NT2 tibric acid
NT1 nicotinic acid
NT1 picolinic acid
NT1 xanthurenic acid

AROMATIC COMPOUNDS
uf *aromatics*
NT1 aromatic acids
NT2 4-pyridoxic acid
NT2 6-chloropicolinic acid
NT2 benzoic acids
NT3 aminobenzoic acids
NT4 p-aminobenzoic acid
NT4 aminosalicylic acid
NT4 hydroxyanthranilic acid
NT3 benzoic acid
NT3 phenolic acids
NT4 4-hydroxybenzoic acid
NT4 dihydroxybenzoic acid
NT4 gallic acid
NT4 hydroxyanthranilic acid
NT4 protocatechuic acid
NT4 salicylic acids
NT5 3,5-dimethoxysalicylic acid
NT5 aminosalicylic acid
NT5 aspirin
NT5 salicylic acid
NT4 syringic acid
NT4 tannins
NT4 vanillic acid
NT3 phthalic acid
NT3 tibric acid
NT2 nicotinic acid
NT2 picolinic acid
NT2 xanthurenic acid
NT1 aromatic hydrocarbons
NT2 azulene
NT2 benzene
NT2 benzopyrene
NT2 biphenyl
NT2 cymenes
NT3 p-cymene
NT2 naphthalene
NT2 phenanthrene
NT2 styrene
NT2 toluene
NT2 xylene
NT1 flavonoids
NT2 anthocyanidins
NT3 cyanidin
NT3 delphinidin
NT3 pelargonidin
NT2 betacyanins
NT2 bioflavonoids
NT3 hesperidin
NT3 naringin
NT3 quercetin
NT3 rutoside

AROMATIC COMPOUNDS *cont.*
NT2 chalcones
NT3 chalcone
NT2 flavanols
NT3 catechin
NT3 epicatechin
NT2 flavones
NT3 flavonols
NT4 isorhamnetin
NT4 kaempferol
NT4 quercetin
NT2 glycoflavones
NT3 anthocyanins
NT4 cyanin
NT4 delphinin
NT4 rubrobrassicin
NT3 hesperidin
NT3 isoquercitrin
NT3 naringin
NT3 phloridzin
NT3 quercitrin
NT3 rutoside
NT3 vitexin
NT2 isoflavans
NT2 isoflavones
NT3 daidzein
NT3 dimethoxyisoflavone
NT3 formononetin
NT3 genistein
NT3 medicarpin
NT3 phaseollin
NT3 pisatin
NT3 rotenoids
NT4 rotenone
NT2 karanjin
NT1 phenolic compounds
NT2 lignans
NT2 phenolic acids
NT3 4-hydroxybenzoic acid
NT3 dihydroxybenzoic acid
NT3 gallic acid
NT3 hydroxyanthranilic acid
NT3 protocatechuic acid
NT3 salicylic acids
NT4 3,5-dimethoxysalicylic acid
NT4 aminosalicylic acid
NT4 aspirin
NT4 salicylic acid
NT3 syringic acid
NT3 tannins
NT3 vanillic acid
NT2 phenols
NT3 2,4,5-trichlorophenol
NT3 2,4-dichlorophenol
NT3 2,4-dinitrophenol
NT3 2-iodophenol
NT3 2-phenylphenol
NT3 creosote
NT3 cresols
NT4 o-cresol
NT4 p-cresol
NT3 dichlorophen
NT3 disophenol
NT3 gossypol
NT3 guaiacol
NT3 hydroquinone
NT3 naphthols
NT4 1-naphthol
NT3 nitrophenols
NT4 o-nitrophenol
NT4 p-nitrophenol
NT3 phenol
NT3 polyphenols
NT3 probucol
NT3 pyrocatechol
NT3 pyrogallol
NT3 resorcinols
NT4 alkylresorcinols
NT4 pinosylvin
NT4 resorcinol
NT4 resorcylic acid lactones
NT5 zearalenol
NT5 zearalenone
NT5 zeranol
NT3 thymol
NT3 vanillin
NT1 quinones
NT2 anthraquinones
NT3 emodin
NT2 benzoquinone

AROMATIC COMPOUNDS *cont.*
NT2 juglone
NT2 naphthoquinone
NT2 quinone fungicides
NT3 benquinox
NT3 chloranil
NT3 dichlone
NT3 dithianon
NT2 rugulosins
NT3 luteoskyrin
NT2 ubiquinones
NT3 ubichromenols
NT1 stilbenes
NT2 diethylstilbestrol
NT2 pinosylvin
rt aroma

AROMATIC FUNGICIDES
BT1 fungicides
BT2 pesticides
NT1 2,4,5-trichlorophenol
NT1 chloroneb
NT1 chlorothalonil
NT1 dicloran
NT1 hexachlorobenzene
NT1 nitrothal-isopropyl
NT1 quintozene
NT1 sodium pentachlorophenoxide
NT1 tecnazene

AROMATIC HYDROCARBONS
uf *hydrocarbons, aromatic*
BT1 aromatic compounds
BT1 hydrocarbons
NT1 azulene
NT1 benzene
NT1 benzopyrene
NT1 biphenyl
NT1 cymenes
NT2 p-cymene
NT1 naphthalene
NT1 phenanthrene
NT1 styrene
NT1 toluene
NT1 xylene
rt essential oils

aromatics
USE **aromatic compounds**

ARONIA
BT1 rosaceae
NT1 aronia melanocarpa
NT1 aronia prunifolia
rt amelanchier

ARONIA MELANOCARPA
uf *amelanchier melanocarpa*
uf *pyrus melanocarpa*
uf *sorbus melanocarpa*
BT1 aronia
BT2 rosaceae
BT1 ornamental woody plants

ARONIA PRUNIFOLIA
uf *pyrus floribunda*
BT1 aronia
BT2 rosaceae
BT1 ornamental woody plants

ARPRINOCID
BT1 coccidiostats
BT2 antiprotozoal agents
BT3 antiparasitic agents
BT4 drugs

ARRACACHA A NEPOVIRUS
HN from 1990
BT1 nepovirus group
BT2 plant viruses
BT3 plant pathogens
BT4 pathogens

ARRACACIA
BT1 umbelliferae
NT1 arracacia xanthorrhiza

ARRACACIA XANTHORRHIZA
BT1 arracacia
BT2 umbelliferae
BT1 root vegetables
BT2 root crops
BT2 vegetables

ARRENURIDAE
BT1 prostigmata
BT2 acari
NT1 arrenurus

ARRENURUS
BT1 arrenuridae
BT2 prostigmata
BT3 acari

ARRHENATHERUM
BT1 gramineae
NT1 arrhenatherum elatius
NT1 arrhenatherum elatius subsp. bulbosum

ARRHENATHERUM ELATIUS
uf *tall oatgrass*
BT1 arrhenatherum
BT2 gramineae
BT1 fodder plants
BT1 pasture plants

ARRHENATHERUM ELATIUS SUBSP. BULBOSUM
uf *arrhenatherum tuberosum*
BT1 arrhenatherum
BT2 gramineae
BT1 weeds

arrhenatherum tuberosum
USE **arrhenatherum elatius subsp. bulbosum**

ARRHENOTOKY
BT1 parthenogenesis
BT2 reproduction

ARRHOSTOXYLUM
BT1 acanthaceae
NT1 arrhostoxylum elegans
rt ornamental woody plants

ARRHOSTOXYLUM ELEGANS
BT1 arrhostoxylum
BT2 acanthaceae

ARRHYTHMIA
BT1 heart diseases
BT2 cardiovascular diseases
BT3 organic diseases
BT4 diseases

ARROWROOT
rt maranta arundinacea

ARSANILIC ACID
BT1 antibacterial agents
BT2 antiinfective agents
BT3 drugs
BT1 growth promoters
BT2 growth regulators
BT2 promoters
BT1 organoarsenical compounds
BT2 arsenicals

ARSENATES
BT1 arsenicals
BT1 inorganic salts
BT2 inorganic compounds
BT2 salts
NT1 calcium arsenate
NT1 copper arsenate
NT1 copper chrome arsenate
NT1 lead arsenate

ARSENIC
BT1 nonmetallic elements
BT2 elements
rt arsenicals

arsenic compounds
USE **arsenicals**

ARSENICAL HERBICIDES
BT1 arsenicals
BT1 herbicides
BT2 pesticides
NT1 cacodylic acid
NT1 cma
NT1 dsma
NT1 hexaflurate
NT1 mama
NT1 msma

ARSENICAL INSECTICIDES
BT1 arsenicals
BT1 insecticides
BT2 pesticides
NT1 calcium arsenate
NT1 copper acetoarsenite
NT1 copper arsenate
NT1 lead arsenate
NT1 sodium arsenite

ARSENICALS
uf *arsenic compounds*
NT1 arsenates
NT2 calcium arsenate
NT2 copper arsenate
NT2 copper chrome arsenate
NT2 lead arsenate
NT1 arsenical herbicides
NT2 cacodylic acid
NT2 cma
NT2 dsma
NT2 hexaflurate
NT2 mama
NT2 msma
NT1 arsenical insecticides
NT2 calcium arsenate
NT2 copper acetoarsenite
NT2 copper arsenate
NT2 lead arsenate
NT2 sodium arsenite
NT1 arsenites
NT2 sodium arsenite
NT1 organoarsenical compounds
NT2 arsanilic acid
NT2 melarsonyl
NT2 melarsoprol
NT2 neoarsphenamine
NT2 roxarsone
NT2 tryparsamide
rt arsenic
rt toxic substances

ARSENITES
BT1 arsenicals
BT1 inorganic salts
BT2 inorganic compounds
BT2 salts
NT1 sodium arsenite

ARSI
HN from 1990
BT1 cattle breeds
BT2 breeds

ARTABOTRYS
BT1 annonaceae
NT1 artabotrys hexapetalus

ARTABOTRYS HEXAPETALUS
uf *artabotrys odoratissimus*
uf *artabotrys uncinatus*
BT1 antifungal plants
BT1 artabotrys
BT2 annonaceae
BT1 medicinal plants

artabotrys odoratissimus
USE **artabotrys hexapetalus**

artabotrys uncinatus
USE **artabotrys hexapetalus**

ARTEFACTS
uf *artifacts*
rt human activity
rt soil micromorphological features

ARTEMETHER
BT1 anthelmintics
BT2 antiparasitic agents
BT3 drugs
BT1 antimalarials
BT2 antiprotozoal agents
BT3 antiparasitic agents
BT4 drugs

ARTEMIA
BT1 anostraca
BT2 branchiopoda
BT3 crustacea
BT4 arthropods
NT1 artemia salina

ARTEMIA SALINA
BT1 artemia
BT2 anostraca
BT3 branchiopoda
BT4 crustacea
BT5 arthropods

ARTEMISIA
BT1 compositae
NT1 artemisia abrotanum
NT1 artemisia absinthium
NT1 artemisia albicerata
NT1 artemisia annua
NT1 artemisia apiacea
NT1 artemisia arbuscula
NT1 artemisia armeniaca
NT1 artemisia aschurbajevii
NT1 artemisia austriaca
NT1 artemisia balchanorum
NT1 artemisia barrelieri
NT1 artemisia californica
NT1 artemisia campestris
NT1 artemisia cana
NT1 artemisia canariensis
NT1 artemisia capillaris
NT1 artemisia compacta
NT1 artemisia diffusa
NT1 artemisia dracunculus
NT1 artemisia filifolia
NT1 artemisia fragrans
NT1 artemisia frigida
NT1 artemisia fukudo
NT1 artemisia heptapotamica
NT1 artemisia herba-alba
NT1 artemisia judaica
NT1 artemisia klotzchiana
NT1 artemisia lercheana
NT1 artemisia leucodes
NT1 artemisia longiloba
NT1 artemisia ludoviciana
NT1 artemisia macrocephala
NT1 artemisia maritima
NT1 artemisia monosperma
NT1 artemisia mutellina
NT1 artemisia pallens
NT1 artemisia pamirica
NT1 artemisia pauciflora
NT1 artemisia pontica
NT1 artemisia princeps
NT1 artemisia pygmaea
NT1 artemisia rutifolia
NT1 artemisia santonina
NT1 artemisia scoparia
NT1 artemisia scopulorum
NT1 artemisia sericea
NT1 artemisia seriphidium
NT1 artemisia spinescens
NT1 artemisia taurica
NT1 artemisia terrae-albae
NT1 artemisia tilesii
NT1 artemisia tridentata
NT1 artemisia tripartita
NT1 artemisia vestita
NT1 artemisia vulgaris
NT1 artemisia xanthophora
NT1 artemisia xerophytica

ARTEMISIA ABROTANUM
BT1 artemisia
BT2 compositae
BT1 insecticidal plants
BT2 pesticidal plants
BT1 medicinal plants

ARTEMISIA ABSINTHIUM
BT1 artemisia
BT2 compositae
BT1 essential oil plants
BT2 oil plants
BT1 insecticidal plants
BT2 pesticidal plants
BT1 medicinal plants

ARTEMISIA ALBICERATA
BT1 artemisia
BT2 compositae

ARTEMISIA ANNUA
BT1 artemisia
BT2 compositae
BT1 essential oil plants
BT2 oil plants

ARTEMISIA ANNUA *cont.*
BT1 medicinal plants

ARTEMISIA APIACEA
BT1 artemisia
BT2 compositae

ARTEMISIA ARBUSCULA
BT1 artemisia
BT2 compositae

ARTEMISIA ARMENIACA
BT1 artemisia
BT2 compositae

ARTEMISIA ASCHURBAJEVII
BT1 artemisia
BT2 compositae

ARTEMISIA AUSTRIACA
BT1 artemisia
BT2 compositae

ARTEMISIA BALCHANORUM
BT1 artemisia
BT2 compositae

ARTEMISIA BARRELIERI
BT1 artemisia
BT2 compositae
BT1 medicinal plants

ARTEMISIA CALIFORNICA
BT1 artemisia
BT2 compositae

ARTEMISIA CAMPESTRIS
BT1 artemisia
BT2 compositae

ARTEMISIA CANA
BT1 artemisia
BT2 compositae
BT1 browse plants

ARTEMISIA CANARIENSIS
BT1 artemisia
BT2 compositae

ARTEMISIA CAPILLARIS
BT1 artemisia
BT2 compositae
BT1 insecticidal plants
BT2 pesticidal plants
BT1 medicinal plants

ARTEMISIA COMPACTA
BT1 artemisia
BT2 compositae

ARTEMISIA DIFFUSA
BT1 artemisia
BT2 compositae

ARTEMISIA DRACUNCULUS
uf *artemisia glauca*
BT1 artemisia
BT2 compositae
BT1 culinary herbs
BT1 essential oil plants
BT2 oil plants
rt tarragon

ARTEMISIA FILIFOLIA
BT1 artemisia
BT2 compositae

ARTEMISIA FRAGRANS
BT1 artemisia
BT2 compositae
BT1 pasture plants

ARTEMISIA FRIGIDA
BT1 artemisia
BT2 compositae
BT1 medicinal plants

ARTEMISIA FUKUDO
BT1 artemisia
BT2 compositae

artemisia glauca
USE **artemisia dracunculus**

ARTEMISIA HEPTAPOTAMICA
BT1 artemisia

ARTEMISIA HEPTAPOTAMICA *cont.*
BT2 compositae

ARTEMISIA HERBA-ALBA
BT1 antibacterial plants
BT1 artemisia
BT2 compositae
BT1 essential oil plants
BT2 oil plants
BT1 medicinal plants

ARTEMISIA JUDAICA
BT1 artemisia
BT2 compositae

ARTEMISIA KLOTZCHIANA
BT1 artemisia
BT2 compositae

ARTEMISIA LERCHEANA
BT1 artemisia
BT2 compositae
BT1 pasture plants

ARTEMISIA LEUCODES
BT1 artemisia
BT2 compositae

ARTEMISIA LONGILOBA
BT1 artemisia
BT2 compositae

ARTEMISIA LUDOVICIANA
BT1 artemisia
BT2 compositae

ARTEMISIA MACROCEPHALA
BT1 artemisia
BT2 compositae

ARTEMISIA MARITIMA
BT1 antifungal plants
BT1 artemisia
BT2 compositae
BT1 essential oil plants
BT2 oil plants
BT1 nematicidal plants
BT2 pesticidal plants

ARTEMISIA MONOSPERMA
BT1 artemisia
BT2 compositae
BT1 insecticidal plants
BT2 pesticidal plants

ARTEMISIA MUTELLINA
uf *artemisia umbelliformis*
BT1 artemisia
BT2 compositae
BT1 essential oil plants
BT2 oil plants

artemisia nova
USE **artemisia tridentata**

ARTEMISIA PALLENS
BT1 artemisia
BT2 compositae
BT1 essential oil plants
BT2 oil plants

ARTEMISIA PAMIRICA
BT1 artemisia
BT2 compositae

ARTEMISIA PAUCIFLORA
BT1 artemisia
BT2 compositae
BT1 pasture plants

ARTEMISIA PONTICA
BT1 artemisia
BT2 compositae

ARTEMISIA PRINCEPS
BT1 artemisia
BT2 compositae
BT1 medicinal plants

ARTEMISIA PYGMAEA
BT1 artemisia
BT2 compositae

ARTEMISIA RUTIFOLIA
BT1 artemisia
BT2 compositae

ARTEMISIA SANTONINA
BT1 artemisia
BT2 compositae

ARTEMISIA SCOPARIA
BT1 artemisia
BT2 compositae

ARTEMISIA SCOPULORUM
BT1 artemisia
BT2 compositae

ARTEMISIA SERICEA
BT1 artemisia
BT2 compositae

ARTEMISIA SERIPHIDIUM
BT1 artemisia
BT2 compositae

ARTEMISIA SPINESCENS
BT1 artemisia
BT2 compositae

ARTEMISIA TAURICA
BT1 artemisia
BT2 compositae

ARTEMISIA TERRAE-ALBAE
BT1 artemisia
BT2 compositae
BT1 pasture plants

ARTEMISIA TILESII
BT1 artemisia
BT2 compositae
BT1 medicinal plants
BT1 pasture plants

ARTEMISIA TRIDENTATA
uf artemisia nova
BT1 artemisia
BT2 compositae
BT1 browse plants
BT1 medicinal plants
BT1 weeds

ARTEMISIA TRIPARTITA
BT1 artemisia
BT2 compositae

artemisia umbelliformis
USE **artemisia mutellina**

ARTEMISIA VESTITA
BT1 artemisia
BT2 compositae

ARTEMISIA VULGARIS
BT1 artemisia
BT2 compositae
BT1 essential oil plants
BT2 oil plants
BT1 medicinal plants

ARTEMISIA XANTHOPHORA
BT1 artemisia
BT2 compositae

ARTEMISIA XEROPHYTICA
BT1 artemisia
BT2 compositae

artemisinin
USE **qinghaosu**

ARTERIES
BT1 blood vessels
BT2 cardiovascular system
BT3 body parts
NT1 aorta
NT1 pulmonary artery
rt aneurysm
rt arteritis
rt blood circulation
rt ergotism

arteriosclerosis
USE **atherosclerosis**

ARTERITIS
BT1 vascular diseases
BT2 cardiovascular diseases
BT3 organic diseases
BT4 diseases
rt arteries

ARTERITIS *cont.*
rt equine arteritis virus

ARTERIVIRUS
BT1 togaviridae
BT2 viruses
NT1 equine arteritis virus

ARTESUNATE
uf qinghaozhi
BT1 antimalarials
BT2 antiprotozoal agents
BT3 antiparasitic agents
BT4 drugs

ARTHRAXON
BT1 gramineae
NT1 arthraxon hispidus

ARTHRAXON HISPIDUS
BT1 arthraxon
BT2 gramineae

ARTHRITIS
BT1 joint diseases
BT2 organic diseases
BT3 diseases
NT1 osteoarthritis
NT1 rheumatoid arthritis
rt aurothioglucose
rt gout
rt inflammation
rt rheumatism

ARTHROBACTER
BT1 firmicutes
BT2 bacteria
BT3 prokaryotes
NT1 arthrobacter crystallopoietes
NT1 arthrobacter fluorescens
NT1 arthrobacter giacomelloi
NT1 arthrobacter globiformis

ARTHROBACTER CRYSTALLOPOIETES
BT1 arthrobacter
BT2 firmicutes
BT3 bacteria
BT4 prokaryotes

ARTHROBACTER FLUORESCENS
BT1 arthrobacter
BT2 firmicutes
BT3 bacteria
BT4 prokaryotes

ARTHROBACTER GIACOMELLOI
BT1 arthrobacter
BT2 firmicutes
BT3 bacteria
BT4 prokaryotes

ARTHROBACTER GLOBIFORMIS
BT1 arthrobacter
BT2 firmicutes
BT3 bacteria
BT4 prokaryotes

ARTHROBOTRYS
BT1 deuteromycotina
NT1 arthrobotrys amerospora
NT1 arthrobotrys botryospora
NT1 arthrobotrys oligospora

ARTHROBOTRYS AMEROSPORA
BT1 arthrobotrys
BT2 deuteromycotina

ARTHROBOTRYS BOTRYOSPORA
BT1 arthrobotrys
BT2 deuteromycotina

ARTHROBOTRYS OLIGOSPORA
BT1 arthrobotrys
BT2 deuteromycotina

ARTHRODERMA
BT1 gymnoascales
NT1 arthroderma ajelloi
NT1 arthroderma benhamiae
NT1 arthroderma flavescens
NT1 arthroderma gertleri
NT1 arthroderma insingulare
NT1 arthroderma lenticularum

ARTHRODERMA *cont.*
NT1 arthroderma quadrifidum
NT1 arthroderma simii
NT1 arthroderma tuberculatum
NT1 arthroderma uncinatum
NT1 arthroderma vanbreuseghemii
rt chrysosporium
rt dermatophytes
rt keratinomyces
rt trichophyton

ARTHRODERMA AJELLOI
BT1 arthroderma
BT2 gymnoascales
rt keratinomyces ajelloi

ARTHRODERMA BENHAMIAE
BT1 arthroderma
BT2 gymnoascales
rt trichophyton mentagrophytes

ARTHRODERMA FLAVESCENS
BT1 arthroderma
BT2 gymnoascales

ARTHRODERMA GERTLERI
BT1 arthroderma
BT2 gymnoascales
rt trichophyton vanbreuseghemii

ARTHRODERMA INSINGULARE
BT1 arthroderma
BT2 gymnoascales
rt trichophyton terrestre

ARTHRODERMA LENTICULARUM
BT1 arthroderma
BT2 gymnoascales
rt trichophyton terrestre

ARTHRODERMA QUADRIFIDUM
BT1 arthroderma
BT2 gymnoascales
rt trichophyton terrestre

ARTHRODERMA SIMII
BT1 arthroderma
BT2 gymnoascales
rt trichophyton simii

ARTHRODERMA TUBERCULATUM
BT1 arthroderma
BT2 gymnoascales

ARTHRODERMA UNCINATUM
BT1 arthroderma
BT2 gymnoascales
rt keratinomyces ajelloi

ARTHRODERMA VANBREUSEGHEMII
BT1 arthroderma
BT2 gymnoascales
rt trichophyton mentagrophytes

ARTHROGRYPOSIS
BT1 congenital abnormalities
BT2 abnormalities

arthropathy
USE **joint diseases**

ARTHROPLASTY
BT1 surgical operations
rt joints (animal)

ARTHROPOD ALLERGIES
HN from 1990
(hypersensitivity to arthropod bites or stings, or to inhaled arthropod parts, etc.)
uf allergy, arthropod
uf allergy, insect
uf insect allergies
BT1 allergies
BT2 immunological diseases
BT3 diseases
rt arthropods
rt house dust mites
rt insect bites
rt stings

ARTHROPOD ALLERGIES *cont.*
rt venoms

ARTHROPOD COMMUNITIES
BT1 communities
NT1 insect communities

ARTHROPOD HORMONES
BT1 hormones
NT1 adipokinetic hormones
NT1 juvenile hormones
NT2 juvenile hormone i
NT2 juvenile hormone ii
NT2 juvenile hormone iii
NT1 moulting hormones
NT2 α-ecdysone
NT2 ecdysterone
NT1 prothoracicotropic hormones

ARTHROPOD PESTS
BT1 pests
NT1 ectoparasites
NT2 feather mites
NT1 haematophagous arthropods
NT2 haematophagous insects
NT1 insect pests
NT2 bark beetles
NT2 boring insects
NT3 stem borers
NT2 haematophagous insects
NT2 leaf miners
NT2 leafhoppers
NT2 locusts
NT2 planthoppers
rt arthropods

arthropoda
USE **arthropods**

ARTHROPODS
(insect families, genera and species are listed elsewhere, consult the scope note at insects; acarine suborders, families, genera and species are listed at acari)
uf arthropoda
NT1 arachnida
NT2 araneae
NT3 agelenidae
NT4 tegenaria
NT5 tegenaria agrestis
NT3 araneidae
NT4 araneus
NT5 araneus diadematus
NT4 argiope
NT5 argiope argentata
NT4 nephila
NT5 nephila clavata
NT3 clubionidae
NT4 cheiracanthium
NT5 cheiracanthium mildei
NT3 ctenidae
NT4 phoneutria
NT3 dipluridae
NT3 heteropodidae
NT4 heteropoda
NT3 hexathelidae
NT4 atrax
NT5 atrax robustus
NT3 linyphiidae
NT4 erigonidium
NT5 erigonidium graminicolum
NT4 oedothorax
NT5 oedothorax insecticeps
NT3 loxoscelidae
NT4 loxosceles
NT5 loxosceles laeta
NT5 loxosceles reclusa
NT5 loxosceles rufescens
NT3 lycosidae
NT4 lycosa
NT5 lycosa pseudoannulata
NT4 trochosa
NT3 oxyopidae
NT4 oxyopes
NT5 oxyopes salticus
NT3 pholcidae
NT4 pholcus
NT5 pholcus phalangioides

ARTHROPODS *cont.*
NT3 tetragnathidae
NT4 tetragnatha
NT5 tetragnatha laboriosa
NT3 theraphosidae
NT4 aphonopelma
NT5 aphonopelma seemanni
NT3 theridiidae
NT4 achaearanea
NT5 achaearanea tepidariorum
NT4 latrodectus
NT5 latrodectus geometricus
NT5 latrodectus hasseltii
NT5 latrodectus hesperus
NT5 latrodectus katipo
NT5 latrodectus mactans
NT5 latrodectus tredecimguttatus
NT4 theridion
NT2 opiliones
NT2 pseudoscorpiones
NT2 scorpiones
NT3 buthidae
NT4 androctonus
NT5 androctonus aeneas
NT5 androctonus amoreuxi
NT5 androctonus australis
NT6 androctonus australis hector
NT5 androctonus mauretanicus
NT4 buthotus
NT5 buthotus minax
NT5 buthotus tamulus
NT4 buthus
NT5 buthus martensi
NT5 buthus occitanus
NT4 centruroides
NT5 centruroides gracilis
NT5 centruroides limpidus
NT6 centruroides limpidus limpidus
NT6 centruroides limpidus tecomanus
NT5 centruroides noxius
NT5 centruroides sculpturatus
NT4 leiurus
NT5 leiurus quinquestriatus
NT4 mesobuthus
NT4 tityus
NT5 tityus serrulatus
NT3 scorpionidae
NT4 heterometrus
NT5 heterometrus bengalensis
NT5 heterometrus fulvipes
NT5 heterometrus scaber
NT4 pandinus
NT2 solifugae
NT1 crustacea
NT2 branchiopoda
NT3 anostraca
NT4 artemia
NT5 artemia salina
NT3 cladocera
NT4 daphnia
NT5 daphnia magna
NT5 daphnia pulex
NT2 branchiura (arthropods)
NT3 argulus
NT2 cirripedia
NT3 thoracica
NT4 balanus
NT4 pollicipes
NT4 semibalanus
NT5 semibalanus balanoides
NT2 copepoda
NT3 calanoida
NT4 acartia
NT5 acartia clausi
NT5 acartia tonsa
NT4 diaptomus
NT4 eudiaptomus
NT5 eudiaptomus gracilis
NT5 eudiaptomus graciloides
NT4 eurytemora
NT5 eurytemora velox

ARTHROPODS *cont.*
NT4 pseudocalanus
NT4 skistodiaptomus
NT5 skistodiaptomus pallidus
NT4 temora
NT3 cyclopoida
NT4 acanthocyclops
NT5 acanthocyclops bicuspidatus
NT6 acanthocyclops bicuspidatus thomasi
NT5 acanthocyclops robustus
NT5 acanthocyclops vernalis
NT5 acanthocyclops viridis
NT4 cyclops
NT5 cyclops strenuus
NT4 lernaea
NT5 lernaea cyprinacea
NT4 mesocyclops
NT5 mesocyclops aspericornis
NT5 mesocyclops leuckarti
NT3 poecilostomatoida
NT4 ergasilus
NT5 ergasilus mirabilis
NT3 siphonostomatoida
NT4 lepeophtheirus
NT5 lepeophtheirus salmonis
NT2 malacostraca
NT3 amphipoda
NT4 corophium
NT4 gammarus
NT5 gammarus fossarum
NT5 gammarus oceanicus
NT5 gammarus pulex
NT3 decapoda
NT4 astacus
NT4 austropotamobius
NT5 austropotamobius pallipes
NT4 callinectes
NT4 cambarus
NT4 cancer
NT4 carcinus
NT5 carcinus aestuarii
NT5 carcinus maenas
NT4 cherax
NT5 cherax destructor
NT4 chionoecetes
NT4 crangon
NT4 homarus
NT5 homarus americanus
NT5 homarus gammarus
NT4 jasus
NT4 macrobrachium
NT5 macrobrachium rosenbergii
NT4 maia
NT4 metapenaeus
NT4 palaemon
NT5 palaemon serratus
NT5 palaemon serrifer
NT4 palaemonetes
NT5 palaemonetes pugio
NT4 pandalus
NT5 pandalus jordani
NT4 panulirus
NT5 panulirus argus
NT4 paralithodes
NT4 penaeus
NT5 penaeus indicus
NT5 penaeus japonicus
NT5 penaeus merguiensis
NT5 penaeus monodon
NT5 penaeus semisulcatus
NT5 penaeus setiferus
NT5 penaeus stylirostris
NT5 penaeus vannamei
NT4 portunus
NT4 potamon
NT5 potamon chinghungense
NT4 procambarus
NT5 procambarus clarkii
NT3 isopoda
NT4 armadillidiidae
NT5 armadillidium

ARTHROPODS *cont.*
NT6 armadillidium vulgare
NT4 asellidae
NT5 asellus
NT6 asellus aquaticus
NT4 ligiidae
NT5 ligia
NT6 ligia oceanica
NT4 oniscidae
NT5 oniscus
NT6 oniscus asellus
NT4 philosciidae
NT5 philoscia
NT6 philoscia muscorum
NT4 porcellionidae
NT5 porcellio
NT6 porcellio scaber
NT4 trichoniscidae
NT5 trichoniscus
NT6 trichoniscus pusillus
NT2 ostracoda
NT3 podocopa
NT4 cyprinotus
NT5 cyprinotus incongruens
NT4 cypris
NT1 insects
NT2 aerial insects
NT2 aquatic insects
NT2 beneficial insects
NT3 dung beetles
NT3 silkworms
NT4 antheraea pernyi
NT4 bombyx mori
NT2 insect pests
NT3 bark beetles
NT3 boring insects
NT4 stem borers
NT3 haematophagous insects
NT3 leaf miners
NT3 leafhoppers
NT3 locusts
NT3 planthoppers
NT2 parasitoids
NT3 hyperparasitoids
NT2 predatory insects
NT2 social insects
NT2 soil insects
NT1 merostomata
NT2 xiphosura
NT3 limulus
NT1 myriapoda
NT2 chilopoda
NT3 lithobiidae
NT4 lithobius
NT5 lithobius forficatus
NT3 scolopendridae
NT4 scolopendra
NT5 scolopendra subspinipes
NT3 scutigeridae
NT4 scutigera
NT5 scutigera coleoptrata
NT2 diplopoda
NT3 blaniulidae
NT4 archiboreoiulus
NT5 archiboreoiulus pallidus
NT4 blaniulus
NT5 blaniulus guttulatus
NT4 ommatoiulus
NT5 ommatoiulus moreleti
NT3 glomeridae
NT4 glomeris
NT5 glomeris marginata
NT3 iulidae
NT4 cylindroiulus
NT3 pachybolidae
NT4 pachybolus
NT5 pachybolus laminatus
NT3 paradoxosomatidae
NT4 oxidus
NT5 oxidus gracilis
NT3 polydesmidae
NT4 polydesmus
NT5 polydesmus inconstans
NT3 polyzoniidae
NT4 polyzonium
NT5 polyzonium germanicum
NT3 rhinocricidae
NT4 rhinocricus

ARTHROPODS *cont.*
NT5 rhinocricus bernardinensis
NT5 rhinocricus nattereri
NT3 trigoniulidae
NT4 trigoniulus
NT5 trigoniulus lumbricinus
NT1 pauropoda
NT1 pentastomida
NT2 cephalobaenida
NT3 raillietiella
NT2 porocephalida
NT3 armillifer
NT4 armillifer armillatus
NT3 linguatula
NT4 linguatula serrata
NT3 porocephalus
NT1 symphylida
NT2 hanseniella
NT3 hanseniella ivorensis
NT2 scutigerella
NT3 scutigerella immaculata
NT1 tardigrada
rt aquatic arthropods
rt arthropod allergies
rt arthropod pests
rt beneficial arthropods
rt invertebrates
rt predatory arthropods

ARTHROSAMANEA
BT1 leguminosae
NT1 arthrosamanea pistaciaefolia

ARTHROSAMANEA PISTACIAEFOLIA
BT1 arthrosamanea
BT2 leguminosae

ARTIBEUS
BT1 phyllostomidae
BT2 chiroptera
BT3 mammals
NT1 artibeus jamaicensis

ARTIBEUS JAMAICENSIS
BT1 artibeus
BT2 phyllostomidae
BT3 chiroptera
BT4 mammals

artichoke, globe
USE **globe artichokes**

ARTICHOKE ITALIAN LATENT NEPOVIRUS
HN from 1990
BT1 nepovirus group
BT2 plant viruses
BT3 plant pathogens
BT4 pathogens

artichoke, jerusalem
USE **jerusalem artichokes**

ARTICHOKE LATENT VIRUS
BT1 miscellaneous plant viruses
BT2 plant viruses
BT3 plant pathogens
BT4 pathogens

ARTICHOKE MOTTLED CRINKLE VIRUS
BT1 miscellaneous plant viruses
BT2 plant viruses
BT3 plant pathogens
BT4 pathogens

ARTICHOKE YELLOW RINGSPOT NEPOVIRUS
HN from 1990
BT1 nepovirus group
BT2 plant viruses
BT3 plant pathogens
BT4 pathogens

ARTICULATED TRACTORS
uf *tractors, articulated*
BT1 tractors
BT2 cross country vehicles
BT3 vehicles

artifacts
USE **artefacts**

ARTIFICIAL COLORS (AGRICOLA)
HN from 1989
BT1 food colorants

artificial defoliation
USE **defoliation**

artificial diets
USE **synthetic diets**

ARTIFICIAL DRYING
BT1 drying
BT2 dehydration
BT3 processing
rt driers

ARTIFICIAL FLAVORS (AGRICOLA)
HN from 1989
BT1 flavorings

ARTIFICIAL FOODS (AGRICOLA)
BT1 foods
rt simulated foods

ARTIFICIAL HONEY
BT1 honey
BT2 hive products
BT3 animal products
BT4 products

ARTIFICIAL INSEMINATION
uf *ai*
BT1 animal breeding methods
BT2 breeding methods
BT3 methodology
NT1 intrauterine insemination
rt age at first insemination
rt ai bulls
rt artificial vagina
rt collection dummy
rt deposition site
rt electroejaculation
rt insemination
rt semen
rt semen diluent additives
rt semen diluents
rt semen preservation
rt teasing

ARTIFICIAL LIGHT
uf *light, artificial*
BT1 light
BT2 electromagnetic radiation
BT3 radiation
rt artificial lighting (agricola)
rt illumination
rt intermittent light
rt lamps
rt light regime
rt lighting
rt natural light
rt supplementary light

ARTIFICIAL LIGHTING (AGRICOLA)
BT1 lighting
rt artificial light
rt illumination

ARTIFICIAL PANCREAS
uf *pancreas, artificial*
BT1 pancreas
BT2 digestive system
BT3 body parts

ARTIFICIAL PRECIPITATION
BT1 precipitation
BT2 meteorological factors
BT3 climatic factors
rt cloud seeding
rt rain
rt weather control

ARTIFICIAL REARING
uf *hand rearing*
BT1 animal husbandry
BT2 husbandry
BT2 zootechny

ARTIFICIAL REGENERATION
uf *regeneration, artificial*
BT1 silviculture
BT2 forestry
rt natural regeneration

ARTIFICIAL REGENERATION *cont.*
rt planting
rt regeneration surveys
rt rehabilitation
rt sowing

ARTIFICIAL RESPIRATION
BT1 therapy
rt respiration

ARTIFICIAL RUMEN
uf *rumen, artificial*
BT1 rumen
BT2 forestomach
BT3 stomach
BT4 digestive system
BT5 body parts

ARTIFICIAL SEEDS
HN from 1990
rt micropropagation
rt plant embryos
rt seeds
rt vegetative propagation

ARTIFICIAL SELECTION
uf *selection, artificial*
BT1 selection
NT1 in vitro selection
rt breeding
rt breeding methods
rt genetic gain
rt natural selection
rt selection criteria
rt selection intensity
rt selection programme
rt selective breeding

ARTIFICIAL SWEETENERS
BT1 sugar substitutes
BT2 substitutes
BT2 sweeteners
BT3 food additives
BT4 additives
NT1 aspartame
NT1 saccharin
NT1 sodium cyclamate
rt polyols
rt stevia rebaudiana
rt sweet tasting compounds
rt synsepalum dulcificum
rt thaumatococcus daniellii

ARTIFICIAL VAGINA
BT1 equipment
rt artificial insemination
rt semen production

ARTIFICIAL VENTILATION
uf *ventilation, artificial*
BT1 ventilation
rt air conditioning
rt cooling systems
rt ventilators

ARTIODACTYLA
BT1 mammals
BT1 ungulates
NT1 ruminantia
NT2 antilocapridae
NT3 antilocapra
NT4 antilocapra americana
NT2 bovidae
NT3 aepyceros
NT4 aepyceros melampus
NT3 alcelaphus
NT4 alcelaphus buselaphus
NT3 ammotragus
NT4 ammotragus lervia
NT3 antidorcas
NT4 antidorcas marsupialis
NT3 antilope
NT4 antilope cervicapra
NT3 bison (genus)
NT4 bison bonasus
NT3 bos
NT4 bos primigenius
NT3 boselaphus
NT4 boselaphus tragocamelus
NT3 bubalus
NT3 capra
NT4 capra ibex

ARTIODACTYLA *cont.*
NT4 capra pyrenaica
NT3 capricornis
NT4 capricornis crispus
NT3 connochaetes
NT4 connochaetes gnou
NT4 connochaetes taurinus
NT3 damaliscus
NT4 damaliscus dorcas
NT3 gazella
NT4 gazella gazella
NT4 gazella granti
NT4 gazella thomsonii
NT3 hippotragus
NT4 hippotragus equinus
NT4 hippotragus niger
NT3 kobus
NT4 kobus ellipsiprymnus
NT4 kobus kob
NT4 kobus leche
NT3 oreamnos
NT4 oreamnos americanus
NT3 oryx
NT4 oryx gazella
NT3 ourebia
NT4 ourebia ourebi
NT3 ovibos
NT4 ovibos moschatus
NT3 ovis
NT4 ovis ammon
NT4 ovis canadensis
NT4 ovis dalli
NT3 pelea (mammals)
NT4 pelea capreolus
NT3 redunca
NT4 redunca arundinum
NT4 redunca fulvorufula
NT4 redunca redunca
NT3 rupicapra
NT3 saiga
NT4 saiga tatarica
NT3 sylvicapra
NT4 sylvicapra grimmia
NT3 synceros
NT4 synceros caffer
NT3 tragelaphus
NT4 tragelaphus oryx
NT4 tragelaphus scriptus
NT4 tragelaphus strepsiceros
NT2 cervidae
NT3 alces
NT4 alces alces
NT3 capreolus
NT4 capreolus capreolus
NT3 cervus
NT4 cervus axis
NT4 cervus elaphus
NT5 cervus elaphus canadensis
NT4 cervus nippon
NT4 cervus porcinus
NT4 cervus timorensis
NT4 cervus unicolor
NT3 muntiacus
NT3 odocoileus
NT4 odocoileus hemionus
NT4 odocoileus virginianus
NT3 rangifer
NT2 giraffidae
NT3 giraffa
NT4 giraffa camelopardalis
NT3 okapia
NT4 okapia johnstoni
NT2 tragulidae
NT1 suiformes
NT2 hippopotamidae
NT3 hippopotamus
NT4 hippopotamus amphibius
NT2 suidae
NT3 phacochoerus
NT4 phacochoerus aethiopicus
NT3 potamochoerus
NT4 potamochoerus porcus
NT3 sus
NT4 sus barbatus
NT4 sus scrofa
NT2 tayassuidae
NT3 tayassu
NT4 tayassu tajacu
NT1 tylopoda

ARTIODACTYLA *cont.*
NT2 camelidae
NT3 camelus
NT3 lama
NT4 lama guanicoe

ARTISTS
BT1 occupations
rt amateurs
rt fine arts
rt performers

ARTOCARPUS
BT1 moraceae
NT1 artocarpus altilis
NT1 artocarpus blancoi
NT1 artocarpus chaplasha
NT1 artocarpus elasticus
NT1 artocarpus heterophyllus
NT1 artocarpus hirsutus
NT1 artocarpus integer
NT1 artocarpus lakoocha
NT1 artocarpus utilis
rt forest trees

ARTOCARPUS ALTILIS
uf *artocarpus communis*
uf *artocarpus incisa*
BT1 artocarpus
BT2 moraceae
rt breadfruits

ARTOCARPUS BLANCOI
BT1 antibacterial plants
BT1 artocarpus
BT2 moraceae

artocarpus champeden
USE **artocarpus integer**

ARTOCARPUS CHAPLASHA
BT1 artocarpus
BT2 moraceae

artocarpus communis
USE **artocarpus altilis**

ARTOCARPUS ELASTICUS
BT1 artocarpus
BT2 moraceae

ARTOCARPUS HETEROPHYLLUS
uf *artocarpus integra*
BT1 artocarpus
BT2 moraceae
rt jackfruits

ARTOCARPUS HIRSUTUS
BT1 artocarpus
BT2 moraceae

artocarpus incisa
USE **artocarpus altilis**

ARTOCARPUS INTEGER
uf *artocarpus champeden*
uf *artocarpus integrifolius*
BT1 artocarpus
BT2 moraceae
BT1 tropical tree fruits
BT2 tree fruits
BT2 tropical fruits
BT3 fruit crops

artocarpus integra
USE **artocarpus heterophyllus**

artocarpus integrifolius
USE **artocarpus integer**

ARTOCARPUS LAKOOCHA
BT1 artocarpus
BT2 moraceae

ARTOCARPUS UTILIS
BT1 artocarpus
BT2 moraceae
BT1 tropical tree fruits
BT2 tree fruits
BT2 tropical fruits
BT3 fruit crops
rt breadfruits

artogeia
USE **pieris (lepidoptera)**

artogeia melete
USE **pieris melete**

artogeia napi
USE **pieris napi**

artogeia rapae
USE **pieris rapae**

ARTONA
BT1 zygaenidae
BT2 lepidoptera
NT1 artona catoxantha

ARTONA CATOXANTHA
BT1 artona
BT2 zygaenidae
BT3 lepidoptera

ARTS
NT1 culinary arts (agricola)
NT2 carving techniques (agricola)
NT1 fine arts
NT2 graphic arts
NT2 plastic arts
NT3 sculpture
NT3 wood carving
NT2 visual arts
NT1 food art (agricola)
NT2 cake decoration (agricola)
NT1 performing arts
NT2 circuses
NT2 concerts
NT2 dancing
NT3 ballet
NT3 folk dancing
NT3 modern dance
NT2 drama
NT3 acting
NT2 music
NT3 classical music
NT3 folk music
NT3 instrumental music
NT4 orchestras
NT3 pop music
NT4 discos
NT3 vocal music
NT4 choirs
NT4 opera
NT4 singing
NT2 theatre
rt arts activities
rt arts centres
rt arts policy
rt cultural activities
rt cultural behaviour
rt literature
rt patronage

ARTS ACTIVITIES
HN from 1989
rt arts
rt cultural activities
rt leisure activities

ARTS CENTERS
HN from 1989
BF arts centres

ARTS CENTRES
HN from 1989
AF arts centers
BT1 cultural facilities
rt arts
rt cultural centres
rt leisure centres

arts exhibitions
USE **cultural exhibitions**

ARTS POLICY
HN from 1989
rt arts
rt cultural policy
rt leisure policy
rt policy

ARTYFECHINOSTOMUM
BT1 echinostomatidae
BT2 digenea
BT3 trematoda
NT1 artyfechinostomum sufrartyfex

ARTYFECHINOSTOMUM SUFRARTYFEX
BT1 artyfechinostomum
BT2 echinostomatidae
BT3 digenea
BT4 trematoda

ARUBA
BT1 netherlands antilles
BT2 caribbean
BT3 america

ARUM
BT1 araceae
NT1 arum italicum
NT1 arum maculatum
NT1 arum orientale

arum campanulatum
USE **amorphophallus campanulatus**

ARUM ITALICUM
BT1 arum
BT2 araceae
BT1 ornamental bulbs
rt tubers

arum lily
USE **zantedeschia aethiopica**

ARUM MACULATUM
BT1 arum
BT2 araceae

ARUM ORIENTALE
BT1 arum
BT2 araceae

ARUNACHAL PRADESH
BT1 india
BT2 south asia
BT3 asia

ARUNDINA
BT1 orchidaceae
NT1 arundina graminifolia

ARUNDINA GRAMINIFOLIA
BT1 arundina
BT2 orchidaceae
BT1 ornamental orchids

ARUNDINARIA
BT1 gramineae
NT1 arundinaria amabilis
NT1 arundinaria disticha
NT1 arundinaria pygmaea
rt bamboos

ARUNDINARIA AMABILIS
BT1 arundinaria
BT2 gramineae
BT1 ornamental woody plants

ARUNDINARIA DISTICHA
uf *pleioblastus distichus*
BT1 arundinaria
BT2 gramineae
BT1 ornamental woody plants

ARUNDINARIA PYGMAEA
uf *sasa pygmaea*
BT1 arundinaria
BT2 gramineae
BT1 ornamental woody plants

arundinaria vagans
USE **sasaella ramosa**

ARUNDINELLA
BT1 gramineae
NT1 arundinella bengalensis

ARUNDINELLA BENGALENSIS
BT1 arundinella
BT2 gramineae

ARUNDO
BT1 gramineae
NT1 arundo donax

ARUNDO DONAX
BT1 arundo
BT2 gramineae
BT1 medicinal plants

ARVICANTHIS
BT1 murinae
BT2 muridae
BT3 rodents
BT4 mammals
NT1 arvicanthis niloticus

ARVICANTHIS NILOTICUS
BT1 arvicanthis
BT2 murinae
BT3 muridae
BT4 rodents
BT5 mammals

ARVICOLA
BT1 microtinae
BT2 muridae
BT3 rodents
BT4 mammals
NT1 arvicola sapidus
NT1 arvicola terrestris
rt voles

ARVICOLA SAPIDUS
BT1 arvicola
BT2 microtinae
BT3 muridae
BT4 rodents
BT5 mammals

ARVICOLA TERRESTRIS
BT1 arvicola
BT2 microtinae
BT3 muridae
BT4 rodents
BT5 mammals

aryl hydrocarbon hydroxylase
USE **unspecific monooxygenase**

ARYLALANINE HERBICIDES
BT1 anilide herbicides
BT2 amide herbicides
BT3 herbicides
BT4 pesticides
NT1 benzoylprop-ethyl
NT1 flamprop

ARYLESTERASE
(ec 3.1.1.2)
uf *phenyl esterase*
BT1 carboxylic ester hydrolases
BT2 esterases
BT3 hydrolases
BT4 enzymes

ARYLOXYPHENOXYPROPIONIC HERBICIDES
BT1 phenoxypropionic herbicides
BT2 phenoxy herbicides
BT3 herbicides
BT4 pesticides
NT1 chlorazifop
NT1 clofop
NT1 diclofop
NT1 fenoxaprop
NT1 fenthiaprop
NT1 fluazifop
NT1 haloxyfop
NT1 propaquizafop
NT1 quizalofop
NT1 trifop

ARYLSULFATASE
(ec 3.1.6.1)
uf *arylsulphatase*
BT1 sulfuric ester hydrolases
BT2 esterases
BT3 hydrolases
BT4 enzymes

arylsulphatase
USE **arylsulfatase**

ASAPHES
BT1 pteromalidae
BT2 hymenoptera
NT1 asaphes lucens
NT1 asaphes vulgaris

ASAPHES LUCENS
BT1 asaphes
BT2 pteromalidae

ASAPHES LUCENS *cont.*
BT3 hymenoptera

ASAPHES VULGARIS
BT1 asaphes
BT2 pteromalidae
BT3 hymenoptera

ASAPHIDION
BT1 carabidae
BT2 coleoptera
NT1 asaphidion flavipes

ASAPHIDION FLAVIPES
BT1 asaphidion
BT2 carabidae
BT3 coleoptera

ASARUM
BT1 aristolochiaceae
NT1 asarum caudatum
NT1 asarum caulescens
NT1 asarum europaeum

ASARUM CAUDATUM
BT1 asarum
BT2 aristolochiaceae
BT1 ornamental herbaceous plants

ASARUM CAULESCENS
BT1 asarum
BT2 aristolochiaceae

ASARUM EUROPAEUM
BT1 asarum
BT2 aristolochiaceae
BT1 medicinal plants
BT1 ornamental herbaceous plants
rt emetics

ASBESTOS
BT1 carcinogens
BT2 toxic substances
BT1 insulating materials
BT2 materials
BT1 nonclay minerals
BT2 minerals
rt fireproofing

ASCARIASIS
BT1 nematode infections
BT2 helminthoses
BT3 parasitoses
BT4 diseases
rt ascarididae

ASCARIDIA
BT1 ascaridiidae
BT2 nematoda
NT1 ascaridia columbae
NT1 ascaridia galli

ASCARIDIA COLUMBAE
BT1 ascaridia
BT2 ascaridiidae
BT3 nematoda

ASCARIDIA GALLI
BT1 ascaridia
BT2 ascaridiidae
BT3 nematoda

ASCARIDIDAE
uf *ascarids*
BT1 nematoda
NT1 ascaris
NT2 ascaris lumbricoides
NT2 ascaris suum
NT1 lagochilascaris
NT1 ophidascaris
NT1 parascaris
NT2 parascaris equorum
NT1 porrocaecum
NT1 toxascaris
NT2 toxascaris leonina
NT1 toxocara
NT2 toxocara canis
NT2 toxocara cati
NT2 toxocara vitulorum
rt animal parasitic nematodes
rt ascariasis
rt ascaridiosis

ASCARIDIIDAE
BT1 nematoda
NT1 ascaridia
NT2 ascaridia columbae
NT2 ascaridia galli
rt animal parasitic nematodes

ASCARIDIOSIS
BT1 nematode infections
BT2 helminthoses
BT3 parasitoses
BT4 diseases
rt ascarididae

ascarids
USE **ascarididae**

ASCARIS
BT1 ascarididae
BT2 nematoda
NT1 ascaris lumbricoides
NT1 ascaris suum

ASCARIS LUMBRICOIDES
BT1 ascaris
BT2 ascarididae
BT3 nematoda

ASCARIS SUUM
BT1 ascaris
BT2 ascarididae
BT3 nematoda

ASCAROPS
BT1 spirocercidae
BT2 nematoda
NT1 ascarops strongylina

ASCAROPS STRONGYLINA
BT1 ascarops
BT2 spirocercidae
BT3 nematoda

ASCENSION
uf *st. helena (ascension)*
BT1 st. helena
BT2 southern africa
BT3 africa south of sahara
BT4 africa

ASCETOSPORA
BT1 protozoa
NT1 bonamia
NT2 bonamia ostreae
NT1 coelosporidium
NT2 coelosporidium chydoricola
NT1 haplosporidium
NT2 haplosporidium lusitanicum
NT2 haplosporidium nelsoni
NT1 marteilia
NT2 marteilia refringens
NT2 marteilia sidneyi
NT1 minchinia
NT2 minchinia armoricana
NT2 minchinia costalis
NT2 minchinia nelsoni
NT1 urosporidium
NT2 urosporidium spisuli

ASCHERSONIA
BT1 deuteromycotina
NT1 aschersonia aleyrodis

ASCHERSONIA ALEYRODIS
BT1 aschersonia
BT2 deuteromycotina

ASCI
BT1 fungal morphology
BT2 morphology
rt ascomycetes

ASCIDAE
BT1 mesostigmata
BT2 acari
NT1 blattisocius
NT2 blattisocius keegani
NT2 blattisocius tarsalis
NT1 melichares
NT1 proctolaelaps
NT2 proctolaelaps pygmaeus

ASCITES
BT1 exudation
rt oedema

ASCLEPIADACEAE
NT1 ampelamus
NT2 ampelamus albidus
NT1 araujia
NT2 araujia hortorum
NT2 araujia sericofera
NT1 asclepias
NT2 asclepias capricornu
NT2 asclepias curassavica
NT2 asclepias fruticosa
NT2 asclepias incarnata
NT2 asclepias syriaca
NT2 asclepias tuberosa
NT2 asclepias verticillata
NT1 calotropis
NT2 calotropis gigantea
NT2 calotropis procera
NT1 caralluma
NT1 cynanchum
NT2 cynanchum caudatum
NT2 cynanchum unifarium
NT1 dischidia
NT1 gomphocarpus
NT1 gymnema
NT2 gymnema sylvestre
NT1 hoya
NT2 hoya australis
NT2 hoya bella
NT2 hoya carnosa
NT1 kanahia
NT2 kanahia laniflora
NT1 leptadenia
NT2 leptadenia pyrotechnica
NT2 leptadenia reticulata
NT1 marsdenia
NT2 marsdenia erecta
NT2 marsdenia latifolia
NT2 marsdenia tenacissima
NT2 marsdenia tinctoria
NT1 morrenia
NT2 morrenia brachystephana
NT2 morrenia odorata
NT1 orbea
NT2 orbea variegata
NT1 sarcostemma
NT2 sarcostemma clausa
NT1 stapelia
NT1 stephanotis
NT2 stephanotis floribunda
NT1 tylophora
NT2 tylophora asthmatica
NT2 tylophora cordifolia
NT2 tylophora dalzelli
NT2 tylophora indica
NT1 vincetoxicum
NT2 vincetoxicum hirundinaria
NT2 vincetoxicum scandens

ASCLEPIAS
BT1 asclepiadaceae
NT1 asclepias capricornu
NT1 asclepias curassavica
NT1 asclepias fruticosa
NT1 asclepias incarnata
NT1 asclepias syriaca
NT1 asclepias tuberosa
NT1 asclepias verticillata
rt gomphocarpus

ASCLEPIAS CAPRICORNU
BT1 asclepias
BT2 asclepiadaceae

ASCLEPIAS CURASSAVICA
BT1 asclepias
BT2 asclepiadaceae

ASCLEPIAS FRUTICOSA
uf *gomphocarpus fruticosus*
BT1 asclepias
BT2 asclepiadaceae
BT1 medicinal plants

ASCLEPIAS INCARNATA
BT1 asclepias
BT2 asclepiadaceae
BT1 ornamental herbaceous plants

ASCLEPIAS SYRIACA
BT1 asclepias
BT2 asclepiadaceae
BT1 weeds

ASCLEPIAS TUBEROSA
BT1 asclepias
BT2 asclepiadaceae
BT1 insecticidal plants
BT2 pesticidal plants

ASCLEPIAS VERTICILLATA
BT1 asclepias
BT2 asclepiadaceae

ASCOCALYX
HN from 1990
BT1 helotiales
rt gremmeniella

ascocalyx abietina
USE **gremmeniella abietina**

ASCOCENDA
BT1 orchidaceae

ASCOCHYTA
BT1 deuteromycotina
NT1 ascochyta agropyri-repentis
NT1 ascochyta fabae
NT1 ascochyta necans
NT1 ascochyta oryzae
NT1 ascochyta pisi
NT1 ascochyta punctata
NT1 ascochyta rabiei
rt apiocarpella
rt ascochytella
rt didymella
rt mycosphaerella
rt phoma
rt phyllosticta

ascochyta adzamethica
USE **didymosphaeria arachidicola**

ASCOCHYTA AGROPYRI-REPENTIS
HN from 1990
uf *apiocarpella agropyri*
BT1 ascochyta
BT2 deuteromycotina

ascochyta ampelina
USE **ascochytella ampelina**

ascochyta chrysanthemi
USE **didymella chrysanthemi**

ascochyta cucumeris
USE **didymella bryoniae**

ASCOCHYTA FABAE
BT1 ascochyta
BT2 deuteromycotina

ascochyta hortorum
USE **phoma exigua**

ascochyta imperfecta
USE **phoma medicaginis**

ascochyta lycopersici
USE **didymella lycopersici**

ASCOCHYTA NECANS
HN from 1990
uf *ascochyta pteridis*
BT1 ascochyta
BT2 deuteromycotina

ASCOCHYTA ORYZAE
BT1 ascochyta
BT2 deuteromycotina

ascochyta pinodella
USE **phoma medicaginis var. pinodella**

ascochyta pinodes
USE **mycosphaerella pinodes**

ASCOCHYTA PISI
BT1 ascochyta
BT2 deuteromycotina

ascochyta pteridis
USE **ascochyta necans**

ASCOCHYTA PUNCTATA
BT1 ascochyta

ASCOCHYTA PUNCTATA *cont.*
BT2 deuteromycotina

ASCOCHYTA RABIEI
uf *didymella rabiei*
uf *phyllosticta rabiei*
BT1 ascochyta
BT2 deuteromycotina

ASCOCHYTELLA
HN from 1990
BT1 deuteromycotina
NT1 ascochytella ampelina
rt ascochyta

ASCOCHYTELLA AMPELINA
HN from 1990
uf *ascochyta ampelina*
BT1 ascochytella
BT2 deuteromycotina

ASCOGASTER
BT1 braconidae
BT2 hymenoptera
NT1 ascogaster quadridentata

ASCOGASTER QUADRIDENTATA
BT1 ascogaster
BT2 braconidae
BT3 hymenoptera
BT1 biological control agents
BT2 beneficial organisms

ASCOGREGARINA
BT1 apicomplexa
BT2 protozoa
NT1 ascogregarina barretti

ASCOGREGARINA BARRETTI
BT1 ascogregarina
BT2 apicomplexa
BT3 protozoa

ASCOMYCETES
rt asci
rt ascospores
rt fungi

ASCORBATE OXIDASE
(ec 1.10.3.3)
uf *ascorbic acid oxidase*
BT1 oxidoreductases
BT2 enzymes

ASCORBIC ACID
uf *vitamin c*
BT1 antioxidants
BT2 additives
BT1 ascorbic acids
BT2 aldonic acids
BT3 sugar acids
BT4 carboxylic acids
BT5 organic acids
BT6 acids
BT4 monosaccharides
BT5 carbohydrates
BT1 water-soluble vitamins
BT2 vitamins
rt scurvy
rt vitamin c antagonists

ascorbic acid oxidase
USE **ascorbate oxidase**

ASCORBIC ACIDS
BT1 aldonic acids
BT2 sugar acids
BT3 carboxylic acids
BT4 organic acids
BT5 acids
BT3 monosaccharides
BT4 carbohydrates
NT1 ascorbic acid
NT1 dehydroascorbic acid
NT1 diketogulonic acid
NT1 isoascorbic acid

ASCOSCHOENGASTIA
uf *eltonella*
BT1 trombiculidae
BT2 prostigmata
BT3 acari

ASCOSPHAERA
BT1 ascosphaerales

ASCOSPHAERA *cont.*
BT1 entomogenous fungi
BT2 entomopathogens
BT3 pathogens
BT2 fungi
NT1 ascosphaera apis

ASCOSPHAERA APIS
BT1 ascosphaera
BT2 ascosphaerales
BT2 entomogenous fungi
BT3 entomopathogens
BT4 pathogens
BT3 fungi
rt chalk brood

ASCOSPHAERALES
NT1 ascosphaera
NT2 ascosphaera apis
rt fungi

ASCOSPORES
BT1 fungal spores
BT2 spores
BT3 cells
rt ascomycetes

ASCOTIS
BT1 geometridae
BT2 lepidoptera
NT1 ascotis selenaria

ASCOTIS SELENARIA
uf boarmia selenaria
BT1 ascotis
BT2 geometridae
BT3 lepidoptera

ASCOVIRUS
BT1 insect viruses
BT2 entomopathogens
BT3 pathogens
BT1 unclassified viruses
BT2 viruses

ASEAN
(association of south east asian nations)
BT1 international organizations
BT2 organizations
rt brunei
rt economic regions
rt indonesia
rt malaysia
rt philippines
rt singapore
rt thailand

ASELLIDAE
BT1 isopoda
BT2 malacostraca
BT3 crustacea
BT4 arthropods
NT1 asellus
NT2 asellus aquaticus

ASELLUS
BT1 asellidae
BT2 isopoda
BT3 malacostraca
BT4 crustacea
BT5 arthropods
NT1 asellus aquaticus

ASELLUS AQUATICUS
BT1 asellus
BT2 asellidae
BT3 isopoda
BT4 malacostraca
BT5 crustacea
BT6 arthropods

ASEPTIC PACKAGING
BT1 packaging
BT2 handling
rt aseptic state (agricola)
rt contamination

ASEPTIC STATE (AGRICOLA)
rt aseptic packaging
rt sterilizing

ASEXUAL REPRODUCTION
uf reproduction, vegetative

ASEXUAL REPRODUCTION *cont.*
uf vegetative reproduction
BT1 reproduction
NT1 apomixis
NT1 parthenocarpy
rt clones
rt sexual reproduction
rt vegetative propagation

ASH
NT1 bone ash
NT1 fly ash
NT1 volcanic ash
NT1 wood ash
rt ashing
rt burning
rt fires

ASH DUMPS
BT1 land types

ash trees
USE **fraxinus**

ASHING
BT1 burning
BT1 sample processing
BT2 processing
rt ash
rt combustion

ASHMEADIELLA
BT1 apidae
BT2 hymenoptera

ASHWORTHIUS
BT1 trichostrongylidae
BT2 nematoda

ASIA
NT1 east asia
NT2 china
NT3 anhui
NT3 beijing
NT3 central southern china
NT3 eastern china
NT3 fujian
NT3 gansu
NT3 guangdong
NT3 guangxi
NT3 guizhou
NT3 hebei
NT3 heilongjiang
NT3 henan
NT3 hubei
NT3 hunan
NT3 jiangsu
NT3 jiangxi
NT3 jilin
NT3 liaoning
NT3 nei menggu
NT3 ningxia
NT3 north eastern china
NT3 north western china
NT3 northern china
NT3 qinghai
NT3 shaanxi
NT3 shandong
NT3 shanghai
NT3 shanxi
NT3 sichuan
NT3 south western china
NT3 tianjin
NT3 tibet
NT3 xinjiang
NT3 yunnan
NT3 zhejiang
NT2 hong kong
NT2 japan
NT3 hokkaido
NT3 honshu
NT3 kyushu
NT3 ryukyu archipelago
NT3 shikoku
NT2 korea democratic people's republic
NT2 korea republic
NT2 macao
NT2 mongolia
NT2 ussr far east
NT1 south asia
NT2 bangladesh
NT3 chittagong

ASIA *cont.*
NT3 dacca
NT3 khulna
NT3 rajshahi
NT2 bhutan
NT2 india
NT3 andaman and nicobar islands
NT3 andhra pradesh
NT3 arunachal pradesh
NT3 assam
NT3 bihar
NT3 chandigarh
NT3 dadra and nagar haveli
NT3 delhi
NT3 goa, daman and diu
NT3 gujarat
NT3 haryana
NT3 himachal pradesh
NT3 indian punjab
NT3 jammu and kashmir
NT3 karnataka
NT3 kerala
NT3 laccadive, minicoy and amindivi is.
NT3 lakshadweep
NT3 madhya pradesh
NT3 maharashtra
NT3 manipur
NT3 meghalaya
NT3 mizoram
NT3 nagaland
NT3 orissa
NT3 pondicherry
NT3 rajasthan
NT3 sikkim
NT3 tamil nadu
NT3 tripura
NT3 uttar pradesh
NT3 west bengal
NT2 maldives
NT2 nepal
NT2 pakistan
NT3 baluchistan
NT3 islamabad
NT3 pakistan northwest frontier
NT3 pakistan punjab
NT3 pakistan tribal areas
NT3 sind
NT2 sri lanka
NT1 south east asia
NT2 brunei
NT2 burma
NT2 cambodia
NT2 indonesia
NT3 bali
NT3 irian jaya
NT3 java
NT3 kalimantan
NT3 lombok
NT3 loro sae
NT3 madura
NT3 maluku
NT3 nusa tenggara
NT3 sulawesi
NT3 sumatra
NT3 sunda islands
NT3 timur
NT2 lao
NT2 malaysia
NT3 peninsular malaysia
NT3 sabah
NT3 sarawak
NT2 philippines
NT2 singapore
NT2 taiwan
NT2 thailand
NT2 vietnam
NT1 west asia
NT2 afghanistan
NT2 cyprus
NT2 iran
NT2 iraq
NT2 israel
NT2 jordan
NT2 lebanon
NT2 oman
NT2 persian gulf states
NT3 bahrain
NT3 kuwait

ASIA *cont.*
NT3 qatar
NT3 united arab emirates
NT4 abu dhabi
NT4 ajman
NT4 dubai
NT4 fujairah
NT4 ras al khaimah
NT4 sharjah
NT4 umm al qaiwain
NT2 saudi arabia
NT2 syria
NT2 turkey
NT2 yemen arab republic
NT2 yemen democratic republic
NT3 socotra
rt developing countries
rt middle east
rt tropical asia

asia, east
USE **east asia**

asia, south
USE **south asia**

asia, south east
USE **south east asia**

asia, west
USE **west asia**

ASIAGO CHEESE
HN from 1989
BT1 cheeses
BT2 milk products
BT3 products

ASIANS (AGRICOLA)
BT1 ethnic groups
BT2 groups

ASIMINA
BT1 annonaceae
NT1 asimina parviflora
NT1 asimina triloba

ASIMINA PARVIFLORA
BT1 asimina
BT2 annonaceae

ASIMINA TRILOBA
uf papaw (asimina)
BT1 asimina
BT2 annonaceae
BT1 ornamental woody plants
BT1 subtropical tree fruits
BT2 subtropical fruits
BT3 fruit crops
BT2 tree fruits

ASIO
BT1 strigidae
BT2 strigiformes
BT3 birds
NT1 asio flammeus
NT1 asio otus

ASIO FLAMMEUS
BT1 asio
BT2 strigidae
BT3 strigiformes
BT4 birds

ASIO OTUS
BT1 asio
BT2 strigidae
BT3 strigiformes
BT4 birds

ASKANIAN
BT1 sheep breeds
BT2 breeds

asolcus
USE **trissolcus**

asolcus semistriatus
USE **trissolcus semistriatus**

ASPARAGINASE
(ec 3.5.1.1)
BT1 amide hydrolases
BT2 hydrolases
BT3 enzymes

ASPARAGINE
BT1 nonessential amino acids
BT2 amino acids
BT3 carboxylic acids
BT4 organic acids
BT5 acids
BT3 organic nitrogen compounds

asparagine aminotransferase
USE **asparagine-oxo-acid aminotransferase**

ASPARAGINE-OXO-ACID AMINOTRANSFERASE
(ec 2.6.1.14)
uf *asparagine aminotransferase*
BT1 aminotransferases
BT2 transferases
BT3 enzymes

asparagine synthetase
USE **aspartate-ammonia ligase**

ASPARAGUS
BT1 liliaceae
NT1 asparagus adscendens
NT1 asparagus densiflorus
NT1 asparagus falcatus
NT1 asparagus myriocladus
NT1 asparagus officinalis
NT1 asparagus racemosus
NT1 asparagus retrofractus
NT1 asparagus setaceus
NT1 asparagus tenuifolius
NT1 asparagus virgatus
rt asparagus 2 ilarvirus
rt spears
rt stem vegetables

ASPARAGUS ADSCENDENS
BT1 asparagus
BT2 liliaceae

ASPARAGUS DENSIFLORUS
uf *asparagus meyeri*
uf *asparagus sprengeri*
BT1 asparagus
BT2 liliaceae
rt ornamental foliage plants

ASPARAGUS FALCATUS
BT1 asparagus
BT2 liliaceae
rt ornamental foliage plants

ASPARAGUS 2 ILARVIRUS
HN from 1990; previously "asparagus virus 2"
uf *asparagus virus 2*
BT1 ilarvirus
rt asparagus

asparagus meyeri
USE **asparagus densiflorus**

ASPARAGUS MYRIOCLADUS
BT1 asparagus
BT2 liliaceae

ASPARAGUS OFFICINALIS
BT1 asparagus
BT2 liliaceae

asparagus plumosus
USE **asparagus setaceus**

ASPARAGUS RACEMOSUS
BT1 antifungal plants
BT1 asparagus
BT2 liliaceae
BT1 medicinal plants

ASPARAGUS RETROFRACTUS
BT1 asparagus
BT2 liliaceae
rt ornamental foliage plants

ASPARAGUS SETACEUS
uf *asparagus plumosus*
BT1 asparagus
BT2 liliaceae
BT1 molluscicidal plants
BT2 pesticidal plants
rt ornamental foliage plants

asparagus sprengeri
USE **asparagus densiflorus**

ASPARAGUS TENUIFOLIUS
BT1 asparagus
BT2 liliaceae
rt ornamental foliage plants

ASPARAGUS VIRGATUS
BT1 asparagus
BT2 liliaceae
rt ornamental foliage plants

asparagus virus 2
USE **asparagus 2 ilarvirus**

ASPARTAME
BT1 artificial sweeteners
BT2 sugar substitutes
BT3 substitutes
BT3 sweeteners
BT4 food additives
BT5 additives
BT1 dipeptides
BT2 oligopeptides
BT3 peptides
BT1 sweet tasting compounds
BT2 flavour compounds

ASPARTATE AMINOTRANSFERASE
(ec 2.6.1.1)
uf *glutamate oxaloacetate transaminase*
uf *glutamic oxaloacetic transaminase*
uf *got*
BT1 aminotransferases
BT2 transferases
BT3 enzymes

ASPARTATE-AMMONIA LIGASE
(ec 6.3.1.1)
uf *asparagine synthetase*
BT1 amide synthases
BT2 ligases
BT3 enzymes

ASPARTIC ACID
BT1 nonessential amino acids
BT2 amino acids
BT3 carboxylic acids
BT4 organic acids
BT5 acids
BT3 organic nitrogen compounds

ASPASIA
BT1 orchidaceae
rt ornamental plants

ASPECT
BT1 topography
rt gradients
rt slope

ASPERGILLIC ACID
BT1 antibacterial agents
BT2 antiinfective agents
BT3 drugs
BT1 antibiotics

ASPERGILLOMA
BT1 aspergillosis
BT2 mycoses
BT3 infectious diseases
BT4 diseases
BT2 respiratory diseases
BT3 organic diseases
BT4 diseases
rt aspergillus

ASPERGILLOSIS
BT1 mycoses
BT2 infectious diseases
BT3 diseases
BT1 respiratory diseases
BT2 organic diseases
BT3 diseases
NT1 allergic bronchopulmonary aspergillosis
NT1 aspergilloma
rt aspergillus

ASPERGILLUS
BT1 deuteromycotina
NT1 aspergillus aculeatus
NT1 aspergillus awamori
NT1 aspergillus bicolor
NT1 aspergillus candidus
NT1 aspergillus corneus
NT1 aspergillus flavipes
NT1 aspergillus flavus
NT1 aspergillus fumigatus
NT1 aspergillus glaucus
NT1 aspergillus nidulans
NT1 aspergillus niger
NT1 aspergillus ochraceus
NT1 aspergillus oryzae
NT1 aspergillus parasiticus
NT1 aspergillus spectabilis
NT1 aspergillus terreus
NT1 aspergillus variecolor
NT1 aspergillus versicolor
rt allergic bronchopulmonary aspergillosis
rt aspergilloma
rt aspergillosis
rt stone brood

ASPERGILLUS ACULEATUS
BT1 aspergillus
BT2 deuteromycotina

ASPERGILLUS AWAMORI
BT1 aspergillus
BT2 deuteromycotina

ASPERGILLUS BICOLOR
BT1 aspergillus
BT2 deuteromycotina

ASPERGILLUS CANDIDUS
BT1 aspergillus
BT2 deuteromycotina

ASPERGILLUS CORNEUS
BT1 aspergillus
BT2 deuteromycotina

ASPERGILLUS FLAVIPES
HN from 1989
BT1 aspergillus
BT2 deuteromycotina

ASPERGILLUS FLAVUS
BT1 aspergillus
BT2 deuteromycotina

ASPERGILLUS FUMIGATUS
BT1 aspergillus
BT2 deuteromycotina

ASPERGILLUS GLAUCUS
BT1 aspergillus
BT2 deuteromycotina

ASPERGILLUS NIDULANS
BT1 aspergillus
BT2 deuteromycotina

ASPERGILLUS NIGER
BT1 aspergillus
BT2 deuteromycotina

ASPERGILLUS OCHRACEUS
BT1 aspergillus
BT2 deuteromycotina

ASPERGILLUS ORYZAE
BT1 aspergillus
BT2 deuteromycotina

ASPERGILLUS PARASITICUS
BT1 aspergillus
BT2 deuteromycotina

ASPERGILLUS SPECTABILIS
BT1 aspergillus
BT2 deuteromycotina

ASPERGILLUS TERREUS
BT1 aspergillus
BT2 deuteromycotina

ASPERGILLUS VARIECOLOR
BT1 aspergillus
BT2 deuteromycotina

ASPERGILLUS VERSICOLOR
BT1 aspergillus
BT2 deuteromycotina

ASPERISPORIUM
uf *pucciniopsis*
BT1 deuteromycotina
NT1 asperisporium caricae

ASPERISPORIUM CARICAE
uf *pucciniopsis caricae*
BT1 asperisporium
BT2 deuteromycotina

asphalt
USE **bitumen**

asphalt emulsions
USE **bitumen emulsions**

ASPHODELUS
BT1 liliaceae
NT1 asphodelus albus
NT1 asphodelus cerasiferus
NT1 asphodelus fistulosus
NT1 asphodelus microcarpus
NT1 asphodelus tenuifolius

ASPHODELUS ALBUS
BT1 asphodelus
BT2 liliaceae

ASPHODELUS CERASIFERUS
BT1 asphodelus
BT2 liliaceae

ASPHODELUS FISTULOSUS
BT1 asphodelus
BT2 liliaceae

ASPHODELUS MICROCARPUS
BT1 asphodelus
BT2 liliaceae
BT1 dye plants

ASPHODELUS TENUIFOLIUS
BT1 asphodelus
BT2 liliaceae

ASPHONDYLIA
BT1 cecidomyiidae
BT2 diptera
NT1 asphondylia sesami

ASPHONDYLIA SESAMI
BT1 asphondylia
BT2 cecidomyiidae
BT3 diptera

ASPHYXIA
BT1 respiratory disorders
BT2 functional disorders
BT3 animal disorders
BT4 disorders
BT2 respiratory diseases
BT3 organic diseases
BT4 diseases
rt oxygen
rt respiration

ASPICULURIS
BT1 heteroxynematidae
BT2 nematoda

ASPIDIACEAE
NT1 arachniodes
NT2 arachniodes adiantiformis
NT1 ctenitis
NT2 ctenitis ampla
NT2 ctenitis apiciflora
NT2 ctenitis clarkei
NT2 ctenitis nidus
NT1 cyrtomium
NT2 cyrtomium falcatum
NT1 dryopteris
NT2 dryopteris affinis
NT2 dryopteris assimilis
NT2 dryopteris carthusiana
NT2 dryopteris chrysocoma
NT2 dryopteris cochleata
NT2 dryopteris erythrosora
NT2 dryopteris filix-mas
NT2 dryopteris marginalis
NT1 matteuccia
NT2 matteuccia struthiopteris

ASPIDIACEAE *cont.*
NT1 peranema
NT2 peranema cyantheoides
NT1 polystichum
NT2 polystichum munitum
NT2 polystichum setiferum
NT1 rumohra
NT1 tectaria
NT2 tectaria variolosa
NT1 woodsia
NT2 woodsia obtusa

aspidiotiphagus
USE **encarsia**

aspidiotiphagus citrinus
USE **encarsia citrina**

ASPIDIOTUS
BT1 diaspididae
BT2 coccoidea
BT3 sternorrhyncha
BT4 homoptera
NT1 aspidiotus destructor
NT1 aspidiotus nerii
rt abgrallaspis
rt quadraspidiotus

aspidiotus cyanophylli
USE **abgrallaspis cyanophylli**

ASPIDIOTUS DESTRUCTOR
BT1 aspidiotus
BT2 diaspididae
BT3 coccoidea
BT4 sternorrhyncha
BT5 homoptera

ASPIDIOTUS NERII
BT1 aspidiotus
BT2 diaspididae
BT3 coccoidea
BT4 sternorrhyncha
BT5 homoptera

aspidiotus perniciosus
USE **quadraspidiotus perniciosus**

ASPIDISTRA
BT1 liliaceae
rt ornamental foliage plants

ASPIDOBOTHRIA
uf *aspidogastrea*
BT1 trematoda
NT1 aspidogasteridae
NT2 aspidogaster
NT3 aspidogaster conchicola
NT2 lobatostoma
NT3 lobatostoma manteri

ASPIDOGASTER
BT1 aspidogasteridae
BT2 aspidobothria
BT3 trematoda
NT1 aspidogaster conchicola

ASPIDOGASTER CONCHICOLA
BT1 aspidogaster
BT2 aspidogasteridae
BT3 aspidobothria
BT4 trematoda

ASPIDOGASTERIDAE
BT1 aspidobothria
BT2 trematoda
NT1 aspidogaster
NT2 aspidogaster conchicola
NT1 lobatostoma
NT2 lobatostoma manteri

aspidogastrea
USE **aspidobothria**

ASPIDOSPERMA
BT1 apocynaceae
NT1 aspidosperma cuspa
NT1 aspidosperma exalatum
NT1 aspidosperma nitidum
NT1 aspidosperma polyneuron
NT1 aspidosperma quebrachoblanco
NT1 aspidosperma rhombeosignatum

ASPIDOSPERMA CUSPA
BT1 aspidosperma
BT2 apocynaceae

ASPIDOSPERMA EXALATUM
BT1 aspidosperma
BT2 apocynaceae

ASPIDOSPERMA NITIDUM
BT1 aspidosperma
BT2 apocynaceae

ASPIDOSPERMA POLYNEURON
BT1 aspidosperma
BT2 apocynaceae

ASPIDOSPERMA QUEBRACHOBLANCO
BT1 aspidosperma
BT2 apocynaceae
BT1 tan plants

ASPIDOSPERMA RHOMBEOSIGNATUM
BT1 aspidosperma
BT2 apocynaceae

ASPIRATED PSYCHROMETERS
BT1 psychrometers
BT2 instruments

ASPIRATION
BT1 respiration
BT2 physiology

ASPIRATIONS
BT1 attitudes
rt career development
rt educational opportunities
rt personal development
rt roles

ASPIRATORS
BT1 equipment
rt air flow
rt respiration
rt seed cleaners
rt separators
rt winnowing seed cleaners

ASPIRIN
uf *acetylsalicylic acid*
BT1 analgesics
BT2 neurotropic drugs
BT3 drugs
BT1 antitranspirants
BT1 salicylic acids
BT2 phenolic acids
BT3 benzoic acids
BT4 aromatic acids
BT5 aromatic compounds
BT5 organic acids
BT6 acids
BT3 phenolic compounds
BT4 aromatic compounds

ASPLENIACEAE
NT1 asplenium
NT2 asplenium adiantum-nigrum
NT2 asplenium bulbiferum
NT2 asplenium exiguum
NT2 asplenium hispidulum
NT2 asplenium nidus
NT2 asplenium platyneuron
NT2 asplenium trichomanes
NT1 phyllitis
NT2 phyllitis scolopendrium

ASPLENIUM
BT1 aspleniaceae
NT1 asplenium adiantum-nigrum
NT1 asplenium bulbiferum
NT1 asplenium exiguum
NT1 asplenium hispidulum
NT1 asplenium nidus
NT1 asplenium platyneuron
NT1 asplenium trichomanes

ASPLENIUM ADIANTUM-NIGRUM
BT1 asplenium
BT2 aspleniaceae

ASPLENIUM BULBIFERUM
BT1 asplenium

ASPLENIUM BULBIFERUM *cont.*
BT2 aspleniaceae
BT1 ornamental ferns
BT2 ferns
BT2 ornamental foliage plants
BT3 foliage plants

ASPLENIUM EXIGUUM
BT1 asplenium
BT2 aspleniaceae

asplenium filix-femina
USE **athyrium filix-femina**

ASPLENIUM HISPIDULUM
BT1 asplenium
BT2 aspleniaceae

ASPLENIUM NIDUS
uf *asplenium nidus-avis*
BT1 asplenium
BT2 aspleniaceae
BT1 ornamental ferns
BT2 ferns
BT2 ornamental foliage plants
BT3 foliage plants

asplenium nidus-avis
USE **asplenium nidus**

ASPLENIUM PLATYNEURON
BT1 asplenium
BT2 aspleniaceae
BT1 ornamental ferns
BT2 ferns
BT2 ornamental foliage plants
BT3 foliage plants

ASPLENIUM TRICHOMANES
BT1 asplenium
BT2 aspleniaceae
BT1 ornamental ferns
BT2 ferns
BT2 ornamental foliage plants
BT3 foliage plants

ass breeds
USE **donkey breeds**

ASSAM
BT1 india
BT2 south asia
BT3 asia

ASSAM HILL
BT1 goat breeds
BT2 breeds

ASSAYS
NT1 bioassays
NT1 immunoassay
NT2 chemiluminescence immunoassays
NT2 enzyme immunoassay
NT3 elisa
NT2 radioimmunoassay
NT3 rast
rt analysis
rt milk testing
rt tests
rt trials

ASSERTIVENESS (AGRICOLA)
uf *assertiveness training*
BT1 behavior
rt behavior modification (agricola)
rt stress management (agricola)

assertiveness training
USE **assertiveness (agricola)**

asses
USE **donkeys**

ASSESSMENT
BT1 estimation
rt controls (experimental)
rt taxes

ASSETS
uf *investments*
NT1 fixed capital
NT1 working capital

ASSETS *cont.*
rt accounts
rt balance sheets
rt book-keeping
rt capital
rt capital formation
rt funds
rt stocks (financial) (agricola)

ASSIMILATION
rt metabolism
rt net assimilation rate

associations
USE **farmers' associations**
OR **organizations**
OR **trade associations**

ASSORTATIVE MATING
HN from 1989
BT1 mating systems

ASSORTMENTS
uf *assortments and assortment tables*
rt mensuration
rt volume tables

assortments and assortment tables
USE **assortments**

ASTACUS
BT1 decapoda
BT2 malacostraca
BT3 crustacea
BT4 arthropods
rt crayfish

ASTASIA
BT1 sarcomastigophora
BT2 protozoa

ASTAXANTHIN
BT1 xanthophylls
BT2 carotenoids
BT3 lipochromes
BT4 pigments
BT3 terpenoids
BT4 isoprenoids
BT5 lipids

ASTELIA
BT1 liliaceae
rt ornamental herbaceous plants

ASTER
uf *michaelmas daisy*
BT1 compositae
NT1 aster alpinus
NT1 aster dumosus
NT1 aster ericoides
NT1 aster lateriflorus
NT1 aster linosyris
NT1 aster novae-angliae
NT1 aster novi-belgii
NT1 aster pilosus
NT1 aster scaber
NT1 aster sibiricus
NT1 aster spathulifolius
NT1 aster spinosus
NT1 aster squamatus
NT1 aster subulatus
NT1 aster tataricus
NT1 aster tripolium
NT1 aster umbellatus
NT1 aster vimineus
rt aster yellows

ASTER ALPINUS
BT1 antifungal plants
BT1 aster
BT2 compositae
BT1 ornamental herbaceous plants

aster, china
USE **callistephus chinensis**

ASTER DUMOSUS
BT1 aster
BT2 compositae

ASTER ERICOIDES
BT1 aster
BT2 compositae

ASTER LATERIFLORUS
BT1 aster
BT2 compositae

ASTER LINOSYRIS
BT1 aster
BT2 compositae
BT1 ornamental herbaceous plants

ASTER NOVAE-ANGLIAE
BT1 aster
BT2 compositae
BT1 ornamental herbaceous plants

ASTER NOVI-BELGII
BT1 aster
BT2 compositae
BT1 ornamental herbaceous plants

ASTER PILOSUS
BT1 aster
BT2 compositae

ASTER SCABER
BT1 aster
BT2 compositae

ASTER SIBIRICUS
BT1 aster
BT2 compositae

ASTER SPATHULIFOLIUS
BT1 aster
BT2 compositae

ASTER SPINOSUS
BT1 aster
BT2 compositae

ASTER SQUAMATUS
BT1 aster
BT2 compositae

ASTER SUBULATUS
BT1 aster
BT2 compositae

ASTER TATARICUS
BT1 aster
BT2 compositae
BT1 medicinal plants

ASTER TRIPOLIUM
BT1 aster
BT2 compositae

ASTER UMBELLATUS
BT1 aster
BT2 compositae

ASTER VIMINEUS
BT1 aster
BT2 compositae

ASTER YELLOWS
BT1 plant diseases
rt aster

asteraceae
USE **compositae**

ASTERIONELLA
BT1 bacillariophyta
BT2 algae
NT1 asterionella formosa

ASTERIONELLA FORMOSA
BT1 asterionella
BT2 bacillariophyta
BT3 algae

ASTEROLECANIIDAE
BT1 coccoidea
BT2 sternorrhyncha
BT3 homoptera
NT1 asterolecanium
NT2 asterolecanium pustulans

ASTEROLECANIUM
BT1 asterolecaniidae
BT2 coccoidea
BT3 sternorrhyncha
BT4 homoptera
NT1 asterolecanium pustulans

ASTEROLECANIUM PUSTULANS
BT1 asterolecanium
BT2 asterolecaniidae
BT3 coccoidea
BT4 sternorrhyncha
BT5 homoptera

ASTEROMELLA
BT1 deuteromycotina
NT1 asteromella mali
rt phyllosticta

ASTEROMELLA MALI
uf *phyllosticta mali*
BT1 asteromella
BT2 deuteromycotina

ASTHMA
BT1 respiratory disorders
BT2 functional disorders
BT3 animal disorders
BT4 disorders
BT2 respiratory diseases
BT3 organic diseases
BT4 diseases
rt atopy
rt immediate hypersensitivity

ASTIGMATA
uf *acaridida*
BT1 acari
NT1 acaridae
NT2 acarus
NT3 acarus farris
NT3 acarus siro
NT2 aleuroglyphus
NT3 aleuroglyphus ovatus
NT2 caloglyphus
NT3 caloglyphus berlesei
NT2 rhizoglyphus
NT3 rhizoglyphus callae
NT3 rhizoglyphus echinopus
NT3 rhizoglyphus robini
NT2 tyrophagus
NT3 tyrophagus longior
NT3 tyrophagus perniciosus
NT3 tyrophagus putrescentiae
NT1 analgidae
NT2 megninia
NT3 megninia cubitalis
NT3 megninia ginglymura
NT1 atopomelidae
NT2 chirodiscoides
NT3 chirodiscoides caviae
NT1 carpoglyphidae
NT2 carpoglyphus
NT3 carpoglyphus lactis
NT1 chortoglyphidae
NT2 chortoglyphus
NT3 chortoglyphus arcuatus
NT1 falculiferidae
NT2 pterophagus
NT3 pterophagus strictus
NT1 glycyphagidae
NT2 blomia
NT3 blomia tjibodas
NT3 blomia tropicalis
NT2 glycyphagus
NT3 glycyphagus domesticus
NT2 gohieria
NT3 gohieria fusca
NT2 lepidoglyphus
NT3 lepidoglyphus destructor
NT1 histiostomatidae
NT2 histiostoma
NT1 knemidokoptidae
NT2 knemidokoptes
NT3 knemidokoptes mutans
NT3 knemidokoptes pilae
NT1 lardoglyphidae
NT2 lardoglyphus
NT3 lardoglyphus konoi
NT1 listrophoridae
NT2 leporacarus
NT3 leporacarus gibbus

ASTIGMATA *cont.*
NT2 listrophorus
NT1 myocoptidae
NT2 myocoptes
NT3 myocoptes musculinus
NT1 psoroptidae
NT2 chorioptes
NT3 chorioptes bovis
NT2 otodectes
NT3 otodectes cynotis
NT2 psoroptes
NT3 psoroptes cuniculi
NT3 psoroptes equi
NT3 psoroptes ovis
NT1 pyroglyphidae
NT2 dermatophagoides
NT3 dermatophagoides farinae
NT3 dermatophagoides microceras
NT3 dermatophagoides pteronyssinus
NT3 dermatophagoides scheremetewskyi
NT2 euroglyphus
NT3 euroglyphus maynei
NT2 hirstia
NT2 sturnophagoides
NT1 sarcoptidae
NT2 notoedres
NT3 notoedres cati
NT2 sarcoptes
NT3 sarcoptes scabiei
NT2 trixacarus
NT3 trixacarus caviae
NT1 winterschmidtiidae
NT2 suidasia
NT3 suidasia pontifica

ASTILBE
BT1 saxifragaceae
rt ornamental herbaceous plants

ASTRAEACEAE
NT1 astraeus
NT2 astraeus hygrometricus

ASTRAEUS
BT1 astraeaceae
NT1 astraeus hygrometricus

ASTRAEUS HYGROMETRICUS
BT1 astraeus
BT2 astraeaceae

ASTRAGALUS
BT1 leguminosae
NT1 astragalus adscendens
NT1 astragalus ammodendron
NT1 astragalus armatus
NT1 astragalus bisulcatus
NT1 astragalus borissovae
NT1 astragalus brachycarpus
NT1 astragalus brachyceras
NT1 astragalus canadensis
NT1 astragalus cicer
NT1 astragalus coluteocarpus
NT1 astragalus crotalariae
NT1 astragalus dasyanthus
NT1 astragalus emoryanus
NT1 astragalus falcatus
NT1 astragalus flexus
NT1 astragalus frigidus
NT1 astragalus galegiformis
NT1 astragalus glycyphylloides
NT1 astragalus glycyphyllos
NT1 astragalus heydei
NT1 astragalus kodschorensis
NT1 astragalus lasiopetalus
NT1 astragalus lentiginosus
NT1 astragalus miser
NT1 astragalus mollissimus
NT1 astragalus praelongus
NT1 astragalus racemosus
NT1 astragalus rhizanthus
NT1 astragalus sclerocarpus
NT1 astragalus severtzovii
NT1 astragalus sieversianus
NT1 astragalus sinicus
NT1 astragalus striatus
NT1 astragalus troitskyi
NT1 astragalus ugamicus

ASTRAGALUS *cont.*
NT1 astragalus wootonii
rt loco weed
rt miserotoxin

ASTRAGALUS ADSCENDENS
BT1 astragalus
BT2 leguminosae

ASTRAGALUS AMMODENDRON
BT1 astragalus
BT2 leguminosae

ASTRAGALUS ARMATUS
BT1 astragalus
BT2 leguminosae

ASTRAGALUS BISULCATUS
BT1 astragalus
BT2 leguminosae

ASTRAGALUS BORISSOVAE
BT1 astragalus
BT2 leguminosae

ASTRAGALUS BRACHYCARPUS
BT1 astragalus
BT2 leguminosae

ASTRAGALUS BRACHYCERAS
BT1 astragalus
BT2 leguminosae

ASTRAGALUS CANADENSIS
BT1 astragalus
BT2 leguminosae

ASTRAGALUS CICER
BT1 astragalus
BT2 leguminosae

ASTRAGALUS COLUTEOCARPUS
BT1 astragalus
BT2 leguminosae
BT1 pasture legumes
BT2 legumes
BT2 pasture plants

ASTRAGALUS CROTALARIAE
BT1 astragalus
BT2 leguminosae
BT1 pasture legumes
BT2 legumes
BT2 pasture plants

ASTRAGALUS DASYANTHUS
BT1 astragalus
BT2 leguminosae
BT1 medicinal plants

ASTRAGALUS EMORYANUS
BT1 astragalus
BT2 leguminosae
BT1 poisonous plants

ASTRAGALUS FALCATUS
BT1 astragalus
BT2 leguminosae

ASTRAGALUS FLEXUS
BT1 astragalus
BT2 leguminosae

ASTRAGALUS FRIGIDUS
BT1 astragalus
BT2 leguminosae

ASTRAGALUS GALEGIFORMIS
BT1 astragalus
BT2 leguminosae

ASTRAGALUS GLYCYPHYLLOIDES
BT1 astragalus
BT2 leguminosae
BT1 pasture legumes
BT2 legumes
BT2 pasture plants

ASTRAGALUS GLYCYPHYLLOS
BT1 astragalus
BT2 leguminosae
BT1 pasture legumes
BT2 legumes
BT2 pasture plants

ASTRAGALUS HEYDEI
BT1 astragalus
BT2 leguminosae
BT1 pasture legumes
BT2 legumes
BT2 pasture plants

ASTRAGALUS KODSCHORENSIS
BT1 astragalus
BT2 leguminosae

ASTRAGALUS LASIOPETALUS
BT1 astragalus
BT2 leguminosae

ASTRAGALUS LENTIGINOSUS
BT1 astragalus
BT2 leguminosae
BT1 poisonous plants

ASTRAGALUS MISER
BT1 astragalus
BT2 leguminosae
BT1 poisonous plants

ASTRAGALUS MOLLISSIMUS
BT1 astragalus
BT2 leguminosae
BT1 poisonous plants

astragalus pilosus
USE **oxytropis pilosa**

ASTRAGALUS PRAELONGUS
BT1 astragalus
BT2 leguminosae
BT1 poisonous plants

ASTRAGALUS RACEMOSUS
BT1 astragalus
BT2 leguminosae
BT1 pasture legumes
BT2 legumes
BT2 pasture plants

ASTRAGALUS RHIZANTHUS
BT1 astragalus
BT2 leguminosae
BT1 pasture legumes
BT2 legumes
BT2 pasture plants

ASTRAGALUS SCLEROCARPUS
BT1 astragalus
BT2 leguminosae

ASTRAGALUS SEVERTZOVII
BT1 astragalus
BT2 leguminosae

ASTRAGALUS SIEVERSIANUS
BT1 astragalus
BT2 leguminosae

ASTRAGALUS SINICUS
BT1 astragalus
BT2 leguminosae
BT1 fodder legumes
BT2 fodder plants
BT2 legumes
BT1 pasture legumes
BT2 legumes
BT2 pasture plants

ASTRAGALUS STRIATUS
BT1 astragalus
BT2 leguminosae

ASTRAGALUS TROITSKYI
BT1 astragalus
BT2 leguminosae

ASTRAGALUS UGAMICUS
BT1 astragalus
BT2 leguminosae

ASTRAGALUS WOOTONII
BT1 astragalus
BT2 leguminosae
BT1 poisonous plants

ASTRANTIA
BT1 umbelliferae
NT1 astrantia major

ASTRANTIA MAJOR
BT1 astrantia
BT2 umbelliferae
BT1 ornamental herbaceous plants

ASTREBLA
BT1 gramineae
NT1 astrebla elymoides
NT1 astrebla lappacea
NT1 astrebla pectinata

ASTREBLA ELYMOIDES
BT1 astrebla
BT2 gramineae
BT1 pasture plants

ASTREBLA LAPPACEA
BT1 astrebla
BT2 gramineae
BT1 pasture plants

ASTREBLA PECTINATA
BT1 astrebla
BT2 gramineae
BT1 pasture plants

ASTRINGENTS
BT1 dermatological agents
BT2 drugs

ASTROCARYUM
BT1 palmae
NT1 astrocaryum aculeatissimum
NT1 astrocaryum jauary
NT1 astrocaryum mexicanum
NT1 astrocaryum murumuru
NT1 astrocaryum tucuma
NT1 astrocaryum vulgare

ASTROCARYUM ACULEATISSIMUM
BT1 astrocaryum
BT2 palmae

ASTROCARYUM JAUARY
BT1 astrocaryum
BT2 palmae
BT1 fibre plants

ASTROCARYUM MEXICANUM
BT1 astrocaryum
BT2 palmae

ASTROCARYUM MURUMURU
BT1 astrocaryum
BT2 palmae
BT1 fibre plants

ASTROCARYUM TUCUMA
BT1 astrocaryum
BT2 palmae
BT1 fibre plants

ASTROCARYUM VULGARE
BT1 astrocaryum
BT2 palmae
BT1 fibre plants

ASTROVIRUS
BT1 unclassified viruses
BT2 viruses
rt insect viruses

ASTURIAN
BT1 cattle breeds
BT2 breeds

ASULAM
BT1 carbamate herbicides
BT2 carbamate pesticides
BT2 herbicides
BT3 pesticides

ASYMMETRY
rt distortion
rt geometry

ASYMPHYLODORA
BT1 monorchiidae
BT2 digenea
BT3 trematoda

ASYNAPSIS
uf *asyndesis*
rt chromosomes

ASYNAPSIS *cont.*
rt desynapsis
rt meiosis

asyndesis
USE **asynapsis**

ASYSTASIA
BT1 acanthaceae
NT1 asystasia gangetica
NT1 asystasia macrocarpa

ASYSTASIA GANGETICA
BT1 asystasia
BT2 acanthaceae

ASYSTASIA MACROCARPA
BT1 asystasia
BT2 acanthaceae

ATALANTIA
BT1 cleomaceae
NT1 atalantia missionis
NT1 atalantia monophylla
NT1 atalantia roxburghiana

ATALANTIA MISSIONIS
BT1 atalantia
BT2 cleomaceae

ATALANTIA MONOPHYLLA
BT1 atalantia
BT2 cleomaceae

ATALANTIA ROXBURGHIANA
BT1 atalantia
BT2 cleomaceae
BT1 medicinal plants

ATALODERA
BT1 heteroderidae
BT2 nematoda

ATAXIA
BT1 movement disorders
BT2 functional disorders
BT3 animal disorders
BT4 disorders
BT1 muscular diseases
BT2 organic diseases
BT3 diseases
NT1 cerebellar ataxia

ataxia, enzootic
USE **swayback**

atebrin
USE **mepacrine**

ATELECTASIS
BT1 respiratory disorders
BT2 functional disorders
BT3 animal disorders
BT4 disorders
BT2 respiratory diseases
BT3 organic diseases
BT4 diseases

ATELERIX
BT1 erinaceidae
BT2 insectivores
BT3 mammals
NT1 atelerix albiventris
rt erinaceus

ATELERIX ALBIVENTRIS
uf *erinaceus albiventris*
BT1 atelerix
BT2 erinaceidae
BT3 insectivores
BT4 mammals

ATELES
uf *spider monkeys*
BT1 cebidae
BT2 primates
BT3 mammals

ATEMOYAS
BT1 subtropical tree fruits
BT2 subtropical fruits
BT3 fruit crops
BT2 tree fruits
rt annona

ATENOLOL
BT1 amino alcohols
BT2 alcohols
BT2 amino compounds
BT3 organic nitrogen compounds
BT1 sympatholytics
BT2 neurotropic drugs
BT3 drugs

ATHALIA
BT1 tenthredinidae
BT2 hymenoptera
NT1 athalia lugens
NT1 athalia rosae

ATHALIA LUGENS
BT1 athalia
BT2 tenthredinidae
BT3 hymenoptera

ATHALIA ROSAE
BT1 athalia
BT2 tenthredinidae
BT3 hymenoptera

ATHELIA
BT1 aphyllophorales
NT1 athelia epiphylla
rt corticium

ATHELIA EPIPHYLLA
uf *corticium centrifugum*
BT1 athelia
BT2 aphyllophorales

ATHENE
BT1 strigidae
BT2 strigiformes
BT3 birds
rt speotyto

athene cunicularia
USE **speotyto cunicularia**

ATHERESTHES
BT1 pleuronectidae
BT2 pleuronectiformes
BT3 osteichthyes
BT4 fishes

ATHERIGONA
BT1 muscidae
BT2 diptera
NT1 atherigona approximata
NT1 atherigona falcata
NT1 atherigona naqvii
NT1 atherigona orientalis
NT1 atherigona oryzae
NT1 atherigona simplex
NT1 atherigona soccata
NT1 atherigona varia

ATHERIGONA APPROXIMATA
BT1 atherigona
BT2 muscidae
BT3 diptera

atherigona bituberculata
USE **atherigona simplex**

ATHERIGONA FALCATA
uf *atherigona nudiseta*
BT1 atherigona
BT2 muscidae
BT3 diptera

ATHERIGONA NAQVII
BT1 atherigona
BT2 muscidae
BT3 diptera

atherigona nudiseta
USE **atherigona falcata**

ATHERIGONA ORIENTALIS
BT1 atherigona
BT2 muscidae
BT3 diptera

ATHERIGONA ORYZAE
BT1 atherigona
BT2 muscidae
BT3 diptera

ATHERIGONA SIMPLEX
uf *atherigona bituberculata*
BT1 atherigona
BT2 muscidae
BT3 diptera

ATHERIGONA SOCCATA
BT1 atherigona
BT2 muscidae
BT3 diptera

ATHERIGONA VARIA
BT1 atherigona
BT2 muscidae
BT3 diptera

ATHERINA
BT1 atherinidae
BT2 atheriniformes
BT3 osteichthyes
BT4 fishes
NT1 atherina forskalii
NT1 atherina mochon
NT2 atherina mochon pontica

ATHERINA FORSKALII
BT1 atherina
BT2 atherinidae
BT3 atheriniformes
BT4 osteichthyes
BT5 fishes

ATHERINA MOCHON
BT1 atherina
BT2 atherinidae
BT3 atheriniformes
BT4 osteichthyes
BT5 fishes
NT1 atherina mochon pontica

ATHERINA MOCHON PONTICA
BT1 atherina mochon
BT2 atherina
BT3 atherinidae
BT4 atheriniformes
BT5 osteichthyes
BT6 fishes

ATHERINIDAE
BT1 atheriniformes
BT2 osteichthyes
BT3 fishes
NT1 atherina
NT2 atherina forskalii
NT2 atherina mochon
NT3 atherina mochon pontica
NT1 chirostoma
NT1 leuresthes
NT1 menidia

ATHERINIFORMES
BT1 osteichthyes
BT2 fishes
NT1 atherinidae
NT2 atherina
NT3 atherina forskalii
NT3 atherina mochon
NT4 atherina mochon pontica
NT2 chirostoma
NT2 leuresthes
NT2 menidia

ATHEROGENESIS
BT1 vascular diseases
BT2 cardiovascular diseases
BT3 organic diseases
BT4 diseases
rt atherogenic diet
rt atheroma
rt atherosclerosis

ATHEROGENIC DIET
BT1 diets
rt atherogenesis
rt atheroma
rt atherosclerosis
rt thrombogenic diet
rt vascular diseases

ATHEROMA
BT1 vascular diseases
BT2 cardiovascular diseases
BT3 organic diseases
BT4 diseases

ATHEROMA *cont.*
rt atherogenesis
rt atherogenic diet
rt atherosclerosis

ATHEROSCLEROSIS
uf *arteriosclerosis*
BT1 vascular diseases
BT2 cardiovascular diseases
BT3 organic diseases
BT4 diseases
NT1 experimental atherosclerosis
rt atherogenesis
rt atherogenic diet
rt atheroma

atherosclerosis, experimental
USE **experimental atherosclerosis**

ATHEROSPERMA
BT1 atherospermataceae
NT1 atherosperma moschatum
rt ornamental woody plants

ATHEROSPERMA MOSCHATUM
HN from 1990
BT1 atherosperma
BT2 atherospermataceae
BT1 forest trees

ATHEROSPERMATACEAE
NT1 atherosperma
NT2 atherosperma moschatum
NT1 doryphora
NT2 doryphora aromatica
NT2 doryphora sassafras
NT1 laurelia
NT2 laurelia philippiana
NT2 laurelia sempervirens

ATHERURUS
BT1 hystricidae
BT2 rodents
BT3 mammals
NT1 atherurus africanus

ATHERURUS AFRICANUS
BT1 atherurus
BT2 hystricidae
BT3 rodents
BT4 mammals

ATHLETES
BT1 performers
rt athletics

ATHLETICS
BT1 physical activity
BT1 sport
rt agonistic behaviour
rt athletes
rt exercise
rt running

ATHOUS
BT1 elateridae
BT2 coleoptera
NT1 athous subfuscus

ATHOUS SUBFUSCUS
BT1 athous
BT2 elateridae
BT3 coleoptera

ATHYRIACEAE
NT1 athyrium
NT2 athyrium filix-femina
NT1 cystopteris
NT2 cystopteris bulbifera
NT2 cystopteris fragilis
NT1 diplazium
NT2 diplazium pycnocarpon

ATHYRIUM
BT1 athyriaceae
NT1 athyrium filix-femina

ATHYRIUM FILIX-FEMINA
uf *asplenium filix-femina*
BT1 antibacterial plants
BT1 athyrium
BT2 athyriaceae
BT1 ornamental ferns
BT2 ferns

ATHYRIUM FILIX-FEMINA *cont.*
BT2 ornamental foliage plants
BT3 foliage plants

athyrium pycnocarpon
USE **diplazium pycnocarpon**

ATLANTIC OCEAN
BT1 marine areas
NT1 black sea
NT1 eastern central atlantic
NT1 mediterranean sea
NT2 adriatic sea
NT1 northeast atlantic
NT2 baltic sea
NT2 irish sea
NT2 north sea
NT1 northwest atlantic
NT1 southeast atlantic
NT1 southwest atlantic
NT1 western central atlantic
NT2 caribbean sea
NT2 gulf of mexico

ATLANTIC SALMON
uf *salmo salar*
BT1 diadromous fishes
BT2 aquatic animals
BT3 animals
BT3 aquatic organisms
BT1 salmon

atlases
USE **maps**

ATMOSPHERE
NT1 anaerobic conditions
rt air
rt atmospheric pressure
rt climatic factors
rt environmental factors
rt meteorological factors

atmospheres, controlled
USE **controlled atmospheres**

atmospheres, protective
USE **protective atmospheres**

atmospheric pollution
USE **air pollution**

ATMOSPHERIC PRESSURE
uf *barometric pressure*
BT1 meteorological factors
BT2 climatic factors
BT1 pressure
BT2 physical properties
BT3 properties
rt altitude
rt atmosphere

atmospheric sciences
USE **climatology**
OR **meteorology**

atmospheric visibility
USE **visibility**

ATOLLS
BT1 islands
BT2 physiographic features
rt coral

ATOMARIA
BT1 cryptophagidae
BT2 coleoptera
NT1 atomaria linearis

ATOMARIA LINEARIS
BT1 atomaria
BT2 cryptophagidae
BT3 coleoptera

ATOMIC ABSORPTION SPECTROPHOTOMETRY
BT1 spectrophotometry
BT2 analytical methods
BT3 methodology
rt atomic absorption spectroscopy

ATOMIC ABSORPTION SPECTROSCOPY
BT1 spectroscopy

ATOMIC ABSORPTION SPECTROSCOPY *cont.*
BT2 analytical methods
BT3 methodology
rt atomic absorption spectrophotometry

ATOMIC FLUORESCENCE SPECTROSCOPY
BT1 spectroscopy
BT2 analytical methods
BT3 methodology
rt fluorescence

ATOMIZATION
BT1 processing
rt atomizers
rt droplet size
rt sprays

ATOMIZERS
uf *nozzles, atomizing*
rt atomization
rt droplet size
rt mist blowers
rt mist sprayers
rt nozzles
rt sprayers
rt sprays

ATOPOMELIDAE
BT1 astigmata
BT2 acari
NT1 chirodiscoides
NT2 chirodiscoides caviae

ATOPY
(genetic predisposition to immediate hypersensitivity reactions)
BT1 immediate hypersensitivity
BT2 hypersensitivity
BT3 immune response
BT4 immunity
rt asthma

atoxoplasma
USE **lankesterella**

ATP
uf *adenosine triphosphate*
BT1 adenosine phosphates
BT2 phosphates (esters)
BT3 esters
BT3 phosphates
BT2 purine nucleotides
BT3 nucleotides
BT4 glycosides
BT5 carbohydrates
rt adenosine triphosphate cycle
rt adenosinetriphosphatase
rt mitochondria

ATP CITRATE LYASE
(ec 4.1.3.8)
BT1 oxo-acid-lyases
BT2 lyases
BT3 enzymes

ATP PYROPHOSPHATASE
(ec 3.6.1.8)
BT1 pyrophosphatases
BT2 acid anhydride hydrolases
BT3 hydrolases
BT4 enzymes

atpase
USE **adenosinetriphosphatase**

ATRACTIDAE
BT1 nematoda
NT1 atractis
NT1 crossocephalus
NT1 cyrtosomum
NT1 probstmayria
NT2 probstmayria vivipara
rt animal parasitic nematodes

ATRACTIS
BT1 atractidae
BT2 nematoda

ATRACTYLODES
BT1 compositae
NT1 atractylodes japonica
NT1 atractylodes lancea

ATRACTYLODES JAPONICA
BT1 atractylodes
BT2 compositae
BT1 medicinal plants

ATRACTYLODES LANCEA
BT1 atractylodes
BT2 compositae

ATRATON
BT1 triazine herbicides
BT2 herbicides
BT3 pesticides
BT2 triazines
BT3 heterocyclic nitrogen compounds
BT4 organic nitrogen compounds

ATRAX
BT1 hexathelidae
BT2 araneae
BT3 arachnida
BT4 arthropods
NT1 atrax robustus

ATRAX ROBUSTUS
BT1 atrax
BT2 hexathelidae
BT3 araneae
BT4 arachnida
BT5 arthropods

ATRAZINE
BT1 antitranspirants
BT1 evaporation suppressants
BT2 soil amendments
BT3 amendments
BT1 triazine herbicides
BT2 herbicides
BT3 pesticides
BT2 triazines
BT3 heterocyclic nitrogen compounds
BT4 organic nitrogen compounds

ATRESIA
BT1 malformations
BT2 abnormalities
rt development

ATRIPLEX
BT1 chenopodiaceae
NT1 atriplex alaskensis
NT1 atriplex canescens
NT1 atriplex confertifolia
NT1 atriplex corrugata
NT1 atriplex gmelinii
NT1 atriplex halimus
NT1 atriplex hastata
NT1 atriplex hortensis
NT1 atriplex hymenelytra
NT1 atriplex lentiformis
NT1 atriplex nummularia
NT1 atriplex nuttalii
NT1 atriplex patula
NT1 atriplex polycarpa
NT1 atriplex repanda
NT1 atriplex semibaccata
NT1 atriplex subspicata

ATRIPLEX ALASKENSIS
BT1 atriplex
BT2 chenopodiaceae

ATRIPLEX CANESCENS
BT1 atriplex
BT2 chenopodiaceae

ATRIPLEX CONFERTIFOLIA
BT1 atriplex
BT2 chenopodiaceae

ATRIPLEX CORRUGATA
BT1 atriplex
BT2 chenopodiaceae

ATRIPLEX GMELINII
BT1 atriplex
BT2 chenopodiaceae

ATRIPLEX HALIMUS
BT1 atriplex
BT2 chenopodiaceae
BT1 browse plants

ATRIPLEX HASTATA
BT1 atriplex
BT2 chenopodiaceae

ATRIPLEX HORTENSIS
BT1 atriplex
BT2 chenopodiaceae
BT1 leafy vegetables
BT2 vegetables

ATRIPLEX HYMENELYTRA
BT1 atriplex
BT2 chenopodiaceae

ATRIPLEX LENTIFORMIS
BT1 atriplex
BT2 chenopodiaceae

ATRIPLEX NUMMULARIA
BT1 atriplex
BT2 chenopodiaceae
BT1 molluscicidal plants
BT2 pesticidal plants

ATRIPLEX NUTTALII
BT1 atriplex
BT2 chenopodiaceae

ATRIPLEX PATULA
BT1 atriplex
BT2 chenopodiaceae

ATRIPLEX POLYCARPA
BT1 atriplex
BT2 chenopodiaceae

ATRIPLEX REPANDA
BT1 atriplex
BT2 chenopodiaceae

ATRIPLEX SEMIBACCATA
BT1 atriplex
BT2 chenopodiaceae
BT1 browse plants

ATRIPLEX SUBSPICATA
BT1 atriplex
BT2 chenopodiaceae

ATROPA
BT1 solanaceae
NT1 atropa acuminata
NT1 atropa baetica
NT1 atropa belladonna
NT1 atropa caucasica
NT1 atropa komarovii
NT1 atropa pallidiflora

ATROPA ACUMINATA
BT1 atropa
BT2 solanaceae

ATROPA BAETICA
BT1 atropa
BT2 solanaceae

ATROPA BELLADONNA
uf *belladonna*
uf *deadly nightshade*
BT1 atropa
BT2 solanaceae
BT1 medicinal plants
rt atropine
rt belladonna mottle tymovirus

ATROPA CAUCASICA
BT1 atropa
BT2 solanaceae

ATROPA KOMAROVII
BT1 atropa
BT2 solanaceae
BT1 medicinal plants

ATROPA PALLIDIFLORA
BT1 atropa

ATROPA PALLIDIFLORA *cont.*
BT2 solanaceae

ATROPHIC GASTRITIS
uf *gastric atrophy*
uf *gastritis, atrophic*
BT1 gastritis
BT2 stomach diseases
BT3 gastrointestinal diseases
BT4 digestive system diseases
BT5 organic diseases
BT6 diseases

ATROPHIC RHINITIS
uf *rhinitis, atrophic*
BT1 rhinitis
BT2 respiratory diseases
BT3 organic diseases
BT4 diseases

ATROPHY
BT1 degeneration
NT1 lupinosis

ATROPINE
BT1 parasympatholytics
BT2 neurotropic drugs
BT3 drugs
BT1 tropane alkaloids
BT2 alkaloids
rt atropa belladonna
rt tropinesterase

atropinesterase
USE **tropinesterase**

ATTA
BT1 formicidae
BT2 hymenoptera
NT1 atta cephalotes
NT1 atta sexdens
NT1 atta texana
NT1 atta vollenweideri

ATTA CEPHALOTES
BT1 atta
BT2 formicidae
BT3 hymenoptera

ATTA SEXDENS
BT1 atta
BT2 formicidae
BT3 hymenoptera

ATTA TEXANA
BT1 atta
BT2 formicidae
BT3 hymenoptera

ATTA VOLLENWEIDERI
BT1 atta
BT2 formicidae
BT3 hymenoptera

ATTACHMENT BEHAVIOR (AGRICOLA)
uf *bonding, social*
uf *social bonding*
BT1 behavior

ATTAGENUS
BT1 dermestidae
BT2 coleoptera
NT1 attagenus unicolor

attagenus megatoma
USE **attagenus unicolor**

attagenus piceus
USE **attagenus unicolor**

ATTAGENUS UNICOLOR
uf *attagenus megatoma*
uf *attagenus piceus*
BT1 attagenus
BT2 dermestidae
BT3 coleoptera

ATTALEA
BT1 palmae
NT1 attalea funifera

ATTALEA FUNIFERA
BT1 attalea

ATTALEA FUNIFERA *cont.*
BT2 palmae

attapulgite
USE **palygorskite**

ATTELABIDAE
BT1 coleoptera
NT1 rhynchites

attenuated vaccines
USE **live vaccines**

ATTENUATION
rt dampers
rt optical properties
rt reduction
rt vaccines
rt virulence

ATTITUDES
NT1 aspirations
NT1 attitudes to leisure
NT1 attitudes to work
NT2 strikes
NT1 consumer attitudes (agricola)
NT1 farmers' attitudes
NT1 political attitudes
rt behaviour
rt ideology
rt posture
rt public opinion
rt resistance to change (agricola)

attitudes, farmers
USE **farmers' attitudes**

attitudes, political
USE **political attitudes**

ATTITUDES TO LEISURE
BT1 attitudes
rt leisure

ATTITUDES TO WORK
BT1 attitudes
NT1 strikes
rt labour
rt student dropouts
rt work satisfaction
rt working conditions

ATTRACTANTS
NT1 baits
NT1 insect attractants
NT2 α-cubebene
NT2 cue-lure
NT2 disparlure
NT2 eugenol
NT2 grandlure
NT2 hexalure
NT2 looplure
NT2 methyl eugenol
NT2 muscalure
NT2 oviposition attractants
NT2 sex attractants
NT2 trimedlure
rt trapping
rt traps

attractants, insect
USE **insect attractants**

attractions, tourist
USE **tourist attractions**

ATYLOSIA
BT1 leguminosae
NT1 atylosia trinervia

ATYLOSIA TRINERVIA
BT1 antibacterial plants
BT1 atylosia
BT2 leguminosae

ATYLOTUS
BT1 tabanidae
BT2 diptera
NT1 atylotus agrestis
rt tabanus

ATYLOTUS AGRESTIS
uf *tabanus agrestis*

ATYLOTUS AGRESTIS *cont.*
BT1 atylotus
BT2 tabanidae
BT3 diptera

AUBERGINES
AF eggplants
uf *brinjal*
BT1 antiviral plants
BT1 fruit vegetables
BT2 vegetables
BT1 medicinal plants
rt eggplant mosaic tymovirus
rt eggplant mottled crinkle tombusvirus
rt eggplant mottled dwarf rhabdovirus
rt solanum melongena

AUBRAC
BT1 cattle breeds
BT2 breeds

AUBRIETA
BT1 cruciferae
NT1 aubrieta deltoidea

AUBRIETA DELTOIDEA
uf *aubrieta graeca*
BT1 aubrieta
BT2 cruciferae
BT1 ornamental herbaceous plants

aubrieta graeca
USE **aubrieta deltoidea**

AUBUES SOIL
BT1 soil types (polygenetic)

AUCHENORRHYNCHA
BT1 homoptera
NT1 cercopoidea
NT2 aphrophoridae
NT3 aphrophora
NT4 aphrophora alni
NT3 philaenus
NT4 philaenus spumarius
NT2 cercopidae
NT3 aeneolamia
NT4 aeneolamia contigua
NT4 aeneolamia selecta
NT4 aeneolamia varia
NT3 deois
NT4 deois flavopicta
NT4 deois schach
NT3 mahanarva
NT4 mahanarva fimbriolata
NT4 mahanarva posticata
NT3 zulia
NT4 zulia colombiana
NT4 zulia entreriana
NT2 machaerotidae
NT3 hindola
NT4 hindola fulva
NT4 hindola striata
NT1 cicadelloidea
NT2 cicadellidae
NT3 agallia
NT4 agallia constricta
NT4 agallia laevis
NT3 alnetoidia
NT4 alnetoidia alneti
NT3 amplicephalus
NT3 amrasca
NT4 amrasca biguttula
NT4 amrasca devastans
NT3 anaceratagallia
NT3 chlorita
NT3 cicadella
NT4 cicadella viridis
NT3 cicadulina
NT4 cicadulina bipunctata
NT4 cicadulina chinai
NT4 cicadulina mbila
NT4 cicadulina parazeae
NT4 cicadulina storeyi
NT3 circulifer
NT4 circulifer tenellus
NT3 cofana
NT4 cofana spectra
NT3 colladonus
NT4 colladonus montanus

AUCHENORRHYNCHA *cont.*
NT3 dalbulus
NT4 dalbulus elimatus
NT4 dalbulus gelbus
NT4 dalbulus maidis
NT3 empoasca
NT4 empoasca decipiens
NT4 empoasca dolichi
NT4 empoasca fabae
NT4 empoasca flavescens
NT4 empoasca kerri
NT4 empoasca kraemeri
NT3 empoascanara
NT4 empoascanara maculifrons
NT3 erythroneura
NT4 erythroneura elegantula
NT3 eupteryx
NT4 eupteryx atropunctata
NT3 euscelis
NT4 euscelis plebeja
NT3 eutettix
NT3 exitianus
NT4 exitianus exitiosus
NT3 fieberiella
NT4 fieberiella florii
NT3 graminella
NT4 graminella nigrifrons
NT3 graphocephala
NT4 graphocephala atropunctata
NT3 hishimonus
NT4 hishimonus phycitis
NT3 idiocerus
NT3 idioscopus
NT4 idioscopus clypealis
NT3 jacobiasca
NT4 jacobiasca lybica
NT3 jacobiella
NT4 jacobiella facialis
NT3 macrosteles
NT4 macrosteles fascifrons
NT4 macrosteles laevis
NT4 macrosteles sexnotatus
NT3 neoaliturus
NT3 nephotettix
NT4 nephotettix cincticeps
NT4 nephotettix malayanus
NT4 nephotettix nigropictus
NT4 nephotettix virescens
NT3 orosius
NT4 orosius argentatus
NT3 psammotettix
NT4 psammotettix striatus
NT3 recilia
NT4 recilia dorsalis
NT3 scaphoideus
NT4 scaphoideus titanus
NT3 scaphytopius
NT4 scaphytopius acutus
NT4 scaphytopius magdalensis
NT3 tettigoniella
NT3 thaia
NT4 thaia oryzivora
NT4 thaia subrufa
NT3 typhlocyba
NT3 zygina
NT3 zyginidia
NT2 membracidae
NT3 ceresa
NT4 ceresa bubalus
NT3 spissistilus
NT4 spissistilus festinus
NT3 stictocephala
NT4 stictocephala bisonia
NT1 cicadoidea
NT2 cicadidae
NT3 magicicada
NT4 magicicada cassinii
NT4 magicicada septendecim
NT4 magicicada septendecula
NT1 fulgoroidea
NT2 cixiidae
NT3 myndus
NT4 myndus crudus
NT2 delphacidae
NT3 delphacodes
NT3 javesella
NT4 javesella pellucida
NT3 laodelphax

AUCHENORRHYNCHA *cont.*
NT4 laodelphax striatella
NT3 nilaparvata
NT4 nilaparvata bakeri
NT4 nilaparvata lugens
NT3 peregrinus
NT4 peregrinus maidis
NT3 perkinsiella
NT4 perkinsiella saccharicida
NT3 sogata
NT3 sogatella
NT4 sogatella furcifera
NT3 sogatodes
NT4 sogatodes cubanus
NT4 sogatodes orizicola
NT3 toya
NT4 toya propinqua
NT2 lophopidae
NT3 pyrilla
NT4 pyrilla perpusilla
NT2 tettigometridae
NT3 hilda
NT4 hilda patruelis
NT2 tropiduchidae
NT3 numicia
NT4 numicia viridis

AUCOUMEA
BT1 burseraceae
NT1 aucoumea klaineana

AUCOUMEA KLAINEANA
BT1 aucoumea
BT2 burseraceae

AUCTIONS
BT1 marketing techniques
BT2 techniques

AUCUBA
BT1 cornaceae
NT1 aucuba japonica

AUCUBA JAPONICA
BT1 aucuba
BT2 cornaceae
BT1 ornamental woody plants

AUCUBIN
BT1 iridoid glycosides
BT2 glycosides
BT3 carbohydrates
BT2 iridoids
BT3 isoprenoids
BT4 lipids

AUDIENCES
uf *spectators*
rt consumers
rt entertainment
rt performing arts
rt target groups

AUDIOTAPES (AGRICOLA)
BT1 audiovisual aids
BT2 teaching materials
rt tape recorders

AUDIOVISUAL AIDS
uf *audiovisual equipment*
uf *instructional media*
uf *visual aids*
BT1 teaching materials
NT1 audiotapes (agricola)
NT1 bulletin boards (agricola)
NT1 educational radio
NT1 educational television
NT1 filmstrips (agricola)
NT1 video recorders
rt extension
rt films
rt radio
rt teaching
rt television

audiovisual equipment
USE **audiovisual aids**

AUDITING
BT1 controls
rt accounting
rt monitoring

AUDITORY THRESHOLD
uf *threshold of hearing*
BT1 hearing
BT2 senses

AUERBACHIA
BT1 myxozoa
BT2 protozoa
NT1 auerbachia pulchra

AUERBACHIA PULCHRA
BT1 auerbachia
BT2 myxozoa
BT3 protozoa

AUGER CONVEYORS
uf *conveyors, auger*
BT1 conveyors
rt augers

AUGERS
BT1 tools
rt auger conveyors
rt combine harvesters
rt screws

AUGITE
BT1 nonclay minerals
BT2 minerals

AUGMENTATION
HN from 1989
BT1 biological control
BT2 pest control
BT3 control
NT1 parasitoid augmentation
NT1 predator augmentation
rt natural enemies

AUGOCHLORA
BT1 apidae
BT2 hymenoptera

AUGOCHLORELLA
BT1 apidae
BT2 hymenoptera

AUGOCHLOROPSIS
BT1 apidae
BT2 hymenoptera

AUJESZKY VIRUS
uf *pseudorabies virus*
BT1 porcine herpesvirus
BT2 herpesviridae
BT3 viruses
rt aujeszky's disease

AUJESZKY'S DISEASE
BT1 viral diseases
BT2 infectious diseases
BT3 diseases
rt aujeszky virus
rt swine diseases

AULACASPIS
BT1 diaspididae
BT2 coccoidea
BT3 sternorrhyncha
BT4 homoptera
NT1 aulacaspis madiunensis
NT1 aulacaspis rosae
NT1 aulacaspis tegalensis
NT1 aulacaspis tubercularis

aulacaspis cinnamomi
USE **aulacaspis tubercularis**

AULACASPIS MADIUNENSIS
BT1 aulacaspis
BT2 diaspididae
BT3 coccoidea
BT4 sternorrhyncha
BT5 homoptera

AULACASPIS ROSAE
BT1 aulacaspis
BT2 diaspididae
BT3 coccoidea
BT4 sternorrhyncha
BT5 homoptera

AULACASPIS TEGALENSIS
BT1 aulacaspis
BT2 diaspididae

AULACASPIS TEGALENSIS *cont.*
BT3 coccoidea
BT4 sternorrhyncha
BT5 homoptera

AULACASPIS TUBERCULARIS
uf *aulacaspis cinnamomi*
BT1 aulacaspis
BT2 diaspididae
BT3 coccoidea
BT4 sternorrhyncha
BT5 homoptera

AULACOMYA
BT1 mytilidae
BT2 bivalvia
BT3 mollusca
NT1 aulacomya ater

AULACOMYA ATER
BT1 aulacomya
BT2 mytilidae
BT3 bivalvia
BT4 mollusca

AULACOPHORA
uf *raphidopalpa*
BT1 chrysomelidae
BT2 coleoptera
NT1 aulacophora foveicollis

AULACOPHORA FOVEICOLLIS
uf *raphidopalpa foveicollis*
BT1 aulacophora
BT2 chrysomelidae
BT3 coleoptera

AULACORTHUM
uf *neomyzus*
BT1 aphididae
BT2 aphidoidea
BT3 sternorrhyncha
BT4 homoptera
NT1 aulacorthum circumflexum
NT1 aulacorthum solani
rt acyrthosiphon
rt macrosiphum

AULACORTHUM CIRCUMFLEXUM
uf *neomyzus circumflexus*
BT1 aulacorthum
BT2 aphididae
BT3 aphidoidea
BT4 sternorrhyncha
BT5 homoptera

AULACORTHUM SOLANI
uf *acyrthosiphon solani*
uf *macrosiphum solani*
BT1 aulacorthum
BT2 aphididae
BT3 aphidoidea
BT4 sternorrhyncha
BT5 homoptera

AULIE-ATA
BT1 cattle breeds
BT2 breeds

AULOSIRA
BT1 cyanobacteria
BT2 prokaryotes
NT1 aulosira prolifica

AULOSIRA PROLIFICA
BT1 aulosira
BT2 cyanobacteria
BT3 prokaryotes

AURAL COMMUNICATION
BT1 communication

aurantiin
USE **naringin**

AUREOBASIDIUM
uf *pullularia*
BT1 deuteromycotina
NT1 aureobasidium pullulans

AUREOBASIDIUM PULLULANS
uf *pullularia pullulans*
BT1 aureobasidium
BT2 deuteromycotina
BT1 mycorrhizal fungi

AUREOBASIDIUM PULLULANS *cont.*
BT2 fungi

AUREOFUNGIN
BT1 antibiotic fungicides
BT2 antibiotics
BT2 fungicides
BT3 pesticides

AUREOLARIA
BT1 scrophulariaceae

aureomycin
USE **chlortetracycline**

AURICULARIA
BT1 auriculariales
NT1 auricularia auricula

AURICULARIA AURICULA
BT1 auricularia
BT2 auriculariales
BT1 edible fungi
BT2 fungi
BT2 vegetables

AURICULARIALES
NT1 auricularia
NT2 auricularia auricula
NT1 helicobasidium
NT2 helicobasidium purpureum
rt fungi

aurochs
USE **bos primigenius**

aurofac
USE **chlortetracycline**

AUROTHIOGLUCOSE
uf *gold thioglucose*
BT1 dermatological agents
BT2 drugs
rt arthritis

AUSCULTATION
BT1 clinical examination
BT2 diagnostic techniques
BT3 techniques

AUSIMI
HN from 1990
BT1 sheep breeds
BT2 breeds

AUSTRALASIA
BT1 oceania
NT1 australia
NT2 australian capital territory
NT2 australian northern territory
NT2 new south wales
NT2 queensland
NT2 south australia
NT2 tasmania
NT2 victoria
NT2 western australia
NT1 melanesia
NT2 fiji
NT2 new caledonia
NT2 solomon islands
NT2 vanuatu
NT1 new zealand
NT1 papua new guinea

AUSTRALIA
BT1 australasia
BT2 oceania
NT1 australian capital territory
NT1 australian northern territory
NT1 new south wales
NT1 queensland
NT1 south australia
NT1 tasmania
NT1 victoria
NT1 western australia
rt christmas island
rt cocos islands
rt commonwealth of nations
rt oecd

AUSTRALIAN CAPITAL TERRITORY
uf *capital territory of australia*
BT1 australia

AUSTRALIAN CAPITAL TERRITORY *cont.*
BT2 australasia
BT3 oceania

AUSTRALIAN FOOTBALL
HN from 1989
BT1 football
BT2 ball games
BT3 games
BT3 sport

australian illawarra shorthorn
USE **illawarra**

AUSTRALIAN MERINO
BT1 sheep breeds
BT2 breeds

AUSTRALIAN NORTHERN TERRITORY
uf *northern territory of australia*
BT1 australia
BT2 australasia
BT3 oceania

AUSTRALIAN OCEANIA
uf *pacific islands (aus)*
BT1 oceania
NT1 christmas island
NT1 cocos islands
NT1 heard and mcdonald islands
NT1 norfolk island
NT1 territory of ashmore and cartier islands
NT1 territory of coral sea islands
rt pacific islands
rt south pacific commission

AUSTRIA
BT1 western europe
BT2 europe
NT1 burgenland
NT1 lower austria
NT1 salzburg
NT1 styria
NT1 tyrol
NT1 upper austria
NT1 vienna
NT1 vorarlberg
rt efta
rt oecd

AUSTRIAN BROWN
BT1 cattle breeds
BT2 breeds

AUSTRIAN SIMMENTAL
BT1 cattle breeds
BT2 breeds

AUSTRIAN YELLOW
BT1 cattle breeds
BT2 breeds

AUSTROBILHARZIA
BT1 schistosomatidae
BT2 digenea
BT3 trematoda

austrocedrus
USE **libocedrus**

AUSTROPOTAMOBIUS
BT1 decapoda
BT2 malacostraca
BT3 crustacea
BT4 arthropods
NT1 austropotamobius pallipes

AUSTROPOTAMOBIUS PALLIPES
BT1 austropotamobius
BT2 decapoda
BT3 malacostraca
BT4 crustacea
BT5 arthropods

AUSTROSIMULIUM
BT1 simuliidae
BT2 diptera

AUTECOLOGY
(ecology of individual species)
BT1 ecology

AUTHORITY
rt corruption
rt leadership
rt political power

AUTOAGGLUTINATION
BT1 agglutination

AUTOANTIBODIES
BT1 antibodies
BT2 immunoglobulins
BT3 glycoproteins
BT4 proteins
BT5 peptides
BT3 immunological factors
rt autoimmune diseases

AUTOANTIGENS
BT1 antigens
BT2 immunological factors

AUTOCLAVING
BT1 sterilizing
rt soil sterilization
rt sterilizers

AUTOCORRELATION
BT1 correlation
rt statistical analysis

AUTOGENOUS VACCINES
BT1 vaccines

AUTOGENY
BT1 reproduction
rt anautogeny
rt gonotrophic cycles

AUTOGRAPHA
BT1 noctuidae
BT2 lepidoptera
NT1 autographa californica
NT1 autographa gamma
NT1 autographa nigrisigna
rt chrysodeixis
rt cornutiplusia
rt phytometra
rt plusia
rt syngrapha

AUTOGRAPHA CALIFORNICA
uf *plusia californica*
BT1 autographa
BT2 noctuidae
BT3 lepidoptera

autographa chalcites
USE **chrysodeixis chalcites**

autographa circumflexa
USE **cornutiplusia circumflexa**

AUTOGRAPHA GAMMA
uf *phytometra gamma*
uf *plusia gamma*
BT1 autographa
BT2 noctuidae
BT3 lepidoptera

AUTOGRAPHA NIGRISIGNA
uf *plusia nigrisigna*
BT1 autographa
BT2 noctuidae
BT3 lepidoptera

AUTOIMMUNE DISEASES
BT1 immunological diseases
BT2 diseases
NT1 autoimmune thyroiditis
rt autoantibodies
rt autoimmunity

AUTOIMMUNE THYROIDITIS
BT1 autoimmune diseases
BT2 immunological diseases
BT3 diseases
BT1 thyroid diseases
BT2 endocrine diseases
BT3 organic diseases
BT4 diseases

AUTOIMMUNITY
HN from 1989
BT1 immunity
rt autoimmune diseases

AUTOMATIC CLUSTER REMOVAL
rt automation
rt clusters
rt milking parlours

AUTOMATIC CONTROL
uf *control, automatic*
BT1 controls
rt automation
rt cybernetics
rt feedback
rt instrumentation
rt robots
rt servomotors
rt thermostats

AUTOMATIC COUPLINGS
uf *couplings, automatic*
BT1 couplings
BT2 components
rt automatic hitches
rt hydraulic couplings
rt mechanical couplings

AUTOMATIC FEED DISPENSERS
BT1 feed dispensers
BT2 dispensers
rt self feeders

AUTOMATIC GUIDANCE
BT1 steering
BT2 guidance
rt driverless vehicles
rt radar
rt radio control
rt remote control
rt sensing
rt servomotors
rt tracking

AUTOMATIC HITCHES
uf *hitches, automatic*
BT1 hitches
BT2 components
rt automatic couplings
rt mechanical couplings
rt safety hitches

AUTOMATIC IRRIGATION SYSTEMS
uf *irrigation systems, automatic*
BT1 irrigation systems
BT2 water systems
BT3 systems

AUTOMATIC STEERING
uf *steering, automatic*
BT1 steering
BT2 guidance

AUTOMATIC TRANSMISSIONS
uf *transmissions, automatic*
BT1 transmissions
BT2 components
rt differential transmissions
rt drives
rt hydromechanical transmissions
rt hydrostatic transmissions
rt synchromesh transmissions

AUTOMATION
rt automatic cluster removal
rt automatic control
rt computers
rt controls
rt cybernetics
rt instrumentation
rt mechanization
rt remote control
rt robots
rt technical progress

AUTOMOBILE INSURANCE (AGRICOLA)
BT1 insurance
NT1 collision insurance (agricola)
NT1 no fault automobile insurance (agricola)

AUTONOMIC NERVOUS SYSTEM
uf *nervous system, autonomic*
uf *parasympathetic system*

AUTONOMIC NERVOUS SYSTEM *cont.*
BT1 nervous system
BT2 body parts
NT1 sympathetic nervous system
NT1 vasomotor system
rt dysautonomia

autopolyploidy
USE **polyploidy**

AUTORADIOGRAPHY
uf *radioautography*
BT1 radiography
BT2 biological techniques
BT3 techniques
BT2 diagnostic techniques
BT3 techniques
rt tracer techniques

autoregressive integrated moving average
USE **arima**

AUTOREGULATION
HN from 1989
BT1 regulation

AUTOSEXING
BT1 sex diagnosis
BT2 diagnosis
BT2 sex differentiation
BT3 differentiation

AUTOSOMES
BT1 chromosomes
BT2 nuclei
BT3 organelles
BT4 cell structure

AUTRANELLA
BT1 sapotaceae
NT1 autranella congolensis

AUTRANELLA CONGOLENSIS
BT1 autranella
BT2 sapotaceae

AUTUMN
BT1 seasons
rt spring
rt summer
rt winter

AUVERGNE
BT1 france
BT2 western europe
BT3 europe

auxiliary personnel
USE **auxiliary workers**

AUXILIARY WORKERS
uf *auxiliary personnel*
BT1 labour
BT1 workers
NT1 medical auxiliaries
NT2 barefoot doctors
NT2 midwives
rt social workers

AUXINS
BT1 plant growth regulators
BT2 growth regulators
NT1 1-naphthol
NT1 2,4,5-t
NT1 2,4-d
NT1 2,4-db
NT1 2,4-dep
NT1 2-naphthoxyacetic acid
NT1 3,5-d
NT1 4-cpa
NT1 dicamba
NT1 dichlorprop
NT1 disul
NT1 fenoprop
NT1 iaa
NT1 iba
NT1 naa
NT1 naphthaleneacetamide
NT1 potassium naphthenate
NT1 sodium naphthenate

AUXOIS
BT1 horse breeds
BT2 breeds

AVAHI
BT1 indriidae
BT2 primates
BT3 mammals
NT1 avahi laniger

AVAHI LANIGER
BT1 avahi
BT2 indriidae
BT3 primates
BT4 mammals

AVAILABILITY
NT1 bioavailability
NT1 nutrient availability

available days
USE **workable days**

AVAILABLE WATER
BT1 soil water categories
BT2 soil water
BT3 water
NT1 water availability
rt available water capacity
rt soil water content

AVAILABLE WATER CAPACITY
BT1 soil water constants
rt available water
rt capacity
rt water availability

AVALANCHE CONTROL (AGRICOLA)
BT1 control
rt avalanches

AVALANCHES
BT1 natural disasters
BT2 disasters
rt avalanche control (agricola)
rt landslides
rt mountains
rt snow
rt snow damage

AVENA
BT1 gramineae
NT1 avena abyssinica
NT1 avena barbata
NT1 avena byzantina
NT1 avena canariensis
NT1 avena clauda
NT1 avena fatua
NT1 avena hirtula
NT1 avena longiglumis
NT1 avena magna
NT1 avena maroccana
NT1 avena murphyi
NT1 avena nuda
NT1 avena persica
NT1 avena pilosa
NT1 avena sativa
NT1 avena sterilis
NT1 avena sterilis subsp. ludoviciana
NT1 avena sterilis subsp. sterilis
NT1 avena ventricosa
NT1 avena wiestii
rt avenin
rt oat blue dwarf virus

AVENA ABYSSINICA
BT1 avena
BT2 gramineae

avena alba var. barbata
USE **avena barbata**

AVENA BARBATA
uf *avena alba var. barbata*
BT1 avena
BT2 gramineae

AVENA BYZANTINA
BT1 avena
BT2 gramineae

AVENA CANARIENSIS
BT1 avena

AVENA CANARIENSIS *cont.*
BT2 gramineae

AVENA CLAUDA
BT1 avena
BT2 gramineae

AVENA FATUA
BT1 avena
BT2 gramineae
BT1 weeds

AVENA HIRTULA
uf *avena prostrata*
BT1 avena
BT2 gramineae
BT1 pasture plants

AVENA LONGIGLUMIS
BT1 avena
BT2 gramineae

avena ludoviciana
USE **avena sterilis subsp. ludoviciana**

avena macrocarpa
USE **avena sterilis subsp. sterilis**

AVENA MAGNA
BT1 avena
BT2 gramineae

AVENA MAROCCANA
BT1 avena
BT2 gramineae

AVENA MURPHYI
BT1 avena
BT2 gramineae

AVENA NUDA
uf *avena strigosa*
BT1 avena
BT2 gramineae

AVENA PERSICA
BT1 avena
BT2 gramineae

AVENA PILOSA
BT1 avena
BT2 gramineae

avena pratensis
USE **avenula pratensis**

avena prostrata
USE **avena hirtula**

avena pubescens
USE **avenula pubescens**

AVENA SATIVA
BT1 avena
BT2 gramineae
BT1 fodder plants
rt oat sterile dwarf fijivirus
rt oats

AVENA STERILIS
BT1 antiviral plants
BT1 avena
BT2 gramineae
BT1 weeds

AVENA STERILIS SUBSP. LUDOVICIANA
uf *avena ludoviciana*
BT1 avena
BT2 gramineae
BT1 weeds

avena sterilis subsp. macrocarpa
USE **avena sterilis subsp. sterilis**

AVENA STERILIS SUBSP. STERILIS
HN from 1990
uf *avena macrocarpa*
uf *avena sterilis subsp. macrocarpa*
BT1 avena
BT2 gramineae

avena strigosa
USE **avena nuda**

AVENA VENTRICOSA
BT1 avena
BT2 gramineae

AVENA WIESTII
BT1 avena
BT2 gramineae

AVENIN
BT1 prolamins
BT2 cereal proteins
BT3 plant proteins
BT4 proteins
BT5 peptides
rt avena

AVENULA
BT1 gramineae
NT1 avenula pratensis
NT1 avenula pubescens

AVENULA PRATENSIS
uf *avena pratensis*
uf *helictotrichon pratensis*
BT1 avenula
BT2 gramineae
BT1 pasture plants

AVENULA PUBESCENS
uf *avena pubescens*
uf *helictotrichon pubescens*
BT1 avenula
BT2 gramineae
BT1 ornamental herbaceous plants
BT1 pasture plants

AVERAGE PRICES
BT1 prices

AVERAGES
rt mathematics
rt statistics

avermectin b1
USE **abamectin**

AVERMECTINS
BT1 antibiotics
NT1 abamectin
NT1 ivermectin

AVERRHOA
BT1 averrhoaceae
NT1 averrhoa bilimbi
NT1 averrhoa carambola

AVERRHOA BILIMBI
uf *bilimbi*
BT1 averrhoa
BT2 averrhoaceae
BT1 tropical tree fruits
BT2 tree fruits
BT2 tropical fruits
BT3 fruit crops

AVERRHOA CARAMBOLA
uf *carambola*
BT1 averrhoa
BT2 averrhoaceae
BT1 tropical tree fruits
BT2 tree fruits
BT2 tropical fruits
BT3 fruit crops

AVERRHOACEAE
NT1 averrhoa
NT2 averrhoa bilimbi
NT2 averrhoa carambola

AVG
BT1 ethylene releasers
BT2 plant growth regulators
BT3 growth regulators

AVIADENOVIRUS
uf *avian adenovirus*
BT1 adenoviridae
BT2 viruses
NT1 haemorrhagic enteritis virus
rt egg drop syndrome

AVIAN ADENO-ASSOCIATED VIRUS
BT1 adeno-associated virus
BT2 parvoviridae
BT3 viruses

avian adenovirus
USE **aviadenovirus**

AVIAN ENCEPHALOMYELITIS VIRUS
BT1 enterovirus
BT2 picornaviridae
BT3 viruses
rt brain disorders
rt encephalitis
rt nervous system diseases

AVIAN ERYTHROBLASTOSIS
BT1 blood disorders
BT2 animal disorders
BT3 disorders

AVIAN HERPESVIRUS
BT1 herpesviridae
BT2 viruses
NT1 avian laryngotracheitis virus
NT1 duck plague virus
NT1 marek's disease virus
NT1 pigeon herpesvirus
NT1 turkey herpesvirus

avian infectious bronchitis virus
USE **infectious bronchitis virus**

AVIAN INFECTIOUS BURSITIS
uf *infectious bursal disease*
BT1 poultry diseases
BT2 animal diseases
BT3 diseases
BT1 viral diseases
BT2 infectious diseases
BT3 diseases
rt bursitis
rt infectious bursal disease virus

AVIAN INFLUENZAVIRUS
BT1 influenzavirus
BT2 orthomyxoviridae
BT3 viruses
NT1 fowl plague virus

AVIAN LARYNGOTRACHEITIS VIRUS
BT1 avian herpesvirus
BT2 herpesviridae
BT3 viruses
rt larynx

AVIAN LEUKOSIS
BT1 leukosis
BT2 leukocyte disorders
BT3 blood disorders
BT4 animal disorders
BT5 disorders
BT1 poultry diseases
BT2 animal diseases
BT3 diseases
rt avian oncovirus

avian leukosis virus
USE **avian oncovirus**

AVIAN MYELOBLASTOSIS
BT1 leukocyte disorders
BT2 blood disorders
BT3 animal disorders
BT4 disorders
rt avian myeloblastosis virus

AVIAN MYELOBLASTOSIS VIRUS
BT1 avian oncovirus
BT2 oncovirus type c
BT3 oncovirinae
BT4 retroviridae
BT5 viruses
rt avian myeloblastosis

AVIAN ONCOVIRUS
uf *avian leukosis virus*
BT1 oncovirus type c
BT2 oncovirinae
BT3 retroviridae

AVIAN ONCOVIRUS *cont.*
BT4 viruses
NT1 avian myeloblastosis virus
NT1 erythroblastosis virus
NT1 myelocytomatosis virus
NT1 reticuloendotheliosis virus
NT1 rous sarcoma virus
rt avian leukosis

AVIAN OSTEOPETROSIS
BT1 osteopetrosis
BT2 bone diseases
BT3 organic diseases
BT4 diseases

AVIAN PARAMYXOVIRUS
BT1 paramyxovirus
BT2 paramyxoviridae
BT3 viruses
NT1 newcastle disease virus
NT1 yucaipa virus

avian poxvirus
USE **avipoxvirus**

AVIAN REOVIRUS
BT1 reovirus
BT2 reoviridae
BT3 viruses

AVIAN RETICULOENDOTHELIOSIS
BT1 viral diseases
BT2 infectious diseases
BT3 diseases
rt reticuloendotheliosis virus

avian viral sarcoma
USE **rous sarcoma**

AVIARIES
BT1 animal housing
rt aviary birds

AVIARY BIRDS
uf *cage birds*
BT1 animals
NT1 budgerigars
NT1 parakeets
rt aviaries
rt aviculture
rt birds
rt canaries
rt ornamental birds

aviation
USE **air transport**

aviation, agricultural
USE **agricultural aviation**

AVICENNIA
BT1 verbenaceae
NT1 avicennia germinans
NT1 avicennia intermedia
NT1 avicennia marina
NT1 avicennia nitida
NT1 avicennia officinalis

AVICENNIA GERMINANS
BT1 avicennia
BT2 verbenaceae
BT1 forest trees

AVICENNIA INTERMEDIA
BT1 avicennia
BT2 verbenaceae

AVICENNIA MARINA
BT1 avicennia
BT2 verbenaceae
BT1 forest trees

AVICENNIA NITIDA
BT1 avicennia
BT2 verbenaceae

AVICENNIA OFFICINALIS
BT1 avicennia
BT2 verbenaceae

AVICIDES
BT1 pesticides
NT1 4-aminopyridine
NT1 chloralose
NT1 endrin

AVICIDES *cont.*
NT1 fenthion
rt bird control
rt birds

AVICULTURE
rt aviary birds
rt birds
rt game birds

AVIDIN
BT1 biotin antagonists
BT2 vitamin b antagonists
BT3 vitamin antagonists
BT4 antagonists
BT5 metabolic inhibitors
BT6 inhibitors
BT1 glycoproteins
BT2 proteins
BT3 peptides
rt egg albumen

AVILENA-BLACK IBERIAN
HN from 1990
BT1 cattle breeds
BT2 breeds

AVIPOXVIRUS
uf *avian poxvirus*
BT1 chordopoxvirinae
BT2 poxviridae
BT3 viruses
NT1 canary pox virus
NT1 fowl pox virus
NT1 turkey pox virus

AVITELLINA
BT1 anoplocephalidae
BT2 eucestoda
BT3 cestoda
NT1 avitellina centripunctata

AVITELLINA CENTRIPUNCTATA
BT1 avitellina
BT2 anoplocephalidae
BT3 eucestoda
BT4 cestoda

AVOCADO SUNBLOTCH VIROID
BT1 viroids
BT2 plant pathogens
BT3 pathogens

AVOCADOS
BT1 antifungal plants
BT1 fatty oil plants
BT2 oil plants
BT1 medicinal plants
BT1 subtropical tree fruits
BT2 subtropical fruits
BT3 fruit crops
BT2 tree fruits
rt black streak
rt carapace spot
rt crick-side
rt persea americana
rt ring-neck

AVOIDANCE CONDITIONING
uf *avoidance learning*
BT1 behaviour

avoidance learning
USE **avoidance conditioning**

AVOPARCIN
uf *avotan*
BT1 antibacterial agents
BT2 antiinfective agents
BT3 drugs
BT1 antibiotics
BT1 growth promoters
BT2 growth regulators
BT2 promoters

avotan
USE **avoparcin**

AVRANCHIN
BT1 sheep breeds
BT2 breeds

AWASSI
BT1 sheep breeds
BT2 breeds

AWNS
BT1 glumes
BT2 inflorescences
BT3 plant
rt gramineae

axerophthol
USE **retinol**

AXES
BT1 tools
rt felling

AXIAGASTUS
BT1 pentatomidae
BT2 heteroptera
NT1 axiagastus cambelli

AXIAGASTUS CAMBELLI
BT1 axiagastus
BT2 pentatomidae
BT3 heteroptera

AXIAL FLOW COMBINE HARVESTERS
BT1 combine harvesters
BT2 harvesters
BT3 farm machinery
BT4 machinery

AXIAL FLOW FANS
uf *fans, axial flow*
BT1 fans
BT2 components
rt centrifugal fans

AXIAL FLOW PUMPS
BT1 pumps
BT2 machinery
NT1 propeller pumps

AXILS
BT1 shoots
BT2 plant
rt phytotelmata

axis
USE **cervus**

axis axis
USE **cervus axis**

axis porcinus
USE **cervus porcinus**

AXLES
BT1 components
rt wheels

AXONCHIUM
BT1 belondiridae
BT2 nematoda

AXONOPUS
BT1 gramineae
NT1 axonopus affinis
NT1 axonopus compressus
NT1 axonopus purpusii

AXONOPUS AFFINIS
BT1 axonopus
BT2 gramineae
BT1 pasture plants

AXONOPUS COMPRESSUS
BT1 axonopus
BT2 gramineae
BT1 pasture plants

AXONOPUS PURPUSII
BT1 axonopus
BT2 gramineae
BT1 pasture plants

AXYLIA
BT1 noctuidae
BT2 lepidoptera
NT1 axylia putris

AXYLIA PUTRIS
BT1 axylia
BT2 noctuidae
BT3 lepidoptera

AXYRIS
BT1 chenopodiaceae

AXYRIS *cont.*
NT1 axyris amaranthoides
NT1 axyris lanata

AXYRIS AMARANTHOIDES
BT1 axyris
BT2 chenopodiaceae

AXYRIS LANATA
BT1 axyris
BT2 chenopodiaceae

AYRSHIRE
BT1 cattle breeds
BT2 breeds

AYU
uf *plecoglossus altivelis*
BT1 freshwater fishes
BT2 aquatic animals
BT3 animals
BT3 aquatic organisms
rt plecoglossidae

AZADIRACHTA
BT1 meliaceae
NT1 azadirachta indica
rt melia

AZADIRACHTA INDICA
uf *melia azadirachta*
uf *neem*
BT1 acaricidal plants
BT2 pesticidal plants
BT1 antibacterial plants
BT1 antifungal plants
BT1 azadirachta
BT2 meliaceae
BT1 forest trees
BT1 gum plants
BT1 insecticidal plants
BT2 pesticidal plants
BT1 medicinal plants
BT1 molluscicidal plants
BT2 pesticidal plants
BT1 nematicidal plants
BT2 pesticidal plants
BT1 oilseed plants
BT2 fatty oil plants
BT3 oil plants
rt azadirachtin
rt neem extracts
rt neem seed cake
rt neem seed extract

AZADIRACHTIN
BT1 allomones
BT2 allelochemicals
BT3 semiochemicals
BT1 meliacins
BT2 triterpenoids
BT3 terpenoids
BT4 isoprenoids
BT5 lipids
rt azadirachta indica

8-AZAGUANINE
BT1 metabolic inhibitors
BT2 inhibitors

azaleas
USE **rhododendron**

AZAMETHIPHOS
BT1 organothiophosphate insecticides
BT2 organophosphorus insecticides
BT3 insecticides
BT4 pesticides
BT3 organophosphorus pesticides
BT4 organophosphorus compounds

AZANZA
BT1 malvaceae
NT1 azanza garckeana

AZANZA GARCKEANA
BT1 azanza
BT2 malvaceae

AZAOUAK
BT1 cattle breeds
BT2 breeds

AZAPERONE
BT1 neuroleptics
BT2 psychotropic drugs
BT3 neurotropic drugs
BT4 drugs

AZASERINE
BT1 antibiotics
BT1 antineoplastic agents
BT2 drugs

AZERBAIDZHAN SSR
uf *ussr in asia*
BT1 ussr
rt ussr in europe

AZERBAIJAN
BT1 horse breeds
BT2 breeds

AZERBAIJAN MOUNTAIN MERINO
BT1 sheep breeds
BT2 breeds

AZERBAIJAN ZEBU
BT1 zebu breeds
BT2 breeds

azide, potassium
USE **potassium azide**

azide, sodium
USE **sodium azide**

AZIDES
BT1 organic nitrogen compounds
NT1 potassium azide
NT1 sodium azide

azidine
USE **diminazene**

AZIMA
BT1 salvadoraceae
NT1 azima tetracantha

AZIMA TETRACANTHA
BT1 azima
BT2 salvadoraceae

AZINE DYES
BT1 dyes

AZINES
BT1 heterocyclic nitrogen compounds
BT2 organic nitrogen compounds
NT1 piperazines
NT2 diethylcarbamazine
NT2 piperazine
NT1 pyrazines

AZINPHOS-ETHYL
BT1 organothiophosphate acaricides
BT2 organophosphorus acaricides
BT3 acaricides
BT4 pesticides
BT3 organophosphorus pesticides
BT4 organophosphorus compounds
BT1 organothiophosphate insecticides
BT2 organophosphorus insecticides
BT3 insecticides
BT4 pesticides
BT3 organophosphorus pesticides
BT4 organophosphorus compounds

AZINPHOS-METHYL
BT1 organothiophosphate acaricides
BT2 organophosphorus acaricides
BT3 acaricides

AZINPHOS-METHYL *cont.*
BT4 pesticides
BT3 organophosphorus pesticides
BT4 organophosphorus compounds
BT1 organothiophosphate insecticides
BT2 organophosphorus insecticides
BT3 insecticides
BT4 pesticides
BT3 organophosphorus pesticides
BT4 organophosphorus compounds

AZIPROTRYNE
BT1 triazine herbicides
BT2 herbicides
BT3 pesticides
BT2 triazines
BT3 heterocyclic nitrogen compounds
BT4 organic nitrogen compounds

aziridine
USE **ethyleneimine**

AZO COMPOUNDS
BT1 organic nitrogen compounds
NT1 p-dimethylaminoazobenzene
rt dyes

AZOCHIS
BT1 pyralidae
BT2 lepidoptera
NT1 azochis gripusalis

AZOCHIS GRIPUSALIS
BT1 azochis
BT2 pyralidae
BT3 lepidoptera

AZOCYCLOTIN
BT1 organotin acaricides
BT2 acaricides
BT3 pesticides
BT2 organotin pesticides
BT3 organotin compounds

AZOLES
BT1 heterocyclic nitrogen compounds
BT2 organic nitrogen compounds
NT1 conazole fungicides
NT2 diclobutrazol
NT2 etaconazole
NT2 imazalil
NT2 penconazole
NT2 prochloraz
NT2 propiconazole
NT2 triadimefon
NT2 triadimenol
NT1 imidazoles
NT2 allantoin
NT2 clotrimazole
NT2 creatinine
NT2 econazole
NT2 etomidate
NT2 fenticonazole
NT2 histamine
NT2 histidine
NT2 imidazole alkaloids
NT3 pilocarpine
NT2 imidazole fungicides
NT3 fenapanil
NT2 imidazolinone herbicides
NT3 imazamethabenz
NT3 imazapyr
NT3 imazaquin
NT3 imazethapyr
NT2 ketoconazole
NT2 metizoline
NT2 metomidate
NT2 miconazole
NT2 nitroimidazoles
NT3 dimetridazole
NT3 ipronidazole
NT3 metronidazole
NT3 ornidazole

AZOLES *cont.*
NT3 ronidazole
NT3 secnidazole
NT3 tinidazole
NT2 urocanic acid
NT1 triazoles
NT2 fluconazole
NT2 triazole fungicides
NT3 bitertanol
NT3 fluotrimazole
NT3 triazbutil
NT2 triazole herbicides
NT3 amitrole
NT3 epronaz

AZOLLA
BT1 azollaceae
NT1 azolla caroliniana
NT1 azolla filiculoides
NT1 azolla imbricata
NT1 azolla pinnata

AZOLLA CAROLINIANA
BT1 azolla
BT2 azollaceae

AZOLLA FILICULOIDES
BT1 azolla
BT2 azollaceae

AZOLLA IMBRICATA
BT1 azolla
BT2 azollaceae

AZOLLA PINNATA
BT1 azolla
BT2 azollaceae
BT1 green manures
BT2 manures
BT3 organic amendments
BT4 soil amendments
BT5 amendments

AZOLLACEAE
NT1 azolla
NT2 azolla caroliniana
NT2 azolla filiculoides
NT2 azolla imbricata
NT2 azolla pinnata

AZOMONAS
BT1 azotobacteraceae
BT2 gracilicutes
BT3 bacteria
BT4 prokaryotes

AZORES
BT1 western europe
BT2 europe
rt portugal

AZOSPIRILLUM
BT1 spirillaceae
BT2 gracilicutes
BT3 bacteria
BT4 prokaryotes
NT1 azospirillum brasilense
NT1 azospirillum lipoferum

AZOSPIRILLUM BRASILENSE
BT1 azospirillum
BT2 spirillaceae
BT3 gracilicutes
BT4 bacteria
BT5 prokaryotes

AZOSPIRILLUM LIPOFERUM
BT1 azospirillum
BT2 spirillaceae
BT3 gracilicutes
BT4 bacteria
BT5 prokaryotes

azotaemia
USE **uraemia**

AZOTOBACTER
BT1 azotobacteraceae
BT2 gracilicutes
BT3 bacteria
BT4 prokaryotes
NT1 azotobacter beijerinckii
NT1 azotobacter chroococcum
NT1 azotobacter vinelandii

AZOTOBACTER BEIJERINCKII
BT1 azotobacter
BT2 azotobacteraceae
BT3 gracilicutes
BT4 bacteria
BT5 prokaryotes

AZOTOBACTER CHROOCOCCUM
BT1 azotobacter
BT2 azotobacteraceae
BT3 gracilicutes
BT4 bacteria
BT5 prokaryotes

AZOTOBACTER VINELANDII
BT1 azotobacter
BT2 azotobacteraceae
BT3 gracilicutes
BT4 bacteria
BT5 prokaryotes

AZOTOBACTERACEAE
BT1 gracilicutes
BT2 bacteria
BT3 prokaryotes
NT1 azomonas
NT1 azotobacter
NT2 azotobacter beijerinckii
NT2 azotobacter chroococcum
NT2 azotobacter vinelandii
NT1 beijerinckia
NT2 beijerinckia indica
NT2 beijerinckia lacticogenes
NT1 derxia

AZOV TSIGAI
BT1 sheep breeds
BT2 breeds

AZOXY COMPOUNDS
BT1 organic nitrogen compounds
NT1 azoxymethane
NT1 cycasin

AZOXYMETHANE
BT1 azoxy compounds
BT2 organic nitrogen compounds

AZTECA
BT1 formicidae
BT2 hymenoptera
NT1 azteca chartifex

AZTECA CHARTIFEX
BT1 azteca
BT2 formicidae
BT3 hymenoptera

AZULENE
BT1 aromatic hydrocarbons
BT2 aromatic compounds
BT2 hydrocarbons

AZYGOPHLEPS
BT1 cossidae
BT2 lepidoptera
NT1 azygophleps scalaris

AZYGOPHLEPS SCALARIS
BT1 azygophleps
BT2 cossidae
BT3 lepidoptera

b cells
USE **b lymphocytes**

B CHROMOSOMES
BT1 accessory chromosomes
BT2 chromosomes
BT3 nuclei
BT4 organelles
BT5 cell structure

B HORIZONS
BT1 horizons
BT2 soil morphological features

B LYMPHOCYTES
uf *b cells*
BT1 lymphocytes
BT2 leukocytes
BT3 blood cells
BT4 cells

ba (plant growth regulator)
USE **benzyladenine**

ba (symbol)
USE **barium**

BABCOCK METHOD
BT1 analytical methods
BT2 methodology
rt milk fat

BABESIA
uf *nuttallia*
uf *redwater fever*
BT1 apicomplexa
BT2 protozoa
NT1 babesia argentina
NT1 babesia beliceri
NT1 babesia bigemina
NT1 babesia bovis
NT1 babesia caballi
NT1 babesia calcaratus
NT1 babesia canis
NT1 babesia capreoli
NT1 babesia caucasica
NT1 babesia colchica
NT1 babesia divergens
NT1 babesia equi
NT1 babesia galagolata
NT1 babesia gibsoni
NT1 babesia herpailuri
NT1 babesia hylomysci
NT1 babesia jakimovi
NT1 babesia major
NT1 babesia microti
NT1 babesia motasi
NT1 babesia musculi
NT1 babesia ovata
NT1 babesia ovis
NT1 babesia rodhaini
NT1 babesia trautmanni
NT1 babesia vesperuginis
NT1 babesia vitalii

BABESIA ARGENTINA
BT1 babesia
BT2 apicomplexa
BT3 protozoa

BABESIA BELICERI
BT1 babesia
BT2 apicomplexa
BT3 protozoa

BABESIA BIGEMINA
BT1 babesia
BT2 apicomplexa
BT3 protozoa

BABESIA BOVIS
BT1 babesia
BT2 apicomplexa
BT3 protozoa

BABESIA CABALLI
BT1 babesia
BT2 apicomplexa
BT3 protozoa

BABESIA CALCARATUS
BT1 babesia
BT2 apicomplexa
BT3 protozoa

BABESIA CANIS
BT1 babesia
BT2 apicomplexa
BT3 protozoa

BABESIA CAPREOLI
BT1 babesia
BT2 apicomplexa
BT3 protozoa

BABESIA CAUCASICA
BT1 babesia
BT2 apicomplexa
BT3 protozoa

BABESIA COLCHICA
BT1 babesia
BT2 apicomplexa
BT3 protozoa

BABESIA DIVERGENS
BT1 babesia
BT2 apicomplexa
BT3 protozoa

BABESIA EQUI
BT1 babesia
BT2 apicomplexa
BT3 protozoa

BABESIA GALAGOLATA
BT1 babesia
BT2 apicomplexa
BT3 protozoa

BABESIA GIBSONI
BT1 babesia
BT2 apicomplexa
BT3 protozoa

BABESIA HERPAILURI
BT1 babesia
BT2 apicomplexa
BT3 protozoa

BABESIA HYLOMYSCI
BT1 babesia
BT2 apicomplexa
BT3 protozoa

BABESIA JAKIMOVI
BT1 babesia
BT2 apicomplexa
BT3 protozoa

BABESIA MAJOR
BT1 babesia
BT2 apicomplexa
BT3 protozoa

BABESIA MICROTI
BT1 babesia
BT2 apicomplexa
BT3 protozoa

BABESIA MOTASI
BT1 babesia
BT2 apicomplexa
BT3 protozoa

BABESIA MUSCULI
BT1 babesia
BT2 apicomplexa
BT3 protozoa

BABESIA OVATA
BT1 babesia
BT2 apicomplexa
BT3 protozoa

BABESIA OVIS
BT1 babesia
BT2 apicomplexa
BT3 protozoa

BABESIA RODHAINI
BT1 babesia
BT2 apicomplexa
BT3 protozoa

BABESIA TRAUTMANNI
BT1 babesia
BT2 apicomplexa
BT3 protozoa

BABESIA VESPERUGINIS
BT1 babesia
BT2 apicomplexa
BT3 protozoa

BABESIA VITALII
BT1 babesia
BT2 apicomplexa
BT3 protozoa

BABESIOSOMA
BT1 apicomplexa
BT2 protozoa

BABIANA
BT1 iridaceae
rt ornamental bulbs

BABOON MILK
uf *milk, baboon*
BT1 milks
BT2 body fluids
BT3 fluids
rt papio

baboons
USE **papio**

baby foods
USE **infant foods**

BACCAUREA
BT1 euphorbiaceae
NT1 baccaurea motleyana
NT1 baccaurea sapida

BACCAUREA MOTLEYANA
BT1 baccaurea
BT2 euphorbiaceae

BACCAUREA SAPIDA
BT1 baccaurea
BT2 euphorbiaceae

BACCHARIS
BT1 compositae
NT1 baccharis articulata
NT1 baccharis cordifolia
NT1 baccharis crispa
NT1 baccharis dracunculifolia
NT1 baccharis halimifolia
NT1 baccharis megapotamica
NT1 baccharis pilularis
NT1 baccharis salicina
NT1 baccharis tricuneata

BACCHARIS ARTICULATA
BT1 baccharis
BT2 compositae

BACCHARIS CORDIFOLIA
BT1 baccharis
BT2 compositae

BACCHARIS CRISPA
BT1 antibacterial plants
BT1 baccharis
BT2 compositae

BACCHARIS DRACUNCULIFOLIA
BT1 baccharis
BT2 compositae

BACCHARIS HALIMIFOLIA
BT1 baccharis
BT2 compositae

BACCHARIS MEGAPOTAMICA
BT1 baccharis
BT2 compositae
BT1 medicinal plants

BACCHARIS PILULARIS
BT1 baccharis
BT2 compositae

BACCHARIS SALICINA
BT1 baccharis
BT2 compositae

BACCHARIS TRICUNEATA
BT1 baccharis
BT2 compositae

BACHAUR
BT1 cattle breeds

BACHAUR *cont.*
BT2 breeds

BACILLACEAE
BT1 firmicutes
BT2 bacteria
BT3 prokaryotes
NT1 bacillus
NT2 bacillus anthracis
NT2 bacillus brevis
NT2 bacillus cereus
NT2 bacillus circulans
NT2 bacillus coagulans
NT2 bacillus larvae
NT2 bacillus licheniformis
NT2 bacillus macerans
NT2 bacillus megaterium
NT2 bacillus mesentericus
NT2 bacillus mycoides
NT2 bacillus natto
NT2 bacillus pantothenicus
NT2 bacillus penetrans
NT2 bacillus piliformis
NT2 bacillus polymyxa
NT2 bacillus popilliae
NT2 bacillus pumilus
NT2 bacillus sphaericus
NT2 bacillus stearothermophilus
NT3 bacillus stearothermophilus var. calidolactis
NT2 bacillus subtilis
NT2 bacillus thuringiensis
NT3 bacillus thuringiensis subsp. aizawai
NT3 bacillus thuringiensis subsp. dendrolimus
NT3 bacillus thuringiensis subsp. galleriae
NT3 bacillus thuringiensis subsp. israelensis
NT3 bacillus thuringiensis subsp. kurstaki
NT3 bacillus thuringiensis subsp. thuringiensis
NT1 clostridium
NT2 clostridium acetobutylicum
NT2 clostridium bifermentans
NT2 clostridium botulinum
NT2 clostridium butyricum
NT2 clostridium chauvoei
NT2 clostridium difficile
NT2 clostridium haemolyticum
NT2 clostridium novyi
NT2 clostridium pasteurianum
NT2 clostridium perfringens
NT2 clostridium septicum
NT2 clostridium sordellii
NT2 clostridium sporogenes
NT2 clostridium tetani
NT2 clostridium thermocellum
NT2 clostridium tyrobutyricum

BACILLARIOPHYTA
uf *diatoms*
BT1 algae
NT1 asterionella
NT2 asterionella formosa
NT1 cyclotella
NT2 cyclotella meneghiniana
NT1 fragilaria
NT2 fragilaria crotonensis
NT1 melosira
NT2 melosira italica
NT1 navicula
NT2 navicula atomus
NT1 nitzschia
NT2 nitzschia dissipata

BACILLIDIUM
BT1 microspora
BT2 protozoa

BACILLUS
BT1 bacillaceae
BT2 firmicutes
BT3 bacteria
BT4 prokaryotes
NT1 bacillus anthracis
NT1 bacillus brevis
NT1 bacillus cereus
NT1 bacillus circulans

BACILLUS *cont.*
NT1 bacillus coagulans
NT1 bacillus larvae
NT1 bacillus licheniformis
NT1 bacillus macerans
NT1 bacillus megaterium
NT1 bacillus mesentericus
NT1 bacillus mycoides
NT1 bacillus natto
NT1 bacillus pantothenicus
NT1 bacillus penetrans
NT1 bacillus piliformis
NT1 bacillus polymyxa
NT1 bacillus popilliae
NT1 bacillus pumilus
NT1 bacillus sphaericus
NT1 bacillus stearothermophilus
NT2 bacillus stearothermophilus var. calidolactis
NT1 bacillus subtilis
NT1 bacillus thuringiensis
NT2 bacillus thuringiensis subsp. aizawai
NT2 bacillus thuringiensis subsp. dendrolimus
NT2 bacillus thuringiensis subsp. galleriae
NT2 bacillus thuringiensis subsp. israelensis
NT2 bacillus thuringiensis subsp. kurstaki
NT2 bacillus thuringiensis subsp. thuringiensis

BACILLUS ANTHRACIS
BT1 bacillus
BT2 bacillaceae
BT3 firmicutes
BT4 bacteria
BT5 prokaryotes
rt anthrax

BACILLUS BREVIS
BT1 bacillus
BT2 bacillaceae
BT3 firmicutes
BT4 bacteria
BT5 prokaryotes

BACILLUS CEREUS
BT1 bacillus
BT2 bacillaceae
BT3 firmicutes
BT4 bacteria
BT5 prokaryotes
BT1 bacterial insecticides
BT2 insecticides
BT3 pesticides
BT2 microbial pesticides
BT3 pesticides

BACILLUS CIRCULANS
BT1 bacillus
BT2 bacillaceae
BT3 firmicutes
BT4 bacteria
BT5 prokaryotes

BACILLUS COAGULANS
BT1 bacillus
BT2 bacillaceae
BT3 firmicutes
BT4 bacteria
BT5 prokaryotes

BACILLUS LARVAE
BT1 bacillus
BT2 bacillaceae
BT3 firmicutes
BT4 bacteria
BT5 prokaryotes
rt american foul brood

BACILLUS LICHENIFORMIS
BT1 bacillus
BT2 bacillaceae
BT3 firmicutes
BT4 bacteria
BT5 prokaryotes

BACILLUS MACERANS
BT1 bacillus
BT2 bacillaceae

BACILLUS MACERANS *cont.*
BT3 firmicutes
BT4 bacteria
BT5 prokaryotes
BT1 plant pathogenic bacteria
BT2 plant pathogens
BT3 pathogens

BACILLUS MEGATERIUM
BT1 bacillus
BT2 bacillaceae
BT3 firmicutes
BT4 bacteria
BT5 prokaryotes
BT1 plant pathogenic bacteria
BT2 plant pathogens
BT3 pathogens

BACILLUS MESENTERICUS
BT1 bacillus
BT2 bacillaceae
BT3 firmicutes
BT4 bacteria
BT5 prokaryotes

BACILLUS MYCOIDES
BT1 bacillus
BT2 bacillaceae
BT3 firmicutes
BT4 bacteria
BT5 prokaryotes

BACILLUS NATTO
BT1 bacillus
BT2 bacillaceae
BT3 firmicutes
BT4 bacteria
BT5 prokaryotes

BACILLUS PANTOTHENICUS
BT1 bacillus
BT2 bacillaceae
BT3 firmicutes
BT4 bacteria
BT5 prokaryotes

BACILLUS PENETRANS
BT1 bacillus
BT2 bacillaceae
BT3 firmicutes
BT4 bacteria
BT5 prokaryotes

BACILLUS PILIFORMIS
uf tyzzer disease agent
BT1 bacillus
BT2 bacillaceae
BT3 firmicutes
BT4 bacteria
BT5 prokaryotes

BACILLUS POLYMYXA
BT1 bacillus
BT2 bacillaceae
BT3 firmicutes
BT4 bacteria
BT5 prokaryotes
BT1 plant pathogenic bacteria
BT2 plant pathogens
BT3 pathogens

BACILLUS POPILLIAE
BT1 bacillus
BT2 bacillaceae
BT3 firmicutes
BT4 bacteria
BT5 prokaryotes
BT1 bacterial insecticides
BT2 insecticides
BT3 pesticides
BT2 microbial pesticides
BT3 pesticides

BACILLUS PUMILUS
BT1 bacillus
BT2 bacillaceae
BT3 firmicutes
BT4 bacteria
BT5 prokaryotes

BACILLUS SPHAERICUS
BT1 bacillus
BT2 bacillaceae
BT3 firmicutes

BACILLUS SPHAERICUS *cont.*
BT4 bacteria
BT5 prokaryotes
BT1 bacterial insecticides
BT2 insecticides
BT3 pesticides
BT2 microbial pesticides
BT3 pesticides

BACILLUS STEAROTHERMOPHILUS
BT1 bacillus
BT2 bacillaceae
BT3 firmicutes
BT4 bacteria
BT5 prokaryotes
NT1 bacillus stearothermophilus var. calidolactis

BACILLUS STEAROTHERMOPHILUS VAR. CALIDOLACTIS
HN from 1989
BT1 bacillus stearothermophilus
BT2 bacillus
BT3 bacillaceae
BT4 firmicutes
BT5 bacteria
BT6 prokaryotes

BACILLUS SUBTILIS
BT1 bacillus
BT2 bacillaceae
BT3 firmicutes
BT4 bacteria
BT5 prokaryotes
BT1 fungal antagonists
BT2 fungicides
BT3 pesticides
BT2 microbial pesticides
BT3 pesticides

BACILLUS THURINGIENSIS
BT1 bacillus
BT2 bacillaceae
BT3 firmicutes
BT4 bacteria
BT5 prokaryotes
NT1 bacillus thuringiensis subsp. aizawai
NT1 bacillus thuringiensis subsp. dendrolimus
NT1 bacillus thuringiensis subsp. galleriae
NT1 bacillus thuringiensis subsp. israelensis
NT1 bacillus thuringiensis subsp. kurstaki
NT1 bacillus thuringiensis subsp. thuringiensis
rt thuringiensin

BACILLUS THURINGIENSIS SUBSP. AIZAWAI
BT1 bacillus thuringiensis
BT2 bacillus
BT3 bacillaceae
BT4 firmicutes
BT5 bacteria
BT6 prokaryotes

BACILLUS THURINGIENSIS SUBSP. DENDROLIMUS
BT1 bacillus thuringiensis
BT2 bacillus
BT3 bacillaceae
BT4 firmicutes
BT5 bacteria
BT6 prokaryotes
BT1 bacterial insecticides
BT2 insecticides
BT3 pesticides
BT2 microbial pesticides
BT3 pesticides

BACILLUS THURINGIENSIS SUBSP. GALLERIAE
BT1 bacillus thuringiensis
BT2 bacillus
BT3 bacillaceae
BT4 firmicutes
BT5 bacteria
BT6 prokaryotes

BACILLUS THURINGIENSIS SUBSP. GALLERIAE *cont.*
BT1 bacterial insecticides
BT2 insecticides
BT3 pesticides
BT2 microbial pesticides
BT3 pesticides

BACILLUS THURINGIENSIS SUBSP. ISRAELENSIS
BT1 bacillus thuringiensis
BT2 bacillus
BT3 bacillaceae
BT4 firmicutes
BT5 bacteria
BT6 prokaryotes
BT1 bacterial insecticides
BT2 insecticides
BT3 pesticides
BT2 microbial pesticides
BT3 pesticides

BACILLUS THURINGIENSIS SUBSP. KURSTAKI
BT1 bacillus thuringiensis
BT2 bacillus
BT3 bacillaceae
BT4 firmicutes
BT5 bacteria
BT6 prokaryotes
BT1 bacterial insecticides
BT2 insecticides
BT3 pesticides
BT2 microbial pesticides
BT3 pesticides

BACILLUS THURINGIENSIS SUBSP. THURINGIENSIS
BT1 bacillus thuringiensis
BT2 bacillus
BT3 bacillaceae
BT4 firmicutes
BT5 bacteria
BT6 prokaryotes
BT1 bacterial insecticides
BT2 insecticides
BT3 pesticides
BT2 microbial pesticides
BT3 pesticides

BACITRACIN
BT1 antibacterial agents
BT2 antiinfective agents
BT3 drugs
BT1 antibiotics
BT1 growth promoters
BT2 growth regulators
BT2 promoters
BT1 polypeptides
BT2 peptides
rt zinc bacitracin

BACK
BT1 body regions
NT1 withers

BACK MUTATIONS
uf mutations, back
BT1 mutations

BACKCROSSES
BT1 crosses
BT2 hybrids
rt backcrossing

BACKCROSSING
BT1 crossing
BT2 breeding
rt backcrosses

BACKFAT
BT1 body fat
BT2 fat

BACKFILLING
rt drainage
rt filling
rt replacement

BACKPACKING (AGRICOLA)
BT1 outdoor recreation
BT2 recreation
rt hiking

BACKUSELLA
BT1 mucorales
NT1 backusella lamprospora
rt mucor

BACKUSELLA LAMPROSPORA
uf mucor lamprosporus
BT1 backusella
BT2 mucorales

BACON
BT1 meat products
BT2 animal products
BT3 products
BT1 pigmeat
BT2 meat
BT3 animal products
BT4 products
BT3 foods
rt ham

BACOPA
uf moniera
BT1 scrophulariaceae
NT1 bacopa monnieri
NT1 bacopa rotundifolia

BACOPA MONNIERI
BT1 bacopa
BT2 scrophulariaceae

BACOPA ROTUNDIFOLIA
BT1 bacopa
BT2 scrophulariaceae

BACTERIA
BT1 prokaryotes
NT1 eubacteriales
NT2 eubacterium
NT1 firmicutes
NT2 actinobacillus
NT3 actinobacillus equuli
NT3 actinobacillus lignieresii
NT3 actinobacillus pleuropneumoniae
NT2 actinomycetales
NT3 actinomycetaceae
NT4 actinomyces
NT5 actinomyces bovis
NT5 actinomyces israelii
NT5 actinomyces naeslundii
NT5 actinomyces odontolyticus
NT5 actinomyces pyogenes
NT5 actinomyces viscosus
NT4 bifidobacterium
NT5 bifidobacterium adolescentis
NT5 bifidobacterium bifidum
NT5 bifidobacterium breve
NT5 bifidobacterium infantum
NT5 bifidobacterium longum
NT4 kineosporia
NT5 kineosporia aurantiaca
NT3 dermatophilaceae
NT4 dermatophilus
NT5 dermatophilus congolensis
NT3 faenia
NT4 faenia rectivirgula
NT3 frankiaceae
NT4 frankia
NT5 frankia ceanothi
NT3 micromonosporaceae
NT4 micropolyspora
NT4 thermoactinomyces
NT5 thermoactinomyces candida
NT5 thermoactinomyces sacchari
NT5 thermoactinomyces vulgaris
NT4 thermopolyspora
NT3 nocardiaceae
NT4 actinomadura
NT5 actinomadura madurae
NT5 actinomadura pelletieri
NT4 nocardia
NT5 nocardia asteroides
NT5 nocardia brasiliensis
NT5 nocardia caviae
NT5 nocardia farcinica

BACTERIA *cont.*
NT4 nocardiopsis
NT4 rhodococcus (bacteria)
NT5 rhodococcus equi
NT5 rhodococcus fascians
NT3 renibacterium
NT4 renibacterium salmoninarum
NT3 streptomycetaceae
NT4 streptomyces
NT5 streptomyces albus
NT5 streptomyces collinus
NT5 streptomyces galbus
NT5 streptomyces griseus
NT5 streptomyces ipomoea
NT5 streptomyces olivocinereus
NT5 streptomyces scabies
NT5 streptomyces somaliensis
NT5 streptomyces viridosporus
NT2 agromyces
NT3 agromyces ramosus
NT2 arthrobacter
NT3 arthrobacter crystallopoietes
NT3 arthrobacter fluorescens
NT3 arthrobacter giacomelloi
NT3 arthrobacter globiformis
NT2 bacillaceae
NT3 bacillus
NT4 bacillus anthracis
NT4 bacillus brevis
NT4 bacillus cereus
NT4 bacillus circulans
NT4 bacillus coagulans
NT4 bacillus larvae
NT4 bacillus licheniformis
NT4 bacillus macerans
NT4 bacillus megaterium
NT4 bacillus mesentericus
NT4 bacillus mycoides
NT4 bacillus natto
NT4 bacillus pantothenicus
NT4 bacillus penetrans
NT4 bacillus piliformis
NT4 bacillus polymyxa
NT4 bacillus popilliae
NT4 bacillus pumilus
NT4 bacillus sphaericus
NT4 bacillus stearothermophilus
NT5 bacillus stearothermophilus var. calidolactis
NT4 bacillus subtilis
NT4 bacillus thuringiensis
NT5 bacillus thuringiensis subsp. aizawai
NT5 bacillus thuringiensis subsp. dendrolimus
NT5 bacillus thuringiensis subsp. galleriae
NT5 bacillus thuringiensis subsp. israelensis
NT5 bacillus thuringiensis subsp. kurstaki
NT5 bacillus thuringiensis subsp. thuringiensis
NT3 clostridium
NT4 clostridium acetobutylicum
NT4 clostridium bifermentans
NT4 clostridium botulinum
NT4 clostridium butyricum
NT4 clostridium chauvoei
NT4 clostridium difficile
NT4 clostridium haemolyticum
NT4 clostridium novyi
NT4 clostridium pasteurianum
NT4 clostridium perfringens
NT4 clostridium septicum
NT4 clostridium sordellii
NT4 clostridium sporogenes
NT4 clostridium tetani
NT4 clostridium thermocellum

BACTERIA *cont.*
NT4 clostridium tyrobutyricum
NT2 cellulomonas
NT2 chlamydiales
NT3 chlamydiaceae
NT4 chlamydia
NT5 chlamydia psittaci
NT5 chlamydia trachomatis
NT2 coryneform group of bacteria
NT3 brevibacteriaceae
NT4 brevibacterium
NT5 brevibacterium linens
NT3 clavibacter
NT4 clavibacter iranicus
NT4 clavibacter michiganensis
NT5 clavibacter michiganensis subsp. insidiosus
NT5 clavibacter michiganensis subsp. michiganensis
NT5 clavibacter michiganensis subsp. nebraskensis
NT5 clavibacter michiganensis subsp. sepedonicus
NT4 clavibacter rathayi
NT4 clavibacter tritici
NT4 clavibacter xyli
NT5 clavibacter xyli subsp. xyli
NT3 corynebacteriaceae
NT4 corynebacterium
NT5 corynebacterium bovis
NT5 corynebacterium ovis
NT5 corynebacterium pseudotuberculosis
NT5 corynebacterium renale
NT3 curtobacterium
NT4 curtobacterium flaccumfaciens
NT5 curtobacterium flaccumfaciens pv. betae
NT5 curtobacterium flaccumfaciens pv. flaccumfaciens
NT5 curtobacterium flaccumfaciens pv. oortii
NT5 curtobacterium flaccumfaciens pv. poinsettiae
NT3 propionibacteriaceae
NT4 propionibacterium
NT5 propionibacterium freudenreichii
NT6 propionibacterium freudenreichii subsp. shermanii
NT2 lactobacillaceae
NT3 erysipelothrix
NT4 erysipelothrix rhusiopathiae
NT3 lactobacillus
NT4 lactobacillus acidophilus
NT4 lactobacillus brevis
NT4 lactobacillus buchneri
NT4 lactobacillus bulgaricus
NT4 lactobacillus casei
NT5 lactobacillus casei subsp. alactosus
NT5 lactobacillus casei subsp. casei
NT5 lactobacillus casei subsp. rhamnosus
NT4 lactobacillus cellobiosus
NT4 lactobacillus delbrueckii
NT4 lactobacillus fermentum
NT4 lactobacillus helveticus
NT4 lactobacillus lactis
NT4 lactobacillus leichmannii
NT4 lactobacillus murinus
NT4 lactobacillus plantarum
NT4 lactobacillus reuteri
NT4 lactobacillus salivarius
NT4 lactobacillus sporogenes

BACTERIA *cont.*
NT4 lactobacillus viridescens
NT3 listeria
NT4 listeria monocytogenes
NT2 melissococcus
NT3 melissococcus pluton
NT2 micrococcaceae
NT3 micrococcus
NT4 micrococcus luteus
NT4 micrococcus varians
NT3 staphylococcus
NT4 staphylococcus albus
NT4 staphylococcus aureus
NT4 staphylococcus caseolyticus
NT4 staphylococcus epidermidis
NT4 staphylococcus hyicus
NT2 mycobacteriaceae
NT3 mycobacterium
NT4 mycobacterium avium
NT4 mycobacterium bovis
NT4 mycobacterium farcinogenes
NT4 mycobacterium paratuberculosis
NT4 mycobacterium phlei
NT4 mycobacterium smegmatis
NT4 mycobacterium tuberculosis
NT2 peptococcaceae
NT3 peptococcus
NT4 peptococcus indolicus
NT3 peptostreptococcus
NT3 ruminococcus
NT4 ruminococcus albus
NT3 sarcina
NT2 streptococcaceae
NT3 enterococcus
NT4 enterococcus faecalis
NT4 enterococcus faecium
NT3 leuconostoc
NT4 leuconostoc cremoris
NT4 leuconostoc dextranicum
NT4 leuconostoc lactis
NT4 leuconostoc mesenteroides
NT3 pediococcus
NT4 pediococcus acidilactici
NT4 pediococcus cerevisiae
NT4 pediococcus pentosaceus
NT3 streptococcus
NT4 streptococcus acetoinicus
NT4 streptococcus agalactiae
NT4 streptococcus bovis
NT4 streptococcus cremoris
NT4 streptococcus durans
NT4 streptococcus dysgalactiae
NT4 streptococcus equi
NT4 streptococcus equisimilis
NT4 streptococcus faecalis
NT4 streptococcus faecium
NT4 streptococcus lactis
NT4 streptococcus mitis
NT4 streptococcus mutans
NT4 streptococcus pneumoniae
NT4 streptococcus pyogenes
NT4 streptococcus salivarius
NT4 streptococcus suis
NT4 streptococcus thermophilus
NT4 streptococcus uberis
NT4 streptococcus viridans
NT4 streptococcus zooepidemicus
NT1 gracilicutes
NT2 acetobacteraceae
NT3 acetobacter
NT4 acetobacter aceti
NT2 alcaligenes
NT3 alcaligenes faecalis
NT3 alcaligenes latus
NT3 alcaligenes paradoxus
NT2 azotobacteraceae
NT3 azomonas
NT3 azotobacter

BACTERIA *cont.*
- **NT4** azotobacter beijerinckii
- **NT4** azotobacter chroococcum
- **NT4** azotobacter vinelandii
- **NT3** beijerinckia
- **NT4** beijerinckia indica
- **NT4** beijerinckia lacticogenes
- **NT3** derxia
- **NT2** bacteroidaceae
- **NT3** bacteroides
- **NT4** bacteroides nodosus
- **NT4** bacteroides ruminicola
- **NT3** butyrivibrio
- **NT4** butyrivibrio fibrisolvens
- **NT3** fusobacterium
- **NT4** fusobacterium necrophorum
- **NT2** bordetella
- **NT3** bordetella avium
- **NT3** bordetella bronchiseptica
- **NT2** brucellaceae
- **NT3** brucella
- **NT4** brucella abortus
- **NT4** brucella canis
- **NT4** brucella melitensis
- **NT4** brucella ovis
- **NT4** brucella suis
- **NT2** caulobacteraceae
- **NT3** gallionella
- **NT2** chromobacterium
- **NT3** chromobacterium lividum
- **NT2** cytophagaceae
- **NT3** cytophaga
- **NT3** flexibacter
- **NT3** saprospira
- **NT4** saprospira alba
- **NT2** desulfovibrio
- **NT3** desulfovibrio desulfuricans
- **NT3** desulfovibrio vulgaris
- **NT2** enterobacteriaceae
- **NT3** citrobacter
- **NT4** citrobacter freundii
- **NT3** edwardsiella
- **NT3** enterobacter
- **NT4** enterobacter aerogenes
- **NT4** enterobacter agglomerans
- **NT4** enterobacter cancerogenus
- **NT4** enterobacter cloacae
- **NT3** erwinia
- **NT4** erwinia amylovora
- **NT4** erwinia ananas
- **NT4** erwinia carotovora
- **NT5** erwinia carotovora subsp. atroseptica
- **NT5** erwinia carotovora subsp. betavasculorum
- **NT5** erwinia carotovora subsp. carotovora
- **NT4** erwinia chrysanthemi
- **NT5** erwinia chrysanthemi pv. chrysanthemi
- **NT5** erwinia chrysanthemi pv. dianthicola
- **NT5** erwinia chrysanthemi pv. dieffenbachiae
- **NT5** erwinia chrysanthemi pv. paradisiaca
- **NT5** erwinia chrysanthemi pv. parthenii
- **NT5** erwinia chrysanthemi pv. zeae
- **NT4** erwinia herbicola
- **NT5** erwinia herbicola pv. millettiae
- **NT4** erwinia rhapontici
- **NT4** erwinia rubrifaciens
- **NT4** erwinia salicis
- **NT4** erwinia stewartii
- **NT4** erwinia tracheiphila
- **NT4** erwinia uredovora
- **NT3** escherichia
- **NT4** escherichia coli
- **NT3** hafnia
- **NT4** hafnia alvei
- **NT3** klebsiella
- **NT4** klebsiella aerogenes
- **NT4** klebsiella oxytoca

BACTERIA *cont.*
- **NT4** klebsiella pneumoniae
- **NT3** morganella
- **NT3** proteus
- **NT4** proteus mirabilis
- **NT4** proteus vulgaris
- **NT3** providencia
- **NT3** salmonella
- **NT4** salmonella abortusequi
- **NT4** salmonella abortusovis
- **NT4** salmonella anatum
- **NT4** salmonella arizonae
- **NT4** salmonella choleraesuis
- **NT4** salmonella dublin
- **NT4** salmonella enteritidis
- **NT4** salmonella gallinarum
- **NT4** salmonella muenster
- **NT4** salmonella pullorum
- **NT4** salmonella typhi
- **NT4** salmonella typhimurium
- **NT3** serratia
- **NT4** serratia liquefasciens
- **NT4** serratia marcescens
- **NT3** shigella
- **NT4** shigella dysenteriae
- **NT4** shigella flexneri
- **NT4** shigella sonnei
- **NT3** xenorhabdus
- **NT4** xenorhabdus luminescens
- **NT4** xenorhabdus nematophilus
- **NT3** yersinia
- **NT4** yersinia enterocolitica
- **NT4** yersinia frederiksenii
- **NT4** yersinia intermedia
- **NT4** yersinia kristensenii
- **NT4** yersinia pseudotuberculosis
- **NT5** yersinia pseudotuberculosis subsp. pestis
- **NT4** yersinia ruckeri
- **NT2** flavobacterium
- **NT3** flavobacterium meningosepticum
- **NT2** francisella
- **NT3** francisella tularensis
- **NT2** legionellaceae
- **NT3** legionella
- **NT4** legionella pneumophila
- **NT2** lysobacterales
- **NT3** lysobacter
- **NT2** neisseriaceae
- **NT3** acinetobacter
- **NT4** acinetobacter calcoaceticus
- **NT3** branhamella
- **NT3** kingella
- **NT3** moraxella
- **NT4** moraxella anatipestifer
- **NT4** moraxella bovis
- **NT3** neisseria
- **NT2** nitrobacteraceae
- **NT3** nitrobacter
- **NT4** nitrobacter agilis
- **NT4** nitrobacter winogradskyi
- **NT3** nitrosolobus
- **NT3** nitrosomonas
- **NT3** paracoccus
- **NT4** paracoccus denitrificans
- **NT2** pasteurellaceae
- **NT3** haemophilus
- **NT4** haemophilus equigenitalis
- **NT4** haemophilus paragallinarum
- **NT4** haemophilus somnus
- **NT3** histophilus
- **NT3** pasteurella
- **NT4** pasteurella haemolytica
- **NT4** pasteurella multocida
- **NT2** pseudomonadaceae
- **NT3** pseudomonas
- **NT4** pseudomonas aeruginosa
- **NT4** pseudomonas andropogonis
- **NT4** pseudomonas avenae
- **NT4** pseudomonas azotogensis

BACTERIA *cont.*
- **NT4** pseudomonas caryophylli
- **NT4** pseudomonas cepacia
- **NT4** pseudomonas cichorii
- **NT4** pseudomonas corrugata
- **NT4** pseudomonas fluorescens
- **NT4** pseudomonas fragi
- **NT4** pseudomonas fuscovaginae
- **NT4** pseudomonas gladioli
- **NT5** pseudomonas gladioli pv. alliicola
- **NT5** pseudomonas gladioli pv. gladioli
- **NT4** pseudomonas glumae
- **NT4** pseudomonas mallei
- **NT4** pseudomonas maltophilia
- **NT4** pseudomonas marginalis
- **NT5** pseudomonas marginalis pv. alfalfae
- **NT5** pseudomonas marginalis pv. marginalis
- **NT5** pseudomonas marginalis pv. pastinaceae
- **NT4** pseudomonas plantarii
- **NT4** pseudomonas pseudoalcaligenes
- **NT5** pseudomonas pseudoalcaligenes subsp. konjaci
- **NT4** pseudomonas pseudomallei
- **NT4** pseudomonas putida
- **NT4** pseudomonas rubrilineans
- **NT4** pseudomonas solanacearum
- **NT4** pseudomonas striata
- **NT4** pseudomonas syringae
- **NT5** pseudomonas syringae pv. aptata
- **NT5** pseudomonas syringae pv. atrofaciens
- **NT5** pseudomonas syringae pv. atropurpurea
- **NT5** pseudomonas syringae pv. coronafaciens
- **NT5** pseudomonas syringae pv. dendropanicis
- **NT5** pseudomonas syringae pv. garcae
- **NT5** pseudomonas syringae pv. glycinea
- **NT5** pseudomonas syringae pv. helianthi
- **NT5** pseudomonas syringae pv. lachrymans
- **NT5** pseudomonas syringae pv. maculicola
- **NT5** pseudomonas syringae pv. mori
- **NT5** pseudomonas syringae pv. morsprunorum
- **NT5** pseudomonas syringae pv. panici
- **NT5** pseudomonas syringae pv. papulans
- **NT5** pseudomonas syringae pv. persicae
- **NT5** pseudomonas syringae pv. phaseolicola
- **NT5** pseudomonas syringae pv. pisi
- **NT5** pseudomonas syringae pv. savastanoi
- **NT5** pseudomonas syringae pv. sesami
- **NT5** pseudomonas syringae pv. syringae
- **NT5** pseudomonas syringae pv. tabaci
- **NT5** pseudomonas syringae pv. tagetis
- **NT5** pseudomonas syringae pv. theae

BACTERIA *cont.*
- **NT5** pseudomonas syringae pv. tomato
- **NT4** pseudomonas syzygii
- **NT4** pseudomonas testeroni
- **NT4** pseudomonas tolaasii
- **NT4** pseudomonas viridiflava
- **NT3** xanthomonas
- **NT4** xanthomonas albilineans
- **NT4** xanthomonas campestris
- **NT5** xanthomonas campestris pv. alfalfae
- **NT5** xanthomonas campestris pv. armoraciae
- **NT5** xanthomonas campestris pv. begoniae
- **NT5** xanthomonas campestris pv. betlicola
- **NT5** xanthomonas campestris pv. cajani
- **NT5** xanthomonas campestris pv. campestris
- **NT5** xanthomonas campestris pv. cassavae
- **NT5** xanthomonas campestris pv. citri
- **NT5** xanthomonas campestris pv. corylina
- **NT5** xanthomonas campestris pv. cyamopsidis
- **NT5** xanthomonas campestris pv. dieffenbachiae
- **NT5** xanthomonas campestris pv. glycines
- **NT5** xanthomonas campestris pv. graminis
- **NT5** xanthomonas campestris pv. hederae
- **NT5** xanthomonas campestris pv. holcicola
- **NT5** xanthomonas campestris pv. hyacinthi
- **NT5** xanthomonas campestris pv. juglandis
- **NT5** xanthomonas campestris pv. malvacearum
- **NT5** xanthomonas campestris pv. mangiferaeindicae
- **NT5** xanthomonas campestris pv. manihotis
- **NT5** xanthomonas campestris pv. oryzae
- **NT5** xanthomonas campestris pv. oryzicola
- **NT5** xanthomonas campestris pv. pelargonii
- **NT5** xanthomonas campestris pv. phaseoli
- **NT5** xanthomonas campestris pv. pruni
- **NT5** xanthomonas campestris pv. ricini
- **NT5** xanthomonas campestris pv. sesami
- **NT5** xanthomonas campestris pv. syngonii
- **NT5** xanthomonas campestris pv. translucens
- **NT5** xanthomonas campestris pv. undulosa
- **NT5** xanthomonas campestris pv. vasculorum

BACTERIA *cont.*
NT5 xanthomonas campestris pv. vesicatoria
NT5 xanthomonas campestris pv. vignaeradiatae
NT5 xanthomonas campestris pv. vignicola
NT4 xanthomonas fragariae
NT4 xanthomonas heterocea
NT4 xanthomonas populi
NT3 xylophilus
NT4 xylophilus ampelinus
NT2 rhizobiaceae
NT3 agrobacterium
NT4 agrobacterium radiobacter
NT4 agrobacterium rhizogenes
NT4 agrobacterium rubi
NT4 agrobacterium tumefaciens
NT3 bradyrhizobium
NT4 bradyrhizobium japonicum
NT3 rhizobium
NT4 rhizobium leguminosarum
NT4 rhizobium lupini
NT4 rhizobium meliloti
NT4 rhizobium phaseoli
NT4 rhizobium trifolii
NT2 selenomonas
NT3 selenomonas ruminantium
NT2 spirillaceae
NT3 azospirillum
NT4 azospirillum brasilense
NT4 azospirillum lipoferum
NT3 bdellovibrio
NT3 campylobacter
NT4 campylobacter fetus
NT4 campylobacter jejuni
NT4 campylobacter sputorum
NT3 spirillum
NT4 spirillum lipoferum
NT2 spirochaetales
NT3 leptospiraceae
NT4 leptospira
NT5 leptospira interrogans
NT3 spirochaetaceae
NT4 borrelia
NT5 borrelia anserina
NT5 borrelia burgdorferi
NT5 borrelia latyschevi
NT5 borrelia persica
NT5 borrelia recurrentis
NT3 treponemataceae
NT4 treponema
NT5 treponema hyodysenteriae
NT2 streptobacillus
NT2 taylorella
NT3 taylorella equigenitalis
NT2 thiobacteriaceae
NT3 thiobacillus
NT4 thiobacillus ferrooxidans
NT4 thiobacillus thiooxidans
NT2 vibrionaceae
NT3 aeromonas
NT4 aeromonas hydrophila
NT4 aeromonas salmonicida
NT3 photobacterium
NT3 plesiomonas
NT3 vibrio
NT4 vibrio anguillarum
NT4 vibrio cholerae
NT2 wolinella
NT2 xylella
NT3 xylella fastidiosa
NT2 zymomonas
NT3 zymomonas mobilis
NT1 mendosicutes
NT2 methanobacteriaceae
NT3 methanobacterium
NT2 methanosarcinaceae
NT3 methanosarcina
NT4 methanosarcina barkeri
NT1 rickettsiales
NT2 anaplasmataceae

BACTERIA *cont.*
NT3 aegyptianella
NT4 aegyptianella pullorum
NT3 anaplasma
NT4 anaplasma centrale
NT4 anaplasma marginale
NT4 anaplasma ovis
NT3 eperythrozoon
NT4 eperythrozoon coccoides
NT4 eperythrozoon felis
NT4 eperythrozoon ovis
NT4 eperythrozoon suis
NT4 eperythrozoon wenyoni
NT3 haemobartonella
NT4 haemobartonella bovis
NT4 haemobartonella canis
NT4 haemobartonella felis
NT4 haemobartonella muris
NT3 paranaplasma
NT4 paranaplasma caudata
NT2 bartonellaceae
NT3 bartonella
NT4 bartonella bacilliformis
NT3 grahamella
NT2 colesiota
NT2 ehrlichiaceae
NT3 cowdria
NT4 cowdria ruminantium
NT3 cytoecetes
NT3 ehrlichia
NT4 ehrlichia canis
NT4 ehrlichia phagocytophila
NT4 ehrlichia risticii
NT3 neorickettsia
NT2 rickettsia-like organisms
NT2 rickettsiaceae
NT3 coxiella
NT4 coxiella burnetii
NT3 rickettsia
NT4 rickettsia conorii
NT4 rickettsia montana
NT4 rickettsia parkeri
NT4 rickettsia prowazekii
NT4 rickettsia rhipicephali
NT4 rickettsia rickettsii
NT4 rickettsia sibirica
NT4 rickettsia tsutsugamushi
NT4 rickettsia typhi
NT2 wolbachiaceae
NT3 wolbachia
NT4 wolbachia pipientis
NT1 tenericutes
NT2 mollicutes
NT3 acholeplasmatales
NT4 acholeplasmataceae
NT5 acholeplasma
NT6 acholeplasma laidlawii
NT3 mycoplasmatales
NT4 mycoplasma-like organisms
NT4 mycoplasmataceae
NT5 mycoplasma
NT6 mycoplasma agalactiae
NT6 mycoplasma alkalescens
NT6 mycoplasma arginini
NT6 mycoplasma bovigenitalium
NT6 mycoplasma bovirhinis
NT6 mycoplasma bovis
NT6 mycoplasma californicum
NT6 mycoplasma canadense
NT6 mycoplasma capricolum
NT6 mycoplasma dispar
NT6 mycoplasma felis
NT6 mycoplasma gallisepticum
NT6 mycoplasma hyopneumoniae
NT6 mycoplasma hyorhinis
NT6 mycoplasma hyosynoviae
NT6 mycoplasma iowae
NT6 mycoplasma meleagridis

BACTERIA *cont.*
NT6 mycoplasma mycoides
NT6 mycoplasma ovipneumoniae
NT6 mycoplasma pulmonis
NT6 mycoplasma putrefasciens
NT6 mycoplasma synoviae
NT5 ureaplasma
NT6 ureaplasma diversum
NT4 spiroplasmataceae
NT5 spiroplasma
NT6 spiroplasma citri
NT6 spiroplasma kunkelii
NT6 spiroplasma phoeniceum
rt antibacterial properties
rt antitoxins
rt bacterial agglutination
rt bacterial antigens
rt bacterial counting
rt bacterial diseases
rt bacterial insecticides
rt bacterial leaching
rt bacterial products
rt bacterial protein
rt bacterial proteins
rt bacterial spores
rt bacterial toxins
rt bactericides
rt bacteriocins
rt bacteriology
rt bacteriophages
rt butyric acid bacteria
rt coliform bacteria
rt culture collections
rt cultures
rt cyanobacteria
rt endotoxins
rt entomopathogenic bacteria
rt fimbriae
rt germfree animals
rt germfree husbandry
rt gram negative bacteria
rt gram positive bacteria
rt ice nucleation
rt lactic acid bacteria
rt microbial flora
rt microorganisms
rt nitrogen fixing bacteria
rt plant pathogenic bacteria
rt propionic acid bacteria
rt psychrophilic bacteria
rt psychrotrophic bacteria
rt rumen bacteria
rt soil bacteria
rt sulfate reducing bacteria
rt thermoduric bacteria
rt thermophilic bacteria

bacteria, coliform
USE **coliform bacteria**

bacteria, psychrophilic
USE **psychrophilic bacteria**

bacteria, psychrotrophic
USE **psychrotrophic bacteria**

bacteria, rumen
USE **rumen bacteria**

bacteria, thermoduric
USE **thermoduric bacteria**

bacteria, thermophilic
USE **thermophilic bacteria**

BACTERIAL AGGLUTINATION
BT1 agglutination
rt bacteria

BACTERIAL ANTIGENS
BT1 antigens
BT2 immunological factors
NT1 tuberculin
rt bacteria

BACTERIAL COUNT
NT1 plate count
rt bacterial counting
rt bacteriology

BACTERIAL COUNT *cont.*
rt microbial flora

BACTERIAL COUNTING
BT1 counting
BT2 recording
rt bacteria
rt bacterial count

BACTERIAL DISEASES
(see also under animal diseases and plant diseases)
uf bacterioses
uf diseases, bacterial
BT1 infectious diseases
BT2 diseases
NT1 actinomycosis
NT2 cervicofacial actinomycosis
NT1 anaplasmosis
NT1 anthrax
NT1 botulism
NT1 brucellosis
NT1 glanders
NT1 heartwater
NT1 leptospirosis
NT1 lyme disease
NT1 mycoplasmosis
NT1 pasteurellosis
NT1 psittacosis
NT1 salmonellosis
NT1 tetanus
NT1 tick pyaemia
NT1 tuberculosis
NT1 typhoid
rt abscesses
rt antibacterial properties
rt bacteria
rt microbial flora
rt pus
rt septicaemia

bacterial flora
USE **microbial flora**

BACTERIAL INSECTICIDES
BT1 insecticides
BT2 pesticides
BT1 microbial pesticides
BT2 pesticides
NT1 bacillus cereus
NT1 bacillus popilliae
NT1 bacillus sphaericus
NT1 bacillus thuringiensis subsp. dendrolimus
NT1 bacillus thuringiensis subsp. galleriae
NT1 bacillus thuringiensis subsp. israelensis
NT1 bacillus thuringiensis subsp. kurstaki
NT1 bacillus thuringiensis subsp. thuringiensis
rt bacteria
rt bacterial products
rt biological control
rt entomopathogenic bacteria

BACTERIAL LEACHING
BT1 mining
BT2 industry
rt bacteria
rt leaching

BACTERIAL PRODUCTS
BT1 products
rt antibiotics
rt bacteria
rt bacterial insecticides

BACTERIAL PROTEIN
BT1 single cell protein
BT2 protein products
BT3 products
rt bacteria

BACTERIAL PROTEINS
HN from 1990
BT1 microbial proteins
BT2 proteins
BT3 peptides
rt bacteria

BACTERIAL SPORES
BT1 spores
BT2 cells
rt bacteria

BACTERIAL TOXINS
BT1 toxins
NT1 phaseolotoxin
NT1 thuringiensin
rt bacteria

bactericidal plants
USE **antibacterial plants**

bactericidal properties
USE **antibacterial properties**

BACTERICIDES
BT1 pesticides
NT1 dehydroacetic acid
NT1 formaldehyde
NT1 nitrapyrin
NT1 streptomycin
rt antibacterial properties
rt bacteria

BACTERIOCINS
BT1 antibiotics
NT1 colicins
rt bacteria
rt bacteriophages

BACTERIOLOGY
BT1 microbiology
BT2 biology
rt bacteria
rt bacterial count
rt biotechnology
rt microbial flora

BACTERIOPHAGES
uf *phages*
BT1 viruses
rt antibacterial properties
rt bacteria
rt bacteriocins
rt lysogeny
rt lysotypes
rt phasmids
rt transduction

bacterioses
USE **bacterial diseases**

BACTEROIDACEAE
BT1 gracilicutes
BT2 bacteria
BT3 prokaryotes
NT1 bacteroides
NT2 bacteroides nodosus
NT2 bacteroides ruminicola
NT1 butyrivibrio
NT2 butyrivibrio fibrisolvens
NT1 fusobacterium
NT2 fusobacterium necrophorum

BACTEROIDES
BT1 bacteroidaceae
BT2 gracilicutes
BT3 bacteria
BT4 prokaryotes
NT1 bacteroides nodosus
NT1 bacteroides ruminicola

BACTEROIDES NODOSUS
uf *fusiformis nodosum*
BT1 bacteroides
BT2 bacteroidaceae
BT3 gracilicutes
BT4 bacteria
BT5 prokaryotes
rt foot rot

BACTEROIDES RUMINICOLA
BT1 bacteroides
BT2 bacteroidaceae
BT3 gracilicutes
BT4 bacteria
BT5 prokaryotes

BACTEROIDS
BT1 microbial flora
BT2 flora

BACTOFUGATION
BT1 milk processing
BT2 processing

BACTRA
BT1 tortricidae
BT2 lepidoptera
NT1 bactra verutana

BACTRA VERUTANA
BT1 bactra
BT2 tortricidae
BT3 lepidoptera

bactrian camels
USE **camels**

BACTRIS
uf *guilielma*
BT1 palmae
NT1 bactris gasipaes

BACTRIS GASIPAES
uf *bactris minor*
uf *guilielma gasipaes*
uf *guilielma speciosa*
uf *guilielma utilis*
BT1 bactris
BT2 palmae
BT1 tropical tree fruits
BT2 tree fruits
BT2 tropical fruits
BT3 fruit crops

bactris minor
USE **bactris gasipaes**

BACTROCERA
HN from 1990
uf *strumeta*
uf *tetradacus*
BT1 tephritidae
BT2 diptera
NT1 bactrocera cacuminata
NT1 bactrocera cucumis
NT1 bactrocera cucurbitae
NT1 bactrocera dorsalis
NT1 bactrocera oleae
NT1 bactrocera tryoni
NT1 bactrocera tsuneonis
NT1 bactrocera zonata
rt dacus

BACTROCERA CACUMINATA
HN from 1989; previously "dacus cacuminatus"
uf *dacus cacuminatus*
BT1 bactrocera
BT2 tephritidae
BT3 diptera

BACTROCERA CUCUMIS
HN from 1989; previously "dacus cucumis"
uf *dacus cucumis*
BT1 bactrocera
BT2 tephritidae
BT3 diptera

BACTROCERA CUCURBITAE
HN from 1989; previously "dacus cucurbitae"
uf *dacus cucurbitae*
uf *strumeta cucurbitae*
BT1 bactrocera
BT2 tephritidae
BT3 diptera

BACTROCERA DORSALIS
HN from 1989; previously "dacus dorsalis"
uf *dacus dorsalis*
uf *dacus ferrugineus*
BT1 bactrocera
BT2 tephritidae
BT3 diptera

BACTROCERA OLEAE
HN from 1989; previously "dacus oleae"
uf *dacus oleae*
BT1 bactrocera
BT2 tephritidae
BT3 diptera

BACTROCERA TRYONI
HN from 1989; previously "dacus tryoni"
uf *dacus tryoni*
uf *strumeta tryoni*
BT1 bactrocera
BT2 tephritidae
BT3 diptera

BACTROCERA TSUNEONIS
HN from 1989; previously "dacus tsuneonis"
uf *dacus citri*
uf *dacus tsuneonis*
uf *tetradacus citri*
BT1 bactrocera
BT2 tephritidae
BT3 diptera

BACTROCERA ZONATA
HN from 1989; previously "dacus zonatus"
uf *dacus zonatus*
BT1 bactrocera
BT2 tephritidae
BT3 diptera

BACULOVIRIDAE
BT1 insect viruses
BT2 entomopathogens
BT3 pathogens
BT1 viruses
NT1 baculovirus
NT2 granulosis viruses
NT2 nuclear polyhedrosis viruses
NT3 baculovirus heliothis

BACULOVIRUS
BT1 baculoviridae
BT2 insect viruses
BT3 entomopathogens
BT4 pathogens
BT2 viruses
NT1 granulosis viruses
NT1 nuclear polyhedrosis viruses
NT2 baculovirus heliothis

BACULOVIRUS HELIOTHIS
BT1 nuclear polyhedrosis viruses
BT2 baculovirus
BT3 baculoviridae
BT4 insect viruses
BT5 entomopathogens
BT6 pathogens
BT4 viruses
BT1 viral insecticides
BT2 insecticides
BT3 pesticides
BT2 microbial pesticides
BT3 pesticides

BADEN-WURTTEMBERG
BT1 german federal republic
BT2 western europe
BT3 europe

BADGERS
BT1 wild animals
BT2 animals
rt meles

BADMINTON
BT1 ball games
BT2 games
BT2 sport

bael
USE **aegle marmelos**

BAG LUNCHES (AGRICOLA)
BT1 lunch (agricola)
BT2 meals

BAGASSA
HN from 1990
BT1 moraceae
NT1 bagassa guianensis

BAGASSA GUIANENSIS
HN from 1990
BT1 bagassa
BT2 moraceae
BT1 forest trees

BAGASSE
BT1 agricultural wastes
BT2 wastes
BT1 plant residues
BT2 residues
NT1 sisal bagasse
NT1 sugarcane bagasse
rt manures

BAGGARA
HN from 1990
BT1 cattle breeds
BT2 breeds

BAGGING
BT1 packaging
BT2 handling
rt packages
rt sacks

BAGRADA
BT1 pentatomidae
BT2 heteroptera
NT1 bagrada hilaris

bagrada cruciferarum
USE **bagrada hilaris**

BAGRADA HILARIS
uf *bagrada cruciferarum*
BT1 bagrada
BT2 pentatomidae
BT3 heteroptera

BAGRE
BT1 ariidae
BT2 siluriformes
BT3 osteichthyes
BT4 fishes

BAGRIDAE
BT1 siluriformes
BT2 osteichthyes
BT3 fishes
NT1 chrysichthys
NT2 chrysichthys walkeri

BAGS (AGRICOLA)
BT1 containers
NT1 paper bags (agricola)

BAHAMAS
BT1 caribbean
BT2 america
rt acp
rt caribbean community
rt commonwealth of nations

bahia grass
USE **paspalum notatum**

BAHRAIN
BT1 persian gulf states
BT2 west asia
BT3 asia
rt arab countries
rt middle east
rt west asia

BAIKIAEA
BT1 leguminosae
NT1 baikiaea insignis
NT1 baikiaea plurijuga
rt browse plants

BAIKIAEA INSIGNIS
BT1 baikiaea
BT2 leguminosae

BAIKIAEA PLURIJUGA
BT1 baikiaea
BT2 leguminosae

BAILEYA
BT1 compositae
NT1 baileya multiradiata
NT1 baileya pauciradiata

BAILEYA MULTIRADIATA
BT1 baileya
BT2 compositae
BT1 medicinal plants

BAILEYA PAUCIRADIATA
BT1 baileya

BAILEYA PAUCIRADIATA *cont.*
BT2 compositae
BT1 medicinal plants

BAISSEA
BT1 apocynaceae

BAIT SPREADERS
BT1 spreaders
BT2 application equipment
BT3 equipment
BT2 farm machinery
BT3 machinery
rt baiting
rt baits

BAIT TRAPS
BT1 traps
BT2 equipment
rt baiting
rt baits
rt insecticides

BAITING
rt bait spreaders
rt bait traps
rt baits
rt control methods
rt trapping

BAITS
BT1 attractants
rt bait spreaders
rt bait traps
rt baiting
rt trapping

bajra
USE **pennisetum americanum**

baked goods
USE **bakery products**

BAKERS (AGRICOLA)
BT1 occupations

BAKERS' CHEESE
BT1 cheeses
BT2 milk products
BT3 products

BAKERS' YEAST
uf *yeast, bakers'*
BT1 yeasts

BAKERY INDUSTRY
BT1 food industry
BT2 industry
rt bakery products
rt baking

BAKERY PRODUCTS
uf *baked goods*
BT1 foods
BT1 products
NT1 biscuits
NT2 wafers
NT1 bread
NT2 gluten free bread
NT2 quick breads (agricola)
NT2 yeast breads (agricola)
NT1 cakes
NT1 muffins (agricola)
NT1 pies (agricola)
NT1 pizzas (agricola)
NT1 tortillas
rt bakery industry
rt baking
rt batters (agricola)
rt breadmaking
rt chapattis
rt doughs (agricola)

BAKHTIARI-LURI
HN from 1990
BT1 sheep breeds
BT2 breeds

BAKING
BT1 processing
rt bakery industry
rt bakery products
rt breadmaking
rt food technology
rt leavening agents (agricola)

baking characteristics
USE **baking quality**

BAKING QUALITY
uf *baking characteristics*
uf *flour quality*
uf *milling and baking quality*
uf *quality for milling and baking*
BT1 food processing quality
BT2 processing quality
BT3 quality
rt milling quality

BALAENA
BT1 balaenidae
BT2 mysticeti
BT3 cetacea
BT4 mammals
NT1 balaena mysticetus

BALAENA MYSTICETUS
BT1 balaena
BT2 balaenidae
BT3 mysticeti
BT4 cetacea
BT5 mammals

BALAENIDAE
BT1 mysticeti
BT2 cetacea
BT3 mammals
NT1 balaena
NT2 balaena mysticetus

BALAENOPTERIDAE
BT1 mysticeti
BT2 cetacea
BT3 mammals
NT1 megaptera
NT2 megaptera novaeangliae

balance of nature
USE **ecological balance**

BALANCE OF PAYMENTS
NT1 terms of trade
rt balance of trade
rt external debt
rt monetary agreements
rt monetary policy
rt public ownership

BALANCE OF TRADE
BT1 trade policy
BT2 economic policy
rt balance of payments
rt supply balance

BALANCE SHEETS
BT1 accounting
NT1 cash flow
rt assets
rt cash flow
rt liabilities

BALANCE STUDIES (AGRICOLA)
BT1 methodology
rt nutrition

BALANCED LETHALS
uf *lethals, balanced*
BT1 heterozygotes
BT2 genotypes
BT1 lethals
BT2 genes

BALANCES
uf *scales (balances)*
BT1 instruments
rt weighbridges
rt weighers
rt weight

BALANGIR
HN from 1990
BT1 sheep breeds
BT2 breeds

balaninus
USE **curculio**

balaninus nucum
USE **curculio nucum**

BALANITES
BT1 zygophyllaceae
NT1 balanites aegyptiaca

BALANITES AEGYPTIACA
uf *balanites roxburghii*
BT1 balanites
BT2 zygophyllaceae
BT1 forest trees
BT1 medicinal plants
BT1 molluscicidal plants
BT2 pesticidal plants
BT1 oilseed plants
BT2 fatty oil plants
BT3 oil plants

balanites roxburghii
USE **balanites aegyptiaca**

BALANITIS
ufa *balanoposthitis*
BT1 male genital diseases
BT2 organic diseases
BT3 diseases

BALANOPHORA
BT1 balanophoraceae

BALANOPHORACEAE
NT1 balanophora

balanoposthitis
USE **balanitis**
AND **posthitis**

BALANTIDIUM
BT1 ciliophora
BT2 protozoa
NT1 balantidium coli
NT1 balantidium ctenopharyngodonis
NT1 balantidium entozoon
NT1 balantidium kakatiyae

BALANTIDIUM COLI
BT1 balantidium
BT2 ciliophora
BT3 protozoa

BALANTIDIUM CTENOPHARYNGODONIS
BT1 balantidium
BT2 ciliophora
BT3 protozoa

BALANTIDIUM ENTOZOON
BT1 balantidium
BT2 ciliophora
BT3 protozoa

BALANTIDIUM KAKATIYAE
BT1 balantidium
BT2 ciliophora
BT3 protozoa

BALANUS
BT1 thoracica
BT2 cirripedia
BT3 crustacea
BT4 arthropods
rt semibalanus

balanus balanoides
USE **semibalanus balanoides**

BALBAS
BT1 sheep breeds
BT2 breeds

BALDUINA
BT1 compositae
NT1 balduina angustifolia

BALDUINA ANGUSTIFOLIA
BT1 balduina
BT2 compositae
BT1 medicinal plants

BALE COLLECTORS
BT1 farm machinery
BT2 machinery
rt bale loaders
rt bale throwers
rt bales

BALE LOADERS
uf *loaders, bale*
BT1 loaders
BT2 handling machinery
BT3 machinery
rt bale collectors
rt bale throwers
rt bales

bale sledges
USE **sledges**

BALE THROWERS
BT1 farm machinery
BT2 machinery
rt bale collectors
rt bale loaders
rt bales
rt conveyors
rt elevators
rt loaders

BALEARIC ISLANDS
HN from 1990
BT1 spain
BT2 western europe
BT3 europe

BALERS
BT1 farm machinery
BT2 machinery
NT1 big balers
NT1 high density balers
NT1 pickup balers
NT1 roll balers
rt bales
rt baling
rt presses
rt straw trussers

balers, big
USE **big balers**

balers, high density
USE **high density balers**

balers, pick up
USE **pickup balers**

balers, roll
USE **roll balers**

BALES
BT1 packages
NT1 high density bales
NT1 large bales
NT1 round bales
NT1 straw bales
rt bale collectors
rt bale loaders
rt bale throwers
rt balers
rt baling

BALFOURODENDRON
BT1 rutaceae
NT1 balfourodendron riedelianum

BALFOURODENDRON RIEDELIANUM
BT1 balfourodendron
BT2 rutaceae

BALI
BT1 indonesia
BT2 south east asia
BT3 asia

BALI (CATTLE BREED)
HN from 1990; previously "balinese"
uf *balinese*
BT1 cattle breeds
BT2 breeds

balinese
USE **bali (cattle breed)**

BALING
BT1 packaging
BT2 handling
rt balers
rt bales
rt pickup balers
rt pressing

BALING *cont.*
rt twine
rt tying devices

BALIOSPERMUM
BT1 euphorbiaceae
NT1 baliospermum axillare

BALIOSPERMUM AXILLARE
uf baliospermum indicum
uf baliospermum montanum
BT1 baliospermum
BT2 euphorbiaceae
BT1 poisonous plants

baliospermum indicum
USE **baliospermum axillare**

baliospermum montanum
USE **baliospermum axillare**

BALIOTHRIPS
uf chloethrips
BT1 thripidae
BT2 thysanoptera
rt stenchaetothrips

baliothrips biformis
USE **stenchaetothrips biformis**

BALISTES
BT1 balistidae
BT2 tetraodontiformes
BT3 osteichthyes
BT4 fishes

BALISTIDAE
uf filefishes
uf monacanthidae
uf triggerfishes
BT1 tetraodontiformes
BT2 osteichthyes
BT3 fishes
NT1 alutera
NT1 balistes
NT1 monacanthus
NT1 xanthichthys

BALKAN ENDEMIC NEPHROPATHY
BT1 mycotoxicoses
BT2 poisoning
BT1 nephropathy
BT2 abnormalities
BT2 kidney diseases
BT3 urinary tract diseases
BT4 organic diseases
BT5 diseases

BALKANS
BT1 europe
rt albania
rt bulgaria
rt eastern europe
rt romania
rt yugoslavia

BALKHI
BT1 sheep breeds
BT2 breeds

BALL GAMES
BT1 games
BT1 sport
NT1 badminton
NT1 baseball
NT1 basketball
NT1 bowling
NT1 cricket
NT1 croquet
NT1 football
NT2 american football
NT2 australian football
NT2 soccer
NT1 golf
NT1 handball
NT1 hockey
NT1 rugby
NT1 squash rackets
NT1 tennis
rt indoor games
rt outdoor games

ball mills
USE **crushing mills**

BALLAST
BT1 traction aids
BT2 components
NT1 wheel weights
rt bulk
rt loading
rt stability
rt tractors
rt tyres
rt water ballasting
rt weights

BALLED STOCK
BT1 planting stock

BALLET
BT1 dancing
BT2 performing arts
BT3 arts

BALLING
BT1 aggressive behaviour
BT2 behaviour
rt queen honeybees
rt worker honeybees

BALLISTOCARDIOGRAPHY
BT1 diagnostic techniques
BT2 techniques
rt heart rate

BALLOON TIRES
BF balloon tyres
BT1 tires

BALLOON TYRES
AF balloon tires
uf tyres, balloon
BT1 tyres
BT2 components

BALLOONS
BT1 aircraft
rt logging

BALLOTA
BT1 labiatae
NT1 ballota lanata
NT1 ballota nigra
NT1 ballota rupestris

ballota foetida
USE **ballota nigra**

ballota hispanica
USE **ballota rupestris**

BALLOTA LANATA
BT1 ballota
BT2 labiatae

BALLOTA NIGRA
uf ballota foetida
BT1 ballota
BT2 labiatae
BT1 medicinal plants

BALLOTA RUPESTRIS
uf ballota hispanica
BT1 ballota
BT2 labiatae
BT1 medicinal plants

BALSAMINACEAE
NT1 impatiens
NT2 impatiens balsamina
NT2 impatiens capensis
NT2 impatiens glandulifera
NT2 impatiens walleriana

BALSAMORHIZA
BT1 compositae
NT1 balsamorhiza careyana

BALSAMORHIZA CAREYANA
BT1 balsamorhiza
BT2 compositae

BALTIC BLACK PIED
BT1 cattle breeds
BT2 breeds

BALTIC SEA
BT1 northeast atlantic
BT2 atlantic ocean
BT3 marine areas

BALTIMORA
BT1 compositae
NT1 baltimora recta

BALTIMORA RECTA
BT1 baltimora
BT2 compositae

BALUCHI
BT1 horse breeds
BT2 breeds
BT1 sheep breeds
BT2 breeds

baluchi (goat breed)
USE **khurasani**

BALUCHISTAN
BT1 pakistan
BT2 south asia
BT3 asia

BAMBARA
BT1 cattle breeds
BT2 breeds

bambara groundnuts
USE **vigna subterranea**

BAMBERMYCIN
uf flavomycin
uf flavophospholipol
BT1 antibacterial agents
BT2 antiinfective agents
BT3 drugs
BT1 antibiotics
BT1 feed additives
BT2 additives

BAMBOO SHOOTS
BT1 plant products
BT2 products
BT1 stem vegetables
BT2 vegetables
rt bambusa

BAMBOOS
rt arundinaria
rt bambusa
rt building materials
rt canes and rattans
rt chusquea
rt dendrocalamus
rt forest products
rt gigantochloa
rt phyllostachys
rt plants
rt sasa
rt shibataea
rt sinarundinaria

BAMBUSA
uf leleba
BT1 gramineae
NT1 bambusa arundinacea
NT1 bambusa balcooa
NT1 bambusa blumeana
NT1 bambusa oldhami
NT1 bambusa tulda
NT1 bambusa vulgaris
rt bamboo shoots
rt bamboos
rt ornamental woody plants

bambusa apus
USE **gigantochloa apus**

BAMBUSA ARUNDINACEA
BT1 bambusa
BT2 gramineae

BAMBUSA BALCOOA
HN from 1990
BT1 bambusa
BT2 gramineae

BAMBUSA BLUMEANA
BT1 bambusa
BT2 gramineae

BAMBUSA OLDHAMI
BT1 bambusa
BT2 gramineae

BAMBUSA TULDA
BT1 bambusa
BT2 gramineae

BAMBUSA VULGARIS
BT1 bambusa
BT2 gramineae

BANANA BUNCHY TOP VIRUS
BT1 unclassified plant viruses
BT2 plant viruses
BT3 plant pathogens
BT4 pathogens
rt bananas
rt musa

BANANA MEAL
BT1 feeds
BT1 meal
rt bananas

BANANA WASTE
BT1 agricultural wastes
BT2 wastes
rt bananas

BANANAS
uf plantains
BT1 medicinal plants
BT1 tropical small fruits
BT2 small fruits
BT2 tropical fruits
BT3 fruit crops
rt banana bunchy top virus
rt banana meal
rt banana waste
rt dehanding
rt maturity bronzing
rt musa paradisiaca
rt pseudostems

BAND DRILLS
uf drills, band
BT1 drills
BT2 farm machinery
BT3 machinery

BAND PLACEMENT
uf banding
BT1 placement
BT2 application methods
BT3 methodology

band saws
USE **bandsaws**

BAND SPRAYERS
uf sprayers, band
BT1 sprayers
BT2 spraying equipment
BT3 application equipment
BT4 equipment

BAND SPRAYING
BT1 spraying
BT2 application methods
BT3 methodology

BANDAGES
rt first aid
rt wounds

BANDEIRAEA
uf griffonia
BT1 leguminosae
NT1 bandeiraea simplicifolia

BANDEIRAEA SIMPLICIFOLIA
uf griffonia simplicifolia
BT1 bandeiraea
BT2 leguminosae

BANDICOTA
BT1 murinae
BT2 muridae
BT3 rodents
BT4 mammals
NT1 bandicota bengalensis
NT1 bandicota indica

BANDICOTA BENGALENSIS
BT1 bandicota
BT2 murinae
BT3 muridae
BT4 rodents
BT5 mammals

BANDICOTA INDICA
BT1 bandicota
BT2 murinae
BT3 muridae
BT4 rodents
BT5 mammals

banding
(fertilizers, pesticides or seeds)
USE **band placement**

banding, chromosome
USE **chromosome banding**

banding of animals
USE **identification**

BANDOLIER FEED MECHANISM
uf *feed mechanism, bandolier*
BT1 feed mechanisms
rt transplanters

BANDSAWS
HN from 1990; previously "band saws"
uf *band saws*
uf *saws, band*
BT1 saws
BT2 forestry machinery
BT3 machinery
BT2 tools

BANGLADESH
BT1 south asia
BT2 asia
NT1 chittagong
NT1 dacca
NT1 khulna
NT1 rajshahi
rt commonwealth of nations
rt developing countries
rt least developed countries

BANISTERIOPSIS
BT1 malpighiaceae
NT1 banisteriopsis caapi

BANISTERIOPSIS CAAPI
BT1 banisteriopsis
BT2 malpighiaceae
BT1 medicinal plants

BANK LOANS
BT1 loans
BT2 credit
BT3 finance
rt private loans

BANKIA
BT1 teredinidae
BT2 bivalvia
BT3 mollusca
NT1 bankia gouldi

BANKIA GOULDI
BT1 bankia
BT2 teredinidae
BT3 bivalvia
BT4 mollusca

banking
USE **banks**

BANKRUPTCY
BT1 debt
rt farm indebtedness

BANKS
uf *banking*
BT1 financial institutions
BT2 organizations
NT1 agricultural banks
NT1 commercial banks
NT1 cooperative banks
NT1 development banks
NT2 inter-american development bank
NT2 world bank

BANKS *cont.*
NT1 investment banks
NT1 savings banks
rt land banks
rt work banks

banks, agricultural
USE **agricultural banks**

banks, commercial
USE **commercial banks**

banks, cooperative
USE **cooperative banks**

banks, development
USE **development banks**

banks, investment
USE **investment banks**

banks, land
USE **land banks**

banks, saving
USE **savings banks**

BANKSIA
BT1 proteaceae
NT1 banksia grandis

BANKSIA GRANDIS
BT1 banksia
BT2 proteaceae
BT1 forest trees

BANQUETS (AGRICOLA)
BT1 meals
rt feasts (agricola)

BANTAMS
BT1 fowls
BT2 poultry
BT3 livestock
BT4 animals

BANTENG
uf *bos banteng*
uf *bos javanicus*
BT1 ruminants
BT2 animals
rt bovidae
rt cattle

bantustan
USE **south african homelands**

BAOULE
BT1 cattle breeds
BT2 breeds

BAPHIA
BT1 leguminosae

BAPTISIA
BT1 leguminosae
NT1 baptisia australis
NT1 baptisia leucophaea
NT1 baptisia psammophila

BAPTISIA AUSTRALIS
BT1 baptisia
BT2 leguminosae

BAPTISIA LEUCOPHAEA
BT1 baptisia
BT2 leguminosae
BT1 pasture legumes
BT2 legumes
BT2 pasture plants

BAPTISIA PSAMMOPHILA
BT1 baptisia
BT2 leguminosae

barathra
USE **mamestra**

barathra brassicae
USE **mamestra brassicae**

BARB
BT1 horse breeds
BT2 breeds

BARBADOS
BT1 caribbean

BARBADOS *cont.*
BT2 america
rt acp
rt caribbean community
rt commonwealth of nations

BARBADOS BLACKBELLY
HN from 1990
BT1 sheep breeds
BT2 breeds

BARBAN
BT1 carbanilate herbicides
BT2 carbamate pesticides
BT2 herbicides
BT3 pesticides

BARBARA
BT1 tortricidae
BT2 lepidoptera
NT1 barbara colfaxiana

BARBARA COLFAXIANA
BT1 barbara
BT2 tortricidae
BT3 lepidoptera

BARBAREA
BT1 cruciferae
NT1 barbarea intermedia
NT1 barbarea stricta
NT1 barbarea verna
NT1 barbarea vulgaris

BARBAREA INTERMEDIA
BT1 barbarea
BT2 cruciferae

barbarea praecox
USE **barbarea verna**

BARBAREA STRICTA
BT1 barbarea
BT2 cruciferae

BARBAREA VERNA
uf *barbarea praecox*
BT1 barbarea
BT2 cruciferae

BARBAREA VULGARIS
BT1 barbarea
BT2 cruciferae

BARBARI
uf *thori*
BT1 goat breeds
BT2 breeds

barberry
USE **berberis**

BARBITURATES
NT1 methitural
NT1 pentobarbital
NT1 phenobarbital
NT1 thiopental
rt anticonvulsants
rt injectable anaesthetics

barbuda
USE **antigua**

BARBUS
BT1 cyprinidae
BT2 cypriniformes
BT3 osteichthyes
BT4 fishes

BARDOKA
BT1 sheep breeds
BT2 breeds

BARE ROOTED STOCK
BT1 planting stock

BAREFOOT DOCTORS
BT1 medical auxiliaries
BT2 auxiliary workers
BT3 labour
BT3 workers
BT2 paraprofessionals
rt health services

BARENTS SEA
BT1 arctic ocean

BARENTS SEA *cont.*
BT2 marine areas

BARGES
BT1 boats

BARGUR
BT1 cattle breeds
BT2 breeds

BARIS
BT1 curculionidae
BT2 coleoptera

BARITE
BT1 nonclay minerals
BT2 minerals

BARIUM
uf *ba (symbol)*
BT1 alkaline earth metals
BT2 metallic elements
BT3 elements
BT3 metals
rt barium sulfate

BARIUM SULFATE
uf *barium sulphate*
BT1 contrast media
BT1 sulfates (inorganic salts)
BT2 inorganic salts
BT3 inorganic compounds
BT3 salts
BT2 sulfates
rt barium

barium sulphate
USE **barium sulfate**

BARK
BT1 growing media
BT1 minor forest products
BT2 forest products
BT3 products
BT1 mulches
BT1 plant residues
BT2 residues
BT1 soil conditioners
BT2 soil amendments
BT3 amendments
NT1 pine bark
rt barkers
rt barking
rt composts
rt cork
rt cortex
rt decortication
rt periderm
rt phloem
rt pulping materials
rt rinds
rt tanstuffs

BARK BEETLES
BT1 insect pests
BT2 arthropod pests
BT3 pests
BT2 insects
BT3 arthropods
rt forest pests
rt platypodidae
rt scolytidae

BARK COMPOST
uf *bark humus*
BT1 composts
BT2 manures
BT3 organic amendments
BT4 soil amendments
BT5 amendments

bark humus
USE **bark compost**

BARKA
HN from 1990
BT1 cattle breeds
BT2 breeds

BARKERS
BT1 forestry machinery
BT2 machinery
rt bark
rt barking

BARKI
BT1 sheep breeds
BT2 breeds

BARKING
uf *debarking*
BT1 primary conversion
BT2 conversion
NT1 hydraulic barking
NT1 manual barking
rt bark
rt barkers
rt logs

BARLERIA
BT1 acanthaceae
NT1 barleria cristata
NT1 barleria prionitis

BARLERIA CRISTATA
BT1 barleria
BT2 acanthaceae
BT1 ornamental woody plants

BARLERIA PRIONITIS
BT1 barleria
BT2 acanthaceae

BARLEY
BT1 cereals
BT2 grain crops
rt barley hay
rt barley meal
rt barley pellets
rt barley silage
rt barley straw
rt barley stripe mosaic hordeivirus
rt barley yellow dwarf luteovirus
rt barley yellow mosaic virus
rt barley yellow striate mosaic rhabdovirus
rt hordeum vulgare
rt malt
rt malting barley

barley flour
USE **barley meal**

BARLEY HAY
BT1 hay
BT2 feeds
rt barley

BARLEY MEAL
uf *barley flour*
uf *ground barley*
BT1 meal
rt barley

BARLEY PELLETS
BT1 cereal products
BT2 plant products
BT3 products
BT1 pellets
rt barley

BARLEY SILAGE
uf *silage, barley*
BT1 silage
BT2 feeds
BT2 fermentation products
BT3 products
rt barley

BARLEY STRAW
uf *straw, barley*
BT1 straw
BT2 agricultural byproducts
BT3 byproducts
BT2 feeds
BT2 plant residues
BT3 residues
rt barley

BARLEY STRIPE MOSAIC HORDEIVIRUS
HN from 1990; previously "barley stripe mosaic virus"
uf *barley stripe mosaic virus*
BT1 hordeivirus group
BT2 plant viruses
BT3 plant pathogens

BARLEY STRIPE MOSAIC HORDEIVIRUS *cont.*
BT4 pathogens
rt barley
rt hordeum vulgare

barley stripe mosaic virus
USE **barley stripe mosaic hordeivirus**

BARLEY YELLOW DWARF LUTEOVIRUS
HN from 1990; previously "barley yellow dwarf virus"
uf *barley yellow dwarf virus*
BT1 luteovirus group
BT2 plant viruses
BT3 plant pathogens
BT4 pathogens
rt barley
rt hordeum vulgare

barley yellow dwarf virus
USE **barley yellow dwarf luteovirus**

BARLEY YELLOW MOSAIC VIRUS
BT1 unclassified plant viruses
BT2 plant viruses
BT3 plant pathogens
BT4 pathogens
rt barley
rt hordeum vulgare

BARLEY YELLOW STRIATE MOSAIC RHABDOVIRUS
HN from 1990
BT1 rhabdovirus group
BT2 plant viruses
BT3 plant pathogens
BT4 pathogens
BT2 rhabdoviridae
BT3 viruses
rt barley
rt hordeum vulgare

BARN DRIERS
AF barn dryers
uf *driers, barn*
BT1 driers
BT2 farm machinery
BT3 machinery
rt barn drying
rt barns

BARN DRYERS
BF barn driers
BT1 dryers

BARN DRYING
BT1 drying
BT2 dehydration
BT3 processing
rt barn driers
rt barns

barnacles
USE **thoracica**

BARNS
BT1 farm buildings
BT2 buildings
BT1 stores
NT1 dutch barns
rt animal housing
rt barn driers
rt barn drying
rt cow housing
rt sheds

barns, dutch
USE **dutch barns**

barnyard grass
USE **echinochloa crus-galli**

barnyard millet
USE **echinochloa frumentacea**

barometric pressure
USE **atmospheric pressure**

BAROSMA
BT1 rutaceae
NT1 barosma betulina

BAROSMA *cont.*
NT1 barosma crenulata
NT1 barosma serratifolia

BAROSMA BETULINA
uf *agathosma betulina*
BT1 barosma
BT2 rutaceae
BT1 essential oil plants
BT2 oil plants

BAROSMA CRENULATA
uf *agathosma crenulata*
BT1 barosma
BT2 rutaceae
BT1 essential oil plants
BT2 oil plants

BAROSMA SERRATIFOLIA
BT1 barosma
BT2 rutaceae
BT1 essential oil plants
BT2 oil plants

BAROTSE
BT1 cattle breeds
BT2 breeds

barracudas
USE **sphyraenidae**

BARRANQUERAS VIRUS
BT1 bunyavirus
BT2 arboviruses
BT3 pathogens
BT2 bunyaviridae
BT3 viruses

barrel medic
USE **medicago truncatula**

BARRIER HUSBANDRY
BT1 animal husbandry
BT2 husbandry
BT2 zootechny

BARRIERS
NT1 dams
NT2 dykes
NT1 fences
NT2 electric fences
NT2 live fences
NT2 slat fences
NT1 plastic barriers
NT1 subsurface barriers
rt blockage
rt flow resistance
rt polystyrene beads
rt screens
rt water conservation

barriers, social
USE **social barriers**

BARRINGTONIA
BT1 barringtoniaceae
NT1 barringtonia acutangula
NT1 barringtonia asiatica

BARRINGTONIA ACUTANGULA
BT1 barringtonia
BT2 barringtoniaceae
rt eugenia acutangula

BARRINGTONIA ASIATICA
uf *barringtonia speciosa*
BT1 barringtonia
BT2 barringtoniaceae
BT1 piscicidal plants

barringtonia speciosa
USE **barringtonia asiatica**

BARRINGTONIACEAE
NT1 barringtonia
NT2 barringtonia acutangula
NT2 barringtonia asiatica

BARROSA
HN from 1990
BT1 cattle breeds
BT2 breeds

BARTER
BT1 trade

BARTONELLA
BT1 bartonellaceae
BT2 rickettsiales
BT3 bacteria
BT4 prokaryotes
NT1 bartonella bacilliformis

BARTONELLA BACILLIFORMIS
BT1 bartonella
BT2 bartonellaceae
BT3 rickettsiales
BT4 bacteria
BT5 prokaryotes

BARTONELLACEAE
BT1 rickettsiales
BT2 bacteria
BT3 prokaryotes
NT1 bartonella
NT2 bartonella bacilliformis
NT1 grahamella

BARTSIA
BT1 scrophulariaceae
NT1 bartsia alpina
NT1 bartsia odontites

BARTSIA ALPINA
BT1 bartsia
BT2 scrophulariaceae

BARTSIA ODONTITES
BT1 bartsia
BT2 scrophulariaceae

BARUWAL
HN from 1990
BT1 sheep breeds
BT2 breeds

BASAL AREA
BT1 area
rt dimensions
rt increment

BASAL DRESSINGS
BT1 application methods
BT2 methodology

basal energy exchange
USE **basal metabolism**

basal metabolic rate
USE **metabolism**

BASAL METABOLISM
uf *basal energy exchange*
uf *energy exchange, basal*
BT1 energy exchange
BT1 metabolism
rt energy relations
rt metabolizable energy

BASAL STEM SPRAYING
uf *sprays, basal stem*
BT1 spraying
BT2 application methods
BT3 methodology

BASALT
BT1 rocks
BT1 soil parent materials
rt basalt soils

BASALT SOILS
BT1 soil types (lithological)
rt basalt

BASALUMINITE
BT1 nonclay minerals
BT2 minerals

BASCO-BEARNAIS
HN from 1990
BT1 sheep breeds
BT2 breeds

BASE SATURATION
BT1 ion exchange
rt bases

BASEBALL
BT1 ball games
BT2 games
BT2 sport

BASELLA
BT1 basellaceae
NT1 basella alba

BASELLA ALBA
uf *basella rubra*
BT1 basella
BT2 basellaceae
rt food colourants

basella rubra
USE **basella alba**

BASELLACEAE
NT1 anredera
NT1 basella
NT2 basella alba
NT1 ullucus
NT2 ullucus tuberosus

BASES
NT1 alkalis
NT2 sodium bicarbonate
NT2 sodium carbonate
NT2 sodium hydroxide
NT1 antacids
NT2 aluminium hydroxide
NT2 aluminium phosphate
NT2 calcium carbonate
NT2 sodium bicarbonate
rt base saturation
rt ph

BASHKIR
BT1 horse breeds
BT2 breeds

basic four
USE **food groups**

basic funds
USE **fixed capital**

BASIC HOMEOWNERS' INSURANCE (AGRICOLA)
BT1 homeowners' insurance (agricola)
BT2 insurance

BASIC HOSPITAL EXPENSE INSURANCE (AGRICOLA)
BT1 insurance

BASIC NEEDS
BT1 living standards
BT2 living conditions
NT1 basic services
NT1 survival rations
rt deprivation
rt hunger
rt need gratification (agricola)
rt needs assessment (agricola)
rt poverty
rt quality of life

BASIC NUTRITION (AGRICOLA)
BT1 nutrition

BASIC SERVICES
BT1 basic needs
BT2 living standards
BT3 living conditions
BT1 services
rt deprivation
rt social services

BASIC SLAG
BT1 phosphorus fertilizers
BT2 fertilizers

BASIDIA
BT1 fungal morphology
BT2 morphology
rt basidiomycetes

BASIDIOBOLUS
BT1 entomophthorales
NT1 basidiobolus haptosporus
NT1 basidiobolus meristosporus
NT1 basidiobolus ranarum
rt subcutaneous phycomycosis

BASIDIOBOLUS HAPTOSPORUS
BT1 basidiobolus
BT2 entomophthorales

BASIDIOBOLUS MERISTOSPORUS
BT1 basidiobolus
BT2 entomophthorales

BASIDIOBOLUS RANARUM
BT1 basidiobolus
BT2 entomophthorales

BASIDIOMYCETES
rt basidia
rt basidiospores
rt fungi

BASIDIOSPORES
BT1 fungal spores
BT2 spores
BT3 cells
rt basidiomycetes

basil
USE **ocimum basilicum**

BASILICATA
BT1 italy
BT2 western europe
BT3 europe

BASIN IRRIGATION
uf *check basin irrigation*
uf *check basins*
uf *irrigation, basin*
BT1 irrigation

BASIROLAIMUS
BT1 hoplolaimidae
BT2 nematoda
rt hoplolaimus

BASKETBALL
BT1 ball games
BT2 games
BT2 sport

BASOPHILS
BT1 granulocytes
BT2 leukocytes
BT3 blood cells
BT4 cells

BASS
BT1 marine fishes
BT2 aquatic animals
BT3 animals
BT3 aquatic organisms
rt sea bass

basse-normande
USE **lower normandy**

BASSIA
BT1 sapotaceae
NT1 bassia astrocarpa
NT1 bassia birchii
NT1 bassia diacantha
NT1 bassia hyssopifolia
NT1 bassia lanicuspis
NT1 bassia latifolia
NT1 bassia ventricosa

BASSIA ASTROCARPA
BT1 bassia
BT2 sapotaceae
BT1 browse plants

BASSIA BIRCHII
BT1 bassia
BT2 sapotaceae

bassia butyracea
USE **diploknema butyracea**

BASSIA DIACANTHA
BT1 bassia
BT2 sapotaceae
BT1 browse plants

BASSIA HYSSOPIFOLIA
BT1 bassia
BT2 sapotaceae

BASSIA LANICUSPIS
BT1 bassia
BT2 sapotaceae
BT1 browse plants

BASSIA LATIFOLIA
BT1 bassia
BT2 sapotaceae
rt mahua seed meal

bassia scoparia
USE **kochia scoparia**

BASSIA VENTRICOSA
BT1 bassia
BT2 sapotaceae
BT1 browse plants

BASSUS
BT1 ichneumonidae
BT2 hymenoptera
rt diplazon

bassus laetatorius
USE **diplazon laetatorius**

BATCH DRIERS
AF batch dryers
uf *driers, batch*
BT1 driers
BT2 farm machinery
BT3 machinery
rt continuous driers
rt floor driers

BATCH DRYERS
BF batch driers
BT1 dryers

BATHYCOELIA
BT1 pentatomidae
BT2 heteroptera
NT1 bathycoelia thalassina

BATHYCOELIA THALASSINA
BT1 bathycoelia
BT2 pentatomidae
BT3 heteroptera

BATHYERGIDAE
BT1 rodents
BT2 mammals
NT1 heterocephalus
NT2 heterocephalus glaber

BATHYMERMIS
BT1 mermithidae
BT2 nematoda

BATHYPLECTES
BT1 ichneumonidae
BT2 hymenoptera
NT1 bathyplectes anurus
NT1 bathyplectes curculionis

BATHYPLECTES ANURUS
BT1 bathyplectes
BT2 ichneumonidae
BT3 hymenoptera

BATHYPLECTES CURCULIONIS
BT1 bathyplectes
BT2 ichneumonidae
BT3 hymenoptera
BT1 biological control agents
BT2 beneficial organisms

BATHYSA
BT1 rubiaceae
NT1 bathysa meridionalis

BATHYSA MERIDIONALIS
BT1 bathysa
BT2 rubiaceae

bathystoma
USE **haemulon**

BATIK (AGRICOLA)
BT1 dyeing (agricola)
BT2 processing

BATISTE (AGRICOLA)
BT1 fabrics
rt textiles

BATRACHEDRA
BT1 cosmopterigidae
BT2 lepidoptera
NT1 batrachedra amydraula
NT1 batrachedra arenosella

BATRACHEDRA AMYDRAULA
BT1 batrachedra
BT2 cosmopterigidae
BT3 lepidoptera

BATRACHEDRA ARENOSELLA
BT1 batrachedra
BT2 cosmopterigidae
BT3 lepidoptera

bats
USE **chiroptera**

BATTER FRIED FOODS (AGRICOLA)
BT1 fried foods (agricola)
BT2 foods

battered women
USE **spouse abuse (agricola)**

BATTERIES
BT1 electrical equipment
BT2 equipment

BATTERS (AGRICOLA)
rt bakery products
rt coatings

BATTERY CAGES
BT1 cages
BT2 animal housing
rt poultry housing

BATTERY HUSBANDRY
uf *battery rearing*
BT1 animal husbandry
BT2 husbandry
BT2 zootechny
BT1 factory farming
BT2 intensive livestock farming
BT3 intensive farming
BT4 farming
BT3 livestock farming
BT4 farming
rt poultry farming

battery rearing
USE **battery husbandry**

bauerella
USE **baueropsis**

BAUEROPSIS
uf *bauerella*
BT1 leguminosae
NT1 baueropsis simplicifolia

BAUEROPSIS SIMPLICIFOLIA
BT1 baueropsis
BT2 leguminosae

BAUHINIA
BT1 leguminosae
NT1 bauhinia acuminata
NT1 bauhinia candicans
NT1 bauhinia galpinii
NT1 bauhinia malabarica
NT1 bauhinia petersiana
NT1 bauhinia purpurea
NT1 bauhinia retusa
NT1 bauhinia rufescens
NT1 bauhinia vahlii
NT1 bauhinia variegata

BAUHINIA ACUMINATA
BT1 bauhinia
BT2 leguminosae
BT1 ornamental woody plants

BAUHINIA CANDICANS
BT1 antifungal plants
BT1 bauhinia
BT2 leguminosae
BT1 medicinal plants
BT1 ornamental woody plants

BAUHINIA GALPINII
BT1 bauhinia
BT2 leguminosae
BT1 ornamental woody plants

BAUHINIA MALABARICA
BT1 bauhinia
BT2 leguminosae

BAUHINIA PETERSIANA
BT1 bauhinia
BT2 leguminosae

BAUHINIA PURPUREA
BT1 bauhinia
BT2 leguminosae
BT1 forest trees
BT1 ornamental woody plants

BAUHINIA RETUSA
BT1 bauhinia
BT2 leguminosae

BAUHINIA RUFESCENS
BT1 bauhinia
BT2 leguminosae
BT1 tan plants

BAUHINIA VAHLII
BT1 bauhinia
BT2 leguminosae

BAUHINIA VARIEGATA
BT1 bauhinia
BT2 leguminosae
BT1 forest trees
BT1 ornamental woody plants
BT1 tan plants

BAUXITE
BT1 clay minerals
BT2 minerals
rt aluminium
rt bauxitic soils
rt bauxitization

BAUXITE RESIDUES
BT1 industrial wastes
BT2 wastes

BAUXITIC SOILS
BT1 soil types (mineralogical)
rt bauxite
rt bauxitization

BAUXITIZATION
BT1 soil formation
rt bauxite
rt bauxitic soils

BAVARIA
uf *bayern*
BT1 german federal republic
BT2 western europe
BT3 europe

bay laurel
USE **laurus nobilis**

BAY OF BENGAL
BT1 eastern indian ocean
BT2 indian ocean
BT3 marine areas

BAYERITE
BT1 nonclay minerals
BT2 minerals

bayern
USE **bavaria**

BAYESIAN THEORY
rt decision making
rt theory

BCG VACCINE
BT1 live vaccines
BT2 vaccines
rt mycobacterium bovis

BDELLIDAE
BT1 prostigmata
BT2 acari
NT1 bdellodes
NT2 bdellodes lapidaria
NT1 biscirus

BDELLODES
BT1 bdellidae
BT2 prostigmata
BT3 acari
NT1 bdellodes lapidaria
rt biscirus

BDELLODES LAPIDARIA
uf *biscirus lapidarius*
BT1 bdellodes
BT2 bdellidae
BT3 prostigmata
BT4 acari

BDELLOVIBRIO
BT1 spirillaceae
BT2 gracilicutes
BT3 bacteria
BT4 prokaryotes

BEACH SOILS
BT1 soil types (physiographic)
rt coastal terrace soils

BEACHES
BT1 physiographic features
rt coasts

BEAK
BT1 head
BT2 body regions
rt birds
rt debeaking

BEAMS
BT1 structural components
BT2 components
rt building construction
rt composite wood assemblies
rt girders
rt laminated wood
rt structural timbers
rt struts

BEAN COMMON MOSAIC POTYVIRUS
HN from 1990; previously "bean common mosaic virus"
uf *bean common mosaic virus*
BT1 potyvirus group
BT2 plant viruses
BT3 plant pathogens
BT4 pathogens

bean common mosaic virus
USE **bean common mosaic potyvirus**

BEAN CURD (AGRICOLA)
BT1 soyabean products
BT2 vegetable products
BT3 plant products
BT4 products
rt tofu

BEAN GOLDEN MOSAIC GEMINIVIRUS
HN from 1990; previously "bean golden mosaic virus"
uf *bean golden mosaic virus*
BT1 geminivirus group
BT2 plant viruses
BT3 plant pathogens
BT4 pathogens

bean golden mosaic virus
USE **bean golden mosaic geminivirus**

BEAN HARVESTERS
uf *harvesters, bean*
BT1 harvesters
BT2 farm machinery
BT3 machinery

BEAN LEAF ROLL LUTEOVIRUS
HN from 1990; previously "bean leaf roll virus"
uf *bean leaf roll virus*
uf *pea leaf roll luteovirus*
uf *pea leaf roll virus*
BT1 luteovirus group
BT2 plant viruses
BT3 plant pathogens
BT4 pathogens

bean leaf roll virus
USE **bean leaf roll luteovirus**

BEAN MEAL
BT1 meal

BEAN MEAL *cont.*
BT1 vegetable products
BT2 plant products
BT3 products

BEAN POD MOTTLE COMOVIRUS
HN from 1990; previously "bean pod mottle virus"
uf *bean pod mottle virus*
BT1 comovirus group
BT2 plant viruses
BT3 plant pathogens
BT4 pathogens

bean pod mottle virus
USE **bean pod mottle comovirus**

BEAN RUGOSE MOSAIC COMOVIRUS
HN from 1990; previously "bean rugose mosaic virus"
uf *bean rugose mosaic virus*
BT1 comovirus group
BT2 plant viruses
BT3 plant pathogens
BT4 pathogens

bean rugose mosaic virus
USE **bean rugose mosaic comovirus**

bean southern mosaic virus
USE **southern bean mosaic sobemovirus**

BEAN STRAW
BT1 straw
BT2 agricultural byproducts
BT3 byproducts
BT2 feeds
BT2 plant residues
BT3 residues

BEAN YELLOW MOSAIC POTYVIRUS
HN from 1990; previously "bean yellow mosaic virus"
uf *bean yellow mosaic virus*
uf *pea mosaic virus*
BT1 potyvirus group
BT2 plant viruses
BT3 plant pathogens
BT4 pathogens

bean yellow mosaic virus
USE **bean yellow mosaic potyvirus**

BEAN YELLOW STIPPLE VIRUS
BT1 miscellaneous plant viruses
BT2 plant viruses
BT3 plant pathogens
BT4 pathogens

BEANS
BT1 foods

beans, broad
USE **faba beans**
OR **vicia faba**

beans (cyamopsis)
USE **cyamopsis tetragonoloba**

beans, french
USE **phaseolus vulgaris**

beans, horse
USE **faba beans**
OR **vicia faba**

beans, kidney
USE **phaseolus vulgaris**

beans (phaseolus)
USE **phaseolus acutifolius**
OR **phaseolus coccineus**
OR **phaseolus lunatus**
OR **phaseolus vulgaris**

beans (vicia)
USE **vicia faba**

BEARING CAPACITY
BT1 bearing characteristics

BEARING CAPACITY *cont.*
BT2 soil mechanics
BT3 soil properties
BT4 properties
rt capacity

bearing capacity (fruiting)
USE **fruiting potential**

BEARING CHARACTERISTICS
BT1 soil mechanics
BT2 soil properties
BT3 properties
NT1 bearing capacity
rt roads
rt soil physics

BEARINGS
uf *bearings and bushes*
BT1 components
NT1 roller bearings
NT2 tapered roller bearings
NT1 thrust bearings
rt lubricants

bearings and bushes
USE **bearings**

bearings, roller
USE **roller bearings**

bearings, tapered roller
USE **tapered roller bearings**

bearings, thrust
USE **thrust bearings**

bears
USE **ursidae**

BEATERS
BT1 components
rt flails
rt threshing
rt threshing drums
rt threshing machines

BEATING UP
HN from 1990
uf *reinforcement planting*
BT1 silviculture
BT2 forestry

BEAUFORT SEA
BT1 arctic ocean
BT2 marine areas

BEAUMONTIA
BT1 apocynaceae
NT1 beaumontia grandiflora

BEAUMONTIA GRANDIFLORA
BT1 beaumontia
BT2 apocynaceae

BEAUTIFICATION (AGRICOLA)
rt aesthetic value

BEAUVERIA
BT1 deuteromycotina
BT1 entomogenous fungi
BT2 entomopathogens
BT3 pathogens
BT2 fungi
NT1 beauveria bassiana
NT1 beauveria brongniartii

BEAUVERIA BASSIANA
uf *beauveria tenella*
BT1 beauveria
BT2 deuteromycotina
BT2 entomogenous fungi
BT3 entomopathogens
BT4 pathogens
BT3 fungi
BT1 fungal insecticides
BT2 insecticides
BT3 pesticides
BT2 microbial pesticides
BT3 pesticides

BEAUVERIA BRONGNIARTII
BT1 beauveria
BT2 deuteromycotina
BT2 entomogenous fungi

BEAUVERIA BRONGNIARTII *cont.*
BT3 entomopathogens
BT4 pathogens
BT3 fungi

beauveria tenella
USE **beauveria bassiana**

beavers
USE **castor**

BECKMANNIA
BT1 gramineae
NT1 beckmannia syzigachne

BECKMANNIA SYZIGACHNE
BT1 beckmannia
BT2 gramineae
BT1 pasture plants

BED AND BREAKFAST ACCOMMODATION
HN from 1989
BT1 holiday accommodation
BT2 accommodation
rt guest houses

BED COVERINGS (AGRICOLA)
NT1 bedspreads (agricola)
rt blankets (agricola)
rt linens (agricola)

BED NETS
BT1 nets
rt application methods
rt culicidae
rt insect control
rt mosquito nets

BED REST
BT1 rest

BEDDERS
BT1 implements

bedding
(for animals)
USE **litter**

BEDDING PLANTS
rt annuals
rt ornamental plants
rt plants

BEDSPREADS (AGRICOLA)
BT1 bed coverings (agricola)
BT1 fabrics

BEE ACUTE PARALYSIS VIRUS
BT1 bee viruses
BT2 insect viruses
BT3 entomopathogens
BT4 pathogens

BEE BLOWERS
BT1 removing
BT2 manipulations
BT3 beekeeping
rt blowers

BEE CHRONIC PARALYSIS VIRUS
BT1 bee viruses
BT2 insect viruses
BT3 entomopathogens
BT4 pathogens

BEE CHRONIC PARALYSIS VIRUS ASSOCIATE
BT1 bee viruses
BT2 insect viruses
BT3 entomopathogens
BT4 pathogens

BEE-COLLECTED POLLEN
BT1 hive products
BT2 animal products
BT3 products
rt pollen
rt pollen loads
rt pollen trapping

bee colonies
USE **honeybee colonies**

BEE DISEASES
BT1 animal diseases

BEE DISEASES *cont.*
BT2 diseases
NT1 acarine disease
NT1 amoeba disease
NT1 apimyiasis
NT1 chalk brood
NT1 foul brood
NT2 american foul brood
NT2 european foul brood
NT1 nosema disease
NT1 rickettsial disease
NT1 stone brood
rt bee viruses
rt honeybees

bee eaters
USE **meropidae**

BEE ESCAPES
BT1 hive parts
BT2 movable-comb hives
BT3 hives

BEE HOUSES
BT1 beekeeping
rt apiaries

BEE HUNTING
BT1 wild honeybee colonies
BT2 honeybee colonies
BT3 honeybees
rt honey hunting

bee lice
USE **braula**

BEE VIRUSES
BT1 insect viruses
BT2 entomopathogens
BT3 pathogens
NT1 arkansas bee virus
NT1 bee acute paralysis virus
NT1 bee chronic paralysis virus
NT1 bee chronic paralysis virus associate
NT1 black queen cell virus
NT1 kashmir bee virus
NT1 sacbrood virus
rt bee diseases
rt honeybees

beech
USE **fagus**
OR **nothofagus**

BEEF
BT1 meat
BT2 animal products
BT3 products
BT2 foods
NT1 ground beef (agricola)
rt beef breeds
rt beef cattle
rt beef production
rt beef quality
rt corned beef (agricola)
rt steers

BEEF BREEDS
BT1 cattle breeds
BT2 breeds
rt beef
rt beef bulls
rt beef cattle
rt beef cows
rt beef herds

BEEF BULLS
BT1 beef cattle
BT2 cattle
BT3 livestock
BT4 animals
BT3 ruminants
BT4 animals
BT3 skin producing animals
BT4 animals
BT2 meat animals
BT3 animals
BT1 bulls
BT2 male animals
BT3 animals
rt beef breeds
rt beef cows
rt beef herds

BEEF CATTLE
BT1 cattle
BT2 livestock
BT3 animals
BT2 ruminants
BT3 animals
BT2 skin producing animals
BT3 animals
BT1 meat animals
BT2 animals
NT1 beef bulls
NT1 beef cows
rt beef
rt beef breeds
rt beef production

BEEF COWS
BT1 beef cattle
BT2 cattle
BT3 livestock
BT4 animals
BT3 ruminants
BT4 animals
BT3 skin producing animals
BT4 animals
BT2 meat animals
BT3 animals
BT1 cows
BT2 female animals
BT3 animals
rt beef breeds
rt beef bulls
rt beef herds

beef fat
USE **tallow**

BEEF HERDS
BT1 herds
BT2 groups
rt beef breeds
rt beef bulls
rt beef cows
rt beef production

BEEF PRODUCTION
BT1 meat production
BT2 animal production
BT3 agricultural production
BT4 production
rt beef
rt beef cattle
rt beef herds
rt beef quality

BEEF QUALITY
BT1 meat quality
BT2 quality
rt beef
rt beef production

BEEF SHORTHORN
BT1 cattle breeds
BT2 breeds

BEEKEEPERS
BT1 occupations
rt beekeepers' associations
rt beekeeping

BEEKEEPERS' ASSOCIATIONS
BT1 interest groups
BT2 groups
BT2 organizations
rt beekeepers
rt beekeeping

BEEKEEPING
uf *apiculture*
NT1 apiaries
NT2 apiary layout
NT2 apiary sites
NT2 apiary size
NT2 out apiaries
NT2 wall apiaries
NT1 bee houses
NT1 commercial beekeeping
NT1 manipulations
NT2 adding
NT2 foundation fitting
NT2 hive relocation
NT2 hiving
NT2 opening

BEEKEEPING *cont.*
NT2 removing
NT3 bee blowers
NT2 smoking
NT2 subduing
NT2 taking swarms
NT2 transferring
NT2 uniting
NT2 wing clipping
NT1 migratory beekeeping
NT1 queen rearing
rt animal husbandry
rt beekeepers
rt beekeepers' associations
rt hive products
rt hives
rt honeybees
rt livestock enterprises

BEERS
BT1 alcoholic beverages
BT2 beverages
NT1 light beer (agricola)
rt brewing
rt brewing industry
rt fermentation products
rt hops
rt wort

bees
USE **apidae**
OR **honeybees**

BEESWAX
BT1 hive products
BT2 animal products
BT3 products
BT1 wax esters
BT2 fatty acid esters
BT3 esters
BT2 waxes
rt beeswax substitutes
rt capping
rt cappings
rt combs
rt foundation
rt honeybees
rt minor forest products
rt rendering
rt solar beeswax extractors

BEESWAX SUBSTITUTES
BT1 substitutes
BT1 waxes
rt beeswax

beet cleaners
USE **root cleaners**

BEET CRYPTIC 1 CRYPTOVIRUS
HN from 1990
BT1 cryptovirus group
BT2 plant viruses
BT3 plant pathogens
BT4 pathogens
rt beta vulgaris

BEET CRYPTIC 2 CRYPTOVIRUS
HN from 1990
BT1 cryptovirus group
BT2 plant viruses
BT3 plant pathogens
BT4 pathogens
rt beta vulgaris

BEET CRYPTIC VIRUS
BT1 miscellaneous plant viruses
BT2 plant viruses
BT3 plant pathogens
BT4 pathogens

BEET CURLY TOP GEMINIVIRUS
HN from 1990; previously "beet curly top virus"
uf *beet curly top virus*
BT1 geminivirus group
BT2 plant viruses
BT3 plant pathogens
BT4 pathogens
rt beta vulgaris

beet curly top virus
USE **beet curly top geminivirus**

beet, fodder
USE **fodder beet**

beet, forage
USE **fodder beet**

BEET HARVESTERS
uf *harvesters, beet*
uf *sugarbeet harvesters*
BT1 root harvesters
BT2 harvesters
BT3 farm machinery
BT4 machinery
NT1 beet lifters
rt beet toppers
rt sugarbeet

BEET LIFTERS
BT1 beet harvesters
BT2 root harvesters
BT3 harvesters
BT4 farm machinery
BT5 machinery
rt beet toppers
rt sugarbeet

beet mild yellowing virus
USE **beet western yellows luteovirus**

beet molasses
USE **molasses**

BEET MOSAIC POTYVIRUS
HN from 1990; previously "beet mosaic virus"
uf *beet mosaic virus*
BT1 potyvirus group
BT2 plant viruses
BT3 plant pathogens
BT4 pathogens
rt beta vulgaris

beet mosaic virus
USE **beet mosaic potyvirus**

BEET NECROTIC YELLOW VEIN VIRUS
BT1 unclassified plant viruses
BT2 plant viruses
BT3 plant pathogens
BT4 pathogens
rt beta vulgaris

BEET PULP
BT1 feeds
BT1 vegetable pulps
BT2 pulps
BT2 vegetable products
BT3 plant products
BT4 products
rt sugarbeet

BEET SUGAR
BT1 sugar
BT2 plant products
BT3 products

beet, sugar
USE **sugarbeet**

BEET TOP SILAGE
BT1 silage
BT2 feeds
BT2 fermentation products
BT3 products
rt fodder beet

BEET TOPPERS
uf *toppers, beet*
BT1 toppers
BT2 farm machinery
BT3 machinery
rt beet harvesters
rt beet lifters
rt feeler wheels
rt sugarbeet

BEET WESTERN YELLOWS LUTEOVIRUS
HN from 1990; previously "beet western yellows virus"
uf *beet mild yellowing virus*
uf *beet western yellows virus*

BEET WESTERN YELLOWS LUTEOVIRUS *cont.*
uf *malva yellows virus*
BT1 luteovirus group
BT2 plant viruses
BT3 plant pathogens
BT4 pathogens
rt beta vulgaris

beet western yellows virus
USE **beet western yellows luteovirus**

BEET YELLOW STUNT CLOSTEROVIRUS
HN from 1990
BT1 closterovirus group
BT2 plant viruses
BT3 plant pathogens
BT4 pathogens

BEET YELLOWS CLOSTEROVIRUS
HN from 1990; previously "beet yellows virus"
uf *beet yellows virus*
uf *sugar beet yellows closterovirus*
BT1 closterovirus group
BT2 plant viruses
BT3 plant pathogens
BT4 pathogens
rt beta vulgaris

beet yellows virus
USE **beet yellows closterovirus**

BEETAL
BT1 goat breeds
BT2 breeds

beetles
USE **coleoptera**

BEETROOTS
AF beets
uf *red beet*
BT1 root vegetables
BT2 root crops
BT2 vegetables
rt beta vulgaris
rt blackheart

BEETS
BF beetroots
rt beta vulgaris

BEGGIATOA
BT1 beggiatoaceae

BEGGIATOACEAE
NT1 beggiatoa

BEGONIA
BT1 begoniaceae
NT1 begonia alice-clarkae
NT1 begonia attenuata
NT1 begonia bogneri
NT1 begonia boweri
NT1 begonia carrieae
NT1 begonia cheimantha
NT1 begonia coccinea
NT1 begonia cubensis
NT1 begonia cucullata
NT1 begonia depauperata
NT1 begonia edmundoi
NT1 begonia epipsila
NT1 begonia fenicis
NT1 begonia fimbristipula
NT1 begonia franconis
NT1 begonia glabra
NT1 begonia grandis
NT1 begonia heracleifolia
NT1 begonia herbacea
NT1 begonia hiemalis
NT1 begonia hispida
NT1 begonia monophylla
NT1 begonia multangula
NT1 begonia multiflora
NT1 begonia nelumbifolia
NT1 begonia odeteiantha
NT1 begonia pavonina
NT1 begonia picta
NT1 begonia repens

BEGONIA *cont.*
NT1 begonia rhopalocarpa
NT1 begonia ricinifolia
NT1 begonia robusta
NT1 begonia roxburghii
NT1 begonia socotrana
NT1 begonia stipulacea
NT1 begonia tuberhybrida
NT1 begonia velloziane
NT1 begonia vitifolia

BEGONIA ALICE-CLARKAE
BT1 begonia
BT2 begoniaceae
BT1 ornamental woody plants

begonia angularis
USE **begonia stipulacea**

BEGONIA ATTENUATA
BT1 begonia
BT2 begoniaceae
BT1 ornamental bulbs
rt rhizomes

BEGONIA BOGNERI
BT1 begonia
BT2 begoniaceae
BT1 ornamental bulbs
rt tubers

BEGONIA BOWERI
BT1 begonia
BT2 begoniaceae
BT1 ornamental bulbs
rt rhizomes

BEGONIA CARRIEAE
BT1 begonia
BT2 begoniaceae
BT1 ornamental bulbs
rt rhizomes

BEGONIA CHEIMANTHA
BT1 begonia
BT2 begoniaceae
BT1 ornamental bulbs
rt tubers

BEGONIA COCCINEA
BT1 begonia
BT2 begoniaceae
BT1 ornamental woody plants

BEGONIA CUBENSIS
BT1 begonia
BT2 begoniaceae

BEGONIA CUCULLATA
uf *begonia semperflorens*
BT1 begonia
BT2 begoniaceae
BT1 ornamental herbaceous plants

BEGONIA DEPAUPERATA
BT1 begonia
BT2 begoniaceae
BT1 ornamental bulbs
rt rhizomes

BEGONIA EDMUNDOI
BT1 begonia
BT2 begoniaceae
BT1 ornamental woody plants

BEGONIA EPIPSILA
BT1 begonia
BT2 begoniaceae
BT1 ornamental woody plants

begonia evansiana
USE **begonia grandis**

BEGONIA FENICIS
BT1 begonia
BT2 begoniaceae
BT1 ornamental bulbs
rt rhizomes

BEGONIA FIMBRISTIPULA
BT1 begonia
BT2 begoniaceae

BEGONIA FRANCONIS
BT1 begonia
BT2 begoniaceae

begonia fusca-sericea
USE **begonia repens**

BEGONIA GLABRA
BT1 begonia
BT2 begoniaceae
BT1 ornamental bulbs
rt rhizomes

BEGONIA GRANDIS
uf *begonia evansiana*
BT1 begonia
BT2 begoniaceae
BT1 ornamental bulbs
rt tubers

BEGONIA HERACLEIFOLIA
BT1 begonia
BT2 begoniaceae
BT1 ornamental bulbs
rt rhizomes

BEGONIA HERBACEA
BT1 begonia
BT2 begoniaceae
BT1 ornamental bulbs
rt rhizomes

BEGONIA HIEMALIS
BT1 begonia
BT2 begoniaceae
BT1 ornamental bulbs
rt tubers

BEGONIA HISPIDA
BT1 begonia
BT2 begoniaceae
rt ornamental foliage plants

BEGONIA MONOPHYLLA
BT1 begonia
BT2 begoniaceae

BEGONIA MULTANGULA
BT1 begonia
BT2 begoniaceae
BT1 ornamental bulbs
rt rhizomes

BEGONIA MULTIFLORA
BT1 begonia
BT2 begoniaceae
BT1 ornamental herbaceous plants

BEGONIA NELUMBIFOLIA
BT1 begonia
BT2 begoniaceae
BT1 ornamental bulbs
rt rhizomes

BEGONIA ODETEIANTHA
BT1 begonia
BT2 begoniaceae
rt ornamental foliage plants

BEGONIA PAVONINA
BT1 begonia
BT2 begoniaceae
rt ornamental foliage plants

BEGONIA PICTA
BT1 begonia
BT2 begoniaceae
BT1 ornamental bulbs
rt rhizomes

BEGONIA REPENS
uf *begonia fusca-sericea*
BT1 begonia
BT2 begoniaceae
BT1 ornamental bulbs
rt rhizomes

BEGONIA RHOPALOCARPA
BT1 begonia
BT2 begoniaceae
BT1 ornamental herbaceous plants

BEGONIA RICINIFOLIA
BT1 begonia
BT2 begoniaceae
BT1 ornamental bulbs
rt rhizomes

BEGONIA ROBUSTA
BT1 begonia
BT2 begoniaceae
BT1 ornamental bulbs
rt rhizomes

BEGONIA ROXBURGHII
BT1 begonia
BT2 begoniaceae
BT1 ornamental bulbs
rt rhizomes

begonia semperflorens
USE **begonia cucullata**

BEGONIA SOCOTRANA
BT1 begonia
BT2 begoniaceae
BT1 ornamental bulbs
rt tubers

BEGONIA STIPULACEA
uf begonia angularis
BT1 begonia
BT2 begoniaceae
BT1 ornamental woody plants

BEGONIA TUBERHYBRIDA
BT1 begonia
BT2 begoniaceae
BT1 ornamental bulbs
rt tubers

BEGONIA VELLOZIANE
BT1 begonia
BT2 begoniaceae
BT1 ornamental bulbs
rt rhizomes

BEGONIA VITIFOLIA
BT1 begonia
BT2 begoniaceae
rt ornamental foliage plants

BEGONIACEAE
NT1 begonia
NT2 begonia alice-clarkae
NT2 begonia attenuata
NT2 begonia bogneri
NT2 begonia boweri
NT2 begonia carrieae
NT2 begonia cheimantha
NT2 begonia coccinea
NT2 begonia cubensis
NT2 begonia cucullata
NT2 begonia depauperata
NT2 begonia edmundoi
NT2 begonia epipsila
NT2 begonia fenicis
NT2 begonia fimbristipula
NT2 begonia franconis
NT2 begonia glabra
NT2 begonia grandis
NT2 begonia heracleifolia
NT2 begonia herbacea
NT2 begonia hiemalis
NT2 begonia hispida
NT2 begonia monophylla
NT2 begonia multangula
NT2 begonia multiflora
NT2 begonia nelumbifolia
NT2 begonia odeteiantha
NT2 begonia pavonina
NT2 begonia picta
NT2 begonia repens
NT2 begonia rhopalocarpa
NT2 begonia ricinifolia
NT2 begonia robusta
NT2 begonia roxburghii
NT2 begonia socotrana
NT2 begonia stipulacea
NT2 begonia tuberhybrida
NT2 begonia velloziane
NT2 begonia vitifolia
NT1 symbegonia

BEHAVIOR
BF behaviour

BEHAVIOR *cont.*
NT1 abnormal behavior
NT2 compulsions (agricola)
NT3 compulsive eating (agricola)
NT1 aggressive behavior
NT1 agonistic behavior
NT1 animal behavior
NT1 assertiveness (agricola)
NT1 attachment behavior (agricola)
NT1 cultural behavior
NT1 drinking behavior
NT1 feeding behavior
NT2 grazing behavior
NT1 human behavior
NT2 antisocial behavior (agricola)
NT3 child abuse
NT3 child neglect (agricola)
NT3 delinquent behavior
NT3 discipline problems (agricola)
NT3 elder abuse (agricola)
NT3 incest (agricola)
NT3 sexual harassment (agricola)
NT3 spouse abuse (agricola)
NT3 theft (agricola)
NT4 employee theft (agricola)
NT2 economic behavior
NT3 consumer behavior
NT2 leisure behavior
NT2 visitor behavior
NT1 maternal behavior
NT1 paternal behavior
NT1 reproductive behavior
NT1 searching behavior
NT2 host-seeking behavior
NT1 seasonal behavior
NT1 sexual behavior
NT2 mating behavior
NT1 social behavior
NT2 economic behavior
NT3 consumer behavior
NT2 group behavior
rt behavior change (agricola)
rt behavior disorders (agricola)
rt behavior modeling (agricola)
rt behavior modification (agricola)
rt behavior patterns (agricola)
rt behavior problems (agricola)
rt behavioral objectives (agricola)
rt behavioral resistance
rt boredom (agricola)

BEHAVIOR CHANGE (AGRICOLA)
rt behavior
rt behavior modeling (agricola)
rt behavior modification (agricola)
rt change

BEHAVIOR DISORDERS (AGRICOLA)
BT1 functional disorders
BT2 animal disorders
BT3 disorders
rt antisocial behavior (agricola)
rt behavior

BEHAVIOR MODELING (AGRICOLA)
rt behavior
rt behavior change (agricola)

BEHAVIOR MODIFICATION (AGRICOLA)
rt assertiveness (agricola)
rt behavior
rt behavior change (agricola)
rt modification

BEHAVIOR PATTERNS (AGRICOLA)
BT1 patterns
rt behavior

BEHAVIOR PROBLEMS (AGRICOLA)
rt antisocial behavior (agricola)

BEHAVIOR PROBLEMS (AGRICOLA) *cont.*
rt behavior
rt discipline problems (agricola)

BEHAVIORAL OBJECTIVES (AGRICOLA)
rt behavior
rt competency based education (agricola)
rt objectives

BEHAVIORAL RESISTANCE
BF behavioural resistance
rt behavior

BEHAVIOUR
AF behavior
NT1 abnormal behaviour
NT2 cannibalism
NT2 feather pecking
NT2 hyperactivity
NT2 tail biting
NT2 vices
NT1 aggressive behaviour
NT2 balling
NT2 colony defence
NT2 fighting
NT2 robbing
NT2 stinging
NT1 agonistic behaviour
NT1 altruism
NT1 animal behaviour
NT2 aggregation
NT2 broodiness
NT2 burrowing
NT2 clustering
NT2 communication between animals
NT3 dances
NT3 piping
NT2 drifting
NT2 dust bathing
NT2 eviction
NT2 fanning
NT2 fearfulness
NT3 gunshyness
NT2 fright
NT2 grooming
NT2 group effect
NT2 imprinting
NT2 mimicry
NT2 nesting
NT2 social dominance
NT2 soil ingestion
NT2 supersedure
NT2 swarming
NT3 absconding
NT3 swarming impulse
NT3 swarming preparations
NT2 tameness
NT2 territoriality
NT1 avoidance conditioning
NT1 drinking behaviour
NT2 thirst control
NT1 enjoyment
NT1 feeding behaviour
NT2 biting rates
NT2 feeding habits
NT3 browsing
NT3 coprophagy
NT4 caecotrophy
NT3 feeding frequency
NT3 feeding preferences
NT4 food preferences
NT5 food beliefs
NT5 salt preference
NT3 foraging
NT4 honey-getting capacity
NT3 haematophagy
NT3 nectar feeding
NT3 overeating
NT3 overfeeding
NT4 hyperalimentation
NT3 sugar feeding
NT2 functional responses
NT2 grazing behaviour
NT3 overgrazing
NT2 trophallaxis
NT1 host guest relations
NT1 human behaviour

BEHAVIOUR *cont.*
NT2 economic behaviour
NT3 consumer behaviour
NT4 complaints
NT4 consumer preferences
NT4 purchasing habits
NT3 economic impact
NT2 leisure behaviour
NT2 visitor behaviour
NT3 visitor impact
NT1 maternal behaviour
NT2 mothering ability
NT1 paternal behaviour
NT1 reproductive behaviour
NT2 reproductive traits
NT1 searching behaviour
NT2 host-seeking behaviour
NT1 seasonal behaviour
NT1 sexual behaviour
NT2 flehmen
NT2 impotence
NT2 libido
NT2 mating behaviour
NT2 nymphomania
NT2 prostitution
NT2 reaction time
NT2 standing reflex
NT2 teasing
NT1 social behaviour
NT2 cultural behaviour
NT3 cultural integration
NT3 cultural interaction
NT2 delinquent behaviour
NT3 addiction
NT4 drug addiction
NT3 vandalism
NT2 economic behaviour
NT3 consumer behaviour
NT4 complaints
NT4 consumer preferences
NT4 purchasing habits
NT3 economic impact
NT2 etiquette (agricola)
NT3 table manners (agricola)
NT2 group behaviour
NT3 group interaction
NT2 non-participation
NT2 social barriers
NT2 social integration
NT2 social interaction
NT2 social mobility
NT3 vertical mobility
NT2 social participation
NT3 social activities
NT1 vocalization
rt antagonism
rt attitudes
rt behavioural resistance
rt conditioned reflexes
rt conditioning
rt consciousness
rt habits
rt mental ability
rt nervous type
rt opinions
rt temperament
rt tractability
rt traits

behaviour, conditioned reflex
USE **conditioned reflexes**

behaviour, consumer
USE **consumer behaviour**

BEHAVIOURAL RESISTANCE
AF behavioral resistance
BT1 resistance
rt behaviour
rt insecticide resistance
rt pest resistance
rt resistance mechanisms

BEIDELLITE
BT1 clay minerals
BT2 minerals

BEIJERINCKIA
BT1 azotobacteraceae
BT2 gracilicutes
BT3 bacteria
BT4 prokaryotes

BEIJERINCKIA *cont.*
NT1 beijerinckia indica
NT1 beijerinckia lacticogenes

BEIJERINCKIA INDICA
BT1 beijerinckia
BT2 azotobacteraceae
BT3 gracilicutes
BT4 bacteria
BT5 prokaryotes

BEIJERINCKIA LACTICOGENES
BT1 beijerinckia
BT2 azotobacteraceae
BT3 gracilicutes
BT4 bacteria
BT5 prokaryotes

BEIJING
uf *china (peking)*
uf *peking municipality*
BT1 china
BT2 east asia
BT3 asia

BEIJING BLACK
HN from 1990
BT1 pig breeds
BT2 breeds

BEILSCHMIEDIA
BT1 lauraceae
NT1 beilschmiedia miersii
NT1 beilschmiedia tawa

BEILSCHMIEDIA MIERSII
BT1 beilschmiedia
BT2 lauraceae

BEILSCHMIEDIA TAWA
BT1 beilschmiedia
BT2 lauraceae

BEL PAESE CHEESE
BT1 cheeses
BT2 milk products
BT3 products

BELAU
BT1 pacific islands trust territory
BT2 american oceania
BT3 oceania

BELGIAN
BT1 horse breeds
BT2 breeds

BELGIAN BLACK PIED
BT1 cattle breeds
BT2 breeds

BELGIAN BLUE
HN from 1990; previously "central and upper belgian"
uf *central and upper belgian*
BT1 cattle breeds
BT2 breeds

BELGIAN FAWN
BT1 goat breeds
BT2 breeds

BELGIAN LANDRACE
BT1 pig breeds
BT2 breeds

BELGIAN LUXEMBOURG
uf *belgium (luxembourg)*
uf *luxembourg (belgian)*
BT1 belgium
BT2 western europe
BT3 europe
rt luxembourg

BELGIAN RED
HN from 1990; previously "west flemish red"
uf *west flemish red*
BT1 cattle breeds
BT2 breeds

BELGIAN RED PIED
HN from 1990; previously "campine red pied"
uf *campine red pied*

BELGIAN RED PIED *cont.*
BT1 cattle breeds
BT2 breeds

BELGIAN WHITE-AND-RED
HN from 1990
BT1 cattle breeds
BT2 breeds

BELGIUM
BT1 western europe
BT2 europe
NT1 antwerp
NT1 belgian luxembourg
NT1 brabant
NT1 east flanders
NT1 hainault
NT1 liege
NT1 limbourg
NT1 namur
NT1 west flanders
rt benelux
rt european communities
rt oecd

belgium (antwerp)
USE **antwerp**

belgium (brabant)
USE **brabant**

belgium (east flanders)
USE **east flanders**

belgium (hainault)
USE **hainault**

belgium (liege)
USE **liege**

belgium (limbourg)
USE **limbourg**

belgium (luxembourg)
USE **belgian luxembourg**

belgium (namur)
USE **namur**

belgium (west flanders)
USE **west flanders**

BELIEFS (AGRICOLA)
NT1 health beliefs (agricola)

BELIZE
uf *british honduras*
uf *honduras, british*
BT1 central america
BT2 america
rt acp
rt caribbean community
rt commonwealth of nations

belladonna
USE **atropa belladonna**

BELLADONNA MOTTLE TYMOVIRUS
HN from 1990; previously "belladonna mottle virus"
uf *belladonna mottle virus*
BT1 tymovirus group
BT2 plant viruses
BT3 plant pathogens
BT4 pathogens
rt atropa belladonna

belladonna mottle virus
USE **belladonna mottle tymovirus**

BELLARDIA
BT1 scrophulariaceae
NT1 bellardia trixago

BELLARDIA TRIXAGO
BT1 bellardia
BT2 scrophulariaceae

BELLARDIOCHLOA
BT1 gramineae
NT1 bellardiochloa violacea
rt poa

BELLARDIOCHLOA VIOLACEA
uf *poa violacea*
BT1 bellardiochloa
BT2 gramineae

BELLARY
BT1 sheep breeds
BT2 breeds

BELLIERIA
BT1 sarcophagidae
BT2 diptera
rt helicophagella

bellieria melanura
USE **helicophagella melanura**

BELLIS
BT1 compositae
NT1 bellis perennis

BELLIS PERENNIS
BT1 bellis
BT2 compositae
BT1 ornamental herbaceous plants

BELLY
BT1 body regions
rt abdomen

BELONDIRA
BT1 belondiridae
BT2 nematoda
NT1 belondira gracile

BELONDIRA GRACILE
BT1 belondira
BT2 belondiridae
BT3 nematoda

BELONDIRIDAE
BT1 nematoda
NT1 acrobelus
NT1 axonchium
NT1 belondira
NT2 belondira gracile
NT1 cephalobus
NT1 chiloplacus
NT1 dorylaimellus
NT1 oxidirus
rt free living nematodes

BELONOLAIMIDAE
BT1 nematoda
NT1 belonolaimus
NT2 belonolaimus longicaudatus
NT1 morulaimus
rt plant parasitic nematodes

BELONOLAIMUS
BT1 belonolaimidae
BT2 nematoda
NT1 belonolaimus longicaudatus

BELONOLAIMUS LONGICAUDATUS
BT1 belonolaimus
BT2 belonolaimidae
BT3 nematoda

BELONTIIDAE
BT1 perciformes
BT2 osteichthyes
BT3 fishes
NT1 trichogaster

BELOPERONE
BT1 acanthaceae
NT1 beloperone guttata

BELOPERONE GUTTATA
BT1 beloperone
BT2 acanthaceae
BT1 ornamental woody plants

belorussian ssr
USE **byelorussian ssr**

BELT CONVEYORS
uf *conveyors, belt*
BT1 conveyors
rt belts

BELT DRIVES
uf *drives, belt*
BT1 drives
BT2 machinery
rt belts

BELT FEED MECHANISM
uf *feed mechanism, belt*
BT1 feed mechanisms
rt belts

BELTED GALLOWAY
BT1 cattle breeds
BT2 breeds

BELTS
BT1 components
rt belt conveyors
rt belt drives
rt belt feed mechanism

BELTSVILLE NO. 1
BT1 pig breeds
BT2 breeds

BELTSVILLE NO. 2
BT1 pig breeds
BT2 breeds

beluga
USE **huso huso**

BEMBECIA
BT1 sesiidae
BT2 lepidoptera
rt pennisetia

bembecia hylaeiformis
USE **pennisetia hylaeiformis**

bembecia marginata
USE **pennisetia marginata**

BEMBIDION
BT1 carabidae
BT2 coleoptera
NT1 bembidion lampros
NT1 bembidion quadrimaculatum

BEMBIDION LAMPROS
BT1 bembidion
BT2 carabidae
BT3 coleoptera

BEMBIDION QUADRIMACULATUM
BT1 bembidion
BT2 carabidae
BT3 coleoptera

BEMISIA
BT1 aleyrodidae
BT2 aleyrodoidea
BT3 sternorrhyncha
BT4 homoptera
NT1 bemisia giffardi
NT1 bemisia tabaci

BEMISIA GIFFARDI
BT1 bemisia
BT2 aleyrodidae
BT3 aleyrodoidea
BT4 sternorrhyncha
BT5 homoptera

bemisia longispina
USE **bemisia tabaci**

BEMISIA TABACI
uf *bemisia longispina*
BT1 bemisia
BT2 aleyrodidae
BT3 aleyrodoidea
BT4 sternorrhyncha
BT5 homoptera

BENACIL
BT1 anthelmintics
BT2 antiparasitic agents
BT3 drugs

BENADIR
HN from 1990
BT1 goat breeds
BT2 breeds

BENALAXYL
BT1 xylylalanine fungicides
BT2 fungicides
BT3 pesticides

BENAZOLIN
BT1 unclassified herbicides
BT2 herbicides
BT3 pesticides

benazoline
USE **metizoline**

BENCH GRAFTS
rt grafting

benches
USE **staging**

BENCHMARK SOILS
BT1 soil types (miscellaneous)
rt technology transfer

BENDING
rt bending strength
rt bentwood
rt brashness
rt deformation
rt epinasty
rt warping
rt woodworking

BENDING STRENGTH
uf *strength, bending*
BT1 strength
BT2 mechanical properties
BT3 properties
rt bending
rt bending stress
rt stresses and sets

BENDING STRESS
uf *stress, bending*
BT1 stresses
rt bending strength

BENDIOCARB
BT1 carbamate insecticides
BT2 carbamate pesticides
BT2 insecticides
BT3 pesticides

BENEDENIA
BT1 capsalidae
BT2 monogenea

BENEFICIAL ARTHROPODS
BT1 beneficial organisms
NT1 beneficial insects
NT2 dung beetles
NT2 silkworms
NT3 antheraea pernyi
NT3 bombyx mori
rt arthropods

BENEFICIAL INSECTS
BT1 beneficial arthropods
BT2 beneficial organisms
BT1 insects
BT2 arthropods
NT1 dung beetles
NT1 silkworms
NT2 antheraea pernyi
NT2 bombyx mori
rt maggot therapy
rt parasitoids

BENEFICIAL ORGANISMS
NT1 beneficial arthropods
NT2 beneficial insects
NT3 dung beetles
NT3 silkworms
NT4 antheraea pernyi
NT4 bombyx mori
NT1 biological control agents
NT2 aceratoneuromyia indica
NT2 agasicles hygrophila
NT2 agathis pumila
NT2 agrypon flaveolatum
NT2 apanteles subandinus
NT2 aphelinus mali
NT2 aphelinus thomsoni
NT2 aphidius smithi
NT2 aphytis chrysomphali

BENEFICIAL ORGANISMS *cont.*
NT2 aphytis holoxanthus
NT2 aphytis lepidosaphes
NT2 aphytis lingnanensis
NT2 aphytis melinus
NT2 aphytis mytilaspidis
NT2 apion antiquum
NT2 apion ulicis
NT2 ascogaster quadridentata
NT2 bathyplectes curculionis
NT2 biosteres fullawayi
NT2 biosteres longicaudatus
NT2 cactoblastis cactorum
NT2 comperiella bifasciata
NT2 compsilura concinnata
NT2 copidosoma koehleri
NT2 cotesia flavipes
NT2 cotesia glomerata
NT2 cryptolaemus montrouzieri
NT2 cyzenis albicans
NT2 dactylopius opuntiae
NT2 encarsia citrina
NT2 encarsia formosa
NT2 epidinocarsis lopezi
NT2 illidops scutellaris
NT2 lixophaga diatraeae
NT2 longitarsus jacobaeae
NT2 lysiphlebus testaceipes
NT2 macrocentrus ancylivorus
NT2 mesoleius tenthredinis
NT2 metagonistylum minense
NT2 metaphycus helvolus
NT2 metaphycus lounsburyi
NT2 meteorus versicolor
NT2 microlarinus lypriformis
NT2 monodontomerus dentipes
NT2 muscidifurax raptor
NT2 neochetina eichhorniae
NT2 neodusmetia sangwani
NT2 olesicampe benefactor
NT2 ooencyrtus kuvanae
NT2 orgilus lepidus
NT2 pachycrepoideus vindemmiae
NT2 paratheresia claripalpis
NT2 pholetesor circumscriptus
NT2 phytoseiulus persimilis
NT2 pleolophus basizonus
NT2 pseudaphycus malinus
NT2 pteromalus puparum
NT2 rhinocyllus conicus
NT2 rhizophagus grandis
NT2 rodolia cardinalis
NT2 sameodes albiguttalis
NT2 scutellista cyanea
NT2 serangium parcesetosum
NT2 spalangia nigra
NT2 teleonemia scrupulosa
NT2 trichogramma japonicum
NT2 trioxys pallidus
NT2 trissolcus basalis
NT2 tyria jacobaeae
NT2 tytthus mundulus
NT2 vogtia malloi
NT1 pollinators
NT2 hummingbirds
rt natural enemies
rt nontarget effects

BENEFICIATION
BT1 fertilizer technology
BT2 technology
rt enrichment

benefits, accident
USE **accident benefits**

benefits, non-market
USE **non-market benefits**

benefits, old age
USE **old age benefits**

benefits, sickness
USE **sickness benefits**

benefits, social
USE **social benefits**

BENELUX
BT1 international organizations
BT2 organizations
rt belgium

BENELUX *cont.*
rt economic regions
rt european communities
rt luxembourg
rt netherlands

BENFLUOREX
BT1 amphetamines
BT2 phenethylamines
BT3 amines
BT4 amino compounds
BT5 organic nitrogen compounds
BT1 anorexiants
BT2 drugs
BT1 enzyme inhibitors
BT2 metabolic inhibitors
BT3 inhibitors

BENFLURALIN
BT1 dinitroaniline herbicides
BT2 herbicides
BT3 pesticides

BENFURACARB
BT1 carbamate insecticides
BT2 carbamate pesticides
BT2 insecticides
BT3 pesticides

BENFURESATE
BT1 benzofuranyl alkylsulfonate herbicides
BT2 herbicides
BT3 pesticides

BENGAL
BT1 goat breeds
BT2 breeds

bengal, west
USE **west bengal**

BENI AHSEN
BT1 sheep breeds
BT2 breeds

BENI GUIL
BT1 sheep breeds
BT2 breeds

BENIGN COURSE
HN from 1990
BT1 disease course

BENIN
uf *benin people's republic*
uf *dahomey*
BT1 west africa
BT2 africa south of sahara
BT3 africa
rt acp
rt developing countries
rt least developed countries

benin (nigeria)
USE **nigeria**

benin people's republic
USE **benin**

BENINCASA
BT1 cucurbitaceae
NT1 benincasa hispida

benincasa cerifera
USE **benincasa hispida**

BENINCASA HISPIDA
uf *benincasa cerifera*
uf *gourd, ash*
BT1 benincasa
BT2 cucurbitaceae
BT1 cucurbit vegetables
BT2 fruit vegetables
BT3 vegetables

beniseed
USE **sesame**

BENODANIL
BT1 benzanilide fungicides
BT2 anilide fungicides
BT3 fungicides
BT4 pesticides

BENOMYL
uf *fundazol*
BT1 antioxidants
BT2 additives
BT1 benzimidazole fungicides
BT2 fungicides
BT3 pesticides
BT1 carbamate acaricides
BT2 acaricides
BT3 pesticides
BT2 carbamate pesticides
BT1 carbamate nematicides
BT2 carbamate pesticides
BT2 nematicides
BT3 pesticides
rt storage dips

BENQUINOX
BT1 quinone fungicides
BT2 fungicides
BT3 pesticides
BT2 quinones
BT3 aromatic compounds

BENSULFURON
BT1 sulfonylurea herbicides
BT2 sulfonylureas
BT3 sulfonamides
BT4 amides
BT5 organic nitrogen compounds
BT4 organic sulfur compounds
BT2 urea herbicides
BT3 herbicides
BT4 pesticides

BENSULIDE
BT1 organophosphorus herbicides
BT2 herbicides
BT3 pesticides
BT2 organophosphorus pesticides
BT3 organophosphorus compounds

bent
USE **agrostis**

BENTAZONE
BT1 unclassified herbicides
BT2 herbicides
BT3 pesticides

benthiocarb
USE **thiobencarb**

BENTHOS
rt aquatic organisms

BENTONITE
BT1 clay minerals
BT2 minerals
BT1 soil conditioners
BT2 soil amendments
BT3 amendments
rt montmorillonite

BENTWOOD
BT1 forest products
BT2 products
BT1 wood
rt bending
rt furniture

BENZADOX
BT1 amide herbicides
BT2 herbicides
BT3 pesticides

BENZALDEHYDE
BT1 aldehydes
BT1 flavour compounds
BT1 solvents
rt dyes

BENZALKONIUM CHLORIDE
BT1 antibacterial agents
BT2 antiinfective agents
BT3 drugs
BT1 antifungal agents
BT2 antiinfective agents
BT3 drugs

BENZALKONIUM CHLORIDE *cont.*
BT1 antiseptics
BT2 antiinfective agents
BT3 drugs
BT1 quaternary ammonium compounds
BT2 ammonium compounds
BT2 organic nitrogen compounds
BT1 surfactants

benzamizole
USE **isoxaben**

BENZANILIDE FUNGICIDES
BT1 anilide fungicides
BT2 fungicides
BT3 pesticides
NT1 benodanil
NT1 flutolanil
NT1 mebenil

BENZENE
BT1 aromatic hydrocarbons
BT2 aromatic compounds
BT2 hydrocarbons
BT1 carcinogens
BT2 toxic substances
BT1 fuels
BT1 solvents

benzene hexachloride
USE **hch**

BENZENEALKANOIC ACIDS
BT1 carboxylic acids
BT2 organic acids
BT3 acids
NT1 homovanillic acid
NT1 mandelic acid
NT1 phenylacetic acid
NT1 phenyllactic acid
NT1 vanillomandelic acid

BENZENEALKENOIC ACIDS
BT1 carboxylic acids
BT2 organic acids
BT3 acids
NT1 cinnamic acid
NT1 coumaric acids
NT2 p-coumaric acid
NT2 caffeic acid
NT2 ferulic acid
NT2 sinapic acid

BENZIMIDAZOLE
BT1 benzimidazoles
BT2 heterocyclic nitrogen compounds
BT3 organic nitrogen compounds
BT1 cytokinins
BT2 plant growth regulators
BT3 growth regulators
BT1 vitamin b antagonists
BT2 vitamin antagonists
BT3 antagonists
BT4 metabolic inhibitors
BT5 inhibitors

BENZIMIDAZOLE FUNGICIDES
BT1 fungicides
BT2 pesticides
NT1 benomyl
NT1 carbendazim
NT1 cypendazole
NT1 fuberidazole
NT1 mecarbinzid
NT1 thiabendazole
NT1 thiophanate
NT1 thiophanate-methyl
rt benzimidazoles

BENZIMIDAZOLES
BT1 heterocyclic nitrogen compounds
BT2 organic nitrogen compounds
NT1 albendazole
NT1 benzimidazole
NT1 cambendazole
NT1 ciclobendazole
NT1 fenbendazole

BENZIMIDAZOLES *cont.*
NT1 flubendazole
NT1 luxabendazole
NT1 mebendazole
NT1 oxfendazole
NT1 oxibendazole
NT1 parbendazole
rt anthelmintics
rt benzimidazole fungicides

BENZIPRAM
BT1 amide herbicides
BT2 herbicides
BT3 pesticides

BENZNIDAZOLE
BT1 trypanocides
BT2 antiprotozoal agents
BT3 antiparasitic agents
BT4 drugs

BENZOATES
NT1 benzoates (esters)
NT2 benzyl benzoate
NT1 benzoates (salts)
NT2 sodium benzoate
rt benzoic acid

BENZOATES (ESTERS)
BT1 benzoates
BT1 esters
NT1 benzyl benzoate

BENZOATES (SALTS)
BT1 benzoates
BT1 organic salts
BT2 salts
NT1 sodium benzoate

BENZOCAINE
BT1 local anaesthetics
BT2 anaesthetics
BT3 neurotropic drugs
BT4 drugs

BENZODIAZEPINES
BT1 heterocyclic nitrogen compounds
BT2 organic nitrogen compounds
NT1 chlordiazepoxide
NT1 diazepam
NT1 elfazepam

BENZOFURANYL ALKYLSULFONATE HERBICIDES
BT1 herbicides
BT2 pesticides
NT1 benfuresate
NT1 ethofumesate

BENZOIC ACID
BT1 benzoic acids
BT2 aromatic acids
BT3 aromatic compounds
BT3 organic acids
BT4 acids
BT1 food preservatives
BT2 preservatives
rt benzoates

BENZOIC ACID HERBICIDES
BT1 aromatic acid herbicides
BT2 herbicides
BT3 pesticides
NT1 2,3,6-tba
NT1 chloramben
NT1 dicamba

BENZOIC ACIDS
BT1 aromatic acids
BT2 aromatic compounds
BT2 organic acids
BT3 acids
NT1 aminobenzoic acids
NT2 p-aminobenzoic acid
NT2 aminosalicylic acid
NT2 hydroxyanthranilic acid
NT1 benzoic acid
NT1 phenolic acids
NT2 4-hydroxybenzoic acid
NT2 dihydroxybenzoic acid
NT2 gallic acid
NT2 hydroxyanthranilic acid

BENZOIC ACIDS *cont.*
NT2 protocatechuic acid
NT2 salicylic acids
NT3 3,5-dimethoxysalicylic acid
NT3 aminosalicylic acid
NT3 aspirin
NT3 salicylic acid
NT2 syringic acid
NT2 tannins
NT2 vanillic acid
NT1 phthalic acid
NT1 tibric acid
rt carboxylic acids

BENZOPYRENE
BT1 aromatic hydrocarbons
BT2 aromatic compounds
BT2 hydrocarbons
BT1 carcinogens
BT2 toxic substances

BENZOQUINONE
BT1 enzyme inhibitors
BT2 metabolic inhibitors
BT3 inhibitors
BT1 quinones
BT2 aromatic compounds

BENZOXIMATE
BT1 unclassified acaricides
BT2 acaricides
BT3 pesticides

BENZOYLPHENYLUREAS
BT1 amides
BT2 organic nitrogen compounds
NT1 chlorfluazuron
NT1 diflubenzuron
NT1 penfluron
NT1 teflubenzuron
NT1 triflumuron
rt chitin synthesis inhibitors

BENZOYLPROP-ETHYL
BT1 arylalanine herbicides
BT2 anilide herbicides
BT3 amide herbicides
BT4 herbicides
BT5 pesticides

BENZTHIAZURON
BT1 urea herbicides
BT2 herbicides
BT3 pesticides

BENZYL ALCOHOL
BT1 alcohols
BT1 flavour compounds
BT1 solvents

BENZYL BENZOATE
BT1 benzoates (esters)
BT2 benzoates
BT2 esters
BT1 bridged diphenyl acaricides
BT2 acaricides
BT3 pesticides
BT1 ectoparasiticides
BT2 antiparasitic agents
BT3 drugs

BENZYL ISOTHIOCYANATE
BT1 cut flower preservatives
BT2 preservatives
BT1 isothiocyanates
BT2 esters
BT2 organic sulfur compounds

BENZYLADENINE
uf *ba (plant growth regulator)*
uf *benzylaminopurine*
BT1 adenines
BT2 purines
BT3 heterocyclic nitrogen compounds
BT4 organic nitrogen compounds
BT1 cytokinins
BT2 plant growth regulators
BT3 growth regulators

benzylaminopurine
USE **benzyladenine**

BEPHENIUM
BT1 anthelmintics
BT2 antiparasitic agents
BT3 drugs
BT1 quaternary ammonium compounds
BT2 ammonium compounds
BT2 organic nitrogen compounds

BERBER
BT1 sheep breeds
BT2 breeds

BERBERENTULUS
BT1 acerentomidae
BT2 protura

BERBERIDACEAE
NT1 berberis
NT2 berberis baluchistanica
NT2 berberis chillanensis
NT2 berberis coriaria
NT2 berberis darwinii
NT2 berberis glaucocarpa
NT2 berberis heteropoda
NT2 berberis hookeri
NT2 berberis integerrima
NT2 berberis jamesiana
NT2 berberis julianae
NT2 berberis nummularia
NT2 berberis orthobotrys
NT2 berberis poiretii
NT2 berberis thunbergii
NT2 berberis trifoliolata
NT2 berberis umbellata
NT2 berberis vulgaris
NT2 berberis zabeliana
NT1 epimedium
NT1 mahonia
NT2 mahonia aquifolium
NT2 mahonia bealei
NT2 mahonia japonica
NT2 mahonia lomariifolia
NT1 plagiorhegma
NT2 plagiorhegma dubium

BERBERIS
uf *barberry*
BT1 berberidaceae
NT1 berberis baluchistanica
NT1 berberis chillanensis
NT1 berberis coriaria
NT1 berberis darwinii
NT1 berberis glaucocarpa
NT1 berberis heteropoda
NT1 berberis hookeri
NT1 berberis integerrima
NT1 berberis jamesiana
NT1 berberis julianae
NT1 berberis nummularia
NT1 berberis orthobotrys
NT1 berberis poiretii
NT1 berberis thunbergii
NT1 berberis trifoliolata
NT1 berberis umbellata
NT1 berberis vulgaris
NT1 berberis zabeliana

berberis aquifolium
USE **mahonia aquifolium**

BERBERIS BALUCHISTANICA
BT1 berberis
BT2 berberidaceae

BERBERIS CHILLANENSIS
BT1 berberis
BT2 berberidaceae

BERBERIS CORIARIA
BT1 berberis
BT2 berberidaceae

BERBERIS DARWINII
BT1 berberis
BT2 berberidaceae
BT1 ornamental woody plants

BERBERIS GLAUCOCARPA
BT1 berberis

BERBERIS GLAUCOCARPA *cont.*
BT2 berberidaceae

BERBERIS HETEROPODA
BT1 berberis
BT2 berberidaceae
BT1 ornamental woody plants

BERBERIS HOOKERI
uf *berberis wallichiana*
BT1 berberis
BT2 berberidaceae
BT1 ornamental woody plants

BERBERIS INTEGERRIMA
BT1 berberis
BT2 berberidaceae

BERBERIS JAMESIANA
BT1 berberis
BT2 berberidaceae

BERBERIS JULIANAE
BT1 berberis
BT2 berberidaceae
BT1 ornamental woody plants

BERBERIS NUMMULARIA
BT1 berberis
BT2 berberidaceae

BERBERIS ORTHOBOTRYS
BT1 berberis
BT2 berberidaceae
BT1 ornamental woody plants

BERBERIS POIRETII
BT1 berberis
BT2 berberidaceae
BT1 medicinal plants
BT1 ornamental woody plants

BERBERIS THUNBERGII
BT1 berberis
BT2 berberidaceae
BT1 ornamental woody plants

BERBERIS TRIFOLIOLATA
BT1 berberis
BT2 berberidaceae

BERBERIS UMBELLATA
BT1 berberis
BT2 berberidaceae
BT1 ornamental woody plants

BERBERIS VULGARIS
BT1 berberis
BT2 berberidaceae
BT1 dye plants

berberis wallichiana
USE **berberis hookeri**

BERBERIS ZABELIANA
BT1 berberis
BT2 berberidaceae
BT1 ornamental woody plants

BERCAEA
BT1 sarcophagidae
BT2 diptera
NT1 bercaea cruentata
rt sarcophaga

BERCAEA CRUENTATA
uf *bercaea haemorrhoidalis*
uf *sarcophaga cruentata*
uf *sarcophaga haemorrhoidalis*
BT1 bercaea
BT2 sarcophagidae
BT3 diptera

bercaea haemorrhoidalis
USE **bercaea cruentata**

berenil
USE **diminazene**

BERGAMASCA
HN from 1990; previously "bergamo"
uf *bergamo*
BT1 sheep breeds
BT2 breeds

bergamo
USE **bergamasca**

bergamot
USE **citrus bergamia**
OR **monarda fistulosa**

BERGENIA
BT1 saxifragaceae
NT1 bergenia ciliata
NT1 bergenia cordifolia
NT1 bergenia crassifolia

BERGENIA CILIATA
uf *bergenia ligulata*
BT1 bergenia
BT2 saxifragaceae
BT1 ornamental herbaceous plants

BERGENIA CORDIFOLIA
BT1 bergenia
BT2 saxifragaceae
BT1 ornamental herbaceous plants

BERGENIA CRASSIFOLIA
uf *bergenia pacifica*
BT1 bergenia
BT2 saxifragaceae
BT1 ornamental herbaceous plants
BT1 tan plants

bergenia ligulata
USE **bergenia ciliata**

bergenia pacifica
USE **bergenia crassifolia**

BERIBERI
BT1 deficiency diseases
BT2 diseases
BT2 nutritional disorders
BT3 animal disorders
BT4 disorders
rt vitamin b complex

BERIBERI HEART DISEASE
BT1 heart diseases
BT2 cardiovascular diseases
BT3 organic diseases
BT4 diseases
rt vitamin b complex

BERING SEA
BT1 northeast pacific
BT2 pacific ocean
BT3 marine areas
BT1 northwest pacific
BT2 pacific ocean
BT3 marine areas

BERKSHIRE
BT1 pig breeds
BT2 breeds

BERLIN
BT1 europe
NT1 east berlin
NT1 west berlin

BERMUDA
BT1 north america
BT2 america
rt cacm

bermuda grass
USE **cynodon dactylon**

BERNE VIRUS
BT1 toroviridae
BT2 viruses

BERNOULLIA
BT1 bombacaceae
NT1 bernoullia flammea

BERNOULLIA FLAMMEA
BT1 bernoullia
BT2 bombacaceae

BERRICHON DU CHER
HN from 1990; previously "cher berrichon"
uf *cher berrichon*

BERRICHON DU CHER *cont.*
BT1 sheep breeds
BT2 breeds

berries
USE **fruits**

berry fruits
USE **small fruits**

BERSAMA
BT1 melianthaceae
NT1 bersama yangambiensis

BERSAMA YANGAMBIENSIS
BT1 bersama
BT2 melianthaceae

berseem
USE **trifolium alexandrinum**

BERTEROA
BT1 cruciferae
NT1 berteroa incana

BERTEROA INCANA
BT1 berteroa
BT2 cruciferae

BERTHOLLETIA
BT1 lecythidaceae
NT1 bertholletia excelsa

BERTHOLLETIA EXCELSA
BT1 bertholletia
BT2 lecythidaceae
rt brazil nuts

BERTIELLA
BT1 anoplocephalidae
BT2 eucestoda
BT3 cestoda
NT1 bertiella studeri

BERTIELLA STUDERI
BT1 bertiella
BT2 anoplocephalidae
BT3 eucestoda
BT4 cestoda

BERULA
BT1 umbelliferae
NT1 berula erecta

BERULA ERECTA
BT1 berula
BT2 umbelliferae

BERYLLIUM
BT1 alkaline earth metals
BT2 metallic elements
BT3 elements
BT3 metals

BERYTIDAE
BT1 heteroptera
NT1 jalysus
NT2 jalysus spinosus

BESCHORNERIA
BT1 agavaceae

BESNOITIA
uf *globidium*
BT1 apicomplexa
BT2 protozoa
NT1 besnoitia besnoiti
NT1 besnoitia darlingi
NT1 besnoitia jellisoni
NT1 besnoitia wallacei

BESNOITIA BESNOITI
BT1 besnoitia
BT2 apicomplexa
BT3 protozoa

BESNOITIA DARLINGI
BT1 besnoitia
BT2 apicomplexa
BT3 protozoa

BESNOITIA JELLISONI
BT1 besnoitia
BT2 apicomplexa
BT3 protozoa

BESNOITIA WALLACEI
BT1 besnoitia
BT2 apicomplexa
BT3 protozoa

BESSA
BT1 tachinidae
BT2 diptera
NT1 bessa harveyi
NT1 bessa parallela
NT1 bessa selecta

bessa fugax
USE **bessa parallela**

BESSA HARVEYI
BT1 bessa
BT2 tachinidae
BT3 diptera

BESSA PARALLELA
uf *bessa fugax*
uf *bessa selecta fugax*
BT1 bessa
BT2 tachinidae
BT3 diptera

BESSA SELECTA
BT1 bessa
BT2 tachinidae
BT3 diptera

bessa selecta fugax
USE **bessa parallela**

BEST LINEAR UNBIASED ESTIMATION
uf *blue*
BT1 estimation

BEST LINEAR UNBIASED PREDICTION
uf *blup*
BT1 estimation

BESTUZHEV
BT1 cattle breeds
BT2 breeds

BETA
BT1 chenopodiaceae
NT1 beta adanensis
NT1 beta bourgaei
NT1 beta macrocarpa
NT1 beta vulgaris
NT1 beta vulgaris var. saccharifera

BETA ADANENSIS
BT1 beta
BT2 chenopodiaceae

BETA-ADRENERGIC AGONISTS
(sorted under adrenergic agonists)

BETA-ADRENERGIC RECEPTORS
(sorted under adrenergic receptors)

BETA-AMYLASE
(sorted under amylase)

BETA-AMYRIN
(sorted under amyrin)

BETA-BLOCKERS
(sorted under blockers)

BETA BOURGAEI
BT1 beta
BT2 chenopodiaceae

BETA-CAROTENE
(sorted under carotene)

BETA-CASEIN
(sorted under casein)

BETA-FRUCTOFURANOSIDASE
(sorted under fructofuranosidase)

BETA-GALACTOSIDASE
(sorted under galactosidase)

BETA-GLUCAN
(sorted under glucan)

BETA-GLUCANASE
(sorted under glucanase)

BETA-GLUCOSIDASE
(sorted under glucosidase)

BETA-GLUCURONIDASE
(sorted under glucuronidase)

BETA-IONONE
(sorted under ionone)

BETA-LACTAMASE
(sorted under lactamase)

BETA-LACTOGLOBULIN
(sorted under lactoglobulin)

BETA MACROCARPA
BT1 beta
BT2 chenopodiaceae

BETA-MANNOSIDASE
(sorted under mannosidase)

BETA-PINENE
(sorted under pinene)

BETA RADIATION
uf *beta rays*
BT1 radiation

beta rays
USE **beta radiation**

BETA-TOCOPHEROL
(sorted under tocopherol)

BETA VULGARIS
BT1 beta
BT2 chenopodiaceae
BT1 fodder plants
rt beet cryptic 1 cryptovirus
rt beet cryptic 2 cryptovirus
rt beet curly top geminivirus
rt beet mosaic potyvirus
rt beet necrotic yellow vein virus
rt beet western yellows luteovirus
rt beet yellows closterovirus
rt beetroots
rt beets
rt fodder beet
rt mangolds
rt spinach beets

BETA VULGARIS VAR. SACCHARIFERA
BT1 beta
BT2 chenopodiaceae
rt sugarbeet

BETA-XYLOSIDASE
(sorted under xylosidase)

BETACYANINS
BT1 flavonoids
BT2 aromatic compounds
BT2 plant pigments
BT3 pigments

BETAINE
uf *glycinebetaine*
BT1 lipotropic factors
BT2 drugs
BT1 quaternary ammonium compounds
BT2 ammonium compounds
BT2 organic nitrogen compounds

BETAMETHASONE
BT1 antiinflammatory agents
BT2 drugs
BT1 dermatological agents
BT2 drugs
BT1 pregnanes
BT2 steroids
BT3 isoprenoids
BT4 lipids
BT1 synthetic glucocorticoids
BT2 synthetic corticoids
BT3 corticoids
BT3 synthetic hormones

BETEL
rt piper betle

BETHANECHOL
uf *urecholine*
BT1 parasympathomimetics
BT2 neurotropic drugs
BT3 drugs
BT1 quaternary ammonium compounds
BT2 ammonium compounds
BT2 organic nitrogen compounds

BETHYLIDAE
BT1 hymenoptera
NT1 cephalonomia
NT1 goniozus
NT2 goniozus nephantidis

betonica
USE **stachys**

betonica grandiflora
USE **stachys grandiflora**

betonica officinalis
USE **stachys officinalis**

betting
USE **gambling**

BETTONGIA
BT1 macropodidae
BT2 marsupials
BT3 mammals
NT1 bettongia gaimardi

BETTONGIA GAIMARDI
BT1 bettongia
BT2 macropodidae
BT3 marsupials
BT4 mammals

BETULA
uf *birch*
BT1 betulaceae
NT1 betula alba
NT1 betula albosinensis
NT1 betula alleghaniensis
NT1 betula caerulea
NT1 betula costata
NT1 betula davurica
NT1 betula ermanii
NT1 betula exilis
NT1 betula glandulosa
NT1 betula jacquemontii
NT1 betula lanata
NT1 betula lenta
NT1 betula litwinowii
NT1 betula maximowicziana
NT1 betula nana
NT1 betula nigra
NT1 betula odorata
NT1 betula papyrifera
NT1 betula pendula
NT2 betula pendula f. carelica
NT1 betula platyphylla
NT1 betula populifolia
NT1 betula pubescens
NT1 betula raddeana
NT1 betula schmidtii
NT1 betula tortuosa
NT1 betula utilis
rt betulafolienetriol

BETULA ALBA
BT1 betula
BT2 betulaceae
BT1 forest trees
rt betula pendula
rt betula pubescens

BETULA ALBOSINENSIS
BT1 betula
BT2 betulaceae
BT1 ornamental woody plants

BETULA ALLEGHANIENSIS
uf *betula lutea*
BT1 betula
BT2 betulaceae
BT1 forest trees
BT1 ornamental woody plants

BETULA CAERULEA
BT1 betula
BT2 betulaceae

BETULA COSTATA
BT1 betula
BT2 betulaceae
BT1 ornamental woody plants

BETULA DAVURICA
BT1 betula
BT2 betulaceae
BT1 ornamental woody plants

BETULA ERMANII
BT1 betula
BT2 betulaceae
BT1 forest trees
BT1 ornamental woody plants

BETULA EXILIS
BT1 betula
BT2 betulaceae

BETULA GLANDULOSA
BT1 betula
BT2 betulaceae

BETULA JACQUEMONTII
BT1 betula
BT2 betulaceae
BT1 ornamental woody plants

BETULA LANATA
BT1 betula
BT2 betulaceae

BETULA LENTA
BT1 betula
BT2 betulaceae
BT1 forest trees
BT1 ornamental woody plants

BETULA LITWINOWII
BT1 betula
BT2 betulaceae

betula lutea
USE **betula alleghaniensis**

betula mandshurica
USE **betula platyphylla**

BETULA MAXIMOWICZIANA
BT1 betula
BT2 betulaceae
BT1 forest trees
BT1 ornamental woody plants

BETULA NANA
BT1 betula
BT2 betulaceae
BT1 forest trees

BETULA NIGRA
BT1 betula
BT2 betulaceae
BT1 forest trees
BT1 ornamental woody plants

BETULA ODORATA
BT1 betula
BT2 betulaceae

BETULA PAPYRIFERA
BT1 betula
BT2 betulaceae
BT1 forest trees
BT1 ornamental woody plants

BETULA PENDULA
uf *betula verrucosa*
BT1 betula
BT2 betulaceae
BT1 forest trees
BT1 medicinal plants
BT1 ornamental woody plants
NT1 betula pendula f. carelica
rt betula alba

BETULA PENDULA F. CARELICA
HN from 1990
BT1 betula pendula
BT2 betula
BT3 betulaceae
BT2 forest trees

BETULA PENDULA F. CARELICA *cont.*
BT2 medicinal plants
BT2 ornamental woody plants
rt grain and figure

BETULA PLATYPHYLLA
uf *betula mandshurica*
BT1 betula
BT2 betulaceae
BT1 forest trees
BT1 ornamental woody plants

BETULA POPULIFOLIA
BT1 betula
BT2 betulaceae
BT1 ornamental woody plants

BETULA PUBESCENS
BT1 betula
BT2 betulaceae
BT1 forest trees
rt betula alba

BETULA RADDEANA
BT1 betula
BT2 betulaceae

BETULA SCHMIDTII
BT1 betula
BT2 betulaceae

BETULA TORTUOSA
BT1 betula
BT2 betulaceae
BT1 forest trees

BETULA UTILIS
HN from 1990
BT1 betula
BT2 betulaceae
BT1 forest trees

betula verrucosa
USE **betula pendula**

BETULACEAE
uf *carpinaceae*
NT1 alnus
NT2 alnus acuminata
NT2 alnus cordata
NT2 alnus crispa
NT2 alnus fauriei
NT2 alnus firmifolia
NT2 alnus formosana
NT2 alnus glutinosa
NT2 alnus hirsuta
NT2 alnus incana
NT2 alnus inokumae
NT2 alnus japonica
NT2 alnus jorullensis
NT2 alnus kamtschatica
NT2 alnus koehnei
NT2 alnus nepalensis
NT2 alnus nitida
NT2 alnus rhombifolia
NT2 alnus rubra
NT2 alnus rugosa
NT2 alnus sinuata
NT2 alnus spaethii
NT2 alnus subcordata
NT2 alnus viridis
NT1 betula
NT2 betula alba
NT2 betula albosinensis
NT2 betula alleghaniensis
NT2 betula caerulea
NT2 betula costata
NT2 betula davurica
NT2 betula ermanii
NT2 betula exilis
NT2 betula glandulosa
NT2 betula jacquemontii
NT2 betula lanata
NT2 betula lenta
NT2 betula litwinowii
NT2 betula maximowicziana
NT2 betula nana
NT2 betula nigra
NT2 betula odorata
NT2 betula papyrifera
NT2 betula pendula
NT3 betula pendula f. carelica

BETULACEAE *cont.*
NT2 betula platyphylla
NT2 betula populifolia
NT2 betula pubescens
NT2 betula raddeana
NT2 betula schmidtii
NT2 betula tortuosa
NT2 betula utilis
NT1 carpinus
NT2 carpinus betulus
NT2 carpinus caroliniana
NT2 carpinus laxiflora
NT2 carpinus orientalis
NT2 carpinus tschonoskii
NT1 ostrya
NT2 ostrya carpinifolia
NT2 ostrya virginiana

BETULAFOLIENETRIOL
BT1 phytosterols
BT2 sterols
BT3 alcohols
BT3 steroids
BT4 isoprenoids
BT5 lipids
rt betula

BETULIN
uf *betulinol*
BT1 triterpenoids
BT2 terpenoids
BT3 isoprenoids
BT4 lipids

betulinol
USE **betulin**

BEVEL GEARS
uf *gears, bevel*
BT1 gears
BT2 components

beverage crops
USE **stimulant plants**

BEVERAGE INDUSTRY
BT1 food industry
BT2 industry
NT1 brewing industry
NT1 coffee industry
NT1 distilling industry
NT1 tea industry
NT1 wine industry
rt alcoholic beverages
rt beverages
rt ethanol
rt postagricultural sector

beverage plants
USE **stimulant plants**

BEVERAGE QUALITY
uf *quality of beverage*
BT1 quality
rt beverages

BEVERAGES
uf *drinks*
NT1 alcoholic beverages
NT2 beers
NT3 light beer (agricola)
NT2 cider
NT2 distilled spirits
NT3 brandy
NT3 gin
NT3 liqueurs
NT4 amaretto (agricola)
NT3 rum
NT3 vodka
NT3 whisky
NT2 mead
NT2 sake
NT2 wines
NT3 champagne and sparkling wines
NT3 quality wine
NT3 table wine
NT1 cocoa beverages
NT1 coffee
NT1 cordials (agricola)
NT1 fruit drinks
NT1 herbal teas (agricola)
NT1 iced tea (agricola)

BEVERAGES *cont.*
NT1 lactic beverages
NT1 mate
NT1 milk shakes
NT1 mineral waters
NT1 soft drinks
NT1 tea
rt beverage industry
rt beverage quality
rt carbonation
rt drinking
rt drinking water
rt food products
rt milk
rt plant products
rt stimulants
rt whey

beverages, alcoholic
USE **alcoholic beverages**

BEZAFIBRATE
BT1 antilipaemics
BT2 haematologic agents
BT3 drugs

BEZOAR
uf *hair balls*
BT1 concretions

bha
USE **butylated hydroxyanisole**

BHADARWAH
BT1 sheep breeds
BT2 breeds

BHADAWARI
HN from 1990
BT1 buffalo breeds
BT2 breeds

BHAGNARI
BT1 cattle breeds
BT2 breeds

BHAKARWAL
BT1 sheep breeds
BT2 breeds

BHANJA VIRUS
BT1 unclassified viruses
BT2 viruses

bhc
USE **hch**

BHOTIA PONY
BT1 horse breeds
BT2 breeds

bht
USE **butylated hydroxytoluene**

BHUJ
HN from 1990; previously "brazilian bhuj"
uf *brazilian bhuj*
BT1 goat breeds
BT2 breeds

BHUTAN
BT1 south asia
BT2 asia
rt developing countries
rt least developed countries

bialaphos
USE **bilanafos**

BIBIO
BT1 bibionidae
BT2 diptera
NT1 bibio hortulanus

BIBIO HORTULANUS
BT1 bibio
BT2 bibionidae
BT3 diptera

BIBIONIDAE
BT1 diptera
NT1 bibio
NT2 bibio hortulanus
NT1 plecia
NT2 plecia nearctica

BIBLIOGRAPHIES
BT1 publications
BT1 reference works

BIBRIK
BT1 sheep breeds
BT2 breeds

BICARBONATE WATER
BT1 irrigation water
BT2 water
rt bicarbonates

BICARBONATES
BT1 inorganic salts
BT2 inorganic compounds
BT2 salts
NT1 ammonium bicarbonate
NT1 carboxylin
NT1 sodium bicarbonate
rt alkali reserve
rt bicarbonate water
rt buffers
rt carbon dioxide

BICONICAL TRAPS
BT1 insect traps
BT2 traps
BT3 equipment
rt glossina

BICYCLING
uf *cycling (recreation)*
BT1 mechanized recreation
BT2 recreation
BT2 sport
rt cycleways

BIDENS
BT1 compositae
NT1 bidens bipinnata
NT1 bidens cernua
NT1 bidens chinensis
NT1 bidens coronala
NT1 bidens frondosa
NT1 bidens pilosa
NT1 bidens tripartita
rt bidens mottle potyvirus

BIDENS BIPINNATA
BT1 bidens
BT2 compositae

BIDENS CERNUA
BT1 bidens
BT2 compositae

BIDENS CHINENSIS
BT1 bidens
BT2 compositae

BIDENS CORONALA
BT1 bidens
BT2 compositae

bidens formosa
USE **cosmos bipinnatus**

BIDENS FRONDOSA
BT1 bidens
BT2 compositae

BIDENS MOTTLE POTYVIRUS
HN from 1990
BT1 potyvirus group
BT2 plant viruses
BT3 plant pathogens
BT4 pathogens
rt bidens

BIDENS PILOSA
BT1 bidens
BT2 compositae
BT1 medicinal plants
BT1 weeds

BIDENS TRIPARTITA
BT1 bidens
BT2 compositae

biella
USE **biellese**

BIELLESE
HN from 1990; previously "biella"
uf *biella*
BT1 sheep breeds
BT2 breeds

biennial bearing
USE **irregular bearing**

BIENNIAL CROPPING
BT1 cropping systems
rt harvesting

BIFENOX
BT1 nitrophenyl ether herbicides
BT2 herbicides
BT3 pesticides

BIFENTHRIN
BT1 pyrethroid acaricides
BT2 acaricides
BT3 pesticides
BT2 pyrethroids
BT1 pyrethroid insecticides
BT2 insecticides
BT3 pesticides
BT2 pyrethroids

BIFIDOBACTERIUM
BT1 actinomycetaceae
BT2 actinomycetales
BT3 firmicutes
BT4 bacteria
BT5 prokaryotes
NT1 bifidobacterium adolescentis
NT1 bifidobacterium bifidum
NT1 bifidobacterium breve
NT1 bifidobacterium infantum
NT1 bifidobacterium longum

BIFIDOBACTERIUM ADOLESCENTIS
HN from 1989
BT1 bifidobacterium
BT2 actinomycetaceae
BT3 actinomycetales
BT4 firmicutes
BT5 bacteria
BT6 prokaryotes

BIFIDOBACTERIUM BIFIDUM
BT1 bifidobacterium
BT2 actinomycetaceae
BT3 actinomycetales
BT4 firmicutes
BT5 bacteria
BT6 prokaryotes

BIFIDOBACTERIUM BREVE
HN from 1989
BT1 bifidobacterium
BT2 actinomycetaceae
BT3 actinomycetales
BT4 firmicutes
BT5 bacteria
BT6 prokaryotes

BIFIDOBACTERIUM INFANTUM
HN from 1989
BT1 bifidobacterium
BT2 actinomycetaceae
BT3 actinomycetales
BT4 firmicutes
BT5 bacteria
BT6 prokaryotes

BIFIDOBACTERIUM LONGUM
HN from 1989
BT1 bifidobacterium
BT2 actinomycetaceae
BT3 actinomycetales
BT4 firmicutes
BT5 bacteria
BT6 prokaryotes

BIFORA
BT1 umbelliferae
NT1 bifora radians

BIFORA RADIANS
BT1 bifora
BT2 umbelliferae

BIG BALERS
uf *balers, big*
BT1 balers
BT2 farm machinery
BT3 machinery
rt large bales

big bluestem
USE **andropogon gerardii**

BIGNONIACEAE
NT1 adenocalymma
NT1 campsis
NT2 campsis grandiflora
NT2 campsis radicans
NT2 campsis tagliabuana
NT1 catalpa
NT2 catalpa bignonioides
NT2 catalpa ovata
NT2 catalpa speciosa
NT1 crescentia
NT2 crescentia cujete
NT1 dolichandrone
NT2 dolichandrone crispa
NT1 eccremocarpus
NT2 eccremocarpus scaber
NT1 godmania
NT2 godmania macrocarpa
NT1 haplophragma
NT2 haplophragma adenophyllum
NT1 heterophragma
NT2 heterophragma quadriloculare
NT1 jacaranda
NT2 jacaranda caucana
NT2 jacaranda copaia
NT2 jacaranda mimosifolia
NT1 kigelia
NT2 kigelia africana
NT2 kigelia pinnata
NT1 millingtonia
NT2 millingtonia hortensis
NT1 oroxylum
NT2 oroxylum indicum
NT1 parmentiera
NT2 parmentiera alata
NT2 parmentiera cerifera
NT2 parmentiera edulis
NT1 phyllarthron
NT2 phyllarthron madagascariense
NT1 pseudocalymma
NT2 pseudocalymma alliaceum
NT1 pyrostegia
NT2 pyrostegia venusta
NT1 spathodea
NT2 spathodea campanulata
NT1 stereospermum
NT2 stereospermum suaveolens
NT1 tabebuia
NT2 tabebuia cassinoides
NT2 tabebuia pallida
NT2 tabebuia pentaphylla
NT2 tabebuia rosea
NT1 tecoma
NT2 tecoma stans
NT1 tecomella
NT2 tecomella undulata
NT1 zeyheria
NT2 zeyheria tuberculosa

BIGUANIDES
BT1 amides
BT2 organic nitrogen compounds
NT1 buformin
NT1 metformin
rt dyes

BIHAR
BT1 india
BT2 south asia
BT3 asia

BIKANERI
BT1 sheep breeds
BT2 breeds

BILANAFOS
uf *bialaphos*
BT1 antibiotic herbicides
BT2 antibiotics

BILANAFOS *cont.*
BT2 herbicides
BT3 pesticides

BILBERRIES
rt vaccinium

BILDERDYKIA
BT1 polygonaceae
rt fallopia

bilderdykia convolvulus
USE **fallopia convolvulus**

BILE
uf *gall*
BT1 body fluids
BT2 fluids
BT1 secretions
rt bile acids
rt bile ducts
rt bile pigments
rt bile salts
rt bile secretion
rt biliary system
rt cholagogues
rt digestive system
rt fats

BILE ACIDS
NT1 chenodeoxycholic acid
NT1 cholic acid
NT1 dehydrocholic acid
NT1 deoxycholic acid
NT1 glycocholic acid
NT1 glycodehydrocholic acid
NT1 hyodeoxycholic acid
NT1 lithocholic acid
NT1 taurocholic acid
NT1 taurodeoxycholic acid
NT1 ursodeoxycholic acid
rt bile
rt bile salts
rt gastrointestinal agents

BILE DUCTS
BT1 biliary system
BT2 digestive system
BT3 body parts
rt bile
rt biliary calculi
rt cholangitis
rt gall bladder
rt liver

BILE PIGMENTS
BT1 pigments
NT1 bilirubin
NT1 biliverdin
rt bile

BILE SALTS
BT1 emulsifiers
BT2 surfactants
BT1 organic salts
BT2 salts
rt bile
rt bile acids

BILE SECRETION
BT1 secretion
BT2 physiological functions
rt bile
rt dehydrocholic acid
rt deoxycholic acid

bilharziasis
USE **schistosomiasis**

BILHARZIELLA
BT1 schistosomatidae
BT2 digenea
BT3 trematoda

BILIARY CALCULI
uf *calculi, biliary*
uf *gallstones*
uf *lithiasis, biliary*
BT1 concretions
rt bile ducts
rt cholelithiasis

BILIARY SYSTEM
BT1 digestive system

BILIARY SYSTEM *cont.*
BT2 body parts
NT1 bile ducts
rt bile
rt liver

bilimbi
USE **averrhoa bilimbi**

BILINGUAL EDUCATION
BT1 education
rt languages

BILIRUBIN
BT1 bile pigments
BT2 pigments
rt hyperbilirubinaemia

BILIVERDIN
BT1 bile pigments
BT2 pigments

BILLBERGIA
BT1 bromeliaceae
NT1 billbergia nutans
NT1 billbergia vittata

BILLBERGIA NUTANS
BT1 billbergia
BT2 bromeliaceae
BT1 ornamental bromeliads

BILLBERGIA VITTATA
BT1 billbergia
BT2 bromeliaceae
BT1 ornamental bromeliads

BILOBA
BT1 gelechiidae
BT2 lepidoptera
rt aproaerema

biloba subsecivella
USE **aproaerema modicella**

BINAPACRYL
BT1 dinitrophenol acaricides
BT2 acaricides
BT3 pesticides
BT1 dinitrophenol fungicides
BT2 fungicides
BT3 pesticides

BINDERS
BT1 harvesters
BT2 farm machinery
BT3 machinery

BINDING
rt additives
rt binding agents
rt cooking

BINDING AGENTS
rt binding
rt stabilizers

BINDING MATERIALS
HN from 1990
rt packaging

BINDING PROTEINS
uf *carrier proteins*
BT1 proteins
BT2 peptides
NT1 blastokinin
NT1 calcium binding proteins
NT2 calbindin
NT2 calmodulin
NT1 chlorophyll a/b binding protein
NT1 dna binding proteins
NT1 neurophysins
NT1 transcobalamins

BINDING SITE
rt immobilization
rt receptors
rt translocation

binge eating
USE **bulimia**

BINGO
BT1 indoor games
BT2 games

BINGO *cont.*
BT2 indoor recreation
BT3 recreation
rt gambling

BINS
BT1 containers
NT1 ventilated bins
rt boxes
rt bunkers
rt clamps
rt cribs
rt hoppers
rt stores

bins, ventilated
USE **ventilated bins**

BIOALLETHRIN
BT1 pyrethroid insecticides
BT2 insecticides
BT3 pesticides
BT2 pyrethroids

BIOASSAYS
BT1 assays
BT1 biological techniques
BT2 techniques

BIOAVAILABILITY
BT1 availability
rt nutrient availability

BIOCENOSIS
BF biocoenosis

biochanin a
USE **genistein**

BIOCHEMICAL GENETICS
uf *genetics, biochemical*
BT1 genetics
BT2 biology
NT1 gene expression
NT1 nucleotide sequences
NT1 restriction mapping
rt biochemistry
rt immunogenetics
rt molecular biology
rt molecular genetics

BIOCHEMICAL PATHWAYS
NT1 adenosine triphosphate cycle
NT1 calvin cycle
NT1 carbon pathways
NT2 cam pathway
NT1 cori cycle
NT1 glyoxylate cycle
NT1 pentose phosphate cycle
NT1 respiratory chain
NT1 tricarboxylic acid cycle
rt glycolysis
rt lipolysis
rt metabolism
rt respiration

BIOCHEMICAL POLYMORPHISM
uf *polymorphism, biochemical*
BT1 polymorphism
NT1 enzyme polymorphism
NT1 potassium types
rt biochemistry
rt erythrocyte potassium types
rt immunogenetics

biochemical taxonomy
USE **chemotaxonomy**

BIOCHEMICAL TECHNIQUES
BT1 techniques
NT1 acetylene reduction
NT1 dna fingerprinting
NT1 dna footprinting
NT1 dna hybridization
NT1 dna libraries
NT1 dna methylation
NT1 dna probes
NT1 dna sequencing
NT2 chromosome walking
NT1 gene splicing
NT1 percolation
NT1 polymerase chain reaction

BIOCHEMICAL TECHNIQUES *cont.*
NT1 respirometry
NT1 rna amplification
NT1 rna probes
rt biochemistry
rt biological techniques

BIOCHEMISTRY
BT1 chemistry
NT1 cytochemistry
NT1 enzymology
NT2 histoenzymology
NT1 neurochemistry
rt biochemical genetics
rt biochemical polymorphism
rt biochemical techniques
rt biology
rt biosynthesis
rt biotechnology
rt physiology
rt serology

BIOCIDES
NT1 antifouling agents
rt antiinfective agents
rt pesticides

BIOCLIMATE
BT1 climate
rt bioclimatic indexes
rt microclimate

BIOCLIMATIC INDEXES
BT1 indexes
rt bioclimate
rt climate
rt climatology
rt dendrochronology
rt ecology

BIOCOENOSIS
AF biocenosis
BT1 communities
rt biota
rt biotopes
rt ecology

BIODEGRADATION
BT1 degradation
NT1 microbial degradation
rt biodeterioration
rt biological treatment
rt waste treatment

BIODETERIORATION
BT1 deterioration
NT1 foxing
NT1 microbial corrosion
rt biodegradation
rt decay
rt decomposition
rt marine fouling
rt protective atmospheres
rt spoilage

BIOELECTRIC POTENTIAL
BT1 electric potential
BT2 electricity
BT3 energy sources

BIOENERGETICS
rt ecology
rt energy

BIOENERGY
BT1 energy

BIOETHANOMETHRIN
BT1 pyrethroid insecticides
BT2 insecticides
BT3 pesticides
BT2 pyrethroids

BIOETHICS
HN from 1990
NT1 animal testing alternatives

BIOFEEDBACK (AGRICOLA)
rt feedback

BIOFERMAL
BT1 feed supplements
BT2 supplements

BIOFILMS
BT1 film
rt biological treatment

BIOFLAVONOIDS
uf *vitamin p*
uf *vitamin p complex*
BT1 flavonoids
BT2 aromatic compounds
BT2 plant pigments
BT3 pigments
BT1 water-soluble vitamins
BT2 vitamins
NT1 hesperidin
NT1 naringin
NT1 quercetin
NT1 rutoside

BIOFOULING
BT1 fouling
BT2 pollution
NT1 marine fouling
rt antifouling agents

BIOFRAL
BT1 feed supplements
BT2 supplements

BIOGAS
BT1 alkanes
BT2 hydrocarbons
BT1 natural gas
BT2 fuels
rt anaerobic digestion
rt methane

BIOGAS SLURRY
BT1 slurries
rt methane

BIOGENIC AMINES
BT1 amines
BT2 amino compounds
BT3 organic nitrogen compounds
NT1 acetylcholine
NT1 cadaverine
NT1 carnitine
NT1 catecholamines
NT2 dopamine
NT2 epinephrine
NT2 norepinephrine
NT1 choline
NT1 histamine
NT1 hordenine
NT1 octopamine
NT1 phenethylamine
NT1 putrescine
NT1 serotonin
NT1 spermine
NT1 tryptamine
NT1 tyramine

BIOGEOCHEMISTRY
HN from 1990
BT1 chemistry
BT1 geology
rt geochemistry

BIOGEOGRAPHY
BT1 geography
NT1 zoogeography
rt ecology
rt fauna
rt flora

BIOGHURT
BT1 cultured milks
BT2 milk products
BT3 products

BIOGRAPHIES
BT1 historical records
BT2 records
rt obituaries

BIOLOGICAL ACTIVITY IN SOIL
BT1 soil biology
BT2 biology

BIOLOGICAL COMPETITION
HN from 1990
uf *competition*
NT1 animal competition

BIOLOGICAL COMPETITION *cont.*
NT1 interspecific competition
NT2 crop weed competition
NT1 intraspecific competition
NT2 mating competitiveness
NT1 plant competition
NT2 crop weed competition
NT2 weed competition
NT1 pollen competition

BIOLOGICAL CONTROL
(pest and weed control by deliberate use of natural enemies)
uf *control, biological*
BT1 pest control
BT2 control
NT1 augmentation
NT2 parasitoid augmentation
NT2 predator augmentation
NT1 encouragement
rt bacterial insecticides
rt biological control agents
rt disease control
rt integrated control
rt parasitism
rt predation
rt release techniques

BIOLOGICAL CONTROL AGENTS
HN from 1990 in agricola; previously "biological control organisms"
(organisms deliberately used for biological control of pests or weeds)
uf *biological control organisms*
BT1 beneficial organisms
NT1 aceratoneuromyia indica
NT1 agasicles hygrophila
NT1 agathis pumila
NT1 agrypon flaveolatum
NT1 apanteles subandinus
NT1 aphelinus mali
NT1 aphelinus thomsoni
NT1 aphidius smithi
NT1 aphytis chrysomphali
NT1 aphytis holoxanthus
NT1 aphytis lepidosaphes
NT1 aphytis lingnanensis
NT1 aphytis melinus
NT1 aphytis mytilaspidis
NT1 apion antiquum
NT1 apion ulicis
NT1 ascogaster quadridentata
NT1 bathyplectes curculionis
NT1 biosteres fullawayi
NT1 biosteres longicaudatus
NT1 cactoblastis cactorum
NT1 comperiella bifasciata
NT1 compsilura concinnata
NT1 copidosoma koehleri
NT1 cotesia flavipes
NT1 cotesia glomerata
NT1 cryptolaemus montrouzieri
NT1 cyzenis albicans
NT1 dactylopius opuntiae
NT1 encarsia citrina
NT1 encarsia formosa
NT1 epidinocarsis lopezi
NT1 illidops scutellaris
NT1 lixophaga diatraeae
NT1 longitarsus jacobaeae
NT1 lysiphlebus testaceipes
NT1 macrocentrus ancylivorus
NT1 mesoleius tenthredinis
NT1 metagonistylum minense
NT1 metaphycus helvolus
NT1 metaphycus lounsburyi
NT1 meteorus versicolor
NT1 microlarinus lypriformis
NT1 monodontomerus dentipes
NT1 muscidifurax raptor
NT1 neochetina eichhorniae
NT1 neodusmetia sangwani
NT1 olesicampe benefactor
NT1 ooencyrtus kuvanae
NT1 orgilus lepidus
NT1 pachycrepoideus vindemmiae
NT1 paratheresia claripalpis
NT1 pholetesor circumscriptus
NT1 phytoseiulus persimilis

BIOLOGICAL CONTROL AGENTS *cont.*
NT1 pleolophus basizonus
NT1 pseudaphycus malinus
NT1 pteromalus puparum
NT1 rhinocyllus conicus
NT1 rhizophagus grandis
NT1 rodolia cardinalis
NT1 sameodes albiguttalis
NT1 scutellista cyanea
NT1 serangium parcesetosum
NT1 spalangia nigra
NT1 teleonemia scrupulosa
NT1 trichogramma japonicum
NT1 trioxys pallidus
NT1 trissolcus basalis
NT1 tyria jacobaeae
NT1 tytthus mundulus
NT1 vogtia malloi
rt biological control
rt entomogenous fungi
rt entomophilic nematodes
rt insect viruses
rt introduction
rt microbial pesticides
rt natural enemies
rt parasites of insect pests (agricola)
rt parasitoids
rt predators
rt predators of insect pests (agricola)

biological control organisms
USE **biological control agents**

BIOLOGICAL DEVELOPMENT
HN from 1990
NT1 cell differentiation
rt development

BIOLOGICAL FILTRATION
BT1 filtration
BT2 processing
NT1 biological fixed-film systems

BIOLOGICAL FIXED-FILM SYSTEMS
BT1 biological filtration
BT2 filtration
BT3 processing

BIOLOGICAL FLUIDS
BT1 fluids
rt body fluids
rt rumen fluid

biological growth rate
USE **growth rate**

BIOLOGICAL INDICATORS
BT1 indicators
NT1 biological tags

BIOLOGICAL OXYGEN DEMAND
BT1 oxygen requirement
BT2 requirements
rt chemical oxygen demand
rt effluents

BIOLOGICAL PRODUCTION
BT1 production
rt biomass
rt fertility
rt food chains
rt productivity
rt trophic levels
rt yields

BIOLOGICAL RHYTHMS
NT1 cardiac rhythm
NT1 circadian rhythm
NT1 menopause
NT1 menstrual cycle
NT2 menarche
NT1 moulting
NT2 apolysis
NT2 ecdysis
NT1 oestrous cycle
NT2 anoestrus
NT2 dioestrus
NT2 menstruation
NT3 amenorrhoea
NT2 metoestrus

BIOLOGICAL RHYTHMS *cont.*
NT2 oestrus
NT2 pro-oestrus
NT2 service period
rt dormancy
rt life cycle
rt rest

biological standardization
USE **standardization**

BIOLOGICAL TAGS
BT1 biological indicators
BT2 indicators
rt identification
rt marking

BIOLOGICAL TECHNIQUES
BT1 techniques
NT1 bioassays
NT1 biopsy
NT1 culture techniques
NT2 in vitro culture
NT3 cell culture
NT3 somatic embryogenesis
NT3 tissue culture
NT4 anther culture
NT4 embryo culture
NT4 organ culture
NT4 ovule culture
NT4 shoot tip culture
NT2 vermiculture
NT1 enumeration
NT1 flow cytometry
NT1 fluorimetry
NT1 qualitative techniques
NT1 quantitative techniques
NT1 radiography
NT2 autoradiography
NT2 microradiography
NT2 tomography
NT3 computed tomography
NT1 rearing techniques
NT2 mass rearing
NT1 rusch method
NT1 sectioning
rt biochemical techniques
rt extraction
rt smears

BIOLOGICAL TREATMENT
BT1 waste treatment
NT1 desulfurization
rt biodegradation
rt biofilms
rt bulking
rt rotating biological contactors
rt waste water treatment

BIOLOGICAL WARFARE
BT1 war
BT2 emergencies
rt yellow rain

BIOLOGISTS
BT1 scientists
BT2 occupations
NT1 cytologists
NT1 taxonomists
rt biology

BIOLOGY
NT1 anatomy
NT2 animal anatomy
NT2 plant anatomy
NT3 seed anatomy
NT3 wood anatomy
NT4 growth rings
NT5 earlywood
NT5 latewood
NT4 latex tubes
NT4 rays
NT4 trabeculae
NT1 botany
NT2 bryology
NT2 ethnobotany
NT2 mycology
NT3 medical mycology
NT3 veterinary mycology
NT2 palaeobotany
NT2 palynology
NT3 pollen analysis

BIOLOGY *cont.*
NT2 weed biology
NT1 cellular biology
NT1 cytology
NT1 embryology
NT1 freshwater biology (agricola)
NT1 genetics
NT2 biochemical genetics
NT3 gene expression
NT3 nucleotide sequences
NT3 restriction mapping
NT2 chloroplast genetics
NT2 complementation
NT2 epigenetics
NT2 gene dosage
NT3 hemizygosity
NT2 gene interaction
NT3 epistasis
NT2 gene location
NT2 gene mapping
NT3 molecular mapping
NT2 genetic engineering
NT3 gene transfer
NT2 genetic regulation
NT2 genetic theory
NT3 fisher's theorem
NT2 genotype environment interaction
NT2 genotype nutrition interaction
NT2 heterozygosity
NT2 homozygosity
NT2 mendelism
NT2 mitochondrial genetics
NT2 molecular genetics
NT2 nucleocytoplasmic interaction
NT2 penetrance
NT2 pleiotropy
NT2 population genetics
NT3 gene flow
NT3 gene frequency
NT3 genetic drift
NT3 genetic equilibrium
NT4 disequilibrium
NT2 quantitative genetics
NT3 diallel analysis
NT2 transduction
NT1 histology
NT2 histochemistry
NT3 immunohistochemistry
NT2 histoenzymology
NT2 plant histology
NT1 hydrobiology
NT1 microbiology
NT2 air microbiology
NT3 air spora
NT2 bacteriology
NT2 food microbiology
NT2 industrial microbiology
NT2 virology
NT2 water microbiology
NT1 molecular biology
NT1 palaeontology
NT2 palaeobotany
NT1 soil biology
NT2 biological activity in soil
NT1 zoology
NT2 acarology
NT2 entomology
NT3 agricultural entomology
NT3 forensic entomology
NT3 medical entomology
NT3 military entomology
NT3 veterinary entomology
NT2 helminthology
NT3 medical helminthology
NT3 nematology
NT3 veterinary helminthology
NT2 herpetology
NT2 protozoology
rt agricultural sciences
rt biochemistry
rt biologists
rt biophysics
rt climatology
rt geology
rt immunology
rt limnology
rt parasitology
rt physiology

BIOLOGY *cont.*
rt taxonomy

biology, weed
USE **weed biology**

BIOMASS
rt biological production
rt biomass production
rt biota
rt energy resources
rt fuel crops
rt fuels
rt productivity
rt renewable resources
rt weight

BIOMASS PRODUCTION
HN from 1989
BT1 production
rt biomass

BIOMETRY
BT1 statistics
rt anthropometric dimensions
rt body measurements
rt height
rt measurement
rt variation
rt weight

BIOMPHALARIA
BT1 planorbidae
BT2 gastropoda
BT3 mollusca
NT1 biomphalaria alexandrina
NT1 biomphalaria glabrata
NT1 biomphalaria pfeifferi
NT1 biomphalaria straminea
NT1 biomphalaria tenagophila

BIOMPHALARIA ALEXANDRINA
BT1 biomphalaria
BT2 planorbidae
BT3 gastropoda
BT4 mollusca

BIOMPHALARIA GLABRATA
BT1 biomphalaria
BT2 planorbidae
BT3 gastropoda
BT4 mollusca

BIOMPHALARIA PFEIFFERI
BT1 biomphalaria
BT2 planorbidae
BT3 gastropoda
BT4 mollusca

BIOMPHALARIA STRAMINEA
BT1 biomphalaria
BT2 planorbidae
BT3 gastropoda
BT4 mollusca

BIOMPHALARIA TENAGOPHILA
BT1 biomphalaria
BT2 planorbidae
BT3 gastropoda
BT4 mollusca

biomycin
USE **chlortetracycline**

BIOPERMETHRIN
BT1 pyrethroid insecticides
BT2 insecticides
BT3 pesticides
BT2 pyrethroids

BIOPHYSICS
BT1 physics
rt biology

BIOPSY
BT1 biological techniques
BT2 techniques
rt diagnosis

BIOPTERIN
BT1 coenzymes
BT1 pteridines
BT2 heterocyclic nitrogen compounds

BIOPTERIN *cont.*
BT3 organic nitrogen compounds
rt royal jelly

BIOREACTORS
HN from 1989
BT1 equipment

BIORESMETHRIN
BT1 pyrethroid insecticides
BT2 insecticides
BT3 pesticides
BT2 pyrethroids

BIOSENSORS
HN from 1989
BT1 sensors

BIOSEQUENCES
BT1 soil sequences

BIOSTERES
BT1 braconidae
BT2 hymenoptera
NT1 biosteres arisanus
NT1 biosteres fullawayi
NT1 biosteres longicaudatus
rt opius

BIOSTERES ARISANUS
uf *biosteres oophilus*
uf *opius oophilus*
BT1 biosteres
BT2 braconidae
BT3 hymenoptera

BIOSTERES FULLAWAYI
uf *opius fullawayi*
BT1 biological control agents
BT2 beneficial organisms
BT1 biosteres
BT2 braconidae
BT3 hymenoptera

BIOSTERES LONGICAUDATUS
uf *opius longicaudatus*
BT1 biological control agents
BT2 beneficial organisms
BT1 biosteres
BT2 braconidae
BT3 hymenoptera

biosteres oophilus
USE **biosteres arisanus**

BIOSTIL PROCESS
HN from 1990
BT1 processing
rt fermentation

BIOSUPER
BT1 phosphorus fertilizers
BT2 fertilizers

BIOSYNTHESIS
BT1 metabolism
BT1 synthesis
NT1 urea biosynthesis
rt biochemistry

BIOSYSTEMATICS
BT1 taxonomy
BT2 classification

BIOTA
rt biocoenosis
rt biomass
rt fauna
rt flora
rt habitats

BIOTECHNOLOGY
BT1 technology
NT1 food biotechnology (agricola)
rt bacteriology
rt biochemistry
rt fermentation
rt genetic engineering
rt microbiology

BIOTIN
BT1 coenzymes
BT1 vitamin b complex

BIOTIN *cont.*
BT2 water-soluble vitamins
BT3 vitamins

BIOTIN ANTAGONISTS
BT1 vitamin b antagonists
BT2 vitamin antagonists
BT3 antagonists
BT4 metabolic inhibitors
BT5 inhibitors
NT1 avidin

BIOTITE
BT1 nonclay minerals
BT2 minerals

BIOTOPES
BT1 habitats
rt biocoenosis

BIOTYPES
NT1 ecotypes
NT1 pathotypes
rt clines
rt genotypes
rt physiological races

BIPARENTAL MATING
BT1 hybridization
BT2 crossing
BT3 breeding
rt mating

BIPHENYL
uf *diphenyl*
BT1 aromatic hydrocarbons
BT2 aromatic compounds
BT2 hydrocarbons
BT1 unclassified fungicides
BT2 fungicides
BT3 pesticides
rt polybrominated biphenyls
rt polychlorinated biphenyls

BIPOLARIS
BT1 deuteromycotina
NT1 bipolaris heveae
NT1 bipolaris incurvata
NT1 bipolaris indica
NT1 bipolaris leersiae
NT1 bipolaris sacchari
NT1 bipolaris sorghicola
NT1 bipolaris stenospila
rt cochliobolus
rt drechslera
rt helminthosporium

bipolaris australiensis
USE **cochliobolus australiensis**

bipolaris cynodontis
USE **cochliobolus cynodontis**

bipolaris ellisii
USE **cochliobolus ellisii**

bipolaris gossypii
USE **drechslera gossypii**

BIPOLARIS HEVEAE
HN from 1990
uf *drechslera heveae*
uf *helminthosporium heveae*
BT1 bipolaris
BT2 deuteromycotina

BIPOLARIS INCURVATA
HN from 1990
uf *drechslera incurvata*
uf *helminthosporium incurvatum*
BT1 bipolaris
BT2 deuteromycotina

BIPOLARIS INDICA
HN from 1990
uf *drechslera indica*
BT1 bipolaris
BT2 deuteromycotina

BIPOLARIS LEERSIAE
HN from 1990
uf *drechslera leersiae*
BT1 bipolaris
BT2 deuteromycotina

bipolaris maydis
USE **cochliobolus heterostrophus**

BIPOLARIS SACCHARI
uf *drechslera sacchari*
uf *helminthosporium sacchari*
BT1 bipolaris
BT2 deuteromycotina

BIPOLARIS SORGHICOLA
HN from 1990
uf *drechslera sorghicola*
uf *helminthosporium sorghicola*
BT1 bipolaris
BT2 deuteromycotina

bipolaris sorokiniana
USE **cochliobolus sativus**

bipolaris spicifera
USE **cochliobolus spicifer**

BIPOLARIS STENOSPILA
HN from 1990
uf *cochliobolus stenospilus*
uf *drechslera stenospila*
uf *helminthosporium stenospilum*
BT1 bipolaris
BT2 deuteromycotina

bipolaris tetramera
USE **cochliobolus spicifer**

bipolaris victoriae
USE **cochliobolus victoriae**

BIPTERIA
BT1 myxozoa
BT2 protozoa

birch
USE **betula**

BIRD CONTROL
BT1 pest control
BT2 control
rt avicides
rt bird repellents
rt bird scarers
rt bird strikes
rt birds
rt plant protection

BIRD REPELLENTS
BT1 repellents
NT1 chloralose
NT1 copper oxychloride
NT1 methiocarb
NT1 trimethacarb
rt bird control
rt bird scarers
rt birds
rt plant protection

BIRD SCARERS
BT1 scarers
BT2 pest control equipment
NT1 scarecrows
rt bird control
rt bird repellents
rt birds

BIRD STRIKES
rt aircraft
rt bird control
rt birds
rt vertebrate pests

BIRDS
(for common names see aviary birds, game birds, ornamental birds, plumage birds, poultry, predatory birds and wild birds)
NT1 anseriformes
NT2 anatidae
NT3 anas
NT4 anas crecca
NT4 anas discors
NT4 anas gibberifrons
NT4 anas platyrhynchos
NT4 anas querquedula
NT3 anser
NT4 anser caerulescens

BIRDS *cont.*
NT3 cairina
NT3 cygnus
NT4 cygnus columbianus
NT4 cygnus cygnus
NT5 cygnus cygnus buccinator
NT4 cygnus olor
NT1 apodiformes
NT2 apodidae
NT3 apus
NT4 apus affinis
NT4 apus apus
NT2 trochilidae
NT1 apterygiformes
NT2 apterygidae
NT3 apteryx
NT1 caprimulgiformes
NT2 podargidae
NT3 podargus
NT1 casuariiformes
NT2 casuariidae
NT3 casuarius
NT2 dromaiidae
NT3 dromaius
NT1 charadriiformes
NT2 alcidae
NT3 aethia
NT3 alca
NT4 alca torda
NT3 cepphus
NT3 fratercula
NT4 fratercula arctica
NT4 fratercula corniculata
NT3 lunda
NT4 lunda cirrhata
NT3 uria
NT4 uria aalge
NT4 uria lomvia
NT2 charadriidae
NT3 charadrius
NT4 charadrius alexandrinus
NT3 pluvialis
NT3 vanellus
NT4 vanellus vanellus
NT2 laridae
NT3 larus
NT4 larus argentatus
NT4 larus dominicanus
NT4 larus ridibundus
NT3 rissa
NT4 rissa tridactyla
NT3 sterna
NT4 sterna hirundo
NT2 scolopacidae
NT3 arenaria (birds)
NT3 calidris
NT4 calidris alpina
NT4 calidris minuta
NT3 gallinago
NT3 limosa
NT4 limosa fedoa
NT4 limosa limosa
NT3 numenius
NT3 scolopax
NT4 scolopax rusticola
NT3 tringa
NT4 tringa glareola
NT4 tringa totanus
NT2 stercorariidae
NT3 catharacta
NT3 stercorarius
NT1 ciconiiformes
NT2 ardeidae
NT3 ardea
NT4 ardea cinerea
NT4 ardea herodias
NT4 ardea purpurea
NT3 ardeola
NT3 bubulcus
NT4 bubulcus ibis
NT5 bubulcus ibis coromandus
NT3 butorides
NT4 butorides striatus
NT3 egretta
NT4 egretta alba
NT4 egretta garzetta
NT3 nycticorax
NT4 nycticorax caledonicus
NT4 nycticorax nycticorax

BIRDS *cont.*
NT2 ciconiidae
NT3 ciconia
NT4 ciconia ciconia
NT3 leptoptilos
NT4 leptoptilos crumeniferus
NT2 phoenicopteridae
NT3 phoenicopterus
NT1 coliiformes
NT1 columbiformes
NT2 columbidae
NT3 columba
NT4 columba palumba
NT3 streptopelia
NT4 streptopelia decaocto
NT4 streptopelia senegalensis
NT1 coraciiformes
NT2 alcedinidae
NT3 alcedo
NT4 alcedo atthis
NT3 halcyon
NT4 halcyon chloris
NT4 halcyon smyrnensis
NT3 pelargopsis
NT4 pelargopsis capensis
NT2 bucerotidae
NT2 meropidae
NT3 merops
NT1 cuculiformes
NT2 cuculidae
NT1 falconiformes
NT2 accipitridae
NT3 accipiter
NT4 accipiter cooperii
NT4 accipiter gentilis
NT4 accipiter striatus
NT3 aquila
NT4 aquila chrysaetos
NT3 circus
NT4 circus cyaneus
NT2 falconidae
NT3 falco
NT4 falco sparverius
NT4 falco tinnunculus
NT2 pandionidae
NT3 pandion
NT4 pandion haliaetus
NT1 galliformes
NT2 cracidae
NT2 megapodiidae
NT2 opisthocomidae
NT3 opisthocomus
NT4 opisthocomus hoatzin
NT2 phasianidae
NT3 alectoris
NT4 alectoris chukar
NT4 alectoris graeca
NT4 alectoris rufa
NT3 colinus
NT4 colinus virginianus
NT3 coturnix
NT3 francolinus
NT3 gallus
NT4 gallus gallus
NT5 gallus gallus spadiceus
NT3 lagopus
NT4 lagopus lagopus
NT5 lagopus lagopus scoticus
NT4 lagopus mutus
NT3 lophortyx
NT4 lophortyx californica
NT4 lophortyx gambelii
NT3 meleagris
NT3 numida
NT3 pavo
NT3 perdix
NT4 perdix perdix
NT3 phasianus
NT4 phasianus colchicus
NT3 tetrao
NT4 tetrao tetrix
NT4 tetrao urogallus
NT1 gaviiformes
NT2 gaviidae
NT3 gavia
NT1 gruiformes
NT2 gruidae
NT3 grus
NT4 grus canadensis

BIRDS *cont.*
NT2 otidae
NT3 choriotis
NT3 otis
NT2 rallidae
NT3 fulica
NT4 fulica americana
NT4 fulica atra
NT3 gallinula
NT4 gallinula chloropus
NT3 rallus
NT4 rallus longirostris
NT1 passeriformes
NT2 alaudidae
NT2 corvidae
NT3 corvus
NT4 corvus brachyrhynchos
NT4 corvus corax
NT4 corvus corone
NT4 corvus frugilegus
NT4 corvus monedula
NT4 corvus splendens
NT3 garrulus
NT4 garrulus glandarius
NT3 pica (genus)
NT4 pica pica
NT2 fringillidae
NT3 carduelis
NT3 fringilla
NT4 fringilla coelebs
NT3 pyrrhula
NT4 pyrrhula pyrrhula
NT3 serinus
NT2 hirundinidae
NT3 delichon
NT4 delichon urbica
NT3 hirundo
NT4 hirundo rustica
NT3 petrochelidon
NT4 petrochelidon pyrrhonota
NT3 riparia
NT4 riparia riparia
NT2 laniidae
NT3 lanius
NT2 muscicapidae
NT3 ficedula
NT3 muscicapa
NT4 muscicapa striata
NT3 oenanthe (birds)
NT4 oenanthe isabellina
NT3 phoenicurus
NT3 phylloscopus
NT4 phylloscopus trochilus
NT3 sylvia
NT3 turdoides
NT4 turdoides striatus
NT3 turdus
NT4 turdus merula
NT4 turdus migratorius
NT4 turdus pilaris
NT2 ploceidae
NT3 passer
NT4 passer domesticus
NT4 passer montanus
NT3 ploceus
NT3 quelea
NT4 quelea quelea
NT2 sturnidae
NT3 acridotheres
NT4 acridotheres ginginianus
NT4 acridotheres tristis
NT3 gracula
NT4 gracula religiosa
NT3 sturnus
NT4 sturnus vulgaris
NT1 pelecaniformes
NT2 pelecanidae
NT3 pelecanus
NT2 phalacrocoracidae
NT3 phalacrocorax
NT4 phalacrocorax aristotelis
NT4 phalacrocorax carbo
NT2 sulidae
NT1 piciformes
NT2 picidae
NT3 dryocopus
NT4 dryocopus martius
NT3 picoides
NT4 picoides borealis
NT4 picoides major

BIRDS *cont.*
NT3 picus
NT2 ramphastidae
NT3 ramphastos
NT4 ramphastos toco
NT1 podicipediformes
NT2 podicipedidae
NT3 podiceps
NT4 podiceps cristatus
NT4 podiceps grisegena
NT3 tachybaptus
NT4 tachybaptus ruficollis
NT1 procellariiformes
NT2 procellariidae
NT3 fulmarus
NT3 puffinus
NT1 psittaciformes
NT2 psittacidae
NT3 agapornis
NT3 amazona
NT3 melopsittacus
NT3 psittacula
NT3 psittacus
NT1 rheiformes
NT2 rheidae
NT3 rhea
NT1 sphenisciformes
NT2 spheniscidae
NT3 aptenodytes
NT3 eudyptula
NT3 pygoscelis
NT3 spheniscus
NT1 strigiformes
NT2 strigidae
NT3 aegolius
NT4 aegolius funereus
NT3 asio
NT4 asio flammeus
NT4 asio otus
NT3 athene
NT3 bubo
NT4 bubo bubo
NT4 bubo virginianus
NT3 nyctea
NT4 nyctea scandiaca
NT3 otus
NT3 speotyto
NT4 speotyto cunicularia
NT3 strix
NT4 strix aluco
NT4 strix occidentalis
NT2 tytonidae
NT3 tyto
NT4 tyto alba
NT1 struthioniformes
NT2 struthionidae
NT3 struthio
NT1 tinamiformes
NT1 trogoniformes
NT2 trogonidae
NT3 trogon
rt aviary birds
rt avicides
rt aviculture
rt beak
rt bird control
rt bird repellents
rt bird scarers
rt bird strikes
rt birds' nests
rt birdwatching
rt edible birdsnests
rt game birds
rt guano
rt nesting
rt nests
rt ornamental birds
rt pest control
rt plant pests
rt plumage
rt plumage birds
rt poultry
rt predatory birds
rt scarecrows
rt vertebrates
rt waterfowl
rt wild birds

birds, game
USE **game birds**

BIRDS' NESTS
BT1 nests
rt birds

birds of prey
USE **predatory birds**

birdsfoot trefoil
USE **lotus corniculatus**

birdsnest, edible
USE **edible birdsnests**

BIRDWATCHING
BT1 outdoor recreation
BT2 recreation
rt birds
rt natural history

birdwood grass
USE **cenchrus setigerus**

BIRNAVIRIDAE
BT1 viruses
NT1 birnavirus
NT2 infectious bursal disease virus
NT2 pancreatic necrosis virus
NT2 trout infectious pancreatitis virus

BIRNAVIRUS
BT1 birnaviridae
BT2 viruses
NT1 infectious bursal disease virus
NT1 pancreatic necrosis virus
NT1 trout infectious pancreatitis virus

BIRNESSITE
BT1 nonclay minerals
BT2 minerals
rt manganese

BIRTH
rt abortion
rt birth control (agricola)
rt birth rate
rt birth weight
rt birthcoat
rt caesarean section
rt childbirth (agricola)
rt illegitimate births (agricola)
rt multiple births
rt parturition
rt postnatal development
rt pregnancy
rt reproductive physiology
rt vital statistics

BIRTH CONTROL (AGRICOLA)
NT1 rhythm method (agricola)
NT1 tubal ligation (agricola)
rt birth
rt contraceptives
rt family planning
rt population control

birth defects
USE **congenital abnormalities**

BIRTH RATE
BT1 vital statistics
rt birth
rt fertility
rt parturition
rt population growth

BIRTH WEIGHT
BT1 body weight
BT2 weight
rt birth
rt low birth weight infants (agricola)
rt postnatal development
rt prematurity

BIRTHCOAT
BT1 coat
rt birth
rt wool

BISABOLANGELONE
BT1 sesquiterpenoid lactones

BISABOLANGELONE *cont.*
BT2 lactones
BT3 heterocyclic oxygen compounds
BT3 ketones
BT2 sesquiterpenoids
BT3 terpenoids
BT4 isoprenoids
BT5 lipids

α-BISABOLOL
(for retrieval spell out "alpha")
BT1 sesquiterpenoids
BT2 terpenoids
BT3 isoprenoids
BT4 lipids
rt commiphora
rt essential oils

BISARO
BT1 pig breeds
BT2 breeds

BISAZIR
BT1 amides
BT2 organic nitrogen compounds
BT1 chemosterilants
BT2 sterilants
BT1 heterocyclic nitrogen compounds
BT2 organic nitrogen compounds

BISCHOFIA
BT1 bischofiaceae
NT1 bischofia javanica

BISCHOFIA JAVANICA
BT1 bischofia
BT2 bischofiaceae
BT1 ornamental woody plants

BISCHOFIACEAE
NT1 bischofia
NT2 bischofia javanica

BISCIRUS
BT1 bdellidae
BT2 prostigmata
BT3 acari
rt bdellodes

biscirus lapidarius
USE **bdellodes lapidaria**

BISCUITS
BT1 bakery products
BT2 foods
BT2 products
NT1 wafers
rt cookies (agricola)
rt crackers (agricola)

1,4-BISDIAZOACETYLBUTANE
BT1 diazo compounds
BT2 organic nitrogen compounds
BT1 mutagens

BISEQUUM SOILS
BT1 soil types (polygenetic)

BISMUTH
BT1 metallic elements
BT2 elements
BT2 metals

BISON
uf *american bison*
uf *american buffaloes*
uf *bison bison*
uf *buffaloes, american*
BT1 meat animals
BT2 animals
BT1 ruminants
BT2 animals
BT1 skin producing animals
BT2 animals
rt bovidae

bison bison
USE **bison**

BISON BONASUS
BT1 bison (genus)
BT2 bovidae
BT3 ruminantia
BT4 artiodactyla
BT5 mammals
BT5 ungulates

BISON (GENUS)
BT1 bovidae
BT2 ruminantia
BT3 artiodactyla
BT4 mammals
BT4 ungulates
NT1 bison bonasus

BISSETIA
BT1 pyralidae
BT2 lepidoptera
NT1 bissetia steniella
rt acigona

BISSETIA STENIELLA
uf *acigona steniellus*
BT1 bissetia
BT2 pyralidae
BT3 lepidoptera

BISTON
BT1 geometridae
BT2 lepidoptera
NT1 biston betularia
rt buzura

BISTON BETULARIA
BT1 biston
BT2 geometridae
BT3 lepidoptera

biston suppressaria
USE **buzura suppressaria**

BISULFITES
uf *bisulphites*
BT1 inorganic salts
BT2 inorganic compounds
BT2 salts
NT1 sodium bisulfite

bisulphites
USE **bisulfites**

BITCHES
BT1 female animals
BT2 animals
rt dogs

BITERTANOL
BT1 triazole fungicides
BT2 fungicides
BT3 pesticides
BT2 triazoles
BT3 azoles
BT4 heterocyclic nitrogen compounds
BT5 organic nitrogen compounds

BITES
BT1 wounds
BT2 trauma
NT1 insect bites
NT1 snake bites
rt aggressive behaviour
rt arachnidism
rt biting rates
rt stings
rt venoms

BITHIONOL
BT1 anthelmintics
BT2 antiparasitic agents
BT3 drugs
BT1 unclassified fungicides
BT2 fungicides
BT3 pesticides

BITHYNIA
uf *parafossarulus*
BT1 bithyniidae
BT2 gastropoda
BT3 mollusca
NT1 bithynia inflata
NT1 bithynia manchourica

BITHYNIA *cont.*
NT1 bithynia tentaculata

BITHYNIA INFLATA
BT1 bithynia
BT2 bithyniidae
BT3 gastropoda
BT4 mollusca

BITHYNIA MANCHOURICA
uf *parafossarulus manchouricus*
BT1 bithynia
BT2 bithyniidae
BT3 gastropoda
BT4 mollusca

BITHYNIA TENTACULATA
BT1 bithynia
BT2 bithyniidae
BT3 gastropoda
BT4 mollusca

BITHYNIIDAE
BT1 gastropoda
BT2 mollusca
NT1 bithynia
NT2 bithynia inflata
NT2 bithynia manchourica
NT2 bithynia tentaculata

BITING RATES
BT1 feeding behaviour
BT2 behaviour
rt bites
rt haematophagous insects

BITIS
BT1 viperidae
BT2 serpentes
BT3 reptiles

BITOSCANATE
BT1 anthelmintics
BT2 antiparasitic agents
BT3 drugs

α-bitter acid
USE **humulon**

β-bitter acid
USE **lupulon**

BITTER ACIDS
NT1 humulon
NT1 lupulon
rt bitterness

bitter gourds
USE **momordica charantia**

BITTER PEPTIDES
BT1 peptides
rt bitterness

BITTER PIT
BT1 plant disorders
BT2 disorders
rt apples
rt capsicum

BITTERNESS
BT1 tastes
BT2 organoleptic traits
BT3 physicochemical properties
BT4 properties
BT3 traits
rt bitter acids
rt bitter peptides
rt cucurbitacins
rt palatability
rt phenylthiourea

BITUMEN
uf *asphalt*
rt bitumen emulsions
rt coal
rt soil conditioners

BITUMEN EMULSIONS
uf *asphalt emulsions*
uf *humofina*
BT1 emulsions
rt bitumen

BITYLENCHUS
HN from 1990
BT1 dolichodoridae
BT2 nematoda

BIURET
BT1 feed additives
BT2 additives
BT1 ureides
BT2 amides
BT3 organic nitrogen compounds
rt biuret digestion

BIURET DIGESTION
BT1 digestion
BT2 physiological functions
rt biuret
rt proteins

BIVALENTS
BT1 chromosomes
BT2 nuclei
BT3 organelles
BT4 cell structure

bivalves
USE **bivalvia**

BIVALVIA
uf *bivalves*
BT1 mollusca
NT1 arcidae
NT2 anadara
NT2 arca
NT1 arcticidae
NT2 arctica
NT3 arctica islandica
NT1 cardiidae
NT2 cardium
NT1 donacidae
NT2 donax
NT1 glycymeridae
NT2 glycymeris
NT1 mactridae
NT2 mactra
NT3 mactra chinensis
NT2 mulinia
NT3 mulinia lateralis
NT2 spisula
NT3 spisula solidissima
NT1 mesodesmatidae
NT2 mesodesma
NT1 myidae
NT2 mya
NT3 mya arenaria
NT1 mytilidae
NT2 aulacomya
NT3 aulacomya ater
NT2 choromytilus
NT2 modiolus
NT2 mytilus
NT3 mytilus edulis
NT3 mytilus galloprovincialis
NT1 ostreidae
NT2 crassostrea
NT3 crassostrea gigas
NT3 crassostrea virginica
NT2 ostrea
NT3 ostrea edulis
NT1 pectinidae
NT2 argopecten
NT3 argopecten irradians
NT2 chlamys
NT3 chlamys islandica
NT2 pecten
NT3 pecten maximus
NT1 solenidae
NT2 ensis
NT2 siliqua
NT2 solen
NT1 teredinidae
NT2 bankia
NT3 bankia gouldi
NT2 teredo
NT1 veneridae
NT2 mercenaria
NT3 mercenaria mercenaria
NT2 meretrix
NT3 meretrix lusoria
NT2 protothaca
NT3 protothaca staminea

BIVALVIA *cont.*
NT3 protothaca thaca
NT2 saxidomus
NT3 saxidomus giganteus
NT3 saxidomus nuttalli
NT2 tapes
NT2 tivela
NT2 venerupis
NT3 venerupis philippinarum
NT2 venus
NT3 venus mortoni

BIXA
BT1 bixaceae
NT1 bixa orellana

BIXA ORELLANA
BT1 bixa
BT2 bixaceae
BT1 dye plants
rt annatto

BIXACEAE
NT1 bixa
NT2 bixa orellana

BIZET
BT1 sheep breeds
BT2 breeds

BJERKANDERA
BT1 aphyllophorales
NT1 bjerkandera adusta

BJERKANDERA ADUSTA
uf *polyporus adustus*
BT1 bjerkandera
BT2 aphyllophorales

BLABERIDAE
BT1 blattaria
BT2 dictyoptera
NT1 blaberus
NT2 blaberus atropos
NT2 blaberus craniifer
NT2 blaberus discoidalis
NT2 blaberus giganteus
NT1 diploptera
NT2 diploptera punctata

BLABERUS
BT1 blaberidae
BT2 blattaria
BT3 dictyoptera
NT1 blaberus atropos
NT1 blaberus craniifer
NT1 blaberus discoidalis
NT1 blaberus giganteus

BLABERUS ATROPOS
BT1 blaberus
BT2 blaberidae
BT3 blattaria
BT4 dictyoptera

BLABERUS CRANIIFER
uf *blaberus fuscus*
BT1 blaberus
BT2 blaberidae
BT3 blattaria
BT4 dictyoptera

BLABERUS DISCOIDALIS
BT1 blaberus
BT2 blaberidae
BT3 blattaria
BT4 dictyoptera

blaberus fuscus
USE **blaberus craniifer**

BLABERUS GIGANTEUS
BT1 blaberus
BT2 blaberidae
BT3 blattaria
BT4 dictyoptera

BLACK BEETLE VIRUS
BT1 nodaviridae
BT2 insect viruses
BT3 entomopathogens
BT4 pathogens
BT2 viruses

black cotton soils
USE **vertisols**

BLACK CURRANT HARVESTERS
uf *harvesters, black current*
BT1 soft fruit harvesters
BT2 harvesters
BT3 farm machinery
BT4 machinery
rt black currants

BLACK CURRANT REVERSION VIRUS
BT1 miscellaneous plant viruses
BT2 plant viruses
BT3 plant pathogens
BT4 pathogens
rt ribes nigrum

BLACK CURRANTS
BT1 antifungal plants
BT1 temperate small fruits
BT2 small fruits
BT2 temperate fruits
BT3 fruit crops
rt black currant harvesters
rt ribes nigrum

black-eared white
USE **blanco orejinegro**

black earths
USE **chernozems**

black-eyed peas
USE **cowpeas**

BLACK GRAM
uf *gram*
uf *gram, black*
rt vigna mungo

BLACK IBERIAN
BT1 pig breeds
BT2 breeds

BLACK MERINO
BT1 sheep breeds
BT2 breeds

black mustard
USE **brassica nigra**

BLACK PEPPER
uf *pepper, black*
BT1 pepper
BT2 condiments

BLACK PIEDRA
BT1 piedra
BT2 mycoses
BT3 infectious diseases
BT4 diseases
rt piedraia

BLACK QUEEN CELL VIRUS
BT1 bee viruses
BT2 insect viruses
BT3 entomopathogens
BT4 pathogens

black rats
USE **rattus rattus**

BLACK SEA
BT1 atlantic ocean
BT2 marine areas

BLACK SOILS
BT1 vertisols
BT2 soil types (genetic)

BLACK SPOT
BT1 plant disorders
BT2 disorders
rt capsicum

BLACK STREAK
BT1 plant disorders
BT2 disorders
rt avocados

black-tailed deer
USE **odocoileus hemionus**

BLACK TONGUE
BT1 deficiency diseases
BT2 diseases
BT2 nutritional disorders
BT3 animal disorders
BT4 disorders
rt pellagra
rt vitamin b complex

BLACK WELSH MOUNTAIN
BT1 sheep breeds
BT2 breeds

BLACKBERRIES
uf *brambles*
BT1 temperate small fruits
BT2 small fruits
BT2 temperate fruits
BT3 fruit crops
rt rubus fruticosus

blackbird
USE **turdus merula**

BLACKEYE COWPEA MOSAIC POTYVIRUS
HN from 1990; previously "blackeye cowpea mosaic virus"
uf *blackeye cowpea mosaic virus*
BT1 potyvirus group
BT2 plant viruses
BT3 plant pathogens
BT4 pathogens
rt cowpeas
rt vigna unguiculata

blackeye cowpea mosaic virus
USE **blackeye cowpea mosaic potyvirus**

BLACKHEAD PERSIAN
BT1 sheep breeds
BT2 breeds

BLACKHEART
BT1 plant disorders
BT2 disorders
rt beetroots
rt celery
rt pineapples

BLACKLINE
BT1 plant disorders
BT2 disorders
rt walnuts

BLACKS (AGRICOLA)
BT1 ethnic groups
BT2 groups

BLACKSIDED TRONDHEIM AND NORDLAND
BT1 cattle breeds
BT2 breeds

BLACKWATER FEVER
BT1 malaria
BT2 human diseases
BT3 diseases
BT2 mosquito-borne diseases
BT3 vector-borne diseases
BT4 diseases
BT2 protozoal infections
BT3 parasitoses
BT4 diseases
rt fever
rt plasmodium

BLADDER
uf *urinary bladder*
BT1 urinary tract
BT2 urogenital system
BT3 body parts
rt bladder diseases

BLADDER CALCULI
uf *calculi, bladder*
BT1 concretions
rt bladder diseases
rt urolithiasis

BLADDER DISEASES
BT1 urinary tract diseases

BLADDER DISEASES *cont.*
BT2 organic diseases
BT3 diseases
NT1 cystitis
rt bladder
rt bladder calculi

BLADE PLOUGHING
AF blade plowing
uf *ploughing, blade*
BT1 ploughing
BT2 tillage
BT3 cultivation
rt ploughs

BLADE PLOWING
BF blade ploughing
BT1 plowing

BLADES
BT1 components
rt cutters
rt implements
rt knives
rt tines
rt vanes

blaeberries
USE **vaccinium myrtillus**

BLAINVILLEA
BT1 compositae
NT1 blainvillea latifolia

BLAINVILLEA LATIFOLIA
BT1 blainvillea
BT2 compositae

blakeslea
USE **choanephora**

BLANC DU MASSIF CENTRAL
BT1 sheep breeds
BT2 breeds

BLANCHING
BT1 processing
rt cultural methods
rt dark
rt earthing up
rt etiolation

BLANCO OREJINEGRO
HN from 1990; previously "black-eared white"
uf *black-eared white*
BT1 cattle breeds
BT2 breeds

BLANIULIDAE
BT1 diplopoda
BT2 myriapoda
BT3 arthropods
NT1 archiboreoiulus
NT2 archiboreoiulus pallidus
NT1 blaniulus
NT2 blaniulus guttulatus
NT1 ommatoiulus
NT2 ommatoiulus moreleti

BLANIULUS
BT1 blaniulidae
BT2 diplopoda
BT3 myriapoda
BT4 arthropods
NT1 blaniulus guttulatus

BLANIULUS GUTTULATUS
BT1 blaniulus
BT2 blaniulidae
BT3 diplopoda
BT4 myriapoda
BT5 arthropods

BLANKETS (AGRICOLA)
rt bed coverings (agricola)

BLAPS
BT1 tenebrionidae
BT2 coleoptera
NT1 blaps halophila

BLAPS HALOPHILA
BT1 blaps
BT2 tenebrionidae

BLAPS HALOPHILA *cont.*
BT3 coleoptera

BLARINA
BT1 soricidae
BT2 insectivores
BT3 mammals
NT1 blarina brevicauda

BLARINA BREVICAUDA
BT1 blarina
BT2 soricidae
BT3 insectivores
BT4 mammals

BLAST FREEZING (AGRICOLA)
BT1 freezing
BT2 change of state
BT2 processing

blast transformation
USE **lymphocyte transformation**

BLASTICIDIN-S
BT1 antibiotic fungicides
BT2 antibiotics
BT2 fungicides
BT3 pesticides
BT1 nucleoside antibiotics
BT2 antibiotics
BT2 nucleosides
BT3 glycosides
BT4 carbohydrates

BLASTOBASIDAE
BT1 lepidoptera
NT1 holcocera
NT1 pseudohypatopa
NT2 pseudohypatopa pulverea

BLASTOCLADIALES
NT1 coelomomyces
NT2 coelomomyces indicus
NT2 coelomomyces psorophorae
NT2 coelomomyces stegomyiae
NT1 physoderma
NT2 physoderma maydis
rt fungi

BLASTOCRITHIDIA
BT1 sarcomastigophora
BT2 protozoa
NT1 blastocrithidia culicis
NT1 blastocrithidia triatomae

BLASTOCRITHIDIA CULICIS
BT1 blastocrithidia
BT2 sarcomastigophora
BT3 protozoa

BLASTOCRITHIDIA TRIATOMAE
BT1 blastocrithidia
BT2 sarcomastigophora
BT3 protozoa
BT1 entomopathogenic protozoa
BT2 entomopathogens
BT3 pathogens

BLASTOCYST
BT1 embryos
NT1 blastomere
rt blastokinin
rt ova

BLASTOCYSTIS
BT1 entomophthorales
NT1 blastocystis hominis

BLASTOCYSTIS HOMINIS
BT1 blastocystis
BT2 entomophthorales

BLASTODINIUM
BT1 sarcomastigophora
BT2 protozoa

blastogenesis
USE **lymphocyte transformation**

BLASTOKININ
uf *uteroglobin*
BT1 binding proteins

BLASTOKININ *cont.*
BT2 proteins
BT3 peptides
BT1 glycoproteins
BT2 proteins
BT3 peptides
BT1 kinins
BT2 hormones
BT2 peptides
rt blastocyst

BLASTOMERE
BT1 blastocyst
BT2 embryos

BLASTOMYCES
BT1 deuteromycotina
NT1 blastomyces dermatitidis
rt ajellomyces

BLASTOMYCES DERMATITIDIS
BT1 blastomyces
BT2 deuteromycotina
rt ajellomyces dermatitidis
rt blastomycosis

BLASTOMYCOSIS
uf *blastomycosis, north american*
uf *north american blastomycosis*
BT1 mycoses
BT2 infectious diseases
BT3 diseases
rt blastomyces dermatitidis

blastomycosis, european
USE **cryptococcosis**

blastomycosis, keloidal
USE **lobomycosis**

blastomycosis, north american
USE **blastomycosis**

blastomycosis, south american
USE **paracoccidioidomycosis**

blastophagus
USE **tomicus**

blastophagus minor
USE **tomicus minor**

blastophagus piniperda
USE **tomicus piniperda**

BLASTOSCHIZOMYCES
BT1 deuteromycotina
NT1 blastoschizomyces capitatus
rt trichosporon

BLASTOSCHIZOMYCES CAPITATUS
uf *trichosporon capitatum*
BT1 blastoschizomyces
BT2 deuteromycotina

BLASTOTHRIX
BT1 encyrtidae
BT2 hymenoptera
NT1 blastothrix longipennis

blastothrix confusa
USE **blastothrix longipennis**

BLASTOTHRIX LONGIPENNIS
uf *blastothrix confusa*
BT1 blastothrix
BT2 encyrtidae
BT3 hymenoptera

BLATTA
BT1 blattidae
BT2 blattaria
BT3 dictyoptera
NT1 blatta orientalis

BLATTA ORIENTALIS
BT1 blatta
BT2 blattidae
BT3 blattaria
BT4 dictyoptera

BLATTARIA
uf *cockroaches*

BLATTARIA *cont.*
uf *roaches*
BT1 dictyoptera
NT1 blaberidae
NT2 blaberus
NT3 blaberus atropos
NT3 blaberus craniifer
NT3 blaberus discoidalis
NT3 blaberus giganteus
NT2 diploptera
NT3 diploptera punctata
NT1 blattellidae
NT2 blattella
NT3 blattella asahinai
NT3 blattella germanica
NT2 parcoblatta
NT2 supella
NT3 supella longipalpa
NT1 blattidae
NT2 blatta
NT3 blatta orientalis
NT2 periplaneta
NT3 periplaneta americana
NT3 periplaneta australasiae
NT3 periplaneta brunnea
NT3 periplaneta fuliginosa
NT3 periplaneta japonica
NT1 oxyhaloidae
NT2 gromphadorhina
NT3 gromphadorhina portentosa
NT2 nauphoeta
NT3 nauphoeta cinerea
NT2 pycnoscelus
NT3 pycnoscelus surinamensis
NT2 rhyparobia
NT3 rhyparobia maderae
NT1 polyphagidae
NT2 polyphaga

BLATTELLA
BT1 blattellidae
BT2 blattaria
BT3 dictyoptera
NT1 blattella asahinai
NT1 blattella germanica

BLATTELLA ASAHINAI
HN from 1989
BT1 blattella
BT2 blattellidae
BT3 blattaria
BT4 dictyoptera

BLATTELLA GERMANICA
BT1 blattella
BT2 blattellidae
BT3 blattaria
BT4 dictyoptera

BLATTELLIDAE
BT1 blattaria
BT2 dictyoptera
NT1 blattella
NT2 blattella asahinai
NT2 blattella germanica
NT1 parcoblatta
NT1 supella
NT2 supella longipalpa

BLATTIDAE
BT1 blattaria
BT2 dictyoptera
NT1 blatta
NT2 blatta orientalis
NT1 periplaneta
NT2 periplaneta americana
NT2 periplaneta australasiae
NT2 periplaneta brunnea
NT2 periplaneta fuliginosa
NT2 periplaneta japonica

BLATTISOCIUS
BT1 ascidae
BT2 mesostigmata
BT3 acari
NT1 blattisocius keegani
NT1 blattisocius tarsalis
rt melichares

BLATTISOCIUS KEEGANI
uf *melichares keegani*
BT1 blattisocius

BLATTISOCIUS KEEGANI *cont.*
BT2 ascidae
BT3 mesostigmata
BT4 acari

BLATTISOCIUS TARSALIS
uf *melichares tarsalis*
BT1 blattisocius
BT2 ascidae
BT3 mesostigmata
BT4 acari

BLEACHING
BT1 processing
rt bleaching agents (agricola)
rt bleaching powder
rt colour
rt oxidants
rt sodium carbonate
rt stain removal
rt stains
rt sulfur dioxide
rt wood technology

BLEACHING AGENTS (AGRICOLA)
rt bleaching
rt bleaching powder
rt whiteners (agricola)

BLEACHING POWDER
uf *chlorinated lime*
BT1 laundry products (agricola)
BT2 non-food products
BT3 products
rt bleaching
rt bleaching agents (agricola)
rt disinfectants

BLECHNACEAE
NT1 blechnum
NT1 stenochlaena
NT2 stenochlaena palustris

BLECHNUM
BT1 blechnaceae
rt ornamental ferns

bleeding
USE **haemorrhage**

BLEEKERIA
BT1 apocynaceae
NT1 bleekeria vitiensis

BLEEKERIA VITIENSIS
BT1 bleekeria
BT2 apocynaceae

BLENDED FOODS (AGRICOLA)
BT1 foods

BLENDERS (AGRICOLA)
BT1 food processing equipment (agricola)
BT2 equipment
rt appliances (agricola)
rt home food preparation (agricola)

BLENDING
BT1 processing
NT1 bulk blending
rt butter
rt buttermaking
rt mixing

BLEPHARELLA
HN from 1989
BT1 tachinidae
BT2 diptera
NT1 blepharella lateralis

BLEPHARELLA LATERALIS
HN from 1989
BT1 blepharella
BT2 tachinidae
BT3 diptera

BLEPHARIGLOTTIS
BT1 orchidaceae
rt ornamental plants

BLEPHARIPA
BT1 tachinidae
BT2 diptera

BLEPHARIPA *cont.*
NT1 blepharipa pratensis
NT1 blepharipa scutellata

BLEPHARIPA PRATENSIS
BT1 blepharipa
BT2 tachinidae
BT3 diptera

BLEPHARIPA SCUTELLATA
BT1 blepharipa
BT2 tachinidae
BT3 diptera

BLEPHARITA
BT1 noctuidae
BT2 lepidoptera
NT1 blepharita solieri

BLEPHARITA SOLIERI
BT1 blepharita
BT2 noctuidae
BT3 lepidoptera

bletia hyacinthina
USE **bletilla striata**

BLETILLA
BT1 orchidaceae
NT1 bletilla striata

bletilla hyacinthina
USE **bletilla striata**

BLETILLA STRIATA
uf *bletia hyacinthina*
uf *bletilla hyacinthina*
BT1 antibacterial plants
BT1 bletilla
BT2 orchidaceae
BT1 ornamental orchids

BLEU DU MAINE
HN from 1990; previously "bluefaced maine"
uf *bluefaced maine*
BT1 sheep breeds
BT2 breeds

BLIGHIA
BT1 sapindaceae
NT1 blighia sapida

BLIGHIA SAPIDA
BT1 blighia
BT2 sapindaceae
BT1 subtropical tree fruits
BT2 subtropical fruits
BT3 fruit crops
BT2 tree fruits
rt hypoglycine a

BLIGHT
BT1 plant disorders
BT2 disorders

BLIND LOOP SYNDROME
BT1 intestinal diseases
BT2 gastrointestinal diseases
BT3 digestive system diseases
BT4 organic diseases
BT5 diseases
rt small intestine

BLINDNESS
BT1 vision disorders
BT2 eye diseases
BT3 organic diseases
BT4 diseases
BT2 sensory disorders
BT3 functional disorders
BT4 animal disorders
BT5 disorders
BT3 nervous system diseases
BT4 animal disorders
BT5 disorders

BLINDS
BT1 screens
BT2 shelter
BT3 protection
rt shading
rt thermal screens

BLISSUS
BT1 lygaeidae
BT2 heteroptera
NT1 blissus insularis
NT1 blissus leucopterus

BLISSUS INSULARIS
BT1 blissus
BT2 lygaeidae
BT3 heteroptera

BLISSUS LEUCOPTERUS
BT1 blissus
BT2 lygaeidae
BT3 heteroptera

BLITOPERTHA
BT1 scarabaeidae
BT2 coleoptera
NT1 blitopertha orientalis
rt anomala

BLITOPERTHA ORIENTALIS
uf *anomala orientalis*
BT1 blitopertha
BT2 scarabaeidae
BT3 coleoptera

BLOAT
uf *blown*
uf *tympanites*
BT1 digestive disorders
BT2 functional disorders
BT3 animal disorders
BT4 disorders
rt antibloat agents
rt flatus

BLOCKAGE
rt barriers
rt emitters
rt flow
rt nozzles

BLOCKBOARD
BT1 panels
BT2 building materials
BT3 materials
rt composite wood assemblies

β-BLOCKERS
HN from 1990
(for retrieval spell out "beta")
uf *adrenergic beta receptor blockaders*
BT1 sympatholytics
BT2 neurotropic drugs
BT3 drugs
NT1 ergot alkaloids
NT2 dihydroergocryptine
NT2 ergometrine
rt β-adrenergic receptors

BLOMIA
BT1 glycyphagidae
BT2 astigmata
BT3 acari
NT1 blomia tjibodas
NT1 blomia tropicalis

BLOMIA TJIBODAS
BT1 blomia
BT2 glycyphagidae
BT3 astigmata
BT4 acari

BLOMIA TROPICALIS
BT1 blomia
BT2 glycyphagidae
BT3 astigmata
BT4 acari

BLONDE D'AQUITAINE
HN from 1990; previously "aquitaine blond"
uf *aquitaine blond*
BT1 cattle breeds
BT2 breeds

BLOOD
BT1 body fluids
BT2 fluids
NT1 blood plasma
NT1 blood serum

BLOOD *cont.*
NT1 cord blood
rt anticoagulants
rt blood analysis (agricola)
rt blood cells
rt blood circulation
rt blood coagulation
rt blood composition
rt blood disorders
rt blood donors
rt blood flow
rt blood group antigens
rt blood groups
rt blood meal
rt blood picture
rt blood pressure
rt blood proteins
rt blood sampling
rt blood sedimentation
rt blood specimen collection
rt blood spots
rt blood transfusion
rt blood vessels
rt blood volume
rt clotting
rt haematocrit
rt haematology
rt haematopoiesis
rt haematuria
rt haemodialysis
rt haemolymph
rt haemolysins
rt hyperaminoacidaemia
rt hyperammonaemia
rt hyperargininaemia
rt hyperbilirubinaemia
rt hypercalcaemia
rt hypercapnia
rt hypercarotenaemia
rt hypercholesterolaemia
rt hyperchylomicronaemia
rt hyperglycaemia
rt hyperglycinaemia
rt hyperinsulinaemia
rt hyperkaliaemia
rt hyperketonaemia
rt hyperlipaemia
rt hyperlipoproteinaemia
rt hypermagnesaemia
rt hypermethioninaemia
rt hypernatraemia
rt hyperphenylalaninaemia
rt hyperphosphataemia
rt hypertriglyceridaemia
rt hyperuricaemia
rt hypocalcaemia
rt hypocholesterolaemia
rt hypocupraemia
rt hypoglycaemia
rt hypokaliaemia
rt hypolipaemia
rt hypomagnesaemia
rt hyponatraemia
rt ketonaemia
rt serum
rt toxaemia

BLOOD ANALYSIS (AGRICOLA)
rt analysis
rt blood

BLOOD CELLS
BT1 cells
NT1 erythrocytes
NT2 reticulocytes
NT1 haemocytes
NT1 leukocytes
NT2 granulocytes
NT3 basophils
NT3 eosinophils
NT3 neutrophils
NT2 lymphocytes
NT3 b lymphocytes
NT3 immunocytes
NT3 melanocytes
NT3 natural killer cells
NT3 t lymphocytes
NT4 cytotoxic t lymphocytes
NT4 suppressor cells
NT3 thymocytes
NT2 macrophages
NT2 monocytes

BLOOD CELLS *cont.*
NT1 phagocytes
NT2 macrophages
NT2 neutrophils
NT1 platelets
rt blood
rt blood composition
rt histiocytosis
rt macrocytic anaemia
rt pernicious anaemia
rt polycythaemia

BLOOD CHEMISTRY
BT1 blood composition
BT2 composition
NT1 alkali reserve
NT1 blood lipids
NT1 blood protein
NT1 blood sugar
NT1 erythrocyte potassium types
rt electrolytes

BLOOD CIRCULATION
uf *blood stream*
BT1 physiological functions
NT1 blood flow
NT1 capillary circulation
NT1 haemodynamics
NT2 blood pressure
NT2 blood volume
NT2 cardiac output
NT3 heart rate
NT2 vasoconstriction
NT2 vasodilation
NT1 portal circulation
NT1 pulse
NT1 venous circulation
rt arteries
rt blood
rt blood coagulation
rt cardiovascular system
rt circulation
rt extracorporeal circulation
rt heart sounds
rt heart valves
rt pulse rate
rt thrombolysis

blood circulation disorders
USE **circulatory disorders**

BLOOD COAGULATION
uf *clotting system*
uf *coagulation, blood*
BT1 blood physiology
BT2 animal physiology
BT3 physiology
BT1 coagulation
rt anticoagulants
rt blood
rt blood circulation
rt blood coagulation disorders
rt blood coagulation factors
rt blood flow
rt fibrin
rt fibrin hydrolysate
rt fibrinogen
rt fibrinolysis
rt haemophilia
rt kallikrein
rt prothrombin
rt syneresis
rt thrombin
rt thromboplastin

BLOOD COAGULATION DISORDERS
BT1 blood disorders
BT2 animal disorders
BT3 disorders
NT1 disseminated intravascular coagulation
NT1 haemophilia
NT1 thrombocythaemia
NT1 thrombocytopenia
NT1 thrombocytopenic purpura
NT1 thrombosis
rt blood coagulation

BLOOD COAGULATION FACTORS
BT1 blood proteins
BT2 animal proteins

BLOOD COAGULATION FACTORS *cont.*
BT3 proteins
BT4 peptides
rt blood coagulation
rt coagulants

BLOOD COMPOSITION
BT1 composition
NT1 blood chemistry
NT2 alkali reserve
NT2 blood lipids
NT2 blood protein
NT2 blood sugar
NT2 erythrocyte potassium types
rt blood
rt blood cells
rt blood donors
rt blood plasma
rt blood proteins
rt blood serum
rt erythrocytes
rt haemoglobin value

BLOOD DISORDERS
BT1 animal disorders
BT2 disorders
NT1 acidaemia
NT2 butyryl acidaemia
NT2 citrullinaemia
NT2 histidinaemia
NT2 methylmalonic acidaemia
NT2 propionic acidaemia
NT1 anaemia
NT2 aplastic anaemia
NT2 equine infectious anaemia
NT2 haemoglobinuria
NT2 haemolytic anaemia
NT2 hypochromic anaemia
NT2 iron deficiency anaemia
NT2 macrocytic anaemia
NT2 megaloblastic anaemia
NT2 microcytic anaemia
NT2 nutritional anaemia
NT2 pernicious anaemia
NT2 sickle cell anaemia
NT2 sideroblastic anaemia
NT2 thalassaemia
NT1 avian erythroblastosis
NT1 blood coagulation disorders
NT2 disseminated intravascular coagulation
NT2 haemophilia
NT2 thrombocythaemia
NT2 thrombocytopenia
NT2 thrombocytopenic purpura
NT2 thrombosis
NT1 blood protein disorders
NT2 hyperproteinaemia
NT3 hyperlipoproteinaemia
NT4 hyperchylomicronaemia
NT3 hyperprolactinaemia
NT2 hypoproteinaemia
NT3 hypoalbuminaemia
NT3 hypogammaglobulinaemia
NT3 hypolipoproteinaemia
NT4 abetalipoproteinaemia
NT3 hypoprothrombinaemia
NT2 methaemoglobinaemia
NT2 myohaemoglobinaemia
NT1 bone marrow disorders
NT2 aplastic anaemia
NT1 haemolysis
NT1 histiocytosis
NT1 hypovolaemia
NT1 leukocyte disorders
NT2 avian myeloblastosis
NT2 chediak-higashi syndrome
NT2 eosinophilia
NT3 tropical eosinophilia
NT2 leukaemia
NT2 leukopenia
NT2 leukosis
NT3 avian leukosis
NT3 bovine leukosis
NT2 monocytosis
NT1 lipaemia
NT1 pancytopenia
NT1 polycythaemia
NT1 polycythaemia vera
rt blood

BLOOD DONORS
BT1 donors
rt blood
rt blood composition
rt blood transfusion

blood feeding
USE **haematophagy**

BLOOD FLOW
BT1 blood circulation
BT2 physiological functions
rt blood
rt blood coagulation
rt blood vessels
rt dextran
rt heart sounds

blood formation
USE **haematopoiesis**

blood glucose
USE **blood sugar**

BLOOD GROUP ANTIGENS
BT1 antigens
BT2 immunological factors
rt blood
rt blood groups
rt blood transfusion

BLOOD GROUPS
rt blood
rt blood group antigens
rt blood transfusion

BLOOD LIPIDS
BT1 blood chemistry
BT2 blood composition
BT3 composition
rt chylomicron lipids
rt hyperlipaemia
rt lipids

BLOOD MEAL
BT1 meal
rt blood
rt blood protein
rt slaughterhouse waste

BLOOD-MEALS
rt anautogeny
rt haematophagous arthropods
rt haematophagy
rt parous rates

blood, packed cell volume
USE **haematocrit**

BLOOD PHYSIOLOGY
BT1 animal physiology
BT2 physiology
NT1 blood coagulation
NT1 haematopoiesis
NT2 erythropoiesis
NT2 thrombocytopoiesis
NT1 haemostasis

BLOOD PICTURE
NT1 erythrocyte count
NT1 erythrocyte survival
NT1 leukocyte count
NT1 platelet count
rt blood
rt erythrocyte sedimentation rate
rt erythrocyte size
rt haematology
rt haemoglobin
rt haemoglobin value

BLOOD PLASMA
uf *plasma (blood)*
BT1 blood
BT2 body fluids
BT3 fluids
rt blood composition
rt blood serum
rt plasma substitutes

blood plasma proteins
HN was a preferred term until 1990
USE **blood proteins**

blood platelets
USE **platelets**

BLOOD PRESSURE
BT1 haemodynamics
BT2 blood circulation
BT3 physiological functions
rt blood
rt cardiac output
rt hypertension
rt hypotension

blood pressure, high
USE **hypertension**

BLOOD PROTEIN
uf *plasma protein*
uf *serum protein*
BT1 animal protein
BT2 protein
BT1 blood chemistry
BT2 blood composition
BT3 composition
rt blood meal

BLOOD PROTEIN DISORDERS
BT1 blood disorders
BT2 animal disorders
BT3 disorders
NT1 hyperproteinaemia
NT2 hyperlipoproteinaemia
NT3 hyperchylomicronaemia
NT2 hyperprolactinaemia
NT1 hypoproteinaemia
NT2 hypoalbuminaemia
NT2 hypogammaglobulinaemia
NT2 hypolipoproteinaemia
NT3 abetalipoproteinaemia
NT2 hypoprothrombinaemia
NT1 methaemoglobinaemia
NT1 myohaemoglobinaemia
rt blood proteins

BLOOD PROTEINS
uf *blood plasma proteins*
uf *blood serum proteins*
BT1 animal proteins
BT2 proteins
BT3 peptides
NT1 α-fetoprotein
NT1 blood coagulation factors
NT1 ceruloplasmin
NT1 erythropoietin
NT1 fibrin
NT1 fibrinogen
NT1 haemoglobin
NT2 haemoglobin a1
NT2 haemoglobin a2
NT2 methaemoglobin
NT1 haptoglobins
NT1 myoglobin
NT1 opsonins
NT1 postalbumin
NT1 prealbumin
NT1 properdin
NT1 prothrombin
NT1 seromucoid
NT1 serum albumin
NT2 bovine serum albumin
NT1 sex-limited protein
NT1 thrombin
NT1 thromboplastin
NT1 transcobalamins
NT1 transferrin
NT1 transthyretin
NT1 x-protein
rt blood
rt blood composition
rt blood protein disorders
rt immunoglobulins

blood red cells
USE **erythrocytes**

BLOOD SAMPLING
BT1 sampling
BT2 techniques
rt blood

BLOOD SEDIMENTATION
BT1 sedimentation
BT2 processing
BT2 techniques

BLOOD SEDIMENTATION *cont.*
rt blood

BLOOD SERUM
BT1 blood
BT2 body fluids
BT3 fluids
BT1 serum
BT2 body fluids
BT3 fluids
rt blood composition
rt blood plasma

blood serum proteins
HN was a preferred term until 1990
USE **blood proteins**

BLOOD SPECIMEN COLLECTION
BT1 sampling
BT2 techniques
rt blood
rt specimens

BLOOD SPOTS
BT1 egg quality
BT2 quality
rt blood
rt eggs

blood stream
USE **blood circulation**

BLOOD SUGAR
uf *blood glucose*
uf *glucose in blood*
uf *glycaemia*
BT1 blood chemistry
BT2 blood composition
BT3 composition
rt diabetes
rt glucose
rt glucose tolerance
rt glucose tolerance test
rt haemoglobin a1
rt hyperglycaemia
rt hypoglycaemia
rt hypoglycaemic agents

blood sugar, low
USE **hypoglycaemia**

blood sugar tolerance
USE **glucose tolerance**

BLOOD TRANSFUSION
BT1 therapy
rt blood
rt blood donors
rt blood group antigens
rt blood groups
rt transfusion

blood vessel disorders
USE **vascular diseases**

BLOOD VESSELS
BT1 cardiovascular system
BT2 body parts
NT1 arteries
NT2 aorta
NT2 pulmonary artery
NT1 capillaries
NT1 coronary vessels
NT1 ductus arteriosus
NT1 veins
NT2 jugular vein
NT2 portal vein
NT2 vena cava
rt blood
rt blood flow
rt endothelium
rt radiography
rt vascular diseases
rt vasomotor system
rt vessels

BLOOD VOLUME
BT1 haemodynamics
BT2 blood circulation
BT3 physiological functions
rt blood
rt cardiac output
rt volume

bloodsucking arthropods
USE **haematophagous arthropods**

BLOSSFELDIA
BT1 cactaceae
rt ornamental succulent plants

BLOSSOM-END ROT
BT1 plant disorders
BT2 disorders
rt tomatoes

blotting, immunological
USE **immunoblotting**

BLOWERS
BT1 machinery
NT1 forage blowers
NT1 mist blowers
NT1 wind machines
rt bee blowers
rt fans
rt ventilators

blowers, forage
USE **forage blowers**

blowers, hay
USE **forage blowers**

blown
USE **bloat**

blue
USE **best linear unbiased estimation**

BLUE CHEESE
BT1 cheeses
BT2 milk products
BT3 products

blue grama
USE **bouteloua gracilis**

blue green algae
USE **cyanobacteria**

BLUE LIGHT
uf *light, blue*
BT1 light
BT2 electromagnetic radiation
BT3 radiation

blue sisal
USE **agave amaniensis**

BLUE STAIN
BT1 fungal stains
BT2 stains
rt stain fungi

blue whiting
USE **micromestistius poutassou**

BLUEBERRIES
rt blueberry leaf mottle nepovirus
rt vaccinium

BLUEBERRY LEAF MOTTLE NEPOVIRUS
HN from 1990
BT1 nepovirus group
BT2 plant viruses
BT3 plant pathogens
BT4 pathogens
rt blueberries
rt vaccinium

blueberry shoestring virus
USE **vaccinium (blueberry) shoestring virus**

BLUEFACED LEICESTER
BT1 sheep breeds
BT2 breeds

bluefaced maine
USE **bleu du maine**

bluegill
USE **lepomis macrochirus**

BLUEGRASS
rt poa

BLUETONGUE VIRUS
BT1 orbivirus
BT2 arboviruses
BT3 pathogens
BT2 reoviridae
BT3 viruses

BLUMEA
BT1 compositae
NT1 blumea balsamifera
NT1 blumea eriantha
NT1 blumea lacera
NT1 blumea malcolmii
NT1 blumea membranacea
NT1 blumea wightiana
rt insecticidal plants

BLUMEA BALSAMIFERA
uf *conyza balsamifera*
BT1 blumea
BT2 compositae

BLUMEA ERIANTHA
BT1 blumea
BT2 compositae

BLUMEA LACERA
BT1 blumea
BT2 compositae

BLUMEA MALCOLMII
BT1 antibacterial plants
BT1 blumea
BT2 compositae

BLUMEA MEMBRANACEA
BT1 blumea
BT2 compositae
BT1 medicinal plants

BLUMEA WIGHTIANA
BT1 blumea
BT2 compositae

BLUMERIA
HN from 1990
BT1 erysiphales
rt erysiphe

blumeria graminis
USE **erysiphe graminis**

BLUMERIELLA
uf *coccomyces*
uf *higginsia*
BT1 helotiales
NT1 blumeriella jaapii
rt cylindrosporium

BLUMERIELLA JAAPII
uf *coccomyces hiemalis*
uf *cylindrosporium hiemale*
uf *cylindrosporium padi*
uf *higginsia hiemalis*
BT1 blumeriella
BT2 helotiales

blup
USE **best linear unbiased prediction**

BOA
BT1 boidae
BT2 serpentes
BT3 reptiles
rt constrictor

boa constrictor
USE **constrictor constrictor**

BOAR FATTENING
BT1 pig fattening
BT2 fattening
BT3 animal feeding
BT4 feeding
rt boars

BOAR FEEDING
BT1 pig feeding
BT2 livestock feeding
BT3 animal feeding
BT4 feeding

BOAR FEEDING *cont.*
rt boars

BOAR PROGENY TESTING
uf *pig progeny testing*
BT1 progeny testing
BT2 animal breeding methods
BT3 breeding methods
BT4 methodology
BT2 testing
rt boars

BOAR TAINT
BT1 taint
BT2 odours
BT3 organoleptic traits
BT4 physicochemical properties
BT5 properties
BT4 traits
rt aroma
rt boars
rt palatability

BOARD GAMES
BT1 indoor games
BT2 games
BT2 indoor recreation
BT3 recreation

BOARDING HOMES (AGRICOLA)
BT1 homes
BT2 housing

boarmia
USE **hypomecis**

boarmia rhomboidaria
USE **peribatodes rhomboidaria**

boarmia selenaria
USE **ascotis selenaria**

BOARS
BT1 male animals
BT2 animals
rt boar fattening
rt boar feeding
rt boar progeny testing
rt boar taint
rt pigs

boars, wild
USE **wild pigs**

BOAT HIRE
AF boat rental
BT1 hiring
BT2 capital leasing
rt boats

BOAT RENTAL
BF boat hire

BOATING
BT1 water recreation
BT2 recreation
NT1 canoeing
NT1 power boating
NT1 rowing
NT1 sailing
rt boats

BOATS
uf *boats and ships*
NT1 barges
NT1 weed cutting launches
rt boat hire
rt boating
rt fishing
rt inland waterways
rt sailing
rt shipbuilding
rt ships
rt water transport
rt waterways
rt wood products

boats and ships
USE **boats**
OR **ships**

bobwhite quail
USE **colinus virginianus**

BOCCONIA
BT1 papaveraceae
NT1 bocconia vulcanica

bocconia cordata
USE **macleaya cordata**

BOCCONIA VULCANICA
BT1 bocconia
BT2 papaveraceae

body
USE **animal anatomy**

body build
USE **somatotype**

BODY CAVITIES
BT1 body parts
NT1 abdominal cavity
NT1 thoracic cavity
rt abdomen
rt pelvis

BODY-CHECKED EGGS
HN from 1989
rt eggs

body components
USE **animal anatomy**

BODY COMPOSITION
(see under body fat, body fluids, body parts, body regions)
rt anatomy
rt body fat
rt carcass composition
rt composition

BODY CONDITION

body conformation
USE **conformation**

BODY DENSITY
BT1 density
rt body measurements
rt body weight
rt bone density

BODY FAT
BT1 fat
NT1 abdominal fat
NT1 backfat
NT1 brown fat
NT1 depot fat
NT1 subcutaneous fat
rt adipocytes
rt adipose tissue
rt body composition
rt carcass composition
rt fat percentage
rt fat thickness
rt obesity

BODY FLUIDS
BT1 fluids
NT1 allantoic fluid
NT1 amniotic fluid
NT1 bile
NT1 blood
NT2 blood plasma
NT2 blood serum
NT2 cord blood
NT1 body water
NT1 cerebrospinal fluid
NT1 colostrum
NT2 cow colostrum
NT2 human colostrum
NT1 digestive juices
NT2 chymosin
NT3 rennet
NT4 microbial rennet
NT2 duodenal fluids
NT2 gastric juices
NT3 gastric acid
NT2 pancreatic juice
NT2 rumen fluid
NT2 saliva
NT1 extracellular fluids
NT1 follicular fluid
NT1 haemolymph
NT1 interstitial fluids
NT1 lymph

BODY FLUIDS *cont.*
NT2 chyle
NT1 metabolic water
NT1 milks
NT2 baboon milk
NT2 buffalo milk
NT2 camel milk
NT2 dog milk
NT2 ewe milk
NT2 goat milk
NT2 human milk
NT2 mare milk
NT2 mouse milk
NT2 pigeon crop milk
NT2 rabbit milk
NT2 rat milk
NT2 seal milk
NT2 sow milk
NT1 placental fluids
NT1 semen
NT2 mixed semen
NT2 seminal plasma
NT1 serum
NT2 blood serum
NT2 immune serum
NT2 pms
NT1 sputum
NT1 sweat
NT1 synovial fluid
NT1 tears
NT1 total body fluid
NT1 urine
rt animal anatomy
rt biological fluids
rt secretions

BODY HEAT LOSS
BT1 heat loss
BT2 losses

BODY IMAGE (AGRICOLA)
BT1 self perception
BT2 perception

BODY LANGUAGE (AGRICOLA)
BT1 nonverbal communication (agricola)
BT2 communication

BODY LEAN MASS
uf *lean body mass*
BT1 body weight
BT2 weight
rt lean

BODY LENGTH
rt body measurements
rt length

BODY MEASUREMENTS
rt anthropometric dimensions
rt biometry
rt body density
rt body length
rt body surface area
rt body weight
rt breast angle
rt growth
rt head dimensions (agricola)
rt heart girth
rt height
rt height-weight tables (agricola)
rt muscle bone ratio
rt nutritional state
rt somatotype
rt thinness
rt underweight
rt weight

BODY PARTS
uf *body systems*
NT1 body cavities
NT2 abdominal cavity
NT2 thoracic cavity
NT1 cardiovascular system
NT2 blood vessels
NT3 arteries
NT4 aorta
NT4 pulmonary artery
NT3 capillaries
NT3 coronary vessels
NT3 ductus arteriosus

BODY PARTS *cont.*
NT3 veins
NT4 jugular vein
NT4 portal vein
NT4 vena cava
NT2 haemolymph nodes
NT2 heart
NT3 endocardium
NT3 heart valves
NT3 ventricles
NT2 lymphatic system
NT3 bursa fabricii
NT3 lymph nodes
NT3 peyer patches
NT3 thoracic duct
NT3 thymus gland
NT2 spleen
NT1 digestive system
NT2 anus
NT3 cloaca
NT2 biliary system
NT3 bile ducts
NT2 digestive tract
NT3 peritrophic membrane
NT2 fat body
NT2 foregut
NT2 gastric glands
NT2 hindgut
NT2 honey sac
NT2 intestines
NT3 jejunum
NT3 large intestine
NT4 caecum
NT4 colon
NT3 midgut
NT3 rectum
NT3 small intestine
NT4 duodenum
NT4 ileum
NT4 villi
NT2 liver
NT3 gall bladder
NT2 mouth
NT3 gingiva
NT3 periodontium
NT3 tongue
NT2 oesophagus
NT3 crop
NT3 reticular groove
NT2 pancreas
NT3 artificial pancreas
NT3 pancreas islets
NT2 pharynx
NT3 palate
NT3 tonsils
NT2 proventriculus
NT2 salivary glands
NT3 mandibular glands
NT3 parotid gland
NT2 stomach
NT3 abomasum
NT3 forestomach
NT4 reticulum
NT4 rumen
NT5 artificial rumen
NT5 omasum
NT3 gizzard
NT1 endocrine system
NT1 excretory system
NT2 malpighian tubules
NT1 glands (animal)
NT2 accessory glands
NT3 bulbo-urethral gland
NT3 prostate
NT3 vesicular gland
NT2 anal glands
NT2 endocrine glands
NT3 adrenal glands
NT4 adrenal cortex
NT4 adrenal medulla
NT3 parathyroid
NT3 pineal body
NT3 pituitary
NT4 anterior pituitary
NT4 posterior pituitary
NT3 thyroid gland
NT3 ultimobranchial body
NT2 endometrial glands
NT2 gastric glands
NT2 hepatopancreas
NT2 hypopharyngeal glands

BODY PARTS *cont.*
NT2 labial glands
NT2 lacrimal apparatus
NT2 mammary glands
NT3 individual quarters
NT3 teat number
NT3 teats
NT4 supernumerary teats
NT3 udders
NT2 mucus glands
NT2 nasonov gland
NT2 poll glands
NT2 preputial glands
NT2 prothoracic glands
NT2 salivary glands
NT3 mandibular glands
NT3 parotid gland
NT2 salt gland
NT2 scent glands
NT2 shell gland
NT2 silk glands
NT2 skin glands
NT3 sweat glands
NT2 tarsal glands
NT2 thymus gland
NT2 venom glands
NT3 alkaline venom gland
NT2 wax glands
NT1 integument
NT2 bristles
NT2 claws
NT2 comb
NT2 feathers
NT3 hamuli
NT2 hair
NT2 hooves
NT2 horns
NT3 antlers
NT4 velvet
NT2 nail
NT2 scales
NT2 shells
NT2 skin
NT3 dermis
NT3 skin folds
NT2 wattles
NT1 mouthparts
NT1 musculoskeletal system
NT2 bones
NT3 bone marrow
NT3 capitulum
NT3 epiphyses
NT3 jaws
NT4 mandible
NT4 teeth
NT5 dentine
NT5 dentition
NT5 enamel
NT5 gubernaculum
NT3 keels
NT3 limb bones
NT4 carpus
NT4 femur
NT4 fibula
NT4 humerus
NT4 metacarpus
NT4 metatarsus
NT4 patella
NT4 phalanges
NT4 radius
NT4 scapula
NT4 tarsometatarsus
NT4 tarsus
NT4 tibia
NT4 ulna
NT3 pelvis
NT3 periosteum
NT3 ribs
NT3 sesamoid bones
NT3 skull
NT4 orbits
NT3 spine
NT4 intervertebral disks
NT3 sternum
NT2 cartilage
NT2 double muscling
NT2 joints (animal)
NT3 elbows
NT3 knees
NT3 ligaments
NT4 gubernaculum

BODY PARTS *cont.*
NT3 stifle
NT3 synovial sheaths
NT2 muscles
NT3 breast muscle
NT3 diaphragm
NT3 longissimus dorsi
NT3 myocardium
NT3 skeletal muscle
NT3 sphincters
NT4 oesophageal sphincter
NT2 skeleton
NT3 exoskeleton
NT2 tendons
NT1 nervous system
NT2 autonomic nervous system
NT3 sympathetic nervous system
NT3 vasomotor system
NT2 central nervous system
NT3 brain
NT4 cerebellum
NT5 amygdala
NT4 cerebral cortex
NT4 cerebral ventricles
NT4 hippocampus
NT4 hypothalamus
NT5 preoptic area
NT4 medulla oblongata
NT4 thalamus
NT3 brain stem
NT3 central nervous system centres
NT3 cerebrospinal tracts
NT3 peripheral nerves
NT4 vagus nerve
NT3 spinal cord
NT3 spinal ganglia
NT2 higher nervous activity
NT2 myoneural junctions
NT2 plexus
NT3 brachial plexus
NT3 choroid plexus
NT1 neurosecretory system
NT2 corpora allata
NT2 corpora cardiaca
NT1 respiratory system
NT2 air sacs
NT3 pneumatophores
NT2 bronchi
NT2 gills
NT2 larynx
NT2 lungs
NT2 nose
NT2 paranasal sinuses
NT2 spiracles
NT2 swim bladder
NT2 trachea
NT1 sense organs
NT2 antennae
NT2 ears
NT3 guttural pouch
NT2 eyes
NT3 compound eyes
NT3 conjunctiva
NT3 cornea
NT3 eye lens
NT3 retina
NT2 ocelli
NT2 olfactory organs
NT3 vomeronasal organ
NT2 photoreceptors
NT2 sensilla
NT2 statoliths
NT1 spurs (poultry)
NT1 tergites
NT1 urogenital system
NT2 genitalia
NT3 female genitalia
NT4 oviducts
NT5 infundibulum
NT5 magnum
NT4 spermatheca
NT4 uterus
NT5 cervix
NT5 endometrium
NT5 muellerian ducts
NT5 myometrium
NT4 vagina
NT4 vulva
NT5 clitoris

BODY PARTS *cont.*
NT3 male genitalia
NT4 accessory glands
NT5 bulbo-urethral gland
NT5 prostate
NT5 vesicular gland
NT4 ductus deferens
NT5 ampulla
NT4 gubernaculum
NT4 penis
NT5 prepuce
NT4 scrotum
NT4 spermatic cord
NT2 urinary tract
NT3 bladder
NT3 kidneys
NT4 glomerulus
NT3 ureter
NT3 urethra
rt animal anatomy
rt body regions
rt organs
rt serosa

BODY PROTEIN
BT1 protein

BODY REGIONS
NT1 abdomen
NT2 umbilicus
NT1 back
NT2 withers
NT1 belly
NT1 head
NT2 beak
NT2 face
NT3 eyelids
NT3 lips
NT2 scalp
NT1 limbs
NT2 feet
NT3 digits
NT3 soles
NT2 hips
NT2 legs
NT3 hocks
NT3 shanks
NT3 shins
NT3 thighs
NT2 shoulders
NT2 wings
NT1 loins
NT1 neck
NT2 throat
NT1 perineum
NT1 rump
NT1 sides
NT1 tail
NT1 thorax
NT2 mediastinum
rt animal anatomy
rt body parts

BODY SURFACE AREA
BT1 surface area
BT2 area
rt body measurements

body systems
USE **body parts**

BODY TEMPERATURE
uf temperature, body
BT1 temperature
rt energy exchange
rt fever
rt heat regulation
rt hyperthermia
rt hypothermia
rt skin temperature
rt sweating

BODY TEMPERATURE REGULATION
BT1 thermoregulation

body type
USE **somatotype**

BODY WATER
uf water, body
BT1 body fluids
BT2 fluids

BODY WATER *cont.*
BT1 water
rt oedema

BODY WEIGHT
BT1 weight
NT1 birth weight
NT1 body lean mass
NT1 muscle weight
NT1 weaning weight
rt body density
rt body measurements
rt fattening performance
rt growth

BOEHMERIA
BT1 urticaceae
NT1 boehmeria caudata
NT1 boehmeria cylindrica
NT1 boehmeria macrophylla
NT1 boehmeria nivea

BOEHMERIA CAUDATA
BT1 boehmeria
BT2 urticaceae
BT1 medicinal plants

BOEHMERIA CYLINDRICA
BT1 antifungal plants
BT1 boehmeria
BT2 urticaceae

BOEHMERIA MACROPHYLLA
BT1 boehmeria
BT2 urticaceae
BT1 fibre plants

BOEHMERIA NIVEA
uf *ramie*
BT1 boehmeria
BT2 urticaceae
BT1 fibre plants

BOEHMITE
BT1 nonclay minerals
BT2 minerals

BOENNINGHAUSENIA
BT1 rutaceae
NT1 boenninghausenia albiflora

BOENNINGHAUSENIA ALBIFLORA
BT1 boenninghausenia
BT2 rutaceae
BT1 essential oil plants
BT2 oil plants
BT1 medicinal plants

BOER
HN from 1990
BT1 goat breeds
BT2 breeds

BOERHAVIA
BT1 nyctaginaceae
NT1 boerhavia diffusa
NT1 boerhavia erecta

BOERHAVIA DIFFUSA
BT1 antiviral plants
BT1 boerhavia
BT2 nyctaginaceae
BT1 medicinal plants

BOERHAVIA ERECTA
BT1 boerhavia
BT2 nyctaginaceae

BOETTCHERISCA
BT1 sarcophagidae
BT2 diptera
NT1 boettcherisca peregrina
rt sarcophaga

BOETTCHERISCA PEREGRINA
uf *sarcophaga peregrina*
BT1 boettcherisca
BT2 sarcophagidae
BT3 diptera

BOG PLANTS
BT1 plant communities
BT2 communities
rt bog soils
rt bogs

BOG PLANTS *cont.*
rt ecology
rt plants

BOG SOILS
BT1 soil types (ecological)
rt bog plants
rt bogs
rt histosols
rt peat soils
rt wetland soils

boglands
USE **bogs**
OR **wetlands**

BOGS
uf *boglands*
BT1 land types
BT1 vegetation types
rt bog plants
rt bog soils
rt boreal forests
rt peat
rt waterlogging
rt wetlands

BOIDAE
BT1 serpentes
BT2 reptiles
NT1 boa
NT1 constrictor
NT2 constrictor constrictor
NT1 python
NT2 python molurus
NT2 python reticulatus

BOIL IN BAG (AGRICOLA)
BT1 cooking methods (agricola)
BT2 methodology

BOILER FEED WATER
HN from 1990
BT1 water
rt boilers

BOILERS
BT1 heaters
BT2 equipment
NT1 steam boilers
rt boiler feed water
rt boiling
rt burners
rt dairy equipment

boilers, steam
USE **steam boilers**

BOILING
BT1 cooking methods (agricola)
BT2 methodology
BT1 processing
rt boilers
rt boiling point
rt condensation
rt heating
rt steam
rt steaming

BOILING OF WOOD
BT1 wood technology
BT2 technology

BOILING POINT
HN from 1990
BT1 physical properties
BT2 properties
rt boiling
rt bpe
rt temperature

boiling point elevation
USE **bpe**

boissiera
USE **bromus**

boissiera squamosa
USE **bromus pumilio**

BOLBITIS
BT1 lomariopsidaceae
NT1 bolbitis presliana
NT1 bolbitis virens

BOLBITIS PRESLIANA
BT1 bolbitis
BT2 lomariopsidaceae
BT1 ornamental ferns
BT2 ferns
BT2 ornamental foliage plants
BT3 foliage plants

BOLBITIS VIRENS
BT1 bolbitis
BT2 lomariopsidaceae
BT1 ornamental ferns
BT2 ferns
BT2 ornamental foliage plants
BT3 foliage plants

BOLBOSCHOENUS
BT1 cyperaceae
NT1 bolboschoenus maritimus

BOLBOSCHOENUS MARITIMUS
BT1 bolboschoenus
BT2 cyperaceae

BOLBOSOMA
BT1 polymorphidae
BT2 acanthocephala

BOLEODORUS
BT1 tylenchidae
BT2 nematoda

BOLETALES
NT1 boletus
NT2 boletus aestivalis
NT2 boletus betulicola
NT2 boletus edulis
NT2 boletus luridus
NT2 boletus pinophilus
NT2 boletus satanas
NT2 boletus sublutens
NT1 leccinum
NT1 paxillus
NT2 paxillus involutus
NT1 suillus
NT2 suillus granulatus
NT2 suillus grevillei
NT2 suillus luteus
rt fungi

BOLETUS
BT1 boletales
NT1 boletus aestivalis
NT1 boletus betulicola
NT1 boletus edulis
NT1 boletus luridus
NT1 boletus pinophilus
NT1 boletus satanas
NT1 boletus sublutens
rt suillus

BOLETUS AESTIVALIS
BT1 boletus
BT2 boletales

BOLETUS BETULICOLA
BT1 boletus
BT2 boletales

BOLETUS EDULIS
BT1 boletus
BT2 boletales
BT1 edible fungi
BT2 fungi
BT2 vegetables

boletus granulatus
USE **suillus granulatus**

boletus grevillei
USE **suillus grevillei**

BOLETUS LURIDUS
BT1 boletus
BT2 boletales

boletus luteus
USE **suillus luteus**

BOLETUS PINOPHILUS
BT1 boletus
BT2 boletales

BOLETUS SATANAS
BT1 boletus

BOLETUS SATANAS *cont.*
BT2 boletales

BOLETUS SUBLUTENS
BT1 boletus
BT2 boletales
BT1 edible fungi
BT2 fungi
BT2 vegetables

BOLIVIA
BT1 south america
BT2 america
rt andean group
rt developing countries

BOLLS
rt cotton
rt fruits

BOLOMYS
BT1 hesperomyinae
BT2 muridae
BT3 rodents
BT4 mammals
NT1 bolomys lasiurus
rt akodon
rt zygodontomys

BOLOMYS LASIURUS
uf *akodon arviculoides*
uf *zygodontomys lasiurus*
BT1 bolomys
BT2 hesperomyinae
BT3 muridae
BT4 rodents
BT5 mammals

BOLTED JOINTS
BT1 joints (timber)
rt woodworking

BOLTING
BT1 flowering
BT2 plant development
rt growth

BOLTS
BT1 structural components
BT2 components
rt building materials

BOLUSES
BT1 application methods
BT2 methodology
rt formulations

BOLUSIELLA
BT1 orchidaceae
NT1 bolusiella imbricata

BOLUSIELLA IMBRICATA
BT1 bolusiella
BT2 orchidaceae
BT1 ornamental orchids

BOMAREA
BT1 alstroemeriaceae
NT1 bomarea cantabrigiensis

BOMAREA CANTABRIGIENSIS
BT1 bomarea
BT2 alstroemeriaceae
BT1 ornamental bulbs

BOMBACACEAE
NT1 adansonia
NT2 adansonia digitata
NT1 bernoullia
NT2 bernoullia flammea
NT1 bombacopsis
NT2 bombacopsis quinata
NT1 bombax
NT2 bombax buonopozence
NT2 bombax costatum
NT2 bombax malabaricum
NT2 bombax sessile
NT1 ceiba
NT2 ceiba pentandra
NT1 durio
NT2 durio zibethinus
NT1 huberodendron
NT2 huberodendron patinoi
NT1 montezuma
NT2 montezuma speciosissima

BOMBACACEAE *cont.*
NT1 ochroma
NT2 ochroma pyramidale
NT1 patinoa
NT1 quararibea
NT2 quararibea cordata

BOMBACOPSIS
BT1 bombacaceae
NT1 bombacopsis quinata

BOMBACOPSIS QUINATA
BT1 bombacopsis
BT2 bombacaceae

BOMBAX
uf *salmalia*
BT1 bombacaceae
NT1 bombax buonopozence
NT1 bombax costatum
NT1 bombax malabaricum
NT1 bombax sessile

BOMBAX BUONOPOZENCE
BT1 bombax
BT2 bombacaceae

bombax ceiba
USE **bombax malabaricum**

BOMBAX COSTATUM
BT1 bombax
BT2 bombacaceae
BT1 medicinal plants

BOMBAX MALABARICUM
uf *bombax ceiba*
BT1 bombax
BT2 bombacaceae
BT1 fibre plants
BT1 forest trees
BT1 medicinal plants

BOMBAX SESSILE
BT1 bombax
BT2 bombacaceae

BOMBESIN
BT1 neuropeptides
BT2 peptides
BT1 polypeptides
BT2 peptides

bombs
USE **gunfire and bomb damage**

BOMBUS
uf *bumble bees*
BT1 apidae
BT2 hymenoptera

BOMBYCIDAE
BT1 lepidoptera
NT1 bombyx
NT2 bombyx mori

BOMBYLIIDAE
BT1 diptera
NT1 villa

BOMBYX
BT1 bombycidae
BT2 lepidoptera
NT1 bombyx mori

BOMBYX MORI
BT1 bombyx
BT2 bombycidae
BT3 lepidoptera
BT1 silkworms
BT2 beneficial insects
BT3 beneficial arthropods
BT4 beneficial organisms
BT3 insects
BT4 arthropods

BONAIRE
BT1 netherlands antilles
BT2 caribbean
BT3 america

BONAMIA
BT1 ascetospora
BT2 protozoa
NT1 bonamia ostreae

BONAMIA OSTREAE
BT1 bonamia
BT2 ascetospora
BT3 protozoa

BONATEA
BT1 orchidaceae
rt ornamental orchids

BOND STRENGTH
BT1 strength
BT2 mechanical properties
BT3 properties
rt adhesion

BONDED FABRICS (AGRICOLA)
BT1 fabrics

BONDED LABOR
BF bonded labour
rt labor

BONDED LABOUR
AF bonded labor
BT1 forced labour
BT2 labour

bonded water
USE **bound water**

bonding, social
USE **attachment behavior (agricola)**

bone age
USE **skeletal age**

BONE ASH
BT1 ash
rt bones

bone calcification
USE **bone formation**

BONE CHAR
HN from 1990
BT1 adsorbents
rt charcoal

BONE DENSITY
BT1 density
rt body density
rt bone formation
rt bones

bone destruction
USE **bone resorption**

BONE DISEASES
uf *bone disorders*
BT1 organic diseases
BT2 diseases
NT1 bone resorption
NT1 calcinosis
NT1 chondrodystrophy
NT1 dyschondroplasia
NT1 dysplasia
NT1 exostoses
NT1 hyperostosis
NT1 navicular disease
NT1 osteitis
NT1 osteochondritis
NT1 osteodystrophy
NT1 osteogenesis imperfecta
NT1 osteomalacia
NT1 osteomyelitis
NT1 osteopetrosis
NT2 avian osteopetrosis
NT1 osteoporosis
NT1 osteosclerosis
NT1 paget's disease
NT1 perosis
NT1 spavin
NT1 spinal diseases
NT2 lordosis
NT2 scoliosis
NT2 spina bifida
NT2 spondylitis
NT2 torticollis
rt bone marrow disorders
rt bones
rt dwarfism
rt hypophosphataemia
rt hypophosphataemic rickets
rt leg weakness

BONE DISEASES *cont.*
rt rickets

bone disorders
USE **bone diseases**

BONE FORMATION
uf *bone calcification*
BT1 skeletal development
rt bone density
rt bone mineralization
rt bone strength
rt bone weight
rt bones
rt calcification
rt skeletal age

BONE FRACTURES
BT1 fractures
BT2 trauma
rt bones
rt fracture fixation

BONE MARROW
uf *marrow, bone*
BT1 bones
BT2 musculoskeletal system
BT3 body parts
rt bone marrow cells
rt bone marrow disorders
rt bone marrow transplant
rt haematopoiesis
rt osteomyelitis
rt thrombocytopoiesis

BONE MARROW CELLS
BT1 cells
rt bone marrow
rt granulocytes
rt haematopoiesis

BONE MARROW DISORDERS
BT1 blood disorders
BT2 animal disorders
BT3 disorders
NT1 aplastic anaemia
rt bone diseases
rt bone marrow

BONE MARROW TRANSPLANT
HN from 1989
BT1 transplantation
BT2 surgical operations
rt bone marrow

BONE MEAL
BT1 meal
BT1 phosphorus fertilizers
BT2 fertilizers
rt bones
rt slaughterhouse waste

BONE MINERALIZATION
BT1 mineralization
rt bone formation
rt bones
rt calcification

BONE RESORPTION
uf *bone destruction*
BT1 bone diseases
BT2 organic diseases
BT3 diseases
rt bones
rt demineralization

BONE STRENGTH
BT1 strength
BT2 mechanical properties
BT3 properties
rt bone formation
rt bones

BONE TISSUE
BT1 animal tissues
BT2 tissues
rt bones

BONE WEIGHT
BT1 weight
rt bone formation
rt bones
rt carcass weight

BONES
BT1 musculoskeletal system
BT2 body parts
NT1 bone marrow
NT1 capitulum
NT1 epiphyses
NT1 jaws
NT2 mandible
NT2 teeth
NT3 dentine
NT3 dentition
NT3 enamel
NT3 gubernaculum
NT1 keels
NT1 limb bones
NT2 carpus
NT2 femur
NT2 fibula
NT2 humerus
NT2 metacarpus
NT2 metatarsus
NT2 patella
NT2 phalanges
NT2 radius
NT2 scapula
NT2 tarsometatarsus
NT2 tarsus
NT2 tibia
NT2 ulna
NT1 pelvis
NT1 periosteum
NT1 ribs
NT1 sesamoid bones
NT1 skull
NT2 orbits
NT1 spine
NT2 intervertebral disks
NT1 sternum
rt bone ash
rt bone density
rt bone diseases
rt bone formation
rt bone fractures
rt bone meal
rt bone mineralization
rt bone resorption
rt bone strength
rt bone tissue
rt bone weight
rt cartilage
rt muscle bone ratio
rt ossification
rt osteitis
rt osteochondritis
rt osteomalacia
rt osteomyelitis
rt osteopetrosis
rt osteosclerosis
rt rickets
rt skeletal age
rt skeleton

BONING (AGRICOLA)
BT1 butchering (agricola)
NT1 hot boning (agricola)

BONITOS
BT1 marine fishes
BT2 aquatic animals
BT3 animals
BT3 aquatic organisms
rt sarda
rt scombridae

bonnetia
USE **linnaemya**

bonnetia comta
USE **linnaemya comta**

BONSAI
rt pruning
rt training

BONSMARA
BT1 cattle breeds
BT2 breeds

BONUSES
uf *premiums*
BT1 incentives
rt wages

BOOK-KEEPING
BT1 accounting
NT1 single entry book-keeping
NT1 stock accounting
rt amortization
rt assets
rt farm accounting
rt inventories

BOOK REVIEWS
BT1 reviews
rt books

bookings
USE **reservations**

BOOKS
BT1 publications
NT1 activity books (agricola)
NT1 coloring books (agricola)
NT1 cookbooks
NT2 children's cookbooks (agricola)
NT1 cookery books
NT1 dictionaries
NT1 guide books
NT2 buyers' guides
NT2 forest guides
NT1 handbooks
NT1 textbooks
NT2 laboratory manuals (agricola)
NT1 workbooks (agricola)
NT1 yearbooks
rt book reviews
rt education
rt libraries
rt literacy
rt reference works

BOOMS
BT1 components
NT1 spray booms
rt sprayers

BOOPHILUS
BT1 ixodidae
BT2 metastigmata
BT3 acari
NT1 boophilus annulatus
NT1 boophilus decoloratus
NT1 boophilus geigyi
NT1 boophilus kohlsi
NT1 boophilus microplus

BOOPHILUS ANNULATUS
uf *boophilus calcaratus*
BT1 boophilus
BT2 ixodidae
BT3 metastigmata
BT4 acari

boophilus calcaratus
USE **boophilus annulatus**

BOOPHILUS DECOLORATUS
BT1 boophilus
BT2 ixodidae
BT3 metastigmata
BT4 acari

BOOPHILUS GEIGYI
BT1 boophilus
BT2 ixodidae
BT3 metastigmata
BT4 acari

BOOPHILUS KOHLSI
HN from 1989
BT1 boophilus
BT2 ixodidae
BT3 metastigmata
BT4 acari

BOOPHILUS MICROPLUS
BT1 boophilus
BT2 ixodidae
BT3 metastigmata
BT4 acari

boophthora
USE **simulium**

boophthora erythrocephala
USE **simulium erythrocephalum**

BOOPIIDAE
BT1 amblycera
BT2 mallophaga
BT3 phthiraptera
NT1 heterodoxus
NT2 heterodoxus longitarsus
NT2 heterodoxus spiniger

BOOTS
BT1 protective clothing
BT2 clothing

BOPHUTHATSWANA
BT1 south african homelands
BT2 south africa
BT3 southern africa
BT4 africa south of sahara
BT5 africa

BORAGINACEAE
NT1 alkanna
NT2 alkanna tuberculata
NT1 amsinckia
NT2 amsinckia hispida
NT2 amsinckia intermedia
NT1 anchusa
NT2 anchusa arvensis
NT2 anchusa officinalis
NT1 arnebia
NT2 arnebia nobilis
NT2 arnebia pulchra
NT1 borago
NT2 borago officinalis
NT1 brunnera
NT1 buglossoides
NT2 buglossoides arvensis
NT2 buglossoides purpurocaerulea
NT1 cordia
NT2 cordia alliodora
NT2 cordia boissieri
NT2 cordia curassavica
NT2 cordia dichotoma
NT2 cordia glabrata
NT2 cordia goeldiana
NT2 cordia myxa
NT2 cordia rothii
NT2 cordia sinensis
NT2 cordia trichotoma
NT2 cordia verbenacea
NT1 cynoglossum
NT2 cynoglossum creticum
NT2 cynoglossum divaricatum
NT2 cynoglossum glochidiatum
NT2 cynoglossum lanceolatum
NT2 cynoglossum nervosum
NT2 cynoglossum officinale
NT1 echium
NT2 echium italicum
NT2 echium plantagineum
NT2 echium vulgare
NT1 heliotropium
NT2 heliotropium arbainense
NT2 heliotropium arborescens
NT2 heliotropium curassavicum
NT2 heliotropium eichwaldii
NT2 heliotropium europaeum
NT2 heliotropium indicum
NT2 heliotropium maris-mortui
NT2 heliotropium rotundifolium
NT1 lindelofia
NT2 lindelofia angustifolia
NT1 lithodora
NT2 lithodora fruticosa
NT1 lithospermum
NT2 lithospermum erythrorhizon
NT2 lithospermum officinale
NT1 macrotomia
NT2 macrotomia cephalotes
NT2 macrotomia euchroma
NT1 myosotis
NT2 myosotis arvensis
NT2 myosotis sylvatica
NT1 pulmonaria
NT2 pulmonaria mollis
NT2 pulmonaria obscura
NT1 symphytum
NT2 symphytum asperum

BORAGINACEAE *cont.*
NT2 symphytum caucasicum
NT2 symphytum officinale
NT2 symphytum peregrinum
NT2 symphytum tuberosum
NT2 symphytum uplandicum
NT1 trichodesma
NT2 trichodesma africana
NT2 trichodesma incanum

BORAGO
BT1 boraginaceae
NT1 borago officinalis

BORAGO OFFICINALIS
BT1 borago
BT2 boraginaceae
BT1 culinary herbs
BT1 medicinal plants

BORAN
BT1 zebu breeds
BT2 breeds

BORASSUS
BT1 palmae
NT1 borassus aethiopum
NT1 borassus flabellifer

BORASSUS AETHIOPUM
BT1 borassus
BT2 palmae

BORASSUS FLABELLIFER
BT1 borassus
BT2 palmae
BT1 ornamental palms
BT1 sugar crops

BORATES
BT1 inorganic salts
BT2 inorganic compounds
BT2 salts
NT1 borax
NT1 sodium borate
rt boric acid

BORAX
BT1 antiseptics
BT2 antiinfective agents
BT3 drugs
BT1 borates
BT2 inorganic salts
BT3 inorganic compounds
BT3 salts
BT1 inorganic herbicides
BT2 herbicides
BT3 pesticides
BT1 nonclay minerals
BT2 minerals
BT1 wood preservatives
BT2 preservatives
rt sodium borate

BORDEAUX MIXTURE
BT1 copper fungicides
BT2 fungicides
BT3 pesticides

BORDER DISEASE
BT1 sheep diseases
BT2 animal diseases
BT3 diseases
BT1 viral diseases
BT2 infectious diseases
BT3 diseases
rt border disease virus

BORDER DISEASE VIRUS
BT1 pestivirus
BT2 togaviridae
BT3 viruses
rt border disease

BORDER EFFECTS
BT1 field experimentation
BT2 trials
BT3 research
rt experimental design
rt experimental plots

BORDER IRRIGATION
uf *irrigation, border*
BT1 irrigation

BORDER LEICESTER
BT1 sheep breeds
BT2 breeds

borders, forest
USE **forest borders**

BORDETELLA
BT1 gracilicutes
BT2 bacteria
BT3 prokaryotes
NT1 bordetella avium
NT1 bordetella bronchiseptica

BORDETELLA AVIUM
BT1 bordetella
BT2 gracilicutes
BT3 bacteria
BT4 prokaryotes

BORDETELLA BRONCHISEPTICA
BT1 bordetella
BT2 gracilicutes
BT3 bacteria
BT4 prokaryotes

BOREAL FORESTS
uf *taiga*
BT1 forests
BT2 vegetation types
rt bogs
rt coniferous forests
rt taiga soils

BOREAVA
BT1 cruciferae

BOREDOM (AGRICOLA)
rt behavior

BOREOGADUS
BT1 gadidae
BT2 gadiformes
BT3 osteichthyes
BT4 fishes

BORERS
BT1 machinery
NT1 plant hole borers
rt boring

borers (insects)
USE **boring insects**

borers, marine
USE **marine borers**

BORGOU
HN from 1990
BT1 cattle breeds
BT2 breeds

BORIC ACID
BT1 inorganic acids
BT2 acids
BT2 inorganic compounds
BT1 wood preservatives
BT2 preservatives
rt borates
rt boron

BORING
uf *drilling (woodworking)*
BT1 woodworking
rt borers
rt drilling

BORING INSECTS
uf *borers (insects)*
BT1 insect pests
BT2 arthropod pests
BT3 pests
BT2 insects
BT3 arthropods
NT1 stem borers

BORNA DISEASE VIRUS
BT1 arboviruses
BT2 pathogens
BT1 unclassified viruses
BT2 viruses

borneo
USE **kalimantan**

BORNEOL
BT1 monoterpenoids
BT2 terpenoids
BT3 isoprenoids
BT4 lipids

BORNHOLM
uf *denmark (bornholm)*
BT1 denmark
BT2 scandinavia
BT3 europe

BORNYL ACETATE
BT1 acetates (esters)
BT2 acetates
BT2 fatty acid esters
BT3 esters

BOROJOA
BT1 rubiaceae
NT1 borojoa patinoi

BOROJOA PATINOI
BT1 borojoa
BT2 rubiaceae

BOROLLS
BT1 chernozems
BT2 soil types (genetic)
BT1 mollisols
BT2 steppic soils
BT3 soil types (genetic)

BORON
BT1 nonmetallic elements
BT2 elements
BT1 trace elements
BT2 elements
rt boric acid
rt boron fertilizers

BORON FERTILIZERS
BT1 trace element fertilizers
BT2 fertilizers
NT1 colemanite
rt boron

BORONELLA
BT1 rutaceae
NT1 boronella verticillata

BORONELLA VERTICILLATA
BT1 boronella
BT2 rutaceae

BORONIA
BT1 rutaceae
NT1 boronia megastigma
NT1 boronia serrulata

BORONIA MEGASTIGMA
BT1 boronia
BT2 rutaceae
BT1 ornamental woody plants

BORONIA SERRULATA
BT1 boronia
BT2 rutaceae
BT1 ornamental woody plants

BORRELIA
BT1 spirochaetaceae
BT2 spirochaetales
BT3 gracilicutes
BT4 bacteria
BT5 prokaryotes
NT1 borrelia anserina
NT1 borrelia burgdorferi
NT1 borrelia latyschevi
NT1 borrelia persica
NT1 borrelia recurrentis

BORRELIA ANSERINA
uf *spirochaeta gallinarum*
uf *spirochaetosis (avian)*
BT1 borrelia
BT2 spirochaetaceae
BT3 spirochaetales
BT4 gracilicutes
BT5 bacteria
BT6 prokaryotes

BORRELIA BURGDORFERI
BT1 borrelia
BT2 spirochaetaceae

BORRELIA BURGDORFERI *cont.*
BT3 spirochaetales
BT4 gracilicutes
BT5 bacteria
BT6 prokaryotes
rt lyme disease

BORRELIA LATYSCHEVI
BT1 borrelia
BT2 spirochaetaceae
BT3 spirochaetales
BT4 gracilicutes
BT5 bacteria
BT6 prokaryotes

BORRELIA PERSICA
BT1 borrelia
BT2 spirochaetaceae
BT3 spirochaetales
BT4 gracilicutes
BT5 bacteria
BT6 prokaryotes

BORRELIA RECURRENTIS
BT1 borrelia
BT2 spirochaetaceae
BT3 spirochaetales
BT4 gracilicutes
BT5 bacteria
BT6 prokaryotes

BORRERIA
BT1 rubiaceae
NT1 borreria alata
NT1 borreria articularis
NT1 borreria hispida
NT1 borreria latifolia
NT1 borreria ocymoides
NT1 borreria verticillata

BORRERIA ALATA
BT1 borreria
BT2 rubiaceae

BORRERIA ARTICULARIS
BT1 borreria
BT2 rubiaceae

BORRERIA HISPIDA
BT1 borreria
BT2 rubiaceae

BORRERIA LATIFOLIA
BT1 borreria
BT2 rubiaceae

BORRERIA OCYMOIDES
BT1 borreria
BT2 rubiaceae

BORRERIA VERTICILLATA
BT1 borreria
BT2 rubiaceae

BOS
BT1 bovidae
BT2 ruminantia
BT3 artiodactyla
BT4 mammals
BT4 ungulates
NT1 bos primigenius

bos banteng
USE **banteng**

bos frontalis
USE **gayals**

bos gaurus
USE **gaur**

bos grunniens
USE **yaks**

bos indicus
USE **zebu**

bos javanicus
USE **banteng**

bos mutus
USE **yaks**

BOS PRIMIGENIUS
uf *aurochs*
BT1 bos

BOS PRIMIGENIUS *cont.*
BT2 bovidae
BT3 ruminantia
BT4 artiodactyla
BT5 mammals
BT5 ungulates

bos taurus
USE **cattle**

BOSCIA
BT1 capparidaceae
NT1 boscia senegalensis

BOSCIA SENEGALENSIS
BT1 boscia
BT2 capparidaceae
BT1 browse plants

BOSELAPHUS
BT1 bovidae
BT2 ruminantia
BT3 artiodactyla
BT4 mammals
BT4 ungulates
NT1 boselaphus tragocamelus

BOSELAPHUS TRAGOCAMELUS
BT1 boselaphus
BT2 bovidae
BT3 ruminantia
BT4 artiodactyla
BT5 mammals
BT5 ungulates

BOSNIAN MOUNTAIN
BT1 sheep breeds
BT2 breeds

BOSNIAN PONY
BT1 horse breeds
BT2 breeds

BOSTRICHIDAE
BT1 coleoptera
NT1 dinoderus
NT2 dinoderus minutus
NT1 prostephanus
NT2 prostephanus truncatus
NT1 rhyzopertha
NT2 rhyzopertha dominica
NT1 sinoxylon
NT2 sinoxylon anale
NT2 sinoxylon sexdentatum

BOSWELLIA
BT1 burseraceae
NT1 boswellia frereana
NT1 boswellia sacra
NT1 boswellia serrata

boswellia carteri
USE **boswellia sacra**

BOSWELLIA FREREANA
HN from 1990
BT1 boswellia
BT2 burseraceae

BOSWELLIA SACRA
uf *boswellia carteri*
BT1 boswellia
BT2 burseraceae
BT1 incense plants
BT1 medicinal plants

BOSWELLIA SERRATA
BT1 antibacterial plants
BT1 boswellia
BT2 burseraceae
BT1 essential oil plants
BT2 oil plants

botanic gardens
USE **botanical gardens**

BOTANICAL COMPOSITION
uf *pasture composition*
BT1 composition
rt botany
rt ecology
rt flora
rt plant communities

BOTANICAL GARDENS
uf *botanic gardens*
uf *gardens, botanic*
BT1 gardens
rt arboreta
rt botany
rt parks
rt plant collections
rt plant introduction
rt public gardens

BOTANICAL INSECTICIDES
BT1 insecticides
BT2 pesticides
NT1 anabasine
NT1 nicotine
NT1 pyrethrins
NT1 rotenone
NT1 sabadilla

BOTANISTS
BT1 scientists
BT2 occupations
rt botany

BOTANOPHILA
uf *pegohylemyia*
BT1 anthomyiidae
BT2 diptera

BOTANY
BT1 biology
NT1 bryology
NT1 ethnobotany
NT1 mycology
NT2 medical mycology
NT2 veterinary mycology
NT1 palaeobotany
NT1 palynology
NT2 pollen analysis
NT1 weed biology
rt agricultural sciences
rt botanical composition
rt botanical gardens
rt botanists
rt microbiology
rt plant collections
rt plant ecology
rt plant physiology
rt taxonomy

botelua
USE **bouteloua**

BOTHIDAE
BT1 pleuronectiformes
BT2 osteichthyes
BT3 fishes
NT1 paralichthys
NT2 paralichthys olivaceus
NT1 scophthalmus
NT2 scophthalmus rhombus
rt flatfishes

BOTHRIOCEPHALIDAE
BT1 eucestoda
BT2 cestoda
NT1 bothriocephalus
NT2 bothriocephalus acheilognathi

BOTHRIOCEPHALUS
BT1 bothriocephalidae
BT2 eucestoda
BT3 cestoda
NT1 bothriocephalus acheilognathi

BOTHRIOCEPHALUS ACHEILOGNATHI
uf *bothriocephalus gowkongensis*
BT1 bothriocephalus
BT2 bothriocephalidae
BT3 eucestoda
BT4 cestoda

bothriocephalus gowkongensis
USE **bothriocephalus acheilognathi**

BOTHRIOCHLOA
BT1 gramineae
NT1 bothriochloa ambigua

BOTHRIOCHLOA *cont.*
NT1 bothriochloa barbinodis
NT1 bothriochloa bladhii
NT1 bothriochloa caucasica
NT1 bothriochloa insculpta
NT1 bothriochloa intermedia
NT1 bothriochloa ischaemum
NT1 bothriochloa macra
NT1 bothriochloa pertusa
rt andropogon

BOTHRIOCHLOA AMBIGUA
BT1 bothriochloa
BT2 gramineae
BT1 pasture plants

BOTHRIOCHLOA BARBINODIS
uf *andropogon barbinodis*
BT1 bothriochloa
BT2 gramineae
BT1 pasture plants

BOTHRIOCHLOA BLADHII
BT1 bothriochloa
BT2 gramineae
BT1 pasture plants

BOTHRIOCHLOA CAUCASICA
uf *dichanthium caucasicum*
BT1 bothriochloa
BT2 gramineae
BT1 pasture plants

BOTHRIOCHLOA INSCULPTA
uf *dichanthium insculptum*
BT1 bothriochloa
BT2 gramineae
BT1 pasture plants

BOTHRIOCHLOA INTERMEDIA
BT1 bothriochloa
BT2 gramineae
BT1 pasture plants

BOTHRIOCHLOA ISCHAEMUM
uf *andropogon ischaemum*
BT1 bothriochloa
BT2 gramineae
BT1 pasture plants

BOTHRIOCHLOA MACRA
BT1 bothriochloa
BT2 gramineae
BT1 pasture plants

BOTHRIOCHLOA PERTUSA
BT1 bothriochloa
BT2 gramineae
BT1 pasture plants

BOTHYNODERES
BT1 curculionidae
BT2 coleoptera
NT1 bothynoderes foveocollis
NT1 bothynoderes punctiventris

BOTHYNODERES FOVEOCOLLIS
BT1 bothynoderes
BT2 curculionidae
BT3 coleoptera

BOTHYNODERES PUNCTIVENTRIS
BT1 bothynoderes
BT2 curculionidae
BT3 coleoptera

BOTHYNUS
BT1 scarabaeidae
BT2 coleoptera
rt ligyrus

bothynus gibbosus
USE **ligyrus gibbosus**

BOTRYODIPLODIA
BT1 deuteromycotina
NT1 botryodiplodia theobromae
rt diplodia

BOTRYODIPLODIA THEOBROMAE
uf *diplodia corchori*
uf *diplodia gossypina*
uf *diplodia natalensis*
uf *diplodia theae-sinensis*
uf *diplodia theobromae*

BOTRYODIPLODIA THEOBROMAE *cont.*
BT1 botryodiplodia
BT2 deuteromycotina

BOTRYOSPHAERIA
BT1 dothideales
NT1 botryosphaeria dothidea
NT1 botryosphaeria obtusa
NT1 botryosphaeria ribis
NT1 botryosphaeria stevensii
rt coccodiella
rt diplodia
rt physalospora
rt sphaeropsis

botryosphaeria banksiae
USE **coccodiella banksiae**

BOTRYOSPHAERIA DOTHIDEA
BT1 botryosphaeria
BT2 dothideales

BOTRYOSPHAERIA OBTUSA
uf *physalospora obtusa*
uf *sphaeropsis malorum*
BT1 botryosphaeria
BT2 dothideales

BOTRYOSPHAERIA RIBIS
BT1 botryosphaeria
BT2 dothideales

BOTRYOSPHAERIA STEVENSII
uf *diplodia mutila*
BT1 botryosphaeria
BT2 dothideales

botryotinia fuckeliana
USE **sclerotinia fuckeliana**

botryotinia narcissicola
USE **sclerotinia narcissicola**

BOTRYTIS
uf *phymatotrichum*
BT1 deuteromycotina
NT1 botrytis allii
NT1 botrytis cinerea
NT1 botrytis fabae
NT1 botrytis tulipae
rt sclerotinia

botrytis aclada
USE **botrytis allii**

BOTRYTIS ALLII
uf *botrytis aclada*
BT1 botrytis
BT2 deuteromycotina

BOTRYTIS CINEREA
uf *botrytis vulgaris*
BT1 botrytis
BT2 deuteromycotina

botrytis convoluta
USE **sclerotinia convoluta**

BOTRYTIS FABAE
BT1 botrytis
BT2 deuteromycotina

botrytis gladiolorum
USE **sclerotinia draytonii**

botrytis narcissicola
USE **sclerotinia narcissicola**

botrytis parasitica
USE **botrytis tulipae**

botrytis squamosa
USE **sclerotinia squamosa**

BOTRYTIS TULIPAE
uf *botrytis parasitica*
BT1 botrytis
BT2 deuteromycotina

botrytis vulgaris
USE **botrytis cinerea**

BOTSWANA
BT1 sadcc countries
BT1 southern africa

BOTSWANA *cont.*
BT2 africa south of sahara
BT3 africa
rt acp
rt anglophone africa
rt commonwealth of nations
rt developing countries
rt kalahari desert
rt least developed countries

BOTTLE FEEDING (AGRICOLA)
BT1 infant feeding
BT2 feeding

bottle gourds
USE **lagenaria siceraria**

BOTTLES
BT1 containers
rt bottling
rt milk bottles

BOTTLING
BT1 packaging
BT2 handling
rt bottles
rt preservation

BOTTOM UNLOADERS
uf *unloaders, bottom*
BT1 unloaders
rt unloading

BOTTOMLAND FORESTS
BT1 forests
BT2 vegetation types
rt floodplains

BOTTOMLAND SOILS
BT1 soil types (physiographic)
rt bottomlands

BOTTOMLANDS
BT1 land types
rt alluvial land
rt bottomland soils
rt floodplains

BOTULISM
BT1 bacterial diseases
BT2 infectious diseases
BT3 diseases
rt clostridium botulinum
rt food poisoning

BOTYRODIPLODIA THEOBROMAE
uf *diplodia manihotis*

BOUCLE (AGRICOLA)
BT1 fabrics

BOUGAINVILLEA
BT1 nyctaginaceae
rt ornamental woody plants

BOULBENE SOILS
BT1 planosols
BT2 soil types (genetic)

BOULDER CLAY SOILS
BT1 soil types (lithological)

BOULONNAIS
BT1 horse breeds
BT2 breeds
BT1 sheep breeds
BT2 breeds

BOUND WATER
uf *bonded water*
uf *matric bound water*
BT1 soil water categories
BT2 soil water
BT3 water

BOUNDARIES
rt ecotones
rt forest borders
rt forest inventories
rt marking
rt soil boundaries

BOURGELATIA
BT1 chabertiidae
BT2 nematoda

bourgogne
USE **burgundy**

bourkina fasso
USE **burkina faso**

BOURLETIELLA
BT1 sminthuridae
BT2 collembola
NT1 bourletiella hortensis

BOURLETIELLA HORTENSIS
BT1 bourletiella
BT2 sminthuridae
BT3 collembola

BOURRERIA
BT1 ehretiaceae
NT1 bourreria aculiata

BOURRERIA ACULIATA
BT1 bourreria
BT2 ehretiaceae

BOUTELOUA
uf *botelua*
BT1 gramineae
NT1 bouteloua chasei
NT1 bouteloua curtipendula
NT1 bouteloua eriopoda
NT1 bouteloua gracilis
NT1 bouteloua hirsuta
NT1 bouteloua rothrockii

BOUTELOUA CHASEI
BT1 bouteloua
BT2 gramineae
BT1 pasture plants

BOUTELOUA CURTIPENDULA
uf *sideoats grama*
BT1 bouteloua
BT2 gramineae
BT1 pasture plants

BOUTELOUA ERIOPODA
BT1 bouteloua
BT2 gramineae
BT1 pasture plants

BOUTELOUA GRACILIS
uf *blue grama*
BT1 bouteloua
BT2 gramineae
BT1 pasture plants

BOUTELOUA HIRSUTA
BT1 bouteloua
BT2 gramineae
BT1 pasture plants

BOUTELOUA ROTHROCKII
BT1 bouteloua
BT2 gramineae

BOUVARDIA
BT1 rubiaceae
rt ornamental woody plants

BOVICOLA
BT1 trichodectidae
BT2 ischnocera
BT3 mallophaga
BT4 phthiraptera
NT1 bovicola bovis
NT1 bovicola caprae
NT1 bovicola crassipes
NT1 bovicola limbata
NT1 bovicola ovis
rt damalinia
rt werneckiella

BOVICOLA BOVIS
uf *damalinia bovis*
BT1 bovicola
BT2 trichodectidae
BT3 ischnocera
BT4 mallophaga
BT5 phthiraptera

BOVICOLA CAPRAE
uf *damalinia caprae*
BT1 bovicola
BT2 trichodectidae
BT3 ischnocera

BOVICOLA CAPRAE *cont.*
BT4 mallophaga
BT5 phthiraptera

BOVICOLA CRASSIPES
uf *damalinia crassipes*
BT1 bovicola
BT2 trichodectidae
BT3 ischnocera
BT4 mallophaga
BT5 phthiraptera

bovicola equi
USE **werneckiella equi**

BOVICOLA LIMBATA
uf *damalinia limbata*
BT1 bovicola
BT2 trichodectidae
BT3 ischnocera
BT4 mallophaga
BT5 phthiraptera

BOVICOLA OVIS
uf *damalinia ovis*
BT1 bovicola
BT2 trichodectidae
BT3 ischnocera
BT4 mallophaga
BT5 phthiraptera

BOVICORNIA
BT1 sminthuridae
BT2 collembola
NT1 bovicornia bidoma

BOVICORNIA BIDOMA
BT1 bovicornia
BT2 sminthuridae
BT3 collembola

BOVIDAE
uf *bovines*
BT1 ruminantia
BT2 artiodactyla
BT3 mammals
BT3 ungulates
NT1 aepyceros
NT2 aepyceros melampus
NT1 alcelaphus
NT2 alcelaphus buselaphus
NT1 ammotragus
NT2 ammotragus lervia
NT1 antidorcas
NT2 antidorcas marsupialis
NT1 antilope
NT2 antilope cervicapra
NT1 bison (genus)
NT2 bison bonasus
NT1 bos
NT2 bos primigenius
NT1 boselaphus
NT2 boselaphus tragocamelus
NT1 bubalus
NT1 capra
NT2 capra ibex
NT2 capra pyrenaica
NT1 capricornis
NT2 capricornis crispus
NT1 connochaetes
NT2 connochaetes gnou
NT2 connochaetes taurinus
NT1 damaliscus
NT2 damaliscus dorcas
NT1 gazella
NT2 gazella gazella
NT2 gazella granti
NT2 gazella thomsonii
NT1 hippotragus
NT2 hippotragus equinus
NT2 hippotragus niger
NT1 kobus
NT2 kobus ellipsiprymnus
NT2 kobus kob
NT2 kobus leche
NT1 oreamnos
NT2 oreamnos americanus
NT1 oryx
NT2 oryx gazella
NT1 ourebia
NT2 ourebia ourebi
NT1 ovibos
NT2 ovibos moschatus

BOVIDAE *cont.*
NT1 ovis
NT2 ovis ammon
NT2 ovis canadensis
NT2 ovis dalli
NT1 pelea (mammals)
NT2 pelea capreolus
NT1 redunca
NT2 redunca arundinum
NT2 redunca fulvorufula
NT2 redunca redunca
NT1 rupicapra
NT1 saiga
NT2 saiga tatarica
NT1 sylvicapra
NT2 sylvicapra grimmia
NT1 synceros
NT2 synceros caffer
NT1 tragelaphus
NT2 tragelaphus oryx
NT2 tragelaphus scriptus
NT2 tragelaphus strepsiceros
rt banteng
rt bison
rt buffaloes
rt cattle
rt chamois
rt gaur
rt gayals
rt goats
rt mouflon
rt sheep
rt yaks
rt zebu

BOVINE ADENOVIRUS
BT1 mastadenovirus
BT2 adenoviridae
BT3 viruses

BOVINE DIARRHEA VIRUS
BF bovine diarrhoea virus
rt diarrhea

BOVINE DIARRHOEA VIRUS
(not to be confused with calf diarrhoea virus)
AF bovine diarrhea virus
uf *mucosal disease virus*
BT1 pestivirus
BT2 togaviridae
BT3 viruses
rt diarrhoea

BOVINE ENTEROVIRUS
BT1 enterovirus
BT2 picornaviridae
BT3 viruses

BOVINE EPHEMERAL FEVER VIRUS
uf *ephemeral fever virus*
BT1 vesiculovirus
BT2 rhabdoviridae
BT3 viruses

BOVINE HERPESVIRUS
BT1 herpesviridae
BT2 viruses
NT1 ibr ipv virus
NT1 malignant catarrhal fever virus
NT1 mammillitis herpesvirus

BOVINE LEUKOSIS
BT1 leukosis
BT2 leukocyte disorders
BT3 blood disorders
BT4 animal disorders
BT5 disorders
rt bovine oncovirus

bovine leukosis virus
USE **bovine oncovirus**

BOVINE MASTITIS
BT1 mastitis
BT2 mammary gland diseases
BT3 organic diseases
BT4 diseases
rt udders

BOVINE ONCOVIRUS
uf *bovine leukosis virus*

BOVINE ONCOVIRUS *cont.*
BT1 mammalian oncovirus
BT2 oncovirus type c
BT3 oncovirinae
BT4 retroviridae
BT5 viruses
rt bovine leukosis

BOVINE ORTHOPOXVIRUS
uf *bovine poxvirus*
BT1 orthopoxvirus
BT2 chordopoxvirinae
BT3 poxviridae
BT4 viruses

BOVINE PAPILLOMAVIRUS
BT1 papillomavirus
BT2 papovaviridae
BT3 viruses

BOVINE PAPULAR STOMATITIS VIRUS
BT1 parapoxvirus
BT2 chordopoxvirinae
BT3 poxviridae
BT4 viruses
rt stomatitis

BOVINE PARAINFLUENZA VIRUS
uf *bovine paramyxovirus*
BT1 paramyxovirus
BT2 paramyxoviridae
BT3 viruses

bovine paramyxovirus
USE **bovine parainfluenza virus**

BOVINE PARVOVIRUS
BT1 parvovirus
BT2 parvoviridae
BT3 viruses

bovine poxvirus
USE **bovine orthopoxvirus**

BOVINE RESPIRATORY SYNCYTIAL VIRUS
BT1 pneumovirus
BT2 paramyxoviridae
BT3 viruses

bovine rhinotracheitis virus
USE **ibr ipv virus**

BOVINE RHINOVIRUS
BT1 rhinovirus
BT2 picornaviridae
BT3 viruses

BOVINE SERUM ALBUMIN
HN from 1989
BT1 serum albumin
BT2 albumins
BT3 proteins
BT4 peptides
BT2 blood proteins
BT3 animal proteins
BT4 proteins
BT5 peptides

BOVINE SPONGIFORM ENCEPHALOPATHY
HN from 1989
uf *bse*
BT1 cattle diseases
BT2 animal diseases
BT3 diseases
BT1 spongiform encephalopathy
BT2 nervous system diseases
BT3 organic diseases
BT4 diseases

BOVINE SYNCYTIAL VIRUS
BT1 spumavirinae
BT2 retroviridae
BT3 viruses

bovines
USE **bovidae**

BOWDICHIA
BT1 leguminosae
NT1 bowdichia virgilioides

BOWDICHIA VIRGILIOIDES
BT1 bowdichia
BT2 leguminosae
BT1 forest trees

BOWKERIA
BT1 scrophulariaceae
NT1 bowkeria citrina

BOWKERIA CITRINA
BT1 bowkeria
BT2 scrophulariaceae

BOWL DRINKERS
uf *drinkers, bowl*
BT1 drinkers
rt drinking
rt water troughs

BOWLING
BT1 ball games
BT2 games
BT2 sport

box
USE **buxus sempervirens**

BOXES
BT1 containers
rt bins
rt bunkers
rt crates
rt cribs
rt cubicles
rt pallet boxes
rt seed boxes

BOXING
BT1 combative sports
BT2 sport

BOYS
BT1 children
BT2 people
rt men
rt sons

BOYSENBERRIES
BT1 temperate small fruits
BT2 small fruits
BT2 temperate fruits
BT3 fruit crops
rt rubus

BOZAKH
BT1 sheep breeds
BT2 breeds

BPE
HN from 1990
(boiling point elevation)
uf *boiling point elevation*
rt boiling point
rt sugar boiling

bpmc
USE **fenobucarb**

BRA CHEESE
HN from 1989
BT1 cheeses
BT2 milk products
BT3 products

BRABANT
uf *belgium (brabant)*
BT1 belgium
BT2 western europe
BT3 europe

BRACHIAL PLEXUS
BT1 plexus
BT2 nervous system
BT3 body parts

BRACHIARIA
BT1 gramineae
NT1 brachiaria brizantha
NT1 brachiaria decumbens
NT1 brachiaria deflexa
NT1 brachiaria dictyoneura
NT1 brachiaria distachya
NT1 brachiaria eruciformis
NT1 brachiaria hagerupii
NT1 brachiaria humidicola

BRACHIARIA *cont.*
NT1 brachiaria jubata
NT1 brachiaria miliiformis
NT1 brachiaria mutica
NT1 brachiaria plantaginea
NT1 brachiaria platyphylla
NT1 brachiaria pubigera
NT1 brachiaria radicans
NT1 brachiaria ramosa
NT1 brachiaria ruziziensis
NT1 brachiaria subquadriparia
rt panicum

BRACHIARIA BRIZANTHA
BT1 brachiaria
BT2 gramineae
BT1 pasture plants

BRACHIARIA DECUMBENS
BT1 brachiaria
BT2 gramineae
BT1 pasture plants

BRACHIARIA DEFLEXA
BT1 brachiaria
BT2 gramineae
BT1 pasture plants

BRACHIARIA DICTYONEURA
BT1 brachiaria
BT2 gramineae
BT1 pasture plants

BRACHIARIA DISTACHYA
BT1 brachiaria
BT2 gramineae
BT1 pasture plants

BRACHIARIA ERUCIFORMIS
BT1 brachiaria
BT2 gramineae
BT1 pasture plants

BRACHIARIA HAGERUPII
BT1 brachiaria
BT2 gramineae
BT1 pasture plants

BRACHIARIA HUMIDICOLA
BT1 brachiaria
BT2 gramineae
BT1 pasture plants

BRACHIARIA JUBATA
BT1 brachiaria
BT2 gramineae
BT1 pasture plants

BRACHIARIA MILIIFORMIS
BT1 brachiaria
BT2 gramineae
BT1 pasture plants

BRACHIARIA MUTICA
uf *brachiaria purpurascens*
uf *panicum purpurascens*
uf *para grass*
BT1 brachiaria
BT2 gramineae
BT1 pasture plants

BRACHIARIA PLANTAGINEA
BT1 brachiaria
BT2 gramineae
BT1 pasture plants
BT1 weeds

BRACHIARIA PLATYPHYLLA
BT1 brachiaria
BT2 gramineae
BT1 pasture plants
BT1 weeds

BRACHIARIA PUBIGERA
BT1 brachiaria
BT2 gramineae
BT1 pasture plants

brachiaria purpurascens
USE **brachiaria mutica**

BRACHIARIA RADICANS
BT1 brachiaria
BT2 gramineae
BT1 pasture plants

BRACHIARIA RAMOSA
BT1 brachiaria
BT2 gramineae
BT1 millets
BT2 cereals
BT3 grain crops
BT1 pasture plants

BRACHIARIA RUZIZIENSIS
BT1 brachiaria
BT2 gramineae
BT1 pasture plants

BRACHIARIA SUBQUADRIPARIA
BT1 brachiaria
BT2 gramineae

BRACHIOPODA
rt invertebrates
rt shellfish

brachistes
USE **eubazus**

brachistes atricornis
USE **eubazus atricornis**

BRACHMIA
BT1 gelechiidae
BT2 lepidoptera
NT1 brachmia triannulella

BRACHMIA TRIANNULELLA
BT1 brachmia
BT2 gelechiidae
BT3 lepidoptera

BRACHYCAUDUS
uf *appelia*
BT1 aphididae
BT2 aphidoidea
BT3 sternorrhyncha
BT4 homoptera
NT1 brachycaudus cardui
NT1 brachycaudus helichrysi
NT1 brachycaudus persicae
NT1 brachycaudus schwartzi
rt aphis

BRACHYCAUDUS CARDUI
BT1 brachycaudus
BT2 aphididae
BT3 aphidoidea
BT4 sternorrhyncha
BT5 homoptera

BRACHYCAUDUS HELICHRYSI
uf *aphis helichrysi*
BT1 brachycaudus
BT2 aphididae
BT3 aphidoidea
BT4 sternorrhyncha
BT5 homoptera

brachycaudus maidiradicis
USE **aphis middletonii**

BRACHYCAUDUS PERSICAE
BT1 brachycaudus
BT2 aphididae
BT3 aphidoidea
BT4 sternorrhyncha
BT5 homoptera

BRACHYCAUDUS SCHWARTZI
uf *appelia schwartzi*
BT1 brachycaudus
BT2 aphididae
BT3 aphidoidea
BT4 sternorrhyncha
BT5 homoptera

BRACHYCHITON
BT1 sterculiaceae
NT1 brachychiton populneus

BRACHYCHITON POPULNEUS
BT1 brachychiton
BT2 sterculiaceae

BRACHYCOLUS
BT1 aphididae
BT2 aphidoidea
BT3 sternorrhyncha
BT4 homoptera

BRACHYCOLUS *cont.*
rt brachycorynella
rt semiaphis

brachycolus asparagi
USE **brachycorynella asparagi**

brachycolus heraclei
USE **semiaphis heraclei**

BRACHYCORYNELLA
BT1 aphididae
BT2 aphidoidea
BT3 sternorrhyncha
BT4 homoptera
NT1 brachycorynella asparagi
rt brachycolus

BRACHYCORYNELLA ASPARAGI
uf *brachycolus asparagi*
BT1 brachycorynella
BT2 aphididae
BT3 aphidoidea
BT4 sternorrhyncha
BT5 homoptera

BRACHYELYTRUM
BT1 gramineae
NT1 brachyelytrum erectum

BRACHYELYTRUM ERECTUM
BT1 brachyelytrum
BT2 gramineae

BRACHYGNATHIA
BT1 congenital abnormalities
BT2 abnormalities

BRACHYLAEMA
BT1 brachylaemidae
BT2 digenea
BT3 trematoda
NT1 brachylaema migrans

BRACHYLAEMA MIGRANS
BT1 brachylaema
BT2 brachylaemidae
BT3 digenea
BT4 trematoda

BRACHYLAEMIDAE
BT1 digenea
BT2 trematoda
NT1 brachylaema
NT2 brachylaema migrans
NT1 leucochloridiomorpha
NT2 leucochloridiomorpha constantiae

BRACHYLAENA
BT1 compositae
NT1 brachylaena hutchinsii

BRACHYLAENA HUTCHINSII
BT1 brachylaena
BT2 compositae

BRACHYLECITHUM
BT1 dicrocoeliidae
BT2 digenea
BT3 trematoda

BRACHYMERIA
BT1 chalcididae
BT2 hymenoptera
NT1 brachymeria intermedia
NT1 brachymeria lasus
NT1 brachymeria podagrica
rt chalcis

BRACHYMERIA INTERMEDIA
BT1 brachymeria
BT2 chalcididae
BT3 hymenoptera

BRACHYMERIA LASUS
BT1 brachymeria
BT2 chalcididae
BT3 hymenoptera

BRACHYMERIA PODAGRICA
uf *chalcis podagrica*
BT1 brachymeria
BT2 chalcididae
BT3 hymenoptera

BRACHYPODIUM
BT1 gramineae
NT1 brachypodium phoenicoides
NT1 brachypodium pinnatum
NT1 brachypodium ramosum
NT1 brachypodium sylvaticum

BRACHYPODIUM PHOENICOIDES
BT1 brachypodium
BT2 gramineae
BT1 pasture plants

BRACHYPODIUM PINNATUM
BT1 brachypodium
BT2 gramineae
BT1 pasture plants

BRACHYPODIUM RAMOSUM
BT1 brachypodium
BT2 gramineae
BT1 pasture plants

BRACHYPODIUM SYLVATICUM
BT1 brachypodium
BT2 gramineae
BT1 pasture plants

brachyrhinus
USE **otiorhynchus**

brachyrhinus ligustici
USE **otiorhynchus ligustici**

BRACHYSTEGIA
BT1 leguminosae
NT1 brachystegia boehmii
NT1 brachystegia spiciformis

BRACHYSTEGIA BOEHMII
BT1 brachystegia
BT2 leguminosae

BRACHYSTEGIA SPICIFORMIS
BT1 brachystegia
BT2 leguminosae

BRACHYSTOMELLA
BT1 hypogastruridae
BT2 collembola

bracken
USE **pteridium aquilinum**

BRACKISH WATER
uf *water, brackish*
BT1 water
rt irrigation water
rt mangrove swamps
rt saline water

BRACKISH WATER FISHES
uf *saltwater fishes*
BT1 aquatic animals
BT2 animals
BT2 aquatic organisms
rt fishes

BRACON
uf *habrobracon*
uf *microbracon*
BT1 braconidae
BT2 hymenoptera
NT1 bracon brevicornis
NT1 bracon gelechiae
NT1 bracon hebetor
NT1 bracon kirkpatricki
NT1 bracon mellitor

BRACON BREVICORNIS
uf *microbracon brevicornis*
BT1 bracon
BT2 braconidae
BT3 hymenoptera

BRACON GELECHIAE
BT1 bracon
BT2 braconidae
BT3 hymenoptera

BRACON HEBETOR
uf *habrobracon hebetor*
uf *microbracon hebetor*
BT1 bracon
BT2 braconidae
BT3 hymenoptera

BRACON KIRKPATRICKI
uf *microbracon kirkpatricki*
BT1 bracon
BT2 braconidae
BT3 hymenoptera

BRACON MELLITOR
BT1 bracon
BT2 braconidae
BT3 hymenoptera

BRACONIDAE
uf *aphidiidae*
BT1 hymenoptera
NT1 agathis (hymenoptera)
NT2 agathis cincta
NT2 agathis gibbosa
NT2 agathis pumila
NT1 aleiodes
NT1 allorhogas
NT1 apanteles
NT2 apanteles diatraeae
NT2 apanteles fumiferanae
NT2 apanteles subandinus
NT1 aphaereta
NT2 aphaereta minuta
NT2 aphaereta pallipes
NT1 aphidius
NT2 aphidius colemani
NT2 aphidius ervi
NT2 aphidius gifuensis
NT2 aphidius matricariae
NT2 aphidius nigripes
NT2 aphidius picipes
NT2 aphidius rhopalosiphi
NT2 aphidius rosae
NT2 aphidius smithi
NT2 aphidius uzbekistanicus
NT1 ascogaster
NT2 ascogaster quadridentata
NT1 biosteres
NT2 biosteres arisanus
NT2 biosteres fullawayi
NT2 biosteres longicaudatus
NT1 bracon
NT2 bracon brevicornis
NT2 bracon gelechiae
NT2 bracon hebetor
NT2 bracon kirkpatricki
NT2 bracon mellitor
NT1 cardiochiles
NT2 cardiochiles nigriceps
NT1 chelonus
NT2 chelonus blackburni
NT2 chelonus insularis
NT1 coeloides
NT2 coeloides vancouverensis
NT1 cotesia
NT2 cotesia flavipes
NT2 cotesia glomerata
NT2 cotesia hyphantriae
NT2 cotesia kurdjumovi
NT2 cotesia marginiventris
NT2 cotesia melanoscelus
NT2 cotesia plutellae
NT2 cotesia rubecula
NT2 cotesia ruficrus
NT2 cotesia telengai
NT2 cotesia tibialis
NT1 dacnusa
NT2 dacnusa sibirica
NT1 dendrosoter
NT2 dendrosoter protuberans
NT1 diaeretiella
NT2 diaeretiella rapae
NT1 diaeretus
NT1 dinocampus
NT2 dinocampus coccinellae
NT1 dolichogenidea
NT2 dolichogenidea albipennis
NT2 dolichogenidea turionellae
NT1 ephedrus
NT2 ephedrus cerasicola
NT2 ephedrus plagiator
NT1 eubazus
NT2 eubazus atricornis
NT1 glabromicroplitis
NT2 glabromicroplitis croceipes
NT1 glyptapanteles
NT2 glyptapanteles africanus
NT2 glyptapanteles militaris
NT2 glyptapanteles pallipes

BRACONIDAE *cont.*
NT2 glyptapanteles porthetriae
NT1 illidops
NT2 illidops scutellaris
NT1 iphiaulax
NT1 leiophron
NT2 leiophron uniformis
NT1 lysiphlebia
NT2 lysiphlebia japonica
NT2 lysiphlebia mirzai
NT1 lysiphlebus
NT2 lysiphlebus confusus
NT2 lysiphlebus fabarum
NT2 lysiphlebus testaceipes
NT1 macrocentrus
NT2 macrocentrus ancylivorus
NT2 macrocentrus collaris
NT2 macrocentrus grandii
NT1 meteorus
NT2 meteorus autographae
NT2 meteorus rubens
NT2 meteorus versicolor
NT1 microctonus
NT2 microctonus aethiopoides
NT1 microdus
NT2 microdus rufipes
NT1 microgaster
NT2 microgaster demolitor
NT2 microgaster mediator
NT2 microgaster rufiventris
NT1 monoctonus
NT2 monoctonus nervosus
NT1 nealiolus
NT2 nealiolus curculionis
NT1 opius
NT2 opius concolor
NT2 opius pallipes
NT1 orgilus
NT2 orgilus lepidus
NT2 orgilus obscurator
NT1 perilitus
NT1 peristenus
NT2 peristenus pallipes
NT2 peristenus stygicus
NT1 phanerotoma
NT2 phanerotoma flavitestacea
NT1 pholetesor
NT2 pholetesor bicolor
NT2 pholetesor circumscriptus
NT2 pholetesor ornigis
NT1 praon
NT2 praon dorsale
NT2 praon volucre
NT1 rogas
NT2 rogas aligharensi
NT2 rogas dimidiatus
NT1 stenobracon
NT2 stenobracon nicevillei
NT1 trioxys
NT2 trioxys complanatus
NT2 trioxys indicus
NT2 trioxys pallidus
NT1 xanthomicrogaster
NT2 xanthomicrogaster dignus
NT1 zele

BRACTS
BT1 plant
rt flowers
rt glumes
rt leaves

BRADYBAENA
BT1 eulotidae
BT2 gastropoda
BT3 mollusca
NT1 bradybaena circulus
NT1 bradybaena similaris

BRADYBAENA CIRCULUS
BT1 bradybaena
BT2 eulotidae
BT3 gastropoda
BT4 mollusca

BRADYBAENA SIMILARIS
BT1 bradybaena
BT2 eulotidae
BT3 gastropoda
BT4 mollusca

BRADYKININ
BT1 kinins
BT2 hormones
BT2 peptides
BT1 neuropeptides
BT2 peptides
BT1 oligopeptides
BT2 peptides
BT1 vasodilator agents
BT2 cardiovascular agents
BT3 drugs

BRADYPODIDAE
BT1 edentata
BT2 mammals
NT1 bradypus
NT2 bradypus variegatus

BRADYPUS
BT1 bradypodidae
BT2 edentata
BT3 mammals
NT1 bradypus variegatus

BRADYPUS VARIEGATUS
BT1 bradypus
BT2 bradypodidae
BT3 edentata
BT4 mammals

BRADYRHIZOBIUM
BT1 rhizobiaceae
BT2 gracilicutes
BT3 bacteria
BT4 prokaryotes
NT1 bradyrhizobium japonicum
rt rhizobium
rt root nodules

BRADYRHIZOBIUM JAPONICUM
uf *rhizobium japonicum*
BT1 bradyrhizobium
BT2 rhizobiaceae
BT3 gracilicutes
BT4 bacteria
BT5 prokaryotes

BRAGANCA GALICIAN
HN from 1990
BT1 sheep breeds
BT2 breeds

BRAHMAN
BT1 zebu breeds
BT2 breeds

BRAIN
uf *cerebrum*
BT1 central nervous system
BT2 nervous system
BT3 body parts
NT1 cerebellum
NT2 amygdala
NT1 cerebral cortex
NT1 cerebral ventricles
NT1 hippocampus
NT1 hypothalamus
NT2 preoptic area
NT1 medulla oblongata
NT1 thalamus
rt brain as food
rt brain disorders
rt brain stem
rt electroencephalograms
rt electroencephalography
rt encephalograms

BRAIN AS FOOD
BT1 offal
BT2 meat byproducts
BT3 agricultural byproducts
BT4 byproducts
rt brain
rt meat

brain cerebellum
USE **cerebellum**

BRAIN DISORDERS
BT1 nervous system diseases
BT2 organic diseases
BT3 diseases
NT1 cerebral palsy
NT1 cerebrovascular disorders

BRAIN DISORDERS *cont.*
NT2 apoplexy
NT2 migraine
NT2 stroke
NT1 encephalitis
NT2 allergic encephalomyelitis
NT2 japanese encephalitis
NT1 encephalomalacia
NT1 encephalopathy
NT2 wernicke's disease
NT2 wernicke-korsakoff syndrome
NT1 epilepsy
NT1 epileptiform attacks
NT1 homocystinuria
NT1 hydrocephalus
NT1 menkes' disease
NT1 myeloencephalopathy
rt avian encephalomyelitis virus
rt brain
rt electroencephalograms
rt electroencephalography
rt paralysis

brain, hippocampus
USE **hippocampus**

brain, hypothalamus
USE **hypothalamus**

BRAIN STEM
BT1 central nervous system
BT2 nervous system
BT3 body parts
rt brain

brain, thalamus
USE **thalamus**

brainstorming
USE **problem analysis**

BRAISING (AGRICOLA)
BT1 cooking methods (agricola)
BT2 methodology

BRAKES
BT1 components
NT1 air brakes
NT1 hydraulic brakes
rt braking
rt vehicles

brakes, air
USE **air brakes**

brakes, hydraulic
USE **hydraulic brakes**

brakes, pneumatic
USE **air brakes**

BRAKING
rt brakes
rt stopping

BRAMA
BT1 bramidae
BT2 perciformes
BT3 osteichthyes
BT4 fishes
NT1 brama brama

BRAMA BRAMA
uf *brama rayi*
BT1 brama
BT2 bramidae
BT3 perciformes
BT4 osteichthyes
BT5 fishes

brama rayi
USE **brama brama**

brambles
USE **blackberries**

BRAMIDAE
BT1 perciformes
BT2 osteichthyes
BT3 fishes
NT1 brama
NT2 brama brama
NT1 taractes

BRAN
BT1 cereal byproducts
BT2 agricultural byproducts
BT3 byproducts
NT1 maize bran
NT1 oat bran (agricola)
NT1 rice bran
NT1 wheat bran
rt aleurone layer
rt fibre
rt pineapple bran
rt roughage
rt testas

BRANCHED-CHAIN-AMINO-ACID AMINOTRANSFERASE
(ec 2.6.1.42)
BT1 aminotransferases
BT2 transferases
BT3 enzymes

BRANCHED CHAIN AMINO ACIDS
uf amino acids, branched chain
BT1 amino acids
BT2 carboxylic acids
BT3 organic acids
BT4 acids
BT2 organic nitrogen compounds
NT1 aminoisobutyric acid
NT1 valine

BRANCHED CHAIN FATTY ACIDS
BT1 fatty acids
BT2 carboxylic acids
BT3 organic acids
BT4 acids
BT2 lipids
NT1 phytanic acid

BRANCHED CHAIN KETO ACIDS
uf keto acids, branched chain
BT1 keto acids
BT2 carboxylic acids
BT3 organic acids
BT4 acids
BT2 ketones

branched chain ketoaciduria
USE **maple syrup urine disease**

BRANCHES
BT1 canopy
NT1 smallwood
rt branching
rt branchwood
rt dead wood
rt knots
rt pruning

BRANCHING
rt apical dominance
rt apical meristems
rt branches
rt buds
rt determinate and indeterminate habit
rt differentiation
rt fasciation
rt growth
rt pruning

BRANCHIOMYCES
BT1 saprolegniales
NT1 branchiomyces sanguinis

BRANCHIOMYCES SANGUINIS
BT1 branchiomyces
BT2 saprolegniales

BRANCHIOPODA
BT1 crustacea
BT2 arthropods
NT1 anostraca
NT2 artemia
NT3 artemia salina
NT1 cladocera
NT2 daphnia
NT3 daphnia magna
NT3 daphnia pulex
rt aquatic animals

branchiura
USE **branchiura (annelida)**
OR **branchiura (arthropods)**

BRANCHIURA (ANNELIDA)
uf branchiura
BT1 tubificidae
BT2 oligochaeta
BT3 annelida
NT1 branchiura sowerbyi

BRANCHIURA (ARTHROPODS)
uf branchiura
BT1 crustacea
BT2 arthropods
NT1 argulus

BRANCHIURA SOWERBYI
BT1 branchiura (annelida)
BT2 tubificidae
BT3 oligochaeta
BT4 annelida

BRANCHWOOD
BT1 wood
rt branches
rt pruning
rt pulping materials
rt smallwood

BRAND NAME PRODUCTS (AGRICOLA)
BT1 products
rt labeling
rt proprietary names (agricola)

BRANDING
BT1 identification

brands
USE **labelling**
OR **trade marks**

BRANDY
BT1 distilled spirits
BT2 alcoholic beverages
BT3 beverages

BRANGUS
HN from 1990
BT1 cattle breeds
BT2 breeds

BRANHAMELLA
BT1 neisseriaceae
BT2 gracilicutes
BT3 bacteria
BT4 prokaryotes

BRASENIA
BT1 cabombaceae
NT1 brasenia schreberi

BRASENIA SCHREBERI
BT1 brasenia
BT2 cabombaceae
BT1 leafy vegetables
BT2 vegetables

brashing
USE **pruning**

BRASHNESS
BT1 wood defects
BT2 defects
rt bending

BRASILIOPUNTIA
BT1 cactaceae
NT1 brasiliopuntia brasiliensis

BRASILIOPUNTIA BRASILIENSIS
uf opuntia brasiliensis
BT1 brasiliopuntia
BT2 cactaceae
BT1 ornamental succulent plants
BT2 succulent plants

BRASS
BT1 non-ferrous alloys
BT2 alloys
BT3 metals
BT3 mixtures
rt copper
rt tin

BRASS *cont.*
rt zinc

brassaia
USE **schefflera**

BRASSAVOLA
BT1 orchidaceae
NT1 brassavola nodosa

BRASSAVOLA NODOSA
BT1 brassavola
BT2 orchidaceae
BT1 ornamental orchids

BRASSICA
BT1 cruciferae
NT1 brassica alboglabra
NT1 brassica barrelieri
NT1 brassica campestris
NT1 brassica campestris var. oleifera
NT1 brassica campestris var. rapa
NT1 brassica campestris var. toria
NT1 brassica carinata
NT1 brassica caulorapa
NT1 brassica cernua
NT1 brassica cheiranthus
NT1 brassica chinensis
NT1 brassica hirta
NT1 brassica japonica
NT1 brassica juncea
NT1 brassica kaber
NT1 brassica kaber var. pinnatifida
NT1 brassica napus
NT1 brassica napus var. dichotoma
NT1 brassica napus var. glauca
NT1 brassica napus var. napobrassica
NT1 brassica napus var. oleifera
NT1 brassica nigra
NT1 brassica oleracea
NT2 brassica oleracea var. botrytis
NT2 brassica oleracea var. capitata
NT2 brassica oleracea var. gemmifera
NT2 brassica oleracea var. gongylodes
NT2 brassica oleracea var. italica
NT2 brassica oleracea var. viridis
NT1 brassica pekinensis
NT1 brassica perviridis
NT1 raphanobrassica

brassica alba
USE **sinapis alba**

BRASSICA ALBOGLABRA
uf chinese kale
BT1 brassica
BT2 cruciferae
BT1 leafy vegetables
BT2 vegetables

BRASSICA BARRELIERI
BT1 brassica
BT2 cruciferae

BRASSICA CAMPESTRIS
uf brassica rapa
BT1 brassica
BT2 cruciferae
BT1 nematicidal plants
BT2 pesticidal plants

BRASSICA CAMPESTRIS VAR. OLEIFERA
BT1 brassica
BT2 cruciferae
rt rape
rt turnip rape

BRASSICA CAMPESTRIS VAR. RAPA
BT1 brassica
BT2 cruciferae

BRASSICA CAMPESTRIS VAR. RAPA *cont.*
BT1 fodder plants
rt turnip crinkle carmovirus
rt turnip mosaic potyvirus
rt turnip rosette sobemovirus
rt turnip yellow mosaic tymovirus
rt turnips

BRASSICA CAMPESTRIS VAR. TORIA
uf brassica napus var. toria
BT1 brassica
BT2 cruciferae
BT1 oilseed plants
BT2 fatty oil plants
BT3 oil plants
rt toria

BRASSICA CARINATA
BT1 brassica
BT2 cruciferae
BT1 leafy vegetables
BT2 vegetables
BT1 oilseed plants
BT2 fatty oil plants
BT3 oil plants

BRASSICA CAULORAPA
BT1 brassica
BT2 cruciferae

BRASSICA CERNUA
BT1 brassica
BT2 cruciferae

BRASSICA CHEIRANTHUS
BT1 brassica
BT2 cruciferae

BRASSICA CHINENSIS
BT1 brassica
BT2 cruciferae
BT1 leafy vegetables
BT2 vegetables

BRASSICA HIRTA
BT1 brassica
BT2 cruciferae

brassica integrifolia
USE **brassica juncea**

BRASSICA JAPONICA
BT1 brassica
BT2 cruciferae
BT1 leafy vegetables
BT2 vegetables

BRASSICA JUNCEA
uf brassica integrifolia
BT1 brassica
BT2 cruciferae
BT1 leafy vegetables
BT2 vegetables
BT1 oilseed plants
BT2 fatty oil plants
BT3 oil plants
rt indian mustard

BRASSICA KABER
BT1 brassica
BT2 cruciferae
rt sinapis arvensis

BRASSICA KABER VAR. PINNATIFIDA
BT1 brassica
BT2 cruciferae

BRASSICA NAPUS
BT1 brassica
BT2 cruciferae
rt sarson

BRASSICA NAPUS VAR. DICHOTOMA
uf brown sarson
BT1 brassica
BT2 cruciferae
BT1 fodder plants
BT1 oilseed plants
BT2 fatty oil plants
BT3 oil plants

BRASSICA NAPUS VAR. GLAUCA
uf *yellow sarson*
BT1 brassica
BT2 cruciferae
BT1 fodder plants
BT1 oilseed plants
BT2 fatty oil plants
BT3 oil plants

BRASSICA NAPUS VAR. NAPOBRASSICA
BT1 brassica
BT2 cruciferae
rt rutabagas
rt swedes

BRASSICA NAPUS VAR. OLEIFERA
BT1 brassica
BT2 cruciferae
rt rape
rt swede rape

brassica napus var. toria
USE **brassica campestris var. toria**

BRASSICA NIGRA
uf *black mustard*
uf *mustard, black*
uf *sinapis nigra*
BT1 brassica
BT2 cruciferae
BT1 insecticidal plants
BT2 pesticidal plants
BT1 oilseed plants
BT2 fatty oil plants
BT3 oil plants
BT1 spice plants
rt mustard
rt sinigrin

BRASSICA OLERACEA
BT1 brassica
BT2 cruciferae
NT1 brassica oleracea var. botrytis
NT1 brassica oleracea var. capitata
NT1 brassica oleracea var. gemmifera
NT1 brassica oleracea var. gongylodes
NT1 brassica oleracea var. italica
NT1 brassica oleracea var. viridis

BRASSICA OLERACEA VAR. BOTRYTIS
BT1 brassica oleracea
BT2 brassica
BT3 cruciferae
rt cauliflower mosaic caulimovirus
rt cauliflowers

BRASSICA OLERACEA VAR. CAPITATA
BT1 brassica oleracea
BT2 brassica
BT3 cruciferae
rt cabbages
rt sauerkraut

BRASSICA OLERACEA VAR. GEMMIFERA
BT1 brassica oleracea
BT2 brassica
BT3 cruciferae
rt brussels sprouts

BRASSICA OLERACEA VAR. GONGYLODES
BT1 brassica oleracea
BT2 brassica
BT3 cruciferae
rt kohlrabi

BRASSICA OLERACEA VAR. ITALICA
BT1 brassica oleracea
BT2 brassica
BT3 cruciferae
rt broccoli

BRASSICA OLERACEA VAR. ITALICA *cont.*
rt broccoli necrotic yellows rhabdovirus

BRASSICA OLERACEA VAR. VIRIDIS
BT1 brassica oleracea
BT2 brassica
BT3 cruciferae
BT1 fodder plants
rt kale

BRASSICA PEKINENSIS
BT1 brassica
BT2 cruciferae
rt chinese cabbages

BRASSICA PERVIRIDIS
BT1 brassica
BT2 cruciferae
BT1 leafy vegetables
BT2 vegetables

brassica rapa
USE **brassica campestris**

brassicaceae
USE **cruciferae**

BRASSIDIC ACID
BT1 docosenoic acids
BT2 long chain fatty acids
BT3 fatty acids
BT4 carboxylic acids
BT5 organic acids
BT6 acids
BT4 lipids
BT2 monoenoic fatty acids
BT3 unsaturated fatty acids
BT4 fatty acids
BT5 carboxylic acids
BT6 organic acids
BT7 acids
BT5 lipids
BT1 trans fatty acids
BT2 fatty acids
BT3 carboxylic acids
BT4 organic acids
BT5 acids
BT3 lipids

BRASSINOLIDE
BT1 brassinosteroids
BT2 phytosterols
BT3 sterols
BT4 alcohols
BT4 steroids
BT5 isoprenoids
BT6 lipids
BT1 growth stimulators
BT2 plant growth regulators
BT3 growth regulators

BRASSINOSTEROIDS
BT1 phytosterols
BT2 sterols
BT3 alcohols
BT3 steroids
BT4 isoprenoids
BT5 lipids
NT1 brassinolide

BRASSOLIS
BT1 nymphalidae
BT2 lepidoptera
NT1 brassolis sophorae

BRASSOLIS SOPHORAE
BT1 brassolis
BT2 nymphalidae
BT3 lepidoptera

BRAULA
uf *bee lice*
BT1 braulidae
BT2 diptera
NT1 braula coeca

BRAULA COECA
BT1 braula
BT2 braulidae
BT3 diptera

BRAULIDAE
BT1 diptera
NT1 braula
NT2 braula coeca

BRAUNSAPIS
BT1 apidae
BT2 hymenoptera

BRAYULINEA
BT1 amaranthaceae
NT1 brayulinea densa

BRAYULINEA DENSA
BT1 brayulinea
BT2 amaranthaceae

BRAZIL
BT1 south america
BT2 america
NT1 central west brazil
NT1 east brazil
NT1 north brazil
NT1 north east brazil
NT1 south brazil
rt developing countries
rt threshold countries

brazil (central west)
USE **central west brazil**

brazil (east)
USE **east brazil**

brazil (north)
USE **north brazil**

brazil (north east)
USE **north east brazil**

BRAZIL NUTS
BT1 tropical tree nuts
BT2 nut crops
rt bertholletia excelsa

brazil (south)
USE **south brazil**

brazilian bhuj
USE **bhuj**

BRAZILIAN COOKERY (AGRICOLA)
BT1 cookery (agricola)

BRAZILIAN GIR
HN from 1990
BT1 cattle breeds
BT2 breeds

BRAZILIAN POLLED
BT1 cattle breeds
BT2 breeds

BRAZILIAN SOMALI
BT1 sheep breeds
BT2 breeds

brd
USE **german federal republic**

BREAD
BT1 bakery products
BT2 foods
BT2 products
NT1 gluten free bread
NT1 quick breads (agricola)
NT1 yeast breads (agricola)
rt breadmaking

bread, gluten free
USE **gluten free bread**

BREADFRUITS
BT1 tropical tree fruits
BT2 tree fruits
BT2 tropical fruits
BT3 fruit crops
rt artocarpus altilis
rt artocarpus utilis

BREADMAKING
BT1 food technology
BT2 technology
rt bakery products
rt baking
rt bread

BREADMAKING *cont.*
rt kneading

BREAK CROPS
rt catch crops
rt crops

BREAK-EVEN POINT
BT1 profitability

BREAKAGE
BT1 damage
NT1 chromosome breakage
rt breaking strength
rt breaking stress
rt cracking
rt fracture
rt rupture

BREAKDOWN
BT1 plant disorders
BT2 disorders
rt fruit crops

BREAKFAST (AGRICOLA)
BT1 meals
rt breakfast cereals
rt school breakfasts (agricola)

BREAKFAST CEREALS
BT1 cereal products
BT2 plant products
BT3 products
BT1 foods
rt breakfast (agricola)

BREAKING STRENGTH
uf *strength, breaking*
BT1 strength
BT2 mechanical properties
BT3 properties
rt breakage
rt breaking stress

BREAKING STRESS
uf *stress, breaking*
BT1 strength
BT2 mechanical properties
BT3 properties
rt breakage
rt breaking strength

bream (freshwater)
USE **abramis brama**

bream, sea
USE **sea bream**

BREAST ANGLE
rt body measurements

BREAST BLISTERS
rt poultry

BREAST FEEDING
BT1 infant feeding
BT2 feeding
rt human milk
rt infant foods
rt lactation
rt preweaning period
rt suckling
rt weaning

breast milk
USE **human milk**

breast milk fat
USE **human milk fat**

BREAST MUSCLE
BT1 muscles
BT2 musculoskeletal system
BT3 body parts

BREATH
BT1 respiration
BT2 physiology
rt respiratory system

breathing
USE **respiration**

BRED HEIFERS
HN from 1989
BT1 heifers

BRED HEIFERS *cont.*
BT2 cows
BT3 female animals
BT4 animals
BT2 young animals
BT3 animals

BREDA VIRUS
BT1 toroviridae
BT2 viruses

BREDEMEYERA
BT1 polygalaceae
NT1 bredemeyera floribunda

BREDEMEYERA FLORIBUNDA
BT1 bredemeyera
BT2 polygalaceae

BREED DIFFERENCES
rt breeds
rt differentiation
rt line differences
rt species differences
rt strain differences

BREEDERS' ASSOCIATIONS
BT1 interest groups
BT2 groups
BT2 organizations
rt breeding
rt cooperative services
rt farmers' associations
rt herd improvement

BREEDERS' RIGHTS
BT1 legal rights
BT2 legal systems
rt animal breeding
rt breeding
rt patents
rt plant breeding

BREEDING
NT1 animal breeding
NT2 horse breeding
NT1 crossing
NT2 backcrossing
NT2 hybridization
NT3 biparental mating
NT3 intergeneric hybridization
NT3 interspecific hybridization
NT3 somatic hybridization
NT3 wide hybridization
NT2 topcrossing
NT1 plant breeding
NT2 tree breeding
NT1 selective breeding
NT2 genetic improvement
rt artificial selection
rt breeders' associations
rt breeders' rights
rt breeding efficiency
rt breeding life
rt breeding methods
rt breeding programmes
rt breeding value
rt breeds
rt castration
rt female fertility
rt genetic markers
rt grandparents
rt hybridization
rt mating
rt mutagens
rt mutants
rt mutations
rt pedigree
rt plus trees
rt reproduction
rt selection

breeding aims
USE **selection criteria**

breeding, animal
USE **animal breeding**

BREEDING EFFICIENCY
BT1 efficiency
NT1 repeat breeders
rt animal breeding
rt breeding
rt progeny testing

BREEDING LIFE
rt animal breeding
rt breeding
rt life
rt lifespan

BREEDING METHODS
BT1 methodology
NT1 animal breeding methods
NT2 artificial insemination
NT3 intrauterine insemination
NT2 crossbreeding
NT2 mating combinations
NT3 polygamy
NT3 polygyny
NT2 outbreeding
NT2 progeny testing
NT3 boar progeny testing
NT3 contemporary comparisons
NT4 improved contemporary comparisons
NT2 sire evaluation
NT3 direct sire comparisons
NT1 plant breeding methods
NT2 emasculation
NT2 graft hybridization
NT2 inbreeding
NT2 outbreeding
NT2 selfing
NT2 vegetative hybridization
rt artificial selection
rt breeding
rt breeding programmes
rt stabilizing selection

BREEDING PLACES
BT1 habitats
rt tree holes

breeding, plant
USE **plant breeding**

BREEDING PROGRAMMES
AF breeding programs
BT1 projects
NT1 group breeding schemes
NT1 nucleus scheme
NT1 upgrading
rt breeding
rt breeding methods
rt breeding season
rt mating combinations

BREEDING PROGRAMS
BF breeding programmes
BT1 programs (agricola)

BREEDING SEASON
rt animal breeding
rt anoestrus
rt breeding programmes
rt oestrous cycle
rt oestrus
rt seasons

breeding, selective
USE **selective breeding**

BREEDING VALUE
rt animal breeding
rt breeding
rt cow indexes
rt elites
rt prepotency
rt progeny testing

BREEDS
NT1 buffalo breeds
NT2 anatolian
NT2 bhadawari
NT2 bulgarian
NT2 egyptian
NT2 european
NT2 italian
NT2 jafarabadi
NT2 kundi
NT2 mehsana
NT2 murrah
NT2 nagpuri
NT2 nili-ravi
NT2 surti
NT2 tarai

BREEDS *cont.*
NT1 cattle breeds
NT2 aberdeen-angus
NT2 abondance
NT2 adamawa
NT2 africander
NT2 ala-tau
NT2 alambadi
NT2 albanian
NT2 american angus
NT2 american brown swiss
NT2 amritmahal
NT2 anatolian black
NT2 andalusian
NT2 andalusian black
NT2 andalusian blond
NT2 angeln
NT2 angoni
NT2 ankole
NT2 aosta
NT2 apulian podolian
NT2 arado
NT2 argentine friesian
NT2 arsi
NT2 asturian
NT2 aubrac
NT2 aulie-ata
NT2 austrian brown
NT2 austrian simmental
NT2 austrian yellow
NT2 avilena-black iberian
NT2 ayrshire
NT2 azaouak
NT2 bachaur
NT2 baggara
NT2 bali (cattle breed)
NT2 baltic black pied
NT2 bambara
NT2 baoule
NT2 bargur
NT2 barka
NT2 barotse
NT2 barrosa
NT2 beef breeds
NT2 beef shorthorn
NT2 belgian black pied
NT2 belgian blue
NT2 belgian red
NT2 belgian red pied
NT2 belgian white-and-red
NT2 belted galloway
NT2 bestuzhev
NT2 bhagnari
NT2 blacksided trondheim and nordland
NT2 blanco orejinegro
NT2 blonde d'aquitaine
NT2 bonsmara
NT2 borgou
NT2 brangus
NT2 brazilian gir
NT2 brazilian polled
NT2 breton black pied
NT2 british friesian
NT2 british white
NT2 brown atlas
NT2 bulgarian brown
NT2 bulgarian red
NT2 bulgarian simmental
NT2 busa
NT2 bushuev
NT2 butana
NT2 byelorussian red
NT2 canadian
NT2 canchim
NT2 caracu
NT2 carpathian brown
NT2 caucasian brown
NT2 charolais
NT2 chianina
NT2 chinese black-and-white
NT2 czech pied
NT2 dairy breeds
NT2 dairy shorthorn
NT2 damascus
NT2 damietta
NT2 danakil
NT2 dangi
NT2 danish black pied
NT2 danish jersey
NT2 danish red

BREEDS *cont.*
NT2 danish red pied
NT2 deoni
NT2 devon
NT2 dexter
NT2 dhanni
NT2 diali
NT2 drakensberger
NT2 droughtmaster
NT2 dual purpose cattle
NT3 dual purpose bull
NT2 dutch black pied
NT2 east anatolian red
NT2 egyptian
NT2 estonian black pied
NT2 estonian red
NT2 fighting bull
NT2 finnish
NT2 finnish ayrshire
NT2 fogera
NT2 french brown
NT2 french friesian
NT2 friesian
NT2 friesland
NT2 galician blond
NT2 galloway
NT2 gaolao
NT2 gelbvieh
NT2 georgian mountain
NT2 german black pied
NT2 german brown
NT2 german red pied
NT2 german simmental
NT2 gobra
NT2 golpayegani
NT2 gorbatov red
NT2 grey alpine
NT2 guernsey
NT2 guzera
NT2 hallikar
NT2 hariana
NT2 hereford
NT2 herens
NT2 highland
NT2 holstein-friesian
NT2 hungarian pied
NT2 hungarian simmental
NT2 hungarofries
NT2 icelandic
NT2 illawarra
NT2 indo-brazilian
NT2 israeli friesian
NT2 istoben
NT2 italian brown
NT2 italian friesian
NT2 italian red pied
NT2 jamaica black
NT2 jamaica hope
NT2 jamaica red
NT2 japanese black
NT2 japanese brown
NT2 japanese poll
NT2 japanese shorthorn
NT2 jersey
NT2 jiddu
NT2 jinnan
NT2 kalmyk
NT2 kangayam
NT2 kankrej
NT2 kazakh
NT2 kazakh whiteheaded
NT2 kedah-kelantan
NT2 kenana
NT2 kenkatha
NT2 kenya boran
NT2 kerry
NT2 keteku
NT2 kherigarh
NT2 khillari
NT2 kholmogory
NT2 korean native
NT2 kostroma
NT2 krishna valley
NT2 kurgan
NT2 kuri
NT2 latvian brown
NT2 lebedin
NT2 lincoln red
NT2 lithuanian black pied
NT2 lithuanian red
NT2 lohani

BREEDS *cont.*
NT2 luxi
NT2 madurese
NT2 maine-anjou
NT2 malvi
NT2 marchigiana
NT2 maremmana
NT2 mashona
NT2 mauritius creole
NT2 mazandarani
NT2 meuse-rhine-yssel
NT2 mewati
NT2 milking shorthorn
NT2 mirandesa
NT2 modicana
NT2 mongolian
NT2 montbeliard
NT2 morucha
NT2 murnau-werdenfels
NT2 murray grey
NT2 n'dama
NT2 nagori
NT2 nanyang
NT2 nelore
NT2 new zealand jersey
NT2 nguni
NT2 nilotic
NT2 nimari
NT2 nkone
NT2 normande
NT2 norwegian red
NT2 ongole
NT2 ovambo
NT2 pie rouge des plaines
NT2 pinzgauer
NT2 pitangueiras
NT2 polish black-and-white lowland
NT2 polish red
NT2 polish red-and-white lowland
NT2 polish simmental
NT2 poll shorthorn
NT2 polled hereford
NT2 ponwan
NT2 pyrenean
NT2 qinchuan
NT2 rath
NT2 red bororo
NT2 red poll
NT2 red sindhi
NT2 red steppe
NT2 retinta
NT2 romagnola
NT2 romanian brown
NT2 romanian red
NT2 romanian simmental
NT2 romanian steppe
NT2 romosinuano
NT2 russian black pied
NT2 russian brown
NT2 russian simmental
NT2 sahiwal
NT2 salers
NT2 san martinero
NT2 santa gertrudis
NT2 sarabi
NT2 shahabadi
NT2 shetland
NT2 shorthorn
NT2 shuwa
NT2 simmental
NT2 sinhala
NT2 siri
NT2 sistani
NT2 slovakian pied
NT2 slovakian pinzgau
NT2 slovenian brown
NT2 sokoto gudali
NT2 south anatolian red
NT2 south devon
NT2 spanish brown
NT2 sudanese fulani
NT2 suksun
NT2 sussex
NT2 swedish friesian
NT2 swedish jersey
NT2 swedish polled
NT2 swedish red-and-white
NT2 swiss black pied
NT2 swiss brown

BREEDS *cont.*
NT2 sychevka
NT2 tagil
NT2 tambov red
NT2 tarentaise
NT2 telemark
NT2 thari
NT2 tonga (cattle breed)
NT2 transylvanian pinzgau
NT2 tropical dairy criollo
NT2 tswana
NT2 tudanca
NT2 tuli
NT2 tuni
NT2 turino
NT2 tyrol grey
NT2 ukrainian grey
NT2 ukrainian whiteheaded
NT2 villard-de-lans
NT2 vorderwald
NT2 vosges
NT2 welsh black
NT2 west african shorthorn
NT2 white caceres
NT2 white fulani
NT2 yaroslavl
NT2 yugoslav pied
NT2 yurino
NT1 donkey breeds
NT2 poitou
NT1 dual purpose breeds
NT1 endangered breeds
NT1 goat breeds
NT2 altai mountain
NT2 anatolian black
NT2 anglo-nubian
NT2 angora
NT2 appenzell
NT2 apulian
NT2 assam hill
NT2 barbari
NT2 beetal
NT2 belgian fawn
NT2 benadir
NT2 bengal
NT2 bhuj
NT2 boer
NT2 british alpine
NT2 british saanen
NT2 british toggenburg
NT2 campine
NT2 canary island
NT2 carpathian
NT2 chamois coloured
NT2 chappar
NT2 charnequeira
NT2 chengde polled
NT2 chengdu brown
NT2 chigu
NT2 damani
NT2 damascus
NT2 dera din panah
NT2 don
NT2 duan
NT2 dutch toggenburg
NT2 dutch white
NT2 french alpine
NT2 french saanen
NT2 gaddi
NT2 garganica
NT2 german improved fawn
NT2 german improved white
NT2 girgentana
NT2 gohilwadi
NT2 granada
NT2 greek
NT2 haimen
NT2 huaipi
NT2 iraqi
NT2 israeli saanen
NT2 jamnapari
NT2 jining grey
NT2 kamori
NT2 kannaiadu
NT2 katjang
NT2 khurasani
NT2 kilis
NT2 kirgiz
NT2 kurdi
NT2 lehri
NT2 leizhou

BREEDS *cont.*
NT2 liaoning cashmere
NT2 malabari
NT2 malaga
NT2 maltese
NT2 mamber
NT2 maradi
NT2 matou
NT2 mehsana
NT2 mingrelian
NT2 murcia-granada
NT2 nachi
NT2 nordic
NT2 orenburg
NT2 osmanabadi
NT2 poitou
NT2 pyrenean
NT2 red bosnian
NT2 red sokoto
NT2 russian white
NT2 saanen
NT2 sahelian
NT2 salt range
NT2 sangamneri
NT2 serpentina
NT2 serrana
NT2 sind desi
NT2 sinhal
NT2 sirli
NT2 sirohi
NT2 small east african
NT2 somali
NT2 southern sudan
NT2 soviet mohair
NT2 sudanese desert
NT2 sudanese nubian
NT2 surti
NT2 telemark
NT2 toggenburg
NT2 valais blackneck
NT2 verata
NT2 verzasca
NT2 west african dwarf
NT2 wuan
NT2 zalawadi
NT2 zaraibi
NT2 zhiwulin black
NT2 zhongwei
NT1 horse breeds
NT2 akhal-teke
NT2 albanian
NT2 altai
NT2 american saddle horse
NT2 american trotter
NT2 anatolian native
NT2 andalusian
NT2 appaloosa
NT2 arab
NT2 argentine criollo
NT2 auxois
NT2 azerbaijan
NT2 baluchi
NT2 barb
NT2 bashkir
NT2 belgian
NT2 bhotia pony
NT2 bosnian pony
NT2 boulonnais
NT2 breton
NT2 budyonny
NT2 byelorussian harness
NT2 campolino
NT2 canadian
NT2 chumysh
NT2 cleveland bay
NT2 clydesdale
NT2 comtois
NT2 connemara pony
NT2 crioulo
NT2 cukurova
NT2 dales pony
NT2 danube
NT2 dartmoor pony
NT2 don
NT2 dongola
NT2 east bulgarian
NT2 east friesian
NT2 edles warmblut
NT2 finnish
NT2 fjord
NT2 frederiksborg

BREEDS *cont.*
NT2 french anglo-arab
NT2 french ardennais
NT2 french saddlebred
NT2 french trotter
NT2 gelderland (horse breed)
NT2 german riding horse
NT2 hackney
NT2 haflinger
NT2 hequ
NT2 holstein
NT2 hungarian draft
NT2 hutsul
NT2 iceland pony
NT2 jinzhou
NT2 karabair
NT2 kathiawari
NT2 kazakh
NT2 kirgiz
NT2 kushum
NT2 kustanai
NT2 lipitsa
NT2 lithuanian heavy draft
NT2 lokai
NT2 malopolski
NT2 mangalarga
NT2 manipuri pony
NT2 marwari
NT2 mingrelian
NT2 morgan
NT2 new kirgiz
NT2 nonius
NT2 noric
NT2 ob
NT2 oldenburg
NT2 orlov trotter
NT2 paint
NT2 palomino
NT2 pechora
NT2 percheron
NT2 pleven
NT2 poitou
NT2 polesian
NT2 quarter horse
NT2 romanian
NT2 rottal
NT2 russian heavy draft
NT2 russian trotter
NT2 sandalwood pony
NT2 schleswig
NT2 shan pony
NT2 shetland pony
NT2 shire
NT2 south german coldblood
NT2 soviet heavy draft
NT2 spiti pony
NT2 suffolk
NT2 swedish ardennes
NT2 tavda
NT2 tennessee walking horse
NT2 tersk
NT2 thoroughbred
NT2 tibetan pony
NT2 tori
NT2 trakehner
NT2 tushin
NT2 ukrainian saddle horse
NT2 vladimir heavy draft
NT2 vyatka
NT2 waziri
NT2 welsh pony
NT2 western sudan pony
NT2 wielkopolski
NT2 wurttemberg
NT2 yakut
NT2 zaniskari pony
NT2 zemaitukai
NT2 zweibrucken
NT1 imported breeds
NT2 exotics
NT1 pig breeds
NT2 alentejana
NT2 american landrace
NT2 american yorkshire
NT2 andalusian blond
NT2 andalusian spotted
NT2 angeln saddleback
NT2 beijing black
NT2 belgian landrace
NT2 beltsville no. 1
NT2 beltsville no. 2

BREEDS *cont.*
NT2 berkshire
NT2 bisaro
NT2 black iberian
NT2 breitov
NT2 british landrace
NT2 british saddleback
NT2 bulgarian white
NT2 byelorussian black pied
NT2 canadian yorkshire
NT2 canastra
NT2 canastrao
NT2 cantonese
NT2 chester white
NT2 czech improved white
NT2 danish landrace
NT2 dermantsi pied
NT2 duroc
NT2 dutch landrace
NT2 dutch yorkshire
NT2 east balkan
NT2 edelschwein
NT2 estonian bacon
NT2 finnish landrace
NT2 french landrace
NT2 french large white
NT2 german landrace
NT2 hainan
NT2 hampshire
NT2 harbin white
NT2 hereford
NT2 huang-huai-hai black
NT2 hungarian white
NT2 jinhua
NT2 kemerovo
NT2 lacombe
NT2 landrace
NT2 large black
NT2 large white
NT2 latvian white
NT2 lithuanian white
NT2 livny
NT2 luchuan
NT2 mangalitsa
NT2 middle white
NT2 min
NT2 minnesota no. 1
NT2 mirgorod
NT2 neijiang
NT2 new huai
NT2 nilo
NT2 ningxiang
NT2 north caucasus
NT2 north siberian
NT2 norwegian landrace
NT2 piau
NT2 pietrain
NT2 pirapitinga
NT2 poland china
NT2 polish landrace
NT2 polish large white
NT2 prestice
NT2 pulawy
NT2 russian large white
NT2 russian long-eared white
NT2 russian short-eared white
NT2 semirechensk
NT2 siena belted
NT2 south african landrace
NT2 south yunnan short-eared
NT2 spotted
NT2 swabian-hall
NT2 swedish landrace
NT2 swiss edelschwein
NT2 swiss improved landrace
NT2 taihu
NT2 tamworth
NT2 taoyuan
NT2 tatu
NT2 turopolje
NT2 ukrainian spotted steppe
NT2 ukrainian white steppe
NT2 urzhum
NT2 welsh
NT2 west french white
NT2 xinjin
NT1 races
NT2 geographical races
NT2 physiological races
NT1 rare breeds
NT1 sheep breeds

BREEDS *cont.*
NT2 abyssinian
NT2 afghan arabi
NT2 alai
NT2 alcarrena
NT2 algarve churro
NT2 algerian arab
NT2 altai
NT2 altamurana
NT2 american merino
NT2 american rambouillet
NT2 american tunis
NT2 appennine
NT2 arabi
NT2 aragonese
NT2 argentine merino
NT2 arles merino
NT2 armenian semicoursewool
NT2 askanian
NT2 ausimi
NT2 australian merino
NT2 avranchin
NT2 awassi
NT2 azerbaijan mountain merino
NT2 azov tsigai
NT2 bakhtiari-luri
NT2 balangir
NT2 balbas
NT2 balkhi
NT2 baluchi
NT2 barbados blackbelly
NT2 bardoka
NT2 barki
NT2 baruwal
NT2 basco-bearnais
NT2 bellary
NT2 beni ahsen
NT2 beni guil
NT2 berber
NT2 bergamasca
NT2 berrichon du cher
NT2 bhadarwah
NT2 bhakarwal
NT2 bibrik
NT2 biellese
NT2 bikaneri
NT2 bizet
NT2 black merino
NT2 black welsh mountain
NT2 blackhead persian
NT2 blanc du massif central
NT2 bleu du maine
NT2 bluefaced leicester
NT2 border leicester
NT2 bosnian mountain
NT2 boulonnais
NT2 bozakh
NT2 braganca galician
NT2 brazilian somali
NT2 buchi
NT2 buryat
NT2 campanian barbary
NT2 campanica
NT2 canadian corriedale
NT2 castilian
NT2 caucasian
NT2 central pyrenean
NT2 charmoise
NT2 charollais
NT2 cheviot
NT2 chios
NT2 chokla
NT2 chotanagpuri
NT2 churra da terra quente
NT2 churro do campo
NT2 chushka
NT2 clun forest
NT2 coimbatore
NT2 columbia
NT2 comisano
NT2 common albanian
NT2 corriedale
NT2 corsican
NT2 cotentin
NT2 criollo
NT2 cyprus fat-tailed
NT2 d'man
NT2 dagestan mountain
NT2 daglic
NT2 dala

BREEDS *cont.*
NT2 dales-bred
NT2 dalmatian-karst
NT2 damani
NT2 danube finewool
NT2 danube merino
NT2 dartmoor
NT2 darvaz
NT2 deccani
NT2 degeres mutton-wool
NT2 derbyshire gritstone
NT2 dorper
NT2 dorset down
NT2 dorset horn
NT2 drysdale
NT2 dubrovnik
NT2 dumbi
NT2 east friesian
NT2 edilbaev
NT2 entre douro e minho
NT2 estonian darkheaded
NT2 exmoor horn
NT2 fabrianese
NT2 finnish landrace
NT2 fulani
NT2 gadik
NT2 galician
NT2 galway
NT2 gansu alpine finewool
NT2 gentile di puglia
NT2 german blackheaded mutton
NT2 german mountain
NT2 german mutton merino
NT2 german whiteheaded mutton
NT2 ghiljai
NT2 gorki
NT2 greek zackel
NT2 grey shirazi
NT2 grozny
NT2 gujarati
NT2 gurez
NT2 hampshire down
NT2 han
NT2 harnai
NT2 hashtnagri
NT2 hassan
NT2 hazaragie
NT2 heidschnucke
NT2 hejazi
NT2 hissar
NT2 hu
NT2 hungarian merino
NT2 icelandic
NT2 ile-de-france
NT2 improved sumava
NT2 improved valachian
NT2 indonesian fat-tailed
NT2 iraq kurdi
NT2 island pramenka
NT2 istrian milk
NT2 jaidara
NT2 jaisalmeri
NT2 jalauni
NT2 javanese thin-tailed
NT2 junin
NT2 kachhi
NT2 kallakui
NT2 kandahari
NT2 karachai
NT2 karagouniko
NT2 karakachan
NT2 karakul
NT2 karayaka
NT2 kargalin fat-rumped
NT2 karnobat finewool
NT2 katsika
NT2 kazakh arkhar-merino
NT2 kazakh fat-rumped
NT2 kazakh finewool
NT2 khorasan kurdi
NT2 kilakarsal
NT2 kirgiz finewool
NT2 kivircik
NT2 kooka
NT2 krasnoyarsk finewool
NT2 kuibyshev
NT2 lacaune
NT2 lacho
NT2 langhe

BREEDS *cont.*
NT2 latvian darkheaded
NT2 leccese
NT2 leicester longwool
NT2 lezgian
NT2 libyan barbary
NT2 lika
NT2 lincoln longwool
NT2 liski
NT2 lithuanian blackheaded
NT2 lohi
NT2 macina
NT2 madras red
NT2 magra
NT2 majorcan
NT2 makui
NT2 malpura
NT2 manchega
NT2 mandya
NT2 manech
NT2 masai
NT2 massese
NT2 mecheri
NT2 mehraban
NT2 menz
NT2 merinolandschaf
NT2 michni
NT2 moghani
NT2 mondegueira
NT2 mongolian
NT2 montesina
NT2 morada nova
NT2 muzzafarnagri
NT2 najdi
NT2 nali
NT2 nellore
NT2 new zealand romney
NT2 north bulgarian semifinewool
NT2 north caucasus mutton-wool
NT2 north country cheviot
NT2 north kazakh merino
NT2 north-east bulgarian finewool
NT2 north-east china finewool
NT2 ojalada
NT2 ossimi
NT2 ovce polje
NT2 oxford down
NT2 pagliarola
NT2 palas merino
NT2 patanwadi
NT2 pelibuey
NT2 pinzirita
NT2 pleven blackhead
NT2 polish merino
NT2 polwarth
NT2 portuguese merino
NT2 prealpes du sud
NT2 precoce
NT2 priangan
NT2 pugal
NT2 rabo largo
NT2 race de l'est a laine merinos
NT2 racka
NT2 rahmani
NT2 rakhshani
NT2 rambouillet
NT2 ramnad white
NT2 rampur bushair
NT2 rava
NT2 red african
NT2 red karaman
NT2 rhon
NT2 ripollesa
NT2 romanov
NT2 romney
NT2 rouge de l'ouest
NT2 rough fell
NT2 roumloukion
NT2 russian longwool
NT2 ryeland
NT2 rygja
NT2 saloia
NT2 salsk
NT2 sangesari
NT2 sanjabi
NT2 santa ines
NT2 sar planina

BREEDS *cont.*
NT2 saraja
NT2 sardi
NT2 sardinian
NT2 sary-ja
NT2 scottish blackface
NT2 segurena
NT2 serra da estrela
NT2 serrai
NT2 shahabadi
NT2 shetland
NT2 shkodra
NT2 shropshire
NT2 shumen
NT2 sicilian barbary
NT2 sjenica
NT2 skopelos
NT2 sokolki
NT2 solcava
NT2 somali
NT2 sonadi
NT2 sopravissana
NT2 south african merino
NT2 south kazakh merino
NT2 south sudanese
NT2 south suffolk
NT2 south ural
NT2 south wales mountain
NT2 southdown
NT2 soviet merino
NT2 soviet mutton-wool
NT2 spaelsau
NT2 spanish churro
NT2 spanish merino
NT2 stavropol
NT2 steigar
NT2 steinschaf
NT2 stogos
NT2 sudan desert
NT2 suffolk
NT2 sumava
NT2 svishtov
NT2 svrljig
NT2 swaledale
NT2 swedish fur sheep
NT2 swedish landrace
NT2 swiss black-brown mountain
NT2 swiss brownheaded mutton
NT2 swiss white alpine
NT2 tadla
NT2 tadmit
NT2 tajik
NT2 talaverana
NT2 tan
NT2 tanzania long-tailed
NT2 tarasconnais
NT2 targhee
NT2 teeswater
NT2 telengit
NT2 texel
NT2 thalli
NT2 thibar
NT2 thones-marthod
NT2 thrace finewool
NT2 tibetan
NT2 timahadite
NT2 tirahi
NT2 tiruchy black
NT2 tong
NT2 transbaikal finewool
NT2 tsigai
NT2 tuareg
NT2 tuj
NT2 tunisian barbary
NT2 turcana
NT2 turki
NT2 turkish merino
NT2 tushin
NT2 tyan shan
NT2 tyrol mountain
NT2 valachian
NT2 valais blacknose
NT2 varese
NT2 velay black
NT2 vembur
NT2 vendeen
NT2 volgograd
NT2 voloshian
NT2 vyatka

BREEDS *cont.*
NT2 waziri
NT2 welsh mountain
NT2 wensleydale
NT2 west african dwarf
NT2 white dorper
NT2 white face dartmoor
NT2 white karaman
NT2 white klementina
NT2 white south bulgarian
NT2 wicklow mountain
NT2 wiltshire horn
NT2 xinjiang finewool
NT2 zaghawa
NT2 zante
NT2 zel
NT2 zemmour
NT2 zeta yellow
NT1 single purpose breeds
NT1 zebu breeds
NT2 azerbaijan zebu
NT2 boran
NT2 brahman
NT2 gir
NT2 haryana zebu
NT2 small east african zebu
NT2 tharparkar
rt ancestry
rt animal breeding
rt breed differences
rt breeding
rt native livestock
rt studbooks

BREI
HN from 1990
rt sample processing
rt sugarbeet

BREINLIA
BT1 onchocercidae
BT2 nematoda

BREITOV
BT1 pig breeds
BT2 breeds

BREMIA
BT1 peronosporales
NT1 bremia lactucae

BREMIA LACTUCAE
BT1 bremia
BT2 peronosporales

bretagne
USE **brittany**

BRETON
BT1 horse breeds
BT2 breeds

BRETON BLACK PIED
BT1 cattle breeds
BT2 breeds

BREVENNIA
BT1 pseudococcidae
BT2 coccoidea
BT3 sternorrhyncha
BT4 homoptera
NT1 brevennia rehi

BREVENNIA REHI
BT1 brevennia
BT2 pseudococcidae
BT3 coccoidea
BT4 sternorrhyncha
BT5 homoptera

BREVIBACTERIACEAE
BT1 coryneform group of bacteria
BT2 firmicutes
BT3 bacteria
BT4 prokaryotes
NT1 brevibacterium
NT2 brevibacterium linens

BREVIBACTERIUM
BT1 brevibacteriaceae
BT2 coryneform group of bacteria
BT3 firmicutes

BREVIBACTERIUM *cont.*
BT4 bacteria
BT5 prokaryotes
NT1 brevibacterium linens

BREVIBACTERIUM LINENS
BT1 brevibacterium
BT2 brevibacteriaceae
BT3 coryneform group of bacteria
BT4 firmicutes
BT5 bacteria
BT6 prokaryotes

BREVICOMIN
BT1 aggregation pheromones
BT2 pheromones
BT3 semiochemicals
rt dendroctonus brevicomis

BREVICORYNE
BT1 aphididae
BT2 aphidoidea
BT3 sternorrhyncha
BT4 homoptera
NT1 brevicoryne brassicae

BREVICORYNE BRASSICAE
BT1 brevicoryne
BT2 aphididae
BT3 aphidoidea
BT4 sternorrhyncha
BT5 homoptera

BREVIPALPUS
BT1 tenuipalpidae
BT2 prostigmata
BT3 acari
NT1 brevipalpus californicus
NT1 brevipalpus lewisi
NT1 brevipalpus obovatus
NT1 brevipalpus phoenicis
rt cenopalpus

BREVIPALPUS CALIFORNICUS
BT1 brevipalpus
BT2 tenuipalpidae
BT3 prostigmata
BT4 acari

BREVIPALPUS LEWISI
BT1 brevipalpus
BT2 tenuipalpidae
BT3 prostigmata
BT4 acari

BREVIPALPUS OBOVATUS
BT1 brevipalpus
BT2 tenuipalpidae
BT3 prostigmata
BT4 acari

BREVIPALPUS PHOENICIS
BT1 brevipalpus
BT2 tenuipalpidae
BT3 prostigmata
BT4 acari

brevipalpus pulcher
USE **cenopalpus pulcher**

BREVOORTIA
BT1 clupeidae
BT2 clupeiformes
BT3 osteichthyes
BT4 fishes

brevoortia tyrannus
USE **menhaden**

BREWERS' GRAINS
BT1 brewery byproducts
BT2 agroindustrial byproducts
BT3 byproducts
BT1 cereal byproducts
BT2 agricultural byproducts
BT3 byproducts
rt brewing industry

BREWERS' YEAST
uf *yeast, brewers'*
BT1 yeasts
rt brewing industry
rt fermentation

BREWERY BYPRODUCTS
BT1 agroindustrial byproducts
BT2 byproducts
NT1 brewers' grains
rt brewing
rt brewing industry

BREWERY EFFLUENT
BT1 factory effluents
BT2 effluents
BT3 wastes
rt brewing
rt brewing industry
rt irrigation water

BREWING
uf *malting and brewing*
BT1 processing
rt alcoholic beverages
rt beers
rt brewery byproducts
rt brewery effluent
rt brewing industry
rt fermentation
rt food technology

BREWING INDUSTRY
BT1 beverage industry
BT2 food industry
BT3 industry
rt beers
rt brewers' grains
rt brewers' yeast
rt brewery byproducts
rt brewery effluent
rt brewing
rt fermentation
rt hopping quality
rt hops
rt vats
rt yeasts

BREWING QUALITY
BT1 quality
rt hopping quality
rt humulon
rt lupulon
rt malting quality

BREXIACEAE
NT1 ixerba
NT2 ixerba brexioides

BREYNIA
BT1 euphorbiaceae
NT1 breynia disticha

BREYNIA DISTICHA
uf *breynia nivosa*
BT1 acaricidal plants
BT2 pesticidal plants
BT1 breynia
BT2 euphorbiaceae

breynia nivosa
USE **breynia disticha**

BRICK CHEESE
BT1 cheeses
BT2 milk products
BT3 products

BRICKS
BT1 building materials
BT2 materials
rt brickwork

BRICKWORK
BT1 building construction
BT2 construction
rt bricks
rt stonework

BRIDELIA
BT1 euphorbiaceae
NT1 bridelia ferruginea

BRIDELIA FERRUGINEA
BT1 bridelia
BT2 euphorbiaceae
BT1 medicinal plants

BRIDGED DIPHENYL ACARICIDES
BT1 acaricides
BT2 pesticides

BRIDGED DIPHENYL ACARICIDES *cont.*
NT1 benzyl benzoate
NT1 bromopropylate
NT1 chlorfenethol
NT1 chlorfenson
NT1 chlorfensulphide
NT1 chlorobenzilate
NT1 chloropropylate
NT1 dicofol
NT1 tetradifon
NT1 tetrasul

BRIDGES
BT1 structures
rt railways
rt rivers
rt roads
rt span

BRIDGING
rt flow

BRIDLE PATHS
BT1 paths
BT2 roads
rt footpaths
rt horse riding

BRIE CHEESE
BT1 cheeses
BT2 milk products
BT3 products

brigades
USE **work teams**

brigalow soils
USE **vertisols**

brill
USE **scophthalmus rhombus**

BRINCKOCHRYSA
BT1 chrysopidae
BT2 neuroptera
NT1 brinckochrysa scelestes
rt chrysopa

BRINCKOCHRYSA SCELESTES
uf *chrysopa scelestes*
BT1 brinckochrysa
BT2 chrysopidae
BT3 neuroptera

BRINE
BT1 food preservatives
BT2 preservatives
BT1 saline water
BT2 water
rt brining
rt salinity
rt salt

BRINING
BT1 processing
rt brine
rt pickling
rt preservation

brinjal
USE **aubergines**

BRIQUETTES
NT1 grass briquettes
rt briquetting
rt controlled release
rt feeds
rt formulations
rt fuels
rt sawdust

BRIQUETTING
BT1 processing
rt briquettes
rt fuels
rt sawdust

BRISTLES
BT1 animal fibres
BT2 animal products
BT3 products
BT2 fibres
BT1 integument
BT2 body parts

BRISTLES *cont.*
rt hair

britain
USE **uk**

BRITISH ALPINE
BT1 goat breeds
BT2 breeds

BRITISH COLUMBIA
BT1 canada
BT2 north america
BT3 america

BRITISH FRIESIAN
BT1 cattle breeds
BT2 breeds

british guiana
USE **guyana**

british honduras
USE **belize**

british indian ocean territory
USE **seychelles**

BRITISH ISLES
BT1 western europe
BT2 europe
NT1 irish republic
NT2 connacht
NT2 leinster
NT2 munster
NT1 uk
NT2 channel islands
NT2 great britain
NT3 england
NT4 east midlands of england
NT4 eastern england
NT4 northern england
NT4 south east england
NT4 south west england
NT4 west midlands of england
NT4 yorkshire and lancashire
NT3 scotland
NT4 eastern scotland
NT4 northern scotland
NT4 scottish highlands and islands
NT4 west scotland
NT3 wales
NT2 isle of man
NT2 northern ireland

BRITISH LANDRACE
BT1 pig breeds
BT2 breeds

BRITISH SAANEN
BT1 goat breeds
BT2 breeds

BRITISH SADDLEBACK
BT1 pig breeds
BT2 breeds

BRITISH STANDARD HIVES
BT1 movable-comb hives
BT2 hives

BRITISH TOGGENBURG
BT1 goat breeds
BT2 breeds

BRITISH VIRGIN ISLANDS
uf *tortola*
uf *virgin islands (uk)*
BT1 caribbean
BT2 america

BRITISH WHITE
BT1 cattle breeds
BT2 breeds

britoa
USE **campomanesia**

BRITTANY
uf *bretagne*
BT1 france
BT2 western europe

BRITTANY *cont.*
BT3 europe

BRITTLENESS
BT1 mechanical properties
BT2 properties
rt cracking
rt failure

BRIX
rt hydrometers
rt sugar

BRIZA
BT1 gramineae
NT1 briza maxima
NT1 briza media
NT1 briza minor

BRIZA MAXIMA
BT1 briza
BT2 gramineae

BRIZA MEDIA
BT1 briza
BT2 gramineae
BT1 ornamental herbaceous plants

BRIZA MINOR
BT1 briza
BT2 gramineae

BROAD BEAN MOSAIC VIRUS
BT1 miscellaneous plant viruses
BT2 plant viruses
BT3 plant pathogens
BT4 pathogens
rt vicia faba

BROAD BEAN MOTTLE BROMOVIRUS
HN from 1990; previously "broad bean mottle virus"
uf *broad bean mottle virus*
BT1 bromovirus group
BT2 plant viruses
BT3 plant pathogens
BT4 pathogens
rt faba beans
rt vicia faba

broad bean mottle virus
USE **broad bean mottle bromovirus**

BROAD BEAN STAIN COMOVIRUS
HN from 1990; previously "broad bean stain virus"
uf *broad bean stain virus*
BT1 comovirus group
BT2 plant viruses
BT3 plant pathogens
BT4 pathogens
rt faba beans
rt vicia faba

broad bean stain virus
USE **broad bean stain comovirus**

BROAD BEAN TRUE MOSAIC COMOVIRUS
HN from 1990; previously "echtes ackerbohnenmosaik virus"
uf *broad bean true mosaic virus*
uf *echtes ackerbohnenmosaik virus*
BT1 comovirus group
BT2 plant viruses
BT3 plant pathogens
BT4 pathogens
rt faba beans
rt vicia faba

broad bean true mosaic virus
USE **broad bean true mosaic comovirus**

BROAD BEAN WILT FABAVIRUS
HN from 1990; previously "broad bean wilt virus"
uf *broad bean wilt virus*

BROAD BEAN WILT FABAVIRUS *cont.*
BT1 fabavirus group
BT2 plant viruses
BT3 plant pathogens
BT4 pathogens
rt faba beans
rt vicia faba

broad bean wilt virus
USE **broad bean wilt fabavirus**

broad beans
USE **faba beans**

BROADCASTING
BT1 application methods
BT2 methodology

BROADCLOTH (AGRICOLA)
BT1 fabrics

BROADLEAVED DECIDUOUS FORESTS
BT1 deciduous forests
BT2 forests
BT3 vegetation types

BROADLEAVED EVERGREEN FORESTS
BT1 forests
BT2 vegetation types

BROADLEAVES
rt forest trees

BROCADE (AGRICOLA)
BT1 fabrics

BROCCOLI
uf *broccoli, sprouting*
uf *calabrese*
uf *sprouting broccoli*
BT1 leafy vegetables
BT2 vegetables
rt brassica oleracea var. italica
rt broccoli necrotic yellows rhabdovirus
rt hollow stem
rt spears

broccoli, heading
USE **cauliflowers**

BROCCOLI NECROTIC YELLOWS RHABDOVIRUS
HN from 1990; previously "broccoli necrotic yellows virus"
uf *broccoli necrotic yellows virus*
BT1 rhabdovirus group
BT2 plant viruses
BT3 plant pathogens
BT4 pathogens
BT2 rhabdoviridae
BT3 viruses
rt brassica oleracea var. italica
rt broccoli

broccoli necrotic yellows virus
USE **broccoli necrotic yellows rhabdovirus**

broccoli, sprouting
USE **broccoli**

BRODIAEA
BT1 alliaceae

brodiaea laxa
USE **triteleia laxa**

brodiaea uniflora
USE **ipheion uniflorum**

BRODIFACOUM
BT1 coumarin rodenticides
BT2 coumarins
BT3 lactones
BT4 heterocyclic oxygen compounds
BT4 ketones
BT2 rodenticides
BT3 pesticides

BROILER LINES
BT1 lines
rt animal breeding

BROILER PERFORMANCE
BT1 performance

BROILER PRODUCTION
BT1 meat production
BT2 animal production
BT3 agricultural production
BT4 production

BROILERS
BT1 fowls
BT2 poultry
BT3 livestock
BT4 animals

BROILERS (KITCHEN APPLIANCE) (AGRICOLA)
BT1 cooking utensils (agricola)
BT2 utensils (agricola)

BROILING (AGRICOLA)
BT1 cooking methods (agricola)
BT2 methodology
rt charcoal broiled foods (agricola)

BROMACIL
BT1 uracil herbicides
BT2 herbicides
BT3 pesticides
BT2 uracil derivatives
BT3 pyrimidines
BT4 heterocyclic nitrogen compounds
BT5 organic nitrogen compounds

BROMADIOLONE
BT1 coumarin rodenticides
BT2 coumarins
BT3 lactones
BT4 heterocyclic oxygen compounds
BT4 ketones
BT2 rodenticides
BT3 pesticides

brome
USE **bromus**

BROME MOSAIC BROMOVIRUS
HN from 1990; previously "brome mosaic virus"
uf *brome mosaic virus*
BT1 bromovirus group
BT2 plant viruses
BT3 plant pathogens
BT4 pathogens
rt bromus

brome mosaic virus
USE **brome mosaic bromovirus**

BROMELIACEAE
uf *bromeliads*
NT1 aechmea
NT2 aechmea arenosa
NT2 aechmea bracteata
NT2 aechmea fasciata
NT2 aechmea magdalenae
NT1 ananas
NT2 ananas comosus
NT1 billbergia
NT2 billbergia nutans
NT2 billbergia vittata
NT1 cryptanthus
NT2 cryptanthus bivittatus
NT1 dyckia
NT1 guzmania
NT2 guzmania lingulata
NT1 hohenbergia
NT1 neoregelia
NT2 neoregelia carolinae
NT1 pitcairnia
NT1 tillandsia
NT2 tillandsia aeranthos
NT2 tillandsia cyanea
NT2 tillandsia lindenii
NT2 tillandsia recurvata
NT2 tillandsia usneoides

BROMELIACEAE *cont.*
NT1 vriesea
NT2 vriesea gigantea
NT2 vriesea malzinei
NT2 vriesea regina
NT2 vriesea splendens
rt ornamental bromeliads
rt phytotelmata

bromeliads
USE **bromeliaceae**

BROMETHALIN
BT1 rodenticides
BT2 pesticides

BROMFENVINFOS
BT1 organophosphate insecticides
BT2 organophosphorus insecticides
BT3 insecticides
BT4 pesticides
BT3 organophosphorus pesticides
BT4 organophosphorus compounds

BROMHEADIA
BT1 orchidaceae
NT1 bromheadia finlaysoniana

BROMHEADIA FINLAYSONIANA
BT1 bromheadia
BT2 orchidaceae
BT1 ornamental orchids

BROMIDE
BT1 anions
BT2 ions
rt bromides
rt bromine

BROMIDES
BT1 halides
BT2 inorganic salts
BT3 inorganic compounds
BT3 salts
NT1 potassium bromide
rt bromide
rt bromine

BROMINE
BT1 halogens
BT2 nonmetallic elements
BT3 elements
BT1 trace elements
BT2 elements
rt bromide
rt bromides
rt organobromine compounds

BROMOACETAMIDE
BT1 molluscicides
BT2 pesticides

BROMOBUTIDE
HN from 1990
BT1 amide herbicides
BT2 herbicides
BT3 pesticides

BROMOCRIPTINE
BT1 hormone antagonists
BT2 antagonists
BT3 metabolic inhibitors
BT4 inhibitors
rt ergot alkaloids
rt prolactin

BROMOCYCLEN
BT1 ectoparasiticides
BT2 antiparasitic agents
BT3 drugs
BT1 organochlorine acaricides
BT2 acaricides
BT3 pesticides
BT2 organochlorine pesticides
BT3 organochlorine compounds
BT4 organic halogen compounds

bromodeoxyuridine
USE **broxuridine**

BROMOFENOFOS
uf *bromofenophos*
BT1 anthelmintics
BT2 antiparasitic agents
BT3 drugs

bromofenophos
USE **bromofenofos**

BROMOFENOXIM
BT1 nitrophenyl ether herbicides
BT2 herbicides
BT3 pesticides

bromofos
USE **bromophos**

bromomethane
USE **methyl bromide**

BROMOPHOS
uf *bromofos*
BT1 anthelmintics
BT2 antiparasitic agents
BT3 drugs
BT1 organothiophosphate insecticides
BT2 organophosphorus insecticides
BT3 insecticides
BT4 pesticides
BT3 organophosphorus pesticides
BT4 organophosphorus compounds

BROMOPHOS-ETHYL
BT1 organothiophosphate insecticides
BT2 organophosphorus insecticides
BT3 insecticides
BT4 pesticides
BT3 organophosphorus pesticides
BT4 organophosphorus compounds

BROMOPROPYLATE
BT1 bridged diphenyl acaricides
BT2 acaricides
BT3 pesticides

bromopsis
USE **bromus**

5-BROMOURACIL
BT1 metabolic inhibitors
BT2 inhibitors
BT1 mutagens
BT1 uracil derivatives
BT2 pyrimidines
BT3 heterocyclic nitrogen compounds
BT4 organic nitrogen compounds

BROMOVIRUS GROUP
HN from 1990
BT1 plant viruses
BT2 plant pathogens
BT3 pathogens
NT1 broad bean mottle bromovirus
NT1 brome mosaic bromovirus
NT1 cassia yellow blotch bromovirus
NT1 cowpea chlorotic mottle bromovirus
NT1 melandrium yellow fleck bromovirus

BROMOXYNIL
BT1 nitrile herbicides
BT2 herbicides
BT3 pesticides

BROMUS
uf *anisantha*
uf *boissiera*
uf *brome*

BROMUS *cont.*
uf *bromopsis*
uf *ceratochloa*
uf *zerna*
BT1 gramineae
NT1 bromus benekenii
NT1 bromus biebersteinii
NT1 bromus brevis
NT1 bromus cappadocicus
NT1 bromus carinatus
NT1 bromus catharticus
NT1 bromus commutatus
NT1 bromus diandrus
NT1 bromus erectus
NT1 bromus hordeaceus
NT1 bromus inermis
NT1 bromus japonicus
NT1 bromus macrostachys
NT1 bromus madritensis
NT1 bromus marginatus
NT1 bromus molliformis
NT1 bromus oxyodon
NT1 bromus pumilio
NT1 bromus racemosus
NT1 bromus rigidus
NT1 bromus riparius
NT1 bromus rubens
NT1 bromus sarothrae
NT1 bromus scoparius
NT1 bromus secalinus
NT1 bromus sericeus
NT1 bromus sitchensis
NT1 bromus sterilis
NT1 bromus tectorum
NT1 bromus tomentellus
NT1 bromus variegatus
rt brome mosaic bromovirus

BROMUS BENEKENII
BT1 bromus
BT2 gramineae

BROMUS BIEBERSTEINII
BT1 bromus
BT2 gramineae
BT1 pasture plants

BROMUS BREVIS
BT1 bromus
BT2 gramineae
BT1 pasture plants

BROMUS CAPPADOCICUS
BT1 bromus
BT2 gramineae
BT1 pasture plants

BROMUS CARINATUS
BT1 bromus
BT2 gramineae
BT1 pasture plants

BROMUS CATHARTICUS
uf *bromus unioloides*
uf *bromus willdenowii*
uf *ceratochloa unioloides*
BT1 bromus
BT2 gramineae
BT1 pasture plants

BROMUS COMMUTATUS
BT1 bromus
BT2 gramineae

BROMUS DIANDRUS
BT1 bromus
BT2 gramineae

BROMUS ERECTUS
BT1 bromus
BT2 gramineae
BT1 pasture plants

BROMUS HORDEACEUS
uf *bromus mollis*
BT1 bromus
BT2 gramineae
BT1 pasture plants

BROMUS INERMIS
BT1 bromus
BT2 gramineae
BT1 pasture plants

BROMUS JAPONICUS
BT1 bromus
BT2 gramineae
BT1 pasture plants

BROMUS MACROSTACHYS
BT1 bromus
BT2 gramineae
BT1 pasture plants

BROMUS MADRITENSIS
BT1 bromus
BT2 gramineae
BT1 pasture plants

BROMUS MARGINATUS
BT1 bromus
BT2 gramineae
BT1 pasture plants

BROMUS MOLLIFORMIS
BT1 bromus
BT2 gramineae
BT1 pasture plants

bromus mollis
USE **bromus hordeaceus**
BT1 pasture plants

BROMUS OXYODON
BT1 bromus
BT2 gramineae
BT1 pasture plants

BROMUS PUMILIO
uf *boissiera squamosa*
BT1 bromus
BT2 gramineae

BROMUS RACEMOSUS
BT1 bromus
BT2 gramineae
BT1 pasture plants

BROMUS RIGIDUS
BT1 bromus
BT2 gramineae

BROMUS RIPARIUS
BT1 bromus
BT2 gramineae
BT1 pasture plants

BROMUS RUBENS
BT1 bromus
BT2 gramineae
BT1 pasture plants

BROMUS SAROTHRAE
BT1 bromus
BT2 gramineae

BROMUS SCOPARIUS
BT1 bromus
BT2 gramineae
BT1 pasture plants

BROMUS SECALINUS
BT1 bromus
BT2 gramineae

BROMUS SERICEUS
BT1 bromus
BT2 gramineae
BT1 pasture plants

BROMUS SITCHENSIS
BT1 bromus
BT2 gramineae
BT1 pasture plants

BROMUS STERILIS
BT1 bromus
BT2 gramineae
BT1 weeds

BROMUS TECTORUM
BT1 bromus
BT2 gramineae
BT1 weeds

BROMUS TOMENTELLUS
BT1 bromus
BT2 gramineae
BT1 pasture plants

bromus unioloides
USE **bromus catharticus**

BROMUS VARIEGATUS
BT1 bromus
BT2 gramineae
BT1 pasture plants

bromus willdenowii
USE **bromus catharticus**

BRONCHI
BT1 respiratory system
BT2 body parts
rt bronchitis

BRONCHITIS
BT1 respiratory diseases
BT2 organic diseases
BT3 diseases
rt bronchi
rt infectious bronchitis virus

BRONCHOALVEOLAR LAVAGE
HN from 1990
BT1 diagnostic techniques
BT2 techniques

BRONCHODILATORS
BT1 respiratory system agents
BT2 drugs
NT1 clenbuterol

BRONCHOPULMONARY DYSPLASIA (AGRICOLA)
BT1 respiratory diseases
BT2 organic diseases
BT3 diseases

BRONCHOSCOPY
HN from 1990
BT1 diagnostic techniques
BT2 techniques

BRONOPOL
BT1 glycols
BT2 alcohols
BT1 preservatives
rt milk preservation

BRONTISPA
BT1 chrysomelidae
BT2 coleoptera
NT1 brontispa longissima

BRONTISPA LONGISSIMA
BT1 brontispa
BT2 chrysomelidae
BT3 coleoptera

BROOD CARE
BT1 brood rearing
rt nurse honeybees

BROOD FOOD
NT1 royal jelly
rt brood rearing

BROOD REARING
NT1 brood care
rt brood food
rt honeybee brood
rt nurse honeybees

BROODERS
BT1 poultry housing
BT2 animal housing
rt broodiness
rt hatcheries
rt incubation
rt incubators

BROODINESS
BT1 animal behaviour
BT2 behaviour
rt brooders
rt incubation

broods
USE **honeybee brood**

brook trout
USE **salvelinus fontinalis**

broom, witches'
USE **witches' brooms**

broomcorn
USE **sorghum bicolor**

BROOMS
BT1 tools

BROSCUS
BT1 carabidae
BT2 coleoptera
NT1 broscus cephalotes

BROSCUS CEPHALOTES
BT1 broscus
BT2 carabidae
BT3 coleoptera

BROSIMUM
BT1 moraceae
NT1 brosimum alicastrum

BROSIMUM ALICASTRUM
BT1 brosimum
BT2 moraceae
BT1 browse plants
BT1 medicinal plants

BROTIANIDE
BT1 anthelmintics
BT2 antiparasitic agents
BT3 drugs

BROTIZOLAM
HN from 1989
BT1 appetite stimulants
BT2 stimulants
BT3 drugs

BROUSSONETIA
BT1 moraceae
NT1 broussonetia kazinoki
NT1 broussonetia papyrifera

broussonetia kaempferi
USE **broussonetia kazinoki**

BROUSSONETIA KAZINOKI
uf *broussonetia kaempferi*
BT1 broussonetia
BT2 moraceae
BT1 ornamental woody plants

BROUSSONETIA PAPYRIFERA
BT1 broussonetia
BT2 moraceae

BROWALLIA
BT1 solanaceae
NT1 browallia speciosa

BROWALLIA SPECIOSA
BT1 browallia
BT2 solanaceae
BT1 ornamental herbaceous plants

BROWN AND SERVE FOODS (AGRICOLA)
BT1 convenience foods
BT2 foods

BROWN ATLAS
HN from 1990
BT1 cattle breeds
BT2 breeds

BROWN COAL
uf *coal, brown*
BT1 coal
BT2 fuels
BT2 growing media
BT2 inoculant carriers
BT3 carriers
BT2 manures
BT3 organic amendments
BT4 soil amendments
BT5 amendments
rt peat

BROWN CORE
BT1 plant disorders
BT2 disorders
rt apples
rt chicory
rt pears

BROWN EARTHS
BT1 cambisols
BT2 soil types (genetic)

BROWN FAT
uf *adipose tissue, brown*
BT1 body fat
BT2 fat

BROWN FOREST SOILS
BT1 cambisols
BT2 soil types (genetic)

BROWN HEART
BT1 plant disorders
BT2 disorders
rt apples
rt radishes
rt swedes

BROWN PODZOLIC SOILS
BT1 podzols
BT2 soil types (genetic)

BROWN RENDZINAS
BT1 rendzinas
BT2 soil types (genetic)

brown sarson
USE **brassica napus var. dichotoma**

BROWN SEAWEEDS
BT1 seaweeds
rt laminaria
rt phaeophyta
rt sargassum

BROWN SUGAR
HN from 1990
BT1 sugar
BT2 plant products
BT3 products

brown swiss
USE **american brown swiss**

BROWN TROUT
uf *salmo trutta fario*
uf *trout, brown*
BT1 freshwater fishes
BT2 aquatic animals
BT3 animals
BT3 aquatic organisms
rt salmonidae

BROWNING
(enzymatic oxidation of phenolic substances in foods; for nonenzymatic browning use "maillard reaction")
rt enzyme activity
rt maillard reaction
rt phenolic compounds

browning reaction
USE **maillard reaction**

BROWSE
(any plant material browsed or fit for browsing)
rt browse plants

BROWSE PLANTS
NT1 acacia homalophylla
NT1 acacia sophorae
NT1 acacia sowdenii
NT1 acacia tetragonophylla
NT1 albizia chinensis
NT1 amelanchier utahensis
NT1 artemisia cana
NT1 artemisia tridentata
NT1 atriplex halimus
NT1 atriplex semibaccata
NT1 bassia astrocarpa
NT1 bassia diacantha
NT1 bassia lanicuspis
NT1 bassia ventricosa
NT1 boscia senegalensis
NT1 brosimum alicastrum
NT1 brunonia australis
NT1 calandrinia remota
NT1 capparis decidua
NT1 capparis tomentosa
NT1 cassia eremophila

BROWSE PLANTS *cont.*
NT1 cassia italica
NT1 cassia leptocarpa
NT1 cassia leurssenii
NT1 cassia notabilis
NT1 cassia orientalis
NT1 cassia peralteana
NT1 cassia sturtii
NT1 cassinia fulvida
NT1 ceanothus cordulatus
NT1 ceanothus fendleri
NT1 ceanothus leucodermis
NT1 ceanothus prostratus
NT1 cercidium microphyllum
NT1 cercis chinensis
NT1 cercocarpus betuloides
NT1 coleogyne ramosissima
NT1 colutea istria
NT1 combretum aculeatum
NT1 combretum zeyheri
NT1 coprosma parviflora
NT1 coprosma propinqua
NT1 cordia rothii
NT1 derris kanjilalii
NT1 dodonaea attenuata
NT1 dodonaea viscosa
NT1 eremophila fraseri
NT1 eremophila gilesii
NT1 eremophila longifolia
NT1 eremophila mitchellii
NT1 eremophila sturtii
NT1 eriogonum fasciculatum
NT1 erythrina indica
NT1 juniperus occidentalis
NT1 juniperus osteosperma
NT1 juniperus scopulorum
NT1 krascheninnikovia ceratoides
NT1 krascheninnikovia lanata
NT1 larrea tridentata
NT1 lonicera japonica
NT1 lotus creticus
NT1 maireana pyramidata
NT1 opuntia microrhiza
NT1 parmentiera cerifera
NT1 prosopis affinis
NT1 prosopis alba
NT1 prosopis chilensis
NT1 prosopis nigra
NT1 prosopis pallida
NT1 prosopis tamarugo
NT1 samanea saman
NT1 sarcobatus vermiculatus
NT1 sesbania grandiflora
NT1 tamarindus indica
rt baikiaea
rt browse
rt browsing
rt feeds
rt fodder
rt fodder crops
rt fodder plants
rt forest trees
rt grazing
rt green fodders
rt herbage
rt plants

BROWSING
uf *browsing behaviour*
BT1 feeding habits
BT2 feeding behaviour
BT3 behaviour
BT2 habits
rt browse plants
rt browsing damage
rt feeding
rt unrestricted feeding

browsing behaviour
USE **browsing**

BROWSING DAMAGE
BT1 damage
rt browsing

BROXURIDINE
uf *bromodeoxyuridine*
BT1 deoxyuridines
BT2 deoxyribonucleosides
BT3 nucleosides
BT4 glycosides
BT5 carbohydrates

BROXURIDINE *cont.*
BT1 metabolic inhibitors
BT2 inhibitors
BT1 mutagens

BRUCEA
BT1 simaroubaceae
NT1 brucea javanica

BRUCEA JAVANICA
BT1 brucea
BT2 simaroubaceae
BT1 medicinal plants

BRUCEANTIN
BT1 quassinoids
BT2 triterpenoids
BT3 terpenoids
BT4 isoprenoids
BT5 lipids

BRUCELLA
BT1 brucellaceae
BT2 gracilicutes
BT3 bacteria
BT4 prokaryotes
NT1 brucella abortus
NT1 brucella canis
NT1 brucella melitensis
NT1 brucella ovis
NT1 brucella suis
rt brucellin

BRUCELLA ABORTUS
BT1 brucella
BT2 brucellaceae
BT3 gracilicutes
BT4 bacteria
BT5 prokaryotes
rt brucellosis

BRUCELLA CANIS
BT1 brucella
BT2 brucellaceae
BT3 gracilicutes
BT4 bacteria
BT5 prokaryotes

BRUCELLA MELITENSIS
BT1 brucella
BT2 brucellaceae
BT3 gracilicutes
BT4 bacteria
BT5 prokaryotes
rt brucellosis

BRUCELLA OVIS
BT1 brucella
BT2 brucellaceae
BT3 gracilicutes
BT4 bacteria
BT5 prokaryotes

BRUCELLA SUIS
BT1 brucella
BT2 brucellaceae
BT3 gracilicutes
BT4 bacteria
BT5 prokaryotes
rt brucellosis

BRUCELLACEAE
BT1 gracilicutes
BT2 bacteria
BT3 prokaryotes
NT1 brucella
NT2 brucella abortus
NT2 brucella canis
NT2 brucella melitensis
NT2 brucella ovis
NT2 brucella suis

BRUCELLIN
BT1 allergens
BT2 antigens
BT3 immunological factors
rt brucella
rt brucellosis

BRUCELLOSIS
BT1 bacterial diseases
BT2 infectious diseases
BT3 diseases
BT1 milkborne diseases

BRUCELLOSIS *cont.*
BT2 diseases
rt abortion
rt brucella abortus
rt brucella melitensis
rt brucella suis
rt brucellin
rt infertility
rt ring test

BRUCHIDAE
BT1 coleoptera
NT1 acanthoscelides
NT2 acanthoscelides obtectus
NT1 bruchidius
NT2 bruchidius atrolineatus
NT2 bruchidius incarnatus
NT1 bruchus
NT2 bruchus emarginatus
NT2 bruchus lentis
NT2 bruchus pisorum
NT2 bruchus rufimanus
NT1 callosobruchus
NT2 callosobruchus analis
NT2 callosobruchus chinensis
NT2 callosobruchus maculatus
NT1 caryedon
NT2 caryedon serratus
NT1 megacerus
NT2 megacerus discoidus
NT1 spermophagus
NT2 spermophagus sericeus
NT1 zabrotes
NT2 zabrotes subfasciatus

BRUCHIDIUS
BT1 bruchidae
BT2 coleoptera
NT1 bruchidius atrolineatus
NT1 bruchidius incarnatus

BRUCHIDIUS ATROLINEATUS
BT1 bruchidius
BT2 bruchidae
BT3 coleoptera

BRUCHIDIUS INCARNATUS
BT1 bruchidius
BT2 bruchidae
BT3 coleoptera

BRUCHOPHAGUS
BT1 eurytomidae
BT2 hymenoptera
NT1 bruchophagus roddi
rt eurytoma

BRUCHOPHAGUS RODDI
uf *eurytoma roddi*
BT1 bruchophagus
BT2 eurytomidae
BT3 hymenoptera

BRUCHUS
BT1 bruchidae
BT2 coleoptera
NT1 bruchus emarginatus
NT1 bruchus lentis
NT1 bruchus pisorum
NT1 bruchus rufimanus
rt callosobruchus

bruchus chinensis
USE **callosobruchus chinensis**

BRUCHUS EMARGINATUS
BT1 bruchus
BT2 bruchidae
BT3 coleoptera

BRUCHUS LENTIS
BT1 bruchus
BT2 bruchidae
BT3 coleoptera

BRUCHUS PISORUM
BT1 bruchus
BT2 bruchidae
BT3 coleoptera

BRUCHUS RUFIMANUS
BT1 bruchus
BT2 bruchidae
BT3 coleoptera

BRUCKENTHALIA
BT1 ericaceae
rt ornamental plants

BRUGIA
BT1 onchocercidae
BT2 nematoda
NT1 brugia malayi
NT1 brugia pahangi
NT1 brugia patei
NT1 brugia timori

BRUGIA MALAYI
BT1 brugia
BT2 onchocercidae
BT3 nematoda

BRUGIA PAHANGI
BT1 brugia
BT2 onchocercidae
BT3 nematoda

BRUGIA PATEI
BT1 brugia
BT2 onchocercidae
BT3 nematoda

BRUGIA TIMORI
BT1 brugia
BT2 onchocercidae
BT3 nematoda

BRUGMANSIA
BT1 solanaceae
NT1 brugmansia aurea
NT1 brugmansia sanguinea

BRUGMANSIA AUREA
BT1 brugmansia
BT2 solanaceae

BRUGMANSIA SANGUINEA
BT1 brugmansia
BT2 solanaceae

BRUGUIERA
BT1 rhizophoraceae
NT1 bruguiera cylindrica
NT1 bruguiera gymnorrhiza
NT1 bruguiera parviflora
NT1 bruguiera sexangula
rt mangroves

BRUGUIERA CYLINDRICA
BT1 bruguiera
BT2 rhizophoraceae
BT1 forest trees

BRUGUIERA GYMNORRHIZA
BT1 bruguiera
BT2 rhizophoraceae
BT1 forest trees

BRUGUIERA PARVIFLORA
BT1 bruguiera
BT2 rhizophoraceae
BT1 forest trees

BRUGUIERA SEXANGULA
BT1 bruguiera
BT2 rhizophoraceae

BRUISES
HN from 1990
(animals and man; for plant material use "bruising")
BT1 trauma

BRUISING
(plant material; for animals and man use "bruises")
BT1 injuries
rt damage
rt handling
rt mechanical damage
rt processing

BRUMOIDES
BT1 coccinellidae
BT2 coleoptera
NT1 brumoides suturalis

BRUMOIDES SUTURALIS
BT1 brumoides
BT2 coccinellidae

BRUMOIDES SUTURALIS *cont.*
BT3 coleoptera

brunchorstia
USE **gremmeniella**

brunchorstia destruens
USE **gremmeniella abietina**

brunchorstia pinea
USE **gremmeniella abietina**

BRUNEI
BT1 south east asia
BT2 asia
rt asean

BRUNFELSIA
BT1 solanaceae
NT1 brunfelsia macrophylla
NT1 brunfelsia pauciflora
NT1 brunfelsia uniflora

brunfelsia calycina
USE **brunfelsia pauciflora**

brunfelsia hopeana
USE **brunfelsia uniflora**

BRUNFELSIA MACROPHYLLA
BT1 brunfelsia
BT2 solanaceae
BT1 ornamental woody plants

BRUNFELSIA PAUCIFLORA
uf *brunfelsia calycina*
BT1 brunfelsia
BT2 solanaceae
BT1 ornamental woody plants

BRUNFELSIA UNIFLORA
uf *brunfelsia hopeana*
BT1 brunfelsia
BT2 solanaceae
BT1 medicinal plants

BRUNISOLIC SOILS
BT1 cambisols
BT2 soil types (genetic)

BRUNIZEMS
BT1 phaeozems
BT2 soil types (genetic)

BRUNNERA
BT1 boraginaceae
rt ornamental herbaceous plants

BRUNNICHIA
BT1 polygonaceae
NT1 brunnichia cirrhosa

BRUNNICHIA CIRRHOSA
BT1 brunnichia
BT2 polygonaceae

BRUNONIA
BT1 brunoniaceae
NT1 brunonia australis

BRUNONIA AUSTRALIS
BT1 browse plants
BT1 brunonia
BT2 brunoniaceae

BRUNONIACEAE
NT1 brunonia
NT2 brunonia australis

BRUNSVIGIA
BT1 amaryllidaceae
NT1 brunsvigia radulosa

BRUNSVIGIA RADULOSA
BT1 brunsvigia
BT2 amaryllidaceae
BT1 medicinal plants
BT1 ornamental bulbs

BRUSH CONTROL
rt brush cutters
rt brushwood
rt herbicides
rt slashing
rt weed control

BRUSH CONTROL *cont.*
rt woody weeds

BRUSH CUTTERS
BT1 forestry machinery
BT2 machinery
rt brush control
rt weed control
rt woody weeds

BRUSHES
rt cleaning
rt forage conditioners
rt root cleaners

BRUSHWOOD
BT1 vegetation types
rt brush control

BRUSSELS SPROUTS
BT1 leafy vegetables
BT2 vegetables
rt brassica oleracea var. gemmifera
rt sprouts

BRYOBIA
BT1 tetranychidae
BT2 prostigmata
BT3 acari
NT1 bryobia praetiosa
NT1 bryobia ribis
NT1 bryobia rubrioculus

BRYOBIA PRAETIOSA
BT1 bryobia
BT2 tetranychidae
BT3 prostigmata
BT4 acari

BRYOBIA RIBIS
BT1 bryobia
BT2 tetranychidae
BT3 prostigmata
BT4 acari

BRYOBIA RUBRIOCULUS
BT1 bryobia
BT2 tetranychidae
BT3 prostigmata
BT4 acari

BRYOLOGY
BT1 botany
BT2 biology
rt bryophyta

BRYONIA
BT1 cucurbitaceae
NT1 bryonia alba
NT1 bryonia cretica

BRYONIA ALBA
BT1 bryonia
BT2 cucurbitaceae

BRYONIA CRETICA
uf *bryonia dioica*
BT1 bryonia
BT2 cucurbitaceae
BT1 medicinal plants

bryonia dioica
USE **bryonia cretica**

BRYOPHYLLUM
BT1 crassulaceae
rt kalanchoe

bryophyllum calycinum
USE **kalanchoe pinnata**

bryophyllum crenatum
USE **kalanchoe laxiflora**

BRYOPHYTA
rt bryology
rt cryptogams
rt liverworts
rt mosses

bryozoa
USE **ectoprocta**
OR **endoprocta**

BRYUM
BT1 mosses

bse
USE **bovine spongiform encephalopathy**

BUBALUS
BT1 bovidae
BT2 ruminantia
BT3 artiodactyla
BT4 mammals
BT4 ungulates

bubalus bubalis
USE **buffaloes**

BUBO
BT1 strigidae
BT2 strigiformes
BT3 birds
NT1 bubo bubo
NT1 bubo virginianus

BUBO BUBO
BT1 bubo
BT2 strigidae
BT3 strigiformes
BT4 birds

BUBO VIRGINIANUS
BT1 bubo
BT2 strigidae
BT3 strigiformes
BT4 birds

BUBULCUS
BT1 ardeidae
BT2 ciconiiformes
BT3 birds
NT1 bubulcus ibis
NT2 bubulcus ibis coromandus
rt ardeola

bubulcus coromandus
USE **bubulcus ibis coromandus**

BUBULCUS IBIS
uf *ardeola ibis*
BT1 bubulcus
BT2 ardeidae
BT3 ciconiiformes
BT4 birds
NT1 bubulcus ibis coromandus

BUBULCUS IBIS COROMANDUS
uf *bubulcus coromandus*
BT1 bubulcus ibis
BT2 bubulcus
BT3 ardeidae
BT4 ciconiiformes
BT5 birds

BUCCINIDAE
BT1 gastropoda
BT2 mollusca
NT1 buccinum
NT2 buccinum undatum

BUCCINUM
BT1 buccinidae
BT2 gastropoda
BT3 mollusca
NT1 buccinum undatum

BUCCINUM UNDATUM
BT1 buccinum
BT2 buccinidae
BT3 gastropoda
BT4 mollusca

BUCCULATRIX
BT1 lyonetiidae
BT2 lepidoptera
NT1 bucculatrix thurberiella

BUCCULATRIX THURBERIELLA
BT1 bucculatrix
BT2 lyonetiidae
BT3 lepidoptera

BUCEPHALIDAE
BT1 digenea
BT2 trematoda
NT1 bucephalus

BUCEPHALIDAE *cont.*
NT1 prosorhynchus
NT1 rhipidocotyle

BUCEPHALUS
BT1 bucephalidae
BT2 digenea
BT3 trematoda

BUCEROTIDAE
uf *hornbills*
BT1 coraciiformes
BT2 birds

BUCHANANIA
BT1 anacardiaceae
NT1 buchanania lanzan

BUCHANANIA LANZAN
BT1 buchanania
BT2 anacardiaceae
BT1 oilseed plants
BT2 fatty oil plants
BT3 oil plants

BUCHI
HN from 1990
BT1 sheep breeds
BT2 breeds

BUCHLOE
BT1 gramineae
NT1 buchloe dactyloides

BUCHLOE DACTYLOIDES
BT1 buchloe
BT2 gramineae
BT1 pasture plants

BUCIDA
BT1 combretaceae
NT1 bucida buceras

BUCIDA BUCERAS
BT1 bucida
BT2 combretaceae
BT1 ornamental woody plants

BUCKET CALF FEEDERS
BT1 calf feeders
BT2 feed dispensers
BT3 dispensers

BUCKET ELEVATORS
uf *elevators, bucket*
BT1 elevators
BT2 conveyors

BUCKET MILKING MACHINES
uf *milking machines, bucket*
BT1 milking machines
BT2 farm machinery
BT3 machinery

BUCKETS
BT1 containers
rt earth moving equipment
rt power shovels
rt scoops

BUCKLEYA
BT1 santalaceae
NT1 buckleya lanceolata

BUCKLEYA LANCEOLATA
BT1 buckleya
BT2 santalaceae

BUCKRAKES
uf *sweeps*
BT1 rakes
BT2 farm machinery
BT3 machinery
rt haymaking

BUCKS
BT1 male animals
BT2 animals

BUCKWHEAT
BT1 green manures
BT2 manures
BT3 organic amendments
BT4 soil amendments
BT5 amendments
BT1 pseudocereals

BUCKWHEAT *cont.*
BT2 grain crops
rt fagopyrum esculentum

BUD CULTURE
HN from 1990
BT1 vegetative propagation
BT2 propagation
rt buds

BUDDING
BT1 grafting
BT2 vegetative propagation
BT3 propagation
rt buds
rt budwood
rt rootstocks
rt unions

BUDDLEJA
BT1 buddlejaceae
NT1 buddleja davidii
NT1 buddleja japonica
NT1 buddleja madagascariensis

BUDDLEJA DAVIDII
BT1 buddleja
BT2 buddlejaceae
BT1 ornamental woody plants
BT1 piscicidal plants

BUDDLEJA JAPONICA
BT1 buddleja
BT2 buddlejaceae
BT1 ornamental woody plants
BT1 piscicidal plants

BUDDLEJA MADAGASCARIENSIS
BT1 buddleja
BT2 buddlejaceae
BT1 ornamental woody plants

BUDDLEJACEAE
NT1 buddleja
NT2 buddleja davidii
NT2 buddleja japonica
NT2 buddleja madagascariensis
NT1 gomphostigma
NT2 gomphostigma virgatum

budennyi
USE **budyonny**

BUDGERIGARS
uf *melopsittacus undulatus*
BT1 aviary birds
BT2 animals
rt pets
rt psittacidae
rt psittaciformes

budget accounting
USE **budgets**
OR **farm budgeting**

BUDGET HOTELS
BT1 hotels
BT2 holiday accommodation
BT3 accommodation

BUDGETARY CONTROL
BT1 budgets

budgeting
USE **farm budgeting**

BUDGETS
uf *budget accounting*
NT1 agricultural budgets
NT1 budgetary control
NT1 family budgets
NT2 household consumption
NT2 household expenditure
NT1 farm budgeting
NT1 household budgets (agricola)

BUDS
uf *flower buds*
uf *leaf buds*
BT1 plant
rt apical meristems
rt branching
rt bud culture
rt budding

BUDS *cont.*
rt budwood
rt bulbils
rt disbudding
rt epicormics
rt flowers
rt fruiting potential
rt leaves
rt propagation materials
rt scions
rt shoots
rt sphaeroblasts
rt sprouts

BUDWOOD
BT1 scions
BT2 propagation materials
rt budding
rt buds
rt shoots
rt topworking

BUDYONNY
HN from 1990; previously "budennyi"
uf *budennyi*
BT1 horse breeds
BT2 breeds

BUFADIENOLIDES
BT1 lactones
BT2 heterocyclic oxygen compounds
BT2 ketones
BT1 steroids
BT2 isoprenoids
BT3 lipids

BUFENCARB
uf *metalkamate*
BT1 carbamate insecticides
BT2 carbamate pesticides
BT2 insecticides
BT3 pesticides

buffalo
USE **buffaloes**

BUFFALO BREEDS
(only important and recognised breeds are listed)
BT1 breeds
NT1 anatolian
NT1 bhadawari
NT1 bulgarian
NT1 egyptian
NT1 european
NT1 italian
NT1 jafarabadi
NT1 kundi
NT1 mehsana
NT1 murrah
NT1 nagpuri
NT1 nili-ravi
NT1 surti
NT1 tarai

BUFFALO CALVES
BT1 young animals
BT2 animals
rt buffaloes

BUFFALO DUNG
BT1 faeces
BT2 excreta
BT3 animal wastes
BT4 wastes
rt buffaloes

BUFFALO FEEDING
BT1 ruminant feeding
BT2 livestock feeding
BT3 animal feeding
BT4 feeding
rt buffaloes

BUFFALO MEAT
BT1 meat
BT2 animal products
BT3 products
BT2 foods
rt buffaloes

BUFFALO MILK
uf *milk, buffalo*
BT1 milks
BT2 body fluids
BT3 fluids
rt buffalo milk fat
rt buffaloes

BUFFALO MILK FAT
BT1 milk fat
BT2 animal fat
BT3 fat
rt buffalo milk
rt buffaloes

BUFFALO POXVIRUS
BT1 orthopoxvirus
BT2 chordopoxvirinae
BT3 poxviridae
BT4 viruses

BUFFALOES
(distinguish from bison and from synceros caffer)
uf *bubalus bubalis*
uf *buffalo*
uf *carabao*
uf *river buffaloes*
uf *swamp buffaloes*
uf *water buffaloes*
BT1 meat animals
BT2 animals
BT1 working animals
BT2 animals
rt bovidae
rt buffalo calves
rt buffalo dung
rt buffalo feeding
rt buffalo meat
rt buffalo milk
rt buffalo milk fat
rt livestock

buffaloes, african
USE **synceros caffer**

buffaloes, american
USE **bison**

buffel grass
USE **cenchrus ciliaris**
OR **urochloa mosambicensis**

BUFFER STOCKS
uf *reserve stocks*
uf *stock piling (economic)*
BT1 stocks
rt market stabilization
rt stabilization
rt stock piling subsidies

BUFFERING CAPACITY
BT1 physicochemical properties
BT2 properties
rt acid base equilibrium
rt buffers
rt capacity
rt ph

BUFFERS
NT1 sodium bicarbonate
rt acid base equilibrium
rt bicarbonates
rt buffering capacity
rt ph

BUFFETS (AGRICOLA)
BT1 food serving methods (agricola)
BT2 methodology

BUFO
BT1 bufonidae
BT2 anura
BT3 amphibia
NT1 bufo bufo
NT1 bufo marinus
NT1 bufo melanostictus
NT1 bufo paracnemis
NT1 bufo regularis
NT1 bufo typhonius
NT1 bufo viridis

BUFO BUFO
BT1 bufo
BT2 bufonidae
BT3 anura
BT4 amphibia

BUFO MARINUS
BT1 bufo
BT2 bufonidae
BT3 anura
BT4 amphibia

BUFO MELANOSTICTUS
BT1 bufo
BT2 bufonidae
BT3 anura
BT4 amphibia

BUFO PARACNEMIS
BT1 bufo
BT2 bufonidae
BT3 anura
BT4 amphibia

BUFO REGULARIS
BT1 bufo
BT2 bufonidae
BT3 anura
BT4 amphibia

BUFO TYPHONIUS
BT1 bufo
BT2 bufonidae
BT3 anura
BT4 amphibia

BUFO VIRIDIS
BT1 bufo
BT2 bufonidae
BT3 anura
BT4 amphibia

BUFONIDAE
BT1 anura
BT2 amphibia
NT1 bufo
NT2 bufo bufo
NT2 bufo marinus
NT2 bufo melanostictus
NT2 bufo paracnemis
NT2 bufo regularis
NT2 bufo typhonius
NT2 bufo viridis

BUFORMIN
BT1 biguanides
BT2 amides
BT3 organic nitrogen compounds
BT1 hypoglycaemic agents
BT2 haematologic agents
BT3 drugs

BUGLOSSOIDES
BT1 boraginaceae
NT1 buglossoides arvensis
NT1 buglossoides purpurocaerulea

BUGLOSSOIDES ARVENSIS
uf *lithospermum arvense*
BT1 buglossoides
BT2 boraginaceae
BT1 medicinal plants

BUGLOSSOIDES PURPUROCAERULEA
uf *lithospermum purpurocaeruleum*
BT1 buglossoides
BT2 boraginaceae
BT1 medicinal plants

bugs
USE **hemiptera**

BUILDING CONSTRUCTION
BT1 construction
NT1 brickwork
NT1 foundations
NT1 stonework
rt architecture
rt beams
rt building materials

BUILDING CONSTRUCTION *cont.*
rt building timbers
rt buildings
rt construction technology
rt engineering
rt girders
rt inflated structures
rt masonry
rt panels
rt partitions
rt prefabricated buildings
rt reinforcement
rt roofs
rt struts
rt walls
rt wind loads
rt windows

BUILDING CONTROLS
BT1 physical planning
BT2 planning
rt buildings
rt farm dwellings
rt land use
rt rural housing
rt zoning

BUILDING INDUSTRY
HN from 1989
BT1 industry
rt building materials

BUILDING MATERIALS
BT1 materials
NT1 bricks
NT1 building timbers
NT1 cement
NT2 wood cement
NT1 cladding
NT2 double cladding
NT2 plastic cladding
NT1 clay
NT2 kaolin
NT2 phosphatic clay
NT1 concrete
NT1 expanded metal
NT1 galvanized iron
NT1 glass
NT2 coated glass
NT2 diffused glass
NT2 glasswool
NT1 glassfibre reinforced plastics
NT1 mortar
NT1 mud
NT1 panels
NT2 blockboard
NT2 composite boards
NT2 fibreboards
NT3 hardboard
NT2 laminated wood
NT3 microlam
NT2 particleboards
NT3 flakeboards
NT3 osb
NT2 plastic panels
NT2 wood panels
NT1 partitions
NT1 plaster
NT2 plaster of paris
NT1 plasterboard
NT1 sawnwood
NT2 slabs
NT1 sheet metal
NT1 shingles
NT1 slabs
NT1 slates
NT1 straw cobs
NT1 strawboards
NT1 tiles
NT1 wallboard
rt bamboos
rt bolts
rt building construction
rt building industry
rt buildings
rt construction
rt construction technology
rt insulating materials
rt poles
rt reinforcement
rt structural components
rt structural steel

building methods
USE **construction technology**

BUILDING TIMBERS
BT1 building materials
BT2 materials
rt building construction
rt construction
rt timber trade

BUILDINGS
NT1 abattoirs
NT1 animal hospitals
NT1 cabins
NT2 log cabins
NT1 churches
NT1 country houses
NT1 factories
NT2 canneries (agricola)
NT2 dairy factories
NT2 sugar refineries
NT2 textile mills (agricola)
NT1 farm buildings
NT2 barns
NT3 dutch barns
NT2 chitting houses
NT2 farm dairies
NT2 greenhouses
NT3 tower greenhouses
NT3 wide span greenhouses
NT2 mushroom houses
NT1 garages
NT1 historic buildings
NT1 honey houses
NT1 hospitals
NT1 libraries
NT1 mobile buildings
NT1 nursing homes
NT1 packhouses
NT1 prefabricated buildings
NT1 recreational buildings
NT2 casinos
NT2 ice rinks
NT2 indoor arenas
NT1 school buildings
NT1 sheds
NT2 tobacco curing sheds
NT1 sports buildings
NT1 temporary buildings
NT1 tropical buildings
NT1 workshops
rt architecture
rt building construction
rt building controls
rt building materials
rt ceilings
rt cellars
rt columns
rt construction technology
rt doors
rt foundations
rt inflated structures
rt lightning conductors
rt roofs
rt span
rt stairs
rt stores
rt structures
rt ventilators
rt walls
rt windows

buildings, agricultural
USE **farm buildings**

buildings, farm
USE **farm buildings**

buildings, mobile
USE **mobile buildings**

buildings, prefabricated
USE **prefabricated buildings**

buildings, temporary
USE **temporary buildings**

buildings, tropical
USE **tropical buildings**

BULB HARVESTERS
uf *harvesters, bulb*
BT1 harvesters

BULB HARVESTERS *cont.*
BT2 farm machinery
BT3 machinery
rt bulbs

BULB PLANTERS
uf *planters, bulb*
BT1 planters
BT2 farm machinery
BT3 machinery
rt bulbs

BULB SCALES
BT1 bulbs
BT2 plant
BT2 propagation materials
rt leaves

BULBECTOMY
HN from 1989
BT1 surgical operations

BULBILS
rt buds
rt bulbs
rt leaves
rt vegetative propagation

BULBO-URETHRAL GLAND
BT1 accessory glands
BT2 glands (animal)
BT3 body parts
BT3 glands
BT2 male genitalia
BT3 genitalia
BT4 urogenital system
BT5 body parts

BULBOCODIUM
BT1 liliaceae

BULBOPHYLLUM
BT1 orchidaceae
NT1 bulbophyllum adenambon
NT1 bulbophyllum garupinum

BULBOPHYLLUM ADENAMBON
BT1 bulbophyllum
BT2 orchidaceae
BT1 ornamental orchids

BULBOPHYLLUM GARUPINUM
BT1 bulbophyllum
BT2 orchidaceae
BT1 ornamental orchids

BULBOUS VEGETABLES
BT1 vegetables
NT1 allium chinense
NT1 allium ledbourianum
NT1 allium ramosum
NT1 allium scorodoprasum
NT1 chives
NT1 garlic
NT1 leeks
NT1 onions
NT1 shallots
NT1 welsh onions
rt plants

BULBS
BT1 plant
BT1 propagation materials
NT1 bulb scales
rt bulb harvesters
rt bulb planters
rt bulbils
rt ornamental bulbs
rt planting stock
rt sets
rt sprouting
rt stems
rt vegetative propagation

bulbs, ornamental
USE **ornamental bulbs**

BULGARIA
BT1 eastern europe
BT2 europe
rt balkans
rt cmea

BULGARIAN
HN from 1990

BULGARIAN *cont.*
BT1 buffalo breeds
BT2 breeds

BULGARIAN BROWN
HN from 1990; previously "sofia brown"
uf *sofia brown*
BT1 cattle breeds
BT2 breeds

BULGARIAN RED
BT1 cattle breeds
BT2 breeds

BULGARIAN SIMMENTAL
HN from 1990
BT1 cattle breeds
BT2 breeds

BULGARIAN WHITE
BT1 pig breeds
BT2 breeds

BULGUR
BT1 foods
rt wheat

BULIMIA
uf *binge eating*
BT1 appetite disorders
BT2 digestive disorders
BT3 functional disorders
BT4 animal disorders
BT5 disorders
rt bulimia nervosa (agricola)
rt compulsive eating (agricola)

BULIMIA NERVOSA (AGRICOLA)
BT1 appetite disorders
BT2 digestive disorders
BT3 functional disorders
BT4 animal disorders
BT5 disorders
rt bulimia

BULINIDAE
BT1 gastropoda
BT2 mollusca
NT1 bulinus
NT2 bulinus africanus
NT2 bulinus forskali
NT2 bulinus globosus
NT2 bulinus rohlfsi
NT2 bulinus senegalensis
NT2 bulinus tropicus
NT2 bulinus truncatus
NT1 indoplanorbis
NT2 indoplanorbis exustus

BULINUS
BT1 bulinidae
BT2 gastropoda
BT3 mollusca
NT1 bulinus africanus
NT1 bulinus forskali
NT1 bulinus globosus
NT1 bulinus rohlfsi
NT1 bulinus senegalensis
NT1 bulinus tropicus
NT1 bulinus truncatus

BULINUS AFRICANUS
BT1 bulinus
BT2 bulinidae
BT3 gastropoda
BT4 mollusca

BULINUS FORSKALI
BT1 bulinus
BT2 bulinidae
BT3 gastropoda
BT4 mollusca

BULINUS GLOBOSUS
BT1 bulinus
BT2 bulinidae
BT3 gastropoda
BT4 mollusca

BULINUS ROHLFSI
BT1 bulinus
BT2 bulinidae
BT3 gastropoda

BULINUS ROHLFSI *cont.*
BT4 mollusca

BULINUS SENEGALENSIS
BT1 bulinus
BT2 bulinidae
BT3 gastropoda
BT4 mollusca

BULINUS TROPICUS
BT1 bulinus
BT2 bulinidae
BT3 gastropoda
BT4 mollusca

BULINUS TRUNCATUS
BT1 bulinus
BT2 bulinidae
BT3 gastropoda
BT4 mollusca

BULK
rt ballast
rt bulk density
rt bulk handling
rt bulk storage
rt bulk trailers
rt bulking agents
rt digestion
rt volume

BULK BLENDING
BT1 blending
BT2 processing
rt bulk blends

BULK BLENDS
rt bulk blending
rt fertilizers

BULK DENSITY
uf density, bulk
BT1 density
rt bulk
rt compacted density
rt soil density

BULK HANDLING
BT1 handling
rt bulk

BULK MILK
uf milk, bulk
BT1 milk
BT2 animal products
BT3 products

BULK STORAGE
uf storage, bulk
BT1 storage
rt bulk

BULK TRAILERS
BT1 trailers
BT2 vehicles
rt bulk

BULKING
rt biological treatment
rt waste water treatment

BULKING AGENTS
BT1 food additives
BT2 additives
NT1 methylcellulose
rt bulk
rt improved wood
rt stabilizers
rt swelling

bull
USE **bulls**

BULL DAMS
HN from 1989
BT1 dams (mothers)
BT2 parents
BT3 ancestry

BULL FATTENING
BT1 cattle fattening
BT2 fattening
BT3 animal feeding
BT4 feeding
rt bulls

BULL FEEDING
BT1 cattle feeding
BT2 ruminant feeding
BT3 livestock feeding
BT4 animal feeding
BT5 feeding
rt bulls

BULL FIGHTING
BT1 spectator events
BT2 entertainment
BT3 leisure activities
BT2 recreational activities
rt tourist attractions

BULLDOZERS
BT1 earth moving equipment
BT2 equipment
rt land levellers

BULLETIN BOARDS (AGRICOLA)
BT1 audiovisual aids
BT2 teaching materials

bullocks
USE **steers**

bullock's heart
USE **annona reticulata**

BULLS
uf bull
BT1 male animals
BT2 animals
NT1 ai bulls
NT1 beef bulls
NT1 dairy bulls
NT1 steers
rt bull fattening
rt bull feeding
rt cattle
rt teasing

bulrush millet
USE **pearl millet**

bumble bees
USE **bombus**

BUMELIA
BT1 sapotaceae
NT1 bumelia lanuginosa

BUMELIA LANUGINOSA
BT1 bumelia
BT2 sapotaceae

BUMINAFOS
HN from 1990
BT1 desiccant herbicides
BT2 desiccants
BT1 organophosphorus herbicides
BT2 herbicides
BT3 pesticides
BT2 organophosphorus pesticides
BT3 organophosphorus compounds

BUNAMIDINE
BT1 amidines
BT2 organic nitrogen compounds
BT1 anthelmintics
BT2 antiparasitic agents
BT3 drugs

BUNCHING
BT1 handling
rt bundling
rt cut flowers
rt cut foliage
rt fasciation
rt felling
rt skidding

BUNDLED WOOD
BT1 wood
rt handling

BUNDLING
BT1 handling
rt bunching
rt collection

BUNDLING *cont.*
rt straw trussers

BUNDS
BT1 ridges
rt water conservation

BUNIAS
BT1 cruciferae
NT1 bunias orientalis

BUNIAS ORIENTALIS
BT1 bunias
BT2 cruciferae
BT1 fodder plants

BUNIUM
BT1 umbelliferae
NT1 bunium bulbocastanum
NT1 bunium persicum

BUNIUM BULBOCASTANUM
uf carum bulbocastanum
BT1 bunium
BT2 umbelliferae

BUNIUM PERSICUM
BT1 bunium
BT2 umbelliferae
BT1 essential oil plants
BT2 oil plants

BUNKER SILOS
uf silos, bunker
BT1 silos
BT2 stores
rt pit silos

BUNKERS
BT1 containers
rt bins
rt boxes
rt hoppers
rt stores

BUNOSTOMUM
BT1 ancylostomatidae
BT2 nematoda
NT1 bunostomum phlebotomum
NT1 bunostomum trigonocephalum

BUNOSTOMUM PHLEBOTOMUM
BT1 bunostomum
BT2 ancylostomatidae
BT3 nematoda

BUNOSTOMUM TRIGONOCEPHALUM
BT1 bunostomum
BT2 ancylostomatidae
BT3 nematoda

BUNYAVIRIDAE
BT1 viruses
NT1 bunyavirus
NT2 akabane virus
NT2 barranqueras virus
NT2 cache valley virus
NT2 california encephalitis virus
NT2 calovo virus
NT2 jamestown canyon virus
NT2 la crosse virus
NT2 oropouche virus
NT2 snowshoe hare virus
NT2 tahyna virus
NT2 trivittatus virus
NT1 hantavirus
NT2 hantaan virus
NT1 nairovirus
NT2 crimean-congo haemorrhagic fever virus
NT2 dugbe virus
NT2 hughes virus
NT2 nairobi sheep disease virus
NT1 phlebovirus
NT2 rift valley fever virus
NT2 sandfly fever viruses
NT3 sandfly fever (naples) virus
NT3 sandfly fever (sicily) virus
NT2 toscana virus
NT1 uukuvirus
NT2 uukuniemi virus

BUNYAVIRIDAE *cont.*
NT2 zaliv terpeniya virus

BUNYAVIRUS
BT1 arboviruses
BT2 pathogens
BT1 bunyaviridae
BT2 viruses
NT1 akabane virus
NT1 barranqueras virus
NT1 cache valley virus
NT1 california encephalitis virus
NT1 calovo virus
NT1 jamestown canyon virus
NT1 la crosse virus
NT1 oropouche virus
NT1 snowshoe hare virus
NT1 tahyna virus
NT1 trivittatus virus

BUPALUS
BT1 geometridae
BT2 lepidoptera
NT1 bupalus piniarius

BUPALUS PINIARIUS
BT1 bupalus
BT2 geometridae
BT3 lepidoptera

BUPARVAQUONE
HN from 1990
BT1 antiprotozoal agents
BT2 antiparasitic agents
BT3 drugs

BUPIRIMATE
BT1 pyrimidine fungicides
BT2 fungicides
BT3 pesticides
BT2 pyrimidines
BT3 heterocyclic nitrogen compounds
BT4 organic nitrogen compounds

BUPLEURUM
BT1 umbelliferae
NT1 bupleurum aureum
NT1 bupleurum falcatum
NT1 bupleurum lancifolium
NT1 bupleurum multinerve
NT1 bupleurum rotundifolium
NT1 bupleurum scorzonerifolium
NT1 bupleurum tenuissimum

BUPLEURUM AUREUM
BT1 bupleurum
BT2 umbelliferae

BUPLEURUM FALCATUM
BT1 bupleurum
BT2 umbelliferae
BT1 medicinal plants

BUPLEURUM LANCIFOLIUM
BT1 bupleurum
BT2 umbelliferae

BUPLEURUM MULTINERVE
BT1 bupleurum
BT2 umbelliferae

BUPLEURUM ROTUNDIFOLIUM
BT1 bupleurum
BT2 umbelliferae

BUPLEURUM SCORZONERIFOLIUM
BT1 bupleurum
BT2 umbelliferae
BT1 medicinal plants

BUPLEURUM TENUISSIMUM
BT1 bupleurum
BT2 umbelliferae

BUPRESTIDAE
BT1 coleoptera
NT1 agrilus
NT2 agrilus anxius
NT1 capnodis
NT2 capnodis miliaris
NT2 capnodis tenebrionis
NT1 chrysobothris
NT1 melanophila

BUPROFEZIN
BT1 chitin synthesis inhibitors
BT2 insect growth regulators
BT3 growth regulators
BT3 insecticides
BT4 pesticides
BT2 metabolic inhibitors
BT3 inhibitors

BUQUINOLATE
BT1 coccidiostats
BT2 antiprotozoal agents
BT3 antiparasitic agents
BT4 drugs
BT1 quinolines
BT2 heterocyclic nitrogen compounds
BT3 organic nitrogen compounds

burbots
USE **lota lota**

BURCKELLA
BT1 sapotaceae
NT1 burckella obovata

BURCKELLA OBOVATA
BT1 burckella
BT2 sapotaceae

BURENELLA
BT1 microspora
BT2 protozoa
NT1 burenella dimorpha

BURENELLA DIMORPHA
BT1 burenella
BT2 microspora
BT3 protozoa

BURGENLAND
BT1 austria
BT2 western europe
BT3 europe

burglar alarms
USE **alarms**

BURGUNDY
uf *bourgogne*
BT1 france
BT2 western europe
BT3 europe

BURGUNDY MIXTURE
BT1 copper fungicides
BT2 fungicides
BT3 pesticides

BURIED SEEDS
HN from 1989
rt seed banks
rt seeds

BURIED SOILS
BT1 soil types (palaeosolic)
rt fossil soils
rt palaeosols

BURKEA
BT1 leguminosae
NT1 burkea africana

BURKEA AFRICANA
BT1 burkea
BT2 leguminosae

BURKINA FASO
uf *bourkina fasso*
uf *upper volta*
BT1 west africa
BT2 africa south of sahara
BT3 africa
rt acp
rt developing countries
rt francophone africa
rt least developed countries

BURMA
BT1 south east asia
BT2 asia
rt developing countries
rt least developed countries

BURNERS
BT1 heaters
BT2 equipment
rt boilers
rt combustion
rt fuels

BURNING
uf *flaming*
NT1 ashing
NT1 controlled burning
NT1 haulm destruction
NT1 straw burning
rt ash
rt cautery
rt combustion
rt fire effects
rt fires
rt flame cultivators
rt ignition
rt kilns
rt shifting cultivation
rt spontaneous ignition
rt toasting
rt wood smoke

BURNOUT (AGRICOLA)
rt mental stress

BURNS
BT1 trauma
rt heat

BURNT SOILS
BT1 soil types (miscellaneous)

BUROZEMS
BT1 xerosols
BT2 soil types (genetic)

BURRAMYIDAE
BT1 marsupials
BT2 mammals
NT1 acrobates

BURRKNOTS
BT1 plant
rt shoots

BURROWING
BT1 animal behaviour
BT2 behaviour
rt animal burrows

BURRS
rt fruits
rt grain and figure
rt wood defects

bursa
USE **serous bursa**

bursa cloacae
USE **bursa fabricii**

BURSA FABRICII
uf *bursa cloacae*
BT1 lymphatic system
BT2 cardiovascular system
BT3 body parts
rt cloaca

BURSAPHELENCHUS
BT1 aphelenchoididae
BT2 nematoda
NT1 bursaphelenchus mucronatus
NT1 bursaphelenchus xylophilus

bursaphelenchus lignicolus
USE **bursaphelenchus xylophilus**

BURSAPHELENCHUS MUCRONATUS
HN from 1990
BT1 bursaphelenchus
BT2 aphelenchoididae
BT3 nematoda

BURSAPHELENCHUS XYLOPHILUS
HN from 1990; previously "bursaphelenchus lignicolus"
uf *bursaphelenchus lignicolus*

BURSAPHELENCHUS XYLOPHILUS *cont.*
BT1 bursaphelenchus
BT2 aphelenchoididae
BT3 nematoda

BURSARIA
BT1 ciliophora
BT2 protozoa
NT1 bursaria truncatella

BURSARIA TRUNCATELLA
BT1 bursaria
BT2 ciliophora
BT3 protozoa

BURSECTOMY
BT1 surgical operations

BURSERA
BT1 burseraceae
NT1 bursera klugii
NT1 bursera morelensis
NT1 bursera penicillata
NT1 bursera schlechtendalii
NT1 bursera simaruba
rt forest trees

bursera delpechiana
USE **bursera penicillata**

BURSERA KLUGII
BT1 bursera
BT2 burseraceae

BURSERA MORELENSIS
BT1 bursera
BT2 burseraceae

BURSERA PENICILLATA
uf *bursera delpechiana*
BT1 antiviral plants
BT1 bursera
BT2 burseraceae
BT1 essential oil plants
BT2 oil plants

BURSERA SCHLECHTENDALII
BT1 bursera
BT2 burseraceae

BURSERA SIMARUBA
BT1 bursera
BT2 burseraceae

BURSERACEAE
NT1 aucoumea
NT2 aucoumea klaineana
NT1 boswellia
NT2 boswellia frereana
NT2 boswellia sacra
NT2 boswellia serrata
NT1 bursera
NT2 bursera klugii
NT2 bursera morelensis
NT2 bursera penicillata
NT2 bursera schlechtendalii
NT2 bursera simaruba
NT1 canarium
NT2 canarium luzonicum
NT2 canarium schweinfurthii
NT2 canarium vitiense
NT2 canarium zeylanicum
NT1 commiphora
NT2 commiphora africana
NT2 commiphora mukul
NT2 commiphora wightii
NT1 garuga
NT2 garuga pinnata

BURSITIS
BT1 joint diseases
BT2 organic diseases
BT3 diseases
rt avian infectious bursitis

BURUNDI
BT1 central africa
BT2 africa south of sahara
BT3 africa
rt acp
rt developing countries
rt francophone africa
rt least developed countries

BURYAT
BT1 sheep breeds
BT2 breeds

BUS TRANSPORT
BT1 transport

BUSA
BT1 cattle breeds
BT2 breeds

bush fallowing
USE **shifting cultivation**

BUSHUEV
HN from 1990
BT1 cattle breeds
BT2 breeds

business management
USE **farm management**
OR **management**

BUSINESS TOURISM
BT1 tourism

BUSINESSES
uf *economic units*
NT1 entrepreneurship
NT1 firms
NT2 companies
NT3 multinational corporations
NT3 private companies
NT3 public companies
NT2 foreign firms
NT2 large firms
NT2 private firms
NT3 partnerships
NT4 limited partnerships (agricola)
NT1 home-based businesses (agricola)
NT1 small businesses
NT2 cottage industry
NT1 travel agents

BUSSEOLA
BT1 noctuidae
BT2 lepidoptera
NT1 busseola fusca

BUSSEOLA FUSCA
BT1 busseola
BT2 noctuidae
BT3 lepidoptera

BUSULFAN
BT1 alkylating agents
BT1 antineoplastic agents
BT2 drugs
BT1 chemosterilants
BT2 sterilants
BT1 sulfonates
BT2 organic sulfur compounds

BUTACARB
BT1 carbamate insecticides
BT2 carbamate pesticides
BT2 insecticides
BT3 pesticides

BUTACHLOR
BT1 chloroacetanilide herbicides
BT2 anilide herbicides
BT3 amide herbicides
BT4 herbicides
BT5 pesticides

BUTADIENE-STYRENE COPOLYMER
BT1 polymers
BT1 soil conditioners
BT2 soil amendments
BT3 amendments

butam
USE **tebutam**

BUTAMIFOS
BT1 organophosphorus herbicides
BT2 herbicides
BT3 pesticides
BT2 organophosphorus pesticides

BUTAMIFOS *cont.*
BT3 organophosphorus compounds

BUTANA
HN from 1990; previously "red butana"
uf *red butana*
BT1 cattle breeds
BT2 breeds

BUTANEDIOL
BT1 glycols
BT2 alcohols

butanoic acid
USE **butyric acid**

BUTANOL
BT1 alcohols

BUTCHERING (AGRICOLA)
NT1 boning (agricola)
NT2 hot boning (agricola)
rt food processing
rt meat cuts
rt slaughtering

BUTEA
BT1 leguminosae
NT1 butea monosperma

butea frondosa
USE **butea monosperma**

BUTEA MONOSPERMA
uf *butea frondosa*
BT1 butea
BT2 leguminosae
BT1 forest trees
BT1 medicinal plants
BT1 nematicidal plants
BT2 pesticidal plants

BUTHIDAE
BT1 scorpiones
BT2 arachnida
BT3 arthropods
NT1 androctonus
NT2 androctonus aeneas
NT2 androctonus amoreuxi
NT2 androctonus australis
NT3 androctonus australis hector
NT2 androctonus mauretanicus
NT1 buthotus
NT2 buthotus minax
NT2 buthotus tamulus
NT1 buthus
NT2 buthus martensi
NT2 buthus occitanus
NT1 centruroides
NT2 centruroides gracilis
NT2 centruroides limpidus
NT3 centruroides limpidus limpidus
NT3 centruroides limpidus tecomanus
NT2 centruroides noxius
NT2 centruroides sculpturatus
NT1 leiurus
NT2 leiurus quinquestriatus
NT1 mesobuthus
NT1 tityus
NT2 tityus serrulatus

BUTHIDAZOLE
BT1 unclassified herbicides
BT2 herbicides
BT3 pesticides

BUTHIOBATE
BT1 pyridine fungicides
BT2 fungicides
BT3 pesticides
BT2 pyridines
BT3 heterocyclic nitrogen compounds
BT4 organic nitrogen compounds

BUTHIURON
BT1 urea herbicides
BT2 herbicides

BUTHIURON *cont.*
BT3 pesticides

BUTHOTUS
BT1 buthidae
BT2 scorpiones
BT3 arachnida
BT4 arthropods
NT1 buthotus minax
NT1 buthotus tamulus
rt buthus

BUTHOTUS MINAX
uf *buthus minax*
BT1 buthotus
BT2 buthidae
BT3 scorpiones
BT4 arachnida
BT5 arthropods

BUTHOTUS TAMULUS
HN from 1990; previously "buthus tamulus"
uf *buthus tamulus*
BT1 buthotus
BT2 buthidae
BT3 scorpiones
BT4 arachnida
BT5 arthropods

BUTHUS
BT1 buthidae
BT2 scorpiones
BT3 arachnida
BT4 arthropods
NT1 buthus martensi
NT1 buthus occitanus
rt buthotus
rt leiurus
rt mesobuthus

BUTHUS MARTENSI
HN from 1989
BT1 buthus
BT2 buthidae
BT3 scorpiones
BT4 arachnida
BT5 arthropods

buthus minax
USE **buthotus minax**

BUTHUS OCCITANUS
BT1 buthus
BT2 buthidae
BT3 scorpiones
BT4 arachnida
BT5 arthropods

buthus quinquestriatus
USE **leiurus quinquestriatus**

buthus tamulus
USE **buthotus tamulus**

BUTIA
BT1 palmae
NT1 butia capitata

BUTIA CAPITATA
BT1 butia
BT2 palmae
BT1 ornamental palms

BUTOCARBOXIM
BT1 oxime carbamate acaricides
BT2 carbamate acaricides
BT3 acaricides
BT4 pesticides
BT3 carbamate pesticides
BT1 oxime carbamate insecticides
BT2 carbamate insecticides
BT3 carbamate pesticides
BT3 insecticides
BT4 pesticides

BUTOMACEAE
NT1 butomus
NT2 butomus umbellatus

BUTOMUS
BT1 butomaceae
NT1 butomus umbellatus

BUTOMUS UMBELLATUS
BT1 butomus
BT2 butomaceae

BUTONATE
BT1 phosphonate insecticides
BT2 organophosphorus insecticides
BT3 insecticides
BT4 pesticides
BT3 organophosphorus pesticides
BT4 organophosphorus compounds

BUTOPYRONOXYL
BT1 insect repellents
BT2 repellents

BUTORIDES
BT1 ardeidae
BT2 ciconiiformes
BT3 birds
NT1 butorides striatus

BUTORIDES STRIATUS
BT1 butorides
BT2 ardeidae
BT3 ciconiiformes
BT4 birds

BUTRALIN
BT1 dinitroaniline herbicides
BT2 herbicides
BT3 pesticides

butt rots
USE **root and butt rots**

BUTTER
BT1 milk products
BT2 products
NT1 whey butter
rt blending
rt butter churns
rt butter oil
rt buttermaking
rt buttermilk
rt clarification
rt clarifiers
rt cooking fats
rt crystallization
rt fats
rt ghee
rt margarine
rt milk fat
rt ripened cream
rt sweet cream

BUTTER CHURNS
BT1 dairy equipment
BT2 equipment
rt butter
rt buttermaking

BUTTER OIL
BT1 animal oils
BT2 fatty oils
BT3 oils
BT1 milk products
BT2 products
rt butter
rt ghee
rt milk fat

butter yellow
USE **p-dimethylaminoazobenzene**

butterfat
USE **milk fat**

butterfish
USE **pholis gunnellus**

BUTTERMAKING
BT1 dairying
NT1 continuous buttermaking
rt blending
rt butter
rt butter churns
rt cream
rt dairy technology
rt milk products

BUTTERMAKING *cont.*
rt ripened cream
rt sweet cream

buttermaking, continuous
USE **continuous buttermaking**

BUTTERMILK
BT1 milk products
BT2 products
rt butter

BUTTRESSES
BT1 trunks
rt spurs
rt stem form

BUTURON
BT1 urea herbicides
BT2 herbicides
BT3 pesticides

BUTYLAMINE
uf *2-aminobutane*
BT1 aliphatic nitrogen fungicides
BT2 fungicides
BT3 pesticides

BUTYLATE
BT1 thiocarbamate herbicides
BT2 carbamate pesticides
BT2 herbicides
BT3 pesticides

BUTYLATED HYDROXYANISOLE
uf *bha*
uf *hydroxyanisole, butylated*
BT1 antioxidants
BT2 additives
BT1 food preservatives
BT2 preservatives

BUTYLATED HYDROXYTOLUENE
uf *bht*
uf *hydroxytoluene, butylated*
BT1 antioxidants
BT2 additives
BT1 food preservatives
BT2 preservatives

BUTYRATES
NT1 butyrates (esters)
NT2 tributyrin
NT1 butyrates (salts)
NT2 sodium butyrate
rt butyric acid

BUTYRATES (ESTERS)
BT1 butyrates
BT1 esters
NT1 tributyrin

BUTYRATES (SALTS)
BT1 butyrates
BT1 organic salts
BT2 salts
NT1 sodium butyrate

BUTYRIC ACID
uf *butanoic acid*
BT1 silage additives
BT2 additives
BT1 volatile fatty acids
BT2 fatty acids
BT3 carboxylic acids
BT4 organic acids
BT5 acids
BT3 lipids
BT2 volatile compounds
rt butyrates
rt butyric acid bacteria

BUTYRIC ACID BACTERIA
BT1 microbial flora
BT2 flora
rt bacteria
rt butyric acid
rt butyrivibrio

BUTYRIVIBRIO
BT1 bacteroidaceae
BT2 gracilicutes
BT3 bacteria
BT4 prokaryotes
NT1 butyrivibrio fibrisolvens

BUTYRIVIBRIO *cont.*
rt butyric acid bacteria

BUTYRIVIBRIO FIBRISOLVENS
BT1 butyrivibrio
BT2 bacteroidaceae
BT3 gracilicutes
BT4 bacteria
BT5 prokaryotes

BUTYROMETERS
BT1 dairy equipment
BT2 equipment
rt milk fat

BUTYROSPERMUM
BT1 sapotaceae

butyrospermum paradoxum
USE **vitellaria paradoxa**

butyrospermum parkii
USE **vitellaria paradoxa**

BUTYRYL ACIDAEMIA
AF butyryl acidemia
BT1 acidaemia
BT2 blood disorders
BT3 animal disorders
BT4 disorders

BUTYRYL ACIDEMIA
BF butyryl acidaemia
BT1 acidemia

BUTYRYL-COA DEHYDROGENASE
(ec 1.3.99.2)
BT1 oxidoreductases
BT2 enzymes

butyrylcholine esterase
USE **cholinesterase**

BUXACEAE
NT1 buxus
NT2 buxus japonica
NT2 buxus madagascarica
NT2 buxus microphylla
NT2 buxus sempervirens
NT2 buxus wallichiana
NT1 pachysandra
NT2 pachysandra procumbens
NT2 pachysandra terminalis

BUXTONELLA
BT1 ciliophora
BT2 protozoa
NT1 buxtonella sulcata

BUXTONELLA SULCATA
BT1 buxtonella
BT2 ciliophora
BT3 protozoa

BUXUS
BT1 buxaceae
NT1 buxus japonica
NT1 buxus madagascarica
NT1 buxus microphylla
NT1 buxus sempervirens
NT1 buxus wallichiana

buxus harlandii
USE **buxus microphylla**

BUXUS JAPONICA
BT1 buxus
BT2 buxaceae

BUXUS MADAGASCARICA
BT1 buxus
BT2 buxaceae

BUXUS MICROPHYLLA
uf *buxus harlandii*
BT1 buxus
BT2 buxaceae
BT1 ornamental woody plants

BUXUS SEMPERVIRENS
uf *box*
BT1 buxus
BT2 buxaceae
BT1 forest trees
BT1 ornamental woody plants

BUXUS WALLICHIANA
BT1 buxus
BT2 buxaceae
BT1 ornamental woody plants

BUYERS' GUIDES
BT1 catalogues
BT2 publications
BT1 guide books
BT2 books
BT3 publications
rt prices

BUYING GROUPS
BT1 groups
BT1 wholesale marketing
BT2 marketing channels
BT3 marketing
rt cooperative marketing
rt cooperative purchasing

BUYING PRICES
uf *prices, buying*
BT1 prices

BUZURA
BT1 geometridae
BT2 lepidoptera
NT1 buzura suppressaria
rt biston

BUZURA SUPPRESSARIA
uf *biston suppressaria*
BT1 buzura
BT2 geometridae
BT3 lepidoptera

BYELORUSSIAN BLACK PIED
HN from 1990; previously "white-russian black pied"
uf *white-russian black pied*
BT1 pig breeds
BT2 breeds

BYELORUSSIAN HARNESS
HN from 1990
BT1 horse breeds
BT2 breeds

BYELORUSSIAN RED
HN from 1990; previously "white-russian red"
uf *white-russian red*
BT1 cattle breeds
BT2 breeds

BYELORUSSIAN SSR
uf *belorussian ssr*
BT1 ussr in europe
BT2 ussr

BYPRODUCTS
NT1 agricultural byproducts
NT2 cereal byproducts
NT3 bran
NT4 maize bran
NT4 oat bran (agricola)
NT4 rice bran
NT4 wheat bran
NT3 brewers' grains
NT3 chaff
NT3 maize byproducts
NT4 maize bran
NT4 maize cobs
NT4 maize stover
NT4 maize straw
NT3 rice byproducts
NT4 rice bran
NT4 rice polishings
NT4 rice straw
NT3 rye middlings
NT2 cocoa byproducts
NT2 meat byproducts
NT3 meat and bone meal
NT3 meat meal
NT4 tendon meal
NT4 whale meal
NT3 offal
NT4 brain as food
NT4 heart as food
NT4 kidneys as food
NT4 livers as food
NT5 foie gras
NT5 goose liver

BYPRODUCTS *cont.*
NT4 sweetbreads
NT2 milk byproducts
NT2 peel
NT3 cassava peel
NT3 orange peel
NT2 straw
NT3 barley straw
NT3 bean straw
NT3 groundnut haulm
NT3 maize straw
NT3 oat straw
NT3 rape straw
NT3 rice straw
NT3 rye straw
NT3 ryegrass straw
NT3 sorghum stalks
NT3 soya straw
NT3 stover
NT4 maize stover
NT3 wheat straw
NT2 sugarcane byproducts
NT3 sugarcane bagasse
NT3 sugarcane pith
NT3 sugarcane tops
NT1 agroindustrial byproducts
NT2 brewery byproducts
NT3 brewers' grains
NT2 hydrol
NT2 milling byproducts
rt products

BYRSONIMA
BT1 malpighiaceae
NT1 byrsonima verbascifolia

BYRSONIMA VERBASCIFOLIA
BT1 byrsonima
BT2 malpighiaceae
BT1 medicinal plants

BYSSOCHLAMYS
BT1 eurotiales
NT1 byssochlamys fulva
NT1 byssochlamys nivea

BYSSOCHLAMYS FULVA
BT1 byssochlamys
BT2 eurotiales

BYSSOCHLAMYS NIVEA
BT1 byssochlamys
BT2 eurotiales

BYTURIDAE
BT1 coleoptera
NT1 byturus
NT2 byturus tomentosus

BYTURUS
BT1 byturidae
BT2 coleoptera
NT1 byturus tomentosus

BYTURUS TOMENTOSUS
BT1 byturus
BT2 byturidae
BT3 coleoptera

C-AMP
uf *adenosine monophosphate, cyclic*
uf *cyclic adenosine monophosphate*
uf *cyclic amp*
BT1 adenosine phosphates
BT2 phosphates (esters)
BT3 esters
BT3 phosphates
BT2 purine nucleotides
BT3 nucleotides
BT4 glycosides
BT5 carbohydrates
BT1 cyclic nucleotides
BT2 nucleotides
BT3 glycosides
BT4 carbohydrates
rt amp

C BANDS
rt chromosome banding
rt chromosomes

C-PEPTIDE
BT1 polypeptides
BT2 peptides
rt insulin

c (symbol)
USE **carbon**

ca (symbol)
USE **calcium**

CAATINGA
HN from 1990
BT1 savanna woodlands
BT2 woodlands
BT3 vegetation types

CAB INTERNATIONAL
uf *commonwealth agricultural bureaux*
BT1 international organizations
BT2 organizations
rt identification services
rt information services

cabbage, chinese
USE **chinese cabbages**

CABBAGE HARVESTERS
uf *harvesters, cabbage*
BT1 harvesters
BT2 farm machinery
BT3 machinery
rt cabbages

cabbage, red
USE **cabbages**

CABBAGES
uf *cabbage, red*
BT1 leafy vegetables
BT2 vegetables
BT1 nematicidal plants
BT2 pesticidal plants
rt brassica oleracea var. capitata
rt cabbage harvesters
rt pepper spot
rt sauerkraut
rt tipburn

CABINS
BT1 buildings
NT1 log cabins
rt holiday chalets

CABLE METHODS
uf *cable traction*
uf *traction, cable*
rt cables
rt cableways
rt forestry machinery
rt logging
rt winches

cable traction
USE **cable methods**

CABLES
BT1 equipment
rt cable methods

CABLES *cont.*
rt cableways
rt forestry machinery
rt grapple methods
rt logging

CABLEWAYS
uf *skyline logging*
BT1 forestry machinery
BT2 machinery
rt cable methods
rt cables
rt conveyors
rt logging

CABOMBA
BT1 cabombaceae
NT1 cabomba caroliniana

CABOMBA CAROLINIANA
BT1 cabomba
BT2 cabombaceae

CABOMBACEAE
NT1 brasenia
NT2 brasenia schreberi
NT1 cabomba
NT2 cabomba caroliniana

CABS
uf *tractor cabs*
BT1 components
NT1 safety cabs
NT1 suspension cabs
rt farm machinery
rt tractors

cacao
USE **cocoa**
OR **theobroma cacao**

CACAO SWOLLEN SHOOT VIRUS
uf *cocoa swollen shoot virus*
BT1 unclassified plant viruses
BT2 plant viruses
BT3 plant pathogens
BT4 pathogens
rt cocoa
rt theobroma cacao

CACAO YELLOW MOSAIC TYMOVIRUS
HN from 1990
BT1 tymovirus group
BT2 plant viruses
BT3 plant pathogens
BT4 pathogens
rt cocoa
rt theobroma cacao

CACHE VALLEY VIRUS
BT1 bunyavirus
BT2 arboviruses
BT3 pathogens
BT2 bunyaviridae
BT3 viruses

CACHEXIA
BT1 human diseases
BT2 diseases
rt anaemia
rt malnutrition

CACIOCAVALLO CHEESE
BT1 cheeses
BT2 milk products
BT3 products

CACM
uf *central american common market*
BT1 common markets
BT2 economic unions
rt bermuda
rt costa rica
rt economic regions
rt el salvador
rt guatemala
rt honduras
rt nicaragua

CACODYLIC ACID
uf *dimethylarsinic acid*
BT1 arboricides

CACODYLIC ACID *cont.*
BT2 herbicides
BT3 pesticides
BT1 arsenical herbicides
BT2 arsenicals
BT2 herbicides
BT3 pesticides

cacoecia
USE **archips**

cacoecia crataegana
USE **archips crataeganus**

cacoecia podana
USE **archips podanus**

cacoecia pronubana
USE **cacoecimorpha pronubana**

cacoecia rosana
USE **archips rosanus**

CACOECIMORPHA
BT1 tortricidae
BT2 lepidoptera
NT1 cacoecimorpha pronubana
rt tortrix

CACOECIMORPHA PRONUBANA
uf *cacoecia pronubana*
uf *tortrix pronubana*
BT1 cacoecimorpha
BT2 tortricidae
BT3 lepidoptera

CACOPAURUS
BT1 paratylenchidae
BT2 nematoda
NT1 cacopaurus pestis

CACOPAURUS PESTIS
BT1 cacopaurus
BT2 paratylenchidae
BT3 nematoda

CACOPSYLLA
BT1 psyllidae
BT2 psylloidea
BT3 sternorrhyncha
BT4 homoptera
NT1 cacopsylla mali
NT1 cacopsylla pyri
NT1 cacopsylla pyricola
NT1 cacopsylla pyrisuga
rt psylla

CACOPSYLLA MALI
uf *psylla mali*
BT1 cacopsylla
BT2 psyllidae
BT3 psylloidea
BT4 sternorrhyncha
BT5 homoptera

CACOPSYLLA PYRI
uf *psylla pyri*
BT1 cacopsylla
BT2 psyllidae
BT3 psylloidea
BT4 sternorrhyncha
BT5 homoptera

CACOPSYLLA PYRICOLA
uf *psylla pyricola*
BT1 cacopsylla
BT2 psyllidae
BT3 psylloidea
BT4 sternorrhyncha
BT5 homoptera

CACOPSYLLA PYRISUGA
BT1 cacopsylla
BT2 psyllidae
BT3 psylloidea
BT4 sternorrhyncha
BT5 homoptera

CACTACEAE
uf *cacti*
NT1 ancistrocactus
NT1 ariocarpus
NT1 blossfeldia
NT1 brasiliopuntia
NT2 brasiliopuntia brasiliensis

CACTACEAE *cont.*
NT1 carnegiea
NT2 carnegiea gigantea
NT1 cephalocereus
NT2 cephalocereus albispinus
NT2 cephalocereus chrysacanthus
NT2 cephalocereus guerreronis
NT2 cephalocereus maxonii
NT2 cephalocereus senilis
NT1 cereus
NT2 cereus jamacaru
NT2 cereus validus
NT1 cleistocactus
NT2 cleistocactus baumannii
NT2 cleistocactus strausii
NT1 coryphantha
NT2 coryphantha calipensis
NT2 coryphantha cladispina
NT2 coryphantha greenwoodii
NT2 coryphantha macromeris
NT2 coryphantha ramillosa
NT2 coryphantha robbinsorum
NT1 discocactus
NT2 discocactus albispinus
NT2 discocactus alteolens
NT2 discocactus araneispinus
NT2 discocactus estevesii
NT2 discocactus horichii
NT2 discocactus lankesteri
NT1 dolichothele
NT2 dolichothele longimamma
NT2 dolichothele sphaerica
NT1 echinocactus
NT2 echinocactus grusonii
NT2 echinocactus horizonthalonius
NT1 echinocereus
NT2 echinocereus cinerascens
NT2 echinocereus engelmannii
NT2 echinocereus knippelianus
NT2 echinocereus nivosus
NT2 echinocereus pectinatus
NT2 echinocereus triglochidiatus
NT2 echinocereus viridiflorus
NT1 echinomastus
NT2 echinomastus intertextus
NT1 echinopsis
NT2 echinopsis kermesina
NT1 epiphyllum
NT1 epithelantha
NT2 epithelantha micromeris
NT1 eriocereus
NT2 eriocereus adscendens
NT2 eriocereus martinii
NT1 escobaria
NT2 escobaria henricksonii
NT2 escobaria strobiliformis
NT2 escobaria vivipara
NT1 escontria
NT1 espostoa
NT2 espostoa huanucensis
NT2 espostoa plumosa
NT1 ferocactus
NT2 ferocactus grusonii
NT2 ferocactus latispinus
NT1 gymnocactus
NT1 hamatocactus
NT2 hamatocactus setispinus
NT1 hatiora
NT2 hatiora salicornioides
NT1 heliabravoa
NT2 heliabravoa chende
NT1 hylocereus
NT2 hylocereus calcaratus
NT2 hylocereus trigonus
NT2 hylocereus undatus
NT1 kotocactus
NT1 lemaireocereus
NT1 leptocladodia
NT2 leptocladodia elongata
NT1 lobivia
NT2 lobivia allegriana
NT2 lobivia aurea
NT2 lobivia backebergii
NT2 lobivia binghamiana
NT2 lobivia huashua
NT2 lobivia pentlandii
NT1 lophocereus
NT2 lophocereus schottii

CACTACEAE *cont.*
NT1 lophophora
NT2 lophophora diffusa
NT2 lophophora fricii
NT2 lophophora jourdaniana
NT2 lophophora williamsii
NT1 machaerocereus
NT1 maihuenia
NT2 maihuenia patagonica
NT2 maihuenia poeppigii
NT1 mammillaria
NT2 mammillaria hexacantha
NT2 mammillaria meridiorosei
NT2 mammillaria microcarpa
NT2 mammillaria parkinsonii
NT2 mammillaria perbella
NT2 mammillaria plumosa
NT2 mammillaria polythele
NT2 mammillaria prolifera
NT2 mammillaria pygmaea
NT2 mammillaria varieaculeata
NT2 mammillaria woodsii
NT1 mitrocereus
NT2 mitrocereus militaris
NT1 myrtillocactus
NT1 neobuxbaumia
NT2 neobuxbaumia euphorbioides
NT1 neolloydia
NT1 notocactus
NT2 notocactus coccinus
NT2 notocactus ottonis
NT2 notocactus submammulosus
NT1 obregonia
NT1 opuntia
NT2 opuntia aurantiaca
NT2 opuntia basilaris
NT2 opuntia boaplandii
NT2 opuntia clavata
NT2 opuntia dillenii
NT2 opuntia elata
NT2 opuntia elatior
NT2 opuntia engelmannii
NT2 opuntia ficus-indica
NT2 opuntia fragilis
NT2 opuntia fulgida
NT2 opuntia imbricata
NT2 opuntia leptocaulis
NT2 opuntia leptocaulis var. leptocauli
NT2 opuntia lindheimeri
NT2 opuntia microrhiza
NT2 opuntia phaeacantha
NT2 opuntia polyacantha
NT2 opuntia robusta
NT2 opuntia schottii
NT2 opuntia spinosior
NT2 opuntia stanlyi
NT2 opuntia stricta
NT2 opuntia tunicata
NT2 opuntia vulgaris
NT1 pachycereus
NT2 pachycereus hollianus
NT2 pachycereus pecten-arboriginum
NT2 pachycereus pringlei
NT1 parodia
NT1 pediocactus
NT1 pelecyphora
NT1 pereskia
NT2 pereskia aculeata
NT2 pereskia grandifolia
NT1 pereskiopsis
NT1 pseudomammillaria
NT2 pseudomammillaria camptotricha
NT1 pterocereus
NT2 pterocereus gaumeri
NT1 rathbunia
NT1 rebutia
NT2 rebutia marsoneri
NT2 rebutia minuscula
NT1 rhipsalidopsis
NT2 rhipsalidopsis gaertneri
NT1 rhipsalis
NT1 schlumbergera
NT2 schlumbergera buckleyi
NT2 schlumbergera orssichiana
NT2 schlumbergera russelliana
NT1 sclerocactus

CACTACEAE *cont.*
NT2 sclerocactus polyancistrus
NT1 selenicereus
NT2 selenicereus atropilosus
NT2 selenicereus macdonaldiae
NT1 stenocereus
NT2 stenocereus weberi
NT1 thelocactus
NT2 thelocactus viereckii
NT1 toumeya
NT1 trichocereus
NT2 trichocereus candicans
NT2 trichocereus pachanoi
NT2 trichocereus pasacana
NT2 trichocereus peruvianus
NT2 trichocereus spachianus
NT1 wigginsia
NT2 wigginsia arechavaletai
rt succulent plants

cacti
USE **cactaceae**

CACTOBLASTIS
BT1 pyralidae
BT2 lepidoptera
NT1 cactoblastis cactorum

CACTOBLASTIS CACTORUM
BT1 biological control agents
BT2 beneficial organisms
BT1 cactoblastis
BT2 pyralidae
BT3 lepidoptera

CACTODERA
BT1 heteroderidae
BT2 nematoda

CACTUS 2 CARLAVIRUS
HN from 1990
BT1 carlavirus group
BT2 plant viruses
BT3 plant pathogens
BT4 pathogens

cactus virus x
USE **cactus x potexvirus**

CACTUS X POTEXVIRUS
HN from 1990; previously "cactus virus x"
uf *cactus virus x*
BT1 potexvirus group
BT2 plant viruses
BT3 plant pathogens
BT4 pathogens

CADASTERS
BF cadastres

CADASTRES
AF cadasters
uf *land registers*
rt land ownership
rt land use
rt registration
rt surveys

CADAVERINE
uf *1,5-pentanediamine*
BT1 biogenic amines
BT2 amines
BT3 amino compounds
BT4 organic nitrogen compounds
BT1 diamines
BT2 amines
BT3 amino compounds
BT4 organic nitrogen compounds
BT1 ptomaines
BT2 organic nitrogen compounds
BT2 toxic substances

CADAVERS
rt forensic entomology
rt man

caddis
USE **trichoptera**

CADIA
BT1 leguminosae
NT1 cadia purpurea

CADIA PURPUREA
BT1 cadia
BT2 leguminosae

CADMIUM
uf *cd (symbol)*
BT1 transition elements
BT2 metallic elements
BT3 elements
BT3 metals

cadra
USE **ephestia**

cadra cautella
USE **ephestia cautella**

cadra figulilella
USE **ephestia figulilella**

CAECOTROPHY
AF cecotrophy
BT1 coprophagy
BT2 feeding habits
BT3 feeding behaviour
BT4 behaviour
BT3 habits
rt caecum
rt cellulose
rt circadian rhythm
rt faeces

CAECUM
AF cecum
BT1 large intestine
BT2 intestines
BT3 digestive system
BT4 body parts
rt caecotrophy

CAENORHABDITIS
BT1 rhabditidae
BT2 nematoda
NT1 caenorhabditis briggsae
NT1 caenorhabditis elegans

CAENORHABDITIS BRIGGSAE
BT1 caenorhabditis
BT2 rhabditidae
BT3 nematoda

CAENORHABDITIS ELEGANS
BT1 caenorhabditis
BT2 rhabditidae
BT3 nematoda

CAERPHILLY CHEESE
BT1 cheeses
BT2 milk products
BT3 products

caerulein
USE **ceruletide**

caeruloplasmin
USE **ceruloplasmin**

CAESALPINIA
BT1 leguminosae
NT1 caesalpinia bonduc
NT1 caesalpinia coriaria
NT1 caesalpinia crista
NT1 caesalpinia decapetala
NT1 caesalpinia echinata
NT1 caesalpinia ferrea
NT1 caesalpinia gilliesii
NT1 caesalpinia peltophoroides
NT1 caesalpinia pulcherrima
NT1 caesalpinia sappan
NT1 caesalpinia tinctoria
NT1 caesalpinia velutina

CAESALPINIA BONDUC
HN from 1990; previously "caesalpinia bonducella"
uf *caesalpinia bonducella*
BT1 caesalpinia
BT2 leguminosae
BT1 ornamental woody plants

caesalpinia bonducella
USE **caesalpinia bonduc**

CAESALPINIA CORIARIA
BT1 algicidal plants
BT1 caesalpinia
BT2 leguminosae
BT1 medicinal plants
BT1 tan plants

CAESALPINIA CRISTA
uf *caesalpinia nigra*
BT1 antibacterial plants
BT1 caesalpinia
BT2 leguminosae

CAESALPINIA DECAPETALA
BT1 caesalpinia
BT2 leguminosae

CAESALPINIA ECHINATA
BT1 caesalpinia
BT2 leguminosae

CAESALPINIA FERREA
BT1 caesalpinia
BT2 leguminosae

CAESALPINIA GILLIESII
BT1 caesalpinia
BT2 leguminosae

caesalpinia nigra
USE **caesalpinia crista**

CAESALPINIA PELTOPHOROIDES
BT1 caesalpinia
BT2 leguminosae

CAESALPINIA PULCHERRIMA
BT1 caesalpinia
BT2 leguminosae
BT1 ornamental woody plants

CAESALPINIA SAPPAN
BT1 caesalpinia
BT2 leguminosae
BT1 medicinal plants

CAESALPINIA TINCTORIA
BT1 caesalpinia
BT2 leguminosae

CAESALPINIA VELUTINA
HN from 1990
BT1 caesalpinia
BT2 leguminosae
BT1 forest trees

CAESAREAN SECTION
BT1 surgical operations
rt birth
rt parturition complications

CAESIUM
AF cesium
uf *cs (symbol)*
BT1 alkali metals
BT2 metallic elements
BT3 elements
BT3 metals

CAFES
BT1 dining facilities (agricola)
rt catering industry
rt restaurants

CAFETERIAS (AGRICOLA)
BT1 dining facilities (agricola)

CAFFEIC ACID
BT1 coumaric acids
BT2 benzenealkenoic acids
BT3 carboxylic acids
BT4 organic acids
BT5 acids

CAFFEINE
BT1 analeptics
BT2 neurotropic drugs
BT3 drugs
BT1 diuretics
BT2 drugs
BT1 stimulants
BT2 drugs
BT1 xanthine alkaloids

CAFFEINE *cont.*
BT2 alkaloids
BT2 xanthines
BT3 purines
BT4 heterocyclic nitrogen compounds
BT5 organic nitrogen compounds
rt camellia sinensis
rt coffea
rt cola acuminata

caffeoylquinic acid
USE **chlorogenic acid**

cage birds
USE **aviary birds**

CAGE DENSITY
rt cages
rt density
rt poultry farming
rt stocking density

CAGE SIZE
rt cages
rt size

CAGE WHEELS
uf *wheels, cage*
BT1 wheels
BT2 components
rt traction aids
rt tractors

CAGES
BT1 animal housing
NT1 battery cages
NT1 flat deck cages
NT1 flight cages
NT1 metabolism cages
NT1 perches
rt cage density
rt cage size
rt poultry housing

caicos islands
USE **turks and caicos islands**

CAIMAN
BT1 alligatoridae
BT2 crocodylia
BT3 reptiles

CAIRINA
BT1 anatidae
BT2 anseriformes
BT3 birds

cairina moschata
USE **muscovy ducks**

CAJANUS
BT1 leguminosae
NT1 cajanus cajan

CAJANUS CAJAN
uf *cajanus indicus*
uf *tur*
BT1 cajanus
BT2 leguminosae
BT1 grain legumes
BT2 grain crops
BT2 legumes
BT1 medicinal plants
rt pigeon pea sterility mosaic virus
rt pigeon peas

cajanus indicus
USE **cajanus cajan**

CAKE DECORATION (AGRICOLA)
BT1 food art (agricola)
BT2 arts
rt cakes

CAKES
BT1 bakery products
BT2 foods
BT2 products
BT1 confectionery
rt cake decoration (agricola)
rt oilseed cakes

CAKING
HN from 1990
rt anticaking agents
rt anticaking treatment
rt hardening

calabrese
USE **broccoli**

CALABRIA
BT1 italy
BT2 western europe
BT3 europe

CALACARUS
BT1 eriophyidae
BT2 prostigmata
BT3 acari
NT1 calacarus carinatus

CALACARUS CARINATUS
BT1 calacarus
BT2 eriophyidae
BT3 prostigmata
BT4 acari

CALADENIA
BT1 orchidaceae
rt ornamental orchids

CALADIUM
BT1 araceae
NT1 caladium hortulanum
NT1 caladium humboldtii

caladium argyrites
USE **caladium humboldtii**

CALADIUM HORTULANUM
BT1 caladium
BT2 araceae
rt ornamental foliage plants

CALADIUM HUMBOLDTII
uf *caladium argyrites*
BT1 caladium
BT2 araceae
rt ornamental foliage plants

CALAMAGROSTIS
uf *reed grass*
BT1 gramineae
NT1 calamagrostis angustifolia
NT1 calamagrostis arctica
NT1 calamagrostis arundinacea
NT1 calamagrostis canadensis
NT1 calamagrostis canescens
NT1 calamagrostis deschampsiodes
NT1 calamagrostis epigejos
NT1 calamagrostis fauriei
NT1 calamagrostis gunniana
NT1 calamagrostis longiseta
NT1 calamagrostis montanensis
NT1 calamagrostis neglecta
NT1 calamagrostis purpurascens
NT1 calamagrostis purpurea
NT1 calamagrostis purpurea subsp. langsdorfii
NT1 calamagrostis rubescens
NT1 calamagrostis villosa

CALAMAGROSTIS ANGUSTIFOLIA
BT1 calamagrostis
BT2 gramineae
BT1 pasture plants

CALAMAGROSTIS ARCTICA
BT1 calamagrostis
BT2 gramineae
BT1 pasture plants

CALAMAGROSTIS ARUNDINACEA
BT1 calamagrostis
BT2 gramineae

CALAMAGROSTIS CANADENSIS
BT1 calamagrostis
BT2 gramineae
BT1 pasture plants

CALAMAGROSTIS CANESCENS
BT1 calamagrostis
BT2 gramineae
BT1 pasture plants

CALAMAGROSTIS DESCHAMPSIODES
BT1 calamagrostis
BT2 gramineae
BT1 pasture plants

CALAMAGROSTIS EPIGEJOS
BT1 calamagrostis
BT2 gramineae
BT1 pasture plants

CALAMAGROSTIS FAURIEI
BT1 calamagrostis
BT2 gramineae
BT1 pasture plants

CALAMAGROSTIS GUNNIANA
BT1 calamagrostis
BT2 gramineae
BT1 pasture plants

calamagrostis langsdorfii
USE **calamagrostis purpurea subsp. langsdorfii**

CALAMAGROSTIS LONGISETA
BT1 calamagrostis
BT2 gramineae
BT1 pasture plants

CALAMAGROSTIS MONTANENSIS
BT1 calamagrostis
BT2 gramineae
BT1 pasture plants

CALAMAGROSTIS NEGLECTA
BT1 calamagrostis
BT2 gramineae
BT1 pasture plants

CALAMAGROSTIS PURPURASCENS
BT1 calamagrostis
BT2 gramineae
BT1 pasture plants

CALAMAGROSTIS PURPUREA
BT1 calamagrostis
BT2 gramineae
BT1 pasture plants

CALAMAGROSTIS PURPUREA SUBSP. LANGSDORFII
uf *calamagrostis langsdorfii*
BT1 calamagrostis
BT2 gramineae
BT1 pasture plants

CALAMAGROSTIS RUBESCENS
BT1 calamagrostis
BT2 gramineae
BT1 pasture plants

CALAMAGROSTIS VILLOSA
BT1 calamagrostis
BT2 gramineae
BT1 pasture plants

CALAMINTHA
BT1 labiatae
NT1 calamintha macrostema
NT1 calamintha officinalis
NT1 calamintha sylvatica

calamintha alpina
USE **acinos alpinus**

calamintha ascendens
USE **calamintha officinalis**

calamintha hortensis
USE **satureja hortensis**

CALAMINTHA MACROSTEMA
BT1 calamintha
BT2 labiatae

CALAMINTHA OFFICINALIS
uf *calamintha ascendens*
BT1 calamintha
BT2 labiatae

calamintha suaveolens
USE **acinos suaveolens**

CALAMINTHA SYLVATICA
uf *satureja calamintha*
BT1 calamintha
BT2 labiatae
BT1 essential oil plants
BT2 oil plants

CALAMONDINS
BT1 citrus fruits
BT2 subtropical tree fruits
BT3 subtropical fruits
BT4 fruit crops
BT3 tree fruits
rt citrus madurensis

CALAMOVILFA
BT1 gramineae
NT1 calamovilfa longifolia

CALAMOVILFA LONGIFOLIA
BT1 calamovilfa
BT2 gramineae
BT1 pasture plants

CALAMUS
BT1 palmae
NT1 calamus manan
NT1 calamus ornatus
NT1 calamus polystachys

CALAMUS MANAN
HN from 1990
BT1 calamus
BT2 palmae

CALAMUS ORNATUS
BT1 calamus
BT2 palmae

CALAMUS POLYSTACHYS
BT1 calamus
BT2 palmae

calandra
USE **sitophilus**

calandra granaria
USE **sitophilus granarius**

calandra oryzae
USE **sitophilus oryzae**

CALANDRIAS
HN from 1990
BT1 steamers
BT2 equipment
rt vacuum pans

CALANDRINIA
BT1 portulacaceae
NT1 calandrinia remota

CALANDRINIA REMOTA
BT1 browse plants
BT1 calandrinia
BT2 portulacaceae

CALANOIDA
BT1 copepoda
BT2 crustacea
BT3 arthropods
NT1 acartia
NT2 acartia clausi
NT2 acartia tonsa
NT1 diaptomus
NT1 eudiaptomus
NT2 eudiaptomus gracilis
NT2 eudiaptomus graciloides
NT1 eurytemora
NT2 eurytemora velox
NT1 pseudocalanus
NT1 skistodiaptomus
NT2 skistodiaptomus pallidus
NT1 temora

CALANTHE
BT1 orchidaceae
NT1 calanthe triplicata

CALANTHE TRIPLICATA
BT1 calanthe
BT2 orchidaceae
BT1 ornamental orchids

CALATHEA
BT1 marantaceae
NT1 calathea allouia
NT1 calathea crocata
NT1 calathea lancifolia
NT1 calathea lutea
NT1 calathea makoyana

CALATHEA ALLOUIA
BT1 calathea
BT2 marantaceae
BT1 root vegetables
BT2 root crops
BT2 vegetables
BT1 starch crops

CALATHEA CROCATA
BT1 calathea
BT2 marantaceae
rt ornamental foliage plants

calathea insignis
USE **calathea lancifolia**

CALATHEA LANCIFOLIA
uf *calathea insignis*
BT1 calathea
BT2 marantaceae
rt ornamental foliage plants

CALATHEA LUTEA
BT1 calathea
BT2 marantaceae

CALATHEA MAKOYANA
uf *maranta makoyana*
BT1 calathea
BT2 marantaceae
rt ornamental foliage plants

CALBINDIN
HN from 1990
BT1 calcium binding proteins
BT2 binding proteins
BT3 proteins
BT4 peptides

CALCAREOUS CHERNOZEMS
BT1 chernozems
BT2 soil types (genetic)

calcareous crusts
USE **calcrete**

CALCAREOUS ROCKS
BT1 soil parent materials

CALCAREOUS SOILS
BT1 soil types (chemical)
BT1 soil types (lithological)
rt calcicoles

CALCEOLARIA
BT1 scrophulariaceae
NT1 calceolaria mexicana

CALCEOLARIA MEXICANA
BT1 calceolaria
BT2 scrophulariaceae
BT1 ornamental herbaceous plants

CALCIC HORIZONS
BT1 horizons
BT2 soil morphological features

CALCICOLES
BT1 plant ecological groups
rt calcareous soils
rt calcifuges
rt ecology
rt ph

CALCIDIOL 1-MONOOXYGENASE
(ec 1.14.13.13)
uf *25-hydroxycholecalciferol 1-hydroxylase*
uf *25-hydroxycholecalciferol 1-monooxygenase*
BT1 oxygenases
BT2 oxidoreductases
BT3 enzymes

calciferol
USE **ergocalciferol**

CALCIFICATION
uf *skeleton calcification*
NT1 teeth calcification
rt bone formation
rt bone mineralization
rt calcinosis
rt calcium
rt lime

CALCIFUGES
BT1 plant ecological groups
rt calcicoles
rt calcium carbonate
rt ecology
rt ph

CALCINATION
BT1 processing
rt fertilizer technology

CALCINED ALUMINIUM PHOSPHATE
AF calcined aluminum phosphate
BT1 calcined phosphates
BT2 phosphorus fertilizers
BT3 fertilizers

CALCINED ALUMINUM PHOSPHATE
BF calcined aluminium phosphate

CALCINED PHOSPHATES
BT1 phosphorus fertilizers
BT2 fertilizers
NT1 calcined aluminium phosphate

CALCINOSIS
uf *enteque seco*
BT1 bone diseases
BT2 organic diseases
BT3 diseases
BT1 mineral metabolism disorders
BT2 metabolic disorders
BT3 animal disorders
BT4 disorders
rt calcification
rt calcium
rt milk alkali syndrome
rt nephrocalcinosis

CALCITE
BT1 nonclay minerals
BT2 minerals
rt calcium carbonate
rt chalk
rt limestone

CALCITONIN
uf *thyrocalcitonin*
BT1 neuropeptides
BT2 peptides
BT1 thyroid hormones
BT2 hormones

CALCITRIOL
uf *1,25-dihydroxycholecalciferol*
uf *1,25-dihydroxyvitamin d*
BT1 hydroxycholecalciferols
BT2 cholecalciferol derivatives
BT3 sterols
BT4 alcohols
BT4 steroids
BT5 isoprenoids
BT6 lipids
BT3 vitamin d
BT4 fat soluble vitamins
BT5 vitamins

CALCIUM
uf *ca (symbol)*
BT1 alkaline earth metals
BT2 metallic elements
BT3 elements
BT3 metals
rt calcification
rt calcinosis
rt calcium absorption
rt calcium arsenate
rt calcium binding proteins

CALCIUM *cont.*
rt calcium carbide
rt calcium carbonate
rt calcium chlorate
rt calcium chloride
rt calcium cyanamide
rt calcium fertilizers
rt calcium fluoride
rt calcium formate
rt calcium fructosate
rt calcium hydroxide
rt calcium ions
rt calcium nitrate
rt calcium oxalate
rt calcium oxide
rt calcium peroxide
rt calcium phosphate
rt calcium polyphosphates
rt calcium polysulfide
rt calcium propionate
rt calcium pyrophosphate
rt calcium silicate
rt calcium sulfate
rt hypercalcaemia
rt hypercalciuria
rt hyperparathyroidism
rt hypocalcaemia
rt hypocalciuria
rt monocalcium phosphate

CALCIUM ABSORPTION
BT1 mineral absorption
BT2 absorption
BT3 sorption
rt calcium

CALCIUM AMMONIUM NITRATE
uf *ammonium nitrate/calcium carbonate*
uf *calcium carbonate/ammonium nitrate*
uf *can*
uf *nitrochalk*
BT1 ammonium fertilizers
BT2 nitrogen fertilizers
BT3 fertilizers
BT1 nitrate fertilizers
BT2 nitrogen fertilizers
BT3 fertilizers

CALCIUM AMMONIUM TRIMETAPHOSPHATE
uf *ammonium calcium trimetaphosphate*
BT1 calcium phosphates
BT2 phosphates (salts)
BT3 inorganic salts
BT4 inorganic compounds
BT4 salts
BT3 phosphates
BT2 phosphorus fertilizers
BT3 fertilizers
BT1 trimetaphosphates
BT2 metaphosphates
BT3 condensed phosphates
BT4 phosphorus fertilizers
BT5 fertilizers
BT3 phosphates (salts)
BT4 inorganic salts
BT5 inorganic compounds
BT5 salts
BT4 phosphates

CALCIUM ARSENATE
BT1 arsenates
BT2 arsenicals
BT2 inorganic salts
BT3 inorganic compounds
BT3 salts
BT1 arsenical insecticides
BT2 arsenicals
BT2 insecticides
BT3 pesticides
BT1 molluscicides
BT2 pesticides
rt calcium

CALCIUM BINDING PROTEINS
BT1 binding proteins
BT2 proteins
BT3 peptides

CALCIUM BINDING PROTEINS *cont.*
NT1 calbindin
NT1 calmodulin
rt calcium

calcium bis(hydrogen methylarsonate)
USE **cma**

CALCIUM CARBIDE
BT1 carbides
BT2 inorganic compounds
rt acetylene
rt calcium

CALCIUM CARBONATE
BT1 antacids
BT2 bases
BT2 gastrointestinal agents
BT3 drugs
BT1 antidiarrhoea agents
BT2 absorbents
BT2 gastrointestinal agents
BT3 drugs
BT1 carbonates
BT2 inorganic salts
BT3 inorganic compounds
BT3 salts
BT1 liming materials
BT2 soil amendments
BT3 amendments
rt calcifuges
rt calcite
rt calcium
rt chalk
rt lime
rt limestone

calcium carbonate/ammonium nitrate
USE **calcium ammonium nitrate**

CALCIUM CHLORATE
BT1 chlorates
BT2 inorganic salts
BT3 inorganic compounds
BT3 salts
BT1 disinfectants
BT1 inorganic herbicides
BT2 herbicides
BT3 pesticides
rt calcium

CALCIUM CHLORIDE
BT1 calcium fertilizers
BT2 fertilizers
BT1 chlorides
BT2 halides
BT3 inorganic salts
BT4 inorganic compounds
BT4 salts
BT1 desiccants
BT1 liming materials
BT2 soil amendments
BT3 amendments
rt calcium
rt refrigeration

CALCIUM CYANAMIDE
BT1 anthelmintics
BT2 antiparasitic agents
BT3 drugs
BT1 defoliants
BT2 plant growth regulators
BT3 growth regulators
BT1 nitrogen fertilizers
BT2 fertilizers
BT1 ovicides and larvicides
BT2 antiparasitic agents
BT3 drugs
BT1 unclassified herbicides
BT2 herbicides
BT3 pesticides
rt calcium
rt cyanamide

CALCIUM FERTILIZERS
BT1 fertilizers
NT1 calcium chloride
NT1 gypsum
NT1 phosphogypsum
rt calcium

CALCIUM FERTILIZERS *cont.*
rt liming materials

CALCIUM FLUORIDE
BT1 fluorides
BT2 halides
BT3 inorganic salts
BT4 inorganic compounds
BT4 salts
rt calcium

CALCIUM FORMATE
BT1 formates (salts)
BT2 formates
BT2 organic salts
BT3 salts
rt calcium

CALCIUM FRUCTOSATE
BT1 organic salts
BT2 salts
rt calcium

calcium hydrogen phosphate
USE **dicalcium phosphate**

CALCIUM HYDROXIDE
BT1 dermatological agents
BT2 drugs
BT1 hydroxides
BT2 inorganic compounds
BT1 liming materials
BT2 soil amendments
BT3 amendments
BT1 ovicides and larvicides
BT2 antiparasitic agents
BT3 drugs
rt calcium
rt lime

CALCIUM IONS
BT1 metal ions
BT2 cations
BT3 ions
rt calcium

CALCIUM NITRATE
BT1 nitrate fertilizers
BT2 nitrogen fertilizers
BT3 fertilizers
BT1 nitrates (inorganic salts)
BT2 inorganic salts
BT3 inorganic compounds
BT3 salts
BT2 nitrates
rt calcium

CALCIUM OXALATE
BT1 oxalates
BT2 organic salts
BT3 salts
rt calcium

CALCIUM OXIDE
BT1 liming materials
BT2 soil amendments
BT3 amendments
BT1 oxides
BT2 inorganic compounds
rt calcium
rt lime

CALCIUM PEROXIDE
BT1 peroxides
BT2 inorganic compounds
rt calcium

CALCIUM PHOSPHATE
BT1 calcium phosphates
BT2 phosphates (salts)
BT3 inorganic salts
BT4 inorganic compounds
BT4 salts
BT3 phosphates
BT2 phosphorus fertilizers
BT3 fertilizers
rt calcium

CALCIUM PHOSPHATES
BT1 phosphates (salts)
BT2 inorganic salts
BT3 inorganic compounds
BT3 salts
BT2 phosphates

CALCIUM PHOSPHATES *cont.*
BT1 phosphorus fertilizers
BT2 fertilizers
NT1 apatite
NT2 phosphorite
NT1 calcium ammonium trimetaphosphate
NT1 calcium phosphate
NT1 calcium polyphosphates
NT2 calcium pyrophosphate
NT1 dicalcium phosphate
NT1 monocalcium phosphate
NT1 octacalcium phosphate
NT1 rock phosphate
NT1 tricalcium phosphate
NT1 triple superphosphate

CALCIUM POLYPHOSPHATES
BT1 calcium phosphates
BT2 phosphates (salts)
BT3 inorganic salts
BT4 inorganic compounds
BT4 salts
BT3 phosphates
BT2 phosphorus fertilizers
BT3 fertilizers
NT1 calcium pyrophosphate
rt calcium

CALCIUM POLYSULFIDE
uf *calcium polysulphide*
uf *lime sulfur*
uf *lime sulphur*
BT1 unclassified fungicides
BT2 fungicides
BT3 pesticides
rt calcium

calcium polysulphide
USE **calcium polysulfide**

CALCIUM PROPIONATE
BT1 food preservatives
BT2 preservatives
BT1 propionates (salts)
BT2 organic salts
BT3 salts
BT2 propionates
rt calcium

CALCIUM PYROPHOSPHATE
BT1 calcium polyphosphates
BT2 calcium phosphates
BT3 phosphates (salts)
BT4 inorganic salts
BT5 inorganic compounds
BT5 salts
BT4 phosphates
BT3 phosphorus fertilizers
BT4 fertilizers
BT1 pyrophosphates
BT2 phosphates (salts)
BT3 inorganic salts
BT4 inorganic compounds
BT4 salts
BT3 phosphates
BT2 polyphosphates
BT3 condensed phosphates
BT4 phosphorus fertilizers
BT5 fertilizers
rt calcium

CALCIUM SILICATE
BT1 liming materials
BT2 soil amendments
BT3 amendments
BT1 silicates
BT2 inorganic salts
BT3 inorganic compounds
BT3 salts
rt calcium
rt cement
rt wollastonite

CALCIUM SULFATE
uf *calcium sulphate*
BT1 liming materials
BT2 soil amendments
BT3 amendments
BT1 sulfates (inorganic salts)
BT2 inorganic salts
BT3 inorganic compounds
BT3 salts

CALCIUM SULFATE *cont.*
BT2 sulfates
rt calcium
rt gypsum

calcium sulphate
USE **calcium sulfate**

CALCRETE
uf *calcareous crusts*
uf *caliche*
uf *crusts, calcareous*
BT1 soil morphological features

CALCULATION
BT1 mathematics
NT1 design calculations
rt computer analysis
rt computers
rt statistical analysis

calculi, biliary
USE **biliary calculi**

calculi, bladder
USE **bladder calculi**

calculi, renal
USE **renal calculi**

calculi, urinary
USE **urinary calculi**

CALENDULA
BT1 compositae
NT1 calendula arvensis
NT1 calendula officinalis

CALENDULA ARVENSIS
BT1 calendula
BT2 compositae
BT1 medicinal plants

CALENDULA OFFICINALIS
uf *marigolds, pot*
BT1 antibacterial plants
BT1 calendula
BT2 compositae
BT1 medicinal plants
BT1 nematicidal plants
BT2 pesticidal plants
BT1 ornamental herbaceous plants

CALEPITRIMERUS
BT1 eriophyidae
BT2 prostigmata
BT3 acari
NT1 calepitrimerus vitis

CALEPITRIMERUS VITIS
BT1 calepitrimerus
BT2 eriophyidae
BT3 prostigmata
BT4 acari

CALES
BT1 aphelinidae
BT2 hymenoptera
NT1 cales noacki

CALES NOACKI
BT1 cales
BT2 aphelinidae
BT3 hymenoptera

calf
USE **calves**

CALF DIARRHEA ROTAVIRUS
BF calf diarrhoea rotavirus
rt diarrhea

CALF DIARRHOEA ROTAVIRUS
AF calf diarrhea rotavirus
BT1 rotavirus
BT2 reoviridae
BT3 viruses
rt calves
rt diarrhoea

CALF DISEASES
BT1 young animal diseases
BT2 animal diseases
BT3 diseases
rt calves

CALF DISEASES *cont.*
rt cattle diseases

CALF FEEDERS
BT1 feed dispensers
BT2 dispensers
NT1 bucket calf feeders
rt calves
rt nipple drinkers

calf feeders, nipple
USE **nipple drinkers**

CALF FEEDING
BT1 cattle feeding
BT2 ruminant feeding
BT3 livestock feeding
BT4 animal feeding
BT5 feeding
rt calves

CALF HOUSING
BT1 cattle housing
BT2 animal housing
rt calves

CALF PRODUCTION
BT1 animal production
BT2 agricultural production
BT3 production
rt calves

CALF REMOVAL
HN from 1990
BT1 removal
NT1 temporary calf removal
rt calves

calf rumen
USE **rumen**

CALIBRATION
BT1 standardization
rt instruments

caliche
USE **calcrete**

CALICIVIRIDAE
BT1 viruses
NT1 calicivirus
NT2 feline calicivirus
NT2 san miguel sealion virus
NT2 vesicular exanthema virus

CALICIVIRUS
BT1 caliciviridae
BT2 viruses
NT1 feline calicivirus
NT1 san miguel sealion virus
NT1 vesicular exanthema virus

CALICOPHORON
BT1 paramphistomatidae
BT2 digenea
BT3 trematoda
NT1 calicophoron calicophorum
NT1 calicophoron microbothrium
NT1 calicophoron raja

CALICOPHORON CALICOPHORUM
BT1 calicophoron
BT2 paramphistomatidae
BT3 digenea
BT4 trematoda

CALICOPHORON MICROBOTHRIUM
BT1 calicophoron
BT2 paramphistomatidae
BT3 digenea
BT4 trematoda

CALICOPHORON RAJA
BT1 calicophoron
BT2 paramphistomatidae
BT3 digenea
BT4 trematoda

CALIDRIS
BT1 scolopacidae
BT2 charadriiformes
BT3 birds
NT1 calidris alpina
NT1 calidris minuta

CALIDRIS ALPINA
BT1 calidris
BT2 scolopacidae
BT3 charadriiformes
BT4 birds

CALIDRIS MINUTA
BT1 calidris
BT2 scolopacidae
BT3 charadriiformes
BT4 birds

CALIFORNIA
BT1 pacific states of usa
BT2 western states of usa
BT3 usa
BT4 north america
BT5 america
rt mojave desert

CALIFORNIA ENCEPHALITIS VIRUS
BT1 bunyavirus
BT2 arboviruses
BT3 pathogens
BT2 bunyaviridae
BT3 viruses

CALIFORNIA MASTITIS TEST
BT1 tests
rt mastitis

california quail
USE **lophortyx californica**

CALIOTHRIPS
uf hercothrips
BT1 thripidae
BT2 thysanoptera
NT1 caliothrips indicus

CALIOTHRIPS INDICUS
BT1 caliothrips
BT2 thripidae
BT3 thysanoptera

CALIROA
BT1 tenthredinidae
BT2 hymenoptera
NT1 caliroa annulipes
NT1 caliroa cerasi

CALIROA ANNULIPES
BT1 caliroa
BT2 tenthredinidae
BT3 hymenoptera

CALIROA CERASI
uf caliroa limacina
BT1 caliroa
BT2 tenthredinidae
BT3 hymenoptera

caliroa limacina
USE **caliroa cerasi**

CALL OPTIONS (AGRICOLA)
BT1 options trading (agricola)
BT2 forward trading (agricola)
BT3 trading (agricola)

CALLA
BT1 araceae
rt zantedeschia

calla aethiopica
USE **zantedeschia aethiopica**

callandrena
USE **andrena**

CALLANTHIDIUM
BT1 apidae
BT2 hymenoptera

CALLIANDRA
BT1 leguminosae
NT1 calliandra calothyrsus
NT1 calliandra surinamensis

CALLIANDRA CALOTHYRSUS
BT1 calliandra
BT2 leguminosae
BT1 forest trees

CALLIANDRA SURINAMENSIS
BT1 calliandra
BT2 leguminosae
BT1 ornamental woody plants

CALLICARPA
BT1 verbenaceae
NT1 callicarpa americana
NT1 callicarpa arborea
NT1 callicarpa candicans
NT1 callicarpa formosana
NT1 callicarpa macrophylla

CALLICARPA AMERICANA
BT1 callicarpa
BT2 verbenaceae

CALLICARPA ARBOREA
BT1 callicarpa
BT2 verbenaceae

CALLICARPA CANDICANS
BT1 antibacterial plants
BT1 callicarpa
BT2 verbenaceae
BT1 insecticidal plants
BT2 pesticidal plants
BT1 poisonous plants

CALLICARPA FORMOSANA
BT1 antibacterial plants
BT1 callicarpa
BT2 verbenaceae

CALLICARPA MACROPHYLLA
BT1 callicarpa
BT2 verbenaceae

CALLICEBUS
BT1 cebidae
BT2 primates
BT3 mammals

CALLIGONUM
BT1 polygonaceae
NT1 calligonum aphyllum
NT1 calligonum comosum
NT1 calligonum polygonoides

CALLIGONUM APHYLLUM
BT1 calligonum
BT2 polygonaceae

CALLIGONUM COMOSUM
BT1 calligonum
BT2 polygonaceae

CALLIGONUM POLYGONOIDES
BT1 calligonum
BT2 polygonaceae

CALLILEPIS
BT1 compositae
NT1 callilepis laureola

CALLILEPIS LAUREOLA
BT1 callilepis
BT2 compositae
BT1 medicinal plants

CALLINECTES
BT1 decapoda
BT2 malacostraca
BT3 crustacea
BT4 arthropods

CALLIOPSIS
BT1 apidae
BT2 hymenoptera

CALLIPERS
BT1 instruments

CALLIPHORA
BT1 calliphoridae
BT2 diptera
NT1 calliphora augur
NT1 calliphora hilli
NT1 calliphora nigribarbis
NT1 calliphora placida
NT1 calliphora stygia
NT1 calliphora uralensis
NT1 calliphora vicina
NT1 calliphora vomitoria
rt aldrichina

CALLIPHORA AUGUR
BT1 calliphora
BT2 calliphoridae
BT3 diptera

calliphora erythrocephala
USE **calliphora vicina**

calliphora grahami
USE **aldrichina grahami**

CALLIPHORA HILLI
BT1 calliphora
BT2 calliphoridae
BT3 diptera

calliphora lata
USE **calliphora nigribarbis**

CALLIPHORA NIGRIBARBIS
uf calliphora lata
BT1 calliphora
BT2 calliphoridae
BT3 diptera

calliphora nociva
USE **calliphora placida**

CALLIPHORA PLACIDA
uf calliphora nociva
BT1 calliphora
BT2 calliphoridae
BT3 diptera

CALLIPHORA STYGIA
BT1 calliphora
BT2 calliphoridae
BT3 diptera

CALLIPHORA URALENSIS
BT1 calliphora
BT2 calliphoridae
BT3 diptera

CALLIPHORA VICINA
uf calliphora erythrocephala
BT1 calliphora
BT2 calliphoridae
BT3 diptera

CALLIPHORA VOMITORIA
BT1 calliphora
BT2 calliphoridae
BT3 diptera

CALLIPHORIDAE
BT1 diptera
NT1 aldrichina
NT2 aldrichina grahami
NT1 calliphora
NT2 calliphora augur
NT2 calliphora hilli
NT2 calliphora nigribarbis
NT2 calliphora placida
NT2 calliphora stygia
NT2 calliphora uralensis
NT2 calliphora vicina
NT2 calliphora vomitoria
NT1 chrysomya
NT2 chrysomya albiceps
NT2 chrysomya bezziana
NT2 chrysomya chloropyga
NT2 chrysomya megacephala
NT2 chrysomya putoria
NT2 chrysomya regalis
NT2 chrysomya rufifacies
NT1 cochliomyia
NT2 cochliomyia hominivorax
NT2 cochliomyia macellaria
NT1 cordylobia
NT2 cordylobia anthropophaga
NT1 hemilucilia
NT2 hemilucilia semidiaphana
NT1 lucilia
NT2 lucilia bufonivora
NT2 lucilia caesar
NT2 lucilia cuprina
NT2 lucilia eximia
NT2 lucilia illustris
NT2 lucilia sericata
NT1 phormia
NT2 phormia regina
NT2 phormia terraenovae
NT1 pollenia

CALLIPHORIDAE *cont.*
NT2 pollenia rudis
rt maggot therapy

CALLIPTAMUS
BT1 acrididae
BT2 orthoptera
NT1 calliptamus italicus

CALLIPTAMUS ITALICUS
BT1 calliptamus
BT2 acrididae
BT3 orthoptera

CALLISTEMON
BT1 myrtaceae
NT1 callistemon citrinus

CALLISTEMON CITRINUS
uf callistemon lanceolatus
BT1 antifungal plants
BT1 callistemon
BT2 myrtaceae
BT1 ornamental woody plants

callistemon lanceolatus
USE **callistemon citrinus**

CALLISTEPHUS
BT1 compositae
NT1 callistephus chinensis

CALLISTEPHUS CHINENSIS
uf aster, china
uf china aster
BT1 callistephus
BT2 compositae
BT1 ornamental herbaceous plants

CALLISTO
BT1 gracillariidae
BT2 lepidoptera
NT1 callisto denticulella

CALLISTO DENTICULELLA
uf ornix guttea
BT1 callisto
BT2 gracillariidae
BT3 lepidoptera

CALLITHRICIDAE
uf callitrichidae
BT1 primates
BT2 mammals
NT1 callithrix
NT2 callithrix jacchus

CALLITHRIX
BT1 callithricidae
BT2 primates
BT3 mammals
NT1 callithrix jacchus
rt marmosets

CALLITHRIX JACCHUS
BT1 callithrix
BT2 callithricidae
BT3 primates
BT4 mammals

CALLITRICHACEAE
NT1 callitriche
NT2 callitriche stagnalis

CALLITRICHE
BT1 callitrichaceae
NT1 callitriche stagnalis

CALLITRICHE STAGNALIS
BT1 callitriche
BT2 callitrichaceae

callitrichidae
USE **callithricidae**

CALLITRIS
BT1 cupressaceae
NT1 callitris columellaris
NT1 callitris intratropica
NT1 callitris rhomboidea

CALLITRIS COLUMELLARIS
uf callitris glauca
uf callitris hugelli
BT1 antibacterial plants

CALLITRIS COLUMELLARIS *cont.*
BT1 callitris
BT2 cupressaceae

callitris cupressiformis
USE **callitris rhomboidea**

callitris glauca
USE **callitris columellaris**

callitris hugelli
USE **callitris columellaris**

CALLITRIS INTRATROPICA
BT1 callitris
BT2 cupressaceae

CALLITRIS RHOMBOIDEA
uf *callitris cupressiformis*
BT1 callitris
BT2 cupressaceae

callitroga
USE **cochliomyia**

callitroga hominivorax
USE **cochliomyia hominivorax**

CALLITULA
BT1 pteromalidae
BT2 hymenoptera
NT1 callitula bicolor

CALLITULA BICOLOR
BT1 callitula
BT2 pteromalidae
BT3 hymenoptera

CALLOPSYLLA
BT1 ceratophyllidae
BT2 siphonaptera

CALLORHINUS
BT1 otariidae
BT2 pinnipedia
BT3 carnivores
BT4 mammals
NT1 callorhinus ursinus

CALLORHINUS URSINUS
BT1 callorhinus
BT2 otariidae
BT3 pinnipedia
BT4 carnivores
BT5 mammals

CALLOSCIURUS
BT1 sciuridae
BT2 rodents
BT3 mammals
NT1 callosciurus erythraeus
NT1 callosciurus notatus

CALLOSCIURUS ERYTHRAEUS
uf *callosciurus flavimanus*
BT1 callosciurus
BT2 sciuridae
BT3 rodents
BT4 mammals

callosciurus flavimanus
USE **callosciurus erythraeus**

CALLOSCIURUS NOTATUS
BT1 callosciurus
BT2 sciuridae
BT3 rodents
BT4 mammals

CALLOSE
BT1 polysaccharides
BT2 carbohydrates
rt callus
rt cell walls
rt phloem
rt sieve plates

CALLOSOBRUCHUS
BT1 bruchidae
BT2 coleoptera
NT1 callosobruchus analis
NT1 callosobruchus chinensis
NT1 callosobruchus maculatus
rt bruchus

CALLOSOBRUCHUS ANALIS
BT1 callosobruchus
BT2 bruchidae
BT3 coleoptera

CALLOSOBRUCHUS CHINENSIS
uf *bruchus chinensis*
BT1 callosobruchus
BT2 bruchidae
BT3 coleoptera

CALLOSOBRUCHUS MACULATUS
BT1 callosobruchus
BT2 bruchidae
BT3 coleoptera

CALLUNA
BT1 ericaceae
NT1 calluna vulgaris

CALLUNA VULGARIS
uf *heather*
uf *ling (plant)*
BT1 calluna
BT2 ericaceae
BT1 medicinal plants

CALLUS
BT1 plant tissues
BT2 plant
BT2 tissues
rt callose
rt tissue culture

CALMODULIN
BT1 calcium binding proteins
BT2 binding proteins
BT3 proteins
BT4 peptides

CALOCARPUM
BT1 sapotaceae
NT1 calocarpum viride

calocarpum mammosum
USE **pouteria sapota**

calocarpum sapota
USE **pouteria sapota**

CALOCARPUM VIRIDE
BT1 calocarpum
BT2 sapotaceae
BT1 tropical tree fruits
BT2 tree fruits
BT2 tropical fruits
BT3 fruit crops

calocedrus
USE **libocedrus**

CALOCERA
BT1 dacrymycetales
NT1 calocera viscosa

CALOCERA VISCOSA
BT1 calocera
BT2 dacrymycetales

CALOCHORTUS
BT1 liliaceae

CALOCORIS
BT1 miridae
BT2 heteroptera
NT1 calocoris angustatus

CALOCORIS ANGUSTATUS
BT1 calocoris
BT2 miridae
BT3 heteroptera

CALOCYBE
BT1 agaricales
NT1 calocybe indica

CALOCYBE INDICA
BT1 calocybe
BT2 agaricales
BT1 edible fungi
BT2 fungi
BT2 vegetables

CALOGLYPHUS
BT1 acaridae
BT2 astigmata

CALOGLYPHUS *cont.*
BT3 acari
NT1 caloglyphus berlesei

CALOGLYPHUS BERLESEI
BT1 caloglyphus
BT2 acaridae
BT3 astigmata
BT4 acari

calomel
USE **mercurous chloride**

CALOMYS
BT1 hesperomyinae
BT2 muridae
BT3 rodents
BT4 mammals
NT1 calomys callosus

CALOMYS CALLOSUS
BT1 calomys
BT2 hesperomyinae
BT3 muridae
BT4 rodents
BT5 mammals

CALONECTRIA
BT1 hypocreales
NT1 calonectria crotalariae
NT1 calonectria ilicicola
NT1 calonectria kyotensis
NT1 calonectria quinqueseptata
NT1 calonectria theae
rt cylindrocladium
rt fusarium
rt nectria

CALONECTRIA CROTALARIAE
BT1 calonectria
BT2 hypocreales

CALONECTRIA ILICICOLA
HN from 1990
uf *cylindrocladium ilicicola*
BT1 calonectria
BT2 hypocreales

CALONECTRIA KYOTENSIS
BT1 calonectria
BT2 hypocreales

calonectria nivalis
USE **monographella nivalis**

CALONECTRIA QUINQUESEPTATA
HN from 1990
uf *cylindrocladium quinqueseptatum*
BT1 calonectria
BT2 hypocreales

calonectria rigidiuscula
USE **nectria rigidiuscula**

CALONECTRIA THEAE
BT1 calonectria
BT2 hypocreales

CALONYCTION
BT1 convolvulaceae
NT1 calonyction album
NT1 calonyction muricatum

calonyction aculeatum
USE **calonyction album**

CALONYCTION ALBUM
uf *calonyction aculeatum*
BT1 calonyction
BT2 convolvulaceae

CALONYCTION MURICATUM
uf *ipomoea muricata*
BT1 calonyction
BT2 convolvulaceae

CALOOSIA
BT1 criconematidae
BT2 nematoda

CALOPHYLLUM
BT1 guttiferae
NT1 calophyllum antillanum
NT1 calophyllum brasiliense

CALOPHYLLUM *cont.*
NT1 calophyllum calaba
NT1 calophyllum elatum
NT1 calophyllum floribundum
NT1 calophyllum inophyllum
NT1 calophyllum mariae

CALOPHYLLUM ANTILLANUM
BT1 calophyllum
BT2 guttiferae

CALOPHYLLUM BRASILIENSE
BT1 calophyllum
BT2 guttiferae
BT1 forest trees

CALOPHYLLUM CALABA
BT1 calophyllum
BT2 guttiferae

CALOPHYLLUM ELATUM
BT1 calophyllum
BT2 guttiferae

CALOPHYLLUM FLORIBUNDUM
BT1 calophyllum
BT2 guttiferae

CALOPHYLLUM INOPHYLLUM
BT1 calophyllum
BT2 guttiferae
BT1 forest trees
BT1 medicinal plants

CALOPHYLLUM MARIAE
BT1 calophyllum
BT2 guttiferae

CALOPOGON
BT1 orchidaceae
rt ornamental orchids

CALOPOGONIUM
BT1 leguminosae
NT1 calopogonium caeruleum
NT1 calopogonium mucunoides

CALOPOGONIUM CAERULEUM
BT1 calopogonium
BT2 leguminosae

CALOPOGONIUM MUCUNOIDES
BT1 calopogonium
BT2 leguminosae
BT1 green manures
BT2 manures
BT3 organic amendments
BT4 soil amendments
BT5 amendments
BT1 pasture legumes
BT2 legumes
BT2 pasture plants

CALOPTERYGIDAE
BT1 odonata
NT1 agrion

CALOPTILIA
BT1 gracillariidae
BT2 lepidoptera

CALORIC DEFICIENCY (AGRICOLA)
BT1 deficiency
rt calories

CALORIC INTAKE (AGRICOLA)
BT1 intake
rt calories
rt energy intake
rt food intake

CALORIC MODIFICATIONS (AGRICOLA)
BT1 diets
rt calories
rt energy intake

CALORIC VALUE
BF calorific value

calorie requirement
USE **energy requirements**

CALORIE-RESTRICTED DIETS (AGRICOLA)

CALORIE-RESTRICTED DIETS (AGRICOLA) *cont.*
BT1 diets
rt calories

calorie value
USE **calorific value**
OR **energy value**

CALORIES
rt caloric deficiency (agricola)
rt caloric intake (agricola)
rt caloric modifications (agricola)
rt calorie-restricted diets (agricola)
rt energy
rt heat
rt specific dynamic action

CALORIFIC VALUE
AF caloric value
uf *calorie value*
NT1 specific dynamic action
rt calorimeters
rt calorimetry
rt energy value
rt heat
rt heat production

calorigenesis
USE **heat production**

CALORIMETERS
BT1 equipment
rt calorific value
rt calorimetry
rt heat production

calorimetric methods
USE **calorimetry**

CALORIMETRY
uf *calorimetric methods*
BT1 methodology
NT1 microcalorimetry
rt calorific value
rt calorimeters
rt heat
rt heat production

CALOSOMA
BT1 carabidae
BT2 coleoptera
NT1 calosoma sycophanta

CALOSOMA SYCOPHANTA
BT1 calosoma
BT2 carabidae
BT3 coleoptera

CALOTHAMNUS
BT1 myrtaceae
NT1 calothamnus gilesii

CALOTHAMNUS GILESII
BT1 calothamnus
BT2 myrtaceae

CALOTHRIX
BT1 cyanobacteria
BT2 prokaryotes
NT1 calothrix brevissima

CALOTHRIX BREVISSIMA
BT1 calothrix
BT2 cyanobacteria
BT3 prokaryotes

CALOTROPIS
BT1 asclepiadaceae
NT1 calotropis gigantea
NT1 calotropis procera

CALOTROPIS GIGANTEA
BT1 calotropis
BT2 asclepiadaceae

CALOTROPIS PROCEA
BT1 insecticidal plants
BT2 pesticidal plants

CALOTROPIS PROCERA
BT1 antifungal plants
BT1 calotropis

CALOTROPIS PROCERA *cont.*
BT2 asclepiadaceae
BT1 fibre plants
BT1 medicinal plants
BT1 nematicidal plants
BT2 pesticidal plants
BT1 weeds

CALOVO VIRUS
BT1 bunyavirus
BT2 arboviruses
BT3 pathogens
BT2 bunyaviridae
BT3 viruses

calpe
USE **calyptra**
OR **oraesia**

calpe emarginata
USE **oraesia emarginata**

calpe thalictri
USE **calyptra thalictri**

CALPODES
BT1 hesperiidae
BT2 lepidoptera
NT1 calpodes ethlius

CALPODES ETHLIUS
BT1 calpodes
BT2 hesperiidae
BT3 lepidoptera

CALPURNIA
BT1 leguminosae
NT1 calpurnia aurea

CALPURNIA AUREA
BT1 calpurnia
BT2 leguminosae
BT1 insecticidal plants
BT2 pesticidal plants
BT1 molluscicidal plants
BT2 pesticidal plants

CALTHA
BT1 ranunculaceae
NT1 caltha palustris

CALTHA PALUSTRIS
uf *caltha polypetala*
BT1 caltha
BT2 ranunculaceae
BT1 medicinal plants
BT1 ornamental herbaceous plants

caltha polypetala
USE **caltha palustris**

CALVATIA
BT1 lycoperdales
NT1 calvatia gigantea

CALVATIA GIGANTEA
uf *lycoperdon giganteum*
BT1 calvatia
BT2 lycoperdales
BT1 edible fungi
BT2 fungi
BT2 vegetables

CALVES
uf *calf*
BT1 young animals
BT2 animals
NT1 veal calves
rt calf diarrhoea rotavirus
rt calf diseases
rt calf feeders
rt calf feeding
rt calf housing
rt calf production
rt calf removal
rt calving
rt calving interval
rt calving rate
rt calving season
rt cattle
rt rennet

CALVIN CYCLE
BT1 biochemical pathways

CALVIN CYCLE *cont.*
rt respiration

CALVING
BT1 parturition
BT2 sexual reproduction
BT3 reproduction
NT1 calving interval
NT1 calving rate
rt age at first calving
rt calves
rt calving season

CALVING INTERVAL
BT1 calving
BT2 parturition
BT3 sexual reproduction
BT4 reproduction
BT1 female fertility
BT2 fertility
BT2 reproductive efficiency
BT3 efficiency
BT3 reproductive performance
BT4 performance
rt calves
rt calving rate
rt calving season
rt dry period

CALVING RATE
BT1 calving
BT2 parturition
BT3 sexual reproduction
BT4 reproduction
BT1 female fertility
BT2 fertility
BT2 reproductive efficiency
BT3 efficiency
BT3 reproductive performance
BT4 performance
rt calves
rt calving interval
rt calving season

CALVING SEASON
rt calves
rt calving
rt calving interval
rt calving rate
rt seasons

CALYCANTHACEAE
NT1 chimonanthus
NT2 chimonanthus praecox

CALYCOMYZA
BT1 agromyzidae
BT2 diptera

CALYCOPHYLLUM
BT1 rubiaceae
NT1 calycophyllum candidissimum

CALYCOPHYLLUM CANDIDISSIMUM
BT1 calycophyllum
BT2 rubiaceae

CALYPSO
BT1 orchidaceae
rt ornamental orchids

CALYPTRA
uf *calpe*
BT1 noctuidae
BT2 lepidoptera
NT1 calyptra thalictri

CALYPTRA THALICTRI
uf *calpe thalictri*
BT1 calyptra
BT2 noctuidae
BT3 lepidoptera

CALYPTROCHILUM
BT1 orchidaceae
rt ornamental plants

calyptus
USE **eubazus**

calyptus atricornis
USE **eubazus atricornis**

CALYSTEGIA
BT1 convolvulaceae
NT1 calystegia japonica
NT1 calystegia sepium
NT1 calystegia silvaticum
NT1 calystegia tuguriorum

CALYSTEGIA JAPONICA
BT1 calystegia
BT2 convolvulaceae

CALYSTEGIA SEPIUM
uf *convolvulus sepium*
BT1 calystegia
BT2 convolvulaceae

CALYSTEGIA SILVATICUM
BT1 calystegia
BT2 convolvulaceae

CALYSTEGIA TUGURIORUM
BT1 calystegia
BT2 convolvulaceae

CALYX
uf *sepals*
BT1 flowers
BT2 inflorescences
BT3 plant

CALYX SPLITTING
BT1 plant disorders
BT2 disorders
rt carnations

CAM PATHWAY
uf *crassulacean acid metabolism*
BT1 carbon pathways
BT2 biochemical pathways
BT2 photosynthesis
BT3 energy metabolism
BT4 metabolism
BT3 plant physiology
BT4 physiology

CAMALLANIDAE
BT1 nematoda
NT1 camallanus
NT2 camallanus oxycephalus
NT1 procamallanus
rt animal parasitic nematodes

CAMALLANUS
BT1 camallanidae
BT2 nematoda
NT1 camallanus oxycephalus

CAMALLANUS OXYCEPHALUS
BT1 camallanus
BT2 camallanidae
BT3 nematoda

CAMAROGRAPHIUM
HN from 1990
BT1 deuteromycotina
rt stegonsporiopsis

camarographium abietis
USE **stegonsporiopsis cenangioides**

CAMASSIA
BT1 liliaceae

CAMBARUS
BT1 decapoda
BT2 malacostraca
BT3 crustacea
BT4 arthropods

CAMBENDAZOLE
BT1 anthelmintics
BT2 antiparasitic agents
BT3 drugs
BT1 benzimidazoles
BT2 heterocyclic nitrogen compounds
BT3 organic nitrogen compounds

CAMBENDICHLOR
BT1 unclassified herbicides
BT2 herbicides
BT3 pesticides

CAMBIC HORIZONS
BT1 horizons
BT2 soil morphological features

CAMBISOLS
BT1 soil types (genetic)
NT1 acid brown soils
NT1 brown earths
NT1 brown forest soils
NT1 brunisolic soils
NT1 cinnamonic soils
NT1 ochrepts
NT1 sod calcareous soils
NT1 tropepts
NT1 xerochrepts
NT1 yellow brown earths
NT1 yellow brown forest soils

CAMBIUM
BT1 plant tissues
BT2 plant
BT2 tissues
rt cell division

CAMBODIA
HN from 1990; previously "kampuchea"
uf *democratic kampuchea*
uf *kampuchea*
uf *khmer republic*
BT1 south east asia
BT2 asia
rt developing countries
rt indochina
rt least developed countries

CAMBRIDGE ROLLERS
uf *rollers, cambridge*
BT1 rollers
BT2 implements

CAMEL MEAT
BT1 meat
BT2 animal products
BT3 products
BT2 foods
rt camels

CAMEL MILK
uf *milk, camel*
BT1 milks
BT2 body fluids
BT3 fluids
rt camels

CAMELIDAE
BT1 tylopoda
BT2 artiodactyla
BT3 mammals
BT3 ungulates
NT1 camelus
NT1 lama
NT2 lama guanicoe
rt alpacas
rt camels
rt dromedaries
rt llamas
rt vicunas

CAMELINA
BT1 cruciferae
NT1 camelina alyssum
NT1 camelina pilosa
NT1 camelina sativa

CAMELINA ALYSSUM
BT1 camelina
BT2 cruciferae

CAMELINA PILOSA
BT1 camelina
BT2 cruciferae

CAMELINA SATIVA
BT1 camelina
BT2 cruciferae
BT1 oilseed plants
BT2 fatty oil plants
BT3 oil plants

CAMELLIA
uf *thea (theaceae)*
BT1 theaceae
NT1 camellia hiemalis

CAMELLIA *cont.*
NT1 camellia japonica
NT1 camellia sasanqua
NT1 camellia sinensis
rt forest trees

CAMELLIA HIEMALIS
BT1 camellia
BT2 theaceae

CAMELLIA JAPONICA
BT1 camellia
BT2 theaceae
BT1 ornamental woody plants

CAMELLIA SASANQUA
BT1 camellia
BT2 theaceae
BT1 ornamental woody plants

CAMELLIA SINENSIS
uf *thea sinensis*
BT1 camellia
BT2 theaceae
rt caffeine
rt tea

CAMELOSTRONGYLUS
BT1 trichostrongylidae
BT2 nematoda
NT1 camelostrongylus mentulatus

CAMELOSTRONGYLUS MENTULATUS
BT1 camelostrongylus
BT2 trichostrongylidae
BT3 nematoda

CAMELS
uf *bactrian camels*
uf *camelus bactrianus*
BT1 working animals
BT2 animals
rt camel meat
rt camel milk
rt camelidae
rt dromedaries

CAMEL'S HAIR (AGRICOLA)
BT1 animal fibres
BT2 animal products
BT3 products
BT2 fibres

CAMELUS
BT1 camelidae
BT2 tylopoda
BT3 artiodactyla
BT4 mammals
BT4 ungulates

camelus bactrianus
USE **camels**

camelus dromedarius
USE **dromedaries**

CAMEMBERT CHEESE
BT1 cheeses
BT2 milk products
BT3 products

CAMERARIA
BT1 gracillariidae
BT2 lepidoptera
NT1 cameraria hamadryadella
rt phyllonorycter

CAMERARIA HAMADRYADELLA
uf *phyllonorycter hamadryadella*
BT1 cameraria
BT2 gracillariidae
BT3 lepidoptera

CAMEROON
BT1 central africa
BT2 africa south of sahara
BT3 africa
rt acp
rt developing countries
rt francophone africa

CAMISIA
BT1 camisiidae
BT2 cryptostigmata
BT3 acari

CAMISIIDAE
BT1 cryptostigmata
BT2 acari
NT1 camisia

CAMNULA
BT1 acrididae
BT2 orthoptera
NT1 camnula pellucida

CAMNULA PELLUCIDA
BT1 camnula
BT2 acrididae
BT3 orthoptera

CAMP SITES
BT1 amenity and recreation areas
BT2 areas
BT1 holiday accommodation
BT2 accommodation
BT1 site types
rt camping

CAMP TEST
BT1 tests
rt mastitis

CAMPANIA
BT1 italy
BT2 western europe
BT3 europe

CAMPANIAN BARBARY
BT1 sheep breeds
BT2 breeds

CAMPANICA
BT1 sheep breeds
BT2 breeds

CAMPANULA
BT1 campanulaceae
NT1 campanula carpatica
NT1 campanula dasyantha
NT1 campanula garganica
NT1 campanula glomerata
NT1 campanula isophylla
NT1 campanula persicifolia
NT1 campanula porscharskyana
NT1 campanula portenschlagiana
NT1 campanula pyrimidalis
NT1 campanula rapunculoides
NT1 campanula rapunculus

CAMPANULA CARPATICA
BT1 campanula
BT2 campanulaceae
BT1 ornamental herbaceous plants

CAMPANULA DASYANTHA
BT1 campanula
BT2 campanulaceae

CAMPANULA GARGANICA
BT1 campanula
BT2 campanulaceae
BT1 ornamental herbaceous plants

CAMPANULA GLOMERATA
BT1 campanula
BT2 campanulaceae
BT1 ornamental herbaceous plants

campanula grandis
USE **campanula persicifolia**

CAMPANULA ISOPHYLLA
BT1 campanula
BT2 campanulaceae
BT1 ornamental herbaceous plants

campanula latiloba
USE **campanula persicifolia**

CAMPANULA PERSICIFOLIA
uf *campanula grandis*
uf *campanula latiloba*
BT1 campanula
BT2 campanulaceae
BT1 ornamental herbaceous plants

CAMPANULA PORSCHARSKYANA
BT1 campanula
BT2 campanulaceae
BT1 ornamental herbaceous plants

CAMPANULA PORTENSCHLAGIANA
BT1 campanula
BT2 campanulaceae
BT1 ornamental herbaceous plants

CAMPANULA PYRIMIDALIS
BT1 campanula
BT2 campanulaceae

CAMPANULA RAPUNCULOIDES
BT1 campanula
BT2 campanulaceae

CAMPANULA RAPUNCULUS
BT1 campanula
BT2 campanulaceae
BT1 ornamental herbaceous plants

CAMPANULACEAE
uf *lobeliaceae*
NT1 adenophora
NT2 adenophora latifolia
NT2 adenophora tetraphylla
NT1 campanula
NT2 campanula carpatica
NT2 campanula dasyantha
NT2 campanula garganica
NT2 campanula glomerata
NT2 campanula isophylla
NT2 campanula persicifolia
NT2 campanula porscharskyana
NT2 campanula portenschlagiana
NT2 campanula pyrimidalis
NT2 campanula rapunculoides
NT2 campanula rapunculus
NT1 codonopsis
NT2 codonopsis ovata
NT1 lobelia
NT2 lobelia affinis
NT2 lobelia cardinalis
NT2 lobelia chinensis
NT2 lobelia erinus
NT2 lobelia fulgens
NT2 lobelia inflata
NT2 lobelia nicotianaefolia
NT2 lobelia puberula
NT2 lobelia siphilitica
NT1 platycodon
NT2 platycodon grandiflorus

CAMPANULOTES
BT1 goniodidae
BT2 ischnocera
BT3 mallophaga
BT4 phthiraptera
NT1 campanulotes bidentatus
NT2 campanulotes bidentatus compar
rt goniocotes

CAMPANULOTES BIDENTATUS
uf *goniocotes bidentatus*
BT1 campanulotes
BT2 goniodidae
BT3 ischnocera
BT4 mallophaga
BT5 phthiraptera
NT1 campanulotes bidentatus compar

CAMPANULOTES BIDENTATUS COMPAR
HN from 1989; previously campanulotes compar
uf *campanulotes compar*

CAMPANULOTES BIDENTATUS COMPAR *cont.*
BT1 campanulotes bidentatus
BT2 campanulotes
BT3 goniodidae
BT4 ischnocera
BT5 mallophaga
BT6 phthiraptera

campanulotes compar
USE **campanulotes bidentatus compar**

CAMPESTEROL
BT1 ergostanes
BT2 steroids
BT3 isoprenoids
BT4 lipids
BT1 phytosterols
BT2 sterols
BT3 alcohols
BT3 steroids
BT4 isoprenoids
BT5 lipids
rt rapeseed oil

CAMPHECHLOR
uf *toxaphene*
BT1 organochlorine insecticides
BT2 insecticides
BT3 pesticides
BT2 organochlorine pesticides
BT3 organochlorine compounds
BT4 organic halogen compounds

CAMPHENE
BT1 monoterpenes
BT2 monoterpenoids
BT3 terpenoids
BT4 isoprenoids
BT5 lipids
rt essential oils

CAMPHOR
BT1 insect repellents
BT2 repellents
BT1 monoterpenoids
BT2 terpenoids
BT3 isoprenoids
BT4 lipids
BT1 plasticizers
BT1 preservatives
rt cinnamomum camphora
rt essential oils

CAMPINA
HN from 1990
BT1 grasslands
BT2 vegetation types

CAMPINE
BT1 goat breeds
BT2 breeds

campine red pied
USE **belgian red pied**

CAMPING
BT1 holidays
BT2 tourism
BT1 outdoor recreation
BT2 recreation
rt ancillary enterprises
rt camp sites
rt forest recreation

CAMPNOSPERMA
BT1 anacardiaceae
NT1 campnosperma panamensis

CAMPNOSPERMA PANAMENSIS
BT1 campnosperma
BT2 anacardiaceae

CAMPOLETIS
uf *anilastus*
uf *ecphoropsis*
BT1 ichneumonidae
BT2 hymenoptera
NT1 campoletis chlorideae
NT1 campoletis flavicincta
NT1 campoletis sonorensis

CAMPOLETIS CHLORIDEAE
BT1 campoletis
BT2 ichneumonidae
BT3 hymenoptera

CAMPOLETIS FLAVICINCTA
uf *campoletis perdistincta*
uf *ecphoropsis perdistinctus*
BT1 campoletis
BT2 ichneumonidae
BT3 hymenoptera

campoletis perdistincta
USE **campoletis flavicincta**

CAMPOLETIS SONORENSIS
BT1 campoletis
BT2 ichneumonidae
BT3 hymenoptera

CAMPOLINO
BT1 horse breeds
BT2 breeds

CAMPOMANESIA
uf *britoa*
BT1 myrtaceae

CAMPONOTUS
BT1 formicidae
BT2 hymenoptera
NT1 camponotus acvapimensis
NT1 camponotus herculeanus
NT1 camponotus pennsylvanicus
NT1 camponotus rufipes

CAMPONOTUS ACVAPIMENSIS
BT1 camponotus
BT2 formicidae
BT3 hymenoptera

CAMPONOTUS HERCULEANUS
BT1 camponotus
BT2 formicidae
BT3 hymenoptera

CAMPONOTUS PENNSYLVANICUS
BT1 camponotus
BT2 formicidae
BT3 hymenoptera

CAMPONOTUS RUFIPES
BT1 camponotus
BT2 formicidae
BT3 hymenoptera

CAMPOPLEX
BT1 ichneumonidae
BT2 hymenoptera
rt sinophorus

campoplex xanthostomus
USE **sinophorus xanthostomus**

CAMPSIS
BT1 bignoniaceae
NT1 campsis grandiflora
NT1 campsis radicans
NT1 campsis tagliabuana

CAMPSIS GRANDIFLORA
BT1 campsis
BT2 bignoniaceae
BT1 ornamental woody plants

CAMPSIS RADICANS
uf *tecoma radicans*
BT1 campsis
BT2 bignoniaceae
BT1 ornamental woody plants

CAMPSIS TAGLIABUANA
BT1 campsis
BT2 bignoniaceae
BT1 ornamental woody plants

CAMPTOCHIRONOMUS
BT1 chironomidae
BT2 diptera
NT1 camptochironomus tentans
rt chironomus

CAMPTOCHIRONOMUS TENTANS
uf *chironomus tentans*
BT1 camptochironomus

CAMPTOCHIRONOMUS TENTANS *cont.*
BT2 chironomidae
BT3 diptera

CAMPTOTHECA
BT1 nyssaceae
NT1 camptotheca acuminata

CAMPTOTHECA ACUMINATA
BT1 camptotheca
BT2 nyssaceae
BT1 insecticidal plants
BT2 pesticidal plants
BT1 medicinal plants

CAMPULIDAE
BT1 digenea
BT2 trematoda
NT1 zalophotrema

CAMPYLANDRA
BT1 liliaceae
NT1 campylandra aurantiaca

CAMPYLANDRA AURANTIACA
BT1 campylandra
BT2 liliaceae

CAMPYLOBACTER
BT1 spirillaceae
BT2 gracilicutes
BT3 bacteria
BT4 prokaryotes
NT1 campylobacter fetus
NT1 campylobacter jejuni
NT1 campylobacter sputorum

CAMPYLOBACTER FETUS
uf *vibrio fetus*
uf *vibriosis in cattle*
BT1 campylobacter
BT2 spirillaceae
BT3 gracilicutes
BT4 bacteria
BT5 prokaryotes

CAMPYLOBACTER JEJUNI
BT1 campylobacter
BT2 spirillaceae
BT3 gracilicutes
BT4 bacteria
BT5 prokaryotes

CAMPYLOBACTER SPUTORUM
BT1 campylobacter
BT2 spirillaceae
BT3 gracilicutes
BT4 bacteria
BT5 prokaryotes

CAMPYLOMMA
BT1 miridae
BT2 heteroptera
NT1 campylomma verbasci

CAMPYLOMMA VERBASCI
BT1 campylomma
BT2 miridae
BT3 heteroptera

CAMS
BT1 components

can
USE **calcium ammonium nitrate**

CAN OPENERS (AGRICOLA)
BT1 household equipment (agricola)
BT2 equipment

CANADA
BT1 north america
BT2 america
NT1 alberta
NT1 british columbia
NT1 canadian northwest territories
NT1 manitoba
NT1 new brunswick
NT1 newfoundland
NT1 nova scotia
NT1 ontario

CANADA *cont.*
NT1 prince edward island
NT1 quebec
NT1 saskatchewan
NT1 yukon
rt commonwealth of nations
rt idrc
rt oecd

CANADIAN
BT1 cattle breeds
BT2 breeds
BT1 horse breeds
BT2 breeds

CANADIAN CORRIEDALE
BT1 sheep breeds
BT2 breeds

CANADIAN NORTHWEST TERRITORIES
uf *northwest territories of canada*
BT1 canada
BT2 north america
BT3 america

CANADIAN YORKSHIRE
HN from 1990
BT1 pig breeds
BT2 breeds

CANAL BANKS
rt canal plantations
rt canals
rt ditch banks

CANAL PLANTATIONS
BT1 plantations
rt canal banks
rt canals
rt forestry
rt linear plantations
rt riverside plantations

canal zone
USE **panama canal zone**

CANALS
BT1 inland waterways
BT2 waterways
rt canal banks
rt canal plantations
rt channels
rt ducts
rt water recreation
rt water transport
rt weirs

CANANGA
BT1 annonaceae
NT1 cananga odorata

CANANGA ODORATA
uf *ylang-ylang*
BT1 cananga
BT2 annonaceae
BT1 essential oil plants
BT2 oil plants

CANARIES
uf *serinus canaria*
BT1 ornamental birds
BT2 animals
rt aviary birds
rt fringillidae

CANARIUM
BT1 burseraceae
NT1 canarium luzonicum
NT1 canarium schweinfurthii
NT1 canarium vitiense
NT1 canarium zeylanicum
rt forest trees

CANARIUM LUZONICUM
BT1 canarium
BT2 burseraceae
BT1 essential oil plants
BT2 oil plants
BT1 medicinal plants

CANARIUM SCHWEINFURTHII
BT1 canarium
BT2 burseraceae

CANARIUM VITIENSE
BT1 canarium
BT2 burseraceae

CANARIUM ZEYLANICUM
BT1 canarium
BT2 burseraceae

canary grass
USE **phalaris canariensis**

CANARY ISLAND
HN from 1990
BT1 goat breeds
BT2 breeds

CANARY ISLANDS
BT1 western europe
BT2 europe
rt spain

CANARY POX VIRUS
BT1 avipoxvirus
BT2 chordopoxvirinae
BT3 poxviridae
BT4 viruses

CANASTRA
BT1 pig breeds
BT2 breeds

CANASTRAO
BT1 pig breeds
BT2 breeds

CANAVALIA
uf *dolichos*
BT1 leguminosae
NT1 canavalia campylocarpa
NT1 canavalia ensiformis
NT1 canavalia gladiata
NT1 canavalia lineata
NT1 canavalia maritima
NT1 canavalia paraguayensis
rt canavanine

CANAVALIA CAMPYLOCARPA
BT1 canavalia
BT2 leguminosae
BT1 green manures
BT2 manures
BT3 organic amendments
BT4 soil amendments
BT5 amendments

CANAVALIA ENSIFORMIS
uf *jack beans*
BT1 canavalia
BT2 leguminosae
BT1 grain legumes
BT2 grain crops
BT2 legumes
BT1 green manures
BT2 manures
BT3 organic amendments
BT4 soil amendments
BT5 amendments
BT1 pasture legumes
BT2 legumes
BT2 pasture plants

CANAVALIA GLADIATA
uf *dolichos gladiata*
BT1 canavalia
BT2 leguminosae
BT1 green manures
BT2 manures
BT3 organic amendments
BT4 soil amendments
BT5 amendments
BT1 pasture legumes
BT2 legumes
BT2 pasture plants

CANAVALIA LINEATA
BT1 canavalia
BT2 leguminosae
BT1 pasture legumes
BT2 legumes
BT2 pasture plants

CANAVALIA MARITIMA
BT1 canavalia
BT2 leguminosae

CANAVALIA PARAGUAYENSIS
BT1 canavalia
BT2 leguminosae

CANAVANINE
BT1 allomones
BT2 allelochemicals
BT3 semiochemicals
BT1 nonprotein amino acids
BT2 amino acids
BT3 carboxylic acids
BT4 organic acids
BT5 acids
BT3 organic nitrogen compounds
rt canavalia

canbra rapeseed oil
USE **rapeseed oil**

CANCER
BT1 decapoda
BT2 malacostraca
BT3 crustacea
BT4 arthropods

cancer (disease)
USE **neoplasms**

CANCHIM
HN from 1990
BT1 cattle breeds
BT2 breeds

CANDICIDIN
BT1 antibiotics
BT1 antifungal agents
BT2 antiinfective agents
BT3 drugs
rt candida

CANDIDA
BT1 deuteromycotina
NT1 candida albicans
NT1 candida claussenii
NT1 candida curvata
NT1 candida cylindracea
NT1 candida guilliermondii
NT1 candida humicola
NT1 candida kefyr
NT1 candida krusei
NT1 candida lipolytica
NT1 candida lusitaniae
NT1 candida muscorum
NT1 candida norvegensis
NT1 candida parapsilosis
NT1 candida rugosa
NT1 candida slooffiae
NT1 candida stellatoidea
NT1 candida tropicalis
NT1 candida utilis
NT1 candida viswanathii
NT1 candida zeylanoides
rt candicidin
rt candidosis
rt pichia
rt torulopsis
rt yeasts

CANDIDA ALBICANS
uf *monilia albicans*
BT1 candida
BT2 deuteromycotina

CANDIDA CLAUSSENII
BT1 candida
BT2 deuteromycotina

CANDIDA CURVATA
HN from 1989
BT1 candida
BT2 deuteromycotina

CANDIDA CYLINDRACEA
HN from 1989
BT1 candida
BT2 deuteromycotina

candida famata
USE **torulopsis candida**

candida glabrata
USE **torulopsis glabrata**

CANDIDA GUILLIERMONDII
BT1 candida
BT2 deuteromycotina

candida holmii
USE **torulopsis holmii**

CANDIDA HUMICOLA
BT1 candida
BT2 deuteromycotina

candida inconspicua
USE **torulopsis inconspicua**

CANDIDA KEFYR
uf *candida pseudotropicalis*
BT1 candida
BT2 deuteromycotina

CANDIDA KRUSEI
uf *candida parakrusei*
BT1 candida
BT2 deuteromycotina

CANDIDA LIPOLYTICA
BT1 candida
BT2 deuteromycotina

CANDIDA LUSITANIAE
HN from 1989
BT1 candida
BT2 deuteromycotina

CANDIDA MUSCORUM
BT1 candida
BT2 deuteromycotina

CANDIDA NORVEGENSIS
HN from 1989
BT1 candida
BT2 deuteromycotina

candida parakrusei
USE **candida krusei**

CANDIDA PARAPSILOSIS
BT1 candida
BT2 deuteromycotina

candida pseudotropicalis
USE **candida kefyr**

CANDIDA RUGOSA
BT1 candida
BT2 deuteromycotina

candida shehatae
USE **pichia stipitis**

CANDIDA SLOOFFIAE
BT1 candida
BT2 deuteromycotina

CANDIDA STELLATOIDEA
BT1 candida
BT2 deuteromycotina

CANDIDA TROPICALIS
BT1 candida
BT2 deuteromycotina

CANDIDA UTILIS
BT1 candida
BT2 deuteromycotina

CANDIDA VISWANATHII
BT1 candida
BT2 deuteromycotina

CANDIDA ZEYLANOIDES
BT1 candida
BT2 deuteromycotina

candidiasis
USE **candidosis**

CANDIDOSIS
uf *candidiasis*
BT1 mycoses
BT2 infectious diseases
BT3 diseases
NT1 chronic mucocutaneous candidosis
rt candida

CANDY
BT1 feeds

CANDY *cont.*
rt sweets

cane mills
USE **roller mills**

cane molasses
USE **molasses**

CANE SUGAR
BT1 sugar
BT2 plant products
BT3 products
rt sucrose

CANE SYRUP
HN from 1990
BT1 sugar industry intermediates
BT1 syrups
BT2 liquids

CANELLACEAE
NT1 cinnamodendron
NT2 cinnamodendron dinisii
NT1 cinnamosma
NT2 cinnamosma madagascariensis

canes
USE **canes and rattans**

CANES AND RATTANS
uf *canes*
uf *rattans*
rt bamboos
rt minor forest products

CANIDAE
BT1 fissipeda
BT2 carnivores
BT3 mammals
NT1 alopex
NT2 alopex lagopus
NT1 canis
NT2 canis aureus
NT2 canis familiaris dingo
NT2 canis mesomelas
NT1 chrysocyon
NT2 chrysocyon brachyurus
NT1 lycaon
NT2 lycaon pictus
NT1 nyctereutes
NT1 vulpes
NT2 vulpes cinereoargenteus
NT2 vulpes vulpes
rt coyotes
rt dogs
rt foxes
rt jackals
rt raccoon dogs
rt wolves

canihua
USE **chenopodium canihua**

CANINE ADENOVIRUS
BT1 mastadenovirus
BT2 adenoviridae
BT3 viruses
NT1 canine hepatitis virus
rt dog diseases

CANINE CORONAVIRUS
BT1 coronavirus
BT2 coronaviridae
BT3 viruses

CANINE HEPATITIS VIRUS
BT1 canine adenovirus
BT2 mastadenovirus
BT3 adenoviridae
BT4 viruses
rt viral hepatitis

CANINE HERPESVIRUS
BT1 herpesviridae
BT2 viruses
rt dog diseases

CANINE PAPILLOMAVIRUS
BT1 papillomavirus
BT2 papovaviridae
BT3 viruses

CANINE PARAINFLUENZA VIRUS
BT1 canine paramyxovirus
BT2 paramyxovirus
BT3 paramyxoviridae
BT4 viruses

CANINE PARAMYXOVIRUS
BT1 paramyxovirus
BT2 paramyxoviridae
BT3 viruses
NT1 canine parainfluenza virus

CANINE PARVOVIRUS
BT1 parvovirus
BT2 parvoviridae
BT3 viruses
rt dog diseases

CANIS
BT1 canidae
BT2 fissipeda
BT3 carnivores
BT4 mammals
NT1 canis aureus
NT1 canis familiaris dingo
NT1 canis mesomelas
rt jackals

CANIS AUREUS
BT1 canis
BT2 canidae
BT3 fissipeda
BT4 carnivores
BT5 mammals

canis dingo
USE **canis familiaris dingo**

canis familiaris
USE **dogs**

CANIS FAMILIARIS DINGO
HN from 1990; previously "canis dingo"
uf *canis dingo*
uf *dingo*
BT1 canis
BT2 canidae
BT3 fissipeda
BT4 carnivores
BT5 mammals

canis latrans
USE **coyotes**

canis lupus
USE **wolves**

CANIS MESOMELAS
BT1 canis
BT2 canidae
BT3 fissipeda
BT4 carnivores
BT5 mammals

CANKERS
BT1 plant disorders
BT2 disorders
rt galls

CANNA
BT1 cannaceae
NT1 canna edulis
NT1 canna glauca
NT1 canna indica

CANNA EDULIS
uf *queensland arrowroot*
BT1 canna
BT2 cannaceae
BT1 fodder plants
BT1 root vegetables
BT2 root crops
BT2 vegetables
BT1 starch crops

CANNA GLAUCA
BT1 canna
BT2 cannaceae

CANNA INDICA
BT1 antifungal plants
BT1 canna
BT2 cannaceae
BT1 ornamental bulbs

CANNA INDICA *cont.*
rt rhizomes

CANNABIDACEAE
NT1 cannabis
NT2 cannabis sativa
NT1 humulus
NT2 humulus japonica
NT2 humulus lupulus

CANNABIDIOL
BT1 cannabinoids
BT2 neurotropic drugs
BT3 drugs
rt cannabis resin

CANNABINOIDS
BT1 neurotropic drugs
BT2 drugs
NT1 cannabidiol
NT1 tetrahydrocannabinol
rt cannabis resin
rt cannabis sativa

CANNABIS
BT1 cannabidaceae
NT1 cannabis sativa

CANNABIS RESIN
BT1 resins
rt cannabidiol
rt cannabinoids

CANNABIS SATIVA
BT1 antifungal plants
BT1 cannabis
BT2 cannabidaceae
BT1 fibre plants
BT1 medicinal plants
BT1 nematicidal plants
BT2 pesticidal plants
BT1 oilseed plants
BT2 fatty oil plants
BT3 oil plants
rt cannabinoids
rt hemp

CANNACEAE
NT1 canna
NT2 canna edulis
NT2 canna glauca
NT2 canna indica

CANNED FISH
BT1 canned products
BT2 products
BT1 fish products
BT2 animal products
BT3 products

canned foods
USE **canned products**

CANNED FRUIT
uf *fruit, canned*
BT1 canned products
BT2 products
BT1 fruit products
BT2 plant products
BT3 products
rt fruit

CANNED MEAT
BT1 canned products
BT2 products
BT1 meat products
BT2 animal products
BT3 products
rt meat

CANNED PRODUCTS
uf *canned foods*
BT1 products
NT1 canned fish
NT1 canned fruit
NT1 canned meat
NT1 canned vegetables
rt canneries (agricola)
rt canning
rt canning industry
rt canning quality
rt processed products

CANNED VEGETABLES
BT1 canned products
BT2 products
BT1 vegetable products
BT2 plant products
BT3 products
rt vegetables

CANNERIES (AGRICOLA)
BT1 factories
BT2 buildings
rt canned products
rt cannery effluent
rt cannery wastes

CANNERY EFFLUENT
BT1 factory effluents
BT2 effluents
BT3 wastes
rt canneries (agricola)
rt cannery wastes
rt canning
rt canning industry

CANNERY WASTES
BT1 industrial wastes
BT2 wastes
rt canneries (agricola)
rt cannery effluent
rt canning
rt canning industry

CANNIBALISM
BT1 abnormal behaviour
BT2 behaviour
rt appetite disorders

CANNING
BT1 packaging
BT2 handling
BT1 processing
rt canned products
rt cannery effluent
rt cannery wastes
rt preservation

CANNING INDUSTRY
BT1 food industry
BT2 industry
rt canned products
rt cannery effluent
rt cannery wastes

CANNING QUALITY
uf *quality for canning*
BT1 food processing quality
BT2 processing quality
BT3 quality
rt canned products

CANNULAE
BT1 instruments
rt cannulation
rt duodenal ulcer

CANNULATION
BT1 techniques
rt cannulae

CANOEING
BT1 boating
BT2 water recreation
BT3 recreation

canola
USE **rape**

CANONICAL ANALYSIS
BT1 multivariate analysis
BT2 statistical analysis
BT3 data analysis
BT3 statistics
rt canonical correlation

CANONICAL CORRELATION
BT1 correlation
rt canonical analysis
rt correlation analysis

CANOPY
uf *crown cover*
uf *leaf canopy*
NT1 branches
NT2 smallwood
rt canopy penetration

CANOPY *cont.*
rt crown
rt foliage
rt foliage area
rt foliar spraying
rt interception
rt leaf area
rt light penetration
rt shade
rt shade trees
rt stemflow

CANOPY PENETRATION
rt canopy
rt penetration
rt spraying

CANS (AGRICOLA)
BT1 containers

CANSCORA
BT1 gentianaceae
NT1 canscora decussata

CANSCORA DECUSSATA
BT1 canscora
BT2 gentianaceae
BT1 medicinal plants

CANSJERA
BT1 opiliaceae
NT1 cansjera rheedii

CANSJERA RHEEDII
BT1 cansjera
BT2 opiliaceae

CANTAL CHEESE
BT1 cheeses
BT2 milk products
BT3 products

cantaloupes
USE **melons**

CANTHARELLALES
NT1 cantharellus
NT2 cantharellus cibarius
rt fungi

CANTHARELLUS
BT1 cantharellales
NT1 cantharellus cibarius

CANTHARELLUS CIBARIUS
BT1 cantharellus
BT2 cantharellales
BT1 edible fungi
BT2 fungi
BT2 vegetables

CANTHARIDIN
BT1 monoterpenoids
BT2 terpenoids
BT3 isoprenoids
BT4 lipids
BT1 toxins

CANTHAXANTHIN
BT1 food colourants
BT2 food additives
BT3 additives
BT1 xanthophylls
BT2 carotenoids
BT3 lipochromes
BT4 pigments
BT3 terpenoids
BT4 isoprenoids
BT5 lipids

CANTHIUM
BT1 rubiaceae
NT1 canthium dicoccum

CANTHIUM DICOCCUM
BT1 canthium
BT2 rubiaceae

CANTHON
BT1 scarabaeidae
BT2 coleoptera
NT1 canthon pilularius

CANTHON PILULARIUS
BT1 canthon

CANTHON PILULARIUS *cont.*
BT2 scarabaeidae
BT3 coleoptera

canton and enderbury islands
USE **kiribati**

CANTONESE
HN from 1990
BT1 pig breeds
BT2 breeds

CANVAS
BT1 textiles
BT2 non-food products
BT3 products

CAP
uf *common agricultural policy*
BT1 agricultural policy
rt european communities

cap (chlormadinone)
USE **chlormadinone**

capability, land
USE **land capability**

CAPACITANCE
BT1 electrical properties
BT2 physical properties
BT3 properties

CAPACITATION
rt spermatozoa

CAPACITY
rt available water capacity
rt bearing capacity
rt buffering capacity
rt capillary capacity
rt carrying capacity
rt cation exchange capacity
rt efficiency
rt field capacity
rt honey-getting capacity
rt ion exchange capacity
rt iron binding capacity
rt maximum water holding capacity
rt rooting capacity
rt spare capacity
rt storage
rt vectorial capacity
rt volume
rt water binding capacity
rt water holding capacity
rt work capacity

cape gooseberries
USE **physalis peruviana**

cape honeybee
USE **apis mellifera capensis**

CAPE VERDE
uf *republic of cape verde*
BT1 west africa
BT2 africa south of sahara
BT3 africa
rt acp
rt developing countries
rt least developed countries

capelin
USE **mallotus villosus**

CAPERONIA
BT1 euphorbiaceae
NT1 caperonia castanaefolia
NT1 caperonia palustris

CAPERONIA CASTANAEFOLIA
BT1 caperonia
BT2 euphorbiaceae

CAPERONIA PALUSTRIS
BT1 caperonia
BT2 euphorbiaceae

CAPERS
BT1 condiments
rt capparis spinosa

CAPILLARIA
BT1 trichuridae

CAPILLARIA *cont.*
BT2 nematoda
NT1 capillaria hepatica
NT1 capillaria obsignata
NT1 capillaria philippinensis

CAPILLARIA HEPATICA
BT1 capillaria
BT2 trichuridae
BT3 nematoda

CAPILLARIA OBSIGNATA
BT1 capillaria
BT2 trichuridae
BT3 nematoda

CAPILLARIA PHILIPPINENSIS
BT1 capillaria
BT2 trichuridae
BT3 nematoda

CAPILLARIES
BT1 blood vessels
BT2 cardiovascular system
BT3 body parts
rt antihistaminics
rt capillary circulation
rt pores

capillarity
USE **capillary rise**

CAPILLARY CAPACITY
BT1 soil water constants
rt capacity

CAPILLARY CIRCULATION
BT1 blood circulation
BT2 physiological functions
rt capillaries

capillary flow
USE **capillary rise**

CAPILLARY FRINGE
BT1 soil water
BT2 water

capillary irrigation
USE **trickle irrigation**

CAPILLARY RISE
uf *capillarity*
uf *capillary flow*
BT1 soil water movement
BT2 movement

CAPILLOVIRUS GROUP
HN from 1990
BT1 plant viruses
BT2 plant pathogens
BT3 pathogens
NT1 apple stem grooving capillovirus
NT1 potato t capillovirus

CAPITAL
uf *investments*
BT1 finance
NT1 fixed capital
NT1 working capital
rt assets
rt capital accounts
rt capital allocation
rt capital formation
rt capital leasing
rt capital market
rt capital productivity
rt capital taxation
rt depreciation
rt economic resources
rt factors of production
rt farm inputs
rt investment
rt owner's equity
rt stocks (financial) (agricola)

CAPITAL ACCOUNTS
BT1 accounts
rt capital
rt economic accounts

CAPITAL ALLOCATION
rt agricultural situation
rt capital

CAPITAL ALLOCATION *cont.*
rt capital leasing

capital, fixed
USE **fixed capital**

CAPITAL FORMATION
BT1 finance
rt assets
rt capital
rt investment
rt savings

capital gains tax
USE **capital taxation**

CAPITAL LEASING
uf *leasing*
NT1 hiring
NT2 boat hire
NT2 car hire
NT2 custom hiring (agricola)
rt capital
rt capital allocation
rt leases

CAPITAL MARKET
uf *factor markets*
BT1 markets
rt capital

capital outlay
USE **investment**

CAPITAL PRODUCTIVITY
BT1 productivity
rt capital

CAPITAL TAXATION
uf *capital gains tax*
uf *capital transfer tax*
uf *taxation, capital*
BT1 direct taxation
BT2 taxes
BT3 fiscal policy
BT4 economic policy
BT4 public finance
NT1 land tax
NT1 rates
rt capital
rt valuation

capital territory of australia
USE **australian capital territory**

capital transfer tax
USE **capital taxation**

capital, working
USE **working capital**

CAPITALISM
BT1 economic systems
BT2 systems
BT1 political systems
BT2 politics
rt capitalist agriculture
rt capitalist countries
rt market economies

CAPITALIST AGRICULTURE
BT1 agriculture
rt capitalism

CAPITALIST COUNTRIES
rt capitalism
rt economic systems
rt market economies
rt mixed economies

CAPITOPHORUS
BT1 aphididae
BT2 aphidoidea
BT3 sternorrhyncha
BT4 homoptera
NT1 capitophorus elaeagni
NT1 capitophorus hippophaes
NT1 capitophorus horni
rt chaetosiphon

CAPITOPHORUS ELAEAGNI
BT1 capitophorus
BT2 aphididae
BT3 aphidoidea
BT4 sternorrhyncha

CAPITOPHORUS ELAEAGNI *cont.*
BT5 homoptera

capitophorus fragaefolii
USE **chaetosiphon fragaefolii**

CAPITOPHORUS HIPPOPHAES
BT1 capitophorus
BT2 aphididae
BT3 aphidoidea
BT4 sternorrhyncha
BT5 homoptera

CAPITOPHORUS HORNI
BT1 capitophorus
BT2 aphididae
BT3 aphidoidea
BT4 sternorrhyncha
BT5 homoptera

CAPITULUM
BT1 bones
BT2 musculoskeletal system
BT3 body parts

capitulums
(botanical)
USE **inflorescences**

CAPNODIS
BT1 buprestidae
BT2 coleoptera
NT1 capnodis miliaris
NT1 capnodis tenebrionis

CAPNODIS MILIARIS
BT1 capnodis
BT2 buprestidae
BT3 coleoptera

CAPNODIS TENEBRIONIS
BT1 capnodis
BT2 buprestidae
BT3 coleoptera

CAPONS
BT1 fowls
BT2 poultry
BT3 livestock
BT4 animals
rt castration

CAPPARIDACEAE
NT1 apophyllum
NT2 apophyllum anomalum
NT1 boscia
NT2 boscia senegalensis
NT1 capparis
NT2 capparis aphylla
NT2 capparis decidua
NT2 capparis ovata
NT2 capparis pringlei
NT2 capparis spinosa
NT2 capparis tomentosa
NT1 cleome
NT2 cleome arabica
NT2 cleome gynandra
NT2 cleome hassleriana
NT2 cleome rutidosperma
NT2 cleome spinosa
NT2 cleome viscosa
NT1 crateva
NT2 crateva religiosa
NT1 maerua
NT2 maerua crassifolia

CAPPARIS
BT1 capparidaceae
NT1 capparis aphylla
NT1 capparis decidua
NT1 capparis ovata
NT1 capparis pringlei
NT1 capparis spinosa
NT1 capparis tomentosa

CAPPARIS APHYLLA
BT1 capparis
BT2 capparidaceae

CAPPARIS DECIDUA
BT1 browse plants
BT1 capparis
BT2 capparidaceae

CAPPARIS OVATA
BT1 capparis
BT2 capparidaceae

CAPPARIS PRINGLEI
BT1 capparis
BT2 capparidaceae

CAPPARIS SPINOSA
BT1 antiviral plants
BT1 capparis
BT2 capparidaceae
BT1 medicinal plants
BT1 spice plants
rt capers

CAPPARIS TOMENTOSA
BT1 browse plants
BT1 capparis
BT2 capparidaceae

CAPPING
rt beeswax

CAPPINGS
BT1 cells (honeybees)
BT2 combs
BT3 hive parts
BT4 movable-comb hives
BT5 hives
rt beeswax
rt honey
rt uncapping

CAPRA
BT1 bovidae
BT2 ruminantia
BT3 artiodactyla
BT4 mammals
BT4 ungulates
NT1 capra ibex
NT1 capra pyrenaica

capra hircus
USE **goats**

CAPRA IBEX
uf ibex
BT1 capra
BT2 bovidae
BT3 ruminantia
BT4 artiodactyla
BT5 mammals
BT5 ungulates
rt wild goats

CAPRA PYRENAICA
BT1 capra
BT2 bovidae
BT3 ruminantia
BT4 artiodactyla
BT5 mammals
BT5 ungulates
rt wild goats

CAPREOLUS
BT1 cervidae
BT2 ruminantia
BT3 artiodactyla
BT4 mammals
BT4 ungulates
NT1 capreolus capreolus

CAPREOLUS CAPREOLUS
uf deer, roe
uf roe deer
BT1 capreolus
BT2 cervidae
BT3 ruminantia
BT4 artiodactyla
BT5 mammals
BT5 ungulates

capric acid
USE **decanoic acid**

CAPRICORNIS
BT1 bovidae
BT2 ruminantia
BT3 artiodactyla
BT4 mammals
BT4 ungulates
NT1 capricornis crispus

CAPRICORNIS CRISPUS
BT1 capricornis
BT2 bovidae
BT3 ruminantia
BT4 artiodactyla
BT5 mammals
BT5 ungulates

CAPRIFOLIACEAE
NT1 abelia
NT2 abelia grandiflora
NT1 diervilla
NT1 dipelta
NT1 kolkwitzia
NT2 kolkwitzia amabilis
NT1 leycesteria
NT2 leycesteria formosa
NT1 lonicera
NT2 lonicera alpigena
NT2 lonicera altaica
NT2 lonicera caerulea
NT2 lonicera caprifolium
NT2 lonicera edulis
NT2 lonicera henryi
NT2 lonicera japonica
NT2 lonicera kesselringii
NT2 lonicera maackii
NT2 lonicera microphylla
NT2 lonicera morrowii
NT2 lonicera nigra
NT2 lonicera nitida
NT2 lonicera periclymenum
NT2 lonicera pileata
NT2 lonicera pyrenaica
NT2 lonicera quinquelocularis
NT2 lonicera regeliana
NT2 lonicera tatarica
NT2 lonicera turczaninowii
NT2 lonicera xylosteum
NT1 symphoricarpos
NT2 symphoricarpos albus
NT2 symphoricarpos occidentalis
NT2 symphoricarpos vaccinioides
NT1 viburnum
NT2 viburnum alnifolium
NT2 viburnum burkwoodii
NT2 viburnum carlesii
NT2 viburnum davidii
NT2 viburnum dilatatum
NT2 viburnum farreri
NT2 viburnum globosum
NT2 viburnum grandiflorum
NT2 viburnum henryi
NT2 viburnum japonicum
NT2 viburnum lantana
NT2 viburnum odoratissimum
NT2 viburnum opulus
NT2 viburnum plicatum
NT2 viburnum schensianum
NT2 viburnum setigerum
NT2 viburnum sieboldii
NT2 viburnum suspensum
NT2 viburnum tinus
NT2 viburnum trilobum
NT1 weigela
NT2 weigela florida

CAPRIMULGIFORMES
BT1 birds
NT1 podargidae
NT2 podargus

CAPRINE ARTHRITIS ENCEPHALITIS VIRUS
BT1 lentivirinae
BT2 retroviridae
BT3 viruses

CAPRIPOXVIRUS
BT1 chordopoxvirinae
BT2 poxviridae
BT3 viruses
NT1 goat pox virus
NT1 lumpy skin disease virus
NT1 sheep pox virus

caproic acid
USE **hexanoic acid**

CAPROMYIDAE
BT1 rodents

CAPROMYIDAE *cont.*
BT2 mammals
NT1 capromys

CAPROMYS
BT1 capromyidae
BT2 rodents
BT3 mammals

caprylic acid
USE **octanoic acid**

CAPSAICIN
BT1 amides
BT2 organic nitrogen compounds
BT1 flavour compounds
rt capsicum

CAPSALA
BT1 capsalidae
BT2 monogenea

CAPSALIDAE
BT1 monogenea
NT1 benedenia
NT1 capsala
NT1 encotyllabe
NT1 entobdella
NT2 entobdella soleae

CAPSANTHIN
BT1 xanthophylls
BT2 carotenoids
BT3 lipochromes
BT4 pigments
BT3 terpenoids
BT4 isoprenoids
BT5 lipids
rt capsicum

CAPSELLA
BT1 cruciferae
NT1 capsella bursa-pastoris

CAPSELLA BURSA-PASTORIS
BT1 capsella
BT2 cruciferae
BT1 insecticidal plants
BT2 pesticidal plants
BT1 weeds

CAPSICUM
uf pepper (capsicum)
uf pepper, red
uf pepper, sweet
BT1 solanaceae
NT1 capsicum angulosum
NT1 capsicum annuum
NT1 capsicum baccatum
NT1 capsicum chinense
NT1 capsicum conicum
NT1 capsicum frutescens
rt bitter pit
rt black spot
rt capsaicin
rt capsanthin
rt capsidiol
rt fruit vegetables
rt pepper veinal mottle potyvirus

CAPSICUM ANGULOSUM
BT1 capsicum
BT2 solanaceae

CAPSICUM ANNUUM
BT1 antiviral plants
BT1 capsicum
BT2 solanaceae
BT1 nematicidal plants
BT2 pesticidal plants
rt chillies
rt paprika

CAPSICUM BACCATUM
BT1 capsicum
BT2 solanaceae

CAPSICUM CHINENSE
BT1 capsicum
BT2 solanaceae

CAPSICUM CONICUM
BT1 capsicum

CAPSICUM CONICUM *cont.*
BT2 solanaceae

CAPSICUM FRUTESCENS
uf red pepper
BT1 capsicum
BT2 solanaceae
BT1 insecticidal plants
BT2 pesticidal plants
rt chillies

CAPSIDIOL
BT1 phytoalexins
BT2 allomones
BT3 allelochemicals
BT4 semiochemicals
BT1 sesquiterpenoids
BT2 terpenoids
BT3 isoprenoids
BT4 lipids
rt capsicum

CAPTAFOL
BT1 dicarboximide fungicides
BT2 fungicides
BT3 pesticides

CAPTAN
BT1 dicarboximide fungicides
BT2 fungicides
BT3 pesticides

CAPTURE OF ANIMALS
rt trapping
rt wildlife conservation
rt zoo animals
rt zoological gardens

capuchin monkeys
USE **cebus**

CAPUT EPIDIDYMIDIS
BT1 epididymis
BT2 testes
BT3 gonads
BT4 reproductive organs

CAPYBARAS
HN from 1990; previously "hydrochaerus hydrochaeris"
uf hydrochaerus hydrochaeris
BT1 meat animals
BT2 animals
rt hydrochaeridae

CAR HIRE
AF car rental
BT1 hiring
BT2 capital leasing
rt motor cars

CAR RENTAL
BF car hire

carabao
USE **buffaloes**

CARABIDAE
BT1 coleoptera
NT1 agonum
NT2 agonum dorsale
NT1 asaphidion
NT2 asaphidion flavipes
NT1 bembidion
NT2 bembidion lampros
NT2 bembidion quadrimaculatum
NT1 broscus
NT2 broscus cephalotes
NT1 calosoma
NT2 calosoma sycophanta
NT1 clivina
NT2 clivina fossor
NT2 clivina impressifrons
NT1 harpalus
NT2 harpalus affinis
NT2 harpalus distinguendus
NT2 harpalus pennsylvanicus
NT2 harpalus rufipes
NT1 loricera
NT2 loricera pilicornis
NT1 nebria
NT2 nebria brevicollis

CARABIDAE *cont.*
NT1 notiophilus
NT2 notiophilus biguttatus
NT1 pterostichus
NT2 pterostichus chalcites
NT2 pterostichus cupreus
NT2 pterostichus madidus
NT2 pterostichus melanarius
NT2 pterostichus oblongopunctatus
NT2 pterostichus sericeus
NT1 trechus
NT2 trechus quadristriatus
NT2 trechus secalis
NT1 zabrus
NT2 zabrus tenebrioides

CARACU
BT1 cattle breeds
BT2 breeds

CARAGANA
BT1 leguminosae
NT1 caragana arborescens
NT1 caragana brevifolia
NT1 caragana frutex
NT1 caragana pygmaea

CARAGANA ARBORESCENS
BT1 caragana
BT2 leguminosae
BT1 forest trees
BT1 ornamental woody plants

CARAGANA BREVIFOLIA
BT1 caragana
BT2 leguminosae

CARAGANA FRUTEX
BT1 caragana
BT2 leguminosae
BT1 ornamental woody plants

CARAGANA PYGMAEA
BT1 caragana
BT2 leguminosae

CARALLUMA
BT1 asclepiadaceae
rt ornamental succulent plants

carambola
USE **averrhoa carambola**

CARAMEL
BT1 flavourings
BT2 food additives
BT3 additives
BT1 food colourants
BT2 food additives
BT3 additives

CARANGA PYGMAEA
BT1 pasture legumes
BT2 legumes
BT2 pasture plants

CARANGIDAE
BT1 perciformes
BT2 osteichthyes
BT3 fishes
NT1 caranx
NT1 decapterus
NT1 seriola
NT1 trachinotus
NT2 trachinotus carolinus
NT2 trachinotus goodei
NT1 trachurus
NT2 trachurus lathami
NT2 trachurus trachurus
NT1 vomer
rt pompanos
rt yellowtails

CARANX
BT1 carangidae
BT2 perciformes
BT3 osteichthyes
BT4 fishes

CARAPA
BT1 meliaceae
NT1 carapa guianensis
NT1 carapa procera

CARAPA GUIANENSIS
BT1 carapa
BT2 meliaceae
BT1 forest trees

CARAPA PROCERA
BT1 carapa
BT2 meliaceae

CARAPACE SPOT
BT1 plant disorders
BT2 disorders
rt avocados

CARASSIUS
BT1 cyprinidae
BT2 cypriniformes
BT3 osteichthyes
BT4 fishes
NT1 carassius carassius

carassius auratus
USE **goldfish**

CARASSIUS CARASSIUS
uf *carp, crucian*
uf *crucian carp*
BT1 carassius
BT2 cyprinidae
BT3 cypriniformes
BT4 osteichthyes
BT5 fishes

CARAUSIUS
BT1 phasmatidae
BT2 phasmida
NT1 carausius morosus

CARAUSIUS MOROSUS
BT1 carausius
BT2 phasmatidae
BT3 phasmida

CARAVAN SITES
BT1 amenity and recreation areas
BT2 areas
BT1 holiday accommodation
BT2 accommodation
BT1 site types
rt ancillary enterprises
rt caravanning

CARAVANNING
BT1 holidays
BT2 tourism
BT1 outdoor recreation
BT2 recreation
rt caravan sites

CARAWAY
rt carum carvi

CARAZOLOL
BT1 sympatholytics
BT2 neurotropic drugs
BT3 drugs

CARBACHOL
uf *carbamoylcholine*
BT1 parasympathomimetics
BT2 neurotropic drugs
BT3 drugs

CARBADOX
BT1 antibacterial agents
BT2 antiinfective agents
BT3 drugs
BT1 growth promoters
BT2 growth regulators
BT2 promoters

CARBAMATE ACARICIDES
BT1 acaricides
BT2 pesticides
BT1 carbamate pesticides
NT1 benomyl
NT1 carbaryl
NT1 metolcarb
NT1 oxime carbamate acaricides
NT2 aldicarb
NT2 butocarboxim
NT1 propoxur

CARBAMATE HERBICIDES
BT1 carbamate pesticides
BT1 herbicides
BT2 pesticides
NT1 asulam
NT1 dichlormate
NT1 karbutilate
NT1 terbucarb

CARBAMATE INSECTICIDES
BT1 carbamate pesticides
BT1 insecticides
BT2 pesticides
NT1 allyxycarb
NT1 aminocarb
NT1 bendiocarb
NT1 benfuracarb
NT1 bufencarb
NT1 butacarb
NT1 carbaryl
NT1 carbofuran
NT1 carbosulfan
NT1 cartap
NT1 cloethocarb
NT1 dimetilan
NT1 dioxacarb
NT1 ethiofencarb
NT1 fenobucarb
NT1 furathiocarb
NT1 isoprocarb
NT1 methiocarb
NT1 metolcarb
NT1 mexacarbate
NT1 oxime carbamate insecticides
NT2 aldicarb
NT2 aldoxycarb
NT2 butocarboxim
NT2 methomyl
NT2 oxamyl
NT2 thiodicarb
NT2 thiofanox
NT1 pirimicarb
NT1 promecarb
NT1 propoxur
NT1 tazimcarb
NT1 trimethacarb

CARBAMATE NEMATICIDES
BT1 carbamate pesticides
BT1 nematicides
BT2 pesticides
NT1 benomyl
NT1 carbofuran
NT1 carbosulfan
NT1 cloethocarb
NT1 oxime carbamate nematicides
NT2 aldicarb
NT2 aldoxycarb
NT2 oxamyl

CARBAMATE PESTICIDES
NT1 carbamate acaricides
NT2 benomyl
NT2 carbaryl
NT2 metolcarb
NT2 oxime carbamate acaricides
NT3 aldicarb
NT3 butocarboxim
NT2 propoxur
NT1 carbamate herbicides
NT2 asulam
NT2 dichlormate
NT2 karbutilate
NT2 terbucarb
NT1 carbamate insecticides
NT2 allyxycarb
NT2 aminocarb
NT2 bendiocarb
NT2 benfuracarb
NT2 bufencarb
NT2 butacarb
NT2 carbaryl
NT2 carbofuran
NT2 carbosulfan
NT2 cartap
NT2 cloethocarb
NT2 dimetilan
NT2 dioxacarb
NT2 ethiofencarb

CARBAMATE PESTICIDES *cont.*
NT2 fenobucarb
NT2 furathiocarb
NT2 isoprocarb
NT2 methiocarb
NT2 metolcarb
NT2 mexacarbate
NT2 oxime carbamate insecticides
NT3 aldicarb
NT3 aldoxycarb
NT3 butocarboxim
NT3 methomyl
NT3 oxamyl
NT3 thiodicarb
NT3 thiofanox
NT2 pirimicarb
NT2 promecarb
NT2 propoxur
NT2 tazimcarb
NT2 trimethacarb
NT1 carbamate nematicides
NT2 benomyl
NT2 carbofuran
NT2 carbosulfan
NT2 cloethocarb
NT2 oxime carbamate nematicides
NT3 aldicarb
NT3 aldoxycarb
NT3 oxamyl
NT1 carbanilate herbicides
NT2 barban
NT2 carbasulam
NT2 carbetamide
NT2 chlorbufam
NT2 chlorpropham
NT2 desmedipham
NT2 phenisopham
NT2 phenmedipham
NT2 phenmedipham-ethyl
NT2 propham
NT2 swep
NT1 dithiocarbamate fungicides
NT2 cufraneb
NT2 cuprobam
NT2 disulfiram
NT2 etem
NT2 ferbam
NT2 mancozeb
NT2 maneb
NT2 metiram
NT2 milneb
NT2 nabam
NT2 polycarbamate
NT2 propineb
NT2 thiram
NT2 zineb
NT2 ziram
NT1 thiocarbamate herbicides
NT2 butylate
NT2 cycloate
NT2 di-allate
NT2 eptc
NT2 esprocarb
NT2 ethiolate
NT2 metham
NT2 methiobencarb
NT2 molinate
NT2 orbencarb
NT2 pebulate
NT2 prosulfocarb
NT2 sulfallate
NT2 thiobencarb
NT2 tiocarbazil
NT2 tri-allate
NT2 vernolate
rt carbamates
rt pesticides

CARBAMATES
BT1 esters
NT1 meprobamate
NT1 physostigmine
NT1 urethane
rt carbamate pesticides

CARBAMOYL-PHOSPHATE SYNTHASE
(ec 6.3.5.5)
BT1 ligases
BT2 enzymes

carbamoylcholine
USE **carbachol**

CARBANILATE HERBICIDES
BT1 carbamate pesticides
BT1 herbicides
BT2 pesticides
NT1 barban
NT1 carbasulam
NT1 carbetamide
NT1 chlorbufam
NT1 chlorpropham
NT1 desmedipham
NT1 phenisopham
NT1 phenmedipham
NT1 phenmedipham-ethyl
NT1 propham
NT1 swep

CARBARYL
BT1 anthelmintics
BT2 antiparasitic agents
BT3 drugs
BT1 carbamate acaricides
BT2 acaricides
BT3 pesticides
BT2 carbamate pesticides
BT1 carbamate insecticides
BT2 carbamate pesticides
BT2 insecticides
BT3 pesticides
BT1 ectoparasiticides
BT2 antiparasitic agents
BT3 drugs
BT1 plant growth regulators
BT2 growth regulators

CARBASULAM
BT1 carbanilate herbicides
BT2 carbamate pesticides
BT2 herbicides
BT3 pesticides

carbathion
USE **metham**

CARBAZOLES
BT1 heterocyclic nitrogen compounds
BT2 organic nitrogen compounds

CARBENDAZIM
uf *carbendazol*
uf *mbc*
BT1 benzimidazole fungicides
BT2 fungicides
BT3 pesticides

carbendazol
USE **carbendazim**

CARBENICILLIN
BT1 penicillins
BT2 antibacterial agents
BT3 antiinfective agents
BT4 drugs
BT2 heterocyclic nitrogen compounds
BT3 organic nitrogen compounds

CARBETAMIDE
BT1 carbanilate herbicides
BT2 carbamate pesticides
BT2 herbicides
BT3 pesticides

CARBIDES
BT1 inorganic compounds
NT1 calcium carbide

CARBOFURAN
BT1 carbamate insecticides
BT2 carbamate pesticides
BT2 insecticides
BT3 pesticides
BT1 carbamate nematicides
BT2 carbamate pesticides
BT2 nematicides
BT3 pesticides

carbohydrases
USE **glycosidases**

CARBOHYDRATE LOADING (AGRICOLA)
BT1 diets
rt carbohydrates

CARBOHYDRATE METABOLISM
BT1 metabolism
NT1 gluconeogenesis
NT1 glycogenolysis
NT1 glycolysis
NT1 glyconeogenesis
rt carbohydrate metabolism disorders
rt carbohydrates

CARBOHYDRATE METABOLISM DISORDERS
uf *carbohydrate sensitivity*
BT1 metabolic disorders
BT2 animal disorders
BT3 disorders
NT1 disaccharidosis
NT1 fructose intolerance
NT1 galactosaemia
NT1 glycogenosis
NT1 glycosuria
NT1 hyperglycaemia
NT1 hypoglycaemia
NT1 lactose intolerance
NT1 mannosidosis
NT1 mucopolysaccharidosis
NT1 sucrose intolerance
rt carbohydrate metabolism
rt carbohydrates

CARBOHYDRATE MODIFICATIONS (AGRICOLA)
BT1 diets
rt carbohydrates

CARBOHYDRATE-RICH FOODS (AGRICOLA)
BT1 foods
rt carbohydrates

carbohydrate sensitivity
USE **carbohydrate metabolism disorders**

CARBOHYDRATES
uf *saccharides*
NT1 glycosides
NT2 aminoglycoside antibiotics
NT3 framycetin
NT3 gentamicin
NT3 kanamycin
NT3 paromomycin
NT3 spiramycin
NT3 streptomycin
NT2 cardiac glycosides
NT3 digitonin
NT3 digitoxin
NT3 digoxin
NT3 lanatosides
NT3 strophanthins
NT4 ouabain
NT2 cerebrosides
NT2 cyanogenic glycosides
NT3 amygdalin
NT3 linamarin
NT3 taxiphyllin
NT2 glucosides
NT3 aesculin
NT3 amygdalin
NT3 chloralose
NT3 cycasin
NT3 fragilin
NT3 glucosinolates
NT4 glucobrassicin
NT4 gluconapin
NT4 progoitrin
NT4 sinigrin
NT3 glycyrrhizin
NT3 isoquercitrin
NT3 linamarin
NT3 methyl glucoside
NT3 oleuropein
NT3 salicin
NT3 tannins
NT3 taxiphyllin
NT3 vicine
NT3 vitexin
NT2 glycoflavones

CARBOHYDRATES *cont.*
NT3 anthocyanins
NT4 cyanin
NT4 delphinin
NT4 rubrobrassicin
NT3 hesperidin
NT3 isoquercitrin
NT3 naringin
NT3 phloridzin
NT3 quercitrin
NT3 rutoside
NT3 vitexin
NT2 iridoid glycosides
NT3 aucubin
NT3 loganin
NT2 locundioside
NT2 neomycin
NT2 nucleosides
NT3 deoxyribonucleosides
NT4 cordycepin
NT4 deoxyadenosine
NT4 deoxyuridines
NT5 broxuridine
NT5 deoxyuridine
NT5 floxuridine
NT5 idoxuridine
NT4 thymidine
NT3 nucleoside antibiotics
NT4 blasticidin-s
NT4 cordycepin
NT4 gougerotin
NT4 nikkomycins
NT4 polyoxins
NT4 puromycin
NT4 toyocamycin
NT3 ribonucleosides
NT4 adenosine
NT4 adenosylhomocysteine
NT4 adenosylmethionine
NT4 cytidine
NT4 guanosine
NT4 inosine
NT4 pseudouridine
NT4 toyocamycin
NT4 uridine
NT2 nucleotides
NT3 cyclic nucleotides
NT4 c-amp
NT3 nucleotide coenzymes
NT4 coenzyme a
NT4 nad
NT4 nadh
NT4 nadp
NT4 nadph
NT4 pyridine nucleotides
NT3 purine nucleotides
NT4 adenosine phosphates
NT5 adp
NT5 amp
NT5 atp
NT5 c-amp
NT4 guanosine diphosphate
NT4 guanosine monophosphate
NT4 guanosine triphosphate
NT3 pyrimidine nucleotides
NT4 cytidine triphosphate
NT4 udp
NT4 ump
NT2 saponins
NT3 glycoalkaloids
NT4 α-tomatine
NT4 lanatosides
NT4 solanine
NT3 steroid saponins
NT4 digitonin
NT4 digitoxin
NT4 digoxin
NT3 triterpenoid saponins
NT1 monosaccharides
NT2 aldoses
NT3 hexoses
NT4 2-deoxy-d-glucose
NT4 fucose
NT4 galactose
NT4 glucose
NT4 mannose
NT4 rhamnose
NT3 pentoses
NT4 arabinose
NT4 ribose

CARBOHYDRATES *cont.*
NT4 xylose
NT3 tetroses
NT4 erythrose
NT3 trioses
NT4 glyceraldehyde
NT2 ketoses
NT3 hexuloses
NT4 fructose
NT4 psicose
NT4 sorbose
NT3 pentuloses
NT4 ribulose
NT4 xylulose
NT2 sugar acids
NT3 aldaric acids
NT4 glucaric acid
NT4 tartaric acid
NT3 aldonic acids
NT4 ascorbic acids
NT5 ascorbic acid
NT5 dehydroascorbic acid
NT5 diketogulonic acid
NT5 isoascorbic acid
NT4 gluconic acid
NT4 neuraminic acid
NT4 sialic acids
NT3 uronic acids
NT4 galacturonic acid
NT4 glucuronic acid
NT2 sugar lactones
NT3 gluconolactone
NT1 oligosaccharides
NT2 disaccharides
NT3 cellobiose
NT3 gentiobiose
NT3 isomaltose
NT3 isomaltulose
NT3 lactose
NT3 lactulose
NT3 leucrose
NT3 maltose
NT3 melibiose
NT3 sucrose
NT3 trehalose
NT2 tetrasaccharides
NT3 nystose
NT3 stachyose
NT2 trisaccharides
NT3 erlose
NT3 kestose
NT3 melezitose
NT3 raffinose
NT1 photosynthates
NT2 glycerate 3-phosphate
NT2 ribulose 1,5-diphosphate
NT1 polysaccharides
NT2 callose
NT2 chitin
NT2 fructans
NT3 inulin
NT3 levan
NT2 galactans
NT3 agar
NT3 agarose
NT3 carrageenan
NT2 glucans
NT3 α-glucan
NT3 β-glucan
NT3 cellulose
NT4 lignocellulose
NT3 dextran
NT3 dextrins
NT4 maltodextrins
NT3 glycogen
NT3 starch
NT4 amylopectin
NT4 amylose
NT4 cassava starch
NT4 maize starch
NT4 potato starch
NT3 xyloglucans
NT2 glucomannans
NT3 konjak mannan
NT2 gums
NT3 dextran
NT3 dextrins
NT4 maltodextrins
NT3 gum arabic
NT3 xanthan
NT3 xylan

CARBOHYDRATES *cont.*
NT2 hemicelluloses
NT2 lipopolysaccharides
NT2 mannans
NT3 galactomannans
NT4 guar gum
NT2 mucilages
NT3 agar
NT3 alginic acid
NT3 carrageenan
NT3 guar gum
NT2 mucopolysaccharides
NT3 acid mucopolysaccharides
NT4 chondroitin sulfate
NT4 heparin
NT4 hyaluronic acid
NT3 chitosan
NT3 glycosaminoglycans
NT2 pentosans
NT3 xylan
NT2 peptidoglycans
NT3 murein
NT2 polyuronides
NT3 alginates
NT3 alginic acid
NT3 pectins
NT2 proteoglycans
NT2 zymosan
NT1 sugar alcohols
NT2 alditols
NT3 arabinitol
NT3 erythritol
NT3 galactitol
NT3 glycerol
NT3 lactitol
NT3 maltitol
NT3 mannitol
NT3 palatinit
NT3 sorbitol
NT3 xylitol
NT2 cyclitols
NT3 myo-inositol
NT3 pinitol
NT1 sugar phosphates
NT2 fructose 6-phosphate
NT2 glucose 1-phosphate
NT2 glucose 6-phosphate
NT2 glyceraldehyde 3-phosphate
NT2 inositol phosphates
NT3 phytic acid
NT2 ribulose 1,5-diphosphate
NT1 sugars
NT2 l-sugars
NT2 amino sugars
NT3 hexosamines
NT4 n-acetylglucosamine
NT4 galactosamine
NT4 glucosamine
NT3 neuraminic acid
NT3 sialic acids
NT2 deoxysugars
NT3 2-deoxy-d-glucose
NT3 fucose
NT3 rhamnose
NT2 gur
NT2 nonreducing sugars
NT3 ketoses
NT4 hexuloses
NT5 fructose
NT5 psicose
NT5 sorbose
NT4 pentuloses
NT5 ribulose
NT5 xylulose
NT3 raffinose
NT3 sucrose
NT3 trehalose
NT2 reducing sugars
NT3 aldoses
NT4 hexoses
NT5 2-deoxy-d-glucose
NT5 fucose
NT5 galactose
NT5 glucose
NT5 mannose
NT5 rhamnose
NT4 pentoses
NT5 arabinose
NT5 ribose
NT5 xylose

CARBOHYDRATES *cont.*
NT4 tetroses
NT5 erythrose
NT4 trioses
NT5 glyceraldehyde
NT3 cellobiose
NT3 gentiobiose
NT3 invert sugar
NT3 lactose
NT3 maltose
NT3 melibiose
NT2 sap sugar
rt carbohydrate loading (agricola)
rt carbohydrate metabolism
rt carbohydrate metabolism disorders
rt carbohydrate modifications (agricola)
rt carbohydrate-rich foods (agricola)
rt dietary carbohydrate
rt nutrients

CARBON
uf *c (symbol)*
BT1 nonmetallic elements
BT2 elements
rt activated carbon
rt carbon dioxide
rt carbon monoxide
rt carbon-nitrogen ratio
rt charcoal

carbon assimilation
USE **photosynthesis**

CARBON CYCLE
HN from 1990
BT1 cycling
rt carbon dioxide

CARBON DIOXIDE
BT1 oxides
BT2 inorganic compounds
BT1 respiratory gases
BT2 gases
rt bicarbonates
rt carbon
rt carbon cycle
rt carbon dioxide enrichment
rt carbonation
rt compensation point
rt fermentation
rt hypercapnia
rt photosynthesis
rt plant nutrition
rt respiratory quotient

CARBON DIOXIDE ENRICHMENT
rt carbon dioxide
rt enrichment

carbon dioxide fixation
USE **photosynthesis**

CARBON DISULFIDE
uf *carbon disulphide*
BT1 fumigant insecticides
BT2 fumigants
BT3 pesticides
BT2 insecticides
BT3 pesticides
BT1 nitrification inhibitors
BT2 metabolic inhibitors
BT3 inhibitors
BT1 soil fumigants
BT2 fumigants
BT3 pesticides
BT1 solvents
BT1 sulfides (organic)
BT2 organic sulfur compounds
BT2 sulfides

carbon disulphide
USE **carbon disulfide**

CARBON MONOXIDE
BT1 oxides
BT2 inorganic compounds
BT1 reducing agents
BT1 toxic gases
BT2 gases

CARBON MONOXIDE *cont.*
BT2 toxic substances
rt carbon
rt exhaust gases

CARBON-NITROGEN RATIO
BT1 ratios
rt carbon
rt nitrogen

CARBON PATHWAYS
BT1 biochemical pathways
BT1 photosynthesis
BT2 energy metabolism
BT3 metabolism
BT2 plant physiology
BT3 physiology
NT1 cam pathway

CARBON TETRACHLORIDE
uf *tetrachloromethane*
BT1 anthelmintics
BT2 antiparasitic agents
BT3 drugs
BT1 chlorinated hydrocarbons
BT2 halogenated hydrocarbons
BT3 organic halogen compounds
BT1 fumigant insecticides
BT2 fumigants
BT3 pesticides
BT2 insecticides
BT3 pesticides
BT1 solvents

CARBONATATION
HN from 1990
BT1 purification
BT2 processing
NT1 precarbonatation
rt defecosaturation
rt saturators

carbonatation mud
USE **filter cake**

CARBONATE
BT1 anions
BT2 ions

CARBONATE DEHYDRATASE
(ec 4.2.1.1)
uf *carbonic anhydrase*
BT1 hydro-lyases
BT2 lyases
BT3 enzymes

CARBONATES
BT1 inorganic salts
BT2 inorganic compounds
BT2 salts
NT1 calcium carbonate
NT1 copper carbonate
NT1 magnesium carbonate
NT1 potassium carbonate
NT1 sodium carbonate

CARBONATION
(adding carbon dioxide to beverages)
BT1 processing
rt aeration
rt beverages
rt carbon dioxide

carbonic anhydrase
USE **carbonate dehydratase**

CARBONYL COMPOUNDS
BT1 organic compounds
BT2 chemicals
rt aldehydes
rt ketones

CARBONYL SULFIDE
uf *carbonyl sulphide*
BT1 sulfides (organic)
BT2 organic sulfur compounds
BT2 sulfides

carbonyl sulphide
USE **carbonyl sulfide**

CARBOPHENOTHION
BT1 organothiophosphate acaricides
BT2 organophosphorus acaricides
BT3 acaricides
BT4 pesticides
BT3 organophosphorus pesticides
BT4 organophosphorus compounds
BT1 organothiophosphate insecticides
BT2 organophosphorus insecticides
BT3 insecticides
BT4 pesticides
BT3 organophosphorus pesticides
BT4 organophosphorus compounds

CARBOSULFAN
BT1 carbamate insecticides
BT2 carbamate pesticides
BT2 insecticides
BT3 pesticides
BT1 carbamate nematicides
BT2 carbamate pesticides
BT2 nematicides
BT3 pesticides

CARBOXIN
uf *dcmo*
BT1 oxathiin fungicides
BT2 anilide fungicides
BT3 fungicides
BT4 pesticides

CARBOXY-LYASES
(ec 4.1.1)
uf *carboxylases*
uf *decarboxylases*
BT1 lyases
BT2 enzymes
NT1 adenosylmethionine decarboxylase
NT1 glutamate decarboxylase
NT1 methylmalonyl-coa decarboxylase
NT1 ornithine decarboxylase
NT1 phosphoenolpyruvate carboxykinase
NT1 phosphoenolpyruvate carboxylase
NT1 pyruvate decarboxylase
NT1 ribulose-bisphosphate carboxylase

γ-CARBOXYGLUTAMIC ACID
(for retrieval spell out "gamma")
BT1 nonessential amino acids
BT2 amino acids
BT3 carboxylic acids
BT4 organic acids
BT5 acids
BT3 organic nitrogen compounds

carboxylases
USE **carboxy-lyases**

CARBOXYLATION
rt carboxylic acids

CARBOXYLESTERASE
(ec 3.1.1.1)
uf *aliesterase*
uf *cocaine esterase*
BT1 carboxylic ester hydrolases
BT2 esterases
BT3 hydrolases
BT4 enzymes

CARBOXYLIC ACIDS
BT1 organic acids
BT2 acids
NT1 amino acids
NT2 branched chain amino acids
NT3 aminoisobutyric acid
NT3 valine
NT2 cyclic amino acids

CARBOXYLIC ACIDS *cont.*
NT3 cycloleucine
NT3 desmosine
NT3 hypoglycine a
NT3 methylhistidine
NT2 diamino amino acids
NT3 diaminopimelic acid
NT2 essential amino acids
NT3 arginine
NT3 histidine
NT3 isoleucine
NT3 leucine
NT3 lysine
NT3 methionine
NT3 phenylalanine
NT3 threonine
NT3 tryptophan
NT3 valine
NT2 iodo amino acids
NT3 diiodothyronine
NT3 iodothyronine
NT3 thyroxine
NT4 d-thyroxine
NT4 l-thyroxine
NT3 triiodothyronine
NT2 limiting amino acids
NT2 nitrosoamino acids
NT2 nonessential amino acids
NT3 γ-carboxyglutamic acid
NT3 alanine
NT3 asparagine
NT3 aspartic acid
NT3 cystine
NT3 glutamic acid
NT3 glutamine
NT3 glycine
NT3 hydroxylysine
NT3 hydroxyproline
NT3 proline
NT3 serine
NT3 tyrosine
NT2 nonprotein amino acids
NT3 α-aminobutyric acid
NT3 γ-aminobutyric acid
NT3 aminoadipic acid
NT3 aminolaevulinic acid
NT3 canavanine
NT3 citrulline
NT3 dopa
NT4 levodopa
NT3 hippuric acid
NT3 homoserine
NT3 kynurenine
NT3 mimosine
NT3 ornithine
NT3 pipecolic acid
NT3 taurine
NT3 thyronine
NT2 seleno amino acids
NT3 selenomethionine
NT2 sulfur amino acids
NT3 cystathionine
NT3 cysteic acid
NT3 cysteine
NT3 cystine
NT3 ethionine
NT3 homocysteine
NT3 methionine
NT3 penicillamine
NT3 taurine
NT1 benzenealkanoic acids
NT2 homovanillic acid
NT2 mandelic acid
NT2 phenylacetic acid
NT2 phenyllactic acid
NT2 vanillomandelic acid
NT1 benzenealkenoic acids
NT2 cinnamic acid
NT2 coumaric acids
NT3 p-coumaric acid
NT3 caffeic acid
NT3 ferulic acid
NT3 sinapic acid
NT1 cyclohexanecarboxylic acids
NT2 chlorogenic acid
NT2 cyclohexanecarboxylic acid
NT2 quinic acid
NT2 shikimic acid
NT1 dicarboxylic acids
NT2 α-ketoglutaric acid
NT2 adipic acid

CARBOXYLIC ACIDS *cont.*
NT2 diferulic acid
NT2 diglycine
NT2 fumaric acid
NT2 glutaric acid
NT2 guanidinosuccinic acid
NT2 malic acid
NT2 malonic acid
NT2 methylmalonic acid
NT2 oxalic acid
NT2 oxaloacetic acid
NT2 phthalic acid
NT2 porphobilinogen
NT2 succinic acid
NT2 tartaric acid
NT1 fatty acids
NT2 branched chain fatty acids
NT3 phytanic acid
NT2 cyclopropenoid fatty acids
NT3 cyclopropenoic acid
NT3 sterculic acid
NT2 essential fatty acids
NT3 arachidonic acid
NT3 linoleic acid
NT3 linolenic acid
NT2 hydroxy fatty acids
NT3 3-hydroxybutyric acid
NT3 ricinoleic acid
NT3 trihydroxyoctadecenoic acid
NT2 long chain fatty acids
NT3 arachidonic acid
NT3 docosenoic acids
NT4 brassidic acid
NT4 erucic acid
NT3 elaidic acid
NT3 gadoleic acid
NT3 linoleic acid
NT3 oleic acid
NT3 palmitic acid
NT3 palmitoleic acid
NT3 pentadecanoic acid
NT3 stearic acid
NT3 tetracosadienoic acid
NT2 medium chain fatty acids
NT3 3,5-tetradecadienoic acid
NT3 decanoic acid
NT3 dodecanoic acid
NT3 myristic acid
NT3 nonanoic acid
NT3 octanoic acid
NT3 tridecanoic acid
NT2 odd chain fatty acids
NT3 nonanoic acid
NT3 pentadecanoic acid
NT3 tridecanoic acid
NT2 saturated fatty acids
NT3 decanoic acid
NT3 dodecanoic acid
NT3 hexanoic acid
NT3 myristic acid
NT3 nonanoic acid
NT3 octanoic acid
NT3 palmitic acid
NT3 pentadecanoic acid
NT3 phytanic acid
NT3 stearic acid
NT3 tridecanoic acid
NT2 short chain fatty acids
NT3 hexanoic acid
NT3 maleic acid
NT3 sorbic acid
NT2 trans fatty acids
NT3 brassidic acid
NT3 elaidic acid
NT2 unsaturated fatty acids
NT3 dienoic fatty acids
NT4 3,5-tetradecadienoic acid
NT4 linoleic acid
NT4 sorbic acid
NT4 tetracosadienoic acid
NT3 monoenoic fatty acids
NT4 docosenoic acids
NT5 brassidic acid
NT5 erucic acid
NT4 elaidic acid
NT4 gadoleic acid
NT4 maleic acid
NT4 oleic acid
NT4 palmitoleic acid

CARBOXYLIC ACIDS *cont.*
NT3 polyenoic fatty acids
NT4 arachidonic acid
NT4 eicosapentaenoic acid
NT4 linolenic acid
NT2 volatile fatty acids
NT3 butyric acid
NT3 isobutyric acid
NT3 valeric acid
NT1 keto acids
NT2 α-ketoglutaric acid
NT2 acetoacetic acid
NT2 aminolaevulinic acid
NT2 branched chain keto acids
NT2 laevulinic acid
NT2 oxaloacetic acid
NT2 phenylpyruvic acid
NT2 pyruvic acid
NT1 lichenic acids
NT1 monocarboxylic acids
NT2 3-nitropropionic acid
NT2 4-pyridoxic acid
NT2 6-aminohexanoic acid
NT2 6-chloropicolinic acid
NT2 acetic acid
NT2 acrylic acid
NT2 allantoic acid
NT2 chlorophenoxyisobutyric acid
NT2 chrysanthemic acid
NT2 fluoroacetic acid
NT2 formic acid
NT2 glycolic acid
NT2 glyoxylic acid
NT2 iodoacetic acid
NT2 jasmonic acid
NT2 kaurenoic acid
NT2 lactic acid
NT2 mevalonic acid
NT2 orotic acid
NT2 peracetic acid
NT2 propionic acid
NT2 retinoic acid
NT2 steviol
NT2 triterpene acids
NT3 oleanolic acid
NT3 ursolic acid
NT2 valproic acid
NT2 xanthurenic acid
NT1 resin acids
NT2 abietic acid
NT2 palustric acid
NT2 pimaric acid
NT1 sugar acids
NT2 aldaric acids
NT3 glucaric acid
NT3 tartaric acid
NT2 aldonic acids
NT3 ascorbic acids
NT4 ascorbic acid
NT4 dehydroascorbic acid
NT4 diketogulonic acid
NT4 isoascorbic acid
NT3 gluconic acid
NT3 neuraminic acid
NT3 sialic acids
NT2 uronic acids
NT3 galacturonic acid
NT3 glucuronic acid
NT1 tricarboxylic acids
NT2 aconitic acid
NT2 citric acid
NT2 isocitric acid
rt benzoic acids
rt carboxylation

CARBOXYLIC ESTER HYDROLASES
(ec 3.1.1)
BT1 esterases
BT2 hydrolases
BT3 enzymes
NT1 acetylcholinesterase
NT1 arylesterase
NT1 carboxylesterase
NT1 chlorophyllase
NT1 cholesterol esterase
NT1 cholinesterase
NT1 lipoprotein lipase
NT1 lysophospholipase
NT1 pectinesterase

CARBOXYLIC ESTER HYDROLASES *cont.*
NT1 phospholipase a
NT1 phospholipase a1
NT1 phospholipase a2
NT1 retinyl-palmitate esterase
NT1 tannase
NT1 triacylglycerol lipase
NT1 tropinesterase

CARBOXYLIN
BT1 bicarbonates
BT2 inorganic salts
BT3 inorganic compounds
BT3 salts
BT1 sulfates (inorganic salts)
BT2 inorganic salts
BT3 inorganic compounds
BT3 salts
BT2 sulfates

CARBOXYMETHYLCELLULOSE
BT1 stabilizers

CARBOXYPEPTIDASE A
(ec 3.4.17.1)
BT1 carboxypeptidases
BT2 peptidases
BT3 peptide hydrolases
BT4 hydrolases
BT5 enzymes

CARBOXYPEPTIDASES
(ec 3.4.16-18)
BT1 peptidases
BT2 peptide hydrolases
BT3 hydrolases
BT4 enzymes
NT1 carboxypeptidase a
NT1 dipeptidyl carboxypeptidases

CARCASS COMPOSITION
NT1 dressing percentage
NT1 fat percentage
NT1 lean
rt body composition
rt body fat
rt carcass quality
rt carcasses
rt meat
rt meat yield
rt offal

CARCASS CONDEMNATION
BT1 meat inspection
BT2 food inspection
BT3 inspection
BT4 quality controls
BT5 consumer protection
BT6 protection
BT5 controls
rt carcass disposal
rt carcasses

CARCASS DISPOSAL
BT1 disposal
rt carcass condemnation
rt carcasses
rt destruction of animals
rt waste disposal

CARCASS GRADING
BT1 grading
rt carcass quality
rt carcasses
rt meat inspection
rt meat quality

CARCASS MEAL
BT1 meal
rt carcasses

CARCASS QUALITY
BT1 quality
rt carcass composition
rt carcass grading
rt carcasses

CARCASS WASTE
BT1 slaughterhouse waste
BT2 animal wastes
BT3 wastes
rt carcasses

CARCASS WEIGHT
BT1 weight
rt bone weight
rt carcass yield
rt carcasses
rt slaughter weight

CARCASS YIELD
BT1 yields
rt carcass weight
rt carcasses
rt slaughter weight

CARCASSES
rt animal fat
rt carcass composition
rt carcass condemnation
rt carcass disposal
rt carcass grading
rt carcass meal
rt carcass quality
rt carcass waste
rt carcass weight
rt carcass yield
rt carrion
rt live estimation
rt meat
rt meat cuts
rt meat yield
rt muscle bone ratio
rt slaughter
rt slaughter weight

CARCELIA
uf *eucarcelia*
BT1 tachinidae
BT2 diptera
NT1 carcelia evolans

CARCELIA EVOLANS
uf *eucarcelia evolans*
BT1 carcelia
BT2 tachinidae
BT3 diptera

CARCHARHINIDAE
BT1 lamniformes
BT2 chondrichthyes
BT3 fishes
NT1 carcharhinus
NT1 galeorhinus
NT1 mustelus
NT1 prionace

CARCHARHINUS
BT1 carcharhinidae
BT2 lamniformes
BT3 chondrichthyes
BT4 fishes

CARCHARODON
BT1 lamnidae
BT2 lamniformes
BT3 chondrichthyes
BT4 fishes

CARCINOGENESIS
rt carcinogens
rt neoplasms

CARCINOGENS
BT1 toxic substances
NT1 n-ethyl-n-nitrosourea
NT1 n-methyl-n-nitrosoguanidine
NT1 n-methyl-n-nitrosourea
NT1 n-nitrosodimethylamine
NT1 1,2-dimethylhydrazine
NT1 acetylaminofluorene
NT1 aflatoxins
NT1 asbestos
NT1 benzene
NT1 benzopyrene
NT1 cycasin
NT1 dactinomycin
NT1 ethionine
NT1 hempa
NT1 lasiocarpine
NT1 nitrosopyrrolidine
NT1 patulin
NT1 penicillic acid
NT1 propiolactone
NT1 sterigmatocystin
rt carcinogenesis

CARCINOGENS *cont.*
rt carcinoma
rt neoplasms
rt nitroso compounds
rt oncogenicity

CARCINOMA
BT1 neoplasms
BT2 diseases
NT1 walker carcinoma
rt carcinogens

CARCINOPS
BT1 histeridae
BT2 coleoptera
NT1 carcinops pumilio

CARCINOPS PUMILIO
BT1 carcinops
BT2 histeridae
BT3 coleoptera

CARCINUS
BT1 decapoda
BT2 malacostraca
BT3 crustacea
BT4 arthropods
NT1 carcinus aestuarii
NT1 carcinus maenas

CARCINUS AESTUARII
uf *carcinus mediterraneus*
BT1 carcinus
BT2 decapoda
BT3 malacostraca
BT4 crustacea
BT5 arthropods

CARCINUS MAENAS
BT1 carcinus
BT2 decapoda
BT3 malacostraca
BT4 crustacea
BT5 arthropods

carcinus mediterraneus
USE **carcinus aestuarii**

CARD GAMES
BT1 indoor games
BT2 games
BT2 indoor recreation
BT3 recreation
rt casinos
rt gambling

CARD SERVICES
BT1 information services
BT2 services

CARDAMINE
BT1 cruciferae
NT1 cardamine hirsuta
NT1 cardamine oligosperma

CARDAMINE HIRSUTA
BT1 cardamine
BT2 cruciferae
BT1 insecticidal plants
BT2 pesticidal plants

CARDAMINE OLIGOSPERMA
BT1 cardamine
BT2 cruciferae

CARDAMOM MOSAIC POTYVIRUS
HN from 1990
BT1 potyvirus group
BT2 plant viruses
BT3 plant pathogens
BT4 pathogens

CARDAMOMS
BT1 spices
BT2 plant products
BT3 products
rt elettaria cardamomum

CARDAN SHAFTS
BT1 shafts
BT2 components
rt drives
rt transmissions

CARDANTHERA
BT1 acanthaceae
NT1 cardanthera triflora

CARDANTHERA TRIFLORA
BT1 cardanthera
BT2 acanthaceae

CARDARIA
BT1 cruciferae
NT1 cardaria chalepensis
NT1 cardaria draba
NT1 cardaria pubescens
rt lepidium

CARDARIA CHALEPENSIS
BT1 cardaria
BT2 cruciferae

CARDARIA DRABA
uf *lepidium draba*
BT1 antibacterial plants
BT1 cardaria
BT2 cruciferae

CARDARIA PUBESCENS
BT1 cardaria
BT2 cruciferae

CARDBOARD (AGRICOLA)
BT1 packaging materials
BT2 materials

CARDED FABRICS (AGRICOLA)
BT1 fabrics

CARDENOLIDES
BT1 lactones
BT2 heterocyclic oxygen compounds
BT2 ketones
BT1 steroids
BT2 isoprenoids
BT3 lipids
NT1 digitoxigenin
NT1 digoxigenin

CARDIAC GLYCOSIDES
BT1 cardiovascular agents
BT2 drugs
BT1 glycosides
BT2 carbohydrates
NT1 digitonin
NT1 digitoxin
NT1 digoxin
NT1 lanatosides
NT1 strophanthins
NT2 ouabain
rt heart

CARDIAC INSUFFICIENCY
BT1 heart diseases
BT2 cardiovascular diseases
BT3 organic diseases
BT4 diseases

cardiac muscle
USE **myocardium**

CARDIAC OUTPUT
uf *heart output*
BT1 haemodynamics
BT2 blood circulation
BT3 physiological functions
NT1 heart rate
rt blood pressure
rt blood volume
rt heart

CARDIAC RHYTHM
BT1 biological rhythms
rt heart

CARDIIDAE
BT1 bivalvia
BT2 mollusca
NT1 cardium

CARDING (AGRICOLA)
BT1 processing
rt cotton system (agricola)
rt textile industry

CARDING MACHINES (AGRICOLA)
BT1 textile machinery (agricola)

CARDING MACHINES (AGRICOLA) *cont.*
BT2 machinery

CARDIOCHILES
BT1 braconidae
BT2 hymenoptera
NT1 cardiochiles nigriceps

CARDIOCHILES NIGRICEPS
BT1 cardiochiles
BT2 braconidae
BT3 hymenoptera

CARDIOCRINUM
BT1 liliaceae
rt ornamental bulbs

CARDIOMEGALY
BT1 heart diseases
BT2 cardiovascular diseases
BT3 organic diseases
BT4 diseases

CARDIOMYOPATHY
BT1 heart diseases
BT2 cardiovascular diseases
BT3 organic diseases
BT4 diseases
rt myocardium

CARDIOSPERMUM
BT1 sapindaceae
NT1 cardiospermum grandiflorum
NT1 cardiospermum halicacabum

CARDIOSPERMUM GRANDIFLORUM
BT1 cardiospermum
BT2 sapindaceae

CARDIOSPERMUM HALICACABUM
BT1 cardiospermum
BT2 sapindaceae

CARDIOVASCULAR AGENTS
BT1 drugs
NT1 antihypertensive agents
NT2 chlorothiazide
NT2 diazoxide
NT2 furosemide
NT2 methyldopa
NT2 phenoxybenzamine
NT1 cardiac glycosides
NT2 digitonin
NT2 digitoxin
NT2 digoxin
NT2 lanatosides
NT2 strophanthins
NT3 ouabain
NT1 myocardial depressants
NT2 disopyramide
NT2 lidocaine
NT2 propranolol
NT2 quinidine
NT1 vasoconstrictor agents
NT1 vasodilator agents
NT2 bradykinin
NT2 chlorpromazine
NT2 dipyridamole
NT2 eledoisin
NT2 erythritol
NT2 isoxsuprine
NT2 kallikrein
NT2 papaverine
NT2 pindolol
NT2 propranolol
NT2 substance p
NT2 theobromine
NT2 theophylline
rt heart

CARDIOVASCULAR DISEASES
BT1 organic diseases
BT2 diseases
NT1 heart diseases
NT2 arrhythmia
NT2 beriberi heart disease
NT2 cardiac insufficiency
NT2 cardiomegaly
NT2 cardiomyopathy
NT2 endocarditis
NT2 myocardial infarction

CARDIOVASCULAR DISEASES *cont.*
NT2 myocardial ischaemia
NT2 myocarditis
NT2 pericardial effusion
NT2 pericarditis
NT1 vascular diseases
NT2 aneurysm
NT2 aortic rupture
NT2 arteritis
NT2 atherogenesis
NT2 atheroma
NT2 atherosclerosis
NT3 experimental atherosclerosis
NT2 cerebrovascular disorders
NT3 apoplexy
NT3 migraine
NT3 stroke
NT2 circulatory disorders
NT3 vasoconstriction
NT2 embolism
NT2 haemorrhoids
NT2 hypertension
NT2 hypotension
NT2 ischaemia
NT2 microangiopathy
NT2 phlebitis
NT2 raynaud's syndrome
rt cardiovascular system

CARDIOVASCULAR SYSTEM
uf *circulatory system*
uf *vascular system (animal)*
BT1 body parts
NT1 blood vessels
NT2 arteries
NT3 aorta
NT3 pulmonary artery
NT2 capillaries
NT2 coronary vessels
NT2 ductus arteriosus
NT2 veins
NT3 jugular vein
NT3 portal vein
NT3 vena cava
NT1 haemolymph nodes
NT1 heart
NT2 endocardium
NT2 heart valves
NT2 ventricles
NT1 lymphatic system
NT2 bursa fabricii
NT2 lymph nodes
NT2 peyer patches
NT2 thoracic duct
NT2 thymus gland
NT1 spleen
rt blood circulation
rt cardiovascular diseases

CARDIOVIRUS
BT1 picornaviridae
BT2 viruses
NT1 encephalomyocarditis virus
NT1 murine encephalomyelitis virus

CARDIUM
BT1 cardiidae
BT2 bivalvia
BT3 mollusca

CARDOONS
BT1 stem vegetables
BT2 vegetables
rt cynara cardunculus

CARDUELIS
BT1 fringillidae
BT2 passeriformes
BT3 birds

CARDUNCELLUS
BT1 compositae
NT1 carduncellus monspeliensium

CARDUNCELLUS MONSPELIENSIUM
BT1 carduncellus
BT2 compositae

CARDUUS
BT1 compositae
NT1 carduus acanthoides
NT1 carduus crispus
NT1 carduus macrocephalus
NT1 carduus nutans
NT1 carduus nutans var. leiophyllus
NT1 carduus pycnocephalus
NT1 carduus tenuiflorus
NT1 carduus thoermeri

CARDUUS ACANTHOIDES
BT1 carduus
BT2 compositae

carduus benedictus
USE **cnicus benedictus**

CARDUUS CRISPUS
BT1 carduus
BT2 compositae

CARDUUS MACROCEPHALUS
BT1 carduus
BT2 compositae

CARDUUS NUTANS
BT1 carduus
BT2 compositae
BT1 weeds

CARDUUS NUTANS VAR. LEIOPHYLLUS
BT1 carduus
BT2 compositae

CARDUUS PYCNOCEPHALUS
BT1 carduus
BT2 compositae

CARDUUS TENUIFLORUS
BT1 carduus
BT2 compositae

CARDUUS THOERMERI
BT1 carduus
BT2 compositae

CARE LABELS (AGRICOLA)
BT1 labeling
rt clothing labels (agricola)

career change
USE **occupational change**

CAREER CHOICE (AGRICOLA)
rt career development
rt career education (agricola)
rt career planning (agricola)
rt careers

CAREER DEVELOPMENT
uf *career ladders*
uf *vocational development*
BT1 personal development
rt aspirations
rt career choice (agricola)
rt career education (agricola)
rt career planning (agricola)
rt careers

CAREER EDUCATION (AGRICOLA)
BT1 education
rt career choice (agricola)
rt career development
rt careers

career ladders
USE **career development**

career opportunities
USE **employment opportunities**

CAREER PLANNING (AGRICOLA)
BT1 planning
rt career choice (agricola)
rt career development
rt careers

CAREERS
rt career choice (agricola)
rt career development
rt career education (agricola)
rt career planning (agricola)

3-CARENE
BT1 monoterpenes
BT2 monoterpenoids
BT3 terpenoids
BT4 isoprenoids
BT5 lipids

CAREPROVIDERS (AGRICOLA)
NT1 child careproviders (agricola)

CARETTA
BT1 cheloniidae
BT2 testudines
BT3 reptiles
NT1 caretta caretta

CARETTA CARETTA
BT1 caretta
BT2 cheloniidae
BT3 testudines
BT4 reptiles

CAREX
BT1 cyperaceae
NT1 carex aquatica
NT1 carex aquatilis
NT1 carex arenaria
NT1 carex bigelowii
NT1 carex brevicollis
NT1 carex breviculmis
NT1 carex brizoides
NT1 carex caespitosa
NT1 carex caryophyllea
NT1 carex chrysopetala
NT1 carex elata
NT1 carex filifolia
NT1 carex flacca
NT1 carex flagellifera
NT1 carex guadichaudiana
NT1 carex heliophila
NT1 carex hoodii
NT1 carex humilis
NT1 carex lacustris
NT1 carex lanuginosa
NT1 carex lasiocarpa
NT1 carex longebrachiata
NT1 carex lynx
NT1 carex nigra
NT1 carex obtusata
NT1 carex pennsylvanica
NT1 carex physodes
NT1 carex praegracilis
NT1 carex riparia
NT1 carex rostrata
NT1 carex sempervirens
NT1 carex stricta var. strictior
NT1 carex subspathacea
NT1 carex vaginata
NT1 carex vulpina

CAREX AQUATICA
BT1 carex
BT2 cyperaceae
BT1 pasture plants

CAREX AQUATILIS
BT1 carex
BT2 cyperaceae
BT1 pasture plants

CAREX ARENARIA
BT1 carex
BT2 cyperaceae
BT1 pasture plants

CAREX BIGELOWII
BT1 carex
BT2 cyperaceae
BT1 pasture plants

CAREX BREVICOLLIS
BT1 carex
BT2 cyperaceae

CAREX BREVICULMIS
BT1 carex
BT2 cyperaceae
BT1 pasture plants

CAREX BRIZOIDES
BT1 carex
BT2 cyperaceae

CAREX CAESPITOSA
BT1 carex
BT2 cyperaceae

CAREX CARYOPHYLLEA
BT1 carex
BT2 cyperaceae
BT1 pasture plants

CAREX CHRYSOPETALA
BT1 carex
BT2 cyperaceae

CAREX ELATA
uf *carex hudsonii*
BT1 carex
BT2 cyperaceae

CAREX FILIFOLIA
BT1 carex
BT2 cyperaceae
BT1 pasture plants

CAREX FLACCA
BT1 carex
BT2 cyperaceae

CAREX FLAGELLIFERA
BT1 carex
BT2 cyperaceae

CAREX GUADICHAUDIANA
BT1 carex
BT2 cyperaceae
BT1 pasture plants

CAREX HELIOPHILA
BT1 carex
BT2 cyperaceae
BT1 pasture plants

CAREX HOODII
BT1 carex
BT2 cyperaceae
BT1 pasture plants

carex hudsonii
USE **carex elata**

CAREX HUMILIS
BT1 carex
BT2 cyperaceae

CAREX LACUSTRIS
BT1 carex
BT2 cyperaceae

CAREX LANUGINOSA
BT1 carex
BT2 cyperaceae

CAREX LASIOCARPA
BT1 carex
BT2 cyperaceae
BT1 pasture plants

CAREX LONGEBRACHIATA
BT1 carex
BT2 cyperaceae

CAREX LYNX
BT1 carex
BT2 cyperaceae

CAREX NIGRA
BT1 carex
BT2 cyperaceae
BT1 pasture plants

CAREX OBTUSATA
BT1 carex
BT2 cyperaceae
BT1 pasture plants

CAREX PENNSYLVANICA
BT1 carex
BT2 cyperaceae

CAREX PHYSODES
BT1 carex
BT2 cyperaceae
BT1 pasture plants

CAREX PRAEGRACILIS
BT1 carex
BT2 cyperaceae

CAREX PRAEGRACILIS *cont.*
BT1 pasture plants

CAREX RIPARIA
BT1 carex
BT2 cyperaceae

CAREX ROSTRATA
BT1 carex
BT2 cyperaceae

CAREX SEMPERVIRENS
BT1 carex
BT2 cyperaceae

CAREX STRICTA VAR. STRICTIOR
BT1 carex
BT2 cyperaceae

CAREX SUBSPATHACEA
BT1 carex
BT2 cyperaceae
BT1 pasture plants

CAREX VAGINATA
BT1 carex
BT2 cyperaceae

CAREX VULPINA
BT1 carex
BT2 cyperaceae
BT1 pasture plants

CARIBBEAN
uf *antilles*
uf *west indies*
BT1 america
NT1 anguilla island
NT1 antigua
NT1 bahamas
NT1 barbados
NT1 british virgin islands
NT1 cayman islands
NT1 cuba
NT1 dominica
NT1 dominican republic
NT1 grenada
NT1 guadeloupe
NT1 haiti
NT1 jamaica
NT1 martinique
NT1 montserrat
NT1 netherlands antilles
NT2 aruba
NT2 bonaire
NT2 curacao
NT2 saba
NT2 st. eustatius
NT2 st. maarten
NT1 puerto rico
NT1 st. kitts-nevis
NT1 st. lucia
NT1 st. vincent and grenadines
NT1 trinidad and tobago
NT1 turks and caicos islands
NT1 united states virgin islands
rt acp
rt developing countries

CARIBBEAN COMMUNITY
uf *caricom*
BT1 common markets
BT2 economic unions
rt antigua
rt bahamas
rt barbados
rt belize
rt dominica
rt economic regions
rt grenada
rt guyana
rt jamaica
rt montserrat
rt st. lucia
rt st. vincent and grenadines
rt trinidad and tobago

CARIBBEAN SEA
BT1 western central atlantic
BT2 atlantic ocean
BT3 marine areas

caribou
USE **reindeer**

CARICA
BT1 caricaceae
NT1 carica papaya
NT1 carica pentagona
NT1 carica pubescens

carica candamarcensis
USE **carica pubescens**

CARICA PAPAYA
BT1 carica
BT2 caricaceae
rt papain
rt papaw ringspot virus
rt papaya mosaic potexvirus
rt pawpaws

CARICA PENTAGONA
BT1 carica
BT2 caricaceae
BT1 subtropical tree fruits
BT2 subtropical fruits
BT3 fruit crops
BT2 tree fruits

CARICA PUBESCENS
uf *carica candamarcensis*
BT1 carica
BT2 caricaceae
BT1 tropical tree fruits
BT2 tree fruits
BT2 tropical fruits
BT3 fruit crops

CARICACEAE
NT1 carica
NT2 carica papaya
NT2 carica pentagona
NT2 carica pubescens
NT1 jacaratia
NT2 jacaratia dodecaphyla
NT1 jarilla
NT2 jarilla chocola

caricom
USE **caribbean community**

caries
USE **dental caries**

CARINIANA
BT1 lecythidaceae
NT1 cariniana estrellensis
NT1 cariniana pyriformis

CARINIANA ESTRELLENSIS
BT1 cariniana
BT2 lecythidaceae

CARINIANA PYRIFORMIS
BT1 cariniana
BT2 lecythidaceae

CARIOGENIC FOODS (AGRICOLA)
BT1 foods
rt dental caries

CARIS
(computerised agricultural research information system fao)
BT1 information services
BT2 services
rt food and agriculture organization
rt research

CARISSA
BT1 apocynaceae
NT1 carissa bispinosa
NT1 carissa carandas
NT1 carissa macrocarpa
NT1 carissa opaea
NT1 carissa ovata
NT1 carissa spinarum

carissa arduina
USE **carissa bispinosa**

CARISSA BISPINOSA
uf *carissa arduina*
BT1 carissa
BT2 apocynaceae

CARISSA BISPINOSA *cont.*
BT1 subtropical small fruits
BT2 small fruits
BT2 subtropical fruits
BT3 fruit crops

CARISSA CARANDAS
BT1 carissa
BT2 apocynaceae

carissa grandiflora
USE **carissa macrocarpa**

CARISSA MACROCARPA
uf *carissa grandiflora*
BT1 carissa
BT2 apocynaceae
BT1 subtropical small fruits
BT2 small fruits
BT2 subtropical fruits
BT3 fruit crops

CARISSA OPAEA
BT1 carissa
BT2 apocynaceae

CARISSA OVATA
BT1 carissa
BT2 apocynaceae

CARISSA SPINARUM
BT1 carissa
BT2 apocynaceae

CARLAVIRUS GROUP
HN from 1990
BT1 plant viruses
BT2 plant pathogens
BT3 pathogens
NT1 cactus 2 carlavirus
NT1 carnation latent carlavirus
NT1 chrysanthemum b carlavirus
NT1 cowpea mild mottle carlavirus
NT1 dandelion latent carlavirus
NT1 elderberry carlavirus
NT1 helenium s carlavirus
NT1 honeysuckle latent carlavirus
NT1 hop latent carlavirus
NT1 hop mosaic carlavirus
NT1 lilac mottle carlavirus
NT1 lily symptomless carlavirus
NT1 mulberry latent carlavirus
NT1 muskmelon vein necrosis carlavirus
NT1 narcissus latent carlavirus
NT1 nerine latent carlavirus
NT1 passiflora latent carlavirus
NT1 pea streak carlavirus
NT1 pepino latent carlavirus
NT1 poplar mosaic carlavirus
NT1 potato m carlavirus
NT1 potato s carlavirus
NT1 red clover vein mosaic carlavirus
NT1 shallot latent carlavirus

CARLINA
BT1 compositae
NT1 carlina acanthifolia
NT1 carlina acaulis
NT1 carlina vulgaris

CARLINA ACANTHIFOLIA
BT1 carlina
BT2 compositae

CARLINA ACAULIS
BT1 carlina
BT2 compositae

CARLINA VULGARIS
BT1 carlina
BT2 compositae

CARLUDOVICA
BT1 cyclanthaceae
NT1 carludovica palmata

CARLUDOVICA PALMATA
BT1 carludovica
BT2 cyclanthaceae

CARMINATIVES
uf *antiflatulents*
BT1 gastrointestinal agents
BT2 drugs
NT1 carvone
NT1 chloroform
NT1 safrole
NT1 turpentine

CARMOVIRUS GROUP
HN from 1990
BT1 plant viruses
BT2 plant pathogens
BT3 pathogens
NT1 carnation mottle carmovirus
NT1 galinsoga mosaic carmovirus
NT1 hibiscus chlorotic ringspot carmovirus
NT1 pelargonium flower break carmovirus
NT1 saguaro cactus carmovirus
NT1 turnip crinkle carmovirus

CARMYERIUS
BT1 gastrothylacidae
BT2 digenea
BT3 trematoda

CARNALLITE
BT1 chlorine fertilizers
BT2 trace element fertilizers
BT3 fertilizers
BT1 magnesium fertilizers
BT2 fertilizers
BT1 potassium fertilizers
BT2 fertilizers

CARNATION CRYPTIC CRYPTOVIRUS
HN from 1990
BT1 cryptovirus group
BT2 plant viruses
BT3 plant pathogens
BT4 pathogens
rt carnations
rt dianthus caryophyllus

CARNATION ETCHED RING CAULIMOVIRUS
HN from 1990; previously "carnation etched ring virus"
uf *carnation etched ring virus*
BT1 caulimovirus group
BT2 plant viruses
BT3 plant pathogens
BT4 pathogens
rt carnations
rt dianthus caryophyllus

carnation etched ring virus
USE **carnation etched ring caulimovirus**

CARNATION LATENT CARLAVIRUS
HN from 1990; previously "carnation latent virus"
uf *carnation latent virus*
BT1 carlavirus group
BT2 plant viruses
BT3 plant pathogens
BT4 pathogens
rt carnations
rt dianthus caryophyllus

carnation latent virus
USE **carnation latent carlavirus**

CARNATION MOTTLE CARMOVIRUS
HN from 1990; previously "carnation mottle virus"
uf *carnation mottle virus*
BT1 carmovirus group
BT2 plant viruses
BT3 plant pathogens
BT4 pathogens
rt carnations
rt dianthus caryophyllus

carnation mottle virus
USE **carnation mottle carmovirus**

CARNATION NECROTIC FLECK CLOSTEROVIRUS
HN from 1990; previously "carnation necrotic fleck virus"
uf *carnation necrotic fleck virus*
BT1 closterovirus group
BT2 plant viruses
BT3 plant pathogens
BT4 pathogens
rt carnations
rt dianthus caryophyllus

carnation necrotic fleck virus
USE **carnation necrotic fleck closterovirus**

CARNATION RINGSPOT DIANTHOVIRUS
HN from 1990; previously "carnation ringspot virus"
uf *carnation ringspot virus*
BT1 dianthovirus group
BT2 plant viruses
BT3 plant pathogens
BT4 pathogens
rt carnations
rt dianthus caryophyllus

carnation ringspot virus
USE **carnation ringspot dianthovirus**

CARNATION VEIN MOTTLE POTYVIRUS
HN from 1990; previously "carnation vein mottle virus"
uf *carnation vein mottle virus*
BT1 potyvirus group
BT2 plant viruses
BT3 plant pathogens
BT4 pathogens
rt carnations
rt dianthus caryophyllus

carnation vein mottle virus
USE **carnation vein mottle potyvirus**

CARNATIONS
BT1 antifungal plants
BT1 antiviral plants
BT1 medicinal plants
BT1 ornamental herbaceous plants
rt calyx splitting
rt carnation cryptic cryptovirus
rt carnation etched ring caulimovirus
rt carnation latent carlavirus
rt carnation mottle carmovirus
rt carnation necrotic fleck closterovirus
rt carnation ringspot dianthovirus
rt carnation vein mottle potyvirus
rt dianthus caryophyllus

CARNEGIEA
BT1 cactaceae
NT1 carnegiea gigantea

CARNEGIEA GIGANTEA
BT1 carnegiea
BT2 cactaceae
rt saguaro cactus carmovirus

carniolan honeybee
USE **apis mellifera carnica**

CARNITINE
BT1 biogenic amines
BT2 amines
BT3 amino compounds
BT4 organic nitrogen compounds

CARNITINE *cont.*
BT1 quaternary ammonium compounds
BT2 ammonium compounds
BT2 organic nitrogen compounds
BT1 vitamin b complex
BT2 water-soluble vitamins
BT3 vitamins

CARNITINE ACETYLTRANSFERASE
(ec 2.3.1.7)
BT1 acyltransferases
BT2 transferases
BT3 enzymes

CARNITINE PALMITOYLTRANSFERASE
(ec 2.3.1.21)
BT1 acyltransferases
BT2 transferases
BT3 enzymes

CARNIVALS
uf *fairs*
BT1 entertainment
BT2 leisure activities
rt festivals
rt funfairs

carnivora
USE **carnivores**

CARNIVORES
uf *carnivora*
BT1 mammals
NT1 fissipeda
NT2 ailuropodidae
NT3 ailuropoda
NT4 ailuropoda melanoleuca
NT3 ailurus
NT4 ailurus fulgens
NT2 canidae
NT3 alopex
NT4 alopex lagopus
NT3 canis
NT4 canis aureus
NT4 canis familiaris dingo
NT4 canis mesomelas
NT3 chrysocyon
NT4 chrysocyon brachyurus
NT3 lycaon
NT4 lycaon pictus
NT3 nyctereutes
NT3 vulpes
NT4 vulpes cinereoargenteus
NT4 vulpes vulpes
NT2 felidae
NT3 acinonyx
NT4 acinonyx jubatus
NT3 felis
NT4 felis bengalensis
NT4 felis concolor
NT4 felis lynx
NT4 felis rufus
NT4 felis silvestris
NT4 felis wiedii
NT3 neofelis
NT4 neofelis nebulosa
NT3 panthera
NT4 panthera uncia
NT2 herpestidae
NT3 herpestes
NT4 herpestes auropunctatus
NT4 herpestes edwardsii
NT2 hyaenidae
NT3 crocuta
NT4 crocuta crocuta
NT3 hyaena
NT2 mustelidae
NT3 enhydra
NT4 enhydra lutris
NT3 gulo
NT4 gulo gulo
NT3 lutra
NT4 lutra canadensis
NT3 martes
NT4 martes americana
NT4 martes foina
NT4 martes martes
NT3 meles

CARNIVORES *cont.*
NT4 meles meles
NT3 mephitis
NT4 mephitis mephitis
NT3 mustela
NT4 mustela altaica
NT4 mustela erminea
NT4 mustela lutreola
NT4 mustela nivalis
NT4 mustela sibirica
NT2 procyonidae
NT3 nasua
NT4 nasua nasua
NT3 potos
NT4 potos flavus
NT3 procyon
NT4 procyon lotor
NT2 ursidae
NT3 helarctos
NT4 helarctos malayanus
NT3 selenarctos
NT4 selenarctos thibetanus
NT3 thalarctos
NT4 thalarctos maritimus
NT3 ursus
NT4 ursus americanus
NT4 ursus arctos
NT2 viverridae
NT3 genetta
NT3 paguma
NT4 paguma larvata
NT1 pinnipedia
NT2 odobenidae
NT3 odobenus
NT4 odobenus rosmarus
NT2 otariidae
NT3 arctocephalus
NT4 arctocephalus pusillus
NT3 callorhinus
NT4 callorhinus ursinus
NT3 eumetopias
NT4 eumetopias jubatus
NT3 neophoca
NT4 neophoca cinerea
NT3 otaria
NT4 otaria bryonia
NT3 zalophus
NT4 zalophus californianus
NT2 phocidae
NT3 hydrurga
NT4 hydrurga leptonyx
NT3 mirounga
NT3 monachus
NT3 phoca
NT4 phoca vitulina

CARNIVOROUS PLANTS
NT1 insectivorous plants
NT2 dionaea muscipula
NT2 pinguicula moranensis
NT2 sarracenia flava
NT2 utricularia inflexa
rt insecticidal plants
rt ornamental plants
rt plants

CARNOSINE
BT1 dipeptides
BT2 oligopeptides
BT3 peptides
BT1 neuropeptides
BT2 peptides

CAROB MEAL
BT1 meal
rt ceratonia siliqua

CAROBS
BT1 gum plants
BT1 subtropical tree fruits
BT2 subtropical fruits
BT3 fruit crops
BT2 tree fruits
rt ceratonia siliqua

α-CAROTENE
(for retrieval spell out "alpha")
BT1 carotenes
BT2 carotenoids
BT3 lipochromes
BT4 pigments
BT3 terpenoids

α-CAROTENE *cont.*
BT4 isoprenoids
BT5 lipids
BT1 provitamins
BT2 precursors

β-CAROTENE
(for retrieval spell out "beta")
BT1 carotenes
BT2 carotenoids
BT3 lipochromes
BT4 pigments
BT3 terpenoids
BT4 isoprenoids
BT5 lipids
BT1 provitamins
BT2 precursors

CAROTENES
BT1 carotenoids
BT2 lipochromes
BT3 pigments
BT2 terpenoids
BT3 isoprenoids
BT4 lipids
NT1 α-carotene
NT1 β-carotene
NT1 lycopene
NT1 phytoene
NT1 phytofluene

CAROTENOIDS
uf *tetraterpenoids*
BT1 lipochromes
BT2 pigments
BT1 terpenoids
BT2 isoprenoids
BT3 lipids
NT1 carotenes
NT2 α-carotene
NT2 β-carotene
NT2 lycopene
NT2 phytoene
NT2 phytofluene
NT1 retinoids
NT2 dehydroretinol
NT2 retinal
NT2 retinoic acid
NT2 retinol
NT2 retinyl esters
NT3 retinyl acetate
NT3 retinyl palmitate
NT1 xanthophylls
NT2 astaxanthin
NT2 canthaxanthin
NT2 capsanthin
NT2 violaxanthin
NT2 xanthophyll
NT2 zeaxanthin

CAROTID BODY
BT1 nerve endings
BT2 nerve tissue
BT3 animal tissues
BT4 tissues

carotid sinus
USE **pressoreceptors**

CARP
uf *cyprinus carpio*
BT1 freshwater fishes
BT2 aquatic animals
BT3 animals
BT3 aquatic organisms
rt cyprinidae

carp, crucian
USE **carassius carassius**

CARPATHIAN
HN from 1990
BT1 goat breeds
BT2 breeds

CARPATHIAN BROWN
HN from 1990
BT1 cattle breeds
BT2 breeds

carpel
USE **gynoecium**

CARPENTARIA
BT1 palmae
NT1 carpentaria acuminata

CARPENTARIA ACUMINATA
BT1 carpentaria
BT2 palmae
BT1 ornamental palms

CARPESIUM
BT1 compositae
NT1 carpesium abrotanoides

CARPESIUM ABROTANOIDES
BT1 carpesium
BT2 compositae

CARPET (AGRICOLA)
BT1 floor coverings (agricola)
NT1 tufted carpet (agricola)
rt rugs (agricola)

carpet shells
USE **veneridae**

carpinaceae
USE **betulaceae**

CARPINUS
BT1 betulaceae
NT1 carpinus betulus
NT1 carpinus caroliniana
NT1 carpinus laxiflora
NT1 carpinus orientalis
NT1 carpinus tschonoskii

CARPINUS BETULUS
uf *hornbeam*
BT1 carpinus
BT2 betulaceae
BT1 forest trees
BT1 ornamental woody plants

CARPINUS CAROLINIANA
BT1 carpinus
BT2 betulaceae
BT1 ornamental woody plants

CARPINUS LAXIFLORA
HN from 1990
BT1 carpinus
BT2 betulaceae
BT1 forest trees

CARPINUS ORIENTALIS
BT1 carpinus
BT2 betulaceae

CARPINUS TSCHONOSKII
HN from 1990
BT1 carpinus
BT2 betulaceae
BT1 forest trees

CARPOBROTUS
BT1 aizoaceae
NT1 carpobrotus edulis
rt mesembryanthemum

CARPOBROTUS EDULIS
uf *mesembryanthemum edule*
BT1 carpobrotus
BT2 aizoaceae
BT1 ornamental succulent plants
BT2 succulent plants
BT1 subtropical small fruits
BT2 small fruits
BT2 subtropical fruits
BT3 fruit crops

CARPOGLYPHIDAE
BT1 astigmata
BT2 acari
NT1 carpoglyphus
NT2 carpoglyphus lactis

CARPOGLYPHUS
BT1 carpoglyphidae
BT2 astigmata
BT3 acari
NT1 carpoglyphus lactis

CARPOGLYPHUS LACTIS
BT1 carpoglyphus
BT2 carpoglyphidae

CARPOGLYPHUS LACTIS *cont.*
BT3 astigmata
BT4 acari

CARPOPHILUS
BT1 nitidulidae
BT2 coleoptera
NT1 carpophilus dimidiatus
NT1 carpophilus hemipterus
NT1 carpophilus mutilatus
rt urophorus

CARPOPHILUS DIMIDIATUS
BT1 carpophilus
BT2 nitidulidae
BT3 coleoptera

CARPOPHILUS HEMIPTERUS
BT1 carpophilus
BT2 nitidulidae
BT3 coleoptera

carpophilus humeralis
USE **urophorus humeralis**

CARPOPHILUS MUTILATUS
BT1 carpophilus
BT2 nitidulidae
BT3 coleoptera

CARPOSINA
BT1 carposinidae
BT2 lepidoptera
NT1 carposina sasakii

CARPOSINA SASAKII
BT1 carposina
BT2 carposinidae
BT3 lepidoptera

CARPOSINIDAE
BT1 lepidoptera
NT1 carposina
NT2 carposina sasakii

CARPUS
BT1 limb bones
BT2 bones
BT3 musculoskeletal system
BT4 body parts

carrageen
USE **chondrus crispus**

CARRAGEENAN
BT1 colloids
BT1 galactans
BT2 polysaccharides
BT3 carbohydrates
BT1 mucilages
BT2 polysaccharides
BT3 carbohydrates
BT1 stabilizers
rt chondrus crispus
rt seaweeds

CARRE DE L'EST CHEESE
BT1 cheeses
BT2 milk products
BT3 products

carrier proteins
USE **binding proteins**

CARRIER STATE
rt disease vectors
rt diseases
rt epidemiology

CARRIERS
NT1 ferredoxin
NT1 fertilizer carriers
NT2 frits
NT1 implement carriers
NT1 inoculant carriers
NT2 coal
NT3 brown coal
NT2 filter cake
NT2 peat
NT1 tool carriers
NT1 trioctanoin

CARRION
rt carcasses

CARROT HARVESTERS
uf *harvesters, carrot*
BT1 root harvesters
BT2 harvesters
BT3 farm machinery
BT4 machinery
rt carrots

CARROT JUICE
BT1 vegetable juices
BT2 juices
BT3 liquids
BT2 vegetable extracts
BT3 plant extracts
BT4 extracts
BT3 vegetable products
BT4 plant products
BT5 products
rt carrots

CARROT MOTTLE VIRUS
BT1 miscellaneous plant viruses
BT2 plant viruses
BT3 plant pathogens
BT4 pathogens

CARROT RED LEAF LUTEOVIRUS
HN from 1990; previously "carrot red leaf virus"
uf *carrot red leaf virus*
BT1 luteovirus group
BT2 plant viruses
BT3 plant pathogens
BT4 pathogens
rt carrots
rt daucus carota

carrot red leaf virus
USE **carrot red leaf luteovirus**

CARROT THIN LEAF POTYVIRUS
HN from 1990
BT1 potyvirus group
BT2 plant viruses
BT3 plant pathogens
BT4 pathogens
rt carrots
rt daucus carota

CARROTS
BT1 antibacterial plants
BT1 antifungal plants
BT1 medicinal plants
BT1 root vegetables
BT2 root crops
BT2 vegetables
rt carrot harvesters
rt carrot juice
rt carrot red leaf luteovirus
rt carrot thin leaf potyvirus
rt cavity spot
rt daucus carota
rt rusty root

carry out foods
USE **takeout foods (agricola)**

CARRYING CAPACITY
rt capacity
rt population density

cars
USE **motor cars**

CARSIDARIDAE
HN from 1989
BT1 psylloidea
BT2 sternorrhyncha
BT3 homoptera
NT1 mesohomotoma
NT2 mesohomotoma tessmanni

CARTAP
BT1 carbamate insecticides
BT2 carbamate pesticides
BT2 insecticides
BT3 pesticides

CARTELS
BT1 monopoly
BT2 imperfect competition
BT3 market competition
rt combines
rt integration

CARTELS *cont.*
rt price controls
rt production controls

CARTHAMUS
BT1 compositae
NT1 carthamus lanatus
NT1 carthamus oxyacantha
NT1 carthamus tinctorius

CARTHAMUS LANATUS
BT1 carthamus
BT2 compositae
BT1 medicinal plants

CARTHAMUS OXYACANTHA
BT1 carthamus
BT2 compositae

CARTHAMUS TINCTORIUS
BT1 carthamus
BT2 compositae
BT1 dye plants
BT1 fodder plants
rt safflower

CARTILAGE
BT1 musculoskeletal system
BT2 body parts
rt bones
rt chondrocytes
rt chondrodystrophy

cartography
USE **mapping**

CARTONBOARD (AGRICOLA)
BT1 packaging materials
BT2 materials

cartons
USE **packages**

CARTOONS (AGRICOLA)
BT1 publications
rt comics (agricola)

CARTS
BT1 vehicles
rt wagons

CARUM
BT1 umbelliferae
NT1 carum carvi
NT1 carum gracile

carum bulbocastanum
USE **bunium bulbocastanum**

CARUM CARVI
BT1 antibacterial plants
BT1 carum
BT2 umbelliferae
BT1 essential oil plants
BT2 oil plants
BT1 spice plants
rt caraway
rt carvone

carum copticum
USE **trachyspermum ammi**

CARUM GRACILE
BT1 carum
BT2 umbelliferae

CARVED WOOD
BT1 works of art
rt wood
rt wood carving
rt woodworking

CARVING TECHNIQUES (AGRICOLA)
BT1 culinary arts (agricola)
BT2 arts

carving, wood
USE **wood carving**

CARVONE
BT1 carminatives
BT2 gastrointestinal agents
BT3 drugs
BT1 flavour compounds
BT1 ketones

CARVONE *cont.*
BT1 monoterpenoids
BT2 terpenoids
BT3 isoprenoids
BT4 lipids
rt carum carvi
rt essential oils

CARYA
uf *hicoria*
BT1 juglandaceae
NT1 carya cordiformis
NT1 carya glabra
NT1 carya illinoensis
NT1 carya lecontei
NT1 carya ovalis
NT1 carya ovata
NT1 carya texana
NT1 carya tomentosa

CARYA CORDIFORMIS
BT1 carya
BT2 juglandaceae
BT1 ornamental woody plants

CARYA GLABRA
BT1 carya
BT2 juglandaceae
BT1 forest trees
BT1 ornamental woody plants

CARYA ILLINOENSIS
uf *carya pecan*
BT1 carya
BT2 juglandaceae
BT1 forest trees
BT1 ornamental woody plants
rt pecans

CARYA LECONTEI
BT1 carya
BT2 juglandaceae

CARYA OVALIS
BT1 carya
BT2 juglandaceae

CARYA OVATA
BT1 carya
BT2 juglandaceae
BT1 forest trees
BT1 ornamental woody plants

carya pecan
USE **carya illinoensis**

CARYA TEXANA
BT1 carya
BT2 juglandaceae

CARYA TOMENTOSA
BT1 carya
BT2 juglandaceae
BT1 forest trees
BT1 ornamental woody plants

CARYEDON
BT1 bruchidae
BT2 coleoptera
NT1 caryedon serratus

caryedon gonagra
USE **caryedon serratus**

CARYEDON SERRATUS
uf *caryedon gonagra*
BT1 caryedon
BT2 bruchidae
BT3 coleoptera

CARYOCAR
BT1 caryocaraceae
NT1 caryocar amygdaliferum
NT1 caryocar coriaceum
NT1 caryocar nuciferum

CARYOCAR AMYGDALIFERUM
BT1 caryocar
BT2 caryocaraceae
BT1 oilseed plants
BT2 fatty oil plants
BT3 oil plants

CARYOCAR CORIACEUM
BT1 caryocar

CARYOCAR CORIACEUM *cont.*
BT2 caryocaraceae
BT1 oilseed plants
BT2 fatty oil plants
BT3 oil plants

CARYOCAR NUCIFERUM
BT1 caryocar
BT2 caryocaraceae
BT1 oilseed plants
BT2 fatty oil plants
BT3 oil plants

CARYOCARACEAE
NT1 caryocar
NT2 caryocar amygdaliferum
NT2 caryocar coriaceum
NT2 caryocar nuciferum

CARYOPHYLLACEAE
NT1 acanthophyllum
NT2 acanthophyllum glandulosum
NT2 acanthophyllum gypsophiloides
NT2 acanthophyllum microcephalum
NT2 acanthophyllum paniculatum
NT2 acanthophyllum sordidum
NT1 agrostemma
NT2 agrostemma githago
NT1 allochrusa
NT2 allochrusa gypsophiloides
NT1 arenaria (caryophyllaceae)
NT1 cerastium
NT2 cerastium arvense
NT2 cerastium atrovirens
NT2 cerastium biebersteinii
NT2 cerastium caespitosum
NT2 cerastium fontanum
NT2 cerastium holosteoides
NT1 cucubalus
NT2 cucubalus baccifer
NT1 dianthus
NT2 dianthus acicularis
NT2 dianthus barbatus
NT2 dianthus caryophyllus
NT2 dianthus chinensis
NT2 dianthus deltoides
NT2 dianthus gratianopolitanus
NT2 dianthus plumarius
NT2 dianthus superbus
NT1 drymaria
NT2 drymaria arenarioides
NT2 drymaria cordata
NT2 drymaria diandra
NT1 gypsophila
NT2 gypsophila elegans
NT2 gypsophila paniculata
NT2 gypsophila perfoliata
NT2 gypsophila trichotoma
NT1 herniaria
NT2 herniaria glabra
NT1 holosteum
NT1 lychnis
NT2 lychnis coronaria
NT2 lychnis flos-cuculi
NT1 malachium
NT2 malachium aquaticum
NT1 myosoton
NT2 myosoton aquaticum
NT1 sagina
NT2 sagina procumbens
NT1 saponaria
NT2 saponaria ocymoides
NT2 saponaria officinalis
NT1 scleranthus
NT2 scleranthus annuus
NT1 silene
NT2 silene anglica
NT2 silene armeria
NT2 silene coeli-rosa
NT2 silene compacta
NT2 silene cucubalus
NT2 silene dioica
NT2 silene latifolia
NT2 silene linicola
NT2 silene noctiflora
NT2 silene praemixta
NT2 silene pratensis
NT2 silene spergulifolia

CARYOPHYLLACEAE *cont.*
NT2 silene uralensis
NT2 silene vulgaris
NT1 spergula
NT2 spergula arvensis
NT2 spergula arvensis var. maxima
NT1 spergularia
NT1 stellaria
NT2 stellaria graminea
NT2 stellaria media
NT2 stellaria uliginosa
NT1 vaccaria
NT2 vaccaria hispanica

CARYOPHYLLAEIDAE
BT1 eucestoda
BT2 cestoda
NT1 khawia
NT2 khawia sinensis

caryophyllus aromaticus
USE **syzygium aromaticum**

caryopses
USE **grass seeds**
OR **seeds**

CARYOPTERIS
BT1 verbenaceae
NT1 caryopteris incana
rt ornamental plants

CARYOPTERIS INCANA
uf *caryopteris tangutica*
BT1 caryopteris
BT2 verbenaceae
BT1 essential oil plants
BT2 oil plants
BT1 ornamental woody plants

caryopteris tangutica
USE **caryopteris incana**

CARYOSPORA
BT1 apicomplexa
BT2 protozoa
NT1 caryospora simplex

CARYOSPORA SIMPLEX
BT1 caryospora
BT2 apicomplexa
BT3 protozoa

CARYOTA
BT1 palmae
NT1 caryota mitis
NT1 caryota urens

CARYOTA MITIS
BT1 caryota
BT2 palmae
BT1 ornamental palms

CARYOTA URENS
BT1 caryota
BT2 palmae
BT1 ornamental palms

CASBENE
BT1 diterpenoids
BT2 terpenoids
BT3 isoprenoids
BT4 lipids
BT1 phytoalexins
BT2 allomones
BT3 allelochemicals
BT4 semiochemicals

CASCADE DRIERS
AF cascade dryers
uf *driers, cascade*
BT1 driers
BT2 farm machinery
BT3 machinery

CASCADE DRYERS
BF cascade driers
BT1 dryers

CASE HARDENING
BT1 surface hardening
BT2 hardening
NT1 nitriding
rt alloys

CASE HARDENING *cont.*
rt drying
rt hardfacing
rt metallurgy

CASE REPORTS
(medical and veterinary only)
BT1 reports
BT2 publications

CASE STUDIES
(for medical and veterinary studies use "case reports")
NT1 longitudinal studies (agricola)
rt feasibility studies
rt research
rt teaching methods
rt trials

CASEIN
BT1 milk proteins
BT2 animal proteins
BT3 proteins
BT4 peptides
BT1 phosphoproteins
BT2 proteins
BT3 peptides
NT1 αs-casein
NT2 αs1-casein
NT2 αs2-casein
NT1 α-casein
NT1 β-casein
NT1 γ-casein
NT1 κ-casein
NT1 λ-casein
rt casein hydrolysate
rt caseinates
rt cheeses
rt micelles
rt milk
rt rennin
rt thyroprotein

CASEIN HYDROLYSATE
BT1 protein hydrolysates
BT2 hydrolysates
rt casein
rt parenteral feeding

α-CASEIN
(for retrieval spell out "alpha")
BT1 casein
BT2 milk proteins
BT3 animal proteins
BT4 proteins
BT5 peptides
BT2 phosphoproteins
BT3 proteins
BT4 peptides

αS-CASEIN
(for retrieval spell out "alpha")
BT1 casein
BT2 milk proteins
BT3 animal proteins
BT4 proteins
BT5 peptides
BT2 phosphoproteins
BT3 proteins
BT4 peptides
NT1 αs1-casein
NT1 αs2-casein

αS1-CASEIN
(for retrieval spell out "alpha")
BT1 αs-casein
BT2 casein
BT3 milk proteins
BT4 animal proteins
BT5 proteins
BT6 peptides
BT3 phosphoproteins
BT4 proteins
BT5 peptides

αS2-CASEIN
(for retrieval spell out "alpha")
BT1 αs-casein
BT2 casein
BT3 milk proteins
BT4 animal proteins
BT5 proteins

αS2-CASEIN *cont.*
BT6 peptides
BT3 phosphoproteins
BT4 proteins
BT5 peptides

β-CASEIN
(for retrieval spell out "beta")
BT1 casein
BT2 milk proteins
BT3 animal proteins
BT4 proteins
BT5 peptides
BT2 phosphoproteins
BT3 proteins
BT4 peptides

γ-CASEIN
(for retrieval spell out "gamma")
BT1 casein
BT2 milk proteins
BT3 animal proteins
BT4 proteins
BT5 peptides
BT2 phosphoproteins
BT3 proteins
BT4 peptides

κ-CASEIN
(for retrieval spell out "kappa")
BT1 casein
BT2 milk proteins
BT3 animal proteins
BT4 proteins
BT5 peptides
BT2 phosphoproteins
BT3 proteins
BT4 peptides

λ-CASEIN
(for retrieval spell out "lambda")
BT1 casein
BT2 milk proteins
BT3 animal proteins
BT4 proteins
BT5 peptides
BT2 phosphoproteins
BT3 proteins
BT4 peptides

CASEINATES
BT1 organic salts
BT2 salts
rt casein

CASH CROPS
rt commercial farming
rt crops
rt marketable surplus

CASH FLOW
BT1 balance sheets
BT2 accounting
rt balance sheets
rt cash flow analysis
rt expenditure
rt income
rt liquidity

CASH FLOW ANALYSIS
uf discounted cash flow
BT1 accounting
BT1 cost analysis
BT2 accounting
rt cash flow

CASH FORWARD CONTRACTING (AGRICOLA)
BT1 forward trading (agricola)
BT2 trading (agricola)

CASHEWS
BT1 antibacterial plants
BT1 antifungal plants
BT1 fatty oil plants
BT2 oil plants
BT1 gum plants
BT1 molluscicidal plants
BT2 pesticidal plants
BT1 tropical tree fruits
BT2 tree fruits
BT2 tropical fruits
BT3 fruit crops
BT1 tropical tree nuts

CASHEWS *cont.*
BT2 nut crops
rt anacardium occidentale

CASHMERE
BT1 animal fibres
BT2 animal products
BT3 products
BT2 fibres
rt pashmina
rt undercoat
rt wool

CASIMIROA
BT1 rutaceae
NT1 casimiroa edulis

CASIMIROA EDULIS
BT1 casimiroa
BT2 rutaceae
BT1 medicinal plants
BT1 subtropical tree fruits
BT2 subtropical fruits
BT3 fruit crops
BT2 tree fruits

CASING
rt cultural methods
rt mushroom casing soils
rt mushrooms

CASINOS
BT1 recreational buildings
BT2 buildings
rt card games
rt gambling

cassandra calyculata
USE **chamaedaphne calyculata**

CASSAVA
uf manioc
BT1 root vegetables
BT2 root crops
BT2 vegetables
BT1 starch crops
rt african cassava mosaic geminivirus
rt cassava common mosaic potexvirus
rt cassava leaf meal
rt cassava leaves
rt cassava meal
rt cassava peel
rt cassava silage
rt cassava starch
rt hydrogen cyanide
rt manihot esculenta
rt tapioca
rt tapioca meal

CASSAVA BROWN STREAK VIRUS
BT1 miscellaneous plant viruses
BT2 plant viruses
BT3 plant pathogens
BT4 pathogens
rt manihot esculenta

CASSAVA COMMON MOSAIC POTEXVIRUS
HN from 1990
BT1 potexvirus group
BT2 plant viruses
BT3 plant pathogens
BT4 pathogens
rt cassava
rt manihot esculenta

cassava latent geminivirus
USE **african cassava mosaic geminivirus**

cassava latent virus
USE **african cassava mosaic geminivirus**

CASSAVA LEAF MEAL
BT1 leaf meal
BT2 meal
rt cassava
rt cassava leaves
rt cassava meal

CASSAVA LEAVES
BT1 feeds
rt cassava
rt cassava leaf meal

CASSAVA MEAL
BT1 meal
rt cassava
rt cassava leaf meal

CASSAVA MOSAIC VIRUS
BT1 miscellaneous plant viruses
BT2 plant viruses
BT3 plant pathogens
BT4 pathogens
rt manihot esculenta

CASSAVA PEEL
BT1 feeds
BT1 peel
BT2 agricultural byproducts
BT3 byproducts
rt cassava

CASSAVA SILAGE
BT1 silage
BT2 feeds
BT2 fermentation products
BT3 products
rt cassava

CASSAVA STARCH
BT1 starch
BT2 absorbents
BT2 glucans
BT3 polysaccharides
BT4 carbohydrates
rt cassava

CASSEROLES (AGRICOLA)
rt meals

CASSETTES
rt mass media
rt video recordings

CASSIA
BT1 leguminosae
NT1 cassia absus
NT1 cassia alata
NT1 cassia angustifolia
NT1 cassia artemisioides
NT1 cassia auriculata
NT1 cassia didymobotrya
NT1 cassia eremophila
NT1 cassia fistula
NT1 cassia glauca
NT1 cassia grandis
NT1 cassia hirsuta
NT1 cassia italica
NT1 cassia javanica
NT1 cassia laevigata
NT1 cassia leptocarpa
NT1 cassia leschenaulthiana
NT1 cassia leurssenii
NT1 cassia marginata
NT1 cassia multijuga
NT1 cassia nemophila
NT1 cassia nodosa
NT1 cassia notabilis
NT1 cassia obtusifolia
NT1 cassia occidentalis
NT1 cassia orientalis
NT1 cassia patellaria
NT1 cassia peralteana
NT1 cassia podocarpa
NT1 cassia quinquangulata
NT1 cassia renigera
NT1 cassia rogeoni
NT1 cassia rotundifolia
NT1 cassia senna
NT1 cassia siamea
NT1 cassia sieberiana
NT1 cassia sophera
NT1 cassia spectabilis
NT1 cassia sturtii
NT1 cassia surattensis
NT1 cassia tora
rt cassia yellow blotch bromovirus
rt senna

CASSIA ABSUS
BT1 cassia
BT2 leguminosae

cassia acutifolia
USE **cassia senna**

CASSIA ALATA
BT1 cassia
BT2 leguminosae
BT1 medicinal plants

CASSIA ANGUSTIFOLIA
BT1 cassia
BT2 leguminosae
BT1 medicinal plants

CASSIA ARTEMISIOIDES
BT1 cassia
BT2 leguminosae

CASSIA AURICULATA
BT1 cassia
BT2 leguminosae
BT1 tan plants

cassia bark
USE **cinnamomum aromaticum**

CASSIA DIDYMOBOTRYA
BT1 cassia
BT2 leguminosae

CASSIA EREMOPHILA
BT1 browse plants
BT1 cassia
BT2 leguminosae

CASSIA FISTULA
BT1 cassia
BT2 leguminosae
BT1 forest trees
BT1 insecticidal plants
BT2 pesticidal plants
BT1 ornamental woody plants

CASSIA GLAUCA
BT1 cassia
BT2 leguminosae
BT1 ornamental woody plants

CASSIA GRANDIS
BT1 cassia
BT2 leguminosae

CASSIA HIRSUTA
BT1 cassia
BT2 leguminosae

CASSIA ITALICA
uf cassia obovata
BT1 browse plants
BT1 cassia
BT2 leguminosae

CASSIA JAVANICA
BT1 cassia
BT2 leguminosae
BT1 tan plants

CASSIA LAEVIGATA
BT1 cassia
BT2 leguminosae

CASSIA LEPTOCARPA
BT1 browse plants
BT1 cassia
BT2 leguminosae

CASSIA LESCHENAULTHIANA
BT1 cassia
BT2 leguminosae
BT1 green manures
BT2 manures
BT3 organic amendments
BT4 soil amendments
BT5 amendments

CASSIA LEURSSENII
BT1 browse plants
BT1 cassia
BT2 leguminosae

CASSIA MARGINATA
BT1 cassia
BT2 leguminosae

CASSIA MULTIJUGA
BT1 cassia
BT2 leguminosae

CASSIA NEMOPHILA
BT1 cassia
BT2 leguminosae

CASSIA NODOSA
BT1 cassia
BT2 leguminosae

CASSIA NOTABILIS
BT1 browse plants
BT1 cassia
BT2 leguminosae

cassia obovata
USE **cassia italica**

CASSIA OBTUSIFOLIA
BT1 antibacterial plants
BT1 cassia
BT2 leguminosae
BT1 weeds

CASSIA OCCIDENTALIS
BT1 antiviral plants
BT1 cassia
BT2 leguminosae

CASSIA ORIENTALIS
BT1 browse plants
BT1 cassia
BT2 leguminosae

CASSIA PATELLARIA
BT1 cassia
BT2 leguminosae

CASSIA PERALTEANA
BT1 browse plants
BT1 cassia
BT2 leguminosae

CASSIA PODOCARPA
BT1 cassia
BT2 leguminosae
BT1 medicinal plants

CASSIA QUINQUANGULATA
BT1 cassia
BT2 leguminosae

CASSIA RENIGERA
BT1 cassia
BT2 leguminosae

CASSIA ROGEONI
BT1 cassia
BT2 leguminosae

CASSIA ROTUNDIFOLIA
HN from 1989
BT1 cassia
BT2 leguminosae

CASSIA SENNA
uf *cassia acutifolia*
BT1 cassia
BT2 leguminosae
BT1 medicinal plants

CASSIA SIAMEA
BT1 antiviral plants
BT1 cassia
BT2 leguminosae
BT1 forest trees
BT1 medicinal plants

CASSIA SIEBERIANA
BT1 cassia
BT2 leguminosae

CASSIA SOPHERA
BT1 cassia
BT2 leguminosae

CASSIA SPECTABILIS
BT1 cassia
BT2 leguminosae
BT1 ornamental woody plants

CASSIA STURTII
BT1 browse plants
BT1 cassia

CASSIA STURTII *cont.*
BT2 leguminosae

CASSIA SURATTENSIS
BT1 cassia
BT2 leguminosae

CASSIA TORA
BT1 cassia
BT2 leguminosae
BT1 medicinal plants

CASSIA YELLOW BLOTCH BROMOVIRUS
HN from 1990
BT1 bromovirus group
BT2 plant viruses
BT3 plant pathogens
BT4 pathogens
rt cassia

CASSIDA
BT1 chrysomelidae
BT2 coleoptera
NT1 cassida nebulosa

CASSIDA NEBULOSA
BT1 cassida
BT2 chrysomelidae
BT3 coleoptera

CASSINE
BT1 celastraceae
NT1 cassine matabelica

CASSINE MATABELICA
BT1 cassine
BT2 celastraceae

CASSINIA
BT1 compositae
NT1 cassinia arcuata
NT1 cassinia fulvida
NT1 cassinia leptophylla

CASSINIA ARCUATA
BT1 cassinia
BT2 compositae

CASSINIA FULVIDA
BT1 browse plants
BT1 cassinia
BT2 compositae

CASSINIA LEPTOPHYLLA
BT1 cassinia
BT2 compositae

CASSIPOUREA
BT1 rhizophoraceae
NT1 cassipourea euryoides
NT1 cassipourea malosana
NT1 cassipourea mollis
NT1 cassipourea mossambicensis
NT1 cassipourea obovata

CASSIPOUREA EURYOIDES
BT1 cassipourea
BT2 rhizophoraceae

CASSIPOUREA MALOSANA
BT1 cassipourea
BT2 rhizophoraceae

CASSIPOUREA MOLLIS
BT1 cassipourea
BT2 rhizophoraceae

CASSIPOUREA MOSSAMBICENSIS
BT1 cassipourea
BT2 rhizophoraceae

CASSIPOUREA OBOVATA
BT1 cassipourea
BT2 rhizophoraceae

CASSYTHA
BT1 lauraceae
NT1 cassytha filiformis

CASSYTHA FILIFORMIS
BT1 cassytha
BT2 lauraceae

CAST IRON
BT1 ferrous alloys
BT2 alloys
BT3 metals
BT3 mixtures

CASTANEA
BT1 fagaceae
NT1 castanea crenata
NT1 castanea dentata
NT1 castanea mollissima
NT1 castanea sativa

CASTANEA CRENATA
BT1 castanea
BT2 fagaceae
BT1 forest trees
BT1 medicinal plants
BT1 ornamental woody plants

CASTANEA DENTATA
BT1 castanea
BT2 fagaceae
BT1 forest trees
BT1 ornamental woody plants
BT1 tan plants

CASTANEA MOLLISSIMA
BT1 castanea
BT2 fagaceae
BT1 forest trees

CASTANEA SATIVA
BT1 castanea
BT2 fagaceae
BT1 forest trees
BT1 ornamental woody plants
rt chestnuts

CASTANOPSIS
uf *shiia*
BT1 fagaceae
NT1 castanopsis cuspidata
NT1 castanopsis indica
NT1 castanopsis sieboldii
NT1 castanopsis tribuloides

CASTANOPSIS CUSPIDATA
BT1 castanopsis
BT2 fagaceae
BT1 forest trees
BT1 ornamental woody plants

CASTANOPSIS INDICA
BT1 castanopsis
BT2 fagaceae

CASTANOPSIS SIEBOLDII
BT1 castanopsis
BT2 fagaceae

CASTANOPSIS TRIBULOIDES
BT1 castanopsis
BT2 fagaceae

CASTANOSPERMUM
HN from 1990
BT1 leguminosae
NT1 castanospermum australe

CASTANOSPERMUM AUSTRALE
HN from 1990
BT1 castanospermum
BT2 leguminosae

CASTE
BT1 social differentiation
BT2 social structure
NT1 caste determination
rt classification
rt social change
rt social classes
rt social status

CASTE DETERMINATION
BT1 caste
BT2 social differentiation
BT3 social structure
rt social insects

CASTILIAN
BT1 sheep breeds
BT2 breeds

CASTILLA
uf *castilloa*
BT1 moraceae
NT1 castilla elastica
NT1 castilla fallax
NT1 castilla ulea

CASTILLA ELASTICA
BT1 castilla
BT2 moraceae

CASTILLA FALLAX
BT1 castilla
BT2 moraceae

CASTILLA ULEA
BT1 castilla
BT2 moraceae

CASTILLEJA
BT1 scrophulariaceae
NT1 castilleja cusickii
NT1 castilleja lutescens
NT1 castilleja rhexifolia
NT1 castilleja sulphurea

CASTILLEJA CUSICKII
BT1 castilleja
BT2 scrophulariaceae

CASTILLEJA LUTESCENS
BT1 castilleja
BT2 scrophulariaceae

CASTILLEJA RHEXIFOLIA
BT1 castilleja
BT2 scrophulariaceae

CASTILLEJA SULPHUREA
BT1 castilleja
BT2 scrophulariaceae

castilloa
USE **castilla**

CASTNIA
BT1 castniidae
BT2 lepidoptera
NT1 castnia licoides
NT1 castnia licus
rt eupalamides

castnia dedalus
USE **eupalamides cyparissias**

CASTNIA LICOIDES
BT1 castnia
BT2 castniidae
BT3 lepidoptera

CASTNIA LICUS
BT1 castnia
BT2 castniidae
BT3 lepidoptera

CASTNIIDAE
BT1 lepidoptera
NT1 castnia
NT2 castnia licoides
NT2 castnia licus
NT1 eupalamides
NT2 eupalamides cyparissias
NT1 lapaeumides

CASTOR
uf *beavers*
BT1 castoridae
BT2 rodents
BT3 mammals
NT1 castor canadensis
NT1 castor fiber

CASTOR BEANS
BT1 oilseeds
BT2 plant products
BT3 products
rt ricinus communis

CASTOR CANADENSIS
BT1 castor
BT2 castoridae
BT3 rodents
BT4 mammals
BT1 furbearing animals
BT2 animals

CASTOR FIBER
BT1 castor
BT2 castoridae
BT3 rodents
BT4 mammals

CASTOR OIL
BT1 purgatives
BT2 gastrointestinal agents
BT3 drugs
BT1 seed oils
BT2 plant oils
BT3 oils
BT3 plant products
BT4 products
rt castor oilmeal
rt ricinus communis

castor oil plants
USE **ricinus communis**

CASTOR OILMEAL
BT1 oilmeals
BT2 feeds
BT2 meal
rt castor oil
rt ricinus communis

CASTORIDAE
BT1 rodents
BT2 mammals
NT1 castor
NT2 castor canadensis
NT2 castor fiber

CASTRATION
BT1 gonadectomy
BT2 surgical operations
rt breeding
rt capons
rt emasculation
rt steers
rt sterilization
rt testes
rt wethers

CASTS
BT1 swarms
BT2 honeybee colonies
BT3 honeybees

CASUARIIDAE
HN from 1989
BT1 casuariiformes
BT2 birds
NT1 casuarius

CASUARIIFORMES
BT1 birds
NT1 casuariidae
NT2 casuarius
NT1 dromaiidae
NT2 dromaius

CASUARINA
BT1 casuarinaceae
NT1 casuarina cristata
NT1 casuarina cunninghamiana
NT1 casuarina equisetifolia
NT1 casuarina glauca
NT1 casuarina junghuhniana
NT1 casuarina littoralis
NT1 casuarina obesa
NT1 casuarina stricta

CASUARINA CRISTATA
BT1 casuarina
BT2 casuarinaceae

CASUARINA CUNNINGHAMIANA
BT1 casuarina
BT2 casuarinaceae
BT1 forest trees
BT1 ornamental woody plants

CASUARINA EQUISETIFOLIA
BT1 casuarina
BT2 casuarinaceae
BT1 forest trees

CASUARINA GLAUCA
BT1 casuarina
BT2 casuarinaceae
BT1 forest trees

CASUARINA GLAUCA *cont.*
BT1 ornamental woody plants

CASUARINA JUNGHUHNIANA
HN from 1990
BT1 casuarina
BT2 casuarinaceae
BT1 forest trees

CASUARINA LITTORALIS
BT1 casuarina
BT2 casuarinaceae

CASUARINA OBESA
HN from 1990
BT1 casuarina
BT2 casuarinaceae
BT1 forest trees

CASUARINA STRICTA
BT1 casuarina
BT2 casuarinaceae

CASUARINACEAE
NT1 casuarina
NT2 casuarina cristata
NT2 casuarina cunninghamiana
NT2 casuarina equisetifolia
NT2 casuarina glauca
NT2 casuarina junghuhniana
NT2 casuarina littoralis
NT2 casuarina obesa
NT2 casuarina stricta

CASUARIUS
BT1 casuariidae
BT2 casuariiformes
BT3 birds

cat
USE **cats**

CAT DISEASES
BT1 animal diseases
BT2 diseases
rt cats

cat face
USE **catfacing**

CAT FAECES
AF cat feces
BT1 faeces
BT2 excreta
BT3 animal wastes
BT4 wastes
rt cats

CAT FECES
BF cat faeces
BT1 feces

CAT FOODS
BT1 pet foods
BT2 feeds
rt cats

CATABOLISM
BT1 metabolism
rt anabolism

CATABROSA
BT1 gramineae
NT1 catabrosa aquatica

CATABROSA AQUATICA
BT1 catabrosa
BT2 gramineae
BT1 pasture plants

CATAGLYPHIS
BT1 formicidae
BT2 hymenoptera
NT1 cataglyphis aenescens

CATAGLYPHIS AENESCENS
BT1 cataglyphis
BT2 formicidae
BT3 hymenoptera

CATALASE
(ec 1.11.1.6)
uf *erythrocyte catalase*
BT1 peroxidases
BT2 oxidoreductases
BT3 enzymes

CATALASE *cont.*
rt catalase test

CATALASE TEST
BT1 tests
rt catalase
rt mastitis

CATALLAGIA
BT1 hystrichopsyllidae
BT2 siphonaptera

CATALOGS
BF catalogues
NT1 culture collection catalogs

CATALOGUES
AF catalogs
BT1 publications
NT1 buyers' guides
NT1 culture collection catalogues
rt checklists
rt inventories
rt taxonomy

CATALPA
BT1 bignoniaceae
NT1 catalpa bignonioides
NT1 catalpa ovata
NT1 catalpa speciosa
rt forest trees

CATALPA BIGNONIOIDES
BT1 catalpa
BT2 bignoniaceae
BT1 ornamental woody plants

CATALPA OVATA
BT1 catalpa
BT2 bignoniaceae
BT1 ornamental woody plants

CATALPA SPECIOSA
BT1 catalpa
BT2 bignoniaceae
BT1 insecticidal plants
BT2 pesticidal plants
BT1 ornamental woody plants

CATALYSTS
rt catalytic activity
rt chemicals

CATALYTIC ACTIVITY
BT1 activity
rt catalysts

CATANANCHE
BT1 compositae
NT1 catananche caerulea

CATANANCHE CAERULEA
BT1 catananche
BT2 compositae

CATAPODIUM
BT1 gramineae

catapodium marinum
USE **desmazeria marina**

CATARACT
BT1 eye diseases
BT2 organic diseases
BT3 diseases

CATASETUM
BT1 orchidaceae
NT1 catasetum barbatum
NT1 catasetum pileatum
NT1 catasetum thylaciochilum

CATASETUM BARBATUM
BT1 catasetum
BT2 orchidaceae
BT1 ornamental orchids

CATASETUM PILEATUM
BT1 catasetum
BT2 orchidaceae
BT1 ornamental orchids

CATASETUM THYLACIOCHILUM
BT1 catasetum
BT2 orchidaceae
BT1 ornamental orchids

CATASTEGA
BT1 tortricidae
BT2 lepidoptera
NT1 catastega aceriella
rt epinotia

CATASTEGA ACERIELLA
uf *epinotia aceriella*
BT1 catastega
BT2 tortricidae
BT3 lepidoptera

CATCH COMPOSITION
BT1 composition
rt fishing

CATCH CROPPING
BT1 cropping systems
rt catch crops
rt intercropping

CATCH CROPS
rt break crops
rt catch cropping

CATCHING FRAMES
BT1 harvesters
BT2 farm machinery
BT3 machinery
rt tree shakers

catchment areas
USE **watersheds**

CATCHMENT HYDROLOGY
BT1 hydrology
rt watersheds

CATECHIN
BT1 flavanols
BT2 alcohols
BT2 flavonoids
BT3 aromatic compounds
BT3 plant pigments
BT4 pigments
rt acacia catechu

catechins
USE **flavanols**

catechol
USE **pyrocatechol**

CATECHOL ESTROGENS
BF catechol oestrogens
BT1 estrogens

CATECHOL OESTROGENS
HN from 1989
AF catechol estrogens
BT1 oestrogens
BT2 sex hormones
BT3 hormones

CATECHOL OXIDASE
(ec 1.10.3.1)
uf *o-diphenol oxidase*
uf *phenolase*
uf *polyphenol oxidase*
uf *tyrosinase*
BT1 oxidoreductases
BT2 enzymes

CATECHOLAMINES
BT1 biogenic amines
BT2 amines
BT3 amino compounds
BT4 organic nitrogen compounds
NT1 dopamine
NT1 epinephrine
NT1 norepinephrine
rt levodopa

CATEGORICAL TRAITS
HN from 1989
BT1 traits

CATENAS
BT1 soil sequences

CATERERS (AGRICOLA)
BT1 occupations
rt catering

CATERING
AF food service
NT1 hospital catering
NT1 hotel catering
NT1 industrial catering
NT1 institutional catering
NT1 military rations
NT1 school meals
NT2 school breakfasts (agricola)
NT2 school lunches (agricola)
NT1 transport catering
rt caterers (agricola)
rt catering industry
rt cooking
rt diets
rt feeding
rt survival rations

CATERING INDUSTRY
AF food service industry
BT1 hospitality industry
BT2 industry
rt cafes
rt catering
rt fast foods
rt food industry
rt hotel catering
rt hotels
rt institutional catering
rt public houses
rt restaurants
rt transport catering

CATFACING
uf cat face
BT1 plant disorders
BT2 disorders
rt tomatoes

catfish, channel
USE **ictalurus punctatus**

CATHA
BT1 celastraceae
NT1 catha edulis

CATHA EDULIS
BT1 catha
BT2 celastraceae
BT1 medicinal plants
rt cathidine

CATHARACTA
BT1 stercorariidae
BT2 charadriiformes
BT3 birds

CATHARANTHUS
BT1 apocynaceae
NT1 catharanthus lanceus
NT1 catharanthus longifolius
NT1 catharanthus ovalis
NT1 catharanthus phyllanthoides
NT1 catharanthus roseus
NT1 catharanthus trichophyllus
rt vinca

CATHARANTHUS LANCEUS
BT1 catharanthus
BT2 apocynaceae

CATHARANTHUS LONGIFOLIUS
BT1 catharanthus
BT2 apocynaceae

CATHARANTHUS OVALIS
BT1 catharanthus
BT2 apocynaceae

CATHARANTHUS PHYLLANTHOIDES
uf catharanthus texana
BT1 catharanthus
BT2 apocynaceae

CATHARANTHUS ROSEUS
uf vinca rosea
BT1 antifungal plants
BT1 catharanthus
BT2 apocynaceae
BT1 insecticidal plants
BT2 pesticidal plants
BT1 medicinal plants
BT1 nematicidal plants

CATHARANTHUS ROSEUS *cont.*
BT2 pesticidal plants
rt vinca rosea proliferation

catharanthus texana
USE **catharanthus phyllanthoides**

CATHARANTHUS TRICHOPHYLLUS
BT1 catharanthus
BT2 apocynaceae

cathartics
USE **purgatives**

CATHCARTIA
BT1 papaveraceae
NT1 cathcartia villosa

CATHCARTIA VILLOSA
BT1 cathcartia
BT2 papaveraceae

CATHEPSINS
(ec 3.4)
BT1 peptidases
BT2 peptide hydrolases
BT3 hydrolases
BT4 enzymes
BT1 proteinases
BT2 peptide hydrolases
BT3 hydrolases
BT4 enzymes

CATHETERIZATION
BT1 diagnostic techniques
BT2 techniques

CATHETERS
BT1 tubes

CATHIDINE
BT1 pyridine alkaloids
BT2 alkaloids
BT2 pyridines
BT3 heterocyclic nitrogen compounds
BT4 organic nitrogen compounds
rt catha edulis

cation-anion balance
USE **ion balance**

CATION EXCHANGE
BT1 ion exchange
rt anion exchange
rt cation exchange capacity
rt cations
rt roots

CATION EXCHANGE CAPACITY
BT1 ion exchange capacity
rt capacity
rt cation exchange
rt cations
rt roots

CATION EXCHANGE RESINS
BT1 ion exchange resins
BT2 resins

CATION SATURATION
BT1 saturation
rt cations
rt sample processing

CATIONS
BT1 ions
NT1 ammonium
NT1 exchangeable cations
NT2 exchangeable sodium
NT1 hydrogen ions
NT1 metal ions
NT2 calcium ions
NT2 ferric ions
NT2 ferrous ions
NT2 silver ions
rt anions
rt cation exchange
rt cation exchange capacity
rt cation saturation

CATLA
BT1 cyprinidae
BT2 cypriniformes
BT3 osteichthyes
BT4 fishes
NT1 catla catla

CATLA CATLA
BT1 catla
BT2 cyprinidae
BT3 cypriniformes
BT4 osteichthyes
BT5 fishes

CATOCHRYSOPS
BT1 lycaenidae
BT2 lepidoptera
rt euchrysops

catochrysops cnejus
USE **euchrysops cnejus**

CATOLACCUS
BT1 pteromalidae
BT2 hymenoptera
NT1 catolaccus aeneoviridis

CATOLACCUS AENEOVIRIDIS
BT1 catolaccus
BT2 pteromalidae
BT3 hymenoptera

CATS
HN until 1990 was "cat" in agricola
uf cat
uf felis catus
BT1 domestic animals
BT2 animals
rt cat diseases
rt cat faeces
rt cat foods
rt felidae
rt kittens
rt laboratory mammals
rt pets

CATTLE
uf bos taurus
uf oxen
BT1 livestock
BT2 animals
BT1 ruminants
BT2 animals
BT1 skin producing animals
BT2 animals
NT1 beef cattle
NT2 beef bulls
NT2 beef cows
NT1 dairy cattle
NT2 dairy bulls
NT2 dairy cows
rt banteng
rt bovidae
rt bulls
rt calves
rt cattle breeds
rt cattle dung
rt cattle farming
rt cattle fattening
rt cattle feeding
rt cattle housing
rt cattle husbandry
rt cows
rt freemartins
rt gaur
rt veal calves
rt zebu

CATTLE BREEDS
(only important and recognised breeds are listed)
BT1 breeds
NT1 aberdeen-angus
NT1 abondance
NT1 adamawa
NT1 africander
NT1 ala-tau
NT1 alambadi
NT1 albanian
NT1 american angus
NT1 american brown swiss
NT1 amritmahal

CATTLE BREEDS *cont.*
NT1 anatolian black
NT1 andalusian
NT1 andalusian black
NT1 andalusian blond
NT1 angeln
NT1 angoni
NT1 ankole
NT1 aosta
NT1 apulian podolian
NT1 arado
NT1 argentine friesian
NT1 arsi
NT1 asturian
NT1 aubrac
NT1 aulie-ata
NT1 austrian brown
NT1 austrian simmental
NT1 austrian yellow
NT1 avilena-black iberian
NT1 ayrshire
NT1 azaouak
NT1 bachaur
NT1 baggara
NT1 bali (cattle breed)
NT1 baltic black pied
NT1 bambara
NT1 baoule
NT1 bargur
NT1 barka
NT1 barotse
NT1 barrosa
NT1 beef breeds
NT1 beef shorthorn
NT1 belgian black pied
NT1 belgian blue
NT1 belgian red
NT1 belgian red pied
NT1 belgian white-and-red
NT1 belted galloway
NT1 bestuzhev
NT1 bhagnari
NT1 blacksided trondheim and nordland
NT1 blanco orejinegro
NT1 blonde d'aquitaine
NT1 bonsmara
NT1 borgou
NT1 brangus
NT1 brazilian gir
NT1 brazilian polled
NT1 breton black pied
NT1 british friesian
NT1 british white
NT1 brown atlas
NT1 bulgarian brown
NT1 bulgarian red
NT1 bulgarian simmental
NT1 busa
NT1 bushuev
NT1 butana
NT1 byelorussian red
NT1 canadian
NT1 canchim
NT1 caracu
NT1 carpathian brown
NT1 caucasian brown
NT1 charolais
NT1 chianina
NT1 chinese black-and-white
NT1 czech pied
NT1 dairy breeds
NT1 dairy shorthorn
NT1 damascus
NT1 damietta
NT1 danakil
NT1 dangi
NT1 danish black pied
NT1 danish jersey
NT1 danish red
NT1 danish red pied
NT1 deoni
NT1 devon
NT1 dexter
NT1 dhanni
NT1 diali
NT1 drakensberger
NT1 droughtmaster
NT1 dual purpose cattle
NT2 dual purpose bull
NT1 dutch black pied

CATTLE BREEDS *cont.*
NT1 east anatolian red
NT1 egyptian
NT1 estonian black pied
NT1 estonian red
NT1 fighting bull
NT1 finnish
NT1 finnish ayrshire
NT1 fogera
NT1 french brown
NT1 french friesian
NT1 friesian
NT1 friesland
NT1 galician blond
NT1 galloway
NT1 gaolao
NT1 gelbvieh
NT1 georgian mountain
NT1 german black pied
NT1 german brown
NT1 german red pied
NT1 german simmental
NT1 gobra
NT1 golpayegani
NT1 gorbatov red
NT1 grey alpine
NT1 guernsey
NT1 guzera
NT1 hallikar
NT1 hariana
NT1 hereford
NT1 herens
NT1 highland
NT1 holstein-friesian
NT1 hungarian pied
NT1 hungarian simmental
NT1 hungarofries
NT1 icelandic
NT1 illawarra
NT1 indo-brazilian
NT1 israeli friesian
NT1 istoben
NT1 italian brown
NT1 italian friesian
NT1 italian red pied
NT1 jamaica black
NT1 jamaica hope
NT1 jamaica red
NT1 japanese black
NT1 japanese brown
NT1 japanese poll
NT1 japanese shorthorn
NT1 jersey
NT1 jiddu
NT1 jinnan
NT1 kalmyk
NT1 kangayam
NT1 kankrej
NT1 kazakh
NT1 kazakh whiteheaded
NT1 kedah-kelantan
NT1 kenana
NT1 kenkatha
NT1 kenya boran
NT1 kerry
NT1 keteku
NT1 kherigarh
NT1 khillari
NT1 kholmogory
NT1 korean native
NT1 kostroma
NT1 krishna valley
NT1 kurgan
NT1 kuri
NT1 latvian brown
NT1 lebedin
NT1 lincoln red
NT1 lithuanian black pied
NT1 lithuanian red
NT1 lohani
NT1 luxi
NT1 madurese
NT1 maine-anjou
NT1 malvi
NT1 marchigiana
NT1 maremmana
NT1 mashona
NT1 mauritius creole
NT1 mazandarani
NT1 meuse-rhine-yssel
NT1 mewati

CATTLE BREEDS *cont.*
NT1 milking shorthorn
NT1 mirandesa
NT1 modicana
NT1 mongolian
NT1 montbeliard
NT1 morucha
NT1 murnau-werdenfels
NT1 murray grey
NT1 n'dama
NT1 nagori
NT1 nanyang
NT1 nelore
NT1 new zealand jersey
NT1 nguni
NT1 nilotic
NT1 nimari
NT1 nkone
NT1 normande
NT1 norwegian red
NT1 ongole
NT1 ovambo
NT1 pie rouge des plaines
NT1 pinzgauer
NT1 pitangueiras
NT1 polish black-and-white lowland
NT1 polish red
NT1 polish red-and-white lowland
NT1 polish simmental
NT1 poll shorthorn
NT1 polled hereford
NT1 ponwan
NT1 pyrenean
NT1 qinchuan
NT1 rath
NT1 red bororo
NT1 red poll
NT1 red sindhi
NT1 red steppe
NT1 retinta
NT1 romagnola
NT1 romanian brown
NT1 romanian red
NT1 romanian simmental
NT1 romanian steppe
NT1 romosinuano
NT1 russian black pied
NT1 russian brown
NT1 russian simmental
NT1 sahiwal
NT1 salers
NT1 san martinero
NT1 santa gertrudis
NT1 sarabi
NT1 shahabadi
NT1 shetland
NT1 shorthorn
NT1 shuwa
NT1 simmental
NT1 sinhala
NT1 siri
NT1 sistani
NT1 slovakian pied
NT1 slovakian pinzgau
NT1 slovenian brown
NT1 sokoto gudali
NT1 south anatolian red
NT1 south devon
NT1 spanish brown
NT1 sudanese fulani
NT1 suksun
NT1 sussex
NT1 swedish friesian
NT1 swedish jersey
NT1 swedish polled
NT1 swedish red-and-white
NT1 swiss black pied
NT1 swiss brown
NT1 sychevka
NT1 tagil
NT1 tambov red
NT1 tarentaise
NT1 telemark
NT1 thari
NT1 tonga (cattle breed)
NT1 transylvanian pinzgau
NT1 tropical dairy criollo
NT1 tswana
NT1 tudanca

CATTLE BREEDS *cont.*
NT1 tuli
NT1 tuni
NT1 turino
NT1 tyrol grey
NT1 ukrainian grey
NT1 ukrainian whiteheaded
NT1 villard-de-lans
NT1 vorderwald
NT1 vosges
NT1 welsh black
NT1 west african shorthorn
NT1 white caceres
NT1 white fulani
NT1 yaroslavl
NT1 yugoslav pied
NT1 yurino
rt cattle
rt dairy bulls
rt dairy cows
rt dairy herds

cattle, dairy
USE **dairy cattle**

CATTLE DISEASES
BT1 animal diseases
BT2 diseases
NT1 anaplasmosis
NT1 anthrax
NT1 bovine spongiform encephalopathy
NT1 foot and mouth disease
NT1 rinderpest
rt calf diseases
rt cerebrocortical necrosis

cattle, dual purpose
USE **dual purpose cattle**

CATTLE DUNG
BT1 faeces
BT2 excreta
BT3 animal wastes
BT4 wastes
rt cattle
rt cattle slurry

CATTLE FARMING
BT1 livestock enterprises
BT2 farm enterprises
BT3 enterprises
BT1 livestock farming
BT2 farming
NT1 dairy farming
rt cattle

CATTLE FATTENING
BT1 fattening
BT2 animal feeding
BT3 feeding
NT1 bull fattening
rt cattle

CATTLE FEEDING
BT1 ruminant feeding
BT2 livestock feeding
BT3 animal feeding
BT4 feeding
NT1 bull feeding
NT1 calf feeding
rt cattle

CATTLE FEEDLOT SOILS
BT1 soil types (anthropogenic)

CATTLE HOUSING
uf *cattle sheds*
BT1 animal housing
NT1 calf housing
NT1 cow housing
NT2 cubicles
rt cattle
rt loose housing
rt tethered housing

CATTLE HUSBANDRY
uf *cattle management*
BT1 animal husbandry
BT2 husbandry
BT2 zootechny
rt cattle

cattle management
USE **cattle husbandry**

CATTLE MANURE
BT1 animal manures
BT2 manures
BT3 organic amendments
BT4 soil amendments
BT5 amendments
rt farmyard manure

cattle rumen
USE **rumen**

cattle sheds
USE **cattle housing**

CATTLE SLURRY
uf *slurry, cattle*
BT1 animal wastes
BT2 wastes
BT1 slurries
rt cattle dung

CATTLE WEIGHERS
uf *weighers, cattle*
BT1 weighers
BT2 instruments

CATTLEYA
BT1 orchidaceae
NT1 cattleya aurantiaca
NT1 cattleya bowringiana
NT1 cattleya dowiana
NT1 cattleya fabingiana
NT1 cattleya forbesii
NT1 cattleya trianaei

CATTLEYA AURANTIACA
BT1 cattleya
BT2 orchidaceae
BT1 ornamental orchids

CATTLEYA BOWRINGIANA
BT1 cattleya
BT2 orchidaceae
BT1 ornamental orchids

CATTLEYA DOWIANA
BT1 cattleya
BT2 orchidaceae
BT1 ornamental orchids

CATTLEYA FABINGIANA
BT1 cattleya
BT2 orchidaceae

CATTLEYA FORBESII
BT1 cattleya
BT2 orchidaceae
BT1 ornamental orchids

CATTLEYA TRIANAEI
BT1 cattleya
BT2 orchidaceae
BT1 ornamental orchids

CAUCASIAN
BT1 sheep breeds
BT2 breeds

CAUCASIAN BROWN
BT1 cattle breeds
BT2 breeds

caucasian honeybee
USE **apis mellifera caucasica**

CAUDA EPIDIDYMIDIS
BT1 epididymis
BT2 testes
BT3 gonads
BT4 reproductive organs

CAUDATA
BT1 amphibia
NT1 ambystomatidae
NT2 ambystoma

CAUDOSPORA
BT1 microspora
BT2 protozoa

CAULIFLOWER MOSAIC CAULIMOVIRUS

CAULIFLOWER MOSAIC CAULIMOVIRUS *cont.*
HN from 1990; previously "cauliflower mosaic virus"
uf *cauliflower mosaic virus*
BT1 caulimovirus group
BT2 plant viruses
BT3 plant pathogens
BT4 pathogens
rt brassica oleracea var. botrytis
rt cauliflowers

cauliflower mosaic virus
USE **cauliflower mosaic caulimovirus**

CAULIFLOWERS
uf *broccoli, heading*
uf *heading broccoli*
BT1 leafy vegetables
BT2 vegetables
rt brassica oleracea var. botrytis
rt cauliflower mosaic caulimovirus
rt curds
rt hollow stem
rt whiptail

CAULIMOVIRUS GROUP
HN from 1990
BT1 plant viruses
BT2 plant pathogens
BT3 pathogens
NT1 carnation etched ring caulimovirus
NT1 cauliflower mosaic caulimovirus
NT1 dahlia mosaic caulimovirus
NT1 figwort mosaic caulimovirus
NT1 mirabilis mosaic caulimovirus
NT1 soybean chlorotic mottle caulimovirus
NT1 strawberry vein banding caulimovirus
NT1 thistle mottle caulimovirus

CAULOBACTERACEAE
BT1 gracilicutes
BT2 bacteria
BT3 prokaryotes
NT1 gallionella

CAUTERY
BT1 instruments
rt burning
rt dichloroacetic acid

CAVARIELLA
BT1 aphididae
BT2 aphidoidea
BT3 sternorrhyncha
BT4 homoptera
NT1 cavariella aegopodii

CAVARIELLA AEGOPODII
BT1 cavariella
BT2 aphididae
BT3 aphidoidea
BT4 sternorrhyncha
BT5 homoptera

CAVE SOILS
BT1 soil types (physiographic)

CAVELERIUS
BT1 lygaeidae
BT2 heteroptera
NT1 cavelerius excavatus
NT1 cavelerius saccharivorus

CAVELERIUS EXCAVATUS
BT1 cavelerius
BT2 lygaeidae
BT3 heteroptera

CAVELERIUS SACCHARIVORUS
BT1 cavelerius
BT2 lygaeidae
BT3 heteroptera

CAVERNICOLA
BT1 reduviidae
BT2 heteroptera
NT1 cavernicola pilosa

CAVERNICOLA PILOSA
BT1 cavernicola
BT2 reduviidae
BT3 heteroptera

CAVES
BT1 physiographic features
rt underground storage

CAVIA
BT1 caviidae
BT2 rodents
BT3 mammals

cavia porcellus
USE **guinea pigs**
OR **guineapigs**

CAVIAR
BT1 fish roe
BT2 fish products
BT3 animal products
BT4 products
rt acipenser

CAVIIDAE
BT1 rodents
BT2 mammals
NT1 cavia
rt guineapigs

CAVITATION
rt flow
rt homogenization

CAVITIES IN TREES
BT1 abnormal development
rt tree holes
rt tree surgery

CAVITY SPOT
BT1 plant disorders
BT2 disorders
rt carrots

CAYMAN ISLANDS
uf *grand cayman*
BT1 caribbean
BT2 america

ccc
USE **chlormequat**

cd (symbol)
USE **cadmium**

cdaa
USE **allidochlor**

CDC LIGHT TRAPS
uf *cdc miniature light traps*
BT1 light traps
BT2 insect traps
BT3 traps
BT4 equipment

cdc miniature light traps
USE **cdc light traps**

CDEA
BT1 amide herbicides
BT2 herbicides
BT3 pesticides

CDU
uf *crotonylidene diurea*
BT1 slow release fertilizers
BT2 fertilizers
BT1 urea fertilizers
BT2 nitrogen fertilizers
BT3 fertilizers

ce (symbol)
USE **cerium**

CEANOTHUS
BT1 rhamnaceae
NT1 ceanothus cordulatus
NT1 ceanothus cuneatus
NT1 ceanothus fendleri
NT1 ceanothus greggi

CEANOTHUS *cont.*
NT1 ceanothus integerrimus
NT1 ceanothus leucodermis
NT1 ceanothus prostratus
NT1 ceanothus sanguineus
NT1 ceanothus thyrsiflorus
NT1 ceanothus velutinus
NT1 ceanothus velutinus var. laevigatus

CEANOTHUS CORDULATUS
BT1 browse plants
BT1 ceanothus
BT2 rhamnaceae

CEANOTHUS CUNEATUS
BT1 ceanothus
BT2 rhamnaceae

CEANOTHUS FENDLERI
BT1 browse plants
BT1 ceanothus
BT2 rhamnaceae

CEANOTHUS GREGGI
BT1 ceanothus
BT2 rhamnaceae

CEANOTHUS INTEGERRIMUS
BT1 ceanothus
BT2 rhamnaceae
BT1 ornamental woody plants

CEANOTHUS LEUCODERMIS
BT1 browse plants
BT1 ceanothus
BT2 rhamnaceae

CEANOTHUS PROSTRATUS
BT1 browse plants
BT1 ceanothus
BT2 rhamnaceae

CEANOTHUS SANGUINEUS
BT1 ceanothus
BT2 rhamnaceae

CEANOTHUS THYRSIFLORUS
BT1 ceanothus
BT2 rhamnaceae
BT1 ornamental woody plants

CEANOTHUS VELUTINUS
BT1 ceanothus
BT2 rhamnaceae
BT1 ornamental woody plants

CEANOTHUS VELUTINUS VAR. LAEVIGATUS
BT1 ceanothus
BT2 rhamnaceae

CEBIDAE
(new-world monkeys)
BT1 primates
BT2 mammals
NT1 alouatta
NT1 aotus
NT2 aotus trivirgatus
NT1 ateles
NT1 callicebus
NT1 cebus
NT2 cebus apella
NT1 saimiri
NT2 saimiri sciureus
rt monkeys

CEBUS
uf *capuchin monkeys*
BT1 cebidae
BT2 primates
BT3 mammals
NT1 cebus apella

CEBUS APELLA
BT1 cebus
BT2 cebidae
BT3 primates
BT4 mammals

CECIDOMYIA
BT1 cecidomyiidae
BT2 diptera

CECIDOMYIIDAE
BT1 diptera
NT1 aphidoletes
NT2 aphidoletes abietis
NT2 aphidoletes aphidimyza
NT1 asphondylia
NT2 asphondylia sesami
NT1 cecidomyia
NT1 contarinia
NT2 contarinia baeri
NT2 contarinia medicaginis
NT2 contarinia nasturtii
NT2 contarinia okadai
NT2 contarinia oregonensis
NT2 contarinia pisi
NT2 contarinia pyrivora
NT2 contarinia schulzi
NT2 contarinia sorghicola
NT2 contarinia tritici
NT1 dasineura
NT2 dasineura brassicae
NT2 dasineura ignorata
NT2 dasineura mali
NT2 dasineura pyri
NT2 dasineura ribis
NT1 haplodiplosis
NT2 haplodiplosis marginata
NT1 heteropeza
NT2 heteropeza pygmaea
NT1 kaltenbachiola
NT2 kaltenbachiola strobi
NT1 kiefferia
NT1 lasioptera
NT1 masakimyia
NT2 masakimyia pustulae
NT1 mayetiola
NT2 mayetiola destructor
NT1 mycophila
NT2 mycophila speyeri
NT1 orseolia
NT2 orseolia oryzae
NT2 orseolia oryzivora
NT1 pachydiplosis
NT1 paradiplosis
NT2 paradiplosis abietis
NT2 paradiplosis tumifex
NT1 plemeliella
NT2 plemeliella abietina
NT1 resseliella
NT2 resseliella theobaldi
NT1 rhopalomyia
NT2 rhopalomyia chrysanthemi
NT1 sitodiplosis
NT2 sitodiplosis mosellana
NT1 thecodiplosis
NT2 thecodiplosis brachyntera
NT2 thecodiplosis japonensis

CECIDOPHYES
BT1 eriophyidae
BT2 prostigmata
BT3 acari
rt cecidophyopsis

cecidophyes ribis
USE **cecidophyopsis ribis**

CECIDOPHYOPSIS
BT1 eriophyidae
BT2 prostigmata
BT3 acari
NT1 cecidophyopsis ribis
rt cecidophyes
rt eriophyes
rt phytoptus

CECIDOPHYOPSIS RIBIS
uf *cecidophyes ribis*
uf *eriophyes ribis*
uf *phytoptus ribis*
BT1 cecidophyopsis
BT2 eriophyidae
BT3 prostigmata
BT4 acari

CECOTROPHY
BF caecotrophy

CECROPIA
BT1 urticaceae
NT1 cecropia concolor
NT1 cecropia dielsiana
NT1 cecropia distachya

CECROPIA *cont.*
NT1 cecropia engleriana
NT1 cecropia ficifolia
NT1 cecropia francisci
NT1 cecropia latiloba
NT1 cecropia membranacea
NT1 cecropia obtusa
NT1 cecropia obtusifolia
NT1 cecropia palmata
NT1 cecropia purpurascens
NT1 cecropia sciadophylla
NT1 cecropia silvae
NT1 cecropia surinamensis
NT1 cecropia ulei
rt forest trees

CECROPIA CONCOLOR
BT1 cecropia
BT2 urticaceae

CECROPIA DIELSIANA
BT1 cecropia
BT2 urticaceae

CECROPIA DISTACHYA
BT1 cecropia
BT2 urticaceae

CECROPIA ENGLERIANA
BT1 cecropia
BT2 urticaceae

CECROPIA FICIFOLIA
BT1 cecropia
BT2 urticaceae

CECROPIA FRANCISCI
BT1 cecropia
BT2 urticaceae

CECROPIA LATILOBA
BT1 cecropia
BT2 urticaceae

CECROPIA MEMBRANACEA
BT1 cecropia
BT2 urticaceae

CECROPIA OBTUSA
BT1 cecropia
BT2 urticaceae

CECROPIA OBTUSIFOLIA
BT1 cecropia
BT2 urticaceae
BT1 medicinal plants

CECROPIA PALMATA
BT1 cecropia
BT2 urticaceae

CECROPIA PURPURASCENS
BT1 cecropia
BT2 urticaceae

CECROPIA SCIADOPHYLLA
BT1 cecropia
BT2 urticaceae

CECROPIA SILVAE
BT1 cecropia
BT2 urticaceae

CECROPIA SURINAMENSIS
BT1 cecropia
BT2 urticaceae

CECROPIA ULEI
BT1 cecropia
BT2 urticaceae

CECUM
BF caecum

cedar
USE **cedrus**

CEDARWOOD OIL
BT1 essential oils
BT2 plant oils
BT3 oils
BT3 plant products
BT4 products

CEDRELA
BT1 meliaceae

CEDRELA *cont.*
NT1 cedrela oaxacensis
NT1 cedrela odorata
NT1 cedrela salvadorensis
NT1 cedrela tonduzii
rt toona

cedrela mexicana
USE **cedrela odorata**

CEDRELA OAXACENSIS
BT1 cedrela
BT2 meliaceae

CEDRELA ODORATA
uf *cedrela mexicana*
BT1 cedrela
BT2 meliaceae
BT1 forest trees

CEDRELA SALVADORENSIS
BT1 cedrela
BT2 meliaceae

cedrela sinensis
USE **toona sinensis**

CEDRELA TONDUZII
BT1 cedrela
BT2 meliaceae

cedrela toona
USE **toona ciliata**

CEDRELINGA
BT1 leguminosae
NT1 cedrelinga catenaeformis

CEDRELINGA CATENAEFORMIS
BT1 cedrelinga
BT2 leguminosae
BT1 forest trees

CEDROBIUM
BT1 aphididae
BT2 aphidoidea
BT3 sternorrhyncha
BT4 homoptera
NT1 cedrobium laportei

CEDROBIUM LAPORTEI
BT1 cedrobium
BT2 aphididae
BT3 aphidoidea
BT4 sternorrhyncha
BT5 homoptera

CEDRUS
uf *cedar*
BT1 pinaceae
NT1 cedrus atlantica
NT1 cedrus brevifolia
NT1 cedrus deodara
NT1 cedrus libani

CEDRUS ATLANTICA
BT1 cedrus
BT2 pinaceae
BT1 forest trees
BT1 ornamental conifers
BT2 conifers
BT2 ornamental woody plants

CEDRUS BREVIFOLIA
BT1 cedrus
BT2 pinaceae

CEDRUS DEODARA
BT1 cedrus
BT2 pinaceae
BT1 forest trees
BT1 ornamental conifers
BT2 conifers
BT2 ornamental woody plants

CEDRUS LIBANI
BT1 cedrus
BT2 pinaceae

CEFAMANDOLE
BT1 antibacterial agents
BT2 antiinfective agents
BT3 drugs
BT1 antibiotics

CEFAZOLIN
BT1 antibacterial agents
BT2 antiinfective agents
BT3 drugs
BT1 antibiotics

CEFOXITIN
BT1 antibacterial agents
BT2 antiinfective agents
BT3 drugs
BT1 antibiotics

CEIBA
uf *eriodendron*
BT1 bombacaceae
NT1 ceiba pentandra

CEIBA PENTANDRA
uf *eriodendron pentandrum*
BT1 antibacterial plants
BT1 ceiba
BT2 bombacaceae
BT1 fibre plants
BT1 forest trees
BT1 oilseed plants
BT2 fatty oil plants
BT3 oil plants
rt kapok

CEILINGS
BT1 roofs
rt buildings

CELAMA
BT1 noctuidae
BT2 lepidoptera
NT1 celama sorghiella
rt nola

CELAMA SORGHIELLA
uf *nola sorghiella*
BT1 celama
BT2 noctuidae
BT3 lepidoptera

CELASTRACEAE
uf *hippocrateaceae*
NT1 cassine
NT2 cassine matabelica
NT1 catha
NT2 catha edulis
NT1 celastrus
NT2 celastrus paniculatus
NT2 celastrus scandens
NT1 elaeodendron
NT2 elaeodendron glaucum
NT1 euonymus
NT2 euonymus alatus
NT2 euonymus bungeanus
NT2 euonymus czernjaevii
NT2 euonymus europaeus
NT2 euonymus fortunei
NT2 euonymus hamiltonianus
NT2 euonymus japonicus
NT2 euonymus kiautschovicus
NT2 euonymus lucidus
NT2 euonymus pendulus
NT2 euonymus radicans
NT1 gymnosporia
NT2 gymnosporia emarginata
NT2 gymnosporia trilocularis
NT2 gymnosporia wallichiana
NT1 kokoona
NT2 kokoona zeylanica
NT1 lophopetalum
NT2 lophopetalum toxicum
NT1 maytenus
NT2 maytenus buxifolia
NT2 maytenus canariensis
NT2 maytenus chuchuhuasca
NT2 maytenus dispermus
NT2 maytenus rothiana
NT2 maytenus senegalensis
NT1 peripterygia
NT2 peripterygia marginata
NT1 pleurostylia
NT2 pleurostylia africana
NT1 putterlickia
NT1 schaefferia
NT2 schaefferia cuneifolia
NT1 tripterygium
NT2 tripterygium wilfordii

CELASTRUS
BT1 celastraceae
NT1 celastrus paniculatus
NT1 celastrus scandens

CELASTRUS PANICULATUS
BT1 celastrus
BT2 celastraceae

CELASTRUS SCANDENS
BT1 celastrus
BT2 celastraceae
BT1 ornamental woody plants

celebes
USE **sulawesi**

CELERIAC
BT1 root vegetables
BT2 root crops
BT2 vegetables
rt apium graveolens var. rapaceum
rt hollow heart

celerio
USE **hyles**

celerio euphorbiae
USE **hyles euphorbiae**

celerio lineata
USE **hyles lineata**

CELERY
BT1 antibacterial plants
BT1 antifungal plants
BT1 leafy vegetables
BT2 vegetables
BT1 medicinal plants
rt apium graveolens
rt blackheart
rt celery mosaic potyvirus
rt pithiness

CELERY MOSAIC POTYVIRUS
HN from 1990; previously "celery mosaic virus"
uf *celery mosaic virus*
BT1 potyvirus group
BT2 plant viruses
BT3 plant pathogens
BT4 pathogens
rt apium graveolens
rt celery

celery mosaic virus
USE **celery mosaic potyvirus**

CELIAC SYNDROME
BF coeliac syndrome
rt steatorrhea

cell count
USE **leukocyte count**

CELL COUNTING
BT1 counting
BT2 recording
rt cells
rt erythrocyte count
rt leukocyte count
rt plate count

CELL CULTURE
BT1 in vitro culture
BT2 culture techniques
BT3 biological techniques
BT4 techniques
rt cell cultures
rt cell suspensions
rt cells
rt somaclonal variation
rt tissue culture

CELL CULTURE VACCINES
BT1 vaccines
rt cell cultures

CELL CULTURES
(properties of cultures; for culture techniques use "cell culture")
BT1 cultures
NT1 cell lines
NT2 hela cells

CELL CULTURES *cont.*
rt cell culture
rt cell culture vaccines

CELL DIFFERENTIATION
HN from 1990
(developmental process leading to specialization in form and function of cells, tissues and organs)
uf *cytodifferentiation*
uf *differentiation, cell*
BT1 biological development

CELL DIVISION
uf *karyokinesis*
NT1 amitosis
NT1 desynapsis
NT1 meiosis
NT1 mitosis
NT1 sporulation
NT2 zoosporogenesis
rt cambium
rt cells
rt chromosome disposition
rt cleavage
rt growth
rt nuclei
rt symplasts

cell elongation
USE **cell growth**

CELL GROWTH
uf *cell elongation*
BT1 growth
rt cells

cell inclusions
USE **cytoplasmic inclusions**

CELL INVASION
HN from 1989
BT1 infection
BT2 disease transmission
BT3 transmission
BT1 invasion
NT1 erythrocyte invasion

CELL LINES
BT1 cell cultures
BT2 cultures
NT1 hela cells

cell mediated hypersensitivity
USE **delayed type hypersensitivity**

CELL MEDIATED IMMUNITY
uf *cellular immunity*
BT1 immunity
NT1 cell mediated lympholysis
NT1 graft versus host reactions
NT1 lymphocyte transformation
rt macrophages
rt t lymphocytes

CELL MEDIATED LYMPHOLYSIS
BT1 cell mediated immunity
BT2 immunity
rt cells

CELL MEMBRANES
BT1 membranes
NT1 microvilli
NT1 tonoplast
rt cell structure
rt cell walls
rt cells
rt egg membranes
rt protoplasm

cell nuclei
USE **nuclei**

CELL STRUCTURE
NT1 cilia
NT1 fimbriae
NT1 flagella
NT1 organelles
NT2 centrosomes
NT3 centrioles
NT2 golgi apparatus
NT2 mitochondria
NT2 nuclei

CELL STRUCTURE *cont.*
NT3 chromosomes
NT4 accessory chromosomes
NT5 b chromosomes
NT4 acrocentric chromosomes
NT4 autosomes
NT4 bivalents
NT4 centromeres
NT5 chromocentres
NT4 chromatids
NT4 loci
NT4 microchromosomes
NT4 nucleolus organizer
NT4 polytene chromosomes
NT4 secondary constrictions
NT4 sex chromosomes
NT5 x chromosome
NT5 y chromosome
NT4 submetacentric
NT4 telocentrics
NT3 nuclear inclusions
NT3 nucleolus
NT3 pronucleus
rt cell membranes
rt cell ultrastructure
rt cell walls
rt cells
rt cellular biology
rt cytology
rt cytoplasm
rt cytoplasmic inclusions
rt structure

CELL SUSPENSIONS
rt cell culture
rt cells
rt tissue culture

CELL ULTRASTRUCTURE
BT1 ultrastructure
NT1 plasmalemma
rt cell structure
rt cells
rt cytology
rt microvilli
rt organelles

CELL WALL COMPONENTS
NT1 murein
rt cell walls

CELL WALLS
rt callose
rt cell membranes
rt cell structure
rt cell wall components
rt cellulose
rt endocytosis
rt glucomannans
rt lignification
rt pits
rt plasmodesmata
rt plasmolysis
rt suberization

CELLANA
BT1 patellidae
BT2 gastropoda
BT3 mollusca
NT1 cellana tramoserica

CELLANA TRAMOSERICA
BT1 cellana
BT2 patellidae
BT3 gastropoda
BT4 mollusca

CELLARS
rt buildings
rt pits
rt storage
rt underground storage

CELLOBIOSE
BT1 disaccharides
BT2 oligosaccharides
BT3 carbohydrates
BT1 reducing sugars
BT2 sugars
BT3 carbohydrates

CELLOPHANE (AGRICOLA)
BT1 packaging materials
BT2 materials

CELLS
NT1 adipocytes
NT1 aleurone cells
NT1 blood cells
NT2 erythrocytes
NT3 reticulocytes
NT2 haemocytes
NT2 leukocytes
NT3 granulocytes
NT4 basophils
NT4 eosinophils
NT4 neutrophils
NT3 lymphocytes
NT4 b lymphocytes
NT4 immunocytes
NT4 melanocytes
NT4 natural killer cells
NT4 t lymphocytes
NT5 cytotoxic t lymphocytes
NT5 suppressor cells
NT4 thymocytes
NT3 macrophages
NT3 monocytes
NT2 phagocytes
NT3 macrophages
NT3 neutrophils
NT2 platelets
NT1 bone marrow cells
NT1 chondrocytes
NT1 embryonic stem cells
NT1 erythroblasts
NT1 eukaryotes
NT1 fibroblasts
NT1 germ cells
NT2 ova
NT3 cumulus oophorus
NT3 helminth ova
NT3 oocytes
NT4 germinal vesicle
NT3 oogonia
NT3 zona pellucida
NT2 spermatogonia
NT2 spermatozoa
NT3 accessory spermatozoa
NT3 acrosome
NT3 midpiece
NT1 giant cells
NT1 gonadotropic cells
NT1 granulosa cells
NT1 histiocytes
NT1 hybridomas
NT1 immunocompetent cells
NT1 liver cells
NT1 luteal cells
NT1 mast cells
NT1 microcell hybrids
NT1 microsomes
NT1 nerve cells
NT2 ganglia
NT1 plasma cells
NT1 spermatids
NT1 spermatocytes
NT1 spores
NT2 bacterial spores
NT2 fungal spores
NT3 aeciospores
NT3 ascospores
NT3 basidiospores
NT3 chlamydospores
NT3 conidia
NT3 oospores
NT3 zoospores
NT1 thecal cells
rt cell counting
rt cell culture
rt cell division
rt cell growth
rt cell mediated lympholysis
rt cell membranes
rt cell structure
rt cell suspensions
rt cell ultrastructure
rt cellular biology
rt cytochemistry
rt cytology
rt cytolysis

CELLS *cont.*
rt cytomixis
rt cytopathogenicity
rt cytoplasm
rt heterokaryosis
rt intercellular spaces
rt nuclei
rt plant tissues
rt protoplasm
rt tissues
rt tyloses

CELLS (HONEYBEES)
BT1 combs
BT2 hive parts
BT3 movable-comb hives
BT4 hives
NT1 cappings
NT1 queen cells
rt honeybees

CELLULAR BIOLOGY
BT1 biology
rt cell structure
rt cells

cellular immunity
USE **cell mediated immunity**

CELLULASE
(ec 3.2.1.4)
BT1 o-glycoside hydrolases
BT2 glycosidases
BT3 hydrolases
BT4 enzymes

CELLULITIS
BT1 skin diseases
BT2 organic diseases
BT3 diseases
rt inflammation

cellulolysis
USE **cellulose digestion**

CELLULOLYTIC MICROORGANISMS
uf *microorganisms, cellulolytic*
BT1 microorganisms
rt cellulose digestion

CELLULOMONAS
BT1 firmicutes
BT2 bacteria
BT3 prokaryotes

CELLULOSE
BT1 glucans
BT2 polysaccharides
BT3 carbohydrates
NT1 lignocellulose
rt caecotrophy
rt cell walls
rt cellulose acetate
rt cellulose digestion
rt cellulosic wastes
rt fibres
rt pulps
rt pyroxylin
rt roughage
rt wood chemistry
rt xylose

CELLULOSE ACETATE
BT1 acetates (esters)
BT2 acetates
BT2 fatty acid esters
BT3 esters
rt cellulose

CELLULOSE DIGESTION
uf *cellulolysis*
BT1 digestion
BT2 physiological functions
rt cellulolytic microorganisms
rt cellulose

cellulose nitrate
USE **pyroxylin**

CELLULOSE XANTHATE
BT1 soil conditioners
BT2 soil amendments
BT3 amendments

CELLULOSIC FIBERS (AGRICOLA)
BT1 textile fibers
BT2 fibers
NT1 acetate (fiber) (agricola)
NT1 rayon (agricola)
NT1 triacetate (agricola)
rt manmade fibers (agricola)
rt natural fibers (agricola)

CELLULOSIC WASTES
BT1 organic wastes
BT2 wastes
rt cellulose

CELOSIA
BT1 amaranthaceae
NT1 celosia argentea
NT1 celosia argentea var. cristata
NT1 celosia argentea var. plumosa
NT1 celosia crenata

CELOSIA ARGENTEA
BT1 celosia
BT2 amaranthaceae

CELOSIA ARGENTEA VAR. CRISTATA
uf *celosia cristata*
BT1 celosia
BT2 amaranthaceae
BT1 ornamental herbaceous plants

CELOSIA ARGENTEA VAR. PLUMOSA
uf *celosia plumosa*
BT1 celosia
BT2 amaranthaceae
BT1 ornamental herbaceous plants

CELOSIA CRENATA
BT1 celosia
BT2 amaranthaceae

celosia cristata
USE **celosia argentea var. cristata**

celosia plumosa
USE **celosia argentea var. plumosa**

CELTIS
BT1 ulmaceae
NT1 celtis laevigata
NT1 celtis latifolia
NT1 celtis mildbraedii
NT1 celtis occidentalis
NT1 celtis pallida
NT1 celtis philippinensis

celtis integrifolia
USE **celtis laevigata**

CELTIS LAEVIGATA
uf *celtis integrifolia*
BT1 celtis
BT2 ulmaceae
BT1 forest trees
BT1 ornamental woody plants

CELTIS LATIFOLIA
BT1 celtis
BT2 ulmaceae

CELTIS MILDBRAEDII
BT1 celtis
BT2 ulmaceae

CELTIS OCCIDENTALIS
BT1 celtis
BT2 ulmaceae
BT1 ornamental woody plants

CELTIS PALLIDA
BT1 celtis
BT2 ulmaceae

CELTIS PHILIPPINENSIS
BT1 celtis
BT2 ulmaceae

CEMENT
BT1 building materials
BT2 materials
BT1 soil conditioners
BT2 soil amendments
BT3 amendments
NT1 wood cement
rt calcium silicate
rt cement dust
rt concrete
rt mortar

CEMENT DUST
BT1 liming materials
BT2 soil amendments
BT3 amendments
BT1 potassium fertilizers
BT2 fertilizers
rt cement

cemented horizons
USE **indurated horizons**

CEMETERY VASES
BT1 water containers
BT2 containers

cemiostoma
USE **leucoptera**

cemiostoma scitella
USE **leucoptera malifoliella**

CENCHRUS
BT1 gramineae
NT1 cenchrus barbatus
NT1 cenchrus biflorus
NT1 cenchrus brownii
NT1 cenchrus ciliaris
NT1 cenchrus echinatus
NT1 cenchrus incertus
NT1 cenchrus longispinus
NT1 cenchrus prieurii
NT1 cenchrus setigerus
rt pennisetum

CENCHRUS BARBATUS
BT1 cenchrus
BT2 gramineae
BT1 pasture plants

CENCHRUS BIFLORUS
BT1 cenchrus
BT2 gramineae
BT1 pasture plants

CENCHRUS BROWNII
BT1 cenchrus
BT2 gramineae

CENCHRUS CILIARIS
uf *buffel grass*
uf *pennisetum ciliare*
BT1 cenchrus
BT2 gramineae
BT1 pasture plants

CENCHRUS ECHINATUS
BT1 cenchrus
BT2 gramineae
BT1 pasture plants
BT1 weeds

CENCHRUS INCERTUS
uf *cenchrus pauciflorus*
BT1 cenchrus
BT2 gramineae

CENCHRUS LONGISPINUS
BT1 cenchrus
BT2 gramineae
BT1 pasture plants

cenchrus pauciflorus
USE **cenchrus incertus**

CENCHRUS PRIEURII
BT1 cenchrus
BT2 gramineae
BT1 pasture plants

CENCHRUS SETIGERUS
uf *birdwood grass*
BT1 cenchrus
BT2 gramineae

CENCHRUS SETIGERUS *cont.*
BT1 pasture plants

CENOCOCCUM
BT1 deuteromycotina
NT1 cenococcum geophilum
NT1 cenococcum graniforme

CENOCOCCUM GEOPHILUM
BT1 cenococcum
BT2 deuteromycotina
BT1 mycorrhizal fungi
BT2 fungi

CENOCOCCUM GRANIFORME
BT1 cenococcum
BT2 deuteromycotina

CENOPALPUS
BT1 tenuipalpidae
BT2 prostigmata
BT3 acari
NT1 cenopalpus pulcher
rt brevipalpus

CENOPALPUS PULCHER
uf *brevipalpus pulcher*
BT1 cenopalpus
BT2 tenuipalpidae
BT3 prostigmata
BT4 acari

CENSUSES
uf *enumeration surveys*
BT1 surveys
NT1 agricultural censuses
NT2 livestock censuses
NT2 world census of agriculture
rt data collection
rt registration
rt statistics

CENTARANTHERA
BT1 scrophulariaceae

CENTAUREA
BT1 compositae
NT1 centaurea americana
NT1 centaurea aspera
NT1 centaurea australis
NT1 centaurea calcitrapa
NT1 centaurea canariensis
NT1 centaurea cyanus
NT1 centaurea depressa
NT1 centaurea diffusa
NT1 centaurea iberica
NT1 centaurea lugdunensis
NT1 centaurea maculosa
NT1 centaurea melitensis
NT1 centaurea montana
NT1 centaurea picris
NT1 centaurea repens
NT1 centaurea scabiosa
NT1 centaurea solstitialis
NT1 centaurea squarrosa
NT1 centaurea webbiana

CENTAUREA AMERICANA
BT1 centaurea
BT2 compositae
BT1 ornamental herbaceous plants

CENTAUREA ASPERA
BT1 centaurea
BT2 compositae

CENTAUREA AUSTRALIS
BT1 centaurea
BT2 compositae

CENTAUREA CALCITRAPA
BT1 centaurea
BT2 compositae

CENTAUREA CANARIENSIS
BT1 centaurea
BT2 compositae

CENTAUREA CYANUS
BT1 centaurea
BT2 compositae
BT1 ornamental herbaceous plants
BT1 weeds

CENTAUREA DEPRESSA
BT1 centaurea
BT2 compositae

CENTAUREA DIFFUSA
BT1 centaurea
BT2 compositae

CENTAUREA IBERICA
BT1 centaurea
BT2 compositae

CENTAUREA LUGDUNENSIS
BT1 centaurea
BT2 compositae

CENTAUREA MACULOSA
BT1 centaurea
BT2 compositae
BT1 weeds

CENTAUREA MELITENSIS
BT1 centaurea
BT2 compositae

CENTAUREA MONTANA
BT1 centaurea
BT2 compositae
BT1 ornamental herbaceous plants

centaurea moschata
USE **amberboa moschata**

CENTAUREA PICRIS
BT1 centaurea
BT2 compositae

CENTAUREA REPENS
BT1 centaurea
BT2 compositae

CENTAUREA SCABIOSA
BT1 centaurea
BT2 compositae

CENTAUREA SOLSTITIALIS
BT1 centaurea
BT2 compositae
BT1 medicinal plants

CENTAUREA SQUARROSA
BT1 centaurea
BT2 compositae

CENTAUREA WEBBIANA
BT1 centaurea
BT2 compositae

CENTAURIUM
BT1 gentianaceae
NT1 centaurium spicatum

CENTAURIUM SPICATUM
BT1 centaurium
BT2 gentianaceae

CENTELLA
BT1 hydrocotylaceae
NT1 centella asiatica

CENTELLA ASIATICA
BT1 centella
BT2 hydrocotylaceae

CENTER OF GRAVITY
BF centre of gravity

CENTER PIVOT IRRIGATION
BF centre pivot irrigation

CENTERS OF DIVERSITY
BF centres of diversity

CENTERS OF ORIGIN
BF centres of origin

centipedes
USE **chilopoda**

CENTRAL AFRICA
uf *africa, central*
BT1 africa south of sahara
BT2 africa
NT1 burundi
NT1 cameroon
NT1 central african republic

CENTRAL AFRICA *cont.*
NT1 chad
NT1 congo
NT1 equatorial guinea
NT1 gabon
NT1 sao tome and principe
NT1 zaire

central african empire
USE **central african republic**

CENTRAL AFRICAN REPUBLIC
uf *central african empire*
BT1 central africa
BT2 africa south of sahara
BT3 africa
rt acp
rt developing countries
rt francophone africa
rt least developed countries

CENTRAL AMERICA
uf *america, central*
BT1 america
NT1 belize
NT1 costa rica
NT1 el salvador
NT1 guatemala
NT1 honduras
NT1 nicaragua
NT1 panama
NT1 panama canal zone
rt developing countries
rt latin america

central american common market
USE **cacm**

central and upper belgian
USE **belgian blue**

CENTRAL FRANCE
BT1 france
BT2 western europe
BT3 europe

CENTRAL GOVERNMENT
BT1 government
NT1 ministries of agriculture
NT2 usda (agricola)

CENTRAL KITCHENS (AGRICOLA)
BT1 kitchens (agricola)

CENTRAL NERVOUS SYSTEM
uf *cns*
uf *nervous system, central*
BT1 nervous system
BT2 body parts
NT1 brain
NT2 cerebellum
NT3 amygdala
NT2 cerebral cortex
NT2 cerebral ventricles
NT2 hippocampus
NT2 hypothalamus
NT3 preoptic area
NT2 medulla oblongata
NT2 thalamus
NT1 brain stem
NT1 central nervous system centres
NT1 cerebrospinal tracts
NT1 peripheral nerves
NT2 vagus nerve
NT1 spinal cord
NT1 spinal ganglia
rt lesch-nyhan syndrome
rt meninges
rt strychnine

CENTRAL NERVOUS SYSTEM CENTERS
BF central nervous system centres

CENTRAL NERVOUS SYSTEM CENTRES
AF central nervous system centers
BT1 central nervous system
BT2 nervous system
BT3 body parts

CENTRAL PLACES
rt geographical distribution
rt location of production
rt location theory
rt spatial equilibrium analysis

CENTRAL PYRENEAN
BT1 sheep breeds
BT2 breeds

CENTRAL SOUTHERN CHINA
uf *china (central southern region)*
uf *wuhan*
BT1 china
BT2 east asia
BT3 asia

CENTRAL WEST BRAZIL
uf *brazil (central west)*
BT1 brazil
BT2 south america
BT3 america

CENTRALIZATION
BT1 socioeconomic organization
rt decentralization
rt regionalization

CENTRALLY PLANNED ECONOMIES
uf *socialist countries*
BT1 economic systems
BT2 systems
rt china
rt cmea
rt mixed economies
rt socialist agriculture

CENTRANTHERA
BT1 scrophulariaceae
NT1 centranthera nepalensis

CENTRANTHERA NEPALENSIS
BT1 centranthera
BT2 scrophulariaceae

CENTRANTHUS
BT1 valerianaceae
NT1 centranthus longiflorus
NT1 centranthus ruber

CENTRANTHUS LONGIFLORUS
BT1 centranthus
BT2 valerianaceae

CENTRANTHUS RUBER
BT1 centranthus
BT2 valerianaceae
BT1 medicinal plants

CENTRARCHIDAE
BT1 perciformes
BT2 osteichthyes
BT3 fishes
NT1 lepomis
NT2 lepomis cyanellus
NT2 lepomis gibbosus
NT2 lepomis macrochirus
rt sunfishes

CENTRATHERUM
BT1 compositae
NT1 centratherum punctatum

CENTRATHERUM PUNCTATUM
BT1 centratherum
BT2 compositae
BT1 medicinal plants

CENTRE OF GRAVITY
AF center of gravity
rt gravity

CENTRE PIVOT IRRIGATION
AF center pivot irrigation
uf *irrigation, centre pivot*
BT1 sprinkler irrigation
BT2 irrigation

CENTRES OF DIVERSITY
AF centers of diversity
rt evolution
rt genetic resources

CENTRES OF ORIGIN
AF centers of origin
rt evolution
rt genetic resources
rt origin
rt sources
rt spread

CENTRIFUGAL FANS
uf *fans, centrifugal*
BT1 fans
BT2 components
rt axial flow fans

CENTRIFUGAL PUMPS
BT1 pumps
BT2 machinery

CENTRIFUGAL SEED CLEANERS
uf *cleaners, centrifugal seed*
BT1 seed cleaners
BT2 cleaners
BT3 machinery

CENTRIFUGALS
HN from 1990
BT1 centrifuges
BT2 separators
BT3 machinery
NT1 continuous centrifugals
rt teapot effect

CENTRIFUGATION
BT1 separation
NT1 density gradient centrifugation
NT1 ultracentrifugation

CENTRIFUGES
BT1 separators
BT2 machinery
NT1 centrifugals
NT2 continuous centrifugals
rt separation

CENTRIOLES
BT1 centrosomes
BT2 organelles
BT3 cell structure
rt mitosis

CENTRIS
uf *hemisia*
BT1 apidae
BT2 hymenoptera

CENTROLOBIUM
BT1 leguminosae
NT1 centrolobium tomentosum

CENTROLOBIUM TOMENTOSUM
BT1 centrolobium
BT2 leguminosae

CENTROMERES
BT1 chromosomes
BT2 nuclei
BT3 organelles
BT4 cell structure
NT1 chromocentres
rt telocentrics

CENTROPOMIDAE
BT1 perciformes
BT2 osteichthyes
BT3 fishes
NT1 centropomus
NT2 centropomus undecimalis
NT1 lates
NT2 lates calcarifer
NT2 lates niloticus

CENTROPOMUS
BT1 centropomidae
BT2 perciformes
BT3 osteichthyes
BT4 fishes
NT1 centropomus undecimalis

CENTROPOMUS UNDECIMALIS
uf *snook*
BT1 centropomus
BT2 centropomidae
BT3 perciformes
BT4 osteichthyes

CENTROPOMUS UNDECIMALIS *cont.*
BT5 fishes

CENTROPRISTIS
BT1 serranidae
BT2 perciformes
BT3 osteichthyes
BT4 fishes

CENTRORHYNCHIDAE
BT1 acanthocephala
NT1 centrorhynchus

CENTRORHYNCHUS
BT1 centrorhynchidae
BT2 acanthocephala

CENTROSCYLLIUM
BT1 squalidae
BT2 squaliformes
BT3 chondrichthyes
BT4 fishes

CENTROSEMA
BT1 leguminosae
NT1 centrosema pascuorum
NT1 centrosema plumieri
NT1 centrosema pubescens

CENTROSEMA PASCUORUM
HN from 1989
BT1 centrosema
BT2 leguminosae

CENTROSEMA PLUMIERI
BT1 centrosema
BT2 leguminosae
BT1 green manures
BT2 manures
BT3 organic amendments
BT4 soil amendments
BT5 amendments

CENTROSEMA PUBESCENS
BT1 centrosema
BT2 leguminosae
BT1 green manures
BT2 manures
BT3 organic amendments
BT4 soil amendments
BT5 amendments
BT1 pasture legumes
BT2 legumes
BT2 pasture plants

CENTROSOMES
BT1 organelles
BT2 cell structure
NT1 centrioles

CENTRUROIDES
BT1 buthidae
BT2 scorpiones
BT3 arachnida
BT4 arthropods
NT1 centruroides gracilis
NT1 centruroides limpidus
NT2 centruroides limpidus limpidus
NT2 centruroides limpidus tecomanus
NT1 centruroides noxius
NT1 centruroides sculpturatus

CENTRUROIDES GRACILIS
BT1 centruroides
BT2 buthidae
BT3 scorpiones
BT4 arachnida
BT5 arthropods

CENTRUROIDES LIMPIDUS
HN from 1990
BT1 centruroides
BT2 buthidae
BT3 scorpiones
BT4 arachnida
BT5 arthropods
NT1 centruroides limpidus limpidus
NT1 centruroides limpidus tecomanus

CENTRUROIDES LIMPIDUS LIMPIDUS
HN from 1990
BT1 centruroides limpidus
BT2 centruroides
BT3 buthidae
BT4 scorpiones
BT5 arachnida
BT6 arthropods

CENTRUROIDES LIMPIDUS TECOMANUS
HN from 1990
BT1 centruroides limpidus
BT2 centruroides
BT3 buthidae
BT4 scorpiones
BT5 arachnida
BT6 arthropods

CENTRUROIDES NOXIUS
HN from 1989
BT1 centruroides
BT2 buthidae
BT3 scorpiones
BT4 arachnida
BT5 arthropods

CENTRUROIDES SCULPTURATUS
BT1 centruroides
BT2 buthidae
BT3 scorpiones
BT4 arachnida
BT5 arthropods

CEPAEA
BT1 helicidae
BT2 gastropoda
BT3 mollusca
NT1 cepaea hortensis
NT1 cepaea nemoralis
rt helix

CEPAEA HORTENSIS
uf *helix hortensis*
BT1 cepaea
BT2 helicidae
BT3 gastropoda
BT4 mollusca

CEPAEA NEMORALIS
HN from 1990
uf *helix nemoralis*
BT1 cepaea
BT2 helicidae
BT3 gastropoda
BT4 mollusca

CEPFAR
(european training and development centre for farming and rural life)
BT1 international organizations
BT2 organizations

CEPHAELIS
BT1 rubiaceae
NT1 cephaelis acuminata
NT1 cephaelis ipecacuanha

CEPHAELIS ACUMINATA
BT1 cephaelis
BT2 rubiaceae

CEPHAELIS IPECACUANHA
uf *psychotria ipecacuanha*
BT1 cephaelis
BT2 rubiaceae

CEPHALANTHERA
BT1 orchidaceae
rt ornamental orchids

CEPHALARIA
BT1 dipsacaceae
NT1 cephalaria gigantea
NT1 cephalaria syriaca

CEPHALARIA GIGANTEA
BT1 cephalaria
BT2 dipsacaceae

CEPHALARIA SYRIACA
BT1 cephalaria
BT2 dipsacaceae

CEPHALASPIDOMORPHI
BT1 fishes
NT1 petromyzontiformes
NT2 petromyzontidae
NT3 lampetra
NT4 lampetra fluviatilis
NT3 petromyzon

CEPHALCIA
BT1 pamphiliidae
BT2 hymenoptera
NT1 cephalcia abietis

CEPHALCIA ABIETIS
BT1 cephalcia
BT2 pamphiliidae
BT3 hymenoptera

CEPHALENCHUS
BT1 tylenchidae
BT2 nematoda
NT1 cephalenchus emarginatus

CEPHALENCHUS EMARGINATUS
BT1 cephalenchus
BT2 tylenchidae
BT3 nematoda

CEPHALETA
uf *anysis*
BT1 pteromalidae
BT2 hymenoptera
NT1 cephaleta brunniventris

cephaleta alcocki
USE **cephaleta brunniventris**

CEPHALETA BRUNNIVENTRIS
HN from 1989
uf *anysis alcocki*
uf *cephaleta alcocki*
BT1 cephaleta
BT2 pteromalidae
BT3 hymenoptera

CEPHALEUROS
BT1 chlorophyta
BT2 algae
NT1 cephaleuros virescens

cephaleuros mycoidea
USE **cephaleuros virescens**

cephaleuros parasiticus
USE **cephaleuros virescens**

CEPHALEUROS VIRESCENS
uf *cephaleuros mycoidea*
uf *cephaleuros parasiticus*
BT1 cephaleuros
BT2 chlorophyta
BT3 algae

CEPHALINS
BT1 glycerophospholipids
BT2 phospholipids
BT3 lipids
NT1 phosphatidylethanolamines
NT1 phosphatidylserines

CEPHALOBAENIDA
BT1 pentastomida
BT2 arthropods
NT1 raillietiella

CEPHALOBIDAE
BT1 nematoda
NT1 acrobeloides
NT1 turbatrix
NT2 turbatrix aceti
rt free living nematodes

CEPHALOBUS
HN from 1990
BT1 belondiridae
BT2 nematoda

CEPHALOCEREUS
uf *pilocereus*
BT1 cactaceae
NT1 cephalocereus albispinus
NT1 cephalocereus chrysacanthus
NT1 cephalocereus guerreronis
NT1 cephalocereus maxonii

CEPHALOCEREUS *cont.*
NT1 cephalocereus senilis

CEPHALOCEREUS ALBISPINUS
BT1 cephalocereus
BT2 cactaceae
BT1 ornamental succulent plants
BT2 succulent plants

CEPHALOCEREUS CHRYSACANTHUS
BT1 cephalocereus
BT2 cactaceae
BT1 ornamental succulent plants
BT2 succulent plants

CEPHALOCEREUS GUERRERONIS
BT1 cephalocereus
BT2 cactaceae
BT1 ornamental succulent plants
BT2 succulent plants

CEPHALOCEREUS MAXONII
BT1 cephalocereus
BT2 cactaceae
BT1 ornamental succulent plants
BT2 succulent plants

CEPHALOCEREUS SENILIS
BT1 cephalocereus
BT2 cactaceae
BT1 ornamental succulent plants
BT2 succulent plants

CEPHALOIDOPHORA
BT1 apicomplexa
BT2 protozoa
NT1 cephaloidophora conformis

CEPHALOIDOPHORA CONFORMIS
BT1 cephaloidophora
BT2 apicomplexa
BT3 protozoa

CEPHALONEMA
BT1 tiliaceae

CEPHALONOMIA
HN from 1989
BT1 bethylidae
BT2 hymenoptera

cephalophora
USE **helenium**

CEPHALOPHYLLUM
BT1 aizoaceae
NT1 cephalophyllum loreum

CEPHALOPHYLLUM LOREUM
BT1 cephalophyllum
BT2 aizoaceae
BT1 ornamental succulent plants
BT2 succulent plants

CEPHALOPINA
BT1 oestridae
BT2 diptera
NT1 cephalopina titillator

CEPHALOPINA TITILLATOR
BT1 cephalopina
BT2 oestridae
BT3 diptera

CEPHALOPODA
BT1 mollusca
NT1 loliginidae
NT2 alloteuthis
NT2 loligo
NT3 loligo reynaudi
NT1 octopodidae
NT2 eledone
NT2 octopus
NT3 octopus vulgaris
NT1 ommastrephidae
NT2 ommastrephes
NT2 todarodes
NT3 todarodes pacificus
NT1 sepiidae
NT2 sepia
NT1 sepiolidae
NT2 sepiola

CEPHALORHYNCHUS
BT1 delphinidae
BT2 odontoceti
BT3 cetacea
BT4 mammals

CEPHALOSPHAERA
BT1 myristicaceae
NT1 cephalosphaera usambarensis

CEPHALOSPHAERA USAMBARENSIS
BT1 cephalosphaera
BT2 myristicaceae

CEPHALOSPORINS
BT1 antibacterial agents
BT2 antiinfective agents
BT3 drugs
BT1 antibiotics

CEPHALOSPORIUM
BT1 deuteromycotina
rt acremonium
rt hymenula
rt phialophora

cephalosporium acremonium
USE **acremonium strictum**

cephalosporium falciforme
USE **acremonium falciforme**

cephalosporium gramineum
USE **hymenula cerealis**

cephalosporium gregatum
USE **phialophora gregata**

cephalosporium kiliense
USE **acremonium kiliense**

cephalosporium recifei
USE **acremonium recifei**

CEPHALOTACEAE
NT1 cephalotus
NT2 cephalotus follicularis

CEPHALOTAXUS
BT1 taxaceae
NT1 cephalotaxus harringtonia
NT1 cephalotaxus mannii
NT1 cephalotaxus oliveri
NT1 cephalotaxus wilsoniana

CEPHALOTAXUS HARRINGTONIA
BT1 cephalotaxus
BT2 taxaceae
BT1 ornamental conifers
BT2 conifers
BT2 ornamental woody plants

CEPHALOTAXUS MANNII
BT1 cephalotaxus
BT2 taxaceae
BT1 medicinal plants

CEPHALOTAXUS OLIVERI
BT1 cephalotaxus
BT2 taxaceae

CEPHALOTAXUS WILSONIANA
BT1 cephalotaxus
BT2 taxaceae

CEPHALOTHECIUM
BT1 deuteromycotina
rt trichothecium

cephalothecium roseum
USE **trichothecium roseum**

cephalotrigona
USE **trigona**

CEPHALOTUS
BT1 cephalotaceae
NT1 cephalotus follicularis

CEPHALOTUS FOLLICULARIS
BT1 cephalotus
BT2 cephalotaceae

CEPHEIDAE
BT1 cryptostigmata

CEPHEIDAE *cont.*
BT2 acari
NT1 eupterotegaeus
NT2 eupterotegaeus rostratus

CEPHENEMYIA
BT1 oestridae
BT2 diptera
NT1 cephenemyia auribarbis
NT1 cephenemyia stimulator
NT1 cephenemyia trompe

CEPHENEMYIA AURIBARBIS
BT1 cephenemyia
BT2 oestridae
BT3 diptera

CEPHENEMYIA STIMULATOR
HN from 1990
BT1 cephenemyia
BT2 oestridae
BT3 diptera

CEPHENEMYIA TROMPE
BT1 cephenemyia
BT2 oestridae
BT3 diptera

CEPHIDAE
BT1 hymenoptera
NT1 cephus
NT2 cephus cinctus
NT2 cephus pygmeus
NT1 trachelus
NT2 trachelus tabidus

CEPHUS
BT1 cephidae
BT2 hymenoptera
NT1 cephus cinctus
NT1 cephus pygmeus

CEPHUS CINCTUS
BT1 cephus
BT2 cephidae
BT3 hymenoptera

CEPHUS PYGMEUS
BT1 cephus
BT2 cephidae
BT3 hymenoptera

CEPPHUS
BT1 alcidae
BT2 charadriiformes
BT3 birds

CERACIA
uf *myothyria*
BT1 tachinidae
BT2 diptera
NT1 ceracia fergusoni

CERACIA FERGUSONI
uf *myothyria fergusoni*
BT1 ceracia
BT2 tachinidae
BT3 diptera

CERAMBYCIDAE
BT1 coleoptera
NT1 arhopalus
NT2 arhopalus rusticus
NT2 arhopalus syriacus
NT1 cerambyx
NT2 cerambyx dux
NT1 dectes
NT2 dectes texanus
NT1 enaphalodes
NT2 enaphalodes rufulus
NT1 hylotrupes
NT2 hylotrupes bajulus
NT1 megacyllene
NT2 megacyllene robiniae
NT1 migdolus
NT2 migdolus fryanus
NT1 monochamus
NT2 monochamus alternatus
NT2 monochamus carolinensis
NT2 monochamus galloprovincialis
NT2 monochamus scutellatus
NT2 monochamus sutor
NT2 monochamus titillator

CERAMBYCIDAE *cont.*
NT2 monochamus urussovii
NT1 oberea
NT1 obereopsis
NT2 obereopsis brevis
NT1 oncideres
NT1 phoracantha
NT2 phoracantha semipunctata
NT1 plocaederus
NT2 plocaederus ferrugineus
NT1 rhagium
NT2 rhagium bifasciatum
NT2 rhagium inquisitor
NT1 saperda
NT2 saperda carcharias
NT2 saperda populnea
NT2 saperda scalaris
NT1 semanotus
NT2 semanotus japonicus
NT1 steirastoma
NT2 steirastoma breve
NT1 tetropium
NT1 xylotrechus
NT2 xylotrechus pyrrhoderus

CERAMBYX
BT1 cerambycidae
BT2 coleoptera
NT1 cerambyx dux

CERAMBYX DUX
BT1 cerambyx
BT2 cerambycidae
BT3 coleoptera

CERAMICS
BT1 materials
rt clay

CERAPHRONIDAE
BT1 hymenoptera
NT1 aphanogmus

CERAPTERYX
BT1 noctuidae
BT2 lepidoptera
NT1 cerapteryx graminis

CERAPTERYX GRAMINIS
BT1 cerapteryx
BT2 noctuidae
BT3 lepidoptera

CERASTIUM
BT1 caryophyllaceae
NT1 cerastium arvense
NT1 cerastium atrovirens
NT1 cerastium biebersteinii
NT1 cerastium caespitosum
NT1 cerastium fontanum
NT1 cerastium holosteoides

CERASTIUM ARVENSE
BT1 cerastium
BT2 caryophyllaceae

CERASTIUM ATROVIRENS
BT1 cerastium
BT2 caryophyllaceae

CERASTIUM BIEBERSTEINII
BT1 cerastium
BT2 caryophyllaceae
BT1 ornamental herbaceous plants

CERASTIUM CAESPITOSUM
BT1 cerastium
BT2 caryophyllaceae

CERASTIUM FONTANUM
BT1 cerastium
BT2 caryophyllaceae

CERASTIUM HOLOSTEOIDES
uf *cerastium vulgatum*
BT1 cerastium
BT2 caryophyllaceae

cerastium vulgatum
USE **cerastium holosteoides**

cerasus
USE **prunus**

CERATINA
BT1 apidae
BT2 hymenoptera

CERATITIS
uf *pterandrus*
BT1 tephritidae
BT2 diptera
NT1 ceratitis capitata
NT1 ceratitis rosa

CERATITIS CAPITATA
BT1 ceratitis
BT2 tephritidae
BT3 diptera

CERATITIS ROSA
uf *pterandrus rosa*
BT1 ceratitis
BT2 tephritidae
BT3 diptera

ceratixodes
USE **ixodes**

ceratixodes putus
USE **ixodes uriae**

CERATOBASIDIUM
HN from 1990
BT1 tulasnellales
NT1 ceratobasidium oryzae-sativae
rt rhizoctonia
rt sclerotium

CERATOBASIDIUM ORYZAE-SATIVAE
HN from 1990
uf *rhizoctonia oryzae-sativae*
uf *sclerotium oryzae-sativae*
BT1 ceratobasidium
BT2 tulasnellales

ceratochaeta
USE **zenillia**

ceratochaeta caudata
USE **phryxe caudata**

ceratochloa
USE **bromus**

ceratochloa unioloides
USE **bromus catharticus**

ceratocide
USE **nystatin**

CERATOCYSTIS
BT1 ophiostomatales
NT1 ceratocystis fagacearum
NT1 ceratocystis fimbriata
NT1 ceratocystis minor
NT1 ceratocystis paradoxa
NT1 ceratocystis piceae
NT1 ceratocystis ulmi
NT1 ceratocystis wageneri
rt ophiostoma
rt thielaviopsis
rt verticicladiella

CERATOCYSTIS FAGACEARUM
BT1 ceratocystis
BT2 ophiostomatales

CERATOCYSTIS FIMBRIATA
BT1 ceratocystis
BT2 ophiostomatales

CERATOCYSTIS MINOR
HN from 1990
uf *ceratocystis pini*
BT1 ceratocystis
BT2 ophiostomatales

CERATOCYSTIS PARADOXA
uf *thielaviopsis paradoxa*
BT1 ceratocystis
BT2 ophiostomatales

CERATOCYSTIS PICEAE
BT1 ceratocystis
BT2 ophiostomatales

ceratocystis pini
USE **ceratocystis minor**

ceratocystis stenoceras
USE **ophiostoma stenoceras**

CERATOCYSTIS ULMI
uf *ophiostoma ulmi*
BT1 ceratocystis
BT2 ophiostomatales
rt ceratoulmin

CERATOCYSTIS WAGENERI
uf *verticicladiella wageneri*
BT1 ceratocystis
BT2 ophiostomatales

ceratoides
USE **krascheninnikovia**

CERATOMYXA
BT1 myxozoa
BT2 protozoa
NT1 ceratomyxa hokarari
NT1 ceratomyxa hopkinsi
NT1 ceratomyxa shasta

CERATOMYXA HOKARARI
BT1 ceratomyxa
BT2 myxozoa
BT3 protozoa

CERATOMYXA HOPKINSI
BT1 ceratomyxa
BT2 myxozoa
BT3 protozoa

CERATOMYXA SHASTA
BT1 ceratomyxa
BT2 myxozoa
BT3 protozoa

CERATONIA
BT1 leguminosae
NT1 ceratonia siliqua

CERATONIA SILIQUA
BT1 ceratonia
BT2 leguminosae
BT1 fodder legumes
BT2 fodder plants
BT2 legumes
rt carob meal
rt carobs
rt food additives

CERATOPHYLLACEAE
NT1 ceratophyllum
NT2 ceratophyllum demersum
NT2 ceratophyllum muricatum
NT2 ceratophyllum submersum

CERATOPHYLLIDAE
BT1 siphonaptera
NT1 callopsylla
NT1 ceratophyllus
NT2 ceratophyllus anisus
NT2 ceratophyllus celsus
NT2 ceratophyllus farreni
NT2 ceratophyllus gallinae
NT2 ceratophyllus hirundinis
NT2 ceratophyllus sciurorum
NT2 ceratophyllus styx
NT1 citellophilus
NT2 citellophilus tesquorum
NT1 megabothris
NT2 megabothris turbidus
NT1 nosopsyllus
NT2 nosopsyllus consimilis
NT2 nosopsyllus fasciatus
NT2 nosopsyllus laeviceps
NT1 orchopeas
NT2 orchopeas howardii
NT2 orchopeas leucopus
NT1 oropsylla
NT1 tarsopsylla
NT2 tarsopsylla octodecimdentata

CERATOPHYLLUM
BT1 ceratophyllaceae
NT1 ceratophyllum demersum
NT1 ceratophyllum muricatum
NT1 ceratophyllum submersum

CERATOPHYLLUM DEMERSUM
BT1 ceratophyllum
BT2 ceratophyllaceae
BT1 weeds

CERATOPHYLLUM MURICATUM
BT1 ceratophyllum
BT2 ceratophyllaceae

CERATOPHYLLUM SUBMERSUM
BT1 ceratophyllum
BT2 ceratophyllaceae

CERATOPHYLLUS
uf *monopsyllus*
BT1 ceratophyllidae
BT2 siphonaptera
NT1 ceratophyllus anisus
NT1 ceratophyllus celsus
NT1 ceratophyllus farreni
NT1 ceratophyllus gallinae
NT1 ceratophyllus hirundinis
NT1 ceratophyllus sciurorum
NT1 ceratophyllus styx
rt citellophilus
rt nosopsyllus

CERATOPHYLLUS ANISUS
uf *monopsyllus anisus*
BT1 ceratophyllus
BT2 ceratophyllidae
BT3 siphonaptera

CERATOPHYLLUS CELSUS
BT1 ceratophyllus
BT2 ceratophyllidae
BT3 siphonaptera

ceratophyllus consimilis
USE **nosopsyllus consimilis**

CERATOPHYLLUS FARRENI
BT1 ceratophyllus
BT2 ceratophyllidae
BT3 siphonaptera

CERATOPHYLLUS GALLINAE
BT1 ceratophyllus
BT2 ceratophyllidae
BT3 siphonaptera

CERATOPHYLLUS HIRUNDINIS
BT1 ceratophyllus
BT2 ceratophyllidae
BT3 siphonaptera

ceratophyllus laeviceps
USE **nosopsyllus laeviceps**

CERATOPHYLLUS SCIURORUM
uf *monopsyllus sciurorum*
BT1 ceratophyllus
BT2 ceratophyllidae
BT3 siphonaptera

CERATOPHYLLUS STYX
BT1 ceratophyllus
BT2 ceratophyllidae
BT3 siphonaptera

ceratophyllus tesquorum
USE **citellophilus tesquorum**

CERATOPOGONIDAE
BT1 diptera
NT1 culicoides
NT2 culicoides arakawai
NT2 culicoides barbosai
NT2 culicoides biguttatus
NT2 culicoides brevitarsis
NT2 culicoides circumscriptus
NT2 culicoides denningi
NT2 culicoides edeni
NT2 culicoides fascipennis
NT2 culicoides furens
NT2 culicoides grisescens
NT2 culicoides hieroglyphicus
NT2 culicoides hollensis
NT2 culicoides imicola
NT2 culicoides impunctatus
NT2 culicoides insignis
NT2 culicoides jamesi
NT2 culicoides kingi
NT2 culicoides melleus
NT2 culicoides mississippiensis

CERATOPOGONIDAE *cont.*
NT2 culicoides nubeculosus
NT2 culicoides obsoletus
NT2 culicoides oxystoma
NT2 culicoides pallidicornis
NT2 culicoides paraensis
NT2 culicoides pulicaris
NT2 culicoides punctatus
NT2 culicoides puncticollis
NT2 culicoides pusillus
NT2 culicoides riethi
NT2 culicoides salinarius
NT2 culicoides schultzei
NT2 culicoides stellifer
NT2 culicoides variipennis
NT2 culicoides venustus
NT2 culicoides wadai
NT1 forcipomyia
NT2 forcipomyia sibirica
NT1 leptoconops
NT2 leptoconops bequaerti
NT2 leptoconops kerteszi

CERATOPTERIS
BT1 parkeriaceae
NT1 ceratopteris thalictroides

CERATOPTERIS THALICTROIDES
BT1 ceratopteris
BT2 parkeriaceae

ceratosphaeria grisea
USE **magnaporthe grisea**

CERATOSTIGMA
BT1 plumbaginaceae
NT1 ceratostigma plumbaginoides

CERATOSTIGMA PLUMBAGINOIDES
BT1 antibacterial plants
BT1 ceratostigma
BT2 plumbaginaceae
BT1 ornamental woody plants

CERATOTHECA
BT1 pedaliaceae
NT1 ceratotheca sesamoides

CERATOTHECA SESAMOIDES
BT1 ceratotheca
BT2 pedaliaceae

CERATOTHERIUM
BT1 rhinocerotidae
BT2 perissodactyla
BT3 mammals
BT3 ungulates
NT1 ceratotherium simum
rt diceros

CERATOTHERIUM SIMUM
uf *diceros simus*
BT1 ceratotherium
BT2 rhinocerotidae
BT3 perissodactyla
BT4 mammals
BT4 ungulates

CERATOULMIN
BT1 mycotoxins
BT2 toxins
rt ceratocystis ulmi

CERATOZAMIA
BT1 zamiaceae
NT1 ceratozamia mexicana

CERATOZAMIA MEXICANA
BT1 ceratozamia
BT2 zamiaceae

CERBERA
BT1 apocynaceae
NT1 cerbera manghas
NT1 cerbera odollam

CERBERA MANGHAS
BT1 cerbera
BT2 apocynaceae
BT1 poisonous plants

CERBERA ODOLLAM
BT1 cerbera

CERBERA ODOLLAM *cont.*
BT2 apocynaceae
BT1 medicinal plants

CERCARIAE
BT1 digenean larvae
BT2 helminth larvae
BT3 helminths
BT4 parasites
BT3 larvae
BT4 developmental stages
rt cercarial dermatitis

CERCARIAL DERMATITIS
uf *swimmer's itch*
BT1 dermatitis
BT2 skin diseases
BT3 organic diseases
BT4 diseases
rt cercariae

CERCIDIPHYLLACEAE
NT1 cercidiphyllum
NT2 cercidiphyllum japonicum

CERCIDIPHYLLUM
BT1 cercidiphyllaceae
NT1 cercidiphyllum japonicum

CERCIDIPHYLLUM JAPONICUM
BT1 cercidiphyllum
BT2 cercidiphyllaceae
BT1 ornamental woody plants

CERCIDIUM
BT1 leguminosae
NT1 cercidium microphyllum

CERCIDIUM MICROPHYLLUM
BT1 browse plants
BT1 cercidium
BT2 leguminosae

CERCIS
BT1 leguminosae
NT1 cercis canadensis
NT1 cercis chinensis
NT1 cercis lutea
NT1 cercis occidentalis
NT1 cercis siliquastrum

CERCIS CANADENSIS
BT1 cercis
BT2 leguminosae
BT1 forest trees
BT1 ornamental woody plants

CERCIS CHINENSIS
BT1 browse plants
BT1 cercis
BT2 leguminosae

CERCIS LUTEA
BT1 cercis
BT2 leguminosae

CERCIS OCCIDENTALIS
BT1 cercis
BT2 leguminosae
BT1 ornamental woody plants

CERCIS SILIQUASTRUM
BT1 cercis
BT2 leguminosae
BT1 ornamental woody plants

CERCOCARPUS
BT1 rosaceae
NT1 cercocarpus betuloides
NT1 cercocarpus breviflorus
NT1 cercocarpus ledifolius
NT1 cercocarpus montanus

CERCOCARPUS BETULOIDES
BT1 browse plants
BT1 cercocarpus
BT2 rosaceae

CERCOCARPUS BREVIFLORUS
BT1 cercocarpus
BT2 rosaceae

CERCOCARPUS LEDIFOLIUS
BT1 cercocarpus
BT2 rosaceae

CERCOCARPUS LEDIFOLIUS *cont.*
BT1 forest trees

CERCOCARPUS MONTANUS
BT1 cercocarpus
BT2 rosaceae

CERCOCEBUS
uf *mangabeys*
BT1 cercopithecidae
BT2 primates
BT3 mammals

CERCOPIDAE
BT1 cercopoidea
BT2 auchenorrhyncha
BT3 homoptera
NT1 aeneolamia
NT2 aeneolamia contigua
NT2 aeneolamia selecta
NT2 aeneolamia varia
NT1 deois
NT2 deois flavopicta
NT2 deois schach
NT1 mahanarva
NT2 mahanarva fimbriolata
NT2 mahanarva posticata
NT1 zulia
NT2 zulia colombiana
NT2 zulia entreriana

CERCOPITHECIDAE
(old-world monkeys)
BT1 primates
BT2 mammals
NT1 cercocebus
NT1 cercopithecus
NT2 cercopithecus aethiops
NT2 cercopithecus mitis
NT1 colobus
NT2 colobus guereza
NT1 erythrocebus
NT2 erythrocebus patas
NT1 macaca
NT2 macaca arctoides
NT2 macaca cyclopis
NT2 macaca fascicularis
NT2 macaca mulatta
NT2 macaca nemestrina
NT2 macaca radiata
NT1 papio
NT2 papio anubis
NT2 papio cynocephalus
NT1 presbytis
NT2 presbytis cristata
NT2 presbytis entellus
NT2 presbytis melalophos
rt monkeys

CERCOPITHECUS
BT1 cercopithecidae
BT2 primates
BT3 mammals
NT1 cercopithecus aethiops
NT1 cercopithecus mitis

CERCOPITHECUS AETHIOPS
uf *cercopithecus pygerythrus*
BT1 cercopithecus
BT2 cercopithecidae
BT3 primates
BT4 mammals

CERCOPITHECUS MITIS
BT1 cercopithecus
BT2 cercopithecidae
BT3 primates
BT4 mammals

cercopithecus pygerythrus
USE **cercopithecus aethiops**

CERCOPOIDEA
BT1 auchenorrhyncha
BT2 homoptera
NT1 aphrophoridae
NT2 aphrophora
NT3 aphrophora alni
NT2 philaenus
NT3 philaenus spumarius
NT1 cercopidae
NT2 aeneolamia
NT3 aeneolamia contigua

CERCOPOIDEA *cont.*
NT3 aeneolamia selecta
NT3 aeneolamia varia
NT2 deois
NT3 deois flavopicta
NT3 deois schach
NT2 mahanarva
NT3 mahanarva fimbriolata
NT3 mahanarva posticata
NT2 zulia
NT3 zulia colombiana
NT3 zulia entreriana
NT1 machaerotidae
NT2 hindola
NT3 hindola fulva
NT3 hindola striata

CERCOSEPTORIA
BT1 deuteromycotina
NT1 cercoseptoria theae
rt mycosphaerella
rt pseudocercospora

cercoseptoria heteromalla
USE **pseudocercospora heteromalla**

cercoseptoria pini-densiflorae
USE **mycosphaerella gibsonii**

CERCOSEPTORIA THEAE
uf *cercospora theae*
BT1 cercoseptoria
BT2 deuteromycotina

CERCOSPORA
BT1 deuteromycotina
NT1 cercospora apii
NT1 cercospora beticola
NT1 cercospora canescens
NT1 cercospora capsici
NT1 cercospora carthami
NT1 cercospora coffeicola
NT1 cercospora effusa
NT1 cercospora elaeidis
NT1 cercospora gossypina
NT1 cercospora kikuchii
NT1 cercospora nicotianae
NT1 cercospora oryzae
NT1 cercospora rodmanii
NT1 cercospora sorghi
NT1 cercospora zeae-maydis
NT1 cercospora zebrina
rt cercosporella
rt cercosporidium
rt mycosphaerella
rt mycovellosiella
rt paracercospora
rt phaeoramularia
rt pseudocercospora
rt sphaerulina

cercospora abelmoschi
USE **pseudocercospora abelmoschi**

cercospora aleuritis
USE **mycosphaerella aleuritis**

CERCOSPORA APII
BT1 cercospora
BT2 deuteromycotina

cercospora arachidicola
USE **mycosphaerella arachidis**

CERCOSPORA BETICOLA
BT1 cercospora
BT2 deuteromycotina

cercospora bischofiae
USE **pseudocercospora bischofiae**

CERCOSPORA CANESCENS
BT1 cercospora
BT2 deuteromycotina

CERCOSPORA CAPSICI
BT1 cercospora
BT2 deuteromycotina

cercospora caribaea
USE **phaeoramularia manihotis**

CERCOSPORA CARTHAMI
BT1 cercospora
BT2 deuteromycotina

CERCOSPORA COFFEICOLA
BT1 cercospora
BT2 deuteromycotina

cercospora concors
USE **mycovellosiella concors**

cercospora cosmicola
USE **pseudocercospora cosmicola**

cercospora cruenta
USE **mycosphaerella cruenta**

cercospora daemiae
USE **pseudocercospora daemiae**

CERCOSPORA EFFUSA
uf *cladosporium effusum*
uf *fusicladium effusum*
BT1 cercospora
BT2 deuteromycotina

cercospora egenula
USE **paracercospora egenula**

CERCOSPORA ELAEIDIS
BT1 cercospora
BT2 deuteromycotina

cercospora ferruginea
USE **mycovellosiella ferruginea**

cercospora fuligena
USE **pseudocercospora fuligena**

CERCOSPORA GOSSYPINA
BT1 cercospora
BT2 deuteromycotina

cercospora grewiae
USE **mycovellosiella grewiae**

cercospora henningsii
USE **mycosphaerella henningsii**

cercospora hibisci
USE **pseudocercospora abelmoschi**

cercospora ipomoeae-purpureae
USE **pseudocercospora ipomoeae-purpureae**

CERCOSPORA KIKUCHII
BT1 cercospora
BT2 deuteromycotina

cercospora koepkei
USE **mycovellosiella koepkei**

cercospora midnapurensis
USE **pseudocercospora midnapurensis**

cercospora murina
USE **mycovellosiella murina**

CERCOSPORA NICOTIANAE
BT1 cercospora
BT2 deuteromycotina

cercospora olivacea
USE **mycovellosiella ferruginea**

CERCOSPORA ORYZAE
uf *sphaerulina oryzina*
BT1 cercospora
BT2 deuteromycotina

cercospora personata
USE **mycosphaerella berkeleyi**

cercospora pini-densiflorae
USE **mycosphaerella gibsonii**

cercospora pongamiae
USE **mycovellosiella pongamiae**

CERCOSPORA RODMANII
BT1 cercospora

CERCOSPORA RODMANII *cont.*
BT2 deuteromycotina
BT1 mycoherbicides
BT2 herbicides
BT3 pesticides
BT2 microbial pesticides
BT3 pesticides

cercospora sesami
USE **mycosphaerella sesamicola**

CERCOSPORA SORGHI
BT1 cercospora
BT2 deuteromycotina

cercospora theae
USE **cercoseptoria theae**

cercospora vaginae
USE **mycovellosiella vaginae**

cercospora viticis
USE **pseudocercospora viticis**

CERCOSPORA ZEAE-MAYDIS
uf *cercosporella zeae-maydis*
BT1 cercospora
BT2 deuteromycotina

CERCOSPORA ZEBRINA
BT1 cercospora
BT2 deuteromycotina

CERCOSPORELLA
BT1 deuteromycotina
rt cercospora
rt mycosphaerella
rt pseudocercosporella

cercosporella brassicae
USE **pseudocercosporella capsellae**

cercosporella herpotrichoides
USE **pseudocercosporella herpotrichoides**

cercosporella persica
USE **mycosphaerella pruni-persicae**

cercosporella zeae-maydis
USE **cercospora zeae-maydis**

CERCOSPORIDIUM
BT1 deuteromycotina
rt cercospora

cercosporidium henningsii
USE **mycosphaerella henningsii**

cercosporidium personatum
USE **mycosphaerella berkeleyi**

CEREAL BYPRODUCTS
BT1 agricultural byproducts
BT2 byproducts
NT1 bran
NT2 maize bran
NT2 oat bran (agricola)
NT2 rice bran
NT2 wheat bran
NT1 brewers' grains
NT1 chaff
NT1 maize byproducts
NT2 maize bran
NT2 maize cobs
NT2 maize stover
NT2 maize straw
NT1 rice byproducts
NT2 rice bran
NT2 rice polishings
NT2 rice straw
NT1 rye middlings
rt cereal products
rt plant products
rt straw

CEREAL FLOURS
BT1 cereal products
BT2 plant products
BT3 products
BT1 flours
BT2 plant products

CEREAL FLOURS *cont.*
BT3 products
NT1 cornflour
NT1 oatmeal
NT1 rice flour
NT1 rye flour
NT1 wheat flour

CEREAL GERMS
BT1 cereal products
BT2 plant products
BT3 products
NT1 maize germ
NT1 wheat germ

CEREAL GRAINS
BT1 cereal products
BT2 plant products
BT3 products

CEREAL PRODUCTS
BT1 plant products
BT2 products
NT1 alimentary pastes
NT1 barley pellets
NT1 breakfast cereals
NT1 cereal flours
NT2 cornflour
NT2 oatmeal
NT2 rice flour
NT2 rye flour
NT2 wheat flour
NT1 cereal germs
NT2 maize germ
NT2 wheat germ
NT1 cereal grains
NT1 malt
NT1 popcorn
NT1 wheat flakes
rt cereal byproducts
rt cereals
rt food products
rt pasta

CEREAL PROTEIN
BT1 plant protein
BT2 protein
NT1 maize protein
NT1 oat protein
NT1 rice protein
NT1 rye protein
NT1 sorghum protein
NT1 wheat protein
rt cereal proteins

CEREAL PROTEINS
BT1 plant proteins
BT2 proteins
BT3 peptides
NT1 glutelins
NT2 glutenins
NT1 gluten
NT2 maize gluten
NT2 wheat gluten
NT1 prolamins
NT2 avenin
NT2 gliadin
NT2 hordein
NT2 zein
rt cereal protein

CEREALS
uf *feed cereals*
BT1 grain crops
NT1 barley
NT1 coix lacryma-jobi
NT1 maize
NT1 millets
NT2 brachiaria ramosa
NT2 digitaria exilis
NT2 digitaria iburua
NT2 echinochloa colonum
NT2 echinochloa decompositum
NT2 echinochloa frumentacea
NT2 eleusine coracana
NT2 eragrostis tef
NT2 panicum miliaceum
NT2 panicum miliare
NT2 paspalum scrobiculatum
NT2 pennisetum americanum
NT2 phalaris canariensis
NT2 setaria italica
NT2 setaria viridis

CEREALS *cont.*
NT1 oats
NT1 rice
NT1 rye
NT1 triticale
NT1 wheat
NT1 zizania aquatica
NT1 zizania palustris
rt cereal products
rt field crops
rt plants
rt sorghum
rt starch crops

CEREBELLAR ATAXIA
BT1 ataxia
BT2 movement disorders
BT3 functional disorders
BT4 animal disorders
BT5 disorders
BT2 muscular diseases
BT3 organic diseases
BT4 diseases

CEREBELLUM
uf *brain cerebellum*
BT1 brain
BT2 central nervous system
BT3 nervous system
BT4 body parts
NT1 amygdala

CEREBRAL CORTEX
BT1 brain
BT2 central nervous system
BT3 nervous system
BT4 body parts

CEREBRAL MALARIA
BT1 malaria
BT2 human diseases
BT3 diseases
BT2 mosquito-borne diseases
BT3 vector-borne diseases
BT4 diseases
BT2 protozoal infections
BT3 parasitoses
BT4 diseases

CEREBRAL PALSY
uf *palsy, cerebral*
BT1 brain disorders
BT2 nervous system diseases
BT3 organic diseases
BT4 diseases

CEREBRAL VENTRICLES
BT1 brain
BT2 central nervous system
BT3 nervous system
BT4 body parts

CEREBROCORTICAL NECROSIS
BT1 necrosis
BT1 nervous system diseases
BT2 organic diseases
BT3 diseases
rt cattle diseases

CEREBROSIDES
uf *galactolipids*
BT1 glycosides
BT2 carbohydrates
BT1 glycosphingolipids
BT2 glycolipids
BT3 lipids
BT2 sphingolipids
BT3 lipids

CEREBROSPINAL FLUID
BT1 body fluids
BT2 fluids

CEREBROSPINAL TRACTS
BT1 central nervous system
BT2 nervous system
BT3 body parts

CEREBROVASCULAR DISORDERS
BT1 brain disorders
BT2 nervous system diseases
BT3 organic diseases
BT4 diseases
BT1 vascular diseases

CEREBROVASCULAR DISORDERS *cont.*
BT2 cardiovascular diseases
BT3 organic diseases
BT4 diseases
NT1 apoplexy
NT1 migraine
NT1 stroke

cerebrum
USE **brain**

CEREMONIAL FOODS (AGRICOLA)
BT1 foods
rt ethnic foods (agricola)

CERESA
BT1 membracidae
BT2 cicadelloidea
BT3 auchenorrhyncha
BT4 homoptera
NT1 ceresa bubalus
rt stictocephala

CERESA BUBALUS
uf *stictocephala bubalus*
BT1 ceresa
BT2 membracidae
BT3 cicadelloidea
BT4 auchenorrhyncha
BT5 homoptera

CEREUS
BT1 cactaceae
NT1 cereus jamacaru
NT1 cereus validus

CEREUS JAMACARU
BT1 cereus
BT2 cactaceae
BT1 ornamental succulent plants
BT2 succulent plants

cereus triangularis
USE **hylocereus undatus**

CEREUS VALIDUS
BT1 cereus
BT2 cactaceae
BT1 ornamental succulent plants
BT2 succulent plants

CERIOPS
BT1 rhizophoraceae
NT1 ceriops decandra
NT1 ceriops tagal

CERIOPS DECANDRA
BT1 ceriops
BT2 rhizophoraceae
BT1 forest trees

CERIOPS TAGAL
BT1 ceriops
BT2 rhizophoraceae
BT1 forest trees
rt mangroves

CERITHIDEA
BT1 potamididae
BT2 gastropoda
BT3 mollusca
rt pomatiopsis

cerithidea californica
USE **pomatiopsis californica**

CERIUM
uf *ce (symbol)*
BT1 rare earth elements
BT2 transition elements
BT3 metallic elements
BT4 elements
BT4 metals

CERNUELLA
BT1 helicidae
BT2 gastropoda
BT3 mollusca
NT1 cernuella cespitum
NT1 cernuella virgata
rt helicella

CERNUELLA CESPITUM
BT1 cernuella

CERNUELLA CESPITUM *cont.*
BT2 helicidae
BT3 gastropoda
BT4 mollusca

CERNUELLA VIRGATA
uf *helicella virgata*
BT1 cernuella
BT2 helicidae
BT3 gastropoda
BT4 mollusca

CEROID
uf *lipochrome pigment*
BT1 pigments
rt lipofuscin

CEROPLASTES
BT1 coccidae
BT2 coccoidea
BT3 sternorrhyncha
BT4 homoptera
NT1 ceroplastes destructor
NT1 ceroplastes floridensis
NT1 ceroplastes japonicus
NT1 ceroplastes rubens
NT1 ceroplastes rusci
rt gascardia

CEROPLASTES DESTRUCTOR
uf *gascardia destructor*
BT1 ceroplastes
BT2 coccidae
BT3 coccoidea
BT4 sternorrhyncha
BT5 homoptera

CEROPLASTES FLORIDENSIS
BT1 ceroplastes
BT2 coccidae
BT3 coccoidea
BT4 sternorrhyncha
BT5 homoptera

CEROPLASTES JAPONICUS
BT1 ceroplastes
BT2 coccidae
BT3 coccoidea
BT4 sternorrhyncha
BT5 homoptera

CEROPLASTES RUBENS
BT1 ceroplastes
BT2 coccidae
BT3 coccoidea
BT4 sternorrhyncha
BT5 homoptera

CEROPLASTES RUSCI
BT1 ceroplastes
BT2 coccidae
BT3 coccoidea
BT4 sternorrhyncha
BT5 homoptera

CEROTOMA
BT1 chrysomelidae
BT2 coleoptera
NT1 cerotoma facialis
NT1 cerotoma ruficornis
NT1 cerotoma trifurcata

CEROTOMA FACIALIS
BT1 cerotoma
BT2 chrysomelidae
BT3 coleoptera

CEROTOMA RUFICORNIS
BT1 cerotoma
BT2 chrysomelidae
BT3 coleoptera

CEROTOMA TRIFURCATA
BT1 cerotoma
BT2 chrysomelidae
BT3 coleoptera

CEROXYLON
BT1 palmae
NT1 ceroxylon andicola

CEROXYLON ANDICOLA
BT1 ceroxylon
BT2 palmae

CERRADO
BT1 scrublands
BT2 savanna woodlands
BT3 woodlands
BT4 vegetation types

CERRADO SOILS
BT1 soil types (ecological)
rt scrubland soils

CERTIFICATES OF DEPOSIT (AGRICOLA)

CERTIFICATION
rt planting stock
rt quality controls
rt seed certification
rt teacher certification (agricola)

certification, seed
USE **seed certification**

cerulein
USE **ceruletide**

CERULETIDE
uf *caerulein*
uf *cerulein*
BT1 oligopeptides
BT2 peptides

CERULOPLASMIN
uf *caeruloplasmin*
BT1 blood proteins
BT2 animal proteins
BT3 proteins
BT4 peptides
BT1 glycoproteins
BT2 proteins
BT3 peptides
BT1 metalloproteins
BT2 proteins
BT3 peptides
rt ferroxidase

CERVICAL MUCUS
BT1 mucus
BT2 secretions
rt cervix

CERVICITIS
BT1 uterine diseases
BT2 female genital diseases
BT3 organic diseases
BT4 diseases
rt cervix

CERVICOFACIAL ACTINOMYCOSIS
BT1 actinomycosis
BT2 bacterial diseases
BT3 infectious diseases
BT4 diseases

CERVIDAE
BT1 ruminantia
BT2 artiodactyla
BT3 mammals
BT3 ungulates
NT1 alces
NT2 alces alces
NT1 capreolus
NT2 capreolus capreolus
NT1 cervus
NT2 cervus axis
NT2 cervus elaphus
NT3 cervus elaphus canadensis
NT2 cervus nippon
NT2 cervus porcinus
NT2 cervus timorensis
NT2 cervus unicolor
NT1 muntiacus
NT1 odocoileus
NT2 odocoileus hemionus
NT2 odocoileus virginianus
NT1 rangifer
rt deer
rt reindeer

CERVIX
BT1 uterus
BT2 female genitalia

CERVIX *cont.*
BT3 genitalia
BT4 urogenital system
BT5 body parts
rt cervical mucus
rt cervicitis

CERVUS
uf *axis*
uf *dama*
BT1 cervidae
BT2 ruminantia
BT3 artiodactyla
BT4 mammals
BT4 ungulates
NT1 cervus axis
NT1 cervus elaphus
NT2 cervus elaphus canadensis
NT1 cervus nippon
NT1 cervus porcinus
NT1 cervus timorensis
NT1 cervus unicolor

CERVUS AXIS
uf *axis axis*
BT1 cervus
BT2 cervidae
BT3 ruminantia
BT4 artiodactyla
BT5 mammals
BT5 ungulates

cervus canadensis
USE **cervus elaphus canadensis**

cervus dama
USE **fallow deer**

CERVUS ELAPHUS
BT1 cervus
BT2 cervidae
BT3 ruminantia
BT4 artiodactyla
BT5 mammals
BT5 ungulates
NT1 cervus elaphus canadensis
rt red deer

CERVUS ELAPHUS CANADENSIS
uf *cervus canadensis*
uf *elks, american*
uf *wapiti*
BT1 cervus elaphus
BT2 cervus
BT3 cervidae
BT4 ruminantia
BT5 artiodactyla
BT6 mammals
BT6 ungulates

CERVUS NIPPON
BT1 cervus
BT2 cervidae
BT3 ruminantia
BT4 artiodactyla
BT5 mammals
BT5 ungulates

CERVUS PORCINUS
uf *axis porcinus*
BT1 cervus
BT2 cervidae
BT3 ruminantia
BT4 artiodactyla
BT5 mammals
BT5 ungulates

CERVUS TIMORENSIS
BT1 cervus
BT2 cervidae
BT3 ruminantia
BT4 artiodactyla
BT5 mammals
BT5 ungulates

CERVUS UNICOLOR
BT1 cervus
BT2 cervidae
BT3 ruminantia
BT4 artiodactyla
BT5 mammals
BT5 ungulates

CESIUM
BF caesium

CESSPITS
HN from 1989
rt sewerage

CESTODA
NT1 cestodaria
NT2 amphilina
NT2 gephyrolina
NT2 gigantolina
NT2 gyrocotyle
NT2 gyrocotyloides
NT2 gyrometra
NT2 hunteroides
NT2 nesolecithus
NT2 schizochoerus
NT1 eucestoda
NT2 amabiliidae
NT3 tatria
NT2 amphicotylidae
NT3 eubothrium
NT2 anoplocephalidae
NT3 andrya
NT3 anoplocephala
NT4 anoplocephala magna
NT4 anoplocephala perfoliata
NT3 avitellina
NT4 avitellina centripunctata
NT3 bertiella
NT4 bertiella studeri
NT3 moniezia
NT4 moniezia autumnalia
NT4 moniezia benedeni
NT4 moniezia expansa
NT3 paranoplocephala
NT4 paranoplocephala mamillana
NT3 stilesia
NT4 stilesia globipunctata
NT4 stilesia hepatica
NT3 thysaniezia
NT4 thysaniezia giardi
NT3 thysanosoma
NT4 thysanosoma actinioides
NT2 bothriocephalidae
NT3 bothriocephalus
NT4 bothriocephalus acheilognathi
NT2 caryophyllaeidae
NT3 khawia
NT4 khawia sinensis
NT2 davaineidae
NT3 cotugnia
NT4 cotugnia digonophora
NT3 davainea
NT4 davainea proglottina
NT3 raillietina
NT4 raillietina cesticillus
NT4 raillietina echinobothrida
NT4 raillietina tetragona
NT2 dilepididae
NT3 amoebotaenia
NT4 amoebotaenia sphenoides
NT3 anomotaenia
NT3 choanotaenia
NT4 choanotaenia infundibulum
NT3 diplopylidium
NT4 diplopylidium nolleri
NT3 dipylidium
NT4 dipylidium caninum
NT3 joyeuxiella
NT4 joyeuxiella echinorhynchoides
NT4 joyeuxiella pasqualei
NT2 diphyllobothriidae
NT3 diphyllobothrium
NT4 diphyllobothrium cordiceps
NT4 diphyllobothrium dendriticum
NT4 diphyllobothrium latum
NT3 diplogonoporus
NT4 diplogonoporus balaenopterae
NT4 diplogonoporus fukuokaensis
NT4 diplogonoporus grandis
NT3 ligula

CESTODA *cont.*
NT4 ligula intestinalis
NT3 schistocephalus
NT4 schistocephalus solidus
NT3 spirometra
NT4 spirometra mansonoides
NT2 hymenolepididae
NT3 aploparaksis
NT3 diorchis
NT3 fimbriaria
NT4 fimbriaria fasciolaris
NT3 hymenolepis
NT4 hymenolepis citelli
NT4 hymenolepis diminuta
NT4 hymenolepis microstoma
NT4 hymenolepis nana
NT3 microsomacanthus
NT3 retinometra
NT3 sobolevicanthus
NT4 sobolevicanthus gracilis
NT3 triodontolepis
NT2 mesocestoidae
NT3 mesocestoides
NT4 mesocestoides corti
NT4 mesocestoides lineatus
NT2 nematoparataeniidae
NT3 gastrotaenia
NT2 onchobothriidae
NT3 acanthobothrium
NT2 proteocephalidae
NT3 proteocephalus
NT2 taeniidae
NT3 echinococcus
NT4 echinococcus granulosus
NT4 echinococcus multilocularis
NT3 taenia
NT4 taenia crassiceps
NT4 taenia hydatigena
NT4 taenia multiceps
NT4 taenia ovis
NT4 taenia pisiformis
NT4 taenia saginata
NT4 taenia serialis
NT4 taenia solium
NT4 taenia taeniaeformis
NT2 triaenophoridae
NT3 triaenophorus
NT4 triaenophorus nodulosus

CESTODARIA
HN from 1990
BT1 cestoda
NT1 amphilina
NT1 gephyrolina
NT1 gigantolina
NT1 gyrocotyle
NT1 gyrocotyloides
NT1 gyrometra
NT1 hunteroides
NT1 nesolecithus
NT1 schizochoerus

CESTODE INFECTIONS
BT1 helminthoses
BT2 parasitoses
BT3 diseases
NT1 cysticercosis
rt eucestoda

CESTODE LARVAE
(developmental stages of a cestode before metamorphosis to a metacestode)
BT1 helminth larvae
BT2 helminths
BT3 parasites
BT2 larvae
BT3 developmental stages
NT1 coracidia
NT1 oncospheres
rt eucestoda
rt metacestodes

cestodes
USE **eucestoda**

CESTRUM
BT1 solanaceae
NT1 cestrum diurnum
NT1 cestrum elegans
NT1 cestrum nocturnum

CESTRUM DIURNUM
BT1 antifungal plants
BT1 cestrum
BT2 solanaceae

CESTRUM ELEGANS
uf *cestrum purpureum*
BT1 cestrum
BT2 solanaceae
BT1 ornamental woody plants

CESTRUM NOCTURNUM
BT1 antiviral plants
BT1 cestrum
BT2 solanaceae
BT1 insecticidal plants
BT2 pesticidal plants

cestrum purpureum
USE **cestrum elegans**

CETACEA
BT1 mammals
NT1 mysticeti
NT2 balaenidae
NT3 balaena
NT4 balaena mysticetus
NT2 balaenopteridae
NT3 megaptera
NT4 megaptera novaeangliae
NT1 odontoceti
NT2 delphinidae
NT3 cephalorhynchus
NT3 delphinus
NT3 lagenorhynchus
NT3 stenella
NT4 stenella coeruleoalba
NT3 tursiops
NT4 tursiops truncatus
NT2 monodontidae
NT3 delphinapterus
NT4 delphinapterus leucas
NT3 monodon
NT4 monodon monoceros
NT2 phocoenidae
NT3 phocoena
NT2 physeteridae
NT3 physeter
NT4 physeter catodon
rt whales

CETORHINUS
BT1 lamnidae
BT2 lamniformes
BT3 chondrichthyes
BT4 fishes
NT1 cetorhinus maximus

CETORHINUS MAXIMUS
BT1 cetorhinus
BT2 lamnidae
BT3 lamniformes
BT4 chondrichthyes
BT5 fishes

CETRARIA
BT1 lichens
BT1 parmeliaceae

CETRIMONIUM
BT1 antiseptics
BT2 antiinfective agents
BT3 drugs
BT1 quaternary ammonium compounds
BT2 ammonium compounds
BT2 organic nitrogen compounds

cetyl alcohol
USE **1-hexadecanol**

ceuthorhynchidius
USE **ceutorhynchus**

ceuthorhynchidius horridus
USE **trichosirocalus horridus**

CEUTORHYNCHUS
uf *ceuthorhynchidius*
BT1 curculionidae
BT2 coleoptera
NT1 ceutorhynchus assimilis
NT1 ceutorhynchus litura

CEUTORHYNCHUS *cont.*
NT1 ceutorhynchus napi
NT1 ceutorhynchus pallidactylus
NT1 ceutorhynchus pleurostigma

CEUTORHYNCHUS ASSIMILIS
BT1 ceutorhynchus
BT2 curculionidae
BT3 coleoptera

CEUTORHYNCHUS LITURA
BT1 ceutorhynchus
BT2 curculionidae
BT3 coleoptera

CEUTORHYNCHUS NAPI
BT1 ceutorhynchus
BT2 curculionidae
BT3 coleoptera

CEUTORHYNCHUS PALLIDACTYLUS
uf *ceutorhynchus quadridens*
BT1 ceutorhynchus
BT2 curculionidae
BT3 coleoptera

CEUTORHYNCHUS PLEUROSTIGMA
BT1 ceutorhynchus
BT2 curculionidae
BT3 coleoptera

ceutorhynchus quadridens
USE **ceutorhynchus pallidactylus**

ceylon
USE **sri lanka**

CGIAR
HN from 1990
BT1 international organizations
BT2 organizations
NT1 cimmyt
NT1 icarda

CHABERTIA
BT1 chabertiidae
BT2 nematoda
NT1 chabertia ovina

CHABERTIA OVINA
BT1 chabertia
BT2 chabertiidae
BT3 nematoda

CHABERTIIDAE
BT1 nematoda
NT1 agriostomum
NT2 agriostomum vryburgi
NT1 bourgelatia
NT1 chabertia
NT2 chabertia ovina
NT1 daubneyia
NT1 oesophagostomum
NT2 oesophagostomum columbianum
NT2 oesophagostomum dentatum
NT2 oesophagostomum quadrispinulatum
NT2 oesophagostomum radiatum
NT2 oesophagostomum venulosum
NT1 ternidens
NT2 ternidens deminutus
rt animal parasitic nematodes

CHAD
uf *tchad*
BT1 central africa
BT2 africa south of sahara
BT3 africa
rt acp
rt developing countries
rt francophone africa
rt least developed countries

CHAENOMELES
BT1 rosaceae
NT1 chaenomeles cardinalis
NT1 chaenomeles japonica

CHAENOMELES *cont.*
rt cydonia

CHAENOMELES CARDINALIS
BT1 chaenomeles
BT2 rosaceae

CHAENOMELES JAPONICA
uf *cydonia japonica*
BT1 chaenomeles
BT2 rosaceae

chaenomeles sinensis
USE **cydonia sinensis**

CHAETOCNEMA
BT1 chrysomelidae
BT2 coleoptera
NT1 chaetocnema concinna
NT1 chaetocnema pulicaria
NT1 chaetocnema tibialis

chaetocnema breviuscula
USE **chaetocnema tibialis**

CHAETOCNEMA CONCINNA
BT1 chaetocnema
BT2 chrysomelidae
BT3 coleoptera

CHAETOCNEMA PULICARIA
BT1 chaetocnema
BT2 chrysomelidae
BT3 coleoptera

CHAETOCNEMA TIBIALIS
uf *chaetocnema breviuscula*
BT1 chaetocnema
BT2 chrysomelidae
BT3 coleoptera

CHAETOGNATHA
NT1 sagitta
NT2 sagitta elegans
rt invertebrates

CHAETOMIUM
BT1 sordariales
NT1 chaetomium globosum
NT1 chaetomium virescens

chaetomium cellulolyticum
USE **chaetomium virescens**

CHAETOMIUM GLOBOSUM
BT1 chaetomium
BT2 sordariales

CHAETOMIUM VIRESCENS
uf *chaetomium cellulolyticum*
BT1 chaetomium
BT2 sordariales

CHAETOPORUS
HN from 1990
BT1 aphyllophorales
NT1 chaetoporus radula
rt poria

CHAETOPORUS RADULA
HN from 1990
uf *poria radula*
BT1 chaetoporus
BT2 aphyllophorales

CHAETOPSINA
BT1 deuteromycotina

CHAETOPSYLLA
BT1 vermipsyllidae
BT2 siphonaptera

chaetoptelius
USE **acrantus**

chaetoptelius vestitus
USE **acrantus vestitus**

CHAETOSIPHON
BT1 aphididae
BT2 aphidoidea
BT3 sternorrhyncha
BT4 homoptera
NT1 chaetosiphon fragaefolii
rt capitophorus

CHAETOSIPHON FRAGAEFOLII
uf *capitophorus fragaefolii*
BT1 chaetosiphon
BT2 aphididae
BT3 aphidoidea
BT4 sternorrhyncha
BT5 homoptera

CHAFF
BT1 cereal byproducts
BT2 agricultural byproducts
BT3 byproducts
BT1 milling residues
BT2 plant residues
BT3 residues

CHAGAS' DISEASE
BT1 human diseases
BT2 diseases
BT1 trypanosomiasis
BT2 protozoal infections
BT3 parasitoses
BT4 diseases
BT2 vector-borne diseases
BT3 diseases
rt trypanosoma cruzi

CHAGASELLA
BT1 apicomplexa
BT2 protozoa

CHAGOS ARCHIPELAGO
BT1 east africa
BT2 africa south of sahara
BT3 africa

CHAIN AND FLIGHT CONVEYORS
uf *conveyors, chain and flight*
BT1 conveyors

chain saws
USE **chainsaws**

CHAINS
rt ropes

CHAINSAWS
HN from 1990; previously "chain saws"
uf *chain saws*
uf *power saws*
uf *saws, chain*
uf *saws, power*
BT1 saws
BT2 forestry machinery
BT3 machinery
BT2 tools

CHALARA
HN from 1990
BT1 deuteromycotina
rt thielaviopsis

chalara elegans
USE **thielaviopsis basicola**

CHALCIDIDAE
BT1 hymenoptera
NT1 brachymeria
NT2 brachymeria intermedia
NT2 brachymeria lasus
NT2 brachymeria podagrica
NT1 chalcis
NT1 dirhinus
NT2 dirhinus giffardii
NT1 spilochalcis
NT2 spilochalcis albifrons
NT2 spilochalcis hirtifemora

CHALCIS
BT1 chalcididae
BT2 hymenoptera
rt brachymeria

chalcis podagrica
USE **brachymeria podagrica**

CHALCODERMUS
BT1 curculionidae
BT2 coleoptera
NT1 chalcodermus aeneus

CHALCODERMUS AENEUS
BT1 chalcodermus
BT2 curculionidae

CHALCODERMUS AENEUS *cont.*
BT3 coleoptera

CHALCOGENS
BT1 nonmetallic elements
BT2 elements
NT1 oxygen
NT1 sulfur
NT1 tellurium

CHALCONE
BT1 chalcones
BT2 flavonoids
BT3 aromatic compounds
BT3 plant pigments
BT4 pigments

chalcone flavanone isomerase
USE **chalcone isomerase**

CHALCONE ISOMERASE
(ec 5.5.1.6)
uf *chalcone flavanone isomerase*
BT1 isomerases
BT2 enzymes

chalcone synthase
USE **naringenin-chalcone synthase**

CHALCONES
BT1 flavonoids
BT2 aromatic compounds
BT2 plant pigments
BT3 pigments
NT1 chalcone

CHALCOPONERA
BT1 formicidae
BT2 hymenoptera
rt rhytidoponera

chalcoponera metallica
USE **rhytidoponera metallica**

CHALICODOMA
BT1 apidae
BT2 hymenoptera

CHALINOLOBUS
BT1 vespertilionidae
BT2 chiroptera
BT3 mammals

CHALK
BT1 liming materials
BT2 soil amendments
BT3 amendments
BT1 soil parent materials
rt calcite
rt calcium carbonate
rt chalk grasslands
rt chalk soils

CHALK BROOD
BT1 bee diseases
BT2 animal diseases
BT3 diseases
rt ascosphaera apis
rt honeybee brood

CHALK GRASSLANDS
uf *grasslands, chalk*
BT1 grasslands
BT2 vegetation types
rt chalk

CHALK SOILS
BT1 soil types (lithological)
rt chalk

CHALLIS (AGRICOLA)
BT1 fabrics

CHAMAECYPARIS
BT1 cupressaceae
NT1 chamaecyparis formosensis
NT1 chamaecyparis lawsoniana
NT1 chamaecyparis nootkatensis
NT1 chamaecyparis obtusa
NT1 chamaecyparis pisifera
NT1 chamaecyparis thyoides

CHAMAECYPARIS FORMOSENSIS
BT1 chamaecyparis
BT2 cupressaceae
BT1 forest trees

chamaecyparis funebris
USE **cupressus funebris**

CHAMAECYPARIS LAWSONIANA
BT1 chamaecyparis
BT2 cupressaceae
BT1 forest trees
BT1 ornamental conifers
BT2 conifers
BT2 ornamental woody plants

CHAMAECYPARIS NOOTKATENSIS
BT1 chamaecyparis
BT2 cupressaceae

CHAMAECYPARIS OBTUSA
uf *chamaecyparis taiwanensis*
BT1 chamaecyparis
BT2 cupressaceae
BT1 essential oil plants
BT2 oil plants
BT1 forest trees
BT1 ornamental conifers
BT2 conifers
BT2 ornamental woody plants

CHAMAECYPARIS PISIFERA
BT1 chamaecyparis
BT2 cupressaceae
BT1 forest trees
BT1 ornamental conifers
BT2 conifers
BT2 ornamental woody plants

chamaecyparis taiwanensis
USE **chamaecyparis obtusa**

CHAMAECYPARIS THYOIDES
BT1 chamaecyparis
BT2 cupressaceae

chamaecytisus
USE **cytisus**

CHAMAEDAPHNE
BT1 ericaceae
NT1 chamaedaphne calyculata

CHAMAEDAPHNE CALYCULATA
uf *cassandra calyculata*
BT1 chamaedaphne
BT2 ericaceae
BT1 ornamental woody plants

CHAMAEDOREA
BT1 palmae
NT1 chamaedorea elegans

CHAMAEDOREA ELEGANS
BT1 chamaedorea
BT2 palmae
BT1 ornamental palms

CHAMAEMELUM
BT1 compositae
NT1 chamaemelum fuscatum
NT1 chamaemelum nobile

CHAMAEMELUM FUSCATUM
BT1 chamaemelum
BT2 compositae

CHAMAEMELUM NOBILE
uf *anthemis nobilis*
uf *chamomile*
BT1 chamaemelum
BT2 compositae
BT1 essential oil plants
BT2 oil plants

CHAMAEMYIIDAE
BT1 diptera
NT1 leucopis
NT2 leucopis interruptovittata

CHAMAENERION
BT1 onagraceae
NT1 chamaenerion angustifolium
rt epilobium

CHAMAENERION ANGUSTIFOLIUM
BT1 chamaenerion
BT2 onagraceae
rt epilobium angustifolium

CHAMAEROPS
BT1 palmae
NT1 chamaerops humilis

CHAMAEROPS HUMILIS
BT1 chamaerops
BT2 palmae
BT1 ornamental palms

CHAMBRAY (AGRICOLA)
BT1 fabrics

CHAMOIS
uf *rupicapra rupicapra*
BT1 antelopes
BT2 ruminants
BT3 animals
BT1 skin producing animals
BT2 animals
rt bovidae

CHAMOIS COLORED
BF chamois coloured

CHAMOIS COLOURED
AF chamois colored
BT1 goat breeds
BT2 breeds

chamomile
USE **chamaemelum nobile**
OR **chamomilla recutita**

CHAMOMILLA
BT1 compositae
NT1 chamomilla recutita
NT1 chamomilla suaveolens

CHAMOMILLA RECUTITA
uf *chamomile*
uf *matricaria chamomilla*
uf *matricaria recutita*
BT1 antiviral plants
BT1 chamomilla
BT2 compositae
BT1 essential oil plants
BT2 oil plants
BT1 insecticidal plants
BT2 pesticidal plants
BT1 medicinal plants
BT1 ornamental herbaceous plants
BT1 weeds

CHAMOMILLA SUAVEOLENS
uf *matricaria matricarioides*
uf *matricaria suaveolens*
BT1 chamomilla
BT2 compositae
BT1 essential oil plants
BT2 oil plants
BT1 medicinal plants
BT1 weeds

CHAMPAGNE AND SPARKLING WINES
BT1 wines
BT2 alcoholic beverages
BT3 beverages

CHAMPAGNE ARDENNES
BT1 france
BT2 western europe
BT3 europe

CHANDIGARH
BT1 india
BT2 south asia
BT3 asia

CHANGE
NT1 climatic change
rt behavior change (agricola)
rt change agents (agricola)
rt change of state
rt clines
rt conversion
rt development
rt educational reform

CHANGE *cont.*
rt genetic change
rt midlife transitions (agricola)
rt modification
rt population change
rt resistance to change (agricola)
rt social change
rt structural change
rt substitution
rt variation

CHANGE AGENTS (AGRICOLA)
NT1 extension agents (agricola)
rt change

CHANGE OF STATE
NT1 condensation
NT1 evaporation
NT2 vacuum evaporation
NT1 freezing
NT2 blast freezing (agricola)
NT2 gelation
NT1 melting
NT1 solidification
NT2 gelation
NT1 thawing
NT1 vaporization
NT1 volatilization
rt change

CHANIDAE
BT1 gonorhynchiformes
BT2 osteichthyes
BT3 fishes
NT1 chanos
NT2 chanos chanos

CHANNA
BT1 channidae
BT2 perciformes
BT3 osteichthyes
BT4 fishes

channel catfish
USE **ictalurus punctatus**

CHANNEL CATFISH VIRUS
BT1 herpesviridae
BT2 viruses
rt ictalurus punctatus

CHANNEL ISLANDS
BT1 uk
BT2 british isles
BT3 western europe
BT4 europe

CHANNELS
NT1 chutes
NT1 culverts
NT1 ditches
NT2 dykes
NT2 oxidation ditches
NT1 drainage channels
NT1 earthworm channels
NT1 irrigation channels
rt canals
rt pipes
rt sluices
rt spillways
rt transmission
rt tubes
rt waterways
rt weirs

CHANNIDAE
BT1 perciformes
BT2 osteichthyes
BT3 fishes
NT1 channa

CHANOS
BT1 chanidae
BT2 gonorhynchiformes
BT3 osteichthyes
BT4 fishes
NT1 chanos chanos

CHANOS CHANOS
uf *milkfish*
BT1 chanos
BT2 chanidae
BT3 gonorhynchiformes

CHANOS CHANOS *cont.*
BT4 osteichthyes
BT5 fishes

chanothar
USE **sonadi**

CHAOBORIDAE
BT1 diptera
NT1 chaoborus
NT1 corethrella
NT2 corethrella brakeleyi
NT1 mochlonyx
NT2 mochlonyx velutinus

CHAOBORUS
BT1 chaoboridae
BT2 diptera

CHAOS
BT1 sarcomastigophora
BT2 protozoa

CHAPARRAL
BT1 scrub
BT2 vegetation types

CHAPARRAL SOILS
BT1 soil types (ecological)
rt scrubland soils

CHAPATTIS
BT1 foods
rt bakery products

chaper
USE **chappar**

CHAPMANIUM
BT1 microspora
BT2 protozoa

CHAPPAR
HN from 1990; previously "chaper"
uf *chaper*
BT1 goat breeds
BT2 breeds

CHARA
BT1 charophyta
BT2 algae
NT1 chara globularis
NT1 chara vulgaris
NT1 chara zeylanica

CHARA GLOBULARIS
BT1 chara
BT2 charophyta
BT3 algae

CHARA VULGARIS
BT1 chara
BT2 charophyta
BT3 algae

CHARA ZEYLANICA
BT1 chara
BT2 charophyta
BT3 algae

CHARACIFORMES
BT1 osteichthyes
BT2 fishes
NT1 curimatidae
NT2 prochilodus

CHARACTERISTICS
NT1 acquired characters
NT1 agronomic characteristics
NT2 plant height
NT2 resistance to penetration
NT2 resistivity
NT2 wind resistance
NT1 individual characteristics (agricola)
NT1 litter traits
NT1 meat characteristics
NT1 milk production characteristics
NT2 milk flow
NT1 quantitative traits
NT1 seed characteristics
NT2 seed longevity
NT2 seed moisture

CHARACTERISTICS *cont.*
NT2 seed size
NT2 seed weight
NT1 semen characters
NT2 ejaculate volume
NT1 sex limited characters
NT1 silvicultural characters
NT1 stand characteristics
NT2 stand density
NT2 stand structure
NT2 stand tables
NT1 style
rt characterization
rt phenotypic correlation
rt prepotency
rt tractability

CHARACTERIZATION
BT1 classification
rt characteristics
rt identification
rt silvicultural characters
rt sorting

CHARADRIIDAE
uf plovers
BT1 charadriiformes
BT2 birds
NT1 charadrius
NT2 charadrius alexandrinus
NT1 pluvialis
NT1 vanellus
NT2 vanellus vanellus

CHARADRIIFORMES
BT1 birds
NT1 alcidae
NT2 aethia
NT2 alca
NT3 alca torda
NT2 cepphus
NT2 fratercula
NT3 fratercula arctica
NT3 fratercula corniculata
NT2 lunda
NT3 lunda cirrhata
NT2 uria
NT3 uria aalge
NT3 uria lomvia
NT1 charadriidae
NT2 charadrius
NT3 charadrius alexandrinus
NT2 pluvialis
NT2 vanellus
NT3 vanellus vanellus
NT1 laridae
NT2 larus
NT3 larus argentatus
NT3 larus dominicanus
NT3 larus ridibundus
NT2 rissa
NT3 rissa tridactyla
NT2 sterna
NT3 sterna hirundo
NT1 scolopacidae
NT2 arenaria (birds)
NT2 calidris
NT3 calidris alpina
NT3 calidris minuta
NT2 gallinago
NT2 limosa
NT3 limosa fedoa
NT3 limosa limosa
NT2 numenius
NT2 scolopax
NT3 scolopax rusticola
NT2 tringa
NT3 tringa glareola
NT3 tringa totanus
NT1 stercorariidae
NT2 catharacta
NT2 stercorarius

CHARADRIUS
BT1 charadriidae
BT2 charadriiformes
BT3 birds
NT1 charadrius alexandrinus

CHARADRIUS ALEXANDRINUS
BT1 charadrius
BT2 charadriidae

CHARADRIUS ALEXANDRINUS *cont.*
BT3 charadriiformes
BT4 birds

CHARCOAL
BT1 adsorbents
BT1 fuels
rt activated carbon
rt bone char
rt carbon
rt destructive distillation
rt forest products

CHARCOAL BROILED FOODS (AGRICOLA)
BT1 foods
rt broiling (agricola)

chard, swiss
USE **spinach beets**

CHARGE ACCOUNTS (AGRICOLA)
rt credit
rt credit cards (agricola)

CHARGE CHARACTERISTICS
BT1 ion exchange

CHARGE DENSITY
BT1 density
rt ion exchange

CHARGES
uf charging
BT1 electrical properties
BT2 physical properties
BT3 properties

charges (costs)
USE **costs**
OR **expenditure**
OR **fees**
OR **prices**

charging
USE **charges**

charging, electrostatic
USE **electrostatic charging**

CHARIPIDAE
BT1 hymenoptera
NT1 alloxysta
NT2 alloxysta victrix

charips
USE **dilyta**

CHARITABLE CONTRIBUTIONS (AGRICOLA)
rt tax credits (agricola)

CHARMOISE
BT1 sheep breeds
BT2 breeds

CHARNEQUEIRA
HN from 1990
BT1 goat breeds
BT2 breeds

CHAROLAIS
BT1 cattle breeds
BT2 breeds

CHAROLLAIS
HN from 1990
BT1 sheep breeds
BT2 breeds

CHAROPHYTA
BT1 algae
NT1 chara
NT2 chara globularis
NT2 chara vulgaris
NT2 chara zeylanica
NT1 nitella
NT2 nitella hookeri

CHAROPS
BT1 ichneumonidae
BT2 hymenoptera

charr
USE **salvelinus alpinus**

CHARTOCERUS
BT1 signiphoridae
BT2 hymenoptera
NT1 chartocerus subaeneus
rt thysanus

CHARTOCERUS SUBAENEUS
uf thysanus subaeneus
BT1 chartocerus
BT2 signiphoridae
BT3 hymenoptera

CHARTREUSIN
uf lambdamycin
BT1 antibiotics

CHARTS (AGRICOLA)
NT1 flipcharts (agricola)
NT1 flow charts (agricola)

CHASMOPODIUM
BT1 gramineae
NT1 chasmopodium caudatum
NT1 chasmopodium purpurascens

CHASMOPODIUM CAUDATUM
BT1 chasmopodium
BT2 gramineae
BT1 pasture plants

CHASMOPODIUM PURPURASCENS
BT1 chasmopodium
BT2 gramineae
BT1 pasture plants

chayote
USE **sechium edule**

check basin irrigation
USE **basin irrigation**

check basins
USE **basin irrigation**

CHECKLISTS
BT1 reference works
rt catalogues
rt taxonomy

CHECKS
BT1 wood defects
BT2 defects

CHEDDAR CHEESE
BT1 cheeses
BT2 milk products
BT3 products
rt cheddaring

CHEDDARING
BT1 cheesemaking
rt cheddar cheese

CHEDIAK-HIGASHI SYNDROME
(phagocyte bactericidal dysfunction)
BT1 leukocyte disorders
BT2 blood disorders
BT3 animal disorders
BT4 disorders
rt immunological diseases

cheese making
USE **cheesemaking**

CHEESE MILK
BT1 milk
BT2 animal products
BT3 products
rt cheesemaking

CHEESE MITES
BT1 mites
BT1 stored products pests
BT2 pests
rt cheeses

CHEESE MOLDS
BF cheese moulds
uf molds, cheese

CHEESE MOULDS
AF cheese molds
uf moulds, cheese

CHEESE MOULDS *cont.*
BT1 dairy equipment
BT2 equipment
rt cheesemaking

CHEESE PRESSES
BT1 dairy equipment
BT2 equipment
BT1 presses
BT2 farm machinery
BT3 machinery
rt cheesemaking

CHEESE QUALITY
BT1 quality
rt cheeses

CHEESE RIPENING
BT1 cheesemaking
NT1 accelerated ripening
rt ripening

CHEESE SLURRY
rt cheesemaking
rt cheeses
rt slurries

CHEESE SPREAD
BT1 milk products
BT2 products
rt cheeses

CHEESE STARTERS
HN from 1990
BT1 starters

CHEESE STORES
BT1 stores
rt cheeses
rt dairy factories

cheese varieties
USE **cheeses**

CHEESE VATS
BT1 dairy equipment
BT2 equipment
rt cheesemaking

CHEESEMAKING
uf cheese making
NT1 cheddaring
NT1 cheese ripening
NT2 accelerated ripening
NT1 continuous cheesemaking
NT1 direct acidification
NT1 moulding
rt cheese milk
rt cheese moulds
rt cheese presses
rt cheese slurry
rt cheese vats
rt cheeses
rt chymosin
rt coagulum
rt curd
rt dairy technology
rt whitening

cheesemaking, continuous
USE **continuous cheesemaking**

CHEESES
uf cheese varieties
BT1 milk products
BT2 products
NT1 appenzell cheese
NT1 asiago cheese
NT1 bakers' cheese
NT1 bel paese cheese
NT1 blue cheese
NT1 bra cheese
NT1 brick cheese
NT1 brie cheese
NT1 caciocavallo cheese
NT1 caerphilly cheese
NT1 camembert cheese
NT1 cantal cheese
NT1 carre de l'est cheese
NT1 cheddar cheese
NT1 cheshire cheese
NT1 colby cheese
NT1 comte cheese
NT1 cottage cheese

CHEESES *cont.*
NT1 cream cheese
NT1 crescenza cheese
NT1 curd
NT1 domiati cheese
NT1 dutch cheese
NT1 edam cheese
NT1 emmental cheese
NT1 feta cheese
NT1 filled cheese
NT1 fondue
NT1 fontina cheese
NT1 gammelost cheese
NT1 gorgonzola cheese
NT1 gouda cheese
NT1 grana cheese
NT1 grated cheese
NT1 gruyere cheese
NT1 italian cheese
NT1 kachkaval cheese
NT1 kareish cheese
NT1 kasseri cheese
NT1 kefalotyri cheese
NT1 limburg cheese
NT1 liptauer cheese
NT1 low fat cheeses
NT1 manchego cheese
NT1 mitzithra cheese
NT1 montasio cheese
NT1 mozzarella cheese
NT1 munster cheese
NT1 neufchatel cheese
NT1 parmesan cheese
NT1 pasta filata cheese
NT1 pecorino cheese
NT1 pickled cheese
NT1 pont-l'eveque cheese
NT1 port du salut cheese
NT1 prato cheese
NT1 processed cheese
NT1 provolone cheese
NT1 queso blanco cheese
NT1 reblochon cheese
NT1 ricotta cheese
NT1 romadur cheese
NT1 romano cheese
NT1 roquefort cheese
NT1 smoked cheese
NT1 soft cheese
NT1 stilton cheese
NT1 svecia cheese
NT1 swiss cheese
NT1 taleggio cheese
NT1 teleme cheese
NT1 tilsit cheese
NT1 trappist cheese
NT1 travnik cheese
NT1 tvorog
NT1 vacherin cheese
NT1 whey cheese
NT1 white cheese
rt casein
rt cheese mites
rt cheese quality
rt cheese slurry
rt cheese spread
rt cheese stores
rt cheesemaking
rt triers

cheetahs
USE **acinonyx jubatus**

CHEFS (AGRICOLA)
BT1 occupations
rt cooks (agricola)

cheghu
USE **chigu**

CHEILANTHES
BT1 pteridophyta

CHEILOMENES
BT1 coccinellidae
BT2 coleoptera
NT1 cheilomenes sexmaculata
rt menochilus

CHEILOMENES SEXMACULATA
uf *menochilus sexmaculatus*
BT1 cheilomenes
BT2 coccinellidae

CHEILOMENES SEXMACULATA *cont.*
BT3 coleoptera

CHEILONEURUS
BT1 encyrtidae
BT2 hymenoptera
NT1 cheiloneurus claviger

CHEILONEURUS CLAVIGER
BT1 cheiloneurus
BT2 encyrtidae
BT3 hymenoptera

CHEILOSIS
BT1 deficiency diseases
BT2 diseases
BT2 nutritional disorders
BT3 animal disorders
BT4 disorders
rt riboflavin deficiency

cheimatobia
USE **operophtera**

cheimatobia brumata
USE **operophtera brumata**

CHEIRACANTHIUM
BT1 clubionidae
BT2 araneae
BT3 arachnida
BT4 arthropods
NT1 cheiracanthium mildei

CHEIRACANTHIUM MILDEI
BT1 cheiracanthium
BT2 clubionidae
BT3 araneae
BT4 arachnida
BT5 arthropods

CHEIRANTHUS
BT1 cruciferae
NT1 cheiranthus cheiri

cheiranthus allionii
USE **erysimum allionii**

CHEIRANTHUS CHEIRI
uf *wallflowers*
BT1 cheiranthus
BT2 cruciferae
BT1 medicinal plants
BT1 ornamental herbaceous plants

CHEIROGALEIDAE
BT1 primates
BT2 mammals
NT1 microcebus
rt lemurs

chekiang
USE **zhejiang**

CHELATES
NT1 zinc edta
rt chelating agents
rt chelation
rt fertilizer carriers
rt metals
rt minor elements
rt soil amendments

CHELATING AGENTS
NT1 deferoxamine
NT1 dimercaprol
NT1 edta
NT1 etidronic acid
NT1 humic acids
NT1 hydroxyquinoline
NT1 nitrilotriacetic acid
NT1 penicillamine
NT1 phytic acid
rt chelates
rt detoxicants

CHELATION
rt chelates
rt combination
rt iron binding capacity
rt metals

CHELETOGENES
BT1 cheyletidae

CHELETOGENES *cont.*
BT2 prostigmata
BT3 acari
NT1 cheletogenes ornatus

CHELETOGENES ORNATUS
BT1 cheletogenes
BT2 cheyletidae
BT3 prostigmata
BT4 acari

CHELIDAE
BT1 testudines
BT2 reptiles
NT1 chelodina
NT2 chelodina longicollis

CHELIDONICHTHYS
BT1 triglidae
BT2 scorpaeniformes
BT3 osteichthyes
BT4 fishes

CHELIDONIUM
BT1 papaveraceae
NT1 chelidonium japonicum
NT1 chelidonium majus

CHELIDONIUM JAPONICUM
BT1 chelidonium
BT2 papaveraceae

CHELIDONIUM MAJUS
BT1 antifungal plants
BT1 chelidonium
BT2 papaveraceae
BT1 medicinal plants

CHELINIDEA
BT1 coreidae
BT2 heteroptera
NT1 chelinidea vittiger

CHELINIDEA VITTIGER
BT1 chelinidea
BT2 coreidae
BT3 heteroptera

chelocnetha
USE **simulium**

CHELODINA
BT1 chelidae
BT2 testudines
BT3 reptiles
NT1 chelodina longicollis

CHELODINA LONGICOLLIS
BT1 chelodina
BT2 chelidae
BT3 testudines
BT4 reptiles

CHELONIA
BT1 cheloniidae
BT2 testudines
BT3 reptiles
NT1 chelonia mydas

CHELONIA MYDAS
BT1 chelonia
BT2 cheloniidae
BT3 testudines
BT4 reptiles

CHELONIIDAE
BT1 testudines
BT2 reptiles
NT1 caretta
NT2 caretta caretta
NT1 chelonia
NT2 chelonia mydas
NT1 eretmochelys

CHELONUS
BT1 braconidae
BT2 hymenoptera
NT1 chelonus blackburni
NT1 chelonus insularis

CHELONUS BLACKBURNI
BT1 chelonus
BT2 braconidae
BT3 hymenoptera

CHELONUS INSULARIS
BT1 chelonus
BT2 braconidae
BT3 hymenoptera

CHELOSTOMA
BT1 apidae
BT2 hymenoptera

CHELYDRA
BT1 chelydridae
BT2 testudines
BT3 reptiles
NT1 chelydra serpentina

CHELYDRA SERPENTINA
BT1 chelydra
BT2 chelydridae
BT3 testudines
BT4 reptiles

CHELYDRIDAE
BT1 testudines
BT2 reptiles
NT1 chelydra
NT2 chelydra serpentina

CHEMICAL ANALYSIS
NT1 protein analysis
NT1 spectral analysis
rt analysis
rt chemical composition
rt chemical precipitation
rt chemistry
rt qualitative techniques
rt quantitative techniques

CHEMICAL COMPOSITION
BT1 composition
NT1 amino nitrogen
NT1 ammonium nitrogen
NT1 dissolved oxygen
NT1 free amino acids
NT1 inorganic phosphorus
NT1 nitrate nitrogen
NT1 nitrogen content
NT1 nonprotein nitrogen
rt chemical analysis

chemical constituents of wood
USE **wood chemistry**

CHEMICAL CONTROL
BT1 control
rt pest control
rt weed control

CHEMICAL DEGRADATION
BT1 degradation
NT1 corrosion
NT2 rust

CHEMICAL ECOLOGY
BT1 ecology
rt secondary metabolites

chemical hybridizing agents
USE **gametocides**

chemical immunosuppression
USE **immunosuppression**

CHEMICAL INDUSTRY
BT1 industry
NT1 fertilizer industry
rt agricultural chemicals
rt chemistry

CHEMICAL MODIFICATION OF WOOD
BT1 chemical treatment
NT1 acetylation
rt improved wood
rt wood chemistry

CHEMICAL OXYGEN DEMAND
BT1 oxygen requirement
BT2 requirements
rt biological oxygen demand
rt effluents
rt pollution

CHEMICAL PRECIPITATION
HN from 1990
uf *precipitation (chemical)*

CHEMICAL PRECIPITATION *cont.*
rt chemical analysis
rt deposition
rt flocculation

CHEMICAL PRESERVATION
BT1 preservation
BT2 techniques
rt chemical treatment
rt preservatives
rt silage additives

CHEMICAL PROPERTIES
uf chemico-physical properties
BT1 properties
NT1 acidity
NT2 saponification number
NT2 soil acidity
NT3 exchange acidity
NT3 titratable acidity
NT1 alkalinity
NT2 soil alkalinity
NT3 titratable basicity
NT1 enzyme activity
NT1 hygroscopicity
NT2 maximum hygroscopicity
NT1 molecular weight
rt physicochemical properties

CHEMICAL PRUNING
uf pruning, chemical
BT1 pruning
rt plant growth regulators

CHEMICAL REACTIONS
HN from 1990
NT1 hydrolysis
NT1 oxidation
NT2 vapour phase oxidation
NT1 redox reactions
NT2 electron transfer
NT1 reduction
NT2 acetylene reduction
NT2 nitrate reduction

chemical residues
USE **residues**

chemical soil types
USE **soil types (chemical)**

CHEMICAL SPECIATION
HN from 1990; previously "speciation"
uf speciation, chemical
rt elements
rt metals
rt minerals

CHEMICAL STIMULANTS
HN from 1990; previously "stimulants"
(stimulants of resin flow; for drugs use "stimulants")
rt resin tapping

CHEMICAL TREATMENT
NT1 chemical modification of wood
NT2 acetylation
NT1 sodium hydroxide treatment
rt chemical preservation
rt scrubbers
rt silage additives
rt treatment

CHEMICAL VS. CULTURAL WEED CONTROL
uf cultural vs. chemical weed control
BT1 weed control
BT2 pest control
BT3 control
rt cultural weed control

CHEMICALS
NT1 nitrogenous compounds
NT1 organic compounds
NT2 carbonyl compounds
NT2 vinyl compounds
NT3 vinyl plastics
rt agricultural chemicals
rt analogues
rt catalysts

CHEMICALS *cont.*
rt sucrochemicals

chemico-physical properties
USE **chemical properties**
OR **physical properties**
OR **physicochemical properties**

CHEMILUMINESCENCE
BT1 luminescence
BT2 radiation
rt chemiluminescence immunoassays

CHEMILUMINESCENCE IMMUNOASSAYS
HN from 1990
uf immunoassays, chemiluminescent
BT1 immunoassay
BT2 assays
BT2 immunological techniques
BT3 techniques
rt chemiluminescence

CHEMIMECHANICAL PULPING
BT1 pulping
BT2 processing

CHEMISTRY
NT1 biochemistry
NT2 cytochemistry
NT2 enzymology
NT3 histoenzymology
NT2 neurochemistry
NT1 biogeochemistry
NT1 dairy chemistry
NT1 food chemistry (agricola)
NT1 geochemistry
NT1 histochemistry
NT2 immunohistochemistry
NT1 physical chemistry
NT1 stereochemistry
NT1 wood chemistry
rt chemical analysis
rt chemical industry
rt chemists
rt crystallography
rt immunochemistry
rt soil chemistry

CHEMISTS
BT1 scientists
BT2 occupations
rt chemistry

CHEMITHERMOMECHANICAL PULPING
HN from 1990
BT1 pulping
BT2 processing

CHEMOPROPHYLAXIS
BT1 prophylaxis
BT2 control methods
BT3 methodology
rt agricultural chemicals
rt disease prevention
rt drug therapy

CHEMORECEPTORS
BT1 receptors

CHEMOSTERILANTS
BT1 sterilants
NT1 apholate
NT1 bisazir
NT1 busulfan
NT1 hemel
NT1 hempa
NT1 metepa
NT1 tepa
NT1 thiohempa
NT1 thiotepa
NT1 tretamine
rt sterilization

CHEMOTAXIS
BT1 taxis
BT2 movement
rt stimulation

CHEMOTAXONOMY
uf biochemical taxonomy
BT1 taxonomy
BT2 classification

chemotherapy
USE **drug therapy**

CHEMOTROPISM
BT1 tropisms
BT2 movement
BT2 plant physiology
BT3 physiology
BT2 responses

CHENGDE POLLED
HN from 1990
BT1 goat breeds
BT2 breeds

CHENGDU BROWN
HN from 1990
BT1 goat breeds
BT2 breeds

chenic acid
USE **chenodeoxycholic acid**

CHENILLE (AGRICOLA)
BT1 fabrics
BT1 yarns (agricola)

CHENODEOXYCHOLIC ACID
uf chenic acid
BT1 bile acids
BT1 cholanes
BT2 steroids
BT3 isoprenoids
BT4 lipids

CHENOPODIACEAE
NT1 allenrolfea
NT2 allenrolfea occidentalis
NT1 anabasis
NT2 anabasis aphylla
NT2 anabasis salsa
NT1 atriplex
NT2 atriplex alaskensis
NT2 atriplex canescens
NT2 atriplex confertifolia
NT2 atriplex corrugata
NT2 atriplex gmelinii
NT2 atriplex halimus
NT2 atriplex hastata
NT2 atriplex hortensis
NT2 atriplex hymenelytra
NT2 atriplex lentiformis
NT2 atriplex nummularia
NT2 atriplex nuttalii
NT2 atriplex patula
NT2 atriplex polycarpa
NT2 atriplex repanda
NT2 atriplex semibaccata
NT2 atriplex subspicata
NT1 axyris
NT2 axyris amaranthoides
NT2 axyris lanata
NT1 beta
NT2 beta adanensis
NT2 beta bourgaei
NT2 beta macrocarpa
NT2 beta vulgaris
NT2 beta vulgaris var. saccharifera
NT1 chenopodium
NT2 chenopodium album
NT2 chenopodium album var. centrorubrum
NT2 chenopodium amaranticolor
NT2 chenopodium ambrosioides
NT2 chenopodium berlandieri
NT2 chenopodium bonus-henricus
NT2 chenopodium botrys
NT2 chenopodium canihua
NT2 chenopodium ficifolium
NT2 chenopodium giganteum
NT2 chenopodium glaucum
NT2 chenopodium hircinum
NT2 chenopodium hybridum
NT2 chenopodium murale
NT2 chenopodium nuttaliae

CHENOPODIACEAE *cont.*
NT2 chenopodium pallidicaule
NT2 chenopodium polyspermum
NT2 chenopodium quinoa
NT2 chenopodium rubrum
NT2 chenopodium serotinum
NT2 chenopodium strictum
NT2 chenopodium suecicum
NT1 enchylaena
NT2 enchylaena tomentosa
NT1 eremosemium
NT2 eremosemium spinosa
NT1 eurotia
NT2 eurotia lanata
NT1 halocnemum
NT2 halocnemum strobilaceum
NT1 halogeton
NT2 halogeton glomeratus
NT1 halostachys
NT2 halostachys caspica
NT1 haloxylon
NT2 haloxylon ammodendron
NT2 haloxylon aphyllum
NT2 haloxylon persicum
NT1 kochia
NT2 kochia americana
NT2 kochia brevifolia
NT2 kochia indica
NT2 kochia prostrata
NT2 kochia pyramidata
NT2 kochia scoparia
NT1 krascheninnikovia
NT2 krascheninnikovia ceratoides
NT2 krascheninnikovia lanata
NT1 maireana
NT2 maireana brevifolia
NT2 maireana pyramidata
NT1 salicornia
NT2 salicornia herbacea
NT1 salsola
NT2 salsola iberica
NT2 salsola kali
NT2 salsola kali var. tenuifolia
NT2 salsola paulsenii
NT2 salsola pestifera
NT2 salsola richteri
NT2 salsola ruthenica
NT2 salsola tragus
NT1 sarcobatus
NT2 sarcobatus vermiculatus
NT1 spinacia
NT2 spinacia oleracea
NT1 suaeda

CHENOPODIUM
BT1 chenopodiaceae
NT1 chenopodium album
NT1 chenopodium album var. centrorubrum
NT1 chenopodium amaranticolor
NT1 chenopodium ambrosioides
NT1 chenopodium berlandieri
NT1 chenopodium bonus-henricus
NT1 chenopodium botrys
NT1 chenopodium canihua
NT1 chenopodium ficifolium
NT1 chenopodium giganteum
NT1 chenopodium glaucum
NT1 chenopodium hircinum
NT1 chenopodium hybridum
NT1 chenopodium murale
NT1 chenopodium nuttaliae
NT1 chenopodium pallidicaule
NT1 chenopodium polyspermum
NT1 chenopodium quinoa
NT1 chenopodium rubrum
NT1 chenopodium serotinum
NT1 chenopodium strictum
NT1 chenopodium suecicum

CHENOPODIUM ALBUM
BT1 chenopodium
BT2 chenopodiaceae
BT1 insecticidal plants
BT2 pesticidal plants
BT1 pseudocereals
BT2 grain crops
BT1 weeds

CHENOPODIUM ALBUM VAR. CENTRORUBRUM
BT1 chenopodium
BT2 chenopodiaceae

CHENOPODIUM AMARANTICOLOR
BT1 antifungal plants
BT1 chenopodium
BT2 chenopodiaceae

CHENOPODIUM AMBROSIOIDES
BT1 chenopodium
BT2 chenopodiaceae
BT1 insecticidal plants
BT2 pesticidal plants
BT1 medicinal plants
BT1 nematicidal plants
BT2 pesticidal plants

CHENOPODIUM BERLANDIERI
BT1 chenopodium
BT2 chenopodiaceae

CHENOPODIUM BONUS-HENRICUS
BT1 chenopodium
BT2 chenopodiaceae

CHENOPODIUM BOTRYS
BT1 chenopodium
BT2 chenopodiaceae

CHENOPODIUM CANIHUA
uf *canihua*
BT1 chenopodium
BT2 chenopodiaceae

CHENOPODIUM FICIFOLIUM
BT1 chenopodium
BT2 chenopodiaceae

CHENOPODIUM GIGANTEUM
BT1 chenopodium
BT2 chenopodiaceae

CHENOPODIUM GLAUCUM
BT1 chenopodium
BT2 chenopodiaceae

CHENOPODIUM HIRCINUM
BT1 chenopodium
BT2 chenopodiaceae

CHENOPODIUM HYBRIDUM
BT1 chenopodium
BT2 chenopodiaceae

CHENOPODIUM MURALE
BT1 chenopodium
BT2 chenopodiaceae
BT1 weeds

CHENOPODIUM NUTTALIAE
BT1 chenopodium
BT2 chenopodiaceae
BT1 pseudocereals
BT2 grain crops

CHENOPODIUM PALLIDICAULE
BT1 chenopodium
BT2 chenopodiaceae

CHENOPODIUM POLYSPERMUM
BT1 chenopodium
BT2 chenopodiaceae

CHENOPODIUM QUINOA
BT1 chenopodium
BT2 chenopodiaceae
BT1 pseudocereals
BT2 grain crops

CHENOPODIUM RUBRUM
BT1 chenopodium
BT2 chenopodiaceae
BT1 weeds

CHENOPODIUM SEROTINUM
BT1 chenopodium
BT2 chenopodiaceae

CHENOPODIUM STRICTUM
BT1 chenopodium
BT2 chenopodiaceae

CHENOPODIUM SUECICUM
BT1 chenopodium
BT2 chenopodiaceae

cher berrichon
USE **berrichon du cher**

CHERAX
BT1 decapoda
BT2 malacostraca
BT3 crustacea
BT4 arthropods
NT1 cherax destructor

CHERAX DESTRUCTOR
BT1 cherax
BT2 decapoda
BT3 malacostraca
BT4 crustacea
BT5 arthropods

CHERIMOYAS
BT1 tropical tree fruits
BT2 tree fruits
BT2 tropical fruits
BT3 fruit crops
rt annona cherimola

chermes
USE **adelges**

CHERNOZEMIC SOILS
BT1 chernozems
BT2 soil types (genetic)

CHERNOZEMS
uf *black earths*
BT1 soil types (genetic)
NT1 borolls
NT1 calcareous chernozems
NT1 chernozemic soils
NT1 compact chernozems
NT1 leached chernozems
NT1 salinized chernozems
NT1 smonitza chernozems
NT1 solonetzic chernozems

CHERRIES
BT1 antiviral plants
BT1 stone fruits
BT2 temperate tree fruits
BT3 temperate fruits
BT4 fruit crops
BT3 tree fruits
rt cherry leaf roll nepovirus
rt prunus avium
rt prunus cerasus

CHERRY LEAF ROLL NEPOVIRUS
HN from 1990; previously "cherry leaf roll virus"
uf *cherry leaf roll virus*
BT1 nepovirus group
BT2 plant viruses
BT3 plant pathogens
BT4 pathogens
rt cherries

cherry leaf roll virus
USE **cherry leaf roll nepovirus**

CHERRY RASP LEAF VIRUS
BT1 miscellaneous plant viruses
BT2 plant viruses
BT3 plant pathogens
BT4 pathogens
rt prunus avium
rt prunus cerasus

cherry salmon
USE **oncorhynchus masou**

chervil
USE **anthriscus cerefolium**

CHESHIRE CHEESE
BT1 cheeses
BT2 milk products
BT3 products

CHESHUNT MIXTURE
BT1 copper fungicides
BT2 fungicides
BT3 pesticides

CHESTER WHITE
BT1 pig breeds
BT2 breeds

CHESTNUT SOILS
BT1 kastanozems
BT2 soil types (genetic)

CHESTNUTS
BT1 medicinal plants
BT1 temperate tree nuts
BT2 nut crops
rt castanea sativa

CHEVIOT
BT1 sheep breeds
BT2 breeds

CHEWING GUM
BT1 confectionery

CHEWING TOBACCO
BT1 plant products
BT2 products
rt tobacco

CHEYLETIA
BT1 cheyletidae
BT2 prostigmata
BT3 acari

CHEYLETIDAE
BT1 prostigmata
BT2 acari
NT1 acaropsellina
NT2 acaropsellina docta
NT1 acaropsis
NT2 acaropsis aegyptiaca
NT1 cheletogenes
NT2 cheletogenes ornatus
NT1 cheyletia
NT1 cheyletus
NT2 cheyletus aversor
NT2 cheyletus eruditus
NT2 cheyletus malaccensis
NT1 hemicheyletia

CHEYLETIELLA
BT1 cheyletiellidae
BT2 prostigmata
BT3 acari
NT1 cheyletiella blakei
NT1 cheyletiella parasitivorax
NT1 cheyletiella yasguri

CHEYLETIELLA BLAKEI
BT1 cheyletiella
BT2 cheyletiellidae
BT3 prostigmata
BT4 acari

CHEYLETIELLA PARASITIVORAX
BT1 cheyletiella
BT2 cheyletiellidae
BT3 prostigmata
BT4 acari

CHEYLETIELLA YASGURI
BT1 cheyletiella
BT2 cheyletiellidae
BT3 prostigmata
BT4 acari

CHEYLETIELLIDAE
BT1 prostigmata
BT2 acari
NT1 cheyletiella
NT2 cheyletiella blakei
NT2 cheyletiella parasitivorax
NT2 cheyletiella yasguri

CHEYLETUS
BT1 cheyletidae
BT2 prostigmata
BT3 acari
NT1 cheyletus aversor
NT1 cheyletus eruditus
NT1 cheyletus malaccensis

CHEYLETUS AVERSOR
BT1 cheyletus
BT2 cheyletidae
BT3 prostigmata
BT4 acari

CHEYLETUS ERUDITUS
BT1 cheyletus
BT2 cheyletidae
BT3 prostigmata
BT4 acari

CHEYLETUS MALACCENSIS
BT1 cheyletus
BT2 cheyletidae
BT3 prostigmata
BT4 acari

CHHANA
BT1 milk products
BT2 products

chiana
USE **chianina**

CHIANINA
HN from 1990; previously "chiana"
uf *chiana*
BT1 cattle breeds
BT2 breeds

CHIASMA FREQUENCY
BT1 frequency
rt chiasmata
rt crossing over

CHIASMATA
rt chiasma frequency
rt crossing over
rt interference

CHICK EMBRYOS
BT1 embryos
rt chicks

CHICK PRODUCTION
HN from 1990
BT1 animal production
BT2 agricultural production
BT3 production
rt chicks

CHICKEN ANAEMIA AGENT
HN from 1990
AF chicken anemia agent
rt anaemia
rt parvoviridae
rt poultry diseases

CHICKEN ANEMIA AGENT
HN from 1990
BF chicken anaemia agent
rt anemia

chicken corn
USE **sorghum**

CHICKEN FAT
BT1 poultry fat
BT2 animal fat
BT3 fat
rt fowls

chicken fattening
USE **fowl fattening**

CHICKEN HOUSING
BT1 poultry housing
BT2 animal housing
rt fowls

CHICKEN MEAT
uf *chickens*
BT1 poultry meat
BT2 meat
BT3 animal products
BT4 products
BT3 foods
rt fowls

chicken pox
USE **varicella**

chickens
USE **chicken meat**
OR **fowls**

CHICKPEAS
rt cicer arietinum

CHICKS
BT1 young animals
BT2 animals
rt chick embryos
rt chick production
rt fowls
rt hatching weight

CHICORY
BT1 leafy vegetables
BT2 vegetables
BT1 nematicidal plants
BT2 pesticidal plants
rt brown core
rt chicory yellow mottle nepovirus
rt cichorium intybus

CHICORY YELLOW MOTTLE NEPOVIRUS
HN from 1990
BT1 nepovirus group
BT2 plant viruses
BT3 plant pathogens
BT4 pathogens
rt chicory
rt cichorium intybus

CHIFFON (AGRICOLA)
BT1 fabrics

CHIGU
HN from 1990; previously "cheghu"
uf *cheghu*
BT1 goat breeds
BT2 breeds

CHIKUNGUNYA VIRUS
BT1 alphavirus
BT2 arboviruses
BT3 pathogens
BT2 togaviridae
BT3 viruses

CHILD ABUSE
BT1 abuse (agricola)
BT1 antisocial behavior (agricola)
BT2 human behavior
BT3 behavior
rt child neglect (agricola)
rt children

CHILD CARE
BT1 social welfare
rt child careproviders (agricola)
rt child day care (agricola)
rt child rearing practices (agricola)
rt child welfare (agricola)
rt children
rt education
rt paediatrics

child care workers
USE **child careproviders (agricola)**

CHILD CAREPROVIDERS (AGRICOLA)
uf *child care workers*
BT1 careproviders (agricola)
rt child care

CHILD CUSTODY (AGRICOLA)
rt divorce (agricola)
rt visitation rights (agricola)

CHILD DAY CARE (AGRICOLA)
BT1 day care (agricola)
NT1 day camp programs (agricola)
rt child care
rt day care centers (agricola)

CHILD DEVELOPMENT (AGRICOLA)
NT1 early childhood development (agricola)
rt child development centers (agricola)
rt children
rt development

CHILD DEVELOPMENT (AGRICOLA) *cont.*
rt infant development (agricola)
rt psychomotor development (agricola)

CHILD DEVELOPMENT CENTERS (AGRICOLA)
rt child development (agricola)
rt early childhood education (agricola)

CHILD FEEDING
BT1 feeding
rt child nutrition (agricola)
rt children
rt diets
rt infant feeding
rt infant foods
rt school meals

CHILD LABOR
BF child labour
rt labor

CHILD LABOUR
AF child labor
BT1 labour
rt children
rt young workers

CHILD NEGLECT (AGRICOLA)
BT1 antisocial behavior (agricola)
BT2 human behavior
BT3 behavior
rt child abuse
rt child welfare (agricola)
rt children
rt parent child relationships

CHILD NUTRITION (AGRICOLA)
BT1 nutrition
rt child feeding
rt children
rt infant nutrition (agricola)

CHILD REARING PRACTICES (AGRICOLA)
rt child care
rt children

CHILD WELFARE (AGRICOLA)
rt child care
rt child neglect (agricola)
rt children

CHILDBIRTH (AGRICOLA)
NT1 home birth (agricola)
NT1 montessori method (agricola)
NT1 natural childbirth (agricola)
rt birth
rt childbirth education (agricola)
rt lamaze childbirth training (agricola)

CHILDBIRTH EDUCATION (AGRICOLA)
BT1 education
rt childbirth (agricola)

CHILDHOOD DISEASES (AGRICOLA)
BT1 human diseases
BT2 diseases
NT1 tay-sachs disease (agricola)
rt children
rt infant disorders
rt pediatrics

CHILDLESSNESS (AGRICOLA)

CHILDREN
uf *offspring*
BT1 people
NT1 adopted children (agricola)
NT1 boys
NT1 exceptional children (agricola)
NT1 foster children (agricola)
NT1 handicapped children (agricola)

CHILDREN *cont.*
NT1 latchkey children (agricola)
NT1 preschool children (agricola)
NT1 school children
rt adolescents
rt child abuse
rt child care
rt child development (agricola)
rt child feeding
rt child labour
rt child neglect (agricola)
rt child nutrition (agricola)
rt child rearing practices (agricola)
rt child welfare (agricola)
rt childhood diseases (agricola)
rt daughters
rt family structure
rt infants
rt paediatrics
rt parent child relationships
rt parents
rt progeny
rt school leavers
rt sons
rt unicef

CHILDREN'S COOKBOOKS (AGRICOLA)
BT1 children's literature (agricola)
BT2 literature
BT1 cookbooks
BT2 books
BT3 publications

CHILDREN'S GAMES
uf *games, children's*
BT1 games
BT1 play
BT2 leisure activities
rt indoor games
rt outdoor games

CHILDREN'S LITERATURE (AGRICOLA)
BT1 literature
NT1 children's cookbooks (agricola)
rt activity books (agricola)
rt coloring books (agricola)
rt comics (agricola)

CHILE
BT1 south america
BT2 america
rt developing countries
rt threshold countries

CHILIOTRICHUM
BT1 compositae
rt ornamental woody plants

CHILLIES
BT1 spices
BT2 plant products
BT3 products
rt capsicum annuum
rt capsicum frutescens

CHILLING
rt chilling requirement
rt cold
rt cooling

CHILLING INJURY
BT1 plant disorders
BT2 disorders

CHILLING REQUIREMENT
BT1 requirements
rt chilling
rt dormancy

CHILO
uf *chilotraea*
uf *proceras*
BT1 pyralidae
BT2 lepidoptera
NT1 chilo agamemnon
NT1 chilo auricilius
NT1 chilo diffusilineus
NT1 chilo infuscatellus

CHILO *cont.*
NT1 chilo luteellus
NT1 chilo orichalcociliellus
NT1 chilo partellus
NT1 chilo polychrysus
NT1 chilo sacchariphagus
NT2 chilo sacchariphagus sacchariphagus
NT1 chilo suppressalis
NT1 chilo zacconius

CHILO AGAMEMNON
BT1 chilo
BT2 pyralidae
BT3 lepidoptera

CHILO AURICILIUS
uf *chilotraea auricilia*
BT1 chilo
BT2 pyralidae
BT3 lepidoptera

CHILO DIFFUSILINEUS
BT1 chilo
BT2 pyralidae
BT3 lepidoptera

CHILO INFUSCATELLUS
uf *chilotraea infuscatella*
BT1 chilo
BT2 pyralidae
BT3 lepidoptera

CHILO IRIDESCENT VIRUS
BT1 iridescent viruses
BT2 iridovirus
BT3 insect viruses
BT4 entomopathogens
BT5 pathogens
BT3 iridoviridae
BT4 viruses

CHILO LUTEELLUS
BT1 chilo
BT2 pyralidae
BT3 lepidoptera

CHILO ORICHALCOCILIELLUS
BT1 chilo
BT2 pyralidae
BT3 lepidoptera

CHILO PARTELLUS
uf *chilo zonellus*
BT1 chilo
BT2 pyralidae
BT3 lepidoptera

CHILO POLYCHRYSUS
uf *chilotraea polychrysa*
BT1 chilo
BT2 pyralidae
BT3 lepidoptera

CHILO SACCHARIPHAGUS
uf *proceras sacchariphagus*
BT1 chilo
BT2 pyralidae
BT3 lepidoptera
NT1 chilo sacchariphagus sacchariphagus

CHILO SACCHARIPHAGUS SACCHARIPHAGUS
uf *chilo sacchariphagus venosatus*
uf *chilo venosatus*
uf *proceras venosatus*
BT1 chilo sacchariphagus
BT2 chilo
BT3 pyralidae
BT4 lepidoptera

chilo sacchariphagus venosatus
USE **chilo sacchariphagus sacchariphagus**

CHILO SUPPRESSALIS
BT1 chilo
BT2 pyralidae
BT3 lepidoptera

chilo venosatus
USE **chilo sacchariphagus sacchariphagus**

CHILO ZACCONIUS
BT1 chilo
BT2 pyralidae
BT3 lepidoptera

chilo zonellus
USE **chilo partellus**

CHILOCORUS
BT1 coccinellidae
BT2 coleoptera
NT1 chilocorus bipustulatus
NT1 chilocorus kuwanae
NT1 chilocorus nigrita

CHILOCORUS BIPUSTULATUS
BT1 chilocorus
BT2 coccinellidae
BT3 coleoptera

CHILOCORUS KUWANAE
BT1 chilocorus
BT2 coccinellidae
BT3 coleoptera

CHILOCORUS NIGRITA
BT1 chilocorus
BT2 coccinellidae
BT3 coleoptera

CHILODONELLA
BT1 ciliophora
BT2 protozoa
NT1 chilodonella algivora
NT1 chilodonella cucullulus
NT1 chilodonella cyprini
NT1 chilodonella hexastichus
NT1 chilodonella uncinata

CHILODONELLA ALGIVORA
BT1 chilodonella
BT2 ciliophora
BT3 protozoa

CHILODONELLA CUCULLULUS
BT1 chilodonella
BT2 ciliophora
BT3 protozoa

CHILODONELLA CYPRINI
BT1 chilodonella
BT2 ciliophora
BT3 protozoa

CHILODONELLA HEXASTICHUS
BT1 chilodonella
BT2 ciliophora
BT3 protozoa

CHILODONELLA UNCINATA
BT1 chilodonella
BT2 ciliophora
BT3 protozoa

CHILOLOBA
BT1 scarabaeidae
BT2 coleoptera
NT1 chiloloba acuta

CHILOLOBA ACUTA
BT1 chiloloba
BT2 scarabaeidae
BT3 coleoptera

CHILOMASTIX
BT1 sarcomastigophora
BT2 protozoa
NT1 chilomastix equi
NT1 chilomastix mesnili

CHILOMASTIX EQUI
BT1 chilomastix
BT2 sarcomastigophora
BT3 protozoa

CHILOMASTIX MESNILI
BT1 chilomastix
BT2 sarcomastigophora
BT3 protozoa

CHILOPLACUS
HN from 1990
BT1 belondiridae
BT2 nematoda

CHILOPODA
uf centipedes
BT1 myriapoda
BT2 arthropods
NT1 lithobiidae
NT2 lithobius
NT3 lithobius forficatus
NT1 scolopendridae
NT2 scolopendra
NT3 scolopendra subspinipes
NT1 scutigeridae
NT2 scutigera
NT3 scutigera coleoptrata

chilotraea
USE **chilo**

chilotraea auricilia
USE **chilo auricilius**

chilotraea infuscatella
USE **chilo infuscatellus**

chilotraea polychrysa
USE **chilo polychrysus**

CHIMAERA
BT1 chimaeridae
BT2 chimaeriformes
BT3 chondrichthyes
BT4 fishes
NT1 chimaera monstrosa

CHIMAERA MONSTROSA
BT1 chimaera
BT2 chimaeridae
BT3 chimaeriformes
BT4 chondrichthyes
BT5 fishes

CHIMAERAS
AF chimeras
uf chimaerism
uf sectoring
rt graft hybridization
rt mixoploidy
rt mosaicism
rt vegetative hybridization

CHIMAERIDAE
BT1 chimaeriformes
BT2 chondrichthyes
BT3 fishes
NT1 chimaera
NT2 chimaera monstrosa
NT1 hydrolagus

CHIMAERIFORMES
BT1 chondrichthyes
BT2 fishes
NT1 chimaeridae
NT2 chimaera
NT3 chimaera monstrosa
NT2 hydrolagus

chimaerism
USE **chimaeras**

CHIMERAS
BF chimaeras
rt chimerism (agricola)

CHIMERISM (AGRICOLA)
rt chimeras

CHIMONANTHUS
BT1 calycanthaceae
NT1 chimonanthus praecox

CHIMONANTHUS PRAECOX
BT1 chimonanthus
BT2 calycanthaceae
BT1 ornamental woody plants

CHIMONOBAMBUSA
BT1 gramineae
NT1 chimonobambusa jaunsarensis

CHIMONOBAMBUSA JAUNSARENSIS
BT1 chimonobambusa
BT2 gramineae

CHIMPANZEES
uf pan troglodytes
BT1 wild animals
BT2 animals
rt pongidae

CHINA
uf china, mainland
uf china, people's republic
uf mainland china
BT1 east asia
BT2 asia
NT1 anhui
NT1 beijing
NT1 central southern china
NT1 eastern china
NT1 fujian
NT1 gansu
NT1 guangdong
NT1 guangxi
NT1 guizhou
NT1 hebei
NT1 heilongjiang
NT1 henan
NT1 hubei
NT1 hunan
NT1 jiangsu
NT1 jiangxi
NT1 jilin
NT1 liaoning
NT1 nei menggu
NT1 ningxia
NT1 north eastern china
NT1 north western china
NT1 northern china
NT1 qinghai
NT1 shaanxi
NT1 shandong
NT1 shanghai
NT1 shanxi
NT1 sichuan
NT1 south western china
NT1 tianjin
NT1 tibet
NT1 xinjiang
NT1 yunnan
NT1 zhejiang
rt centrally planned economies
rt developing countries
rt gobi desert
rt least developed countries
rt peoples' communes

china (anhwei)
USE **anhui**

china aster
USE **callistephus chinensis**

china (central southern region)
USE **central southern china**

china (chekiang)
USE **zhejiang**

china (chinghai)
USE **qinghai**

china (eastern region)
USE **eastern china**

china (fukien)
USE **fujian**

china (heilungkiang)
USE **heilongjiang**

china (hopei)
USE **hebei**

china (hunan)
USE **hunan**

china (hupei)
USE **hubei**

china (inner mongolia)
USE **nei menggu**

china (kansu)
USE **gansu**

china (kiangsi)
USE **jiangxi**

china (kiangsu)
USE **jiangsu**

china (kirin)
USE **jilin**

china (kwangsi)
USE **guangxi**

china (kwantung)
USE **guangdong**

china (kweichow)
USE **guizhou**

china (liaoning)
USE **liaoning**

china, mainland
USE **china**

china (ningsia-hui)
USE **ningxia**

china (north eastern region)
USE **north eastern china**

china (north western region)
USE **north western china**

china (northern region)
USE **northern china**

china (peking)
USE **beijing**
OR **northern china**

china, people's republic
USE **china**

china (shanghai)
USE **eastern china**
OR **shanghai**

china (shansi)
USE **shanxi**

china (shantung)
USE **shandong**

china (shensi)
USE **shaanxi**

china (sinkiang)
USE **xinjiang**

china (south western region)
USE **south western china**

china (szechwan)
USE **sichuan**

china (taiwan)
USE **taiwan**

china (tibet)
USE **tibet**

china (tientsin)
USE **tianjin**

china (xizhang)
USE **tibet**

china (yunnan)
USE **yunnan**

CHINCHILLA
BT1 chinchillidae
BT2 rodents
BT3 mammals

chinchilla laniger
USE **chinchillas**

CHINCHILLAS
uf chinchilla laniger
BT1 furbearing animals
BT2 animals
rt chinchillidae

CHINCHILLIDAE
BT1 rodents
BT2 mammals
NT1 chinchilla
NT1 lagidium
NT2 lagidium peruanum
NT1 lagostomus

CHINCHILLIDAE *cont.*
NT2 lagostomus maximus
rt chinchillas

CHINESE BLACK-AND-WHITE
HN from 1990
BT1 cattle breeds
BT2 breeds

CHINESE CABBAGES
uf *cabbage, chinese*
BT1 leafy vegetables
BT2 vegetables
rt brassica pekinensis

CHINESE COOKERY (AGRICOLA)
BT1 cookery (agricola)

chinese gooseberries
USE **actinidia deliciosa**
OR **kiwifruits**

chinese hamster
USE **cricetulus barabensis**

chinese jujube
USE **ziziphus sativa**

chinese kale
USE **brassica alboglabra**

CHINESE RESTAURANT SYNDROME
BT1 digestive disorders
BT2 functional disorders
BT3 animal disorders
BT4 disorders
BT1 food poisoning
BT2 poisoning
rt monosodium glutamate

chinghai
USE **qinghai**

CHINOMETHIONAT
uf *oxythioquinox*
uf *quinomethionate*
BT1 quinoxaline acaricides
BT2 acaricides
BT3 pesticides
BT2 quinoxalines
BT3 heterocyclic nitrogen compounds
BT4 organic nitrogen compounds
BT1 quinoxaline fungicides
BT2 fungicides
BT3 pesticides
BT2 quinoxalines
BT3 heterocyclic nitrogen compounds
BT4 organic nitrogen compounds

chinosol
USE **hydroxyquinoline**

CHINTZ (AGRICOLA)
BT1 fabrics

CHIONACHNE
BT1 gramineae

CHIONASPIS
uf *phenacaspis*
BT1 diaspididae
BT2 coccoidea
BT3 sternorrhyncha
BT4 homoptera
NT1 chionaspis pinifoliae
NT1 chionaspis salicis

CHIONASPIS PINIFOLIAE
uf *phenacaspis pinifoliae*
BT1 chionaspis
BT2 diaspididae
BT3 coccoidea
BT4 sternorrhyncha
BT5 homoptera

CHIONASPIS SALICIS
BT1 chionaspis
BT2 diaspididae
BT3 coccoidea
BT4 sternorrhyncha

CHIONASPIS SALICIS *cont.*
BT5 homoptera

CHIONOCHLOA
BT1 gramineae
NT1 chionochloa antarctica
NT1 chionochloa crassiuscula
NT1 chionochloa flavescens
NT1 chionochloa juncea
NT1 chionochloa macra
NT1 chionochloa pallens
NT1 chionochloa rigida
NT1 chionochloa rubra

CHIONOCHLOA ANTARCTICA
BT1 chionochloa
BT2 gramineae
BT1 pasture plants

CHIONOCHLOA CRASSIUSCULA
BT1 chionochloa
BT2 gramineae
BT1 pasture plants

CHIONOCHLOA FLAVESCENS
BT1 chionochloa
BT2 gramineae
BT1 pasture plants

CHIONOCHLOA JUNCEA
BT1 chionochloa
BT2 gramineae
BT1 pasture plants

CHIONOCHLOA MACRA
BT1 chionochloa
BT2 gramineae
BT1 pasture plants

CHIONOCHLOA PALLENS
BT1 chionochloa
BT2 gramineae
BT1 pasture plants

CHIONOCHLOA RIGIDA
BT1 chionochloa
BT2 gramineae
BT1 pasture plants

CHIONOCHLOA RUBRA
BT1 chionochloa
BT2 gramineae
BT1 pasture plants

CHIONODOXA
BT1 liliaceae
rt ornamental bulbs

CHIONOECETES
BT1 decapoda
BT2 malacostraca
BT3 crustacea
BT4 arthropods

CHIOS
BT1 sheep breeds
BT2 breeds

chipboards
USE **particleboards**

chipmunk
USE **tamias**

CHIPPING
uf *comminution of wood*
BT1 processing
rt wood chips

CHIPPING HEADRIGS
BT1 forestry machinery
BT2 machinery
rt logs
rt sawmilling

chips
USE **chips (french fries)**
OR **wood chips**

CHIPS (FRENCH FRIES)
AF french fries
uf *chips*
BT1 potato products
BT2 vegetable products
BT3 plant products
BT4 products

CHIPS (FRENCH FRIES) *cont.*
rt crisps
rt potatoes

chips, wood
USE **wood chips**

CHIRANTHODENDRON
BT1 sterculiaceae
NT1 chiranthodendron pentadactylon

CHIRANTHODENDRON PENTADACTYLON
BT1 chiranthodendron
BT2 sterculiaceae

CHIRODISCOIDES
BT1 atopomelidae
BT2 astigmata
BT3 acari
NT1 chirodiscoides caviae

CHIRODISCOIDES CAVIAE
BT1 chirodiscoides
BT2 atopomelidae
BT3 astigmata
BT4 acari

CHIRONJAS
BT1 citrus fruits
BT2 subtropical tree fruits
BT3 subtropical fruits
BT4 fruit crops
BT3 tree fruits
rt citrus

CHIRONOMIDAE
BT1 diptera
NT1 camptochironomus
NT2 camptochironomus tentans
NT1 chironomus
NT2 chironomus anthracinus
NT2 chironomus crassicaudatus
NT2 chironomus decorus
NT2 chironomus plumosus
NT2 chironomus riparius
NT3 chironomus riparius piger
NT3 chironomus riparius riparius
NT2 chironomus staegeri
NT2 chironomus yoshimatsui
NT1 cladotanytarsus
NT2 cladotanytarsus lewisi
NT1 dicrotendipes
NT2 dicrotendipes californicus
NT1 glyptotendipes
NT2 glyptotendipes paripes
NT1 procladius
NT1 tanytarsus
NT1 tokunagayusurika
NT2 tokunagayusurika akamusi

CHIRONOMUS
BT1 chironomidae
BT2 diptera
NT1 chironomus anthracinus
NT1 chironomus crassicaudatus
NT1 chironomus decorus
NT1 chironomus plumosus
NT1 chironomus riparius
NT2 chironomus riparius piger
NT2 chironomus riparius riparius
NT1 chironomus staegeri
NT1 chironomus yoshimatsui
rt camptochironomus
rt dicrotendipes

CHIRONOMUS ANTHRACINUS
BT1 chironomus
BT2 chironomidae
BT3 diptera

chironomus californicus
USE **dicrotendipes californicus**

CHIRONOMUS CRASSICAUDATUS
BT1 chironomus
BT2 chironomidae
BT3 diptera

CHIRONOMUS DECORUS
BT1 chironomus

CHIRONOMUS DECORUS *cont.*
BT2 chironomidae
BT3 diptera

CHIRONOMUS PLUMOSUS
BT1 chironomus
BT2 chironomidae
BT3 diptera

CHIRONOMUS RIPARIUS
uf *chironomus thummi*
BT1 chironomus
BT2 chironomidae
BT3 diptera
NT1 chironomus riparius piger
NT1 chironomus riparius riparius

CHIRONOMUS RIPARIUS PIGER
HN from 1990
BT1 chironomus riparius
BT2 chironomus
BT3 chironomidae
BT4 diptera

CHIRONOMUS RIPARIUS RIPARIUS
HN from 1990
BT1 chironomus riparius
BT2 chironomus
BT3 chironomidae
BT4 diptera

CHIRONOMUS STAEGERI
BT1 chironomus
BT2 chironomidae
BT3 diptera

chironomus tentans
USE **camptochironomus tentans**

chironomus thummi
USE **chironomus riparius**

CHIRONOMUS YOSHIMATSUI
BT1 chironomus
BT2 chironomidae
BT3 diptera

CHIROPTERA
uf *bats*
BT1 mammals
NT1 emballonuridae
NT2 taphozous
NT3 taphozous perforatus
NT1 hipposideridae
NT2 hipposideros
NT1 molossidae
NT2 molossus
NT3 molossus molossus
NT2 tadarida
NT3 tadarida plicata
NT1 noctilionidae
NT2 noctilio
NT1 phyllostomidae
NT2 artibeus
NT3 artibeus jamaicensis
NT2 desmodus
NT1 pteropodidae
NT2 cynopterus
NT2 pteropus
NT3 pteropus poliocephalus
NT2 rousettus
NT3 rousettus aegyptiacus
NT1 rhinolophidae
NT2 rhinolophus
NT3 rhinolophus cornutus
NT3 rhinolophus ferrumequinum
NT1 rhinopomatidae
NT2 rhinopoma
NT3 rhinopoma microphyllum
NT1 vespertilionidae
NT2 chalinolobus
NT2 eptesicus
NT3 eptesicus fuscus
NT3 eptesicus serotinus
NT2 lasiurus (mammals)
NT3 lasiurus cinereus
NT2 miniopterus
NT3 miniopterus schreibersi
NT2 myotis
NT3 myotis blythii

CHIROPTERA *cont.*
NT3 myotis daubentonii
NT3 myotis lucifugus
NT3 myotis macrodactylus
NT3 myotis myotis
NT3 myotis mystacinus
NT2 nyctalus
NT2 pipistrellus
NT3 pipistrellus kuhli
NT3 pipistrellus pipistrellus
NT2 plecotus
NT3 plecotus auritus
NT2 scotophilus
NT3 scotophilus heathii
NT2 vespertilio

CHIROSTOMA
BT1 atherinidae
BT2 atheriniformes
BT3 osteichthyes
BT4 fishes

CHISEL PLOUGHS
AF chisel plows
uf *ploughs, chisel*
BT1 ploughs
BT2 implements
rt chisel shares
rt chiselling
rt subsoilers

CHISEL PLOWS
BF chisel ploughs
BT1 plows

CHISEL SHARES
uf *shares, chisel*
BT1 shares
BT2 components
rt chisel ploughs

CHISELLING
BT1 tillage
BT2 cultivation
rt chisel ploughs

CHISELS
BT1 tools

CHISOCHETON
BT1 meliaceae
NT1 chisocheton paniculatus

CHISOCHETON PANICULATUS
BT1 chisocheton
BT2 meliaceae

CHITIN
BT1 polysaccharides
BT2 carbohydrates
rt chitin synthesis inhibitors
rt chitosan
rt cuticle

CHITIN SYNTHESIS INHIBITORS
BT1 insect growth regulators
BT2 growth regulators
BT2 insecticides
BT3 pesticides
BT1 metabolic inhibitors
BT2 inhibitors
NT1 buprofezin
NT1 chlorfluazuron
NT1 cyromazine
NT1 diflubenzuron
NT1 flufenoxuron
NT1 penfluron
NT1 teflubenzuron
NT1 triflumuron
rt benzoylphenylureas
rt chitin
rt nikkomycins
rt polyoxins

CHITINASE
(ec 3.2.1.14)
BT1 o-glycoside hydrolases
BT2 glycosidases
BT3 hydrolases
BT4 enzymes

CHITOSAN
BT1 mucopolysaccharides
BT2 polysaccharides

CHITOSAN *cont.*
BT3 carbohydrates
rt chitin

CHITTAGONG
BT1 bangladesh
BT2 south asia
BT3 asia

CHITTING
BT1 sprouting
BT2 plant development
rt chitting houses
rt potatoes
rt tuber sprouting

CHITTING HOUSES
BT1 farm buildings
BT2 buildings
rt chitting
rt pregermination

CHIVES
BT1 bulbous vegetables
BT2 vegetables
rt allium schoenoprasum

CHLAMYDIA
BT1 chlamydiaceae
BT2 chlamydiales
BT3 firmicutes
BT4 bacteria
BT5 prokaryotes
NT1 chlamydia psittaci
NT1 chlamydia trachomatis

chlamydia ovis
USE **chlamydia psittaci**

CHLAMYDIA PSITTACI
uf *chlamydia ovis*
uf *ornithosis*
BT1 chlamydia
BT2 chlamydiaceae
BT3 chlamydiales
BT4 firmicutes
BT5 bacteria
BT6 prokaryotes
rt psittacosis

CHLAMYDIA TRACHOMATIS
BT1 chlamydia
BT2 chlamydiaceae
BT3 chlamydiales
BT4 firmicutes
BT5 bacteria
BT6 prokaryotes

CHLAMYDIACEAE
BT1 chlamydiales
BT2 firmicutes
BT3 bacteria
BT4 prokaryotes
NT1 chlamydia
NT2 chlamydia psittaci
NT2 chlamydia trachomatis

CHLAMYDIALES
BT1 firmicutes
BT2 bacteria
BT3 prokaryotes
NT1 chlamydiaceae
NT2 chlamydia
NT3 chlamydia psittaci
NT3 chlamydia trachomatis

CHLAMYDOMONAS
BT1 chlorophyta
BT2 algae
NT1 chlamydomonas eugametos
NT1 chlamydomonas reinhardtii

CHLAMYDOMONAS EUGAMETOS
BT1 chlamydomonas
BT2 chlorophyta
BT3 algae

CHLAMYDOMONAS REINHARDTII
BT1 chlamydomonas
BT2 chlorophyta
BT3 algae

CHLAMYDOSPORES
BT1 fungal spores
BT2 spores

CHLAMYDOSPORES *cont.*
BT3 cells

CHLAMYS
BT1 pectinidae
BT2 bivalvia
BT3 mollusca
NT1 chlamys islandica
rt scallops

CHLAMYS ISLANDICA
BT1 chlamys
BT2 pectinidae
BT3 bivalvia
BT4 mollusca

chloethrips
USE **baliothrips**

chloethrips oryzae
USE **stenchaetothrips biformis**

CHLOMETHOXYFEN
HN from 1990
BT1 nitrophenyl ether herbicides
BT2 herbicides
BT3 pesticides

CHLORAL HYDRATE
BT1 injectable anaesthetics
BT2 anaesthetics
BT3 neurotropic drugs
BT4 drugs

CHLORALOSE
BT1 avicides
BT2 pesticides
BT1 bird repellents
BT2 repellents
BT1 glucosides
BT2 glycosides
BT3 carbohydrates
BT1 neuroleptics
BT2 psychotropic drugs
BT3 neurotropic drugs
BT4 drugs
BT1 rodenticides
BT2 pesticides

CHLORAMBEN
BT1 benzoic acid herbicides
BT2 aromatic acid herbicides
BT3 herbicides
BT4 pesticides
BT1 urease inhibitors
BT2 enzyme inhibitors
BT3 metabolic inhibitors
BT4 inhibitors

CHLORAMPHENICOL
BT1 antibacterial agents
BT2 antiinfective agents
BT3 drugs
BT1 antibiotics
BT1 antiprotozoal agents
BT2 antiparasitic agents
BT3 drugs
BT1 nitrification inhibitors
BT2 metabolic inhibitors
BT3 inhibitors
BT1 protein synthesis inhibitors
BT2 metabolic inhibitors
BT3 inhibitors

CHLORAMPHENICOL ACETYLTRANSFERASE
HN from 1990
(ec 2.3.1.28)
BT1 acyltransferases
BT2 transferases
BT3 enzymes

CHLORANIFORMETHAN
BT1 unclassified fungicides
BT2 fungicides
BT3 pesticides

CHLORANIL
BT1 quinone fungicides
BT2 fungicides
BT3 pesticides
BT2 quinones
BT3 aromatic compounds

CHLORANOCRYL
BT1 anilide herbicides
BT2 amide herbicides
BT3 herbicides
BT4 pesticides

CHLORANTHACEAE
NT1 chloranthus
NT2 chloranthus japonicus

CHLORANTHUS
BT1 chloranthaceae
NT1 chloranthus japonicus

CHLORANTHUS JAPONICUS
BT1 antifungal plants
BT1 chloranthus
BT2 chloranthaceae

CHLORATES
BT1 inorganic salts
BT2 inorganic compounds
BT2 salts
NT1 calcium chlorate
NT1 sodium chlorate
rt chlorine

CHLORAZIFOP
BT1 aryloxyphenoxypropionic herbicides
BT2 phenoxypropionic herbicides
BT3 phenoxy herbicides
BT4 herbicides
BT5 pesticides

CHLORBROMURON
BT1 urea herbicides
BT2 herbicides
BT3 pesticides

CHLORBUFAM
BT1 carbanilate herbicides
BT2 carbamate pesticides
BT2 herbicides
BT3 pesticides

CHLORDANE
BT1 cyclodiene insecticides
BT2 organochlorine insecticides
BT3 insecticides
BT4 pesticides
BT3 organochlorine pesticides
BT4 organochlorine compounds
BT5 organic halogen compounds

CHLORDECONE
BT1 cyclodiene insecticides
BT2 organochlorine insecticides
BT3 insecticides
BT4 pesticides
BT3 organochlorine pesticides
BT4 organochlorine compounds
BT5 organic halogen compounds

CHLORDIAZEPOXIDE
BT1 benzodiazepines
BT2 heterocyclic nitrogen compounds
BT3 organic nitrogen compounds
BT1 neuroleptics
BT2 psychotropic drugs
BT3 neurotropic drugs
BT4 drugs

CHLORDIMEFORM
BT1 formamidine acaricides
BT2 acaricides
BT3 pesticides
BT1 formamidine insecticides
BT2 insecticides
BT3 pesticides

CHLORELLA
BT1 chlorophyta
BT2 algae
NT1 chlorella ellipsoidea
NT1 chlorella pyrenoidosa
NT1 chlorella sorokiniana

CHLORELLA *cont.*
NT1 chlorella vulgaris

CHLORELLA ELLIPSOIDEA
BT1 chlorella
BT2 chlorophyta
BT3 algae

CHLORELLA PYRENOIDOSA
BT1 chlorella
BT2 chlorophyta
BT3 algae

CHLORELLA SOROKINIANA
BT1 chlorella
BT2 chlorophyta
BT3 algae

CHLORELLA VULGARIS
BT1 chlorella
BT2 chlorophyta
BT3 algae

CHLORETURON
BT1 urea herbicides
BT2 herbicides
BT3 pesticides

CHLORFENAC
BT1 unclassified herbicides
BT2 herbicides
BT3 pesticides

CHLORFENETHOL
BT1 bridged diphenyl acaricides
BT2 acaricides
BT3 pesticides

CHLORFENPROP-METHYL
BT1 unclassified herbicides
BT2 herbicides
BT3 pesticides

CHLORFENSON
BT1 bridged diphenyl acaricides
BT2 acaricides
BT3 pesticides

CHLORFENSULPHIDE
BT1 bridged diphenyl acaricides
BT2 acaricides
BT3 pesticides

CHLORFENVINPHOS
BT1 organophosphate insecticides
BT2 organophosphorus insecticides
BT3 insecticides
BT4 pesticides
BT3 organophosphorus pesticides
BT4 organophosphorus compounds

CHLORFLUAZURON
BT1 benzoylphenylureas
BT2 amides
BT3 organic nitrogen compounds
BT1 chitin synthesis inhibitors
BT2 insect growth regulators
BT3 growth regulators
BT3 insecticides
BT4 pesticides
BT2 metabolic inhibitors
BT3 inhibitors

chlorflurecol
USE **chlorflurenol**

CHLORFLURENOL
uf *chlorflurecol*
BT1 morphactins
BT2 growth inhibitors
BT3 inhibitors
BT3 plant growth regulators
BT4 growth regulators
BT1 unclassified herbicides
BT2 herbicides
BT3 pesticides

chlorguanide
USE **proguanil**

CHLORIDAZON
uf *pyrazone*
BT1 pyridazinone herbicides
BT2 herbicides
BT3 pesticides
BT2 pyridazines
BT3 heterocyclic nitrogen compounds
BT4 organic nitrogen compounds

CHLORIDE
BT1 anions
BT2 ions
rt chlorides
rt chlorine

chloridea
USE **heliothis**

chloridea assulta
USE **helicoverpa assulta**

chloridea dipsacea
USE **heliothis viriplaca**

chloridea maritima
USE **heliothis maritima**

chloridea viriplaca
USE **heliothis viriplaca**

CHLORIDES
BT1 halides
BT2 inorganic salts
BT3 inorganic compounds
BT3 salts
NT1 ammonium chloride
NT1 calcium chloride
NT1 mercuric chloride
NT1 mercurous chloride
NT1 potassium chloride
NT1 sodium chloride
rt chloride
rt chlorine

CHLORIMURON
HN from 1990
BT1 sulfonylurea herbicides
BT2 sulfonylureas
BT3 sulfonamides
BT4 amides
BT5 organic nitrogen compounds
BT4 organic sulfur compounds
BT2 urea herbicides
BT3 herbicides
BT4 pesticides

CHLORINATED FATTY ACIDS
BT1 organochlorine compounds
BT2 organic halogen compounds
NT1 dalapon
NT1 dichloroacetic acid
NT1 tca
rt fatty acids

CHLORINATED HYDROCARBONS
BT1 halogenated hydrocarbons
BT2 organic halogen compounds
NT1 carbon tetrachloride
NT1 chloroform
NT1 ethylene dichloride
NT1 hexachloroparaxylene
NT1 methylene chloride
NT1 polychlorinated biphenyls
NT1 polychlorinated terphenyls
rt organochlorine pesticides

chlorinated lime
USE **bleaching powder**

chlorinated sucrose
USE **sucralose**

CHLORINE
BT1 disinfectants
BT1 gases
BT1 halogens
BT2 nonmetallic elements
BT3 elements

CHLORINE *cont.*
rt chlorates
rt chloride
rt chlorides
rt chlorine fertilizers
rt chlorites
rt organochlorine compounds

CHLORINE FERTILIZERS
BT1 trace element fertilizers
BT2 fertilizers
NT1 ammonium chloride
NT1 carnallite
NT1 potassium chloride
NT1 sodium chloride
NT1 sylvinite
rt chlorine

CHLORIS
BT1 gramineae
NT1 chloris barbata
NT1 chloris crinita
NT1 chloris gayana
NT1 chloris pilosa
NT1 chloris prieurii
NT1 chloris truncata
NT1 chloris virgata
rt chloris striate mosaic geminivirus

CHLORIS BARBATA
BT1 chloris
BT2 gramineae
BT1 pasture plants

CHLORIS CRINITA
BT1 chloris
BT2 gramineae
BT1 pasture plants

CHLORIS GAYANA
uf *rhodes grass*
BT1 chloris
BT2 gramineae
BT1 pasture plants

CHLORIS PILOSA
BT1 chloris
BT2 gramineae

CHLORIS PRIEURII
BT1 chloris
BT2 gramineae
BT1 pasture plants

CHLORIS STRIATE MOSAIC GEMINIVIRUS
HN from 1990
BT1 geminivirus group
BT2 plant viruses
BT3 plant pathogens
BT4 pathogens
rt chloris

CHLORIS TRUNCATA
BT1 chloris
BT2 gramineae
BT1 pasture plants

CHLORIS VIRGATA
BT1 chloris
BT2 gramineae
BT1 pasture plants

CHLORITA
BT1 cicadellidae
BT2 cicadelloidea
BT3 auchenorrhyncha
BT4 homoptera
rt empoasca

chlorita flavescens
USE **empoasca flavescens**

CHLORITE
BT1 clay minerals
BT2 minerals

CHLORITES
BT1 inorganic salts
BT2 inorganic compounds
BT2 salts
rt chlorine

CHLORMADINONE
uf *cap (chlormadinone)*
BT1 oral contraceptives
BT2 contraceptives
BT2 drugs
BT1 pregnanes
BT2 steroids
BT3 isoprenoids
BT4 lipids
BT1 synthetic progestogens
BT2 synthetic hormones

CHLORMEPHOS
BT1 organothiophosphate insecticides
BT2 organophosphorus insecticides
BT3 insecticides
BT4 pesticides
BT3 organophosphorus pesticides
BT4 organophosphorus compounds

CHLORMEQUAT
uf *ccc*
uf *chlorocholine chloride*
BT1 antitranspirants
BT1 growth retardants
BT2 plant growth regulators
BT3 growth regulators
BT2 retardants
BT1 quaternary ammonium compounds
BT2 ammonium compounds
BT2 organic nitrogen compounds

CHLORNITROFEN
BT1 nitrophenyl ether herbicides
BT2 herbicides
BT3 pesticides

CHLOROACETANILIDE HERBICIDES
BT1 anilide herbicides
BT2 amide herbicides
BT3 herbicides
BT4 pesticides
NT1 acetochlor
NT1 alachlor
NT1 butachlor
NT1 delachlor
NT1 diethatyl
NT1 dimethachlor
NT1 metazachlor
NT1 metolachlor
NT1 pretilachlor
NT1 propachlor
NT1 prynachlor
NT1 terbuchlor

CHLOROBENZILATE
BT1 bridged diphenyl acaricides
BT2 acaricides
BT3 pesticides

chlorocholine chloride
USE **chlormequat**

CHLOROCHROA
uf *rhytidolomia*
BT1 pentatomidae
BT2 heteroptera
NT1 chlorochroa ligata

CHLOROCHROA LIGATA
uf *rhytidolomia ligata*
BT1 chlorochroa
BT2 pentatomidae
BT3 heteroptera

CHLOROCOCCUM
BT1 chlorophyta
BT2 algae
NT1 chlorococcum hypnosporum

CHLOROCOCCUM HYPNOSPORUM
BT1 chlorococcum
BT2 chlorophyta
BT3 algae

(2-chloroethyl)phosphonic acid
USE **ethephon**

CHLOROFORM
BT1 carminatives
BT2 gastrointestinal agents
BT3 drugs
BT1 chlorinated hydrocarbons
BT2 halogenated hydrocarbons
BT3 organic halogen compounds
BT1 solvents

chlorofos
USE **trichlorfon**

CHLOROGALUM
BT1 liliaceae

CHLOROGENIC ACID
uf *caffeoylquinic acid*
BT1 allomones
BT2 allelochemicals
BT3 semiochemicals
BT1 cyclohexanecarboxylic acids
BT2 carboxylic acids
BT3 organic acids
BT4 acids
BT1 esters

CHLOROHYDRA
BT1 coelenterata
NT1 chlorohydra viridissima

CHLOROHYDRA VIRIDISSIMA
BT1 chlorohydra
BT2 coelenterata

α-CHLOROHYDRIN
(for retrieval spell out "alpha")
BT1 rodenticides
BT2 pesticides

CHLOROMETHIURON
BT1 ectoparasiticides
BT2 antiparasitic agents
BT3 drugs
BT1 unclassified acaricides
BT2 acaricides
BT3 pesticides

(4-chloro-2-methylphenoxy)acetic acid
USE **mcpa**

CHLOROMYXUM
BT1 myxozoa
BT2 protozoa
NT1 chloromyxum catostomi
NT1 chloromyxum dubium
NT1 chloromyxum esocinum
NT1 chloromyxum musculoliquefaciens
NT1 chloromyxum ovatum
NT1 chloromyxum trijugum
NT1 chloromyxum truttae

CHLOROMYXUM CATOSTOMI
BT1 chloromyxum
BT2 myxozoa
BT3 protozoa

CHLOROMYXUM DUBIUM
BT1 chloromyxum
BT2 myxozoa
BT3 protozoa

CHLOROMYXUM ESOCINUM
BT1 chloromyxum
BT2 myxozoa
BT3 protozoa

CHLOROMYXUM MUSCULOLIQUEFACIENS
BT1 chloromyxum
BT2 myxozoa
BT3 protozoa

CHLOROMYXUM OVATUM
BT1 chloromyxum
BT2 myxozoa
BT3 protozoa

CHLOROMYXUM TRIJUGUM
BT1 chloromyxum

CHLOROMYXUM TRIJUGUM *cont.*
BT2 myxozoa
BT3 protozoa

CHLOROMYXUM TRUTTAE
BT1 chloromyxum
BT2 myxozoa
BT3 protozoa

CHLORONEB
BT1 aromatic fungicides
BT2 fungicides
BT3 pesticides

CHLOROPHACINONE
BT1 rodenticides
BT2 pesticides

(4-chlorophenoxy)acetic acid
USE **4-cpa**

CHLOROPHENOXYISOBUTYRIC ACID
BT1 antiauxins
BT2 plant growth regulators
BT3 growth regulators
BT1 monocarboxylic acids
BT2 carboxylic acids
BT3 organic acids
BT4 acids

CHLOROPHORA
BT1 moraceae
NT1 chlorophora excelsa
NT1 chlorophora tinctoria
rt forest trees

CHLOROPHORA EXCELSA
BT1 chlorophora
BT2 moraceae

CHLOROPHORA TINCTORIA
BT1 chlorophora
BT2 moraceae

chlorophos
USE **trichlorfon**

chlorophyceae
USE **chlorophyta**

CHLOROPHYLL
BT1 lipochromes
BT2 pigments
BT1 porphyrins
BT2 heterocyclic nitrogen compounds
BT3 organic nitrogen compounds
rt chlorophyll a/b binding protein
rt chlorophyllase
rt chloroplasts
rt chlorosis
rt greening
rt protochlorophyll
rt protochlorophyllides

CHLOROPHYLL A/B BINDING PROTEIN
HN from 1990
BT1 binding proteins
BT2 proteins
BT3 peptides
rt chlorophyll
rt photosynthesis

CHLOROPHYLLASE
(ec 3.1.1.14)
BT1 carboxylic ester hydrolases
BT2 esterases
BT3 hydrolases
BT4 enzymes
rt chlorophyll

CHLOROPHYLLIDES
BT1 porphyrins
BT2 heterocyclic nitrogen compounds
BT3 organic nitrogen compounds

CHLOROPHYTA
uf *chlorophyceae*
BT1 algae

CHLOROPHYTA *cont.*
NT1 ankistrodesmus
NT2 ankistrodesmus falcatus
NT1 cephaleuros
NT2 cephaleuros virescens
NT1 chlamydomonas
NT2 chlamydomonas eugametos
NT2 chlamydomonas reinhardtii
NT1 chlorella
NT2 chlorella ellipsoidea
NT2 chlorella pyrenoidosa
NT2 chlorella sorokiniana
NT2 chlorella vulgaris
NT1 chlorococcum
NT2 chlorococcum hypnosporum
NT1 cladophora
NT2 cladophora glomerata
NT1 cystobia
NT1 diplodina
NT1 dunaliella
NT2 dunaliella tertiolecta
NT1 eudorina
NT2 eudorina elegans
NT1 gonospora
NT1 hydrodictyon
NT2 hydrodictyon reticulatum
NT1 pithophora
NT2 pithophora oedogonia
NT1 prototheca
NT2 prototheca wickerhamii
NT2 prototheca zopfii
NT1 pterospora
NT1 rhizoclonium
NT2 rhizoclonium hieroglyphicum
NT1 scenedesmus
NT2 scenedesmus bijugatus
NT2 scenedesmus quadricauda
NT1 stigeoclonium
NT2 stigeoclonium tenue
rt green seaweeds
rt seaweeds

CHLOROPHYTUM
BT1 liliaceae
NT1 chlorophytum arundinaceum
NT1 chlorophytum capense
NT1 chlorophytum comosum

CHLOROPHYTUM ARUNDINACEUM
BT1 chlorophytum
BT2 liliaceae
rt ornamental foliage plants

CHLOROPHYTUM CAPENSE
uf *chlorophytum elatum*
BT1 chlorophytum
BT2 liliaceae
rt ornamental foliage plants

CHLOROPHYTUM COMOSUM
BT1 chlorophytum
BT2 liliaceae
rt ornamental foliage plants

chlorophytum elatum
USE **chlorophytum capense**

6-CHLOROPICOLINIC ACID
BT1 aromatic acids
BT2 aromatic compounds
BT2 organic acids
BT3 acids
BT1 monocarboxylic acids
BT2 carboxylic acids
BT3 organic acids
BT4 acids

CHLOROPICRIN
uf *trichloronitromethane*
BT1 soil fumigants
BT2 fumigants
BT3 pesticides
BT1 unclassified fungicides
BT2 fungicides
BT3 pesticides
BT1 unclassified nematicides
BT2 nematicides
BT3 pesticides

CHLOROPIDAE
BT1 diptera
NT1 chlorops
NT2 chlorops oryzae
NT2 chlorops pumilionis
NT1 hippelates
NT1 liohippelates
NT2 liohippelates collusor
NT2 liohippelates pusio
NT1 meromyza
NT1 oscinella
NT2 oscinella frit
NT2 oscinella pusilla
NT2 oscinella vastator

CHLOROPLAST GENETICS
BT1 genetics
BT2 biology
rt chloroplasts
rt cytoplasmic inheritance
rt molecular genetics

CHLOROPLASTS
BT1 plastids
BT2 cytoplasmic inclusions
BT3 cytoplasm
BT4 protoplasm
NT1 etioplasts
NT1 thylakoids
rt chlorophyll
rt chloroplast genetics

CHLOROPROPYLATE
BT1 bridged diphenyl acaricides
BT2 acaricides
BT3 pesticides

CHLOROPS
BT1 chloropidae
BT2 diptera
NT1 chlorops oryzae
NT1 chlorops pumilionis

CHLOROPS ORYZAE
BT1 chlorops
BT2 chloropidae
BT3 diptera

CHLOROPS PUMILIONIS
BT1 chlorops
BT2 chloropidae
BT3 diptera

CHLOROPULVINARIA
BT1 coccidae
BT2 coccoidea
BT3 sternorrhyncha
BT4 homoptera
NT1 chloropulvinaria aurantii
NT1 chloropulvinaria floccifera
NT1 chloropulvinaria psidii
rt pulvinaria

CHLOROPULVINARIA AURANTII
BT1 chloropulvinaria
BT2 coccidae
BT3 coccoidea
BT4 sternorrhyncha
BT5 homoptera

CHLOROPULVINARIA FLOCCIFERA
uf *pulvinaria floccifera*
BT1 chloropulvinaria
BT2 coccidae
BT3 coccoidea
BT4 sternorrhyncha
BT5 homoptera

CHLOROPULVINARIA PSIDII
uf *pulvinaria psidii*
BT1 chloropulvinaria
BT2 coccidae
BT3 coccoidea
BT4 sternorrhyncha
BT5 homoptera

CHLOROQUINE
BT1 aminoquinolines
BT2 quinolines
BT3 heterocyclic nitrogen compounds
BT4 organic nitrogen compounds
BT1 antimalarials

CHLOROQUINE *cont.*
BT2 antiprotozoal agents
BT3 antiparasitic agents
BT4 drugs

CHLOROSIS
BT1 plant disorders
BT2 disorders
rt chlorophyll
rt colour
rt mineral deficiencies
rt tentoxin
rt yellow leaf disease

CHLOROTHALONIL
BT1 aromatic fungicides
BT2 fungicides
BT3 pesticides

CHLOROTHIAZIDE
BT1 antihypertensive agents
BT2 cardiovascular agents
BT3 drugs
BT1 diuretics
BT2 drugs

CHLOROTOLUENE
BT1 solvents

CHLOROTOLURON
uf *chlortoluron*
BT1 urea herbicides
BT2 herbicides
BT3 pesticides

CHLOROXURON
BT1 urea herbicides
BT2 herbicides
BT3 pesticides

CHLORPHONIUM
BT1 growth inhibitors
BT2 inhibitors
BT2 plant growth regulators
BT3 growth regulators
BT1 quaternary ammonium compounds
BT2 ammonium compounds
BT2 organic nitrogen compounds

CHLORPHOXIM
BT1 organothiophosphate insecticides
BT2 organophosphorus insecticides
BT3 insecticides
BT4 pesticides
BT3 organophosphorus pesticides
BT4 organophosphorus compounds

CHLORPROGUANIL
BT1 antimalarials
BT2 antiprotozoal agents
BT3 antiparasitic agents
BT4 drugs

CHLORPROMAZINE
uf *aminazine*
BT1 antiemetics
BT2 gastrointestinal agents
BT3 drugs
BT1 phenothiazines
BT2 heterocyclic nitrogen compounds
BT3 organic nitrogen compounds
BT1 vasodilator agents
BT2 cardiovascular agents
BT3 drugs

CHLORPROPAMIDE
BT1 hypoglycaemic agents
BT2 haematologic agents
BT3 drugs
BT1 sulfonamides
BT2 amides
BT3 organic nitrogen compounds
BT2 organic sulfur compounds

CHLORPROPHAM
BT1 carbanilate herbicides
BT2 carbamate pesticides
BT2 herbicides
BT3 pesticides
BT1 growth inhibitors
BT2 inhibitors
BT2 plant growth regulators
BT3 growth regulators

CHLORPYRIFOS
BT1 ectoparasiticides
BT2 antiparasitic agents
BT3 drugs
BT1 organothiophosphate insecticides
BT2 organophosphorus insecticides
BT3 insecticides
BT4 pesticides
BT3 organophosphorus pesticides
BT4 organophosphorus compounds
BT1 organothiophosphate nematicides
BT2 organophosphorus nematicides
BT3 nematicides
BT4 pesticides
BT3 organophosphorus pesticides
BT4 organophosphorus compounds

CHLORPYRIFOS-METHYL
BT1 organothiophosphate insecticides
BT2 organophosphorus insecticides
BT3 insecticides
BT4 pesticides
BT3 organophosphorus pesticides
BT4 organophosphorus compounds

CHLORQUINOX
BT1 quinoxaline fungicides
BT2 fungicides
BT3 pesticides
BT2 quinoxalines
BT3 heterocyclic nitrogen compounds
BT4 organic nitrogen compounds

CHLORSULFURON
BT1 sulfonylurea herbicides
BT2 sulfonylureas
BT3 sulfonamides
BT4 amides
BT5 organic nitrogen compounds
BT4 organic sulfur compounds
BT2 urea herbicides
BT3 herbicides
BT4 pesticides

CHLORTETRACYCLINE
uf *aureomycin*
uf *aurofac*
uf *biomycin*
BT1 antibacterial agents
BT2 antiinfective agents
BT3 drugs
BT1 antibiotics
BT1 antiprotozoal agents
BT2 antiparasitic agents
BT3 drugs
BT1 tetracyclines

CHLORTHAL-DIMETHYL
uf *dcpa*
BT1 unclassified herbicides
BT2 herbicides
BT3 pesticides

CHLORTHIAMID
BT1 amide herbicides
BT2 herbicides
BT3 pesticides

chlortoluron
USE **chlorotoluron**

chloxyle
USE **hexachloroparaxylene**

CHOANEPHORA
uf *blakeslea*
BT1 mucorales
NT1 choanephora cucurbitarum
NT1 choanephora trispora

CHOANEPHORA CUCURBITARUM
BT1 choanephora
BT2 mucorales

CHOANEPHORA TRISPORA
BT1 choanephora
BT2 mucorales

CHOANOTAENIA
BT1 dilepididae
BT2 eucestoda
BT3 cestoda
NT1 choanotaenia infundibulum

CHOANOTAENIA INFUNDIBULUM
BT1 choanotaenia
BT2 dilepididae
BT3 eucestoda
BT4 cestoda

CHOCOLATE
BT1 confectionery
rt chocolate milk
rt cocoa products

chocolate industry
USE **cocoa industry**

CHOCOLATE MILK
BT1 flavoured milk
BT2 milk products
BT3 products
rt chocolate

choetospila
USE **theocolax**

choetospila elegans
USE **theocolax elegans**

choice
USE **decision making**

CHOICE OF SPECIES
BT1 selection
rt afforestation
rt exotics
rt plantations
rt selectivity
rt species

CHOIRS
BT1 vocal music
BT2 music
BT3 performing arts
BT4 arts
rt cultural activities

CHOISYA
BT1 rutaceae
NT1 choisya ternata

CHOISYA TERNATA
BT1 choisya
BT2 rutaceae
BT1 ornamental woody plants

CHOKLA
HN from 1990
BT1 sheep breeds
BT2 breeds

CHOLAGOGUES
BT1 gastrointestinal agents
BT2 drugs
rt bile

CHOLANES
BT1 steroids
BT2 isoprenoids
BT3 lipids
NT1 chenodeoxycholic acid
NT1 cholic acid
NT1 dehydrocholic acid

CHOLANES *cont.*
NT1 lithocholic acid
NT1 ursodeoxycholic acid

CHOLANGITIS
BT1 digestive system diseases
BT2 organic diseases
BT3 diseases
rt bile ducts

CHOLECALCIFEROL
uf *vitamin d3*
BT1 vitamin d
BT2 fat soluble vitamins
BT3 vitamins
rt cholecalciferol derivatives

CHOLECALCIFEROL DERIVATIVES
BT1 sterols
BT2 alcohols
BT2 steroids
BT3 isoprenoids
BT4 lipids
BT1 vitamin d
BT2 fat soluble vitamins
BT3 vitamins
NT1 hydroxycholecalciferols
NT2 1α-hydroxycholecalciferol
NT2 24,25-dihydroxycholecalciferol
NT2 25,26-dihydroxycholecalciferol
NT2 calcitriol
rt cholecalciferol

CHOLECYSTECTOMY
uf *gall bladder removal*
BT1 surgical operations
rt gall bladder

CHOLECYSTITIS
BT1 gall bladder diseases
BT2 digestive system diseases
BT3 organic diseases
BT4 diseases
rt inflammation

cholecystokinin
USE **pancreozymin**

CHOLELITHIASIS
BT1 gall bladder diseases
BT2 digestive system diseases
BT3 organic diseases
BT4 diseases
rt biliary calculi

CHOLERA
BT1 human diseases
BT2 diseases
rt vibrio cholerae

CHOLESTANES
BT1 steroids
BT2 isoprenoids
BT3 lipids
NT1 α-ecdysone
NT1 cholesterol
NT1 coprostanol
NT1 ecdysterone

CHOLESTASIS
BT1 obstruction
BT2 digestive disorders
BT3 functional disorders
BT4 animal disorders
BT5 disorders
rt gall bladder diseases

cholesterase
USE **cholesterol esterase**

CHOLESTEROL
BT1 cholestanes
BT2 steroids
BT3 isoprenoids
BT4 lipids
BT1 sterols
BT2 alcohols
BT2 steroids
BT3 isoprenoids
BT4 lipids
rt anticholesteremic agents (agricola)

CHOLESTEROL *cont.*
rt cholesterol metabolism
rt cholesteryl esters
rt clofibrate
rt colestipol
rt hypercholesterolaemia
rt hyperlipaemia
rt hypocholesterolaemia
rt low cholesterol diets (agricola)

CHOLESTEROL ACYLTRANSFERASE
(ec 2.3.1.26)
BT1 acyltransferases
BT2 transferases
BT3 enzymes

cholesterol atherosclerosis
USE **experimental atherosclerosis**

CHOLESTEROL ESTERASE
(ec 3.1.1.13)
uf *cholesterase*
BT1 carboxylic ester hydrolases
BT2 esterases
BT3 hydrolases
BT4 enzymes

cholesterol esters
USE **cholesteryl esters**

cholesterol 7α-hydroxylase
USE **cholesterol 7α-monooxygenase**

CHOLESTEROL METABOLISM
BT1 metabolism
rt cholesterol

CHOLESTEROL METABOLISM DISORDERS
BT1 lipid metabolism disorders
BT2 metabolic disorders
BT3 animal disorders
BT4 disorders
NT1 hypercholesterolaemia
NT1 hypocholesterolaemia

CHOLESTEROL 7α-MONOOXYGENASE
(ec 1.14.13.7)
(for retrieval spell out "alpha")
uf *cholesterol 7α-hydroxylase*
BT1 oxygenases
BT2 oxidoreductases
BT3 enzymes

CHOLESTERYL ESTERS
uf *cholesterol esters*
BT1 sterol esters
BT2 esters
BT2 steroids
BT3 isoprenoids
BT4 lipids
rt cholesterol

cholestyramine
USE **colestyramine**

CHOLIC ACID
BT1 bile acids
BT1 cholanes
BT2 steroids
BT3 isoprenoids
BT4 lipids
BT1 digestants
BT2 gastrointestinal agents
BT3 drugs
rt taurocholic acid

CHOLINE
BT1 biogenic amines
BT2 amines
BT3 amino compounds
BT4 organic nitrogen compounds
BT1 lipotropic factors
BT2 drugs
BT1 ptomaines
BT2 organic nitrogen compounds
BT2 toxic substances

CHOLINE *cont.*
BT1 quaternary ammonium compounds
BT2 ammonium compounds
BT2 organic nitrogen compounds
BT1 vitamin b complex
BT2 water-soluble vitamins
BT3 vitamins
rt acetylcholine
rt choline acetyltransferase
rt perosis

CHOLINE ACETYLTRANSFERASE
(ec 2.3.1.6)
BT1 acyltransferases
BT2 transferases
BT3 enzymes
rt choline

CHOLINE KINASE
(ec 2.7.1.32)
BT1 kinases
BT2 transferases
BT3 enzymes

CHOLINE-PHOSPHATE CYTIDYLYLTRANSFERASE
(ec 2.7.7.15)
BT1 nucleotidyltransferases
BT2 transferases
BT3 enzymes

CHOLINERGIC MECHANISMS
rt acetylcholine
rt cholinesterase
rt decamethonium
rt dopamine
rt inhibition

CHOLINERGIC RECEPTORS
BT1 receptors

CHOLINESTERASE
(ec 3.1.1.8)
uf *butyrylcholine esterase*
BT1 carboxylic ester hydrolases
BT2 esterases
BT3 hydrolases
BT4 enzymes
rt cholinergic mechanisms
rt cholinesterase inhibitors

CHOLINESTERASE INHIBITORS
BT1 enzyme inhibitors
BT2 metabolic inhibitors
BT3 inhibitors
BT1 neurotropic drugs
BT2 drugs
NT1 neostigmine
NT1 physostigmine
rt cholinesterase

CHOLODKOVSKYA
BT1 adelgidae
BT2 aphidoidea
BT3 sternorrhyncha
BT4 homoptera
NT1 cholodkovskya viridana
rt adelges

CHOLODKOVSKYA VIRIDANA
uf *adelges viridanus*
BT1 cholodkovskya
BT2 adelgidae
BT3 aphidoidea
BT4 sternorrhyncha
BT5 homoptera

CHOLOEPUS
BT1 megalonychidae
BT2 edentata
BT3 mammals
NT1 choloepus didactylus

CHOLOEPUS DIDACTYLUS
BT1 choloepus
BT2 megalonychidae
BT3 edentata
BT4 mammals

CHONDRICHTHYES
BT1 fishes
NT1 chimaeriformes

CHONDRICHTHYES *cont.*
NT2 chimaeridae
NT3 chimaera
NT4 chimaera monstrosa
NT3 hydrolagus
NT1 hexanchiformes
NT2 hexanchidae
NT3 hexanchus
NT1 lamniformes
NT2 carcharhinidae
NT3 carcharhinus
NT3 galeorhinus
NT3 mustelus
NT3 prionace
NT2 lamnidae
NT3 alopias
NT3 carcharodon
NT3 cetorhinus
NT4 cetorhinus maximus
NT3 isurus
NT3 lamna
NT2 odontaspididae
NT3 odontaspis
NT2 scyliorhinidae
NT3 galeus
NT3 scyliorhinus
NT1 rajiformes
NT2 dasyatidae
NT3 dasyatis
NT2 pristidae
NT3 pristis
NT2 rajidae
NT3 raja
NT1 squaliformes
NT2 pristiophoridae
NT3 pristiophorus
NT2 squalidae
NT3 centroscyllium
NT3 squalus
NT4 squalus acanthias
NT2 squatinidae
NT3 squatina

CHONDRILLA
BT1 compositae
NT1 chondrilla juncea

CHONDRILLA JUNCEA
BT1 chondrilla
BT2 compositae
BT1 weeds

CHONDROCYTES
BT1 cells
rt cartilage

CHONDRODYSTROPHY
BT1 bone diseases
BT2 organic diseases
BT3 diseases
rt cartilage

CHONDROITIN SULFATE
uf *chondroitin sulphate*
BT1 acid mucopolysaccharides
BT2 mucopolysaccharides
BT3 polysaccharides
BT4 carbohydrates

chondroitin sulphate
USE **chondroitin sulfate**

CHONDRORHYNCHA
BT1 orchidaceae
NT1 chondrorhyncha discolor

CHONDRORHYNCHA DISCOLOR
BT1 chondrorhyncha
BT2 orchidaceae
BT1 ornamental orchids

CHONDROSTEREUM
BT1 aphyllophorales
NT1 chondrostereum purpureum
rt stereum

CHONDROSTEREUM PURPUREUM
uf *stereum purpureum*
BT1 chondrostereum
BT2 aphyllophorales

CHONDRUS
BT1 rhodophyta
BT2 algae

CHONDRUS *cont.*
NT1 chondrus crispus
rt red seaweeds
rt seaweeds

CHONDRUS CRISPUS
uf *carrageen*
BT1 chondrus
BT2 rhodophyta
BT3 algae
rt carrageenan

chongquing
USE **south western china**

CHOP LENGTH
rt choppers

CHOPPERS
BT1 farm machinery
BT2 machinery
rt chop length
rt chopping

CHOPPING
BT1 cutting
rt choppers

CHORDATA
NT1 urochordata
NT1 vertebrates

CHORDOPOXVIRINAE
BT1 poxviridae
BT2 viruses
NT1 avipoxvirus
NT2 canary pox virus
NT2 fowl pox virus
NT2 turkey pox virus
NT1 capripoxvirus
NT2 goat pox virus
NT2 lumpy skin disease virus
NT2 sheep pox virus
NT1 leporipoxvirus
NT2 myxoma virus
NT1 orthopoxvirus
NT2 bovine orthopoxvirus
NT2 buffalo poxvirus
NT2 ectromelia virus
NT2 rabbit orthopoxvirus
NT2 vaccinia virus
NT1 parapoxvirus
NT2 bovine papular stomatitis virus
NT2 contagious ecthyma virus
NT1 suipoxvirus
NT2 swine pox virus

CHOREUTIDAE
BT1 lepidoptera
NT1 anthophila
NT1 choreutis
NT2 choreutis pariana

CHOREUTIS
uf *eutromula*
BT1 choreutidae
BT2 lepidoptera
NT1 choreutis pariana
rt anthophila

CHOREUTIS PARIANA
uf *anthophila pariana*
uf *eutromula pariana*
uf *simaethis pariana*
BT1 choreutis
BT2 choreutidae
BT3 lepidoptera

CHORINAEUS
BT1 ichneumonidae
BT2 hymenoptera

CHORIOALLANTOIC MEMBRANE
BT1 membranes
rt fetus
rt placenta

choriogonadotropin
USE **chorionic gonadotropin**

CHORIOMAMMOTROPIN
uf *chorionic somatomammotropin*
uf *lactogen*

CHORIOMAMMOTROPIN *cont.*
uf *placental lactogen*
uf *somatomammotropin, chorionic*
BT1 placental hormones
BT2 hormones

CHORION
HN from 1989
BT1 fetal membranes
BT2 membranes

CHORIONIC GONADOTROPIN
uf *choriogonadotropin*
uf *gonadotropin, chorionic*
BT1 gonadotropins
BT2 glycoproteins
BT3 proteins
BT4 peptides
BT2 sex hormones
BT3 hormones
BT1 placental hormones
BT2 hormones
NT1 hcg

chorionic gonadotropin, human
USE **hcg**

chorionic somatomammotropin
USE **choriomammotropin**

CHORIOPTES
BT1 psoroptidae
BT2 astigmata
BT3 acari
NT1 chorioptes bovis

CHORIOPTES BOVIS
uf *chorioptes equi*
uf *chorioptes ovis*
BT1 chorioptes
BT2 psoroptidae
BT3 astigmata
BT4 acari

chorioptes equi
USE **chorioptes bovis**

chorioptes ovis
USE **chorioptes bovis**

CHORIOTIS
BT1 otidae
BT2 gruiformes
BT3 birds

CHORISPORA
BT1 cruciferae
NT1 chorispora tenella

CHORISPORA TENELLA
BT1 chorispora
BT2 cruciferae

CHORISTONEURA
BT1 tortricidae
BT2 lepidoptera
NT1 choristoneura biennis
NT1 choristoneura conflictana
NT1 choristoneura diversana
NT1 choristoneura fumiferana
NT1 choristoneura murinana
NT1 choristoneura occidentalis
NT1 choristoneura pinus
NT1 choristoneura retiniana
NT1 choristoneura rosaceana

CHORISTONEURA BIENNIS
BT1 choristoneura
BT2 tortricidae
BT3 lepidoptera

CHORISTONEURA CONFLICTANA
BT1 choristoneura
BT2 tortricidae
BT3 lepidoptera

CHORISTONEURA DIVERSANA
BT1 choristoneura
BT2 tortricidae
BT3 lepidoptera

CHORISTONEURA FUMIFERANA
BT1 choristoneura
BT2 tortricidae

CHORISTONEURA FUMIFERANA *cont.*
BT3 lepidoptera

CHORISTONEURA MURINANA
BT1 choristoneura
BT2 tortricidae
BT3 lepidoptera

CHORISTONEURA OCCIDENTALIS
BT1 choristoneura
BT2 tortricidae
BT3 lepidoptera

CHORISTONEURA PINUS
BT1 choristoneura
BT2 tortricidae
BT3 lepidoptera

CHORISTONEURA RETINIANA
BT1 choristoneura
BT2 tortricidae
BT3 lepidoptera

CHORISTONEURA ROSACEANA
BT1 choristoneura
BT2 tortricidae
BT3 lepidoptera

chorizagrotis
USE **euxoa**

chorizagrotis auxiliaris
USE **euxoa auxiliaris**

CHOROID PLEXUS
BT1 plexus
BT2 nervous system
BT3 body parts

CHOROMYTILUS
BT1 mytilidae
BT2 bivalvia
BT3 mollusca

CHORTHIPPUS
BT1 acrididae
BT2 orthoptera
NT1 chorthippus brunneus

CHORTHIPPUS BRUNNEUS
BT1 chorthippus
BT2 acrididae
BT3 orthoptera

CHORTOGLYPHIDAE
BT1 astigmata
BT2 acari
NT1 chortoglyphus
NT2 chortoglyphus arcuatus

CHORTOGLYPHUS
BT1 chortoglyphidae
BT2 astigmata
BT3 acari
NT1 chortoglyphus arcuatus

CHORTOGLYPHUS ARCUATUS
BT1 chortoglyphus
BT2 chortoglyphidae
BT3 astigmata
BT4 acari

CHORTOICETES
BT1 acrididae
BT2 orthoptera
NT1 chortoicetes terminifera

CHORTOICETES TERMINIFERA
BT1 chortoicetes
BT2 acrididae
BT3 orthoptera

chortophila
USE **phorbia**

chortophila brassicae
USE **delia radicum**

chortophila floralis
USE **delia floralis**

chortophila laricicola
USE **strobilomyia laricicola**

CHOTANAGPURI
HN from 1990
BT1 sheep breeds
BT2 breeds

CHRISTISONIA
BT1 orobanchaceae
NT1 christisonia subacaulis

CHRISTISONIA SUBACAULIS
BT1 christisonia
BT2 orobanchaceae

CHRISTMAS ISLAND
BT1 australian oceania
BT2 oceania
rt australia

christmas islands (pacific)
USE **kiribati**

CHRISTMAS TREES
BT1 minor forest products
BT2 forest products
BT3 products

CHROMADORIDAE
BT1 nematoda
NT1 chromadorina
NT2 chromadorina bioculata
rt free living nematodes
rt marine nematodes

CHROMADORINA
BT1 chromadoridae
BT2 nematoda
NT1 chromadorina bioculata

CHROMADORINA BIOCULATA
BT1 chromadorina
BT2 chromadoridae
BT3 nematoda

CHROMAPHIS
BT1 aphididae
BT2 aphidoidea
BT3 sternorrhyncha
BT4 homoptera
NT1 chromaphis juglandicola

CHROMAPHIS JUGLANDICOLA
BT1 chromaphis
BT2 aphididae
BT3 aphidoidea
BT4 sternorrhyncha
BT5 homoptera

CHROMATIDS
BT1 chromosomes
BT2 nuclei
BT3 organelles
BT4 cell structure
rt chromatin
rt meiosis
rt mitosis
rt sister chromatid exchange

CHROMATIN
BT1 nucleoproteins
BT2 proteins
BT3 peptides
NT1 euchromatin
NT1 heterochromatin
NT1 sex chromatin
rt chromatids
rt nuclei
rt nucleic acids

CHROMATOGRAPHY
BT1 analytical methods
BT2 methodology
NT1 gas chromatography
NT2 pyrolysis gas chromatography
NT1 gas liquid chromatography
NT1 gel filtration chromatography
NT1 ion exchange chromatography
NT1 liquid chromatography
NT2 hplc
NT1 lysimetric chromatography
NT1 paper chromatography
NT2 northern blotting

CHROMATOGRAPHY *cont.*
NT2 southern blotting
NT1 spot test chromatography
NT1 thin layer chromatography

chromatography, thin layer
USE **thin layer chromatography**

CHROMATOMYIA
BT1 agromyzidae
BT2 diptera
NT1 chromatomyia horticola
NT1 chromatomyia nigra
NT1 chromatomyia syngenesiae
rt agromyza
rt phytomyza

CHROMATOMYIA HORTICOLA
uf *agromyza atricornis*
uf *phytomyza atricornis*
uf *phytomyza horticola*
BT1 chromatomyia
BT2 agromyzidae
BT3 diptera

CHROMATOMYIA NIGRA
uf *phytomyza nigra*
BT1 chromatomyia
BT2 agromyzidae
BT3 diptera

CHROMATOMYIA SYNGENESIAE
uf *agromyza atricornis*
uf *phytomyza atricornis*
uf *phytomyza syngenesiae*
BT1 chromatomyia
BT2 agromyzidae
BT3 diptera

CHROMIC LUVISOLS
BT1 luvisols
BT2 soil types (genetic)

CHROMIC OXIDE
BT1 digestibility markers
BT2 markers
BT1 oxides
BT2 inorganic compounds
rt chromium

CHROMIUM
uf *cr*
BT1 trace elements
BT2 elements
BT1 transition elements
BT2 metallic elements
BT3 elements
BT3 metals
rt chromic oxide
rt copper chrome arsenate

CHROMOBACTERIUM
BT1 gracilicutes
BT2 bacteria
BT3 prokaryotes
NT1 chromobacterium lividum

CHROMOBACTERIUM LIVIDUM
BT1 chromobacterium
BT2 gracilicutes
BT3 bacteria
BT4 prokaryotes

CHROMOBLASTOMYCOSIS
BT1 mycoses
BT2 infectious diseases
BT3 diseases
rt chromomycosis

CHROMOCENTERS
BF chromocentres

CHROMOCENTRES
AF chromocenters
BT1 centromeres
BT2 chromosomes
BT3 nuclei
BT4 organelles
BT5 cell structure
rt heterochromatin

CHROMOLAENA
BT1 compositae
rt eupatorium

chromolaena odorata
USE **eupatorium odoratum**

CHROMOMYCOSIS
uf *phaeohyphomycosis*
BT1 mycoses
BT2 infectious diseases
BT3 diseases
rt chromoblastomycosis

CHROMONES
BT1 pigments

CHROMOSOME ABERRATIONS
uf *chromosome abnormalities*
rt chromosome breakage
rt chromosomes
rt mutagens
rt sister chromatid exchange

chromosome abnormalities
USE **chromosome aberrations**

CHROMOSOME ADDITION
BT1 cytogenetics
rt addition lines
rt chromosome number
rt chromosome substitution
rt chromosomes

CHROMOSOME ANALYSIS
BT1 genetic analysis
rt analysis
rt chromosomes

chromosome arrangement
USE **chromosome disposition**

CHROMOSOME BANDING
uf *banding, chromosome*
BT1 staining
BT2 techniques
rt c bands
rt chromosome morphology
rt chromosomes
rt cytology

CHROMOSOME BREAKAGE
BT1 breakage
BT2 damage
rt chromosome aberrations
rt chromosomes

CHROMOSOME DISPOSITION
uf *chromosome arrangement*
rt cell division
rt chromosomes

CHROMOSOME ELIMINATION
rt chromosome number
rt chromosomes
rt haploidy

CHROMOSOME MAPS
BT1 cytogenetics
BT1 maps
rt chromosomes
rt gene location
rt gene mapping
rt linkage

CHROMOSOME MORPHOLOGY
uf *idiogram*
rt chromosome banding
rt chromosomes
rt cytology
rt karyotypes

CHROMOSOME NUMBER
rt aneuploidy
rt chromosome addition
rt chromosome elimination
rt chromosomes
rt cytology
rt haploids
rt karyotypes
rt ploidy
rt tetraploidy

CHROMOSOME PAIRING
rt chromosomes
rt cytology
rt genome analysis
rt meiosis
rt synapsis

CHROMOSOME PAIRING *cont.*
rt synaptonemal complex

CHROMOSOME POLYMORPHISM
BT1 polymorphism
rt chromosomes
rt cytology

CHROMOSOME SUBSTITUTION
BT1 cytogenetics
rt chromosome addition
rt chromosomes
rt substitution lines

CHROMOSOME TRANSLOCATION
uf *interchange*
uf *translocation, chromosome*
rt chromosomes
rt crossing over
rt deletions
rt inversion
rt translocation lines

CHROMOSOME TRANSMISSION
rt chromosomes

CHROMOSOME WALKING
HN from 1990
BT1 dna sequencing
BT2 biochemical techniques
BT3 techniques
rt chromosomes

CHROMOSOMES
BT1 nuclei
BT2 organelles
BT3 cell structure
NT1 accessory chromosomes
NT2 b chromosomes
NT1 acrocentric chromosomes
NT1 autosomes
NT1 bivalents
NT1 centromeres
NT2 chromocentres
NT1 chromatids
NT1 loci
NT1 microchromosomes
NT1 nucleolus organizer
NT1 polytene chromosomes
NT1 secondary constrictions
NT1 sex chromosomes
NT2 x chromosome
NT2 y chromosome
NT1 submetacentric
NT1 telocentrics
rt asynapsis
rt c bands
rt chromosome aberrations
rt chromosome addition
rt chromosome analysis
rt chromosome banding
rt chromosome breakage
rt chromosome disposition
rt chromosome elimination
rt chromosome maps
rt chromosome morphology
rt chromosome number
rt chromosome pairing
rt chromosome polymorphism
rt chromosome substitution
rt chromosome translocation
rt chromosome transmission
rt chromosome walking
rt crossing over
rt cytogenetics
rt cytology
rt dna
rt genes
rt genomes
rt karyotypes
rt non-disjunction
rt nuclei
rt polyteny
rt position effect
rt rna
rt segregation
rt tetraploidy
rt trisomy
rt x-y separation

chromosomes, accessory
USE **accessory chromosomes**

chromosomes, sex
USE **sex chromosomes**

CHRONIC COURSE
HN from 1990
BT1 disease course

CHRONIC MUCOCUTANEOUS CANDIDOSIS
BT1 candidosis
BT2 mycoses
BT3 infectious diseases
BT4 diseases

CHRONOSEQUENCES
BT1 soil sequences

CHROTOGONUS
BT1 acrididae
BT2 orthoptera
NT1 chrotogonus trachypterus

CHROTOGONUS TRACHYPTERUS
BT1 chrotogonus
BT2 acrididae
BT3 orthoptera

CHROZOPHORA
BT1 euphorbiaceae
NT1 chrozophora rottleri

CHROZOPHORA ROTTLERI
BT1 chrozophora
BT2 euphorbiaceae

CHRYSALIDOCARPUS
BT1 palmae
NT1 chrysalidocarpus lutescens

CHRYSALIDOCARPUS LUTESCENS
BT1 chrysalidocarpus
BT2 palmae
BT1 ornamental palms

CHRYSANTHEMIC ACID
BT1 monocarboxylic acids
BT2 carboxylic acids
BT3 organic acids
BT4 acids
BT1 monoterpenoids
BT2 terpenoids
BT3 isoprenoids
BT4 lipids
rt dyes
rt pyrethroids

CHRYSANTHEMOIDES
BT1 compositae
NT1 chrysanthemoides moniliferum

CHRYSANTHEMOIDES MONILIFERUM
BT1 chrysanthemoides
BT2 compositae

CHRYSANTHEMUM
uf *pyrethrum (genus)*
BT1 compositae
NT1 chrysanthemum alpinum
NT1 chrysanthemum carinatum
NT1 chrysanthemum coronarium
NT1 chrysanthemum frutescens
NT1 chrysanthemum parthenifolium
NT1 chrysanthemum prealtum
NT1 chrysanthemum segetum
rt chrysanthemum chlorotic mottle viroid
rt chrysanthemum stunt viroid

CHRYSANTHEMUM ALPINUM
BT1 antifungal plants
BT1 chrysanthemum
BT2 compositae
BT1 ornamental herbaceous plants

CHRYSANTHEMUM B CARLAVIRUS
HN from 1990
BT1 carlavirus group
BT2 plant viruses
BT3 plant pathogens

CHRYSANTHEMUM B CARLAVIRUS *cont.*
BT4 pathogens

CHRYSANTHEMUM CARINATUM
BT1 chrysanthemum
BT2 compositae
BT1 ornamental herbaceous plants

CHRYSANTHEMUM CHLOROTIC MOTTLE VIROID
BT1 viroids
BT2 plant pathogens
BT3 pathogens
rt chrysanthemum

chrysanthemum cinerariifolium
USE **tanacetum cinerariifolium**

chrysanthemum coccineum
USE **tanacetum coccineum**

CHRYSANTHEMUM CORONARIUM
BT1 chrysanthemum
BT2 compositae
BT1 insecticidal plants
BT2 pesticidal plants
BT1 leafy vegetables
BT2 vegetables
BT1 ornamental herbaceous plants

CHRYSANTHEMUM FRUTESCENS
BT1 chrysanthemum
BT2 compositae

chrysanthemum indicum
USE **dendranthema indicum**

chrysanthemum leucanthemum
USE **leucanthemum vulgare**

chrysanthemum maximum
USE **leucanthemum maximum**

chrysanthemum morifolium
USE **dendranthema morifolium**

CHRYSANTHEMUM PARTHENIFOLIUM
BT1 chrysanthemum
BT2 compositae

chrysanthemum parthenium
USE **tanacetum parthenium**

CHRYSANTHEMUM PREALTUM
BT1 chrysanthemum
BT2 compositae
BT1 ornamental herbaceous plants

CHRYSANTHEMUM SEGETUM
BT1 chrysanthemum
BT2 compositae
BT1 leafy vegetables
BT2 vegetables

CHRYSANTHEMUM STUNT VIROID
BT1 viroids
BT2 plant pathogens
BT3 pathogens
rt chrysanthemum

CHRYSANTHEMUMS
BT1 antibacterial plants
BT1 antifungal plants
BT1 insecticidal plants
BT2 pesticidal plants
BT1 medicinal plants
BT1 ornamental herbaceous plants
rt dendranthema indicum
rt dendranthema morifolium

CHRYSEMYS
BT1 emydidae
BT2 testudines
BT3 reptiles
NT1 chrysemys picta

CHRYSEMYS PICTA
BT1 chrysemys
BT2 emydidae

CHRYSEMYS PICTA *cont.*
BT3 testudines
BT4 reptiles

CHRYSICHTHYS
BT1 bagridae
BT2 siluriformes
BT3 osteichthyes
BT4 fishes
NT1 chrysichthys walkeri

CHRYSICHTHYS WALKERI
BT1 chrysichthys
BT2 bagridae
BT3 siluriformes
BT4 osteichthyes
BT5 fishes

CHRYSOBALANACEAE
NT1 chrysobalanus
NT2 chrysobalanus icaco
NT1 couepia
NT2 couepia polyandra
NT1 licania
NT2 licania densiflora
NT2 licania platypus
NT2 licania rigida
NT1 parinari
NT2 parinari capense
NT2 parinari curatellifolia

CHRYSOBALANUS
BT1 chrysobalanaceae
NT1 chrysobalanus icaco

CHRYSOBALANUS ICACO
BT1 chrysobalanus
BT2 chrysobalanaceae
BT1 tropical tree fruits
BT2 tree fruits
BT2 tropical fruits
BT3 fruit crops

CHRYSOBOTHRIS
BT1 buprestidae
BT2 coleoptera

CHRYSOCHARIS
BT1 eulophidae
BT2 hymenoptera
NT1 chrysocharis nitetis
NT1 chrysocharis parksi

CHRYSOCHARIS NITETIS
BT1 chrysocharis
BT2 eulophidae
BT3 hymenoptera

CHRYSOCHARIS PARKSI
BT1 chrysocharis
BT2 eulophidae
BT3 hymenoptera

CHRYSOCYON
BT1 canidae
BT2 fissipeda
BT3 carnivores
BT4 mammals
NT1 chrysocyon brachyurus

CHRYSOCYON BRACHYURUS
BT1 chrysocyon
BT2 canidae
BT3 fissipeda
BT4 carnivores
BT5 mammals

CHRYSODEIXIS
uf *pseudoplusia*
BT1 noctuidae
BT2 lepidoptera
NT1 chrysodeixis agnata
NT1 chrysodeixis chalcites
NT1 chrysodeixis eriosoma
NT1 chrysodeixis includens
rt autographa
rt plusia

CHRYSODEIXIS AGNATA
HN from 1989; previously acanthoplusia agnata
uf *acanthoplusia agnata*
BT1 chrysodeixis
BT2 noctuidae

CHRYSODEIXIS AGNATA *cont.*
BT3 lepidoptera

CHRYSODEIXIS CHALCITES
uf *autographa chalcites*
uf *plusia chalcites*
BT1 chrysodeixis
BT2 noctuidae
BT3 lepidoptera

CHRYSODEIXIS ERIOSOMA
BT1 chrysodeixis
BT2 noctuidae
BT3 lepidoptera

CHRYSODEIXIS INCLUDENS
HN from 1989; previously pseudoplusia includens
uf *pseudoplusia includens*
BT1 chrysodeixis
BT2 noctuidae
BT3 lepidoptera

CHRYSOLINA
BT1 chrysomelidae
BT2 coleoptera

CHRYSOMELA
uf *melasoma*
BT1 chrysomelidae
BT2 coleoptera
NT1 chrysomela aenea
NT1 chrysomela populi
rt leptinotarsa

CHRYSOMELA AENEA
uf *melasoma aenea*
BT1 chrysomela
BT2 chrysomelidae
BT3 coleoptera

chrysomela decemlineata
USE **leptinotarsa decemlineata**

CHRYSOMELA POPULI
uf *melasoma populi*
BT1 chrysomela
BT2 chrysomelidae
BT3 coleoptera

CHRYSOMELIDAE
BT1 coleoptera
NT1 acalymma
NT2 acalymma vittatum
NT1 agasicles
NT2 agasicles hygrophila
NT1 agelastica
NT2 agelastica alni
NT1 altica
NT2 altica carduorum
NT1 aphthona
NT2 aphthona abdominalis
NT2 aphthona euphorbiae
NT1 aulacophora
NT2 aulacophora foveicollis
NT1 brontispa
NT2 brontispa longissima
NT1 cassida
NT2 cassida nebulosa
NT1 cerotoma
NT2 cerotoma facialis
NT2 cerotoma ruficornis
NT2 cerotoma trifurcata
NT1 chaetocnema
NT2 chaetocnema concinna
NT2 chaetocnema pulicaria
NT2 chaetocnema tibialis
NT1 chrysolina
NT1 chrysomela
NT2 chrysomela aenea
NT2 chrysomela populi
NT1 coelaenomenodera
NT2 coelaenomenodera elaeidis
NT1 colaspis
NT2 colaspis ornata
NT1 diabrotica
NT2 diabrotica balteata
NT2 diabrotica barberi
NT2 diabrotica longicornis
NT2 diabrotica speciosa
NT2 diabrotica undecimpunctata

CHRYSOMELIDAE *cont.*
NT3 diabrotica undecimpunctata howardi
NT2 diabrotica virgifera
NT1 dicladispa
NT2 dicladispa armigera
NT1 disonycha
NT2 disonycha argentinensis
NT1 entomoscelis
NT2 entomoscelis americana
NT1 epitrix
NT2 epitrix hirtipennis
NT1 galeruca
NT1 galerucella
NT1 gonioctena
NT1 lema
NT1 leptinotarsa
NT2 leptinotarsa decemlineata
NT1 leptispa
NT2 leptispa pygmaea
NT1 lochmaea
NT2 lochmaea caprea
NT2 lochmaea suturalis
NT1 longitarsus
NT2 longitarsus jacobaeae
NT2 longitarsus nigripennis
NT2 longitarsus parvulus
NT1 madurasia
NT2 madurasia obscurella
NT1 monolepta
NT2 monolepta signata
NT1 nisotra
NT2 nisotra sjostedti
NT1 odontota
NT2 odontota dorsalis
NT1 ootheca
NT2 ootheca bennigseni
NT2 ootheca mutabilis
NT1 oulema
NT2 oulema lichenis
NT2 oulema melanopus
NT2 oulema oryzae
NT1 paropsis
NT2 paropsis atomaria
NT2 paropsis charybdis
NT1 phaedon
NT2 phaedon cochleariae
NT1 phyllotreta
NT2 phyllotreta atra
NT2 phyllotreta cruciferae
NT2 phyllotreta nemorum
NT2 phyllotreta striolata
NT2 phyllotreta undulata
NT1 plagiodera
NT2 plagiodera versicolora
NT1 podagrica
NT2 podagrica uniformis
NT1 psylliodes
NT2 psylliodes attenuata
NT2 psylliodes chrysocephala
NT2 psylliodes punctulata
NT1 pyrrhalta
NT2 pyrrhalta luteola
NT1 systena
NT1 trirhabda
NT2 trirhabda borealis
NT2 trirhabda virgata
NT1 uroplata
NT2 uroplata girardi
NT1 xenochalepus
NT1 zygogramma
NT2 zygogramma suturalis

CHRYSOMPHALUS
BT1 diaspididae
BT2 coccoidea
BT3 sternorrhyncha
BT4 homoptera
NT1 chrysomphalus aonidum
NT1 chrysomphalus dictyospermi

CHRYSOMPHALUS AONIDUM
uf *chrysomphalus ficus*
BT1 chrysomphalus
BT2 diaspididae
BT3 coccoidea
BT4 sternorrhyncha
BT5 homoptera

CHRYSOMPHALUS DICTYOSPERMI
BT1 chrysomphalus

CHRYSOMPHALUS DICTYOSPERMI *cont.*
BT2 diaspididae
BT3 coccoidea
BT4 sternorrhyncha
BT5 homoptera

chrysomphalus ficus
USE **chrysomphalus aonidum**

CHRYSOMYA
BT1 calliphoridae
BT2 diptera
NT1 chrysomya albiceps
NT1 chrysomya bezziana
NT1 chrysomya chloropyga
NT1 chrysomya megacephala
NT1 chrysomya putoria
NT1 chrysomya regalis
NT1 chrysomya rufifacies

CHRYSOMYA ALBICEPS
BT1 chrysomya
BT2 calliphoridae
BT3 diptera

CHRYSOMYA BEZZIANA
BT1 chrysomya
BT2 calliphoridae
BT3 diptera

CHRYSOMYA CHLOROPYGA
BT1 chrysomya
BT2 calliphoridae
BT3 diptera

CHRYSOMYA MEGACEPHALA
BT1 chrysomya
BT2 calliphoridae
BT3 diptera

CHRYSOMYA PUTORIA
BT1 chrysomya
BT2 calliphoridae
BT3 diptera

CHRYSOMYA REGALIS
HN from 1990
BT1 chrysomya
BT2 calliphoridae
BT3 diptera

CHRYSOMYA RUFIFACIES
BT1 chrysomya
BT2 calliphoridae
BT3 diptera

CHRYSOMYXA
BT1 uredinales
NT1 chrysomyxa ledi
NT1 chrysomyxa ledicola

CHRYSOMYXA LEDI
BT1 chrysomyxa
BT2 uredinales

CHRYSOMYXA LEDICOLA
BT1 chrysomyxa
BT2 uredinales

CHRYSONOTOMYIA
uf *achrysocharella*
uf *achrysocharis*
BT1 eulophidae
BT2 hymenoptera
NT1 chrysonotomyia formosa

CHRYSONOTOMYIA FORMOSA
uf *achrysocharella formosa*
BT1 chrysonotomyia
BT2 eulophidae
BT3 hymenoptera

CHRYSOPA
BT1 chrysopidae
BT2 neuroptera
NT1 chrysopa perla
rt brinckochrysa
rt chrysoperla
rt mallada

chrysopa boninensis
USE **mallada boninensis**

chrysopa carnea
USE **chrysoperla carnea**

CHRYSOPA PERLA
BT1 chrysopa
BT2 chrysopidae
BT3 neuroptera

chrysopa rufilabris
USE **chrysoperla rufilabris**

chrysopa scelestes
USE **brinckochrysa scelestes**

chrysopa vulgaris
USE **chrysoperla carnea**

CHRYSOPERLA
BT1 chrysopidae
BT2 neuroptera
NT1 chrysoperla carnea
NT1 chrysoperla rufilabris
rt anisochrysa
rt chrysopa

CHRYSOPERLA CARNEA
uf *anisochrysa carnea*
uf *chrysopa carnea*
uf *chrysopa vulgaris*
uf *chrysoperla vulgaris*
BT1 chrysoperla
BT2 chrysopidae
BT3 neuroptera

CHRYSOPERLA RUFILABRIS
uf *chrysopa rufilabris*
BT1 chrysoperla
BT2 chrysopidae
BT3 neuroptera

chrysoperla vulgaris
USE **chrysoperla carnea**

CHRYSOPHANIC ACID
BT1 organic acids
BT2 acids

CHRYSOPHRYS
BT1 sparidae
BT2 perciformes
BT3 osteichthyes
BT4 fishes
NT1 chrysophrys sarba
rt pagrus

chrysophrys aurata
USE **pagrus aurata**

CHRYSOPHRYS SARBA
BT1 chrysophrys
BT2 sparidae
BT3 perciformes
BT4 osteichthyes
BT5 fishes

chrysophyceae
USE **chrysophyta**

CHRYSOPHYLLUM
BT1 sapotaceae
NT1 chrysophyllum cainito

CHRYSOPHYLLUM CAINITO
uf *star apple*
BT1 chrysophyllum
BT2 sapotaceae
BT1 ornamental woody plants
BT1 tropical tree fruits
BT2 tree fruits
BT2 tropical fruits
BT3 fruit crops

CHRYSOPHYTA
uf *chrysophyceae*
BT1 algae
NT1 prymnesium
NT2 prymnesium parvum

CHRYSOPIDAE
BT1 neuroptera
NT1 anisochrysa
NT1 brinckochrysa
NT2 brinckochrysa scelestes
NT1 chrysopa
NT2 chrysopa perla

CHRYSOPIDAE *cont.*
NT1 chrysoperla
NT2 chrysoperla carnea
NT2 chrysoperla rufilabris
NT1 mallada
NT2 mallada boninensis

CHRYSOPOGON
BT1 gramineae
NT1 chrysopogon aucheri
NT1 chrysopogon echinulatus
NT1 chrysopogon fallax
NT1 chrysopogon fulvus
NT1 chrysopogon gryllus
NT1 chrysopogon serrulatus
rt andropogon

CHRYSOPOGON AUCHERI
BT1 chrysopogon
BT2 gramineae
BT1 pasture plants

CHRYSOPOGON ECHINULATUS
BT1 chrysopogon
BT2 gramineae
BT1 pasture plants

CHRYSOPOGON FALLAX
BT1 chrysopogon
BT2 gramineae
BT1 pasture plants

CHRYSOPOGON FULVUS
BT1 chrysopogon
BT2 gramineae

CHRYSOPOGON GRYLLUS
uf *andropogon gryllus*
BT1 chrysopogon
BT2 gramineae

CHRYSOPOGON SERRULATUS
BT1 chrysopogon
BT2 gramineae
BT1 pasture plants

CHRYSOPS
BT1 tabanidae
BT2 diptera
NT1 chrysops atlanticus
NT1 chrysops excitans
NT1 chrysops fuliginosus
NT1 chrysops furcatus
NT1 chrysops mlokosiewiczi
NT1 chrysops suavis
NT1 chrysops vanderwulpi

CHRYSOPS ATLANTICUS
BT1 chrysops
BT2 tabanidae
BT3 diptera

CHRYSOPS EXCITANS
BT1 chrysops
BT2 tabanidae
BT3 diptera

CHRYSOPS FULIGINOSUS
BT1 chrysops
BT2 tabanidae
BT3 diptera

CHRYSOPS FURCATUS
BT1 chrysops
BT2 tabanidae
BT3 diptera

CHRYSOPS MLOKOSIEWICZI
BT1 chrysops
BT2 tabanidae
BT3 diptera

CHRYSOPS SUAVIS
BT1 chrysops
BT2 tabanidae
BT3 diptera

CHRYSOPS VANDERWULPI
BT1 chrysops
BT2 tabanidae
BT3 diptera

chrysosarus
USE **megachile**

CHRYSOSPORIUM
BT1 deuteromycotina
NT1 chrysosporium evolceanui
NT1 chrysosporium keratinophilum
NT1 chrysosporium tropicum
rt arthroderma
rt emmonsia
rt myceliophthora

CHRYSOSPORIUM EVOLCEANUI
BT1 chrysosporium
BT2 deuteromycotina

CHRYSOSPORIUM KERATINOPHILUM
BT1 chrysosporium
BT2 deuteromycotina

chrysosporium parvum
USE **emmonsia parva**

chrysosporium thermophilum
USE **myceliophthora thermophila**

CHRYSOSPORIUM TROPICUM
BT1 chrysosporium
BT2 deuteromycotina

CHRYSOTEUCHIA
BT1 pyralidae
BT2 lepidoptera
NT1 chrysoteuchia topiaria

CHRYSOTEUCHIA TOPIARIA
BT1 chrysoteuchia
BT2 pyralidae
BT3 lepidoptera

CHRYSOTHAMNUS
BT1 compositae
NT1 chrysothamnus nauseosus
NT1 chrysothamnus parryi
NT1 chrysothamnus viscidiflorus

CHRYSOTHAMNUS NAUSEOSUS
BT1 chrysothamnus
BT2 compositae
BT1 insecticidal plants
BT2 pesticidal plants
BT1 rubber plants

CHRYSOTHAMNUS PARRYI
BT1 chrysothamnus
BT2 compositae

CHRYSOTHAMNUS VISCIDIFLORUS
BT1 chrysothamnus
BT2 compositae

chub
USE **leuciscus cephalus**

chufa
USE **cyperus esculentus**

CHUKRASIA
BT1 meliaceae
NT1 chukrasia tabularis

CHUKRASIA TABULARIS
BT1 chukrasia
BT2 meliaceae

CHUMYSH
BT1 horse breeds
BT2 breeds

CHUNK HONEY
BT1 honey
BT2 hive products
BT3 animal products
BT4 products
rt comb honey
rt section honey

CHUQUIRAGA
BT1 compositae
NT1 chuquiraga chontalensis

CHUQUIRAGA CHONTALENSIS
BT1 chuquiraga
BT2 compositae
BT1 medicinal plants

CHURCHES
BT1 buildings
rt organizations
rt religion

CHURRA DA TERRA QUENTE
HN from 1990
BT1 sheep breeds
BT2 breeds

CHURRO DO CAMPO
BT1 sheep breeds
BT2 breeds

CHUSHKA
BT1 sheep breeds
BT2 breeds

CHUSQUEA
BT1 gramineae
NT1 chusquea quila
rt bamboos
rt ornamental woody plants

CHUSQUEA QUILA
BT1 chusquea
BT2 gramineae

CHUTES
uf *flumes*
BT1 channels
rt slopes
rt spillways

CHUZAN VIRUS
HN from 1990
BT1 orbivirus
BT2 arboviruses
BT3 pathogens
BT2 reoviridae
BT3 viruses

CHYLE
BT1 lymph
BT2 body fluids
BT3 fluids

CHYLOMICRON LIPIDS
uf *chylomicrons*
BT1 lipoproteins
BT2 proteins
BT3 peptides
rt blood lipids
rt hyperchylomicronaemia

chylomicrons
USE **chylomicron lipids**

CHYLOTHORAX
BT1 respiratory diseases
BT2 organic diseases
BT3 diseases
rt lymph

CHYLURIA
BT1 urinary tract diseases
BT2 organic diseases
BT3 diseases
rt lymph
rt urine

chyme
USE **digesta**

CHYMOSIN
uf *milk clotting enzyme*
uf *rennin*
BT1 digestive juices
BT2 body fluids
BT3 fluids
NT1 rennet
NT2 microbial rennet
rt cheesemaking
rt milk

CHYMOTRYPSIN
(ec 3.4.21.1)
BT1 proteinases
BT2 peptide hydrolases
BT3 hydrolases
BT4 enzymes
rt chymotrypsin inhibitors
rt chymotrypsinogen

CHYMOTRYPSIN INHIBITORS
BT1 proteinase inhibitors
BT2 enzyme inhibitors
BT3 metabolic inhibitors
BT4 inhibitors
rt chymotrypsin

CHYMOTRYPSINOGEN
BT1 enzyme precursors
BT2 precursors
rt chymotrypsin

CHYTRIDIALES
NT1 olpidium
NT2 olpidium brassicae
NT1 synchytrium
NT2 synchytrium endobioticum
rt fungi

CHYTRIDIOPSIS
BT1 microspora
BT2 protozoa

CICADELLA
uf *tettigella*
BT1 cicadellidae
BT2 cicadelloidea
BT3 auchenorrhyncha
BT4 homoptera
NT1 cicadella viridis

CICADELLA VIRIDIS
BT1 cicadella
BT2 cicadellidae
BT3 cicadelloidea
BT4 auchenorrhyncha
BT5 homoptera

CICADELLIDAE
BT1 cicadelloidea
BT2 auchenorrhyncha
BT3 homoptera
NT1 agallia
NT2 agallia constricta
NT2 agallia laevis
NT1 alnetoidia
NT2 alnetoidia alneti
NT1 amplicephalus
NT1 amrasca
NT2 amrasca biguttula
NT2 amrasca devastans
NT1 anaceratagallia
NT1 chlorita
NT1 cicadella
NT2 cicadella viridis
NT1 cicadulina
NT2 cicadulina bipunctata
NT2 cicadulina chinai
NT2 cicadulina mbila
NT2 cicadulina parazeae
NT2 cicadulina storeyi
NT1 circulifer
NT2 circulifer tenellus
NT1 cofana
NT2 cofana spectra
NT1 colladonus
NT2 colladonus montanus
NT1 dalbulus
NT2 dalbulus elimatus
NT2 dalbulus gelbus
NT2 dalbulus maidis
NT1 empoasca
NT2 empoasca decipiens
NT2 empoasca dolichi
NT2 empoasca fabae
NT2 empoasca flavescens
NT2 empoasca kerri
NT2 empoasca kraemeri
NT1 empoascanara
NT2 empoascanara maculifrons
NT1 erythroneura
NT2 erythroneura elegantula
NT1 eupteryx
NT2 eupteryx atropunctata
NT1 euscelis
NT2 euscelis plebeja
NT1 eutettix
NT1 exitianus
NT2 exitianus exitiosus
NT1 fieberiella
NT2 fieberiella florii
NT1 graminella
NT2 graminella nigrifrons

CICADELLIDAE *cont.*
NT1 graphocephala
NT2 graphocephala atropunctata
NT1 hishimonus
NT2 hishimonus phycitis
NT1 idiocerus
NT1 idioscopus
NT2 idioscopus clypealis
NT1 jacobiasca
NT2 jacobiasca lybica
NT1 jacobiella
NT2 jacobiella facialis
NT1 macrosteles
NT2 macrosteles fascifrons
NT2 macrosteles laevis
NT2 macrosteles sexnotatus
NT1 neoaliturus
NT1 nephotettix
NT2 nephotettix cincticeps
NT2 nephotettix malayanus
NT2 nephotettix nigropictus
NT2 nephotettix virescens
NT1 orosius
NT2 orosius argentatus
NT1 psammotettix
NT2 psammotettix striatus
NT1 recilia
NT2 recilia dorsalis
NT1 scaphoideus
NT2 scaphoideus titanus
NT1 scaphytopius
NT2 scaphytopius acutus
NT2 scaphytopius magdalensis
NT1 tettigoniella
NT1 thaia
NT2 thaia oryzivora
NT2 thaia subrufa
NT1 typhlocyba
NT1 zygina
NT1 zyginidia

CICADELLOIDEA
BT1 auchenorrhyncha
BT2 homoptera
NT1 cicadellidae
NT2 agallia
NT3 agallia constricta
NT3 agallia laevis
NT2 alnetoidia
NT3 alnetoidia alneti
NT2 amplicephalus
NT2 amrasca
NT3 amrasca biguttula
NT3 amrasca devastans
NT2 anaceratagallia
NT2 chlorita
NT2 cicadella
NT3 cicadella viridis
NT2 cicadulina
NT3 cicadulina bipunctata
NT3 cicadulina chinai
NT3 cicadulina mbila
NT3 cicadulina parazeae
NT3 cicadulina storeyi
NT2 circulifer
NT3 circulifer tenellus
NT2 cofana
NT3 cofana spectra
NT2 colladonus
NT3 colladonus montanus
NT2 dalbulus
NT3 dalbulus elimatus
NT3 dalbulus gelbus
NT3 dalbulus maidis
NT2 empoasca
NT3 empoasca decipiens
NT3 empoasca dolichi
NT3 empoasca fabae
NT3 empoasca flavescens
NT3 empoasca kerri
NT3 empoasca kraemeri
NT2 empoascanara
NT3 empoascanara maculifrons
NT2 erythroneura
NT3 erythroneura elegantula
NT2 eupteryx
NT3 eupteryx atropunctata
NT2 euscelis
NT3 euscelis plebeja

CICADELLOIDEA *cont.*
NT2 eutettix
NT2 exitianus
NT3 exitianus exitiosus
NT2 fieberiella
NT3 fieberiella florii
NT2 graminella
NT3 graminella nigrifrons
NT2 graphocephala
NT3 graphocephala atropunctata
NT2 hishimonus
NT3 hishimonus phycitis
NT2 idiocerus
NT2 idioscopus
NT3 idioscopus clypealis
NT2 jacobiasca
NT3 jacobiasca lybica
NT2 jacobiella
NT3 jacobiella facialis
NT2 macrosteles
NT3 macrosteles fascifrons
NT3 macrosteles laevis
NT3 macrosteles sexnotatus
NT2 neoaliturus
NT2 nephotettix
NT3 nephotettix cincticeps
NT3 nephotettix malayanus
NT3 nephotettix nigropictus
NT3 nephotettix virescens
NT2 orosius
NT3 orosius argentatus
NT2 psammotettix
NT3 psammotettix striatus
NT2 recilia
NT3 recilia dorsalis
NT2 scaphoideus
NT3 scaphoideus titanus
NT2 scaphytopius
NT3 scaphytopius acutus
NT3 scaphytopius magdalensis
NT2 tettigoniella
NT2 thaia
NT3 thaia oryzivora
NT3 thaia subrufa
NT2 typhlocyba
NT2 zygina
NT2 zyginidia
NT1 membracidae
NT2 ceresa
NT3 ceresa bubalus
NT2 spissistilus
NT3 spissistilus festinus
NT2 stictocephala
NT3 stictocephala bisonia

CICADIDAE
BT1 cicadoidea
BT2 auchenorrhyncha
BT3 homoptera
NT1 magicicada
NT2 magicicada cassinii
NT2 magicicada septendecim
NT2 magicicada septendecula

CICADOIDEA
BT1 auchenorrhyncha
BT2 homoptera
NT1 cicadidae
NT2 magicicada
NT3 magicicada cassinii
NT3 magicicada septendecim
NT3 magicicada septendecula

CICADULINA
BT1 cicadellidae
BT2 cicadelloidea
BT3 auchenorrhyncha
BT4 homoptera
NT1 cicadulina bipunctata
NT1 cicadulina chinai
NT1 cicadulina mbila
NT1 cicadulina parazeae
NT1 cicadulina storeyi

CICADULINA BIPUNCTATA
BT1 cicadulina
BT2 cicadellidae
BT3 cicadelloidea
BT4 auchenorrhyncha
BT5 homoptera

CICADULINA CHINAI
BT1 cicadulina
BT2 cicadellidae
BT3 cicadelloidea
BT4 auchenorrhyncha
BT5 homoptera

CICADULINA MBILA
BT1 cicadulina
BT2 cicadellidae
BT3 cicadelloidea
BT4 auchenorrhyncha
BT5 homoptera

CICADULINA PARAZEAE
BT1 cicadulina
BT2 cicadellidae
BT3 cicadelloidea
BT4 auchenorrhyncha
BT5 homoptera

CICADULINA STOREYI
BT1 cicadulina
BT2 cicadellidae
BT3 cicadelloidea
BT4 auchenorrhyncha
BT5 homoptera

CICER
BT1 leguminosae
NT1 cicer arietinum

CICER ARIETINUM
BT1 cicer
BT2 leguminosae
BT1 grain legumes
BT2 grain crops
BT2 legumes
rt chickpeas

CICHLIDAE
BT1 perciformes
BT2 osteichthyes
BT3 fishes
NT1 tilapia
NT2 tilapia aurea
NT2 tilapia mossambica
NT2 tilapia nilotica
NT2 tilapia zillii

CICHLIDOGYRUS
BT1 dactylogyridae
BT2 monogenea

CICHORIUM
BT1 compositae
NT1 cichorium endivia
NT1 cichorium intybus
NT1 cichorium pumilum

CICHORIUM ENDIVIA
BT1 cichorium
BT2 compositae
rt endives

CICHORIUM INTYBUS
BT1 cichorium
BT2 compositae
rt chicory
rt chicory yellow mottle nepovirus

CICHORIUM PUMILUM
BT1 cichorium
BT2 compositae

CICINNOBOLUS
HN from 1990
BT1 deuteromycotina
rt ampelomyces

cicinnobolus cesati
USE **ampelomyces quisqualis**

CICLOBENDAZOLE
BT1 anthelmintics
BT2 antiparasitic agents
BT3 drugs
BT1 benzimidazoles
BT2 heterocyclic nitrogen compounds
BT3 organic nitrogen compounds

CICONIA
BT1 ciconiidae
BT2 ciconiiformes
BT3 birds
NT1 ciconia ciconia

CICONIA CICONIA
BT1 ciconia
BT2 ciconiidae
BT3 ciconiiformes
BT4 birds

CICONIIDAE
uf storks
BT1 ciconiiformes
BT2 birds
NT1 ciconia
NT2 ciconia ciconia
NT1 leptoptilos
NT2 leptoptilos crumeniferus

CICONIIFORMES
uf ardeiformes
BT1 birds
NT1 ardeidae
NT2 ardea
NT3 ardea cinerea
NT3 ardea herodias
NT3 ardea purpurea
NT2 ardeola
NT2 bubulcus
NT3 bubulcus ibis
NT4 bubulcus ibis coromandus
NT2 butorides
NT3 butorides striatus
NT2 egretta
NT3 egretta alba
NT3 egretta garzetta
NT2 nycticorax
NT3 nycticorax caledonicus
NT3 nycticorax nycticorax
NT1 ciconiidae
NT2 ciconia
NT3 ciconia ciconia
NT2 leptoptilos
NT3 leptoptilos crumeniferus
NT1 phoenicopteridae
NT2 phoenicopterus

CICUTA
BT1 umbelliferae
NT1 cicuta douglasii
NT1 cicuta maculata
NT1 cicuta virosa

CICUTA DOUGLASII
BT1 cicuta
BT2 umbelliferae

CICUTA MACULATA
BT1 cicuta
BT2 umbelliferae

CICUTA VIROSA
BT1 cicuta
BT2 umbelliferae

CIDER
BT1 alcoholic beverages
BT2 beverages
rt apple juice
rt apple pomace
rt apples

CIGUATERA
BT1 fish toxins
BT2 toxins
rt poisoning

CILIA
BT1 cell structure

CILIATES
rt ciliophora

CILIOPHORA
uf opalinata
BT1 protozoa
NT1 allantosoma
NT1 ancistrocoma
NT1 ancistrum
NT2 ancistrum mytili
NT1 anophrys

CILIOPHORA *cont.*
NT1 anoplophrya
NT1 apiosoma
NT2 apiosoma piscicola
NT1 balantidium
NT2 balantidium coli
NT2 balantidium ctenopharyngodonis
NT2 balantidium entozoon
NT2 balantidium kakatiyae
NT1 bursaria
NT2 bursaria truncatella
NT1 buxtonella
NT2 buxtonella sulcata
NT1 chilodonella
NT2 chilodonella algivora
NT2 chilodonella cucullulus
NT2 chilodonella cyprini
NT2 chilodonella hexastichus
NT2 chilodonella uncinata
NT1 colpoda
NT2 colpoda steini
NT1 conidophrys
NT1 cothurnia
NT2 cothurnia variabilis
NT1 cryptocaryon
NT2 cryptocaryon irritans
NT1 cyathodinium
NT1 cycloposthium
NT1 dasytricha
NT2 dasytricha ruminantium
NT1 diplodinium
NT1 drilocineta
NT1 entodinium
NT2 entodinium bursa
NT2 entodinium caudatum
NT2 entodinium longinucleatum
NT1 epidinium
NT2 epidinium caudatum
NT2 epidinium ecaudatum
NT1 epistylis
NT2 epistylis horizontalis
NT2 epistylis lwoffi
NT2 epistylis niagarae
NT1 eudiplodinium
NT1 foettingeria
NT1 glossatella
NT1 haptophrya
NT2 haptophrya gigantica
NT1 heterocinetopsis
NT1 holotrichia (protozoa)
NT1 hyalophysa
NT1 ichthyophthirius
NT2 ichthyophthirius multifiliis
NT1 infundibulorium
NT1 isotricha
NT2 isotricha intestinalis
NT2 isotricha prostoma
NT1 lagenophrys
NT1 lambornella
NT1 metadinium
NT1 metaradiophrya
NT1 myxophyllum
NT1 nyctotheroides
NT1 nyctotherus
NT1 opalina
NT1 opercularia
NT1 oxytricha
NT1 paraisotricha
NT1 paramecium
NT1 paranophrys
NT1 paratrichodina
NT1 peritrichia
NT1 plagiotoma
NT1 polyplastron
NT1 pronyctotherus
NT1 ptychostomum
NT1 rhabdostyla
NT1 scyphidia
NT1 semitrichodina
NT2 semitrichodina sphaeronuclea
NT1 sphenophrya
NT1 spirotrichia
NT1 synophrya
NT1 tetrahymena
NT2 tetrahymena corlissi
NT2 tetrahymena geleei
NT2 tetrahymena paravorax
NT2 tetrahymena pyriformis
NT2 tetrahymena stegomyiae

CILIOPHORA *cont.*
NT2 tetrahymena thermophila
NT1 trichodina
NT2 trichodina domerguei
NT2 trichodina pediculus
NT2 trichodina perforata
NT1 trichodinella
NT2 trichodinella subtilis
NT1 trichophrya
NT1 tripartiella
NT2 tripartiella bulbosa
NT1 troglodytella
NT2 troglodytella abrassarti
NT1 urceolaria
NT1 zelleriella
rt ciliates

CIMETIDINE
BT1 antihistaminics
BT2 drugs
BT1 guanidines
BT2 organic nitrogen compounds

CIMEX
BT1 cimicidae
BT2 heteroptera
NT1 cimex hemipterus
NT1 cimex lectularius

CIMEX HEMIPTERUS
BT1 cimex
BT2 cimicidae
BT3 heteroptera

CIMEX LECTULARIUS
BT1 cimex
BT2 cimicidae
BT3 heteroptera

CIMICIDAE
BT1 heteroptera
NT1 cimex
NT2 cimex hemipterus
NT2 cimex lectularius
NT1 oeciacus
NT2 oeciacus hirundinis

CIMMYT
(centro internacional de mejoramiento de maiz y trigo)
BT1 cgiar
BT2 international organizations
BT3 organizations
rt maize
rt wheat

CINARA
BT1 aphididae
BT2 aphidoidea
BT3 sternorrhyncha
BT4 homoptera
NT1 cinara pinea
NT1 cinara pini

CINARA PINEA
BT1 cinara
BT2 aphididae
BT3 aphidoidea
BT4 sternorrhyncha
BT5 homoptera

CINARA PINI
BT1 cinara
BT2 aphididae
BT3 aphidoidea
BT4 sternorrhyncha
BT5 homoptera

CINCHONA
BT1 rubiaceae
NT1 cinchona ledgeriana
NT1 cinchona pubescens
rt quinine
rt quinolines

CINCHONA LEDGERIANA
BT1 cinchona
BT2 rubiaceae
BT1 medicinal plants

CINCHONA PUBESCENS
uf cinchona succirubra
BT1 cinchona

CINCHONA PUBESCENS *cont.*
BT2 rubiaceae
BT1 medicinal plants

cinchona succirubra
USE **cinchona pubescens**

CINEMA
AF motion pictures
BT1 mass media
BT2 communication
rt films
rt recreational buildings
rt theatre

cineole
USE **eucalyptol**

cineraria
USE **senecio cruentus**
OR **senecio hybridus**

CINMETHYLIN
BT1 unclassified herbicides
BT2 herbicides
BT3 pesticides

CINNAMIC ACID
BT1 anthelmintics
BT2 antiparasitic agents
BT3 drugs
BT1 benzenealkenoic acids
BT2 carboxylic acids
BT3 organic acids
BT4 acids
rt perfumery

CINNAMODENDRON
BT1 canellaceae
NT1 cinnamodendron dinisii

CINNAMODENDRON DINISII
BT1 cinnamodendron
BT2 canellaceae
BT1 medicinal plants

CINNAMOMUM
BT1 lauraceae
NT1 cinnamomum aromaticum
NT1 cinnamomum burmanii
NT1 cinnamomum camphora
NT1 cinnamomum doederleinii
NT1 cinnamomum japonicum
NT1 cinnamomum laubattii
NT1 cinnamomum mercadoi
NT1 cinnamomum mindanaense
NT1 cinnamomum sieboldii
NT1 cinnamomum tamala
NT1 cinnamomum zeylanicum

CINNAMOMUM AROMATICUM
uf cassia bark
uf cinnamomum cassia
BT1 cinnamomum
BT2 lauraceae
BT1 essential oil plants
BT2 oil plants
BT1 medicinal plants
BT1 spice plants

CINNAMOMUM BURMANII
BT1 cinnamomum
BT2 lauraceae
BT1 essential oil plants
BT2 oil plants

CINNAMOMUM CAMPHORA
BT1 cinnamomum
BT2 lauraceae
BT1 essential oil plants
BT2 oil plants
BT1 forest trees
rt camphor

cinnamomum cassia
USE **cinnamomum aromaticum**

CINNAMOMUM DOEDERLEINII
BT1 cinnamomum
BT2 lauraceae

CINNAMOMUM JAPONICUM
BT1 cinnamomum
BT2 lauraceae

CINNAMOMUM LAUBATTII
BT1 cinnamomum
BT2 lauraceae

CINNAMOMUM MERCADOI
BT1 cinnamomum
BT2 lauraceae

CINNAMOMUM MINDANAENSE
BT1 cinnamomum
BT2 lauraceae

CINNAMOMUM SIEBOLDII
BT1 cinnamomum
BT2 lauraceae

CINNAMOMUM TAMALA
BT1 antibacterial plants
BT1 cinnamomum
BT2 lauraceae
rt cinnamon

cinnamomum verum
USE **cinnamomum zeylanicum**

CINNAMOMUM ZEYLANICUM
uf cinnamomum verum
BT1 antibacterial plants
BT1 cinnamomum
BT2 lauraceae
BT1 essential oil plants
BT2 oil plants
BT1 medicinal plants
BT1 spice plants
rt cinnamon

CINNAMON
BT1 spices
BT2 plant products
BT3 products
rt cinnamomum tamala
rt cinnamomum zeylanicum

CINNAMON BROWN SOILS
BT1 luvisols
BT2 soil types (genetic)

CINNAMONIC SOILS
BT1 cambisols
BT2 soil types (genetic)
BT1 luvisols
BT2 soil types (genetic)

CINNAMOSMA
BT1 canellaceae
NT1 cinnamosma madagascariensis

CINNAMOSMA MADAGASCARIENSIS
BT1 cinnamosma
BT2 canellaceae

CINTRACTIA
HN from 1990
BT1 ustilaginales
rt anthracoidea

cintractia caricis
USE **anthracoidea caricis**

cintractia subinclusa
USE **anthracoidea subinclusa**

CIRCADIAN RHYTHM
BT1 biological rhythms
rt caecotrophy

CIRCINELLA
BT1 mucorales
NT1 circinella circinans

CIRCINELLA CIRCINANS
BT1 circinella
BT2 mucorales

CIRCINOTRICHUM
BT1 deuteromycotina

CIRCUITS
NT1 electric circuits
NT1 integrated circuits
rt electricity
rt switches

circuits, electric
USE **electric circuits**

CIRCULAR SAWS
uf saws, circular
BT1 saws
BT2 forestry machinery
BT3 machinery
BT2 tools

CIRCULATING ANTIGENS
BT1 antigens
BT2 immunological factors

CIRCULATION
NT1 extracorporeal circulation
NT1 lymph flow
rt blood circulation

circulatory diseases
USE **circulatory disorders**

CIRCULATORY DISORDERS
uf blood circulation disorders
uf circulatory diseases
BT1 functional disorders
BT2 animal disorders
BT3 disorders
BT1 vascular diseases
BT2 cardiovascular diseases
BT3 organic diseases
BT4 diseases
NT1 vasoconstriction
rt haemorrhage

circulatory system
USE **cardiovascular system**

CIRCULIFER
BT1 cicadellidae
BT2 cicadelloidea
BT3 auchenorrhyncha
BT4 homoptera
NT1 circulifer tenellus

CIRCULIFER TENELLUS
BT1 circulifer
BT2 cicadellidae
BT3 cicadelloidea
BT4 auchenorrhyncha
BT5 homoptera

CIRCUMSPOROZOITE PROTEINS
HN from 1989
BT1 animal proteins
BT2 proteins
BT3 peptides
rt malaria
rt plasmodium
rt vaccines

CIRCUS
BT1 accipitridae
BT2 falconiformes
BT3 birds
NT1 circus cyaneus

CIRCUS ANIMALS
uf performing animals
BT1 working animals
BT2 animals
rt circuses

CIRCUS CYANEUS
BT1 circus
BT2 accipitridae
BT3 falconiformes
BT4 birds

CIRCUSES
BT1 performing arts
BT2 arts
rt circus animals
rt spectator events
rt theatre

cirphis
USE **mythimna**
OR **spodoptera**

CIRRHOPETALUM
BT1 orchidaceae
rt ornamental orchids

CIRRHOSIS
uf liver cirrhosis
BT1 degeneration
BT1 liver diseases
BT2 digestive system diseases
BT3 organic diseases
BT4 diseases
rt fibrosis

CIRRIPEDIA
BT1 crustacea
BT2 arthropods
NT1 thoracica
NT2 balanus
NT2 pollicipes
NT2 semibalanus
NT3 semibalanus balanoides

CIRROSPILUS
BT1 eulophidae
BT2 hymenoptera
NT1 cirrospilus vittatus

CIRROSPILUS VITTATUS
BT1 cirrospilus
BT2 eulophidae
BT3 hymenoptera

CIRSIUM
BT1 compositae
NT1 cirsium acaule
NT1 cirsium arvense
NT1 cirsium canum
NT1 cirsium erisithales
NT1 cirsium heterophyllum
NT1 cirsium japonicum
NT1 cirsium oleraceum
NT1 cirsium palustre
NT1 cirsium setosum
NT1 cirsium undulatum
NT1 cirsium vulgare

CIRSIUM ACAULE
BT1 cirsium
BT2 compositae

CIRSIUM ARVENSE
BT1 cirsium
BT2 compositae
BT1 weeds

CIRSIUM CANUM
BT1 cirsium
BT2 compositae

CIRSIUM ERISITHALES
BT1 cirsium
BT2 compositae

CIRSIUM HETEROPHYLLUM
BT1 cirsium
BT2 compositae

CIRSIUM JAPONICUM
BT1 cirsium
BT2 compositae
BT1 nematicidal plants
BT2 pesticidal plants

CIRSIUM OLERACEUM
BT1 cirsium
BT2 compositae

CIRSIUM PALUSTRE
BT1 cirsium
BT2 compositae

CIRSIUM SETOSUM
BT1 cirsium
BT2 compositae

CIRSIUM UNDULATUM
BT1 cirsium
BT2 compositae

CIRSIUM VULGARE
BT1 cirsium
BT2 compositae

CISKEI
BT1 south african homelands
BT2 south africa
BT3 southern africa
BT4 africa south of sahara
BT5 africa

CISMETHRIN
BT1 pyrethroid insecticides
BT2 insecticides
BT3 pesticides
BT2 pyrethroids

CISSAMPELOS
BT1 menispermaceae
NT1 cissampelos pareira

CISSAMPELOS PAREIRA
BT1 cissampelos
BT2 menispermaceae

CISSUS
BT1 vitidaceae
NT1 cissus antarctica
NT1 cissus quadrangula
NT1 cissus rhombifolia

CISSUS ANTARCTICA
BT1 cissus
BT2 vitidaceae
BT1 ornamental foliage plants
BT2 foliage plants

CISSUS QUADRANGULA
BT1 cissus
BT2 vitidaceae
BT1 ornamental succulent plants
BT2 succulent plants
BT1 poisonous plants
rt ornamental foliage plants

CISSUS RHOMBIFOLIA
uf rhoicissus rhomboidea
BT1 cissus
BT2 vitidaceae
rt ornamental foliage plants

CISTACEAE
NT1 cistus
NT2 cistus incanus subsp. creticus
NT2 cistus ladanifer
NT2 cistus laurifolius
NT2 cistus monspeliensis
NT1 helianthemum
NT2 helianthemum ledifolium

CISTANCHE
BT1 orobanchaceae
NT1 cistanche tinctoria
NT1 cistanche tubulosa
NT1 cistanche violacea

CISTANCHE TINCTORIA
BT1 cistanche
BT2 orobanchaceae

CISTANCHE TUBULOSA
BT1 cistanche
BT2 orobanchaceae
BT1 parasitic plants
BT2 parasites

CISTANCHE VIOLACEA
BT1 cistanche
BT2 orobanchaceae

CISTRONS
BT1 genes
rt complementation
rt dna
rt genetic code
rt molecular genetics
rt rna

CISTUS
BT1 cistaceae
NT1 cistus incanus subsp. creticus
NT1 cistus ladanifer
NT1 cistus laurifolius
NT1 cistus monspeliensis

CISTUS INCANUS SUBSP. CRETICUS
uf cistus villosus
BT1 cistus
BT2 cistaceae
BT1 ornamental woody plants

CISTUS LADANIFER
BT1 cistus

CISTUS LADANIFER *cont.*
BT2 cistaceae
BT1 essential oil plants
BT2 oil plants
BT1 ornamental woody plants

CISTUS LAURIFOLIUS
BT1 antifungal plants
BT1 cistus
BT2 cistaceae
BT1 ornamental woody plants

CISTUS MONSPELIENSIS
BT1 cistus
BT2 cistaceae
BT1 ornamental woody plants

cistus villosus
USE **cistus incanus subsp. creticus**

CITELLOPHILUS
BT1 ceratophyllidae
BT2 siphonaptera
NT1 citellophilus tesquorum
rt ceratophyllus

CITELLOPHILUS TESQUORUM
uf ceratophyllus tesquorum
BT1 citellophilus
BT2 ceratophyllidae
BT3 siphonaptera

citellus
USE **spermophilus**

citellus fulvus
USE **spermophilus fulvus**

citizen participation
USE **social participation**

CITRADIAS
BT1 citrus fruits
BT2 subtropical tree fruits
BT3 subtropical fruits
BT4 fruit crops
BT3 tree fruits
rt citrus aurantium x poncirus trifoliata

CITRAL
BT1 aldehydes
BT1 monoterpenoids
BT2 terpenoids
BT3 isoprenoids
BT4 lipids
NT1 geranial
NT1 neral
rt essential oils
rt perfumery

CITRANDARINS
BT1 citrus fruits
BT2 subtropical tree fruits
BT3 subtropical fruits
BT4 fruit crops
BT3 tree fruits

CITRANGEQUATS
BT1 citrus fruits
BT2 subtropical tree fruits
BT3 subtropical fruits
BT4 fruit crops
BT3 tree fruits
rt citrus
rt fortunella
rt poncirus trifoliata

CITRANGES
BT1 citrus fruits
BT2 subtropical tree fruits
BT3 subtropical fruits
BT4 fruit crops
BT3 tree fruits
rt citrangors
rt citrus sinensis x poncirus trifoliata

CITRANGORS
BT1 citrus fruits
BT2 subtropical tree fruits
BT3 subtropical fruits
BT4 fruit crops
BT3 tree fruits

CITRANGORS *cont.*
rt citranges

CITRATES
BT1 organic salts
BT2 salts
NT1 sodium citrate
rt citric acid

CITREMONS
BT1 citrus fruits
BT2 subtropical tree fruits
BT3 subtropical fruits
BT4 fruit crops
BT3 tree fruits
rt citrus limon x poncirus trifoliata

CITREOVIRIDIN
BT1 mycotoxins
BT2 toxins

CITRIC ACID
BT1 acidulants
BT2 food additives
BT3 additives
BT1 antioxidants
BT2 additives
BT1 tricarboxylic acids
BT2 carboxylic acids
BT3 organic acids
BT4 acids
rt citrates
rt isocitric acid

citric acid cycle
USE **tricarboxylic acid cycle**

CITRININ
BT1 antibiotics
BT1 mycotoxins
BT2 toxins

CITROBACTER
BT1 enterobacteriaceae
BT2 gracilicutes
BT3 bacteria
BT4 prokaryotes
NT1 citrobacter freundii

CITROBACTER FREUNDII
BT1 citrobacter
BT2 enterobacteriaceae
BT3 gracilicutes
BT4 bacteria
BT5 prokaryotes

CITRONS
BT1 citrus fruits
BT2 subtropical tree fruits
BT3 subtropical fruits
BT4 fruit crops
BT3 tree fruits
rt citrus limonimedica
rt citrus medica

CITROPSIS
BT1 rutaceae
NT1 citropsis daweana
NT1 citropsis gabunensis
NT1 citropsis gilletiana
NT1 citropsis schweinfurthii
rt citrus fruits

CITROPSIS DAWEANA
BT1 citropsis
BT2 rutaceae

CITROPSIS GABUNENSIS
BT1 citropsis
BT2 rutaceae

CITROPSIS GILLETIANA
BT1 citropsis
BT2 rutaceae

CITROPSIS SCHWEINFURTHII
BT1 citropsis
BT2 rutaceae

citrovorum factor
USE **folinic acid**

CITRULLINAEMIA
AF citrullinemia

CITRULLINAEMIA *cont.*
BT1 acidaemia
BT2 blood disorders
BT3 animal disorders
BT4 disorders
rt epilepsy
rt mental disorders

CITRULLINE
BT1 nonprotein amino acids
BT2 amino acids
BT3 carboxylic acids
BT4 organic acids
BT5 acids
BT3 organic nitrogen compounds

CITRULLINEMIA
BF citrullinaemia
BT1 acidemia

CITRULLUS
BT1 cucurbitaceae
NT1 citrullus colocynthis
NT1 citrullus lanatus
NT1 citrullus lanatus var. fistulosus

CITRULLUS COLOCYNTHIS
uf colocynthis vulgaris
BT1 citrullus
BT2 cucurbitaceae
BT1 cucurbit vegetables
BT2 fruit vegetables
BT3 vegetables
BT1 medicinal plants
BT1 oilseed plants
BT2 fatty oil plants
BT3 oil plants

CITRULLUS LANATUS
uf citrullus vulgaris
uf colocynthis citrullus
BT1 citrullus
BT2 cucurbitaceae
rt watermelon mosaic virus
rt watermelons

CITRULLUS LANATUS VAR. FISTULOSUS
uf citrullus vulgaris var. fistulosus
uf gourd, round
BT1 citrullus
BT2 cucurbitaceae

citrullus vulgaris
USE **citrullus lanatus**

citrullus vulgaris var. fistulosus
USE **citrullus lanatus var. fistulosus**

CITRUMELOS
BT1 citrus fruits
BT2 subtropical tree fruits
BT3 subtropical fruits
BT4 fruit crops
BT3 tree fruits
rt citrus paradisi x poncirus trifoliata

CITRUS
BT1 rutaceae
NT1 citrus amblycarpa
NT1 citrus assamensis
NT1 citrus aurantiifolia
NT1 citrus aurantium
NT1 citrus aurantium x poncirus trifoliata
NT1 citrus bergamia
NT1 citrus clementina
NT1 citrus deliciosa
NT1 citrus depressa
NT1 citrus glaberrima
NT1 citrus hassaku
NT1 citrus hystrix
NT1 citrus ichangensis
NT1 citrus intermedia
NT1 citrus iyo
NT1 citrus jambhiri
NT1 citrus junos
NT1 citrus kabusu
NT1 citrus karna

CITRUS *cont.*
NT1 citrus kotokan
NT1 citrus latifolia
NT1 citrus limettioides
NT1 citrus limon
NT1 citrus limon x poncirus trifoliata
NT1 citrus limonia
NT1 citrus limonimedica
NT1 citrus macrophylla
NT1 citrus macroptera
NT1 citrus maderaspatana
NT1 citrus madurensis
NT1 citrus maxima
NT1 citrus medica
NT1 citrus medioglobosa
NT1 citrus megaloxycarpa
NT1 citrus meyeri
NT1 citrus miaray
NT1 citrus myrtifolia
NT1 citrus natsudaidai
NT1 citrus nobilis
NT1 citrus oblonga
NT1 citrus obovoidea
NT1 citrus otachibana
NT1 citrus papuana
NT1 citrus paradisi
NT1 citrus paradisi x citrus reticulata
NT1 citrus paradisi x poncirus trifoliata
NT1 citrus pennivesiculata
NT1 citrus poonensis
NT1 citrus pseudolimon
NT1 citrus reshni
NT1 citrus reticulata
NT1 citrus sinensis
NT1 citrus sinensis x citrus reticulata
NT1 citrus sinensis x poncirus trifoliata
NT1 citrus sudachi
NT1 citrus sulcata
NT1 citrus sunki
NT1 citrus tachibana
NT1 citrus taiwanica
NT1 citrus takuma-sudachi
NT1 citrus tamurana
NT1 citrus tankan
NT1 citrus tengu
NT1 citrus ujikitsu
NT1 citrus unshiu
NT1 citrus volkameriana
NT1 citrus wilsonii
NT1 citrus yuko
rt chironjas
rt citrangequats
rt citrus exocortis viroid
rt citrus fruits
rt citrus greening
rt citrus impietratura virus
rt citrus infectious variegation virus
rt citrus leaf rugose ilarvirus
rt citrus mosaic virus
rt citrus psorosis virus
rt citrus pulp
rt citrus seedling yellows virus
rt citrus tatter leaf virus
rt citrus tristeza closterovirus
rt citrus variegation ilarvirus
rt citrus vein enation virus
rt citrus xyloporosis virus

CITRUS AMBLYCARPA
BT1 citrus
BT2 rutaceae

CITRUS ASSAMENSIS
BT1 citrus
BT2 rutaceae

CITRUS AURANTIIFOLIA
BT1 citrus
BT2 rutaceae
rt limes
rt procimequats

CITRUS AURANTIUM
BT1 citrus
BT2 rutaceae
BT1 essential oil plants

CITRUS AURANTIUM *cont.*
BT2 oil plants
rt sour oranges

CITRUS AURANTIUM X PONCIRUS TRIFOLIATA
BT1 citrus
BT2 rutaceae
rt citradias

CITRUS BERGAMIA
uf *bergamot*
BT1 citrus
BT2 rutaceae
BT1 essential oil plants
BT2 oil plants

CITRUS CLEMENTINA
BT1 citrus
BT2 rutaceae
rt clementines

citrus decumana
USE **citrus maxima**

CITRUS DELICIOSA
HN from 1990
BT1 citrus
BT2 rutaceae
rt mandarins

CITRUS DEPRESSA
BT1 citrus
BT2 rutaceae

CITRUS EXOCORTIS VIROID
BT1 viroids
BT2 plant pathogens
BT3 pathogens
rt citrus

CITRUS FRUITS
BT1 subtropical tree fruits
BT2 subtropical fruits
BT3 fruit crops
BT2 tree fruits
NT1 calamondins
NT1 chironjas
NT1 citradias
NT1 citrandarins
NT1 citrangequats
NT1 citranges
NT1 citrangors
NT1 citremons
NT1 citrons
NT1 citrumelos
NT1 clementines
NT1 grapefruits
NT1 kumquats
NT1 lemons
NT1 limes
NT1 mandarins
NT1 natsudaidais
NT1 oranges
NT1 ortaniques
NT1 procimequats
NT1 pummelos
NT1 rough lemons
NT1 satsumas
NT1 sour oranges
NT1 tangelos
NT1 tangors
rt citropsis
rt citrus
rt citrus harvesters
rt creasing
rt degreening
rt fortunella
rt fruit puffing
rt granulation
rt marmalade
rt oleocellosis
rt plants
rt poncirus
rt rind pitting

CITRUS GLABERRIMA
BT1 citrus
BT2 rutaceae

citrus grandis
USE **citrus maxima**

CITRUS GREENING
HN from 1990
BT1 greening disease
BT2 plant diseases
rt citrus

CITRUS HARVESTERS
uf *harvesters, citrus*
BT1 harvesters
BT2 farm machinery
BT3 machinery
rt citrus fruits

CITRUS HASSAKU
BT1 citrus
BT2 rutaceae

CITRUS HYSTRIX
BT1 citrus
BT2 rutaceae

CITRUS ICHANGENSIS
BT1 citrus
BT2 rutaceae

CITRUS IMPIETRATURA VIRUS
BT1 miscellaneous plant viruses
BT2 plant viruses
BT3 plant pathogens
BT4 pathogens
rt citrus

CITRUS INFECTIOUS VARIEGATION VIRUS
BT1 miscellaneous plant viruses
BT2 plant viruses
BT3 plant pathogens
BT4 pathogens
rt citrus

CITRUS INTERMEDIA
BT1 citrus
BT2 rutaceae

CITRUS IYO
BT1 citrus
BT2 rutaceae

CITRUS JAMBHIRI
BT1 citrus
BT2 rutaceae
rt rough lemons

CITRUS JUNOS
uf *yuzu*
BT1 citrus
BT2 rutaceae
BT1 medicinal plants

CITRUS KABUSU
BT1 citrus
BT2 rutaceae

CITRUS KARNA
BT1 citrus
BT2 rutaceae

CITRUS KOTOKAN
BT1 citrus
BT2 rutaceae

CITRUS LATIFOLIA
uf *persian limes*
uf *tahiti limes*
BT1 citrus
BT2 rutaceae

CITRUS LEAF RUGOSE ILARVIRUS
HN from 1990; previously "citrus leaf rugose virus"
uf *citrus leaf rugose virus*
BT1 ilarvirus group
BT2 plant viruses
BT3 plant pathogens
BT4 pathogens
rt citrus

citrus leaf rugose virus
USE **citrus leaf rugose ilarvirus**

CITRUS LIMETTIOIDES
uf *palestine limes*
uf *sweet limes*
BT1 citrus

CITRUS LIMETTIOIDES *cont.*
BT2 rutaceae

CITRUS LIMON
BT1 citrus
BT2 rutaceae
rt lemons

CITRUS LIMON X PONCIRUS TRIFOLIATA
BT1 citrus
BT2 rutaceae
rt citremons

CITRUS LIMONIA
uf *rangpur limes*
BT1 citrus
BT2 rutaceae

CITRUS LIMONIMEDICA
BT1 citrus
BT2 rutaceae
rt citrons

CITRUS MACROPHYLLA
BT1 citrus
BT2 rutaceae

CITRUS MACROPTERA
BT1 citrus
BT2 rutaceae

CITRUS MADERASPATANA
BT1 citrus
BT2 rutaceae

CITRUS MADURENSIS
uf *citrus mitis*
BT1 citrus
BT2 rutaceae
rt calamondins

CITRUS MAXIMA
uf *citrus decumana*
uf *citrus grandis*
BT1 citrus
BT2 rutaceae
rt pummelos

CITRUS MEDICA
BT1 citrus
BT2 rutaceae
rt citrons

CITRUS MEDIOGLOBOSA
BT1 citrus
BT2 rutaceae

CITRUS MEGALOXYCARPA
BT1 citrus
BT2 rutaceae

CITRUS MEYERI
uf *lemons, meyer*
uf *meyer lemons*
BT1 citrus
BT2 rutaceae
BT1 essential oil plants
BT2 oil plants

CITRUS MIARAY
BT1 citrus
BT2 rutaceae

citrus mitis
USE **citrus madurensis**

CITRUS MOSAIC VIRUS
BT1 miscellaneous plant viruses
BT2 plant viruses
BT3 plant pathogens
BT4 pathogens
rt citrus

CITRUS MYRTIFOLIA
BT1 citrus
BT2 rutaceae

CITRUS NATSUDAIDAI
BT1 citrus
BT2 rutaceae
rt natsudaidais

CITRUS NOBILIS
BT1 citrus
BT2 rutaceae

CITRUS OBLONGA
BT1 citrus
BT2 rutaceae
rt oranges

CITRUS OBOVOIDEA
BT1 citrus
BT2 rutaceae

CITRUS OTACHIBANA
BT1 citrus
BT2 rutaceae

CITRUS PAPUANA
BT1 citrus
BT2 rutaceae

CITRUS PARADISI
BT1 citrus
BT2 rutaceae
rt grapefruits

CITRUS PARADISI X CITRUS RETICULATA
BT1 citrus
BT2 rutaceae
rt tangelos

CITRUS PARADISI X PONCIRUS TRIFOLIATA
BT1 citrus
BT2 rutaceae
rt citrumelos

CITRUS PENNIVESICULATA
BT1 citrus
BT2 rutaceae

CITRUS POONENSIS
BT1 citrus
BT2 rutaceae
BT1 insecticidal plants
BT2 pesticidal plants

CITRUS PSEUDOLIMON
BT1 citrus
BT2 rutaceae

CITRUS PSOROSIS VIRUS
BT1 miscellaneous plant viruses
BT2 plant viruses
BT3 plant pathogens
BT4 pathogens
rt citrus

CITRUS PULP
BT1 fruit pulp
BT2 fruit products
BT3 plant products
BT4 products
BT2 pulps
NT1 orange pulp
rt citrus

CITRUS RESHNI
BT1 citrus
BT2 rutaceae
rt mandarins

CITRUS RETICULATA
BT1 citrus
BT2 rutaceae
rt mandarins

CITRUS SEEDLING YELLOWS VIRUS
BT1 miscellaneous plant viruses
BT2 plant viruses
BT3 plant pathogens
BT4 pathogens
rt citrus

CITRUS SINENSIS
BT1 citrus
BT2 rutaceae
rt oranges

CITRUS SINENSIS X CITRUS RETICULATA
BT1 citrus
BT2 rutaceae
rt tangors

CITRUS SINENSIS X PONCIRUS TRIFOLIATA

CITRUS SINENSIS X PONCIRUS TRIFOLIATA *cont.*
BT1 citrus
BT2 rutaceae
rt citranges

CITRUS SOILS
BT1 soil types (cultural)

CITRUS SUDACHI
BT1 citrus
BT2 rutaceae
BT1 medicinal plants

CITRUS SULCATA
BT1 citrus
BT2 rutaceae

CITRUS SUNKI
BT1 citrus
BT2 rutaceae

CITRUS TACHIBANA
BT1 citrus
BT2 rutaceae

CITRUS TAIWANICA
BT1 citrus
BT2 rutaceae

CITRUS TAKUMA-SUDACHI
BT1 citrus
BT2 rutaceae

CITRUS TAMURANA
BT1 citrus
BT2 rutaceae

CITRUS TANKAN
BT1 citrus
BT2 rutaceae

CITRUS TATTER LEAF VIRUS
BT1 miscellaneous plant viruses
BT2 plant viruses
BT3 plant pathogens
BT4 pathogens
rt citrus

CITRUS TENGU
BT1 citrus
BT2 rutaceae

CITRUS TRISTEZA CLOSTEROVIRUS
HN from 1990; previously "citrus tristeza virus"
uf *citrus tristeza virus*
uf *tristeza*
BT1 closterovirus group
BT2 plant viruses
BT3 plant pathogens
BT4 pathogens
rt citrus

citrus tristeza virus
USE **citrus tristeza closterovirus**

CITRUS UJIKITSU
BT1 citrus
BT2 rutaceae

CITRUS UNSHIU
BT1 citrus
BT2 rutaceae
rt satsumas

CITRUS VARIEGATION ILARVIRUS
HN from 1990
BT1 ilarvirus group
BT2 plant viruses
BT3 plant pathogens
BT4 pathogens
rt citrus

CITRUS VEIN ENATION VIRUS
BT1 miscellaneous plant viruses
BT2 plant viruses
BT3 plant pathogens
BT4 pathogens
rt citrus

CITRUS VOLKAMERIANA
BT1 citrus
BT2 rutaceae

CITRUS WILSONII
BT1 citrus
BT2 rutaceae

CITRUS XYLOPOROSIS VIRUS
BT1 miscellaneous plant viruses
BT2 plant viruses
BT3 plant pathogens
BT4 pathogens
rt citrus

CITRUS YUKO
BT1 citrus
BT2 rutaceae

civets
USE **viverridae**

CIVIL DEFENSE (AGRICOLA)
rt emergencies
rt war

CIVIL ENGINEERING
BT1 engineering

CIVIL RIGHTS
BT1 human rights

CIXIIDAE
BT1 fulgoroidea
BT2 auchenorrhyncha
BT3 homoptera
NT1 myndus
NT2 myndus crudus

CLADDING
BT1 building materials
BT2 materials
NT1 double cladding
NT1 plastic cladding
rt glazing
rt greenhouses
rt panels

cladding, double
USE **double cladding**

cladding, plastic
USE **plastic cladding**

CLADIUM
BT1 cyperaceae
NT1 cladium jamaicense

CLADIUM JAMAICENSE
BT1 cladium
BT2 cyperaceae

CLADOBOTRYUM
HN from 1990
BT1 deuteromycotina
NT1 cladobotryum verticillatum
rt verticillium

CLADOBOTRYUM VERTICILLATUM
HN from 1990
uf *verticillium agaricinum*
BT1 cladobotryum
BT2 deuteromycotina

CLADOCERA
BT1 branchiopoda
BT2 crustacea
BT3 arthropods
NT1 daphnia
NT2 daphnia magna
NT2 daphnia pulex

CLADONIA
BT1 lecanorales

CLADOPHORA
BT1 chlorophyta
BT2 algae
NT1 cladophora glomerata
rt seaweeds

CLADOPHORA GLOMERATA
BT1 cladophora
BT2 chlorophyta
BT3 algae

CLADOSPORIUM
uf *heterosporium*
BT1 deuteromycotina

CLADOSPORIUM *cont.*
NT1 cladosporium carrionii
NT1 cladosporium cladosporioides
NT1 cladosporium cucumerinum
NT1 cladosporium herbarum
NT1 cladosporium phlei
rt phaeoannellomyces
rt venturia (dothideales)
rt xylohypha

cladosporium bantianum
USE **xylohypha bantiana**

cladosporium carpophilum
USE **venturia carpophila**

CLADOSPORIUM CARRIONII
BT1 cladosporium
BT2 deuteromycotina

CLADOSPORIUM CLADOSPORIOIDES
BT1 cladosporium
BT2 deuteromycotina

CLADOSPORIUM CUCUMERINUM
BT1 cladosporium
BT2 deuteromycotina

cladosporium effusum
USE **cercospora effusa**

cladosporium fulvum
USE **fulvia fulva**

CLADOSPORIUM HERBARUM
BT1 cladosporium
BT2 deuteromycotina

CLADOSPORIUM PHLEI
uf *heterosporium phlei*
BT1 cladosporium
BT2 deuteromycotina

cladosporium resinae
USE **amorphotheca resinae**

cladosporium trichoides
USE **xylohypha bantiana**

cladosporium werneckii
USE **phaeoannellomyces werneckii**

CLADOTANYTARSUS
BT1 chironomidae
BT2 diptera
NT1 cladotanytarsus lewisi

CLADOTANYTARSUS LEWISI
BT1 cladotanytarsus
BT2 chironomidae
BT3 diptera

CLADRASTIS
BT1 leguminosae
NT1 cladrastis kentukea
NT1 cladrastis platycarpa
NT1 cladrastis shikokiana

CLADRASTIS KENTUKEA
uf *cladrastis lutea*
BT1 cladrastis
BT2 leguminosae
BT1 dye plants
BT1 ornamental woody plants

cladrastis lutea
USE **cladrastis kentukea**

CLADRASTIS PLATYCARPA
BT1 cladrastis
BT2 leguminosae

CLADRASTIS SHIKOKIANA
BT1 cladrastis
BT2 leguminosae

CLAMPS
BT1 stores
rt bins
rt containers
rt silos
rt storage

CLAMS
BT1 seafoods
BT2 foods
BT1 shellfish
BT2 aquatic invertebrates
BT3 aquatic animals
BT4 animals
BT4 aquatic organisms
NT1 hard clams
NT1 surf clams

CLAPPERTONIA
BT1 tiliaceae

CLARIAS
BT1 clariidae
BT2 siluriformes
BT3 osteichthyes
BT4 fishes
NT1 clarias lazera

CLARIAS LAZERA
BT1 clarias
BT2 clariidae
BT3 siluriformes
BT4 osteichthyes
BT5 fishes

CLARIFICATION
uf *clarifying*
BT1 milk processing
BT2 processing
BT1 purification
BT2 processing
rt butter
rt clarifiers
rt gelatin
rt ghee
rt separation

clarification mud
USE **filter cake**

CLARIFIERS
BT1 dairy equipment
BT2 equipment
rt butter
rt clarification
rt cyclohexanecarboxylic acid
rt ghee
rt kaolin
rt purification
rt separation
rt separators

clarifying
USE **clarification**

CLARIIDAE
BT1 siluriformes
BT2 osteichthyes
BT3 fishes
NT1 clarias
NT2 clarias lazera

CLARKIA
uf *godetia*
BT1 onagraceae
NT1 clarkia amoena
NT1 clarkia exilis
NT1 clarkia tembloriensis
NT1 clarkia unguiculata

CLARKIA AMOENA
BT1 clarkia
BT2 onagraceae
BT1 ornamental herbaceous plants

clarkia elegans
USE **clarkia unguiculata**

CLARKIA EXILIS
BT1 clarkia
BT2 onagraceae

CLARKIA TEMBLORIENSIS
BT1 clarkia
BT2 onagraceae

CLARKIA UNGUICULATA
uf *clarkia elegans*
BT1 clarkia
BT2 onagraceae

CLARKIA UNGUICULATA *cont.*
BT1 ornamental herbaceous plants

CLASS ACTIVITIES (AGRICOLA)
rt learning activities (agricola)
rt teaching methods

CLASS CONFLICT
BT1 conflict
BT2 social unrest
BT3 social change
rt social classes

classical complement pathway
USE **complement activation**

CLASSICAL ECONOMICS
uf *economics, classical*
BT1 economics
rt division of labour
rt neoclassical economics

CLASSICAL MUSIC
BT1 music
BT2 performing arts
BT3 arts

CLASSIFICATION
uf *typology*
NT1 characterization
NT1 land classification
NT1 ranking
NT1 soil classification
NT2 soil taxonomy
NT1 taxonomy
NT2 biosystematics
NT2 chemotaxonomy
NT2 cytotaxonomy
NT2 immunotaxonomy
NT2 numerical taxonomy
NT2 variety classification
NT1 terrain classification
rt caste
rt genera
rt information processing
rt sorting
rt species

classification, land
USE **land classification**

classroom materials
USE **teaching materials**

clasterosporium
USE **stigmina**

clasterosporium carpophilum
USE **stigmina carpophila**

CLASTOGENS
BT1 mutagens

CLAUS PROCESS
BT1 fertilizer technology
BT2 technology

CLAUSENA
BT1 rutaceae
NT1 clausena anisata
NT1 clausena dentata
NT1 clausena indica
NT1 clausena lansium
NT1 clausena pentaphylla

CLAUSENA ANISATA
BT1 clausena
BT2 rutaceae
BT1 medicinal plants
BT1 molluscicidal plants
BT2 pesticidal plants

CLAUSENA DENTATA
BT1 clausena
BT2 rutaceae

CLAUSENA INDICA
BT1 clausena
BT2 rutaceae

CLAUSENA LANSIUM
BT1 clausena
BT2 rutaceae
BT1 medicinal plants

CLAUSENA LANSIUM *cont.*
BT1 subtropical tree fruits
BT2 subtropical fruits
BT3 fruit crops
BT2 tree fruits

CLAUSENA PENTAPHYLLA
BT1 clausena
BT2 rutaceae
BT1 medicinal plants

CLAVIBACTER
BT1 coryneform group of bacteria
BT2 firmicutes
BT3 bacteria
BT4 prokaryotes
BT1 plant pathogenic bacteria
BT2 plant pathogens
BT3 pathogens
NT1 clavibacter iranicus
NT1 clavibacter michiganensis
NT2 clavibacter michiganensis subsp. insidiosus
NT2 clavibacter michiganensis subsp. michiganensis
NT2 clavibacter michiganensis subsp. nebraskensis
NT2 clavibacter michiganensis subsp. sepedonicus
NT1 clavibacter rathayi
NT1 clavibacter tritici
NT1 clavibacter xyli
NT2 clavibacter xyli subsp. xyli
rt corynebacterium

CLAVIBACTER IRANICUS
uf *corynebacterium michiganense pv. iranicum*
BT1 clavibacter
BT2 coryneform group of bacteria
BT3 firmicutes
BT4 bacteria
BT5 prokaryotes
BT2 plant pathogenic bacteria
BT3 plant pathogens
BT4 pathogens

CLAVIBACTER MICHIGANENSIS
uf *corynebacterium michiganense*
BT1 clavibacter
BT2 coryneform group of bacteria
BT3 firmicutes
BT4 bacteria
BT5 prokaryotes
BT2 plant pathogenic bacteria
BT3 plant pathogens
BT4 pathogens
NT1 clavibacter michiganensis subsp. insidiosus
NT1 clavibacter michiganensis subsp. michiganensis
NT1 clavibacter michiganensis subsp. nebraskensis
NT1 clavibacter michiganensis subsp. sepedonicus

CLAVIBACTER MICHIGANENSIS SUBSP. INSIDIOSUS
uf *corynebacterium michiganense pv. insidiosum*
BT1 clavibacter michiganensis
BT2 clavibacter
BT3 coryneform group of bacteria
BT4 firmicutes
BT5 bacteria
BT6 prokaryotes
BT3 plant pathogenic bacteria
BT4 plant pathogens
BT5 pathogens

CLAVIBACTER MICHIGANENSIS SUBSP. MICHIGANENSIS
uf *corynebacterium michiganense pv. michiganense*
BT1 clavibacter michiganensis
BT2 clavibacter

CLAVIBACTER MICHIGANENSIS SUBSP. MICHIGANENSIS *cont.*
BT3 coryneform group of bacteria
BT4 firmicutes
BT5 bacteria
BT6 prokaryotes
BT3 plant pathogenic bacteria
BT4 plant pathogens
BT5 pathogens

CLAVIBACTER MICHIGANENSIS SUBSP. NEBRASKENSIS
uf *corynebacterium michiganense pv. nebraskense*
uf *corynebacterium nebraskense*
BT1 clavibacter michiganensis
BT2 clavibacter
BT3 coryneform group of bacteria
BT4 firmicutes
BT5 bacteria
BT6 prokaryotes
BT3 plant pathogenic bacteria
BT4 plant pathogens
BT5 pathogens

CLAVIBACTER MICHIGANENSIS SUBSP. SEPEDONICUS
uf *corynebacterium michiganense pv. sepedonicum*
uf *corynebacterium sepedonicum*
BT1 clavibacter michiganensis
BT2 clavibacter
BT3 coryneform group of bacteria
BT4 firmicutes
BT5 bacteria
BT6 prokaryotes
BT3 plant pathogenic bacteria
BT4 plant pathogens
BT5 pathogens

CLAVIBACTER RATHAYI
uf *corynebacterium rathayi*
BT1 clavibacter
BT2 coryneform group of bacteria
BT3 firmicutes
BT4 bacteria
BT5 prokaryotes
BT2 plant pathogenic bacteria
BT3 plant pathogens
BT4 pathogens

CLAVIBACTER TRITICI
uf *corynebacterium michiganense pv. tritici*
BT1 clavibacter
BT2 coryneform group of bacteria
BT3 firmicutes
BT4 bacteria
BT5 prokaryotes
BT2 plant pathogenic bacteria
BT3 plant pathogens
BT4 pathogens

CLAVIBACTER XYLI
BT1 clavibacter
BT2 coryneform group of bacteria
BT3 firmicutes
BT4 bacteria
BT5 prokaryotes
BT2 plant pathogenic bacteria
BT3 plant pathogens
BT4 pathogens
NT1 clavibacter xyli subsp. xyli

CLAVIBACTER XYLI SUBSP. XYLI
BT1 clavibacter xyli
BT2 clavibacter
BT3 coryneform group of bacteria
BT4 firmicutes
BT5 bacteria
BT6 prokaryotes
BT3 plant pathogenic bacteria

CLAVIBACTER XYLI SUBSP. XYLI *cont.*
BT4 plant pathogens
BT5 pathogens

CLAVICEPS
BT1 clavicipitales
NT1 claviceps fusiformis
NT1 claviceps paspali
NT1 claviceps purpurea
NT1 claviceps sorghi
rt sphacelia

CLAVICEPS FUSIFORMIS
BT1 claviceps
BT2 clavicipitales

claviceps microcephala
USE **claviceps purpurea**

CLAVICEPS PASPALI
BT1 claviceps
BT2 clavicipitales

CLAVICEPS PURPUREA
uf *claviceps microcephala*
BT1 claviceps
BT2 clavicipitales
rt ergot
rt ergot alkaloids
rt ergotism

CLAVICEPS SORGHI
HN from 1990
uf *sphacelia sorghi*
BT1 claviceps
BT2 clavicipitales

CLAVICIPITALES
NT1 apiocrea
NT2 apiocrea chrysosperma
NT1 claviceps
NT2 claviceps fusiformis
NT2 claviceps paspali
NT2 claviceps purpurea
NT2 claviceps sorghi
NT1 cordyceps
NT2 cordyceps militaris
NT1 epichloe
NT1 hypomyces
NT2 hypomyces rosellus
rt fungi

CLAVIGRALLA
uf *acanthomia*
BT1 coreidae
BT2 heteroptera
NT1 clavigralla gibbosa
NT1 clavigralla horrida
NT1 clavigralla tomentosicollis

CLAVIGRALLA GIBBOSA
BT1 clavigralla
BT2 coreidae
BT3 heteroptera

CLAVIGRALLA HORRIDA
uf *acanthomia horrida*
BT1 clavigralla
BT2 coreidae
BT3 heteroptera

CLAVIGRALLA TOMENTOSICOLLIS
uf *acanthomia tomentosicollis*
BT1 clavigralla
BT2 coreidae
BT3 heteroptera

CLAWS
uf *hoof and claw*
uf *hooves and claws*
BT1 integument
BT2 body parts

CLAY
BT1 building materials
BT2 materials
BT1 soil parent materials
NT1 kaolin
NT1 phosphatic clay
rt ceramics
rt clay fraction
rt clay minerals

CLAY *cont.*
rt clay soils
rt puddling
rt soil texture
rt tiles

CLAY FRACTION
BT1 soil separates
rt clay

clay illuviation
USE **argilluviation**

CLAY LOAM SOILS
BT1 soil types (textural)

CLAY MINERALS
uf minerals, clay
BT1 minerals
NT1 allophane
NT1 anauxite
NT1 bauxite
NT1 beidellite
NT1 bentonite
NT1 chlorite
NT1 dickite
NT1 glauconite
NT1 halloysite
NT1 hectorite
NT1 illite
NT1 imogolite
NT1 intergrade minerals
NT1 interstratified minerals
NT1 kaolinite
NT1 montmorillonite
NT1 nontronite
NT1 palygorskite
NT1 sepiolite
NT1 smectites
NT1 vermiculite
rt clay
rt soil types (mineralogical)

CLAY SOILS
uf heavy soils
BT1 soil types (textural)
rt clay
rt claypan soils
rt drainage

CLAY TRANSLOCATION
BT1 soil formation
rt argillans
rt argilluviation
rt translocation

CLAYPAN SOILS
BT1 soil types (structural)
rt clay soils
rt drainage

CLAYTONIA
BT1 portulacaceae
NT1 claytonia perfoliata

CLAYTONIA PERFOLIATA
uf montia perfoliata
BT1 claytonia
BT2 portulacaceae
BT1 leafy vegetables
BT2 vegetables

CLEAN YIELD
BT1 yields
rt cleaning
rt dirt tare

CLEANERS
BT1 machinery
NT1 air cleaners
NT1 root cleaners
NT1 seed cleaners
NT2 centrifugal seed cleaners
NT2 electrical seed cleaners
NT2 electrostatic seed cleaners
NT2 flat sieve seed cleaners
NT2 flotation seed cleaners
NT2 frictional seed cleaners
NT2 indented cylinder seed cleaners
NT2 magnetic seed cleaners
NT2 precleaners
NT2 winnowing seed cleaners
NT1 steam cleaners

CLEANERS *cont.*
rt cleaning
rt washers

cleaners, beet
USE **root cleaners**

cleaners, centrifugal seed
USE **centrifugal seed cleaners**

cleaners, electrical seed
USE **electrical seed cleaners**

cleaners, electrostatic seed
USE **electrostatic seed cleaners**

cleaners, flat sieve seed
USE **flat sieve seed cleaners**

cleaners, flotation seed
USE **flotation seed cleaners**

cleaners, frictional seed
USE **frictional seed cleaners**

cleaners, indented cylinder seed
USE **indented cylinder seed cleaners**

cleaners, magnetic seed
USE **magnetic seed cleaners**

cleaners, root
USE **root cleaners**

cleaners, seed
USE **seed cleaners**

cleaners, steam
USE **steam cleaners**

cleaners, winnowing seed
USE **winnowing seed cleaners**

CLEANING
BT1 processing
NT1 dry cleaning (agricola)
rt brushes
rt clean yield
rt cleaners
rt cleaning and sterilization
rt cleaning equipment (agricola)
rt controlled burning
rt detergents
rt disinfection
rt dredging
rt hygiene
rt laundry (agricola)
rt silviculture
rt slash
rt sterilizing
rt washing
rt weed control

CLEANING AND STERILIZATION
NT1 disinfection
NT1 disinfestation
rt cleaning
rt disinfectants
rt sterilizing

CLEANING EQUIPMENT (AGRICOLA)
BT1 equipment
rt cleaning
rt household equipment (agricola)

cleanliness
USE **hygiene**

CLEAR FELLING
AF clearcutting
BT1 felling
BT2 forestry practices
BT3 forestry
BT1 silvicultural systems
NT1 stump removal
rt clear strip felling
rt deforestation
rt grubbing
rt land clearance
rt logging
rt logging effects

CLEAR FELLING *cont.*
rt shifting cultivation
rt site preparation
rt stump pullers
rt stumps

CLEAR STRIP FELLING
BT1 felling
BT2 forestry practices
BT3 forestry
BT1 silvicultural systems
rt clear felling
rt logging
rt site preparation
rt strip cropping

CLEARANCE
uf ground clearance
rt dimensions
rt specifications

CLEARCUTTING
BF clear felling

CLEARING
BT1 processing
rt staining

clearing (land)
USE **land clearance**

CLEARING SAWS
BT1 saws
BT2 forestry machinery
BT3 machinery
BT2 tools

CLEAVAGE
BT1 embryonic development
rt cell division
rt mitosis
rt ova
rt zygotes

CLEAVAGE STRENGTH
HN from 1990; previously "cleavage"
rt wood strength

cleaving
USE **log splitters**
OR **splitting**

CLEFT PALATE
uf palatoschisis
BT1 congenital abnormalities
BT2 abnormalities
rt palate

CLEISTANTHUS
BT1 euphorbiaceae
NT1 cleistanthus collinus

CLEISTANTHUS COLLINUS
BT1 cleistanthus
BT2 euphorbiaceae
BT1 poisonous plants

CLEISTES
BT1 orchidaceae

CLEISTOCACTUS
BT1 cactaceae
NT1 cleistocactus baumannii
NT1 cleistocactus strausii

CLEISTOCACTUS BAUMANNII
BT1 cleistocactus
BT2 cactaceae
BT1 ornamental succulent plants
BT2 succulent plants

CLEISTOCACTUS STRAUSII
BT1 cleistocactus
BT2 cactaceae
BT1 ornamental succulent plants
BT2 succulent plants

CLEISTOGAMY
BT1 fertilization
BT2 sexual reproduction
BT3 reproduction
BT1 pollination
rt self pollination

CLEMATIS
BT1 ranunculaceae
NT1 clematis alpina
NT1 clematis barbellata
NT1 clematis buchaniana
NT1 clematis connata
NT1 clematis gouriana
NT1 clematis grata
NT1 clematis grossa
NT1 clematis hexapetala
NT1 clematis integrifolia
NT1 clematis jackmanii
NT1 clematis languinosa
NT1 clematis mandshurica
NT1 clematis montana
NT1 clematis montevidensis
NT1 clematis orientalis
NT1 clematis paniculata
NT1 clematis tangutica
NT1 clematis viorna
NT1 clematis vitalba
NT1 clematis viticella

CLEMATIS ALPINA
uf clematis sibirica
BT1 clematis
BT2 ranunculaceae
BT1 ornamental woody plants

CLEMATIS BARBELLATA
BT1 clematis
BT2 ranunculaceae

CLEMATIS BUCHANIANA
BT1 clematis
BT2 ranunculaceae

CLEMATIS CONNATA
BT1 clematis
BT2 ranunculaceae

CLEMATIS GOURIANA
BT1 antifungal plants
BT1 clematis
BT2 ranunculaceae

CLEMATIS GRATA
BT1 clematis
BT2 ranunculaceae
BT1 ornamental woody plants

CLEMATIS GROSSA
BT1 clematis
BT2 ranunculaceae

CLEMATIS HEXAPETALA
BT1 clematis
BT2 ranunculaceae

CLEMATIS INTEGRIFOLIA
BT1 clematis
BT2 ranunculaceae
BT1 ornamental herbaceous plants

CLEMATIS JACKMANII
BT1 clematis
BT2 ranunculaceae
BT1 ornamental woody plants

CLEMATIS LANGUINOSA
BT1 clematis
BT2 ranunculaceae

CLEMATIS MANDSHURICA
BT1 clematis
BT2 ranunculaceae

CLEMATIS MONTANA
BT1 clematis
BT2 ranunculaceae
BT1 ornamental woody plants

CLEMATIS MONTEVIDENSIS
BT1 clematis
BT2 ranunculaceae
BT1 poisonous plants

CLEMATIS ORIENTALIS
BT1 clematis
BT2 ranunculaceae
BT1 ornamental woody plants

CLEMATIS PANICULATA
BT1 clematis

CLEMATIS PANICULATA *cont.*
BT2 ranunculaceae
BT1 ornamental woody plants

clematis sibirica
USE **clematis alpina**

CLEMATIS TANGUTICA
BT1 clematis
BT2 ranunculaceae
BT1 ornamental woody plants

CLEMATIS VIORNA
BT1 clematis
BT2 ranunculaceae

CLEMATIS VITALBA
BT1 clematis
BT2 ranunculaceae
BT1 ornamental woody plants

CLEMATIS VITICELLA
BT1 clematis
BT2 ranunculaceae
BT1 ornamental woody plants

CLEMENTINES
BT1 citrus fruits
BT2 subtropical tree fruits
BT3 subtropical fruits
BT4 fruit crops
BT3 tree fruits
rt citrus clementina

CLENBUTEROL
BT1 bronchodilators
BT2 respiratory system agents
BT3 drugs
BT1 sympathomimetics
BT2 neurotropic drugs
BT3 drugs

CLEOMACEAE
NT1 atalantia
NT2 atalantia missionis
NT2 atalantia monophylla
NT2 atalantia roxburghiana

CLEOME
BT1 capparidaceae
NT1 cleome arabica
NT1 cleome gynandra
NT1 cleome hassleriana
NT1 cleome rutidosperma
NT1 cleome spinosa
NT1 cleome viscosa

CLEOME ARABICA
BT1 cleome
BT2 capparidaceae
BT1 medicinal plants

CLEOME GYNANDRA
BT1 cleome
BT2 capparidaceae

CLEOME HASSLERIANA
BT1 cleome
BT2 capparidaceae
BT1 ornamental herbaceous plants

CLEOME RUTIDOSPERMA
BT1 cleome
BT2 capparidaceae

CLEOME SPINOSA
BT1 cleome
BT2 capparidaceae
BT1 ornamental herbaceous plants

CLEOME VISCOSA
BT1 cleome
BT2 capparidaceae
BT1 medicinal plants

CLEONIA
BT1 labiatae
NT1 cleonia lusitanica

CLEONIA LUSITANICA
BT1 cleonia
BT2 labiatae

CLEPSIS
BT1 tortricidae
BT2 lepidoptera
NT1 clepsis spectrana

CLEPSIS SPECTRANA
BT1 clepsis
BT2 tortricidae
BT3 lepidoptera

cleptoparasitism
USE **kleptoparasitism**

CLERIDAE
BT1 coleoptera
NT1 enoclerus
NT1 necrobia
NT2 necrobia rufipes
NT1 thanasimus
NT2 thanasimus dubius
NT2 thanasimus femoralis
NT2 thanasimus formicarius
NT2 thanasimus undatulus
NT1 trichodes

clerodendron
USE **clerodendrum**

CLERODENDRUM
uf *clerodendron*
BT1 verbenaceae
NT1 clerodendrum colebrookianum
NT1 clerodendrum fragrans
NT1 clerodendrum inerme
NT1 clerodendrum infortunatum
NT1 clerodendrum macrosiphon
NT1 clerodendrum paniculatum
NT1 clerodendrum phlomoides
NT1 clerodendrum serratum
NT1 clerodendrum splendens
NT1 clerodendrum squamatum
NT1 clerodendrum thomsoniae
NT1 clerodendrum trichotomum
rt insecticidal plants

CLERODENDRUM COLEBROOKIANUM
BT1 clerodendrum
BT2 verbenaceae

CLERODENDRUM FRAGRANS
BT1 clerodendrum
BT2 verbenaceae
BT1 ornamental woody plants

CLERODENDRUM INERME
BT1 clerodendrum
BT2 verbenaceae
BT1 medicinal plants

CLERODENDRUM INFORTUNATUM
uf *clerodendrum viscosum*
BT1 clerodendrum
BT2 verbenaceae
BT1 ornamental woody plants

CLERODENDRUM MACROSIPHON
BT1 clerodendrum
BT2 verbenaceae
BT1 ornamental woody plants

CLERODENDRUM PANICULATUM
BT1 clerodendrum
BT2 verbenaceae

CLERODENDRUM PHLOMOIDES
BT1 clerodendrum
BT2 verbenaceae

CLERODENDRUM SERRATUM
BT1 clerodendrum
BT2 verbenaceae

CLERODENDRUM SPLENDENS
BT1 clerodendrum
BT2 verbenaceae
BT1 ornamental woody plants

CLERODENDRUM SQUAMATUM
BT1 clerodendrum
BT2 verbenaceae

CLERODENDRUM THOMSONIAE
BT1 clerodendrum
BT2 verbenaceae
BT1 ornamental woody plants

CLERODENDRUM TRICHOTOMUM
BT1 clerodendrum
BT2 verbenaceae

clerodendrum viscosum
USE **clerodendrum infortunatum**

CLETHRA
BT1 clethraceae
NT1 clethra barbinervis

CLETHRA BARBINERVIS
BT1 clethra
BT2 clethraceae

CLETHRACEAE
NT1 clethra
NT2 clethra barbinervis

CLETHRIONOMYS
BT1 microtinae
BT2 muridae
BT3 rodents
BT4 mammals
NT1 clethrionomys gapperi
NT1 clethrionomys glareolus
NT1 clethrionomys rufocanus
NT1 clethrionomys rutilus
rt voles

CLETHRIONOMYS GAPPERI
BT1 clethrionomys
BT2 microtinae
BT3 muridae
BT4 rodents
BT5 mammals

CLETHRIONOMYS GLAREOLUS
BT1 clethrionomys
BT2 microtinae
BT3 muridae
BT4 rodents
BT5 mammals

CLETHRIONOMYS RUFOCANUS
BT1 clethrionomys
BT2 microtinae
BT3 muridae
BT4 rodents
BT5 mammals

CLETHRIONOMYS RUTILUS
BT1 clethrionomys
BT2 microtinae
BT3 muridae
BT4 rodents
BT5 mammals

CLETUS
BT1 coreidae
BT2 heteroptera
NT1 cletus punctiger

CLETUS PUNCTIGER
BT1 cletus
BT2 coreidae
BT3 heteroptera

CLEVELAND BAY
BT1 horse breeds
BT2 breeds

CLEYERA
BT1 theaceae
NT1 cleyera japonica

CLEYERA JAPONICA
uf *cleyera ochnacea*
uf *eurya japonica*
BT1 cleyera
BT2 theaceae
BT1 ornamental woody plants

cleyera ochnacea
USE **cleyera japonica**

CLIANTHUS
BT1 leguminosae
NT1 clianthus formosus

CLIANTHUS FORMOSUS
BT1 clianthus
BT2 leguminosae
BT1 ornamental woody plants

CLIDEMIA
BT1 melastomataceae
NT1 clidemia hirta

CLIDEMIA HIRTA
BT1 clidemia
BT2 melastomataceae

CLIDINIUM
BT1 parasympatholytics
BT2 neurotropic drugs
BT3 drugs
BT1 quaternary ammonium compounds
BT2 ammonium compounds
BT2 organic nitrogen compounds

CLIFFORTIA
BT1 rosaceae
NT1 cliffortia linearifolia
NT1 cliffortia paucistaminea

CLIFFORTIA LINEARIFOLIA
BT1 cliffortia
BT2 rosaceae

CLIFFORTIA PAUCISTAMINEA
BT1 cliffortia
BT2 rosaceae

CLIMATE
NT1 arid climate
NT1 bioclimate
NT1 mediterranean climate
NT1 mesoclimate
NT1 microclimate
NT1 oceanic climate
NT1 quaternary palaeoclimates
NT1 semiarid climate
NT1 temperate climate
NT1 tropical climate
rt acclimatization
rt adaptation
rt agricultural meteorology
rt bioclimatic indexes
rt climatic change
rt climatic factors
rt climatic zones
rt climatology
rt climosequences
rt environmental factors
rt forest influences
rt meteorological factors
rt phenology
rt site factors
rt soil types (climatic)
rt weather
rt weather data
rt weather forecasting
rt weather patterns
rt weather reports

climatic areas
USE **climatic zones**

CLIMATIC CHANGE
BT1 change
rt climate

CLIMATIC FACTORS
NT1 drought
NT1 freeze thaw cycles
NT1 meteorological factors
NT2 atmospheric pressure
NT2 dew
NT2 frost
NT2 hurricanes
NT2 insolation
NT2 precipitation
NT3 artificial precipitation
NT3 hail
NT3 rain
NT3 snow
NT3 throughfall
NT2 storms
NT3 dust storms
NT2 turbulence
NT2 whirlwinds

CLIMATIC FACTORS *cont.*
NT2 wind
NT2 wind speed
rt adaptation
rt agricultural disasters
rt agricultural meteorology
rt atmosphere
rt climate
rt environmental factors
rt frozen conditions
rt temperature
rt weathering
rt weathering sequences

climatic soil types
USE **soil types (climatic)**

CLIMATIC ZONES
uf *climatic areas*
NT1 arid zones
NT2 arid regions
NT3 deserts
NT4 gobi desert
NT4 kalahari desert
NT4 mojave desert
NT4 sahara desert
NT3 sahel
NT1 cold zones
NT2 polar regions
NT2 tundra
NT3 arctic tundra
NT1 humid zones
NT2 humid tropics
NT1 semiarid zones
NT1 subtropics
NT1 temperate zones
NT1 tropical zones
NT1 tropics
NT2 humid tropics
NT2 tropical africa
NT2 tropical america
NT2 tropical asia
NT2 tropical oceania
rt climate
rt weather patterns

CLIMATOLOGY
uf *atmospheric sciences*
NT1 agroclimatology
NT1 dendroclimatology
NT1 microclimatology
NT1 palaeoclimatology
rt bioclimatic indexes
rt biology
rt climate
rt meteorology
rt physical geography
rt precipitation
rt weather data
rt weather patterns

CLIMAX COMMUNITIES
BT1 plant communities
BT2 communities

CLIMBERS
(plants)
uf *climbing plants*
uf *lianes*
NT1 heterophragma quadriloculare
rt support trees
rt tendrils

CLIMBING
BT1 active recreation
BT2 recreation
rt climbing devices
rt ladders

CLIMBING DEVICES
BT1 equipment
rt climbing

climbing plants
USE **climbers**

CLIMOSEQUENCES
BT1 soil sequences
rt climate

CLINDAMYCIN
BT1 antibacterial agents
BT2 antiinfective agents

CLINDAMYCIN *cont.*
BT3 drugs
BT1 antiprotozoal agents
BT2 antiparasitic agents
BT3 drugs
BT1 macrolide antibiotics
BT2 antibiotics
BT2 lactones
BT3 heterocyclic oxygen compounds
BT3 ketones

CLINES
rt biotypes
rt change
rt ecotypes
rt gradients

clinical assessment
USE **diagnosis**

CLINICAL EXAMINATION
BT1 diagnostic techniques
BT2 techniques
NT1 auscultation
NT1 palpation
NT2 rectal palpation
rt prognosis

CLINICAL EXPERIENCE (AGRICOLA)
BT1 learning experiences (agricola)
BT2 learning

CLINICAL INVESTIGATIONS (AGRICOLA)
BT1 methodology

CLINICAL NUTRITION (AGRICOLA)
BT1 nutrition

CLINICAL TRIALS
BT1 trials
BT2 research

clinics
USE **health centres**

clinics, animal
USE **animal clinics**

CLINOPODIUM
BT1 labiatae
NT1 clinopodium vulgare

CLINOPODIUM VULGARE
uf *satureja vulgaris*
BT1 clinopodium
BT2 labiatae

CLINOPTILOLITE
BT1 nonclay minerals
BT2 minerals
BT1 potassium fertilizers
BT2 fertilizers

CLINOSEQUENCES
BT1 soil sequences

CLINOSTOMIDAE
BT1 digenea
BT2 trematoda
NT1 clinostomum
NT2 clinostomum complanatum
NT1 euclinostomum
NT2 euclinostomum heterostomum

CLINOSTOMUM
BT1 clinostomidae
BT2 digenea
BT3 trematoda
NT1 clinostomum complanatum

CLINOSTOMUM COMPLANATUM
BT1 clinostomum
BT2 clinostomidae
BT3 digenea
BT4 trematoda

CLIODINATE
BT1 pyridine herbicides
BT2 herbicides
BT3 pesticides

CLIODINATE *cont.*
BT2 pyridines
BT3 heterocyclic nitrogen compounds
BT4 organic nitrogen compounds

CLIOQUINOL
BT1 amoebicides
BT2 antiprotozoal agents
BT3 antiparasitic agents
BT4 drugs

CLIOXANIDE
BT1 anthelmintics
BT2 antiparasitic agents
BT3 drugs

CLIPPERS
BT1 tools
rt clipping

CLIPPING
BT1 cutting
rt clippers

CLITOCYBE
BT1 agaricales
NT1 clitocybe geotropa
NT1 clitocybe illudens
NT1 clitocybe nebularis
rt armillaria

CLITOCYBE GEOTROPA
BT1 clitocybe
BT2 agaricales
BT1 medicinal plants

CLITOCYBE ILLUDENS
BT1 clitocybe
BT2 agaricales
BT1 medicinal plants

CLITOCYBE NEBULARIS
BT1 clitocybe
BT2 agaricales
BT1 medicinal plants

clitocybe tabescens
USE **armillaria tabescens**

CLITORIA
BT1 leguminosae
NT1 clitoria biflora
NT1 clitoria ternatea
rt clitoria yellow vein tymovirus

CLITORIA BIFLORA
BT1 clitoria
BT2 leguminosae
BT1 pasture legumes
BT2 legumes
BT2 pasture plants

CLITORIA TERNATEA
BT1 clitoria
BT2 leguminosae
BT1 ornamental herbaceous plants

CLITORIA YELLOW VEIN TYMOVIRUS
HN from 1990
BT1 tymovirus group
BT2 plant viruses
BT3 plant pathogens
BT4 pathogens
rt clitoria

CLITORIDECTOMY
BT1 surgical operations
rt clitoris

CLITORIS
HN from 1989
BT1 vulva
BT2 female genitalia
BT3 genitalia
BT4 urogenital system
BT5 body parts
rt clitoridectomy

CLIVIA
BT1 amaryllidaceae

CLIVIA *cont.*
NT1 clivia miniata
NT1 clivia nobilis

CLIVIA MINIATA
BT1 antiviral plants
BT1 clivia
BT2 amaryllidaceae
BT1 ornamental bulbs

CLIVIA NOBILIS
BT1 clivia
BT2 amaryllidaceae
BT1 ornamental bulbs

CLIVINA
BT1 carabidae
BT2 coleoptera
NT1 clivina fossor
NT1 clivina impressifrons

CLIVINA FOSSOR
BT1 clivina
BT2 carabidae
BT3 coleoptera

CLIVINA IMPRESSIFRONS
BT1 clivina
BT2 carabidae
BT3 coleoptera

CLOACA
BT1 anus
BT2 digestive system
BT3 body parts
rt bursa fabricii

CLOCHES
rt plastic tunnels
rt protected cultivation
rt tunnels

CLOD CRUSHERS
BT1 crushers
BT2 farm machinery
BT3 machinery
rt clods
rt crumblers
rt cultivators

CLODS
BT1 soil structural units
BT2 soil structure
BT3 soil physical properties
BT4 soil properties
BT5 properties
rt clod crushers
rt tillage

CLOETHOCARB
BT1 carbamate insecticides
BT2 carbamate pesticides
BT2 insecticides
BT3 pesticides
BT1 carbamate nematicides
BT2 carbamate pesticides
BT2 nematicides
BT3 pesticides

CLOFENTEZINE
BT1 mite growth regulators
BT2 acaricides
BT3 pesticides
BT2 growth regulators

CLOFIBRATE
BT1 antilipaemics
BT2 haematologic agents
BT3 drugs
rt cholesterol

CLOFOP
BT1 aryloxyphenoxypropionic herbicides
BT2 phenoxypropionic herbicides
BT3 phenoxy herbicides
BT4 herbicides
BT5 pesticides

CLOMAZONE
HN from 1990
BT1 unclassified herbicides
BT2 herbicides
BT3 pesticides

CLOMEPROP
HN from 1990
BT1 anilide herbicides
BT2 amide herbicides
BT3 herbicides
BT4 pesticides

CLOMIFENE
HN from 1989
uf *clomiphene*
BT1 fertility agents
BT2 drugs

clomiphene
USE **clomifene**

CLONAL VARIATION
BT1 variation
rt clones
rt somaclonal variation
rt vegetative propagation

CLONES
NT1 nucellar clones
rt asexual reproduction
rt clonal variation
rt cloning
rt degeneration
rt vegetative propagation

clones, nucellar
USE **nucellar clones**

CLONING
rt clones
rt genetics

CLONORCHIS
BT1 opisthorchiidae
BT2 digenea
BT3 trematoda
NT1 clonorchis sinensis

CLONORCHIS SINENSIS
BT1 clonorchis
BT2 opisthorchiidae
BT3 digenea
BT4 trematoda
rt liver flukes

CLOPIDOL
uf *meticlorpindol*
BT1 coccidiostats
BT2 antiprotozoal agents
BT3 antiparasitic agents
BT4 drugs
BT1 pyridines
BT2 heterocyclic nitrogen compounds
BT3 organic nitrogen compounds

CLOPROP
BT1 phenoxypropionic herbicides
BT2 phenoxy herbicides
BT3 herbicides
BT4 pesticides

CLOPROSTENOL
BT1 synthetic prostaglandins
BT2 synthetic hormones

CLOPROXYDIM
BT1 cyclohexene oxime herbicides
BT2 herbicides
BT3 pesticides

CLOPYRALID
uf *3,6-dichloropicolinic acid*
BT1 picolinic acid herbicides
BT2 aromatic acid herbicides
BT3 herbicides
BT4 pesticides

CLORSULON
BT1 anthelmintics
BT2 antiparasitic agents
BT3 drugs

CLOSANTEL
BT1 ectoparasiticides
BT2 antiparasitic agents
BT3 drugs
BT1 unclassified acaricides

CLOSANTEL *cont.*
BT2 acaricides
BT3 pesticides

CLOSED SYSTEMS
HN from 1990
BT1 systems

CLOSTERA
uf *pygaera*
BT1 notodontidae
BT2 lepidoptera
NT1 clostera anastomosis

CLOSTERA ANASTOMOSIS
uf *pygaera anastomosis*
BT1 clostera
BT2 notodontidae
BT3 lepidoptera

CLOSTEROVIRUS GROUP
HN from 1990
BT1 plant viruses
BT2 plant pathogens
BT3 pathogens
NT1 beet yellow stunt closterovirus
NT1 beet yellows closterovirus
NT1 carnation necrotic fleck closterovirus
NT1 citrus tristeza closterovirus
NT1 lilac chlorotic leafspot closterovirus
NT1 wheat yellow leaf closterovirus

CLOSTRIDIUM
BT1 bacillaceae
BT2 firmicutes
BT3 bacteria
BT4 prokaryotes
NT1 clostridium acetobutylicum
NT1 clostridium bifermentans
NT1 clostridium botulinum
NT1 clostridium butyricum
NT1 clostridium chauvoei
NT1 clostridium difficile
NT1 clostridium haemolyticum
NT1 clostridium novyi
NT1 clostridium pasteurianum
NT1 clostridium perfringens
NT1 clostridium septicum
NT1 clostridium sordellii
NT1 clostridium sporogenes
NT1 clostridium tetani
NT1 clostridium thermocellum
NT1 clostridium tyrobutyricum

CLOSTRIDIUM ACETOBUTYLICUM
BT1 clostridium
BT2 bacillaceae
BT3 firmicutes
BT4 bacteria
BT5 prokaryotes

CLOSTRIDIUM BIFERMENTANS
BT1 clostridium
BT2 bacillaceae
BT3 firmicutes
BT4 bacteria
BT5 prokaryotes

CLOSTRIDIUM BOTULINUM
BT1 clostridium
BT2 bacillaceae
BT3 firmicutes
BT4 bacteria
BT5 prokaryotes
rt botulism

CLOSTRIDIUM BUTYRICUM
BT1 clostridium
BT2 bacillaceae
BT3 firmicutes
BT4 bacteria
BT5 prokaryotes

CLOSTRIDIUM CHAUVOEI
BT1 clostridium
BT2 bacillaceae
BT3 firmicutes
BT4 bacteria
BT5 prokaryotes

CLOSTRIDIUM DIFFICILE
BT1 clostridium
BT2 bacillaceae
BT3 firmicutes
BT4 bacteria
BT5 prokaryotes

CLOSTRIDIUM HAEMOLYTICUM
BT1 clostridium
BT2 bacillaceae
BT3 firmicutes
BT4 bacteria
BT5 prokaryotes

CLOSTRIDIUM NOVYI
BT1 clostridium
BT2 bacillaceae
BT3 firmicutes
BT4 bacteria
BT5 prokaryotes

CLOSTRIDIUM PASTEURIANUM
BT1 clostridium
BT2 bacillaceae
BT3 firmicutes
BT4 bacteria
BT5 prokaryotes

CLOSTRIDIUM PERFRINGENS
uf *welchia perfringens*
BT1 clostridium
BT2 bacillaceae
BT3 firmicutes
BT4 bacteria
BT5 prokaryotes

CLOSTRIDIUM SEPTICUM
BT1 clostridium
BT2 bacillaceae
BT3 firmicutes
BT4 bacteria
BT5 prokaryotes

CLOSTRIDIUM SORDELLII
BT1 clostridium
BT2 bacillaceae
BT3 firmicutes
BT4 bacteria
BT5 prokaryotes

CLOSTRIDIUM SPOROGENES
BT1 clostridium
BT2 bacillaceae
BT3 firmicutes
BT4 bacteria
BT5 prokaryotes

CLOSTRIDIUM TETANI
BT1 clostridium
BT2 bacillaceae
BT3 firmicutes
BT4 bacteria
BT5 prokaryotes
rt tetanus

CLOSTRIDIUM THERMOCELLUM
BT1 clostridium
BT2 bacillaceae
BT3 firmicutes
BT4 bacteria
BT5 prokaryotes

CLOSTRIDIUM TYROBUTYRICUM
BT1 clostridium
BT2 bacillaceae
BT3 firmicutes
BT4 bacteria
BT5 prokaryotes

CLOSURES (AGRICOLA)
NT1 corks (agricola)
NT1 lids (agricola)
NT1 pull tabs (agricola)
NT1 stoppers (agricola)
rt packaging

closures, farm
USE **farm closures**

cloth
USE **textiles**

CLOTHING
uf *apparel*
NT1 functional clothing (agricola)

CLOTHING *cont.*
NT1 protective clothing
NT2 boots
NT2 hearing protectors
NT2 masks
NT2 roguing gloves
NT1 recycled clothing (agricola)
NT1 working clothing
rt clothing construction (agricola)
rt clothing design (agricola)
rt clothing instruction (agricola)
rt costume (agricola)
rt hang tag (agricola)
rt woolens (agricola)

CLOTHING CONSTRUCTION (AGRICOLA)
NT1 pressing (clothing construction) (agricola)
NT1 tailoring (agricola)
rt clothing
rt clothing design (agricola)

CLOTHING DESIGN (AGRICOLA)
rt clothing
rt clothing construction (agricola)
rt design
rt pattern alterations (agricola)

CLOTHING INSTRUCTION (AGRICOLA)
BT1 instruction (agricola)
rt clothing

CLOTHING LABELS (AGRICOLA)
BT1 labeling
rt care labels (agricola)

clothing, working and protective
USE **protective clothing**
OR **working clothing**

CLOTRIMAZOLE
BT1 antifungal agents
BT2 antiinfective agents
BT3 drugs
BT1 antiprotozoal agents
BT2 antiparasitic agents
BT3 drugs
BT1 imidazoles
BT2 azoles
BT3 heterocyclic nitrogen compounds
BT4 organic nitrogen compounds

CLOTTING
BT1 coagulation
rt blood
rt embolism
rt haemophilia
rt thrombin
rt thrombolysis
rt thrombosis

clotting system
USE **blood coagulation**

CLOUD FORESTS
HN from 1990
uf *mist forests*
BT1 forests
BT2 vegetation types

CLOUD SEEDING
BT1 weather control
BT2 control
rt artificial precipitation
rt clouds
rt hail guns

cloudberry
USE **rubus chamaemorus**

CLOUDS
rt cloud seeding
rt mists

clover, alsike
USE **trifolium hybridum**

clover, crimson
USE **trifolium incarnatum**

clover, egyptian
USE **trifolium alexandrinum**

CLOVER HAY
BT1 hay
BT2 feeds
rt trifolium

CLOVER MEAL
BT1 meal
rt trifolium

clover, red
USE **trifolium pratense**

CLOVER SILAGE
BT1 silage
BT2 feeds
BT2 fermentation products
BT3 products
rt trifolium

clover, subterranean
USE **trifolium subterraneum**

clover, subterranean, redleaf virus
USE **subterranean clover red leaf virus**

clover, sweet
USE **melilotus alba**
OR **melilotus indica**
OR **melilotus officinalis**

clover, white
USE **trifolium repens**

CLOVER YELLOW MOSAIC POTEXVIRUS
HN from 1990
BT1 potexvirus group
BT2 plant viruses
BT3 plant pathogens
BT4 pathogens
rt clovers
rt trifolium

CLOVER YELLOW VEIN POTYVIRUS
HN from 1990; previously "clover yellow vein virus"
uf *clover yellow vein virus*
BT1 potyvirus group
BT2 plant viruses
BT3 plant pathogens
BT4 pathogens
rt clovers
rt trifolium

clover yellow vein virus
USE **clover yellow vein potyvirus**

CLOVERS
rt clover yellow mosaic potexvirus
rt clover yellow vein potyvirus
rt trifolium

CLOVES
rt sumatra disease
rt syzygium aromaticum

CLOXACILLIN
BT1 penicillins
BT2 antibacterial agents
BT3 antiinfective agents
BT4 drugs
BT2 heterocyclic nitrogen compounds
BT3 organic nitrogen compounds

CLUBIONIDAE
BT1 araneae
BT2 arachnida
BT3 arthropods
NT1 cheiracanthium
NT2 cheiracanthium mildei

CLUBS
uf *societies*

CLUBS *cont.*
BT1 interest groups
BT2 groups
BT2 organizations
BT1 recreational facilities
NT1 4-h clubs (agricola)
NT1 health clubs
rt entertainment
rt farmers' associations
rt night clubs
rt private organizations

CLUN FOREST
BT1 sheep breeds
BT2 breeds

CLUPEA
BT1 clupeidae
BT2 clupeiformes
BT3 osteichthyes
BT4 fishes
NT1 clupea ilisha
rt sardina

clupea harengus
USE **herrings**

CLUPEA ILISHA
BT1 clupea
BT2 clupeidae
BT3 clupeiformes
BT4 osteichthyes
BT5 fishes

clupea pilchardus
USE **sardines**

clupea sprattus
USE **sprats**

CLUPEIDAE
BT1 clupeiformes
BT2 osteichthyes
BT3 fishes
NT1 alosa
NT2 alosa pseudoharengus
NT2 alosa sapidissima
NT1 brevoortia
NT1 clupea
NT2 clupea ilisha
NT1 dorosoma
NT1 etrumeus
NT2 etrumeus teres
NT1 hilsa
NT1 sardina
NT1 sardinella
NT1 sardinops
NT1 sprattus
rt herrings
rt menhaden
rt sardines
rt sprats

CLUPEIFORMES
BT1 osteichthyes
BT2 fishes
NT1 clupeidae
NT2 alosa
NT3 alosa pseudoharengus
NT3 alosa sapidissima
NT2 brevoortia
NT2 clupea
NT3 clupea ilisha
NT2 dorosoma
NT2 etrumeus
NT3 etrumeus teres
NT2 hilsa
NT2 sardina
NT2 sardinella
NT2 sardinops
NT2 sprattus
NT1 engraulidae
NT2 anchoa
NT2 coilia
NT2 engraulis

clusiaceae
USE **guttiferae**

CLUSTER ANALYSIS
BT1 statistical analysis
BT2 data analysis
BT2 statistics

CLUSTER BEANS
rt cyamopsis tetragonoloba

cluster, seed
USE **seed clusters**

CLUSTERING
BT1 animal behaviour
BT2 behaviour
BT1 heat regulation
rt honeybee colonies
rt winter cluster

CLUSTERS
NT1 seed clusters
rt automatic cluster removal
rt milking machines
rt teatcups

CLUTCHES
(for clutches of eggs, use "egg clutches")
BT1 control components
BT2 components
NT1 friction clutches
NT1 steering clutches
rt drives
rt engines
rt overload protection
rt transmissions
rt vehicles

clutches, friction
USE **friction clutches**

CLYDESDALE
BT1 horse breeds
BT2 breeds

CLYMENIA
BT1 rutaceae
NT1 clymenia polyandra

CLYMENIA POLYANDRA
BT1 clymenia
BT2 rutaceae

CLYPEOPORTHE
HN from 1990
BT1 diaporthales
NT1 clypeoporthe iliau
rt gnomonia

CLYPEOPORTHE ILIAU
HN from 1990
uf *gnomonia iliau*
BT1 clypeoporthe
BT2 diaporthales

clysia
USE **eupoecilia**

clysia ambiguella
USE **eupoecilia ambiguella**

CLYTIOMYA
BT1 tachinidae
BT2 diptera
NT1 clytiomya helluo

CLYTIOMYA HELLUO
BT1 clytiomya
BT2 tachinidae
BT3 diptera

CMA
uf *calcium bis(hydrogen methylarsonate)*
BT1 arsenical herbicides
BT2 arsenicals
BT2 herbicides
BT3 pesticides

CMEA
(council for mutual economic assistance)
uf *comecon*
BT1 economic unions
BT1 international organizations
BT2 organizations
rt bulgaria
rt centrally planned economies
rt cuba
rt czechoslovakia
rt economic regions

CMEA *cont.*
rt german democratic republic
rt hungary
rt mongolia
rt poland
rt romania
rt ussr
rt vietnam

CMI DESCRIPTIONS
BT1 descriptions
rt plant pathogens

CMI DISTRIBUTION MAPS
BT1 maps
rt plant diseases

CMI/AAB DESCRIPTIONS
BT1 descriptions
rt plant viruses

cmpp
USE **mecoprop**

cmu
USE **monuron**

CNAPHALOCROCIS
BT1 pyralidae
BT2 lepidoptera
NT1 cnaphalocrocis medinalis

CNAPHALOCROCIS MEDINALIS
BT1 cnaphalocrocis
BT2 pyralidae
BT3 lepidoptera

cnemidocoptes
USE **knemidokoptes**

CNEORACEAE
NT1 cneorum
NT2 cneorum tricoccon
NT1 neochamaelea
NT2 neochamaelea pulverulenta

CNEORUM
BT1 cneoraceae
NT1 cneorum tricoccon

cneorum pulverulentum
USE **neochamaelea pulverulenta**

CNEORUM TRICOCCON
BT1 antibacterial plants
BT1 cneorum
BT2 cneoraceae
BT1 medicinal plants
BT1 ornamental woody plants

CNEPHASIA
BT1 tortricidae
BT2 lepidoptera
NT1 cnephasia asseclana
NT1 cnephasia pasiuana
NT1 cnephasia pumicana

CNEPHASIA ASSECLANA
uf *cnephasia interjectana*
BT1 cnephasia
BT2 tortricidae
BT3 lepidoptera

cnephasia interjectana
USE **cnephasia asseclana**

CNEPHASIA PASIUANA
BT1 cnephasia
BT2 tortricidae
BT3 lepidoptera

CNEPHASIA PUMICANA
BT1 cnephasia
BT2 tortricidae
BT3 lepidoptera

CNEPHIA
BT1 simuliidae
BT2 diptera
NT1 cnephia dacotensis
NT1 cnephia ornithophilia
rt simulium
rt stegopterna

CNEPHIA DACOTENSIS
BT1 cnephia
BT2 simuliidae
BT3 diptera

cnephia mutata
USE **stegopterna mutata**

CNEPHIA ORNITHOPHILIA
HN from 1990
BT1 cnephia
BT2 simuliidae
BT3 diptera

cnephia ovtshinnikovi
USE **simulium ovtshinnikovi**

CNESTIS
BT1 connaraceae
NT1 cnestis ferruginea

CNESTIS FERRUGINEA
BT1 cnestis
BT2 connaraceae
BT1 medicinal plants

CNICUS
BT1 compositae
NT1 cnicus benedictus

CNICUS BENEDICTUS
uf *carduus benedictus*
BT1 cnicus
BT2 compositae
BT1 oilseed plants
BT2 fatty oil plants
BT3 oil plants

CNIDIUM
BT1 umbelliferae
NT1 cnidium officinale
rt ligusticum

CNIDIUM OFFICINALE
uf *ligusticum officinale*
BT1 cnidium
BT2 umbelliferae
BT1 medicinal plants

CNIDOSCOLUS
BT1 euphorbiaceae
NT1 cnidoscolus chayamansa
NT1 cnidoscolus elasticus

CNIDOSCOLUS CHAYAMANSA
BT1 cnidoscolus
BT2 euphorbiaceae

CNIDOSCOLUS ELASTICUS
BT1 cnidoscolus
BT2 euphorbiaceae
BT1 rubber plants

cns
USE **central nervous system**

co-ownership
USE **coownership**

co-responsibility levies
USE **levies**

co (symbol)
USE **cobalt**

COACHING
rt teaching methods

COAGULANTS
rt blood coagulation factors
rt coagulation

COAGULASE TEST
BT1 tests
rt staphylococcus

COAGULATION
NT1 blood coagulation
NT1 clotting
rt anticoagulants
rt coagulants
rt heat stability
rt syneresis

coagulation, blood
USE **blood coagulation**

COAGULUM
NT1 curd
rt cheesemaking

COAL
BT1 fuels
BT1 growing media
BT1 inoculant carriers
BT2 carriers
BT1 manures
BT2 organic amendments
BT3 soil amendments
BT4 amendments
NT1 brown coal
rt anthracite waste
rt bitumen
rt coke
rt leonardite

coal, brown
USE **brown coal**

COAL MINE SPOIL
HN from 1989; previously colliery spoil
uf *colliery spoil*
BT1 mine spoil
BT2 spoil
BT3 industrial wastes
BT4 wastes

COAL MINED LAND
HN from 1989
BT1 mined land
BT2 land types

coalfish
USE **pollachius virens**

COANCESTRY
BT1 ancestry

COARSE GRAINS
BT1 feed grains
BT2 feeds
BT2 grain

COARSE TEXTURED SOILS
BT1 soil types (textural)

COASTAL AREAS
BT1 areas
NT1 heritage coasts
rt coasts
rt physiographic features
rt tides

COASTAL DUNE SOILS
BT1 soil types (physiographic)

COASTAL PLAIN SOILS
BT1 soil types (physiographic)

COASTAL PLAINS
BT1 plains
BT2 physiographic features
rt coasts

COASTAL PLANT COMMUNITIES
BT1 plant communities
BT2 communities
rt coasts

COASTAL RESORTS
BT1 resorts
rt coasts

COASTAL SOILS
BT1 soil types (physiographic)
rt coasts

COASTAL TERRACE SOILS
uf *raised beach soils*
BT1 soil types (physiographic)
rt beach soils

COASTS
BT1 physiographic features
rt beaches
rt coastal areas
rt coastal plains
rt coastal plant communities
rt coastal resorts
rt coastal soils

COAT
uf *pelage*
NT1 birthcoat
NT1 undercoat
NT2 pashmina
rt curl
rt epidermis
rt fur
rt pelts
rt shedding
rt wool

COAT PROTEINS
BT1 viral proteins
BT2 microbial proteins
BT3 proteins
BT4 peptides

COATED GLASS
uf *glass, coated*
BT1 glass
BT2 building materials
BT3 materials
rt coatings
rt protective coatings

COATINGS
NT1 enamel
NT1 galvanizing
NT1 glazes (agricola)
NT1 lacquers (agricola)
NT1 protective coatings
NT2 epoxides
NT2 paints
NT2 polishes
NT3 floor polishes
NT3 leaf polishes
NT2 varnishes
NT2 whitewash
NT1 wax coatings
rt batters (agricola)
rt coated glass
rt covers
rt film
rt galvanized iron
rt sputter coating

cobalamin
USE **vitamin b12**

COBALT
uf *co (symbol)*
BT1 trace elements
BT2 elements
BT1 transition elements
BT2 metallic elements
BT3 elements
BT3 metals
rt cobalt fertilizers

COBALT FERTILIZERS
BT1 trace element fertilizers
BT2 fertilizers
rt cobalt

COBAMAMIDE
BT1 vitamin b12
BT2 lipotropic factors
BT3 drugs
BT2 vitamin b complex
BT3 water-soluble vitamins
BT4 vitamins

COBB-DOUGLAS FUNCTIONS
BT1 production functions
BT2 econometrics
BT2 production economics
BT3 economics

COBITIDIDAE
BT1 cypriniformes
BT2 osteichthyes
BT3 fishes
NT1 misgurnus
NT2 misgurnus anguillicaudatus

cobnuts
USE **hazelnuts**

COBWEB MODELS
uf *models, cobweb*
BT1 mathematical models
BT2 models
BT2 optimization methods

COBWEB MODELS *cont.*
BT3 optimization
rt price stabilization

coca
USE **erythroxylum coca**

COCAINE
BT1 tropane alkaloids
BT2 alkaloids
rt erythroxylum coca
rt neurotropic drugs

cocaine esterase
USE **carboxylesterase**
OR **tropinesterase**

COCCIDAE
BT1 coccoidea
BT2 sternorrhyncha
BT3 homoptera
NT1 anapulvinaria
NT2 anapulvinaria pistaciae
NT1 ceroplastes
NT2 ceroplastes destructor
NT2 ceroplastes floridensis
NT2 ceroplastes japonicus
NT2 ceroplastes rubens
NT2 ceroplastes rusci
NT1 chloropulvinaria
NT2 chloropulvinaria aurantii
NT2 chloropulvinaria floccifera
NT2 chloropulvinaria psidii
NT1 coccus
NT2 coccus hesperidum
NT2 coccus perlatus
NT2 coccus viridis
NT1 eulecanium
NT2 eulecanium tiliae
NT1 gascardia
NT1 kilifia
NT2 kilifia acuminata
NT1 palaeolecanium
NT2 palaeolecanium bituberculatum
NT1 parasaissetia
NT2 parasaissetia nigra
NT1 parthenolecanium
NT2 parthenolecanium corni
NT1 protopulvinaria
NT2 protopulvinaria pyriformis
NT1 pulvinaria
NT2 pulvinaria mesembryanthemi
NT2 pulvinaria regalis
NT1 pulvinariella
NT1 rhodococcus (homoptera)
NT2 rhodococcus turanicus
NT1 saissetia
NT2 saissetia coffeae
NT2 saissetia oleae
NT1 sphaerolecanium
NT2 sphaerolecanium prunastri

COCCIDIA
BT1 parasites
rt apicomplexa
rt coccidiosis

COCCIDIOIDES
BT1 deuteromycotina
NT1 coccidioides immitis

COCCIDIOIDES IMMITIS
BT1 coccidioides
BT2 deuteromycotina
rt coccidioidin
rt coccidioidomycosis
rt spherulin

COCCIDIOIDIN
BT1 fungal antigens
BT2 antigens
BT3 immunological factors
rt coccidioides immitis
rt spherulin

COCCIDIOIDOMYCOSIS
uf *coccidiomycosis*
BT1 mycoses
BT2 infectious diseases
BT3 diseases
rt coccidioides immitis

coccidiomycosis
USE **coccidioidomycosis**

COCCIDIOSIS
BT1 protozoal infections
BT2 parasitoses
BT3 diseases
rt coccidia
rt coccidiostats
rt eimeria

COCCIDIOSTATS
uf *anticoccidials*
BT1 antiprotozoal agents
BT2 antiparasitic agents
BT3 drugs
NT1 aminitrozole
NT1 amprolium
NT1 arprinocid
NT1 buquinolate
NT1 clopidol
NT1 decoquinate
NT1 diaveridine
NT1 dinitolmide
NT1 ethopabate
NT1 halofuginone
NT1 lasalocid
NT1 monensin
NT1 narasin
NT1 nequinate
NT1 nicarbazin
NT1 nitrofural
NT1 ormetoprim
NT1 parvaquone
NT1 robenidine
NT1 salinomycin
NT1 sulfadimethoxine
NT1 sulfadimidine
NT1 sulfanitran
NT1 sulfaquinoxaline
NT1 toltrazuril
rt coccidiosis

COCCIDOPHILUS
uf *cryptoweisea*
BT1 coccinellidae
BT2 coleoptera

COCCIDOXENOIDES
BT1 encyrtidae
BT2 hymenoptera
NT1 coccidoxenoides peregrinus
rt pauridia

COCCIDOXENOIDES PEREGRINUS
uf *pauridia peregrina*
BT1 coccidoxenoides
BT2 encyrtidae
BT3 hymenoptera

COCCINELLA
BT1 coccinellidae
BT2 coleoptera
NT1 coccinella quinquepunctata
NT1 coccinella septempunctata
NT1 coccinella transversalis
NT1 coccinella transversoguttata
NT1 coccinella undecimpunctata
rt adalia
rt coccinula
rt harmonia
rt oenopia

coccinella axyridis
USE **harmonia axyridis**

coccinella bipunctata
USE **adalia bipunctata**

coccinella conglobata
USE **oenopia conglobata**

coccinella decempunctata
USE **adalia decempunctata**

coccinella quatuordecimpustulata
USE **coccinula quatuordecimpustulata**

COCCINELLA QUINQUEPUNCTATA
BT1 coccinella
BT2 coccinellidae
BT3 coleoptera

coccinella repanda
USE **coccinella transversalis**

COCCINELLA SEPTEMPUNCTATA
BT1 coccinella
BT2 coccinellidae
BT3 coleoptera

COCCINELLA TRANSVERSALIS
uf *coccinella repanda*
BT1 coccinella
BT2 coccinellidae
BT3 coleoptera

COCCINELLA TRANSVERSOGUTTATA
BT1 coccinella
BT2 coccinellidae
BT3 coleoptera

COCCINELLA UNDECIMPUNCTATA
BT1 coccinella
BT2 coccinellidae
BT3 coleoptera

COCCINELLIDAE
uf *ladybirds*
BT1 coleoptera
NT1 adalia
NT2 adalia bipunctata
NT2 adalia decempunctata
NT1 brumoides
NT2 brumoides suturalis
NT1 cheilomenes
NT2 cheilomenes sexmaculata
NT1 chilocorus
NT2 chilocorus bipustulatus
NT2 chilocorus kuwanae
NT2 chilocorus nigrita
NT1 coccidophilus
NT1 coccinella
NT2 coccinella quinquepunctata
NT2 coccinella septempunctata
NT2 coccinella transversalis
NT2 coccinella transversoguttata
NT2 coccinella undecimpunctata
NT1 coccinula
NT2 coccinula quatuordecimpustulata
NT1 coleomegilla
NT2 coleomegilla maculata
NT1 cryptolaemus
NT2 cryptolaemus montrouzieri
NT1 cycloneda
NT2 cycloneda sanguinea
NT1 epilachna
NT2 epilachna dodecastigma
NT2 epilachna varivestis
NT2 epilachna vigintioctomaculata
NT2 epilachna vigintioctopunctata
NT1 eriopis
NT2 eriopis connexa
NT1 exochomus
NT2 exochomus flavipes
NT2 exochomus quadripustulatus
NT1 harmonia
NT2 harmonia axyridis
NT2 harmonia octomaculata
NT1 hippodamia
NT2 hippodamia convergens
NT2 hippodamia oculata
NT2 hippodamia parenthesis
NT2 hippodamia tredecimpunctata
NT2 hippodamia variegata
NT1 hyperaspis
NT1 lioadalia
NT2 lioadalia flavomaculata
NT1 menochilus
NT1 nephus
NT2 nephus reunioni
NT1 oenopia
NT2 oenopia conglobata
NT1 propylea
NT2 propylea japonica

COCCINELLIDAE *cont.*
NT2 propylea quattuordecimpunctata
NT1 psyllobora
NT2 psyllobora vigintiduopunctata
NT1 rhyzobius
NT2 rhyzobius lophanthae
NT1 rodolia
NT2 rodolia cardinalis
NT1 scymnus
NT2 scymnus coccivora
NT2 scymnus hoffmanni
NT2 scymnus syriacus
NT1 serangium
NT2 serangium parcesetosum
NT1 stethorus
NT2 stethorus bifidus
NT2 stethorus nigripes
NT2 stethorus pauperculus
NT2 stethorus punctillum
NT2 stethorus punctum
NT1 subcoccinella
NT2 subcoccinella vigintiquattuorpunctata
NT1 telsimia
NT1 tytthaspis
NT2 tytthaspis sedecimpunctata

COCCINIA
BT1 cucurbitaceae
NT1 coccinia grandis

COCCINIA GRANDIS
uf *coccinia indica*
BT1 coccinia
BT2 cucurbitaceae
BT1 cucurbit fruits
BT2 fruit crops
BT1 medicinal plants

coccinia indica
USE **coccinia grandis**

COCCINULA
BT1 coccinellidae
BT2 coleoptera
NT1 coccinula quatuordecimpustulata
rt coccinella

COCCINULA QUATUORDECIMPUSTULATA
uf *coccinella quatuordecimpustulata*
BT1 coccinula
BT2 coccinellidae
BT3 coleoptera

COCCOBIUS
BT1 aphelinidae
BT2 hymenoptera
NT1 coccobius fulvus

COCCOBIUS FULVUS
BT1 coccobius
BT2 aphelinidae
BT3 hymenoptera

COCCODIELLA
HN from 1990
BT1 dothideales
NT1 coccodiella banksiae
rt botryosphaeria
rt coccostroma

COCCODIELLA BANKSIAE
HN from 1990
uf *botryosphaeria banksiae*
uf *coccostroma banksiae*
BT1 coccodiella
BT2 dothideales

COCCOIDEA
BT1 sternorrhyncha
BT2 homoptera
NT1 aclerdidae
NT2 aclerda
NT3 aclerda campinensis
NT1 asterolecaniidae
NT2 asterolecanium
NT3 asterolecanium pustulans
NT1 coccidae

COCCOIDEA *cont.*
NT2 anapulvinaria
NT3 anapulvinaria pistaciae
NT2 ceroplastes
NT3 ceroplastes destructor
NT3 ceroplastes floridensis
NT3 ceroplastes japonicus
NT3 ceroplastes rubens
NT3 ceroplastes rusci
NT2 chloropulvinaria
NT3 chloropulvinaria aurantii
NT3 chloropulvinaria floccifera
NT3 chloropulvinaria psidii
NT2 coccus
NT3 coccus hesperidum
NT3 coccus perlatus
NT3 coccus viridis
NT2 eulecanium
NT3 eulecanium tiliae
NT2 gascardia
NT2 kilifia
NT3 kilifia acuminata
NT2 palaeolecanium
NT3 palaeolecanium bituberculatum
NT2 parasaissetia
NT3 parasaissetia nigra
NT2 parthenolecanium
NT3 parthenolecanium corni
NT2 protopulvinaria
NT3 protopulvinaria pyriformis
NT2 pulvinaria
NT3 pulvinaria mesembryanthemi
NT3 pulvinaria regalis
NT2 pulvinariella
NT2 rhodococcus (homoptera)
NT3 rhodococcus turanicus
NT2 saissetia
NT3 saissetia coffeae
NT3 saissetia oleae
NT2 sphaerolecanium
NT3 sphaerolecanium prunastri
NT1 dactylopiidae
NT2 dactylopius
NT3 dactylopius ceylonicus
NT3 dactylopius opuntiae
NT1 diaspididae
NT2 abgrallaspis
NT3 abgrallaspis cyanophylli
NT2 aonidiella
NT3 aonidiella aurantii
NT3 aonidiella citrina
NT3 aonidiella orientalis
NT2 aonidomytilus
NT3 aonidomytilus albus
NT2 aspidiotus
NT3 aspidiotus destructor
NT3 aspidiotus nerii
NT2 aulacaspis
NT3 aulacaspis madiunensis
NT3 aulacaspis rosae
NT3 aulacaspis tegalensis
NT3 aulacaspis tubercularis
NT2 chionaspis
NT3 chionaspis pinifoliae
NT3 chionaspis salicis
NT2 chrysomphalus
NT3 chrysomphalus aonidum
NT3 chrysomphalus dictyospermi
NT2 diaspidiotus
NT2 diaspis
NT3 diaspis bromeliae
NT2 fiorinia
NT3 fiorinia theae
NT2 hemiberlesia
NT3 hemiberlesia lataniae
NT3 hemiberlesia rapax
NT2 insulaspis
NT2 lepidosaphes
NT3 lepidosaphes beckii
NT3 lepidosaphes gloverii
NT3 lepidosaphes ulmi
NT2 leucaspis
NT2 melanaspis
NT3 melanaspis glomerata
NT2 parlatoria
NT3 parlatoria blanchardii
NT3 parlatoria oleae
NT3 parlatoria pergandii

COCCOIDEA *cont.*
NT3 parlatoria ziziphi
NT2 pinnaspis
NT3 pinnaspis strachani
NT2 pseudaonidia
NT2 pseudaulacaspis
NT3 pseudaulacaspis pentagona
NT2 quadraspidiotus
NT3 quadraspidiotus ostreaeformis
NT3 quadraspidiotus perniciosus
NT2 selenaspidus
NT3 selenaspidus articulatus
NT2 unaspis
NT3 unaspis citri
NT3 unaspis euonymi
NT3 unaspis yanonensis
NT1 eriococcidae
NT2 cryptococcus (homoptera)
NT3 cryptococcus fagisuga
NT1 kermesidae
NT2 kermes
NT1 kerriidae
NT2 kerria (homoptera)
NT3 kerria lacca
NT1 margarodidae
NT2 icerya
NT3 icerya aegyptiaca
NT3 icerya purchasi
NT2 margarodes
NT2 matsucoccus
NT3 matsucoccus feytaudi
NT3 matsucoccus massonianae
NT3 matsucoccus matsumurae
NT3 matsucoccus pini
NT3 matsucoccus resinosae
NT2 porphyrophora
NT3 porphyrophora hamelii
NT1 pseudococcidae
NT2 antonina
NT3 antonina graminis
NT2 brevennia
NT3 brevennia rehi
NT2 dysmicoccus
NT3 dysmicoccus brevipes
NT2 eurycoccus
NT2 ferrisia
NT3 ferrisia virgata
NT2 hypogeococcus
NT2 maconellicoccus
NT3 maconellicoccus hirsutus
NT2 nipaecoccus
NT3 nipaecoccus viridis
NT2 phenacoccus
NT3 phenacoccus gossypii
NT3 phenacoccus herreni
NT3 phenacoccus manihoti
NT3 phenacoccus solani
NT2 planococcoides
NT3 planococcoides njalensis
NT2 planococcus
NT3 planococcus citri
NT3 planococcus ficus
NT2 pseudococcus
NT3 pseudococcus adonidum
NT3 pseudococcus affinis
NT3 pseudococcus calceolariae
NT3 pseudococcus comstocki
NT3 pseudococcus longispinus
NT3 pseudococcus maritimus
NT2 rastrococcus
NT3 rastrococcus iceryoides
NT3 rastrococcus invadens
NT2 rhizoecus
NT3 rhizoecus cacticans
NT2 saccharicoccus
NT3 saccharicoccus sacchari
NT2 trionymus

COCCOLOBA
BT1 polygonaceae
NT1 coccoloba diversifolia
NT1 coccoloba uvifera

COCCOLOBA DIVERSIFOLIA
BT1 coccoloba
BT2 polygonaceae

COCCOLOBA UVIFERA
BT1 coccoloba
BT2 polygonaceae
BT1 ornamental woody plants

coccomyces
USE **blumeriella**

coccomyces hiemalis
USE **blumeriella jaapii**

COCCOPHAGUS
BT1 aphelinidae
BT2 hymenoptera
NT1 coccophagus cowperi
NT1 coccophagus lycimnia

COCCOPHAGUS COWPERI
BT1 coccophagus
BT2 aphelinidae
BT3 hymenoptera

COCCOPHAGUS LYCIMNIA
BT1 coccophagus
BT2 aphelinidae
BT3 hymenoptera

COCCOSTROMA
HN from 1990
BT1 dothideales
rt coccodiella

coccostroma banksiae
USE **coccodiella banksiae**

COCCULUS
BT1 menispermaceae
NT1 cocculus laurifolius
NT1 cocculus macrocarpus
NT1 cocculus pendulus

COCCULUS LAURIFOLIUS
BT1 cocculus
BT2 menispermaceae
BT1 medicinal plants
BT1 poisonous plants

COCCULUS MACROCARPUS
BT1 cocculus
BT2 menispermaceae

COCCULUS PENDULUS
BT1 cocculus
BT2 menispermaceae
BT1 medicinal plants

COCCUS
uf *lecanium*
BT1 coccidae
BT2 coccoidea
BT3 sternorrhyncha
BT4 homoptera
NT1 coccus hesperidum
NT1 coccus perlatus
NT1 coccus viridis
rt saissetia

COCCUS HESPERIDUM
BT1 coccus
BT2 coccidae
BT3 coccoidea
BT4 sternorrhyncha
BT5 homoptera

coccus oleae
USE **saissetia oleae**

COCCUS PERLATUS
uf *lecanium deltae*
BT1 coccus
BT2 coccidae
BT3 coccoidea
BT4 sternorrhyncha
BT5 homoptera

COCCUS VIRIDIS
BT1 coccus
BT2 coccidae
BT3 coccoidea
BT4 sternorrhyncha
BT5 homoptera

coccygomimus
USE **pimpla**

coccygomimus disparis
USE **pimpla disparis**

COCHLEARIA
BT1 cruciferae
NT1 cochlearia anglica
NT1 cochlearia officinalis

COCHLEARIA ANGLICA
BT1 cochlearia
BT2 cruciferae

cochlearia armoracia
USE **armoracia rusticana**

COCHLEARIA OFFICINALIS
BT1 cochlearia
BT2 cruciferae

cochlearia rusticana
USE **armoracia rusticana**

COCHLICELLA
BT1 helicidae
BT2 gastropoda
BT3 mollusca
NT1 cochlicella acuta
NT1 cochlicella ventricosa

COCHLICELLA ACUTA
BT1 cochlicella
BT2 helicidae
BT3 gastropoda
BT4 mollusca

COCHLICELLA VENTRICOSA
BT1 cochlicella
BT2 helicidae
BT3 gastropoda
BT4 mollusca

COCHLIOBOLUS
BT1 dothideales
NT1 cochliobolus australiensis
NT1 cochliobolus carbonum
NT1 cochliobolus cynodontis
NT1 cochliobolus ellisii
NT1 cochliobolus eragrostidis
NT1 cochliobolus geniculatus
NT1 cochliobolus hawaiiensis
NT1 cochliobolus heterostrophus
NT1 cochliobolus intermedius
NT1 cochliobolus lunatus
NT1 cochliobolus miyabeanus
NT1 cochliobolus nodulosus
NT1 cochliobolus pallescens
NT1 cochliobolus ravenelii
NT1 cochliobolus sativus
NT1 cochliobolus setariae
NT1 cochliobolus spicifer
NT1 cochliobolus verruculosus
NT1 cochliobolus victoriae
rt bipolaris
rt curvularia
rt drechslera
rt helminthosporium
rt pseudocochliobolus

COCHLIOBOLUS AUSTRALIENSIS
HN from 1990
uf *bipolaris australiensis*
uf *drechslera australiensis*
uf *pseudocochliobolus australiensis*
BT1 cochliobolus
BT2 dothideales

COCHLIOBOLUS CARBONUM
uf *drechslera zeicola*
uf *helminthosporium carbonum*
BT1 cochliobolus
BT2 dothideales

COCHLIOBOLUS CYNODONTIS
uf *bipolaris cynodontis*
uf *helminthosporium cynodontis*
BT1 cochliobolus
BT2 dothideales

COCHLIOBOLUS ELLISII
HN from 1990
uf *bipolaris ellisii*
uf *drechslera ellisii*

COCHLIOBOLUS ELLISII *cont.*
BT1 cochliobolus
BT2 dothideales

COCHLIOBOLUS ERAGROSTIDIS
HN from 1990
uf *curvularia eragrostidis*
uf *curvularia maculans*
BT1 cochliobolus
BT2 dothideales

COCHLIOBOLUS GENICULATUS
uf *curvularia geniculata*
BT1 cochliobolus
BT2 dothideales

COCHLIOBOLUS HAWAIIENSIS
uf *drechslera hawaiiensis*
uf *helminthosporium hawaiiense*
BT1 cochliobolus
BT2 dothideales

COCHLIOBOLUS HETEROSTROPHUS
uf *bipolaris maydis*
uf *drechslera maydis*
uf *helminthosporium maydis*
BT1 cochliobolus
BT2 dothideales

COCHLIOBOLUS INTERMEDIUS
uf *curvularia intermedia*
BT1 cochliobolus
BT2 dothideales

COCHLIOBOLUS LUNATUS
uf *curvularia lunata*
BT1 cochliobolus
BT2 dothideales

COCHLIOBOLUS MIYABEANUS
uf *drechslera oryzae*
uf *helminthosporium oryzae*
BT1 cochliobolus
BT2 dothideales

COCHLIOBOLUS NODULOSUS
uf *helminthosporium leucostylum*
uf *helminthosporium nodulosum*
BT1 cochliobolus
BT2 dothideales

COCHLIOBOLUS PALLESCENS
HN from 1990
uf *curvularia pallescens*
BT1 cochliobolus
BT2 dothideales

COCHLIOBOLUS RAVENELII
HN from 1990
uf *drechslera ravenelii*
BT1 cochliobolus
BT2 dothideales

COCHLIOBOLUS SATIVUS
uf *bipolaris sorokiniana*
uf *drechslera sorokiniana*
uf *helminthosporium sativum*
uf *helminthosporium sorokinianum*
BT1 cochliobolus
BT2 dothideales

COCHLIOBOLUS SETARIAE
uf *drechslera setariae*
uf *helminthosporium setariae*
BT1 cochliobolus
BT2 dothideales

COCHLIOBOLUS SPICIFER
uf *bipolaris spicifera*
uf *bipolaris tetramera*
uf *drechslera spicifer*
uf *drechslera tetramera*
uf *helminthosporium spiciferum*
uf *helminthosporium tetramera*
BT1 cochliobolus
BT2 dothideales

cochliobolus stenospilus
USE **bipolaris stenospila**

COCHLIOBOLUS VERRUCULOSUS
HN from 1990
uf *curvularia verruculosa*
BT1 cochliobolus
BT2 dothideales

COCHLIOBOLUS VICTORIAE
uf *bipolaris victoriae*
uf *helminthosporium victoriae*
BT1 cochliobolus
BT2 dothideales
rt victorin

COCHLIOMYIA
uf *callitroga*
BT1 calliphoridae
BT2 diptera
NT1 cochliomyia hominivorax
NT1 cochliomyia macellaria

COCHLIOMYIA HOMINIVORAX
uf *callitroga hominivorax*
BT1 cochliomyia
BT2 calliphoridae
BT3 diptera

COCHLIOMYIA MACELLARIA
BT1 cochliomyia
BT2 calliphoridae
BT3 diptera

COCHLONEMA
BT1 entomophthorales

COCHYLIDAE
HN from 1989
BT1 lepidoptera
NT1 cochylis

COCHYLIS
HN from 1989
BT1 cochylidae
BT2 lepidoptera

cockerels
USE **cocks**

cockroaches
USE **blattaria**

COCKS
uf *cockerels*
BT1 male animals
BT2 animals
rt fowls

cocksfoot
USE **dactylis glomerata**

COCKSFOOT MILD MOSAIC VIRUS
BT1 miscellaneous plant viruses
BT2 plant viruses
BT3 plant pathogens
BT4 pathogens
rt dactylis glomerata

COCKSFOOT MOTTLE VIRUS
BT1 miscellaneous plant viruses
BT2 plant viruses
BT3 plant pathogens
BT4 pathogens
rt dactylis glomerata

COCKSFOOT STREAK POTYVIRUS
HN from 1990; previously "cocksfoot streak virus"
uf *cocksfoot streak virus*
BT1 potyvirus group
BT2 plant viruses
BT3 plant pathogens
BT4 pathogens
rt dactylis glomerata

cocksfoot streak virus
USE **cocksfoot streak potyvirus**

COCOA
uf *cacao*
BT1 medicinal plants
BT1 nematicidal plants
BT2 pesticidal plants
BT1 oilseed plants

COCOA *cont.*
BT2 fatty oil plants
BT3 oil plants
BT1 stimulant plants
rt cacao swollen shoot virus
rt cacao yellow mosaic tymovirus
rt cocoa beans
rt cocoa beverages
rt cocoa byproducts
rt cocoa husks
rt cocoa industry
rt cocoa pod meal
rt cocoa products
rt theobroma cacao

COCOA BEANS
rt cocoa

COCOA BEVERAGES
BT1 beverages
rt cocoa

COCOA BYPRODUCTS
BT1 agricultural byproducts
BT2 byproducts
rt cocoa

COCOA HUSKS
BT1 husks
BT2 plant residues
BT3 residues
rt cocoa

COCOA INDUSTRY
uf *chocolate industry*
BT1 food industry
BT2 industry
rt cocoa
rt cocoa products
rt confectionery industry

COCOA POD MEAL
BT1 meal
rt cocoa

COCOA PRODUCTS
BT1 plant products
BT2 products
rt chocolate
rt cocoa
rt cocoa industry

cocoa swollen shoot virus
USE **cacao swollen shoot virus**

COCONUT CADANG-CADANG VIROID
BT1 viroids
BT2 plant pathogens
BT3 pathogens
rt coconuts

coconut fibre
USE **coir**

COCONUT LETHAL YELLOWING
BT1 plant diseases
rt coconuts

COCONUT MILK
BT1 coconut products
BT2 nut products
BT3 plant products
BT4 products
rt coconuts

COCONUT OIL
BT1 coconut products
BT2 nut products
BT3 plant products
BT4 products
BT1 seed oils
BT2 plant oils
BT3 oils
BT3 plant products
BT4 products
rt coconut oilmeal

COCONUT OILMEAL
BT1 oilmeals
BT2 feeds
BT2 meal
rt coconut oil
rt coconuts

coconut palms
USE **cocos nucifera**

COCONUT PRODUCTS
BT1 nut products
BT2 plant products
BT3 products
NT1 coconut milk
NT1 coconut oil
NT1 coir
NT1 copra
NT1 desiccated coconut
rt coconuts

COCONUT PROTEIN
BT1 plant protein
BT2 protein
rt coconuts

COCONUTS
BT1 antifungal plants
BT1 fibre plants
BT1 insecticidal plants
BT2 pesticidal plants
BT1 oilseed plants
BT2 fatty oil plants
BT3 oil plants
BT1 tropical tree nuts
BT2 nut crops
rt coconut cadang-cadang viroid
rt coconut lethal yellowing
rt coconut milk
rt coconut oilmeal
rt coconut products
rt coconut protein
rt cocos nucifera
rt coir
rt copra
rt desiccated coconut
rt root (wilt)

COCOONS
HN from 1990
rt pupae
rt silk

COCOS
BT1 palmae
NT1 cocos nucifera

cocos island (pacific)
USE **costa rica**

COCOS ISLANDS
uf *cocos islands (indian ocean)*
uf *keeling islands*
BT1 australian oceania
BT2 oceania
rt australia

cocos islands (indian ocean)
USE **cocos islands**

COCOS NUCIFERA
uf *coconut palms*
BT1 cocos
BT2 palmae
BT1 forest trees
rt coconuts

cocoyam
USE **colocasia esculenta**

COD
uf *gadus morhua*
BT1 marine fishes
BT2 aquatic animals
BT3 animals
BT3 aquatic organisms
rt cod liver oil
rt gadidae

COD LIVER OIL
BT1 fish liver oils
BT2 fish oils
BT3 animal oils
BT4 fatty oils
BT5 oils
BT3 fish products
BT4 animal products
BT5 products
rt cod

cod, poor
USE **trisopterus minutus**

CODARIOCALYX
BT1 leguminosae
NT1 codariocalyx gyroides
NT1 codariocalyx motorius

CODARIOCALYX GYROIDES
uf *desmodium gyroides*
BT1 codariocalyx
BT2 leguminosae
BT1 pasture legumes
BT2 legumes
BT2 pasture plants

CODARIOCALYX MOTORIUS
uf *desmodium gyrans*
BT1 codariocalyx
BT2 leguminosae
BT1 pasture legumes
BT2 legumes
BT2 pasture plants

CODE OF PRACTICE
rt practice
rt regulations

CODEINE
BT1 analgesics
BT2 neurotropic drugs
BT3 drugs
BT1 opium alkaloids
BT2 alkaloids
rt papaver somniferum

CODEX ALIMENTARIUS (AGRICOLA)
BT1 standards
rt foods

CODIAEUM
BT1 euphorbiaceae
NT1 codiaeum variegatum

CODIAEUM VARIEGATUM
uf *croton variegatus*
BT1 codiaeum
BT2 euphorbiaceae
rt ornamental foliage plants

CODINAEA
BT1 deuteromycotina

CODONANTHE
BT1 gesneriaceae
NT1 codonanthe gracilis

CODONANTHE GRACILIS
BT1 codonanthe
BT2 gesneriaceae
BT1 ornamental herbaceous plants

CODONOPSIS
BT1 campanulaceae
NT1 codonopsis ovata

CODONOPSIS OVATA
BT1 codonopsis
BT2 campanulaceae
BT1 ornamental herbaceous plants

COEFFICIENT OF LINEAR EXTENSIBILITY
BT1 soil mechanics
BT2 soil properties
BT3 properties

COEFFICIENT OF RELATIONSHIP
BT1 correlation

COELAENOMENODERA
BT1 chrysomelidae
BT2 coleoptera
NT1 coelaenomenodera elaeidis

COELAENOMENODERA ELAEIDIS
BT1 coelaenomenodera
BT2 chrysomelidae
BT3 coleoptera

COELENTERATA
NT1 chlorohydra
NT2 chlorohydra viridissima

COELENTERATA *cont.*
NT1 corals
NT1 hydra
rt invertebrates

coeliac disease
USE **coeliac syndrome**

COELIAC SYNDROME
AF celiac syndrome
uf *coeliac disease*
BT1 intestinal diseases
BT2 gastrointestinal diseases
BT3 digestive system diseases
BT4 organic diseases
BT5 diseases
rt gluten free bread
rt gluten free diet
rt sprue
rt steatorrhoea

COELIOXYS
BT1 apidae
BT2 hymenoptera

COELOGYNE
BT1 orchidaceae
NT1 coelogyne cristata
NT1 coelogyne judithiae
NT1 coelogyne nitida

COELOGYNE CRISTATA
BT1 coelogyne
BT2 orchidaceae
BT1 ornamental orchids

COELOGYNE JUDITHIAE
BT1 coelogyne
BT2 orchidaceae
BT1 ornamental orchids

COELOGYNE NITIDA
uf *coelogyne ochracea*
BT1 coelogyne
BT2 orchidaceae
BT1 ornamental orchids

coelogyne ochracea
USE **coelogyne nitida**

COELOIDES
BT1 braconidae
BT2 hymenoptera
NT1 coeloides vancouverensis

coeloides brunneri
USE **coeloides vancouverensis**

COELOIDES VANCOUVERENSIS
uf *coeloides brunneri*
BT1 coeloides
BT2 braconidae
BT3 hymenoptera

COELOMOMYCES
BT1 blastocladiales
BT1 entomogenous fungi
BT2 entomopathogens
BT3 pathogens
BT2 fungi
NT1 coelomomyces indicus
NT1 coelomomyces psorophorae
NT1 coelomomyces stegomyiae

COELOMOMYCES INDICUS
BT1 coelomomyces
BT2 blastocladiales
BT2 entomogenous fungi
BT3 entomopathogens
BT4 pathogens
BT3 fungi

COELOMOMYCES PSOROPHORAE
BT1 coelomomyces
BT2 blastocladiales
BT2 entomogenous fungi
BT3 entomopathogens
BT4 pathogens
BT3 fungi

COELOMOMYCES STEGOMYIAE
BT1 coelomomyces
BT2 blastocladiales
BT2 entomogenous fungi
BT3 entomopathogens

COELOMOMYCES STEGOMYIAE *cont.*
BT4 pathogens
BT3 fungi

COELOPA
HN from 1989
BT1 coelopidae
BT2 diptera

COELOPIDAE
HN from 1989
BT1 diptera
NT1 coelopa

COELORACHIS
BT1 gramineae

COELOSPORIDIUM
BT1 ascetospora
BT2 protozoa
NT1 coelosporidium chydoricola

COELOSPORIDIUM CHYDORICOLA
BT1 coelosporidium
BT2 ascetospora
BT3 protozoa

COELOTROPHA
BT1 apicomplexa
BT2 protozoa

COENDOU
BT1 erethizontidae
BT2 rodents
BT3 mammals

COENURI
BT1 metacestodes
BT2 developmental stages

coenurus
USE **taenia**

coenurus cerebralis
USE **taenia multiceps**

COENZYME A
BT1 nucleotide coenzymes
BT2 coenzymes
BT2 nucleotides
BT3 glycosides
BT4 carbohydrates
rt acetyl coenzyme a
rt pantothenic acid

coenzyme q
USE **ubiquinones**

COENZYMES
NT1 biopterin
NT1 biotin
NT1 glutathione
NT1 methylcobalamin
NT1 nucleotide coenzymes
NT2 coenzyme a
NT2 nad
NT2 nadh
NT2 nadp
NT2 nadph
NT2 pyridine nucleotides
NT1 pyridoxal phosphate
NT1 thioctic acid
NT1 ubiquinones
NT2 ubichromenols
rt enzyme activators
rt enzymes

COFANA
BT1 cicadellidae
BT2 cicadelloidea
BT3 auchenorrhyncha
BT4 homoptera
NT1 cofana spectra
rt tettigoniella

COFANA SPECTRA
uf *tettigella spectra*
uf *tettigoniella spectra*
BT1 cofana
BT2 cicadellidae
BT3 cicadelloidea
BT4 auchenorrhyncha
BT5 homoptera

COFFEA
BT1 rubiaceae
NT1 coffea arabica
NT1 coffea bengalensis
NT1 coffea canephora
NT1 coffea congensis
NT1 coffea eugenioides
NT1 coffea kapakata
NT1 coffea liberica
NT1 coffea racemosa
NT1 coffea stenophylla
NT1 coffea zanquebariae
rt caffeine

COFFEA ARABICA
BT1 coffea
BT2 rubiaceae
rt coffee

COFFEA BENGALENSIS
BT1 coffea
BT2 rubiaceae

COFFEA CANEPHORA
uf *coffea robusta*
BT1 coffea
BT2 rubiaceae
rt coffee

COFFEA CONGENSIS
BT1 coffea
BT2 rubiaceae
rt coffee

COFFEA EUGENIOIDES
BT1 coffea
BT2 rubiaceae

coffea excelsa
USE **coffea liberica**

COFFEA KAPAKATA
BT1 coffea
BT2 rubiaceae

COFFEA LIBERICA
uf *coffea excelsa*
BT1 coffea
BT2 rubiaceae
rt coffee

COFFEA RACEMOSA
BT1 coffea
BT2 rubiaceae
rt coffee

coffea robusta
USE **coffea canephora**

COFFEA STENOPHYLLA
BT1 coffea
BT2 rubiaceae
rt coffee

COFFEA ZANQUEBARIAE
BT1 coffea
BT2 rubiaceae

COFFEE
uf *robusta coffee*
BT1 antifungal plants
BT1 beverages
BT1 stimulant plants
rt coffea arabica
rt coffea canephora
rt coffea congensis
rt coffea liberica
rt coffea racemosa
rt coffea stenophylla
rt coffee cream
rt coffee industry
rt coffee meal
rt coffee milk
rt coffee pulp
rt coffee whitener
rt coffeemakers (agricola)
rt instant coffee

COFFEE CREAM
BT1 cream
BT2 milk products
BT3 products
rt coffee

COFFEE INDUSTRY
BT1 beverage industry
BT2 food industry
BT3 industry
rt coffee

coffee, instant
USE **instant coffee**

COFFEE MEAL
BT1 meal
rt coffee

COFFEE MILK
BT1 flavoured milk
BT2 milk products
BT3 products
rt coffee

COFFEE PULP
BT1 pulps
rt coffee

COFFEE WHITENER
BT1 milk products
BT2 products
rt coffee
rt milk substitutes

COFFEEMAKERS (AGRICOLA)
BT1 appliances (agricola)
rt coffee
rt household equipment (agricola)

COGNITIVE DEVELOPMENT (AGRICOLA)
uf *mental development*
rt development
rt mental ability

COHESION
BT1 soil mechanics
BT2 soil properties
BT3 properties
rt adhesion

coho salmon
USE **oncorhynchus kisutch**

COILIA
BT1 engraulidae
BT2 clupeiformes
BT3 osteichthyes
BT4 fishes
rt anchovies

COIMBATORE
HN from 1990
BT1 sheep breeds
BT2 breeds

COIR
uf *coconut fibre*
BT1 coconut products
BT2 nut products
BT3 plant products
BT4 products
BT1 plant fibres
BT2 fibres
rt coconuts

coitus
USE **copulation**

COIX
BT1 gramineae
NT1 coix lacryma-jobi

coix lachryma-jobi
USE **coix lacryma-jobi**

COIX LACRYMA-JOBI
uf *adlay*
uf *coix lachryma-jobi*
uf *job's tears*
BT1 cereals
BT2 grain crops
BT1 coix
BT2 gramineae
BT1 fodder plants
BT1 medicinal plants
BT1 ornamental herbaceous plants

COKE
BT1 fuels
rt coal

COLA
BT1 sterculiaceae
NT1 cola acuminata
NT1 cola nitida

COLA ACUMINATA
uf kola
BT1 cola
BT2 sterculiaceae
BT1 stimulant plants
BT1 tropical tree nuts
BT2 nut crops
rt caffeine
rt kola nuts

cola beverages
USE **soft drinks**

COLA NITIDA
BT1 cola
BT2 sterculiaceae
BT1 stimulant plants

COLASPIS
uf maecolaspis
BT1 chrysomelidae
BT2 coleoptera
NT1 colaspis ornata

COLASPIS ORNATA
uf maecolaspis ornata
BT1 colaspis
BT2 chrysomelidae
BT3 coleoptera

COLBY CHEESE
BT1 cheeses
BT2 milk products
BT3 products

colchamine
USE **demecolcine**

COLCHICINE
BT1 isoquinoline alkaloids
BT2 alkaloids
BT1 mutagens
rt demecolcine

COLCHICUM
BT1 liliaceae
NT1 colchicum autumnale
NT1 colchicum dorfleri
NT1 colchicum kesselringii
NT1 colchicum latifolium
NT1 colchicum luteum
NT1 colchicum macedonicum
NT1 colchicum speciosum
NT1 colchicum szovitsii

COLCHICUM AUTUMNALE
BT1 colchicum
BT2 liliaceae
BT1 insecticidal plants
BT2 pesticidal plants
BT1 ornamental bulbs
rt corms

COLCHICUM DORFLERI
BT1 colchicum
BT2 liliaceae

COLCHICUM KESSELRINGII
BT1 colchicum
BT2 liliaceae

COLCHICUM LATIFOLIUM
BT1 colchicum
BT2 liliaceae

COLCHICUM LUTEUM
BT1 colchicum
BT2 liliaceae
BT1 ornamental bulbs
rt corms

COLCHICUM MACEDONICUM
BT1 colchicum
BT2 liliaceae

COLCHICUM SPECIOSUM
BT1 colchicum
BT2 liliaceae
BT1 ornamental bulbs
rt corms

COLCHICUM SZOVITSII
BT1 colchicum
BT2 liliaceae

COLD
rt chilling
rt cold hardening
rt cold injury
rt cold resistance
rt cold shock
rt cold storage
rt cold stores
rt cold stress
rt cold tolerance
rt cold zones
rt cryogenics
rt freezing
rt frost
rt hypothermia
rt psychrophilic bacteria
rt raynaud's syndrome
rt shelter
rt snow
rt temperature
rt temperature resistance
rt vernalization
rt winter hardiness

COLD HARDENING
BT1 hardening
rt cold

cold hardiness
USE **cold resistance**

COLD INJURY
BT1 injuries
rt cold
rt cold resistance
rt frost injury
rt plant disorders

COLD PLATTERS (AGRICOLA)
rt meals

cold regions
USE **cold zones**

COLD RESISTANCE
uf cold hardiness
BT1 temperature resistance
BT2 resistance
rt cold
rt cold injury
rt cold tolerance
rt frost resistance
rt hardening
rt hardiness
rt winter hardiness

COLD SHOCK
BT1 shock
rt cold

COLD STORAGE
uf storage, cold
BT1 storage
rt cold
rt cold stores
rt frozen storage
rt refrigeration

COLD STORES
uf stores, cold
BT1 stores
rt cold
rt cold storage
rt fruit stores

COLD STRESS
BT1 stress
NT1 hypothermia
rt cold

COLD TOLERANCE
BT1 tolerance
rt cold
rt cold resistance

COLD TOLERANCE *cont.*
rt energy exchange
rt frost resistance
rt psychrophilic bacteria
rt winter hardiness

COLD ZONES
uf arctic zones
uf cold regions
BT1 climatic zones
NT1 polar regions
NT1 tundra
NT2 arctic tundra
rt antarctica
rt arctic regions
rt cold

COLEMANITE
BT1 boron fertilizers
BT2 trace element fertilizers
BT3 fertilizers

COLEOGYNE
BT1 rosaceae
NT1 coleogyne ramosissima

COLEOGYNE RAMOSISSIMA
BT1 browse plants
BT1 coleogyne
BT2 rosaceae

COLEOMEGILLA
BT1 coccinellidae
BT2 coleoptera
NT1 coleomegilla maculata

COLEOMEGILLA MACULATA
BT1 coleomegilla
BT2 coccinellidae
BT3 coleoptera

COLEOPHORA
BT1 coleophoridae
BT2 lepidoptera
NT1 coleophora frischella
NT1 coleophora laricella
NT1 coleophora serratella

COLEOPHORA FRISCHELLA
BT1 coleophora
BT2 coleophoridae
BT3 lepidoptera

coleophora fuscedinella
USE **coleophora serratella**

COLEOPHORA LARICELLA
BT1 coleophora
BT2 coleophoridae
BT3 lepidoptera

COLEOPHORA SERRATELLA
uf coleophora fuscedinella
BT1 coleophora
BT2 coleophoridae
BT3 lepidoptera

COLEOPHORIDAE
BT1 lepidoptera
NT1 coleophora
NT2 coleophora frischella
NT2 coleophora laricella
NT2 coleophora serratella

COLEOPTERA
uf beetles
NT1 anobiidae
NT2 anobium
NT3 anobium punctatum
NT2 hadrobregmus
NT3 hadrobregmus pertinax
NT2 lasioderma
NT3 lasioderma serricorne
NT2 stegobium
NT3 stegobium paniceum
NT1 anthribidae
NT2 araecerus
NT3 araecerus fasciculatus
NT1 apionidae
NT2 apion
NT3 apion antiquum
NT3 apion apricans
NT3 apion assimile
NT3 apion corchori

COLEOPTERA *cont.*
NT3 apion fulvipes
NT3 apion seniculus
NT3 apion trifolii
NT3 apion ulicis
NT3 apion virens
NT3 apion vorax
NT2 cylas
NT3 cylas formicarius
NT4 cylas formicarius elegantulus
NT3 cylas puncticollis
NT1 attelabidae
NT2 rhynchites
NT1 bostrichidae
NT2 dinoderus
NT3 dinoderus minutus
NT2 prostephanus
NT3 prostephanus truncatus
NT2 rhyzopertha
NT3 rhyzopertha dominica
NT2 sinoxylon
NT3 sinoxylon anale
NT3 sinoxylon sexdentatum
NT1 bruchidae
NT2 acanthoscelides
NT3 acanthoscelides obtectus
NT2 bruchidius
NT3 bruchidius atrolineatus
NT3 bruchidius incarnatus
NT2 bruchus
NT3 bruchus emarginatus
NT3 bruchus lentis
NT3 bruchus pisorum
NT3 bruchus rufimanus
NT2 callosobruchus
NT3 callosobruchus analis
NT3 callosobruchus chinensis
NT3 callosobruchus maculatus
NT2 caryedon
NT3 caryedon serratus
NT2 megacerus
NT3 megacerus discoidus
NT2 spermophagus
NT3 spermophagus sericeus
NT2 zabrotes
NT3 zabrotes subfasciatus
NT1 buprestidae
NT2 agrilus
NT3 agrilus anxius
NT2 capnodis
NT3 capnodis miliaris
NT3 capnodis tenebrionis
NT2 chrysobothris
NT2 melanophila
NT1 byturidae
NT2 byturus
NT3 byturus tomentosus
NT1 carabidae
NT2 agonum
NT3 agonum dorsale
NT2 asaphidion
NT3 asaphidion flavipes
NT2 bembidion
NT3 bembidion lampros
NT3 bembidion quadrimaculatum
NT2 broscus
NT3 broscus cephalotes
NT2 calosoma
NT3 calosoma sycophanta
NT2 clivina
NT3 clivina fossor
NT3 clivina impressifrons
NT2 harpalus
NT3 harpalus affinis
NT3 harpalus distinguendus
NT3 harpalus pennsylvanicus
NT3 harpalus rufipes
NT2 loricera
NT3 loricera pilicornis
NT2 nebria
NT3 nebria brevicollis
NT2 notiophilus
NT3 notiophilus biguttatus
NT2 pterostichus
NT3 pterostichus chalcites
NT3 pterostichus cupreus
NT3 pterostichus madidus
NT3 pterostichus melanarius

COLEOPTERA *cont.*
NT3 pterostichus oblongopunctatus
NT3 pterostichus sericeus
NT2 trechus
NT3 trechus quadristriatus
NT3 trechus secalis
NT2 zabrus
NT3 zabrus tenebrioides
NT1 cerambycidae
NT2 arhopalus
NT3 arhopalus rusticus
NT3 arhopalus syriacus
NT2 cerambyx
NT3 cerambyx dux
NT2 dectes
NT3 dectes texanus
NT2 enaphalodes
NT3 enaphalodes rufulus
NT2 hylotrupes
NT3 hylotrupes bajulus
NT2 megacyllene
NT3 megacyllene robiniae
NT2 migdolus
NT3 migdolus fryanus
NT2 monochamus
NT3 monochamus alternatus
NT3 monochamus carolinensis
NT3 monochamus galloprovincialis
NT3 monochamus scutellatus
NT3 monochamus sutor
NT3 monochamus titillator
NT3 monochamus urussovii
NT2 oberea
NT2 obereopsis
NT3 obereopsis brevis
NT2 oncideres
NT2 phoracantha
NT3 phoracantha semipunctata
NT2 plocaederus
NT3 plocaederus ferrugineus
NT2 rhagium
NT3 rhagium bifasciatum
NT3 rhagium inquisitor
NT2 saperda
NT3 saperda carcharias
NT3 saperda populnea
NT3 saperda scalaris
NT2 semanotus
NT3 semanotus japonicus
NT2 steirastoma
NT3 steirastoma breve
NT2 tetropium
NT2 xylotrechus
NT3 xylotrechus pyrrhoderus
NT1 chrysomelidae
NT2 acalymma
NT3 acalymma vittatum
NT2 agasicles
NT3 agasicles hygrophila
NT2 agelastica
NT3 agelastica alni
NT2 altica
NT3 altica carduorum
NT2 aphthona
NT3 aphthona abdominalis
NT3 aphthona euphorbiae
NT2 aulacophora
NT3 aulacophora foveicollis
NT2 brontispa
NT3 brontispa longissima
NT2 cassida
NT3 cassida nebulosa
NT2 cerotoma
NT3 cerotoma facialis
NT3 cerotoma ruficornis
NT3 cerotoma trifurcata
NT2 chaetocnema
NT3 chaetocnema concinna
NT3 chaetocnema pulicaria
NT3 chaetocnema tibialis
NT2 chrysolina
NT2 chrysomela
NT3 chrysomela aenea
NT3 chrysomela populi
NT2 coelaenomenodera
NT3 coelaenomenodera elaeidis
NT2 colaspis

COLEOPTERA *cont.*
NT3 colaspis ornata
NT2 diabrotica
NT3 diabrotica balteata
NT3 diabrotica barberi
NT3 diabrotica longicornis
NT3 diabrotica speciosa
NT3 diabrotica undecimpunctata
NT4 diabrotica undecimpunctata howardi
NT3 diabrotica virgifera
NT2 dicladispa
NT3 dicladispa armigera
NT2 disonycha
NT3 disonycha argentinensis
NT2 entomoscelis
NT3 entomoscelis americana
NT2 epitrix
NT3 epitrix hirtipennis
NT2 galeruca
NT2 galerucella
NT2 gonioctena
NT2 lema
NT2 leptinotarsa
NT3 leptinotarsa decemlineata
NT2 leptispa
NT3 leptispa pygmaea
NT2 lochmaea
NT3 lochmaea caprea
NT3 lochmaea suturalis
NT2 longitarsus
NT3 longitarsus jacobaeae
NT3 longitarsus nigripennis
NT3 longitarsus parvulus
NT2 madurasia
NT3 madurasia obscurella
NT2 monolepta
NT3 monolepta signata
NT2 nisotra
NT3 nisotra sjostedti
NT2 odontota
NT3 odontota dorsalis
NT2 ootheca
NT3 ootheca bennigseni
NT3 ootheca mutabilis
NT2 oulema
NT3 oulema lichenis
NT3 oulema melanopus
NT3 oulema oryzae
NT2 paropsis
NT3 paropsis atomaria
NT3 paropsis charybdis
NT2 phaedon
NT3 phaedon cochleariae
NT2 phyllotreta
NT3 phyllotreta atra
NT3 phyllotreta cruciferae
NT3 phyllotreta nemorum
NT3 phyllotreta striolata
NT3 phyllotreta undulata
NT2 plagiodera
NT3 plagiodera versicolora
NT2 podagrica
NT3 podagrica uniformis
NT2 psylliodes
NT3 psylliodes attenuata
NT3 psylliodes chrysocephala
NT3 psylliodes punctulata
NT2 pyrrhalta
NT3 pyrrhalta luteola
NT2 systena
NT2 trirhabda
NT3 trirhabda borealis
NT3 trirhabda virgata
NT2 uroplata
NT3 uroplata girardi
NT2 xenochalepus
NT2 zygogramma
NT3 zygogramma suturalis
NT1 cleridae
NT2 enoclerus
NT2 necrobia
NT3 necrobia rufipes
NT2 thanasimus
NT3 thanasimus dubius
NT3 thanasimus femoralis
NT3 thanasimus formicarius
NT3 thanasimus undatulus
NT2 trichodes

COLEOPTERA *cont.*
NT1 coccinellidae
NT2 adalia
NT3 adalia bipunctata
NT3 adalia decempunctata
NT2 brumoides
NT3 brumoides suturalis
NT2 cheilomenes
NT3 cheilomenes sexmaculata
NT2 chilocorus
NT3 chilocorus bipustulatus
NT3 chilocorus kuwanae
NT3 chilocorus nigrita
NT2 coccidophilus
NT2 coccinella
NT3 coccinella quinquepunctata
NT3 coccinella septempunctata
NT3 coccinella transversalis
NT3 coccinella transversoguttata
NT3 coccinella undecimpunctata
NT2 coccinula
NT3 coccinula quatuordecimpustulata
NT2 coleomegilla
NT3 coleomegilla maculata
NT2 cryptolaemus
NT3 cryptolaemus montrouzieri
NT2 cycloneda
NT3 cycloneda sanguinea
NT2 epilachna
NT3 epilachna dodecastigma
NT3 epilachna varivestis
NT3 epilachna vigintioctomaculata
NT3 epilachna vigintioctopunctata
NT2 eriopis
NT3 eriopis connexa
NT2 exochomus
NT3 exochomus flavipes
NT3 exochomus quadripustulatus
NT2 harmonia
NT3 harmonia axyridis
NT3 harmonia octomaculata
NT2 hippodamia
NT3 hippodamia convergens
NT3 hippodamia oculata
NT3 hippodamia parenthesis
NT3 hippodamia tredecimpunctata
NT3 hippodamia variegata
NT2 hyperaspis
NT2 lioadalia
NT3 lioadalia flavomaculata
NT2 menochilus
NT2 nephus
NT3 nephus reunioni
NT2 oenopia
NT3 oenopia conglobata
NT2 propylea
NT3 propylea japonica
NT3 propylea quattuordecimpunctata
NT2 psyllobora
NT3 psyllobora vigintiduopunctata
NT2 rhyzobius
NT3 rhyzobius lophanthae
NT2 rodolia
NT3 rodolia cardinalis
NT2 scymnus
NT3 scymnus coccivora
NT3 scymnus hoffmanni
NT3 scymnus syriacus
NT2 serangium
NT3 serangium parcesetosum
NT2 stethorus
NT3 stethorus bifidus
NT3 stethorus nigripes
NT3 stethorus pauperculus
NT3 stethorus punctillum
NT3 stethorus punctum
NT2 subcoccinella
NT3 subcoccinella vigintiquattuorpunctata

COLEOPTERA *cont.*
NT2 telsimia
NT2 tytthaspis
NT3 tytthaspis sedecimpunctata
NT1 cryptophagidae
NT2 atomaria
NT3 atomaria linearis
NT1 cucujidae
NT2 cryptolestes
NT3 cryptolestes ferrugineus
NT3 cryptolestes pusillus
NT2 laemophloeus
NT1 curculionidae
NT2 alcidodes
NT3 alcidodes haemopterus
NT2 anthonomus
NT3 anthonomus grandis
NT3 anthonomus pomorum
NT3 anthonomus rubi
NT2 baris
NT2 bothynoderes
NT3 bothynoderes foveocollis
NT3 bothynoderes punctiventris
NT2 ceutorhynchus
NT3 ceutorhynchus assimilis
NT3 ceutorhynchus litura
NT3 ceutorhynchus napi
NT3 ceutorhynchus pallidactylus
NT3 ceutorhynchus pleurostigma
NT2 chalcodermus
NT3 chalcodermus aeneus
NT2 conorhynchus
NT2 conotrachelus
NT3 conotrachelus nenuphar
NT2 cosmopolites
NT3 cosmopolites sordidus
NT2 cryptorhynchus
NT3 cryptorhynchus lapathi
NT2 curculio
NT3 curculio caryae
NT3 curculio elephas
NT3 curculio nucum
NT2 cylindrocopturus
NT3 cylindrocopturus adspersus
NT2 cyrtobagous
NT3 cyrtobagous salviniae
NT3 cyrtobagous singularis
NT2 diaprepes
NT3 diaprepes abbreviatus
NT2 echinocnemus
NT2 elaeidobius
NT3 elaeidobius kamerunicus
NT2 gonipterus
NT3 gonipterus scutellatus
NT2 graphognathus
NT3 graphognathus leucoloma
NT3 graphognathus peregrinus
NT2 hylobius
NT3 hylobius abietis
NT3 hylobius pales
NT2 hypera
NT3 hypera meles
NT3 hypera nigrirostris
NT3 hypera postica
NT2 larinus
NT2 lissorhoptrus
NT3 lissorhoptrus oryzophilus
NT2 listronotus
NT3 listronotus bonariensis
NT3 listronotus oregonensis
NT2 lixomorphus
NT3 lixomorphus algirus
NT2 lixus
NT3 lixus juncii
NT3 lixus speciosus
NT2 metamasius
NT3 metamasius hemipterus
NT2 microlarinus
NT3 microlarinus lypriformis
NT2 mylloceru
NT3 myllocerus curvicornis
NT3 myllocerus discolor
NT3 myllocerus subfasciatus
NT3 myllocerus undecimpustulatus
NT2 naupactus

COLEOPTERA *cont.*
NT3 naupactus xanthographus
NT2 neochetina
NT3 neochetina bruchi
NT3 neochetina eichhorniae
NT2 otiorhynchus
NT3 otiorhynchus ligustici
NT3 otiorhynchus ovatus
NT3 otiorhynchus rugosostriatus
NT3 otiorhynchus singularis
NT3 otiorhynchus sulcatus
NT2 pachnaeus
NT3 pachnaeus litus
NT3 pachnaeus opalus
NT2 pachylobius
NT3 pachylobius picivorus
NT2 pantomorus
NT3 pantomorus cervinus
NT2 pentarthrum
NT3 pentarthrum huttoni
NT2 phyllobius
NT3 phyllobius argentatus
NT3 phyllobius pyri
NT2 pissodes
NT3 pissodes castaneus
NT3 pissodes nemorensis
NT3 pissodes piceae
NT3 pissodes pini
NT3 pissodes strobi
NT3 pissodes validirostris
NT2 premnotrypes
NT2 psalidium
NT3 psalidium maxillosum
NT2 rhabdoscelus
NT3 rhabdoscelus obscurus
NT2 rhinocyllus
NT3 rhinocyllus conicus
NT2 rhynchaenus
NT3 rhynchaenus fagi
NT3 rhynchaenus mangiferae
NT2 rhynchophorus
NT3 rhynchophorus ferrugineus
NT3 rhynchophorus palmarum
NT2 sitona
NT3 sitona callosus
NT3 sitona cylindricollis
NT3 sitona discoideus
NT3 sitona hispidulus
NT3 sitona humeralis
NT3 sitona lepidus
NT3 sitona lineatus
NT3 sitona macularius
NT3 sitona puncticollis
NT3 sitona sulcifrons
NT2 sitophilus
NT3 sitophilus granarius
NT3 sitophilus oryzae
NT3 sitophilus zeamais
NT2 smicronyx
NT3 smicronyx fulvus
NT3 smicronyx jungermanniae
NT2 sphenophorus
NT3 sphenophorus callosus
NT3 sphenophorus parvulus
NT2 sternochetus
NT3 sternochetus mangiferae
NT2 tanymecus
NT3 tanymecus dilaticollis
NT3 tanymecus palliatus
NT2 trichosirocalus
NT3 trichosirocalus horridus
NT2 tychius
NT3 tychius flavus
NT3 tychius picirostris
NT1 dermestidae
NT2 anthrenus
NT3 anthrenus flavipes
NT3 anthrenus fuscus
NT3 anthrenus verbasci
NT2 attagenus
NT3 attagenus unicolor
NT2 dermestes
NT3 dermestes ater
NT3 dermestes lardarius
NT3 dermestes maculatus
NT2 trogoderma
NT3 trogoderma glabrum
NT3 trogoderma granarium
NT3 trogoderma inclusum

COLEOPTERA *cont.*
NT3 trogoderma variabile
NT1 dytiscidae
NT2 cybister
NT2 rhantus
NT1 elateridae
NT2 adelocera
NT3 adelocera subcostata
NT2 agriotes
NT3 agriotes brevis
NT3 agriotes gurgistanus
NT3 agriotes lineatus
NT3 agriotes obscurus
NT3 agriotes sordidus
NT3 agriotes sputator
NT3 agriotes squalidus
NT3 agriotes ustulatus
NT2 athous
NT3 athous subfuscus
NT2 conoderus
NT3 conoderus exsul
NT3 conoderus falli
NT3 conoderus scalaris
NT3 conoderus vespertinus
NT2 ctenicera
NT3 ctenicera destructor
NT2 lacon
NT2 limonius
NT3 limonius californicus
NT2 melanotus
NT3 melanotus communis
NT2 selatosomus
NT3 selatosomus aeneus
NT3 selatosomus latus
NT1 geotrupidae
NT2 geotrupes
NT3 geotrupes stercorarius
NT3 geotrupes stercorosus
NT1 histeridae
NT2 carcinops
NT3 carcinops pumilio
NT2 hister
NT2 teretriosoma
NT3 teretriosoma nigrescens
NT1 lagriidae
NT2 lagria
NT3 lagria villosa
NT1 lathridiidae
NT2 lathridius
NT3 lathridius minutus
NT1 lyctidae
NT2 lyctus
NT3 lyctus brunneus
NT2 minthea
NT3 minthea rugicollis
NT1 lymexylidae
NT2 hylecoetus
NT3 hylecoetus dermestoides
NT1 meloidae
NT2 epicauta
NT3 epicauta vittata
NT2 lytta
NT2 mylabris
NT3 mylabris pustulata
NT1 mycetophagidae
NT2 typhaea
NT3 typhaea stercorea
NT1 nitidulidae
NT2 carpophilus
NT3 carpophilus dimidiatus
NT3 carpophilus hemipterus
NT3 carpophilus mutilatus
NT2 cybocephalus
NT2 glischrochilus
NT3 glischrochilus quadrisignatus
NT2 meligethes
NT3 meligethes aeneus
NT2 stelidota
NT3 stelidota geminata
NT2 urophorus
NT3 urophorus humeralis
NT1 platypodidae
NT2 platypus
NT1 ptinidae
NT2 gibbium
NT3 gibbium psylloides
NT2 ptinus
NT3 ptinus tectus
NT1 rhizophagidae
NT2 rhizophagus (coleoptera)

COLEOPTERA *cont.*
NT3 rhizophagus grandis
NT1 scarabaeidae
NT2 adoretus
NT2 amphimallon
NT3 amphimallon majalis
NT3 amphimallon solstitiale
NT2 anisoplia
NT3 anisoplia segetum
NT2 anomala
NT3 anomala cuprea
NT3 anomala cupripes
NT2 antitrogus
NT3 antitrogus mussoni
NT2 aphodius
NT3 aphodius fimetarius
NT3 aphodius rufipes
NT3 aphodius tasmaniae
NT2 apogonia
NT2 blitopertha
NT3 blitopertha orientalis
NT2 bothynus
NT2 canthon
NT3 canthon pilularius
NT2 chiloloba
NT3 chiloloba acuta
NT2 copris
NT2 costelytra
NT3 costelytra zealandica
NT2 cyclocephala
NT3 cyclocephala parallela
NT2 heteronychus
NT3 heteronychus arator
NT2 holotrichia (coleoptera)
NT3 holotrichia consanguinea
NT3 holotrichia morosa
NT3 holotrichia serrata
NT2 hoplochelus
NT3 hoplochelus marginalis
NT2 kheper
NT3 kheper lamarcki
NT2 ligyrus
NT3 ligyrus gibbosus
NT3 ligyrus subtropicus
NT2 melolontha
NT3 melolontha hippocastani
NT3 melolontha melolontha
NT2 mimela
NT3 mimela testaceipes
NT2 oniticellus
NT3 oniticellus intermedius
NT2 onitis
NT3 onitis alexis
NT3 onitis caffer
NT2 onthophagus
NT3 onthophagus binodis
NT3 onthophagus ferox
NT3 onthophagus gazella
NT3 onthophagus granulatus
NT3 onthophagus taurus
NT2 oryctes
NT3 oryctes boas
NT3 oryctes elegans
NT3 oryctes gigas
NT3 oryctes monoceros
NT3 oryctes rhinoceros
NT2 oxythyrea
NT3 oxythyrea funesta
NT2 phyllopertha
NT3 phyllopertha horticola
NT2 phyllophaga
NT3 phyllophaga anxia
NT3 phyllophaga crinita
NT2 polyphylla
NT3 polyphylla fullo
NT2 popillia
NT3 popillia japonica
NT2 rhopaea
NT2 scapanes
NT3 scapanes australis
NT2 scarabaeus
NT2 sericesthis
NT3 sericesthis geminata
NT3 sericesthis nigrolineata
NT2 xylotrupes
NT3 xylotrupes gideon
NT1 scolytidae
NT2 acrantus
NT3 acrantus vestitus
NT2 conophthorus
NT3 conophthorus ponderosae

COLEOPTERA *cont.*
NT3 conophthorus resinosae
NT2 corthylus
NT2 cryphalus
NT3 cryphalus piceae
NT2 dendroctonus
NT3 dendroctonus adjunctus
NT3 dendroctonus brevicomis
NT3 dendroctonus frontalis
NT3 dendroctonus micans
NT3 dendroctonus ponderosae
NT3 dendroctonus pseudotsugae
NT3 dendroctonus rufipennis
NT3 dendroctonus terebrans
NT3 dendroctonus valens
NT2 dryocoetes
NT3 dryocoetes affaber
NT3 dryocoetes autographus
NT2 euwallacea
NT3 euwallacea fornicatus
NT2 gnathotrichus
NT3 gnathotrichus retusus
NT3 gnathotrichus sulcatus
NT2 hylastes
NT3 hylastes ater
NT2 hylesinus
NT3 hylesinus varius
NT2 hylurgopinus
NT3 hylurgopinus rufipes
NT2 hylurgops
NT3 hylurgops palliatus
NT2 hypothenemus
NT3 hypothenemus hampei
NT2 ips
NT3 ips acuminatus
NT3 ips amitinus
NT3 ips avulsus
NT3 ips calligraphus
NT3 ips cembrae
NT3 ips grandicollis
NT3 ips paraconfusus
NT3 ips pini
NT3 ips sexdentatus
NT3 ips typographus
NT2 orthotomicus
NT3 orthotomicus erosus
NT2 phloeosinus
NT3 phloeosinus aubei
NT2 pityogenes
NT3 pityogenes bidentatus
NT3 pityogenes calcaratus
NT3 pityogenes chalcographus
NT2 pityokteines
NT3 pityokteines curvidens
NT2 pityophthorus
NT3 pityophthorus pityographus
NT2 scolytus
NT3 scolytus intricatus
NT3 scolytus laevis
NT3 scolytus multistriatus
NT3 scolytus pygmaeus
NT3 scolytus rugulosus
NT3 scolytus scolytus
NT3 scolytus ventralis
NT2 tomicus
NT3 tomicus minor
NT3 tomicus piniperda
NT2 trypodendron
NT3 trypodendron domesticum
NT3 trypodendron lineatum
NT3 trypodendron signatum
NT2 xyleborinus
NT3 xyleborinus saxeseni
NT2 xyleborus
NT3 xyleborus dispar
NT3 xyleborus ferrugineus
NT3 xyleborus similis
NT2 xylosandrus
NT3 xylosandrus compactus
NT3 xylosandrus germanus
NT1 silphidae
NT2 aclypea
NT3 aclypea opaca
NT2 nicrophorus
NT2 silpha
NT1 silvanidae
NT2 ahasverus
NT3 ahasverus advena

COLEOPTERA *cont.*
NT2 oryzaephilus
NT3 oryzaephilus mercator
NT3 oryzaephilus surinamensis
NT2 silvanus
NT1 staphylinidae
NT2 aleochara
NT3 aleochara bilineata
NT3 aleochara bimaculata
NT3 aleochara bipustulata
NT2 paederus
NT3 paederus alfierii
NT3 paederus fuscipes
NT2 philonthus
NT3 philonthus splendens
NT2 tachyporus
NT3 tachyporus hypnorum
NT1 tenebrionidae
NT2 alphitobius
NT3 alphitobius diaperinus
NT3 alphitobius laevigatus
NT2 blaps
NT3 blaps halophila
NT2 eleodes
NT2 gonocephalum
NT2 latheticus
NT3 latheticus oryzae
NT2 opatrum
NT3 opatrum sabulosum
NT2 tenebrio
NT3 tenebrio molitor
NT3 tenebrio obscurus
NT2 tribolium
NT3 tribolium castaneum
NT3 tribolium confusum
NT3 tribolium destructor
NT3 tribolium madens
NT1 trogossitidae
NT2 temnoscheila
NT3 temnoscheila virescens
NT2 tenebroides
NT3 tenebroides mauritanicus
rt insects

COLEOPTILES
BT1 seedlings
rt leaves
rt mesocotyls
rt seeds

COLEOSPORIUM
HN from 1990
BT1 uredinales
NT1 coleosporium domingense

COLEOSPORIUM DOMINGENSE
HN from 1990
uf *coleosporium plumeriae*
BT1 coleosporium
BT2 uredinales

coleosporium plumeriae
USE **coleosporium domingense**

COLEOTECHNITES
BT1 gelechiidae
BT2 lepidoptera
rt pulicalvaria

coleotechnites thujaella
USE **pulicalvaria thujaella**

COLESIOTA
BT1 rickettsiales
BT2 bacteria
BT3 prokaryotes

COLESTIPOL
BT1 anion exchange resins
BT2 ion exchange resins
BT3 resins
BT1 antilipaemics
BT2 haematologic agents
BT3 drugs
BT1 polyamines
BT2 amines
BT3 amino compounds
BT4 organic nitrogen compounds
rt cholesterol

COLESTYRAMINE
uf *cholestyramine*

COLESTYRAMINE *cont.*
BT1 antilipaemics
BT2 haematologic agents
BT3 drugs
BT1 ion exchange resins
BT2 resins

COLEUS
BT1 labiatae
NT1 coleus amboinicus
NT1 coleus blumei
NT1 coleus forskohlii
NT1 coleus rotundifolius
NT1 coleus scutellarioides

COLEUS AMBOINICUS
BT1 coleus
BT2 labiatae
rt ornamental foliage plants

coleus barbatus
USE **coleus forskohlii**

COLEUS BLUMEI
BT1 coleus
BT2 labiatae
BT1 medicinal plants
rt ornamental foliage plants

COLEUS FORSKOHLII
uf *coleus barbatus*
BT1 coleus
BT2 labiatae
BT1 medicinal plants

coleus parviflorus
USE **coleus rotundifolius**

COLEUS ROTUNDIFOLIUS
uf *coleus parviflorus*
BT1 coleus
BT2 labiatae
BT1 root vegetables
BT2 root crops
BT2 vegetables
rt ornamental foliage plants

COLEUS SCUTELLARIOIDES
BT1 coleus
BT2 labiatae
rt ornamental foliage plants

coley
USE **pollachius virens**

COLIAS
BT1 pieridae
BT2 lepidoptera
NT1 colias eurytheme

COLIAS EURYTHEME
BT1 colias
BT2 pieridae
BT3 lepidoptera

colibacteriosis
USE **escherichia coli**

COLIC
BT1 digestive disorders
BT2 functional disorders
BT3 animal disorders
BT4 disorders
BT1 pain
rt intussusception
rt paints
rt reproductive disorders
rt urinary tract diseases

COLICINS
BT1 bacteriocins
BT2 antibiotics

COLIFORM BACTERIA
uf *bacteria, coliform*
BT1 microbial flora
BT2 flora
NT1 faecal coliforms
rt bacteria
rt coliform count
rt enterobacteriaceae

COLIFORM COUNT
BT1 milk testing
BT2 testing

COLIFORM COUNT *cont.*
rt coliform bacteria

COLIIFORMES
BT1 birds

COLINUS
BT1 phasianidae
BT2 galliformes
BT3 birds
NT1 colinus virginianus

COLINUS VIRGINIANUS
uf *bobwhite quail*
uf *quail, bobwhite*
BT1 colinus
BT2 phasianidae
BT3 galliformes
BT4 birds

colipase
USE **triacylglycerol lipase**

COLITIS
BT1 intestinal diseases
BT2 gastrointestinal diseases
BT3 digestive system diseases
BT4 organic diseases
BT5 diseases
NT1 ulcerative colitis
rt colon
rt enterocolitis

colitis, ulcerative
USE **ulcerative colitis**

colladonia
USE **heptaptera**

colladonia triquetra
USE **heptaptera triquetra**

COLLADONUS
BT1 cicadellidae
BT2 cicadelloidea
BT3 auchenorrhyncha
BT4 homoptera
NT1 colladonus montanus

COLLADONUS MONTANUS
BT1 colladonus
BT2 cicadellidae
BT3 cicadelloidea
BT4 auchenorrhyncha
BT5 homoptera

COLLAGEN
BT1 glycoproteins
BT2 proteins
BT3 peptides
BT1 scleroproteins
BT2 proteins
BT3 peptides
rt connective tissue
rt gelatin

COLLAGENASE
(ec 3.4.24.3)
BT1 proteinases
BT2 peptide hydrolases
BT3 hydrolases
BT4 enzymes

COLLAPSE
BT1 functional disorders
BT2 animal disorders
BT3 disorders

COLLAPSE (DRYING)
HN from 1990; previously "collapse"
BT1 wood defects
BT2 defects

collards
USE **kale**

COLLECTION
NT1 aerial collection
NT1 data collection
NT2 interviews
NT2 questionnaires
NT1 faeces collection
NT1 milk collection
NT1 seed collection

COLLECTION *cont.*
rt bundling
rt collectors
rt transport

COLLECTION DUMMY
BT1 equipment
rt artificial insemination
rt semen

COLLECTIONS
NT1 culture collections
NT1 plant collections
NT2 arboreta
NT2 herbaria
rt groups
rt museums
rt specimens
rt zoological gardens

collections, plant
USE **plant collections**

COLLECTIVE AGREEMENTS
BT1 contract legislation
BT2 legislation
BT3 legal systems
NT1 wage agreements
rt arbitration
rt contracts
rt wages

collective behavior
USE **group behavior**

collective behaviour
USE **group behaviour**

COLLECTIVE FARMS
uf *farms, collective*
BT1 farms
NT1 ejidos
NT1 kibbutzim
NT1 kolkhozy
NT1 moshavim
rt communes
rt cooperative farms
rt cooperatives
rt producer cooperatives
rt state farms

COLLECTIVIZATION
BT1 tenure systems
rt agrarian reform
rt ownership

COLLECTORS
BT1 equipment
NT1 egg collectors
NT1 solar collectors
rt collection

COLLECTORS (OCCUPATION) (AGRICOLA)
HN from 1990
BT1 occupations

collectors, solar
USE **solar collectors**

COLLEGE CURRICULUM (AGRICOLA)
BT1 curriculum
BT2 educational courses
rt colleges (agricola)

COLLEGE FOOD SERVICE (AGRICOLA)
BT1 food service
rt colleges (agricola)

COLLEGE PROGRAMS (AGRICOLA)
BT1 programs (agricola)
rt colleges (agricola)
rt higher education

COLLEGE STUDENTS (AGRICOLA)
BT1 students
BT2 people
rt colleges (agricola)

COLLEGES (AGRICOLA)
BT1 educational institutions
NT1 medical schools (agricola)

COLLEGES (AGRICOLA) *cont.*
rt agricultural colleges
rt college curriculum (agricola)
rt college food service (agricola)
rt college programs (agricola)
rt college students (agricola)
rt higher education
rt universities

COLLEMBOLA
uf *springtails*
NT1 entomobryidae
NT2 dicranorchesella
NT2 tomocerus
NT3 tomocerus minor
NT1 hypogastruridae
NT2 anurida
NT3 anurida granulata
NT2 brachystomella
NT2 hypogastrura
NT3 hypogastrura tullbergi
NT1 isotomidae
NT2 cryptopygus
NT3 cryptopygus antarcticus
NT2 folsomia
NT3 folsomia candida
NT2 folsomides
NT2 isotoma
NT2 parisotoma
NT2 proisotoma
NT3 proisotoma minuta
NT1 onychiuridae
NT2 onychiurus
NT3 onychiurus fimatus
NT3 onychiurus pseudarmatus
NT1 sminthuridae
NT2 bourletiella
NT3 bourletiella hortensis
NT2 bovicornia
NT3 bovicornia bidoma
NT2 sminthurus
NT3 sminthurus viridis
rt insects

COLLENCHYMA
BT1 plant tissues
BT2 plant
BT2 tissues

COLLETES
BT1 apidae
BT2 hymenoptera

COLLETOTRICHUM
BT1 deuteromycotina
NT1 colletotrichum acutatum
NT1 colletotrichum capsici
NT1 colletotrichum circinans
NT1 colletotrichum coccodes
NT1 colletotrichum crassipes
NT1 colletotrichum dematium
NT1 colletotrichum destructivum
NT1 colletotrichum graminicola
NT1 colletotrichum lindemuthianum
NT1 colletotrichum lini
NT1 colletotrichum manihotis
NT1 colletotrichum musae
NT1 colletotrichum orbiculare
NT1 colletotrichum tabacum
NT1 colletotrichum trifolii
NT1 colletotrichum truncatum
rt gloeosporium
rt glomerella

COLLETOTRICHUM ACUTATUM
BT1 colletotrichum
BT2 deuteromycotina

colletotrichum atramentarium
USE **colletotrichum coccodes**

COLLETOTRICHUM CAPSICI
BT1 colletotrichum
BT2 deuteromycotina

COLLETOTRICHUM CIRCINANS
BT1 colletotrichum
BT2 deuteromycotina

COLLETOTRICHUM COCCODES
uf *colletotrichum atramentarium*
BT1 colletotrichum
BT2 deuteromycotina

colletotrichum coffeanum
USE **glomerella cingulata**

COLLETOTRICHUM CRASSIPES
BT1 colletotrichum
BT2 deuteromycotina

COLLETOTRICHUM DEMATIUM
BT1 colletotrichum
BT2 deuteromycotina

colletotrichum dematium var. truncatum
USE **colletotrichum truncatum**

COLLETOTRICHUM DESTRUCTIVUM
BT1 colletotrichum
BT2 deuteromycotina

colletotrichum falcatum
USE **glomerella tucumanensis**

colletotrichum fragariae
USE **glomerella cingulata**

colletotrichum gloeosporioides
USE **glomerella cingulata**

colletotrichum glycines
USE **glomerella glycines**

colletotrichum gossypii
USE **glomerella gossypii**

COLLETOTRICHUM GRAMINICOLA
BT1 colletotrichum
BT2 deuteromycotina

colletotrichum lagenarium
USE **colletotrichum orbiculare**

COLLETOTRICHUM LINDEMUTHIANUM
BT1 colletotrichum
BT2 deuteromycotina

COLLETOTRICHUM LINI
uf *colletotrichum linicola*
BT1 colletotrichum
BT2 deuteromycotina

colletotrichum linicola
USE **colletotrichum lini**

COLLETOTRICHUM MANIHOTIS
BT1 colletotrichum
BT2 deuteromycotina

COLLETOTRICHUM MUSAE
uf *gloeosporium musarum*
BT1 colletotrichum
BT2 deuteromycotina

COLLETOTRICHUM ORBICULARE
uf *colletotrichum lagenarium*
uf *glomerella cingulata var. orbiculare*
BT1 colletotrichum
BT2 deuteromycotina

colletotrichum phomoides
USE **glomerella phomoides**

COLLETOTRICHUM TABACUM
BT1 colletotrichum
BT2 deuteromycotina

COLLETOTRICHUM TRIFOLII
BT1 colletotrichum
BT2 deuteromycotina

COLLETOTRICHUM TRUNCATUM
uf *colletotrichum dematium var. truncatum*
BT1 colletotrichum
BT2 deuteromycotina

colliery spoil
USE **coal mine spoil**

COLLIGUAJA
BT1 euphorbiaceae
NT1 colliguaja odorifera

COLLIGUAJA ODORIFERA
BT1 colliguaja
BT2 euphorbiaceae

COLLISION INSURANCE (AGRICOLA)
BT1 automobile insurance (agricola)
BT2 insurance
rt traffic accidents

COLLOIDAL PROPERTIES
BT1 physicochemical properties
BT2 properties
rt colloids
rt flocculation
rt isoelectric point
rt soil colloid chemistry
rt swelling

COLLOIDS
NT1 aerosols
NT1 carrageenan
NT1 petrolatum
rt agar
rt alginic acid
rt colloidal properties
rt dispersion
rt emulsions
rt micelles
rt soil colloid chemistry

COLLOSPERMUM
BT1 liliaceae

COLLUVIAL DEPOSITS
BT1 soil parent materials

COLLUVIAL SOILS
BT1 soil types (lithological)

COLLYBIA
BT1 agaricales
NT1 collybia velutipes

COLLYBIA VELUTIPES
BT1 collybia
BT2 agaricales
BT1 edible fungi
BT2 fungi
BT2 vegetables

COLOBOMA
BT1 congenital abnormalities
BT2 abnormalities

COLOBUS
BT1 cercopithecidae
BT2 primates
BT3 mammals
NT1 colobus guereza

COLOBUS GUEREZA
BT1 colobus
BT2 cercopithecidae
BT3 primates
BT4 mammals

COLOCASIA
BT1 araceae
NT1 colocasia antiquorum
NT1 colocasia esculenta

COLOCASIA ANTIQUORUM
BT1 colocasia
BT2 araceae

COLOCASIA ESCULENTA
uf *cocoyam*
uf *dasheen*
uf *taro*
BT1 colocasia
BT2 araceae
BT1 root vegetables
BT2 root crops
BT2 vegetables
rt dasheen mosaic potyvirus

COLOCERAS
BT1 philopteridae
BT2 ischnocera

COLOCERAS *cont.*
BT3 mallophaga
BT4 phthiraptera

colocynthis citrullus
USE **citrullus lanatus**

colocynthis vulgaris
USE **citrullus colocynthis**

COLOLABIS
BT1 scomberesocidae
BT2 cyprinodontiformes
BT3 osteichthyes
BT4 fishes

COLOMBIA
BT1 south america
BT2 america
rt andean group
rt developing countries

COLOMBO PLAN
BT1 international organizations
BT2 organizations
rt usa

COLOMERUS
BT1 eriophyidae
BT2 prostigmata
BT3 acari
NT1 colomerus vitis
rt eriophyes

COLOMERUS VITIS
uf *eriophyes vitis*
BT1 colomerus
BT2 eriophyidae
BT3 prostigmata
BT4 acari

COLON
BT1 large intestine
BT2 intestines
BT3 digestive system
BT4 body parts
rt colitis
rt colostomy
rt diverticulosis
rt irritable colon
rt megacolon

COLONIALISM
BT1 imperialism
BT2 political systems
BT3 politics
rt colonies

COLONIES
BT1 countries
BT1 groups
rt colonialism
rt developing countries
rt imperialism

COLONIZATION
rt settlement

colonization, plant
USE **plant colonization**

COLONIZING ABILITY
rt competitive ability
rt ecology
rt pioneer species
rt plant colonization
rt revegetation
rt spread

COLONY DEFENCE
AF colony defense
BT1 aggressive behaviour
BT2 behaviour
BT1 defence
rt honeybee colonies
rt stinging

COLONY DEFENSE
BF colony defence
BT1 defense

COLOPHOSPERMUM
BT1 leguminosae
NT1 colophospermum mopane

COLOPHOSPERMUM MOPANE
BT1 colophospermum
BT2 leguminosae

COLOR
BF colour
rt color fading (agricola)
rt color matching (agricola)
rt color patterns
rt color photography
rt color sorters
rt color sorting
rt color varieties
rt colored sticky traps
rt coloring
rt egg yolk color
rt food colorants
rt soil color

COLOR FADING (AGRICOLA)
rt color
rt fastness (agricola)

color fastness
USE **fastness (agricola)**

COLOR MATCHING (AGRICOLA)
rt color

COLOR PATTERNS
BF colour patterns
rt color

COLOR PHOTOGRAPHY
BF colour photography
rt color

COLOR SORTERS
BF colour sorters
rt color
rt color sorting

COLOR SORTING
BF colour sorting
rt color
rt color sorters

COLOR VARIETIES
BF colour varieties
rt color

COLORADO
BT1 mountain states of usa
BT2 western states of usa
BT3 usa
BT4 north america
BT5 america

COLORADO TICK FEVER VIRUS
BT1 orbivirus
BT2 arboviruses
BT3 pathogens
BT2 reoviridae
BT3 viruses

COLORED STICKY TRAPS
BF coloured sticky traps
rt color

COLORIMETRY
BT1 analytical methods
BT2 methodology

COLORING
BF colouring
rt color

COLORING BOOKS (AGRICOLA)
BT1 books
BT2 publications
rt children's literature (agricola)

COLOSTOMY
BT1 surgical operations
rt anus
rt colon

colostral antibody
USE **colostral immunity**

COLOSTRAL IMMUNITY
uf *colostral antibody*
BT1 maternal immunity
BT2 passive immunity
BT3 immunity

COLOSTRAL IMMUNITY *cont.*
rt colostrum

COLOSTRUM
ufa *colostrum, ewe*
ufa *colostrum, mare*
ufa *colostrum, sow*
ufa *ewe colostrum*
ufa *goat colostrum*
ufa *mare colostrum*
ufa *rabbit colostrum*
ufa *sow colostrum*
BT1 body fluids
BT2 fluids
NT1 cow colostrum
NT1 human colostrum
rt colostral immunity
rt milk

colostrum, cow
USE **cow colostrum**

colostrum, ewe
USE **colostrum**
AND **ewes**

colostrum, mare
USE **colostrum**
AND **mares**

colostrum, sow
USE **colostrum**
AND **sows**

COLOUR
AF color
BT1 optical properties
BT2 physical properties
BT3 properties
rt bleaching
rt chlorosis
rt colour patterns
rt colour photography
rt colour sorters
rt colour sorting
rt colour varieties
rt coloured sticky traps
rt colouring
rt discoloration
rt egg yolk colour
rt pigmentation
rt pigments
rt soil colour

COLOUR PATTERNS
AF color patterns
BT1 patterns
rt colour

COLOUR PHOTOGRAPHY
AF color photography
uf *aerial colour photography*
BT1 photography
BT2 techniques
rt colour
rt mapping
rt surveying

COLOUR SORTERS
AF color sorters
uf *sorters, colour*
BT1 sorters
rt colour

COLOUR SORTING
AF color sorting
BT1 sorting
BT2 grading
BT2 processing
BT2 separation
rt colour

COLOUR VARIETIES
AF color varieties
BT1 varieties
rt colour

COLOURE
BT1 plant disorders
BT2 disorders
rt grapes

COLOURED STICKY TRAPS
AF colored sticky traps

COLOURED STICKY TRAPS *cont.*
BT1 insect traps
BT2 traps
BT3 equipment
rt colour

COLOURING
AF coloring
rt colour

colouring compounds
USE **dyes**
OR **pigments**

colourings
USE **dyes**
OR **pigments**

COLPOCEPHALUM
BT1 menoponidae
BT2 amblycera
BT3 mallophaga
BT4 phthiraptera
NT1 colpocephalum turbinatum

COLPOCEPHALUM TURBINATUM
BT1 colpocephalum
BT2 menoponidae
BT3 amblycera
BT4 mallophaga
BT5 phthiraptera

COLPODA
BT1 ciliophora
BT2 protozoa
NT1 colpoda steini

COLPODA STEINI
BT1 colpoda
BT2 ciliophora
BT3 protozoa

COLPOMA
BT1 rhytismatales
NT1 colpoma quercinum

COLPOMA QUERCINUM
BT1 colpoma
BT2 rhytismatales

COLTRICIA
uf *xanthochrous*
BT1 aphyllophorales
NT1 coltricia tomentosa
rt polyporus

COLTRICIA TOMENTOSA
uf *polyporus tomentosus*
BT1 coltricia
BT2 aphyllophorales

COLTS
BT1 young animals
BT2 animals
rt foals
rt horses

COLUBER
BT1 colubridae
BT2 serpentes
BT3 reptiles

COLUBRIDAE
BT1 serpentes
BT2 reptiles
NT1 coluber
NT1 elaphe
NT2 elaphe obsoleta
NT1 natrix
NT2 natrix piscator
NT1 thamnophis

COLUBRINA
BT1 rhamnaceae
NT1 colubrina faralaotra
NT1 colubrina texensis

COLUBRINA FARALAOTRA
BT1 colubrina
BT2 rhamnaceae

COLUBRINA TEXENSIS
BT1 colubrina
BT2 rhamnaceae

COLUMBA
BT1 columbidae
BT2 columbiformes
BT3 birds
NT1 columba palumba

columba livia
USE **pigeons**

COLUMBA PALUMBA
BT1 columba
BT2 columbidae
BT3 columbiformes
BT4 birds

COLUMBIA
BT1 sheep breeds
BT2 breeds

COLUMBICOLA
BT1 philopteridae
BT2 ischnocera
BT3 mallophaga
BT4 phthiraptera
NT1 columbicola columbae

COLUMBICOLA COLUMBAE
BT1 columbicola
BT2 philopteridae
BT3 ischnocera
BT4 mallophaga
BT5 phthiraptera

COLUMBIDAE
BT1 columbiformes
BT2 birds
NT1 columba
NT2 columba palumba
NT1 streptopelia
NT2 streptopelia decaocto
NT2 streptopelia senegalensis

COLUMBIFORMES
BT1 birds
NT1 columbidae
NT2 columba
NT3 columba palumba
NT2 streptopelia
NT3 streptopelia decaocto
NT3 streptopelia senegalensis
rt pigeons

columbus grass
USE **sorghum almum**

COLUMNEA
BT1 gesneriaceae
NT1 columnea stavanger

COLUMNEA STAVANGER
BT1 columnea
BT2 gesneriaceae
BT1 ornamental woody plants

COLUMNS
BT1 structural components
BT2 components
rt buildings

COLUTEA
BT1 leguminosae
NT1 colutea istria

COLUTEA ISTRIA
BT1 browse plants
BT1 colutea
BT2 leguminosae

colza
USE **rape**

COMA
BT1 dysregulation
BT2 functional disorders
BT3 animal disorders
BT4 disorders
NT1 diabetic coma

COMB
(of birds)
BT1 integument
BT2 body parts
rt head
rt wattles

COMB HONEY
BT1 honey
BT2 hive products
BT3 animal products
BT4 products
rt chunk honey
rt section honey

COMB STARTERS
BT1 combs
BT2 hive parts
BT3 movable-comb hives
BT4 hives

COMB TYPE
BT1 combs
BT2 hive parts
BT3 movable-comb hives
BT4 hives

COMBATIVE SPORTS
BT1 sport
NT1 boxing
NT1 judo
NT1 wrestling

COMBINATION
rt agglutination
rt chelation
rt synergism

COMBINE DRILLS
uf drills, combine
BT1 drills
BT2 farm machinery
BT3 machinery
rt drilling
rt fertilizer distributors

COMBINE HARVESTERS
uf harvesters, combine
uf harvesters, grain
BT1 harvesters
BT2 farm machinery
BT3 machinery
NT1 axial flow combine harvesters
NT1 concaves
NT1 grain tanks
rt augers
rt combine harvesting
rt grain loss monitors
rt maize pickers
rt reels
rt swath harvesting
rt tailboards

combine harvesters, plot
USE **plot harvesters**

COMBINE HARVESTING
uf harvesting, combine
BT1 harvesting
rt combine harvesters

COMBINED VACCINES
HN from 1990
(mixtures of vaccines intended to protect against different species of infectious organisms)
uf mixed vaccines
BT1 vaccines

COMBINES
BT1 cooperative activities
rt cartels
rt integration
rt monopoly

COMBING
HN from 1990
BT1 harvesting

COMBINING ABILITY
NT1 general combining ability
NT1 specific combining ability
rt crossing
rt genetic parameters
rt heterosis
rt hybridization

COMBRETACEAE
NT1 anogeissus
NT2 anogeissus acuminata

COMBRETACEAE *cont.*
NT2 anogeissus latifolia
NT2 anogeissus leiocarpus
NT2 anogeissus pendula
NT1 bucida
NT2 bucida buceras
NT1 combretum
NT2 combretum aculeatum
NT2 combretum apiculatum
NT2 combretum caffrum
NT2 combretum collinum
NT2 combretum erythrophyllum
NT2 combretum fragrans
NT2 combretum geitonophyllum
NT2 combretum hartmannianum
NT2 combretum hypopilinum
NT2 combretum molle
NT2 combretum nigricans
NT2 combretum psidioides
NT2 combretum zeyheri
NT1 conocarpus
NT2 conocarpus erectus
NT2 conocarpus lancifolius
NT1 guiera
NT2 guiera senegalensis
NT1 laguncularia
NT2 laguncularia racemosa
NT1 lumnitzera
NT2 lumnitzera racemosa
NT1 quisqualis
NT2 quisqualis indica
NT1 terminalia
NT2 terminalia arjuna
NT2 terminalia bellirica
NT2 terminalia bialata
NT2 terminalia calamansanai
NT2 terminalia catappa
NT2 terminalia chebula
NT2 terminalia edulis
NT2 terminalia horrida
NT2 terminalia ivorensis
NT2 terminalia procera
NT2 terminalia sericea
NT2 terminalia stenostachya
NT2 terminalia superba
NT2 terminalia tomentosa

COMBRETUM
BT1 combretaceae
NT1 combretum aculeatum
NT1 combretum apiculatum
NT1 combretum caffrum
NT1 combretum collinum
NT1 combretum erythrophyllum
NT1 combretum fragrans
NT1 combretum geitonophyllum
NT1 combretum hartmannianum
NT1 combretum hypopilinum
NT1 combretum molle
NT1 combretum nigricans
NT1 combretum psidioides
NT1 combretum zeyheri

COMBRETUM ACULEATUM
BT1 browse plants
BT1 combretum
BT2 combretaceae

COMBRETUM APICULATUM
BT1 combretum
BT2 combretaceae

COMBRETUM CAFFRUM
BT1 combretum
BT2 combretaceae
BT1 medicinal plants

COMBRETUM COLLINUM
BT1 combretum
BT2 combretaceae

COMBRETUM ERYTHROPHYLLUM
BT1 combretum
BT2 combretaceae

COMBRETUM FRAGRANS
BT1 combretum
BT2 combretaceae

COMBRETUM GEITONOPHYLLUM
BT1 combretum
BT2 combretaceae

COMBRETUM HARTMANNIANUM
BT1 combretum
BT2 combretaceae

COMBRETUM HYPOPILINUM
BT1 combretum
BT2 combretaceae

COMBRETUM MOLLE
BT1 combretum
BT2 combretaceae

COMBRETUM NIGRICANS
BT1 combretum
BT2 combretaceae

COMBRETUM PSIDIOIDES
BT1 combretum
BT2 combretaceae

COMBRETUM ZEYHERI
BT1 browse plants
BT1 combretum
BT2 combretaceae

COMBS
BT1 hive parts
BT2 movable-comb hives
BT3 hives
NT1 cells (honeybees)
NT2 cappings
NT2 queen cells
NT1 comb starters
NT1 comb type
NT1 foundation
NT2 plastic foundation
NT1 framed combs
NT1 plastic combs
rt beeswax
rt frames
rt rendering
rt solar beeswax extractors

COMBUSTION
rt ashing
rt burners
rt burning
rt fireproofing
rt fires
rt heating
rt ignition
rt producer gas
rt smoke

comecon
USE **cmea**

COMESOMATIDAE
BT1 nematoda
NT1 sabateria
rt marine nematodes

COMETOIDES
BT1 apicomplexa
BT2 protozoa

comfrey
USE **symphytum officinale**

COMICS (AGRICOLA)
BT1 publications
rt cartoons (agricola)
rt children's literature (agricola)

COMISANO
HN from 1990; previously "comiso"
uf comiso
BT1 sheep breeds
BT2 breeds

comiso
USE **comisano**

COMMELINA
BT1 commelinaceae
NT1 commelina benghalensis
NT1 commelina communis
NT1 commelina diffusa
NT1 commelina elegans
NT1 commelina erecta
NT1 commelina forskaeli
NT1 commelina nudiflora
rt commelina mosaic potyvirus

COMMELINA *cont.*
rt commelina x potexvirus

COMMELINA BENGHALENSIS
BT1 commelina
BT2 commelinaceae
BT1 ornamental herbaceous plants

COMMELINA COMMUNIS
BT1 commelina
BT2 commelinaceae
BT1 weeds

COMMELINA DIFFUSA
BT1 commelina
BT2 commelinaceae

COMMELINA ELEGANS
BT1 commelina
BT2 commelinaceae

COMMELINA ERECTA
BT1 commelina
BT2 commelinaceae

COMMELINA FORSKAELI
BT1 commelina
BT2 commelinaceae

COMMELINA MOSAIC POTYVIRUS
HN from 1990
BT1 potyvirus group
BT2 plant viruses
BT3 plant pathogens
BT4 pathogens
rt commelina

COMMELINA NUDIFLORA
BT1 commelina
BT2 commelinaceae

COMMELINA X POTEXVIRUS
HN from 1990
BT1 potexvirus group
BT2 plant viruses
BT3 plant pathogens
BT4 pathogens
rt commelina

COMMELINACEAE
NT1 aneilema
NT2 aneilema japonicum
NT2 aneilema keisak
NT1 commelina
NT2 commelina benghalensis
NT2 commelina communis
NT2 commelina diffusa
NT2 commelina elegans
NT2 commelina erecta
NT2 commelina forskaeli
NT2 commelina nudiflora
NT1 cyanotis
NT2 cyanotis axillaris
NT1 rhoeo
NT2 rhoeo spathacea
NT1 tradescantia
NT2 tradescantia albiflora
NT2 tradescantia fluminensis
NT2 tradescantia ohiensis
NT2 tradescantia paludosa
NT2 tradescantia virginiana
NT1 zebrina
NT2 zebrina pendula

COMMENSALS
HN from 1989
rt symbionts

COMMERCIAL BANKS
uf banks, commercial
BT1 banks
BT2 financial institutions
BT3 organizations

COMMERCIAL BEEKEEPING
BT1 beekeeping

COMMERCIAL FARMING
BT1 farming
rt cash crops

COMMERCIAL FOOD SERVICE (AGRICOLA)

COMMERCIAL FOOD SERVICE (AGRICOLA) *cont.*
BT1 food service
NT1 contract food service (agricola)

COMMERCIAL HYBRIDS
HN from 1989
BT1 hybrids

COMMERCIAL SOIL ADDITIVES
BT1 soil amendments
BT2 amendments

comminution of wood
USE **chipping**
OR **wood chips**

COMMIPHORA
BT1 burseraceae
NT1 commiphora africana
NT1 commiphora mukul
NT1 commiphora wightii
rt α-bisabolol

COMMIPHORA AFRICANA
BT1 commiphora
BT2 burseraceae
BT1 gum plants
BT1 medicinal plants

COMMIPHORA MUKUL
BT1 antifungal plants
BT1 commiphora
BT2 burseraceae
BT1 medicinal plants

COMMIPHORA WIGHTII
BT1 commiphora
BT2 burseraceae

COMMISSARIES (AGRICOLA)
BT1 shops
BT2 retail marketing
BT3 marketing channels
BT4 marketing
rt food service

COMMITTEES (AGRICOLA)
NT1 advisory committees (agricola)
rt hearings (agricola)

COMMODITIES
rt agricultural products
rt agricultural trade
rt commodity exchanges
rt commodity markets
rt international agreements
rt market stabilization
rt primary products
rt products
rt world markets

commodity agreements
USE **international agreements**

COMMODITY EXCHANGES
BT1 marketing channels
BT2 marketing
NT1 futures trading
rt commodities
rt trade

COMMODITY MARKETS
uf *markets, commodity*
uf *product markets*
BT1 markets
rt commodities
rt trade
rt wholesale marketing

COMMON AFRO-MAURITIAN ORGANIZATION
uf *ocam*
BT1 international organizations
BT2 organizations

common agricultural policy
USE **cap**

COMMON ALBANIAN
BT1 sheep breeds
BT2 breeds

COMMON COLD
BT1 human diseases
BT2 diseases
BT1 viral diseases
BT2 infectious diseases
BT3 diseases
rt rhinovirus

common grazing
USE **common lands**

COMMON LANDS
uf *common grazing*
BT1 land types
rt coownership
rt land
rt public ownership
rt right of access

common market
USE **european communities**

COMMON MARKETS
BT1 economic unions
NT1 cacm
NT1 caribbean community
NT1 european communities
rt customs unions
rt markets
rt single market

common millet
USE **panicum miliaceum**

commonwealth
USE **commonwealth of nations**

commonwealth agricultural bureaux
USE **cab international**

COMMONWEALTH OF NATIONS
uf *commonwealth*
rt antigua
rt australia
rt bahamas
rt bangladesh
rt barbados
rt belize
rt botswana
rt canada
rt cyprus
rt dominica
rt economic unions
rt fiji
rt gambia
rt ghana
rt grenada
rt guyana
rt india
rt international organizations
rt jamaica
rt kenya
rt kiribati
rt lesotho
rt malawi
rt malaysia
rt maldives
rt malta
rt mauritius
rt nauru
rt new zealand
rt nigeria
rt papua new guinea
rt seychelles
rt sierra leone
rt singapore
rt solomon islands
rt sri lanka
rt st. kitts-nevis
rt st. lucia
rt st. vincent and grenadines
rt swaziland
rt tanzania
rt tonga
rt trinidad and tobago
rt tuvalu
rt uganda
rt uk
rt vanuatu
rt western samoa
rt zambia
rt zimbabwe

COMMUNAL FEEDING
uf *feeding, communal*
BT1 feeding

communal ownership
USE **coownership**

COMMUNES
BT1 rural communities
BT2 communities
NT1 panchayats
NT1 peoples' communes
NT1 ujamaa villages
rt collective farms
rt cooperation
rt kibbutzim
rt socioeconomic organization

communes, peoples
USE **peoples' communes**

COMMUNICABLE DISEASES (AGRICOLA)
BT1 diseases
rt infectious diseases

COMMUNICATION
NT1 aural communication
NT1 communication between animals
NT2 dances
NT2 piping
NT1 cybernetics
NT1 data communication
NT2 telemetry
NT1 mass media
NT2 cinema
NT2 compact discs
NT2 disc recordings
NT2 films
NT2 newspapers
NT2 radio
NT3 educational radio
NT2 television
NT3 educational television
NT2 video recordings
NT3 videodiscs (agricola)
NT3 videotapes (agricola)
NT1 nonverbal communication (agricola)
NT2 body language (agricola)
NT2 sign language (agricola)
NT1 oral communication (agricola)
NT1 telecommunications
NT2 telephones
NT1 verbal communication (agricola)
NT2 public speaking (agricola)
NT2 speech (agricola)
rt communication skills (agricola)
rt communication theory
rt extension
rt information services
rt letters (correspondence) (agricola)
rt radio control
rt railways
rt sounds
rt traffic
rt transport

COMMUNICATION BETWEEN ANIMALS
BT1 animal behaviour
BT2 behaviour
BT1 communication
NT1 dances
NT1 piping
rt pheromones

COMMUNICATION SKILLS (AGRICOLA)
BT1 skills (agricola)
rt communication

COMMUNICATION THEORY
rt communication
rt information science
rt learning
rt theory

COMMUNISM
BT1 economic systems
BT2 systems
BT1 political systems
BT2 politics

COMMUNITIES
NT1 aquatic communities
NT2 plankton
NT3 krill
NT3 phytoplankton
NT3 zooplankton
NT2 pleuston
NT2 seston
NT1 arthropod communities
NT2 insect communities
NT1 biocoenosis
NT1 neighbourhoods
NT1 plant communities
NT2 bog plants
NT2 climax communities
NT2 coastal plant communities
NT2 desert plants
NT2 ecotones
NT2 old fields
NT2 serpentine communities
NT2 weed associations
NT1 rural communities
NT2 communes
NT3 panchayats
NT3 peoples' communes
NT3 ujamaa villages
rt community action
rt community ecology
rt synecology

communities, plant
USE **plant communities**

COMMUNITY ACTION
rt communities
rt community development
rt community involvement (agricola)
rt community programs (agricola)
rt social participation

COMMUNITY CENTERS
BF community centres
NT1 community feeding centers (agricola)

COMMUNITY CENTRES
AF community centers
BT1 cultural facilities
BT1 recreational facilities
rt recreational buildings

COMMUNITY DEVELOPMENT
BT1 rural development
NT1 rural animation
rt animation
rt community action
rt community education
rt extension
rt public services
rt rural communities
rt self help

COMMUNITY ECOLOGY
BT1 ecology
rt communities

COMMUNITY EDUCATION
uf *education, community*
BT1 education
NT1 population education
rt community development
rt non-formal education
rt public services
rt rural communities

COMMUNITY FEEDING CENTERS (AGRICOLA)
uf *congregate meals*
BT1 community centers
rt food service

COMMUNITY FORESTRY
(community-executed tree planting programmes on common or public land with only limited state input)
BT1 forestry

COMMUNITY FORESTRY *cont.*
- **rt** agroforestry
- **rt** farm forestry
- **rt** social forestry

COMMUNITY HEALTH SERVICES (AGRICOLA)
- **BT1** health services
- **BT2** social services
- **BT3** social welfare

COMMUNITY INVOLVEMENT (AGRICOLA)
- **BT1** participation
- **rt** community action
- **rt** social participation

COMMUNITY NUTRITION (AGRICOLA)
- **BT1** nutrition

COMMUNITY PROGRAMS (AGRICOLA)
- **BT1** programs (agricola)
- **rt** community action

community services
- USE **public services**

COMMUTING
- **rt** labour mobility
- **rt** migration

COMOROS
- *uf* *angouan*
- *uf* *great comoro*
- *uf* *moheli*
- **BT1** southern africa
- **BT2** africa south of sahara
- **BT3** africa
- **rt** acp
- **rt** developing countries
- **rt** francophone africa
- **rt** least developed countries

COMOVIRUS GROUP
- **HN** from 1990
- **BT1** plant viruses
- **BT2** plant pathogens
- **BT3** pathogens
- **NT1** andean potato mottle comovirus
- **NT1** bean pod mottle comovirus
- **NT1** bean rugose mosaic comovirus
- **NT1** broad bean stain comovirus
- **NT1** broad bean true mosaic comovirus
- **NT1** cowpea mosaic comovirus
- **NT1** cowpea severe mosaic comovirus
- **NT1** glycine mosaic comovirus
- **NT1** pea mild mosaic comovirus
- **NT1** quail pea mosaic comovirus
- **NT1** radish mosaic comovirus
- **NT1** red clover mottle comovirus
- **NT1** squash mosaic comovirus
- **NT1** ullucus c comovirus

COMPACT CHERNOZEMS
- **BT1** chernozems
- **BT2** soil types (genetic)

COMPACT DISCS
- **HN** from 1989
- **BT1** mass media
- **BT2** communication

COMPACT SOILS
- **BT1** soil types (structural)

COMPACT TRACTORS
- **HN** from 1990
- **BT1** tractors
- **BT2** cross country vehicles
- **BT3** vehicles

COMPACTED DENSITY
- *uf* *density, compacted*
- **BT1** density
- **rt** bulk density
- **rt** compaction
- **rt** compressibility

COMPACTION
- **NT1** soil compaction
- **rt** compacted density
- **rt** compressibility
- **rt** compression
- **rt** compressors
- **rt** contraction
- **rt** trafficability
- **rt** trampling

COMPANIES
- *uf* *corporations*
- **BT1** firms
- **BT2** businesses
- **NT1** multinational corporations
- **NT1** private companies
- **NT1** public companies
- **rt** company law
- **rt** company tax

COMPANION CROPS
- *uf* *nurse crops*
- **rt** crops
- **rt** intercropping
- **rt** intercrops
- **rt** mixed cropping
- **rt** nurse trees
- **rt** underplanting
- **rt** undersowing

COMPANY LAW
- **BT1** law
- **BT2** legal systems
- **rt** companies

COMPANY TAX
- *uf* *tax, company*
- **BT1** direct taxation
- **BT2** taxes
- **BT3** fiscal policy
- **BT4** economic policy
- **BT4** public finance
- **rt** companies

comparative advantage
- USE **terms of trade**

COMPARISONS
- **HN** from 1990

COMPARTMENTS
- **BT1** divisions
- **rt** plantations
- **rt** walls

COMPATIBILITY
- *uf* *sterility and fertility*
- **NT1** histocompatibility
- **NT1** self compatibility
- **rt** acceptability
- **rt** antagonism
- **rt** fertility
- **rt** grafting
- **rt** incompatibility
- **rt** pollination

COMPENSATION
- *uf* *indemnification*
- **NT1** compensatory amounts
- **NT1** workmen's compensation (agricola)
- **rt** agricultural disasters
- **rt** compulsory purchase
- **rt** indivisible estates
- **rt** legal liability
- **rt** valuation

COMPENSATION POINT
- **rt** carbon dioxide
- **rt** light
- **rt** photosynthesis
- **rt** respiration
- **rt** temperature

COMPENSATORY AMOUNTS
- *uf* *mca*
- *uf* *monetary compensatory amounts*
- *uf* *transitional compensatory amounts*
- **BT1** compensation
- **BT1** monetary parity
- **BT2** monetary situation
- **rt** european communities

COMPENSATORY GROWTH
- **HN** from 1989
- **BT1** growth

COMPERIELLA
- **BT1** encyrtidae
- **BT2** hymenoptera
- **NT1** comperiella bifasciata

COMPERIELLA BIFASCIATA
- **BT1** biological control agents
- **BT2** beneficial organisms
- **BT1** comperiella
- **BT2** encyrtidae
- **BT3** hymenoptera

competence, immunological
- USE **immune competence**

COMPETENCY BASED EDUCATION (AGRICOLA)
- **BT1** education
- **rt** academic standards (agricola)
- **rt** behavioral objectives (agricola)

competition
- (consult also the narrower and related terms of the following)
- USE **biological competition**
- OR **competitive ability**
- OR **market competition**
- OR **role conflicts**

competition, plant
- USE **plant competition**

competition, weed
- USE **weed competition**

COMPETITIVE ABILITY
- *uf* *competition*
- **rt** allelopathy
- **rt** colonizing ability
- **rt** ecology

COMPLAINTS
- **BT1** consumer behaviour
- **BT2** economic behaviour
- **BT3** human behaviour
- **BT4** behaviour
- **BT3** social behaviour
- **BT4** behaviour

COMPLEMENT
- *uf* *alexin*
- **BT1** immunological factors
- **rt** complement activation
- **rt** haemolysins
- **rt** immune response

COMPLEMENT ACTIVATION
- **HN** from 1990; previously "complement fixation"
- *uf* *activation, complement*
- *uf* *alternative complement pathway*
- *uf* *classical complement pathway*
- *uf* *complement pathways*
- *uf* *pathways, complement*
- **rt** complement

COMPLEMENT FIXATION TESTS
- **BT1** immunological techniques
- **BT2** techniques
- **BT1** tests

complement pathways
- USE **complement activation**

COMPLEMENTARY GENES
- **BT1** multiple genes
- **BT2** genes

COMPLEMENTARY PROTEINS (AGRICOLA)
- **BT1** proteins
- **BT2** peptides

COMPLEMENTATION
- **BT1** genetics
- **BT2** biology
- **rt** cistrons

COMPLETE FEEDS
- **BT1** feeds
- **rt** feed mixing

complex carbohydrates
- USE **polysaccharides**

COMPLEX LOCI
- **BT1** genes
- **rt** genetics

COMPLICATIONS
- **HN** from 1990
- **BT1** disease course
- **NT1** postoperative complications

COMPONENT ANALYSIS
- **BT1** statistical analysis
- **BT2** data analysis
- **BT2** statistics
- **rt** factorial analysis

COMPONENTS
- *uf* *parts*
- **NT1** axles
- **NT1** bearings
- **NT2** roller bearings
- **NT3** tapered roller bearings
- **NT2** thrust bearings
- **NT1** beaters
- **NT1** belts
- **NT1** blades
- **NT1** booms
- **NT2** spray booms
- **NT1** brakes
- **NT2** air brakes
- **NT2** hydraulic brakes
- **NT1** cabs
- **NT2** safety cabs
- **NT2** suspension cabs
- **NT1** cams
- **NT1** control components
- **NT2** clutches
- **NT3** friction clutches
- **NT3** steering clutches
- **NT1** coulters
- **NT2** disc coulters
- **NT2** skims
- **NT2** suffolk coulters
- **NT1** couplings
- **NT2** automatic couplings
- **NT2** hydraulic couplings
- **NT2** mechanical couplings
- **NT1** crankshafts
- **NT1** cutter bars
- **NT1** cylinders
- **NT1** dampers
- **NT1** dies
- **NT1** distributors
- **NT1** drawbars
- **NT1** drums
- **NT1** electrodes
- **NT2** specific ion electrodes
- **NT1** fans
- **NT2** axial flow fans
- **NT2** centrifugal fans
- **NT2** cross flow fans
- **NT1** feelers
- **NT2** feeler wheels
- **NT1** filter cloths
- **NT1** flails
- **NT1** gears
- **NT2** bevel gears
- **NT2** differential gears
- **NT2** planetary gears
- **NT2** spur gears
- **NT2** worm and wheel gears
- **NT1** governors
- **NT1** ground drive
- **NT2** driven wheels
- **NT1** handles
- **NT1** hitches
- **NT2** automatic hitches
- **NT2** safety hitches
- **NT1** linkages
- **NT1** lugs
- **NT1** motors
- **NT2** electric motors
- **NT2** hydraulic motors
- **NT2** servomotors
- **NT1** mouldboards
- **NT1** nozzles

COMPONENTS *cont.*
NT2 cone nozzles
NT2 fan nozzles
NT2 spinning disc nozzles
NT1 pipes
NT2 concrete pipes
NT2 drain pipes
NT2 plastic pipes
NT3 corrugated plastic pipes
NT1 pistons
NT1 power takeoffs
NT1 propellers
NT1 radiators
NT1 rams (machinery)
NT2 hydraulic rams
NT1 reels
NT1 regulators
NT2 pendulums
NT2 pressure regulators
NT2 vacuum regulators
NT1 rotors
NT1 saw teeth
NT1 scoops
NT1 seats
NT2 infant car seats (agricola)
NT2 reversible seats
NT2 suspension seats
NT1 shafts
NT2 cardan shafts
NT1 shares
NT2 chisel shares
NT2 disc shares
NT2 self sharpening shares
NT1 shock absorbers
NT1 spare parts
NT1 sparking plugs
NT1 spinning discs
NT1 springs
NT1 sprockets
NT1 straw walkers
NT1 structural components
NT2 beams
NT2 bolts
NT2 columns
NT2 decks
NT2 frames
NT2 girders
NT2 struts
NT1 sumps
NT1 superchargers
NT1 suspension systems
NT1 switches
NT2 time switches
NT1 tailboards
NT1 threshing drums
NT1 throttles
NT1 tines
NT2 spring loaded tines
NT2 spring tines
NT1 torque converters
NT1 track links
NT1 track plates
NT1 track rods
NT1 tracks
NT2 grousers
NT2 rubber tracks
NT2 wheel tracks
NT1 traction aids
NT2 ballast
NT3 wheel weights
NT2 strakes
NT2 tyre girdles
NT1 transmissions
NT2 automatic transmissions
NT2 differential transmissions
NT2 hydraulic transmissions
NT2 hydromechanical transmissions
NT2 hydrostatic transmissions
NT2 synchromesh transmissions
NT1 tyres
NT2 balloon tyres
NT2 crossply tyres
NT2 dual tyres
NT2 radial tyres
NT2 rigid tyres
NT1 valves
NT1 vanes
NT1 ventilators
NT2 vents

COMPONENTS *cont.*
NT1 weights
NT2 wheel weights
NT1 wheels
NT2 cage wheels
NT2 depth wheels
NT2 driven wheels
NT2 press wheels
NT2 skeleton wheels
NT2 tandem wheels
rt engines
rt equipment
rt instruments
rt knives
rt machinery
rt tools

COMPOSITAE
uf *asteraceae*
NT1 acanthospermum
NT2 acanthospermum australe
NT2 acanthospermum glabratum
NT2 acanthospermum hispidum
NT1 achillea
NT2 achillea ageratum
NT2 achillea asiatica
NT2 achillea biebersteinii
NT2 achillea cartilaginea
NT2 achillea eriophora
NT2 achillea filipendulina
NT2 achillea kitaibeliana
NT2 achillea millefolium
NT2 achillea ptarmica
NT2 achillea santolina
NT2 achillea setacea
NT2 achillea vermicularis
NT1 acroptilon
NT2 acroptilon repens
NT1 adenocaulon
NT2 adenocaulon himalaicum
NT1 adenostemma
NT2 adenostemma lavenia
NT1 ageratina
NT2 ageratina riparia
NT1 ageratum
NT2 ageratum conyzoides
NT2 ageratum houstonianum
NT1 amberboa
NT2 amberboa moschata
NT1 ambrosia
NT2 ambrosia ambrosioides
NT2 ambrosia artemisiifolia
NT2 ambrosia bidentata
NT2 ambrosia chenopodiifolia
NT2 ambrosia coronopifolia
NT2 ambrosia deltoidea
NT2 ambrosia dumosa
NT2 ambrosia eriocentra
NT2 ambrosia ilicifolia
NT2 ambrosia psilostachya
NT2 ambrosia pumila
NT2 ambrosia trifida
NT1 anaphalis
NT2 anaphalis contorta
NT2 anaphalis morrisonicola
NT1 antennaria
NT2 antennaria dioica
NT2 antennaria microphylla
NT1 anthemis
NT2 anthemis arvensis
NT2 anthemis austriaca
NT2 anthemis cotula
NT2 anthemis jailensis
NT2 anthemis pseudocotula
NT2 anthemis tinctoria
NT1 anvillea
NT2 anvillea garcini
NT1 arctium
NT2 arctium lappa
NT1 arctotheca
NT2 arctotheca calendula
NT1 arctotis
NT2 arctotis stoechadifolia
NT1 argyroxiphium
NT2 argyroxiphium kauense
NT2 argyroxiphium sandwicence
NT1 arnica
NT2 arnica amplexicaulis
NT2 arnica chamissonis

COMPOSITAE *cont.*
NT2 arnica foliosa
NT2 arnica lanceolata
NT2 arnica longifolia
NT2 arnica montana
NT2 arnica parryi
NT2 arnica sachalinensis
NT1 artemisia
NT2 artemisia abrotanum
NT2 artemisia absinthium
NT2 artemisia albicerata
NT2 artemisia annua
NT2 artemisia apiacea
NT2 artemisia arbuscula
NT2 artemisia armeniaca
NT2 artemisia aschurbajevii
NT2 artemisia austriaca
NT2 artemisia balchanorum
NT2 artemisia barrelieri
NT2 artemisia californica
NT2 artemisia campestris
NT2 artemisia cana
NT2 artemisia canariensis
NT2 artemisia capillaris
NT2 artemisia compacta
NT2 artemisia diffusa
NT2 artemisia dracunculus
NT2 artemisia filifolia
NT2 artemisia fragrans
NT2 artemisia frigida
NT2 artemisia fukudo
NT2 artemisia heptapotamica
NT2 artemisia herba-alba
NT2 artemisia judaica
NT2 artemisia klotzchiana
NT2 artemisia lercheana
NT2 artemisia leucodes
NT2 artemisia longiloba
NT2 artemisia ludoviciana
NT2 artemisia macrocephala
NT2 artemisia maritima
NT2 artemisia monosperma
NT2 artemisia mutellina
NT2 artemisia pallens
NT2 artemisia pamirica
NT2 artemisia pauciflora
NT2 artemisia pontica
NT2 artemisia princeps
NT2 artemisia pygmaea
NT2 artemisia rutifolia
NT2 artemisia santonina
NT2 artemisia scoparia
NT2 artemisia scopulorum
NT2 artemisia sericea
NT2 artemisia seriphidium
NT2 artemisia spinescens
NT2 artemisia taurica
NT2 artemisia terrae-albae
NT2 artemisia tilesii
NT2 artemisia tridentata
NT2 artemisia tripartita
NT2 artemisia vestita
NT2 artemisia vulgaris
NT2 artemisia xanthophora
NT2 artemisia xerophytica
NT1 aster
NT2 aster alpinus
NT2 aster dumosus
NT2 aster ericoides
NT2 aster lateriflorus
NT2 aster linosyris
NT2 aster novae-angliae
NT2 aster novi-belgii
NT2 aster pilosus
NT2 aster scaber
NT2 aster sibiricus
NT2 aster spathulifolius
NT2 aster spinosus
NT2 aster squamatus
NT2 aster subulatus
NT2 aster tataricus
NT2 aster tripolium
NT2 aster umbellatus
NT2 aster vimineus
NT1 atractylodes
NT2 atractylodes japonica
NT2 atractylodes lancea
NT1 baccharis
NT2 baccharis articulata
NT2 baccharis cordifolia
NT2 baccharis crispa

COMPOSITAE *cont.*
NT2 baccharis dracunculifolia
NT2 baccharis halimifolia
NT2 baccharis megapotamica
NT2 baccharis pilularis
NT2 baccharis salicina
NT2 baccharis tricuneata
NT1 baileya
NT2 baileya multiradiata
NT2 baileya pauciradiata
NT1 balduina
NT2 balduina angustifolia
NT1 balsamorhiza
NT2 balsamorhiza careyana
NT1 baltimora
NT2 baltimora recta
NT1 bellis
NT2 bellis perennis
NT1 bidens
NT2 bidens bipinnata
NT2 bidens cernua
NT2 bidens chinensis
NT2 bidens coronala
NT2 bidens frondosa
NT2 bidens pilosa
NT2 bidens tripartita
NT1 blainvillea
NT2 blainvillea latifolia
NT1 blumea
NT2 blumea balsamifera
NT2 blumea eriantha
NT2 blumea lacera
NT2 blumea malcolmii
NT2 blumea membranacea
NT2 blumea wightiana
NT1 brachylaena
NT2 brachylaena hutchinsii
NT1 calendula
NT2 calendula arvensis
NT2 calendula officinalis
NT1 callilepis
NT2 callilepis laureola
NT1 callistephus
NT2 callistephus chinensis
NT1 carduncellus
NT2 carduncellus monspeliensium
NT1 carduus
NT2 carduus acanthoides
NT2 carduus crispus
NT2 carduus macrocephalus
NT2 carduus nutans
NT2 carduus nutans var. leiophyllus
NT2 carduus pycnocephalus
NT2 carduus tenuiflorus
NT2 carduus thoermeri
NT1 carlina
NT2 carlina acanthifolia
NT2 carlina acaulis
NT2 carlina vulgaris
NT1 carpesium
NT2 carpesium abrotanoides
NT1 carthamus
NT2 carthamus lanatus
NT2 carthamus oxyacantha
NT2 carthamus tinctorius
NT1 cassinia
NT2 cassinia arcuata
NT2 cassinia fulvida
NT2 cassinia leptophylla
NT1 catananche
NT2 catananche caerulea
NT1 centaurea
NT2 centaurea americana
NT2 centaurea aspera
NT2 centaurea australis
NT2 centaurea calcitrapa
NT2 centaurea canariensis
NT2 centaurea cyanus
NT2 centaurea depressa
NT2 centaurea diffusa
NT2 centaurea iberica
NT2 centaurea lugdunensis
NT2 centaurea maculosa
NT2 centaurea melitensis
NT2 centaurea montana
NT2 centaurea picris
NT2 centaurea repens
NT2 centaurea scabiosa
NT2 centaurea solstitialis

COMPOSITAE *cont.*
NT2 centaurea squarrosa
NT2 centaurea webbiana
NT1 centratherum
NT2 centratherum punctatum
NT1 chamaemelum
NT2 chamaemelum fuscatum
NT2 chamaemelum nobile
NT1 chamomilla
NT2 chamomilla recutita
NT2 chamomilla suaveolens
NT1 chiliotrichum
NT1 chondrilla
NT2 chondrilla juncea
NT1 chromolaena
NT1 chrysanthemoides
NT2 chrysanthemoides moniliferum
NT1 chrysanthemum
NT2 chrysanthemum alpinum
NT2 chrysanthemum carinatum
NT2 chrysanthemum coronarium
NT2 chrysanthemum frutescens
NT2 chrysanthemum parthenifolium
NT2 chrysanthemum prealtum
NT2 chrysanthemum segetum
NT1 chrysothamnus
NT2 chrysothamnus nauseosus
NT2 chrysothamnus parryi
NT2 chrysothamnus viscidiflorus
NT1 chuquiraga
NT2 chuquiraga chontalensis
NT1 cichorium
NT2 cichorium endivia
NT2 cichorium intybus
NT2 cichorium pumilum
NT1 cirsium
NT2 cirsium acaule
NT2 cirsium arvense
NT2 cirsium canum
NT2 cirsium erisithales
NT2 cirsium heterophyllum
NT2 cirsium japonicum
NT2 cirsium oleraceum
NT2 cirsium palustre
NT2 cirsium setosum
NT2 cirsium undulatum
NT2 cirsium vulgare
NT1 cnicus
NT2 cnicus benedictus
NT1 conyza
NT2 conyza aegyptiaca
NT2 conyza albida
NT2 conyza bilbaoana
NT2 conyza bonariensis
NT2 conyza canadensis
NT2 conyza dioscoridis
NT2 conyza linifolia
NT2 conyza parva
NT2 conyza stricta
NT1 coreopsis
NT2 coreopsis auriculata
NT2 coreopsis basalis
NT2 coreopsis grandiflora
NT2 coreopsis nuecensis
NT2 coreopsis saxicola
NT2 coreopsis tinctoria
NT2 coreopsis tripteris
NT1 cosmos
NT2 cosmos bipinnatus
NT1 cotula
NT2 cotula cinerea
NT1 crassocephalum
NT2 crassocephalum crepidioides
NT1 crepis
NT2 crepis rhoeadifolia
NT2 crepis rubra
NT2 crepis tectorum
NT1 crupina
NT2 crupina vulgaris
NT1 cryptostemma
NT2 cryptostemma calendula
NT1 cynara
NT2 cynara cardunculus
NT2 cynara scolymus
NT1 dahlia
NT2 dahlia pinnata

COMPOSITAE *cont.*
NT1 dendranthema
NT2 dendranthema indicum
NT2 dendranthema morifolium
NT1 dimorphotheca
NT2 dimorphotheca sinuata
NT1 doronicum
NT2 doronicum columnae
NT2 doronicum macrophyllum
NT2 doronicum oblongifolium
NT1 echinacea
NT2 echinacea angustifolia
NT2 echinacea purpurea
NT1 echinops
NT2 echinops echinatus
NT2 echinops ellenbecki
NT2 echinops latifolia
NT2 echinops ritro
NT2 echinops sphaerocephalus
NT2 echinops spinosus
NT1 eclipta
NT2 eclipta alba
NT2 eclipta prostrata
NT1 elephantopus
NT2 elephantopus mollis
NT2 elephantopus scaber
NT2 elephantopus tomentosus
NT1 eleutheranthera
NT2 eleutheranthera ruderalis
NT1 emilia
NT2 emilia flammea
NT2 emilia javanica
NT2 emilia sonchifolia
NT1 enydra
NT2 enydra fluctuans
NT1 erechtites
NT2 erechtites hieracifolia
NT1 eremanthus
NT2 eremanthus elaeagnus
NT2 eremanthus goyazensis
NT1 ericameria
NT2 ericameria austrotexana
NT1 erigeron
NT2 erigeron annuus
NT2 erigeron linifolius
NT2 erigeron sumatrensis
NT1 eriocephalus
NT2 eriocephalus punctulatus
NT1 eriophyllum
NT2 eriophyllum confertiflorum
NT1 eupatorium
NT2 eupatorium africanum
NT2 eupatorium altissimum
NT2 eupatorium anomalum
NT2 eupatorium ayapana
NT2 eupatorium cannabinum
NT2 eupatorium capillifolium
NT2 eupatorium coelestinum
NT2 eupatorium compositifolium
NT2 eupatorium correlliorum
NT2 eupatorium dubium
NT2 eupatorium formosanum
NT2 eupatorium hyssopifolium
NT2 eupatorium inulaefolium
NT2 eupatorium japonicum
NT2 eupatorium laevigatum
NT2 eupatorium ligustrinum
NT2 eupatorium mohrii
NT2 eupatorium odoratum
NT2 eupatorium perfoliatum
NT2 eupatorium pilosum
NT2 eupatorium purpureum
NT2 eupatorium repandum
NT2 eupatorium riparium
NT2 eupatorium rotundifolium
NT2 eupatorium rugosum
NT2 eupatorium semiserratum
NT2 eupatorium stoechadosmum
NT2 eupatorium trapezoideum
NT1 fabiana
NT2 fabiana imbricata
NT1 felicia
NT2 felicia echinata
NT1 filaginella
NT2 filaginella uliginosa
NT1 flaveria
NT2 flaveria bidentis
NT1 flourensia
NT2 flourensia annua

COMPOSITAE *cont.*
NT2 flourensia oolepis
NT1 franseria
NT2 franseria acanthicarpa
NT2 franseria deltoidea
NT2 franseria dumosa
NT2 franseria tenuifolia
NT2 franseria tomentosa
NT1 gaillardia
NT2 gaillardia pulchella
NT1 galinsoga
NT2 galinsoga ciliata
NT2 galinsoga parviflora
NT2 galinsoga quadriradiata
NT1 gamolepis
NT2 gamolepis chrysanthemoides
NT1 gazania
NT2 gazania rigens
NT1 geigeria
NT1 gerbera
NT2 gerbera jamesonii
NT1 glossocardia
NT2 glossocardia bosvallia
NT1 gnaphalium
NT2 gnaphalium obtusifolium
NT2 gnaphalium pellitum
NT2 gnaphalium purpureum
NT1 gnaphalium obtusifolium
NT1 grangea
NT2 grangea maderaspatana
NT1 grindelia
NT2 grindelia aphanactis
NT2 grindelia integrifolia
NT2 grindelia robusta
NT2 grindelia squarrosa
NT1 grossheimia
NT2 grossheimia macrocephala
NT1 guizotia
NT2 guizotia abyssinica
NT1 gutierrezia
NT2 gutierrezia dracunculoides
NT2 gutierrezia lucida
NT2 gutierrezia sarothrae
NT1 gynura
NT2 gynura crepidioides
NT2 gynura procumbens
NT1 haplopappus
NT2 haplopappus ciliatus
NT2 haplopappus helix
NT2 haplopappus pinifolius
NT2 haplopappus tenuisectus
NT1 helenium
NT2 helenium amarum
NT2 helenium aromaticum
NT2 helenium autumnale
NT2 helenium hoopesii
NT2 helenium microcephalum
NT2 helenium puberulum
NT1 helianthus
NT2 helianthus annuus
NT2 helianthus annuus var. ruderalis
NT2 helianthus argophyllus
NT2 helianthus bolanderi
NT2 helianthus ciliaris
NT2 helianthus debilis
NT2 helianthus exilis
NT2 helianthus petiolaris
NT2 helianthus pumilus
NT2 helianthus scaberrimus
NT2 helianthus tuberosus
NT1 helichrysum
NT2 helichrysum arenarium
NT2 helichrysum bracteatum
NT2 helichrysum italicum
NT2 helichrysum plicatum
NT1 heliopsis
NT2 heliopsis helianthoides
NT1 helipterum
NT1 helminthia
NT1 hertia
NT1 heteropappus
NT1 heterotheca
NT2 heterotheca grandiflora
NT2 heterotheca ruthii
NT2 heterotheca subaxillaris
NT1 hieracium
NT2 hieracium aurantiacum
NT2 hieracium florentinum
NT2 hieracium floribundum

COMPOSITAE *cont.*
NT2 hieracium murorum
NT2 hieracium pilosella
NT2 hieracium piloselloides
NT2 hieracium pratense
NT1 holocarpha
NT1 hymenoxys
NT2 hymenoxys odorata
NT1 hypochoeris
NT2 hypochoeris glabra
NT2 hypochoeris radicata
NT1 inula
NT2 inula bifrons
NT2 inula britannica
NT2 inula cappa
NT2 inula conyza
NT2 inula grandis
NT2 inula helenium
NT2 inula magnifica
NT2 inula obtusifolia
NT2 inula racemosa
NT2 inula royleana
NT2 inula salicina
NT2 inula spiraeifolia
NT2 inula viscosa
NT1 isocoma
NT2 isocoma coronopifolia
NT2 isocoma drummondii
NT2 isocoma wrightii
NT1 iva
NT2 iva axillaris
NT2 iva xanthiifolia
NT1 jasonia
NT2 jasonia glutinosa
NT1 jurinea
NT2 jurinea alata
NT2 jurinea macrocephala
NT1 lactuca
NT2 lactuca indica
NT2 lactuca orientalis
NT2 lactuca sativa
NT2 lactuca serriola
NT2 lactuca tatarica
NT2 lactuca virosa
NT1 lagascea
NT2 lagascea mollis
NT1 laggera
NT2 laggera aurita
NT1 lapsana
NT2 lapsana apogonoides
NT2 lapsana communis
NT1 launaea
NT1 layia
NT2 layia platyglossa
NT1 leontodon
NT2 leontodon autumnalis
NT2 leontodon hispidus
NT1 leontopodium
NT2 leontopodium alpinum
NT2 leontopodium leontopodioides
NT2 leontopodium souliei
NT1 lepidospartum
NT2 lepidospartum latisquamum
NT1 leucanthemum
NT2 leucanthemum maximum
NT2 leucanthemum vulgare
NT1 leuzea
NT2 leuzea carthamoides
NT2 leuzea rhapontica
NT1 liatris
NT2 liatris pycnostachya
NT2 liatris spicata
NT1 ligularia
NT2 ligularia hiberniflora
NT2 ligularia japonica
NT2 ligularia macrophylla
NT2 ligularia thyrsoidea
NT2 ligularia tussilaginea
NT1 lonas
NT2 lonas annua
NT1 lychnophora
NT2 lychnophora affinis
NT1 macowania
NT2 macowania corymbosa
NT2 macowania glandulosa
NT2 macowania hamata
NT1 madia
NT2 madia glomerata
NT1 matricaria

COMPOSITAE *cont.*
NT2 matricaria perforata
NT1 megalodonta
NT2 megalodonta beckii
NT1 melampodium
NT2 melampodium hispidum
NT1 mikania
NT2 mikania cordata
NT2 mikania micrantha
NT2 mikania oblongifolia
NT2 mikania scandens
NT1 montanoa
NT2 montanoa frutescens
NT1 nassauvia
NT1 notobasis
NT2 notobasis syriaca
NT1 olearia
NT2 olearia macrodonta
NT2 olearia muelleri
NT1 onopordum
NT2 onopordum acanthium
NT2 onopordum alexandrinum
NT2 onopordum illyricum
NT1 osteospermum
NT2 osteospermum ecklonis
NT2 osteospermum fruticosum
NT1 otanthus
NT2 otanthus maritimus
NT1 parthenium
NT2 parthenium argentatum
NT2 parthenium hysterophorus
NT2 parthenium incanum
NT1 petasites
NT2 petasites albus
NT2 petasites hybridus
NT2 petasites japonicus
NT2 petasites paradoxus
NT1 phagnalon
NT2 phagnalon rupestra
NT1 picris
NT2 picris echioides
NT2 picris hieracioides
NT1 piptocarpha
NT2 piptocarpha chontalensis
NT1 piqueria
NT2 piqueria trinervia
NT1 pluchea
NT2 pluchea chingoyo
NT2 pluchea sagittalis
NT1 polymnia
NT2 polymnia sonchifolia
NT1 porophyllum
NT2 porophyllum lanceolatum
NT1 pseudelephantopus
NT2 pseudelephantopus spicatus
NT1 psiadia
NT2 psiadia salviifolia
NT1 psila (compositae)
NT2 psila spartioides
NT1 psilostrophe
NT2 psilostrophe villosa
NT1 pterocaulon
NT2 pterocaulon virgatum
NT1 pulicaria
NT2 pulicaria crispa
NT1 pyrrhopappus
NT1 rhaponticum
NT2 rhaponticum carthamoides
NT2 rhaponticum integrifolium
NT1 rudbeckia
NT2 rudbeckia hirta
NT2 rudbeckia laciniata
NT2 rudbeckia occidentalis
NT1 santolina
NT2 santolina chamaecyparissus
NT2 santolina rosmarinifolia
NT1 sanvitalia
NT2 sanvitalia procumbens
NT1 saussurea
NT2 saussurea elegans
NT2 saussurea lappa
NT1 scolymus
NT2 scolymus hispanicus
NT2 scolymus maculatus
NT1 scorzonera
NT2 scorzonera hispanica
NT1 senecio
NT2 senecio adonidifolius
NT2 senecio aquaticus

COMPOSITAE *cont.*
NT2 senecio articulatus
NT2 senecio bicolor
NT2 senecio bipinnatisectus
NT2 senecio congestus
NT2 senecio cruentus
NT2 senecio doronicum
NT2 senecio douglasii var. longilobus
NT2 senecio elegans
NT2 senecio erucifolius
NT2 senecio glabellus
NT2 senecio greyi
NT2 senecio grisebachii
NT2 senecio hybridus
NT2 senecio jacobaea
NT2 senecio lautus
NT2 senecio laxifolius
NT2 senecio longilobus
NT2 senecio nemorensis
NT2 senecio othonnae
NT2 senecio paludaffinis
NT2 senecio pampeanus
NT2 senecio platyphylloides
NT2 senecio procerus
NT2 senecio rhombifolius
NT2 senecio riddellii
NT2 senecio rowleyanus
NT2 senecio serpens
NT2 senecio spathulatus
NT2 senecio squalidus
NT2 senecio sylvaticus
NT2 senecio tweedei
NT2 senecio vernalis
NT2 senecio viscosus
NT2 senecio vulgaris
NT2 senecio vulgaris f. radiatus
NT2 senecio vulgaris f. vulgaris
NT1 serratula
NT2 serratula sogdiana
NT1 sigesbeckia
NT2 sigesbeckia orientalis
NT2 sigesbeckia pubescens
NT1 silphium
NT2 silphium perfoliatum
NT1 silybum
NT2 silybum eburneum
NT2 silybum marianum
NT1 solidago
NT2 solidago altissima
NT2 solidago canadensis
NT2 solidago graminifolia
NT2 solidago nemoralis
NT2 solidago odora
NT2 solidago rigida
NT2 solidago rugosa
NT2 solidago virgaurea
NT1 soliva
NT2 soliva anthemifolia
NT2 soliva pterosperma
NT2 soliva sessilis
NT2 soliva valdiviana
NT1 sonchus
NT2 sonchus arvensis
NT2 sonchus asper
NT2 sonchus hierrensis
NT2 sonchus jacquini
NT2 sonchus oleraceus
NT2 sonchus palustris
NT2 sonchus tuberifer
NT1 spilanthes
NT2 spilanthes urens
NT1 stevia
NT2 stevia purpurea
NT2 stevia rebaudiana
NT1 stokesia
NT2 stokesia laevis
NT1 synedrella
NT2 synedrella nodiflora
NT1 tagetes
NT2 tagetes erecta
NT2 tagetes florida
NT2 tagetes lucida
NT2 tagetes minuta
NT2 tagetes patula
NT2 tagetes tenuifolia
NT1 tanacetum
NT2 tanacetum balsamita
NT2 tanacetum boreale
NT2 tanacetum cinerariifolium
NT2 tanacetum coccineum

COMPOSITAE *cont.*
NT2 tanacetum parthenifolium
NT2 tanacetum parthenium
NT2 tanacetum pseudoachillea
NT2 tanacetum vulgare
NT1 taraxacum
NT2 taraxacum cordatum
NT2 taraxacum kok-saghyz
NT2 taraxacum officinale
NT1 tarchonanthus
NT2 tarchonanthus camphoratus
NT1 tessaria
NT2 tessaria integrifolia
NT1 tetragonotheca
NT2 tetragonotheca helianthoides
NT2 tetragonotheca ludoviciana
NT2 tetragonotheca repanda
NT2 tetragonotheca texana
NT1 tithonia
NT2 tithonia diversifolia
NT2 tithonia rotundifolia
NT1 tragopogon
NT2 tragopogon porrifolius
NT1 tricholepis
NT2 tricholepis glaberrima
NT1 tridax
NT2 tridax procumbens
NT1 tripleurospermum
NT1 tussilago
NT2 tussilago farfara
NT1 ursinia
NT2 ursinia anthemoides
NT2 ursinia chrysanthemoides
NT1 varthemia
NT2 varthemia candicans
NT1 venidium
NT1 verbesina
NT2 verbesina encelioides
NT1 vernonia
NT2 vernonia altissima
NT2 vernonia amygdalina
NT2 vernonia anthelmintica
NT2 vernonia baldwinii
NT2 vernonia cinerea
NT2 vernonia flexuosa
NT2 vernonia nudiflora
NT2 vernonia patens
NT2 vernonia pectoralis
NT2 vernonia polyanthes
NT2 vernonia saltensis
NT2 vernonia scorpioides
NT2 vernonia trifloculosa
NT2 vernonia wessiniana
NT1 vittadinia
NT2 vittadinia australis
NT1 wedelia
NT2 wedelia asperrima
NT2 wedelia glauca
NT2 wedelia scaberrima
NT2 wedelia trilobata
NT1 wyethia
NT1 xanthium
NT2 xanthium californicum
NT2 xanthium cavanillesii
NT2 xanthium chinense
NT2 xanthium italicum
NT2 xanthium pensylvanicum
NT2 xanthium pungens
NT2 xanthium spinosum
NT2 xanthium strumarium
NT1 xanthocephalum
NT1 zaluzania
NT2 zaluzania robinsonii
NT1 zinnia

COMPOSITE BOARDS
BT1 panels
BT2 building materials
BT3 materials
rt plywood

COMPOSITE VARIETIES
BT1 varieties
NT1 multiline varieties
rt genotype mixtures

COMPOSITE WOOD ASSEMBLIES
rt beams
rt blockboard
rt decks

COMPOSITE WOOD ASSEMBLIES *cont.*
rt wood

COMPOSITION
(not normally used as a primary or leading descriptor)
NT1 blood composition
NT2 blood chemistry
NT3 alkali reserve
NT3 blood lipids
NT3 blood protein
NT3 blood sugar
NT3 erythrocyte potassium types
NT1 botanical composition
NT1 catch composition
NT1 chemical composition
NT2 amino nitrogen
NT2 ammonium nitrogen
NT2 dissolved oxygen
NT2 free amino acids
NT2 inorganic phosphorus
NT2 nitrate nitrogen
NT2 nitrogen content
NT2 nonprotein nitrogen
NT1 dry matter
NT1 egg composition
NT2 egg protein
NT2 egg yolk composition
NT1 faeces composition
NT1 fibre content
NT1 food composition
NT1 grease content
NT1 meat composition
NT2 lean
NT2 leanness
NT1 milk composition
NT2 milk fat percentage
NT2 milk protein percentage
NT2 solids not fat
NT2 total solids
NT1 mineral content
NT1 moisture content
NT2 equilibrium moisture content
NT2 seed moisture
NT1 nutrient content
NT1 plant composition
NT1 protein composition
NT1 protein content
NT2 protein status
NT1 vitamin content
NT1 water content
NT2 equilibrium moisture content
NT2 soil water content
rt body composition
rt constituents
rt dissociation
rt feed composition tables
rt normal values
rt plant analysis

COMPOSTING
BT1 processing
NT1 vermicomposting
rt composts
rt waste disposal
rt waste treatment

COMPOSTS
BT1 manures
BT2 organic amendments
BT3 soil amendments
BT4 amendments
NT1 bark compost
NT1 leaf mould
NT1 mushroom compost
NT1 refuse compost
rt bark
rt composting
rt growing media
rt straw disposal

COMPOUND EYES
BT1 eyes
BT2 sense organs
BT3 body parts

COMPOUND FEEDS
BT1 feeds

COMPOUND FERTILIZERS
BT1 fertilizers
NT1 nitrogen-phosphorus fertilizers
NT2 ammonium phosphates
NT3 ammonium metaphosphates
NT3 ammonium polyphosphates
NT4 ammonium polyphosphate sulfate
NT4 ammonium pyrophosphate
NT4 ammonium tripolyphosphate
NT4 diammonium pyrophosphate
NT4 tetraammonium pyrophosphate
NT4 triammonium pyrophosphate
NT4 urea ammonium polyphosphate
NT3 diammonium phosphate
NT3 magnesium ammonium phosphate
NT3 monoammonium phosphate
NT3 triammonium phosphate
NT3 urea ammonium phosphate
NT3 urea ammonium pyrophosphate
NT2 nitroammophoska
NT2 nitrophosphates
NT1 nitrogen-potassium fertilizers
NT2 nitrokalimag
NT2 potassium nitrate
NT1 npk fertilizers
NT2 urea potassium pyrophosphate
NT1 phosphorus-potassium fertilizers
NT2 potassium phosphates
NT3 dipotassium hydrogen phosphate
NT3 potassium dihydrogen phosphate
NT3 potassium metaphosphate
NT3 potassium polyphosphates
NT4 potassium dihydrogen triphosphate
NT4 potassium hydrogen tripolyphosphates
NT4 potassium pyrophosphate
NT4 urea potassium pyrophosphate

COMPOUND HIVES
BT1 hives
rt multiple-queen colonies

COMPREHENSIVE HOMEOWNERS' INSURANCE (AGRICOLA)
BT1 homeowners' insurance (agricola)
BT2 insurance

COMPRESSED WOOD
BT1 improved wood
BT2 wood
rt compression
rt wood technology

COMPRESSIBILITY
BT1 mechanical properties
BT2 properties
rt compacted density
rt compaction
rt compression
rt compressors
rt pressure
rt pressure treatment

COMPRESSION
rt compaction
rt compressed wood
rt compressibility

COMPRESSION *cont.*
rt compression ratio
rt compressive strength
rt compressors
rt contraction
rt reaction wood

COMPRESSION DRYING
HN from 1990
BT1 drying
BT2 dehydration
BT3 processing

COMPRESSION RATIO
BT1 ratios
rt compression
rt engines

compression strength
USE **compressive strength**

compression wood
USE **reaction wood**

COMPRESSIONAL WAVE VELOCITY
BT1 acoustic properties
BT2 physical properties
BT3 properties
BT1 velocity

COMPRESSIVE STRENGTH
uf compression strength
uf crushing strength
uf strength, compressive
BT1 strength
BT2 mechanical properties
BT3 properties
rt compression

COMPRESSORS
BT1 machinery
rt compaction
rt compressibility
rt compression
rt refrigeration
rt superchargers

COMPSILURA
BT1 tachinidae
BT2 diptera
NT1 compsilura concinnata

COMPSILURA CONCINNATA
BT1 biological control agents
BT2 beneficial organisms
BT1 compsilura
BT2 tachinidae
BT3 diptera

COMPTONIA
BT1 myricaceae
NT1 comptonia asplenifolia
NT1 comptonia peregrina

COMPTONIA ASPLENIFOLIA
BT1 comptonia
BT2 myricaceae

COMPTONIA PEREGRINA
BT1 comptonia
BT2 myricaceae
BT1 medicinal plants

COMPULSIONS (AGRICOLA)
BT1 abnormal behavior
BT2 behavior
NT1 compulsive eating (agricola)

COMPULSIVE EATING (AGRICOLA)
BT1 appetite disorders
BT2 digestive disorders
BT3 functional disorders
BT4 animal disorders
BT5 disorders
BT1 compulsions (agricola)
BT2 abnormal behavior
BT3 behavior
rt bulimia

compulsory labour
USE **forced labour**

COMPULSORY PURCHASE
uf expropriation of forests and land
BT1 land transfers
BT2 land ownership
BT3 ownership
BT4 tenure systems
BT1 purchasing
BT2 acquisition of ownership
BT3 acquisition
rt compensation
rt ownership limitations
rt valuation

COMPUTED TOMOGRAPHY
HN from 1989
BT1 tomography
BT2 radiography
BT3 biological techniques
BT4 techniques
BT3 diagnostic techniques
BT4 techniques

COMPUTER ANALYSIS
rt algorithms
rt analysis
rt calculation
rt computer hardware
rt computer programming
rt computer software
rt computer techniques
rt computers
rt statistical analysis

computer applications
USE **computer techniques**

COMPUTER ASSISTED INSTRUCTION (AGRICOLA)
rt computers
rt programmed learning
rt teaching methods

COMPUTER GAMES
BT1 indoor games
BT2 games
BT2 indoor recreation
BT3 recreation
rt mechanized recreation
rt play

COMPUTER GRAPHICS
BT1 computer techniques
BT2 techniques
rt computer software
rt computers
rt design
rt graphs

COMPUTER HARDWARE
uf terminals
BT1 computers
NT1 microcomputers
NT1 minicomputers
rt computer analysis

computer mapping
USE **computer techniques**
AND **mapping**

COMPUTER PROGRAMMING
uf programming, computer
BT1 programming
BT2 optimization methods
BT3 optimization
rt computer analysis
rt computer software
rt computers
rt systems analysis

computer programs
USE **computer software**

COMPUTER SIMULATION
BT1 simulation
rt computers
rt simulation models

COMPUTER SOFTWARE
uf computer programs
uf programs
BT1 computers
NT1 expert systems
rt computer analysis

COMPUTER SOFTWARE *cont.*
rt computer graphics
rt computer programming
rt computer techniques

COMPUTER TECHNIQUES
uf computer applications
ufa computer mapping
BT1 techniques
NT1 computer graphics
rt animal testing alternatives
rt computer analysis
rt computer software
rt computers

COMPUTERS
NT1 computer hardware
NT2 microcomputers
NT2 minicomputers
NT1 computer software
NT2 expert systems
rt analogues
rt automation
rt calculation
rt computer analysis
rt computer assisted instruction (agricola)
rt computer graphics
rt computer programming
rt computer simulation
rt computer techniques
rt data processing
rt electronics
rt information systems
rt microprocessors

COMTE CHEESE
HN from 1989
BT1 cheeses
BT2 milk products
BT3 products

COMTOIS
BT1 horse breeds
BT2 breeds

CONALBUMIN
BT1 egg proteins
BT2 animal proteins
BT3 proteins
BT4 peptides
BT1 siderophilins
BT2 glycoproteins
BT3 proteins
BT4 peptides
rt egg albumen

CONANDRON
BT1 gesneriaceae
NT1 conandron ramondioides

CONANDRON RAMONDIOIDES
BT1 conandron
BT2 gesneriaceae

CONAZOLE FUNGICIDES
BT1 azoles
BT2 heterocyclic nitrogen compounds
BT3 organic nitrogen compounds
BT1 fungicides
BT2 pesticides
NT1 diclobutrazol
NT1 etaconazole
NT1 imazalil
NT1 penconazole
NT1 prochloraz
NT1 propiconazole
NT1 triadimefon
NT1 triadimenol
rt imidazole fungicides
rt triazole fungicides

CONCANAVALIN A
BT1 lipoproteins
BT2 proteins
BT3 peptides
BT1 phytohaemagglutinins
BT2 lectins
BT3 agglutinins
BT4 antibodies
BT5 immunoglobulins

CONCANAVALIN A *cont.*
BT6 glycoproteins
BT7 proteins
BT6 immunological factors
BT3 mitogens
BT3 plant proteins
BT4 proteins
BT5 peptides
BT2 phytotoxins
BT3 toxins

CONCAVES
BT1 combine harvesters
BT2 harvesters
BT3 farm machinery
BT4 machinery
BT1 threshing machines
BT2 farm machinery
BT3 machinery
rt cylinders
rt threshing
rt threshing drums

CONCENTRATED MILK
uf milk, concentrated
BT1 milk products
BT2 products

CONCENTRATED SUPERPHOSPHATE
BT1 superphosphates
BT2 phosphorus fertilizers
BT3 fertilizers

CONCENTRATES
uf protein feeds
BT1 feeds
BT1 foods
NT1 protein concentrates
NT2 animal protein concentrates
NT2 fish protein concentrate
NT2 leaf protein concentrate
NT2 lucerne protein concentrate
NT2 mustard protein concentrate
NT2 potato protein concentrate
NT2 rapeseed protein concentrate
NT1 uromol
rt livestock feeding
rt protein hydrolysates
rt protein sources

CONCENTRATING
HN from 1990
BT1 processing

CONCENTRATION
(in economics, use "concentration of production")
rt condensation

CONCENTRATION OF PRODUCTION
BT1 socioeconomic organization
NT1 farm amalgamations
NT1 integration
NT2 horizontal integration
NT2 mergers
NT2 social integration
NT2 vertical integration
rt agricultural structure

CONCEPTION
BT1 sexual reproduction
BT2 reproduction
NT1 conception rate
NT2 pregnancy rate
rt fertilization
rt pregnancy

CONCEPTION RATE
BT1 conception
BT2 sexual reproduction
BT3 reproduction
NT1 pregnancy rate
rt female fertility

CONCEPTUS
HN from 1990
rt embryos
rt fetus

CONCERTS
BT1 performing arts
BT2 arts
rt music

CONCESSIONS
BT1 permits
rt forest administration
rt forest policy
rt licences

CONCHOPHTHIRIUS
BT1 apicomplexa
BT2 protozoa

CONCRETE
BT1 building materials
BT2 materials
rt cement
rt concrete pipes
rt concrete roads
rt reinforcement
rt slabs

CONCRETE PIPES
BT1 pipes
BT2 components
rt concrete

CONCRETE ROADS
uf roads, concrete
BT1 roads
rt concrete

CONCRETIONS
NT1 bezoar
NT1 biliary calculi
NT1 bladder calculi
NT1 renal calculi
NT1 urinary calculi
rt digestive disorders
rt minerals
rt soil micromorphological features

CONCURRENT FLOW DRIERS
AF concurrent flow dryers
uf driers, concurrent flow
BT1 driers
BT2 farm machinery
BT3 machinery
rt cross flow driers

CONCURRENT FLOW DRYERS
BF concurrent flow driers
BT1 dryers

CONDALIA
BT1 rhamnaceae
NT1 condalia obtusifolia

CONDALIA OBTUSIFOLIA
BT1 condalia
BT2 rhamnaceae

CONDENSATES
BT1 liquids
NT1 dew
rt condensation
rt condensers
rt evaporation
rt moisture

CONDENSATION
BT1 change of state
rt boiling
rt concentration
rt condensates
rt condensers
rt dewpoint
rt milk processing

CONDENSED MILK
uf milk, condensed
uf milk, sweetened condensed
uf sweetened condensed milk
BT1 milk products
BT2 products
rt evaporated milk

CONDENSED PHOSPHATES
BT1 phosphorus fertilizers
BT2 fertilizers
NT1 metaphosphates
NT2 ammonium metaphosphates
NT2 potassium metaphosphate
NT2 trimetaphosphates
NT3 calcium ammonium trimetaphosphate
NT1 octacalcium phosphate
NT1 polyphosphates
NT2 ammonium polyphosphate sulfate
NT2 potassium polyphosphates
NT3 potassium dihydrogen triphosphate
NT3 potassium hydrogen tripolyphosphates
NT3 potassium pyrophosphate
NT3 urea potassium pyrophosphate
NT2 pyrophosphates
NT3 ammonium pyrophosphate
NT3 calcium pyrophosphate
NT3 diammonium pyrophosphate
NT3 potassium pyrophosphate
NT3 sodium pyrophosphate
NT3 tetraammonium pyrophosphate
NT3 triammonium pyrophosphate
NT3 urea ammonium pyrophosphate
NT3 urea potassium pyrophosphate
NT2 tripolyphosphates
NT3 potassium dihydrogen triphosphate
NT3 potassium hydrogen tripolyphosphates
NT3 sodium tripolyphosphate
NT2 urea ammonium polyphosphate

CONDENSER WATER
HN from 1990
BT1 water
rt condensers

CONDENSERS
HN from 1990
BT1 equipment
rt condensates
rt condensation
rt condenser water

CONDIMENTS
uf seasonings
NT1 capers
NT1 mustard
NT1 pepper
NT2 black pepper
NT1 sodium chloride
NT1 vinegar
rt culinary herbs
rt flavour compounds
rt sauces

CONDITIONED REFLEXES
uf behaviour, conditioned reflex
BT1 reflexes
BT2 physiological functions
BT1 responses
rt animal behaviour
rt behaviour
rt conditioning

CONDITIONING
NT1 forage conditioning
rt behaviour
rt conditioned reflexes
rt drying
rt soil conditioners

conditions, living
USE **living conditions**

conditions, social
USE **living conditions**

conditions, working
USE **working conditions**

CONDOMINIUMS (AGRICOLA)
BT1 homes
BT2 housing

CONDOMS (AGRICOLA)
BT1 contraceptives

conductance
USE **electrical conductance**

CONDUCTION ANAESTHESIA
AF conduction anesthesia
uf epidural anaesthesia
BT1 anaesthesia
rt local anaesthesia

CONDUCTION ANESTHESIA
BF conduction anaesthesia
BT1 anesthesia

CONDUCTIVITY
BT1 physical properties
BT2 properties
NT1 electrical conductivity
NT1 hydraulic conductivity
NT2 saturated hydraulic conductivity
NT2 unsaturated hydraulic conductivity
NT1 thermal conductivity
rt diffusivity
rt flow
rt resistance
rt transmission

conductivity, thermal
USE **thermal conductivity**

CONE NOZZLES
uf nozzles, cone
BT1 nozzles
BT2 components
BT2 spraying equipment
BT3 application equipment
BT4 equipment

CONE WITHERING
BT1 plant disorders
BT2 disorders
rt hops

CONES
NT1 seed cones
rt coniferae
rt hops
rt inflorescences

cones, ice cream
USE **ice cream cones**

CONFECTIONERY
NT1 cakes
NT1 chewing gum
NT1 chocolate
NT1 ice cream
NT2 water ices
NT1 milk ice
NT1 sugar confectionery
NT1 sweets
rt confectionery industry
rt gelatin
rt liquorice
rt plant products

CONFECTIONERY INDUSTRY
BT1 food industry
BT2 industry
rt cocoa industry
rt confectionery
rt sugar industry

CONFERENCE FACILITIES
rt conferences

CONFERENCE TOURISM
BT1 tourism

CONFERENCES
uf congresses
uf meetings
uf proceedings
uf seminars
uf symposia
rt conference facilities

CONFLICT
BT1 social unrest
BT2 social change
NT1 class conflict
NT1 generation conflict
NT1 role conflicts
rt social disintegration
rt strikes

CONFORMATION
uf body conformation
BT1 types
NT1 somatotype
rt structure
rt type score

CONGENERS
BT1 species
rt genotypes

CONGENIC STRAINS
HN from 1990
BT1 strains

CONGENITAL ABNORMALITIES
uf birth defects
uf congenital malformations
uf malformations, congenital
BT1 abnormalities
NT1 anorectal atresia
NT1 aplasia
NT2 anencephaly
NT2 segmental aplasia
NT2 taillessness
NT2 wolffian duct aplasia
NT1 arthrogryposis
NT1 brachygnathia
NT1 cleft palate
NT1 coloboma
NT1 congenital functional anomalies
NT2 strabismus
NT1 congenital goitre
NT1 congenital hernia
NT2 spina bifida
NT1 congenital metabolic anomalies
NT2 retinal atrophy
NT1 congenital neoplasms
NT1 congenital tremor
NT1 down's syndrome
NT1 ectopia
NT1 epitheliogenesis imperfecta
NT1 genetic disorders
NT1 hepatolenticular degeneration
NT1 hip dysplasia
NT1 hyperplasia
NT2 interdigital hyperplasia
NT2 mammary hyperplasia
NT2 megacolon
NT1 hypoplasia
NT2 hypotrichosis
NT2 microphthalmia
NT1 musculoskeletal anomalies
NT1 organ duplication
NT1 phimosis
NT1 prader-willi syndrome
NT1 schizosoma reflexum
NT1 sex differentiation disorders
NT2 dysgenesis
NT2 intersexuality
NT3 freemartinism
NT3 pseudohermaphroditism
NT2 sex reversal
NT2 testicular feminization
NT1 sickle cell anaemia
NT1 supernumerary organs
NT2 polydactylia
NT1 syndactyly
NT1 teratogenesis
rt hereditary diseases
rt inheritance

CONGENITAL EDEMA
BF congenital oedema
BT1 edema

CONGENITAL FUNCTIONAL ANOMALIES
BT1 congenital abnormalities
BT2 abnormalities
NT1 strabismus

CONGENITAL FUNCTIONAL ANOMALIES *cont.*
rt functional disorders
rt splayleg

CONGENITAL GOITER
BF congenital goitre
BT1 goiter

CONGENITAL GOITRE
AF congenital goiter
uf goitre, congenital
BT1 congenital abnormalities
BT2 abnormalities
BT1 goitre
BT2 thyroid diseases
BT3 endocrine diseases
BT4 organic diseases
BT5 diseases

CONGENITAL HERNIA
BT1 congenital abnormalities
BT2 abnormalities
BT1 hernia
NT1 spina bifida

CONGENITAL INFECTION
uf prenatal infection
BT1 infection
BT2 disease transmission
BT3 transmission

congenital malformations
USE **congenital abnormalities**

CONGENITAL METABOLIC ANOMALIES
BT1 congenital abnormalities
BT2 abnormalities
NT1 retinal atrophy
rt metabolic disorders

CONGENITAL NEOPLASMS
BT1 congenital abnormalities
BT2 abnormalities
BT1 neoplasms
BT2 diseases

CONGENITAL OEDEMA
AF congenital edema
BT1 oedema
BT2 water metabolism disorders
BT3 metabolic disorders
BT4 animal disorders
BT5 disorders
NT1 hydrocephalus

CONGENITAL TREMOR
BT1 congenital abnormalities
BT2 abnormalities
BT1 tremor
BT2 dysregulation
BT3 functional disorders
BT4 animal disorders
BT5 disorders

CONGLUTINATION
rt antigen antibody reactions

CONGO
uf congo brazzaville
uf congo pr
BT1 central africa
BT2 africa south of sahara
BT3 africa
rt acp
rt francophone africa

congo brazzaville
USE **congo**

congo democratic republic
USE **zaire**

congo kinshasa
USE **zaire**

congo leopoldville
USE **zaire**

congo pr
USE **congo**

congo virus
USE **crimean-congo haemorrhagic fever virus**

CONGREGATE LIVING (AGRICOLA)

congregate meals
USE **community feeding centers (agricola)**

congresses
USE **conferences**

CONIDIA
BT1 fungal spores
BT2 spores
BT3 cells

CONIDIOBOLUS
BT1 entomophthorales
NT1 conidiobolus coronatus
NT1 conidiobolus obscurus
NT1 conidiobolus thromboides
rt entomophthora

CONIDIOBOLUS CORONATUS
uf entomophthora coronata
BT1 conidiobolus
BT2 entomophthorales

CONIDIOBOLUS OBSCURUS
BT1 conidiobolus
BT2 entomophthorales

CONIDIOBOLUS THROMBOIDES
BT1 conidiobolus
BT2 entomophthorales

CONIDOPHRYS
BT1 ciliophora
BT2 protozoa

CONIELLA
BT1 deuteromycotina
NT1 coniella diplodiella
rt coniothyrium

CONIELLA DIPLODIELLA
uf coniothyrium diplodiella
BT1 coniella
BT2 deuteromycotina

CONIESTA
HN from 1989
BT1 pyralidae
BT2 lepidoptera
NT1 coniesta ignefusalis
rt acigona

CONIESTA IGNEFUSALIS
HN from 1989; previously acigona ignefusalis
uf acigona ignefusalis
BT1 coniesta
BT2 pyralidae
BT3 lepidoptera

CONIFER MEAL
BT1 meal
rt conifers

CONIFER NEEDLES
BT1 leaves
BT2 plant
BT1 plant residues
BT2 residues
NT1 pine needles
rt conifers

CONIFERAE
rt araucariaceae
rt cones
rt conifers
rt cupressaceae
rt ginkgoaceae
rt gymnosperms
rt lythraceae
rt pinaceae
rt podocarpaceae
rt taxaceae
rt taxodiaceae

CONIFEROUS FORESTS
BT1 forests

CONIFEROUS FORESTS *cont.*
BT2 vegetation types
rt boreal forests
rt conifers

CONIFERS
NT1 ornamental conifers
NT2 abies alba
NT2 abies balsamea
NT2 abies concolor
NT2 abies grandis
NT2 abies procera
NT2 araucaria angustifolia
NT2 araucaria araucana
NT2 araucaria heterophylla
NT2 cedrus atlantica
NT2 cedrus deodara
NT2 cephalotaxus harringtonia
NT2 chamaecyparis lawsoniana
NT2 chamaecyparis obtusa
NT2 chamaecyparis pisifera
NT2 cryptomeria japonica
NT2 cupressocyparis leylandii
NT2 cupressus arizonica
NT2 cupressus funebris
NT2 cupressus lusitanica
NT2 cupressus macrocarpa
NT2 ginkgo biloba
NT2 juniperus chinensis
NT2 juniperus communis
NT2 juniperus conferta
NT2 juniperus horizontalis
NT2 juniperus procumbens
NT2 juniperus sabina
NT2 juniperus scopulorum
NT2 larix decidua
NT2 lawsonia inermis
NT2 libocedrus decurrens
NT2 metasequoia glyptostroboides
NT2 picea abies
NT2 picea engelmannii
NT2 picea glauca
NT2 picea jezoensis
NT2 picea omorika
NT2 picea pungens
NT2 picea sitchensis
NT2 pinus canariensis
NT2 pinus cembra
NT2 pinus densiflora
NT2 pinus engelmannii
NT2 pinus halepensis
NT2 pinus monticola
NT2 pinus mugo
NT2 pinus nigra
NT2 pinus pinaster
NT2 pinus radiata
NT2 pinus resinosa
NT2 pinus rigida
NT2 pinus strobus
NT2 pinus sylvestris
NT2 pinus taeda
NT2 pinus thunbergii
NT2 podocarpus macrophyllus
NT2 podocarpus nagi
NT2 podocarpus nivalis
NT2 pseudolarix amabilis
NT2 sequoia sempervirens
NT2 sequoiadendron giganteum
NT2 taxodium ascendens
NT2 taxodium distichum
NT2 taxus baccata
NT2 taxus canadensis
NT2 taxus cuspidata
NT2 taxus media
NT2 thuja occidentalis
NT2 thuja orientalis
NT2 thuja plicata
NT2 torreya californica
NT2 torreya grandis
NT2 torreya nucifera
NT2 tsuga canadensis
rt conifer meal
rt conifer needles
rt coniferae
rt coniferous forests
rt plants

CONIOPHORA
BT1 aphyllophorales
NT1 coniophora puteana

coniophora cerebella
USE **coniophora puteana**

CONIOPHORA PUTEANA
uf *coniophora cerebella*
BT1 coniophora
BT2 aphyllophorales

CONIOPTERYGIDAE
BT1 neuroptera
NT1 conwentzia

CONIOSELINUM
BT1 umbelliferae

CONIOTHYRIUM
BT1 deuteromycotina
NT1 coniothyrium clematidis-rectae
NT1 coniothyrium fuckelii
NT1 coniothyrium minitans
NT1 coniothyrium pyrinum
rt coniella
rt phyllosticta

CONIOTHYRIUM CLEMATIDIS-RECTAE
BT1 coniothyrium
BT2 deuteromycotina

coniothyrium diplodiella
USE **coniella diplodiella**

CONIOTHYRIUM FUCKELII
BT1 coniothyrium
BT2 deuteromycotina

CONIOTHYRIUM MINITANS
BT1 coniothyrium
BT2 deuteromycotina

CONIOTHYRIUM PYRINUM
uf *phyllosticta pirina*
BT1 coniothyrium
BT2 deuteromycotina

CONIUM
BT1 umbelliferae
NT1 conium maculatum

CONIUM MACULATUM
BT1 conium
BT2 umbelliferae
BT1 poisonous plants

CONJUNCTIVA
BT1 eyes
BT2 sense organs
BT3 body parts
rt conjunctivitis
rt keratoconjunctivitis

CONJUNCTIVITIS
BT1 eye diseases
BT2 organic diseases
BT3 diseases
rt conjunctiva

CONNACHT
BT1 irish republic
BT2 british isles
BT3 western europe
BT4 europe

CONNARACEAE
NT1 agelaea
NT2 agelaea obliqua
NT1 cnestis
NT2 cnestis ferruginea
NT1 jaundea
NT2 jaundea pinnata
NT1 manotes
NT2 manotes longiflora

CONNECTICUT
BT1 new england
BT2 northeastern states of usa
BT3 usa
BT4 north america
BT5 america

CONNECTIVE TISSUE
BT1 animal tissues
BT2 tissues
rt collagen

CONNECTIVE TISSUE *cont.*
rt elastin

connectors, timber
USE **timber connectors**

CONNEMARA PONY
BT1 horse breeds
BT2 breeds

CONNOCHAETES
uf *wildebeest*
BT1 bovidae
BT2 ruminantia
BT3 artiodactyla
BT4 mammals
BT4 ungulates
NT1 connochaetes gnou
NT1 connochaetes taurinus

CONNOCHAETES GNOU
BT1 connochaetes
BT2 bovidae
BT3 ruminantia
BT4 artiodactyla
BT5 mammals
BT5 ungulates

CONNOCHAETES TAURINUS
BT1 connochaetes
BT2 bovidae
BT3 ruminantia
BT4 artiodactyla
BT5 mammals
BT5 ungulates

CONOCARPUS
BT1 combretaceae
NT1 conocarpus erectus
NT1 conocarpus lancifolius

CONOCARPUS ERECTUS
BT1 conocarpus
BT2 combretaceae
BT1 forest trees
BT1 ornamental woody plants

CONOCARPUS LANCIFOLIUS
BT1 conocarpus
BT2 combretaceae

CONOCYBE
BT1 agaricales
NT1 conocybe smithii

CONOCYBE SMITHII
BT1 conocybe
BT2 agaricales

CONODERUS
BT1 elateridae
BT2 coleoptera
NT1 conoderus exsul
NT1 conoderus falli
NT1 conoderus scalaris
NT1 conoderus vespertinus

CONODERUS EXSUL
BT1 conoderus
BT2 elateridae
BT3 coleoptera

CONODERUS FALLI
BT1 conoderus
BT2 elateridae
BT3 coleoptera

CONODERUS SCALARIS
BT1 conoderus
BT2 elateridae
BT3 coleoptera

CONODERUS VESPERTINUS
BT1 conoderus
BT2 elateridae
BT3 coleoptera

CONOPHOLIS
BT1 orobanchaceae
NT1 conopholis americana

CONOPHOLIS AMERICANA
BT1 conopholis
BT2 orobanchaceae

CONOPHTHORUS
BT1 scolytidae
BT2 coleoptera
NT1 conophthorus ponderosae
NT1 conophthorus resinosae

CONOPHTHORUS PONDEROSAE
BT1 conophthorus
BT2 scolytidae
BT3 coleoptera

CONOPHTHORUS RESINOSAE
BT1 conophthorus
BT2 scolytidae
BT3 coleoptera

CONOPHYTUM
BT1 aizoaceae

conopia
USE **synanthedon**

conopia myopaeformis
USE **synanthedon myopaeformis**

conopia spheciformis
USE **synanthedon spheciformis**

CONOPOMORPHA
BT1 gracillariidae
BT2 lepidoptera
NT1 conopomorpha cramerella
rt acrocercops

CONOPOMORPHA CRAMERELLA
uf *acrocercops cramerella*
BT1 conopomorpha
BT2 gracillariidae
BT3 lepidoptera

CONORHYNCHUS
BT1 curculionidae
BT2 coleoptera

CONOTRACHELUS
BT1 curculionidae
BT2 coleoptera
NT1 conotrachelus nenuphar

CONOTRACHELUS NENUPHAR
BT1 conotrachelus
BT2 curculionidae
BT3 coleoptera

CONRADINA
BT1 labiatae
NT1 conradina verticillata

CONRADINA VERTICILLATA
BT1 conradina
BT2 labiatae

CONSCIENTIZATION
BT1 social consciousness
BT2 socialization

CONSCIOUSNESS
rt behaviour

CONSERVATION
NT1 energy conservation
NT1 environmental protection
NT1 grain conservation
NT1 heat conservation
NT2 heat retention
NT3 waste heat utilization
NT1 landscape conservation
NT1 nature conservation
NT2 protected species
NT2 wildlife conservation
NT1 resource conservation
NT1 soil conservation
NT2 grass waterways
NT2 levelling
NT2 riverbank protection
NT2 soil stabilization
NT3 sand dune stabilization
NT3 sand stabilization
NT2 terraces
NT1 water conservation
NT2 microwatersheds
NT2 ponding
NT2 subsurface barriers
NT2 subsurface troughs

CONSERVATION *cont.*
NT2 water harvesting
NT2 water spreading
NT1 wood conservation

CONSERVATION AREAS
BT1 areas
NT1 areas of outstanding natural beauty
rt landscape conservation

CONSERVATION TILLAGE
HN from 1990
BT1 tillage
BT2 cultivation
rt no-tillage
rt soil conservation

CONSERVING QUALITY
uf *quality for conserving*
BT1 food processing quality
BT2 processing quality
BT3 quality
NT1 pickling quality
NT1 salting quality
rt jams

CONSISTENCY
BT1 physical properties
BT2 properties
rt density
rt firmness

CONSOLIDA
BT1 ranunculaceae
NT1 consolida ambigua
NT1 consolida regalis

CONSOLIDA AMBIGUA
uf *delphinium ajacis*
BT1 consolida
BT2 ranunculaceae
BT1 ornamental herbaceous plants

CONSOLIDA REGALIS
uf *delphinium consolida*
BT1 consolida
BT2 ranunculaceae

consolidation of land holdings
USE **land consolidation**

CONSORTIA
BT1 groups

CONSTIPATION
BT1 digestive disorders
BT2 functional disorders
BT3 animal disorders
BT4 disorders

CONSTITUENTS
HN from 1989
rt composition

CONSTITUTION
(for legal constitution, use "constitution and law")
BT1 health
rt genotypes
rt haemorrhagic diathesis
rt reconstitution
rt strength
rt type score

CONSTITUTION AND LAW
HN from 1990
BT1 government
BT1 law
BT2 legal systems

CONSTRAINTS
rt disincentives
rt efficiency

CONSTRICTOR
BT1 boidae
BT2 serpentes
BT3 reptiles
NT1 constrictor constrictor
rt boa

CONSTRICTOR CONSTRICTOR
uf *boa constrictor*

CONSTRICTOR CONSTRICTOR *cont.*
BT1 constrictor
BT2 boidae
BT3 serpentes
BT4 reptiles

CONSTRUCTION
uf *construction and maintenance*
NT1 building construction
NT2 brickwork
NT2 foundations
NT2 stonework
NT1 road construction
NT1 terracing
rt building materials
rt building timbers
rt construction technology
rt texture

construction and maintenance
USE **construction**
OR **maintenance**

CONSTRUCTION TECHNOLOGY
uf *building methods*
BT1 technology
NT1 cooperage
NT1 modules
NT1 moulding
NT1 prefabrication
rt building construction
rt building materials
rt buildings
rt construction
rt girders
rt structural components
rt wall pressure
rt welding
rt wood technology

CONSULTANTS
BT1 occupations
rt advisory committees (agricola)
rt specialization

consumer advocacy
USE **consumer protection**

CONSUMER ATTITUDES (AGRICOLA)
BT1 attitudes
rt consumer behavior
rt consumers

CONSUMER BEHAVIOR
BF consumer behaviour
BT1 economic behavior
BT2 human behavior
BT3 behavior
BT2 social behavior
BT3 behavior
rt consumer attitudes (agricola)

CONSUMER BEHAVIOUR
AF consumer behavior
uf *behaviour, consumer*
BT1 economic behaviour
BT2 human behaviour
BT3 behaviour
BT2 social behaviour
BT3 behaviour
NT1 complaints
NT1 consumer preferences
NT1 purchasing habits
rt consumer expenditure
rt consumer panels
rt consumer protection
rt consumer surveys
rt consumers
rt feeding habits
rt household consumption
rt market research

CONSUMER COOPERATIVES
BT1 cooperatives
rt consumer expenditure
rt consumer information
rt consumer prices
rt consumer protection
rt consumers

CONSUMER COOPERATIVES *cont.*
rt cooperative marketing
rt retail marketing

CONSUMER ECONOMICS (AGRICOLA)
BT1 economics
rt consumers

CONSUMER EDUCATION (AGRICOLA)
BT1 education
rt consumer protection
rt consumers

CONSUMER EXPENDITURE
uf *expenditure, consumer*
BT1 aggregate data
BT1 expenditure
NT1 household expenditure
NT1 tourist expenditure
NT2 souvenirs
rt consumer behaviour
rt consumer cooperatives
rt consumer surveys
rt consumers
rt economic sociology
rt household consumption

CONSUMER INFORMATION
BT1 consumer protection
BT2 protection
BT1 information
NT1 open dating (agricola)
rt consumer cooperatives
rt consumer prices
rt consumers

CONSUMER PANELS
BT1 consumer surveys
BT2 market surveys
BT3 market research
BT4 market intelligence
BT5 market transparency
BT6 market economics
BT7 economics
BT4 research
BT3 surveys
rt consumer behaviour
rt consumer preferences
rt consumers
rt taste panels (agricola)

CONSUMER PREFERENCES
BT1 consumer behaviour
BT2 economic behaviour
BT3 human behaviour
BT4 behaviour
BT3 social behaviour
BT4 behaviour
rt consumer panels
rt consumers
rt market research

CONSUMER PRICE INDEX
BT1 consumer prices
BT2 retail prices
BT3 market prices
BT4 prices
rt consumers

CONSUMER PRICES
uf *prices, consumer*
BT1 retail prices
BT2 market prices
BT3 prices
NT1 consumer price index
rt consumer cooperatives
rt consumer information
rt consumers
rt food prices
rt market prices

CONSUMER PROTECTION
uf *consumer advocacy*
BT1 protection
NT1 consumer information
NT2 open dating (agricola)
NT1 price discrimination
NT2 price elasticities
NT1 quality controls
NT2 inspection
NT3 food inspection

CONSUMER PROTECTION *cont.*
NT4 meat inspection
NT5 antemortem examinations (agricola)
NT5 carcass condemnation
NT2 labelling controls
NT2 quality circles (agricola)
NT2 quality standards
NT3 gradeability
rt consumer behaviour
rt consumer cooperatives
rt consumer education (agricola)
rt consumers
rt food inspection
rt grading
rt labelling
rt legislation
rt market regulations
rt merchandise information (agricola)
rt price controls
rt standard labelling
rt standardization
rt unit pricing
rt universal product codes (agricola)
rt warranties (agricola)

CONSUMER SATISFACTION
rt consumers
rt enjoyment

CONSUMER SURPLUS
BT1 welfare economics
BT2 economics
rt consumers
rt cost benefit analysis

CONSUMER SURVEYS
BT1 market surveys
BT2 market research
BT3 market intelligence
BT4 market transparency
BT5 market economics
BT6 economics
BT3 research
BT2 surveys
NT1 consumer panels
rt consumer behaviour
rt consumer expenditure
rt consumers
rt household consumption
rt household expenditure

CONSUMERS
rt audiences
rt consumer attitudes (agricola)
rt consumer behaviour
rt consumer cooperatives
rt consumer economics (agricola)
rt consumer education (agricola)
rt consumer expenditure
rt consumer information
rt consumer panels
rt consumer preferences
rt consumer price index
rt consumer prices
rt consumer protection
rt consumer satisfaction
rt consumer surplus
rt consumer surveys
rt customer relations (agricola)

CONSUMPTION
NT1 consumption functions
NT1 consumption per caput
NT1 domestic consumption
NT1 egg consumption
NT1 energy consumption
NT1 fat consumption
NT1 fish consumption
NT1 food consumption
NT2 milk consumption
NT1 fuel consumption
NT2 specific fuel consumption
NT1 heat consumption
NT1 household consumption
NT1 on-farm consumption

CONSUMPTION *cont.*
rt demand
rt expenditure
rt final consumption

CONSUMPTION FUNCTIONS
BT1 consumption
BT1 econometrics
rt economic analysis

CONSUMPTION PATTERNS (AGRICOLA)
BT1 patterns
rt eating
rt food consumption

CONSUMPTION PER CAPUT
BT1 consumption

CONTACT ANGLE
uf *angle of wetting*
rt interface
rt surface tension
rt wettability
rt wetting

CONTACT LENSES
NT1 soft contact lenses
rt eye lens

contagious agalactia agent
USE **mycoplasma agalactiae**

CONTAGIOUS ECTHYMA VIRUS
uf *orf virus*
BT1 parapoxvirus
BT2 chordopoxvirinae
BT3 poxviridae
BT4 viruses

CONTAGIOUS EQUINE METRITIS
BT1 horse diseases
BT2 animal diseases
BT3 diseases

CONTAINER GROWN PLANTS
rt containers
rt planting stock
rt plants
rt pot plants

CONTAINER TRANSPORT
uf *transport, container*
BT1 transport
rt containers

CONTAINERS
uf *plastic containers*
uf *storage containers*
NT1 bags (agricola)
NT2 paper bags (agricola)
NT1 bins
NT2 ventilated bins
NT1 bottles
NT1 boxes
NT1 buckets
NT1 bunkers
NT1 cans (agricola)
NT1 crates
NT1 cribs
NT2 maize cribs
NT1 cups
NT1 foil pouches (agricola)
NT1 gas holders
NT1 hanging baskets
NT1 hoppers
NT1 jars (agricola)
NT1 mangers
NT1 milk containers
NT2 milk bottles
NT2 milk cans
NT2 milk cartons
NT2 milk tanks
NT1 packing containers
NT1 pallet boxes
NT1 pots
NT1 refuse containers
NT1 retort pouches (agricola)
NT1 retort trays (agricola)
NT1 sachets
NT1 sacks
NT1 seed boxes
NT1 tankers
NT2 milk tankers

CONTAINERS *cont.*
NT2 slurry tankers
NT1 tanks
NT2 fuel tanks
NT2 milk tanks
NT2 vacuum tanks
NT1 trays (agricola)
NT1 troughs
NT2 feed troughs
NT2 subsurface troughs
NT2 water troughs
NT1 vats
NT1 water containers
NT2 cemetery vases
NT1 window boxes
rt clamps
rt container grown plants
rt container transport
rt cooperage
rt packages
rt packaging
rt packing
rt racks
rt stores
rt sumps

CONTAMINANTS
NT1 foreign bodies
NT1 polybrominated biphenyls
NT1 polychlorinated dibenzofurans
NT1 polychlorinated terphenyls
rt adulterants
rt contamination
rt pollutants
rt polychlorinated biphenyls

CONTAMINATION
NT1 food contamination
NT1 microbial contamination
NT1 seed contamination
rt adulteration
rt aseptic packaging
rt contaminants
rt decontamination
rt dockage
rt infection
rt pollution

contamination, genetic
USE **genetic contamination**

CONTARINIA
BT1 cecidomyiidae
BT2 diptera
NT1 contarinia baeri
NT1 contarinia medicaginis
NT1 contarinia nasturtii
NT1 contarinia okadai
NT1 contarinia oregonensis
NT1 contarinia pisi
NT1 contarinia pyrivora
NT1 contarinia schulzi
NT1 contarinia sorghicola
NT1 contarinia tritici

CONTARINIA BAERI
BT1 contarinia
BT2 cecidomyiidae
BT3 diptera

CONTARINIA MEDICAGINIS
BT1 contarinia
BT2 cecidomyiidae
BT3 diptera

CONTARINIA NASTURTII
BT1 contarinia
BT2 cecidomyiidae
BT3 diptera

CONTARINIA OKADAI
BT1 contarinia
BT2 cecidomyiidae
BT3 diptera

CONTARINIA OREGONENSIS
BT1 contarinia
BT2 cecidomyiidae
BT3 diptera

CONTARINIA PISI
BT1 contarinia
BT2 cecidomyiidae

CONTARINIA PISI *cont.*
BT3 diptera

CONTARINIA PYRIVORA
BT1 contarinia
BT2 cecidomyiidae
BT3 diptera

CONTARINIA SCHULZI
BT1 contarinia
BT2 cecidomyiidae
BT3 diptera

CONTARINIA SORGHICOLA
BT1 contarinia
BT2 cecidomyiidae
BT3 diptera

CONTARINIA TRITICI
BT1 contarinia
BT2 cecidomyiidae
BT3 diptera

CONTEMPORARY COMPARISONS
BT1 progeny testing
BT2 animal breeding methods
BT3 breeding methods
BT4 methodology
BT2 testing
NT1 improved contemporary comparisons

CONTEMPORARY SOCIETY
rt social change

CONTINUING EDUCATION
uf education, further
uf further education
BT1 adult education
BT2 education
NT1 professional continuing education (agricola)
rt apprenticeship
rt inservice training
rt school leavers
rt secondary education

CONTINUOUS BUTTERMAKING
uf buttermaking, continuous
BT1 buttermaking
BT2 dairying

CONTINUOUS CENTRIFUGALS
HN from 1990
BT1 centrifugals
BT2 centrifuges
BT3 separators
BT4 machinery

CONTINUOUS CHEESEMAKING
uf cheesemaking, continuous
BT1 cheesemaking

CONTINUOUS CROPPING
uf monocropping
BT1 cropping systems
rt perennial cropping

CONTINUOUS DRIERS
AF continuous dryers
uf driers, continuous
BT1 driers
BT2 farm machinery
BT3 machinery
rt batch driers

CONTINUOUS DRYERS
BF continuous driers
BT1 dryers

CONTINUOUS VACUUM PANS
HN from 1990
BT1 vacuum pans
BT2 equipment

CONTORTYLENCHUS
BT1 allantonematidae
BT2 nematoda

CONTOUR CULTIVATION
BT1 cultivation
rt soil conservation

CONTOUR RIDGING
(including ridging and terracing)

CONTOUR RIDGING *cont.*
BT1 ridging
BT2 cultivation
rt terracing
rt trenching

CONTRACAECUM
BT1 anisakidae
BT2 nematoda

CONTRACEPTION
BT1 family planning
BT2 population control
BT3 control

CONTRACEPTIVES
NT1 condoms (agricola)
NT1 diaphragms (agricola)
NT1 intrauterine devices
NT1 oral contraceptives
NT2 chlormadinone
NT2 medroxyprogesterone
NT2 megestrol
NT2 mestranol
NT2 norethisterone
NT1 spermicides (agricola)
rt birth control (agricola)
rt diethylstilbestrol
rt steroids

contraceptives, oral
USE **oral contraceptives**

CONTRACT FARMING
BT1 farming
rt agribusiness
rt contracts
rt vertical integration

CONTRACT FOOD SERVICE (AGRICOLA)
BT1 commercial food service (agricola)
BT2 food service

CONTRACT LEGISLATION
BT1 legislation
BT2 legal systems
NT1 collective agreements
NT2 wage agreements
rt agricultural law
rt contracts
rt integration

CONTRACTILE PROTEINS
BT1 proteins
BT2 peptides
NT1 actin
NT1 myosin

CONTRACTION
uf expansion and contraction
rt compaction
rt compression
rt involution
rt plasmolysis
rt reduction
rt shrinkage

CONTRACTORS
BT1 occupations
rt contracts
rt hiring

CONTRACTS
NT1 franchises
NT1 labour contracts
rt arbitration
rt collective agreements
rt contract farming
rt contract legislation
rt contractors
rt legislation
rt tendering
rt wage agreements

CONTRAST MEDIA
uf media, contrast
NT1 barium sulfate
NT1 metrizamide
rt opacity
rt organoiodine compounds
rt x radiation

CONTROL
NT1 avalanche control (agricola)
NT1 chemical control
NT1 cost control (agricola)
NT1 cultural control
NT1 disease control
NT2 plant disease control
NT2 quarantine
NT2 supervised control
NT2 tree surgery
NT3 delimbing
NT1 draught control
NT1 dust control
NT1 environmental control
NT1 erosion control
NT2 riverbank protection
NT1 fire control
NT2 fire fighting
NT2 fire suppression
NT1 flood control
NT1 fungus control
NT1 pest control
NT2 biological control
NT3 augmentation
NT4 parasitoid augmentation
NT4 predator augmentation
NT3 encouragement
NT2 bird control
NT2 environmental management
NT2 genetic control
NT2 insect control
NT3 aggregation disruption
NT3 mating disruption
NT3 mules' operation
NT3 sterile insect release
NT2 integrated control
NT2 mite control
NT2 mollusc control
NT2 nematode control
NT2 pest management
NT3 integrated pest management
NT2 poisoning of animal pests
NT2 predator control (agricola)
NT2 quarantine
NT2 rodent control
NT2 supervised control
NT2 systemic action
NT2 vermin control
NT2 weed control
NT3 chemical vs. cultural weed control
NT3 cultural weed control
NT3 electrical weed control
NT3 manual weed control
NT3 non-crop weed control
NT3 slashing
NT3 weeding
NT1 physical control
NT1 population control
NT2 family planning
NT3 contraception
NT1 portion control (agricola)
NT1 project control
NT1 scrub control
NT1 sex control
NT1 thirst control
NT1 weather control
NT2 cloud seeding
NT1 weight control (agricola)
rt control methods
rt prevention
rt protection
rt river regulation

control, automatic
USE **automatic control**

control, biological
USE **biological control**

CONTROL COMPONENTS
BT1 components
NT1 clutches
NT2 friction clutches
NT2 steering clutches

CONTROL METHODS
uf pest control methods
BT1 methodology
NT1 prophylaxis

CONTROL METHODS *cont.*
NT2 chemoprophylaxis
NT1 trapping
rt baiting
rt control

CONTROL PROGRAMMES
HN from 1989
AF control programs
rt disease control
rt pest control

CONTROL PROGRAMS
HN from 1989
BF control programmes
BT1 programs (agricola)

control, remote
USE **remote control**

CONTROLLED ATMOSPHERE STORAGE
(storage in an atmosphere that is monitored and controlled)
uf *storage, controlled atmosphere*
BT1 storage
rt controlled atmosphere stores
rt controlled atmospheres
rt environmental control
rt insect control
rt modified atmosphere storage

CONTROLLED ATMOSPHERE STORES
uf *stores, controlled atmosphere*
BT1 stores
rt controlled atmosphere storage
rt controlled atmospheres
rt fruit stores

CONTROLLED ATMOSPHERES
uf *atmospheres, controlled*
NT1 protective atmospheres
rt controlled atmosphere storage
rt controlled atmosphere stores

CONTROLLED BURNING
AF prescribed burning
BT1 burning
rt cleaning
rt fire control
rt shifting cultivation

CONTROLLED DROPLET APPLICATION
BT1 spraying
BT2 application methods
BT3 methodology
rt droplets
rt low volume spraying
rt ultralow volume sprayers

CONTROLLED GRAZING
uf *grazing, controlled*
uf *grazing, paddock*
uf *paddock grazing*
BT1 grazing systems
BT2 grazing
rt grazing intensity
rt grazing time
rt sward renovation

CONTROLLED PRICES
uf *prices, controlled*
BT1 prices
NT1 minimum prices
rt price controls

CONTROLLED RELEASE
uf *slow release*
uf *sustained release*
BT1 application methods
BT2 methodology
rt briquettes
rt formulations
rt microencapsulation
rt pesticides

CONTROLLED TRAFFIC
HN from 1990
rt traffic

CONTROLLERS
NT1 actuators
rt controls
rt regulators

CONTROLLING ELEMENTS
BT1 genes
rt mutator genes
rt transposable elements

CONTROLS
uf *pedals*
NT1 accelerators
NT1 auditing
NT1 automatic control
NT1 credit control
NT2 discount rates
NT2 interest rates
NT3 preferential interest rates
NT1 electrical control
NT1 export controls
NT1 hormonal control
NT2 gonadotropin release
NT2 neurohormonal control
NT1 import controls
NT2 customs regulations
NT2 import levies
NT2 import quotas
NT2 non-tariff barriers to trade
NT3 tax agreements
NT2 tariffs
NT3 duty free allowances
NT3 preferential tariffs
NT1 one man operation
NT1 quality controls
NT2 inspection
NT3 food inspection
NT4 meat inspection
NT5 antemortem examinations (agricola)
NT5 carcass condemnation
NT2 labelling controls
NT2 quality circles (agricola)
NT2 quality standards
NT3 gradeability
NT1 radio control
NT1 remote control
NT1 steering wheels
NT1 taps
rt automation
rt controllers
rt displays
rt drivers
rt feedback
rt handles
rt instrumentation
rt levers
rt manual operation
rt power steering
rt production controls
rt regulations
rt signals
rt steerability
rt steering
rt symbols
rt thermistors
rt thyristors
rt time switches
rt vehicles

CONTROLS (EXPERIMENTAL)
rt assessment
rt experiments

controls, labelling
USE **labelling controls**

controls, production
USE **production controls**

controls, quality
USE **quality controls**

controls, quantity
USE **quantity controls**

CONVALLARIA
BT1 liliaceae
NT1 convallaria keiskei

CONVALLARIA *cont.*
NT1 convallaria majalis

CONVALLARIA KEISKEI
BT1 convallaria
BT2 liliaceae
BT1 ornamental bulbs
rt rhizomes

CONVALLARIA MAJALIS
uf *lily of the valley*
BT1 convallaria
BT2 liliaceae
BT1 essential oil plants
BT2 oil plants
BT1 medicinal plants
BT1 ornamental bulbs
rt rhizomes

CONVECTION
rt air temperature
rt convection driers
rt heat flow
rt heat transfer
rt temperature inversion
rt transport processes

CONVECTION DRIERS
AF convection dryers
uf *driers, convection*
BT1 driers
BT2 farm machinery
BT3 machinery
rt convection

CONVECTION DRYERS
BF convection driers
BT1 dryers

CONVECTION OVENS (AGRICOLA)
BT1 ovens (agricola)

CONVENIENCE FOODS
BT1 foods
NT1 brown and serve foods (agricola)
NT1 instant coffee
NT1 instant foods
NT1 instant milk
NT1 prepared foods

CONVERSION
NT1 energy conversion
NT1 feed conversion
NT2 fattening performance
NT1 food conversion
NT1 primary conversion
NT2 barking
NT3 hydraulic barking
NT3 manual barking
NT2 cross cutting
NT2 delimbing
NT1 resolution
NT1 silvicultural conversion
rt change
rt conversion tables
rt outturn
rt pressure transducers
rt transducers
rt transfer
rt utilization

conversion, feed
USE **feed conversion**

conversion, silvicultural
USE **silvicultural conversion**

CONVERSION TABLES
HN from 1990; previously "conversion tables and factors"
uf *conversion tables and factors*
BT1 measurement tables
rt conversion

conversion tables and factors
USE **conversion tables**

CONVEYOR DRIERS
AF conveyor dryers
uf *driers, conveyor*
BT1 driers

CONVEYOR DRIERS *cont.*
BT2 farm machinery
BT3 machinery
rt conveyors

CONVEYOR DRYERS
BF conveyor driers
BT1 dryers

CONVEYORS
NT1 auger conveyors
NT1 belt conveyors
NT1 chain and flight conveyors
NT1 elevators
NT2 bucket elevators
NT1 hoists
NT1 pneumatic conveyors
NT1 roller conveyors
NT1 scraper conveyors
NT1 shaker conveyors
NT1 sorting conveyors
rt bale throwers
rt cableways
rt conveyor driers
rt forage blowers
rt gantries
rt loaders
rt trolleys

conveyors, auger
USE **auger conveyors**

conveyors, belt
USE **belt conveyors**

conveyors, chain and flight
USE **chain and flight conveyors**

conveyors, pneumatic
USE **pneumatic conveyors**

conveyors, roller
USE **roller conveyors**

conveyors, scraper
USE **scraper conveyors**

conveyors, shaker
USE **shaker conveyors**

conveyors, sorting
USE **sorting conveyors**

CONVOLVULACEAE
NT1 argyreia
NT2 argyreia nervosa
NT2 argyreia splendens
NT1 calonyction
NT2 calonyction album
NT2 calonyction muricatum
NT1 calystegia
NT2 calystegia japonica
NT2 calystegia sepium
NT2 calystegia silvaticum
NT2 calystegia tuguriorum
NT1 convolvulus
NT2 convolvulus arvensis
NT2 convolvulus betonicifolius
NT2 convolvulus microphyllus
NT1 cressa
NT2 cressa cretica
NT1 dichondra
NT2 dichondra micrantha
NT2 dichondra repens
NT2 dichondra sativa
NT1 evolvulus
NT2 evolvulus alsinoides
NT1 exogonium
NT2 exogonium purga
NT1 ipomoea
NT2 ipomoea aculeata
NT2 ipomoea aquatica
NT2 ipomoea arborescens
NT2 ipomoea aristolochiaefolia
NT2 ipomoea batatas
NT2 ipomoea cairica
NT2 ipomoea carnea
NT2 ipomoea congesta
NT2 ipomoea fastigiata
NT2 ipomoea heptaphylla
NT2 ipomoea hirsutula
NT2 ipomoea lacunosa
NT2 ipomoea obscura

CONVOLVULACEAE *cont.*
NT2 ipomoea operculata
NT2 ipomoea pandurata
NT2 ipomoea parasitica
NT2 ipomoea pentaphylla
NT2 ipomoea pes-caprae
NT2 ipomoea pes-tigridis
NT2 ipomoea plebeia
NT2 ipomoea repens
NT2 ipomoea rubra
NT2 ipomoea sepiaria
NT2 ipomoea stolonifera
NT2 ipomoea trichocarpa
NT2 ipomoea tricolor
NT2 ipomoea triloba
NT2 ipomoea turbinata
NT2 ipomoea wrightii
NT1 jacquemontia
NT2 jacquemontia tamnifolia
NT1 merremia
NT2 merremia gangetica
NT2 merremia tuberosa
NT1 operculina
NT2 operculina turpethum
NT1 pharbitis
NT2 pharbitis hederacea
NT2 pharbitis learii
NT2 pharbitis nil
NT2 pharbitis purpurea
NT1 quamoclit
NT2 quamoclit coccinea
NT2 quamoclit hederifolia
NT2 quamoclit vulgaris
NT1 stictocardia
NT2 stictocardia campanulata

CONVOLVULUS
uf morning glory
BT1 convolvulaceae
NT1 convolvulus arvensis
NT1 convolvulus betonicifolius
NT1 convolvulus microphyllus

CONVOLVULUS ARVENSIS
BT1 convolvulus
BT2 convolvulaceae
BT1 weeds

CONVOLVULUS BETONICIFOLIUS
BT1 convolvulus
BT2 convolvulaceae

CONVOLVULUS MICROPHYLLUS
BT1 convolvulus
BT2 convolvulaceae

convolvulus nervosus
USE **argyreia nervosa**

convolvulus sepium
USE **calystegia sepium**

convolvulus splendens
USE **argyreia splendens**

CONVULSIONS
BT1 dysregulation
BT2 functional disorders
BT3 animal disorders
BT4 disorders
BT1 nervous system diseases
BT2 organic diseases
BT3 diseases
rt anticonvulsants
rt epilepsy

CONWENTZIA
BT1 coniopterygidae
BT2 neuroptera

CONYZA
BT1 compositae
NT1 conyza aegyptiaca
NT1 conyza albida
NT1 conyza bilbaoana
NT1 conyza bonariensis
NT1 conyza canadensis
NT1 conyza dioscoridis
NT1 conyza linifolia
NT1 conyza parva
NT1 conyza stricta

CONYZA AEGYPTIACA
BT1 conyza

CONYZA AEGYPTIACA *cont.*
BT2 compositae

CONYZA ALBIDA
BT1 conyza
BT2 compositae

conyza balsamifera
USE **blumea balsamifera**

CONYZA BILBAOANA
BT1 conyza
BT2 compositae

CONYZA BONARIENSIS
BT1 conyza
BT2 compositae

CONYZA CANADENSIS
uf erigeron canadensis
BT1 conyza
BT2 compositae
BT1 essential oil plants
BT2 oil plants
BT1 medicinal plants
BT1 weeds

CONYZA DIOSCORIDIS
BT1 conyza
BT2 compositae

CONYZA LINIFOLIA
BT1 conyza
BT2 compositae

CONYZA PARVA
BT1 conyza
BT2 compositae

CONYZA STRICTA
BT1 conyza
BT2 compositae

COOK-CHILL SYSTEM (AGRICOLA)
BT1 food preparation (agricola)

COOK-FREEZE SYSTEM (AGRICOLA)
BT1 food preparation (agricola)

COOK ISLANDS
BT1 new zealand oceania
BT2 oceania

COOKBOOKS
BF cookery books
BT1 books
BT2 publications
NT1 children's cookbooks (agricola)

COOKERY (AGRICOLA)
NT1 brazilian cookery (agricola)
NT1 chinese cookery (agricola)
NT1 french cookery (agricola)
NT1 gourmet cookery (agricola)
NT1 indian cookery (agricola)
NT1 italian cookery (agricola)
NT1 mexican cookery (agricola)
NT1 middle eastern cookery (agricola)
NT1 oven cookery (agricola)
NT1 vegetarian cookery (agricola)
rt cooking
rt culinary arts (agricola)
rt home economics
rt recipes (agricola)

COOKERY BOOKS
AF cookbooks
BT1 books
BT2 publications
rt cooking

COOKIES (AGRICOLA)
rt biscuits

COOKING
BT1 processing
NT1 outdoor cooking (agricola)
rt binding
rt catering
rt cookery (agricola)

COOKING *cont.*
rt cookery books
rt cooking fats
rt cooking instruction (agricola)
rt cooking losses (agricola)
rt cooking methods (agricola)
rt cooking oils
rt cooking quality
rt cooking utensils (agricola)
rt cooks (agricola)
rt feed steamers
rt heat treatment
rt heating
rt home economics

COOKING FATS
BT1 fat products
BT2 products
NT1 lard
NT1 margarine
NT1 suet
rt butter
rt cooking
rt cooking oils

COOKING INSTRUCTION (AGRICOLA)
BT1 instruction (agricola)
rt cooking

COOKING LOSSES (AGRICOLA)
BT1 losses
rt cooking

COOKING METHODS (AGRICOLA)
BT1 methodology
NT1 boil in bag (agricola)
NT1 boiling
NT1 braising (agricola)
NT1 broiling (agricola)
NT1 frying
NT2 deep fat frying (agricola)
NT2 stir frying (agricola)
NT1 grilling (agricola)
NT1 microwave cooking
NT1 roasting
NT1 sauteing (agricola)
NT1 simmering (agricola)
NT1 steaming
NT1 stewing (agricola)
NT1 toasting
rt cooking
rt food preparation (agricola)

COOKING OILS
BT1 oils
NT1 sunflower oil
rt animal oils
rt cooking
rt cooking fats
rt plant oils

COOKING QUALITY
uf quality for cooking
BT1 food processing quality
BT2 processing quality
BT3 quality
rt cooking

COOKING UTENSILS (AGRICOLA)
BT1 utensils (agricola)
NT1 broilers (kitchen appliance) (agricola)
NT1 pressure cookers (agricola)
rt cooking
rt household equipment (agricola)

COOKS (AGRICOLA)
BT1 occupations
rt chefs (agricola)
rt cooking

COOLERS
NT1 cooling towers
NT1 evaporative coolers
NT1 hydrocoolers
NT1 ice bank coolers
NT1 milk coolers
NT1 precoolers
rt cooling
rt cooling systems

COOLERS *cont.*
rt dairy equipment

coolers, evaporative
USE **evaporative coolers**

coolers, ice bank
USE **ice bank coolers**

COOLING
NT1 egg cooling
NT1 evaporative cooling
NT1 milk cooling
rt chilling
rt coolers
rt cooling systems
rt cooling towers
rt environmental control
rt fans
rt freezing
rt heat transfer
rt precooling
rt radiators
rt refrigeration
rt ventilation

COOLING SYSTEMS
BT1 systems
rt artificial ventilation
rt coolers
rt cooling
rt cooling towers
rt fans
rt radiators
rt water cooled engines
rt water supply

COOLING TOWERS
BT1 coolers
rt cooling
rt cooling systems
rt wood

COOMBS TEST
BT1 haemagglutination tests
BT2 agglutination tests
BT3 immunological techniques
BT4 techniques
BT3 tests
rt immunology

COOPERAGE
BT1 construction technology
BT2 technology
rt containers

COOPERATION
uf mutual help
BT1 socioeconomic organization
NT1 international cooperation
NT2 international agreements
NT3 lome convention
NT3 monetary agreements
NT3 trade agreements
NT4 gatt
NT4 trade negotiations
NT4 trade preferences
NT3 treaty of rome
rt communes
rt cooperative activities
rt cooperative extension service
rt cooperative farm enterprises
rt cooperative farming
rt cooperatives
rt coownership
rt economic unions
rt integration
rt socialization
rt work sharing

COOPERATIVE ACTIVITIES
NT1 combines
NT1 cooperative farming
NT1 cooperative marketing
NT2 cooperative bargaining
NT2 cooperative selling
NT1 cooperative processing
NT1 cooperative purchasing
NT1 cooperative services
NT2 cooperative banks

COOPERATIVE ACTIVITIES *cont.*
- **NT2** cooperative extension service
- **NT2** cooperative insurance
- **NT2** farm helper services
- **NT2** work banks
- **rt** cooperation
- **rt** cooperatives
- **rt** multipurpose cooperatives
- **rt** producer cooperatives

COOPERATIVE BANKS
- *uf* *banks, cooperative*
- **BT1** banks
- **BT2** financial institutions
- **BT3** organizations
- **BT1** cooperative services
- **BT2** cooperative activities
- **BT2** services
- **rt** cooperative credit

COOPERATIVE BARGAINING
- **BT1** cooperative marketing
- **BT2** cooperative activities
- **BT2** marketing
- **rt** strikes
- **rt** working conditions

COOPERATIVE CREDIT
- *uf* *credit, cooperative*
- **BT1** credit
- **BT2** finance
- **rt** agricultural credit
- **rt** cooperative banks
- **rt** cooperative services

COOPERATIVE EXTENSION SERVICE
- **BT1** cooperative services
- **BT2** cooperative activities
- **BT2** services
- **BT1** extension
- **rt** cooperation

COOPERATIVE FARM ENTERPRISES
(cooperation on a single crop or livestock activity)
- *uf* *enterprises, cooperative farm*
- *uf* *inter-farm enterprises*
- *uf* *intercooperative enterprises*
- *uf* *joint enterprises*
- **BT1** farm enterprises
- **BT2** enterprises
- **NT1** gaec
- **NT1** livestock groups
- **NT1** safer
- **rt** cooperation
- **rt** cooperative farming

COOPERATIVE FARMING
- *uf* *group farming*
- *uf* *joint farming*
- **BT1** cooperative activities
- **BT1** farming
- **rt** cooperation
- **rt** cooperative farm enterprises
- **rt** machinery cooperatives
- **rt** moshavim
- **rt** panchayats

COOPERATIVE FARMS
- **BT1** farms
- **rt** collective farms

COOPERATIVE HOUSING (AGRICOLA)
- **BT1** housing
- **rt** cooperatives

COOPERATIVE INSURANCE
- **BT1** cooperative services
- **BT2** cooperative activities
- **BT2** services
- **BT1** insurance
- **rt** agricultural insurance

COOPERATIVE MARKETING
- *uf* *marketing cooperatives*
- *uf* *marketing, cooperative*
- **BT1** cooperative activities
- **BT1** marketing

COOPERATIVE MARKETING *cont.*
- **NT1** cooperative bargaining
- **NT1** cooperative selling
- **rt** buying groups
- **rt** consumer cooperatives
- **rt** producer groups

COOPERATIVE PROCESSING
- **BT1** cooperative activities
- **BT1** processing

COOPERATIVE PURCHASING
- *uf* *supply cooperatives*
- **BT1** cooperative activities
- **rt** buying groups

COOPERATIVE SELLING
- **BT1** cooperative marketing
- **BT2** cooperative activities
- **BT2** marketing

COOPERATIVE SERVICES
- *uf* *services, cooperative*
- **BT1** cooperative activities
- **BT1** services
- **NT1** cooperative banks
- **NT1** cooperative extension service
- **NT1** cooperative insurance
- **NT1** farm helper services
- **NT1** work banks
- **rt** breeders' associations
- **rt** cooperative credit
- **rt** cooperatives
- **rt** farmers' associations
- **rt** machinery cooperatives
- **rt** public services

COOPERATIVES
- **NT1** consumer cooperatives
- **NT1** dairy cooperatives
- **NT1** food cooperatives (agricola)
- **NT1** machinery cooperatives
- **NT1** multipurpose cooperatives
- **NT1** producer cooperatives
- **NT1** viticulture cooperatives
- **rt** collective farms
- **rt** cooperation
- **rt** cooperative activities
- **rt** cooperative housing (agricola)
- **rt** cooperative services

cooperatives, dairy
- USE **dairy cooperatives**

cooperatives, multipurpose
- USE **multipurpose cooperatives**

cooperatives, viticulture
- USE **viticulture cooperatives**

COOPERIA
- **BT1** trichostrongylidae
- **BT2** nematoda
- **NT1** cooperia curticei
- **NT1** cooperia oncophora
- **NT1** cooperia pectinata
- **NT1** cooperia punctata
- **NT1** cooperia spatulata
- **NT1** cooperia surnabada

COOPERIA CURTICEI
- **BT1** cooperia
- **BT2** trichostrongylidae
- **BT3** nematoda

COOPERIA ONCOPHORA
- **BT1** cooperia
- **BT2** trichostrongylidae
- **BT3** nematoda

COOPERIA PECTINATA
- **BT1** cooperia
- **BT2** trichostrongylidae
- **BT3** nematoda

COOPERIA PUNCTATA
- **BT1** cooperia
- **BT2** trichostrongylidae
- **BT3** nematoda

COOPERIA SPATULATA
- **BT1** cooperia

COOPERIA SPATULATA *cont.*
- **BT2** trichostrongylidae
- **BT3** nematoda

COOPERIA SURNABADA
- **BT1** cooperia
- **BT2** trichostrongylidae
- **BT3** nematoda

COORDINATION
- **BT1** correlation
- **BT1** socioeconomic organization

COOWNERSHIP
- *uf* *co-ownership*
- *uf* *communal ownership*
- *uf* *joint ownership*
- **BT1** ownership
- **BT2** tenure systems
- **rt** common lands
- **rt** cooperation

COPAIFERA
- **BT1** leguminosae
- **rt** forest trees

COPAL
- **BT1** minor forest products
- **BT2** forest products
- **BT3** products
- **BT1** resins

COPEPODA
- **BT1** crustacea
- **BT2** arthropods
- **NT1** calanoida
- **NT2** acartia
- **NT3** acartia clausi
- **NT3** acartia tonsa
- **NT2** diaptomus
- **NT2** eudiaptomus
- **NT3** eudiaptomus gracilis
- **NT3** eudiaptomus graciloides
- **NT2** eurytemora
- **NT3** eurytemora velox
- **NT2** pseudocalanus
- **NT2** skistodiaptomus
- **NT3** skistodiaptomus pallidus
- **NT2** temora
- **NT1** cyclopoida
- **NT2** acanthocyclops
- **NT3** acanthocyclops bicuspidatus
- **NT4** acanthocyclops bicuspidatus thomasi
- **NT3** acanthocyclops robustus
- **NT3** acanthocyclops vernalis
- **NT3** acanthocyclops viridis
- **NT2** cyclops
- **NT3** cyclops strenuus
- **NT2** lernaea
- **NT3** lernaea cyprinacea
- **NT2** mesocyclops
- **NT3** mesocyclops aspericornis
- **NT3** mesocyclops leuckarti
- **NT1** poecilostomatoida
- **NT2** ergasilus
- **NT3** ergasilus mirabilis
- **NT1** siphonostomatoida
- **NT2** lepeophtheirus
- **NT3** lepeophtheirus salmonis

COPERNICIA
- **BT1** palmae
- **NT1** copernicia prunifera

copernicia cerifera
- USE **copernicia prunifera**

COPERNICIA PRUNIFERA
- *uf* *copernicia cerifera*
- **BT1** copernicia
- **BT2** palmae

COPIDOSOMA
- **BT1** encyrtidae
- **BT2** hymenoptera
- **NT1** copidosoma koehleri
- **NT1** copidosoma truncatellum
- **rt** litomastix

COPIDOSOMA KOEHLERI
- **BT1** biological control agents
- **BT2** beneficial organisms

COPIDOSOMA KOEHLERI *cont.*
- **BT1** copidosoma
- **BT2** encyrtidae
- **BT3** hymenoptera

COPIDOSOMA TRUNCATELLUM
- *uf* *litomastix truncatella*
- **BT1** copidosoma
- **BT2** encyrtidae
- **BT3** hymenoptera

COPPER
- *uf* *cu (symbol)*
- **BT1** trace elements
- **BT2** elements
- **BT1** transition elements
- **BT2** metallic elements
- **BT3** elements
- **BT3** metals
- **rt** brass
- **rt** copper acetoarsenite
- **rt** copper arsenate
- **rt** copper carbonate
- **rt** copper chrome arsenate
- **rt** copper fertilizers
- **rt** copper fungicides
- **rt** copper hydroxide
- **rt** copper naphthenate
- **rt** copper oxychloride
- **rt** copper sulfate
- **rt** copper trichlorophenolate
- **rt** cuprous oxide
- **rt** hepatolenticular degeneration
- **rt** hypocupraemia
- **rt** menkes' disease
- **rt** organocopper compounds

COPPER ACETOARSENITE
- *uf* *paris green*
- **BT1** arsenical insecticides
- **BT2** arsenicals
- **BT2** insecticides
- **BT3** pesticides
- **rt** copper

COPPER ARSENATE
- **BT1** arsenates
- **BT2** arsenicals
- **BT2** inorganic salts
- **BT3** inorganic compounds
- **BT3** salts
- **BT1** arsenical insecticides
- **BT2** arsenicals
- **BT2** insecticides
- **BT3** pesticides
- **BT1** wood preservatives
- **BT2** preservatives
- **rt** copper

COPPER CARBONATE
- **BT1** carbonates
- **BT2** inorganic salts
- **BT3** inorganic compounds
- **BT3** salts
- **BT1** copper fungicides
- **BT2** fungicides
- **BT3** pesticides
- **rt** copper

COPPER CHROME ARSENATE
- **BT1** arsenates
- **BT2** arsenicals
- **BT2** inorganic salts
- **BT3** inorganic compounds
- **BT3** salts
- **BT1** wood preservatives
- **BT2** preservatives
- **rt** chromium
- **rt** copper

COPPER FERTILIZERS
- **BT1** trace element fertilizers
- **BT2** fertilizers
- **NT1** copper sulfate
- **rt** copper

COPPER FUNGICIDES
- **BT1** fungicides
- **BT2** pesticides
- **NT1** bordeaux mixture
- **NT1** burgundy mixture
- **NT1** cheshunt mixture

COPPER FUNGICIDES *cont.*
NT1 copper carbonate
NT1 copper hydroxide
NT1 copper naphthenate
NT1 copper oxychloride
NT1 copper sulfate
NT1 copper trichlorophenolate
NT1 cufraneb
NT1 cuprobam
NT1 cuprous oxide
NT1 oxine-copper
rt copper

COPPER HYDROXIDE
BT1 copper fungicides
BT2 fungicides
BT3 pesticides
BT1 hydroxides
BT2 inorganic compounds
rt copper

COPPER NAPHTHENATE
BT1 copper fungicides
BT2 fungicides
BT3 pesticides
BT1 naphthenates
BT2 organic salts
BT3 salts
BT1 wood preservatives
BT2 preservatives
rt copper

COPPER OXYCHLORIDE
BT1 bird repellents
BT2 repellents
BT1 copper fungicides
BT2 fungicides
BT3 pesticides
rt copper

COPPER SULFATE
uf *copper sulphate*
BT1 anthelmintics
BT2 antiparasitic agents
BT3 drugs
BT1 copper fertilizers
BT2 trace element fertilizers
BT3 fertilizers
BT1 copper fungicides
BT2 fungicides
BT3 pesticides
BT1 molluscicides
BT2 pesticides
BT1 ovicides and larvicides
BT2 antiparasitic agents
BT3 drugs
BT1 sulfates (inorganic salts)
BT2 inorganic salts
BT3 inorganic compounds
BT3 salts
BT2 sulfates
rt copper

copper sulphate
USE **copper sulfate**

COPPER TRICHLOROPHENOLATE
BT1 copper fungicides
BT2 fungicides
BT3 pesticides
BT1 phenoxides
BT2 organic salts
BT3 salts
rt copper

COPPICE
BT1 silvicultural systems
NT1 coppice with standards
rt coppicing
rt natural regeneration
rt shoots

COPPICE WITH STANDARDS
BT1 coppice
BT2 silvicultural systems

COPPICING
BT1 forestry practices
BT2 forestry
rt coppice
rt natural regeneration
rt osiers
rt pollarding

COPPICING *cont.*
rt shoots
rt stooling
rt suckering
rt withies

COPRA
BT1 coconut products
BT2 nut products
BT3 plant products
BT4 products
rt coconuts
rt copra meal

COPRA MEAL
BT1 oilmeals
BT2 feeds
BT2 meal
rt copra

COPRECIPITATES
BT1 milk products
BT2 products

COPRECIPITATION
BT1 analytical methods
BT2 methodology

COPRINUS
BT1 agaricales
NT1 coprinus aratus
NT1 coprinus atramentarius
NT1 coprinus comatus
NT1 coprinus micaceus

COPRINUS ARATUS
BT1 coprinus
BT2 agaricales
BT1 edible fungi
BT2 fungi
BT2 vegetables

COPRINUS ATRAMENTARIUS
BT1 coprinus
BT2 agaricales
BT1 edible fungi
BT2 fungi
BT2 vegetables

COPRINUS COMATUS
BT1 coprinus
BT2 agaricales
BT1 edible fungi
BT2 fungi
BT2 vegetables

COPRINUS MICACEUS
BT1 coprinus
BT2 agaricales
BT1 edible fungi
BT2 fungi
BT2 vegetables

COPRIS
BT1 scarabaeidae
BT2 coleoptera

COPROICA
HN from 1989
BT1 sphaeroceridae
BT2 diptera
NT1 coproica hirtula
rt leptocera

COPROICA HIRTULA
HN from 1989
uf *leptocera hirtula*
BT1 coproica
BT2 sphaeroceridae
BT3 diptera

COPROMYZA
BT1 sphaeroceridae
BT2 diptera

COPROPHAGY
BT1 feeding habits
BT2 feeding behaviour
BT3 behaviour
BT2 habits
NT1 caecotrophy
rt faeces

COPROSMA
BT1 rubiaceae

COPROSMA *cont.*
NT1 coprosma mensiesii
NT1 coprosma parviflora
NT1 coprosma propinqua
NT1 coprosma pyrifolia
NT1 coprosma repens

COPROSMA MENSIESII
BT1 coprosma
BT2 rubiaceae

COPROSMA PARVIFLORA
BT1 browse plants
BT1 coprosma
BT2 rubiaceae

COPROSMA PROPINQUA
BT1 browse plants
BT1 coprosma
BT2 rubiaceae

COPROSMA PYRIFOLIA
BT1 coprosma
BT2 rubiaceae

COPROSMA REPENS
BT1 coprosma
BT2 rubiaceae
BT1 ornamental woody plants

COPROSTANOL
BT1 cholestanes
BT2 steroids
BT3 isoprenoids
BT4 lipids
BT1 sterols
BT2 alcohols
BT2 steroids
BT3 isoprenoids
BT4 lipids
rt faeces

COPTIS
BT1 ranunculaceae

COPTOPSYLLA
BT1 coptopsyllidae
BT2 siphonaptera

COPTOPSYLLIDAE
BT1 siphonaptera
NT1 coptopsylla

COPTOTERMES
BT1 rhinotermitidae
BT2 isoptera
NT1 coptotermes acinaciformis
NT1 coptotermes formosanus

COPTOTERMES ACINACIFORMIS
BT1 coptotermes
BT2 rhinotermitidae
BT3 isoptera

COPTOTERMES FORMOSANUS
BT1 coptotermes
BT2 rhinotermitidae
BT3 isoptera

COPULATION
uf *coitus*
BT1 mating
BT2 sexual reproduction
BT3 reproduction
NT1 intromission
NT1 transport in female genitalia
rt ejaculation
rt fertilization
rt impregnation
rt insemination
rt natural mating
rt service crates
rt service period
rt sexual behaviour

COQUILLETTIDIA
BT1 culicidae
BT2 diptera
NT1 coquillettidia crassipes
NT1 coquillettidia perturbans
NT1 coquillettidia richiardii
rt mansonia (diptera)

COQUILLETTIDIA CRASSIPES
BT1 coquillettidia

COQUILLETTIDIA CRASSIPES *cont.*
BT2 culicidae
BT3 diptera

COQUILLETTIDIA PERTURBANS
uf *mansonia perturbans*
BT1 coquillettidia
BT2 culicidae
BT3 diptera

COQUILLETTIDIA RICHIARDII
uf *mansonia richiardii*
BT1 coquillettidia
BT2 culicidae
BT3 diptera

CORACIDIA
BT1 cestode larvae
BT2 helminth larvae
BT3 helminths
BT4 parasites
BT3 larvae
BT4 developmental stages

CORACIIFORMES
BT1 birds
NT1 alcedinidae
NT2 alcedo
NT3 alcedo atthis
NT2 halcyon
NT3 halcyon chloris
NT3 halcyon smyrnensis
NT2 pelargopsis
NT3 pelargopsis capensis
NT1 bucerotidae
NT1 meropidae
NT2 merops

CORAL
BT1 rocks
rt atolls

CORAL SEA
BT1 western central pacific
BT2 pacific ocean
BT3 marine areas

CORAL SOILS
BT1 soil types (lithological)

CORALLORRHIZA
BT1 orchidaceae
rt ornamental orchids

CORALS
BT1 coelenterata

CORCHORUS
BT1 tiliaceae
NT1 corchorus acutangulus
NT1 corchorus capsularis
NT1 corchorus fascicularis
NT1 corchorus olitorius
NT1 corchorus trilocularis

CORCHORUS ACUTANGULUS
BT1 corchorus
BT2 tiliaceae

CORCHORUS CAPSULARIS
BT1 corchorus
BT2 tiliaceae
BT1 leafy vegetables
BT2 vegetables
rt jute

CORCHORUS FASCICULARIS
BT1 corchorus
BT2 tiliaceae

CORCHORUS OLITORIUS
BT1 corchorus
BT2 tiliaceae
BT1 leafy vegetables
BT2 vegetables
BT1 weeds
rt jute

CORCHORUS TRILOCULARIS
BT1 corchorus
BT2 tiliaceae

CORCYRA
BT1 pyralidae
BT2 lepidoptera

CORCYRA *cont.*
NT1 corcyra cephalonica

CORCYRA CEPHALONICA
BT1 corcyra
BT2 pyralidae
BT3 lepidoptera

CORD BLOOD
BT1 blood
BT2 body fluids
BT3 fluids
rt neonates

CORDANA
BT1 deuteromycotina
NT1 cordana musae

CORDANA MUSAE
BT1 cordana
BT2 deuteromycotina

CORDEAUXIA
BT1 leguminosae
NT1 cordeauxia edulis

CORDEAUXIA EDULIS
BT1 cordeauxia
BT2 leguminosae

CORDIA
BT1 boraginaceae
NT1 cordia alliodora
NT1 cordia boissieri
NT1 cordia curassavica
NT1 cordia dichotoma
NT1 cordia glabrata
NT1 cordia goeldiana
NT1 cordia myxa
NT1 cordia rothii
NT1 cordia sinensis
NT1 cordia trichotoma
NT1 cordia verbenacea

CORDIA ALLIODORA
BT1 cordia
BT2 boraginaceae
BT1 forest trees

CORDIA BOISSIERI
BT1 cordia
BT2 boraginaceae

CORDIA CURASSAVICA
uf *cordia cylindrostachys*
BT1 cordia
BT2 boraginaceae

cordia cylindrostachys
USE **cordia curassavica**

CORDIA DICHOTOMA
uf *cordia obliqua*
BT1 cordia
BT2 boraginaceae
BT1 nematicidal plants
BT2 pesticidal plants
BT1 oilseed plants
BT2 fatty oil plants
BT3 oil plants

CORDIA GLABRATA
BT1 cordia
BT2 boraginaceae

CORDIA GOELDIANA
BT1 cordia
BT2 boraginaceae
BT1 forest trees

CORDIA MYXA
BT1 cordia
BT2 boraginaceae
BT1 nematicidal plants
BT2 pesticidal plants

cordia obliqua
USE **cordia dichotoma**

CORDIA ROTHII
BT1 browse plants
BT1 cordia
BT2 boraginaceae

CORDIA SINENSIS
BT1 cordia

CORDIA SINENSIS *cont.*
BT2 boraginaceae

CORDIA TRICHOTOMA
BT1 cordia
BT2 boraginaceae

CORDIA VERBENACEA
BT1 cordia
BT2 boraginaceae
BT1 oilseed plants
BT2 fatty oil plants
BT3 oil plants

CORDIALS (AGRICOLA)
BT1 beverages

CORDUROY (AGRICOLA)
BT1 fabrics

CORDWOOD
BT1 roundwood
BT2 forest products
BT3 products
BT2 wood
NT1 fuelwood
rt pulpwood production

CORDYCEPIN
BT1 deoxyribonucleosides
BT2 nucleosides
BT3 glycosides
BT4 carbohydrates
BT1 mycotoxins
BT2 toxins
BT1 nucleoside antibiotics
BT2 antibiotics
BT2 nucleosides
BT3 glycosides
BT4 carbohydrates
rt cordyceps militaris

CORDYCEPS
BT1 clavicipitales
BT1 entomogenous fungi
BT2 entomopathogens
BT3 pathogens
BT2 fungi
NT1 cordyceps militaris

CORDYCEPS MILITARIS
BT1 cordyceps
BT2 clavicipitales
BT2 entomogenous fungi
BT3 entomopathogens
BT4 pathogens
BT3 fungi
rt cordycepin

CORDYLA
BT1 leguminosae
NT1 cordyla africana

CORDYLA AFRICANA
BT1 cordyla
BT2 leguminosae

CORDYLINE
BT1 agavaceae
NT1 cordyline australis
NT1 cordyline cannifolia
NT1 cordyline fruticosa
NT1 cordyline indivisa

CORDYLINE AUSTRALIS
BT1 cordyline
BT2 agavaceae

CORDYLINE CANNIFOLIA
BT1 cordyline
BT2 agavaceae

CORDYLINE FRUTICOSA
uf *cordyline terminalis*
BT1 cordyline
BT2 agavaceae
BT1 ornamental woody plants

CORDYLINE INDIVISA
BT1 cordyline
BT2 agavaceae
BT1 fibre plants
BT1 ornamental woody plants
rt ornamental foliage plants

cordyline terminalis
USE **cordyline fruticosa**

CORDYLOBIA
BT1 calliphoridae
BT2 diptera
NT1 cordylobia anthropophaga

CORDYLOBIA ANTHROPOPHAGA
BT1 cordylobia
BT2 calliphoridae
BT3 diptera

CORE CURRICULUM (AGRICOLA)
BT1 curriculum
BT2 educational courses

CORE FLUSH
BT1 plant disorders
BT2 disorders
rt apples

CORE SAMPLERS
uf *samplers, core*
BT1 samplers
BT2 equipment
rt core sampling

CORE SAMPLING
BT1 sampling
BT2 techniques
rt core samplers

COREGONUS
BT1 salmonidae
BT2 salmoniformes
BT3 osteichthyes
BT4 fishes

COREIDAE
BT1 heteroptera
NT1 amblypelta
NT2 amblypelta cocophaga
NT2 amblypelta lutescens
NT2 amblypelta nitida
NT2 amblypelta theobromae
NT1 anoplocnemis
NT2 anoplocnemis curvipes
NT1 chelinidea
NT2 chelinidea vittiger
NT1 clavigralla
NT2 clavigralla gibbosa
NT2 clavigralla horrida
NT2 clavigralla tomentosicollis
NT1 cletus
NT2 cletus punctiger
NT1 gonocerus
NT2 gonocerus acuteangulatus
NT1 leptocorisa
NT2 leptocorisa acuta
NT2 leptocorisa chinensis
NT2 leptocorisa oratorius
NT1 leptoglossus
NT1 pseudotheraptus
NT2 pseudotheraptus devastans
NT1 riptortus
NT2 riptortus clavatus
NT2 riptortus dentipes
NT2 riptortus linearis
NT1 veneza
NT2 veneza corculus
NT2 veneza phyllopus

COREOPSIS
BT1 compositae
NT1 coreopsis auriculata
NT1 coreopsis basalis
NT1 coreopsis grandiflora
NT1 coreopsis nuecensis
NT1 coreopsis saxicola
NT1 coreopsis tinctoria
NT1 coreopsis tripteris

COREOPSIS AURICULATA
BT1 coreopsis
BT2 compositae

COREOPSIS BASALIS
BT1 coreopsis
BT2 compositae

COREOPSIS GRANDIFLORA
BT1 coreopsis

COREOPSIS GRANDIFLORA *cont.*
BT2 compositae
BT1 ornamental herbaceous plants

COREOPSIS NUECENSIS
BT1 coreopsis
BT2 compositae

COREOPSIS SAXICOLA
BT1 coreopsis
BT2 compositae

COREOPSIS TINCTORIA
BT1 coreopsis
BT2 compositae
BT1 ornamental herbaceous plants

COREOPSIS TRIPTERIS
BT1 coreopsis
BT2 compositae

CORETHRELLA
BT1 chaoboridae
BT2 diptera
NT1 corethrella brakeleyi

CORETHRELLA BRAKELEYI
BT1 corethrella
BT2 chaoboridae
BT3 diptera

CORI CYCLE
BT1 biochemical pathways
rt metabolism

coriander
USE **coriandrum sativum**

CORIANDRUM
BT1 umbelliferae
NT1 coriandrum sativum

CORIANDRUM SATIVUM
uf *coriander*
BT1 antibacterial plants
BT1 antifungal plants
BT1 coriandrum
BT2 umbelliferae
BT1 essential oil plants
BT2 oil plants
BT1 medicinal plants
BT1 spice plants

CORIARIA
BT1 coriariaceae
NT1 coriaria japonica
NT1 coriaria myrtifolia

CORIARIA JAPONICA
BT1 coriaria
BT2 coriariaceae
BT1 ornamental woody plants

CORIARIA MYRTIFOLIA
BT1 coriaria
BT2 coriariaceae
BT1 ornamental woody plants

CORIARIACEAE
NT1 coriaria
NT2 coriaria japonica
NT2 coriaria myrtifolia

CORIOLUS
BT1 aphyllophorales
NT1 coriolus hirsutus
NT1 coriolus versicolor
rt polyporus
rt polystictus
rt pycnoporus
rt trametes

CORIOLUS HIRSUTUS
uf *polyporus hirsutus*
uf *polystictus hirsutus*
uf *trametes hirsuta*
BT1 coriolus
BT2 aphyllophorales

coriolus sanguineus
USE **pycnoporus sanguineus**

CORIOLUS VERSICOLOR
uf *polyporus versicolor*

CORIOLUS VERSICOLOR *cont.*
uf *polystictus versicolor*
uf *trametes versicolor*
BT1 coriolus
BT2 aphyllophorales
BT1 edible fungi
BT2 fungi
BT2 vegetables

CORK
BT1 minor forest products
BT2 forest products
BT3 products
rt bark
rt corks (agricola)
rt periderm
rt quercus suber
rt suberin
rt suberization

CORK SPOT
BT1 plant disorders
BT2 disorders
rt apples
rt pears

CORKING
BT1 plant disorders
BT2 disorders
rt apples

CORKS (AGRICOLA)
BT1 closures (agricola)
rt cork

cormorants
USE **phalacrocorax**

CORMS
BT1 plant
BT1 propagation materials
NT1 seed corms
rt acidanthera bicolor
rt colchicum autumnale
rt colchicum luteum
rt colchicum speciosum
rt crocosmia crocosmiiflora
rt crocosmia masoniorum
rt crocus boryi
rt crocus kotschyanus
rt crocus laevigatus
rt crocus olivieri
rt crocus pallasii
rt crocus sativus
rt crocus tommasinianus
rt crocus tournefortii
rt freesia
rt gladiolus atroviolaceus
rt gladiolus communis
rt gladiolus illyricus
rt gladiolus imbricatus
rt gladiolus italicus
rt gladiolus natalensis
rt gladiolus palustris
rt homoglossum
rt ixia polystachya
rt lapeirousia laxa
rt romulea rosea
rt sparaxis grandiflora
rt sparaxis tricolor
rt stems
rt tritonia crocata
rt vegetative propagation

corn
USE **maize**
OR **zea mays**

CORN BELT OF USA
BT1 north central states of usa
BT2 usa
BT3 north america
BT4 america
NT1 illinois
NT1 indiana
NT1 iowa
NT1 missouri
NT1 ohio

corn oil
USE **maize oil**

corn salad
USE **valerianella locusta**

CORN-SOY-MILK (AGRICOLA)
uf *csm*
BT1 milk substitutes
BT2 products
BT2 substitutes

CORN SYRUP
uf *maize syrup*
BT1 glucose syrups
BT2 syrups
BT3 liquids
rt maize

CORNACEAE
NT1 aucuba
NT2 aucuba japonica
NT1 cornus
NT2 cornus alba
NT2 cornus amomum
NT2 cornus canadensis
NT2 cornus controversa
NT2 cornus disciflora
NT2 cornus excelsa
NT2 cornus florida
NT2 cornus kousa
NT2 cornus mas
NT2 cornus nuttallii
NT2 cornus sanguinea
NT2 cornus sericea
NT2 cornus stolonifera
NT2 cornus suecica

CORNEA
uf *eye cornea*
BT1 eyes
BT2 sense organs
BT3 body parts
rt keratitis
rt keratoconjunctivitis
rt keratomalacia
rt xerophthalmia

CORNED BEEF (AGRICOLA)
BT1 cured meats (agricola)
BT2 cured products (agricola)
BT3 foods
BT3 products
BT2 meat products
BT3 animal products
BT4 products
rt beef

CORNFLOUR
BT1 cereal flours
BT2 cereal products
BT3 plant products
BT4 products
BT2 flours
BT3 plant products
BT4 products
rt maize

CORNUS
BT1 cornaceae
NT1 cornus alba
NT1 cornus amomum
NT1 cornus canadensis
NT1 cornus controversa
NT1 cornus disciflora
NT1 cornus excelsa
NT1 cornus florida
NT1 cornus kousa
NT1 cornus mas
NT1 cornus nuttallii
NT1 cornus sanguinea
NT1 cornus sericea
NT1 cornus stolonifera
NT1 cornus suecica

CORNUS ALBA
uf *thelycrania alba*
BT1 cornus
BT2 cornaceae
BT1 ornamental woody plants

CORNUS AMOMUM
BT1 cornus
BT2 cornaceae
BT1 ornamental woody plants

CORNUS CANADENSIS
BT1 cornus
BT2 cornaceae

CORNUS CONTROVERSA
BT1 cornus
BT2 cornaceae
BT1 ornamental woody plants

CORNUS DISCIFLORA
BT1 cornus
BT2 cornaceae

CORNUS EXCELSA
BT1 cornus
BT2 cornaceae

CORNUS FLORIDA
BT1 cornus
BT2 cornaceae
BT1 forest trees

CORNUS KOUSA
BT1 cornus
BT2 cornaceae
BT1 ornamental woody plants

CORNUS MAS
BT1 cornus
BT2 cornaceae
BT1 ornamental woody plants

CORNUS NUTTALLII
BT1 cornus
BT2 cornaceae
BT1 ornamental woody plants

CORNUS SANGUINEA
BT1 cornus
BT2 cornaceae
BT1 ornamental woody plants

CORNUS SERICEA
BT1 cornus
BT2 cornaceae
BT1 ornamental woody plants

CORNUS STOLONIFERA
BT1 cornus
BT2 cornaceae
BT1 ornamental woody plants

CORNUS SUECICA
BT1 cornus
BT2 cornaceae

CORNUTIPLUSIA
HN from 1989
BT1 noctuidae
BT2 lepidoptera
NT1 cornutiplusia circumflexa
rt autographa
rt phytometra
rt syngrapha

CORNUTIPLUSIA CIRCUMFLEXA
HN from 1989; previously syngrapha circumflexa
uf *autographa circumflexa*
uf *phytometra circumflexa*
uf *syngrapha circumflexa*
BT1 cornutiplusia
BT2 noctuidae
BT3 lepidoptera

COROLLA
uf *petals*
BT1 flowers
BT2 inflorescences
BT3 plant

CORONA DISCHARGE
BT1 electric discharges
BT2 discharges
rt ionizing radiation

coronary diseases
USE **heart diseases**

CORONARY VESSELS
BT1 blood vessels
BT2 cardiovascular system
BT3 body parts

CORONAVIRIDAE
BT1 viruses
NT1 coronavirus
NT2 canine coronavirus
NT2 feline peritonitis virus

CORONAVIRIDAE *cont.*
NT2 human coronavirus
NT2 infectious bronchitis virus
NT2 murine hepatitis virus
NT2 porcine coronavirus
NT3 transmissible gastroenteritis virus
NT2 sialodacryoadenitis virus
NT2 turkey bluecomb disease virus

CORONAVIRUS
BT1 coronaviridae
BT2 viruses
NT1 canine coronavirus
NT1 feline peritonitis virus
NT1 human coronavirus
NT1 infectious bronchitis virus
NT1 murine hepatitis virus
NT1 porcine coronavirus
NT2 transmissible gastroenteritis virus
NT1 sialodacryoadenitis virus
NT1 turkey bluecomb disease virus

CORONILLA
BT1 leguminosae
NT1 coronilla emerus
NT1 coronilla valentina
NT1 coronilla varia

CORONILLA EMERUS
BT1 coronilla
BT2 leguminosae
BT1 fodder legumes
BT2 fodder plants
BT2 legumes
BT1 pasture legumes
BT2 legumes
BT2 pasture plants

coronilla glauca
USE **coronilla valentina**

CORONILLA VALENTINA
uf *coronilla glauca*
BT1 coronilla
BT2 leguminosae
BT1 ornamental woody plants

CORONILLA VARIA
uf *crown vetch*
BT1 coronilla
BT2 leguminosae
BT1 fodder legumes
BT2 fodder plants
BT2 legumes
BT1 medicinal plants
BT1 pasture legumes
BT2 legumes
BT2 pasture plants
BT1 weeds

CORONOPUS
BT1 cruciferae
NT1 coronopus didymus

CORONOPUS DIDYMUS
BT1 coronopus
BT2 cruciferae

COROPHIUM
BT1 amphipoda
BT2 malacostraca
BT3 crustacea
BT4 arthropods

COROZO
BT1 palmae

corozo oleifera
USE **elaeis oleifera**

CORPORA ALLATA
BT1 neurosecretory system
BT2 body parts

CORPORA CARDIACA
BT1 neurosecretory system
BT2 body parts

corporations
USE **companies**

CORPUS EPIDIDYMIDIS
BT1 epididymis
BT2 testes
BT3 gonads
BT4 reproductive organs

CORPUS LUTEUM
BT1 ovaries
BT2 gonads
BT3 reproductive organs
rt enucleation
rt luteal cells
rt luteinization
rt oestrous cycle
rt sex hormones

CORPUS LUTEUM HORMONES
BT1 sex hormones
BT2 hormones
NT1 progesterone
NT1 relaxin

CORREA
BT1 rutaceae

CORRECTION FACTORS
rt accuracy
rt measurement

CORRECTIONAL INSTITUTIONS
uf *prisons*
BT1 institutions (agricola)
rt crime

CORRELATED RESPONSES
BT1 selection responses
rt correlation

CORRELATED TRAITS
BT1 traits
rt correlation

CORRELATION
NT1 autocorrelation
NT1 canonical correlation
NT1 coefficient of relationship
NT1 coordination
NT1 covariance
NT2 genetic covariance
NT1 genetic correlation
NT1 phenotypic correlation
NT1 yield correlations
rt correlated responses
rt correlated traits
rt correlation analysis
rt relationships

CORRELATION ANALYSIS
BT1 statistical analysis
BT2 data analysis
BT2 statistics
NT1 transect correlograms
rt canonical correlation
rt correlation
rt regression analysis

CORRESPONDENCE COURSES
BT1 educational courses
rt distance teaching

CORRIDOR SYSTEMS
BT1 fallow systems
BT2 cropping systems
BT1 shifting cultivation
BT2 cropping systems
rt agroforestry systems

CORRIEDALE
BT1 sheep breeds
BT2 breeds

CORROSION
BT1 chemical degradation
BT2 degradation
NT1 rust
rt corrosion protection
rt corrosion resistance
rt metallurgy
rt microbial corrosion
rt wear

corrosion in soil
USE **deterioration of materials in soil**

CORROSION PROTECTION
BT1 protection
rt corrosion
rt corrosion resistance
rt methenamine
rt preservation
rt protective coatings

CORROSION RESISTANCE
BT1 resistance
rt corrosion
rt corrosion protection
rt protective coatings

CORRUGATED PLASTIC PIPES
BT1 plastic pipes
BT2 irrigation equipment
BT3 equipment
BT2 pipes
BT3 components

CORRUGATIONS
rt ridges

CORRUPTION
BT1 political power
BT2 politics
rt authority
rt crime

CORSICA
BT1 france
BT2 western europe
BT3 europe

CORSICAN
BT1 sheep breeds
BT2 breeds

CORTADERIA
BT1 gramineae
NT1 cortaderia fulvida
NT1 cortaderia jubata
NT1 cortaderia selloana

CORTADERIA FULVIDA
BT1 cortaderia
BT2 gramineae

CORTADERIA JUBATA
BT1 cortaderia
BT2 gramineae

CORTADERIA SELLOANA
BT1 cortaderia
BT2 gramineae
BT1 ornamental herbaceous plants
BT1 poisonous plants

CORTEX
BT1 plant tissues
BT2 plant
BT2 tissues
rt bark
rt parenchyma

CORTHYLUS
BT1 scolytidae
BT2 coleoptera

CORTICIUM
BT1 aphyllophorales
NT1 corticium fuciforme
NT1 corticium galactinum
NT1 corticium invisum
NT1 corticium rolfsii
NT1 corticium salmonicolor
NT1 corticium theae
rt athelia
rt koleroga
rt pellicularia
rt sclerotium
rt thanatephorus

corticium centrifugum
USE **athelia epiphylla**

CORTICIUM FUCIFORME
BT1 corticium
BT2 aphyllophorales

CORTICIUM GALACTINUM
BT1 corticium
BT2 aphyllophorales

CORTICIUM INVISUM
BT1 corticium
BT2 aphyllophorales

corticium koleroga
USE **koleroga noxius**

corticium praticola
USE **thanatephorus praticola**

CORTICIUM ROLFSII
uf *sclerotium rolfsii*
BT1 corticium
BT2 aphyllophorales

CORTICIUM SALMONICOLOR
BT1 corticium
BT2 aphyllophorales

corticium sasakii
USE **thanatephorus sasakii**

corticium solani
USE **thanatephorus cucumeris**

CORTICIUM THEAE
BT1 corticium
BT2 aphyllophorales

CORTICOIDS
uf *corticosteroids*
NT1 adrenal cortex hormones
NT2 glucocorticoids
NT3 corticosterone
NT3 cortisone
NT3 hydrocortisone
NT2 mineralocorticoids
NT3 aldosterone
NT3 corticosterone
NT3 cortisone
NT3 desoxycortone
NT3 hydrocortisone
NT1 synthetic corticoids
NT2 synthetic glucocorticoids
NT3 betamethasone
NT3 dexamethasone
NT3 fludrocortisone
NT3 flumetasone
NT3 prednisolone
NT3 prednisone
NT3 triamcinolone
NT2 synthetic mineralocorticoids

CORTICOLIBERIN
uf *corticotropin releasing factor*
uf *corticotropin releasing hormone*
BT1 hypothalamic releasing hormones
BT2 hormones
BT1 neuropeptides
BT2 peptides
rt corticotropin

corticosteroids
USE **corticoids**

CORTICOSTERONE
BT1 glucocorticoids
BT2 adrenal cortex hormones
BT3 corticoids
BT3 hormones
BT1 mineralocorticoids
BT2 adrenal cortex hormones
BT3 corticoids
BT3 hormones
BT1 pregnanes
BT2 steroids
BT3 isoprenoids
BT4 lipids

CORTICOTROPIN
uf *acth*
uf *adrenocorticotropic hormone*
uf *adrenocorticotropin*
BT1 neuropeptides
BT2 peptides
BT1 pituitary hormones
BT2 hormones
rt corticoliberin

corticotropin releasing factor
USE **corticoliberin**

corticotropin releasing hormone
USE **corticoliberin**

CORTINARIUS
BT1 agaricales
NT1 cortinarius armillatus

CORTINARIUS ARMILLATUS
BT1 cortinarius
BT2 agaricales

cortisol
USE **hydrocortisone**

CORTISONE
BT1 glucocorticoids
BT2 adrenal cortex hormones
BT3 corticoids
BT3 hormones
BT1 mineralocorticoids
BT2 adrenal cortex hormones
BT3 corticoids
BT3 hormones
BT1 pregnanes
BT2 steroids
BT3 isoprenoids
BT4 lipids

CORVIDAE
BT1 passeriformes
BT2 birds
NT1 corvus
NT2 corvus brachyrhynchos
NT2 corvus corax
NT2 corvus corone
NT2 corvus frugilegus
NT2 corvus monedula
NT2 corvus splendens
NT1 garrulus
NT2 garrulus glandarius
NT1 pica (genus)
NT2 pica pica

CORVUS
uf *crows*
BT1 corvidae
BT2 passeriformes
BT3 birds
NT1 corvus brachyrhynchos
NT1 corvus corax
NT1 corvus corone
NT1 corvus frugilegus
NT1 corvus monedula
NT1 corvus splendens

CORVUS BRACHYRHYNCHOS
BT1 corvus
BT2 corvidae
BT3 passeriformes
BT4 birds

CORVUS CORAX
uf *raven*
BT1 corvus
BT2 corvidae
BT3 passeriformes
BT4 birds

CORVUS CORONE
BT1 corvus
BT2 corvidae
BT3 passeriformes
BT4 birds

CORVUS FRUGILEGUS
uf *rook*
BT1 corvus
BT2 corvidae
BT3 passeriformes
BT4 birds

CORVUS MONEDULA
BT1 corvus
BT2 corvidae
BT3 passeriformes
BT4 birds

CORVUS SPLENDENS
BT1 corvus
BT2 corvidae
BT3 passeriformes

CORVUS SPLENDENS *cont.*
BT4 birds

CORYANTHES
BT1 orchidaceae
NT1 coryanthes yohimbe

CORYANTHES YOHIMBE
BT1 coryanthes
BT2 orchidaceae
BT1 medicinal plants

CORYDALIS
BT1 fumariaceae
NT1 corydalis cava
NT1 corydalis gigantea
NT1 corydalis govaniana
NT1 corydalis incisa
NT1 corydalis ledebouriana
NT1 corydalis lutea
NT1 corydalis marschalliana
NT1 corydalis ochotensis
NT1 corydalis ophiocarpa
NT1 corydalis remota
NT1 corydalis rosea
NT1 corydalis solida
NT1 corydalis vaginans

corydalis bulbosa
USE **corydalis cava**

CORYDALIS CAVA
uf *corydalis bulbosa*
BT1 corydalis
BT2 fumariaceae

CORYDALIS GIGANTEA
BT1 corydalis
BT2 fumariaceae

CORYDALIS GOVANIANA
BT1 corydalis
BT2 fumariaceae

CORYDALIS INCISA
BT1 corydalis
BT2 fumariaceae

CORYDALIS LEDEBOURIANA
BT1 corydalis
BT2 fumariaceae

CORYDALIS LUTEA
BT1 corydalis
BT2 fumariaceae
BT1 ornamental bulbs
rt tubers

CORYDALIS MARSCHALLIANA
BT1 corydalis
BT2 fumariaceae

CORYDALIS OCHOTENSIS
BT1 corydalis
BT2 fumariaceae

CORYDALIS OPHIOCARPA
BT1 corydalis
BT2 fumariaceae

CORYDALIS REMOTA
BT1 corydalis
BT2 fumariaceae

CORYDALIS ROSEA
BT1 corydalis
BT2 fumariaceae

CORYDALIS SOLIDA
BT1 corydalis
BT2 fumariaceae

CORYDALIS VAGINANS
BT1 corydalis
BT2 fumariaceae

CORYLACEAE
NT1 corylus
NT2 corylus avellana
NT2 corylus colurna
NT2 corylus cornuta
NT2 corylus heterophylla
NT2 corylus maxima
NT2 corylus sieboldiana

CORYLOBIUM
BT1 aphididae
BT2 aphidoidea
BT3 sternorrhyncha
BT4 homoptera
NT1 corylobium avellanae

CORYLOBIUM AVELLANAE
BT1 corylobium
BT2 aphididae
BT3 aphidoidea
BT4 sternorrhyncha
BT5 homoptera

CORYLOPSIS
BT1 hamamelidaceae

CORYLUS
BT1 corylaceae
NT1 corylus avellana
NT1 corylus colurna
NT1 corylus cornuta
NT1 corylus heterophylla
NT1 corylus maxima
NT1 corylus sieboldiana
rt withies

CORYLUS AVELLANA
BT1 corylus
BT2 corylaceae
BT1 forest trees
rt hazelnuts

CORYLUS COLURNA
BT1 corylus
BT2 corylaceae

CORYLUS CORNUTA
BT1 corylus
BT2 corylaceae
BT1 ornamental woody plants

CORYLUS HETEROPHYLLA
BT1 corylus
BT2 corylaceae

CORYLUS MAXIMA
BT1 corylus
BT2 corylaceae
BT1 forest trees

CORYLUS SIEBOLDIANA
BT1 corylus
BT2 corylaceae

CORYNANTHE
BT1 rubiaceae
NT1 corynanthe mayumbensis

CORYNANTHE MAYUMBENSIS
BT1 corynanthe
BT2 rubiaceae

CORYNEBACTERIACEAE
BT1 coryneform group of bacteria
BT2 firmicutes
BT3 bacteria
BT4 prokaryotes
NT1 corynebacterium
NT2 corynebacterium bovis
NT2 corynebacterium ovis
NT2 corynebacterium pseudotuberculosis
NT2 corynebacterium renale

CORYNEBACTERIUM
BT1 corynebacteriaceae
BT2 coryneform group of bacteria
BT3 firmicutes
BT4 bacteria
BT5 prokaryotes
NT1 corynebacterium bovis
NT1 corynebacterium ovis
NT1 corynebacterium pseudotuberculosis
NT1 corynebacterium renale
rt clavibacter
rt curtobacterium
rt rhodococcus (bacteria)

CORYNEBACTERIUM BOVIS
BT1 corynebacterium
BT2 corynebacteriaceae

CORYNEBACTERIUM BOVIS *cont.*
BT3 coryneform group of bacteria
BT4 firmicutes
BT5 bacteria
BT6 prokaryotes

corynebacterium equi
USE **rhodococcus equi**

corynebacterium fascians
USE **rhodococcus fascians**

corynebacterium flaccumfaciens
USE **curtobacterium flaccumfaciens**

corynebacterium michiganense
USE **clavibacter michiganensis**

corynebacterium michiganense pv. insidiosum
USE **clavibacter michiganensis subsp. insidiosus**

corynebacterium michiganense pv. iranicum
USE **clavibacter iranicus**

corynebacterium michiganense pv. michiganense
USE **clavibacter michiganensis subsp. michiganensis**

corynebacterium michiganense pv. nebraskense
USE **clavibacter michiganensis subsp. nebraskensis**

corynebacterium michiganense pv. sepedonicum
USE **clavibacter michiganensis subsp. sepedonicus**

corynebacterium michiganense pv. tritici
USE **clavibacter tritici**

corynebacterium nebraskense
USE **clavibacter michiganensis subsp. nebraskensis**

CORYNEBACTERIUM OVIS
uf *ulcerative lymphangitis agent*
BT1 corynebacterium
BT2 corynebacteriaceae
BT3 coryneform group of bacteria
BT4 firmicutes
BT5 bacteria
BT6 prokaryotes

CORYNEBACTERIUM PSEUDOTUBERCULOSIS
BT1 corynebacterium
BT2 corynebacteriaceae
BT3 coryneform group of bacteria
BT4 firmicutes
BT5 bacteria
BT6 prokaryotes

corynebacterium pyogenes
USE **actinomyces pyogenes**

corynebacterium rathayi
USE **clavibacter rathayi**

CORYNEBACTERIUM RENALE
BT1 corynebacterium
BT2 corynebacteriaceae
BT3 coryneform group of bacteria
BT4 firmicutes
BT5 bacteria
BT6 prokaryotes

corynebacterium sepedonicum
USE **clavibacter michiganensis subsp. sepedonicus**

CORYNEFORM GROUP OF BACTERIA
BT1 firmicutes
BT2 bacteria

CORYNEFORM GROUP OF BACTERIA *cont.*
BT3 prokaryotes
NT1 brevibacteriaceae
NT2 brevibacterium
NT3 brevibacterium linens
NT1 clavibacter
NT2 clavibacter iranicus
NT2 clavibacter michiganensis
NT3 clavibacter michiganensis subsp. insidiosus
NT3 clavibacter michiganensis subsp. michiganensis
NT3 clavibacter michiganensis subsp. nebraskensis
NT3 clavibacter michiganensis subsp. sepedonicus
NT2 clavibacter rathayi
NT2 clavibacter tritici
NT2 clavibacter xyli
NT3 clavibacter xyli subsp. xyli
NT1 corynebacteriaceae
NT2 corynebacterium
NT3 corynebacterium bovis
NT3 corynebacterium ovis
NT3 corynebacterium pseudotuberculosis
NT3 corynebacterium renale
NT1 curtobacterium
NT2 curtobacterium flaccumfaciens
NT3 curtobacterium flaccumfaciens pv. betae
NT3 curtobacterium flaccumfaciens pv. flaccumfaciens
NT3 curtobacterium flaccumfaciens pv. oortii
NT3 curtobacterium flaccumfaciens pv. poinsettiae
NT1 propionibacteriaceae
NT2 propionibacterium
NT3 propionibacterium freudenreichii
NT4 propionibacterium freudenreichii subsp. shermanii

CORYNEPHORUS
BT1 gramineae
NT1 corynephorus canescens

CORYNEPHORUS CANESCENS
BT1 corynephorus
BT2 gramineae

CORYNESPORA
BT1 deuteromycotina
NT1 corynespora cassiicola

CORYNESPORA CASSIICOLA
uf *corynespora melonis*
BT1 corynespora
BT2 deuteromycotina

corynespora melonis
USE **corynespora cassiicola**

CORYNEUM
BT1 deuteromycotina
rt seiridium
rt stigmina

coryneum beijerinckii
USE **stigmina carpophila**

coryneum cardinale
USE **seiridium cardinale**

CORYPHA
BT1 palmae
NT1 corypha umbraculifera
NT1 corypha utan

corypha elata
USE **corypha utan**

CORYPHA UMBRACULIFERA
BT1 corypha
BT2 palmae

CORYPHA UTAN
uf *corypha elata*
BT1 corypha
BT2 palmae
BT1 fibre plants
BT1 sugar crops

CORYPHANTHA
BT1 cactaceae
NT1 coryphantha calipensis
NT1 coryphantha cladispina
NT1 coryphantha greenwoodii
NT1 coryphantha macromeris
NT1 coryphantha ramillosa
NT1 coryphantha robbinsorum

CORYPHANTHA CALIPENSIS
BT1 coryphantha
BT2 cactaceae
BT1 ornamental succulent plants
BT2 succulent plants

CORYPHANTHA CLADISPINA
BT1 coryphantha
BT2 cactaceae
BT1 ornamental succulent plants
BT2 succulent plants

CORYPHANTHA GREENWOODII
BT1 coryphantha
BT2 cactaceae
BT1 ornamental succulent plants
BT2 succulent plants

CORYPHANTHA MACROMERIS
BT1 coryphantha
BT2 cactaceae
BT1 ornamental succulent plants
BT2 succulent plants

CORYPHANTHA RAMILLOSA
BT1 coryphantha
BT2 cactaceae
BT1 ornamental succulent plants
BT2 succulent plants

CORYPHANTHA ROBBINSORUM
BT1 coryphantha
BT2 cactaceae
BT1 ornamental succulent plants
BT2 succulent plants

coryphantha vivipara
USE **escobaria vivipara**

CORYTHUCHA
BT1 tingidae
BT2 heteroptera
NT1 corythucha ciliata

CORYTHUCHA CILIATA
BT1 corythucha
BT2 tingidae
BT3 heteroptera

CORYZA
BT1 respiratory diseases
BT2 organic diseases
BT3 diseases
rt rhinitis

COSCINIUM
BT1 menispermaceae
NT1 coscinium fenestratum

COSCINIUM FENESTRATUM
BT1 coscinium
BT2 menispermaceae
BT1 dye plants
BT1 medicinal plants

COSLENCHUS
BT1 tylenchidae
BT2 nematoda
NT1 coslenchus costatus
rt aglenchus

COSLENCHUS COSTATUS
uf *aglenchus costatus*
BT1 coslenchus
BT2 tylenchidae
BT3 nematoda

COSMETIC SURGERY
BT1 surgery

COSMETIC SURGERY *cont.*
BT2 medicine

COSMETICS
HN from 1989
BT1 non-food products
BT2 products

COSMIDS
HN from 1990
BT1 vectors

COSMOCERCA
BT1 cosmocercidae
BT2 nematoda

COSMOCERCIDAE
BT1 nematoda
NT1 cosmocerca
rt animal parasitic nematodes

cosmophila
USE **anomis**

cosmophila flava
USE **anomis flava**

COSMOPOLITES
BT1 curculionidae
BT2 coleoptera
NT1 cosmopolites sordidus

COSMOPOLITES SORDIDUS
BT1 cosmopolites
BT2 curculionidae
BT3 coleoptera

COSMOPTERIGIDAE
BT1 lepidoptera
NT1 batrachedra
NT2 batrachedra amydraula
NT2 batrachedra arenosella
NT1 pyroderces
NT2 pyroderces simplex

COSMOS
BT1 compositae
NT1 cosmos bipinnatus

COSMOS BIPINNATUS
uf *bidens formosa*
BT1 cosmos
BT2 compositae
BT1 nematicidal plants
BT2 pesticidal plants
BT1 ornamental herbaceous plants

COSMOTRICHE
BT1 lasiocampidae
BT2 lepidoptera
NT1 cosmotriche lunigera

COSMOTRICHE LUNIGERA
BT1 cosmotriche
BT2 lasiocampidae
BT3 lepidoptera

COSSETTES
HN from 1990
rt juice extraction
rt sugarbeet

COSSIDAE
BT1 lepidoptera
NT1 azygophleps
NT2 azygophleps scalaris
NT1 cossus
NT2 cossus cossus
NT1 prionoxystus
NT2 prionoxystus robiniae
NT1 zeuzera
NT2 zeuzera coffeae
NT2 zeuzera pyrina

COSSUS
BT1 cossidae
BT2 lepidoptera
NT1 cossus cossus

COSSUS COSSUS
BT1 cossus
BT2 cossidae
BT3 lepidoptera

COST ANALYSIS
uf *costing*
BT1 accounting
NT1 cash flow analysis
NT1 returns
NT2 marginal returns
rt costs
rt economic analysis

COST BENEFIT ANALYSIS
BT1 economic analysis
NT1 non-market benefits
NT2 externalities
NT1 shadow prices
rt consumer surplus
rt cost effectiveness analysis (agricola)
rt costs
rt economic thresholds
rt externalities
rt feasibility studies
rt opportunity costs
rt project appraisal
rt returns
rt social accounting
rt social costs

COST CONTROL (AGRICOLA)
BT1 control
rt costs

COST EFFECTIVENESS ANALYSIS (AGRICOLA)
BT1 economic analysis
rt cost benefit analysis

cost of living
USE **living standards**

COSTA RICA
uf *cocos island (pacific)*
BT1 central america
BT2 america
rt cacm
rt developing countries
rt threshold countries

COSTACEAE
NT1 costus
NT2 costus megalobractea
NT2 costus speciosus

COSTELYTRA
BT1 scarabaeidae
BT2 coleoptera
NT1 costelytra zealandica

COSTELYTRA ZEALANDICA
BT1 costelytra
BT2 scarabaeidae
BT3 coleoptera

costia necatrix
USE **ichthyobodo necator**

costing
USE **cost analysis**

costings
USE **costs**

COSTS
uf *charges (costs)*
uf *costings*
NT1 energy cost of activities
NT1 energy cost of maintenance
NT1 energy cost of production
NT1 estimated costs
NT1 food costs (agricola)
NT1 health care costs (agricola)
NT1 heating costs (agricola)
NT1 housing costs (agricola)
NT1 labour costs
NT1 operating costs
NT1 opportunity costs
NT1 production costs
NT2 fixed costs
NT2 milk production costs
NT2 special costs
NT2 variable costs
NT1 rental costs (agricola)
NT1 social costs
NT1 specific costs
NT1 total costs

COSTS *cont.*
NT1 transport costs (agricola)
NT1 unit costs
NT1 utility costs (agricola)
NT1 water costs
rt cost analysis
rt cost benefit analysis
rt cost control (agricola)
rt farm results
rt profitability

costs, estimated
USE **estimated costs**

costs, fixed
USE **fixed costs**

costs, operating
USE **operating costs**

costs, production
USE **production costs**

costs, social
USE **social costs**

costs, specific
USE **specific costs**

costs, total
USE **total costs**

costs, variable
USE **variable costs**

COSTUME (AGRICOLA)
rt clothing
rt costume history (agricola)

COSTUME HISTORY (AGRICOLA)
rt costume (agricola)

COSTUS
BT1 costaceae
NT1 costus megalobractea
NT1 costus speciosus

COSTUS MEGALOBRACTEA
BT1 costus
BT2 costaceae

COSTUS SPECIOSUS
BT1 costus
BT2 costaceae

COT DEATH
AF sudden infant death
BT1 death
rt infants

cote d'ivoire
USE **ivory coast**

COTENTIN
BT1 sheep breeds
BT2 breeds

COTESIA
BT1 braconidae
BT2 hymenoptera
NT1 cotesia flavipes
NT1 cotesia glomerata
NT1 cotesia hyphantriae
NT1 cotesia kurdjumovi
NT1 cotesia marginiventris
NT1 cotesia melanoscelus
NT1 cotesia plutellae
NT1 cotesia rubecula
NT1 cotesia ruficrus
NT1 cotesia telengai
NT1 cotesia tibialis
rt apanteles

cotesia congesta
USE **cotesia tibialis**

COTESIA FLAVIPES
HN from 1990; previously "apanteles flavipes"
uf *apanteles flavipes*
BT1 biological control agents
BT2 beneficial organisms
BT1 cotesia
BT2 braconidae
BT3 hymenoptera

COTESIA GLOMERATA
HN from 1990; previously "apanteles glomeratus"
uf *apanteles glomeratus*
BT1 biological control agents
BT2 beneficial organisms
BT1 cotesia
BT2 braconidae
BT3 hymenoptera

COTESIA HYPHANTRIAE
HN from 1990; previously "apanteles hyphantriae"
uf *apanteles hyphantriae*
BT1 cotesia
BT2 braconidae
BT3 hymenoptera

COTESIA KURDJUMOVI
HN from 1990; previously "apanteles kurdjumovi"
uf *apanteles kurdjumovi*
BT1 cotesia
BT2 braconidae
BT3 hymenoptera

COTESIA MARGINIVENTRIS
HN from 1990; previously "apanteles marginiventris"
uf *apanteles marginiventris*
BT1 cotesia
BT2 braconidae
BT3 hymenoptera

COTESIA MELANOSCELUS
HN from 1990; previously "apanteles melanoscelus"
uf *apanteles melanoscelus*
BT1 cotesia
BT2 braconidae
BT3 hymenoptera

COTESIA PLUTELLAE
HN from 1990; previously "apanteles plutellae"
uf *apanteles plutellae*
BT1 cotesia
BT2 braconidae
BT3 hymenoptera

COTESIA RUBECULA
HN from 1990; previously "apanteles rubecula"
uf *apanteles rubecula*
BT1 cotesia
BT2 braconidae
BT3 hymenoptera

COTESIA RUFICRUS
HN from 1990; previously "apanteles ruficrus"
uf *apanteles ruficrus*
BT1 cotesia
BT2 braconidae
BT3 hymenoptera

COTESIA TELENGAI
HN from 1990; previously "apanteles telengai"
uf *apanteles telengai*
BT1 cotesia
BT2 braconidae
BT3 hymenoptera

COTESIA TIBIALIS
HN from 1990; previously "apanteles tibialis"
uf *apanteles congestus*
uf *apanteles tibialis*
uf *cotesia congesta*
BT1 cotesia
BT2 braconidae
BT3 hymenoptera

COTHURNIA
BT1 ciliophora
BT2 protozoa
NT1 cothurnia variabilis

COTHURNIA VARIABILIS
BT1 cothurnia
BT2 ciliophora
BT3 protozoa

COTINUS
BT1 anacardiaceae
NT1 cotinus coggygria
NT1 cotinus obovatus

COTINUS COGGYGRIA
uf *rhus cotinus*
BT1 cotinus
BT2 anacardiaceae
BT1 ornamental woody plants
BT1 tan plants

COTINUS OBOVATUS
BT1 cotinus
BT2 anacardiaceae
BT1 ornamental woody plants

COTONEASTER
BT1 rosaceae
NT1 cotoneaster acutifolius
NT1 cotoneaster apiculatus
NT1 cotoneaster congestus
NT1 cotoneaster conspicuus
NT1 cotoneaster dammeri
NT1 cotoneaster divaricatus
NT1 cotoneaster glaucophyllus
NT1 cotoneaster horizontalis
NT1 cotoneaster lucidus
NT1 cotoneaster salicifolius
NT1 cotoneaster simonsii

COTONEASTER ACUTIFOLIUS
BT1 cotoneaster
BT2 rosaceae
BT1 ornamental woody plants

COTONEASTER APICULATUS
BT1 cotoneaster
BT2 rosaceae
BT1 ornamental woody plants

COTONEASTER CONGESTUS
BT1 cotoneaster
BT2 rosaceae

COTONEASTER CONSPICUUS
BT1 cotoneaster
BT2 rosaceae

COTONEASTER DAMMERI
BT1 cotoneaster
BT2 rosaceae

COTONEASTER DIVARICATUS
BT1 cotoneaster
BT2 rosaceae
BT1 ornamental woody plants

COTONEASTER GLAUCOPHYLLUS
BT1 cotoneaster
BT2 rosaceae

COTONEASTER HORIZONTALIS
BT1 cotoneaster
BT2 rosaceae
BT1 ornamental woody plants

COTONEASTER LUCIDUS
BT1 cotoneaster
BT2 rosaceae
BT1 ornamental woody plants

COTONEASTER SALICIFOLIUS
BT1 cotoneaster
BT2 rosaceae

COTONEASTER SIMONSII
BT1 cotoneaster
BT2 rosaceae

COTTAGE CHEESE
BT1 cheeses
BT2 milk products
BT3 products

COTTAGE INDUSTRY
uf *home manufacture*
uf *home production*
BT1 industry
BT1 small businesses
BT2 businesses
rt rural industry

COTTIDAE
BT1 scorpaeniformes

COTTIDAE *cont.*
BT2 osteichthyes
BT3 fishes
NT1 cottus
NT1 icelinus
NT1 leptocottus
NT1 myoxocephalus
NT1 scorpaenichthys

COTTING
HN from 1989
BT1 defects
rt wool

COTTON
BT1 fibre plants
BT1 oilseed plants
BT2 fatty oil plants
BT3 oil plants
rt bolls
rt cotton ginning
rt cotton industry
rt cotton pickers
rt cotton system (agricola)
rt cotton waste
rt cottonseed
rt fuzz
rt gossypium arboreum
rt gossypium barbadense
rt gossypium herbaceum
rt gossypium hirsutum
rt gossypol

COTTON GIN TRASH
uf *gin trash*
BT1 industrial wastes
BT2 wastes
rt cotton gins

COTTON GINNING
BT1 cotton industry
BT2 textile industry
BT3 non-food industries
BT4 industry
BT1 ginning
BT2 processing
rt cotton
rt cotton gins

COTTON GINS
BT1 gins
BT2 farm machinery
BT3 machinery
rt cotton gin trash
rt cotton ginning

COTTON INDUSTRY
BT1 textile industry
BT2 non-food industries
BT3 industry
NT1 cotton ginning
NT1 cotton system (agricola)
rt cotton

COTTON PICKERS
uf *harvesters, cotton*
BT1 harvesters
BT2 farm machinery
BT3 machinery
rt cotton

cotton rats
USE **sigmodon**

COTTON SYSTEM (AGRICOLA)
BT1 cotton industry
BT2 textile industry
BT3 non-food industries
BT4 industry
rt carding (agricola)
rt cotton

COTTON WASTE
BT1 agricultural wastes
BT2 wastes
BT1 soil conditioners
BT2 soil amendments
BT3 amendments
rt cotton

COTTONSEED
BT1 oilseeds
BT2 plant products
BT3 products

COTTONSEED *cont.*
rt cotton
rt cottonseed husks
rt cottonseed oil
rt cottonseed oilmeal
rt cottonseed products
rt cottonseed protein
rt cottonseed residues

COTTONSEED HUSKS
BT1 husks
BT2 plant residues
BT3 residues
rt cottonseed

COTTONSEED OIL
BT1 seed oils
BT2 plant oils
BT3 oils
BT3 plant products
BT4 products
rt cottonseed
rt cottonseed oilmeal

COTTONSEED OILMEAL
BT1 oilmeals
BT2 feeds
BT2 meal
rt cottonseed
rt cottonseed oil

COTTONSEED PRODUCTS
BT1 plant products
BT2 products
rt cottonseed

COTTONSEED PROTEIN
BT1 plant protein
BT2 protein
rt cottonseed

COTTONSEED RESIDUES
BT1 oilseed residues
BT2 plant residues
BT3 residues
rt cottonseed

cottontail
USE **sylvilagus**

COTTUS
BT1 cottidae
BT2 scorpaeniformes
BT3 osteichthyes
BT4 fishes

COTUGNIA
BT1 davaineidae
BT2 eucestoda
BT3 cestoda
NT1 cotugnia digonophora

COTUGNIA DIGONOPHORA
BT1 cotugnia
BT2 davaineidae
BT3 eucestoda
BT4 cestoda

COTULA
BT1 compositae
NT1 cotula cinerea

COTULA CINEREA
BT1 cotula
BT2 compositae
BT1 medicinal plants

COTURNIX
BT1 phasianidae
BT2 galliformes
BT3 birds

coturnix coturnix
USE **quails**

coturnix coturnix japonica
USE **japanese quails**

coturnix japonica
USE **japanese quails**

COTYLEDONS
BT1 seedlings
NT1 mesocotyls
rt epicotyls

COTYLEDONS *cont.*
rt hypocotyls
rt leaves
rt mesocotyls
rt plumules
rt scutellum
rt seeds

COTYLOPHORON
BT1 paramphistomatidae
BT2 digenea
BT3 trematoda
NT1 cotylophoron cotylophorum

COTYLOPHORON COTYLOPHORUM
BT1 cotylophoron
BT2 paramphistomatidae
BT3 digenea
BT4 trematoda

COTYLURUS
BT1 strigeidae
BT2 digenea
BT3 trematoda
NT1 cotylurus flabelliformis

COTYLURUS FLABELLIFORMIS
BT1 cotylurus
BT2 strigeidae
BT3 digenea
BT4 trematoda

couch
USE **elymus repens**

COUEPIA
BT1 chrysobalanaceae
NT1 couepia polyandra

COUEPIA POLYANDRA
BT1 couepia
BT2 chrysobalanaceae

cougars
USE **felis concolor**

COUGH
BT1 respiratory disorders
BT2 functional disorders
BT3 animal disorders
BT4 disorders
BT2 respiratory diseases
BT3 organic diseases
BT4 diseases

cough suppressants
USE **antitussive agents**

COULTERS
BT1 components
NT1 disc coulters
NT1 skims
NT1 suffolk coulters
rt drills
rt furrow openers
rt ploughs
rt seed tubes
rt tramlining

coulters, disc
USE **disc coulters**

coulters, suffolk
USE **suffolk coulters**

COUMA
BT1 apocynaceae
NT1 couma macrocarpa

COUMA MACROCARPA
BT1 couma
BT2 apocynaceae

COUMACHLOR
BT1 coumarin rodenticides
BT2 coumarins
BT3 lactones
BT4 heterocyclic oxygen compounds
BT4 ketones
BT2 rodenticides
BT3 pesticides

coumafos
USE **coumaphos**

COUMAPHOS
uf *coumafos*
BT1 anthelmintics
BT2 antiparasitic agents
BT3 drugs
BT1 ectoparasiticides
BT2 antiparasitic agents
BT3 drugs
BT1 organothiophosphate acaricides
BT2 organophosphorus acaricides
BT3 acaricides
BT4 pesticides
BT3 organophosphorus pesticides
BT4 organophosphorus compounds
BT1 organothiophosphate insecticides
BT2 organophosphorus insecticides
BT3 insecticides
BT4 pesticides
BT3 organophosphorus pesticides
BT4 organophosphorus compounds

P-COUMARIC ACID
BT1 coumaric acids
BT2 benzenealkenoic acids
BT3 carboxylic acids
BT4 organic acids
BT5 acids
BT1 phytoalexins
BT2 allomones
BT3 allelochemicals
BT4 semiochemicals
BT1 plant growth regulators
BT2 growth regulators

COUMARIC ACIDS
uf *hydroxycinnamic acids*
BT1 benzenealkenoic acids
BT2 carboxylic acids
BT3 organic acids
BT4 acids
NT1 p-coumaric acid
NT1 caffeic acid
NT1 ferulic acid
NT1 sinapic acid

COUMARIN
BT1 coumarins
BT2 lactones
BT3 heterocyclic oxygen compounds
BT3 ketones
BT1 flavour compounds

COUMARIN RODENTICIDES
BT1 coumarins
BT2 lactones
BT3 heterocyclic oxygen compounds
BT3 ketones
BT1 rodenticides
BT2 pesticides
NT1 brodifacoum
NT1 bromadiolone
NT1 coumachlor
NT1 coumatetralyl
NT1 difenacoum
NT1 flocoumafen
NT1 warfarin

COUMARINS
BT1 lactones
BT2 heterocyclic oxygen compounds
BT2 ketones
NT1 coumarin
NT1 coumarin rodenticides
NT2 brodifacoum
NT2 bromadiolone
NT2 coumachlor
NT2 coumatetralyl
NT2 difenacoum
NT2 flocoumafen

COUMARINS *cont.*
NT2 warfarin
NT1 coumoestrol
NT1 dicoumarol
rt ammi
rt anticoagulants
rt dyes
rt perfumery
rt trifolium

COUMATETRALYL
BT1 coumarin rodenticides
BT2 coumarins
BT3 lactones
BT4 heterocyclic oxygen compounds
BT4 ketones
BT2 rodenticides
BT3 pesticides

COUMESTROL
BF coumoestrol
BT1 plant estrogens
BT2 estrogens

COUMOESTROL
AF coumestrol
BT1 coumarins
BT2 lactones
BT3 heterocyclic oxygen compounds
BT3 ketones
BT1 plant oestrogens
BT2 oestrogens
BT3 sex hormones
BT4 hormones

COUNSELING (AGRICOLA)
NT1 diet counseling (agricola)
NT1 family counseling (agricola)
NT1 group counseling (agricola)
NT1 individual counseling (agricola)
NT1 leisure counseling
NT1 marriage counseling (agricola)

COUNTERFLOW DRIERS
AF counterflow dryers
uf *driers, counter flow*
BT1 driers
BT2 farm machinery
BT3 machinery
rt cross flow driers

COUNTERFLOW DRYERS
BF counterflow driers
BT1 dryers

COUNTERIMMUNOELECTROPHORESIS
BT1 immunoelectrophoresis
BT2 electrophoresis
BT3 analytical methods
BT4 methodology
BT2 immunoprecipitation tests
BT3 immunological techniques
BT4 techniques
BT3 tests

COUNTERS
BT1 recording instruments
BT2 instruments
NT1 seed counters
rt counting

counters, seed
USE **seed counters**

COUNTING
BT1 recording
NT1 bacterial counting
NT1 cell counting
rt counters
rt enumeration

COUNTRIES
NT1 agrarian countries
NT1 colonies
NT1 developed countries
NT2 industrial countries
NT1 developing countries
NT2 least developed countries
NT2 threshold countries
rt geography

COUNTRIES *cont.*
rt nations

COUNTRY HOUSES
BT1 buildings
rt rural housing

COUNTRY PARKS
BT1 parks

countryside planning
USE **rural planning**

COUPLINGS
BT1 components
NT1 automatic couplings
NT1 hydraulic couplings
NT1 mechanical couplings
rt drives
rt farm machinery
rt hitches
rt joints (transmissions)
rt linkages
rt pins
rt tractors

couplings, automatic
USE **automatic couplings**

couplings, hydraulic
USE **hydraulic couplings**

couplings, mechanical
USE **mechanical couplings**

COUPONS (AGRICOLA)
uf *food coupons*
rt nutrition programs

courgettes
USE **marrows**

COURTS (AGRICOLA)
NT1 juvenile court (agricola)
rt legal systems

COUTINIA
BT1 apocynaceae
NT1 coutinia succuba

COUTINIA SUCCUBA
BT1 coutinia
BT2 apocynaceae
BT1 medicinal plants

COVARIANCE
BT1 correlation
NT1 genetic covariance
rt analysis of covariance
rt variance covariance matrix

covariance analysis
USE **analysis of covariance**

COVER CROPS
rt crops
rt green manures
rt ground cover plants
rt live mulches
rt plants

COVERAGE
NT1 overlap
rt covers
rt distribution
rt operating range
rt spraying
rt spreading

COVERS
rt coatings
rt coverage
rt mulches

COVERT (AGRICOLA)
BT1 fabrics

cow
USE **cows**

COW COLOSTRUM
uf *colostrum, cow*
BT1 colostrum
BT2 body fluids
BT3 fluids

COW HOUSING
uf *cowsheds*
uf *dairy cattle housing*
BT1 cattle housing
BT2 animal housing
NT1 cubicles
rt barns
rt cows
rt dairy cattle

COW INDEXES
BT1 performance indexes
BT2 indexes
rt breeding value
rt cows
rt performance testing
rt progeny testing

cow lactation
USE **lactation**

cow milk
USE **milk**

COWANIA
BT1 rosaceae
NT1 cowania mexicana

COWANIA MEXICANA
uf *cowania stausburiana*
BT1 cowania
BT2 rosaceae

cowania stausburiana
USE **cowania mexicana**

COWDRIA
BT1 ehrlichiaceae
BT2 rickettsiales
BT3 bacteria
BT4 prokaryotes
NT1 cowdria ruminantium

COWDRIA RUMINANTIUM
BT1 cowdria
BT2 ehrlichiaceae
BT3 rickettsiales
BT4 bacteria
BT5 prokaryotes
rt heartwater

COWPEA APHID-BORNE MOSAIC VIRUS
BT1 miscellaneous plant viruses
BT2 plant viruses
BT3 plant pathogens
BT4 pathogens
rt vigna unguiculata

COWPEA BANDING MOSAIC VIRUS
BT1 miscellaneous plant viruses
BT2 plant viruses
BT3 plant pathogens
BT4 pathogens
rt vigna unguiculata

COWPEA CHLOROTIC MOTTLE BROMOVIRUS
HN from 1990; previously "cowpea chlorotic mottle virus"
uf *cowpea chlorotic mottle virus*
BT1 bromovirus group
BT2 plant viruses
BT3 plant pathogens
BT4 pathogens
rt cowpeas
rt vigna unguiculata

cowpea chlorotic mottle virus
USE **cowpea chlorotic mottle bromovirus**

COWPEA CHLOROTIC SPOT VIRUS
BT1 miscellaneous plant viruses
BT2 plant viruses
BT3 plant pathogens
BT4 pathogens
rt vigna unguiculata

COWPEA HAY
BT1 hay

COWPEA HAY *cont.*
BT2 feeds
rt vigna unguiculata

COWPEA MEAL
BT1 meal
rt vigna unguiculata

COWPEA MILD MOTTLE CARLAVIRUS
HN from 1990; previously "cowpea mild mottle virus"
uf *cowpea mild mottle virus*
BT1 carlavirus group
BT2 plant viruses
BT3 plant pathogens
BT4 pathogens
rt cowpeas
rt vigna unguiculata

cowpea mild mottle virus
USE **cowpea mild mottle carlavirus**

COWPEA MOSAIC COMOVIRUS
HN from 1990; previously "cowpea mosaic virus"
uf *cowpea mosaic virus*
BT1 comovirus group
BT2 plant viruses
BT3 plant pathogens
BT4 pathogens
rt cowpeas
rt vigna unguiculata

cowpea mosaic virus
USE **cowpea mosaic comovirus**

COWPEA SEVERE MOSAIC COMOVIRUS
HN from 1990; previously "cowpea severe mosaic virus"
uf *cowpea severe mosaic virus*
BT1 comovirus group
BT2 plant viruses
BT3 plant pathogens
BT4 pathogens
rt cowpeas
rt vigna unguiculata

cowpea severe mosaic virus
USE **cowpea severe mosaic comovirus**

COWPEA SILAGE
BT1 silage
BT2 feeds
BT2 fermentation products
BT3 products
rt vigna unguiculata

COWPEA YELLOW MOSAIC VIRUS
BT1 miscellaneous plant viruses
BT2 plant viruses
BT3 plant pathogens
BT4 pathogens
rt vigna unguiculata

COWPEAS
uf *black-eyed peas*
uf *peas, southern*
uf *southern peas*
rt blackeye cowpea mosaic potyvirus
rt cowpea chlorotic mottle bromovirus
rt cowpea mild mottle carlavirus
rt cowpea mosaic comovirus
rt cowpea severe mosaic comovirus
rt vigna unguiculata

COWS
uf *cow*
BT1 female animals
BT2 animals
NT1 beef cows
NT1 dairy cows
NT1 heifers
NT2 bred heifers

COWS *cont.*
NT1 nurse cows
rt cattle
rt cow housing
rt cow indexes
rt dams (mothers)
rt milk production
rt steaming up

cowsheds
USE **cow housing**

COX DISEASE
BT1 plant disorders
BT2 disorders
rt apples

COX SPOT
BT1 plant disorders
BT2 disorders
rt apples

COXIELLA
BT1 rickettsiaceae
BT2 rickettsiales
BT3 bacteria
BT4 prokaryotes
NT1 coxiella burnetii
rt q fever

COXIELLA BURNETII
BT1 coxiella
BT2 rickettsiaceae
BT3 rickettsiales
BT4 bacteria
BT5 prokaryotes

COXSACKIE VIRUS
BT1 enterovirus
BT2 picornaviridae
BT3 viruses

COYOTES
uf *canis latrans*
BT1 wild animals
BT2 animals
rt canidae

coypu
USE **nutria**

4-CPA
uf *(4-chlorophenoxy)acetic acid*
BT1 auxins
BT2 plant growth regulators
BT3 growth regulators
BT1 phenoxyacetic herbicides
BT2 phenoxy herbicides
BT3 herbicides
BT4 pesticides

cr
USE **chromium**

CRAB MEAT
BT1 meat
BT2 animal products
BT3 products
BT2 foods
rt crabs

CRAB WASTE
BT1 animal wastes
BT2 wastes
BT1 liming materials
BT2 soil amendments
BT3 amendments
rt crabs

CRABS
BT1 shellfish
BT2 aquatic invertebrates
BT3 aquatic animals
BT4 animals
BT4 aquatic organisms
rt crab meat
rt crab waste
rt decapoda

CRACIDAE
BT1 galliformes
BT2 birds

CRACKERS (AGRICOLA)
rt biscuits

CRACKING
rt breakage
rt brittleness
rt cracks
rt fracture
rt soil mechanics

CRACKS
BT1 soil morphological features
BT1 wood defects
BT2 defects
rt cracking

CRAFTS
rt handicrafts

CRAMBE
BT1 cruciferae
NT1 crambe abyssinica
NT1 crambe cordifolia
NT1 crambe hispanica
NT1 crambe maritima
NT1 crambe pontica
NT1 crambe steveniana
NT1 crambe tatarica
rt crambe meal
rt crambe seeds

CRAMBE ABYSSINICA
BT1 crambe
BT2 cruciferae
BT1 oilseed plants
BT2 fatty oil plants
BT3 oil plants

CRAMBE CORDIFOLIA
BT1 crambe
BT2 cruciferae

CRAMBE HISPANICA
BT1 crambe
BT2 cruciferae

CRAMBE MARITIMA
uf *sea kale*
BT1 crambe
BT2 cruciferae
BT1 leafy vegetables
BT2 vegetables

CRAMBE MEAL
BT1 meal
rt crambe

CRAMBE PONTICA
BT1 crambe
BT2 cruciferae

CRAMBE SEEDS
rt crambe
rt seeds

CRAMBE STEVENIANA
BT1 crambe
BT2 cruciferae

CRAMBE TATARICA
BT1 crambe
BT2 cruciferae

CRAMBUS
BT1 pyralidae
BT2 lepidoptera

CRANBERRIES
rt vaccinium

CRANES
BT1 machinery
rt elevators
rt forestry machinery
rt grabs
rt hoists
rt lifting
rt loaders

CRANGON
BT1 decapoda
BT2 malacostraca
BT3 crustacea
BT4 arthropods
rt prawns

CRANKSHAFTS
BT1 components

CRASSOCEPHALUM
BT1 compositae
NT1 crassocephalum crepidioides

CRASSOCEPHALUM CREPIDIOIDES
BT1 crassocephalum
BT2 compositae

CRASSOSTREA
BT1 ostreidae
BT2 bivalvia
BT3 mollusca
NT1 crassostrea gigas
NT1 crassostrea virginica

CRASSOSTREA GIGAS
BT1 crassostrea
BT2 ostreidae
BT3 bivalvia
BT4 mollusca

CRASSOSTREA VIRGINICA
BT1 crassostrea
BT2 ostreidae
BT3 bivalvia
BT4 mollusca

CRASSULA
BT1 crassulaceae
NT1 crassula muscosa
NT1 crassula ovata
NT1 crassula perfoliata

crassula argentea
USE **crassula ovata**

crassula falcata
USE **crassula perfoliata**

crassula lycopodioides
USE **crassula muscosa**

CRASSULA MUSCOSA
uf *crassula lycopodioides*
BT1 crassula
BT2 crassulaceae
BT1 ornamental succulent plants
BT2 succulent plants

crassula obliqua
USE **crassula ovata**

CRASSULA OVATA
uf *crassula argentea*
uf *crassula obliqua*
BT1 crassula
BT2 crassulaceae
BT1 ornamental succulent plants
BT2 succulent plants

CRASSULA PERFOLIATA
uf *crassula falcata*
BT1 crassula
BT2 crassulaceae
BT1 ornamental succulent plants
BT2 succulent plants

CRASSULACEAE
NT1 bryophyllum
NT1 crassula
NT2 crassula muscosa
NT2 crassula ovata
NT2 crassula perfoliata
NT1 cremnophila
NT2 cremnophila nutans
NT1 echeveria
NT2 echeveria agavoides
NT2 echeveria chihuahuaensis
NT2 echeveria coccinea
NT2 echeveria colorata
NT2 echeveria elegans
NT2 echeveria harmsii
NT2 echeveria nayaritensis
NT2 echeveria prolifica
NT1 graptopetalum
NT2 graptopetalum paraguayense
NT1 graptoveria
NT1 kalanchoe
NT2 kalanchoe blossfeldiana
NT2 kalanchoe crenata
NT2 kalanchoe daigremontiana
NT2 kalanchoe fedtschenkoi

CRASSULACEAE *cont.*
NT2 kalanchoe gastonisbonnieri
NT2 kalanchoe laciniata
NT2 kalanchoe laxiflora
NT2 kalanchoe pinnata
NT2 kalanchoe porphyrocalyx
NT2 kalanchoe tubiflora
NT2 kalanchoe verticillata
NT1 rhodiola
NT2 rhodiola algida
NT2 rhodiola gelida
NT2 rhodiola heterodonta
NT2 rhodiola litvinovii
NT2 rhodiola pinnatifida
NT2 rhodiola rosea
NT1 sedum
NT2 sedum acre
NT2 sedum aizoon
NT2 sedum album
NT2 sedum burrito
NT2 sedum carpaticum
NT2 sedum caucasicum
NT2 sedum formosanum
NT2 sedum hybridum
NT2 sedum lydium
NT2 sedum oppositifolium
NT2 sedum pallidum
NT2 sedum populifolium
NT2 sedum praealtum
NT2 sedum suaveolens
NT2 sedum telephioides
NT2 sedum telephium
NT1 sempervivum

crassulacean acid metabolism
USE **cam pathway**

CRATAEGUS
BT1 rosaceae
NT1 crataegus arnoldiana
NT1 crataegus bullata
NT1 crataegus curvisepala
NT1 crataegus laevigata
NT1 crataegus monogyna
NT1 crataegus pedicellata
NT1 crataegus pentagyna
NT1 crataegus pubescens
NT1 crataegus sanguinea
NT1 crataegus songarica
NT1 crataegus submollis

CRATAEGUS ARNOLDIANA
BT1 crataegus
BT2 rosaceae
BT1 ornamental woody plants

CRATAEGUS BULLATA
BT1 crataegus
BT2 rosaceae

crataegus coccinea
USE **crataegus pedicellata**

CRATAEGUS CURVISEPALA
BT1 crataegus
BT2 rosaceae

CRATAEGUS LAEVIGATA
uf *crataegus oxyacantha*
uf *hawthorn*
BT1 crataegus
BT2 rosaceae
BT1 medicinal plants
BT1 ornamental woody plants

CRATAEGUS MONOGYNA
BT1 crataegus
BT2 rosaceae
BT1 forest trees
BT1 medicinal plants
BT1 ornamental woody plants

crataegus oxyacantha
USE **crataegus laevigata**

CRATAEGUS PEDICELLATA
uf *crataegus coccinea*
BT1 crataegus
BT2 rosaceae
BT1 ornamental woody plants

CRATAEGUS PENTAGYNA
BT1 crataegus
BT2 rosaceae

CRATAEGUS PUBESCENS
BT1 crataegus
BT2 rosaceae

CRATAEGUS SANGUINEA
BT1 crataegus
BT2 rosaceae

CRATAEGUS SONGARICA
BT1 crataegus
BT2 rosaceae

CRATAEGUS SUBMOLLIS
BT1 crataegus
BT2 rosaceae
BT1 ornamental woody plants

CRATES
BT1 containers
rt boxes
rt packages
rt pallet boxes

CRATEVA
BT1 capparidaceae
NT1 crateva religiosa

crateva nurvala
USE **crateva religiosa**

CRATEVA RELIGIOSA
uf *crateva nurvala*
BT1 crateva
BT2 capparidaceae

CRAYFISH
BT1 shellfish
BT2 aquatic invertebrates
BT3 aquatic animals
BT4 animals
BT4 aquatic organisms
rt astacus
rt procambarus

crayfish plague fungus
USE **aphanomyces astaci**

CREAM
BT1 milk products
BT2 products
NT1 coffee cream
NT1 cultured cream
NT1 dried cream
NT1 frozen cream
NT1 ripened cream
NT1 sterilized cream
NT1 sweet cream
NT1 whipped cream
NT1 whipping cream
rt buttermaking
rt creaming
rt imitation cream

CREAM CHEESE
BT1 cheeses
BT2 milk products
BT3 products

cream, cultured
USE **cultured cream**

cream, dried
USE **dried cream**

cream, frozen
USE **frozen cream**

cream, imitation
USE **imitation cream**

cream, ripened
USE **ripened cream**

cream, sterilized
USE **sterilized cream**

cream substitutes
USE **imitation cream**
OR **milk substitutes**

cream, sweet
USE **sweet cream**

cream, whipped
USE **whipped cream**

cream, whipping
USE **whipping cream**

CREAMED HONEY
BT1 honey
BT2 hive products
BT3 animal products
BT4 products
rt extracted honey
rt granulated honey

CREAMING
BT1 processing
rt cream

crease resistant finishes
USE **wrinkle resistant finishes (agricola)**

CREASING
BT1 plant disorders
BT2 disorders
rt citrus fruits

CREATINE
BT1 guanidines
BT2 organic nitrogen compounds
rt phosphocreatine

CREATINE KINASE
(ec 2.7.3.2)
uf *creatine phosphokinase*
BT1 kinases
BT2 transferases
BT3 enzymes

creatine phosphate
USE **phosphocreatine**

creatine phosphokinase
USE **creatine kinase**

CREATININE
BT1 imidazoles
BT2 azoles
BT3 heterocyclic nitrogen compounds
BT4 organic nitrogen compounds

CREDENTIALS (AGRICOLA)
rt qualifications

CREDIT
uf *credit transactions*
uf *credits and subsidies*
BT1 finance
NT1 agricultural credit
NT1 cooperative credit
NT1 export credits
NT1 installment credit (agricola)
NT1 loans
NT2 bank loans
NT2 international loans
NT2 private loans
NT2 public loans
NT1 long term credit
NT2 mortgages
NT3 zero rate mortgages (agricola)
NT1 short term credit
rt charge accounts (agricola)
rt credit insurance
rt credit policy
rt financial institutions
rt tax credits (agricola)

credit, agricultural
USE **agricultural credit**

CREDIT CARDS (AGRICOLA)
rt charge accounts (agricola)
rt credit sales

CREDIT CONTROL
BT1 controls
NT1 discount rates
NT1 interest rates
NT2 preferential interest rates
rt credit policy
rt fiscal policy

credit, cooperative
USE **cooperative credit**

CREDIT INSURANCE
BT1 insurance
NT1 export credits
rt credit

CREDIT POLICY
uf policy, credit
BT1 economic policy
rt credit
rt credit control
rt loans
rt policy

CREDIT SALES
BT1 marketing techniques
BT2 techniques
rt credit cards (agricola)

credit, short term
USE **short term credit**

credit transactions
USE **credit**

credits and subsidies
USE **credit**
OR **subsidies**

credits, export
USE **export credits**

CREEP
BT1 movement
rt creep strength
rt plasticity
rt soil creep

CREEP FEEDING
BT1 feeding
rt creep grazing
rt creeps

CREEP GRAZING
BT1 grazing systems
BT2 grazing
rt creep feeding

CREEP STRENGTH
uf strength, creep
BT1 strength
BT2 mechanical properties
BT3 properties
rt creep

creeping eruption
USE **larva migrans**

CREEPS
BT1 animal housing
rt creep feeding
rt farrowing pens

CREMASTUS
BT1 ichneumonidae
BT2 hymenoptera
rt temelucha

cremastus interruptor
USE **temelucha interruptor**

CREMATOGASTER
BT1 formicidae
BT2 hymenoptera
NT1 crematogaster scutellaris

CREMATOGASTER SCUTELLARIS
BT1 crematogaster
BT2 formicidae
BT3 hymenoptera

CREMNOMYS
BT1 murinae
BT2 muridae
BT3 rodents
BT4 mammals
NT1 cremnomys blanfordi
rt rattus

CREMNOMYS BLANFORDI
uf rattus blanfordi
BT1 cremnomys
BT2 murinae
BT3 muridae
BT4 rodents
BT5 mammals

CREMNOPHILA
BT1 crassulaceae
NT1 cremnophila nutans

CREMNOPHILA NUTANS
uf sedum cremnophila
uf sedum nutans
BT1 cremnophila
BT2 crassulaceae
BT1 ornamental succulent plants
BT2 succulent plants

CRENOSOMA
BT1 crenosomatidae
BT2 nematoda
NT1 crenosoma vulpis

CRENOSOMA VULPIS
BT1 crenosoma
BT2 crenosomatidae
BT3 nematoda

CRENOSOMATIDAE
BT1 nematoda
NT1 crenosoma
NT2 crenosoma vulpis
rt animal parasitic nematodes

CREOSOTE
BT1 anthelmintics
BT2 antiparasitic agents
BT3 drugs
BT1 expectorants
BT2 antitussive agents
BT3 respiratory system agents
BT4 drugs
BT1 phenols
BT2 alcohols
BT2 phenolic compounds
BT3 aromatic compounds
BT1 wood preservatives
BT2 preservatives
rt wood tar

CREPE (AGRICOLA)
BT1 fabrics

CREPIDOSTOMUM
BT1 allocreadiidae
BT2 digenea
BT3 trematoda
NT1 crepidostomum farionis
NT1 crepidostomum metoecus

CREPIDOSTOMUM FARIONIS
BT1 crepidostomum
BT2 allocreadiidae
BT3 digenea
BT4 trematoda

CREPIDOSTOMUM METOECUS
BT1 crepidostomum
BT2 allocreadiidae
BT3 digenea
BT4 trematoda

CREPIS
BT1 compositae
NT1 crepis rhoeadifolia
NT1 crepis rubra
NT1 crepis tectorum

CREPIS RHOEADIFOLIA
BT1 crepis
BT2 compositae

CREPIS RUBRA
BT1 crepis
BT2 compositae

CREPIS TECTORUM
BT1 crepis
BT2 compositae
BT1 medicinal plants

CRESCENTIA
BT1 bignoniaceae
NT1 crescentia cujete

CRESCENTIA CUJETE
BT1 crescentia
BT2 bignoniaceae

CRESCENZA CHEESE
BT1 cheeses

CRESCENZA CHEESE *cont.*
BT2 milk products
BT3 products

O-CRESOL
uf 2-methylphenol
BT1 cresols
BT2 phenols
BT3 alcohols
BT3 phenolic compounds
BT4 aromatic compounds
BT1 disinfectants
BT1 solvents

P-CRESOL
uf 4-methylphenol
BT1 cresols
BT2 phenols
BT3 alcohols
BT3 phenolic compounds
BT4 aromatic compounds

CRESOLS
uf methylphenols
BT1 phenols
BT2 alcohols
BT2 phenolic compounds
BT3 aromatic compounds
NT1 o-cresol
NT1 p-cresol

CRESS
BT1 leafy vegetables
BT2 vegetables
rt lepidium sativum

cress, water
USE **watercress**

CRESSA
BT1 convolvulaceae
NT1 cressa cretica

CRESSA CRETICA
BT1 cressa
BT2 convolvulaceae

CRETINISM
BT1 thyroid diseases
BT2 endocrine diseases
BT3 organic diseases
BT4 diseases
rt mental disorders

CRIBS
BT1 containers
NT1 maize cribs
rt bins
rt boxes
rt stores

CRICETINAE
BT1 muridae
BT2 rodents
BT3 mammals
NT1 cricetulus
NT2 cricetulus barabensis
NT2 cricetulus longicaudatus
NT2 cricetulus migratorius
NT1 cricetus
NT2 cricetus cricetus
NT1 mesocricetus
NT1 phodopus
NT2 phodopus sungorus

CRICETOMYINAE
BT1 muridae
BT2 rodents
BT3 mammals
NT1 cricetomys

CRICETOMYS
BT1 cricetomyinae
BT2 muridae
BT3 rodents
BT4 mammals

CRICETULUS
BT1 cricetinae
BT2 muridae
BT3 rodents
BT4 mammals
NT1 cricetulus barabensis
NT1 cricetulus longicaudatus

CRICETULUS *cont.*
NT1 cricetulus migratorius

CRICETULUS BARABENSIS
uf chinese hamster
uf hamster, chinese
BT1 cricetulus
BT2 cricetinae
BT3 muridae
BT4 rodents
BT5 mammals

CRICETULUS LONGICAUDATUS
BT1 cricetulus
BT2 cricetinae
BT3 muridae
BT4 rodents
BT5 mammals

CRICETULUS MIGRATORIUS
BT1 cricetulus
BT2 cricetinae
BT3 muridae
BT4 rodents
BT5 mammals

CRICETUS
BT1 cricetinae
BT2 muridae
BT3 rodents
BT4 mammals
NT1 cricetus cricetus

cricetus auratus
USE **golden hamsters**

CRICETUS CRICETUS
uf european hamster
BT1 cricetus
BT2 cricetinae
BT3 muridae
BT4 rodents
BT5 mammals

CRICK-SIDE
BT1 plant disorders
BT2 disorders
rt avocados

CRICKET
BT1 ball games
BT2 games
BT2 sport

crickets
USE **gryllidae**

CRICONEMA
BT1 criconematidae
BT2 nematoda
NT1 criconema palmatus

CRICONEMA PALMATUS
BT1 criconema
BT2 criconematidae
BT3 nematoda

CRICONEMATIDAE
BT1 nematoda
NT1 caloosia
NT1 criconema
NT2 criconema palmatus
NT1 criconemella
NT2 criconemella parva
NT1 criconemoides
NT2 criconemoides morgensis
NT1 crossonema
NT1 discocriconemella
NT1 hemicriconemoides
NT2 hemicriconemoides chitwoodi
NT2 hemicriconemoides cocophilus
NT2 hemicriconemoides mangiferae
NT1 hemicycliophora
NT2 hemicycliophora arenaria
NT1 lobocriconema
NT1 macroposthonia
NT2 macroposthonia curvata
NT2 macroposthonia sphaerocephala
NT2 macroposthonia xenoplax
NT1 ogma

CRICONEMATIDAE *cont.*
rt plant parasitic nematodes

CRICONEMELLA
BT1 criconematidae
BT2 nematoda
NT1 criconemella parva
rt criconemoides

CRICONEMELLA PARVA
BT1 criconemella
BT2 criconematidae
BT3 nematoda

CRICONEMOIDES
BT1 criconematidae
BT2 nematoda
NT1 criconemoides morgensis
rt criconemella
rt macroposthonia

CRICONEMOIDES MORGENSIS
BT1 criconemoides
BT2 criconematidae
BT3 nematoda

criconemoides xenoplax
USE **macroposthonia xenoplax**

CRIME
NT1 terrorism
NT1 theft (agricola)
NT2 employee theft (agricola)
rt correctional institutions
rt corruption
rt crime protection (agricola)
rt delinquent behaviour
rt law enforcement (agricola)
rt punishment (agricola)
rt vandalism

CRIME PROTECTION (AGRICOLA)
rt crime
rt crimewatch (agricola)

CRIMEAN-CONGO HAEMORRHAGIC FEVER VIRUS
HN from 1990; previously "congo virus"
AF crimean-congo hemorrhagic fever virus
uf *congo virus*
BT1 nairovirus
BT2 arboviruses
BT3 pathogens
BT2 bunyaviridae
BT3 viruses

CRIMEAN-CONGO HEMORRHAGIC FEVER VIRUS
HN from 1990
BF crimean-congo haemorrhagic fever virus

CRIMEWATCH (AGRICOLA)
rt crime protection (agricola)

CRIMIDINE
BT1 rodenticides
BT2 pesticides

CRIMP
rt crimpers
rt wool

CRIMPERS
BT1 farm machinery
BT2 machinery
rt crimp
rt forage conditioners
rt mower conditioners

crimson clover
USE **trifolium incarnatum**

CRIMSON CLOVER LATENT NEPOVIRUS
HN from 1990
BT1 nepovirus group
BT2 plant viruses
BT3 plant pathogens
BT4 pathogens
rt trifolium incarnatum

CRINIPELLIS
BT1 agaricales
NT1 crinipellis perniciosa

CRINIPELLIS PERNICIOSA
uf *marasmius perniciosus*
BT1 crinipellis
BT2 agaricales

CRINODENDRON
BT1 elaeocarpaceae
NT1 crinodendron hookerianum

CRINODENDRON HOOKERIANUM
BT1 crinodendron
BT2 elaeocarpaceae
BT1 ornamental woody plants

CRINUM
BT1 amaryllidaceae
NT1 crinum asiaticum
NT1 crinum bulbispermum
NT1 crinum moorei

CRINUM ASIATICUM
BT1 crinum
BT2 amaryllidaceae
BT1 ornamental bulbs

CRINUM BULBISPERMUM
uf *crinum longifolium*
BT1 crinum
BT2 amaryllidaceae
BT1 ornamental bulbs

crinum longifolium
USE **crinum bulbispermum**

CRINUM MOOREI
BT1 antifungal plants
BT1 crinum
BT2 amaryllidaceae
BT1 ornamental bulbs

criocephalus
USE **arhopalus**

criocephalus rusticus
USE **arhopalus rusticus**

criocephalus syriacus
USE **arhopalus syriacus**

CRIOCERAS
BT1 apocynaceae
NT1 crioceras dipladeniiflorus

CRIOCERAS DIPLADENIIFLORUS
BT1 crioceras
BT2 apocynaceae

CRIOLLO
HN from 1990
BT1 sheep breeds
BT2 breeds

CRIOULO
BT1 horse breeds
BT2 breeds

CRISES (AGRICOLA)
NT1 agricultural crises
NT1 economic crises
NT2 economic depression
NT3 inflation
NT1 family crises (agricola)

CRISPS
AF potato chips
BT1 potato products
BT2 vegetable products
BT3 plant products
BT4 products
rt chips (french fries)

CRISTULARIELLA
BT1 deuteromycotina
rt grovesinia

cristulariella pyramidalis
USE **grovesinia pyramidalis**

criteria, selection
USE **selection criteria**

CRITHIDIA
BT1 sarcomastigophora
BT2 protozoa
NT1 crithidia acanthocephali
NT1 crithidia deanei
NT1 crithidia fasciculata
NT1 crithidia harmosa
NT1 crithidia hyalommae
NT1 crithidia luciliae
NT1 crithidia oncopelti

CRITHIDIA ACANTHOCEPHALI
BT1 crithidia
BT2 sarcomastigophora
BT3 protozoa

CRITHIDIA DEANEI
BT1 crithidia
BT2 sarcomastigophora
BT3 protozoa

CRITHIDIA FASCICULATA
BT1 crithidia
BT2 sarcomastigophora
BT3 protozoa

CRITHIDIA HARMOSA
BT1 crithidia
BT2 sarcomastigophora
BT3 protozoa

CRITHIDIA HYALOMMAE
BT1 crithidia
BT2 sarcomastigophora
BT3 protozoa

CRITHIDIA LUCILIAE
BT1 crithidia
BT2 sarcomastigophora
BT3 protozoa

CRITHIDIA ONCOPELTI
BT1 crithidia
BT2 sarcomastigophora
BT3 protozoa

CRITICAL PATH ANALYSIS
HN from 1990
BT1 network analysis
BT2 optimization methods
BT3 optimization
BT1 path analysis
BT2 statistical analysis
BT3 data analysis
BT3 statistics

CRITICAL TEMPERATURE
uf *temperature, critical*
BT1 temperature

crivellia
USE **przhevalskiana**

crivellia silenus
USE **przhevalskiana silenus**

CROCHET (AGRICOLA)
BT1 needlework
BT2 handicrafts

CROCIDOLOMIA
BT1 pyralidae
BT2 lepidoptera
NT1 crocidolomia binotalis

CROCIDOLOMIA BINOTALIS
BT1 crocidolomia
BT2 pyralidae
BT3 lepidoptera

CROCIDURA
BT1 soricidae
BT2 insectivores
BT3 mammals
NT1 crocidura russula
NT1 crocidura suaveolens

CROCIDURA RUSSULA
BT1 crocidura
BT2 soricidae
BT3 insectivores
BT4 mammals

CROCIDURA SUAVEOLENS
BT1 crocidura

CROCIDURA SUAVEOLENS *cont.*
BT2 soricidae
BT3 insectivores
BT4 mammals

CROCODILES
BT1 aquatic animals
BT2 animals
BT2 aquatic organisms
BT1 skin producing animals
BT2 animals
rt crocodylia
rt reptiles

CROCODYLIA
BT1 reptiles
NT1 alligatoridae
NT2 alligator
NT2 caiman
NT1 crocodylidae
NT2 crocodylus
NT3 crocodylus porosus
NT1 gavialidae
NT2 gavialis
NT3 gavialis gangeticus
rt crocodiles

CROCODYLIDAE
BT1 crocodylia
BT2 reptiles
NT1 crocodylus
NT2 crocodylus porosus

CROCODYLUS
BT1 crocodylidae
BT2 crocodylia
BT3 reptiles
NT1 crocodylus porosus

CROCODYLUS POROSUS
BT1 crocodylus
BT2 crocodylidae
BT3 crocodylia
BT4 reptiles

CROCOSMIA
BT1 iridaceae
NT1 crocosmia crocosmiiflora
NT1 crocosmia crocosmiifolia
NT1 crocosmia masoniorum

CROCOSMIA CROCOSMIIFLORA
BT1 crocosmia
BT2 iridaceae
BT1 ornamental bulbs
rt corms

CROCOSMIA CROCOSMIIFOLIA
BT1 crocosmia
BT2 iridaceae

CROCOSMIA MASONIORUM
BT1 crocosmia
BT2 iridaceae
BT1 ornamental bulbs
rt corms

CROCUS
BT1 iridaceae
NT1 crocus asumaniae
NT1 crocus boryi
NT1 crocus kotschyanus
NT1 crocus laevigatus
NT1 crocus olivieri
NT1 crocus pallasii
NT1 crocus sativus
NT1 crocus tommasinianus
NT1 crocus tournefortii

CROCUS ASUMANIAE
BT1 crocus
BT2 iridaceae

CROCUS BORYI
BT1 crocus
BT2 iridaceae
BT1 ornamental bulbs
rt corms

crocus cancellatus
USE **crocus kotschyanus**

CROCUS KOTSCHYANUS
uf *crocus cancellatus*
BT1 crocus

CROCUS KOTSCHYANUS *cont.*
BT2 iridaceae
BT1 ornamental bulbs
rt corms

CROCUS LAEVIGATUS
BT1 crocus
BT2 iridaceae
BT1 ornamental bulbs
rt corms

CROCUS OLIVIERI
BT1 crocus
BT2 iridaceae
BT1 ornamental bulbs
rt corms

CROCUS PALLASII
BT1 crocus
BT2 iridaceae
BT1 ornamental bulbs
rt corms

CROCUS SATIVUS
BT1 crocus
BT2 iridaceae
BT1 dye plants
BT1 ornamental bulbs
BT1 spice plants
rt corms
rt saffron

CROCUS TOMMASINIANUS
BT1 crocus
BT2 iridaceae
BT1 ornamental bulbs
rt corms

CROCUS TOURNEFORTII
BT1 crocus
BT2 iridaceae
BT1 ornamental bulbs
rt corms

CROCUTA
BT1 hyaenidae
BT2 fissipeda
BT3 carnivores
BT4 mammals
NT1 crocuta crocuta

CROCUTA CROCUTA
BT1 crocuta
BT2 hyaenidae
BT3 fissipeda
BT4 carnivores
BT5 mammals

CROFTS
BT1 small farms
BT2 farms

CROHN'S DISEASE
BT1 intestinal diseases
BT2 gastrointestinal diseases
BT3 digestive system diseases
BT4 organic diseases
BT5 diseases

CRONARTIUM
BT1 uredinales
NT1 cronartium coleosporioides
NT1 cronartium comandrae
NT1 cronartium comptoniae
NT1 cronartium flaccidum
NT1 cronartium fusiforme
NT1 cronartium quercuum
NT1 cronartium ribicola
rt endocronartium

cronartium asclepiadeum
USE **cronartium flaccidum**

CRONARTIUM COLEOSPORIOIDES
BT1 cronartium
BT2 uredinales

CRONARTIUM COMANDRAE
BT1 cronartium
BT2 uredinales

CRONARTIUM COMPTONIAE
BT1 cronartium
BT2 uredinales

CRONARTIUM FLACCIDUM
uf *cronartium asclepiadeum*
BT1 cronartium
BT2 uredinales

CRONARTIUM FUSIFORME
uf *cronartium quercuum f.sp. fusiforme*
BT1 cronartium
BT2 uredinales

cronartium harknessii
USE **endocronartium harknessii**

CRONARTIUM QUERCUUM
BT1 cronartium
BT2 uredinales

cronartium quercuum f.sp. fusiforme
USE **cronartium fusiforme**

CRONARTIUM RIBICOLA
BT1 cronartium
BT2 uredinales

CROOK
BT1 stem form

CROOKED NECK
BT1 abnormalities
BT1 deformities
rt neck

CROP
BT1 oesophagus
BT2 digestive system
BT3 body parts

CROP DAMAGE
uf *crop injury*
BT1 damage
NT1 lodging
rt crop losses
rt crops

CROP DENSITY
uf *density, crop*
uf *density, planting*
BT1 plant density
BT2 density
NT1 row spacing
rt crops
rt spacing
rt stand characteristics
rt stand density
rt thinning

CROP ENTERPRISES
BT1 farm enterprises
BT2 enterprises
rt crops
rt diversification
rt farm sector

CROP ESTABLISHMENT
uf *establishment, crop*
BT1 establishment
BT1 planting

CROP GROWTH STAGE
NT1 filling period
rt crops
rt developmental stages
rt growth stages
rt plant development

CROP HUSBANDRY
BT1 husbandry
rt agronomy
rt crop management
rt crop production
rt cropping systems
rt crops
rt cultivation
rt plant protection

crop injury
USE **crop damage**

CROP INSURANCE
BT1 agricultural insurance
BT2 insurance
rt agricultural disasters

CROP INSURANCE *cont.*
rt crops

CROP LIFTERS
BT1 harvesters
BT2 farm machinery
BT3 machinery
rt crops

CROP LOSSES
BT1 losses
rt crop damage
rt crops
rt windfalls
rt yield losses

CROP MANAGEMENT
rt crop husbandry
rt crops
rt management

crop maturation
USE **maturation**

CROP MIXTURES
uf *mixtures, crop*
BT1 mixtures
rt crops
rt genotype mixtures
rt intercropping
rt mixed cropping
rt mixed pastures

crop plants
USE **crops**
OR **plants**

CROP PLANTS AS WEEDS (AGRICOLA)
HN from 1989
rt weeds

CROP PRODUCTION
uf *plant production*
ufa *cut-flower production*
BT1 agricultural production
BT2 production
rt crop husbandry
rt crop yield

crop products
USE **plant products**

crop protection
USE **plant protection**

CROP QUALITY
BT1 quality
rt crops

CROP RESIDUES
BT1 plant residues
BT2 residues
NT1 stubble
NT2 sorghum stubble
rt agricultural wastes
rt crops
rt fuels
rt stubble

crop rotation
USE **rotations**

CROP WEED COMPETITION
BT1 interspecific competition
BT2 biological competition
BT1 plant competition
BT2 biological competition
rt crops
rt weeds

CROP YIELD
BT1 yields
rt crop production
rt growth yield relationship (agricola)

CROPPING SYSTEMS
NT1 biennial cropping
NT1 catch cropping
NT1 continuous cropping
NT1 double cropping
NT1 dry farming
NT1 fallow
NT2 summer fallow

CROPPING SYSTEMS *cont.*
NT1 fallow systems
NT2 corridor systems
NT2 improved fallow
NT1 intensive cropping
NT1 intercropping
NT2 alley cropping
NT1 mixed cropping
NT2 interplanting
NT1 monoculture
NT1 multiple cropping
NT1 perennial cropping
NT1 ratooning
NT1 relay cropping
NT1 rotations
NT1 seasonal cropping
NT1 sequential cropping
NT1 shifting cultivation
NT2 corridor systems
NT1 sole cropping
NT1 strip cropping
NT2 grass strips
rt arable farming
rt crop husbandry
rt cultivation
rt farming systems
rt production structure
rt protected cultivation

CROPS
(individual species are listed under browse plants, culinary herbs, dye plants, fibre plants, fodder plants, fruit crops, grain crops, gum plants, incense plants, industrial crops, medicinal plants, nut crops, oil plants, pasture plants, pesticidal plants, root crops, rubber plants, spice plants, starch crops, stimulant plants, sugar crops, tan plants and vegetables)
uf *crop plants*
rt break crops
rt cash crops
rt companion crops
rt cover crops
rt crop damage
rt crop density
rt crop enterprises
rt crop growth stage
rt crop husbandry
rt crop insurance
rt crop lifters
rt crop losses
rt crop management
rt crop mixtures
rt crop quality
rt crop residues
rt crop weed competition
rt cut flowers
rt cut foliage
rt domestication
rt field crops
rt fodder crops
rt food crops
rt forest trees
rt fuel crops
rt green manures
rt greenhouse crops
rt horticultural crops
rt intensive crops
rt intercrops
rt ornamental plants
rt plantation crops
rt plants
rt rescue crops
rt rowcrops
rt seed crops
rt stubble crops
rt subtropical crops
rt tropical crops

crops, stubble
USE **stubble crops**

CROQUET
BT1 ball games
BT2 games
BT2 sport

CROSS AGE TEACHING (AGRICOLA)

CROSS AGE TEACHING (AGRICOLA) *cont.*
BT1 teaching methods
BT2 methodology

CROSS ARMS
BT1 poles

CROSS COUNTRY VEHICLES
uf *vehicles, cross country*
BT1 vehicles
NT1 off road vehicles
NT1 tractors
NT2 articulated tractors
NT2 compact tractors
NT2 floating tractors
NT2 four wheel drive tractors
NT2 high clearance tractors
NT2 hillside tractors
NT2 low profile tractors
NT2 rowcrop tractors
NT2 tandem tractors
NT2 track laying tractors
NT2 two way tractors
NT2 vineyard tractors
NT2 walking tractors
NT2 wheeled tractors
rt earth moving equipment
rt low ground pressure vehicles
rt tracked vehicles
rt trafficability

CROSS CULTURAL STUDIES
BT1 cultural research
BT2 culture
BT2 research
rt international comparisons

CROSS CULTURAL TRAINING (AGRICOLA)
BT1 training
rt culture

CROSS CUTTING
BT1 primary conversion
BT2 conversion
rt logging

CROSS DYEING (AGRICOLA)
BT1 dyeing (agricola)
BT2 processing

CROSS FLOW DRIERS
AF cross flow dryers
BT1 driers
BT2 farm machinery
BT3 machinery
rt concurrent flow driers
rt counterflow driers
rt grain driers

CROSS FLOW DRYERS
BF cross flow driers
BT1 dryers

CROSS FLOW FANS
BT1 fans
BT2 components

CROSS IMMUNITY
HN from 1990
BT1 immunity
rt cross immunization
rt cross reaction

CROSS IMMUNIZATION
BT1 immunization
BT2 immunostimulation
BT3 immunotherapy
BT4 therapy
rt cross immunity

CROSS INFECTION
BT1 infection
BT2 disease transmission
BT3 transmission

CROSS POLLINATION
uf *pollination, cross*
BT1 pollination
rt crossing
rt outcrossing

CROSS REACTION
(reaction of an antibody with an antigen that was used to induce it)
BT1 antigen antibody reactions
BT2 immune response
BT3 immunity
rt cross immunity

CROSS RESISTANCE
BT1 pesticide resistance
BT2 resistance
rt insecticide resistance

CROSSANDRA
BT1 acanthaceae
NT1 crossandra infundibuliformis

CROSSANDRA INFUNDIBULIFORMIS
uf *crossandra undulifolia*
BT1 crossandra
BT2 acanthaceae
BT1 ornamental woody plants

crossandra undulifolia
USE **crossandra infundibuliformis**

CROSSBRED PROGENY
BT1 progeny
rt crossbreds

CROSSBREDS
BT1 crosses
BT2 hybrids
rt crossbred progeny

CROSSBREEDING
(animals)
BT1 animal breeding methods
BT2 breeding methods
BT3 methodology

crossbreeding (plants)
USE **hybridization**

CROSSES
BT1 hybrids
NT1 backcrosses
NT1 crossbreds
rt crossing

CROSSING
BT1 breeding
NT1 backcrossing
NT1 hybridization
NT2 biparental mating
NT2 intergeneric hybridization
NT2 interspecific hybridization
NT2 somatic hybridization
NT2 wide hybridization
NT1 topcrossing
rt combining ability
rt cross pollination
rt crosses
rt hybridization

CROSSING OVER
NT1 interference
rt chiasma frequency
rt chiasmata
rt chromosome translocation
rt chromosomes
rt recombination
rt segregation

CROSSKILL ROLLERS
uf *rollers, crosskill*
BT1 rollers
BT2 implements

CROSSOCEPHALUS
BT1 atractidae
BT2 nematoda

CROSSONEMA
BT1 criconematidae
BT2 nematoda

CROSSONEPHELIS
BT1 sapindaceae
NT1 crossonephelis adamii

CROSSONEPHELIS ADAMII
BT1 crossonephelis

CROSSONEPHELIS ADAMII *cont.*
BT2 sapindaceae

CROSSOPTERYX
BT1 rubiaceae
NT1 crossopteryx febrifuga

CROSSOPTERYX FEBRIFUGA
BT1 crossopteryx
BT2 rubiaceae
BT1 medicinal plants

CROSSPLY TIRES
BF crossply tyres
BT1 tires

CROSSPLY TYRES
AF crossply tires
uf *tyres, crossply*
BT1 tyres
BT2 components
rt radial tyres

CROTALARIA
BT1 leguminosae
NT1 crotalaria aegyptiaca
NT1 crotalaria anagyroides
NT1 crotalaria brevidens
NT1 crotalaria burhia
NT1 crotalaria candicans
NT1 crotalaria incana
NT1 crotalaria juncea
NT1 crotalaria laburnoides
NT1 crotalaria leschnaultii
NT1 crotalaria madurensis
NT1 crotalaria medicaginea
NT1 crotalaria mucronata
NT1 crotalaria mysorensis
NT1 crotalaria pallida
NT1 crotalaria pumila
NT1 crotalaria retusa
NT1 crotalaria sericea
NT1 crotalaria spectabilis
NT1 crotalaria triquetra
NT1 crotalaria verrucosa

CROTALARIA AEGYPTIACA
BT1 crotalaria
BT2 leguminosae

CROTALARIA ANAGYROIDES
BT1 crotalaria
BT2 leguminosae
BT1 green manures
BT2 manures
BT3 organic amendments
BT4 soil amendments
BT5 amendments
BT1 poisonous plants

CROTALARIA BREVIDENS
BT1 crotalaria
BT2 leguminosae
BT1 leafy vegetables
BT2 vegetables

CROTALARIA BURHIA
BT1 crotalaria
BT2 leguminosae
BT1 medicinal plants

CROTALARIA CANDICANS
BT1 crotalaria
BT2 leguminosae
BT1 fodder legumes
BT2 fodder plants
BT2 legumes

CROTALARIA INCANA
BT1 crotalaria
BT2 leguminosae

CROTALARIA JUNCEA
BT1 crotalaria
BT2 leguminosae
BT1 fibre plants
BT1 green manures
BT2 manures
BT3 organic amendments
BT4 soil amendments
BT5 amendments
rt hemp
rt sunn hemp
rt sunn hemp rosette virus

CROTALARIA JUNCEA *cont.*
rt sunn-hemp mosaic tobamovirus

CROTALARIA LABURNOIDES
BT1 crotalaria
BT2 leguminosae
BT1 fodder legumes
BT2 fodder plants
BT2 legumes

CROTALARIA LESCHNAULTII
BT1 crotalaria
BT2 leguminosae

CROTALARIA MADURENSIS
BT1 antifungal plants
BT1 crotalaria
BT2 leguminosae
BT1 medicinal plants

CROTALARIA MEDICAGINEA
BT1 crotalaria
BT2 leguminosae

CROTALARIA MUCRONATA
uf *crotalaria striata*
BT1 crotalaria
BT2 leguminosae

CROTALARIA MYSORENSIS
BT1 crotalaria
BT2 leguminosae
BT1 fodder legumes
BT2 fodder plants
BT2 legumes

CROTALARIA PALLIDA
BT1 crotalaria
BT2 leguminosae
BT1 fodder legumes
BT2 fodder plants
BT2 legumes

CROTALARIA PUMILA
BT1 crotalaria
BT2 leguminosae
BT1 fodder legumes
BT2 fodder plants
BT2 legumes

CROTALARIA RETUSA
BT1 crotalaria
BT2 leguminosae
BT1 fibre plants
BT1 medicinal plants

CROTALARIA SERICEA
BT1 crotalaria
BT2 leguminosae
BT1 fodder legumes
BT2 fodder plants
BT2 legumes

CROTALARIA SPECTABILIS
BT1 crotalaria
BT2 leguminosae
BT1 weeds

crotalaria striata
USE **crotalaria mucronata**

CROTALARIA TRIQUETRA
BT1 crotalaria
BT2 leguminosae

CROTALARIA VERRUCOSA
BT1 crotalaria
BT2 leguminosae
BT1 medicinal plants

CROTALUS
BT1 viperidae
BT2 serpentes
BT3 reptiles

CROTAMITON
BT1 ectoparasiticides
BT2 antiparasitic agents
BT3 drugs
BT1 unclassified acaricides
BT2 acaricides
BT3 pesticides
BT1 unclassified insecticides
BT2 insecticides

CROTAMITON *cont.*
BT3 pesticides

CROTON
BT1 euphorbiaceae
NT1 croton bonplandianus
NT1 croton cajucara
NT1 croton californicus
NT1 croton corylifolius
NT1 croton draconoides
NT1 croton flavens
NT1 croton lechleri
NT1 croton lobatus
NT1 croton macrostachys
NT1 croton megalocarpus
NT1 croton niveus
NT1 croton sonderianus
NT1 croton sparsiflorus
NT1 croton sublyratus
NT1 croton texensis
NT1 croton tiglium
NT1 croton zehntneri

CROTON BONPLANDIANUS
BT1 croton
BT2 euphorbiaceae
BT1 nematicidal plants
BT2 pesticidal plants

CROTON CAJUCARA
BT1 croton
BT2 euphorbiaceae

CROTON CALIFORNICUS
BT1 croton
BT2 euphorbiaceae

CROTON CORYLIFOLIUS
BT1 croton
BT2 euphorbiaceae

CROTON DRACONOIDES
BT1 croton
BT2 euphorbiaceae

CROTON FLAVENS
BT1 croton
BT2 euphorbiaceae

CROTON LECHLERI
BT1 croton
BT2 euphorbiaceae
BT1 medicinal plants

CROTON LOBATUS
BT1 croton
BT2 euphorbiaceae

CROTON MACROSTACHYS
BT1 croton
BT2 euphorbiaceae

CROTON MEGALOCARPUS
BT1 croton
BT2 euphorbiaceae

CROTON NIVEUS
BT1 croton
BT2 euphorbiaceae

CROTON SONDERIANUS
BT1 antibacterial plants
BT1 croton
BT2 euphorbiaceae
BT1 medicinal plants

CROTON SPARSIFLORUS
BT1 croton
BT2 euphorbiaceae

CROTON SUBLYRATUS
BT1 croton
BT2 euphorbiaceae
BT1 medicinal plants

CROTON TEXENSIS
BT1 croton
BT2 euphorbiaceae

CROTON TIGLIUM
BT1 croton
BT2 euphorbiaceae
BT1 insecticidal plants
BT2 pesticidal plants
BT1 medicinal plants

croton variegatus
USE **codiaeum variegatum**

CROTON ZEHNTNERI
BT1 croton
BT2 euphorbiaceae

crotonylidene diurea
USE **cdu**

CROTOXYPHOS
BT1 ectoparasiticides
BT2 antiparasitic agents
BT3 drugs
BT1 organophosphate acaricides
BT2 organophosphorus acaricides
BT3 acaricides
BT4 pesticides
BT3 organophosphorus pesticides
BT4 organophosphorus compounds
BT1 organophosphate insecticides
BT2 organophosphorus insecticides
BT3 insecticides
BT4 pesticides
BT3 organophosphorus pesticides
BT4 organophosphorus compounds

CROWDING
HN from 1989
rt overcrowding
rt population density
rt stocking density

CROWN
rt canopy
rt foliage
rt trees

crown cover
USE **canopy**

CROWN GALL
BT1 galls
BT2 plant disorders
BT3 disorders
rt agrobacterium tumefaciens

crown vetch
USE **coronilla varia**

crows
USE **corvus**

CROZOPHORA
BT1 euphorbiaceae
NT1 crozophora tinctoria

CROZOPHORA TINCTORIA
BT1 crozophora
BT2 euphorbiaceae

crucian carp
USE **carassius carassius**

CRUCIFERAE
uf *brassicaceae*
NT1 alliaria
NT2 alliaria petiolata
NT1 alyssum
NT2 alyssum argentum
NT1 arabidopsis
NT2 arabidopsis thaliana
NT1 arabis
NT2 arabis alpina
NT2 arabis caucasica
NT1 armoracia
NT2 armoracia rusticana
NT1 aubrieta
NT2 aubrieta deltoidea
NT1 barbarea
NT2 barbarea intermedia
NT2 barbarea stricta
NT2 barbarea verna
NT2 barbarea vulgaris
NT1 berteroa
NT2 berteroa incana
NT1 boreava

CRUCIFERAE *cont.*
NT1 brassica
NT2 brassica alboglabra
NT2 brassica barrelieri
NT2 brassica campestris
NT2 brassica campestris var. oleifera
NT2 brassica campestris var. rapa
NT2 brassica campestris var. toria
NT2 brassica carinata
NT2 brassica caulorapa
NT2 brassica cernua
NT2 brassica cheiranthus
NT2 brassica chinensis
NT2 brassica hirta
NT2 brassica japonica
NT2 brassica juncea
NT2 brassica kaber
NT2 brassica kaber var. pinnatifida
NT2 brassica napus
NT2 brassica napus var. dichotoma
NT2 brassica napus var. glauca
NT2 brassica napus var. napobrassica
NT2 brassica napus var. oleifera
NT2 brassica nigra
NT2 brassica oleracea
NT3 brassica oleracea var. botrytis
NT3 brassica oleracea var. capitata
NT3 brassica oleracea var. gemmifera
NT3 brassica oleracea var. gongylodes
NT3 brassica oleracea var. italica
NT3 brassica oleracea var. viridis
NT2 brassica pekinensis
NT2 brassica perviridis
NT2 raphanobrassica
NT1 bunias
NT2 bunias orientalis
NT1 camelina
NT2 camelina alyssum
NT2 camelina pilosa
NT2 camelina sativa
NT1 capsella
NT2 capsella bursa-pastoris
NT1 cardamine
NT2 cardamine hirsuta
NT2 cardamine oligosperma
NT1 cardaria
NT2 cardaria chalepensis
NT2 cardaria draba
NT2 cardaria pubescens
NT1 cheiranthus
NT2 cheiranthus cheiri
NT1 chorispora
NT2 chorispora tenella
NT1 cochlearia
NT2 cochlearia anglica
NT2 cochlearia officinalis
NT1 coronopus
NT2 coronopus didymus
NT1 crambe
NT2 crambe abyssinica
NT2 crambe cordifolia
NT2 crambe hispanica
NT2 crambe maritima
NT2 crambe pontica
NT2 crambe steveniana
NT2 crambe tatarica
NT1 degenia
NT2 degenia velebitica
NT1 descurainia
NT2 descurainia pinnata
NT2 descurainia sophia
NT1 diplotaxis
NT2 diplotaxis tenuifolia
NT1 draba
NT2 draba verna
NT1 eruca
NT2 eruca vesicaria
NT1 erucaria

CRUCIFERAE *cont.*
NT1 erucastrum
NT2 erucastrum gallicum
NT1 erysimum
NT2 erysimum allionii
NT2 erysimum aureum
NT2 erysimum cheiranthoides
NT2 erysimum crepidifolium
NT2 erysimum cuspidatum
NT2 erysimum diffusum
NT2 erysimum perovskianum
NT2 erysimum pieninicum
NT2 erysimum repandum
NT2 erysimum sibiculosa
NT1 eutrema
NT2 eutrema wasabi
NT1 hesperis
NT2 hesperis matronalis
NT1 hutchinsia
NT2 hutchinsia alpina
NT1 iberis
NT2 iberis sempervirens
NT1 isatis
NT2 isatis tinctoria
NT1 lepidium
NT2 lepidium campestre
NT2 lepidium fremontii
NT2 lepidium latifolium
NT2 lepidium meyenii
NT2 lepidium perfoliatum
NT2 lepidium ruderale
NT2 lepidium sativum
NT2 lepidium syvaschium
NT2 lepidium virginicum
NT1 lesquerella
NT1 lobularia
NT2 lobularia maritima
NT1 lunaria
NT2 lunaria annua
NT1 malcolmia
NT2 malcolmia maritima
NT1 matthiola
NT2 matthiola incana
NT1 nasturtium
NT2 nasturtium officinale
NT1 pringlea
NT2 pringlea antiscorbutica
NT1 raphanus
NT2 raphanus raphanistrum
NT2 raphanus sativus
NT1 rapistrum
NT2 rapistrum rugosum
NT1 rorippa
NT2 rorippa amphibia
NT2 rorippa islandica
NT2 rorippa palustris
NT2 rorippa sylvestris
NT2 rorippa teres
NT1 sibara
NT2 sibara virginica
NT1 sinapis
NT2 sinapis alba
NT2 sinapis arvensis
NT2 sinapis glauca
NT1 sisymbrium
NT2 sisymbrium altissimum
NT2 sisymbrium irio
NT2 sisymbrium officinale
NT1 stanleya
NT2 stanleya pinnata
NT1 syrenia
NT2 syrenia sessiliflora
NT1 thlaspi
NT2 thlaspi arvense
NT2 thlaspi perfoliatum
NT1 zilla

CRUDE FIBER
BF crude fibre
BT1 fiber

CRUDE FIBRE
AF crude fiber
uf *fibre, crude*
BT1 nutrients
rt fibre
rt fibre content

CRUDE PROTEIN
BT1 protein

CRUFOMATE
BT1 anthelmintics
BT2 antiparasitic agents
BT3 drugs
BT1 ectoparasiticides
BT2 antiparasitic agents
BT3 drugs
BT1 phosphoramidate insecticides
BT2 organophosphorus insecticides
BT3 insecticides
BT4 pesticides
BT3 organophosphorus pesticides
BT4 organophosphorus compounds

CRUISES
BT1 holidays
BT2 tourism
rt water recreation

cruising
USE **forest inventories**

CRUMBLERS
BT1 implements
rt clod crushers
rt crumbs
rt crushers
rt harrows

CRUMBS
BT1 soil structural units
BT2 soil structure
BT3 soil physical properties
BT4 soil properties
BT5 properties
rt crumblers

CRUMENULA
BT1 helotiales
rt crumenulopsis
rt gremmeniella

crumenula abietina
USE **gremmeniella abietina**

crumenula pinicola
USE **crumenulopsis pinicola**

crumenula sororia
USE **crumenulopsis sororia**

CRUMENULOPSIS
BT1 helotiales
NT1 crumenulopsis pinicola
NT1 crumenulopsis sororia
rt crumenula

CRUMENULOPSIS PINICOLA
uf *crumenula pinicola*
BT1 crumenulopsis
BT2 helotiales

CRUMENULOPSIS SORORIA
uf *crumenula sororia*
BT1 crumenulopsis
BT2 helotiales

CRUPINA
BT1 compositae
NT1 crupina vulgaris

CRUPINA VULGARIS
BT1 crupina
BT2 compositae

CRUSH RESISTANT FINISHES (AGRICOLA)
BT1 textile finishes (agricola)
BT2 finishes

CRUSHERS
BT1 farm machinery
BT2 machinery
NT1 clod crushers
rt crumblers
rt crushing
rt crushing mills
rt grinders
rt macerators
rt mills

CRUSHING
uf *grinding*
BT1 processing
rt crushers
rt crushing mills
rt milling

CRUSHING MILLS
uf *ball mills*
uf *mills, crushing*
BT1 mills
BT2 machinery
rt crushers
rt crushing
rt milling

crushing strength
USE **compressive strength**

CRUSTACEA
BT1 arthropods
NT1 branchiopoda
NT2 anostraca
NT3 artemia
NT4 artemia salina
NT2 cladocera
NT3 daphnia
NT4 daphnia magna
NT4 daphnia pulex
NT1 branchiura (arthropods)
NT2 argulus
NT1 cirripedia
NT2 thoracica
NT3 balanus
NT3 pollicipes
NT3 semibalanus
NT4 semibalanus balanoides
NT1 copepoda
NT2 calanoida
NT3 acartia
NT4 acartia clausi
NT4 acartia tonsa
NT3 diaptomus
NT3 eudiaptomus
NT4 eudiaptomus gracilis
NT4 eudiaptomus graciloides
NT3 eurytemora
NT4 eurytemora velox
NT3 pseudocalanus
NT3 skistodiaptomus
NT4 skistodiaptomus pallidus
NT3 temora
NT2 cyclopoida
NT3 acanthocyclops
NT4 acanthocyclops bicuspidatus
NT5 acanthocyclops bicuspidatus thomasi
NT4 acanthocyclops robustus
NT4 acanthocyclops vernalis
NT4 acanthocyclops viridis
NT3 cyclops
NT4 cyclops strenuus
NT3 lernaea
NT4 lernaea cyprinacea
NT3 mesocyclops
NT4 mesocyclops aspericornis
NT4 mesocyclops leuckarti
NT2 poecilostomatoida
NT3 ergasilus
NT4 ergasilus mirabilis
NT2 siphonostomatoida
NT3 lepeophtheirus
NT4 lepeophtheirus salmonis
NT1 malacostraca
NT2 amphipoda
NT3 corophium
NT3 gammarus
NT4 gammarus fossarum
NT4 gammarus oceanicus
NT4 gammarus pulex
NT2 decapoda
NT3 astacus
NT3 austropotamobius
NT4 austropotamobius pallipes
NT3 callinectes
NT3 cambarus
NT3 cancer
NT3 carcinus
NT4 carcinus aestuarii

CRUSTACEA *cont.*
NT4 carcinus maenas
NT3 cherax
NT4 cherax destructor
NT3 chionoecetes
NT3 crangon
NT3 homarus
NT4 homarus americanus
NT4 homarus gammarus
NT3 jasus
NT3 macrobrachium
NT4 macrobrachium rosenbergii
NT3 maia
NT3 metapenaeus
NT3 palaemon
NT4 palaemon serratus
NT4 palaemon serrifer
NT3 palaemonetes
NT4 palaemonetes pugio
NT3 pandalus
NT4 pandalus jordani
NT3 panulirus
NT4 panulirus argus
NT3 paralithodes
NT3 penaeus
NT4 penaeus indicus
NT4 penaeus japonicus
NT4 penaeus merguiensis
NT4 penaeus monodon
NT4 penaeus semisulcatus
NT4 penaeus setiferus
NT4 penaeus stylirostris
NT4 penaeus vannamei
NT3 portunus
NT3 potamon
NT4 potamon chinghungense
NT3 procambarus
NT4 procambarus clarkii
NT2 isopoda
NT3 armadillidiidae
NT4 armadillidium
NT5 armadillidium vulgare
NT3 asellidae
NT4 asellus
NT5 asellus aquaticus
NT3 ligiidae
NT4 ligia
NT5 ligia oceanica
NT3 oniscidae
NT4 oniscus
NT5 oniscus asellus
NT3 philosciidae
NT4 philoscia
NT5 philoscia muscorum
NT3 porcellionidae
NT4 porcellio
NT5 porcellio scaber
NT3 trichoniscidae
NT4 trichoniscus
NT5 trichoniscus pusillus
NT1 ostracoda
NT2 podocopa
NT3 cyprinotus
NT4 cyprinotus incongruens
NT3 cypris
rt plankton
rt shellfish

crusted scabies
USE **hyperkeratotic scabies**

CRUSTS
BT1 soil morphological features
NT1 lichen crusts

crusts, calcareous
USE **calcrete**

crymodes
USE **apamea**

crymodes devastator
USE **apamea devastatrix**

CRYOGENIC FEATURES
BT1 soil morphological features

CRYOGENIC PROCESSES
BT1 soil formation

CRYOGENIC SOILS
BT1 soil types (genetic)

CRYOGENIC SURGERY
BT1 surgery
BT2 medicine
rt cryogenics

CRYOGENICS
rt cold
rt cryogenic surgery
rt cryopreservation

CRYOLITE
BT1 fluorides
BT2 halides
BT3 inorganic salts
BT4 inorganic compounds
BT4 salts
BT1 fluorine insecticides
BT2 insecticides
BT3 pesticides
rt aluminium
rt sodium

cryophytum crystallinum
USE **mesembryanthemum crystallinum**

CRYOPRESERVATION
BT1 preservation
BT2 techniques
rt cryogenics
rt cryoprotectants
rt freezing

CRYOPROTECTANTS
BT1 protectants
NT1 dimethyl sulfoxide
NT1 glycerol
rt cryopreservation
rt frost protection

CRYORTHODS
BT1 spodosols
BT2 podzols
BT3 soil types (genetic)

CRYPHALUS
BT1 scolytidae
BT2 coleoptera
NT1 cryphalus piceae

CRYPHALUS PICEAE
BT1 cryphalus
BT2 scolytidae
BT3 coleoptera

CRYPHONECTRIA
BT1 diaporthales
NT1 cryphonectria cubensis
NT1 cryphonectria gyrosa
NT1 cryphonectria havanensis
NT1 cryphonectria parasitica
rt cryptosporella
rt endothia

CRYPHONECTRIA CUBENSIS
uf *cryphonectria eugeniae*
uf *cryptosporella eugeniae*
uf *endothia eugeniae*
BT1 cryphonectria
BT2 diaporthales

cryphonectria eugeniae
USE **cryphonectria cubensis**

CRYPHONECTRIA GYROSA
HN from 1990
uf *endothia tropicalis*
BT1 cryphonectria
BT2 diaporthales

CRYPHONECTRIA HAVANENSIS
HN from 1990
uf *endothia havanensis*
BT1 cryphonectria
BT2 diaporthales

CRYPHONECTRIA PARASITICA
uf *endothia parasitica*
BT1 cryphonectria
BT2 diaporthales

CRYPSIS
BT1 gramineae
NT1 crypsis schoenoides

CRYPSIS SCHOENOIDES
BT1 crypsis
BT2 gramineae
BT1 pasture plants

CRYPTANTHUS
BT1 bromeliaceae
NT1 cryptanthus bivittatus

CRYPTANTHUS BIVITTATUS
BT1 cryptanthus
BT2 bromeliaceae
BT1 ornamental bromeliads

CRYPTAPHELENCHUS
BT1 aphelenchoididae
BT2 nematoda

CRYPTERONIACEAE
NT1 dactylocladus
NT2 dactylocladus stenostachys

CRYPTOBIA
BT1 sarcomastigophora
BT2 protozoa
NT1 cryptobia salmositica

CRYPTOBIA SALMOSITICA
BT1 cryptobia
BT2 sarcomastigophora
BT3 protozoa

CRYPTOBLABES
BT1 pyralidae
BT2 lepidoptera
NT1 cryptoblabes gnidiella

CRYPTOBLABES GNIDIELLA
BT1 cryptoblabes
BT2 pyralidae
BT3 lepidoptera

CRYPTOCARYA
BT1 lauraceae
NT1 cryptocarya alba
NT1 cryptocarya laevigata
NT1 cryptocarya pleurosperma

CRYPTOCARYA ALBA
BT1 cryptocarya
BT2 lauraceae

CRYPTOCARYA LAEVIGATA
BT1 cryptocarya
BT2 lauraceae

CRYPTOCARYA PLEUROSPERMA
BT1 cryptocarya
BT2 lauraceae

CRYPTOCARYON
BT1 ciliophora
BT2 protozoa
NT1 cryptocaryon irritans

CRYPTOCARYON IRRITANS
BT1 cryptocaryon
BT2 ciliophora
BT3 protozoa

cryptococcidae
USE **eriococcidae**

CRYPTOCOCCOSIS
uf *blastomycosis, european*
uf *european blastomycosis*
BT1 mycoses
BT2 infectious diseases
BT3 diseases
rt cryptococcus neoformans

cryptococcus
USE **cryptococcus (deuteromycotina)**
OR **cryptococcus (homoptera)**

CRYPTOCOCCUS ALBIDUS
BT1 cryptococcus (deuteromycotina)
BT2 deuteromycotina

CRYPTOCOCCUS BACILLISPORUS
BT1 cryptococcus (deuteromycotina)
BT2 deuteromycotina

CRYPTOCOCCUS BACILLISPORUS *cont.*
rt filobasidiella bacillispora

CRYPTOCOCCUS (DEUTEROMYCOTINA)
uf *cryptococcus*
BT1 deuteromycotina
NT1 cryptococcus albidus
NT1 cryptococcus bacillisporus
NT1 cryptococcus laurentii
NT1 cryptococcus neoformans
rt filobasidiella
rt yeasts

CRYPTOCOCCUS FAGISUGA
BT1 cryptococcus (homoptera)
BT2 eriococcidae
BT3 coccoidea
BT4 sternorrhyncha
BT5 homoptera

CRYPTOCOCCUS (HOMOPTERA)
uf *cryptococcus*
BT1 eriococcidae
BT2 coccoidea
BT3 sternorrhyncha
BT4 homoptera
NT1 cryptococcus fagisuga

CRYPTOCOCCUS LAURENTII
BT1 cryptococcus (deuteromycotina)
BT2 deuteromycotina

CRYPTOCOCCUS NEOFORMANS
BT1 cryptococcus (deuteromycotina)
BT2 deuteromycotina
rt cryptococcosis
rt filobasidiella neoformans

CRYPTOCOTYLE
BT1 heterophyidae
BT2 digenea
BT3 trematoda
NT1 cryptocotyle lingua

CRYPTOCOTYLE LINGUA
BT1 cryptocotyle
BT2 heterophyidae
BT3 digenea
BT4 trematoda

CRYPTODIAPORTHE
uf *dothichiza*
BT1 diaporthales
NT1 cryptodiaporthe populea

CRYPTODIAPORTHE POPULEA
uf *dothichiza populea*
BT1 cryptodiaporthe
BT2 diaporthales

CRYPTOGAMS
rt bryophyta
rt plants
rt pteridophyta
rt thallophyta

CRYPTOLAEMUS
BT1 coccinellidae
BT2 coleoptera
NT1 cryptolaemus montrouzieri

CRYPTOLAEMUS MONTROUZIERI
BT1 biological control agents
BT2 beneficial organisms
BT1 cryptolaemus
BT2 coccinellidae
BT3 coleoptera

CRYPTOLEPIS
BT1 periplocaceae
NT1 cryptolepis buchanani
NT1 cryptolepis sanguinolenta

CRYPTOLEPIS BUCHANANI
BT1 cryptolepis
BT2 periplocaceae
BT1 medicinal plants

CRYPTOLEPIS SANGUINOLENTA
BT1 cryptolepis
BT2 periplocaceae

CRYPTOLEPIS SANGUINOLENTA *cont.*
BT1 medicinal plants

CRYPTOLESTES
BT1 cucujidae
BT2 coleoptera
NT1 cryptolestes ferrugineus
NT1 cryptolestes pusillus
rt laemophloeus

CRYPTOLESTES FERRUGINEUS
BT1 cryptolestes
BT2 cucujidae
BT3 coleoptera

CRYPTOLESTES PUSILLUS
uf *laemophloeus minutus*
BT1 cryptolestes
BT2 cucujidae
BT3 coleoptera

CRYPTOMERIA
BT1 taxodiaceae
NT1 cryptomeria japonica

CRYPTOMERIA JAPONICA
BT1 cryptomeria
BT2 taxodiaceae
BT1 forest trees
BT1 ornamental conifers
BT2 conifers
BT2 ornamental woody plants

CRYPTONE
BT1 ketones
rt essential oils

CRYPTOPHAGIDAE
BT1 coleoptera
NT1 atomaria
NT2 atomaria linearis

CRYPTOPHLEBIA
BT1 tortricidae
BT2 lepidoptera
NT1 cryptophlebia leucotreta
NT1 cryptophlebia ombrodelta

CRYPTOPHLEBIA LEUCOTRETA
BT1 cryptophlebia
BT2 tortricidae
BT3 lepidoptera

CRYPTOPHLEBIA OMBRODELTA
BT1 cryptophlebia
BT2 tortricidae
BT3 lepidoptera

CRYPTOPYGUS
BT1 isotomidae
BT2 collembola
NT1 cryptopygus antarcticus

CRYPTOPYGUS ANTARCTICUS
BT1 cryptopygus
BT2 isotomidae
BT3 collembola

CRYPTORCHIDISM
BT1 abnormalities
BT1 reproductive disorders
BT2 functional disorders
BT3 animal disorders
BT4 disorders
rt testes

CRYPTORHYNCHUS
BT1 curculionidae
BT2 coleoptera
NT1 cryptorhynchus lapathi
rt sternochetus

CRYPTORHYNCHUS LAPATHI
BT1 cryptorhynchus
BT2 curculionidae
BT3 coleoptera

cryptorhynchus mangiferae
USE **sternochetus mangiferae**

CRYPTOSPORELLA
BT1 diaporthales
rt cryphonectria
rt phomopsis

cryptosporella eugeniae
USE **cryphonectria cubensis**

cryptosporella viticola
USE **phomopsis viticola**

cryptosporidia
USE **cryptosporidium**

CRYPTOSPORIDIUM
uf *cryptosporidia*
BT1 apicomplexa
BT2 protozoa

CRYPTOSPORIOPSIS
BT1 deuteromycotina
rt pezicula

cryptosporiopsis corticola
USE **pezicula corticola**

cryptosporiopsis malicorticis
USE **pezicula malicorticis**

CRYPTOSTEMMA
BT1 compositae
NT1 cryptostemma calendula

CRYPTOSTEMMA CALENDULA
BT1 cryptostemma
BT2 compositae

CRYPTOSTIGMATA
uf *oribatei*
uf *oribatida*
BT1 acari
NT1 camisiidae
NT2 camisia
NT1 cepheidae
NT2 eupterotegaeus
NT3 eupterotegaeus rostratus
NT1 damaeidae
NT2 epidamaeus
NT1 phthiracaridae
NT2 steganacarus
NT3 steganacarus magnus
NT1 scheloribatidae
NT2 scheloribates
NT3 scheloribates latipes

CRYPTOSTROMA
BT1 deuteromycotina
NT1 cryptostroma corticale

CRYPTOSTROMA CORTICALE
BT1 cryptostroma
BT2 deuteromycotina

CRYPTOTAENIA
BT1 umbelliferae
NT1 cryptotaenia japonica

CRYPTOTAENIA JAPONICA
BT1 cryptotaenia
BT2 umbelliferae
BT1 leafy vegetables
BT2 vegetables

CRYPTOTERMES
BT1 kalotermitidae
BT2 isoptera
NT1 cryptotermes brevis

CRYPTOTERMES BREVIS
BT1 cryptotermes
BT2 kalotermitidae
BT3 isoptera

CRYPTOVIRUS GROUP
HN from 1990
BT1 plant viruses
BT2 plant pathogens
BT3 pathogens
NT1 beet cryptic 1 cryptovirus
NT1 beet cryptic 2 cryptovirus
NT1 carnation cryptic cryptovirus
NT1 hop trefoil cryptic 1 cryptovirus
NT1 hop trefoil cryptic 2 cryptovirus
NT1 radish yellow edge cryptovirus
NT1 red clover cryptic 2 cryptovirus
NT1 ryegrass cryptic cryptovirus

CRYPTOVIRUS GROUP *cont.*
NT1 spinach temperate cryptovirus
NT1 vicia cryptic cryptovirus
NT1 white clover cryptic 1 cryptovirus
NT1 white clover cryptic 2 cryptovirus
NT1 white clover cryptic 3 cryptovirus

cryptoweisea
USE **coccidophilus**

CRYSTAL (AGRICOLA)
rt dinnerware (agricola)
rt glassware (agricola)
rt household equipment (agricola)
rt table settings (agricola)

CRYSTAL INCLUSIONS
HN from 1990
rt crystallization

crystal violet
USE **gentian violet**

CRYSTALLINS
HN from 1990
BT1 proteins
BT2 peptides
rt eye lens

CRYSTALLIZATION
BT1 processing
rt butter
rt crystal inclusions
rt crystallography
rt crystals
rt evaporation
rt false grain
rt massecuites
rt nucleation
rt recrystallization
rt seeding

CRYSTALLOGRAPHY
BT1 mineralogy
BT2 geology
rt chemistry
rt crystallization
rt crystals
rt x ray diffraction

CRYSTALS
NT1 false grain
rt crystallization
rt crystallography
rt minerals
rt opal phytoliths

cs (symbol)
USE **caesium**

csm
USE **corn-soy-milk (agricola)**

CTENICERA
BT1 elateridae
BT2 coleoptera
NT1 ctenicera destructor
rt selatosomus

ctenicera aenea
USE **selatosomus aeneus**

CTENICERA DESTRUCTOR
BT1 ctenicera
BT2 elateridae
BT3 coleoptera

CTENICHNEUMON
BT1 ichneumonidae
BT2 hymenoptera
NT1 ctenichneumon panzeri
rt amblyteles

CTENICHNEUMON PANZERI
uf *amblyteles panzeri*
BT1 ctenichneumon
BT2 ichneumonidae
BT3 hymenoptera

CTENIDAE
HN from 1989
BT1 araneae
BT2 arachnida
BT3 arthropods
NT1 phoneutria

CTENITIS
BT1 aspidiaceae
NT1 ctenitis ampla
NT1 ctenitis apiciflora
NT1 ctenitis clarkei
NT1 ctenitis nidus

CTENITIS AMPLA
BT1 ctenitis
BT2 aspidiaceae
BT1 ornamental ferns
BT2 ferns
BT2 ornamental foliage plants
BT3 foliage plants

CTENITIS APICIFLORA
BT1 ctenitis
BT2 aspidiaceae

CTENITIS CLARKEI
BT1 ctenitis
BT2 aspidiaceae

CTENITIS NIDUS
BT1 ctenitis
BT2 aspidiaceae

CTENOCEPHALIDES
uf *ctenocephalus*
BT1 pulicidae
BT2 siphonaptera
NT1 ctenocephalides canis
NT1 ctenocephalides felis

CTENOCEPHALIDES CANIS
uf *ctenocephalus canis*
BT1 ctenocephalides
BT2 pulicidae
BT3 siphonaptera

CTENOCEPHALIDES FELIS
BT1 ctenocephalides
BT2 pulicidae
BT3 siphonaptera

ctenocephalus
USE **ctenocephalides**

ctenocephalus canis
USE **ctenocephalides canis**

CTENOLEPISMA
BT1 lepismatidae
BT2 thysanura

CTENOMYIDAE
uf *tuco-tucos*
BT1 rodents
BT2 mammals
NT1 ctenomys

CTENOMYS
BT1 ctenomyidae
BT2 rodents
BT3 mammals

CTENOPHTHALMUS
BT1 hystrichopsyllidae
BT2 siphonaptera
NT1 ctenophthalmus agyrtes
NT1 ctenophthalmus baeticus
NT1 ctenophthalmus dolichus
NT1 ctenophthalmus pseudagyrtes
NT1 ctenophthalmus wladimiri

CTENOPHTHALMUS AGYRTES
BT1 ctenophthalmus
BT2 hystrichopsyllidae
BT3 siphonaptera

CTENOPHTHALMUS BAETICUS
BT1 ctenophthalmus
BT2 hystrichopsyllidae
BT3 siphonaptera

CTENOPHTHALMUS DOLICHUS
BT1 ctenophthalmus

CTENOPHTHALMUS DOLICHUS *cont.*
BT2 hystrichopsyllidae
BT3 siphonaptera

CTENOPHTHALMUS PSEUDAGYRTES
BT1 ctenophthalmus
BT2 hystrichopsyllidae
BT3 siphonaptera

CTENOPHTHALMUS WLADIMIRI
BT1 ctenophthalmus
BT2 hystrichopsyllidae
BT3 siphonaptera

CTENOPLECTRA
BT1 apidae
BT2 hymenoptera

CTENOPLUSIA
uf *acanthoplusia*
BT1 noctuidae
BT2 lepidoptera

CTENOPSEUSTIS
BT1 tortricidae
BT2 lepidoptera
NT1 ctenopseustis obliquana

CTENOPSEUSTIS OBLIQUANA
BT1 ctenopseustis
BT2 tortricidae
BT3 lepidoptera

cu (symbol)
USE **copper**

CUBA
BT1 caribbean
BT2 america
rt cmea
rt developing countries

α-CUBEBENE
(for retrieval spell out "alpha")
BT1 insect attractants
BT2 attractants

CUBES
NT1 hay cubes
rt cubing
rt cubing machines

CUBICLES
BT1 cow housing
BT2 cattle housing
BT3 animal housing
rt boxes
rt stalls

CUBING
BT1 processing
rt cubes
rt cubing machines
rt pelleting
rt wafering

CUBING MACHINES
BT1 farm machinery
BT2 machinery
rt cubes
rt cubing
rt dies
rt wafering machines

CUBITERMES
BT1 termitidae
BT2 isoptera

cuckoos
USE **cuculidae**

CUCLOTOGASTER
BT1 philopteridae
BT2 ischnocera
BT3 mallophaga
BT4 phthiraptera
NT1 cuclotogaster heterographa

CUCLOTOGASTER HETEROGRAPHA
HN from 1989
BT1 cuclotogaster
BT2 philopteridae
BT3 ischnocera

CUCLOTOGASTER HETEROGRAPHA *cont.*
BT4 mallophaga
BT5 phthiraptera

CUCUBALUS
BT1 caryophyllaceae
NT1 cucubalus baccifer

CUCUBALUS BACCIFER
BT1 cucubalus
BT2 caryophyllaceae
BT1 medicinal plants

CUCUJIDAE
BT1 coleoptera
NT1 cryptolestes
NT2 cryptolestes ferrugineus
NT2 cryptolestes pusillus
NT1 laemophloeus

CUCULIDAE
uf *cuckoos*
BT1 cuculiformes
BT2 birds

CUCULIFORMES
BT1 birds
NT1 cuculidae

CUCUMARIA
BT1 holothuroidea
BT2 echinodermata

CUCUMBER GREEN MOTTLE MOSAIC TOBAMOVIRUS
HN from 1990; previously "cucumber green mottle mosaic virus"
uf *cucumber green mottle mosaic virus*
BT1 tobamovirus group
BT2 plant viruses
BT3 plant pathogens
BT4 pathogens
rt cucumbers
rt cucumis sativus

cucumber green mottle mosaic virus
USE **cucumber green mottle mosaic tobamovirus**

CUCUMBER MOSAIC CUCUMOVIRUS
HN from 1990; previously "cucumber mosaic virus"
uf *cucumber mosaic virus*
BT1 cucumovirus group
BT2 plant viruses
BT3 plant pathogens
BT4 pathogens
rt cucumbers
rt cucumis sativus

cucumber mosaic virus
USE **cucumber mosaic cucumovirus**

CUCUMBER 4 TOBAMOVIRUS
HN from 1990
BT1 tobamovirus group
BT2 plant viruses
BT3 plant pathogens
BT4 pathogens
rt cucumbers
rt cucumis sativus

CUCUMBERS
uf *gherkins*
BT1 cucurbit vegetables
BT2 fruit vegetables
BT3 vegetables
rt cucumber 4 tobamovirus
rt cucumber green mottle mosaic tobamovirus
rt cucumber mosaic cucumovirus
rt cucumis sativus

CUCUMEROPSIS
BT1 cucurbitaceae
NT1 cucumeropsis edulis
NT1 cucumeropsis mannii

CUCUMEROPSIS EDULIS
BT1 cucumeropsis
BT2 cucurbitaceae
BT1 cucurbit vegetables
BT2 fruit vegetables
BT3 vegetables
BT1 oilseed plants
BT2 fatty oil plants
BT3 oil plants

CUCUMEROPSIS MANNII
BT1 cucumeropsis
BT2 cucurbitaceae
BT1 cucurbit vegetables
BT2 fruit vegetables
BT3 vegetables
BT1 oilseed plants
BT2 fatty oil plants
BT3 oil plants

CUCUMIS
BT1 cucurbitaceae
NT1 cucumis anguria
NT1 cucumis melo
NT1 cucumis metuliferus
NT1 cucumis prophetarum
NT1 cucumis sativus
NT1 cucumis trigonus

CUCUMIS ANGURIA
BT1 cucumis
BT2 cucurbitaceae
BT1 cucurbit vegetables
BT2 fruit vegetables
BT3 vegetables

CUCUMIS MELO
BT1 cucumis
BT2 cucurbitaceae
rt melons

CUCUMIS METULIFERUS
BT1 cucumis
BT2 cucurbitaceae

CUCUMIS PROPHETARUM
BT1 cucumis
BT2 cucurbitaceae

CUCUMIS SATIVUS
BT1 cucumis
BT2 cucurbitaceae
rt cucumber 4 tobamovirus
rt cucumber green mottle mosaic tobamovirus
rt cucumber mosaic cucumovirus
rt cucumbers

CUCUMIS TRIGONUS
BT1 cucumis
BT2 cucurbitaceae
BT1 medicinal plants

CUCUMOVIRUS GROUP
HN from 1990
BT1 plant viruses
BT2 plant pathogens
BT3 pathogens
NT1 cucumber mosaic cucumovirus
NT1 peanut stunt cucumovirus
NT1 tomato aspermy cucumovirus

CUCURBIT FRUITS
BT1 fruit crops
NT1 coccinia grandis
NT1 melons
NT1 watermelons
rt cucurbitaceae
rt plants
rt vegetables

CUCURBIT VEGETABLES
BT1 fruit vegetables
BT2 vegetables
NT1 benincasa hispida
NT1 citrullus colocynthis
NT1 cucumbers
NT1 cucumeropsis edulis
NT1 cucumeropsis mannii
NT1 cucumis anguria
NT1 cucurbita ficifolia

CUCURBIT VEGETABLES *cont.*
NT1 cucurbita maxima
NT1 cucurbita mixta
NT1 cucurbita moschata
NT1 cucurbita pepo
NT1 lagenaria siceraria
NT1 luffa acutangula
NT1 luffa aegyptiaca
NT1 marrows
NT1 momordica charantia
NT1 momordica cochinchinensis
NT1 momordica dioica
NT1 pumpkins
NT1 sechium edule
NT1 squashes
NT2 winter squash
NT1 trichosanthes cucumerina
NT1 trichosanthes dioica
rt cucurbitaceae
rt plants

CUCURBITA
BT1 cucurbitaceae
NT1 cucurbita ficifolia
NT1 cucurbita foetidissima
NT1 cucurbita lundelliana
NT1 cucurbita maxima
NT1 cucurbita mixta
NT1 cucurbita moschata
NT1 cucurbita pepo
NT1 cucurbita texana
rt nematicidal plants
rt pumpkins
rt squash leaf curl geminivirus
rt squash mosaic comovirus
rt squashes
rt winter squash

CUCURBITA FICIFOLIA
uf gourd, siam
BT1 cucurbit vegetables
BT2 fruit vegetables
BT3 vegetables
BT1 cucurbita
BT2 cucurbitaceae

CUCURBITA FOETIDISSIMA
BT1 cucurbita
BT2 cucurbitaceae
BT1 oilseed plants
BT2 fatty oil plants
BT3 oil plants

CUCURBITA LUNDELLIANA
BT1 cucurbita
BT2 cucurbitaceae

CUCURBITA MAXIMA
BT1 cucurbit vegetables
BT2 fruit vegetables
BT3 vegetables
BT1 cucurbita
BT2 cucurbitaceae

CUCURBITA MIXTA
BT1 cucurbit vegetables
BT2 fruit vegetables
BT3 vegetables
BT1 cucurbita
BT2 cucurbitaceae

CUCURBITA MOSCHATA
BT1 cucurbit vegetables
BT2 fruit vegetables
BT3 vegetables
BT1 cucurbita
BT2 cucurbitaceae

CUCURBITA PEPO
BT1 cucurbit vegetables
BT2 fruit vegetables
BT3 vegetables
BT1 cucurbita
BT2 cucurbitaceae
BT1 medicinal plants
BT1 oilseed plants
BT2 fatty oil plants
BT3 oil plants
rt marrows
rt zucchini yellow mosaic potyvirus

CUCURBITA TEXANA
BT1 cucurbita
BT2 cucurbitaceae

CUCURBITACEAE
uf cucurbits
NT1 acanthosicyos
NT2 acanthosicyos horridus
NT1 apodanthera
NT2 apodanthera undulata
NT1 benincasa
NT2 benincasa hispida
NT1 bryonia
NT2 bryonia alba
NT2 bryonia cretica
NT1 citrullus
NT2 citrullus colocynthis
NT2 citrullus lanatus
NT2 citrullus lanatus var. fistulosus
NT1 coccinia
NT2 coccinia grandis
NT1 cucumeropsis
NT2 cucumeropsis edulis
NT2 cucumeropsis mannii
NT1 cucumis
NT2 cucumis anguria
NT2 cucumis melo
NT2 cucumis metuliferus
NT2 cucumis prophetarum
NT2 cucumis sativus
NT2 cucumis trigonus
NT1 cucurbita
NT2 cucurbita ficifolia
NT2 cucurbita foetidissima
NT2 cucurbita lundelliana
NT2 cucurbita maxima
NT2 cucurbita mixta
NT2 cucurbita moschata
NT2 cucurbita pepo
NT2 cucurbita texana
NT1 cyclanthera
NT2 cyclanthera brachystachya
NT1 ecballium
NT2 ecballium elaterium
NT1 echinocystis
NT2 echinocystis lobata
NT1 lagenaria
NT2 lagenaria siceraria
NT1 luffa
NT2 luffa acutangula
NT2 luffa aegyptiaca
NT2 luffa echinata
NT1 marah
NT2 marah macrocarpus
NT2 marah oreganus
NT1 melothria
NT2 melothria pendula
NT1 momordica
NT2 momordica cabrei
NT2 momordica charantia
NT2 momordica cochinchinensis
NT2 momordica dioica
NT2 momordica foetida
NT1 sechium
NT2 sechium edule
NT1 sicyos
NT2 sicyos angulatus
NT2 sicyos polyacanthus
NT1 telfairia
NT2 telfairia occidentalis
NT2 telfairia pedata
NT1 thladiantha
NT2 thladiantha grosvenorii
NT1 trichosanthes
NT2 trichosanthes bracteata
NT2 trichosanthes cucumerina
NT2 trichosanthes dioica
NT2 trichosanthes kirilowii
NT2 trichosanthes ovigera
NT1 zehneria
NT2 zehneria maysorensis
rt cucurbit fruits
rt cucurbit vegetables
rt gourds

CUCURBITACINS
BT1 phytosterols
BT2 sterols
BT3 alcohols
BT3 steroids
BT4 isoprenoids

CUCURBITACINS *cont.*
BT5 lipids
BT1 triterpenoids
BT2 terpenoids
BT3 isoprenoids
BT4 lipids
rt bitterness

cucurbits
USE **cucurbitaceae**

CUDRANIA
BT1 moraceae
NT1 cudrania chochinchinensis
NT1 cudrania tricuspidata

CUDRANIA CHOCHINCHINENSIS
BT1 cudrania
BT2 moraceae

CUDRANIA TRICUSPIDATA
BT1 cudrania
BT2 moraceae

CUE-LURE
BT1 insect attractants
BT2 attractants

CUFRANEB
BT1 copper fungicides
BT2 fungicides
BT3 pesticides
BT1 dithiocarbamate fungicides
BT2 carbamate pesticides
BT2 fungicides
BT3 pesticides

CUKUROVA
BT1 horse breeds
BT2 breeds

CULAEA
BT1 gasterosteidae
BT2 gasterosteiformes
BT3 osteichthyes
BT4 fishes
NT1 culaea inconstans

CULAEA INCONSTANS
BT1 culaea
BT2 gasterosteidae
BT3 gasterosteiformes
BT4 osteichthyes
BT5 fishes

CULEX
BT1 culicidae
BT2 diptera
NT1 culex annulirostris
NT1 culex annulus
NT1 culex antennatus
NT1 culex australicus
NT1 culex bitaeniorhynchus
NT1 culex cinereus
NT1 culex coronator
NT1 culex decens
NT1 culex erraticus
NT1 culex erythrothorax
NT1 culex fuscanus
NT1 culex fuscocephalus
NT1 culex gelidus
NT1 culex hayashii
NT1 culex modestus
NT1 culex neavei
NT1 culex nebulosus
NT1 culex nigripalpus
NT1 culex orientalis
NT1 culex peus
NT1 culex pipiens
NT2 culex pipiens pallens
NT2 culex pipiens pipiens
NT1 culex portesi
NT1 culex pseudovishnui
NT1 culex quinquefasciatus
NT1 culex restuans
NT1 culex salinarius
NT1 culex sitiens
NT1 culex taeniopus
NT1 culex tarsalis
NT1 culex territans
NT1 culex thalassius
NT1 culex theileri
NT1 culex tigripes
NT1 culex torrentium

CULEX *cont.*
NT1 culex tritaeniorhynchus
NT1 culex univittatus
NT1 culex vishnui
rt culiseta

CULEX ANNULIROSTRIS
BT1 culex
BT2 culicidae
BT3 diptera

CULEX ANNULUS
BT1 culex
BT2 culicidae
BT3 diptera

CULEX ANTENNATUS
BT1 culex
BT2 culicidae
BT3 diptera

CULEX AUSTRALICUS
HN from 1989
BT1 culex
BT2 culicidae
BT3 diptera

CULEX BITAENIORHYNCHUS
BT1 culex
BT2 culicidae
BT3 diptera

CULEX CINEREUS
BT1 culex
BT2 culicidae
BT3 diptera

CULEX CORONATOR
BT1 culex
BT2 culicidae
BT3 diptera

CULEX DECENS
BT1 culex
BT2 culicidae
BT3 diptera

CULEX ERRATICUS
BT1 culex
BT2 culicidae
BT3 diptera

CULEX ERYTHROTHORAX
BT1 culex
BT2 culicidae
BT3 diptera

culex fatigans
USE **culex quinquefasciatus**

CULEX FUSCANUS
BT1 culex
BT2 culicidae
BT3 diptera

CULEX FUSCOCEPHALUS
BT1 culex
BT2 culicidae
BT3 diptera

CULEX GELIDUS
BT1 culex
BT2 culicidae
BT3 diptera

CULEX HAYASHII
BT1 culex
BT2 culicidae
BT3 diptera

culex incidens
USE **culiseta incidens**

CULEX MODESTUS
BT1 culex
BT2 culicidae
BT3 diptera

CULEX NEAVEI
BT1 culex
BT2 culicidae
BT3 diptera

CULEX NEBULOSUS
BT1 culex
BT2 culicidae

CULEX NEBULOSUS *cont.*
BT3 diptera

CULEX NIGRIPALPUS
BT1 culex
BT2 culicidae
BT3 diptera

CULEX ORIENTALIS
BT1 culex
BT2 culicidae
BT3 diptera

CULEX PEUS
BT1 culex
BT2 culicidae
BT3 diptera

CULEX PIPIENS
BT1 culex
BT2 culicidae
BT3 diptera
NT1 culex pipiens pallens
NT1 culex pipiens pipiens

culex pipiens fatigans
USE **culex quinquefasciatus**

CULEX PIPIENS PALLENS
HN from 1989
BT1 culex pipiens
BT2 culex
BT3 culicidae
BT4 diptera

CULEX PIPIENS PIPIENS
HN from 1989
BT1 culex pipiens
BT2 culex
BT3 culicidae
BT4 diptera

CULEX PORTESI
BT1 culex
BT2 culicidae
BT3 diptera

CULEX PSEUDOVISHNUI
BT1 culex
BT2 culicidae
BT3 diptera

CULEX QUINQUEFASCIATUS
uf *culex fatigans*
uf *culex pipiens fatigans*
BT1 culex
BT2 culicidae
BT3 diptera

CULEX RESTUANS
BT1 culex
BT2 culicidae
BT3 diptera

CULEX SALINARIUS
BT1 culex
BT2 culicidae
BT3 diptera

CULEX SITIENS
BT1 culex
BT2 culicidae
BT3 diptera

CULEX TAENIOPUS
BT1 culex
BT2 culicidae
BT3 diptera

CULEX TARSALIS
BT1 culex
BT2 culicidae
BT3 diptera

CULEX TERRITANS
BT1 culex
BT2 culicidae
BT3 diptera

CULEX THALASSIUS
BT1 culex
BT2 culicidae
BT3 diptera

CULEX THEILERI
BT1 culex

CULEX THEILERI *cont.*
BT2 culicidae
BT3 diptera

CULEX TIGRIPES
BT1 culex
BT2 culicidae
BT3 diptera

CULEX TORRENTIUM
BT1 culex
BT2 culicidae
BT3 diptera

CULEX TRITAENIORHYNCHUS
BT1 culex
BT2 culicidae
BT3 diptera

CULEX UNIVITTATUS
BT1 culex
BT2 culicidae
BT3 diptera

CULEX VISHNUI
BT1 culex
BT2 culicidae
BT3 diptera

CULICIDAE
uf *mosquitoes*
BT1 diptera
NT1 aedeomyia
NT2 aedeomyia squamipennis
NT1 aedes
NT2 aedes abserratus
NT2 aedes aegypti
NT2 aedes africanus
NT2 aedes albifasciatus
NT2 aedes albopictus
NT2 aedes alcasidi
NT2 aedes ambreensis
NT2 aedes angustivittatus
NT2 aedes annulipes
NT2 aedes apicoargenteus
NT2 aedes atlanticus
NT2 aedes atropalpus
NT2 aedes campestris
NT2 aedes canadensis
NT2 aedes cantans
NT2 aedes cantator
NT2 aedes caspius
NT2 aedes cataphylla
NT2 aedes cinereus
NT2 aedes circumluteolus
NT2 aedes communis
NT2 aedes cooki
NT2 aedes cumminsii
NT2 aedes cyprius
NT2 aedes dentatus
NT2 aedes detritus
NT2 aedes diantaeus
NT2 aedes dorsalis
NT2 aedes durbanensis
NT2 aedes echinus
NT2 aedes epactius
NT2 aedes esoensis
NT2 aedes euedes
NT2 aedes excrucians
NT2 aedes fitchii
NT2 aedes flavescens
NT2 aedes flavopictus
NT2 aedes fluviatilis
NT2 aedes fryeri
NT2 aedes fulvus
NT2 aedes furcifer
NT2 aedes galloisi
NT2 aedes geniculatus
NT2 aedes guamensis
NT2 aedes hebrideus
NT2 aedes hendersoni
NT2 aedes hexodontus
NT2 aedes impiger
NT2 aedes implicatus
NT2 aedes increpitus
NT2 aedes infirmatus
NT2 aedes ingrami
NT2 aedes intrudens
NT2 aedes japonicus
NT2 aedes juppi
NT2 aedes kochi
NT2 aedes koreicoides
NT2 aedes koreicus

CULICIDAE *cont.*
NT2 aedes leucomelas
NT2 aedes lineatopennis
NT2 aedes luridus
NT2 aedes luteocephalus
NT2 aedes mariae
NT2 aedes mascarensis
NT2 aedes mediovittatus
NT2 aedes melanimon
NT2 aedes metallicus
NT2 aedes montchadskyi
NT2 aedes monticola
NT2 aedes nevadensis
NT2 aedes nigripes
NT2 aedes nigromaculis
NT2 aedes nipponicus
NT2 aedes notoscriptus
NT2 aedes novalbopictus
NT2 aedes opok
NT2 aedes pembaensis
NT2 aedes phoeniciae
NT2 aedes pionips
NT2 aedes poicilia
NT2 aedes polynesiensis
NT2 aedes pseudalbopictus
NT2 aedes pseudoscutellaris
NT2 aedes pulchritarsis
NT2 aedes pullatus
NT2 aedes punctodes
NT2 aedes punctor
NT2 aedes refiki
NT2 aedes riparius
NT2 aedes rusticus
NT2 aedes samoanus
NT2 aedes scapularis
NT2 aedes scutellaris
NT3 aedes scutellaris katherinensis
NT3 aedes scutellaris malayensis
NT2 aedes seatoi
NT2 aedes serratus
NT2 aedes sierrensis
NT2 aedes simpsoni
NT2 aedes sollicitans
NT2 aedes spencerii
NT2 aedes squamiger
NT2 aedes sticticus
NT2 aedes stimulans
NT2 aedes stokesi
NT2 aedes subdiversus
NT2 aedes taeniorhynchus
NT2 aedes tarsalis
NT2 aedes taylori
NT2 aedes terrens
NT2 aedes thelcter
NT2 aedes thibaulti
NT2 aedes togoi
NT2 aedes tormentor
NT2 aedes triseriatus
NT2 aedes trivittatus
NT2 aedes unidentatus
NT2 aedes varipalpus
NT2 aedes vexans
NT2 aedes vigilax
NT2 aedes vittatus
NT2 aedes w-albus
NT2 aedes watteni
NT2 aedes zoosophus
NT1 anopheles
NT2 anopheles aconitus
NT2 anopheles albimanus
NT2 anopheles albitarsis
NT2 anopheles algeriensis
NT2 anopheles amictus
NT2 anopheles annularis
NT2 anopheles annulipes
NT2 anopheles aquasalis
NT2 anopheles arabiensis
NT2 anopheles atroparvus
NT2 anopheles atropos
NT2 anopheles balabacensis
NT2 anopheles bancroftii
NT2 anopheles barberi
NT2 anopheles barbirostris
NT2 anopheles beklemishevi
NT2 anopheles bellator
NT2 anopheles bradleyi
NT2 anopheles campestris
NT2 anopheles claviger
NT2 anopheles coustani

CULICIDAE *cont.*
NT2 anopheles crucians
NT2 anopheles cruzii
NT2 anopheles culicifacies
NT2 anopheles darlingi
NT2 anopheles demeilloni
NT2 anopheles dirus
NT2 anopheles dthali
NT2 anopheles earlei
NT2 anopheles farauti
NT2 anopheles flavirostris
NT2 anopheles fluviatilis
NT2 anopheles freeborni
NT2 anopheles funestus
NT2 anopheles gambiae
NT2 anopheles hancocki
NT2 anopheles hargreavesi
NT2 anopheles hilli
NT2 anopheles hispaniola
NT2 anopheles hyrcanus
NT2 anopheles jamesii
NT2 anopheles koliensis
NT2 anopheles labranchiae
NT2 anopheles lesteri
NT3 anopheles lesteri anthropophagus
NT2 anopheles leucosphyrus
NT2 anopheles lindesayi
NT2 anopheles litoralis
NT2 anopheles maculatus
NT2 anopheles maculipennis
NT2 anopheles marshallii
NT2 anopheles mascarensis
NT2 anopheles melanoon
NT2 anopheles melas
NT2 anopheles merus
NT2 anopheles messeae
NT2 anopheles minimus
NT2 anopheles multicolor
NT2 anopheles neivai
NT2 anopheles nigerrimus
NT2 anopheles nili
NT2 anopheles nivipes
NT2 anopheles nuneztovari
NT2 anopheles occidentalis
NT2 anopheles oswaldoi
NT2 anopheles pharoensis
NT2 anopheles philippinensis
NT2 anopheles plumbeus
NT2 anopheles pretoriensis
NT2 anopheles pseudopunctipennis
NT3 anopheles pseudopunctipennis franciscanus
NT2 anopheles pulcherrimus
NT2 anopheles punctimacula
NT2 anopheles punctipennis
NT2 anopheles punctulatus
NT2 anopheles quadriannulatus
NT2 anopheles quadrimaculatus
NT2 anopheles rivulorum
NT2 anopheles rufipes
NT2 anopheles sacharovi
NT2 anopheles sergentii
NT2 anopheles sinensis
NT2 anopheles splendidus
NT2 anopheles squamosus
NT2 anopheles stephensi
NT2 anopheles subalpinus
NT2 anopheles subpictus
NT2 anopheles sundaicus
NT2 anopheles superpictus
NT2 anopheles tenebrosus
NT2 anopheles tessellatus
NT2 anopheles theobaldi
NT2 anopheles triannulatus
NT2 anopheles turkhudi
NT2 anopheles vagus
NT2 anopheles wellcomei
NT2 anopheles ziemanni
NT1 armigeres
NT2 armigeres subalbatus
NT1 coquillettidia
NT2 coquillettidia crassipes
NT2 coquillettidia perturbans
NT2 coquillettidia richiardii
NT1 culex
NT2 culex annulirostris
NT2 culex annulus
NT2 culex antennatus

CULICIDAE *cont.*
NT2 culex australicus
NT2 culex bitaeniorhynchus
NT2 culex cinereus
NT2 culex coronator
NT2 culex decens
NT2 culex erraticus
NT2 culex erythrothorax
NT2 culex fuscanus
NT2 culex fuscocephalus
NT2 culex gelidus
NT2 culex hayashii
NT2 culex modestus
NT2 culex neavei
NT2 culex nebulosus
NT2 culex nigripalpus
NT2 culex orientalis
NT2 culex peus
NT2 culex pipiens
NT3 culex pipiens pallens
NT3 culex pipiens pipiens
NT2 culex portesi
NT2 culex pseudovishnui
NT2 culex quinquefasciatus
NT2 culex restuans
NT2 culex salinarius
NT2 culex sitiens
NT2 culex taeniopus
NT2 culex tarsalis
NT2 culex territans
NT2 culex thalassius
NT2 culex theileri
NT2 culex tigripes
NT2 culex torrentium
NT2 culex tritaeniorhynchus
NT2 culex univittatus
NT2 culex vishnui
NT1 culiseta
NT2 culiseta alaskaensis
NT2 culiseta annulata
NT2 culiseta bergrothi
NT2 culiseta incidens
NT2 culiseta inornata
NT2 culiseta longiareolata
NT2 culiseta melanura
NT2 culiseta morsitans
NT2 culiseta ochroptera
NT2 culiseta subochrea
NT1 deinocerites
NT2 deinocerites cancer
NT2 deinocerites pseudes
NT1 eretmapodites
NT2 eretmapodites quinquevittatus
NT1 ficalbia
NT1 haemagogus
NT2 haemagogus capricornii
NT2 haemagogus celeste
NT2 haemagogus equinus
NT2 haemagogus janthinomys
NT2 haemagogus leucocelaenus
NT1 mansonia (diptera)
NT2 mansonia africana
NT2 mansonia annulata
NT2 mansonia annulifera
NT2 mansonia bonneae
NT2 mansonia dives
NT2 mansonia dyari
NT2 mansonia indiana
NT2 mansonia titillans
NT2 mansonia uniformis
NT1 opifex
NT2 opifex fuscus
NT1 orthopodomyia
NT2 orthopodomyia signifera
NT1 psorophora
NT2 psorophora ciliata
NT2 psorophora columbiae
NT2 psorophora confinnis
NT2 psorophora cyanescens
NT2 psorophora discolor
NT2 psorophora ferox
NT2 psorophora signipennis
NT1 sabethes
NT1 topomyia
NT1 toxorhynchites
NT2 toxorhynchites amboinensis
NT2 toxorhynchites brevipalpis
NT2 toxorhynchites gravelyi
NT2 toxorhynchites rutilus

CULICIDAE *cont.*
NT3 toxorhynchites rutilus septentrionalis
NT2 toxorhynchites splendens
NT2 toxorhynchites theobaldi
NT1 trichoprosopon
NT1 tripteroides
NT2 tripteroides bambusa
NT1 uranotaenia
NT2 uranotaenia lowii
NT2 uranotaenia sapphirina
NT2 uranotaenia unguiculata
NT1 wyeomyia
NT2 wyeomyia mitchellii
NT2 wyeomyia smithii
NT2 wyeomyia vanduzeei
rt bed nets
rt mosquito coils
rt mosquito nets
rt overcrowding factors

CULICINOMYCES
BT1 deuteromycotina
BT1 entomogenous fungi
BT2 entomopathogens
BT3 pathogens
BT2 fungi
NT1 culicinomyces clavisporus

CULICINOMYCES CLAVISPORUS
BT1 culicinomyces
BT2 deuteromycotina
BT2 entomogenous fungi
BT3 entomopathogens
BT4 pathogens
BT3 fungi

CULICOIDES
BT1 ceratopogonidae
BT2 diptera
NT1 culicoides arakawai
NT1 culicoides barbosai
NT1 culicoides biguttatus
NT1 culicoides brevitarsis
NT1 culicoides circumscriptus
NT1 culicoides denningi
NT1 culicoides edeni
NT1 culicoides fascipennis
NT1 culicoides furens
NT1 culicoides grisescens
NT1 culicoides hieroglyphicus
NT1 culicoides hollensis
NT1 culicoides imicola
NT1 culicoides impunctatus
NT1 culicoides insignis
NT1 culicoides jamesi
NT1 culicoides kingi
NT1 culicoides melleus
NT1 culicoides mississippiensis
NT1 culicoides nubeculosus
NT1 culicoides obsoletus
NT1 culicoides oxystoma
NT1 culicoides pallidicornis
NT1 culicoides paraensis
NT1 culicoides pulicaris
NT1 culicoides punctatus
NT1 culicoides puncticollis
NT1 culicoides pusillus
NT1 culicoides riethi
NT1 culicoides salinarius
NT1 culicoides schultzei
NT1 culicoides stellifer
NT1 culicoides variipennis
NT1 culicoides venustus
NT1 culicoides wadai

CULICOIDES ARAKAWAI
BT1 culicoides
BT2 ceratopogonidae
BT3 diptera

CULICOIDES BARBOSAI
BT1 culicoides
BT2 ceratopogonidae
BT3 diptera

CULICOIDES BIGUTTATUS
BT1 culicoides
BT2 ceratopogonidae
BT3 diptera

CULICOIDES BREVITARSIS
BT1 culicoides

CULICOIDES BREVITARSIS *cont.*
BT2 ceratopogonidae
BT3 diptera

CULICOIDES CIRCUMSCRIPTUS
BT1 culicoides
BT2 ceratopogonidae
BT3 diptera

CULICOIDES DENNINGI
BT1 culicoides
BT2 ceratopogonidae
BT3 diptera

CULICOIDES EDENI
HN from 1989
BT1 culicoides
BT2 ceratopogonidae
BT3 diptera

CULICOIDES FASCIPENNIS
BT1 culicoides
BT2 ceratopogonidae
BT3 diptera

CULICOIDES FURENS
BT1 culicoides
BT2 ceratopogonidae
BT3 diptera

CULICOIDES GRISESCENS
BT1 culicoides
BT2 ceratopogonidae
BT3 diptera

CULICOIDES HIEROGLYPHICUS
BT1 culicoides
BT2 ceratopogonidae
BT3 diptera

CULICOIDES HOLLENSIS
BT1 culicoides
BT2 ceratopogonidae
BT3 diptera

CULICOIDES IMICOLA
uf culicoides pallidipennis
BT1 culicoides
BT2 ceratopogonidae
BT3 diptera

CULICOIDES IMPUNCTATUS
BT1 culicoides
BT2 ceratopogonidae
BT3 diptera

CULICOIDES INSIGNIS
HN from 1989
BT1 culicoides
BT2 ceratopogonidae
BT3 diptera

CULICOIDES JAMESI
BT1 culicoides
BT2 ceratopogonidae
BT3 diptera

CULICOIDES KINGI
HN from 1990
BT1 culicoides
BT2 ceratopogonidae
BT3 diptera

CULICOIDES MELLEUS
BT1 culicoides
BT2 ceratopogonidae
BT3 diptera

CULICOIDES MISSISSIPPIENSIS
BT1 culicoides
BT2 ceratopogonidae
BT3 diptera

CULICOIDES NUBECULOSUS
BT1 culicoides
BT2 ceratopogonidae
BT3 diptera

CULICOIDES OBSOLETUS
BT1 culicoides
BT2 ceratopogonidae
BT3 diptera

CULICOIDES OXYSTOMA
HN from 1990; previously sunk to culicoides schultzei

CULICOIDES OXYSTOMA *cont.*
BT1 culicoides
BT2 ceratopogonidae
BT3 diptera

CULICOIDES PALLIDICORNIS
BT1 culicoides
BT2 ceratopogonidae
BT3 diptera

culicoides pallidipennis
USE **culicoides imicola**

CULICOIDES PARAENSIS
BT1 culicoides
BT2 ceratopogonidae
BT3 diptera

CULICOIDES PULICARIS
BT1 culicoides
BT2 ceratopogonidae
BT3 diptera

CULICOIDES PUNCTATUS
BT1 culicoides
BT2 ceratopogonidae
BT3 diptera

CULICOIDES PUNCTICOLLIS
BT1 culicoides
BT2 ceratopogonidae
BT3 diptera

CULICOIDES PUSILLUS
HN from 1990
BT1 culicoides
BT2 ceratopogonidae
BT3 diptera

CULICOIDES RIETHI
BT1 culicoides
BT2 ceratopogonidae
BT3 diptera

CULICOIDES SALINARIUS
BT1 culicoides
BT2 ceratopogonidae
BT3 diptera

CULICOIDES SCHULTZEI
BT1 culicoides
BT2 ceratopogonidae
BT3 diptera

CULICOIDES STELLIFER
HN from 1989
BT1 culicoides
BT2 ceratopogonidae
BT3 diptera

CULICOIDES VARIIPENNIS
BT1 culicoides
BT2 ceratopogonidae
BT3 diptera

CULICOIDES VENUSTUS
BT1 culicoides
BT2 ceratopogonidae
BT3 diptera

CULICOIDES WADAI
HN from 1989
BT1 culicoides
BT2 ceratopogonidae
BT3 diptera

CULINARY ARTS (AGRICOLA)
BT1 arts
NT1 carving techniques (agricola)
rt cookery (agricola)
rt food art (agricola)

CULINARY HERBS
uf *flavouring crops*
uf *herbs, culinary*
NT1 anethum graveolens
NT1 angelica archangelica
NT1 anthriscus cerefolium
NT1 armoracia rusticana
NT1 artemisia dracunculus
NT1 borago officinalis
NT1 fennel
NT1 laurus nobilis
NT1 melissa officinalis
NT1 mentha piperita

CULINARY HERBS *cont.*
NT1 mentha spicata
NT1 ocimum basilicum
NT1 origanum majorana
NT1 origanum onites
NT1 origanum vulgare
NT1 petroselinum crispum
NT1 rosmarinus officinalis
NT1 salvia officinalis
NT1 satureja hortensis
NT1 satureja montana
NT1 thymus citriodorus
NT1 thymus vulgaris
rt condiments
rt essential oil plants
rt flavourings
rt horticultural crops
rt industrial crops
rt medicinal plants
rt plants
rt spice plants

CULISETA
uf *allotheobaldia*
uf *theobaldia*
BT1 culicidae
BT2 diptera
NT1 culiseta alaskaensis
NT1 culiseta annulata
NT1 culiseta bergrothi
NT1 culiseta incidens
NT1 culiseta inornata
NT1 culiseta longiareolata
NT1 culiseta melanura
NT1 culiseta morsitans
NT1 culiseta ochroptera
NT1 culiseta subochrea
rt culex

CULISETA ALASKAENSIS
BT1 culiseta
BT2 culicidae
BT3 diptera

CULISETA ANNULATA
uf *theobaldia annulata*
BT1 culiseta
BT2 culicidae
BT3 diptera

CULISETA BERGROTHI
BT1 culiseta
BT2 culicidae
BT3 diptera

CULISETA INCIDENS
uf *culex incidens*
BT1 culiseta
BT2 culicidae
BT3 diptera

CULISETA INORNATA
BT1 culiseta
BT2 culicidae
BT3 diptera

CULISETA LONGIAREOLATA
uf *allotheobaldia longiareolata*
BT1 culiseta
BT2 culicidae
BT3 diptera

CULISETA MELANURA
BT1 culiseta
BT2 culicidae
BT3 diptera

CULISETA MORSITANS
BT1 culiseta
BT2 culicidae
BT3 diptera

CULISETA OCHROPTERA
uf *theobaldia ochroptera*
BT1 culiseta
BT2 culicidae
BT3 diptera

CULISETA SUBOCHREA
HN from 1989
BT1 culiseta
BT2 culicidae
BT3 diptera

CULL TREES
BT1 trees
rt culling
rt forest trees
rt thinning

CULLING
BT1 selection
NT1 roguing
rt cull trees
rt grading
rt replacement rate
rt sorting
rt wastage

culms
USE **stems**

CULTIVAR AUTHENTICITY
HN from 1990
BT1 seed testing
rt cultivars

CULTIVAR IDENTIFICATION
HN from 1990
BT1 seed testing
rt cultivars
rt identification

CULTIVARS
uf *cultivated varieties*
uf *varieties, cultivated*
BT1 varieties
NT1 dessert cultivars
NT1 dwarf cultivars
NT1 edible cultivars
NT1 leafless cultivars
NT1 miniature cultivars
NT1 wine cultivars
rt cultivar authenticity
rt cultivar identification
rt types
rt variety classification
rt variety trials

cultivated varieties
USE **cultivars**

CULTIVATION
uf *culture, plant*
NT1 contour cultivation
NT1 digging
NT1 earthing up
NT1 hilling
NT1 interrow cultivation
NT1 no-tillage
NT1 ridging
NT2 contour ridging
NT2 tio ridging
NT1 seedbed preparation
NT1 stubble cultivation
NT1 tillage
NT2 chiselling
NT2 conservation tillage
NT2 deep tillage
NT2 discing
NT2 harrowing
NT2 hoeing
NT2 minimum tillage
NT2 ploughing
NT3 blade ploughing
NT3 deep ploughing
NT2 puddling
NT2 ripping
NT2 rolling
NT2 rotary cultivation
NT2 row tillage
NT2 subsoiling
NT1 vertical topsoiling
rt crop husbandry
rt cropping systems
rt cultivators
rt cultural methods
rt site preparation
rt soil management
rt spacing
rt sward renovation
rt weeding

cultivation, protected
USE **protected cultivation**

cultivation under glass or plastic
USE **protected cultivation**

CULTIVATORS
BT1 implements
NT1 disc cultivators
NT1 rippers
NT1 rotary cultivators
NT1 rotary diggers
NT1 seeder cultivators
NT1 tine cultivators
NT2 spring loaded tine cultivators
NT2 spring tine cultivators
rt clod crushers
rt cultivation
rt depth wheels
rt discs
rt flame cultivators
rt furrow openers
rt furrow presses
rt incorporators
rt ploughs
rt scarifiers
rt stone pickers
rt subsoilers
rt subsoiling attachments
rt tines

cultivators, disc
USE **disc cultivators**

cultivators, rotary
USE **rotary cultivators**

cultivators, spring loaded tine
USE **spring loaded tine cultivators**

cultivators, spring tine
USE **spring tine cultivators**

CULTURAL ACTIVITIES
uf *activities, cultural*
BT1 culture
BT1 entertainment
BT2 leisure activities
NT1 cultural exhibitions
NT1 cultural tourism
NT1 festivals
rt animation
rt arts
rt arts activities
rt choirs
rt cultural behaviour
rt leisure activities
rt recreational activities
rt television

cultural anthropology
USE **social anthropology**

CULTURAL BEHAVIOR
BF cultural behaviour
BT1 behavior

CULTURAL BEHAVIOUR
AF cultural behavior
BT1 culture
BT1 social behaviour
BT2 behaviour
NT1 cultural integration
NT1 cultural interaction
rt arts
rt cultural activities
rt leisure behaviour
rt religion
rt social customs

CULTURAL CENTERS
BF cultural centres

CULTURAL CENTRES
AF cultural centers
BT1 cultural facilities
rt arts centres
rt culture
rt leisure centres
rt museums
rt recreational buildings
rt recreational facilities

CULTURAL CHANGE
BT1 cultural development

CULTURAL CHANGE *cont.*
rt culture
rt modernization

CULTURAL CONTROL
BT1 control
rt pest control
rt weed control

CULTURAL DEVELOPMENT
NT1 cultural change
rt culture
rt development
rt social anthropology
rt unesco

CULTURAL DIFFERENTIATION
rt cultural environment
rt cultural integration
rt culture

CULTURAL ENVIRONMENT
uf *cultural influences*
BT1 environment
NT1 acculturation
NT1 cultural heritage
rt cultural differentiation
rt cultural integration
rt culture
rt quality of life

CULTURAL EXHIBITIONS
uf *arts exhibitions*
BT1 cultural activities
BT2 culture
BT2 entertainment
BT3 leisure activities
BT1 exhibitions
BT2 entertainment
BT3 leisure activities

CULTURAL FACILITIES
NT1 arts centres
NT1 community centres
NT1 cultural centres
NT1 libraries
NT1 museums
NT2 open air museums
rt leisure centres
rt recreational facilities
rt tourist attractions

CULTURAL HERITAGE
uf *cultural influences*
BT1 cultural environment
BT2 environment
rt ancient monuments
rt culture
rt heritage areas
rt historic buildings
rt libraries
rt museums
rt social customs
rt traditions

cultural influences
USE **cultural environment**
OR **cultural heritage**

CULTURAL INTEGRATION
BT1 cultural behaviour
BT2 culture
BT2 social behaviour
BT3 behaviour
rt cultural differentiation
rt cultural environment
rt culture
rt social integration

CULTURAL INTERACTION
BT1 cultural behaviour
BT2 culture
BT2 social behaviour
BT3 behaviour
rt social participation

CULTURAL METHODS
NT1 forcing
NT1 low energy cultivation
NT1 organic culture
NT1 pot culture
NT1 protected cultivation
NT2 greenhouse culture
NT1 soilless culture

CULTURAL METHODS *cont.*
NT2 hydroponics
NT2 nutrient film techniques
NT1 two year culture
rt blanching
rt casing
rt cultivation
rt handling
rt harvesting
rt irrigation
rt plant nutrition
rt plant protection
rt planting
rt propagation
rt pruning
rt shading
rt soil management
rt sowing
rt staking
rt storage
rt training
rt vertical mulching
rt weed control

CULTURAL POLICY
BT1 culture
rt arts policy
rt social policy

CULTURAL RESEARCH
BT1 culture
BT1 research
NT1 cross cultural studies
rt cultural sociology

CULTURAL SOCIOLOGY
BT1 culture
BT1 sociology
rt cultural research

cultural soil types
USE **soil types (cultural)**

CULTURAL TOURISM
BT1 cultural activities
BT2 culture
BT2 entertainment
BT3 leisure activities
BT1 tourism

CULTURAL VALUES
BT1 culture
BT1 value systems
rt values

cultural vs. chemical weed control
USE **chemical vs. cultural weed control**

CULTURAL WEED CONTROL
uf *weed control, cultural*
BT1 weed control
BT2 pest control
BT3 control
rt chemical vs. cultural weed control

CULTURE
(civilization)
NT1 cultural activities
NT2 cultural exhibitions
NT2 cultural tourism
NT2 festivals
NT1 cultural behaviour
NT2 cultural integration
NT2 cultural interaction
NT1 cultural policy
NT1 cultural research
NT2 cross cultural studies
NT1 cultural sociology
NT1 cultural values
NT1 folk culture
NT2 folk dancing
NT2 folk music
NT1 popular culture
rt acculturation
rt cross cultural training (agricola)
rt cultural centres
rt cultural change
rt cultural development
rt cultural differentiation
rt cultural environment

CULTURE *cont.*
rt cultural heritage
rt cultural integration
rt leisure
rt recreation
rt unesco

CULTURE COLLECTION CATALOGS
BF culture collection catalogues
BT1 catalogs

CULTURE COLLECTION CATALOGUES
AF culture collection catalogs
BT1 catalogues
BT2 publications
rt culture collections

CULTURE COLLECTIONS
BT1 collections
rt bacteria
rt culture collection catalogues
rt cultures
rt fungi

CULTURE FILTRATES
BT1 filtrates
BT2 liquids
rt cultures
rt microorganisms

culture, folk
USE **folk culture**

CULTURE MEDIA
uf *media (propagation)*
uf *media, culture*
NT1 agar
rt cultures
rt substrates
rt tissue culture

culture, plant
USE **cultivation**

culture, popular
USE **popular culture**

CULTURE TECHNIQUES
BT1 biological techniques
BT2 techniques
NT1 in vitro culture
NT2 cell culture
NT2 somatic embryogenesis
NT2 tissue culture
NT3 anther culture
NT3 embryo culture
NT3 organ culture
NT3 ovule culture
NT3 shoot tip culture
NT1 vermiculture
rt animal testing alternatives
rt cultures
rt laboratory methods

CULTURED CREAM
uf *cream, cultured*
BT1 cream
BT2 milk products
BT3 products

CULTURED MILK STARTERS
HN from 1990
BT1 starters
rt cultured milks

CULTURED MILKS
uf *fermented milk*
uf *milk, fermented*
BT1 milk products
BT2 products
NT1 acidified milk
NT1 acidophilin
NT1 acidophilus milk
NT1 bioghurt
NT1 dahi
NT1 kefir
NT1 koumiss
NT1 leben
NT1 prostokvasha
NT1 ryazhenka
NT1 smetana
NT1 sour milk

CULTURED MILKS *cont.*
NT1 ymer
NT1 yoghurt
rt cultured milk starters

CULTURED PRODUCT STARTERS
HN from 1990
BT1 starters
rt cultured products

CULTURED PRODUCTS
BT1 products
rt algal cultures
rt cultured product starters

CULTURES
(properties of organic cultures; for culture techniques use "culture techniques" or one of its narrower terms)
NT1 algal cultures
NT1 cell cultures
NT2 cell lines
NT3 hela cells
NT1 tissue cultures
rt bacteria
rt culture collections
rt culture filtrates
rt culture media
rt culture techniques
rt fungi
rt vaccines

CULVERTS
BT1 channels

cumin
USE **cuminum cyminum**

CUMINUM
BT1 umbelliferae
NT1 cuminum cyminum

CUMINUM CYMINUM
uf *cumin*
BT1 cuminum
BT2 umbelliferae
BT1 essential oil plants
BT2 oil plants
BT1 insecticidal plants
BT2 pesticidal plants
BT1 spice plants

cumulative effects
USE **residual effects**

cumulative temperature
USE **heat sums**

CUMULUS OOPHORUS
BT1 ova
BT2 gametes
BT2 germ cells
BT3 cells

CUNAXA
BT1 cunaxidae
BT2 prostigmata
BT3 acari

CUNAXIDAE
BT1 prostigmata
BT2 acari
NT1 cunaxa
NT1 rubroscirus

cuniculus
USE **agouti**

CUNNINGHAMELLA
BT1 mucorales
NT1 cunninghamella bertholletiae
NT1 cunninghamella elegans

CUNNINGHAMELLA BERTHOLLETIAE
BT1 cunninghamella
BT2 mucorales

CUNNINGHAMELLA ELEGANS
BT1 cunninghamella
BT2 mucorales

CUNNINGHAMIA
BT1 taxodiaceae

CUNNINGHAMIA *cont.*
NT1 cunninghamia konishii
NT1 cunninghamia lanceolata

CUNNINGHAMIA KONISHII
BT1 cunninghamia
BT2 taxodiaceae

CUNNINGHAMIA LANCEOLATA
BT1 cunninghamia
BT2 taxodiaceae
BT1 forest trees

CUNONIACEAE
NT1 weinmannia
NT2 weinmannia racemosa
NT2 weinmannia trichosperma

CUNURIA
BT1 euphorbiaceae
NT1 cunuria spruceana

CUNURIA SPRUCEANA
BT1 cunuria
BT2 euphorbiaceae
BT1 medicinal plants

CUP FEED MECHANISM
uf *feed mechanism, cup*
BT1 feed mechanisms
rt drills

CUPHEA
BT1 lythraceae
NT1 cuphea carthagenensis
NT1 cuphea hyssopifolia
NT1 cuphea racemosa

CUPHEA CARTHAGENENSIS
BT1 cuphea
BT2 lythraceae

CUPHEA HYSSOPIFOLIA
BT1 cuphea
BT2 lythraceae

CUPHEA RACEMOSA
BT1 cuphea
BT2 lythraceae

CUPRESSACEAE
NT1 callitris
NT2 callitris columellaris
NT2 callitris intratropica
NT2 callitris rhomboidea
NT1 chamaecyparis
NT2 chamaecyparis formosensis
NT2 chamaecyparis lawsoniana
NT2 chamaecyparis nootkatensis
NT2 chamaecyparis obtusa
NT2 chamaecyparis pisifera
NT2 chamaecyparis thyoides
NT1 cupressocyparis
NT2 cupressocyparis leylandii
NT1 cupressus
NT2 cupressus arizonica
NT2 cupressus atlantica
NT2 cupressus dupreziana
NT2 cupressus forbesii
NT2 cupressus funebris
NT2 cupressus lusitanica
NT2 cupressus macrocarpa
NT2 cupressus pygmaea
NT2 cupressus sempervirens
NT2 cupressus torulosa
NT1 fitzroya
NT2 fitzroya cupressoides
NT1 fokienia
NT2 fokienia hodginsii
NT1 juniperus
NT2 juniperus ashei
NT2 juniperus brevifolia
NT2 juniperus chinensis
NT2 juniperus communis
NT2 juniperus conferta
NT2 juniperus drupacea
NT2 juniperus excelsa
NT2 juniperus foetidissima
NT2 juniperus horizontalis
NT2 juniperus macropoda
NT2 juniperus monosperma
NT2 juniperus occidentalis
NT2 juniperus osteosperma

CUPRESSACEAE *cont.*
NT2 juniperus oxycedrus
NT2 juniperus phoenicea
NT2 juniperus pinchotii
NT2 juniperus procera
NT2 juniperus procumbens
NT2 juniperus ramulosa
NT2 juniperus recurva
NT2 juniperus rigida
NT2 juniperus sabina
NT2 juniperus scopulorum
NT2 juniperus thurifera
NT2 juniperus turkestanica
NT2 juniperus virginiana
NT1 libocedrus
NT2 libocedrus bidwillii
NT2 libocedrus decurrens
NT1 thuja
NT2 thuja occidentalis
NT2 thuja orientalis
NT2 thuja plicata
NT1 thujopsis
NT2 thujopsis dolabrata
rt coniferae

CUPRESSOCYPARIS
BT1 cupressaceae
NT1 cupressocyparis leylandii

CUPRESSOCYPARIS LEYLANDII
BT1 cupressocyparis
BT2 cupressaceae
BT1 forest trees
BT1 ornamental conifers
BT2 conifers
BT2 ornamental woody plants

CUPRESSUS
uf *cypresses*
BT1 cupressaceae
NT1 cupressus arizonica
NT1 cupressus atlantica
NT1 cupressus dupreziana
NT1 cupressus forbesii
NT1 cupressus funebris
NT1 cupressus lusitanica
NT1 cupressus macrocarpa
NT1 cupressus pygmaea
NT1 cupressus sempervirens
NT1 cupressus torulosa

CUPRESSUS ARIZONICA
uf *cupressus glabra*
uf *cupressus nevadensis*
BT1 cupressus
BT2 cupressaceae
BT1 forest trees
BT1 ornamental conifers
BT2 conifers
BT2 ornamental woody plants

CUPRESSUS ATLANTICA
BT1 cupressus
BT2 cupressaceae

CUPRESSUS DUPREZIANA
BT1 cupressus
BT2 cupressaceae

CUPRESSUS FORBESII
BT1 cupressus
BT2 cupressaceae

CUPRESSUS FUNEBRIS
HN until 1989 was "see chamaecyparis funebris"
uf *chamaecyparis funebris*
BT1 cupressus
BT2 cupressaceae
BT1 ornamental conifers
BT2 conifers
BT2 ornamental woody plants

cupressus glabra
USE **cupressus arizonica**

cupressus lindleyi
USE **cupressus lusitanica**

CUPRESSUS LUSITANICA
uf *cupressus lindleyi*
BT1 cupressus
BT2 cupressaceae
BT1 forest trees

CUPRESSUS LUSITANICA *cont.*
BT1 ornamental conifers
BT2 conifers
BT2 ornamental woody plants

CUPRESSUS MACROCARPA
BT1 cupressus
BT2 cupressaceae
BT1 forest trees
BT1 ornamental conifers
BT2 conifers
BT2 ornamental woody plants

cupressus nevadensis
USE **cupressus arizonica**

CUPRESSUS PYGMAEA
BT1 cupressus
BT2 cupressaceae

CUPRESSUS SEMPERVIRENS
BT1 cupressus
BT2 cupressaceae
BT1 essential oil plants
BT2 oil plants
BT1 forest trees

CUPRESSUS TORULOSA
BT1 antifungal plants
BT1 cupressus
BT2 cupressaceae
BT1 forest trees

CUPRIFEROUS SOILS
BT1 soil types (chemical)

CUPROBAM
BT1 copper fungicides
BT2 fungicides
BT3 pesticides
BT1 dithiocarbamate fungicides
BT2 carbamate pesticides
BT2 fungicides
BT3 pesticides

CUPROUS OXIDE
BT1 copper fungicides
BT2 fungicides
BT3 pesticides
BT1 oxides
BT2 inorganic compounds
rt copper

CUPS
BT1 containers

CURACAO
BT1 netherlands antilles
BT2 caribbean
BT3 america

curasol
USE **poly(vinyl acetate)**

CURATELLA
BT1 dilleniaceae
NT1 curatella americana

CURATELLA AMERICANA
BT1 curatella
BT2 dilleniaceae
BT1 medicinal plants
BT1 tan plants

CURCULIGO
BT1 hypoxidaceae
NT1 curculigo orchioides

CURCULIGO ORCHIOIDES
BT1 curculigo
BT2 hypoxidaceae

CURCULIO
uf *balaninus*
BT1 curculionidae
BT2 coleoptera
NT1 curculio caryae
NT1 curculio elephas
NT1 curculio nucum

CURCULIO CARYAE
BT1 curculio
BT2 curculionidae
BT3 coleoptera

CURCULIO ELEPHAS
BT1 curculio
BT2 curculionidae
BT3 coleoptera

CURCULIO NUCUM
uf *balaninus nucum*
BT1 curculio
BT2 curculionidae
BT3 coleoptera

CURCULIONIDAE
uf *weevils*
BT1 coleoptera
NT1 alcidodes
NT2 alcidodes haemopterus
NT1 anthonomus
NT2 anthonomus grandis
NT2 anthonomus pomorum
NT2 anthonomus rubi
NT1 baris
NT1 bothynoderes
NT2 bothynoderes foveocollis
NT2 bothynoderes punctiventris
NT1 ceutorhynchus
NT2 ceutorhynchus assimilis
NT2 ceutorhynchus litura
NT2 ceutorhynchus napi
NT2 ceutorhynchus pallidactylus
NT2 ceutorhynchus pleurostigma
NT1 chalcodermus
NT2 chalcodermus aeneus
NT1 conorhynchus
NT1 conotrachelus
NT2 conotrachelus nenuphar
NT1 cosmopolites
NT2 cosmopolites sordidus
NT1 cryptorhynchus
NT2 cryptorhynchus lapathi
NT1 curculio
NT2 curculio caryae
NT2 curculio elephas
NT2 curculio nucum
NT1 cylindrocopturus
NT2 cylindrocopturus adspersus
NT1 cyrtobagous
NT2 cyrtobagous salviniae
NT2 cyrtobagous singularis
NT1 diaprepes
NT2 diaprepes abbreviatus
NT1 echinocnemus
NT1 elaeidobius
NT2 elaeidobius kamerunicus
NT1 gonipterus
NT2 gonipterus scutellatus
NT1 graphognathus
NT2 graphognathus leucoloma
NT2 graphognathus peregrinus
NT1 hylobius
NT2 hylobius abietis
NT2 hylobius pales
NT1 hypera
NT2 hypera meles
NT2 hypera nigrirostris
NT2 hypera postica
NT1 larinus
NT1 lissorhoptrus
NT2 lissorhoptrus oryzophilus
NT1 listronotus
NT2 listronotus bonariensis
NT2 listronotus oregonensis
NT1 lixomorphus
NT2 lixomorphus algirus
NT1 lixus
NT2 lixus juncii
NT2 lixus speciosus
NT1 metamasius
NT2 metamasius hemipterus
NT1 microlarinus
NT2 microlarinus lypriformis
NT1 myllocerus
NT2 myllocerus curvicornis
NT2 myllocerus discolor
NT2 myllocerus subfasciatus
NT2 myllocerus undecimpustulatus
NT1 naupactus
NT2 naupactus xanthographus
NT1 neochetina
NT2 neochetina bruchi

CURCULIONIDAE *cont.*
NT2 neochetina eichhorniae
NT1 otiorhynchus
NT2 otiorhynchus ligustici
NT2 otiorhynchus ovatus
NT2 otiorhynchus rugosostriatus
NT2 otiorhynchus singularis
NT2 otiorhynchus sulcatus
NT1 pachnaeus
NT2 pachnaeus litus
NT2 pachnaeus opalus
NT1 pachylobius
NT2 pachylobius picivorus
NT1 pantomorus
NT2 pantomorus cervinus
NT1 pentarthrum
NT2 pentarthrum huttoni
NT1 phyllobius
NT2 phyllobius argentatus
NT2 phyllobius pyri
NT1 pissodes
NT2 pissodes castaneus
NT2 pissodes nemorensis
NT2 pissodes piceae
NT2 pissodes pini
NT2 pissodes strobi
NT2 pissodes validirostris
NT1 premnotrypes
NT1 psalidium
NT2 psalidium maxillosum
NT1 rhabdoscelus
NT2 rhabdoscelus obscurus
NT1 rhinocyllus
NT2 rhinocyllus conicus
NT1 rhynchaenus
NT2 rhynchaenus fagi
NT2 rhynchaenus mangiferae
NT1 rhynchophorus
NT2 rhynchophorus ferrugineus
NT2 rhynchophorus palmarum
NT1 sitona
NT2 sitona callosus
NT2 sitona cylindricollis
NT2 sitona discoideus
NT2 sitona hispidulus
NT2 sitona humeralis
NT2 sitona lepidus
NT2 sitona lineatus
NT2 sitona macularius
NT2 sitona puncticollis
NT2 sitona sulcifrons
NT1 sitophilus
NT2 sitophilus granarius
NT2 sitophilus oryzae
NT2 sitophilus zeamais
NT1 smicronyx
NT2 smicronyx fulvus
NT2 smicronyx jungermanniae
NT1 sphenophorus
NT2 sphenophorus callosus
NT2 sphenophorus parvulus
NT1 sternochetus
NT2 sternochetus mangiferae
NT1 tanymecus
NT2 tanymecus dilaticollis
NT2 tanymecus palliatus
NT1 trichosirocalus
NT2 trichosirocalus horridus
NT1 tychius
NT2 tychius flavus
NT2 tychius picirostris

CURCUMA
BT1 zingiberaceae
NT1 curcuma amada
NT1 curcuma angustifolia
NT1 curcuma aromatica
NT1 curcuma caesia
NT1 curcuma longa
NT1 curcuma mangga
NT1 curcuma xanthorrhiza
NT1 curcuma zeodaria

CURCUMA AMADA
BT1 antifungal plants
BT1 curcuma
BT2 zingiberaceae

CURCUMA ANGUSTIFOLIA
BT1 antifungal plants
BT1 curcuma

CURCUMA ANGUSTIFOLIA *cont.*
BT2 zingiberaceae
BT1 starch crops

CURCUMA AROMATICA
BT1 antifungal plants
BT1 curcuma
BT2 zingiberaceae

CURCUMA CAESIA
BT1 curcuma
BT2 zingiberaceae

curcuma domestica
USE **curcuma longa**

CURCUMA LONGA
uf *curcuma domestica*
BT1 antibacterial plants
BT1 antifungal plants
BT1 curcuma
BT2 zingiberaceae
BT1 dye plants
BT1 insecticidal plants
BT2 pesticidal plants
BT1 medicinal plants
BT1 spice plants
rt turmeric

CURCUMA MANGGA
BT1 curcuma
BT2 zingiberaceae

CURCUMA XANTHORRHIZA
BT1 curcuma
BT2 zingiberaceae
BT1 medicinal plants
BT1 starch crops

CURCUMA ZEODARIA
BT1 curcuma
BT2 zingiberaceae
BT1 medicinal plants
BT1 root vegetables
BT2 root crops
BT2 vegetables

CURCUMIN
BT1 dyes

CURD
BT1 cheeses
BT2 milk products
BT3 products
BT1 coagulum
rt cheesemaking
rt whey

CURDS
rt cauliflowers
rt inflorescences

CURED MEATS (AGRICOLA)
BT1 cured products (agricola)
BT2 foods
BT2 products
BT1 meat products
BT2 animal products
BT3 products
NT1 corned beef (agricola)

CURED PRODUCTS (AGRICOLA)
BT1 foods
BT1 products
NT1 cured meats (agricola)
NT2 corned beef (agricola)

CURIMATIDAE
BT1 characiformes
BT2 osteichthyes
BT3 fishes
NT1 prochilodus

CURING
BT1 processing
NT1 flue curing
rt drying
rt preservation

CURIUM
BT1 actinides
BT2 transition elements
BT3 metallic elements
BT4 elements
BT4 metals

CURL
rt coat
rt fleece
rt wool

CURRENCIES
uf *monetary systems*
NT1 european units of account
NT1 foreign exchange
NT1 green money
NT1 national currencies
rt monetary policy

current
USE **electric current**

CURRICULUM
BT1 educational courses
NT1 college curriculum (agricola)
NT1 core curriculum (agricola)
NT1 high school curriculum (agricola)
rt curriculum guides (agricola)
rt education
rt educational planning
rt educational reform
rt environmental education
rt schools

CURRICULUM GUIDES (AGRICOLA)
rt curriculum
rt teaching materials

CURRY (AGRICOLA)
rt meals

CURTAINS
rt screens

CURTOBACTERIUM
BT1 coryneform group of bacteria
BT2 firmicutes
BT3 bacteria
BT4 prokaryotes
NT1 curtobacterium flaccumfaciens
NT2 curtobacterium flaccumfaciens pv. betae
NT2 curtobacterium flaccumfaciens pv. flaccumfaciens
NT2 curtobacterium flaccumfaciens pv. oortii
NT2 curtobacterium flaccumfaciens pv. poinsettiae
rt corynebacterium

CURTOBACTERIUM FLACCUMFACIENS
uf *corynebacterium flaccumfaciens*
BT1 curtobacterium
BT2 coryneform group of bacteria
BT3 firmicutes
BT4 bacteria
BT5 prokaryotes
BT1 plant pathogenic bacteria
BT2 plant pathogens
BT3 pathogens
NT1 curtobacterium flaccumfaciens pv. betae
NT1 curtobacterium flaccumfaciens pv. flaccumfaciens
NT1 curtobacterium flaccumfaciens pv. oortii
NT1 curtobacterium flaccumfaciens pv. poinsettiae

CURTOBACTERIUM FLACCUMFACIENS PV. BETAE
BT1 curtobacterium flaccumfaciens
BT2 curtobacterium
BT3 coryneform group of bacteria
BT4 firmicutes
BT5 bacteria

CURTOBACTERIUM FLACCUMFACIENS PV. BETAE *cont.*
BT6 prokaryotes
BT2 plant pathogenic bacteria
BT3 plant pathogens
BT4 pathogens

CURTOBACTERIUM FLACCUMFACIENS PV. FLACCUMFACIENS
BT1 curtobacterium flaccumfaciens
BT2 curtobacterium
BT3 coryneform group of bacteria
BT4 firmicutes
BT5 bacteria
BT6 prokaryotes
BT2 plant pathogenic bacteria
BT3 plant pathogens
BT4 pathogens

CURTOBACTERIUM FLACCUMFACIENS PV. OORTII
BT1 curtobacterium flaccumfaciens
BT2 curtobacterium
BT3 coryneform group of bacteria
BT4 firmicutes
BT5 bacteria
BT6 prokaryotes
BT2 plant pathogenic bacteria
BT3 plant pathogens
BT4 pathogens

CURTOBACTERIUM FLACCUMFACIENS PV. POINSETTIAE
BT1 curtobacterium flaccumfaciens
BT2 curtobacterium
BT3 coryneform group of bacteria
BT4 firmicutes
BT5 bacteria
BT6 prokaryotes
BT2 plant pathogenic bacteria
BT3 plant pathogens
BT4 pathogens

CURVULARIA
BT1 deuteromycotina
NT1 curvularia inaequalis
NT1 curvularia penniseti
NT1 curvularia spicata
NT1 curvularia tuberculata
rt cochliobolus

curvularia eragrostidis
USE **cochliobolus eragrostidis**

curvularia geniculata
USE **cochliobolus geniculatus**

CURVULARIA INAEQUALIS
BT1 curvularia
BT2 deuteromycotina

curvularia intermedia
USE **cochliobolus intermedius**

curvularia lunata
USE **cochliobolus lunatus**

curvularia maculans
USE **cochliobolus eragrostidis**

curvularia pallescens
USE **cochliobolus pallescens**

CURVULARIA PENNISETI
BT1 curvularia
BT2 deuteromycotina

CURVULARIA SPICATA
BT1 curvularia
BT2 deuteromycotina

CURVULARIA TUBERCULATA
BT1 curvularia
BT2 deuteromycotina

curvularia verruculosa
USE **cochliobolus verruculosus**

CUSCUTA
BT1 cuscutaceae
NT1 cuscuta approximata
NT1 cuscuta australis
NT1 cuscuta californica
NT1 cuscuta campestris
NT1 cuscuta chinensis
NT1 cuscuta epithymum
NT1 cuscuta europaea
NT1 cuscuta europaea var. indica
NT1 cuscuta gronovii
NT1 cuscuta hyalina
NT1 cuscuta indecora
NT1 cuscuta jungermanniae
NT1 cuscuta lehmaniana
NT1 cuscuta lupuliformis
NT1 cuscuta minor
NT1 cuscuta monogyna
NT1 cuscuta nevadensis
NT1 cuscuta odorata
NT1 cuscuta pedicellata
NT1 cuscuta pentagona
NT1 cuscuta planiflora
NT1 cuscuta pulchella
NT1 cuscuta reflexa
NT1 cuscuta reflexa var. brachystigma
NT1 cuscuta subinclusa
NT1 cuscuta trifolii

CUSCUTA APPROXIMATA
BT1 cuscuta
BT2 cuscutaceae

cuscuta arvensis
USE **cuscuta campestris**

CUSCUTA AUSTRALIS
BT1 cuscuta
BT2 cuscutaceae
BT1 parasitic plants
BT2 parasites

CUSCUTA CALIFORNICA
BT1 cuscuta
BT2 cuscutaceae

CUSCUTA CAMPESTRIS
uf *cuscuta arvensis*
BT1 cuscuta
BT2 cuscutaceae
BT1 parasitic plants
BT2 parasites
BT1 weeds

CUSCUTA CHINENSIS
BT1 cuscuta
BT2 cuscutaceae
BT1 medicinal plants

CUSCUTA EPITHYMUM
BT1 cuscuta
BT2 cuscutaceae
BT1 parasitic plants
BT2 parasites

CUSCUTA EUROPAEA
BT1 cuscuta
BT2 cuscutaceae
BT1 parasitic plants
BT2 parasites

CUSCUTA EUROPAEA VAR. INDICA
BT1 cuscuta
BT2 cuscutaceae

CUSCUTA GRONOVII
BT1 cuscuta
BT2 cuscutaceae

CUSCUTA HYALINA
BT1 cuscuta
BT2 cuscutaceae
BT1 parasitic plants
BT2 parasites

CUSCUTA INDECORA
BT1 cuscuta
BT2 cuscutaceae

CUSCUTA JUNGERMANNIAE
BT1 cuscuta

CUSCUTA JUNGERMANNIAE *cont.*
BT2 cuscutaceae

CUSCUTA LEHMANIANA
BT1 cuscuta
BT2 cuscutaceae

CUSCUTA LUPULIFORMIS
BT1 cuscuta
BT2 cuscutaceae
BT1 parasitic plants
BT2 parasites

CUSCUTA MINOR
BT1 cuscuta
BT2 cuscutaceae

CUSCUTA MONOGYNA
BT1 cuscuta
BT2 cuscutaceae

CUSCUTA NEVADENSIS
BT1 cuscuta
BT2 cuscutaceae

CUSCUTA ODORATA
BT1 cuscuta
BT2 cuscutaceae

CUSCUTA PEDICELLATA
BT1 cuscuta
BT2 cuscutaceae

CUSCUTA PENTAGONA
BT1 cuscuta
BT2 cuscutaceae

CUSCUTA PLANIFLORA
BT1 cuscuta
BT2 cuscutaceae

CUSCUTA PULCHELLA
BT1 cuscuta
BT2 cuscutaceae

CUSCUTA REFLEXA
BT1 antiviral plants
BT1 cuscuta
BT2 cuscutaceae
BT1 parasitic plants
BT2 parasites

CUSCUTA REFLEXA VAR. BRACHYSTIGMA
BT1 cuscuta
BT2 cuscutaceae

CUSCUTA SUBINCLUSA
BT1 cuscuta
BT2 cuscutaceae

CUSCUTA TRIFOLII
BT1 cuscuta
BT2 cuscutaceae

CUSCUTACEAE
NT1 cuscuta
NT2 cuscuta approximata
NT2 cuscuta australis
NT2 cuscuta californica
NT2 cuscuta campestris
NT2 cuscuta chinensis
NT2 cuscuta epithymum
NT2 cuscuta europaea
NT2 cuscuta europaea var. indica
NT2 cuscuta gronovii
NT2 cuscuta hyalina
NT2 cuscuta indecora
NT2 cuscuta jungermanniae
NT2 cuscuta lehmaniana
NT2 cuscuta lupuliformis
NT2 cuscuta minor
NT2 cuscuta monogyna
NT2 cuscuta nevadensis
NT2 cuscuta odorata
NT2 cuscuta pedicellata
NT2 cuscuta pentagona
NT2 cuscuta planiflora
NT2 cuscuta pulchella
NT2 cuscuta reflexa
NT2 cuscuta reflexa var. brachystigma
NT2 cuscuta subinclusa
NT2 cuscuta trifolii

CUSCUTACEAE *cont.*
NT1 monogynella
NT2 monogynella lehmanniana

CUSHING'S SYNDROME
BT1 adrenal gland diseases
BT2 endocrine diseases
BT3 organic diseases
BT4 diseases

CUSSONIA
BT1 araliaceae
NT1 cussonia barteri

CUSSONIA BARTERI
BT1 cussonia
BT2 araliaceae
BT1 medicinal plants

CUSTARD
BT1 milk products
BT2 products

custard apples
USE **annona reticulata**

CUSTOM HIRING (AGRICOLA)
BT1 hiring
BT2 capital leasing
rt hired labor

CUSTOM-MADE EQUIPMENT (AGRICOLA)
BT1 equipment

CUSTOMARY LAW
BT1 law
BT2 legal systems

CUSTOMER RELATIONS (AGRICOLA)
rt consumers
rt relationships

customs duties
USE **tariffs**

CUSTOMS REGULATIONS
BT1 import controls
BT2 controls
BT2 trade barriers
BT3 trade protection
BT4 trade policy
BT5 economic policy

CUSTOMS UNIONS
BT1 economic unions
NT1 efta
rt common markets

CUT FLOWER PRESERVATIVES
BT1 preservatives
NT1 8-hydroxyquinoline citrate
NT1 benzyl isothiocyanate
NT1 silver thiosulfate
rt cut flowers
rt vase life

CUT-FLOWER PRODUCTION
HN was used until 1990 in agricola
USE **crop production**
AND **cut flowers**

CUT FLOWERS
uf *flowers, cut*
ufa *cut-flower production*
NT1 dried flowers
rt bunching
rt crops
rt cut flower preservatives
rt cut foliage
rt floriculture
rt flowers
rt ornamental plants
rt vase life

CUT FOLIAGE
uf *decorative greenery*
uf *foliage, cut*
rt bunching
rt crops
rt cut flowers
rt foliage plants
rt leaves

CUT FOLIAGE *cont.*
rt minor forest products
rt ornamental plants
rt preservatives
rt vase life

CUT SETS
BT1 propagation materials
rt sets
rt tubers

CUTANEOUS APPLICATION
BT1 application methods
BT2 methodology
rt skin

CUTANS
BT1 soil micromorphological features
BT2 soil morphological features
NT1 argillans
NT1 gel coatings
NT1 organic coatings
NT1 sesquans

CUTEREBRA
BT1 cuterebridae
BT2 diptera
NT1 cuterebra fontinella
NT2 cuterebra fontinella grisea
NT1 cuterebra tenebrosa

CUTEREBRA FONTINELLA
HN from 1989
BT1 cuterebra
BT2 cuterebridae
BT3 diptera
NT1 cuterebra fontinella grisea

CUTEREBRA FONTINELLA GRISEA
HN from 1989; previously cuterebra grisea
uf *cuterebra grisea*
BT1 cuterebra fontinella
BT2 cuterebra
BT3 cuterebridae
BT4 diptera

cuterebra grisea
USE **cuterebra fontinella grisea**

CUTEREBRA TENEBROSA
BT1 cuterebra
BT2 cuterebridae
BT3 diptera

CUTEREBRIDAE
BT1 diptera
NT1 cuterebra
NT2 cuterebra fontinella
NT3 cuterebra fontinella grisea
NT2 cuterebra tenebrosa
NT1 dermatobia
NT2 dermatobia hominis

CUTICLE
BT1 epidermis
BT2 animal tissues
BT3 tissues
BT2 plant tissues
BT3 plant
BT3 tissues
rt chitin
rt cutin
rt integument
rt skin

CUTIN
BT1 vegetable fat
BT2 fat
BT2 plant products
BT3 products
rt cuticle
rt epidermis

cuts
USE **meat cuts**

CUTTER BAR MOWERS
uf *mowers, cutter bar*
BT1 mowers
BT2 farm machinery
BT3 machinery

CUTTER BAR MOWERS *cont.*
rt cutter bars
rt cutting

CUTTER BARS
BT1 components
rt cutter bar mowers
rt dividers

CUTTER LOADERS
BT1 harvesters
BT2 farm machinery
BT3 machinery
BT1 loaders
BT2 handling machinery
BT3 machinery

CUTTERS
BT1 farm machinery
BT2 machinery
NT1 hedge cutters
NT1 scrub cutters
NT1 shears
NT2 logging shears
NT2 pruning shears
NT1 silage cutters
NT1 trench cutters
rt blades
rt cutting
rt forestry machinery
rt knives
rt mowing
rt woodworking

cutthroat trout
USE **salmo clarki**

CUTTING
NT1 chopping
NT1 clipping
NT1 cutting programmes
NT1 mowing
NT1 rotary cutting
NT1 shear cutting
NT1 shearing
NT1 slicing
rt cutter bar mowers
rt cutters
rt cutting date
rt cutting frequency
rt cutting height
rt cutting methods
rt harvesting
rt outturn

CUTTING DATE
BT1 harvesting date
rt cutting
rt date

CUTTING FREQUENCY
BT1 harvesting frequency
BT2 frequency
rt cutting

CUTTING HEIGHT
rt cutting
rt mowing

CUTTING METHODS
BT1 methodology
rt cutting

CUTTING PROGRAMMES
AF cutting programs
BT1 cutting
rt sawmilling

CUTTING PROGRAMS
BF cutting programmes

CUTTINGS
BT1 propagation materials
NT1 leaf bud cuttings
NT1 leaf cuttings
NT1 root cuttings
NT1 shoot cuttings
NT1 summer cuttings
NT1 winter cuttings
rt offshoots
rt sets
rt slips
rt suckers
rt vegetative propagation

cutworms
USE **noctuidae**

CYACETACIDE
uf *cyacetazide*
BT1 anthelmintics
BT2 antiparasitic agents
BT3 drugs

cyacetazide
USE **cyacetacide**

CYADOX
BT1 growth promoters
BT2 growth regulators
BT2 promoters

CYAMOPSIS
BT1 leguminosae
NT1 cyamopsis tetragonoloba

cyamopsis psoraloides
USE **cyamopsis tetragonoloba**

CYAMOPSIS TETRAGONOLOBA
uf *beans (cyamopsis)*
uf *cyamopsis psoraloides*
BT1 cyamopsis
BT2 leguminosae
BT1 grain legumes
BT2 grain crops
BT2 legumes
BT1 medicinal plants
BT1 vegetable legumes
BT2 fruit vegetables
BT3 vegetables
BT2 legumes
rt cluster beans
rt guar
rt guar gum
rt guar meal
rt guar oil

CYANAMIDE
BT1 imides
BT2 organic nitrogen compounds
rt calcium cyanamide

CYANATES
BT1 inorganic salts
BT2 inorganic compounds
BT2 salts
NT1 potassium cyanate

CYANATRYN
BT1 triazine herbicides
BT2 herbicides
BT3 pesticides
BT2 triazines
BT3 heterocyclic nitrogen compounds
BT4 organic nitrogen compounds

CYANAZINE
BT1 triazine herbicides
BT2 herbicides
BT3 pesticides
BT2 triazines
BT3 heterocyclic nitrogen compounds
BT4 organic nitrogen compounds

CYANIDE SENSITIVE RESPIRATION
BT1 respiration
BT2 physiology

CYANIDES
BT1 inorganic salts
BT2 inorganic compounds
BT2 salts
NT1 potassium cyanide
rt nitriles

CYANIDIN
BT1 anthocyanidins
BT2 flavonoids
BT3 aromatic compounds
BT3 plant pigments
BT4 pigments
rt cyanin

CYANIN
BT1 anthocyanins
BT2 glycoflavones
BT3 flavonoids
BT4 aromatic compounds
BT4 plant pigments
BT5 pigments
BT3 glycosides
BT4 carbohydrates
rt cyanidin

CYANOBACTERIA
uf *blue green algae*
uf *cyanochloronta*
uf *cyanophyta*
BT1 prokaryotes
NT1 anabaena
NT2 anabaena azollae
NT2 anabaena circinalis
NT2 anabaena cylindrica
NT2 anabaena doliolum
NT2 anabaena flos-aquae
NT2 anabaena hassalii
NT2 anabaena scheremetievi
NT2 anabaena variabilis
NT1 anacystis
NT2 anacystis cyanea
NT2 anacystis incerta
NT2 anacystis nidulans
NT1 aphanizomenon
NT2 aphanizomenon flos-aquae
NT2 aphanizomenon hoisatica
NT1 aphanocapsa
NT1 aulosira
NT2 aulosira prolifica
NT1 calothrix
NT2 calothrix brevissima
NT1 gloeocapsa
NT2 gloeocapsa alpicola
NT1 lyngbya
NT2 lyngbya birgei
NT1 microcoleus
NT1 microcystis
NT2 microcystis aeruginosa
NT2 microcystis pulverea
NT1 myxosarcina
NT2 myxosarcina spectabilis
NT1 nostoc
NT2 nostoc muscorum
NT1 nostochopsis
NT2 nostochopsis lobatus
NT1 oscillatoria
NT2 oscillatoria agardhii
NT2 oscillatoria lutea
NT2 oscillatoria redekei
NT2 oscillatoria rubescens
NT1 phormidium
NT2 phormidium luridum
NT2 phormidium uncinatum
NT1 plectonema
NT2 plectonema boryganum
NT1 spirulina
NT1 synechococcus
NT2 synechococcus leopoliensis
NT1 tolypothrix
NT2 tolypothrix tenuis
rt bacteria

cyanochloronta
USE **cyanobacteria**

CYANOCOBALAMIN
BT1 vitamin b12
BT2 lipotropic factors
BT3 drugs
BT2 vitamin b complex
BT3 water-soluble vitamins
BT4 vitamins

CYANOFENPHOS
BT1 phosphonothioate insecticides
BT2 organophosphorus insecticides
BT3 insecticides
BT4 pesticides
BT3 organophosphorus pesticides
BT4 organophosphorus compounds

CYANOGEN
BT1 nitriles
BT2 organic nitrogen compounds

CYANOGENESIS
rt cyanogens
rt hydrogen cyanide

CYANOGENIC GLYCOSIDES
uf *nitrilosides*
BT1 cyanogens
BT2 toxic substances
BT1 glycosides
BT2 carbohydrates
NT1 amygdalin
NT1 linamarin
NT1 taxiphyllin
rt hydrogen cyanide

CYANOGENS
BT1 toxic substances
NT1 cyanogenic glycosides
NT2 amygdalin
NT2 linamarin
NT2 taxiphyllin
rt cyanogenesis

cyanoguanidine
USE **dicyandiamide**

CYANOPHOS
BT1 organothiophosphate insecticides
BT2 organophosphorus insecticides
BT3 insecticides
BT4 pesticides
BT3 organophosphorus pesticides
BT4 organophosphorus compounds

cyanophyta
USE **cyanobacteria**

CYANOTIS
BT1 commelinaceae
NT1 cyanotis axillaris

CYANOTIS AXILLARIS
BT1 cyanotis
BT2 commelinaceae

CYATHODINIUM
BT1 ciliophora
BT2 protozoa

CYATHOSTOMA
uf *trichonema*
BT1 syngamidae
BT2 nematoda
NT1 cyathostoma bronchialis

CYATHOSTOMA BRONCHIALIS
BT1 cyathostoma
BT2 syngamidae
BT3 nematoda

CYATHOSTOMINAE
uf *small strongyles*
uf *strongyles, small*
BT1 strongylidae
BT2 nematoda
NT1 cyathostomum
NT1 cylicocyclus
NT1 cylicodontophorus
NT1 cylicostephanus

CYATHOSTOMUM
BT1 cyathostominae
BT2 strongylidae
BT3 nematoda

CYBERNETICS
BT1 communication
rt automatic control
rt automation
rt robots

CYBERNINS
BT1 hormones

CYBISTER
BT1 dytiscidae

CYBISTER *cont.*
BT2 coleoptera

CYBOCEPHALUS
BT1 nitidulidae
BT2 coleoptera

CYCADACEAE
uf cycads
NT1 cycas
NT2 cycas circinalis
NT2 cycas revoluta

cycads
USE **cycadaceae**

CYCAS
BT1 cycadaceae
NT1 cycas circinalis
NT1 cycas revoluta
rt cycas necrotic stunt nepovirus

cycas beddomei
USE **cycas circinalis**

CYCAS CIRCINALIS
uf cycas beddomei
BT1 cycas
BT2 cycadaceae

CYCAS NECROTIC STUNT NEPOVIRUS
HN from 1990
BT1 nepovirus group
BT2 plant viruses
BT3 plant pathogens
BT4 pathogens
rt cycas

CYCAS REVOLUTA
BT1 antiviral plants
BT1 cycas
BT2 cycadaceae

CYCASIN
BT1 azoxy compounds
BT2 organic nitrogen compounds
BT1 carcinogens
BT2 toxic substances
BT1 glucosides
BT2 glycosides
BT3 carbohydrates

CYCLAFURAMID
BT1 furanilide fungicides
BT2 anilide fungicides
BT3 fungicides
BT4 pesticides

CYCLAMATES
BT1 organic salts
BT2 salts
NT1 sodium cyclamate

CYCLAMEN
BT1 primulaceae
NT1 cyclamen graecum
NT1 cyclamen hederifolium
NT1 cyclamen persicum
NT1 cyclamen purpurascens

cyclamen colchicum
USE **cyclamen purpurascens**

cyclamen europaeum
USE **cyclamen purpurascens**

cyclamen fatrense
USE **cyclamen purpurascens**

CYCLAMEN GRAECUM
BT1 cyclamen
BT2 primulaceae
BT1 ornamental bulbs
rt tubers

CYCLAMEN HEDERIFOLIUM
uf cyclamen neapolitanum
BT1 cyclamen
BT2 primulaceae
BT1 ornamental bulbs
rt tubers

cyclamen indicum
USE **cyclamen persicum**

cyclamen neapolitanum
USE **cyclamen hederifolium**

CYCLAMEN PERSICUM
uf cyclamen indicum
BT1 cyclamen
BT2 primulaceae
BT1 ornamental bulbs
rt tubers

CYCLAMEN PURPURASCENS
uf cyclamen colchicum
uf cyclamen europaeum
uf cyclamen fatrense
BT1 cyclamen
BT2 primulaceae
BT1 ornamental bulbs
rt tubers

CYCLANEUSMA
BT1 rhytismatales
NT1 cyclaneusma minus
NT1 cyclaneusma niveum
rt naemacyclus

CYCLANEUSMA MINUS
HN from 1990
uf naemacyclus minor
BT1 cyclaneusma
BT2 rhytismatales

CYCLANEUSMA NIVEUM
uf naemacyclus niveus
BT1 cyclaneusma
BT2 rhytismatales

CYCLANTHACEAE
uf synanthae
NT1 carludovica
NT2 carludovica palmata

CYCLANTHERA
BT1 cucurbitaceae
NT1 cyclanthera brachystachya

CYCLANTHERA BRACHYSTACHYA
uf cyclanthera explodens
BT1 cyclanthera
BT2 cucurbitaceae
BT1 ornamental herbaceous plants

cyclanthera explodens
USE **cyclanthera brachystachya**

CYCLE MENUS (AGRICOLA)
BT1 menus

CYCLEA
BT1 menispermaceae
NT1 cyclea barbata
NT1 cyclea hypoglauca

CYCLEA BARBATA
BT1 cyclea
BT2 menispermaceae

CYCLEA HYPOGLAUCA
BT1 cyclea
BT2 menispermaceae

cycles, nutrient
USE **cycling**

CYCLEWAYS
BT1 paths
BT2 roads
rt bicycling
rt footpaths

cyclic adenosine monophosphate
USE **c-amp**

CYCLIC AMINO ACIDS
BT1 amino acids
BT2 carboxylic acids
BT3 organic acids
BT4 acids
BT2 organic nitrogen compounds
NT1 cycloleucine

CYCLIC AMINO ACIDS *cont.*
NT1 desmosine
NT1 hypoglycine a
NT1 methylhistidine

cyclic amp
USE **c-amp**

CYCLIC FLUCTUATIONS
BT1 fluctuations

CYCLIC NUCLEOTIDES
BT1 nucleotides
BT2 glycosides
BT3 carbohydrates
NT1 c-amp

CYCLIC PEPTIDES
BT1 oligopeptides
BT2 peptides
NT1 cyclosporins
NT1 gramicidin s
NT1 polymyxin b
NT1 somatostatin
NT1 tentoxin
NT1 valinomycin
NT1 virginiamycin

CYCLING
(for cycles other than carbon and nitrogen, use "cycling" and the name of the chemical)
uf cycles, nutrient
uf cycling in ecosystems
uf nutrient cycles
uf nutrient cycling
NT1 carbon cycle
NT1 nitrogen cycle

cycling in ecosystems
USE **cycling**

cycling (recreation)
USE **bicycling**

CYCLITOLS
BT1 sugar alcohols
BT2 carbohydrates
BT2 polyols
BT3 alcohols
NT1 myo-inositol
NT1 pinitol

CYCLOATE
BT1 thiocarbamate herbicides
BT2 carbamate pesticides
BT2 herbicides
BT3 pesticides

CYCLOCEPHALA
BT1 scarabaeidae
BT2 coleoptera
NT1 cyclocephala parallela

CYCLOCEPHALA PARALLELA
BT1 cyclocephala
BT2 scarabaeidae
BT3 coleoptera

CYCLOCOELIDAE
BT1 digenea
BT2 trematoda
NT1 cyclocoelum

CYCLOCOELUM
BT1 cyclocoelidae
BT2 digenea
BT3 trematoda

CYCLOCONIUM
BT1 deuteromycotina
rt spilocaea

cycloconium oleagina
USE **spilocaea oleagina**

CYCLODIENE INSECTICIDES
BT1 organochlorine insecticides
BT2 insecticides
BT3 pesticides
BT2 organochlorine pesticides
BT3 organochlorine compounds
BT4 organic halogen compounds

CYCLODIENE INSECTICIDES *cont.*
NT1 aldrin
NT1 chlordane
NT1 chlordecone
NT1 dieldrin
NT1 dilor
NT1 endosulfan
NT1 endrin
NT1 heptachlor
NT1 isobenzan
NT1 kelevan
NT1 mirex

CYCLOGUANIL EMBONATE
BT1 antimalarials
BT2 antiprotozoal agents
BT3 antiparasitic agents
BT4 drugs

CYCLOHEXANECARBOXYLIC ACID
BT1 cyclohexanecarboxylic acids
BT2 carboxylic acids
BT3 organic acids
BT4 acids
rt clarifiers

CYCLOHEXANECARBOXYLIC ACIDS
BT1 carboxylic acids
BT2 organic acids
BT3 acids
NT1 chlorogenic acid
NT1 cyclohexanecarboxylic acid
NT1 quinic acid
NT1 shikimic acid

CYCLOHEXENE OXIME HERBICIDES
BT1 herbicides
BT2 pesticides
NT1 alloxydim
NT1 cloproxydim
NT1 cycloxydim
NT1 sethoxydim
NT1 tralkoxydim

CYCLOHEXIMIDE
BT1 antibiotic fungicides
BT2 antibiotics
BT2 fungicides
BT3 pesticides
BT1 antifungal agents
BT2 antiinfective agents
BT3 drugs
BT1 metabolic inhibitors
BT2 inhibitors

CYCLOLEUCINE
BT1 amino acid antagonists
BT2 antagonists
BT3 metabolic inhibitors
BT4 inhibitors
BT1 cyclic amino acids
BT2 amino acids
BT3 carboxylic acids
BT4 organic acids
BT5 acids
BT3 organic nitrogen compounds

CYCLONEDA
BT1 coccinellidae
BT2 coleoptera
NT1 cycloneda sanguinea

CYCLONEDA SANGUINEA
BT1 cycloneda
BT2 coccinellidae
BT3 coleoptera

CYCLONES
BT1 separators
BT2 machinery
rt dust extractors
rt filtration
rt separation

CYCLOPHOSPHAMIDE
uf cyclophosphane
BT1 antineoplastic agents
BT2 drugs
BT1 immunosuppressive agents
BT2 drugs

CYCLOPHOSPHAMIDE *cont.*
BT1 organophosphorus compounds

cyclophosphane
USE **cyclophosphamide**

CYCLOPIAZONIC ACID
BT1 mycotoxins
BT2 toxins

CYCLOPOIDA
BT1 copepoda
BT2 crustacea
BT3 arthropods
NT1 acanthocyclops
NT2 acanthocyclops bicuspidatus
NT3 acanthocyclops bicuspidatus thomasi
NT2 acanthocyclops robustus
NT2 acanthocyclops vernalis
NT2 acanthocyclops viridis
NT1 cyclops
NT2 cyclops strenuus
NT1 lernaea
NT2 lernaea cyprinacea
NT1 mesocyclops
NT2 mesocyclops aspericornis
NT2 mesocyclops leuckarti

CYCLOPOSTHIUM
BT1 ciliophora
BT2 protozoa

CYCLOPROPENOIC ACID
BT1 cyclopropenoid fatty acids
BT2 fatty acids
BT3 carboxylic acids
BT4 organic acids
BT5 acids
BT3 lipids

CYCLOPROPENOID FATTY ACIDS
BT1 fatty acids
BT2 carboxylic acids
BT3 organic acids
BT4 acids
BT2 lipids
NT1 cyclopropenoic acid
NT1 sterculic acid

CYCLOPS
BT1 cyclopoida
BT2 copepoda
BT3 crustacea
BT4 arthropods
NT1 cyclops strenuus
rt acanthocyclops

cyclops bicuspidatus
USE **acanthocyclops bicuspidatus**

CYCLOPS STRENUUS
BT1 cyclops
BT2 cyclopoida
BT3 copepoda
BT4 crustacea
BT5 arthropods

CYCLOPTERIDAE
BT1 scorpaeniformes
BT2 osteichthyes
BT3 fishes
NT1 cyclopterus

CYCLOPTERUS
BT1 cyclopteridae
BT2 scorpaeniformes
BT3 osteichthyes
BT4 fishes

CYCLOSERINE
uf *oxamycin*
BT1 antibacterial agents
BT2 antiinfective agents
BT3 drugs
BT1 antibiotics
BT1 metabolic inhibitors
BT2 inhibitors

CYCLOSPORINS
BT1 antibiotics

CYCLOSPORINS *cont.*
BT1 cyclic peptides
BT2 oligopeptides
BT3 peptides

CYCLOTELLA
BT1 bacillariophyta
BT2 algae
NT1 cyclotella meneghiniana

CYCLOTELLA MENEGHINIANA
BT1 cyclotella
BT2 bacillariophyta
BT3 algae

CYCLOXYDIM
BT1 cyclohexene oxime herbicides
BT2 herbicides
BT3 pesticides

CYCLURON
BT1 urea herbicides
BT2 herbicides
BT3 pesticides

CYCNIUM
BT1 scrophulariaceae
NT1 cycnium veronicifolium
NT1 cycnium volkensii

CYCNIUM VERONICIFOLIUM
BT1 cycnium
BT2 scrophulariaceae

CYCNIUM VOLKENSII
BT1 cycnium
BT2 scrophulariaceae

CYDIA
uf *grapholita*
uf *laspeyresia*
BT1 tortricidae
BT2 lepidoptera
NT1 cydia caryana
NT1 cydia critica
NT1 cydia delineana
NT1 cydia funebrana
NT1 cydia latiferreana
NT1 cydia leucostoma
NT1 cydia medicaginis
NT1 cydia molesta
NT1 cydia nigricana
NT1 cydia pactolana
NT1 cydia pomonella
NT1 cydia pyrivora
NT1 cydia splendana
NT1 cydia strobilella
rt leguminivora

CYDIA CARYANA
uf *laspeyresia caryana*
BT1 cydia
BT2 tortricidae
BT3 lepidoptera

CYDIA CRITICA
BT1 cydia
BT2 tortricidae
BT3 lepidoptera

CYDIA DELINEANA
uf *grapholita delineana*
BT1 cydia
BT2 tortricidae
BT3 lepidoptera

CYDIA FUNEBRANA
uf *grapholita funebrana*
BT1 cydia
BT2 tortricidae
BT3 lepidoptera

CYDIA LATIFERREANA
BT1 cydia
BT2 tortricidae
BT3 lepidoptera

CYDIA LEUCOSTOMA
BT1 cydia
BT2 tortricidae
BT3 lepidoptera

CYDIA MEDICAGINIS
BT1 cydia

CYDIA MEDICAGINIS *cont.*
BT2 tortricidae
BT3 lepidoptera

CYDIA MOLESTA
uf *grapholita molesta*
uf *laspeyresia molesta*
BT1 cydia
BT2 tortricidae
BT3 lepidoptera

CYDIA NIGRICANA
uf *laspeyresia nigricana*
BT1 cydia
BT2 tortricidae
BT3 lepidoptera

CYDIA PACTOLANA
uf *laspeyresia pactolana*
BT1 cydia
BT2 tortricidae
BT3 lepidoptera

CYDIA POMONELLA
uf *laspeyresia pomonella*
BT1 cydia
BT2 tortricidae
BT3 lepidoptera

cydia ptychora
USE **leguminivora ptychora**

CYDIA PYRIVORA
uf *laspeyresia pyrivora*
BT1 cydia
BT2 tortricidae
BT3 lepidoptera

CYDIA SPLENDANA
BT1 cydia
BT2 tortricidae
BT3 lepidoptera

CYDIA STROBILELLA
uf *cydia youngana*
uf *laspeyresia strobilella*
uf *laspeyresia youngana*
BT1 cydia
BT2 tortricidae
BT3 lepidoptera

cydia youngana
USE **cydia strobilella**

CYDNIDAE
BT1 heteroptera
NT1 cyrtomenus
NT2 cyrtomenus bergi

CYDONIA
BT1 rosaceae
NT1 cydonia oblonga
NT1 cydonia sinensis
rt chaenomeles

cydonia japonica
USE **chaenomeles japonica**

CYDONIA OBLONGA
uf *cydonia vulgaris*
BT1 cydonia
BT2 rosaceae
rt quinces

CYDONIA SINENSIS
uf *chaenomeles sinensis*
BT1 cydonia
BT2 rosaceae
BT1 ornamental woody plants

cydonia vulgaris
USE **cydonia oblonga**

CYFLUTHRIN
BT1 pyrethroid insecticides
BT2 insecticides
BT3 pesticides
BT2 pyrethroids

CYGNUS
BT1 anatidae
BT2 anseriformes
BT3 birds
NT1 cygnus columbianus
NT1 cygnus cygnus

CYGNUS *cont.*
NT2 cygnus cygnus buccinator
NT1 cygnus olor
rt swans

cygnus buccinator
USE **cygnus cygnus buccinator**

CYGNUS COLUMBIANUS
BT1 cygnus
BT2 anatidae
BT3 anseriformes
BT4 birds

CYGNUS CYGNUS
BT1 cygnus
BT2 anatidae
BT3 anseriformes
BT4 birds
NT1 cygnus cygnus buccinator

CYGNUS CYGNUS BUCCINATOR
uf *cygnus buccinator*
BT1 cygnus cygnus
BT2 cygnus
BT3 anatidae
BT4 anseriformes
BT5 birds

CYGNUS OLOR
BT1 cygnus
BT2 anatidae
BT3 anseriformes
BT4 birds

CYHALOTHRIN
BT1 ectoparasiticides
BT2 antiparasitic agents
BT3 drugs
BT1 pyrethroid insecticides
BT2 insecticides
BT3 pesticides
BT2 pyrethroids
rt lambda-cyhalothrin

LAMBDA-CYHALOTHRIN
HN from 1990
BT1 pyrethroid insecticides
BT2 insecticides
BT3 pesticides
BT2 pyrethroids
rt cyhalothrin

CYHEXATIN
BT1 organotin acaricides
BT2 acaricides
BT3 pesticides
BT2 organotin pesticides
BT3 organotin compounds

CYLAS
BT1 apionidae
BT2 coleoptera
NT1 cylas formicarius
NT2 cylas formicarius elegantulus
NT1 cylas puncticollis

CYLAS FORMICARIUS
BT1 cylas
BT2 apionidae
BT3 coleoptera
NT1 cylas formicarius elegantulus

CYLAS FORMICARIUS ELEGANTULUS
BT1 cylas formicarius
BT2 cylas
BT3 apionidae
BT4 coleoptera

CYLAS PUNCTICOLLIS
BT1 cylas
BT2 apionidae
BT3 coleoptera

CYLICOCYCLUS
BT1 cyathostominae
BT2 strongylidae
BT3 nematoda

CYLICODONTOPHORUS
BT1 cyathostominae
BT2 strongylidae

CYLICODONTOPHORUS *cont.*
BT3 nematoda

CYLICOSPIRURA
BT1 spirocercidae
BT2 nematoda

CYLICOSTEPHANUS
uf trichonema
BT1 cyathostominae
BT2 strongylidae
BT3 nematoda

CYLINDER MOWERS
uf mowers, cylinder
BT1 mowers
BT2 farm machinery
BT3 machinery

CYLINDERS
BT1 components
rt concaves
rt engines
rt pistons

CYLINDROCARPON
BT1 deuteromycotina
rt nectria

cylindrocarpon destructans
USE **nectria radicicola**

cylindrocarpon mali
USE **nectria galligena**

cylindrocarpon radicicola
USE **nectria radicicola**

CYLINDROCLADIUM
BT1 deuteromycotina
NT1 cylindrocladium clavatum
NT1 cylindrocladium crotalariae
NT1 cylindrocladium scoparium
NT1 cylindrocladium theae
rt calonectria

CYLINDROCLADIUM CLAVATUM
BT1 cylindrocladium
BT2 deuteromycotina

CYLINDROCLADIUM CROTALARIAE
BT1 cylindrocladium
BT2 deuteromycotina

cylindrocladium ilicicola
USE **calonectria ilicicola**

cylindrocladium quinqueseptatum
USE **calonectria quinqueseptata**

CYLINDROCLADIUM SCOPARIUM
BT1 cylindrocladium
BT2 deuteromycotina

CYLINDROCLADIUM THEAE
BT1 cylindrocladium
BT2 deuteromycotina

CYLINDROCOPTURUS
BT1 curculionidae
BT2 coleoptera
NT1 cylindrocopturus adspersus

CYLINDROCOPTURUS ADSPERSUS
BT1 cylindrocopturus
BT2 curculionidae
BT3 coleoptera

CYLINDROIULUS
BT1 iulidae
BT2 diplopoda
BT3 myriapoda
BT4 arthropods

CYLINDROSPORIUM
BT1 deuteromycotina
NT1 cylindrosporium filipendulae
NT1 cylindrosporium maculans
rt blumeriella
rt phloeosporella
rt pyrenopeziza

cylindrosporium concentricum
USE **pyrenopeziza brassicae**

CYLINDROSPORIUM FILIPENDULAE
HN from 1990
uf phloeosporella filipendulae
BT1 cylindrosporium
BT2 deuteromycotina

cylindrosporium hiemale
USE **blumeriella jaapii**

CYLINDROSPORIUM MACULANS
BT1 cylindrosporium
BT2 deuteromycotina

cylindrosporium padi
USE **blumeriella jaapii**

CYLISTA
BT1 leguminosae
NT1 cylista scariosa

CYLISTA SCARIOSA
BT1 cylista
BT2 leguminosae

CYMADOTHEA
uf polythrincium
BT1 dothideales
NT1 cymadothea trifolii

CYMADOTHEA TRIFOLII
uf polythrincium trifolii
BT1 cymadothea
BT2 dothideales

CYMBALARIA
BT1 scrophulariaceae
NT1 cymbalaria muralis

CYMBALARIA MURALIS
uf linaria cymbalaria
BT1 cymbalaria
BT2 scrophulariaceae

CYMBIDIUM
BT1 orchidaceae
NT1 cymbidium giganteum
NT1 cymbidium grandiflorum
NT1 cymbidium tigrinum
rt antifungal plants
rt cymbidium mosaic potexvirus
rt cymbidium ringspot tombusvirus

CYMBIDIUM GIGANTEUM
BT1 cymbidium
BT2 orchidaceae
BT1 medicinal plants
BT1 ornamental orchids

CYMBIDIUM GRANDIFLORUM
uf cymbidium hookerianum
BT1 cymbidium
BT2 orchidaceae
BT1 ornamental orchids

cymbidium hookerianum
USE **cymbidium grandiflorum**

CYMBIDIUM MOSAIC POTEXVIRUS
HN from 1990; previously "cymbidium mosaic virus"
uf cymbidium mosaic virus
BT1 potexvirus group
BT2 plant viruses
BT3 plant pathogens
BT4 pathogens
rt cymbidium

cymbidium mosaic virus
USE **cymbidium mosaic potexvirus**

CYMBIDIUM RINGSPOT TOMBUSVIRUS
HN from 1990; previously "cymbidium ringspot virus"
uf cymbidium ringspot virus
BT1 tombusvirus group
BT2 plant viruses

CYMBIDIUM RINGSPOT TOMBUSVIRUS *cont.*
BT3 plant pathogens
BT4 pathogens
rt cymbidium

cymbidium ringspot virus
USE **cymbidium ringspot tombusvirus**

CYMBIDIUM TIGRINUM
BT1 cymbidium
BT2 orchidaceae
BT1 ornamental orchids

CYMBOPETALUM
BT1 annonaceae
NT1 cymbopetalum baillonii

CYMBOPETALUM BAILLONII
BT1 cymbopetalum
BT2 annonaceae

CYMBOPOGON
BT1 gramineae
NT1 cymbopogon afronardus
NT1 cymbopogon caesius
NT1 cymbopogon citratus
NT1 cymbopogon commutatus
NT1 cymbopogon confertiflorus
NT1 cymbopogon distans
NT1 cymbopogon excavatus
NT1 cymbopogon flexuosus
NT1 cymbopogon jwarancusa
NT1 cymbopogon khasianus
NT1 cymbopogon martinii
NT1 cymbopogon nardus
NT1 cymbopogon nervatus
NT1 cymbopogon parkeri
NT1 cymbopogon pendulus
NT1 cymbopogon proximus
NT1 cymbopogon refractus
NT1 cymbopogon schoenanthus
NT1 cymbopogon winterianus

CYMBOPOGON AFRONARDUS
BT1 cymbopogon
BT2 gramineae

CYMBOPOGON CAESIUS
BT1 cymbopogon
BT2 gramineae
BT1 insecticidal plants
BT2 pesticidal plants

CYMBOPOGON CITRATUS
uf lemon grass
BT1 antibacterial plants
BT1 cymbopogon
BT2 gramineae
BT1 essential oil plants
BT2 oil plants
BT1 medicinal plants

CYMBOPOGON COMMUTATUS
BT1 cymbopogon
BT2 gramineae

CYMBOPOGON CONFERTIFLORUS
BT1 cymbopogon
BT2 gramineae

CYMBOPOGON DISTANS
BT1 cymbopogon
BT2 gramineae

CYMBOPOGON EXCAVATUS
BT1 cymbopogon
BT2 gramineae

CYMBOPOGON FLEXUOSUS
BT1 antifungal plants
BT1 cymbopogon
BT2 gramineae
BT1 essential oil plants
BT2 oil plants

CYMBOPOGON JWARANCUSA
BT1 cymbopogon
BT2 gramineae
BT1 essential oil plants
BT2 oil plants

CYMBOPOGON KHASIANUS
BT1 cymbopogon

CYMBOPOGON KHASIANUS *cont.*
BT2 gramineae

CYMBOPOGON MARTINII
BT1 antifungal plants
BT1 cymbopogon
BT2 gramineae
BT1 essential oil plants
BT2 oil plants

CYMBOPOGON NARDUS
BT1 cymbopogon
BT2 gramineae
BT1 essential oil plants
BT2 oil plants

CYMBOPOGON NERVATUS
BT1 antibacterial plants
BT1 cymbopogon
BT2 gramineae
BT1 medicinal plants

CYMBOPOGON PARKERI
BT1 cymbopogon
BT2 gramineae
BT1 pasture plants

CYMBOPOGON PENDULUS
BT1 cymbopogon
BT2 gramineae

CYMBOPOGON PROXIMUS
BT1 cymbopogon
BT2 gramineae

CYMBOPOGON REFRACTUS
BT1 cymbopogon
BT2 gramineae
BT1 pasture plants

CYMBOPOGON SCHOENANTHUS
BT1 cymbopogon
BT2 gramineae
BT1 pasture plants

CYMBOPOGON WINTERIANUS
BT1 antifungal plants
BT1 cymbopogon
BT2 gramineae
BT1 essential oil plants
BT2 oil plants

P-CYMENE
BT1 cymenes
BT2 aromatic hydrocarbons
BT3 aromatic compounds
BT3 hydrocarbons
rt essential oils

CYMENES
BT1 aromatic hydrocarbons
BT2 aromatic compounds
BT2 hydrocarbons
NT1 p-cymene

CYMODOCEA
BT1 cymodoceaceae
NT1 cymodocea isoetifolia

CYMODOCEA ISOETIFOLIA
BT1 cymodocea
BT2 cymodoceaceae

CYMODOCEACEAE
NT1 cymodocea
NT2 cymodocea isoetifolia

CYMOPTERUS
BT1 umbelliferae
NT1 cymopterus acualis
NT1 cymopterus terbinthinus

CYMOPTERUS ACUALIS
BT1 cymopterus
BT2 umbelliferae

CYMOPTERUS TERBINTHINUS
BT1 cymopterus
BT2 umbelliferae

CYMOXANIL
BT1 aliphatic nitrogen fungicides
BT2 fungicides
BT3 pesticides

CYNANCHUM
BT1 asclepiadaceae
NT1 cynanchum caudatum
NT1 cynanchum unifarium

CYNANCHUM CAUDATUM
BT1 cynanchum
BT2 asclepiadaceae
BT1 medicinal plants

CYNANCHUM UNIFARIUM
BT1 cynanchum
BT2 asclepiadaceae

cynanchum vincetoxicum
USE **vincetoxicum hirundinaria**

CYNARA
BT1 compositae
NT1 cynara cardunculus
NT1 cynara scolymus

CYNARA CARDUNCULUS
BT1 cynara
BT2 compositae
BT1 weeds
rt cardoons

CYNARA SCOLYMUS
BT1 cynara
BT2 compositae
rt globe artichokes

CYNIPIDAE
BT1 hymenoptera
NT1 andricus
NT1 dilyta
NT1 diplolepis
NT1 dryocosmus
NT2 dryocosmus kuriphilus
NT1 synergus

CYNOCEPHALIDAE
BT1 dermoptera
BT2 mammals
NT1 cynocephalus

CYNOCEPHALUS
BT1 cynocephalidae
BT2 dermoptera
BT3 mammals

CYNODON
BT1 gramineae
NT1 cynodon aethiopicus
NT1 cynodon dactylon
NT1 cynodon magennisii
NT1 cynodon nlemfuensis
NT1 cynodon plectostachyus

CYNODON AETHIOPICUS
BT1 cynodon
BT2 gramineae
BT1 pasture plants

CYNODON DACTYLON
uf bermuda grass
uf doob
BT1 cynodon
BT2 gramineae
BT1 lawns and turf
BT1 pasture plants
BT1 weeds

CYNODON MAGENNISII
BT1 cynodon
BT2 gramineae

CYNODON NLEMFUENSIS
BT1 cynodon
BT2 gramineae

CYNODON PLECTOSTACHYUS
BT1 cynodon
BT2 gramineae
BT1 pasture plants

CYNOGLOSSUM
BT1 boraginaceae
NT1 cynoglossum creticum
NT1 cynoglossum divaricatum
NT1 cynoglossum glochidiatum
NT1 cynoglossum lanceolatum
NT1 cynoglossum nervosum
NT1 cynoglossum officinale

CYNOGLOSSUM CRETICUM
BT1 cynoglossum
BT2 boraginaceae

CYNOGLOSSUM DIVARICATUM
BT1 cynoglossum
BT2 boraginaceae

CYNOGLOSSUM GLOCHIDIATUM
BT1 cynoglossum
BT2 boraginaceae

CYNOGLOSSUM LANCEOLATUM
BT1 cynoglossum
BT2 boraginaceae

CYNOGLOSSUM NERVOSUM
BT1 cynoglossum
BT2 boraginaceae

CYNOGLOSSUM OFFICINALE
BT1 antibacterial plants
BT1 cynoglossum
BT2 boraginaceae
BT1 medicinal plants

CYNOMETRA
BT1 leguminosae
NT1 cynometra retusa

CYNOMETRA RETUSA
BT1 cynometra
BT2 leguminosae

CYNOMYS
BT1 sciuridae
BT2 rodents
BT3 mammals
NT1 cynomys ludovicianus

CYNOMYS LUDOVICIANUS
BT1 cynomys
BT2 sciuridae
BT3 rodents
BT4 mammals

CYNOPTERUS
BT1 pteropodidae
BT2 chiroptera
BT3 mammals

CYNOSCION
BT1 sciaenidae
BT2 perciformes
BT3 osteichthyes
BT4 fishes
NT1 cynoscion leiarchus
NT1 cynoscion regalis

CYNOSCION LEIARCHUS
BT1 cynoscion
BT2 sciaenidae
BT3 perciformes
BT4 osteichthyes
BT5 fishes

CYNOSCION REGALIS
uf weakfish
BT1 cynoscion
BT2 sciaenidae
BT3 perciformes
BT4 osteichthyes
BT5 fishes

CYNOSURUS
BT1 gramineae
NT1 cynosurus cristatus
NT1 cynosurus echinatus

CYNOSURUS CRISTATUS
BT1 cynosurus
BT2 gramineae
BT1 lawns and turf
BT1 pasture plants

CYNOSURUS ECHINATUS
BT1 cynosurus
BT2 gramineae
BT1 pasture plants

CYNTHIA
BT1 nymphalidae
BT2 lepidoptera
NT1 cynthia cardui

CYNTHIA CARDUI
BT1 cynthia
BT2 nymphalidae
BT3 lepidoptera

CYOMETRINIL
BT1 herbicide safeners
BT2 safeners

CYPENDAZOLE
BT1 benzimidazole fungicides
BT2 fungicides
BT3 pesticides

CYPERACEAE
NT1 bolboschoenus
NT2 bolboschoenus maritimus
NT1 carex
NT2 carex aquatica
NT2 carex aquatilis
NT2 carex arenaria
NT2 carex bigelowii
NT2 carex brevicollis
NT2 carex breviculmis
NT2 carex brizoides
NT2 carex caespitosa
NT2 carex caryophyllea
NT2 carex chrysopetala
NT2 carex elata
NT2 carex filifolia
NT2 carex flacca
NT2 carex flagellifera
NT2 carex guadichaudiana
NT2 carex heliophila
NT2 carex hoodii
NT2 carex humilis
NT2 carex lacustris
NT2 carex lanuginosa
NT2 carex lasiocarpa
NT2 carex longebrachiata
NT2 carex lynx
NT2 carex nigra
NT2 carex obtusata
NT2 carex pennsylvanica
NT2 carex physodes
NT2 carex praegracilis
NT2 carex riparia
NT2 carex rostrata
NT2 carex sempervirens
NT2 carex stricta var. strictior
NT2 carex subspathacea
NT2 carex vaginata
NT2 carex vulpina
NT1 cladium
NT2 cladium jamaicense
NT1 cyperus
NT2 cyperus alternifolius
NT2 cyperus amuricus
NT2 cyperus antiquorum
NT2 cyperus aromaticus
NT2 cyperus articulatus
NT2 cyperus brevifolius
NT2 cyperus bulbosus
NT2 cyperus compressus
NT2 cyperus dentatus
NT2 cyperus difformis
NT2 cyperus digitatus
NT2 cyperus elegans
NT2 cyperus esculentus
NT2 cyperus fastigiatus
NT2 cyperus flavus
NT2 cyperus haspan
NT2 cyperus imbricatus
NT2 cyperus immensus
NT2 cyperus inflexus
NT2 cyperus iria
NT2 cyperus ligularis
NT2 cyperus longus
NT2 cyperus malaccensis
NT2 cyperus microiria
NT2 cyperus ochraceus
NT2 cyperus odoratus
NT2 cyperus papyrus
NT2 cyperus rigidifolius
NT2 cyperus rotundus
NT2 cyperus scariosus
NT2 cyperus serotinus
NT2 cyperus tuberosus
NT2 cyperus zollingeri
NT1 eleocharis
NT2 eleocharis acicularis
NT2 eleocharis coloradoensis

CYPERACEAE *cont.*
NT2 eleocharis congesta
NT2 eleocharis dulcis
NT2 eleocharis kuroguwai
NT2 eleocharis palustris
NT2 eleocharis parvula
NT2 eleocharis plantaginea
NT2 eleocharis sphacelata
NT2 eleocharis tuberosa
NT1 eriophorum
NT2 eriophorum vaginatum
NT1 fimbristylis
NT2 fimbristylis ferruginea
NT2 fimbristylis globulosa
NT2 fimbristylis littoralis
NT2 fimbristylis miliacea
NT1 fuirena
NT2 fuirena ciliaris
NT2 fuirena pubescens
NT1 kobresia
NT2 kobresia simpliciuscula
NT1 kyllinga
NT2 kyllinga bulbosa
NT1 schoenoplectus
NT1 scirpus
NT2 scirpus acutus
NT2 scirpus compactus
NT2 scirpus erectus
NT2 scirpus fluviatilis
NT2 scirpus grossus
NT2 scirpus heterochaetus
NT2 scirpus juncoides
NT2 scirpus juncoides var. hotarui
NT2 scirpus juncoides var. juncoides
NT2 scirpus juncoides var. ohwianus
NT2 scirpus lacustris
NT2 scirpus lateriflorus
NT2 scirpus maritimus
NT2 scirpus mucronatus
NT2 scirpus subterminalis
NT2 scirpus validus
NT2 scirpus wallichii
NT1 sedges

CYPERMETHRIN
BT1 ectoparasiticides
BT2 antiparasitic agents
BT3 drugs
BT1 pyrethroid acaricides
BT2 acaricides
BT3 pesticides
BT2 pyrethroids
BT1 pyrethroid insecticides
BT2 insecticides
BT3 pesticides
BT2 pyrethroids
rt alpha-cypermethrin

ALPHA-CYPERMETHRIN
HN from 1990
BT1 pyrethroid insecticides
BT2 insecticides
BT3 pesticides
BT2 pyrethroids
rt cypermethrin

CYPERQUAT
BT1 quaternary ammonium herbicides
BT2 herbicides
BT3 pesticides
BT2 quaternary ammonium compounds
BT3 ammonium compounds
BT3 organic nitrogen compounds

CYPERUS
BT1 cyperaceae
NT1 cyperus alternifolius
NT1 cyperus amuricus
NT1 cyperus antiquorum
NT1 cyperus aromaticus
NT1 cyperus articulatus
NT1 cyperus brevifolius
NT1 cyperus bulbosus
NT1 cyperus compressus
NT1 cyperus dentatus
NT1 cyperus difformis

CYPERUS *cont.*
NT1 cyperus digitatus
NT1 cyperus elegans
NT1 cyperus esculentus
NT1 cyperus fastigiatus
NT1 cyperus flavus
NT1 cyperus haspan
NT1 cyperus imbricatus
NT1 cyperus immensus
NT1 cyperus inflexus
NT1 cyperus iria
NT1 cyperus ligularis
NT1 cyperus longus
NT1 cyperus malaccensis
NT1 cyperus microiria
NT1 cyperus ochraceus
NT1 cyperus odoratus
NT1 cyperus papyrus
NT1 cyperus rigidifolius
NT1 cyperus rotundus
NT1 cyperus scariosus
NT1 cyperus serotinus
NT1 cyperus tuberosus
NT1 cyperus zollingeri

CYPERUS ALTERNIFOLIUS
BT1 cyperus
BT2 cyperaceae
BT1 ornamental herbaceous plants

CYPERUS AMURICUS
BT1 cyperus
BT2 cyperaceae

CYPERUS ANTIQUORUM
BT1 cyperus
BT2 cyperaceae

CYPERUS AROMATICUS
BT1 cyperus
BT2 cyperaceae

CYPERUS ARTICULATUS
BT1 cyperus
BT2 cyperaceae

CYPERUS BREVIFOLIUS
BT1 cyperus
BT2 cyperaceae

CYPERUS BULBOSUS
BT1 cyperus
BT2 cyperaceae

CYPERUS COMPRESSUS
BT1 cyperus
BT2 cyperaceae

CYPERUS DENTATUS
BT1 cyperus
BT2 cyperaceae

CYPERUS DIFFORMIS
BT1 cyperus
BT2 cyperaceae
BT1 weeds

CYPERUS DIGITATUS
BT1 cyperus
BT2 cyperaceae

CYPERUS ELEGANS
BT1 cyperus
BT2 cyperaceae

CYPERUS ESCULENTUS
uf *chufa*
BT1 cyperus
BT2 cyperaceae
BT1 pasture plants
BT1 root vegetables
BT2 root crops
BT2 vegetables
BT1 weeds

CYPERUS FASTIGIATUS
BT1 cyperus
BT2 cyperaceae

CYPERUS FLAVUS
BT1 cyperus
BT2 cyperaceae

CYPERUS HASPAN
BT1 cyperus
BT2 cyperaceae

CYPERUS IMBRICATUS
BT1 cyperus
BT2 cyperaceae

CYPERUS IMMENSUS
BT1 cyperus
BT2 cyperaceae

CYPERUS INFLEXUS
BT1 cyperus
BT2 cyperaceae

CYPERUS IRIA
BT1 cyperus
BT2 cyperaceae
BT1 weeds

CYPERUS LIGULARIS
BT1 cyperus
BT2 cyperaceae

CYPERUS LONGUS
BT1 cyperus
BT2 cyperaceae

CYPERUS MALACCENSIS
BT1 cyperus
BT2 cyperaceae

CYPERUS MICROIRIA
BT1 cyperus
BT2 cyperaceae

CYPERUS OCHRACEUS
BT1 cyperus
BT2 cyperaceae

CYPERUS ODORATUS
BT1 cyperus
BT2 cyperaceae

CYPERUS PAPYRUS
BT1 cyperus
BT2 cyperaceae

CYPERUS RIGIDIFOLIUS
BT1 cyperus
BT2 cyperaceae

CYPERUS ROTUNDUS
BT1 cyperus
BT2 cyperaceae
BT1 nematicidal plants
BT2 pesticidal plants
BT1 weeds

CYPERUS SCARIOSUS
BT1 antifungal plants
BT1 cyperus
BT2 cyperaceae
BT1 essential oil plants
BT2 oil plants

CYPERUS SEROTINUS
BT1 cyperus
BT2 cyperaceae
BT1 weeds

CYPERUS TUBEROSUS
BT1 cyperus
BT2 cyperaceae

CYPERUS ZOLLINGERI
BT1 cyperus
BT2 cyperaceae

CYPHOMANDRA
BT1 solanaceae
NT1 cyphomandra betacea

CYPHOMANDRA BETACEA
BT1 cyphomandra
BT2 solanaceae
rt tamarillos

CYPRAZINE
HN from 1990
BT1 triazine herbicides
BT2 herbicides
BT3 pesticides
BT2 triazines

CYPRAZINE *cont.*
BT3 heterocyclic nitrogen compounds
BT4 organic nitrogen compounds

CYPRAZOLE
BT1 amide herbicides
BT2 herbicides
BT3 pesticides

cypresses
USE **cupressus**

cyprian honeybee
USE **apis mellifera cypria**

CYPRINIDAE
BT1 cypriniformes
BT2 osteichthyes
BT3 fishes
NT1 abramis
NT2 abramis brama
NT1 barbus
NT1 carassius
NT2 carassius carassius
NT1 catla
NT2 catla catla
NT1 cyprinus
NT1 gobio
NT2 gobio gobio
NT1 labeo
NT1 leucaspius
NT1 leuciscus
NT2 leuciscus cephalus
NT2 leuciscus idus
NT2 leuciscus leuciscus
NT1 notemigonus
NT1 phoxinus
NT2 phoxinus phoxinus
NT1 pimephales
NT2 pimephales promelas
NT1 rutilus
NT2 rutilus rutilus
NT1 semotilus
NT1 tinca
rt carp
rt goldfish

CYPRINIFORMES
BT1 osteichthyes
BT2 fishes
NT1 cobitididae
NT2 misgurnus
NT3 misgurnus anguillicaudatus
NT1 cyprinidae
NT2 abramis
NT3 abramis brama
NT2 barbus
NT2 carassius
NT3 carassius carassius
NT2 catla
NT3 catla catla
NT2 cyprinus
NT2 gobio
NT3 gobio gobio
NT2 labeo
NT2 leucaspius
NT2 leuciscus
NT3 leuciscus cephalus
NT3 leuciscus idus
NT3 leuciscus leuciscus
NT2 notemigonus
NT2 phoxinus
NT3 phoxinus phoxinus
NT2 pimephales
NT3 pimephales promelas
NT2 rutilus
NT3 rutilus rutilus
NT2 semotilus
NT2 tinca

CYPRINODONTIDAE
BT1 cyprinodontiformes
BT2 osteichthyes
BT3 fishes
NT1 fundulus
NT2 fundulus heteroclitus
NT2 fundulus kansae

CYPRINODONTIFORMES
BT1 osteichthyes

CYPRINODONTIFORMES *cont.*
BT2 fishes
NT1 aplocheilidae
NT2 aplocheilus
NT3 aplocheilus latipes
NT1 cyprinodontidae
NT2 fundulus
NT3 fundulus heteroclitus
NT3 fundulus kansae
NT1 exocoetidae
NT2 cypselurus
NT2 exocoetus
NT2 prognichthys
NT1 hemiramphidae
NT2 hemiramphus
NT3 hemiramphus brachynopterus
NT2 hyporhamphus
NT1 poeciliidae
NT2 gambusia
NT3 gambusia affinis
NT2 poecilia
NT3 poecilia reticulata
NT1 scomberesocidae
NT2 cololabis
NT2 scomberesox

CYPRINOTUS
BT1 podocopa
BT2 ostracoda
BT3 crustacea
BT4 arthropods
NT1 cyprinotus incongruens

CYPRINOTUS INCONGRUENS
BT1 cyprinotus
BT2 podocopa
BT3 ostracoda
BT4 crustacea
BT5 arthropods

CYPRINUS
BT1 cyprinidae
BT2 cypriniformes
BT3 osteichthyes
BT4 fishes

cyprinus carpio
USE **carp**

CYPRIPEDIUM
BT1 orchidaceae
NT1 cypripedium calceolus
NT1 cypripedium reginae

CYPRIPEDIUM CALCEOLUS
BT1 cypripedium
BT2 orchidaceae
BT1 ornamental orchids

CYPRIPEDIUM REGINAE
BT1 cypripedium
BT2 orchidaceae
BT1 ornamental orchids

CYPRIS
BT1 podocopa
BT2 ostracoda
BT3 crustacea
BT4 arthropods

CYPROFURAM
BT1 anilide fungicides
BT2 fungicides
BT3 pesticides

CYPROHEPTADINE
BT1 antihistaminics
BT2 drugs
BT1 piperidines
BT2 heterocyclic nitrogen compounds
BT3 organic nitrogen compounds

CYPROMID
BT1 anilide herbicides
BT2 amide herbicides
BT3 herbicides
BT4 pesticides

CYPRUS
BT1 west asia
BT2 asia

CYPRUS *cont.*
rt commonwealth of nations
rt developing countries
rt mediterranean countries
rt middle east
rt threshold countries

CYPRUS FAT-TAILED
BT1 sheep breeds
BT2 breeds

CYPSELURUS
BT1 exocoetidae
BT2 cyprinodontiformes
BT3 osteichthyes
BT4 fishes

CYROMAZINE
BT1 chitin synthesis inhibitors
BT2 insect growth regulators
BT3 growth regulators
BT3 insecticides
BT4 pesticides
BT2 metabolic inhibitors
BT3 inhibitors
BT1 ectoparasiticides
BT2 antiparasitic agents
BT3 drugs

CYRTACANTHACRIS
BT1 acrididae
BT2 orthoptera
rt patanga
rt valanga

cyrtacanthacris nigricornis
USE **valanga nigricornis**

cyrtacanthacris septemfasciata
USE **patanga septemfasciata**

CYRTANTHUS
BT1 amaryllidaceae
NT1 cyrtanthus elatus

CYRTANTHUS ELATUS
uf *vallota purpurea*
uf *vallota speciosa*
BT1 cyrtanthus
BT2 amaryllidaceae
BT1 ornamental bulbs

CYRTOBAGOUS
BT1 curculionidae
BT2 coleoptera
NT1 cyrtobagous salviniae
NT1 cyrtobagous singularis

CYRTOBAGOUS SALVINIAE
BT1 cyrtobagous
BT2 curculionidae
BT3 coleoptera

CYRTOBAGOUS SINGULARIS
BT1 cyrtobagous
BT2 curculionidae
BT3 coleoptera

CYRTOCARPA
BT1 anacardiaceae

CYRTOCOCCUM
BT1 gramineae
NT1 cyrtococcum patens

CYRTOCOCCUM PATENS
BT1 cyrtococcum
BT2 gramineae

CYRTOMENUS
BT1 cydnidae
BT2 heteroptera
NT1 cyrtomenus bergi

CYRTOMENUS BERGI
BT1 cyrtomenus
BT2 cydnidae
BT3 heteroptera

CYRTOMIUM
BT1 aspidiaceae
NT1 cyrtomium falcatum
rt phanerophlebia

CYRTOMIUM FALCATUM
uf *phanerophlebia falcata*

CYRTOMIUM FALCATUM *cont.*
BT1 acaricidal plants
BT2 pesticidal plants
BT1 cyrtomium
BT2 aspidiaceae

CYRTOPELTIS
uf *nesidiocoris*
BT1 miridae
BT2 heteroptera
NT1 cyrtopeltis tenuis

CYRTOPELTIS TENUIS
HN from 1990; previously "nesidiocoris tenuis"
uf *nesidiocoris tenuis*
BT1 cyrtopeltis
BT2 miridae
BT3 heteroptera

CYRTOPODIUM
BT1 orchidaceae
rt ornamental orchids

CYRTOPTYX
BT1 pteromalidae
BT2 hymenoptera

CYRTORHINUS
BT1 miridae
BT2 heteroptera
NT1 cyrtorhinus lividipennis

CYRTORHINUS LIVIDIPENNIS
BT1 cyrtorhinus
BT2 miridae
BT3 heteroptera

CYRTOSOMUM
BT1 atractidae
BT2 nematoda

CYRTOSPERMA
BT1 araceae
NT1 cyrtosperma chamissonis

CYRTOSPERMA CHAMISSONIS
uf *cyrtosperma edule*
BT1 cyrtosperma
BT2 araceae

cyrtosperma edule
USE **cyrtosperma chamissonis**

CYSTACANTHS
BT1 acanthocephalan larvae
BT2 helminth larvae
BT3 helminths
BT4 parasites
BT3 larvae
BT4 developmental stages

CYSTATHIONINE
BT1 sulfur amino acids
BT2 amino acids
BT3 carboxylic acids
BT4 organic acids
BT5 acids
BT3 organic nitrogen compounds
BT2 organic sulfur compounds

CYSTATHIONINE γ-LYASE
(ec 4.4.1.1)
(for retrieval spell out "gamma")
uf *homoserine dehydratase*
BT1 lyases
BT2 enzymes

CYSTATHIONINE β-SYNTHASE
(ec 4.2.1.22)
(for retrieval spell out "beta")
BT1 hydro-lyases
BT2 lyases
BT3 enzymes

CYSTEAMINE
uf *mercaptamine*
BT1 amino alcohols
BT2 alcohols
BT2 amino compounds
BT3 organic nitrogen compounds
BT1 thiols
BT2 organic sulfur compounds

CYSTEIC ACID
BT1 sulfur amino acids
BT2 amino acids
BT3 carboxylic acids
BT4 organic acids
BT5 acids
BT3 organic nitrogen compounds
BT2 organic sulfur compounds

CYSTEINE
BT1 sulfur amino acids
BT2 amino acids
BT3 carboxylic acids
BT4 organic acids
BT5 acids
BT3 organic nitrogen compounds
BT2 organic sulfur compounds
rt cysteinesulfinic acid
rt folcysteine
rt mecysteine

CYSTEINE DIOXYGENASE
(ec 1.13.11.20)
BT1 oxygenases
BT2 oxidoreductases
BT3 enzymes

CYSTEINESULFINIC ACID
uf *cysteinesulphinic acid*
BT1 amino acid derivatives
BT2 amino compounds
BT3 organic nitrogen compounds
rt cysteine

cysteinesulphinic acid
USE **cysteinesulfinic acid**

CYSTIC DEGENERATION
BT1 degeneration
rt cysts

CYSTIC FIBROSIS
BT1 fibrosis
BT2 respiratory diseases
BT3 organic diseases
BT4 diseases
rt pancreas

CYSTICERCI
BT1 metacestodes
BT2 developmental stages

CYSTICERCOIDS
BT1 metacestodes
BT2 developmental stages

CYSTICERCOSIS
BT1 cestode infections
BT2 helminthoses
BT3 parasitoses
BT4 diseases

cysticercus
USE **taenia**

cysticercus bovis
USE **taenia saginata**

cysticercus cellulosae
USE **taenia solium**

cysticercus fasciolaris
USE **taenia taeniaeformis**

cysticercus longicollis
USE **taenia crassiceps**

cysticercus ovis
USE **taenia ovis**

cysticercus pisiformis
USE **taenia pisiformis**

cysticercus tenuicollis
USE **taenia hydatigena**

CYSTINE
BT1 nonessential amino acids
BT2 amino acids
BT3 carboxylic acids
BT4 organic acids
BT5 acids

CYSTINE *cont.*
BT3 organic nitrogen compounds
BT1 sulfur amino acids
BT2 amino acids
BT3 carboxylic acids
BT4 organic acids
BT5 acids
BT3 organic nitrogen compounds
BT2 organic sulfur compounds
rt cystinosis
rt cystinuria

CYSTINOSIS
BT1 kidney diseases
BT2 urinary tract diseases
BT3 organic diseases
BT4 diseases
rt cystine

CYSTINURIA
BT1 aminoaciduria
BT2 aciduria
BT3 metabolic disorders
BT4 animal disorders
BT5 disorders
rt cystine
rt urine

CYSTITIS
BT1 bladder diseases
BT2 urinary tract diseases
BT3 organic diseases
BT4 diseases

CYSTOBIA
BT1 apicomplexa
BT2 protozoa
BT1 chlorophyta
BT2 algae

CYSTOCAULUS
BT1 protostrongylidae
BT2 nematoda
NT1 cystocaulus ocreatus
rt lungworms

CYSTOCAULUS OCREATUS
BT1 cystocaulus
BT2 protostrongylidae
BT3 nematoda

CYSTOISOSPORA
BT1 apicomplexa
BT2 protozoa

CYSTOPAGE
BT1 entomophthorales

CYSTOPTERIS
BT1 athyriaceae
NT1 cystopteris bulbifera
NT1 cystopteris fragilis

CYSTOPTERIS BULBIFERA
BT1 cystopteris
BT2 athyriaceae
BT1 ornamental ferns
BT2 ferns
BT2 ornamental foliage plants
BT3 foliage plants

CYSTOPTERIS FRAGILIS
BT1 antibacterial plants
BT1 cystopteris
BT2 athyriaceae
BT1 ornamental ferns
BT2 ferns
BT2 ornamental foliage plants
BT3 foliage plants

CYSTS
NT1 ovarian cysts
rt cystic degeneration
rt encystment

CYTAUXZOON
BT1 apicomplexa
BT2 protozoa
NT1 cytauxzoon felis

CYTAUXZOON FELIS
BT1 cytauxzoon
BT2 apicomplexa

CYTAUXZOON FELIS *cont.*
BT3 protozoa

CYTHIOATE
BT1 ectoparasiticides
BT2 antiparasitic agents
BT3 drugs
BT1 organothiophosphate insecticides
BT2 organophosphorus insecticides
BT3 insecticides
BT4 pesticides
BT3 organophosphorus pesticides
BT4 organophosphorus compounds

CYTIDINE
BT1 ribonucleosides
BT2 nucleosides
BT3 glycosides
BT4 carbohydrates

CYTIDINE TRIPHOSPHATE
BT1 pyrimidine nucleotides
BT2 nucleotides
BT3 glycosides
BT4 carbohydrates
rt cytosine
rt degeneration

CYTISUS
uf *chamaecytisus*
uf *sarothamnus*
BT1 leguminosae
NT1 cytisus austriacus
NT1 cytisus commutatus
NT1 cytisus ingramii
NT1 cytisus monspessulanus
NT1 cytisus nigricans
NT1 cytisus praecox
NT1 cytisus purgans
NT1 cytisus racemosus
NT1 cytisus scoparius
NT1 cytisus serotinus
NT1 cytisus sessilifolius
NT1 cytisus striatus

CYTISUS AUSTRIACUS
BT1 cytisus
BT2 leguminosae
BT1 ornamental woody plants

CYTISUS COMMUTATUS
BT1 cytisus
BT2 leguminosae
BT1 pasture legumes
BT2 legumes
BT2 pasture plants

CYTISUS INGRAMII
BT1 cytisus
BT2 leguminosae
BT1 pasture legumes
BT2 legumes
BT2 pasture plants

CYTISUS MONSPESSULANUS
BT1 cytisus
BT2 leguminosae

CYTISUS NIGRICANS
BT1 cytisus
BT2 leguminosae

CYTISUS PRAECOX
BT1 cytisus
BT2 leguminosae
BT1 ornamental woody plants

CYTISUS PURGANS
BT1 cytisus
BT2 leguminosae
BT1 ornamental woody plants

CYTISUS RACEMOSUS
BT1 cytisus
BT2 leguminosae

CYTISUS SCOPARIUS
BT1 cytisus
BT2 leguminosae
BT1 medicinal plants

CYTISUS SCOPARIUS *cont.*
BT1 ornamental woody plants

CYTISUS SEROTINUS
BT1 cytisus
BT2 leguminosae

CYTISUS SESSILIFOLIUS
BT1 cytisus
BT2 leguminosae

CYTISUS STRIATUS
BT1 cytisus
BT2 leguminosae

CYTOADHERENCE
HN from 1990
BT1 host parasite relationships

CYTOCHALASIN B
HN from 1989
BT1 metabolic inhibitors
BT2 inhibitors

CYTOCHEMISTRY
BT1 biochemistry
BT2 chemistry
rt cells
rt cytology

CYTOCHROME B
BT1 cytochromes
BT2 metalloproteins
BT3 proteins
BT4 peptides
BT2 porphyrins
BT3 heterocyclic nitrogen compounds
BT4 organic nitrogen compounds

CYTOCHROME C
BT1 cytochromes
BT2 metalloproteins
BT3 proteins
BT4 peptides
BT2 porphyrins
BT3 heterocyclic nitrogen compounds
BT4 organic nitrogen compounds

CYTOCHROME-C OXIDASE
(ec 1.9.3.1)
uf *cytochrome oxidase*
BT1 oxidoreductases
BT2 enzymes

CYTOCHROME-C PEROXIDASE
(ec 1.11.1.5)
BT1 peroxidases
BT2 oxidoreductases
BT3 enzymes

cytochrome-c reductase
USE **nadh dehydrogenase**

cytochrome oxidase
USE **cytochrome-c oxidase**

CYTOCHROME P-450
BT1 cytochromes
BT2 metalloproteins
BT3 proteins
BT4 peptides
BT2 porphyrins
BT3 heterocyclic nitrogen compounds
BT4 organic nitrogen compounds

CYTOCHROMES
BT1 metalloproteins
BT2 proteins
BT3 peptides
BT1 porphyrins
BT2 heterocyclic nitrogen compounds
BT3 organic nitrogen compounds
NT1 cytochrome b
NT1 cytochrome c
NT1 cytochrome p-450
rt respiration

cytodifferentiation
USE **cell differentiation**

CYTOECETES
BT1 ehrlichiaceae
BT2 rickettsiales
BT3 bacteria
BT4 prokaryotes
rt ehrlichia

cytoecetes phagocytophila
USE **ehrlichia phagocytophila**

CYTOGENETICS
NT1 chromosome addition
NT1 chromosome maps
NT1 chromosome substitution
rt chromosomes
rt cytology

CYTOKININS
BT1 plant growth regulators
BT2 growth regulators
NT1 benzimidazole
NT1 benzyladenine
NT1 kinetin
NT1 zeatin
rt kinins

CYTOLOGISTS
BT1 biologists
BT2 scientists
BT3 occupations

CYTOLOGY
BT1 biology
rt cell structure
rt cell ultrastructure
rt cells
rt chromosome banding
rt chromosome morphology
rt chromosome number
rt chromosome pairing
rt chromosome polymorphism
rt chromosomes
rt cytochemistry
rt cytogenetics
rt cytotaxonomy
rt heterokaryosis
rt protoplasts
rt sectioning

CYTOLYSIS
HN from 1990
BT1 lysis
rt cells

CYTOMEGALOVIRUS
BT1 herpesviridae
BT2 viruses

CYTOMIXIS
rt cells

cytopathic effects
USE **cytopathogenicity**
OR **cytotoxicity**

CYTOPATHOGENICITY
uf *cytopathic effects*
BT1 pathogenicity
rt cells
rt cytotoxicity

CYTOPHAGA
BT1 cytophagaceae
BT2 gracilicutes
BT3 bacteria
BT4 prokaryotes

CYTOPHAGACEAE
BT1 gracilicutes
BT2 bacteria
BT3 prokaryotes
NT1 cytophaga
NT1 flexibacter
NT1 saprospira
NT2 saprospira alba

CYTOPLASM
BT1 protoplasm
NT1 cytoplasmic inclusions
NT2 cytoplasmic reticulum
NT2 liposomes
NT2 lysosomes

CYTOPLASM *cont.*
NT2 microfilaments
NT2 plasmids
NT2 plastids
NT3 chloroplasts
NT4 etioplasts
NT4 thylakoids
NT2 ribosomes
NT2 secretory granules
NT1 cytosol
NT1 endoplasmic reticulum
NT1 plasmodesmata
rt cell structure
rt cells
rt cytoplasmic male sterility
rt microsomes
rt mitochondria
rt tyloses
rt vacuoles

CYTOPLASMIC INCLUSIONS
uf *cell inclusions*
uf *inclusion bodies*
BT1 cytoplasm
BT2 protoplasm
NT1 cytoplasmic reticulum
NT1 liposomes
NT1 lysosomes
NT1 microfilaments
NT1 plasmids
NT1 plastids
NT2 chloroplasts
NT3 etioplasts
NT3 thylakoids
NT1 ribosomes
NT1 secretory granules
rt cell structure

CYTOPLASMIC INHERITANCE
BT1 inheritance
rt chloroplast genetics
rt cytoplasmic male sterility
rt maternal effects
rt mitochondrial genetics
rt nucleocytoplasmic interaction
rt plasmagenes
rt reciprocal effects

CYTOPLASMIC MALE STERILITY
uf *sterility, male cytoplasmic*
BT1 male sterility
BT2 sterility
rt cytoplasm
rt cytoplasmic inheritance
rt nucleocytoplasmic interaction

CYTOPLASMIC POLYHEDROSIS VIRUSES
BT1 insect viruses
BT2 entomopathogens
BT3 pathogens
BT1 reoviridae
BT2 viruses

CYTOPLASMIC RETICULUM
BT1 cytoplasmic inclusions
BT2 cytoplasm
BT3 protoplasm

CYTOSINE
BT1 pyrimidines
BT2 heterocyclic nitrogen compounds
BT3 organic nitrogen compounds
rt cytidine triphosphate
rt flucytosine

CYTOSOL
HN from 1989
BT1 cytoplasm
BT2 protoplasm

CYTOSOL AMINOPEPTIDASE
(ec 3.4.11.1)
uf *aminopeptidase (cytosol)*
uf *leucine aminopeptidase*
uf *leucine arylaminopeptidase*
BT1 aminopeptidases
BT2 peptidases
BT3 peptide hydrolases

CYTOSOL AMINOPEPTIDASE *cont.*
BT4 hydrolases
BT5 enzymes

CYTOSPORA
uf *leucocytospora*
BT1 deuteromycotina
NT1 cytospora sacchari
rt leucostoma
rt valsa

cytospora chrysosperma
USE **valsa sordida**

cytospora cincta
USE **leucostoma cinctum**

cytospora leucostoma
USE **leucostoma persoonii**

cytospora nivea
USE **leucostoma niveum**

CYTOSPORA SACCHARI
BT1 cytospora
BT2 deuteromycotina

CYTOTAXONOMY
BT1 taxonomy
BT2 classification
rt cytology

cytotoxic agents
USE **antineoplastic agents**

CYTOTOXIC COMPOUNDS
BT1 toxic substances
rt antineoplastic agents
rt cytotoxicity

CYTOTOXIC T LYMPHOCYTES
HN from 1989
BT1 t lymphocytes
BT2 lymphocytes
BT3 leukocytes
BT4 blood cells
BT5 cells

CYTOTOXICITY
uf *cytopathic effects*
BT1 toxicity
rt cytopathogenicity
rt cytotoxic compounds

CYZENIS
BT1 tachinidae
BT2 diptera
NT1 cyzenis albicans

CYZENIS ALBICANS
BT1 biological control agents
BT2 beneficial organisms
BT1 cyzenis
BT2 tachinidae
BT3 diptera

CZECH IMPROVED WHITE
HN from 1990; previously "czechoslovakian improved white"
uf *czechoslovakian improved white*
BT1 pig breeds
BT2 breeds

CZECH PIED
BT1 cattle breeds
BT2 breeds

CZECHOSLOVAKIA
BT1 eastern europe
BT2 europe
rt cmea

czechoslovakian improved white
USE **czech improved white**

2,4-D
uf *(2,4-dichlorophenoxy)acetic acid*
BT1 auxins
BT2 plant growth regulators
BT3 growth regulators
BT1 desiccant herbicides
BT2 desiccants
BT1 phenoxyacetic herbicides
BT2 phenoxy herbicides
BT3 herbicides
BT4 pesticides

3,5-D
uf *(3,5-dichlorophenoxy)acetic acid*
BT1 auxins
BT2 plant growth regulators
BT3 growth regulators

DABOECIA
BT1 ericaceae
rt ornamental woody plants

DACCA
BT1 bangladesh
BT2 south asia
BT3 asia

dace
USE **leuciscus leuciscus**

DACNUSA
BT1 braconidae
BT2 hymenoptera
NT1 dacnusa sibirica

DACNUSA SIBIRICA
BT1 dacnusa
BT2 braconidae
BT3 hymenoptera

dacron
USE **polyesters (agricola)**

DACRYDIUM
BT1 podocarpaceae
NT1 dacrydium bidwillii
NT1 dacrydium colensoi
NT1 dacrydium cupressinum
NT1 dacrydium intermedium

DACRYDIUM BIDWILLII
BT1 dacrydium
BT2 podocarpaceae

DACRYDIUM COLENSOI
BT1 dacrydium
BT2 podocarpaceae

DACRYDIUM CUPRESSINUM
BT1 dacrydium
BT2 podocarpaceae
BT1 forest trees
BT1 tan plants

DACRYDIUM INTERMEDIUM
BT1 dacrydium
BT2 podocarpaceae

DACRYMYCETALES
NT1 calocera
NT2 calocera viscosa
rt fungi

DACTINOMYCIN
uf *actinomycin d*
BT1 antibiotics
BT1 antineoplastic agents
BT2 drugs
BT1 carcinogens
BT2 toxic substances

DACTULIOPHORA
BT1 deuteromycotina
NT1 dactuliophora tarrii

DACTULIOPHORA TARRII
BT1 dactuliophora
BT2 deuteromycotina

DACTYELLA
BT1 deuteromycotina
NT1 dactyella brochopaga
NT1 dactyella oviparasitica

DACTYELLA BROCHOPAGA
BT1 dactyella
BT2 deuteromycotina

DACTYELLA OVIPARASITICA
BT1 dactyella
BT2 deuteromycotina

DACTYLIS
BT1 gramineae
NT1 dactylis glomerata

DACTYLIS GLOMERATA
uf *cocksfoot*
uf *orchardgrass*
BT1 dactylis
BT2 gramineae
BT1 lawns and turf
BT1 pasture plants
rt cocksfoot mild mosaic virus
rt cocksfoot mottle virus
rt cocksfoot streak potyvirus

dactylium
USE **hypomyces**

dactylium dendroides
USE **hypomyces rosellus**

DACTYLOCLADUS
BT1 crypteroniaceae
NT1 dactylocladus stenostachys

DACTYLOCLADUS STENOSTACHYS
BT1 dactylocladus
BT2 crypteroniaceae

DACTYLOCTENIUM
BT1 gramineae
NT1 dactyloctenium aegyptium
NT1 dactyloctenium ctenoides
NT1 dactyloctenium geminatum
NT1 dactyloctenium pilosum
NT1 dactyloctenium sindicum

DACTYLOCTENIUM AEGYPTIUM
BT1 dactyloctenium
BT2 gramineae
BT1 pasture plants
BT1 weeds

DACTYLOCTENIUM CTENOIDES
BT1 dactyloctenium
BT2 gramineae
BT1 pasture plants

DACTYLOCTENIUM GEMINATUM
BT1 dactyloctenium
BT2 gramineae
BT1 pasture plants

DACTYLOCTENIUM PILOSUM
BT1 dactyloctenium
BT2 gramineae
BT1 pasture plants

DACTYLOCTENIUM SINDICUM
BT1 dactyloctenium
BT2 gramineae

DACTYLOGYRIDAE
BT1 monogenea
NT1 amphibdella
NT1 ancyrocephalus
NT1 cichlidogyrus
NT1 dactylogyrus
NT2 dactylogyrus lamellatus
NT2 dactylogyrus vastator
NT1 haliotrema
NT1 neodactylogyrus
NT1 oncocleidus
NT1 urocleidus

DACTYLOGYRUS
BT1 dactylogyridae
BT2 monogenea
NT1 dactylogyrus lamellatus
NT1 dactylogyrus vastator

DACTYLOGYRUS LAMELLATUS
BT1 dactylogyrus
BT2 dactylogyridae
BT3 monogenea

DACTYLOGYRUS VASTATOR
BT1 dactylogyrus
BT2 dactylogyridae
BT3 monogenea

DACTYLOPHORUS
BT1 apicomplexa
BT2 protozoa

DACTYLOPIIDAE
BT1 coccoidea
BT2 sternorrhyncha
BT3 homoptera
NT1 dactylopius
NT2 dactylopius ceylonicus
NT2 dactylopius opuntiae

DACTYLOPIUS
BT1 dactylopiidae
BT2 coccoidea
BT3 sternorrhyncha
BT4 homoptera
NT1 dactylopius ceylonicus
NT1 dactylopius opuntiae

DACTYLOPIUS CEYLONICUS
uf *dactylopius indicus*
BT1 dactylopius
BT2 dactylopiidae
BT3 coccoidea
BT4 sternorrhyncha
BT5 homoptera

dactylopius indicus
USE **dactylopius ceylonicus**

DACTYLOPIUS OPUNTIAE
BT1 biological control agents
BT2 beneficial organisms
BT1 dactylopius
BT2 dactylopiidae
BT3 coccoidea
BT4 sternorrhyncha
BT5 homoptera

DACTYLOPTERIDAE
uf *gurnards, flying*
BT1 dactylopteriformes
BT2 osteichthyes
BT3 fishes
NT1 dactylopterus

DACTYLOPTERIFORMES
BT1 osteichthyes
BT2 fishes
NT1 dactylopteridae
NT2 dactylopterus

DACTYLOPTERUS
BT1 dactylopteridae
BT2 dactylopteriformes
BT3 osteichthyes
BT4 fishes

dactylorchis
USE **dactylorhiza**

DACTYLORHIZA
uf *dactylorchis*
BT1 orchidaceae
NT1 dactylorhiza majalis
NT1 dactylorhiza purpurella

DACTYLORHIZA MAJALIS
uf *orchis latifolia*
BT1 dactylorhiza
BT2 orchidaceae
BT1 ornamental orchids

DACTYLORHIZA PURPURELLA
BT1 dactylorhiza
BT2 orchidaceae
BT1 ornamental orchids

DACTYLOSOMA
BT1 apicomplexa
BT2 protozoa
NT1 dactylosoma ranarum

DACTYLOSOMA RANARUM
BT1 dactylosoma
BT2 apicomplexa
BT3 protozoa

dactynotus
USE **uroleucon**

dactynotus ambrosiae
USE **uroleucon ambrosiae**

dactynotus compositae
USE **uroleucon compositae**

DACUS
uf *didacus*
BT1 tephritidae
BT2 diptera
NT1 dacus ciliatus
rt bactrocera

dacus cacuminatus
USE **bactrocera cacuminata**

DACUS CILIATUS
uf *didacus ciliatus*
BT1 dacus
BT2 tephritidae
BT3 diptera

dacus citri
USE **bactrocera tsuneonis**

dacus cucumis
USE **bactrocera cucumis**

dacus cucurbitae
USE **bactrocera cucurbitae**

dacus dorsalis
USE **bactrocera dorsalis**

dacus ferrugineus
USE **bactrocera dorsalis**

dacus oleae
USE **bactrocera oleae**

dacus tryoni
USE **bactrocera tryoni**

dacus tsuneonis
USE **bactrocera tsuneonis**

dacus zonatus
USE **bactrocera zonata**

DADRA AND NAGAR HAVELI
BT1 india
BT2 south asia
BT3 asia

DAEDALACANTHUS
BT1 acanthaceae
rt eranthemum

daedalacanthus nervosus
USE **eranthemum pulchellum**

DAEDALEA
BT1 aphyllophorales
NT1 daedalea quercina

DAEDALEA QUERCINA
BT1 daedalea
BT2 aphyllophorales

DAEMONOROPS
BT1 palmae
NT1 daemonorops draco
NT1 daemonorops ursina

DAEMONOROPS DRACO
BT1 antifungal plants
BT1 daemonorops
BT2 palmae
BT1 medicinal plants

DAEMONOROPS URSINA
BT1 daemonorops
BT2 palmae

daffodils
USE **narcissus**

DAGESTAN MOUNTAIN
BT1 sheep breeds
BT2 breeds

DAGLIC
BT1 sheep breeds
BT2 breeds

DAHI
BT1 cultured milks
BT2 milk products
BT3 products

DAHLBOMINUS
BT1 eulophidae
BT2 hymenoptera

DAHLIA
BT1 compositae
NT1 dahlia pinnata
rt dahlia mosaic caulimovirus
rt ornamental bulbs
rt tubers

DAHLIA MOSAIC CAULIMOVIRUS
HN from 1990
BT1 caulimovirus group
BT2 plant viruses
BT3 plant pathogens
BT4 pathogens
rt dahlia

DAHLIA PINNATA
uf *dahlia variabilis*
BT1 dahlia
BT2 compositae
BT1 ornamental bulbs
rt tubers

dahlia variabilis
USE **dahlia pinnata**

dahomey
USE **benin**

DAIDZEIN
BT1 isoflavones
BT2 flavonoids
BT3 aromatic compounds
BT3 plant pigments
BT4 pigments

DAILY LIVING SKILLS (AGRICOLA)
HN from 1990
(personal management and social skills which are necessary for adequate functioning on an independent basis)
uf *life skills*
BT1 skills (agricola)

DAIRIES
NT1 farm dairies
rt dairy cattle
rt dairy cooperatives
rt dairy education
rt dairy effluent
rt dairy engineering
rt dairy equipment
rt dairy factories
rt dairy farming
rt dairy performance
rt dairy research
rt dairy science
rt dairy statistics
rt dairy technology
rt dairy wastes
rt dairying
rt milk products
rt milking parlours

dairies, farm
USE **farm dairies**

DAIRY BREEDS
BT1 cattle breeds
BT2 breeds
rt dairy cattle
rt dairy traits

DAIRY BULLS
BT1 bulls
BT2 male animals
BT3 animals
BT1 dairy cattle
BT2 cattle
BT3 livestock
BT4 animals
BT3 ruminants
BT4 animals
BT3 skin producing animals
BT4 animals

DAIRY BULLS *cont.*
rt cattle breeds

dairy byproducts
USE **milk byproducts**

DAIRY CATTLE
uf *cattle, dairy*
BT1 cattle
BT2 livestock
BT3 animals
BT2 ruminants
BT3 animals
BT2 skin producing animals
BT3 animals
NT1 dairy bulls
NT1 dairy cows
rt cow housing
rt dairies
rt dairy breeds

dairy cattle housing
USE **cow housing**

dairy cattle wastes
USE **dairy wastes**

DAIRY CHEMISTRY
BT1 chemistry
rt dairy science

DAIRY COOPERATIVES
uf *cooperatives, dairy*
BT1 cooperatives
rt dairies
rt dairy factories
rt international dairy federation

DAIRY COWS
BT1 cows
BT2 female animals
BT3 animals
BT1 dairy cattle
BT2 cattle
BT3 livestock
BT4 animals
BT3 ruminants
BT4 animals
BT3 skin producing animals
BT4 animals
BT1 milk-yielding animals
BT2 animals
rt cattle breeds

DAIRY EDUCATION
BT1 agricultural education
BT2 education
rt dairies
rt dairy industry
rt dairy science
rt dairy technology

DAIRY EFFLUENT
BT1 effluents
BT2 wastes
rt dairies
rt dairy wastes
rt manures

DAIRY ENGINEERING
BT1 engineering
rt dairies
rt dairy equipment
rt dairy factories
rt dairy technology

DAIRY EQUIPMENT
BT1 equipment
NT1 butter churns
NT1 butyrometers
NT1 cheese moulds
NT1 cheese presses
NT1 cheese vats
NT1 clarifiers
NT1 homogenizers
NT1 milk crates
NT1 milk filters
NT1 milk meters
NT1 milk pipelines
NT1 milk pumps
NT1 milk tankers
NT1 milk tanks
NT1 pasteurizers

DAIRY EQUIPMENT *cont.*
NT1 triers
rt boilers
rt coolers
rt dairies
rt dairy engineering
rt dairy factories
rt separators
rt washers

DAIRY FACTORIES
BT1 factories
BT2 buildings
rt cheese stores
rt dairies
rt dairy cooperatives
rt dairy engineering
rt dairy equipment
rt dairy technology

DAIRY FARMING
BT1 cattle farming
BT2 livestock enterprises
BT3 farm enterprises
BT4 enterprises
BT2 livestock farming
BT3 farming
rt dairies

DAIRY FARMS
BT1 farms
rt dairying

DAIRY HERDS
BT1 herds
BT2 groups
rt cattle breeds

DAIRY HYGIENE
HN from 1990
BT1 hygiene
rt milk hygiene

DAIRY INDUSTRY
BT1 food industry
BT2 industry
rt dairy education
rt dairy statistics
rt milk prices
rt milk production
rt milk production costs
rt milk supply

dairy parlours
USE **milking parlours**

DAIRY PERFORMANCE
BT1 performance
NT1 milk yield
NT2 milk fat yield
NT2 milk protein yield
NT1 milking rate
NT2 milk flow
rt dairies
rt milk production

dairy products
USE **milk products**

DAIRY RESEARCH
BT1 agricultural research
BT2 research
rt dairies
rt dairy science

DAIRY SCIENCE
BT1 agricultural sciences
rt dairies
rt dairy chemistry
rt dairy education
rt dairy research
rt dairy technology

DAIRY SHORTHORN
BT1 cattle breeds
BT2 breeds

DAIRY STATISTICS
BT1 agricultural statistics
BT2 statistics
rt dairies
rt dairy industry

DAIRY TECHNOLOGY
BT1 technology

DAIRY TECHNOLOGY *cont.*
rt buttermaking
rt cheesemaking
rt dairies
rt dairy education
rt dairy engineering
rt dairy factories
rt dairy science
rt milk processing

DAIRY TRAITS
BT1 traits
rt dairy breeds

DAIRY WASTES
uf *dairy cattle wastes*
BT1 agricultural wastes
BT2 wastes
rt dairies
rt dairy effluent

DAIRYING
NT1 buttermaking
NT2 continuous buttermaking
NT1 milking
NT2 hand milking
NT2 machine milking
NT2 milking interval
rt dairies
rt dairy farms
rt milkers

daktulosphaira
USE **phylloxera**
OR **viteus**

daktulosphaira vitifoliae
USE **viteus vitifoliae**

DALA
BT1 sheep breeds
BT2 breeds

DALACA
BT1 hepialidae
BT2 lepidoptera
NT1 dalaca dimidiata
rt hepialus

DALACA DIMIDIATA
uf *hepialus dimidiatus*
BT1 dalaca
BT2 hepialidae
BT3 lepidoptera

DALAPON
uf *2,2-dichloropropionic acid*
BT1 chlorinated fatty acids
BT2 organochlorine compounds
BT3 organic halogen compounds
BT1 halogenated aliphatic herbicides
BT2 herbicides
BT3 pesticides

DALBERGIA
BT1 leguminosae
NT1 dalbergia cochinchinensis
NT1 dalbergia decipularis
NT1 dalbergia latifolia
NT1 dalbergia melanoxylon
NT1 dalbergia nigra
NT1 dalbergia nitidula
NT1 dalbergia oliveri
NT1 dalbergia paniculata
NT1 dalbergia retusa
NT1 dalbergia sericea
NT1 dalbergia sissoo
NT1 dalbergia volubilis

DALBERGIA COCHINCHINENSIS
BT1 dalbergia
BT2 leguminosae

DALBERGIA DECIPULARIS
BT1 dalbergia
BT2 leguminosae

DALBERGIA LATIFOLIA
BT1 dalbergia
BT2 leguminosae
BT1 forest trees

DALBERGIA MELANOXYLON
BT1 dalbergia
BT2 leguminosae

DALBERGIA NIGRA
BT1 dalbergia
BT2 leguminosae

DALBERGIA NITIDULA
BT1 dalbergia
BT2 leguminosae

DALBERGIA OLIVERI
BT1 dalbergia
BT2 leguminosae

DALBERGIA PANICULATA
BT1 dalbergia
BT2 leguminosae
BT1 ornamental woody plants

DALBERGIA RETUSA
BT1 dalbergia
BT2 leguminosae

DALBERGIA SERICEA
BT1 dalbergia
BT2 leguminosae

DALBERGIA SISSOO
BT1 dalbergia
BT2 leguminosae
BT1 forest trees

DALBERGIA VOLUBILIS
BT1 dalbergia
BT2 leguminosae

DALBULUS
BT1 cicadellidae
BT2 cicadelloidea
BT3 auchenorrhyncha
BT4 homoptera
NT1 dalbulus elimatus
NT1 dalbulus gelbus
NT1 dalbulus maidis

DALBULUS ELIMATUS
BT1 dalbulus
BT2 cicadellidae
BT3 cicadelloidea
BT4 auchenorrhyncha
BT5 homoptera

DALBULUS GELBUS
BT1 dalbulus
BT2 cicadellidae
BT3 cicadelloidea
BT4 auchenorrhyncha
BT5 homoptera

DALBULUS MAIDIS
BT1 dalbulus
BT2 cicadellidae
BT3 cicadelloidea
BT4 auchenorrhyncha
BT5 homoptera

DALES-BRED
BT1 sheep breeds
BT2 breeds

DALES PONY
BT1 horse breeds
BT2 breeds

dallis grass
USE **paspalum dilatatum**

DALMATIAN-KARST
BT1 sheep breeds
BT2 breeds

dama
USE **cervus**

dama dama
USE **fallow deer**

DAMAEIDAE
BT1 cryptostigmata
BT2 acari
NT1 epidamaeus

DAMAGE
NT1 adverse effects

DAMAGE *cont.*
NT1 breakage
NT2 chromosome breakage
NT1 browsing damage
NT1 crop damage
NT2 lodging
NT1 forest damage
NT1 gunfire and bomb damage
NT1 hail damage
NT1 ice damage
NT1 mechanical damage
NT1 rain damage
NT1 snow damage
NT1 threshing damage
NT1 wind damage
NT2 lodging
rt abiotic injuries
rt agricultural disasters
rt bruising
rt deformities
rt economic thresholds
rt handling
rt injuries
rt rupture
rt safety
rt salvage felling and logging
rt seed injury
rt wear
rt wounds

damage thresholds
USE **economic thresholds**

DAMALINIA
BT1 trichodectidae
BT2 ischnocera
BT3 mallophaga
BT4 phthiraptera
rt bovicola
rt werneckiella

damalinia bovis
USE **bovicola bovis**

damalinia caprae
USE **bovicola caprae**

damalinia crassipes
USE **bovicola crassipes**

damalinia equi
USE **werneckiella equi**

damalinia limbata
USE **bovicola limbata**

damalinia ovis
USE **bovicola ovis**

DAMALISCUS
BT1 bovidae
BT2 ruminantia
BT3 artiodactyla
BT4 mammals
BT4 ungulates
NT1 damaliscus dorcas

DAMALISCUS DORCAS
BT1 damaliscus
BT2 bovidae
BT3 ruminantia
BT4 artiodactyla
BT5 mammals
BT5 ungulates

DAMANI
BT1 goat breeds
BT2 breeds
BT1 sheep breeds
BT2 breeds

DAMASCUS
BT1 cattle breeds
BT2 breeds
BT1 goat breeds
BT2 breeds

DAMASK (AGRICOLA)
BT1 fabrics

DAMASONIUM
BT1 hydrocharitaceae
NT1 damasonium minus

DAMASONIUM MINUS
BT1 damasonium
BT2 hydrocharitaceae

DAMIETTA
BT1 cattle breeds
BT2 breeds

DAMINOZIDE
uf *n-(dimethylamino)succinamic acid*
uf *sadh*
uf *succinic acid 2,2-dimethylhydrazide*
BT1 growth retardants
BT2 plant growth regulators
BT3 growth regulators
BT2 retardants
BT1 hydrazides
BT2 organic nitrogen compounds

DAMPERS
BT1 components
rt attenuation
rt damping
rt shock absorbers
rt suppression

DAMPING
rt dampers
rt hysteresis
rt noise abatement
rt reduction
rt suppression

DAMPING OFF
BT1 fungal diseases
BT2 plant diseases
rt seedlings

DAMS
uf *reservoirs, ponds and dams*
BT1 barriers
NT1 dykes
rt hydraulic engineering
rt hydraulic structures
rt water reservoirs

DAMS (MOTHERS)
BT1 parents
BT2 ancestry
NT1 bull dams
rt cows
rt ewes
rt mares
rt maternal behaviour
rt maternal effects
rt maternity
rt mothers
rt sires
rt sows

DAMSONS
BT1 stone fruits
BT2 temperate tree fruits
BT3 temperate fruits
BT4 fruit crops
BT3 tree fruits
rt plums
rt prunus insititia

DANAE
BT1 ruscaceae
NT1 danae racemosa

DANAE RACEMOSA
BT1 danae
BT2 ruscaceae
BT1 ornamental woody plants

DANAKIL
HN from 1990
BT1 cattle breeds
BT2 breeds

DANAUS
BT1 nymphalidae
BT2 lepidoptera
NT1 danaus plexippus

DANAUS PLEXIPPUS
BT1 danaus

DANAUS PLEXIPPUS *cont.*
BT2 nymphalidae
BT3 lepidoptera

DANCES
BT1 communication between animals
BT2 animal behaviour
BT3 behaviour
BT2 communication
rt worker honeybees

DANCING
(recreational activity)
BT1 performing arts
BT2 arts
NT1 ballet
NT1 folk dancing
NT1 modern dance

DANDELION LATENT CARLAVIRUS
HN from 1990
BT1 carlavirus group
BT2 plant viruses
BT3 plant pathogens
BT4 pathogens

DANGEROUS TREES
BT1 trees
rt forest trees

DANGI
BT1 cattle breeds
BT2 breeds

DANIELLIA
BT1 leguminosae
NT1 daniellia oliveri

DANIELLIA OLIVERI
BT1 daniellia
BT2 leguminosae

DANISH BLACK PIED
BT1 cattle breeds
BT2 breeds

DANISH JERSEY
HN from 1990
BT1 cattle breeds
BT2 breeds

DANISH LANDRACE
BT1 pig breeds
BT2 breeds

DANISH RED
BT1 cattle breeds
BT2 breeds

DANISH RED PIED
BT1 cattle breeds
BT2 breeds

DANLOS SYNDROME
BT1 skin diseases
BT2 organic diseases
BT3 diseases

DANTHONIA
BT1 gramineae
NT1 danthonia caespitosa
NT1 danthonia compressa
NT1 danthonia decumbens
NT1 danthonia linkii
NT1 danthonia penicillata
NT1 danthonia richardsonii
NT1 danthonia sericea
NT1 danthonia spicata
NT1 danthonia vestita

DANTHONIA CAESPITOSA
BT1 danthonia
BT2 gramineae
BT1 pasture plants

DANTHONIA COMPRESSA
BT1 danthonia
BT2 gramineae

DANTHONIA DECUMBENS
uf *sieglingia decumbens*
BT1 danthonia
BT2 gramineae

DANTHONIA DECUMBENS *cont.*
BT1 pasture plants

DANTHONIA LINKII
BT1 danthonia
BT2 gramineae
BT1 pasture plants

DANTHONIA PENICILLATA
BT1 danthonia
BT2 gramineae
BT1 pasture plants

DANTHONIA RICHARDSONII
BT1 danthonia
BT2 gramineae
BT1 pasture plants

DANTHONIA SERICEA
BT1 danthonia
BT2 gramineae
BT1 pasture plants

DANTHONIA SPICATA
BT1 danthonia
BT2 gramineae
BT1 pasture plants

DANTHONIA VESTITA
BT1 danthonia
BT2 gramineae
BT1 pasture plants

DANUBE
HN from 1990
BT1 horse breeds
BT2 breeds

DANUBE FINEWOOL
HN from 1990
BT1 sheep breeds
BT2 breeds

DANUBE MERINO
BT1 sheep breeds
BT2 breeds

DAPHNE
BT1 thymelaeaceae
NT1 daphne acuminata
NT1 daphne burkwoodii
NT1 daphne cneorum
NT1 daphne genkwa
NT1 daphne mezereum
NT1 daphne odora
NT1 daphne papyracea
NT1 daphne petraea
NT1 daphne retusa
rt daphne x potexvirus

DAPHNE ACUMINATA
BT1 daphne
BT2 thymelaeaceae

DAPHNE BURKWOODII
BT1 daphne
BT2 thymelaeaceae
BT1 ornamental woody plants

DAPHNE CNEORUM
BT1 daphne
BT2 thymelaeaceae
BT1 ornamental woody plants

DAPHNE GENKWA
BT1 daphne
BT2 thymelaeaceae
BT1 medicinal plants
BT1 ornamental woody plants

DAPHNE MEZEREUM
BT1 daphne
BT2 thymelaeaceae
BT1 ornamental woody plants
BT1 poisonous plants

DAPHNE ODORA
BT1 daphne
BT2 thymelaeaceae
BT1 ornamental woody plants

DAPHNE PAPYRACEA
BT1 daphne
BT2 thymelaeaceae
BT1 medicinal plants

DAPHNE PAPYRACEA *cont.*
BT1 ornamental woody plants

DAPHNE PETRAEA
BT1 daphne
BT2 thymelaeaceae
BT1 ornamental woody plants

DAPHNE RETUSA
BT1 daphne
BT2 thymelaeaceae
BT1 ornamental woody plants

DAPHNE X POTEXVIRUS
HN from 1990
BT1 potexvirus group
BT2 plant viruses
BT3 plant pathogens
BT4 pathogens
rt daphne

DAPHNIA
BT1 cladocera
BT2 branchiopoda
BT3 crustacea
BT4 arthropods
NT1 daphnia magna
NT1 daphnia pulex

DAPHNIA MAGNA
BT1 daphnia
BT2 cladocera
BT3 branchiopoda
BT4 crustacea
BT5 arthropods

DAPHNIA PULEX
BT1 daphnia
BT2 cladocera
BT3 branchiopoda
BT4 crustacea
BT5 arthropods

DAPHNIPHYLLUM
BT1 euphorbiaceae
NT1 daphniphyllum teysmannii

DAPHNIPHYLLUM TEYSMANNII
BT1 daphniphyllum
BT2 euphorbiaceae

DAPSONE
BT1 antibacterial agents
BT2 antiinfective agents
BT3 drugs
BT1 antimalarials
BT2 antiprotozoal agents
BT3 antiparasitic agents
BT4 drugs
BT1 sulfonamides
BT2 amides
BT3 organic nitrogen compounds
BT2 organic sulfur compounds

DARK
uf *darkness*
rt blanching
rt dark adaptation
rt etiolation
rt light
rt photoperiodism

DARK ADAPTATION
BT1 adaptation
rt dark
rt night blindness

DARK CHESTNUT SOILS
BT1 kastanozems
BT2 soil types (genetic)

DARK CUTTING MEAT
HN from 1990
uf *dark firm dry meat*
BT1 meat
BT2 animal products
BT3 products
BT2 foods

dark firm dry meat
USE **dark cutting meat**

DARK FIXATION
BT1 photosynthesis

DARK FIXATION *cont.*
BT2 energy metabolism
BT3 metabolism
BT2 plant physiology
BT3 physiology

darkness
USE **dark**

DARLINGIA
BT1 proteaceae
NT1 darlingia darlingiana

DARLINGIA DARLINGIANA
BT1 darlingia
BT2 proteaceae

darluca
USE **eudarluca**

darluca filum
USE **eudarluca caricis**

DARNA
BT1 limacodidae
BT2 lepidoptera
NT1 darna trima

DARNA TRIMA
BT1 darna
BT2 limacodidae
BT3 lepidoptera

DARTMOOR
BT1 sheep breeds
BT2 breeds

DARTMOOR PONY
BT1 horse breeds
BT2 breeds

DARTS
BT1 indoor games
BT2 games
BT2 indoor recreation
BT3 recreation

DARVAZ
BT1 sheep breeds
BT2 breeds

DASCYLLUS
BT1 pomacentridae
BT2 perciformes
BT3 osteichthyes
BT4 fishes

dasheen
USE **colocasia esculenta**

DASHEEN MOSAIC POTYVIRUS
HN from 1990; previously "dasheen mosaic virus"
uf *dasheen mosaic virus*
BT1 potyvirus group
BT2 plant viruses
BT3 plant pathogens
BT4 pathogens
rt colocasia esculenta

dasheen mosaic virus
USE **dasheen mosaic potyvirus**

DASINEURA
BT1 cecidomyiidae
BT2 diptera
NT1 dasineura brassicae
NT1 dasineura ignorata
NT1 dasineura mali
NT1 dasineura pyri
NT1 dasineura ribis

DASINEURA BRASSICAE
BT1 dasineura
BT2 cecidomyiidae
BT3 diptera

DASINEURA IGNORATA
BT1 dasineura
BT2 cecidomyiidae
BT3 diptera

DASINEURA MALI
BT1 dasineura
BT2 cecidomyiidae
BT3 diptera

DASINEURA PYRI
BT1 dasineura
BT2 cecidomyiidae
BT3 diptera

DASINEURA RIBIS
BT1 dasineura
BT2 cecidomyiidae
BT3 diptera

DASYATIDAE
BT1 rajiformes
BT2 chondrichthyes
BT3 fishes
NT1 dasyatis

DASYATIS
BT1 dasyatidae
BT2 rajiformes
BT3 chondrichthyes
BT4 fishes

DASYCHIRA
BT1 lymantriidae
BT2 lepidoptera

DASYLIRION
BT1 agavaceae

DASYPODA
BT1 apidae
BT2 hymenoptera

DASYPODIDAE
uf *armadillos*
BT1 edentata
BT2 mammals
NT1 dasypus
NT2 dasypus novemcinctus
NT1 euphractus
NT2 euphractus sexcinctus

DASYPROCTIDAE
BT1 rodents
BT2 mammals
NT1 agouti

DASYPUS
BT1 dasypodidae
BT2 edentata
BT3 mammals
NT1 dasypus novemcinctus

DASYPUS NOVEMCINCTUS
BT1 dasypus
BT2 dasypodidae
BT3 edentata
BT4 mammals

dasypus sexcinctus
USE **euphractus sexcinctus**

DASYPYRUM
uf *haynaldia*
BT1 gramineae
NT1 dasypyrum villosum

DASYPYRUM VILLOSUM
HN from 1989; previously haynaldia villosa
uf *haynaldia villosa*
BT1 dasypyrum
BT2 gramineae

DASYSCYPHA
HN from 1990
BT1 helotiales
rt trichoscyphella

dasyscypha willkommii
USE **trichoscyphella willkommii**

DASYTRICHA
BT1 ciliophora
BT2 protozoa
NT1 dasytricha ruminantium

DASYTRICHA RUMINANTIUM
BT1 dasytricha
BT2 ciliophora
BT3 protozoa

DASYURIDAE
BT1 marsupials
BT2 mammals

DASYURIDAE *cont.*
NT1 antechinus
NT2 antechinus swainsonii
NT1 phascogale

DATA ANALYSIS
NT1 statistical analysis
NT2 analysis of covariance
NT2 analysis of variance
NT2 cluster analysis
NT2 component analysis
NT2 correlation analysis
NT3 transect correlograms
NT2 decision analysis
NT2 diallel analysis
NT2 discriminant analysis
NT2 factorial analysis
NT2 finite element analysis
NT2 gini coefficient
NT2 least squares
NT2 maximum likelihood
NT2 motad
NT2 multiple comparison test
NT2 multivariate analysis
NT3 canonical analysis
NT2 path analysis
NT3 critical path analysis
NT2 principal component analysis
NT2 probability analysis
NT2 probit analysis
NT2 regression analysis
NT3 arima
NT3 multiple regression
NT3 stepwise regression
NT2 standard deviation
NT2 statistical inference
NT2 student's test
NT2 time series
NT2 unbiased estimates
NT2 unbiased estimator
NT2 variance
rt data processing

DATA BANKS
BT1 information systems
BT2 systems
NT1 nutrient databanks (agricola)

DATA COLLECTION
uf data logging
BT1 collection
NT1 interviews
NT1 questionnaires
rt censuses
rt data communication
rt information systems
rt instrumentation
rt inventories
rt monitoring
rt recording
rt sampling
rt surveys

DATA COMMUNICATION
BT1 communication
NT1 telemetry
rt data collection
rt data processing
rt instrumentation
rt telecommunications

data logging
USE **data collection**

DATA PROCESSING
uf electronic data processing
BT1 information processing
BT2 information
rt computers
rt data analysis
rt data communication
rt microprocessors
rt on line
rt statistics

data storage
USE **information storage**

DATABASES
BT1 information systems
BT2 systems

DATABASES *cont.*
rt information storage

DATE
rt application date
rt cutting date
rt flowering date
rt harvesting date
rt hatching date
rt heading date
rt planting date
rt sowing date

date palms
USE **dates**
OR **phoenix dactylifera**

DATE STAMPING
BT1 standardization
rt open dating (agricola)

DATES
uf date palms
BT1 subtropical tree fruits
BT2 subtropical fruits
BT3 fruit crops
BT2 tree fruits
rt phoenix dactylifera

DATISCA
BT1 datiscaceae
NT1 datisca cannabina
NT1 datisca glomerata

DATISCA CANNABINA
BT1 datisca
BT2 datiscaceae
BT1 dye plants
BT1 medicinal plants

DATISCA GLOMERATA
BT1 datisca
BT2 datiscaceae

DATISCACEAE
NT1 datisca
NT2 datisca cannabina
NT2 datisca glomerata

DATURA
BT1 solanaceae
NT1 datura candida
NT1 datura ceratocaula
NT1 datura composita
NT1 datura deltoidea
NT1 datura discolor
NT1 datura fastuosa
NT1 datura ferox
NT1 datura metel
NT1 datura quercifolia
NT1 datura sanguinea
NT1 datura stramonium
NT1 datura suaveolens
NT1 datura wrightii
rt datura shoestring potyvirus

datura alba
USE **datura metel**

DATURA CANDIDA
BT1 datura
BT2 solanaceae
BT1 poisonous plants

DATURA CERATOCAULA
BT1 datura
BT2 solanaceae

DATURA COMPOSITA
BT1 datura
BT2 solanaceae

DATURA DELTOIDEA
BT1 datura
BT2 solanaceae

DATURA DISCOLOR
BT1 datura
BT2 solanaceae

DATURA FASTUOSA
uf datura innoxia
uf datura meteloides
BT1 antiviral plants
BT1 datura

DATURA FASTUOSA *cont.*
BT2 solanaceae
BT1 dye plants
BT1 medicinal plants

DATURA FEROX
BT1 datura
BT2 solanaceae

datura godronii
USE **datura stramonium**

datura inermis
USE **datura stramonium**

datura innoxia
USE **datura fastuosa**

DATURA METEL
uf datura alba
BT1 antifungal plants
BT1 antiviral plants
BT1 datura
BT2 solanaceae
BT1 nematicidal plants
BT2 pesticidal plants

datura meteloides
USE **datura fastuosa**

DATURA QUERCIFOLIA
BT1 datura
BT2 solanaceae
BT1 medicinal plants

DATURA SANGUINEA
BT1 datura
BT2 solanaceae

DATURA SHOESTRING POTYVIRUS
HN from 1990
BT1 potyvirus group
BT2 plant viruses
BT3 plant pathogens
BT4 pathogens
rt datura

DATURA STRAMONIUM
uf datura godronii
uf datura inermis
uf datura tatula
BT1 antifungal plants
BT1 antiviral plants
BT1 datura
BT2 solanaceae
BT1 insecticidal plants
BT2 pesticidal plants
BT1 medicinal plants
BT1 poisonous plants
BT1 weeds

DATURA SUAVEOLENS
BT1 datura
BT2 solanaceae

datura tatula
USE **datura stramonium**

DATURA WRIGHTII
BT1 datura
BT2 solanaceae

DAUBENTONIA
BT1 leguminosae
NT1 daubentonia punicea
NT1 daubentonia texana

DAUBENTONIA PUNICEA
BT1 daubentonia
BT2 leguminosae

DAUBENTONIA TEXANA
BT1 daubentonia
BT2 leguminosae

DAUBNEYIA
BT1 chabertiidae
BT2 nematoda

DAUCUS
BT1 umbelliferae
NT1 daucus carota

DAUCUS CAROTA
BT1 daucus

DAUCUS CAROTA *cont.*
BT2 umbelliferae
rt carrot red leaf luteovirus
rt carrot thin leaf potyvirus
rt carrots

DAUGHTERS
BT1 female animals
BT2 animals
BT1 progeny
rt children
rt girls
rt siblings

DAVAINEA
BT1 davaineidae
BT2 eucestoda
BT3 cestoda
NT1 davainea proglottina

DAVAINEA PROGLOTTINA
BT1 davainea
BT2 davaineidae
BT3 eucestoda
BT4 cestoda

DAVAINEIDAE
BT1 eucestoda
BT2 cestoda
NT1 cotugnia
NT2 cotugnia digonophora
NT1 davainea
NT2 davainea proglottina
NT1 raillietina
NT2 raillietina cesticillus
NT2 raillietina echinobothrida
NT2 raillietina tetragona

DAVALLIA
BT1 davalliaceae
rt ornamental ferns

DAVALLIACEAE
NT1 davallia

DAVISIA
BT1 myxozoa
BT2 protozoa

DAY CAMP PROGRAMS (AGRICOLA)
BT1 child day care (agricola)
BT2 day care (agricola)
rt summer programs (agricola)

DAY CARE (AGRICOLA)
NT1 adult day care (agricola)
NT1 child day care (agricola)
NT2 day camp programs (agricola)
NT1 family day care (agricola)

DAY CARE CENTERS (AGRICOLA)
rt child day care (agricola)
rt early childhood education (agricola)

day-degrees
USE **heat sums**

DAY VISITS
BT1 visits
BT2 travel

daylength
USE **photoperiod**

DAYLIGHT
BT1 light
BT2 electromagnetic radiation
BT3 radiation
rt solar radiation
rt sunshine hours

DAZOMET
BT1 soil fumigants
BT2 fumigants
BT3 pesticides
BT1 unclassified fungicides
BT2 fungicides
BT3 pesticides
BT1 unclassified herbicides
BT2 herbicides
BT3 pesticides
BT1 unclassified nematicides

DAZOMET *cont.*
BT2 nematicides
BT3 pesticides

2,4-DB
uf *4-(2,4-dichlorophenoxy)butyric acid*
BT1 auxins
BT2 plant growth regulators
BT3 growth regulators
BT1 phenoxybutyric herbicides
BT2 phenoxy herbicides
BT3 herbicides
BT4 pesticides

DBCP
uf *dibromochloropropane*
BT1 soil fumigants
BT2 fumigants
BT3 pesticides
BT1 unclassified nematicides
BT2 nematicides
BT3 pesticides

dbr
USE **german federal republic**

dcd
USE **dicyandiamide**

dcmo
USE **carboxin**

dcmu
USE **diuron**

dcna
USE **dicloran**

dcpa
USE **chlorthal-dimethyl**

dcu
USE **dichloralurea**

ddr
USE **german democratic republic**

DDT
uf *dicophane*
BT1 ectoparasiticides
BT2 antiparasitic agents
BT3 drugs
BT1 organochlorine acaricides
BT2 acaricides
BT3 pesticides
BT2 organochlorine pesticides
BT3 organochlorine compounds
BT4 organic halogen compounds
BT1 organochlorine insecticides
BT2 insecticides
BT3 pesticides
BT2 organochlorine pesticides
BT3 organochlorine compounds
BT4 organic halogen compounds

DDT-DEHYDROCHLORINASE
(ec 4.5.1.1)
BT1 lyases
BT2 enzymes

ddvp
USE **dichlorvos**

DEAD TREES
BT1 trees
rt death
rt decay
rt forest trees
rt salvage felling and logging
rt sanitation fellings

DEAD WOOD
BT1 wood
rt branches
rt decay
rt decayed wood

deadly nightshade
USE **atropa belladonna**

deaf
USE **deafness**

DEAFNESS
uf *deaf*
BT1 hearing impairment
BT2 sensory disorders
BT3 functional disorders
BT4 animal disorders
BT5 disorders
BT3 nervous system diseases
BT4 organic diseases
BT5 diseases
rt ear diseases
rt hearing

DEAMINATION
BT1 protein metabolism
BT2 metabolism
rt amino compounds
rt urea

DEATH
NT1 cot death
NT1 electrocution
NT1 euthanasia
NT1 fetal death
NT2 mummification
rt aging
rt dead trees
rt death and dying (agricola)
rt mortality
rt necrosis
rt obituaries
rt postmortem changes
rt postmortem examinations
rt slaughter

DEATH AND DYING (AGRICOLA)
NT1 sudden infant death
rt death
rt fetal death
rt hospices (agricola)
rt suicide (agricola)

death rate
USE **mortality**

debarking
USE **barking**

DEBARYOMYCES
BT1 endomycetales
NT1 debaryomyces hansenii

DEBARYOMYCES HANSENII
HN from 1989
BT1 debaryomyces
BT2 endomycetales

DEBEAKING
BT1 surgical operations
rt amputation
rt beak

DEBLOSSOMING
BT1 thinning
rt abscission
rt flowers
rt shedding
rt stopping

debre-fanconi syndrome
USE **fanconi syndrome**

DEBT
uf *indebtedness*
NT1 bankruptcy
NT1 external debt
NT1 farm indebtedness
rt liabilities
rt loans
rt losses

DECAFENTIN
BT1 organotin fungicides
BT2 fungicides
BT3 pesticides
BT2 organotin pesticides
BT3 organotin compounds

DECAMETHONIUM
BT1 muscle relaxants
BT2 neurotropic drugs
BT3 drugs

DECAMETHONIUM *cont.*
BT1 quaternary ammonium compounds
BT2 ammonium compounds
BT2 organic nitrogen compounds
rt cholinergic mechanisms

1-DECANAMINE
BT1 monoamines
BT2 amines
BT3 amino compounds
BT4 organic nitrogen compounds
BT1 primary amines
BT2 amines
BT3 amino compounds
BT4 organic nitrogen compounds

DECANE
BT1 alkanes
BT2 hydrocarbons

DECANOIC ACID
uf *capric acid*
BT1 medium chain fatty acids
BT2 fatty acids
BT3 carboxylic acids
BT4 organic acids
BT5 acids
BT3 lipids
BT1 saturated fatty acids
BT2 fatty acids
BT3 carboxylic acids
BT4 organic acids
BT5 acids
BT3 lipids

1-DECANOL
BT1 alcohols

DECAPITATION
rt head

DECAPODA
BT1 malacostraca
BT2 crustacea
BT3 arthropods
NT1 astacus
NT1 austropotamobius
NT2 austropotamobius pallipes
NT1 callinectes
NT1 cambarus
NT1 cancer
NT1 carcinus
NT2 carcinus aestuarii
NT2 carcinus maenas
NT1 cherax
NT2 cherax destructor
NT1 chionoecetes
NT1 crangon
NT1 homarus
NT2 homarus americanus
NT2 homarus gammarus
NT1 jasus
NT1 macrobrachium
NT2 macrobrachium rosenbergii
NT1 maia
NT1 metapenaeus
NT1 palaemon
NT2 palaemon serratus
NT2 palaemon serrifer
NT1 palaemonetes
NT2 palaemonetes pugio
NT1 pandalus
NT2 pandalus jordani
NT1 panulirus
NT2 panulirus argus
NT1 paralithodes
NT1 penaeus
NT2 penaeus indicus
NT2 penaeus japonicus
NT2 penaeus merguiensis
NT2 penaeus monodon
NT2 penaeus semisulcatus
NT2 penaeus setiferus
NT2 penaeus stylirostris
NT2 penaeus vannamei
NT1 portunus
NT1 potamon
NT2 potamon chinghungense
NT1 procambarus

DECAPODA *cont.*
NT2 procambarus clarkii
rt crabs
rt lobsters

DECAPPING
BT1 processing
rt hulling
rt strawberries
rt uncapping

DECAPTERUS
BT1 carangidae
BT2 perciformes
BT3 osteichthyes
BT4 fishes

decarboxylases
USE **carboxy-lyases**

DECARYIA
BT1 didiereaceae
NT1 decaryia madagascariensis

DECARYIA MADAGASCARIENSIS
BT1 decaryia
BT2 didiereaceae
BT1 ornamental succulent plants
BT2 succulent plants

DECAY
BT1 decomposition
BT1 deterioration
NT1 fruit rots
NT1 postharvest decay
NT2 spoilage
NT3 food spoilage
NT2 storage decay
NT1 root and butt rots
rt biodeterioration
rt dead trees
rt dead wood
rt decay fungi
rt decayed wood
rt dental caries
rt durability
rt postmortem changes
rt salvage felling and logging
rt sanitation fellings
rt saprophytes
rt wastes

DECAY FUNGI
uf *rot fungi*
BT1 fungi
BT1 saprophytes
rt decay

DECAYED WOOD
BT1 wood
rt dead wood
rt decay

DECCANI
BT1 sheep breeds
BT2 breeds

DECENTRALIZATION
BT1 socioeconomic organization
rt centralization

DECIDUOUS FORESTS
BT1 forests
BT2 vegetation types
NT1 broadleaved deciduous forests

DECISION ANALYSIS
HN from 1989
BT1 statistical analysis
BT2 data analysis
BT2 statistics

DECISION MAKING
uf *choice*
rt bayesian theory
rt management
rt managers

DECKS
BT1 structural components
BT2 components
rt composite wood assemblies
rt flat deck cages

DECLINE
BT1 plant diseases

DECODON
BT1 lythraceae
NT1 decodon verticillatus

DECODON VERTICILLATUS
BT1 decodon
BT2 lythraceae

DECOLORIZATION
HN from 1990
BT1 purification
BT2 processing
rt electrofiltration
rt sugar refining

DECOMPOSITION
NT1 decay
NT2 fruit rots
NT2 postharvest decay
NT3 spoilage
NT4 food spoilage
NT3 storage decay
NT2 root and butt rots
NT1 dissociation
NT1 fibrinolysis
NT1 glycogenolysis
NT1 glycolysis
rt biodeterioration
rt deterioration

DECONTAMINATION
BT1 hygiene
rt contamination
rt disinfection
rt sterilizing

DECOQUINATE
BT1 coccidiostats
BT2 antiprotozoal agents
BT3 antiparasitic agents
BT4 drugs

DECORATIVE DESIGN (AGRICOLA)
rt design

DECORATIVE FABRICS (AGRICOLA)
BT1 fabrics

decorative greenery
USE **cut foliage**

DECORTICATION
BT1 processing
NT1 husking
rt bark
rt decorticators
rt hulling
rt peeling
rt rinds
rt shelling

DECORTICATORS
BT1 farm machinery
BT2 machinery
rt decortication

DECTES
BT1 cerambycidae
BT2 coleoptera
NT1 dectes texanus

DECTES TEXANUS
BT1 dectes
BT2 cerambycidae
BT3 coleoptera

DEEP BED DRIERS
AF deep bed dryers
uf *driers, deep bed*
BT1 driers
BT2 farm machinery
BT3 machinery
rt grain driers

DEEP BED DRYERS
BF deep bed driers
BT1 dryers

deep cultivation
USE **deep tillage**

DEEP FAT FRYING (AGRICOLA)
BT1 frying
BT2 cooking methods (agricola)
BT3 methodology

DEEP LITTER HOUSING
BT1 animal housing
rt litter

DEEP PLACEMENT
BT1 placement
BT2 application methods
BT3 methodology

DEEP PLOUGHING
AF deep plowing
uf *ploughing, deep*
BT1 ploughing
BT2 tillage
BT3 cultivation
rt deep tillage
rt subsoiling

DEEP PLOWING
BF deep ploughing
BT1 plowing

DEEP TILLAGE
uf *deep cultivation*
BT1 tillage
BT2 cultivation
rt deep ploughing
rt subsoiling

DEEP WATER RICE
rt rice

DEER
BT1 meat animals
BT2 animals
BT1 ruminants
BT2 animals
NT1 fallow deer
NT1 red deer
NT1 reindeer
rt cervidae
rt deer farming
rt deer feeding
rt venison

deer, black-tailed
USE **odocoileus hemionus**

DEER FARMING
BT1 game farming
BT2 livestock farming
BT3 farming
rt deer

DEER FEEDING
BT1 ruminant feeding
BT2 livestock feeding
BT3 animal feeding
BT4 feeding
rt deer

deer meat
USE **venison**

deer, mule
USE **odocoileus hemionus**

deer, roe
USE **capreolus capreolus**

deer, white-tailed
USE **odocoileus virginianus**

deermice
USE **peromyscus**

deet
USE **diethyltoluamide**

DEFAECATION
AF defecation
BT1 excretion
BT2 physiological functions
rt digestive system
rt excreta
rt faeces

DEFECATION
BF defaecation
rt feces

DEFECOSATURATION
HN from 1990
BT1 purification
BT2 processing
rt carbonatation
rt sugar refining

DEFECTS
NT1 cotting
NT1 egg shell defects
NT1 genetic defects
NT2 genetic disorders
NT2 phenylketonuria
NT1 wood defects
NT2 abnormal heartwood
NT2 brashness
NT2 checks
NT2 collapse (drying)
NT2 cracks
NT2 honeycombing
NT2 knots
NT2 resin pockets
NT2 shakes
NT2 splits
NT2 warping
rt abnormalities

defects in wood
USE **wood defects**

DEFENCE
AF defense
NT1 colony defence
NT1 defence mechanisms
rt defensive secretions

DEFENCE MECHANISMS
AF defense mechanisms
BT1 defence
rt defensive secretions
rt disease resistance
rt host parasite relationships
rt naturally acquired immunity
rt phagocytosis

DEFENSE
BF defence
NT1 colony defense
NT1 defense mechanisms

DEFENSE MECHANISMS
BF defence mechanisms
BT1 defense

DEFENSIVE SECRETIONS
BT1 allomones
BT2 allelochemicals
BT3 semiochemicals
rt defence
rt defence mechanisms

DEFEROXAMINE
uf *desferrioxamine*
BT1 chelating agents
rt iron

deferred utilization
USE **stock piling**

DEFICIENCY
NT1 caloric deficiency (agricola)
NT1 enzyme deficiencies
NT2 hypophosphatasia
NT2 lactase deficiency
NT1 immunological deficiency
NT2 viral immunosuppression
NT3 acquired immune deficiency syndrome
NT1 nutrient deficiencies
NT2 fat deficiencies
NT2 mineral deficiencies
NT2 protein deficiencies
NT2 trace element deficiencies
NT2 vitamin deficiencies
NT3 folic acid deficiency
NT3 riboflavin deficiency
NT3 vitamin a deficiency

DEFICIENCY DISEASES
BT1 diseases
BT1 nutritional disorders
BT2 animal disorders
BT3 disorders
NT1 beriberi

DEFICIENCY DISEASES *cont.*
NT1 black tongue
NT1 cheilosis
NT1 iron deficiency anaemia
NT1 kwashiorkor
NT1 mulberry heart disease
NT1 night blindness
NT1 pellagra
NT1 perosis
NT1 phrynoderma
NT1 scurvy
NT1 xerophthalmia
rt enzyme deficiencies
rt functional disorders
rt malnutrition
rt mineral deficiencies
rt nutrient deficiencies
rt protein deficiencies
rt vitamin deficiencies
rt xerosis

deficiency, nutrient
USE **nutrient deficiencies**

DEFICIENCY PAYMENTS
BT1 support measures

DEFLATION
BT1 monetary parity
BT2 monetary situation
rt economic depression
rt inflation

DEFLUORINATED ROCK PHOSPHATE
BT1 phosphorus fertilizers
BT2 fertilizers
rt rock phosphate

DEFOAMING
BT1 processing
rt defoaming agents
rt foaming
rt foams

DEFOAMING AGENTS
rt defoaming
rt food additives
rt surfactants

DEFOLIANTS
BT1 plant growth regulators
BT2 growth regulators
NT1 s,s,s-tributyl phosphorotrithioate
NT1 calcium cyanamide
NT1 endothal
NT1 ethephon
NT1 metoxuron
NT1 pentachlorophenol
NT1 thidiazuron
rt abscission
rt defoliation
rt herbicides
rt leaves

DEFOLIATION
(artificial)
uf *artificial defoliation*
uf *leaf removal*
rt defoliants
rt leaf fall
rt leaves

DEFORESTATION
BT1 forestry practices
BT2 forestry
rt agricultural land
rt clear felling

DEFORMATION
rt bending
rt deformities
rt plastic limit
rt plasticity
rt rheological properties
rt soil mechanics
rt strain

DEFORMITIES
NT1 crooked neck
rt abnormalities
rt damage
rt deformation

DEFORMITIES *cont.*
rt orthopaedics

DEGASSING
BT1 processing

DEGENERATION
NT1 atrophy
NT2 lupinosis
NT1 cirrhosis
NT1 cystic degeneration
NT1 fatty degeneration
NT1 hepatolenticular degeneration
rt clones
rt cytidine triphosphate
rt development
rt regression

DEGENIA
BT1 cruciferae
NT1 degenia velebitica

DEGENIA VELEBITICA
BT1 degenia
BT2 cruciferae

degeres
USE **degeres mutton-wool**

DEGERES MUTTON-WOOL
HN from 1990; previously "degeres"
uf *degeres*
BT1 sheep breeds
BT2 breeds

DEGLUTITION
uf *swallowing*
BT1 physiological functions

DEGRADATION
NT1 biodegradation
NT2 microbial degradation
NT1 chemical degradation
NT2 corrosion
NT3 rust
NT1 environmental degradation
NT1 protein degradation
NT2 proteolysis
NT1 soil degradation
NT1 thermal degradation

degradation, photolytic
USE **photolysis**

DEGRADED FORESTS
BT1 forests
BT2 vegetation types

degree-days
USE **heat sums**

DEGREENING
BT1 processing
rt citrus fruits
rt ripening

DEGUMMING
BT1 processing
rt gums

DEHANDING
BT1 handling
rt bananas

DEHESA GRASSLANDS
HN from 1990
BT1 grasslands
BT2 vegetation types

DEHISCENCE
rt fruits
rt ripening

DEHORNING
uf *polling*
BT1 surgical operations
rt polled condition

DEHUMIDIFICATION
BT1 drying
BT2 dehydration
BT3 processing

dehydratases
USE **hydro-lyases**

DEHYDRATED FODDERS
BT1 feeds

DEHYDRATED FOODS (AGRICOLA)
BT1 foods
rt dried foods

DEHYDRATION
BT1 processing
NT1 drying
NT2 air drying
NT2 artificial drying
NT2 barn drying
NT2 compression drying
NT2 dehumidification
NT2 drying methods
NT2 drying schedules
NT2 drying under restraint
NT2 end coating
NT2 field drying
NT2 fluidized bed drying
NT2 forced air drying
NT2 freeze drying
NT2 grain drying
NT3 drieration
NT2 high frequency drying
NT2 intermittent drying
NT2 jet drying
NT2 low temperature drying
NT2 natural drying
NT2 platen drying
NT2 roller drying
NT2 solar drying
NT2 solvent drying
NT2 spray drying
NT2 vacuum drying
NT2 vapour drying
rt rehydration
rt water deprivation

DEHYDRATION (PHYSIOLOGICAL)
BT1 water metabolism disorders
BT2 metabolic disorders
BT3 animal disorders
BT4 disorders
rt water deprivation

DEHYDROACETIC ACID
BT1 antifungal agents
BT2 antiinfective agents
BT3 drugs
BT1 bactericides
BT2 pesticides
BT1 plasticizers
BT1 unclassified fungicides
BT2 fungicides
BT3 pesticides

DEHYDROASCORBIC ACID
BT1 ascorbic acids
BT2 aldonic acids
BT3 sugar acids
BT4 carboxylic acids
BT5 organic acids
BT6 acids
BT4 monosaccharides
BT5 carbohydrates
BT1 vitamin c antagonists
BT2 vitamin antagonists
BT3 antagonists
BT4 metabolic inhibitors
BT5 inhibitors
rt scurvy

DEHYDROCHOLIC ACID
BT1 bile acids
BT1 cholanes
BT2 steroids
BT3 isoprenoids
BT4 lipids
rt bile secretion

DEHYDROEMETINE
BT1 amoebicides
BT2 antiprotozoal agents
BT3 antiparasitic agents
BT4 drugs
BT1 isoquinoline alkaloids
BT2 alkaloids

dehydroepiandrosterone
USE **prasterone**

dehydrogenases
USE **oxidoreductases**

DEHYDRORETINOL
uf *vitamin a2*
BT1 retinoids
BT2 carotenoids
BT3 lipochromes
BT4 pigments
BT3 terpenoids
BT4 isoprenoids
BT5 lipids
BT2 fat soluble vitamins
BT3 vitamins
rt fish liver oils
rt vision disorders

DEIGHTONIELLA
BT1 deuteromycotina
NT1 deightoniella torulosa
rt helminthosporium

DEIGHTONIELLA TORULOSA
uf *helminthosporium torulosum*
BT1 deightoniella
BT2 deuteromycotina

DEINOCERITES
BT1 culicidae
BT2 diptera
NT1 deinocerites cancer
NT1 deinocerites pseudes

DEINOCERITES CANCER
BT1 deinocerites
BT2 culicidae
BT3 diptera

DEINOCERITES PSEUDES
BT1 deinocerites
BT2 culicidae
BT3 diptera

DEIODINATION
BT1 processing
rt iodination

DELACHLOR
BT1 chloroacetanilide herbicides
BT2 anilide herbicides
BT3 amide herbicides
BT4 herbicides
BT5 pesticides

DELADENUS
BT1 neotylenchidae
BT2 nematoda

DELAWARE
BT1 appalachian states of usa
BT2 southern states of usa
BT3 usa
BT4 north america
BT5 america

delayed hypersensitivity
USE **delayed type hypersensitivity**

DELAYED PARENTHOOD (AGRICOLA)
BT1 parenthood (agricola)

DELAYED TYPE HYPERSENSITIVITY
uf *cell mediated hypersensitivity*
uf *delayed hypersensitivity*
uf *tuberculin reaction*
BT1 hypersensitivity
BT2 immune response
BT3 immunity
rt t lymphocytes

DELETIONS
rt chromosome translocation

DELHI
BT1 india
BT2 south asia
BT3 asia

DELIA
uf *erioischia*
uf *leptohylemyia*
BT1 anthomyiidae
BT2 diptera
NT1 delia antiqua
NT1 delia coarctata
NT1 delia floralis
NT1 delia florilega
NT1 delia platura
NT1 delia radicum
rt hylemya
rt phorbia

DELIA ANTIQUA
uf *hylemya antiqua*
uf *phorbia antiqua*
BT1 delia
BT2 anthomyiidae
BT3 diptera

delia brassicae
USE **delia radicum**

DELIA COARCTATA
uf *hylemya coarctata*
uf *leptohylemyia coarctata*
uf *phorbia coarctata*
BT1 delia
BT2 anthomyiidae
BT3 diptera

DELIA FLORALIS
uf *chortophila floralis*
uf *erioischia floralis*
uf *hylemya floralis*
uf *phorbia floralis*
BT1 delia
BT2 anthomyiidae
BT3 diptera

DELIA FLORILEGA
uf *hylemya florilega*
uf *hylemya liturata*
uf *phorbia florilega*
BT1 delia
BT2 anthomyiidae
BT3 diptera

DELIA PLATURA
uf *hylemya cilicrura*
uf *hylemya platura*
BT1 delia
BT2 anthomyiidae
BT3 diptera

DELIA RADICUM
uf *chortophila brassicae*
uf *delia brassicae*
uf *erioischia brassicae*
uf *hylemya brassicae*
uf *phorbia brassicae*
BT1 delia
BT2 anthomyiidae
BT3 diptera

DELICHON
BT1 hirundinidae
BT2 passeriformes
BT3 birds
NT1 delichon urbica

DELICHON URBICA
BT1 delichon
BT2 hirundinidae
BT3 passeriformes
BT4 birds

DELIMBING
BT1 primary conversion
BT2 conversion
BT1 tree surgery
BT2 disease control
BT3 control
BT2 pruning
rt silviculture

delinquency
USE **delinquent behaviour**

DELINQUENT BEHAVIOR
BF delinquent behaviour
BT1 antisocial behavior (agricola)
BT2 human behavior

DELINQUENT BEHAVIOR *cont.*
  BT3 behavior

DELINQUENT BEHAVIOUR
AF delinquent behavior
uf *delinquency*
BT1 social behaviour
  BT2 behaviour
NT1 addiction
  NT2 drug addiction
NT1 vandalism
rt crime
rt social unrest

DELINTING
BT1 processing
rt lint

DELONIX
BT1 leguminosae
NT1 delonix elata
NT1 delonix regia

DELONIX ELATA
BT1 delonix
  BT2 leguminosae

DELONIX REGIA
BT1 delonix
  BT2 leguminosae
BT1 forest trees
BT1 ornamental woody plants

DELOSPERMA
BT1 aizoaceae
NT1 delosperma alba

DELOSPERMA ALBA
BT1 delosperma
  BT2 aizoaceae
BT1 ornamental succulent plants
  BT2 succulent plants

DELPHACIDAE
BT1 fulgoroidea
  BT2 auchenorrhyncha
    BT3 homoptera
NT1 delphacodes
NT1 javesella
  NT2 javesella pellucida
NT1 laodelphax
  NT2 laodelphax striatella
NT1 nilaparvata
  NT2 nilaparvata bakeri
  NT2 nilaparvata lugens
NT1 peregrinus
  NT2 peregrinus maidis
NT1 perkinsiella
  NT2 perkinsiella saccharicida
NT1 sogata
NT1 sogatella
  NT2 sogatella furcifera
NT1 sogatodes
  NT2 sogatodes cubanus
  NT2 sogatodes orizicola
NT1 toya
  NT2 toya propinqua

DELPHACODES
BT1 delphacidae
  BT2 fulgoroidea
    BT3 auchenorrhyncha
      BT4 homoptera
rt toya

delphacodes propinqua
USE **toya propinqua**

DELPHI METHOD
BT1 forecasts
BT1 statistics
rt prediction

DELPHINAPTERUS
BT1 monodontidae
  BT2 odontoceti
    BT3 cetacea
      BT4 mammals
NT1 delphinapterus leucas

DELPHINAPTERUS LEUCAS
BT1 delphinapterus
  BT2 monodontidae
    BT3 odontoceti

DELPHINAPTERUS LEUCAS *cont.*
      BT4 cetacea
        BT5 mammals

DELPHINIDAE
BT1 odontoceti
  BT2 cetacea
    BT3 mammals
NT1 cephalorhynchus
NT1 delphinus
NT1 lagenorhynchus
NT1 stenella
  NT2 stenella coeruleoalba
NT1 tursiops
  NT2 tursiops truncatus
rt dolphins

DELPHINIDIN
BT1 anthocyanidins
  BT2 flavonoids
    BT3 aromatic compounds
    BT3 plant pigments
      BT4 pigments

DELPHININ
BT1 anthocyanins
  BT2 glycoflavones
    BT3 flavonoids
      BT4 aromatic compounds
      BT4 plant pigments
        BT5 pigments
    BT3 glycosides
      BT4 carbohydrates

DELPHINIUM
BT1 ranunculaceae
NT1 delphinium barbeyi
NT1 delphinium bicolor
NT1 delphinium biternatum
NT1 delphinium brachycentrum
NT1 delphinium cardiopetalum
NT1 delphinium cashmerianum
NT1 delphinium crassifolium
NT1 delphinium dictyocarpum
NT1 delphinium elisabethae
NT1 delphinium geyeri
NT1 delphinium glaucescens
NT1 delphinium grandiflorum
NT1 delphinium maackianum
NT1 delphinium occidentale
NT1 delphinium pentagynum
NT1 delphinium semibarbatum
NT1 delphinium staphisagria
NT1 delphinium tamarae
NT1 delphinium tricorne
NT1 delphinium triste

delphinium ajacis
USE **consolida ambigua**

DELPHINIUM BARBEYI
BT1 delphinium
  BT2 ranunculaceae

DELPHINIUM BICOLOR
BT1 delphinium
  BT2 ranunculaceae
BT1 ornamental herbaceous plants

DELPHINIUM BITERNATUM
BT1 delphinium
  BT2 ranunculaceae

DELPHINIUM BRACHYCENTRUM
BT1 delphinium
  BT2 ranunculaceae

DELPHINIUM CARDIOPETALUM
BT1 delphinium
  BT2 ranunculaceae

DELPHINIUM CASHMERIANUM
BT1 delphinium
  BT2 ranunculaceae
BT1 ornamental herbaceous plants

delphinium consolida
USE **consolida regalis**

DELPHINIUM CRASSIFOLIUM
BT1 delphinium
  BT2 ranunculaceae

DELPHINIUM DICTYOCARPUM
BT1 delphinium
  BT2 ranunculaceae

DELPHINIUM ELISABETHAE
BT1 delphinium
  BT2 ranunculaceae

DELPHINIUM GEYERI
BT1 delphinium
  BT2 ranunculaceae

DELPHINIUM GLAUCESCENS
BT1 delphinium
  BT2 ranunculaceae

DELPHINIUM GRANDIFLORUM
BT1 delphinium
  BT2 ranunculaceae
BT1 ornamental herbaceous plants

DELPHINIUM MAACKIANUM
BT1 delphinium
  BT2 ranunculaceae

DELPHINIUM OCCIDENTALE
BT1 delphinium
  BT2 ranunculaceae

DELPHINIUM PENTAGYNUM
BT1 delphinium
  BT2 ranunculaceae

DELPHINIUM SEMIBARBATUM
BT1 delphinium
  BT2 ranunculaceae

DELPHINIUM STAPHISAGRIA
BT1 delphinium
  BT2 ranunculaceae
BT1 insecticidal plants
  BT2 pesticidal plants
BT1 poisonous plants

DELPHINIUM TAMARAE
BT1 delphinium
  BT2 ranunculaceae

DELPHINIUM TRICORNE
BT1 delphinium
  BT2 ranunculaceae

DELPHINIUM TRISTE
BT1 delphinium
  BT2 ranunculaceae

DELPHINUS
BT1 delphinidae
  BT2 odontoceti
    BT3 cetacea
      BT4 mammals

DELTA SOILS
BT1 soil types (physiographic)

DELTA STATES OF USA
BT1 southern states of usa
  BT2 usa
    BT3 north america
      BT4 america
NT1 arkansas
NT1 louisiana
NT1 mississippi

deltaic areas
USE **deltas**

DELTAMETHRIN
BT1 ectoparasiticides
  BT2 antiparasitic agents
    BT3 drugs
BT1 pyrethroid insecticides
  BT2 insecticides
    BT3 pesticides
  BT2 pyrethroids

DELTAS
uf *deltaic areas*
BT1 physiographic features
rt alluvial land
rt rivers
rt wetlands

DELUSORY PARASITOSES
BT1 psychoses

DELUSORY PARASITOSES *cont.*
  BT2 mental disorders
    BT3 functional disorders
      BT4 animal disorders
        BT5 disorders
rt ectoparasitoses
rt parasitoses

DEMAND
BT1 supply balance
  BT2 market economics
    BT3 economics
rt consumption
rt supply

DEMAND ELASTICITIES
BT1 elasticities
  BT2 econometrics
rt price elasticities

DEMAND FUNCTIONS
BT1 econometrics
rt economic analysis

dematophora
USE **rosellinia**

dematophora necatrix
USE **rosellinia necatrix**

DEMECOLCINE
uf *colchamine*
BT1 antineoplastic agents
  BT2 drugs
BT1 isoquinoline alkaloids
  BT2 alkaloids
rt colchicine

DEMETON
BT1 organothiophosphate insecticides
  BT2 organophosphorus insecticides
    BT3 insecticides
      BT4 pesticides
    BT3 organophosphorus pesticides
      BT4 organophosphorus compounds

DEMETON-O-METHYL
BT1 organothiophosphate insecticides
  BT2 organophosphorus insecticides
    BT3 insecticides
      BT4 pesticides
    BT3 organophosphorus pesticides
      BT4 organophosphorus compounds

DEMETON-S-METHYL
BT1 organothiophosphate acaricides
  BT2 organophosphorus acaricides
    BT3 acaricides
      BT4 pesticides
    BT3 organophosphorus pesticides
      BT4 organophosphorus compounds
BT1 organothiophosphate insecticides
  BT2 organophosphorus insecticides
    BT3 insecticides
      BT4 pesticides
    BT3 organophosphorus pesticides
      BT4 organophosphorus compounds

DEMETON-S-METHYLSULPHON
BT1 organothiophosphate acaricides
  BT2 organophosphorus acaricides
    BT3 acaricides
      BT4 pesticides
    BT3 organophosphorus pesticides

DEMETON-S-METHYLSULPHON *cont.*
BT4 organophosphorus compounds
BT1 organothiophosphate insecticides
BT2 organophosphorus insecticides
BT3 insecticides
BT4 pesticides
BT3 organophosphorus pesticides
BT4 organophosphorus compounds

DEMINERALIZATION
BT1 processing
rt bone resorption
rt desalinization

DEMOCRACY
BT1 political systems
BT2 politics
rt parliament

democratic kampuchea
USE **cambodia**

democratic yemen
USE **yemen democratic republic**

DEMODEX
BT1 demodicidae
BT2 prostigmata
BT3 acari
NT1 demodex bovis
NT1 demodex brevis
NT1 demodex canis
NT1 demodex caprae
NT1 demodex cati
NT1 demodex criceti
NT1 demodex folliculorum
NT1 demodex kutzeri
NT1 demodex ovis
NT1 demodex phylloides

DEMODEX BOVIS
BT1 demodex
BT2 demodicidae
BT3 prostigmata
BT4 acari

DEMODEX BREVIS
BT1 demodex
BT2 demodicidae
BT3 prostigmata
BT4 acari

DEMODEX CANIS
BT1 demodex
BT2 demodicidae
BT3 prostigmata
BT4 acari

DEMODEX CAPRAE
BT1 demodex
BT2 demodicidae
BT3 prostigmata
BT4 acari

DEMODEX CATI
HN from 1989
BT1 demodex
BT2 demodicidae
BT3 prostigmata
BT4 acari

DEMODEX CRICETI
HN from 1989
BT1 demodex
BT2 demodicidae
BT3 prostigmata
BT4 acari

DEMODEX FOLLICULORUM
BT1 demodex
BT2 demodicidae
BT3 prostigmata
BT4 acari

DEMODEX KUTZERI
HN from 1990
BT1 demodex
BT2 demodicidae

DEMODEX KUTZERI *cont.*
BT3 prostigmata
BT4 acari

DEMODEX OVIS
HN from 1989
BT1 demodex
BT2 demodicidae
BT3 prostigmata
BT4 acari

DEMODEX PHYLLOIDES
HN from 1990
BT1 demodex
BT2 demodicidae
BT3 prostigmata
BT4 acari

DEMODICIDAE
BT1 prostigmata
BT2 acari
NT1 demodex
NT2 demodex bovis
NT2 demodex brevis
NT2 demodex canis
NT2 demodex caprae
NT2 demodex cati
NT2 demodex criceti
NT2 demodex folliculorum
NT2 demodex kutzeri
NT2 demodex ovis
NT2 demodex phylloides

DEMOGRAPHY
BT1 statistics
NT1 population distribution
rt migration
rt populations

DEMONSTRATION FARMS
BT1 advisory centres
BT2 information centres
BT3 information services
BT4 services
BT1 farms
rt displays
rt open days
rt pilot farms

DEMONSTRATION FORESTS
(for demonstration and instructional purposes)
BT1 forests
BT2 vegetation types
rt extension

DEMOSPONGIA
BT1 parazoa

DEMYELINATION
BT1 nervous system diseases
BT2 organic diseases
BT3 diseases
rt myelin

DENATURATION
BT1 processing
rt proteins

DENDRANTHEMA
BT1 compositae
NT1 dendranthema indicum
NT1 dendranthema morifolium

DENDRANTHEMA INDICUM
uf *chrysanthemum indicum*
BT1 dendranthema
BT2 compositae
rt chrysanthemums

DENDRANTHEMA MORIFOLIUM
uf *chrysanthemum morifolium*
BT1 dendranthema
BT2 compositae
rt chrysanthemums

DENDROBAENA
BT1 lumbricidae
BT2 oligochaeta
BT3 annelida
rt dendrodrilus

dendrobaena rubida
USE **dendrodrilus rubidus**

dendrobaena rubida tenuis
USE **dendrodrilus rubidus**

DENDROBIUM
BT1 orchidaceae
NT1 dendrobium aduncum
NT1 dendrobium aphyllum
NT1 dendrobium barbulatum
NT1 dendrobium codonosepalum
NT1 dendrobium crumenatum
NT1 dendrobium densiflorum
NT1 dendrobium farmeri
NT1 dendrobium fimbriatum
NT1 dendrobium isochiloides
NT1 dendrobium lichenastrum
NT1 dendrobium moniliforme
NT1 dendrobium nobile
NT1 dendrobium ochreatum
NT1 dendrobium palpebrae
NT1 dendrobium phalaenopsis
NT1 dendrobium punamense
NT1 dendrobium ruppianum

DENDROBIUM ADUNCUM
BT1 dendrobium
BT2 orchidaceae
BT1 ornamental orchids

dendrobium amoenum
USE **dendrobium aphyllum**

DENDROBIUM APHYLLUM
uf *dendrobium amoenum*
BT1 dendrobium
BT2 orchidaceae
BT1 ornamental orchids

DENDROBIUM BARBULATUM
BT1 dendrobium
BT2 orchidaceae
BT1 ornamental orchids

DENDROBIUM CODONOSEPALUM
BT1 dendrobium
BT2 orchidaceae
BT1 ornamental orchids

DENDROBIUM CRUMENATUM
BT1 dendrobium
BT2 orchidaceae
BT1 ornamental orchids

DENDROBIUM DENSIFLORUM
uf *dendrobium thyrsiflorum*
BT1 dendrobium
BT2 orchidaceae
BT1 ornamental orchids

DENDROBIUM FARMERI
BT1 dendrobium
BT2 orchidaceae
BT1 ornamental orchids

DENDROBIUM FIMBRIATUM
BT1 dendrobium
BT2 orchidaceae
BT1 ornamental orchids

DENDROBIUM ISOCHILOIDES
BT1 dendrobium
BT2 orchidaceae
BT1 ornamental orchids

DENDROBIUM LICHENASTRUM
BT1 dendrobium
BT2 orchidaceae
BT1 ornamental orchids

dendrobium monile
USE **dendrobium moniliforme**

DENDROBIUM MONILIFORME
uf *dendrobium monile*
BT1 dendrobium
BT2 orchidaceae
BT1 ornamental orchids

DENDROBIUM NOBILE
BT1 dendrobium
BT2 orchidaceae
BT1 medicinal plants
BT1 ornamental orchids

DENDROBIUM OCHREATUM
BT1 dendrobium

DENDROBIUM OCHREATUM *cont.*
BT2 orchidaceae
BT1 ornamental orchids

DENDROBIUM PALPEBRAE
BT1 dendrobium
BT2 orchidaceae
BT1 ornamental orchids

DENDROBIUM PHALAENOPSIS
BT1 dendrobium
BT2 orchidaceae
BT1 ornamental orchids

DENDROBIUM PUNAMENSE
BT1 dendrobium
BT2 orchidaceae
BT1 ornamental orchids

DENDROBIUM RUPPIANUM
BT1 dendrobium
BT2 orchidaceae
BT1 ornamental orchids

dendrobium thyrsiflorum
USE **dendrobium densiflorum**

DENDROCALAMUS
BT1 gramineae
NT1 dendrocalamus giganteus
NT1 dendrocalamus hamiltonii
NT1 dendrocalamus latiflorus
NT1 dendrocalamus strictus
rt bamboos
rt sinocalamus

DENDROCALAMUS GIGANTEUS
HN from 1990
BT1 dendrocalamus
BT2 gramineae

DENDROCALAMUS HAMILTONII
HN from 1990
BT1 dendrocalamus
BT2 gramineae

DENDROCALAMUS LATIFLORUS
uf *sinocalamus latiflorus*
BT1 dendrocalamus
BT2 gramineae

DENDROCALAMUS STRICTUS
BT1 dendrocalamus
BT2 gramineae

DENDROCERUS
BT1 megaspilidae
BT2 hymenoptera
NT1 dendrocerus carpenteri

DENDROCERUS CARPENTERI
BT1 dendrocerus
BT2 megaspilidae
BT3 hymenoptera

DENDROCHRONOLOGY
BT1 age determination
BT2 determination
BT3 techniques
rt age
rt bioclimatic indexes
rt growth rings
rt time

DENDROCLIMATOLOGY
BT1 climatology
rt growth rings

DENDROCOELIDAE
BT1 tricladida
BT2 turbellaria
NT1 dendrocoelum

DENDROCOELUM
BT1 dendrocoelidae
BT2 tricladida
BT3 turbellaria

DENDROCTONUS
BT1 scolytidae
BT2 coleoptera
NT1 dendroctonus adjunctus
NT1 dendroctonus brevicomis
NT1 dendroctonus frontalis
NT1 dendroctonus micans

DENDROCTONUS *cont.*
NT1 dendroctonus ponderosae
NT1 dendroctonus pseudotsugae
NT1 dendroctonus rufipennis
NT1 dendroctonus terebrans
NT1 dendroctonus valens

DENDROCTONUS ADJUNCTUS
BT1 dendroctonus
BT2 scolytidae
BT3 coleoptera

DENDROCTONUS BREVICOMIS
BT1 dendroctonus
BT2 scolytidae
BT3 coleoptera
rt brevicomin

DENDROCTONUS FRONTALIS
BT1 dendroctonus
BT2 scolytidae
BT3 coleoptera
rt frontalin

DENDROCTONUS MICANS
BT1 dendroctonus
BT2 scolytidae
BT3 coleoptera

dendroctonus obesus
USE **dendroctonus rufipennis**

DENDROCTONUS PONDEROSAE
BT1 dendroctonus
BT2 scolytidae
BT3 coleoptera

DENDROCTONUS PSEUDOTSUGAE
BT1 dendroctonus
BT2 scolytidae
BT3 coleoptera

DENDROCTONUS RUFIPENNIS
uf *dendroctonus obesus*
BT1 dendroctonus
BT2 scolytidae
BT3 coleoptera

DENDROCTONUS TEREBRANS
BT1 dendroctonus
BT2 scolytidae
BT3 coleoptera

DENDROCTONUS VALENS
BT1 dendroctonus
BT2 scolytidae
BT3 coleoptera

DENDRODOCHIUM
BT1 deuteromycotina
NT1 dendrodochium toxicum

DENDRODOCHIUM TOXICUM
BT1 dendrodochium
BT2 deuteromycotina

DENDRODRILUS
BT1 lumbricidae
BT2 oligochaeta
BT3 annelida
NT1 dendrodrilus rubidus
rt dendrobaena

DENDRODRILUS RUBIDUS
uf *dendrobaena rubida*
uf *dendrobaena rubida tenuis*
BT1 dendrodrilus
BT2 lumbricidae
BT3 oligochaeta
BT4 annelida

DENDROLIMUS
BT1 lasiocampidae
BT2 lepidoptera
NT1 dendrolimus pini
NT1 dendrolimus punctatus
NT1 dendrolimus sibiricus
NT1 dendrolimus spectabilis
NT1 dendrolimus superans

DENDROLIMUS PINI
BT1 dendrolimus
BT2 lasiocampidae
BT3 lepidoptera

DENDROLIMUS PUNCTATUS
BT1 dendrolimus
BT2 lasiocampidae
BT3 lepidoptera

DENDROLIMUS SIBIRICUS
BT1 dendrolimus
BT2 lasiocampidae
BT3 lepidoptera

DENDROLIMUS SPECTABILIS
BT1 dendrolimus
BT2 lasiocampidae
BT3 lepidoptera

DENDROLIMUS SUPERANS
BT1 dendrolimus
BT2 lasiocampidae
BT3 lepidoptera

dendrology
USE **silvicultural characters**

DENDROMETERS
BT1 instruments
rt diameter
rt mensuration

DENDROPHOMA
HN from 1990
BT1 deuteromycotina
rt phomopsis

dendrophoma obscurans
USE **phomopsis obscurans**

DENDROPHTHOE
BT1 loranthaceae
NT1 dendrophthoe falcata
rt mistletoes

DENDROPHTHOE FALCATA
BT1 dendrophthoe
BT2 loranthaceae

DENDROSOTER
BT1 braconidae
BT2 hymenoptera
NT1 dendrosoter protuberans

DENDROSOTER PROTUBERANS
BT1 dendrosoter
BT2 braconidae
BT3 hymenoptera

DENERVATION
BT1 surgical operations

DENGUE
BT1 human diseases
BT2 diseases
BT1 mosquito-borne diseases
BT2 vector-borne diseases
BT3 diseases
BT1 viral diseases
BT2 infectious diseases
BT3 diseases
NT1 dengue haemorrhagic fever
rt dengue virus

DENGUE HAEMORRHAGIC FEVER
AF dengue hemorrhagic fever
BT1 dengue
BT2 human diseases
BT3 diseases
BT2 mosquito-borne diseases
BT3 vector-borne diseases
BT4 diseases
BT2 viral diseases
BT3 infectious diseases
BT4 diseases
rt fever

DENGUE HEMORRHAGIC FEVER
BF dengue haemorrhagic fever

DENGUE VIRUS
BT1 flavivirus
BT2 arboviruses
BT3 pathogens
BT2 flaviviridae
BT3 viruses
rt dengue

DENIM (AGRICOLA)
BT1 fabrics

DENITRIFICATION
rt denitrifying microorganisms
rt nitrogen
rt soil biology

DENITRIFYING MICROORGANISMS
uf *microorganisms, denitrifying*
BT1 microorganisms
rt denitrification

DENMARK
BT1 scandinavia
BT2 europe
NT1 bornholm
NT1 fyn
NT1 jutland
NT1 lolland falster
NT1 zealand
rt european communities
rt faroe islands
rt greenland
rt oecd

denmark (bornholm)
USE **bornholm**

denmark (fyn)
USE **fyn**

denmark (jutland)
USE **jutland**

denmark (lolland falster)
USE **lolland falster**

denmark (zealand)
USE **zealand**

DENNETTIA
BT1 annonaceae
NT1 dennettia tripetala

DENNETTIA TRIPETALA
BT1 dennettia
BT2 annonaceae

DENNSTAEDTIA
BT1 dennstaedtiaceae
NT1 dennstaedtia punctilobula

DENNSTAEDTIA PUNCTILOBULA
BT1 dennstaedtia
BT2 dennstaedtiaceae

DENNSTAEDTIACEAE
NT1 dennstaedtia
NT2 dennstaedtia punctilobula
NT1 pteridium
NT2 pteridium aquilinum
NT2 pteridium aquilinum var. esculentum
NT2 pteridium aquilinum var. pubescens

DENSITOMETERS
BT1 instruments
rt absorbance
rt densitometry

DENSITOMETRY
BT1 analytical methods
BT2 methodology
rt absorbance
rt densitometers

DENSITY
NT1 body density
NT1 bone density
NT1 bulk density
NT1 charge density
NT1 compacted density
NT1 nutrient density (agricola)
NT1 plant density
NT2 crop density
NT3 row spacing
NT2 stand density
NT1 population density
NT1 soil density
NT2 aggregate density
NT2 particle density
NT1 stocking density

DENSITY *cont.*
NT1 wood density
rt cage density
rt consistency
rt density gradient centrifugation
rt inoculum density
rt mass
rt specific gravity
rt stand characteristics
rt thermogravimetry

density, bulk
USE **bulk density**

density, compacted
USE **compacted density**

density, crop
USE **crop density**

DENSITY DEPENDENT SELECTION
HN from 1989
BT1 selection

DENSITY GRADIENT CENTRIFUGATION
BT1 centrifugation
BT2 separation
rt density

density of stocking
USE **stocking density**

density, optical
USE **absorbance**

density, planting
USE **crop density**
OR **spacing**

DENSONUCLEOSIS VIRUSES
BT1 densovirus
BT2 insect viruses
BT3 entomopathogens
BT4 pathogens
BT2 parvoviridae
BT3 viruses

DENSOVIRUS
BT1 insect viruses
BT2 entomopathogens
BT3 pathogens
BT1 parvoviridae
BT2 viruses
NT1 densonucleosis viruses

DENT MAIZE
rt maize

DENTAL CARIES
uf *caries*
uf *teeth caries*
BT1 tooth diseases
BT2 mouth diseases
BT3 organic diseases
BT4 diseases
rt cariogenic foods (agricola)
rt decay
rt fluoridation
rt teeth

DENTAL HEALTH (AGRICOLA)
BT1 health
NT1 nursing bottle syndrome (agricola)
rt dentists (agricola)
rt tooth diseases

DENTAL PLAQUE
uf *plaque*
BT1 tooth diseases
BT2 mouth diseases
BT3 organic diseases
BT4 diseases
rt teeth

dental prostheses
USE **dentures**

DENTINE
BT1 teeth
BT2 jaws
BT3 bones
BT4 musculoskeletal system

DENTINE *cont.*
BT5 body parts
rt enamel

DENTISTRY
BT1 occupations
NT1 preventive dentistry (agricola)
rt dentists (agricola)
rt teeth

DENTISTS (AGRICOLA)
BT1 people
rt dental health (agricola)
rt dentistry

DENTITION
BT1 teeth
BT2 jaws
BT3 bones
BT4 musculoskeletal system
BT5 body parts

DENTURES
uf *dental prostheses*
BT1 prostheses
rt teeth

DEODORIZING
BT1 processing
rt odour abatement
rt odours
rt sodium bicarbonate

DEOIS
BT1 cercopidae
BT2 cercopoidea
BT3 auchenorrhyncha
BT4 homoptera
NT1 deois flavopicta
NT1 deois schach

DEOIS FLAVOPICTA
BT1 deois
BT2 cercopidae
BT3 cercopoidea
BT4 auchenorrhyncha
BT5 homoptera

DEOIS SCHACH
BT1 deois
BT2 cercopidae
BT3 cercopoidea
BT4 auchenorrhyncha
BT5 homoptera

DEONI
BT1 cattle breeds
BT2 breeds

DEOXYADENOSINE
BT1 deoxyribonucleosides
BT2 nucleosides
BT3 glycosides
BT4 carbohydrates

DEOXYCHOLIC ACID
uf *glycodehydroxycholic acid*
BT1 bile acids
BT1 digestants
BT2 gastrointestinal agents
BT3 drugs
rt bile secretion

deoxycorticosterone
USE **desoxycortone**

2-DEOXY-D-GLUCOSE
BT1 deoxysugars
BT2 sugars
BT3 carbohydrates
BT1 hexoses
BT2 aldoses
BT3 monosaccharides
BT4 carbohydrates
BT3 reducing sugars
BT4 sugars
BT5 carbohydrates
rt glucose

deoxynivalenol
USE **vomitoxin**

4-DEOXYPYRIDOXINE
BT1 vitamin b antagonists

4-DEOXYPYRIDOXINE *cont.*
BT2 vitamin antagonists
BT3 antagonists
BT4 metabolic inhibitors
BT5 inhibitors

DEOXYRIBONUCLEASE I
(ec 3.1.21.1)
uf *dnase*
BT1 nucleases
BT2 esterases
BT3 hydrolases
BT4 enzymes
rt dna

deoxyribonucleic acid
USE **dna**

DEOXYRIBONUCLEOSIDES
BT1 nucleosides
BT2 glycosides
BT3 carbohydrates
NT1 cordycepin
NT1 deoxyadenosine
NT1 deoxyuridines
NT2 broxuridine
NT2 deoxyuridine
NT2 floxuridine
NT2 idoxuridine
NT1 thymidine

DEOXYSUGARS
BT1 sugars
BT2 carbohydrates
NT1 2-deoxy-d-glucose
NT1 fucose
NT1 rhamnose

DEOXYURIDINE
BT1 deoxyuridines
BT2 deoxyribonucleosides
BT3 nucleosides
BT4 glycosides
BT5 carbohydrates

DEOXYURIDINES
BT1 deoxyribonucleosides
BT2 nucleosides
BT3 glycosides
BT4 carbohydrates
NT1 broxuridine
NT1 deoxyuridine
NT1 floxuridine
NT1 idoxuridine

2,4-DEP
BT1 auxins
BT2 plant growth regulators
BT3 growth regulators
BT1 phenoxy herbicides
BT2 herbicides
BT3 pesticides

DEPLETION
BT1 exhaustion
NT1 protein depletion

depopulation
USE **rural depopulation**

DEPOSITION
NT1 spore deposition
rt chemical precipitation
rt deposition site
rt placement

deposition, sediment
USE **geological sedimentation**

DEPOSITION SITE
rt artificial insemination
rt deposition

DEPOT FAT
BT1 body fat
BT2 fat

DEPRECIATION
(reduction in value of tangible assets as a result of aging)
rt accounting
rt capital

DEPRESSARIA
BT1 oecophoridae

DEPRESSARIA *cont.*
BT2 lepidoptera

DEPRESSION
BT1 mental disorders
BT2 functional disorders
BT3 animal disorders
BT4 disorders
rt antidepressants
rt doping
rt economic depression

DEPRIVATION
NT1 energy deprivation
NT1 food deprivation
rt basic needs
rt basic services
rt fasting
rt living conditions
rt poverty
rt protein deprivation
rt starvation

DEPTH
BT1 dimensions
rt application depth
rt depth wheels
rt planting depth
rt rooting depth
rt soil depth
rt sowing depth

DEPTH WHEELS
BT1 wheels
BT2 components
rt cultivators
rt depth
rt draught control
rt ploughs

DERA DIN PANAH
HN from 1990
BT1 goat breeds
BT2 breeds

DERAEOCORIS
BT1 miridae
BT2 heteroptera
NT1 deraeocoris brevis

DERAEOCORIS BREVIS
BT1 deraeocoris
BT2 miridae
BT3 heteroptera

DERBYSHIRE GRITSTONE
BT1 sheep breeds
BT2 breeds

DEREGULATION
rt regulations
rt transport

DERELICT LAND
BT1 land types

DERIVATIVES

DERMACENTOR
BT1 ixodidae
BT2 metastigmata
BT3 acari
NT1 dermacentor albipictus
NT1 dermacentor andersoni
NT1 dermacentor auratus
NT1 dermacentor daghestanicus
NT1 dermacentor marginatus
NT1 dermacentor nuttalli
NT1 dermacentor occidentalis
NT1 dermacentor parumapertus
NT1 dermacentor pictus
NT1 dermacentor reticulatus
NT1 dermacentor silvarum
NT1 dermacentor variabilis
rt anocentor

DERMACENTOR ALBIPICTUS
BT1 dermacentor
BT2 ixodidae
BT3 metastigmata
BT4 acari

DERMACENTOR ANDERSONI
BT1 dermacentor
BT2 ixodidae

DERMACENTOR ANDERSONI *cont.*
BT3 metastigmata
BT4 acari

DERMACENTOR AURATUS
HN from 1989
BT1 dermacentor
BT2 ixodidae
BT3 metastigmata
BT4 acari

DERMACENTOR DAGHESTANICUS
BT1 dermacentor
BT2 ixodidae
BT3 metastigmata
BT4 acari

DERMACENTOR MARGINATUS
BT1 dermacentor
BT2 ixodidae
BT3 metastigmata
BT4 acari

dermacentor nitens
USE **anocentor nitens**

DERMACENTOR NUTTALLI
BT1 dermacentor
BT2 ixodidae
BT3 metastigmata
BT4 acari

DERMACENTOR OCCIDENTALIS
BT1 dermacentor
BT2 ixodidae
BT3 metastigmata
BT4 acari

DERMACENTOR PARUMAPERTUS
HN from 1989
BT1 dermacentor
BT2 ixodidae
BT3 metastigmata
BT4 acari

DERMACENTOR PICTUS
BT1 dermacentor
BT2 ixodidae
BT3 metastigmata
BT4 acari

DERMACENTOR RETICULATUS
BT1 dermacentor
BT2 ixodidae
BT3 metastigmata
BT4 acari

DERMACENTOR SILVARUM
BT1 dermacentor
BT2 ixodidae
BT3 metastigmata
BT4 acari

DERMACENTOR VARIABILIS
BT1 dermacentor
BT2 ixodidae
BT3 metastigmata
BT4 acari

DERMANTSI PIED
BT1 pig breeds
BT2 breeds

DERMANYSSIDAE
BT1 mesostigmata
BT2 acari
NT1 dermanyssus
NT2 dermanyssus gallinae
NT2 dermanyssus hirundinis
NT1 liponyssoides

DERMANYSSUS
BT1 dermanyssidae
BT2 mesostigmata
BT3 acari
NT1 dermanyssus gallinae
NT1 dermanyssus hirundinis

DERMANYSSUS GALLINAE
BT1 dermanyssus
BT2 dermanyssidae
BT3 mesostigmata
BT4 acari

DERMANYSSUS HIRUNDINIS
HN from 1990
BT1 dermanyssus
BT2 dermanyssidae
BT3 mesostigmata
BT4 acari

DERMAPTERA
NT1 anisolabiidae
NT2 anisolabis
NT2 euborellia
NT3 euborellia annulipes
NT1 forficulidae
NT2 doru
NT3 doru lineare
NT2 forficula
NT3 forficula auricularia
NT1 labiduridae
NT2 labidura
NT3 labidura riparia
NT2 nala
NT3 nala lividipes
rt insects

DERMATITIS
BT1 skin diseases
BT2 organic diseases
BT3 diseases
NT1 acrodermatitis
NT2 acrodermatitis enteropathica
NT1 cercarial dermatitis
NT1 dermatitis herpetiformis
NT1 interdigital dermatitis
NT1 pododermatitis
NT1 sunburn
rt eczema
rt sweet itch

DERMATITIS HERPETIFORMIS
BT1 dermatitis
BT2 skin diseases
BT3 organic diseases
BT4 diseases

DERMATOBIA
BT1 cuterebridae
BT2 diptera
NT1 dermatobia hominis

DERMATOBIA HOMINIS
BT1 dermatobia
BT2 cuterebridae
BT3 diptera

DERMATOLOGICAL AGENTS
uf skin dressings
BT1 drugs
NT1 allantoin
NT1 astringents
NT1 aurothioglucose
NT1 betamethasone
NT1 calcium hydroxide
NT1 dexamethasone
NT1 dichloroacetic acid
NT1 formic acid
NT1 hydrocortisone
NT1 linseed oil
NT1 olive oil
NT1 petrolatum
NT1 pyrogallol triacetate
NT1 resorcinol
NT1 retinoic acid
NT1 salicylic acid
NT1 turpentine
rt antiinfective agents
rt antiinflammatory agents
rt dermatology
rt ointments

DERMATOLOGY
BT1 medicine
rt dermatological agents
rt skin diseases

DERMATOMYCOSES
BT1 mycoses
BT2 infectious diseases
BT3 diseases
BT1 skin diseases
BT2 organic diseases
BT3 diseases
NT1 pityriasis versicolor

DERMATOMYCOSES *cont.*
NT1 tinea nigra
rt dermatophytes

DERMATOPHAGOIDES
BT1 pyroglyphidae
BT2 astigmata
BT3 acari
NT1 dermatophagoides farinae
NT1 dermatophagoides microceras
NT1 dermatophagoides pteronyssinus
NT1 dermatophagoides scheremetewskyi
rt house dust mites

dermatophagoides culinae
USE **dermatophagoides farinae**

DERMATOPHAGOIDES FARINAE
uf dermatophagoides culinae
BT1 dermatophagoides
BT2 pyroglyphidae
BT3 astigmata
BT4 acari

DERMATOPHAGOIDES MICROCERAS
HN from 1989
BT1 dermatophagoides
BT2 pyroglyphidae
BT3 astigmata
BT4 acari

DERMATOPHAGOIDES PTERONYSSINUS
BT1 dermatophagoides
BT2 pyroglyphidae
BT3 astigmata
BT4 acari

DERMATOPHAGOIDES SCHEREMETEWSKYI
BT1 dermatophagoides
BT2 pyroglyphidae
BT3 astigmata
BT4 acari

DERMATOPHILACEAE
BT1 actinomycetales
BT2 firmicutes
BT3 bacteria
BT4 prokaryotes
NT1 dermatophilus
NT2 dermatophilus congolensis

DERMATOPHILUS
BT1 dermatophilaceae
BT2 actinomycetales
BT3 firmicutes
BT4 bacteria
BT5 prokaryotes
NT1 dermatophilus congolensis

DERMATOPHILUS CONGOLENSIS
uf dermatophilus dermatonomus
BT1 dermatophilus
BT2 dermatophilaceae
BT3 actinomycetales
BT4 firmicutes
BT5 bacteria
BT6 prokaryotes

dermatophilus dermatonomus
USE **dermatophilus congolensis**

DERMATOPHYTES
rt arthroderma
rt dermatomycoses
rt epidermophyton
rt keratinophilic fungi
rt microsporum
rt nannizzia
rt trichophyton

dermatoses
USE **skin diseases**

DERMESTES
BT1 dermestidae
BT2 coleoptera

DERMESTES *cont.*
NT1 dermestes ater
NT1 dermestes lardarius
NT1 dermestes maculatus

DERMESTES ATER
BT1 dermestes
BT2 dermestidae
BT3 coleoptera

DERMESTES LARDARIUS
BT1 dermestes
BT2 dermestidae
BT3 coleoptera

DERMESTES MACULATUS
uf dermestes vulpinus
BT1 dermestes
BT2 dermestidae
BT3 coleoptera

dermestes vulpinus
USE **dermestes maculatus**

DERMESTIDAE
BT1 coleoptera
NT1 anthrenus
NT2 anthrenus flavipes
NT2 anthrenus fuscus
NT2 anthrenus verbasci
NT1 attagenus
NT2 attagenus unicolor
NT1 dermestes
NT2 dermestes ater
NT2 dermestes lardarius
NT2 dermestes maculatus
NT1 trogoderma
NT2 trogoderma glabrum
NT2 trogoderma granarium
NT2 trogoderma inclusum
NT2 trogoderma variabile

DERMIS
BT1 skin
BT2 integument
BT3 body parts

DERMOCHELYIDAE
BT1 testudines
BT2 reptiles
NT1 dermochelys

DERMOCHELYS
BT1 dermochelyidae
BT2 testudines
BT3 reptiles

DERMOCYSTIDIUM
BT1 apicomplexa
BT2 protozoa
NT1 dermocystidium anguillae

DERMOCYSTIDIUM ANGUILLAE
BT1 dermocystidium
BT2 apicomplexa
BT3 protozoa

DERMOPTERA
BT1 mammals
NT1 cynocephalidae
NT2 cynocephalus

DERNOPODZOLIC SOILS
BT1 podzoluvisols
BT2 soil types (genetic)

DEROCERAS
uf agriolimax
BT1 limacidae
BT2 gastropoda
BT3 mollusca
NT1 deroceras laeve
NT1 deroceras panormitanum
NT1 deroceras reticulatum

deroceras caruanae
USE **deroceras panormitanum**

DEROCERAS LAEVE
BT1 deroceras
BT2 limacidae
BT3 gastropoda
BT4 mollusca

DEROCERAS PANORMITANUM
HN from 1990
uf deroceras caruanae
BT1 deroceras
BT2 limacidae
BT3 gastropoda
BT4 mollusca

DEROCERAS RETICULATUM
uf agriolimax reticulatus
BT1 deroceras
BT2 limacidae
BT3 gastropoda
BT4 mollusca

DEROGENES
BT1 hemiuridae
BT2 digenea
BT3 trematoda
NT1 derogenes ruber

DEROGENES RUBER
BT1 derogenes
BT2 hemiuridae
BT3 digenea
BT4 trematoda

DERRIS
BT1 leguminosae
NT1 derris brevipes
NT1 derris elliptica
NT1 derris indica
NT1 derris kanjilalii
NT1 derris obtusa
NT1 derris robusta
NT1 derris scandens
NT1 derris uliginosa
rt piscicidal plants
rt rotenone

derris (botanical insecticide)
USE **rotenone**

DERRIS BREVIPES
BT1 derris
BT2 leguminosae

DERRIS ELLIPTICA
BT1 derris
BT2 leguminosae
BT1 insecticidal plants
BT2 pesticidal plants
rt rotenone

DERRIS INDICA
BT1 derris
BT2 leguminosae

DERRIS KANJILALII
BT1 browse plants
BT1 derris
BT2 leguminosae

DERRIS OBTUSA
BT1 derris
BT2 leguminosae

DERRIS ROBUSTA
BT1 derris
BT2 leguminosae

DERRIS SCANDENS
BT1 derris
BT2 leguminosae

DERRIS ULIGINOSA
BT1 derris
BT2 leguminosae
BT1 insecticidal plants
BT2 pesticidal plants

DERXIA
BT1 azotobacteraceae
BT2 gracilicutes
BT3 bacteria
BT4 prokaryotes

2,4-des
USE **disul**

DESALINIZATION
BT1 processing
BT1 soil formation
rt demineralization
rt inorganic salts

DESALINIZATION *cont.*
rt salinity

DESCHAMPSIA
BT1 gramineae
NT1 deschampsia cespitosa
NT1 deschampsia flexuosa
NT1 deschampsia setacea

DESCHAMPSIA CESPITOSA
BT1 deschampsia
BT2 gramineae
BT1 pasture plants

DESCHAMPSIA FLEXUOSA
BT1 deschampsia
BT2 gramineae
BT1 ornamental herbaceous plants
BT1 pasture plants

DESCHAMPSIA SETACEA
uf *aristavena setacea*
BT1 deschampsia
BT2 gramineae

DESCRIPTIONS
NT1 cmi descriptions
NT1 cmi/aab descriptions
NT1 redescriptions
rt illustrations
rt taxonomy

DESCRIPTIVE STATISTICS
uf *statistics, descriptive*
BT1 statistics
NT1 time series
NT1 weighting
rt agricultural censuses
rt agricultural statistics

DESCURAINIA
BT1 cruciferae
NT1 descurainia pinnata
NT1 descurainia sophia

DESCURAINIA PINNATA
BT1 descurainia
BT2 cruciferae

DESCURAINIA SOPHIA
BT1 descurainia
BT2 cruciferae
BT1 insecticidal plants
BT2 pesticidal plants

desensitization, immunologic
USE **immune desensitization**

DESERT ANIMALS
BT1 animals
NT1 desert rodents
rt deserts

desert climate
USE **arid climate**

DESERT PAVEMENT
BT1 soil morphological features
rt wind erosion

DESERT PLANTS
BT1 plant communities
BT2 communities
rt alhagi
rt deserts
rt plants
rt semi-desert scrub

DESERT RODENTS
uf *rodents, desert*
BT1 desert animals
BT2 animals
rt rodents

DESERT SOILS
BT1 soil types (climatic)
BT1 yermosols
BT2 soil types (genetic)
rt arid soils
rt deserts

DESERT VARNISH
rt oxides
rt rocks

DESERT VARNISH *cont.*
rt soil morphology

DESERTIFICATION
rt arid regions
rt arid soils
rt drought
rt erosion
rt soil degradation

DESERTS
BT1 arid regions
BT2 arid zones
BT3 climatic zones
BT1 land types
NT1 gobi desert
NT1 kalahari desert
NT1 mojave desert
NT1 sahara desert
rt arid climate
rt desert animals
rt desert plants
rt desert soils
rt oases
rt wilderness

desferrioxamine
USE **deferoxamine**

DESICCANT HERBICIDES
BT1 desiccants
NT1 2,4-d
NT1 buminafos
NT1 dinoseb
NT1 diquat
NT1 endothal
NT1 ethephon
NT1 formic acid
NT1 glyphosate
NT1 metoxuron
NT1 paraquat
rt herbicides

DESICCANTS
NT1 calcium chloride
NT1 desiccant herbicides
NT2 2,4-d
NT2 buminafos
NT2 dinoseb
NT2 diquat
NT2 endothal
NT2 ethephon
NT2 formic acid
NT2 glyphosate
NT2 metoxuron
NT2 paraquat
NT1 propionic acid
NT1 silica gel
NT1 tributyl phosphate
rt desiccation
rt driers
rt drying

DESICCATED COCONUT
BT1 coconut products
BT2 nut products
BT3 plant products
BT4 products
rt coconuts

DESICCATION
BT1 plant water relations
BT2 plant physiology
BT3 physiology
rt desiccants
rt drying

DESIGN
NT1 plant design
rt architecture
rt clothing design (agricola)
rt computer graphics
rt decorative design (agricola)
rt design calculations
rt engineering
rt ergonomics
rt experimental design
rt fashion designers (agricola)
rt interior design (agricola)
rt layout
rt menu design (agricola)
rt planning
rt programming

DESIGN *cont.*
rt structural design (agricola)

DESIGN CALCULATIONS
BT1 calculation
BT2 mathematics
rt design
rt mathematical models

design, experimental
USE **experimental design**

DESIPRAMINE
BT1 antidepressants
BT2 psychotropic drugs
BT3 neurotropic drugs
BT4 drugs
BT2 stimulants
BT3 drugs

DESMANTHUS
BT1 leguminosae
NT1 desmanthus virgatus

DESMANTHUS VIRGATUS
BT1 desmanthus
BT2 leguminosae
BT1 pasture legumes
BT2 legumes
BT2 pasture plants

DESMAZERIA
BT1 gramineae
NT1 desmazeria marina
NT1 desmazeria rigida

DESMAZERIA MARINA
uf *catapodium marinum*
BT1 desmazeria
BT2 gramineae
BT1 pasture plants

DESMAZERIA RIGIDA
BT1 desmazeria
BT2 gramineae
BT1 pasture plants

DESMEDIPHAM
BT1 carbanilate herbicides
BT2 carbamate pesticides
BT2 herbicides
BT3 pesticides

DESMETRYN
uf *desmetryne*
BT1 triazine herbicides
BT2 herbicides
BT3 pesticides
BT2 triazines
BT3 heterocyclic nitrogen compounds
BT4 organic nitrogen compounds

desmetryne
USE **desmetryn**

DESMODIUM
BT1 leguminosae
NT1 desmodium ampliflorum
NT1 desmodium arechavaletae
NT1 desmodium canum
NT1 desmodium diffusum
NT1 desmodium discolor
NT1 desmodium floribundum
NT1 desmodium frutescens
NT1 desmodium heterophyllum
NT1 desmodium intortum
NT1 desmodium leiocarpum
NT1 desmodium ovalifolium
NT1 desmodium tiliaefolium
NT1 desmodium tortuosum
NT1 desmodium triflorum
NT1 desmodium uncinatum
rt desmodium yellow mottle tymovirus

DESMODIUM AMPLIFLORUM
BT1 desmodium
BT2 leguminosae
BT1 pasture legumes
BT2 legumes
BT2 pasture plants

DESMODIUM ARECHAVALETAE
BT1 desmodium
BT2 leguminosae
BT1 pasture legumes
BT2 legumes
BT2 pasture plants

DESMODIUM CANUM
BT1 desmodium
BT2 leguminosae

DESMODIUM DIFFUSUM
BT1 desmodium
BT2 leguminosae

DESMODIUM DISCOLOR
BT1 desmodium
BT2 leguminosae
BT1 pasture legumes
BT2 legumes
BT2 pasture plants

DESMODIUM FLORIBUNDUM
BT1 desmodium
BT2 leguminosae

DESMODIUM FRUTESCENS
BT1 desmodium
BT2 leguminosae
BT1 pasture legumes
BT2 legumes
BT2 pasture plants

desmodium gyrans
USE **codariocalyx motorius**

desmodium gyroides
USE **codariocalyx gyroides**

DESMODIUM HETEROPHYLLUM
BT1 desmodium
BT2 leguminosae
BT1 pasture legumes
BT2 legumes
BT2 pasture plants

DESMODIUM INTORTUM
BT1 desmodium
BT2 leguminosae
BT1 pasture legumes
BT2 legumes
BT2 pasture plants

DESMODIUM LEIOCARPUM
BT1 desmodium
BT2 leguminosae

DESMODIUM OVALIFOLIUM
BT1 desmodium
BT2 leguminosae

DESMODIUM TILIAEFOLIUM
BT1 desmodium
BT2 leguminosae

DESMODIUM TORTUOSUM
BT1 desmodium
BT2 leguminosae
BT1 green manures
BT2 manures
BT3 organic amendments
BT4 soil amendments
BT5 amendments
BT1 weeds

DESMODIUM TRIFLORUM
BT1 desmodium
BT2 leguminosae
BT1 pasture legumes
BT2 legumes
BT2 pasture plants

DESMODIUM UNCINATUM
BT1 desmodium
BT2 leguminosae
BT1 pasture legumes
BT2 legumes
BT2 pasture plants

DESMODIUM YELLOW MOTTLE TYMOVIRUS
HN from 1990; previously "desmodium yellow mottle virus"

DESMODIUM YELLOW MOTTLE TYMOVIRUS *cont.*
uf *desmodium yellow mottle virus*
BT1 tymovirus group
BT2 plant viruses
BT3 plant pathogens
BT4 pathogens
rt desmodium

desmodium yellow mottle virus
USE **desmodium yellow mottle tymovirus**

DESMODORA
BT1 desmodoridae
BT2 nematoda

DESMODORIDAE
BT1 nematoda
NT1 desmodora
rt free living nematodes
rt marine nematodes

DESMODUS
BT1 phyllostomidae
BT2 chiroptera
BT3 mammals

DESMOSCOLECIDAE
BT1 nematoda
NT1 desmoscolex
rt marine nematodes

DESMOSCOLEX
BT1 desmoscolecidae
BT2 nematoda

DESMOSINE
BT1 cyclic amino acids
BT2 amino acids
BT3 carboxylic acids
BT4 organic acids
BT5 acids
BT3 organic nitrogen compounds
BT1 pyridines
BT2 heterocyclic nitrogen compounds
BT3 organic nitrogen compounds
rt elastin

DESMOSTACHYA
BT1 gramineae
NT1 desmostachya bipinnata

DESMOSTACHYA BIPINNATA
BT1 desmostachya
BT2 gramineae

DESORPTION
rt absorption
rt adsorption

DESOXYCORTONE
uf *deoxycorticosterone*
uf *doca*
BT1 mineralocorticoids
BT2 adrenal cortex hormones
BT3 corticoids
BT3 hormones
BT1 pregnanes
BT2 steroids
BT3 isoprenoids
BT4 lipids

DESSERT CULTIVARS
BT1 cultivars
BT2 varieties
rt fruit crops

DESSERTS
BT1 foods
NT1 frozen desserts

DESTABILIZING SELECTION
HN from 1989
BT1 selection

DESTINATIONS
BT1 travel
rt holidays
rt tourism
rt tourism impact

DESTINATIONS *cont.*
rt visits

DESTRUCTION
NT1 destruction of animals
NT2 euthanasia
NT1 habitat destruction
NT1 haulm destruction
NT1 sward destruction
rt fire effects

DESTRUCTION OF ANIMALS
(killing of animals for purposes other than obtaining products; not to be confused with "slaughter")
BT1 destruction
NT1 euthanasia
rt carcass disposal
rt slaughter

DESTRUCTIVE DISTILLATION
uf *distillation, destructive*
uf *gas production from wood*
BT1 distillation
BT2 processing
rt charcoal
rt wood chemical industry
rt wood liquefaction

DESTRUXIN B
HN from 1990
BT1 destruxins
BT2 mycotoxins
BT3 toxins

DESTRUXIN E
HN from 1990
BT1 destruxins
BT2 mycotoxins
BT3 toxins

DESTRUXINS
HN from 1990
BT1 mycotoxins
BT2 toxins
NT1 destruxin b
NT1 destruxin e
rt antibiotic insecticides
rt metarhizium anisopliae

DESULFOVIBRIO
BT1 gracilicutes
BT2 bacteria
BT3 prokaryotes
NT1 desulfovibrio desulfuricans
NT1 desulfovibrio vulgaris

DESULFOVIBRIO DESULFURICANS
BT1 desulfovibrio
BT2 gracilicutes
BT3 bacteria
BT4 prokaryotes

DESULFOVIBRIO VULGARIS
BT1 desulfovibrio
BT2 gracilicutes
BT3 bacteria
BT4 prokaryotes

DESULFURIZATION
uf *desulphurization*
BT1 biological treatment
BT2 waste treatment
rt sulfur

desulphurization
USE **desulfurization**

DESWEETENING
HN from 1990
BT1 processing
rt washing

DESYNAPSIS
BT1 cell division
rt asynapsis
rt meiosis

DETECTION
NT1 fire detection
NT1 sensing
NT2 remote sensing
rt analysis
rt detectors
rt monitoring

DETECTORS
BT1 sensors
NT1 metal detectors
rt detection
rt feeler wheels
rt feelers
rt gypsum blocks
rt instruments
rt monitors
rt transducers

DETERGENTS
BT1 laundry products (agricola)
BT2 non-food products
BT3 products
BT1 surfactants
NT1 teepol
rt acacia concinna
rt cleaning
rt disinfectants
rt presoaks (agricola)
rt soaps
rt washing
rt wetters

DETERIORATION
NT1 biodeterioration
NT2 foxing
NT2 microbial corrosion
NT1 decay
NT2 fruit rots
NT2 postharvest decay
NT3 spoilage
NT4 food spoilage
NT3 storage decay
NT2 root and butt rots
NT1 deterioration of materials in soil
NT1 inbreeding depression
rt decomposition
rt grain mottling
rt quality

deterioration in storage
USE **storage decay**

DETERIORATION OF MATERIALS IN SOIL
uf *corrosion in soil*
BT1 deterioration

DETERMINATE AND INDETERMINATE HABIT
BT1 habit
rt apical dominance
rt branching

DETERMINATION
BT1 techniques
NT1 age determination
NT2 dendrochronology
NT2 radiocarbon dating
NT1 fertilizer requirement determination
NT1 volume determination
NT1 weight determination
rt analysis
rt measurement

DETERMINISTIC MODELS
uf *models, deterministic*
BT1 simulation models
BT2 models

DETOXICANTS
BT1 drugs
NT1 4-aminopyridine
NT1 antidotes
NT2 dimercaprol
NT2 glutathione
NT2 methylene blue
NT2 pralidoxime
NT1 enzyme activators
NT2 pralidoxime
NT1 narcotic antagonists
NT2 diprenorphine
NT2 nad
NT2 naloxone
NT1 yohimbine
rt chelating agents
rt detoxification
rt safeners
rt toxic substances

DETOXIFICATION
BT1 processing
rt detoxicants
rt metabolic detoxification
rt toxic substances

DETRITIVORES
BT1 herbivores
rt detritus
rt feeding

DETRITUS
BT1 residues
rt detritivores
rt litter

DEUDORIX
BT1 lycaenidae
BT2 lepidoptera

DEUTERIUM
BT1 hydrogen
BT2 gases
BT2 nonmetallic elements
BT3 elements
BT1 isotopes
BT1 tracers
rt deuterium oxide

DEUTERIUM OXIDE
BT1 tracers
BT1 water
rt deuterium

DEUTEROMYCOTINA
uf *fungi imperfecti*
NT1 acremonium
NT2 acremonium coenophialum
NT2 acremonium diospyri
NT2 acremonium falciforme
NT2 acremonium kiliense
NT2 acremonium recifei
NT2 acremonium strictum
NT1 acrocylindrium
NT1 acrosporium
NT1 alternaria
NT2 alternaria alternata
NT2 alternaria brassicae
NT2 alternaria brassicicola
NT2 alternaria burnsii
NT2 alternaria carthami
NT2 alternaria cheiranthi
NT2 alternaria cichorii
NT2 alternaria citri
NT2 alternaria crassa
NT2 alternaria dauci
NT2 alternaria helianthi
NT2 alternaria kikuchiana
NT2 alternaria longipes
NT2 alternaria longissima
NT2 alternaria macrospora
NT2 alternaria mali
NT2 alternaria padwickii
NT2 alternaria panax
NT2 alternaria porri
NT2 alternaria radicina
NT2 alternaria raphani
NT2 alternaria solani
NT2 alternaria tagetica
NT2 alternaria tenuissima
NT2 alternaria triticina
NT2 alternaria zinniae
NT1 ampelomyces
NT2 ampelomyces quisqualis
NT1 anguillospora
NT1 apiocarpella
NT1 arthrobotrys
NT2 arthrobotrys amerospora
NT2 arthrobotrys botryospora
NT2 arthrobotrys oligospora
NT1 aschersonia
NT2 aschersonia aleyrodis
NT1 ascochyta
NT2 ascochyta agropyri-repentis
NT2 ascochyta fabae
NT2 ascochyta necans
NT2 ascochyta oryzae
NT2 ascochyta pisi
NT2 ascochyta punctata
NT2 ascochyta rabiei
NT1 ascochytella
NT2 ascochytella ampelina

DEUTEROMYCOTINA *cont.*
NT1 aspergillus
NT2 aspergillus aculeatus
NT2 aspergillus awamori
NT2 aspergillus bicolor
NT2 aspergillus candidus
NT2 aspergillus corneus
NT2 aspergillus flavipes
NT2 aspergillus flavus
NT2 aspergillus fumigatus
NT2 aspergillus glaucus
NT2 aspergillus nidulans
NT2 aspergillus niger
NT2 aspergillus ochraceus
NT2 aspergillus oryzae
NT2 aspergillus parasiticus
NT2 aspergillus spectabilis
NT2 aspergillus terreus
NT2 aspergillus variecolor
NT2 aspergillus versicolor
NT1 asperisporium
NT2 asperisporium caricae
NT1 asteromella
NT2 asteromella mali
NT1 aureobasidium
NT2 aureobasidium pullulans
NT1 beauveria
NT2 beauveria bassiana
NT2 beauveria brongniartii
NT1 bipolaris
NT2 bipolaris heveae
NT2 bipolaris incurvata
NT2 bipolaris indica
NT2 bipolaris leersiae
NT2 bipolaris sacchari
NT2 bipolaris sorghicola
NT2 bipolaris stenospila
NT1 blastomyces
NT2 blastomyces dermatitidis
NT1 blastoschizomyces
NT2 blastoschizomyces capitatus
NT1 botryodiplodia
NT2 botryodiplodia theobromae
NT1 botrytis
NT2 botrytis allii
NT2 botrytis cinerea
NT2 botrytis fabae
NT2 botrytis tulipae
NT1 camarographium
NT1 candida
NT2 candida albicans
NT2 candida claussenii
NT2 candida curvata
NT2 candida cylindracea
NT2 candida guilliermondii
NT2 candida humicola
NT2 candida kefyr
NT2 candida krusei
NT2 candida lipolytica
NT2 candida lusitaniae
NT2 candida muscorum
NT2 candida norvegensis
NT2 candida parapsilosis
NT2 candida rugosa
NT2 candida slooffiae
NT2 candida stellatoidea
NT2 candida tropicalis
NT2 candida utilis
NT2 candida viswanathii
NT2 candida zeylanoides
NT1 cenococcum
NT2 cenococcum geophilum
NT2 cenococcum graniforme
NT1 cephalosporium
NT1 cephalothecium
NT1 cercoseptoria
NT2 cercoseptoria theae
NT1 cercospora
NT2 cercospora apii
NT2 cercospora beticola
NT2 cercospora canescens
NT2 cercospora capsici
NT2 cercospora carthami
NT2 cercospora coffeicola
NT2 cercospora effusa
NT2 cercospora elaeidis
NT2 cercospora gossypina
NT2 cercospora kikuchii
NT2 cercospora nicotianae
NT2 cercospora oryzae

DEUTEROMYCOTINA *cont.*
NT2 cercospora rodmanii
NT2 cercospora sorghi
NT2 cercospora zeae-maydis
NT2 cercospora zebrina
NT1 cercosporella
NT1 cercosporidium
NT1 chaetopsina
NT1 chalara
NT1 chrysosporium
NT2 chrysosporium evolceanui
NT2 chrysosporium keratinophilum
NT2 chrysosporium tropicum
NT1 cicinnobolus
NT1 circinotrichum
NT1 cladobotryum
NT2 cladobotryum verticillatum
NT1 cladosporium
NT2 cladosporium carrionii
NT2 cladosporium cladosporioides
NT2 cladosporium cucumerinum
NT2 cladosporium herbarum
NT2 cladosporium phlei
NT1 coccidioides
NT2 coccidioides immitis
NT1 codinaea
NT1 colletotrichum
NT2 colletotrichum acutatum
NT2 colletotrichum capsici
NT2 colletotrichum circinans
NT2 colletotrichum coccodes
NT2 colletotrichum crassipes
NT2 colletotrichum dematium
NT2 colletotrichum destructivum
NT2 colletotrichum graminicola
NT2 colletotrichum lindemuthianum
NT2 colletotrichum lini
NT2 colletotrichum manihotis
NT2 colletotrichum musae
NT2 colletotrichum orbiculare
NT2 colletotrichum tabacum
NT2 colletotrichum trifolii
NT2 colletotrichum truncatum
NT1 coniella
NT2 coniella diplodiella
NT1 coniothyrium
NT2 coniothyrium clematidis-rectae
NT2 coniothyrium fuckelii
NT2 coniothyrium minitans
NT2 coniothyrium pyrinum
NT1 cordana
NT2 cordana musae
NT1 corynespora
NT2 corynespora cassiicola
NT1 coryneum
NT1 cristulariella
NT1 cryptococcus (deuteromycotina)
NT2 cryptococcus albidus
NT2 cryptococcus bacillisporus
NT2 cryptococcus laurentii
NT2 cryptococcus neoformans
NT1 cryptosporiopsis
NT1 cryptostroma
NT2 cryptostroma corticale
NT1 culicinomyces
NT2 culicinomyces clavisporus
NT1 curvularia
NT2 curvularia inaequalis
NT2 curvularia penniseti
NT2 curvularia spicata
NT2 curvularia tuberculata
NT1 cycloconium
NT1 cylindrocarpon
NT1 cylindrocladium
NT2 cylindrocladium clavatum
NT2 cylindrocladium crotalariae
NT2 cylindrocladium scoparium
NT2 cylindrocladium theae
NT1 cylindrosporium
NT2 cylindrosporium filipendulae
NT2 cylindrosporium maculans
NT1 cytospora
NT2 cytospora sacchari
NT1 dactuliophora

DEUTEROMYCOTINA *cont.*
NT2 dactuliophora tarrii
NT1 dactyella
NT2 dactyella brochopaga
NT2 dactyella oviparasitica
NT1 deightoniella
NT2 deightoniella torulosa
NT1 dendrodochium
NT2 dendrodochium toxicum
NT1 dendrophoma
NT1 deuterophoma
NT2 deuterophoma tracheiphila
NT1 diheterospora
NT1 diplodia
NT2 diplodia pinea
NT1 dothistroma
NT1 drechslera
NT2 drechslera biseptata
NT2 drechslera cactivora
NT2 drechslera catenaria
NT2 drechslera gossypii
NT2 drechslera phlei
NT2 drechslera poae
NT2 drechslera portulacae
NT2 drechslera triseptata
NT1 embellisia
NT2 embellisia hyacinthi
NT1 emmonsia
NT2 emmonsia crescens
NT2 emmonsia parva
NT1 entomosporium
NT1 epicoccum
NT2 epicoccum nigrum
NT1 epidermophyton
NT2 epidermophyton floccosum
NT1 exophiala
NT1 exserohilum
NT1 fonsecaea
NT2 fonsecaea compacta
NT2 fonsecaea pedrosoi
NT1 fulvia
NT2 fulvia fulva
NT1 fusarium
NT2 fusarium arthrosporioides
NT2 fusarium chlamydosporum
NT2 fusarium concolor
NT2 fusarium culmorum
NT2 fusarium equiseti
NT2 fusarium oxysporum
NT3 fusarium oxysporum f.sp. apii
NT3 fusarium oxysporum f.sp. cepae
NT3 fusarium oxysporum f.sp. ciceris
NT3 fusarium oxysporum f.sp. cubense
NT3 fusarium oxysporum f.sp. cucumerinum
NT3 fusarium oxysporum f.sp. dianthi
NT3 fusarium oxysporum f.sp. lini
NT3 fusarium oxysporum f.sp. lycopersici
NT3 fusarium oxysporum f.sp. medicaginis
NT3 fusarium oxysporum f.sp. niveum
NT3 fusarium oxysporum f.sp. pisi
NT3 fusarium oxysporum f.sp. vasinfectum
NT3 fusarium oxysporum var. redolens
NT2 fusarium pallidoroseum
NT2 fusarium poae
NT2 fusarium proliferatum
NT2 fusarium roseum
NT2 fusarium solani
NT3 fusarium solani f.sp. coeruleum
NT3 fusarium solani f.sp. phaseoli
NT3 fusarium solani f.sp. pisi
NT3 fusarium solani var. coeruleum
NT2 fusarium sporotrichioides
NT2 fusarium tricinctum
NT2 fusarium udum
NT1 fusicoccum

DEUTEROMYCOTINA *cont.*
NT1 gelarchia
NT1 geotrichum
NT2 geotrichum candidum
NT3 geotrichum candidum var. citri-aurantii
NT1 gilmaniella
NT2 gilmaniella subornata
NT1 gliocladium
NT2 gliocladium roseum
NT2 gliocladium virens
NT1 gloeocercospora
NT2 gloeocercospora sorghi
NT1 gloeosporium
NT2 gloeosporium amygdalinum
NT2 gloeosporium minus
NT1 haplobasidion
NT2 haplobasidion musae
NT1 harposporium
NT2 harposporium arcuatum
NT1 helminthosporium
NT2 helminthosporium solani
NT2 helminthosporium tucumense
NT1 hendersonula
NT1 hirsutella
NT2 hirsutella thompsonii
NT1 histoplasma
NT2 histoplasma capsulatum
NT2 histoplasma duboisii
NT2 histoplasma farciminosum
NT1 hormoconis
NT1 humicola
NT2 humicola fuscoatra
NT2 humicola lanuginosa
NT1 hymenula
NT2 hymenula cerealis
NT1 isaria
NT2 isaria sinclairii
NT1 kabatiella
NT2 kabatiella caulivora
NT2 kabatiella lini
NT2 kabatiella zeae
NT1 kabatina
NT2 kabatina thujae
NT1 keratinomyces
NT2 keratinomyces ajelloi
NT1 lecanosticta
NT1 macroallantina
NT1 macrophomina
NT2 macrophomina phaseolina
NT1 madurella
NT2 madurella grisea
NT2 madurella mycetomatis
NT1 malassezia
NT2 malassezia furfur
NT2 malassezia pachydermatis
NT1 marssonina
NT1 metarhizium
NT2 metarhizium anisopliae
NT2 metarhizium flavoviride
NT1 microdochium
NT2 microdochium dimerum
NT2 microdochium panattonianum
NT2 microdochium tabacinum
NT1 microsporum
NT2 microsporum amazonicum
NT2 microsporum audouinii
NT2 microsporum canis
NT2 microsporum cookei
NT2 microsporum distortum
NT2 microsporum equinum
NT2 microsporum ferrugineum
NT2 microsporum fulvum
NT2 microsporum gypseum
NT2 microsporum nanum
NT2 microsporum persicolor
NT2 microsporum racemosum
NT2 microsporum vanbreuseghemii
NT1 monilia
NT1 moniliopsis
NT2 moniliopsis aderholdii
NT1 monochaetia
NT1 myceliophthora
NT2 myceliophthora thermophila
NT1 mycocentrospora
NT2 mycocentrospora acerina
NT1 mycogone

DEUTEROMYCOTINA *cont.*
NT2 mycogone perniciosa
NT1 mycovellosiella
NT2 mycovellosiella concors
NT2 mycovellosiella ferruginea
NT2 mycovellosiella grewiae
NT2 mycovellosiella koepkei
NT2 mycovellosiella murina
NT2 mycovellosiella oryzae
NT2 mycovellosiella phaseoli
NT2 mycovellosiella pongamiae
NT2 mycovellosiella vaginae
NT1 myrothecium
NT2 myrothecium leucotrichum
NT2 myrothecium roridum
NT2 myrothecium verrucaria
NT1 nattrassia
NT2 nattrassia mangiferae
NT1 nigrospora
NT2 nigrospora sphaerica
NT1 nomuraea
NT2 nomuraea rileyi
NT1 oidiopsis
NT1 oidium
NT2 oidium heveae
NT2 oidium lini
NT2 oidium mangiferae
NT1 ozonium
NT2 ozonium texanum
NT1 paecilomyces
NT2 paecilomyces farinosus
NT2 paecilomyces fumosoroseus
NT2 paecilomyces lilacinus
NT2 paecilomyces varioti
NT1 paracercospora
NT2 paracercospora egenula
NT1 paracoccidioides
NT2 paracoccidioides brasiliensis
NT1 penicillium
NT2 penicillium aurantiogriseum
NT2 penicillium brevicompactum
NT2 penicillium camembertii
NT2 penicillium chrysogenum
NT2 penicillium citreoviride
NT2 penicillium citrinum
NT2 penicillium commune
NT2 penicillium corymbiferum
NT2 penicillium digitatum
NT2 penicillium expansum
NT2 penicillium funiculosum
NT2 penicillium gladioli
NT2 penicillium granulatum
NT2 penicillium islandicum
NT2 penicillium italicum
NT2 penicillium janthinellum
NT2 penicillium marneffei
NT2 penicillium martensii
NT2 penicillium nigricans
NT2 penicillium notatum
NT2 penicillium oxalicum
NT2 penicillium palitans
NT2 penicillium purpurogenum
NT2 penicillium roquefortii
NT2 penicillium rubrum
NT2 penicillium rugulosum
NT2 penicillium stoloniferum
NT2 penicillium variabile
NT2 penicillium verruculosum
NT2 penicillium viridicatum
NT1 periconia
NT2 periconia circinata
NT2 periconia manihoticola
NT1 periconiella
NT2 periconiella musae
NT1 pestalotia
NT1 pestalotiopsis
NT2 pestalotiopsis dichaeta
NT2 pestalotiopsis funerea
NT2 pestalotiopsis paeoniae
NT2 pestalotiopsis palmarum
NT2 pestalotiopsis psidii
NT2 pestalotiopsis versicolor
NT1 phacidiopycnis
NT2 phacidiopycnis padwickii
NT1 phaeoannellomyces
NT2 phaeoannellomyces werneckii
NT1 phaeocytostroma

DEUTEROMYCOTINA *cont.*
NT2 phaeocytostroma sacchari
NT1 phaeoisariopsis
NT2 phaeoisariopsis griseola
NT1 phaeoramularia
NT2 phaeoramularia manihotis
NT1 phaeotrichoconis
NT2 phaeotrichoconis crotalaria
NT1 phialophora
NT2 phialophora cinerescens
NT2 phialophora graminicola
NT2 phialophora gregata
NT2 phialophora melinii
NT2 phialophora mutabilis
NT2 phialophora radicicola
NT2 phialophora richardsiae
NT2 phialophora verrucosa
NT1 phloeosporella
NT1 phoma
NT2 phoma destructiva
NT2 phoma exigua
NT3 phoma exigua var. exigua
NT3 phoma exigua var. foveata
NT2 phoma medicaginis
NT3 phoma medicaginis var. pinodella
NT2 phoma sorghina
NT2 phoma violacea
NT2 phoma zingiberis
NT1 phomopsis
NT2 phomopsis amygdali
NT2 phomopsis juniperivora
NT2 phomopsis obscurans
NT2 phomopsis sclerotioides
NT2 phomopsis theae
NT2 phomopsis viticola
NT1 phyllosticta
NT2 phyllosticta gerbericola
NT1 phymatotrichopsis
NT2 phymatotrichopsis omnivora
NT1 piggotia
NT2 piggotia coryli
NT1 pithomyces
NT2 pithomyces chartarum
NT1 pleiochaeta
NT2 pleiochaeta setosa
NT1 polyscytalum
NT2 polyscytalum pustulans
NT1 polyspora
NT2 polyspora lini
NT1 pseudocercospora
NT2 pseudocercospora abelmoschi
NT2 pseudocercospora bischofiae
NT2 pseudocercospora cosmicola
NT2 pseudocercospora daemiae
NT2 pseudocercospora fuligena
NT2 pseudocercospora heteromalla
NT2 pseudocercospora ipomoeae-purpureae
NT2 pseudocercospora midnapurensis
NT2 pseudocercospora viticis
NT1 pseudocercosporella
NT2 pseudocercosporella brassicae
NT2 pseudocercosporella capsellae
NT2 pseudocercosporella herpotrichoides
NT1 pseudoseptoria
NT2 pseudoseptoria donacis
NT1 pyrenochaeta
NT2 pyrenochaeta lycopersici
NT2 pyrenochaeta romeroi
NT2 pyrenochaeta terrestris
NT1 pyricularia
NT2 pyricularia oryzae
NT2 pyricularia penniseti
NT2 pyricularia setariae
NT1 pyriculariopsis
NT2 pyriculariopsis parasitica
NT1 ramularia
NT2 ramularia carthami
NT2 ramularia collo-cygni
NT2 ramularia gossypii

DEUTEROMYCOTINA *cont.*
NT1 ramulispora
NT2 ramulispora sorghi
NT1 rhodotorula
NT2 rhodotorula glutinis
NT2 rhodotorula rubra
NT1 rhynchosporium
NT2 rhynchosporium orthosporum
NT2 rhynchosporium secalis
NT1 sarcinomyces
NT2 sarcinomyces crustaceus
NT1 sarocladium
NT2 sarocladium oryzae
NT1 sclerophoma
NT1 scopulariopsis
NT2 scopulariopsis brevicaulis
NT1 scytalidium
NT2 scytalidium dimidiatum
NT2 scytalidium lignicola
NT1 seiridium
NT2 seiridium cardinale
NT2 seiridium unicorne
NT1 selenophoma
NT1 sepedonium
NT1 septoria
NT2 septoria apiicola
NT2 septoria lycopersici
NT1 sirococcus
NT2 sirococcus conigenus
NT1 sphacelia
NT1 sphaceloma
NT1 sphaeropsis
NT1 spilocaea
NT2 spilocaea oleagina
NT2 spilocaea pyracanthae
NT1 sporidesmium
NT1 sporothrix
NT2 sporothrix cyanescens
NT2 sporothrix schenckii
NT1 sporotrichum
NT1 stachybotrys
NT2 stachybotrys atra
NT1 stachylidium
NT1 stagonospora
NT2 stagonospora sacchari
NT1 stegonsporiopsis
NT2 stegonsporiopsis cenangioides
NT1 stemphylium
NT2 stemphylium sarciniforme
NT2 stemphylium vesicarium
NT1 stenocarpella
NT2 stenocarpella macrospora
NT2 stenocarpella maydis
NT1 stigmina
NT2 stigmina carpophila
NT1 teratosperma
NT2 teratosperma sclerotivora
NT1 thielaviopsis
NT2 thielaviopsis basicola
NT1 tolypocladium
NT2 tolypocladium cylindrosporum
NT2 tolypocladium niveum
NT1 torula
NT1 torulopsis
NT2 torulopsis candida
NT2 torulopsis glabrata
NT2 torulopsis holmii
NT2 torulopsis inconspicua
NT1 trichoconis
NT1 trichoderma
NT2 trichoderma hamatum
NT2 trichoderma harzianum
NT2 trichoderma koningii
NT2 trichoderma longibrachiatum
NT2 trichoderma pseudokoningii
NT2 trichoderma viride
NT1 trichophyton
NT2 trichophyton concentricum
NT2 trichophyton equinum
NT2 trichophyton erinacei
NT2 trichophyton gallinae
NT2 trichophyton interdigitale
NT2 trichophyton megninii
NT2 trichophyton mentagrophytes
NT2 trichophyton quinckeanum
NT2 trichophyton rubrum

DEUTEROMYCOTINA *cont.*
NT2 trichophyton schoenleinii
NT2 trichophyton simii
NT2 trichophyton soudanense
NT2 trichophyton terrestre
NT2 trichophyton tonsurans
NT2 trichophyton vanbreuseghemii
NT2 trichophyton verrucosum
NT2 trichophyton violaceum
NT2 trichophyton yaoundei
NT1 trichosporon
NT2 trichosporon beigelii
NT1 trichothecium
NT2 trichothecium roseum
NT1 tritirachium
NT2 tritirachium album
NT1 truncatella
NT2 truncatella hartigii
NT1 ustilaginoidea
NT2 ustilaginoidea virens
NT1 verticicladiella
NT2 verticicladiella abietina
NT2 verticicladiella procera
NT1 verticillium
NT2 verticillium albo-atrum
NT2 verticillium dahliae
NT2 verticillium fungicola
NT2 verticillium lecanii
NT2 verticillium nigrescens
NT2 verticillium theobromae
NT1 wangiella
NT2 wangiella dermatitidis
NT1 xylohypha
NT2 xylohypha bantiana
rt fungi

DEUTEROPHOMA
BT1 deuteromycotina
NT1 deuterophoma tracheiphila
rt phoma

DEUTEROPHOMA TRACHEIPHILA
uf *phoma tracheiphila*
BT1 deuterophoma
BT2 deuteromycotina

DEUTZIA
BT1 philadelphaceae
NT1 deutzia crenata
NT1 deutzia scabra

DEUTZIA CRENATA
BT1 deutzia
BT2 philadelphaceae
BT1 ornamental woody plants

DEUTZIA SCABRA
BT1 deutzia
BT2 philadelphaceae
BT1 ornamental woody plants

DEVALUATION
BT1 monetary parity
BT2 monetary situation
rt foreign exchange

DEVELOPED COUNTRIES
BT1 countries
NT1 industrial countries

DEVELOPING COUNTRIES
uf *less developed countries*
uf *third world*
uf *underdeveloped countries*
BT1 countries
NT1 least developed countries
NT1 threshold countries
rt acp
rt afghanistan
rt africa
rt agrarian countries
rt algeria
rt angola
rt argentina
rt asia
rt bangladesh
rt benin
rt bhutan
rt bolivia
rt botswana
rt brazil
rt burkina faso

DEVELOPING COUNTRIES *cont.*
rt burma
rt burundi
rt cambodia
rt cameroon
rt cape verde
rt caribbean
rt central african republic
rt central america
rt chad
rt chile
rt china
rt colombia
rt colonies
rt comoros
rt costa rica
rt cuba
rt cyprus
rt dominican republic
rt ecuador
rt egypt
rt el salvador
rt ethiopia
rt gambia
rt ghana
rt guatemala
rt guinea
rt guyana
rt haiti
rt hong kong
rt indonesia
rt iran
rt iraq
rt ivory coast
rt jamaica
rt jordan
rt kenya
rt korea democratic people's republic
rt korea republic
rt lao
rt latin america
rt lebanon
rt lesotho
rt liberia
rt madagascar
rt malawi
rt malaysia
rt maldives
rt mali
rt malta
rt mauritania
rt mexico
rt mongolia
rt morocco
rt mozambique
rt nepal
rt nicaragua
rt niger
rt nigeria
rt oceania
rt pakistan
rt panama
rt papua new guinea
rt paraguay
rt peru
rt philippines
rt rwanda
rt senegal
rt sierra leone
rt singapore
rt somalia
rt south america
rt sri lanka
rt sudan
rt syria
rt tanzania
rt thailand
rt togo
rt trinidad and tobago
rt tunisia
rt uganda
rt uruguay
rt venezuela
rt vietnam
rt yemen arab republic
rt yemen democratic republic
rt zaire
rt zambia
rt zimbabwe

DEVELOPMENT
(use of a more specific term is recommended; consult the terms listed below)
rt abnormal development
rt adolescent development (agricola)
rt adult development (agricola)
rt agricultural development
rt atresia
rt biological development
rt change
rt child development (agricola)
rt cognitive development (agricola)
rt cultural development
rt degeneration
rt development agencies
rt development policy
rt development projects
rt development rights
rt development studies
rt development theory
rt developmental stages
rt differentiation
rt economic development
rt embryonic development
rt evolution
rt farm development
rt fetal development
rt forestry development
rt growth
rt infant development (agricola)
rt land development
rt mammary development
rt management development (agricola)
rt metamorphosis
rt moral development (agricola)
rt motor development (agricola)
rt neonatal development (agricola)
rt ontogeny
rt organizational development (agricola)
rt organogenesis
rt ovarian development
rt personal development
rt physical development (agricola)
rt plant development
rt postnatal development
rt prenatal development (agricola)
rt product development (agricola)
rt program development (agricola)
rt psychomotor development (agricola)
rt regional development
rt resource development (agricola)
rt rumen development
rt rural development
rt seasonal development
rt sectoral development
rt sex differentiation
rt sexual development
rt skeletal development
rt social development
rt social emotional development (agricola)
rt stand development
rt technical progress
rt tourism development
rt unido
rt urban development

development, abnormal
USE **abnormal development**

DEVELOPMENT AGENCIES
BT1 organizations
NT1 development banks
NT2 inter-american development bank
NT2 world bank
NT1 oxfam

DEVELOPMENT AGENCIES *cont.*
NT1 unicef
rt development
rt development aid
rt idrc
rt ifad

development, agricultural
USE **agricultural development**

DEVELOPMENT AID
uf *aid*
NT1 food aid
NT2 food for work programmes
NT1 technical aid
rt development agencies
rt development banks
rt development policy
rt development projects
rt funds
rt ifad
rt international agreements
rt international cooperation
rt rural development

DEVELOPMENT BANKS
uf *banks, development*
BT1 banks
BT2 financial institutions
BT3 organizations
BT1 development agencies
BT2 organizations
NT1 inter-american development bank
NT1 world bank
rt development aid
rt investment
rt investment banks

development, economic
USE **economic development**

development, forestry
USE **forestry development**

DEVELOPMENT PLANNING
NT1 institution building

DEVELOPMENT PLANS
BT1 planning
rt development policy
rt development projects
rt farm planning

DEVELOPMENT POLICY
NT1 new international economic order
rt agricultural development
rt development
rt development aid
rt development plans
rt development rights
rt economic development
rt economic policy
rt inter-american development bank
rt oecd
rt policy
rt rural development
rt social change
rt unctad

DEVELOPMENT PROJECTS
BT1 projects
NT1 package programmes
rt development
rt development aid
rt development plans
rt project appraisal
rt undp

development, regional
USE **regional development**

DEVELOPMENT RIGHTS
BT1 legal rights
BT2 legal systems
rt development
rt development policy
rt land development
rt planning

development, rural
USE **rural development**

DEVELOPMENT STUDIES
BT1 social sciences
rt development

DEVELOPMENT THEORY
BT1 economic theory
BT2 economics
NT1 economic dualism
rt development
rt economic development

developmental biology
USE **ontogeny**

DEVELOPMENTAL STAGES
uf *growth phase*
NT1 larvae
NT2 helminth larvae
NT3 acanthocephalan larvae
NT4 acanthellae
NT4 acanthors
NT4 cystacanths
NT3 cestode larvae
NT4 coracidia
NT4 oncospheres
NT3 digenean larvae
NT4 cercariae
NT4 diplostomula
NT4 metacercariae
NT4 miracidia
NT4 rediae
NT4 schistosomula
NT4 sporocysts
NT3 monogenean larvae
NT4 oncomiracidia
NT3 nematode larvae
NT4 microfilariae
NT2 nematode juveniles
NT1 maturation period
NT1 maturity stage
NT1 menarche
NT1 metacestodes
NT2 coenuri
NT2 cysticerci
NT2 cysticercoids
NT2 hydatids
NT3 alveolar hydatids
NT3 unilocular hydatids
NT2 plerocerci
NT2 plerocercoids
NT2 procercoids
NT2 protoscoleces
NT2 spargana
NT2 strobilocerci
NT2 strobilocercoids
NT2 tetrathyridia
NT1 morphs
NT1 nymphs
NT1 oocysts
NT1 postweaning interval
NT1 preweaning period
NT1 pupae
NT2 prepupae
NT1 schizonts
NT1 senescence
NT1 smoltification
NT1 sporozoites
NT1 sucklings
rt crop growth stage
rt development
rt growth
rt growth period
rt growth stages
rt plant development
rt postnatal development
rt prematurity
rt sexual maturity
rt transstadial transmission

deviant behaviour
USE **abnormal behaviour**

DEVON
BT1 cattle breeds
BT2 breeds

devorgilla
USE **venturia (hymenoptera)**

DEW
BT1 condensates
BT2 liquids
BT1 meteorological factors

DEW *cont.*
BT2 climatic factors
rt dewpoint
rt relative humidity
rt vapour

DEWATERING
BT1 processing
rt drying
rt separation
rt water

dewberries
USE **rubus caesius**

DEWPOINT
BT1 temperature
rt condensation
rt dew
rt relative humidity
rt vapour
rt water vapour

DEXAMETHASONE
BT1 antiinflammatory agents
BT2 drugs
BT1 dermatological agents
BT2 drugs
BT1 pregnanes
BT2 steroids
BT3 isoprenoids
BT4 lipids
BT1 synthetic glucocorticoids
BT2 synthetic corticoids
BT3 corticoids
BT3 synthetic hormones

DEXTER
BT1 cattle breeds
BT2 breeds

DEXTRAN
BT1 food additives
BT2 additives
BT1 glucans
BT2 polysaccharides
BT3 carbohydrates
BT1 gums
BT2 polysaccharides
BT3 carbohydrates
rt blood flow
rt malt

DEXTRANASE
(ec 3.2.1.11)
BT1 o-glycoside hydrolases
BT2 glycosidases
BT3 hydrolases
BT4 enzymes

DEXTRANSUCRASE
HN from 1990
(ec 2.4.1.5)
BT1 hexosyltransferases
BT2 glycosyltransferases
BT3 transferases
BT4 enzymes

dextrin maltose
USE **maltodextrins**

DEXTRINS
uf *starch gum*
BT1 glucans
BT2 polysaccharides
BT3 carbohydrates
BT1 gums
BT2 polysaccharides
BT3 carbohydrates
BT1 sweet tasting compounds
BT2 flavour compounds
NT1 maltodextrins
rt glycogen
rt starch

dextroerythrose sodium
USE **erythrose**

dextrose
USE **glucose**

DEYEUXIA
BT1 gramineae
NT1 deyeuxia youngii

DEYEUXIA YOUNGII
BT1 deyeuxia
BT2 gramineae
BT1 pasture plants

dhal
USE **lentils**
OR **pigeon peas**

DHANNI
HN from 1990
BT1 cattle breeds
BT2 breeds

DI-ALLATE
BT1 thiocarbamate herbicides
BT2 carbamate pesticides
BT2 herbicides
BT3 pesticides

DIABETES
BT1 metabolic disorders
BT2 animal disorders
BT3 disorders
NT1 diabetes insipidus
NT1 diabetes mellitus
NT1 diabetic acidosis
NT1 diabetic neuropathy
NT1 experimental diabetes
rt alloxan
rt blood sugar
rt diabetic coma
rt diabetic diets (agricola)
rt glucose tolerance
rt glucose tolerance test
rt hyperglycaemia
rt hypoglycaemic agents
rt insulin
rt obesity hyperglycaemia syndrome
rt pancreas islets

diabetes, experimental
USE **experimental diabetes**

DIABETES INSIPIDUS
BT1 diabetes
BT2 metabolic disorders
BT3 animal disorders
BT4 disorders
rt thirst
rt urination

DIABETES MELLITUS
BT1 diabetes
BT2 metabolic disorders
BT3 animal disorders
BT4 disorders

DIABETIC ACIDOSIS
BT1 acidosis
BT2 acid base disorders
BT3 metabolic disorders
BT4 animal disorders
BT5 disorders
BT1 diabetes
BT2 metabolic disorders
BT3 animal disorders
BT4 disorders

DIABETIC COMA
BT1 coma
BT2 dysregulation
BT3 functional disorders
BT4 animal disorders
BT5 disorders
rt diabetes

DIABETIC DIETS (AGRICOLA)
BT1 diets
rt diabetes

DIABETIC NEUROPATHY
uf *neuropathy, diabetic*
BT1 diabetes
BT2 metabolic disorders
BT3 animal disorders
BT4 disorders

DIABROTICA
BT1 chrysomelidae
BT2 coleoptera
NT1 diabrotica balteata
NT1 diabrotica barberi

DIABROTICA *cont.*
NT1 diabrotica longicornis
NT1 diabrotica speciosa
NT1 diabrotica undecimpunctata
NT2 diabrotica undecimpunctata howardi
NT1 diabrotica virgifera

DIABROTICA BALTEATA
BT1 diabrotica
BT2 chrysomelidae
BT3 coleoptera

DIABROTICA BARBERI
BT1 diabrotica
BT2 chrysomelidae
BT3 coleoptera

DIABROTICA LONGICORNIS
BT1 diabrotica
BT2 chrysomelidae
BT3 coleoptera

DIABROTICA SPECIOSA
BT1 diabrotica
BT2 chrysomelidae
BT3 coleoptera

DIABROTICA UNDECIMPUNCTATA
BT1 diabrotica
BT2 chrysomelidae
BT3 coleoptera
NT1 diabrotica undecimpunctata howardi

DIABROTICA UNDECIMPUNCTATA HOWARDI
BT1 diabrotica undecimpunctata
BT2 diabrotica
BT3 chrysomelidae
BT4 coleoptera

DIABROTICA VIRGIFERA
BT1 diabrotica
BT2 chrysomelidae
BT3 coleoptera

DIACETOXYSCIRPENOL
BT1 trichothecenes
BT2 mycotoxins
BT3 toxins

DIACETYL
BT1 flavour compounds
BT1 ketones
rt aroma

DIACHRYSIA
BT1 noctuidae
BT2 lepidoptera
rt thysanoplusia

diachrysia orichalcea
USE **thysanoplusia orichalcea**

DIACRISIA
BT1 arctiidae
BT2 lepidoptera
rt spilosoma

diacrisia casigneta
USE **spilosoma casigneta**

diacrisia obliqua
USE **spilosoma obliqua**

diacrisia virginica
USE **spilosoma virginica**

diacylglycerol lipase
USE **lipoprotein lipase**

DIACYLGLYCEROLS
uf *diglycerides*
BT1 acylglycerols
BT2 fatty acid esters
BT3 esters
BT2 neutral fats
BT3 fats
BT4 lipids

DIADASIA
BT1 apidae
BT2 hymenoptera

DIADEGMA
uf *horogenes*
uf *nythobia*
BT1 ichneumonidae
BT2 hymenoptera
NT1 diadegma armillata
NT1 diadegma eucerophaga
NT1 diadegma fenestralis
NT1 diadegma insularis

DIADEGMA ARMILLATA
uf *nythobia armillata*
BT1 diadegma
BT2 ichneumonidae
BT3 hymenoptera

DIADEGMA EUCEROPHAGA
BT1 diadegma
BT2 ichneumonidae
BT3 hymenoptera

DIADEGMA FENESTRALIS
uf *horogenes fenestralis*
uf *nythobia fenestralis*
BT1 diadegma
BT2 ichneumonidae
BT3 hymenoptera

DIADEGMA INSULARIS
uf *nythobia insularis*
BT1 diadegma
BT2 ichneumonidae
BT3 hymenoptera

DIADROMOUS FISHES
BT1 aquatic animals
BT2 animals
BT2 aquatic organisms
NT1 atlantic salmon
NT1 european eels
NT1 lampreys
NT1 sturgeons
rt fishes

DIADROMUS
BT1 ichneumonidae
BT2 hymenoptera
NT1 diadromus pulchellus

DIADROMUS PULCHELLUS
BT1 diadromus
BT2 ichneumonidae
BT3 hymenoptera

DIAERETIELLA
BT1 braconidae
BT2 hymenoptera
NT1 diaeretiella rapae
rt aphidius
rt diaeretus

DIAERETIELLA RAPAE
uf *aphidius brassicae*
uf *diaeretus rapae*
BT1 diaeretiella
BT2 braconidae
BT3 hymenoptera

DIAERETUS
BT1 braconidae
BT2 hymenoptera
rt diaeretiella

diaeretus rapae
USE **diaeretiella rapae**

DIAGNOSIS
uf *clinical assessment*
NT1 differential diagnosis
NT1 immunodiagnosis
NT1 laboratory diagnosis
NT1 pregnancy diagnosis
NT2 rectal palpation
NT1 prenatal diagnosis
NT1 sex diagnosis
NT2 autosexing
NT1 ultrasonic diagnosis
NT1 xenodiagnosis
rt biopsy
rt diagnostic techniques
rt diagnostic value
rt identification
rt prognosis
rt skin fold thickness

DIAGNOSIS *cont.*
rt symptoms

diagnosis, serological
USE **immunodiagnosis**

DIAGNOSTIC HORIZONS
BT1 horizons
BT2 soil morphological features

DIAGNOSTIC TECHNIQUES
BT1 techniques
NT1 amniocentesis
NT1 ballistocardiography
NT1 bronchoalveolar lavage
NT1 bronchoscopy
NT1 catheterization
NT1 clinical examination
NT2 auscultation
NT2 palpation
NT3 rectal palpation
NT1 dris
NT1 echocardiography
NT1 endoscopy
NT1 hair analysis (agricola)
NT1 laparoscopy
NT1 liver function tests
NT1 ophthalmoscopy
NT1 platelet count
NT1 radiography
NT2 autoradiography
NT2 microradiography
NT2 tomography
NT3 computed tomography
NT1 renal function tests
NT1 smears
NT2 vaginal smears
NT1 thermography
NT1 thyroid function tests
NT1 ultrasonography
NT1 urine analysis (agricola)
NT1 whiteside test
NT1 wisconsin mastitis test
rt diagnosis
rt skin fold thickness
rt symptoms
rt virus indicators

DIAGNOSTIC VALUE
rt diagnosis

DIALEURODES
BT1 aleyrodidae
BT2 aleyrodoidea
BT3 sternorrhyncha
BT4 homoptera
NT1 dialeurodes citri
NT1 dialeurodes citrifolii

DIALEURODES CITRI
BT1 dialeurodes
BT2 aleyrodidae
BT3 aleyrodoidea
BT4 sternorrhyncha
BT5 homoptera

DIALEURODES CITRIFOLII
BT1 dialeurodes
BT2 aleyrodidae
BT3 aleyrodoidea
BT4 sternorrhyncha
BT5 homoptera

DIALI
HN from 1990
BT1 cattle breeds
BT2 breeds

DIALICTUS
BT1 apidae
BT2 hymenoptera

dialifor
USE **dialifos**

DIALIFOS
uf *dialifor*
BT1 organothiophosphate acaricides
BT2 organophosphorus acaricides
BT3 acaricides
BT4 pesticides

DIALIFOS *cont.*
BT3 organophosphorus pesticides
BT4 organophosphorus compounds
BT1 organothiophosphate insecticides
BT2 organophosphorus insecticides
BT3 insecticides
BT4 pesticides
BT3 organophosphorus pesticides
BT4 organophosphorus compounds

DIALIUM
BT1 leguminosae
NT1 dialium engleranum
NT1 dialium guianense

DIALIUM ENGLERANUM
BT1 dialium
BT2 leguminosae

DIALIUM GUIANENSE
BT1 dialium
BT2 leguminosae

DIALLEL ANALYSIS
BT1 quantitative genetics
BT2 genetics
BT3 biology
BT1 statistical analysis
BT2 data analysis
BT2 statistics

DIALYANTHERA
BT1 myristicaceae

DIALYSIS
BT1 processing
BT1 separation
NT1 electrodialysis
NT1 haemodialysis
rt membranes
rt permeability
rt renal failure

DIAMETER
BT1 dimensions
rt dendrometers
rt form quotients
rt girth
rt increment

DIAMFENETIDE
BT1 anthelmintics
BT2 antiparasitic agents
BT3 drugs

diamine oxidase
USE **amine oxidase (copper-containing)**

DIAMINES
BT1 amines
BT2 amino compounds
BT3 organic nitrogen compounds
NT1 cadaverine
NT1 putrescine
rt polyamines

DIAMINO AMINO ACIDS
BT1 amino acids
BT2 carboxylic acids
BT3 organic acids
BT4 acids
BT2 organic nitrogen compounds
NT1 diaminopimelic acid

DIAMINOPIMELIC ACID
BT1 diamino amino acids
BT2 amino acids
BT3 carboxylic acids
BT4 organic acids
BT5 acids
BT3 organic nitrogen compounds
rt lysine

DIAMMONIUM PHOSPHATE
BT1 ammonium phosphates
BT2 ammonium fertilizers
BT3 nitrogen fertilizers
BT4 fertilizers
BT2 ammonium salts
BT3 ammonium compounds
BT2 nitrogen-phosphorus fertilizers
BT3 compound fertilizers
BT4 fertilizers
BT2 phosphates (salts)
BT3 inorganic salts
BT4 inorganic compounds
BT4 salts
BT3 phosphates
BT2 phosphorus fertilizers
BT3 fertilizers
BT1 feed additives
BT2 additives
rt protein supplements

DIAMMONIUM PYROPHOSPHATE
BT1 ammonium polyphosphates
BT2 ammonium phosphates
BT3 ammonium fertilizers
BT4 nitrogen fertilizers
BT5 fertilizers
BT3 ammonium salts
BT4 ammonium compounds
BT3 nitrogen-phosphorus fertilizers
BT4 compound fertilizers
BT5 fertilizers
BT3 phosphates (salts)
BT4 inorganic salts
BT5 inorganic compounds
BT5 salts
BT4 phosphates
BT3 phosphorus fertilizers
BT4 fertilizers
BT1 pyrophosphates
BT2 phosphates (salts)
BT3 inorganic salts
BT4 inorganic compounds
BT4 salts
BT3 phosphates
BT2 polyphosphates
BT3 condensed phosphates
BT4 phosphorus fertilizers
BT5 fertilizers

dianabol
USE **metandienone**

DIANTHIDIUM
BT1 apidae
BT2 hymenoptera

DIANTHOVIRUS GROUP
HN from 1990
BT1 plant viruses
BT2 plant pathogens
BT3 pathogens
NT1 carnation ringspot dianthovirus
NT1 red clover necrotic mosaic dianthovirus
NT1 sweet clover necrotic mosaic dianthovirus

DIANTHUS
BT1 caryophyllaceae
NT1 dianthus acicularis
NT1 dianthus barbatus
NT1 dianthus caryophyllus
NT1 dianthus chinensis
NT1 dianthus deltoides
NT1 dianthus gratianopolitanus
NT1 dianthus plumarius
NT1 dianthus superbus

DIANTHUS ACICULARIS
BT1 dianthus
BT2 caryophyllaceae

DIANTHUS BARBATUS
uf *sweet william*
BT1 dianthus
BT2 caryophyllaceae
BT1 ornamental herbaceous plants

DIANTHUS CARYOPHYLLUS
BT1 antiviral plants
BT1 dianthus
BT2 caryophyllaceae
rt carnation cryptic cryptovirus
rt carnation etched ring caulimovirus
rt carnation latent carlavirus
rt carnation mottle carmovirus
rt carnation necrotic fleck closterovirus
rt carnation ringspot dianthovirus
rt carnation vein mottle potyvirus
rt carnations

DIANTHUS CHINENSIS
BT1 dianthus
BT2 caryophyllaceae
BT1 medicinal plants
BT1 ornamental herbaceous plants

DIANTHUS DELTOIDES
BT1 dianthus
BT2 caryophyllaceae
BT1 ornamental herbaceous plants

DIANTHUS GRATIANOPOLITANUS
BT1 dianthus
BT2 caryophyllaceae
BT1 ornamental herbaceous plants

DIANTHUS PLUMARIUS
BT1 dianthus
BT2 caryophyllaceae
BT1 ornamental herbaceous plants

DIANTHUS SUPERBUS
BT1 dianthus
BT2 caryophyllaceae
BT1 medicinal plants
BT1 ornamental herbaceous plants

DIAPAUSE
BT1 dormancy
rt hibernation
rt metamorphosis

DIAPHANIA
BT1 pyralidae
BT2 lepidoptera
NT1 diaphania hyalinata
NT1 diaphania nitidalis

DIAPHANIA HYALINATA
BT1 diaphania
BT2 pyralidae
BT3 lepidoptera

DIAPHANIA NITIDALIS
BT1 diaphania
BT2 pyralidae
BT3 lepidoptera

DIAPHEROMERA
BT1 phasmatidae
BT2 phasmida
NT1 diapheromera femorata

DIAPHEROMERA FEMORATA
BT1 diapheromera
BT2 phasmatidae
BT3 phasmida

DIAPHORINA
BT1 aphalaridae
BT2 psylloidea
BT3 sternorrhyncha
BT4 homoptera
NT1 diaphorina citri

DIAPHORINA CITRI
BT1 diaphorina
BT2 aphalaridae
BT3 psylloidea
BT4 sternorrhyncha
BT5 homoptera

DIAPHRAGM
BT1 muscles
BT2 musculoskeletal system
BT3 body parts

DIAPHRAGM PUMPS
BT1 pumps
BT2 machinery

DIAPHRAGMS (AGRICOLA)
BT1 contraceptives

DIAPORTHALES
NT1 apiognomonia
NT2 apiognomonia errabunda
NT2 apiognomonia veneta
NT1 clypeoporthe
NT2 clypeoporthe iliau
NT1 cryphonectria
NT2 cryphonectria cubensis
NT2 cryphonectria gyrosa
NT2 cryphonectria havanensis
NT2 cryphonectria parasitica
NT1 cryptodiaporthe
NT2 cryptodiaporthe populea
NT1 cryptosporella
NT1 diaporthe
NT2 diaporthe citri
NT2 diaporthe eres
NT2 diaporthe helianthi
NT2 diaporthe perniciosa
NT2 diaporthe phaseolorum
NT3 diaporthe phaseolorum var. sojae
NT2 diaporthe woodii
NT1 endothia
NT1 gaeumannomyces
NT2 gaeumannomyces graminis
NT3 gaeumannomyces graminis var. graminis
NT1 gnomonia
NT2 gnomonia fructicola
NT2 gnomonia leptostyla
NT2 gnomonia platani
NT1 leucostoma
NT2 leucostoma cinctum
NT2 leucostoma niveum
NT2 leucostoma persoonii
NT1 valsa
NT2 valsa iranica
NT2 valsa kunzei
NT2 valsa mali
NT2 valsa sordida
rt fungi

DIAPORTHE
BT1 diaporthales
NT1 diaporthe citri
NT1 diaporthe eres
NT1 diaporthe helianthi
NT1 diaporthe perniciosa
NT1 diaporthe phaseolorum
NT2 diaporthe phaseolorum var. sojae
NT1 diaporthe woodii
rt phomopsis

DIAPORTHE CITRI
uf *phomopsis citri*
BT1 diaporthe
BT2 diaporthales

DIAPORTHE ERES
BT1 diaporthe
BT2 diaporthales

DIAPORTHE HELIANTHI
HN from 1990
uf *phomopsis helianthi*
BT1 diaporthe
BT2 diaporthales

DIAPORTHE PERNICIOSA
uf *phomopsis mali*
BT1 diaporthe
BT2 diaporthales

DIAPORTHE PHASEOLORUM
BT1 diaporthe
BT2 diaporthales
NT1 diaporthe phaseolorum var. sojae

DIAPORTHE PHASEOLORUM VAR. SOJAE
HN from 1990
uf *phomopsis sojae*
BT1 diaporthe phaseolorum
BT2 diaporthe
BT3 diaporthales

DIAPORTHE WOODII
uf *phomopsis leptostromiformis*
uf *phomopsis rossiana*
BT1 diaporthe
BT2 diaporthales
rt phomopsins

DIAPREPES
BT1 curculionidae
BT2 coleoptera
NT1 diaprepes abbreviatus

DIAPREPES ABBREVIATUS
BT1 diaprepes
BT2 curculionidae
BT3 coleoptera

DIAPRIIDAE
BT1 hymenoptera

DIAPTOMUS
BT1 calanoida
BT2 copepoda
BT3 crustacea
BT4 arthropods
rt skistodiaptomus

diaptomus pallidus
USE **skistodiaptomus pallidus**

DIARRHEA
BF diarrhoea
rt antidiarrhea agents
rt bovine diarrhea virus
rt calf diarrhea rotavirus

DIARRHENA
BT1 gramineae

DIARRHOEA
AF diarrhea
uf *scouring*
BT1 digestive disorders
BT2 functional disorders
BT3 animal disorders
BT4 disorders
NT1 giardiasis
rt antidiarrhoea agents
rt bovine diarrhoea virus
rt calf diarrhoea rotavirus
rt enteritis
rt oral rehydration solutions
rt oral rehydration therapy

DIASPIDIDAE
BT1 coccoidea
BT2 sternorrhyncha
BT3 homoptera
NT1 abgrallaspis
NT2 abgrallaspis cyanophylli
NT1 aonidiella
NT2 aonidiella aurantii
NT2 aonidiella citrina
NT2 aonidiella orientalis
NT1 aonidomytilus
NT2 aonidomytilus albus
NT1 aspidiotus
NT2 aspidiotus destructor
NT2 aspidiotus nerii
NT1 aulacaspis
NT2 aulacaspis madiunensis
NT2 aulacaspis rosae
NT2 aulacaspis tegalensis
NT2 aulacaspis tubercularis
NT1 chionaspis
NT2 chionaspis pinifoliae
NT2 chionaspis salicis
NT1 chrysomphalus
NT2 chrysomphalus aonidum
NT2 chrysomphalus dictyospermi
NT1 diaspidiotus
NT1 diaspis
NT2 diaspis bromeliae
NT1 fiorinia

DIASPIDIDAE *cont.*
NT2 fiorinia theae
NT1 hemiberlesia
NT2 hemiberlesia lataniae
NT2 hemiberlesia rapax
NT1 insulaspis
NT1 lepidosaphes
NT2 lepidosaphes beckii
NT2 lepidosaphes gloverii
NT2 lepidosaphes ulmi
NT1 leucaspis
NT1 melanaspis
NT2 melanaspis glomerata
NT1 parlatoria
NT2 parlatoria blanchardii
NT2 parlatoria oleae
NT2 parlatoria pergandii
NT2 parlatoria ziziphi
NT1 pinnaspis
NT2 pinnaspis strachani
NT1 pseudaonidia
NT1 pseudaulacaspis
NT2 pseudaulacaspis pentagona
NT1 quadraspidiotus
NT2 quadraspidiotus ostreaeformis
NT2 quadraspidiotus perniciosus
NT1 selenaspidus
NT2 selenaspidus articulatus
NT1 unaspis
NT2 unaspis citri
NT2 unaspis euonymi
NT2 unaspis yanonensis

DIASPIDIOTUS
BT1 diaspididae
BT2 coccoidea
BT3 sternorrhyncha
BT4 homoptera

DIASPIS
BT1 diaspididae
BT2 coccoidea
BT3 sternorrhyncha
BT4 homoptera
NT1 diaspis bromeliae

DIASPIS BROMELIAE
BT1 diaspis
BT2 diaspididae
BT3 coccoidea
BT4 sternorrhyncha
BT5 homoptera

DIASPORE
BT1 nonclay minerals
BT2 minerals

diastase
USE **α-glucosidase**

diataraxia
USE **lacanobia**

diataraxia oleracea
USE **lacanobia oleracea**

DIATHESES
NT1 exudative diathesis
NT1 haemorrhagic diathesis
rt susceptibility

diathesis, exudative
USE **exudative diathesis**

diathesis, haemorrhagic
USE **haemorrhagic diathesis**

diatomaceous earth
USE **diatomite**

DIATOMITE
uf *diatomaceous earth*
BT1 nonclay minerals
BT2 minerals
NT1 kieselguhr
rt silica

diatoms
USE **bacillariophyta**

DIATRAEA
BT1 pyralidae
BT2 lepidoptera

DIATRAEA *cont.*
NT1 diatraea centrella
NT1 diatraea grandiosella
NT1 diatraea impersonatella
NT1 diatraea lineolata
NT1 diatraea saccharalis

DIATRAEA CENTRELLA
BT1 diatraea
BT2 pyralidae
BT3 lepidoptera

DIATRAEA GRANDIOSELLA
BT1 diatraea
BT2 pyralidae
BT3 lepidoptera

DIATRAEA IMPERSONATELLA
BT1 diatraea
BT2 pyralidae
BT3 lepidoptera

DIATRAEA LINEOLATA
BT1 diatraea
BT2 pyralidae
BT3 lepidoptera

DIATRAEA SACCHARALIS
BT1 diatraea
BT2 pyralidae
BT3 lepidoptera

DIATRYPALES
NT1 eutypa
NT2 eutypa armeniacae
NT2 eutypa japonica
NT2 eutypa vexans
NT1 eutypella
NT2 eutypella parasitica
rt fungi

DIAVERIDINE
BT1 coccidiostats
BT2 antiprotozoal agents
BT3 antiparasitic agents
BT4 drugs

DIAZEPAM
BT1 benzodiazepines
BT2 heterocyclic nitrogen compounds
BT3 organic nitrogen compounds
BT1 neuroleptics
BT2 psychotropic drugs
BT3 neurotropic drugs
BT4 drugs

DIAZINON
BT1 ectoparasiticides
BT2 antiparasitic agents
BT3 drugs
BT1 organothiophosphate acaricides
BT2 organophosphorus acaricides
BT3 acaricides
BT4 pesticides
BT3 organophosphorus pesticides
BT4 organophosphorus compounds
BT1 organothiophosphate insecticides
BT2 organophosphorus insecticides
BT3 insecticides
BT4 pesticides
BT3 organophosphorus pesticides
BT4 organophosphorus compounds

DIAZO COMPOUNDS
BT1 organic nitrogen compounds
NT1 1,4-bisdiazoacetylbutane

DIAZOXIDE
BT1 antihypertensive agents
BT2 cardiovascular agents
BT3 drugs

DIBBERS
BT1 farm machinery

DIBBERS *cont.*
BT2 machinery
rt planting
rt precision drills

dibothriocephalus
USE **diphyllobothrium**

DIBOTRYON
HN from 1990
BT1 dothideales
rt apiosporina

dibotryon morbosum
USE **apiosporina morbosa**

DIBRACHYS
BT1 pteromalidae
BT2 hymenoptera
NT1 dibrachys cavus

DIBRACHYS CAVUS
BT1 dibrachys
BT2 pteromalidae
BT3 hymenoptera

dibromochloropropane
USE **dbcp**

1,2-dibromoethane
USE **ethylene dibromide**

DIBUTYL PHTHALATE
BT1 insect repellents
BT2 repellents
BT1 phthalates
BT2 esters
BT1 plasticizers

DICALCIUM PHOSPHATE
uf *calcium hydrogen phosphate*
BT1 calcium phosphates
BT2 phosphates (salts)
BT3 inorganic salts
BT4 inorganic compounds
BT4 salts
BT3 phosphates
BT2 phosphorus fertilizers
BT3 fertilizers

DICAMBA
BT1 auxins
BT2 plant growth regulators
BT3 growth regulators
BT1 benzoic acid herbicides
BT2 aromatic acid herbicides
BT3 herbicides
BT4 pesticides

DICARBOXIMIDE FUNGICIDES
BT1 fungicides
BT2 pesticides
NT1 captafol
NT1 captan
NT1 folpet
NT1 iprodione
NT1 procymidone
NT1 vinclozolin

DICARBOXYLIC ACIDS
BT1 carboxylic acids
BT2 organic acids
BT3 acids
NT1 α-ketoglutaric acid
NT1 adipic acid
NT1 diferulic acid
NT1 diglycine
NT1 fumaric acid
NT1 glutaric acid
NT1 guanidinosuccinic acid
NT1 malic acid
NT1 malonic acid
NT1 methylmalonic acid
NT1 oxalic acid
NT1 oxaloacetic acid
NT1 phthalic acid
NT1 porphobilinogen
NT1 succinic acid
NT1 tartaric acid

DICENTRA
BT1 fumariaceae
NT1 dicentra spectabilis

DICENTRA SPECTABILIS
BT1 dicentra
BT2 fumariaceae
BT1 ornamental herbaceous plants

DICENTRARCHUS
BT1 percichthyidae
BT2 perciformes
BT3 osteichthyes
BT4 fishes
rt morone

dicentrarchus labrax
USE **sea bass**

diceratosmia
USE **osmia**

DICERORHINUS
BT1 rhinocerotidae
BT2 perissodactyla
BT3 mammals
BT3 ungulates
NT1 dicerorhinus sumatrensis

DICERORHINUS SUMATRENSIS
BT1 dicerorhinus
BT2 rhinocerotidae
BT3 perissodactyla
BT4 mammals
BT4 ungulates

DICEROS
BT1 rhinocerotidae
BT2 perissodactyla
BT3 mammals
BT3 ungulates
NT1 diceros bicornis
rt ceratotherium

DICEROS BICORNIS
BT1 diceros
BT2 rhinocerotidae
BT3 perissodactyla
BT4 mammals
BT4 ungulates

diceros simus
USE **ceratotherium simum**

dichanthelium oligosanthes
USE **panicum oligosanthes**

DICHANTHIUM
BT1 gramineae
NT1 dichanthium annulatum
NT1 dichanthium aristatum
NT1 dichanthium caricosum
NT1 dichanthium contortum
NT1 dichanthium sericeum

DICHANTHIUM ANNULATUM
BT1 dichanthium
BT2 gramineae
BT1 pasture plants

DICHANTHIUM ARISTATUM
BT1 dichanthium
BT2 gramineae
BT1 pasture plants

DICHANTHIUM CARICOSUM
BT1 dichanthium
BT2 gramineae

dichanthium caucasicum
USE **bothriochloa caucasica**

DICHANTHIUM CONTORTUM
BT1 dichanthium
BT2 gramineae

dichanthium insculptum
USE **bothriochloa insculpta**

DICHANTHIUM SERICEUM
BT1 dichanthium
BT2 gramineae
BT1 pasture plants

DICHAPETALACEAE
NT1 dichapetalum
NT2 dichapetalum cymosum

DICHAPETALUM
BT1 dichapetalaceae
NT1 dichapetalum cymosum

DICHAPETALUM CYMOSUM
BT1 dichapetalum
BT2 dichapetalaceae

DICHELACHNE
BT1 gramineae
NT1 dichelachne sciurea

DICHELACHNE SCIUREA
BT1 dichelachne
BT2 gramineae
BT1 pasture plants

DICHLOBENIL
BT1 nitrile herbicides
BT2 herbicides
BT3 pesticides

DICHLOFENTHION
BT1 organothiophosphate insecticides
BT2 organophosphorus insecticides
BT3 insecticides
BT4 pesticides
BT3 organophosphorus pesticides
BT4 organophosphorus compounds
BT1 organothiophosphate nematicides
BT2 organophosphorus nematicides
BT3 nematicides
BT4 pesticides
BT3 organophosphorus pesticides
BT4 organophosphorus compounds

DICHLOFLUANID
BT1 phenylsulfamide fungicides
BT2 fungicides
BT3 pesticides

DICHLONE
BT1 quinone fungicides
BT2 fungicides
BT3 pesticides
BT2 quinones
BT3 aromatic compounds

DICHLORALUREA
uf *dcu*
BT1 urea herbicides
BT2 herbicides
BT3 pesticides

DICHLORFLURENOL
BT1 morphactins
BT2 growth inhibitors
BT3 inhibitors
BT3 plant growth regulators
BT4 growth regulators

DICHLORMATE
BT1 carbamate herbicides
BT2 carbamate pesticides
BT2 herbicides
BT3 pesticides

DICHLORMID
BT1 herbicide safeners
BT2 safeners

DICHLOROACETIC ACID
BT1 chlorinated fatty acids
BT2 organochlorine compounds
BT3 organic halogen compounds
BT1 dermatological agents
BT2 drugs
rt cautery

3,4-DICHLOROANILINE
BT1 pesticide residues
BT2 residues

PARA-DICHLOROBENZENE
BT1 fumigant insecticides
BT2 fumigants

PARA-DICHLOROBENZENE *cont.*
BT3 pesticides
BT2 insecticides
BT3 pesticides

1,2-dichloroethane
USE **ethylene dichloride**

2,3-DICHLOROISOBUTYRIC ACID
BT1 gametocides
BT2 plant growth regulators
BT3 growth regulators
BT1 growth retardants
BT2 plant growth regulators
BT3 growth regulators
BT2 retardants

dichloromethane
USE **methylene chloride**

DICHLOROPHEN
BT1 anthelmintics
BT2 antiparasitic agents
BT3 drugs
BT1 antiprotozoal agents
BT2 antiparasitic agents
BT3 drugs
BT1 phenols
BT2 alcohols
BT2 phenolic compounds
BT3 aromatic compounds
BT1 unclassified fungicides
BT2 fungicides
BT3 pesticides

2,4-DICHLOROPHENOL
BT1 phenols
BT2 alcohols
BT2 phenolic compounds
BT3 aromatic compounds

(2,4-dichlorophenoxy)acetic acid
USE **2,4-d**

(3,5-dichlorophenoxy)acetic acid
USE **3,5-d**

4-(2,4-dichlorophenoxy)butyric acid
USE **2,4-db**

3,6-dichloropicolinic acid
USE **clopyralid**

1,2-DICHLOROPROPANE
BT1 soil fumigants
BT2 fumigants
BT3 pesticides
BT1 solvents
BT1 unclassified nematicides
BT2 nematicides
BT3 pesticides

1,3-DICHLOROPROPENE
BT1 soil fumigants
BT2 fumigants
BT3 pesticides
BT1 unclassified nematicides
BT2 nematicides
BT3 pesticides

2,2-dichloropropionic acid
USE **dalapon**

DICHLORPROP
BT1 auxins
BT2 plant growth regulators
BT3 growth regulators
BT1 phenoxypropionic herbicides
BT2 phenoxy herbicides
BT3 herbicides
BT4 pesticides

DICHLORVOS
uf *ddvp*
BT1 anthelmintics
BT2 antiparasitic agents
BT3 drugs
BT1 ectoparasiticides
BT2 antiparasitic agents
BT3 drugs
BT1 organophosphate insecticides
BT2 organophosphorus insecticides

DICHLORVOS *cont.*
BT3 insecticides
BT4 pesticides
BT3 organophosphorus pesticides
BT4 organophosphorus compounds

DICHLOZOLINE
BT1 oxazole fungicides
BT2 fungicides
BT3 pesticides

DICHOCROCIS
BT1 pyralidae
BT2 lepidoptera
NT1 dichocrocis punctiferalis

DICHOCROCIS PUNCTIFERALIS
BT1 dichocrocis
BT2 pyralidae
BT3 lepidoptera

DICHONDRA
BT1 convolvulaceae
NT1 dichondra micrantha
NT1 dichondra repens
NT1 dichondra sativa

DICHONDRA MICRANTHA
BT1 dichondra
BT2 convolvulaceae
BT1 ornamental herbaceous plants

DICHONDRA REPENS
BT1 dichondra
BT2 convolvulaceae
BT1 ornamental herbaceous plants

DICHONDRA SATIVA
BT1 dichondra
BT2 convolvulaceae
BT1 ornamental herbaceous plants

DICHROA
BT1 hydrangeaceae
NT1 dichroa febrifuga

DICHROA FEBRIFUGA
BT1 dichroa
BT2 hydrangeaceae

DICHROSTACHYS
BT1 leguminosae
NT1 dichrostachys cinerea
NT1 dichrostachys glomerata

DICHROSTACHYS CINEREA
BT1 dichrostachys
BT2 leguminosae

DICHROSTACHYS GLOMERATA
BT1 dichrostachys
BT2 leguminosae
BT1 pasture legumes
BT2 legumes
BT2 pasture plants

DICKITE
BT1 clay minerals
BT2 minerals

DICLADISPA
uf *hispa*
BT1 chrysomelidae
BT2 coleoptera
NT1 dicladispa armigera

DICLADISPA ARMIGERA
uf *hispa armigera*
BT1 dicladispa
BT2 chrysomelidae
BT3 coleoptera

DICLADOCERUS
BT1 eulophidae
BT2 hymenoptera
NT1 dicladocerus westwoodii

DICLADOCERUS WESTWOODII
BT1 dicladocerus
BT2 eulophidae

DICLADOCERUS WESTWOODII *cont.*
BT3 hymenoptera

DICLIDOPHORA
BT1 diclidophoridae
BT2 monogenea

DICLIDOPHORIDAE
BT1 monogenea
NT1 diclidophora

DICLOBUTRAZOL
BT1 conazole fungicides
BT2 azoles
BT3 heterocyclic nitrogen compounds
BT4 organic nitrogen compounds
BT2 fungicides
BT3 pesticides

DICLOFOP
BT1 aryloxyphenoxypropionic herbicides
BT2 phenoxypropionic herbicides
BT3 phenoxy herbicides
BT4 herbicides
BT5 pesticides

DICLORAN
uf *dcna*
BT1 aromatic fungicides
BT2 fungicides
BT3 pesticides

DICOFOL
BT1 bridged diphenyl acaricides
BT2 acaricides
BT3 pesticides

dicophane
USE **ddt**

DICORYNIA
BT1 leguminosae
NT1 dicorynia guianensis

DICORYNIA GUIANENSIS
BT1 dicorynia
BT2 leguminosae

DICOTYLEDONS
rt monocotyledons
rt plants
rt seeds

DICOUMAROL
BT1 anticoagulants
BT2 haematologic agents
BT3 drugs
BT1 coumarins
BT2 lactones
BT3 heterocyclic oxygen compounds
BT3 ketones
BT1 vitamin k antagonists
BT2 vitamin antagonists
BT3 antagonists
BT4 metabolic inhibitors
BT5 inhibitors

DICRANOPTERIS
BT1 gleicheniaceae
NT1 dicranopteris linearis

DICRANOPTERIS LINEARIS
BT1 dicranopteris
BT2 gleicheniaceae
BT1 ornamental ferns
BT2 ferns
BT2 ornamental foliage plants
BT3 foliage plants

DICRANORCHESELLA
BT1 entomobryidae
BT2 collembola

DICRANOSTIGMA
BT1 papaveraceae
NT1 dicranostigma franchetianum

DICRANOSTIGMA FRANCHETIANUM

DICRANOSTIGMA FRANCHETIANUM *cont.*
BT1 dicranostigma
BT2 papaveraceae

DICROCOELIIDAE
BT1 digenea
BT2 trematoda
NT1 brachylecithum
NT1 dicrocoelium
NT2 dicrocoelium hospes
NT2 dicrocoelium lanceolatum
NT1 eurytrema
NT2 eurytrema coelomaticum
NT2 eurytrema pancreaticum
NT1 platynosomum

DICROCOELIUM
BT1 dicrocoeliidae
BT2 digenea
BT3 trematoda
NT1 dicrocoelium hospes
NT1 dicrocoelium lanceolatum

dicrocoelium dendriticum
USE **dicrocoelium lanceolatum**

DICROCOELIUM HOSPES
BT1 dicrocoelium
BT2 dicrocoeliidae
BT3 digenea
BT4 trematoda

DICROCOELIUM LANCEOLATUM
uf *dicrocoelium dendriticum*
BT1 dicrocoelium
BT2 dicrocoeliidae
BT3 digenea
BT4 trematoda
rt liver flukes

DICROSTACHYS
BT1 leguminosae

DICROSTONYX
BT1 microtinae
BT2 muridae
BT3 rodents
BT4 mammals
rt lemmings

DICROTENDIPES
BT1 chironomidae
BT2 diptera
NT1 dicrotendipes californicus
rt chironomus

DICROTENDIPES CALIFORNICUS
uf *chironomus californicus*
BT1 dicrotendipes
BT2 chironomidae
BT3 diptera

DICROTOPHOS
BT1 organophosphate insecticides
BT2 organophosphorus insecticides
BT3 insecticides
BT4 pesticides
BT3 organophosphorus pesticides
BT4 organophosphorus compounds

DICTAMNUS
BT1 rutaceae
NT1 dictamnus albus
NT1 dictamnus caucasica
NT1 dictamnus gymnostylis
NT1 dictamnus tadshikorum

DICTAMNUS ALBUS
BT1 dictamnus
BT2 rutaceae

DICTAMNUS CAUCASICA
BT1 dictamnus
BT2 rutaceae

DICTAMNUS GYMNOSTYLIS
BT1 dictamnus
BT2 rutaceae

DICTAMNUS TADSHIKORUM
BT1 dictamnus
BT2 rutaceae

DICTATORSHIP
BT1 political systems
BT2 politics

DICTIONARIES
BT1 books
BT2 publications
BT1 reference works
rt glossaries
rt terminology

DICTYOCAULIDAE
BT1 nematoda
NT1 dictyocaulus
NT2 dictyocaulus arnfieldi
NT2 dictyocaulus cameli
NT2 dictyocaulus filaria
NT2 dictyocaulus viviparus
rt animal parasitic nematodes

DICTYOCAULUS
BT1 dictyocaulidae
BT2 nematoda
NT1 dictyocaulus arnfieldi
NT1 dictyocaulus cameli
NT1 dictyocaulus filaria
NT1 dictyocaulus viviparus

DICTYOCAULUS ARNFIELDI
BT1 dictyocaulus
BT2 dictyocaulidae
BT3 nematoda

DICTYOCAULUS CAMELI
BT1 dictyocaulus
BT2 dictyocaulidae
BT3 nematoda

DICTYOCAULUS FILARIA
BT1 dictyocaulus
BT2 dictyocaulidae
BT3 nematoda
rt lungworms

DICTYOCAULUS VIVIPARUS
BT1 dictyocaulus
BT2 dictyocaulidae
BT3 nematoda
rt lungworms

DICTYOPHORA
BT1 phallales

DICTYOPTERA
NT1 blattaria
NT2 blaberidae
NT3 blaberus
NT4 blaberus atropos
NT4 blaberus craniifer
NT4 blaberus discoidalis
NT4 blaberus giganteus
NT3 diploptera
NT4 diploptera punctata
NT2 blattellidae
NT3 blattella
NT4 blattella asahinai
NT4 blattella germanica
NT3 parcoblatta
NT3 supella
NT4 supella longipalpa
NT2 blattidae
NT3 blatta
NT4 blatta orientalis
NT3 periplaneta
NT4 periplaneta americana
NT4 periplaneta australasiae
NT4 periplaneta brunnea
NT4 periplaneta fuliginosa
NT4 periplaneta japonica
NT2 oxyhaloidae
NT3 gromphadorhina
NT4 gromphadorhina portentosa
NT3 nauphoeta
NT4 nauphoeta cinerea
NT3 pycnoscelus
NT4 pycnoscelus surinamensis
NT3 rhyparobia
NT4 rhyparobia maderae

DICTYOPTERA *cont.*
NT2 polyphagidae
NT3 polyphaga
NT1 mantodea
NT2 mantidae
NT3 mantis
NT4 mantis religiosa
NT3 tenodera
NT4 tenodera angustipennis
NT4 tenodera aridifolia
rt insects

DICTYOSOMES
BT1 protoplasm

DICTYOSTELIALES
NT1 dictyostelium
rt fungi

DICTYOSTELIUM
BT1 dictyosteliales

DICYANDIAMIDE
uf *cyanoguanidine*
uf *dcd*
BT1 guanidines
BT2 organic nitrogen compounds
BT1 nitrification inhibitors
BT2 metabolic inhibitors
BT3 inhibitors

DICYANODIAMIDINE
BT1 guanidines
BT2 organic nitrogen compounds
BT1 nitrogen fertilizers
BT2 fertilizers
BT1 slow release fertilizers
BT2 fertilizers

DICYANODIAMIDINE SULFATE
uf *dicyanodiamidine sulphate*
BT1 nitrogen fertilizers
BT2 fertilizers
BT1 sulfates (organic salts)
BT2 organic salts
BT3 salts
BT2 sulfates
BT1 sulfur fertilizers
BT2 fertilizers

dicyanodiamidine sulphate
USE **dicyanodiamidine sulfate**

dicyclomine
USE **dicycloverine**

DICYCLOVERINE
uf *dicyclomine*
BT1 parasympatholytics
BT2 neurotropic drugs
BT3 drugs

DIDACTIC DRAWINGS
BT1 teaching methods
BT2 methodology

didacus
USE **dacus**

didacus ciliatus
USE **dacus ciliatus**

DIDELPHIDAE
BT1 marsupials
BT2 mammals
NT1 didelphis
NT2 didelphis albiventris
NT2 didelphis marsupialis
NT2 didelphis virginiana
NT1 marmosa
NT1 metachirus
NT2 metachirus nudicaudatus
NT1 monodelphis
NT2 monodelphis domestica
NT1 philander
NT2 philander opossum
rt opossums

DIDELPHIS
BT1 didelphidae
BT2 marsupials
BT3 mammals
NT1 didelphis albiventris

DIDELPHIS *cont.*
NT1 didelphis marsupialis
NT1 didelphis virginiana

DIDELPHIS ALBIVENTRIS
BT1 didelphis
BT2 didelphidae
BT3 marsupials
BT4 mammals

DIDELPHIS MARSUPIALIS
BT1 didelphis
BT2 didelphidae
BT3 marsupials
BT4 mammals

DIDELPHIS VIRGINIANA
BT1 didelphis
BT2 didelphidae
BT3 marsupials
BT4 mammals

DIDIEREA
BT1 didiereaceae
NT1 didierea madagascariensis

DIDIEREA MADAGASCARIENSIS
BT1 didierea
BT2 didiereaceae

DIDIEREACEAE
NT1 alluaudia
NT2 alluaudia dumosa
NT2 alluaudia procera
NT1 alluaudiopsis
NT2 alluaudiopsis marnierana
NT1 decaryia
NT2 decaryia madagascariensis
NT1 didierea
NT2 didierea madagascariensis

DIDISCUS
BT1 umbelliferae
NT1 didiscus caeruleus

DIDISCUS CAERULEUS
uf *trachymene caerulea*
BT1 didiscus
BT2 umbelliferae
BT1 ornamental herbaceous plants

DIDYMELLA
BT1 dothideales
NT1 didymella applanata
NT1 didymella bryoniae
NT1 didymella chrysanthemi
NT1 didymella lycopersici
rt ascochyta
rt mycosphaerella
rt phoma

DIDYMELLA APPLANATA
BT1 didymella
BT2 dothideales

DIDYMELLA BRYONIAE
uf *ascochyta cucumeris*
uf *mycosphaerella citrullina*
uf *mycosphaerella melonis*
BT1 didymella
BT2 dothideales

DIDYMELLA CHRYSANTHEMI
uf *ascochyta chrysanthemi*
uf *mycosphaerella ligulicola*
BT1 didymella
BT2 dothideales

DIDYMELLA LYCOPERSICI
uf *ascochyta lycopersici*
uf *phoma lycopersici*
BT1 didymella
BT2 dothideales

didymella pinodes
USE **mycosphaerella pinodes**

didymella rabiei
USE **ascochyta rabiei**

DIDYMOCARPUS
BT1 gesneriaceae
NT1 didymocarpus oblonga
NT1 didymocarpus pedicellata

DIDYMOCARPUS OBLONGA
BT1 didymocarpus
BT2 gesneriaceae

DIDYMOCARPUS PEDICELLATA
BT1 didymocarpus
BT2 gesneriaceae

DIDYMOPANAX
BT1 araliaceae
NT1 didymopanax morototoni

DIDYMOPANAX MOROTOTONI
BT1 didymopanax
BT2 araliaceae
BT1 forest trees

DIDYMOPHYES
BT1 apicomplexa
BT2 protozoa
NT1 didymophyes gigantea

DIDYMOPHYES GIGANTEA
BT1 didymophyes
BT2 apicomplexa
BT3 protozoa

DIDYMOSPHAERIA
BT1 dothideales
NT1 didymosphaeria arachidicola

DIDYMOSPHAERIA ARACHIDICOLA
uf *ascochyta adzamethica*
uf *mycosphaerella arachidicola*
uf *mycosphaerella argentinensis*
uf *phoma arachidicola*
BT1 didymosphaeria
BT2 dothideales

DIEBACK
BT1 plant disorders
BT2 disorders

DIECTOMIS
BT1 gramineae
NT1 diectomis fastigiata

DIECTOMIS FASTIGIATA
BT1 diectomis
BT2 gramineae
BT1 pasture plants

DIEFFENBACHIA
BT1 araceae
NT1 dieffenbachia amoena
NT1 dieffenbachia bausei
NT1 dieffenbachia exotica
NT1 dieffenbachia maculata

DIEFFENBACHIA AMOENA
BT1 dieffenbachia
BT2 araceae
BT1 medicinal plants
rt ornamental foliage plants

DIEFFENBACHIA BAUSEI
BT1 dieffenbachia
BT2 araceae
rt ornamental foliage plants

DIEFFENBACHIA EXOTICA
BT1 dieffenbachia
BT2 araceae
rt ornamental foliage plants

DIEFFENBACHIA MACULATA
uf *dieffenbachia picta*
BT1 dieffenbachia
BT2 araceae
rt ornamental foliage plants

dieffenbachia picta
USE **dieffenbachia maculata**

DIEHLIOMYCES
BT1 gymnoascales
NT1 diehliomyces microsporus

DIEHLIOMYCES MICROSPORUS
BT1 diehliomyces
BT2 gymnoascales

DIELDRIN
BT1 cyclodiene insecticides

DIELDRIN *cont.*
BT2 organochlorine insecticides
BT3 insecticides
BT4 pesticides
BT3 organochlorine pesticides
BT4 organochlorine compounds
BT5 organic halogen compounds

DIELECTRIC CONSTANT
uf *permittivity*
BT1 dielectric properties
BT2 physicochemical properties
BT3 properties
rt electrical properties

DIELECTRIC PROPERTIES
BT1 physicochemical properties
BT2 properties
NT1 dielectric constant

DIELECTRICS
BT1 insulating materials
BT2 materials
rt electrical conductance
rt electrical resistance

DIENOCHLOR
BT1 organochlorine acaricides
BT2 acaricides
BT3 pesticides
BT2 organochlorine pesticides
BT3 organochlorine compounds
BT4 organic halogen compounds

DIENOIC FATTY ACIDS
BT1 unsaturated fatty acids
BT2 fatty acids
BT3 carboxylic acids
BT4 organic acids
BT5 acids
BT3 lipids
NT1 3,5-tetradecadienoic acid
NT1 linoleic acid
NT1 sorbic acid
NT1 tetracosadienoic acid

DIENTAMOEBA
BT1 sarcomastigophora
BT2 protozoa
NT1 dientamoeba fragilis

DIENTAMOEBA FRAGILIS
BT1 dientamoeba
BT2 sarcomastigophora
BT3 protozoa

DIERVILLA
BT1 caprifoliaceae
rt weigela

diervilla florida
USE **weigela florida**

DIES
BT1 components
rt cubing machines
rt pressing
rt wafering

DIESEL ENGINES
uf *engines, diesel*
BT1 engines
BT2 machinery
rt diesel oil
rt fuel injection

DIESEL OIL
uf *oil, diesel*
BT1 fuel oils
BT2 mineral oils
BT3 oils
rt diesel engines
rt petroleum

DIESTRUS
BF dioestrus
BT1 estrous cycle

DIET
uf *dietary factors*
rt diet clubs (agricola)

DIET *cont.*
rt diet counseling (agricola)
rt diet prescription (agricola)
rt dietary guidelines (agricola)
rt dietary surveys (agricola)
rt dieting (agricola)
rt food restriction
rt meals
rt religious dietary laws (agricola)

DIET CLUBS (AGRICOLA)
BT1 organizations
rt diet
rt dieting (agricola)
rt weight control (agricola)

DIET COUNSELING (AGRICOLA)
BT1 counseling (agricola)
rt diet

diet, elemental
USE **elemental diets**

DIET PLANNING
BT1 planning
rt diets
rt meal patterns
rt unconventional foods

diet preferences
USE **food preferences**

DIET PRESCRIPTION (AGRICOLA)
rt diet

diet, semipurified
USE **semipurified diets**

DIET STUDIES
BT1 dietetics
rt diet study techniques
rt diets
rt nutritional state

DIET STUDY TECHNIQUES
BT1 techniques
NT1 dietary history (agricola)
rt diet studies
rt dietetics

diet, synthetic
USE **synthetic diets**

diet therapy
USE **therapeutic diets**

DIET TREATMENT
rt diets
rt treatment

DIETARY CARBOHYDRATE
BT1 nutrients
rt carbohydrates

dietary factors
HN was used until 1990 in agricola
USE **diet**

DIETARY FAT
uf *source fat*
BT1 nutrients
rt fat

DIETARY GUIDELINES (AGRICOLA)
rt diet

DIETARY HISTORY (AGRICOLA)
uf *dietary recall*
uf *food history*
BT1 diet study techniques
BT2 techniques

DIETARY MINERALS
BT1 nutrients
rt mineral nutrition

DIETARY PROTEIN
BT1 nutrients
BT1 protein

dietary recall
USE **dietary history (agricola)**

dietary standards
USE **nutrient requirements**

DIETARY SURVEYS (AGRICOLA)
BT1 nutrition surveys
BT2 nutrition research
BT3 research
BT2 surveys
rt diet

DIETETIC EDUCATION (AGRICOLA)
BT1 education
rt dietetic interns (agricola)
rt dietetics

DIETETIC FOODS
BT1 foods
rt dietetics
rt therapeutic diets

DIETETIC INTERNS (AGRICOLA)
uf *dietetic internship programs*
BT1 students
BT2 people
rt dietetic education (agricola)
rt dietetics

dietetic internship programs
USE **dietetic interns (agricola)**

DIETETIC TECHNICIANS (AGRICOLA)
BT1 technicians
BT2 occupations
BT2 skilled labour
BT3 labour
rt dietetics

DIETETICS
NT1 diet studies
rt diet study techniques
rt dietetic education (agricola)
rt dietetic foods
rt dietetic interns (agricola)
rt dietetic technicians (agricola)
rt dietitians
rt diets
rt nutrition

DIETHAMQUAT
BT1 quaternary ammonium herbicides
BT2 herbicides
BT3 pesticides
BT2 quaternary ammonium compounds
BT3 ammonium compounds
BT3 organic nitrogen compounds

DIETHATYL
BT1 chloroacetanilide herbicides
BT2 anilide herbicides
BT3 amide herbicides
BT4 herbicides
BT5 pesticides

DIETHOLATE
BT1 herbicide safeners
BT2 safeners

diethyl ether
USE **ethyl ether**

DIETHYL SULFATE
uf *diethyl sulphate*
BT1 mutagens
BT1 sulfates (esters)
BT2 esters
BT2 sulfates

diethyl sulphate
USE **diethyl sulfate**

diethyl sulphide
USE **ethyl sulfide**

DIETHYLAMINE
BT1 secondary amines
BT2 amines
BT3 amino compounds
BT4 organic nitrogen compounds

DIETHYLCARBAMAZINE
BT1 anthelmintics
BT2 antiparasitic agents
BT3 drugs
BT1 piperazines
BT2 azines
BT3 heterocyclic nitrogen compounds
BT4 organic nitrogen compounds

DIETHYLSTILBESTROL
uf *diethylstilboestrol*
uf *stilboestrol*
BT1 growth promoters
BT2 growth regulators
BT2 promoters
BT1 stilbenes
BT2 aromatic compounds
BT1 synthetic oestrogens
BT2 synthetic hormones
rt contraceptives

diethylstilboestrol
USE **diethylstilbestrol**

DIETHYLTOLUAMIDE
uf *deet*
BT1 amides
BT2 organic nitrogen compounds
BT1 insect repellents
BT2 repellents

DIETING (AGRICOLA)
rt diet
rt diet clubs (agricola)
rt weight control (agricola)

DIETITIANS
BT1 occupations
rt dietetics
rt diets

DIETS
NT1 atherogenic diet
NT1 caloric modifications (agricola)
NT1 calorie-restricted diets (agricola)
NT1 carbohydrate loading (agricola)
NT1 carbohydrate modifications (agricola)
NT1 diabetic diets (agricola)
NT1 elemental diets
NT1 elimination diets (agricola)
NT1 experimental diets (agricola)
NT1 fad diets (agricola)
NT1 formula diets (agricola)
NT1 gluten free diet
NT1 high fiber diets (agricola)
NT1 hospital diets
NT1 ketogenic diets (agricola)
NT1 liquid diets
NT2 liquid protein diets (agricola)
NT1 low cholesterol diets (agricola)
NT1 metabolic diets (agricola)
NT1 phenylalanine restricted diets (agricola)
NT1 renal diets (agricola)
NT1 semipurified diets
NT1 synthetic diets
NT1 therapeutic diets
NT2 fat restricted diets (agricola)
NT2 fiber restricted diets (agricola)
NT2 protein modifications (agricola)
NT2 sodium-restricted diets (agricola)
NT2 ulcer diets (agricola)
NT1 thrombogenic diet
NT1 vegetarian diets (agricola)
NT1 weight loss diets (agricola)
rt catering
rt child feeding
rt diet planning
rt diet studies
rt diet treatment

DIETS *cont.*
rt dietetics
rt dietitians
rt feeding
rt foods
rt meal patterns
rt nutrition
rt nutrition programmes
rt protein requirement
rt survival rations
rt unconventional foods
rt vegetarians

diets in hospital
USE **hospital diets**

diets, semipurified
USE **semipurified diets**

DIFENACOUM
BT1 coumarin rodenticides
BT2 coumarins
BT3 lactones
BT4 heterocyclic oxygen compounds
BT4 ketones
BT2 rodenticides
BT3 pesticides

DIFENOPENTEN
BT1 phenoxybutyric herbicides
BT2 phenoxy herbicides
BT3 herbicides
BT4 pesticides

DIFENOXURON
BT1 urea herbicides
BT2 herbicides
BT3 pesticides

DIFENZOQUAT
BT1 quaternary ammonium herbicides
BT2 herbicides
BT3 pesticides
BT2 quaternary ammonium compounds
BT3 ammonium compounds
BT3 organic nitrogen compounds

DIFERULIC ACID
BT1 dicarboxylic acids
BT2 carboxylic acids
BT3 organic acids
BT4 acids
rt ferulic acid

DIFFERENTIAL DIAGNOSIS
BT1 diagnosis

DIFFERENTIAL GEARS
uf *gears, differential*
BT1 gears
BT2 components
rt transmissions

DIFFERENTIAL PRICING
BT1 price fixing
BT2 price policy
BT3 economic policy
NT1 payment basis
rt price discrimination

DIFFERENTIAL RENT
BT1 rent
rt rent theory

DIFFERENTIAL STAINING
BT1 staining
BT2 techniques
rt microscopy

DIFFERENTIAL TRANSMISSIONS
uf *transmissions, differential*
BT1 transmissions
BT2 components
rt automatic transmissions

DIFFERENTIATION
NT1 sex differentiation
NT2 dioecy
NT2 sex diagnosis
NT3 autosexing
rt branching

DIFFERENTIATION *cont.*
rt breed differences
rt development
rt discrimination
rt embryology
rt growth
rt heterothallism
rt meristems
rt polarity
rt separation
rt sex hormones
rt strain differences

differentiation, cell
USE **cell differentiation**

DIFFRACTION
HN from 1990
BT1 optical properties
BT2 physical properties
BT3 properties

DIFFUSED GLASS
uf glass, diffused
BT1 glass
BT2 building materials
BT3 materials
rt diffusion

DIFFUSER FEED WATER
HN from 1990
BT1 water
rt diffusers

DIFFUSERS
HN from 1990
BT1 extractors
BT2 equipment
rt diffuser feed water

DIFFUSION
NT1 thermal diffusion
rt diffused glass
rt diffusion models
rt diffusion resistance
rt diffusivity
rt electrodiffusion
rt extraction
rt juice extraction
rt leaf diffusion resistance
rt osmosis
rt permeability
rt transport processes

diffusion coefficient
USE **diffusivity**

DIFFUSION MODELS
BT1 models
rt diffusion

DIFFUSION OF INFORMATION
uf information dissemination
BT1 information services
BT2 services
NT1 diffusion of research
rt information
rt mass media
rt technical progress
rt technology transfer

DIFFUSION OF RESEARCH
BT1 diffusion of information
BT2 information services
BT3 services
BT1 research policy
BT1 technical progress
rt agrep
rt implementation of research
rt research
rt research institutes
rt technology transfer

DIFFUSION RESISTANCE
BT1 resistance
NT1 leaf diffusion resistance
rt diffusion
rt diffusivity

DIFFUSIVITY
uf diffusion coefficient
BT1 physical properties
BT2 properties
NT1 thermal diffusivity

DIFFUSIVITY *cont.*
rt conductivity
rt diffusion
rt diffusion resistance
rt soil water movement

DIFLUBENZURON
BT1 benzoylphenylureas
BT2 amides
BT3 organic nitrogen compounds
BT1 chitin synthesis inhibitors
BT2 insect growth regulators
BT3 growth regulators
BT3 insecticides
BT4 pesticides
BT2 metabolic inhibitors
BT3 inhibitors

DIFLUFENICAN
HN from 1990
BT1 anilide herbicides
BT2 amide herbicides
BT3 herbicides
BT4 pesticides

DIGENEA
BT1 trematoda
NT1 acanthostomidae
NT2 acanthostomum
NT1 allocreadiidae
NT2 allocreadium
NT2 crepidostomum
NT3 crepidostomum farionis
NT3 crepidostomum metoecus
NT1 brachylaemidae
NT2 brachylaema
NT3 brachylaema migrans
NT2 leucochloridiomorpha
NT3 leucochloridiomorpha constantiae
NT1 bucephalidae
NT2 bucephalus
NT2 prosorhynchus
NT2 rhipidocotyle
NT1 campulidae
NT2 zalophotrema
NT1 clinostomidae
NT2 clinostomum
NT3 clinostomum complanatum
NT2 euclinostomum
NT3 euclinostomum heterostomum
NT1 cyclocoelidae
NT2 cyclocoelum
NT1 dicrocoeliidae
NT2 brachylecithum
NT2 dicrocoelium
NT3 dicrocoelium hospes
NT3 dicrocoelium lanceolatum
NT2 eurytrema
NT3 eurytrema coelomaticum
NT3 eurytrema pancreaticum
NT2 platynosomum
NT1 diplostomidae
NT2 alaria
NT3 alaria alata
NT2 diplostomum
NT3 diplostomum phoxini
NT3 diplostomum spathaceum
NT2 neodiplostomum
NT2 posthodiplostomum
NT1 echinostomatidae
NT2 artyfechinostomum
NT3 artyfechinostomum sufrartyfex
NT2 echinochasmus
NT2 echinoparyphium
NT2 echinostoma
NT3 echinostoma audyi
NT3 echinostoma hystricosum
NT3 echinostoma ilocanum
NT3 echinostoma lindoense
NT3 echinostoma revolutum
NT2 euparyphium
NT2 himasthla
NT2 paryphostomum
NT2 patagifer
NT2 petasiger
NT1 eucotylidae
NT2 eucotyle

DIGENEA *cont.*
NT3 eucotyle nephritica
NT2 tanaisia
NT3 tanaisia zarudnyi
NT1 fasciolidae
NT2 fasciola
NT3 fasciola gigantica
NT3 fasciola hepatica
NT2 fascioloides
NT3 fascioloides magna
NT2 fasciolopsis
NT3 fasciolopsis buski
NT2 parafasciolopsis
NT1 gastrothylacidae
NT2 carmyerius
NT2 fischoederius
NT3 fischoederius elongatus
NT2 gastrothylax
NT3 gastrothylax crumenifer
NT1 gorgoderidae
NT2 gorgoderina
NT3 gorgoderina vitelliloba
NT2 phyllodistomum
NT1 hemiuridae
NT2 derogenes
NT3 derogenes ruber
NT2 dinurus
NT2 halipegus
NT2 lecithaster
NT2 lecithocladium
NT2 sterrhurus
NT1 heterophyidae
NT2 apophallus
NT2 cryptocotyle
NT3 cryptocotyle lingua
NT2 galactosomum
NT2 haplorchis
NT3 haplorchis pumilio
NT2 heterophyes
NT3 heterophyes heterophyes
NT2 metagonimus
NT3 metagonimus yokogawai
NT2 procerovum
NT3 procerovum calderoni
NT1 isoparorchiidae
NT2 isoparorchis
NT1 lecithodendriidae
NT2 lecithodendrium
NT2 phaneropsolus
NT2 pleurogenes
NT2 prosthodendrium
NT1 maseniidae
NT2 eumasenia
NT2 masenia
NT1 microphallidae
NT2 gymnophallus
NT3 gymnophallus fossarum
NT2 maritrema
NT1 monorchiidae
NT2 asymphylodora
NT1 nanophyetidae
NT2 nanophyetus
NT3 nanophyetus salmincola
NT1 notocotylidae
NT2 notocotylus
NT1 opisthorchiidae
NT2 clonorchis
NT3 clonorchis sinensis
NT2 metorchis
NT3 metorchis albidus
NT2 opisthorchis
NT3 opisthorchis felineus
NT3 opisthorchis viverrini
NT1 paragonimidae
NT2 paragonimus
NT3 paragonimus iloktsuenensis
NT3 paragonimus kellicotti
NT3 paragonimus miyazakii
NT3 paragonimus ohirai
NT3 paragonimus peruvianus
NT3 paragonimus uterobilateralis
NT3 paragonimus westermani
NT1 paramphistomatidae
NT2 calicophoron
NT3 calicophoron calicophorum
NT3 calicophoron microbothrium
NT3 calicophoron raja

DIGENEA *cont.*
NT2 cotylophoron
NT3 cotylophoron cotylophorum
NT2 explanatum
NT2 gastrodiscoides
NT3 gastrodiscoides hominis
NT2 gastrodiscus
NT3 gastrodiscus aegyptiacus
NT3 gastrodiscus secundus
NT2 gigantocotyle
NT3 gigantocotyle explanatum
NT3 gigantocotyle symmeri
NT2 homalogaster
NT3 homalogaster paloniae
NT2 orthocoelium
NT3 orthocoelium dicranocoelium
NT3 orthocoelium orthocoelium
NT3 orthocoelium scoliocoelium
NT2 paramphistomum
NT3 paramphistomum cervi
NT3 paramphistomum epiclitum
NT3 paramphistomum leydeni
NT2 stephanopharynx
NT3 stephanopharynx compactus
NT1 philophthalmidae
NT2 philophthalmus
NT1 plagiorchiidae
NT2 plagiorchis
NT3 plagiorchis fastuosus
NT3 plagiorchis laricola
NT1 prosthogonimidae
NT2 prosthogonimus
NT3 prosthogonimus ovatus
NT1 psilostomidae
NT2 sphaeridiotrema
NT3 sphaeridiotrema globulus
NT1 sanguinicolidae
NT2 sanguinicola
NT1 schistosomatidae
NT2 austrobilharzia
NT2 bilharziella
NT2 heterobilharzia
NT3 heterobilharzia americana
NT2 ornithobilharzia
NT3 ornithobilharzia turkestanicum
NT2 schistosoma
NT3 schistosoma bovis
NT3 schistosoma haematobium
NT3 schistosoma incognitum
NT3 schistosoma intercalatum
NT3 schistosoma japonicum
NT3 schistosoma mansoni
NT3 schistosoma margrebowiei
NT3 schistosoma mattheei
NT3 schistosoma mekongi
NT3 schistosoma nasalis
NT3 schistosoma rodhaini
NT3 schistosoma spindale
NT2 trichobilharzia
NT3 trichobilharzia brevis
NT1 strigeidae
NT2 apatemon
NT3 apatemon gracilis
NT2 cotylurus
NT3 cotylurus flabelliformis
rt digenean larvae

DIGENEAN LARVAE
BT1 helminth larvae
BT2 helminths
BT3 parasites
BT2 larvae
BT3 developmental stages
NT1 cercariae
NT1 diplostomula
NT1 metacercariae
NT1 miracidia
NT1 rediae
NT1 schistosomula
NT1 sporocysts
rt digenea
rt trematoda

DIGERA
BT1 amaranthaceae
NT1 digera alternifolia
NT1 digera arvensis

DIGERA ALTERNIFOLIA
BT1 digera
BT2 amaranthaceae

DIGERA ARVENSIS
BT1 digera
BT2 amaranthaceae
BT1 pasture plants

DIGESTA
uf *chyme*
uf *digestive tract contents*
rt antibloat agents
rt digestibility
rt digestive juices

DIGESTANTS
BT1 gastrointestinal agents
BT2 drugs
NT1 cholic acid
NT1 deoxycholic acid
NT1 hydrochloric acid
NT1 pancreatin
NT1 taurocholic acid
NT1 ursodeoxycholic acid

DIGESTERS
BT1 equipment
NT1 anaerobic digesters
rt manures
rt methane production
rt slurries
rt waste utilization

DIGESTIBILITY
uf *feed digestibility*
NT1 energy digestibility
NT1 feed conversion efficiency
NT1 in vitro digestibility
NT1 nutritive ratio
NT1 protein digestibility
rt digesta
rt digestibility markers
rt digestion
rt digestive system

digestibility in vitro
USE **in vitro digestibility**

DIGESTIBILITY MARKERS
BT1 markers
NT1 chromic oxide
rt digestibility

DIGESTIBLE ENERGY
BT1 energy
rt energy digestibility

DIGESTION
BT1 physiological functions
NT1 biuret digestion
NT1 cellulose digestion
NT1 digestive absorption
NT2 intestinal absorption
NT1 fat mobilization
NT1 protein digestion
NT1 rumen digestion
NT2 rumen fermentation
NT2 rumination
NT3 sheep rumination
NT1 starch digestion
NT1 stomach emptying
rt acid base disorders
rt acid base equilibrium
rt acidosis
rt alkali treatment
rt bulk
rt digestibility
rt digestive disorders
rt digestive system
rt digestive tract
rt digestive tract motility
rt faeces
rt feed conversion
rt fermentation
rt gastric juices
rt rumen bacteria
rt ruminant symbionts
rt transit time

digestion in rumen
USE **rumen digestion**

DIGESTIVE ABSORPTION
BT1 digestion
BT2 physiological functions
NT1 intestinal absorption
rt absorption
rt digestive tract mucosa

DIGESTIVE DISORDERS
uf *gastrointestinal disorders*
BT1 functional disorders
BT2 animal disorders
BT3 disorders
NT1 appetite disorders
NT2 anorexia
NT3 anorexia nervosa
NT2 bulimia
NT2 bulimia nervosa (agricola)
NT2 compulsive eating (agricola)
NT2 geophagia
NT2 pica
NT1 bloat
NT1 chinese restaurant syndrome
NT1 colic
NT1 constipation
NT1 diarrhoea
NT2 giardiasis
NT1 dyspepsia
NT1 flatus
NT1 gizzard erosion
NT1 grass sickness
NT1 hyperacidity (agricola)
NT1 malabsorption
NT1 milk intolerance
NT1 obstruction
NT2 cholestasis
NT2 intestinal obstruction
NT3 duodenal obstruction
NT3 intussusception
NT1 phytobezoariasis
NT1 sialuria
NT1 vomiting
NT2 hyperemesis gravidarum
NT2 nausea
rt antacids
rt antibloat agents
rt concretions
rt digestion
rt nutritional disorders

DIGESTIVE JUICES
BT1 body fluids
BT2 fluids
NT1 chymosin
NT2 rennet
NT3 microbial rennet
NT1 duodenal fluids
NT1 gastric juices
NT2 gastric acid
NT1 pancreatic juice
NT1 rumen fluid
NT1 saliva
rt digesta
rt digestive system
rt gastric glands
rt secretions

DIGESTIVE SYSTEM
uf *alimentary tract*
uf *gastrointestinal system*
BT1 body parts
NT1 anus
NT2 cloaca
NT1 biliary system
NT2 bile ducts
NT1 digestive tract
NT2 peritrophic membrane
NT1 fat body
NT1 foregut
NT1 gastric glands
NT1 hindgut
NT1 honey sac
NT1 intestines
NT2 jejunum
NT2 large intestine
NT3 caecum
NT3 colon
NT2 midgut

DIGESTIVE SYSTEM *cont.*
NT2 rectum
NT2 small intestine
NT3 duodenum
NT3 ileum
NT3 villi
NT1 liver
NT2 gall bladder
NT1 mouth
NT2 gingiva
NT2 periodontium
NT2 tongue
NT1 oesophagus
NT2 crop
NT2 reticular groove
NT1 pancreas
NT2 artificial pancreas
NT2 pancreas islets
NT1 pharynx
NT2 palate
NT2 tonsils
NT1 proventriculus
NT1 salivary glands
NT2 mandibular glands
NT2 parotid gland
NT1 stomach
NT2 abomasum
NT2 forestomach
NT3 reticulum
NT3 rumen
NT4 artificial rumen
NT4 omasum
NT2 gizzard
rt bile
rt defaecation
rt digestibility
rt digestion
rt digestive juices
rt faeces collection
rt gastric inhibitory polypeptides
rt gastrin
rt gastrointestinal hormones
rt hydrochloric acid secretion
rt short bowel syndrome

DIGESTIVE SYSTEM DISEASES
BT1 organic diseases
BT2 diseases
NT1 cholangitis
NT1 enterotoxaemia
NT1 gall bladder diseases
NT2 cholecystitis
NT2 cholelithiasis
NT1 gastrointestinal diseases
NT2 dumping syndrome
NT2 intestinal diseases
NT3 appendicitis (agricola)
NT3 blind loop syndrome
NT3 coeliac syndrome
NT3 colitis
NT4 ulcerative colitis
NT3 crohn's disease
NT3 diverticulosis
NT3 dysentery
NT4 swine dysentery
NT3 enteritis
NT3 enterocolitis
NT3 gastroenteritis
NT3 haemorrhagic enteritis
NT3 irritable colon
NT3 short bowel syndrome
NT3 sprue
NT3 steatorrhoea
NT3 tropical sprue
NT3 typhlitis
NT2 peptic ulcer
NT3 duodenal ulcer
NT2 stomach diseases
NT3 achlorhydria
NT3 gastritis
NT4 atrophic gastritis
NT3 rumenitis
NT3 stomach ulcer
NT1 liver diseases
NT2 cirrhosis
NT2 fatty liver
NT2 fatty liver haemorrhagic syndrome
NT2 hepatitis
NT3 reye's syndrome

DIGESTIVE SYSTEM DISEASES *cont.*
NT3 viral hepatitis
NT2 hepatolenticular degeneration
NT2 hepatoma
NT2 hepatomegaly
NT2 jaundice
NT3 toxaemic jaundice
NT2 liver abscess
NT1 oesophageal diseases
NT1 pancreatic diseases
NT2 pancreatitis
NT2 zollinger-ellison syndrome
NT1 peritonitis
NT1 pharyngitis

DIGESTIVE TRACT
uf *gastrointestinal tract*
BT1 digestive system
BT2 body parts
NT1 peritrophic membrane
rt digestion
rt digestive tract mucosa
rt faeces

digestive tract contents
USE **digesta**

DIGESTIVE TRACT MOTILITY
uf *gastrointestinal motility*
BT1 motility
BT2 movement
NT1 intestinal motility
NT1 peristalsis
NT1 regurgitation
NT1 rumen motility
NT1 stomach motility
rt digestion
rt rumination

DIGESTIVE TRACT MUCOSA
BT1 mucosa
BT2 membranes
NT1 intestinal mucosa
NT1 stomach mucosa
rt digestive absorption
rt digestive tract

DIGGING
BT1 cultivation
rt elevator diggers
rt rotary diggers

DIGITAL DISPLAYS
uf *displays, digital*
BT1 displays
rt indicating instruments
rt liquid crystal displays

DIGITALIS
BT1 scrophulariaceae
NT1 digitalis ciliata
NT1 digitalis ferruginea
NT1 digitalis grandiflora
NT1 digitalis lamarckii
NT1 digitalis lanata
NT1 digitalis lutea
NT1 digitalis purpurea
NT1 digitalis schischkinii
NT1 digitalis thapsi
NT1 digitalis trojana
NT1 digitalis viridiflora
rt digoxin

digitalis ambigua
USE **digitalis grandiflora**

DIGITALIS CILIATA
BT1 digitalis
BT2 scrophulariaceae

DIGITALIS FERRUGINEA
BT1 digitalis
BT2 scrophulariaceae

DIGITALIS GRANDIFLORA
uf *digitalis ambigua*
BT1 antifungal plants
BT1 digitalis
BT2 scrophulariaceae
BT1 medicinal plants

DIGITALIS LAMARCKII
BT1 digitalis

DIGITALIS LAMARCKII *cont.*
BT2 scrophulariaceae

DIGITALIS LANATA
BT1 digitalis
BT2 scrophulariaceae

DIGITALIS LUTEA
BT1 digitalis
BT2 scrophulariaceae

DIGITALIS PURPUREA
uf *foxglove*
BT1 digitalis
BT2 scrophulariaceae
BT1 medicinal plants
BT1 ornamental herbaceous plants
rt digitonin

DIGITALIS SCHISCHKINII
BT1 digitalis
BT2 scrophulariaceae

DIGITALIS THAPSI
BT1 digitalis
BT2 scrophulariaceae

DIGITALIS TROJANA
BT1 digitalis
BT2 scrophulariaceae

DIGITALIS VIRIDIFLORA
BT1 digitalis
BT2 scrophulariaceae

DIGITARIA
BT1 gramineae
NT1 digitaria aegyptiaca
NT1 digitaria brownei
NT1 digitaria californica
NT1 digitaria ciliaris
NT1 digitaria cruciata
NT1 digitaria decumbens
NT1 digitaria didactyla
NT1 digitaria divaricatissima
NT1 digitaria exilis
NT1 digitaria filiformis
NT1 digitaria horizontalis
NT1 digitaria iburua
NT1 digitaria insularis
NT1 digitaria ischaemum
NT1 digitaria longiflora
NT1 digitaria macroblephara
NT1 digitaria macroglossa
NT1 digitaria marginata
NT1 digitaria milanjiana
NT1 digitaria monodactyla
NT1 digitaria pentzii
NT1 digitaria sanguinalis
NT1 digitaria scalarum
NT1 digitaria serotina
NT1 digitaria setivalva
NT1 digitaria smutsii
NT1 digitaria swazilandensis
NT1 digitaria tricholaenoides
NT1 digitaria velutina
NT1 digitaria violescens

digitaria adscendens
USE **digitaria ciliaris**

DIGITARIA AEGYPTIACA
BT1 digitaria
BT2 gramineae
BT1 pasture plants

DIGITARIA BROWNEI
BT1 digitaria
BT2 gramineae
BT1 pasture plants

DIGITARIA CALIFORNICA
BT1 digitaria
BT2 gramineae

DIGITARIA CILIARIS
uf *digitaria adscendens*
BT1 digitaria
BT2 gramineae
BT1 pasture plants

DIGITARIA CRUCIATA
BT1 digitaria
BT2 gramineae

DIGITARIA CRUCIATA *cont.*
BT1 pasture plants

DIGITARIA DECUMBENS
uf *pangola grass*
BT1 digitaria
BT2 gramineae
BT1 pasture plants
rt pangola stunt fijivirus

DIGITARIA DIDACTYLA
BT1 digitaria
BT2 gramineae
BT1 pasture plants

DIGITARIA DIVARICATISSIMA
BT1 digitaria
BT2 gramineae
BT1 pasture plants

DIGITARIA EXILIS
BT1 digitaria
BT2 gramineae
BT1 millets
BT2 cereals
BT3 grain crops
BT1 pasture plants

DIGITARIA FILIFORMIS
BT1 digitaria
BT2 gramineae

DIGITARIA HORIZONTALIS
BT1 digitaria
BT2 gramineae

DIGITARIA IBURUA
BT1 digitaria
BT2 gramineae
BT1 millets
BT2 cereals
BT3 grain crops

DIGITARIA INSULARIS
BT1 digitaria
BT2 gramineae

DIGITARIA ISCHAEMUM
BT1 digitaria
BT2 gramineae
BT1 pasture plants
BT1 weeds

DIGITARIA LONGIFLORA
BT1 digitaria
BT2 gramineae
BT1 pasture plants

DIGITARIA MACROBLEPHARA
BT1 digitaria
BT2 gramineae
BT1 pasture plants

DIGITARIA MACROGLOSSA
BT1 digitaria
BT2 gramineae
BT1 pasture plants

DIGITARIA MARGINATA
BT1 digitaria
BT2 gramineae

DIGITARIA MILANJIANA
BT1 digitaria
BT2 gramineae
BT1 pasture plants

DIGITARIA MONODACTYLA
BT1 digitaria
BT2 gramineae
BT1 pasture plants

DIGITARIA PENTZII
BT1 digitaria
BT2 gramineae
BT1 pasture plants

DIGITARIA SANGUINALIS
BT1 digitaria
BT2 gramineae
BT1 pasture plants
BT1 weeds

DIGITARIA SCALARUM
BT1 digitaria
BT2 gramineae

DIGITARIA SCALARUM *cont.*
BT1 pasture plants

DIGITARIA SEROTINA
BT1 digitaria
BT2 gramineae
BT1 pasture plants

DIGITARIA SETIVALVA
BT1 digitaria
BT2 gramineae
BT1 pasture plants

DIGITARIA SMUTSII
BT1 digitaria
BT2 gramineae
BT1 pasture plants

DIGITARIA SWAZILANDENSIS
BT1 digitaria
BT2 gramineae
BT1 pasture plants

DIGITARIA TRICHOLAENOIDES
BT1 digitaria
BT2 gramineae
BT1 pasture plants

DIGITARIA VELUTINA
BT1 digitaria
BT2 gramineae
BT1 pasture plants

DIGITARIA VIOLESCENS
BT1 digitaria
BT2 gramineae
BT1 pasture plants

DIGITONIN
BT1 cardiac glycosides
BT2 cardiovascular agents
BT3 drugs
BT2 glycosides
BT3 carbohydrates
BT1 steroid saponins
BT2 saponins
BT3 glycosides
BT4 carbohydrates
rt digitalis purpurea

DIGITOXIGENIN
BT1 cardenolides
BT2 lactones
BT3 heterocyclic oxygen compounds
BT3 ketones
BT2 steroids
BT3 isoprenoids
BT4 lipids
rt digitoxin

DIGITOXIN
BT1 cardiac glycosides
BT2 cardiovascular agents
BT3 drugs
BT2 glycosides
BT3 carbohydrates
BT1 steroid saponins
BT2 saponins
BT3 glycosides
BT4 carbohydrates
rt digitoxigenin

DIGITS
BT1 feet
BT2 limbs
BT3 body regions

diglycerides
USE **diacylglycerols**

DIGLYCINE
BT1 dicarboxylic acids
BT2 carboxylic acids
BT3 organic acids
BT4 acids

DIGLYPHUS
BT1 eulophidae
BT2 hymenoptera
NT1 diglyphus begini
NT1 diglyphus intermedius
NT1 diglyphus isaea

DIGLYPHUS BEGINI
BT1 diglyphus
BT2 eulophidae
BT3 hymenoptera

DIGLYPHUS INTERMEDIUS
BT1 diglyphus
BT2 eulophidae
BT3 hymenoptera

DIGLYPHUS ISAEA
BT1 diglyphus
BT2 eulophidae
BT3 hymenoptera

DIGOXIGENIN
BT1 cardenolides
BT2 lactones
BT3 heterocyclic oxygen compounds
BT3 ketones
BT2 steroids
BT3 isoprenoids
BT4 lipids
rt digoxin

DIGOXIN
BT1 cardiac glycosides
BT2 cardiovascular agents
BT3 drugs
BT2 glycosides
BT3 carbohydrates
BT1 steroid saponins
BT2 saponins
BT3 glycosides
BT4 carbohydrates
rt digitalis
rt digoxigenin

DIHETEROPOGON
BT1 gramineae

DIHETEROSPORA
BT1 deuteromycotina

DIHYDROCARVONE
BT1 monoterpenoids
BT2 terpenoids
BT3 isoprenoids
BT4 lipids

DIHYDROERGOCRYPTINE
BT1 ergot alkaloids
BT2 β-blockers
BT3 sympatholytics
BT4 neurotropic drugs
BT5 drugs
BT2 indole alkaloids
BT3 alkaloids
BT3 indoles

DIHYDROFOLATE REDUCTASE
(ec 1.5.1.3)
uf *tetrahydrofolate dehydrogenase*
BT1 amine oxidoreductases
BT2 oxidoreductases
BT3 enzymes

DIHYDROPHASEIC ACID
BT1 sesquiterpenoids
BT2 terpenoids
BT3 isoprenoids
BT4 lipids
rt abscisic acid

DIHYDROPTERIDINE REDUCTASE
(ec 1.6.99.7)
BT1 oxidoreductases
BT2 enzymes

DIHYDROSTREPTOMYCIN
BT1 antibacterial agents
BT2 antiinfective agents
BT3 drugs
BT1 antibiotics

DIHYDROTACHYSTEROL
uf *hydrotachysterol*
BT1 ergostanes
BT2 steroids
BT3 isoprenoids
BT4 lipids
BT1 sterols

DIHYDROTACHYSTEROL *cont.*
BT2 alcohols
BT2 steroids
BT3 isoprenoids
BT4 lipids
BT1 vitamin d
BT2 fat soluble vitamins
BT3 vitamins

DIHYDROXYBENZOIC ACID
BT1 phenolic acids
BT2 benzoic acids
BT3 aromatic acids
BT4 aromatic compounds
BT4 organic acids
BT5 acids
BT2 phenolic compounds
BT3 aromatic compounds

1,25-dihydroxycholecalciferol
USE **calcitriol**

24,25-DIHYDROXYCHOLECALCIFEROL
BT1 hydroxycholecalciferols
BT2 cholecalciferol derivatives
BT3 sterols
BT4 alcohols
BT4 steroids
BT5 isoprenoids
BT6 lipids
BT3 vitamin d
BT4 fat soluble vitamins
BT5 vitamins

25,26-DIHYDROXYCHOLECALCIFEROL
BT1 hydroxycholecalciferols
BT2 cholecalciferol derivatives
BT3 sterols
BT4 alcohols
BT4 steroids
BT5 isoprenoids
BT6 lipids
BT3 vitamin d
BT4 fat soluble vitamins
BT5 vitamins

3,4-dihydroxyphenylalanine
USE **dopa**

1,25-dihydroxyvitamin d
USE **calcitriol**

DIIODOHYDROXYQUINOLINE
BT1 antiprotozoal agents
BT2 antiparasitic agents
BT3 drugs
BT1 quinolines
BT2 heterocyclic nitrogen compounds
BT3 organic nitrogen compounds

DIIODOTHYRONINE
BT1 iodo amino acids
BT2 amino acids
BT3 carboxylic acids
BT4 organic acids
BT5 acids
BT3 organic nitrogen compounds
BT2 organoiodine compounds
BT3 organic halogen compounds
rt thyroxine

DIKEGULAC
BT1 growth inhibitors
BT2 inhibitors
BT2 plant growth regulators
BT3 growth regulators

DIKES
BF dykes

DIKETOGULONIC ACID
BT1 ascorbic acids
BT2 aldonic acids
BT3 sugar acids
BT4 carboxylic acids
BT5 organic acids
BT6 acids
BT4 monosaccharides

DIKETOGULONIC ACID *cont.*
BT5 carbohydrates

DILATION
BT1 techniques

DILATIONAL WAVE VELOCITY
BT1 acoustic properties
BT2 physical properties
BT3 properties

DILEPIDIDAE
BT1 eucestoda
BT2 cestoda
NT1 amoebotaenia
NT2 amoebotaenia sphenoides
NT1 anomotaenia
NT1 choanotaenia
NT2 choanotaenia infundibulum
NT1 diplopylidium
NT2 diplopylidium nolleri
NT1 dipylidium
NT2 dipylidium caninum
NT1 joyeuxiella
NT2 joyeuxiella echinorhynchoides
NT2 joyeuxiella pasqualei

DILL
rt anethum graveolens

DILLENIA
BT1 dilleniaceae
NT1 dillenia indica
NT1 dillenia pentagyna

DILLENIA INDICA
BT1 dillenia
BT2 dilleniaceae

DILLENIA PENTAGYNA
BT1 dillenia
BT2 dilleniaceae

DILLENIACEAE
NT1 curatella
NT2 curatella americana
NT1 dillenia
NT2 dillenia indica
NT2 dillenia pentagyna
NT1 hibbertia

DILOR
BT1 cyclodiene insecticides
BT2 organochlorine insecticides
BT3 insecticides
BT4 pesticides
BT3 organochlorine pesticides
BT4 organochlorine compounds
BT5 organic halogen compounds

DILOXANIDE
BT1 amoebicides
BT2 antiprotozoal agents
BT3 antiparasitic agents
BT4 drugs

DILUDIN
BT1 antioxidants
BT2 additives

DILUENTS
NT1 semen diluents
rt dilution

DILUTION
NT1 isotope dilution
rt diluents
rt solutions

DILYTA
uf *charips*
BT1 cynipidae
BT2 hymenoptera

DIMBOA
BT1 allomones
BT2 allelochemicals
BT3 semiochemicals
BT1 ketones

DIMEFURON
BT1 urea herbicides

DIMEFURON *cont.*
BT2 herbicides
BT3 pesticides

DIMENSIONAL ANALYSIS
rt analysis

DIMENSIONS
NT1 anthropometric dimensions
NT2 arm circumference (agricola)
NT1 depth
NT1 diameter
NT1 girth
NT2 heart girth
NT1 height
NT2 plant height
NT1 length
NT1 particle shape
NT1 thickness
NT2 egg shell thickness
NT1 thinness
NT1 width
rt basal area
rt clearance
rt distortion
rt geometry
rt measurement
rt mensuration
rt shape
rt shrinkage
rt size
rt specifications
rt wheelbase

DIMEPIPERATE
HN from 1990
BT1 unclassified herbicides
BT2 herbicides
BT3 pesticides

DIMERCAPROL
BT1 antidotes
BT2 detoxicants
BT3 drugs
BT1 chelating agents

DIMETHACHLOR
BT1 chloroacetanilide herbicides
BT2 anilide herbicides
BT3 amide herbicides
BT4 herbicides
BT5 pesticides

DIMETHAMETRYN
BT1 triazine herbicides
BT2 herbicides
BT3 pesticides
BT2 triazines
BT3 heterocyclic nitrogen compounds
BT4 organic nitrogen compounds

DIMETHIRIMOL
BT1 pyrimidine fungicides
BT2 fungicides
BT3 pesticides
BT2 pyrimidines
BT3 heterocyclic nitrogen compounds
BT4 organic nitrogen compounds

DIMETHOATE
BT1 organothiophosphate insecticides
BT2 organophosphorus insecticides
BT3 insecticides
BT4 pesticides
BT3 organophosphorus pesticides
BT4 organophosphorus compounds
BT1 organothiophosphate nematicides
BT2 organophosphorus nematicides
BT3 nematicides
BT4 pesticides
BT3 organophosphorus pesticides

DIMETHOATE *cont.*
BT4 organophosphorus compounds

DIMETHOXYISOFLAVONE
BT1 isoflavones
BT2 flavonoids
BT3 aromatic compounds
BT3 plant pigments
BT4 pigments
BT1 phytoalexins
BT2 allomones
BT3 allelochemicals
BT4 semiochemicals

3,5-DIMETHOXYSALICYLIC ACID
BT1 salicylic acids
BT2 phenolic acids
BT3 benzoic acids
BT4 aromatic acids
BT5 aromatic compounds
BT5 organic acids
BT6 acids
BT3 phenolic compounds
BT4 aromatic compounds

DIMETHYL PHTHALATE
BT1 insect repellents
BT2 repellents
BT1 phthalates
BT2 esters

DIMETHYL SULFATE
uf *dimethyl sulphate*
BT1 alkylating agents
BT1 mutagens
BT1 sulfates (esters)
BT2 esters
BT2 sulfates

DIMETHYL SULFOXIDE
uf *dimethyl sulphoxide*
uf *dmso*
BT1 cryoprotectants
BT2 protectants
BT1 organic sulfur compounds
BT1 solvents

dimethyl sulphate
USE **dimethyl sulfate**

dimethyl sulphide
USE **methyl sulfide**

dimethyl sulphoxide
USE **dimethyl sulfoxide**

DIMETHYLAMINE
BT1 secondary amines
BT2 amines
BT3 amino compounds
BT4 organic nitrogen compounds

P-DIMETHYLAMINOAZOBENZENE
uf *butter yellow*
BT1 azo compounds
BT2 organic nitrogen compounds
BT1 dyes
BT1 food colourants
BT2 food additives
BT3 additives

n-(dimethylamino)succinamic acid
USE **daminozide**

dimethylarsinic acid
USE **cacodylic acid**

dimethylbenzene
USE **xylene**

DIMETHYLFORMAMIDE
BT1 amides
BT2 organic nitrogen compounds
BT1 solvents

1,2-DIMETHYLHYDRAZINE
BT1 carcinogens
BT2 toxic substances
BT1 hydrazines
BT2 organic nitrogen compounds

dimethylnitrosamine
USE **n-nitrosodimethylamine**

dimethylpolysiloxane
USE **simethicone**

DIMETILAN
BT1 carbamate insecticides
BT2 carbamate pesticides
BT2 insecticides
BT3 pesticides

DIMETRIDAZOLE
BT1 antiprotozoal agents
BT2 antiparasitic agents
BT3 drugs
BT1 nitroimidazoles
BT2 imidazoles
BT3 azoles
BT4 heterocyclic nitrogen compounds
BT5 organic nitrogen compounds

dimexan
USE **dimexano**

DIMEXANO
uf *dimexan*
BT1 thiocarbonate herbicides
BT2 herbicides
BT3 pesticides

DIMIDAZON
BT1 pyridazinone herbicides
BT2 herbicides
BT3 pesticides
BT2 pyridazines
BT3 heterocyclic nitrogen compounds
BT4 organic nitrogen compounds

DIMINAZENE
uf *azidine*
uf *berenil*
BT1 amidines
BT2 organic nitrogen compounds
BT1 trypanocides
BT2 antiprotozoal agents
BT3 antiparasitic agents
BT4 drugs

DIMOCARPUS
uf *euphoria*
BT1 sapindaceae
NT1 dimocarpus longan

DIMOCARPUS LONGAN
uf *euphoria longana*
uf *nephelium longana*
BT1 dimocarpus
BT2 sapindaceae
rt longans

DIMORPHOTHECA
BT1 compositae
NT1 dimorphotheca sinuata

dimorphotheca aurantiaca
USE **dimorphotheca sinuata**

dimorphotheca ecklonis
USE **osteospermum ecklonis**

DIMORPHOTHECA SINUATA
uf *dimorphotheca aurantiaca*
BT1 dimorphotheca
BT2 compositae
BT1 ornamental herbaceous plants

DINA
BT1 erpobdellidae
BT2 hirudinea
BT3 annelida
NT1 dina anoculata

DINA ANOCULATA
BT1 dina
BT2 erpobdellidae
BT3 hirudinea
BT4 annelida

DINEBRA
BT1 gramineae
NT1 dinebra retroflexa

DINEBRA RETROFLEXA
BT1 dinebra
BT2 gramineae

DINEMA
BT1 sarcomastigophora
BT2 protozoa

DINEMINA
BT1 sarcomastigophora
BT2 protozoa

DINEMULA
BT1 sarcomastigophora
BT2 protozoa

dingo
USE **canis familiaris dingo**

DINING FACILITIES (AGRICOLA)
NT1 cafes
NT1 cafeterias (agricola)
NT1 restaurants
NT2 fast food restaurants
NT2 speciality restaurants
NT2 takeout restaurants
NT2 theme restaurants
rt eating out (agricola)
rt food service

DINITOLMIDE
uf *zoalene*
BT1 coccidiostats
BT2 antiprotozoal agents
BT3 antiparasitic agents
BT4 drugs

DINITRAMINE
BT1 dinitroaniline herbicides
BT2 herbicides
BT3 pesticides

DINITROANILINE HERBICIDES
BT1 herbicides
BT2 pesticides
NT1 benfluralin
NT1 butralin
NT1 dinitramine
NT1 ethalfluralin
NT1 fluchloralin
NT1 isopropalin
NT1 methalpropalin
NT1 nitralin
NT1 oryzalin
NT1 pendimethalin
NT1 prodiamine
NT1 profluralin
NT1 trifluralin

dinitrocarbolineum
USE **dnoc**

dinitro-o-cresol
USE **dnoc**

2,4-DINITROPHENOL
BT1 metabolic inhibitors
BT2 inhibitors
BT1 phenols
BT2 alcohols
BT2 phenolic compounds
BT3 aromatic compounds

DINITROPHENOL ACARICIDES
BT1 acaricides
BT2 pesticides
NT1 binapacryl
NT1 dinobuton
NT1 dinocap

DINITROPHENOL FUNGICIDES
BT1 fungicides
BT2 pesticides
NT1 binapacryl
NT1 dinobuton
NT1 dinocap
NT1 dinocton
NT1 dinopenton
NT1 dinosulfon
NT1 dinoterbon

DINITROPHENOL HERBICIDES
BT1 herbicides
BT2 pesticides
NT1 dinoseb
NT1 dinoterb
NT1 dnoc
NT1 medinoterb

DINITROPHENOL INSECTICIDES
BT1 insecticides
BT2 pesticides
NT1 dnoc

DINNER (AGRICOLA)
BT1 meals

DINNERWARE (AGRICOLA)
rt crystal (agricola)
rt dishes (agricola)
rt flatware (agricola)
rt household equipment (agricola)
rt table settings (agricola)

DINOBUTON
BT1 dinitrophenol acaricides
BT2 acaricides
BT3 pesticides
BT1 dinitrophenol fungicides
BT2 fungicides
BT3 pesticides

DINOCAMPUS
BT1 braconidae
BT2 hymenoptera
NT1 dinocampus coccinellae
rt perilitus

DINOCAMPUS COCCINELLAE
uf *perilitus coccinellae*
BT1 dinocampus
BT2 braconidae
BT3 hymenoptera

DINOCAP
BT1 dinitrophenol acaricides
BT2 acaricides
BT3 pesticides
BT1 dinitrophenol fungicides
BT2 fungicides
BT3 pesticides

DINOCHLOA
BT1 gramineae
NT1 dinochloa scandens

DINOCHLOA SCANDENS
BT1 dinochloa
BT2 gramineae

DINOCTON
BT1 dinitrophenol fungicides
BT2 fungicides
BT3 pesticides

DINODERUS
BT1 bostrichidae
BT2 coleoptera
NT1 dinoderus minutus

DINODERUS MINUTUS
BT1 dinoderus
BT2 bostrichidae
BT3 coleoptera

DINOPENTON
BT1 dinitrophenol fungicides
BT2 fungicides
BT3 pesticides

DINOPHYTA
BT1 algae
NT1 amphidinium
NT1 gymnodinium
NT1 peridinium
NT2 peridinium cinctum
NT2 peridinium cinctum f. westii

dinoprost
USE **prostaglandins**

DINOSEB
uf *dnbp*
BT1 desiccant herbicides

DINOSEB *cont.*
BT2 desiccants
BT1 dinitrophenol herbicides
BT2 herbicides
BT3 pesticides

DINOSULFON
BT1 dinitrophenol fungicides
BT2 fungicides
BT3 pesticides

DINOTERB
BT1 dinitrophenol herbicides
BT2 herbicides
BT3 pesticides

DINOTERBON
BT1 dinitrophenol fungicides
BT2 fungicides
BT3 pesticides

DINURUS
BT1 hemiuridae
BT2 digenea
BT3 trematoda

DIOCTOPHYMATIDAE
BT1 nematoda
NT1 dioctophyme
NT2 dioctophyme renale
NT1 eustrongylides
rt animal parasitic nematodes

DIOCTOPHYME
BT1 dioctophymatidae
BT2 nematoda
NT1 dioctophyme renale

DIOCTOPHYME RENALE
BT1 dioctophyme
BT2 dioctophymatidae
BT3 nematoda

dioctyl sodium sulphosuccinate
USE **docusate sodium**

DIOECY
BT1 sex differentiation
BT2 differentiation
rt flowers
rt sex

DIOESTRUS
AF diestrus
BT1 oestrous cycle
BT2 biological rhythms
BT2 sexual reproduction
BT3 reproduction

DIONAEA
BT1 droseraceae
NT1 dionaea muscipula

DIONAEA MUSCIPULA
BT1 dionaea
BT2 droseraceae
BT1 insectivorous plants
BT2 carnivorous plants
BT1 ornamental herbaceous plants

DIONCOPHYLLACEAE
NT1 triphyophyllum
NT2 triphyophyllum peltatum

DIONYSIA
BT1 primulaceae
NT1 dionysia hissarica

DIONYSIA HISSARICA
BT1 dionysia
BT2 primulaceae

DIOPSIDAE
BT1 diptera
NT1 diopsis
NT2 diopsis apicalis
NT2 diopsis collaris

DIOPSIS
BT1 diopsidae
BT2 diptera
NT1 diopsis apicalis
NT1 diopsis collaris

DIOPSIS APICALIS
BT1 diopsis
BT2 diopsidae
BT3 diptera

DIOPSIS COLLARIS
BT1 diopsis
BT2 diopsidae
BT3 diptera

DIOPTIDAE
BT1 lepidoptera
NT1 phryganidia
NT2 phryganidia californica

DIORCHIS
BT1 hymenolepididae
BT2 eucestoda
BT3 cestoda

DIORITE SOILS
BT1 soil types (lithological)

DIORYCTRIA
BT1 pyralidae
BT2 lepidoptera
NT1 dioryctria abietella
NT1 dioryctria abietivorella
NT1 dioryctria amatella
NT1 dioryctria clarioralis
NT1 dioryctria reniculelloides
NT1 dioryctria resinosella
NT1 dioryctria sylvestrella
NT1 dioryctria taedae

DIORYCTRIA ABIETELLA
BT1 dioryctria
BT2 pyralidae
BT3 lepidoptera

DIORYCTRIA ABIETIVORELLA
uf dioryctria reniculella
BT1 dioryctria
BT2 pyralidae
BT3 lepidoptera

DIORYCTRIA AMATELLA
BT1 dioryctria
BT2 pyralidae
BT3 lepidoptera

DIORYCTRIA CLARIORALIS
BT1 dioryctria
BT2 pyralidae
BT3 lepidoptera

dioryctria reniculella
USE **dioryctria abietivorella**

DIORYCTRIA RENICULELLOIDES
BT1 dioryctria
BT2 pyralidae
BT3 lepidoptera

DIORYCTRIA RESINOSELLA
BT1 dioryctria
BT2 pyralidae
BT3 lepidoptera

dioryctria splendidella
USE **dioryctria sylvestrella**

DIORYCTRIA SYLVESTRELLA
uf dioryctria splendidella
BT1 dioryctria
BT2 pyralidae
BT3 lepidoptera

DIORYCTRIA TAEDAE
BT1 dioryctria
BT2 pyralidae
BT3 lepidoptera

DIOSCOREA
BT1 dioscoreaceae
NT1 dioscorea alata
NT1 dioscorea bartlettii
NT1 dioscorea belizensis
NT1 dioscorea bernoulliana
NT1 dioscorea bulbifera
NT1 dioscorea burkiliana
NT1 dioscorea caucasica
NT1 dioscorea cayenensis
NT1 dioscorea chingii
NT1 dioscorea composita

DIOSCOREA *cont.*
NT1 dioscorea convolvulacea
NT1 dioscorea deltoidea
NT1 dioscorea dumetorum
NT1 dioscorea esculenta
NT1 dioscorea floribunda
NT1 dioscorea friedrichsthalii
NT1 dioscorea glandulosa
NT1 dioscorea hispida
NT1 dioscorea mangenotiana
NT1 dioscorea mexicana
NT1 dioscorea nelsonii
NT1 dioscorea nipponica
NT1 dioscorea nummularia
NT1 dioscorea opposita
NT1 dioscorea pentaphylla
NT1 dioscorea prazeri
NT1 dioscorea preussii
NT1 dioscorea rotundata
NT1 dioscorea tokoro
NT1 dioscorea trifida
NT1 dioscorea villosa
NT1 dioscorea zingiberensis
rt dioscorea latent potexvirus
rt diosgenin
rt yams

DIOSCOREA ALATA
BT1 dioscorea
BT2 dioscoreaceae
BT1 root vegetables
BT2 root crops
BT2 vegetables

DIOSCOREA BARTLETTII
BT1 dioscorea
BT2 dioscoreaceae

DIOSCOREA BELIZENSIS
BT1 dioscorea
BT2 dioscoreaceae

DIOSCOREA BERNOULLIANA
BT1 dioscorea
BT2 dioscoreaceae

DIOSCOREA BULBIFERA
uf dioscorea sativa
BT1 dioscorea
BT2 dioscoreaceae
BT1 medicinal plants
BT1 root vegetables
BT2 root crops
BT2 vegetables

DIOSCOREA BURKILIANA
BT1 dioscorea
BT2 dioscoreaceae

DIOSCOREA CAUCASICA
BT1 dioscorea
BT2 dioscoreaceae

DIOSCOREA CAYENENSIS
BT1 dioscorea
BT2 dioscoreaceae
BT1 root vegetables
BT2 root crops
BT2 vegetables

DIOSCOREA CHINGII
BT1 dioscorea
BT2 dioscoreaceae

DIOSCOREA COMPOSITA
BT1 dioscorea
BT2 dioscoreaceae

DIOSCOREA CONVOLVULACEA
BT1 dioscorea
BT2 dioscoreaceae

DIOSCOREA DELTOIDEA
BT1 dioscorea
BT2 dioscoreaceae
BT1 medicinal plants

DIOSCOREA DUMETORUM
BT1 dioscorea
BT2 dioscoreaceae
BT1 root vegetables
BT2 root crops
BT2 vegetables

DIOSCOREA ESCULENTA
BT1 dioscorea
BT2 dioscoreaceae
BT1 root vegetables
BT2 root crops
BT2 vegetables

DIOSCOREA FLORIBUNDA
BT1 antiviral plants
BT1 dioscorea
BT2 dioscoreaceae
BT1 medicinal plants

DIOSCOREA FRIEDRICHSTHALII
BT1 dioscorea
BT2 dioscoreaceae

DIOSCOREA GLANDULOSA
BT1 dioscorea
BT2 dioscoreaceae
BT1 root vegetables
BT2 root crops
BT2 vegetables

DIOSCOREA HISPIDA
BT1 dioscorea
BT2 dioscoreaceae
BT1 poisonous plants

DIOSCOREA LATENT POTEXVIRUS
HN from 1990
BT1 potexvirus group
BT2 plant viruses
BT3 plant pathogens
BT4 pathogens
rt dioscorea

DIOSCOREA MANGENOTIANA
BT1 dioscorea
BT2 dioscoreaceae

DIOSCOREA MEXICANA
BT1 dioscorea
BT2 dioscoreaceae

DIOSCOREA NELSONII
BT1 dioscorea
BT2 dioscoreaceae

DIOSCOREA NIPPONICA
BT1 dioscorea
BT2 dioscoreaceae

DIOSCOREA NUMMULARIA
BT1 dioscorea
BT2 dioscoreaceae

DIOSCOREA OPPOSITA
BT1 dioscorea
BT2 dioscoreaceae

DIOSCOREA PENTAPHYLLA
BT1 dioscorea
BT2 dioscoreaceae

DIOSCOREA PRAZERI
BT1 dioscorea
BT2 dioscoreaceae

DIOSCOREA PREUSSII
BT1 dioscorea
BT2 dioscoreaceae

DIOSCOREA ROTUNDATA
BT1 dioscorea
BT2 dioscoreaceae
BT1 insecticidal plants
BT2 pesticidal plants
BT1 root vegetables
BT2 root crops
BT2 vegetables

dioscorea sativa
USE **dioscorea bulbifera**

DIOSCOREA TOKORO
BT1 dioscorea
BT2 dioscoreaceae

DIOSCOREA TRIFIDA
BT1 dioscorea
BT2 dioscoreaceae
BT1 root vegetables
BT2 root crops
BT2 vegetables

DIOSCOREA VILLOSA
BT1 dioscorea
BT2 dioscoreaceae

DIOSCOREA ZINGIBERENSIS
BT1 dioscorea
BT2 dioscoreaceae

DIOSCOREACEAE
NT1 dioscorea
NT2 dioscorea alata
NT2 dioscorea bartlettii
NT2 dioscorea belizensis
NT2 dioscorea bernoulliana
NT2 dioscorea bulbifera
NT2 dioscorea burkiliana
NT2 dioscorea caucasica
NT2 dioscorea cayenensis
NT2 dioscorea chingii
NT2 dioscorea composita
NT2 dioscorea convolvulacea
NT2 dioscorea deltoidea
NT2 dioscorea dumetorum
NT2 dioscorea esculenta
NT2 dioscorea floribunda
NT2 dioscorea friedrichsthalii
NT2 dioscorea glandulosa
NT2 dioscorea hispida
NT2 dioscorea mangenotiana
NT2 dioscorea mexicana
NT2 dioscorea nelsonii
NT2 dioscorea nipponica
NT2 dioscorea nummularia
NT2 dioscorea opposita
NT2 dioscorea pentaphylla
NT2 dioscorea prazeri
NT2 dioscorea preussii
NT2 dioscorea rotundata
NT2 dioscorea tokoro
NT2 dioscorea trifida
NT2 dioscorea villosa
NT2 dioscorea zingiberensis
NT1 tamus
NT2 tamus communis

DIOSCOREOPHYLLUM
BT1 menispermaceae
NT1 dioscoreophyllum cumminsii

DIOSCOREOPHYLLUM CUMMINSII
BT1 dioscoreophyllum
BT2 menispermaceae
BT1 industrial crops
BT1 medicinal plants

DIOSGENIN
BT1 sapogenins
rt dioscorea

DIOSPYROS
BT1 ebenaceae
NT1 diospyros bipindensis
NT1 diospyros blancoi
NT1 diospyros cinnabarina
NT1 diospyros cornii
NT1 diospyros ebenaster
NT1 diospyros ferra
NT1 diospyros graciliensis
NT1 diospyros grascilescens
NT1 diospyros guianensis
NT1 diospyros kaki
NT1 diospyros kirkii
NT1 diospyros lotus
NT1 diospyros melanoxylon
NT1 diospyros mespiliformis
NT1 diospyros mollis
NT1 diospyros montana
NT1 diospyros obliquifolia
NT1 diospyros peregrina
NT1 diospyros sapota
NT1 diospyros texana
NT1 diospyros usambarensis
NT1 diospyros virginiana
rt antifungal plants
rt insecticidal plants

DIOSPYROS BIPINDENSIS
BT1 diospyros
BT2 ebenaceae

DIOSPYROS BLANCOI
BT1 diospyros
BT2 ebenaceae

DIOSPYROS CINNABARINA
BT1 diospyros
BT2 ebenaceae

DIOSPYROS CORNII
BT1 diospyros
BT2 ebenaceae

diospyros digyna
USE **diospyros ebenaster**

DIOSPYROS EBENASTER
uf diospyros digyna
BT1 diospyros
BT2 ebenaceae
BT1 subtropical tree fruits
BT2 subtropical fruits
BT3 fruit crops
BT2 tree fruits

DIOSPYROS FERRA
BT1 diospyros
BT2 ebenaceae

DIOSPYROS GRACILIENSIS
BT1 diospyros
BT2 ebenaceae

DIOSPYROS GRASCILESCENS
BT1 diospyros
BT2 ebenaceae

DIOSPYROS GUIANENSIS
BT1 diospyros
BT2 ebenaceae

DIOSPYROS KAKI
uf kaki
BT1 diospyros
BT2 ebenaceae
rt persimmons

DIOSPYROS KIRKII
BT1 diospyros
BT2 ebenaceae

DIOSPYROS LOTUS
BT1 diospyros
BT2 ebenaceae
rt persimmons

DIOSPYROS MELANOXYLON
BT1 diospyros
BT2 ebenaceae
BT1 forest trees

DIOSPYROS MESPILIFORMIS
BT1 diospyros
BT2 ebenaceae

DIOSPYROS MOLLIS
BT1 diospyros
BT2 ebenaceae

DIOSPYROS MONTANA
BT1 diospyros
BT2 ebenaceae
BT1 medicinal plants

DIOSPYROS OBLIQUIFOLIA
BT1 diospyros
BT2 ebenaceae

DIOSPYROS PEREGRINA
BT1 diospyros
BT2 ebenaceae

DIOSPYROS SAPOTA
BT1 diospyros
BT2 ebenaceae

DIOSPYROS TEXANA
BT1 diospyros
BT2 ebenaceae

DIOSPYROS USAMBARENSIS
BT1 diospyros
BT2 ebenaceae
BT1 medicinal plants

DIOSPYROS VIRGINIANA
BT1 diospyros
BT2 ebenaceae
rt persimmons

DIOXABENZOFOS
uf salithion
BT1 organothiophosphate insecticides
BT2 organophosphorus insecticides
BT3 insecticides
BT4 pesticides
BT3 organophosphorus pesticides
BT4 organophosphorus compounds

DIOXACARB
BT1 carbamate insecticides
BT2 carbamate pesticides
BT2 insecticides
BT3 pesticides

DIOXANE
BT1 heterocyclic oxygen compounds
BT1 solvents
rt dispersion

DIOXATHION
BT1 ectoparasiticides
BT2 antiparasitic agents
BT3 drugs
BT1 organothiophosphate acaricides
BT2 organophosphorus acaricides
BT3 acaricides
BT4 pesticides
BT3 organophosphorus pesticides
BT4 organophosphorus compounds
BT1 organothiophosphate insecticides
BT2 organophosphorus insecticides
BT3 insecticides
BT4 pesticides
BT3 organophosphorus pesticides
BT4 organophosphorus compounds

dioxyphenylalanine
USE **dopa**

DIPAROPSIS
BT1 noctuidae
BT2 lepidoptera
NT1 diparopsis castanea
NT1 diparopsis watersi

DIPAROPSIS CASTANEA
BT1 diparopsis
BT2 noctuidae
BT3 lepidoptera

DIPAROPSIS WATERSI
BT1 diparopsis
BT2 noctuidae
BT3 lepidoptera

DIPELTA
BT1 caprifoliaceae

DIPEPTIDASE
(ec 3.4.13.11)
BT1 peptidases
BT2 peptide hydrolases
BT3 hydrolases
BT4 enzymes

DIPEPTIDES
BT1 oligopeptides
BT2 peptides
NT1 γ-glutamylcysteine
NT1 aspartame
NT1 carnosine
NT1 glycylglycine
NT1 glycylproline
NT1 glycylsarcosine
NT1 lysinoalanine

DIPEPTIDYL CARBOXYPEPTIDASES
BT1 carboxypeptidases
BT2 peptidases

DIPEPTIDYL CARBOXYPEPTIDASES *cont.*
BT3 peptide hydrolases
BT4 hydrolases
BT5 enzymes

DIPETALOGASTER
BT1 reduviidae
BT2 heteroptera
NT1 dipetalogaster maxima

DIPETALOGASTER MAXIMA
HN from 1989
BT1 dipetalogaster
BT2 reduviidae
BT3 heteroptera

DIPETALONEMA
BT1 onchocercidae
BT2 nematoda
NT1 dipetalonema dessetae
NT1 dipetalonema reconditum
NT1 dipetalonema viteae

DIPETALONEMA DESSETAE
BT1 dipetalonema
BT2 onchocercidae
BT3 nematoda

dipetalonema perstans
USE **mansonella perstans**

DIPETALONEMA RECONDITUM
BT1 dipetalonema
BT2 onchocercidae
BT3 nematoda

dipetalonema streptocerca
USE **mansonella streptocerca**

DIPETALONEMA VITEAE
uf dipetalonema wite
BT1 dipetalonema
BT2 onchocercidae
BT3 nematoda

dipetalonema wite
USE **dipetalonema viteae**

DIPHACINONE
BT1 rodenticides
BT2 pesticides

DIPHENAMID
BT1 amide herbicides
BT2 herbicides
BT3 pesticides

o-diphenol oxidase
USE **catechol oxidase**

diphenyl
USE **biphenyl**

DIPHENYLAMINE
BT1 secondary amines
BT2 amines
BT3 amino compounds
BT4 organic nitrogen compounds
BT1 unclassified fungicides
BT2 fungicides
BT3 pesticides

diphenylhydantoin
USE **phenytoin**

DIPHOSPHATIDYLGLYCEROLS
uf glycerophosphatides
uf phosphatidylglycerols
BT1 glycerophospholipids
BT2 phospholipids
BT3 lipids

diphosphoglycerate
USE **glycerate 2,3-bis(phosphate)**

DIPHYLLOBOTHRIIDAE
BT1 eucestoda
BT2 cestoda
NT1 diphyllobothrium
NT2 diphyllobothrium cordiceps
NT2 diphyllobothrium dendriticum
NT2 diphyllobothrium latum

DIPHYLLOBOTHRIIDAE *cont.*
NT1 diplogonoporus
NT2 diplogonoporus balaenopterae
NT2 diplogonoporus fukuokaensis
NT2 diplogonoporus grandis
NT1 ligula
NT2 ligula intestinalis
NT1 schistocephalus
NT2 schistocephalus solidus
NT1 spirometra
NT2 spirometra mansonoides

DIPHYLLOBOTHRIUM
uf dibothriocephalus
BT1 diphyllobothriidae
BT2 eucestoda
BT3 cestoda
NT1 diphyllobothrium cordiceps
NT1 diphyllobothrium dendriticum
NT1 diphyllobothrium latum

DIPHYLLOBOTHRIUM CORDICEPS
BT1 diphyllobothrium
BT2 diphyllobothriidae
BT3 eucestoda
BT4 cestoda

DIPHYLLOBOTHRIUM DENDRITICUM
BT1 diphyllobothrium
BT2 diphyllobothriidae
BT3 eucestoda
BT4 cestoda

DIPHYLLOBOTHRIUM LATUM
BT1 diphyllobothrium
BT2 diphyllobothriidae
BT3 eucestoda
BT4 cestoda

DIPHYSA
BT1 leguminosae
rt ornamental woody plants

DIPLACHNE
BT1 gramineae
NT1 diplachne fusca

DIPLACHNE FUSCA
BT1 diplachne
BT2 gramineae

DIPLADENIA
BT1 apocynaceae
NT1 dipladenia sanderi

DIPLADENIA SANDERI
BT1 dipladenia
BT2 apocynaceae
BT1 ornamental woody plants

DIPLAZIUM
BT1 athyriaceae
NT1 diplazium pycnocarpon

DIPLAZIUM PYCNOCARPON
uf athyrium pycnocarpon
BT1 diplazium
BT2 athyriaceae
BT1 ornamental ferns
BT2 ferns
BT2 ornamental foliage plants
BT3 foliage plants

DIPLAZON
BT1 ichneumonidae
BT2 hymenoptera
NT1 diplazon laetatorius
rt bassus

DIPLAZON LAETATORIUS
uf bassus laetatorius
BT1 diplazon
BT2 ichneumonidae
BT3 hymenoptera

DIPLECTRUM
BT1 serranidae
BT2 perciformes
BT3 osteichthyes
BT4 fishes

DIPLOCARPON
BT1 helotiales
NT1 diplocarpon earlianum
NT1 diplocarpon mespili
NT1 diplocarpon rosae
rt entomosporium
rt fabraea

diplocarpon earliana
USE **diplocarpon earlianum**

DIPLOCARPON EARLIANUM
uf *diplocarpon earliana*
BT1 diplocarpon
BT2 helotiales

DIPLOCARPON MESPILI
HN from 1990
uf *diplocarpon soraueri*
uf *entomosporium maculatum*
uf *fabraea maculata*
BT1 diplocarpon
BT2 helotiales

DIPLOCARPON ROSAE
BT1 diplocarpon
BT2 helotiales

diplocarpon soraueri
USE **diplocarpon mespili**

diplococcus pneumoniae
USE **streptococcus pneumoniae**

DIPLOCYSTIS
BT1 apicomplexa
BT2 protozoa
NT1 diplocystis clerci
NT1 diplocystis johnsoni
NT1 diplocystis major
NT1 diplocystis metselaari
NT1 diplocystis minor
NT1 diplocystis oxyxani
NT1 diplocystis schneideri
NT1 diplocystis zootermopsidis

DIPLOCYSTIS CLERCI
BT1 diplocystis
BT2 apicomplexa
BT3 protozoa

DIPLOCYSTIS JOHNSONI
BT1 diplocystis
BT2 apicomplexa
BT3 protozoa

DIPLOCYSTIS MAJOR
BT1 diplocystis
BT2 apicomplexa
BT3 protozoa

DIPLOCYSTIS METSELAARI
BT1 diplocystis
BT2 apicomplexa
BT3 protozoa

DIPLOCYSTIS MINOR
BT1 diplocystis
BT2 apicomplexa
BT3 protozoa

DIPLOCYSTIS OXYXANI
BT1 diplocystis
BT2 apicomplexa
BT3 protozoa

DIPLOCYSTIS SCHNEIDERI
BT1 diplocystis
BT2 apicomplexa
BT3 protozoa

DIPLOCYSTIS ZOOTERMOPSIDIS
BT1 diplocystis
BT2 apicomplexa
BT3 protozoa

DIPLODIA
BT1 deuteromycotina
NT1 diplodia pinea
rt botryodiplodia
rt botryosphaeria
rt macrophomina
rt physalospora
rt sphaeropsis

DIPLODIA *cont.*
rt stenocarpella

diplodia corchori
USE **botryodiplodia theobromae**

diplodia frumenti
USE **physalospora zeicola**

diplodia gossypina
USE **botryodiplodia theobromae**

diplodia macrospora
USE **stenocarpella macrospora**

diplodia manihotis
USE **botyrodiplodia theobromae**

diplodia maydis
USE **stenocarpella maydis**

diplodia mutila
USE **botryosphaeria stevensii**

diplodia natalensis
USE **botryodiplodia theobromae**

DIPLODIA PINEA
uf *macrophoma pinea*
uf *macrophomina pinea*
uf *sphaeropsis pinea*
BT1 diplodia
BT2 deuteromycotina

diplodia theae-sinensis
USE **botryodiplodia theobromae**

diplodia theobromae
USE **botryodiplodia theobromae**

diplodia zeae
USE **stenocarpella maydis**

DIPLODINA
BT1 apicomplexa
BT2 protozoa
BT1 chlorophyta
BT2 algae

DIPLODINIUM
BT1 ciliophora
BT2 protozoa

DIPLODISCUS
BT1 tiliaceae
NT1 diplodiscus paniculatus

DIPLODISCUS PANICULATUS
BT1 antibacterial plants
BT1 diplodiscus
BT2 tiliaceae

DIPLOGONOPORUS
BT1 diphyllobothriidae
BT2 eucestoda
BT3 cestoda
NT1 diplogonoporus balaenopterae
NT1 diplogonoporus fukuokaensis
NT1 diplogonoporus grandis

DIPLOGONOPORUS BALAENOPTERAE
BT1 diplogonoporus
BT2 diphyllobothriidae
BT3 eucestoda
BT4 cestoda

DIPLOGONOPORUS FUKUOKAENSIS
BT1 diplogonoporus
BT2 diphyllobothriidae
BT3 eucestoda
BT4 cestoda

DIPLOGONOPORUS GRANDIS
BT1 diplogonoporus
BT2 diphyllobothriidae
BT3 eucestoda

DIPLOGONOPORUS GRANDIS *cont.*
BT4 cestoda

diploids
USE **diploidy**

DIPLOIDY
uf *diploids*
BT1 ploidy

DIPLOKNEMA
BT1 sapotaceae
NT1 diploknema butyracea

DIPLOKNEMA BUTYRACEA
uf *bassia butyracea*
uf *madhuca butyracea*
BT1 diploknema
BT2 sapotaceae
BT1 oilseed plants
BT2 fatty oil plants
BT3 oil plants

DIPLOLEPIS
BT1 cynipidae
BT2 hymenoptera

DIPLOON
BT1 sapotaceae
NT1 diploon cuspidatum

DIPLOON CUSPIDATUM
BT1 diploon
BT2 sapotaceae

DIPLOPODA
uf *millepedes*
BT1 myriapoda
BT2 arthropods
NT1 blaniulidae
NT2 archiboreoiulus
NT3 archiboreoiulus pallidus
NT2 blaniulus
NT3 blaniulus guttulatus
NT2 ommatoiulus
NT3 ommatoiulus moreleti
NT1 glomeridae
NT2 glomeris
NT3 glomeris marginata
NT1 iulidae
NT2 cylindroiulus
NT1 pachybolidae
NT2 pachybolus
NT3 pachybolus laminatus
NT1 paradoxosomatidae
NT2 oxidus
NT3 oxidus gracilis
NT1 polydesmidae
NT2 polydesmus
NT3 polydesmus inconstans
NT1 polyzoniidae
NT2 polyzonium
NT3 polyzonium germanicum
NT1 rhinocricidae
NT2 rhinocricus
NT3 rhinocricus bernardinensis
NT3 rhinocricus nattereri
NT1 trigoniulidae
NT2 trigoniulus
NT3 trigoniulus lumbricinus

DIPLOPTERA
BT1 blaberidae
BT2 blattaria
BT3 dictyoptera
NT1 diploptera punctata

DIPLOPTERA PUNCTATA
BT1 diploptera
BT2 blaberidae
BT3 blattaria
BT4 dictyoptera

DIPLOPYLIDIUM
BT1 dilepididae
BT2 eucestoda
BT3 cestoda
NT1 diplopylidium nolleri

DIPLOPYLIDIUM NOLLERI
BT1 diplopylidium
BT2 dilepididae
BT3 eucestoda
BT4 cestoda

diplostomatidae
USE **diplostomidae**

DIPLOSTOMIDAE
uf *diplostomatidae*
BT1 digenea
BT2 trematoda
NT1 alaria
NT2 alaria alata
NT1 diplostomum
NT2 diplostomum phoxini
NT2 diplostomum spathaceum
NT1 neodiplostomum
NT1 posthodiplostomum

DIPLOSTOMULA
BT1 digenean larvae
BT2 helminth larvae
BT3 helminths
BT4 parasites
BT3 larvae
BT4 developmental stages

DIPLOSTOMUM
BT1 diplostomidae
BT2 digenea
BT3 trematoda
NT1 diplostomum phoxini
NT1 diplostomum spathaceum

DIPLOSTOMUM PHOXINI
BT1 diplostomum
BT2 diplostomidae
BT3 digenea
BT4 trematoda

DIPLOSTOMUM SPATHACEUM
BT1 diplostomum
BT2 diplostomidae
BT3 digenea
BT4 trematoda

DIPLOTAXIS
BT1 cruciferae
NT1 diplotaxis tenuifolia

DIPLOTAXIS TENUIFOLIA
BT1 diplotaxis
BT2 cruciferae

diplothemium
USE **allagoptera**

DIPLOTROPIS
BT1 leguminosae
NT1 diplotropis purpurea

DIPLOTROPIS PURPUREA
BT1 diplotropis
BT2 leguminosae

DIPLOZOIDAE
BT1 monogenea
NT1 diplozoon
NT2 diplozoon paradoxum

DIPLOZOON
BT1 diplozoidae
BT2 monogenea
NT1 diplozoon paradoxum

DIPLOZOON PARADOXUM
BT1 diplozoon
BT2 diplozoidae
BT3 monogenea

DIPLURIDAE
BT1 araneae
BT2 arachnida
BT3 arthropods

DIPODIDAE
BT1 rodents
BT2 mammals
NT1 allactaga
NT2 allactaga sibirica
NT1 dipus
NT2 dipus sagitta
NT1 notomys
NT2 notomys alexis

DIPODOMYS
uf *kangaroo rats*
BT1 heteromyidae
BT2 rodents

DIPODOMYS *cont.*
BT3 mammals

DIPOTASSIUM HYDROGEN PHOSPHATE
BT1 potassium phosphates
BT2 phosphates (salts)
BT3 inorganic salts
BT4 inorganic compounds
BT4 salts
BT3 phosphates
BT2 phosphorus fertilizers
BT3 fertilizers
BT2 phosphorus-potassium fertilizers
BT3 compound fertilizers
BT4 fertilizers
BT2 potassium fertilizers
BT3 fertilizers

DIPPING
BT1 application methods
BT2 methodology
rt dips
rt sheep dipping races

DIPRENORPHINE
BT1 analeptics
BT2 neurotropic drugs
BT3 drugs
BT1 narcotic antagonists
BT2 detoxicants
BT3 drugs
BT1 neuroleptics
BT2 psychotropic drugs
BT3 neurotropic drugs
BT4 drugs

DIPRION
BT1 diprionidae
BT2 hymenoptera
NT1 diprion pini
NT1 diprion similis
rt gilpinia
rt neodiprion

diprion frutetorum
USE **gilpinia frutetorum**

diprion hercyniae
USE **gilpinia hercyniae**

DIPRION PINI
BT1 diprion
BT2 diprionidae
BT3 hymenoptera

diprion sertifer
USE **neodiprion sertifer**

DIPRION SIMILIS
BT1 diprion
BT2 diprionidae
BT3 hymenoptera

DIPRIONIDAE
BT1 hymenoptera
NT1 diprion
NT2 diprion pini
NT2 diprion similis
NT1 gilpinia
NT2 gilpinia frutetorum
NT2 gilpinia hercyniae
NT1 neodiprion
NT2 neodiprion abietis
NT2 neodiprion lecontei
NT2 neodiprion nanulus
NT2 neodiprion pratti
NT2 neodiprion sertifer
NT2 neodiprion swainei
NT2 neodiprion taedae
NT2 neodiprion tsugae
NT1 nesodiprion

DIPROPETRYN
BT1 triazine herbicides
BT2 herbicides
BT3 pesticides
BT2 triazines
BT3 heterocyclic nitrogen compounds
BT4 organic nitrogen compounds

DIPS
NT1 storage dips
NT1 teat dip
rt dipping
rt ectoparasiticides
rt sheep dipping races

DIPSACACEAE
NT1 cephalaria
NT2 cephalaria gigantea
NT2 cephalaria syriaca
NT1 dipsacus
NT2 dipsacus fullonum
NT2 dipsacus sylvestris
NT1 scabiosa
NT2 scabiosa caucasica
NT2 scabiosa comosa
NT2 scabiosa ochroleuca

DIPSACUS
BT1 dipsacaceae
NT1 dipsacus fullonum
NT1 dipsacus sylvestris

DIPSACUS FULLONUM
BT1 dipsacus
BT2 dipsacaceae
rt wool industry

DIPSACUS SYLVESTRIS
BT1 dipsacus
BT2 dipsacaceae

DIPTERA
uf *flies*
NT1 agromyzidae
NT2 agromyza
NT3 agromyza frontella
NT3 agromyza oryzae
NT2 calycomyza
NT2 chromatomyia
NT3 chromatomyia horticola
NT3 chromatomyia nigra
NT3 chromatomyia syngenesiae
NT2 liriomyza
NT3 liriomyza bryoniae
NT3 liriomyza cepae
NT3 liriomyza cicerina
NT3 liriomyza huidobrensis
NT3 liriomyza sativae
NT3 liriomyza trifoliearum
NT3 liriomyza trifolii
NT2 melanagromyza
NT3 melanagromyza obtusa
NT3 melanagromyza sojae
NT2 napomyza
NT3 napomyza carotae
NT2 ophiomyia
NT3 ophiomyia centrosematis
NT3 ophiomyia lantanae
NT3 ophiomyia phaseoli
NT3 ophiomyia shibatsujii
NT3 ophiomyia simplex
NT2 phytobia
NT2 phytomyza
NT3 phytomyza ilicicola
NT3 phytomyza orobanchia
NT3 phytomyza ranunculi
NT2 tropicomyia
NT3 tropicomyia theae
NT1 anthomyiidae
NT2 botanophila
NT2 delia
NT3 delia antiqua
NT3 delia coarctata
NT3 delia floralis
NT3 delia florilega
NT3 delia platura
NT3 delia radicum
NT2 hylemya
NT2 lasiomma
NT2 pegomya
NT3 pegomya betae
NT3 pegomya hyoscyami
NT2 phorbia
NT3 phorbia haberlandti
NT3 phorbia securis
NT2 strobilomyia
NT3 strobilomyia anthracina
NT3 strobilomyia laricicola
NT3 strobilomyia melania

DIPTERA *cont.*
NT1 bibionidae
NT2 bibio
NT3 bibio hortulanus
NT2 plecia
NT3 plecia nearctica
NT1 bombyliidae
NT2 villa
NT1 braulidae
NT2 braula
NT3 braula coeca
NT1 calliphoridae
NT2 aldrichina
NT3 aldrichina grahami
NT2 calliphora
NT3 calliphora augur
NT3 calliphora hilli
NT3 calliphora nigribarbis
NT3 calliphora placida
NT3 calliphora stygia
NT3 calliphora uralensis
NT3 calliphora vicina
NT3 calliphora vomitoria
NT2 chrysomya
NT3 chrysomya albiceps
NT3 chrysomya bezziana
NT3 chrysomya chloropyga
NT3 chrysomya megacephala
NT3 chrysomya putoria
NT3 chrysomya regalis
NT3 chrysomya rufifacies
NT2 cochliomyia
NT3 cochliomyia hominivorax
NT3 cochliomyia macellaria
NT2 cordylobia
NT3 cordylobia anthropophaga
NT2 hemilucilia
NT3 hemilucilia semidiaphana
NT2 lucilia
NT3 lucilia bufonivora
NT3 lucilia caesar
NT3 lucilia cuprina
NT3 lucilia eximia
NT3 lucilia illustris
NT3 lucilia sericata
NT2 phormia
NT3 phormia regina
NT3 phormia terraenovae
NT2 pollenia
NT3 pollenia rudis
NT1 cecidomyiidae
NT2 aphidoletes
NT3 aphidoletes abietis
NT3 aphidoletes aphidimyza
NT2 asphondylia
NT3 asphondylia sesami
NT2 cecidomyia
NT2 contarinia
NT3 contarinia baeri
NT3 contarinia medicaginis
NT3 contarinia nasturtii
NT3 contarinia okadai
NT3 contarinia oregonensis
NT3 contarinia pisi
NT3 contarinia pyrivora
NT3 contarinia schulzi
NT3 contarinia sorghicola
NT3 contarinia tritici
NT2 dasineura
NT3 dasineura brassicae
NT3 dasineura ignorata
NT3 dasineura mali
NT3 dasineura pyri
NT3 dasineura ribis
NT2 haplodiplosis
NT3 haplodiplosis marginata
NT2 heteropeza
NT3 heteropeza pygmaea
NT2 kaltenbachiola
NT3 kaltenbachiola strobi
NT2 kiefferia
NT2 lasioptera
NT2 masakimyia
NT3 masakimyia pustulae
NT2 mayetiola
NT3 mayetiola destructor
NT2 mycophila
NT3 mycophila speyeri
NT2 orseolia
NT3 orseolia oryzae
NT3 orseolia oryzivora

DIPTERA *cont.*
NT2 pachydiplosis
NT2 paradiplosis
NT3 paradiplosis abietis
NT3 paradiplosis tumifex
NT2 plemeliella
NT3 plemeliella abietina
NT2 resseliella
NT3 resseliella theobaldi
NT2 rhopalomyia
NT3 rhopalomyia chrysanthemi
NT2 sitodiplosis
NT3 sitodiplosis mosellana
NT2 thecodiplosis
NT3 thecodiplosis brachyntera
NT3 thecodiplosis japonensis
NT1 ceratopogonidae
NT2 culicoides
NT3 culicoides arakawai
NT3 culicoides barbosai
NT3 culicoides biguttatus
NT3 culicoides brevitarsis
NT3 culicoides circumscriptus
NT3 culicoides denningi
NT3 culicoides edeni
NT3 culicoides fascipennis
NT3 culicoides furens
NT3 culicoides grisescens
NT3 culicoides hieroglyphicus
NT3 culicoides hollensis
NT3 culicoides imicola
NT3 culicoides impunctatus
NT3 culicoides insignis
NT3 culicoides jamesi
NT3 culicoides kingi
NT3 culicoides melleus
NT3 culicoides mississippiensis
NT3 culicoides nubeculosus
NT3 culicoides obsoletus
NT3 culicoides oxystoma
NT3 culicoides pallidicornis
NT3 culicoides paraensis
NT3 culicoides pulicaris
NT3 culicoides punctatus
NT3 culicoides puncticollis
NT3 culicoides pusillus
NT3 culicoides riethi
NT3 culicoides salinarius
NT3 culicoides schultzei
NT3 culicoides stellifer
NT3 culicoides variipennis
NT3 culicoides venustus
NT3 culicoides wadai
NT2 forcipomyia
NT3 forcipomyia sibirica
NT2 leptoconops
NT3 leptoconops bequaerti
NT3 leptoconops kerteszi
NT1 chamaemyiidae
NT2 leucopis
NT3 leucopis interruptovittata
NT1 chaoboridae
NT2 chaoborus
NT2 corethrella
NT3 corethrella brakeleyi
NT2 mochlonyx
NT3 mochlonyx velutinus
NT1 chironomidae
NT2 camptochironomus
NT3 camptochironomus tentans
NT2 chironomus
NT3 chironomus anthracinus
NT3 chironomus crassicaudatus
NT3 chironomus decorus
NT3 chironomus plumosus
NT3 chironomus riparius
NT4 chironomus riparius piger
NT4 chironomus riparius riparius
NT3 chironomus staegeri
NT3 chironomus yoshimatsui
NT2 cladotanytarsus
NT3 cladotanytarsus lewisi
NT2 dicrotendipes
NT3 dicrotendipes californicus
NT2 glyptotendipes
NT3 glyptotendipes paripes

DIPTERA *cont.*
NT2 procladius
NT2 tanytarsus
NT2 tokunagayusurika
NT3 tokunagayusurika akamusi
NT1 chloropidae
NT2 chlorops
NT3 chlorops oryzae
NT3 chlorops pumilionis
NT2 hippelates
NT2 liohippelates
NT3 liohippelates collusor
NT3 liohippelates pusio
NT2 meromyza
NT2 oscinella
NT3 oscinella frit
NT3 oscinella pusilla
NT3 oscinella vastator
NT1 coelopidae
NT2 coelopa
NT1 culicidae
NT2 aedeomyia
NT3 aedeomyia squamipennis
NT2 aedes
NT3 aedes abserratus
NT3 aedes aegypti
NT3 aedes africanus
NT3 aedes albifasciatus
NT3 aedes albopictus
NT3 aedes alcasidi
NT3 aedes ambreensis
NT3 aedes angustivittatus
NT3 aedes annulipes
NT3 aedes apicoargenteus
NT3 aedes atlanticus
NT3 aedes atropalpus
NT3 aedes campestris
NT3 aedes canadensis
NT3 aedes cantans
NT3 aedes cantator
NT3 aedes caspius
NT3 aedes cataphylla
NT3 aedes cinereus
NT3 aedes circumluteolus
NT3 aedes communis
NT3 aedes cooki
NT3 aedes cumminsii
NT3 aedes cyprius
NT3 aedes dentatus
NT3 aedes detritus
NT3 aedes diantaeus
NT3 aedes dorsalis
NT3 aedes durbanensis
NT3 aedes echinus
NT3 aedes epactius
NT3 aedes esoensis
NT3 aedes euedes
NT3 aedes excrucians
NT3 aedes fitchii
NT3 aedes flavescens
NT3 aedes flavopictus
NT3 aedes fluviatilis
NT3 aedes fryeri
NT3 aedes fulvus
NT3 aedes furcifer
NT3 aedes galloisi
NT3 aedes geniculatus
NT3 aedes guamensis
NT3 aedes hebrideus
NT3 aedes hendersoni
NT3 aedes hexodontus
NT3 aedes impiger
NT3 aedes implicatus
NT3 aedes increpitus
NT3 aedes infirmatus
NT3 aedes ingrami
NT3 aedes intrudens
NT3 aedes japonicus
NT3 aedes juppi
NT3 aedes kochi
NT3 aedes koreicoides
NT3 aedes koreicus
NT3 aedes leucomelas
NT3 aedes lineatopennis
NT3 aedes luridus
NT3 aedes luteocephalus
NT3 aedes mariae
NT3 aedes mascarensis
NT3 aedes mediovittatus
NT3 aedes melanimon

DIPTERA *cont.*
NT3 aedes metallicus
NT3 aedes montchadskyi
NT3 aedes monticola
NT3 aedes nevadensis
NT3 aedes nigripes
NT3 aedes nigromaculis
NT3 aedes nipponicus
NT3 aedes notoscriptus
NT3 aedes novalbopictus
NT3 aedes opok
NT3 aedes pembaensis
NT3 aedes phoeniciae
NT3 aedes pionips
NT3 aedes poicilia
NT3 aedes polynesiensis
NT3 aedes pseudalbopictus
NT3 aedes pseudoscutellaris
NT3 aedes pulchritarsis
NT3 aedes pullatus
NT3 aedes punctodes
NT3 aedes punctor
NT3 aedes refiki
NT3 aedes riparius
NT3 aedes rusticus
NT3 aedes samoanus
NT3 aedes scapularis
NT3 aedes scutellaris
NT4 aedes scutellaris katherinensis
NT4 aedes scutellaris malayensis
NT3 aedes seatoi
NT3 aedes serratus
NT3 aedes sierrensis
NT3 aedes simpsoni
NT3 aedes sollicitans
NT3 aedes spencerii
NT3 aedes squamiger
NT3 aedes sticticus
NT3 aedes stimulans
NT3 aedes stokesi
NT3 aedes subdiversus
NT3 aedes taeniorhynchus
NT3 aedes tarsalis
NT3 aedes taylori
NT3 aedes terrens
NT3 aedes thelcter
NT3 aedes thibaulti
NT3 aedes togoi
NT3 aedes tormentor
NT3 aedes triseriatus
NT3 aedes trivittatus
NT3 aedes unidentatus
NT3 aedes varipalpus
NT3 aedes vexans
NT3 aedes vigilax
NT3 aedes vittatus
NT3 aedes w-albus
NT3 aedes watteni
NT3 aedes zoosophus
NT2 anopheles
NT3 anopheles aconitus
NT3 anopheles albimanus
NT3 anopheles albitarsis
NT3 anopheles algeriensis
NT3 anopheles amictus
NT3 anopheles annularis
NT3 anopheles annulipes
NT3 anopheles aquasalis
NT3 anopheles arabiensis
NT3 anopheles atroparvus
NT3 anopheles atropos
NT3 anopheles balabacensis
NT3 anopheles bancroftii
NT3 anopheles barberi
NT3 anopheles barbirostris
NT3 anopheles beklemishevi
NT3 anopheles bellator
NT3 anopheles bradleyi
NT3 anopheles campestris
NT3 anopheles claviger
NT3 anopheles coustani
NT3 anopheles crucians
NT3 anopheles cruzii
NT3 anopheles culicifacies
NT3 anopheles darlingi
NT3 anopheles demeilloni
NT3 anopheles dirus
NT3 anopheles dthali
NT3 anopheles earlei

DIPTERA *cont.*
NT3 anopheles farauti
NT3 anopheles flavirostris
NT3 anopheles fluviatilis
NT3 anopheles freeborni
NT3 anopheles funestus
NT3 anopheles gambiae
NT3 anopheles hancocki
NT3 anopheles hargreavesi
NT3 anopheles hilli
NT3 anopheles hispaniola
NT3 anopheles hyrcanus
NT3 anopheles jamesii
NT3 anopheles koliensis
NT3 anopheles labranchiae
NT3 anopheles lesteri
NT4 anopheles lesteri anthropophagus
NT3 anopheles leucosphyrus
NT3 anopheles lindesayi
NT3 anopheles litoralis
NT3 anopheles maculatus
NT3 anopheles maculipennis
NT3 anopheles marshallii
NT3 anopheles mascarensis
NT3 anopheles melanoon
NT3 anopheles melas
NT3 anopheles merus
NT3 anopheles messeae
NT3 anopheles minimus
NT3 anopheles multicolor
NT3 anopheles neivai
NT3 anopheles nigerrimus
NT3 anopheles nili
NT3 anopheles nivipes
NT3 anopheles nuneztovari
NT3 anopheles occidentalis
NT3 anopheles oswaldoi
NT3 anopheles pharoensis
NT3 anopheles philippinensis
NT3 anopheles plumbeus
NT3 anopheles pretoriensis
NT3 anopheles pseudopunctipennis
NT4 anopheles pseudopunctipennis franciscanus
NT3 anopheles pulcherrimus
NT3 anopheles punctimacula
NT3 anopheles punctipennis
NT3 anopheles punctulatus
NT3 anopheles quadriannulatus
NT3 anopheles quadrimaculatus
NT3 anopheles rivulorum
NT3 anopheles rufipes
NT3 anopheles sacharovi
NT3 anopheles sergentii
NT3 anopheles sinensis
NT3 anopheles splendidus
NT3 anopheles squamosus
NT3 anopheles stephensi
NT3 anopheles subalpinus
NT3 anopheles subpictus
NT3 anopheles sundaicus
NT3 anopheles superpictus
NT3 anopheles tenebrosus
NT3 anopheles tessellatus
NT3 anopheles theobaldi
NT3 anopheles triannulatus
NT3 anopheles turkhudi
NT3 anopheles vagus
NT3 anopheles wellcomei
NT3 anopheles ziemanni
NT2 armigeres
NT3 armigeres subalbatus
NT2 coquillettidia
NT3 coquillettidia crassipes
NT3 coquillettidia perturbans
NT3 coquillettidia richiardii
NT2 culex
NT3 culex annulirostris
NT3 culex annulus
NT3 culex antennatus
NT3 culex australicus
NT3 culex bitaeniorhynchus
NT3 culex cinereus
NT3 culex coronator
NT3 culex decens
NT3 culex erraticus

DIPTERA *cont.*
NT3 culex erythrothorax
NT3 culex fuscanus
NT3 culex fuscocephalus
NT3 culex gelidus
NT3 culex hayashii
NT3 culex modestus
NT3 culex neavei
NT3 culex nebulosus
NT3 culex nigripalpus
NT3 culex orientalis
NT3 culex peus
NT3 culex pipiens
NT4 culex pipiens pallens
NT4 culex pipiens pipiens
NT3 culex portesi
NT3 culex pseudovishnui
NT3 culex quinquefasciatus
NT3 culex restuans
NT3 culex salinarius
NT3 culex sitiens
NT3 culex taeniopus
NT3 culex tarsalis
NT3 culex territans
NT3 culex thalassius
NT3 culex theileri
NT3 culex tigripes
NT3 culex torrentium
NT3 culex tritaeniorhynchus
NT3 culex univittatus
NT3 culex vishnui
NT2 culiseta
NT3 culiseta alaskaensis
NT3 culiseta annulata
NT3 culiseta bergrothi
NT3 culiseta incidens
NT3 culiseta inornata
NT3 culiseta longiareolata
NT3 culiseta melanura
NT3 culiseta morsitans
NT3 culiseta ochroptera
NT3 culiseta subochrea
NT2 deinocerites
NT3 deinocerites cancer
NT3 deinocerites pseudes
NT2 eretmapodites
NT3 eretmapodites quinquevittatus
NT2 ficalbia
NT2 haemagogus
NT3 haemagogus capricornii
NT3 haemagogus celeste
NT3 haemagogus equinus
NT3 haemagogus janthinomys
NT3 haemagogus leucocelaenus
NT2 mansonia (diptera)
NT3 mansonia africana
NT3 mansonia annulata
NT3 mansonia annulifera
NT3 mansonia bonneae
NT3 mansonia dives
NT3 mansonia dyari
NT3 mansonia indiana
NT3 mansonia titillans
NT3 mansonia uniformis
NT2 opifex
NT3 opifex fuscus
NT2 orthopodomyia
NT3 orthopodomyia signifera
NT2 psorophora
NT3 psorophora ciliata
NT3 psorophora columbiae
NT3 psorophora confinnis
NT3 psorophora cyanescens
NT3 psorophora discolor
NT3 psorophora ferox
NT3 psorophora signipennis
NT2 sabethes
NT2 topomyia
NT2 toxorhynchites
NT3 toxorhynchites amboinensis
NT3 toxorhynchites brevipalpis
NT3 toxorhynchites gravelyi
NT3 toxorhynchites rutilus
NT4 toxorhynchites rutilus septentrionalis
NT3 toxorhynchites splendens
NT3 toxorhynchites theobaldi
NT2 trichoprosopon

DIPTERA *cont.*
NT2 tripteroides
NT3 tripteroides bambusa
NT2 uranotaenia
NT3 uranotaenia lowii
NT3 uranotaenia sapphirina
NT3 uranotaenia unguiculata
NT2 wyeomyia
NT3 wyeomyia mitchellii
NT3 wyeomyia smithii
NT3 wyeomyia vanduzeei
NT1 cuterebridae
NT2 cuterebra
NT3 cuterebra fontinella
NT4 cuterebra fontinella grisea
NT3 cuterebra tenebrosa
NT2 dermatobia
NT3 dermatobia hominis
NT1 diopsidae
NT2 diopsis
NT3 diopsis apicalis
NT3 diopsis collaris
NT1 dolichopodidae
NT2 medetera
NT1 drosophilidae
NT2 drosophila
NT3 drosophila melanogaster
NT3 drosophila pseudoobscura
NT3 drosophila simulans
NT3 drosophila subobscura
NT3 drosophila virilis
NT2 scaptomyza
NT1 dryomyzidae
NT2 dryomyza
NT3 dryomyza anilis
NT1 ephydridae
NT2 ephydra
NT2 hydrellia
NT3 hydrellia griseola
NT3 hydrellia philippina
NT1 fanniidae
NT2 fannia
NT3 fannia canicularis
NT3 fannia femoralis
NT3 fannia pusio
NT3 fannia scalaris
NT1 gasterophilidae
NT2 gasterophilus
NT3 gasterophilus haemorrhoidalis
NT3 gasterophilus inermis
NT3 gasterophilus intestinalis
NT3 gasterophilus meridionalis
NT3 gasterophilus nasalis
NT3 gasterophilus nigricornis
NT3 gasterophilus pecorum
NT3 gasterophilus ternicinctus
NT1 glossinidae
NT2 glossina
NT3 glossina austeni
NT3 glossina brevipalpis
NT3 glossina fusca
NT3 glossina fuscipes
NT4 glossina fuscipes fuscipes
NT4 glossina fuscipes quanzensis
NT3 glossina longipalpis
NT3 glossina longipennis
NT3 glossina medicorum
NT3 glossina morsitans
NT4 glossina morsitans centralis
NT4 glossina morsitans morsitans
NT4 glossina morsitans submorsitans
NT3 glossina nigrofusca
NT3 glossina pallicera
NT3 glossina pallidipes
NT3 glossina palpalis
NT4 glossina palpalis gambiensis
NT4 glossina palpalis palpalis
NT3 glossina swynnertoni
NT3 glossina tabaniformis
NT3 glossina tachinoides
NT1 hippoboscidae
NT2 hippobosca
NT3 hippobosca camelina

DIPTERA *cont.*
NT3 hippobosca equina
NT3 hippobosca longipennis
NT2 lipoptena
NT3 lipoptena cervi
NT2 melophagus
NT3 melophagus ovinus
NT2 pseudolynchia
NT3 pseudolynchia canariensis
NT1 lonchaeidae
NT2 neosilba
NT3 neosilba pendula
NT2 silba
NT3 silba adipata
NT3 silba virescens
NT1 muscidae
NT2 atherigona
NT3 atherigona approximata
NT3 atherigona falcata
NT3 atherigona naqvii
NT3 atherigona orientalis
NT3 atherigona oryzae
NT3 atherigona simplex
NT3 atherigona soccata
NT3 atherigona varia
NT2 haematobia
NT3 haematobia irritans
NT4 haematobia irritans exigua
NT4 haematobia irritans irritans
NT3 haematobia thirouxi
NT4 haematobia thirouxi potans
NT3 haematobia titillans
NT2 haematobosca
NT3 haematobosca stimulans
NT2 hydrotaea
NT3 hydrotaea aenescens
NT3 hydrotaea ignava
NT3 hydrotaea irritans
NT3 hydrotaea meteorica
NT2 morellia
NT3 morellia hortorum
NT3 morellia simplex
NT2 musca
NT3 musca autumnalis
NT3 musca conducens
NT3 musca crassirostris
NT3 musca domestica
NT4 musca domestica domestica
NT3 musca lusoria
NT3 musca nevilli
NT3 musca osiris
NT3 musca sorbens
NT3 musca vetustissima
NT3 musca vitripennis
NT3 musca xanthomelas
NT2 muscina
NT3 muscina levida
NT3 muscina stabulans
NT2 neomyia
NT3 neomyia cornicina
NT2 orthellia
NT2 stomoxys
NT3 stomoxys calcitrans
NT3 stomoxys niger
NT1 oestridae
NT2 cephalopina
NT3 cephalopina titillator
NT2 cephenemyia
NT3 cephenemyia auribarbis
NT3 cephenemyia stimulator
NT3 cephenemyia trompe
NT2 gedoelstia
NT2 hypoderma
NT3 hypoderma bovis
NT3 hypoderma diana
NT3 hypoderma lineatum
NT3 hypoderma tarandi
NT2 oestrus (diptera)
NT3 oestrus ovis
NT2 pharyngomyia
NT3 pharyngomyia picta
NT2 przhevalskiana
NT3 przhevalskiana silenus
NT2 rhinoestrus
NT3 rhinoestrus latifrons
NT3 rhinoestrus purpureus

DIPTERA *cont.*
NT3 rhinoestrus usbekistanicus
NT1 opomyzidae
NT2 geomyza
NT3 geomyza tripunctata
NT2 opomyza
NT3 opomyza florum
NT1 otitidae
NT2 euxesta
NT3 euxesta notata
NT2 tetanops
NT3 tetanops myopaeformis
NT1 phoridae
NT2 megaselia
NT3 megaselia halterata
NT3 megaselia scalaris
NT1 piophilidae
NT2 piophila
NT3 piophila casei
NT1 platystomatidae
NT2 rivellia
NT3 rivellia quadrifasciata
NT1 psilidae
NT2 psila (diptera)
NT3 psila rosae
NT1 psychodidae
NT2 phlebotominae
NT3 grassomyia
NT4 grassomyia squamipleuris
NT3 lutzomyia
NT4 lutzomyia anduzei
NT4 lutzomyia anthophora
NT4 lutzomyia ayrozai
NT4 lutzomyia carrerai
NT5 lutzomyia carrerai carrerai
NT4 lutzomyia diabolica
NT4 lutzomyia fischeri
NT4 lutzomyia flaviscutellata
NT4 lutzomyia gomezi
NT4 lutzomyia hirsuta
NT4 lutzomyia intermedia
NT4 lutzomyia longipalpis
NT4 lutzomyia migonei
NT4 lutzomyia olmeca
NT5 lutzomyia olmeca bicolor
NT4 lutzomyia ovallesi
NT4 lutzomyia panamensis
NT4 lutzomyia pessoai
NT4 lutzomyia sanguinaria
NT4 lutzomyia shannoni
NT4 lutzomyia sordellii
NT4 lutzomyia townsendi
NT4 lutzomyia trapidoi
NT4 lutzomyia trinidadensis
NT4 lutzomyia umbratilis
NT4 lutzomyia vespertilionis
NT4 lutzomyia vexator
NT4 lutzomyia wellcomei
NT4 lutzomyia whitmani
NT4 lutzomyia ylephiletrix
NT3 phlebotomus
NT4 phlebotomus alexandri
NT4 phlebotomus andrejevi
NT4 phlebotomus argentipes
NT4 phlebotomus ariasi
NT4 phlebotomus bergeroti
NT4 phlebotomus caucasicus
NT4 phlebotomus chinensis
NT4 phlebotomus duboscqi
NT4 phlebotomus langeroni
NT4 phlebotomus longipes
NT4 phlebotomus major
NT4 phlebotomus martini
NT4 phlebotomus mongolensis
NT4 phlebotomus papatasi
NT4 phlebotomus pedifer
NT4 phlebotomus perfiliewi
NT4 phlebotomus perniciosus
NT4 phlebotomus sergenti
NT4 phlebotomus simici
NT4 phlebotomus smirnovi
NT4 phlebotomus tobbi
NT3 sergentomyia
NT4 sergentomyia adleri
NT4 sergentomyia africana
NT4 sergentomyia antennata

DIPTERA *cont.*
NT5 sergentomyia antennata form sintoni
NT4 sergentomyia babu
NT4 sergentomyia baghdadis
NT4 sergentomyia bailyi
NT4 sergentomyia bedfordi
NT4 sergentomyia clydei
NT4 sergentomyia dentata
NT4 sergentomyia garnhami
NT4 sergentomyia grekovi
NT4 sergentomyia ingrami
NT4 sergentomyia minuta
NT4 sergentomyia murgabiensis
NT4 sergentomyia schwetzi
NT4 sergentomyia sogdiana
NT2 psychodinae
NT3 psychoda
NT4 psychoda alternata
NT4 psychoda cinerea
NT3 telmatoscopus
NT1 sarcophagidae
NT2 acridiophaga
NT2 agria
NT3 agria housei
NT2 bellieria
NT2 bercaea
NT3 bercaea cruentata
NT2 boettcherisca
NT3 boettcherisca peregrina
NT2 helicophagella
NT3 helicophagella melanura
NT2 neobellieria
NT3 neobellieria bullata
NT2 parasarcophaga
NT3 parasarcophaga albiceps
NT3 parasarcophaga argyrostoma
NT3 parasarcophaga crassipalpis
NT3 parasarcophaga misera
NT3 parasarcophaga ruficornis
NT2 ravinia
NT2 sarcophaga
NT3 sarcophaga carnaria
NT2 senotainia
NT2 wohlfahrtia
NT3 wohlfahrtia magnifica
NT3 wohlfahrtia vigil
NT1 scathophagidae
NT2 nanna
NT2 scathophaga
NT3 scathophaga stercoraria
NT1 sciaridae
NT2 lycoriella
NT3 lycoriella auripila
NT3 lycoriella mali
NT2 sciara
NT1 sciomyzidae
NT2 elgiva
NT2 knutsonia
NT3 knutsonia albiseta
NT2 sepedon
NT3 sepedon fuscipennis
NT1 sepsidae
NT2 sepsis (diptera)
NT1 simuliidae
NT2 austrosimulium
NT2 cnephia
NT3 cnephia dacotensis
NT3 cnephia ornithophilia
NT2 metacnephia
NT3 metacnephia pallipes
NT2 prosimulium
NT3 prosimulium fuscum
NT3 prosimulium mixtum
NT2 simulium
NT3 simulium adersi
NT3 simulium albellum
NT3 simulium amazonicum
NT3 simulium angustipes
NT3 simulium angustitarse
NT3 simulium aokii
NT3 simulium arcticum
NT3 simulium argyreatum
NT3 simulium aureum
NT3 simulium bezzii
NT3 simulium bivittatum
NT3 simulium callidum
NT3 simulium canadense

DIPTERA *cont.*
NT3 simulium congareenarum
NT3 simulium costatum
NT3 simulium damnosum
NT3 simulium decorum
NT3 simulium equinum
NT3 simulium erythrocephalum
NT3 simulium euryadminiculum
NT3 simulium exiguum
NT3 simulium guianense
NT3 simulium hargreavesi
NT3 simulium horacioi
NT3 simulium jenningsi
NT3 simulium latigonium
NT3 simulium latipes
NT3 simulium latizonum
NT3 simulium limbatum
NT3 simulium lineatum
NT3 simulium maculatum
NT3 simulium metallicum
NT3 simulium mexicanum
NT3 simulium monticola
NT3 simulium morsitans
NT3 simulium neavei
NT3 simulium nitidifrons
NT3 simulium noelleri
NT3 simulium ochraceum
NT3 simulium ornatum
NT3 simulium ovtshinnikovi
NT3 simulium oyapockense
NT3 simulium paynei
NT3 simulium pictipes
NT3 simulium pintoi
NT3 simulium pontinum
NT3 simulium pseudequinum
NT3 simulium pusillum
NT3 simulium reptans
NT3 simulium rugglesi
NT3 simulium sanctipauli
NT3 simulium sanguineum
NT3 simulium schoutedeni
NT3 simulium sirbanum
NT3 simulium slossonae
NT3 simulium soubrense
NT3 simulium squamosum
NT3 simulium takahasii
NT3 simulium tuberosum
NT3 simulium uchidai
NT3 simulium venustum
NT3 simulium verecundum
NT3 simulium vittatum
NT3 simulium voilensis
NT3 simulium vorax
NT3 simulium yahense
NT2 stegopterna
NT3 stegopterna mutata
NT1 sphaeroceridae
NT2 coproica
NT3 coproica hirtula
NT2 copromyza
NT2 leptocera
NT1 stratiomyidae
NT2 hermetia
NT3 hermetia illucens
NT2 inopus
NT3 inopus rubriceps
NT1 syrphidae
NT2 allograpta
NT3 allograpta obliqua
NT3 allograpta pulchra
NT2 epistrophe
NT2 episyrphus
NT3 episyrphus balteatus
NT2 eristalis
NT3 eristalis tenax
NT2 eumerus
NT2 eupeodes
NT3 eupeodes corollae
NT2 ischiodon
NT3 ischiodon aegyptius
NT2 melanostoma
NT2 merodon
NT3 merodon equestris
NT2 scaeva
NT3 scaeva pyrastri
NT2 sphaerophoria
NT3 sphaerophoria scripta
NT2 syrphus
NT3 syrphus ribesii

DIPTERA *cont.*
NT3 syrphus vitripennis
NT2 xanthogramma
NT1 tabanidae
NT2 atylotus
NT3 atylotus agrestis
NT2 chrysops
NT3 chrysops atlanticus
NT3 chrysops excitans
NT3 chrysops fuliginosus
NT3 chrysops furcatus
NT3 chrysops mlokosiewiczi
NT3 chrysops suavis
NT3 chrysops vanderwulpi
NT2 haematopota
NT3 haematopota crassicornis
NT3 haematopota italica
NT3 haematopota pluvialis
NT3 haematopota subcylindrica
NT2 hirosia
NT3 hirosia iyoensis
NT2 hybomitra
NT3 hybomitra arpadi
NT3 hybomitra bimaculata
NT3 hybomitra borealis
NT3 hybomitra caucasica
NT3 hybomitra lasiophthalma
NT3 hybomitra montana
NT3 hybomitra tarandina
NT2 phaeotabanus
NT3 phaeotabanus cajennensis
NT2 tabanus
NT3 tabanus abactor
NT3 tabanus atratus
NT3 tabanus autumnalis
NT3 tabanus bromius
NT3 tabanus chrysurus
NT3 tabanus fuscicostatus
NT3 tabanus glaucopis
NT3 tabanus importunus
NT3 tabanus infestus
NT3 tabanus lineola
NT3 tabanus nigrovittatus
NT3 tabanus nipponicus
NT3 tabanus occidentalis
NT4 tabanus occidentalis var. dorsovittatus
NT3 tabanus punctifer
NT3 tabanus quinquevittatus
NT3 tabanus rufidens
NT3 tabanus sulcifrons
NT3 tabanus taeniola
NT3 tabanus taiwanus
NT3 tabanus trigeminus
NT3 tabanus trigonus
NT1 tachinidae
NT2 actia
NT3 actia nudibasis
NT2 alophora
NT3 alophora subcoleoptrata
NT2 anagonia
NT3 anagonia anguliventris
NT2 archytas
NT3 archytas marmoratus
NT2 bessa
NT3 bessa harveyi
NT3 bessa parallela
NT3 bessa selecta
NT2 blepharella
NT3 blepharella lateralis
NT2 blepharipa
NT3 blepharipa pratensis
NT3 blepharipa scutellata
NT2 carcelia
NT3 carcelia evolans
NT2 ceracia
NT3 ceracia fergusoni
NT2 clytiomya
NT3 clytiomya helluo
NT2 compsilura
NT3 compsilura concinnata
NT2 cyzenis
NT3 cyzenis albicans
NT2 drino
NT2 ectophasia
NT3 ectophasia crassipennis
NT2 eucelatoria
NT2 exorista
NT3 exorista fallax
NT3 exorista fasciata

DIPTERA *cont.*
NT3 exorista larvarum
NT3 exorista rossica
NT3 exorista segregata
NT2 gonia
NT2 goniophthalmus
NT3 goniophthalmus halli
NT2 lespesia
NT3 lespesia archippivora
NT2 linnaemya
NT3 linnaemya comta
NT2 lixophaga
NT3 lixophaga diatraeae
NT3 lixophaga mediocris
NT2 lydella
NT3 lydella thompsoni
NT2 meigenia
NT2 metagonistylum
NT3 metagonistylum minense
NT2 myiopharus
NT3 myiopharus doryphorae
NT2 nemorilla
NT3 nemorilla maculosa
NT2 pales
NT3 pales pavida
NT2 palexorista
NT3 palexorista imberbis
NT2 paratheresia
NT3 paratheresia claripalpis
NT2 phasia
NT2 phryxe
NT3 phryxe caudata
NT3 phryxe vulgaris
NT2 pseudogonia
NT3 pseudogonia rufifrons
NT2 pseudoperichaeta
NT3 pseudoperichaeta nigrolineata
NT2 siphona
NT2 tachina
NT2 voria
NT3 voria ruralis
NT2 winthemia
NT2 zenillia
NT1 tephritidae
NT2 acanthiophilus
NT3 acanthiophilus helianthi
NT2 anastrepha
NT3 anastrepha fraterculus
NT3 anastrepha ludens
NT3 anastrepha obliqua
NT3 anastrepha pickeli
NT3 anastrepha suspensa
NT2 bactrocera
NT3 bactrocera cacuminata
NT3 bactrocera cucumis
NT3 bactrocera cucurbitae
NT3 bactrocera dorsalis
NT3 bactrocera oleae
NT3 bactrocera tryoni
NT3 bactrocera tsuneonis
NT3 bactrocera zonata
NT2 ceratitis
NT3 ceratitis capitata
NT3 ceratitis rosa
NT2 dacus
NT3 dacus ciliatus
NT2 euleia
NT3 euleia heraclii
NT2 eurosta
NT3 eurosta solidaginis
NT2 orellia
NT2 pardalaspis
NT2 rhagoletis
NT3 rhagoletis cerasi
NT3 rhagoletis completa
NT3 rhagoletis fausta
NT3 rhagoletis indifferens
NT3 rhagoletis mendax
NT3 rhagoletis pomonella
NT2 tephritis
NT3 tephritis dilacerata
NT2 terellia
NT3 terellia ruficauda
NT2 toxotrypana
NT3 toxotrypana curvicauda
NT2 trirhithromyia
NT3 trirhithromyia cyanescens
NT2 urophora
NT3 urophora affinis
NT3 urophora cardui

DIPTERA *cont.*
NT3 urophora quadrifasciata
NT1 tipulidae
NT2 tipula
NT3 tipula paludosa
rt insects
rt myiasis

DIPTEROCARPACEAE
NT1 anisoptera
NT2 anisoptera thurifera
NT1 dipterocarpus
NT2 dipterocarpus gracilis
NT2 dipterocarpus grandiflorus
NT2 dipterocarpus hasseltii
NT1 dryobalanops
NT2 dryobalanops aromatica
NT1 hopea
NT1 parashorea
NT2 parashorea malaanonan
NT2 parashorea stellata
NT2 parashorea tomentella
NT1 pentacme
NT2 pentacme burmanica
NT2 pentacme contorta
NT1 shorea
NT2 shorea acuminata
NT2 shorea javanica
NT2 shorea leprosula
NT2 shorea negrosensis
NT2 shorea ovalis
NT2 shorea parvifolia
NT2 shorea robusta
NT2 shorea worthingtonii
NT1 vateria
NT2 vateria indica
NT1 vatica
NT2 vatica obscura

DIPTEROCARPUS
BT1 dipterocarpaceae
NT1 dipterocarpus gracilis
NT1 dipterocarpus grandiflorus
NT1 dipterocarpus hasseltii

DIPTEROCARPUS GRACILIS
BT1 dipterocarpus
BT2 dipterocarpaceae

DIPTEROCARPUS GRANDIFLORUS
BT1 dipterocarpus
BT2 dipterocarpaceae

DIPTEROCARPUS HASSELTII
HN from 1990
BT1 dipterocarpus
BT2 dipterocarpaceae
BT1 forest trees

DIPTERYX
BT1 leguminosae
NT1 dipteryx odorata
NT1 dipteryx panamensis

DIPTERYX ODORATA
BT1 dipteryx
BT2 leguminosae

DIPTERYX PANAMENSIS
HN from 1990
BT1 dipteryx
BT2 leguminosae
BT1 forest trees

DIPUS
BT1 dipodidae
BT2 rodents
BT3 mammals
NT1 dipus sagitta

DIPUS SAGITTA
BT1 dipus
BT2 dipodidae
BT3 rodents
BT4 mammals

DIPYLIDIUM
BT1 dilepididae
BT2 eucestoda
BT3 cestoda
NT1 dipylidium caninum

DIPYLIDIUM CANINUM
BT1 dipylidium

DIPYLIDIUM CANINUM *cont.*
BT2 dilepididae
BT3 eucestoda
BT4 cestoda

DIPYRIDAMOLE
BT1 vasodilator agents
BT2 cardiovascular agents
BT3 drugs

DIQUAT
BT1 desiccant herbicides
BT2 desiccants
BT1 quaternary ammonium herbicides
BT2 herbicides
BT3 pesticides
BT2 quaternary ammonium compounds
BT3 ammonium compounds
BT3 organic nitrogen compounds

DIRECT ACIDIFICATION
BT1 cheesemaking

DIRECT DNA UPTAKE
HN from 1989
rt electroporation
rt genetic engineering

direct drilling
USE **direct sowing**

DIRECT MARKETING
uf *market, direct*
BT1 retail marketing
BT2 marketing channels
BT3 marketing
NT1 farmers' markets (agricola)

DIRECT MICROSCOPIC COUNT
BT1 analytical methods
BT2 methodology
rt plate count

DIRECT SIRE COMPARISONS
uf *mixed model method*
BT1 sire evaluation
BT2 animal breeding methods
BT3 breeding methods
BT4 methodology

DIRECT SOWING
uf *direct drilling*
uf *drilling, direct*
uf *sowing, direct*
BT1 drilling
BT2 application methods
BT3 methodology
BT2 sowing methods
BT3 sowing
BT4 planting
rt furrow openers
rt minimum tillage
rt no-tillage
rt seeder cultivators
rt sod seeders
rt sod sowing

DIRECT TAXATION
uf *taxation, direct*
BT1 taxes
BT2 fiscal policy
BT3 economic policy
BT3 public finance
NT1 capital taxation
NT2 land tax
NT2 rates
NT1 company tax
NT1 income tax
NT1 inheritance tax

DIRECTIVES
BT1 legislation
BT2 legal systems
rt regulations

DIRECTORIES
BT1 publications
BT1 reference works

DIRHINUS
BT1 chalcididae

DIRHINUS *cont.*
BT2 hymenoptera
NT1 dirhinus giffardii

DIRHINUS GIFFARDII
BT1 dirhinus
BT2 chalcididae
BT3 hymenoptera

DIROFILARIA
uf *heartworm*
BT1 onchocercidae
BT2 nematoda
NT1 dirofilaria immitis
NT1 dirofilaria repens

DIROFILARIA IMMITIS
BT1 dirofilaria
BT2 onchocercidae
BT3 nematoda

DIROFILARIA REPENS
BT1 dirofilaria
BT2 onchocercidae
BT3 nematoda

DIRT TARE
BT1 tare
BT2 weight
rt clean yield

DISA
BT1 orchidaceae
NT1 disa uniflora
NT1 disa veitchii

DISA UNIFLORA
BT1 disa
BT2 orchidaceae
BT1 ornamental orchids

DISA VEITCHII
BT1 disa
BT2 orchidaceae
BT1 ornamental orchids

DISABILITY INSURANCE (AGRICOLA)
BT1 insurance

disabled persons
USE **handicapped persons**

DISABLED VETERANS (AGRICOLA)
BT1 handicapped persons
BT2 people
rt veterans (agricola)

DISACCHARIDASES
BT1 o-glycoside hydrolases
BT2 glycosidases
BT3 hydrolases
BT4 enzymes
rt disaccharides

DISACCHARIDES
BT1 oligosaccharides
BT2 carbohydrates
NT1 cellobiose
NT1 gentiobiose
NT1 isomaltose
NT1 isomaltulose
NT1 lactose
NT1 lactulose
NT1 leucrose
NT1 maltose
NT1 melibiose
NT1 sucrose
NT1 trehalose
rt disaccharidases

DISACCHARIDOSIS
BT1 carbohydrate metabolism disorders
BT2 metabolic disorders
BT3 animal disorders
BT4 disorders

DISADVANTAGED (AGRICOLA)
NT1 disadvantaged youth (agricola)
NT1 economically disadvantaged

DISADVANTAGED YOUTH (AGRICOLA)
BT1 disadvantaged (agricola)
BT1 youth
BT2 age groups
BT3 groups

DISANTHUS
BT1 hamamelidaceae

DISASSORTATIVE MATING
HN from 1989
BT1 mating systems

DISASTERS
NT1 agricultural disasters
NT2 agricultural crises
NT1 natural disasters
NT2 avalanches
NT2 earthquakes
NT2 famine
NT2 flooding
NT2 landslides
NT2 storms
NT3 dust storms
NT2 volcanic activity
rt drought

disasters, agricultural
USE **agricultural disasters**

disasters, natural
USE **natural disasters**

DISBUDDING
BT1 stopping
BT2 pruning
rt buds

DISC COULTERS
uf *coulters, disc*
BT1 coulters
BT2 components
rt discs

DISC CULTIVATORS
uf *cultivators, disc*
BT1 cultivators
BT2 implements
rt discs

DISC HARROWS
uf *harrows, disc*
BT1 harrows
BT2 implements
rt discs

DISC PLOUGHS
AF disc plows
uf *ploughs, disc*
BT1 ploughs
BT2 implements
rt discs

DISC PLOWS
BF disc ploughs
BT1 plows

DISC RECORDINGS
BT1 mass media
BT2 communication

DISC RIDGERS
uf *ridgers, disc*
BT1 ridgers
BT2 implements
rt discs

DISC SHARES
uf *shares, disc*
BT1 shares
BT2 components
rt discs

DISCARIA
BT1 rhamnaceae
NT1 discaria crenata
NT1 discaria toumatu

DISCARIA CRENATA
BT1 discaria
BT2 rhamnaceae

DISCARIA TOUMATU
BT1 discaria

DISCARIA TOUMATU *cont.*
BT2 rhamnaceae

DISCESTRA
BT1 noctuidae
BT2 lepidoptera
NT1 discestra trifolii
rt mamestra

DISCESTRA TRIFOLII
uf *mamestra trifolii*
BT1 discestra
BT2 noctuidae
BT3 lepidoptera

DISCHARGE

DISCHARGES
NT1 electric discharges
NT2 corona discharge
rt exudates

DISCHIDIA
BT1 asclepiadaceae

DISCING
BT1 tillage
BT2 cultivation

DISCIPLINE (AGRICOLA)
rt discipline problems (agricola)
rt punishment (agricola)

DISCIPLINE PROBLEMS (AGRICOLA)
BT1 antisocial behavior (agricola)
BT2 human behavior
BT3 behavior
rt behavior problems (agricola)
rt discipline (agricola)

DISCOCACTUS
BT1 cactaceae
NT1 discocactus albispinus
NT1 discocactus alteolens
NT1 discocactus araneispinus
NT1 discocactus estevesii
NT1 discocactus horichii
NT1 discocactus lankesteri

DISCOCACTUS ALBISPINUS
BT1 discocactus
BT2 cactaceae
BT1 ornamental succulent plants
BT2 succulent plants

DISCOCACTUS ALTEOLENS
BT1 discocactus
BT2 cactaceae
BT1 ornamental succulent plants
BT2 succulent plants

DISCOCACTUS ARANEISPINUS
BT1 discocactus
BT2 cactaceae
BT1 ornamental succulent plants
BT2 succulent plants

DISCOCACTUS ESTEVESII
BT1 discocactus
BT2 cactaceae
BT1 ornamental succulent plants
BT2 succulent plants

DISCOCACTUS HORICHII
BT1 discocactus
BT2 cactaceae
BT1 ornamental succulent plants
BT2 succulent plants

DISCOCACTUS LANKESTERI
BT1 discocactus
BT2 cactaceae
BT1 ornamental succulent plants
BT2 succulent plants

DISCOCRICONEMELLA
BT1 criconematidae
BT2 nematoda

DISCOLORATION
BT1 stains
rt colour

DISCOS
BT1 pop music
BT2 music
BT3 performing arts
BT4 arts

DISCOUNT RATES
BT1 credit control
BT2 controls

discounted cash flow
USE **cash flow analysis**

DISCOUNTS
BT1 marketing techniques
BT2 techniques
rt sales promotion

DISCOVERY TEACHING METHOD (AGRICOLA)
BT1 teaching methods
BT2 methodology

discrete programming
USE **integer programming**

DISCRIMINANT ANALYSIS
uf *multiple discriminant analysis*
BT1 statistical analysis
BT2 data analysis
BT2 statistics

DISCRIMINATION
NT1 racial discrimination
NT1 sexual discrimination
rt differentiation
rt price discrimination
rt selection
rt trade discrimination

DISCS
uf *disks*
rt cultivators
rt disc coulters
rt disc cultivators
rt disc harrows
rt disc ploughs
rt disc ridgers
rt disc shares

DISCUS
BT1 endodontidae
BT2 gastropoda
BT3 mollusca
NT1 discus cronkhitei

DISCUS CRONKHITEI
BT1 discus
BT2 endodontidae
BT3 gastropoda
BT4 mollusca

DISCUSSION GROUPS
BT1 groups
BT1 teaching methods
BT2 methodology

DISEASE CONTROL
uf *elimination*
uf *eradication*
BT1 control
NT1 plant disease control
NT1 quarantine
NT1 supervised control
NT1 tree surgery
NT2 delimbing
rt biological control
rt control programmes
rt disease prevention
rt diseases
rt disinfection
rt fungus control
rt health protection
rt pest control
rt plant protection
rt sanitation fellings
rt spraying
rt tree injection

DISEASE COURSE
HN from 1990
NT1 acute course
NT1 benign course

DISEASE COURSE *cont.*
NT1 chronic course
NT1 complications
NT2 postoperative complications
NT1 malignant course
NT1 metastasis
NT1 neoplasm regression
NT1 relapse
rt diseases
rt pathogenesis
rt prognosis

DISEASE DISTRIBUTION
BT1 distribution
rt aetiology
rt diseases
rt epidemiology
rt spread

DISEASE MODELS
BT1 models
rt animal models
rt diseases
rt symptoms

DISEASE PREVALENCE
rt diseases

DISEASE PREVENTION
(measures to prevent the introduction of a disease into areas or organisms)
BT1 prevention
rt chemoprophylaxis
rt disease control
rt diseases
rt plant protection
rt prophylaxis
rt quarantine
rt sanitation

DISEASE RESISTANCE
uf *plant resistance*
uf *resistance to disease*
BT1 resistance
NT1 genetic resistance
NT1 induced resistance
NT1 nonspecific resistance
rt defence mechanisms
rt diseases
rt immunity
rt naturally acquired immunity
rt phytoalexins
rt plant disease control
rt predisposition
rt serology
rt susceptibility

DISEASE STATISTICS
BT1 statistics
rt animal diseases

disease surveillance
USE **disease surveys**

DISEASE SURVEYS
uf *disease surveillance*
BT1 surveys
rt diseases
rt epidemiological surveys
rt epidemiology
rt serological surveys

DISEASE TRANSMISSION
BT1 transmission
NT1 infection
NT2 accidental infection
NT2 airborne infection
NT2 cell invasion
NT3 erythrocyte invasion
NT2 congenital infection
NT2 cross infection
NT2 experimental infection
NT2 microbial contamination
NT2 reinfection
NT2 trickle infection
NT1 mechanical transmission
NT1 sexual transmission
NT1 transovarial transmission
NT1 transplacental transmission
NT1 transstadial transmission
NT1 vertical transmission

DISEASE TRANSMISSION *cont.*
rt aetiology
rt diseases
rt epidemiology
rt hereditary diseases
rt vectorial capacity
rt vectors

DISEASE VECTORS
BT1 vectors
rt arboviruses
rt carrier state
rt intermediate hosts
rt vector competence
rt vectorial capacity

DISEASES
NT1 animal diseases
NT2 bee diseases
NT3 acarine disease
NT3 amoeba disease
NT3 apimyiasis
NT3 chalk brood
NT3 foul brood
NT4 american foul brood
NT4 european foul brood
NT3 nosema disease
NT3 rickettsial disease
NT3 stone brood
NT2 cat diseases
NT2 cattle diseases
NT3 anaplasmosis
NT3 anthrax
NT3 bovine spongiform encephalopathy
NT3 foot and mouth disease
NT3 rinderpest
NT2 dog diseases
NT2 fish diseases
NT2 goat diseases
NT2 horse diseases
NT3 african horse sickness
NT3 contagious equine metritis
NT3 dourine
NT3 equine infectious anaemia
NT3 glanders
NT3 sweet itch
NT2 mink diseases
NT3 aleutian disease
NT3 wet belly disease
NT2 poultry diseases
NT3 avian infectious bursitis
NT3 avian leukosis
NT3 duck diseases
NT3 egg drop syndrome
NT3 fowl diseases
NT3 marek's disease
NT3 newcastle disease
NT2 rabbit diseases
NT2 sheep diseases
NT3 border disease
NT3 foot rot
NT3 scrapie
NT3 sheep pox
NT2 swine diseases
NT3 african swine fever
NT3 foot and mouth disease
NT3 porcine stress syndrome
NT3 swine dysentery
NT3 swine fever
NT2 young animal diseases
NT3 calf diseases
NT3 foal diseases
NT3 lamb diseases
NT3 omphalitis
NT3 piglet diseases
NT1 communicable diseases (agricola)
NT1 deficiency diseases
NT2 beriberi
NT2 black tongue
NT2 cheilosis
NT2 iron deficiency anaemia
NT2 kwashiorkor
NT2 mulberry heart disease
NT2 night blindness
NT2 pellagra
NT2 perosis
NT2 phrynoderma
NT2 scurvy
NT2 xerophthalmia

DISEASES *cont.*
NT1 foodborne diseases
NT1 hereditary diseases
NT2 lesch-nyhan syndrome
NT1 human diseases
NT2 acquired immune deficiency syndrome
NT2 alcoholism
NT2 alzheimer's disease
NT2 appendicitis (agricola)
NT2 cachexia
NT2 chagas' disease
NT2 childhood diseases (agricola)
NT3 tay-sachs disease (agricola)
NT2 cholera
NT2 common cold
NT2 dengue
NT3 dengue haemorrhagic fever
NT2 farmer's lung
NT2 favism
NT2 hodgkin's disease
NT2 infant disorders
NT2 lyme disease
NT2 malaria
NT3 airport malaria
NT3 blackwater fever
NT3 cerebral malaria
NT2 measles
NT2 psittacosis
NT2 q fever
NT2 schistosomiasis
NT2 sclerosis
NT2 sickle cell anaemia
NT2 sjogren's syndrome
NT2 typhoid
NT2 varicella
NT2 venereal diseases (agricola)
NT3 gonorrhea (agricola)
NT3 syphilis (agricola)
NT2 yaws
NT2 yellow fever
NT1 iatrogenic diseases
NT1 immunological diseases
NT2 allergic encephalomyelitis
NT2 allergies
NT3 arthropod allergies
NT3 drug allergies
NT3 farmer's lung
NT3 food allergies
NT4 milk allergy
NT3 humidifier disease
NT2 autoimmune diseases
NT3 autoimmune thyroiditis
NT2 immune complex diseases
NT2 immunological deficiency
NT3 viral immunosuppression
NT4 acquired immune deficiency syndrome
NT2 wasting disease
NT1 infectious diseases
NT2 algal diseases
NT3 protothecosis
NT2 bacterial diseases
NT3 actinomycosis
NT4 cervicofacial actinomycosis
NT3 anaplasmosis
NT3 anthrax
NT3 botulism
NT3 brucellosis
NT3 glanders
NT3 heartwater
NT3 leptospirosis
NT3 lyme disease
NT3 mycoplasmosis
NT3 pasteurellosis
NT3 psittacosis
NT3 salmonellosis
NT3 tetanus
NT3 tick pyaemia
NT3 tuberculosis
NT3 typhoid
NT2 mycoses
NT3 adiaspiromycosis
NT3 aspergillosis
NT4 allergic bronchopulmonary aspergillosis

DISEASES *cont.*
NT4 aspergilloma
NT3 blastomycosis
NT3 candidosis
NT4 chronic mucocutaneous candidosis
NT3 chromoblastomycosis
NT3 chromomycosis
NT3 coccidioidomycosis
NT3 cryptococcosis
NT3 dermatomycoses
NT4 pityriasis versicolor
NT4 tinea nigra
NT3 epizootic lymphangitis
NT3 geotrichosis
NT3 histoplasmosis
NT4 african histoplasmosis
NT3 lobomycosis
NT3 mycetoma
NT3 mycotic abortion
NT3 mycotic keratitis
NT3 mycotic mastitis
NT3 oculomycosis
NT3 paracoccidioidomycosis
NT3 phycomycosis
NT4 zygomycosis
NT5 subcutaneous phycomycosis
NT3 piedra
NT4 black piedra
NT4 white piedra
NT3 rhinosporidiosis
NT3 sporotrichosis
NT2 viral diseases
NT3 acquired immune deficiency syndrome
NT3 african horse sickness
NT3 african swine fever
NT3 aleutian disease
NT3 aujeszky's disease
NT3 avian infectious bursitis
NT3 avian reticuloendotheliosis
NT3 border disease
NT3 common cold
NT3 dengue
NT4 dengue haemorrhagic fever
NT3 foot and mouth disease
NT3 haemorrhagic enteritis
NT3 influenza
NT3 japanese encephalitis
NT3 malignant catarrhal fever
NT3 marek's disease
NT3 newcastle disease
NT3 puffinosis
NT3 rabies
NT3 rinderpest
NT3 sheep pox
NT3 swine fever
NT3 varicella
NT3 viral hepatitis
NT3 yellow fever
NT1 milkborne diseases
NT2 brucellosis
NT1 neoplasms
NT2 adenoma
NT2 angioma
NT2 carcinoma
NT3 walker carcinoma
NT2 congenital neoplasms
NT2 fibroma
NT2 hepatoma
NT2 leukaemia
NT2 lipoma
NT2 lymphoma
NT3 lymphosarcoma
NT2 mammary gland neoplasms
NT2 melanoma
NT2 myeloma
NT2 papillomas
NT2 sarcoma
NT3 rous sarcoma
NT2 transmissible venereal tumour
NT1 organic diseases
NT2 bone diseases
NT3 bone resorption
NT3 calcinosis
NT3 chondrodystrophy

DISEASES *cont.*
NT3 dyschondroplasia
NT3 dysplasia
NT3 exostoses
NT3 hyperostosis
NT3 navicular disease
NT3 osteitis
NT3 osteochondritis
NT3 osteodystrophy
NT3 osteogenesis imperfecta
NT3 osteomalacia
NT3 osteomyelitis
NT3 osteopetrosis
NT4 avian osteopetrosis
NT3 osteoporosis
NT3 osteosclerosis
NT3 paget's disease
NT3 perosis
NT3 spavin
NT3 spinal diseases
NT4 lordosis
NT4 scoliosis
NT4 spina bifida
NT4 spondylitis
NT4 torticollis
NT2 cardiovascular diseases
NT3 heart diseases
NT4 arrhythmia
NT4 beriberi heart disease
NT4 cardiac insufficiency
NT4 cardiomegaly
NT4 cardiomyopathy
NT4 endocarditis
NT4 myocardial infarction
NT4 myocardial ischaemia
NT4 myocarditis
NT4 pericardial effusion
NT4 pericarditis
NT3 vascular diseases
NT4 aneurysm
NT4 aortic rupture
NT4 arteritis
NT4 atherogenesis
NT4 atheroma
NT4 atherosclerosis
NT5 experimental atherosclerosis
NT4 cerebrovascular disorders
NT5 apoplexy
NT5 migraine
NT5 stroke
NT4 circulatory disorders
NT5 vasoconstriction
NT4 embolism
NT4 haemorrhoids
NT4 hypertension
NT4 hypotension
NT4 ischaemia
NT4 microangiopathy
NT4 phlebitis
NT4 raynaud's syndrome
NT2 digestive system diseases
NT3 cholangitis
NT3 enterotoxaemia
NT3 gall bladder diseases
NT4 cholecystitis
NT4 cholelithiasis
NT3 gastrointestinal diseases
NT4 dumping syndrome
NT4 intestinal diseases
NT5 appendicitis (agricola)
NT5 blind loop syndrome
NT5 coeliac syndrome
NT5 colitis
NT6 ulcerative colitis
NT5 crohn's disease
NT5 diverticulosis
NT5 dysentery
NT6 swine dysentery
NT5 enteritis
NT5 enterocolitis
NT5 gastroenteritis
NT5 haemorrhagic enteritis
NT5 irritable colon
NT5 short bowel syndrome
NT5 sprue
NT5 steatorrhoea
NT5 tropical sprue
NT5 typhlitis
NT4 peptic ulcer

DISEASES *cont.*
NT5 duodenal ulcer
NT4 stomach diseases
NT5 achlorhydria
NT5 gastritis
NT6 atrophic gastritis
NT5 rumenitis
NT5 stomach ulcer
NT3 liver diseases
NT4 cirrhosis
NT4 fatty liver
NT4 fatty liver haemorrhagic syndrome
NT4 hepatitis
NT5 reye's syndrome
NT5 viral hepatitis
NT4 hepatolenticular degeneration
NT4 hepatoma
NT4 hepatomegaly
NT4 jaundice
NT5 toxaemic jaundice
NT4 liver abscess
NT3 oesophageal diseases
NT3 pancreatic diseases
NT4 pancreatitis
NT4 zollinger-ellison syndrome
NT3 peritonitis
NT3 pharyngitis
NT2 ear diseases
NT3 otitis
NT2 endocrine diseases
NT3 adrenal gland diseases
NT4 cushing's syndrome
NT3 gonadal disorders
NT4 hermaphroditism
NT4 hypogonadism
NT3 hyperinsulinism
NT3 parathyroid diseases
NT4 hyperparathyroidism
NT4 hypoparathyroidism
NT3 pituitary diseases
NT4 acromegaly
NT4 hypophysation
NT3 thyroid diseases
NT4 autoimmune thyroiditis
NT4 cretinism
NT4 goitre
NT5 congenital goitre
NT5 endemic goitre
NT4 hyperthyroidism
NT4 hypothyroidism
NT2 eye diseases
NT3 cataract
NT3 conjunctivitis
NT3 exophthalmos
NT3 eyelid diseases
NT4 entropion
NT3 glaucoma
NT3 keratitis
NT4 mycotic keratitis
NT3 keratoconjunctivitis
NT3 keratomalacia
NT3 oculomycosis
NT3 ophthalmia
NT3 retinal atrophy
NT3 retinitis
NT3 retinitis pigmentosa
NT3 retinopathy
NT3 strabismus
NT3 vision disorders
NT4 blindness
NT4 night blindness
NT3 xerophthalmia
NT2 female genital diseases
NT3 ovarian diseases
NT4 ovarian cysts
NT3 salpingitis
NT3 uterine diseases
NT4 cervicitis
NT4 endometritis
NT4 pyometra
NT4 uterine prolapse
NT4 uterine torsion
NT3 vaginal diseases
NT4 vaginal prolapse
NT4 vaginitis
NT3 vulvitis
NT2 foot diseases
NT3 laminitis

DISEASES *cont.*
NT3 pododermatitis
NT2 joint diseases
NT3 ankylosis
NT3 arthritis
NT4 osteoarthritis
NT4 rheumatoid arthritis
NT3 bursitis
NT3 synovitis
NT2 lymphatic diseases
NT3 lymphadenitis
NT3 lymphangitis
NT4 epizootic lymphangitis
NT3 sarcoid
NT3 splenic diseases
NT4 splenomegaly
NT3 thymus diseases
NT3 tonsillitis
NT2 male genital diseases
NT3 balanitis
NT3 epididymitis
NT3 hydrocele
NT3 posthitis
NT3 testicular diseases
NT4 orchitis
NT2 mammary gland diseases
NT3 mammary gland neoplasms
NT3 mammary oedema
NT3 mastitis
NT4 bovine mastitis
NT4 mycotic mastitis
NT4 summer mastitis
NT3 teat diseases
NT2 mouth diseases
NT3 periodontal diseases
NT4 gingivitis
NT3 salivary gland diseases
NT3 stomatitis
NT3 tongue diseases
NT4 glossitis
NT4 tongue lesions
NT3 tooth diseases
NT4 dental caries
NT4 dental plaque
NT2 muscular diseases
NT3 ataxia
NT4 cerebellar ataxia
NT3 muscular dystrophy
NT4 nutritional muscular dystrophy
NT3 myositis
NT3 neuromuscular diseases
NT4 myasthenia gravis
NT4 myotonia
NT3 splayleg
NT3 tenosynovitis
NT2 nervous system diseases
NT3 alzheimer's disease
NT3 brain disorders
NT4 cerebral palsy
NT4 cerebrovascular disorders
NT5 apoplexy
NT5 migraine
NT5 stroke
NT4 encephalitis
NT5 allergic encephalomyelitis
NT5 japanese encephalitis
NT4 encephalomalacia
NT4 encephalopathy
NT5 wernicke's disease
NT5 wernicke-korsakoff syndrome
NT4 epilepsy
NT4 epileptiform attacks
NT4 homocystinuria
NT4 hydrocephalus
NT4 menkes' disease
NT4 myeloencephalopathy
NT3 cerebrocortical necrosis
NT3 convulsions
NT3 demyelination
NT3 dysautonomia
NT4 grass sickness
NT3 meningitis
NT3 multiple sclerosis
NT3 myelitis
NT3 neuritis
NT3 neuromuscular diseases

DISEASES *cont.*
NT4 myasthenia gravis
NT4 myotonia
NT3 paralysis
NT4 paraplegia
NT4 paresis
NT5 parturient paresis
NT4 tick paralysis
NT3 polioencephalomalacia
NT3 poliomyelitis
NT3 refsum's syndrome
NT3 sensory disorders
NT4 anosmia
NT4 hearing impairment
NT5 deafness
NT4 vision disorders
NT5 blindness
NT5 night blindness
NT3 shingles (disease)
NT3 spongiform encephalopathy
NT4 bovine spongiform encephalopathy
NT3 staggers
NT4 phalaris staggers
NT4 ryegrass staggers
NT2 respiratory diseases
NT3 aspergillosis
NT4 allergic bronchopulmonary aspergillosis
NT4 aspergilloma
NT3 bronchitis
NT3 bronchopulmonary dysplasia (agricola)
NT3 chylothorax
NT3 coryza
NT3 farmer's lung
NT3 fibrosis
NT4 cystic fibrosis
NT4 silicosis
NT3 hydrothorax
NT3 laryngitis
NT3 laryngotracheitis
NT3 pleurisy
NT3 pleuropneumonia
NT3 pneumonia
NT3 pneumothorax
NT3 pulmonary adenomatosis
NT3 pulmonary emphysema
NT3 respiratory disorders
NT4 asphyxia
NT4 asthma
NT4 atelectasis
NT4 cough
NT4 dyspnoea
NT4 hypercapnia
NT4 hypoxia
NT3 rhinitis
NT4 atrophic rhinitis
NT3 rhinotracheitis
NT3 sarcoid
NT3 siderosis
NT3 sinusitis
NT3 tracheitis
NT2 skin diseases
NT3 acanthosis
NT3 acne
NT3 alopecia
NT3 amyloidosis
NT3 cellulitis
NT3 danlos syndrome
NT3 dermatitis
NT4 acrodermatitis
NT5 acrodermatitis enteropathica
NT4 cercarial dermatitis
NT4 dermatitis herpetiformis
NT4 interdigital dermatitis
NT4 pododermatitis
NT4 sunburn
NT3 dermatomycoses
NT4 pityriasis versicolor
NT4 tinea nigra
NT3 eczema
NT4 facial eczema
NT3 exanthema
NT3 furunculosis
NT3 hyperkeratosis
NT3 hypohidrosis
NT3 keratomalacia

DISEASES *cont.*
NT3 keratosis
NT4 parakeratosis
NT3 mange
NT3 pemphigus (skin disease) (agricola)
NT3 photosensitivity
NT3 psoriasis
NT3 sarcoid
NT3 scabies
NT4 hyperkeratotic scabies
NT3 scleroderma
NT3 seborrhoea
NT3 shingles (disease)
NT3 urticaria
NT3 xanthomatosis
NT3 xerosis
NT3 yaws
NT2 urinary tract diseases
NT3 bladder diseases
NT4 cystitis
NT3 chyluria
NT3 haematuria
NT3 kidney diseases
NT4 cystinosis
NT4 fanconi syndrome
NT4 fatty kidney
NT4 glomerulopathy
NT5 glomerulonephritis
NT4 nephritis
NT4 nephrocalcinosis
NT4 nephrolithiasis
NT4 nephropathy
NT5 balkan endemic nephropathy
NT4 nephrosis
NT4 nephrotic syndrome
NT4 pyelitis
NT4 pyelonephritis
NT4 renal failure
NT4 uraemia
NT3 proteinuria
NT4 haemoglobinuria
NT4 myoglobinuria
NT3 urination disorders
NT4 polyuria
NT4 urinary incontinence
NT3 urolithiasis
NT1 parasitoses
NT2 ectoparasitoses
NT3 mange
NT3 myiasis
NT4 apimyiasis
NT3 scabies
NT4 hyperkeratotic scabies
NT3 tick infestations
NT2 helminthoses
NT3 cestode infections
NT4 cysticercosis
NT3 nematode infections
NT4 ascariasis
NT4 ascaridiosis
NT4 elephantiasis
NT4 filariasis
NT5 onchocerciasis
NT4 heterakidosis
NT4 larva migrans
NT5 visceral larva migrans
NT3 trematode infections
NT4 fascioliasis
NT4 schistosomiasis
NT2 pentastomiasis
NT2 protozoal infections
NT3 coccidiosis
NT3 giardiasis
NT3 leishmaniasis
NT3 malaria
NT4 airport malaria
NT4 blackwater fever
NT4 cerebral malaria
NT3 toxoplasmosis
NT3 trypanosomiasis
NT4 chagas' disease
NT4 dourine
NT1 systemic diseases
NT2 sclerosis
NT1 tropical diseases
NT1 vector-borne diseases
NT2 african horse sickness
NT2 filariasis
NT3 onchocerciasis

DISEASES *cont.*
NT2 leishmaniasis
NT2 mosquito-borne diseases
NT3 dengue
NT4 dengue haemorrhagic fever
NT3 japanese encephalitis
NT3 malaria
NT4 airport malaria
NT4 blackwater fever
NT4 cerebral malaria
NT3 yellow fever
NT2 plague
NT2 snail-borne diseases
NT3 fascioliasis
NT3 schistosomiasis
NT2 tickborne diseases
NT3 anaplasmosis
NT3 lyme disease
NT3 q fever
NT3 tick pyaemia
NT3 tickborne fever
NT2 trypanosomiasis
NT3 chagas' disease
NT3 dourine
NT1 waterborne diseases
NT1 zoonoses
rt aetiology
rt carrier state
rt disease control
rt disease course
rt disease distribution
rt disease models
rt disease prevalence
rt disease prevention
rt disease resistance
rt disease surveys
rt disease transmission
rt disorders
rt epidemics
rt health
rt illness (agricola)
rt morbidity
rt outbreaks
rt pathogenesis
rt pathogens
rt pathology
rt plant diseases
rt preincubation period
rt seasonal cycle
rt therapy

diseases, bacterial
USE **bacterial diseases**

diseases, plant
USE **plant diseases**

DISEQUILIBRIUM
BT1 genetic equilibrium
BT2 population genetics
BT3 genetics
BT4 biology
rt equilibrium

disguised unemployment
USE **underemployment**

DISHES (AGRICOLA)
rt dinnerware (agricola)
rt household equipment (agricola)
rt table settings (agricola)

DISHWASHERS (AGRICOLA)
BT1 appliances (agricola)
rt dishwashing (agricola)
rt household equipment (agricola)

DISHWASHING (AGRICOLA)
rt dishwashers (agricola)

DISINCENTIVES
BT1 motivation
rt constraints
rt incentives

DISINFECTANTS
NT1 o-cresol
NT1 8-hydroxyquinoline citrate
NT1 calcium chlorate
NT1 chlorine

DISINFECTANTS *cont.*
NT1 ethacridine
NT1 formaldehyde
NT1 hydroxyquinoline
NT1 iodine
NT1 iodophors
NT1 mercuric chloride
NT1 methylene blue
NT1 paraformaldehyde
NT1 peracetic acid
NT1 phenol
NT1 propiolactone
NT1 propylene glycol
NT1 sodium hypochlorite
NT1 sulfur dioxide
rt antiseptics
rt bleaching powder
rt cleaning and sterilization
rt detergents
rt disinfection
rt infections
rt oxidants
rt teat dip

DISINFECTION
BT1 cleaning and sterilization
rt antiinfective agents
rt cleaning
rt decontamination
rt disease control
rt disinfectants
rt fumigation
rt hygiene

DISINFESTATION
BT1 cleaning and sterilization
rt pesticides

DISINTEGRATORS
HN from 1990
BT1 equipment

disks
USE **discs**

DISLOCATIONS
BT1 trauma
rt joints (animal)

disodium methylarsonate
USE **dsma**

DISONYCHA
BT1 chrysomelidae
BT2 coleoptera
NT1 disonycha argentinensis

DISONYCHA ARGENTINENSIS
BT1 disonycha
BT2 chrysomelidae
BT3 coleoptera

DISOPHENOL
BT1 anthelmintics
BT2 antiparasitic agents
BT3 drugs
BT1 ovicides and larvicides
BT2 antiparasitic agents
BT3 drugs
BT1 phenols
BT2 alcohols
BT2 phenolic compounds
BT3 aromatic compounds

DISOPYRAMIDE
BT1 myocardial depressants
BT2 cardiovascular agents
BT3 drugs
BT1 pyridines
BT2 heterocyclic nitrogen compounds
BT3 organic nitrogen compounds

DISORDERS
NT1 animal disorders
NT2 blood disorders
NT3 acidaemia
NT4 butyryl acidaemia
NT4 citrullinaemia
NT4 histidinaemia
NT4 methylmalonic acidaemia
NT4 propionic acidaemia

DISORDERS *cont.*
NT3 anaemia
NT4 aplastic anaemia
NT4 equine infectious anaemia
NT4 haemoglobinuria
NT4 haemolytic anaemia
NT4 hypochromic anaemia
NT4 iron deficiency anaemia
NT4 macrocytic anaemia
NT4 megaloblastic anaemia
NT4 microcytic anaemia
NT4 nutritional anaemia
NT4 pernicious anaemia
NT4 sickle cell anaemia
NT4 sideroblastic anaemia
NT4 thalassaemia
NT3 avian erythroblastosis
NT3 blood coagulation disorders
NT4 disseminated intravascular coagulation
NT4 haemophilia
NT4 thrombocythaemia
NT4 thrombocytopenia
NT4 thrombocytopenic purpura
NT4 thrombosis
NT3 blood protein disorders
NT4 hyperproteinaemia
NT5 hyperlipoproteinaemia
NT6 hyperchylomicronaemia
NT5 hyperprolactinaemia
NT4 hypoproteinaemia
NT5 hypoalbuminaemia
NT5 hypogammaglobulinaemia
NT5 hypolipoproteinaemia
NT6 abetalipoproteinaemia
NT5 hypoprothrombinaemia
NT4 methaemoglobinaemia
NT4 myohaemoglobinaemia
NT3 bone marrow disorders
NT4 aplastic anaemia
NT3 haemolysis
NT3 histiocytosis
NT3 hypovolaemia
NT3 leukocyte disorders
NT4 avian myeloblastosis
NT4 chediak-higashi syndrome
NT4 eosinophilia
NT5 tropical eosinophilia
NT4 leukaemia
NT4 leukopenia
NT4 leukosis
NT5 avian leukosis
NT5 bovine leukosis
NT4 monocytosis
NT3 lipaemia
NT3 pancytopenia
NT3 polycythaemia
NT3 polycythaemia vera
NT2 fetal development disorders
NT2 functional disorders
NT3 behavior disorders (agricola)
NT3 circulatory disorders
NT4 vasoconstriction
NT3 collapse
NT3 digestive disorders
NT4 appetite disorders
NT5 anorexia
NT6 anorexia nervosa
NT5 bulimia
NT5 bulimia nervosa (agricola)
NT5 compulsive eating (agricola)
NT5 geophagia
NT5 pica
NT4 bloat
NT4 chinese restaurant syndrome
NT4 colic
NT4 constipation
NT4 diarrhoea
NT5 giardiasis
NT4 dyspepsia
NT4 flatus
NT4 gizzard erosion

DISORDERS *cont.*
NT4 grass sickness
NT4 hyperacidity (agricola)
NT4 malabsorption
NT4 milk intolerance
NT4 obstruction
NT5 cholestasis
NT5 intestinal obstruction
NT6 duodenal obstruction
NT6 intussusception
NT4 phytobezoariasis
NT4 sialuria
NT4 vomiting
NT5 hyperemesis gravidarum
NT5 nausea
NT3 dysregulation
NT4 coma
NT5 diabetic coma
NT4 convulsions
NT4 spasms
NT4 spastic paresis
NT4 tremor
NT5 congenital tremor
NT3 equilibrium disorders
NT3 fever
NT3 mental disorders
NT4 depression
NT4 down's syndrome
NT4 emotional disturbances (agricola)
NT4 mental retardation
NT4 neuroses
NT4 psychoses
NT5 alzheimer's disease
NT5 delusory parasitoses
NT5 schizophrenia
NT3 movement disorders
NT4 ataxia
NT5 cerebellar ataxia
NT4 lameness
NT5 navicular disease
NT4 staggers
NT5 phalaris staggers
NT5 ryegrass staggers
NT4 swayback
NT3 polydipsia
NT3 reproductive disorders
NT4 abortion
NT5 mycotic abortion
NT5 spontaneous abortion (agricola)
NT4 cryptorchidism
NT4 eclampsia
NT4 embryo malpositions
NT4 endometritis
NT4 female infertility
NT5 pseudopregnancy
NT4 male infertility
NT5 impotence
NT5 spermiostasis
NT4 nymphomania
NT4 parturition complications
NT5 dystocia
NT5 uterine torsion
NT4 pregnancy complications
NT5 extrauterine pregnancy
NT5 hydramnios
NT5 preeclampsia
NT4 puerperal disorders
NT5 lactation disorders
NT6 agalactia
NT6 galactorrhoea
NT6 lactation persistency
NT5 parturient paresis
NT5 placental retention
NT5 pregnancy toxaemia
NT4 sex differentiation disorders
NT5 dysgenesis
NT5 intersexuality
NT6 freemartinism
NT6 pseudohermaphroditism
NT5 sex reversal
NT5 testicular feminization
NT3 respiratory disorders
NT4 asphyxia
NT4 asthma
NT4 atelectasis
NT4 cough
NT4 dyspnoea

DISORDERS *cont.*
NT4 hypercapnia
NT4 hypoxia
NT3 sensory disorders
NT4 anosmia
NT4 hearing impairment
NT5 deafness
NT4 vision disorders
NT5 blindness
NT5 night blindness
NT3 urination disorders
NT4 polyuria
NT4 urinary incontinence
NT2 growth disorders
NT3 dwarfism
NT3 gigantism
NT3 hypotrophy
NT3 metaplasia
NT3 runting
NT2 metabolic disorders
NT3 acid base disorders
NT4 acidosis
NT5 diabetic acidosis
NT5 ketoacidosis
NT5 ketosis
NT5 lactic acidosis
NT4 alkalosis
NT3 aciduria
NT4 aminoaciduria
NT5 cystinuria
NT5 homocystinuria
NT4 argininosuccinic aciduria
NT4 glutaric aciduria
NT4 methylglutaconic aciduria
NT4 methylmalonic aciduria
NT4 orotic aciduria
NT4 oxaluria
NT3 amino acid disorders
NT4 alkaptonuria
NT5 ochronosis
NT4 hyperaminoacidaemia
NT5 hyperargininaemia
NT5 hyperglycinaemia
NT5 hypermethioninaemia
NT5 hyperphenylalaninaemia
NT4 hyperaminoaciduria
NT4 ketonuria
NT5 phenylketonuria
NT4 maple syrup urine disease
NT3 carbohydrate metabolism disorders
NT4 disaccharidosis
NT4 fructose intolerance
NT4 galactosaemia
NT4 glycogenosis
NT4 glycosuria
NT4 hyperglycaemia
NT4 hypoglycaemia
NT4 lactose intolerance
NT4 mannosidosis
NT4 mucopolysaccharidosis
NT4 sucrose intolerance
NT3 diabetes
NT4 diabetes insipidus
NT4 diabetes mellitus
NT4 diabetic acidosis
NT4 diabetic neuropathy
NT4 experimental diabetes
NT3 food-related disorders (agricola)
NT3 gout
NT3 hepatolenticular degeneration
NT3 hyperammonaemia
NT3 hyperbilirubinaemia
NT3 hyperinsulinaemia
NT3 hyperketonaemia
NT3 hyperoxaluria
NT3 hyperoxia
NT3 hyperuricaemia
NT3 ketonaemia
NT3 lesch-nyhan syndrome
NT3 lipid metabolism disorders
NT4 cholesterol metabolism disorders
NT5 hypercholesterolaemia
NT5 hypocholesterolaemia
NT4 fatty degeneration

DISORDERS *cont.*
NT4 fatty kidney
NT4 gaucher's disease
NT4 hyperlipaemia
NT5 hypercarotenaemia
NT5 hypercholesterolaemia
NT5 hyperlipoproteinaemia
NT6 hyperchylomicron-aemia
NT5 hypertriglyceridaemia
NT4 hypolipaemia
NT5 hypocholesterolaemia
NT5 hypolipoproteinaemia
NT6 abetalipoproteinaemia
NT4 lipidosis
NT5 sphingolipidosis
NT6 gangliosidosis
NT4 triglyceride storage disease
NT3 menkes' disease
NT3 milk alkali syndrome
NT3 mineral metabolism disorders
NT4 calcinosis
NT4 haemochromatosis
NT4 hypercalciuria
NT4 hypermagnesaemia
NT4 hyperphosphataemia
NT4 hyperphosphaturia
NT4 hypocalciuria
NT4 hypocupraemia
NT4 hypomagnesaemia
NT5 grass tetany
NT4 hypophosphataemia
NT4 pseudohypopara-thyroidism
NT4 rickets
NT5 experimental rickets
NT5 hypophosphataemic rickets
NT5 scurvy rickets
NT5 vitamin resistant rickets
NT3 obesity hyperglycaemia syndrome
NT3 protein metabolism disorders
NT4 protein intolerance
NT3 proteinuria
NT4 haemoglobinuria
NT4 myoglobinuria
NT3 rheumatism
NT3 water metabolism disorders
NT4 dehydration (physiological)
NT4 hydrops
NT4 oedema
NT5 congenital oedema
NT6 hydrocephalus
NT5 nutritional oedema
NT3 water-electrolyte imbalance
NT4 hypercalcaemia
NT4 hyperkaliaemia
NT4 hypernatraemia
NT4 hypocalcaemia
NT5 tetany
NT4 hypokaliaemia
NT4 hyponatraemia
NT3 xanthomatosis
NT2 nutritional disorders
NT3 deficiency diseases
NT4 beriberi
NT4 black tongue
NT4 cheilosis
NT4 iron deficiency anaemia
NT4 kwashiorkor
NT4 mulberry heart disease
NT4 night blindness
NT4 pellagra
NT4 perosis
NT4 phrynoderma
NT4 scurvy
NT4 xerophthalmia
NT3 emaciation
NT3 nutritional anaemia
NT3 obesity
NT4 prader-willi syndrome
NT3 osteodystrophy

DISORDERS *cont.*
NT3 protein energy malnutrition
NT4 marasmus
NT2 occupational disorders
NT2 pigmentation disorders
NT3 albinism
NT3 haemochromatosis
NT3 melanosis
NT3 porphyria
NT3 vitiligo
NT1 plant disorders
NT2 bitter pit
NT2 black spot
NT2 black streak
NT2 blackheart
NT2 blackline
NT2 blight
NT2 blossom-end rot
NT2 breakdown
NT2 brown core
NT2 brown heart
NT2 calyx splitting
NT2 cankers
NT2 carapace spot
NT2 catfacing
NT2 cavity spot
NT2 chilling injury
NT2 chlorosis
NT2 coloure
NT2 cone withering
NT2 core flush
NT2 cork spot
NT2 corking
NT2 cox disease
NT2 cox spot
NT2 creasing
NT2 crick-side
NT2 dieback
NT2 flesh browning
NT2 flesh hardening
NT2 fruit cracking
NT2 fruit puffing
NT2 galls
NT3 crown gall
NT3 witches' brooms
NT4 sweet potato witches' broom
NT2 glassiness
NT2 grain shrivelling
NT2 granulation
NT2 greenback
NT2 gummosis
NT2 hollow heart
NT2 hollow stem
NT2 internal browning
NT2 leaf spotting
NT2 marsh spot
NT2 maturity bronzing
NT2 mealy endosperm
NT2 millerandage
NT2 necroses
NT3 hybrid necrosis
NT3 internal bark necrosis
NT2 oleocellosis
NT2 pepper spot
NT2 petal shatter
NT2 phyllody
NT2 pithiness
NT2 rind pitting
NT2 ring-neck
NT2 root (wilt)
NT2 russeting
NT2 rusty root
NT2 scald
NT2 scarfskin
NT2 scorch
NT2 short life
NT2 speckle bottom disease
NT2 split-pit
NT2 spongy tissue
NT2 stalk necrosis
NT2 stem end bleeding
NT2 sunburn
NT2 sunscald
NT2 tipburn
NT2 tumours
NT2 vitrification
NT2 water core
NT2 whiptail
NT2 woolliness

DISORDERS *cont.*
NT2 yellow leaf disease
rt diseases

disorders, plant
USE **plant disorders**

DISPARITY
BT1 income distribution
rt parity

DISPARLURE
BT1 insect attractants
BT2 attractants

DISPATCHER SYSTEMS
BT1 information services
BT2 services
BT1 organization of work

DISPENSERS
NT1 feed dispensers
NT2 automatic feed dispensers
NT2 calf feeders
NT3 bucket calf feeders
NT2 liquid feed dispensers
NT2 mobile feeders
NT2 nipple feed dispensers
NT2 pig feeders
NT2 programmed feed dispensers
NT2 self feeders
NT2 sheep feeders
NT2 troughs
NT3 feed troughs
NT3 subsurface troughs
NT3 water troughs
NT1 milk dispensers
rt troughs

DISPERSAL
rt migration
rt seed dispersal
rt spore dispersal

dispersal, seed
USE **seed dispersal**

DISPERSION
NT1 hydrodynamic dispersion
NT1 spore dispersal
NT2 sporulation
NT3 zoosporogenesis
NT1 spreading
NT2 water spreading
NT1 thrombolysis
NT1 time series
NT1 ultrasonic dispersion
rt aerosol sprayers
rt colloids
rt dioxane
rt distribution
rt redistribution
rt sample processing
rt solutions
rt suspensions
rt vapour

dispharynx nasuta
USE **synhimantus nasuta**

DISPLACED HOMEMAKERS (AGRICOLA)
BT1 homemakers (agricola)
rt reentry workers (agricola)

DISPLACEMENT
NT1 hydrodynamic displacement

DISPLAYS
NT1 digital displays
NT1 liquid crystal displays
rt controls
rt demonstration farms
rt indicating instruments
rt symbols

displays, digital
USE **digital displays**

displays, liquid crystal
USE **liquid crystal displays**

DISPOSABLES (AGRICOLA)
NT1 non-returnable items (agricola)

DISPOSAL
NT1 carcass disposal
NT1 prunings disposal
NT1 straw disposal
NT1 waste disposal
NT2 municipal refuse disposal
NT2 sewage effluent disposal
NT2 sewerage
rt non-returnable items (agricola)
rt storage

DISRUPTION
HN from 1989
NT1 aggregation disruption
NT1 mating disruption

DISSEMINATED INFECTIONS
HN from 1989
BT1 infections

DISSEMINATED INTRAVASCULAR COAGULATION
HN from 1990
BT1 blood coagulation disorders
BT2 blood disorders
BT3 animal disorders
BT4 disorders

dissertations
USE **theses**

DISSOCIATION
BT1 decomposition
rt anaesthesia
rt composition
rt psychological factors
rt psychoses

DISSOLVED OXYGEN
BT1 chemical composition
BT2 composition
rt oxygen

DISSOLVING
BT1 processing
rt heat of solution
rt solutions
rt solvents

DISSOTIS
BT1 melastomataceae
NT1 dissotis rotundifolia

dissotis plumosa
USE **dissotis rotundifolia**

DISSOTIS ROTUNDIFOLIA
uf *dissotis plumosa*
BT1 dissotis
BT2 melastomataceae
BT1 ornamental woody plants

DISTANCE TEACHING
BT1 teaching methods
BT2 methodology
rt correspondence courses
rt educational radio
rt educational television
rt non-formal education

DISTANCE TRAVELLED
rt long distance transport
rt travel

DISTANTIELLA
BT1 miridae
BT2 heteroptera
NT1 distantiella theobroma

DISTANTIELLA THEOBROMA
BT1 distantiella
BT2 miridae
BT3 heteroptera

DISTEMONANTHUS
BT1 leguminosae
NT1 distemonanthus benthamianus

DISTEMONANTHUS BENTHAMIANUS
BT1 distemonanthus
BT2 leguminosae

DISTEMPER VIRUS
BT1 morbillivirus
BT2 paramyxoviridae
BT3 viruses

DISTICHLIS
BT1 gramineae
NT1 distichlis spicata
NT1 distichlis stricta

DISTICHLIS SPICATA
BT1 distichlis
BT2 gramineae

DISTICHLIS STRICTA
BT1 distichlis
BT2 gramineae

DISTILLATES
rt distillation
rt distilled spirits
rt distilling industry

DISTILLATION
BT1 processing
NT1 destructive distillation
NT1 vacuum distillation
rt distillates
rt distillers' grains
rt distillers' residues
rt distillers' solubles
rt distillers' spent wash
rt distillery effluent
rt distilling
rt distilling industry
rt purification

distillation, destructive
USE **destructive distillation**

DISTILLED SPIRITS
uf *spirits, distilled*
BT1 alcoholic beverages
BT2 beverages
NT1 brandy
NT1 gin
NT1 liqueurs
NT2 amaretto (agricola)
NT1 rum
NT1 vodka
NT1 whisky
rt distillates
rt distilling industry

DISTILLERS' GRAINS
BT1 distillers' residues
BT2 residues
rt distillation
rt distilling industry

DISTILLERS' RESIDUES
BT1 residues
NT1 distillers' grains
NT1 distillers' solubles
NT2 maize fermentation solubles
NT2 molasses distillers' solubles
NT1 distillers' spent wash
rt distillation
rt distilling industry

DISTILLERS' SOLUBLES
BT1 distillers' residues
BT2 residues
BT1 vinasse
BT2 feed supplements
BT3 supplements
BT2 fermentation wastes
BT3 wastes
NT1 maize fermentation solubles
NT1 molasses distillers' solubles
rt distillation
rt distilling industry

DISTILLERS' SPENT WASH
BT1 distillers' residues
BT2 residues
rt distillation

DISTILLERS' SPENT WASH *cont.*
rt distilling industry

DISTILLERS' YEAST
uf yeast, distillers'
BT1 yeasts
rt distilling industry

DISTILLERY EFFLUENT
BT1 factory effluents
BT2 effluents
BT3 wastes
rt distillation
rt distilling industry

DISTILLING
BT1 processing
rt distillation
rt distilling industry
rt evaporation
rt fractionation

DISTILLING INDUSTRY
BT1 beverage industry
BT2 food industry
BT3 industry
rt alcoholic beverages
rt distillates
rt distillation
rt distilled spirits
rt distillers' grains
rt distillers' residues
rt distillers' solubles
rt distillers' spent wash
rt distillers' yeast
rt distillery effluent
rt distilling
rt maize fermentation solubles

DISTORTION
NT1 segregation distortion
rt asymmetry
rt dimensions

DISTRIBUTION
NT1 disease distribution
NT1 dry matter distribution
NT1 frequency distribution
NT1 geographical distribution
NT1 longitudinal distribution
NT1 spatial distribution
NT1 time series
NT1 transverse distribution
NT1 variance
NT1 water distribution
rt coverage
rt dispersion
rt food delivery systems (agricola)
rt overlap
rt redistribution
rt spreading
rt statistics
rt tertiary sector
rt transport

distribution, longitudinal
USE **longitudinal distribution**

distribution, particle size
USE **particle size distribution**

distribution, transverse
USE **transverse distribution**

DISTRIBUTORS
BT1 components
rt engines
rt internal combustion engines
rt liquid fertilizer distributors

DISTRICT OF COLUMBIA
BT1 appalachian states of usa
BT2 southern states of usa
BT3 usa
BT4 north america
BT5 america

DISTURBED LAND
BT1 land types

DISTURBED PROFILES
BT1 soil morphological features

DISTURBED SOILS
BT1 soil types (anthropogenic)

DISTYLIUM
BT1 hamamelidaceae
NT1 distylium racemosum

DISTYLIUM RACEMOSUM
BT1 distylium
BT2 hamamelidaceae

DISUL
uf 2,4-des
BT1 auxins
BT2 plant growth regulators
BT3 growth regulators
BT1 phenoxy herbicides
BT2 herbicides
BT3 pesticides

DISULFIRAM
BT1 dithiocarbamate fungicides
BT2 carbamate pesticides
BT2 fungicides
BT3 pesticides

DISULFOTON
BT1 organothiophosphate insecticides
BT2 organophosphorus insecticides
BT3 insecticides
BT4 pesticides
BT3 organophosphorus pesticides
BT4 organophosphorus compounds

DITALIMFOS
BT1 organophosphorus fungicides
BT2 fungicides
BT3 pesticides
BT2 organophosphorus pesticides
BT3 organophosphorus compounds

DITCH BANKS
BT1 ridges
rt canal banks
rt ditches

DITCH CLEANERS
BT1 drainage equipment
BT2 equipment
BT1 farm machinery
BT2 machinery
rt ditches
rt drainage
rt excavators
rt scoops

DITCHES
BT1 channels
NT1 dykes
NT1 oxidation ditches
rt ditch banks
rt ditch cleaners
rt drainage
rt drainage channels

DITERPENES
BT1 diterpenoids
BT2 terpenoids
BT3 isoprenoids
BT4 lipids

DITERPENOIDS
BT1 terpenoids
BT2 isoprenoids
BT3 lipids
NT1 abietic acid
NT1 casbene
NT1 diterpenes
NT1 duvanes
NT1 gibberellins
NT2 gibberellic acid
NT1 kaurene
NT1 kaurenoic acid
NT1 phytol
NT1 pimaric acid
NT1 pyrethrins
NT1 steviol

DITHIANON
BT1 quinone fungicides
BT2 fungicides
BT3 pesticides
BT2 quinones
BT3 aromatic compounds

DITHIAZANINE IODIDE
BT1 anthelmintics
BT2 antiparasitic agents
BT3 drugs
BT1 heterocyclic nitrogen compounds
BT2 organic nitrogen compounds

DITHIOCARBAMATE FUNGICIDES
BT1 carbamate pesticides
BT1 fungicides
BT2 pesticides
NT1 cufraneb
NT1 cuprobam
NT1 disulfiram
NT1 etem
NT1 ferbam
NT1 mancozeb
NT1 maneb
NT1 metiram
NT1 milneb
NT1 nabam
NT1 polycarbamate
NT1 propineb
NT1 thiram
NT1 zineb
NT1 ziram

DITHIONITE
BT1 anions
BT2 ions

ditilin
USE **suxamethonium**

DITYLENCHUS
BT1 anguinidae
BT2 nematoda
NT1 ditylenchus angustus
NT1 ditylenchus destructor
NT1 ditylenchus dipsaci
NT1 ditylenchus myceliophagus

DITYLENCHUS ANGUSTUS
BT1 ditylenchus
BT2 anguinidae
BT3 nematoda

DITYLENCHUS DESTRUCTOR
BT1 ditylenchus
BT2 anguinidae
BT3 nematoda

DITYLENCHUS DIPSACI
BT1 ditylenchus
BT2 anguinidae
BT3 nematoda

DITYLENCHUS MYCELIOPHAGUS
BT1 ditylenchus
BT2 anguinidae
BT3 nematoda

DIURAPHIS
BT1 aphididae
BT2 aphidoidea
BT3 sternorrhyncha
BT4 homoptera
NT1 diuraphis noxia

DIURAPHIS NOXIA
BT1 diuraphis
BT2 aphididae
BT3 aphidoidea
BT4 sternorrhyncha
BT5 homoptera

diureidoisobutane
USE **ibdu**

DIURESIS
rt diuretics
rt kidneys
rt osmolarity
rt urine
rt water excretion

DIURETICS
BT1 drugs
NT1 acetazolamide
NT1 aminophylline
NT1 ammonium chloride
NT1 caffeine
NT1 chlorothiazide
NT1 formononetin
NT1 furosemide
NT1 hydrochlorothiazide
NT1 mannitol
NT1 mersalyl
NT1 potassium nitrate
NT1 sodium citrate
NT1 sorbitol
NT1 spironolactone
NT1 theobromine
NT1 theophylline
NT1 triamterene
NT1 urea
rt antihypertensive agents
rt diuresis
rt urine
rt water excretion

DIURIS
BT1 orchidaceae
NT1 diuris punctata

DIURIS PUNCTATA
BT1 diuris
BT2 orchidaceae
BT1 ornamental orchids

DIURNAL ACTIVITY
rt activity
rt nocturnal activity

DIURNAL VARIATION
BT1 temporal variation
BT2 variation

DIURON
uf dcmu
BT1 urea herbicides
BT2 herbicides
BT3 pesticides

divers (birds)
USE **gavia**

DIVERSIFICATION
BT1 socioeconomic organization
NT1 export diversification
rt ancillary enterprises
rt crop enterprises
rt farming systems
rt integration
rt mixed cropping

DIVERSITY

DIVERTICULOSIS
BT1 intestinal diseases
BT2 gastrointestinal diseases
BT3 digestive system diseases
BT4 organic diseases
BT5 diseases
rt colon

DIVIDERS
BT1 harvesters
BT2 farm machinery
BT3 machinery
BT1 instruments
rt cutter bars

DIVING
BT1 water recreation
BT2 recreation
rt swimming

DIVISION OF LABOR
BF division of labour
rt labor

DIVISION OF LABOUR
AF division of labor
BT1 labour economics
BT2 economics
rt classical economics
rt international trade
rt specialization

DIVISION OF PROPERTY (AGRICOLA)
rt divorce (agricola)
rt inheritance of property
rt property

DIVISIONS
NT1 compartments
NT1 polarization
NT1 steps
rt partitions
rt walls

DIVORCE (AGRICOLA)
NT1 no-fault divorce (agricola)
rt annulment (agricola)
rt child custody (agricola)
rt division of property (agricola)
rt divorce law (agricola)
rt marital separation (agricola)
rt marriage

DIVORCE LAW (AGRICOLA)
BT1 law
BT2 legal systems
rt divorce (agricola)

DIZYGOTHECA
BT1 araliaceae
NT1 dizygotheca elegantissima

DIZYGOTHECA ELEGANTISSIMA
uf *aralia elegantissima*
BT1 dizygotheca
BT2 araliaceae
BT1 ornamental woody plants
rt ornamental foliage plants

DJIBOUTI
uf *afars and issas territory*
uf *french somaliland*
uf *french territory of the afars and the issas*
uf *jibuti*
BT1 east africa
BT2 africa south of sahara
BT3 africa
rt acp
rt arab countries
rt francophone africa

D'MAN
HN from 1990
BT1 sheep breeds
BT2 breeds

DMPA
BT1 organophosphorus herbicides
BT2 herbicides
BT3 pesticides
BT2 organophosphorus pesticides
BT3 organophosphorus compounds

dmso
USE **dimethyl sulfoxide**

DNA
uf *deoxyribonucleic acid*
BT1 nucleic acids
BT2 organic acids
BT3 acids
NT1 antisense dna
NT1 mitochondrial dna
NT1 recombinant dna
NT1 repetitive dna
NT1 ribosomal dna
NT1 satellite dna
NT2 minisatellites
NT1 z dna
rt alternative splicing
rt chromosomes
rt cistrons
rt deoxyribonuclease i
rt dna amplification
rt dna binding proteins
rt dna conformation
rt dna fingerprinting
rt dna footprinting
rt dna hybridization
rt dna libraries

DNA *cont.*
rt dna methylation
rt dna modification
rt dna nucleotidylexotransferase
rt dna polymerase
rt dna probes
rt dna repair
rt dna replication
rt dna sequencing
rt dna slippage
rt exons
rt genetic code
rt genetic transformation
rt introns
rt molecular mapping
rt promoters
rt southern blotting
rt transcription
rt transduction
rt transfection

DNA AMPLIFICATION
HN from 1989
(amplification in vivo; for amplification in vitro use the name of the technique, e.g. "polymerase chain reaction")
uf *amplification, dna*
BT1 amplification
rt dna
rt polymerase chain reaction

DNA BINDING PROTEINS
HN from 1990
BT1 binding proteins
BT2 proteins
BT3 peptides
rt dna

DNA CONFORMATION
HN from 1989
rt dna

DNA FINGERPRINTING
HN from 1989
BT1 biochemical techniques
BT2 techniques
rt dna

DNA FOOTPRINTING
HN from 1990
BT1 biochemical techniques
BT2 techniques
rt dna

DNA HYBRIDIZATION
HN from 1989
BT1 biochemical techniques
BT2 techniques
rt dna
rt hybridization

DNA LIBRARIES
HN from 1989
BT1 biochemical techniques
BT2 techniques
rt dna
rt dna probes

DNA METHYLATION
HN from 1989
BT1 biochemical techniques
BT2 techniques
rt dna

DNA MODIFICATION
HN from 1990
rt dna

DNA NUCLEOTIDYLEXOTRANSFERASE
(ec 2.7.7.31)
BT1 nucleotidyltransferases
BT2 transferases
BT3 enzymes
rt dna

DNA POLYMERASE
(ec 2.7.7.7 and 2.7.7.49)
BT1 nucleotidyltransferases
BT2 transferases
BT3 enzymes
NT1 reverse transcriptase

DNA POLYMERASE *cont.*
rt dna

DNA PROBES
BT1 biochemical techniques
BT2 techniques
rt dna
rt dna libraries
rt taxonomy

DNA REPAIR
rt dna

DNA REPLICATION
HN from 1990
BT1 replication
rt dna

dna sequences
USE **nucleotide sequences**

DNA SEQUENCING
HN from 1989
BT1 biochemical techniques
BT2 techniques
NT1 chromosome walking
rt dna
rt nucleotide sequences

DNA SLIPPAGE
HN from 1990
rt dna

dnase
USE **deoxyribonuclease i**

dnbp
USE **dinoseb**

DNOC
uf *dinitro-o-cresol*
uf *dinitrocarbolineum*
BT1 dinitrophenol herbicides
BT2 herbicides
BT3 pesticides
BT1 dinitrophenol insecticides
BT2 insecticides
BT3 pesticides

DO IT YOURSELF ACTIVITIES
BT1 home based leisure
BT2 leisure activities
rt hobbies
rt home economics

doca
USE **desoxycortone**

DOCIOSTAURUS
BT1 acrididae
BT2 orthoptera
NT1 dociostaurus maroccanus

DOCIOSTAURUS MAROCCANUS
BT1 dociostaurus
BT2 acrididae
BT3 orthoptera

DOCKAGE
rt contamination
rt foreign bodies

DOCKING
BT1 surgical operations
rt tail

DOCOSENOIC ACIDS
BT1 long chain fatty acids
BT2 fatty acids
BT3 carboxylic acids
BT4 organic acids
BT5 acids
BT3 lipids
BT1 monoenoic fatty acids
BT2 unsaturated fatty acids
BT3 fatty acids
BT4 carboxylic acids
BT5 organic acids
BT6 acids
BT4 lipids
NT1 brassidic acid
NT1 erucic acid

DOCUMENTATION
rt literature

DOCUMENTATION *cont.*
rt publications

DOCUSATE SODIUM
uf *dioctyl sodium sulphosuccinate*
BT1 laxatives
BT2 gastrointestinal agents
BT3 drugs

DOCYNIA
BT1 rosaceae
NT1 docynia hookeriana

DOCYNIA HOOKERIANA
BT1 docynia
BT2 rosaceae

1-DODECANAMINE
BT1 monoamines
BT2 amines
BT3 amino compounds
BT4 organic nitrogen compounds
BT1 primary amines
BT2 amines
BT3 amino compounds
BT4 organic nitrogen compounds

DODECANOIC ACID
uf *lauric acid*
BT1 medium chain fatty acids
BT2 fatty acids
BT3 carboxylic acids
BT4 organic acids
BT5 acids
BT3 lipids
BT1 saturated fatty acids
BT2 fatty acids
BT3 carboxylic acids
BT4 organic acids
BT5 acids
BT3 lipids
rt trilaurin

1-DODECANOL
uf *lauryl alcohol*
BT1 fatty alcohols
BT2 alcohols
BT2 lipids

DODECYL BENZENESULFONATE
uf *dodecyl benzenesulphonate*
BT1 sulfonates
BT2 organic sulfur compounds
BT1 surfactants

dodecyl benzenesulphonate
USE **dodecyl benzenesulfonate**

DODEMORPH
BT1 morpholine fungicides
BT2 fungicides
BT3 pesticides

DODICIN
BT1 aliphatic nitrogen fungicides
BT2 fungicides
BT3 pesticides
BT1 antiseptics
BT2 antiinfective agents
BT3 drugs

DODINE
uf *doguadine*
BT1 aliphatic nitrogen fungicides
BT2 fungicides
BT3 pesticides

DODONAEA
BT1 sapindaceae
NT1 dodonaea attenuata
NT1 dodonaea viscosa

DODONAEA ATTENUATA
BT1 browse plants
BT1 dodonaea
BT2 sapindaceae

DODONAEA VISCOSA
BT1 browse plants
BT1 dodonaea
BT2 sapindaceae
BT1 oilseed plants

DODONAEA VISCOSA *cont.*
BT2 fatty oil plants
BT3 oil plants

doe
USE **female animals**

dog
USE **dogs**

DOG DISEASES
BT1 animal diseases
BT2 diseases
rt canine adenovirus
rt canine herpesvirus
rt canine parvovirus
rt dogs
rt spavin

DOG FAECES
AF dog feces
BT1 faeces
BT2 excreta
BT3 animal wastes
BT4 wastes
rt dogs

DOG FECES
BF dog faeces
BT1 feces

DOG FEEDING
BT1 animal feeding
BT2 feeding
rt dogs

DOG FOODS
BT1 pet foods
BT2 feeds
rt dogs

DOG MILK
uf milk, dog
BT1 milks
BT2 body fluids
BT3 fluids
rt dogs

DOGFISHES
uf rock salmon
BT1 marine fishes
BT2 aquatic animals
BT3 animals
BT3 aquatic organisms
rt scyliorhinidae
rt squalidae

DOGS
uf canis familiaris
uf dog
BT1 domestic animals
BT2 animals
rt bitches
rt canidae
rt dog diseases
rt dog faeces
rt dog feeding
rt dog foods
rt dog milk
rt greyhounds
rt guard dogs
rt guide dogs
rt hunting dogs
rt kennels
rt pets
rt puppies
rt sheep dogs

doguadine
USE **dodine**

DOLICHANDRONE
BT1 bignoniaceae
NT1 dolichandrone crispa

DOLICHANDRONE CRISPA
BT1 dolichandrone
BT2 bignoniaceae

DOLICHODERA
BT1 heteroderidae
BT2 nematoda

DOLICHODORIDAE
BT1 nematoda

DOLICHODORIDAE *cont.*
NT1 amplimerlinius
NT1 bitylenchus
NT1 dolichodorus
NT2 dolichodorus heterocephalus
NT1 geocenamus
NT1 histotylenchus
NT1 merlinius
NT2 merlinius brevidens
NT1 nagelus
NT1 paratrophurus
NT1 quinisulcius
NT2 quinisulcius capitatus
NT1 scutylenchus
NT2 scutylenchus quadrifer
NT1 telotylenchus
NT1 trichotylenchus
NT1 trophurus
NT2 trophurus imperialis
NT1 tylenchorhynchus
NT2 tylenchorhynchus annulatus
NT2 tylenchorhynchus claytoni
NT2 tylenchorhynchus cylindricus
NT2 tylenchorhynchus dubius
rt plant parasitic nematodes

DOLICHODORUS
BT1 dolichodoridae
BT2 nematoda
NT1 dolichodorus heterocephalus

DOLICHODORUS HETEROCEPHALUS
BT1 dolichodorus
BT2 dolichodoridae
BT3 nematoda

DOLICHOGENIDEA
HN from 1990
BT1 braconidae
BT2 hymenoptera
NT1 dolichogenidea albipennis
NT1 dolichogenidea turionellae
rt apanteles

DOLICHOGENIDEA ALBIPENNIS
HN from 1990; previously "apanteles albipennis"
uf apanteles albipennis
BT1 dolichogenidea
BT2 braconidae
BT3 hymenoptera

DOLICHOGENIDEA TURIONELLAE
HN from 1990; previously "apanteles turionellae"
uf apanteles turionellae
BT1 dolichogenidea
BT2 braconidae
BT3 hymenoptera

DOLICHOLS
BT1 polyprenols
BT2 alcohols
BT2 isoprenoids
BT3 lipids

DOLICHOMITUS
BT1 ichneumonidae
BT2 hymenoptera
NT1 dolichomitus populneus
rt ephialtes

DOLICHOMITUS POPULNEUS
uf ephialtes populneus
BT1 dolichomitus
BT2 ichneumonidae
BT3 hymenoptera

DOLICHOPODIDAE
BT1 diptera
NT1 medetera

dolichos
USE **canavalia**
OR **lablab**
OR **macrotyloma**
OR **pseudovigna**
OR **vigna**

dolichos angularis
USE **vigna angularis**

dolichos argenteus
USE **pseudovigna argentea**

dolichos axillaris
USE **macrotyloma axillare**

dolichos bean
USE **lablab purpureus**

dolichos biflorus
USE **macrotyloma uniflorum**

DOLICHOS ENATION MOSAIC VIRUS
BT1 miscellaneous plant viruses
BT2 plant viruses
BT3 plant pathogens
BT4 pathogens
rt lablab

dolichos gladiata
USE **canavalia gladiata**

dolichos lablab
USE **lablab purpureus**

DOLICHOTHELE
BT1 cactaceae
NT1 dolichothele longimamma
NT1 dolichothele sphaerica
rt mammillaria

DOLICHOTHELE LONGIMAMMA
uf mammillaria longimamma
uf mammillaria uberiformis
BT1 dolichothele
BT2 cactaceae
BT1 ornamental succulent plants
BT2 succulent plants

DOLICHOTHELE SPHAERICA
uf mammillaria sphaerica
BT1 dolichothele
BT2 cactaceae
BT1 ornamental succulent plants
BT2 succulent plants

DOLICHOVESPULA
BT1 vespidae
BT2 hymenoptera
NT1 dolichovespula arenaria
NT1 dolichovespula maculata
NT1 dolichovespula sylvestris
rt vespula

DOLICHOVESPULA ARENARIA
BT1 dolichovespula
BT2 vespidae
BT3 hymenoptera

dolichovespula germanica
USE **vespula germanica**

DOLICHOVESPULA MACULATA
BT1 dolichovespula
BT2 vespidae
BT3 hymenoptera

DOLICHOVESPULA SYLVESTRIS
BT1 dolichovespula
BT2 vespidae
BT3 hymenoptera

DOLIOCYSTIS
BT1 apicomplexa
BT2 protozoa

DOLOMITE
BT1 liming materials
BT2 soil amendments
BT3 amendments
BT1 magnesium fertilizers
BT2 fertilizers
BT1 nonclay minerals
BT2 minerals
BT1 soil parent materials

dolomitic limestone
USE **magnesian limestone**

DOLPHINS
BT1 marine mammals
BT2 aquatic animals

DOLPHINS *cont.*
BT3 animals
BT3 aquatic organisms
rt delphinidae

DOLYCORIS
BT1 pentatomidae
BT2 heteroptera
NT1 dolycoris baccarum
NT1 dolycoris indicus

DOLYCORIS BACCARUM
BT1 dolycoris
BT2 pentatomidae
BT3 heteroptera

DOLYCORIS INDICUS
BT1 dolycoris
BT2 pentatomidae
BT3 heteroptera

DOM
(departements et territoires d'outre mer)
BT1 france
BT2 western europe
BT3 europe
rt french guiana
rt martinique
rt mayotte
rt reunion
rt st. pierre and miquelon

DOMESTIC ANIMALS
BT1 animals
NT1 cats
NT1 dogs
rt domestication
rt livestock
rt mammals
rt pets
rt poultry

DOMESTIC CONSUMPTION
BT1 consumption
rt self sufficiency

DOMESTIC GARDENS
(small gardens, usually on the grounds of one's residence, in which vegetables, fruits and flowers are grown for home use; for agroforestry systems use "home gardens")
uf gardens, domestic
uf home farming plots
uf kitchen gardens
BT1 gardens
NT1 allotments
rt home gardens
rt horticulture

domestic geese
USE **geese**

DOMESTIC MARKETS
uf markets, domestic
BT1 markets

DOMESTIC PRODUCTION
uf production, domestic
BT1 production
rt self sufficiency
rt supply

domestic science
USE **home economics**

DOMESTIC TOURISM
BT1 tourism
rt recreation

DOMESTIC TRADE
uf trade, domestic
BT1 trade

domesticated birds
USE **poultry**

DOMESTICATION
rt crops
rt domestic animals
rt evolution

DOMIATI CHEESE
BT1 cheeses
BT2 milk products
BT3 products

DOMINANCE
NT1 overdominance
NT1 semidominance
rt alleles
rt dominant lethals
rt genetics

dominance, social
USE **social dominance**

DOMINANT LETHALS
uf lethals, dominant
BT1 lethals
BT2 genes
rt dominance

DOMINICA
BT1 caribbean
BT2 america
rt acp
rt caribbean community
rt commonwealth of nations

DOMINICAN REPUBLIC
BT1 caribbean
BT2 america
rt developing countries
rt threshold countries

DON
BT1 goat breeds
BT2 breeds
BT1 horse breeds
BT2 breeds

DONACIDAE
BT1 bivalvia
BT2 mollusca
NT1 donax

DONAX
BT1 donacidae
BT2 bivalvia
BT3 mollusca

DONGOLA
BT1 horse breeds
BT2 breeds

donkey
USE **donkeys**

DONKEY BREEDS
(only important and recognised breeds are listed)
uf ass breeds
BT1 breeds
NT1 poitou

DONKEYS
uf asses
uf donkey
uf equus asinus
BT1 working animals
BT2 animals
rt equidae
rt hinnies
rt horses
rt mules

DONORS
HN from 1990
(for development aid donors, use "development agencies")
NT1 blood donors
rt recipients
rt transplantation

doob
USE **cynodon dactylon**

DOORS
rt buildings
rt gates

DOPA
uf 3,4-dihydroxyphenylalanine
uf dioxyphenylalanine
BT1 nonprotein amino acids
BT2 amino acids

DOPA *cont.*
BT3 carboxylic acids
BT4 organic acids
BT5 acids
BT3 organic nitrogen compounds
NT1 levodopa

DOPAMINE
BT1 catecholamines
BT2 biogenic amines
BT3 amines
BT4 amino compounds
BT5 organic nitrogen compounds
BT1 neurotransmitters
rt cholinergic mechanisms
rt dopamine β-monooxygenase

DOPAMINE β-MONOOXYGENASE
(ec 1.14.17.1)
(for retrieval spell out "beta")
BT1 oxygenases
BT2 oxidoreductases
BT3 enzymes
rt dopamine

DOPATRIUM
BT1 scrophulariaceae
NT1 dopatrium junceum

DOPATRIUM JUNCEUM
BT1 dopatrium
BT2 scrophulariaceae

dope dyeing
USE **solution dyeing (agricola)**

DOPING
rt depression
rt racing animals
rt stimulation

doralis
USE **aphis**

doralis fabae
USE **aphis fabae**

DORITIS
BT1 orchidaceae
NT1 doritis pulcherrima

DORITIS PULCHERRIMA
BT1 doritis
BT2 orchidaceae
BT1 ornamental orchids

DORMANCY
NT1 aestivation
NT1 anhydrobiosis
NT1 diapause
NT1 hibernation
NT1 seed dormancy
NT1 torpor
rt biological rhythms
rt chilling requirement
rt dormancy breaking
rt hard seeds
rt plant development
rt rest
rt sleep
rt stratification
rt vernalization

DORMANCY BREAKING
rt after-ripening
rt dormancy

DORONICUM
BT1 compositae
NT1 doronicum columnae
NT1 doronicum macrophyllum
NT1 doronicum oblongifolium

DORONICUM COLUMNAE
uf doronicum cordifolium
BT1 doronicum
BT2 compositae
BT1 ornamental herbaceous plants

doronicum cordifolium
USE **doronicum columnae**

DORONICUM MACROPHYLLUM
BT1 doronicum
BT2 compositae
BT1 medicinal plants

DORONICUM OBLONGIFOLIUM
BT1 doronicum
BT2 compositae

DOROSOMA
BT1 clupeidae
BT2 clupeiformes
BT3 osteichthyes
BT4 fishes

DOROTHEANTHUS
BT1 aizoaceae
NT1 dorotheanthus bellidiformis

DOROTHEANTHUS BELLIDIFORMIS
uf mesembryanthemum criniflorum
BT1 dorotheanthus
BT2 aizoaceae
BT1 ornamental succulent plants
BT2 succulent plants

DORPER
BT1 sheep breeds
BT2 breeds

DORSET DOWN
BT1 sheep breeds
BT2 breeds

DORSET HORN
BT1 sheep breeds
BT2 breeds

DORU
BT1 forficulidae
BT2 dermaptera
NT1 doru lineare

DORU LINEARE
BT1 doru
BT2 forficulidae
BT3 dermaptera

DORYALIS
uf dovyalis
BT1 flacourtiaceae
NT1 doryalis caffra

DORYALIS CAFFRA
uf dovyalis caffra
BT1 doryalis
BT2 flacourtiaceae

DORYANTHES
BT1 amaryllidaceae

DORYLAIMELLUS
HN from 1990
BT1 belondiridae
BT2 nematoda

DORYLAIMIDAE
BT1 nematoda
NT1 enchodelus
NT1 eudorylaimus
NT1 mesodorylaimus
rt free living nematodes

DORYLUS
BT1 formicidae
BT2 hymenoptera

DORYPHORA
BT1 atherospermataceae
NT1 doryphora aromatica
NT1 doryphora sassafras

DORYPHORA AROMATICA
BT1 doryphora
BT2 atherospermataceae

DORYPHORA SASSAFRAS
HN from 1990
BT1 doryphora
BT2 atherospermataceae
BT1 forest trees

doryphorophaga
USE **myiopharus**

doryphorophaga doryphorae
USE **myiopharus doryphorae**

DOSAGE
(in genetics, use "gene dosage")
NT1 lethal dose
rt dosage effects
rt overdose (agricola)

DOSAGE COMPENSATION
rt dosage effects
rt gene dosage
rt genes

DOSAGE EFFECTS
BT1 effects
rt application rates
rt dosage
rt dosage compensation

dothichiza
USE **cryptodiaporthe**

dothichiza populea
USE **cryptodiaporthe populea**

DOTHIDEALES
NT1 apiosporina
NT2 apiosporina morbosa
NT1 botryosphaeria
NT2 botryosphaeria dothidea
NT2 botryosphaeria obtusa
NT2 botryosphaeria ribis
NT2 botryosphaeria stevensii
NT1 coccodiella
NT2 coccodiella banksiae
NT1 coccostroma
NT1 cochliobolus
NT2 cochliobolus australiensis
NT2 cochliobolus carbonum
NT2 cochliobolus cynodontis
NT2 cochliobolus ellisii
NT2 cochliobolus eragrostidis
NT2 cochliobolus geniculatus
NT2 cochliobolus hawaiiensis
NT2 cochliobolus heterostrophus
NT2 cochliobolus intermedius
NT2 cochliobolus lunatus
NT2 cochliobolus miyabeanus
NT2 cochliobolus nodulosus
NT2 cochliobolus pallescens
NT2 cochliobolus ravenelii
NT2 cochliobolus sativus
NT2 cochliobolus setariae
NT2 cochliobolus spicifer
NT2 cochliobolus verruculosus
NT2 cochliobolus victoriae
NT1 cymadothea
NT2 cymadothea trifolii
NT1 dibotryon
NT1 didymella
NT2 didymella applanata
NT2 didymella bryoniae
NT2 didymella chrysanthemi
NT2 didymella lycopersici
NT1 didymosphaeria
NT2 didymosphaeria arachidicola
NT1 dothidella
NT1 elsinoe
NT2 elsinoe ampelina
NT2 elsinoe batatas
NT2 elsinoe brasiliensis
NT2 elsinoe fawcettii
NT2 elsinoe veneta
NT1 eudarluca
NT2 eudarluca caricis
NT1 fusicladium
NT1 guignardia
NT2 guignardia bidwellii
NT2 guignardia citricarpa
NT1 keissleriella
NT1 leptosphaeria
NT2 leptosphaeria avenaria
NT2 leptosphaeria coniothyrium
NT2 leptosphaeria libanotis
NT2 leptosphaeria maculans
NT2 leptosphaeria nodorum
NT2 leptosphaeria senegalensis
NT1 leptosphaerulina
NT2 leptosphaerulina trifolii
NT1 microcyclus

DOTHIDEALES *cont.*
NT2 microcyclus ulei
NT1 mycosphaerella
NT2 mycosphaerella aleuritis
NT2 mycosphaerella arachidis
NT2 mycosphaerella berkeleyi
NT2 mycosphaerella brassicicola
NT2 mycosphaerella citri
NT2 mycosphaerella cruenta
NT2 mycosphaerella dearnessii
NT2 mycosphaerella fijiensis
NT2 mycosphaerella fragariae
NT2 mycosphaerella gibsonii
NT2 mycosphaerella graminicola
NT2 mycosphaerella henningsii
NT2 mycosphaerella linicola
NT2 mycosphaerella maculiformis
NT2 mycosphaerella musae
NT2 mycosphaerella musicola
NT2 mycosphaerella pini
NT2 mycosphaerella pinodes
NT2 mycosphaerella populorum
NT2 mycosphaerella pruni-persicae
NT2 mycosphaerella sesamicola
NT2 mycosphaerella zeae-maydis
NT1 neotestudina
NT2 neotestudina rosatii
NT1 paraphaeosphaeria
NT2 paraphaeosphaeria michotii
NT1 phaeocryptopus
NT2 phaeocryptopus gaeumannii
NT1 piedraia
NT2 piedraia hortae
NT1 pleosphaerulina
NT2 pleosphaerulina sojicola
NT1 pleospora
NT2 pleospora betae
NT2 pleospora herbarum
NT2 pleospora infectoria
NT2 pleospora papaveracea
NT1 pseudocochliobolus
NT1 pyrenophora
NT2 pyrenophora avenae
NT2 pyrenophora bromi
NT2 pyrenophora chaetomioides
NT2 pyrenophora dictyoides
NT2 pyrenophora erythrospila
NT2 pyrenophora graminea
NT2 pyrenophora lolii
NT2 pyrenophora semeniperda
NT2 pyrenophora teres
NT2 pyrenophora tritici-repentis
NT1 scirrhia
NT1 setosphaeria
NT2 setosphaeria holmii
NT2 setosphaeria monoceras
NT2 setosphaeria pedicellata
NT2 setosphaeria rostrata
NT2 setosphaeria turcica
NT1 sphaerulina
NT1 sydowia
NT2 sydowia polyspora
NT1 venturia (dothideales)
NT2 venturia carpophila
NT2 venturia chlorospora
NT2 venturia inaequalis
NT2 venturia macularis
NT2 venturia pirina
NT2 venturia saliciperda
rt fungi
rt sooty moulds

DOTHIDELLA
BT1 dothideales
rt microcyclus

dothidella ulei
USE **microcyclus ulei**

DOTHISTROMA
BT1 deuteromycotina
rt mycosphaerella

dothistroma pini
USE **mycosphaerella pini**

dothistroma septospora
USE **mycosphaerella pini**

1-DOTRIACONTANOL
BT1 fatty alcohols
BT2 alcohols
BT2 lipids

DOUBLE CLADDING
uf *cladding, double*
BT1 cladding
BT2 building materials
BT3 materials
rt double glazing
rt greenhouses
rt windows

DOUBLE CROPPING
BT1 cropping systems

DOUBLE GLAZING
uf *glazing, double*
BT1 glazing
rt double cladding
rt glass
rt greenhouses
rt thermal pane windows (agricola)
rt windows

DOUBLE INSEMINATION
HN from 1989
BT1 insemination
BT2 mating
BT3 sexual reproduction
BT4 reproduction

DOUBLE MUSCLING
BT1 musculoskeletal system
BT2 body parts
rt muscles
rt muscular hypertrophy

double options
USE **options trading (agricola)**

DOUBLE SUPERPHOSPHATE
BT1 superphosphates
BT2 phosphorus fertilizers
BT3 fertilizers

DOUBLE-WALLED HIVES
BT1 movable-comb hives
BT2 hives

DOUGHS (AGRICOLA)
uf *pastry*
rt bakery products

douglas fir
USE **pseudotsuga menziesii**

doum palm
USE **hyphaene thebaica**

DOURINE
BT1 horse diseases
BT2 animal diseases
BT3 diseases
BT1 trypanosomiasis
BT2 protozoal infections
BT3 parasitoses
BT4 diseases
BT2 vector-borne diseases
BT3 diseases
rt trypanosoma equiperdum

dourine trypanosome
USE **trypanosoma equiperdum**

DOVER SOLES
uf *sole, dover*
uf *solea solea*
BT1 flatfishes
BT2 marine fishes
BT3 aquatic animals
BT4 animals
BT4 aquatic organisms

dovyalis
USE **doryalis**

dovyalis caffra
USE **doryalis caffra**

DOWELLED JOINTS
BT1 joints (timber)

DOWN
BT1 plumage
rt feathers
rt undercoat

DOWN THE ROW THINNERS
uf *thinners, down the row*
BT1 thinners
BT2 farm machinery
BT3 machinery

DOWN'S SYNDROME
uf *mongolism*
BT1 congenital abnormalities
BT2 abnormalities
BT1 mental disorders
BT2 functional disorders
BT3 animal disorders
BT4 disorders

DOWNWARD MOVEMENT
HN from 1989
BT1 transport processes

DOXAPRAM
BT1 analeptics
BT2 neurotropic drugs
BT3 drugs

DOXORUBICIN
uf *adriamycin*
BT1 antibiotics
BT1 antineoplastic agents
BT2 drugs

DOXYCYCLINE
BT1 antimalarials
BT2 antiprotozoal agents
BT3 antiparasitic agents
BT4 drugs

DOXYLAMINE
BT1 antihistaminics
BT2 drugs

DRABA
BT1 cruciferae
NT1 draba verna

DRABA VERNA
BT1 draba
BT2 cruciferae

DRACAENA
BT1 agavaceae
NT1 dracaena angustifolia
NT1 dracaena deremensis
NT1 dracaena fragrans
NT1 dracaena marginata
NT1 dracaena sanderiana

DRACAENA ANGUSTIFOLIA
BT1 dracaena
BT2 agavaceae

DRACAENA DEREMENSIS
BT1 dracaena
BT2 agavaceae
BT1 ornamental succulent plants
BT2 succulent plants
rt ornamental foliage plants

DRACAENA FRAGRANS
BT1 dracaena
BT2 agavaceae
BT1 ornamental succulent plants
BT2 succulent plants
rt ornamental foliage plants

DRACAENA MARGINATA
BT1 dracaena
BT2 agavaceae
BT1 ornamental succulent plants
BT2 succulent plants
rt ornamental foliage plants

DRACAENA SANDERIANA
BT1 dracaena
BT2 agavaceae
BT1 ornamental succulent plants
BT2 succulent plants
rt ornamental foliage plants

DRACOCEPHALUM
BT1 labiatae
NT1 dracocephalum fruticulosum
NT1 dracocephalum moldavica
NT1 dracocephalum renati

DRACOCEPHALUM FRUTICULOSUM
BT1 dracocephalum
BT2 labiatae

DRACOCEPHALUM MOLDAVICA
BT1 dracocephalum
BT2 labiatae

DRACOCEPHALUM RENATI
BT1 dracocephalum
BT2 labiatae

DRACUNCULIDAE
BT1 nematoda
NT1 dracunculus
NT2 dracunculus insignis
NT2 dracunculus medinensis
rt animal parasitic nematodes

DRACUNCULUS
BT1 dracunculidae
BT2 nematoda
NT1 dracunculus insignis
NT1 dracunculus medinensis

DRACUNCULUS INSIGNIS
BT1 dracunculus
BT2 dracunculidae
BT3 nematoda

DRACUNCULUS MEDINENSIS
BT1 dracunculus
BT2 dracunculidae
BT3 nematoda

DRAFT
BF draught
rt draft animals
rt draft control

DRAFT ANIMALS
BF draught animals
rt draft

DRAFT CONTROL
BF draught control
rt draft

DRAG
uf *air resistance*
BT1 flow resistance
BT2 resistance
rt air flow
rt turbulence

dragonflies
USE **odonata**

DRAIN LAYERS
BT1 drainage equipment
BT2 equipment
rt drain laying
rt subsurface drainage

DRAIN LAYING
rt drain layers
rt drain pipes
rt installation
rt subsurface drainage

DRAIN PIPES
BT1 drainage equipment
BT2 equipment
BT1 pipes
BT2 components
rt drain laying
rt subsurface drainage

DRAIN PLOUGHS
AF drain plows
BT1 drainage equipment
BT2 equipment
BT1 ploughs
BT2 implements
rt subsurface drainage

DRAIN PLOWS
BF drain ploughs

DRAIN PLOWS *cont.*
BT1 plows

DRAINAGE
NT1 gravel tunnel drains
NT1 mole drainage
NT1 pipe drainage
NT1 stone drains
NT1 subsurface drainage
NT1 surface drainage
NT1 tile drainage
NT1 well drainage
rt backfilling
rt clay soils
rt claypan soils
rt ditch cleaners
rt ditches
rt drainage equipment
rt drainage systems
rt drainage water
rt drained conditions
rt dredging
rt envelope materials
rt flow to drains
rt hydraulic engineering
rt impeded drainage
rt internal drainage
rt land improvement
rt lysimetry
rt runoff water
rt seepage
rt site factors
rt soil management
rt water management
rt waterlogging

DRAINAGE CHANNELS
BT1 channels
rt ditches
rt flow to drains
rt surface drainage
rt waterways

DRAINAGE EQUIPMENT
BT1 equipment
NT1 ditch cleaners
NT1 drain layers
NT1 drain pipes
NT1 drain ploughs
NT1 dredgers
rt drainage
rt earth moving equipment
rt pumps

drainage, mole
USE **mole drainage**

drainage, pipe
USE **pipe drainage**

drainage, subsurface
USE **subsurface drainage**

drainage, surface
USE **surface drainage**

DRAINAGE SYSTEMS
BT1 systems
rt drainage

drainage, tile
USE **tile drainage**

DRAINAGE WATER
BT1 water
NT1 runoff water
rt drainage
rt flow to drains

DRAINED CONDITIONS
BT1 soil water regimes
rt drainage

drained weight
USE **net weight (agricola)**

DRAKENSBERGER
BT1 cattle breeds
BT2 breeds

DRAMA
BT1 performing arts
BT2 arts
NT1 acting
rt opera

DRAMA *cont.*
rt performers
rt theatre

DRAPE (AGRICOLA)
rt fabrics

DRASCHIA
BT1 habronematidae
BT2 nematoda

DRAUGHT
AF draft
uf *implement draught*
uf *plough draught*
rt draught animals
rt draught control
rt soil mechanics
rt traction
rt tractors

DRAUGHT ANIMALS
AF draft animals
BT1 working animals
BT2 animals
rt animal power
rt draught

DRAUGHT CONTROL
AF draft control
BT1 control
rt depth wheels
rt draught
rt traction

DRAWBAR POWER
BT1 power
rt drawbars
rt traction
rt tractors

DRAWBARS
BT1 components
rt drawbar power
rt traction
rt tractors

DRAWIDA
BT1 moniligastridae
BT2 oligochaeta
BT3 annelida

DRAZOXOLON
BT1 oxazole fungicides
BT2 fungicides
BT3 pesticides

DREAD DISEASE INSURANCE (AGRICOLA)
BT1 insurance

DRECHSLERA
BT1 deuteromycotina
NT1 drechslera biseptata
NT1 drechslera cactivora
NT1 drechslera catenaria
NT1 drechslera gossypii
NT1 drechslera phlei
NT1 drechslera poae
NT1 drechslera portulacae
NT1 drechslera triseptata
rt bipolaris
rt cochliobolus
rt helminthosporium
rt pyrenophora
rt setosphaeria

drechslera australiensis
USE **cochliobolus australiensis**

drechslera avenacea
USE **pyrenophora chaetomioides**

DRECHSLERA BISEPTATA
HN from 1990
uf *helminthosporium biseptatum*
BT1 drechslera
BT2 deuteromycotina

DRECHSLERA CACTIVORA
BT1 drechslera
BT2 deuteromycotina

drechslera campanulata
USE **pyrenophora semeniperda**

DRECHSLERA CATENARIA
BT1 drechslera
BT2 deuteromycotina

drechslera dictyoides
USE **pyrenophora dictyoides**

drechslera ellisii
USE **cochliobolus ellisii**

drechslera erythrospila
USE **pyrenophora erythrospila**

DRECHSLERA GOSSYPII
HN from 1990
uf *bipolaris gossypii*
uf *helminthosporium gossypii*
BT1 drechslera
BT2 deuteromycotina

drechslera halodes
USE **setosphaeria rostrata**

drechslera hawaiiensis
USE **cochliobolus hawaiiensis**

drechslera heveae
USE **bipolaris heveae**

drechslera holmii
USE **setosphaeria holmii**

drechslera incurvata
USE **bipolaris incurvata**

drechslera indica
USE **bipolaris indica**

drechslera leersiae
USE **bipolaris leersiae**

drechslera maydis
USE **cochliobolus heterostrophus**

drechslera monoceras
USE **setosphaeria monoceras**

drechslera oryzae
USE **cochliobolus miyabeanus**

DRECHSLERA PHLEI
HN from 1990
uf *helminthosporium dictyoides var. phlei*
BT1 drechslera
BT2 deuteromycotina

DRECHSLERA POAE
uf *helminthosporium vagans*
BT1 drechslera
BT2 deuteromycotina

DRECHSLERA PORTULACAE
HN from 1990
uf *helminthosporium portulacae*
BT1 drechslera
BT2 deuteromycotina

drechslera ravenelii
USE **cochliobolus ravenelii**

drechslera rostrata
USE **setosphaeria rostrata**

drechslera sacchari
USE **bipolaris sacchari**

drechslera setariae
USE **cochliobolus setariae**

drechslera siccans
USE **pyrenophora lolii**

drechslera sorghicola
USE **bipolaris sorghicola**

drechslera sorokiniana
USE **cochliobolus sativus**

drechslera spicifer
USE **cochliobolus spicifer**

drechslera stenospila
USE **bipolaris stenospila**

drechslera teres
USE **pyrenophora teres**

drechslera tetramera
USE **cochliobolus spicifer**

DRECHSLERA TRISEPTATA
HN from 1990
uf *helminthosporium triseptatum*
BT1 drechslera
BT2 deuteromycotina

drechslera turcica
USE **setosphaeria turcica**

drechslera verticillata
USE **pyrenophora semeniperda**

drechslera zeicola
USE **cochliobolus carbonum**

DREDGERS
BT1 drainage equipment
BT2 equipment
rt dredging
rt excavators

DREDGING
rt cleaning
rt drainage
rt dredgers
rt dredgings

DREDGINGS
BT1 soil parent materials
BT1 spoil
BT2 industrial wastes
BT3 wastes
rt alluvium
rt dredging
rt mud
rt sapropel

DREMOMYS
BT1 sciuridae
BT2 rodents
BT3 mammals
NT1 dremomys pernyi

DREMOMYS PERNYI
BT1 dremomys
BT2 sciuridae
BT3 rodents
BT4 mammals

DRENTHE
uf *netherlands (drenthe)*
BT1 netherlands
BT2 western europe
BT3 europe

DREPANOPEZIZA
BT1 helotiales
NT1 drepanopeziza populorum
NT1 drepanopeziza punctiformis
NT1 drepanopeziza ribis
rt marssonina
rt pseudopeziza

DREPANOPEZIZA POPULORUM
HN from 1990
uf *marssonina populi*
BT1 drepanopeziza
BT2 helotiales

DREPANOPEZIZA PUNCTIFORMIS
uf *marssonina brunnea*
BT1 drepanopeziza
BT2 helotiales

DREPANOPEZIZA RIBIS
uf *pseudopeziza ribis*
BT1 drepanopeziza
BT2 helotiales

DREPANOSIPHUM
BT1 aphididae
BT2 aphidoidea
BT3 sternorrhyncha
BT4 homoptera
NT1 drepanosiphum dixoni

DREPANOSIPHUM *cont.*
NT1 drepanosiphum platanoidis

DREPANOSIPHUM DIXONI
BT1 drepanosiphum
BT2 aphididae
BT3 aphidoidea
BT4 sternorrhyncha
BT5 homoptera

DREPANOSIPHUM PLATANOIDIS
BT1 drepanosiphum
BT2 aphididae
BT3 aphidoidea
BT4 sternorrhyncha
BT5 homoptera

DRESSING PERCENTAGE
BT1 carcass composition

DRESSINGS
BT1 application methods
BT2 methodology
rt annual dressings
rt seed dressings
rt top dressings

DREYFUSIA
BT1 adelgidae
BT2 aphidoidea
BT3 sternorrhyncha
BT4 homoptera
NT1 dreyfusia nordmannianae
NT1 dreyfusia piceae
rt adelges

DREYFUSIA NORDMANNIANAE
uf adelges nordmannianae
uf dreyfusia nuesslini
BT1 dreyfusia
BT2 adelgidae
BT3 aphidoidea
BT4 sternorrhyncha
BT5 homoptera

dreyfusia nuesslini
USE **dreyfusia nordmannianae**

DREYFUSIA PICEAE
uf adelges piceae
BT1 dreyfusia
BT2 adelgidae
BT3 aphidoidea
BT4 sternorrhyncha
BT5 homoptera

DRIED ALFALFA
BF dried lucerne
rt alfalfa

DRIED CREAM
uf cream, dried
BT1 cream
BT2 milk products
BT3 products
BT1 dried foods
BT2 foods

DRIED EGG
uf egg powder
uf egg, dried
BT1 dried foods
BT2 foods
BT1 egg products
BT2 poultry products
BT3 animal products
BT4 products
rt eggs

DRIED FISH
uf fish, dried
BT1 dried foods
BT2 foods
BT1 fish products
BT2 animal products
BT3 products

DRIED FLOWERS
BT1 cut flowers

DRIED FODDERS
BT1 feeds

DRIED FOODS
BT1 foods

DRIED FOODS *cont.*
NT1 dried cream
NT1 dried egg
NT1 dried fish
NT1 dried fruit
NT2 prunes
NT2 raisins
NT1 dried meat
NT1 dried milk
NT1 dried milk products
NT2 dried skim milk
NT2 dried whey
NT1 dry beans (agricola)
rt dehydrated foods (agricola)
rt dried honey
rt processed products

DRIED FRUIT
uf fruit, dried
BT1 dried foods
BT2 foods
BT1 fruit products
BT2 plant products
BT3 products
NT1 prunes
NT1 raisins
rt grapes

DRIED HONEY
BT1 honey
BT2 hive products
BT3 animal products
BT4 products
rt dried foods
rt drying

DRIED LUCERNE
AF dried alfalfa
uf lucerne, dried
BT1 feeds
rt lucerne

DRIED MEAT
BT1 dried foods
BT2 foods
BT1 meat products
BT2 animal products
BT3 products
rt meat

DRIED MILK
uf milk powder
uf milk, dried
BT1 dried foods
BT2 foods
BT1 milk products
BT2 products
rt dried milk products

DRIED MILK PRODUCTS
BT1 dried foods
BT2 foods
BT1 milk products
BT2 products
NT1 dried skim milk
NT1 dried whey
rt dried milk

DRIED SKIM MILK
uf milk, skimmed dried
uf nonfat dry milk
uf skim milk, dried
BT1 dried milk products
BT2 dried foods
BT3 foods
BT2 milk products
BT3 products
rt filled milk
rt skim milk

DRIED WHEY
uf whey powder
uf whey, dried
BT1 dried milk products
BT2 dried foods
BT3 foods
BT2 milk products
BT3 products
rt whey

DRIERATION
BT1 grain drying
BT2 drying

DRIERATION *cont.*
BT3 dehydration
BT4 processing
rt ventilation

DRIERS
AF dryers
uf drying machinery
BT1 farm machinery
BT2 machinery
NT1 barn driers
NT1 batch driers
NT1 cascade driers
NT1 concurrent flow driers
NT1 continuous driers
NT1 convection driers
NT1 conveyor driers
NT1 counterflow driers
NT1 cross flow driers
NT1 deep bed driers
NT1 drum driers
NT1 electric driers
NT1 forage driers
NT1 grain driers
NT2 floor driers
NT1 high temperature driers
NT1 infrared driers
NT1 microwave driers
NT1 roller driers
NT1 shallow bed driers
NT1 spray driers
NT1 tower driers
NT1 tray driers
NT1 tunnel driers
NT1 ventilated bin driers
NT1 ventilated silo driers
rt air drying
rt artificial drying
rt desiccants
rt drying air
rt fluidized beds
rt kilns

driers, barn
USE **barn driers**

driers, batch
USE **batch driers**

driers, cascade
USE **cascade driers**

driers, concurrent flow
USE **concurrent flow driers**

driers, continuous
USE **continuous driers**

driers, convection
USE **convection driers**

driers, conveyor
USE **conveyor driers**

driers, counter flow
USE **counterflow driers**

driers, deep bed
USE **deep bed driers**

driers, drum
USE **drum driers**

driers, electric
USE **electric driers**

driers, floor
USE **floor driers**

driers, grain
USE **grain driers**

driers, high temperature
USE **high temperature driers**

driers, infrared
USE **infrared driers**

driers, microwave
USE **microwave driers**

driers, roller
USE **roller driers**

driers, shallow bed
USE **shallow bed driers**

driers, spray
USE **spray driers**

driers, tower
USE **tower driers**

driers, ventilated bin
USE **ventilated bin driers**

driers, ventilated silo
USE **ventilated silo driers**

DRIFT
uf spray drift
NT1 simulated spray drift
rt air flow
rt drift spraying
rt pollution
rt segregation distortion
rt spraying

DRIFT SPRAYING
uf spraying, drift
BT1 spraying
BT2 application methods
BT3 methodology
rt drift

DRIFTING
BT1 animal behaviour
BT2 behaviour
rt fighting
rt honeybee colonies
rt orientation

DRILLING
BT1 application methods
BT2 methodology
BT1 sowing methods
BT2 sowing
BT3 planting
NT1 direct sowing
NT1 precision drilling
rt boring
rt combine drills
rt drills
rt placement
rt woodworking

drilling, direct
USE **direct sowing**

drilling, precision
USE **precision drilling**

drilling (woodworking)
USE **boring**

DRILLS
uf seeders
BT1 farm machinery
BT2 machinery
NT1 band drills
NT1 combine drills
NT1 fluid drills
NT1 grain drills
NT1 plot drills
NT1 pneumatic drills
NT1 precision drills
NT1 press drills
NT1 ridge drills
NT1 root drills
NT1 seed coverers
NT1 seed drills
NT1 seed tubes
NT1 seeder cultivators
NT1 sod seeders
rt coulters
rt cup feed mechanism
rt drilling
rt fertilizer distributors
rt fluted roller feed mechanism
rt furrow openers
rt planters
rt pneumatic feed mechanism
rt press wheels
rt seed broadcasters
rt tramlining

drills, band
USE **band drills**

drills, combine
USE **combine drills**

drills, fertilizer
USE **fertilizer distributors**

drills, fluid
USE **fluid drills**

drills, grain
USE **grain drills**

drills, plot
USE **plot drills**

drills, pneumatic
USE **pneumatic drills**

drills, precision
USE **precision drills**

drills, press
USE **press drills**

drills, ridge
USE **ridge drills**

drills, root
USE **root drills**

DRILOCINETA
BT1 ciliophora
BT2 protozoa

DRIMYS
BT1 winteraceae
NT1 drimys confertifolia
NT1 drimys winteri

DRIMYS CONFERTIFOLIA
BT1 drimys
BT2 winteraceae

DRIMYS WINTERI
BT1 drimys
BT2 winteraceae

DRINKERS
NT1 bowl drinkers
NT1 nipple drinkers
NT1 troughs
NT2 feed troughs
NT2 subsurface troughs
NT2 water troughs
rt drinking
rt mangers

drinkers, bowl
USE **bowl drinkers**

drinkers, nipple
USE **nipple drinkers**

DRINKING
rt beverages
rt bowl drinkers
rt drinkers
rt drinking behaviour
rt drinking water
rt polydipsia
rt thirst
rt water intake
rt water troughs

DRINKING BEHAVIOR
BF drinking behaviour
BT1 behavior

DRINKING BEHAVIOUR
AF drinking behavior
uf *drinking habits*
BT1 behaviour
NT1 thirst control
rt drinking

drinking habits
USE **drinking behaviour**

DRINKING WATER
uf *water, drinking*
BT1 water
rt beverages
rt drinking
rt tap water
rt water hardness
rt water intake

DRINKING WATER *cont.*
rt water troughs

drinks
USE **beverages**

DRINO
BT1 tachinidae
BT2 diptera

drino imberbis
USE **palexorista imberbis**

drip dry finishes
USE **wrinkle resistant finishes (agricola)**

drip irrigation
USE **trickle irrigation**

DRIS
BT1 diagnostic techniques
BT2 techniques

DRIVEN WHEELS
uf *wheels, driven*
BT1 ground drive
BT2 components
BT1 wheels
BT2 components
rt drives

DRIVERLESS VEHICLES
BT1 vehicles
rt automatic guidance
rt robots

DRIVERS
BT1 technicians
BT2 occupations
BT2 skilled labour
BT3 labour
rt controls
rt one man operation
rt operators

DRIVES
BT1 machinery
NT1 belt drives
NT1 electric drives
NT1 power takeoffs
NT1 tandem drives
NT1 torque
NT1 variable speed drives
rt automatic transmissions
rt cardan shafts
rt clutches
rt couplings
rt driven wheels
rt gears
rt ground drive
rt hydraulic power systems
rt motors
rt overload protection
rt propellers
rt torque converters
rt transmissions

drives, belt
USE **belt drives**

drives, electric
USE **electric drives**

drives, tandem
USE **tandem drives**

drives, variable speed
USE **variable speed drives**

DROMAIIDAE
BT1 casuariiformes
BT2 birds
NT1 dromaius
rt emus

DROMAIUS
BT1 dromaiidae
BT2 casuariiformes
BT3 birds

dromaius novaehollandiae
USE **emus**

DROMEDARIES
uf *camelus dromedarius*

DROMEDARIES *cont.*
BT1 working animals
BT2 animals
rt camelidae
rt camels

DRONE CONGREGATION AREAS
BT1 drone honeybees
BT2 honeybees
rt mating

DRONE HONEYBEES
uf *drones*
BT1 honeybees
NT1 drone congregation areas
rt eviction
rt polymorphism

drones
USE **drone honeybees**

DROP
rt abscission
rt windfalls

drop size
USE **droplet size**

DROPERIDOL
BT1 neuroleptics
BT2 psychotropic drugs
BT3 neurotropic drugs
BT4 drugs

DROPLET SIZE
uf *drop size*
rt atomization
rt atomizers
rt droplet studies
rt droplets
rt particle size
rt size
rt sprays

DROPLET STUDIES
BT1 research
rt droplet size
rt droplets
rt spraying

DROPLETS
rt controlled droplet application
rt droplet size
rt droplet studies
rt silt droplets
rt spraying
rt sprays

DROSANTHEMUM
BT1 aizoaceae
NT1 drosanthemum hispidum

DROSANTHEMUM HISPIDUM
BT1 drosanthemum
BT2 aizoaceae
BT1 ornamental succulent plants
BT2 succulent plants

DROSERA
BT1 droseraceae

DROSERACEAE
NT1 dionaea
NT2 dionaea muscipula
NT1 drosera

DROSOPHILA
BT1 drosophilidae
BT2 diptera
NT1 drosophila melanogaster
NT1 drosophila pseudoobscura
NT1 drosophila simulans
NT1 drosophila subobscura
NT1 drosophila virilis

DROSOPHILA MELANOGASTER
BT1 drosophila
BT2 drosophilidae
BT3 diptera

DROSOPHILA PSEUDOOBSCURA
BT1 drosophila
BT2 drosophilidae
BT3 diptera

DROSOPHILA SIMULANS
BT1 drosophila
BT2 drosophilidae
BT3 diptera

DROSOPHILA SUBOBSCURA
BT1 drosophila
BT2 drosophilidae
BT3 diptera

DROSOPHILA VIRILIS
BT1 drosophila
BT2 drosophilidae
BT3 diptera

DROSOPHILIDAE
BT1 diptera
NT1 drosophila
NT2 drosophila melanogaster
NT2 drosophila pseudoobscura
NT2 drosophila simulans
NT2 drosophila subobscura
NT2 drosophila virilis
NT1 scaptomyza

DROUGHT
BT1 climatic factors
rt arid climate
rt desertification
rt disasters
rt drought injury
rt drought resistance
rt dry conditions
rt dry season
rt plant water relations
rt stress
rt water deprivation
rt water requirements
rt water stress

DROUGHT INJURY
BT1 injuries
rt drought
rt drought resistance

DROUGHT RESISTANCE
uf *drought tolerance*
uf *heat and drought resistance*
BT1 resistance
rt drought
rt drought injury
rt heat resistance
rt plant water relations

drought tolerance
USE **drought resistance**

DROUGHTMASTER
BT1 cattle breeds
BT2 breeds

drug abuse
USE **substance abuse (agricola)**

drug action
USE **pharmacodynamics**

DRUG ADDICTION
BT1 addiction
BT2 delinquent behaviour
BT3 social behaviour
BT4 behaviour
rt drugs
rt intravenous drug users

DRUG ALLERGIES
HN from 1990
uf *allergy, drug*
uf *drug hypersensitivity*
uf *hypersensitivity, drug*
BT1 allergies
BT2 immunological diseases
BT3 diseases
rt drugs

DRUG ANTAGONISM
BT1 antagonism
BT2 incompatibility
rt narcotic antagonists

DRUG COMBINATIONS
rt drug synergy
rt drug therapy
rt drugs

DRUG COMBINATIONS *cont.*
rt mixtures

DRUG DELIVERY SYSTEMS
HN from 1989
BT1 application methods
BT2 methodology
rt drugs

DRUG EFFECTS (AGRICOLA)
BT1 effects
rt drugs

DRUG EXCRETION
BT1 excretion
BT2 physiological functions
rt drugs

DRUG FORMULATIONS
BT1 formulations
NT1 ointments
rt drug therapy
rt drugs
rt generics (agricola)
rt pharmacy

drug hypersensitivity
USE **drug allergies**

DRUG METABOLISM
BT1 metabolism
rt drugs

drug plants
USE **medicinal plants**

DRUG RESIDUES
BT1 residues
NT1 antibiotic residues
rt drugs

DRUG RESISTANCE
uf *resistance, drug*
BT1 resistance
rt drug therapy
rt drugs
rt resistance mechanisms

drug resistance mechanisms
USE **resistance mechanisms**

DRUG SYNERGY
BT1 synergism
rt drug combinations
rt drug therapy
rt drugs
rt synergists

DRUG THERAPY
uf *chemotherapy*
BT1 therapy
rt chemoprophylaxis
rt drug combinations
rt drug formulations
rt drug resistance
rt drug synergy
rt drugs
rt pharmacodynamics
rt pharmacokinetics
rt pharmacology

DRUG TOXICITY
BT1 toxicity
rt drugs

DRUGS
uf *medicines*
uf *pharmaceuticals*
NT1 anorexiants
NT2 benfluorex
NT2 fenfluramine
NT2 satietin
NT1 antihistaminics
NT2 cimetidine
NT2 cyproheptadine
NT2 doxylamine
NT2 promethazine
NT1 antiinfective agents
NT2 antibacterial agents
NT3 aminosalicylic acid
NT3 antimycobacterial agents
NT3 apramycin
NT3 arsanilic acid
NT3 aspergillic acid
NT3 avoparcin

DRUGS *cont.*
NT3 bacitracin
NT3 bambermycin
NT3 benzalkonium chloride
NT3 carbadox
NT3 cefamandole
NT3 cefazolin
NT3 cefoxitin
NT3 cephalosporins
NT3 chloramphenicol
NT3 chlortetracycline
NT3 clindamycin
NT3 cycloserine
NT3 dapsone
NT3 dihydrostreptomycin
NT3 erythromycin
NT3 framycetin
NT3 furaltadone
NT3 gentamicin
NT3 gentian violet
NT3 gloxazone
NT3 gougerotin
NT3 gramicidin
NT3 gramicidin s
NT3 isoniazid
NT3 kanamycin
NT3 kasugamycin
NT3 lincomycin
NT3 nalidixic acid
NT3 neomycin
NT3 nifuroxazide
NT3 nitrofurantoin
NT3 nitrovin
NT3 novobiocin
NT3 oleandomycin
NT3 oxytetracycline
NT3 penicillins
NT4 amoxicillin
NT4 ampicillin
NT4 carbenicillin
NT4 cloxacillin
NT4 oxacillin
NT3 polymyxin b
NT3 rifampicin
NT3 rifamycin
NT3 roxarsone
NT3 spectinomycin
NT3 spiramycin
NT3 streptomycin
NT3 sulfachlorpyridazine
NT3 sulfadiazine
NT3 sulfadimethoxine
NT3 sulfadimidine
NT3 sulfadoxine
NT3 sulfafurazole
NT3 sulfamerazine
NT3 sulfamethoxazole
NT3 sulfamethoxypyridazine
NT3 sulfamonomethoxine
NT3 sulfanilamide
NT3 sulfapyrazole
NT3 sulfapyridine
NT3 sulfathiazole
NT3 tetracycline
NT3 thiopeptin
NT3 tiamulin
NT3 trimethoprim
NT3 turimycins
NT3 tylosin
NT3 virginiamycin
NT3 xantocillin
NT3 zinc bacitracin
NT2 antifungal agents
NT3 amphotericin b
NT3 benzalkonium chloride
NT3 candicidin
NT3 clotrimazole
NT3 cycloheximide
NT3 dehydroacetic acid
NT3 econazole
NT3 fenticonazole
NT3 fluconazole
NT3 flucytosine
NT3 gentian violet
NT3 griseofulvin
NT3 itraconazole
NT3 ketoconazole
NT3 miconazole
NT3 monensin
NT3 natamycin
NT3 nystatin

DRUGS *cont.*
NT3 oligomycin
NT3 partricin
NT3 phenylmercury nitrate
NT3 propionic acid
NT3 terbinafine
NT3 thiomersal
NT3 tolnaftate
NT3 trichodermin
NT2 antiseptics
NT3 acriflavine
NT3 aluminium sulfate
NT3 benzalkonium chloride
NT3 borax
NT3 cetrimonium
NT3 dodicin
NT3 formaldehyde
NT3 iodine
NT3 malachite green
NT3 mandelic acid
NT3 mercuric chloride
NT3 mercuric oxide
NT3 methylene blue
NT3 naphthalene
NT3 potassium permanganate
NT3 safrole
NT3 thiram
NT2 antiviral agents
NT3 amantadine
NT3 floxuridine
NT3 hygromycin b
NT3 idoxuridine
NT3 imanin
NT3 interferon
NT3 lysozyme
NT1 antiinflammatory agents
NT2 betamethasone
NT2 dexamethasone
NT2 fludrocortisone
NT2 flumetasone
NT2 flunixin
NT2 hydrocortisone
NT2 indometacin
NT2 oxyphenbutazone
NT2 prednisolone
NT2 prednisone
NT2 triamcinolone
NT1 antineoplastic agents
NT2 allopurinol
NT2 alloxan
NT2 aminopterin
NT2 azaserine
NT2 busulfan
NT2 cyclophosphamide
NT2 dactinomycin
NT2 demecolcine
NT2 doxorubicin
NT2 floxuridine
NT2 fluorouracil
NT2 hydroxycarbamide
NT2 melengestrol
NT2 methotrexate
NT2 mitomycin
NT2 puromycin
NT2 spectinomycin
NT2 tenuazonic acid
NT2 tretamine
NT2 trichodermin
NT2 urethane
NT2 vinblastine
NT1 antiparasitic agents
NT2 anthelmintics
NT3 abamectin
NT3 acetarsol
NT3 albendazole
NT3 amoscanate
NT3 anthiolimine
NT3 antimony potassium tartrate
NT3 arecoline
NT3 artemether
NT3 benacil
NT3 bephenium
NT3 bithionol
NT3 bitoscanate
NT3 bromofenofos
NT3 bromophos
NT3 brotianide
NT3 bunamidine
NT3 calcium cyanamide
NT3 cambendazole

DRUGS *cont.*
NT3 carbaryl
NT3 carbon tetrachloride
NT3 ciclobendazole
NT3 cinnamic acid
NT3 clioxanide
NT3 clorsulon
NT3 copper sulfate
NT3 coumaphos
NT3 creosote
NT3 crufomate
NT3 cyacetacide
NT3 diamfenetide
NT3 dichlorophen
NT3 dichlorvos
NT3 diethylcarbamazine
NT3 disophenol
NT3 dithiazanine iodide
NT3 emetine
NT3 febantel
NT3 fenbendazole
NT3 flubendazole
NT3 furapyrimidone
NT3 gentian violet
NT3 halofuginone
NT3 haloxon
NT3 hexachloroethane
NT3 hexachloroparaxylene
NT3 hexachlorophene
NT3 hexylresorcinol
NT3 hycanthone
NT3 hygromycin b
NT3 ivermectin
NT3 kamala
NT3 lucanthone
NT3 luxabendazole
NT3 mebendazole
NT3 medamine
NT3 melarsonyl
NT3 metronidazole
NT3 metyridine
NT3 milbemycin d
NT3 mitomycin
NT3 morantel
NT3 naftalofos
NT3 niclofolan
NT3 niclosamide
NT3 nicotine
NT3 niridazole
NT3 nitroscanate
NT3 nitroxinil
NT3 novel anthelmintics
NT3 oxamniquine
NT3 oxantel
NT3 oxfendazole
NT3 oxyclozanide
NT3 parbendazole
NT3 phenothiazine
NT3 piperazine
NT3 praziquantel
NT3 pyrantel
NT3 pyrvinium chloride
NT3 rafoxanide
NT3 sodium stibocaptate
NT3 stibophen
NT3 suramin
NT3 tetramisole
NT4 levamisole
NT3 thiabendazole
NT3 thiacetarsamide sodium
NT3 thiofuradene
NT3 tribromsalan
NT3 trichlorfon
NT3 triclabendazole
NT2 antiprotozoal agents
NT3 acetarsol
NT3 acriflavine
NT3 allopurinol
NT3 amicarbalide
NT3 amoebicides
NT4 clioquinol
NT4 dehydroemetine
NT4 diloxanide
NT4 emetine
NT4 metronidazole
NT4 ornidazole
NT4 paromomycin
NT4 secnidazole
NT4 tetracycline
NT4 tinidazole
NT3 amphotericin b

DRUGS *cont.*
NT3 antimalarials
NT4 amodiaquine
NT4 artemether
NT4 artesunate
NT4 chloroquine
NT4 chlorproguanil
NT4 cycloguanil embonate
NT4 dapsone
NT4 doxycycline
NT4 floxacrine
NT4 halofantrine
NT4 mefloquine
NT4 menoctone
NT4 mepacrine
NT4 piperaquine
NT4 primaquine
NT4 proguanil
NT4 pyrimethamine
NT4 pyronaridine
NT4 qinghaosu
NT4 quinine
NT4 sulfadoxine
NT4 sulfalene
NT3 buparvaquone
NT3 chloramphenicol
NT3 chlortetracycline
NT3 clindamycin
NT3 clotrimazole
NT3 coccidiostats
NT4 aminitrozole
NT4 amprolium
NT4 arprinocid
NT4 buquinolate
NT4 clopidol
NT4 decoquinate
NT4 diaveridine
NT4 dinitolmide
NT4 ethopabate
NT4 halofuginone
NT4 lasalocid
NT4 monensin
NT4 narasin
NT4 nequinate
NT4 nicarbazin
NT4 nitrofural
NT4 ormetoprim
NT4 parvaquone
NT4 robenidine
NT4 salinomycin
NT4 sulfadimethoxine
NT4 sulfadimidine
NT4 sulfanitran
NT4 sulfaquinoxaline
NT4 toltrazuril
NT3 dichlorophen
NT3 diiodohydroxyquinoline
NT3 dimetridazole
NT3 fumagillin
NT3 furazolidone
NT3 imidocarb
NT3 ipronidazole
NT3 meglumine antimonate
NT3 miconazole
NT3 mitomycin
NT3 neoarsphenamine
NT3 nimorazole
NT3 novel antiprotozoal agents
NT3 oxytetracycline
NT3 partricin
NT3 pentamidine
NT3 quinuronium sulfate
NT3 ronidazole
NT3 secnidazole
NT3 sodium stibogluconate
NT3 spiramycin
NT3 sulfadiazine
NT3 sulfamethoxazole
NT3 sulfamonomethoxine
NT3 tinidazole
NT3 trimethoprim
NT3 trypanocides
NT4 benznidazole
NT4 diminazene
NT4 gossypol
NT4 homidium
NT4 isometamidium
NT4 melarsonyl
NT4 melarsoprol
NT4 nifurtimox

DRUGS *cont.*
NT4 nitrofural
NT4 pentamidine
NT4 puromycin
NT4 pyritidium
NT4 quinapyramine
NT4 suramin
NT4 tryparsamide
NT2 ectoparasiticides
NT3 amitraz
NT3 benzyl benzoate
NT3 bromocyclen
NT3 carbaryl
NT3 chloromethiuron
NT3 chlorpyrifos
NT3 closantel
NT3 coumaphos
NT3 crotamiton
NT3 crotoxyphos
NT3 crufomate
NT3 cyhalothrin
NT3 cypermethrin
NT3 cyromazine
NT3 cythioate
NT3 ddt
NT3 deltamethrin
NT3 diazinon
NT3 dichlorvos
NT3 dioxathion
NT3 ethion
NT3 famphur
NT3 fenchlorphos
NT3 fenthion
NT3 fenvalerate
NT3 flucythrinate
NT3 flumethrin
NT3 ivermectin
NT3 lindane
NT3 malathion
NT3 metolcarb
NT3 nifluridide
NT3 permethrin
NT3 phosalone
NT3 phosmet
NT3 phoxim
NT3 propetamphos
NT3 propoxur
NT3 quintiofos
NT3 rafoxanide
NT3 tetrachlorvinphos
NT3 trichlorfon
NT2 ovicides and larvicides
NT3 calcium cyanamide
NT3 calcium hydroxide
NT3 copper sulfate
NT3 disophenol
NT1 antipyretics
NT2 acetaminophen
NT1 cardiovascular agents
NT2 antihypertensive agents
NT3 chlorothiazide
NT3 diazoxide
NT3 furosemide
NT3 methyldopa
NT3 phenoxybenzamine
NT2 cardiac glycosides
NT3 digitonin
NT3 digitoxin
NT3 digoxin
NT3 lanatosides
NT3 strophanthins
NT4 ouabain
NT2 myocardial depressants
NT3 disopyramide
NT3 lidocaine
NT3 propranolol
NT3 quinidine
NT2 vasoconstrictor agents
NT2 vasodilator agents
NT3 bradykinin
NT3 chlorpromazine
NT3 dipyridamole
NT3 eledoisin
NT3 erythritol
NT3 isoxsuprine
NT3 kallikrein
NT3 papaverine
NT3 pindolol
NT3 propranolol
NT3 substance p
NT3 theobromine

DRUGS *cont.*
NT3 theophylline
NT1 dermatological agents
NT2 allantoin
NT2 astringents
NT2 aurothioglucose
NT2 betamethasone
NT2 calcium hydroxide
NT2 dexamethasone
NT2 dichloroacetic acid
NT2 formic acid
NT2 hydrocortisone
NT2 linseed oil
NT2 olive oil
NT2 petrolatum
NT2 pyrogallol triacetate
NT2 resorcinol
NT2 retinoic acid
NT2 salicylic acid
NT2 turpentine
NT1 detoxicants
NT2 4-aminopyridine
NT2 antidotes
NT3 dimercaprol
NT3 glutathione
NT3 methylene blue
NT3 pralidoxime
NT2 enzyme activators
NT3 pralidoxime
NT2 narcotic antagonists
NT3 diprenorphine
NT3 nad
NT3 naloxone
NT2 yohimbine
NT1 diuretics
NT2 acetazolamide
NT2 aminophylline
NT2 ammonium chloride
NT2 caffeine
NT2 chlorothiazide
NT2 formononetin
NT2 furosemide
NT2 hydrochlorothiazide
NT2 mannitol
NT2 mersalyl
NT2 potassium nitrate
NT2 sodium citrate
NT2 sorbitol
NT2 spironolactone
NT2 theobromine
NT2 theophylline
NT2 triamterene
NT2 urea
NT1 fertility agents
NT2 clomifene
NT1 gastrointestinal agents
NT2 antacids
NT3 aluminium hydroxide
NT3 aluminium phosphate
NT3 calcium carbonate
NT3 sodium bicarbonate
NT2 antibloat agents
NT3 simethicone
NT2 antidiarrhoea agents
NT3 calcium carbonate
NT3 kaolin
NT3 pectins
NT2 antiemetics
NT3 chlorpromazine
NT2 carminatives
NT3 carvone
NT3 chloroform
NT3 safrole
NT3 turpentine
NT2 cholagogues
NT2 digestants
NT3 cholic acid
NT3 deoxycholic acid
NT3 hydrochloric acid
NT3 pancreatin
NT3 taurocholic acid
NT3 ursodeoxycholic acid
NT2 emetics
NT3 apomorphine
NT2 laxatives
NT3 agar
NT3 docusate sodium
NT3 lactulose
NT3 linseed oil
NT3 liquid paraffin
NT3 methylcellulose

DRUGS *cont.*
NT3 olive oil
NT3 sorbitol
NT2 pentagastrin
NT2 purgatives
NT3 castor oil
NT3 emodin
NT3 germanium
NT3 magnesium sulfate
NT4 epsom salts
NT3 senna
NT3 sodium sulfate
NT2 tetragastrin
NT1 generics (agricola)
NT1 haematologic agents
NT2 anticoagulants
NT3 dicoumarol
NT3 edta
NT3 heparin
NT3 sodium citrate
NT3 warfarin
NT2 antilipaemics
NT3 d-thyroxine
NT3 3-hydroxy-3-methylglutaric acid
NT3 bezafibrate
NT3 clofibrate
NT3 colestipol
NT3 colestyramine
NT3 halofenate
NT3 niceritrol
NT3 ornithine
NT3 probucol
NT3 sucrose polyester
NT2 hypoglycaemic agents
NT3 buformin
NT3 chlorpropamide
NT3 glibenclamide
NT3 gliclazide
NT3 glipizide
NT3 glucagon
NT3 hypoglycine a
NT3 insulin
NT3 metformin
NT3 tolbutamide
NT2 hypolipaemic agents
NT3 orotic acid
NT2 plasma substitutes
NT3 polyvidona
NT2 prothrombin
NT2 thromboplastin
NT1 homeopathic drugs
NT1 immunosuppressive agents
NT2 cyclophosphamide
NT1 lipotropic factors
NT2 myo-inositol
NT2 betaine
NT2 choline
NT2 folic acid
NT2 konjak mannan
NT2 methionine
NT2 phosphatidylcholines
NT2 vitamin b12
NT3 cobamamide
NT3 cyanocobalamin
NT3 hydroxocobalamin
NT1 neurotropic drugs
NT2 anaesthetics
NT3 inhaled anaesthetics
NT4 ethyl ether
NT4 halothane
NT4 methoxyflurane
NT4 nitrous oxide
NT3 injectable anaesthetics
NT4 chloral hydrate
NT4 etomidate
NT4 etorphine
NT4 fentanyl
NT4 ketamine
NT4 methadone
NT4 methitural
NT4 metomidate
NT4 pentobarbital
NT4 phencyclidine
NT4 phenobarbital
NT4 thiopental
NT4 urethane
NT3 local anaesthetics
NT4 benzocaine
NT4 lidocaine
NT4 procaine

DRUGS *cont.*
NT2 analeptics
NT3 amfetamine
NT3 caffeine
NT3 diprenorphine
NT3 doxapram
NT3 strychnine
NT2 analgesics
NT3 acetaminophen
NT3 aspirin
NT3 codeine
NT3 etorphine
NT3 eugenol
NT3 fentanyl
NT3 indometacin
NT3 metergoline
NT3 methadone
NT3 morphine
NT3 opium
NT3 oxyphenbutazone
NT3 pethidine
NT3 phenacetin
NT3 phenazone
NT3 phenylbutazone
NT3 quinine
NT3 salicin
NT3 salicylamide
NT3 sodium salicylate
NT3 xylazine
NT2 anticonvulsants
NT3 magnesium sulfate
NT4 epsom salts
NT3 phenobarbital
NT3 phenytoin
NT3 sultroponium
NT3 valproic acid
NT2 cannabinoids
NT3 cannabidiol
NT3 tetrahydrocannabinol
NT2 cholinesterase inhibitors
NT3 neostigmine
NT3 physostigmine
NT2 muscle relaxants
NT3 decamethonium
NT3 gallamine triethiodide
NT3 guaifenesin
NT3 isoxsuprine
NT3 meprobamate
NT3 papaverine
NT3 suxamethonium
NT2 opioids
NT2 parasympatholytics
NT3 atropine
NT3 clidinium
NT3 dicycloverine
NT3 fenpipramide
NT3 levodopa
NT3 nicotine
NT3 papaverine
NT3 sultroponium
NT2 parasympathomimetics
NT3 acetylcholine
NT3 arecoline
NT3 bethanechol
NT3 carbachol
NT3 neostigmine
NT3 nicotine
NT3 physostigmine
NT3 pilocarpine
NT2 psychotropic drugs
NT3 antidepressants
NT4 desipramine
NT3 hallucinogens
NT4 psilocin
NT4 psilocybine
NT3 neuroleptics
NT4 azaperone
NT4 chloralose
NT4 chlordiazepoxide
NT4 diazepam
NT4 diprenorphine
NT4 droperidol
NT4 elfazepam
NT4 fentanyl
NT4 haloperidol
NT4 meprobamate
NT4 pimozide
NT4 promazine
NT4 propiomazine
NT4 reserpine
NT4 thalidomide

DRUGS *cont.*
NT4 triflupromazine
NT4 valerian
NT2 sympatholytics
NT3 β-blockers
NT4 ergot alkaloids
NT5 dihydroergocryptine
NT5 ergometrine
NT3 atenolol
NT3 carazolol
NT3 metoprolol
NT3 oxprenolol
NT3 pindolol
NT3 propranolol
NT3 reserpine
NT3 yohimbine
NT2 sympathomimetics
NT3 clenbuterol
NT3 ephedrine
NT3 fenfluramine
NT3 isoprenaline
NT3 methoxamine
NT3 metizoline
NT3 norepinephrine
NT3 tyramine
NT1 new drugs
NT1 oral contraceptives
NT2 chlormadinone
NT2 medroxyprogesterone
NT2 megestrol
NT2 mestranol
NT2 norethisterone
NT1 respiratory system agents
NT2 antitussive agents
NT3 expectorants
NT4 ammonium bicarbonate
NT4 ammonium chloride
NT4 creosote
NT4 eucalyptol
NT4 guaiacol
NT4 guaifenesin
NT4 potassium iodide
NT4 turpentine
NT2 bronchodilators
NT3 clenbuterol
NT1 stimulants
NT2 antidepressants
NT3 desipramine
NT2 appetite stimulants
NT3 brotizolam
NT3 elfazepam
NT2 caffeine
NT2 phagostimulants
NT2 strychnine
NT2 tonics
NT1 traditional medicines
rt drug addiction
rt drug allergies
rt drug combinations
rt drug delivery systems
rt drug effects (agricola)
rt drug excretion
rt drug formulations
rt drug metabolism
rt drug residues
rt drug resistance
rt drug synergy
rt drug therapy
rt drug toxicity
rt hormone antagonists
rt immunostimulants
rt medicinal plants
rt mode of action
rt nutrient drug interactions (agricola)
rt pharmacology
rt pharmacy
rt placebos (agricola)
rt prescriptions
rt structure activity relationships
rt usage

DRUM DRIERS
AF drum dryers
uf driers, drum
BT1 driers
BT2 farm machinery
BT3 machinery

DRUM DRYERS
BF drum driers

DRUM DRYERS *cont.*
BT1 dryers

DRUMS
BT1 components

DRY BEANS (AGRICOLA)
BT1 dried foods
BT2 foods

DRY CLEANING (AGRICOLA)
BT1 cleaning
BT2 processing

DRY CONDITIONS
BT1 soil water regimes
rt arid climate
rt arid regions
rt drought
rt soil water regimes

DRY FARMING
uf dryland farming
BT1 cropping systems
rt arid regions

DRY FEEDING
uf feeding, dry
BT1 feeding
rt dry feeds

DRY FEEDS
BT1 feeds
rt dry feeding

DRY LOT FEEDING
BT1 fattening
BT2 animal feeding
BT3 feeding
rt feedlots

DRY MATTER
BT1 composition
rt dry matter accumulation
rt dry matter distribution
rt moisture content
rt water content

DRY MATTER ACCUMULATION
rt dry matter
rt dry matter distribution

DRY MATTER DISTRIBUTION
HN from 1989
BT1 distribution
rt dry matter
rt dry matter accumulation

DRY PERIOD
uf drying off
rt calving interval
rt lactation
rt lactation duration

DRY ROT
rt wood destroying fungi

DRY SEASON
BT1 seasons
rt drought

DRYANDRA
BT1 euphorbiaceae
NT1 dryandra praemorsa

DRYANDRA PRAEMORSA
BT1 dryandra
BT2 euphorbiaceae
BT1 ornamental woody plants

DRYERS
BF driers
NT1 barn dryers
NT1 batch dryers
NT1 cascade dryers
NT1 concurrent flow dryers
NT1 continuous dryers
NT1 convection dryers
NT1 conveyor dryers
NT1 counterflow dryers
NT1 cross flow dryers
NT1 deep bed dryers
NT1 drum dryers
NT1 electric dryers
NT1 floor dryers

DRYERS *cont.*
NT1 forage dryers
NT1 grain dryers
NT1 high temperature dryers
NT1 infrared dryers
NT1 microwave dryers
NT1 roller dryers
NT1 shallow bed dryers
NT1 spray dryers
NT1 tower dryers
NT1 tray dryers
NT1 tunnel dryers
NT1 ventilated bin dryers
NT1 ventilated silo dryers

DRYING
uf seasoning
BT1 dehydration
BT2 processing
NT1 air drying
NT1 artificial drying
NT1 barn drying
NT1 compression drying
NT1 dehumidification
NT1 drying methods
NT1 drying schedules
NT1 drying under restraint
NT1 end coating
NT1 field drying
NT1 fluidized bed drying
NT1 forced air drying
NT1 freeze drying
NT1 grain drying
NT2 drieration
NT1 high frequency drying
NT1 intermittent drying
NT1 jet drying
NT1 low temperature drying
NT1 natural drying
NT1 platen drying
NT1 roller drying
NT1 solar drying
NT1 solvent drying
NT1 spray drying
NT1 vacuum drying
NT1 vapour drying
rt case hardening
rt conditioning
rt curing
rt desiccants
rt desiccation
rt dewatering
rt dried honey
rt drying air
rt drying front
rt drying quality
rt drying temperature
rt evaporation
rt forage conditioning
rt haymaking
rt heating
rt kiln schedules
rt kilns
rt preservation
rt soil water balance
rt stickers
rt storage
rt windrows

DRYING AIR
BT1 air
BT2 gases
rt air drying
rt driers
rt drying

drying, freeze
USE **freeze drying**

DRYING FRONT
rt drying
rt soil water movement

drying, intermittent
USE **intermittent drying**

drying machinery
USE **driers**

DRYING METHODS
BT1 drying
BT2 dehydration
BT3 processing

DRYING METHODS *cont.*
BT1 methodology

drying off
USE **dry period**

DRYING OILS
BT1 fatty oils
BT2 oils
NT1 tung oil

DRYING QUALITY
uf *quality for drying*
BT1 food processing quality
BT2 processing quality
BT3 quality
rt drying

DRYING SCHEDULES
BT1 drying
BT2 dehydration
BT3 processing

DRYING TEMPERATURE
BT1 temperature
rt drying

DRYING UNDER RESTRAINT
BT1 drying
BT2 dehydration
BT3 processing

dryland farming
USE **dry farming**

DRYMARIA
BT1 caryophyllaceae
NT1 drymaria arenarioides
NT1 drymaria cordata
NT1 drymaria diandra

DRYMARIA ARENARIOIDES
BT1 drymaria
BT2 caryophyllaceae

DRYMARIA CORDATA
BT1 drymaria
BT2 caryophyllaceae

DRYMARIA DIANDRA
BT1 drymaria
BT2 caryophyllaceae

DRYOBALANOPS
BT1 dipterocarpaceae
NT1 dryobalanops aromatica

DRYOBALANOPS AROMATICA
BT1 dryobalanops
BT2 dipterocarpaceae
BT1 forest trees

DRYOCOETES
BT1 scolytidae
BT2 coleoptera
NT1 dryocoetes affaber
NT1 dryocoetes autographus

DRYOCOETES AFFABER
BT1 dryocoetes
BT2 scolytidae
BT3 coleoptera

DRYOCOETES AUTOGRAPHUS
BT1 dryocoetes
BT2 scolytidae
BT3 coleoptera

DRYOCOPUS
BT1 picidae
BT2 piciformes
BT3 birds
NT1 dryocopus martius

DRYOCOPUS MARTIUS
BT1 dryocopus
BT2 picidae
BT3 piciformes
BT4 birds

DRYOCOSMUS
BT1 cynipidae
BT2 hymenoptera
NT1 dryocosmus kuriphilus

DRYOCOSMUS KURIPHILUS
BT1 dryocosmus
BT2 cynipidae
BT3 hymenoptera

DRYOMYZA
BT1 dryomyzidae
BT2 diptera
NT1 dryomyza anilis

DRYOMYZA ANILIS
BT1 dryomyza
BT2 dryomyzidae
BT3 diptera

DRYOMYZIDAE
BT1 diptera
NT1 dryomyza
NT2 dryomyza anilis

DRYOPTERIS
BT1 aspidiaceae
NT1 dryopteris affinis
NT1 dryopteris assimilis
NT1 dryopteris carthusiana
NT1 dryopteris chrysocoma
NT1 dryopteris cochleata
NT1 dryopteris erythrosora
NT1 dryopteris filix-mas
NT1 dryopteris marginalis
rt antibacterial plants

DRYOPTERIS AFFINIS
uf *dryopteris borreri*
BT1 dryopteris
BT2 aspidiaceae
BT1 ornamental ferns
BT2 ferns
BT2 ornamental foliage plants
BT3 foliage plants

DRYOPTERIS ASSIMILIS
BT1 dryopteris
BT2 aspidiaceae

dryopteris borreri
USE **dryopteris affinis**

DRYOPTERIS CARTHUSIANA
BT1 antibacterial plants
BT1 dryopteris
BT2 aspidiaceae

DRYOPTERIS CHRYSOCOMA
BT1 dryopteris
BT2 aspidiaceae

DRYOPTERIS COCHLEATA
BT1 dryopteris
BT2 aspidiaceae
BT1 ornamental ferns
BT2 ferns
BT2 ornamental foliage plants
BT3 foliage plants

DRYOPTERIS ERYTHROSORA
BT1 dryopteris
BT2 aspidiaceae
BT1 ornamental ferns
BT2 ferns
BT2 ornamental foliage plants
BT3 foliage plants

DRYOPTERIS FILIX-MAS
BT1 antibacterial plants
BT1 dryopteris
BT2 aspidiaceae
BT1 ornamental ferns
BT2 ferns
BT2 ornamental foliage plants
BT3 foliage plants

DRYOPTERIS MARGINALIS
BT1 dryopteris
BT2 aspidiaceae

DRYPETES
uf *putranjiva*
BT1 euphorbiaceae
NT1 drypetes roxburghii

DRYPETES ROXBURGHII
uf *putranjiva roxburghii*
BT1 drypetes
BT2 euphorbiaceae

DRYPETES ROXBURGHII *cont.*
BT1 ornamental woody plants

DRYSDALE
HN from 1990
BT1 sheep breeds
BT2 breeds

DSMA
uf *disodium methylarsonate*
BT1 arsenical herbicides
BT2 arsenicals
BT2 herbicides
BT3 pesticides

DUABANGA
BT1 sonneratiaceae
NT1 duabanga grandiflora

DUABANGA GRANDIFLORA
BT1 duabanga
BT2 sonneratiaceae

DUAL PURPOSE BREEDS
BT1 breeds
rt dual purpose cattle

DUAL PURPOSE BULL
BT1 dual purpose cattle
BT2 cattle breeds
BT3 breeds

DUAL PURPOSE CATTLE
uf *cattle, dual purpose*
BT1 cattle breeds
BT2 breeds
NT1 dual purpose bull
rt dual purpose breeds
rt multiple use

DUAL TIRES
BF dual tyres
BT1 tires

DUAL TYRES
AF dual tires
uf *tyres, dual*
BT1 tyres
BT2 components

dualism, economic
USE **economic dualism**

DUAN
HN from 1990
BT1 goat breeds
BT2 breeds

DUBAI
BT1 united arab emirates
BT2 persian gulf states
BT3 west asia
BT4 asia

DUBOISIA
BT1 orchidaceae
NT1 duboisia hopwoodii
NT1 duboisia leichhardtii
NT1 duboisia myoporoides

DUBOISIA HOPWOODII
BT1 duboisia
BT2 orchidaceae
BT1 medicinal plants

DUBOISIA LEICHHARDTII
BT1 duboisia
BT2 orchidaceae

DUBOISIA MYOPOROIDES
BT1 duboisia
BT2 orchidaceae

DUBOSCQIA
BT1 microspora
BT2 protozoa

DUBROVNIK
BT1 sheep breeds
BT2 breeds

DUCHESNEA
BT1 rosaceae
NT1 duchesnea indica

DUCHESNEA INDICA
BT1 duchesnea
BT2 rosaceae

duck
USE **ducks**

DUCK (AGRICOLA)
BT1 fabrics

duck-billed platypus
USE **ornithorhynchus anatinus**

DUCK DISEASES
BT1 poultry diseases
BT2 animal diseases
BT3 diseases
rt ducks

DUCK EGGS
uf *egg, duck*
BT1 eggs
BT2 poultry products
BT3 animal products
BT4 products
rt ducks

duck enteritis virus
USE **duck plague virus**

DUCK FATTENING
BT1 poultry fattening
BT2 fattening
BT3 animal feeding
BT4 feeding
rt ducks

DUCK FEEDING
BT1 poultry feeding
BT2 livestock feeding
BT3 animal feeding
BT4 feeding
rt ducks

DUCK HEPATITIS VIRUS
BT1 enterovirus
BT2 picornaviridae
BT3 viruses
rt hepatitis
rt poultry diseases

DUCK MEAT
BT1 poultry meat
BT2 meat
BT3 animal products
BT4 products
BT3 foods
rt ducks

DUCK PLAGUE VIRUS
uf *duck enteritis virus*
BT1 avian herpesvirus
BT2 herpesviridae
BT3 viruses
rt poultry diseases

DUCKLINGS
BT1 young animals
BT2 animals
rt ducks

DUCKS
uf *duck*
BT1 poultry
BT2 livestock
BT3 animals
NT1 muscovy ducks
rt anatidae
rt duck diseases
rt duck eggs
rt duck fattening
rt duck feeding
rt duck meat
rt ducklings

ducks, muscovy
USE **muscovy ducks**

ductless glands
USE **endocrine glands**

DUCTS
BT1 tubes
NT1 plastic ducts
rt canals

DUCTS *cont.*
rt pipes
rt vessels

ducts, plastic
USE **plastic ducts**

DUCTUS ARTERIOSUS
BT1 blood vessels
BT2 cardiovascular system
BT3 body parts
rt fetus

DUCTUS DEFERENS
uf vas deferens
BT1 male genitalia
BT2 genitalia
BT3 urogenital system
BT4 body parts
NT1 ampulla
rt epididymis
rt vasectomy

duff
USE **forest litter**

DUFOUREA
BT1 apidae
BT2 hymenoptera

DUGBE VIRUS
BT1 nairovirus
BT2 arboviruses
BT3 pathogens
BT2 bunyaviridae
BT3 viruses

DUGESIA
BT1 planariidae
BT2 tricladida
BT3 turbellaria
NT1 dugesia dorotocephala
NT1 dugesia tigrina

DUGESIA DOROTOCEPHALA
HN from 1990
BT1 dugesia
BT2 planariidae
BT3 tricladida
BT4 turbellaria

DUGESIA TIGRINA
BT1 dugesia
BT2 planariidae
BT3 tricladida
BT4 turbellaria

DUGONG
BT1 dugongidae
BT2 sirenia
BT3 mammals
NT1 dugong dugon

DUGONG DUGON
BT1 dugong
BT2 dugongidae
BT3 sirenia
BT4 mammals

DUGONGIDAE
BT1 sirenia
BT2 mammals
NT1 dugong
NT2 dugong dugon

DUGUETIA
BT1 annonaceae
NT1 duguetia calycina

DUGUETIA CALYCINA
BT1 duguetia
BT2 annonaceae

DULCAMARA MOTTLE TYMOVIRUS
HN from 1990
BT1 tymovirus group
BT2 plant viruses
BT3 plant pathogens
BT4 pathogens

DULCE DE LECHE
BT1 milk products
BT2 products

dulcitol
USE **galactitol**

DUMBI
HN from 1990
BT1 sheep breeds
BT2 breeds

DUMMIES
NT1 anthropometric dummies
rt physical models

DUMPING
rt export subsidies
rt price discrimination

DUMPING SYNDROME
BT1 gastrointestinal diseases
BT2 digestive system diseases
BT3 organic diseases
BT4 diseases
rt gastrectomy

DUNALIELLA
BT1 chlorophyta
BT2 algae
NT1 dunaliella tertiolecta

DUNALIELLA TERTIOLECTA
BT1 dunaliella
BT2 chlorophyta
BT3 algae

DUNE GRASSLANDS
uf grasslands, dune
BT1 grasslands
BT2 vegetation types
rt duneland plants
rt dunes

DUNE SAND
BT1 soil parent materials
rt sand

DUNE SLACK SOILS
BT1 soil types (physiographic)
rt dune soils

DUNE SOILS
BT1 soil types (physiographic)
rt dune slack soils
rt duneland soils
rt dunes

DUNELAND
BT1 land types
rt dunes

DUNELAND PLANTS
rt dune grasslands
rt dunes
rt plant communities
rt plants
rt sand dune stabilization

DUNELAND SOILS
BT1 soil types (physiographic)
rt dune soils
rt dunes

DUNES
uf sand dunes
BT1 physiographic features
rt dune grasslands
rt dune soils
rt duneland
rt duneland plants
rt duneland soils
rt mounds
rt sand
rt sand dune stabilization
rt sandy soils

dung
USE **faeces**
OR **farmyard manure**

DUNG BEETLES
BT1 beneficial insects
BT2 beneficial arthropods
BT3 beneficial organisms
BT2 insects
BT3 arthropods

DUODENAL FLUIDS
BT1 digestive juices
BT2 body fluids
BT3 fluids
rt duodenum

DUODENAL OBSTRUCTION
BT1 intestinal obstruction
BT2 obstruction
BT3 digestive disorders
BT4 functional disorders
BT5 animal disorders
BT6 disorders
rt duodenum

DUODENAL ULCER
uf ulcer, duodenal
BT1 peptic ulcer
BT2 gastrointestinal diseases
BT3 digestive system diseases
BT4 organic diseases
BT5 diseases
BT2 ulcers
BT3 symptoms
rt cannulae
rt duodenum
rt gastric ulcer

DUODENUM
BT1 small intestine
BT2 intestines
BT3 digestive system
BT4 body parts
rt duodenal fluids
rt duodenal obstruction
rt duodenal ulcer

DUPLEX SOILS
BT1 argilluvic soils
BT2 soil types (genetic)

DUPLICATION
BT1 replication

DUPONTIA
BT1 gramineae
NT1 dupontia fisheri

DUPONTIA FISHERI
BT1 dupontia
BT2 gramineae
BT1 pasture plants

DURABILITY
rt decay
rt heartwood
rt longevity
rt resistance
rt service life
rt wear

durable press finishes
USE **wrinkle resistant finishes (agricola)**

DURANTA
BT1 verbenaceae
NT1 duranta repens

duranta plumieri
USE **duranta repens**

DURANTA REPENS
uf duranta plumieri
BT1 duranta
BT2 verbenaceae
BT1 insecticidal plants
BT2 pesticidal plants
BT1 ornamental woody plants

DURATION
BT1 time
NT1 gestation period
NT1 lactation duration
NT1 leaf duration
NT1 postpartum period
NT1 preimplantation period
NT1 prenatal period
NT2 preincubation period
NT1 preovulatory period
NT1 prepartum period
NT1 preweaning period
rt age
rt length

DURATION *cont.*
rt operating time

DURIANS
BT1 tropical tree fruits
BT2 tree fruits
BT2 tropical fruits
BT3 fruit crops
rt durio zibethinus

DURICRUSTS
uf lateritic crusts
BT1 soil morphological features

DURIO
BT1 bombacaceae
NT1 durio zibethinus

DURIO ZIBETHINUS
BT1 durio
BT2 bombacaceae
rt durians

DURIPANS
BT1 soil morphological features

DUROC
BT1 pig breeds
BT2 breeds

durras
USE **sorghum bicolor**

DUST
NT1 grain dust
NT1 house dust
NT1 sugar dust
NT1 wood dust
rt dust control
rt dust extractors
rt dust storms
rt dusts
rt particles
rt silicosis
rt smoke

DUST BATHING
HN from 1989
BT1 animal behaviour
BT2 behaviour

DUST CONTROL
BT1 control
rt dust
rt dust extractors

DUST EXTRACTORS
BT1 extractors
BT2 equipment
rt air cleaners
rt air conditioners
rt cyclones
rt dust
rt dust control
rt separators

DUST STORMS
BT1 storms
BT2 meteorological factors
BT3 climatic factors
BT2 natural disasters
BT3 disasters
rt dust

dustbins
USE **refuse containers**

DUSTING
BT1 application methods
BT2 methodology
rt dusts

DUSTS
BT1 formulations
rt dust
rt dusting
rt powders

DUTCH BARNS
uf barns, dutch
BT1 barns
BT2 farm buildings
BT3 buildings
BT2 stores

DUTCH BLACK PIED
BT1 cattle breeds
BT2 breeds

DUTCH CHEESE
BT1 cheeses
BT2 milk products
BT3 products

dutch guyana
USE **surinam**

DUTCH LANDRACE
BT1 pig breeds
BT2 breeds

dutch lights
USE **frames**

DUTCH TOGGENBURG
HN from 1990
BT1 goat breeds
BT2 breeds

DUTCH WHITE
HN from 1990
BT1 goat breeds
BT2 breeds

DUTCH YORKSHIRE
BT1 pig breeds
BT2 breeds

DUTY FREE ALLOWANCES
BT1 tariffs
BT2 import controls
BT3 controls
BT3 trade barriers
BT4 trade protection
BT5 trade policy
BT6 economic policy

DUVANES
BT1 diterpenoids
BT2 terpenoids
BT3 isoprenoids
BT4 lipids

DWARF CULTIVARS
BT1 cultivars
BT2 varieties

DWARFING
(plants)
rt growth retardants
rt rootstocks

DWARFISM
(animals)
BT1 growth disorders
BT2 animal disorders
BT3 disorders
rt bone diseases
rt height

DWELLINGS
uf houses
BT1 housing

DYCKIA
BT1 bromeliaceae

DYE BINDING
BT1 analytical methods
BT2 methodology
NT1 amido black method

DYE LABELING
BF dye labelling
BT1 labeling

DYE LABELLING
AF dye labeling
BT1 techniques
rt dyes

DYE PLANTS
NT1 acacia catechu
NT1 acacia harpophylla
NT1 adenanthera pavonina
NT1 aegle marmelos
NT1 agrimonia eupatoria
NT1 alkanna tuberculata
NT1 anthemis tinctoria
NT1 arcangelisia flava
NT1 asphodelus microcarpus

DYE PLANTS *cont.*
NT1 berberis vulgaris
NT1 bixa orellana
NT1 carthamus tinctorius
NT1 cladrastis kentukea
NT1 coscinium fenestratum
NT1 crocus sativus
NT1 curcuma longa
NT1 datisca cannabina
NT1 datura fastuosa
NT1 enantia polycarpa
NT1 euclea natalensis
NT1 garcinia cambogia
NT1 garcinia xanthochymus
NT1 genista tinctoria
NT1 gentiana pneumonanthe
NT1 glycyrrhiza glabra
NT1 indigofera anil
NT1 indigofera arrecta
NT1 indigofera tinctoria
NT1 iris pseudacorus
NT1 isatis tinctoria
NT1 koelreuteria paniculata
NT1 lannea coromandelica
NT1 lawsonia inermis
NT1 leonurus cardiaca
NT1 lithospermum erythrorhizon
NT1 maclura pomifera
NT1 mallotus philippensis
NT1 marsdenia tinctoria
NT1 morinda tinctoria
NT1 oldenlandia corymbosa
NT1 papaver rhoeas
NT1 quercus velutina
NT1 reseda luteola
NT1 rivina humilis
NT1 roemeria refracta
NT1 rubia cordifolia
NT1 rubia iberica
NT1 rubia tinctorum
NT1 toddalia asiatica
NT1 uncaria gambir
rt dyes
rt horticultural crops
rt industrial crops
rt plants

DYEING (AGRICOLA)
BT1 processing
NT1 batik (agricola)
NT1 cross dyeing (agricola)
NT1 piece dyeing (agricola)
NT1 solid dyeing (agricola)
NT1 solution dyeing (agricola)
NT1 stock dyeing (agricola)
NT1 tie dyeing (agricola)
NT1 union dyeing (agricola)
NT1 yarn dyeing (agricola)
rt textile industry

DYERA
BT1 apocynaceae
NT1 dyera costulata

DYERA COSTULATA
BT1 dyera
BT2 apocynaceae

DYES
uf colouring compounds
uf colourings
uf dyestuffs
NT1 p-dimethylaminoazobenzene
NT1 amaranth dye
NT1 azine dyes
NT1 curcumin
NT1 eosine
NT1 erythrosine
NT1 ferrous sulfate
NT1 fluorescein
NT1 fluorescent dyes
NT1 gentian violet
NT1 malachite green
NT1 pyrogallol
NT1 quercitrin
NT1 rose bengal
NT1 tetrazolium dyes
NT2 2,3,5-triphenyltetrazolium chloride
NT2 nitroblue tetrazolium
NT1 trypan blue
rt acridines

DYES *cont.*
rt azo compounds
rt benzaldehyde
rt biguanides
rt chrysanthemic acid
rt coumarins
rt dye labelling
rt dye plants
rt fastness (agricola)
rt food additives
rt food colourants
rt non-food products
rt pigments
rt plant products
rt vats

dyestuffs
USE **dyes**

DYKES
AF dikes
BT1 dams
BT2 barriers
BT1 ditches
BT2 channels
BT1 ridges

DYNAMIC LOADS
uf loads, dynamic
BT1 loads
rt dynamics
rt static loads

DYNAMIC MODELS
uf models, dynamic
BT1 mathematical models
BT2 models
BT2 optimization methods
BT3 optimization

DYNAMIC PROGRAMMING
uf programming, dynamic
BT1 programming
BT2 optimization methods
BT3 optimization
rt recursive programming

DYNAMIC TESTING
uf testing, dynamic
BT1 testing
rt dynamics

DYNAMICS
BT1 mechanics
BT2 physics
NT1 aerodynamics
NT1 hydrodynamics
rt dynamic loads
rt dynamic testing
rt forces
rt kinematics
rt kinetics
rt momentum
rt population dynamics
rt statics

DYNAMOMETERS
BT1 instruments
rt forces
rt loads
rt power
rt traction

DYSAPHIS
BT1 aphididae
BT2 aphidoidea
BT3 sternorrhyncha
BT4 homoptera
NT1 dysaphis crataegi
NT1 dysaphis devecta
NT1 dysaphis plantaginea
NT1 dysaphis pyri
NT1 dysaphis reaumuri
rt anuraphis

DYSAPHIS CRATAEGI
BT1 dysaphis
BT2 aphididae
BT3 aphidoidea
BT4 sternorrhyncha
BT5 homoptera

DYSAPHIS DEVECTA
uf anuraphis devecta

DYSAPHIS DEVECTA *cont.*
BT1 dysaphis
BT2 aphididae
BT3 aphidoidea
BT4 sternorrhyncha
BT5 homoptera

dysaphis mali
USE **dysaphis plantaginea**

DYSAPHIS PLANTAGINEA
uf dysaphis mali
BT1 dysaphis
BT2 aphididae
BT3 aphidoidea
BT4 sternorrhyncha
BT5 homoptera

DYSAPHIS PYRI
BT1 dysaphis
BT2 aphididae
BT3 aphidoidea
BT4 sternorrhyncha
BT5 homoptera

DYSAPHIS REAUMURI
BT1 dysaphis
BT2 aphididae
BT3 aphidoidea
BT4 sternorrhyncha
BT5 homoptera

DYSAUTONOMIA
HN from 1990
uf feline dysautonomia
uf key-gaskell syndrome
BT1 nervous system diseases
BT2 organic diseases
BT3 diseases
NT1 grass sickness
rt autonomic nervous system

DYSCHONDROPLASIA
BT1 bone diseases
BT2 organic diseases
BT3 diseases

DYSDERCUS
BT1 pyrrhocoridae
BT2 heteroptera
NT1 dysdercus cingulatus
NT1 dysdercus fasciatus
NT1 dysdercus intermedius
NT1 dysdercus koenigii
NT1 dysdercus superstitiosus
NT1 dysdercus voelkeri

DYSDERCUS CINGULATUS
uf dysdercus megalopygus
BT1 dysdercus
BT2 pyrrhocoridae
BT3 heteroptera

DYSDERCUS FASCIATUS
BT1 dysdercus
BT2 pyrrhocoridae
BT3 heteroptera

DYSDERCUS INTERMEDIUS
BT1 dysdercus
BT2 pyrrhocoridae
BT3 heteroptera

DYSDERCUS KOENIGII
BT1 dysdercus
BT2 pyrrhocoridae
BT3 heteroptera

dysdercus megalopygus
USE **dysdercus cingulatus**

DYSDERCUS SUPERSTITIOSUS
BT1 dysdercus
BT2 pyrrhocoridae
BT3 heteroptera

DYSDERCUS VOELKERI
BT1 dysdercus
BT2 pyrrhocoridae
BT3 heteroptera

DYSENTERY
BT1 intestinal diseases
BT2 gastrointestinal diseases
BT3 digestive system diseases

DYSENTERY *cont.*
BT4 organic diseases
BT5 diseases
NT1 swine dysentery
rt enteritis
rt intestines

DYSGENESIS
HN from 1989
BT1 sex differentiation disorders
BT2 congenital abnormalities
BT3 abnormalities
BT2 reproductive disorders
BT3 functional disorders
BT4 animal disorders
BT5 disorders

DYSMICOCCUS
BT1 pseudococcidae
BT2 coccoidea
BT3 sternorrhyncha
BT4 homoptera
NT1 dysmicoccus brevipes

DYSMICOCCUS BREVIPES
BT1 dysmicoccus
BT2 pseudococcidae
BT3 coccoidea
BT4 sternorrhyncha
BT5 homoptera

DYSOXYLUM
BT1 meliaceae
NT1 dysoxylum binectariferum
NT1 dysoxylum malabaricum
rt antibacterial plants
rt piscicidal plants

DYSOXYLUM BINECTARIFERUM
BT1 dysoxylum
BT2 meliaceae

DYSOXYLUM MALABARICUM
BT1 dysoxylum
BT2 meliaceae

DYSPEPSIA
uf *indigestion*
BT1 digestive disorders
BT2 functional disorders
BT3 animal disorders
BT4 disorders

DYSPLASIA
BT1 abnormalities
BT1 bone diseases
BT2 organic diseases
BT3 diseases

DYSPNEA
BF dyspnoea

DYSPNOEA
AF dyspnea
BT1 respiratory disorders
BT2 functional disorders
BT3 animal disorders
BT4 disorders
BT2 respiratory diseases
BT3 organic diseases
BT4 diseases

DYSREGULATION
BT1 functional disorders
BT2 animal disorders
BT3 disorders
NT1 coma
NT2 diabetic coma
NT1 convulsions
NT1 spasms
NT1 spastic paresis
NT1 tremor
NT2 congenital tremor
rt retention

DYSTOCIA
BT1 parturition complications
BT2 reproductive disorders
BT3 functional disorders
BT4 animal disorders
BT5 disorders
rt parturition

DYSTRANDEPTS
BT1 andepts
BT2 andosols
BT3 soil types (genetic)

dystrophy, muscular
USE **muscular dystrophy**

DYTISCIDAE
BT1 coleoptera
NT1 cybister
NT1 rhantus

E VALUES
BT1 indexes of nutrient availability
BT2 indexes

EAGGF
(european agricultural and guarantee fund)
uf *feoga*
BT1 funds
BT1 international organizations
BT2 organizations
rt european communities

EAGLES
BT1 predatory birds
BT2 predators
rt accipitridae

EAR CROPPING
BT1 surgical operations
rt ears
rt identification

EAR DISEASES
BT1 organic diseases
BT2 diseases
NT1 otitis
rt deafness
rt ears
rt equilibrium disorders
rt hearing impairment

ear muffs
USE **hearing protectors**

EAR TAGS
BT1 application methods
BT2 methodology
rt ectoparasiticides
rt formulations

EARIAS
BT1 noctuidae
BT2 lepidoptera
NT1 earias biplaga
NT1 earias cupreoviridis
NT1 earias insulana
NT1 earias vittella

EARIAS BIPLAGA
BT1 earias
BT2 noctuidae
BT3 lepidoptera

EARIAS CUPREOVIRIDIS
BT1 earias
BT2 noctuidae
BT3 lepidoptera

earias fabia
USE **earias vittella**

EARIAS INSULANA
BT1 earias
BT2 noctuidae
BT3 lepidoptera

EARIAS VITTELLA
uf *earias fabia*
BT1 earias
BT2 noctuidae
BT3 lepidoptera

EARLINESS
BT1 growth period
rt flowering date
rt forcing

early and late wood
USE **earlywood**
OR **latewood**

EARLY CHILDHOOD DEVELOPMENT (AGRICOLA)
BT1 child development (agricola)
rt early childhood education (agricola)
rt infant development (agricola)

EARLY CHILDHOOD EDUCATION (AGRICOLA)
BT1 education

EARLY CHILDHOOD EDUCATION (AGRICOLA) *cont.*
rt child development centers (agricola)
rt day care centers (agricola)
rt early childhood development (agricola)
rt infant stimulation centers (agricola)
rt kindergarten (agricola)
rt nursery schools (agricola)
rt preschool education
rt primary education

EARLY POTATOES
rt potatoes

EARLY PREGNANCY FACTOR
HN from 1990
BT1 animal proteins
BT2 proteins
BT3 peptides

EARLY SELECTION
uf *selection, early*
BT1 selection
rt selection criteria

EARLY WEANING
uf *weaning, early*
BT1 weaning

early wood
USE **earlywood**

EARLYWOOD
HN from 1990; previously "early wood"
uf *early and late wood*
uf *early wood*
BT1 growth rings
BT2 wood anatomy
BT3 plant anatomy
BT4 anatomy
BT5 biology
rt wood density

EARNED INCOME
uf *remunerations*
BT1 income
NT1 wages
NT2 piece work wages
NT2 time wages
NT2 wages in kind
rt farm results
rt fees

EARS
BT1 sense organs
BT2 body parts
NT1 guttural pouch
rt ear cropping
rt ear diseases
rt hearing

ears (plant)
USE **maize ears**
OR **spikes**

EARTH MOVING EQUIPMENT
BT1 equipment
NT1 bulldozers
NT1 excavators
NT1 land levellers
NT1 power shovels
NT1 scrapers
NT1 trench cutters
rt buckets
rt cross country vehicles
rt drainage equipment
rt farm machinery
rt scoops

earth tremors
USE **earthquakes**

EARTHING
BT1 electrical engineering
BT2 engineering
rt electric current
rt electrical safety
rt lightning conductors

EARTHING UP
BT1 cultivation
rt blanching
rt ridging

EARTHQUAKES
uf *earth tremors*
BT1 natural disasters
BT2 disasters
rt tectonics

earthworm casts
USE **worm casts**

EARTHWORM CHANNELS
BT1 channels
BT1 soil micromorphological features
BT2 soil morphological features
rt earthworms

EARTHWORMS
BT1 soil invertebrates
BT2 soil fauna
BT3 fauna
rt earthworm channels
rt oligochaeta
rt vermicomposting
rt vermiculture
rt worm casts

EAST AFRICA
uf *africa, east*
BT1 africa south of sahara
BT2 africa
NT1 chagos archipelago
NT1 djibouti
NT1 ethiopia
NT1 kenya
NT1 malawi
NT1 rwanda
NT1 seychelles
NT1 somalia
NT1 sudan
NT1 tanzania
NT2 zanzibar
NT1 uganda
rt sadcc countries

EAST ANATOLIAN RED
HN from 1990
BT1 cattle breeds
BT2 breeds

EAST ASIA
uf *asia, east*
BT1 asia
NT1 china
NT2 anhui
NT2 beijing
NT2 central southern china
NT2 eastern china
NT2 fujian
NT2 gansu
NT2 guangdong
NT2 guangxi
NT2 guizhou
NT2 hebei
NT2 heilongjiang
NT2 henan
NT2 hubei
NT2 hunan
NT2 jiangsu
NT2 jiangxi
NT2 jilin
NT2 liaoning
NT2 nei menggu
NT2 ningxia
NT2 north eastern china
NT2 north western china
NT2 northern china
NT2 qinghai
NT2 shaanxi
NT2 shandong
NT2 shanghai
NT2 shanxi
NT2 sichuan
NT2 south western china
NT2 tianjin
NT2 tibet
NT2 xinjiang
NT2 yunnan
NT2 zhejiang

EAST ASIA *cont.*
NT1 hong kong
NT1 japan
NT2 hokkaido
NT2 honshu
NT2 kyushu
NT2 ryukyu archipelago
NT2 shikoku
NT1 korea democratic people's republic
NT1 korea republic
NT1 macao
NT1 mongolia
NT1 ussr far east
rt ussr

EAST BALKAN
BT1 pig breeds
BT2 breeds

EAST BERLIN
BT1 berlin
BT2 europe
rt german democratic republic

EAST BRAZIL
uf *brazil (east)*
BT1 brazil
BT2 south america
BT3 america

EAST BULGARIAN
BT1 horse breeds
BT2 breeds

EAST CHINA SEA
BT1 northwest pacific
BT2 pacific ocean
BT3 marine areas

east coast fever
USE **theileria parva**

EAST FLANDERS
uf *belgium (east flanders)*
uf *flanders, east*
uf *oost-vlanderen*
BT1 belgium
BT2 western europe
BT3 europe

EAST FRIESIAN
BT1 horse breeds
BT2 breeds
BT1 sheep breeds
BT2 breeds

east germany
USE **german democratic republic**

EAST MIDLANDS OF ENGLAND
BT1 england
BT2 great britain
BT3 uk
BT4 british isles
BT5 western europe
BT6 europe

east timor
USE **loro sae**

EASTERN CENTRAL ATLANTIC
BT1 atlantic ocean
BT2 marine areas

EASTERN CENTRAL PACIFIC
BT1 pacific ocean
BT2 marine areas

EASTERN CHINA
uf *china (eastern region)*
uf *china (shanghai)*
uf *shanghai region*
BT1 china
BT2 east asia
BT3 asia

EASTERN ENGLAND
BT1 england
BT2 great britain
BT3 uk
BT4 british isles
BT5 western europe
BT6 europe

EASTERN EQUINE ENCEPHALITIS VIRUS
BT1 equine encephalomyelitis virus
BT2 alphavirus
BT3 arboviruses
BT4 pathogens
BT3 togaviridae
BT4 viruses

EASTERN EUROPE
BT1 europe
NT1 albania
NT1 bulgaria
NT1 czechoslovakia
NT1 german democratic republic
NT1 hungary
NT1 poland
NT1 romania
NT1 yugoslavia
rt balkans
rt ussr

EASTERN INDIAN OCEAN
BT1 indian ocean
BT2 marine areas
NT1 bay of bengal

EASTERN SCOTLAND
BT1 scotland
BT2 great britain
BT3 uk
BT4 british isles
BT5 western europe
BT6 europe

EATING
NT1 mastication
rt consumption patterns (agricola)
rt eating rates (agricola)
rt feeding behaviour
rt ingestion

eating disorders
USE **appetite disorders**

eating habits
HN was a preferred term until 1990
USE **feeding habits**

EATING OUT (AGRICOLA)
rt dining facilities (agricola)

EATING PATTERNS (AGRICOLA)
BT1 patterns
rt food consumption
rt meal patterns

EATING RATES (AGRICOLA)
rt eating
rt food consumption
rt food intake

EBENACEAE
NT1 diospyros
NT2 diospyros bipindensis
NT2 diospyros blancoi
NT2 diospyros cinnabarina
NT2 diospyros cornii
NT2 diospyros ebenaster
NT2 diospyros ferra
NT2 diospyros graciliensis
NT2 diospyros grascilescens
NT2 diospyros guianensis
NT2 diospyros kaki
NT2 diospyros kirkii
NT2 diospyros lotus
NT2 diospyros melanoxylon
NT2 diospyros mespiliformis
NT2 diospyros mollis
NT2 diospyros montana
NT2 diospyros obliquifolia
NT2 diospyros peregrina
NT2 diospyros sapota
NT2 diospyros texana
NT2 diospyros usambarensis
NT2 diospyros virginiana
NT1 euclea
NT2 euclea divinorum
NT2 euclea natalensis
NT1 maba
NT2 maba buxifolia

EBOLA VIRUS
BT1 filovirus
BT2 filoviridae
BT3 viruses

ec
USE **european communities**

EC REGULATIONS
BT1 regulations
rt european communities

ECBALLIUM
BT1 cucurbitaceae
NT1 ecballium elaterium

ECBALLIUM ELATERIUM
BT1 ecballium
BT2 cucurbitaceae

ECCENTRICITIES
BT1 abnormalities
rt form factors

eccoptogaster
USE **scolytus**

eccoptogaster rugulosus
USE **scolytus rugulosus**

ECCREMOCARPUS
BT1 bignoniaceae
NT1 eccremocarpus scaber

ECCREMOCARPUS SCABER
BT1 eccremocarpus
BT2 bignoniaceae
BT1 ornamental woody plants

ECDYSIS
BT1 moulting
BT2 biological rhythms
BT2 shedding
rt sclerotization

α-ECDYSONE
(for retrieval spell out "alpha")
BT1 cholestanes
BT2 steroids
BT3 isoprenoids
BT4 lipids
BT1 moulting hormones
BT2 arthropod hormones
BT3 hormones

β-ecdysone
USE **ecdysterone**

ecdysones
USE **moulting hormones**

ecdysteroids
USE **moulting hormones**

ECDYSTERONE
uf *20-hydroxyecdysone*
uf *β-ecdysone*
BT1 cholestanes
BT2 steroids
BT3 isoprenoids
BT4 lipids
BT1 moulting hormones
BT2 arthropod hormones
BT3 hormones

ecg
USE **electrocardiograms**

ECHEVERIA
BT1 crassulaceae
NT1 echeveria agavoides
NT1 echeveria chihuahuensis
NT1 echeveria coccinea
NT1 echeveria colorata
NT1 echeveria elegans
NT1 echeveria harmsii
NT1 echeveria nayaritensis
NT1 echeveria prolifica

ECHEVERIA AGAVOIDES
BT1 echeveria
BT2 crassulaceae
BT1 ornamental succulent plants
BT2 succulent plants

ECHEVERIA CHIHUAHUAENSIS
BT1 echeveria
BT2 crassulaceae
BT1 ornamental succulent plants
BT2 succulent plants

ECHEVERIA COCCINEA
BT1 echeveria
BT2 crassulaceae
BT1 ornamental succulent plants
BT2 succulent plants

ECHEVERIA COLORATA
BT1 echeveria
BT2 crassulaceae
BT1 ornamental succulent plants
BT2 succulent plants

ECHEVERIA ELEGANS
BT1 echeveria
BT2 crassulaceae
BT1 ornamental succulent plants
BT2 succulent plants

ECHEVERIA HARMSII
BT1 echeveria
BT2 crassulaceae
BT1 ornamental succulent plants
BT2 succulent plants

ECHEVERIA NAYARITENSIS
BT1 echeveria
BT2 crassulaceae
BT1 ornamental succulent plants
BT2 succulent plants

ECHEVERIA PROLIFICA
BT1 echeveria
BT2 crassulaceae
BT1 ornamental succulent plants
BT2 succulent plants

echidnas
USE **tachyglossidae**

ECHIDNOPHAGA
BT1 pulicidae
BT2 siphonaptera
NT1 echidnophaga gallinacea

ECHIDNOPHAGA GALLINACEA
BT1 echidnophaga
BT2 pulicidae
BT3 siphonaptera

ECHIMYIDAE
BT1 rodents
BT2 mammals
NT1 proechimys
NT2 proechimys iheringi

ECHINACEA
BT1 compositae
NT1 echinacea angustifolia
NT1 echinacea purpurea

ECHINACEA ANGUSTIFOLIA
BT1 echinacea
BT2 compositae
BT1 insecticidal plants
BT2 pesticidal plants

ECHINACEA PURPUREA
uf *rudbeckia purpurea*
BT1 echinacea
BT2 compositae

ECHINOCACTUS
BT1 cactaceae
NT1 echinocactus grusonii
NT1 echinocactus horizonthalonius

ECHINOCACTUS GRUSONII
BT1 echinocactus
BT2 cactaceae
BT1 ornamental succulent plants
BT2 succulent plants

ECHINOCACTUS HORIZONTHALONIUS
BT1 echinocactus
BT2 cactaceae
BT1 ornamental succulent plants
BT2 succulent plants

ECHINOCEREUS
BT1 cactaceae
NT1 echinocereus cinerascens
NT1 echinocereus engelmannii
NT1 echinocereus knippelianus
NT1 echinocereus nivosus
NT1 echinocereus pectinatus
NT1 echinocereus triglochidiatus
NT1 echinocereus viridiflorus

echinocereus chloranthus
USE **echinocereus viridiflorus**

ECHINOCEREUS CINERASCENS
BT1 echinocereus
BT2 cactaceae
BT1 ornamental succulent plants
BT2 succulent plants

ECHINOCEREUS ENGELMANNII
BT1 echinocereus
BT2 cactaceae
BT1 ornamental succulent plants
BT2 succulent plants

ECHINOCEREUS KNIPPELIANUS
BT1 echinocereus
BT2 cactaceae
BT1 ornamental succulent plants
BT2 succulent plants

ECHINOCEREUS NIVOSUS
BT1 echinocereus
BT2 cactaceae
BT1 ornamental succulent plants
BT2 succulent plants

ECHINOCEREUS PECTINATUS
uf *echinocereus reichenbachii*
BT1 echinocereus
BT2 cactaceae
BT1 ornamental succulent plants
BT2 succulent plants

echinocereus reichenbachii
USE **echinocereus pectinatus**

ECHINOCEREUS TRIGLOCHIDIATUS
BT1 echinocereus
BT2 cactaceae
BT1 medicinal plants
BT1 ornamental succulent plants
BT2 succulent plants

ECHINOCEREUS VIRIDIFLORUS
uf *echinocereus chloranthus*
BT1 echinocereus
BT2 cactaceae
BT1 ornamental succulent plants
BT2 succulent plants

ECHINOCHASMUS
BT1 echinostomatidae
BT2 digenea
BT3 trematoda

ECHINOCHLOA
BT1 gramineae
NT1 echinochloa colonum
NT1 echinochloa crus-galli
NT1 echinochloa crus-pavonis
NT1 echinochloa decompositum
NT1 echinochloa frumentacea
NT1 echinochloa glabrescens
NT1 echinochloa hispidula
NT1 echinochloa hostii
NT1 echinochloa muricata
NT1 echinochloa oryzoides
NT1 echinochloa polystachya
NT1 echinochloa pyramidalis
NT1 echinochloa spiralis
NT1 echinochloa stagnina
NT1 echinochloa turnerana
rt panicum

ECHINOCHLOA COLONUM
uf *panicum colonum*
BT1 echinochloa
BT2 gramineae
BT1 millets
BT2 cereals
BT3 grain crops
BT1 pasture plants

ECHINOCHLOA CRUS-GALLI
uf *barnyard grass*
BT1 echinochloa
BT2 gramineae
BT1 insecticidal plants
BT2 pesticidal plants
BT1 pasture plants
BT1 weeds

ECHINOCHLOA CRUS-PAVONIS
BT1 echinochloa
BT2 gramineae
BT1 pasture plants

ECHINOCHLOA DECOMPOSITUM
BT1 echinochloa
BT2 gramineae
BT1 millets
BT2 cereals
BT3 grain crops

ECHINOCHLOA FRUMENTACEA
uf *barnyard millet*
BT1 echinochloa
BT2 gramineae
BT1 millets
BT2 cereals
BT3 grain crops

ECHINOCHLOA GLABRESCENS
BT1 echinochloa
BT2 gramineae
BT1 pasture plants

ECHINOCHLOA HISPIDULA
BT1 echinochloa
BT2 gramineae
BT1 pasture plants

ECHINOCHLOA HOSTII
BT1 echinochloa
BT2 gramineae

ECHINOCHLOA MURICATA
BT1 echinochloa
BT2 gramineae
BT1 pasture plants

echinochloa oryzicola
USE **echinochloa oryzoides**

ECHINOCHLOA ORYZOIDES
uf *echinochloa oryzicola*
uf *echinochloa phyllopogon*
BT1 echinochloa
BT2 gramineae
BT1 pasture plants
BT1 weeds

echinochloa phyllopogon
USE **echinochloa oryzoides**

ECHINOCHLOA POLYSTACHYA
BT1 echinochloa
BT2 gramineae
BT1 pasture plants

ECHINOCHLOA PYRAMIDALIS
BT1 echinochloa
BT2 gramineae
BT1 pasture plants

ECHINOCHLOA SPIRALIS
BT1 echinochloa
BT2 gramineae

ECHINOCHLOA STAGNINA
BT1 echinochloa
BT2 gramineae

ECHINOCHLOA TURNERANA
BT1 echinochloa
BT2 gramineae
BT1 pasture plants

ECHINOCNEMUS
BT1 curculionidae
BT2 coleoptera

ECHINOCOCCUS
BT1 taeniidae
BT2 eucestoda
BT3 cestoda
NT1 echinococcus granulosus
NT1 echinococcus multilocularis

ECHINOCOCCUS *cont.*
rt hydatids

ECHINOCOCCUS GRANULOSUS
BT1 echinococcus
BT2 taeniidae
BT3 eucestoda
BT4 cestoda
rt unilocular hydatids

ECHINOCOCCUS MULTILOCULARIS
BT1 echinococcus
BT2 taeniidae
BT3 eucestoda
BT4 cestoda
rt alveolar hydatids

ECHINOCYSTIS
BT1 cucurbitaceae
NT1 echinocystis lobata

echinocystis echinata
USE **echinocystis lobata**

ECHINOCYSTIS LOBATA
uf *echinocystis echinata*
BT1 echinocystis
BT2 cucurbitaceae

ECHINODERMATA
NT1 echinoidea
NT2 echinus
NT2 heliocidaris
NT2 loxechinus
NT2 pseudocentrotus
NT2 strongylocentrotus
NT1 holothuroidea
NT2 cucumaria
NT2 stichopus
rt aquatic animals
rt invertebrates

ECHINODORUS
BT1 alismataceae
NT1 echinodorus rostratus

ECHINODORUS ROSTRATUS
BT1 echinodorus
BT2 alismataceae

ECHINOIDEA
uf *sea urchins*
BT1 echinodermata
NT1 echinus
NT1 heliocidaris
NT1 loxechinus
NT1 pseudocentrotus
NT1 strongylocentrotus

echinolaelaps
USE **laelaps**

echinolaelaps echidnina
USE **laelaps echidnina**

ECHINOMASTUS
BT1 cactaceae
NT1 echinomastus intertextus

ECHINOMASTUS INTERTEXTUS
BT1 echinomastus
BT2 cactaceae
BT1 ornamental succulent plants
BT2 succulent plants

ECHINOMERA
BT1 apicomplexa
BT2 protozoa

ECHINONYSSUS
BT1 laelapidae
BT2 mesostigmata
BT3 acari

ECHINOPANAX
BT1 araliaceae

echinopanax elatus
USE **oplopanax elatus**

echinopanax horridus
USE **oplopanax horridus**

ECHINOPARYPHIUM
BT1 echinostomatidae

ECHINOPARYPHIUM *cont.*
BT2 digenea
BT3 trematoda

ECHINOPS
BT1 compositae
NT1 echinops echinatus
NT1 echinops ellenbecki
NT1 echinops latifolia
NT1 echinops ritro
NT1 echinops sphaerocephalus
NT1 echinops spinosus

ECHINOPS ECHINATUS
BT1 echinops
BT2 compositae

ECHINOPS ELLENBECKI
BT1 echinops
BT2 compositae

ECHINOPS LATIFOLIA
BT1 echinops
BT2 compositae
BT1 medicinal plants

ECHINOPS RITRO
BT1 echinops
BT2 compositae

ECHINOPS SPHAEROCEPHALUS
BT1 echinops
BT2 compositae

ECHINOPS SPINOSUS
BT1 echinops
BT2 compositae

ECHINOPSIS
BT1 cactaceae
NT1 echinopsis kermesina

ECHINOPSIS KERMESINA
BT1 echinopsis
BT2 cactaceae

ECHINORHYNCHIDAE
BT1 acanthocephala
NT1 acanthocephalus
NT1 echinorhynchus
NT2 echinorhynchus truttae

ECHINORHYNCHUS
BT1 echinorhynchidae
BT2 acanthocephala
NT1 echinorhynchus truttae

ECHINORHYNCHUS TRUTTAE
BT1 echinorhynchus
BT2 echinorhynchidae
BT3 acanthocephala

ECHINOSOPHORA
BT1 leguminosae
NT1 echinosophora koreensis

ECHINOSOPHORA KOREENSIS
BT1 echinosophora
BT2 leguminosae

ECHINOSTOMA
BT1 echinostomatidae
BT2 digenea
BT3 trematoda
NT1 echinostoma audyi
NT1 echinostoma hystricosum
NT1 echinostoma ilocanum
NT1 echinostoma lindoense
NT1 echinostoma revolutum

ECHINOSTOMA AUDYI
BT1 echinostoma
BT2 echinostomatidae
BT3 digenea
BT4 trematoda

ECHINOSTOMA HYSTRICOSUM
BT1 echinostoma
BT2 echinostomatidae
BT3 digenea
BT4 trematoda

ECHINOSTOMA ILOCANUM
BT1 echinostoma
BT2 echinostomatidae
BT3 digenea

ECHINOSTOMA ILOCANUM *cont.*
BT4 trematoda

ECHINOSTOMA LINDOENSE
BT1 echinostoma
BT2 echinostomatidae
BT3 digenea
BT4 trematoda

ECHINOSTOMA REVOLUTUM
BT1 echinostoma
BT2 echinostomatidae
BT3 digenea
BT4 trematoda

ECHINOSTOMATIDAE
uf *echinostomatids*
BT1 digenea
BT2 trematoda
NT1 artyfechinostomum
NT2 artyfechinostomum sufrartyfex
NT1 echinochasmus
NT1 echinoparyphium
NT1 echinostoma
NT2 echinostoma audyi
NT2 echinostoma hystricosum
NT2 echinostoma ilocanum
NT2 echinostoma lindoense
NT2 echinostoma revolutum
NT1 euparyphium
NT1 himasthla
NT1 paryphostomum
NT1 patagifer
NT1 petasiger

echinostomatids
USE **echinostomatidae**

ECHINURIA
BT1 acuariidae
BT2 nematoda
NT1 echinuria uncinata

ECHINURIA UNCINATA
BT1 echinuria
BT2 acuariidae
BT3 nematoda

ECHINUS
BT1 echinoidea
BT2 echinodermata

ECHITES
BT1 apocynaceae
NT1 echites hirsuta

ECHITES HIRSUTA
BT1 echites
BT2 apocynaceae

ECHIUM
BT1 boraginaceae
NT1 echium italicum
NT1 echium plantagineum
NT1 echium vulgare

ECHIUM ITALICUM
BT1 echium
BT2 boraginaceae

echium lycopsis
USE **echium plantagineum**

ECHIUM PLANTAGINEUM
uf *echium lycopsis*
BT1 echium
BT2 boraginaceae
BT1 ornamental herbaceous plants
BT1 poisonous plants
BT1 weeds

ECHIUM VULGARE
BT1 echium
BT2 boraginaceae

ECHIUROIDEA
rt invertebrates

echlomezol
USE **etridiazole**

ECHOCARDIOGRAPHY
BT1 diagnostic techniques

ECHOCARDIOGRAPHY *cont.*
BT2 techniques

echtes ackerbohnenmosaik virus
USE **broad bean true mosaic comovirus**

ECLAMPSIA
BT1 reproductive disorders
BT2 functional disorders
BT3 animal disorders
BT4 disorders
rt parturition
rt preeclampsia
rt pregnancy
rt pregnancy toxaemia

ECLIPTA
BT1 compositae
NT1 eclipta alba
NT1 eclipta prostrata

ECLIPTA ALBA
BT1 antiviral plants
BT1 eclipta
BT2 compositae
BT1 medicinal plants
BT1 nematicidal plants
BT2 pesticidal plants

ECLIPTA PROSTRATA
BT1 eclipta
BT2 compositae
BT1 medicinal plants

eco-agriculture
USE **organic farming**

ECOLOGICAL BALANCE
uf balance of nature
uf natural balance
BT1 ecology
rt ecosystems
rt vegetation management

ecological soil types
USE **soil types (ecological)**

ECOLOGISTS
BT1 scientists
BT2 occupations
rt ecology

ECOLOGY
NT1 autecology
NT1 chemical ecology
NT1 community ecology
NT1 ecological balance
NT1 fire ecology
NT1 forest ecology
NT1 freshwater ecology
NT1 human ecology
NT1 landscape ecology
NT1 marine ecology
NT1 palaeoecology
NT1 plant ecology
NT1 plant succession
NT1 population ecology
NT1 synecology
NT2 layer structure
NT2 species diversity
rt bioclimatic indexes
rt biocoenosis
rt bioenergetics
rt biogeography
rt bog plants
rt botanical composition
rt calcicoles
rt calcifuges
rt colonizing ability
rt competitive ability
rt ecologists
rt ecotypes
rt environmental degradation
rt environmental factors
rt habitat selection
rt habitats
rt nature tourism
rt phenology
rt plant communities
rt plant competition
rt plant interaction
rt soil types (ecological)
rt sustainability

ECOLOGY *cont.*
rt vegetation types
rt weed associations
rt zoogeography

ECONAZOLE
BT1 antifungal agents
BT2 antiinfective agents
BT3 drugs
BT1 imidazoles
BT2 azoles
BT3 heterocyclic nitrogen compounds
BT4 organic nitrogen compounds

ECONOMETRIC MODELS
uf models, econometric
BT1 mathematical models
BT2 models
BT2 optimization methods
BT3 optimization
rt econometrics

ECONOMETRICS
NT1 consumption functions
NT1 demand functions
NT1 elasticities
NT2 demand elasticities
NT2 income elasticities
NT2 price elasticities
NT2 supply elasticities
NT1 parametric programming
NT1 production functions
NT2 cobb-douglas functions
NT2 multiple objective functions
NT1 profit functions
NT1 savings functions
NT1 spatial equilibrium analysis
NT1 supply functions
NT1 utility functions
rt econometric models
rt economic analysis
rt economic evaluation
rt economic systems
rt economic theory
rt economics

ECONOMIC ACCOUNTS
BT1 accounts
rt aggregate accounts
rt capital accounts
rt economics
rt farm accounts
rt national accounting
rt regional accounting

ECONOMIC ANALYSIS
NT1 cost benefit analysis
NT2 non-market benefits
NT3 externalities
NT2 shadow prices
NT1 cost effectiveness analysis (agricola)
NT1 macroeconomic analysis
NT2 input output analysis
NT3 shift share analysis
NT1 marginal analysis
NT2 marginal returns
NT1 microeconomic analysis
NT2 gross margins analysis
NT1 savings functions
NT1 sectoral analysis
rt analysis
rt consumption functions
rt cost analysis
rt demand functions
rt econometrics
rt economics
rt factor analysis
rt factors of production
rt gross margins
rt national accounting
rt regional accounting

ECONOMIC BEHAVIOR
BF economic behaviour
BT1 human behavior
BT2 behavior
BT1 social behavior
BT2 behavior
NT1 consumer behavior

ECONOMIC BEHAVIOUR
AF economic behavior
BT1 human behaviour
BT2 behaviour
BT1 social behaviour
BT2 behaviour
NT1 consumer behaviour
NT2 complaints
NT2 consumer preferences
NT2 purchasing habits
NT1 economic impact
rt economics

ECONOMIC CRISES
HN from 1990
BT1 crises (agricola)
NT1 economic depression
NT2 inflation

ECONOMIC DEPENDENCE
BT1 economic development
rt economic situation

ECONOMIC DEPRESSION
uf recession
BT1 economic crises
BT2 crises (agricola)
BT1 economic situation
NT1 inflation
rt agricultural crises
rt deflation
rt depression
rt economic recovery
rt economics
rt social disintegration
rt trade cycles

ECONOMIC DEVELOPMENT
uf development, economic
NT1 economic dependence
NT1 economic dualism
NT1 economic growth
NT1 industrialization
NT2 industrial methods
rt agricultural development
rt development
rt development policy
rt development theory
rt economics
rt regional development
rt rural development
rt social change

ECONOMIC DUALISM
uf dualism, economic
BT1 development theory
BT2 economic theory
BT3 economics
BT1 economic development

ECONOMIC EVALUATION
BT1 evaluation
NT1 economic viability
rt econometrics
rt economics

ECONOMIC GROWTH
uf growth, economic
BT1 economic development
rt economics
rt growth theory

ECONOMIC IMPACT
BT1 economic behaviour
BT2 human behaviour
BT3 behaviour
BT2 social behaviour
BT3 behaviour

ECONOMIC INDICATORS
BT1 indicators
BT1 statistics
rt economics

economic infrastructure
USE **economic situation**

economic laws
USE **economic theory**
OR **economics**

economic life
USE **productive life**

economic loss
USE **losses**

ECONOMIC POLICY
uf supply policy
NT1 credit policy
NT1 fiscal policy
NT2 taxes
NT3 direct taxation
NT4 capital taxation
NT5 land tax
NT5 rates
NT4 company tax
NT4 income tax
NT4 inheritance tax
NT3 forest taxation
NT3 indirect taxation
NT4 stamp duty
NT4 value added tax
NT3 property taxes (agricola)
NT3 sales tax (agricola)
NT1 investment policy
NT2 investment promotion
NT2 investment requirements
NT1 marketing policy
NT2 market planning
NT2 marketing orders (agricola)
NT1 monetary policy
NT2 monetary agreements
NT1 price policy
NT2 price fixing
NT3 differential pricing
NT4 payment basis
NT2 price formation
NT3 price discrimination
NT4 price elasticities
NT3 price stabilization
NT4 price controls
NT3 price support
NT1 production policy
NT2 adjustment of production
NT3 agricultural adjustment
NT2 location of production
NT2 production controls
NT3 land diversion
NT4 land banks
NT3 price controls
NT3 quantity controls
NT4 quotas
NT5 import quotas
NT1 trade policy
NT2 balance of trade
NT2 export promotion
NT3 export credits
NT3 export refunds
NT3 export subsidies
NT2 import substitution
NT2 market stabilization
NT3 stabex
NT2 trade agreements
NT3 gatt
NT3 trade negotiations
NT3 trade preferences
NT2 trade diversion
NT2 trade liberalization
NT3 free trade
NT2 trade protection
NT3 trade barriers
NT4 export controls
NT4 import controls
NT5 customs regulations
NT5 import levies
NT5 import quotas
NT5 non-tariff barriers to trade
NT6 tax agreements
NT5 tariffs
NT6 duty free allowances
NT6 preferential tariffs
NT4 trade sanctions
NT2 trade relations
rt agricultural policy
rt development policy
rt economic systems
rt economic theory
rt economics
rt fiscal policy
rt policy
rt regional policy

ECONOMIC RECOVERY
BT1 economic situation

ECONOMIC RECOVERY *cont.*
rt economic depression
rt economics
rt trade cycles

ECONOMIC REGIONS
uf exclusive economic zones
BT1 regions
rt acp
rt andean group
rt asean
rt benelux
rt cacm
rt caribbean community
rt cmea
rt economic unions
rt economics
rt efta
rt lafta
rt oecd

ECONOMIC RESOURCES
BT1 resources
rt capital
rt economics
rt energy
rt human resources
rt labour
rt land
rt production possibilities

economic schools
USE **economic theory**

ECONOMIC SECTORS
uf sectors of production
NT1 primary sector
NT1 private sector
NT1 public sector
NT1 secondary sector
NT1 tertiary sector
NT1 voluntary sector
rt agroindustrial sector
rt economics
rt intersectoral planning
rt marketing
rt sectoral analysis
rt sectoral development
rt sectoral planning

ECONOMIC SITUATION
uf economic infrastructure
NT1 economic depression
NT2 inflation
NT1 economic recovery
NT1 trade cycles
rt agricultural situation
rt economic dependence
rt economic systems
rt economics

ECONOMIC SOCIOLOGY
BT1 sociology
rt consumer expenditure
rt economics
rt farmers' attitudes
rt marxist sociology
rt rural sociology
rt socioeconomic status
rt sociology of work

ECONOMIC SYSTEMS
BT1 systems
NT1 capitalism
NT1 centrally planned economies
NT1 communism
NT1 feudalism
NT1 market economies
NT1 mixed economies
rt capitalist countries
rt econometrics
rt economic policy
rt economic situation
rt economic theory
rt economics
rt imperialism
rt political systems
rt socialism

ECONOMIC THEORY
uf economic laws
uf economic schools
BT1 economics

ECONOMIC THEORY *cont.*
NT1 development theory
NT2 economic dualism
NT1 economies of scale
NT1 equilibrium theory
NT1 growth theory
NT1 location theory
NT1 value theory
rt econometrics
rt economic policy
rt economic systems
rt theory

ECONOMIC THRESHOLDS
uf damage thresholds
rt cost benefit analysis
rt damage
rt losses
rt pest control

ECONOMIC UNIONS
NT1 cmea
NT1 common markets
NT2 cacm
NT2 caribbean community
NT2 european communities
NT1 customs unions
NT2 efta
rt acp
rt andean group
rt commonwealth of nations
rt cooperation
rt economic regions
rt economics
rt integration
rt monetary policy
rt oecd
rt organizations

economic units
USE **businesses**
OR **farms**
OR **firms**

ECONOMIC VIABILITY
uf viability, financial
BT1 economic evaluation
BT2 evaluation
rt feasibility
rt profitability

ECONOMICALLY DISADVANTAGED
BT1 disadvantaged (agricola)
rt poverty

ECONOMICS
uf economic laws
NT1 agricultural economics
NT1 classical economics
NT1 consumer economics (agricola)
NT1 economic theory
NT2 development theory
NT3 economic dualism
NT2 economies of scale
NT2 equilibrium theory
NT2 growth theory
NT2 location theory
NT2 value theory
NT1 economics of control
NT1 forest economics
NT1 genetic economics
NT1 labour economics
NT2 division of labour
NT2 labour costs
NT2 labour market
NT3 labour mobility
NT3 labour requirements
NT2 wage agreements
NT2 work planning
NT3 workable days
NT3 working plans
NT1 macroeconomics
NT1 market economics
NT2 market transparency
NT3 market intelligence
NT4 market research
NT5 market surveys
NT6 consumer surveys
NT7 consumer panels
NT2 supply balance
NT3 demand

ECONOMICS *cont.*
NT3 supply
NT3 supply functions
NT3 supply response
NT3 surpluses
NT1 marxist economics
NT1 microeconomics
NT1 natural resource economics
NT1 neoclassical economics
NT1 production economics
NT2 factors of production
NT2 production functions
NT3 cobb-douglas functions
NT3 multiple objective functions
NT1 welfare economics
NT2 consumer surplus
rt econometrics
rt economic accounts
rt economic analysis
rt economic behaviour
rt economic depression
rt economic development
rt economic evaluation
rt economic growth
rt economic indicators
rt economic policy
rt economic recovery
rt economic regions
rt economic resources
rt economic sectors
rt economic situation
rt economic sociology
rt economic systems
rt economic unions
rt forest management
rt social sciences
rt socioeconomic advisers
rt stabilization

economics, agricultural
USE **agricultural economics**

economics, classical
USE **classical economics**

economics, marxist
USE **marxist economics**

economics, neoclassical
USE **neoclassical economics**

ECONOMICS OF CONTROL
BT1 economics

economics of labour
USE **labour economics**

economics of marketing
USE **market economics**

economics of production
USE **production economics**

ECONOMIES OF SCALE
BT1 economic theory
BT2 economics

ECONOMY HOTELS
BT1 hotels
BT2 holiday accommodation
BT3 accommodation

ECOSYSTEMS
NT1 aquatic environment
NT1 marine environment
rt ecological balance
rt environment
rt food chains
rt plant communities
rt sustainability
rt trophic levels
rt vegetation

ECOTONES
BT1 plant communities
BT2 communities
rt boundaries
rt synecology

ECOTYPES
BT1 biotypes
rt clines
rt ecology

ECOTYPES *cont.*
rt habitats
rt natural selection
rt races

ecphoropsis
USE **campoletis**

ecphoropsis perdistinctus
USE **campoletis flavicincta**

ECTOEDEMIA
BT1 nepticulidae
BT2 lepidoptera

ECTOMYCORRHIZAS
HN from 1989
BT1 mycorrhizas

ECTOMYELOIS
BT1 pyralidae
BT2 lepidoptera
NT1 ectomyelois ceratoniae
rt myelois

ECTOMYELOIS CERATONIAE
uf myelois ceratoniae
BT1 ectomyelois
BT2 pyralidae
BT3 lepidoptera

ECTOPARASITES
uf parasitic insects
BT1 arthropod pests
BT2 pests
BT1 parasites
NT1 feather mites
rt ectoparasiticides
rt ectoparasitoses
rt haematophagous arthropods
rt hippoboscidae
rt host parasite relationships
rt metastigmata
rt phthiraptera
rt psoroptidae
rt sarcoptidae
rt siphonaptera

ECTOPARASITICIDES
BT1 antiparasitic agents
BT2 drugs
NT1 amitraz
NT1 benzyl benzoate
NT1 bromocyclen
NT1 carbaryl
NT1 chloromethiuron
NT1 chlorpyrifos
NT1 closantel
NT1 coumaphos
NT1 crotamiton
NT1 crotoxyphos
NT1 crufomate
NT1 cyhalothrin
NT1 cypermethrin
NT1 cyromazine
NT1 cythioate
NT1 ddt
NT1 deltamethrin
NT1 diazinon
NT1 dichlorvos
NT1 dioxathion
NT1 ethion
NT1 famphur
NT1 fenchlorphos
NT1 fenthion
NT1 fenvalerate
NT1 flucythrinate
NT1 flumethrin
NT1 ivermectin
NT1 lindane
NT1 malathion
NT1 metolcarb
NT1 nifluridide
NT1 permethrin
NT1 phosalone
NT1 phosmet
NT1 phoxim
NT1 propetamphos
NT1 propoxur
NT1 quintiofos
NT1 rafoxanide
NT1 tetrachlorvinphos

ECTOPARASITICIDES *cont.*
NT1 trichlorfon
rt acaricides
rt dips
rt ear tags
rt ectoparasites
rt insecticides
rt shampoos

ECTOPARASITOSES
BT1 parasitoses
BT2 diseases
NT1 mange
NT1 myiasis
NT2 apimyiasis
NT1 scabies
NT2 hyperkeratotic scabies
NT1 tick infestations
rt delusory parasitoses
rt ectoparasites

ECTOPHASIA
BT1 tachinidae
BT2 diptera
NT1 ectophasia crassipennis
rt phasia

ECTOPHASIA CRASSIPENNIS
uf *phasia crassipennis*
BT1 ectophasia
BT2 tachinidae
BT3 diptera

ECTOPIA
BT1 congenital abnormalities
BT2 abnormalities

ECTOPROCTA
uf *bryozoa*
uf *polyzoa*
rt invertebrates

ECTOPSOCIDAE
BT1 psocoptera
NT1 ectopsocus
NT2 ectopsocus briggsi

ECTOPSOCUS
BT1 ectopsocidae
BT2 psocoptera
NT1 ectopsocus briggsi

ECTOPSOCUS BRIGGSI
BT1 ectopsocus
BT2 ectopsocidae
BT3 psocoptera

ECTROMELIA VIRUS
BT1 orthopoxvirus
BT2 chordopoxvirinae
BT3 poxviridae
BT4 viruses

ECUADOR
BT1 south america
BT2 america
NT1 galapagos islands
rt andean group
rt developing countries
rt opec
rt threshold countries

ecuador (galapagos islands)
USE **galapagos islands**

ECZEMA
BT1 skin diseases
BT2 organic diseases
BT3 diseases
NT1 facial eczema
rt dermatitis

eczema, facial
USE **facial eczema**

EDAM CHEESE
BT1 cheeses
BT2 milk products
BT3 products

EDAPHIC FACTORS
rt environmental factors
rt site factors
rt soil
rt soil properties

edb
USE **ethylene dibromide**

EDELSCHWEIN
HN from 1990; previously "german yorkshire"
uf *german yorkshire*
BT1 pig breeds
BT2 breeds

EDEMA
BF oedema
NT1 congenital edema
NT1 mammary edema
NT1 nutritional edema

EDENTATA
BT1 mammals
NT1 bradypodidae
NT2 bradypus
NT3 bradypus variegatus
NT1 dasypodidae
NT2 dasypus
NT3 dasypus novemcinctus
NT2 euphractus
NT3 euphractus sexcinctus
NT1 megalonychidae
NT2 choloepus
NT3 choloepus didactylus
NT1 myrmecophagidae
NT2 myrmecophaga
NT3 myrmecophaga tridactyla
NT2 tamandua

edetic acid
USE **edta**

EDGEWORTHIA
BT1 thymelaeaceae
NT1 edgeworthia gardneri

EDGEWORTHIA GARDNERI
BT1 edgeworthia
BT2 thymelaeaceae

EDGING
BT1 sawmilling
rt resawing
rt trimming

EDIBLE BIRDSNESTS
uf *birdsnest, edible*
BT1 nests
BT1 unconventional foods
BT2 foods
rt birds

EDIBLE CULTIVARS
BT1 cultivars
BT2 varieties
rt foods

EDIBLE FUNGI
BT1 fungi
BT1 vegetables
NT1 agaricus arvensis
NT1 agaricus bitorquis
NT1 agaricus chionodermus
NT1 agaricus macrocarpus
NT1 agaricus macrosporoides
NT1 agaricus purpurescens
NT1 agaricus silvicola
NT1 agaricus subedulis
NT1 agrocybe aegerita
NT1 auricularia auricula
NT1 boletus edulis
NT1 boletus sublutens
NT1 calocybe indica
NT1 calvatia gigantea
NT1 cantharellus cibarius
NT1 collybia velutipes
NT1 coprinus aratus
NT1 coprinus atramentarius
NT1 coprinus comatus
NT1 coprinus micaceus
NT1 coriolus versicolor
NT1 flammulina velutipes
NT1 helvella esculenta
NT1 kuehneromyces mutabilis
NT1 lactarius chrysorrus
NT1 lactarius rufus
NT1 lactarius sanguifluus
NT1 lactarius torminosus
NT1 lentinula edodes

EDIBLE FUNGI *cont.*
NT1 lepiota naucina
NT1 lyophyllum decastes
NT1 macrolepiota zeyheri
NT1 morchella crassipes
NT1 morchella esculenta
NT1 mushrooms
NT1 peziza auburounii
NT1 pholiota mutabilis
NT1 pholiota squarrosa
NT1 pleurotus cornucopiae
NT1 pleurotus eous
NT1 pleurotus eryngii
NT1 pleurotus flabellatus
NT1 pleurotus florida
NT1 pleurotus ostreatus
NT1 pleurotus sajor-caju
NT1 pleurotus salignus
NT1 pleurotus sapidus
NT1 pleurotus tuber-regium
NT1 podaxis pistillaris
NT1 schizophyllum commune
NT1 stropharia hornemannii
NT1 stropharia rugoso-annulata
NT1 terfezia calveryi
NT1 terfezia hafizi
NT1 tirmania nivea
NT1 tirmania pinoyi
NT1 tremella fuciformis
NT1 tricholoma matsutake
NT1 tricholoma nudum
NT1 truffles
NT1 volvariella diplasia
NT1 volvariella esculenta
NT1 volvariella speciosa
NT1 volvariella volvacea
rt forest products
rt leccinum
rt plants
rt termitomyces

edible insects
USE **insects as food**

EDIBLE SPECIES
BT1 species
rt feeds
rt foods
rt meat
rt meat products
rt plants

EDIBLE SYRUP
HN from 1990
uf *golden syrup*
uf *table syrup*
BT1 syrups
BT2 liquids

edible weeds
USE **wild foods (agricola)**

EDIFENPHOS
uf *edpp*
BT1 organophosphorus fungicides
BT2 fungicides
BT3 pesticides
BT2 organophosphorus pesticides
BT3 organophosphorus compounds

EDILBAEV
BT1 sheep breeds
BT2 breeds

EDITORIALS
BT1 publications

EDLES WARMBLUT
HN from 1990
BT1 horse breeds
BT2 breeds

EDOVUM
BT1 eulophidae
BT2 hymenoptera
NT1 edovum puttleri

EDOVUM PUTTLERI
BT1 edovum
BT2 eulophidae
BT3 hymenoptera

edpp
USE **edifenphos**

EDTA
uf *edetic acid*
uf *ethylenediaminetetraacetic acid*
BT1 anticoagulants
BT2 haematologic agents
BT3 drugs
BT1 chelating agents

EDUCATION
NT1 adult education
NT2 continuing education
NT3 professional continuing education (agricola)
NT2 non-formal education
NT2 parent education (agricola)
NT2 practical education
NT1 agricultural education
NT2 dairy education
NT1 bilingual education
NT1 career education (agricola)
NT1 childbirth education (agricola)
NT1 community education
NT2 population education
NT1 competency based education (agricola)
NT1 consumer education (agricola)
NT1 dietetic education (agricola)
NT1 early childhood education (agricola)
NT1 educational opportunities
NT2 study leave
NT1 educational theory
NT1 elementary education (agricola)
NT1 environmental education
NT1 extension education (agricola)
NT1 family life education (agricola)
NT2 parenthood education (agricola)
NT1 health education
NT2 prenatal education (agricola)
NT1 higher education
NT2 graduate study (agricola)
NT2 veterinary schools
NT1 leisure education
NT1 management education (agricola)
NT1 nutrition education
NT1 patient education (agricola)
NT1 physical education
NT1 postsecondary education (agricola)
NT1 preschool education
NT1 primary education
NT1 professional education (agricola)
NT2 home economics education (agricola)
NT2 medical education (agricola)
NT2 professional continuing education (agricola)
NT1 science education
NT1 secondary education
NT1 sex education (agricola)
NT1 special education (agricola)
NT1 veterinary education
rt academic achievement (agricola)
rt animation
rt books
rt child care
rt curriculum
rt educational courses
rt educational games (agricola)
rt educational grants
rt educational innovation (agricola)
rt educational institutions
rt educational methods (agricola)
rt educational objectives (agricola)

EDUCATION *cont.*
rt educational policy
rt educational programs (agricola)
rt educational radio
rt educational reform
rt educational research
rt educational resources (agricola)
rt educational technology (agricola)
rt educational television
rt educational theory
rt educational toys (agricola)
rt extension
rt field trips (agricola)
rt learning
rt literacy
rt net program (agricola)
rt qualifications
rt schools
rt services
rt social sciences
rt social services
rt students
rt teachers
rt teaching
rt training
rt unesco

education, adult
USE **adult education**

education, agricultural
USE **agricultural education**

education, community
USE **community education**

education, further
USE **continuing education**

education, higher
USE **higher education**

EDUCATIONAL ATTENDANCE
uf *school attendance*
BT1 educational performance
rt student dropouts

educational change
USE **educational reform**

EDUCATIONAL COURSES
NT1 correspondence courses
NT1 curriculum
NT2 college curriculum (agricola)
NT2 core curriculum (agricola)
NT2 high school curriculum (agricola)
rt education

EDUCATIONAL GAMES (AGRICOLA)
BT1 games
rt education

EDUCATIONAL GRANTS
BT1 grants
BT2 support measures
rt education
rt educational opportunities
rt educational policy

EDUCATIONAL INNOVATION (AGRICOLA)
rt education
rt educational reform
rt educational technology (agricola)
rt innovations

EDUCATIONAL INSTITUTIONS
NT1 agricultural colleges
NT1 colleges (agricola)
NT2 medical schools (agricola)
NT1 schools
NT2 elementary schools (agricola)
NT2 high schools (agricola)
NT2 nursery schools (agricola)
NT2 open classrooms (agricola)
NT2 private schools (agricola)

EDUCATIONAL INSTITUTIONS *cont.*
NT3 parochial schools (agricola)
NT2 public schools (agricola)
NT1 training centres
NT1 universities
rt advisory centres
rt education
rt social institutions

EDUCATIONAL METHODS (AGRICOLA)
BT1 methodology
rt education
rt teaching methods

EDUCATIONAL OBJECTIVES (AGRICOLA)
BT1 objectives
rt education
rt educational policy

EDUCATIONAL OPPORTUNITIES
BT1 education
NT1 study leave
rt aspirations
rt educational grants
rt occupational change

EDUCATIONAL PERFORMANCE
uf *performance, educational*
NT1 educational attendance
NT1 qualifications

EDUCATIONAL PLANNING
BT1 educational policy
BT1 planning
NT1 educational reform
rt curriculum

EDUCATIONAL POLICY
uf *policy, educational*
NT1 educational planning
NT2 educational reform
rt education
rt educational grants
rt educational objectives (agricola)
rt policy
rt study leave
rt training levies
rt unesco

EDUCATIONAL PROGRAMS (AGRICOLA)
BT1 programs (agricola)
rt education

EDUCATIONAL RADIO
BT1 audiovisual aids
BT2 teaching materials
BT1 radio
BT2 mass media
BT3 communication
rt distance teaching
rt education

EDUCATIONAL REFORM
uf *educational change*
BT1 educational planning
BT2 educational policy
BT2 planning
rt change
rt curriculum
rt education
rt educational innovation (agricola)

EDUCATIONAL RESEARCH
BT1 research
rt education

EDUCATIONAL RESOURCES (AGRICOLA)
BT1 resources
rt education
rt resource materials (agricola)
rt teaching materials

EDUCATIONAL TECHNOLOGY (AGRICOLA)
BT1 technology
rt education

EDUCATIONAL TECHNOLOGY (AGRICOLA) *cont.*
rt educational innovation (agricola)
rt teaching materials

EDUCATIONAL TELEVISION
BT1 audiovisual aids
BT2 teaching materials
BT1 television
BT2 mass media
BT3 communication
rt distance teaching
rt education

EDUCATIONAL THEORY
BT1 education
rt education
rt learning theory (agricola)
rt theory

EDUCATIONAL TOYS (AGRICOLA)
BT1 toys
BT2 recreation equipment
BT3 equipment
rt education

EDWARDSIELLA
BT1 enterobacteriaceae
BT2 gracilicutes
BT3 bacteria
BT4 prokaryotes

eec
USE **european communities**

eeg
USE **electroencephalography**

EEL CULTURE
BT1 fish culture
BT2 aquaculture
BT3 enterprises
BT2 fish farming
BT3 farming

eel, european
USE **european eels**

eel, moray
USE **muraena helena**

EELS
BT1 marine fishes
BT2 aquatic animals
BT3 animals
BT3 aquatic organisms
rt anguilla
rt anguillidae
rt european eels

eelworms
USE **plant parasitic nematodes**

EFFECTIVE POPULATION SIZE
HN from 1989
BT1 population structure

EFFECTS
NT1 adverse effects
NT1 dosage effects
NT1 drug effects (agricola)
NT1 fire effects
NT1 genetic effects
NT1 growth effects
NT1 logging effects
NT1 maternal effects
NT1 nontarget effects
NT1 paternal effects
NT1 plant effects
NT1 reciprocal effects
NT1 residual effects
NT1 sublethal effects
NT1 teapot effect
NT1 wind effects
rt environmental impact

EFFICIENCY
NT1 breeding efficiency
NT2 repeat breeders
NT1 reproductive efficiency
NT2 female fertility
NT3 calving interval
NT3 calving rate
NT3 lambing rate

EFFICIENCY *cont.*
NT1 thermal efficiency
NT1 tractive efficiency
NT1 use efficiency
NT2 water use efficiency
rt capacity
rt constraints
rt performance
rt productivity
rt program effectiveness (agricola)
rt rationalization
rt reproductive performance
rt utilization
rt wastage
rt work capacity

EFFLORESCENCES
BT1 soil morphological features

effluent, factory
USE **factory effluents**

effluent, sewage
USE **sewage effluent**

effluent, silage
USE **silage effluent**

EFFLUENTS
BT1 wastes
NT1 dairy effluent
NT1 factory effluents
NT2 brewery effluent
NT2 cannery effluent
NT2 distillery effluent
NT2 kraft mill effluent
NT2 meatworks effluent
NT2 palm oil mill effluent
NT2 potato factory effluent
NT2 pulp mill effluent
NT1 feedlot effluent
NT1 piggery effluent
NT1 septic tank effluent
NT1 sewage effluent
NT1 silage effluent
rt biological oxygen demand
rt chemical oxygen demand
rt liquids
rt pollution
rt waste disposal
rt waste gases
rt waste liquors

EFFLUX
BT1 plant physiology
BT2 physiology
rt excretion
rt exudation

EFTA
uf *european free trade associations*
BT1 customs unions
BT2 economic unions
BT1 international organizations
BT2 organizations
rt austria
rt economic regions
rt finland
rt iceland
rt liechtenstein
rt norway
rt portugal
rt sweden
rt switzerland

EGERIA
BT1 rubiaceae
NT1 egeria densa

EGERIA DENSA
BT1 egeria
BT2 rubiaceae

EGG ALBUMEN
uf *albumen*
uf *egg white*
BT1 albumins
BT2 proteins
BT3 peptides
BT1 egg proteins
BT2 animal proteins
BT3 proteins

EGG ALBUMEN *cont.*
BT4 peptides
rt avidin
rt conalbumin
rt ovalbumin

EGG CHARACTERS
BT1 egg quality
BT2 quality
rt eggs

EGG CLUTCHES
HN from 1990

EGG COLLECTORS
BT1 collectors
BT2 equipment
rt eggs
rt poultry housing

EGG COMPOSITION
BT1 composition
NT1 egg protein
NT1 egg yolk composition
rt egg quality
rt eggs

EGG CONSUMPTION
BT1 consumption
rt eggs

EGG COOLING
BT1 cooling
rt eggs

egg, dried
USE **dried egg**

EGG DROP SYNDROME
BT1 poultry diseases
BT2 animal diseases
BT3 diseases
rt aviadenovirus

egg, duck
USE **duck eggs**

EGG FERTILITY
BT1 fertility
NT1 egg hatchability
NT2 turkey egg hatchability
NT1 turkey egg fertility
rt eggs

EGG FLAVOR
BF egg flavour
BT1 flavor

EGG FLAVOUR
AF egg flavor
BT1 egg quality
BT2 quality
BT1 flavour
BT2 organoleptic traits
BT3 physicochemical properties
BT4 properties
BT3 traits
rt eggs

EGG FORMATION
BT1 physiological functions
NT1 egg shell formation
rt eggs
rt oogenesis
rt shell gland

EGG GRADERS
uf *graders, egg*
BT1 graders
rt eggs

EGG HATCHABILITY
uf *hatchability*
BT1 egg fertility
BT2 fertility
NT1 turkey egg hatchability
rt egg turning
rt eggs

EGG MASS
BT1 egg quality
BT2 quality
rt egg weight

EGG MEMBRANES
rt cell membranes
rt eggs

egg powder
USE **dried egg**

EGG PRODUCTION
BT1 animal production
BT2 agricultural production
BT3 production
NT1 turkey egg production
rt age at first egg
rt eggs
rt fecundity
rt laying performance
rt laying test
rt oviposition

EGG PRODUCTS
BT1 poultry products
BT2 animal products
BT3 products
NT1 dried egg
rt eggs
rt food products

EGG PROTEIN
BT1 animal protein
BT2 protein
BT1 egg composition
BT2 composition
rt egg proteins
rt eggs

EGG PROTEINS
BT1 animal proteins
BT2 proteins
BT3 peptides
NT1 conalbumin
NT1 egg albumen
NT1 lysozyme
NT1 ovalbumin
NT1 ovoglobulin
NT1 vitellins
rt egg protein

EGG QUALITY
BT1 quality
NT1 blood spots
NT1 egg characters
NT1 egg flavour
NT1 egg mass
NT1 egg shape
NT1 egg shell defects
NT1 egg shell quality
NT2 egg shell thickness
NT1 egg weight
NT1 egg yolk colour
rt egg composition
rt eggs

EGG SHAPE
BT1 egg quality
BT2 quality
rt eggs

EGG SHELL
rt egg shell defects
rt egg shell formation
rt egg shell meal
rt egg shell quality
rt egg shell thickness
rt eggs
rt shell-less eggs
rt shells

EGG SHELL DEFECTS
BT1 defects
BT1 egg quality
BT2 quality
rt egg shell
rt eggs
rt shell-less eggs
rt soft shelled eggs

EGG SHELL FORMATION
BT1 egg formation
BT2 physiological functions
rt egg shell
rt eggs

EGG SHELL MEAL
BT1 meal

EGG SHELL MEAL *cont.*
rt egg shell
rt eggs

EGG SHELL QUALITY
BT1 egg quality
BT2 quality
NT1 egg shell thickness
rt egg shell
rt eggs

EGG SHELL THICKNESS
BT1 egg shell quality
BT2 egg quality
BT3 quality
BT1 thickness
BT2 dimensions
rt egg shell
rt eggs

EGG TURNING
BT1 incubation
rt egg hatchability
rt eggs

EGG WEIGHT
BT1 egg quality
BT2 quality
rt egg mass
rt eggs

egg white
USE **egg albumen**

EGG YOLK
uf *vitellus*
uf *yolk*
rt egg yolk colour
rt egg yolk composition
rt eggs
rt vitellogenesis

EGG YOLK COLOR
BF egg yolk colour
rt color

EGG YOLK COLOUR
AF egg yolk color
BT1 egg quality
BT2 quality
rt colour
rt egg yolk
rt eggs

EGG YOLK COMPOSITION
BT1 egg composition
BT2 composition
rt egg yolk
rt eggs

EGGPLANT LITTLE LEAF
BT1 plant diseases
rt solanum melongena

EGGPLANT MOSAIC TYMOVIRUS
HN from 1990
BT1 tymovirus group
BT2 plant viruses
BT3 plant pathogens
BT4 pathogens
rt aubergines
rt solanum melongena

EGGPLANT MOTTLED CRINKLE TOMBUSVIRUS
HN from 1990
BT1 tombusvirus group
BT2 plant viruses
BT3 plant pathogens
BT4 pathogens
rt aubergines
rt solanum melongena

EGGPLANT MOTTLED DWARF RHABDOVIRUS
HN from 1990
BT1 rhabdovirus group
BT2 plant viruses
BT3 plant pathogens
BT4 pathogens
BT2 rhabdoviridae
BT3 viruses
rt aubergines
rt solanum melongena

EGGPLANTS
BF aubergines
rt solanum melongena

EGGS
(for eggs as germ cells use ova)
uf *hen eggs*
BT1 poultry products
BT2 animal products
BT3 products
NT1 duck eggs
NT1 goose eggs
NT1 turkey eggs
rt age at first egg
rt blood spots
rt body-checked eggs
rt dried egg
rt egg characters
rt egg collectors
rt egg composition
rt egg consumption
rt egg cooling
rt egg fertility
rt egg flavour
rt egg formation
rt egg graders
rt egg hatchability
rt egg membranes
rt egg production
rt egg products
rt egg protein
rt egg quality
rt egg shape
rt egg shell
rt egg shell defects
rt egg shell formation
rt egg shell meal
rt egg shell quality
rt egg shell thickness
rt egg turning
rt egg weight
rt egg yolk
rt egg yolk colour
rt egg yolk composition
rt food products
rt hatching
rt nests
rt omelets (agricola)
rt preincubation period
rt shell-less eggs
rt soft shelled eggs
rt vitelline membrane

eggs, goose
USE **goose eggs**

EGRETTA
BT1 ardeidae
BT2 ciconiiformes
BT3 birds
NT1 egretta alba
NT1 egretta garzetta

EGRETTA ALBA
BT1 egretta
BT2 ardeidae
BT3 ciconiiformes
BT4 birds

EGRETTA GARZETTA
BT1 egretta
BT2 ardeidae
BT3 ciconiiformes
BT4 birds

EGYPT
uf *arab republic of egypt*
BT1 north africa
BT2 africa
rt arab countries
rt developing countries
rt mediterranean countries
rt middle east

EGYPTIAN
BT1 buffalo breeds
BT2 breeds
BT1 cattle breeds
BT2 breeds

egyptian clover
USE **trifolium alexandrinum**

egyptian honeybees
USE **apis mellifera lamarckii**

EHRETIACEAE
NT1 bourreria
NT2 bourreria aculiata

EHRHARTA
BT1 gramineae
NT1 ehrharta calycina

EHRHARTA CALYCINA
BT1 ehrharta
BT2 gramineae
rt sand stabilization

EHRLICHIA
BT1 ehrlichiaceae
BT2 rickettsiales
BT3 bacteria
BT4 prokaryotes
NT1 ehrlichia canis
NT1 ehrlichia phagocytophila
NT1 ehrlichia risticii
rt cytoecetes

EHRLICHIA CANIS
BT1 ehrlichia
BT2 ehrlichiaceae
BT3 rickettsiales
BT4 bacteria
BT5 prokaryotes

EHRLICHIA PHAGOCYTOPHILA
HN from 1990; previously "cytoecetes phagocytophila"
uf *cytoecetes phagocytophila*
BT1 ehrlichia
BT2 ehrlichiaceae
BT3 rickettsiales
BT4 bacteria
BT5 prokaryotes
rt tickborne fever

EHRLICHIA RISTICII
HN from 1990
uf *potomac horse fever*
BT1 ehrlichia
BT2 ehrlichiaceae
BT3 rickettsiales
BT4 bacteria
BT5 prokaryotes

EHRLICHIACEAE
BT1 rickettsiales
BT2 bacteria
BT3 prokaryotes
NT1 cowdria
NT2 cowdria ruminantium
NT1 cytoecetes
NT1 ehrlichia
NT2 ehrlichia canis
NT2 ehrlichia phagocytophila
NT2 ehrlichia risticii
NT1 neorickettsia

EICHHORNIA
BT1 pontederiaceae
NT1 eichhornia crassipes
NT1 eichhornia heterosperma

EICHHORNIA CRASSIPES
uf *eichhornia speciosa*
BT1 eichhornia
BT2 pontederiaceae
BT1 weeds

EICHHORNIA HETEROSPERMA
BT1 eichhornia
BT2 pontederiaceae

eichhornia speciosa
USE **eichhornia crassipes**

EICOSANOIDS
BT1 lipids
BT1 organic acids
BT2 acids
NT1 leukotrienes
NT1 prostaglandins
NT2 prostacyclin
NT1 thromboxanes

EICOSAPENTAENOIC ACID
BT1 polyenoic fatty acids
BT2 unsaturated fatty acids
BT3 fatty acids
BT4 carboxylic acids
BT5 organic acids
BT6 acids
BT4 lipids

eicosatetraenoic acid
USE **arachidonic acid**

eicosenoic acid
USE **gadoleic acid**

EIMERIA
BT1 apicomplexa
BT2 protozoa
NT1 eimeria acervulina
NT1 eimeria adenoeides
NT1 eimeria ahsata
NT1 eimeria alabamensis
NT1 eimeria andreusi
NT1 eimeria anguillae
NT1 eimeria anseris
NT1 eimeria arabiana
NT1 eimeria arloingi
NT1 eimeria auburnensis
NT1 eimeria bareillyi
NT1 eimeria bateri
NT1 eimeria bistratum
NT1 eimeria bovis
NT1 eimeria brasiliensis
NT1 eimeria brunetti
NT1 eimeria bukidnonensis
NT1 eimeria cameli
NT1 eimeria canadensis
NT1 eimeria canis
NT1 eimeria capreoli
NT1 eimeria carpelli
NT1 eimeria caviae
NT1 eimeria cerdonis
NT1 eimeria citelli
NT1 eimeria clupearum
NT1 eimeria coecicola
NT1 eimeria colchici
NT1 eimeria columbarum
NT1 eimeria confusa
NT1 eimeria contorta
NT1 eimeria debliecki
NT1 eimeria dericksoni
NT1 eimeria dispersa
NT1 eimeria dukei
NT1 eimeria dunsingi
NT1 eimeria duodenalis
NT1 eimeria ellipsoidalis
NT1 eimeria environ
NT1 eimeria europaea
NT1 eimeria falciformis
NT1 eimeria faurei
NT1 eimeria ferrisi
NT1 eimeria funduli
NT1 eimeria gadi
NT1 eimeria gallopavonis
NT1 eimeria granulosa
NT1 eimeria grenieri
NT1 eimeria gruis
NT1 eimeria hagani
NT1 eimeria hungarica
NT1 eimeria indentata
NT1 eimeria intestinalis
NT1 eimeria iroquoina
NT1 eimeria irresidua
NT1 eimeria keilini
NT1 eimeria kotlani
NT1 eimeria kriygsmanni
NT1 eimeria labbeana
NT1 eimeria lancasterensis
NT1 eimeria leporis
NT1 eimeria leuckarti
NT1 eimeria magna
NT1 eimeria marsica
NT1 eimeria mascoutini
NT1 eimeria matsubayashii
NT1 eimeria maxima
NT1 eimeria media
NT1 eimeria meleagrimitis
NT1 eimeria minima
NT1 eimeria mitis
NT1 eimeria mivati
NT1 eimeria myopotami
NT1 eimeria necatrix

EIMERIA *cont.*
NT1 eimeria neodebliecki
NT1 eimeria nieschulzi
NT1 eimeria ninakohlyakimovae
NT1 eimeria ontarioensis
NT1 eimeria os
NT1 eimeria ovina
NT1 eimeria pacifica
NT1 eimeria panda
NT1 eimeria papillata
NT1 eimeria parva
NT1 eimeria pellerdyi
NT1 eimeria pellita
NT1 eimeria pellucida
NT1 eimeria perforans
NT1 eimeria perminuta
NT1 eimeria phasiani
NT1 eimeria pintoensis
NT1 eimeria poljanskyi
NT1 eimeria ponderosa
NT1 eimeria praecox
NT1 eimeria pragensis
NT1 eimeria procyonis
NT1 eimeria reichenowi
NT1 eimeria robertsoni
NT1 eimeria ruficaudati
NT1 eimeria sardinae
NT1 eimeria sciurorum
NT1 eimeria semisculpta
NT1 eimeria separata
NT1 eimeria septentrionalis
NT1 eimeria sigmodontis
NT1 eimeria smithi
NT1 eimeria solipedum
NT1 eimeria somateriae
NT1 eimeria spinosa
NT1 eimeria stiedai
NT1 eimeria subspherica
NT1 eimeria suis
NT1 eimeria superba
NT1 eimeria tenella
NT1 eimeria tetartooimia
NT1 eimeria tetricis
NT1 eimeria townsendi
NT1 eimeria truncata
NT1 eimeria uniungulati
NT1 eimeria utahensis
NT1 eimeria variabilis
NT1 eimeria vermiformis
NT1 eimeria vison
NT1 eimeria wenrichi
NT1 eimeria weybridgensis
NT1 eimeria wyomingensis
NT1 eimeria zapi
NT1 eimeria zuernii
rt coccidiosis

EIMERIA ACERVULINA
BT1 eimeria
BT2 apicomplexa
BT3 protozoa

EIMERIA ADENOEIDES
BT1 eimeria
BT2 apicomplexa
BT3 protozoa

EIMERIA AHSATA
BT1 eimeria
BT2 apicomplexa
BT3 protozoa

EIMERIA ALABAMENSIS
BT1 eimeria
BT2 apicomplexa
BT3 protozoa

EIMERIA ANDREUSI
BT1 eimeria
BT2 apicomplexa
BT3 protozoa

EIMERIA ANGUILLAE
BT1 eimeria
BT2 apicomplexa
BT3 protozoa

EIMERIA ANSERIS
BT1 eimeria
BT2 apicomplexa
BT3 protozoa

EIMERIA ARABIANA
BT1 eimeria
BT2 apicomplexa
BT3 protozoa

EIMERIA ARLOINGI
BT1 eimeria
BT2 apicomplexa
BT3 protozoa

EIMERIA AUBURNENSIS
BT1 eimeria
BT2 apicomplexa
BT3 protozoa

EIMERIA BAREILLYI
BT1 eimeria
BT2 apicomplexa
BT3 protozoa

EIMERIA BATERI
BT1 eimeria
BT2 apicomplexa
BT3 protozoa

EIMERIA BISTRATUM
BT1 eimeria
BT2 apicomplexa
BT3 protozoa

EIMERIA BOVIS
BT1 eimeria
BT2 apicomplexa
BT3 protozoa

EIMERIA BRASILIENSIS
BT1 eimeria
BT2 apicomplexa
BT3 protozoa

EIMERIA BRUNETTI
BT1 eimeria
BT2 apicomplexa
BT3 protozoa

EIMERIA BUKIDNONENSIS
BT1 eimeria
BT2 apicomplexa
BT3 protozoa

EIMERIA CAMELI
BT1 eimeria
BT2 apicomplexa
BT3 protozoa

EIMERIA CANADENSIS
BT1 eimeria
BT2 apicomplexa
BT3 protozoa

EIMERIA CANIS
BT1 eimeria
BT2 apicomplexa
BT3 protozoa

EIMERIA CAPREOLI
BT1 eimeria
BT2 apicomplexa
BT3 protozoa

EIMERIA CARPELLI
BT1 eimeria
BT2 apicomplexa
BT3 protozoa

EIMERIA CAVIAE
BT1 eimeria
BT2 apicomplexa
BT3 protozoa

EIMERIA CERDONIS
BT1 eimeria
BT2 apicomplexa
BT3 protozoa

EIMERIA CITELLI
BT1 eimeria
BT2 apicomplexa
BT3 protozoa

EIMERIA CLUPEARUM
BT1 eimeria
BT2 apicomplexa
BT3 protozoa

EIMERIA COECICOLA
BT1 eimeria
BT2 apicomplexa
BT3 protozoa

EIMERIA COLCHICI
BT1 eimeria
BT2 apicomplexa
BT3 protozoa

EIMERIA COLUMBARUM
BT1 eimeria
BT2 apicomplexa
BT3 protozoa

EIMERIA CONFUSA
BT1 eimeria
BT2 apicomplexa
BT3 protozoa

EIMERIA CONTORTA
BT1 eimeria
BT2 apicomplexa
BT3 protozoa

EIMERIA DEBLIECKI
BT1 eimeria
BT2 apicomplexa
BT3 protozoa

EIMERIA DERICKSONI
BT1 eimeria
BT2 apicomplexa
BT3 protozoa

EIMERIA DISPERSA
BT1 eimeria
BT2 apicomplexa
BT3 protozoa

EIMERIA DUKEI
BT1 eimeria
BT2 apicomplexa
BT3 protozoa

EIMERIA DUNSINGI
BT1 eimeria
BT2 apicomplexa
BT3 protozoa

EIMERIA DUODENALIS
BT1 eimeria
BT2 apicomplexa
BT3 protozoa

EIMERIA ELLIPSOIDALIS
BT1 eimeria
BT2 apicomplexa
BT3 protozoa

EIMERIA ENVIRON
BT1 eimeria
BT2 apicomplexa
BT3 protozoa

EIMERIA EUROPAEA
BT1 eimeria
BT2 apicomplexa
BT3 protozoa

EIMERIA FALCIFORMIS
BT1 eimeria
BT2 apicomplexa
BT3 protozoa

EIMERIA FAUREI
BT1 eimeria
BT2 apicomplexa
BT3 protozoa

EIMERIA FERRISI
BT1 eimeria
BT2 apicomplexa
BT3 protozoa

EIMERIA FUNDULI
BT1 eimeria
BT2 apicomplexa
BT3 protozoa

EIMERIA GADI
BT1 eimeria
BT2 apicomplexa
BT3 protozoa

EIMERIA GALLOPAVONIS
BT1 eimeria
BT2 apicomplexa
BT3 protozoa

EIMERIA GRANULOSA
BT1 eimeria
BT2 apicomplexa
BT3 protozoa

EIMERIA GRENIERI
BT1 eimeria
BT2 apicomplexa
BT3 protozoa

EIMERIA GRUIS
BT1 eimeria
BT2 apicomplexa
BT3 protozoa

EIMERIA HAGANI
BT1 eimeria
BT2 apicomplexa
BT3 protozoa

EIMERIA HUNGARICA
BT1 eimeria
BT2 apicomplexa
BT3 protozoa

EIMERIA INDENTATA
BT1 eimeria
BT2 apicomplexa
BT3 protozoa

EIMERIA INTESTINALIS
BT1 eimeria
BT2 apicomplexa
BT3 protozoa

EIMERIA IROQUOINA
BT1 eimeria
BT2 apicomplexa
BT3 protozoa

EIMERIA IRRESIDUA
BT1 eimeria
BT2 apicomplexa
BT3 protozoa

EIMERIA KEILINI
BT1 eimeria
BT2 apicomplexa
BT3 protozoa

EIMERIA KOTLANI
BT1 eimeria
BT2 apicomplexa
BT3 protozoa

EIMERIA KRIYGSMANNI
BT1 eimeria
BT2 apicomplexa
BT3 protozoa

EIMERIA LABBEANA
BT1 eimeria
BT2 apicomplexa
BT3 protozoa

EIMERIA LANCASTERENSIS
BT1 eimeria
BT2 apicomplexa
BT3 protozoa

EIMERIA LEPORIS
BT1 eimeria
BT2 apicomplexa
BT3 protozoa

EIMERIA LEUCKARTI
BT1 eimeria
BT2 apicomplexa
BT3 protozoa

EIMERIA MAGNA
BT1 eimeria
BT2 apicomplexa
BT3 protozoa

EIMERIA MARSICA
BT1 eimeria
BT2 apicomplexa
BT3 protozoa

EIMERIA MASCOUTINI
BT1 eimeria
BT2 apicomplexa
BT3 protozoa

EIMERIA MATSUBAYASHII
BT1 eimeria
BT2 apicomplexa
BT3 protozoa

EIMERIA MAXIMA
BT1 eimeria
BT2 apicomplexa
BT3 protozoa

EIMERIA MEDIA
BT1 eimeria
BT2 apicomplexa
BT3 protozoa

EIMERIA MELEAGRIMITIS
BT1 eimeria
BT2 apicomplexa
BT3 protozoa

EIMERIA MINIMA
BT1 eimeria
BT2 apicomplexa
BT3 protozoa

EIMERIA MITIS
BT1 eimeria
BT2 apicomplexa
BT3 protozoa

EIMERIA MIVATI
BT1 eimeria
BT2 apicomplexa
BT3 protozoa

EIMERIA MYOPOTAMI
BT1 eimeria
BT2 apicomplexa
BT3 protozoa

EIMERIA NECATRIX
BT1 eimeria
BT2 apicomplexa
BT3 protozoa

EIMERIA NEODEBLIECKI
BT1 eimeria
BT2 apicomplexa
BT3 protozoa

EIMERIA NIESCHULZI
BT1 eimeria
BT2 apicomplexa
BT3 protozoa

EIMERIA NINAKOHLYAKIMOVAE
BT1 eimeria
BT2 apicomplexa
BT3 protozoa

EIMERIA ONTARIOENSIS
BT1 eimeria
BT2 apicomplexa
BT3 protozoa

EIMERIA OS
BT1 eimeria
BT2 apicomplexa
BT3 protozoa

EIMERIA OVINA
BT1 eimeria
BT2 apicomplexa
BT3 protozoa

EIMERIA PACIFICA
BT1 eimeria
BT2 apicomplexa
BT3 protozoa

EIMERIA PANDA
BT1 eimeria
BT2 apicomplexa
BT3 protozoa

EIMERIA PAPILLATA
BT1 eimeria
BT2 apicomplexa
BT3 protozoa

EIMERIA PARVA
BT1 eimeria
BT2 apicomplexa
BT3 protozoa

EIMERIA PELLERDYI
BT1 eimeria
BT2 apicomplexa
BT3 protozoa

EIMERIA PELLITA
BT1 eimeria
BT2 apicomplexa
BT3 protozoa

EIMERIA PELLUCIDA
BT1 eimeria
BT2 apicomplexa
BT3 protozoa

EIMERIA PERFORANS
BT1 eimeria
BT2 apicomplexa
BT3 protozoa

EIMERIA PERMINUTA
BT1 eimeria
BT2 apicomplexa
BT3 protozoa

EIMERIA PHASIANI
BT1 eimeria
BT2 apicomplexa
BT3 protozoa

EIMERIA PINTOENSIS
BT1 eimeria
BT2 apicomplexa
BT3 protozoa

EIMERIA POLJANSKYI
BT1 eimeria
BT2 apicomplexa
BT3 protozoa

EIMERIA PONDEROSA
BT1 eimeria
BT2 apicomplexa
BT3 protozoa

EIMERIA PRAECOX
BT1 eimeria
BT2 apicomplexa
BT3 protozoa

EIMERIA PRAGENSIS
BT1 eimeria
BT2 apicomplexa
BT3 protozoa

EIMERIA PROCYONIS
BT1 eimeria
BT2 apicomplexa
BT3 protozoa

EIMERIA REICHENOWI
BT1 eimeria
BT2 apicomplexa
BT3 protozoa

EIMERIA ROBERTSONI
BT1 eimeria
BT2 apicomplexa
BT3 protozoa

EIMERIA RUFICAUDATI
BT1 eimeria
BT2 apicomplexa
BT3 protozoa

EIMERIA SARDINAE
BT1 eimeria
BT2 apicomplexa
BT3 protozoa

EIMERIA SCIURORUM
BT1 eimeria
BT2 apicomplexa
BT3 protozoa

EIMERIA SEMISCULPTA
BT1 eimeria
BT2 apicomplexa
BT3 protozoa

EIMERIA SEPARATA
BT1 eimeria
BT2 apicomplexa
BT3 protozoa

EIMERIA SEPTENTRIONALIS
BT1 eimeria
BT2 apicomplexa
BT3 protozoa

EIMERIA SIGMODONTIS
BT1 eimeria
BT2 apicomplexa
BT3 protozoa

EIMERIA SMITHI
BT1 eimeria
BT2 apicomplexa
BT3 protozoa

EIMERIA SOLIPEDUM
BT1 eimeria
BT2 apicomplexa
BT3 protozoa

EIMERIA SOMATERIAE
BT1 eimeria
BT2 apicomplexa
BT3 protozoa

EIMERIA SPINOSA
BT1 eimeria
BT2 apicomplexa
BT3 protozoa

EIMERIA STIEDAI
BT1 eimeria
BT2 apicomplexa
BT3 protozoa

EIMERIA SUBSPHERICA
BT1 eimeria
BT2 apicomplexa
BT3 protozoa

EIMERIA SUIS
BT1 eimeria
BT2 apicomplexa
BT3 protozoa

EIMERIA SUPERBA
BT1 eimeria
BT2 apicomplexa
BT3 protozoa

EIMERIA TENELLA
BT1 eimeria
BT2 apicomplexa
BT3 protozoa

EIMERIA TETARTOOIMIA
BT1 eimeria
BT2 apicomplexa
BT3 protozoa

EIMERIA TETRICIS
BT1 eimeria
BT2 apicomplexa
BT3 protozoa

EIMERIA TOWNSENDI
BT1 eimeria
BT2 apicomplexa
BT3 protozoa

EIMERIA TRUNCATA
BT1 eimeria
BT2 apicomplexa
BT3 protozoa

EIMERIA UNIUNGULATI
BT1 eimeria
BT2 apicomplexa
BT3 protozoa

EIMERIA UTAHENSIS
BT1 eimeria
BT2 apicomplexa
BT3 protozoa

EIMERIA VARIABILIS
BT1 eimeria
BT2 apicomplexa
BT3 protozoa

EIMERIA VERMIFORMIS
BT1 eimeria
BT2 apicomplexa
BT3 protozoa

EIMERIA VISON
BT1 eimeria
BT2 apicomplexa
BT3 protozoa

EIMERIA WENRICHI
BT1 eimeria
BT2 apicomplexa
BT3 protozoa

EIMERIA WEYBRIDGENSIS
BT1 eimeria
BT2 apicomplexa
BT3 protozoa

EIMERIA WYOMINGENSIS
BT1 eimeria
BT2 apicomplexa
BT3 protozoa

EIMERIA ZAPI
BT1 eimeria
BT2 apicomplexa
BT3 protozoa

EIMERIA ZUERNII
BT1 eimeria
BT2 apicomplexa
BT3 protozoa

eire
USE **irish republic**

EISENIA
BT1 lumbricidae
BT2 oligochaeta
BT3 annelida
NT1 eisenia fetida
NT1 eisenia nordenskioldi

EISENIA FETIDA
BT1 eisenia
BT2 lumbricidae
BT3 oligochaeta
BT4 annelida

EISENIA NORDENSKIOLDI
BT1 eisenia
BT2 lumbricidae
BT3 oligochaeta
BT4 annelida

EJACULATE VOLUME
BT1 semen characters
BT2 characteristics
rt ejaculation
rt volume

EJACULATION
NT1 ejaculation latency
NT1 electroejaculation
NT1 transport in male genitalia
rt copulation
rt ejaculate volume
rt sexual behaviour

EJACULATION LATENCY
BT1 ejaculation

EJIDOS
BT1 collective farms
BT2 farms

EKEBERGIA
BT1 meliaceae
NT1 ekebergia benguelensis
NT1 ekebergia capensis

EKEBERGIA BENGUELENSIS
BT1 ekebergia
BT2 meliaceae

EKEBERGIA CAPENSIS
BT1 ekebergia
BT2 meliaceae

EKTAPHELENCHUS
BT1 aphelenchoididae
BT2 nematoda

EL SALVADOR
uf salvador
BT1 central america
BT2 america
rt cacm
rt developing countries

ELAEAGNACEAE
NT1 elaeagnus
NT2 elaeagnus angustifolia
NT2 elaeagnus commutata
NT2 elaeagnus macrophylla
NT2 elaeagnus multiflora
NT2 elaeagnus oldhami
NT2 elaeagnus pungens
NT2 elaeagnus umbellata
NT2 elaeagnus villosa
NT1 hippophae
NT2 hippophae rhamnoides
NT1 shepherdia
NT2 shepherdia argentea

ELAEAGNUS
BT1 elaeagnaceae
NT1 elaeagnus angustifolia
NT1 elaeagnus commutata
NT1 elaeagnus macrophylla
NT1 elaeagnus multiflora
NT1 elaeagnus oldhami
NT1 elaeagnus pungens
NT1 elaeagnus umbellata
NT1 elaeagnus villosa

ELAEAGNUS ANGUSTIFOLIA
BT1 elaeagnus
BT2 elaeagnaceae
BT1 forest trees
BT1 ornamental woody plants

ELAEAGNUS COMMUTATA
BT1 elaeagnus
BT2 elaeagnaceae
BT1 ornamental woody plants

ELAEAGNUS MACROPHYLLA
BT1 elaeagnus
BT2 elaeagnaceae
BT1 ornamental woody plants

ELAEAGNUS MULTIFLORA
BT1 elaeagnus
BT2 elaeagnaceae
BT1 ornamental woody plants

ELAEAGNUS OLDHAMI
BT1 elaeagnus
BT2 elaeagnaceae

ELAEAGNUS PUNGENS
BT1 elaeagnus
BT2 elaeagnaceae
BT1 ornamental woody plants

ELAEAGNUS UMBELLATA
BT1 elaeagnus
BT2 elaeagnaceae
BT1 forest trees
BT1 ornamental woody plants

ELAEAGNUS VILLOSA
BT1 elaeagnus
BT2 elaeagnaceae

ELAEIDOBIUS
BT1 curculionidae
BT2 coleoptera
NT1 elaeidobius kamerunicus

ELAEIDOBIUS KAMERUNICUS
BT1 elaeidobius
BT2 curculionidae
BT3 coleoptera

ELAEIS
BT1 palmae
NT1 elaeis guineensis
NT1 elaeis oleifera

ELAEIS GUINEENSIS
BT1 elaeis
BT2 palmae
rt oil palms

ELAEIS OLEIFERA
uf american oil palm

ELAEIS OLEIFERA *cont.*
uf corozo oleifera
BT1 elaeis
BT2 palmae
rt oil palms

ELAEOCARPACEAE
NT1 aristotelia
NT2 aristotelia chilensis
NT2 aristotelia serrata
NT1 crinodendron
NT2 crinodendron hookerianum
NT1 elaeocarpus
NT2 elaeocarpus floribundus
NT2 elaeocarpus ganitrus

ELAEOCARPUS
BT1 elaeocarpaceae
NT1 elaeocarpus floribundus
NT1 elaeocarpus ganitrus

ELAEOCARPUS FLORIBUNDUS
BT1 elaeocarpus
BT2 elaeocarpaceae

ELAEOCARPUS GANITRUS
BT1 elaeocarpus
BT2 elaeocarpaceae

ELAEODENDRON
BT1 celastraceae
NT1 elaeodendron glaucum

ELAEODENDRON GLAUCUM
BT1 elaeodendron
BT2 celastraceae
BT1 poisonous plants

ELAEOPHORA
BT1 onchocercidae
BT2 nematoda
NT1 elaeophora poeli
NT1 elaeophora sagitta
NT1 elaeophora schneideri

ELAEOPHORA POELI
BT1 elaeophora
BT2 onchocercidae
BT3 nematoda

ELAEOPHORA SAGITTA
BT1 elaeophora
BT2 onchocercidae
BT3 nematoda

ELAEOPHORA SCHNEIDERI
BT1 elaeophora
BT2 onchocercidae
BT3 nematoda

ELAEOPHORBIA
BT1 euphorbiaceae

ELAIDIC ACID
BT1 long chain fatty acids
BT2 fatty acids
BT3 carboxylic acids
BT4 organic acids
BT5 acids
BT3 lipids
BT1 monoenoic fatty acids
BT2 unsaturated fatty acids
BT3 fatty acids
BT4 carboxylic acids
BT5 organic acids
BT6 acids
BT4 lipids
BT1 trans fatty acids
BT2 fatty acids
BT3 carboxylic acids
BT4 organic acids
BT5 acids
BT3 lipids

eland
USE **tragelaphus oryx**

ELAPHE
BT1 colubridae
BT2 serpentes
BT3 reptiles
NT1 elaphe obsoleta

ELAPHE OBSOLETA
BT1 elaphe

ELAPHE OBSOLETA *cont.*
BT2 colubridae
BT3 serpentes
BT4 reptiles

ELAPHOSTRONGYLUS
BT1 protostrongylidae
BT2 nematoda
NT1 elaphostrongylus cervi
NT1 elaphostrongylus rangiferi

ELAPHOSTRONGYLUS CERVI
BT1 elaphostrongylus
BT2 protostrongylidae
BT3 nematoda

ELAPHOSTRONGYLUS RANGIFERI
BT1 elaphostrongylus
BT2 protostrongylidae
BT3 nematoda

ELAPIDAE
BT1 serpentes
BT2 reptiles
NT1 naja

ELASMIDAE
BT1 hymenoptera
NT1 elasmus

ELASMOLOMUS
BT1 lygaeidae
BT2 heteroptera
NT1 elasmolomus sordidus
rt aphanus

ELASMOLOMUS SORDIDUS
uf *aphanus sordidus*
BT1 elasmolomus
BT2 lygaeidae
BT3 heteroptera

ELASMOPALPUS
BT1 pyralidae
BT2 lepidoptera
NT1 elasmopalpus lignosellus

ELASMOPALPUS LIGNOSELLUS
BT1 elasmopalpus
BT2 pyralidae
BT3 lepidoptera

ELASMUS
BT1 elasmidae
BT2 hymenoptera

ELASTASE
(ec 3.4.21.11)
BT1 proteinases
BT2 peptide hydrolases
BT3 hydrolases
BT4 enzymes

ELASTICITIES
BT1 econometrics
NT1 demand elasticities
NT1 income elasticities
NT1 price elasticities
NT1 supply elasticities
rt substitution
rt supply response

elasticities, price
USE **price elasticities**

ELASTICITY
BT1 rheological properties
BT2 mechanical properties
BT3 properties
NT1 modulus of elasticity
rt flexibility
rt resonance wood
rt viscoelasticity

ELASTIN
BT1 glycoproteins
BT2 proteins
BT3 peptides
BT1 scleroproteins
BT2 proteins
BT3 peptides
rt connective tissue
rt desmosine

ELATERIDAE
uf *wireworms*
BT1 coleoptera
NT1 adelocera
NT2 adelocera subcostata
NT1 agriotes
NT2 agriotes brevis
NT2 agriotes gurgistanus
NT2 agriotes lineatus
NT2 agriotes obscurus
NT2 agriotes sordidus
NT2 agriotes sputator
NT2 agriotes squalidus
NT2 agriotes ustulatus
NT1 athous
NT2 athous subfuscus
NT1 conoderus
NT2 conoderus exsul
NT2 conoderus falli
NT2 conoderus scalaris
NT2 conoderus vespertinus
NT1 ctenicera
NT2 ctenicera destructor
NT1 lacon
NT1 limonius
NT2 limonius californicus
NT1 melanotus
NT2 melanotus communis
NT1 selatosomus
NT2 selatosomus aeneus
NT2 selatosomus latus

ELATINACEAE
NT1 elatine
NT2 elatine triandra

ELATINE
BT1 elatinaceae
NT1 elatine triandra

ELATINE TRIANDRA
BT1 elatine
BT2 elatinaceae

ELATOBIUM
BT1 aphididae
BT2 aphidoidea
BT3 sternorrhyncha
BT4 homoptera
NT1 elatobium abietinum

ELATOBIUM ABIETINUM
BT1 elatobium
BT2 aphididae
BT3 aphidoidea
BT4 sternorrhyncha
BT5 homoptera

ELBOWS
BT1 joints (animal)
BT2 musculoskeletal system
BT3 body parts
rt limbs

ELDANA
BT1 pyralidae
BT2 lepidoptera
NT1 eldana saccharina

ELDANA SACCHARINA
BT1 eldana
BT2 pyralidae
BT3 lepidoptera

ELDER ABUSE (AGRICOLA)
BT1 abuse (agricola)
BT1 antisocial behavior (agricola)
BT2 human behavior
BT3 behavior

elderberry a virus
USE **elderberry carlavirus**

ELDERBERRY CARLAVIRUS
HN from 1990
uf *elderberry a virus*
BT1 carlavirus group
BT2 plant viruses
BT3 plant pathogens
BT4 pathogens

ELDERLY (AGRICOLA)
uf *aged*
uf *older adults*

ELDERLY (AGRICOLA) *cont.*
uf *senior citizens*
BT1 people
rt elderly nutrition (agricola)
rt old age
rt retired people
rt senior citizen centers (agricola)

ELDERLY NUTRITION (AGRICOLA)
BT1 nutrition
rt elderly (agricola)

elders
USE **sambucus**

ELECTRIC CIRCUITS
uf *circuits, electric*
BT1 circuits
rt electric current
rt electrical conductance
rt electrical conductivity
rt electrical properties
rt electrical resistance
rt electricity
rt electrodes

ELECTRIC CURRENT
uf *current*
uf *electrical current*
NT1 telluric currents
rt earthing
rt electric circuits
rt electric fences
rt electrical activity
rt electrical conductance
rt electrical conductivity
rt electrical resistance
rt electrical safety
rt electricity
rt electricity generators
rt electrolysis
rt power lines
rt stray voltage
rt transformers

ELECTRIC DISCHARGES
BT1 discharges
NT1 corona discharge
rt electric power
rt electrical activity
rt electricity
rt sparks

ELECTRIC DRIERS
AF electric dryers
uf *driers, electric*
BT1 driers
BT2 farm machinery
BT3 machinery
BT1 electrical equipment
BT2 equipment
rt electric heating
rt electricity

ELECTRIC DRIVES
uf *drives, electric*
BT1 drives
BT2 machinery
rt electric motors
rt electric power
rt electric traction
rt electricity

ELECTRIC DRYERS
BF electric driers
BT1 dryers

ELECTRIC FENCES
uf *fences, electric*
BT1 electrical equipment
BT2 equipment
BT1 fences
BT2 barriers
BT2 fencing
rt electric current
rt electricity

ELECTRIC FIELD
BT1 electrical properties
BT2 physical properties
BT3 properties
rt electric potential
rt electricity

ELECTRIC FIELD *cont.*
rt magnetic field

ELECTRIC HEATERS
uf *heaters, electric*
BT1 heaters
BT2 equipment

ELECTRIC HEATING
BT1 heating
rt electric driers
rt electrical resistance
rt electricity

ELECTRIC MOTORS
uf *motors, electric*
BT1 electrical equipment
BT2 equipment
BT1 motors
BT2 components
rt electric drives
rt electric power
rt electric starters
rt electric traction
rt electricity

ELECTRIC POTENTIAL
uf *electrical potential*
BT1 electricity
BT2 energy sources
NT1 bioelectric potential
NT1 external electric potential
NT1 internal electric potential
rt electric field

ELECTRIC POWER
BT1 power
rt electric discharges
rt electric drives
rt electric motors
rt electric traction
rt electrical energy
rt electrical engineering
rt electricity
rt electricity generators
rt electrification
rt power lines

ELECTRIC STARTERS
uf *starters, electric*
rt electric motors
rt electricity
rt engines

ELECTRIC TRACTION
uf *traction, electric*
BT1 traction
rt electric drives
rt electric motors
rt electric power
rt electricity

ELECTRICAL ACTIVITY
BT1 electrical properties
BT2 physical properties
BT3 properties
rt electric current
rt electric discharges
rt electricity

electrical anaesthesia
USE **electronarcosis**

ELECTRICAL CONDUCTANCE
uf *conductance*
BT1 electrical properties
BT2 physical properties
BT3 properties
NT1 electrical conductivity
rt dielectrics
rt electric circuits
rt electric current
rt electrical resistance
rt electricity
rt electrodes
rt power lines

ELECTRICAL CONDUCTIVITY
BT1 conductivity
BT2 physical properties
BT3 properties
BT1 electrical conductance
BT2 electrical properties
BT3 physical properties

ELECTRICAL CONDUCTIVITY *cont.*
BT4 properties
rt electric circuits
rt electric current
rt electrical resistance
rt electricity

ELECTRICAL CONTROL
BT1 controls
rt electricity

electrical current
USE **electric current**

ELECTRICAL DOUBLE LAYER
BT1 electrical properties
BT2 physical properties
BT3 properties
BT1 ion exchange
rt electricity
rt electrolysis

ELECTRICAL ENERGY
BT1 energy
rt electric power

ELECTRICAL ENGINEERING
uf *engineering, electrical*
BT1 engineering
NT1 earthing
NT1 electrification
NT1 hydroelectric schemes
rt electric power
rt electricity
rt electricity generators

ELECTRICAL EQUIPMENT
BT1 equipment
NT1 batteries
NT1 electric driers
NT1 electric fences
NT1 electric motors
NT1 microphones
NT1 photoelectric cells
NT1 photovoltaic cells
NT1 potentiometers
NT1 solenoids
NT1 thermistors
NT1 thyristors
NT1 transformers
NT1 transponders
NT1 windings
rt electricity
rt electrocution
rt electrodialysis
rt electroejaculation
rt electrofocusing
rt electronics
rt sensors
rt switches
rt telephones
rt transducers

ELECTRICAL MOISTURE METERS
uf *moisture meters, electrical*
BT1 moisture meters
BT2 meters
BT3 instruments
rt electricity

ELECTRICAL PHENOMENA IN TREES
BT1 electrical properties
BT2 physical properties
BT3 properties

electrical potential
USE **electric potential**

ELECTRICAL PROPERTIES
BT1 physical properties
BT2 properties
NT1 capacitance
NT1 charges
NT1 electric field
NT1 electrical activity
NT1 electrical conductance
NT2 electrical conductivity
NT1 electrical double layer
NT1 electrical phenomena in trees
NT1 electrical resistance
NT1 electrokinetic potential
NT1 hysteresis

ELECTRICAL PROPERTIES *cont.*
NT1 impedance
NT1 polarization
NT1 resistivity
NT1 streaming potential
rt dielectric constant
rt electric circuits
rt electrical weed control
rt electricity
rt magnetic properties
rt polarity
rt potentiometric titration

ELECTRICAL RESISTANCE
BT1 electrical properties
BT2 physical properties
BT3 properties
BT1 resistance
rt dielectrics
rt electric circuits
rt electric current
rt electric heating
rt electrical conductance
rt electrical conductivity
rt electricity
rt resistivity

ELECTRICAL SAFETY
BT1 safety
rt earthing
rt electric current
rt electricity
rt electrocution
rt power lines
rt safety devices
rt shock
rt stray voltage

ELECTRICAL SEED CLEANERS
uf *cleaners, electrical seed*
uf *seed cleaners, electrical*
BT1 seed cleaners
BT2 cleaners
BT3 machinery
rt electricity

ELECTRICAL STIMULATION
HN from 1989
BT1 stimulation
rt electricity

ELECTRICAL TREATMENT
rt electricity
rt treatment

ELECTRICAL WEED CONTROL
uf *weed control, electrical*
BT1 weed control
BT2 pest control
BT3 control
rt electrical properties
rt electricity

ELECTRICITY
BT1 energy sources
NT1 electric potential
NT2 bioelectric potential
NT2 external electric potential
NT2 internal electric potential
NT1 sparks
rt circuits
rt electric circuits
rt electric current
rt electric discharges
rt electric driers
rt electric drives
rt electric fences
rt electric field
rt electric heating
rt electric motors
rt electric power
rt electric starters
rt electric traction
rt electrical activity
rt electrical conductance
rt electrical conductivity
rt electrical control
rt electrical double layer
rt electrical engineering
rt electrical equipment
rt electrical moisture meters
rt electrical properties
rt electrical resistance

ELECTRICITY *cont.*
rt electrical safety
rt electrical seed cleaners
rt electrical stimulation
rt electrical treatment
rt electrical weed control
rt electricity generators
rt electricity supplies
rt electrification
rt electrokinetic potential
rt electronics
rt electrons
rt fuels

ELECTRICITY GENERATORS
uf *generators, electricity*
BT1 generators
BT2 machinery
NT1 standby generators
NT1 turbines
rt electric current
rt electric power
rt electrical engineering
rt electricity
rt hydroelectric schemes
rt photoelectric cells

ELECTRICITY SUPPLIES
BT1 supplies
rt electricity
rt public utilities

ELECTRIFICATION
BT1 electrical engineering
BT2 engineering
rt electric power
rt electricity
rt mechanization
rt power lines

ELECTROANTENNOGRAMS
HN from 1990
BT1 recordings
rt antennae

ELECTROCARDIOGRAMS
uf *ecg*
BT1 recordings
rt electrocardiography
rt recording instruments

ELECTROCARDIOGRAPHY
BT1 recording
rt electrocardiograms

ELECTROCUTING GRIDS
BT1 grids
rt electrocuting traps

ELECTROCUTING TRAPS
BT1 insect traps
BT2 traps
BT3 equipment
rt electrocuting grids

ELECTROCUTION
BT1 death
rt accidents
rt electrical equipment
rt electrical safety
rt electronarcosis

ELECTRODES
BT1 components
NT1 specific ion electrodes
rt electric circuits
rt electrical conductance
rt electrolysis
rt electrolytes

ELECTRODIALYSIS
BT1 dialysis
BT2 processing
BT2 separation
rt electrical equipment

ELECTRODIFFUSION
HN from 1990
BT1 processing
rt diffusion
rt extraction

ELECTROEJACULATION
BT1 ejaculation

ELECTROEJACULATION *cont.*
BT1 semen production
rt artificial insemination
rt electrical equipment

ELECTROENCEPHALOGRAMS
BT1 encephalograms
BT2 recordings
rt brain
rt brain disorders
rt electroencephalography

ELECTROENCEPHALOGRAPHY
uf *eeg*
BT1 recording
rt brain
rt brain disorders
rt electroencephalograms

ELECTROFILTRATION
HN from 1990
BT1 filtration
BT2 processing
rt decolorization

ELECTROFOCUSING
rt electrical equipment

ELECTROFUSION
HN from 1990
BT1 techniques

ELECTROKINETIC POTENTIAL
uf *zeta potential*
BT1 electrical properties
BT2 physical properties
BT3 properties
rt electricity

ELECTROLYSIS
NT1 polarization
rt electric current
rt electrical double layer
rt electrodes
rt galvanizing
rt ion transport
rt specific ion electrodes

ELECTROLYTES
rt acid base equilibrium
rt blood chemistry
rt electrodes
rt ions
rt solutions

ELECTROMAGNETIC FIELD
BT1 magnetism
rt magnetic field

ELECTROMAGNETIC RADIATION
BT1 radiation
NT1 gamma radiation
NT1 infrared radiation
NT1 light
NT2 artificial light
NT2 blue light
NT2 daylight
NT2 far red light
NT2 fluorescent light
NT2 intermittent light
NT2 moonlight
NT2 natural light
NT2 polarized light
NT2 red light
NT2 supplementary light
NT2 white light
NT1 microwave radiation
NT1 radio waves
NT1 terrestrial radiation
NT1 thermal radiation
NT1 ultraviolet radiation
NT1 x radiation

ELECTROMETRIC METHODS
BT1 analytical methods
BT2 methodology

ELECTROMYOGRAPHY
BT1 recording
rt muscles

electron flow
USE **electron transfer**

ELECTRON MICROSCOPES
uf *microscopes, electron*
BT1 microscopes
BT2 instruments
NT1 scanning electron microscopes
rt electrons

ELECTRON MICROSCOPY
BT1 microscopy
BT2 techniques
NT1 scanning electron microscopy
NT1 transmission electron microscopy
rt electrons
rt ultramicroscopy

ELECTRON PARAMAGNETIC RESONANCE SPECTROSCOPY
BT1 spectroscopy
BT2 analytical methods
BT3 methodology

ELECTRON TRANSFER
uf *electron flow*
uf *electron transport*
BT1 redox reactions
BT2 chemical reactions
rt electrons
rt energy metabolism

electron transport
USE **electron transfer**

ELECTRONARCOSIS
uf *electrical anaesthesia*
BT1 anaesthesia
rt electrocution
rt narcosis

electronic data processing
USE **data processing**

electronic engineering
USE **electronics**

ELECTRONIC SCANNING (AGRICOLA)
rt universal product codes (agricola)

ELECTRONIC SEPARATION
BT1 analytical methods
BT2 methodology
BT1 separation
rt electronics

ELECTRONICS
uf *electronic engineering*
uf *engineering, electronic*
BT1 physics
rt computers
rt electrical equipment
rt electricity
rt electronic separation
rt instruments
rt integrated circuits
rt liquid crystal displays
rt microprocessors
rt television

ELECTRONS
rt electricity
rt electron microscopes
rt electron microscopy
rt electron transfer

ELECTROPHORESIS
BT1 analytical methods
BT2 methodology
NT1 immunoelectrophoresis
NT2 counterimmunoelectrophoresis
NT1 isoelectric focusing
NT1 northern blotting
NT1 page
NT2 sds-page
NT1 pulsed field electrophoresis
NT1 southern blotting
rt ionophores

ELECTROPHYSIOLOGY
HN from 1990
BT1 physiology

ELECTROPHYSIOLOGY *cont.*
rt recordings

ELECTROPORATION
HN from 1989
rt direct dna uptake
rt genetic engineering

ELECTRORETINOGRAMS
BT1 recordings
rt retina

ELECTROSTATIC CHARGING
uf *charging, electrostatic*
rt electrostatic spraying
rt sprays

ELECTROSTATIC SEED CLEANERS
uf *cleaners, electrostatic seed*
uf *seed cleaners, electrostatic*
BT1 seed cleaners
BT2 cleaners
BT3 machinery

ELECTROSTATIC SEPARATION
BT1 analytical methods
BT2 methodology
BT1 separation

ELECTROSTATIC SPRAYERS
HN from 1990
BT1 sprayers
BT2 spraying equipment
BT3 application equipment
BT4 equipment
rt electrostatic spraying

ELECTROSTATIC SPRAYING
uf *spraying, electrostatic*
BT1 spraying
BT2 application methods
BT3 methodology
rt electrostatic charging
rt electrostatic sprayers
rt ultralow volume sprayers

ELECTROULTRAFILTRATION
BT1 analytical methods
BT2 methodology
BT1 ultrafiltration
BT2 filtration
BT3 processing

ELEDOISIN
BT1 kinins
BT2 hormones
BT2 peptides
BT1 vasodilator agents
BT2 cardiovascular agents
BT3 drugs

ELEDONE
BT1 octopodidae
BT2 cephalopoda
BT3 mollusca

ELEGINUS
BT1 gadidae
BT2 gadiformes
BT3 osteichthyes
BT4 fishes

ELEMENTAL DIETS
uf *diet, elemental*
BT1 diets

elemental sulphur
USE **sulfur**

ELEMENTARY EDUCATION (AGRICOLA)
uf *elementary grades*
uf *intermediate grades*
BT1 education
rt elementary schools (agricola)
rt primary education

elementary grades
USE **elementary education (agricola)**

ELEMENTARY SCHOOLS (AGRICOLA)

ELEMENTARY SCHOOLS (AGRICOLA) *cont.*
BT1 schools
BT2 educational institutions
rt elementary education (agricola)

ELEMENTS
NT1 heavy metals
NT1 major elements
NT1 metallic elements
NT2 alkali metals
NT3 caesium
NT3 lithium
NT3 potassium
NT3 rubidium
NT3 sodium
NT2 alkaline earth metals
NT3 barium
NT3 beryllium
NT3 calcium
NT3 magnesium
NT3 radium
NT3 strontium
NT2 aluminium
NT2 antimony
NT2 bismuth
NT2 gallium
NT2 germanium
NT2 indium
NT2 lead
NT2 thallium
NT2 tin
NT2 transition elements
NT3 actinides
NT4 americium
NT4 curium
NT4 neptunium
NT4 plutonium
NT4 protactinium
NT4 thorium
NT4 uranium
NT3 cadmium
NT3 chromium
NT3 cobalt
NT3 copper
NT3 gold
NT3 iron
NT3 manganese
NT3 mercury
NT3 molybdenum
NT3 nickel
NT3 niobium
NT3 palladium
NT3 platinum
NT3 polonium
NT3 rare earth elements
NT4 cerium
NT4 europium
NT4 lanthanum
NT4 samarium
NT4 terbium
NT4 ytterbium
NT3 rhodium
NT3 ruthenium
NT3 scandium
NT3 silver
NT3 tantalum
NT3 technetium
NT3 titanium
NT3 tungsten
NT3 vanadium
NT3 yttrium
NT3 zinc
NT3 zirconium
NT1 minor elements
NT1 nonmetallic elements
NT2 arsenic
NT2 boron
NT2 carbon
NT2 chalcogens
NT3 oxygen
NT3 sulfur
NT3 tellurium
NT2 halogens
NT3 bromine
NT3 chlorine
NT3 fluorine
NT3 iodine
NT2 hydrogen
NT3 deuterium

ELEMENTS *cont.*
NT3 tritium
NT2 nitrogen
NT2 noble gases
NT3 argon
NT3 helium
NT3 radon
NT3 xenon
NT2 phosphorus
NT3 red phosphorus
NT3 yellow phosphorus
NT2 selenium
NT2 silicon
NT1 trace elements
NT2 boron
NT2 bromine
NT2 chromium
NT2 cobalt
NT2 copper
NT2 fluorine
NT2 iodine
NT2 iron
NT2 manganese
NT2 molybdenum
NT2 rubidium
NT2 selenium
NT2 strontium
NT2 tungsten
NT2 vanadium
NT2 zinc
rt chemical speciation
rt semimetals

ELENCHIDAE
BT1 strepsiptera
NT1 elenchus

ELENCHUS
BT1 elenchidae
BT2 strepsiptera

ELEOCHARIS
BT1 cyperaceae
NT1 eleocharis acicularis
NT1 eleocharis coloradoensis
NT1 eleocharis congesta
NT1 eleocharis dulcis
NT1 eleocharis kuroguwai
NT1 eleocharis palustris
NT1 eleocharis parvula
NT1 eleocharis plantaginea
NT1 eleocharis sphacelata
NT1 eleocharis tuberosa

ELEOCHARIS ACICULARIS
BT1 eleocharis
BT2 cyperaceae

ELEOCHARIS COLORADOENSIS
BT1 eleocharis
BT2 cyperaceae

ELEOCHARIS CONGESTA
BT1 eleocharis
BT2 cyperaceae

ELEOCHARIS DULCIS
BT1 eleocharis
BT2 cyperaceae

ELEOCHARIS KUROGUWAI
BT1 eleocharis
BT2 cyperaceae

ELEOCHARIS PALUSTRIS
BT1 eleocharis
BT2 cyperaceae

ELEOCHARIS PARVULA
BT1 eleocharis
BT2 cyperaceae

ELEOCHARIS PLANTAGINEA
BT1 eleocharis
BT2 cyperaceae

ELEOCHARIS SPHACELATA
BT1 eleocharis
BT2 cyperaceae

ELEOCHARIS TUBEROSA
BT1 eleocharis
BT2 cyperaceae
BT1 root vegetables

ELEOCHARIS TUBEROSA *cont.*
BT2 root crops
BT2 vegetables

ELEODES
BT1 tenebrionidae
BT2 coleoptera

ELEOTRIDAE
BT1 perciformes
BT2 osteichthyes
BT3 fishes
NT1 gobiomorus

elephant grass
USE **pennisetum purpureum**

ELEPHANTIASIS
HN from 1990
BT1 nematode infections
BT2 helminthoses
BT3 parasitoses
BT4 diseases
rt filariasis

ELEPHANTIDAE
BT1 proboscidea (mammals)
BT2 mammals
NT1 elephas
NT2 elephas maximus
NT1 loxodonta
NT2 loxodonta africana

ELEPHANTOPUS
BT1 compositae
NT1 elephantopus mollis
NT1 elephantopus scaber
NT1 elephantopus tomentosus

ELEPHANTOPUS MOLLIS
BT1 elephantopus
BT2 compositae
BT1 medicinal plants

ELEPHANTOPUS SCABER
BT1 elephantopus
BT2 compositae

ELEPHANTOPUS TOMENTOSUS
BT1 elephantopus
BT2 compositae
BT1 medicinal plants

ELEPHANTS
BT1 wild animals
BT2 animals
rt proboscidea (mammals)

ELEPHANTULUS
BT1 macroscelididae
BT2 macroscelidea
BT3 mammals

ELEPHAS
BT1 elephantidae
BT2 proboscidea (mammals)
BT3 mammals
NT1 elephas maximus

elephas indicus
USE **elephas maximus**

ELEPHAS MAXIMUS
uf *elephas indicus*
uf *indian elephants*
BT1 elephas
BT2 elephantidae
BT3 proboscidea (mammals)
BT4 mammals

ELETTARIA
BT1 zingiberaceae
NT1 elettaria cardamomum

ELETTARIA CARDAMOMUM
uf *amomum cardamomum*
BT1 antibacterial plants
BT1 antifungal plants
BT1 elettaria
BT2 zingiberaceae
BT1 essential oil plants
BT2 oil plants
BT1 insecticidal plants
BT2 pesticidal plants
BT1 medicinal plants

ELETTARIA CARDAMOMUM *cont.*
BT1 spice plants
rt cardamoms

ELEUSINE
BT1 gramineae
NT1 eleusine aegyptiaca
NT1 eleusine compressa
NT1 eleusine coracana
NT1 eleusine indica
NT1 eleusine jaegeri
NT1 eleusine kigeziensis
NT1 eleusine semisterilis

ELEUSINE AEGYPTIACA
BT1 eleusine
BT2 gramineae
BT1 pasture plants

eleusine africana
USE **eleusine indica**

ELEUSINE COMPRESSA
uf *eleusine flagellifera*
BT1 eleusine
BT2 gramineae
BT1 pasture plants

ELEUSINE CORACANA
BT1 eleusine
BT2 gramineae
BT1 millets
BT2 cereals
BT3 grain crops
BT1 pasture plants
rt finger millet

eleusine flagellifera
USE **eleusine compressa**

ELEUSINE INDICA
uf *eleusine africana*
BT1 eleusine
BT2 gramineae
BT1 pasture plants
BT1 weeds

ELEUSINE JAEGERI
BT1 eleusine
BT2 gramineae
BT1 pasture plants

ELEUSINE KIGEZIENSIS
BT1 eleusine
BT2 gramineae
BT1 pasture plants

ELEUSINE SEMISTERILIS
BT1 eleusine
BT2 gramineae
BT1 pasture plants

ELEUTHERANTHERA
BT1 compositae
NT1 eleutheranthera ruderalis

ELEUTHERANTHERA RUDERALIS
BT1 eleutheranthera
BT2 compositae

ELEUTHEROCOCCUS
BT1 araliaceae
NT1 eleutherococcus senticosus
NT1 eleutherococcus sieboldianus
rt acanthopanax

ELEUTHEROCOCCUS SENTICOSUS
uf *acanthopanax senticosus*
BT1 eleutherococcus
BT2 araliaceae
BT1 medicinal plants

ELEUTHEROCOCCUS SIEBOLDIANUS
uf *acanthopanax sieboldianus*
BT1 eleutherococcus
BT2 araliaceae
BT1 ornamental woody plants

ELEUTHERONEMA
BT1 polynemidae
BT2 perciformes
BT3 osteichthyes

ELEUTHERONEMA *cont.*
BT4 fishes

elevation
USE **altitude**
OR **height**

ELEVATOR DIGGERS
rt digging
rt harvesters
rt potato harvesters

ELEVATORS
BT1 conveyors
NT1 bucket elevators
rt bale throwers
rt cranes
rt harvesters
rt hoists
rt loaders

elevators, bucket
USE **bucket elevators**

ELFAZEPAM
BT1 appetite stimulants
BT2 stimulants
BT3 drugs
BT1 benzodiazepines
BT2 heterocyclic nitrogen compounds
BT3 organic nitrogen compounds
BT1 neuroleptics
BT2 psychotropic drugs
BT3 neurotropic drugs
BT4 drugs

ELFIN WOODLANDS
HN from 1989
BT1 woodlands
BT2 vegetation types

ELGIVA
HN from 1989
uf *ilione*
BT1 sciomyzidae
BT2 diptera

ELIGIBILITY (AGRICOLA)
HN from 1989

elimination
(consult also narrower and related terms of the following)
USE **disease control**
OR **excretion**
OR **pest control**

ELIMINATION DIETS (AGRICOLA)
BT1 diets
rt food allergies

ELIOMYS
BT1 gliridae
BT2 rodents
BT3 mammals
NT1 eliomys quercinus

ELIOMYS QUERCINUS
BT1 eliomys
BT2 gliridae
BT3 rodents
BT4 mammals

ELIONURUS
uf *elyonurus*
BT1 gramineae
NT1 elionurus argenteus
NT1 elionurus muticus
NT1 elionurus viridulus

ELIONURUS ARGENTEUS
BT1 elionurus
BT2 gramineae
BT1 pasture plants

ELIONURUS MUTICUS
BT1 elionurus
BT2 gramineae

ELIONURUS VIRIDULUS
BT1 elionurus
BT2 gramineae

ELISA
uf *enzyme linked immunosorbent assay*
BT1 enzyme immunoassay
BT2 immunoassay
BT3 assays
BT3 immunological techniques
BT4 techniques
BT2 immunoenzyme techniques
BT3 immunological techniques
BT4 techniques

ELITES
BT1 high yielding varieties
BT2 varieties
NT1 plus trees
rt breeding value
rt performance
rt selection criteria
rt selective breeding

ELIZABETHA
BT1 leguminosae
NT1 elizabetha princeps

ELIZABETHA PRINCEPS
BT1 elizabetha
BT2 leguminosae

elks, american
USE **cervus elaphus canadensis**

elks, european
USE **alces alces**

ELLAGIC ACID
BT1 organic acids
BT2 acids
rt tannins

ellice islands
USE **tuvalu**

ELLIOTTIA
BT1 ericaceae
NT1 elliottia bracteata
NT1 elliottia paniculata
NT1 elliottia pyroliflora
NT1 elliottia racemosa

ELLIOTTIA BRACTEATA
BT1 elliottia
BT2 ericaceae

ELLIOTTIA PANICULATA
BT1 elliottia
BT2 ericaceae

ELLIOTTIA PYROLIFLORA
BT1 elliottia
BT2 ericaceae

ELLIOTTIA RACEMOSA
BT1 elliottia
BT2 ericaceae

ELM MOTTLE ILARVIRUS
HN from 1990
BT1 ilarvirus group
BT2 plant viruses
BT3 plant pathogens
BT4 pathogens
rt ulmus

elms
USE **ulmus**

ELODEA
BT1 hydrocharitaceae
NT1 elodea canadensis
NT1 elodea nodosus
NT1 elodea nuttallii

ELODEA CANADENSIS
BT1 elodea
BT2 hydrocharitaceae

ELODEA NODOSUS
BT1 elodea
BT2 hydrocharitaceae

ELODEA NUTTALLII
BT1 elodea
BT2 hydrocharitaceae

ELOPIDAE
BT1 elopiformes
BT2 osteichthyes
BT3 fishes
NT1 elops

ELOPIFORMES
BT1 osteichthyes
BT2 fishes
NT1 elopidae
NT2 elops
NT1 megalopidae
NT2 megalops
NT3 megalops atlanticus
NT3 megalops cyprinoides

ELOPS
BT1 elopidae
BT2 elopiformes
BT3 osteichthyes
BT4 fishes

ELSHOLTZIA
BT1 labiatae
NT1 elsholtzia blanda
NT1 elsholtzia ciliata

ELSHOLTZIA BLANDA
BT1 elsholtzia
BT2 labiatae

ELSHOLTZIA CILIATA
uf *elsholtzia patrinii*
BT1 elsholtzia
BT2 labiatae
BT1 essential oil plants
BT2 oil plants

elsholtzia patrinii
USE **elsholtzia ciliata**

ELSINOE
BT1 dothideales
NT1 elsinoe ampelina
NT1 elsinoe batatas
NT1 elsinoe brasiliensis
NT1 elsinoe fawcettii
NT1 elsinoe veneta
rt gloeosporium
rt sphaceloma

ELSINOE AMPELINA
uf *gloeosporium ampelina*
uf *gloeosporium ampelophagum*
uf *sphaceloma ampelinum*
BT1 elsinoe
BT2 dothideales

ELSINOE BATATAS
uf *sphaceloma batatas*
BT1 elsinoe
BT2 dothideales

ELSINOE BRASILIENSIS
BT1 elsinoe
BT2 dothideales

ELSINOE FAWCETTII
BT1 elsinoe
BT2 dothideales

ELSINOE VENETA
BT1 elsinoe
BT2 dothideales

eltonella
USE **ascoschoengastia**

ELUVIATION
BT1 soil formation
rt illuviation
rt leaching

ELYMUS
uf *elytrigia*
BT1 gramineae
NT1 elymus canadensis
NT1 elymus caninus
NT1 elymus dahuricus
NT1 elymus dentatus
NT1 elymus elongatus
NT1 elymus farctus
NT1 elymus fibrosus
NT1 elymus hispidus

ELYMUS *cont.*
NT1 elymus hispidus subsp. barbulatus
NT1 elymus kronokensis
NT1 elymus lanceolatus
NT1 elymus mutabilis
NT1 elymus pungens
NT1 elymus repens
NT1 elymus sibiricus
NT1 elymus smithii
NT1 elymus spicatus
NT1 elymus trachycaulus
rt taeniatherum
rt thinopyrum

elymus ajanensis
USE **leymus ajanensis**

elymus angustus
USE **leymus angustus**

elymus arenarius
USE **leymus arenarius**

elymus asper
USE **taeniatherum caput-medusae**

ELYMUS CANADENSIS
BT1 elymus
BT2 gramineae
BT1 pasture plants

ELYMUS CANINUS
uf *agropyron caninum*
BT1 elymus
BT2 gramineae
BT1 pasture plants

elymus caput-medusae
USE **taeniatherum caput-medusae**

elymus chinensis
USE **leymus chinensis**

ELYMUS DAHURICUS
BT1 elymus
BT2 gramineae
BT1 pasture plants

ELYMUS DENTATUS
uf *agropyron dentatum*
BT1 elymus
BT2 gramineae
BT1 pasture plants

ELYMUS ELONGATUS
uf *agropyron elongatum*
uf *elytrigia pontica*
uf *thinopyrum ponticum*
BT1 elymus
BT2 gramineae
BT1 pasture plants

ELYMUS FARCTUS
uf *agropyron junceiforme*
uf *elytrigia juncea*
BT1 elymus
BT2 gramineae
BT1 pasture plants

ELYMUS FIBROSUS
uf *agropyron fibrosum*
BT1 elymus
BT2 gramineae
BT1 pasture plants

ELYMUS HISPIDUS
uf *agropyron glaucum*
uf *agropyron intermedium*
uf *elytrigia intermedia*
uf *thinopyrum intermedium*
BT1 elymus
BT2 gramineae
BT1 pasture plants

ELYMUS HISPIDUS SUBSP. BARBULATUS
uf *agropyron trichophorum*
BT1 elymus
BT2 gramineae
BT1 pasture plants

elymus innovatus
USE **leymus innovatus**

elymus jacutensis
USE **leymus jacutensis**

elymus junceus
USE **psathyrostachys juncea**

ELYMUS KRONOKENSIS
uf *agropyron latiglume*
BT1 elymus
BT2 gramineae
BT1 pasture plants

ELYMUS LANCEOLATUS
uf *agropyron dasystachyum*
uf *agropyron riparium*
BT1 elymus
BT2 gramineae
BT1 pasture plants

ELYMUS MUTABILIS
BT1 elymus
BT2 gramineae
BT1 pasture plants

ELYMUS PUNGENS
uf *agropyron pungens*
uf *elytrigia pungens*
BT1 elymus
BT2 gramineae
BT1 pasture plants

elymus ramosus
USE **leymus ramosus**

ELYMUS REPENS
uf *agropyron repens*
uf *couch*
uf *elytrigia repens*
BT1 elymus
BT2 gramineae
BT1 pasture plants
BT1 weeds

elymus secalinus
USE **leymus secalinus**

ELYMUS SIBIRICUS
BT1 elymus
BT2 gramineae
BT1 pasture plants

ELYMUS SMITHII
uf *agropyron smithii*
BT1 elymus
BT2 gramineae
BT1 pasture plants

ELYMUS SPICATUS
uf *agropyron spicatum*
uf *elytrigia spicata*
BT1 elymus
BT2 gramineae
BT1 pasture plants

ELYMUS TRACHYCAULUS
uf *agropyron tenerum*
uf *agropyron trachycaulum*
BT1 elymus
BT2 gramineae
BT1 pasture plants

elymus triticoides
USE **leymus triticoides**

elyonurus
USE **elionurus**

elytrigia
USE **elymus**

elytrigia intermedia
USE **elymus hispidus**

elytrigia juncea
USE **elymus farctus**

elytrigia pontica
USE **elymus elongatus**

elytrigia pungens
USE **elymus pungens**

elytrigia repens
USE **elymus repens**

elytrigia spicata
USE **elymus spicatus**

EMACIATION
BT1 nutritional disorders
BT2 animal disorders
BT3 disorders
rt wasting disease

EMASCULATION
BT1 plant breeding methods
BT2 breeding methods
BT3 methodology
rt castration

EMBALLONURIDAE
BT1 chiroptera
BT2 mammals
NT1 taphozous
NT2 taphozous perforatus

EMBARGOES
BT1 trade discrimination
BT2 imperfect competition
BT3 market competition
BT2 protection
rt trade sanctions

EMBELIA
BT1 myrsinaceae
NT1 embelia ribes

EMBELIA RIBES
BT1 antiviral plants
BT1 embelia
BT2 myrsinaceae
BT1 medicinal plants

EMBELLISIA
BT1 deuteromycotina
NT1 embellisia hyacinthi

EMBELLISIA HYACINTHI
BT1 embellisia
BT2 deuteromycotina

EMBIOPTERA
rt insects

EMBLICA
BT1 euphorbiaceae
rt phyllanthus

emblica officinalis
USE **phyllanthus emblica**

EMBOLISM
BT1 vascular diseases
BT2 cardiovascular diseases
BT3 organic diseases
BT4 diseases
rt clotting
rt thrombosis

EMBOSSED FABRICS (AGRICOLA)
BT1 fabrics

EMBOTHRIUM
BT1 proteaceae
NT1 embothrium coccineum

EMBOTHRIUM COCCINEUM
BT1 embothrium
BT2 proteaceae
BT1 ornamental woody plants

EMBROIDERY (AGRICOLA)
BT1 needlework
BT2 handicrafts

EMBRYO CULTURE
BT1 tissue culture
BT2 in vitro culture
BT3 culture techniques
BT4 biological techniques
BT5 techniques

embryo development
USE **embryonic development**

embryo growth
USE **embryonic development**

EMBRYO IMPLANTATION
HN from 1990
(natural process)
uf *implantation, embryo*
uf *implantation, ovum*
uf *nidation*
BT1 pregnancy
BT2 sexual reproduction
BT3 reproduction
rt preimplantation period

EMBRYO MALPOSITIONS
BT1 malpositions
BT2 abnormalities
BT1 reproductive disorders
BT2 functional disorders
BT3 animal disorders
BT4 disorders
rt embryos

EMBRYO MORTALITY
BT1 mortality
BT2 vital statistics
rt embryos
rt fetal death

EMBRYO NUTRITION
BT1 animal nutrition
BT2 nutrition
rt embryos

EMBRYO SAC
rt embryos
rt gametes
rt reproduction

EMBRYO TRANSFER
rt animal breeding
rt embryos

EMBRYOCOLA
BT1 sarcomastigophora
BT2 protozoa

EMBRYOGENESIS
(plants)
BT1 organogenesis
BT2 plant development
rt embryonic development

EMBRYOLOGY
BT1 biology
rt differentiation
rt embryonic development
rt embryos
rt growth

EMBRYONIC DEVELOPMENT
(animals and man)
uf *embryo development*
uf *embryo growth*
NT1 cleavage
NT1 polyembryony
rt development
rt embryogenesis
rt embryology
rt fetal development disorders
rt fetal growth
rt growth
rt morphogenesis
rt pregnancy
rt reproduction

EMBRYONIC RESORPTION
BT1 resorption
rt embryos

EMBRYONIC STEM CELLS
HN from 1989
BT1 cells
rt embryos

EMBRYOS
(of animals and man)
NT1 blastocyst
NT2 blastomere
NT1 chick embryos
NT1 fetus
NT1 morula
NT1 wolffian duct
rt conceptus
rt embryo malpositions
rt embryo mortality
rt embryo nutrition

EMBRYOS *cont.*
rt embryo sac
rt embryo transfer
rt embryology
rt embryonic resorption
rt embryonic stem cells
rt embryotomy

embryos, plant
USE **plant embryos**

EMBRYOTOMY
BT1 surgical operations
rt embryos
rt obstetrics

EMERGENCE
BT1 plant development
rt germination
rt seedling emergence
rt seedlings

EMERGENCIES
NT1 war
NT2 biological warfare
rt civil defense (agricola)
rt emergency feeding (agricola)
rt food aid
rt food rationing
rt natural disasters
rt refugees

EMERGENCY FEEDING (AGRICOLA)
BT1 feeding
rt emergencies

EMETICS
BT1 gastrointestinal agents
BT2 drugs
NT1 apomorphine
rt antiemetics
rt asarum europaeum
rt vomiting

EMETINE
BT1 amoebicides
BT2 antiprotozoal agents
BT3 antiparasitic agents
BT4 drugs
BT1 anthelmintics
BT2 antiparasitic agents
BT3 drugs
BT1 isoquinoline alkaloids
BT2 alkaloids

EMEX
BT1 polygonaceae
NT1 emex australis
NT1 emex spinosus

EMEX AUSTRALIS
BT1 emex
BT2 polygonaceae

EMEX SPINOSUS
BT1 emex
BT2 polygonaceae

EMIGRATION
BT1 migration

EMILIA
BT1 compositae
NT1 emilia flammea
NT1 emilia javanica
NT1 emilia sonchifolia

EMILIA FLAMMEA
BT1 emilia
BT2 compositae
BT1 medicinal plants

EMILIA JAVANICA
uf *emilia sagittalis*
BT1 emilia
BT2 compositae

EMILIA ROMAGNA
BT1 italy
BT2 western europe
BT3 europe

emilia sagittalis
USE **emilia javanica**

EMILIA SONCHIFOLIA
BT1 emilia
BT2 compositae

EMISSION
NT1 odour emission

EMITTERS
BT1 irrigation equipment
BT2 equipment
rt blockage
rt nozzles

EMMENTAL CHEESE
BT1 cheeses
BT2 milk products
BT3 products

EMMONSIA
uf *haplosporangium*
BT1 deuteromycotina
NT1 emmonsia crescens
NT1 emmonsia parva
rt adiaspiromycosis
rt chrysosporium

EMMONSIA CRESCENS
BT1 emmonsia
BT2 deuteromycotina

EMMONSIA PARVA
uf *chrysosporium parvum*
uf *haplosporangium parvum*
BT1 emmonsia
BT2 deuteromycotina

emmonsiella
USE **ajellomyces**

emmonsiella capsulata
USE **ajellomyces capsulatus**

EMODIN
uf *archin*
BT1 anthraquinones
BT2 quinones
BT3 aromatic compounds
BT1 mycotoxins
BT2 toxins
BT1 purgatives
BT2 gastrointestinal agents
BT3 drugs

EMOTIONAL DEVELOPMENT (AGRICOLA)
BT1 personal development
rt emotions (agricola)
rt social emotional development (agricola)

EMOTIONAL DISTURBANCES (AGRICOLA)
BT1 mental disorders
BT2 functional disorders
BT3 animal disorders
BT4 disorders
rt emotions (agricola)

EMOTIONS (AGRICOLA)
uf *affective behaviour*
rt emotional development (agricola)
rt emotional disturbances (agricola)

EMPETRACEAE
NT1 empetrum
NT2 empetrum nigrum

EMPETRUM
BT1 empetraceae
NT1 empetrum nigrum

EMPETRUM NIGRUM
BT1 empetrum
BT2 empetraceae
BT1 ornamental woody plants

EMPHOROPSIS
BT1 apidae
BT2 hymenoptera

emphysema, pulmonary
USE **pulmonary emphysema**

EMPLOYED PARENTS (AGRICOLA)
BT1 parents
BT2 ancestry
rt employment
rt labor

EMPLOYED WOMEN (AGRICOLA)
uf *working women*
BT1 women
BT2 adults
rt employment
rt labor

employee participation
USE **participative management (agricola)**

EMPLOYEE THEFT (AGRICOLA)
BT1 theft (agricola)
BT2 antisocial behavior (agricola)
BT3 human behavior
BT4 behavior
BT2 crime

employees
USE **personnel**

EMPLOYER EMPLOYEE RELATIONSHIPS (AGRICOLA)
rt labor relations
rt participative management (agricola)
rt relationships

EMPLOYMENT
uf *jobs*
NT1 off-farm employment
NT1 part time employment (agricola)
NT1 underemployment
NT1 unemployment
NT2 rural unemployment
NT3 agricultural unemployment
NT2 seasonal unemployment
NT2 structural unemployment
rt employed parents (agricola)
rt employed women (agricola)
rt employment opportunities
rt job sharing (agricola)
rt labour
rt labour economics
rt labour market
rt labour requirements
rt occupational change
rt occupations
rt personnel
rt working life
rt working population

EMPLOYMENT OPPORTUNITIES
uf *career opportunities*
rt employment

EMPOASCA
BT1 cicadellidae
BT2 cicadelloidea
BT3 auchenorrhyncha
BT4 homoptera
NT1 empoasca decipiens
NT1 empoasca dolichi
NT1 empoasca fabae
NT1 empoasca flavescens
NT1 empoasca kerri
NT1 empoasca kraemeri
rt amrasca
rt chlorita
rt jacobiasca
rt jacobiella

empoasca biguttula
USE **amrasca biguttula**

EMPOASCA DECIPIENS
BT1 empoasca
BT2 cicadellidae
BT3 cicadelloidea
BT4 auchenorrhyncha
BT5 homoptera

empoasca devastans
USE **amrasca devastans**

EMPOASCA DOLICHI
BT1 empoasca
BT2 cicadellidae
BT3 cicadelloidea
BT4 auchenorrhyncha
BT5 homoptera

EMPOASCA FABAE
BT1 empoasca
BT2 cicadellidae
BT3 cicadelloidea
BT4 auchenorrhyncha
BT5 homoptera

empoasca facialis
USE **jacobiella facialis**

EMPOASCA FLAVESCENS
uf chlorita flavescens
BT1 empoasca
BT2 cicadellidae
BT3 cicadelloidea
BT4 auchenorrhyncha
BT5 homoptera

EMPOASCA KERRI
BT1 empoasca
BT2 cicadellidae
BT3 cicadelloidea
BT4 auchenorrhyncha
BT5 homoptera

EMPOASCA KRAEMERI
BT1 empoasca
BT2 cicadellidae
BT3 cicadelloidea
BT4 auchenorrhyncha
BT5 homoptera

empoasca lybica
USE **jacobiasca lybica**

EMPOASCANARA
uf vietnara
BT1 cicadellidae
BT2 cicadelloidea
BT3 auchenorrhyncha
BT4 homoptera
NT1 empoascanara maculifrons
rt zygina

EMPOASCANARA MACULIFRONS
uf vietnara maculifrons
uf zygina maculifrons
BT1 empoascanara
BT2 cicadellidae
BT3 cicadelloidea
BT4 auchenorrhyncha
BT5 homoptera

EMPTY NEST SYNDROME (AGRICOLA)
rt family life

empusa
USE **entomophthora**

empusa fresenii
USE **neozygites fresenii**

EMULSIFIABLE CONCENTRATES
BT1 formulations
rt emulsification
rt emulsions

EMULSIFICATION
BT1 processing
rt emulsifiable concentrates
rt emulsifiers
rt emulsions
rt mixing
rt suspensions
rt whipping

EMULSIFIERS
BT1 surfactants
NT1 alginates
NT1 bile salts
NT1 phosphatidylcholines
NT1 xanthan
rt emulsification
rt food additives

EMULSIFIERS *cont.*
rt stabilizers

EMULSIFYING
BT1 processing
rt emulsions

EMULSIONS
NT1 bitumen emulsions
NT1 fat emulsions
NT2 fat globules
NT2 intralipid
rt colloids
rt emulsifiable concentrates
rt emulsification
rt emulsifying

EMUS
uf dromaius novaehollandiae
BT1 plumage birds
BT2 animals
rt dromaiidae

EMYDIDAE
BT1 testudines
BT2 reptiles
NT1 chrysemys
NT2 chrysemys picta
NT1 pseudemys
NT2 pseudemys nelsoni
NT2 pseudemys scripta

ENAMEL
BT1 coatings
BT1 teeth
BT2 jaws
BT3 bones
BT4 musculoskeletal system
BT5 body parts
rt dentine
rt paints

ENANTIA
BT1 annonaceae
NT1 enantia polycarpa

ENANTIA POLYCARPA
BT1 dye plants
BT1 enantia
BT2 annonaceae

ENANTIOMERS
HN from 1989
uf optical isomers
BT1 isomers

ENAPHALODES
BT1 cerambycidae
BT2 coleoptera
NT1 enaphalodes rufulus

ENAPHALODES RUFULUS
BT1 enaphalodes
BT2 cerambycidae
BT3 coleoptera

ENARMONIA
BT1 tortricidae
BT2 lepidoptera
NT1 enarmonia formosana

ENARMONIA FORMOSANA
uf laspeyresia woeberiana
BT1 enarmonia
BT2 tortricidae
BT3 lepidoptera

ENCAPSULATION
rt fertilizer technology
rt formulations

ENCARSIA
uf aspidiotiphagus
uf prospaltella
BT1 aphelinidae
BT2 hymenoptera
NT1 encarsia berlesei
NT1 encarsia citrina
NT1 encarsia formosa
NT1 encarsia lahorensis
NT1 encarsia lutea
NT1 encarsia perniciosi

ENCARSIA BERLESEI
uf prospaltella berlesei

ENCARSIA BERLESEI *cont.*
BT1 encarsia
BT2 aphelinidae
BT3 hymenoptera

ENCARSIA CITRINA
uf aspidiotiphagus citrinus
BT1 biological control agents
BT2 beneficial organisms
BT1 encarsia
BT2 aphelinidae
BT3 hymenoptera

ENCARSIA FORMOSA
BT1 biological control agents
BT2 beneficial organisms
BT1 encarsia
BT2 aphelinidae
BT3 hymenoptera

ENCARSIA LAHORENSIS
uf prospaltella lahorensis
BT1 encarsia
BT2 aphelinidae
BT3 hymenoptera

ENCARSIA LUTEA
BT1 encarsia
BT2 aphelinidae
BT3 hymenoptera

ENCARSIA PERNICIOSI
uf prospaltella perniciosi
BT1 encarsia
BT2 aphelinidae
BT3 hymenoptera

ENCEPHALARTOS
BT1 zamiaceae
NT1 encephalartos umbeluziensis

ENCEPHALARTOS UMBELUZIENSIS
BT1 encephalartos
BT2 zamiaceae

encephalins
USE **enkephalins**

ENCEPHALITIS
uf encephalomyelitis
BT1 brain disorders
BT2 nervous system diseases
BT3 organic diseases
BT4 diseases
NT1 allergic encephalomyelitis
NT1 japanese encephalitis
rt avian encephalomyelitis virus
rt equine encephalomyelitis virus

ENCEPHALITOZOON
BT1 microspora
BT2 protozoa
NT1 encephalitozoon cuniculi

ENCEPHALITOZOON CUNICULI
BT1 encephalitozoon
BT2 microspora
BT3 protozoa

ENCEPHALOGRAMS
BT1 recordings
NT1 electroencephalograms
rt brain
rt x radiation

ENCEPHALOMALACIA
BT1 brain disorders
BT2 nervous system diseases
BT3 organic diseases
BT4 diseases

encephalomyelitis
USE **encephalitis**

encephalomyelopathy
USE **myeloencephalopathy**

ENCEPHALOMYOCARDITIS VIRUS
BT1 cardiovirus
BT2 picornaviridae
BT3 viruses

ENCEPHALOPATHY
BT1 brain disorders
BT2 nervous system diseases
BT3 organic diseases
BT4 diseases
NT1 wernicke's disease
NT1 wernicke-korsakoff syndrome
rt reye's syndrome

ENCHODELUS
BT1 dorylaimidae
BT2 nematoda

ENCHYLAENA
BT1 chenopodiaceae
NT1 enchylaena tomentosa

ENCHYLAENA TOMENTOSA
BT1 enchylaena
BT2 chenopodiaceae

ENCHYTRAEIDAE
BT1 oligochaeta
BT2 annelida
NT1 enchytraeus
NT2 enchytraeus albidus
NT1 fridericia
NT2 fridericia galba

ENCHYTRAEUS
BT1 enchytraeidae
BT2 oligochaeta
BT3 annelida
NT1 enchytraeus albidus

ENCHYTRAEUS ALBIDUS
BT1 enchytraeus
BT2 enchytraeidae
BT3 oligochaeta
BT4 annelida

ENCOTYLLABE
BT1 capsalidae
BT2 monogenea

ENCOURAGEMENT
HN from 1989
BT1 biological control
BT2 pest control
BT3 control
rt natural enemies

ENCYCLIA
BT1 orchidaceae
NT1 encyclia inaguensis
NT1 encyclia tampensis

ENCYCLIA INAGUENSIS
BT1 encyclia
BT2 orchidaceae
BT1 ornamental orchids

ENCYCLIA TAMPENSIS
uf epidendrum tampense
BT1 encyclia
BT2 orchidaceae
BT1 ornamental orchids

ENCYCLOPEDIAS (AGRICOLA)
BT1 reference works

ENCYRTIDAE
BT1 hymenoptera
NT1 ageniaspis
NT2 ageniaspis fuscicollis
NT1 alamella
NT2 alamella kerrichi
NT1 anabrolepis
NT2 anabrolepis zetterstedtii
NT1 anagyrus
NT2 anagyrus fusciventris
NT2 anagyrus pseudococci
NT1 aphidencyrtus
NT2 aphidencyrtus africanus
NT2 aphidencyrtus aphidivorus
NT1 aphycus
NT1 blastothrix
NT2 blastothrix longipennis
NT1 cheiloneurus
NT2 cheiloneurus claviger
NT1 coccidoxenoides
NT2 coccidoxenoides peregrinus
NT1 comperiella

ENCYRTIDAE *cont.*
NT2 comperiella bifasciata
NT1 copidosoma
NT2 copidosoma koehleri
NT2 copidosoma truncatellum
NT1 encyrtus
NT1 epidinocarsis
NT2 epidinocarsis lopezi
NT1 gyranusoidea
NT2 gyranusoidea tebygi
NT1 habrolepis
NT1 holcothorax
NT2 holcothorax testaceipes
NT1 ixodiphagus
NT2 ixodiphagus hookeri
NT1 leptomastix
NT2 leptomastix dactylopii
NT1 litomastix
NT1 metaphycus
NT2 metaphycus bartletti
NT2 metaphycus flavus
NT2 metaphycus helvolus
NT2 metaphycus insidiosus
NT2 metaphycus lounsburyi
NT2 metaphycus punctipes
NT1 microterys
NT1 neodusmetia
NT2 neodusmetia sangwani
NT1 ooencyrtus
NT2 ooencyrtus clisiocampae
NT2 ooencyrtus ennomophagus
NT2 ooencyrtus kuvanae
NT1 pauridia
NT1 pseudaphycus
NT2 pseudaphycus malinus
NT1 psyllaephagus
NT1 syrphophagus
NT2 syrphophagus aeruginosus
NT1 trichomasthus
NT2 trichomasthus albimanus

ENCYRTUS
BT1 encyrtidae
BT2 hymenoptera

ENCYSTMENT
rt cysts

END COATING
BT1 drying
BT2 dehydration
BT3 processing

ENDAMOEBA
BT1 sarcomastigophora
BT2 protozoa

ENDANGERED BREEDS
HN from 1989
BT1 breeds
rt endangered species

ENDANGERED SPECIES
BT1 species
rt endangered breeds
rt nature conservation
rt wild animals
rt wild plants
rt wildlife

ENDEMIC GOITER
BF endemic goitre
BT1 goiter

ENDEMIC GOITRE
AF endemic goiter
uf *goitre, endemic*
BT1 goitre
BT2 thyroid diseases
BT3 endocrine diseases
BT4 organic diseases
BT5 diseases

ENDIVES
BT1 leafy vegetables
BT2 vegetables
rt cichorium endivia

ENDLICHERIA
BT1 lauraceae
NT1 endlicheria verticillata

ENDLICHERIA VERTICILLATA
BT1 endlicheria

ENDLICHERIA VERTICILLATA *cont.*
BT2 lauraceae

ENDOCARDITIS
BT1 heart diseases
BT2 cardiovascular diseases
BT3 organic diseases
BT4 diseases
rt endocardium

ENDOCARDIUM
BT1 heart
BT2 cardiovascular system
BT3 body parts
rt endocarditis

endocrine control
USE **hormonal control**

ENDOCRINE DISEASES
uf *endocrine disorders*
BT1 organic diseases
BT2 diseases
NT1 adrenal gland diseases
NT2 cushing's syndrome
NT1 gonadal disorders
NT2 hermaphroditism
NT2 hypogonadism
NT1 hyperinsulinism
NT1 parathyroid diseases
NT2 hyperparathyroidism
NT2 hypoparathyroidism
NT1 pituitary diseases
NT2 acromegaly
NT2 hypophysation
NT1 thyroid diseases
NT2 autoimmune thyroiditis
NT2 cretinism
NT2 goitre
NT3 congenital goitre
NT3 endemic goitre
NT2 hyperthyroidism
NT2 hypothyroidism

endocrine disorders
USE **endocrine diseases**

endocrine function
USE **hormone secretion**

ENDOCRINE GLANDS
uf *ductless glands*
BT1 glands (animal)
BT2 body parts
BT2 glands
NT1 adrenal glands
NT2 adrenal cortex
NT2 adrenal medulla
NT1 parathyroid
NT1 pineal body
NT1 pituitary
NT2 anterior pituitary
NT2 posterior pituitary
NT1 thyroid gland
NT1 ultimobranchial body
rt endocrine system
rt endocrinology
rt hormones

endocrine secretion
USE **hormone secretion**

ENDOCRINE SYSTEM
BT1 body parts
rt endocrine glands

ENDOCRINOLOGY
BT1 animal physiology
BT2 physiology
rt endocrine glands
rt hormones

ENDOCRONARTIUM
BT1 uredinales
NT1 endocronartium harknessii
NT1 endocronartium pini
rt cronartium
rt peridermium

ENDOCRONARTIUM HARKNESSII
uf *cronartium harknessii*
uf *peridermium cerebroides*
uf *peridermium harknessii*
BT1 endocronartium

ENDOCRONARTIUM HARKNESSII *cont.*
BT2 uredinales

ENDOCRONARTIUM PINI
uf *peridermium pini*
BT1 endocronartium
BT2 uredinales

ENDOCYTOSIS
BT1 absorption
BT2 sorption
rt cell walls

ENDODONTIDAE
BT1 gastropoda
BT2 mollusca
NT1 discus
NT2 discus cronkhitei

ENDOGENOUS GROWTH REGULATORS
HN from 1989
BT1 plant growth regulators
BT2 growth regulators

endogenous opiates
USE **opioid peptides**

ENDOGENOUS PROTEIN
BT1 protein

ENDOGONALES
NT1 acaulospora
NT2 acaulospora elegans
NT2 acaulospora laevis
NT2 acaulospora spinosa
NT2 acaulospora trappei
NT1 endogone
NT2 endogone calospora
NT2 endogone mosseae
NT1 gigaspora
NT2 gigaspora calospora
NT2 gigaspora margarita
NT1 glomus
NT2 glomus aggregatum
NT2 glomus caledonium
NT2 glomus clarum
NT2 glomus deserticola
NT2 glomus etunicatum
NT2 glomus fasciculatum
NT2 glomus intraradices
NT2 glomus macrocarpum
NT2 glomus manihotis
NT2 glomus microcarpum
NT2 glomus microsporum
NT2 glomus monosporum
NT2 glomus mosseae
NT2 glomus occultum
NT2 glomus tenue
NT2 glomus tubiforme
NT2 glomus versiforme
NT1 rhizophagus (endogonales)
NT2 rhizophagus tenuis
rt fungi

ENDOGONE
BT1 endogonales
NT1 endogone calospora
NT1 endogone mosseae

ENDOGONE CALOSPORA
BT1 endogone
BT2 endogonales

ENDOGONE MOSSEAE
BT1 endogone
BT2 endogonales

ENDOLIMAX
BT1 sarcomastigophora
BT2 protozoa
NT1 endolimax nana

ENDOLIMAX NANA
BT1 endolimax
BT2 sarcomastigophora
BT3 protozoa

endometrial area
USE **endometrium**

ENDOMETRIAL GLANDS
BT1 glands (animal)
BT2 body parts

ENDOMETRIAL GLANDS *cont.*
BT2 glands

ENDOMETRITIS
uf *metritis*
BT1 reproductive disorders
BT2 functional disorders
BT3 animal disorders
BT4 disorders
BT1 uterine diseases
BT2 female genital diseases
BT3 organic diseases
BT4 diseases
rt endometrium

ENDOMETRIUM
uf *endometrial area*
BT1 uterus
BT2 female genitalia
BT3 genitalia
BT4 urogenital system
BT5 body parts
rt endometritis

ENDOMITOSIS
uf *endopolyploidy*
rt mitosis
rt polyploidy

ENDOMYCETALES
NT1 debaryomyces
NT2 debaryomyces hansenii
NT1 hansenula
NT1 kluyveromyces
NT2 kluyveromyces bulgaricus
NT2 kluyveromyces fragilis
NT2 kluyveromyces marxianus
NT3 kluyveromyces marxianus var. lactis
NT3 kluyveromyces marxianus var. marxianus
NT1 pichia
NT2 pichia membranaefaciens
NT2 pichia stipitis
NT1 saccharomyces
NT2 saccharomyces cerevisiae
NT2 saccharomyces fragilis
NT2 saccharomyces uvarum
NT1 saccharomycopsis
rt fungi

ENDOMYCORRHIZAS
HN from 1989
BT1 mycorrhizas

ENDOPEPTIDASES
BT1 proteinases
BT2 peptide hydrolases
BT3 hydrolases
BT4 enzymes

ENDOPHYTES
rt epiphytes
rt parasitic plants

ENDOPLASMIC RETICULUM
BT1 cytoplasm
BT2 protoplasm
rt golgi apparatus
rt microsomes

endopolygalacturonase
USE **polygalacturonase**

endopolyploidy
USE **endomitosis**

ENDOPROCTA
uf *bryozoa*
uf *polyzoa*
rt invertebrates

ENDORIMOSPORA
BT1 apicomplexa
BT2 protozoa

ENDORPHINS
BT1 neuropeptides
BT2 peptides
BT1 neurotransmitters
BT1 opioid peptides
BT2 peptides

ENDOSCOPY
BT1 diagnostic techniques

ENDOSCOPY *cont.*
BT2 techniques

ENDOSPERM
rt albumins
rt aleurone cells
rt seeds

ENDOSULFAN
BT1 cyclodiene insecticides
BT2 organochlorine insecticides
BT3 insecticides
BT4 pesticides
BT3 organochlorine pesticides
BT4 organochlorine compounds
BT5 organic halogen compounds
BT1 organochlorine acaricides
BT2 acaricides
BT3 pesticides
BT2 organochlorine pesticides
BT3 organochlorine compounds
BT4 organic halogen compounds

ENDOTHAL
BT1 defoliants
BT2 plant growth regulators
BT3 growth regulators
BT1 desiccant herbicides
BT2 desiccants
BT1 plant growth regulators
BT2 growth regulators
BT1 unclassified herbicides
BT2 herbicides
BT3 pesticides

ENDOTHELIUM
BT1 animal tissues
BT2 tissues
NT1 reticuloendothelial system
rt blood vessels

ENDOTHIA
BT1 diaporthales
rt cryphonectria

endothia eugeniae
USE **cryphonectria cubensis**

endothia havanensis
USE **cryphonectria havanensis**

endothia parasitica
USE **cryphonectria parasitica**

endothia tropicalis
USE **cryphonectria gyrosa**

ENDOTOXINS
BT1 toxins
rt bacteria
rt intestines
rt microorganisms

ENDOTRYPANUM
BT1 sarcomastigophora
BT2 protozoa

ENDRIN
BT1 avicides
BT2 pesticides
BT1 cyclodiene insecticides
BT2 organochlorine insecticides
BT3 insecticides
BT4 pesticides
BT3 organochlorine pesticides
BT4 organochlorine compounds
BT5 organic halogen compounds

ENDURANCE (AGRICOLA)

ENDURANCE TESTING
uf *testing, endurance*
BT1 testing
rt wear

ENDYMION
BT1 liliaceae
rt hyacinthoides

endymion hispanicus
USE **hyacinthoides hispanica**

endymion non-scriptus
USE **hyacinthoides non-scripta**

endymion nutans
USE **hyacinthoides non-scripta**

ENERGY
NT1 bioenergy
NT1 digestible energy
NT1 electrical energy
NT1 geothermal energy
NT1 kinetic energy
NT1 net energy
NT1 nuclear energy
NT1 potential energy
NT2 hydraulic potential
NT2 metabolizable energy
NT1 solar energy
NT1 thermal energy
rt bioenergetics
rt calories
rt economic resources
rt energy balance
rt energy conservation
rt energy consumption
rt energy content
rt energy conversion
rt energy cost of activities
rt energy cost of maintenance
rt energy cost of production
rt energy deprivation
rt energy digestibility
rt energy exchange
rt energy expenditure (agricola)
rt energy imbalance
rt energy intake
rt energy metabolism
rt energy policy
rt energy relations
rt energy requirements
rt energy resources
rt energy retention
rt energy sources
rt energy value
rt nutritive ratio
rt physical activity
rt power
rt protein energy deficiency
rt stimulation
rt thermodynamics
rt vigour
rt work
rt work capacity

ENERGY BALANCE
BT1 energy relations
rt energy
rt energy consumption
rt energy imbalance
rt energy sources
rt insolation

ENERGY CONSERVATION
BT1 conservation
rt energy
rt energy recovery
rt heat conservation
rt heat exchangers
rt insulation

ENERGY CONSUMPTION
uf *energy use*
uf *energy utilization*
BT1 consumption
BT1 energy relations
rt energy
rt energy balance
rt energy expenditure (agricola)
rt energy requirements
rt fuel consumption

ENERGY CONTENT
rt energy

ENERGY CONVERSION
BT1 conversion
rt energy
rt prime movers

ENERGY COST OF ACTIVITIES
BT1 costs
rt energy

ENERGY COST OF MAINTENANCE
BT1 costs
rt energy
rt maintenance

ENERGY COST OF PRODUCTION
BT1 costs
rt energy
rt production

ENERGY DEPRIVATION
BT1 deprivation
rt energy

energy derivation
USE **energy sources**

ENERGY DIGESTIBILITY
BT1 digestibility
rt digestible energy
rt energy
rt energy exchange

ENERGY EXCHANGE
NT1 basal metabolism
NT1 oxygen consumption
NT1 resting energy exchange
rt body temperature
rt cold tolerance
rt energy
rt energy digestibility
rt energy metabolism
rt ergometers
rt heat regulation
rt respiration rate
rt respiratory quotient
rt specific dynamic action
rt thermal neutrality

energy exchange, basal
USE **basal metabolism**

energy exchange, resting
USE **resting energy exchange**

ENERGY EXPENDITURE (AGRICOLA)
rt energy
rt energy consumption

energy, geothermal
USE **geothermal energy**

ENERGY IMBALANCE
BT1 energy relations
rt energy
rt energy balance

ENERGY INTAKE
BT1 energy relations
BT1 intake
rt caloric intake (agricola)
rt caloric modifications (agricola)
rt energy
rt energy relations
rt energy sources
rt food intake

energy, kinetic
USE **kinetic energy**

ENERGY METABOLISM
BT1 metabolism
NT1 oxidative phosphorylation
NT1 photorespiration
NT2 glycolate pathways
NT1 photosynthesis
NT2 carbon pathways
NT3 cam pathway
NT2 dark fixation
NT2 photophosphorylation
NT2 photosystem i
NT2 photosystem ii
NT2 source sink relations
NT1 specific dynamic action
rt electron transfer
rt energy
rt energy exchange
rt metabolizable energy
rt redox reactions

energy, metabolizable
USE **metabolizable energy**

ENERGY POLICY
rt energy
rt policy

energy, potential
USE **potential energy**

energy protein ratio
USE **nutritive ratio**

ENERGY RECOVERY
BT1 energy sources
BT1 recovery
rt energy conservation
rt energy retention

ENERGY RELATIONS
NT1 energy balance
NT1 energy consumption
NT1 energy imbalance
NT1 energy intake
NT1 energy requirements
NT1 energy retention
rt basal metabolism
rt energy
rt energy intake
rt phosphocreatine
rt relationships

ENERGY REQUIREMENTS
uf *calorie requirement*
BT1 energy relations
BT1 requirements
rt energy
rt energy consumption
rt nutrient requirements
rt power requirement

ENERGY RESOURCES
(quantitative estimates of energy available from one or more energy sources)
uf *resources, energy*
BT1 resources
rt biomass
rt energy

ENERGY RETENTION
BT1 energy relations
BT1 retention
rt energy
rt energy recovery

energy, solar
USE **solar energy**

ENERGY SOURCES
uf *energy derivation*
uf *renewable energy*
NT1 electricity
NT2 electric potential
NT3 bioelectric potential
NT3 external electric potential
NT3 internal electric potential
NT2 sparks
NT1 energy recovery
NT1 water power
NT1 wind power
rt energy
rt energy balance
rt energy intake
rt energy value
rt fuels
rt geothermal energy
rt renewable resources

energy, thermal
USE **thermal energy**

energy use
USE **energy consumption**

energy utilization
USE **energy consumption**

ENERGY VALUE
uf *calorie value*
NT1 starch equivalent
rt calorific value
rt energy
rt energy sources
rt nutritive value

ENGELHARDTIA
BT1 juglandaceae
NT1 engelhardtia mexicana
NT1 engelhardtia spicata

ENGELHARDTIA MEXICANA
BT1 engelhardtia
BT2 juglandaceae

ENGELHARDTIA SPICATA
BT1 engelhardtia
BT2 juglandaceae
BT1 tan plants

ENGINEERING
NT1 agricultural engineering
NT1 civil engineering
NT1 dairy engineering
NT1 electrical engineering
NT2 earthing
NT2 electrification
NT2 hydroelectric schemes
NT1 food engineering (agricola)
NT1 forestry engineering
NT1 hydraulic engineering
NT2 hydroelectric schemes
NT1 public health engineering
NT2 sanitation
NT3 septic tanks
rt building construction
rt design
rt engineers
rt machinery
rt shipbuilding

engineering, electrical
USE **electrical engineering**

engineering, electronic
USE **electronics**

engineering, hydraulic
USE **hydraulic engineering**

engineering properties of soil
USE **soil mechanics**

ENGINEERS
BT1 occupations
rt engineering
rt scientists

ENGINES
BT1 machinery
NT1 air cooled engines
NT1 diesel engines
NT1 exhaust systems
NT2 silencers
NT1 gas engines
NT1 gas turbine engines
NT1 internal combustion engines
NT2 spark ignition engines
NT1 rotary engines
NT1 steam engines
NT1 stirling engines
NT1 wankel engines
NT1 water cooled engines
rt clutches
rt components
rt compression ratio
rt cylinders
rt distributors
rt electric starters
rt farm machinery
rt fuel consumption
rt gears
rt governors
rt locomotion
rt lubrication
rt motors
rt overload protection
rt pistons
rt power
rt prime movers
rt radiators
rt rotational speed
rt silencers
rt throttles
rt transmissions
rt vehicles

engines, air cooled
USE **air cooled engines**

engines, diesel
USE **diesel engines**

engines, gas
USE **gas engines**

engines, gas turbine
USE **gas turbine engines**

engines, internal combustion
USE **internal combustion engines**

engines, rotary
USE **rotary engines**

engines, spark ignition
USE **spark ignition engines**

engines, steam
USE **steam engines**

engines, stirling
USE **stirling engines**

engines, wankel
USE **wankel engines**

engines, water cooled
USE **water cooled engines**

ENGLAND
BT1 great britain
BT2 uk
BT3 british isles
BT4 western europe
BT5 europe
NT1 east midlands of england
NT1 eastern england
NT1 northern england
NT1 south east england
NT1 south west england
NT1 west midlands of england
NT1 yorkshire and lancashire

english football
USE **soccer**

english speaking africa
USE **anglophone africa**

ENGORGEMENT

ENGRAULIDAE
BT1 clupeiformes
BT2 osteichthyes
BT3 fishes
NT1 anchoa
NT1 coilia
NT1 engraulis
rt anchovies

ENGRAULIS
BT1 engraulidae
BT2 clupeiformes
BT3 osteichthyes
BT4 fishes
rt anchovies

ENHANCERS
NT1 flavour enhancers
NT2 monosodium glutamate

ENHYDRA
BT1 mustelidae
BT2 fissipeda
BT3 carnivores
BT4 mammals
NT1 enhydra lutris
rt otters

enhydra (compositae)
USE **enydra**

ENHYDRA LUTRIS
BT1 enhydra
BT2 mustelidae
BT3 fissipeda
BT4 carnivores
BT5 mammals

ENICOSTEMA
BT1 gentianaceae
NT1 enicostema hyssopifolium
NT1 enicostema litorale

ENICOSTEMA HYSSOPIFOLIUM
BT1 enicostema
BT2 gentianaceae

ENICOSTEMA LITORALE
BT1 enicostema
BT2 gentianaceae

ENJOYMENT
BT1 behaviour
rt consumer satisfaction
rt entertainment
rt leisure

ENKEPHALINS
uf *encephalins*
BT1 neuropeptides
BT2 peptides
BT1 opioid peptides
BT2 peptides

ENKIANTHUS
BT1 ericaceae
NT1 enkianthus perulatus

ENKIANTHUS PERULATUS
BT1 antifungal plants
BT1 enkianthus
BT2 ericaceae

ENNEAPOGON
BT1 gramineae
NT1 enneapogon avenaceus
NT1 enneapogon cenchroides
NT1 enneapogon polyphyllus

ENNEAPOGON AVENACEUS
BT1 enneapogon
BT2 gramineae
BT1 pasture plants

ENNEAPOGON CENCHROIDES
BT1 enneapogon
BT2 gramineae
BT1 pasture plants

ENNEAPOGON POLYPHYLLUS
BT1 enneapogon
BT2 gramineae
BT1 pasture plants

ENNOMOS
BT1 geometridae
BT2 lepidoptera
NT1 ennomos subsignarius

ENNOMOS SUBSIGNARIUS
BT1 ennomos
BT2 geometridae
BT3 lepidoptera

ENOCLERUS
BT1 cleridae
BT2 coleoptera

ENOPLIDAE
BT1 nematoda
NT1 enoplus
rt free living nematodes
rt marine nematodes

ENOPLUS
BT1 enoplidae
BT2 nematoda

ENRICHMENT
rt beneficiation
rt carbon dioxide enrichment
rt improvement planting
rt marriage enrichment (agricola)
rt protein enriched milk

ENSETE
BT1 musaceae
NT1 ensete ventricosum

ENSETE VENTRICOSUM
BT1 ensete
BT2 musaceae

ensilage
USE **silage making**

ensiling
USE **silage making**

ensiling losses
USE **silage losses**

ENSIS
BT1 solenidae
BT2 bivalvia
BT3 mollusca

ENTADA
BT1 leguminosae
NT1 entada africana

ENTADA AFRICANA
BT1 antibacterial plants
BT1 entada
BT2 leguminosae

ENTAMOEBA
BT1 sarcomastigophora
BT2 protozoa
NT1 entamoeba bovis
NT1 entamoeba coli
NT1 entamoeba curens
NT1 entamoeba fulva
NT1 entamoeba gingivalis
NT1 entamoeba hartmanni
NT1 entamoeba histolytica
NT1 entamoeba ilowaiskii
NT1 entamoeba invadens
NT1 entamoeba moshkovskii
NT1 entamoeba polecki
NT1 entamoeba pyrrogaster
NT1 entamoeba ranarum

ENTAMOEBA BOVIS
BT1 entamoeba
BT2 sarcomastigophora
BT3 protozoa

ENTAMOEBA COLI
BT1 entamoeba
BT2 sarcomastigophora
BT3 protozoa

ENTAMOEBA CURENS
BT1 entamoeba
BT2 sarcomastigophora
BT3 protozoa

ENTAMOEBA FULVA
BT1 entamoeba
BT2 sarcomastigophora
BT3 protozoa

ENTAMOEBA GINGIVALIS
BT1 entamoeba
BT2 sarcomastigophora
BT3 protozoa

ENTAMOEBA HARTMANNI
BT1 entamoeba
BT2 sarcomastigophora
BT3 protozoa

ENTAMOEBA HISTOLYTICA
uf *amoebic dysentry*
BT1 entamoeba
BT2 sarcomastigophora
BT3 protozoa
rt liver abscess

ENTAMOEBA ILOWAISKII
BT1 entamoeba
BT2 sarcomastigophora
BT3 protozoa

ENTAMOEBA INVADENS
BT1 entamoeba
BT2 sarcomastigophora
BT3 protozoa

ENTAMOEBA MOSHKOVSKII
BT1 entamoeba
BT2 sarcomastigophora
BT3 protozoa

ENTAMOEBA POLECKI
BT1 entamoeba
BT2 sarcomastigophora
BT3 protozoa

ENTAMOEBA PYRROGASTER
BT1 entamoeba
BT2 sarcomastigophora
BT3 protozoa

ENTAMOEBA RANARUM
BT1 entamoeba
BT2 sarcomastigophora
BT3 protozoa

ENTANDROPHRAGMA
BT1 meliaceae
NT1 entandrophragma candollei
NT1 entandrophragma caudatum
NT1 entandrophragma cylindricum
NT1 entandrophragma utile

ENTANDROPHRAGMA CANDOLLEI
BT1 entandrophragma
BT2 meliaceae

ENTANDROPHRAGMA CAUDATUM
BT1 entandrophragma
BT2 meliaceae

ENTANDROPHRAGMA CYLINDRICUM
BT1 entandrophragma
BT2 meliaceae
BT1 forest trees

ENTANDROPHRAGMA UTILE
BT1 entandrophragma
BT2 meliaceae
BT1 forest trees

ENTAPHELENCHIDAE
BT1 nematoda
NT1 entaphelenchus
rt entomophilic nematodes

ENTAPHELENCHUS
BT1 entaphelenchidae
BT2 nematoda

enteque seco
USE **calcinosis**

ENTERAL FEEDING
BT1 feeding
NT1 tube feeding
rt nutritional support (agricola)
rt parenteral feeding

ENTERITIS
uf *ileitis*
uf *jejunitis*
BT1 intestinal diseases
BT2 gastrointestinal diseases
BT3 digestive system diseases
BT4 organic diseases
BT5 diseases
rt diarrhoea
rt dysentery
rt enterocolitis
rt gastroenteritis
rt haemorrhagic enteritis

ENTEROBACTER
uf *aerobacter*
BT1 enterobacteriaceae
BT2 gracilicutes
BT3 bacteria
BT4 prokaryotes
NT1 enterobacter aerogenes
NT1 enterobacter agglomerans
NT1 enterobacter cancerogenus
NT1 enterobacter cloacae

ENTEROBACTER AEROGENES
uf *aerobacter aerogenes*
BT1 enterobacter
BT2 enterobacteriaceae
BT3 gracilicutes
BT4 bacteria
BT5 prokaryotes

ENTEROBACTER AGGLOMERANS
BT1 enterobacter
BT2 enterobacteriaceae
BT3 gracilicutes
BT4 bacteria
BT5 prokaryotes

ENTEROBACTER CANCEROGENUS
HN from 1990
uf *erwinia cancerogena*
BT1 enterobacter

ENTEROBACTER CANCEROGENUS *cont.*
BT2 enterobacteriaceae
BT3 gracilicutes
BT4 bacteria
BT5 prokaryotes
BT1 plant pathogenic bacteria
BT2 plant pathogens
BT3 pathogens

ENTEROBACTER CLOACAE
BT1 enterobacter
BT2 enterobacteriaceae
BT3 gracilicutes
BT4 bacteria
BT5 prokaryotes

ENTEROBACTERIACEAE
BT1 gracilicutes
BT2 bacteria
BT3 prokaryotes
NT1 citrobacter
NT2 citrobacter freundii
NT1 edwardsiella
NT1 enterobacter
NT2 enterobacter aerogenes
NT2 enterobacter agglomerans
NT2 enterobacter cancerogenus
NT2 enterobacter cloacae
NT1 erwinia
NT2 erwinia amylovora
NT2 erwinia ananas
NT2 erwinia carotovora
NT3 erwinia carotovora subsp. atroseptica
NT3 erwinia carotovora subsp. betavasculorum
NT3 erwinia carotovora subsp. carotovora
NT2 erwinia chrysanthemi
NT3 erwinia chrysanthemi pv. chrysanthemi
NT3 erwinia chrysanthemi pv. dianthicola
NT3 erwinia chrysanthemi pv. dieffenbachiae
NT3 erwinia chrysanthemi pv. paradisiaca
NT3 erwinia chrysanthemi pv. parthenii
NT3 erwinia chrysanthemi pv. zeae
NT2 erwinia herbicola
NT3 erwinia herbicola pv. millettiae
NT2 erwinia rhapontici
NT2 erwinia rubrifaciens
NT2 erwinia salicis
NT2 erwinia stewartii
NT2 erwinia tracheiphila
NT2 erwinia uredovora
NT1 escherichia
NT2 escherichia coli
NT1 hafnia
NT2 hafnia alvei
NT1 klebsiella
NT2 klebsiella aerogenes
NT2 klebsiella oxytoca
NT2 klebsiella pneumoniae
NT1 morganella
NT1 proteus
NT2 proteus mirabilis
NT2 proteus vulgaris
NT1 providencia
NT1 salmonella
NT2 salmonella abortusequi
NT2 salmonella abortusovis
NT2 salmonella anatum
NT2 salmonella arizonae
NT2 salmonella choleraesuis
NT2 salmonella dublin
NT2 salmonella enteritidis
NT2 salmonella gallinarum
NT2 salmonella muenster
NT2 salmonella pullorum
NT2 salmonella typhi
NT2 salmonella typhimurium
NT1 serratia
NT2 serratia liquefasciens
NT2 serratia marcescens
NT1 shigella
NT2 shigella dysenteriae

ENTEROBACTERIACEAE *cont.*
NT2 shigella flexneri
NT2 shigella sonnei
NT1 xenorhabdus
NT2 xenorhabdus luminescens
NT2 xenorhabdus nematophilus
NT1 yersinia
NT2 yersinia enterocolitica
NT2 yersinia frederiksenii
NT2 yersinia intermedia
NT2 yersinia kristensenii
NT2 yersinia pseudotuberculosis
NT3 yersinia pseudotuberculosis subsp. pestis
NT2 yersinia ruckeri
rt coliform bacteria

ENTEROBIUS
BT1 oxyuridae
BT2 nematoda
NT1 enterobius vermicularis

ENTEROBIUS VERMICULARIS
BT1 enterobius
BT2 oxyuridae
BT3 nematoda

ENTEROCOCCUS
BT1 streptococcaceae
BT2 firmicutes
BT3 bacteria
BT4 prokaryotes
NT1 enterococcus faecalis
NT1 enterococcus faecium
rt streptococcus

ENTEROCOCCUS FAECALIS
uf *streptococcus faecalis*
BT1 enterococcus
BT2 streptococcaceae
BT3 firmicutes
BT4 bacteria
BT5 prokaryotes

ENTEROCOCCUS FAECIUM
uf *streptococcus faecium*
BT1 enterococcus
BT2 streptococcaceae
BT3 firmicutes
BT4 bacteria
BT5 prokaryotes

ENTEROCOLITIS
BT1 intestinal diseases
BT2 gastrointestinal diseases
BT3 digestive system diseases
BT4 organic diseases
BT5 diseases
rt colitis
rt enteritis

ENTEROCYSTIS
BT1 apicomplexa
BT2 protozoa
NT1 enterocystis ensis
NT1 enterocystis ephemerae
NT1 enterocystis fungoides
NT1 enterocystis grassei
NT1 enterocystis hydrophili
NT1 enterocystis palmata
NT1 enterocystis racovitza
NT1 enterocystis rhithrogenae

ENTEROCYSTIS ENSIS
BT1 enterocystis
BT2 apicomplexa
BT3 protozoa

ENTEROCYSTIS EPHEMERAE
BT1 enterocystis
BT2 apicomplexa
BT3 protozoa

ENTEROCYSTIS FUNGOIDES
BT1 enterocystis
BT2 apicomplexa
BT3 protozoa

ENTEROCYSTIS GRASSEI
BT1 enterocystis
BT2 apicomplexa
BT3 protozoa

ENTEROCYSTIS HYDROPHILI
BT1 enterocystis
BT2 apicomplexa
BT3 protozoa

ENTEROCYSTIS PALMATA
BT1 enterocystis
BT2 apicomplexa
BT3 protozoa

ENTEROCYSTIS RACOVITZA
BT1 enterocystis
BT2 apicomplexa
BT3 protozoa

ENTEROCYSTIS RHITHROGENAE
BT1 enterocystis
BT2 apicomplexa
BT3 protozoa

enterokinase
USE **enteropeptidase**

ENTEROLOBIUM
BT1 leguminosae
NT1 enterolobium contortisiliquum
NT1 enterolobium cyclocarpum

ENTEROLOBIUM CONTORTISILIQUUM
BT1 enterolobium
BT2 leguminosae
BT1 forest trees

ENTEROLOBIUM CYCLOCARPUM
BT1 enterolobium
BT2 leguminosae
BT1 forest trees
BT1 medicinal plants

enteropathy
USE **intestinal diseases**

ENTEROPEPTIDASE
(cc 3.4.21.9)
uf *enterokinase*
BT1 proteinases
BT2 peptide hydrolases
BT3 hydrolases
BT4 enzymes

ENTEROPOGON
BT1 gramineae
rt pasture plants

ENTEROTOXAEMIA
AF enterotoxemia
BT1 digestive system diseases
BT2 organic diseases
BT3 diseases
BT1 toxaemia
BT2 poisoning
rt enterotoxins
rt intestinal diseases
rt toxins

ENTEROTOXEMIA
BF enterotoxaemia
BT1 toxemia

ENTEROTOXINS
BT1 toxins
rt enterotoxaemia
rt intestinal diseases
rt intestines

ENTEROVIRUS
BT1 picornaviridae
BT2 viruses
NT1 avian encephalomyelitis virus
NT1 bovine enterovirus
NT1 coxsackie virus
NT1 duck hepatitis virus
NT1 hepatitis a virus
NT1 murine enterovirus
NT1 polioviruses
NT1 porcine enterovirus
NT2 porcine encephalomyelitis virus
NT2 swine vesicular disease virus

ENTERPRISES
NT1 aquaculture
NT2 algae culture
NT2 fish culture
NT3 eel culture
NT3 salmon culture
NT2 frog culture
NT2 seaweed culture
NT2 shellfish culture
NT3 lobster culture
NT3 mollusc culture
NT4 mussel culture
NT4 oyster culture
NT3 shrimp culture
NT2 turtle culture
NT1 farm enterprises
NT2 ancillary enterprises
NT3 farm holidays
NT3 on-farm processing
NT2 cooperative farm enterprises
NT3 gaec
NT3 livestock groups
NT3 safer
NT2 crop enterprises
NT2 livestock enterprises
NT3 cattle farming
NT4 dairy farming
NT3 goat keeping
NT3 pig farming
NT3 poultry farming
NT3 sheep farming
NT3 small animal rearing
NT2 vegetable growing
NT1 nationalized enterprises

enterprises, ancillary
USE **ancillary enterprises**

enterprises, cooperative farm
USE **cooperative farm enterprises**

enterprises, farm
USE **farm enterprises**

ENTERTAINMENT
uf *amusements*
BT1 leisure activities
NT1 amusement machines
NT1 carnivals
NT1 cultural activities
NT2 cultural exhibitions
NT2 cultural tourism
NT2 festivals
NT1 exhibitions
NT2 cultural exhibitions
NT2 museums
NT3 open air museums
NT1 festivals
NT1 funfairs
NT1 night clubs
NT1 spectator events
NT2 bull fighting
NT2 shows
rt audiences
rt clubs
rt enjoyment
rt films
rt gambling
rt performing arts
rt radio
rt recreational activities
rt sport
rt television

ENTOBDELLA
BT1 capsalidae
BT2 monogenea
NT1 entobdella soleae

ENTOBDELLA SOLEAE
BT1 entobdella
BT2 capsalidae
BT3 monogenea

ENTODINIUM
BT1 ciliophora
BT2 protozoa
NT1 entodinium bursa
NT1 entodinium caudatum
NT1 entodinium longinucleatum

ENTODINIUM BURSA
BT1 entodinium
BT2 ciliophora
BT3 protozoa

ENTODINIUM CAUDATUM
BT1 entodinium
BT2 ciliophora
BT3 protozoa

ENTODINIUM LONGINUCLEATUM
BT1 entodinium
BT2 ciliophora
BT3 protozoa

ENTOLASIA
BT1 gramineae
NT1 entolasia imbricata

ENTOLASIA IMBRICATA
BT1 entolasia
BT2 gramineae
BT1 pasture plants

ENTOMOBRYIDAE
BT1 collembola
NT1 dicranorchesella
NT1 tomocerus
NT2 tomocerus minor

ENTOMOGENOUS FUNGI
BT1 entomopathogens
BT2 pathogens
BT1 fungi
NT1 ascosphaera
NT2 ascosphaera apis
NT1 beauveria
NT2 beauveria bassiana
NT2 beauveria brongniartii
NT1 coelomomyces
NT2 coelomomyces indicus
NT2 coelomomyces psorophorae
NT2 coelomomyces stegomyiae
NT1 cordyceps
NT2 cordyceps militaris
NT1 culicinomyces
NT2 culicinomyces clavisporus
NT1 entomophaga
NT2 entomophaga aulicae
NT2 entomophaga grylli
NT1 entomophthora
NT2 entomophthora muscae
NT2 entomophthora planchoniana
NT1 erynia
NT2 erynia aphidis
NT2 erynia conica
NT2 erynia delphacis
NT2 erynia gammae
NT2 erynia neoaphidis
NT2 erynia phalloides
NT2 erynia phytonomi
NT2 erynia radicans
NT1 hirsutella
NT2 hirsutella thompsonii
NT1 lagenidium
NT2 lagenidium giganteum
NT1 massospora
NT1 metarhizium
NT2 metarhizium anisopliae
NT2 metarhizium flavoviride
NT1 neozygites
NT2 neozygites floridana
NT2 neozygites fresenii
NT2 neozygites parvispora
NT1 nomuraea
NT2 nomuraea rileyi
NT1 paecilomyces farinosus
NT1 paecilomyces fumosoroseus
NT1 verticillium lecanii
rt biological control agents
rt fungal acaricides
rt fungal insecticides
rt parasites of insect pests (agricola)
rt pest control

ENTOMOLOGY
BT1 zoology
BT2 biology
NT1 agricultural entomology
NT1 forensic entomology

ENTOMOLOGY *cont.*
NT1 medical entomology
NT1 military entomology
NT1 veterinary entomology
rt agricultural sciences
rt insects
rt pest control

ENTOMOPATHOGENIC BACTERIA
BT1 entomopathogens
BT2 pathogens
NT1 xenorhabdus luminescens
NT1 xenorhabdus nematophilus
rt bacteria
rt bacterial insecticides
rt parasites of insect pests (agricola)

ENTOMOPATHOGENIC PROTOZOA
BT1 entomopathogens
BT2 pathogens
NT1 adelina tribolii
NT1 blastocrithidia triatomae
NT1 farinocystis tribolii
NT1 lankesteria culicis
NT1 malamoeba locustae
NT1 malpighamoeba mellificae
NT1 mattesia dispora
NT1 nosema algerae
NT1 nosema apis
NT1 nosema bombycis
NT1 nosema carpocapsae
NT1 nosema disstriae
NT1 nosema equestris
NT1 nosema fumiferanae
NT1 nosema locustae
NT1 nosema plodiae
NT1 nosema pyrausta
NT1 nosema whitei
NT1 nosema yponomeutae
NT1 pleistophora schubergi
NT1 pleistophora simulii
NT1 tuzetia debaisieuxi
NT1 vairimorpha necatrix
NT1 vairimorpha plodiae
NT1 vavraia culicis
rt parasites of insect pests (agricola)
rt protozoa

ENTOMOPATHOGENS
BT1 pathogens
NT1 entomogenous fungi
NT2 ascosphaera
NT3 ascosphaera apis
NT2 beauveria
NT3 beauveria bassiana
NT3 beauveria brongniartii
NT2 coelomomyces
NT3 coelomomyces indicus
NT3 coelomomyces psorophorae
NT3 coelomomyces stegomyiae
NT2 cordyceps
NT3 cordyceps militaris
NT2 culicinomyces
NT3 culicinomyces clavisporus
NT2 entomophaga
NT3 entomophaga aulicae
NT3 entomophaga grylli
NT2 entomophthora
NT3 entomophthora muscae
NT3 entomophthora planchoniana
NT2 erynia
NT3 erynia aphidis
NT3 erynia conica
NT3 erynia delphacis
NT3 erynia gammae
NT3 erynia neoaphidis
NT3 erynia phalloides
NT3 erynia phytonomi
NT3 erynia radicans
NT2 hirsutella
NT3 hirsutella thompsonii
NT2 lagenidium
NT3 lagenidium giganteum
NT2 massospora
NT2 metarhizium
NT3 metarhizium anisopliae

ENTOMOPATHOGENS *cont.*
NT3 metarhizium flavoviride
NT2 neozygites
NT3 neozygites floridana
NT3 neozygites fresenii
NT3 neozygites parvispora
NT2 nomuraea
NT3 nomuraea rileyi
NT2 paecilomyces farinosus
NT2 paecilomyces fumosoroseus
NT2 verticillium lecanii
NT1 entomopathogenic bacteria
NT2 xenorhabdus luminescens
NT2 xenorhabdus nematophilus
NT1 entomopathogenic protozoa
NT2 adelina tribolii
NT2 blastocrithidia triatomae
NT2 farinocystis tribolii
NT2 lankesteria culicis
NT2 malamoeba locustae
NT2 malpighamoeba mellificae
NT2 mattesia dispora
NT2 nosema algerae
NT2 nosema apis
NT2 nosema bombycis
NT2 nosema carpocapsae
NT2 nosema disstriae
NT2 nosema equestris
NT2 nosema fumiferanae
NT2 nosema locustae
NT2 nosema plodiae
NT2 nosema pyrausta
NT2 nosema whitei
NT2 nosema yponomeutae
NT2 pleistophora schubergi
NT2 pleistophora simulii
NT2 tuzetia debaisieuxi
NT2 vairimorpha necatrix
NT2 vairimorpha plodiae
NT2 vavraia culicis
NT1 entomophilic nematodes
NT1 insect viruses
NT2 ascovirus
NT2 baculoviridae
NT3 baculovirus
NT4 granulosis viruses
NT4 nuclear polyhedrosis viruses
NT5 baculovirus heliothis
NT2 bee viruses
NT3 arkansas bee virus
NT3 bee acute paralysis virus
NT3 bee chronic paralysis virus
NT3 bee chronic paralysis virus associate
NT3 black queen cell virus
NT3 kashmir bee virus
NT3 sacbrood virus
NT2 cytoplasmic polyhedrosis viruses
NT2 densovirus
NT3 densonucleosis viruses
NT2 entomopoxvirinae
NT3 entomopoxvirus
NT2 iridovirus
NT3 iridescent viruses
NT4 chilo iridescent virus
NT4 regular mosquito iridescent virus
NT4 turquoise mosquito iridescent virus
NT2 nodaviridae
NT3 black beetle virus
NT3 nodamura virus
NT2 polydnaviridae
NT3 polydnavirus
NT2 sigmavirus
rt insects
rt natural enemies

ENTOMOPHAGA
BT1 entomogenous fungi
BT2 entomopathogens
BT3 pathogens
BT2 fungi
BT1 entomophthorales
NT1 entomophaga aulicae
NT1 entomophaga grylli
rt entomophthora

ENTOMOPHAGA AULICAE
HN from 1989; previously entomophthora aulicae
uf entomophthora aulicae
BT1 entomophaga
BT2 entomogenous fungi
BT3 entomopathogens
BT4 pathogens
BT3 fungi
BT2 entomophthorales

ENTOMOPHAGA GRYLLI
BT1 entomophaga
BT2 entomogenous fungi
BT3 entomopathogens
BT4 pathogens
BT3 fungi
BT2 entomophthorales

ENTOMOPHILIC NEMATODES
uf insect nematodes
uf nematodes, insect
BT1 entomopathogens
BT2 pathogens
rt allantonematidae
rt aphelenchidae
rt aphelenchoididae
rt biological control agents
rt entaphelenchidae
rt helminth insecticides
rt heterorhabditidae
rt mermithidae
rt myenchidae
rt nematoda
rt neotylenchidae
rt parasites of insect pests (agricola)
rt sphaerulariidae
rt steinernematidae
rt tetradonematidae
rt thelastomatidae

ENTOMOPHTHORA
uf empusa
BT1 entomogenous fungi
BT2 entomopathogens
BT3 pathogens
BT2 fungi
BT1 entomophthorales
NT1 entomophthora muscae
NT1 entomophthora planchoniana
rt conidiobolus
rt entomophaga
rt neozygites

entomophthora aphidis
USE **erynia aphidis**

entomophthora aulicae
USE **entomophaga aulicae**

entomophthora coronata
USE **conidiobolus coronatus**

entomophthora floridana
USE **neozygites floridana**

entomophthora fresenii
USE **neozygites fresenii**

entomophthora gammae
USE **erynia gammae**

ENTOMOPHTHORA MUSCAE
BT1 entomophthora
BT2 entomogenous fungi
BT3 entomopathogens
BT4 pathogens
BT3 fungi
BT2 entomophthorales

ENTOMOPHTHORA PLANCHONIANA
BT1 entomophthora
BT2 entomogenous fungi
BT3 entomopathogens
BT4 pathogens
BT3 fungi
BT2 entomophthorales

ENTOMOPHTHORALES
NT1 basidiobolus
NT2 basidiobolus haptosporus

ENTOMOPHTHORALES *cont.*
NT2 basidiobolus meristosporus
NT2 basidiobolus ranarum
NT1 blastocystis
NT2 blastocystis hominis
NT1 cochlonema
NT1 conidiobolus
NT2 conidiobolus coronatus
NT2 conidiobolus obscurus
NT2 conidiobolus thromboides
NT1 cystopage
NT1 entomophaga
NT2 entomophaga aulicae
NT2 entomophaga grylli
NT1 entomophthora
NT2 entomophthora muscae
NT2 entomophthora planchoniana
NT1 erynia
NT2 erynia aphidis
NT2 erynia conica
NT2 erynia delphacis
NT2 erynia gammae
NT2 erynia neoaphidis
NT2 erynia phalloides
NT2 erynia phytonomi
NT2 erynia radicans
NT1 ichthyophonus
NT2 ichthyophonus hoferi
NT1 massospora
NT1 neozygites
NT2 neozygites floridana
NT2 neozygites fresenii
NT2 neozygites parvispora
rt fungi

ENTOMOPOXVIRINAE
BT1 insect viruses
BT2 entomopathogens
BT3 pathogens
BT1 poxviridae
BT2 viruses
NT1 entomopoxvirus

ENTOMOPOXVIRUS
BT1 entomopoxvirinae
BT2 insect viruses
BT3 entomopathogens
BT4 pathogens
BT2 poxviridae
BT3 viruses

ENTOMOSCELIS
BT1 chrysomelidae
BT2 coleoptera
NT1 entomoscelis americana

ENTOMOSCELIS AMERICANA
BT1 entomoscelis
BT2 chrysomelidae
BT3 coleoptera

ENTOMOSPORIUM
HN from 1990
BT1 deuteromycotina
rt diplocarpon

entomosporium maculatum
USE **diplocarpon mespili**

ENTOPOLYPOIDES
BT1 apicomplexa
BT2 protozoa

ENTRAPPED AIR
BT1 soil air
rt air

ENTRE DOURO E MINHO
HN from 1990; previously "entre minho e douro"
uf entre minho e douro
BT1 sheep breeds
BT2 breeds

entre minho e douro
USE **entre douro e minho**

ENTREE (AGRICOLA)
uf main dish
BT1 meals

ENTREPRENEURSHIP
BT1 businesses

ENTREPRENEURSHIP *cont.*
rt management
rt risk

ENTROPION
BT1 eyelid diseases
BT2 eye diseases
BT3 organic diseases
BT4 diseases

ENTROPY
HN from 1990
rt thermodynamics

ENTRY FEES
BT1 fees

ENTYLOMA
BT1 ustilaginales
NT1 entyloma dahliae
NT1 entyloma oryzae

ENTYLOMA DAHLIAE
BT1 entyloma
BT2 ustilaginales

ENTYLOMA ORYZAE
BT1 entyloma
BT2 ustilaginales

ENUCLEATION
BT1 surgical operations
rt corpus luteum
rt eyes

ENUMERATION
BT1 biological techniques
BT2 techniques
rt counting
rt inventories
rt leukocyte count
rt livestock censuses

enumeration surveys
USE **censuses**
OR **surveys**

ENVELOPE MATERIALS
rt drainage

ENVENOMATION
HN from 1989
rt arachnidism
rt stings
rt venoms

ENVIRONMENT
NT1 aquatic environment
NT1 cultural environment
NT2 acculturation
NT2 cultural heritage
NT1 marine environment
NT1 microenvironments
NT1 rural environment
NT1 social environment
NT2 family environment (agricola)
NT1 urban environment
rt ecosystems
rt environmental assessment
rt environmental control
rt environmental degradation
rt environmental education
rt environmental factors
rt environmental impact
rt environmental legislation
rt environmental policy
rt environmental protection
rt environmental temperature
rt forest influences
rt genotype environment interaction
rt habitats
rt landscape
rt nature tourism
rt unep

ENVIRONMENTAL ASSESSMENT
BT1 surveys
rt environment

ENVIRONMENTAL CONTROL
BT1 control
rt air conditioning
rt alarms

ENVIRONMENTAL CONTROL *cont.*
rt controlled atmosphere storage
rt cooling
rt environment
rt growth chambers
rt heat transfer
rt heating
rt humidifiers
rt microclimate

ENVIRONMENTAL DEGRADATION
BT1 degradation
rt ecology
rt environment
rt fertility
rt logging effects

ENVIRONMENTAL EDUCATION
BT1 education
rt curriculum
rt environment
rt nutrition education
rt science education

environmental effects
USE **environmental impact**

ENVIRONMENTAL FACTORS
rt adaptation
rt atmosphere
rt climate
rt climatic factors
rt ecology
rt edaphic factors
rt environment
rt phenology
rt phenotypes
rt phenotypic correlation
rt treelines

ENVIRONMENTAL IMPACT
uf environmental effects
rt effects
rt environment
rt environmental impact reporting (agricola)
rt logging effects
rt pollution

ENVIRONMENTAL IMPACT REPORTING (AGRICOLA)
rt environmental impact

ENVIRONMENTAL LEGISLATION
BT1 legislation
BT2 legal systems
NT1 public health legislation
NT2 food legislation
rt environment

ENVIRONMENTAL MANAGEMENT
HN from 1989
BT1 pest control
BT2 control
rt habitat destruction
rt management

ENVIRONMENTAL POLICY
uf policy, environmental
rt environment
rt environmental protection
rt forest policy
rt landscape conservation
rt policy
rt pollution
rt resource conservation

environmental pollution
USE **pollution**

ENVIRONMENTAL PROTECTION
BT1 conservation
rt environment
rt environmental policy

ENVIRONMENTAL TEMPERATURE
uf temperature, environmental
BT1 temperature
rt air temperature
rt environment
rt microclimate

ENYDRA
uf *enhydra (compositae)*
BT1 compositae
NT1 enydra fluctuans

ENYDRA FLUCTUANS
BT1 enydra
BT2 compositae

enzootic ataxia
USE **swayback**

ENZYME ACTIVATORS
BT1 detoxicants
BT2 drugs
NT1 pralidoxime
rt coenzymes
rt enzyme activity
rt enzymes

ENZYME ACTIVITY
BT1 chemical properties
BT2 properties
rt browning
rt enzyme activators
rt enzyme inhibitors
rt enzymes

ENZYME DEFICIENCIES
BT1 deficiency
NT1 hypophosphatasia
NT1 lactase deficiency
rt deficiency diseases
rt enzymes

enzyme histochemistry
USE **histoenzymology**

ENZYME IMMUNOASSAY
BT1 immunoassay
BT2 assays
BT2 immunological techniques
BT3 techniques
BT1 immunoenzyme techniques
BT2 immunological techniques
BT3 techniques
NT1 elisa

ENZYME INHIBITORS
BT1 metabolic inhibitors
BT2 inhibitors
NT1 n-ethylmaleimide
NT1 acetazolamide
NT1 allopurinol
NT1 aminopterin
NT1 benfluorex
NT1 benzoquinone
NT1 cholinesterase inhibitors
NT2 neostigmine
NT2 physostigmine
NT1 glucaric acid
NT1 iodoacetic acid
NT1 nitrate reductase inhibitors
NT1 nordihydroguaiaretic acid
NT1 oligomycin
NT1 phaseolotoxin
NT1 proteinase inhibitors
NT2 chymotrypsin inhibitors
NT2 pepstatin
NT2 trypsin inhibitors
NT3 antitrypsin
NT1 urease inhibitors
NT2 ammonium thiosulfate
NT2 chloramben
NT2 phenyl phosphorodiamidate
NT1 valinomycin
rt enzyme activity
rt enzymes

enzyme linked immunosorbent assay
USE **elisa**

ENZYME POLYMORPHISM
BT1 biochemical polymorphism
BT2 polymorphism
rt enzymes
rt isoenzymes

ENZYME PRECURSORS
BT1 precursors
NT1 chymotrypsinogen
NT1 pepsinogen

ENZYME PRECURSORS *cont.*
NT1 plasminogen
NT1 prothrombin
NT1 trypsinogen
rt enzymes

ENZYME PREPARATIONS
BT1 food additives
BT2 additives
rt enzymes

ENZYMES
NT1 hydrolases
NT2 acid anhydride hydrolases
NT3 adenosinetriphosphatase
NT3 pyrophosphatases
NT4 atp pyrophosphatase
NT4 inorganic pyrophosphatase
NT2 amide hydrolases
NT3 β-lactamase
NT3 amidase
NT3 asparaginase
NT3 glutaminase
NT3 urease
NT2 amidine hydrolases
NT3 adenosine deaminase
NT3 amp deaminase
NT3 arginase
NT3 formiminoglutamase
NT3 guanine deaminase
NT2 epoxide hydrolase
NT2 esterases
NT3 carboxylic ester hydrolases
NT4 acetylcholinesterase
NT4 arylesterase
NT4 carboxylesterase
NT4 chlorophyllase
NT4 cholesterol esterase
NT4 cholinesterase
NT4 lipoprotein lipase
NT4 lysophospholipase
NT4 pectinesterase
NT4 phospholipase a
NT4 phospholipase a1
NT4 phospholipase a2
NT4 retinyl-palmitate esterase
NT4 tannase
NT4 triacylglycerol lipase
NT4 tropinesterase
NT3 nucleases
NT4 deoxyribonuclease i
NT4 ribonucleases
NT3 phosphoric diester hydrolases
NT4 phosphodiesterase i
NT4 phospholipase c
NT3 phosphoric monoester hydrolases
NT4 acid phosphatase
NT4 alkaline phosphatase
NT4 fructose-bisphosphatase
NT4 glucose-6-phosphatase
NT4 nucleotidase
NT4 phosphatidate phosphatase
NT4 phosphoprotein phosphatase
NT4 phosphorylase phosphatase
NT4 phytase
NT3 sulfuric ester hydrolases
NT4 arylsulfatase
NT3 thiolester hydrolases
NT4 palmitoyl-coa hydrolase
NT2 fumarylacetoacetase
NT2 glycosidases
NT3 n-glycoside hydrolases
NT4 n-acetyl-β-glucosaminidase
NT4 β-n-acetylhexosaminidase
NT4 nucleosidases
NT3 o-glycoside hydrolases
NT4 β-fructofuranosidase
NT4 β-glucanase
NT4 β-glucuronidase
NT4 amylases
NT5 α-amylase
NT5 β-amylase

ENZYMES *cont.*
NT4 cellulase
NT4 chitinase
NT4 dextranase
NT4 disaccharidases
NT4 galactosidases
NT5 α-galactosidase
NT5 β-galactosidase
NT4 glucosidases
NT5 α-glucosidase
NT5 β-glucosidase
NT5 glucan 1,4-α-glucosidase
NT5 oligo-1,6-glucosidase
NT5 sucrose α-glucosidase
NT4 hyaluronidase
NT4 hyaluronoglucosaminidase
NT4 inulinase
NT4 isoamylase
NT4 lichenase
NT4 lysozyme
NT4 mannosidases
NT5 α-mannosidase
NT5 β-mannosidase
NT4 polygalacturonase
NT4 pullulanase
NT4 sialidase
NT4 trehalase
NT4 xylan 1,4-β-xylosidase
NT3 s-glycoside hydrolases
NT4 thioglucosidase
NT2 pancreatin
NT2 peptide hydrolases
NT3 peptidases
NT4 aminoacyl-histidine dipeptidase
NT4 aminopeptidases
NT5 aminopeptidase
NT5 cytosol aminopeptidase
NT5 microsomal aminopeptidase
NT4 carboxypeptidases
NT5 carboxypeptidase a
NT5 dipeptidyl carboxypeptidases
NT4 cathepsins
NT4 dipeptidase
NT4 proline dipeptidase
NT3 proteinases
NT4 γ-glutamyl hydrolase
NT4 acrosin
NT4 cathepsins
NT4 chymotrypsin
NT4 collagenase
NT4 elastase
NT4 endopeptidases
NT4 enteropeptidase
NT4 kallikrein
NT4 papain
NT4 pepsin
NT4 plasmin
NT4 plasminogen activator
NT4 renin
NT4 thrombin
NT4 trypsin
NT2 thiaminase
NT1 isoenzymes
NT1 isomerases
NT2 aldose 1-epimerase
NT2 chalcone isomerase
NT2 glucose-6-phosphate isomerase
NT2 mannose-6-phosphate isomerase
NT2 methylmalonyl-coa mutase
NT2 phosphotransferases
NT3 phosphoglucomutase
NT1 ligases
NT2 acetyl-coa carboxylase
NT2 acid-thiol ligases
NT3 acetate-coa ligase
NT3 long-chain-fatty-acid-coa ligase
NT2 amide synthases
NT3 aspartate-ammonia ligase
NT3 glutamate-ammonia ligase
NT2 argininosuccinate synthase
NT2 carbamoyl-phosphate synthase
NT2 glutathione synthase

ENZYMES *cont.*
NT2 propionyl-coa carboxylase
NT2 pyruvate carboxylase
NT1 lyases
NT2 aldehyde-lyases
NT3 fructose-bisphosphate aldolase
NT2 amidine-lyases
NT3 argininosuccinate lyase
NT2 ammonia-lyases
NT3 histidine ammonia-lyase
NT3 phenylalanine ammonia-lyase
NT2 carboxy-lyases
NT3 adenosylmethionine decarboxylase
NT3 glutamate decarboxylase
NT3 methylmalonyl-coa decarboxylase
NT3 ornithine decarboxylase
NT3 phosphoenolpyruvate carboxykinase
NT3 phosphoenolpyruvate carboxylase
NT3 pyruvate decarboxylase
NT3 ribulose-bisphosphate carboxylase
NT2 cystathionine γ-lyase
NT2 ddt-dehydrochlorinase
NT2 hydro-lyases
NT3 carbonate dehydratase
NT3 cystathionine β-synthase
NT3 porphobilinogen synthase
NT3 serine dehydratase
NT3 urocanate hydratase
NT2 oxo-acid-lyases
NT3 atp citrate lyase
NT3 hydroxymethylglutaryl-coa lyase
NT3 isocitrate lyase
NT2 pectate lyase
NT2 phosphorus-oxygen lyases
NT3 adenylate cyclase
NT3 guanylate cyclase
NT2 tyrosine phenol-lyase
NT1 oxidoreductases
NT2 3-hydroxyanthranilate oxidase
NT2 acyl-coa dehydrogenase
NT2 alcohol oxidoreductases
NT3 (s)-2-hydroxy-acid oxidase
NT3 l-gulonolactone oxidase
NT3 l-iditol dehydrogenase
NT3 alcohol dehydrogenase
NT3 glucose oxidase
NT3 glucose-6-phosphate dehydrogenase
NT3 glycerol dehydrogenase
NT3 glycerol-3-phosphate dehydrogenase
NT3 hydroxymethylglutaryl-coa reductase
NT3 hydroxysteroid dehydrogenase
NT3 isocitrate dehydrogenase
NT3 lactate dehydrogenase
NT3 malate dehydrogenase
NT3 malate oxidase
NT3 malic enzyme
NT3 methylenetetrahydro-folate reductase
NT3 phosphogluconate dehydrogenase
NT3 xanthine dehydrogenase
NT3 xanthine oxidase
NT2 aldehyde oxidoreductases
NT3 2-oxoisovalerate dehydrogenase (lipoamide)
NT3 aldehyde dehydrogenase
NT3 glyceraldehyde-3-phosphate dehydrogenase
NT3 pyruvate dehydrogenase (lipoamide)
NT3 pyruvate oxidase
NT2 amine oxidoreductases
NT3 l-amino-acid oxidase
NT3 alanine dehydrogenase

ENZYMES *cont.*
NT3 amine oxidase (copper-containing)
NT3 amine oxidase (flavin-containing)
NT3 dihydrofolate reductase
NT3 glutamate dehydrogenase
NT3 glutamate synthase
NT3 pyridoxamine-phosphate oxidase
NT3 saccharopine dehydrogenase
NT2 ascorbate oxidase
NT2 butyryl-coa dehydrogenase
NT2 catechol oxidase
NT2 cytochrome-c oxidase
NT2 dihydropteridine reductase
NT2 ferroxidase
NT2 glutaryl-coa dehydrogenase
NT2 glutathione reductase (nad(p)h)
NT2 hydrogenase
NT2 iaa oxidase
NT2 laccase
NT2 mixed function oxidase
NT2 nadh dehydrogenase
NT2 nadph-cytochrome-c2 reductase
NT2 nitrate reductase
NT2 nitrite reductase
NT2 nitrogenase
NT2 oxygenases
NT3 acyl-coa desaturase
NT3 calcidiol 1-monooxygenase
NT3 cholesterol 7α-monooxygenase
NT3 cysteine dioxygenase
NT3 dopamine β-monooxygenase
NT3 heme oxygenase (decyclizing)
NT3 lipoxygenase
NT3 luciferase
NT3 monophenol monooxygenase
NT3 phenylalanine 4-monooxygenase
NT3 procollagen-proline,2-oxoglutarate 4-dioxygenase
NT3 prostaglandin synthase
NT3 tryptophan 2,3-dioxygenase
NT3 tryptophan 5-monooxygenase
NT3 tyrosine 3-monooxygenase
NT3 unspecific monooxygenase
NT2 peroxidases
NT3 catalase
NT3 cytochrome-c peroxidase
NT3 glutathione peroxidase
NT3 peroxidase
NT4 lactoperoxidase
NT2 ribonucleotide reductase
NT2 succinate dehydrogenase
NT2 sulfite oxidase
NT2 superoxide dismutase
NT1 soil enzymes
NT1 transferases
NT2 acyltransferases
NT3 5-aminolevulinate synthase
NT3 acetyl-coa acetyltransferase
NT3 aminoacyltransferases
NT4 d-glutamyltransferase
NT4 γ-glutamylcyclotransferase
NT4 γ-glutamyltransferase
NT4 peptidyltransferase
NT3 carnitine acetyltransferase
NT3 carnitine palmitoyltransferase
NT3 chloramphenicol acetyltransferase

ENZYMES *cont.*
NT3 cholesterol acyltransferase
NT3 choline acetyltransferase
NT3 fatty-acid synthase
NT3 glycerol-3-phosphate acyltransferase
NT3 naringenin-chalcone synthase
NT3 phosphatidylcholine-sterol acyltransferase
NT2 alkyl (aryl) transferases
NT3 glutathione transferase
NT3 methionine adenosyltransferase
NT2 aminotransferases
NT3 alanine aminotransferase
NT3 asparagine-oxo-acid aminotransferase
NT3 aspartate aminotransferase
NT3 branched-chain-amino-acid aminotransferase
NT3 leucine aminotransferase
NT3 ornithine-oxo-acid aminotransferase
NT3 tyrosine aminotransferase
NT2 glycosyltransferases
NT3 hexosyltransferases
NT4 dextransucrase
NT4 glycogen (starch) synthase
NT4 lactose synthase
NT4 levansucrase
NT4 phosphorylase
NT5 glycogen phosphorylase
NT4 sucrose synthase
NT3 pentosyltransferases
NT4 adenine phosphoribosyltransferase
NT4 amidophosphoribosyl-transferase
NT4 purine-nucleoside phosphorylase
NT2 kinases
NT3 adenylate kinase
NT3 choline kinase
NT3 creatine kinase
NT3 ethanolamine kinase
NT3 fructokinase
NT3 galactokinase
NT3 glucokinase
NT3 glycerol kinase
NT3 hexokinase
NT3 phosphofructokinase
NT3 phosphoglycerate kinase
NT3 phosphoglycerate kinase (gtp)
NT3 phosphorylase kinase
NT3 protamine kinase
NT3 protein kinase
NT3 pyruvate kinase
NT3 riboflavin kinase
NT3 thiamin pyrophosphokinase
NT3 thymidine kinase
NT3 uridine kinase
NT2 nucleotidyltransferases
NT3 choline-phosphate cytidylyltransferase
NT3 dna nucleotidylexotransferase
NT3 dna polymerase
NT4 reverse transcriptase
NT3 rna polymerase
NT3 utp-hexose-1-phosphate uridylyltransferase
NT2 ornithine carbamoyltransferase
NT2 thiosulfate sulfurtransferase
NT2 transaldolase
NT2 transketolase
NT1 urea cycle enzymes
NT2 arginase
NT2 argininosuccinate lyase
NT2 argininosuccinate synthase
NT2 ornithine carbamoyltransferase
rt coenzymes

ENZYMES *cont.*
rt enzyme activators
rt enzyme activity
rt enzyme deficiencies
rt enzyme inhibitors
rt enzyme polymorphism
rt enzyme precursors
rt enzyme preparations
rt enzymology
rt lysosomes
rt microsomes
rt peptides
rt proteins
rt saliva
rt serology

ENZYMOLOGY
BT1 biochemistry
BT2 chemistry
NT1 histoenzymology
rt enzymes

EOLIAN DEPOSITS
BF aeolian deposits
NT1 eolian sands

EOLIAN SANDS
BF aeolian sands
BT1 eolian deposits

EOLIAN SOILS
BF aeolian soils

eomenacanthus
USE **menacanthus**

eomenacanthus stramineus
USE **menacanthus stramineus**

EOREUMA
BT1 pyralidae
BT2 lepidoptera
NT1 eoreuma loftini

EOREUMA LOFTINI
BT1 eoreuma
BT2 pyralidae
BT3 lepidoptera

EOSENTOMIDAE
BT1 protura
NT1 eosentomon

EOSENTOMON
BT1 eosentomidae
BT2 protura

EOSINE
BT1 dyes

eosinophil leukocytes
USE **eosinophils**

EOSINOPHILIA
BT1 leukocyte disorders
BT2 blood disorders
BT3 animal disorders
BT4 disorders
NT1 tropical eosinophilia

eosinophilia, tropical
USE **tropical eosinophilia**

EOSINOPHILS
uf *eosinophil leukocytes*
uf *leukocytes, eosinophil*
BT1 granulocytes
BT2 leukocytes
BT3 blood cells
BT4 cells

EOTETRANYCHUS
BT1 tetranychidae
BT2 prostigmata
BT3 acari
NT1 eotetranychus carpini
NT1 eotetranychus hicoriae
NT1 eotetranychus pruni
NT1 eotetranychus sexmaculatus
NT1 eotetranychus willamettei
rt schizotetranychus

EOTETRANYCHUS CARPINI
BT1 eotetranychus
BT2 tetranychidae

EOTETRANYCHUS CARPINI *cont.*
BT3 prostigmata
BT4 acari

EOTETRANYCHUS HICORIAE
BT1 eotetranychus
BT2 tetranychidae
BT3 prostigmata
BT4 acari

EOTETRANYCHUS PRUNI
uf *schizotetranychus pruni*
BT1 eotetranychus
BT2 tetranychidae
BT3 prostigmata
BT4 acari

EOTETRANYCHUS SEXMACULATUS
BT1 eotetranychus
BT2 tetranychidae
BT3 prostigmata
BT4 acari

EOTETRANYCHUS WILLAMETTEI
BT1 eotetranychus
BT2 tetranychidae
BT3 prostigmata
BT4 acari

EOTHENOMYS
BT1 microtinae
BT2 muridae
BT3 rodents
BT4 mammals
NT1 eothenomys melanogaster
rt voles

EOTHENOMYS MELANOGASTER
BT1 eothenomys
BT2 microtinae
BT3 muridae
BT4 rodents
BT5 mammals

EPACRIDACEAE
NT1 melichrus
NT1 pentachondra

EPEOLUS
BT1 apidae
BT2 hymenoptera

EPERUA
BT1 leguminosae
NT1 eperua leucantha

EPERUA LEUCANTHA
BT1 eperua
BT2 leguminosae

EPERYTHROZOON
BT1 anaplasmataceae
BT2 rickettsiales
BT3 bacteria
BT4 prokaryotes
NT1 eperythrozoon coccoides
NT1 eperythrozoon felis
NT1 eperythrozoon ovis
NT1 eperythrozoon suis
NT1 eperythrozoon wenyoni

EPERYTHROZOON COCCOIDES
BT1 eperythrozoon
BT2 anaplasmataceae
BT3 rickettsiales
BT4 bacteria
BT5 prokaryotes

EPERYTHROZOON FELIS
BT1 eperythrozoon
BT2 anaplasmataceae
BT3 rickettsiales
BT4 bacteria
BT5 prokaryotes

EPERYTHROZOON OVIS
BT1 eperythrozoon
BT2 anaplasmataceae
BT3 rickettsiales
BT4 bacteria
BT5 prokaryotes

EPERYTHROZOON SUIS
BT1 eperythrozoon

EPERYTHROZOON SUIS *cont.*
BT2 anaplasmataceae
BT3 rickettsiales
BT4 bacteria
BT5 prokaryotes

EPERYTHROZOON WENYONI
BT1 eperythrozoon
BT2 anaplasmataceae
BT3 rickettsiales
BT4 bacteria
BT5 prokaryotes

EPHEDRA
BT1 ephedraceae
NT1 ephedra distachya
NT1 ephedra equisetina
NT1 ephedra foliata
NT1 ephedra gerardiana
NT1 ephedra intermedia
NT1 ephedra major
NT1 ephedra pachyclada
NT1 ephedra sinica
NT1 ephedra viridis

EPHEDRA DISTACHYA
uf *ephedra helvetica*
BT1 ephedra
BT2 ephedraceae
BT1 medicinal plants

EPHEDRA EQUISETINA
BT1 ephedra
BT2 ephedraceae

EPHEDRA FOLIATA
BT1 ephedra
BT2 ephedraceae

EPHEDRA GERARDIANA
BT1 ephedra
BT2 ephedraceae
BT1 medicinal plants

ephedra helvetica
USE **ephedra distachya**

EPHEDRA INTERMEDIA
BT1 ephedra
BT2 ephedraceae

EPHEDRA MAJOR
uf *ephedra nebrodensis*
BT1 ephedra
BT2 ephedraceae
BT1 medicinal plants

ephedra nebrodensis
USE **ephedra major**

EPHEDRA PACHYCLADA
BT1 ephedra
BT2 ephedraceae

EPHEDRA SINICA
BT1 ephedra
BT2 ephedraceae
BT1 medicinal plants

EPHEDRA VIRIDIS
BT1 ephedra
BT2 ephedraceae

EPHEDRACEAE
NT1 ephedra
NT2 ephedra distachya
NT2 ephedra equisetina
NT2 ephedra foliata
NT2 ephedra gerardiana
NT2 ephedra intermedia
NT2 ephedra major
NT2 ephedra pachyclada
NT2 ephedra sinica
NT2 ephedra viridis

EPHEDRINE
BT1 amino alcohols
BT2 alcohols
BT2 amino compounds
BT3 organic nitrogen compounds
BT1 sympathomimetics
BT2 neurotropic drugs
BT3 drugs

EPHEDRUS
BT1 braconidae
BT2 hymenoptera
NT1 ephedrus cerasicola
NT1 ephedrus plagiator

EPHEDRUS CERASICOLA
BT1 ephedrus
BT2 braconidae
BT3 hymenoptera

EPHEDRUS PLAGIATOR
BT1 ephedrus
BT2 braconidae
BT3 hymenoptera

ephemeral fever virus
USE **bovine ephemeral fever virus**

EPHEMEROPTERA
uf *plectoptera*
rt insects

EPHESTIA
uf *anagasta*
uf *cadra*
BT1 pyralidae
BT2 lepidoptera
NT1 ephestia cautella
NT1 ephestia elutella
NT1 ephestia figulilella
NT1 ephestia kuehniella

EPHESTIA CAUTELLA
uf *cadra cautella*
BT1 ephestia
BT2 pyralidae
BT3 lepidoptera

EPHESTIA ELUTELLA
BT1 ephestia
BT2 pyralidae
BT3 lepidoptera

EPHESTIA FIGULILELLA
uf *cadra figulilella*
BT1 ephestia
BT2 pyralidae
BT3 lepidoptera

EPHESTIA KUEHNIELLA
uf *anagasta kuehniella*
BT1 ephestia
BT2 pyralidae
BT3 lepidoptera

EPHIALTES
uf *eremochila*
BT1 ichneumonidae
BT2 hymenoptera
NT1 ephialtes ontario
rt apechthis
rt dolichomitus
rt exeristes
rt gregopimpla
rt liotryphon
rt scambus

ephialtes brevicornis
USE **scambus brevicornis**

ephialtes calobatus
USE **scambus calobatus**

ephialtes comstockii
USE **exeristes comstockii**

ephialtes extensor
USE **liotryphon punctulatus**

EPHIALTES ONTARIO
uf *apechthis ontario*
BT1 ephialtes
BT2 ichneumonidae
BT3 hymenoptera

ephialtes populneus
USE **dolichomitus populneus**

ephialtes punctulatus
USE **liotryphon punctulatus**

ephialtes roborator
USE **exeristes roborator**

EPHYDRA
BT1 ephydridae
BT2 diptera

EPHYDRIDAE
BT1 diptera
NT1 ephydra
NT1 hydrellia
NT2 hydrellia griseola
NT2 hydrellia philippina

EPIBLEMA
BT1 tortricidae
BT2 lepidoptera
NT1 epiblema scudderiana
rt epinotia
rt eucosma

epiblema nigricana
USE **epinotia nigricana**

EPIBLEMA SCUDDERIANA
uf *eucosma scudderiana*
BT1 epiblema
BT2 tortricidae
BT3 lepidoptera

epiblema tedella
USE **epinotia tedella**

EPICATECHIN
BT1 flavanols
BT2 alcohols
BT2 flavonoids
BT3 aromatic compounds
BT3 plant pigments
BT4 pigments
rt tanstuffs

EPICAUTA
BT1 meloidae
BT2 coleoptera
NT1 epicauta vittata

EPICAUTA VITTATA
BT1 epicauta
BT2 meloidae
BT3 coleoptera

EPICHARIS
BT1 apidae
BT2 hymenoptera

EPICHLOE
BT1 clavicipitales
rt acremonium

epichloe typhina
USE **acremonium coenophialum**

EPICHORISTODES
BT1 tortricidae
BT2 lepidoptera
NT1 epichoristodes acerbella

EPICHORISTODES ACERBELLA
BT1 epichoristodes
BT2 tortricidae
BT3 lepidoptera

EPICOCCUM
BT1 deuteromycotina
NT1 epicoccum nigrum

EPICOCCUM NIGRUM
uf *epicoccum purpurascens*
BT1 epicoccum
BT2 deuteromycotina

epicoccum purpurascens
USE **epicoccum nigrum**

EPICORMICS
rt buds
rt shoots

EPICOTYLS
BT1 seedlings
rt cotyledons
rt hypocotyls
rt plumules

EPIDAMAEUS
BT1 damaeidae
BT2 cryptostigmata

EPIDAMAEUS *cont.*
BT3 acari

EPIDEMICS
BT1 outbreaks
rt diseases
rt epidemiology

EPIDEMIOLOGICAL SURVEYS
(surveys for something other than the presence of a disease, e.g. antibodies)
BT1 surveys
rt disease surveys
rt epidemiology

EPIDEMIOLOGY
NT1 epizootiology
rt aetiology
rt carrier state
rt disease distribution
rt disease surveys
rt disease transmission
rt epidemics
rt epidemiological surveys
rt morbidity

EPIDENDRUM
BT1 orchidaceae
NT1 epidendrum anceps
NT1 epidendrum difforme
NT1 epidendrum fehlingii
NT1 epidendrum ibaguense
NT1 epidendrum marmoratum
NT1 epidendrum prostratum
NT1 epidendrum withneri

EPIDENDRUM ANCEPS
BT1 epidendrum
BT2 orchidaceae
BT1 ornamental orchids

EPIDENDRUM DIFFORME
BT1 epidendrum
BT2 orchidaceae
BT1 ornamental orchids

EPIDENDRUM FEHLINGII
BT1 epidendrum
BT2 orchidaceae
BT1 ornamental orchids

EPIDENDRUM IBAGUENSE
uf *epidendrum radicans*
BT1 epidendrum
BT2 orchidaceae

EPIDENDRUM MARMORATUM
BT1 epidendrum
BT2 orchidaceae
BT1 ornamental orchids

EPIDENDRUM PROSTRATUM
BT1 epidendrum
BT2 orchidaceae
BT1 ornamental orchids

epidendrum radicans
USE **epidendrum ibaguense**

epidendrum tampense
USE **encyclia tampensis**

EPIDENDRUM WITHNERI
BT1 epidendrum
BT2 orchidaceae
BT1 ornamental orchids

EPIDERMAL GROWTH FACTOR
BT1 growth factors
BT2 hormones
BT1 polypeptides
BT2 peptides
rt urogastrone

EPIDERMIS
BT1 animal tissues
BT2 tissues
BT1 plant tissues
BT2 plant
BT2 tissues
NT1 cuticle
rt coat
rt cutin
rt guard cells

EPIDERMIS *cont.*
rt guard hairs
rt keratinization
rt keratosis
rt nail
rt periderm
rt plant hairs
rt rhizoplane
rt root hairs
rt stomata

EPIDERMOPHYTON
BT1 deuteromycotina
NT1 epidermophyton floccosum
rt dermatophytes

EPIDERMOPHYTON FLOCCOSUM
BT1 epidermophyton
BT2 deuteromycotina

epidermophyton rubrum
USE **trichophyton rubrum**

EPIDIDYMIS
BT1 testes
BT2 gonads
BT3 reproductive organs
NT1 caput epididymidis
NT1 cauda epididymidis
NT1 corpus epididymidis
rt ductus deferens
rt epididymitis

EPIDIDYMITIS
BT1 male genital diseases
BT2 organic diseases
BT3 diseases
rt epididymis

EPIDINIUM
BT1 ciliophora
BT2 protozoa
NT1 epidinium caudatum
NT1 epidinium ecaudatum

EPIDINIUM CAUDATUM
BT1 epidinium
BT2 ciliophora
BT3 protozoa

EPIDINIUM ECAUDATUM
BT1 epidinium
BT2 ciliophora
BT3 protozoa

EPIDINOCARSIS
uf *apoanagyrus*
BT1 encyrtidae
BT2 hymenoptera
NT1 epidinocarsis lopezi

EPIDINOCARSIS LOPEZI
uf *apoanagyrus lopezi*
BT1 biological control agents
BT2 beneficial organisms
BT1 epidinocarsis
BT2 encyrtidae
BT3 hymenoptera

epidural anaesthesia
USE **conduction anaesthesia**

EPIFAGUS
BT1 orobanchaceae
NT1 epifagus virginiana

EPIFAGUS VIRGINIANA
BT1 epifagus
BT2 orobanchaceae

EPIGENETICS
BT1 genetics
BT2 biology
rt genotypes
rt phenotypes

EPILACHNA
uf *henosepilachna*
BT1 coccinellidae
BT2 coleoptera
NT1 epilachna dodecastigma
NT1 epilachna varivestis
NT1 epilachna vigintioctomaculata

EPILACHNA *cont.*
NT1 epilachna vigintioctopunctata

EPILACHNA DODECASTIGMA
BT1 epilachna
BT2 coccinellidae
BT3 coleoptera

EPILACHNA VARIVESTIS
BT1 epilachna
BT2 coccinellidae
BT3 coleoptera

EPILACHNA VIGINTIOCTOMACULATA
BT1 epilachna
BT2 coccinellidae
BT3 coleoptera

EPILACHNA VIGINTIOCTOPUNCTATA
uf *henosepilachna vigintioctopunctata*
BT1 epilachna
BT2 coccinellidae
BT3 coleoptera

EPILEPSY
BT1 brain disorders
BT2 nervous system diseases
BT3 organic diseases
BT4 diseases
rt anticonvulsants
rt citrullinaemia
rt convulsions
rt epileptiform attacks
rt phenytoin

EPILEPTIFORM ATTACKS
BT1 brain disorders
BT2 nervous system diseases
BT3 organic diseases
BT4 diseases
rt epilepsy
rt phenytoin

EPILOBIUM
BT1 onagraceae
NT1 epilobium angustifolium
NT1 epilobium hirsutum
NT1 epilobium montanum
NT1 epilobium pyrricholophum
NT1 epilobium rosemarinifolium
NT1 epilobium roseum
rt chamaenerion

EPILOBIUM ANGUSTIFOLIUM
BT1 epilobium
BT2 onagraceae
rt chamaenerion angustifolium

EPILOBIUM HIRSUTUM
BT1 epilobium
BT2 onagraceae

EPILOBIUM MONTANUM
BT1 epilobium
BT2 onagraceae

EPILOBIUM PYRRICHOLOPHUM
BT1 epilobium
BT2 onagraceae

EPILOBIUM ROSEMARINIFOLIUM
BT1 epilobium
BT2 onagraceae

EPILOBIUM ROSEUM
BT1 epilobium
BT2 onagraceae

EPIMEDIUM
BT1 berberidaceae
rt ornamental herbaceous plants

EPINASTY
BT1 plant development
rt bending

EPINEPHELUS
BT1 serranidae
BT2 perciformes
BT3 osteichthyes

EPINEPHELUS *cont.*
BT4 fishes
NT1 epinephelus aeneus
NT1 epinephelus akaara
NT1 epinephelus tauvina
rt groupers

EPINEPHELUS AENEUS
BT1 epinephelus
BT2 serranidae
BT3 perciformes
BT4 osteichthyes
BT5 fishes

EPINEPHELUS AKAARA
BT1 epinephelus
BT2 serranidae
BT3 perciformes
BT4 osteichthyes
BT5 fishes

EPINEPHELUS TAUVINA
BT1 epinephelus
BT2 serranidae
BT3 perciformes
BT4 osteichthyes
BT5 fishes

EPINEPHRINE
uf *adrenaline*
BT1 adrenal medulla hormones
BT2 hormones
BT1 catecholamines
BT2 biogenic amines
BT3 amines
BT4 amino compounds
BT5 organic nitrogen compounds

EPINOTIA
BT1 tortricidae
BT2 lepidoptera
NT1 epinotia aporema
NT1 epinotia nanana
NT1 epinotia nigricana
NT1 epinotia tedella
rt catastega
rt epiblema
rt eucosma

epinotia aceriella
USE **catastega aceriella**

EPINOTIA APOREMA
BT1 epinotia
BT2 tortricidae
BT3 lepidoptera

EPINOTIA NANANA
BT1 epinotia
BT2 tortricidae
BT3 lepidoptera

EPINOTIA NIGRICANA
uf *epiblema nigricana*
BT1 epinotia
BT2 tortricidae
BT3 lepidoptera

EPINOTIA TEDELLA
uf *epiblema tedella*
uf *eucosma tedella*
BT1 epinotia
BT2 tortricidae
BT3 lepidoptera

EPIPACTIS
BT1 orchidaceae
NT1 epipactis atropurpurea

EPIPACTIS ATROPURPUREA
BT1 epipactis
BT2 orchidaceae
BT1 ornamental orchids

EPIPHYAS
BT1 tortricidae
BT2 lepidoptera
NT1 epiphyas postvittana

EPIPHYAS POSTVITTANA
BT1 epiphyas
BT2 tortricidae
BT3 lepidoptera

EPIPHYLLUM
BT1 cactaceae
rt ornamental succulent plants

EPIPHYSES
BT1 bones
BT2 musculoskeletal system
BT3 body parts

EPIPHYTES
rt endophytes
rt parasitic plants
rt support trees
rt symbionts
rt symbiosis

EPIPREMNUM
BT1 araceae
NT1 epipremnum pinnatum

epipremnum aureum
USE **epipremnum pinnatum**

EPIPREMNUM PINNATUM
uf *epipremnum aureum*
uf *rhaphidophora aurea*
uf *scindapsus aureus*
BT1 epipremnum
BT2 araceae
BT1 ornamental foliage plants
BT2 foliage plants

EPIPYROPIDAE
HN from 1989
BT1 lepidoptera
NT1 epipyrops
NT1 epiricania
NT2 epiricania melanoleuca

EPIPYROPS
HN from 1989
BT1 epipyropidae
BT2 lepidoptera
rt epiricania

epipyrops melanoleuca
USE **epiricania melanoleuca**

EPIRICANIA
HN from 1989
BT1 epipyropidae
BT2 lepidoptera
NT1 epiricania melanoleuca
rt epipyrops

EPIRICANIA MELANOLEUCA
HN from 1989
uf *epipyrops melanoleuca*
BT1 epiricania
BT2 epipyropidae
BT3 lepidoptera

EPIRRITA
uf *oporinia*
BT1 geometridae
BT2 lepidoptera
NT1 epirrita autumnata

EPIRRITA AUTUMNATA
uf *oporinia autumnata*
BT1 epirrita
BT2 geometridae
BT3 lepidoptera

EPISCIA
BT1 gesneriaceae
NT1 episcia cupreata

EPISCIA CUPREATA
BT1 episcia
BT2 gesneriaceae
BT1 ornamental herbaceous plants

episcia punctata
USE **alsobia punctata**

episcia tesselata
USE **nautilocalyx bullatus**

EPISTASIS
uf *hypostasis*
BT1 gene interaction
BT2 genetics
BT3 biology

EPISTASIS *cont.*
rt genes

EPISTAXIS
BT1 haemorrhage
BT2 symptoms
rt nose

EPISTROPHE
BT1 syrphidae
BT2 diptera
rt episyrphus

epistrophe balteata
USE **episyrphus balteatus**

EPISTYLIS
BT1 ciliophora
BT2 protozoa
NT1 epistylis horizontalis
NT1 epistylis lwoffi
NT1 epistylis niagarae

EPISTYLIS HORIZONTALIS
BT1 epistylis
BT2 ciliophora
BT3 protozoa

EPISTYLIS LWOFFI
BT1 epistylis
BT2 ciliophora
BT3 protozoa

EPISTYLIS NIAGARAE
BT1 epistylis
BT2 ciliophora
BT3 protozoa

EPISYRPHUS
BT1 syrphidae
BT2 diptera
NT1 episyrphus balteatus
rt epistrophe
rt syrphus

EPISYRPHUS BALTEATUS
uf epistrophe balteata
uf syrphus balteatus
BT1 episyrphus
BT2 syrphidae
BT3 diptera

EPITHELANTHA
BT1 cactaceae
NT1 epithelantha micromeris

EPITHELANTHA MICROMERIS
BT1 epithelantha
BT2 cactaceae
BT1 ornamental succulent plants
BT2 succulent plants

EPITHELIOCYSTIS
rt fish diseases

EPITHELIOGENESIS IMPERFECTA
BT1 congenital abnormalities
BT2 abnormalities
rt epithelium

EPITHELIUM
BT1 animal tissues
BT2 tissues
NT1 rumen epithelium
NT2 rumen mucosa
NT1 spermatogenic epithelium
rt epitheliogenesis imperfecta
rt skin

EPITRIMERUS
BT1 eriophyidae
BT2 prostigmata
BT3 acari
NT1 epitrimerus pyri

EPITRIMERUS PYRI
BT1 epitrimerus
BT2 eriophyidae
BT3 prostigmata
BT4 acari

EPITRIX
BT1 chrysomelidae
BT2 coleoptera
NT1 epitrix hirtipennis

EPITRIX HIRTIPENNIS
BT1 epitrix
BT2 chrysomelidae
BT3 coleoptera

epiurus
USE **scambus**

epiurus calobatus
USE **scambus calobatus**

epiurus euphrantae
USE **scambus brevicornis**

EPIZOOTIC HAEMORRHAGIC DISEASE OF DEER VIRUS
AF epizootic hemorrhagic disease of deer virus
BT1 orbivirus
BT2 arboviruses
BT3 pathogens
BT2 reoviridae
BT3 viruses

EPIZOOTIC HEMORRHAGIC DISEASE OF DEER VIRUS
BF epizootic haemorrhagic disease of deer virus

EPIZOOTIC LYMPHANGITIS
BT1 lymphangitis
BT2 lymphatic diseases
BT3 organic diseases
BT4 diseases
BT1 mycoses
BT2 infectious diseases
BT3 diseases
rt histoplasma farciminosum

EPIZOOTIOLOGY
BT1 epidemiology

EPN
BT1 phosphonothioate insecticides
BT2 organophosphorus insecticides
BT3 insecticides
BT4 pesticides
BT3 organophosphorus pesticides
BT4 organophosphorus compounds

EPOFENONANE
BT1 juvenile hormone analogues
BT2 insect growth regulators
BT3 growth regulators
BT3 insecticides
BT4 pesticides

epoxide hydrase
USE **epoxide hydrolase**

EPOXIDE HYDROLASE
(ec 3.3.2.3)
uf epoxide hydrase
BT1 hydrolases
BT2 enzymes

EPOXIDES
HN from 1990
BT1 protective coatings
BT2 coatings

1,2-epoxymenthyl acetate
USE **eucalyptol**

EPRONAZ
BT1 triazole herbicides
BT2 herbicides
BT3 pesticides
BT2 triazoles
BT3 azoles
BT4 heterocyclic nitrogen compounds
BT5 organic nitrogen compounds

EPSOM SALTS
BT1 magnesium sulfate
BT2 anticonvulsants
BT3 neurotropic drugs
BT4 drugs
BT2 magnesium fertilizers

EPSOM SALTS *cont.*
BT3 fertilizers
BT2 nonclay minerals
BT3 minerals
BT2 purgatives
BT3 gastrointestinal agents
BT4 drugs
BT2 sulfates (inorganic salts)
BT3 inorganic salts
BT4 inorganic compounds
BT4 salts
BT3 sulfates

EPSTEIN-BARR VIRUS
BT1 human herpesvirus
BT2 herpesviridae
BT3 viruses

EPTC
BT1 thiocarbamate herbicides
BT2 carbamate pesticides
BT2 herbicides
BT3 pesticides

EPTESICUS
BT1 vespertilionidae
BT2 chiroptera
BT3 mammals
NT1 eptesicus fuscus
NT1 eptesicus serotinus

EPTESICUS FUSCUS
BT1 eptesicus
BT2 vespertilionidae
BT3 chiroptera
BT4 mammals

EPTESICUS SEROTINUS
BT1 eptesicus
BT2 vespertilionidae
BT3 chiroptera
BT4 mammals

EQUATIONS
NT1 green and ampt equation
NT1 universal soil loss equation
rt mathematics

EQUATORIAL FOREST SOILS
uf forest soils, equatorial
BT1 soil types (ecological)

EQUATORIAL GUINEA
uf fernando po
uf guinea, equatorial
uf rio muni
uf spanish guinea
BT1 central africa
BT2 africa south of sahara
BT3 africa
rt acp

EQUIDAE
uf equines
BT1 perissodactyla
BT2 mammals
BT2 ungulates
NT1 equus
NT2 equus burchellii
NT2 equus hemionus
NT2 equus zebra
rt donkeys
rt hinnies
rt horses
rt mules
rt przewalski's horse

EQUILIBRATION
BT1 techniques
rt equilibration time
rt semen

EQUILIBRATION TIME
BT1 time
rt equilibration

EQUILIBRIUM
NT1 acid base equilibrium
rt disequilibrium
rt equilibrium disorders
rt homeostasis

EQUILIBRIUM DISORDERS
BT1 functional disorders

EQUILIBRIUM DISORDERS *cont.*
BT2 animal disorders
BT3 disorders
rt ear diseases
rt equilibrium

EQUILIBRIUM MOISTURE CONTENT
BT1 moisture content
BT2 composition
BT1 water content
BT2 composition
BT2 water relations
rt wood moisture

EQUILIBRIUM THEORY
BT1 economic theory
BT2 economics

EQUINE ADENOVIRUS
BT1 mastadenovirus
BT2 adenoviridae
BT3 viruses

EQUINE ARTERITIS VIRUS
BT1 arterivirus
BT2 togaviridae
BT3 viruses
rt arteritis

EQUINE ENCEPHALOMYELITIS VIRUS
BT1 alphavirus
BT2 arboviruses
BT3 pathogens
BT2 togaviridae
BT3 viruses
NT1 eastern equine encephalitis virus
NT1 venezuelan equine encephalitis virus
NT1 western equine encephalitis virus
rt encephalitis

EQUINE HERPESVIRUS
BT1 herpesviridae
BT2 viruses
NT1 equine rhinopneumonitis virus

EQUINE INFECTIOUS ANAEMIA
AF equine infectious anemia
BT1 anaemia
BT2 blood disorders
BT3 animal disorders
BT4 disorders
BT1 horse diseases
BT2 animal diseases
BT3 diseases
rt equine infectious anaemia virus

EQUINE INFECTIOUS ANAEMIA VIRUS
AF equine infectious anemia virus
BT1 lentivirinae
BT2 retroviridae
BT3 viruses
rt equine infectious anaemia

EQUINE INFECTIOUS ANEMIA
BF equine infectious anaemia
BT1 anemia
rt equine infectious anemia virus

EQUINE INFECTIOUS ANEMIA VIRUS
BF equine infectious anaemia virus
rt equine infectious anemia

EQUINE INFLUENZAVIRUS
BT1 influenzavirus
BT2 orthomyxoviridae
BT3 viruses

EQUINE ONCOVIRUS
BT1 mammalian oncovirus
BT2 oncovirus type c
BT3 oncovirinae
BT4 retroviridae

EQUINE ONCOVIRUS *cont.*
BT5 viruses

EQUINE RHINOPNEUMONITIS VIRUS
BT1 equine herpesvirus
BT2 herpesviridae
BT3 viruses

EQUINE RHINOVIRUS
BT1 rhinovirus
BT2 picornaviridae
BT3 viruses

equines
USE **equidae**

EQUIPMENT
uf plant (industrial)
NT1 agitators
NT1 air conditioners
NT1 ancillary equipment
NT1 apparatus
NT1 application equipment
NT2 applicators
NT3 wiper applicators
NT2 fertilizer distributors
NT3 liquid fertilizer distributors
NT2 fumigation equipment
NT2 injectors
NT3 soil injectors
NT3 tree injectors
NT2 spraying equipment
NT3 lances
NT3 nozzles
NT4 cone nozzles
NT4 fan nozzles
NT4 spinning disc nozzles
NT3 spray guns
NT3 spray races
NT3 sprayers
NT4 aerial sprayers
NT4 aerosol sprayers
NT4 air assisted sprayers
NT4 band sprayers
NT4 electrostatic sprayers
NT4 field sprayers
NT4 high volume sprayers
NT4 logarithmic sprayers
NT4 low volume sprayers
NT5 ultralow volume sprayers
NT4 mist blowers
NT4 mist sprayers
NT4 orchard sprayers
NT4 overhead sprayers
NT4 plot sprayers
NT5 small plot sprayers
NT4 portable sprayers
NT5 knapsack sprayers
NT4 recirculatory sprayers
NT4 tower sprayers
NT3 spraylines
NT2 spreaders
NT3 bait spreaders
NT3 lime spreaders
NT3 manure spreaders
NT3 slurry spreaders
NT1 artificial vagina
NT1 aspirators
NT1 bioreactors
NT1 cables
NT1 calorimeters
NT1 cleaning equipment (agricola)
NT1 climbing devices
NT1 collection dummy
NT1 collectors
NT2 egg collectors
NT2 solar collectors
NT1 condensers
NT1 custom-made equipment (agricola)
NT1 dairy equipment
NT2 butter churns
NT2 butyrometers
NT2 cheese moulds
NT2 cheese presses
NT2 cheese vats
NT2 clarifiers
NT2 homogenizers
NT2 milk crates

EQUIPMENT *cont.*
NT2 milk filters
NT2 milk meters
NT2 milk pipelines
NT2 milk pumps
NT2 milk tankers
NT2 milk tanks
NT2 pasteurizers
NT2 triers
NT1 digesters
NT2 anaerobic digesters
NT1 disintegrators
NT1 drainage equipment
NT2 ditch cleaners
NT2 drain layers
NT2 drain pipes
NT2 drain ploughs
NT2 dredgers
NT1 earth moving equipment
NT2 bulldozers
NT2 excavators
NT2 land levellers
NT2 power shovels
NT2 scrapers
NT2 trench cutters
NT1 electrical equipment
NT2 batteries
NT2 electric driers
NT2 electric fences
NT2 electric motors
NT2 microphones
NT2 photoelectric cells
NT2 photovoltaic cells
NT2 potentiometers
NT2 solenoids
NT2 thermistors
NT2 thyristors
NT2 transformers
NT2 transponders
NT2 windings
NT1 evaporators
NT1 evaporimeters
NT1 experimental equipment
NT2 experimental rigs
NT2 plot sprayers
NT3 small plot sprayers
NT2 rain shelters
NT2 rainfall simulators
NT2 shear boxes
NT2 soil bins
NT2 test rigs
NT3 wind tunnels
NT1 extractors
NT2 diffusers
NT2 dust extractors
NT2 solar beeswax extractors
NT1 farm equipment
NT1 fishing gear
NT2 floats
NT1 food processing equipment (agricola)
NT2 blenders (agricola)
NT2 mixers (kitchen appliance) (agricola)
NT1 freezers
NT1 germination cabinets
NT1 grafting equipment
NT1 growth chambers
NT1 hail guns
NT1 heat exchangers
NT1 heaters
NT2 air heaters
NT2 boilers
NT3 steam boilers
NT2 burners
NT2 electric heaters
NT2 heat lamps
NT2 infrared heaters
NT1 hoses
NT1 household equipment (agricola)
NT2 can openers (agricola)
NT2 garbage disposals (agricola)
NT2 irons (agricola)
NT1 humidifiers
NT1 hydraulic equipment
NT2 hydraulic brakes
NT2 hydraulic couplings
NT2 hydraulic jacks
NT2 hydraulic motors

EQUIPMENT *cont.*
NT2 hydraulic rams
NT2 hydraulic transmissions
NT1 image processors
NT1 irrigation equipment
NT2 emitters
NT2 plastic pipes
NT3 corrugated plastic pipes
NT1 laboratory equipment
NT1 ladders
NT2 steps
NT1 microprocessors
NT1 mobile equipment (agricola)
NT1 neutron probes
NT1 pollen dispensers
NT1 recreation equipment
NT2 recreational vehicles
NT2 signboards and signposts
NT2 toys
NT3 educational toys (agricola)
NT1 samplers
NT2 core samplers
NT1 saturators
NT1 sericultural equipment
NT1 serving equipment (agricola)
NT1 skidding equipment
NT2 sledges
NT3 skidders
NT2 winches
NT1 slaughtering equipment
NT1 sports equipment
NT1 standby equipment
NT2 standby generators
NT1 steamers
NT2 calandrias
NT2 feed steamers
NT1 sterilizers
NT1 storage equipment (agricola)
NT1 stoves
NT1 surgical equipment
NT2 sutures
NT1 traps
NT2 bait traps
NT2 insect traps
NT3 biconical traps
NT3 coloured sticky traps
NT3 electrocuting traps
NT3 funnel traps
NT3 light traps
NT4 cdc light traps
NT4 new jersey light traps
NT3 malaise traps
NT3 manitoba traps
NT3 oviposition traps
NT3 pheromone traps
NT3 pitfall traps
NT3 sex attractant traps
NT3 sound traps
NT3 sticky traps
NT3 suction traps
NT3 trap bands
NT3 trap crops
NT3 trap trees
NT3 visual traps
NT3 water traps
NT3 yellow sticky traps
NT3 yellow traps
NT1 vacuum pans
NT2 continuous vacuum pans
NT1 veterinary equipment
rt components
rt farm machinery
rt implements
rt instruments
rt machinery
rt tools
rt workshops

EQUIPMENT/FURNITURE ARRANGEMENT (AGRICOLA)
uf furniture arrangement
rt furniture
rt layout
rt space utilization (agricola)

EQUISETACEAE
NT1 equisetum
NT2 equisetum arvense
NT2 equisetum fluviatile
NT2 equisetum hyemale
NT2 equisetum palustre

EQUISETACEAE *cont.*
NT2 equisetum prealtum
NT2 equisetum sylvaticum
NT2 equisetum telmateia

EQUISETUM
BT1 equisetaceae
NT1 equisetum arvense
NT1 equisetum fluviatile
NT1 equisetum hyemale
NT1 equisetum palustre
NT1 equisetum prealtum
NT1 equisetum sylvaticum
NT1 equisetum telmateia

EQUISETUM ARVENSE
BT1 equisetum
BT2 equisetaceae
BT1 weeds

EQUISETUM FLUVIATILE
BT1 equisetum
BT2 equisetaceae

EQUISETUM HYEMALE
BT1 equisetum
BT2 equisetaceae

EQUISETUM PALUSTRE
BT1 equisetum
BT2 equisetaceae
BT1 weeds

EQUISETUM PREALTUM
BT1 equisetum
BT2 equisetaceae

EQUISETUM SYLVATICUM
BT1 equisetum
BT2 equisetaceae

EQUISETUM TELMATEIA
BT1 equisetum
BT2 equisetaceae
BT1 medicinal plants

EQUUS
BT1 equidae
BT2 perissodactyla
BT3 mammals
BT3 ungulates
NT1 equus burchellii
NT1 equus hemionus
NT1 equus zebra

equus asinus
USE **donkeys**

equus asinus x equus caballus
USE **hinnies**

EQUUS BURCHELLII
BT1 equus
BT2 equidae
BT3 perissodactyla
BT4 mammals
BT4 ungulates
rt zebras

equus caballus
USE **horses**

equus caballus przewalskii
USE **przewalski's horse**

equus caballus x equus asinus
USE **mules**

EQUUS HEMIONUS
BT1 equus
BT2 equidae
BT3 perissodactyla
BT4 mammals
BT4 ungulates

equus przewalskii
USE **przewalski's horse**

EQUUS ZEBRA
BT1 equus
BT2 equidae
BT3 perissodactyla
BT4 mammals
BT4 ungulates
rt zebras

eradication
(consult also narrower and related terms of "disease control" and "pest control")
USE **disease control**
OR **pest control**

ERAGROSTIS
BT1 gramineae
NT1 eragrostis amabilis
NT1 eragrostis arida
NT1 eragrostis barrelieri
NT1 eragrostis bipinnata
NT1 eragrostis boehmii
NT1 eragrostis capensis
NT1 eragrostis chloromelas
NT1 eragrostis cilianensis
NT1 eragrostis ciliaris
NT1 eragrostis curvula
NT1 eragrostis decumbens
NT1 eragrostis dielsii
NT1 eragrostis elegantissima
NT1 eragrostis eriopoda
NT1 eragrostis exasperata
NT1 eragrostis falcata
NT1 eragrostis ferruginea
NT1 eragrostis heteromera
NT1 eragrostis lehmanniana
NT1 eragrostis lugens
NT1 eragrostis megastachya
NT1 eragrostis minor
NT1 eragrostis multicaulis
NT1 eragrostis oxylepis
NT1 eragrostis pallens
NT1 eragrostis pilosa
NT1 eragrostis plana
NT1 eragrostis racemosa
NT1 eragrostis setifolia
NT1 eragrostis subequiglumis
NT1 eragrostis superba
NT1 eragrostis tef
NT1 eragrostis tenella
NT1 eragrostis tremula
NT1 eragrostis trichodes
NT1 eragrostis unioloides
NT1 eragrostis viscosa

eragrostis abyssinica
USE **eragrostis tef**

ERAGROSTIS AMABILIS
BT1 eragrostis
BT2 gramineae
BT1 pasture plants

ERAGROSTIS ARIDA
BT1 eragrostis
BT2 gramineae
BT1 pasture plants

ERAGROSTIS BARRELIERI
BT1 eragrostis
BT2 gramineae
BT1 pasture plants

ERAGROSTIS BIPINNATA
BT1 eragrostis
BT2 gramineae

ERAGROSTIS BOEHMII
BT1 eragrostis
BT2 gramineae
BT1 pasture plants

ERAGROSTIS CAPENSIS
BT1 eragrostis
BT2 gramineae
BT1 pasture plants

ERAGROSTIS CHLOROMELAS
BT1 eragrostis
BT2 gramineae
BT1 pasture plants

ERAGROSTIS CILIANENSIS
uf *eragrostis major*
BT1 eragrostis
BT2 gramineae
BT1 pasture plants

ERAGROSTIS CILIARIS
BT1 eragrostis
BT2 gramineae
BT1 pasture plants

ERAGROSTIS CURVULA
BT1 eragrostis
BT2 gramineae
BT1 nematicidal plants
BT2 pesticidal plants
BT1 pasture plants

ERAGROSTIS DECUMBENS
BT1 eragrostis
BT2 gramineae
BT1 pasture plants

ERAGROSTIS DIELSII
BT1 eragrostis
BT2 gramineae
BT1 pasture plants

ERAGROSTIS ELEGANTISSIMA
BT1 eragrostis
BT2 gramineae
BT1 pasture plants

ERAGROSTIS ERIOPODA
BT1 eragrostis
BT2 gramineae
BT1 pasture plants

ERAGROSTIS EXASPERATA
BT1 eragrostis
BT2 gramineae
BT1 pasture plants

ERAGROSTIS FALCATA
BT1 eragrostis
BT2 gramineae
BT1 pasture plants

ERAGROSTIS FERRUGINEA
BT1 eragrostis
BT2 gramineae
BT1 pasture plants

ERAGROSTIS HETEROMERA
BT1 eragrostis
BT2 gramineae
BT1 pasture plants

ERAGROSTIS LEHMANNIANA
BT1 eragrostis
BT2 gramineae
BT1 pasture plants

ERAGROSTIS LUGENS
BT1 eragrostis
BT2 gramineae
BT1 pasture plants

eragrostis major
USE **eragrostis cilianensis**

ERAGROSTIS MEGASTACHYA
BT1 eragrostis
BT2 gramineae

ERAGROSTIS MINOR
uf *eragrostis poaeoides*
BT1 eragrostis
BT2 gramineae
BT1 pasture plants

ERAGROSTIS MULTICAULIS
BT1 eragrostis
BT2 gramineae
BT1 pasture plants

ERAGROSTIS OXYLEPIS
BT1 eragrostis
BT2 gramineae
BT1 pasture plants

ERAGROSTIS PALLENS
BT1 eragrostis
BT2 gramineae
BT1 pasture plants

ERAGROSTIS PILOSA
BT1 eragrostis
BT2 gramineae

ERAGROSTIS PLANA
BT1 eragrostis
BT2 gramineae
BT1 pasture plants

eragrostis poaeoides
USE **eragrostis minor**

ERAGROSTIS RACEMOSA
BT1 eragrostis
BT2 gramineae
BT1 pasture plants

ERAGROSTIS SETIFOLIA
BT1 eragrostis
BT2 gramineae
BT1 pasture plants

ERAGROSTIS SUBEQUIGLUMIS
BT1 eragrostis
BT2 gramineae
BT1 pasture plants

ERAGROSTIS SUPERBA
BT1 eragrostis
BT2 gramineae
BT1 pasture plants

ERAGROSTIS TEF
uf *eragrostis abyssinica*
BT1 eragrostis
BT2 gramineae
BT1 millets
BT2 cereals
BT3 grain crops
BT1 pasture plants

ERAGROSTIS TENELLA
BT1 eragrostis
BT2 gramineae
BT1 pasture plants

ERAGROSTIS TREMULA
BT1 eragrostis
BT2 gramineae
BT1 pasture plants

ERAGROSTIS TRICHODES
BT1 eragrostis
BT2 gramineae
BT1 pasture plants

ERAGROSTIS UNIOLOIDES
BT1 eragrostis
BT2 gramineae

ERAGROSTIS VISCOSA
BT1 eragrostis
BT2 gramineae
BT1 pasture plants

ERANNIS
BT1 geometridae
BT2 lepidoptera
NT1 erannis defoliaria

ERANNIS DEFOLIARIA
BT1 erannis
BT2 geometridae
BT3 lepidoptera

ERANTHEMUM
BT1 acanthaceae
NT1 eranthemum pulchellum
NT1 eranthemum tricolor
rt daedalacanthus

eranthemum nervosum
USE **eranthemum pulchellum**

ERANTHEMUM PULCHELLUM
uf *daedalacanthus nervosus*
uf *eranthemum nervosum*
BT1 eranthemum
BT2 acanthaceae
BT1 ornamental woody plants

ERANTHEMUM TRICOLOR
BT1 eranthemum
BT2 acanthaceae
BT1 ornamental woody plants

ERANTHIS
BT1 ranunculaceae
NT1 eranthis hyemalis

ERANTHIS HYEMALIS
BT1 eranthis
BT2 ranunculaceae
BT1 ornamental bulbs
rt tubers

ERBON
BT1 phenoxy herbicides

ERBON *cont.*
BT2 herbicides
BT3 pesticides

ERECHTITES
BT1 compositae
NT1 erechtites hieracifolia

ERECHTITES HIERACIFOLIA
BT1 erechtites
BT2 compositae

EREMAEOPSIS
BT1 myrtaceae

EREMANTHUS
BT1 compositae
NT1 eremanthus elaeagnus
NT1 eremanthus goyazensis

EREMANTHUS ELAEAGNUS
BT1 eremanthus
BT2 compositae

EREMANTHUS GOYAZENSIS
BT1 eremanthus
BT2 compositae

EREMOCARPUS
BT1 euphorbiaceae
NT1 eremocarpus setigerus

EREMOCARPUS SETIGERUS
BT1 eremocarpus
BT2 euphorbiaceae

eremochila
USE **ephialtes**

EREMOCHLOA
BT1 gramineae
NT1 eremochloa ophiuroides

EREMOCHLOA OPHIUROIDES
BT1 eremochloa
BT2 gramineae
BT1 lawns and turf
BT1 pasture plants

EREMOCITRUS
BT1 rutaceae
NT1 eremocitrus glauca

EREMOCITRUS GLAUCA
BT1 eremocitrus
BT2 rutaceae

EREMOPHILA
BT1 myoporaceae
NT1 eremophila fraseri
NT1 eremophila gilesii
NT1 eremophila longifolia
NT1 eremophila mitchellii
NT1 eremophila rotundifolia
NT1 eremophila sturtii

EREMOPHILA FRASERI
BT1 browse plants
BT1 eremophila
BT2 myoporaceae

EREMOPHILA GILESII
BT1 browse plants
BT1 eremophila
BT2 myoporaceae

EREMOPHILA LONGIFOLIA
BT1 browse plants
BT1 eremophila
BT2 myoporaceae

EREMOPHILA MITCHELLII
BT1 antibacterial plants
BT1 browse plants
BT1 eremophila
BT2 myoporaceae

EREMOPHILA ROTUNDIFOLIA
BT1 eremophila
BT2 myoporaceae

EREMOPHILA STURTII
BT1 browse plants
BT1 eremophila
BT2 myoporaceae

eremopyrum
USE **agropyron**

EREMOSEMIUM
uf *grayia*
BT1 chenopodiaceae
NT1 eremosemium spinosa

EREMOSEMIUM SPINOSA
BT1 eremosemium
BT2 chenopodiaceae
BT1 ornamental woody plants

EREMURUS
BT1 liliaceae
NT1 eremurus altaicus
NT1 eremurus stenophyllus

EREMURUS ALTAICUS
BT1 eremurus
BT2 liliaceae
BT1 ornamental bulbs
rt tubers

eremurus bungei
USE **eremurus stenophyllus**

EREMURUS STENOPHYLLUS
uf *eremurus bungei*
BT1 eremurus
BT2 liliaceae
BT1 ornamental bulbs
rt tubers

ERETHIZON
uf *erithizon*
BT1 erethizontidae
BT2 rodents
BT3 mammals
NT1 erethizon dorsatum

ERETHIZON DORSATUM
BT1 erethizon
BT2 erethizontidae
BT3 rodents
BT4 mammals

ERETHIZONTIDAE
BT1 rodents
BT2 mammals
NT1 coendou
NT1 erethizon
NT2 erethizon dorsatum
rt porcupines

ERETMAPODITES
BT1 culicidae
BT2 diptera
NT1 eretmapodites quinquevittatus

ERETMAPODITES QUINQUEVITTATUS
BT1 eretmapodites
BT2 culicidae
BT3 diptera

ERETMOCERUS
BT1 aphelinidae
BT2 hymenoptera
NT1 eretmocerus haldemani
NT1 eretmocerus mundus

ERETMOCERUS HALDEMANI
BT1 eretmocerus
BT2 aphelinidae
BT3 hymenoptera

ERETMOCERUS MUNDUS
BT1 eretmocerus
BT2 aphelinidae
BT3 hymenoptera

ERETMOCHELYS
BT1 cheloniidae
BT2 testudines
BT3 reptiles

ERGASILUS
HN from 1990
BT1 poecilostomatoida
BT2 copepoda
BT3 crustacea
BT4 arthropods
NT1 ergasilus mirabilis

ERGASILUS MIRABILIS
HN from 1990
BT1 ergasilus
BT2 poecilostomatoida
BT3 copepoda
BT4 crustacea
BT5 arthropods

ERGOCALCIFEROL
uf *calciferol*
uf *vitamin d2*
BT1 ergostanes
BT2 steroids
BT3 isoprenoids
BT4 lipids
BT1 rodenticides
BT2 pesticides
BT1 vitamin d
BT2 fat soluble vitamins
BT3 vitamins
rt ergosterol

ERGOMETERS
BT1 instruments
rt energy exchange
rt ergonomics

ERGOMETRINE
uf *ergonovine*
BT1 ergot alkaloids
BT2 β-blockers
BT3 sympatholytics
BT4 neurotropic drugs
BT5 drugs
BT2 indole alkaloids
BT3 alkaloids
BT3 indoles

ERGONOMICS
uf *human engineering*
rt accidents
rt alarms
rt anthropometric dimensions
rt anthropometric dummies
rt design
rt ergometers
rt fatigue
rt health
rt health protection
rt heat stress
rt man
rt noise abatement
rt occupational disorders
rt operator comfort
rt organization of work
rt perception
rt physical strain
rt posture
rt ride comfort
rt safety
rt seats
rt signals
rt visibility
rt whole body vibration

ergonovine
USE **ergometrine**

ERGOSTANES
BT1 steroids
BT2 isoprenoids
BT3 lipids
NT1 campesterol
NT1 dihydrotachysterol
NT1 ergocalciferol
NT1 ergosterol

ERGOSTEROL
BT1 ergostanes
BT2 steroids
BT3 isoprenoids
BT4 lipids
BT1 provitamins
BT2 precursors
BT1 sterols
BT2 alcohols
BT2 steroids
BT3 isoprenoids
BT4 lipids
rt ergocalciferol
rt fats

ERGOT
BT1 fungal diseases
BT2 plant diseases
rt claviceps purpurea
rt ergot alkaloids
rt ergotism

ERGOT ALKALOIDS
uf *ergot derivatives*
BT1 β-blockers
BT2 sympatholytics
BT3 neurotropic drugs
BT4 drugs
BT1 indole alkaloids
BT2 alkaloids
BT2 indoles
BT3 heterocyclic nitrogen compounds
BT4 organic nitrogen compounds
NT1 dihydroergocryptine
NT1 ergometrine
rt bromocriptine
rt claviceps purpurea
rt ergot
rt ergotism
rt mycotoxins

ergot derivatives
USE **ergot alkaloids**

ERGOTISM
BT1 mycotoxicoses
BT2 poisoning
rt arteries
rt claviceps purpurea
rt ergot
rt ergot alkaloids
rt rye

ERHARDORINA
BT1 apicomplexa
BT2 protozoa

ERIA
BT1 orchidaceae

ERIACHNE
BT1 gramineae
NT1 eriachne mucronata

ERIACHNE MUCRONATA
BT1 eriachne
BT2 gramineae
BT1 pasture plants

ERIANTHUS
BT1 gramineae

ERICA
BT1 ericaceae
NT1 erica arborea
NT1 erica cinerea
NT1 erica gracilis
NT1 erica herbacea
NT1 erica hiemalis
NT1 erica lusitanica
NT1 erica tetralix
NT1 erica vagans

ERICA ARBOREA
BT1 erica
BT2 ericaceae
BT1 ornamental woody plants

erica carnea
USE **erica herbacea**

ERICA CINEREA
BT1 erica
BT2 ericaceae
BT1 ornamental woody plants

ERICA GRACILIS
BT1 erica
BT2 ericaceae
BT1 ornamental woody plants

ERICA HERBACEA
uf *erica carnea*
BT1 erica
BT2 ericaceae
BT1 ornamental woody plants

ERICA HIEMALIS
BT1 erica
BT2 ericaceae
BT1 ornamental woody plants

ERICA LUSITANICA
BT1 erica
BT2 ericaceae
BT1 ornamental woody plants

ERICA TETRALIX
BT1 erica
BT2 ericaceae
BT1 ornamental woody plants

ERICA VAGANS
BT1 erica
BT2 ericaceae
BT1 ornamental woody plants

ERICACEAE
NT1 andromeda
NT2 andromeda polifolia
NT1 arbutus
NT2 arbutus andrachne
NT2 arbutus menziesii
NT2 arbutus unedo
NT1 arctostaphylos
NT2 arctostaphylos alpinus
NT2 arctostaphylos columbiana
NT2 arctostaphylos crustacea
NT2 arctostaphylos glandulosa
NT2 arctostaphylos nummularia
NT2 arctostaphylos patula
NT2 arctostaphylos pungens
NT2 arctostaphylos uva-ursi
NT1 bruckenthalia
NT1 calluna
NT2 calluna vulgaris
NT1 chamaedaphne
NT2 chamaedaphne calyculata
NT1 daboecia
NT1 elliottia
NT2 elliottia bracteata
NT2 elliottia paniculata
NT2 elliottia pyroliflora
NT2 elliottia racemosa
NT1 enkianthus
NT2 enkianthus perulatus
NT1 erica
NT2 erica arborea
NT2 erica cinerea
NT2 erica gracilis
NT2 erica herbacea
NT2 erica hiemalis
NT2 erica lusitanica
NT2 erica tetralix
NT2 erica vagans
NT1 gaulnettya
NT1 gaultheria
NT2 gaultheria fragrantissima
NT2 gaultheria nummularioides
NT2 gaultheria procumbens
NT1 gaylussacia
NT2 gaylussacia baccata
NT2 gaylussacia dumosa
NT2 gaylussacia frondosa
NT1 kalmia
NT2 kalmia angustifolia
NT2 kalmia cuneata
NT2 kalmia latifolia
NT1 kalmiopsis
NT2 kalmiopsis leachiana
NT1 ledum
NT2 ledum palustre
NT1 leucothoe
NT2 leucothoe axillaris
NT2 leucothoe grayana
NT2 leucothoe walteri
NT1 lyonia
NT2 lyonia ovalifolia
NT1 oxydendrum
NT2 oxydendrum arboreum
NT1 pernettya
NT1 phylliopsis
NT2 phylliopsis hillieri
NT1 phyllodoce
NT2 phyllodoce empetriformis
NT1 pieris (ericaceae)
NT2 pieris floribunda
NT2 pieris japonica
NT2 pieris phillyreifolia

ERICACEAE *cont.*
NT1 rhododendron
NT2 rhododendron albiflorum
NT2 rhododendron anthopogon
NT2 rhododendron arborescens
NT2 rhododendron arboreum
NT2 rhododendron brachycarpum
NT2 rhododendron canadense
NT2 rhododendron catawbiense
NT2 rhododendron chionoides
NT2 rhododendron dabanshanense
NT2 rhododendron forrestii
NT2 rhododendron glaucophyllum
NT2 rhododendron lepidotum
NT2 rhododendron linearifolium
NT2 rhododendron luteum
NT2 rhododendron maximum
NT2 rhododendron obtusum
NT2 rhododendron ponticum
NT2 rhododendron simsii
NT2 rhododendron smirnowii
NT2 rhododendron thymifolium
NT2 rhododendron triflorum
NT1 tripetaleia
NT1 vaccinium
NT2 vaccinium angustifolium
NT2 vaccinium arboreum
NT2 vaccinium ashei
NT2 vaccinium corymbosum
NT2 vaccinium darrowii
NT2 vaccinium deliciosum
NT2 vaccinium elliottii
NT2 vaccinium fuscatum
NT2 vaccinium macrocarpon
NT2 vaccinium myrsinites
NT2 vaccinium myrtillus
NT2 vaccinium ovatum
NT2 vaccinium oxycoccus
NT2 vaccinium pallidum
NT2 vaccinium uliginosum
NT2 vaccinium vitis-idaea

ERICAMERIA
BT1 compositae
NT1 ericameria austrotexana

ERICAMERIA AUSTROTEXANA
BT1 ericameria
BT2 compositae

ERIGERON
BT1 compositae
NT1 erigeron annuus
NT1 erigeron linifolius
NT1 erigeron sumatrensis

ERIGERON ANNUUS
BT1 erigeron
BT2 compositae

erigeron canadensis
USE **conyza canadensis**

ERIGERON LINIFOLIUS
BT1 erigeron
BT2 compositae

ERIGERON SUMATRENSIS
BT1 erigeron
BT2 compositae

ERIGONIDIUM
BT1 linyphiidae
BT2 araneae
BT3 arachnida
BT4 arthropods
NT1 erigonidium graminicolum

ERIGONIDIUM GRAMINICOLUM
BT1 erigonidium
BT2 linyphiidae
BT3 araneae
BT4 arachnida
BT5 arthropods

ERINACEIDAE
uf *hedgehogs*
BT1 insectivores
BT2 mammals
NT1 atelerix
NT2 atelerix albiventris

ERINACEIDAE *cont.*
NT1 erinaceus
NT2 erinaceus europaeus
NT1 hemiechinus
NT2 hemiechinus auritus

ERINACEUS
BT1 erinaceidae
BT2 insectivores
BT3 mammals
NT1 erinaceus europaeus
rt atelerix

erinaceus albiventris
USE **atelerix albiventris**

ERINACEUS EUROPAEUS
BT1 erinaceus
BT2 erinaceidae
BT3 insectivores
BT4 mammals

ERINNYIS
BT1 sphingidae
BT2 lepidoptera
NT1 erinnyis ello

ERINNYIS ELLO
BT1 erinnyis
BT2 sphingidae
BT3 lepidoptera

ERIOBOTRYA
BT1 rosaceae
NT1 eriobotrya japonica

ERIOBOTRYA JAPONICA
BT1 eriobotrya
BT2 rosaceae
rt loquats

ERIOCAULACEAE
NT1 eriocaulon
NT2 eriocaulon cinereum
NT2 eriocaulon robustinus

ERIOCAULON
BT1 eriocaulaceae
NT1 eriocaulon cinereum
NT1 eriocaulon robustinus

ERIOCAULON CINEREUM
BT1 eriocaulon
BT2 eriocaulaceae

ERIOCAULON ROBUSTINUS
BT1 eriocaulon
BT2 eriocaulaceae

ERIOCEPHALUS
BT1 compositae
NT1 eriocephalus punctulatus

ERIOCEPHALUS PUNCTULATUS
BT1 eriocephalus
BT2 compositae
BT1 essential oil plants
BT2 oil plants

ERIOCEREUS
BT1 cactaceae
NT1 eriocereus adscendens
NT1 eriocereus martinii

ERIOCEREUS ADSCENDENS
BT1 eriocereus
BT2 cactaceae

ERIOCEREUS MARTINII
BT1 eriocereus
BT2 cactaceae

ERIOCHLOA
BT1 gramineae
NT1 eriochloa contracta
NT1 eriochloa gracilis
NT1 eriochloa polystachya
NT1 eriochloa procera
NT1 eriochloa villosa

ERIOCHLOA CONTRACTA
BT1 eriochloa
BT2 gramineae

ERIOCHLOA GRACILIS
BT1 eriochloa

ERIOCHLOA GRACILIS *cont.*
BT2 gramineae

ERIOCHLOA POLYSTACHYA
BT1 eriochloa
BT2 gramineae

ERIOCHLOA PROCERA
BT1 eriochloa
BT2 gramineae

ERIOCHLOA VILLOSA
BT1 eriochloa
BT2 gramineae
BT1 pasture plants

ERIOCOCCIDAE
uf *cryptococcidae*
BT1 coccoidea
BT2 sternorrhyncha
BT3 homoptera
NT1 cryptococcus (homoptera)
NT2 cryptococcus fagisuga

eriodendron
USE **ceiba**

eriodendron pentandrum
USE **ceiba pentandra**

ERIOGLOSSUM
BT1 sapindaceae
NT1 erioglossum edule

ERIOGLOSSUM EDULE
BT1 erioglossum
BT2 sapindaceae

ERIOGONUM
BT1 polygonaceae
NT1 eriogonum fasciculatum
NT1 eriogonum wrightii

ERIOGONUM FASCICULATUM
BT1 browse plants
BT1 eriogonum
BT2 polygonaceae

ERIOGONUM WRIGHTII
BT1 eriogonum
BT2 polygonaceae

erioischia
USE **delia**

erioischia brassicae
USE **delia radicum**

erioischia floralis
USE **delia floralis**

ERIOLAENA
BT1 sterculiaceae
NT1 eriolaena hookeriana

ERIOLAENA HOOKERIANA
BT1 eriolaena
BT2 sterculiaceae

ERIONEURON
BT1 gramineae
NT1 erioneuron pulchellum

ERIONEURON PULCHELLUM
BT1 erioneuron
BT2 gramineae
BT1 pasture plants

ERIONOTA
BT1 hesperiidae
BT2 lepidoptera
NT1 erionota thrax

ERIONOTA THRAX
BT1 erionota
BT2 hesperiidae
BT3 lepidoptera

ERIOPHORUM
BT1 cyperaceae
NT1 eriophorum vaginatum

ERIOPHORUM VAGINATUM
BT1 eriophorum
BT2 cyperaceae
BT1 pasture plants

ERIOPHYES
BT1 eriophyidae
BT2 prostigmata
BT3 acari
NT1 eriophyes pyri
rt acalitus
rt aceria
rt cecidophyopsis
rt colomerus
rt phyllocoptes
rt phytoptus

eriophyes essigi
USE **acalitus essigi**

eriophyes gracilis
USE **phyllocoptes gracilis**

eriophyes guerreronis
USE **aceria guerreronis**

eriophyes litchii
USE **aceria litchii**

eriophyes mangiferae
USE **aceria mangiferae**

eriophyes oleae
USE **aceria oleae**

eriophyes phloeocoptes
USE **acalitus phloeocoptes**

ERIOPHYES PYRI
uf *phytoptus pyri*
BT1 eriophyes
BT2 eriophyidae
BT3 prostigmata
BT4 acari

eriophyes ribis
USE **cecidophyopsis ribis**

eriophyes sheldoni
USE **aceria sheldoni**

eriophyes tulipae
USE **aceria tulipae**

eriophyes vitis
USE **colomerus vitis**

ERIOPHYIDAE
BT1 prostigmata
BT2 acari
NT1 abacarus
NT2 abacarus hystrix
NT1 acalitus
NT2 acalitus essigi
NT2 acalitus phloeocoptes
NT1 acaphylla
NT2 acaphylla theae
NT1 aceria
NT2 aceria chondrillae
NT2 aceria eriobotryae
NT2 aceria guerreronis
NT2 aceria litchii
NT2 aceria mangiferae
NT2 aceria oleae
NT2 aceria sheldoni
NT2 aceria tritici
NT2 aceria tulipae
NT1 aculops
NT2 aculops lycopersici
NT2 aculops pelekassi
NT1 aculus
NT2 aculus fockeui
NT2 aculus schlechtendali
NT1 calacarus
NT2 calacarus carinatus
NT1 calepitrimerus
NT2 calepitrimerus vitis
NT1 cecidophyes
NT1 cecidophyopsis
NT2 cecidophyopsis ribis
NT1 colomerus
NT2 colomerus vitis
NT1 epitrimerus
NT2 epitrimerus pyri
NT1 eriophyes
NT2 eriophyes pyri
NT1 metaculus
NT2 metaculus mangiferae
NT1 oxycenus

ERIOPHYIDAE *cont.*
NT2 oxycenus maxwelli
NT1 phyllocoptes
NT2 phyllocoptes gracilis
NT1 phyllocoptruta
NT2 phyllocoptruta oleivora
NT1 tegonotus
NT1 vasates

ERIOPHYLLUM
BT1 compositae
NT1 eriophyllum confertiflorum
rt antiviral plants

ERIOPHYLLUM CONFERTIFLORUM
BT1 eriophyllum
BT2 compositae
BT1 medicinal plants

ERIOPIS
BT1 coccinellidae
BT2 coleoptera
NT1 eriopis connexa

ERIOPIS CONNEXA
BT1 eriopis
BT2 coccinellidae
BT3 coleoptera

ERIOSOMA
BT1 aphididae
BT2 aphidoidea
BT3 sternorrhyncha
BT4 homoptera
NT1 eriosoma lanigerum
NT1 eriosoma ulmi

ERIOSOMA LANIGERUM
BT1 eriosoma
BT2 aphididae
BT3 aphidoidea
BT4 sternorrhyncha
BT5 homoptera

ERIOSOMA ULMI
BT1 eriosoma
BT2 aphididae
BT3 aphidoidea
BT4 sternorrhyncha
BT5 homoptera

ERIOSTEMON
BT1 rutaceae
NT1 eriostemon myoporoides

ERIOSTEMON MYOPOROIDES
BT1 eriostemon
BT2 rutaceae
BT1 ornamental woody plants

ERISTALIS
BT1 syrphidae
BT2 diptera
NT1 eristalis tenax

ERISTALIS TENAX
BT1 eristalis
BT2 syrphidae
BT3 diptera

erithizon
USE **erethizon**

ERLOSE
HN from 1990
BT1 trisaccharides
BT2 oligosaccharides
BT3 carbohydrates

eroded sites
USE **eroded soils**

ERODED SOILS
uf *eroded sites*
uf *wind blown soils*
BT1 soil types (anthropogenic)
rt erosion

ERODIBILITY
BT1 soil properties
BT2 properties
rt erosion

ERODIUM
BT1 geraniaceae

ERODIUM *cont.*
NT1 erodium botrys
NT1 erodium cicutarium
NT1 erodium moschatum

ERODIUM BOTRYS
BT1 erodium
BT2 geraniaceae

ERODIUM CICUTARIUM
BT1 erodium
BT2 geraniaceae
BT1 insecticidal plants
BT2 pesticidal plants

ERODIUM MOSCHATUM
BT1 erodium
BT2 geraniaceae

EROSION
uf *soil erosion*
NT1 gully erosion
NT1 stream erosion
NT1 tunnel erosion
NT1 water erosion
NT2 interrill erosion
NT2 rill erosion
NT2 splash erosion
NT1 wind erosion
rt desertification
rt eroded soils
rt erodibility
rt erosion control
rt erosivity
rt geological sedimentation
rt mud flows
rt sediment yield
rt soil conservation
rt soil movement
rt soil stabilization
rt universal soil loss equation

EROSION CONTROL
BT1 control
NT1 riverbank protection
rt erosion
rt soil conservation

erosion, gully
USE **gully erosion**

erosion, interrill
USE **interrill erosion**

erosion, rill
USE **rill erosion**

erosion, splash
USE **splash erosion**

erosion, stream
USE **stream erosion**

erosion, tunnel
USE **tunnel erosion**

erosion, water
USE **water erosion**

erosion, wind
USE **wind erosion**

EROSIVITY
rt erosion
rt rain
rt wind

ERPOBDELLA
uf *herpobdella*
BT1 erpobdellidae
BT2 hirudinea
BT3 annelida
NT1 erpobdella octoculata

ERPOBDELLA OCTOCULATA
BT1 erpobdella
BT2 erpobdellidae
BT3 hirudinea
BT4 annelida

ERPOBDELLIDAE
BT1 hirudinea
BT2 annelida
NT1 dina
NT2 dina anoculata

ERPOBDELLIDAE *cont.*
NT1 erpobdella
NT2 erpobdella octoculata

ERRORS

ERUCA
BT1 cruciferae
NT1 eruca vesicaria

eruca sativa
USE **eruca vesicaria**

ERUCA VESICARIA
uf *eruca sativa*
BT1 eruca
BT2 cruciferae
BT1 insecticidal plants
BT2 pesticidal plants
BT1 oilseed plants
BT2 fatty oil plants
BT3 oil plants

ERUCARIA
BT1 cruciferae

ERUCASTRUM
BT1 cruciferae
NT1 erucastrum gallicum

ERUCASTRUM GALLICUM
BT1 erucastrum
BT2 cruciferae

ERUCIC ACID
BT1 docosenoic acids
BT2 long chain fatty acids
BT3 fatty acids
BT4 carboxylic acids
BT5 organic acids
BT6 acids
BT4 lipids
BT2 monoenoic fatty acids
BT3 unsaturated fatty acids
BT4 fatty acids
BT5 carboxylic acids
BT6 organic acids
BT7 acids
BT5 lipids
rt rapeseed

ERVATAMIA
BT1 apocynaceae
NT1 ervatamia heyneana
NT1 ervatamia lifnana
NT1 ervatamia orientalis

ervatamia coronaria
USE **tabernaemontana coronaria**

ervatamia crassa
USE **tabernaemontana crassa**

ERVATAMIA HEYNEANA
BT1 ervatamia
BT2 apocynaceae
BT1 medicinal plants

ERVATAMIA LIFNANA
BT1 ervatamia
BT2 apocynaceae

ERVATAMIA ORIENTALIS
BT1 ervatamia
BT2 apocynaceae

ERWINIA
BT1 enterobacteriaceae
BT2 gracilicutes
BT3 bacteria
BT4 prokaryotes
NT1 erwinia amylovora
NT1 erwinia ananas
NT1 erwinia carotovora
NT2 erwinia carotovora subsp. atroseptica
NT2 erwinia carotovora subsp. betavasculorum
NT2 erwinia carotovora subsp. carotovora
NT1 erwinia chrysanthemi
NT2 erwinia chrysanthemi pv. chrysanthemi

ERWINIA *cont.*
NT2 erwinia chrysanthemi pv. dianthicola
NT2 erwinia chrysanthemi pv. dieffenbachiae
NT2 erwinia chrysanthemi pv. paradisiaca
NT2 erwinia chrysanthemi pv. parthenii
NT2 erwinia chrysanthemi pv. zeae
NT1 erwinia herbicola
NT2 erwinia herbicola pv. millettiae
NT1 erwinia rhapontici
NT1 erwinia rubrifaciens
NT1 erwinia salicis
NT1 erwinia stewartii
NT1 erwinia tracheiphila
NT1 erwinia uredovora

ERWINIA AMYLOVORA
BT1 erwinia
BT2 enterobacteriaceae
BT3 gracilicutes
BT4 bacteria
BT5 prokaryotes
BT1 plant pathogenic bacteria
BT2 plant pathogens
BT3 pathogens

ERWINIA ANANAS
BT1 erwinia
BT2 enterobacteriaceae
BT3 gracilicutes
BT4 bacteria
BT5 prokaryotes
BT1 plant pathogenic bacteria
BT2 plant pathogens
BT3 pathogens

erwinia aroideae
USE **erwinia carotovora subsp. carotovora**

erwinia atroseptica
USE **erwinia carotovora subsp. atroseptica**

erwinia cancerogena
USE **enterobacter cancerogenus**

ERWINIA CAROTOVORA
BT1 erwinia
BT2 enterobacteriaceae
BT3 gracilicutes
BT4 bacteria
BT5 prokaryotes
BT1 plant pathogenic bacteria
BT2 plant pathogens
BT3 pathogens
NT1 erwinia carotovora subsp. atroseptica
NT1 erwinia carotovora subsp. betavasculorum
NT1 erwinia carotovora subsp. carotovora

ERWINIA CAROTOVORA SUBSP. ATROSEPTICA
uf *erwinia atroseptica*
BT1 erwinia carotovora
BT2 erwinia
BT3 enterobacteriaceae
BT4 gracilicutes
BT5 bacteria
BT6 prokaryotes
BT2 plant pathogenic bacteria
BT3 plant pathogens
BT4 pathogens

ERWINIA CAROTOVORA SUBSP. BETAVASCULORUM
HN from 1990
BT1 erwinia carotovora
BT2 erwinia
BT3 enterobacteriaceae
BT4 gracilicutes
BT5 bacteria
BT6 prokaryotes
BT2 plant pathogenic bacteria
BT3 plant pathogens

ERWINIA CAROTOVORA SUBSP. BETAVASCULORUM *cont.*
BT4 pathogens

ERWINIA CAROTOVORA SUBSP. CAROTOVORA
uf *erwinia aroideae*
BT1 erwinia carotovora
BT2 erwinia
BT3 enterobacteriaceae
BT4 gracilicutes
BT5 bacteria
BT6 prokaryotes
BT2 plant pathogenic bacteria
BT3 plant pathogens
BT4 pathogens

ERWINIA CHRYSANTHEMI
BT1 erwinia
BT2 enterobacteriaceae
BT3 gracilicutes
BT4 bacteria
BT5 prokaryotes
BT1 plant pathogenic bacteria
BT2 plant pathogens
BT3 pathogens
NT1 erwinia chrysanthemi pv. chrysanthemi
NT1 erwinia chrysanthemi pv. dianthicola
NT1 erwinia chrysanthemi pv. dieffenbachiae
NT1 erwinia chrysanthemi pv. paradisiaca
NT1 erwinia chrysanthemi pv. parthenii
NT1 erwinia chrysanthemi pv. zeae

ERWINIA CHRYSANTHEMI PV. CHRYSANTHEMI
BT1 erwinia chrysanthemi
BT2 erwinia
BT3 enterobacteriaceae
BT4 gracilicutes
BT5 bacteria
BT6 prokaryotes
BT2 plant pathogenic bacteria
BT3 plant pathogens
BT4 pathogens

ERWINIA CHRYSANTHEMI PV. DIANTHICOLA
BT1 erwinia chrysanthemi
BT2 erwinia
BT3 enterobacteriaceae
BT4 gracilicutes
BT5 bacteria
BT6 prokaryotes
BT2 plant pathogenic bacteria
BT3 plant pathogens
BT4 pathogens

ERWINIA CHRYSANTHEMI PV. DIEFFENBACHIAE
BT1 erwinia chrysanthemi
BT2 erwinia
BT3 enterobacteriaceae
BT4 gracilicutes
BT5 bacteria
BT6 prokaryotes
BT2 plant pathogenic bacteria
BT3 plant pathogens
BT4 pathogens

ERWINIA CHRYSANTHEMI PV. PARADISIACA
BT1 erwinia chrysanthemi
BT2 erwinia
BT3 enterobacteriaceae
BT4 gracilicutes
BT5 bacteria
BT6 prokaryotes
BT2 plant pathogenic bacteria
BT3 plant pathogens
BT4 pathogens

ERWINIA CHRYSANTHEMI PV. PARTHENII
BT1 erwinia chrysanthemi
BT2 erwinia
BT3 enterobacteriaceae
BT4 gracilicutes

ERWINIA CHRYSANTHEMI PV. PARTHENII *cont.*
BT5 bacteria
BT6 prokaryotes
BT2 plant pathogenic bacteria
BT3 plant pathogens
BT4 pathogens

ERWINIA CHRYSANTHEMI PV. ZEAE
BT1 erwinia chrysanthemi
BT2 erwinia
BT3 enterobacteriaceae
BT4 gracilicutes
BT5 bacteria
BT6 prokaryotes
BT2 plant pathogenic bacteria
BT3 plant pathogens
BT4 pathogens

ERWINIA HERBICOLA
BT1 erwinia
BT2 enterobacteriaceae
BT3 gracilicutes
BT4 bacteria
BT5 prokaryotes
BT1 plant pathogenic bacteria
BT2 plant pathogens
BT3 pathogens
NT1 erwinia herbicola pv. millettiae

ERWINIA HERBICOLA PV. MILLETTIAE
HN from 1990
BT1 erwinia herbicola
BT2 erwinia
BT3 enterobacteriaceae
BT4 gracilicutes
BT5 bacteria
BT6 prokaryotes
BT2 plant pathogenic bacteria
BT3 plant pathogens
BT4 pathogens

ERWINIA RHAPONTICI
BT1 erwinia
BT2 enterobacteriaceae
BT3 gracilicutes
BT4 bacteria
BT5 prokaryotes
BT1 plant pathogenic bacteria
BT2 plant pathogens
BT3 pathogens

ERWINIA RUBRIFACIENS
BT1 erwinia
BT2 enterobacteriaceae
BT3 gracilicutes
BT4 bacteria
BT5 prokaryotes
BT1 plant pathogenic bacteria
BT2 plant pathogens
BT3 pathogens

ERWINIA SALICIS
BT1 erwinia
BT2 enterobacteriaceae
BT3 gracilicutes
BT4 bacteria
BT5 prokaryotes
BT1 plant pathogenic bacteria
BT2 plant pathogens
BT3 pathogens

ERWINIA STEWARTII
BT1 erwinia
BT2 enterobacteriaceae
BT3 gracilicutes
BT4 bacteria
BT5 prokaryotes
BT1 plant pathogenic bacteria
BT2 plant pathogens
BT3 pathogens

ERWINIA TRACHEIPHILA
HN from 1990
BT1 erwinia
BT2 enterobacteriaceae
BT3 gracilicutes
BT4 bacteria
BT5 prokaryotes
BT1 plant pathogenic bacteria

ERWINIA TRACHEIPHILA *cont.*
BT2 plant pathogens
BT3 pathogens

ERWINIA UREDOVORA
HN from 1990
BT1 erwinia
BT2 enterobacteriaceae
BT3 gracilicutes
BT4 bacteria
BT5 prokaryotes
BT1 plant pathogenic bacteria
BT2 plant pathogens
BT3 pathogens

ERYNGIUM
BT1 umbelliferae
NT1 eryngium amethystinum
NT1 eryngium bromeliifolium
NT1 eryngium creticum
NT1 eryngium maritimum
NT1 eryngium planum

ERYNGIUM AMETHYSTINUM
BT1 eryngium
BT2 umbelliferae

ERYNGIUM BROMELIIFOLIUM
BT1 eryngium
BT2 umbelliferae

ERYNGIUM CRETICUM
BT1 eryngium
BT2 umbelliferae

ERYNGIUM MARITIMUM
BT1 eryngium
BT2 umbelliferae
BT1 medicinal plants
BT1 ornamental herbaceous plants

ERYNGIUM PLANUM
BT1 eryngium
BT2 umbelliferae

ERYNIA
uf *zoophthora*
BT1 entomogenous fungi
BT2 entomopathogens
BT3 pathogens
BT2 fungi
BT1 entomophthorales
NT1 erynia aphidis
NT1 erynia conica
NT1 erynia delphacis
NT1 erynia gammae
NT1 erynia neoaphidis
NT1 erynia phalloides
NT1 erynia phytonomi
NT1 erynia radicans

ERYNIA APHIDIS
HN from 1989; previously zoophthora aphidis
uf *entomophthora aphidis*
uf *zoophthora aphidis*
BT1 erynia
BT2 entomogenous fungi
BT3 entomopathogens
BT4 pathogens
BT3 fungi
BT2 entomophthorales

ERYNIA CONICA
HN from 1990
BT1 erynia
BT2 entomogenous fungi
BT3 entomopathogens
BT4 pathogens
BT3 fungi
BT2 entomophthorales

ERYNIA DELPHACIS
HN from 1990
BT1 erynia
BT2 entomogenous fungi
BT3 entomopathogens
BT4 pathogens
BT3 fungi
BT2 entomophthorales

ERYNIA GAMMAE
HN from 1989; previously entomophthora gammae
uf *entomophthora gammae*
BT1 erynia
BT2 entomogenous fungi
BT3 entomopathogens
BT4 pathogens
BT3 fungi
BT2 entomophthorales

ERYNIA NEOAPHIDIS
uf *zoophthora neoaphidis*
BT1 erynia
BT2 entomogenous fungi
BT3 entomopathogens
BT4 pathogens
BT3 fungi
BT2 entomophthorales

ERYNIA PHALLOIDES
HN from 1989; previously zoophthora phalloides
uf *zoophthora phalloides*
BT1 erynia
BT2 entomogenous fungi
BT3 entomopathogens
BT4 pathogens
BT3 fungi
BT2 entomophthorales

ERYNIA PHYTONOMI
HN from 1989; previously zoophthora phytonomi
uf *zoophthora phytonomi*
BT1 erynia
BT2 entomogenous fungi
BT3 entomopathogens
BT4 pathogens
BT3 fungi
BT2 entomophthorales

ERYNIA RADICANS
HN from 1989; previously zoophthora radicans
uf *zoophthora radicans*
BT1 erynia
BT2 entomogenous fungi
BT3 entomopathogens
BT4 pathogens
BT3 fungi
BT2 entomophthorales

ERYSIMUM
BT1 cruciferae
NT1 erysimum allionii
NT1 erysimum aureum
NT1 erysimum cheiranthoides
NT1 erysimum crepidifolium
NT1 erysimum cuspidatum
NT1 erysimum diffusum
NT1 erysimum perovskianum
NT1 erysimum pieninicum
NT1 erysimum repandum
NT1 erysimum sibiculosa
rt erysimum latent tymovirus

ERYSIMUM ALLIONII
uf *cheiranthus allionii*
BT1 erysimum
BT2 cruciferae
BT1 ornamental herbaceous plants

ERYSIMUM AUREUM
BT1 erysimum
BT2 cruciferae

ERYSIMUM CHEIRANTHOIDES
BT1 erysimum
BT2 cruciferae

ERYSIMUM CREPIDIFOLIUM
BT1 erysimum
BT2 cruciferae

ERYSIMUM CUSPIDATUM
BT1 erysimum
BT2 cruciferae

ERYSIMUM DIFFUSUM
BT1 erysimum
BT2 cruciferae

ERYSIMUM LATENT TYMOVIRUS
HN from 1990
BT1 tymovirus group
BT2 plant viruses
BT3 plant pathogens
BT4 pathogens
rt erysimum

ERYSIMUM PEROVSKIANUM
BT1 erysimum
BT2 cruciferae

ERYSIMUM PIENINICUM
BT1 erysimum
BT2 cruciferae

ERYSIMUM REPANDUM
BT1 erysimum
BT2 cruciferae

ERYSIMUM SIBICULOSA
BT1 erysimum
BT2 cruciferae

ERYSIPELOTHRIX
BT1 lactobacillaceae
BT2 firmicutes
BT3 bacteria
BT4 prokaryotes
NT1 erysipelothrix rhusiopathiae

ERYSIPELOTHRIX RHUSIOPATHIAE
HN from 1990
BT1 erysipelothrix
BT2 lactobacillaceae
BT3 firmicutes
BT4 bacteria
BT5 prokaryotes

ERYSIPHALES
NT1 blumeria
NT1 erysiphe
NT2 erysiphe betae
NT2 erysiphe cichoracearum
NT3 erysiphe cichoracearum var. fischeri
NT2 erysiphe communis
NT2 erysiphe cruciferarum
NT2 erysiphe graminis
NT2 erysiphe pisi
NT2 erysiphe polygoni
NT2 erysiphe trifolii
NT1 leveillula
NT2 leveillula taurica
NT1 microsphaera
NT2 microsphaera alphitoides
NT2 microsphaera polonica
NT1 podosphaera
NT2 podosphaera leucotricha
NT2 podosphaera tridactyla
NT1 sphaerotheca
NT2 sphaerotheca fuliginea
NT2 sphaerotheca macularis
NT2 sphaerotheca mors-uvae
NT2 sphaerotheca pannosa
NT1 uncinula
NT2 uncinula necator
rt fungi

ERYSIPHE
BT1 erysiphales
NT1 erysiphe betae
NT1 erysiphe cichoracearum
NT2 erysiphe cichoracearum var. fischeri
NT1 erysiphe communis
NT1 erysiphe cruciferarum
NT1 erysiphe graminis
NT1 erysiphe pisi
NT1 erysiphe polygoni
NT1 erysiphe trifolii
rt blumeria

ERYSIPHE BETAE
BT1 erysiphe
BT2 erysiphales

ERYSIPHE CICHORACEARUM
BT1 erysiphe
BT2 erysiphales
NT1 erysiphe cichoracearum var. fischeri

ERYSIPHE CICHORACEARUM VAR. FISCHERI
HN from 1990
uf *erysiphe fischeri*
BT1 erysiphe cichoracearum
BT2 erysiphe
BT3 erysiphales

ERYSIPHE COMMUNIS
BT1 erysiphe
BT2 erysiphales

ERYSIPHE CRUCIFERARUM
BT1 erysiphe
BT2 erysiphales

erysiphe fischeri
USE **erysiphe cichoracearum var. fischeri**

ERYSIPHE GRAMINIS
uf *blumeria graminis*
BT1 erysiphe
BT2 erysiphales

ERYSIPHE PISI
BT1 erysiphe
BT2 erysiphales

ERYSIPHE POLYGONI
BT1 erysiphe
BT2 erysiphales

ERYSIPHE TRIFOLII
BT1 erysiphe
BT2 erysiphales

ERYTHEA
BT1 palmae
NT1 erythea edulis

ERYTHEA EDULIS
BT1 erythea
BT2 palmae

erythorbic acid
USE **isoascorbic acid**

ERYTHRINA
BT1 leguminosae
NT1 erythrina arborescens
NT1 erythrina caffra
NT1 erythrina corallodendrum
NT1 erythrina crista-galli
NT1 erythrina flabelliformis
NT1 erythrina folkersii
NT1 erythrina indica
NT1 erythrina lithosperma
NT1 erythrina poeppigiana
NT1 erythrina senegalensis
NT1 erythrina suberosa
NT1 erythrina variegata
NT1 erythrina velutina

ERYTHRINA ARBORESCENS
BT1 erythrina
BT2 leguminosae

ERYTHRINA CAFFRA
BT1 erythrina
BT2 leguminosae
BT1 ornamental woody plants

ERYTHRINA CORALLODENDRUM
BT1 erythrina
BT2 leguminosae
BT1 medicinal plants
BT1 ornamental woody plants

ERYTHRINA CRISTA-GALLI
BT1 erythrina
BT2 leguminosae
BT1 ornamental woody plants

ERYTHRINA FLABELLIFORMIS
BT1 erythrina
BT2 leguminosae
BT1 ornamental woody plants

ERYTHRINA FOLKERSII
BT1 erythrina
BT2 leguminosae

ERYTHRINA INDICA
BT1 browse plants
BT1 erythrina

ERYTHRINA INDICA *cont.*
BT2 leguminosae

ERYTHRINA LITHOSPERMA
BT1 erythrina
BT2 leguminosae

ERYTHRINA POEPPIGIANA
HN from 1990
BT1 erythrina
BT2 leguminosae
BT1 forest trees

ERYTHRINA SENEGALENSIS
BT1 erythrina
BT2 leguminosae
BT1 medicinal plants
BT1 ornamental woody plants

ERYTHRINA SUBEROSA
BT1 erythrina
BT2 leguminosae
BT1 forest trees

ERYTHRINA VARIEGATA
BT1 erythrina
BT2 leguminosae
BT1 ornamental woody plants

ERYTHRINA VELUTINA
BT1 erythrina
BT2 leguminosae

ERYTHRITOL
BT1 alditols
BT2 sugar alcohols
BT3 carbohydrates
BT3 polyols
BT4 alcohols
BT1 vasodilator agents
BT2 cardiovascular agents
BT3 drugs

ERYTHROBLASTOSIS VIRUS
BT1 avian oncovirus
BT2 oncovirus type c
BT3 oncovirinae
BT4 retroviridae
BT5 viruses

ERYTHROBLASTS
BT1 cells

ERYTHROCEBUS
BT1 cercopithecidae
BT2 primates
BT3 mammals
NT1 erythrocebus patas

ERYTHROCEBUS PATAS
BT1 erythrocebus
BT2 cercopithecidae
BT3 primates
BT4 mammals

ERYTHROCHITON
BT1 rutaceae
NT1 erythrochiton brasiliensis

ERYTHROCHITON BRASILIENSIS
BT1 erythrochiton
BT2 rutaceae

erythrocyte catalase
USE **catalase**

ERYTHROCYTE COUNT
BT1 blood picture
rt cell counting
rt erythrocytes

ERYTHROCYTE FRAGILITY
rt erythrocyte survival
rt erythrocytes
rt haemolysis

ERYTHROCYTE INVASION
HN from 1989
BT1 cell invasion
BT2 infection
BT3 disease transmission
BT4 transmission
BT2 invasion
rt erythrocytes

ERYTHROCYTE POTASSIUM TYPES
BT1 blood chemistry
BT2 blood composition
BT3 composition
rt biochemical polymorphism
rt erythrocytes
rt potassium

ERYTHROCYTE SEDIMENTATION RATE
rt blood picture
rt erythrocytes
rt sedimentation

ERYTHROCYTE SIZE
rt blood picture
rt erythrocytes
rt size

ERYTHROCYTE SURVIVAL
BT1 blood picture
BT1 survival
rt erythrocyte fragility
rt erythrocytes

ERYTHROCYTES
uf *blood red cells*
uf *red blood cells*
BT1 blood cells
BT2 cells
NT1 reticulocytes
rt anaemia
rt blood composition
rt erythrocyte count
rt erythrocyte fragility
rt erythrocyte invasion
rt erythrocyte potassium types
rt erythrocyte sedimentation rate
rt erythrocyte size
rt erythrocyte survival
rt erythropoiesis
rt erythropoietin
rt haemagglutination
rt heinz bodies
rt polycythaemia
rt polycythaemia vera

ERYTHRODES
BT1 orchidaceae

ERYTHROMYCIN
BT1 antibacterial agents
BT2 antiinfective agents
BT3 drugs
BT1 macrolide antibiotics
BT2 antibiotics
BT2 lactones
BT3 heterocyclic oxygen compounds
BT3 ketones

ERYTHRONEURA
BT1 cicadellidae
BT2 cicadelloidea
BT3 auchenorrhyncha
BT4 homoptera
NT1 erythroneura elegantula

ERYTHRONEURA ELEGANTULA
BT1 erythroneura
BT2 cicadellidae
BT3 cicadelloidea
BT4 auchenorrhyncha
BT5 homoptera

ERYTHRONIUM
BT1 liliaceae
NT1 erythronium caucasicum
NT1 erythronium japonicum
NT1 erythronium sibiricum

ERYTHRONIUM CAUCASICUM
BT1 erythronium
BT2 liliaceae

ERYTHRONIUM JAPONICUM
BT1 erythronium
BT2 liliaceae
BT1 ornamental bulbs
rt tubers

ERYTHRONIUM SIBIRICUM
BT1 erythronium
BT2 liliaceae
BT1 ornamental bulbs
rt tubers

ERYTHROPHLEUM
BT1 leguminosae
NT1 erythrophleum africanum
NT1 erythrophleum chlorostachys
NT1 erythrophleum couminga
NT1 erythrophleum suaveolens

ERYTHROPHLEUM AFRICANUM
BT1 erythrophleum
BT2 leguminosae
BT1 poisonous plants

ERYTHROPHLEUM CHLOROSTACHYS
BT1 erythrophleum
BT2 leguminosae

ERYTHROPHLEUM COUMINGA
BT1 erythrophleum
BT2 leguminosae
BT1 poisonous plants

erythrophleum guineense
USE **erythrophleum suaveolens**

ERYTHROPHLEUM SUAVEOLENS
uf *erythrophleum guineense*
BT1 erythrophleum
BT2 leguminosae

ERYTHROPOIESIS
BT1 haematopoiesis
BT2 blood physiology
BT3 animal physiology
BT4 physiology
rt erythrocytes
rt erythropoietin

ERYTHROPOIETIN
BT1 blood proteins
BT2 animal proteins
BT3 proteins
BT4 peptides
BT1 glycoproteins
BT2 proteins
BT3 peptides
BT1 renal hormones
BT2 hormones
rt erythrocytes
rt erythropoiesis

ERYTHROSE
uf *dextroerythrose sodium*
BT1 tetroses
BT2 aldoses
BT3 monosaccharides
BT4 carbohydrates
BT3 reducing sugars
BT4 sugars
BT5 carbohydrates

ERYTHROSINE
uf *erythrosine b*
BT1 dyes
BT1 food colourants
BT2 food additives
BT3 additives
BT1 stains

erythrosine b
USE **erythrosine**

ERYTHROXYLACEAE
NT1 erythroxylum
NT2 erythroxylum australe
NT2 erythroxylum coca
NT2 erythroxylum novogranatense

ERYTHROXYLUM
BT1 erythroxylaceae
NT1 erythroxylum australe
NT1 erythroxylum coca
NT1 erythroxylum novogranatense

ERYTHROXYLUM AUSTRALE
BT1 erythroxylum
BT2 erythroxylaceae

ERYTHROXYLUM COCA
uf *coca*
BT1 erythroxylum
BT2 erythroxylaceae
BT1 medicinal plants
rt cocaine

ERYTHROXYLUM NOVOGRANATENSE
BT1 erythroxylum
BT2 erythroxylaceae

ESCALLONIA
BT1 escalloniaceae
NT1 escallonia rubra
NT1 escallonia rubra var. macrantha

escallonia macrantha
USE **escallonia rubra var. macrantha**

ESCALLONIA RUBRA
BT1 escallonia
BT2 escalloniaceae
BT1 ornamental woody plants

ESCALLONIA RUBRA VAR. MACRANTHA
uf *escallonia macrantha*
BT1 escallonia
BT2 escalloniaceae
BT1 ornamental woody plants

ESCALLONIACEAE
NT1 escallonia
NT2 escallonia rubra
NT2 escallonia rubra var. macrantha

ESCHERICHIA
BT1 enterobacteriaceae
BT2 gracilicutes
BT3 bacteria
BT4 prokaryotes
NT1 escherichia coli

ESCHERICHIA COLI
uf *colibacteriosis*
BT1 escherichia
BT2 enterobacteriaceae
BT3 gracilicutes
BT4 bacteria
BT5 prokaryotes

ESCHSCHOLZIA
BT1 papaveraceae
NT1 eschscholzia californica

ESCHSCHOLZIA CALIFORNICA
BT1 eschscholzia
BT2 papaveraceae
BT1 ornamental herbaceous plants

ESCHWEILERA
BT1 lecythidaceae
NT1 eschweilera grata

ESCHWEILERA GRATA
BT1 eschweilera
BT2 lecythidaceae

ESCOBARIA
BT1 cactaceae
NT1 escobaria henricksonii
NT1 escobaria strobiliformis
NT1 escobaria vivipara

ESCOBARIA HENRICKSONII
BT1 escobaria
BT2 cactaceae
BT1 ornamental succulent plants
BT2 succulent plants

ESCOBARIA STROBILIFORMIS
uf *escobaria tuberculosa*
BT1 escobaria
BT2 cactaceae
BT1 ornamental succulent plants
BT2 succulent plants

escobaria tuberculosa
USE **escobaria strobiliformis**

ESCOBARIA VIVIPARA
uf *coryphantha vivipara*
BT1 escobaria
BT2 cactaceae
BT1 ornamental succulent plants
BT2 succulent plants

ESCONTRIA
BT1 cactaceae

ESCULIN
BF aesculin

esculoside
USE **aesculin**

ESENBECKIA
BT1 rutaceae
NT1 esenbeckia berlandieri

ESENBECKIA BERLANDIERI
BT1 esenbeckia
BT2 rutaceae
BT1 ornamental woody plants

eskimos
USE **inuit**

ESOCIDAE
BT1 salmoniformes
BT2 osteichthyes
BT3 fishes
NT1 esox
rt pike

ESOPHAGEAL DISEASES
BF oesophageal diseases
rt esophagus

ESOPHAGEAL SPHINCTER
BF oesophageal sphincter
rt esophagus

ESOPHAGUS
BF oesophagus
rt esophageal diseases
rt esophageal sphincter

ESOX
BT1 esocidae
BT2 salmoniformes
BT3 osteichthyes
BT4 fishes

esox lucius
USE **pike**

ESPOSTOA
BT1 cactaceae
NT1 espostoa huanucensis
NT1 espostoa plumosa

ESPOSTOA HUANUCENSIS
BT1 espostoa
BT2 cactaceae
BT1 ornamental succulent plants
BT2 succulent plants

ESPOSTOA PLUMOSA
BT1 espostoa
BT2 cactaceae
BT1 ornamental succulent plants
BT2 succulent plants

ESPROCARB
HN from 1990
BT1 thiocarbamate herbicides
BT2 carbamate pesticides
BT2 herbicides
BT3 pesticides

ESSAYS (AGRICOLA)
BT1 publications

ESSENTIAL AMINO ACIDS
uf *amino acids, essential*
BT1 amino acids
BT2 carboxylic acids
BT3 organic acids
BT4 acids
BT2 organic nitrogen compounds
NT1 arginine

ESSENTIAL AMINO ACIDS *cont.*
NT1 histidine
NT1 isoleucine
NT1 leucine
NT1 lysine
NT1 methionine
NT1 phenylalanine
NT1 threonine
NT1 tryptophan
NT1 valine

essential fatty acid deficiency
USE **fat deficiencies**

ESSENTIAL FATTY ACIDS
BT1 fatty acids
BT2 carboxylic acids
BT3 organic acids
BT4 acids
BT2 lipids
NT1 arachidonic acid
NT1 linoleic acid
NT1 linolenic acid

essential oil crops
USE **essential oil plants**

ESSENTIAL OIL PLANTS
uf *essential oil crops*
uf *flavouring crops*
BT1 oil plants
NT1 abelmoschus moschatus
NT1 abies alba
NT1 acacia farnesiana
NT1 achillea millefolium
NT1 acinos alpinus
NT1 acinos suaveolens
NT1 ageratum conyzoides
NT1 aloysia triphylla
NT1 alpinia galanga
NT1 alpinia officinarum
NT1 alpinia zerumbet
NT1 anethum graveolens
NT1 anethum sowa
NT1 angelica archangelica
NT1 artemisia absinthium
NT1 artemisia annua
NT1 artemisia dracunculus
NT1 artemisia herba-alba
NT1 artemisia maritima
NT1 artemisia mutellina
NT1 artemisia pallens
NT1 artemisia vulgaris
NT1 barosma betulina
NT1 barosma crenulata
NT1 barosma serratifolia
NT1 boenninghausenia albiflora
NT1 boswellia serrata
NT1 bunium persicum
NT1 bursera penicillata
NT1 calamintha sylvatica
NT1 cananga odorata
NT1 canarium luzonicum
NT1 carum carvi
NT1 caryopteris incana
NT1 chamaecyparis obtusa
NT1 chamaemelum nobile
NT1 chamomilla recutita
NT1 chamomilla suaveolens
NT1 cinnamomum aromaticum
NT1 cinnamomum burmanii
NT1 cinnamomum camphora
NT1 cinnamomum zeylanicum
NT1 cistus ladanifer
NT1 citrus aurantium
NT1 citrus bergamia
NT1 citrus meyeri
NT1 convallaria majalis
NT1 conyza canadensis
NT1 coriandrum sativum
NT1 cuminum cyminum
NT1 cupressus sempervirens
NT1 cymbopogon citratus
NT1 cymbopogon flexuosus
NT1 cymbopogon jwarancusa
NT1 cymbopogon martinii
NT1 cymbopogon nardus
NT1 cymbopogon winterianus
NT1 cyperus scariosus
NT1 elettaria cardamomum
NT1 elsholtzia ciliata
NT1 eriocephalus punctulatus

ESSENTIAL OIL PLANTS *cont.*
NT1 eucalyptus citriodora
NT1 eucalyptus globulus
NT1 fennel
NT1 geranium macrorrhizum
NT1 grapes
NT1 hedeoma pulegioides
NT1 helichrysum italicum
NT1 hyacinths
NT1 hyssopus seravschanicus
NT1 illicium verum
NT1 inula helenium
NT1 iris germanica
NT1 jasminum auriculatum
NT1 jasminum grandiflorum
NT1 jasminum odoratissimum
NT1 jasminum officinale
NT1 juniperus communis
NT1 laurus nobilis
NT1 lavandula angustifolia
NT1 leeks
NT1 lemons
NT1 limes
NT1 lindera benzoin
NT1 mandarins
NT1 melaleuca alternifolia
NT1 melissa officinalis
NT1 mentha arvensis
NT1 mentha piperita
NT1 mentha pulegium
NT1 mentha spicata
NT1 monarda citriodora
NT1 monarda didyma
NT1 monarda russeliana
NT1 monodora myristica
NT1 myosoton aquaticum
NT1 myristica argentea
NT1 myristica beddomei
NT1 myristica fragrans
NT1 myroxylon balsamum
NT1 myrtus communis
NT1 nardostachys chinensis
NT1 nardostachys jatamansi
NT1 ocimum basilicum
NT1 ocimum gratissimum
NT1 ocimum sanctum
NT1 onions
NT1 oranges
NT1 origanum majorana
NT1 origanum onites
NT1 origanum smyrnaeum
NT1 origanum vulgare
NT1 panax pseudoginseng
NT1 panax quinquefolius
NT1 pelargonium graveolens
NT1 pelargonium roseum
NT1 petroselinum crispum
NT1 peumus boldus
NT1 phyllanthus emblica
NT1 pimenta dioica
NT1 pimenta racemosa
NT1 pimpinella anisum
NT1 piper nigrum
NT1 pistacia lentiscus
NT1 pogostemon cablin
NT1 rosa damascena
NT1 roses
NT1 rosmarinus officinalis
NT1 ruta graveolens
NT1 ruta montana
NT1 salvia lavandulifolia
NT1 salvia officinalis
NT1 salvia sclarea
NT1 santalum album
NT1 satureja hortensis
NT1 satureja montana
NT1 saussurea lappa
NT1 sour oranges
NT1 syringa vulgaris
NT1 syzygium aromaticum
NT1 syzygium cumini
NT1 tanacetum vulgare
NT1 thymus capitatus
NT1 thymus satureioides
NT1 thymus serpyllum
NT1 thymus vulgaris
NT1 thymus zygis
NT1 valeriana officinalis
NT1 vanilla planifolia
NT1 verbena triphylla
NT1 vetiveria zizanioides

ESSENTIAL OIL PLANTS *cont.*
NT1 viola odorata
NT1 zingiber officinale
rt culinary herbs
rt essential oils
rt flavourings
rt horticultural crops
rt incense plants
rt industrial crops
rt medicinal plants
rt perfumery
rt plants
rt spice plants
rt woody plants

ESSENTIAL OILS
uf *oils, essential*
BT1 plant oils
BT2 oils
BT2 plant products
BT3 products
NT1 cedarwood oil
NT1 turpentine
rt p-cymene
rt α-bisabolol
rt α-pinene
rt β-pinene
rt aromatic hydrocarbons
rt camphene
rt camphor
rt carvone
rt citral
rt cryptone
rt essential oil plants
rt eucalyptol
rt eugenol
rt farnesol
rt flavour compounds
rt furfural
rt geraniol
rt linalool
rt menthol
rt methyl eugenol
rt myrcene
rt oleoresins
rt resins
rt sabinene
rt safrole
rt terpenoids
rt thymol

ESTABLISHMENT
uf *plant establishment*
NT1 crop establishment
NT1 rooting
NT1 stand establishment

establishment, crop
USE **crop establishment**

estate duty
USE **inheritance tax**

ESTATE PLANNING (AGRICOLA)
BT1 planning

ESTATES
BT1 property
NT1 indivisible estates
rt land
rt land management
rt land ownership
rt landowners
rt ownership

ESTERASES
(ec 3.1)
BT1 hydrolases
BT2 enzymes
NT1 carboxylic ester hydrolases
NT2 acetylcholinesterase
NT2 arylesterase
NT2 carboxylesterase
NT2 chlorophyllase
NT2 cholesterol esterase
NT2 cholinesterase
NT2 lipoprotein lipase
NT2 lysophospholipase
NT2 pectinesterase
NT2 phospholipase a
NT2 phospholipase a1
NT2 phospholipase a2
NT2 retinyl-palmitate esterase

ESTERASES *cont.*
NT2 tannase
NT2 triacylglycerol lipase
NT2 tropinesterase
NT1 nucleases
NT2 deoxyribonuclease i
NT2 ribonucleases
NT1 phosphoric diester hydrolases
NT2 phosphodiesterase i
NT2 phospholipase c
NT1 phosphoric monoester hydrolases
NT2 acid phosphatase
NT2 alkaline phosphatase
NT2 fructose-bisphosphatase
NT2 glucose-6-phosphatase
NT2 nucleotidase
NT2 phosphatidate phosphatase
NT2 phosphoprotein phosphatase
NT2 phosphorylase phosphatase
NT2 phytase
NT1 sulfuric ester hydrolases
NT2 arylsulfatase
NT1 thiolester hydrolases
NT2 palmitoyl-coa hydrolase

ESTERIFICATION
BT1 processing
rt esters

ESTERS
NT1 acetyl coenzyme a
NT1 benzoates (esters)
NT2 benzyl benzoate
NT1 butyrates (esters)
NT2 tributyrin
NT1 carbamates
NT2 meprobamate
NT2 physostigmine
NT2 urethane
NT1 chlorogenic acid
NT1 fatty acid esters
NT2 acetates (esters)
NT3 bornyl acetate
NT3 cellulose acetate
NT3 isopentyl acetate
NT3 retinyl acetate
NT3 sucrose octaacetate
NT3 triacetin
NT2 acylglycerols
NT3 diacylglycerols
NT3 monoacylglycerols
NT4 monoolein
NT3 olein
NT3 stearin
NT3 sucroglycerides
NT3 triacylglycerols
NT4 long chain triacylglycerols
NT5 triolein
NT4 medium chain triacylglycerols
NT5 trilaurin
NT5 trioctanoin
NT4 short chain triacylglycerols
NT5 triacetin
NT5 tributyrin
NT2 ethyl octanoate
NT2 palmitates
NT3 retinyl palmitate
NT2 propionates (esters)
NT3 phenethyl propionate
NT2 wax esters
NT3 beeswax
NT3 lanolin
NT1 formates (esters)
NT2 ethyl formate
NT1 isothiocyanates
NT2 allyl isothiocyanate
NT2 benzyl isothiocyanate
NT2 methyl isothiocyanate
NT1 nitrates (esters)
NT2 peroxyacetyl nitrate
NT1 phosphates (esters)
NT2 adenosine phosphates
NT3 adp
NT3 amp

ESTERS *cont.*
NT3 atp
NT3 c-amp
NT2 glycerate 2,3-bis(phosphate)
NT2 glycerate 2-phosphate
NT2 glycerate 3-phosphate
NT2 glycerol 3-phosphate
NT2 pyridoxal phosphate
NT2 sugar phosphates
NT3 fructose 6-phosphate
NT3 glucose 1-phosphate
NT3 glucose 6-phosphate
NT3 glyceraldehyde 3-phosphate
NT3 inositol phosphates
NT4 phytic acid
NT3 ribulose 1,5-diphosphate
NT2 thiamin phosphates
NT2 tributyl phosphate
NT1 phthalates
NT2 dibutyl phthalate
NT2 dimethyl phthalate
NT1 propyl gallate
NT1 sinapine
NT1 sterol esters
NT2 cholesteryl esters
NT1 sucrose esters
NT2 sucrose octaacetate
NT2 sucrose polyester
NT1 sulfates (esters)
NT2 diethyl sulfate
NT2 dimethyl sulfate
NT1 sulfites (esters)
NT2 sulfite ester acaricides
NT3 propargite
rt esterification
rt lactones
rt organic compounds

ESTIGMENE
BT1 arctiidae
BT2 lepidoptera
NT1 estigmene acraea

ESTIGMENE ACRAEA
BT1 estigmene
BT2 arctiidae
BT3 lepidoptera

ESTIMATED COSTS
uf *costs, estimated*
uf *imputed costs*
BT1 costs

ESTIMATES
uf *estimations*
NT1 unbiased estimates
rt forecasts
rt quantitative analysis

ESTIMATION
NT1 assessment
NT1 best linear unbiased estimation
NT1 best linear unbiased prediction
NT1 forecasting
NT2 prediction
NT2 weather forecasting
NT3 weather reports
NT2 yield forecasting
NT1 live estimation

estimations
USE **estimates**

ESTIVATION
BF aestivation

ESTONIAN BACON
BT1 pig breeds
BT2 breeds

ESTONIAN BLACK PIED
HN from 1990
BT1 cattle breeds
BT2 breeds

ESTONIAN DARKHEADED
BT1 sheep breeds
BT2 breeds

ESTONIAN RED
BT1 cattle breeds
BT2 breeds

ESTONIAN SSR
BT1 ussr in europe
BT2 ussr

ESTRADIOL
uf oestradiol
BT1 oestranes
BT2 steroids
BT3 isoprenoids
BT4 lipids
BT1 oestrogens
BT2 sex hormones
BT3 hormones

ESTRANES
BF oestranes

ESTRIOL
uf oestriol
BT1 oestranes
BT2 steroids
BT3 isoprenoids
BT4 lipids
BT1 oestrogens
BT2 sex hormones
BT3 hormones

ESTROGEN RECEPTORS
BF oestrogen receptors
rt estrogens

ESTROGENIC PROPERTIES
BF oestrogenic properties
rt estrogens

ESTROGENS
BF oestrogens
NT1 catechol estrogens
NT1 plant estrogens
NT2 coumestrol
rt estrogen receptors
rt estrogenic properties
rt synthetic estrogens

ESTRONE
uf oestrol
uf oestrone
BT1 oestranes
BT2 steroids
BT3 isoprenoids
BT4 lipids
BT1 oestrogens
BT2 sex hormones
BT3 hormones

ESTROUS CYCLE
BF oestrous cycle
NT1 anestrus
NT1 diestrus
NT1 estrus
NT1 metestrus
NT1 proestrus

ESTRUS
BF oestrus
BT1 estrous cycle

ESTUARIES
BT1 physiographic features
rt estuarine soils
rt rivers

ESTUARINE SOILS
BT1 soil types (physiographic)
rt estuaries

ETACELASIL
BT1 plant growth regulators
BT2 growth regulators

ETACONAZOLE
BT1 conazole fungicides
BT2 azoles
BT3 heterocyclic nitrogen compounds
BT4 organic nitrogen compounds
BT2 fungicides
BT3 pesticides

ETEM
BT1 dithiocarbamate fungicides
BT2 carbamate pesticides
BT2 fungicides
BT3 pesticides

ETHACRIDINE
BT1 acridines
BT2 heterocyclic nitrogen compounds
BT3 organic nitrogen compounds
BT1 disinfectants

ETHALFLURALIN
BT1 dinitroaniline herbicides
BT2 herbicides
BT3 pesticides

ETHANE
BT1 alkanes
BT2 hydrocarbons
BT1 fuels
BT1 gases

ethane-1-hydroxy-1,1-diphosphonic acid
USE **etidronic acid**

ETHANOL
uf alcohol, ethyl
uf ethyl alcohol
BT1 alcohols
BT1 solvents
BT1 sugar products
BT2 plant products
BT3 products
rt alcohol test
rt alcoholic beverages
rt beverage industry
rt ethanol production

ETHANOL PRODUCTION
HN from 1990
rt ethanol
rt fermentation

ETHANOLAMINE
BT1 amino alcohols
BT2 alcohols
BT2 amino compounds
BT3 organic nitrogen compounds

ETHANOLAMINE KINASE
(ec 2.7.1.82)
BT1 kinases
BT2 transferases
BT3 enzymes

ethazol
USE **etridiazole**

ETHEOSTOMA
BT1 percidae
BT2 perciformes
BT3 osteichthyes
BT4 fishes

ETHEPHON
uf (2-chloroethyl)phosphonic acid
BT1 defoliants
BT2 plant growth regulators
BT3 growth regulators
BT1 desiccant herbicides
BT2 desiccants
BT1 ethylene releasers
BT2 plant growth regulators
BT3 growth regulators

ether
USE **ethers**
OR **ethyl ether**

ETHER EXTRACTS
BT1 extracts
rt ethyl ether

ETHERS
uf ether
NT1 ethyl ether
NT1 methoxyflurane
NT1 sucrose ethers
NT2 sucrose polyethers

ETHICS
BT1 philosophy
NT1 professional ethics

ETHIDIMURON
BT1 urea herbicides
BT2 herbicides
BT3 pesticides

ethidium
USE **homidium**

ETHINYLESTRADIOL
BT1 pregnanes
BT2 steroids
BT3 isoprenoids
BT4 lipids
BT1 synthetic oestrogens
BT2 synthetic hormones

ETHIOFENCARB
BT1 carbamate insecticides
BT2 carbamate pesticides
BT2 insecticides
BT3 pesticides

ETHIOLATE
BT1 thiocarbamate herbicides
BT2 carbamate pesticides
BT2 herbicides
BT3 pesticides

ETHION
BT1 ectoparasiticides
BT2 antiparasitic agents
BT3 drugs
BT1 organothiophosphate acaricides
BT2 organophosphorus acaricides
BT3 acaricides
BT4 pesticides
BT3 organophosphorus pesticides
BT4 organophosphorus compounds

ETHIONINE
BT1 carcinogens
BT2 toxic substances
BT1 metabolic inhibitors
BT2 inhibitors
BT1 sulfur amino acids
BT2 amino acids
BT3 carboxylic acids
BT4 organic acids
BT5 acids
BT3 organic nitrogen compounds
BT2 organic sulfur compounds

ETHIOPIA
uf abyssinia
BT1 east africa
BT2 africa south of sahara
BT3 africa
rt acp
rt developing countries
rt least developed countries

ethiopian region
USE **afrotropical region**

ETHIRIMOL
BT1 pyrimidine fungicides
BT2 fungicides
BT3 pesticides
BT2 pyrimidines
BT3 heterocyclic nitrogen compounds
BT4 organic nitrogen compounds

ethnic differences
USE **ethnicity**

ETHNIC FOODS (AGRICOLA)
BT1 foods
rt ceremonial foods (agricola)

ETHNIC GROUPS
BT1 groups
NT1 american indians
NT1 asians (agricola)

ETHNIC GROUPS *cont.*
NT1 blacks (agricola)
NT1 hispanics (agricola)
NT1 inuit
NT1 jews (agricola)
NT1 mexican-americans (agricola)
rt ethnicity
rt ethnography (agricola)
rt minorities
rt race relations
rt social structure

ETHNICITY
uf ethnic differences
rt ethnic groups

ETHNOBOTANY
BT1 anthropology
BT2 social sciences
BT1 botany
BT2 biology

ETHNOGRAPHY (AGRICOLA)
rt ethnic groups

ethofenprox
USE **etofenprox**

ETHOFUMESATE
BT1 benzofuranyl alkylsulfonate herbicides
BT2 herbicides
BT3 pesticides

ETHOHEXADIOL
uf ethyl hexanediol
BT1 insect repellents
BT2 repellents

ETHOPABATE
BT1 coccidiostats
BT2 antiprotozoal agents
BT3 antiparasitic agents
BT4 drugs

ethoprop
USE **ethoprophos**

ETHOPROPHOS
uf ethoprop
uf prophos
BT1 organothiophosphate insecticides
BT2 organophosphorus insecticides
BT3 insecticides
BT4 pesticides
BT3 organophosphorus pesticides
BT4 organophosphorus compounds
BT1 organothiophosphate nematicides
BT2 organophosphorus nematicides
BT3 nematicides
BT4 pesticides
BT3 organophosphorus pesticides
BT4 organophosphorus compounds

ETHOXYQUIN
uf santoquin
BT1 antioxidants
BT2 additives
BT1 feed additives
BT2 additives
BT1 food preservatives
BT2 preservatives
BT1 plant growth regulators
BT2 growth regulators
BT1 quinoline fungicides
BT2 fungicides
BT3 pesticides
BT2 quinolines
BT3 heterocyclic nitrogen compounds
BT4 organic nitrogen compounds

ethyl alcohol
USE **ethanol**

ethyl caprylate
USE **ethyl octanoate**

ETHYL-DDD
BT1 organochlorine insecticides
BT2 insecticides
BT3 pesticides
BT2 organochlorine pesticides
BT3 organochlorine compounds
BT4 organic halogen compounds

ETHYL ETHER
uf *diethyl ether*
uf *ether*
BT1 ethers
BT1 inhaled anaesthetics
BT2 anaesthetics
BT3 neurotropic drugs
BT4 drugs
BT1 solvents
rt ether extracts

ETHYL FORMATE
BT1 formates (esters)
BT2 esters
BT2 formates
BT1 fumigant insecticides
BT2 fumigants
BT3 pesticides
BT2 insecticides
BT3 pesticides

ethyl hexanediol
USE **ethohexadiol**

ETHYL METHANESULFONATE
uf *ethyl methanesulphonate*
BT1 alkylating agents
BT1 mutagens
BT1 sulfonates
BT2 organic sulfur compounds

ethyl methanesulphonate
USE **ethyl methanesulfonate**

ETHYL OCTANOATE
uf *ethyl caprylate*
BT1 fatty acid esters
BT2 esters
BT1 flavour compounds

ethyl-parathion
USE **parathion**

ETHYL SULFIDE
uf *diethyl sulphide*
uf *ethyl sulphide*
BT1 sulfides (organic)
BT2 organic sulfur compounds
BT2 sulfides

ethyl sulphide
USE **ethyl sulfide**

ETHYLENE
uf *ethylene and ethylene releasers*
BT1 alkenes
BT2 hydrocarbons
BT1 plant growth regulators
BT2 growth regulators
rt ethylene production
rt ripening

ethylene and ethylene releasers
USE **ethylene**
OR **ethylene releasers**

ETHYLENE CHLOROHYDRIN
BT1 solvents

ETHYLENE DIBROMIDE
uf *1,2-dibromoethane*
uf *edb*
BT1 fumigant insecticides
BT2 fumigants
BT3 pesticides
BT2 insecticides
BT3 pesticides
BT1 halogenated hydrocarbons
BT2 organic halogen compounds
BT1 soil fumigants

ETHYLENE DIBROMIDE *cont.*
BT2 fumigants
BT3 pesticides

ETHYLENE DICHLORIDE
uf *1,2-dichloroethane*
BT1 chlorinated hydrocarbons
BT2 halogenated hydrocarbons
BT3 organic halogen compounds
BT1 fumigant insecticides
BT2 fumigants
BT3 pesticides
BT2 insecticides
BT3 pesticides
BT1 solvents

ETHYLENE DIUREA
BT1 antioxidants
BT2 additives

ETHYLENE GLYCOL
BT1 glycols
BT2 alcohols
BT1 solvents

ETHYLENE OXIDE
uf *oxirane*
BT1 heterocyclic oxygen compounds
BT1 mutagens

ETHYLENE PRODUCTION
BT1 gas production
rt ethylene

ETHYLENE RELEASERS
uf *ethylene and ethylene releasers*
BT1 plant growth regulators
BT2 growth regulators
NT1 acc
NT1 avg
NT1 ethephon

ethylenediaminetetraacetic acid
USE **edta**

ETHYLENEIMINE
uf *aziridine*
BT1 alkylating agents
BT1 heterocyclic nitrogen compounds
BT2 organic nitrogen compounds
BT1 mutagens

N-ETHYLMALEIMIDE
BT1 enzyme inhibitors
BT2 metabolic inhibitors
BT3 inhibitors

ETHYLMERCURY CHLORIDE
BT1 organomercury fungicides
BT2 mercury fungicides
BT3 fungicides
BT4 pesticides
BT2 organomercurial compounds
BT3 mercury compounds

ETHYLMERCURY PHOSPHATE
BT1 organomercury fungicides
BT2 mercury fungicides
BT3 fungicides
BT4 pesticides
BT2 organomercurial compounds
BT3 mercury compounds

N-ETHYL-N-NITROSOUREA
uf *n-nitroso-n-ethylurea*
BT1 carcinogens
BT2 toxic substances
BT1 mutagens
BT1 nitroso compounds
BT2 organic nitrogen compounds

ethylurethane
USE **urethane**

ethyne
USE **acetylene**

ETIDRONIC ACID
uf *ethane-1-hydroxy-1,1-diphosphonic acid*
BT1 chelating agents

ETIELLA
BT1 pyralidae
BT2 lepidoptera
NT1 etiella zinckenella

ETIELLA ZINCKENELLA
BT1 etiella
BT2 pyralidae
BT3 lepidoptera

ETIOLATION
rt blanching
rt dark
rt greening
rt vegetative propagation

ETIOLOGY
BF aetiology

ETIOPLASTS
BT1 chloroplasts
BT2 plastids
BT3 cytoplasmic inclusions
BT4 cytoplasm
BT5 protoplasm

ETIQUETTE (AGRICOLA)
BT1 social behaviour
BT2 behaviour
NT1 table manners (agricola)

ETNIPROMID
BT1 phenoxy herbicides
BT2 herbicides
BT3 pesticides

ETOFENPROX
uf *ethofenprox*
BT1 pyrethroid ether insecticides
BT2 pyrethroid insecticides
BT3 insecticides
BT4 pesticides
BT3 pyrethroids

ETOMIDATE
BT1 imidazoles
BT2 azoles
BT3 heterocyclic nitrogen compounds
BT4 organic nitrogen compounds
BT1 injectable anaesthetics
BT2 anaesthetics
BT3 neurotropic drugs
BT4 drugs

ETORPHINE
BT1 analgesics
BT2 neurotropic drugs
BT3 drugs
BT1 injectable anaesthetics
BT2 anaesthetics
BT3 neurotropic drugs
BT4 drugs

ETRIDIAZOLE
uf *echlomezol*
uf *ethazol*
BT1 nitrification inhibitors
BT2 metabolic inhibitors
BT3 inhibitors
BT1 thiazole fungicides
BT2 fungicides
BT3 pesticides
BT2 thiazoles
BT3 organic sulfur compounds

ETRIMFOS
BT1 organothiophosphate insecticides
BT2 organophosphorus insecticides
BT3 insecticides
BT4 pesticides
BT3 organophosphorus pesticides
BT4 organophosphorus compounds

ETRUMEUS
BT1 clupeidae
BT2 clupeiformes
BT3 osteichthyes
BT4 fishes
NT1 etrumeus teres

ETRUMEUS TERES
uf *round herring*
BT1 etrumeus
BT2 clupeidae
BT3 clupeiformes
BT4 osteichthyes
BT5 fishes

eua
USE **european units of account**

EUASPIS
BT1 apidae
BT2 hymenoptera

EUBACTERIALES
BT1 bacteria
BT2 prokaryotes
NT1 eubacterium

EUBACTERIUM
BT1 eubacteriales
BT2 bacteria
BT3 prokaryotes

EUBAZUS
uf *brachistes*
uf *calyptus*
BT1 braconidae
BT2 hymenoptera
NT1 eubazus atricornis

EUBAZUS ATRICORNIS
uf *brachistes atricornis*
uf *calyptus atricornis*
BT1 eubazus
BT2 braconidae
BT3 hymenoptera

EUBLEMMA
BT1 noctuidae
BT2 lepidoptera
NT1 eublemma amabilis

EUBLEMMA AMABILIS
BT1 eublemma
BT2 noctuidae
BT3 lepidoptera

EUBORELLIA
BT1 anisolabiidae
BT2 dermaptera
NT1 euborellia annulipes
rt anisolabis

EUBORELLIA ANNULIPES
uf *anisolabis annulipes*
BT1 euborellia
BT2 anisolabiidae
BT3 dermaptera

EUBOTHRIUM
BT1 amphicotylidae
BT2 eucestoda
BT3 cestoda

EUCALLIPTERUS
BT1 aphididae
BT2 aphidoidea
BT3 sternorrhyncha
BT4 homoptera
NT1 eucallipterus tiliae

EUCALLIPTERUS TILIAE
BT1 eucallipterus
BT2 aphididae
BT3 aphidoidea
BT4 sternorrhyncha
BT5 homoptera

EUCALYPTOL
uf *1,2-epoxymenthyl acetate*
uf *cineole*
BT1 expectorants
BT2 antitussive agents
BT3 respiratory system agents
BT4 drugs

EUCALYPTOL *cont.*
BT1 monoterpenoids
BT2 terpenoids
BT3 isoprenoids
BT4 lipids
rt essential oils

EUCALYPTUS
BT1 myrtaceae
NT1 eucalyptus acies
NT1 eucalyptus alba
NT1 eucalyptus amygdalina
NT1 eucalyptus astringens
NT1 eucalyptus australiana
NT1 eucalyptus balladoniensis
NT1 eucalyptus barberi
NT1 eucalyptus baxteri
NT1 eucalyptus beardiana
NT1 eucalyptus bicostata
NT1 eucalyptus blakelyi
NT1 eucalyptus botryoides
NT1 eucalyptus brassiana
NT1 eucalyptus bridgesiana
NT1 eucalyptus brookerana
NT1 eucalyptus calophylla
NT1 eucalyptus camaldulensis
NT1 eucalyptus cambageana
NT1 eucalyptus cerasiformis
NT1 eucalyptus cinerea
NT1 eucalyptus citriodora
NT1 eucalyptus cladocalyx
NT1 eucalyptus clelandii
NT1 eucalyptus cloeziana
NT1 eucalyptus crenulata
NT1 eucalyptus cypellocarpa
NT1 eucalyptus dalrympleana
NT1 eucalyptus deanei
NT1 eucalyptus decaisneana
NT1 eucalyptus deflexa
NT1 eucalyptus deglupta
NT1 eucalyptus delegatensis
NT1 eucalyptus diversicolor
NT1 eucalyptus dives
NT1 eucalyptus drepanophylla
NT1 eucalyptus dunnii
NT1 eucalyptus effusa
NT1 eucalyptus elata
NT1 eucalyptus eremophila
NT1 eucalyptus erythrocorys
NT1 eucalyptus exserta
NT1 eucalyptus fastigata
NT1 eucalyptus fibrosa
NT1 eucalyptus ficifolia
NT1 eucalyptus forrestiana
NT1 eucalyptus fraxinoides
NT1 eucalyptus fruticetorum
NT1 eucalyptus georgei
NT1 eucalyptus gittinsii
NT1 eucalyptus globoidea
NT1 eucalyptus globulus
NT1 eucalyptus gomphocephala
NT1 eucalyptus grandis
NT1 eucalyptus gunnii
NT1 eucalyptus intermedia
NT1 eucalyptus johnsoniana
NT1 eucalyptus johnstonii
NT1 eucalyptus kirtoniana
NT1 eucalyptus kombolgiensis
NT1 eucalyptus koolpinensis
NT1 eucalyptus largiflorens
NT1 eucalyptus leptocalyx
NT1 eucalyptus leucophloia
NT1 eucalyptus leucoxylon
NT1 eucalyptus lucens
NT1 eucalyptus macarthurii
NT1 eucalyptus macrandra
NT1 eucalyptus macrocarpa
NT1 eucalyptus macrorhyncha
NT1 eucalyptus maculata
NT1 eucalyptus maidenii
NT1 eucalyptus marginata
NT1 eucalyptus melanophloia
NT1 eucalyptus melliodora
NT1 eucalyptus merrickiae
NT1 eucalyptus micrantha
NT1 eucalyptus microcarpa
NT1 eucalyptus microcorys
NT1 eucalyptus microtheca
NT1 eucalyptus miniata
NT1 eucalyptus mysore hybrid
NT1 eucalyptus naudiniana

EUCALYPTUS *cont.*
NT1 eucalyptus nesophila
NT1 eucalyptus nicholii
NT1 eucalyptus nitens
NT1 eucalyptus nova-anglica
NT1 eucalyptus obliqua
NT1 eucalyptus occidentalis
NT1 eucalyptus oleosa
NT1 eucalyptus oreades
NT1 eucalyptus ovata
NT1 eucalyptus paliformis
NT1 eucalyptus panda
NT1 eucalyptus paniculata
NT1 eucalyptus papuana
NT1 eucalyptus pauciflora
NT1 eucalyptus pellita
NT1 eucalyptus pilularis
NT1 eucalyptus platycorys
NT1 eucalyptus platyphylla
NT1 eucalyptus platypus
NT1 eucalyptus polyanthemos
NT1 eucalyptus polybractea
NT1 eucalyptus populnea
NT1 eucalyptus prominens
NT1 eucalyptus propinqua
NT1 eucalyptus pseudo-globulus
NT1 eucalyptus ptychocarpa
NT1 eucalyptus pulverulenta
NT1 eucalyptus punctata
NT1 eucalyptus pyrocarpa
NT1 eucalyptus quadrangulata
NT1 eucalyptus radiata
NT1 eucalyptus regnans
NT1 eucalyptus resinifera
NT1 eucalyptus rhodantha
NT1 eucalyptus robertsonii
NT1 eucalyptus robusta
NT1 eucalyptus rossii
NT1 eucalyptus rubida
NT1 eucalyptus rudderi
NT1 eucalyptus rudis
NT1 eucalyptus rummeryi
NT1 eucalyptus saligna
NT1 eucalyptus salubris
NT1 eucalyptus sepulcralis
NT1 eucalyptus sideroxylon
NT1 eucalyptus sieberi
NT1 eucalyptus signata
NT1 eucalyptus smithii
NT1 eucalyptus staigerana
NT1 eucalyptus tereticornis
NT1 eucalyptus tessellaris
NT1 eucalyptus tetrodonta
NT1 eucalyptus torelliana
NT1 eucalyptus torquata
NT1 eucalyptus umbra
NT1 eucalyptus urnigera
NT1 eucalyptus urophylla
NT1 eucalyptus viminalis
NT1 eucalyptus viridis
NT1 eucalyptus wandoo
rt insecticidal plants

EUCALYPTUS ACIES
BT1 eucalyptus
BT2 myrtaceae

EUCALYPTUS ALBA
BT1 eucalyptus
BT2 myrtaceae
BT1 forest trees

EUCALYPTUS AMYGDALINA
BT1 eucalyptus
BT2 myrtaceae

EUCALYPTUS ASTRINGENS
BT1 eucalyptus
BT2 myrtaceae
BT1 tan plants

EUCALYPTUS AUSTRALIANA
BT1 eucalyptus
BT2 myrtaceae

EUCALYPTUS BALLADONIENSIS
BT1 eucalyptus
BT2 myrtaceae

EUCALYPTUS BARBERI
BT1 eucalyptus
BT2 myrtaceae

EUCALYPTUS BAXTERI
BT1 eucalyptus
BT2 myrtaceae

EUCALYPTUS BEARDIANA
BT1 eucalyptus
BT2 myrtaceae

EUCALYPTUS BICOSTATA
BT1 eucalyptus
BT2 myrtaceae

EUCALYPTUS BLAKELYI
BT1 eucalyptus
BT2 myrtaceae
BT1 forest trees

EUCALYPTUS BOTRYOIDES
BT1 eucalyptus
BT2 myrtaceae

EUCALYPTUS BRASSIANA
BT1 eucalyptus
BT2 myrtaceae

EUCALYPTUS BRIDGESIANA
BT1 eucalyptus
BT2 myrtaceae

EUCALYPTUS BROOKERANA
BT1 eucalyptus
BT2 myrtaceae

EUCALYPTUS CALOPHYLLA
BT1 eucalyptus
BT2 myrtaceae
BT1 forest trees

EUCALYPTUS CAMALDULENSIS
BT1 eucalyptus
BT2 myrtaceae
BT1 forest trees

EUCALYPTUS CAMBAGEANA
BT1 eucalyptus
BT2 myrtaceae

EUCALYPTUS CERASIFORMIS
BT1 eucalyptus
BT2 myrtaceae

EUCALYPTUS CINEREA
BT1 eucalyptus
BT2 myrtaceae
BT1 forest trees

EUCALYPTUS CITRIODORA
BT1 antibacterial plants
BT1 antifungal plants
BT1 essential oil plants
BT2 oil plants
BT1 eucalyptus
BT2 myrtaceae
BT1 forest trees
BT1 nematicidal plants
BT2 pesticidal plants
BT1 ornamental woody plants

EUCALYPTUS CLADOCALYX
BT1 eucalyptus
BT2 myrtaceae

EUCALYPTUS CLELANDII
BT1 eucalyptus
BT2 myrtaceae

EUCALYPTUS CLOEZIANA
BT1 eucalyptus
BT2 myrtaceae
BT1 forest trees

EUCALYPTUS CRENULATA
BT1 eucalyptus
BT2 myrtaceae

EUCALYPTUS CYPELLOCARPA
BT1 eucalyptus
BT2 myrtaceae

EUCALYPTUS DALRYMPLEANA
BT1 eucalyptus
BT2 myrtaceae
BT1 forest trees
BT1 ornamental woody plants

EUCALYPTUS DEANEI
BT1 eucalyptus
BT2 myrtaceae

EUCALYPTUS DECAISNEANA
BT1 eucalyptus
BT2 myrtaceae

EUCALYPTUS DEFLEXA
BT1 eucalyptus
BT2 myrtaceae

EUCALYPTUS DEGLUPTA
BT1 eucalyptus
BT2 myrtaceae
BT1 forest trees
BT1 insecticidal plants
BT2 pesticidal plants

EUCALYPTUS DELEGATENSIS
BT1 eucalyptus
BT2 myrtaceae
BT1 forest trees

EUCALYPTUS DIVERSICOLOR
BT1 eucalyptus
BT2 myrtaceae
BT1 forest trees

EUCALYPTUS DIVES
BT1 antibacterial plants
BT1 eucalyptus
BT2 myrtaceae

EUCALYPTUS DREPANOPHYLLA
BT1 eucalyptus
BT2 myrtaceae

EUCALYPTUS DUNNII
BT1 eucalyptus
BT2 myrtaceae

EUCALYPTUS EFFUSA
BT1 eucalyptus
BT2 myrtaceae

EUCALYPTUS ELATA
BT1 eucalyptus
BT2 myrtaceae

EUCALYPTUS EREMOPHILA
BT1 eucalyptus
BT2 myrtaceae

EUCALYPTUS ERYTHROCORYS
BT1 eucalyptus
BT2 myrtaceae

EUCALYPTUS EXSERTA
HN from 1990
BT1 eucalyptus
BT2 myrtaceae
BT1 forest trees

EUCALYPTUS FASTIGATA
BT1 eucalyptus
BT2 myrtaceae
BT1 forest trees

EUCALYPTUS FIBROSA
BT1 eucalyptus
BT2 myrtaceae

EUCALYPTUS FICIFOLIA
BT1 eucalyptus
BT2 myrtaceae
BT1 ornamental woody plants

EUCALYPTUS FORRESTIANA
BT1 eucalyptus
BT2 myrtaceae

EUCALYPTUS FRAXINOIDES
BT1 eucalyptus
BT2 myrtaceae

EUCALYPTUS FRUTICETORUM
BT1 eucalyptus
BT2 myrtaceae

EUCALYPTUS GEORGEI
BT1 eucalyptus
BT2 myrtaceae

EUCALYPTUS GITTINSII
BT1 eucalyptus

EUCALYPTUS GITTINSII *cont.*
BT2 myrtaceae

EUCALYPTUS GLOBOIDEA
BT1 eucalyptus
BT2 myrtaceae

EUCALYPTUS GLOBULUS
BT1 essential oil plants
BT2 oil plants
BT1 eucalyptus
BT2 myrtaceae
BT1 forest trees
BT1 medicinal plants
BT1 ornamental woody plants

EUCALYPTUS GOMPHOCEPHALA
BT1 eucalyptus
BT2 myrtaceae
BT1 forest trees

EUCALYPTUS GRANDIS
BT1 eucalyptus
BT2 myrtaceae
BT1 forest trees

EUCALYPTUS GUNNII
BT1 eucalyptus
BT2 myrtaceae
BT1 forest trees
BT1 ornamental woody plants

EUCALYPTUS INTERMEDIA
BT1 eucalyptus
BT2 myrtaceae

EUCALYPTUS JOHNSONIANA
BT1 eucalyptus
BT2 myrtaceae

EUCALYPTUS JOHNSTONII
BT1 eucalyptus
BT2 myrtaceae

EUCALYPTUS KIRTONIANA
BT1 eucalyptus
BT2 myrtaceae

EUCALYPTUS KOMBOLGIENSIS
BT1 eucalyptus
BT2 myrtaceae

EUCALYPTUS KOOLPINENSIS
BT1 eucalyptus
BT2 myrtaceae

EUCALYPTUS LARGIFLORENS
BT1 eucalyptus
BT2 myrtaceae

EUCALYPTUS LEPTOCALYX
BT1 eucalyptus
BT2 myrtaceae

EUCALYPTUS LEUCOPHLOIA
BT1 eucalyptus
BT2 myrtaceae

EUCALYPTUS LEUCOXYLON
BT1 eucalyptus
BT2 myrtaceae
BT1 forest trees
BT1 ornamental woody plants

EUCALYPTUS LUCENS
BT1 eucalyptus
BT2 myrtaceae

EUCALYPTUS MACARTHURII
BT1 eucalyptus
BT2 myrtaceae
BT1 forest trees

EUCALYPTUS MACRANDRA
BT1 eucalyptus
BT2 myrtaceae

EUCALYPTUS MACROCARPA
BT1 eucalyptus
BT2 myrtaceae

EUCALYPTUS MACRORHYNCHA
BT1 eucalyptus
BT2 myrtaceae
BT1 forest trees

EUCALYPTUS MACULATA
BT1 eucalyptus
BT2 myrtaceae
BT1 forest trees

EUCALYPTUS MAIDENII
BT1 eucalyptus
BT2 myrtaceae
BT1 forest trees

EUCALYPTUS MARGINATA
BT1 eucalyptus
BT2 myrtaceae
BT1 forest trees

EUCALYPTUS MELANOPHLOIA
BT1 eucalyptus
BT2 myrtaceae

EUCALYPTUS MELLIODORA
BT1 eucalyptus
BT2 myrtaceae
BT1 forest trees

EUCALYPTUS MERRICKIAE
BT1 eucalyptus
BT2 myrtaceae

EUCALYPTUS MICRANTHA
BT1 eucalyptus
BT2 myrtaceae

EUCALYPTUS MICROCARPA
BT1 eucalyptus
BT2 myrtaceae

EUCALYPTUS MICROCORYS
BT1 eucalyptus
BT2 myrtaceae
BT1 forest trees

EUCALYPTUS MICROTHECA
BT1 eucalyptus
BT2 myrtaceae
BT1 forest trees

EUCALYPTUS MINIATA
BT1 eucalyptus
BT2 myrtaceae

EUCALYPTUS MYSORE HYBRID
BT1 eucalyptus
BT2 myrtaceae

EUCALYPTUS NAUDINIANA
BT1 eucalyptus
BT2 myrtaceae

EUCALYPTUS NESOPHILA
BT1 eucalyptus
BT2 myrtaceae

EUCALYPTUS NICHOLII
BT1 eucalyptus
BT2 myrtaceae
BT1 ornamental woody plants

EUCALYPTUS NITENS
BT1 eucalyptus
BT2 myrtaceae
BT1 forest trees

EUCALYPTUS NOVA-ANGLICA
BT1 eucalyptus
BT2 myrtaceae

EUCALYPTUS OBLIQUA
BT1 eucalyptus
BT2 myrtaceae
BT1 forest trees

EUCALYPTUS OCCIDENTALIS
BT1 eucalyptus
BT2 myrtaceae

EUCALYPTUS OLEOSA
BT1 eucalyptus
BT2 myrtaceae

EUCALYPTUS OREADES
BT1 eucalyptus
BT2 myrtaceae

EUCALYPTUS OVATA
BT1 eucalyptus
BT2 myrtaceae

EUCALYPTUS OVATA *cont.*
BT1 forest trees

EUCALYPTUS PALIFORMIS
BT1 eucalyptus
BT2 myrtaceae

EUCALYPTUS PANDA
BT1 eucalyptus
BT2 myrtaceae

EUCALYPTUS PANICULATA
BT1 eucalyptus
BT2 myrtaceae
BT1 forest trees

EUCALYPTUS PAPUANA
BT1 eucalyptus
BT2 myrtaceae

EUCALYPTUS PAUCIFLORA
BT1 eucalyptus
BT2 myrtaceae
BT1 forest trees
BT1 ornamental woody plants

EUCALYPTUS PELLITA
BT1 eucalyptus
BT2 myrtaceae
BT1 forest trees

EUCALYPTUS PILULARIS
BT1 eucalyptus
BT2 myrtaceae
BT1 forest trees

EUCALYPTUS PLATYCORYS
BT1 eucalyptus
BT2 myrtaceae

EUCALYPTUS PLATYPHYLLA
BT1 eucalyptus
BT2 myrtaceae

EUCALYPTUS PLATYPUS
BT1 eucalyptus
BT2 myrtaceae

EUCALYPTUS POLYANTHEMOS
BT1 eucalyptus
BT2 myrtaceae

EUCALYPTUS POLYBRACTEA
BT1 antibacterial plants
BT1 eucalyptus
BT2 myrtaceae

EUCALYPTUS POPULNEA
BT1 eucalyptus
BT2 myrtaceae

EUCALYPTUS PROMINENS
BT1 eucalyptus
BT2 myrtaceae

EUCALYPTUS PROPINQUA
BT1 eucalyptus
BT2 myrtaceae
BT1 forest trees

EUCALYPTUS PSEUDO-GLOBULUS
BT1 eucalyptus
BT2 myrtaceae

EUCALYPTUS PTYCHOCARPA
BT1 eucalyptus
BT2 myrtaceae

EUCALYPTUS PULVERULENTA
BT1 eucalyptus
BT2 myrtaceae
BT1 ornamental woody plants

EUCALYPTUS PUNCTATA
BT1 eucalyptus
BT2 myrtaceae

EUCALYPTUS PYROCARPA
BT1 eucalyptus
BT2 myrtaceae

EUCALYPTUS QUADRANGULATA
BT1 eucalyptus
BT2 myrtaceae

EUCALYPTUS RADIATA
BT1 antibacterial plants

EUCALYPTUS RADIATA *cont.*
BT1 eucalyptus
BT2 myrtaceae
BT1 forest trees

EUCALYPTUS REGNANS
BT1 eucalyptus
BT2 myrtaceae
BT1 forest trees

EUCALYPTUS RESINIFERA
BT1 eucalyptus
BT2 myrtaceae

EUCALYPTUS RHODANTHA
BT1 eucalyptus
BT2 myrtaceae

EUCALYPTUS ROBERTSONII
BT1 eucalyptus
BT2 myrtaceae

EUCALYPTUS ROBUSTA
BT1 eucalyptus
BT2 myrtaceae
BT1 forest trees

EUCALYPTUS ROSSII
BT1 eucalyptus
BT2 myrtaceae

EUCALYPTUS RUBIDA
BT1 eucalyptus
BT2 myrtaceae

EUCALYPTUS RUDDERI
BT1 eucalyptus
BT2 myrtaceae

EUCALYPTUS RUDIS
BT1 eucalyptus
BT2 myrtaceae
BT1 forest trees

EUCALYPTUS RUMMERYI
BT1 eucalyptus
BT2 myrtaceae

EUCALYPTUS SALIGNA
BT1 eucalyptus
BT2 myrtaceae
BT1 forest trees
BT1 insecticidal plants
BT2 pesticidal plants

EUCALYPTUS SALUBRIS
BT1 eucalyptus
BT2 myrtaceae

EUCALYPTUS SEPULCRALIS
BT1 eucalyptus
BT2 myrtaceae

EUCALYPTUS SIDEROXYLON
BT1 eucalyptus
BT2 myrtaceae
BT1 forest trees

EUCALYPTUS SIEBERI
BT1 eucalyptus
BT2 myrtaceae
BT1 forest trees

EUCALYPTUS SIGNATA
BT1 eucalyptus
BT2 myrtaceae

EUCALYPTUS SMITHII
BT1 eucalyptus
BT2 myrtaceae

EUCALYPTUS STAIGERANA
BT1 eucalyptus
BT2 myrtaceae

EUCALYPTUS TERETICORNIS
BT1 eucalyptus
BT2 myrtaceae
BT1 forest trees

EUCALYPTUS TESSELLARIS
BT1 eucalyptus
BT2 myrtaceae

EUCALYPTUS TETRODONTA
BT1 eucalyptus

EUCALYPTUS TETRODONTA *cont.*
BT2 myrtaceae

EUCALYPTUS TORELLIANA
BT1 eucalyptus
BT2 myrtaceae

EUCALYPTUS TORQUATA
BT1 eucalyptus
BT2 myrtaceae

EUCALYPTUS UMBRA
BT1 eucalyptus
BT2 myrtaceae

EUCALYPTUS URNIGERA
BT1 eucalyptus
BT2 myrtaceae
BT1 ornamental woody plants

EUCALYPTUS UROPHYLLA
BT1 eucalyptus
BT2 myrtaceae
BT1 forest trees

EUCALYPTUS VIMINALIS
BT1 eucalyptus
BT2 myrtaceae
BT1 forest trees

EUCALYPTUS VIRIDIS
BT1 eucalyptus
BT2 myrtaceae

EUCALYPTUS WANDOO
BT1 eucalyptus
BT2 myrtaceae
BT1 forest trees

eucarcelia
USE **carcelia**

eucarcelia evolans
USE **carcelia evolans**

EUCELATORIA
BT1 tachinidae
BT2 diptera

EUCERA
BT1 apidae
BT2 hymenoptera

EUCESTODA
HN from 1990
uf *cestodes*
uf *tapeworms*
BT1 cestoda
NT1 amabiliidae
NT2 tatria
NT1 amphicotylidae
NT2 eubothrium
NT1 anoplocephalidae
NT2 andrya
NT2 anoplocephala
NT3 anoplocephala magna
NT3 anoplocephala perfoliata
NT2 avitellina
NT3 avitellina centripunctata
NT2 bertiella
NT3 bertiella studeri
NT2 moniezia
NT3 moniezia autumnalia
NT3 moniezia benedeni
NT3 moniezia expansa
NT2 paranoplocephala
NT3 paranoplocephala mamillana
NT2 stilesia
NT3 stilesia globipunctata
NT3 stilesia hepatica
NT2 thysaniezia
NT3 thysaniezia giardi
NT2 thysanosoma
NT3 thysanosoma actinioides
NT1 bothriocephalidae
NT2 bothriocephalus
NT3 bothriocephalus acheilognathi
NT1 caryophyllaeidae
NT2 khawia
NT3 khawia sinensis
NT1 davaineidae
NT2 cotugnia

EUCESTODA *cont.*
NT3 cotugnia digonophora
NT2 davainea
NT3 davainea proglottina
NT2 raillietina
NT3 raillietina cesticillus
NT3 raillietina echinobothrida
NT3 raillietina tetragona
NT1 dilepididae
NT2 amoebotaenia
NT3 amoebotaenia sphenoides
NT2 anomotaenia
NT2 choanotaenia
NT3 choanotaenia infundibulum
NT2 diplopylidium
NT3 diplopylidium nolleri
NT2 dipylidium
NT3 dipylidium caninum
NT2 joyeuxiella
NT3 joyeuxiella echinorhynchoides
NT3 joyeuxiella pasqualei
NT1 diphyllobothriidae
NT2 diphyllobothrium
NT3 diphyllobothrium cordiceps
NT3 diphyllobothrium dendriticum
NT3 diphyllobothrium latum
NT2 diplogonoporus
NT3 diplogonoporus balaenopterae
NT3 diplogonoporus fukuokaensis
NT3 diplogonoporus grandis
NT2 ligula
NT3 ligula intestinalis
NT2 schistocephalus
NT3 schistocephalus solidus
NT2 spirometra
NT3 spirometra mansonoides
NT1 hymenolepididae
NT2 aploparaksis
NT2 diorchis
NT2 fimbriaria
NT3 fimbriaria fasciolaris
NT2 hymenolepis
NT3 hymenolepis citelli
NT3 hymenolepis diminuta
NT3 hymenolepis microstoma
NT3 hymenolepis nana
NT2 microsomacanthus
NT2 retinometra
NT2 sobolevicanthus
NT3 sobolevicanthus gracilis
NT2 triodontolepis
NT1 mesocestoidae
NT2 mesocestoides
NT3 mesocestoides corti
NT3 mesocestoides lineatus
NT1 nematoparataeniidae
NT2 gastrotaenia
NT1 onchobothriidae
NT2 acanthobothrium
NT1 proteocephalidae
NT2 proteocephalus
NT1 taeniidae
NT2 echinococcus
NT3 echinococcus granulosus
NT3 echinococcus multilocularis
NT2 taenia
NT3 taenia crassiceps
NT3 taenia hydatigena
NT3 taenia multiceps
NT3 taenia ovis
NT3 taenia pisiformis
NT3 taenia saginata
NT3 taenia serialis
NT3 taenia solium
NT3 taenia taeniaeformis
NT1 triaenophoridae
NT2 triaenophorus
NT3 triaenophorus nodulosus
rt cestode infections
rt cestode larvae
rt helminths
rt metacestodes
rt platyhelminthes

EUCHARIS
BT1 amaryllidaceae
rt urceolina

eucharis amazonica
USE **urceolina amazonica**

eucharis grandiflora
USE **urceolina grandiflora**

euchlaena
USE **zea**

EUCHRESTA
BT1 leguminosae
NT1 euchresta horsfeldii
NT1 euchresta japonica

EUCHRESTA HORSFELDII
BT1 euchresta
BT2 leguminosae

EUCHRESTA JAPONICA
BT1 euchresta
BT2 leguminosae

EUCHROMATIN
BT1 chromatin
BT2 nucleoproteins
BT3 proteins
BT4 peptides

EUCHRYSOPS
BT1 lycaenidae
BT2 lepidoptera
NT1 euchrysops cnejus
rt catochrysops

EUCHRYSOPS CNEJUS
uf *catochrysops cnejus*
BT1 euchrysops
BT2 lycaenidae
BT3 lepidoptera

EUCLEA
BT1 ebenaceae
NT1 euclea divinorum
NT1 euclea natalensis

EUCLEA DIVINORUM
BT1 euclea
BT2 ebenaceae

EUCLEA NATALENSIS
BT1 dye plants
BT1 euclea
BT2 ebenaceae

EUCLINOSTOMUM
BT1 clinostomidae
BT2 digenea
BT3 trematoda
NT1 euclinostomum heterostomum

EUCLINOSTOMUM HETEROSTOMUM
BT1 euclinostomum
BT2 clinostomidae
BT3 digenea
BT4 trematoda

EUCOILIDAE
BT1 hymenoptera
NT1 ganaspis
NT1 leptopilina
NT2 leptopilina boulardi
NT2 leptopilina heterotoma
NT1 trybliographa
NT2 trybliographa rapae

EUCOMIS
BT1 liliaceae
NT1 eucomis autumnalis

EUCOMIS AUTUMNALIS
uf *eucomis undulata*
BT1 eucomis
BT2 liliaceae
BT1 ornamental bulbs

eucomis undulata
USE **eucomis autumnalis**

EUCOMMIA
BT1 eucommiaceae

EUCOMMIA *cont.*
NT1 eucommia ulmoides

EUCOMMIA ULMOIDES
BT1 eucommia
BT2 eucommiaceae

EUCOMMIACEAE
NT1 eucommia
NT2 eucommia ulmoides

EUCOSMA
BT1 tortricidae
BT2 lepidoptera
NT1 eucosma cocana
NT1 eucosma conterminana
rt epiblema
rt epinotia
rt tetramoera

EUCOSMA COCANA
BT1 eucosma
BT2 tortricidae
BT3 lepidoptera

EUCOSMA CONTERMINANA
BT1 eucosma
BT2 tortricidae
BT3 lepidoptera

eucosma schistaceana
USE **tetramoera schistaceana**

eucosma scudderiana
USE **epiblema scudderiana**

eucosma tedella
USE **epinotia tedella**

EUCOTYLE
BT1 eucotylidae
BT2 digenea
BT3 trematoda
NT1 eucotyle nephritica

EUCOTYLE NEPHRITICA
BT1 eucotyle
BT2 eucotylidae
BT3 digenea
BT4 trematoda

EUCOTYLIDAE
BT1 digenea
BT2 trematoda
NT1 eucotyle
NT2 eucotyle nephritica
NT1 tanaisia
NT2 tanaisia zarudnyi

EUCRYPHIA
BT1 eucryphiaceae
NT1 eucryphia cordifolia
NT1 eucryphia lucida

EUCRYPHIA CORDIFOLIA
BT1 eucryphia
BT2 eucryphiaceae
BT1 ornamental woody plants
BT1 tan plants

EUCRYPHIA LUCIDA
HN from 1990
BT1 eucryphia
BT2 eucryphiaceae
BT1 forest trees

EUCRYPHIACEAE
NT1 eucryphia
NT2 eucryphia cordifolia
NT2 eucryphia lucida

EUDARLUCA
uf *darluca*
BT1 dothideales
NT1 eudarluca caricis

EUDARLUCA CARICIS
uf *darluca filum*
BT1 eudarluca
BT2 dothideales

EUDIAPTOMUS
BT1 calanoida
BT2 copepoda
BT3 crustacea
BT4 arthropods

EUDIAPTOMUS *cont.*
NT1 eudiaptomus gracilis
NT1 eudiaptomus graciloides

EUDIAPTOMUS GRACILIS
BT1 eudiaptomus
BT2 calanoida
BT3 copepoda
BT4 crustacea
BT5 arthropods

EUDIAPTOMUS GRACILOIDES
BT1 eudiaptomus
BT2 calanoida
BT3 copepoda
BT4 crustacea
BT5 arthropods

EUDIPLODINIUM
BT1 ciliophora
BT2 protozoa

EUDOCIMA
HN from 1989
uf *othreis*
BT1 noctuidae
BT2 lepidoptera
NT1 eudocima fullonia

EUDOCIMA FULLONIA
HN from 1989; previously othreis fullonia
uf *othreis fullonia*
BT1 eudocima
BT2 noctuidae
BT3 lepidoptera

EUDORINA
BT1 chlorophyta
BT2 algae
NT1 eudorina elegans

EUDORINA ELEGANS
BT1 eudorina
BT2 chlorophyta
BT3 algae

EUDORYLAIMUS
BT1 dorylaimidae
BT2 nematoda

EUDYPTULA
BT1 spheniscidae
BT2 sphenisciformes
BT3 birds

eufriesia
USE **euglossa**

EUGEISSONA
BT1 palmae
NT1 eugeissona tristis

EUGEISSONA TRISTIS
BT1 eugeissona
BT2 palmae

EUGENIA
BT1 myrtaceae
NT1 eugenia acutangula
NT1 eugenia aquea
NT1 eugenia cabelludo
NT1 eugenia dombeyi
NT1 eugenia grandis
NT1 eugenia henyana
NT1 eugenia javanica
NT1 eugenia maire
NT1 eugenia malaccensis
NT1 eugenia onesima
NT1 eugenia pitanga
NT1 eugenia tierneyana
NT1 eugenia tomentosa
NT1 eugenia uniflora
rt syzygium

EUGENIA ACUTANGULA
BT1 eugenia
BT2 myrtaceae
rt barringtonia acutangula

EUGENIA AQUEA
BT1 eugenia
BT2 myrtaceae

eugenia aromatica
USE **syzygium aromaticum**

eugenia brasiliensis
USE **eugenia dombeyi**

EUGENIA CABELLUDO
BT1 eugenia
BT2 myrtaceae

eugenia caryophyllus
USE **syzygium aromaticum**

eugenia cumini
USE **syzygium cumini**

EUGENIA DOMBEYI
uf *eugenia brasiliensis*
BT1 eugenia
BT2 myrtaceae
BT1 subtropical tree fruits
BT2 subtropical fruits
BT3 fruit crops
BT2 tree fruits
BT1 tropical tree fruits
BT2 tree fruits
BT2 tropical fruits
BT3 fruit crops

EUGENIA GRANDIS
BT1 eugenia
BT2 myrtaceae
BT1 ornamental woody plants

EUGENIA HENYANA
BT1 eugenia
BT2 myrtaceae

eugenia jambolana
USE **syzygium cumini**

eugenia jambos
USE **syzygium jambos**

EUGENIA JAVANICA
uf *syzygium javanicum*
BT1 eugenia
BT2 myrtaceae

EUGENIA MAIRE
BT1 eugenia
BT2 myrtaceae

EUGENIA MALACCENSIS
BT1 eugenia
BT2 myrtaceae
BT1 tropical tree fruits
BT2 tree fruits
BT2 tropical fruits
BT3 fruit crops

eugenia michelii
USE **eugenia uniflora**

EUGENIA ONESIMA
BT1 eugenia
BT2 myrtaceae

EUGENIA PITANGA
BT1 eugenia
BT2 myrtaceae

EUGENIA TIERNEYANA
BT1 eugenia
BT2 myrtaceae

EUGENIA TOMENTOSA
BT1 eugenia
BT2 myrtaceae

EUGENIA UNIFLORA
uf *eugenia michelii*
BT1 eugenia
BT2 myrtaceae
BT1 ornamental woody plants
BT1 tropical tree fruits
BT2 tree fruits
BT2 tropical fruits
BT3 fruit crops

EUGENOL
BT1 analgesics
BT2 neurotropic drugs
BT3 drugs
BT1 insect attractants
BT2 attractants

EUGENOL *cont.*
BT1 monoterpenoids
BT2 terpenoids
BT3 isoprenoids
BT4 lipids
rt essential oils

EUGLENA
BT1 euglenophyta
BT2 algae
NT1 euglena gracilis

EUGLENA GRACILIS
BT1 euglena
BT2 euglenophyta
BT3 algae

EUGLENOPHYTA
BT1 algae
NT1 euglena
NT2 euglena gracilis

EUGLOSSA
uf *eufriesia*
BT1 apidae
BT2 hymenoptera

EUKARYOTES
uf *eukaryotic cells*
BT1 cells

eukaryotic cells
USE **eukaryotes**

EULACHNUS
BT1 aphididae
BT2 aphidoidea
BT3 sternorrhyncha
BT4 homoptera
NT1 eulachnus rileyi

EULACHNUS RILEYI
BT1 eulachnus
BT2 aphididae
BT3 aphidoidea
BT4 sternorrhyncha
BT5 homoptera

EULAELAPS
HN from 1989
BT1 laelapidae
BT2 mesostigmata
BT3 acari
NT1 eulaelaps stabularis

EULAELAPS STABULARIS
HN from 1989
BT1 eulaelaps
BT2 laelapidae
BT3 mesostigmata
BT4 acari

EULAEMA
BT1 apidae
BT2 hymenoptera

EULECANIUM
BT1 coccidae
BT2 coccoidea
BT3 sternorrhyncha
BT4 homoptera
NT1 eulecanium tiliae
rt palaeolecanium
rt sphaerolecanium

eulecanium bituberculatum
USE **palaeolecanium bituberculatum**

eulecanium coryli
USE **eulecanium tiliae**

eulecanium prunastri
USE **sphaerolecanium prunastri**

EULECANIUM TILIAE
uf *eulecanium coryli*
BT1 eulecanium
BT2 coccidae
BT3 coccoidea
BT4 sternorrhyncha
BT5 homoptera

EULEIA
BT1 tephritidae
BT2 diptera
NT1 euleia heraclii

EULEIA HERACLII
BT1 euleia
BT2 tephritidae
BT3 diptera

EULONCHOPRIA
BT1 apidae
BT2 hymenoptera

EULOPHIDAE
BT1 hymenoptera
NT1 aceratoneuromyia
NT2 aceratoneuromyia indica
NT1 achrysocharoides
NT1 aprostocetus
NT2 aprostocetus diplosidis
NT2 aprostocetus galactopus
NT2 aprostocetus hagenowii
NT2 aprostocetus purpureus
NT2 aprostocetus venustus
NT1 chrysocharis
NT2 chrysocharis nitetis
NT2 chrysocharis parksi
NT1 chrysonotomyia
NT2 chrysonotomyia formosa
NT1 cirrospilus
NT2 cirrospilus vittatus
NT1 dahlbominus
NT1 dicladocerus
NT2 dicladocerus westwoodii
NT1 diglyphus
NT2 diglyphus begini
NT2 diglyphus intermedius
NT2 diglyphus isaea
NT1 edovum
NT2 edovum puttleri
NT1 euplectrus
NT1 hemiptarsenus
NT1 minotetrastichus
NT2 minotetrastichus ecus
NT1 necremnus
NT1 pediobius
NT2 pediobius foveolatus
NT1 pnigalio
NT2 pnigalio agraules
NT2 pnigalio pectinicornis
NT1 sympiesis
NT2 sympiesis gordius
NT2 sympiesis marylandensis
NT2 sympiesis sericeicornis
NT1 tamarixia
NT2 tamarixia dryi
NT1 tetrastichus
NT2 tetrastichus blastophagi
NT2 tetrastichus brontispae
NT2 tetrastichus evonymellae
NT2 tetrastichus gallerucae
NT2 tetrastichus julis
NT2 tetrastichus pyrillae
NT2 tetrastichus rapo
NT2 tetrastichus schoenobii
NT2 tetrastichus servadeii
NT2 tetrastichus sokolowskii
NT1 trichospilus
NT2 trichospilus diatraeae

EULOPHIDIUM
BT1 orchidaceae

EULOTIDAE
BT1 gastropoda
BT2 mollusca
NT1 bradybaena
NT2 bradybaena circulus
NT2 bradybaena similaris

EUMASENIA
BT1 maseniidae
BT2 digenea
BT3 trematoda

EUMERUS
BT1 syrphidae
BT2 diptera

EUMETOPIAS
BT1 otariidae
BT2 pinnipedia

EUMETOPIAS *cont.*
BT3 carnivores
BT4 mammals
NT1 eumetopias jubatus
rt sealions

EUMETOPIAS JUBATUS
BT1 eumetopias
BT2 otariidae
BT3 pinnipedia
BT4 carnivores
BT5 mammals

EUODIA
uf *evodia*
BT1 rutaceae
NT1 euodia anisodora

EUODIA ANISODORA
BT1 euodia
BT2 rutaceae

euodia daniellii
USE **tetradium daniellii**

euodia hupehensis
USE **tetradium daniellii**

euodia meliaefolia
USE **tetradium glabrifolium**

euodia officinalis
USE **tetradium ruticarpum**

euodia rutaecarpa
USE **tetradium ruticarpum**

euoniticellus
USE **oniticellus**

EUONYMUS
BT1 celastraceae
NT1 euonymus alatus
NT1 euonymus bungeanus
NT1 euonymus czernjaevii
NT1 euonymus europaeus
NT1 euonymus fortunei
NT1 euonymus hamiltonianus
NT1 euonymus japonicus
NT1 euonymus kiautschovicus
NT1 euonymus lucidus
NT1 euonymus pendulus
NT1 euonymus radicans

EUONYMUS ALATUS
BT1 euonymus
BT2 celastraceae
BT1 insecticidal plants
BT2 pesticidal plants
BT1 ornamental woody plants

EUONYMUS BUNGEANUS
BT1 euonymus
BT2 celastraceae
BT1 ornamental woody plants

EUONYMUS CZERNJAEVII
BT1 euonymus
BT2 celastraceae

EUONYMUS EUROPAEUS
BT1 euonymus
BT2 celastraceae
BT1 ornamental woody plants

EUONYMUS FORTUNEI
BT1 euonymus
BT2 celastraceae
BT1 ornamental woody plants

EUONYMUS HAMILTONIANUS
uf *euonymus sieboldianus*
BT1 euonymus
BT2 celastraceae
BT1 ornamental woody plants

EUONYMUS JAPONICUS
BT1 euonymus
BT2 celastraceae
BT1 ornamental woody plants

EUONYMUS KIAUTSCHOVICUS
BT1 euonymus
BT2 celastraceae
BT1 ornamental woody plants

EUONYMUS LUCIDUS
BT1 euonymus
BT2 celastraceae
BT1 ornamental woody plants

EUONYMUS PENDULUS
BT1 euonymus
BT2 celastraceae

EUONYMUS RADICANS
BT1 euonymus
BT2 celastraceae
BT1 ornamental woody plants

euonymus sieboldianus
USE **euonymus hamiltonianus**

EUPALAMIDES
BT1 castniidae
BT2 lepidoptera
NT1 eupalamides cyparissias
rt castnia
rt lapaeumides

EUPALAMIDES CYPARISSIAS
uf *castnia dedalus*
uf *lapaeumides dedalus*
BT1 eupalamides
BT2 castniidae
BT3 lepidoptera

EUPARYPHIUM
BT1 echinostomatidae
BT2 digenea
BT3 trematoda

EUPATORIOPICRIN
BT1 sesquiterpenoid lactones
BT2 lactones
BT3 heterocyclic oxygen compounds
BT3 ketones
BT2 sesquiterpenoids
BT3 terpenoids
BT4 isoprenoids
BT5 lipids

EUPATORIUM
BT1 compositae
NT1 eupatorium africanum
NT1 eupatorium altissimum
NT1 eupatorium anomalum
NT1 eupatorium ayapana
NT1 eupatorium cannabinum
NT1 eupatorium capillifolium
NT1 eupatorium coelestinum
NT1 eupatorium compositifolium
NT1 eupatorium correlliorum
NT1 eupatorium dubium
NT1 eupatorium formosanum
NT1 eupatorium hyssopifolium
NT1 eupatorium inulaefolium
NT1 eupatorium japonicum
NT1 eupatorium laevigatum
NT1 eupatorium ligustrinum
NT1 eupatorium mohrii
NT1 eupatorium odoratum
NT1 eupatorium perfoliatum
NT1 eupatorium pilosum
NT1 eupatorium purpureum
NT1 eupatorium repandum
NT1 eupatorium riparium
NT1 eupatorium rotundifolium
NT1 eupatorium rugosum
NT1 eupatorium semiserratum
NT1 eupatorium stoechadosmum
NT1 eupatorium trapezoideum
rt chromolaena

eupatorium adenophorum
USE **eupatorium trapezoideum**

EUPATORIUM AFRICANUM
BT1 eupatorium
BT2 compositae

EUPATORIUM ALTISSIMUM
BT1 eupatorium
BT2 compositae
BT1 medicinal plants

EUPATORIUM ANOMALUM
BT1 eupatorium
BT2 compositae

EUPATORIUM AYAPANA
BT1 antibacterial plants
BT1 eupatorium
BT2 compositae

EUPATORIUM CANNABINUM
BT1 eupatorium
BT2 compositae

EUPATORIUM CAPILLIFOLIUM
BT1 antibacterial plants
BT1 eupatorium
BT2 compositae

EUPATORIUM COELESTINUM
BT1 eupatorium
BT2 compositae

EUPATORIUM COMPOSITIFOLIUM
BT1 eupatorium
BT2 compositae

EUPATORIUM CORRELLIORUM
BT1 eupatorium
BT2 compositae

EUPATORIUM DUBIUM
BT1 eupatorium
BT2 compositae

EUPATORIUM FORMOSANUM
BT1 eupatorium
BT2 compositae
BT1 medicinal plants

EUPATORIUM HYSSOPIFOLIUM
BT1 eupatorium
BT2 compositae

EUPATORIUM INULAEFOLIUM
BT1 eupatorium
BT2 compositae

EUPATORIUM JAPONICUM
BT1 eupatorium
BT2 compositae
BT1 insecticidal plants
BT2 pesticidal plants

EUPATORIUM LAEVIGATUM
BT1 eupatorium
BT2 compositae

EUPATORIUM LIGUSTRINUM
uf *eupatorium micranthum*
BT1 eupatorium
BT2 compositae

eupatorium micranthum
USE **eupatorium ligustrinum**

EUPATORIUM MOHRII
BT1 eupatorium
BT2 compositae

EUPATORIUM ODORATUM
uf *chromolaena odorata*
BT1 antibacterial plants
BT1 antifungal plants
BT1 eupatorium
BT2 compositae
BT1 medicinal plants
BT1 weeds

EUPATORIUM PERFOLIATUM
BT1 eupatorium
BT2 compositae
BT1 medicinal plants

EUPATORIUM PILOSUM
BT1 eupatorium
BT2 compositae

EUPATORIUM PURPUREUM
BT1 eupatorium
BT2 compositae

EUPATORIUM REPANDUM
BT1 eupatorium
BT2 compositae

EUPATORIUM RIPARIUM
BT1 eupatorium
BT2 compositae

EUPATORIUM ROTUNDIFOLIUM
BT1 eupatorium
BT2 compositae

EUPATORIUM RUGOSUM
BT1 eupatorium
BT2 compositae

EUPATORIUM SEMISERRATUM
BT1 eupatorium
BT2 compositae
BT1 medicinal plants

EUPATORIUM STOECHADOSMUM
BT1 eupatorium
BT2 compositae

EUPATORIUM TRAPEZOIDEUM
uf *eupatorium adenophorum*
BT1 eupatorium
BT2 compositae

EUPELMIDAE
BT1 hymenoptera
NT1 anastatus
NT2 anastatus bifasciatus
NT2 anastatus gastropachae
NT2 anastatus japonicus
NT1 eupelmus
NT2 eupelmus australiensis
NT2 eupelmus tachardiae
NT2 eupelmus urozonus
NT1 neanastatus
NT2 neanastatus cinctiventris

EUPELMUS
BT1 eupelmidae
BT2 hymenoptera
NT1 eupelmus australiensis
NT1 eupelmus tachardiae
NT1 eupelmus urozonus

EUPELMUS AUSTRALIENSIS
HN from 1989; previously eupelmus popa
uf *eupelmus popa*
BT1 eupelmus
BT2 eupelmidae
BT3 hymenoptera

eupelmus popa
USE **eupelmus australiensis**

EUPELMUS TACHARDIAE
BT1 eupelmus
BT2 eupelmidae
BT3 hymenoptera

EUPELMUS UROZONUS
BT1 eupelmus
BT2 eupelmidae
BT3 hymenoptera

EUPEODES
uf *metasyrphus*
BT1 syrphidae
BT2 diptera
NT1 eupeodes corollae
rt syrphus

EUPEODES COROLLAE
uf *metasyrphus corollae*
uf *syrphus corollae*
BT1 eupeodes
BT2 syrphidae
BT3 diptera

EUPETERSIA
BT1 apidae
BT2 hymenoptera

EUPHORBIA
BT1 euphorbiaceae
NT1 euphorbia antisyphilitica
NT1 euphorbia balsamifera
NT1 euphorbia cap-saintemariensis
NT1 euphorbia caudicifolia
NT1 euphorbia coerulescens
NT1 euphorbia cyanthophora
NT1 euphorbia cyparissias
NT1 euphorbia dentata
NT1 euphorbia dracunculoides
NT1 euphorbia esula
NT1 euphorbia exigua

EUPHORBIA *cont.*
NT1 euphorbia fulgens
NT1 euphorbia geniculata
NT1 euphorbia glyptosperma
NT1 euphorbia helioscopia
NT1 euphorbia heterophylla
NT1 euphorbia hirta
NT1 euphorbia hypericifolia
NT1 euphorbia lathyris
NT1 euphorbia leucocephala
NT1 euphorbia maculata
NT1 euphorbia milii
NT1 euphorbia monostula
NT1 euphorbia myrsinites
NT1 euphorbia paralias
NT1 euphorbia peplus
NT1 euphorbia pilulifera
NT1 euphorbia poissonii
NT1 euphorbia prostrata
NT1 euphorbia prunifolia
NT1 euphorbia pulcherrima
NT1 euphorbia salicifolia
NT1 euphorbia seguieriana
NT1 euphorbia supina
NT1 euphorbia terracina
NT1 euphorbia thymifolia
NT1 euphorbia tinctoria
NT1 euphorbia tirucalli
NT1 euphorbia trigona
NT1 euphorbia wallichii
rt euphorbia mosaic geminivirus

EUPHORBIA ANTISYPHILITICA
BT1 euphorbia
BT2 euphorbiaceae

EUPHORBIA BALSAMIFERA
BT1 euphorbia
BT2 euphorbiaceae

EUPHORBIA CAP-SAINTEMARIENSIS
BT1 euphorbia
BT2 euphorbiaceae

EUPHORBIA CAUDICIFOLIA
BT1 euphorbia
BT2 euphorbiaceae

EUPHORBIA COERULESCENS
BT1 euphorbia
BT2 euphorbiaceae

EUPHORBIA CYANTHOPHORA
BT1 euphorbia
BT2 euphorbiaceae

EUPHORBIA CYPARISSIAS
BT1 euphorbia
BT2 euphorbiaceae

EUPHORBIA DENTATA
BT1 euphorbia
BT2 euphorbiaceae

EUPHORBIA DRACUNCULOIDES
BT1 euphorbia
BT2 euphorbiaceae

EUPHORBIA ESULA
BT1 euphorbia
BT2 euphorbiaceae
BT1 poisonous plants
BT1 weeds

EUPHORBIA EXIGUA
BT1 euphorbia
BT2 euphorbiaceae

EUPHORBIA FULGENS
BT1 euphorbia
BT2 euphorbiaceae
BT1 ornamental woody plants

EUPHORBIA GENICULATA
BT1 euphorbia
BT2 euphorbiaceae

EUPHORBIA GLYPTOSPERMA
BT1 euphorbia
BT2 euphorbiaceae

EUPHORBIA HELIOSCOPIA
BT1 euphorbia

EUPHORBIA HELIOSCOPIA *cont.*
BT2 euphorbiaceae

euphorbia hermentiana
USE **euphorbia trigona**

EUPHORBIA HETEROPHYLLA
BT1 euphorbia
BT2 euphorbiaceae
BT1 ornamental herbaceous plants
BT1 weeds

EUPHORBIA HIRTA
BT1 antiviral plants
BT1 euphorbia
BT2 euphorbiaceae
BT1 medicinal plants

EUPHORBIA HYPERICIFOLIA
BT1 euphorbia
BT2 euphorbiaceae

EUPHORBIA LATHYRIS
BT1 euphorbia
BT2 euphorbiaceae
BT1 industrial crops
BT1 pasture plants

EUPHORBIA LEUCOCEPHALA
BT1 euphorbia
BT2 euphorbiaceae
rt ornamental foliage plants

EUPHORBIA MACULATA
BT1 euphorbia
BT2 euphorbiaceae

EUPHORBIA MILII
uf *euphorbia splendens*
BT1 euphorbia
BT2 euphorbiaceae
BT1 medicinal plants
BT1 ornamental succulent plants
BT2 succulent plants

EUPHORBIA MONOSTULA
BT1 euphorbia
BT2 euphorbiaceae

EUPHORBIA MOSAIC GEMINIVIRUS
HN from 1990
BT1 geminivirus group
BT2 plant viruses
BT3 plant pathogens
BT4 pathogens
rt euphorbia

EUPHORBIA MYRSINITES
BT1 euphorbia
BT2 euphorbiaceae
BT1 ornamental succulent plants
BT2 succulent plants

EUPHORBIA PARALIAS
BT1 euphorbia
BT2 euphorbiaceae

EUPHORBIA PEPLUS
BT1 euphorbia
BT2 euphorbiaceae

EUPHORBIA PILULIFERA
BT1 euphorbia
BT2 euphorbiaceae
BT1 medicinal plants

EUPHORBIA POISSONII
BT1 euphorbia
BT2 euphorbiaceae

EUPHORBIA PROSTRATA
BT1 euphorbia
BT2 euphorbiaceae
BT1 medicinal plants

EUPHORBIA PRUNIFOLIA
BT1 euphorbia
BT2 euphorbiaceae

EUPHORBIA PULCHERRIMA
BT1 euphorbia
BT2 euphorbiaceae
rt poinsettias

EUPHORBIA SALICIFOLIA
BT1 euphorbia
BT2 euphorbiaceae

EUPHORBIA SEGUIERIANA
BT1 euphorbia
BT2 euphorbiaceae

euphorbia splendens
USE **euphorbia milii**

EUPHORBIA SUPINA
BT1 euphorbia
BT2 euphorbiaceae

EUPHORBIA TERRACINA
BT1 euphorbia
BT2 euphorbiaceae

EUPHORBIA THYMIFOLIA
BT1 euphorbia
BT2 euphorbiaceae

EUPHORBIA TINCTORIA
BT1 euphorbia
BT2 euphorbiaceae

EUPHORBIA TIRUCALLI
BT1 euphorbia
BT2 euphorbiaceae
BT1 molluscicidal plants
BT2 pesticidal plants
BT1 nematicidal plants
BT2 pesticidal plants
BT1 ornamental succulent plants
BT2 succulent plants

EUPHORBIA TRIGONA
uf *euphorbia hermentiana*
BT1 euphorbia
BT2 euphorbiaceae
BT1 ornamental succulent plants
BT2 succulent plants

EUPHORBIA WALLICHII
BT1 euphorbia
BT2 euphorbiaceae
BT1 medicinal plants

EUPHORBIACEAE
NT1 acalypha
NT2 acalypha australis
NT2 acalypha macrophylla
NT2 acalypha wilkesiana
NT1 aextoxicon
NT2 aextoxicon punctatum
NT1 alchornea
NT2 alchornea cordifolia
NT1 aleurites
NT2 aleurites fordii
NT2 aleurites moluccana
NT2 aleurites montana
NT1 antidesma
NT2 antidesma bunius
NT2 antidesma dallachryanum
NT2 antidesma frutescens
NT2 antidesma menasu
NT1 baccaurea
NT2 baccaurea motleyana
NT2 baccaurea sapida
NT1 baliospermum
NT2 baliospermum axillare
NT1 breynia
NT2 breynia disticha
NT1 bridelia
NT2 bridelia ferruginea
NT1 caperonia
NT2 caperonia castanaefolia
NT2 caperonia palustris
NT1 chrozophora
NT2 chrozophora rottleri
NT1 cleistanthus
NT2 cleistanthus collinus
NT1 cnidoscolus
NT2 cnidoscolus chayamansa
NT2 cnidoscolus elasticus
NT1 codiaeum
NT2 codiaeum variegatum
NT1 colliguaja
NT2 colliguaja odorifera
NT1 croton
NT2 croton bonplandianus
NT2 croton cajucara
NT2 croton californicus

EUPHORBIACEAE *cont.*
NT2 croton corylifolius
NT2 croton draconoides
NT2 croton flavens
NT2 croton lechleri
NT2 croton lobatus
NT2 croton macrostachys
NT2 croton megalocarpus
NT2 croton niveus
NT2 croton sonderianus
NT2 croton sparsiflorus
NT2 croton sublyratus
NT2 croton texensis
NT2 croton tiglium
NT2 croton zehntneri
NT1 crozophora
NT2 crozophora tinctoria
NT1 cunuria
NT2 cunuria spruceana
NT1 daphniphyllum
NT2 daphniphyllum teysmannii
NT1 dryandra
NT2 dryandra praemorsa
NT1 drypetes
NT2 drypetes roxburghii
NT1 elaeophorbia
NT1 emblica
NT1 eremocarpus
NT2 eremocarpus setigerus
NT1 euphorbia
NT2 euphorbia antisyphilitica
NT2 euphorbia balsamifera
NT2 euphorbia cap-saintemariensis
NT2 euphorbia caudicifolia
NT2 euphorbia coerulescens
NT2 euphorbia cyanthophora
NT2 euphorbia cyparissias
NT2 euphorbia dentata
NT2 euphorbia dracunculoides
NT2 euphorbia esula
NT2 euphorbia exigua
NT2 euphorbia fulgens
NT2 euphorbia geniculata
NT2 euphorbia glyptosperma
NT2 euphorbia helioscopia
NT2 euphorbia heterophylla
NT2 euphorbia hirta
NT2 euphorbia hypericifolia
NT2 euphorbia lathyris
NT2 euphorbia leucocephala
NT2 euphorbia maculata
NT2 euphorbia milii
NT2 euphorbia monostula
NT2 euphorbia myrsinites
NT2 euphorbia paralias
NT2 euphorbia peplus
NT2 euphorbia pilulifera
NT2 euphorbia poissonii
NT2 euphorbia prostrata
NT2 euphorbia prunifolia
NT2 euphorbia pulcherrima
NT2 euphorbia salicifolia
NT2 euphorbia seguieriana
NT2 euphorbia supina
NT2 euphorbia terracina
NT2 euphorbia thymifolia
NT2 euphorbia tinctoria
NT2 euphorbia tirucalli
NT2 euphorbia trigona
NT2 euphorbia wallichii
NT1 excoecaria
NT2 excoecaria cochinchinensis
NT1 hevea
NT2 hevea brasiliensis
NT2 hevea guianensis
NT1 hieronyma
NT2 hieronyma chocoensis
NT1 homalanthus
NT2 homalanthus populifolius
NT1 hura
NT2 hura crepitans
NT1 jatropha
NT2 jatropha costaricensis
NT2 jatropha curcas
NT2 jatropha glandulifera
NT2 jatropha gossypiifolia
NT2 jatropha heterophylla
NT2 jatropha heynii
NT2 jatropha macrorhiza
NT2 jatropha podagrica

EUPHORBIACEAE *cont.*
NT1 macaranga
NT2 macaranga peltata
NT1 mallotus (euphorbiaceae)
NT2 mallotus japonicus
NT2 mallotus philippensis
NT2 mallotus repandus
NT1 manihot
NT2 manihot esculenta
NT2 manihot glaziovii
NT1 mercurialis
NT2 mercurialis annua
NT2 mercurialis perennis
NT1 nealchornea
NT2 nealchornea yapurensis
NT1 phyllanthus
NT2 phyllanthus acidus
NT2 phyllanthus emblica
NT2 phyllanthus niruri
NT2 phyllanthus orbiculatus
NT2 phyllanthus reticulatus
NT2 phyllanthus simplex
NT2 phyllanthus urinaria
NT1 pycnocoma
NT2 pycnocoma cornuta
NT1 ricinodendron
NT2 ricinodendron heudelotii
NT2 ricinodendron rautanenii
NT1 ricinus
NT2 ricinus communis
NT1 sapium
NT2 sapium baccatum
NT2 sapium sebiferum
NT1 sauropus
NT2 sauropus albicans
NT1 securinega
NT2 securinega suffruticosa
NT1 synadenium
NT2 synadenium grantii

euphoria
USE **dimocarpus**

euphoria longana
USE **dimocarpus longan**

EUPHRACTUS
BT1 dasypodidae
BT2 edentata
BT3 mammals
NT1 euphractus sexcinctus

EUPHRACTUS SEXCINCTUS
uf *dasypus sexcinctus*
BT1 euphractus
BT2 dasypodidae
BT3 edentata
BT4 mammals

EUPHRASIA
BT1 scrophulariaceae
NT1 euphrasia condensata
NT1 euphrasia officinalis

EUPHRASIA CONDENSATA
BT1 euphrasia
BT2 scrophulariaceae

EUPHRASIA OFFICINALIS
BT1 euphrasia
BT2 scrophulariaceae

EUPHYLLURA
BT1 psyllidae
BT2 psylloidea
BT3 sternorrhyncha
BT4 homoptera
NT1 euphyllura olivina

EUPHYLLURA OLIVINA
BT1 euphyllura
BT2 psyllidae
BT3 psylloidea
BT4 sternorrhyncha
BT5 homoptera

EUPLECTRUS
HN from 1989
BT1 eulophidae
BT2 hymenoptera

EUPLOIDY
BT1 polyploidy
BT2 heteroploidy

EUPLOIDY *cont.*
BT2 ploidy

EUPODIDAE
BT1 prostigmata
BT2 acari
NT1 halotydeus
NT2 halotydeus destructor

EUPOECILIA
uf *clysia*
BT1 tortricidae
BT2 lepidoptera
NT1 eupoecilia ambiguella

EUPOECILIA AMBIGUELLA
uf *clysia ambiguella*
BT1 eupoecilia
BT2 tortricidae
BT3 lepidoptera

EUPOMATIA
BT1 eupomatiaceae
NT1 eupomatia laurina

EUPOMATIA LAURINA
BT1 eupomatia
BT2 eupomatiaceae

EUPOMATIACEAE
NT1 eupomatia
NT2 eupomatia laurina

EUPROCTIS
uf *porthesia*
BT1 lymantriidae
BT2 lepidoptera
NT1 euproctis chrysorrhoea
NT1 euproctis lunata
NT1 euproctis subnotata
NT1 euproctis taiwana
NT1 euproctis xanthorrhoea
rt sphrageidus

EUPROCTIS CHRYSORRHOEA
BT1 euproctis
BT2 lymantriidae
BT3 lepidoptera

EUPROCTIS LUNATA
BT1 euproctis
BT2 lymantriidae
BT3 lepidoptera

euproctis similis
USE **sphrageidus similis**

EUPROCTIS SUBNOTATA
BT1 euproctis
BT2 lymantriidae
BT3 lepidoptera

EUPROCTIS TAIWANA
uf *porthesia taiwana*
BT1 euproctis
BT2 lymantriidae
BT3 lepidoptera

EUPROCTIS XANTHORRHOEA
BT1 euproctis
BT2 lymantriidae
BT3 lepidoptera

eupteromalus
USE **trichomalopsis**

EUPTEROTEGAEUS
BT1 cepheidae
BT2 cryptostigmata
BT3 acari
NT1 eupterotegaeus rostratus

EUPTEROTEGAEUS ROSTRATUS
BT1 eupterotegaeus
BT2 cepheidae
BT3 cryptostigmata
BT4 acari

EUPTERYX
BT1 cicadellidae
BT2 cicadelloidea
BT3 auchenorrhyncha
BT4 homoptera
NT1 eupteryx atropunctata

EUPTERYX ATROPUNCTATA
BT1 eupteryx
BT2 cicadellidae
BT3 cicadelloidea
BT4 auchenorrhyncha
BT5 homoptera

EUROGLYPHUS
BT1 pyroglyphidae
BT2 astigmata
BT3 acari
NT1 euroglyphus maynei

EUROGLYPHUS MAYNEI
BT1 euroglyphus
BT2 pyroglyphidae
BT3 astigmata
BT4 acari

EUROPE
NT1 balkans
NT1 berlin
NT2 east berlin
NT2 west berlin
NT1 eastern europe
NT2 albania
NT2 bulgaria
NT2 czechoslovakia
NT2 german democratic republic
NT2 hungary
NT2 poland
NT2 romania
NT2 yugoslavia
NT1 scandinavia
NT2 denmark
NT3 bornholm
NT3 fyn
NT3 jutland
NT3 lolland falster
NT3 zealand
NT2 faroe islands
NT2 finland
NT2 iceland
NT2 norway
NT2 sweden
NT1 western europe
NT2 andorra
NT2 austria
NT3 burgenland
NT3 lower austria
NT3 salzburg
NT3 styria
NT3 tyrol
NT3 upper austria
NT3 vienna
NT3 vorarlberg
NT2 azores
NT2 belgium
NT3 antwerp
NT3 belgian luxembourg
NT3 brabant
NT3 east flanders
NT3 hainault
NT3 liege
NT3 limbourg
NT3 namur
NT3 west flanders
NT2 british isles
NT3 irish republic
NT4 connacht
NT4 leinster
NT4 munster
NT3 uk
NT4 channel islands
NT4 great britain
NT5 england
NT6 east midlands of england
NT6 eastern england
NT6 northern england
NT6 south east england
NT6 south west england
NT6 west midlands of england
NT6 yorkshire and lancashire
NT5 scotland
NT6 eastern scotland
NT6 northern scotland
NT6 scottish highlands and islands

EUROPE *cont.*
NT6 west scotland
NT5 wales
NT4 isle of man
NT4 northern ireland
NT2 canary islands
NT2 france
NT3 alsace
NT3 aquitaine
NT3 auvergne
NT3 brittany
NT3 burgundy
NT3 central france
NT3 champagne ardennes
NT3 corsica
NT3 dom
NT3 franche comte
NT3 ile de france
NT3 languedoc roussillon
NT3 limousin
NT3 lorraine
NT3 lower normandy
NT3 midi pyrenees
NT3 nord pas de calais
NT3 pays de la loire
NT3 picardy
NT3 poitou charentes
NT3 provence-alpes-cote d'azur
NT3 rhone alpes
NT3 upper normandy
NT2 german federal republic
NT3 baden-wurttemberg
NT3 bavaria
NT3 hesse
NT3 lower saxony
NT3 north rhine-westphalia
NT3 rhineland palatinate
NT3 saarland
NT3 schleswig-holstein
NT2 gibraltar
NT2 greece
NT2 italy
NT3 abruzzi
NT3 apulia
NT3 basilicata
NT3 calabria
NT3 campania
NT3 emilia romagna
NT3 friuli-venezia giulia
NT3 italian marches
NT3 latium
NT3 liguria
NT3 lombardy
NT3 molise
NT3 piedmont
NT3 sardinia
NT3 sicily
NT3 trentino-alto adige
NT3 tuscany
NT3 umbria
NT3 valle d'aosta
NT3 veneto
NT2 liechtenstein
NT2 luxembourg
NT2 madeira
NT2 malta
NT2 monaco
NT2 netherlands
NT3 drenthe
NT3 friesland
NT3 gelderland
NT3 groningen
NT3 noord-brabant
NT3 noord-holland
NT3 overijssel
NT3 utrecht
NT3 zeeland
NT3 zuid-holland
NT3 zuid-limbourg
NT2 portugal
NT2 san marino
NT2 spain
NT3 balearic islands
NT2 switzerland
NT2 vatican
rt mediterranean countries

EUROPEAN
BT1 buffalo breeds
BT2 breeds

european blastomycosis
USE **cryptococcosis**

EUROPEAN COMMUNITIES
uf *common market*
uf *ec*
uf *eec*
uf *european economic communities*
BT1 common markets
BT2 economic unions
BT1 international organizations
BT2 organizations
rt acp
rt belgium
rt benelux
rt cap
rt compensatory amounts
rt denmark
rt eaggf
rt ec regulations
rt european farm accounting network
rt european parliament
rt european regional development fund
rt european social fund
rt european units of account
rt france
rt german federal republic
rt greece
rt green money
rt intracommunity trade
rt irish republic
rt italy
rt lome convention
rt luxembourg
rt netherlands
rt portugal
rt single market
rt spain
rt stabex
rt treaty of rome
rt uk
rt western europe

european economic communities
USE **european communities**

EUROPEAN EELS
uf *anguilla anguilla*
uf *eel, european*
BT1 diadromous fishes
BT2 aquatic animals
BT3 animals
BT3 aquatic organisms
rt eels

EUROPEAN FARM ACCOUNTING NETWORK
uf *fadn*
uf *rica*
BT1 farm surveys
BT2 surveys
BT1 international organizations
BT2 organizations
rt agricultural censuses
rt european communities
rt farm accounts
rt farm income

EUROPEAN FOUL BROOD
BT1 foul brood
BT2 bee diseases
BT3 animal diseases
BT4 diseases
rt honeybee brood
rt melissococcus pluton

european free trade associations
USE **efta**

european hamster
USE **cricetus cricetus**

EUROPEAN PARLIAMENT
BT1 international organizations
BT2 organizations
rt european communities
rt parliament

EUROPEAN REGIONAL DEVELOPMENT FUND

EUROPEAN REGIONAL DEVELOPMENT FUND *cont.*
BT1 funds
BT1 international organizations
BT2 organizations
rt european communities
rt regional development

EUROPEAN SOCIAL FUND
BT1 funds
BT1 international organizations
BT2 organizations
rt european communities
rt social policy

EUROPEAN SOCIETY FOR RURAL SOCIOLOGY
BT1 international organizations
BT2 organizations
rt rural sociology

EUROPEAN UNITS OF ACCOUNT
uf *eua*
BT1 currencies
rt european communities
rt green money

EUROPIUM
BT1 rare earth elements
BT2 transition elements
BT3 metallic elements
BT4 elements
BT4 metals

EUROSTA
BT1 tephritidae
BT2 diptera
NT1 eurosta solidaginis

EUROSTA SOLIDAGINIS
BT1 eurosta
BT2 tephritidae
BT3 diptera

EUROTIA
BT1 chenopodiaceae
NT1 eurotia lanata
rt krascheninnikovia

EUROTIA LANATA
BT1 eurotia
BT2 chenopodiaceae

EUROTIALES
NT1 byssochlamys
NT2 byssochlamys fulva
NT2 byssochlamys nivea
NT1 eurotium
NT2 eurotium echinulatum
NT1 talaromyces
NT2 talaromyces dupontii
NT2 talaromyces flavus
rt fungi

EUROTIUM
BT1 eurotiales
NT1 eurotium echinulatum

EUROTIUM ECHINULATUM
BT1 eurotium
BT2 eurotiales

EURYA
BT1 theaceae

eurya japonica
USE **cleyera japonica**

EURYCOCCUS
BT1 pseudococcidae
BT2 coccoidea
BT3 sternorrhyncha
BT4 homoptera
rt maconellicoccus

EURYCOMA
BT1 simaroubaceae
NT1 eurycoma longifolia

EURYCOMA LONGIFOLIA
BT1 eurycoma
BT2 simaroubaceae

EURYGASTER
BT1 pentatomidae

EURYGASTER *cont.*
BT2 heteroptera
NT1 eurygaster austriaca
NT1 eurygaster integriceps
NT1 eurygaster maura

EURYGASTER AUSTRIACA
BT1 eurygaster
BT2 pentatomidae
BT3 heteroptera

EURYGASTER INTEGRICEPS
BT1 eurygaster
BT2 pentatomidae
BT3 heteroptera

EURYGASTER MAURA
BT1 eurygaster
BT2 pentatomidae
BT3 heteroptera

EURYGLOSSA
BT1 apidae
BT2 hymenoptera

eurymella
USE **megachile**

EURYTEMORA
BT1 calanoida
BT2 copepoda
BT3 crustacea
BT4 arthropods
NT1 eurytemora velox

EURYTEMORA VELOX
BT1 eurytemora
BT2 calanoida
BT3 copepoda
BT4 crustacea
BT5 arthropods

EURYTOMA
BT1 eurytomidae
BT2 hymenoptera
NT1 eurytoma martellii
rt bruchophagus

EURYTOMA MARTELLII
BT1 eurytoma
BT2 eurytomidae
BT3 hymenoptera

eurytoma roddi
USE **bruchophagus roddi**

EURYTOMIDAE
BT1 hymenoptera
NT1 bruchophagus
NT2 bruchophagus roddi
NT1 eurytoma
NT2 eurytoma martellii

EURYTREMA
BT1 dicrocoeliidae
BT2 digenea
BT3 trematoda
NT1 eurytrema coelomaticum
NT1 eurytrema pancreaticum

EURYTREMA COELOMATICUM
BT1 eurytrema
BT2 dicrocoeliidae
BT3 digenea
BT4 trematoda

EURYTREMA PANCREATICUM
BT1 eurytrema
BT2 dicrocoeliidae
BT3 digenea
BT4 trematoda

EUSCELIS
BT1 cicadellidae
BT2 cicadelloidea
BT3 auchenorrhyncha
BT4 homoptera
NT1 euscelis plebeja

EUSCELIS PLEBEJA
BT1 euscelis
BT2 cicadellidae
BT3 cicadelloidea
BT4 auchenorrhyncha
BT5 homoptera

EUSCHISTUS
BT1 pentatomidae
BT2 heteroptera
NT1 euschistus heros
NT1 euschistus servus

EUSCHISTUS HEROS
BT1 euschistus
BT2 pentatomidae
BT3 heteroptera

EUSCHISTUS SERVUS
BT1 euschistus
BT2 pentatomidae
BT3 heteroptera

EUSCHOENGASTIA
BT1 trombiculidae
BT2 prostigmata
BT3 acari

EUSCYRTUS
BT1 gryllidae
BT2 orthoptera
NT1 euscyrtus concinnus

EUSCYRTUS CONCINNUS
BT1 euscyrtus
BT2 gryllidae
BT3 orthoptera

EUSEIUS
BT1 phytoseiidae
BT2 mesostigmata
BT3 acari
NT1 euseius finlandicus
NT1 euseius gossipi
NT1 euseius hibisci
rt amblyseius
rt typhlodromus

EUSEIUS FINLANDICUS
uf *amblyseius finlandicus*
uf *typhlodromus finlandicus*
BT1 euseius
BT2 phytoseiidae
BT3 mesostigmata
BT4 acari

EUSEIUS GOSSIPI
uf *amblyseius gossipi*
uf *typhlodromus gossipi*
BT1 euseius
BT2 phytoseiidae
BT3 mesostigmata
BT4 acari

EUSEIUS HIBISCI
uf *amblyseius hibisci*
BT1 euseius
BT2 phytoseiidae
BT3 mesostigmata
BT4 acari

EUSIDEROXYLON
BT1 lauraceae
NT1 eusideroxylon zwageri

EUSIDEROXYLON ZWAGERI
BT1 eusideroxylon
BT2 lauraceae
BT1 forest trees

eusimulium
USE **simulium**

eusimulium aureum
USE **simulium aureum**

eusimulium costatum
USE **simulium costatum**

eusimulium latipes
USE **simulium latipes**

eusimulium latizonum
USE **simulium latizonum**

eusimulium pusillum
USE **simulium pusillum**

EUSPONGIA
BT1 parazoa

EUSTACHYS
BT1 gramineae

EUSTACHYS *cont.*
rt pasture plants

EUSTOMA
BT1 gentianaceae
NT1 eustoma grandiflorum

EUSTOMA GRANDIFLORUM
uf *eustoma russelianum*
BT1 eustoma
BT2 gentianaceae

eustoma russelianum
USE **eustoma grandiflorum**

EUSTRONGYLIDES
BT1 dioctophymatidae
BT2 nematoda

eutamias
USE **tamias**

eutamias sibiricus
USE **tamias sibiricus**

EUTERPE
BT1 palmae
NT1 euterpe edulis
NT1 euterpe oleracea

EUTERPE EDULIS
BT1 euterpe
BT2 palmae

EUTERPE OLERACEA
BT1 euterpe
BT2 palmae

EUTETRANYCHUS
BT1 tetranychidae
BT2 prostigmata
BT3 acari
NT1 eutetranychus banksi
NT1 eutetranychus orientalis

EUTETRANYCHUS BANKSI
BT1 eutetranychus
BT2 tetranychidae
BT3 prostigmata
BT4 acari

EUTETRANYCHUS ORIENTALIS
BT1 eutetranychus
BT2 tetranychidae
BT3 prostigmata
BT4 acari

EUTETTIX
BT1 cicadellidae
BT2 cicadelloidea
BT3 auchenorrhyncha
BT4 homoptera
rt hishimonus

eutettix phycitis
USE **hishimonus phycitis**

EUTHANASIA
uf *mercy killing*
BT1 death
BT1 destruction of animals
BT2 destruction
rt pain

EUTHYNNUS
BT1 scombridae
BT2 perciformes
BT3 osteichthyes
BT4 fishes
rt tuna

EUTREMA
uf *wasabia*
BT1 cruciferae
NT1 eutrema wasabi

EUTREMA WASABI
BT1 eutrema
BT2 cruciferae

EUTRICHOSIPHUM
BT1 aphididae
BT2 aphidoidea
BT3 sternorrhyncha
BT4 homoptera

EUTROMBICULA
BT1 trombiculidae
BT2 prostigmata
BT3 acari
NT1 eutrombicula alfreddugesi
NT1 eutrombicula splendens

EUTROMBICULA ALFREDDUGESI
HN from 1989
BT1 eutrombicula
BT2 trombiculidae
BT3 prostigmata
BT4 acari

EUTROMBICULA SPLENDENS
HN from 1990
BT1 eutrombicula
BT2 trombiculidae
BT3 prostigmata
BT4 acari

eutromula
USE **choreutis**

eutromula pariana
USE **choreutis pariana**

EUTROPHICATION
rt nutrients

EUTYPA
BT1 diatrypales
NT1 eutypa armeniacae
NT1 eutypa japonica
NT1 eutypa vexans

EUTYPA ARMENIACAE
BT1 eutypa
BT2 diatrypales

EUTYPA JAPONICA
BT1 eutypa
BT2 diatrypales

EUTYPA VEXANS
BT1 eutypa
BT2 diatrypales

EUTYPELLA
BT1 diatrypales
NT1 eutypella parasitica

EUTYPELLA PARASITICA
BT1 eutypella
BT2 diatrypales

EUWALLACEA
HN from 1989
BT1 scolytidae
BT2 coleoptera
NT1 euwallacea fornicatus
rt xyleborus

EUWALLACEA FORNICATUS
HN from 1989; previously "xyleborus fornicatus"
uf *xyleborus fornicatus*
BT1 euwallacea
BT2 scolytidae
BT3 coleoptera

euxanthis
USE **agapeta**

EUXESTA
BT1 otitidae
BT2 diptera
NT1 euxesta notata

EUXESTA NOTATA
BT1 euxesta
BT2 otitidae
BT3 diptera

EUXOA
uf *chorizagrotis*
BT1 noctuidae
BT2 lepidoptera
NT1 euxoa auxiliaris
NT1 euxoa detersa
NT1 euxoa messoria
NT1 euxoa ochrogaster
rt agrotis

EUXOA AUXILIARIS
uf *chorizagrotis auxiliaris*

EUXOA AUXILIARIS *cont.*
BT1 euxoa
BT2 noctuidae
BT3 lepidoptera

EUXOA DETERSA
BT1 euxoa
BT2 noctuidae
BT3 lepidoptera

EUXOA MESSORIA
BT1 euxoa
BT2 noctuidae
BT3 lepidoptera

EUXOA OCHROGASTER
BT1 euxoa
BT2 noctuidae
BT3 lepidoptera

euxoa segetum
USE **agrotis segetum**

euxoa spinifera
USE **agrotis biconica**

EUZOPHERA
BT1 pyralidae
BT2 lepidoptera

EVALUATION
NT1 economic evaluation
NT2 economic viability
NT1 feasibility studies
NT1 feed evaluation
NT2 feed composition tables
NT1 land evaluation
NT1 nutritional assessment (agricola)
NT1 program evaluation (agricola)
NT1 project appraisal
NT2 plan implementation and evaluation
NT2 rapid rural appraisal
NT1 sensory evaluation
NT2 organolepsis
NT1 subjective evaluation
rt performance appraisals (agricola)
rt performance indexes
rt quality
rt selection
rt testing

EVANIA
BT1 evaniidae
BT2 hymenoptera
NT1 evania appendigaster

EVANIA APPENDIGASTER
BT1 evania
BT2 evaniidae
BT3 hymenoptera

EVANIIDAE
BT1 hymenoptera
NT1 evania
NT2 evania appendigaster
NT1 prosevania

EVAPORATED MILK
uf *milk, evaporated*
BT1 milk products
BT2 products
rt condensed milk

EVAPORATION
uf *soil water evaporation*
BT1 change of state
NT1 vacuum evaporation
rt condensates
rt crystallization
rt distilling
rt drying
rt evaporation suppressants
rt evaporative coolers
rt evaporimeters
rt evapotranspiration
rt interception
rt meteorology

EVAPORATION SUPPRESSANTS
BT1 soil amendments

EVAPORATION SUPPRESSANTS *cont.*
BT2 amendments
NT1 atrazine
rt antitranspirants
rt evaporation
rt mulches
rt mulching
rt suppression

EVAPORATIVE COOLERS
uf *coolers, evaporative*
BT1 coolers
rt evaporation

EVAPORATIVE COOLING
BT1 cooling
rt latent heat

evaporative demand
USE **water balance**

EVAPORATORS
BT1 equipment
rt sterilizers

EVAPORIMETERS
BT1 equipment
BT1 instruments
rt evaporation
rt wind

EVAPOTRANSPIRATION
rt evaporation
rt hydrological factors
rt interception
rt meteorology
rt plant water relations
rt soil water balance
rt transpiration

events
USE **tourist attractions**

EVERBEARING HABIT
BT1 habit

EVERGESTIS
BT1 pyralidae
BT2 lepidoptera
NT1 evergestis forficalis

EVERGESTIS FORFICALIS
BT1 evergestis
BT2 pyralidae
BT3 lepidoptera

evetria
USE **petrova**
OR **rhyacionia**

evetria buoliana
USE **rhyacionia buoliana**

evetria cristata
USE **petrova cristata**

evetria resinella
USE **petrova resinella**

EVICTION
BT1 animal behaviour
BT2 behaviour
rt drone honeybees
rt honeybee colonies

EVISCERATION
BT1 processing
rt slaughter

evodia
USE **euodia**

EVOLUTION
uf *history and evolution*
NT1 evolutionarily stable strategy
NT1 founder effect
NT1 natural selection
NT1 phylogeny
NT1 speciation
rt adaptation
rt centres of diversity
rt centres of origin
rt development
rt domestication

EVOLUTION *cont.*
rt gene flow
rt lamarckism
rt palaeontology

EVOLUTIONARILY STABLE STRATEGY
HN from 1990
BT1 evolution

EVOLVULUS
BT1 convolvulaceae
NT1 evolvulus alsinoides

EVOLVULUS ALSINOIDES
BT1 evolvulus
BT2 convolvulaceae

evylaeus
USE **lasioglossum**

ewe colostrum
USE **colostrum**
AND **ewes**

EWE FEEDING
BT1 sheep feeding
BT2 ruminant feeding
BT3 livestock feeding
BT4 animal feeding
BT5 feeding
rt ewes

EWE LACTATION
uf *lactation, ewe*
BT1 lactation
rt ewes

EWE MILK
uf *milk, ewe*
uf *milk, sheep*
uf *sheep milk*
BT1 milks
BT2 body fluids
BT3 fluids
rt ewes

EWES
ufa *colostrum, ewe*
ufa *ewe colostrum*
BT1 female animals
BT2 animals
rt dams (mothers)
rt ewe feeding
rt ewe lactation
rt ewe milk
rt rams
rt sheep

EX-FERM PROCESS
HN from 1990
BT1 fermentation

EXACUM
BT1 gentianaceae
NT1 exacum affine

EXACUM AFFINE
BT1 exacum
BT2 gentianaceae
BT1 ornamental herbaceous plants

EXAERETE
BT1 apidae
BT2 hymenoptera

EXANTHEMA
BT1 skin diseases
BT2 organic diseases
BT3 diseases
rt vesicular exanthema virus

EXCAVATORS
BT1 earth moving equipment
BT2 equipment
rt ditch cleaners
rt dredgers
rt power shovels

EXCEPTIONAL CHILDREN (AGRICOLA)
BT1 children
BT2 people
rt gifted persons (agricola)

EXCHANGE ACIDITY
BT1 ion exchange
BT1 soil acidity
BT2 acidity
BT3 chemical properties
BT4 properties
BT2 soil chemistry

EXCHANGE LISTS (AGRICOLA)
rt food composition
rt nutritive value

exchange rates
USE **foreign exchange**
OR **monetary parity**

exchange, seed
USE **seed exchange**

EXCHANGEABLE CATIONS
BT1 cations
BT2 ions
NT1 exchangeable sodium
rt ion exchange

EXCHANGEABLE SODIUM
uf *sodium, exchangeable*
BT1 exchangeable cations
BT2 cations
BT3 ions
rt gypsum requirement
rt sodium

EXCISION
BT1 surgical operations

exclusive economic zones
USE **economic regions**

EXCOECARIA
BT1 euphorbiaceae
NT1 excoecaria cochinchinensis

excoecaria bicolor
USE **excoecaria cochinchinensis**

EXCOECARIA COCHINCHINENSIS
uf *excoecaria bicolor*
BT1 excoecaria
BT2 euphorbiaceae

EXCRETA
BT1 animal wastes
BT2 wastes
NT1 faeces
NT2 buffalo dung
NT2 cat faeces
NT2 cattle dung
NT2 dog faeces
NT2 horse dung
NT2 human faeces
NT2 poultry droppings
NT2 rabbit droppings
NT2 sheep dung
NT1 urine
rt defaecation
rt excretion
rt manures

EXCRETION
uf *elimination*
BT1 physiological functions
NT1 defaecation
NT1 drug excretion
NT1 urination
NT1 water excretion
NT2 plasmolysis
rt efflux
rt excreta
rt exudation
rt malpighian tubules
rt renal clearance

EXCRETORY SYSTEM
BT1 body parts
NT1 malpighian tubules

excursions
USE **visits**

EXD
BT1 thiocarbonate herbicides
BT2 herbicides
BT3 pesticides

EXELASTIS
BT1 pterophoridae
BT2 lepidoptera
NT1 exelastis atomosa

EXELASTIS ATOMOSA
BT1 exelastis
BT2 pterophoridae
BT3 lepidoptera

EXERCISE
BT1 physical activity
rt athletics
rt fatigue
rt gait
rt sweat
rt sweating

EXERISTES
BT1 ichneumonidae
BT2 hymenoptera
NT1 exeristes comstockii
NT1 exeristes roborator
rt ephialtes
rt pimpla

EXERISTES COMSTOCKII
uf *ephialtes comstockii*
BT1 exeristes
BT2 ichneumonidae
BT3 hymenoptera

EXERISTES ROBORATOR
uf *ephialtes roborator*
uf *pimpla roborator*
BT1 exeristes
BT2 ichneumonidae
BT3 hymenoptera

exhaust
USE **exhaust gases**
OR **exhaust systems**

EXHAUST GASES
uf *exhaust*
BT1 air pollutants
BT2 pollutants
BT1 gases
rt carbon monoxide
rt exhaust systems
rt silencers
rt smoke
rt toxic gases
rt waste gases

EXHAUST SYSTEMS
uf *exhaust*
BT1 engines
BT2 machinery
NT1 silencers
rt exhaust gases

EXHAUSTION
NT1 depletion
NT2 protein depletion
NT1 heat exhaustion
NT1 soil exhaustion
rt fatigue
rt losses

EXHIBITIONS
BT1 entertainment
BT2 leisure activities
NT1 cultural exhibitions
NT1 museums
NT2 open air museums
rt shows
rt trade fairs

EXITIANUS
BT1 cicadellidae
BT2 cicadelloidea
BT3 auchenorrhyncha
BT4 homoptera
NT1 exitianus exitiosus

EXITIANUS EXITIOSUS
BT1 exitianus
BT2 cicadellidae
BT3 cicadelloidea
BT4 auchenorrhyncha
BT5 homoptera

EXMOOR HORN
BT1 sheep breeds
BT2 breeds

EXOANTIGEN TESTS
BT1 immunological techniques
BT2 techniques
rt exoantigens

EXOANTIGENS
BT1 antigens
BT2 immunological factors
rt exoantigen tests

EXOBASIDIALES
NT1 exobasidium
NT2 exobasidium japonicum
NT2 exobasidium vexans
rt fungi

EXOBASIDIUM
BT1 exobasidiales
NT1 exobasidium japonicum
NT1 exobasidium vexans

EXOBASIDIUM JAPONICUM
BT1 exobasidium
BT2 exobasidiales

EXOBASIDIUM VEXANS
BT1 exobasidium
BT2 exobasidiales

EXOCHOMUS
BT1 coccinellidae
BT2 coleoptera
NT1 exochomus flavipes
NT1 exochomus quadripustulatus

EXOCHOMUS FLAVIPES
BT1 exochomus
BT2 coccinellidae
BT3 coleoptera

EXOCHOMUS QUADRIPUSTULATUS
BT1 exochomus
BT2 coccinellidae
BT3 coleoptera

EXOCHORDA
BT1 rosaceae
NT1 exochorda giraldii
NT1 exochorda korolkowii
NT1 exochorda racemosa

exochorda albertii
USE **exochorda korolkowii**

EXOCHORDA GIRALDII
BT1 exochorda
BT2 rosaceae
BT1 ornamental woody plants

EXOCHORDA KOROLKOWII
uf *exochorda albertii*
BT1 exochorda
BT2 rosaceae
BT1 ornamental woody plants

EXOCHORDA RACEMOSA
BT1 exochorda
BT2 rosaceae
BT1 ornamental woody plants

EXOCOETIDAE
uf *flying fishes*
BT1 cyprinodontiformes
BT2 osteichthyes
BT3 fishes
NT1 cypselurus
NT1 exocoetus
NT1 prognichthys

EXOCOETUS
BT1 exocoetidae
BT2 cyprinodontiformes
BT3 osteichthyes
BT4 fishes

EXOGONIUM
BT1 convolvulaceae
NT1 exogonium purga

EXOGONIUM PURGA
uf *ipomoea purga*

EXOGONIUM PURGA *cont.*
BT1 exogonium
BT2 convolvulaceae

EXOMALOPSIS
uf *lanthanomelissa*
BT1 apidae
BT2 hymenoptera

EXONEURA
uf *exoneurella*
BT1 apidae
BT2 hymenoptera

exoneurella
USE **exoneura**

EXONS
HN from 1990
rt dna
rt introns
rt transcription

exopeptidases
USE **peptidases**

EXOPHIALA
BT1 deuteromycotina
rt phaeoannellomyces
rt wangiella

exophiala dermatitidis
USE **wangiella dermatitidis**

exophiala werneckii
USE **phaeoannellomyces werneckii**

EXOPHTHALMOS
BT1 eye diseases
BT2 organic diseases
BT3 diseases

EXORISTA
uf *thrycolyga*
BT1 tachinidae
BT2 diptera
NT1 exorista fallax
NT1 exorista fasciata
NT1 exorista larvarum
NT1 exorista rossica
NT1 exorista segregata
rt tachina

EXORISTA FALLAX
BT1 exorista
BT2 tachinidae
BT3 diptera

EXORISTA FASCIATA
BT1 exorista
BT2 tachinidae
BT3 diptera

EXORISTA LARVARUM
uf *tachina larvarum*
BT1 exorista
BT2 tachinidae
BT3 diptera

EXORISTA ROSSICA
BT1 exorista
BT2 tachinidae
BT3 diptera

EXORISTA SEGREGATA
BT1 exorista
BT2 tachinidae
BT3 diptera

EXOSKELETON
BT1 skeleton
BT2 musculoskeletal system
BT3 body parts
rt sclerotization

EXOSTOSES
BT1 bone diseases
BT2 organic diseases
BT3 diseases

EXOTELEIA
BT1 gelechiidae
BT2 lepidoptera

EXOTICS
BT1 imported breeds
BT2 breeds
rt choice of species

EXOTOXINS
BT1 toxins

EXPANDED METAL
BT1 building materials
BT2 materials
BT1 grids

EXPANSION
uf *expansion and contraction*
rt spread
rt swelling
rt thermal expansion

expansion and contraction
USE **contraction**
OR **expansion**

EXPECTORANTS
BT1 antitussive agents
BT2 respiratory system agents
BT3 drugs
NT1 ammonium bicarbonate
NT1 ammonium chloride
NT1 creosote
NT1 eucalyptol
NT1 guaiacol
NT1 guaifenesin
NT1 potassium iodide
NT1 turpentine

EXPENDITURE
uf *charges (costs)*
NT1 consumer expenditure
NT2 household expenditure
NT2 tourist expenditure
NT3 souvenirs
NT1 national expenditure
NT1 public expenditure
rt cash flow
rt consumption
rt fees

expenditure, consumer
USE **consumer expenditure**

expenditure, household
USE **household expenditure**

expenditure, national
USE **national expenditure**

expenditure, public
USE **public expenditure**

expenditure, tourist
USE **tourist expenditure**

EXPERIMENTAL ATHEROSCLEROSIS
uf *atherosclerosis, experimental*
uf *cholesterol atherosclerosis*
BT1 atherosclerosis
BT2 vascular diseases
BT3 cardiovascular diseases
BT4 organic diseases
BT5 diseases

EXPERIMENTAL DESIGN
uf *design, experimental*
uf *plot design*
rt border effects
rt design
rt experimental plots
rt experiments
rt field experimentation
rt layout
rt missing hills
rt statistical analysis
rt trials

EXPERIMENTAL DIABETES
uf *diabetes, experimental*
BT1 diabetes
BT2 metabolic disorders
BT3 animal disorders
BT4 disorders

EXPERIMENTAL DIETS (AGRICOLA)
BT1 diets

EXPERIMENTAL EQUIPMENT
BT1 equipment
NT1 experimental rigs
NT1 plot sprayers
NT2 small plot sprayers
NT1 rain shelters
NT1 rainfall simulators
NT1 shear boxes
NT1 soil bins
NT1 test rigs
NT2 wind tunnels
rt experiments
rt instrumentation
rt plot drills
rt research
rt test tracks

EXPERIMENTAL INFECTION
BT1 infection
BT2 disease transmission
BT3 transmission
rt animal experiments

EXPERIMENTAL INFECTIONS
BT1 infections

EXPERIMENTAL PLOTS
uf *plots, experimental*
uf *trial plots*
BT1 field experimentation
BT2 trials
BT3 research
rt border effects
rt experimental design
rt plastic barriers
rt plot drills
rt plot harvesters
rt plot size
rt plot sprayers
rt sample plot technique
rt subsurface barriers

EXPERIMENTAL RICKETS
uf *rickets, experimental*
BT1 rickets
BT2 mineral metabolism disorders
BT3 metabolic disorders
BT4 animal disorders
BT5 disorders

EXPERIMENTAL RIGS
BT1 experimental equipment
BT2 equipment
rt experiments
rt laboratory tests
rt soil bins
rt test rigs

EXPERIMENTAL STATIONS
BT1 research institutes
BT2 organizations
rt experiments

EXPERIMENTAL SURGERY
BT1 surgery
BT2 medicine

EXPERIMENTS
NT1 animal experiments
NT1 grazing experiments
NT2 grazing trials
NT1 long term experiments
NT1 pot experimentation
rt controls (experimental)
rt experimental design
rt experimental equipment
rt experimental rigs
rt experimental stations
rt field experimentation
rt in vitro
rt research
rt trials

experiments, long term
USE **long term experiments**

EXPERT SYSTEMS
BT1 computer software
BT2 computers

EXPERTS
rt specialization

EXPLANATUM
BT1 paramphistomatidae
BT2 digenea
BT3 trematoda

EXPLANTS
rt micropropagation
rt tissue culture
rt vegetative propagation

EXPLOITABLE AGE OR SIZE
BT1 forest policy
rt age
rt size

EXPLORATION
rt surveys

EXPLOSIONS
rt explosive hazard
rt explosives
rt ignition

EXPLOSIVE HAZARD
BT1 hazards
rt explosions
rt safety

EXPLOSIVES
rt explosions
rt potassium nitrate

EXPORT CONTROLS
BT1 controls
BT1 trade barriers
BT2 trade protection
BT3 trade policy
BT4 economic policy
rt exports

EXPORT CREDITS
uf *credits, export*
BT1 credit
BT2 finance
BT1 credit insurance
BT2 insurance
BT1 export promotion
BT2 trade policy
BT3 economic policy
rt exports

EXPORT DIVERSIFICATION
BT1 diversification
BT2 socioeconomic organization
BT1 exports
BT2 international trade
BT3 trade
rt trade policy

EXPORT PROMOTION
BT1 trade policy
BT2 economic policy
NT1 export credits
NT1 export refunds
NT1 export subsidies
rt exports

EXPORT REFUNDS
BT1 export promotion
BT2 trade policy
BT3 economic policy
rt export subsidies
rt exports

EXPORT SUBSIDIES
uf *subsidies, export*
BT1 export promotion
BT2 trade policy
BT3 economic policy
BT1 subsidies
BT2 support measures
rt dumping
rt export refunds
rt exports

EXPORTS
BT1 international trade
BT2 trade
NT1 export diversification
rt export controls
rt export credits
rt export promotion

EXPORTS *cont.*
rt export refunds
rt export subsidies
rt imports

EXPOSURE

EXPRESSIVITY
BT1 phenotypes
rt genes

expropriation of forests and land
USE **compulsory purchase**

EXSEROHILUM
HN from 1990
BT1 deuteromycotina
rt setosphaeria

exserohilum holmii
USE **setosphaeria holmii**

exserohilum turcicum
USE **setosphaeria turcica**

EXTENDED FAMILIES
uf families, extended
BT1 families
rt family size
rt family structure
rt tribes

EXTENSION
uf advisory services
uf extension activities
NT1 animation
NT2 rural animation
NT1 cooperative extension service
NT1 leisure counselling
rt advisory centres
rt advisory officers
rt agricultural shows
rt audiovisual aids
rt communication
rt community development
rt demonstration forests
rt education
rt extension education (agricola)
rt open days
rt pilot farms
rt public relations
rt publicity
rt services
rt teaching methods
rt training officers

extension activities
USE **extension**

EXTENSION AGENTS (AGRICOLA)
BT1 change agents (agricola)
rt extension education (agricola)

EXTENSION EDUCATION (AGRICOLA)
BT1 education
rt adult education
rt extension
rt extension agents (agricola)

EXTENSION FACTORS
rt genes
rt spread

EXTENSIVE FARMING
BT1 extensive production
BT2 agricultural production
BT3 production
BT1 farming
NT1 extensive husbandry
NT1 extensive livestock farming
NT2 ranching

EXTENSIVE HUSBANDRY
BT1 extensive farming
BT2 extensive production
BT3 agricultural production
BT4 production
BT2 farming
BT1 husbandry
rt animal husbandry

EXTENSIVE LIVESTOCK FARMING
uf livestock farming, extensive
BT1 extensive farming
BT2 extensive production
BT3 agricultural production
BT4 production
BT2 farming
BT1 livestock farming
BT2 farming
NT1 ranching
rt transhumance

EXTENSIVE PRODUCTION
uf production, extensive
BT1 agricultural production
BT2 production
NT1 extensive farming
NT2 extensive husbandry
NT2 extensive livestock farming
NT3 ranching

EXTERNAL DEBT
BT1 debt
rt balance of payments

EXTERNAL ELECTRIC POTENTIAL
BT1 electric potential
BT2 electricity
BT3 energy sources

EXTERNALITIES
BT1 non-market benefits
BT2 cost benefit analysis
BT3 economic analysis
rt cost benefit analysis
rt social benefits

EXTIRPATION
BT1 surgical operations

EXTRACELLULAR FLUIDS
BT1 body fluids
BT2 fluids

EXTRACELLULAR SPACES

EXTRACORPOREAL CIRCULATION
BT1 circulation
rt blood circulation
rt haemodialysis

EXTRACTANTS
HN from 1989
rt extraction
rt extracts

EXTRACTED HONEY
BT1 extracted products
BT2 products
BT1 honey
BT2 hive products
BT3 animal products
BT4 products
rt creamed honey
rt granulated honey
rt strained honey

EXTRACTED PRODUCTS
BT1 products
NT1 extracted honey
NT1 yeast extracts
rt extraction
rt extracts
rt meat extracts
rt spleen extract

EXTRACTION
BT1 processing
NT1 juice extraction
NT1 protein extraction
NT1 resin extraction
rt analytical methods
rt biological techniques
rt diffusion
rt electrodiffusion
rt extractants
rt extracted products
rt extracts
rt isolation
rt meat extracts
rt milling
rt plant extracts
rt pressing
rt separation

EXTRACTION *cont.*
rt tissue extracts

EXTRACTIVES
BT1 plant products
BT2 products

EXTRACTORS
BT1 equipment
NT1 diffusers
NT1 dust extractors
NT1 solar beeswax extractors

EXTRACTS
NT1 ether extracts
NT1 liver extracts
NT1 meat extracts
NT1 parathyroid extract
NT1 plant extracts
NT2 lucerne juice
NT2 neem extracts
NT3 neem seed extract
NT2 opium
NT2 pyrethrins
NT2 sweet potato extract
NT2 vegetable extracts
NT3 vegetable juices
NT4 carrot juice
NT4 tomato juice
NT2 wood extracts
NT3 wood hemicellulose extract
NT3 wood molasses
NT2 wort
NT2 yeast extracts
NT1 spleen extract
NT1 tissue extracts
NT2 thyroid extract
rt extractants
rt extracted products
rt extraction
rt saturation extract

extracts, plant
USE **plant extracts**

EXTRASEASONAL OCCURRENCE
HN from 1989
BT1 occurrence

extraterrestrial soil types
USE **soil types (extraterrestrial)**

EXTRAUTERINE PREGNANCY
BT1 pregnancy complications
BT2 reproductive disorders
BT3 functional disorders
BT4 animal disorders
BT5 disorders

EXTRUDED FOODS (AGRICOLA)
BT1 foods

EXTRUSION
BT1 processing
rt moulding
rt plastics

EXUDATES
NT1 root exudates
NT1 toxic exudates
rt discharges
rt exudation
rt plant products
rt resins
rt secretions

EXUDATION
NT1 ascites
NT1 guttation
rt efflux
rt excretion
rt exudates
rt exudative diathesis
rt oedema

EXUDATIVE DIATHESIS
uf diathesis, exudative
BT1 diatheses
rt exudation

EXUDATIVE MEAT
uf exudative meat, pale soft

EXUDATIVE MEAT *cont.*
uf pale soft exudative meat
rt meat quality
rt pigmeat
rt porcine stress syndrome

exudative meat, pale soft
USE **exudative meat**

eye cornea
USE **cornea**

EYE DISEASES
uf eye disorders
BT1 organic diseases
BT2 diseases
NT1 cataract
NT1 conjunctivitis
NT1 exophthalmos
NT1 eyelid diseases
NT2 entropion
NT1 glaucoma
NT1 keratitis
NT2 mycotic keratitis
NT1 keratoconjunctivitis
NT1 keratomalacia
NT1 oculomycosis
NT1 ophthalmia
NT1 retinal atrophy
NT1 retinitis
NT1 retinitis pigmentosa
NT1 retinopathy
NT1 strabismus
NT1 vision disorders
NT2 blindness
NT2 night blindness
NT1 xerophthalmia
rt eyes
rt hyperkeratosis

eye disorders
USE **eye diseases**

EYE LENS
uf lens, eye
BT1 eyes
BT2 sense organs
BT3 body parts
rt contact lenses
rt crystallins

eye muscle
USE **longissimus dorsi**

EYELID DISEASES
BT1 eye diseases
BT2 organic diseases
BT3 diseases
NT1 entropion
rt eyelids

EYELIDS
BT1 face
BT2 head
BT3 body regions
rt eyelid diseases

EYES
BT1 sense organs
BT2 body parts
NT1 compound eyes
NT1 conjunctiva
NT1 cornea
NT1 eye lens
NT1 retina
rt enucleation
rt eye diseases
rt face
rt ophthalmoscopy
rt tears
rt vision

EYPREPOCNEMIS
BT1 acrididae
BT2 orthoptera
NT1 eyprepocnemis plorans

EYPREPOCNEMIS PLORANS
BT1 eyprepocnemis
BT2 acrididae
BT3 orthoptera

EYSENHARDTIA
BT1 leguminosae

EYSENHARDTIA *cont.*
NT1 eysenhardtia texana

EYSENHARDTIA TEXANA
BT1 eysenhardtia
BT2 leguminosae

f-2 toxin
USE **zearalenone**

FABA BEANS
uf *beans, broad*
uf *beans, horse*
uf *broad beans*
uf *field bean (vicia)*
uf *horse beans*
rt broad bean mottle bromovirus
rt broad bean stain comovirus
rt broad bean true mosaic comovirus
rt broad bean wilt fabavirus
rt vicia faba

fabaceae
USE **leguminosae**

FABAVIRUS GROUP
HN from 1990
BT1 plant viruses
BT2 plant pathogens
BT3 pathogens
NT1 broad bean wilt fabavirus
NT1 lamium mild mosaic fabavirus

FABESPORA
BT1 myxozoa
BT2 protozoa

FABIANA
BT1 compositae
NT1 fabiana imbricata

FABIANA IMBRICATA
BT1 fabiana
BT2 compositae

FABRAEA
HN from 1990
BT1 helotiales
rt diplocarpon

fabraea maculata
USE **diplocarpon mespili**

FABRIANESE
HN from 1990
BT1 sheep breeds
BT2 breeds

FABRIC
(not to be used for fabrics (cloth))
uf *soil fabric*
rt soil micromorphological features
rt structure
rt texture

FABRIC CONSTRUCTION (AGRICOLA)
rt fabrics

FABRICS
NT1 batiste (agricola)
NT1 bedspreads (agricola)
NT1 bonded fabrics (agricola)
NT1 boucle (agricola)
NT1 broadcloth (agricola)
NT1 brocade (agricola)
NT1 carded fabrics (agricola)
NT1 challis (agricola)
NT1 chambray (agricola)
NT1 chenille (agricola)
NT1 chiffon (agricola)
NT1 chintz (agricola)
NT1 corduroy (agricola)
NT1 covert (agricola)
NT1 crepe (agricola)
NT1 damask (agricola)
NT1 decorative fabrics (agricola)
NT1 denim (agricola)
NT1 duck (agricola)
NT1 embossed fabrics (agricola)
NT1 faille (agricola)
NT1 felt (agricola)
NT1 flannel (agricola)
NT1 georgette (agricola)
NT1 gingham (agricola)
NT1 impregnated fabrics
NT1 lace (agricola)

FABRICS *cont.*
NT1 lawn (agricola)
NT1 linen (agricola)
NT1 madras (fabric) (agricola)
NT1 marquisette (agricola)
NT1 muslin (agricola)
NT1 organdy (agricola)
NT1 percale (agricola)
NT1 plisse (agricola)
NT1 poplin (agricola)
NT1 sailcloth (agricola)
NT1 sateen (agricola)
NT1 seersucker (agricola)
NT1 serge (agricola)
NT1 shantung (agricola)
NT1 taffeta (agricola)
NT1 terry cloth (agricola)
NT1 tufted fabrics (agricola)
NT1 velour (agricola)
NT1 velveteen (agricola)
NT1 voile (agricola)
rt drape (agricola)
rt fabric construction (agricola)
rt luster (agricola)
rt nap (agricola)
rt pilling (agricola)
rt pucker (agricola)
rt textiles
rt weaves (agricola)
rt wet strength (agricola)

FACE
BT1 head
BT2 body regions
NT1 eyelids
NT1 lips
rt eyes
rt mouth
rt nose

FACIAL ECZEMA
uf *eczema, facial*
BT1 eczema
BT2 skin diseases
BT3 organic diseases
BT4 diseases
BT1 mycotoxicoses
BT2 poisoning
rt pithomyces chartarum
rt sporidesmins

FACTOR ANALYSIS
rt analysis
rt economic analysis
rt factors of production
rt genetics

factor markets
USE **capital market**
OR **labour market**
OR **land markets**

FACTORIAL ANALYSIS
BT1 statistical analysis
BT2 data analysis
BT2 statistics
rt component analysis

FACTORIES
BT1 buildings
NT1 canneries (agricola)
NT1 dairy factories
NT1 sugar refineries
NT1 textile mills (agricola)
rt industry
rt mills

FACTORS OF PRODUCTION
uf *production factors*
BT1 production economics
BT2 economics
rt capital
rt economic analysis
rt factor analysis
rt farm inputs
rt labour
rt land
rt production

FACTORY EFFLUENTS
uf *effluent, factory*
BT1 effluents
BT2 wastes

FACTORY EFFLUENTS *cont.*
NT1 brewery effluent
NT1 cannery effluent
NT1 distillery effluent
NT1 kraft mill effluent
NT1 meatworks effluent
NT1 palm oil mill effluent
NT1 potato factory effluent
NT1 pulp mill effluent
rt factory fumes
rt industrial wastes

FACTORY FARMING
BT1 intensive livestock farming
BT2 intensive farming
BT3 farming
BT2 livestock farming
BT3 farming
NT1 battery husbandry

FACTORY FUMES
BT1 air pollutants
BT2 pollutants
BT1 fumes
BT1 waste gases
BT2 gases
BT2 industrial wastes
BT3 wastes
rt air pollution
rt factory effluents

FACTORY WORKERS
BT1 labour
BT1 workers
rt industrialization

FAD DIETS (AGRICOLA)
BT1 diets
rt food fads (agricola)

fadn
USE **european farm accounting network**

FAECAL COLIFORMS
AF fecal coliforms
BT1 coliform bacteria
BT2 microbial flora
BT3 flora
BT1 faecal flora
BT2 microbial flora
BT3 flora
rt faeces

FAECAL FLORA
AF fecal flora
BT1 microbial flora
BT2 flora
NT1 faecal coliforms
rt faeces

FAECES
AF feces
uf *dung*
BT1 excreta
BT2 animal wastes
BT3 wastes
NT1 buffalo dung
NT1 cat faeces
NT1 cattle dung
NT1 dog faeces
NT1 horse dung
NT1 human faeces
NT1 poultry droppings
NT1 rabbit droppings
NT1 sheep dung
rt caecotrophy
rt coprophagy
rt coprostanol
rt defaecation
rt digestion
rt digestive tract
rt faecal coliforms
rt faecal flora
rt faeces collection
rt faeces composition
rt feeds
rt guano
rt night soil
rt sewerage

FAECES COLLECTION
AF feces collection

FAECES COLLECTION *cont.*
BT1 collection
rt digestive system
rt faeces

FAECES COMPOSITION
AF feces composition
BT1 composition
rt faeces

FAENIA
BT1 actinomycetales
BT2 firmicutes
BT3 bacteria
BT4 prokaryotes
NT1 faenia rectivirgula
rt micropolyspora
rt thermopolyspora

FAENIA RECTIVIRGULA
uf *micropolyspora faeni*
uf *thermopolyspora polyspora*
BT1 faenia
BT2 actinomycetales
BT3 firmicutes
BT4 bacteria
BT5 prokaryotes
rt farmer's lung

FAGACEAE
NT1 castanea
NT2 castanea crenata
NT2 castanea dentata
NT2 castanea mollissima
NT2 castanea sativa
NT1 castanopsis
NT2 castanopsis cuspidata
NT2 castanopsis indica
NT2 castanopsis sieboldii
NT2 castanopsis tribuloides
NT1 fagus
NT2 fagus crenata
NT2 fagus grandifolia
NT2 fagus japonica
NT2 fagus moesiaca
NT2 fagus orientalis
NT2 fagus sylvatica
NT1 lithocarpus
NT2 lithocarpus densiflorus
NT2 lithocarpus edulis
NT1 nothofagus
NT2 nothofagus antarctica
NT2 nothofagus betuloides
NT2 nothofagus cunninghamii
NT2 nothofagus dombeyi
NT2 nothofagus fusca
NT2 nothofagus menziesii
NT2 nothofagus moorei
NT2 nothofagus nitida
NT2 nothofagus obliqua
NT2 nothofagus procera
NT2 nothofagus pumilio
NT2 nothofagus solandri
NT3 nothofagus solandri var. cliffortioides
NT2 nothofagus truncata
NT1 quercus
NT2 quercus acuta
NT2 quercus acutissima
NT2 quercus agrifolia
NT2 quercus alba
NT2 quercus canariensis
NT2 quercus castaneifolia
NT2 quercus cerris
NT2 quercus coccifera
NT2 quercus coccinea
NT2 quercus crispula
NT2 quercus dentata
NT2 quercus douglasii
NT2 quercus dumosa
NT2 quercus dumosa var. dumosa
NT2 quercus durandii
NT2 quercus ellipsoidalis
NT2 quercus faginea
NT2 quercus falcata
NT3 quercus falcata var. pagodifolia
NT2 quercus floribunda
NT2 quercus frainetto
NT2 quercus gambelii
NT2 quercus garryana

FAGACEAE *cont.*
NT2 quercus gilva
NT2 quercus glauca
NT2 quercus hartwissiana
NT2 quercus havardii
NT2 quercus hispanica
NT2 quercus iberica
NT2 quercus ilex
NT2 quercus ilicifolia
NT2 quercus incana
NT2 quercus ithaburensis
NT2 quercus kelloggii
NT2 quercus kewensis
NT2 quercus laevis
NT2 quercus leucotrichophora
NT2 quercus longipes
NT2 quercus lyrata
NT2 quercus macranthera
NT2 quercus macrocarpa
NT2 quercus marilandica
NT2 quercus mongolica
NT2 quercus montana
NT2 quercus muehlenbergii
NT2 quercus myrsinaefolia
NT2 quercus nigra
NT2 quercus palustris
NT2 quercus pedunculiflora
NT2 quercus petraea
NT2 quercus phellos
NT2 quercus phillyraeoides
NT2 quercus prinus
NT2 quercus pubescens
NT2 quercus pyrenaica
NT2 quercus robur
NT2 quercus rubra
NT2 quercus semecarpifolia
NT2 quercus serrata
NT2 quercus shumardii
NT2 quercus stellata
NT2 quercus suber
NT2 quercus turbinella
NT2 quercus turneri
NT2 quercus velutina
NT2 quercus virginiana
NT2 quercus wislizenii

FAGARA
BT1 rutaceae
NT1 fagara chalybea
NT1 fagara lemairei
NT1 fagara leprieurii
NT1 fagara mayu
NT1 fagara rubescens
NT1 fagara tessmannii
NT1 fagara zanthoxyloides

FAGARA CHALYBEA
BT1 fagara
BT2 rutaceae

FAGARA LEMAIREI
BT1 fagara
BT2 rutaceae

FAGARA LEPRIEURII
BT1 fagara
BT2 rutaceae

FAGARA MAYU
BT1 fagara
BT2 rutaceae

FAGARA RUBESCENS
BT1 fagara
BT2 rutaceae

FAGARA TESSMANNII
BT1 fagara
BT2 rutaceae

FAGARA ZANTHOXYLOIDES
BT1 antibacterial plants
BT1 fagara
BT2 rutaceae
BT1 medicinal plants

FAGOPYRUM
BT1 polygonaceae
NT1 fagopyrum cymosum
NT1 fagopyrum emarginatum
NT1 fagopyrum esculentum
NT1 fagopyrum tataricum

FAGOPYRUM CYMOSUM
BT1 fagopyrum
BT2 polygonaceae

FAGOPYRUM EMARGINATUM
BT1 fagopyrum
BT2 polygonaceae

FAGOPYRUM ESCULENTUM
uf *polygonum fagopyrum*
BT1 fagopyrum
BT2 polygonaceae
rt buckwheat

FAGOPYRUM TATARICUM
uf *polygonum tataricum*
BT1 fagopyrum
BT2 polygonaceae

FAGUS
uf *beech*
BT1 fagaceae
NT1 fagus crenata
NT1 fagus grandifolia
NT1 fagus japonica
NT1 fagus moesiaca
NT1 fagus orientalis
NT1 fagus sylvatica

FAGUS CRENATA
BT1 fagus
BT2 fagaceae
BT1 forest trees

FAGUS GRANDIFOLIA
BT1 fagus
BT2 fagaceae
BT1 forest trees

FAGUS JAPONICA
HN from 1990
BT1 fagus
BT2 fagaceae
BT1 forest trees

FAGUS MOESIACA
BT1 fagus
BT2 fagaceae

FAGUS ORIENTALIS
BT1 fagus
BT2 fagaceae
BT1 forest trees

FAGUS SYLVATICA
BT1 fagus
BT2 fagaceae
BT1 forest trees
BT1 medicinal plants
BT1 ornamental woody plants

faidherbia
USE **acacia**

faidherbia albida
USE **acacia albida**

FAILLE (AGRICOLA)
BT1 fabrics

FAILURE
rt brittleness
rt fracture

FAILURE TO THRIVE (AGRICOLA)
rt health
rt infant disorders

fairs
USE **carnivals**
OR **funfairs**
OR **shows**

FALCARIA
BT1 umbelliferae
NT1 falcaria vulgaris

FALCARIA VULGARIS
BT1 falcaria
BT2 umbelliferae

FALCAUSTRA
BT1 kathlaniidae
BT2 nematoda

FALCO
BT1 falconidae
BT2 falconiformes
BT3 birds
NT1 falco sparverius
NT1 falco tinnunculus

FALCO SPARVERIUS
uf *kestrel, american*
BT1 falco
BT2 falconidae
BT3 falconiformes
BT4 birds

FALCO TINNUNCULUS
uf *kestrel, common*
BT1 falco
BT2 falconidae
BT3 falconiformes
BT4 birds

FALCONIDAE
uf *falcons*
BT1 falconiformes
BT2 birds
NT1 falco
NT2 falco sparverius
NT2 falco tinnunculus

FALCONIFORMES
BT1 birds
NT1 accipitridae
NT2 accipiter
NT3 accipiter cooperii
NT3 accipiter gentilis
NT3 accipiter striatus
NT2 aquila
NT3 aquila chrysaetos
NT2 circus
NT3 circus cyaneus
NT1 falconidae
NT2 falco
NT3 falco sparverius
NT3 falco tinnunculus
NT1 pandionidae
NT2 pandion
NT3 pandion haliaetus

falcons
USE **falconidae**

FALCULIFERIDAE
BT1 astigmata
BT2 acari
NT1 pterophagus
NT2 pterophagus strictus

FALKLAND ISLANDS
uf *malvinas*
uf *south sandwich islands*
BT1 south america
BT2 america

FALLOPIA
BT1 polygonaceae
NT1 fallopia baldschuanica
NT1 fallopia convolvulus
rt bilderdykia
rt polygonum

FALLOPIA BALDSCHUANICA
uf *polygonum baldschuanicum*
BT1 fallopia
BT2 polygonaceae
BT1 ornamental woody plants

FALLOPIA CONVOLVULUS
HN from 1990
uf *bilderdykia convolvulus*
uf *polygonum convolvulus*
BT1 fallopia
BT2 polygonaceae
BT1 weeds

fallopian tube
USE **oviducts**

FALLOUT
uf *radioactive fallout*
rt air pollution
rt radioactivity

FALLOW
uf *fallowing*

FALLOW *cont.*
BT1 cropping systems
NT1 summer fallow
rt abandoned land
rt fallow systems
rt improved fallow
rt shifting cultivation
rt soil conservation
rt water conservation

FALLOW DEER
uf *cervus dama*
uf *dama dama*
BT1 deer
BT2 meat animals
BT3 animals
BT2 ruminants
BT3 animals

fallow, summer
USE **summer fallow**

FALLOW SYSTEMS
BT1 cropping systems
NT1 corridor systems
NT1 improved fallow
rt fallow

fallowing
USE **fallow**

FALLS (AGRICOLA)
BT1 accidents

FALSE GRAIN
HN from 1990
BT1 crystals
rt crystallization
rt sugar boiling

FAMILIAL INCIDENCE
rt families
rt family structure
rt incidence
rt inheritance
rt relationships

FAMILIES
NT1 extended families
NT1 farm families
NT1 foster family (agricola)
NT1 stepfamily (agricola)
rt familial incidence
rt family counseling (agricola)
rt family crises (agricola)
rt family day care (agricola)
rt family disintegration
rt family farms
rt family labour
rt family life
rt family planning
rt family size
rt family structure
rt grandparents
rt households
rt men
rt parents
rt population structure
rt siblings
rt taxonomy
rt widows
rt women

families, extended
USE **extended families**

families, farm
USE **farm families**

families, nuclear
USE **nuclear families**

FAMILY ALLOWANCES
BT1 allowances
BT1 social security
rt family budgets
rt family size

family breakdown
USE **family disintegration**

FAMILY BUDGETS
BT1 budgets
NT1 household consumption
NT1 household expenditure

FAMILY BUDGETS *cont.*
rt family allowances
rt household budgets (agricola)
rt income

FAMILY COUNSELING (AGRICOLA)
BT1 counseling (agricola)
rt families
rt family problems (agricola)

FAMILY CRISES (AGRICOLA)
BT1 crises (agricola)
rt families
rt family problems (agricola)

FAMILY DAY CARE (AGRICOLA)
BT1 day care (agricola)
rt families

FAMILY DISINTEGRATION
uf family breakdown
rt families
rt relationships

FAMILY ENVIRONMENT (AGRICOLA)
BT1 social environment
BT2 environment
BT2 social systems
rt family life

family farming
USE **family farms**

FAMILY FARMS
uf family farming
BT1 farms
rt families
rt family labour
rt farm families
rt ownership
rt private farms
rt private ownership
rt small farms

FAMILY LABOR
BF family labour
rt labor

FAMILY LABOUR
AF family labor
uf labour, family
BT1 labour
rt families
rt family farms
rt family life
rt farm families
rt farm workers
rt female labour

FAMILY LIFE
rt empty nest syndrome (agricola)
rt families
rt family environment (agricola)
rt family labour
rt family life education (agricola)
rt family planning
rt family problems (agricola)
rt generation conflict
rt marital interaction (agricola)
rt marital separation (agricola)
rt parent child relationships
rt woman's status

FAMILY LIFE EDUCATION (AGRICOLA)
BT1 education
NT1 parenthood education (agricola)
rt family life

FAMILY PLANNING
uf planning, family
BT1 population control
BT2 control
NT1 contraception
rt birth control (agricola)
rt families
rt family life

FAMILY PLANNING *cont.*
rt family size
rt human fertility
rt population education

FAMILY PROBLEMS (AGRICOLA)
rt family counseling (agricola)
rt family crises (agricola)
rt family life

FAMILY SIZE
rt extended families
rt families
rt family allowances
rt family planning
rt size

FAMILY STRUCTURE
NT1 heads of families
NT1 kinship
NT1 marriage
NT2 intermarriage (agricola)
NT2 polygamy
NT2 remarriage (agricola)
NT1 matriarchy
NT1 nuclear families
rt children
rt extended families
rt familial incidence
rt families
rt parents
rt population structure
rt relationships
rt structure

FAMILY STYLE SERVING (AGRICOLA)
BT1 food serving methods (agricola)
BT2 methodology

FAMINE
BT1 natural disasters
BT2 disasters
rt food supply
rt hunger
rt nutrition
rt oxfam
rt starvation

famine oedema
USE **nutritional oedema**

FAMPHUR
BT1 ectoparasiticides
BT2 antiparasitic agents
BT3 drugs
BT1 organothiophosphate insecticides
BT2 organophosphorus insecticides
BT3 insecticides
BT4 pesticides
BT3 organophosphorus pesticides
BT4 organophosphorus compounds

FAN NOZZLES
uf nozzles, fan
BT1 nozzles
BT2 components
BT2 spraying equipment
BT3 application equipment
BT4 equipment
rt spraying

FANCONI SYNDROME
uf debre-fanconi syndrome
uf toni-debre-fanconi syndrome
BT1 kidney diseases
BT2 urinary tract diseases
BT3 organic diseases
BT4 diseases
rt rickets

FANNIA
BT1 fanniidae
BT2 diptera
NT1 fannia canicularis
NT1 fannia femoralis
NT1 fannia pusio
NT1 fannia scalaris

FANNIA CANICULARIS
BT1 fannia
BT2 fanniidae
BT3 diptera

FANNIA FEMORALIS
BT1 fannia
BT2 fanniidae
BT3 diptera

FANNIA PUSIO
BT1 fannia
BT2 fanniidae
BT3 diptera

FANNIA SCALARIS
BT1 fannia
BT2 fanniidae
BT3 diptera

FANNIIDAE
BT1 diptera
NT1 fannia
NT2 fannia canicularis
NT2 fannia femoralis
NT2 fannia pusio
NT2 fannia scalaris

FANNING
BT1 animal behaviour
BT2 behaviour
BT1 heat regulation
rt honeybee colonies
rt nasonov gland

FANS
BT1 components
NT1 axial flow fans
NT1 centrifugal fans
NT1 cross flow fans
rt air flow
rt blowers
rt cooling
rt cooling systems
rt heat regulation
rt ventilation
rt ventilators
rt wind
rt winnowing seed cleaners

fans, axial flow
USE **axial flow fans**

fans, centrifugal
USE **centrifugal fans**

fao
USE **food and agriculture organization**

far east ussr
USE **ussr far east**

FAR RED LIGHT
uf light, far red
BT1 light
BT2 electromagnetic radiation
BT3 radiation
rt infrared radiation

FARES
rt transport

FARINOCYSTIS
BT1 apicomplexa
BT2 protozoa
NT1 farinocystis tribolii

FARINOCYSTIS TRIBOLII
BT1 entomopathogenic protozoa
BT2 entomopathogens
BT3 pathogens
BT1 farinocystis
BT2 apicomplexa
BT3 protozoa

FARM ACCOUNTING
BT1 accounting
rt book-keeping
rt farm accounts
rt farm budgeting

FARM ACCOUNTS
BT1 accounts
NT1 farm results

FARM ACCOUNTS *cont.*
NT2 farm comparisons
NT2 farm indebtedness
NT2 gross margins
rt economic accounts
rt european farm accounting network
rt farm accounting
rt farm budgeting
rt farm management
rt returns

FARM AMALGAMATIONS
uf amalgamations
BT1 concentration of production
BT2 socioeconomic organization
rt agricultural structure
rt farm size
rt farm structure
rt mergers
rt partnerships

FARM AREA
BT1 area
BT1 farm size
rt acreage

FARM BUDGETING
uf budget accounting
uf budgeting
BT1 budgets
BT1 farm planning
BT2 planning
rt farm accounting
rt farm accounts
rt farm management

FARM BUILDINGS
uf agricultural buildings
uf buildings, agricultural
uf buildings, farm
BT1 buildings
NT1 barns
NT2 dutch barns
NT1 chitting houses
NT1 farm dairies
NT1 greenhouses
NT2 tower greenhouses
NT2 wide span greenhouses
NT1 mushroom houses
rt animal housing
rt farm dwellings
rt farm inputs
rt farm structure
rt fixed capital
rt silos

FARM CLOSURES
uf closures, farm
BT1 agricultural structure
rt abandoned land
rt severance allowances
rt structural policy

FARM COMPARISONS
BT1 farm results
BT2 farm accounts
BT3 accounts

FARM DAIRIES
uf dairies, farm
BT1 dairies
BT1 farm buildings
BT2 buildings
rt milk production

FARM DEVELOPMENT
BT1 farm planning
BT2 planning
rt development
rt improvement grants

FARM DWELLINGS
BT1 rural housing
BT2 housing
NT1 tied cottages
rt agricultural households
rt building controls
rt farm buildings
rt farm families

FARM ENTERPRISES
uf enterprises, farm
uf production units

FARM ENTERPRISES *cont.*
BT1 enterprises
NT1 ancillary enterprises
NT2 farm holidays
NT2 on-farm processing
NT1 cooperative farm enterprises
NT2 gaec
NT2 livestock groups
NT2 safer
NT1 crop enterprises
NT1 livestock enterprises
NT2 cattle farming
NT3 dairy farming
NT2 goat keeping
NT2 pig farming
NT2 poultry farming
NT2 sheep farming
NT2 small animal rearing
NT1 vegetable growing
rt farming

FARM ENTRANTS
BT1 farmers
BT2 occupations
rt agricultural structure
rt farm leases
rt setting up grants
rt structural policy

FARM EQUIPMENT
BT1 equipment
rt farm inputs
rt farm machinery
rt fixed capital
rt mechanization

FARM FAMILIES
uf *families, farm*
BT1 families
rt agricultural households
rt family farms
rt family labour
rt farm dwellings
rt farmers

FARM FORESTRY
(tree planting by farmers on private land also used for agriculture)
BT1 farming
BT1 forestry
rt agroforestry
rt agrosilvicultural systems
rt community forestry
rt farm woodlands
rt social forestry

FARM HELPER SERVICES
uf *mutual help*
uf *services, farm helper*
BT1 cooperative services
BT2 cooperative activities
BT2 services
rt farm workers
rt work banks

FARM HOLIDAYS
uf *farm recreation*
BT1 ancillary enterprises
BT2 farm enterprises
BT3 enterprises
BT1 holidays
BT2 tourism
rt farmhouse accommodation

FARM INCOME
uf *income, farm*
BT1 farmers' income
BT2 income
rt european farm accounting network
rt farm results

FARM INDEBTEDNESS
BT1 debt
BT1 farm results
BT2 farm accounts
BT3 accounts
rt agricultural situation
rt bankruptcy

FARM INPUTS
uf *input prices*
uf *production materials*
rt agricultural chemicals
rt capital
rt factors of production
rt farm buildings
rt farm equipment
rt farm machinery
rt farm management
rt fertilizers
rt fuels
rt labour
rt seeds
rt tools

FARM LEASES
uf *leases, farm*
BT1 leases
BT2 tenancy
BT3 tenure systems
rt farm entrants

FARM MACHINERY
BT1 machinery
NT1 bale collectors
NT1 bale throwers
NT1 balers
NT2 big balers
NT2 high density balers
NT2 pickup balers
NT2 roll balers
NT1 choppers
NT1 crimpers
NT1 crushers
NT2 clod crushers
NT1 cubing machines
NT1 cutters
NT2 hedge cutters
NT2 scrub cutters
NT2 shears
NT3 logging shears
NT3 pruning shears
NT2 silage cutters
NT2 trench cutters
NT1 decorticators
NT1 dibbers
NT1 ditch cleaners
NT1 driers
NT2 barn driers
NT2 batch driers
NT2 cascade driers
NT2 concurrent flow driers
NT2 continuous driers
NT2 convection driers
NT2 conveyor driers
NT2 counterflow driers
NT2 cross flow driers
NT2 deep bed driers
NT2 drum driers
NT2 electric driers
NT2 forage driers
NT2 grain driers
NT3 floor driers
NT2 high temperature driers
NT2 infrared driers
NT2 microwave driers
NT2 roller driers
NT2 shallow bed driers
NT2 spray driers
NT2 tower driers
NT2 tray driers
NT2 tunnel driers
NT2 ventilated bin driers
NT2 ventilated silo driers
NT1 drills
NT2 band drills
NT2 combine drills
NT2 fluid drills
NT2 grain drills
NT2 plot drills
NT2 pneumatic drills
NT2 precision drills
NT2 press drills
NT2 ridge drills
NT2 root drills
NT2 seed coverers
NT2 seed drills
NT2 seed tubes
NT2 seeder cultivators
NT2 sod seeders
NT1 fertilizer distributors

FARM MACHINERY *cont.*
NT2 liquid fertilizer distributors
NT1 forage boxes
NT1 forage conditioners
NT2 mower conditioners
NT2 tedders
NT1 gantries
NT1 gins
NT2 cotton gins
NT1 grinders
NT1 harvesters
NT2 aquatic plant harvesters
NT2 bean harvesters
NT2 binders
NT2 bulb harvesters
NT2 cabbage harvesters
NT2 catching frames
NT2 citrus harvesters
NT2 combine harvesters
NT3 axial flow combine harvesters
NT3 concaves
NT3 grain tanks
NT2 cotton pickers
NT2 crop lifters
NT2 cutter loaders
NT2 dividers
NT2 flax pullers
NT2 forage harvesters
NT2 grape harvesters
NT2 groundnut harvesters
NT2 header harvesters
NT2 hemp harvesters
NT2 hop harvesters
NT2 lettuce harvesters
NT2 maize pickers
NT2 melon harvesters
NT2 nut harvesters
NT2 onion harvesters
NT2 pea viners
NT2 plot harvesters
NT2 root harvesters
NT3 beet harvesters
NT4 beet lifters
NT3 carrot harvesters
NT3 potato harvesters
NT4 potato diggers
NT5 shaker diggers
NT3 turnip harvesters
NT2 self propelled harvesters
NT2 soft fruit harvesters
NT3 black currant harvesters
NT3 raspberry harvesters
NT3 strawberry harvesters
NT2 sugarcane harvesters
NT2 tea harvesters
NT2 tobacco harvesters
NT2 tomato harvesters
NT2 vegetable harvesters
NT1 haulm strippers
NT1 implement carriers
NT1 incorporators
NT1 milking machines
NT2 bucket milking machines
NT2 pulsators
NT2 teatcup liner
NT2 teatcups
NT1 mowers
NT2 cutter bar mowers
NT2 cylinder mowers
NT2 flail mowers
NT2 mower conditioners
NT2 rotary mowers
NT1 mulch layers
NT1 picking platforms
NT1 planters
NT2 bulb planters
NT2 potato planters
NT1 presses
NT2 cheese presses
NT2 screw presses
NT1 rakes
NT2 buckrakes
NT1 seed broadcasters
NT1 seed dressers
NT1 shaker diggers
NT1 shearing machines
NT1 soil block makers
NT1 spreaders
NT2 bait spreaders
NT2 lime spreaders

FARM MACHINERY *cont.*
NT2 manure spreaders
NT2 slurry spreaders
NT1 stalk pullers
NT1 stone pickers
NT1 stump pullers
NT1 swath aerators
NT1 swath turners
NT1 thinners
NT2 down the row thinners
NT2 selective thinners
NT1 threshing machines
NT2 concaves
NT1 toppers
NT2 beet toppers
NT1 transplanters
NT1 tree shakers
NT1 wafering machines
NT1 washers
NT2 power washers
NT2 vegetable washers
NT1 windrowers
rt agricultural engineering
rt agricultural machinery industry
rt cabs
rt couplings
rt earth moving equipment
rt engines
rt equipment
rt farm equipment
rt farm inputs
rt mechanization
rt mobile units

FARM MANAGEMENT
uf *business management*
uf *management, farm*
rt farm accounts
rt farm budgeting
rt farm inputs
rt farm planning
rt farmers
rt grassland management
rt land management
rt management
rt managers
rt range management

farm models
USE **models**

FARM NUMBERS
BT1 agricultural structure
rt agricultural censuses
rt structural change

FARM PLANNING
uf *planning, farm*
BT1 planning
NT1 farm budgeting
NT1 farm development
NT1 gross margins analysis
rt agricultural planning
rt development plans
rt farm management
rt farm surveys
rt financial planning
rt investment planning
rt structural policy

farm recreation
USE **farm holidays**
OR **recreation**

FARM RESULTS
BT1 farm accounts
BT2 accounts
NT1 farm comparisons
NT1 farm indebtedness
NT1 gross margins
rt costs
rt earned income
rt farm income
rt returns

FARM ROADS
uf *roads, farm*
BT1 rural roads
BT2 roads
rt intrafarm transport

FARM SECTOR
BT1 agricultural sector
BT2 agroindustrial sector
rt crop enterprises
rt livestock farming

FARM SIZE
NT1 farm area
rt farm amalgamations
rt farm structure
rt farm surveys
rt land consolidation
rt large farms
rt livestock numbers
rt medium sized farms
rt size
rt small farms
rt structural policy

FARM STORAGE
BT1 storage

FARM STRUCTURE
NT1 land consolidation
rt farm amalgamations
rt farm buildings
rt farm size
rt farmyards
rt feedlots
rt field shape
rt field size
rt fields
rt fragmentation
rt livestock numbers
rt mergers
rt structural change
rt structure

FARM SURVEYS
BT1 surveys
NT1 european farm accounting network
rt agricultural censuses
rt farm planning
rt farm size

FARM TESTS
BT1 tests
rt performance testing

FARM TRAILS
BT1 trails
BT2 paths
BT3 roads

farm wastes
USE **agricultural wastes**

FARM WOODLANDS
(woodlands on private farmland)
BT1 woodlands
BT2 vegetation types
rt agroforestry
rt farm forestry

FARM WORKERS
uf agricultural workers
BT1 agricultural manpower
BT2 labour
BT1 workers
NT1 milkers
rt agricultural trade unions
rt family labour
rt farm helper services

farmer participatory research
USE **farming systems research**

FARMERS
BT1 occupations
NT1 farm entrants
NT1 growers
rt farm families
rt farm management
rt farmers' associations
rt farmers' attitudes
rt farmers' income

FARMERS' ASSOCIATIONS
uf agricultural societies
uf associations
uf farmers' circles
BT1 interest groups
BT2 groups

FARMERS' ASSOCIATIONS *cont.*
BT2 organizations
rt agricultural trade unions
rt breeders' associations
rt clubs
rt cooperative services
rt farmers

FARMERS' ATTITUDES
uf attitudes, farmers
BT1 attitudes
rt economic sociology
rt farmers

farmers' circles
USE **farmers' associations**

FARMERS' INCOME
uf income, farmers'
BT1 income
NT1 farm income
NT1 non-farm income
rt farmers

FARMER'S LUNG
BT1 allergies
BT2 immunological diseases
BT3 diseases
BT1 human diseases
BT2 diseases
BT1 respiratory diseases
BT2 organic diseases
BT3 diseases
rt faenia rectivirgula
rt hay

FARMERS' MARKETS (AGRICOLA)
BT1 direct marketing
BT2 retail marketing
BT3 marketing channels
BT4 marketing

FARMHOUSE ACCOMMODATION
BT1 holiday accommodation
BT2 accommodation
rt ancillary enterprises
rt farm holidays
rt rural housing

FARMING
NT1 alternative farming
NT2 organic farming
NT1 arable farming
NT1 commercial farming
NT1 contract farming
NT1 cooperative farming
NT1 extensive farming
NT2 extensive husbandry
NT2 extensive livestock farming
NT3 ranching
NT1 farm forestry
NT1 fish farming
NT2 fish culture
NT3 eel culture
NT3 salmon culture
NT1 full time farming
NT1 intensive farming
NT2 intensive livestock farming
NT3 factory farming
NT4 battery husbandry
NT1 irrigated farming
NT1 ley farming
NT1 livestock farming
NT2 cattle farming
NT3 dairy farming
NT2 extensive livestock farming
NT3 ranching
NT2 free range husbandry
NT2 fur farming
NT2 game farming
NT3 deer farming
NT2 intensive livestock farming
NT3 factory farming
NT4 battery husbandry
NT2 pig farming
NT2 poultry farming
NT2 sheep farming
NT1 mixed farming
NT1 part time farming
NT1 peasant farming
NT1 runoff farming
NT1 specialized farming
NT1 subsistence farming

FARMING *cont.*
NT1 traditional farming
NT1 transitional farming
rt agricultural production
rt agriculture
rt farm enterprises
rt farming systems
rt husbandry
rt primary sector

FARMING SYSTEMS
uf agricultural systems
BT1 agricultural structure
rt cropping systems
rt diversification
rt farming
rt farming systems research
rt farms
rt grazing systems
rt intensification
rt prehistoric agriculture

FARMING SYSTEMS RESEARCH
HN from 1990
uf farmer participatory research
BT1 agricultural research
BT2 research
rt farming systems

FARMLAND
BT1 agricultural land
BT2 land resources
BT3 non-renewable resources
BT4 natural resources
BT5 resources
BT2 land types
rt agricultural land
rt farms

FARMS
uf economic units
uf production units
NT1 collective farms
NT2 ejidos
NT2 kibbutzim
NT2 kolkhozy
NT2 moshavim
NT1 cooperative farms
NT1 dairy farms
NT1 demonstration farms
NT1 family farms
NT1 fish farms
NT1 large farms
NT1 marginal farms
NT1 market gardens
NT1 medium sized farms
NT1 pilot farms
NT1 private farms
NT1 small farms
NT2 crofts
NT1 state farms
NT2 sovkhozy
rt farming systems
rt farmland
rt farmyards
rt fields

farms, collective
USE **collective farms**

farms, large
USE **large farms**

farms, marginal
USE **marginal farms**

farms, medium sized
USE **medium sized farms**

farms, pilot
USE **pilot farms**

farms, private
USE **private farms**

farms, small
USE **small farms**

farms, state
USE **state farms**

FARMYARD MANURE
uf dung

FARMYARD MANURE *cont.*
uf fym
uf stable manure
BT1 animal manures
BT2 manures
BT3 organic amendments
BT4 soil amendments
BT5 amendments
rt cattle manure
rt organic culture
rt poultry manure
rt sheep manure

FARMYARDS
BT1 yards
rt farm structure
rt farms

FARNESOL
BT1 antitranspirants
BT1 fatty alcohols
BT2 alcohols
BT2 lipids
BT1 sesquiterpenoids
BT2 terpenoids
BT3 isoprenoids
BT4 lipids
rt essential oils
rt perfumery

FAROE ISLANDS
BT1 scandinavia
BT2 europe
rt denmark

FARROWING
BT1 parturition
BT2 sexual reproduction
BT3 reproduction
NT1 farrowing interval
NT1 farrowing rate
rt farrowing houses
rt farrowing pens
rt farrowing season
rt pig farming
rt piglets
rt pigs

FARROWING HOUSES
BT1 pig housing
BT2 animal housing
rt farrowing
rt farrowing pens
rt pigs

FARROWING INTERVAL
BT1 farrowing
BT2 parturition
BT3 sexual reproduction
BT4 reproduction

FARROWING PENS
BT1 pens
BT2 animal housing
rt creeps
rt farrowing
rt farrowing houses
rt pig housing
rt pigs

FARROWING RATE
BT1 farrowing
BT2 parturition
BT3 sexual reproduction
BT4 reproduction

FARROWING SEASON
rt farrowing
rt seasons

FASCIATION
BT1 abnormal development
rt branching
rt bunching

FASCIOLA
BT1 fasciolidae
BT2 digenea
BT3 trematoda
NT1 fasciola gigantica
NT1 fasciola hepatica
rt fascioliasis

FASCIOLA GIGANTICA
BT1 fasciola
BT2 fasciolidae
BT3 digenea
BT4 trematoda
rt liver flukes

FASCIOLA HEPATICA
BT1 fasciola
BT2 fasciolidae
BT3 digenea
BT4 trematoda
rt liver flukes

FASCIOLIASIS
BT1 snail-borne diseases
BT2 vector-borne diseases
BT3 diseases
BT1 trematode infections
BT2 helminthoses
BT3 parasitoses
BT4 diseases
rt fasciola

FASCIOLIDAE
BT1 digenea
BT2 trematoda
NT1 fasciola
NT2 fasciola gigantica
NT2 fasciola hepatica
NT1 fascioloides
NT2 fascioloides magna
NT1 fasciolopsis
NT2 fasciolopsis buski
NT1 parafasciolopsis

FASCIOLOIDES
BT1 fasciolidae
BT2 digenea
BT3 trematoda
NT1 fascioloides magna

FASCIOLOIDES MAGNA
BT1 fascioloides
BT2 fasciolidae
BT3 digenea
BT4 trematoda
rt liver flukes

FASCIOLOPSIS
BT1 fasciolidae
BT2 digenea
BT3 trematoda
NT1 fasciolopsis buski

FASCIOLOPSIS BUSKI
BT1 fasciolopsis
BT2 fasciolidae
BT3 digenea
BT4 trematoda

FASHION (AGRICOLA)
rt fashion designers (agricola)
rt fashion illustration (agricola)
rt fashion merchandising (agricola)

FASHION DESIGNERS (AGRICOLA)
BT1 occupations
rt design
rt fashion (agricola)

FASHION ILLUSTRATION (AGRICOLA)
rt fashion (agricola)
rt illustrations

FASHION MERCHANDISING (AGRICOLA)
rt fashion (agricola)
rt sales promotion

FAST FOOD RESTAURANTS
BT1 restaurants
BT2 dining facilities (agricola)
rt fast foods

FAST FOODS
BT1 foods
NT1 sandwiches (agricola)
rt catering industry
rt fast food restaurants

FASTING
BT1 underfeeding

FASTING *cont.*
BT2 feeding
rt deprivation
rt hunger
rt starvation
rt undernutrition
rt underweight

FASTNESS (AGRICOLA)
uf color fastness
rt color fading (agricola)
rt dyes
rt textile fibers

FAT
NT1 animal fat
NT2 milk fat
NT3 buffalo milk fat
NT3 human milk fat
NT2 mutton fat
NT2 myelin
NT2 pig fat
NT3 lard
NT2 poultry fat
NT3 chicken fat
NT2 suet
NT2 tallow
NT1 body fat
NT2 abdominal fat
NT2 backfat
NT2 brown fat
NT2 depot fat
NT2 subcutaneous fat
NT1 protected fat
NT1 vegetable fat
NT2 cutin
NT2 shea butter
rt dietary fat
rt fat restricted diets (agricola)
rt fats
rt nutrients

FAT ABSORPTION
BT1 absorption
BT2 sorption
rt fats

FAT BODY
BT1 digestive system
BT2 body parts
rt metabolism

FAT CELL THEORY (AGRICOLA)
rt adipocytes
rt obesity
rt theory

fat cells
USE **adipocytes**

FAT CONSUMPTION
BT1 consumption
rt fats
rt nutrition

FAT DEFICIENCIES
uf essential fatty acid deficiency
BT1 nutrient deficiencies
BT2 deficiency
rt fats
rt nutrient balance

FAT EMULSIONS
BT1 emulsions
NT1 fat globules
NT1 intralipid
rt fats
rt parenteral feeding

FAT GLOBULES
BT1 fat emulsions
BT2 emulsions
rt milk fat

FAT METABOLISM
BT1 lipid metabolism
BT2 metabolism
rt fats

fat metabolism disorders
USE **lipid metabolism disorders**

FAT METERS
BT1 meters
BT2 instruments
NT1 ultrasonic fat meters
rt fat thickness
rt fats
rt subcutaneous fat

fat meters, ultrasonic
USE **ultrasonic fat meters**

FAT MOBILIZATION
BT1 digestion
BT2 physiological functions
rt fats
rt lipotropin

fat mobilizing hormone
USE **lipotropin**

FAT PERCENTAGE
BT1 carcass composition
rt body fat
rt fat thickness

FAT PRODUCTS
BT1 products
NT1 cooking fats
NT2 lard
NT2 margarine
NT2 suet
NT1 heated fat
NT1 hydrogenated fats
rt animal fat
rt animal products
rt low fat products
rt oil products

FAT RESTRICTED DIETS (AGRICOLA)
BT1 therapeutic diets
BT2 diets
rt fat

FAT SOLUBLE VITAMINS
uf vitamins, fat soluble
BT1 vitamins
NT1 retinoids
NT2 dehydroretinol
NT2 retinal
NT2 retinoic acid
NT2 retinol
NT2 retinyl esters
NT3 retinyl acetate
NT3 retinyl palmitate
NT1 vitamin d
NT2 25-hydroxyergocalciferol
NT2 cholecalciferol
NT2 cholecalciferol derivatives
NT3 hydroxycholecalciferols
NT4 1α-hydroxycholecalciferol
NT4 24,25-dihydroxycholecalciferol
NT4 25,26-dihydroxycholecalciferol
NT4 calcitriol
NT2 dihydrotachysterol
NT2 ergocalciferol
NT2 tachysterol
NT1 vitamin e
NT2 tocopherols
NT3 α-tocopherol
NT3 β-tocopherol
NT2 tocotrienols
NT2 vitamin e acetate
NT1 vitamin k compounds
NT2 menadione sodium bisulfite
NT2 menaquinones
NT3 menadione
NT2 phylloquinone
NT2 vitamin k
rt fats

FAT THICKNESS
rt body fat
rt fat meters
rt fat percentage

FATHERS
BT1 parents
BT2 ancestry
rt mothers

FATHERS *cont.*
rt parentage
rt paternal behaviour
rt paternity
rt sires

FATIGUE
rt ergonomics
rt exercise
rt exhaustion
rt fatigue strength
rt physical activity

FATIGUE STRENGTH
uf strength, fatigue
BT1 strength
BT2 mechanical properties
BT3 properties
rt fatigue
rt metals

fatness
USE **obesity**

FATOUA
BT1 moraceae
NT1 fatoua villosa

FATOUA VILLOSA
BT1 fatoua
BT2 moraceae

FATS
BT1 lipids
NT1 neutral fats
NT2 acylglycerols
NT3 diacylglycerols
NT3 monoacylglycerols
NT4 monoolein
NT3 olein
NT3 stearin
NT3 sucroglycerides
NT3 triacylglycerols
NT4 long chain triacylglycerols
NT5 triolein
NT4 medium chain triacylglycerols
NT5 trilaurin
NT5 trioctanoin
NT4 short chain triacylglycerols
NT5 triacetin
NT5 tributyrin
NT2 saturated fats
NT2 unsaturated fats
NT3 polyunsaturated fats
NT1 oxidized fats
rt bile
rt butter
rt ergosterol
rt fat
rt fat absorption
rt fat consumption
rt fat deficiencies
rt fat emulsions
rt fat metabolism
rt fat meters
rt fat mobilization
rt fat soluble vitamins
rt fatty acids
rt fatty degeneration
rt fatty oil plants
rt fatty oils
rt filled milk
rt iodine value
rt lipaemia
rt lipotropin
rt low fat products
rt oils and fats industry
rt saponification number
rt soapstock
rt steatorrhoea
rt ultrasonic fat meters

FATSHEDERA
BT1 araliaceae
NT1 fatshedera lizei

FATSHEDERA LIZEI
BT1 fatshedera
BT2 araliaceae
BT1 ornamental woody plants

FATSHEDERA LIZEI *cont.*
rt ornamental foliage plants

FATSIA
BT1 araliaceae
NT1 fatsia japonica

FATSIA JAPONICA
uf aralia japonica
uf aralia sieboldii
BT1 fatsia
BT2 araliaceae
BT1 ornamental woody plants
rt ornamental foliage plants

FATTENING
BT1 animal feeding
BT2 feeding
NT1 cattle fattening
NT2 bull fattening
NT1 dry lot feeding
NT1 flushing
NT1 pig fattening
NT2 boar fattening
NT2 piglet fattening
NT1 poultry fattening
NT2 duck fattening
NT2 fowl fattening
NT2 goose fattening
NT2 guineafowl fattening
NT2 turkey fattening
NT1 rabbit fattening
NT1 sheep fattening
NT2 lamb fattening
rt fattening performance
rt feeding
rt livestock farming

FATTENING PERFORMANCE
BT1 feed conversion
BT2 conversion
BT1 performance
rt body weight
rt fattening
rt growth

fatty acid desaturase
USE **acyl-coa desaturase**

FATTY ACID ESTERS
BT1 esters
NT1 acetates (esters)
NT2 bornyl acetate
NT2 cellulose acetate
NT2 isopentyl acetate
NT2 retinyl acetate
NT2 sucrose octaacetate
NT2 triacetin
NT1 acylglycerols
NT2 diacylglycerols
NT2 monoacylglycerols
NT3 monoolein
NT2 olein
NT2 stearin
NT2 sucroglycerides
NT2 triacylglycerols
NT3 long chain triacylglycerols
NT4 triolein
NT3 medium chain triacylglycerols
NT4 trilaurin
NT4 trioctanoin
NT3 short chain triacylglycerols
NT4 triacetin
NT4 tributyrin
NT1 ethyl octanoate
NT1 palmitates
NT2 retinyl palmitate
NT1 propionates (esters)
NT2 phenethyl propionate
NT1 wax esters
NT2 beeswax
NT2 lanolin
rt animal oils
rt fatty acids
rt plant oils

FATTY-ACID SYNTHASE
(ec 2.3.1.85)
BT1 acyltransferases
BT2 transferases
BT3 enzymes

FATTY ACIDS
uf free fatty acids
uf nonesterified fatty acids
BT1 carboxylic acids
BT2 organic acids
BT3 acids
BT1 lipids
NT1 branched chain fatty acids
NT2 phytanic acid
NT1 cyclopropenoid fatty acids
NT2 cyclopropenoic acid
NT2 sterculic acid
NT1 essential fatty acids
NT2 arachidonic acid
NT2 linoleic acid
NT2 linolenic acid
NT1 hydroxy fatty acids
NT2 3-hydroxybutyric acid
NT2 ricinoleic acid
NT2 trihydroxyoctadecenoic acid
NT1 long chain fatty acids
NT2 arachidonic acid
NT2 docosenoic acids
NT3 brassidic acid
NT3 erucic acid
NT2 elaidic acid
NT2 gadoleic acid
NT2 linoleic acid
NT2 oleic acid
NT2 palmitic acid
NT2 palmitoleic acid
NT2 pentadecanoic acid
NT2 stearic acid
NT2 tetracosadienoic acid
NT1 medium chain fatty acids
NT2 3,5-tetradecadienoic acid
NT2 decanoic acid
NT2 dodecanoic acid
NT2 myristic acid
NT2 nonanoic acid
NT2 octanoic acid
NT2 tridecanoic acid
NT1 odd chain fatty acids
NT2 nonanoic acid
NT2 pentadecanoic acid
NT2 tridecanoic acid
NT1 saturated fatty acids
NT2 decanoic acid
NT2 dodecanoic acid
NT2 hexanoic acid
NT2 myristic acid
NT2 nonanoic acid
NT2 octanoic acid
NT2 palmitic acid
NT2 pentadecanoic acid
NT2 phytanic acid
NT2 stearic acid
NT2 tridecanoic acid
NT1 short chain fatty acids
NT2 hexanoic acid
NT2 maleic acid
NT2 sorbic acid
NT1 trans fatty acids
NT2 brassidic acid
NT2 elaidic acid
NT1 unsaturated fatty acids
NT2 dienoic fatty acids
NT3 3,5-tetradecadienoic acid
NT3 linoleic acid
NT3 sorbic acid
NT3 tetracosadienoic acid
NT2 monoenoic fatty acids
NT3 docosenoic acids
NT4 brassidic acid
NT4 erucic acid
NT3 elaidic acid
NT3 gadoleic acid
NT3 maleic acid
NT3 oleic acid
NT3 palmitoleic acid
NT2 polyenoic fatty acids
NT3 arachidonic acid
NT3 eicosapentaenoic acid
NT3 linolenic acid
NT1 volatile fatty acids
NT2 butyric acid
NT2 isobutyric acid
NT2 valeric acid
rt chlorinated fatty acids
rt fats

FATTY ACIDS *cont.*
rt fatty acid esters

FATTY ALCOHOLS
BT1 alcohols
BT1 lipids
NT1 1-dodecanol
NT1 1-dotriacontanol
NT1 1-hexadecanol
NT1 farnesol
NT1 triacontanol

FATTY DEGENERATION
uf yellow fat disease
BT1 degeneration
BT1 lipid metabolism disorders
BT2 metabolic disorders
BT3 animal disorders
BT4 disorders
rt fats
rt fatty liver
rt fatty liver haemorrhagic syndrome

FATTY KIDNEY
BT1 kidney diseases
BT2 urinary tract diseases
BT3 organic diseases
BT4 diseases
BT1 lipid metabolism disorders
BT2 metabolic disorders
BT3 animal disorders
BT4 disorders

FATTY LIVER
uf steatosis
BT1 liver diseases
BT2 digestive system diseases
BT3 organic diseases
BT4 diseases
rt fatty degeneration
rt foie gras
rt reye's syndrome

FATTY LIVER HAEMORRHAGIC SYNDROME
AF fatty liver hemorrhagic syndrome
BT1 liver diseases
BT2 digestive system diseases
BT3 organic diseases
BT4 diseases
rt fatty degeneration
rt haemorrhage

FATTY LIVER HEMORRHAGIC SYNDROME
BF fatty liver haemorrhagic syndrome
rt hemorrhage

FATTY OIL PLANTS
BT1 oil plants
NT1 avocados
NT1 cashews
NT1 juniperus virginiana
NT1 oilseed plants
NT2 acrocomia sclerocarpa
NT2 argania spinosa
NT2 argemone mexicana
NT2 azadirachta indica
NT2 balanites aegyptiaca
NT2 brassica campestris var. toria
NT2 brassica carinata
NT2 brassica juncea
NT2 brassica napus var. dichotoma
NT2 brassica napus var. glauca
NT2 brassica nigra
NT2 buchanania lanzan
NT2 camelina sativa
NT2 cannabis sativa
NT2 caryocar amygdaliferum
NT2 caryocar coriaceum
NT2 caryocar nuciferum
NT2 ceiba pentandra
NT2 citrullus colocynthis
NT2 cnicus benedictus
NT2 cocoa
NT2 coconuts
NT2 cordia dichotoma
NT2 cordia verbenacea

FATTY OIL PLANTS *cont.*
NT2 cotton
NT2 crambe abyssinica
NT2 cucumeropsis edulis
NT2 cucumeropsis mannii
NT2 cucurbita foetidissima
NT2 cucurbita pepo
NT2 diploknema butyracea
NT2 dodonaea viscosa
NT2 eruca vesicaria
NT2 grapes
NT2 groundnuts
NT2 guizotia abyssinica
NT2 hazelnuts
NT2 hevea brasiliensis
NT2 hibiscus syriacus
NT2 hildegardia barteri
NT2 irvingia gabonensis
NT2 jatropha glandulifera
NT2 jessenia bataua
NT2 kigelia africana
NT2 licania rigida
NT2 linum usitatissimum
NT2 madhuca latifolia
NT2 madhuca longifolia
NT2 maize
NT2 mangoes
NT2 mimusops elengi
NT2 moringa aptera
NT2 moringa concanensis
NT2 moringa oleifera
NT2 moringa peregrina
NT2 mucuna sloanei
NT2 ochna squarrosa
NT2 oenothera biennis
NT2 oil palms
NT2 okras
NT2 orbignya martiana
NT2 orbignya oleifera
NT2 papaver somniferum
NT2 pentaclethra macrophylla
NT2 pentadesma butyracea
NT2 perilla frutescens
NT2 pongamia pinnata
NT2 psophocarpus tetragonolobus
NT2 quassia simarouba
NT2 rape
NT2 rice
NT2 ricinodendron heudelotii
NT2 ricinodendron rautanenii
NT2 ricinus communis
NT2 safflower
NT2 sapium sebiferum
NT2 schleichera oleosa
NT2 schleichera trijuga
NT2 sesame
NT2 shorea robusta
NT2 simmondsia chinensis
NT2 sinapis alba
NT2 soyabeans
NT2 sunflowers
NT2 swede rape
NT2 syagrus oleracea
NT2 tea
NT2 telfairia pedata
NT2 tomatoes
NT2 trichilia emetica
NT2 tung
NT2 turnip rape
NT2 vateria indica
NT2 vernonia anthelmintica
NT2 virola surinamensis
NT2 vitellaria paradoxa
NT2 walnuts
NT2 watermelons
NT2 zeyheria tuberculosa
NT1 olives
NT1 raphia hookeri
NT1 raphia regalis
NT1 raphia sudanica
NT1 raphia vinifera
rt fats
rt fatty oils
rt horticultural crops
rt industrial crops
rt lipids
rt plants
rt woody plants

FATTY OILS
BT1 oils
NT1 animal oils
NT2 butter oil
NT2 fish oils
NT3 fish liver oils
NT4 anchovy oil
NT4 cod liver oil
NT4 menhaden oil
NT3 herring oil
NT1 drying oils
NT2 tung oil
rt fats
rt fatty oil plants
rt plant oils

FAUCARIA
BT1 aizoaceae
NT1 faucaria bosscheana

FAUCARIA BOSSCHEANA
BT1 faucaria
BT2 aizoaceae
BT1 ornamental succulent plants
BT2 succulent plants

FAUNA
NT1 soil fauna
NT2 soil invertebrates
NT3 earthworms
NT3 soil arthropods
NT4 soil insects
rt biogeography
rt biota
rt wildlife

FAVISM
BT1 human diseases
BT2 diseases
rt vicia faba

FEARFULNESS
HN from 1989
BT1 animal behaviour
BT2 behaviour
NT1 gunshyness

FEASIBILITY
rt economic viability

FEASIBILITY STUDIES
BT1 evaluation
BT1 trials
BT2 research
rt case studies
rt cost benefit analysis
rt implementation of research
rt pilot projects
rt project appraisal
rt trials

FEASTS (AGRICOLA)
BT1 meals
rt banquets (agricola)

FEATHER MEAL
BT1 meal
rt feathers

FEATHER MITES
HN from 1990
BT1 ectoparasites
BT2 arthropod pests
BT3 pests
BT2 parasites
BT1 mites
rt feathers

FEATHER PECKING
BT1 abnormal behaviour
BT2 behaviour
rt feathers

FEATHERING RATE
rt feathers
rt plumage birds

FEATHERS
(bird)
BT1 integument
BT2 body parts
NT1 hamuli
rt down
rt feather meal

FEATHERS *cont.*
rt feather mites
rt feather pecking
rt feathering rate
rt moult
rt plumage
rt wings

FEBANTEL
BT1 anthelmintics
BT2 antiparasitic agents
BT3 drugs

FECAL COLIFORMS
BF faecal coliforms
BT1 fecal flora
rt feces

FECAL FLORA
BF faecal flora
NT1 fecal coliforms
rt feces

FECES
BF faeces
NT1 cat feces
NT1 dog feces
NT1 human feces
rt defecation
rt fecal coliforms
rt fecal flora
rt feces collection
rt feces composition

FECES COLLECTION
BF faeces collection
rt feces

FECES COMPOSITION
BF faeces composition
rt feces

FECUNDITY
rt egg production
rt fertility
rt litter size

FEDERAL AID (AGRICOLA)
BT1 support measures
rt federal programs (agricola)

FEDERAL GOVERNMENT (AGRICOLA)
HN from 1989
BT1 government

FEDERAL PROGRAMS (AGRICOLA)
BT1 programs (agricola)
rt federal aid (agricola)

FEDERALISM
BT1 political systems
BT2 politics

FEDERATED STATES OF MICRONESIA
BT1 pacific islands trust territory
BT2 american oceania
BT3 oceania

FEDIA
BT1 valerianaceae

FEED ADDITIVES
BT1 additives
NT1 bambermycin
NT1 biuret
NT1 diammonium phosphate
NT1 ethoxyquin
NT1 methionine hydroxy analogue
NT1 monensin
NT1 probiotics
NT1 thiopeptin
NT1 tiamulin
rt antibiotics
rt antioxidants
rt feed industry
rt feed supplements
rt feeds
rt food additives
rt growth promoters
rt medicated feeds
rt mineral supplements

FEED ADDITIVES *cont.*
rt minerals
rt nutrients
rt silage additives
rt sucrose

feed cereals
USE **cereals**

FEED COMPOSITION TABLES
BT1 feed evaluation
BT2 evaluation
rt composition
rt feed formulation
rt feeding standards
rt feeds
rt quality controls

FEED CONVERSION
uf *conversion, feed*
BT1 conversion
NT1 fattening performance
rt digestion
rt feed conversion efficiency
rt feed rations
rt feeds
rt food conversion

FEED CONVERSION EFFICIENCY
BT1 digestibility
rt feed conversion
rt feeds

feed crops
USE **fodder crops**

feed digestibility
USE **digestibility**

FEED DISPENSERS
uf *feeders*
BT1 dispensers
NT1 automatic feed dispensers
NT1 calf feeders
NT2 bucket calf feeders
NT1 liquid feed dispensers
NT1 mobile feeders
NT1 nipple feed dispensers
NT1 pig feeders
NT1 programmed feed dispensers
NT1 self feeders
NT1 sheep feeders
NT1 troughs
NT2 feed troughs
NT2 subsurface troughs
NT2 water troughs
rt feed troughs
rt feeder mixer wagons
rt feeds
rt mangers
rt tube feeding

FEED EVALUATION
BT1 evaluation
NT1 feed composition tables
rt feeds

FEED FORMULATION
BT1 feed mixing
BT2 mixing
BT2 processing
BT1 feeding standards
BT2 standards
rt feed composition tables
rt feed industry
rt feeder mixer wagons
rt feeds

FEED GRAINS
uf *grain feed*
BT1 feeds
BT1 grain
NT1 coarse grains
rt food grains
rt grain conservation
rt grain driers
rt grain drills
rt grain drying
rt grain dust
rt grain loss monitors
rt grain mottling
rt grain stores

feed habits
USE **feeding habits**

FEED INDUSTRY
BT1 input industries
BT2 industry
rt feed additives
rt feed formulation
rt milling industry

FEED INTAKE
BT1 intake
NT1 plane of nutrition
rt feeds
rt food restriction

FEED LEGUMES
BT1 leguminosae
rt feeds

FEED MEALS
BT1 oilmeals
BT2 feeds
BT2 meal
rt feeds

feed mechanism, bandolier
USE **bandolier feed mechanism**

feed mechanism, belt
USE **belt feed mechanism**

feed mechanism, cup
USE **cup feed mechanism**

feed mechanism, fluted roller
USE **fluted roller feed mechanism**

feed mechanism, pneumatic
USE **pneumatic feed mechanism**

FEED MECHANISMS
uf *feeding mechanism*
NT1 bandolier feed mechanism
NT1 belt feed mechanism
NT1 cup feed mechanism
NT1 fluted roller feed mechanism
NT1 pneumatic feed mechanism

FEED MIXING
BT1 mixing
BT1 processing
NT1 feed formulation
rt complete feeds
rt feeder mixer wagons
rt feeds

FEED OF ANIMAL ORIGIN
BT1 feeds

feed preferences
USE **feeding preferences**

feed products
HN was used until 1990 in agricola
USE **feeds**

FEED RATIONS
BT1 feed requirements
BT2 requirements
rt feed conversion

FEED REQUIREMENTS
BT1 requirements
NT1 feed rations
rt feeding habits
rt feeding standards
rt feeds

FEED ROOTS
BT1 root crops
NT1 fodder beet
NT1 swedes
NT1 turnips
rt feeds
rt plants

FEED STEAMERS
uf *steamers, feed*
BT1 steamers
BT2 equipment
rt cooking

FEED STEAMERS *cont.*
rt feeds

FEED SUPPLEMENTS
uf *antibiotic supplements*
BT1 supplements
NT1 biofermal
NT1 biofral
NT1 molasses
NT1 protein concentrates
NT2 animal protein concentrates
NT2 fish protein concentrate
NT2 leaf protein concentrate
NT2 lucerne protein concentrate
NT2 mustard protein concentrate
NT2 potato protein concentrate
NT2 rapeseed protein concentrate
NT1 protein supplements
NT1 starea
NT1 vinasse
NT2 distillers' solubles
NT3 maize fermentation solubles
NT3 molasses distillers' solubles
NT1 vitamin supplements
rt feed additives
rt food supplements

FEED TROUGHS
uf *troughs, feed*
BT1 troughs
BT2 containers
BT2 drinkers
BT2 feed dispensers
BT3 dispensers
rt feed dispensers
rt feeds

FEEDBACK
rt automatic control
rt biofeedback (agricola)
rt controls
rt sensing
rt servomotors
rt tracking

FEEDER MIXER WAGONS
BT1 wagons
BT2 vehicles
rt feed dispensers
rt feed formulation
rt feed mixing
rt feeds
rt mixers
rt self unloading trailers
rt trailers

feeders
USE **feed dispensers**

FEEDING
NT1 animal feeding
NT2 dog feeding
NT2 fattening
NT3 cattle fattening
NT4 bull fattening
NT3 dry lot feeding
NT3 flushing
NT3 pig fattening
NT4 boar fattening
NT4 piglet fattening
NT3 poultry fattening
NT4 duck fattening
NT4 fowl fattening
NT4 goose fattening
NT4 guineafowl fattening
NT4 turkey fattening
NT3 rabbit fattening
NT3 sheep fattening
NT4 lamb fattening
NT2 livestock feeding
NT3 horse feeding
NT4 mare feeding
NT3 pig feeding
NT4 boar feeding
NT4 piglet feeding
NT4 sow feeding
NT3 poultry feeding

FEEDING *cont.*
NT4 duck feeding
NT4 fowl feeding
NT4 goose feeding
NT4 guineafowl feeding
NT4 hen feeding
NT4 turkey feeding
NT5 turkey hen feeding
NT5 turkey poult feeding
NT3 ruminant feeding
NT4 buffalo feeding
NT4 cattle feeding
NT5 bull feeding
NT5 calf feeding
NT4 deer feeding
NT4 goat feeding
NT5 kid feeding
NT4 sheep feeding
NT5 ewe feeding
NT5 lamb feeding
NT2 rabbit feeding
NT2 rat feeding
NT2 suckling
NT1 child feeding
NT1 communal feeding
NT1 creep feeding
NT1 dry feeding
NT1 emergency feeding (agricola)
NT1 enteral feeding
NT2 tube feeding
NT1 fish feeding
NT1 force feeding
NT1 high plane feeding
NT1 individual feeding
NT1 infant feeding
NT2 bottle feeding (agricola)
NT2 breast feeding
NT2 postweaning interval
NT1 low plane feeding
NT1 mastication
NT1 overfeeding
NT2 hyperalimentation
NT1 parenteral feeding
NT1 refeeding
NT1 restricted feeding
NT1 self feeding
NT1 solid feeding (agricola)
NT1 steaming up
NT1 sucking
NT1 supplementary feeding
NT1 underfeeding
NT2 fasting
NT1 unrestricted feeding
NT1 wet feeding
rt animal nutrition
rt antifeedants
rt browsing
rt catering
rt detritivores
rt diets
rt fattening
rt feeding behaviour
rt feeding frequency
rt feeding habits
rt feeding standards
rt feedlots
rt feeds
rt food chains
rt foods
rt grazing
rt hospital diets
rt livestock farming
rt malnutrition
rt nutrition

FEEDING BEHAVIOR
BF feeding behaviour
BT1 behavior
NT1 grazing behavior
rt host-seeking behavior

FEEDING BEHAVIOUR
AF feeding behavior
BT1 behaviour
NT1 biting rates
NT1 feeding habits
NT2 browsing
NT2 coprophagy
NT3 caecotrophy
NT2 feeding frequency
NT2 feeding preferences

FEEDING BEHAVIOUR *cont.*
NT3 food preferences
NT4 food beliefs
NT4 salt preference
NT2 foraging
NT3 honey-getting capacity
NT2 haematophagy
NT2 nectar feeding
NT2 overeating
NT2 overfeeding
NT3 hyperalimentation
NT2 sugar feeding
NT1 functional responses
NT1 grazing behaviour
NT2 overgrazing
NT1 trophallaxis
rt eating
rt feeding
rt food preferences
rt host-seeking behaviour

feeding, communal
USE **communal feeding**

feeding deterrents
USE **antifeedants**

feeding, dry
USE **dry feeding**

FEEDING FREQUENCY
BT1 feeding habits
BT2 feeding behaviour
BT3 behaviour
BT2 habits
rt feeding
rt overfeeding

FEEDING HABITS
uf *eating habits*
uf *feed habits*
uf *food habits*
BT1 feeding behaviour
BT2 behaviour
BT1 habits
NT1 browsing
NT1 coprophagy
NT2 caecotrophy
NT1 feeding frequency
NT1 feeding preferences
NT2 food preferences
NT3 food beliefs
NT3 salt preference
NT1 foraging
NT2 honey-getting capacity
NT1 haematophagy
NT1 nectar feeding
NT1 overeating
NT1 overfeeding
NT2 hyperalimentation
NT1 sugar feeding
rt consumer behaviour
rt feed requirements
rt feeding
rt meal patterns

feeding inhibitors
USE **antifeedants**

feeding mechanism
USE **feed mechanisms**

feeding, parenteral
USE **parenteral feeding**

FEEDING PREFERENCES
HN from 1990; previously "feed preferences"
uf *feed preferences*
BT1 feeding habits
BT2 feeding behaviour
BT3 behaviour
BT2 habits
NT1 food preferences
NT2 food beliefs
NT2 salt preference

feeding programs
USE **nutrition programs**

FEEDING STANDARDS
BT1 standards
NT1 feed formulation
rt feed composition tables

FEEDING STANDARDS *cont.*
rt feed requirements
rt feeding

feeding stimulants
USE **phagostimulants**

feeding stuffs
USE **feeds**

feeding, wet
USE **wet feeding**

FEEDLOT EFFLUENT
BT1 effluents
BT2 wastes
BT1 manures
BT2 organic amendments
BT3 soil amendments
BT4 amendments
rt feedlot wastes
rt feedlots

FEEDLOT WASTES
BT1 animal wastes
BT2 wastes
BT1 manures
BT2 organic amendments
BT3 soil amendments
BT4 amendments
rt feedlot effluent
rt feedlots

FEEDLOTS
BT1 yards
rt dry lot feeding
rt farm structure
rt feeding
rt feedlot effluent
rt feedlot wastes
rt fields
rt intensive livestock farming

FEEDS
uf *feed products*
uf *feeding stuffs*
uf *fodders*
NT1 ammoniated feeds
NT1 banana meal
NT1 beet pulp
NT1 candy
NT1 cassava leaves
NT1 cassava peel
NT1 complete feeds
NT1 compound feeds
NT1 concentrates
NT2 protein concentrates
NT3 animal protein concentrates
NT3 fish protein concentrate
NT3 leaf protein concentrate
NT3 lucerne protein concentrate
NT3 mustard protein concentrate
NT3 potato protein concentrate
NT3 rapeseed protein concentrate
NT2 uromol
NT1 dehydrated fodders
NT1 dried fodders
NT1 dried lucerne
NT1 dry feeds
NT1 feed grains
NT2 coarse grains
NT1 feed of animal origin
NT1 fish meal
NT2 anchovy meal
NT1 fodder beet
NT1 gluten feed
NT1 grass pellets
NT1 green feed
NT1 green fodders
NT1 groundnuts
NT1 hay
NT2 barley hay
NT2 clover hay
NT2 cowpea hay
NT2 lucerne hay
NT3 lucerne haylage
NT2 lupin hay
NT2 oat hay

FEEDS *cont.*
NT2 ryegrass hay
NT2 sainfoin hay
NT2 sorghum hay
NT2 soya hay
NT1 haylage
NT1 manufactured feeds
NT1 meat meal
NT2 tendon meal
NT2 whale meal
NT1 medicated feeds
NT1 middlings
NT1 oilmeals
NT2 castor oilmeal
NT2 coconut oilmeal
NT2 copra meal
NT2 cottonseed oilmeal
NT2 feed meals
NT2 groundnut oilmeal
NT2 kapok seed meal
NT2 linseed oilmeal
NT2 mustard oilmeal
NT2 oilseed cakes
NT3 neem seed cake
NT3 olive cake
NT3 palm kernel cake
NT2 rapeseed oilmeal
NT2 safflower oilmeal
NT2 sal seed meal
NT2 sesame oilmeal
NT2 soyabean oilmeal
NT2 sunflower oilmeal
NT1 pelleted feeds
NT2 straw pellets
NT1 pet foods
NT2 cat foods
NT2 dog foods
NT1 pollen substitutes
NT1 protected fat
NT1 protected protein
NT1 roughage
NT1 silage
NT2 barley silage
NT2 beet top silage
NT2 cassava silage
NT2 clover silage
NT2 cowpea silage
NT2 fish silage
NT2 grass silage
NT2 groundnut silage
NT2 haylage
NT2 legume silage
NT2 lucerne silage
NT2 lupin silage
NT2 maize silage
NT2 oat silage
NT2 pea haulm silage
NT2 potato silage
NT2 rape silage
NT2 rye silage
NT2 ryegrass silage
NT2 sorghum silage
NT2 soya silage
NT2 sugarcane silage
NT2 sunflower silage
NT2 vacuum silage
NT2 wheat silage
NT2 whole crop silage
NT1 straw
NT2 barley straw
NT2 bean straw
NT2 groundnut haulm
NT2 maize straw
NT2 oat straw
NT2 rape straw
NT2 rice straw
NT2 rye straw
NT2 ryegrass straw
NT2 sorghum stalks
NT2 soya straw
NT2 stover
NT3 maize stover
NT2 wheat straw
NT1 supplementary feeds
NT1 wafers
rt animal feeding
rt animal nutrition
rt briquettes
rt browse plants
rt edible species
rt faeces

FEEDS *cont.*
rt feed additives
rt feed composition tables
rt feed conversion
rt feed conversion efficiency
rt feed dispensers
rt feed evaluation
rt feed formulation
rt feed intake
rt feed legumes
rt feed meals
rt feed mixing
rt feed requirements
rt feed roots
rt feed steamers
rt feed troughs
rt feeder mixer wagons
rt feeding
rt fodder
rt fodder plants
rt foods
rt haymaking
rt livestock feeding
rt rumen contents
rt weaning

FEELER WHEELS
BT1 feelers
BT2 components
rt beet toppers
rt detectors
rt wheels

FEELERS
BT1 components
NT1 feeler wheels
rt detectors
rt sensors
rt tracking

FEES
uf *charges (costs)*
NT1 entry fees
rt earned income
rt expenditure
rt income

FEET
uf *foot*
BT1 limbs
BT2 body regions
NT1 digits
NT1 soles
rt treading

FEIJOA
BT1 myrtaceae
rt acca

feijoa sellowiana
USE **acca sellowiana**

FEIJOAS
BT1 subtropical tree fruits
BT2 subtropical fruits
BT3 fruit crops
BT2 tree fruits
rt acca sellowiana

FELDSPAR
BF felspar

FELICIA
BT1 compositae
NT1 felicia echinata

FELICIA ECHINATA
BT1 felicia
BT2 compositae

FELIDAE
BT1 fissipeda
BT2 carnivores
BT3 mammals
NT1 acinonyx
NT2 acinonyx jubatus
NT1 felis
NT2 felis bengalensis
NT2 felis concolor
NT2 felis lynx
NT2 felis rufus
NT2 felis silvestris
NT2 felis wiedii
NT1 neofelis

FELIDAE *cont.*
NT2 neofelis nebulosa
NT1 panthera
NT2 panthera uncia
rt cats
rt jaguars
rt leopards
rt lions
rt ocelots
rt tigers

FELINE CALICIVIRUS
BT1 calicivirus
BT2 caliciviridae
BT3 viruses

feline dysautonomia
USE **dysautonomia**

FELINE HERPESVIRUS
BT1 herpesviridae
BT2 viruses
NT1 feline rhinotracheitis virus

FELINE IMMUNODEFICIENCY VIRUS
HN from 1990
BT1 lentivirinae
BT2 retroviridae
BT3 viruses

feline leukosis
USE **leukaemia**

feline leukosis virus
USE **feline oncovirus**

FELINE ONCOVIRUS
uf *feline leukosis virus*
BT1 mammalian oncovirus
BT2 oncovirus type c
BT3 oncovirinae
BT4 retroviridae
BT5 viruses

FELINE PANLEUKOPENIA VIRUS
uf *panleukopenia virus*
BT1 parvovirus
BT2 parvoviridae
BT3 viruses

FELINE PERITONITIS VIRUS
BT1 coronavirus
BT2 coronaviridae
BT3 viruses

FELINE RHINOTRACHEITIS VIRUS
BT1 feline herpesvirus
BT2 herpesviridae
BT3 viruses

FELINE SYNCYTIAL VIRUS
BT1 spumavirinae
BT2 retroviridae
BT3 viruses

FELIS
uf *lynx (genus)*
BT1 felidae
BT2 fissipeda
BT3 carnivores
BT4 mammals
NT1 felis bengalensis
NT1 felis concolor
NT1 felis lynx
NT1 felis rufus
NT1 felis silvestris
NT1 felis wiedii

FELIS BENGALENSIS
BT1 felis
BT2 felidae
BT3 fissipeda
BT4 carnivores
BT5 mammals

felis catus
USE **cats**

FELIS CONCOLOR
uf *cougars*
uf *pumas*
BT1 felis
BT2 felidae
BT3 fissipeda

FELIS CONCOLOR *cont.*
BT4 carnivores
BT5 mammals

FELIS LYNX
uf *lynx (species)*
uf *lynx lynx*
BT1 felis
BT2 felidae
BT3 fissipeda
BT4 carnivores
BT5 mammals

felis pardalis
USE **ocelots**

FELIS RUFUS
uf *lynx rufus*
BT1 felis
BT2 felidae
BT3 fissipeda
BT4 carnivores
BT5 mammals

FELIS SILVESTRIS
BT1 felis
BT2 felidae
BT3 fissipeda
BT4 carnivores
BT5 mammals

FELIS WIEDII
BT1 felis
BT2 felidae
BT3 fissipeda
BT4 carnivores
BT5 mammals

FELLER BUNCHERS
BT1 forestry machinery
BT2 machinery
rt logging machines

FELLERS
BT1 forestry machinery
BT2 machinery
rt logging machines

FELLING
BT1 forestry practices
BT2 forestry
NT1 clear felling
NT2 stump removal
NT1 clear strip felling
NT1 illicit felling
NT1 improvement fellings
NT1 liberation felling
NT1 sour felling
rt axes
rt bunching
rt grubbing
rt harvesting
rt logging
rt selective felling
rt site preparation
rt timber trade

FELSPAR
AF feldspar
BT1 nonclay minerals
BT2 minerals

FELT (AGRICOLA)
BT1 fabrics

FELTIA
BT1 noctuidae
BT2 lepidoptera
NT1 feltia jaculifera
NT1 feltia subterranea

feltia ducens
USE **feltia jaculifera**

FELTIA JACULIFERA
uf *feltia ducens*
BT1 feltia
BT2 noctuidae
BT3 lepidoptera

FELTIA SUBTERRANEA
BT1 feltia
BT2 noctuidae
BT3 lepidoptera

FEMALE ANIMALS
  uf *doe*
  BT1 animals
  NT1 bitches
  NT1 cows
    NT2 beef cows
    NT2 dairy cows
    NT2 heifers
      NT3 bred heifers
    NT2 nurse cows
  NT1 daughters
  NT1 ewes
  NT1 gilts
  NT1 hens
  NT1 lactating females
  NT1 mares
  NT1 ovariectomized females
  NT1 prepubertal females
  NT1 queens
    NT2 queen honeybees
      NT3 mated queen honeybees
      NT3 virgin queen honeybees
  NT1 sows
  NT1 superovulated females
  NT1 synchronized females
  rt females
  rt milk-yielding animals

FEMALE FERTILITY
  uf *fertility, female*
  BT1 fertility
  BT1 reproductive efficiency
    BT2 efficiency
    BT2 reproductive performance
      BT3 performance
  NT1 calving interval
  NT1 calving rate
  NT1 lambing rate
  rt breeding
  rt conception rate
  rt fertilizing ability
  rt service period
  rt superovulated females

FEMALE GENITAL DISEASES
  uf *genital system diseases*
  BT1 organic diseases
    BT2 diseases
  NT1 ovarian diseases
    NT2 ovarian cysts
  NT1 salpingitis
  NT1 uterine diseases
    NT2 cervicitis
    NT2 endometritis
    NT2 pyometra
    NT2 uterine prolapse
    NT2 uterine torsion
  NT1 vaginal diseases
    NT2 vaginal prolapse
    NT2 vaginitis
  NT1 vulvitis
  rt female genitalia

female genital system
  USE **female genitalia**

FEMALE GENITALIA
  uf *female genital system*
  uf *genital system, female*
  uf *genitalia, female*
  BT1 genitalia
    BT2 urogenital system
      BT3 body parts
  NT1 oviducts
    NT2 infundibulum
    NT2 magnum
  NT1 spermatheca
  NT1 uterus
    NT2 cervix
    NT2 endometrium
    NT2 muellerian ducts
    NT2 myometrium
  NT1 vagina
  NT1 vulva
    NT2 clitoris
  rt female genital diseases
  rt luteinization
  rt reproductive organs

FEMALE INFERTILITY
  (animals and man; for plants use "female sterility")

FEMALE INFERTILITY *cont.*
  BT1 infertility
  BT1 reproductive disorders
    BT2 functional disorders
      BT3 animal disorders
        BT4 disorders
  NT1 pseudopregnancy
  rt nymphomania

FEMALE LABOR
  BF female labour
  rt labor

FEMALE LABOUR
  AF female labor
  uf *labour, female*
  BT1 labour
  rt family labour
  rt rural women
  rt women

FEMALE STERILITY
  (plants; for animals and man use "female infertility")
  uf *sterility, female*
  BT1 sterility

FEMALES
  NT1 virgin females
  rt female animals
  rt widows

FEMUR
  BT1 limb bones
    BT2 bones
      BT3 musculoskeletal system
        BT4 body parts

FEN SOILS
  BT1 soil types (ecological)

FENAMINOSULF
  BT1 unclassified fungicides
    BT2 fungicides
      BT3 pesticides

FENAMIPHOS
  uf *phenamiphos*
  BT1 organophosphate nematicides
    BT2 organophosphorus nematicides
      BT3 nematicides
        BT4 pesticides
      BT3 organophosphorus pesticides
        BT4 organophosphorus compounds

FENAPANIL
  BT1 imidazole fungicides
    BT2 fungicides
      BT3 pesticides
    BT2 imidazoles
      BT3 azoles
        BT4 heterocyclic nitrogen compounds
          BT5 organic nitrogen compounds

FENARIMOL
  BT1 pyrimidine fungicides
    BT2 fungicides
      BT3 pesticides
    BT2 pyrimidines
      BT3 heterocyclic nitrogen compounds
        BT4 organic nitrogen compounds

FENBENDAZOLE
  BT1 anthelmintics
    BT2 antiparasitic agents
      BT3 drugs
  BT1 benzimidazoles
    BT2 heterocyclic nitrogen compounds
      BT3 organic nitrogen compounds

FENBUTATIN OXIDE
  BT1 organotin acaricides
    BT2 acaricides
      BT3 pesticides

FENBUTATIN OXIDE *cont.*
    BT2 organotin pesticides
      BT3 organotin compounds

FENCE LINES
  BT1 fencing

FENCE POSTS
  BT1 posts
    BT2 fencing
    BT2 staking
  rt fences

FENCES
  BT1 barriers
  BT1 fencing
  NT1 electric fences
  NT1 live fences
  NT1 slat fences
  rt fence posts
  rt hedges

fences, electric
  USE **electric fences**

FENCHLORPHOS
  uf *fenclofos*
  uf *ronnel*
  BT1 ectoparasiticides
    BT2 antiparasitic agents
      BT3 drugs
  BT1 organothiophosphate insecticides
    BT2 organophosphorus insecticides
      BT3 insecticides
        BT4 pesticides
      BT3 organophosphorus pesticides
        BT4 organophosphorus compounds

FENCING
  NT1 fence lines
  NT1 fences
    NT2 electric fences
    NT2 live fences
    NT2 slat fences
  NT1 gates
  NT1 posts
    NT2 fence posts
  rt hedges
  rt walls

fenclofos
  USE **fenchlorphos**

FENCLORIM
  BT1 herbicide safeners
    BT2 safeners

FENESTRARIA
  BT1 aizoaceae

FENFLURAMINE
  BT1 amphetamines
    BT2 phenethylamines
      BT3 amines
        BT4 amino compounds
          BT5 organic nitrogen compounds
  BT1 anorexiants
    BT2 drugs
  BT1 sympathomimetics
    BT2 neurotropic drugs
      BT3 drugs

FENFURAM
  BT1 furanilide fungicides
    BT2 anilide fungicides
      BT3 fungicides
        BT4 pesticides

FENITROTHION
  BT1 organothiophosphate insecticides
    BT2 organophosphorus insecticides
      BT3 insecticides
        BT4 pesticides
      BT3 organophosphorus pesticides
        BT4 organophosphorus compounds

FENLAND SOILS
  BT1 soil types (physiographic)

fennecus
  USE **vulpes**

FENNEL
  BT1 culinary herbs
  BT1 essential oil plants
    BT2 oil plants
  BT1 insecticidal plants
    BT2 pesticidal plants
  BT1 medicinal plants
  BT1 stem vegetables
    BT2 vegetables
  rt foeniculum vulgare

FENOBUCARB
  uf *bpmc*
  BT1 carbamate insecticides
    BT2 carbamate pesticides
    BT2 insecticides
      BT3 pesticides

FENOPROP
  uf *2,4,5-tp*
  BT1 auxins
    BT2 plant growth regulators
      BT3 growth regulators
  BT1 phenoxypropionic herbicides
    BT2 phenoxy herbicides
      BT3 herbicides
        BT4 pesticides

FENOXAPROP
  BT1 aryloxyphenoxypropionic herbicides
    BT2 phenoxypropionic herbicides
      BT3 phenoxy herbicides
        BT4 herbicides
          BT5 pesticides

FENOXYCARB
  BT1 juvenile hormone analogues
    BT2 insect growth regulators
      BT3 growth regulators
      BT3 insecticides
        BT4 pesticides

FENPIPRAMIDE
  BT1 parasympatholytics
    BT2 neurotropic drugs
      BT3 drugs

FENPROPATHRIN
  BT1 pyrethroid acaricides
    BT2 acaricides
      BT3 pesticides
    BT2 pyrethroids
  BT1 pyrethroid insecticides
    BT2 insecticides
      BT3 pesticides
    BT2 pyrethroids

FENPROPIMORPH
  BT1 morpholine fungicides
    BT2 fungicides
      BT3 pesticides

FENRIDAZON
  BT1 plant growth regulators
    BT2 growth regulators

FENS
  BT1 land types
  BT1 vegetation types
  rt floodplains
  rt wetlands

FENSULFOTHION
  BT1 organothiophosphate insecticides
    BT2 organophosphorus insecticides
      BT3 insecticides
        BT4 pesticides
      BT3 organophosphorus pesticides
        BT4 organophosphorus compounds
  BT1 organothiophosphate nematicides

FENSULFOTHION *cont.*
BT2 organophosphorus nematicides
BT3 nematicides
BT4 pesticides
BT3 organophosphorus pesticides
BT4 organophosphorus compounds

FENTANYL
BT1 analgesics
BT2 neurotropic drugs
BT3 drugs
BT1 injectable anaesthetics
BT2 anaesthetics
BT3 neurotropic drugs
BT4 drugs
BT1 neuroleptics
BT2 psychotropic drugs
BT3 neurotropic drugs
BT4 drugs

FENTERACOL
BT1 phenoxy herbicides
BT2 herbicides
BT3 pesticides

FENTHIAPROP
BT1 aryloxyphenoxypropionic herbicides
BT2 phenoxypropionic herbicides
BT3 phenoxy herbicides
BT4 herbicides
BT5 pesticides

FENTHION
BT1 avicides
BT2 pesticides
BT1 ectoparasiticides
BT2 antiparasitic agents
BT3 drugs
BT1 organothiophosphate insecticides
BT2 organophosphorus insecticides
BT3 insecticides
BT4 pesticides
BT3 organophosphorus pesticides
BT4 organophosphorus compounds

FENTICONAZOLE
HN from 1989
BT1 antifungal agents
BT2 antiinfective agents
BT3 drugs
BT1 imidazoles
BT2 azoles
BT3 heterocyclic nitrogen compounds
BT4 organic nitrogen compounds

FENTIN ACETATE
uf triphenyltin acetate
BT1 antifeedants
BT2 inhibitors
BT1 organotin fungicides
BT2 fungicides
BT3 pesticides
BT2 organotin pesticides
BT3 organotin compounds

FENTIN CHLORIDE
BT1 antifeedants
BT2 inhibitors
BT1 organotin fungicides
BT2 fungicides
BT3 pesticides
BT2 organotin pesticides
BT3 organotin compounds

FENTIN HYDROXIDE
uf tpth
BT1 algicides
BT2 herbicides
BT3 pesticides
BT1 antifeedants
BT2 inhibitors
BT1 molluscicides

FENTIN HYDROXIDE *cont.*
BT2 pesticides
BT1 organotin fungicides
BT2 fungicides
BT3 pesticides
BT2 organotin pesticides
BT3 organotin compounds

FENUGREEK
rt trigonella foenum-graecum

FENURON
BT1 urea herbicides
BT2 herbicides
BT3 pesticides

FENUSA
BT1 tenthredinidae
BT2 hymenoptera
NT1 fenusa pusilla

FENUSA PUSILLA
BT1 fenusa
BT2 tenthredinidae
BT3 hymenoptera

FENVALERATE
BT1 ectoparasiticides
BT2 antiparasitic agents
BT3 drugs
BT1 pyrethroid insecticides
BT2 insecticides
BT3 pesticides
BT2 pyrethroids

feoga
USE **eaggf**

FERAL HERDS
HN from 1989
BT1 herds
BT2 groups

FERBAM
BT1 dithiocarbamate fungicides
BT2 carbamate pesticides
BT2 fungicides
BT3 pesticides

FERETIA
BT1 rubiaceae
NT1 feretia apodanthera
NT1 feretia apondanthera

FERETIA APODANTHERA
BT1 feretia
BT2 rubiaceae

FERETIA APONDANTHERA
BT1 feretia
BT2 rubiaceae

FERGUSOBIA
BT1 neotylenchidae
BT2 nematoda

FERMENTATION
NT1 ex-ferm process
NT1 rumen fermentation
NT1 silage fermentation
rt biostil process
rt biotechnology
rt brewers' yeast
rt brewing
rt brewing industry
rt carbon dioxide
rt digestion
rt ethanol production
rt fermentation products
rt fermented fish
rt fermented foods
rt methane production
rt processing
rt silage making
rt starters
rt winemaking
rt yeasts

FERMENTATION PRODUCTS
BT1 products
NT1 fermented foods
NT2 fermented fish
NT2 fermented honey
NT3 mead
NT2 miso

FERMENTATION PRODUCTS *cont.*
NT2 natto
NT2 sauerkraut
NT2 tempeh
NT2 yoghurt
NT1 maize fermentation solubles
NT1 maize steep liquor
NT1 silage
NT2 barley silage
NT2 beet top silage
NT2 cassava silage
NT2 clover silage
NT2 cowpea silage
NT2 fish silage
NT2 grass silage
NT2 groundnut silage
NT2 haylage
NT2 legume silage
NT2 lucerne silage
NT2 lupin silage
NT2 maize silage
NT2 oat silage
NT2 pea haulm silage
NT2 potato silage
NT2 rape silage
NT2 rye silage
NT2 ryegrass silage
NT2 sorghum silage
NT2 soya silage
NT2 sugarcane silage
NT2 sunflower silage
NT2 vacuum silage
NT2 wheat silage
NT2 whole crop silage
rt beers
rt fermentation
rt fermented products (agricola)

fermentation, silage
USE **silage fermentation**

FERMENTATION WASTES
BT1 wastes
NT1 vinasse
NT2 distillers' solubles
NT3 maize fermentation solubles
NT3 molasses distillers' solubles
rt manures

FERMENTED FISH
uf fish, fermented
BT1 fermented foods
BT2 fermentation products
BT3 products
BT2 foods
BT1 fish products
BT2 animal products
BT3 products
rt fermentation

FERMENTED FOODS
BT1 fermentation products
BT2 products
BT1 foods
NT1 fermented fish
NT1 fermented honey
NT2 mead
NT1 miso
NT1 natto
NT1 sauerkraut
NT1 tempeh
NT1 yoghurt
rt fermentation

FERMENTED HONEY
BT1 fermented foods
BT2 fermentation products
BT3 products
BT2 foods
NT1 mead
rt honey

fermented milk
USE **cultured milks**

FERMENTED PRODUCTS (AGRICOLA)
rt fermentation products

fernando po
USE **equatorial guinea**

FERNS
NT1 ornamental ferns
NT2 adiantum capillus-veneris
NT2 adiantum hispidulum
NT2 adiantum pedatum
NT2 adiantum tenerum
NT2 arachniodes adiantiformis
NT2 asplenium bulbiferum
NT2 asplenium nidus
NT2 asplenium platyneuron
NT2 asplenium trichomanes
NT2 athyrium filix-femina
NT2 bolbitis presliana
NT2 bolbitis virens
NT2 ctenitis ampla
NT2 cystopteris bulbifera
NT2 cystopteris fragilis
NT2 dicranopteris linearis
NT2 diplazium pycnocarpon
NT2 dryopteris affinis
NT2 dryopteris cochleata
NT2 dryopteris erythrosora
NT2 dryopteris filix-mas
NT2 goniophlebium subauriculatum
NT2 matteuccia struthiopteris
NT2 nephrolepis biserrata
NT2 nephrolepis cordifolia
NT2 nephrolepis exaltata
NT2 oleandra wallichii
NT2 osmunda claytoniana
NT2 osmunda regalis
NT2 pachypodium lamerei
NT2 pellaea viridis
NT2 peranema cyantheoides
NT2 phlebodium aureum
NT2 phyllitis scolopendrium
NT2 pityrogramma austroamericana
NT2 pityrogramma calomelanos
NT2 pityrogramma chrysophylla
NT2 pityrogramma lehmannii
NT2 platycerium bifurcatum
NT2 platycerium coronarium
NT2 polypodium leucotomos
NT2 polypodium subpetiolatum
NT2 polypodium vulgare
NT2 polystichum munitum
NT2 polystichum setiferum
NT2 pteris cretica
NT2 pteris ensiformis
NT2 pteris tremula
NT2 pteris umbrosa
NT2 pteris wallichiana
NT2 stenochlaena palustris
NT2 tectaria variolosa
NT2 thelypteris noveboracensis
NT2 thelypteris palustris
NT2 woodsia obtusa
rt plants
rt pteridophyta

FEROCACTUS
BT1 cactaceae
NT1 ferocactus grusonii
NT1 ferocactus latispinus

FEROCACTUS GRUSONII
BT1 ferocactus
BT2 cactaceae
BT1 ornamental succulent plants
BT2 succulent plants

FEROCACTUS LATISPINUS
BT1 ferocactus
BT2 cactaceae
BT1 ornamental succulent plants
BT2 succulent plants

feronia (coleoptera)
USE **pterostichus**

feronia limonia
USE **limonia acidissima**

feronia madidus
USE **pterostichus madidus**

feronia melanaria
USE **pterostichus melanarius**

feronia (rutaceae)
USE **limonia**

FERRALLITIC SOILS
BT1 ferralsols
BT2 soil types (genetic)
rt ferrallitization

FERRALLITIZATION
uf laterization
BT1 soil formation
rt ferrallitic soils

FERRALSOLS
uf laterite soils
BT1 soil types (genetic)
NT1 ferrallitic soils
NT1 lateritic soils
NT1 latosols
NT2 red latosols
NT1 oxisols
rt red soils

FERRARIA
BT1 apicomplexa
BT2 protozoa

FERREDOXIN
BT1 carriers
BT1 metalloproteins
BT2 proteins
BT3 peptides

FERRETS
uf mustela furo
uf mustela putorius furo
BT1 working animals
BT2 animals
rt mustelidae

FERRIC HYDROXIDE
BT1 iron hydroxides
BT2 hydroxides
BT3 inorganic compounds

FERRIC IONS
BT1 metal ions
BT2 cations
BT3 ions
rt iron

FERRIC PHOSPHATE
BT1 iron phosphates
BT2 phosphates (salts)
BT3 inorganic salts
BT4 inorganic compounds
BT4 salts
BT3 phosphates
BT2 phosphorus fertilizers
BT3 fertilizers
BT1 nonclay minerals
BT2 minerals
rt strengite

FERRIC SULFATE
uf ferric sulphate
BT1 soil conditioners
BT2 soil amendments
BT3 amendments
BT1 sulfates (inorganic salts)
BT2 inorganic salts
BT3 inorganic compounds
BT3 salts
BT2 sulfates
rt iron

ferric sulphate
USE **ferric sulfate**

FERRIHYDRITE
BT1 nonclay minerals
BT2 minerals

FERRISIA
uf ferrisiana
BT1 pseudococcidae
BT2 coccoidea
BT3 sternorrhyncha
BT4 homoptera
NT1 ferrisia virgata

FERRISIA VIRGATA
uf ferrisiana virgata
BT1 ferrisia
BT2 pseudococcidae

FERRISIA VIRGATA *cont.*
BT3 coccoidea
BT4 sternorrhyncha
BT5 homoptera

ferrisiana
USE **ferrisia**

ferrisiana virgata
USE **ferrisia virgata**

FERRITIN
BT1 metalloproteins
BT2 proteins
BT3 peptides
rt iron binding capacity

FERROCYANIDES
HN from 1990
BT1 inorganic salts
BT2 inorganic compounds
BT2 salts

FERROUS ALLOYS
uf alloys, ferrous
BT1 alloys
BT2 metals
BT2 mixtures
NT1 cast iron
NT1 steel
NT2 stainless steel
NT2 structural steel
rt iron

FERROUS IONS
uf ferrous iron
BT1 metal ions
BT2 cations
BT3 ions
rt iron

ferrous iron
USE **ferrous ions**

FERROUS SULFATE
uf ferrous sulphate
BT1 dyes
BT1 soil amendments
BT2 amendments
BT1 sulfates (inorganic salts)
BT2 inorganic salts
BT3 inorganic compounds
BT3 salts
BT2 sulfates
BT1 unclassified herbicides
BT2 herbicides
BT3 pesticides
rt iron
rt wood preservatives

ferrous sulphate
USE **ferrous sulfate**

FERROXIDASE
(ec 1.16.3.1)
uf iron reductase
BT1 oxidoreductases
BT2 enzymes
rt ceruloplasmin

FERRUGINIZATION
uf rubefaction
BT1 soil formation

FERSIALLITIC SOILS
BT1 luvisols
BT2 soil types (genetic)

FERTIGATION
uf fertirrigation
rt fertilizers
rt irrigation
rt plant nutrition

FERTILITY
uf sterility and fertility
NT1 egg fertility
NT2 egg hatchability
NT3 turkey egg hatchability
NT2 turkey egg fertility
NT1 female fertility
NT2 calving interval
NT2 calving rate
NT2 lambing rate
NT1 fertilizing ability

FERTILITY *cont.*
NT1 human fertility
NT1 male fertility
rt 6-aminohexanoic acid
rt biological production
rt birth rate
rt compatibility
rt environmental degradation
rt fecundity
rt infertility
rt laying worker honeybees
rt mineral deficiencies
rt nutrient balance
rt nutritional state
rt reproduction
rt soil fertility
rt sterility

FERTILITY AGENTS
HN from 1989
BT1 drugs
NT1 clomifene

fertility, female
USE **female fertility**

fertility, human
USE **human fertility**

fertility, male
USE **male fertility**

fertility, soil
USE **soil fertility**

FERTILIZATION
(reproduction)
uf fertilizing
BT1 sexual reproduction
BT2 reproduction
NT1 cleistogamy
NT1 selective fertilization
rt conception
rt copulation
rt parthenogenesis
rt pollen competition
rt pollen germination
rt pollen tubes
rt pollination
rt polyembryony
rt polygyny
rt polyspermy
rt prepotency
rt reproductive performance
rt zygotes

FERTILIZER ANALYSIS
rt analysis
rt fertilizers

FERTILIZER CARRIERS
BT1 carriers
NT1 frits
rt application methods
rt chelates
rt fertilizers
rt ion exchange resins

FERTILIZER DISTRIBUTORS
uf drills, fertilizer
uf pneumatic fertilizer distributors
BT1 application equipment
BT2 equipment
BT1 farm machinery
BT2 machinery
NT1 liquid fertilizer distributors
rt combine drills
rt drills
rt lime spreaders
rt manure spreaders
rt spinning discs
rt spreaders
rt tramlining

fertilizer distributors, liquid
USE **liquid fertilizer distributors**

FERTILIZER HERBICIDE COMBINATIONS
uf fertilizer herbicide mixtures
uf herbicide fertilizer mixtures

FERTILIZER HERBICIDE COMBINATIONS *cont.*
BT1 fertilizer pesticide combinations
BT2 pesticide mixtures
BT3 mixtures
BT3 pesticides
BT1 herbicide mixtures
BT2 herbicides
BT3 pesticides
BT2 pesticide mixtures
BT3 mixtures
BT3 pesticides
rt fertilizers

fertilizer herbicide mixtures
USE **fertilizer herbicide combinations**

FERTILIZER INDUSTRY
BT1 chemical industry
BT2 industry
BT1 input industries
BT2 industry
rt fertilizer technology
rt fertilizers

FERTILIZER INJURY
BT1 injuries
rt fertilizers
rt phytotoxicity

FERTILIZER PESTICIDE COMBINATIONS
BT1 pesticide mixtures
BT2 mixtures
BT2 pesticides
NT1 fertilizer herbicide combinations
rt fertilizers

fertilizer placement
USE **placement**

FERTILIZER REQUIREMENT DETERMINATION
HN from 1990
BT1 determination
BT2 techniques
rt application rates
rt nutrient requirements
rt plant analysis
rt soil analysis

FERTILIZER TECHNOLOGY
BT1 technology
NT1 acidulation
NT1 beneficiation
NT1 claus process
NT1 steam reforming
rt ammonia synthesis gas
rt calcination
rt encapsulation
rt fertilizer industry
rt fertilizers
rt gasification
rt plant design
rt prilling

FERTILIZERS
NT1 calcium fertilizers
NT2 calcium chloride
NT2 gypsum
NT2 phosphogypsum
NT1 compound fertilizers
NT2 nitrogen-phosphorus fertilizers
NT3 ammonium phosphates
NT4 ammonium metaphosphates
NT4 ammonium polyphosphates
NT5 ammonium polyphosphate sulfate
NT5 ammonium pyrophosphate
NT5 ammonium tripolyphosphate
NT5 diammonium pyrophosphate
NT5 tetraammonium pyrophosphate

FERTILIZERS *cont.*
NT5 triammonium pyrophosphate
NT5 urea ammonium polyphosphate
NT4 diammonium phosphate
NT4 magnesium ammonium phosphate
NT4 monoammonium phosphate
NT4 triammonium phosphate
NT4 urea ammonium phosphate
NT4 urea ammonium pyrophosphate
NT3 nitroammophoska
NT3 nitrophosphates
NT2 nitrogen-potassium fertilizers
NT3 nitrokalimag
NT3 potassium nitrate
NT2 npk fertilizers
NT3 urea potassium pyrophosphate
NT2 phosphorus-potassium fertilizers
NT3 potassium phosphates
NT4 dipotassium hydrogen phosphate
NT4 potassium dihydrogen phosphate
NT4 potassium metaphosphate
NT4 potassium polyphosphates
NT5 potassium dihydrogen triphosphate
NT5 potassium hydrogen tripolyphosphates
NT5 potassium pyrophosphate
NT5 urea potassium pyrophosphate
NT1 liquid fertilizers
NT1 magnesium fertilizers
NT2 carnallite
NT2 dolomite
NT2 glauconite
NT2 magnesian limestone
NT2 magnesian marl
NT2 magnesium nitrate
NT2 magnesium oxide
NT2 magnesium phosphates
NT3 magnesium ammonium phosphate
NT3 magnesium hydrogen phosphate
NT2 magnesium silicate
NT2 magnesium sulfate
NT3 epsom salts
NT2 nitrokalimag
NT2 potassium magnesium sulfate
NT2 serpentine
NT2 urea magnesium nitrate
NT1 nitrogen fertilizers
NT2 ammonium fertilizers
NT3 ammoniated superphosphate
NT3 ammoniated triple superphosphate
NT3 ammoniated vermiculite
NT3 ammonium bicarbonate
NT3 ammonium chloride
NT3 ammonium lignosulfonate
NT3 ammonium nitrate
NT3 ammonium phosphates
NT4 ammonium metaphosphates
NT4 ammonium polyphosphates
NT5 ammonium polyphosphate sulfate
NT5 ammonium pyrophosphate
NT5 ammonium tripolyphosphate
NT5 diammonium pyrophosphate
NT5 tetraammonium pyrophosphate

FERTILIZERS *cont.*
NT5 triammonium pyrophosphate
NT5 urea ammonium polyphosphate
NT4 diammonium phosphate
NT4 magnesium ammonium phosphate
NT4 monoammonium phosphate
NT4 triammonium phosphate
NT4 urea ammonium phosphate
NT4 urea ammonium pyrophosphate
NT3 ammonium sulfate
NT3 anhydrous ammonia
NT3 aqueous ammonia
NT3 calcium ammonium nitrate
NT3 urea ammonium nitrate
NT3 urea ammonium sulfate
NT2 calcium cyanamide
NT2 dicyanodiamidine
NT2 dicyanodiamidine sulfate
NT2 methenamine
NT2 nitrate fertilizers
NT3 ammonium nitrate
NT3 calcium ammonium nitrate
NT3 calcium nitrate
NT3 guanidine nitrate
NT3 magnesium nitrate
NT3 potassium nitrate
NT3 sodium nitrate
NT3 urea nitrates
NT4 urea ammonium nitrate
NT4 urea magnesium nitrate
NT4 urea nitrate
NT2 nitroammophoska
NT2 nitrokalimag
NT2 nitrophosphates
NT2 oxamide
NT2 phthalimide
NT2 urea fertilizers
NT3 cdu
NT3 ibdu
NT3 methylenediurea
NT3 neem cake coated urea
NT3 shellac coated urea
NT3 urea
NT3 urea aldehyde polymers
NT4 urea formaldehyde
NT4 urea furfural condensates
NT3 urea nitrates
NT4 urea ammonium nitrate
NT4 urea magnesium nitrate
NT4 urea nitrate
NT3 urea phosphates
NT4 urea ammonium phosphate
NT4 urea ammonium polyphosphate
NT4 urea ammonium pyrophosphate
NT4 urea metaphosphates
NT4 urea nitric phosphates
NT4 urea potassium pyrophosphate
NT3 urea sulfur fertilizers
NT4 sulfur coated urea
NT4 urea ammonium sulfate
NT1 organic fertilizers
NT2 humates
NT3 ammonium humate
NT3 nitrohumates
NT3 sodium humate
NT1 organomineral fertilizers
NT1 phosphorus fertilizers
NT2 acidulated phosphates
NT2 aluminium phosphate
NT2 ammonium phosphates
NT3 ammonium metaphosphates
NT3 ammonium polyphosphates
NT4 ammonium polyphosphate sulfate
NT4 ammonium pyrophosphate

FERTILIZERS *cont.*
NT4 ammonium tripolyphosphate
NT4 diammonium pyrophosphate
NT4 tetraammonium pyrophosphate
NT4 triammonium pyrophosphate
NT4 urea ammonium polyphosphate
NT3 diammonium phosphate
NT3 magnesium ammonium phosphate
NT3 monoammonium phosphate
NT3 triammonium phosphate
NT3 urea ammonium phosphate
NT3 urea ammonium pyrophosphate
NT2 basic slag
NT2 biosuper
NT2 bone meal
NT2 calcined phosphates
NT3 calcined aluminium phosphate
NT2 calcium phosphates
NT3 apatite
NT4 phosphorite
NT3 calcium ammonium trimetaphosphate
NT3 calcium phosphate
NT3 calcium polyphosphates
NT4 calcium pyrophosphate
NT3 dicalcium phosphate
NT3 monocalcium phosphate
NT3 octacalcium phosphate
NT3 rock phosphate
NT3 tricalcium phosphate
NT3 triple superphosphate
NT2 condensed phosphates
NT3 metaphosphates
NT4 ammonium metaphosphates
NT4 potassium metaphosphate
NT4 trimetaphosphates
NT5 calcium ammonium trimetaphosphate
NT3 octacalcium phosphate
NT3 polyphosphates
NT4 ammonium polyphosphate sulfate
NT4 potassium polyphosphates
NT5 potassium dihydrogen triphosphate
NT5 potassium hydrogen tripolyphosphates
NT5 potassium pyrophosphate
NT5 urea potassium pyrophosphate
NT4 pyrophosphates
NT5 ammonium pyrophosphate
NT5 calcium pyrophosphate
NT5 diammonium pyrophosphate
NT5 potassium pyrophosphate
NT5 sodium pyrophosphate
NT5 tetraammonium pyrophosphate
NT5 triammonium pyrophosphate
NT5 urea ammonium pyrophosphate
NT5 urea potassium pyrophosphate
NT4 tripolyphosphates
NT5 potassium dihydrogen triphosphate
NT5 potassium hydrogen tripolyphosphates
NT5 sodium tripolyphosphate
NT4 urea ammonium polyphosphate

FERTILIZERS *cont.*
NT2 defluorinated rock phosphate
NT2 fused phosphates
NT3 fused calcium magnesium phosphate
NT3 fused magnesium phosphate
NT2 iron phosphates
NT3 ferric phosphate
NT2 magnesium phosphates
NT3 magnesium ammonium phosphate
NT3 magnesium hydrogen phosphate
NT2 nitroammophoska
NT2 nitrophosphates
NT2 partially acidulated rock phosphate
NT2 phosphobacterin
NT2 potassium phosphates
NT3 dipotassium hydrogen phosphate
NT3 potassium dihydrogen phosphate
NT3 potassium metaphosphate
NT3 potassium polyphosphates
NT4 potassium dihydrogen triphosphate
NT4 potassium hydrogen tripolyphosphates
NT4 potassium pyrophosphate
NT4 urea potassium pyrophosphate
NT2 red phosphorus
NT2 rhenania phosphate
NT2 silicon phosphate
NT2 sodium phosphate
NT2 sodium pyrophosphate
NT2 superphosphates
NT3 ammoniated superphosphate
NT3 ammoniated triple superphosphate
NT3 concentrated superphosphate
NT3 double superphosphate
NT3 superphosphate
NT3 triple superphosphate
NT2 tahoua phosphate
NT2 thermophosphate
NT2 urea phosphates
NT3 urea ammonium phosphate
NT3 urea ammonium polyphosphate
NT3 urea ammonium pyrophosphate
NT3 urea metaphosphates
NT3 urea nitric phosphates
NT3 urea potassium pyrophosphate
NT2 yellow phosphorus
NT1 potassium fertilizers
NT2 carnallite
NT2 cement dust
NT2 clinoptilolite
NT2 glauconite
NT2 nitrokalimag
NT2 potassium chloride
NT2 potassium magnesium sulfate
NT2 potassium nitrate
NT2 potassium phosphates
NT3 dipotassium hydrogen phosphate
NT3 potassium dihydrogen phosphate
NT3 potassium metaphosphate
NT3 potassium polyphosphates
NT4 potassium dihydrogen triphosphate
NT4 potassium hydrogen tripolyphosphates
NT4 potassium pyrophosphate

FERTILIZERS *cont.*
NT4 urea potassium pyrophosphate
NT2 potassium silicates
NT3 potassium metasilicate
NT2 potassium sulfate
NT2 schoenite
NT2 straw ash
NT2 sylvinite
NT1 slow release fertilizers
NT2 cdu
NT2 dicyanodiamidine
NT2 ibdu
NT2 neem cake coated urea
NT2 oxamide
NT2 phthalimide
NT2 rubber coated fertilizers
NT2 shellac coated urea
NT2 sulfur coated urea
NT2 urea aldehyde polymers
NT3 urea formaldehyde
NT3 urea furfural condensates
NT1 sulfur fertilizers
NT2 ammonium polyphosphate sulfate
NT2 ammonium sulfate
NT2 dicyanodiamidine sulfate
NT2 potassium magnesium sulfate
NT2 potassium sulfate
NT2 sodium sulfate
NT2 sulfur
NT2 thiourea
NT2 urea sulfur fertilizers
NT3 sulfur coated urea
NT3 urea ammonium sulfate
NT2 zinc sulfate
NT1 trace element fertilizers
NT2 boron fertilizers
NT3 colemanite
NT2 chlorine fertilizers
NT3 ammonium chloride
NT3 carnallite
NT3 potassium chloride
NT3 sodium chloride
NT3 sylvinite
NT2 cobalt fertilizers
NT2 copper fertilizers
NT3 copper sulfate
NT2 fly ash
NT2 iron fertilizers
NT2 manganese fertilizers
NT3 manganous sulfate
NT2 molybdenum fertilizers
NT2 selenium fertilizers
NT2 silicon fertilizers
NT3 ammoniated vermiculite
NT3 glauconite
NT3 potassium silicates
NT4 potassium metasilicate
NT3 silicon phosphate
NT2 slags
NT2 sodium fertilizers
NT3 sodium chloride
NT3 sodium nitrate
NT3 sodium phosphate
NT3 sodium pyrophosphate
NT3 sodium tripolyphosphate
NT2 vanadium fertilizers
NT2 zinc fertilizers
NT3 zinc edta
NT3 zinc oxide
NT3 zinc sulfate
rt anticaking agents
rt bulk blends
rt farm inputs
rt fertigation
rt fertilizer analysis
rt fertilizer carriers
rt fertilizer herbicide combinations
rt fertilizer industry
rt fertilizer injury
rt fertilizer pesticide combinations
rt fertilizer technology
rt growth promoters
rt manures
rt nutrients
rt plant nutrition
rt soil chemistry

FERTILIZERS *cont.*
rt usage
rt use efficiency

fertilizing
USE **fertilization**

FERTILIZING ABILITY
BT1 fertility
rt female fertility
rt male fertility

fertirrigation
USE **fertigation**

FERULA
BT1 umbelliferae
NT1 ferula assa-foetida
NT1 ferula persica
NT1 ferula pseudooreoselinum
NT1 ferula schutschurowskiana
NT1 ferula syreitschikowii
NT1 ferula szowitsiana
NT1 ferula violacea
NT1 ferula xeromorpha

ferula asafoetida
USE **ferula assa-foetida**

FERULA ASSA-FOETIDA
uf *ferula asafoetida*
BT1 ferula
BT2 umbelliferae
BT1 medicinal plants

FERULA PERSICA
BT1 ferula
BT2 umbelliferae

FERULA PSEUDOOREOSELINUM
BT1 ferula
BT2 umbelliferae

FERULA SCHUTSCHUROWSKIANA
BT1 ferula
BT2 umbelliferae

FERULA SYREITSCHIKOWII
BT1 ferula
BT2 umbelliferae

FERULA SZOWITSIANA
BT1 ferula
BT2 umbelliferae

FERULA VIOLACEA
BT1 ferula
BT2 umbelliferae

FERULA XEROMORPHA
BT1 ferula
BT2 umbelliferae

FERULIC ACID
BT1 coumaric acids
BT2 benzenealkenoic acids
BT3 carboxylic acids
BT4 organic acids
BT5 acids
BT1 phytoalexins
BT2 allomones
BT3 allelochemicals
BT4 semiochemicals
rt diferulic acid

fescue
USE **festuca**

FESSISENTIDAE
BT1 acanthocephala
NT1 fessisentis

FESSISENTIS
BT1 fessisentidae
BT2 acanthocephala

FESTIVALS
BT1 cultural activities
BT2 culture
BT2 entertainment
BT3 leisure activities
BT1 entertainment
BT2 leisure activities
rt carnivals
rt shows
rt spectator events

FESTUCA
uf *fescue*
BT1 gramineae
NT1 festuca airoides
NT1 festuca altaica
NT1 festuca ampla
NT1 festuca arizonica
NT1 festuca arundinacea
NT1 festuca campestris
NT1 festuca filiformis
NT1 festuca gautieri
NT1 festuca gigantea
NT1 festuca glauca
NT1 festuca halleri
NT1 festuca hallii
NT1 festuca heterophylla
NT1 festuca idahoensis
NT1 festuca longifolia
NT1 festuca nigrescens
NT1 festuca novae-zelandiae
NT1 festuca occidentalis
NT1 festuca ovina
NT1 festuca paniculata
NT1 festuca pratensis
NT1 festuca pseudovina
NT1 festuca rubra
NT1 festuca rupicola
NT1 festuca scabrella
NT1 festuca trachyphylla
NT1 festuca valesiaca
NT1 festuca varia
NT1 festuca vivipara
rt festuca leaf streak rhabdovirus

FESTUCA AIROIDES
uf *festuca supina*
BT1 festuca
BT2 gramineae
BT1 pasture plants

FESTUCA ALTAICA
BT1 festuca
BT2 gramineae
BT1 pasture plants

FESTUCA AMPLA
BT1 festuca
BT2 gramineae
BT1 lawns and turf
BT1 pasture plants

FESTUCA ARIZONICA
BT1 festuca
BT2 gramineae

FESTUCA ARUNDINACEA
uf *tall fescue*
BT1 festuca
BT2 gramineae
BT1 lawns and turf
BT1 pasture plants

FESTUCA CAMPESTRIS
BT1 festuca
BT2 gramineae
BT1 pasture plants

festuca capillata
USE **festuca filiformis**

festuca duriuscula
USE **festuca longifolia**

festuca fallax
USE **festuca rubra**

FESTUCA FILIFORMIS
uf *festuca capillata*
uf *festuca tenuifolia*
BT1 festuca
BT2 gramineae
BT1 lawns and turf

FESTUCA GAUTIERI
uf *festuca scoparia*
BT1 festuca
BT2 gramineae
BT1 ornamental herbaceous plants
BT1 pasture plants

FESTUCA GIGANTEA
BT1 festuca

FESTUCA GIGANTEA *cont.*
BT2 gramineae
BT1 pasture plants

FESTUCA GLAUCA
BT1 festuca
BT2 gramineae
BT1 ornamental herbaceous plants

FESTUCA HALLERI
BT1 festuca
BT2 gramineae
BT1 pasture plants

FESTUCA HALLII
BT1 festuca
BT2 gramineae
BT1 pasture plants

FESTUCA HETEROPHYLLA
BT1 festuca
BT2 gramineae
BT1 lawns and turf

FESTUCA IDAHOENSIS
BT1 festuca
BT2 gramineae
BT1 pasture plants

FESTUCA LEAF STREAK RHABDOVIRUS
HN from 1990
BT1 rhabdovirus group
BT2 plant viruses
BT3 plant pathogens
BT4 pathogens
BT2 rhabdoviridae
BT3 viruses
rt festuca

FESTUCA LONGIFOLIA
uf *festuca duriuscula*
BT1 festuca
BT2 gramineae
BT1 lawns and turf
BT1 pasture plants

festuca megalura
USE **vulpia megalura**

festuca myuros
USE **vulpia myuros**

FESTUCA NIGRESCENS
uf *festuca rubra subsp. commutata*
BT1 festuca
BT2 gramineae
BT1 pasture plants

FESTUCA NOVAE-ZELANDIAE
BT1 festuca
BT2 gramineae
BT1 pasture plants

FESTUCA OCCIDENTALIS
BT1 festuca
BT2 gramineae
BT1 pasture plants

FESTUCA OVINA
BT1 festuca
BT2 gramineae
BT1 lawns and turf
BT1 pasture plants

festuca ovina var. duriuscula
USE **festuca trachyphylla**

FESTUCA PANICULATA
uf *festuca spadicea*
BT1 festuca
BT2 gramineae
BT1 pasture plants

FESTUCA PRATENSIS
uf *meadow fescue*
BT1 festuca
BT2 gramineae
BT1 lawns and turf
BT1 pasture plants

FESTUCA PSEUDOVINA
BT1 festuca

FESTUCA PSEUDOVINA *cont.*
BT2 gramineae
BT1 lawns and turf
BT1 pasture plants

FESTUCA RUBRA
uf *festuca fallax*
uf *red fescue*
BT1 festuca
BT2 gramineae
BT1 lawns and turf
BT1 pasture plants

festuca rubra subsp. commutata
USE **festuca nigrescens**

FESTUCA RUPICOLA
uf *festuca sulcata*
BT1 festuca
BT2 gramineae
BT1 pasture plants

FESTUCA SCABRELLA
BT1 festuca
BT2 gramineae
BT1 pasture plants

festuca scoparia
USE **festuca gautieri**

festuca spadicea
USE **festuca paniculata**

festuca sulcata
USE **festuca rupicola**

festuca supina
USE **festuca airoides**

festuca tenuifolia
USE **festuca filiformis**

FESTUCA TRACHYPHYLLA
uf *festuca ovina var. duriuscula*
BT1 festuca
BT2 gramineae
BT1 lawns and turf

FESTUCA VALESIACA
BT1 festuca
BT2 gramineae
BT1 lawns and turf
BT1 pasture plants

FESTUCA VARIA
BT1 festuca
BT2 gramineae
BT1 pasture plants

FESTUCA VIVIPARA
BT1 festuca
BT2 gramineae
BT1 pasture plants

FETA CHEESE
BT1 cheeses
BT2 milk products
BT3 products

FETAL ALCOHOL SYNDROME (AGRICOLA)
rt alcoholism
rt fetus

FETAL DEATH
uf *foetal death*
uf *stillbirth*
BT1 death
NT1 mummification
rt abortion
rt death and dying (agricola)
rt embryo mortality
rt fetus
rt stillbirths

FETAL DEVELOPMENT
rt development
rt fetal development disorders
rt fetus
rt maternal-fetal exchange (agricola)
rt prenatal development (agricola)

FETAL DEVELOPMENT DISORDERS
uf *foetal development disorders*
BT1 animal disorders
BT2 disorders
rt embryonic development
rt fetal development
rt fetus

FETAL GROWTH
uf *foetal growth*
BT1 growth
rt embryonic development
rt fetus

FETAL MEMBRANES
uf *foetal membranes*
BT1 membranes
NT1 allantois
NT1 amnion
NT1 chorion
NT1 yolk sac
rt fetus

FETAL PROTEINS
BT1 proteins
BT2 peptides
NT1 α-fetoprotein
rt fetus

FETAL RESORPTION
BT1 resorption
rt fetus

α-FETOPROTEIN
(for retrieval spell out "alpha")
uf *α-foetoprotein*
uf *fetuin*
BT1 blood proteins
BT2 animal proteins
BT3 proteins
BT4 peptides
BT1 fetal proteins
BT2 proteins
BT3 peptides
BT1 globulins
BT2 proteins
BT3 peptides

fetuin
USE **α-fetoprotein**

FETUS
uf *foetus*
BT1 embryos
rt amniotic fluid
rt chorioallantoic membrane
rt conceptus
rt ductus arteriosus
rt fetal alcohol syndrome (agricola)
rt fetal death
rt fetal development
rt fetal development disorders
rt fetal growth
rt fetal membranes
rt fetal proteins
rt fetal resorption
rt placenta
rt pregnancy
rt reproduction
rt sire of fetus
rt urachus

FEUDALISM
BT1 economic systems
BT2 systems
BT1 political systems
BT2 politics

FEVER
uf *pyrexia*
BT1 functional disorders
BT2 animal disorders
BT3 disorders
rt antipyretics
rt blackwater fever
rt body temperature
rt dengue haemorrhagic fever
rt malignant catarrhal fever
rt pyrogens
rt tickborne fever

FIBER
BF fibre
uf *food fiber*
NT1 crude fiber
rt fiber content
rt fiber restricted diets (agricola)

FIBER CONTENT
BF fibre content
rt fiber

fiber dyeing
USE **stock dyeing (agricola)**

FIBER OPTICS
BF fibre optics

FIBER PLANTS
BF fibre plants
rt plant fibers

FIBER QUALITY
BF fibre quality
rt fibers

FIBER RESTRICTED DIETS (AGRICOLA)
BT1 therapeutic diets
BT2 diets
rt fiber

FIBER SATURATION
BF fibre saturation

FIBERBOARDS
BF fibreboards

FIBERGLASS
BF glassfibre
BT1 noncellulosic fibers (agricola)
BT2 manmade fibers (agricola)
BT3 textile fibers
BT4 fibers
rt fiberglass reinforced plastics

FIBERGLASS REINFORCED PLASTICS
HN from 1989
BF glassfibre reinforced plastics
rt fiberglass

FIBERS
BF fibres
NT1 animal fibers
NT1 plant fibers
NT2 hard fibers
NT2 soft fibers
NT1 synthetic fibers
NT1 textile fibers
NT2 cellulosic fibers (agricola)
NT3 acetate (fiber) (agricola)
NT3 rayon (agricola)
NT3 triacetate (agricola)
NT2 manmade fibers (agricola)
NT3 acetate (fiber) (agricola)
NT3 noncellulosic fibers (agricola)
NT4 acrylics (agricola)
NT5 acrilan (agricola)
NT4 fiberglass
NT4 modacrylics (agricola)
NT4 nylon
NT4 olefin (agricola)
NT4 polyesters (agricola)
NT4 polyurethanes (agricola)
NT4 spandex (agricola)
NT4 vinyl (agricola)
NT3 rayon (agricola)
NT3 triacetate (agricola)
NT2 natural fibers (agricola)
NT2 protein fibers (agricola)
NT2 stock dyed fibers (agricola)
rt fiber quality

FIBRAUREA
BT1 menispermaceae
NT1 fibraurea chloroleuca

FIBRAUREA CHLOROLEUCA
BT1 fibraurea
BT2 menispermaceae

FIBRE
AF fiber
rt bran
rt crude fibre
rt fibre content
rt roughage

FIBRE CONTENT
AF fiber content
BT1 composition
rt crude fibre
rt fibre

fibre crops
USE **fibre plants**

fibre, crude
USE **crude fibre**

fibre flax
USE **linum usitatissimum**

FIBRE OPTICS
AF fiber optics
rt light
rt optical instruments

FIBRE PLANTS
AF fiber plants
uf *fibre crops*
NT1 abelmoschus moschatus
NT1 abelmoschus sativa
NT1 abutilon asiaticum
NT1 abutilon polyandrum
NT1 acrocomia lasiopatha
NT1 acrocomia sclerocarpa
NT1 agave amaniensis
NT1 agave cantala
NT1 agave falcata
NT1 agave fourcroydes
NT1 agave funkiana
NT1 agave lechuguilla
NT1 agave rigida
NT1 agave sisalana
NT1 astrocaryum jauary
NT1 astrocaryum murumuru
NT1 astrocaryum tucuma
NT1 astrocaryum vulgare
NT1 boehmeria macrophylla
NT1 boehmeria nivea
NT1 bombax malabaricum
NT1 calotropis procera
NT1 cannabis sativa
NT1 ceiba pentandra
NT1 coconuts
NT1 cordyline indivisa
NT1 corypha utan
NT1 cotton
NT1 crotalaria juncea
NT1 crotalaria retusa
NT1 furcraea foetida
NT1 furcraea macrophylla
NT1 furcraea marginata
NT1 hibiscus cannabinus
NT1 hibiscus sabdariffa
NT1 hibiscus surattensis
NT1 hibiscus vitifolius
NT1 jute
NT1 linum usitatissimum
NT1 mauritia flexuosa
NT1 mauritia minor
NT1 musa textilis
NT1 nypa fruticans
NT1 oenocarpus bacaba
NT1 phormium tenax
NT1 phragmites australis
NT1 pineapples
NT1 raphia farinifera
NT1 raphia hookeri
NT1 raphia regalis
NT1 raphia sudanica
NT1 raphia vinifera
NT1 sabal palmetto
NT1 sesbania sesban
NT1 sida cordifolia
NT1 stipa tenacissima
NT1 urena lobata
rt fibres
rt field crops
rt hesperaloe
rt horticultural crops
rt industrial crops
rt plant fibres

FIBRE PLANTS *cont.*
rt plants
rt sansevieria
rt yucca

FIBRE QUALITY
AF fiber quality
uf quality of fibre
BT1 quality
NT1 staple
rt fibres

FIBRE SATURATION
HN from 1990
AF fiber saturation
BT1 saturation
rt wood moisture

FIBREBOARDS
AF fiberboards
BT1 forest products
 BT2 products
BT1 panels
 BT2 building materials
  BT3 materials
NT1 hardboard

FIBRES
AF fibers
NT1 animal fibres
 NT2 bristles
 NT2 camel's hair (agricola)
 NT2 cashmere
 NT2 mohair
 NT2 silk
 NT2 wool
  NT3 finewool
  NT3 reprocessed wool (agricola)
  NT3 reused wool (agricola)
  NT3 semifine wool
  NT3 virgin wool (agricola)
NT1 plant fibres
 NT2 coir
 NT2 hard fibres
 NT2 hemp
 NT2 kapok
 NT2 lint
 NT2 soft fibres
NT1 synthetic fibres
 NT2 nylon
 NT2 polyacrylonitrile
NT1 textile fibres
NT1 threads
NT1 wood wool
rt cellulose
rt fibre plants
rt fibre quality
rt fibroblasts
rt lignin
rt medullation
rt non-food products
rt reticulin
rt staple
rt wood pulp

FIBRIN
BT1 blood proteins
 BT2 animal proteins
  BT3 proteins
   BT4 peptides
rt blood coagulation
rt fibrin hydrolysate
rt fibrinogen
rt fibrinolysis
rt plasmin
rt thrombin

FIBRIN HYDROLYSATE
BT1 protein hydrolysates
 BT2 hydrolysates
rt blood coagulation
rt fibrin

FIBRINOGEN
BT1 blood proteins
 BT2 animal proteins
  BT3 proteins
   BT4 peptides
rt blood coagulation
rt fibrin
rt thrombin

FIBRINOLYSIS
BT1 decomposition
BT1 lysis
rt blood coagulation
rt fibrin
rt plasmin
rt thrombolysis

FIBROBLASTS
BT1 cells
rt fibres

FIBROINS
BT1 scleroproteins
 BT2 proteins
  BT3 peptides

FIBROMA
BT1 neoplasms
 BT2 diseases

FIBRONECTINS
BT1 glycoproteins
 BT2 proteins
  BT3 peptides

FIBROSIS
BT1 respiratory diseases
 BT2 organic diseases
  BT3 diseases
NT1 cystic fibrosis
NT1 silicosis
rt cirrhosis
rt scars

FIBULA
BT1 limb bones
 BT2 bones
  BT3 musculoskeletal system
   BT4 body parts

FICALBIA
BT1 culicidae
 BT2 diptera

FICEDULA
BT1 muscicapidae
 BT2 passeriformes
  BT3 birds

FICUS
BT1 moraceae
NT1 ficus benghalensis
NT1 ficus benjamina
NT1 ficus capreaefolia
NT1 ficus carica
NT1 ficus cyathistipula
NT1 ficus decora
NT1 ficus deltoidea
NT1 ficus elastica
NT1 ficus erecta
NT1 ficus glomerata
NT1 ficus hederacea
NT1 ficus hispida
NT1 ficus insipida
NT1 ficus leprieurii
NT1 ficus lucida
NT1 ficus lyrata
NT1 ficus macrophylla
NT1 ficus natalensis
NT1 ficus nekbudu
NT1 ficus nipponica
NT1 ficus platyphylla
NT1 ficus pumila
NT1 ficus racemosa
NT1 ficus religiosa
NT1 ficus retusa
NT1 ficus robusta
NT1 ficus rumphii
NT1 ficus sagittata
NT1 ficus salificolia
NT1 ficus sarmentosa
NT1 ficus septica
NT1 ficus sycomorus
NT1 ficus thonningii
NT1 ficus thunbergii
NT1 ficus villosa
NT1 ficus vogelii
NT1 ficus wassa
NT1 ficus yoponensis

FICUS BENGHALENSIS
uf ficus indica
BT1 ficus

FICUS BENGHALENSIS *cont.*
 BT2 moraceae
BT1 forest trees
BT1 medicinal plants

FICUS BENJAMINA
uf ficus nitida
BT1 ficus
 BT2 moraceae
BT1 medicinal plants
BT1 ornamental woody plants

FICUS CAPREAEFOLIA
BT1 ficus
 BT2 moraceae

FICUS CARICA
BT1 ficus
 BT2 moraceae
rt figs

FICUS CYATHISTIPULA
BT1 ficus
 BT2 moraceae

FICUS DECORA
BT1 ficus
 BT2 moraceae
BT1 ornamental woody plants
rt ornamental foliage plants

FICUS DELTOIDEA
BT1 ficus
 BT2 moraceae
BT1 ornamental woody plants
rt ornamental foliage plants

FICUS ELASTICA
BT1 ficus
 BT2 moraceae
BT1 nematicidal plants
 BT2 pesticidal plants
BT1 ornamental woody plants
rt ornamental foliage plants

FICUS ERECTA
BT1 ficus
 BT2 moraceae

FICUS GLOMERATA
BT1 ficus
 BT2 moraceae
BT1 medicinal plants

FICUS HEDERACEA
BT1 ficus
 BT2 moraceae
BT1 ornamental woody plants
rt ornamental foliage plants

FICUS HISPIDA
BT1 ficus
 BT2 moraceae
BT1 medicinal plants

ficus indica
USE **ficus benghalensis**

FICUS INSIPIDA
BT1 ficus
 BT2 moraceae

FICUS LEPRIEURII
uf ficus triangularis
BT1 ficus
 BT2 moraceae
BT1 ornamental woody plants

FICUS LUCIDA
BT1 ficus
 BT2 moraceae
BT1 ornamental woody plants
rt ornamental foliage plants

FICUS LYRATA
uf ficus pandurata
BT1 ficus
 BT2 moraceae
BT1 ornamental woody plants
rt ornamental foliage plants

FICUS MACROPHYLLA
BT1 ficus
 BT2 moraceae
BT1 ornamental woody plants

FICUS NATALENSIS
BT1 ficus
 BT2 moraceae

FICUS NEKBUDU
BT1 ficus
 BT2 moraceae

FICUS NIPPONICA
BT1 ficus
 BT2 moraceae
BT1 ornamental woody plants

ficus nitida
USE **ficus benjamina**

ficus pandurata
USE **ficus lyrata**

FICUS PLATYPHYLLA
BT1 ficus
 BT2 moraceae

FICUS PUMILA
uf ficus stipulata
BT1 ficus
 BT2 moraceae
BT1 ornamental woody plants

FICUS RACEMOSA
BT1 ficus
 BT2 moraceae
BT1 medicinal plants

FICUS RELIGIOSA
BT1 ficus
 BT2 moraceae
BT1 forest trees
BT1 medicinal plants
BT1 nematicidal plants
 BT2 pesticidal plants
BT1 ornamental woody plants
rt sericulture
rt silkworms

FICUS RETUSA
BT1 ficus
 BT2 moraceae
BT1 ornamental woody plants
rt ornamental foliage plants

FICUS ROBUSTA
BT1 ficus
 BT2 moraceae
BT1 ornamental woody plants
rt ornamental foliage plants

FICUS RUMPHII
BT1 ficus
 BT2 moraceae

FICUS SAGITTATA
BT1 ficus
 BT2 moraceae
BT1 ornamental woody plants
rt ornamental foliage plants

FICUS SALIFICOLIA
BT1 ficus
 BT2 moraceae

FICUS SARMENTOSA
BT1 ficus
 BT2 moraceae
BT1 ornamental woody plants
rt ornamental foliage plants

FICUS SEPTICA
BT1 ficus
 BT2 moraceae

ficus stipulata
USE **ficus pumila**

FICUS SYCOMORUS
BT1 ficus
 BT2 moraceae

FICUS THONNINGII
BT1 ficus
 BT2 moraceae

FICUS THUNBERGII
BT1 ficus
 BT2 moraceae

ficus triangularis
USE **ficus leprieurii**

FICUS VILLOSA
BT1 ficus
BT2 moraceae
BT1 ornamental woody plants
rt ornamental foliage plants

FICUS VOGELII
BT1 ficus
BT2 moraceae

FICUS WASSA
BT1 ficus
BT2 moraceae

FICUS YOPONENSIS
BT1 ficus
BT2 moraceae

FIEBERIELLA
BT1 cicadellidae
BT2 cicadelloidea
BT3 auchenorrhyncha
BT4 homoptera
NT1 fieberiella florii

FIEBERIELLA FLORII
BT1 fieberiella
BT2 cicadellidae
BT3 cicadelloidea
BT4 auchenorrhyncha
BT5 homoptera

field bean (phaseolus)
USE **phaseolus vulgaris**

field bean (vicia)
USE **faba beans**
OR **vicia faba**

FIELD CAPACITY
BT1 soil water constants
rt capacity

FIELD CROPS
rt cereals
rt crops
rt fibre plants
rt grain crops
rt horticultural crops
rt industrial crops
rt oilseed plants
rt plants
rt pseudocereals
rt root crops
rt starch crops
rt sugar crops
rt vegetables

field curing
USE **field drying**
OR **haymaking**

FIELD DRYING
uf *field curing*
BT1 drying
BT2 dehydration
BT3 processing
rt wilting

FIELD EXPERIMENTATION
BT1 trials
BT2 research
NT1 border effects
NT1 experimental plots
NT1 site selection
rt experimental design
rt experiments
rt plot size
rt rain shelters

field mice
USE **apodemus**

FIELD SHAPE
rt farm structure
rt fields
rt land consolidation

FIELD SIZE
rt farm structure
rt fields
rt land consolidation

FIELD SIZE *cont.*
rt size

FIELD SPRAYERS
uf *sprayers, field*
BT1 sprayers
BT2 spraying equipment
BT3 application equipment
BT4 equipment

FIELD TESTS
uf *tests, field*
BT1 pedological techniques
BT2 techniques
BT1 tests

FIELD TRIPS (AGRICOLA)
BT1 visits
BT2 travel
rt education

FIELD WATER BALANCE
uf *soil field water balance*
BT1 soil water balance
BT2 water balance

FIELDS
NT1 old fields
NT1 paddocks
rt farm structure
rt farms
rt feedlots
rt field shape
rt field size
rt pastures

FIGHTING
BT1 aggressive behaviour
BT2 behaviour
rt drifting
rt honeybee colonies

FIGHTING BULL
BT1 cattle breeds
BT2 breeds

FIGS
BT1 medicinal plants
BT1 temperate tree fruits
BT2 temperate fruits
BT3 fruit crops
BT2 tree fruits
rt ficus carica

figure in wood
USE **grain and figure**

FIGWORT MOSAIC CAULIMOVIRUS
HN from 1990
BT1 caulimovirus group
BT2 plant viruses
BT3 plant pathogens
BT4 pathogens
rt scrophularia

FIJI
BT1 melanesia
BT2 australasia
BT3 oceania
rt acp
rt commonwealth of nations
rt south pacific commission

fiji disease fijivirus
USE **sugarcane fiji disease fijivirus**

FIJIVIRUS GROUP
HN from 1990
BT1 plant viruses
BT2 plant pathogens
BT3 pathogens
BT1 reoviridae
BT2 viruses
NT1 maize rough dwarf fijivirus
NT1 oat sterile dwarf fijivirus
NT1 pangola stunt fijivirus
NT1 rice black-streaked dwarf fijivirus
NT1 sugarcane fiji disease fijivirus

FILAGINELLA
BT1 compositae

FILAGINELLA *cont.*
NT1 filaginella uliginosa

FILAGINELLA ULIGINOSA
uf *gnaphalium uliginosum*
BT1 filaginella
BT2 compositae
BT1 weeds

FILARIASIS
BT1 nematode infections
BT2 helminthoses
BT3 parasitoses
BT4 diseases
BT1 vector-borne diseases
BT2 diseases
NT1 onchocerciasis
rt elephantiasis

FILARIIDAE
BT1 nematoda
NT1 parafilaria
NT2 parafilaria bovicola
NT2 parafilaria multipapillosa
NT1 pseudofilaria
NT1 stephanofilaria
NT2 stephanofilaria assamensis
NT2 stephanofilaria dedoesi
NT2 stephanofilaria kaeli
NT2 stephanofilaria stilesi
NT2 stephanofilaria zaheeri
NT1 suifilaria
NT2 suifilaria suis
rt animal parasitic nematodes

FILARIIDS
(unspecified agents of filariasis)
BT1 helminths
BT2 parasites

FILARIOPSIS
BT1 filaroididae
BT2 nematoda

FILAROIDES
BT1 filaroididae
BT2 nematoda
NT1 filaroides hirthi
NT1 filaroides martis
rt lungworms
rt oslerus

FILAROIDES HIRTHI
BT1 filaroides
BT2 filaroididae
BT3 nematoda

FILAROIDES MARTIS
BT1 filaroides
BT2 filaroididae
BT3 nematoda

filaroides osleri
USE **oslerus osleri**

FILAROIDIDAE
BT1 nematoda
NT1 filariopsis
NT1 filaroides
NT2 filaroides hirthi
NT2 filaroides martis
NT1 oslerus
NT2 oslerus osleri
rt animal parasitic nematodes

filberts
USE **hazelnuts**

filefishes
USE **balistidae**

FILENCHUS
HN from 1990
BT1 tylenchidae
BT2 nematoda

FILICOLLIDAE
BT1 acanthocephala
NT1 filicollis
NT2 filicollis anatis

FILICOLLIS
BT1 filicollidae
BT2 acanthocephala
NT1 filicollis anatis

FILICOLLIS ANATIS
BT1 filicollis
BT2 filicollidae
BT3 acanthocephala

FILIPENDULA
BT1 rosaceae
NT1 filipendula denudata
NT1 filipendula palmata
NT1 filipendula stepposa
NT1 filipendula ulmaria

FILIPENDULA DENUDATA
BT1 filipendula
BT2 rosaceae

FILIPENDULA PALMATA
BT1 filipendula
BT2 rosaceae

FILIPENDULA STEPPOSA
BT1 filipendula
BT2 rosaceae

FILIPENDULA ULMARIA
BT1 filipendula
BT2 rosaceae
BT1 medicinal plants
BT1 ornamental herbaceous plants

FILLED CHEESE
BT1 cheeses
BT2 milk products
BT3 products

FILLED MILK
uf *milk, filled*
BT1 milk products
BT2 products
rt dried skim milk
rt fats

FILLERS
BT1 handling machinery
BT2 machinery
rt filling

FILLING
rt backfilling
rt fillers

FILLING PERIOD
BT1 crop growth stage

FILM
NT1 biofilms
NT1 plastic film
NT2 polyethylene film
NT1 solar film (agricola)
rt coatings

film, plastic
USE **plastic film**

FILM WATER
BT1 soil water categories
BT2 soil water
BT3 water

FILMS
BT1 mass media
BT2 communication
rt audiovisual aids
rt cinema
rt entertainment
rt performing arts

FILMSTRIPS (AGRICOLA)
BT1 audiovisual aids
BT2 teaching materials

FILOBASIDIELLA
BT1 sporidiales
NT1 filobasidiella bacillispora
NT1 filobasidiella neoformans
rt cryptococcus (deuteromycotina)

FILOBASIDIELLA BACILLISPORA
BT1 filobasidiella
BT2 sporidiales
rt cryptococcus bacillisporus

FILOBASIDIELLA NEOFORMANS
BT1 filobasidiella

FILOBASIDIELLA NEOFORMANS *cont.*
BT2 sporidiales
rt cryptococcus neoformans

FILOPODIUM
BT1 apicomplexa
BT2 protozoa

FILOVIRIDAE
BT1 viruses
NT1 filovirus
NT2 ebola virus
NT2 marburg virus

FILOVIRUS
BT1 filoviridae
BT2 viruses
NT1 ebola virus
NT1 marburg virus

FILTER AIDS
HN from 1990
NT1 kieselguhr
NT1 perlite
rt filters
rt filtration

FILTER BEDS
BT1 filters

FILTER CAKE
uf carbonatation mud
uf clarification mud
uf mud (sugar refining)
BT1 inoculant carriers
BT2 carriers
BT1 manures
BT2 organic amendments
BT3 soil amendments
BT4 amendments
rt filterability
rt filters

FILTER CLOTHS
HN from 1990
BT1 components
rt filters

FILTERABILITY
HN from 1990
rt filter cake
rt permeability

FILTERS
NT1 air filters
NT1 filter beds
NT1 milk filters
NT1 water filters
rt activated carbon
rt filter aids
rt filter cake
rt filter cloths
rt filtrates
rt filtration
rt sieves

filters, air
USE **air filters**

filters, milk
USE **milk filters**

filters, water
USE **water filters**

FILTRATES
BT1 liquids
NT1 culture filtrates
rt filters
rt filtration
rt retentates

FILTRATION
BT1 processing
NT1 biological filtration
NT2 biological fixed-film systems
NT1 electrofiltration
NT1 glomerular filtration
NT2 glomerular filtration rate
NT1 percolation
NT1 ultrafiltration
NT2 electroultrafiltration
rt cyclones

FILTRATION *cont.*
rt filter aids
rt filters
rt filtrates
rt separation

FIMBRIAE
BT1 cell structure
rt bacteria

FIMBRIARIA
BT1 hymenolepididae
BT2 eucestoda
BT3 cestoda
NT1 fimbriaria fasciolaris

FIMBRIARIA FASCIOLARIS
BT1 fimbriaria
BT2 hymenolepididae
BT3 eucestoda
BT4 cestoda

FIMBRISTYLIS
BT1 cyperaceae
NT1 fimbristylis ferruginea
NT1 fimbristylis globulosa
NT1 fimbristylis littoralis
NT1 fimbristylis miliacea

FIMBRISTYLIS FERRUGINEA
BT1 fimbristylis
BT2 cyperaceae

FIMBRISTYLIS GLOBULOSA
BT1 fimbristylis
BT2 cyperaceae

FIMBRISTYLIS LITTORALIS
BT1 fimbristylis
BT2 cyperaceae
BT1 weeds

FIMBRISTYLIS MILIACEA
BT1 fimbristylis
BT2 cyperaceae
BT1 weeds

FINAL CONSUMPTION
BT1 aggregate data
rt consumption

FINAL PRODUCTION
BT1 aggregate data
rt production

FINANCE
NT1 capital
NT2 fixed capital
NT2 working capital
NT1 capital formation
NT1 credit
NT2 agricultural credit
NT2 cooperative credit
NT2 export credits
NT2 installment credit (agricola)
NT2 loans
NT3 bank loans
NT3 international loans
NT3 private loans
NT3 public loans
NT2 long term credit
NT3 mortgages
NT4 zero rate mortgages (agricola)
NT2 short term credit
NT1 reserve funds
NT1 savings
NT1 self finance
rt financial institutions
rt financial planning
rt investment
rt monetary policy
rt public finance
rt tertiary sector

FINANCIAL INSTITUTIONS
BT1 organizations
NT1 banks
NT2 agricultural banks
NT2 commercial banks
NT2 cooperative banks
NT2 development banks
NT3 inter-american development bank

FINANCIAL INSTITUTIONS *cont.*
NT3 world bank
NT2 investment banks
NT2 savings banks
NT1 international monetary fund
NT1 mortgage financiers (agricola)
rt credit
rt finance
rt funds

FINANCIAL PLANNING
uf planning, financial
BT1 planning
rt agricultural budgets
rt agricultural financial policy
rt farm planning
rt finance

financial policy
USE **agricultural financial policy**
OR **fiscal policy**
OR **investment policy**

financial yields
USE **profits**
OR **returns**

financing research
USE **research support**

finches
USE **fringillidae**

FINE ARTS
BT1 arts
NT1 graphic arts
NT1 plastic arts
NT2 sculpture
NT2 wood carving
NT1 visual arts
rt artists
rt works of art

FINE FRACTION
BT1 soil separates

fine liquor
USE **sugar liquors**

FINE MOTOR DEVELOPMENT (AGRICOLA)
BT1 motor development (agricola)

FINENESS
BT1 physical properties
BT2 properties
rt size graders
rt thinness

FINEWOOL
BT1 wool
BT2 animal fibres
BT3 animal products
BT4 products
BT3 fibres

FINGER MILLET
rt eleusine coracana

FINISHES
NT1 textile finishes (agricola)
NT2 abrasion resistant finishes (agricola)
NT2 antiseptic finishes (agricola)
NT2 antistatic finish (agricola)
NT2 crush resistant finishes (agricola)
NT2 flame retardant finishes (agricola)
NT2 fume fading resistant finishes (agricola)
NT2 insulation finishes (agricola)
NT2 mildew resistant finishes (agricola)
NT2 moire (agricola)
NT2 moth resistant finishes (agricola)
NT2 opaque finishes (agricola)

FINISHES *cont.*
NT2 perspiration resistant finishes (agricola)
NT2 shrink resistant finishes (agricola)
NT2 slip resistant finishes (agricola)
NT2 soil release finishes (agricola)
NT2 stain resistant finishes (agricola)
NT2 water repellent finishes (agricola)
NT2 waterproof finishes (agricola)
NT2 wrinkle resistant finishes (agricola)
rt lacquers (agricola)
rt overlays
rt paints
rt staining
rt surface quality
rt veneering
rt woodworking

FINITE ELEMENT ANALYSIS
BT1 statistical analysis
BT2 data analysis
BT2 statistics

FINLAND
BT1 scandinavia
BT2 europe
rt efta
rt oecd

FINNISH
BT1 cattle breeds
BT2 breeds
BT1 horse breeds
BT2 breeds

FINNISH AYRSHIRE
BT1 cattle breeds
BT2 breeds

FINNISH LANDRACE
BT1 pig breeds
BT2 breeds
BT1 sheep breeds
BT2 breeds

FIORINIA
BT1 diaspididae
BT2 coccoidea
BT3 sternorrhyncha
BT4 homoptera
NT1 fiorinia theae

FIORINIA THEAE
BT1 fiorinia
BT2 diaspididae
BT3 coccoidea
BT4 sternorrhyncha
BT5 homoptera

FIRE
rt fire resistance

FIRE BEHAVIOR (AGRICOLA)
HN from 1989
rt fires

FIRE CAUSES
HN from 1989
rt fires
rt spontaneous ignition

FIRE CONTROL
BT1 control
NT1 fire fighting
NT1 fire suppression
rt controlled burning
rt fire danger
rt fire prevention
rt fires
rt forest fires

FIRE DANGER
BT1 hazards
rt fire control
rt fire effects
rt fire prevention
rt fires

FIRE DANGER *cont.*
rt forest fires
rt spontaneous ignition

FIRE DETECTION
HN from 1990
uf fire detection and reporting
BT1 detection
rt fires

fire detection and reporting
USE **fire detection**

FIRE ECOLOGY
HN from 1989
BT1 ecology
rt fires

FIRE EFFECTS
BT1 effects
rt burning
rt destruction
rt fire danger
rt fires
rt stress factors

FIRE EXTINGUISHERS (AGRICOLA)
rt fire suppression

FIRE FIGHTING
BT1 fire control
BT2 control
rt fire suppression
rt fires

FIRE PREVENTION
BT1 prevention
NT1 firebreaks
NT1 fireproofing
rt alarms
rt fire control
rt fire danger
rt fires
rt mirex
rt miserotoxin
rt safety
rt safety devices
rt spark arresters

FIRE RESISTANCE
BT1 resistance
rt fire
rt fireproofing

FIRE RETARDANTS (AGRICOLA)
rt fireproofing

FIRE SUPPRESSION
BT1 fire control
BT2 control
rt fire extinguishers (agricola)
rt fire fighting
rt firebreaks
rt fires
rt miserotoxin

FIRE WEATHER
HN from 1989
BT1 weather
rt fires

FIREBREAKS
uf firelines
uf fuelbreaks
BT1 fire prevention
BT2 prevention
rt fire suppression
rt fires
rt forest fires

firelines
USE **firebreaks**

FIREPLACES (AGRICOLA)
rt fires

FIREPROOFING
BT1 fire prevention
BT2 prevention
rt asbestos
rt combustion
rt fire resistance
rt fire retardants (agricola)
rt fires

FIRES
NT1 forest fires
NT1 sparks
NT1 wildfires (agricola)
rt ash
rt burning
rt combustion
rt fire behavior (agricola)
rt fire causes
rt fire control
rt fire danger
rt fire detection
rt fire ecology
rt fire effects
rt fire fighting
rt fire prevention
rt fire suppression
rt fire weather
rt firebreaks
rt fireplaces (agricola)
rt fireproofing
rt fuel consumption
rt heat
rt smoke
rt spontaneous ignition
rt wood smoke

fires, forest
USE **forest fires**

firewood
USE **fuelwood**

FIRMICUTES
BT1 bacteria
BT2 prokaryotes
NT1 actinobacillus
NT2 actinobacillus equuli
NT2 actinobacillus lignieresii
NT2 actinobacillus pleuropneumoniae
NT1 actinomycetales
NT2 actinomycetaceae
NT3 actinomyces
NT4 actinomyces bovis
NT4 actinomyces israelii
NT4 actinomyces naeslundii
NT4 actinomyces odontolyticus
NT4 actinomyces pyogenes
NT4 actinomyces viscosus
NT3 bifidobacterium
NT4 bifidobacterium adolescentis
NT4 bifidobacterium bifidum
NT4 bifidobacterium breve
NT4 bifidobacterium infantum
NT4 bifidobacterium longum
NT3 kineosporia
NT4 kineosporia aurantiaca
NT2 dermatophilaceae
NT3 dermatophilus
NT4 dermatophilus congolensis
NT2 faenia
NT3 faenia rectivirgula
NT2 frankiaceae
NT3 frankia
NT4 frankia ceanothi
NT2 micromonosporaceae
NT3 micropolyspora
NT3 thermoactinomyces
NT4 thermoactinomyces candida
NT4 thermoactinomyces sacchari
NT4 thermoactinomyces vulgaris
NT3 thermopolyspora
NT2 nocardiaceae
NT3 actinomadura
NT4 actinomadura madurae
NT4 actinomadura pelletieri
NT3 nocardia
NT4 nocardia asteroides
NT4 nocardia brasiliensis
NT4 nocardia caviae
NT4 nocardia farcinica
NT3 nocardiopsis
NT3 rhodococcus (bacteria)
NT4 rhodococcus equi
NT4 rhodococcus fascians

FIRMICUTES *cont.*
NT2 renibacterium
NT3 renibacterium salmoninarum
NT2 streptomycetaceae
NT3 streptomyces
NT4 streptomyces albus
NT4 streptomyces collinus
NT4 streptomyces galbus
NT4 streptomyces griseus
NT4 streptomyces ipomoea
NT4 streptomyces olivocinereus
NT4 streptomyces scabies
NT4 streptomyces somaliensis
NT4 streptomyces viridosporus
NT1 agromyces
NT2 agromyces ramosus
NT1 arthrobacter
NT2 arthrobacter crystallopoietes
NT2 arthrobacter fluorescens
NT2 arthrobacter giacomelloi
NT2 arthrobacter globiformis
NT1 bacillaceae
NT2 bacillus
NT3 bacillus anthracis
NT3 bacillus brevis
NT3 bacillus cereus
NT3 bacillus circulans
NT3 bacillus coagulans
NT3 bacillus larvae
NT3 bacillus licheniformis
NT3 bacillus macerans
NT3 bacillus megaterium
NT3 bacillus mesentericus
NT3 bacillus mycoides
NT3 bacillus natto
NT3 bacillus pantothenicus
NT3 bacillus penetrans
NT3 bacillus piliformis
NT3 bacillus polymyxa
NT3 bacillus popilliae
NT3 bacillus pumilus
NT3 bacillus sphaericus
NT3 bacillus stearothermophilus
NT4 bacillus stearothermophilus var. calidolactis
NT3 bacillus subtilis
NT3 bacillus thuringiensis
NT4 bacillus thuringiensis subsp. aizawai
NT4 bacillus thuringiensis subsp. dendrolimus
NT4 bacillus thuringiensis subsp. galleriae
NT4 bacillus thuringiensis subsp. israelensis
NT4 bacillus thuringiensis subsp. kurstaki
NT4 bacillus thuringiensis subsp. thuringiesis
NT2 clostridium
NT3 clostridium acetobutylicum
NT3 clostridium bifermentans
NT3 clostridium botulinum
NT3 clostridium butyricum
NT3 clostridium chauvoei
NT3 clostridium difficile
NT3 clostridium haemolyticum
NT3 clostridium novyi
NT3 clostridium pasteurianum
NT3 clostridium perfringens
NT3 clostridium septicum
NT3 clostridium sordellii
NT3 clostridium sporogenes
NT3 clostridium tetani
NT3 clostridium thermocellum
NT3 clostridium tyrobutyricum
NT1 cellulomonas
NT1 chlamydiales
NT2 chlamydiaceae
NT3 chlamydia
NT4 chlamydia psittaci
NT4 chlamydia trachomatis

FIRMICUTES *cont.*
NT1 coryneform group of bacteria
NT2 brevibacteriaceae
NT3 brevibacterium
NT4 brevibacterium linens
NT2 clavibacter
NT3 clavibacter iranicus
NT3 clavibacter michiganensis
NT4 clavibacter michiganensis subsp. insidiosus
NT4 clavibacter michiganensis subsp. michiganensis
NT4 clavibacter michiganensis subsp. nebraskensis
NT4 clavibacter michiganensis subsp. sepedonicus
NT3 clavibacter rathayi
NT3 clavibacter tritici
NT3 clavibacter xyli
NT4 clavibacter xyli subsp. xyli
NT2 corynebacteriaceae
NT3 corynebacterium
NT4 corynebacterium bovis
NT4 corynebacterium ovis
NT4 corynebacterium pseudotuberculosis
NT4 corynebacterium renale
NT2 curtobacterium
NT3 curtobacterium flaccumfaciens
NT4 curtobacterium flaccumfaciens pv. betae
NT4 curtobacterium flaccumfaciens pv. flaccumfaciens
NT4 curtobacterium flaccumfaciens pv. oortii
NT4 curtobacterium flaccumfaciens pv. poinsettiae
NT2 propionibacteriaceae
NT3 propionibacterium
NT4 propionibacterium freudenreichii
NT5 propionibacterium freudenreichii subsp. shermanii
NT1 lactobacillaceae
NT2 erysipelothrix
NT3 erysipelothrix rhusiopathiae
NT2 lactobacillus
NT3 lactobacillus acidophilus
NT3 lactobacillus brevis
NT3 lactobacillus buchneri
NT3 lactobacillus bulgaricus
NT3 lactobacillus casei
NT4 lactobacillus casei subsp. alactosus
NT4 lactobacillus casei subsp. casei
NT4 lactobacillus casei subsp. rhamnosus
NT3 lactobacillus cellobiosus
NT3 lactobacillus delbrueckii
NT3 lactobacillus fermentum
NT3 lactobacillus helveticus
NT3 lactobacillus lactis
NT3 lactobacillus leichmannii
NT3 lactobacillus murinus
NT3 lactobacillus plantarum
NT3 lactobacillus reuteri
NT3 lactobacillus salivarius
NT3 lactobacillus sporogenes
NT3 lactobacillus viridescens
NT2 listeria
NT3 listeria monocytogenes
NT1 melissococcus
NT2 melissococcus pluton
NT1 micrococcaceae
NT2 micrococcus
NT3 micrococcus luteus
NT3 micrococcus varians
NT2 staphylococcus
NT3 staphylococcus albus

FIRMICUTES *cont.*
NT3 staphylococcus aureus
NT3 staphylococcus caseolyticus
NT3 staphylococcus epidermidis
NT3 staphylococcus hyicus
NT1 mycobacteriaceae
NT2 mycobacterium
NT3 mycobacterium avium
NT3 mycobacterium bovis
NT3 mycobacterium farcinogenes
NT3 mycobacterium paratuberculosis
NT3 mycobacterium phlei
NT3 mycobacterium smegmatis
NT3 mycobacterium tuberculosis
NT1 peptococcaceae
NT2 peptococcus
NT3 peptococcus indolicus
NT2 peptostreptococcus
NT2 ruminococcus
NT3 ruminococcus albus
NT2 sarcina
NT1 streptococcaceae
NT2 enterococcus
NT3 enterococcus faecalis
NT3 enterococcus faecium
NT2 leuconostoc
NT3 leuconostoc cremoris
NT3 leuconostoc dextranicum
NT3 leuconostoc lactis
NT3 leuconostoc mesenteroides
NT2 pediococcus
NT3 pediococcus acidilactici
NT3 pediococcus cerevisiae
NT3 pediococcus pentosaceus
NT2 streptococcus
NT3 streptococcus acetoinicus
NT3 streptococcus agalactiae
NT3 streptococcus bovis
NT3 streptococcus cremoris
NT3 streptococcus durans
NT3 streptococcus dysgalactiae
NT3 streptococcus equi
NT3 streptococcus equisimilis
NT3 streptococcus faecalis
NT3 streptococcus faecium
NT3 streptococcus lactis
NT3 streptococcus mitis
NT3 streptococcus mutans
NT3 streptococcus pneumoniae
NT3 streptococcus pyogenes
NT3 streptococcus salivarius
NT3 streptococcus suis
NT3 streptococcus thermophilus
NT3 streptococcus uberis
NT3 streptococcus viridans
NT3 streptococcus zooepidemicus
rt gram positive bacteria

FIRMNESS
rt consistency
rt hardness
rt rheological properties
rt ripening
rt tenderness
rt texture

FIRMS
uf *economic units*
uf *makes*
uf *production units*
BT1 businesses
NT1 companies
NT2 multinational corporations
NT2 private companies
NT2 public companies
NT1 foreign firms
NT1 large firms
NT1 private firms
NT2 partnerships
NT3 limited partnerships (agricola)

firs
USE **abies**

FIRST AID
rt accidents
rt bandages
rt wound treatment

FISCAL POLICY
uf *financial policy*
uf *policy, fiscal*
uf *taxation policy*
BT1 economic policy
BT1 public finance
NT1 taxes
NT2 direct taxation
NT3 capital taxation
NT4 land tax
NT4 rates
NT3 company tax
NT3 income tax
NT3 inheritance tax
NT2 forest taxation
NT2 indirect taxation
NT3 stamp duty
NT3 value added tax
NT2 property taxes (agricola)
NT2 sales tax (agricola)
rt agricultural financial policy
rt credit control
rt economic policy
rt income transfers
rt monetary policy
rt support measures

FISCHOEDERIUS
BT1 gastrothylacidae
BT2 digenea
BT3 trematoda
NT1 fischoederius elongatus

FISCHOEDERIUS ELONGATUS
BT1 fischoederius
BT2 gastrothylacidae
BT3 digenea
BT4 trematoda

FISH
uf *fish as food*
BT1 fish products
BT2 animal products
BT3 products
rt fish consumption
rt fish culture
rt fish farming
rt fish farms
rt fish industry
rt fish manure
rt fish ponds
rt fish processing
rt fish production
rt fish scrap
rt fish silage
rt fish solubles
rt fish sticks (agricola)
rt fisheries
rt fishing
rt fishing gear
rt food products
rt fresh products
rt frozen fish
rt smoked fish

fish as food
USE **fish**

FISH CONSUMPTION
BT1 consumption
rt fish
rt fish industry

FISH CULTURE
BT1 aquaculture
BT2 enterprises
BT1 fish farming
BT2 farming
NT1 eel culture
NT1 salmon culture
rt aquarium fishes
rt fish
rt fish farms
rt fish feeding

FISH DISEASES
BT1 animal diseases
BT2 diseases
rt epitheliocystis
rt fishes

fish, dried
USE **dried fish**

FISH FARMING
uf *agropisciculture*
BT1 farming
NT1 fish culture
NT2 eel culture
NT2 salmon culture
rt aquaculture
rt fish
rt fish farms
rt fish feeding
rt fishes
rt livestock enterprises
rt nets

FISH FARMS
uf *fish hatcheries*
BT1 farms
rt aquaculture
rt fish
rt fish culture
rt fish farming
rt fish feeding
rt fisheries

FISH FEEDING
BT1 feeding
rt fish culture
rt fish farming
rt fish farms

fish, fermented
USE **fermented fish**

fish hatcheries
USE **fish farms**

FISH INDUSTRY
(processing of fish)
BT1 industry
rt fish
rt fish consumption
rt fish liver oils
rt fish manure
rt fish meal
rt fish oils
rt fish pastes
rt fish processing
rt fish production
rt fish products
rt fishing
rt food industry
rt shellfish
rt shellfish culture
rt shellfish fisheries

FISH LIVER OILS
BT1 fish oils
BT2 animal oils
BT3 fatty oils
BT4 oils
BT2 fish products
BT3 animal products
BT4 products
NT1 anchovy oil
NT1 cod liver oil
NT1 menhaden oil
rt dehydroretinol
rt fish industry
rt fish processing

FISH LIVERS
BT1 fish products
BT2 animal products
BT3 products
rt fish processing
rt livers as food

FISH MANURE
BT1 animal manures
BT2 manures
BT3 organic amendments
BT4 soil amendments
BT5 amendments
rt fish
rt fish industry

FISH MANURE *cont.*
rt fish scrap

FISH MEAL
BT1 feeds
BT1 fish products
BT2 animal products
BT3 products
BT1 meal
NT1 anchovy meal
rt fish industry
rt fish processing

FISH OILS
BT1 animal oils
BT2 fatty oils
BT3 oils
BT1 fish products
BT2 animal products
BT3 products
NT1 fish liver oils
NT2 anchovy oil
NT2 cod liver oil
NT2 menhaden oil
NT1 herring oil
rt fish industry
rt fish processing

FISH PASTES
BT1 fish products
BT2 animal products
BT3 products
rt fish industry
rt fish processing

FISH POISONS
uf *piscicides*
BT1 toxic substances
rt industrial crops
rt piscicidal plants

FISH POND SOILS
BT1 soil types (anthropogenic)
rt fish ponds
rt subaqueous soils

FISH PONDS
BT1 fisheries
BT1 ponds
BT2 open water
BT3 water
BT2 physiographic features
rt fish
rt fish pond soils

FISH PROCESSING
BT1 processing
rt fish
rt fish industry
rt fish liver oils
rt fish livers
rt fish meal
rt fish oils
rt fish pastes

FISH PRODUCTION
uf *fishery production*
rt fish
rt fish industry
rt fishery resources (agricola)

FISH PRODUCTS
uf *fishery products*
BT1 animal products
BT2 products
NT1 canned fish
NT1 dried fish
NT1 fermented fish
NT1 fish
NT1 fish livers
NT1 fish meal
NT2 anchovy meal
NT1 fish oils
NT2 fish liver oils
NT3 anchovy oil
NT3 cod liver oil
NT3 menhaden oil
NT2 herring oil
NT1 fish pastes
NT1 fish protein concentrate
NT1 fish protein hydrolysate
NT1 fish roe
NT2 caviar

FISH PRODUCTS *cont.*
NT1 fish sticks (agricola)
NT1 frozen fish
NT1 salted fish
NT1 smoked fish
rt fish industry
rt fish scrap
rt fishes
rt food products

FISH PROTEIN CONCENTRATE
BT1 fish products
BT2 animal products
BT3 products
BT1 protein concentrates
BT2 concentrates
BT3 feeds
BT3 foods
BT2 feed supplements
BT3 supplements

FISH PROTEIN HYDROLYSATE
BT1 fish products
BT2 animal products
BT3 products
BT1 protein hydrolysates
BT2 hydrolysates

FISH RHABDOVIRUS
BT1 vesiculovirus
BT2 rhabdoviridae
BT3 viruses
NT1 haematopoietic necrosis virus
NT1 haemorrhagic septicaemia virus

FISH ROE
uf *roes*
BT1 fish products
BT2 animal products
BT3 products
NT1 caviar
rt ova
rt ovaries
rt testes

fish, salted
USE **salted fish**

FISH SCRAP
uf *fish waste*
BT1 animal wastes
BT2 wastes
rt fish
rt fish manure
rt fish products

FISH SILAGE
BT1 silage
BT2 feeds
BT2 fermentation products
BT3 products
rt fish

FISH SOLUBLES
BT1 residues
rt fish

FISH STICKS (AGRICOLA)
BT1 fish products
BT2 animal products
BT3 products
rt fish

FISH TOXINS
BT1 toxins
NT1 ciguatera

fish waste
USE **fish scrap**

FISHERIES
NT1 fish ponds
NT1 shellfish fisheries
rt aquaculture
rt fish
rt fish farms
rt fishery management (agricola)
rt fishery resources (agricola)
rt hydrobiology
rt shellfish

FISHERMEN
BT1 occupations
rt fishing
rt seamen

FISHER'S THEOREM
(of natural selection)
BT1 genetic theory
BT2 genetics
BT3 biology
rt natural selection

FISHERY MANAGEMENT (AGRICOLA)
HN from 1990
rt fisheries
rt management

fishery production
USE **fish production**

fishery products
USE **fish products**

FISHERY RESOURCES (AGRICOLA)
HN from 1990
BT1 renewable resources
BT2 natural resources
BT3 resources
rt fish production
rt fisheries
rt fishes

FISHES
(for common names see freshwater fishes, marine fishes, diadromous fishes and game fishes)
NT1 cephalaspidomorphi
NT2 petromyzontiformes
NT3 petromyzontidae
NT4 lampetra
NT5 lampetra fluviatilis
NT4 petromyzon
NT1 chondrichthyes
NT2 chimaeriformes
NT3 chimaeridae
NT4 chimaera
NT5 chimaera monstrosa
NT4 hydrolagus
NT2 hexanchiformes
NT3 hexanchidae
NT4 hexanchus
NT2 lamniformes
NT3 carcharhinidae
NT4 carcharhinus
NT4 galeorhinus
NT4 mustelus
NT4 prionace
NT3 lamnidae
NT4 alopias
NT4 carcharodon
NT4 cetorhinus
NT5 cetorhinus maximus
NT4 isurus
NT4 lamna
NT3 odontaspididae
NT4 odontaspis
NT3 scyliorhinidae
NT4 galeus
NT4 scyliorhinus
NT2 rajiformes
NT3 dasyatidae
NT4 dasyatis
NT3 pristidae
NT4 pristis
NT3 rajidae
NT4 raja
NT2 squaliformes
NT3 pristiophoridae
NT4 pristiophorus
NT3 squalidae
NT4 centroscyllium
NT4 squalus
NT5 squalus acanthias
NT3 squatinidae
NT4 squatina
NT1 osteichthyes
NT2 acipenseriformes
NT3 acipenseridae
NT4 acipenser
NT5 acipenser gueldenstaedti

FISHES *cont.*
NT5 acipenser ruthenus
NT5 acipenser stellatus
NT5 acipenser transmontanus
NT4 huso
NT5 huso huso
NT3 polyodontidae
NT4 polyodon
NT2 anguilliformes
NT3 anguillidae
NT4 anguilla
NT5 anguilla japonica
NT5 anguilla reinhardtii
NT5 anguilla rostrata
NT3 muraenidae
NT4 gymnothorax
NT4 muraena
NT5 muraena helena
NT2 atheriniformes
NT3 atherinidae
NT4 atherina
NT5 atherina forskalii
NT5 atherina mochon
NT6 atherina mochon pontica
NT4 chirostoma
NT4 leuresthes
NT4 menidia
NT2 characiformes
NT3 curimatidae
NT4 prochilodus
NT2 clupeiformes
NT3 clupeidae
NT4 alosa
NT5 alosa pseudoharengus
NT5 alosa sapidissima
NT4 brevoortia
NT4 clupea
NT5 clupea ilisha
NT4 dorosoma
NT4 etrumeus
NT5 etrumeus teres
NT4 hilsa
NT4 sardina
NT4 sardinella
NT4 sardinops
NT4 sprattus
NT3 engraulidae
NT4 anchoa
NT4 coilia
NT4 engraulis
NT2 cypriniformes
NT3 cobitididae
NT4 misgurnus
NT5 misgurnus anguillicaudatus
NT3 cyprinidae
NT4 abramis
NT5 abramis brama
NT4 barbus
NT4 carassius
NT5 carassius carassius
NT4 catla
NT5 catla catla
NT4 cyprinus
NT4 gobio
NT5 gobio gobio
NT4 labeo
NT4 leucaspius
NT4 leuciscus
NT5 leuciscus cephalus
NT5 leuciscus idus
NT5 leuciscus leuciscus
NT4 notemigonus
NT4 phoxinus
NT5 phoxinus phoxinus
NT4 pimephales
NT5 pimephales promelas
NT4 rutilus
NT5 rutilus rutilus
NT4 semotilus
NT4 tinca
NT2 cyprinodontiformes
NT3 aplocheilidae
NT4 aplocheilus
NT5 aplocheilus latipes
NT3 cyprinodontidae
NT4 fundulus
NT5 fundulus heteroclitus
NT5 fundulus kansae

FISHES *cont.*
NT3 exocoetidae
NT4 cypselurus
NT4 exocoetus
NT4 prognichthys
NT3 hemiramphidae
NT4 hemiramphus
NT5 hemiramphus brachynopterus
NT4 hyporhamphus
NT3 poeciliidae
NT4 gambusia
NT5 gambusia affinis
NT4 poecilia
NT5 poecilia reticulata
NT3 scomberesocidae
NT4 cololabis
NT4 scomberesox
NT2 dactylopteriformes
NT3 dactylopteridae
NT4 dactylopterus
NT2 elopiformes
NT3 elopidae
NT4 elops
NT3 megalopidae
NT4 megalops
NT5 megalops atlanticus
NT5 megalops cyprinoides
NT2 gadiformes
NT3 gadidae
NT4 boreogadus
NT4 eleginus
NT4 gadus
NT5 gadus aeglefinus
NT4 lota
NT5 lota lota
NT4 melanogrammus
NT4 merlangius
NT4 microgadus
NT4 micromestistius
NT5 micromestistius poutassou
NT4 molva
NT5 molva molva
NT4 pollachius
NT5 pollachius pollachius
NT5 pollachius virens
NT4 trisopterus
NT5 trisopterus minutus
NT4 urophycis
NT3 merlucciidae
NT4 merluccius
NT5 merluccius capensis
NT5 merluccius productus
NT2 gasterosteiformes
NT3 gasterosteidae
NT4 culaea
NT5 culaea inconstans
NT4 gasterosteus
NT5 gasterosteus aculeatus
NT2 gonorhynchiformes
NT3 chanidae
NT4 chanos
NT5 chanos chanos
NT2 lampriformes
NT3 lampridae
NT4 lampris
NT5 lampris guttatus
NT2 lepisosteiformes
NT3 lepisosteidae
NT4 lepisosteus
NT2 lophiiformes
NT3 lophiidae
NT4 lophius
NT5 lophius piscatorius
NT2 ophidiiformes
NT3 ophidiidae
NT4 genypterus
NT5 genypterus blacodes
NT2 perciformes
NT3 ammodytidae
NT4 ammodytes
NT4 hyperoplus
NT3 anabantidae
NT4 anabas
NT5 anabas testudineus
NT3 anarhichadidae
NT4 anarhichas
NT3 belontiidae
NT4 trichogaster
NT3 bramidae

FISHES *cont.*
NT4 brama
NT5 brama brama
NT4 taractes
NT3 carangidae
NT4 caranx
NT4 decapterus
NT4 seriola
NT4 trachinotus
NT5 trachinotus carolinus
NT5 trachinotus goodei
NT4 trachurus
NT5 trachurus lathami
NT5 trachurus trachurus
NT4 vomer
NT3 centrarchidae
NT4 lepomis
NT5 lepomis cyanellus
NT5 lepomis gibbosus
NT5 lepomis macrochirus
NT3 centropomidae
NT4 centropomus
NT5 centropomus undecimalis
NT4 lates
NT5 lates calcarifer
NT5 lates niloticus
NT3 channidae
NT4 channa
NT3 cichlidae
NT4 tilapia
NT5 tilapia aurea
NT5 tilapia mossambica
NT5 tilapia nilotica
NT5 tilapia zillii
NT3 eleotridae
NT4 gobiomorus
NT3 haemulidae
NT4 anisotremus
NT4 haemulon
NT5 haemulon sciurus
NT4 orthopristis
NT4 pomadasys
NT5 pomadasys jubelini
NT5 pomadasys maculatus
NT3 istiophoridae
NT4 istiophorus
NT5 istiophorus platypterus
NT4 makaira
NT4 tetrapturus
NT3 kyphosidae
NT4 girella
NT4 kyphosus
NT5 kyphosus cinerascens
NT3 labridae
NT4 lachnolaimus
NT4 pimelometopon
NT4 tautogolabrus
NT4 thalassoma
NT3 lethrinidae
NT4 lethrinus
NT5 lethrinus mahsena
NT5 lethrinus nebulosus
NT3 lutjanidae
NT4 apsilus
NT4 lutjanus
NT4 ocyurus
NT4 rhomboplites
NT3 mugilidae
NT4 mugil
NT5 mugil cephalus
NT5 mugil waigiensis
NT4 valamugil
NT3 mullidae
NT4 mullus
NT4 upeneus
NT3 percichthyidae
NT4 dicentrarchus
NT4 lateolabrax
NT5 lateolabrax japonicus
NT4 morone
NT5 morone saxatilis
NT4 polyprion
NT4 stereolepis
NT3 percidae
NT4 etheostoma
NT4 perca
NT5 perca flavescens
NT4 stizostedion
NT5 stizostedion canadense
NT5 stizostedion vitreum

FISHES *cont.*
NT3 pholididae
NT4 pholis
NT5 pholis gunnellus
NT3 polynemidae
NT4 eleutheronema
NT4 polydactylus
NT4 polynemus
NT3 pomacentridae
NT4 dascyllus
NT3 pomatomidae
NT4 pomatomus
NT3 sciaenidae
NT4 aplodinotus
NT4 argyrosomus
NT5 argyrosomus argentatus
NT5 argyrosomus hololepidotus
NT4 cynoscion
NT5 cynoscion leiarchus
NT5 cynoscion regalis
NT4 genyonemus
NT4 menticirrhus
NT4 micropogon (fishes)
NT4 pogonias
NT4 sciaenops
NT4 umbrina
NT3 scombridae
NT4 euthynnus
NT4 rastrelliger
NT5 rastrelliger kanagurta
NT4 sarda
NT4 scomber
NT4 scomberomorus
NT4 thunnus
NT3 serranidae
NT4 centropristis
NT4 diplectrum
NT4 epinephelus
NT5 epinephelus aeneus
NT5 epinephelus akaara
NT5 epinephelus tauvina
NT4 mycteroperca
NT4 paralabrax
NT4 serranus
NT5 serranus cabrilla
NT3 sillaginidae
NT4 sillago
NT3 sparidae
NT4 archosargus
NT4 chrysophrys
NT5 chrysophrys sarba
NT4 pagrus
NT5 pagrus aurata
NT5 pagrus major
NT4 sparus
NT3 sphyraenidae
NT4 sphyraena
NT3 stromateidae
NT4 pampus
NT5 pampus argenteus
NT4 stromateus
NT5 stromateus cinereus
NT3 teraponidae
NT4 terapon
NT5 terapon jarbua
NT5 terapon theraps
NT3 trachinidae
NT4 trachinus
NT5 trachinus draco
NT5 trachinus vipera
NT3 trichiuridae
NT4 lepidopus
NT4 trichiurus
NT3 xiphiidae
NT4 xiphias
NT5 xiphias gladius
NT2 percopsiformes
NT3 percopsidae
NT4 percopsis
NT2 pleuronectiformes
NT3 bothidae
NT4 paralichthys
NT5 paralichthys olivaceus
NT4 scophthalmus
NT5 scophthalmus rhombus
NT3 pleuronectidae
NT4 atheresthes
NT4 glyptocephalus

FISHES *cont.*
NT5 glyptocephalus cynoglossus
NT4 hippoglossoides
NT4 hippoglossus
NT4 limanda
NT5 limanda limanda
NT4 liopsetta
NT4 platichthys
NT5 platichthys flesus
NT4 pleuronectes
NT4 pseudopleuronectes
NT4 reinhardtius
NT5 reinhardtius hippoglossoides
NT3 soleidae
NT4 solea
NT2 salmoniformes
NT3 argentinidae
NT4 argentina (fishes)
NT3 esocidae
NT4 esox
NT3 osmeridae
NT4 mallotus (fishes)
NT5 mallotus villosus
NT4 osmerus
NT3 plecoglossidae
NT4 plecoglossus
NT3 salmonidae
NT4 coregonus
NT4 hucho
NT5 hucho hucho
NT4 oncorhynchus
NT5 oncorhynchus gorbuscha
NT5 oncorhynchus keta
NT5 oncorhynchus kisutch
NT5 oncorhynchus masou
NT5 oncorhynchus nerka
NT5 oncorhynchus rhodurus
NT5 oncorhynchus tshawytscha
NT4 salmo
NT5 salmo clarki
NT5 salmo trutta
NT4 salvelinus
NT5 salvelinus alpinus
NT5 salvelinus fontinalis
NT4 thymallus
NT5 thymallus arcticus
NT5 thymallus thymallus
NT2 scorpaeniformes
NT3 anoplopomatidae
NT4 anoplopoma
NT5 anoplopoma fimbria
NT3 cottidae
NT4 cottus
NT4 icelinus
NT4 leptocottus
NT4 myoxocephalus
NT4 scorpaenichthys
NT3 cyclopteridae
NT4 cyclopterus
NT3 platycephalidae
NT4 platycephalus
NT3 scorpaenidae
NT4 scorpaena
NT4 sebastes
NT5 sebastes marinus
NT3 triglidae
NT4 chelidonichthys
NT4 prionotus
NT4 trigla
NT2 siluriformes
NT3 ariidae
NT4 arius
NT4 bagre
NT3 bagridae
NT4 chrysichthys
NT5 chrysichthys walkeri
NT3 clariidae
NT4 clarias
NT5 clarias lazera
NT3 ictaluridae
NT4 ictalurus
NT5 ictalurus nebulosus
NT5 ictalurus punctatus
NT3 pimelodidae
NT4 rhamdia
NT3 plotosidae
NT4 tandanus

FISHES *cont.*
NT5 tandanus tandanus
NT3 siluridae
NT4 silurus
NT5 silurus glanis
NT4 wallago
NT4 wallagonia
NT5 wallagonia attu
NT2 syngnathiformes
NT3 syngnathidae
NT4 hippocampus (genus)
NT2 tetraodontiformes
NT3 balistidae
NT4 alutera
NT4 balistes
NT4 monacanthus
NT4 xanthichthys
NT3 molidae
NT4 masturus
NT4 mola
NT3 tetraodontidae
NT4 sphoeroides
NT2 zeiformes
NT3 zeidae
NT4 zeus
NT5 zeus faber
rt aquarium fishes
rt brackish water fishes
rt diadromous fishes
rt fish diseases
rt fish farming
rt fish products
rt fishery resources (agricola)
rt freshwater fishes
rt fry
rt game fishes
rt gills
rt herbivorous fishes
rt marine fishes
rt ornamental fishes
rt scales
rt smoltification
rt spawning
rt vertebrates

fishes, herbivorous
USE **herbivorous fishes**

FISHING
(commercial fishing; for recreational fishing use "angling")
rt boats
rt catch composition
rt fish
rt fish industry
rt fishermen
rt fishing gear
rt fishing vessels
rt nets
rt put and take
rt ships

FISHING GEAR
BT1 equipment
NT1 floats
rt fish
rt fishing

fishing, recreational
USE **angling**

FISHING VESSELS
BT1 ships
rt fishing

FISSIPEDA
BT1 carnivores
BT2 mammals
NT1 ailuropodidae
NT2 ailuropoda
NT3 ailuropoda melanoleuca
NT2 ailurus
NT3 ailurus fulgens
NT1 canidae
NT2 alopex
NT3 alopex lagopus
NT2 canis
NT3 canis aureus
NT3 canis familiaris dingo
NT3 canis mesomelas
NT2 chrysocyon
NT3 chrysocyon brachyurus
NT2 lycaon

FISSIPEDA *cont.*
NT3 lycaon pictus
NT2 nyctereutes
NT2 vulpes
NT3 vulpes cinereoargenteus
NT3 vulpes vulpes
NT1 felidae
NT2 acinonyx
NT3 acinonyx jubatus
NT2 felis
NT3 felis bengalensis
NT3 felis concolor
NT3 felis lynx
NT3 felis rufus
NT3 felis silvestris
NT3 felis wiedii
NT2 neofelis
NT3 neofelis nebulosa
NT2 panthera
NT3 panthera uncia
NT1 herpestidae
NT2 herpestes
NT3 herpestes auropunctatus
NT3 herpestes edwardsii
NT1 hyaenidae
NT2 crocuta
NT3 crocuta crocuta
NT2 hyaena
NT1 mustelidae
NT2 enhydra
NT3 enhydra lutris
NT2 gulo
NT3 gulo gulo
NT2 lutra
NT3 lutra canadensis
NT2 martes
NT3 martes americana
NT3 martes foina
NT3 martes martes
NT2 meles
NT3 meles meles
NT2 mephitis
NT3 mephitis mephitis
NT2 mustela
NT3 mustela altaica
NT3 mustela erminea
NT3 mustela lutreola
NT3 mustela nivalis
NT3 mustela sibirica
NT1 procyonidae
NT2 nasua
NT3 nasua nasua
NT2 potos
NT3 potos flavus
NT2 procyon
NT3 procyon lotor
NT1 ursidae
NT2 helarctos
NT3 helarctos malayanus
NT2 selenarctos
NT3 selenarctos thibetanus
NT2 thalarctos
NT3 thalarctos maritimus
NT2 ursus
NT3 ursus americanus
NT3 ursus arctos
NT1 viverridae
NT2 genetta
NT2 paguma
NT3 paguma larvata

FISTULA
BT1 abnormalities
rt fistulation

FISTULATION
BT1 surgical operations
rt fistula

FITNESS
BT1 health
rt physical fitness

FITTONIA
BT1 acanthaceae
NT1 fittonia verschaffeltii

FITTONIA VERSCHAFFELTII
BT1 fittonia
BT2 acanthaceae
rt ornamental foliage plants

FITZROYA
BT1 cupressaceae
NT1 fitzroya cupressoides

FITZROYA CUPRESSOIDES
BT1 fitzroya
BT2 cupressaceae

FIXATION
NT1 ammonium fixation
NT1 immobilization
NT2 inactivation
NT1 nitrogen fixation
rt genes

FIXED AMMONIUM
rt ammonium
rt ammonium fixation
rt soil chemistry

FIXED CAPITAL
uf *basic funds*
uf *capital, fixed*
BT1 assets
BT1 capital
BT2 finance
rt farm buildings
rt farm equipment

FIXED-COMB HIVES
BT1 hives
NT1 skeps

FIXED COSTS
uf *costs, fixed*
BT1 production costs
BT2 costs

FJORD
BT1 horse breeds
BT2 breeds

FLABELLULA
BT1 sarcomastigophora
BT2 protozoa

FLACOURTIA
BT1 flacourtiaceae
NT1 flacourtia indica
NT1 flacourtia sepiaria

FLACOURTIA INDICA
BT1 flacourtia
BT2 flacourtiaceae
BT1 ornamental woody plants

FLACOURTIA SEPIARIA
BT1 flacourtia
BT2 flacourtiaceae

FLACOURTIACEAE
NT1 doryalis
NT2 doryalis caffra
NT1 flacourtia
NT2 flacourtia indica
NT2 flacourtia sepiaria
NT1 hydnocarpus
NT2 hydnocarpus kurzii
NT2 hydnocarpus odorata
NT2 hydnocarpus wightiana
NT1 laetia
NT2 laetia thamnia
NT1 ryania
NT2 ryania speciosa
NT1 xylosma
NT2 xylosma congesta
NT2 xylosma velutina

FLAG LEAF
uf *leaf, flag*
BT1 plant
rt leaves

FLAGELLA
BT1 cell structure

FLAGELLATES
rt sarcomastigophora

FLAIL MOWERS
uf *mowers, flail*
BT1 mowers
BT2 farm machinery
BT3 machinery
rt flails

FLAILS
BT1 components
rt beaters
rt flail mowers
rt threshing

FLAKEBOARDS
BT1 particleboards
BT2 forest products
BT3 products
BT2 panels
BT3 building materials
BT4 materials

FLAKING
BT1 processing

FLAME CULTIVATORS
uf *flame weeders*
uf *weeders, flame*
rt burning
rt cultivators
rt weeders

FLAME PHOTOMETRY
BT1 photometry
BT2 analytical methods
BT3 methodology
NT1 absorption flame photometry

FLAME RETARDANT FINISHES (AGRICOLA)
BT1 textile finishes (agricola)
BT2 finishes

flame weeders
USE **flame cultivators**

flaming
USE **burning**

flamingoes
USE **phoenicopteridae**

FLAMMULINA
BT1 agaricales
NT1 flammulina velutipes

FLAMMULINA VELUTIPES
BT1 edible fungi
BT2 fungi
BT2 vegetables
BT1 flammulina
BT2 agaricales

FLAMPROP
BT1 arylalanine herbicides
BT2 anilide herbicides
BT3 amide herbicides
BT4 herbicides
BT5 pesticides

flanders, east
USE **east flanders**

FLANDERS VIRUS
BT1 vesiculovirus
BT2 rhabdoviridae
BT3 viruses

flanders, west
USE **west flanders**

FLANNEL (AGRICOLA)
BT1 fabrics

FLAT DECK CAGES
BT1 cages
BT2 animal housing
rt decks

FLAT SIEVE SEED CLEANERS
uf *cleaners, flat sieve seed*
uf *seed cleaners, flat sieve*
BT1 seed cleaners
BT2 cleaners
BT3 machinery

FLATFISHES
BT1 marine fishes
BT2 aquatic animals
BT3 animals
BT3 aquatic organisms
NT1 dover soles
NT1 flounder

FLATFISHES *cont.*
NT1 halibut
NT1 plaice
NT1 turbot
rt bothidae
rt pleuronectidae
rt soleidae

flatheads
USE **platycephalidae**

FLATULENCE (AGRICOLA)
rt flatus

FLATUS
BT1 digestive disorders
BT2 functional disorders
BT3 animal disorders
BT4 disorders
rt bloat
rt flatulence (agricola)

FLATWARE (AGRICOLA)
rt dinnerware (agricola)
rt household equipment (agricola)
rt table settings (agricola)

FLAVANOLS
uf *catechins*
BT1 alcohols
BT1 flavonoids
BT2 aromatic compounds
BT2 plant pigments
BT3 pigments
NT1 catechin
NT1 epicatechin

FLAVERIA
BT1 compositae
NT1 flaveria bidentis

FLAVERIA BIDENTIS
BT1 flaveria
BT2 compositae

FLAVIVIRIDAE
BT1 viruses
NT1 flavivirus
NT2 dengue virus
NT2 japanese encephalitis virus
NT2 kumlinge virus
NT2 kyasanur forest disease virus
NT2 louping ill virus
NT2 murray valley encephalitis virus
NT2 powassan virus
NT2 rocio virus
NT2 st. louis encephalitis virus
NT2 tickborne encephalitis virus
NT2 tyuleniy virus
NT2 wesselsbron virus
NT2 west nile virus
NT2 yellow fever virus

FLAVIVIRUS
BT1 arboviruses
BT2 pathogens
BT1 flaviviridae
BT2 viruses
NT1 dengue virus
NT1 japanese encephalitis virus
NT1 kumlinge virus
NT1 kyasanur forest disease virus
NT1 louping ill virus
NT1 murray valley encephalitis virus
NT1 powassan virus
NT1 rocio virus
NT1 st. louis encephalitis virus
NT1 tickborne encephalitis virus
NT1 tyuleniy virus
NT1 wesselsbron virus
NT1 west nile virus
NT1 yellow fever virus

FLAVOBACTERIUM
BT1 gracilicutes
BT2 bacteria
BT3 prokaryotes
NT1 flavobacterium meningosepticum

FLAVOBACTERIUM MENINGOSEPTICUM
HN from 1989
BT1 flavobacterium
BT2 gracilicutes
BT3 bacteria
BT4 prokaryotes

flavomycin
USE **bambermycin**

FLAVONES
BT1 flavonoids
BT2 aromatic compounds
BT2 plant pigments
BT3 pigments
NT1 flavonols
NT2 isorhamnetin
NT2 kaempferol
NT2 quercetin

FLAVONOIDS
BT1 aromatic compounds
BT1 plant pigments
BT2 pigments
NT1 anthocyanidins
NT2 cyanidin
NT2 delphinidin
NT2 pelargonidin
NT1 betacyanins
NT1 bioflavonoids
NT2 hesperidin
NT2 naringin
NT2 quercetin
NT2 rutoside
NT1 chalcones
NT2 chalcone
NT1 flavanols
NT2 catechin
NT2 epicatechin
NT1 flavones
NT2 flavonols
NT3 isorhamnetin
NT3 kaempferol
NT3 quercetin
NT1 glycoflavones
NT2 anthocyanins
NT3 cyanin
NT3 delphinin
NT3 rubrobrassicin
NT2 hesperidin
NT2 isoquercitrin
NT2 naringin
NT2 phloridzin
NT2 quercitrin
NT2 rutoside
NT2 vitexin
NT1 isoflavans
NT1 isoflavones
NT2 daidzein
NT2 dimethoxyisoflavone
NT2 formononetin
NT2 genistein
NT2 medicarpin
NT2 phaseollin
NT2 pisatin
NT2 rotenoids
NT3 rotenone
NT1 karanjin

FLAVONOLS
BT1 alcohols
BT1 flavones
BT2 flavonoids
BT3 aromatic compounds
BT3 plant pigments
BT4 pigments
NT1 isorhamnetin
NT1 kaempferol
NT1 quercetin

flavophospholipol
USE **bambermycin**

flavoprotein-linked monooxygenase
USE **unspecific monooxygenase**

FLAVOR
BF flavour
NT1 egg flavor
NT1 milk flavor

FLAVOR *cont.*
NT1 oxidized flavor
rt flavor compounds
rt flavor enhancers

FLAVOR COMPOUNDS
BF flavour compounds
rt flavor

FLAVOR ENHANCERS
BF flavour enhancers
rt flavor

FLAVORED MILK
BF flavoured milk

FLAVORING
BF flavouring
rt flavorings

FLAVORINGS
BF flavourings
NT1 artificial flavors (agricola)
rt flavoring

FLAVOUR
AF flavor
BT1 organoleptic traits
BT2 physicochemical properties
BT3 properties
BT2 traits
NT1 egg flavour
NT1 milk flavour
NT1 oxidized flavour
rt acidity
rt aroma
rt flavour compounds
rt flavour enhancers
rt flavourings
rt organolepsis
rt tastes

FLAVOUR COMPOUNDS
AF flavor compounds
NT1 benzaldehyde
NT1 benzyl alcohol
NT1 capsaicin
NT1 carvone
NT1 coumarin
NT1 diacetyl
NT1 ethyl octanoate
NT1 limonin
NT1 maltol
NT1 menthol
NT1 salt
NT2 iodized salt
NT1 sweet tasting compounds
NT2 aspartame
NT2 dextrins
NT3 maltodextrins
NT2 glycyrrhizin
NT2 lactose
NT2 lactulose
NT2 maltodextrins
NT2 maltose
NT2 sorbitol
NT2 sucrose
NT1 vanillin
rt condiments
rt essential oils
rt flavour
rt flavour enhancers
rt flavourings
rt tastes

FLAVOUR ENHANCERS
AF flavor enhancers
BT1 enhancers
BT1 food additives
BT2 additives
NT1 monosodium glutamate
rt flavour
rt flavour compounds
rt flavouring

FLAVOURED MILK
AF flavored milk
uf *milk, flavoured*
BT1 milk products
BT2 products
NT1 chocolate milk
NT1 coffee milk

FLAVOURING
AF flavoring
BT1 processing
rt flavour enhancers
rt flavourings

flavouring crops
USE **culinary herbs**
OR **essential oil plants**
OR **spice plants**

FLAVOURINGS
AF flavorings
uf *seasonings*
BT1 food additives
BT2 additives
NT1 caramel
rt culinary herbs
rt essential oil plants
rt flavour
rt flavour compounds
rt flavouring
rt sauces
rt spice plants
rt spices
rt sweet tasting compounds

FLAX
uf *oilseed flax*
rt flax pullers
rt linamarin
rt linseed
rt linum usitatissimum

FLAX PULLERS
uf *harvesters, flax*
BT1 harvesters
BT2 farm machinery
BT3 machinery
rt flax
rt stalk pullers

FLEA COLLARS
BT1 application methods
BT2 methodology
rt formulations
rt insecticides
rt siphonaptera

fleas
USE **siphonaptera**

FLEECE
rt animal fibres
rt curl
rt fleece weight
rt shearing
rt shearing machines
rt shears
rt shedding
rt undercoat
rt wool

FLEECE WEIGHT
BT1 weight
rt fleece

fleecing
USE **shearing**

FLEHMEN
HN from 1990
BT1 sexual behaviour
BT2 behaviour

FLEMINGIA
uf *maughania*
BT1 leguminosae
NT1 flemingia lineata

FLEMINGIA LINEATA
BT1 flemingia
BT2 leguminosae

FLESH BROWNING
BT1 plant disorders
BT2 disorders
rt apples

FLESH HARDENING
BT1 plant disorders
BT2 disorders
rt pears

flesh side
USE **hide scrapings**

FLEXIBACTER
BT1 cytophagaceae
BT2 gracilicutes
BT3 bacteria
BT4 prokaryotes

FLEXIBILITY
BT1 mechanical properties
BT2 properties
rt elasticity
rt plasticity

FLEXIBLE PACKAGING (AGRICOLA)
BT1 packaging
BT2 handling

FLEXIBLE SILOS
uf *silos, flexible*
BT1 silos
BT2 stores

flies
USE **diptera**

FLIGHT
rt movement
rt wings

FLIGHT CAGES
BT1 cages
BT2 animal housing

FLINDERSIA
BT1 flindersiaceae
NT1 flindersia brayleyana
NT1 flindersia fournieri

FLINDERSIA BRAYLEYANA
BT1 flindersia
BT2 flindersiaceae

FLINDERSIA FOURNIERI
BT1 flindersia
BT2 flindersiaceae

FLINDERSIACEAE
NT1 flindersia
NT2 flindersia brayleyana
NT2 flindersia fournieri

FLIPCHARTS (AGRICOLA)
BT1 charts (agricola)

FLOATING
uf *rafting*
BT1 water transport
BT2 transport

FLOATING RICE
rt rice

FLOATING TRACTORS
BT1 tractors
BT2 cross country vehicles
BT3 vehicles

FLOATS
BT1 fishing gear
BT2 equipment

FLOCCULANTS
rt flocculation

FLOCCULATION
BT1 analytical methods
BT2 methodology
BT1 processing
rt chemical precipitation
rt colloidal properties
rt flocculants

flocculation tests
USE **immunoprecipitation tests**

FLOCKBOOKS
BT1 herdbooks

FLOCKS
rt goats
rt herds
rt livestock numbers
rt sheep

FLOCOUMAFEN
BT1 coumarin rodenticides
BT2 coumarins
BT3 lactones
BT4 heterocyclic oxygen compounds
BT4 ketones
BT2 rodenticides
BT3 pesticides

FLOOD CONTROL
BT1 control
BT1 water management
rt flooding
rt floods
rt hydraulic structures

FLOOD IRRIGATION
BT1 irrigation

FLOOD MEADOWS
BT1 floodlands
BT2 land types
BT1 meadows
BT2 grasslands
BT3 vegetation types

flood plains
USE **floodplains**

flooded conditions
USE **flooding**

FLOODED LAND
BT1 floodlands
BT2 land types
BT1 wetlands
BT2 land types

FLOODED RICE
rt flooding
rt rice

FLOODING
uf flooded conditions
BT1 natural disasters
BT2 disasters
BT1 water management
rt flood control
rt flooded rice
rt flooding tolerance
rt floodlands
rt floodplains
rt plant water relations
rt stress factors
rt submergence
rt water spreading
rt waterlogging

FLOODING TOLERANCE
HN from 1989
BT1 tolerance
rt flooding

FLOODLANDS
BT1 land types
NT1 flood meadows
NT1 flooded land
rt flooding
rt floodplains
rt floods

FLOODPLAINS
HN previously "flood plains"
uf flood plains
BT1 plains
BT2 physiographic features
rt alluvial land
rt bottomland forests
rt bottomlands
rt fens
rt flooding
rt floodlands

FLOODS
rt flood control
rt floodlands
rt natural disasters

FLOOR AREA
rt area
rt floors

FLOOR COVERINGS (AGRICOLA)
NT1 carpet (agricola)

FLOOR COVERINGS (AGRICOLA) *cont.*
NT2 tufted carpet (agricola)
NT1 rugs (agricola)
rt soft surface flooring (agricola)

FLOOR DRIERS
AF floor dryers
uf driers, floor
BT1 grain driers
BT2 driers
BT3 farm machinery
BT4 machinery
rt batch driers

FLOOR DRYERS
BF floor driers
BT1 dryers

FLOOR HUSBANDRY
BT1 animal husbandry
BT2 husbandry
BT2 zootechny

FLOOR PENS
HN from 1989
BT1 pens
BT2 animal housing

FLOOR PLANS (AGRICOLA)
rt floors
rt planning

FLOOR POLISHES
BT1 polishes
BT2 protective coatings
BT3 coatings

FLOOR SPACE
rt animal housing
rt floors

FLOOR TYPE
rt floors

FLOORS
NT1 grid floors
NT1 permeable floors
NT1 slatted floors
NT1 threshing floors
rt floor area
rt floor plans (agricola)
rt floor space
rt floor type
rt hard surface flooring (agricola)
rt litter
rt mats
rt resilient flooring (agricola)
rt soft surface flooring (agricola)

FLORA
NT1 microbial flora
NT2 bacteroids
NT2 butyric acid bacteria
NT2 coliform bacteria
NT3 faecal coliforms
NT2 faecal flora
NT3 faecal coliforms
NT2 gram negative bacteria
NT2 gram positive bacteria
NT2 intestinal microorganisms
NT2 iron oxidizing bacteria
NT2 lactic acid bacteria
NT2 lipolytic bacteria
NT2 nitrogen fixing bacteria
NT2 propionic acid bacteria
NT2 psychrophilic bacteria
NT2 psychrotrophic bacteria
NT2 rumen flora
NT3 rumen bacteria
NT3 ruminant symbionts
NT2 sporeforming bacteria
NT2 sulfate reducing bacteria
NT2 thermoduric bacteria
NT2 thermophilic bacteria
NT3 thermophilic actinomycetes
NT1 soil flora
NT2 soil bacteria
NT2 soil fungi
NT1 wild flowers

FLORA *cont.*
NT1 wild plants
rt biogeography
rt biota
rt botanical composition
rt microorganisms
rt plants
rt vegetation
rt vegetation types

flores
USE **nusa tenggara**

FLORICULTURE
BT1 horticulture
BT2 agricultural sciences
rt cut flowers
rt ornamental plants
rt pot plants

FLORIDA
BT1 southeastern states of usa
BT2 southern states of usa
BT3 usa
BT4 north america
BT5 america

FLOTATION
BT1 processing
rt separation

FLOTATION SEED CLEANERS
uf cleaners, flotation seed
uf seed cleaners, flotation
BT1 seed cleaners
BT2 cleaners
BT3 machinery

FLOUNDER
HN from 1989
BT1 flatfishes
BT2 marine fishes
BT3 aquatic animals
BT4 animals
BT4 aquatic organisms
rt platichthys flesus

FLOUR MILLS
BT1 mills
BT2 machinery
rt flours

flour quality
USE **baking quality**
OR **milling quality**

FLOURENSIA
BT1 compositae
NT1 flourensia annua
NT1 flourensia oolepis

FLOURENSIA ANNUA
BT1 flourensia
BT2 compositae

FLOURENSIA OOLEPIS
BT1 flourensia
BT2 compositae

FLOURS
BT1 plant products
BT2 products
NT1 cereal flours
NT2 cornflour
NT2 oatmeal
NT2 rice flour
NT2 rye flour
NT2 wheat flour
NT1 groundnut flour
NT1 sago flour
NT1 soyabean flour
NT1 sweet potato flour
rt flour mills
rt meal

FLOW
BT1 movement
NT1 air flow
NT1 flow constants
NT1 flow from roots
NT1 flow to drains
NT1 flow to roots
NT1 groundwater flow
NT1 heat flow

FLOW *cont.*
NT1 horizontal flow
NT1 laminar flow
NT1 macropore flow
NT1 mass flow
NT1 overland flow
NT1 return flow
NT1 root zone flux
NT1 stemflow
NT1 stream flow
NT1 transient flow
NT1 turbulent flow
NT1 two dimensional flow
NT1 unsaturated flow
NT1 water flow
rt blockage
rt bridging
rt cavitation
rt conductivity
rt flow meters
rt fluid mechanics
rt fluids
rt jets
rt rheological properties
rt rivers
rt saturated flow
rt shedding
rt soil water movement
rt stagnation
rt streams
rt taps
rt throughput
rt venturi tubes
rt viscoelasticity
rt water advance
rt water flow resistance
rt water management
rt waterways

FLOW CHARTS (AGRICOLA)
BT1 charts (agricola)

FLOW CONSTANTS
BT1 flow
BT2 movement
rt air flow
rt laminar flow
rt turbulent flow

FLOW CYTOMETRY
HN from 1989
BT1 biological techniques
BT2 techniques

FLOW FROM ROOTS
BT1 flow
BT2 movement
rt roots

FLOW METERS
BT1 meters
BT2 instruments
NT1 venturi tubes
rt air flow
rt flow

flow, nonsteady
USE **transient flow**

FLOW RESISTANCE
BT1 resistance
NT1 drag
NT1 water flow resistance
rt air flow
rt barriers
rt laminar flow
rt viscosity

FLOW SORTING
HN from 1989
BT1 sorting
BT2 grading
BT2 processing
BT2 separation

FLOW TO DRAINS
BT1 flow
BT2 movement
BT1 soil water movement
BT2 movement
rt drainage
rt drainage channels
rt drainage water

FLOW TO ROOTS
BT1 flow
BT2 movement
rt roots

flower buds
USE **buds**

FLOWER GRADERS
uf graders, flower
BT1 graders
rt flowers

flower pots
USE **pots**

FLOWER PRIMORDIA
BT1 plant
rt flowers

FLOWERING
uf anthesis
BT1 plant development
NT1 bolting
NT1 flowering date
rt flowers
rt maturation
rt precocity
rt spur types
rt spurs
rt vernalization

FLOWERING DATE
BT1 flowering
BT2 plant development
rt date
rt earliness
rt flowers
rt maturation

FLOWERS
BT1 inflorescences
BT2 plant
NT1 androecium
NT2 stamens
NT3 anthers
NT4 pollen
NT1 calyx
NT1 corolla
NT1 gynoecium
NT2 ovules
NT2 stigma
NT2 styles
NT1 perianths
rt aestivation
rt bracts
rt buds
rt cut flowers
rt deblossoming
rt dioecy
rt flower graders
rt flower primordia
rt flowering
rt flowering date
rt pollination

flowers, cut
USE **cut flowers**

flowers, wild
USE **wild flowers**

FLOXACRINE
BT1 antimalarials
BT2 antiprotozoal agents
BT3 antiparasitic agents
BT4 drugs

FLOXURIDINE
uf fluorodeoxyuridine
BT1 antineoplastic agents
BT2 drugs
BT1 antiviral agents
BT2 antiinfective agents
BT3 drugs
BT1 deoxyuridines
BT2 deoxyribonucleosides
BT3 nucleosides
BT4 glycosides
BT5 carbohydrates
BT1 mutagens

FLUAZIFOP
BT1 aryloxyphenoxypropionic herbicides
BT2 phenoxypropionic herbicides
BT3 phenoxy herbicides
BT4 herbicides
BT5 pesticides

FLUBENDAZOLE
BT1 anthelmintics
BT2 antiparasitic agents
BT3 drugs
BT1 benzimidazoles
BT2 heterocyclic nitrogen compounds
BT3 organic nitrogen compounds

FLUBENZIMINE
BT1 mite growth regulators
BT2 acaricides
BT3 pesticides
BT2 growth regulators

FLUCHLORALIN
BT1 dinitroaniline herbicides
BT2 herbicides
BT3 pesticides

FLUCONAZOLE
HN from 1989
BT1 antifungal agents
BT2 antiinfective agents
BT3 drugs
BT1 triazoles
BT2 azoles
BT3 heterocyclic nitrogen compounds
BT4 organic nitrogen compounds

FLUCTUATIONS
NT1 cyclic fluctuations
NT1 seasonal fluctuations
NT2 seasonal cycle
NT2 seasonal development
NT3 seasonal growth
NT4 lammas growth
rt movement
rt periodicity
rt trade cycles
rt trends

FLUCYTHRINATE
BT1 ectoparasiticides
BT2 antiparasitic agents
BT3 drugs
BT1 pyrethroid acaricides
BT2 acaricides
BT3 pesticides
BT2 pyrethroids
BT1 pyrethroid insecticides
BT2 insecticides
BT3 pesticides
BT2 pyrethroids

FLUCYTOSINE
uf 5-fluorocytosine
BT1 antifungal agents
BT2 antiinfective agents
BT3 drugs
BT1 pyrimidines
BT2 heterocyclic nitrogen compounds
BT3 organic nitrogen compounds
rt cytosine

FLUDROCORTISONE
BT1 antiinflammatory agents
BT2 drugs
BT1 pregnanes
BT2 steroids
BT3 isoprenoids
BT4 lipids
BT1 synthetic glucocorticoids
BT2 synthetic corticoids
BT3 corticoids
BT3 synthetic hormones

FLUE CURING
BT1 curing

FLUE CURING *cont.*
BT2 processing
rt tobacco curing sheds

FLUFENOXURON
BT1 chitin synthesis inhibitors
BT2 insect growth regulators
BT3 growth regulators
BT3 insecticides
BT4 pesticides
BT2 metabolic inhibitors
BT3 inhibitors
BT1 mite growth regulators
BT2 acaricides
BT3 pesticides
BT2 growth regulators

FLUGESTONE
uf fluorogestone acetate
BT1 pregnanes
BT2 steroids
BT3 isoprenoids
BT4 lipids
BT1 synthetic progestogens
BT2 synthetic hormones

FLUID DRILLS
uf drills, fluid
BT1 drills
BT2 farm machinery
BT3 machinery

FLUID INTAKE (AGRICOLA)
BT1 intake
rt water intake

FLUID MECHANICS
BT1 mechanics
BT2 physics
rt flow
rt hydraulics
rt rheology
rt turbulence
rt turbulent flow

FLUID THERAPY
uf rehydration therapy
BT1 therapy
NT1 oral rehydration therapy
rt rehydration

FLUIDIZED BED DRYING
HN from 1989
BT1 drying
BT2 dehydration
BT3 processing
rt fluidized beds

FLUIDIZED BED WASTES
BT1 industrial wastes
BT2 wastes
BT1 liming materials
BT2 soil amendments
BT3 amendments
rt fluidized beds

FLUIDIZED BEDS
rt driers
rt fluidized bed drying
rt fluidized bed wastes

FLUIDS
NT1 biological fluids
NT1 body fluids
NT2 allantoic fluid
NT2 amniotic fluid
NT2 bile
NT2 blood
NT3 blood plasma
NT3 blood serum
NT3 cord blood
NT2 body water
NT2 cerebrospinal fluid
NT2 colostrum
NT3 cow colostrum
NT3 human colostrum
NT2 digestive juices
NT3 chymosin
NT4 rennet
NT5 microbial rennet
NT3 duodenal fluids
NT3 gastric juices
NT4 gastric acid
NT3 pancreatic juice

FLUIDS *cont.*
NT3 rumen fluid
NT3 saliva
NT2 extracellular fluids
NT2 follicular fluid
NT2 haemolymph
NT2 interstitial fluids
NT2 lymph
NT3 chyle
NT2 metabolic water
NT2 milks
NT3 baboon milk
NT3 buffalo milk
NT3 camel milk
NT3 dog milk
NT3 ewe milk
NT3 goat milk
NT3 human milk
NT3 mare milk
NT3 mouse milk
NT3 pigeon crop milk
NT3 rabbit milk
NT3 rat milk
NT3 seal milk
NT3 sow milk
NT2 placental fluids
NT2 semen
NT3 mixed semen
NT3 seminal plasma
NT2 serum
NT3 blood serum
NT3 immune serum
NT3 pms
NT2 sputum
NT2 sweat
NT2 synovial fluid
NT2 tears
NT2 total body fluid
NT2 urine
NT1 metal working fluids
rt flow
rt gases
rt hydraulics
rt jets
rt laminar flow
rt liquids
rt reservoirs

FLUME WATER
HN from 1990
BT1 water

flumes
USE **chutes**

FLUMETASONE
uf flumethasone
BT1 antiinflammatory agents
BT2 drugs
BT1 pregnanes
BT2 steroids
BT3 isoprenoids
BT4 lipids
BT1 synthetic glucocorticoids
BT2 synthetic corticoids
BT3 corticoids
BT3 synthetic hormones

flumethasone
USE **flumetasone**

FLUMETHRIN
BT1 ectoparasiticides
BT2 antiparasitic agents
BT3 drugs
BT1 pyrethroid acaricides
BT2 acaricides
BT3 pesticides
BT2 pyrethroids

FLUNIXIN
BT1 antiinflammatory agents
BT2 drugs

FLUOMETURON
BT1 urea herbicides
BT2 herbicides
BT3 pesticides

FLUORAPATITE
BT1 nonclay minerals
BT2 minerals
rt rock phosphate

FLUORESCEIN
BT1 dyes
rt immunofluorescence

FLUORESCENCE
BT1 luminescence
BT2 radiation
BT1 optical properties
BT2 physical properties
BT3 properties
NT1 x ray fluorescence
rt atomic fluorescence spectroscopy
rt fluorescence emission spectroscopy
rt fluorescence microscopy
rt fluorescent dyes
rt fluorescent lamps
rt fluorescent light
rt fluorescent powders
rt fluorescent tracers
rt immunofluorescence

FLUORESCENCE EMISSION SPECTROSCOPY
BT1 spectroscopy
BT2 analytical methods
BT3 methodology
rt fluorescence

fluorescence, immunological
USE **immunofluorescence**

FLUORESCENCE MICROSCOPY
BT1 microscopy
BT2 techniques
rt fluorescence

fluorescent antibody technique
USE **immunofluorescence**

FLUORESCENT DYES
BT1 dyes
rt fluorescence

FLUORESCENT LAMPS
uf *lamps, fluorescent*
BT1 lamps
rt fluorescence

FLUORESCENT LIGHT
BT1 light
BT2 electromagnetic radiation
BT3 radiation
rt fluorescence
rt illumination

FLUORESCENT POWDERS
HN from 1990
BT1 powders
BT2 formulations
rt fluorescence

FLUORESCENT TRACERS
uf *tracers, fluorescent*
BT1 tracers
rt fluorescence

FLUORIDAMID
BT1 growth inhibitors
BT2 inhibitors
BT2 plant growth regulators
BT3 growth regulators

FLUORIDATION
rt dental caries
rt fluorides
rt teeth
rt water

FLUORIDE
BT1 anions
BT2 ions
rt fluorides
rt fluorine

FLUORIDES
BT1 halides
BT2 inorganic salts
BT3 inorganic compounds
BT3 salts
NT1 ammonium fluoride
NT1 calcium fluoride
NT1 cryolite
NT1 sodium fluoride

FLUORIDES *cont.*
rt fluoridation
rt fluoride
rt fluorine

FLUORIMETRY
BT1 biological techniques
BT2 techniques
rt fluorine

FLUORINE
BT1 gases
BT1 halogens
BT2 nonmetallic elements
BT3 elements
BT1 trace elements
BT2 elements
rt fluoride
rt fluorides
rt fluorimetry
rt fluorosis
rt freons
rt organofluorine compounds

FLUORINE INSECTICIDES
BT1 insecticides
BT2 pesticides
NT1 cryolite
NT1 sodium hexafluorosilicate

FLUOROACETAMIDE
BT1 organofluorine compounds
BT2 organic halogen compounds
BT1 rodenticides
BT2 pesticides

FLUOROACETIC ACID
BT1 monocarboxylic acids
BT2 carboxylic acids
BT3 organic acids
BT4 acids
BT1 organofluorine compounds
BT2 organic halogen compounds
rt sodium fluoroacetate

5-fluorocytosine
USE **flucytosine**

fluorodeoxyuridine
USE **floxuridine**

FLUORODIFEN
BT1 nitrophenyl ether herbicides
BT2 herbicides
BT3 pesticides

fluorogestone acetate
USE **flugestone**

FLUOROGLYCOFEN
HN from 1990
BT1 nitrophenyl ether herbicides
BT2 herbicides
BT3 pesticides

FLUOROMIDINE
uf *fluromidine*
BT1 unclassified herbicides
BT2 herbicides
BT3 pesticides

FLUORONITROFEN
BT1 nitrophenyl ether herbicides
BT2 herbicides
BT3 pesticides

P-FLUOROPHENYLALANINE
BT1 amino acid antagonists
BT2 antagonists
BT3 metabolic inhibitors
BT4 inhibitors
rt phenylalanine

FLUOROSIS
BT1 poisoning
rt fluorine
rt osteopetrosis
rt teeth

FLUOROURACIL
uf *5-fluorouracil*
BT1 antineoplastic agents
BT2 drugs

FLUOROURACIL *cont.*
BT1 metabolic inhibitors
BT2 inhibitors
BT1 uracil derivatives
BT2 pyrimidines
BT3 heterocyclic nitrogen compounds
BT4 organic nitrogen compounds

5-fluorouracil
USE **fluorouracil**

FLUOTHIURON
uf *thiochlormethyl*
BT1 urea herbicides
BT2 herbicides
BT3 pesticides

FLUOTRIMAZOLE
BT1 triazole fungicides
BT2 fungicides
BT3 pesticides
BT2 triazoles
BT3 azoles
BT4 heterocyclic nitrogen compounds
BT5 organic nitrogen compounds

FLUPROPADINE
BT1 rodenticides
BT2 pesticides

FLUPROPANATE
uf *tetrapion*
BT1 halogenated aliphatic herbicides
BT2 herbicides
BT3 pesticides

FLURAZOLE
BT1 herbicide safeners
BT2 safeners

flurecol
USE **flurenol**

FLURENOL
uf *flurecol*
BT1 morphactins
BT2 growth inhibitors
BT3 inhibitors
BT3 plant growth regulators
BT4 growth regulators

FLURIDONE
BT1 unclassified herbicides
BT2 herbicides
BT3 pesticides

FLUROCHLORIDONE
HN from 1990
BT1 unclassified herbicides
BT2 herbicides
BT3 pesticides

fluromidine
USE **fluoromidine**

FLUROXYPYR
BT1 pyridine herbicides
BT2 herbicides
BT3 pesticides
BT2 pyridines
BT3 heterocyclic nitrogen compounds
BT4 organic nitrogen compounds

FLURPRIMIDOL
BT1 growth retardants
BT2 plant growth regulators
BT3 growth regulators
BT2 retardants

FLURTAMONE
HN from 1990
BT1 unclassified herbicides
BT2 herbicides
BT3 pesticides

FLUSHING
BT1 fattening
BT2 animal feeding

FLUSHING *cont.*
BT3 feeding
rt animal nutrition
rt washing

FLUTED ROLLER FEED MECHANISM
uf *feed mechanism, fluted roller*
BT1 feed mechanisms
rt drills

FLUTOLANIL
BT1 benzanilide fungicides
BT2 anilide fungicides
BT3 fungicides
BT4 pesticides

FLUVALINATE
BT1 pyrethroid acaricides
BT2 acaricides
BT3 pesticides
BT2 pyrethroids
BT1 pyrethroid insecticides
BT2 insecticides
BT3 pesticides
BT2 pyrethroids

FLUVIAL SOILS
BT1 fluvisols
BT2 soil types (genetic)

FLUVIOGLACIAL SANDS
BT1 soil parent materials

FLUVIOGLACIAL SOILS
BT1 soil types (lithological)

FLUVISOLS
uf *marsh soils*
BT1 soil types (genetic)
NT1 acid sulfate soils
NT1 alluvial soils
NT1 fluvial soils
NT1 salt marsh soils
NT1 slate alluvial soils
NT1 thionic fluvisols
rt alluvial land
rt mangrove soils

FLY ASH
uf *pulverized fuel ash*
BT1 ash
BT1 liming materials
BT2 soil amendments
BT3 amendments
BT1 trace element fertilizers
BT2 fertilizers

flying fishes
USE **exocoetidae**

FLYING HONEYBEES
BT1 worker honeybees
BT2 honeybees
rt foraging
rt scout honeybees

fmd virus
USE **aphthovirus**

FOAL DISEASES
BT1 young animal diseases
BT2 animal diseases
BT3 diseases
rt foals
rt horse diseases

FOAL PRODUCTION
HN from 1990
BT1 animal production
BT2 agricultural production
BT3 production
rt foals

FOALING
BT1 parturition
BT2 sexual reproduction
BT3 reproduction
NT1 foaling interval
NT1 foaling rate
rt foaling season
rt foals
rt mares

FOALING INTERVAL
BT1 foaling
BT2 parturition
BT3 sexual reproduction
BT4 reproduction

FOALING RATE
BT1 foaling
BT2 parturition
BT3 sexual reproduction
BT4 reproduction

FOALING SEASON
rt foaling
rt seasons

FOALS
BT1 young animals
BT2 animals
rt colts
rt foal diseases
rt foal production
rt foaling
rt horses

FOAM MARKERS
uf markers, foam
BT1 markers
rt foams

FOAMING
rt defoaming
rt foams

FOAMS
BT1 suspensions
BT2 formulations
NT1 plastic foam
rt defoaming
rt foam markers
rt foaming

FODDER
rt browse plants
rt feeds
rt fodder crops
rt fodder plants
rt forage
rt pasture plants

fodder banks
USE **stock piling**

FODDER BEET
uf beet, fodder
uf beet, forage
uf forage beet
BT1 feed roots
BT2 root crops
BT1 feeds
rt beet top silage
rt beta vulgaris
rt mangolds

FODDER CROPS
uf feed crops
uf forage crops
rt browse plants
rt crops
rt fodder
rt fodder plants
rt green crop fractionation
rt hay
rt pasture plants
rt plants
rt silage plants

FODDER LEGUMES
uf forage legumes
BT1 fodder plants
BT1 legumes
NT1 alysicarpus rugosus
NT1 alysicarpus vaginalis
NT1 arachis glabrata
NT1 arachis hypogaea
NT1 arachis pintoi
NT1 astragalus sinicus
NT1 ceratonia siliqua
NT1 coronilla emerus
NT1 coronilla varia
NT1 crotalaria candicans
NT1 crotalaria laburnoides
NT1 crotalaria mysorensis
NT1 crotalaria pallida

FODDER LEGUMES *cont.*
NT1 crotalaria pumila
NT1 crotalaria sericea
NT1 glycine max
NT1 hedysarum coronarium
NT1 lablab purpureus
NT1 lupinus albus
NT1 lupinus angustifolius
NT1 lupinus luteus
NT1 lupinus mutabilis
NT1 lupinus nootkatensis
NT1 lupinus sparsiflorus
NT1 macroptilium atropurpureum
NT1 macroptilium lathyroides
NT1 macrotyloma axillare
NT1 macrotyloma uniflorum
NT1 medicago sativa
NT1 melilotus alba
NT1 melilotus indica
NT1 melilotus officinalis
NT1 mucuna aterrima
NT1 mucuna deeringiana
NT1 mucuna pruriens
NT1 neonotonia wightii
NT1 onobrychis viciifolia
NT1 pisum abyssinicum
NT1 pisum sativum
NT1 pueraria phaseoloides
NT1 pueraria thunbergiana
NT1 sesbania cannabina
NT1 trifolium alexandrinum
NT1 trifolium hybridum
NT1 trifolium incarnatum
NT1 trifolium pratense
NT1 trifolium resupinatum
NT1 trigonella foenum-graecum
NT1 vicia articulata
NT1 vicia benghalensis
NT1 vicia cracca
NT1 vicia ervilia
NT1 vicia faba
NT1 vicia narbonensis
NT1 vicia pannonica
NT1 vicia sativa
NT1 vicia sativa subsp. nigra
NT1 vicia villosa
NT1 vigna aconitifolia
NT1 vigna angularis
NT1 vigna frutescens
NT1 vigna luteola
NT1 vigna marina
NT1 vigna oblongifolia
NT1 vigna parkeri
NT1 vigna radiata
NT1 vigna schimperi
NT1 vigna umbellata
NT1 vigna unguiculata
NT1 vigna vexillata
rt plants

fodder peas
USE **pisum sativum**

FODDER PLANTS
NT1 arrhenatherum elatius
NT1 avena sativa
NT1 beta vulgaris
NT1 brassica campestris var. rapa
NT1 brassica napus var. dichotoma
NT1 brassica napus var. glauca
NT1 brassica oleracea var. viridis
NT1 bunias orientalis
NT1 canna edulis
NT1 carthamus tinctorius
NT1 coix lacryma-jobi
NT1 fodder legumes
NT2 alysicarpus rugosus
NT2 alysicarpus vaginalis
NT2 arachis glabrata
NT2 arachis hypogaea
NT2 arachis pintoi
NT2 astragalus sinicus
NT2 ceratonia siliqua
NT2 coronilla emerus
NT2 coronilla varia
NT2 crotalaria candicans
NT2 crotalaria laburnoides
NT2 crotalaria mysorensis
NT2 crotalaria pallida
NT2 crotalaria pumila

FODDER PLANTS *cont.*
NT2 crotalaria sericea
NT2 glycine max
NT2 hedysarum coronarium
NT2 lablab purpureus
NT2 lupinus albus
NT2 lupinus angustifolius
NT2 lupinus luteus
NT2 lupinus mutabilis
NT2 lupinus nootkatensis
NT2 lupinus sparsiflorus
NT2 macroptilium atropurpureum
NT2 macroptilium lathyroides
NT2 macrotyloma axillare
NT2 macrotyloma uniflorum
NT2 medicago sativa
NT2 melilotus alba
NT2 melilotus indica
NT2 melilotus officinalis
NT2 mucuna aterrima
NT2 mucuna deeringiana
NT2 mucuna pruriens
NT2 neonotonia wightii
NT2 onobrychis viciifolia
NT2 pisum abyssinicum
NT2 pisum sativum
NT2 pueraria phaseoloides
NT2 pueraria thunbergiana
NT2 sesbania cannabina
NT2 trifolium alexandrinum
NT2 trifolium hybridum
NT2 trifolium incarnatum
NT2 trifolium pratense
NT2 trifolium resupinatum
NT2 trigonella foenum-graecum
NT2 vicia articulata
NT2 vicia benghalensis
NT2 vicia cracca
NT2 vicia ervilia
NT2 vicia faba
NT2 vicia narbonensis
NT2 vicia pannonica
NT2 vicia sativa
NT2 vicia sativa subsp. nigra
NT2 vicia villosa
NT2 vigna aconitifolia
NT2 vigna angularis
NT2 vigna frutescens
NT2 vigna luteola
NT2 vigna marina
NT2 vigna oblongifolia
NT2 vigna parkeri
NT2 vigna radiata
NT2 vigna schimperi
NT2 vigna umbellata
NT2 vigna unguiculata
NT2 vigna vexillata
NT1 helianthus annuus
NT1 helianthus tuberosus
NT1 kochia scoparia
NT1 marsilea drummondii
NT1 panicum miliaceum
NT1 pastinaca sativa
NT1 pennisetum purpureum
NT1 phalaris canariensis
NT1 pistia stratiotes
NT1 saccharum officinarum
NT1 saccharum sinense
NT1 saccharum spontaneum
NT1 secale cereale
NT1 sorghum almum
NT1 sorghum bicolor
NT1 sorghum halepense
NT1 sorghum sudanense
NT1 spergula arvensis var. maxima
NT1 symphytum uplandicum
NT1 tripsacum dactyloides
NT1 tripsacum laxum
NT1 zea mays
NT1 zea mexicana
NT1 zea perennis
rt animal nutrition
rt browse plants
rt feeds
rt fodder
rt fodder crops
rt foggage
rt forage
rt green feed

FODDER PLANTS *cont.*
rt green fodders
rt hay
rt herbage
rt livestock feeding
rt pasture plants
rt plants
rt silage plants

fodder yeasts
USE **yeasts**

fodders
USE **feeds**

fodders, green
USE **green fodders**

FOENICULUM
BT1 umbelliferae
NT1 foeniculum vulgare

foeniculum dulce
USE **foeniculum vulgare**

FOENICULUM VULGARE
uf foeniculum dulce
BT1 foeniculum
BT2 umbelliferae
BT1 spice plants
rt fennel

foetal death
USE **fetal death**

foetal development disorders
USE **fetal development disorders**

foetal growth
USE **fetal growth**

foetal membranes
USE **fetal membranes**

α-foetoprotein
USE **α-fetoprotein**

FOETTINGERIA
BT1 ciliophora
BT2 protozoa

foetus
USE **fetus**

FOG
rt mists
rt relative humidity
rt weather

FOGERA
HN from 1990
BT1 cattle breeds
BT2 breeds

FOGGAGE
rt fodder plants
rt grasslands
rt grazing
rt herbage
rt stock piling
rt winter

FOGGING
BT1 application methods
BT2 methodology
rt irrigation
rt protected cultivation
rt vegetative propagation

FOGS
BT1 formulations
rt aerosol sprayers
rt aerosols

FOIE GRAS
BT1 livers as food
BT2 foods
BT2 offal
BT3 meat byproducts
BT4 agricultural byproducts
BT5 byproducts
rt fatty liver
rt goose liver

FOIL
BT1 mulches
BT1 packaging materials
BT2 materials
NT1 aluminium foil

foil, aluminium
USE **aluminium foil**

FOIL POUCHES (AGRICOLA)
BT1 containers

FOKIENIA
BT1 cupressaceae
NT1 fokienia hodginsii

FOKIENIA HODGINSII
BT1 fokienia
BT2 cupressaceae

folacin
USE **folic acid**

folate
USE **folic acid**

FOLATE ANTAGONISTS
BT1 vitamin b antagonists
BT2 vitamin antagonists
BT3 antagonists
BT4 metabolic inhibitors
BT5 inhibitors
NT1 aminopterin
NT1 methotrexate
rt folic acid

folate conjugase
USE **γ-glutamyl hydrolase**

FOLCYSTEINE
BT1 amino acid derivatives
BT2 amino compounds
BT3 organic nitrogen compounds
BT1 growth stimulators
BT2 plant growth regulators
BT3 growth regulators
rt cysteine
rt folic acid

FOLIAGE
rt canopy
rt crown
rt foliage area
rt foliar application
rt leaves

FOLIAGE AREA
BT1 area
rt canopy
rt foliage

foliage, cut
USE **cut foliage**

foliage diagnosis
USE **foliar diagnosis**

FOLIAGE PLANTS
NT1 ornamental foliage plants
NT2 cissus antarctica
NT2 epipremnum pinnatum
NT2 ornamental ferns
NT3 adiantum capillus-veneris
NT3 adiantum hispidulum
NT3 adiantum pedatum
NT3 adiantum tenerum
NT3 arachniodes adiantiformis
NT3 asplenium bulbiferum
NT3 asplenium nidus
NT3 asplenium platyneuron
NT3 asplenium trichomanes
NT3 athyrium filix-femina
NT3 bolbitis presliana
NT3 bolbitis virens
NT3 ctenitis ampla
NT3 cystopteris bulbifera
NT3 cystopteris fragilis
NT3 dicranopteris linearis
NT3 diplazium pycnocarpon
NT3 dryopteris affinis
NT3 dryopteris cochleata
NT3 dryopteris erythrosora
NT3 dryopteris filix-mas

FOLIAGE PLANTS *cont.*
NT3 goniophlebium subauriculatum
NT3 matteuccia struthiopteris
NT3 nephrolepis biserrata
NT3 nephrolepis cordifolia
NT3 nephrolepis exaltata
NT3 oleandra wallichii
NT3 osmunda claytoniana
NT3 osmunda regalis
NT3 pachypodium lamerei
NT3 pellaea viridis
NT3 peranema cyantheoides
NT3 phlebodium aureum
NT3 phyllitis scolopendrium
NT3 pityrogramma austroamericana
NT3 pityrogramma calomelanos
NT3 pityrogramma chrysophylla
NT3 pityrogramma lehmannii
NT3 platycerium bifurcatum
NT3 platycerium coronarium
NT3 polypodium leucotomos
NT3 polypodium subpetiolatum
NT3 polypodium vulgare
NT3 polystichum munitum
NT3 polystichum setiferum
NT3 pteris cretica
NT3 pteris ensiformis
NT3 pteris tremula
NT3 pteris umbrosa
NT3 pteris wallichiana
NT3 stenochlaena palustris
NT3 tectaria variolosa
NT3 thelypteris noveboracensis
NT3 thelypteris palustris
NT3 woodsia obtusa
rt cut foliage
rt plants

FOLIAR APPLICATION
uf *foliar methods*
BT1 application methods
BT2 methodology
rt foliage
rt foliar nutrition
rt foliar spraying
rt foliar uptake

FOLIAR DIAGNOSIS
uf *foliage diagnosis*
uf *leaf analysis*
uf *petiole analysis*
uf *tissue analysis*
BT1 plant analysis
rt leaves

foliar methods
USE **foliar application**

FOLIAR NUTRITION
BT1 plant nutrition
BT2 nutrition
rt foliar application
rt foliar spraying
rt foliar uptake
rt leaves

FOLIAR SPRAYING
uf *spraying, foliar*
BT1 spraying
BT2 application methods
BT3 methodology
rt canopy
rt foliar application
rt foliar nutrition
rt foliar uptake
rt leaves

FOLIAR UPTAKE
BT1 uptake
rt foliar application
rt foliar nutrition
rt foliar spraying
rt leaves

FOLIC ACID
uf *folacin*
uf *folate*

FOLIC ACID *cont.*
uf *pteroylglutamic acid*
BT1 lipotropic factors
BT2 drugs
BT1 vitamin b complex
BT2 water-soluble vitamins
BT3 vitamins
rt folate antagonists
rt folcysteine
rt folic acid deficiency

FOLIC ACID DEFICIENCY
BT1 vitamin deficiencies
BT2 nutrient deficiencies
BT3 deficiency
rt folic acid
rt sprue

FOLINIC ACID
uf *citrovorum factor*
uf *leucovorin*
BT1 vitamin b complex
BT2 water-soluble vitamins
BT3 vitamins

FOLK CULTURE
uf *culture, folk*
BT1 culture
NT1 folk dancing
NT1 folk music

FOLK DANCING
BT1 dancing
BT2 performing arts
BT3 arts
BT1 folk culture
BT2 culture

FOLK MEDICINE (AGRICOLA)
BT1 medicine

FOLK MUSIC
BT1 folk culture
BT2 culture
BT1 music
BT2 performing arts
BT3 arts

folliberin
USE **fshrh**

follicle stimulating hormone
USE **fsh**

FOLLICLES
NT1 graafian follicles
NT1 hair follicles
rt follicular fluid
rt maturation
rt s p ratio
rt wool

FOLLICULAR FLUID
BT1 body fluids
BT2 fluids
rt follicles

folliculostatin
USE **inhibin**

follitropin
USE **fsh**

FOLPET
BT1 dicarboximide fungicides
BT2 fungicides
BT3 pesticides

FOLSOMIA
BT1 isotomidae
BT2 collembola
NT1 folsomia candida

FOLSOMIA CANDIDA
BT1 folsomia
BT2 isotomidae
BT3 collembola

FOLSOMIDES
BT1 isotomidae
BT2 collembola

FOMES
BT1 aphyllophorales
NT1 fomes fomentarius

FOMES *cont.*
NT1 fomes hartigii
NT1 fomes tremulae
rt fomitopsis
rt ganoderma
rt heterobasidion
rt phellinus
rt rigidoporus

fomes annosus
USE **heterobasidion annosum**

fomes applanatus
USE **ganoderma applanatum**

FOMES FOMENTARIUS
BT1 fomes
BT2 aphyllophorales

FOMES HARTIGII
BT1 fomes
BT2 aphyllophorales

fomes igniarius
USE **phellinus igniarius**

fomes lignosus
USE **rigidoporus lignosus**

fomes lucidus
USE **ganoderma lucidum**

fomes marginatus
USE **fomitopsis pinicola**

fomes noxius
USE **phellinus noxius**

fomes pini
USE **phellinus pini**

fomes pinicola
USE **fomitopsis pinicola**

fomes pomaceus
USE **phellinus pomaceus**

fomes robustus
USE **phellinus robustus**

fomes roseus
USE **fomitopsis rosea**

FOMES TREMULAE
BT1 fomes
BT2 aphyllophorales

fomes ulmarius
USE **rigidoporus ulmarius**

FOMESAFEN
BT1 amide herbicides
BT2 herbicides
BT3 pesticides

FOMITOPSIS
BT1 aphyllophorales
NT1 fomitopsis pinicola
NT1 fomitopsis rosea
rt fomes
rt heterobasidion
rt polyporus

fomitopsis annosa
USE **heterobasidion annosum**

FOMITOPSIS PINICOLA
uf *fomes marginatus*
uf *fomes pinicola*
BT1 fomitopsis
BT2 aphyllophorales

FOMITOPSIS ROSEA
uf *fomes roseus*
uf *polyporus roseus*
BT1 fomitopsis
BT2 aphyllophorales

FONDUE
BT1 cheeses
BT2 milk products
BT3 products

FONOFOS
BT1 phosphonothioate insecticides

FONOFOS *cont.*
BT2 organophosphorus insecticides
BT3 insecticides
BT4 pesticides
BT3 organophosphorus pesticides
BT4 organophosphorus compounds

FONSECAEA
BT1 deuteromycotina
NT1 fonsecaea compacta
NT1 fonsecaea pedrosoi
rt phialophora

FONSECAEA COMPACTA
uf *phialophora compacta*
BT1 fonsecaea
BT2 deuteromycotina

FONSECAEA PEDROSOI
uf *phialophora pedrosoi*
BT1 fonsecaea
BT2 deuteromycotina

FONTINA CHEESE
HN from 1989
BT1 cheeses
BT2 milk products
BT3 products

FOOD
rt food analysis (agricola)
rt food and nutrition controversies (agricola)
rt food cooperatives (agricola)
rt food costs (agricola)
rt food data sources (agricola)
rt food distribution programs (agricola)
rt food grades (agricola)
rt food groups
rt food irradiation
rt food marketing
rt food misinformation (agricola)
rt food plans (agricola)
rt food preparation (agricola)
rt food purchasing (agricola)
rt food shortages (agricola)
rt food storage (agricola)
rt food stores (agricola)
rt food symbolism (agricola)
rt food tables (agricola)
rt foodways (agricola)
rt prey

FOOD ACCEPTABILITY (AGRICOLA)
BT1 acceptability

FOOD ADDITIVES
BT1 additives
NT1 acidulants
NT2 citric acid
NT2 fumaric acid
NT2 gluconolactone
NT2 tartaric acid
NT1 bulking agents
NT2 methylcellulose
NT1 dextran
NT1 enzyme preparations
NT1 flavour enhancers
NT2 monosodium glutamate
NT1 flavourings
NT2 caramel
NT1 food colourants
NT2 p-dimethylaminoazobenzene
NT2 annatto
NT2 canthaxanthin
NT2 caramel
NT2 erythrosine
NT2 tartrazine
NT1 leavening agents (agricola)
NT1 modified starches
NT1 sweeteners
NT2 sugar substitutes
NT3 artificial sweeteners
NT4 aspartame
NT4 saccharin
NT4 sodium cyclamate

FOOD ADDITIVES *cont.*
NT3 high fructose corn syrup
NT1 tenderizers (agricola)
NT1 thickeners
rt ceratonia siliqua
rt defoaming agents
rt dyes
rt emulsifiers
rt feed additives
rt food enrichment
rt food supplements
rt foods
rt mineral supplements
rt preservatives
rt stabilizers

FOOD ADVERTISING (AGRICOLA)
BT1 advertising
BT2 marketing techniques
BT3 techniques
rt food merchandising (agricola)

FOOD AID
BT1 development aid
NT1 food for work programmes
rt emergencies
rt food prices
rt food supply

FOOD ALLERGIES
uf *allergy, food*
uf *anaphylaxis, food*
uf *food anaphylaxis*
uf *food hypersensitivity*
uf *food sensitivity*
uf *hypersensitivity, food*
uf *sensitivity, food*
BT1 allergies
BT2 immunological diseases
BT3 diseases
NT1 milk allergy
rt elimination diets (agricola)
rt food intolerance (agricola)
rt food-related disorders (agricola)
rt foods

FOOD ANALYSIS (AGRICOLA)
uf *nutrient content determination*
NT1 proximate analysis (agricola)
rt analysis
rt food

food anaphylaxis
USE **food allergies**

food and agricultural sector
USE **agroindustrial sector**

FOOD AND AGRICULTURE ORGANIZATION
uf *fao*
BT1 un
BT2 international organizations
BT3 organizations
NT1 world food council
NT1 world food programme
rt agris
rt caris

FOOD AND NUTRITION CONTROVERSIES (AGRICOLA)
rt food
rt nutrition

FOOD ART (AGRICOLA)
BT1 arts
NT1 cake decoration (agricola)
rt culinary arts (agricola)
rt garnishes (agricola)

food attitudes
USE **food beliefs**

food aversion
USE **food preferences**

FOOD BELIEFS
uf *food attitudes*
BT1 food preferences
BT2 feeding preferences
BT3 feeding habits

FOOD BELIEFS *cont.*
BT4 feeding behaviour
BT5 behaviour
BT4 habits
rt foods
rt foodways (agricola)
rt religion
rt religious dietary laws (agricola)

FOOD BIOTECHNOLOGY (AGRICOLA)
BT1 biotechnology
BT2 technology
rt food technology

FOOD CHAINS
rt biological production
rt ecosystems
rt feeding
rt foods
rt sequences
rt trophic levels

FOOD CHEMISTRY (AGRICOLA)
BT1 chemistry
rt food technology

food choices
USE **food preferences**

FOOD COLORANTS
BF food colourants
NT1 artificial colors (agricola)
rt color

FOOD COLOURANTS
AF food colorants
BT1 food additives
BT2 additives
NT1 p-dimethylaminoazobenzene
NT1 annatto
NT1 canthaxanthin
NT1 caramel
NT1 erythrosine
NT1 tartrazine
rt basella alba
rt dyes
rt foods
rt pigments

FOOD COMPOSITION
BT1 composition
rt exchange lists (agricola)
rt food composition tables (agricola)
rt foods
rt index of nutritional quality (agricola)
rt nutrients

FOOD COMPOSITION TABLES (AGRICOLA)
BT1 food tables (agricola)
rt food composition

FOOD CONSUMPTION
BT1 consumption
NT1 milk consumption
rt consumption patterns (agricola)
rt eating patterns (agricola)
rt eating rates (agricola)
rt food diaries (agricola)
rt food intake
rt food production
rt food rationing
rt foods

food contaminants
USE **food contamination**

FOOD CONTAMINATION
uf *food contaminants*
BT1 contamination
rt food hygiene
rt food safety (agricola)
rt microbial contamination

FOOD CONVERSION
BT1 conversion
rt feed conversion
rt foods

FOOD COOPERATIVES (AGRICOLA)
BT1 cooperatives
rt food

FOOD COSTS (AGRICOLA)
BT1 costs
rt food
rt food purchasing (agricola)

food coupons
USE **coupons (agricola)**

FOOD CROPS
rt crops
rt foods

FOOD DATA SOURCES (AGRICOLA)
BT1 sources
rt food
rt information

FOOD DELIVERY SYSTEMS (AGRICOLA)
rt distribution
rt transport

FOOD DEPRIVATION
BT1 deprivation

FOOD DIARIES (AGRICOLA)
BT1 records
rt food consumption
rt weight control (agricola)

food dislikes
USE **food preferences**

food distribution and marketing
USE **food marketing**

FOOD DISTRIBUTION PROGRAMS (AGRICOLA)
BT1 programs (agricola)
rt food
rt home delivered meals (agricola)

FOOD ENGINEERING (AGRICOLA)
BT1 engineering
rt food technology

FOOD ENRICHMENT
BT1 food technology
BT2 technology
rt food additives
rt foods
rt vitamins

FOOD FADS (AGRICOLA)
rt fad diets (agricola)
rt food preferences

food fiber
USE **fiber**

FOOD FOR WORK PROGRAMMES
AF food for work programs
BT1 food aid
BT2 development aid

FOOD FOR WORK PROGRAMS
BF food for work programmes
BT1 programs (agricola)

FOOD GRADES (AGRICOLA)
uf *usda grades*
NT1 meat grades (agricola)
rt food
rt grading
rt quality standards

FOOD GRAINS
BT1 foods
BT1 grain
NT1 whole grains (agricola)
rt feed grains
rt grain conservation
rt grain driers
rt grain drills
rt grain drying
rt grain dust
rt grain loss monitors
rt grain mottling
rt grain stores

FOOD GROUPS
uf *basic four*
rt food

food habits
HN was a preferred term until 1990
USE **feeding habits**

FOOD HANDLING (AGRICOLA)
BT1 handling
rt food hygiene
rt food preparation (agricola)

food history
USE **dietary history (agricola)**

FOOD HOLDING SYSTEMS (AGRICOLA)
BT1 food service

FOOD HYGIENE
BT1 hygiene
NT1 meat hygiene
NT1 milk hygiene
rt food contamination
rt food handling (agricola)
rt food inspection
rt food safety (agricola)
rt food sanitation (agricola)
rt foods

food hypersensitivity
USE **food allergies**

FOOD INDUSTRY
BT1 industry
NT1 bakery industry
NT1 beverage industry
NT2 brewing industry
NT2 coffee industry
NT2 distilling industry
NT2 tea industry
NT2 wine industry
NT1 canning industry
NT1 cocoa industry
NT1 confectionery industry
NT1 dairy industry
NT1 frozen foods industry
NT1 infant food industry (agricola)
NT1 oils and fats industry
NT1 sugar industry
rt agroindustrial sector
rt catering industry
rt fish industry
rt food policy
rt food technology
rt foods
rt milling industry
rt postagricultural sector
rt starch industry

FOOD INSPECTION
BT1 inspection
BT2 quality controls
BT3 consumer protection
BT4 protection
BT3 controls
NT1 meat inspection
NT2 antemortem examinations (agricola)
NT2 carcass condemnation
rt consumer protection
rt food hygiene
rt public health
rt quality controls
rt sensory evaluation

FOOD INTAKE
BT1 intake
NT1 ingestion
rt appetite
rt appetite control
rt caloric intake (agricola)
rt eating rates (agricola)
rt energy intake
rt food consumption
rt food restriction
rt foods
rt satiety

FOOD INTOLERANCE (AGRICOLA)
uf *food sensitivity*

FOOD INTOLERANCE (AGRICOLA) *cont.*
BT1 intolerance
rt food allergies
rt food-related disorders (agricola)

FOOD IRRADIATION
BT1 irradiation
rt food
rt food preservation (agricola)

FOOD LEGISLATION
BT1 public health legislation
BT2 environmental legislation
BT3 legislation
BT4 legal systems
rt food policy
rt foods

FOOD MARKETING
HN from 1990
uf *food distribution and marketing*
BT1 marketing
rt food
rt foods

FOOD MERCHANDISING (AGRICOLA)
BT1 sales promotion
BT2 marketing techniques
BT3 techniques
rt food advertising (agricola)
rt food service

FOOD MICROBIOLOGY
BT1 microbiology
BT2 biology
rt foods

FOOD MISINFORMATION (AGRICOLA)
BT1 misinformation (agricola)
NT1 food quackery (agricola)
rt food

FOOD PACKAGING (AGRICOLA)
BT1 packaging
BT2 handling
rt food technology

FOOD PLANS (AGRICOLA)
rt food

FOOD PLANTS
(of phytophagous organisms)
BT1 hosts

FOOD POISONING
BT1 poisoning
NT1 chinese restaurant syndrome
rt botulism
rt foods
rt gastroenteritis
rt poisonous fungi
rt poisonous plants
rt toxic substances
rt toxins

FOOD POLICY
uf *policy, food*
uf *policy, supply*
uf *supply policy*
NT1 nutrition programmes
NT2 food stamp program
rt agricultural policy
rt food industry
rt food legislation
rt food supply
rt foods
rt nutrition
rt policy

FOOD PREFERENCES
uf *diet preferences*
uf *food aversion*
uf *food choices*
uf *food dislikes*
uf *taste preferences*
BT1 feeding preferences
BT2 feeding habits
BT3 feeding behaviour

FOOD PREFERENCES *cont.*
BT4 behaviour
BT3 habits
NT1 food beliefs
NT1 salt preference
rt feeding behaviour
rt food fads (agricola)
rt foods

FOOD PREPARATION (AGRICOLA)
NT1 cook-chill system (agricola)
NT1 cook-freeze system (agricola)
NT1 home food preparation (agricola)
NT1 on-site food preparation (agricola)
NT1 quantity food preparation (agricola)
rt cooking methods (agricola)
rt food
rt food handling (agricola)
rt food technology
rt ingredient room (agricola)
rt ingredients (agricola)
rt recipes (agricola)

FOOD PRESERVATION (AGRICOLA)
BT1 preservation
BT2 techniques
NT1 home food preservation (agricola)
rt food irradiation
rt food preservatives

FOOD PRESERVATIVES
BT1 preservatives
NT1 acetic acid
NT1 benzoic acid
NT1 brine
NT1 butylated hydroxyanisole
NT1 butylated hydroxytoluene
NT1 calcium propionate
NT1 ethoxyquin
NT1 humulon
NT1 isoascorbic acid
NT1 lupulon
NT1 methylparaben
NT1 nisin
NT1 potassium sorbate
NT1 sodium benzoate
NT1 sodium bisulfite
NT1 sodium metabisulfite
NT1 sodium propionate
NT1 sorbic acid
NT1 sucrose
NT1 sulfur dioxide
NT1 vinegar
rt antioxidants
rt food preservation (agricola)

FOOD PRICES
uf *prices, food*
BT1 prices
NT1 milk prices
rt consumer prices
rt food aid
rt foods

FOOD PROCESSING
BT1 processing
NT1 radappertization (agricola)
rt butchering (agricola)
rt food processing equipment (agricola)
rt food technology

FOOD PROCESSING EQUIPMENT (AGRICOLA)
BT1 equipment
NT1 blenders (agricola)
NT1 mixers (kitchen appliance) (agricola)
rt food processing
rt food technology

FOOD PROCESSING QUALITY
uf *quality for food processing*
BT1 processing quality
BT2 quality
NT1 baking quality
NT1 canning quality

FOOD PROCESSING QUALITY *cont.*
NT1 conserving quality
NT2 pickling quality
NT2 salting quality
NT1 cooking quality
NT1 drying quality
NT1 freezing quality
NT1 milling quality
NT1 popping quality
NT1 smoking quality
rt foods

FOOD PRODUCTION
BT1 production
rt food consumption
rt food supply

FOOD PRODUCTS
BT1 products
rt beverages
rt cereal products
rt egg products
rt eggs
rt fish
rt fish products
rt foods
rt fruit products
rt hive products
rt meat
rt meat products
rt milk products
rt nut products
rt oil plants
rt processed products
rt sugar
rt sweeteners
rt vegetable products

food programs
USE **nutrition programs**

FOOD PURCHASING (AGRICOLA)
BT1 purchasing
BT2 acquisition of ownership
BT3 acquisition
rt food
rt food costs (agricola)

FOOD QUACKERY (AGRICOLA)
BT1 food misinformation (agricola)
BT2 misinformation (agricola)
BT1 quackery (agricola)

FOOD QUALITY
BT1 quality

FOOD RATIONING
BT1 food supply
rt emergencies
rt food consumption

FOOD-RELATED DISORDERS (AGRICOLA)
BT1 metabolic disorders
BT2 animal disorders
BT3 disorders
rt food allergies
rt food intolerance (agricola)

FOOD REQUIREMENTS
BT1 requirements
rt foods

FOOD RESEARCH
BT1 research
rt foods

FOOD RESTRICTION
rt diet
rt feed intake
rt food intake
rt foodways (agricola)

FOOD SAFETY (AGRICOLA)
BT1 safety
rt food contamination
rt food hygiene

FOOD SANITATION (AGRICOLA)
rt food hygiene
rt sanitation

FOOD SCIENCES
rt foods

food sensitivity
USE **food allergies**
OR **food intolerance (agricola)**

FOOD SERVICE
BF catering
NT1 college food service (agricola)
NT1 commercial food service (agricola)
NT2 contract food service (agricola)
NT1 food holding systems (agricola)
NT1 hospital food service
NT1 hotel food service
NT1 industrial food service
NT1 institutional food service
NT1 school food service (agricola)
NT1 transport food service
NT1 volume feeding (agricola)
rt commissaries (agricola)
rt community feeding centers (agricola)
rt dining facilities (agricola)
rt food merchandising (agricola)
rt food service industry
rt food service management (agricola)
rt food service training (agricola)
rt food serving methods (agricola)
rt portion control (agricola)
rt portion size (agricola)
rt waiters and waitresses (agricola)

FOOD SERVICE INDUSTRY
BF catering industry
rt food service

FOOD SERVICE MANAGEMENT (AGRICOLA)
rt food service
rt management

FOOD SERVICE TRAINING (AGRICOLA)
BT1 vocational training
BT2 training
rt food service

FOOD SERVING METHODS (AGRICOLA)
BT1 methodology
NT1 buffets (agricola)
NT1 family style serving (agricola)
NT1 offer versus serve (agricola)
NT1 salad bars (agricola)
NT1 self service units (agricola)
rt food service
rt serving equipment (agricola)
rt table settings (agricola)

FOOD SHORTAGES (AGRICOLA)
rt food
rt food supply

FOOD SPOILAGE
BT1 spoilage
BT2 losses
BT2 postharvest decay
BT3 decay
BT4 decomposition
BT4 deterioration

FOOD STAMP PROGRAM
BT1 nutrition programmes
BT2 food policy
rt poverty

FOOD STORAGE (AGRICOLA)
rt food
rt food storage losses (agricola)
rt food stores (agricola)
rt storage

FOOD STORAGE LOSSES (AGRICOLA)
BT1 storage losses
BT2 postharvest losses
BT3 losses
rt food storage (agricola)

FOOD STORES (AGRICOLA)
BT1 stores
rt food
rt food storage (agricola)

FOOD SUPPLEMENTS
BT1 supplements
NT1 protein supplements
NT1 vitamin supplements
rt feed supplements
rt food additives

FOOD SUPPLY
NT1 food rationing
NT1 milk supply
rt famine
rt food aid
rt food policy
rt food production
rt food shortages (agricola)
rt foods
rt procurement planning
rt supply balance

FOOD SYMBOLISM (AGRICOLA)
rt food

FOOD TABLES (AGRICOLA)
NT1 food composition tables (agricola)
rt food

FOOD TECHNOLOGY
BT1 technology
NT1 breadmaking
NT1 food enrichment
NT1 winemaking
rt baking
rt brewing
rt food biotechnology (agricola)
rt food chemistry (agricola)
rt food engineering (agricola)
rt food industry
rt food packaging (agricola)
rt food preparation (agricola)
rt food processing
rt food processing equipment (agricola)
rt foods
rt packaging

FOOD WASTES
BT1 wastes
rt kitchen waste
rt leftovers (agricola)
rt plate waste (agricola)

FOODBORNE DISEASES
BT1 diseases

FOODS
NT1 artificial foods (agricola)
NT1 bakery products
NT2 biscuits
NT3 wafers
NT2 bread
NT3 gluten free bread
NT3 quick breads (agricola)
NT3 yeast breads (agricola)
NT2 cakes
NT2 muffins (agricola)
NT2 pies (agricola)
NT2 pizzas (agricola)
NT2 tortillas
NT1 beans
NT1 blended foods (agricola)
NT1 breakfast cereals
NT1 bulgur
NT1 carbohydrate-rich foods (agricola)
NT1 cariogenic foods (agricola)
NT1 ceremonial foods (agricola)
NT1 chapattis
NT1 charcoal broiled foods (agricola)

FOODS *cont.*
NT1 concentrates
NT2 protein concentrates
NT3 animal protein concentrates
NT3 fish protein concentrate
NT3 leaf protein concentrate
NT3 lucerne protein concentrate
NT3 mustard protein concentrate
NT3 potato protein concentrate
NT3 rapeseed protein concentrate
NT2 uromol
NT1 convenience foods
NT2 brown and serve foods (agricola)
NT2 instant coffee
NT2 instant foods
NT2 instant milk
NT2 prepared foods
NT1 cured products (agricola)
NT2 cured meats (agricola)
NT3 corned beef (agricola)
NT1 dehydrated foods (agricola)
NT1 desserts
NT2 frozen desserts
NT1 dietetic foods
NT1 dried foods
NT2 dried cream
NT2 dried egg
NT2 dried fish
NT2 dried fruit
NT3 prunes
NT3 raisins
NT2 dried meat
NT2 dried milk
NT2 dried milk products
NT3 dried skim milk
NT3 dried whey
NT2 dry beans (agricola)
NT1 ethnic foods (agricola)
NT1 extruded foods (agricola)
NT1 fast foods
NT2 sandwiches (agricola)
NT1 fermented foods
NT2 fermented fish
NT2 fermented honey
NT3 mead
NT2 miso
NT2 natto
NT2 sauerkraut
NT2 tempeh
NT2 yoghurt
NT1 food grains
NT2 whole grains (agricola)
NT1 fried foods (agricola)
NT2 batter fried foods (agricola)
NT1 frozen foods
NT2 frozen desserts
NT2 frozen fish
NT2 frozen fruit
NT2 frozen meat
NT2 frozen vegetables
NT1 fruit
NT1 health foods
NT1 heart as food
NT1 infant foods
NT2 infant formulae
NT1 insects as food
NT1 junk foods (agricola)
NT1 kosher food (agricola)
NT1 livers as food
NT2 foie gras
NT2 goose liver
NT1 low acid foods (agricola)
NT1 low calorie foods (agricola)
NT1 meat
NT2 beef
NT3 ground beef (agricola)
NT2 buffalo meat
NT2 camel meat
NT2 crab meat
NT2 dark cutting meat
NT2 game meat
NT2 goat meat
NT2 horse meat
NT2 pigmeat

FOODS *cont.*
NT3 bacon
NT3 ham
NT2 poultry meat
NT3 chicken meat
NT3 duck meat
NT3 goose meat
NT3 turkey meat
NT2 rabbit meat
NT2 seal meat
NT2 sheepmeat
NT3 lamb (meat)
NT3 mutton
NT2 turtle meat
NT2 variety meats (agricola)
NT2 veal
NT2 venison
NT2 whale meat
NT1 molasses
NT1 natural foods (agricola)
NT1 novel foods (agricola)
NT1 omelets (agricola)
NT1 organic foods (agricola)
NT1 pasta
NT2 noodles
NT2 spaghetti (agricola)
NT1 patties (agricola)
NT1 pickled foods (agricola)
NT1 precooked foods (agricola)
NT1 preserves (agricola)
NT1 protein foods
NT2 incaprina
NT2 protein sources
NT1 puddings
NT1 raw foods (agricola)
NT1 salads (agricola)
NT1 seafoods
NT2 clams
NT3 hard clams
NT3 surf clams
NT2 squids
NT1 simulated foods
NT2 imitation cream
NT2 imitation milk
NT2 margarine
NT2 meat analogues
NT3 textured proteins
NT1 soups
NT1 spreads (agricola)
NT1 takeout foods (agricola)
NT1 tropical foods (agricola)
NT1 unconventional foods
NT2 edible birdsnests
NT1 welfare foods
NT1 whole foods (agricola)
NT1 wild foods (agricola)
rt codex alimentarius (agricola)
rt diets
rt edible cultivars
rt edible species
rt feeding
rt feeds
rt food additives
rt food allergies
rt food beliefs
rt food chains
rt food colourants
rt food composition
rt food consumption
rt food conversion
rt food crops
rt food enrichment
rt food hygiene
rt food industry
rt food intake
rt food legislation
rt food marketing
rt food microbiology
rt food poisoning
rt food policy
rt food preferences
rt food prices
rt food processing quality
rt food products
rt food requirements
rt food research
rt food sciences
rt food supply
rt food technology
rt nutrition
rt products

FOODS *cont.*
rt vegetables
rt weaning
rt whey

FOODWAYS (AGRICOLA)
rt food
rt food beliefs
rt food restriction

foot
USE **feet**

FOOT AND MOUTH DISEASE
BT1 cattle diseases
BT2 animal diseases
BT3 diseases
BT1 swine diseases
BT2 animal diseases
BT3 diseases
BT1 viral diseases
BT2 infectious diseases
BT3 diseases
rt aphthovirus

foot and mouth disease virus
USE **aphthovirus**

FOOT DISEASES
uf hoof and claw diseases
BT1 organic diseases
BT2 diseases
NT1 laminitis
NT1 pododermatitis
rt interdigital dermatitis
rt interdigital hyperplasia

FOOT ROT
BT1 plant diseases
BT1 sheep diseases
BT2 animal diseases
BT3 diseases
rt bacteroides nodosus

FOOTBALL
BT1 ball games
BT2 games
BT2 sport
NT1 american football
NT1 australian football
NT1 soccer

FOOTPATHS
BT1 paths
BT2 roads
NT1 long distance footpaths
NT1 towpaths
rt bridle paths
rt cycleways
rt trails

FORAGE
rt fodder
rt fodder plants
rt foraging
rt haymaking
rt honeybee forage
rt roughage

forage beet
USE **fodder beet**

FORAGE BLOWERS
uf blowers, forage
uf blowers, hay
uf hay blowers
BT1 blowers
BT2 machinery
rt conveyors

FORAGE BOXES
BT1 farm machinery
BT2 machinery

FORAGE CONDITIONERS
BT1 farm machinery
BT2 machinery
NT1 mower conditioners
NT1 tedders
rt brushes
rt crimpers
rt forage driers
rt forage harvesters

FORAGE CONDITIONING
BT1 conditioning
rt drying
rt harvesting

forage crops
USE **fodder crops**

FORAGE DRIERS
AF forage dryers
BT1 driers
BT2 farm machinery
BT3 machinery
rt forage conditioners

FORAGE DRYERS
BF forage driers
BT1 dryers

FORAGE HARVESTERS
uf harvesters, forage
BT1 harvesters
BT2 farm machinery
BT3 machinery
rt forage conditioners
rt mowers

forage legumes
USE **fodder legumes**

FORAGING
BT1 feeding habits
BT2 feeding behaviour
BT3 behaviour
BT2 habits
NT1 honey-getting capacity
rt flying honeybees
rt forage
rt foraging period
rt robbing
rt scout honeybees
rt weed palatability

FORAGING PERIOD
BT1 periodicity
rt foraging
rt honeybee colonies
rt seasonal cycle

FORCE FEEDING
BT1 feeding

FORCED AIR DRYING
BT1 drying
BT2 dehydration
BT3 processing

FORCED LABOR
BF forced labour
rt labor

FORCED LABOUR
HN from 1990; previously "compulsory labour"
AF forced labor
uf compulsory labour
BT1 labour
NT1 bonded labour

FORCES
NT1 gravity
NT2 zero gravity
NT1 thrust
NT1 tractive effort
rt dynamics
rt dynamometers
rt kinetics
rt levers
rt power
rt shear
rt statics
rt strength
rt torque
rt trajectories

FORCING
BT1 cultural methods
rt earliness
rt protected cultivation

FORCIPOMYIA
uf lasiohelea
BT1 ceratopogonidae
BT2 diptera
NT1 forcipomyia sibirica

FORCIPOMYIA SIBIRICA
uf lasiohelea sibirica
BT1 forcipomyia
BT2 ceratopogonidae
BT3 diptera

FORECASTING
BT1 estimation
NT1 prediction
NT1 weather forecasting
NT2 weather reports
NT1 yield forecasting
rt forecasts
rt risk
rt time series

FORECASTS
NT1 delphi method
NT1 population forecasts
NT1 projections
NT2 trends
rt estimates
rt forecasting
rt prediction

FOREGUT
BT1 digestive system
BT2 body parts

FOREIGN BODIES
BT1 contaminants
rt adulterants
rt dockage
rt metal detectors

FOREIGN EXCHANGE
uf exchange rates
BT1 currencies
rt devaluation

FOREIGN FIRMS
BT1 firms
BT2 businesses

FOREIGN INVESTMENT
BT1 investment

FOREIGN STUDENTS
BT1 students
BT2 people

foreign workers
USE **migrant labour**

FORENSIC ENTOMOLOGY
BT1 entomology
BT2 zoology
BT3 biology
BT1 forensic science
rt cadavers

FORENSIC MEDICINE
BT1 forensic science
BT1 medicine

FORENSIC SCIENCE
NT1 forensic entomology
NT1 forensic medicine

FOREST ADMINISTRATION
BT1 administration
rt concessions
rt forest management
rt forest policy
rt forestry
rt forests
rt management units

FOREST BORDERS
uf borders, forest
rt boundaries
rt forests

FOREST DAMAGE
BT1 damage
rt forests

FOREST ECOLOGY
BT1 ecology
rt forests
rt plant communities
rt plant ecological groups

FOREST ECONOMICS
HN from 1990

FOREST ECONOMICS *cont.*
BT1 economics
rt forestry

FOREST FIRES
uf fires, forest
BT1 fires
rt fire control
rt fire danger
rt firebreaks
rt forests
rt fuel appraisals (agricola)

forest floor
USE **forest litter**

FOREST GARDENS
(agroforestry systems on private land outside villages with planted trees and sometimes additional perennial crops)
BT1 agrosilvicultural systems
BT2 agroforestry systems
rt home gardens
rt mixed gardens
rt tree gardens
rt village forest gardens

FOREST GUIDES
BT1 guide books
BT2 books
BT3 publications
BT1 maps
rt forestry
rt forests

forest industry
USE **forest products industries**

FOREST INFLUENCES
rt climate
rt environment
rt forests
rt microclimate
rt pollution
rt synecology
rt water resources

FOREST INVENTORIES
uf cruising
uf inventories, forest
BT1 inventories
NT1 angle count
rt boundaries
rt forest statistics
rt forest surveys
rt forestry
rt forests
rt relascopes

FOREST LITTER
uf duff
uf forest floor
BT1 litter (plant)
rt forests
rt humus
rt soil morphological features
rt soil organic matter

FOREST MANAGEMENT
uf management, forest
NT1 management units
NT1 protection of forests
NT1 yield regulation
rt economics
rt forest administration
rt forest policy
rt forestry
rt forests
rt growing stock
rt increment
rt management
rt mensuration
rt multiple use
rt planning
rt recruitment
rt rotations
rt silvicultural systems
rt silviculture
rt site class assessment
rt working plans

FOREST NURSERIES
BT1 nurseries

FOREST NURSERIES *cont.*
rt forests
rt seedlings
rt transplanting

FOREST NURSERY SOILS
BT1 soil types (cultural)

FOREST OWNERSHIP
BT1 ownership
BT2 tenure systems
rt forests

FOREST PESTS
BT1 pests
rt bark beetles
rt plant pests

FOREST PLANTATIONS
BT1 plantations
rt forests

FOREST POLICY
uf policy, forest
NT1 exploitable age or size
rt agricultural policy
rt amenity value of forests
rt concessions
rt environmental policy
rt forest administration
rt forest management
rt forestry
rt forestry development
rt forests
rt land use
rt legislation
rt policy
rt private forestry
rt social forestry

FOREST PRAIRIE ECOTONE SOILS
BT1 soil types (ecological)
rt forests

FOREST PRODUCTS
BT1 products
NT1 bentwood
NT1 fibreboards
NT2 hardboard
NT1 laminated wood
NT2 microlam
NT1 mine timbers
NT1 minor forest products
NT2 amber
NT2 bark
NT3 pine bark
NT2 christmas trees
NT2 copal
NT2 cork
NT2 kinos
NT2 rosin
NT2 turpentine
NT2 wood extracts
NT3 wood hemicellulose extract
NT3 wood molasses
NT1 moulded products
NT1 osiers
NT1 particleboards
NT2 flakeboards
NT2 osb
NT1 plywood
NT1 roundwood
NT2 cordwood
NT3 fuelwood
NT2 logs
NT3 frozen logs
NT2 pulpwood
NT1 sawdust
NT1 sawnwood
NT2 slabs
NT1 veneers
NT1 waferboards
NT1 wood chips
NT2 whole tree chips
NT1 wood flour
NT1 wood products
NT2 wood panels
NT2 wood wool
NT1 wood shavings
rt bamboos
rt charcoal
rt edible fungi

FOREST PRODUCTS *cont.*
rt forest products industries
rt forest trees
rt forestry
rt forests
rt non-food products
rt panels
rt resins
rt timber trade
rt timberyards

FOREST PRODUCTS INDUSTRIES
uf forest industry
uf wood industry
BT1 industry
NT1 wood chemical industry
rt forest products
rt match manufacture

FOREST RAILWAYS
BT1 railways
rt forestry

FOREST RECREATION
BT1 amenity value of forests
BT1 outdoor recreation
BT2 recreation
rt amenity forests
rt amenity value of forests
rt camping
rt forests
rt hunting
rt orienteering

FOREST RESOURCES
BT1 renewable resources
BT2 natural resources
BT3 resources
rt forest surveys
rt forests
rt land resources
rt water resources

FOREST SOILS
BT1 soil types (ecological)
rt forestry development
rt forests

forest soils, equatorial
USE **equatorial forest soils**

forest soils, taiga
USE **taiga soils**

FOREST STATISTICS
BT1 statistics
rt forest inventories
rt forest surveys
rt forests
rt mensuration

FOREST STEPPE
BT1 vegetation types
rt forest steppe soils
rt steppes

FOREST STEPPE SOILS
BT1 soil types (ecological)
rt forest steppe
rt forests

FOREST SURVEYS
BT1 surveys
rt forest inventories
rt forest resources
rt forest statistics
rt regeneration surveys

FOREST TAXATION
HN from 1990
BT1 taxes
BT2 fiscal policy
BT3 economic policy
BT3 public finance
rt forestry

FOREST TRAILS
BT1 trails
BT2 paths
BT3 roads

FOREST TREES
(important species for forestry and forest products)
NT1 abies alba

FOREST TREES *cont.*
NT1 abies amabilis
NT1 abies balsamea
NT1 abies cephalonica
NT1 abies concolor
NT1 abies firma
NT1 abies fraseri
NT1 abies grandis
NT1 abies holophylla
NT1 abies lasiocarpa
NT1 abies magnifica
NT1 abies mariesii
NT1 abies nordmanniana
NT1 abies pindrow
NT1 abies procera
NT1 abies sachalinensis
NT1 abies sibirica
NT1 abies veitchii
NT1 acacia albida
NT1 acacia aneura
NT1 acacia aulacocarpa
NT1 acacia auriculiformis
NT1 acacia catechu
NT1 acacia confusa
NT1 acacia crassicarpa
NT1 acacia cyclops
NT1 acacia dealbata
NT1 acacia decurrens
NT1 acacia farnesiana
NT1 acacia holosericea
NT1 acacia karroo
NT1 acacia koa
NT1 acacia leucophloea
NT1 acacia longifolia
NT1 acacia mangium
NT1 acacia mearnsii
NT1 acacia melanoxylon
NT1 acacia modesta
NT1 acacia nilotica
NT1 acacia pulchella
NT1 acacia saligna
NT1 acacia senegal
NT1 acacia tortilis
NT1 acacia victoriae
NT1 acer campestre
NT1 acer macrophyllum
NT1 acer mono
NT1 acer negundo
NT1 acer pensylvanicum
NT1 acer platanoides
NT1 acer pseudoplatanus
NT1 acer rubrum
NT1 acer saccharinum
NT1 acer saccharum
NT1 acer spicatum
NT1 adansonia digitata
NT1 adenanthera pavonina
NT1 aesculus hippocastanum
NT1 aesculus indica
NT1 agathis australis
NT1 agathis dammara
NT1 agathis macrophylla
NT1 ailanthus altissima
NT1 ailanthus triphysa
NT1 albizia falcataria
NT1 albizia julibrissin
NT1 albizia lebbek
NT1 albizia odoratissima
NT1 albizia procera
NT1 aleurites fordii
NT1 aleurites montana
NT1 alnus acuminata
NT1 alnus cordata
NT1 alnus crispa
NT1 alnus formosana
NT1 alnus glutinosa
NT1 alnus hirsuta
NT1 alnus incana
NT1 alnus japonica
NT1 alnus nepalensis
NT1 alnus rubra
NT1 alnus rugosa
NT1 altingia excelsa
NT1 anacardium occidentale
NT1 anadenanthera macrocarpa
NT1 anogeissus latifolia
NT1 anthocephalus chinensis
NT1 araucaria angustifolia
NT1 araucaria araucana
NT1 araucaria cunninghamii
NT1 araucaria hunsteinii

FOREST TREES *cont.*
NT1 arbutus menziesii
NT1 atherosperma moschatum
NT1 avicennia germinans
NT1 avicennia marina
NT1 azadirachta indica
NT1 bagassa guianensis
NT1 balanites aegyptiaca
NT1 banksia grandis
NT1 bauhinia purpurea
NT1 bauhinia variegata
NT1 betula alba
NT1 betula alleghaniensis
NT1 betula ermanii
NT1 betula lenta
NT1 betula maximowicziana
NT1 betula nana
NT1 betula nigra
NT1 betula papyrifera
NT1 betula pendula
NT2 betula pendula f. carelica
NT1 betula platyphylla
NT1 betula pubescens
NT1 betula tortuosa
NT1 betula utilis
NT1 bombax malabaricum
NT1 bowdichia virgilioides
NT1 bruguiera cylindrica
NT1 bruguiera gymnorrhiza
NT1 bruguiera parviflora
NT1 butea monosperma
NT1 buxus sempervirens
NT1 caesalpinia velutina
NT1 calliandra calothyrsus
NT1 calophyllum brasiliense
NT1 calophyllum inophyllum
NT1 caragana arborescens
NT1 carapa guianensis
NT1 carpinus betulus
NT1 carpinus laxiflora
NT1 carpinus tschonoskii
NT1 carya glabra
NT1 carya illinoensis
NT1 carya ovata
NT1 carya tomentosa
NT1 cassia fistula
NT1 cassia siamea
NT1 castanea crenata
NT1 castanea dentata
NT1 castanea mollissima
NT1 castanea sativa
NT1 castanopsis cuspidata
NT1 casuarina cunninghamiana
NT1 casuarina equisetifolia
NT1 casuarina glauca
NT1 casuarina junghuhniana
NT1 casuarina obesa
NT1 cedrela odorata
NT1 cedrelinga catenaeformis
NT1 cedrus atlantica
NT1 cedrus deodara
NT1 ceiba pentandra
NT1 celtis laevigata
NT1 cercis canadensis
NT1 cercocarpus ledifolius
NT1 ceriops decandra
NT1 ceriops tagal
NT1 chamaecyparis formosensis
NT1 chamaecyparis lawsoniana
NT1 chamaecyparis obtusa
NT1 chamaecyparis pisifera
NT1 cinnamomum camphora
NT1 cocos nucifera
NT1 conocarpus erectus
NT1 cordia alliodora
NT1 cordia goeldiana
NT1 cornus florida
NT1 corylus avellana
NT1 corylus maxima
NT1 crataegus monogyna
NT1 cryptomeria japonica
NT1 cunninghamia lanceolata
NT1 cupressocyparis leylandii
NT1 cupressus arizonica
NT1 cupressus lusitanica
NT1 cupressus macrocarpa
NT1 cupressus sempervirens
NT1 cupressus torulosa
NT1 dacrydium cupressinum
NT1 dalbergia latifolia
NT1 dalbergia sissoo

FOREST TREES *cont.*
NT1 delonix regia
NT1 didymopanax morototoni
NT1 diospyros melanoxylon
NT1 dipterocarpus hasseltii
NT1 dipteryx panamensis
NT1 doryphora sassafras
NT1 dryobalanops aromatica
NT1 elaeagnus angustifolia
NT1 elaeagnus umbellata
NT1 entandrophragma cylindricum
NT1 entandrophragma utile
NT1 enterolobium contortisiliquum
NT1 enterolobium cyclocarpum
NT1 erythrina poeppigiana
NT1 erythrina suberosa
NT1 eucalyptus alba
NT1 eucalyptus blakelyi
NT1 eucalyptus calophylla
NT1 eucalyptus camaldulensis
NT1 eucalyptus cinerea
NT1 eucalyptus citriodora
NT1 eucalyptus cloeziana
NT1 eucalyptus dalrympleana
NT1 eucalyptus deglupta
NT1 eucalyptus delegatensis
NT1 eucalyptus diversicolor
NT1 eucalyptus exserta
NT1 eucalyptus fastigata
NT1 eucalyptus globulus
NT1 eucalyptus gomphocephala
NT1 eucalyptus grandis
NT1 eucalyptus gunnii
NT1 eucalyptus leucoxylon
NT1 eucalyptus macarthurii
NT1 eucalyptus macrorhyncha
NT1 eucalyptus maculata
NT1 eucalyptus maidenii
NT1 eucalyptus marginata
NT1 eucalyptus melliodora
NT1 eucalyptus microcorys
NT1 eucalyptus microtheca
NT1 eucalyptus nitens
NT1 eucalyptus obliqua
NT1 eucalyptus ovata
NT1 eucalyptus paniculata
NT1 eucalyptus pauciflora
NT1 eucalyptus pellita
NT1 eucalyptus pilularis
NT1 eucalyptus propinqua
NT1 eucalyptus radiata
NT1 eucalyptus regnans
NT1 eucalyptus robusta
NT1 eucalyptus rudis
NT1 eucalyptus saligna
NT1 eucalyptus sideroxylon
NT1 eucalyptus sieberi
NT1 eucalyptus tereticornis
NT1 eucalyptus urophylla
NT1 eucalyptus viminalis
NT1 eucalyptus wandoo
NT1 eucryphia lucida
NT1 eusideroxylon zwageri
NT1 fagus crenata
NT1 fagus grandifolia
NT1 fagus japonica
NT1 fagus orientalis
NT1 fagus sylvatica
NT1 ficus benghalensis
NT1 ficus religiosa
NT1 fraxinus americana
NT1 fraxinus excelsior
NT1 fraxinus mandshurica
NT1 fraxinus pennsylvanica
NT1 ginkgo biloba
NT1 gleditsia triacanthos
NT1 gliricidia sepium
NT1 gmelina arborea
NT1 goupia glabra
NT1 grevillea robusta
NT1 guazuma ulmifolia
NT1 haloxylon aphyllum
NT1 hevea brasiliensis
NT1 hippophae rhamnoides
NT1 holoptelea integrifolia
NT1 hymenaea courbaril
NT1 ilex aquifolium
NT1 juglans mandshurica
NT1 juglans nigra

FOREST TREES *cont.*
NT1 juglans regia
NT1 juniperus chinensis
NT1 juniperus communis
NT1 juniperus excelsa
NT1 juniperus horizontalis
NT1 juniperus monosperma
NT1 juniperus osteosperma
NT1 juniperus scopulorum
NT1 juniperus virginiana
NT1 kalopanax pictus
NT1 khaya nyasica
NT1 laguncularia racemosa
NT1 larix decidua
NT1 larix eurolepis
NT1 larix gmelinii
NT1 larix kamtchatica
NT1 larix laricina
NT1 larix leptolepis
NT1 larix occidentalis
NT1 larix olgensis
NT1 larix sibirica
NT1 larix sukaczewii
NT1 leucaena diversifolia
NT1 leucaena leucocephala
NT1 libocedrus decurrens
NT1 liquidambar styraciflua
NT1 liriodendron tulipifera
NT1 lithocarpus edulis
NT1 macadamia hildebrandii
NT1 mallotus japonicus
NT1 mallotus philippensis
NT1 mangifera indica
NT1 manilkara zapota
NT1 melaleuca leucadendron
NT1 melia azedarach
NT1 metasequoia glyptostroboides
NT1 metrosideros polymorpha
NT1 metrosideros umbellata
NT1 michelia champaca
NT1 mimosa scabrella
NT1 morus alba
NT1 morus cathayana
NT1 nothofagus cunninghamii
NT1 nothofagus dombeyi
NT1 nothofagus fusca
NT1 nothofagus menziesii
NT1 nothofagus moorei
NT1 nothofagus pumilio
NT1 nothofagus solandri
NT2 nothofagus solandri var. cliffortioides
NT1 nyssa aquatica
NT1 nyssa sylvatica
NT1 ochroma pyramidale
NT1 olea europaea
NT1 ougeinia dalbergioides
NT1 parashorea malaanonan
NT1 parkinsonia aculeata
NT1 paulownia tomentosa
NT1 peltophorum dubium
NT1 pentaclethra macroloba
NT1 phyllanthus emblica
NT1 phyllocladus trichomanoides
NT1 picea abies
NT1 picea engelmannii
NT1 picea glauca
NT1 picea jezoensis
NT1 picea koyamai
NT1 picea mariana
NT1 picea obovata
NT1 picea omorika
NT1 picea orientalis
NT1 picea pungens
NT1 picea rubens
NT1 picea sitchensis
NT1 picea smithiana
NT1 pinus albicaulis
NT1 pinus aristata
NT1 pinus attenuata
NT1 pinus ayacahuite
NT1 pinus banksiana
NT1 pinus brutia
NT1 pinus bungeana
NT1 pinus canariensis
NT1 pinus caribaea
NT1 pinus cembra
NT1 pinus cembroides
NT1 pinus clausa
NT1 pinus contorta

FOREST TREES *cont.*
NT1 pinus coulteri
NT1 pinus cubensis
NT1 pinus densiflora
NT1 pinus echinata
NT1 pinus edulis
NT1 pinus eldarica
NT1 pinus elliottii
NT1 pinus flexilis
NT1 pinus halepensis
NT1 pinus hartwegii
NT1 pinus jeffreyi
NT1 pinus kesiya
NT1 pinus koraiensis
NT1 pinus lambertiana
NT1 pinus leiophylla
NT1 pinus maestrensis
NT1 pinus massoniana
NT1 pinus merkusii
NT1 pinus monophylla
NT1 pinus montezumae
NT1 pinus monticola
NT1 pinus mugo
NT1 pinus muricata
NT1 pinus nigra
NT1 pinus oocarpa
NT1 pinus palustris
NT1 pinus patula
NT1 pinus peuce
NT1 pinus pinaster
NT1 pinus pinea
NT1 pinus ponderosa
NT1 pinus pseudostrobus
NT1 pinus pumila
NT1 pinus radiata
NT1 pinus resinosa
NT1 pinus rigida
NT1 pinus roxburghii
NT1 pinus sabiniana
NT1 pinus sibirica
NT1 pinus strobus
NT1 pinus sylvestris
NT1 pinus tabulaeformis
NT1 pinus taeda
NT1 pinus taiwanensis
NT1 pinus teocote
NT1 pinus thunbergii
NT1 pinus uncinata
NT1 pinus virginiana
NT1 pinus wallichiana
NT1 pinus yunnanensis
NT1 pithecellobium dulce
NT1 platanus acerifolia
NT1 platanus occidentalis
NT1 platanus orientalis
NT1 podocarpus dacrydioides
NT1 pongamia pinnata
NT1 populus alba
NT1 populus balsamifera
NT1 populus canadensis
NT1 populus canescens
NT1 populus ciliata
NT1 populus deltoides
NT1 populus euphratica
NT1 populus grandidentata
NT1 populus interamericana
NT1 populus jackii
NT1 populus maximowiczii
NT1 populus nigra
NT1 populus simonii
NT1 populus tomentosa
NT1 populus tremula
NT1 populus tremuloides
NT1 populus trichocarpa
NT1 prosopis alba
NT1 prosopis chilensis
NT1 prosopis cineraria
NT1 prosopis glandulosa
NT1 prosopis juliflora
NT1 prosopis tamarugo
NT1 prunus avium
NT1 prunus padus
NT1 prunus pensylvanica
NT1 prunus serotina
NT1 prunus virginiana
NT1 pseudotsuga menziesii
NT1 psidium guajava
NT1 pterocarpus indicus
NT1 pterocarpus marsupium
NT1 quassia simarouba
NT1 quercus acutissima

FOREST TREES *cont.*
NT1 quercus agrifolia
NT1 quercus alba
NT1 quercus cerris
NT1 quercus coccifera
NT1 quercus coccinea
NT1 quercus crispula
NT1 quercus faginea
NT1 quercus falcata
NT2 quercus falcata var. pagodifolia
NT1 quercus floribunda
NT1 quercus gambelii
NT1 quercus garryana
NT1 quercus glauca
NT1 quercus hartwissiana
NT1 quercus ilex
NT1 quercus incana
NT1 quercus kelloggii
NT1 quercus leucotrichophora
NT1 quercus macrocarpa
NT1 quercus mongolica
NT1 quercus muehlenbergii
NT1 quercus myrsinaefolia
NT1 quercus nigra
NT1 quercus palustris
NT1 quercus petraea
NT1 quercus prinus
NT1 quercus pubescens
NT1 quercus pyrenaica
NT1 quercus robur
NT1 quercus rubra
NT1 quercus semecarpifolia
NT1 quercus serrata
NT1 quercus shumardii
NT1 quercus stellata
NT1 quercus suber
NT1 quercus variabilis
NT1 quercus velutina
NT1 quercus virginiana
NT1 rhizophora apiculata
NT1 rhizophora mangle
NT1 rhizophora mucronata
NT1 rhizophora stylosa
NT1 rhododendron arboreum
NT1 ricinocarpodendron polystachyum
NT1 ricinodendron rautanenii
NT1 robinia pseudoacacia
NT1 salix alaxensis
NT1 salix alba
NT1 salix aquatica
NT1 salix babylonica
NT1 salix caprea
NT1 salix cinerea
NT1 salix dasyclados
NT1 salix lasiolepis
NT1 salix nigra
NT1 salix pentandra
NT1 salix triandra
NT1 salix viminalis
NT1 samanea saman
NT1 sambucus nigra
NT1 santalum album
NT1 sapindus mukorossi
NT1 sapium sebiferum
NT1 schima superba
NT1 schima wallichii
NT1 schinus terebinthifolius
NT1 schizolobium parahybum
NT1 sciadopitys verticillata
NT1 sequoia sempervirens
NT1 sequoiadendron giganteum
NT1 sesbania grandiflora
NT1 sesbania sesban
NT1 shorea acuminata
NT1 shorea javanica
NT1 shorea leprosula
NT1 shorea ovalis
NT1 shorea parvifolia
NT1 shorea robusta
NT1 sonneratia alba
NT1 sophora japonica
NT1 sorbus aucuparia
NT1 swietenia macrophylla
NT1 swietenia mahagoni
NT1 syringa vulgaris
NT1 syzygium cumini
NT1 tabebuia rosea
NT1 taiwania cryptomerioides
NT1 tamarindus indica

FOREST TREES *cont.*
NT1 tamarix aphylla
NT1 tamarix chinensis
NT1 taxodium distichum
NT1 taxus baccata
NT1 taxus cuspidata
NT1 tectona grandis
NT1 terminalia arjuna
NT1 terminalia calamansanai
NT1 terminalia catappa
NT1 terminalia ivorensis
NT1 terminalia tomentosa
NT1 thuja occidentalis
NT1 thuja orientalis
NT1 thuja plicata
NT1 tilia americana
NT1 tilia cordata
NT1 tilia platyphyllos
NT1 tilia tomentosa
NT1 triplochiton scleroxylon
NT1 tsuga canadensis
NT1 tsuga diversifolia
NT1 tsuga heterophylla
NT1 tsuga mertensiana
NT1 tsuga sieboldii
NT1 ulmus americana
NT1 ulmus glabra
NT1 ulmus laevis
NT1 ulmus minor
NT1 ulmus parvifolia
NT1 ulmus procera
NT1 ulmus pumila
NT2 ulmus pumila var. arborea
NT1 washingtonia filifera
NT1 weinmannia racemosa
NT1 xylocarpus granatum
NT1 zelkova serrata
NT1 ziziphus sativa
rt angophora
rt anisoptera
rt artocarpus
rt broadleaves
rt browse plants
rt bursera
rt camellia
rt canarium
rt catalpa
rt cecropia
rt chlorophora
rt copaifera
rt crops
rt cull trees
rt dangerous trees
rt dead trees
rt forest products
rt garcinia
rt grewia
rt heritiera
rt hopea
rt inga
rt koompassia
rt lagerstroemia
rt leptospermum
rt litsea
rt maclura
rt madhuca
rt manglietia
rt mesua
rt michelia
rt mimosa
rt ocotea
rt ostrya
rt palaquium
rt parinari
rt parkia
rt piptadenia
rt pistacia
rt plants
rt pyrus
rt rhamnus
rt rhus
rt sterculia
rt stryphnodendron
rt swintonia
rt tabernaemontana
rt torreya
rt trees
rt vitex
rt zanthoxylum

FORESTIERA
BT1 oleaceae
NT1 forestiera acuminata

FORESTIERA ACUMINATA
BT1 forestiera
BT2 oleaceae

FORESTOMACH
BT1 stomach
BT2 digestive system
BT3 body parts
NT1 reticulum
NT1 rumen
NT2 artificial rumen
NT2 omasum

FORESTRY
NT1 agroforestry
NT1 arboriculture
NT1 community forestry
NT1 farm forestry
NT1 forestry practices
NT2 coppicing
NT2 deforestation
NT2 felling
NT3 clear felling
NT4 stump removal
NT3 clear strip felling
NT3 illicit felling
NT3 improvement fellings
NT3 liberation felling
NT3 sour felling
NT2 girdling
NT2 logging
NT3 shortwood logging
NT3 tree length logging
NT3 whole tree logging
NT2 pollarding
NT2 root pruning
NT2 tending
NT1 private forestry
NT1 silviculture
NT2 artificial regeneration
NT2 beating up
NT2 intensive silviculture
NT2 pulpwood production
NT2 taungya
NT1 social forestry
NT1 urban forestry
rt agriculture
rt canal plantations
rt forest administration
rt forest economics
rt forest guides
rt forest inventories
rt forest management
rt forest policy
rt forest products
rt forest railways
rt forest taxation
rt forestry development
rt forestry engineering
rt forestry law
rt forestry machinery
rt forests
rt iufro
rt mixtures
rt primary sector
rt wood

FORESTRY DEVELOPMENT
uf *development, forestry*
NT1 afforestation
rt development
rt forest policy
rt forest soils
rt forestry

FORESTRY ENGINEERING
HN from 1990
BT1 engineering
rt forestry

FORESTRY LAW
HN from 1990
BT1 law
BT2 legal systems
rt forestry

FORESTRY MACHINERY
BT1 machinery
NT1 barkers

FORESTRY MACHINERY *cont.*
NT1 brush cutters
NT1 cableways
NT1 chipping headrigs
NT1 feller bunchers
NT1 fellers
NT1 forwarders
NT1 logging machines
NT2 processors
NT1 saws
NT2 bandsaws
NT2 chainsaws
NT2 circular saws
NT2 clearing saws
NT2 frame saws
NT2 hand saws
NT1 scrub cutters
NT1 skidders
NT1 trimmers
rt cable methods
rt cables
rt cranes
rt cutters
rt forestry
rt skidding equipment

forestry operations
USE **forestry practices**

FORESTRY PRACTICES
uf *forestry operations*
BT1 forestry
NT1 coppicing
NT1 deforestation
NT1 felling
NT2 clear felling
NT3 stump removal
NT2 clear strip felling
NT2 illicit felling
NT2 improvement fellings
NT2 liberation felling
NT2 sour felling
NT1 girdling
NT1 logging
NT2 shortwood logging
NT2 tree length logging
NT2 whole tree logging
NT1 pollarding
NT1 root pruning
NT1 tending
rt afforestation
rt silviculture
rt site preparation

FORESTS
BT1 vegetation types
NT1 amenity forests
NT1 boreal forests
NT1 bottomland forests
NT1 broadleaved evergreen forests
NT1 cloud forests
NT1 coniferous forests
NT1 deciduous forests
NT2 broadleaved deciduous forests
NT1 degraded forests
NT1 demonstration forests
NT1 mangrove forests
NT1 mixed forests
NT1 mountain forests
NT1 national forests (agricola)
NT1 protection forests
NT1 pygmy forests
NT1 rain forests
NT2 tropical rain forests
NT1 reserved forests
NT1 riparian forests
NT1 sclerophyllous forests
NT1 secondary forests
NT1 selection forests
NT1 state forests (agricola)
NT1 subalpine forests
NT1 tropical forests
NT2 tropical rain forests
NT1 virgin forests
rt forest administration
rt forest borders
rt forest damage
rt forest ecology
rt forest fires
rt forest guides

FORESTS *cont.*
rt forest influences
rt forest inventories
rt forest litter
rt forest management
rt forest nurseries
rt forest ownership
rt forest plantations
rt forest policy
rt forest prairie ecotone soils
rt forest products
rt forest recreation
rt forest resources
rt forest soils
rt forest statistics
rt forest steppe soils
rt forestry
rt undergrowth
rt underwood

FORFICULA
BT1 forficulidae
BT2 dermaptera
NT1 forficula auricularia

FORFICULA AURICULARIA
BT1 forficula
BT2 forficulidae
BT3 dermaptera

FORFICULIDAE
BT1 dermaptera
NT1 doru
NT2 doru lineare
NT1 forficula
NT2 forficula auricularia

FORK LIFTS
BT1 handling machinery
BT2 machinery
rt handling
rt loaders
rt pallets
rt stackers

FORKING AND MULTIPLE STEMS
HN from 1989
BT1 stem form

FORKS
BT1 hand tools
BT2 tools

FORM FACTORS
rt eccentricities
rt stem form

FORM QUOTIENTS
rt diameter
rt girth
rt stem form
rt trunks

FORMAL GARDENS
BT1 gardens
rt parks

FORMALDEHYDE
BT1 aldehydes
BT1 antiseptics
BT2 antiinfective agents
BT3 drugs
BT1 bactericides
BT2 pesticides
BT1 disinfectants
BT1 preservatives
BT1 silage additives
BT2 additives
BT1 soil fumigants
BT2 fumigants
BT3 pesticides
BT1 unclassified fungicides
BT2 fungicides
BT3 pesticides
rt paraformaldehyde

FORMAMIDINE ACARICIDES
BT1 acaricides
BT2 pesticides
NT1 amitraz
NT1 chlordimeform
NT1 formetanate

FORMAMIDINE INSECTICIDES
BT1 insecticides
BT2 pesticides
NT1 amitraz
NT1 chlordimeform

FORMATES
NT1 formates (esters)
NT2 ethyl formate
NT1 formates (salts)
NT2 ammonium formate
NT2 calcium formate
NT2 sodium formate
rt formic acid

FORMATES (ESTERS)
BT1 esters
BT1 formates
NT1 ethyl formate

FORMATES (SALTS)
BT1 formates
BT1 organic salts
BT2 salts
NT1 ammonium formate
NT1 calcium formate
NT1 sodium formate

FORMATION

FORMETANATE
BT1 formamidine acaricides
BT2 acaricides
BT3 pesticides

FORMIC ACID
BT1 dermatological agents
BT2 drugs
BT1 desiccant herbicides
BT2 desiccants
BT1 monocarboxylic acids
BT2 carboxylic acids
BT3 organic acids
BT4 acids
BT1 silage additives
BT2 additives
rt formates

FORMICA
BT1 formicidae
BT2 hymenoptera
NT1 formica fusca
NT1 formica lugubris
NT1 formica nigricans
NT1 formica polyctena
NT1 formica pratensis
NT1 formica rufa
NT1 formica sanguinea
NT1 formica yessensis

FORMICA FUSCA
BT1 formica
BT2 formicidae
BT3 hymenoptera

FORMICA LUGUBRIS
BT1 formica
BT2 formicidae
BT3 hymenoptera

FORMICA NIGRICANS
BT1 formica
BT2 formicidae
BT3 hymenoptera

FORMICA POLYCTENA
BT1 formica
BT2 formicidae
BT3 hymenoptera

FORMICA PRATENSIS
BT1 formica
BT2 formicidae
BT3 hymenoptera

FORMICA RUFA
BT1 formica
BT2 formicidae
BT3 hymenoptera

FORMICA SANGUINEA
BT1 formica
BT2 formicidae
BT3 hymenoptera

FORMICA YESSENSIS
BT1 formica
BT2 formicidae
BT3 hymenoptera

formicapis
USE **hoplitis**

FORMICIDAE
uf *ants*
BT1 hymenoptera
NT1 acromyrmex
NT2 acromyrmex octospinosus
NT1 anoplolepis
NT2 anoplolepis custodiens
NT2 anoplolepis longipes
NT1 atta
NT2 atta cephalotes
NT2 atta sexdens
NT2 atta texana
NT2 atta vollenweideri
NT1 azteca
NT2 azteca chartifex
NT1 camponotus
NT2 camponotus acvapimensis
NT2 camponotus herculeanus
NT2 camponotus pennsylvanicus
NT2 camponotus rufipes
NT1 cataglyphis
NT2 cataglyphis aenescens
NT1 chalcoponera
NT1 crematogaster
NT2 crematogaster scutellaris
NT1 dorylus
NT1 formica
NT2 formica fusca
NT2 formica lugubris
NT2 formica nigricans
NT2 formica polyctena
NT2 formica pratensis
NT2 formica rufa
NT2 formica sanguinea
NT2 formica yessensis
NT1 iridomyrmex
NT2 iridomyrmex humilis
NT2 iridomyrmex purpureus
NT1 lasius
NT2 lasius brunneus
NT2 lasius fuliginosus
NT2 lasius niger
NT1 messor
NT1 monomorium
NT2 monomorium destructor
NT2 monomorium minimum
NT2 monomorium pharaonis
NT1 myrmecia
NT2 myrmecia gulosa
NT2 myrmecia pilosula
NT1 myrmica
NT2 myrmica rubra
NT2 myrmica ruginodis
NT2 myrmica sabuleti
NT2 myrmica scabrinodis
NT2 myrmica sulcinodis
NT1 myrmicaria
NT2 myrmicaria striata
NT1 oecophylla
NT2 oecophylla longinoda
NT2 oecophylla smaragdina
NT1 pheidole
NT2 pheidole dentata
NT2 pheidole megacephala
NT1 pogonomyrmex
NT2 pogonomyrmex badius
NT2 pogonomyrmex occidentalis
NT2 pogonomyrmex rugosus
NT1 rhytidoponera
NT2 rhytidoponera metallica
NT1 solenopsis
NT2 solenopsis geminata
NT2 solenopsis invicta
NT2 solenopsis richteri
NT2 solenopsis saevissima
NT2 solenopsis xyloni
NT1 technomyrmex
NT2 technomyrmex albipes
NT1 tetramorium
NT2 tetramorium caespitum
NT1 veromessor
NT2 veromessor pergandei

FORMICIDAE *cont.*
rt social insects

FORMIMINOGLUTAMASE
(ec 3.5.3.8)
BT1 amidine hydrolases
BT2 hydrolases
BT3 enzymes

FORMIMINOGLUTAMIC ACID
BT1 amino acid derivatives
BT2 amino compounds
BT3 organic nitrogen compounds

FORMOL TITRATION METHOD
BT1 titration
BT2 analytical methods
BT3 methodology
rt milk protein

FORMONONETIN
BT1 diuretics
BT2 drugs
BT1 isoflavones
BT2 flavonoids
BT3 aromatic compounds
BT3 plant pigments
BT4 pigments
BT1 plant oestrogens
BT2 oestrogens
BT3 sex hormones
BT4 hormones

formosa
USE **taiwan**

FORMOTHION
BT1 organothiophosphate acaricides
BT2 organophosphorus acaricides
BT3 acaricides
BT4 pesticides
BT3 organophosphorus pesticides
BT4 organophosphorus compounds
BT1 organothiophosphate insecticides
BT2 organophosphorus insecticides
BT3 insecticides
BT4 pesticides
BT3 organophosphorus pesticides
BT4 organophosphorus compounds

FORMULA DIETS (AGRICOLA)
BT1 diets

FORMULATIONS
NT1 aqueous concentrates
NT1 drug formulations
NT2 ointments
NT1 dusts
NT1 emulsifiable concentrates
NT1 fogs
NT1 mosquito coils
NT1 oil miscible concentrates
NT1 pour-on formulations
NT1 powders
NT2 fluorescent powders
NT2 water dispersible powders
NT2 water-soluble powders
NT2 wettable powders
NT1 smokes
NT1 suspensions
NT2 foams
NT3 plastic foam
rt agricultural chemicals
rt boluses
rt briquettes
rt controlled release
rt ear tags
rt encapsulation
rt flea collars
rt gels
rt granules
rt microencapsulation
rt pesticides
rt shampoos

FORMULATIONS *cont.*
rt solutions
rt sprays

FORMWORK
HN from 1989
uf *shuttering*
rt structures
rt wood

FORSYTHIA
BT1 oleaceae
NT1 forsythia europaea
NT1 forsythia intermedia
NT1 forsythia japonica
NT1 forsythia suspensa
NT1 forsythia viridissima

FORSYTHIA EUROPAEA
BT1 forsythia
BT2 oleaceae
BT1 ornamental woody plants

FORSYTHIA INTERMEDIA
BT1 forsythia
BT2 oleaceae
BT1 ornamental woody plants

FORSYTHIA JAPONICA
BT1 forsythia
BT2 oleaceae
BT1 ornamental woody plants

forsythia koreana
USE **forsythia viridissima**

FORSYTHIA SUSPENSA
BT1 antibacterial plants
BT1 forsythia
BT2 oleaceae
BT1 medicinal plants
BT1 ornamental woody plants

FORSYTHIA VIRIDISSIMA
uf *forsythia koreana*
BT1 forsythia
BT2 oleaceae
BT1 ornamental woody plants

FORTIFICATION
BT1 processing

fortrel
USE **polyesters (agricola)**

FORTUNEARIA
BT1 hamamelidaceae

FORTUNELLA
BT1 rutaceae
NT1 fortunella japonica
NT1 fortunella margarita
rt citrangequats
rt citrus fruits
rt kumquats

FORTUNELLA JAPONICA
BT1 fortunella
BT2 rutaceae

FORTUNELLA MARGARITA
BT1 fortunella
BT2 rutaceae

FORWARD SPEED
uf *speed*
rt rotational speed
rt velocity

FORWARD TRADING (AGRICOLA)
BT1 trading (agricola)
NT1 cash forward contracting (agricola)
NT1 options trading (agricola)
NT2 call options (agricola)
NT2 put options (agricola)

FORWARDERS
BT1 forestry machinery
BT2 machinery

FOSAMINE
BT1 organophosphorus herbicides
BT2 herbicides
BT3 pesticides

FOSAMINE *cont.*
BT2 organophosphorus pesticides
BT3 organophosphorus compounds

FOSETYL
uf aluminium ethyl phosphite
BT1 organophosphorus fungicides
BT2 fungicides
BT3 pesticides
BT2 organophosphorus pesticides
BT3 organophosphorus compounds

FOSMETHILAN
BT1 organothiophosphate insecticides
BT2 organophosphorus insecticides
BT3 insecticides
BT4 pesticides
BT3 organophosphorus pesticides
BT4 organophosphorus compounds

FOSSIL SOILS
BT1 soil types (palaeosolic)
rt buried soils
rt palaeosols

fossil wood
USE **old and fossil wood**

FOSTER CHILDREN (AGRICOLA)
BT1 children
BT2 people
rt adopted children (agricola)
rt foster family (agricola)
rt foster homes (agricola)
rt fostering

FOSTER FAMILY (AGRICOLA)
BT1 families
rt foster children (agricola)
rt foster homes (agricola)
rt fostering

FOSTER HOMES (AGRICOLA)
BT1 homes
BT2 housing
rt foster children (agricola)
rt foster family (agricola)
rt fostering

FOSTERING
rt foster children (agricola)
rt foster family (agricola)
rt foster homes (agricola)

FOTHERGILLA
BT1 hamamelidaceae
NT1 fothergilla gardenii
NT1 fothergilla major

FOTHERGILLA GARDENII
BT1 fothergilla
BT2 hamamelidaceae
BT1 ornamental woody plants

FOTHERGILLA MAJOR
BT1 fothergilla
BT2 hamamelidaceae
BT1 ornamental woody plants

FOUL BROOD
BT1 bee diseases
BT2 animal diseases
BT3 diseases
NT1 american foul brood
NT1 european foul brood
rt honeybee brood

FOULING
BT1 pollution
NT1 biofouling
NT2 marine fouling
rt milk deposits
rt toxic substances

FOUNDATION
BT1 combs

FOUNDATION *cont.*
BT2 hive parts
BT3 movable-comb hives
BT4 hives
NT1 plastic foundation
rt beeswax

FOUNDATION FITTING
BT1 manipulations
BT2 beekeeping

FOUNDATIONS
BT1 building construction
BT2 construction
rt buildings

FOUNDER EFFECT
BT1 evolution
rt populations

FOUQUIERIA
BT1 fouquieriaceae
NT1 fouquieria shrevei
NT1 fouquieria splendens

FOUQUIERIA SHREVEI
BT1 fouquieria
BT2 fouquieriaceae
BT1 ornamental woody plants

FOUQUIERIA SPLENDENS
BT1 fouquieria
BT2 fouquieriaceae
BT1 ornamental woody plants

FOUQUIERIACEAE
NT1 fouquieria
NT2 fouquieria shrevei
NT2 fouquieria splendens

FOUR WHEEL DRIVE TRACTORS
BT1 tractors
BT2 cross country vehicles
BT3 vehicles

FOWL DISEASES
BT1 poultry diseases
BT2 animal diseases
BT3 diseases
rt fowls

FOWL FATTENING
HN from 1990; previously "chicken fattening"
uf chicken fattening
BT1 poultry fattening
BT2 fattening
BT3 animal feeding
BT4 feeding
rt fowls

FOWL FEEDING
HN from 1990
BT1 poultry feeding
BT2 livestock feeding
BT3 animal feeding
BT4 feeding
rt fowls

FOWL PLAGUE VIRUS
BT1 avian influenzavirus
BT2 influenzavirus
BT3 orthomyxoviridae
BT4 viruses

FOWL POX VIRUS
BT1 avipoxvirus
BT2 chordopoxvirinae
BT3 poxviridae
BT4 viruses

FOWLS
uf chickens
uf gallus gallus domesticus
BT1 poultry
BT2 livestock
BT3 animals
NT1 bantams
NT1 broilers
NT1 capons
rt chicken fat
rt chicken housing
rt chicken meat
rt chicks
rt cocks

FOWLS *cont.*
rt fowl diseases
rt fowl fattening
rt fowl feeding
rt galliformes
rt hens
rt phasianidae
rt pullets

FOXES
BT1 furbearing animals
BT2 animals
rt canidae

foxes, arctic
USE **alopex lagopus**

foxglove
USE **digitalis purpurea**

FOXING
BT1 biodeterioration
BT2 deterioration
rt paper

FOXTAIL MILLET
uf millet, foxtail
rt setaria italica

FOXTAIL MOSAIC POTEXVIRUS
HN from 1990
BT1 potexvirus group
BT2 plant viruses
BT3 plant pathogens
BT4 pathogens

FRACTIONATION
BT1 analytical methods
BT2 methodology
BT1 separation
rt distilling
rt green crop fractionation

FRACTURE
rt breakage
rt cracking
rt failure
rt rupture
rt shear
rt wood strength

FRACTURE FIXATION
BT1 surgical operations
rt bone fractures

FRACTURES
BT1 trauma
NT1 bone fractures

FRAGARIA
BT1 rosaceae
NT1 fragaria ananassa
NT1 fragaria chiloensis
NT1 fragaria indica
NT1 fragaria moschata
NT1 fragaria vesca
NT1 fragaria virginiana

FRAGARIA ANANASSA
HN from 1989; previously fragaria magna
uf fragaria magna
BT1 fragaria
BT2 rosaceae
rt strawberries

FRAGARIA CHILOENSIS
BT1 fragaria
BT2 rosaceae
rt strawberries

fragaria elatior
USE **fragaria moschata**

FRAGARIA INDICA
BT1 fragaria
BT2 rosaceae

fragaria magna
USE **fragaria ananassa**

FRAGARIA MOSCHATA
uf fragaria elatior
BT1 fragaria
BT2 rosaceae

FRAGARIA VESCA
BT1 fragaria
BT2 rosaceae
rt strawberries
rt strawberry crinkle rhabdovirus
rt strawberry latent ringspot virus
rt strawberry mild yellow edge virus
rt strawberry mottle virus
rt strawberry vein banding caulimovirus

FRAGARIA VIRGINIANA
BT1 fragaria
BT2 rosaceae

FRAGILARIA
BT1 bacillariophyta
BT2 algae
NT1 fragilaria crotonensis

FRAGILARIA CROTONENSIS
BT1 fragilaria
BT2 bacillariophyta
BT3 algae

FRAGILIN
BT1 glucosides
BT2 glycosides
BT3 carbohydrates

FRAGIPANS
BT1 pans
BT2 soil morphological features

FRAGIUDALFS
BT1 udalfs
BT2 luvisols
BT3 soil types (genetic)

FRAGMENTATION
rt farm structure

FRAGRANCE
BT1 organoleptic traits
BT2 physicochemical properties
BT3 properties
BT2 traits
rt aroma

FRAME SAWS
uf saws, frame
BT1 saws
BT2 forestry machinery
BT3 machinery
BT2 tools

FRAMED COMBS
BT1 combs
BT2 hive parts
BT3 movable-comb hives
BT4 hives
rt frames

FRAMES
uf dutch lights
BT1 structural components
BT2 components
rt combs
rt framed combs
rt greenhouses
rt hive parts
rt protected cultivation
rt structures

FRAMYCETIN
uf neomycin b
BT1 aminoglycoside antibiotics
BT2 antibiotics
BT2 glycosides
BT3 carbohydrates
BT1 antibacterial agents
BT2 antiinfective agents
BT3 drugs
rt neomycin

FRANCE
BT1 western europe
BT2 europe
NT1 alsace
NT1 aquitaine
NT1 auvergne

FRANCE *cont.*
NT1 brittany
NT1 burgundy
NT1 central france
NT1 champagne ardennes
NT1 corsica
NT1 dom
NT1 franche comte
NT1 ile de france
NT1 languedoc roussillon
NT1 limousin
NT1 lorraine
NT1 lower normandy
NT1 midi pyrenees
NT1 nord pas de calais
NT1 pays de la loire
NT1 picardy
NT1 poitou charentes
NT1 provence-alpes-cote d`azur
NT1 rhone alpes
NT1 upper normandy
rt andorra
rt european communities
rt francophone africa
rt mediterranean countries
rt oecd

FRANCHE COMTE
BT1 france
BT2 western europe
BT3 europe

FRANCHISES
BT1 contracts

FRANCISELLA
BT1 gracilicutes
BT2 bacteria
BT3 prokaryotes
NT1 francisella tularensis

FRANCISELLA TULARENSIS
uf *pasteurella tularensis*
uf *tularaemia*
BT1 francisella
BT2 gracilicutes
BT3 bacteria
BT4 prokaryotes

FRANCOLINUS
BT1 phasianidae
BT2 galliformes
BT3 birds

FRANCOPHONE AFRICA
uf *africa, french speaking*
rt africa
rt africa south of sahara
rt algeria
rt anglophone africa
rt burkina faso
rt burundi
rt cameroon
rt central african republic
rt chad
rt comoros
rt congo
rt djibouti
rt france
rt gabon
rt guinea
rt ivory coast
rt madagascar
rt mali
rt mauritania
rt mayotte
rt morocco
rt niger
rt reunion
rt rwanda
rt senegal
rt togo
rt tunisia
rt zaire

FRANGIPANI MOSAIC TOBAMOVIRUS
HN from 1990
BT1 tobamovirus group
BT2 plant viruses
BT3 plant pathogens
BT4 pathogens
rt plumeria rubra

FRANGULA
BT1 rhamnaceae
rt rhamnus

frangula alnus
USE **rhamnus frangula**

frankfurters
USE **hot dogs (agricola)**

FRANKIA
BT1 frankiaceae
BT2 actinomycetales
BT3 firmicutes
BT4 bacteria
BT5 prokaryotes
NT1 frankia ceanothi

FRANKIA CEANOTHI
BT1 frankia
BT2 frankiaceae
BT3 actinomycetales
BT4 firmicutes
BT5 bacteria
BT6 prokaryotes

FRANKIACEAE
BT1 actinomycetales
BT2 firmicutes
BT3 bacteria
BT4 prokaryotes
NT1 frankia
NT2 frankia ceanothi

FRANKLINIA
BT1 theaceae
NT1 franklinia alatamaha

FRANKLINIA ALATAMAHA
BT1 franklinia
BT2 theaceae
BT1 ornamental woody plants

FRANKLINIELLA
BT1 thripidae
BT2 thysanoptera
NT1 frankliniella fusca
NT1 frankliniella intonsa
NT1 frankliniella occidentalis
NT1 frankliniella schultzei
NT1 frankliniella tritici
NT1 frankliniella williamsi

frankliniella dampfi
USE **frankliniella schultzei**

FRANKLINIELLA FUSCA
BT1 frankliniella
BT2 thripidae
BT3 thysanoptera

FRANKLINIELLA INTONSA
BT1 frankliniella
BT2 thripidae
BT3 thysanoptera

FRANKLINIELLA OCCIDENTALIS
BT1 frankliniella
BT2 thripidae
BT3 thysanoptera

FRANKLINIELLA SCHULTZEI
uf *frankliniella dampfi*
BT1 frankliniella
BT2 thripidae
BT3 thysanoptera

FRANKLINIELLA TRITICI
BT1 frankliniella
BT2 thripidae
BT3 thysanoptera

FRANKLINIELLA WILLIAMSI
BT1 frankliniella
BT2 thripidae
BT3 thysanoptera

FRANSERIA
BT1 compositae
NT1 franseria acanthicarpa
NT1 franseria deltoidea
NT1 franseria dumosa
NT1 franseria tenuifolia
NT1 franseria tomentosa

FRANSERIA ACANTHICARPA
BT1 franseria
BT2 compositae

FRANSERIA DELTOIDEA
BT1 franseria
BT2 compositae

FRANSERIA DUMOSA
BT1 franseria
BT2 compositae

FRANSERIA TENUIFOLIA
BT1 franseria
BT2 compositae

FRANSERIA TOMENTOSA
BT1 franseria
BT2 compositae

FRATERCULA
BT1 alcidae
BT2 charadriiformes
BT3 birds
NT1 fratercula arctica
NT1 fratercula corniculata
rt lunda

FRATERCULA ARCTICA
BT1 fratercula
BT2 alcidae
BT3 charadriiformes
BT4 birds

fratercula cirrhata
USE **lunda cirrhata**

FRATERCULA CORNICULATA
BT1 fratercula
BT2 alcidae
BT3 charadriiformes
BT4 birds

FRAXINUS
uf *ash trees*
BT1 oleaceae
NT1 fraxinus americana
NT1 fraxinus angustifolia
NT1 fraxinus caroliniana
NT1 fraxinus excelsior
NT1 fraxinus japonica
NT1 fraxinus mandshurica
NT1 fraxinus nigra
NT1 fraxinus ornus
NT1 fraxinus pennsylvanica
NT1 fraxinus uhdei
NT1 fraxinus velutina
NT1 fraxinus viridis

FRAXINUS AMERICANA
BT1 forest trees
BT1 fraxinus
BT2 oleaceae
BT1 ornamental woody plants

FRAXINUS ANGUSTIFOLIA
uf *fraxinus oxycarpa*
BT1 fraxinus
BT2 oleaceae

FRAXINUS CAROLINIANA
BT1 fraxinus
BT2 oleaceae

FRAXINUS EXCELSIOR
BT1 forest trees
BT1 fraxinus
BT2 oleaceae
BT1 ornamental woody plants

FRAXINUS JAPONICA
BT1 fraxinus
BT2 oleaceae

FRAXINUS MANDSHURICA
BT1 forest trees
BT1 fraxinus
BT2 oleaceae
BT1 ornamental woody plants

FRAXINUS NIGRA
BT1 fraxinus
BT2 oleaceae
BT1 ornamental woody plants

FRAXINUS ORNUS
BT1 fraxinus
BT2 oleaceae
BT1 ornamental woody plants

fraxinus oxycarpa
USE **fraxinus angustifolia**

FRAXINUS PENNSYLVANICA
uf *fraxinus pubescens*
BT1 forest trees
BT1 fraxinus
BT2 oleaceae
BT1 ornamental woody plants

fraxinus pubescens
USE **fraxinus pennsylvanica**

FRAXINUS UHDEI
BT1 fraxinus
BT2 oleaceae

FRAXINUS VELUTINA
BT1 fraxinus
BT2 oleaceae
BT1 ornamental woody plants

FRAXINUS VIRIDIS
BT1 fraxinus
BT2 oleaceae

FREDERIKSBORG
BT1 horse breeds
BT2 breeds

FREE AMINO ACIDS
uf *amino acids, free*
BT1 chemical composition
BT2 composition
rt amino acids

free fatty acids
USE **fatty acids**

FREE LIVING NEMATODES
uf *nematodes, free living*
uf *soil nematodes*
rt aphelenchidae
rt aphelenchoididae
rt araeolaimidae
rt belondiridae
rt cephalobidae
rt chromadoridae
rt desmodoridae
rt dorylaimidae
rt enoplidae
rt monhysteridae
rt mononchidae
rt nematoda
rt nygolaimidae
rt panagrolaimidae
rt rhabditidae
rt tripylidae

FREE RADICALS
BT1 radicals

FREE RANGE HUSBANDRY
BT1 animal husbandry
BT2 husbandry
BT2 zootechny
BT1 livestock farming
BT2 farming
rt poultry farming

FREE TIME
BT1 time
rt leisure
rt time allocation

FREE TRADE
BT1 trade liberalization
BT2 trade policy
BT3 economic policy

FREEMARTINISM
BT1 intersexuality
BT2 sex differentiation disorders
BT3 congenital abnormalities
BT4 abnormalities
BT3 reproductive disorders
BT4 functional disorders
BT5 animal disorders
BT6 disorders

FREEMARTINISM *cont.*
rt freemartins

FREEMARTINS
rt cattle
rt freemartinism
rt sex differentiation disorders

FREESIA
BT1 iridaceae
rt corms
rt freesia mosaic virus
rt ornamental bulbs

FREESIA MOSAIC VIRUS
BT1 miscellaneous plant viruses
BT2 plant viruses
BT3 plant pathogens
BT4 pathogens
rt freesia

FREEZABILITY
BT1 physicochemical properties
BT2 properties
rt freeze drying
rt freezing
rt freezing quality
rt freezing techniques
rt semen

FREEZE DRYING
uf *drying, freeze*
uf *lyophilization*
BT1 drying
BT2 dehydration
BT3 processing
rt freezability
rt freezers
rt freezing
rt freezing techniques

FREEZE ETCHING

FREEZE THAW CYCLES
BT1 climatic factors
BT1 soil thermal regimes

FREEZERS
BT1 equipment
rt freeze drying
rt freezing
rt freezing techniques

FREEZING
BT1 change of state
BT1 processing
NT1 blast freezing (agricola)
NT1 gelation
rt cold
rt cooling
rt cryopreservation
rt freezability
rt freeze drying
rt freezers
rt freezing point
rt freezing quality
rt freezing techniques
rt frost
rt frozen conditions
rt ice
rt ice damage
rt ice nucleation
rt refrigeration
rt soil water
rt thawing
rt water

FREEZING POINT
BT1 physical properties
BT2 properties
rt freezing
rt temperature

FREEZING QUALITY
uf *quality for freezing*
BT1 food processing quality
BT2 processing quality
BT3 quality
rt freezability
rt freezing
rt freezing techniques

FREEZING TECHNIQUES
BT1 techniques

FREEZING TECHNIQUES *cont.*
rt freezability
rt freeze drying
rt freezers
rt freezing
rt freezing quality
rt processing

fremontia
USE **fremontodendron**

FREMONTODENDRON
uf *fremontia*
BT1 sterculiaceae
NT1 fremontodendron californicum

FREMONTODENDRON CALIFORNICUM
BT1 fremontodendron
BT2 sterculiaceae
BT1 ornamental woody plants

FRENCH ALPINE
HN from 1990
BT1 goat breeds
BT2 breeds

FRENCH ANGLO-ARAB
HN from 1990
BT1 horse breeds
BT2 breeds

FRENCH ARDENNAIS
HN from 1990
BT1 horse breeds
BT2 breeds

french beans
USE **phaseolus vulgaris**

FRENCH BROWN
HN from 1990
BT1 cattle breeds
BT2 breeds

FRENCH COOKERY (AGRICOLA)
BT1 cookery (agricola)

FRENCH FRIES
BF chips (french fries)

FRENCH FRIESIAN
BT1 cattle breeds
BT2 breeds

FRENCH GUIANA
BT1 south america
BT2 america
rt dom

FRENCH LANDRACE
HN from 1990
BT1 pig breeds
BT2 breeds

FRENCH LARGE WHITE
HN from 1990
BT1 pig breeds
BT2 breeds

FRENCH POLYNESIA
uf *pacific islands (french)*
uf *polynesia, french*
BT1 polynesia
BT2 oceania
NT1 gambier islands
NT1 marquesas islands
NT1 society islands
NT1 tuamotu
NT1 tubuai islands
rt pacific islands
rt south pacific commission

FRENCH SAANEN
HN from 1990
BT1 goat breeds
BT2 breeds

FRENCH SADDLEBRED
HN from 1990
BT1 horse breeds
BT2 breeds

french somaliland
USE **djibouti**

french territory of the afars and the issas
USE **djibouti**

FRENCH TROTTER
HN from 1990
BT1 horse breeds
BT2 breeds

french west indies
USE **guadeloupe**
OR **martinique**

FRENKELIA
BT1 apicomplexa
BT2 protozoa
NT1 frenkelia clethrionomyobuteonis
NT1 frenkelia glareoli

FRENKELIA CLETHRIONOMYOBUTEONIS
BT1 frenkelia
BT2 apicomplexa
BT3 protozoa

FRENKELIA GLAREOLI
BT1 frenkelia
BT2 apicomplexa
BT3 protozoa

FREONS
BT1 halogenated hydrocarbons
BT2 organic halogen compounds
rt aerosols
rt fluorine
rt refrigeration

FREQUENCY
NT1 chiasma frequency
NT1 harvesting frequency
NT2 cutting frequency
NT1 mating frequency
rt frequency distribution
rt incidence
rt oscillation
rt statistics
rt vibration

FREQUENCY DEPENDENT SELECTION
HN from 1989
BT1 selection

FREQUENCY DISTRIBUTION
BT1 distribution
rt frequency

FRESH PRODUCTS
BT1 products
rt fish
rt fruit
rt meat
rt perishable products
rt vegetables

FRESH WATER
uf *water, fresh*
BT1 water

FRESHWATER BIOLOGY (AGRICOLA)
BT1 biology
rt aquatic organisms
rt freshwater ecology

FRESHWATER CATFISHES
BT1 freshwater fishes
BT2 aquatic animals
BT3 animals
BT3 aquatic organisms
rt ictaluridae
rt tandanus tandanus

FRESHWATER ECOLOGY
BT1 ecology
rt aquatic animals
rt aquatic communities
rt aquatic organisms
rt aquatic plants
rt freshwater biology (agricola)
rt limnology

FRESHWATER FISHES
BT1 aquatic animals
BT2 animals
BT2 aquatic organisms
NT1 ayu
NT1 brown trout
NT1 carp
NT1 freshwater catfishes
NT1 goldfish
NT1 perch
NT1 pike
NT1 pike perch
NT1 rainbow trout
rt fishes

FRESHWATER MOLLUSCS
BT1 aquatic invertebrates
BT2 aquatic animals
BT3 animals
BT3 aquatic organisms
rt mollusca

FRESHWATER STRUCTURES
HN from 1989
BT1 structures

FREYLINIA
BT1 scrophulariaceae
NT1 freylinia lanceolata

FREYLINIA LANCEOLATA
BT1 freylinia
BT2 scrophulariaceae

FRICASSEE (AGRICOLA)
rt meals

FRICTION
uf *friction coefficient*
BT1 mechanical properties
BT2 properties
NT1 sliding friction
rt adhesion
rt angle of repose
rt lubrication
rt tribology
rt wear

FRICTION CLUTCHES
uf *clutches, friction*
BT1 clutches
BT2 control components
BT3 components

friction coefficient
USE **friction**

friction, sliding
USE **sliding friction**

FRICTIONAL SEED CLEANERS
uf *cleaners, frictional seed*
uf *seed cleaners, frictional*
BT1 seed cleaners
BT2 cleaners
BT3 machinery

FRIDERICIA
BT1 enchytraeidae
BT2 oligochaeta
BT3 annelida
NT1 fridericia galba

FRIDERICIA GALBA
BT1 fridericia
BT2 enchytraeidae
BT3 oligochaeta
BT4 annelida

FRIED FOODS (AGRICOLA)
BT1 foods
NT1 batter fried foods (agricola)
rt frying

FRIESIAN
BT1 cattle breeds
BT2 breeds

FRIESLAND
HN from 1990
uf *netherlands (friesland)*
BT1 cattle breeds
BT2 breeds
BT1 netherlands
BT2 western europe

FRIESLAND *cont.*
BT3 europe

FRIGHT
BT1 animal behaviour
BT2 behaviour

FRIGID SOILS
uf *arctic soils*
BT1 soil types (climatic)
rt permafrost
rt subarctic soils

FRILLING
BT1 ringing
BT2 pruning
rt weed control

FRINGE BENEFITS (AGRICOLA)
BT1 remuneration
rt sick leave (agricola)

FRINGILLA
BT1 fringillidae
BT2 passeriformes
BT3 birds
NT1 fringilla coelebs

FRINGILLA COELEBS
BT1 fringilla
BT2 fringillidae
BT3 passeriformes
BT4 birds

FRINGILLIDAE
uf *finches*
BT1 passeriformes
BT2 birds
NT1 carduelis
NT1 fringilla
NT2 fringilla coelebs
NT1 pyrrhula
NT2 pyrrhula pyrrhula
NT1 serinus
rt canaries

FRITILLARIA
uf *korolkowia*
uf *petilium*
uf *rhinopetalum*
BT1 liliaceae
NT1 fritillaria bucharica
NT1 fritillaria camschatcensis
NT1 fritillaria eduardii
NT1 fritillaria imperialis
NT1 fritillaria meleagris
NT1 fritillaria pallidiflora
NT1 fritillaria persica
NT1 fritillaria roylei
NT1 fritillaria severtzovii

FRITILLARIA BUCHARICA
BT1 fritillaria
BT2 liliaceae
BT1 ornamental bulbs

FRITILLARIA CAMSCHATCENSIS
BT1 fritillaria
BT2 liliaceae
BT1 ornamental bulbs

FRITILLARIA EDUARDII
BT1 fritillaria
BT2 liliaceae

FRITILLARIA IMPERIALIS
BT1 fritillaria
BT2 liliaceae
BT1 ornamental bulbs

FRITILLARIA MELEAGRIS
BT1 fritillaria
BT2 liliaceae
BT1 ornamental bulbs

FRITILLARIA PALLIDIFLORA
BT1 fritillaria
BT2 liliaceae
BT1 ornamental bulbs

FRITILLARIA PERSICA
BT1 fritillaria
BT2 liliaceae
BT1 ornamental bulbs

FRITILLARIA ROYLEI
BT1 fritillaria
BT2 liliaceae
BT1 ornamental bulbs

FRITILLARIA SEVERTZOVII
BT1 fritillaria
BT2 liliaceae
BT1 ornamental bulbs

FRITS
BT1 fertilizer carriers
BT2 carriers

FRIULI-VENEZIA GIULIA
BT1 italy
BT2 western europe
BT3 europe

FROG CULTURE
BT1 aquaculture
BT2 enterprises
rt frogs

FROG MEAL
BT1 meal
rt frogs

FROGS
BT1 aquatic animals
BT2 animals
BT2 aquatic organisms
rt amphibia
rt anura
rt frog culture
rt frog meal
rt meat animals
rt spawning

FRONT END LOADERS
uf *loaders, front end*
BT1 loaders
BT2 handling machinery
BT3 machinery
rt rear loaders

FRONT MOUNTING
rt mounted implements

FRONTALIN
BT1 aggregation pheromones
BT2 pheromones
BT3 semiochemicals
rt dendroctonus frontalis

FRONTIER AREAS
BT1 areas

FRONTOPSYLLA
BT1 leptopsyllidae
BT2 siphonaptera
NT1 frontopsylla frontalis

FRONTOPSYLLA FRONTALIS
BT1 frontopsylla
BT2 leptopsyllidae
BT3 siphonaptera

FROST
BT1 meteorological factors
BT2 climatic factors
rt cold
rt freezing
rt frost heave
rt frost injury
rt frost protection
rt frost resistance
rt frost structures
rt frozen conditions
rt ice
rt patterned ground
rt stress factors
rt winter hardiness

frost damage
USE **frost injury**

FROST HEAVE
BT1 soil movement
rt frost

FROST INJURY
uf *frost damage*
BT1 injuries
rt cold injury

FROST INJURY *cont.*
rt frost
rt frost protection
rt frost resistance
rt frostbite
rt temperature resistance

FROST PROTECTION
BT1 protection
rt cryoprotectants
rt frost
rt frost injury
rt wind machines

FROST RESISTANCE
BT1 resistance
rt cold resistance
rt cold tolerance
rt frost
rt frost injury
rt hardening
rt hardiness
rt susceptibility
rt temperature resistance
rt winter hardiness

FROST STRUCTURES
BT1 soil morphological features
rt frost
rt periglacial features
rt pingos

FROSTBITE
rt frost injury

FROZEN CONDITIONS
BT1 soil thermal regimes
rt climatic factors
rt freezing
rt frost
rt patterned ground
rt permafrost

FROZEN CREAM
uf *cream, frozen*
BT1 cream
BT2 milk products
BT3 products

FROZEN DESSERTS
BT1 desserts
BT2 foods
BT1 frozen foods
BT2 foods

FROZEN FISH
BT1 fish products
BT2 animal products
BT3 products
BT1 frozen foods
BT2 foods
rt fish

FROZEN FOODS
BT1 foods
NT1 frozen desserts
NT1 frozen fish
NT1 frozen fruit
NT1 frozen meat
NT1 frozen vegetables
rt frozen foods industry

FROZEN FOODS INDUSTRY
BT1 food industry
BT2 industry
rt frozen foods

FROZEN FRUIT
BT1 frozen foods
BT2 foods
BT1 fruit products
BT2 plant products
BT3 products
rt fruit

FROZEN LOGS
BT1 logs
BT2 roundwood
BT3 forest products
BT4 products
BT3 wood
rt wood technology

FROZEN MEAT
BT1 frozen foods
BT2 foods
BT1 meat products
BT2 animal products
BT3 products
rt meat

FROZEN MILK
uf *milk, frozen*
BT1 milk products
BT2 products

FROZEN SEMEN
HN from 1990
rt semen

FROZEN STORAGE
BT1 storage
rt cold storage

FROZEN VEGETABLES
BT1 frozen foods
BT2 foods
BT1 vegetable products
BT2 plant products
BT3 products
rt vegetables

FROZEN WOOD
BT1 wood
rt wood technology

FRUCTANS
HN from 1990; previously "fructosans"
uf *fructosans*
BT1 polysaccharides
BT2 carbohydrates
NT1 inulin
NT1 levan

FRUCTIFICATION
BT1 plant development
rt fungi

β-FRUCTOFURANOSIDASE
(ec 3.2.1.26)
(for retrieval spell out "beta")
uf *β-d-fructofuranosidase*
uf *invertase*
uf *sucrase*
BT1 o-glycoside hydrolases
BT2 glycosidases
BT3 hydrolases
BT4 enzymes

β-d-fructofuranosidase
USE **β-fructofuranosidase**

FRUCTOKINASE
(ec 2.7.1.4)
BT1 kinases
BT2 transferases
BT3 enzymes

fructosans
USE **fructans**

FRUCTOSE
uf *laevulose*
uf *levulose*
BT1 hexuloses
BT2 ketoses
BT3 monosaccharides
BT4 carbohydrates
BT3 nonreducing sugars
BT4 sugars
BT5 carbohydrates
rt fructose 6-phosphate
rt fructose intolerance
rt high fructose corn syrup
rt invert sugar
rt syrups

FRUCTOSE-BISPHOSPHATASE
(ec 3.1.3.11)
BT1 phosphoric monoester hydrolases
BT2 esterases
BT3 hydrolases
BT4 enzymes

FRUCTOSE-BISPHOSPHATE ALDOLASE

FRUCTOSE-BISPHOSPHATE ALDOLASE *cont.*
(ec 4.1.2.13)
BT1 aldehyde-lyases
BT2 lyases
BT3 enzymes

FRUCTOSE INTOLERANCE
BT1 carbohydrate metabolism disorders
BT2 metabolic disorders
BT3 animal disorders
BT4 disorders
rt fructose

FRUCTOSE 6-PHOSPHATE
BT1 sugar phosphates
BT2 carbohydrates
BT2 phosphates (esters)
BT3 esters
BT3 phosphates
rt fructose

FRUCTOSE SYRUP
HN from 1990
BT1 syrups
BT2 liquids
rt high fructose corn syrup

FRUIT
BT1 foods
BT1 plant products
BT2 products
rt canned fruit
rt fresh products
rt frozen fruit
rt fruit crops
rt fruit growing
rt fruit products
rt fruits

fruit, canned
USE **canned fruit**

FRUIT CRACKING
BT1 plant disorders
BT2 disorders

FRUIT CROPS
NT1 cucurbit fruits
NT2 coccinia grandis
NT2 melons
NT2 watermelons
NT1 grapes
NT1 subtropical fruits
NT2 subtropical small fruits
NT3 carissa bispinosa
NT3 carissa macrocarpa
NT3 carpobrotus edulis
NT3 opuntia ficus-indica
NT3 passion fruits
NT3 pereskia aculeata
NT3 physalis peruviana
NT3 solanum muricatum
NT3 tamarillos
NT2 subtropical tree fruits
NT3 aegle marmelos
NT3 asimina triloba
NT3 atemoyas
NT3 avocados
NT3 blighia sapida
NT3 carica pentagona
NT3 carobs
NT3 casimiroa edulis
NT3 citrus fruits
NT4 calamondins
NT4 chironjas
NT4 citradias
NT4 citrandarins
NT4 citrangequats
NT4 citranges
NT4 citrangors
NT4 citremons
NT4 citrons
NT4 citrumelos
NT4 clementines
NT4 grapefruits
NT4 kumquats
NT4 lemons
NT4 limes
NT4 mandarins
NT4 natsudaidais
NT4 oranges

FRUIT CROPS *cont.*
NT4 ortaniques
NT4 procimequats
NT4 pummelos
NT4 rough lemons
NT4 satsumas
NT4 sour oranges
NT4 tangelos
NT4 tangors
NT3 clausena lansium
NT3 dates
NT3 diospyros ebenaster
NT3 eugenia dombeyi
NT3 feijoas
NT3 longans
NT3 loquats
NT3 malpighia glabra
NT3 olives
NT3 persimmons
NT3 pomegranates
NT1 temperate fruits
NT2 temperate small fruits
NT3 akebia lobata
NT3 arctostaphylos uva-ursi
NT3 black currants
NT3 blackberries
NT3 boysenberries
NT3 gaylussacia baccata
NT3 gaylussacia dumosa
NT3 gaylussacia frondosa
NT3 gooseberries
NT3 hippophae rhamnoides
NT3 kiwifruits
NT3 loganberries
NT3 raspberries
NT3 red currants
NT3 roses
NT3 rubus allegheniensis
NT3 rubus arcticus
NT3 rubus caesius
NT3 rubus chamaemorus
NT3 rubus phoenicolasius
NT3 strawberries
NT3 tayberries
NT3 vaccinium angustifolium
NT3 vaccinium ashei
NT3 vaccinium corymbosum
NT3 vaccinium darrowii
NT3 vaccinium macrocarpon
NT3 vaccinium myrtillus
NT3 vaccinium oxycoccus
NT3 vaccinium uliginosum
NT3 vaccinium vitis-idaea
NT3 white currants
NT2 temperate tree fruits
NT3 figs
NT3 mulberries
NT3 pome fruits
NT4 apples
NT4 medlars
NT4 pears
NT4 pyrus pyrifolia
NT4 quinces
NT3 sambucus caerulea
NT3 sambucus canadensis
NT3 sambucus nigra
NT3 stone fruits
NT4 apricots
NT4 cherries
NT4 damsons
NT4 nectarines
NT4 peaches
NT4 plums
NT4 prunus spinosa
NT1 tropical fruits
NT2 tropical small fruits
NT3 antidesma bunias
NT3 antidesma dallachryanum
NT3 bananas
NT3 hibiscus sabdariffa
NT3 pineapples
NT3 solanum quitoense
NT2 tropical tree fruits
NT3 annona diversifolia
NT3 annona montana
NT3 annona muricata
NT3 annona purpurea
NT3 annona reticulata
NT3 annona squamosa
NT3 artocarpus integer
NT3 artocarpus utilis

FRUIT CROPS *cont.*
NT3 averrhoa bilimbi
NT3 averrhoa carambola
NT3 bactris gasipaes
NT3 breadfruits
NT3 calocarpum viride
NT3 carica pubescens
NT3 cashews
NT3 cherimoyas
NT3 chrysobalanus icaco
NT3 chrysophyllum cainito
NT3 durians
NT3 eugenia dombeyi
NT3 eugenia malaccensis
NT3 eugenia uniflora
NT3 guavas
NT3 jackfruits
NT3 lansium domesticum
NT3 limonia acidissima
NT3 mammea africana
NT3 mammea americana
NT3 mammea longifolia
NT3 mangoes
NT3 mangosteens
NT3 melicoccus bijugatus
NT3 nephelium mutabile
NT3 pawpaws
NT3 phyllanthus acidus
NT3 pouteria caimito
NT3 pouteria campechiana
NT3 pouteria lucuma
NT3 pouteria sapota
NT3 rambutans
NT3 sandoricum koetjape
NT3 sapodillas
NT3 spondias dulcis
NT3 spondias mombin
NT3 spondias pinnata
NT3 spondias purpurea
NT3 syzygium cumini
NT3 syzygium jambos
NT3 tamarinds
NT3 ziziphus mauritiana
NT3 ziziphus sativa
rt breakdown
rt dessert cultivars
rt fruit
rt fruit graders
rt fruit growing
rt fruit picking aids
rt fruit products
rt fruit trees
rt horticultural crops
rt hulling
rt plants
rt russeting
rt small fruits
rt sunscald
rt tree fruits
rt windfalls
rt woolliness

fruit, dried
USE **dried fruit**

FRUIT DRINKS
BT1 beverages
rt fruit juices
rt fruit products

fruit extracts
USE **fruit juices**

FRUIT GRADERS
uf *graders, fruit*
uf *sorters, fruit*
BT1 graders
rt fruit crops

FRUIT GROWING
BT1 horticulture
BT2 agricultural sciences
rt fruit
rt fruit crops

FRUIT JUICES
uf *fruit extracts*
BT1 fruit products
BT2 plant products
BT3 products
BT1 juices
BT2 liquids
NT1 apple juice

FRUIT JUICES *cont.*
NT1 grape juice
NT2 grape must
NT1 grapefruit juice
NT1 lemon juice
NT1 orange juice
NT1 pineapple juice
rt fruit drinks
rt soft drinks

FRUIT PICKING AIDS
rt fruit crops
rt harvesting
rt picking platforms

FRUIT PRODUCTS
BT1 plant products
BT2 products
NT1 canned fruit
NT1 dried fruit
NT2 prunes
NT2 raisins
NT1 frozen fruit
NT1 fruit juices
NT2 apple juice
NT2 grape juice
NT3 grape must
NT2 grapefruit juice
NT2 lemon juice
NT2 orange juice
NT2 pineapple juice
NT1 fruit pulp
NT2 citrus pulp
NT3 orange pulp
NT2 mango pulp
NT2 olive pulp
NT1 fruit syrups
NT1 grape press cake
NT1 jams
NT2 marmalade
NT1 pomace
NT2 apple pomace
NT2 grape pomace
NT2 tomato pomace
NT1 rose hips
rt food products
rt fruit
rt fruit crops
rt fruit drinks
rt juices

FRUIT PUFFING
BT1 plant disorders
BT2 disorders
rt citrus fruits

FRUIT PULP
BT1 fruit products
BT2 plant products
BT3 products
BT1 pulps
NT1 citrus pulp
NT2 orange pulp
NT1 mango pulp
NT1 olive pulp
rt pomace

FRUIT ROTS
BT1 decay
BT2 decomposition
BT2 deterioration
rt plant diseases

FRUIT STORES
uf *stores, fruit*
BT1 stores
rt cold stores
rt controlled atmosphere stores

FRUIT SYRUPS
BT1 fruit products
BT2 plant products
BT3 products
BT1 syrups
BT2 liquids

FRUIT TREES
BT1 trees
NT1 spur types
rt fruit crops
rt tree fruits

FRUIT VEGETABLES
BT1 vegetables
NT1 aubergines
NT1 cucurbit vegetables
NT2 benincasa hispida
NT2 citrullus colocynthis
NT2 cucumbers
NT2 cucumeropsis edulis
NT2 cucumeropsis mannii
NT2 cucumis anguria
NT2 cucurbita ficifolia
NT2 cucurbita maxima
NT2 cucurbita mixta
NT2 cucurbita moschata
NT2 cucurbita pepo
NT2 lagenaria siceraria
NT2 luffa acutangula
NT2 luffa aegyptiaca
NT2 marrows
NT2 momordica charantia
NT2 momordica cochinchinensis
NT2 momordica dioica
NT2 pumpkins
NT2 sechium edule
NT2 squashes
NT3 winter squash
NT2 trichosanthes cucumerina
NT2 trichosanthes dioica
NT1 okras
NT1 sweetcorn
NT1 tomatoes
NT1 trapa natans
NT1 treculia africana
NT1 vegetable legumes
NT2 cyamopsis tetragonoloba
NT2 peas
NT2 phaseolus acutifolius
NT2 phaseolus coccineus
NT2 phaseolus lunatus
NT2 phaseolus vulgaris
NT2 psophocarpus tetragonolobus
NT2 vicia faba
rt capsicum
rt plants

FRUITING
BT1 plant development
NT1 irregular bearing
NT1 set
NT2 seed set
rt parthenocarpy
rt pollination

fruiting, biennial
USE **irregular bearing**

fruiting, irregular
USE **irregular bearing**

FRUITING POTENTIAL
uf bearing capacity (fruiting)
BT1 reproductive performance
BT2 performance
rt buds

FRUITS
uf berries
BT1 plant
NT1 pericarp
NT2 mesocarp
NT1 seeds
NT2 testas
rt bolls
rt burrs
rt dehiscence
rt fruit
rt hulls
rt naked grain
rt nuts
rt parthenocarpy
rt pods
rt ripening
rt rose hips
rt russeting
rt set
rt windfalls

FRY
HN from 1989
BT1 young animals
BT2 animals
rt fishes

FRYING
BT1 cooking methods (agricola)
BT2 methodology
NT1 deep fat frying (agricola)
NT1 stir frying (agricola)
rt fried foods (agricola)

FSH
uf follicle stimulating hormone
uf follitropin
BT1 pituitary gonadotropins
BT2 gonadotropins
BT3 glycoproteins
BT4 proteins
BT5 peptides
BT3 sex hormones
BT4 hormones
BT2 pituitary hormones
BT3 hormones
rt fshrh
rt gonadotropin release

fsh releasing hormone
USE **fshrh**

FSHRH
uf folliberin
uf fsh releasing hormone
BT1 hypothalamic releasing hormones
BT2 hormones
rt fsh

FUBERIDAZOLE
BT1 benzimidazole fungicides
BT2 fungicides
BT3 pesticides

FUCHSIA
BT1 onagraceae
NT1 fuchsia excorticata

FUCHSIA EXCORTICATA
BT1 fuchsia
BT2 onagraceae

FUCOSE
BT1 deoxysugars
BT2 sugars
BT3 carbohydrates
BT1 hexoses
BT2 aldoses
BT3 monosaccharides
BT4 carbohydrates
BT3 reducing sugars
BT4 sugars
BT5 carbohydrates

FUEL APPRAISALS (AGRICOLA)
HN from 1989
rt forest fires
rt fuels

FUEL CONSUMPTION
BT1 consumption
NT1 specific fuel consumption
rt energy consumption
rt engines
rt fires
rt fuels
rt heat
rt power requirement

fuel consumption, specific
USE **specific fuel consumption**

FUEL CROPS
rt biomass
rt crops
rt fuel plantations
rt industrial crops
rt plants
rt sugar

FUEL INJECTION
rt diesel engines
rt fuels
rt internal combustion engines

FUEL OILS
BT1 mineral oils
BT2 oils
NT1 diesel oil
NT1 petroleum

FUEL OILS *cont.*
rt oil refinery wastes

FUEL PLANTATIONS
HN from 1989
BT1 plantations
rt fuel crops
rt fuelwood

fuel resources
USE **fuels**

FUEL TANKS
uf tanks, fuel
BT1 stores
BT1 tanks
BT2 containers
rt fuels

fuelbreaks
USE **firebreaks**

FUELS
uf fuel resources
NT1 benzene
NT1 charcoal
NT1 coal
NT2 brown coal
NT1 coke
NT1 ethane
NT1 fuelwood
NT1 kerosene
NT1 lignite
NT1 liquid petroleum gas
NT1 metaldehyde
NT1 natural gas
NT2 biogas
NT1 peat
NT1 producer gas
NT1 town gas
NT1 wood gas
rt biomass
rt briquettes
rt briquetting
rt burners
rt crop residues
rt electricity
rt energy sources
rt farm inputs
rt fuel appraisals (agricola)
rt fuel consumption
rt fuel injection
rt fuel tanks
rt methane
rt methanol
rt power
rt specific fuel consumption
rt waste utilization
rt wood chemical industry

FUELWOOD
uf firewood
BT1 cordwood
BT2 roundwood
BT3 forest products
BT4 products
BT3 wood
BT1 fuels
rt fuel plantations

fugus
USE **tetraodontidae**

FUIRENA
BT1 cyperaceae
NT1 fuirena ciliaris
NT1 fuirena pubescens

FUIRENA CILIARIS
BT1 fuirena
BT2 cyperaceae

FUIRENA PUBESCENS
BT1 fuirena
BT2 cyperaceae

FUJAIRAH
BT1 united arab emirates
BT2 persian gulf states
BT3 west asia
BT4 asia

FUJIAN
uf china (fukien)

FUJIAN *cont.*
uf fukien
BT1 china
BT2 east asia
BT3 asia

fukien
USE **fujian**

FULANI
BT1 sheep breeds
BT2 breeds

FULGOROIDEA
BT1 auchenorrhyncha
BT2 homoptera
NT1 cixiidae
NT2 myndus
NT3 myndus crudus
NT1 delphacidae
NT2 delphacodes
NT2 javesella
NT3 javesella pellucida
NT2 laodelphax
NT3 laodelphax striatella
NT2 nilaparvata
NT3 nilaparvata bakeri
NT3 nilaparvata lugens
NT2 peregrinus
NT3 peregrinus maidis
NT2 perkinsiella
NT3 perkinsiella saccharicida
NT2 sogata
NT2 sogatella
NT3 sogatella furcifera
NT2 sogatodes
NT3 sogatodes cubanus
NT3 sogatodes orizicola
NT2 toya
NT3 toya propinqua
NT1 lophopidae
NT2 pyrilla
NT3 pyrilla perpusilla
NT1 tettigometridae
NT2 hilda
NT3 hilda patruelis
NT1 tropiduchidae
NT2 numicia
NT3 numicia viridis

FULICA
BT1 rallidae
BT2 gruiformes
BT3 birds
NT1 fulica americana
NT1 fulica atra

FULICA AMERICANA
BT1 fulica
BT2 rallidae
BT3 gruiformes
BT4 birds

FULICA ATRA
BT1 fulica
BT2 rallidae
BT3 gruiformes
BT4 birds

FULL TIME FARMING
BT1 farming

FULMARUS
BT1 procellariidae
BT2 procellariiformes
BT3 birds

FULVIA
BT1 deuteromycotina
NT1 fulvia fulva

FULVIA FULVA
uf cladosporium fulvum
BT1 fulvia
BT2 deuteromycotina

FULVIC ACIDS
BT1 humus
BT2 soil organic matter
BT3 organic matter
BT3 soil chemistry
BT1 organic acids
BT2 acids
rt pigments

FUMAGILLIN
BT1 antibiotics
BT1 antiprotozoal agents
BT2 antiparasitic agents
BT3 drugs
rt honeybees

FUMARIA
BT1 fumariaceae
NT1 fumaria hygrometrica
NT1 fumaria indica
NT1 fumaria kralikii
NT1 fumaria muralis
NT1 fumaria officinalis
NT1 fumaria parviflora
NT1 fumaria vaillentii

FUMARIA HYGROMETRICA
BT1 fumaria
BT2 fumariaceae

FUMARIA INDICA
BT1 fumaria
BT2 fumariaceae

FUMARIA KRALIKII
BT1 fumaria
BT2 fumariaceae

FUMARIA MURALIS
BT1 fumaria
BT2 fumariaceae

FUMARIA OFFICINALIS
BT1 antiviral plants
BT1 fumaria
BT2 fumariaceae
BT1 weeds

FUMARIA PARVIFLORA
BT1 fumaria
BT2 fumariaceae
BT1 medicinal plants

FUMARIA VAILLENTII
BT1 fumaria
BT2 fumariaceae

FUMARIACEAE
NT1 corydalis
NT2 corydalis cava
NT2 corydalis gigantea
NT2 corydalis govaniana
NT2 corydalis incisa
NT2 corydalis ledebouriana
NT2 corydalis lutea
NT2 corydalis marschalliana
NT2 corydalis ochotensis
NT2 corydalis ophiocarpa
NT2 corydalis remota
NT2 corydalis rosea
NT2 corydalis solida
NT2 corydalis vaginans
NT1 dicentra
NT2 dicentra spectabilis
NT1 fumaria
NT2 fumaria hygrometrica
NT2 fumaria indica
NT2 fumaria kralikii
NT2 fumaria muralis
NT2 fumaria officinalis
NT2 fumaria parviflora
NT2 fumaria vaillentii

FUMARIC ACID
BT1 acidulants
BT2 food additives
BT3 additives
BT1 antioxidants
BT2 additives
BT1 dicarboxylic acids
BT2 carboxylic acids
BT3 organic acids
BT4 acids

FUMARYLACETOACETASE
(ec 3.7.1.2)
BT1 hydrolases
BT2 enzymes

FUME FADING RESISTANT FINISHES (AGRICOLA)
BT1 textile finishes (agricola)
BT2 finishes

FUMES
uf gases and fumes
NT1 factory fumes
NT1 volcanic fumes
rt gases
rt smoke
rt wood smoke

FUMIGANT INSECTICIDES
BT1 fumigants
BT2 pesticides
BT1 insecticides
BT2 pesticides
NT1 para-dichlorobenzene
NT1 acetaldehyde
NT1 carbon disulfide
NT1 carbon tetrachloride
NT1 ethyl formate
NT1 ethylene dibromide
NT1 ethylene dichloride
NT1 hydrogen cyanide
NT1 methyl bromide
NT1 methylene chloride
NT1 phosphine
NT1 sulfuryl fluoride

FUMIGANTS
BT1 pesticides
NT1 fumigant insecticides
NT2 para-dichlorobenzene
NT2 acetaldehyde
NT2 carbon disulfide
NT2 carbon tetrachloride
NT2 ethyl formate
NT2 ethylene dibromide
NT2 ethylene dichloride
NT2 hydrogen cyanide
NT2 methyl bromide
NT2 methylene chloride
NT2 phosphine
NT2 sulfuryl fluoride
NT1 soil fumigants
NT2 1,2-dichloropropane
NT2 1,3-dichloropropene
NT2 carbon disulfide
NT2 chloropicrin
NT2 dazomet
NT2 dbcp
NT2 ethylene dibromide
NT2 formaldehyde
NT2 metham
NT2 methyl bromide
NT2 methyl isothiocyanate
NT2 propylene oxide
rt fumigation
rt fumigation equipment
rt gases
rt smokes
rt wood preservatives

FUMIGATION
BT1 application methods
BT2 methodology
NT1 soil fumigation
rt disinfection
rt fumigants
rt fumigation equipment

FUMIGATION EQUIPMENT
BT1 application equipment
BT2 equipment
rt fumigants
rt fumigation

fumigation, soil
USE **soil fumigation**

FUMITREMORGINS
HN from 1989
BT1 mycotoxins
BT2 toxins

FUNAMBULUS
BT1 sciuridae
BT2 rodents
BT3 mammals
NT1 funambulus palmarum

FUNAMBULUS PALMARUM
BT1 funambulus
BT2 sciuridae
BT3 rodents
BT4 mammals

FUNCTIONAL CLOTHING (AGRICOLA)
BT1 clothing
rt working clothing

FUNCTIONAL DISORDERS
(of animals and man)
uf physiological disorders
BT1 animal disorders
BT2 disorders
NT1 behavior disorders (agricola)
NT1 circulatory disorders
NT2 vasoconstriction
NT1 collapse
NT1 digestive disorders
NT2 appetite disorders
NT3 anorexia
NT4 anorexia nervosa
NT3 bulimia
NT3 bulimia nervosa (agricola)
NT3 compulsive eating (agricola)
NT3 geophagia
NT3 pica
NT2 bloat
NT2 chinese restaurant syndrome
NT2 colic
NT2 constipation
NT2 diarrhoea
NT3 giardiasis
NT2 dyspepsia
NT2 flatus
NT2 gizzard erosion
NT2 grass sickness
NT2 hyperacidity (agricola)
NT2 malabsorption
NT2 milk intolerance
NT2 obstruction
NT3 cholestasis
NT3 intestinal obstruction
NT4 duodenal obstruction
NT4 intussusception
NT2 phytobezoariasis
NT2 sialuria
NT2 vomiting
NT3 hyperemesis gravidarum
NT3 nausea
NT1 dysregulation
NT2 coma
NT3 diabetic coma
NT2 convulsions
NT2 spasms
NT2 spastic paresis
NT2 tremor
NT3 congenital tremor
NT1 equilibrium disorders
NT1 fever
NT1 mental disorders
NT2 depression
NT2 down's syndrome
NT2 emotional disturbances (agricola)
NT2 mental retardation
NT2 neuroses
NT2 psychoses
NT3 alzheimer's disease
NT3 delusory parasitoses
NT3 schizophrenia
NT1 movement disorders
NT2 ataxia
NT3 cerebellar ataxia
NT2 lameness
NT3 navicular disease
NT2 staggers
NT3 phalaris staggers
NT3 ryegrass staggers
NT2 swayback
NT1 polydipsia
NT1 reproductive disorders
NT2 abortion
NT3 mycotic abortion
NT3 spontaneous abortion (agricola)
NT2 cryptorchidism
NT2 eclampsia
NT2 embryo malpositions
NT2 endometritis
NT2 female infertility
NT3 pseudopregnancy
NT2 male infertility

FUNCTIONAL DISORDERS *cont.*
NT3 impotence
NT3 spermiostasis
NT2 nymphomania
NT2 parturition complications
NT3 dystocia
NT3 uterine torsion
NT2 pregnancy complications
NT3 extrauterine pregnancy
NT3 hydramnios
NT3 preeclampsia
NT2 puerperal disorders
NT3 lactation disorders
NT4 agalactia
NT4 galactorrhoea
NT4 lactation persistency
NT3 parturient paresis
NT3 placental retention
NT3 pregnancy toxaemia
NT2 sex differentiation disorders
NT3 dysgenesis
NT3 intersexuality
NT4 freemartinism
NT4 pseudohermaphroditism
NT3 sex reversal
NT3 testicular feminization
NT1 respiratory disorders
NT2 asphyxia
NT2 asthma
NT2 atelectasis
NT2 cough
NT2 dyspnoea
NT2 hypercapnia
NT2 hypoxia
NT1 sensory disorders
NT2 anosmia
NT2 hearing impairment
NT3 deafness
NT2 vision disorders
NT3 blindness
NT3 night blindness
NT1 urination disorders
NT2 polyuria
NT2 urinary incontinence
rt congenital functional anomalies
rt deficiency diseases
rt hypersecretion

FUNCTIONAL RESPONSES
BT1 feeding behaviour
BT2 behaviour
rt parasitoids
rt predators

fundazol
USE **benomyl**

funding, research
USE **research support**

FUNDS
NT1 eaggf
NT1 european regional development fund
NT1 european social fund
NT1 ifad
NT1 international monetary fund
NT1 mutual funds (agricola)
NT1 reserve funds
NT1 stabilization funds
rt assets
rt development aid
rt financial institutions
rt investment promotion

FUNDULUS
BT1 cyprinodontidae
BT2 cyprinodontiformes
BT3 osteichthyes
BT4 fishes
NT1 fundulus heteroclitus
NT1 fundulus kansae

FUNDULUS HETEROCLITUS
BT1 fundulus
BT2 cyprinodontidae
BT3 cyprinodontiformes
BT4 osteichthyes
BT5 fishes

FUNDULUS KANSAE
BT1 fundulus
BT2 cyprinodontidae
BT3 cyprinodontiformes
BT4 osteichthyes
BT5 fishes

FUNFAIRS
uf fairs
BT1 entertainment
BT2 leisure activities
rt carnivals
rt theme parks

FUNGAL ACARICIDES
BT1 acaricides
BT2 pesticides
BT1 microbial pesticides
BT2 pesticides
NT1 hirsutella thompsonii
rt entomogenous fungi

FUNGAL ANTAGONISTS
BT1 fungicides
BT2 pesticides
BT1 microbial pesticides
BT2 pesticides
NT1 agrobacterium radiobacter
NT1 bacillus subtilis
NT1 gaeumannomyces graminis var. graminis
NT1 gliocladium virens
NT1 pseudomonas fluorescens
NT1 scytalidium lignicola
NT1 talaromyces flavus
NT1 trichoderma hamatum
NT1 trichoderma harzianum
NT1 trichoderma viride
rt antagonists

FUNGAL ANTIGENS
BT1 antigens
BT2 immunological factors
NT1 coccidioidin
NT1 histoplasmin
NT1 spherulin

FUNGAL DISEASES
(for diseases of animals use mycoses)
BT1 plant diseases
NT1 damping off
NT1 ergot
NT1 rust diseases
rt antifungal properties
rt fungi
rt mycoses

FUNGAL INSECTICIDES
BT1 insecticides
BT2 pesticides
BT1 microbial pesticides
BT2 pesticides
NT1 beauveria bassiana
NT1 metarhizium anisopliae
NT1 verticillium lecanii
rt entomogenous fungi

FUNGAL MORPHOLOGY
BT1 morphology
NT1 appressoria
NT1 asci
NT1 basidia
NT1 haustoria
NT1 hyphae
NT1 pycnidia
NT1 sclerotia
NT1 sporangia
rt fungal spores
rt fungi
rt mycelium

FUNGAL PROTEIN
BT1 single cell protein
BT2 protein products
BT3 products
NT1 pekilo protein
rt fungi

FUNGAL SPORES
BT1 spores
BT2 cells
NT1 aeciospores

FUNGAL SPORES *cont.*
NT1 ascospores
NT1 basidiospores
NT1 chlamydospores
NT1 conidia
NT1 oospores
NT1 zoospores
rt fungal morphology

FUNGAL STAINS
uf stains, fungal
BT1 stains
NT1 blue stain
rt fungi
rt stain fungi

fungal toxins
USE **mycotoxins**

FUNGI
(fungal species and genera are listed under orders or deuteromycotina; orders are listed as related terms)
NT1 aquatic fungi
NT1 decay fungi
NT1 edible fungi
NT2 agaricus arvensis
NT2 agaricus bitorquis
NT2 agaricus chionodermus
NT2 agaricus macrocarpus
NT2 agaricus macrosporoides
NT2 agaricus purpurescens
NT2 agaricus silvicola
NT2 agaricus subedulis
NT2 agrocybe aegerita
NT2 auricularia auricula
NT2 boletus edulis
NT2 boletus sublutens
NT2 calocybe indica
NT2 calvatia gigantea
NT2 cantharellus cibarius
NT2 collybia velutipes
NT2 coprinus aratus
NT2 coprinus atramentarius
NT2 coprinus comatus
NT2 coprinus micaceus
NT2 coriolus versicolor
NT2 flammulina velutipes
NT2 helvella esculenta
NT2 kuehneromyces mutabilis
NT2 lactarius chrysorrus
NT2 lactarius rufus
NT2 lactarius sanguifluus
NT2 lactarius torminosus
NT2 lentinula edodes
NT2 lepiota naucina
NT2 lyophyllum decastes
NT2 macrolepiota zeyheri
NT2 morchella crassipes
NT2 morchella esculenta
NT2 mushrooms
NT2 peziza auburounii
NT2 pholiota mutabilis
NT2 pholiota squarrosa
NT2 pleurotus cornucopiae
NT2 pleurotus eous
NT2 pleurotus eryngii
NT2 pleurotus flabellatus
NT2 pleurotus florida
NT2 pleurotus ostreatus
NT2 pleurotus sajor-caju
NT2 pleurotus salignus
NT2 pleurotus sapidus
NT2 pleurotus tuber-regium
NT2 podaxis pistillaris
NT2 schizophyllum commune
NT2 stropharia hornemannii
NT2 stropharia rugoso-annulata
NT2 terfezia calveryi
NT2 terfezia hafizi
NT2 tirmania nivea
NT2 tirmania pinoyi
NT2 tremella fuciformis
NT2 tricholoma matsutake
NT2 tricholoma nudum
NT2 truffles
NT2 volvariella diplasia
NT2 volvariella esculenta
NT2 volvariella speciosa
NT2 volvariella volvacea
NT1 entomogenous fungi

FUNGI *cont.*
NT2 ascosphaera
NT3 ascosphaera apis
NT2 beauveria
NT3 beauveria bassiana
NT3 beauveria brongniartii
NT2 coelomomyces
NT3 coelomomyces indicus
NT3 coelomomyces psorophorae
NT3 coelomomyces stegomyiae
NT2 cordyceps
NT3 cordyceps militaris
NT2 culicinomyces
NT3 culicinomyces clavisporus
NT2 entomophaga
NT3 entomophaga aulicae
NT3 entomophaga grylli
NT2 entomophthora
NT3 entomophthora muscae
NT3 entomophthora planchoniana
NT2 erynia
NT3 erynia aphidis
NT3 erynia conica
NT3 erynia delphacis
NT3 erynia gammae
NT3 erynia neoaphidis
NT3 erynia phalloides
NT3 erynia phytonomi
NT3 erynia radicans
NT2 hirsutella
NT3 hirsutella thompsonii
NT2 lagenidium
NT3 lagenidium giganteum
NT2 massospora
NT2 metarhizium
NT3 metarhizium anisopliae
NT3 metarhizium flavoviride
NT2 neozygites
NT3 neozygites floridana
NT3 neozygites fresenii
NT3 neozygites parvispora
NT2 nomuraea
NT3 nomuraea rileyi
NT2 paecilomyces farinosus
NT2 paecilomyces fumosoroseus
NT2 verticillium lecanii
NT1 hallucinogenic fungi
NT2 amanita muscaria
NT2 psilocybe caerulescens
NT1 keratinophilic fungi
NT1 marine fungi
NT1 mildews
NT2 moulds
NT3 snow moulds
NT3 sooty moulds
NT1 mycorrhizal fungi
NT2 acaulospora
NT3 acaulospora elegans
NT3 acaulospora laevis
NT3 acaulospora spinosa
NT3 acaulospora trappei
NT2 aureobasidium pullulans
NT2 cenococcum geophilum
NT2 gigaspora
NT3 gigaspora calospora
NT3 gigaspora margarita
NT2 glomus
NT3 glomus aggregatum
NT3 glomus caledonium
NT3 glomus clarum
NT3 glomus deserticola
NT3 glomus etunicatum
NT3 glomus fasciculatum
NT3 glomus intraradices
NT3 glomus macrocarpum
NT3 glomus manihotis
NT3 glomus microcarpum
NT3 glomus microsporum
NT3 glomus monosporum
NT3 glomus mosseae
NT3 glomus occultum
NT3 glomus tenue
NT3 glomus tubiforme
NT3 glomus versiforme
NT2 hebeloma crustuliniforme
NT2 pisolithus tinctorius
NT2 thelephora terrestris

FUNGI *cont.*
NT2 tuber aestivum
NT2 tuber albidum
NT2 tuber melanosporum
NT1 nematophagous fungi
NT1 phycomycetes
NT1 phylloplane fungi
NT1 plant pathogenic fungi
NT1 poisonous fungi
NT2 amanita muscaria
NT2 amanita pantherina
NT2 amanita phalloides
NT2 amanita virosa
NT2 gyromitra esculenta
NT2 paxillus involutus
NT1 rhizosphere fungi
NT1 rumen fungi
NT1 seedborne fungi
NT1 soil fungi
NT1 stain fungi
NT1 thermophilic fungi
NT1 toxinogenic fungi
NT1 wood destroying fungi
rt agaricales
rt agonomycetales
rt amoeboaphelidium
rt anastomosis groups
rt antifungal properties
rt aphyllophorales
rt ascomycetes
rt ascosphaerales
rt auriculariales
rt basidiomycetes
rt blastocladiales
rt boletales
rt cantharellales
rt chytridiales
rt clavicipitales
rt culture collections
rt cultures
rt dacrymycetales
rt deuteromycotina
rt diaporthales
rt diatrypales
rt dictyosteliales
rt dothideales
rt endogonales
rt endomycetales
rt entomophthorales
rt erysiphales
rt eurotiales
rt exobasidiales
rt fructification
rt fungal diseases
rt fungal morphology
rt fungal protein
rt fungal stains
rt fungicidal properties
rt fungus control
rt galls
rt gymnoascales
rt helotiales
rt hymenogastrales
rt hypocreales
rt lagenidiales
rt lecanorales
rt lichens
rt lycoperdales
rt microascales
rt microorganisms
rt mucorales
rt mycelium
rt mycology
rt mycotoxicoses
rt mycotoxins
rt ophiostomatales
rt peronosporales
rt pezizales
rt phytoalexins
rt plants
rt plasmodiophorales
rt podaxales
rt polystigmatales
rt pyrenulales
rt rhytismatales
rt root and butt rots
rt saprolegniales
rt sclerodermatales
rt sordariales
rt spawn
rt sphaeriales

FUNGI *cont.*
rt sporidiales
rt sporobolomycetales
rt stipes
rt taphrinales
rt tremellales
rt tuberales
rt tulasnellales
rt uredinales
rt ustilaginales
rt yeasts

fungi imperfecti
USE **deuteromycotina**

FUNGI INCERTAE SEDIS
NT1 loboa
NT2 loboa loboi
NT1 rhinosporidium
NT2 rhinosporidium seeberi

fungicidal plants
USE **antifungal plants**

FUNGICIDAL PROPERTIES
BT1 pesticidal properties
BT2 properties
rt antifungal plants
rt antifungal properties
rt fungi
rt fungicides

fungicide resistance
USE **fungicide tolerance**

FUNGICIDE TOLERANCE
uf *fungicide resistance*
BT1 pesticide resistance
BT2 resistance
rt fungicides

FUNGICIDES
(for therapeutic agents use antifungal agents)
uf *fungistats*
BT1 pesticides
NT1 aliphatic nitrogen fungicides
NT2 butylamine
NT2 cymoxanil
NT2 dodicin
NT2 dodine
NT2 guazatine
NT2 propamocarb
NT2 prothiocarb
NT1 anilide fungicides
NT2 benzanilide fungicides
NT3 benodanil
NT3 flutolanil
NT3 mebenil
NT2 cyprofuram
NT2 furanilide fungicides
NT3 cyclafuramid
NT3 fenfuram
NT3 furcarbanil
NT3 furmecyclox
NT2 ofurace
NT2 oxadixyl
NT2 oxathiin fungicides
NT3 carboxin
NT3 oxycarboxin
NT2 pyracarbolid
NT1 antibiotic fungicides
NT2 aureofungin
NT2 blasticidin-s
NT2 cycloheximide
NT2 griseofulvin
NT2 kasugamycin
NT2 natamycin
NT2 polyoxins
NT2 validamycin
NT1 aromatic fungicides
NT2 2,4,5-trichlorophenol
NT2 chloroneb
NT2 chlorothalonil
NT2 dicloran
NT2 hexachlorobenzene
NT2 nitrothal-isopropyl
NT2 quintozene
NT2 sodium pentachlorophenoxide
NT2 tecnazene
NT1 benzimidazole fungicides
NT2 benomyl

FUNGICIDES *cont.*
NT2 carbendazim
NT2 cypendazole
NT2 fuberidazole
NT2 mecarbinzid
NT2 thiabendazole
NT2 thiophanate
NT2 thiophanate-methyl
NT1 conazole fungicides
NT2 diclobutrazol
NT2 etaconazole
NT2 imazalil
NT2 penconazole
NT2 prochloraz
NT2 propiconazole
NT2 triadimefon
NT2 triadimenol
NT1 copper fungicides
NT2 bordeaux mixture
NT2 burgundy mixture
NT2 cheshunt mixture
NT2 copper carbonate
NT2 copper hydroxide
NT2 copper naphthenate
NT2 copper oxychloride
NT2 copper sulfate
NT2 copper trichlorophenolate
NT2 cufraneb
NT2 cuprobam
NT2 cuprous oxide
NT2 oxine-copper
NT1 dicarboximide fungicides
NT2 captafol
NT2 captan
NT2 folpet
NT2 iprodione
NT2 procymidone
NT2 vinclozolin
NT1 dinitrophenol fungicides
NT2 binapacryl
NT2 dinobuton
NT2 dinocap
NT2 dinocton
NT2 dinopenton
NT2 dinosulfon
NT2 dinoterbon
NT1 dithiocarbamate fungicides
NT2 cufraneb
NT2 cuprobam
NT2 disulfiram
NT2 etem
NT2 ferbam
NT2 mancozeb
NT2 maneb
NT2 metiram
NT2 milneb
NT2 nabam
NT2 polycarbamate
NT2 propineb
NT2 thiram
NT2 zineb
NT2 ziram
NT1 fungal antagonists
NT2 agrobacterium radiobacter
NT2 bacillus subtilis
NT2 gaeumannomyces graminis var. graminis
NT2 gliocladium virens
NT2 pseudomonas fluorescens
NT2 scytalidium lignicola
NT2 talaromyces flavus
NT2 trichoderma hamatum
NT2 trichoderma harzianum
NT2 trichoderma viride
NT1 imidazole fungicides
NT2 fenapanil
NT1 mercury fungicides
NT2 inorganic mercury fungicides
NT3 mercuric chloride
NT3 mercuric oxide
NT2 organomercury fungicides
NT3 2-methoxyethylmercury chloride
NT3 ethylmercury chloride
NT3 ethylmercury phosphate
NT3 methylmercury dicyandiamide
NT3 phenylmercury acetate
NT3 phenylmercury chloride
NT3 phenylmercury nitrate

FUNGICIDES *cont.*
NT3 thiomersal
NT3 tolylmercury acetate
NT1 morpholine fungicides
NT2 dodemorph
NT2 fenpropimorph
NT2 tridemorph
NT1 organophosphorus fungicides
NT2 ditalimfos
NT2 edifenphos
NT2 fosetyl
NT2 hexylthiofos
NT2 iprobenfos
NT2 pyrazophos
NT2 tolclofos-methyl
NT2 triamiphos
NT1 organotin fungicides
NT2 decafentin
NT2 fentin acetate
NT2 fentin chloride
NT2 fentin hydroxide
NT2 tributyltin oxide
NT1 oxazole fungicides
NT2 dichlozoline
NT2 drazoxolon
NT2 hymexazol
NT2 metazoxolon
NT2 myclozolin
NT1 phenylsulfamide fungicides
NT2 dichlofluanid
NT2 tolylfluanid
NT1 pyridine fungicides
NT2 buthiobate
NT2 pyridinitril
NT1 pyrimidine fungicides
NT2 bupirimate
NT2 dimethirimol
NT2 ethirimol
NT2 fenarimol
NT2 nuarimol
NT2 triarimol
NT1 quinoline fungicides
NT2 8-hydroxyquinoline sulfate
NT2 ethoxyquin
NT2 halacrinate
NT2 quinacetol sulfate
NT1 quinone fungicides
NT2 benquinox
NT2 chloranil
NT2 dichlone
NT2 dithianon
NT1 quinoxaline fungicides
NT2 chinomethionat
NT2 chlorquinox
NT2 thioquinox
NT1 thiazole fungicides
NT2 etridiazole
NT2 tcmtb
NT1 triazole fungicides
NT2 bitertanol
NT2 fluotrimazole
NT2 triazbutil
NT1 unclassified fungicides
NT2 2-phenylphenol
NT2 anilazine
NT2 biphenyl
NT2 bithionol
NT2 calcium polysulfide
NT2 chloraniformethan
NT2 chloropicrin
NT2 dazomet
NT2 dehydroacetic acid
NT2 dichlorophen
NT2 diphenylamine
NT2 fenaminosulf
NT2 formaldehyde
NT2 hexachlorobutadiene
NT2 isoprothiolane
NT2 methyl bromide
NT2 methyl isothiocyanate
NT2 pencycuron
NT2 quinazamid
NT2 sodium orthophenylphenoxide
NT2 sulfur
NT2 tricyclazole
NT2 triforine
NT1 xylylalanine fungicides
NT2 benalaxyl
NT2 furalaxyl

FUNGICIDES *cont.*
NT2 metalaxyl
rt antifungal agents
rt antifungal plants
rt antifungal properties
rt fungicidal properties
rt fungicide tolerance
rt fungus control
rt plant disease control
rt seed dressings
rt soil fumigants
rt storage dips

FUNGISTASIS
NT1 soil fungistasis

fungistats
USE **fungicides**

FUNGUS CONTROL
BT1 control
rt disease control
rt fungi
rt fungicides

FUNNEL TRAPS
BT1 insect traps
BT2 traps
BT3 equipment

FUNTUMIA
BT1 apocynaceae
NT1 funtumia elastica

FUNTUMIA ELASTICA
BT1 funtumia
BT2 apocynaceae

FUR
rt coat
rt hair
rt undercoat

FUR FARMING
BT1 livestock farming
BT2 farming
rt furbearing animals
rt furs
rt livestock enterprises

FUR QUALITY
BT1 quality
rt furs

FURALAXYL
BT1 xylylalanine fungicides
BT2 fungicides
BT3 pesticides

FURALTADONE
BT1 antibacterial agents
BT2 antiinfective agents
BT3 drugs
BT1 nitrofurans
BT2 furans
BT3 heterocyclic oxygen compounds

FURANILIDE FUNGICIDES
BT1 anilide fungicides
BT2 fungicides
BT3 pesticides
NT1 cyclafuramid
NT1 fenfuram
NT1 furcarbanil
NT1 furmecyclox

FURANS
BT1 heterocyclic oxygen compounds
NT1 furfural
NT1 hmf
NT1 nitrofurans
NT2 furaltadone
NT2 furazolidone
NT2 nifuroxazide
NT2 nitrofural
NT2 nitrofurantoin
NT2 nitrovin
NT2 thiofuradene

FURAPYRIMIDONE
BT1 anthelmintics
BT2 antiparasitic agents
BT3 drugs

FURATHIOCARB
BT1 carbamate insecticides
BT2 carbamate pesticides
BT2 insecticides
BT3 pesticides

FURAZOLIDONE
BT1 antiprotozoal agents
BT2 antiparasitic agents
BT3 drugs
BT1 nitrofurans
BT2 furans
BT3 heterocyclic oxygen compounds

furbearers
USE **furbearing animals**

FURBEARING ANIMALS
uf *furbearers*
BT1 animals
NT1 alopex lagopus
NT1 castor canadensis
NT1 chinchillas
NT1 foxes
NT1 mink
NT1 nutria
NT1 ocelots
NT1 polecats
NT1 rabbits
NT1 sables
NT1 skunks
rt fur farming
rt furs
rt mammals
rt skin producing animals
rt wool-producing animals

FURCARBANIL
BT1 furanilide fungicides
BT2 anilide fungicides
BT3 fungicides
BT4 pesticides

FURCRAEA
BT1 agavaceae
NT1 furcraea cabuya
NT1 furcraea foetida
NT1 furcraea macrophylla
NT1 furcraea marginata
rt hemp

FURCRAEA CABUYA
BT1 furcraea
BT2 agavaceae

FURCRAEA FOETIDA
uf *furcraea gigantea*
BT1 fibre plants
BT1 furcraea
BT2 agavaceae
BT1 molluscicidal plants
BT2 pesticidal plants

furcraea gigantea
USE **furcraea foetida**

FURCRAEA MACROPHYLLA
BT1 fibre plants
BT1 furcraea
BT2 agavaceae

FURCRAEA MARGINATA
BT1 fibre plants
BT1 furcraea
BT2 agavaceae

FURFURAL
BT1 aldehydes
BT1 furans
BT2 heterocyclic oxygen compounds
BT1 solvents
rt essential oils

FURMECYCLOX
BT1 furanilide fungicides
BT2 anilide fungicides
BT3 fungicides
BT4 pesticides

FURNACES
NT1 kilns

FURNITURE
ufa *furniture making (woodworking)*
rt bentwood
rt equipment/furniture arrangement (agricola)
rt furniture reconditioning (agricola)
rt seats

furniture arrangement
USE **equipment/furniture arrangement (agricola)**

furniture making (woodworking)
USE **furniture**
AND **woodworking**

FURNITURE RECONDITIONING (AGRICOLA)
BT1 reconditioning
NT1 reupholstery (agricola)
rt furniture

FUROSEMIDE
BT1 antihypertensive agents
BT2 cardiovascular agents
BT3 drugs
BT1 diuretics
BT2 drugs
BT1 sulfanilamides
BT2 sulfonamides
BT3 amides
BT4 organic nitrogen compounds
BT3 organic sulfur compounds

FUROVIRUS GROUP
HN from 1990
BT1 plant viruses
BT2 plant pathogens
BT3 pathogens
NT1 peanut clump furovirus
NT1 potato mop top furovirus
NT1 soil-borne wheat mosaic furovirus

FURROW IRRIGATION
uf *irrigation, furrow*
BT1 irrigation
rt surface irrigation

FURROW OPENERS
BT1 implements
rt coulters
rt cultivators
rt direct sowing
rt drills

FURROW PRESSES
BT1 implements
rt cultivators
rt press drills
rt rollers
rt seedbed preparation

FURROWS
rt ploughing

FURS
BT1 animal products
BT2 products
rt fur farming
rt fur quality
rt furbearing animals
rt hides and skins
rt pelts

further education
USE **continuing education**

FURUNCULOSIS
BT1 skin diseases
BT2 organic diseases
BT3 diseases

FURYLOXYFEN
HN from 1990
BT1 nitrophenyl ether herbicides
BT2 herbicides
BT3 pesticides

FUSAEA
BT1 annonaceae
NT1 fusaea longifolia

FUSAEA LONGIFOLIA
BT1 fusaea
BT2 annonaceae

FUSARENON-X
BT1 trichothecenes
BT2 mycotoxins
BT3 toxins

FUSARIC ACID
HN from 1989
BT1 antibiotics
BT1 mycotoxins
BT2 toxins

FUSARINS
HN from 1989
BT1 mycotoxins
BT2 toxins

fusariotoxin
USE **t-2 toxin**

FUSARIUM
BT1 deuteromycotina
NT1 fusarium arthrosporioides
NT1 fusarium chlamydosporum
NT1 fusarium concolor
NT1 fusarium culmorum
NT1 fusarium equiseti
NT1 fusarium oxysporum
NT2 fusarium oxysporum f.sp. apii
NT2 fusarium oxysporum f.sp. cepae
NT2 fusarium oxysporum f.sp. ciceris
NT2 fusarium oxysporum f.sp. cubense
NT2 fusarium oxysporum f.sp. cucumerinum
NT2 fusarium oxysporum f.sp. dianthi
NT2 fusarium oxysporum f.sp. lini
NT2 fusarium oxysporum f.sp. lycopersici
NT2 fusarium oxysporum f.sp. medicaginis
NT2 fusarium oxysporum f.sp. niveum
NT2 fusarium oxysporum f.sp. pisi
NT2 fusarium oxysporum f.sp. vasinfectum
NT2 fusarium oxysporum var. redolens
NT1 fusarium pallidoroseum
NT1 fusarium poae
NT1 fusarium proliferatum
NT1 fusarium roseum
NT1 fusarium solani
NT2 fusarium solani f.sp. coeruleum
NT2 fusarium solani f.sp. phaseoli
NT2 fusarium solani f.sp. pisi
NT2 fusarium solani var. coeruleum
NT1 fusarium sporotrichioides
NT1 fusarium tricinctum
NT1 fusarium udum
rt calonectria
rt gibberella
rt microdochium
rt monographella
rt nectria
rt t-2 toxin
rt trichothecenes
rt vomitoxin

fusarium acuminatum
USE **gibberella acuminata**

FUSARIUM ARTHROSPORIOIDES
BT1 fusarium
BT2 deuteromycotina

fusarium avenaceum
USE **gibberella avenacea**

fusarium bulbigenum
USE **fusarium oxysporum**

FUSARIUM CHLAMYDOSPORUM
uf *fusarium fusarioides*
BT1 fusarium
BT2 deuteromycotina

fusarium coccophilum
USE **nectria flammea**

fusarium coeruleum
USE **fusarium solani var. coeruleum**

FUSARIUM CONCOLOR
BT1 fusarium
BT2 deuteromycotina

FUSARIUM CULMORUM
BT1 fusarium
BT2 deuteromycotina

fusarium decemcellulare
USE **nectria rigidiuscula**

fusarium dimerum
USE **microdochium dimerum**

fusarium effusum
USE **gibberella avenacea**

FUSARIUM EQUISETI
uf *fusarium gibbosum*
BT1 fusarium
BT2 deuteromycotina

fusarium fusarioides
USE **fusarium chlamydosporum**

fusarium gibbosum
USE **fusarium equiseti**

fusarium graminearum
USE **gibberella zeae**

fusarium heterosporium
USE **gibberella gordonii**

fusarium javanicum
USE **fusarium solani**

fusarium lateritium
USE **gibberella baccata**

fusarium martii var. pisi
USE **fusarium solani f.sp. pisi**

fusarium moniliforme
USE **gibberella fujikuroi**

fusarium nivale
USE **monographella nivalis**

fusarium orthoceras
USE **fusarium oxysporum**

FUSARIUM OXYSPORUM
uf *fusarium bulbigenum*
uf *fusarium orthoceras*
BT1 fusarium
BT2 deuteromycotina
NT1 fusarium oxysporum f.sp. apii
NT1 fusarium oxysporum f.sp. cepae
NT1 fusarium oxysporum f.sp. ciceris
NT1 fusarium oxysporum f.sp. cubense
NT1 fusarium oxysporum f.sp. cucumerinum
NT1 fusarium oxysporum f.sp. dianthi
NT1 fusarium oxysporum f.sp. lini
NT1 fusarium oxysporum f.sp. lycopersici
NT1 fusarium oxysporum f.sp. medicaginis
NT1 fusarium oxysporum f.sp. niveum
NT1 fusarium oxysporum f.sp. pisi
NT1 fusarium oxysporum f.sp. vasinfectum
NT1 fusarium oxysporum var. redolens

FUSARIUM OXYSPORUM F.SP. APII
BT1 fusarium oxysporum
BT2 fusarium
BT3 deuteromycotina

FUSARIUM OXYSPORUM F.SP. CEPAE
BT1 fusarium oxysporum
BT2 fusarium
BT3 deuteromycotina

FUSARIUM OXYSPORUM F.SP. CICERIS
BT1 fusarium oxysporum
BT2 fusarium
BT3 deuteromycotina

FUSARIUM OXYSPORUM F.SP. CUBENSE
BT1 fusarium oxysporum
BT2 fusarium
BT3 deuteromycotina

FUSARIUM OXYSPORUM F.SP. CUCUMERINUM
BT1 fusarium oxysporum
BT2 fusarium
BT3 deuteromycotina

FUSARIUM OXYSPORUM F.SP. DIANTHI
BT1 fusarium oxysporum
BT2 fusarium
BT3 deuteromycotina

FUSARIUM OXYSPORUM F.SP. LINI
BT1 fusarium oxysporum
BT2 fusarium
BT3 deuteromycotina

FUSARIUM OXYSPORUM F.SP. LYCOPERSICI
BT1 fusarium oxysporum
BT2 fusarium
BT3 deuteromycotina

FUSARIUM OXYSPORUM F.SP. MEDICAGINIS
BT1 fusarium oxysporum
BT2 fusarium
BT3 deuteromycotina

FUSARIUM OXYSPORUM F.SP. NIVEUM
BT1 fusarium oxysporum
BT2 fusarium
BT3 deuteromycotina

FUSARIUM OXYSPORUM F.SP. PISI
BT1 fusarium oxysporum
BT2 fusarium
BT3 deuteromycotina

fusarium oxysporum f.sp. udum
USE **fusarium udum**

FUSARIUM OXYSPORUM F.SP. VASINFECTUM
BT1 fusarium oxysporum
BT2 fusarium
BT3 deuteromycotina

FUSARIUM OXYSPORUM VAR. REDOLENS
HN from 1990
uf *fusarium redolens*
BT1 fusarium oxysporum
BT2 fusarium
BT3 deuteromycotina

FUSARIUM PALLIDOROSEUM
uf *fusarium semitectum*
BT1 fusarium
BT2 deuteromycotina

FUSARIUM POAE
uf *fusarium tricinctum f.sp. poae*
BT1 fusarium
BT2 deuteromycotina

FUSARIUM PROLIFERATUM
HN from 1990
uf *fusarium proliferatum var. proliferatum*
BT1 fusarium
BT2 deuteromycotina

fusarium proliferatum var. proliferatum
USE **fusarium proliferatum**

fusarium redolens
USE **fusarium oxysporum var. redolens**

fusarium rigidiuscula
USE **nectria rigidiuscula**

FUSARIUM ROSEUM
BT1 fusarium
BT2 deuteromycotina

fusarium sambucinum
USE **gibberella pulicaris**

fusarium semitectum
USE **fusarium pallidoroseum**

FUSARIUM SOLANI
uf *fusarium javanicum*
BT1 fusarium
BT2 deuteromycotina
NT1 fusarium solani f.sp. coeruleum
NT1 fusarium solani f.sp. phaseoli
NT1 fusarium solani f.sp. pisi
NT1 fusarium solani var. coeruleum

FUSARIUM SOLANI F.SP. COERULEUM
BT1 fusarium solani
BT2 fusarium
BT3 deuteromycotina

FUSARIUM SOLANI F.SP. PHASEOLI
BT1 fusarium solani
BT2 fusarium
BT3 deuteromycotina

FUSARIUM SOLANI F.SP. PISI
uf *fusarium martii var. pisi*
BT1 fusarium solani
BT2 fusarium
BT3 deuteromycotina

FUSARIUM SOLANI VAR. COERULEUM
HN from 1990
uf *fusarium coeruleum*
BT1 fusarium solani
BT2 fusarium
BT3 deuteromycotina

fusarium sporotrichiella
USE **fusarium sporotrichioides**

FUSARIUM SPOROTRICHIOIDES
uf *fusarium sporotrichiella*
BT1 fusarium
BT2 deuteromycotina

fusarium stilboides
USE **gibberella stilboides**

fusarium subglutinans
USE **gibberella fujikuroi var. subglutinans**

fusarium sulphureum
USE **gibberella cyanogena**

fusarium tabacinum
USE **microdochium tabacinum**

FUSARIUM TRICINCTUM
BT1 fusarium
BT2 deuteromycotina

fusarium tricinctum f.sp. poae
USE **fusarium poae**

FUSARIUM UDUM
uf *fusarium oxysporum f.sp. udum*
BT1 fusarium
BT2 deuteromycotina

FUSED CALCIUM MAGNESIUM PHOSPHATE
BT1 fused phosphates
BT2 phosphorus fertilizers
BT3 fertilizers

FUSED MAGNESIUM PHOSPHATE
BT1 fused phosphates
BT2 phosphorus fertilizers
BT3 fertilizers

FUSED PHOSPHATES
BT1 phosphorus fertilizers
BT2 fertilizers
NT1 fused calcium magnesium phosphate
NT1 fused magnesium phosphate

FUSICLADIUM
BT1 dothideales
rt spilocaea
rt venturia (dothideales)

fusicladium dentriticum
USE **venturia inaequalis**

fusicladium effusum
USE **cercospora effusa**

fusicladium pyracanthae
USE **spilocaea pyracanthae**

fusicladium radiosum
USE **venturia macularis**

fusicladium saliciperdum
USE **venturia chlorospora**

FUSICOCCIN
BT1 mycotoxins
BT2 toxins
BT1 plant growth regulators
BT2 growth regulators
rt fusicoccum

FUSICOCCUM
BT1 deuteromycotina
rt fusicoccin
rt phomopsis

fusicoccum amygdali
USE **phomopsis amygdali**

fusiformis necrophorus
USE **fusobacterium necrophorum**

fusiformis nodosum
USE **bacteroides nodosus**

FUSOBACTERIUM
BT1 bacteroidaceae
BT2 gracilicutes
BT3 bacteria
BT4 prokaryotes
NT1 fusobacterium necrophorum

FUSOBACTERIUM NECROPHORUM
HN from 1990
uf *fusiformis necrophorus*
uf *sphaerophorus necrophorus*
BT1 fusobacterium
BT2 bacteroidaceae
BT3 gracilicutes
BT4 bacteria
BT5 prokaryotes

FUTURES TRADING
uf *hedging*
BT1 commodity exchanges
BT2 marketing channels
BT3 marketing
rt price stabilization

FUZZ
BT1 plant hairs
BT2 plant
rt cotton

fym
USE **farmyard manure**

FYN
uf *denmark (fyn)*
BT1 denmark
BT2 scandinavia
BT3 europe

FYNBOS
HN from 1989
BT1 savanna woodlands
BT2 woodlands
BT3 vegetation types

ga (plant growth regulator)
USE **gibberellic acid**

ga (symbol)
USE **gallium**

gaba
USE **γ-aminobutyric acid**

GABBRO SOILS
BT1 soil types (lithological)

GABON
BT1 central africa
BT2 africa south of sahara
BT3 africa
rt acp
rt francophone africa
rt opec

GADDI
BT1 goat breeds
BT2 breeds

GADIDAE
BT1 gadiformes
BT2 osteichthyes
BT3 fishes
NT1 boreogadus
NT1 eleginus
NT1 gadus
NT2 gadus aeglefinus
NT1 lota
NT2 lota lota
NT1 melanogrammus
NT1 merlangius
NT1 microgadus
NT1 micromestistius
NT2 micromestistius poutassou
NT1 molva
NT2 molva molva
NT1 pollachius
NT2 pollachius pollachius
NT2 pollachius virens
NT1 trisopterus
NT2 trisopterus minutus
NT1 urophycis
rt cod
rt haddock
rt hake
rt whiting

GADIFORMES
BT1 osteichthyes
BT2 fishes
NT1 gadidae
NT2 boreogadus
NT2 eleginus
NT2 gadus
NT3 gadus aeglefinus
NT2 lota
NT3 lota lota
NT2 melanogrammus
NT2 merlangius
NT2 microgadus
NT2 micromestistius
NT3 micromestistius poutassou
NT2 molva
NT3 molva molva
NT2 pollachius
NT3 pollachius pollachius
NT3 pollachius virens
NT2 trisopterus
NT3 trisopterus minutus
NT2 urophycis
NT1 merlucciidae
NT2 merluccius
NT3 merluccius capensis
NT3 merluccius productus

GADIK
HN from 1990
BT1 sheep breeds
BT2 breeds

GADOLEIC ACID
uf *eicosenoic acid*
BT1 long chain fatty acids
BT2 fatty acids
BT3 carboxylic acids
BT4 organic acids
BT5 acids

GADOLEIC ACID *cont.*
BT3 lipids
BT1 monoenoic fatty acids
BT2 unsaturated fatty acids
BT3 fatty acids
BT4 carboxylic acids
BT5 organic acids
BT6 acids
BT4 lipids

GADUS
BT1 gadidae
BT2 gadiformes
BT3 osteichthyes
BT4 fishes
NT1 gadus aeglefinus
rt micromestistius
rt pollachius
rt trisopterus

GADUS AEGLEFINUS
BT1 gadus
BT2 gadidae
BT3 gadiformes
BT4 osteichthyes
BT5 fishes

gadus merlangus
USE **whiting**

gadus minutus
USE **trisopterus minutus**

gadus morhua
USE **cod**

gadus poutassou
USE **micromestistius poutassou**

gadus virens
USE **pollachius virens**

GAEC
uf *groupements agricoles d'exploitation en commun*
BT1 cooperative farm enterprises
BT2 farm enterprises
BT3 enterprises

GAESISCHIA
BT1 apidae
BT2 hymenoptera

GAEUMANNOMYCES
uf *ophiobolus*
BT1 diaporthales
NT1 gaeumannomyces graminis
NT2 gaeumannomyces graminis var. graminis

GAEUMANNOMYCES GRAMINIS
uf *ophiobolus graminis*
BT1 gaeumannomyces
BT2 diaporthales
NT1 gaeumannomyces graminis var. graminis

GAEUMANNOMYCES GRAMINIS VAR. GRAMINIS
BT1 fungal antagonists
BT2 fungicides
BT3 pesticides
BT2 microbial pesticides
BT3 pesticides
BT1 gaeumannomyces graminis
BT2 gaeumannomyces
BT3 diaporthales

GAIGERIA
BT1 ancylostomatidae
BT2 nematoda
NT1 gaigeria pachyscelis

GAIGERIA PACHYSCELIS
BT1 gaigeria
BT2 ancylostomatidae
BT3 nematoda

GAILLARDIA
BT1 compositae
NT1 gaillardia pulchella

GAILLARDIA PULCHELLA
BT1 gaillardia
BT2 compositae
BT1 ornamental herbaceous plants

GAIT
BT1 locomotion
NT1 trotting
rt exercise
rt steps
rt velocity

GALACTANS
BT1 polysaccharides
BT2 carbohydrates
NT1 agar
NT1 agarose
NT1 carrageenan

GALACTIA
BT1 leguminosae
NT1 galactia striata

GALACTIA STRIATA
BT1 galactia
BT2 leguminosae
BT1 pasture legumes
BT2 legumes
BT2 pasture plants

GALACTITOL
uf *dulcitol*
BT1 alditols
BT2 sugar alcohols
BT3 carbohydrates
BT3 polyols
BT4 alcohols

GALACTOKINASE
(ec 2.7.1.6)
BT1 kinases
BT2 transferases
BT3 enzymes

galactolipids
USE **cerebrosides**

GALACTOMANNANS
BT1 mannans
BT2 polysaccharides
BT3 carbohydrates
NT1 guar gum

GALACTORRHEA
BF galactorrhoea

GALACTORRHOEA
AF galactorrhea
BT1 lactation disorders
BT2 puerperal disorders
BT3 reproductive disorders
BT4 functional disorders
BT5 animal disorders
BT6 disorders

GALACTOSAEMIA
HN from 1989
AF galactosemia
BT1 carbohydrate metabolism disorders
BT2 metabolic disorders
BT3 animal disorders
BT4 disorders
rt galactose

GALACTOSAMINE
BT1 hexosamines
BT2 amino sugars
BT3 amino compounds
BT4 organic nitrogen compounds
BT3 sugars
BT4 carbohydrates

GALACTOSE
BT1 hexoses
BT2 aldoses
BT3 monosaccharides
BT4 carbohydrates
BT3 reducing sugars
BT4 sugars
BT5 carbohydrates
rt galactosaemia

galactose-1-phosphate uridylyltransferase
USE **utp-hexose-1-phosphate uridylyltransferase**

GALACTOSEMIA
HN from 1989
BF galactosaemia

β-d-galactosidase deficiency
USE **lactase deficiency**

α-GALACTOSIDASE
(ec 3.2.1.22)
(for retrieval spell out "alpha")
uf *α-d-galactosidase*
BT1 galactosidases
BT2 o-glycoside hydrolases
BT3 glycosidases
BT4 hydrolases
BT5 enzymes

α-d-galactosidase
USE **α-galactosidase**

β-GALACTOSIDASE
(ec 3.2.1.23)
(for retrieval spell out "beta")
uf *β-d-galactosidase*
uf *lactase*
BT1 galactosidases
BT2 o-glycoside hydrolases
BT3 glycosidases
BT4 hydrolases
BT5 enzymes
rt lactase deficiency

β-d-galactosidase
USE **β-galactosidase**

GALACTOSIDASES
BT1 o-glycoside hydrolases
BT2 glycosidases
BT3 hydrolases
BT4 enzymes
NT1 α-galactosidase
NT1 β-galactosidase

GALACTOSOMUM
BT1 heterophyidae
BT2 digenea
BT3 trematoda

GALACTURONIC ACID
BT1 uronic acids
BT2 sugar acids
BT3 carboxylic acids
BT4 organic acids
BT5 acids
BT3 monosaccharides
BT4 carbohydrates

GALAGO
BT1 lorisidae
BT2 primates
BT3 mammals

GALANTHUS
BT1 amaryllidaceae
NT1 galanthus nivalis

GALANTHUS NIVALIS
BT1 galanthus
BT2 amaryllidaceae
BT1 ornamental bulbs

GALAPAGOS ISLANDS
uf *ecuador (galapagos islands)*
BT1 ecuador
BT2 south america
BT3 america

GALEGA
BT1 leguminosae
NT1 galega officinalis

GALEGA OFFICINALIS
BT1 galega
BT2 leguminosae
BT1 poisonous plants

galeichthys
USE **arius**

galendromus
USE **typhlodromus**

GALENIA
BT1 aizoaceae
NT1 galenia pubescens

GALENIA PUBESCENS
BT1 galenia
BT2 aizoaceae

GALEOPSIS
BT1 labiatae
NT1 galeopsis angustifolia
NT1 galeopsis ladanum
NT1 galeopsis segetum
NT1 galeopsis speciosa
NT1 galeopsis tetrahit

GALEOPSIS ANGUSTIFOLIA
BT1 galeopsis
BT2 labiatae
BT1 medicinal plants

GALEOPSIS LADANUM
BT1 galeopsis
BT2 labiatae

galeopsis ochroleuca
USE **galeopsis segetum**

GALEOPSIS SEGETUM
uf *galeopsis ochroleuca*
BT1 galeopsis
BT2 labiatae
BT1 medicinal plants

GALEOPSIS SPECIOSA
BT1 galeopsis
BT2 labiatae

GALEOPSIS TETRAHIT
BT1 galeopsis
BT2 labiatae

GALEORHINUS
BT1 carcharhinidae
BT2 lamniformes
BT3 chondrichthyes
BT4 fishes

GALERUCA
BT1 chrysomelidae
BT2 coleoptera

GALERUCELLA
BT1 chrysomelidae
BT2 coleoptera

GALEUS
BT1 scyliorhinidae
BT2 lamniformes
BT3 chondrichthyes
BT4 fishes

GALICIAN
HN from 1990
BT1 sheep breeds
BT2 breeds

GALICIAN BLOND
BT1 cattle breeds
BT2 breeds

GALINSOGA
BT1 compositae
NT1 galinsoga ciliata
NT1 galinsoga parviflora
NT1 galinsoga quadriradiata
rt galinsoga mosaic carmovirus

GALINSOGA CILIATA
BT1 galinsoga
BT2 compositae
BT1 weeds

GALINSOGA MOSAIC CARMOVIRUS
HN from 1990
BT1 carmovirus group
BT2 plant viruses
BT3 plant pathogens
BT4 pathogens
rt galinsoga

GALINSOGA PARVIFLORA
BT1 galinsoga
BT2 compositae
BT1 weeds

GALINSOGA QUADRIRADIATA
BT1 galinsoga
BT2 compositae

GALIUM
BT1 rubiaceae
NT1 galium aparine
NT1 galium boreale
NT1 galium hercynicum
NT1 galium mollugo
NT1 galium odoratum
NT1 galium saxatile
NT1 galium spurium
NT1 galium verum

GALIUM APARINE
BT1 galium
BT2 rubiaceae
BT1 weeds

GALIUM BOREALE
BT1 galium
BT2 rubiaceae

GALIUM HERCYNICUM
BT1 galium
BT2 rubiaceae

GALIUM MOLLUGO
BT1 galium
BT2 rubiaceae

GALIUM ODORATUM
BT1 galium
BT2 rubiaceae

GALIUM SAXATILE
BT1 galium
BT2 rubiaceae

GALIUM SPURIUM
BT1 galium
BT2 rubiaceae

GALIUM VERUM
BT1 galium
BT2 rubiaceae

gall
USE **bile**

GALL BLADDER
BT1 liver
BT2 digestive system
BT3 body parts
rt bile ducts
rt cholecystectomy
rt gall bladder diseases

GALL BLADDER DISEASES
BT1 digestive system diseases
BT2 organic diseases
BT3 diseases
NT1 cholecystitis
NT1 cholelithiasis
rt cholestasis
rt gall bladder

gall bladder removal
USE **cholecystectomy**

GALLACANTHUS
BT1 menoponidae
BT2 amblycera
BT3 mallophaga
BT4 phthiraptera
NT1 gallacanthus cornutus
rt menacanthus

GALLACANTHUS CORNUTUS
uf *menacanthus cornutus*
BT1 gallacanthus
BT2 menoponidae
BT3 amblycera
BT4 mallophaga
BT5 phthiraptera

GALLAMINE TRIETHIODIDE
BT1 muscle relaxants
BT2 neurotropic drugs

GALLAMINE TRIETHIODIDE *cont.*
BT3 drugs
BT1 quaternary ammonium compounds
BT2 ammonium compounds
BT2 organic nitrogen compounds

GALLERIA
BT1 pyralidae
BT2 lepidoptera
NT1 galleria mellonella

GALLERIA MELLONELLA
uf *wax moths*
BT1 galleria
BT2 pyralidae
BT3 lepidoptera

GALLIC ACID
BT1 phenolic acids
BT2 benzoic acids
BT3 aromatic acids
BT4 aromatic compounds
BT4 organic acids
BT5 acids
BT2 phenolic compounds
BT3 aromatic compounds
rt propyl gallate

GALLIFORMES
BT1 birds
NT1 cracidae
NT1 megapodiidae
NT1 opisthocomidae
NT2 opisthocomus
NT3 opisthocomus hoatzin
NT1 phasianidae
NT2 alectoris
NT3 alectoris chukar
NT3 alectoris graeca
NT3 alectoris rufa
NT2 colinus
NT3 colinus virginianus
NT2 coturnix
NT2 francolinus
NT2 gallus
NT3 gallus gallus
NT4 gallus gallus spadiceus
NT2 lagopus
NT3 lagopus lagopus
NT4 lagopus lagopus scoticus
NT3 lagopus mutus
NT2 lophortyx
NT3 lophortyx californica
NT3 lophortyx gambelii
NT2 meleagris
NT2 numida
NT2 pavo
NT2 perdix
NT3 perdix perdix
NT2 phasianus
NT3 phasianus colchicus
NT2 tetrao
NT3 tetrao tetrix
NT3 tetrao urogallus
rt fowls
rt game birds
rt guineafowls

GALLINAGO
uf *snipes*
BT1 scolopacidae
BT2 charadriiformes
BT3 birds

GALLINULA
BT1 rallidae
BT2 gruiformes
BT3 birds
NT1 gallinula chloropus

GALLINULA CHLOROPUS
BT1 gallinula
BT2 rallidae
BT3 gruiformes
BT4 birds

GALLIONELLA
BT1 caulobacteraceae
BT2 gracilicutes
BT3 bacteria

GALLIONELLA *cont.*
BT4 prokaryotes

GALLIUM
uf *ga (symbol)*
BT1 metallic elements
BT2 elements
BT2 metals

GALLOWAY
BT1 cattle breeds
BT2 breeds

GALLS
BT1 plant disorders
BT2 disorders
NT1 crown gall
NT1 witches' brooms
NT2 sweet potato witches' broom
rt cankers
rt fungi
rt pests

gallstones
USE **biliary calculi**

GALLUS
BT1 phasianidae
BT2 galliformes
BT3 birds
NT1 gallus gallus
NT2 gallus gallus spadiceus
rt jungle fowls

GALLUS GALLUS
BT1 gallus
BT2 phasianidae
BT3 galliformes
BT4 birds
NT1 gallus gallus spadiceus

gallus gallus domesticus
USE **fowls**

GALLUS GALLUS SPADICEUS
BT1 gallus gallus
BT2 gallus
BT3 phasianidae
BT4 galliformes
BT5 birds

GALPHIMIA
BT1 malpighiaceae

GALVANIZED IRON
uf *iron, galvanized*
BT1 building materials
BT2 materials
rt coatings
rt galvanizing
rt iron
rt zinc

GALVANIZING
BT1 coatings
rt electrolysis
rt galvanized iron
rt iron
rt zinc

GALWAY
BT1 sheep breeds
BT2 breeds

GAMASELLUS
BT1 rhodacaridae
BT2 mesostigmata
BT3 acari
NT1 gamasellus racovitzai

GAMASELLUS RACOVITZAI
BT1 gamasellus
BT2 rhodacaridae
BT3 mesostigmata
BT4 acari

gamasida
USE **mesostigmata**

GAMBIA
uf *the gambia*
BT1 west africa
BT2 africa south of sahara
BT3 africa

GAMBIA *cont.*
rt acp
rt anglophone africa
rt commonwealth of nations
rt developing countries
rt least developed countries

GAMBIER ISLANDS
BT1 french polynesia
BT2 polynesia
BT3 oceania

GAMBLING
uf betting
uf gaming
rt addiction
rt amusement machines
rt bingo
rt card games
rt casinos
rt entertainment
rt game theory
rt games
rt horse racing
rt risk

gambling machines
USE **amusement machines**

GAMBUSIA
BT1 poeciliidae
BT2 cyprinodontiformes
BT3 osteichthyes
BT4 fishes
NT1 gambusia affinis

GAMBUSIA AFFINIS
BT1 gambusia
BT2 poeciliidae
BT3 cyprinodontiformes
BT4 osteichthyes
BT5 fishes

GAME ANIMALS
uf game mammals
BT1 animals
NT1 game birds
NT2 grouse
NT2 partridges
NT2 pheasants
rt antelopes
rt game fishes
rt game meat

GAME BIRDS
uf birds, game
BT1 game animals
BT2 animals
NT1 grouse
NT1 partridges
NT1 pheasants
rt aviculture
rt birds
rt galliformes
rt game meat
rt waterfowl

GAME FARMING
uf game ranching
BT1 livestock farming
BT2 farming
NT1 deer farming
rt hunting

GAME FISHES
BT1 aquatic animals
BT2 animals
BT2 aquatic organisms
NT1 trout
rt angling
rt fishes
rt game animals

game mammals
USE **game animals**

GAME MEAT
BT1 meat
BT2 animal products
BT3 products
BT2 foods
rt game animals
rt game birds

game ranching
USE **game farming**

GAME RESERVES
uf reserves
rt hunting
rt nature reserves

GAME THEORY
rt gambling
rt statistical analysis
rt theory

GAMES
NT1 ball games
NT2 badminton
NT2 baseball
NT2 basketball
NT2 bowling
NT2 cricket
NT2 croquet
NT2 football
NT3 american football
NT3 australian football
NT3 soccer
NT2 golf
NT2 handball
NT2 hockey
NT2 rugby
NT2 squash rackets
NT2 tennis
NT1 children's games
NT1 educational games (agricola)
NT1 indoor games
NT2 bingo
NT2 board games
NT2 card games
NT2 computer games
NT2 darts
NT1 management games
NT1 outdoor games
NT1 puzzles (agricola)
rt gambling
rt indoor recreation
rt leisure activities
rt play

games, children's
USE **children's games**

GAMETES
NT1 ova
NT2 cumulus oophorus
NT2 helminth ova
NT2 oocytes
NT3 germinal vesicle
NT2 oogonia
NT2 zona pellucida
NT1 spermatozoa
NT2 accessory spermatozoa
NT2 acrosome
NT2 midpiece
NT1 unreduced gametes
rt embryo sac
rt gametogenesis
rt germ cells
rt megasporogenesis
rt meiosis
rt oogenesis
rt pollen
rt pollen tubes
rt sexual reproduction
rt zygotes

GAMETIC MODELS
HN from 1990
BT1 models
rt population genetics

GAMETOCIDES
uf chemical hybridizing agents
BT1 plant growth regulators
BT2 growth regulators
NT1 2,3-dichloroisobutyric acid
NT1 maleic hydrazide

GAMETOGENESIS
BT1 sexual reproduction
BT2 reproduction
NT1 oogenesis
NT2 vitellogenesis
NT1 spermatogenesis
NT2 spermiation

GAMETOGENESIS *cont.*
rt gametes
rt ova
rt pollen
rt spermatozoa

gaming
USE **gambling**

GAMMA-AMINOBUTYRIC ACID
(sorted under aminobutyric acid)

GAMMA ATTENUATION
BT1 analytical methods
BT2 methodology
rt gamma radiation

GAMMA-CARBOXYGLUTAMIC ACID
(sorted under carboxyglutamic acid)

GAMMA-CASEIN
(sorted under casein)

GAMMA-GLUTAMYL HYDROLASE
(sorted under glutamyl hydrolase)

GAMMA-GLUTAMYLCYCLOTRANSFERASE
(sorted under glutamylcyclotransferase)

GAMMA-GLUTAMYLCYSTEINE
(sorted under glutamylcysteine)

GAMMA-GLUTAMYLTRANSFERASE
(sorted under glutamyltransferase)

GAMMA-HYDROXYORNITHINE
(sorted under hydroxyornithine)

GAMMA RADIATION
uf gamma rays
uf radiation, gamma
BT1 electromagnetic radiation
BT2 radiation
rt gamma attenuation
rt gamma spectrometry

gamma rays
USE **gamma radiation**

GAMMA SPECTROMETRY
uf gamma spectroscopy
uf spectrometry, gamma
BT1 spectrometry
BT2 techniques
rt gamma radiation

gamma spectroscopy
USE **gamma spectrometry**

GAMMARUS
BT1 amphipoda
BT2 malacostraca
BT3 crustacea
BT4 arthropods
NT1 gammarus fossarum
NT1 gammarus oceanicus
NT1 gammarus pulex

GAMMARUS FOSSARUM
BT1 gammarus
BT2 amphipoda
BT3 malacostraca
BT4 crustacea
BT5 arthropods

GAMMARUS OCEANICUS
BT1 gammarus
BT2 amphipoda
BT3 malacostraca
BT4 crustacea
BT5 arthropods

GAMMARUS PULEX
BT1 gammarus
BT2 amphipoda
BT3 malacostraca
BT4 crustacea
BT5 arthropods

GAMMELOST CHEESE
HN from 1989

GAMMELOST CHEESE *cont.*
BT1 cheeses
BT2 milk products
BT3 products

GAMOLEPIS
BT1 compositae
NT1 gamolepis chrysanthemoides

GAMOLEPIS CHRYSANTHEMOIDES
BT1 gamolepis
BT2 compositae
BT1 ornamental herbaceous plants

GANASPIS
BT1 eucoilidae
BT2 hymenoptera
rt leptopilina

ganaspis subnuda
USE **leptopilina heterotoma**

GANGLIA
BT1 nerve cells
BT2 cells

ganglionic blockaders
USE **parasympatholytics**

GANGLIOSIDES
BT1 glycosphingolipids
BT2 glycolipids
BT3 lipids
BT2 sphingolipids
BT3 lipids

GANGLIOSIDOSIS
BT1 sphingolipidosis
BT2 lipidosis
BT3 lipid metabolism disorders
BT4 metabolic disorders
BT5 animal disorders
BT6 disorders

gangrene
USE **necrosis**

GANGS
BT1 work teams
BT2 teams

gannets
USE **sulidae**

GANODERMA
BT1 aphyllophorales
NT1 ganoderma applanatum
NT1 ganoderma lucidum
NT1 ganoderma philippii
rt fomes

GANODERMA APPLANATUM
uf fomes applanatus
BT1 ganoderma
BT2 aphyllophorales

GANODERMA LUCIDUM
uf fomes lucidus
BT1 ganoderma
BT2 aphyllophorales

GANODERMA PHILIPPII
uf ganoderma pseudoferreum
BT1 ganoderma
BT2 aphyllophorales

ganoderma pseudoferreum
USE **ganoderma philippii**

GANSU
uf china (kansu)
uf kansu
BT1 china
BT2 east asia
BT3 asia

GANSU ALPINE FINEWOOL
HN from 1990
BT1 sheep breeds
BT2 breeds

GANTRIES
BT1 farm machinery

GANTRIES *cont.*
BT2 machinery
rt conveyors
rt implement carriers
rt picking platforms
rt self propelled machines
rt traffic lanes

GANYMEDES
BT1 apicomplexa
BT2 protozoa
NT1 ganymedes anaspidis

GANYMEDES ANASPIDIS
BT1 ganymedes
BT2 apicomplexa
BT3 protozoa

GAOLAO
BT1 cattle breeds
BT2 breeds

GAP JUNCTIONS
HN from 1990
BT1 nerve tissue
BT2 animal tissues
BT3 tissues

gappers
USE **thinners**

GARAGES
BT1 buildings
rt maintenance
rt vehicles
rt workshops

garbage
USE **kitchen waste**
OR **refuse**
OR **wastes**

GARBAGE DISPOSALS (AGRICOLA)
BT1 household equipment (agricola)
BT2 equipment

GARBAGE DUMPS
HN from 1990
BF refuse tips

GARCINIA
BT1 guttiferae
NT1 garcinia afzelii
NT1 garcinia cambogia
NT1 garcinia epunctata
NT1 garcinia hanburyi
NT1 garcinia kola
NT1 garcinia mangostana
NT1 garcinia mannii
NT1 garcinia subelliptica
NT1 garcinia xanthochymus
rt forest trees

GARCINIA AFZELII
BT1 garcinia
BT2 guttiferae

GARCINIA CAMBOGIA
BT1 dye plants
BT1 garcinia
BT2 guttiferae

GARCINIA EPUNCTATA
BT1 garcinia
BT2 guttiferae

GARCINIA HANBURYI
BT1 garcinia
BT2 guttiferae

GARCINIA KOLA
BT1 antibacterial plants
BT1 antifungal plants
BT1 garcinia
BT2 guttiferae
BT1 medicinal plants

GARCINIA MANGOSTANA
BT1 garcinia
BT2 guttiferae
rt mangosteens

GARCINIA MANNII
BT1 garcinia
BT2 guttiferae

GARCINIA SUBELLIPTICA
BT1 garcinia
BT2 guttiferae

GARCINIA XANTHOCHYMUS
BT1 dye plants
BT1 garcinia
BT2 guttiferae

GARDENIA
BT1 rubiaceae
NT1 gardenia gummifera
NT1 gardenia jasminoides
NT1 gardenia lucida

GARDENIA GUMMIFERA
BT1 gardenia
BT2 rubiaceae

GARDENIA JASMINOIDES
BT1 gardenia
BT2 rubiaceae
BT1 ornamental woody plants

GARDENIA LUCIDA
BT1 gardenia
BT2 rubiaceae

GARDENING
BT1 home based leisure
BT2 leisure activities
rt gardens
rt horticulture
rt landscape gardening

GARDENS
NT1 botanical gardens
NT1 domestic gardens
NT2 allotments
NT1 formal gardens
NT1 public gardens
NT1 rock gardens
NT1 zoological gardens
rt gardening
rt market gardens
rt parks
rt public parks

gardens, botanic
USE **botanical gardens**

gardens, domestic
USE **domestic gardens**

GARDNERIA
BT1 strychnaceae
NT1 gardneria liukiuensis
NT1 gardneria multiflora

GARDNERIA LIUKIUENSIS
BT1 gardneria
BT2 strychnaceae

GARDNERIA MULTIFLORA
BT1 gardneria
BT2 strychnaceae

GARGANICA
HN from 1990
BT1 goat breeds
BT2 breeds

GARLIC
BT1 antibacterial plants
BT1 antifungal plants
BT1 bulbous vegetables
BT2 vegetables
BT1 insecticidal plants
BT2 pesticidal plants
BT1 medicinal plants
rt allium sativum

GARLIC MOSAIC VIRUS
BT1 miscellaneous plant viruses
BT2 plant viruses
BT3 plant pathogens
BT4 pathogens

GARNISHES (AGRICOLA)
rt food art (agricola)

GARRIGUE
HN from 1989
BT1 matorral
BT2 savanna woodlands
BT3 woodlands
BT4 vegetation types

GARRULUS
BT1 corvidae
BT2 passeriformes
BT3 birds
NT1 garrulus glandarius

GARRULUS GLANDARIUS
uf *jay*
BT1 garrulus
BT2 corvidae
BT3 passeriformes
BT4 birds

GARRYA
BT1 garryaceae

GARRYACEAE
NT1 garrya

GARUGA
BT1 burseraceae
NT1 garuga pinnata

GARUGA PINNATA
BT1 garuga
BT2 burseraceae

GAS CHROMATOGRAPHY
BT1 chromatography
BT2 analytical methods
BT3 methodology
NT1 pyrolysis gas chromatography

GAS ENGINES
uf *engines, gas*
BT1 engines
BT2 machinery
rt gas turbine engines

GAS EXCHANGE
rt gases
rt photosynthesis
rt respiration

GAS FLUSHING
BT1 processing
rt gases

GAS HOLDERS
BT1 containers
rt gases
rt methane production

GAS LIQUID CHROMATOGRAPHY
BT1 chromatography
BT2 analytical methods
BT3 methodology

gas, natural
USE **natural gas**

GAS PRODUCTION
NT1 ethylene production
NT1 methane production
rt gases
rt producer gas
rt town gas
rt waste utilization

gas production from wood
USE **destructive distillation**

GAS TURBINE ENGINES
uf *engines, gas turbine*
BT1 engines
BT2 machinery
rt gas engines

GASCARDIA
BT1 coccidae
BT2 coccoidea
BT3 sternorrhyncha
BT4 homoptera
rt ceroplastes

gascardia destructor
USE **ceroplastes destructor**

GASES
uf *gases and fumes*
NT1 air
NT2 drying air
NT1 ammonia
NT1 ammonia synthesis gas
NT1 chlorine
NT1 ethane
NT1 exhaust gases
NT1 fluorine
NT1 hydrogen
NT2 deuterium
NT2 tritium
NT1 hydrogen sulfide
NT1 inert gases
NT2 nitrogen
NT2 noble gases
NT3 argon
NT3 helium
NT3 radon
NT3 xenon
NT1 methane
NT1 nitric oxide
NT1 nitrogen dioxide
NT1 producer gas
NT1 propane
NT1 propylene
NT1 respiratory gases
NT2 carbon dioxide
NT2 oxygen
NT1 rumen gases
NT1 sulfur dioxide
NT1 town gas
NT1 toxic gases
NT2 carbon monoxide
NT1 vapour
NT2 water vapour
NT3 steam
NT4 aerated steam
NT1 waste gases
NT2 factory fumes
NT1 wood gas
rt fluids
rt fumes
rt fumigants
rt gas exchange
rt gas flushing
rt gas holders
rt gas production
rt vapour pressure

gases and fumes
USE **fumes**
OR **gases**

gases, inert
USE **inert gases**

gases, toxic
USE **toxic gases**

GASIFICATION
BT1 processing
rt fertilizer technology

gasoline
USE **petroleum**

GASTERIA
BT1 liliaceae
NT1 gasteria humilis
NT1 gasteria liliputana
NT1 gasteria nigricans
NT1 gasteria verrucosa

GASTERIA HUMILIS
BT1 gasteria
BT2 liliaceae
BT1 ornamental succulent plants
BT2 succulent plants

GASTERIA LILIPUTANA
BT1 gasteria
BT2 liliaceae
BT1 ornamental succulent plants
BT2 succulent plants

GASTERIA NIGRICANS
BT1 gasteria
BT2 liliaceae

GASTERIA VERRUCOSA
BT1 gasteria
BT2 liliaceae

GASTERIA VERRUCOSA *cont.*
BT1 ornamental succulent plants
BT2 succulent plants

GASTEROPHILIDAE
BT1 diptera
NT1 gasterophilus
NT2 gasterophilus haemorrhoidalis
NT2 gasterophilus inermis
NT2 gasterophilus intestinalis
NT2 gasterophilus meridionalis
NT2 gasterophilus nasalis
NT2 gasterophilus nigricornis
NT2 gasterophilus pecorum
NT2 gasterophilus ternicinctus

GASTEROPHILUS
BT1 gasterophilidae
BT2 diptera
NT1 gasterophilus haemorrhoidalis
NT1 gasterophilus inermis
NT1 gasterophilus intestinalis
NT1 gasterophilus meridionalis
NT1 gasterophilus nasalis
NT1 gasterophilus nigricornis
NT1 gasterophilus pecorum
NT1 gasterophilus ternicinctus

gasterophilus equi
USE **gasterophilus intestinalis**

GASTEROPHILUS HAEMORRHOIDALIS
BT1 gasterophilus
BT2 gasterophilidae
BT3 diptera

GASTEROPHILUS INERMIS
BT1 gasterophilus
BT2 gasterophilidae
BT3 diptera

GASTEROPHILUS INTESTINALIS
uf gasterophilus equi
BT1 gasterophilus
BT2 gasterophilidae
BT3 diptera

GASTEROPHILUS MERIDIONALIS
HN from 1989
BT1 gasterophilus
BT2 gasterophilidae
BT3 diptera

GASTEROPHILUS NASALIS
uf gasterophilus veterinus
BT1 gasterophilus
BT2 gasterophilidae
BT3 diptera

GASTEROPHILUS NIGRICORNIS
BT1 gasterophilus
BT2 gasterophilidae
BT3 diptera

GASTEROPHILUS PECORUM
BT1 gasterophilus
BT2 gasterophilidae
BT3 diptera

GASTEROPHILUS TERNICINCTUS
HN from 1989
BT1 gasterophilus
BT2 gasterophilidae
BT3 diptera

gasterophilus veterinus
USE **gasterophilus nasalis**

GASTEROSTEIDAE
BT1 gasterosteiformes
BT2 osteichthyes
BT3 fishes
NT1 culaea
NT2 culaea inconstans
NT1 gasterosteus
NT2 gasterosteus aculeatus

GASTEROSTEIFORMES
BT1 osteichthyes
BT2 fishes
NT1 gasterosteidae
NT2 culaea
NT3 culaea inconstans
NT2 gasterosteus
NT3 gasterosteus aculeatus

GASTEROSTEUS
BT1 gasterosteidae
BT2 gasterosteiformes
BT3 osteichthyes
BT4 fishes
NT1 gasterosteus aculeatus

GASTEROSTEUS ACULEATUS
BT1 gasterosteus
BT2 gasterosteidae
BT3 gasterosteiformes
BT4 osteichthyes
BT5 fishes

GASTRECTOMY
uf stomach removal
BT1 surgical operations
rt dumping syndrome
rt stomach

GASTRIC ACID
BT1 gastric juices
BT2 digestive juices
BT3 body fluids
BT4 fluids
BT1 inorganic acids
BT2 acids
BT2 inorganic compounds
rt hydrochloric acid
rt hydrochloric acid secretion

gastric atrophy
USE **atrophic gastritis**

GASTRIC BYPASS
BT1 surgical operations
rt stomach

GASTRIC GLANDS
BT1 digestive system
BT2 body parts
BT1 glands (animal)
BT2 body parts
BT2 glands
rt digestive juices
rt stomach

gastric hormones
USE **gastrointestinal hormones**

GASTRIC INHIBITORY POLYPEPTIDES
BT1 neuropeptides
BT2 peptides
BT1 polypeptides
BT2 peptides
rt digestive system
rt inhibition

GASTRIC JUICES
uf stomach secretion
BT1 digestive juices
BT2 body fluids
BT3 fluids
NT1 gastric acid
rt digestion
rt hyperacidity (agricola)

GASTRIC ULCER
uf ulcer, gastric
BT1 ulcers
BT2 symptoms
rt duodenal ulcer
rt stomach ulcer

GASTRIDIUM
BT1 gramineae
NT1 gastridium ventricosum
rt alopecurus

GASTRIDIUM VENTRICOSUM
uf alopecurus ventricosus
BT1 gastridium
BT2 gramineae

GASTRIN
BT1 gastrointestinal hormones
BT2 hormones
BT1 neuropeptides
BT2 peptides
BT1 polypeptides
BT2 peptides
rt digestive system
rt pentagastrin
rt secretin
rt tetragastrin

GASTRITIS
BT1 stomach diseases
BT2 gastrointestinal diseases
BT3 digestive system diseases
BT4 organic diseases
BT5 diseases
NT1 atrophic gastritis
rt gastroenteritis
rt inflammation

gastritis, atrophic
USE **atrophic gastritis**

GASTRODIA
BT1 orchidaceae
NT1 gastrodia elata

GASTRODIA ELATA
BT1 gastrodia
BT2 orchidaceae
BT1 ornamental orchids

GASTRODISCOIDES
BT1 paramphistomatidae
BT2 digenea
BT3 trematoda
NT1 gastrodiscoides hominis

GASTRODISCOIDES HOMINIS
BT1 gastrodiscoides
BT2 paramphistomatidae
BT3 digenea
BT4 trematoda

GASTRODISCUS
BT1 paramphistomatidae
BT2 digenea
BT3 trematoda
NT1 gastrodiscus aegyptiacus
NT1 gastrodiscus secundus

GASTRODISCUS AEGYPTIACUS
BT1 gastrodiscus
BT2 paramphistomatidae
BT3 digenea
BT4 trematoda

GASTRODISCUS SECUNDUS
BT1 gastrodiscus
BT2 paramphistomatidae
BT3 digenea
BT4 trematoda

GASTROENTERITIS
uf gastroenteropathy
BT1 intestinal diseases
BT2 gastrointestinal diseases
BT3 digestive system diseases
BT4 organic diseases
BT5 diseases
rt enteritis
rt food poisoning
rt gastritis
rt transmissible gastroenteritis virus

gastroenteropathy
USE **gastroenteritis**
OR **intestinal diseases**
OR **stomach diseases**

GASTROINTESTINAL AGENTS
BT1 drugs
NT1 antacids
NT2 aluminium hydroxide
NT2 aluminium phosphate
NT2 calcium carbonate
NT2 sodium bicarbonate
NT1 antibloat agents
NT2 simethicone
NT1 antidiarrhoea agents
NT2 calcium carbonate
NT2 kaolin
NT2 pectins
NT1 antiemetics
NT2 chlorpromazine

GASTROINTESTINAL AGENTS *cont.*
NT1 carminatives
NT2 carvone
NT2 chloroform
NT2 safrole
NT2 turpentine
NT1 cholagogues
NT1 digestants
NT2 cholic acid
NT2 deoxycholic acid
NT2 hydrochloric acid
NT2 pancreatin
NT2 taurocholic acid
NT2 ursodeoxycholic acid
NT1 emetics
NT2 apomorphine
NT1 laxatives
NT2 agar
NT2 docusate sodium
NT2 lactulose
NT2 linseed oil
NT2 liquid paraffin
NT2 methylcellulose
NT2 olive oil
NT2 sorbitol
NT1 pentagastrin
NT1 purgatives
NT2 castor oil
NT2 emodin
NT2 germanium
NT2 magnesium sulfate
NT3 epsom salts
NT2 senna
NT2 sodium sulfate
NT1 tetragastrin
rt bile acids
rt gastrointestinal hormones

GASTROINTESTINAL DISEASES
uf gastrointestinal disorders
BT1 digestive system diseases
BT2 organic diseases
BT3 diseases
NT1 dumping syndrome
NT1 intestinal diseases
NT2 appendicitis (agricola)
NT2 blind loop syndrome
NT2 coeliac syndrome
NT2 colitis
NT3 ulcerative colitis
NT2 crohn's disease
NT2 diverticulosis
NT2 dysentery
NT3 swine dysentery
NT2 enteritis
NT2 enterocolitis
NT2 gastroenteritis
NT2 haemorrhagic enteritis
NT2 irritable colon
NT2 short bowel syndrome
NT2 sprue
NT2 steatorrhoea
NT2 tropical sprue
NT2 typhlitis
NT1 peptic ulcer
NT2 duodenal ulcer
NT1 stomach diseases
NT2 achlorhydria
NT2 gastritis
NT3 atrophic gastritis
NT2 rumenitis
NT2 stomach ulcer

gastrointestinal disorders
USE **digestive disorders**
OR **gastrointestinal diseases**

GASTROINTESTINAL HORMONES
uf gastric hormones
BT1 hormones
NT1 gastrin
NT1 motilin
NT1 pancreozymin
NT1 secretin
NT1 substance p
NT1 urogastrone
NT1 vasoactive intestinal peptide
rt digestive system
rt gastrointestinal agents

gastrointestinal motility
USE **digestive tract motility**

gastrointestinal system
USE **digestive system**

gastrointestinal tract
USE **digestive tract**

GASTROLOBIUM
BT1 leguminosae

GASTROMERMIS
BT1 mermithidae
BT2 nematoda

GASTROPODA
uf *gastropods*
BT1 mollusca
NT1 achatinidae
NT2 achatina
NT3 achatina fulica
NT2 rumina
NT3 rumina decollata
NT1 ampullariidae
NT2 marisa
NT3 marisa cornuarietis
NT2 pila
NT3 pila globosa
NT2 pomacea
NT1 ancylidae
NT2 ancylus
NT3 ancylus fluviatilis
NT1 arionidae
NT2 arion
NT3 arion ater
NT3 arion circumscriptus
NT3 arion distinctus
NT3 arion fasciatus
NT3 arion hortensis
NT3 arion intermedius
NT3 arion silvaticus
NT3 arion subfuscus
NT1 bithyniidae
NT2 bithynia
NT3 bithynia inflata
NT3 bithynia manchourica
NT3 bithynia tentaculata
NT1 buccinidae
NT2 buccinum
NT3 buccinum undatum
NT1 bulinidae
NT2 bulinus
NT3 bulinus africanus
NT3 bulinus forskali
NT3 bulinus globosus
NT3 bulinus rohlfsi
NT3 bulinus senegalensis
NT3 bulinus tropicus
NT3 bulinus truncatus
NT2 indoplanorbis
NT3 indoplanorbis exustus
NT1 endodontidae
NT2 discus
NT3 discus cronkhitei
NT1 eulotidae
NT2 bradybaena
NT3 bradybaena circulus
NT3 bradybaena similaris
NT1 haliotidae
NT2 haliotis
NT3 haliotis discus
NT3 haliotis rufescens
NT1 helicidae
NT2 cepaea
NT3 cepaea hortensis
NT3 cepaea nemoralis
NT2 cernuella
NT3 cernuella cespitum
NT3 cernuella virgata
NT2 cochlicella
NT3 cochlicella acuta
NT3 cochlicella ventricosa
NT2 helicella
NT3 helicella candaharica
NT3 helicella itala
NT2 helix
NT3 helix aspersa
NT3 helix pomatia
NT2 monacha
NT3 monacha cartusiana
NT2 theba
NT3 theba pisana
NT1 hydrobiidae
NT2 hydrobia

GASTROPODA *cont.*
NT3 hydrobia ulvae
NT1 limacidae
NT2 ariolimax
NT3 ariolimax columbianus
NT2 deroceras
NT3 deroceras laeve
NT3 deroceras panormitanum
NT3 deroceras reticulatum
NT2 lehmannia
NT2 limax
NT3 limax flavus
NT3 limax maximus
NT3 limax valentianus
NT2 milax
NT3 milax gagates
NT2 tandonia
NT3 tandonia budapestensis
NT3 tandonia sowerbyi
NT1 littorinidae
NT2 littorina
NT3 littorina littorea
NT3 littorina obtusata
NT3 littorina rudis
NT3 littorina saxatilis
NT1 lymnaeidae
NT2 lymnaea
NT3 lymnaea acuminata
NT3 lymnaea auricularia
NT3 lymnaea caillaudi
NT3 lymnaea columella
NT3 lymnaea cubensis
NT3 lymnaea glabra
NT3 lymnaea luteola
NT3 lymnaea natalensis
NT3 lymnaea peregra
NT3 lymnaea rubiginosa
NT3 lymnaea stagnalis
NT3 lymnaea truncatula
NT1 neritidae
NT2 theodoxus
NT3 theodoxus danubialis
NT1 patellidae
NT2 cellana
NT3 cellana tramoserica
NT1 physidae
NT2 physa
NT3 physa acuta
NT3 physa fontinalis
NT3 physa gyrina
NT1 planorbidae
NT2 biomphalaria
NT3 biomphalaria alexandrina
NT3 biomphalaria glabrata
NT3 biomphalaria pfeifferi
NT3 biomphalaria straminea
NT3 biomphalaria tenagophila
NT2 gyraulus
NT3 gyraulus convexiusculus
NT2 helisoma
NT3 helisoma duryi
NT3 helisoma trivolvis
NT2 planorbarius
NT3 planorbarius corneus
NT3 planorbarius metidjensis
NT3 planorbarius purpura
NT2 planorbis
NT3 planorbis planorbis
NT1 pleuroceridae
NT2 semisulcospira
NT3 semisulcospira libertina
NT1 pomatiopsidae
NT2 oncomelania
NT3 oncomelania hupensis
NT3 oncomelania quadrasi
NT2 pomatiopsis
NT3 pomatiopsis californica
NT2 robertsiella
NT3 robertsiella kaporensis
NT2 tricula
NT3 tricula aperta
NT3 tricula bollingi
NT1 potamididae
NT2 cerithidea
NT2 pirenella
NT3 pirenella conica
NT1 succineidae
NT2 succinea
NT3 succinea altaica
NT1 testacellidae
NT2 testacella

GASTROPODA *cont.*
NT1 thiaridae
NT2 melanoides
NT3 melanoides tuberculata
NT2 thiara
NT1 valloniidae
NT2 vallonia
NT3 vallonia pulchella
NT1 veronicellidae
NT2 laevicaulis
NT3 laevicaulis alte
NT2 vaginulus
NT1 vitrinidae
NT2 vitrina
NT3 vitrina limpida
NT1 viviparidae
NT2 viviparus
NT3 viviparus viviparus
NT1 zonitidae
NT2 zonitoides
NT3 zonitoides arboreus
NT3 zonitoides nitidus
rt slugs
rt snails

gastropods
USE **gastropoda**

GASTROTAENIA
BT1 nematoparataeniidae
BT2 eucestoda
BT3 cestoda

GASTROTHYLACIDAE
BT1 digenea
BT2 trematoda
NT1 carmyerius
NT1 fischoederius
NT2 fischoederius elongatus
NT1 gastrothylax
NT2 gastrothylax crumenifer

GASTROTHYLAX
BT1 gastrothylacidae
BT2 digenea
BT3 trematoda
NT1 gastrothylax crumenifer

GASTROTHYLAX CRUMENIFER
BT1 gastrothylax
BT2 gastrothylacidae
BT3 digenea
BT4 trematoda

GATES
BT1 fencing
rt doors

GATT
(general agreement on tariffs and trade)
BT1 international organizations
BT2 organizations
BT1 trade agreements
BT2 international agreements
BT3 international cooperation
BT4 cooperation
BT5 socioeconomic organization
BT2 trade policy
BT3 economic policy
rt trade negotiations

GAUCHER'S DISEASE
BT1 lipid metabolism disorders
BT2 metabolic disorders
BT3 animal disorders
BT4 disorders
rt anaemia
rt spleen

GAUDICHAUDIA
BT1 malpighiaceae

GAUGES
BT1 instruments
NT1 humidity gauges
NT1 level gauges
NT1 pressure gauges
NT1 rain gauges
NT1 strain gauges
NT1 vacuum gauges
rt indicating instruments
rt meters

gauges, level
USE **level gauges**

gauges, pressure
USE **pressure gauges**

gauges, strain
USE **strain gauges**

gauges, temperature
USE **temperature gauges**

GAULNETTYA
BT1 ericaceae

GAULTHERIA
BT1 ericaceae
NT1 gaultheria fragrantissima
NT1 gaultheria nummularioides
NT1 gaultheria procumbens

GAULTHERIA FRAGRANTISSIMA
BT1 gaultheria
BT2 ericaceae

GAULTHERIA NUMMULARIOIDES
BT1 gaultheria
BT2 ericaceae
BT1 medicinal plants

GAULTHERIA PROCUMBENS
BT1 gaultheria
BT2 ericaceae

GAUR
uf *bos gaurus*
BT1 wild animals
BT2 animals
rt bovidae
rt cattle

GAVIA
uf *divers (birds)*
BT1 gaviidae
BT2 gaviiformes
BT3 birds

GAVIALIDAE
BT1 crocodylia
BT2 reptiles
NT1 gavialis
NT2 gavialis gangeticus

GAVIALIS
BT1 gavialidae
BT2 crocodylia
BT3 reptiles
NT1 gavialis gangeticus

GAVIALIS GANGETICUS
BT1 gavialis
BT2 gavialidae
BT3 crocodylia
BT4 reptiles

GAVIIDAE
BT1 gaviiformes
BT2 birds
NT1 gavia

GAVIIFORMES
BT1 birds
NT1 gaviidae
NT2 gavia

GAYALS
uf *bos frontalis*
BT1 ruminants
BT2 animals
rt bovidae

GAYLUSSACIA
uf *huckleberries*
BT1 ericaceae
NT1 gaylussacia baccata
NT1 gaylussacia dumosa
NT1 gaylussacia frondosa

GAYLUSSACIA BACCATA
BT1 gaylussacia
BT2 ericaceae
BT1 temperate small fruits
BT2 small fruits
BT2 temperate fruits
BT3 fruit crops

GAYLUSSACIA DUMOSA
BT1 gaylussacia
BT2 ericaceae
BT1 temperate small fruits
BT2 small fruits
BT2 temperate fruits
BT3 fruit crops

GAYLUSSACIA FRONDOSA
BT1 gaylussacia
BT2 ericaceae
BT1 temperate small fruits
BT2 small fruits
BT2 temperate fruits
BT3 fruit crops

GAZANIA
BT1 compositae
NT1 gazania rigens

GAZANIA RIGENS
uf *gazania splendens*
uf *gazania uniflora*
BT1 gazania
BT2 compositae
BT1 ornamental herbaceous plants

gazania splendens
USE **gazania rigens**

gazania uniflora
USE **gazania rigens**

GAZELLA
uf *gazelles*
BT1 bovidae
BT2 ruminantia
BT3 artiodactyla
BT4 mammals
BT4 ungulates
NT1 gazella gazella
NT1 gazella granti
NT1 gazella thomsonii

GAZELLA GAZELLA
BT1 gazella
BT2 bovidae
BT3 ruminantia
BT4 artiodactyla
BT5 mammals
BT5 ungulates

GAZELLA GRANTI
uf *grant's gazelle*
BT1 gazella
BT2 bovidae
BT3 ruminantia
BT4 artiodactyla
BT5 mammals
BT5 ungulates

GAZELLA THOMSONII
BT1 gazella
BT2 bovidae
BT3 ruminantia
BT4 artiodactyla
BT5 mammals
BT5 ungulates

gazelles
USE **gazella**

gb
USE **great britain**

gdr
USE **german democratic republic**

GEAR PUMPS
BT1 pumps
BT2 machinery

GEARS
BT1 components
NT1 bevel gears
NT1 differential gears
NT1 planetary gears
NT1 spur gears
NT1 worm and wheel gears
rt drives
rt engines
rt sprockets
rt synchromesh transmissions

GEARS *cont.*
rt torque converters
rt transmissions

gears, bevel
USE **bevel gears**

gears, differential
USE **differential gears**

gears, planetary
USE **planetary gears**

gears, spur
USE **spur gears**

gears, worm and wheel
USE **worm and wheel gears**

GEDOELSTIA
BT1 oestridae
BT2 diptera

GEESE
uf *anser domesticus*
uf *domestic geese*
uf *goose*
BT1 poultry
BT2 livestock
BT3 animals
rt anatidae
rt goose eggs
rt goose fattening
rt goose feeding
rt goose liver
rt goose meat
rt goslings

GEIGERIA
BT1 compositae
rt poisonous plants

GEIJERA
BT1 rutaceae
NT1 geijera parviflora

GEIJERA PARVIFLORA
BT1 geijera
BT2 rutaceae

GEKKONIDAE
BT1 sauria
BT2 reptiles
NT1 hemidactylus
NT2 hemidactylus flaviviridis

GEL COATINGS
BT1 cutans
BT2 soil micromorphological features
BT3 soil morphological features

gel diffusion tests
USE **immunodiffusion tests**

GEL FILTRATION CHROMATOGRAPHY
BT1 chromatography
BT2 analytical methods
BT3 methodology

gel precipitation tests
USE **immunodiffusion tests**

GELARCHIA
HN from 1990
BT1 deuteromycotina
rt monographella

gelarchia nivalis
USE **monographella nivalis**

gelarchia oryzae
USE **monographella albescens**

GELASINOSPORA
BT1 sordariales
NT1 gelasinospora cerealis

GELASINOSPORA CEREALIS
BT1 gelasinospora
BT2 sordariales

GELATIN
BT1 glycoproteins

GELATIN *cont.*
BT2 proteins
BT3 peptides
BT1 scleroproteins
BT2 proteins
BT3 peptides
BT1 stabilizers
rt agar
rt clarification
rt collagen
rt confectionery

GELATION
BT1 freezing
BT2 change of state
BT2 processing
BT1 solidification
BT2 change of state
rt pectins
rt physical chemistry

GELBVIEH
HN from 1990; previously "german yellow"
uf *german yellow*
BT1 cattle breeds
BT2 breeds

GELDERLAND
uf *netherlands (gelderland)*
BT1 netherlands
BT2 western europe
BT3 europe

GELDERLAND (HORSE BREED)
BT1 horse breeds
BT2 breeds

GELECHIA
BT1 gelechiidae
BT2 lepidoptera

GELECHIIDAE
BT1 lepidoptera
NT1 anarsia
NT2 anarsia ephippias
NT2 anarsia lineatella
NT1 aproaerema
NT2 aproaerema modicella
NT1 biloba
NT1 brachmia
NT2 brachmia triannulella
NT1 coleotechnites
NT1 exoteleia
NT1 gelechia
NT1 keiferia
NT2 keiferia lycopersicella
NT1 pectinophora
NT2 pectinophora gossypiella
NT2 pectinophora scutigera
NT1 phthorimaea
NT2 phthorimaea operculella
NT1 platyedra
NT1 pulicalvaria
NT2 pulicalvaria thujaella
NT1 recurvaria
NT2 recurvaria nanella
NT1 scrobipalpa
NT2 scrobipalpa heliopa
NT2 scrobipalpa ocellatella
NT1 scrobipalpula
NT2 scrobipalpula absoluta
NT1 sitotroga
NT2 sitotroga cerealella
NT1 stomopteryx
NT1 symmetrischema
NT2 symmetrischema plaesiosema

GELS
rt formulations

GELSEMIUM
BT1 loganiaceae
NT1 gelsemium sempervirens

GELSEMIUM SEMPERVIRENS
BT1 gelsemium
BT2 loganiaceae

GEMINIVIRUS GROUP
HN from 1990
BT1 plant viruses
BT2 plant pathogens

GEMINIVIRUS GROUP *cont.*
BT3 pathogens
NT1 african cassava mosaic geminivirus
NT1 bean golden mosaic geminivirus
NT1 beet curly top geminivirus
NT1 chloris striate mosaic geminivirus
NT1 euphorbia mosaic geminivirus
NT1 maize streak geminivirus
NT1 mung bean yellow mosaic geminivirus
NT1 squash leaf curl geminivirus
NT1 tobacco leaf curl geminivirus
NT1 tobacco yellow dwarf geminivirus
NT1 tomato golden mosaic geminivirus
NT1 tomato yellow leaf curl geminivirus
NT1 wheat dwarf geminivirus

gene amplification
(for amplification of dna in vivo use "dna amplification"; for amplification of dna in vitro use the name of the technique, e.g. "polymerase chain reaction")
USE **amplification**
AND **genes**

GENE BANKS
uf *germplasm banks*
BT1 genetic resources
BT2 renewable resources
BT3 natural resources
BT4 resources
rt genes
rt plant breeding
rt plant collections
rt plant introduction
rt seed exchange

GENE CONVERSION
BT1 genetic change
rt genes

GENE DOSAGE
BT1 genetics
BT2 biology
NT1 hemizygosity
rt dosage compensation
rt genes
rt polyploidy

GENE EXPRESSION
BT1 biochemical genetics
BT2 genetics
BT3 biology
rt genes
rt molecular genetics

GENE FLOW
BT1 population genetics
BT2 genetics
BT3 biology
rt evolution
rt genes

GENE FREQUENCY
BT1 population genetics
BT2 genetics
BT3 biology
rt genes
rt genetic drift
rt genetic equilibrium

GENE INTERACTION
BT1 genetics
BT2 biology
NT1 epistasis
rt genes
rt inhibitor genes
rt modifiers

GENE LOCATION
uf *monosomic analysis*
uf *nullisomic analysis*
BT1 genetics
BT2 biology

GENE LOCATION *cont.*
rt chromosome maps
rt genes
rt linkage

gene locus
USE **genes**

GENE MAPPING
BT1 genetics
BT2 biology
NT1 molecular mapping
rt chromosome maps
rt genes
rt genetic code
rt linkage
rt molecular genetics
rt restriction mapping

gene resources
USE **genetic resources**

GENE SPLICING
HN from 1990
BT1 biochemical techniques
BT2 techniques
rt recombinant dna

GENE SYMBOLS
BT1 symbols
rt genes

GENE THERAPY
HN from 1990
BT1 therapy
rt genes
rt genetic engineering

GENE TRANSFER
HN from 1989
BT1 genetic engineering
BT2 genetics
BT3 biology
rt genes
rt genetic transformation
rt reporter genes
rt vectors

GENERA
rt classification
rt taxonomy

GENERAL COMBINING ABILITY
BT1 combining ability

GENERALIZED INFECTIONS
BT1 infections

GENERALLY RECOGNIZED AS SAFE LIST (AGRICOLA)

GENERATION CONFLICT
BT1 conflict
BT2 social unrest
BT3 social change
rt age differences
rt family life
rt generations

GENERATION INTERVAL
rt generations

GENERATIONS
NT1 overlapping generations
rt generation conflict
rt generation interval
rt parent child relationships

GENERATORS
BT1 machinery
NT1 electricity generators
NT2 standby generators
NT2 turbines

generators, electricity
USE **electricity generators**

generators, standby
USE **standby generators**

GENERICS (AGRICOLA)
BT1 drugs
rt drug formulations

GENES
uf *gene locus*

GENES *cont.*
ufa *gene amplification*
NT1 alleles
NT2 multiple alleles
NT2 neutral alleles
NT2 rare alleles
NT1 cistrons
NT1 complex loci
NT1 controlling elements
NT1 immunoglobulin structural genes
NT1 inhibitor genes
NT1 lethals
NT2 balanced lethals
NT2 dominant lethals
NT2 recessive lethals
NT1 major genes
NT1 marker genes
NT1 modifiers
NT1 multigene families
NT1 multiple genes
NT2 complementary genes
NT1 mutator genes
NT1 non-h-2 complex
NT1 non-rt1 complex
NT1 oncogenes
NT1 plasmagenes
NT1 proto-oncogenes
NT1 pseudogenes
NT1 recessive genes
NT1 reporter genes
NT1 retrogenes
NT1 semidominant genes
NT1 structural genes
NT1 synthetic genes
NT1 transposable elements
rt chromosomes
rt dosage compensation
rt epistasis
rt expressivity
rt extension factors
rt fixation
rt gene banks
rt gene conversion
rt gene dosage
rt gene expression
rt gene flow
rt gene frequency
rt gene interaction
rt gene location
rt gene mapping
rt gene symbols
rt gene therapy
rt gene transfer
rt genetic code
rt genetic distance
rt genetic load
rt genetics
rt genotypes
rt germplasm
rt hemizygosity
rt heterozygosity
rt heterozygotes
rt homozygosity
rt homozygotes
rt inheritance
rt introns
rt linkage
rt loci
rt molecular mapping
rt penetrance
rt pleiotropy
rt polygenic inheritance
rt position effect
rt recombination
rt segregation
rt sex linkage
rt sublethal factors
rt subvital factors
rt transgression

GENETIC ALGEBRAS
rt genetics

GENETIC ANALYSIS
NT1 chromosome analysis
rt analysis
rt genetics

GENETIC CHANGE
NT1 gene conversion
NT1 genetic trend

GENETIC CHANGE *cont.*
NT1 genetic variation
NT2 genetic differences
NT2 genetic polymorphism
NT2 heterogeneity
NT1 recombination
NT2 homologous recombination
NT2 intragenic recombination
NT2 mitotic recombination
rt change
rt genetics
rt mutations

GENETIC CODE
rt cistrons
rt dna
rt gene mapping
rt genes
rt genetic transformation
rt messenger rna
rt molecular genetics
rt rna

GENETIC CONTAMINATION
HN from 1990
uf *contamination, genetic*
rt strains

GENETIC CONTROL
(for regulation by genes, use "genetic regulation")
BT1 pest control
BT2 control
rt sterile insect release

GENETIC CORRELATION
BT1 correlation
BT1 genetic parameters

GENETIC COVARIANCE
BT1 covariance
BT2 correlation
BT1 genetic parameters
rt genetic variance

GENETIC DEFECTS
uf *hereditary defects*
BT1 abnormalities
BT1 defects
NT1 genetic disorders
NT1 phenylketonuria
rt genetics
rt hereditary diseases
rt lethals

GENETIC DIFFERENCES
BT1 genetic variation
BT2 genetic change
BT2 mutations
BT2 variation
rt genetic markers
rt genetics
rt heterozygotes
rt mutants

GENETIC DISORDERS
BT1 congenital abnormalities
BT2 abnormalities
BT1 genetic defects
BT2 abnormalities
BT2 defects
rt prenatal diagnosis

GENETIC DISTANCE
BT1 genetic parameters
rt genes
rt genetic variation
rt genetics

GENETIC DRIFT
BT1 population genetics
BT2 genetics
BT3 biology
rt gene frequency
rt genetics

GENETIC ECONOMICS
BT1 economics
rt genetics

GENETIC EFFECTS
HN from 1989
BT1 effects
rt inheritance

GENETIC ENGINEERING
uf *genetic manipulation*
BT1 genetics
BT2 biology
NT1 gene transfer
rt biotechnology
rt direct dna uptake
rt electroporation
rt gene therapy
rt genetic transformation
rt molecular genetics
rt transduction
rt transgenics

GENETIC EQUILIBRIUM
BT1 population genetics
BT2 genetics
BT3 biology
NT1 disequilibrium
rt gene frequency
rt genetics

GENETIC FACTORS
NT1 sublethal factors
NT1 subvital factors
rt genetics

GENETIC GAIN
rt artificial selection
rt genetics
rt selection responses

GENETIC IMPROVEMENT
BT1 selective breeding
BT2 breeding

GENETIC LOAD
rt genes
rt genetics
rt lethals

genetic manipulation
USE **genetic engineering**

GENETIC MARKERS
BT1 markers
rt breeding
rt genetic differences
rt genetic variation
rt genetics
rt marker genes
rt potassium types

GENETIC MODELS
BT1 models
rt genetics

GENETIC PARAMETERS
NT1 genetic correlation
NT1 genetic covariance
NT1 genetic distance
NT1 genetic variance
NT1 heterosis
rt combining ability
rt genetics

GENETIC POLYMORPHISM
uf *polymorphism, genetic*
BT1 genetic variation
BT2 genetic change
BT2 mutations
BT2 variation
BT1 polymorphism
rt allotypes
rt genetics

genetic recombination
USE **recombination**

GENETIC REGULATION
HN from 1990
BT1 genetics
BT2 biology
rt inheritance
rt mutations

GENETIC RESISTANCE
BT1 disease resistance
BT2 resistance

GENETIC RESOURCES
uf *gene resources*
BT1 renewable resources
BT2 natural resources
BT3 resources

GENETIC RESOURCES *cont.*
NT1 gene banks
rt centres of diversity
rt centres of origin
rt genetics
rt germplasm
rt germplasm releases
rt plant introduction

genetic soil types
USE **soil types (genetic)**

GENETIC THEORY
BT1 genetics
BT2 biology
NT1 fisher's theorem
rt theory

GENETIC TRANSFORMATION
rt dna
rt gene transfer
rt genetic code
rt genetic engineering
rt genetics
rt molecular genetics
rt transduction
rt transformation

GENETIC TREND
BT1 genetic change
rt genetics
rt selection
rt trends

GENETIC VARIANCE
BT1 genetic parameters
rt genetic covariance
rt genetic variation
rt heritability

GENETIC VARIATION
BT1 genetic change
BT1 mutations
BT1 variation
NT1 genetic differences
NT1 genetic polymorphism
NT1 heterogeneity
rt genetic distance
rt genetic markers
rt genetic variance
rt genetics

GENETICS
uf *heredity*
BT1 biology
NT1 biochemical genetics
NT2 gene expression
NT2 nucleotide sequences
NT2 restriction mapping
NT1 chloroplast genetics
NT1 complementation
NT1 epigenetics
NT1 gene dosage
NT2 hemizygosity
NT1 gene interaction
NT2 epistasis
NT1 gene location
NT1 gene mapping
NT2 molecular mapping
NT1 genetic engineering
NT2 gene transfer
NT1 genetic regulation
NT1 genetic theory
NT2 fisher's theorem
NT1 genotype environment interaction
NT1 genotype nutrition interaction
NT1 heterozygosity
NT1 homozygosity
NT1 mendelism
NT1 mitochondrial genetics
NT1 molecular genetics
NT1 nucleocytoplasmic interaction
NT1 penetrance
NT1 pleiotropy
NT1 population genetics
NT2 gene flow
NT2 gene frequency
NT2 genetic drift
NT2 genetic equilibrium
NT3 disequilibrium

GENETICS *cont.*
NT1 quantitative genetics
NT2 diallel analysis
NT1 transduction
rt acquired characters
rt agricultural sciences
rt cloning
rt complex loci
rt dominance
rt factor analysis
rt genes
rt genetic algebras
rt genetic analysis
rt genetic change
rt genetic defects
rt genetic differences
rt genetic distance
rt genetic drift
rt genetic economics
rt genetic equilibrium
rt genetic factors
rt genetic gain
rt genetic load
rt genetic markers
rt genetic models
rt genetic parameters
rt genetic polymorphism
rt genetic resources
rt genetic transformation
rt genetic trend
rt genetic variation
rt genotrophs
rt genotypes
rt heritability
rt immunogenetics
rt inheritance
rt lamarckism
rt paternal effects
rt reciprocal effects
rt sex limited characters
rt transposable elements

genetics, biochemical
USE **biochemical genetics**

genets
USE **genetta**

GENETTA
uf *genets*
BT1 viverridae
BT2 fissipeda
BT3 carnivores
BT4 mammals

GENISTA
BT1 leguminosae
NT1 genista carinalis
NT1 genista lydia
NT1 genista morisii
NT1 genista tinctoria

GENISTA CARINALIS
BT1 genista
BT2 leguminosae

GENISTA LYDIA
BT1 genista
BT2 leguminosae
BT1 ornamental woody plants

GENISTA MORISII
BT1 genista
BT2 leguminosae

GENISTA TINCTORIA
BT1 dye plants
BT1 genista
BT2 leguminosae
BT1 ornamental woody plants

GENISTEIN
uf *biochanin a*
BT1 isoflavones
BT2 flavonoids
BT3 aromatic compounds
BT3 plant pigments
BT4 pigments

genital system diseases
USE **female genital diseases**
OR **male genital diseases**

genital system, female
USE **female genitalia**

genital system, male
USE **male genitalia**

GENITALIA
BT1 urogenital system
BT2 body parts
NT1 female genitalia
NT2 oviducts
NT3 infundibulum
NT3 magnum
NT2 spermatheca
NT2 uterus
NT3 cervix
NT3 endometrium
NT3 muellerian ducts
NT3 myometrium
NT2 vagina
NT2 vulva
NT3 clitoris
NT1 male genitalia
NT2 accessory glands
NT3 bulbo-urethral gland
NT3 prostate
NT3 vesicular gland
NT2 ductus deferens
NT3 ampulla
NT2 gubernaculum
NT2 penis
NT3 prepuce
NT2 scrotum
NT2 spermatic cord

genitalia, female
USE **female genitalia**

genitalia, male
USE **male genitalia**

GENOME ANALYSIS
rt analysis
rt chromosome pairing
rt genomes

GENOMES
NT1 major histocompatibility complex
rt chromosomes
rt genome analysis

GENOTROPHS
rt acquired characters
rt genetics

GENOTYPE ENVIRONMENT INTERACTION
BT1 genetics
BT2 biology
rt environment
rt genotypes
rt interactions
rt relationships
rt stability

GENOTYPE MIXTURES
uf *mixtures, genotype*
BT1 mixtures
rt composite varieties
rt crop mixtures
rt genotypes
rt multiline varieties

GENOTYPE NUTRITION INTERACTION
HN from 1989
BT1 genetics
BT2 biology
rt interactions

GENOTYPES
NT1 haplotypes
NT1 heterozygotes
NT2 balanced lethals
NT1 homozygotes
rt agronomic characteristics
rt allotypes
rt biotypes
rt congeners
rt constitution
rt epigenetics
rt genes
rt genetics

GENOTYPES *cont.*
rt genotype environment interaction
rt genotype mixtures
rt heterogeneity
rt phenotypes

GENTAMICIN
BT1 aminoglycoside antibiotics
BT2 antibiotics
BT2 glycosides
BT3 carbohydrates
BT1 antibacterial agents
BT2 antiinfective agents
BT3 drugs

GENTIAN VIOLET
uf *crystal violet*
uf *methylrosanilinium*
BT1 anthelmintics
BT2 antiparasitic agents
BT3 drugs
BT1 antibacterial agents
BT2 antiinfective agents
BT3 drugs
BT1 antifungal agents
BT2 antiinfective agents
BT3 drugs
BT1 dyes
BT1 stains

GENTIANA
BT1 gentianaceae
NT1 gentiana acaulis
NT1 gentiana algida
NT1 gentiana argentea
NT1 gentiana asclepiadea
NT1 gentiana barbata
NT1 gentiana crinita
NT1 gentiana cruciata
NT1 gentiana decumbens
NT1 gentiana depressa
NT1 gentiana elwesii
NT1 gentiana fischeri
NT1 gentiana lutea
NT1 gentiana macrophylla
NT1 gentiana makinoi
NT1 gentiana pannonica
NT1 gentiana pedicellata
NT1 gentiana pneumonanthe
NT1 gentiana prolata
NT1 gentiana punctata
NT1 gentiana purpurea
NT1 gentiana septemfida
NT1 gentiana sikkimensis

GENTIANA ACAULIS
BT1 gentiana
BT2 gentianaceae
BT1 ornamental herbaceous plants

GENTIANA ALGIDA
BT1 gentiana
BT2 gentianaceae
BT1 medicinal plants

GENTIANA ARGENTEA
BT1 gentiana
BT2 gentianaceae

GENTIANA ASCLEPIADEA
BT1 gentiana
BT2 gentianaceae
BT1 ornamental herbaceous plants

GENTIANA BARBATA
BT1 gentiana
BT2 gentianaceae
BT1 medicinal plants

GENTIANA CRINITA
BT1 gentiana
BT2 gentianaceae
BT1 ornamental herbaceous plants

GENTIANA CRUCIATA
BT1 gentiana
BT2 gentianaceae
BT1 ornamental herbaceous plants

GENTIANA DECUMBENS
BT1 gentiana
BT2 gentianaceae

GENTIANA DEPRESSA
BT1 gentiana
BT2 gentianaceae

GENTIANA ELWESII
BT1 gentiana
BT2 gentianaceae

GENTIANA FISCHERI
BT1 gentiana
BT2 gentianaceae

GENTIANA LUTEA
BT1 gentiana
BT2 gentianaceae
BT1 medicinal plants

GENTIANA MACROPHYLLA
BT1 gentiana
BT2 gentianaceae

GENTIANA MAKINOI
BT1 gentiana
BT2 gentianaceae
BT1 ornamental herbaceous plants

GENTIANA PANNONICA
BT1 gentiana
BT2 gentianaceae

GENTIANA PEDICELLATA
BT1 gentiana
BT2 gentianaceae
BT1 medicinal plants

GENTIANA PNEUMONANTHE
BT1 dye plants
BT1 gentiana
BT2 gentianaceae

GENTIANA PROLATA
BT1 gentiana
BT2 gentianaceae

GENTIANA PUNCTATA
BT1 gentiana
BT2 gentianaceae

GENTIANA PURPUREA
BT1 gentiana
BT2 gentianaceae

GENTIANA SEPTEMFIDA
BT1 gentiana
BT2 gentianaceae
BT1 ornamental herbaceous plants

GENTIANA SIKKIMENSIS
BT1 gentiana
BT2 gentianaceae

GENTIANACEAE
NT1 canscora
NT2 canscora decussata
NT1 centaurium
NT2 centaurium spicatum
NT1 enicostema
NT2 enicostema hyssopifolium
NT2 enicostema litorale
NT1 eustoma
NT2 eustoma grandiflorum
NT1 exacum
NT2 exacum affine
NT1 gentiana
NT2 gentiana acaulis
NT2 gentiana algida
NT2 gentiana argentea
NT2 gentiana asclepiadea
NT2 gentiana barbata
NT2 gentiana crinita
NT2 gentiana cruciata
NT2 gentiana decumbens
NT2 gentiana depressa
NT2 gentiana elwesii
NT2 gentiana fischeri
NT2 gentiana lutea
NT2 gentiana macrophylla
NT2 gentiana makinoi
NT2 gentiana pannonica

GENTIANACEAE *cont.*
NT2 gentiana pedicellata
NT2 gentiana pneumonanthe
NT2 gentiana prolata
NT2 gentiana punctata
NT2 gentiana purpurea
NT2 gentiana septemfida
NT2 gentiana sikkimensis
NT1 hoppea
NT2 hoppea dichotoma
NT1 lomatogonium
NT2 lomatogonium carinthiacum
NT1 swertia
NT2 swertia alata
NT2 swertia angustifolia
NT2 swertia chirata
NT2 swertia connata
NT2 swertia decussata
NT2 swertia hookeri
NT2 swertia iberica
NT2 swertia japonica
NT2 swertia obtusa
NT2 swertia paniculata
NT2 swertia purpurascens

GENTILE DI PUGLIA
HN from 1990; previously "apulian merino"
uf apulian merino
BT1 sheep breeds
BT2 breeds

GENTIOBIOSE
BT1 disaccharides
BT2 oligosaccharides
BT3 carbohydrates
BT1 reducing sugars
BT2 sugars
BT3 carbohydrates

GENYONEMUS
BT1 sciaenidae
BT2 perciformes
BT3 osteichthyes
BT4 fishes

GENYPTERUS
BT1 ophidiidae
BT2 ophidiiformes
BT3 osteichthyes
BT4 fishes
NT1 genypterus blacodes

GENYPTERUS BLACODES
uf ling (fishes)
BT1 genypterus
BT2 ophidiidae
BT3 ophidiiformes
BT4 osteichthyes
BT5 fishes

GEOCENAMUS
BT1 dolichodoridae
BT2 nematoda

GEOCHELONE
BT1 testudinidae
BT2 testudines
BT3 reptiles
NT1 geochelone carbonaria

GEOCHELONE CARBONARIA
BT1 geochelone
BT2 testudinidae
BT3 testudines
BT4 reptiles

GEOCHEMICAL PROSPECTING
BT1 surveying
rt geology

GEOCHEMISTRY
BT1 chemistry
BT1 geology
rt biogeochemistry

GEOCORIS
BT1 lygaeidae
BT2 heteroptera
NT1 geocoris bullatus
NT1 geocoris pallens
NT1 geocoris punctipes

GEOCORIS BULLATUS
BT1 geocoris
BT2 lygaeidae
BT3 heteroptera

GEOCORIS PALLENS
BT1 geocoris
BT2 lygaeidae
BT3 heteroptera

GEOCORIS PUNCTIPES
BT1 geocoris
BT2 lygaeidae
BT3 heteroptera

GEODORUM
BT1 orchidaceae
NT1 geodorum densiflorum

GEODORUM DENSIFLORUM
BT1 geodorum
BT2 orchidaceae
BT1 ornamental orchids

GEOFFROEA
BT1 leguminosae
NT1 geoffroea decorticans

GEOFFROEA DECORTICANS
BT1 geoffroea
BT2 leguminosae

GEOGRAPHERS
BT1 scientists
BT2 occupations
rt geography

GEOGRAPHICAL DISTRIBUTION
uf geographical location
BT1 distribution
rt central places
rt geography
rt location theory
rt new geographic records
rt population distribution
rt regional planning
rt spread
rt sympatric species
rt zoogeographical regions
rt zoogeography

geographical location
USE **geographical distribution**

geographical origin (varieties)
USE **provenance**

GEOGRAPHICAL RACES
BT1 races
BT2 breeds
rt geography

GEOGRAPHY
NT1 agricultural geography
NT1 biogeography
NT2 zoogeography
NT1 physical geography
NT1 rural economy
NT1 social geography
rt countries
rt geographers
rt geographical distribution
rt geographical races
rt geomorphology
rt human ecology
rt landscape
rt maps

GEOLOGICAL SEDIMENTATION
HN from 1990
uf deposition, sediment
uf sediment deposition
uf sediment transport
uf sedimentation, geological
uf transport, sediment
rt erosion
rt sediment

GEOLOGISTS
BT1 scientists
BT2 occupations
rt geology

GEOLOGY
NT1 biogeochemistry

GEOLOGY *cont.*
NT1 geochemistry
NT1 mineralogy
NT2 crystallography
NT1 stratigraphy
NT1 tectonics
rt aquifers
rt biology
rt geochemical prospecting
rt geologists
rt geomorphology
rt geothermal energy
rt old and fossil wood
rt palaeontology
rt pedology
rt physiographic features
rt rocks
rt soil parent materials

GEOMETRIDAE
BT1 lepidoptera
NT1 abraxas
NT2 abraxas grossulariata
NT1 alsophila
NT2 alsophila pometaria
NT1 anacamptodes
NT2 anacamptodes clivinaria
NT1 ascotis
NT2 ascotis selenaria
NT1 biston
NT2 biston betularia
NT1 bupalus
NT2 bupalus piniarius
NT1 buzura
NT2 buzura suppressaria
NT1 ennomos
NT2 ennomos subsignarius
NT1 epirrita
NT2 epirrita autumnata
NT1 erannis
NT2 erannis defoliaria
NT1 hypomecis
NT1 lambdina
NT2 lambdina fiscellaria
NT1 lycia
NT2 lycia hirtaria
NT1 nepytia
NT2 nepytia freemani
NT1 operophtera
NT2 operophtera bruceata
NT2 operophtera brumata
NT1 peribatodes
NT2 peribatodes rhomboidaria
NT1 semiothisa
NT2 semiothisa cyda

GEOMETRY
BT1 mathematics
rt asymmetry
rt dimensions

GEOMORPHOLOGY
rt geography
rt geology
rt landforms
rt landscape
rt physical geography
rt physiographic features
rt terrain
rt topography

GEOMYIDAE
uf pocket gophers
BT1 rodents
BT2 mammals
NT1 geomys
NT2 geomys bursarius
NT1 thomomys
NT2 thomomys bottae
NT2 thomomys talpoides

GEOMYS
BT1 geomyidae
BT2 rodents
BT3 mammals
NT1 geomys bursarius

GEOMYS BURSARIUS
BT1 geomys
BT2 geomyidae
BT3 rodents
BT4 mammals

GEOMYZA
BT1 opomyzidae
BT2 diptera
NT1 geomyza tripunctata

GEOMYZA TRIPUNCTATA
BT1 geomyza
BT2 opomyzidae
BT3 diptera

GEOPHAGIA
BT1 appetite disorders
BT2 digestive disorders
BT3 functional disorders
BT4 animal disorders
BT5 disorders
rt pica

GEOPLANIDAE
BT1 tricladida
BT2 turbellaria

GEORGETTE (AGRICOLA)
BT1 fabrics

GEORGIA
BT1 southeastern states of usa
BT2 southern states of usa
BT3 usa
BT4 north america
BT5 america

GEORGIAN MOUNTAIN
HN from 1990
BT1 cattle breeds
BT2 breeds

GEORGIAN SSR
uf *ussr in asia*
BT1 ussr
rt ussr in europe

GEOTAXIS
BT1 taxis
BT2 movement
rt gravity

GEOTHERMAL ENERGY
uf *energy, geothermal*
BT1 energy
rt energy sources
rt geology
rt heat

GEOTRICHOSIS
BT1 mycoses
BT2 infectious diseases
BT3 diseases
rt geotrichum candidum

GEOTRICHUM
BT1 deuteromycotina
NT1 geotrichum candidum
NT2 geotrichum candidum var. citri-aurantii

GEOTRICHUM CANDIDUM
uf *oospora lactis*
BT1 geotrichum
BT2 deuteromycotina
NT1 geotrichum candidum var. citri-aurantii
rt geotrichosis

GEOTRICHUM CANDIDUM VAR. CITRI-AURANTII
HN from 1990
uf *oospora citri-aurantii*
BT1 geotrichum candidum
BT2 geotrichum
BT3 deuteromycotina

geotrigona
USE **trigona**

GEOTROPISM
BT1 tropisms
BT2 movement
BT2 plant physiology
BT3 physiology
BT2 responses
rt roots

GEOTRUPES
BT1 geotrupidae

GEOTRUPES *cont.*
BT2 coleoptera
NT1 geotrupes stercorarius
NT1 geotrupes stercorosus

GEOTRUPES STERCORARIUS
BT1 geotrupes
BT2 geotrupidae
BT3 coleoptera

GEOTRUPES STERCOROSUS
BT1 geotrupes
BT2 geotrupidae
BT3 coleoptera

GEOTRUPIDAE
BT1 coleoptera
NT1 geotrupes
NT2 geotrupes stercorarius
NT2 geotrupes stercorosus

GEPHYROLINA
HN from 1990
BT1 cestodaria
BT2 cestoda

GERANIACEAE
NT1 erodium
NT2 erodium botrys
NT2 erodium cicutarium
NT2 erodium moschatum
NT1 geranium
NT2 geranium carolinianum
NT2 geranium collinum
NT2 geranium macrorrhizum
NT2 geranium maculatum
NT2 geranium pratense
NT2 geranium rectum
NT2 geranium sanguineum
NT2 geranium sibiricum
NT2 geranium thunbergii
NT2 geranium tripartitum
NT2 geranium tuberosum
NT2 geranium wilfordii
NT2 geranium yoshinoi
NT1 pelargonium
NT2 pelargonium australe
NT2 pelargonium capitatum
NT2 pelargonium crispum
NT2 pelargonium denticulatum
NT2 pelargonium glutinosum
NT2 pelargonium graveolens
NT2 pelargonium hortorum
NT2 pelargonium peltatum
NT2 pelargonium quercifolium
NT2 pelargonium radens
NT2 pelargonium roseum
NT2 pelargonium tomentosum
NT2 pelargonium zonale

GERANIAL
BT1 citral
BT2 aldehydes
BT2 monoterpenoids
BT3 terpenoids
BT4 isoprenoids
BT5 lipids

GERANIOL
BT1 alcohols
BT1 monoterpenoids
BT2 terpenoids
BT3 isoprenoids
BT4 lipids
rt essential oils
rt linalool

GERANIUM
BT1 geraniaceae
NT1 geranium carolinianum
NT1 geranium collinum
NT1 geranium macrorrhizum
NT1 geranium maculatum
NT1 geranium pratense
NT1 geranium rectum
NT1 geranium sanguineum
NT1 geranium sibiricum
NT1 geranium thunbergii
NT1 geranium tripartitum
NT1 geranium tuberosum
NT1 geranium wilfordii
NT1 geranium yoshinoi

GERANIUM CAROLINIANUM
BT1 geranium
BT2 geraniaceae

GERANIUM COLLINUM
BT1 geranium
BT2 geraniaceae

GERANIUM MACRORRHIZUM
BT1 essential oil plants
BT2 oil plants
BT1 geranium
BT2 geraniaceae
BT1 ornamental herbaceous plants

GERANIUM MACULATUM
BT1 geranium
BT2 geraniaceae

GERANIUM PRATENSE
BT1 geranium
BT2 geraniaceae
BT1 ornamental herbaceous plants

GERANIUM RECTUM
BT1 geranium
BT2 geraniaceae

GERANIUM SANGUINEUM
BT1 geranium
BT2 geraniaceae
BT1 ornamental herbaceous plants

GERANIUM SIBIRICUM
BT1 geranium
BT2 geraniaceae

GERANIUM THUNBERGII
BT1 geranium
BT2 geraniaceae
BT1 medicinal plants

GERANIUM TRIPARTITUM
BT1 geranium
BT2 geraniaceae

GERANIUM TUBEROSUM
BT1 geranium
BT2 geraniaceae

GERANIUM WILFORDII
BT1 geranium
BT2 geraniaceae

GERANIUM YOSHINOI
BT1 geranium
BT2 geraniaceae

geraniums
USE **pelargonium**

GERBER METHOD
BT1 analytical methods
BT2 methodology
rt amyl alcohol
rt milk fat

GERBERA
BT1 compositae
NT1 gerbera jamesonii

GERBERA JAMESONII
BT1 gerbera
BT2 compositae
BT1 ornamental herbaceous plants

GERBILLINAE
BT1 muridae
BT2 rodents
BT3 mammals
NT1 gerbillus
NT1 meriones
NT2 meriones crassus
NT2 meriones hurrianae
NT2 meriones libycus
NT2 meriones meridianus
NT2 meriones unguiculatus
NT1 psammomys
NT2 psammomys obesus
NT1 rhombomys
NT2 rhombomys opimus

GERBILLINAE *cont.*
NT1 tatera
NT2 tatera robusta

GERBILLUS
BT1 gerbillinae
BT2 muridae
BT3 rodents
BT4 mammals
rt gerbils

GERBILS
uf *sand rats*
BT1 laboratory mammals
BT2 laboratory animals
BT3 animals
BT1 pets
BT2 animals
rt gerbillus
rt meriones
rt muridae
rt rhombomys
rt tatera

GERIATRICS
uf *gerontology*
BT1 medicine
rt aging
rt old age

GERM CELLS
BT1 cells
NT1 ova
NT2 cumulus oophorus
NT2 helminth ova
NT2 oocytes
NT3 germinal vesicle
NT2 oogonia
NT2 zona pellucida
NT1 spermatogonia
NT1 spermatozoa
NT2 accessory spermatozoa
NT2 acrosome
NT2 midpiece
rt gametes
rt germ line
rt germinal epithelium
rt haploidy
rt meiosis
rt monogerm seeds
rt pollen
rt sexual reproduction

germ free state
USE **germfree state**

GERM LINE
rt germ cells

GERMAN BLACK PIED
BT1 cattle breeds
BT2 breeds

GERMAN BLACKHEADED MUTTON
BT1 sheep breeds
BT2 breeds

GERMAN BROWN
BT1 cattle breeds
BT2 breeds

GERMAN DEMOCRATIC REPUBLIC
uf *ddr*
uf *east germany*
uf *gdr*
uf *germany dr*
BT1 eastern europe
BT2 europe
rt cmea
rt east berlin

GERMAN FEDERAL REPUBLIC
uf *brd*
uf *dbr*
uf *germany fr*
uf *gfr*
uf *west germany*
BT1 western europe
BT2 europe
NT1 baden-wurttemberg
NT1 bavaria
NT1 hesse
NT1 lower saxony

GERMAN FEDERAL REPUBLIC *cont.*
NT1 north rhine-westphalia
NT1 rhineland palatinate
NT1 saarland
NT1 schleswig-holstein
rt european communities
rt oecd
rt west berlin

german heath
USE **heidschnucke**

GERMAN IMPROVED FAWN
BT1 goat breeds
BT2 breeds

GERMAN IMPROVED WHITE
BT1 goat breeds
BT2 breeds

GERMAN LANDRACE
BT1 pig breeds
BT2 breeds

GERMAN MOUNTAIN
HN from 1990
BT1 sheep breeds
BT2 breeds

GERMAN MUTTON MERINO
BT1 sheep breeds
BT2 breeds

GERMAN RED PIED
BT1 cattle breeds
BT2 breeds

GERMAN RIDING HORSE
HN from 1990
BT1 horse breeds
BT2 breeds

GERMAN SIMMENTAL
BT1 cattle breeds
BT2 breeds

GERMAN WHITEHEADED MUTTON
HN from 1990
BT1 sheep breeds
BT2 breeds

german yellow
USE **gelbvieh**

german yorkshire
USE **edelschwein**

GERMANIUM
BT1 metallic elements
BT2 elements
BT2 metals
BT1 purgatives
BT2 gastrointestinal agents
BT3 drugs

germany dr
USE **german democratic republic**

germany fr
USE **german federal republic**

GERMFREE ANIMALS
uf *pathogen-free animals*
BT1 laboratory animals
BT2 animals
rt bacteria
rt germfree husbandry
rt germfree state
rt gnotobiotic animals

GERMFREE HUSBANDRY
BT1 husbandry
rt bacteria
rt germfree animals
rt laboratory methods
rt laboratory rearing

GERMFREE STATE
HN from 1990; previously "germ free state"
uf *germ free state*
rt germfree animals

GERMINAL EPITHELIUM
BT1 ovaries
BT2 gonads
BT3 reproductive organs
rt germ cells

GERMINAL VESICLE
HN from 1990
BT1 oocytes
BT2 ova
BT3 gametes
BT3 germ cells
BT4 cells

GERMINATION
NT1 pollen germination
NT1 seed germination
NT1 spore germination
NT1 vivipary
rt after-ripening
rt emergence
rt germination cabinets
rt germination inhibitors
rt preharvest sprouting
rt seed testing
rt seed treatment
rt seeds
rt sprouting
rt viability

GERMINATION CABINETS
HN from 1990
BT1 equipment
rt germination
rt seed testing

GERMINATION INHIBITORS
BT1 growth inhibitors
BT2 inhibitors
BT2 plant growth regulators
BT3 growth regulators
rt germination

germination, pollen
USE **pollen germination**

GERMPLASM
rt genes
rt genetic resources
rt inheritance
rt protoplasm

germplasm banks
USE **gene banks**

GERMPLASM RELEASES
rt genetic resources
rt plant breeding
rt varieties

gerontology
USE **geriatrics**

GESNERIACEAE
NT1 achimenes
NT1 aeschynanthus
NT2 aeschynanthus hildebrandii
NT2 aeschynanthus radicans
NT2 aeschynanthus speciosus
NT1 alloplectus
NT2 alloplectus schlimii
NT1 alsobia
NT2 alsobia punctata
NT1 codonanthe
NT2 codonanthe gracilis
NT1 columnea
NT2 columnea stavanger
NT1 conandron
NT2 conandron ramondioides
NT1 didymocarpus
NT2 didymocarpus oblonga
NT2 didymocarpus pedicellata
NT1 episcia
NT2 episcia cupreata
NT1 gloxinia
NT2 gloxinia sylvatica
NT1 hypocyrta
NT2 hypocyrta glabra
NT1 jankaea
NT2 jankaea vandedemii
NT1 kohleria
NT2 kohleria eriantha
NT1 nautilocalyx
NT2 nautilocalyx bullatus

GESNERIACEAE *cont.*
NT1 nematanthus
NT2 nematanthus gregarius
NT1 rechsteineria
NT1 rehmannia
NT2 rehmannia glutinosa
NT1 saintpaulia
NT1 seemannia
NT1 sinningia
NT2 sinningia cardinalis
NT2 sinningia speciosa
NT1 smithiantha
NT2 smithiantha multiflora
NT1 streptocarpus
NT2 streptocarpus gardenii
NT2 streptocarpus hybridus
NT2 streptocarpus nobilis
NT2 streptocarpus rexii

gestation
USE **pregnancy**

gestation length
USE **gestation period**

GESTATION PERIOD
(length of time from conception to birth)
uf *gestation length*
uf *pregnancy duration*
BT1 duration
BT2 time
rt pregnancy

GETAH VIRUS
BT1 alphavirus
BT2 arboviruses
BT3 pathogens
BT2 togaviridae
BT3 viruses

GEUM
BT1 rosaceae
NT1 geum alepicum
NT1 geum bulgaricum
NT1 geum intermedium
NT1 geum montanum
NT1 geum rosii
NT1 geum urbanum

GEUM ALEPICUM
BT1 geum
BT2 rosaceae

GEUM BULGARICUM
BT1 geum
BT2 rosaceae

GEUM INTERMEDIUM
BT1 geum
BT2 rosaceae

GEUM MONTANUM
BT1 geum
BT2 rosaceae

GEUM ROSII
BT1 geum
BT2 rosaceae

GEUM URBANUM
BT1 geum
BT2 rosaceae

gfr
USE **german federal republic**

GHANA
BT1 west africa
BT2 africa south of sahara
BT3 africa
rt acp
rt anglophone africa
rt commonwealth of nations
rt developing countries
rt least developed countries

GHEE
BT1 milk products
BT2 products
rt butter
rt butter oil
rt clarification
rt clarifiers

gherkins
USE **cucumbers**

GHILJAI
HN from 1990
BT1 sheep breeds
BT2 breeds

GIANT CELLS
BT1 cells

GIARDIA
BT1 sarcomastigophora
BT2 protozoa
NT1 giardia canis
NT1 giardia caviae
NT1 giardia lamblia
NT1 giardia microti
NT1 giardia muris
NT1 giardia simoni

GIARDIA CANIS
BT1 giardia
BT2 sarcomastigophora
BT3 protozoa

GIARDIA CAVIAE
BT1 giardia
BT2 sarcomastigophora
BT3 protozoa

GIARDIA LAMBLIA
BT1 giardia
BT2 sarcomastigophora
BT3 protozoa
rt giardiasis

GIARDIA MICROTI
BT1 giardia
BT2 sarcomastigophora
BT3 protozoa

GIARDIA MURIS
BT1 giardia
BT2 sarcomastigophora
BT3 protozoa

GIARDIA SIMONI
BT1 giardia
BT2 sarcomastigophora
BT3 protozoa

GIARDIASIS
BT1 diarrhoea
BT2 digestive disorders
BT3 functional disorders
BT4 animal disorders
BT5 disorders
BT1 protozoal infections
BT2 parasitoses
BT3 diseases
rt giardia lamblia

GIBBERELLA
BT1 hypocreales
NT1 gibberella acuminata
NT1 gibberella avenacea
NT1 gibberella baccata
NT1 gibberella cyanogena
NT1 gibberella fujikuroi
NT2 gibberella fujikuroi var. subglutinans
NT1 gibberella gordonii
NT1 gibberella intricans
NT1 gibberella pulicaris
NT1 gibberella stilboides
NT1 gibberella zeae
rt fusarium

GIBBERELLA ACUMINATA
uf *fusarium acuminatum*
BT1 gibberella
BT2 hypocreales

GIBBERELLA AVENACEA
uf *fusarium avenaceum*
uf *fusarium effusum*
BT1 gibberella
BT2 hypocreales

GIBBERELLA BACCATA
uf *fusarium lateritium*
BT1 gibberella
BT2 hypocreales
BT1 mycoherbicides

GIBBERELLA BACCATA *cont.*
BT2 herbicides
BT3 pesticides
BT2 microbial pesticides
BT3 pesticides

gibberella cyanea
USE **gibberella gordonii**

GIBBERELLA CYANOGENA
uf *fusarium sulphureum*
BT1 gibberella
BT2 hypocreales

GIBBERELLA FUJIKUROI
uf *fusarium moniliforme*
BT1 gibberella
BT2 hypocreales
NT1 gibberella fujikuroi var. subglutinans

GIBBERELLA FUJIKUROI VAR. SUBGLUTINANS
uf *fusarium subglutinans*
BT1 gibberella fujikuroi
BT2 gibberella
BT3 hypocreales

GIBBERELLA GORDONII
uf *fusarium heterosporium*
uf *gibberella cyanea*
BT1 gibberella
BT2 hypocreales

GIBBERELLA INTRICANS
BT1 gibberella
BT2 hypocreales

GIBBERELLA PULICARIS
uf *fusarium sambucinum*
BT1 gibberella
BT2 hypocreales

GIBBERELLA STILBOIDES
uf *fusarium stilboides*
BT1 gibberella
BT2 hypocreales

GIBBERELLA ZEAE
uf *fusarium graminearum*
BT1 gibberella
BT2 hypocreales

GIBBERELLIC ACID
uf *ga (plant growth regulator)*
BT1 gibberellins
BT2 diterpenoids
BT3 terpenoids
BT4 isoprenoids
BT5 lipids
BT2 plant growth regulators
BT3 growth regulators

GIBBERELLINS
BT1 diterpenoids
BT2 terpenoids
BT3 isoprenoids
BT4 lipids
BT1 plant growth regulators
BT2 growth regulators
NT1 gibberellic acid

GIBBIUM
BT1 ptinidae
BT2 coleoptera
NT1 gibbium psylloides

GIBBIUM PSYLLOIDES
BT1 gibbium
BT2 ptinidae
BT3 coleoptera

GIBBSITE
BT1 nonclay minerals
BT2 minerals
rt aluminium

GIBRALTAR
BT1 western europe
BT2 europe
rt mediterranean countries

GIEMSA STAINING
BT1 staining
BT2 techniques

GIEMSA STAINING *cont.*
rt microscopy

GIFTED PERSONS (AGRICOLA)
rt exceptional children (agricola)

GIGADUCTUS
BT1 apicomplexa
BT2 protozoa

GIGANTISM
BT1 growth disorders
BT2 animal disorders
BT3 disorders

GIGANTOCHLOA
BT1 gramineae
NT1 gigantochloa apus
NT1 gigantochloa levis
rt bamboos

GIGANTOCHLOA APUS
uf *bambusa apus*
BT1 gigantochloa
BT2 gramineae

GIGANTOCHLOA LEVIS
BT1 gigantochloa
BT2 gramineae

GIGANTOCOTYLE
BT1 paramphistomatidae
BT2 digenea
BT3 trematoda
NT1 gigantocotyle explanatum
NT1 gigantocotyle symmeri

GIGANTOCOTYLE EXPLANATUM
BT1 gigantocotyle
BT2 paramphistomatidae
BT3 digenea
BT4 trematoda

GIGANTOCOTYLE SYMMERI
BT1 gigantocotyle
BT2 paramphistomatidae
BT3 digenea
BT4 trematoda

GIGANTOLINA
HN from 1990
BT1 cestodaria
BT2 cestoda

GIGANTORHYNCHIDAE
BT1 acanthocephala
NT1 mediorhynchus

GIGASPORA
BT1 endogonales
BT1 mycorrhizal fungi
BT2 fungi
NT1 gigaspora calospora
NT1 gigaspora margarita

GIGASPORA CALOSPORA
BT1 gigaspora
BT2 endogonales
BT2 mycorrhizal fungi
BT3 fungi

GIGASPORA MARGARITA
BT1 gigaspora
BT2 endogonales
BT2 mycorrhizal fungi
BT3 fungi

gilbert islands
USE **kiribati**

GILGAI RELIEF
BT1 soil morphological features
rt patterned ground

GILLETTEELLA
BT1 adelgidae
BT2 aphidoidea
BT3 sternorrhyncha
BT4 homoptera
NT1 gilletteella cooleyi
rt adelges

GILLETTEELLA COOLEYI
uf *adelges cooleyi*
BT1 gilletteella

GILLETTEELLA COOLEYI *cont.*
BT2 adelgidae
BT3 aphidoidea
BT4 sternorrhyncha
BT5 homoptera

GILLS
BT1 respiratory system
BT2 body parts
rt fishes

GILMANIELLA
BT1 deuteromycotina
NT1 gilmaniella subornata

GILMANIELLA SUBORNATA
BT1 gilmaniella
BT2 deuteromycotina

GILPINIA
BT1 diprionidae
BT2 hymenoptera
NT1 gilpinia frutetorum
NT1 gilpinia hercyniae
rt diprion

GILPINIA FRUTETORUM
uf *diprion frutetorum*
BT1 gilpinia
BT2 diprionidae
BT3 hymenoptera

GILPINIA HERCYNIAE
uf *diprion hercyniae*
BT1 gilpinia
BT2 diprionidae
BT3 hymenoptera

GILTS
BT1 female animals
BT2 animals
rt pigs
rt sows

GIN
BT1 distilled spirits
BT2 alcoholic beverages
BT3 beverages

gin trash
USE **cotton gin trash**

GINGER
BT1 spices
BT2 plant products
BT3 products
rt zingiber officinale

GINGHAM (AGRICOLA)
BT1 fabrics

GINGIDIUM
BT1 umbelliferae

GINGIVA
uf *gums (mouth)*
BT1 mouth
BT2 digestive system
BT3 body parts
rt gingivitis
rt teeth

GINGIVITIS
BT1 periodontal diseases
BT2 mouth diseases
BT3 organic diseases
BT4 diseases
rt gingiva
rt inflammation

GINI COEFFICIENT
BT1 statistical analysis
BT2 data analysis
BT2 statistics

GINKGO
BT1 ginkgoaceae
NT1 ginkgo biloba

GINKGO BILOBA
BT1 antibacterial plants
BT1 antifungal plants
BT1 forest trees
BT1 ginkgo
BT2 ginkgoaceae

GINKGO BILOBA *cont.*
BT1 medicinal plants
BT1 ornamental conifers
BT2 conifers
BT2 ornamental woody plants

GINKGOACEAE
NT1 ginkgo
NT2 ginkgo biloba
rt coniferae

GINNING
BT1 processing
NT1 cotton ginning
rt gins
rt kapok
rt lint

GINS
BT1 farm machinery
BT2 machinery
NT1 cotton gins
rt ginning
rt kapok
rt traps

ginseng
USE **panax pseudoginseng**

GIR
BT1 zebu breeds
BT2 breeds

GIRAFFA
BT1 giraffidae
BT2 ruminantia
BT3 artiodactyla
BT4 mammals
BT4 ungulates
NT1 giraffa camelopardalis

GIRAFFA CAMELOPARDALIS
uf *giraffes*
BT1 giraffa
BT2 giraffidae
BT3 ruminantia
BT4 artiodactyla
BT5 mammals
BT5 ungulates

giraffes
USE **giraffa camelopardalis**

GIRAFFIDAE
BT1 ruminantia
BT2 artiodactyla
BT3 mammals
BT3 ungulates
NT1 giraffa
NT2 giraffa camelopardalis
NT1 okapia
NT2 okapia johnstoni

GIRDERS
BT1 structural components
BT2 components
rt beams
rt building construction
rt construction technology
rt struts

GIRDLING
HN from 1989; previously ringing
BT1 forestry practices
BT2 forestry
rt ringing

GIRELLA
BT1 kyphosidae
BT2 perciformes
BT3 osteichthyes
BT4 fishes

GIRGENTANA
HN from 1990
BT1 goat breeds
BT2 breeds

GIRLS
rt daughters
rt man

GIRTH
BT1 dimensions

GIRTH *cont.*
NT1 heart girth
rt diameter
rt form quotients
rt increment
rt size

GISEKIA
BT1 aizoaceae
NT1 gisekia pharmacoides

GISEKIA PHARMACOIDES
BT1 gisekia
BT2 aizoaceae

GIZZARD
uf *ventriculus muscularis*
BT1 stomach
BT2 digestive system
BT3 body parts
rt gizzard erosion

GIZZARD EROSION
BT1 digestive disorders
BT2 functional disorders
BT3 animal disorders
BT4 disorders
rt gizzard

GLABROMICROPLITIS
BT1 braconidae
BT2 hymenoptera
NT1 glabromicroplitis croceipes
rt microgaster

GLABROMICROPLITIS CROCEIPES
uf *microgaster croceipes*
uf *microplitis croceipes*
BT1 glabromicroplitis
BT2 braconidae
BT3 hymenoptera

GLACIAL DEPOSITS
BT1 soil parent materials
rt glacial till

GLACIAL SOILS
BT1 soil types (lithological)
rt glacial till soils
rt moraine soils
rt periglacial features

GLACIAL TILL
BT1 soil parent materials
rt glacial deposits
rt glacial till soils

GLACIAL TILL SOILS
BT1 soil types (lithological)
rt glacial soils
rt glacial till

GLADIOLUS
BT1 iridaceae
NT1 gladiolus atroviolaceus
NT1 gladiolus communis
NT1 gladiolus illyricus
NT1 gladiolus imbricatus
NT1 gladiolus italicus
NT1 gladiolus natalensis
NT1 gladiolus palustris

GLADIOLUS ATROVIOLACEUS
BT1 gladiolus
BT2 iridaceae
BT1 ornamental bulbs
rt corms

GLADIOLUS COMMUNIS
BT1 gladiolus
BT2 iridaceae
BT1 ornamental bulbs
rt corms

GLADIOLUS ILLYRICUS
BT1 gladiolus
BT2 iridaceae
BT1 ornamental bulbs
rt corms

GLADIOLUS IMBRICATUS
BT1 gladiolus
BT2 iridaceae
BT1 ornamental bulbs
rt corms

GLADIOLUS ITALICUS
BT1 gladiolus
BT2 iridaceae
BT1 ornamental bulbs
rt corms

GLADIOLUS NATALENSIS
uf *gladiolus psittacinus*
BT1 gladiolus
BT2 iridaceae
BT1 ornamental bulbs
rt corms

GLADIOLUS PALUSTRIS
BT1 gladiolus
BT2 iridaceae
BT1 ornamental bulbs
rt corms

gladiolus psittacinus
USE **gladiolus natalensis**

GLAEBULES
BT1 soil micromorphological features
BT2 soil morphological features
NT1 septaria

GLANDERS
BT1 bacterial diseases
BT2 infectious diseases
BT3 diseases
BT1 horse diseases
BT2 animal diseases
BT3 diseases
rt pseudomonas mallei

GLANDS
NT1 glands (animal)
NT2 accessory glands
NT3 bulbo-urethral gland
NT3 prostate
NT3 vesicular gland
NT2 anal glands
NT2 endocrine glands
NT3 adrenal glands
NT4 adrenal cortex
NT4 adrenal medulla
NT3 parathyroid
NT3 pineal body
NT3 pituitary
NT4 anterior pituitary
NT4 posterior pituitary
NT3 thyroid gland
NT3 ultimobranchial body
NT2 endometrial glands
NT2 gastric glands
NT2 hepatopancreas
NT2 hypopharyngeal glands
NT2 labial glands
NT2 lacrimal apparatus
NT2 mammary glands
NT3 individual quarters
NT3 teat number
NT3 teats
NT4 supernumerary teats
NT3 udders
NT2 mucus glands
NT2 nasonov gland
NT2 poll glands
NT2 preputial glands
NT2 prothoracic glands
NT2 salivary glands
NT3 mandibular glands
NT3 parotid gland
NT2 salt gland
NT2 scent glands
NT2 shell gland
NT2 silk glands
NT2 skin glands
NT3 sweat glands
NT2 tarsal glands
NT2 thymus gland
NT2 venom glands
NT3 alkaline venom gland
NT2 wax glands
NT1 plant glands
NT2 salt glands

GLANDS (ANIMAL)
BT1 body parts
BT1 glands
NT1 accessory glands

GLANDS (ANIMAL) *cont.*
NT2 bulbo-urethral gland
NT2 prostate
NT2 vesicular gland
NT1 anal glands
NT1 endocrine glands
NT2 adrenal glands
NT3 adrenal cortex
NT3 adrenal medulla
NT2 parathyroid
NT2 pineal body
NT2 pituitary
NT3 anterior pituitary
NT3 posterior pituitary
NT2 thyroid gland
NT2 ultimobranchial body
NT1 endometrial glands
NT1 gastric glands
NT1 hepatopancreas
NT1 hypopharyngeal glands
NT1 labial glands
NT1 lacrimal apparatus
NT1 mammary glands
NT2 individual quarters
NT2 teat number
NT2 teats
NT3 supernumerary teats
NT2 udders
NT1 mucus glands
NT1 nasonov gland
NT1 poll glands
NT1 preputial glands
NT1 prothoracic glands
NT1 salivary glands
NT2 mandibular glands
NT2 parotid gland
NT1 salt gland
NT1 scent glands
NT1 shell gland
NT1 silk glands
NT1 skin glands
NT2 sweat glands
NT1 tarsal glands
NT1 thymus gland
NT1 venom glands
NT2 alkaline venom gland
NT1 wax glands
rt gonads

glands, plant
USE **plant glands**

GLASS
BT1 building materials
BT2 materials
NT1 coated glass
NT1 diffused glass
NT1 glasswool
rt double glazing
rt glazing
rt windows

glass, coated
USE **coated glass**

glass, diffused
USE **diffused glass**

GLASSFIBRE
AF fiberglass
BT1 insulating materials
BT2 materials
rt glassfibre reinforced plastics

GLASSFIBRE REINFORCED PLASTICS
AF fiberglass reinforced plastics
uf *plastics, glassfibre reinforced*
BT1 building materials
BT2 materials
BT1 plastics
rt glassfibre

glasshouses
USE **greenhouses**

GLASSINESS
BT1 plant disorders
BT2 disorders
rt lettuces

GLASSWARE (AGRICOLA)
rt crystal (agricola)
rt table settings (agricola)

GLASSWOOL
BT1 glass
BT2 building materials
BT3 materials
BT1 insulating materials
BT2 materials
rt rockwool

GLAUCIUM
BT1 papaveraceae
NT1 glaucium contortuplicatum
NT1 glaucium fimbrilligerum
NT1 glaucium flavum
NT1 glaucium oxylobum
NT1 glaucium pulchrum
NT1 glaucium vitellinum

GLAUCIUM CONTORTUPLICATUM
BT1 glaucium
BT2 papaveraceae

GLAUCIUM FIMBRILLIGERUM
BT1 glaucium
BT2 papaveraceae

GLAUCIUM FLAVUM
BT1 glaucium
BT2 papaveraceae

GLAUCIUM OXYLOBUM
BT1 glaucium
BT2 papaveraceae

GLAUCIUM PULCHRUM
BT1 glaucium
BT2 papaveraceae

GLAUCIUM VITELLINUM
BT1 glaucium
BT2 papaveraceae

GLAUCOMA
BT1 eye diseases
BT2 organic diseases
BT3 diseases
rt acetazolamide

GLAUCOMYS
BT1 sciuridae
BT2 rodents
BT3 mammals

GLAUCONITE
BT1 clay minerals
BT2 minerals
BT1 magnesium fertilizers
BT2 fertilizers
BT1 potassium fertilizers
BT2 fertilizers
BT1 silicon fertilizers
BT2 trace element fertilizers
BT3 fertilizers

glaze
USE **ice damage**

GLAZES (AGRICOLA)
BT1 coatings

GLAZING
NT1 double glazing
rt cladding
rt glass
rt plastic cladding

glazing, double
USE **double glazing**

GLECHOMA
BT1 labiatae
NT1 glechoma hederacea

GLECHOMA HEDERACEA
BT1 glechoma
BT2 labiatae

gleditschia
USE **gleditsia**

GLEDITSIA
uf *gleditschia*
BT1 leguminosae

GLEDITSIA *cont.*
NT1 gleditsia caspica
NT1 gleditsia triacanthos

GLEDITSIA CASPICA
BT1 gleditsia
BT2 leguminosae
BT1 ornamental woody plants

GLEDITSIA TRIACANTHOS
BT1 forest trees
BT1 gleditsia
BT2 leguminosae
BT1 ornamental woody plants

GLEICHENIA
BT1 gleicheniaceae
NT1 gleichenia glauca
NT1 gleichenia japonica

GLEICHENIA GLAUCA
BT1 gleichenia
BT2 gleicheniaceae

GLEICHENIA JAPONICA
BT1 gleichenia
BT2 gleicheniaceae

GLEICHENIACEAE
NT1 dicranopteris
NT2 dicranopteris linearis
NT1 gleichenia
NT2 gleichenia glauca
NT2 gleichenia japonica

GLEY PODZOLS
BT1 podzols
BT2 soil types (genetic)

GLEY SOILS
uf *meadow soils*
BT1 gleysols
BT2 soil types (genetic)
rt gleyification

GLEYIFICATION
BT1 soil formation
rt gley soils

GLEYS
BT1 gleysols
BT2 soil types (genetic)

GLEYSOLS
BT1 soil types (genetic)
NT1 gley soils
NT1 gleys
NT1 humic gleysols
NT1 stagnohumic gley soils
NT1 tarai soils
NT1 thionic gleys
NT1 tundra soils
NT1 tundric gleysols

GLIADIN
BT1 prolamins
BT2 cereal proteins
BT3 plant proteins
BT4 proteins
BT5 peptides
rt gliadin antibodies

GLIADIN ANTIBODIES
BT1 antibodies
BT2 immunoglobulins
BT3 glycoproteins
BT4 proteins
BT5 peptides
BT3 immunological factors
rt gliadin

GLIBENCLAMIDE
uf *glyburide*
BT1 hypoglycaemic agents
BT2 haematologic agents
BT3 drugs
BT1 sulfonylureas
BT2 sulfonamides
BT3 amides
BT4 organic nitrogen compounds
BT3 organic sulfur compounds

GLICLAZIDE
BT1 hypoglycaemic agents

GLICLAZIDE *cont.*
BT2 haematologic agents
BT3 drugs
BT1 sulfonylureas
BT2 sulfonamides
BT3 amides
BT4 organic nitrogen compounds
BT3 organic sulfur compounds

GLIDING
BT1 aerosports
BT2 outdoor recreation
BT3 recreation
BT2 sport
NT1 hang gliding

GLIOCLADIUM
BT1 deuteromycotina
NT1 gliocladium roseum
NT1 gliocladium virens

GLIOCLADIUM ROSEUM
BT1 gliocladium
BT2 deuteromycotina

GLIOCLADIUM VIRENS
BT1 fungal antagonists
BT2 fungicides
BT3 pesticides
BT2 microbial pesticides
BT3 pesticides
BT1 gliocladium
BT2 deuteromycotina

GLIPIZIDE
BT1 hypoglycaemic agents
BT2 haematologic agents
BT3 drugs
BT1 sulfonylureas
BT2 sulfonamides
BT3 amides
BT4 organic nitrogen compounds
BT3 organic sulfur compounds

GLIRICIDIA
BT1 leguminosae
NT1 gliricidia maculata
NT1 gliricidia sepium

GLIRICIDIA MACULATA
BT1 gliricidia
BT2 leguminosae

GLIRICIDIA SEPIUM
BT1 forest trees
BT1 gliricidia
BT2 leguminosae
BT1 poisonous plants

GLIRICOLA
BT1 gyropidae
BT2 amblycera
BT3 mallophaga
BT4 phthiraptera
NT1 gliricola porcelli
rt gyropus

GLIRICOLA PORCELLI
uf *gyropus gracilis*
BT1 gliricola
BT2 gyropidae
BT3 amblycera
BT4 mallophaga
BT5 phthiraptera

GLIRIDAE
uf *muscardinidae*
BT1 rodents
BT2 mammals
NT1 eliomys
NT2 eliomys quercinus
NT1 glis
NT2 glis glis

GLIS
BT1 gliridae
BT2 rodents
BT3 mammals
NT1 glis glis

GLIS GLIS
BT1 glis

GLIS GLIS *cont.*
BT2 gliridae
BT3 rodents
BT4 mammals

GLISCHROCHILUS
BT1 nitidulidae
BT2 coleoptera
NT1 glischrochilus quadrisignatus

GLISCHROCHILUS QUADRISIGNATUS
BT1 glischrochilus
BT2 nitidulidae
BT3 coleoptera

GLOBE ARTICHOKES
uf *artichoke, globe*
BT1 leafy vegetables
BT2 vegetables
BT1 medicinal plants
rt cynara scolymus

globidium
USE **besnoitia**

GLOBINS
HN from 1990
BT1 histones
BT2 proteins
BT3 peptides
rt haemoglobin
rt myoglobin

GLOBOCEPHALUS
BT1 ancylostomatidae
BT2 nematoda
NT1 globocephalus urosubulatus

GLOBOCEPHALUS UROSUBULATUS
BT1 globocephalus
BT2 ancylostomatidae
BT3 nematoda

GLOBODERA
BT1 heteroderidae
BT2 nematoda
NT1 globodera pallida
NT1 globodera rostochiensis
NT1 globodera solanacearum
rt heterodera

GLOBODERA PALLIDA
uf *heterodera pallida*
BT1 globodera
BT2 heteroderidae
BT3 nematoda

GLOBODERA ROSTOCHIENSIS
uf *heterodera rostochiensis*
BT1 globodera
BT2 heteroderidae
BT3 nematoda

GLOBODERA SOLANACEARUM
uf *heterodera solanacearum*
BT1 globodera
BT2 heteroderidae
BT3 nematoda

GLOBULARIA
BT1 globulariaceae
NT1 globularia alypum

GLOBULARIA ALYPUM
BT1 globularia
BT2 globulariaceae

GLOBULARIACEAE
NT1 globularia
NT2 globularia alypum

GLOBULE MEMBRANE
BT1 membranes
rt milk fat

GLOBULINS
BT1 proteins
BT2 peptides
NT1 α-fetoprotein
NT1 actin
NT1 arachins
NT1 haemopexin
NT1 lactoglobulins

GLOBULINS *cont.*
NT2 β-lactoglobulin
NT1 legumin
NT1 microglobulins
NT1 myosin
NT1 ovoglobulin
NT1 phaseolin
NT1 thyroglobulin
NT1 transcobalamins
NT1 vicilin
rt hypogammaglobulinaemia

γ-globulins
USE **immunoglobulins**

GLOEOCAPSA
BT1 cyanobacteria
BT2 prokaryotes
NT1 gloeocapsa alpicola

GLOEOCAPSA ALPICOLA
BT1 gloeocapsa
BT2 cyanobacteria
BT3 prokaryotes

GLOEOCERCOSPORA
BT1 deuteromycotina
NT1 gloeocercospora sorghi

GLOEOCERCOSPORA SORGHI
BT1 gloeocercospora
BT2 deuteromycotina

GLOEOPHYLLUM
HN from 1990
BT1 aphyllophorales
NT1 gloeophyllum sepiarium
NT1 gloeophyllum trabeum
rt lenzites

GLOEOPHYLLUM SEPIARIUM
HN from 1990
uf *lenzites sepiaria*
BT1 gloeophyllum
BT2 aphyllophorales

GLOEOPHYLLUM TRABEUM
HN from 1990
uf *lenzites trabea*
BT1 gloeophyllum
BT2 aphyllophorales

GLOEOSPORIUM
BT1 deuteromycotina
NT1 gloeosporium amygdalinum
NT1 gloeosporium minus
rt colletotrichum
rt elsinoe
rt glomerella
rt pezicula
rt piggotia
rt pyrenopeziza

gloeosporium alborubrum
USE **glomerella cingulata**

gloeosporium album
USE **pezicula alba**

gloeosporium ampelina
USE **elsinoe ampelina**

gloeosporium ampelophagum
USE **elsinoe ampelina**

GLOEOSPORIUM AMYGDALINUM
BT1 gloeosporium
BT2 deuteromycotina

gloeosporium concentricum
USE **pyrenopeziza brassicae**

gloeosporium coryli
USE **piggotia coryli**

gloeosporium fructigenum
USE **glomerella cingulata**

gloeosporium laeticolor
USE **glomerella cingulata**

GLOEOSPORIUM MINUS
BT1 gloeosporium
BT2 deuteromycotina

gloeosporium musarum
USE **colletotrichum musae**

gloeosporium perennans
USE **pezicula malicorticis**

gloeosporium piperatum
USE **glomerella cingulata**

GLOMERELLA
BT1 polystigmatales
NT1 glomerella cingulata
NT2 glomerella cingulata f.sp. aeschynomene
NT1 glomerella glycines
NT1 glomerella gossypii
NT1 glomerella phomoides
NT1 glomerella tucumanensis
rt colletotrichum
rt gloeosporium
rt physalospora

GLOMERELLA CINGULATA
uf *colletotrichum coffeanum*
uf *colletotrichum fragariae*
uf *colletotrichum gloeosporioides*
uf *gloeosporium alborubrum*
uf *gloeosporium fructigenum*
uf *gloeosporium laeticolor*
uf *gloeosporium piperatum*
BT1 glomerella
BT2 polystigmatales
NT1 glomerella cingulata f.sp. aeschynomene

GLOMERELLA CINGULATA F.SP. AESCHYNOMENE
BT1 glomerella cingulata
BT2 glomerella
BT3 polystigmatales
BT1 mycoherbicides
BT2 herbicides
BT3 pesticides
BT2 microbial pesticides
BT3 pesticides

glomerella cingulata var. orbiculare
USE **colletotrichum orbiculare**

GLOMERELLA GLYCINES
uf *colletotrichum glycines*
BT1 glomerella
BT2 polystigmatales

GLOMERELLA GOSSYPII
uf *colletotrichum gossypii*
BT1 glomerella
BT2 polystigmatales

GLOMERELLA PHOMOIDES
uf *colletotrichum phomoides*
BT1 glomerella
BT2 polystigmatales

GLOMERELLA TUCUMANENSIS
uf *colletotrichum falcatum*
uf *helminthosporium tucumanensis*
uf *physalospora tucumanensis*
BT1 glomerella
BT2 polystigmatales

GLOMERIDAE
BT1 diplopoda
BT2 myriapoda
BT3 arthropods
NT1 glomeris
NT2 glomeris marginata

GLOMERIS
BT1 glomeridae
BT2 diplopoda
BT3 myriapoda
BT4 arthropods
NT1 glomeris marginata

GLOMERIS MARGINATA
BT1 glomeris
BT2 glomeridae
BT3 diplopoda
BT4 myriapoda
BT5 arthropods

GLOMERULAR FILTRATION
BT1 filtration
BT2 processing
NT1 glomerular filtration rate
rt kidneys
rt renal clearance

GLOMERULAR FILTRATION RATE
BT1 glomerular filtration
BT2 filtration
BT3 processing

GLOMERULONEPHRITIS
BT1 glomerulopathy
BT2 kidney diseases
BT3 urinary tract diseases
BT4 organic diseases
BT5 diseases
rt nephritis

GLOMERULOPATHY
HN from 1990
BT1 kidney diseases
BT2 urinary tract diseases
BT3 organic diseases
BT4 diseases
NT1 glomerulonephritis
rt glomerulus

GLOMERULUS
HN from 1989
BT1 kidneys
BT2 urinary tract
BT3 urogenital system
BT4 body parts
rt glomerulopathy

GLOMUS
BT1 endogonales
BT1 mycorrhizal fungi
BT2 fungi
NT1 glomus aggregatum
NT1 glomus caledonium
NT1 glomus clarum
NT1 glomus deserticola
NT1 glomus etunicatum
NT1 glomus fasciculatum
NT1 glomus intraradices
NT1 glomus macrocarpum
NT1 glomus manihotis
NT1 glomus microcarpum
NT1 glomus microsporum
NT1 glomus monosporum
NT1 glomus mosseae
NT1 glomus occultum
NT1 glomus tenue
NT1 glomus tubiforme
NT1 glomus versiforme

GLOMUS AGGREGATUM
HN from 1990
BT1 glomus
BT2 endogonales
BT2 mycorrhizal fungi
BT3 fungi

GLOMUS CALEDONIUM
BT1 glomus
BT2 endogonales
BT2 mycorrhizal fungi
BT3 fungi

GLOMUS CLARUM
HN from 1990
BT1 glomus
BT2 endogonales
BT2 mycorrhizal fungi
BT3 fungi

GLOMUS DESERTICOLA
HN from 1990
BT1 glomus
BT2 endogonales
BT2 mycorrhizal fungi
BT3 fungi

glomus epigaeum
USE **glomus versiforme**

GLOMUS ETUNICATUM
BT1 glomus
BT2 endogonales
BT2 mycorrhizal fungi
BT3 fungi

GLOMUS FASCICULATUM
BT1 glomus
BT2 endogonales
BT2 mycorrhizal fungi
BT3 fungi

GLOMUS INTRARADICES
HN from 1990
BT1 glomus
BT2 endogonales
BT2 mycorrhizal fungi
BT3 fungi

GLOMUS MACROCARPUM
uf *glomus macrocarpus*
BT1 glomus
BT2 endogonales
BT2 mycorrhizal fungi
BT3 fungi

glomus macrocarpus
USE **glomus macrocarpum**

GLOMUS MANIHOTIS
HN from 1990
BT1 glomus
BT2 endogonales
BT2 mycorrhizal fungi
BT3 fungi

GLOMUS MICROCARPUM
uf *glomus microcarpus*
BT1 glomus
BT2 endogonales
BT2 mycorrhizal fungi
BT3 fungi

glomus microcarpus
USE **glomus microcarpum**

GLOMUS MICROSPORUM
BT1 glomus
BT2 endogonales
BT2 mycorrhizal fungi
BT3 fungi

GLOMUS MONOSPORUM
BT1 glomus
BT2 endogonales
BT2 mycorrhizal fungi
BT3 fungi

GLOMUS MOSSEAE
BT1 glomus
BT2 endogonales
BT2 mycorrhizal fungi
BT3 fungi

GLOMUS OCCULTUM
HN from 1990
BT1 glomus
BT2 endogonales
BT2 mycorrhizal fungi
BT3 fungi

GLOMUS TENUE
BT1 glomus
BT2 endogonales
BT2 mycorrhizal fungi
BT3 fungi

GLOMUS TUBIFORME
HN from 1990
BT1 glomus
BT2 endogonales
BT2 mycorrhizal fungi
BT3 fungi

GLOMUS VERSIFORME
HN from 1990
uf *glomus epigaeum*
BT1 glomus
BT2 endogonales
BT2 mycorrhizal fungi
BT3 fungi

GLORIOSA
BT1 liliaceae
NT1 gloriosa rothschildiana
NT1 gloriosa superba

GLORIOSA ROTHSCHILDIANA
BT1 gloriosa
BT2 liliaceae
BT1 ornamental bulbs

GLORIOSA ROTHSCHILDIANA *cont.*
rt tubers

GLORIOSA SUPERBA
BT1 gloriosa
BT2 liliaceae
BT1 ornamental bulbs
BT1 poisonous plants
rt tubers

GLOSSARIES
uf *terminologies*
BT1 publications
rt dictionaries
rt nomenclature
rt terminology

GLOSSATELLA
BT1 ciliophora
BT2 protozoa

GLOSSINA
uf *tsetse fly*
BT1 glossinidae
BT2 diptera
NT1 glossina austeni
NT1 glossina brevipalpis
NT1 glossina fusca
NT1 glossina fuscipes
NT2 glossina fuscipes fuscipes
NT2 glossina fuscipes quanzensis
NT1 glossina longipalpis
NT1 glossina longipennis
NT1 glossina medicorum
NT1 glossina morsitans
NT2 glossina morsitans centralis
NT2 glossina morsitans morsitans
NT2 glossina morsitans submorsitans
NT1 glossina nigrofusca
NT1 glossina pallicera
NT1 glossina pallidipes
NT1 glossina palpalis
NT2 glossina palpalis gambiensis
NT2 glossina palpalis palpalis
NT1 glossina swynnertoni
NT1 glossina tabaniformis
NT1 glossina tachinoides
rt biconical traps
rt tsetse screens

GLOSSINA AUSTENI
BT1 glossina
BT2 glossinidae
BT3 diptera

GLOSSINA BREVIPALPIS
BT1 glossina
BT2 glossinidae
BT3 diptera

GLOSSINA FUSCA
BT1 glossina
BT2 glossinidae
BT3 diptera

GLOSSINA FUSCIPES
BT1 glossina
BT2 glossinidae
BT3 diptera
NT1 glossina fuscipes fuscipes
NT1 glossina fuscipes quanzensis

GLOSSINA FUSCIPES FUSCIPES
BT1 glossina fuscipes
BT2 glossina
BT3 glossinidae
BT4 diptera

GLOSSINA FUSCIPES QUANZENSIS
BT1 glossina fuscipes
BT2 glossina
BT3 glossinidae
BT4 diptera

GLOSSINA LONGIPALPIS
BT1 glossina
BT2 glossinidae
BT3 diptera

GLOSSINA LONGIPENNIS
BT1 glossina
BT2 glossinidae
BT3 diptera

GLOSSINA MEDICORUM
HN from 1989
BT1 glossina
BT2 glossinidae
BT3 diptera

GLOSSINA MORSITANS
BT1 glossina
BT2 glossinidae
BT3 diptera
NT1 glossina morsitans centralis
NT1 glossina morsitans morsitans
NT1 glossina morsitans submorsitans

GLOSSINA MORSITANS CENTRALIS
BT1 glossina morsitans
BT2 glossina
BT3 glossinidae
BT4 diptera

GLOSSINA MORSITANS MORSITANS
BT1 glossina morsitans
BT2 glossina
BT3 glossinidae
BT4 diptera

GLOSSINA MORSITANS SUBMORSITANS
BT1 glossina morsitans
BT2 glossina
BT3 glossinidae
BT4 diptera

GLOSSINA NIGROFUSCA
BT1 glossina
BT2 glossinidae
BT3 diptera

GLOSSINA PALLICERA
BT1 glossina
BT2 glossinidae
BT3 diptera

GLOSSINA PALLIDIPES
BT1 glossina
BT2 glossinidae
BT3 diptera

GLOSSINA PALPALIS
BT1 glossina
BT2 glossinidae
BT3 diptera
NT1 glossina palpalis gambiensis
NT1 glossina palpalis palpalis

GLOSSINA PALPALIS GAMBIENSIS
BT1 glossina palpalis
BT2 glossina
BT3 glossinidae
BT4 diptera

GLOSSINA PALPALIS PALPALIS
BT1 glossina palpalis
BT2 glossina
BT3 glossinidae
BT4 diptera

GLOSSINA SWYNNERTONI
BT1 glossina
BT2 glossinidae
BT3 diptera

GLOSSINA TABANIFORMIS
BT1 glossina
BT2 glossinidae
BT3 diptera

GLOSSINA TACHINOIDES
BT1 glossina
BT2 glossinidae
BT3 diptera

GLOSSINIDAE
BT1 diptera
NT1 glossina

GLOSSINIDAE *cont.*
NT2 glossina austeni
NT2 glossina brevipalpis
NT2 glossina fusca
NT2 glossina fuscipes
NT3 glossina fuscipes fuscipes
NT3 glossina fuscipes quanzensis
NT2 glossina longipalpis
NT2 glossina longipennis
NT2 glossina medicorum
NT2 glossina morsitans
NT3 glossina morsitans centralis
NT3 glossina morsitans morsitans
NT3 glossina morsitans submorsitans
NT2 glossina nigrofusca
NT2 glossina pallicera
NT2 glossina pallidipes
NT2 glossina palpalis
NT3 glossina palpalis gambiensis
NT3 glossina palpalis palpalis
NT2 glossina swynnertoni
NT2 glossina tabaniformis
NT2 glossina tachinoides

GLOSSIPHONIA
BT1 glossiphoniidae
BT2 hirudinea
BT3 annelida
NT1 glossiphonia complanata

GLOSSIPHONIA COMPLANATA
BT1 glossiphonia
BT2 glossiphoniidae
BT3 hirudinea
BT4 annelida

GLOSSIPHONIIDAE
BT1 hirudinea
BT2 annelida
NT1 glossiphonia
NT2 glossiphonia complanata
NT1 haementeria
NT1 helobdella
NT2 helobdella stagnalis
NT1 placobdella
NT1 theromyzon
NT2 theromyzon rude

GLOSSITIS
BT1 tongue diseases
BT2 mouth diseases
BT3 organic diseases
BT4 diseases

GLOSSOCARDIA
BT1 compositae
NT1 glossocardia bosvallia

GLOSSOCARDIA BOSVALLIA
BT1 antibacterial plants
BT1 antifungal plants
BT1 glossocardia
BT2 compositae

GLOSSOSCOLECIDAE
BT1 oligochaeta
BT2 annelida
NT1 pontoscolex
NT2 pontoscolex corethrurus

GLOXAZONE
BT1 antibacterial agents
BT2 antiinfective agents
BT3 drugs

GLOXINIA
BT1 gesneriaceae
NT1 gloxinia sylvatica
rt seemannia
rt sinningia speciosa

GLOXINIA SYLVATICA
uf seemannia sylvatica
BT1 gloxinia
BT2 gesneriaceae
BT1 ornamental bulbs
rt rhizomes

GLUCAGON
BT1 hypoglycaemic agents
BT2 haematologic agents
BT3 drugs
BT1 pancreatic hormones
BT2 hormones
BT1 polypeptides
BT2 peptides
rt hyperglycaemia
rt pancreas

GLUCAN 1,4-α-GLUCOSIDASE
(ec 3.2.1.3)
(for retrieval spell out "alpha")
uf exo-1,4-α-glucosidase
uf amyloglucosidase
uf glucoamylase
BT1 glucosidases
BT2 o-glycoside hydrolases
BT3 glycosidases
BT4 hydrolases
BT5 enzymes

α-GLUCAN
(for retrieval spell out "alpha")
BT1 glucans
BT2 polysaccharides
BT3 carbohydrates

β-GLUCAN
(for retrieval spell out "beta")
BT1 glucans
BT2 polysaccharides
BT3 carbohydrates

β-GLUCANASE
(for retrieval spell out "beta")
BT1 o-glycoside hydrolases
BT2 glycosidases
BT3 hydrolases
BT4 enzymes

GLUCANS
BT1 polysaccharides
BT2 carbohydrates
NT1 α-glucan
NT1 β-glucan
NT1 cellulose
NT2 lignocellulose
NT1 dextran
NT1 dextrins
NT2 maltodextrins
NT1 glycogen
NT1 starch
NT2 amylopectin
NT2 amylose
NT2 cassava starch
NT2 maize starch
NT2 potato starch
NT1 xyloglucans

GLUCARIC ACID
BT1 aldaric acids
BT2 sugar acids
BT3 carboxylic acids
BT4 organic acids
BT5 acids
BT3 monosaccharides
BT4 carbohydrates
BT1 enzyme inhibitors
BT2 metabolic inhibitors
BT3 inhibitors

glucoamylase
USE **glucan 1,4-α-glucosidase**

GLUCOBRASSICIN
BT1 glucosinolates
BT2 glucosides
BT3 glycosides
BT4 carbohydrates

GLUCOCORTICOIDS
(not including synthetic glucocorticoids)
BT1 adrenal cortex hormones
BT2 corticoids
BT2 hormones
NT1 corticosterone
NT1 cortisone
NT1 hydrocortisone
rt synthetic glucocorticoids

GLUCOKINASE
(ec 2.7.1.2)
BT1 kinases
BT2 transferases
BT3 enzymes

GLUCOMANNANS
BT1 polysaccharides
BT2 carbohydrates
NT1 konjak mannan
rt cell walls

GLUCONAPIN
BT1 glucosinolates
BT2 glucosides
BT3 glycosides
BT4 carbohydrates

GLUCONEOGENESIS
BT1 carbohydrate metabolism
BT2 metabolism
rt amino acids
rt glucose

GLUCONIC ACID
BT1 aldonic acids
BT2 sugar acids
BT3 carboxylic acids
BT4 organic acids
BT5 acids
BT3 monosaccharides
BT4 carbohydrates
rt gluconolactone

glucono-δ-lactone
USE **gluconolactone**

GLUCONOLACTONE
uf glucono-δ-lactone
BT1 acidulants
BT2 food additives
BT3 additives
BT1 sugar lactones
BT2 lactones
BT3 heterocyclic oxygen compounds
BT3 ketones
BT2 monosaccharides
BT3 carbohydrates
rt gluconic acid

GLUCOSAMINE
BT1 hexosamines
BT2 amino sugars
BT3 amino compounds
BT4 organic nitrogen compounds
BT3 sugars
BT4 carbohydrates

GLUCOSE
uf dextrose
BT1 hexoses
BT2 aldoses
BT3 monosaccharides
BT4 carbohydrates
BT3 reducing sugars
BT4 sugars
BT5 carbohydrates
rt 2-deoxy-d-glucose
rt blood sugar
rt gluconeogenesis
rt glucose 1-phosphate
rt glucose 6-phosphate
rt glucose tolerance
rt glucose tolerance test
rt glucosuria
rt glycolysis
rt glycosuria
rt high fructose corn syrup
rt invert sugar
rt syrups

glucose in blood
USE **blood sugar**

glucose in urine
USE **glucosuria**

glucose isomerase
USE **glucose-6-phosphate isomerase**

GLUCOSE OXIDASE
(ec 1.1.3.4)
BT1 alcohol oxidoreductases
BT2 oxidoreductases
BT3 enzymes

GLUCOSE-6-PHOSPHATASE
(ec 3.1.3.9)
BT1 phosphoric monoester hydrolases
BT2 esterases
BT3 hydrolases
BT4 enzymes
rt glucose 6-phosphate

GLUCOSE-6-PHOSPHATE DEHYDROGENASE
(ec 1.1.1.49)
BT1 alcohol oxidoreductases
BT2 oxidoreductases
BT3 enzymes
rt glucose 6-phosphate

GLUCOSE-6-PHOSPHATE ISOMERASE
(ec 5.3.1.9)
uf *glucose isomerase*
uf *phosphoglucose isomerase*
uf *phosphohexose isomerase*
BT1 isomerases
BT2 enzymes
rt glucose 6-phosphate

GLUCOSE 1-PHOSPHATE
BT1 sugar phosphates
BT2 carbohydrates
BT2 phosphates (esters)
BT3 esters
BT3 phosphates
rt glucose

GLUCOSE 6-PHOSPHATE
BT1 sugar phosphates
BT2 carbohydrates
BT2 phosphates (esters)
BT3 esters
BT3 phosphates
rt glucose
rt glucose-6-phosphatase
rt glucose-6-phosphate dehydrogenase
rt glucose-6-phosphate isomerase

GLUCOSE SYRUPS
HN from 1990
BT1 syrups
BT2 liquids
NT1 corn syrup

GLUCOSE TOLERANCE
uf *blood sugar tolerance*
BT1 tolerance
rt blood sugar
rt diabetes
rt glucose
rt glucose tolerance test
rt insulin

GLUCOSE TOLERANCE TEST
BT1 tests
rt blood sugar
rt diabetes
rt glucose
rt glucose tolerance

α-GLUCOSIDASE
(ec 3.2.1.20)
(for retrieval spell out "alpha")
uf *α-d-glucosidase*
uf *diastase*
uf *maltase*
BT1 glucosidases
BT2 o-glycoside hydrolases
BT3 glycosidases
BT4 hydrolases
BT5 enzymes

α-d-glucosidase
USE **α-glucosidase**

exo-1,4-α-glucosidase
USE **glucan 1,4-α-glucosidase**

β-GLUCOSIDASE
(ec 3.2.1.21)
(for retrieval spell out "beta")
BT1 glucosidases
BT2 o-glycoside hydrolases
BT3 glycosidases
BT4 hydrolases
BT5 enzymes

GLUCOSIDASES
BT1 o-glycoside hydrolases
BT2 glycosidases
BT3 hydrolases
BT4 enzymes
NT1 α-glucosidase
NT1 β-glucosidase
NT1 glucan 1,4-α-glucosidase
NT1 oligo-1,6-glucosidase
NT1 sucrose α-glucosidase

GLUCOSIDES
BT1 glycosides
BT2 carbohydrates
NT1 aesculin
NT1 amygdalin
NT1 chloralose
NT1 cycasin
NT1 fragilin
NT1 glucosinolates
NT2 glucobrassicin
NT2 gluconapin
NT2 progoitrin
NT2 sinigrin
NT1 glycyrrhizin
NT1 isoquercitrin
NT1 linamarin
NT1 methyl glucoside
NT1 oleuropein
NT1 salicin
NT1 tannins
NT1 taxiphyllin
NT1 vicine
NT1 vitexin

GLUCOSINOLATES
BT1 glucosides
BT2 glycosides
BT3 carbohydrates
NT1 glucobrassicin
NT1 gluconapin
NT1 progoitrin
NT1 sinigrin

GLUCOSURIA
uf *glucose in urine*
rt glucose
rt glycosuria
rt urine

GLUCURONIC ACID
BT1 uronic acids
BT2 sugar acids
BT3 carboxylic acids
BT4 organic acids
BT5 acids
BT3 monosaccharides
BT4 carbohydrates

β-GLUCURONIDASE
(ec 3.2.1.31)
(for retrieval spell out "beta")
BT1 o-glycoside hydrolases
BT2 glycosidases
BT3 hydrolases
BT4 enzymes

GLUED JOINTS
BT1 joints (timber)
rt woodworking

glues
USE **adhesives**

GLUFOSINATE
uf *phosphinothricin*
BT1 antibiotic herbicides
BT2 antibiotics
BT2 herbicides
BT3 pesticides

GLUGEA
BT1 microspora
BT2 protozoa
NT1 glugea anomala

GLUGEA *cont.*
NT1 glugea branchiale
NT1 glugea gasti
NT1 glugea habrodesmi
NT1 glugea hertwigi
NT1 glugea polymorpha
NT1 glugea stephani

GLUGEA ANOMALA
BT1 glugea
BT2 microspora
BT3 protozoa

GLUGEA BRANCHIALE
BT1 glugea
BT2 microspora
BT3 protozoa

GLUGEA GASTI
BT1 glugea
BT2 microspora
BT3 protozoa

GLUGEA HABRODESMI
BT1 glugea
BT2 microspora
BT3 protozoa

GLUGEA HERTWIGI
BT1 glugea
BT2 microspora
BT3 protozoa

GLUGEA POLYMORPHA
BT1 glugea
BT2 microspora
BT3 protozoa

GLUGEA STEPHANI
BT1 glugea
BT2 microspora
BT3 protozoa

GLUING
BT1 processing
rt adhesives
rt joints (timber)
rt laminated wood
rt panels
rt plywood

glulam
USE **laminated wood**

GLUMES
BT1 inflorescences
BT2 plant
NT1 awns
rt bracts
rt gramineae
rt rice husks

GLUTAMATE-AMMONIA LIGASE
(ec 6.3.1.2)
uf *glutamine synthetase*
BT1 amide synthases
BT2 ligases
BT3 enzymes

GLUTAMATE DECARBOXYLASE
(ec 4.1.1.15)
BT1 carboxy-lyases
BT2 lyases
BT3 enzymes

GLUTAMATE DEHYDROGENASE
(ec 1.4.1.4)
BT1 amine oxidoreductases
BT2 oxidoreductases
BT3 enzymes

glutamate oxaloacetate transaminase
USE **aspartate aminotransferase**

glutamate pyruvate transaminase
USE **alanine aminotransferase**

GLUTAMATE SYNTHASE
(ec 1.4.7.1)
BT1 amine oxidoreductases
BT2 oxidoreductases
BT3 enzymes

GLUTAMATES
BT1 organic salts
BT2 salts
NT1 monosodium glutamate
rt glutamic acid

GLUTAMIC ACID
BT1 neurotransmitters
BT1 nonessential amino acids
BT2 amino acids
BT3 carboxylic acids
BT4 organic acids
BT5 acids
BT3 organic nitrogen compounds
rt glutamates

glutamic oxaloacetic transaminase
USE **aspartate aminotransferase**

glutamic pyruvic transaminase
USE **alanine aminotransferase**

GLUTAMINASE
(ec 3.5.1.2)
BT1 amide hydrolases
BT2 hydrolases
BT3 enzymes

GLUTAMINE
BT1 nonessential amino acids
BT2 amino acids
BT3 carboxylic acids
BT4 organic acids
BT5 acids
BT3 organic nitrogen compounds

glutamine synthetase
USE **glutamate-ammonia ligase**

γ-GLUTAMYL HYDROLASE
(ec 3.4.22.12)
(for retrieval spell out "gamma")
uf *folate conjugase*
BT1 proteinases
BT2 peptide hydrolases
BT3 hydrolases
BT4 enzymes

glutamyl transferase
USE **γ-glutamyltransferase**

γ-GLUTAMYLCYCLOTRANSFERASE
(ec 2.3.2.4)
(for retrieval spell out "gamma")
BT1 aminoacyltransferases
BT2 acyltransferases
BT3 transferases
BT4 enzymes

γ-GLUTAMYLCYSTEINE
(for retrieval spell out "gamma")
BT1 dipeptides
BT2 oligopeptides
BT3 peptides

γ-GLUTAMYLTRANSFERASE
(ec 2.3.2.2)
(for retrieval spell out "gamma")
uf *glutamyl transferase*
BT1 aminoacyltransferases
BT2 acyltransferases
BT3 transferases
BT4 enzymes

D-GLUTAMYLTRANSFERASE
(ec 2.3.2.1)
BT1 aminoacyltransferases
BT2 acyltransferases
BT3 transferases
BT4 enzymes

GLUTARIC ACID
BT1 dicarboxylic acids
BT2 carboxylic acids
BT3 organic acids
BT4 acids
rt glutaric aciduria

GLUTARIC ACIDURIA
BT1 aciduria
BT2 metabolic disorders

GLUTARIC ACIDURIA *cont.*
BT3 animal disorders
BT4 disorders
rt glutaric acid

GLUTARYL-COA DEHYDROGENASE
(ec 1.3.99.7)
BT1 oxidoreductases
BT2 enzymes

GLUTATHIONE
BT1 antidotes
BT2 detoxicants
BT3 drugs
BT1 coenzymes
BT1 oligopeptides
BT2 peptides

GLUTATHIONE PEROXIDASE
(ec 1.11.1.9)
BT1 peroxidases
BT2 oxidoreductases
BT3 enzymes

GLUTATHIONE REDUCTASE (NAD(P)H)
(ec 1.6.4.2)
BT1 oxidoreductases
BT2 enzymes

GLUTATHIONE SYNTHASE
(ec 6.3.2.3)
BT1 ligases
BT2 enzymes

GLUTATHIONE TRANSFERASE
(ec 2.5.1.18)
uf *ligandin*
BT1 alkyl (aryl) transferases
BT2 transferases
BT3 enzymes

GLUTELINS
BT1 cereal proteins
BT2 plant proteins
BT3 proteins
BT4 peptides
NT1 glutenins

GLUTEN
BT1 cereal proteins
BT2 plant proteins
BT3 proteins
BT4 peptides
NT1 maize gluten
NT1 wheat gluten
rt gluten feed
rt gluten free bread
rt gluten free diet

GLUTEN FEED
BT1 feeds
rt gluten

GLUTEN FREE BREAD
uf *bread, gluten free*
BT1 bread
BT2 bakery products
BT3 foods
BT3 products
rt coeliac syndrome
rt gluten
rt gluten free diet

GLUTEN FREE DIET
BT1 diets
rt coeliac syndrome
rt gluten
rt gluten free bread

GLUTENINS
BT1 glutelins
BT2 cereal proteins
BT3 plant proteins
BT4 proteins
BT5 peptides

glyburide
USE **glibenclamide**

glycaemia
USE **blood sugar**

GLYCERALDEHYDE
BT1 trioses
BT2 aldoses
BT3 monosaccharides
BT4 carbohydrates
BT3 reducing sugars
BT4 sugars
BT5 carbohydrates
rt glyceraldehyde 3-phosphate

GLYCERALDEHYDE 3-PHOSPHATE
BT1 sugar phosphates
BT2 carbohydrates
BT2 phosphates (esters)
BT3 esters
BT3 phosphates
rt glyceraldehyde

GLYCERALDEHYDE-3-PHOSPHATE DEHYDROGENASE
(ec 1.2.1.9)
BT1 aldehyde oxidoreductases
BT2 oxidoreductases
BT3 enzymes

GLYCERATE 2,3-BIS(PHOSPHATE)
uf *diphosphoglycerate*
BT1 phosphates (esters)
BT2 esters
BT2 phosphates

GLYCERATE 2-PHOSPHATE
uf *phosphoglyceric acid*
BT1 phosphates (esters)
BT2 esters
BT2 phosphates

GLYCERATE 3-PHOSPHATE
uf *phosphoglyceric acid*
BT1 phosphates (esters)
BT2 esters
BT2 phosphates
BT1 photosynthates
BT2 carbohydrates

GLYCERIA
uf *reed grass*
BT1 gramineae
NT1 glyceria fluitans
NT1 glyceria maxima

glyceria aquatica
USE **glyceria maxima**

GLYCERIA FLUITANS
BT1 glyceria
BT2 gramineae
BT1 pasture plants

GLYCERIA MAXIMA
uf *glyceria aquatica*
BT1 glyceria
BT2 gramineae
BT1 pasture plants

glycerides
USE **acylglycerols**

GLYCEROL
BT1 alditols
BT2 sugar alcohols
BT3 carbohydrates
BT3 polyols
BT4 alcohols
BT1 cryoprotectants
BT2 protectants
rt glycerol 3-phosphate

GLYCEROL DEHYDROGENASE
(ec 1.1.1.6)
BT1 alcohol oxidoreductases
BT2 oxidoreductases
BT3 enzymes

glycerol ester hydrolase
USE **triacylglycerol lipase**

glycerol esters
USE **acylglycerols**

GLYCEROL KINASE
(ec 2.7.1.30)
BT1 kinases
BT2 transferases
BT3 enzymes

GLYCEROL 3-PHOSPHATE
uf *α-glycerophosphate*
BT1 phosphates (esters)
BT2 esters
BT2 phosphates
rt glycerol

GLYCEROL-3-PHOSPHATE ACYLTRANSFERASE
(ec 2.3.1.15)
BT1 acyltransferases
BT2 transferases
BT3 enzymes

GLYCEROL-3-PHOSPHATE DEHYDROGENASE
(ec 1.1.99.5)
BT1 alcohol oxidoreductases
BT2 oxidoreductases
BT3 enzymes

GLYCEROLIPIDS
BT1 lipids

α-glycerophosphate
USE **glycerol 3-phosphate**

glycerophosphatides
USE **diphosphatidylglycerols**

GLYCEROPHOSPHOLIPIDS
uf *phosphatides*
uf *phosphoglycerides*
BT1 phospholipids
BT2 lipids
NT1 cephalins
NT2 phosphatidylethanolamines
NT2 phosphatidylserines
NT1 diphosphatidylglycerols
NT1 lysophosphatidylcholines
NT1 phosphatidic acids
NT1 phosphatidylcholines
NT1 phosphatidylinositols
NT1 plasmalogens

glyceryl triacetate
USE **triacetin**

GLYCINE
uf *glycocoll*
BT1 nonessential amino acids
BT2 amino acids
BT3 carboxylic acids
BT4 organic acids
BT5 acids
BT3 organic nitrogen compounds
rt hyperglycinaemia

glycine javanica
USE **neonotonia wightii**

GLYCINE KOIDZUMII
BT1 glycine (leguminosae)
BT2 leguminosae

GLYCINE (LEGUMINOSAE)
uf *soja*
BT1 leguminosae
NT1 glycine koidzumii
NT1 glycine max
NT1 glycine soja

GLYCINE MAX
uf *soja max*
BT1 fodder legumes
BT2 fodder plants
BT2 legumes
BT1 glycine (leguminosae)
BT2 leguminosae
rt indonesian soybean dwarf luteovirus
rt soyabean stunt virus
rt soyabeans
rt soybean chlorotic mottle caulimovirus
rt soybean dwarf luteovirus
rt soybean mosaic potyvirus
rt soybeans

GLYCINE MOSAIC COMOVIRUS
HN from 1990
BT1 comovirus group
BT2 plant viruses

GLYCINE MOSAIC COMOVIRUS *cont.*
BT3 plant pathogens
BT4 pathogens

GLYCINE SOJA
BT1 glycine (leguminosae)
BT2 leguminosae
rt soyabeans

glycine wightii
USE **neonotonia wightii**

glycinebetaine
USE **betaine**

GLYCOALKALOIDS
BT1 saponins
BT2 glycosides
BT3 carbohydrates
BT1 steroid alkaloids
BT2 alkaloids
NT1 α-tomatine
NT1 lanatosides
NT1 solanine

GLYCOCHOLIC ACID
BT1 bile acids

glycocoll
USE **glycine**

GLYCODEHYDROCHOLIC ACID
BT1 bile acids

glycodehydroxycholic acid
USE **deoxycholic acid**

GLYCOFLAVONES
BT1 flavonoids
BT2 aromatic compounds
BT2 plant pigments
BT3 pigments
BT1 glycosides
BT2 carbohydrates
NT1 anthocyanins
NT2 cyanin
NT2 delphinin
NT2 rubrobrassicin
NT1 hesperidin
NT1 isoquercitrin
NT1 naringin
NT1 phloridzin
NT1 quercitrin
NT1 rutoside
NT1 vitexin

GLYCOGEN
BT1 glucans
BT2 polysaccharides
BT3 carbohydrates
rt dextrins
rt glycogen body
rt glycogenolysis
rt glycogenosis
rt glycolysis

GLYCOGEN BODY
BT1 animal tissues
BT2 tissues
rt glycogen

GLYCOGEN PHOSPHORYLASE
(ec 2.4.1.1)
BT1 phosphorylase
BT2 hexosyltransferases
BT3 glycosyltransferases
BT4 transferases
BT5 enzymes

GLYCOGEN (STARCH) SYNTHASE
(ec 2.4.1.11)
uf *glycogen synthase*
BT1 hexosyltransferases
BT2 glycosyltransferases
BT3 transferases
BT4 enzymes

glycogen storage disease
USE **glycogenosis**

glycogen synthase
USE **glycogen (starch) synthase**

GLYCOGENOLYSIS
BT1 carbohydrate metabolism
BT2 metabolism
BT1 decomposition
rt glycogen
rt lactic acid

GLYCOGENOSIS
uf *glycogen storage disease*
uf *pompe's disease*
uf *von gierke's disease*
BT1 carbohydrate metabolism disorders
BT2 metabolic disorders
BT3 animal disorders
BT4 disorders
rt glycogen

glycolate
USE **glycolic acid**

glycolate oxidase
USE **(s)-2-hydroxy-acid oxidase**

GLYCOLATE PATHWAYS
BT1 photorespiration
BT2 energy metabolism
BT3 metabolism
BT2 plant physiology
BT3 physiology
BT2 respiration
BT3 physiology

GLYCOLIC ACID
uf *glycolate*
BT1 monocarboxylic acids
BT2 carboxylic acids
BT3 organic acids
BT4 acids

GLYCOLIPIDS
BT1 lipids
NT1 glycophospholipids
NT2 phosphatidylinositols
NT1 glycosphingolipids
NT2 cerebrosides
NT2 gangliosides

GLYCOLS
BT1 alcohols
NT1 bronopol
NT1 butanediol
NT1 ethylene glycol
NT1 polyethylene glycol
NT1 propanediols
NT2 propylene glycol
NT1 sphingosine
NT1 styrene glycol

GLYCOLYSIS
BT1 carbohydrate metabolism
BT2 metabolism
BT1 decomposition
rt biochemical pathways
rt glucose
rt glycogen

GLYCONEOGENESIS
BT1 carbohydrate metabolism
BT2 metabolism

GLYCOPEPTIDES
BT1 peptides

glycophene
USE **iprodione**

GLYCOPHOSPHOLIPIDS
BT1 glycolipids
BT2 lipids
BT1 phospholipids
BT2 lipids
NT1 phosphatidylinositols

GLYCOPHYTES
BT1 plant ecological groups
rt halophytes
rt sodium chloride

GLYCOPROTEINS
BT1 proteins
BT2 peptides
NT1 amyloid
NT1 avidin

GLYCOPROTEINS *cont.*
NT1 blastokinin
NT1 ceruloplasmin
NT1 collagen
NT1 elastin
NT1 erythropoietin
NT1 fibronectins
NT1 gelatin
NT1 gonadotropins
NT2 chorionic gonadotropin
NT3 hcg
NT2 human menopausal gonadotropin
NT2 pituitary gonadotropins
NT3 fsh
NT3 lh
NT2 pmsg
NT1 haemopexin
NT1 haptoglobins
NT1 immunoglobulins
NT2 antibodies
NT3 agglutinins
NT4 haemagglutinins
NT5 viral haemagglutinins
NT4 lectins
NT5 phytohaemagglutinins
NT6 concanavalin a
NT6 limulins
NT6 ricin
NT3 antitoxins
NT3 autoantibodies
NT3 gliadin antibodies
NT3 haemolysins
NT4 melittin
NT3 local antibodies
NT3 maternal antibodies
NT3 natural antibodies
NT3 opsonins
NT3 precipitins
NT2 idiotypes
NT2 iga
NT2 ige
NT2 igg
NT2 igm
NT2 monoclonal antibodies
NT2 secretory component
NT1 inhibin
NT1 mucoproteins
NT2 intrinsic factor
NT2 mucins
NT2 seromucoid
NT2 uromucoids
NT1 proteoglycans
NT1 prothrombin
NT1 satietin
NT1 siderophilins
NT2 conalbumin
NT2 lactoferrin
NT2 transferrin
NT1 thrombopoietin
NT1 thyroglobulin
NT1 thyrotropin
NT1 tubulin
NT1 variant surface glycoproteins
rt glycosaminoglycans

GLYCOSAMINOGLYCANS
BT1 mucopolysaccharides
BT2 polysaccharides
BT3 carbohydrates
rt glycoproteins

GLYCOSIDASES
(ec 3.2)
uf *carbohydrases*
BT1 hydrolases
BT2 enzymes
NT1 n-glycoside hydrolases
NT2 n-acetyl-β-glucosaminidase
NT2 β-n-acetylhexosaminidase
NT2 nucleosidases
NT1 o-glycoside hydrolases
NT2 β-fructofuranosidase
NT2 β-glucanase
NT2 β-glucuronidase
NT2 amylases
NT3 α-amylase
NT3 β-amylase
NT2 cellulase
NT2 chitinase
NT2 dextranase

GLYCOSIDASES *cont.*
NT2 disaccharidases
NT2 galactosidases
NT3 α-galactosidase
NT3 β-galactosidase
NT2 glucosidases
NT3 α-glucosidase
NT3 β-glucosidase
NT3 glucan 1,4-α-glucosidase
NT3 oligo-1,6-glucosidase
NT3 sucrose α-glucosidase
NT2 hyaluronidase
NT2 hyaluronoglucosaminidase
NT2 inulinase
NT2 isoamylase
NT2 lichenase
NT2 lysozyme
NT2 mannosidases
NT3 α-mannosidase
NT3 β-mannosidase
NT2 polygalacturonase
NT2 pullulanase
NT2 sialidase
NT2 trehalase
NT2 xylan 1,4-β-xylosidase
NT1 s-glycoside hydrolases
NT2 thioglucosidase

N-GLYCOSIDE HYDROLASES
(ec 3.2.2)
BT1 glycosidases
BT2 hydrolases
BT3 enzymes
NT1 n-acetyl-β-glucosaminidase
NT1 β-n-acetylhexosaminidase
NT1 nucleosidases

O-GLYCOSIDE HYDROLASES
(ec 3.2.1)
BT1 glycosidases
BT2 hydrolases
BT3 enzymes
NT1 β-fructofuranosidase
NT1 β-glucanase
NT1 β-glucuronidase
NT1 amylases
NT2 α-amylase
NT2 β-amylase
NT1 cellulase
NT1 chitinase
NT1 dextranase
NT1 disaccharidases
NT1 galactosidases
NT2 α-galactosidase
NT2 β-galactosidase
NT1 glucosidases
NT2 α-glucosidase
NT2 β-glucosidase
NT2 glucan 1,4-α-glucosidase
NT2 oligo-1,6-glucosidase
NT2 sucrose α-glucosidase
NT1 hyaluronidase
NT1 hyaluronoglucosaminidase
NT1 inulinase
NT1 isoamylase
NT1 lichenase
NT1 lysozyme
NT1 mannosidases
NT2 α-mannosidase
NT2 β-mannosidase
NT1 polygalacturonase
NT1 pullulanase
NT1 sialidase
NT1 trehalase
NT1 xylan 1,4-β-xylosidase

S-GLYCOSIDE HYDROLASES
(ec 3.2.3)
BT1 glycosidases
BT2 hydrolases
BT3 enzymes
NT1 thioglucosidase

GLYCOSIDES
uf *heterosides*
BT1 carbohydrates
NT1 aminoglycoside antibiotics
NT2 framycetin
NT2 gentamicin
NT2 kanamycin
NT2 paromomycin
NT2 spiramycin

GLYCOSIDES *cont.*
NT2 streptomycin
NT1 cardiac glycosides
NT2 digitonin
NT2 digitoxin
NT2 digoxin
NT2 lanatosides
NT2 strophanthins
NT3 ouabain
NT1 cerebrosides
NT1 cyanogenic glycosides
NT2 amygdalin
NT2 linamarin
NT2 taxiphyllin
NT1 glucosides
NT2 aesculin
NT2 amygdalin
NT2 chloralose
NT2 cycasin
NT2 fragilin
NT2 glucosinolates
NT3 glucobrassicin
NT3 gluconapin
NT3 progoitrin
NT3 sinigrin
NT2 glycyrrhizin
NT2 isoquercitrin
NT2 linamarin
NT2 methyl glucoside
NT2 oleuropein
NT2 salicin
NT2 tannins
NT2 taxiphyllin
NT2 vicine
NT2 vitexin
NT1 glycoflavones
NT2 anthocyanins
NT3 cyanin
NT3 delphinin
NT3 rubrobrassicin
NT2 hesperidin
NT2 isoquercitrin
NT2 naringin
NT2 phloridzin
NT2 quercitrin
NT2 rutoside
NT2 vitexin
NT1 iridoid glycosides
NT2 aucubin
NT2 loganin
NT1 locundioside
NT1 neomycin
NT1 nucleosides
NT2 deoxyribonucleosides
NT3 cordycepin
NT3 deoxyadenosine
NT3 deoxyuridines
NT4 broxuridine
NT4 deoxyuridine
NT4 floxuridine
NT4 idoxuridine
NT3 thymidine
NT2 nucleoside antibiotics
NT3 blasticidin-s
NT3 cordycepin
NT3 gougerotin
NT3 nikkomycins
NT3 polyoxins
NT3 puromycin
NT3 toyocamycin
NT2 ribonucleosides
NT3 adenosine
NT3 adenosylhomocysteine
NT3 adenosylmethionine
NT3 cytidine
NT3 guanosine
NT3 inosine
NT3 pseudouridine
NT3 toyocamycin
NT3 uridine
NT1 nucleotides
NT2 cyclic nucleotides
NT3 c-amp
NT2 nucleotide coenzymes
NT3 coenzyme a
NT3 nad
NT3 nadh
NT3 nadp
NT3 nadph
NT3 pyridine nucleotides
NT2 purine nucleotides

GLYCOSIDES *cont.*
NT3 adenosine phosphates
NT4 adp
NT4 amp
NT4 atp
NT4 c-amp
NT3 guanosine diphosphate
NT3 guanosine monophosphate
NT3 guanosine triphosphate
NT2 pyrimidine nucleotides
NT3 cytidine triphosphate
NT3 udp
NT3 ump
NT1 saponins
NT2 glycoalkaloids
NT3 α-tomatine
NT3 lanatosides
NT3 solanine
NT2 steroid saponins
NT3 digitonin
NT3 digitoxin
NT3 digoxin
NT2 triterpenoid saponins

GLYCOSMIS
BT1 rutaceae
NT1 glycosmis pentaphylla

GLYCOSMIS PENTAPHYLLA
BT1 antibacterial plants
BT1 glycosmis
BT2 rutaceae

GLYCOSPHINGOLIPIDS
BT1 glycolipids
BT2 lipids
BT1 sphingolipids
BT2 lipids
NT1 cerebrosides
NT1 gangliosides

GLYCOSURIA
BT1 carbohydrate metabolism disorders
BT2 metabolic disorders
BT3 animal disorders
BT4 disorders
rt glucose
rt glucosuria
rt urine

GLYCOSYLTRANSFERASES
(ec 2.4)
BT1 transferases
BT2 enzymes
NT1 hexosyltransferases
NT2 dextransucrase
NT2 glycogen (starch) synthase
NT2 lactose synthase
NT2 levansucrase
NT2 phosphorylase
NT3 glycogen phosphorylase
NT2 sucrose synthase
NT1 pentosyltransferases
NT2 adenine phosphoribosyltransferase
NT2 amidophosphoribosyl-transferase
NT2 purine-nucleoside phosphorylase

GLYCYLGLYCINE
BT1 dipeptides
BT2 oligopeptides
BT3 peptides

GLYCYLPROLINE
BT1 dipeptides
BT2 oligopeptides
BT3 peptides

GLYCYLSARCOSINE
BT1 dipeptides
BT2 oligopeptides
BT3 peptides

GLYCYMERIDAE
BT1 bivalvia
BT2 mollusca
NT1 glycymeris

GLYCYMERIS
BT1 glycymeridae

GLYCYMERIS *cont.*
BT2 bivalvia
BT3 mollusca

GLYCYPHAGIDAE
BT1 astigmata
BT2 acari
NT1 blomia
NT2 blomia tjibodas
NT2 blomia tropicalis
NT1 glycyphagus
NT2 glycyphagus domesticus
NT1 gohieria
NT2 gohieria fusca
NT1 lepidoglyphus
NT2 lepidoglyphus destructor

GLYCYPHAGUS
BT1 glycyphagidae
BT2 astigmata
BT3 acari
NT1 glycyphagus domesticus
rt lepidoglyphus

glycyphagus destructor
USE **lepidoglyphus destructor**

GLYCYPHAGUS DOMESTICUS
BT1 glycyphagus
BT2 glycyphagidae
BT3 astigmata
BT4 acari

GLYCYRRHIZA
BT1 leguminosae
NT1 glycyrrhiza aspera
NT1 glycyrrhiza echinata
NT1 glycyrrhiza glabra
NT1 glycyrrhiza lepidota
NT1 glycyrrhiza macedonica
NT1 glycyrrhiza pallidiflora
NT1 glycyrrhiza uralensis

GLYCYRRHIZA ASPERA
BT1 glycyrrhiza
BT2 leguminosae

GLYCYRRHIZA ECHINATA
BT1 glycyrrhiza
BT2 leguminosae

GLYCYRRHIZA GLABRA
BT1 antibacterial plants
BT1 antifungal plants
BT1 antiviral plants
BT1 dye plants
BT1 glycyrrhiza
BT2 leguminosae
BT1 insecticidal plants
BT2 pesticidal plants
BT1 medicinal plants
rt liquorice

GLYCYRRHIZA LEPIDOTA
BT1 antibacterial plants
BT1 glycyrrhiza
BT2 leguminosae

GLYCYRRHIZA MACEDONICA
BT1 glycyrrhiza
BT2 leguminosae

GLYCYRRHIZA PALLIDIFLORA
BT1 glycyrrhiza
BT2 leguminosae

GLYCYRRHIZA URALENSIS
BT1 glycyrrhiza
BT2 leguminosae

GLYCYRRHIZIN
BT1 glucosides
BT2 glycosides
BT3 carbohydrates
BT1 sweet tasting compounds
BT2 flavour compounds
rt liquorice

GLYOXIME
BT1 oximes
BT2 organic nitrogen compounds
BT1 plant growth regulators
BT2 growth regulators
rt abscission

glyoxylate
USE **glyoxylic acid**

GLYOXYLATE CYCLE
BT1 biochemical pathways
rt glyoxylic acid

GLYOXYLIC ACID
uf glyoxylate
BT1 monocarboxylic acids
BT2 carboxylic acids
BT3 organic acids
BT4 acids
rt glyoxylate cycle

GLYPHIPTERIGIDAE
BT1 lepidoptera
NT1 sagalassa
NT2 sagalassa valida

GLYPHOSATE
BT1 desiccant herbicides
BT2 desiccants
BT1 organophosphorus herbicides
BT2 herbicides
BT3 pesticides
BT2 organophosphorus pesticides
BT3 organophosphorus compounds

GLYPHOSINE
BT1 growth inhibitors
BT2 inhibitors
BT2 plant growth regulators
BT3 growth regulators

GLYPTA
BT1 ichneumonidae
BT2 hymenoptera
NT1 glypta fumiferanae

GLYPTA FUMIFERANAE
BT1 glypta
BT2 ichneumonidae
BT3 hymenoptera

GLYPTAPANTELES
HN from 1990
BT1 braconidae
BT2 hymenoptera
NT1 glyptapanteles africanus
NT1 glyptapanteles militaris
NT1 glyptapanteles pallipes
NT1 glyptapanteles porthetriae
rt apanteles

GLYPTAPANTELES AFRICANUS
HN from 1990; previously "apanteles africanus"
uf apanteles africanus
BT1 glyptapanteles
BT2 braconidae
BT3 hymenoptera

GLYPTAPANTELES MILITARIS
HN from 1990; previously "apanteles militaris"
uf apanteles militaris
BT1 glyptapanteles
BT2 braconidae
BT3 hymenoptera

GLYPTAPANTELES PALLIPES
HN from 1990; previously "apanteles pallipes"
uf apanteles pallipes
BT1 glyptapanteles
BT2 braconidae
BT3 hymenoptera

GLYPTAPANTELES PORTHETRIAE
HN from 1990; previously "apanteles porthetriae"
uf apanteles porthetriae
BT1 glyptapanteles
BT2 braconidae
BT3 hymenoptera

GLYPTOCEPHALUS
BT1 pleuronectidae
BT2 pleuronectiformes
BT3 osteichthyes

GLYPTOCEPHALUS *cont.*
BT4 fishes
NT1 glyptocephalus cynoglossus

GLYPTOCEPHALUS CYNOGLOSSUS
uf witch (fish)
BT1 glyptocephalus
BT2 pleuronectidae
BT3 pleuronectiformes
BT4 osteichthyes
BT5 fishes

GLYPTOTENDIPES
BT1 chironomidae
BT2 diptera
NT1 glyptotendipes paripes

GLYPTOTENDIPES PARIPES
BT1 glyptotendipes
BT2 chironomidae
BT3 diptera

GLYPTOTERMES
BT1 kalotermitidae
BT2 isoptera
NT1 glyptotermes dilatatus

GLYPTOTERMES DILATATUS
BT1 glyptotermes
BT2 kalotermitidae
BT3 isoptera

GMELINA
BT1 verbenaceae
NT1 gmelina arborea

GMELINA ARBOREA
BT1 forest trees
BT1 gmelina
BT2 verbenaceae

gmp
USE **guanosine monophosphate**

GNAPHALIUM
BT1 compositae
NT1 gnaphalium obtusifolium
NT1 gnaphalium pellitum
NT1 gnaphalium purpureum

gnaphalium dioicum
USE **antennaria dioica**

GNAPHALIUM OBTUSIFOLIUM
BT1 compositae
BT1 gnaphalium
BT2 compositae

GNAPHALIUM PELLITUM
BT1 gnaphalium
BT2 compositae

GNAPHALIUM PURPUREUM
BT1 gnaphalium
BT2 compositae

gnaphalium uliginosum
USE **filaginella uliginosa**

GNATHOSTOMA
BT1 gnathostomatidae
BT2 nematoda
NT1 gnathostoma doloresi
NT1 gnathostoma spinigerum

GNATHOSTOMA DOLORESI
BT1 gnathostoma
BT2 gnathostomatidae
BT3 nematoda

GNATHOSTOMA SPINIGERUM
BT1 gnathostoma
BT2 gnathostomatidae
BT3 nematoda

GNATHOSTOMATIDAE
BT1 nematoda
NT1 gnathostoma
NT2 gnathostoma doloresi
NT2 gnathostoma spinigerum
rt animal parasitic nematodes

GNATHOTRICHUS
BT1 scolytidae

GNATHOTRICHUS *cont.*
BT2 coleoptera
NT1 gnathotrichus retusus
NT1 gnathotrichus sulcatus

GNATHOTRICHUS RETUSUS
BT1 gnathotrichus
BT2 scolytidae
BT3 coleoptera

GNATHOTRICHUS SULCATUS
BT1 gnathotrichus
BT2 scolytidae
BT3 coleoptera

GNEISS
BT1 rocks

GNEISS SOILS
BT1 soil types (lithological)

GNETACEAE
NT1 gnetum
NT2 gnetum gnemon
NT2 gnetum leyboldii
NT2 gnetum nodiflorum
NT2 gnetum paniculatum
NT2 gnetum schwackeanum
NT2 gnetum urens
NT2 gnetum venosum
NT1 welwitschia
NT2 welwitschia mirabilis

GNETUM
BT1 gnetaceae
NT1 gnetum gnemon
NT1 gnetum leyboldii
NT1 gnetum nodiflorum
NT1 gnetum paniculatum
NT1 gnetum schwackeanum
NT1 gnetum urens
NT1 gnetum venosum

GNETUM GNEMON
BT1 gnetum
BT2 gnetaceae

GNETUM LEYBOLDII
BT1 gnetum
BT2 gnetaceae

GNETUM NODIFLORUM
BT1 gnetum
BT2 gnetaceae

GNETUM PANICULATUM
BT1 gnetum
BT2 gnetaceae

GNETUM SCHWACKEANUM
BT1 gnetum
BT2 gnetaceae

GNETUM URENS
BT1 gnetum
BT2 gnetaceae

GNETUM VENOSUM
BT1 gnetum
BT2 gnetaceae

GNOMONIA
BT1 diaporthales
NT1 gnomonia fructicola
NT1 gnomonia leptostyla
NT1 gnomonia platani
rt apiognomonia
rt clypeoporthe
rt marssonina

GNOMONIA FRUCTICOLA
BT1 gnomonia
BT2 diaporthales

gnomonia iliau
USE **clypeoporthe iliau**

GNOMONIA LEPTOSTYLA
uf *marssonina juglandis*
BT1 gnomonia
BT2 diaporthales

GNOMONIA PLATANI
BT1 gnomonia
BT2 diaporthales

gnomonia tiliae
USE **apiognomonia errabunda**

gnomonia veneta
USE **apiognomonia veneta**

gnorimoschema
USE **phthorimaea**
OR **scrobipalpa**

gnorimoschema ocellatella
USE **scrobipalpa ocellatella**

gnorimoschema operculella
USE **phthorimaea operculella**

GNOTOBIOTIC ANIMALS
BT1 laboratory animals
BT2 animals
rt germfree animals

GNRH
uf *gonadoliberin*
uf *gonadotropin releasing hormone*
BT1 hypothalamic releasing hormones
BT2 hormones

GOA, DAMAN AND DIU
BT1 india
BT2 south asia
BT3 asia

goals
HN was used until 1990 in agricola
USE **objectives**

goat
USE **goats**

GOAT BREEDS
(only important and recognised breeds are listed)
BT1 breeds
NT1 altai mountain
NT1 anatolian black
NT1 anglo-nubian
NT1 angora
NT1 appenzell
NT1 apulian
NT1 assam hill
NT1 barbari
NT1 beetal
NT1 belgian fawn
NT1 benadir
NT1 bengal
NT1 bhuj
NT1 boer
NT1 british alpine
NT1 british saanen
NT1 british toggenburg
NT1 campine
NT1 canary island
NT1 carpathian
NT1 chamois coloured
NT1 chappar
NT1 charnequeira
NT1 chengde polled
NT1 chengdu brown
NT1 chigu
NT1 damani
NT1 damascus
NT1 dera din panah
NT1 don
NT1 duan
NT1 dutch toggenburg
NT1 dutch white
NT1 french alpine
NT1 french saanen
NT1 gaddi
NT1 garganica
NT1 german improved fawn
NT1 german improved white
NT1 girgentana
NT1 gohilwadi
NT1 granada
NT1 greek
NT1 haimen
NT1 huaipi
NT1 iraqi
NT1 israeli saanen
NT1 jamnapari

GOAT BREEDS *cont.*
NT1 jining grey
NT1 kamori
NT1 kannaiadu
NT1 katjang
NT1 khurasani
NT1 kilis
NT1 kirgiz
NT1 kurdi
NT1 lehri
NT1 leizhou
NT1 liaoning cashmere
NT1 malabari
NT1 malaga
NT1 maltese
NT1 mamber
NT1 maradi
NT1 matou
NT1 mehsana
NT1 mingrelian
NT1 murcia-granada
NT1 nachi
NT1 nordic
NT1 orenburg
NT1 osmanabadi
NT1 poitou
NT1 pyrenean
NT1 red bosnian
NT1 red sokoto
NT1 russian white
NT1 saanen
NT1 sahelian
NT1 salt range
NT1 sangamneri
NT1 serpentina
NT1 serrana
NT1 sind desi
NT1 sinhal
NT1 sirli
NT1 sirohi
NT1 small east african
NT1 somali
NT1 southern sudan
NT1 soviet mohair
NT1 sudanese desert
NT1 sudanese nubian
NT1 surti
NT1 telemark
NT1 toggenburg
NT1 valais blackneck
NT1 verata
NT1 verzasca
NT1 west african dwarf
NT1 wuan
NT1 zalawadi
NT1 zaraibi
NT1 zhiwulin black
NT1 zhongwei
rt goats

goat colostrum
USE **colostrum**
AND **goats**

GOAT DISEASES
BT1 animal diseases
BT2 diseases
rt goats

GOAT FEEDING
BT1 ruminant feeding
BT2 livestock feeding
BT3 animal feeding
BT4 feeding
NT1 kid feeding
rt goats

goat flesh
USE **goat meat**

GOAT HOUSING
BT1 animal housing
rt goats

GOAT KEEPING
BT1 animal husbandry
BT2 husbandry
BT2 zootechny
BT1 livestock enterprises
BT2 farm enterprises
BT3 enterprises
rt goats

GOAT MEAT
uf *goat flesh*
BT1 meat
BT2 animal products
BT3 products
BT2 foods
rt goats

GOAT MILK
uf *milk, goat*
BT1 milks
BT2 body fluids
BT3 fluids
rt goats

GOAT POX VIRUS
BT1 capripoxvirus
BT2 chordopoxvirinae
BT3 poxviridae
BT4 viruses

goatfishes
USE **mullidae**

GOATS
uf *capra hircus*
uf *goat*
ufa *goat colostrum*
BT1 livestock
BT2 animals
BT1 meat animals
BT2 animals
BT1 ruminants
BT2 animals
BT1 skin producing animals
BT2 animals
BT1 wool-producing animals
BT2 animals
rt bovidae
rt flocks
rt goat breeds
rt goat diseases
rt goat feeding
rt goat housing
rt goat keeping
rt goat meat
rt goat milk
rt kidding
rt kids
rt mohair
rt wild goats

goats, wild
USE **wild goats**

GOBI DESERT
BT1 deserts
BT2 arid regions
BT3 arid zones
BT4 climatic zones
BT2 land types
rt china
rt mongolia

GOBIO
BT1 cyprinidae
BT2 cypriniformes
BT3 osteichthyes
BT4 fishes
NT1 gobio gobio

GOBIO GOBIO
BT1 gobio
BT2 cyprinidae
BT3 cypriniformes
BT4 osteichthyes
BT5 fishes

GOBIOMORUS
BT1 eleotridae
BT2 perciformes
BT3 osteichthyes
BT4 fishes

GOBRA
HN from 1990; previously "senegal fulani"
uf *senegal fulani*
BT1 cattle breeds
BT2 breeds

godetia
USE **clarkia**

GODMANIA
BT1 bignoniaceae
NT1 godmania macrocarpa

GODMANIA MACROCARPA
BT1 godmania
BT2 bignoniaceae

GOEBELIA
BT1 leguminosae
NT1 goebelia pachycarpa

goebelia alopecuroides
USE **sophora alopecuroides**

GOEBELIA PACHYCARPA
BT1 goebelia
BT2 leguminosae

GOETHITE
uf *limonite*
BT1 iron oxyhydroxides
BT2 inorganic compounds
BT2 nonclay minerals
BT3 minerals

GOHIERIA
BT1 glycyphagidae
BT2 astigmata
BT3 acari
NT1 gohieria fusca

GOHIERIA FUSCA
BT1 gohieria
BT2 glycyphagidae
BT3 astigmata
BT4 acari

GOHILWADI
HN from 1990
BT1 goat breeds
BT2 breeds

GOITER
BF goitre
NT1 congenital goiter
NT1 endemic goiter

GOITRE
AF goiter
BT1 thyroid diseases
BT2 endocrine diseases
BT3 organic diseases
BT4 diseases
NT1 congenital goitre
NT1 endemic goitre
rt goitrin

goitre, congenital
USE **congenital goitre**

goitre, endemic
USE **endemic goitre**

GOITRIN
uf *vinylthiooxazolidone*
BT1 oxazolidinethiones
BT2 heterocyclic nitrogen compounds
BT3 organic nitrogen compounds
BT1 thyroid antagonists
BT2 hormone antagonists
BT3 antagonists
BT4 metabolic inhibitors
BT5 inhibitors
rt goitre
rt progoitrin

goitrogens
USE **thyroid antagonists**

GOLD
BT1 transition elements
BT2 metallic elements
BT3 elements
BT3 metals

gold thioglucose
USE **aurothioglucose**

GOLDEN HAMSTERS
uf *cricetus auratus*
uf *mesocricetus auratus*
BT1 hamsters

GOLDEN HAMSTERS *cont.*
BT2 laboratory mammals
BT3 laboratory animals
BT4 animals
BT2 pets
BT3 animals
rt muridae

golden syrup
USE **edible syrup**

GOLDFISH
uf *carassius auratus*
BT1 freshwater fishes
BT2 aquatic animals
BT3 animals
BT3 aquatic organisms
BT1 pets
BT2 animals
rt cyprinidae

GOLF
BT1 ball games
BT2 games
BT2 sport
rt golf courses

GOLF COURSES
BT1 recreational facilities
BT1 sports facilities
rt golf
rt golf green soils
rt lawns and turf
rt sports grounds

GOLF GREEN SOILS
BT1 soil types (anthropogenic)
rt golf courses

GOLGI APPARATUS
BT1 organelles
BT2 cell structure
rt endoplasmic reticulum

GOLPAYEGANI
HN from 1990
BT1 cattle breeds
BT2 breeds

GOLUNDA
BT1 murinae
BT2 muridae
BT3 rodents
BT4 mammals
NT1 golunda ellioti

GOLUNDA ELLIOTI
BT1 golunda
BT2 murinae
BT3 muridae
BT4 rodents
BT5 mammals

GOMPHOCARPUS
BT1 asclepiadaceae
rt asclepias

gomphocarpus fruticosus
USE **asclepias fruticosa**

GOMPHOSTIGMA
BT1 buddlejaceae
NT1 gomphostigma virgatum

GOMPHOSTIGMA VIRGATUM
BT1 gomphostigma
BT2 buddlejaceae

GOMPHRENA
BT1 amaranthaceae
NT1 gomphrena celosioides
NT1 gomphrena globosa

GOMPHRENA CELOSIOIDES
BT1 gomphrena
BT2 amaranthaceae

GOMPHRENA GLOBOSA
BT1 gomphrena
BT2 amaranthaceae
BT1 ornamental herbaceous plants

GONADAL DISORDERS
HN from 1990

GONADAL DISORDERS *cont.*
BT1 endocrine diseases
BT2 organic diseases
BT3 diseases
NT1 hermaphroditism
NT1 hypogonadism
rt gonads

GONADECTOMY
BT1 surgical operations
NT1 castration
NT1 ovariectomy
rt gonads
rt sterilization

gonadoliberin
USE **gnrh**

GONADORELIN
BT1 hypothalamic releasing hormones
BT2 hormones

GONADOSOMATIC INDEX
BT1 indexes
rt gonads

gonadotropes
USE **gonadotropic cells**

gonadotrophs
USE **gonadotropic cells**

GONADOTROPIC CELLS
HN from 1989
uf *gonadotropes*
uf *gonadotrophs*
BT1 cells

gonadotropin, chorionic
USE **chorionic gonadotropin**

gonadotropin, human chorionic
USE **hcg**

GONADOTROPIN RELEASE
BT1 hormonal control
BT2 controls
rt fsh
rt gonadotropins

gonadotropin releasing hormone
USE **gnrh**

GONADOTROPINS
BT1 glycoproteins
BT2 proteins
BT3 peptides
BT1 sex hormones
BT2 hormones
NT1 chorionic gonadotropin
NT2 hcg
NT1 human menopausal gonadotropin
NT1 pituitary gonadotropins
NT2 fsh
NT2 lh
NT1 pmsg
rt gonadotropin release
rt horse anterior pituitary extract
rt pms

gonadotropins, pituitary
USE **pituitary gonadotropins**

GONADS
BT1 reproductive organs
NT1 ovaries
NT2 corpus luteum
NT2 germinal epithelium
NT2 graafian follicles
NT2 ovarioles
NT2 thecal cells
NT1 testes
NT2 epididymis
NT3 caput epididymidis
NT3 cauda epididymidis
NT3 corpus epididymidis
NT2 leydig cells
NT2 rete testis
NT2 seminiferous epithelium
NT2 seminiferous tubules
NT2 sertoli cells
rt glands (animal)

GONADS *cont.*
rt gonadal disorders
rt gonadectomy
rt gonadosomatic index

GONATOCERUS
BT1 mymaridae
BT2 hymenoptera

GONGYLONEMA
BT1 gongylonematidae
BT2 nematoda
NT1 gongylonema ingluvicola
NT1 gongylonema pulchrum
NT1 gongylonema verrucosum

GONGYLONEMA INGLUVICOLA
BT1 gongylonema
BT2 gongylonematidae
BT3 nematoda

GONGYLONEMA PULCHRUM
BT1 gongylonema
BT2 gongylonematidae
BT3 nematoda

GONGYLONEMA VERRUCOSUM
BT1 gongylonema
BT2 gongylonematidae
BT3 nematoda

GONGYLONEMATIDAE
BT1 nematoda
NT1 gongylonema
NT2 gongylonema ingluvicola
NT2 gongylonema pulchrum
NT2 gongylonema verrucosum
rt animal parasitic nematodes

GONIA
BT1 tachinidae
BT2 diptera
rt pseudogonia

gonia cinerascens
USE **pseudogonia rufifrons**

gonimbrasia
USE **imbrasia**

gonimbrasia belina
USE **imbrasia belina**

GONIOCOTES
BT1 goniodidae
BT2 ischnocera
BT3 mallophaga
BT4 phthiraptera
NT1 goniocotes gallinae
rt campanulotes
rt goniodes

goniocotes bidentatus
USE **campanulotes bidentatus**

GONIOCOTES GALLINAE
uf *goniocotes hologaster*
BT1 goniocotes
BT2 goniodidae
BT3 ischnocera
BT4 mallophaga
BT5 phthiraptera

goniocotes gigas
USE **goniodes gigas**

goniocotes hologaster
USE **goniocotes gallinae**

GONIOCTENA
BT1 chrysomelidae
BT2 coleoptera

GONIODES
BT1 goniodidae
BT2 ischnocera
BT3 mallophaga
BT4 phthiraptera
NT1 goniodes gigas
rt goniocotes

GONIODES GIGAS
uf *goniocotes gigas*
BT1 goniodes
BT2 goniodidae
BT3 ischnocera

GONIODES GIGAS *cont.*
BT4 mallophaga
BT5 phthiraptera

GONIODIDAE
BT1 ischnocera
BT2 mallophaga
BT3 phthiraptera
NT1 campanulotes
NT2 campanulotes bidentatus
NT3 campanulotes bidentatus compar
NT1 goniocotes
NT2 goniocotes gallinae
NT1 goniodes
NT2 goniodes gigas

GONIOLIMON
BT1 plumbaginaceae
NT1 goniolimon tataricum

GONIOLIMON TATARICUM
uf *limonium tataricum*
BT1 goniolimon
BT2 plumbaginaceae
BT1 ornamental herbaceous plants

GONIONCHUS
BT1 xyalidae
BT2 nematoda

GONIOPHLEBIUM
BT1 polypodiaceae
NT1 goniophlebium subauriculatum

GONIOPHLEBIUM SUBAURICULATUM
uf *polypodium subauriculatum*
BT1 goniophlebium
BT2 polypodiaceae
BT1 ornamental ferns
BT2 ferns
BT2 ornamental foliage plants
BT3 foliage plants

GONIOPHTHALMUS
BT1 tachinidae
BT2 diptera
NT1 goniophthalmus halli

GONIOPHTHALMUS HALLI
BT1 goniophthalmus
BT2 tachinidae
BT3 diptera

GONIOTHALAMUS
BT1 annonaceae
NT1 goniothalamus andersonii
NT1 goniothalamus macrophyllus
NT1 goniothalamus malayanus
NT1 goniothalamus velutinus

GONIOTHALAMUS ANDERSONII
BT1 goniothalamus
BT2 annonaceae

GONIOTHALAMUS MACROPHYLLUS
BT1 goniothalamus
BT2 annonaceae

GONIOTHALAMUS MALAYANUS
BT1 goniothalamus
BT2 annonaceae

GONIOTHALAMUS VELUTINUS
BT1 goniothalamus
BT2 annonaceae

GONIOZUS
uf *parasierola*
uf *perisierola*
BT1 bethylidae
BT2 hymenoptera
NT1 goniozus nephantidis

GONIOZUS NEPHANTIDIS
uf *parasierola nephantidis*
uf *perisierola nephantidis*
BT1 goniozus
BT2 bethylidae
BT3 hymenoptera

GONIPTERUS
BT1 curculionidae
BT2 coleoptera
NT1 gonipterus scutellatus

GONIPTERUS SCUTELLATUS
BT1 gonipterus
BT2 curculionidae
BT3 coleoptera

GONOCEPHALUM
BT1 tenebrionidae
BT2 coleoptera

GONOCERUS
BT1 coreidae
BT2 heteroptera
NT1 gonocerus acuteangulatus

GONOCERUS ACUTEANGULATUS
BT1 gonocerus
BT2 coreidae
BT3 heteroptera

GONOMETA
BT1 lasiocampidae
BT2 lepidoptera
NT1 gonometa podocarpi

GONOMETA PODOCARPI
BT1 gonometa
BT2 lasiocampidae
BT3 lepidoptera

GONORHYNCHIFORMES
BT1 osteichthyes
BT2 fishes
NT1 chanidae
NT2 chanos
NT3 chanos chanos

GONORRHEA (AGRICOLA)
BT1 venereal diseases (agricola)
BT2 human diseases
BT3 diseases

GONOSPORA
BT1 apicomplexa
BT2 protozoa
BT1 chlorophyta
BT2 algae

GONOTROPHIC CYCLES
BT1 ovarian development
rt autogeny
rt haematophagous arthropods
rt parous rates

GONYSTYLUS
BT1 thymelaeaceae
NT1 gonystylus bancanus
NT1 gonystylus macrophyllus

GONYSTYLUS BANCANUS
BT1 gonystylus
BT2 thymelaeaceae

GONYSTYLUS MACROPHYLLUS
BT1 gonystylus
BT2 thymelaeaceae

GOODYERA
BT1 orchidaceae
NT1 goodyera pubescens

GOODYERA PUBESCENS
BT1 goodyera
BT2 orchidaceae
BT1 ornamental orchids

goose
USE **geese**

GOOSE EGGS
uf *eggs, goose*
BT1 eggs
BT2 poultry products
BT3 animal products
BT4 products
rt geese

GOOSE FATTENING
BT1 poultry fattening
BT2 fattening
BT3 animal feeding

GOOSE FATTENING *cont.*
BT4 feeding
rt geese

GOOSE FEEDING
BT1 poultry feeding
BT2 livestock feeding
BT3 animal feeding
BT4 feeding
rt geese

goose hepatitis virus
USE **goose parvovirus**

GOOSE LIVER
uf *liver, goose*
BT1 livers as food
BT2 foods
BT2 offal
BT3 meat byproducts
BT4 agricultural byproducts
BT5 byproducts
rt foie gras
rt geese

GOOSE MEAT
BT1 poultry meat
BT2 meat
BT3 animal products
BT4 products
BT3 foods
rt geese

GOOSE PARVOVIRUS
uf *goose hepatitis virus*
BT1 parvovirus
BT2 parvoviridae
BT3 viruses

GOOSEBERRIES
BT1 temperate small fruits
BT2 small fruits
BT2 temperate fruits
BT3 fruit crops
rt ribes uva-crispa

GOPHERUS
BT1 testudinidae
BT2 testudines
BT3 reptiles

GORBATOV RED
BT1 cattle breeds
BT2 breeds

GORDONIA
BT1 theaceae
NT1 gordonia lasianthus

GORDONIA LASIANTHUS
BT1 gordonia
BT2 theaceae

GORGODERIDAE
BT1 digenea
BT2 trematoda
NT1 gorgoderina
NT2 gorgoderina vitelliloba
NT1 phyllodistomum

GORGODERINA
BT1 gorgoderidae
BT2 digenea
BT3 trematoda
NT1 gorgoderina vitelliloba

GORGODERINA VITELLILOBA
BT1 gorgoderina
BT2 gorgoderidae
BT3 digenea
BT4 trematoda

GORGONZOLA CHEESE
BT1 cheeses
BT2 milk products
BT3 products

GORILLA
BT1 pongidae
BT2 primates
BT3 mammals

gorilla gorilla
USE **gorillas**

GORILLAS
uf *gorilla gorilla*
BT1 wild animals
BT2 animals
rt pongidae

GORKI
HN from 1990
BT1 sheep breeds
BT2 breeds

GORTYNA
BT1 noctuidae
BT2 lepidoptera
NT1 gortyna xanthenes

GORTYNA XANTHENES
BT1 gortyna
BT2 noctuidae
BT3 lepidoptera

GOSLINGS
BT1 young animals
BT2 animals
rt geese

GOSSWEILERODENDRON
BT1 leguminosae
NT1 gossweilerodendron balsamiferum

GOSSWEILERODENDRON BALSAMIFERUM
BT1 gossweilerodendron
BT2 leguminosae

GOSSYPIUM
BT1 malvaceae
NT1 gossypium arboreum
NT1 gossypium barbadense
NT1 gossypium herbaceum
NT1 gossypium hirsutum
NT1 gossypium tomentosum

GOSSYPIUM ARBOREUM
BT1 gossypium
BT2 malvaceae
rt cotton

GOSSYPIUM BARBADENSE
BT1 gossypium
BT2 malvaceae
rt cotton

GOSSYPIUM HERBACEUM
BT1 gossypium
BT2 malvaceae
rt cotton

GOSSYPIUM HIRSUTUM
BT1 gossypium
BT2 malvaceae
rt cotton

GOSSYPIUM TOMENTOSUM
BT1 gossypium
BT2 malvaceae

GOSSYPOL
BT1 allomones
BT2 allelochemicals
BT3 semiochemicals
BT1 phenols
BT2 alcohols
BT2 phenolic compounds
BT3 aromatic compounds
BT1 pigments
BT1 triterpenoids
BT2 terpenoids
BT3 isoprenoids
BT4 lipids
BT1 trypanocides
BT2 antiprotozoal agents
BT3 antiparasitic agents
BT4 drugs
rt cotton

got
USE **aspartate aminotransferase**

GOUANIA
BT1 rhamnaceae
NT1 gouania lupuloides

GOUANIA LUPULOIDES
BT1 gouania
BT2 rhamnaceae

GOUDA CHEESE
BT1 cheeses
BT2 milk products
BT3 products

GOUGEROTIN
BT1 antibacterial agents
BT2 antiinfective agents
BT3 drugs
BT1 nucleoside antibiotics
BT2 antibiotics
BT2 nucleosides
BT3 glycosides
BT4 carbohydrates

GOULDIA
BT1 rubiaceae
NT1 gouldia terminalis

GOULDIA TERMINALIS
BT1 gouldia
BT2 rubiaceae

GOUPIA
BT1 goupiaceae
NT1 goupia glabra

GOUPIA GLABRA
BT1 forest trees
BT1 goupia
BT2 goupiaceae

GOUPIACEAE
NT1 goupia
NT2 goupia glabra

gourd, ash
USE **benincasa hispida**

gourd, bitter
USE **momordica charantia**

gourd, bottle
USE **lagenaria siceraria**

gourd, pointed
USE **trichosanthes dioica**

gourd, ridge
USE **luffa acutangula**

gourd, round
USE **citrullus lanatus var. fistulosus**

gourd, siam
USE **cucurbita ficifolia**

gourd, snake
USE **trichosanthes cucumerina**

gourd, sponge
USE **luffa acutangula**

GOURDS
BT1 vessels
rt cucurbitaceae

GOURMET COOKERY (AGRICOLA)
BT1 cookery (agricola)

GOUSSIA
BT1 apicomplexa
BT2 protozoa

GOUT
BT1 metabolic disorders
BT2 animal disorders
BT3 disorders
rt allopurinol
rt arthritis

GOVERNMENT
NT1 central government
NT2 ministries of agriculture
NT3 usda (agricola)
NT1 constitution and law
NT1 federal government (agricola)
NT1 local government
NT1 parliament
NT1 public authorities

GOVERNMENT *cont.*
NT1 regional government
NT1 state government (agricola)
rt administration
rt government organizations
rt government research

government agencies
USE **public agencies (agricola)**

GOVERNMENT ORGANIZATIONS
BT1 organizations
NT1 marketing boards
NT2 milk marketing boards
NT1 ministries of agriculture
NT2 usda (agricola)
rt government
rt semiprivate organizations
rt social institutions

GOVERNMENT RESEARCH
uf *research, government*
BT1 research
rt government
rt organization of research
rt research institutes

GOVERNORS
BT1 components
rt engines

GOYAZITE
BT1 nonclay minerals
BT2 minerals

gpt
USE **alanine aminotransferase**

GRAAFIAN FOLLICLES
uf *ovarian follicles*
BT1 follicles
BT1 ovaries
BT2 gonads
BT3 reproductive organs
rt ovulation
rt reproduction

GRABS
BT1 machinery
rt cranes
rt handling

GRACILACUS
BT1 paratylenchidae
BT2 nematoda
NT1 gracilacus acicula

GRACILACUS ACICULA
BT1 gracilacus
BT2 paratylenchidae
BT3 nematoda

GRACILENTULUS
BT1 acerentomidae
BT2 protura

GRACILICUTES
BT1 bacteria
BT2 prokaryotes
NT1 acetobacteraceae
NT2 acetobacter
NT3 acetobacter aceti
NT1 alcaligenes
NT2 alcaligenes faecalis
NT2 alcaligenes latus
NT2 alcaligenes paradoxus
NT1 azotobacteraceae
NT2 azomonas
NT2 azotobacter
NT3 azotobacter beijerinckii
NT3 azotobacter chroococcum
NT3 azotobacter vinelandii
NT2 beijerinckia
NT3 beijerinckia indica
NT3 beijerinckia lacticogenes
NT2 derxia
NT1 bacteroidaceae
NT2 bacteroides
NT3 bacteroides nodosus
NT3 bacteroides ruminicola
NT2 butyrivibrio
NT3 butyrivibrio fibrisolvens
NT2 fusobacterium

GRACILICUTES *cont.*
NT3 fusobacterium necrophorum
NT1 bordetella
NT2 bordetella avium
NT2 bordetella bronchiseptica
NT1 brucellaceae
NT2 brucella
NT3 brucella abortus
NT3 brucella canis
NT3 brucella melitensis
NT3 brucella ovis
NT3 brucella suis
NT1 caulobacteraceae
NT2 gallionella
NT1 chromobacterium
NT2 chromobacterium lividum
NT1 cytophagaceae
NT2 cytophaga
NT2 flexibacter
NT2 saprospira
NT3 saprospira alba
NT1 desulfovibrio
NT2 desulfovibrio desulfuricans
NT2 desulfovibrio vulgaris
NT1 enterobacteriaceae
NT2 citrobacter
NT3 citrobacter freundii
NT2 edwardsiella
NT2 enterobacter
NT3 enterobacter aerogenes
NT3 enterobacter agglomerans
NT3 enterobacter cancerogenus
NT3 enterobacter cloacae
NT2 erwinia
NT3 erwinia amylovora
NT3 erwinia ananas
NT3 erwinia carotovora
NT4 erwinia carotovora subsp. atroseptica
NT4 erwinia carotovora subsp. betavasculorum
NT4 erwinia carotovora subsp. carotovora
NT3 erwinia chrysanthemi
NT4 erwinia chrysanthemi pv. chrysanthemi
NT4 erwinia chrysanthemi pv. dianthicola
NT4 erwinia chrysanthemi pv. dieffenbachiae
NT4 erwinia chrysanthemi pv. paradisiaca
NT4 erwinia chrysanthemi pv. parthenii
NT4 erwinia chrysanthemi pv. zeae
NT3 erwinia herbicola
NT4 erwinia herbicola pv. millettiae
NT3 erwinia rhapontici
NT3 erwinia rubrifaciens
NT3 erwinia salicis
NT3 erwinia stewartii
NT3 erwinia tracheiphila
NT3 erwinia uredovora
NT2 escherichia
NT3 escherichia coli
NT2 hafnia
NT3 hafnia alvei
NT2 klebsiella
NT3 klebsiella aerogenes
NT3 klebsiella oxytoca
NT3 klebsiella pneumoniae
NT2 morganella
NT2 proteus
NT3 proteus mirabilis
NT3 proteus vulgaris
NT2 providencia
NT2 salmonella
NT3 salmonella abortusequi
NT3 salmonella abortusovis
NT3 salmonella anatum
NT3 salmonella arizonae
NT3 salmonella choleraesuis
NT3 salmonella dublin
NT3 salmonella enteritidis
NT3 salmonella gallinarum
NT3 salmonella muenster
NT3 salmonella pullorum

GRACILICUTES *cont.*
NT3 salmonella typhi
NT3 salmonella typhimurium
NT2 serratia
NT3 serratia liquefasciens
NT3 serratia marcescens
NT2 shigella
NT3 shigella dysenteriae
NT3 shigella flexneri
NT3 shigella sonnei
NT2 xenorhabdus
NT3 xenorhabdus luminescens
NT3 xenorhabdus nematophilus
NT2 yersinia
NT3 yersinia enterocolitica
NT3 yersinia frederiksenii
NT3 yersinia intermedia
NT3 yersinia kristensenii
NT3 yersinia pseudotuberculosis
NT4 yersinia pseudotuberculosis subsp. pestis
NT3 yersinia ruckeri
NT1 flavobacterium
NT2 flavobacterium meningosepticum
NT1 francisella
NT2 francisella tularensis
NT1 legionellaceae
NT2 legionella
NT3 legionella pneumophila
NT1 lysobacterales
NT2 lysobacter
NT1 neisseriaceae
NT2 acinetobacter
NT3 acinetobacter calcoaceticus
NT2 branhamella
NT2 kingella
NT2 moraxella
NT3 moraxella anatipestifer
NT3 moraxella bovis
NT2 neisseria
NT1 nitrobacteraceae
NT2 nitrobacter
NT3 nitrobacter agilis
NT3 nitrobacter winogradskyi
NT2 nitrosolobus
NT2 nitrosomonas
NT2 paracoccus
NT3 paracoccus denitrificans
NT1 pasteurellaceae
NT2 haemophilus
NT3 haemophilus equigenitalis
NT3 haemophilus paragallinarum
NT3 haemophilus somnus
NT2 histophilus
NT2 pasteurella
NT3 pasteurella haemolytica
NT3 pasteurella multocida
NT1 pseudomonadaceae
NT2 pseudomonas
NT3 pseudomonas aeruginosa
NT3 pseudomonas andropogonis
NT3 pseudomonas avenae
NT3 pseudomonas azotogensis
NT3 pseudomonas caryophylli
NT3 pseudomonas cepacia
NT3 pseudomonas cichorii
NT3 pseudomonas corrugata
NT3 pseudomonas fluorescens
NT3 pseudomonas fragi
NT3 pseudomonas fuscovaginae
NT3 pseudomonas gladioli
NT4 pseudomonas gladioli pv. alliicola
NT4 pseudomonas gladioli pv. gladioli
NT3 pseudomonas glumae
NT3 pseudomonas mallei
NT3 pseudomonas maltophilia
NT3 pseudomonas marginalis
NT4 pseudomonas marginalis pv. alfalfae

GRACILICUTES *cont.*
NT4 pseudomonas marginalis pv. marginalis
NT4 pseudomonas marginalis pv. pastinaceae
NT3 pseudomonas plantarii
NT3 pseudomonas pseudoalcaligenes
NT4 pseudomonas pseudoalcaligenes subsp. konjaci
NT3 pseudomonas pseudomallei
NT3 pseudomonas putida
NT3 pseudomonas rubrilineans
NT3 pseudomonas solanacearum
NT3 pseudomonas striata
NT3 pseudomonas syringae
NT4 pseudomonas syringae pv. aptata
NT4 pseudomonas syringae pv. atrofaciens
NT4 pseudomonas syringae pv. atropurpurea
NT4 pseudomonas syringae pv. coronafaciens
NT4 pseudomonas syringae pv. dendropanicis
NT4 pseudomonas syringae pv. garcae
NT4 pseudomonas syringae pv. glycinea
NT4 pseudomonas syringae pv. helianthi
NT4 pseudomonas syringae pv. lachrymans
NT4 pseudomonas syringae pv. maculicola
NT4 pseudomonas syringae pv. mori
NT4 pseudomonas syringae pv. morsprunorum
NT4 pseudomonas syringae pv. panici
NT4 pseudomonas syringae pv. papulans
NT4 pseudomonas syringae pv. persicae
NT4 pseudomonas syringae pv. phaseolicola
NT4 pseudomonas syringae pv. pisi
NT4 pseudomonas syringae pv. savastanoi
NT4 pseudomonas syringae pv. sesami
NT4 pseudomonas syringae pv. syringae
NT4 pseudomonas syringae pv. tabaci
NT4 pseudomonas syringae pv. tagetis
NT4 pseudomonas syringae pv. theae
NT4 pseudomonas syringae pv. tomato
NT3 pseudomonas syzygii
NT3 pseudomonas testeroni
NT3 pseudomonas tolaasii
NT3 pseudomonas viridiflava
NT2 xanthomonas
NT3 xanthomonas albilineans
NT3 xanthomonas campestris
NT4 xanthomonas campestris pv. alfalfae
NT4 xanthomonas campestris pv. armoraciae
NT4 xanthomonas campestris pv. begoniae
NT4 xanthomonas campestris pv. betlicola
NT4 xanthomonas campestris pv. cajani
NT4 xanthomonas campestris pv. campestris
NT4 xanthomonas campestris pv. cassavae
NT4 xanthomonas campestris pv. citri

GRACILICUTES *cont.*
NT4 xanthomonas campestris pv. corylina
NT4 xanthomonas campestris pv. cyamopsidis
NT4 xanthomonas campestris pv. dieffenbachiae
NT4 xanthomonas campestris pv. glycines
NT4 xanthomonas campestris pv. graminis
NT4 xanthomonas campestris pv. hederae
NT4 xanthomonas campestris pv. holcicola
NT4 xanthomonas campestris pv. hyacinthi
NT4 xanthomonas campestris pv. juglandis
NT4 xanthomonas campestris pv. malvacearum
NT4 xanthomonas campestris pv. mangiferaeindicae
NT4 xanthomonas campestris pv. manihotis
NT4 xanthomonas campestris pv. oryzae
NT4 xanthomonas campestris pv. oryzicola
NT4 xanthomonas campestris pv. pelargonii
NT4 xanthomonas campestris pv. phaseoli
NT4 xanthomonas campestris pv. pruni
NT4 xanthomonas campestris pv. ricini
NT4 xanthomonas campestris pv. sesami
NT4 xanthomonas campestris pv. syngonii
NT4 xanthomonas campestris pv. translucens
NT4 xanthomonas campestris pv. undulosa
NT4 xanthomonas campestris pv. vasculorum
NT4 xanthomonas campestris pv. vesicatoria
NT4 xanthomonas campestris pv. vignaeradiatae
NT4 xanthomonas campestris pv. vignicola
NT3 xanthomonas fragariae
NT3 xanthomonas heterocea
NT3 xanthomonas populi
NT2 xylophilus
NT3 xylophilus ampelinus
NT1 rhizobiaceae
NT2 agrobacterium
NT3 agrobacterium radiobacter
NT3 agrobacterium rhizogenes
NT3 agrobacterium rubi
NT3 agrobacterium tumefaciens
NT2 bradyrhizobium
NT3 bradyrhizobium japonicum
NT2 rhizobium
NT3 rhizobium leguminosarum
NT3 rhizobium lupini
NT3 rhizobium meliloti
NT3 rhizobium phaseoli
NT3 rhizobium trifolii
NT1 selenomonas
NT2 selenomonas ruminantium
NT1 spirillaceae
NT2 azospirillum
NT3 azospirillum brasilense
NT3 azospirillum lipoferum
NT2 bdellovibrio
NT2 campylobacter
NT3 campylobacter fetus
NT3 campylobacter jejuni
NT3 campylobacter sputorum
NT2 spirillum
NT3 spirillum lipoferum
NT1 spirochaetales
NT2 leptospiraceae
NT3 leptospira
NT4 leptospira interrogans

GRACILICUTES *cont.*
NT2 spirochaetaceae
NT3 borrelia
NT4 borrelia anserina
NT4 borrelia burgdorferi
NT4 borrelia latyschevi
NT4 borrelia persica
NT4 borrelia recurrentis
NT2 treponemataceae
NT3 treponema
NT4 treponema hyodysenteriae
NT1 streptobacillus
NT1 taylorella
NT2 taylorella equigenitalis
NT1 thiobacteriaceae
NT2 thiobacillus
NT3 thiobacillus ferrooxidans
NT3 thiobacillus thiooxidans
NT1 vibrionaceae
NT2 aeromonas
NT3 aeromonas hydrophila
NT3 aeromonas salmonicida
NT2 photobacterium
NT2 plesiomonas
NT2 vibrio
NT3 vibrio anguillarum
NT3 vibrio cholerae
NT1 wolinella
NT1 xylella
NT2 xylella fastidiosa
NT1 zymomonas
NT2 zymomonas mobilis
rt gram negative bacteria

GRACILLARIIDAE
BT1 lepidoptera
NT1 acrocercops
NT2 acrocercops syngramma
NT2 acrocercops zygonoma
NT1 callisto
NT2 callisto denticulella
NT1 caloptilia
NT1 cameraria
NT2 cameraria hamadryadella
NT1 conopomorpha
NT2 conopomorpha cramerella
NT1 parornix
NT1 phyllonorycter
NT2 phyllonorycter blancardella
NT2 phyllonorycter corylifoliella
NT2 phyllonorycter crataegella
NT2 phyllonorycter cydoniella
NT2 phyllonorycter pomonella
NT2 phyllonorycter pyrifoliella
NT2 phyllonorycter ringoniella

GRACULA
BT1 sturnidae
BT2 passeriformes
BT3 birds
NT1 gracula religiosa

GRACULA RELIGIOSA
BT1 gracula
BT2 sturnidae
BT3 passeriformes
BT4 birds

GRADEABILITY
BT1 quality standards
BT2 quality controls
BT3 consumer protection
BT4 protection
BT3 controls
BT2 standards
rt gradients
rt operation on slopes
rt tractors

GRADERS
NT1 egg graders
NT1 flower graders
NT1 fruit graders
NT1 potato graders
NT1 size graders
NT1 tomato graders
NT1 weight graders
rt grading
rt rotary screens
rt sorters

graders, egg
USE **egg graders**

graders, flower
USE **flower graders**

graders, fruit
USE **fruit graders**

graders, potato
USE **potato graders**

graders, size
USE **size graders**

graders, tomato
USE **tomato graders**

graders, weight
USE **weight graders**

GRADIENTS
NT1 temperature gradients
rt aspect
rt clines
rt gradeability
rt operation on slopes
rt slopes

gradients, temperature
USE **temperature gradients**

GRADING
uf *grading and sorting*
NT1 carcass grading
NT1 sieving
NT1 sorting
NT2 colour sorting
NT2 flow sorting
NT2 magnetic separation
NT1 stress grading
NT1 visual grading
rt consumer protection
rt culling
rt food grades (agricola)
rt graders
rt land forming
rt levelling
rt log grade
rt meat grades (agricola)
rt quality
rt selection
rt standardization
rt standards
rt tree classes

grading and sorting
USE **grading**
OR **sorting**

GRADUATE STUDY (AGRICOLA)
BT1 higher education
BT2 education
rt graduates
rt universities

GRADUATES
rt graduate study (agricola)
rt qualifications
rt students
rt universities

GRAEFFEA
BT1 phasmatidae
BT2 phasmida
NT1 graeffea crouanii

GRAEFFEA CROUANII
BT1 graeffea
BT2 phasmatidae
BT3 phasmida

GRAFT HYBRIDIZATION
uf *hybridization, graft*
BT1 plant breeding methods
BT2 breeding methods
BT3 methodology
rt chimaeras
rt hybridization
rt vegetative hybridization

GRAFT REJECTION
BT1 incompatibility
rt graft versus host reactions
rt grafts

GRAFT REJECTION *cont.*
rt histocompatibility
rt major histocompatibility complex

graft unions
USE **unions**

GRAFT VERSUS HOST REACTIONS
BT1 cell mediated immunity
BT2 immunity
rt graft rejection
rt grafts

GRAFTING
(plants)
BT1 vegetative propagation
BT2 propagation
NT1 budding
NT1 inarching
NT1 topworking
rt bench grafts
rt compatibility
rt grafting equipment
rt grafts
rt interstocks
rt rootstock scion relationships
rt rootstocks
rt scions
rt ties
rt unions

GRAFTING EQUIPMENT
BT1 equipment
rt grafting

GRAFTS
(animals)
NT1 allografts
rt graft rejection
rt graft versus host reactions
rt grafting

GRAHAMELLA
BT1 bartonellaceae
BT2 rickettsiales
BT3 bacteria
BT4 prokaryotes

GRAIN
HN from 1989
NT1 feed grains
NT2 coarse grains
NT1 food grains
NT2 whole grains (agricola)

grain amaranths
USE **amaranthus**

GRAIN AND FIGURE
uf *figure in wood*
BT1 structure
BT1 texture
BT2 physical properties
BT3 properties
BT1 wood
NT1 spiral grain
rt betula pendula f. carelica
rt burrs
rt knots

GRAIN CONSERVATION
BT1 conservation
rt feed grains
rt food grains
rt grain stores

GRAIN CROPS
NT1 cereals
NT2 barley
NT2 coix lacryma-jobi
NT2 maize
NT2 millets
NT3 brachiaria ramosa
NT3 digitaria exilis
NT3 digitaria iburua
NT3 echinochloa colonum
NT3 echinochloa decompositum
NT3 echinochloa frumentacea
NT3 eleusine coracana
NT3 eragrostis tef

GRAIN CROPS *cont.*
NT3 panicum miliaceum
NT3 panicum miliare
NT3 paspalum scrobiculatum
NT3 pennisetum americanum
NT3 phalaris canariensis
NT3 setaria italica
NT3 setaria viridis
NT2 oats
NT2 rice
NT2 rye
NT2 triticale
NT2 wheat
NT2 zizania aquatica
NT2 zizania palustris
NT1 grain legumes
NT2 cajanus cajan
NT2 canavalia ensiformis
NT2 cicer arietinum
NT2 cyamopsis tetragonoloba
NT2 groundnuts
NT2 lablab purpureus
NT2 lathyrus sativus
NT2 lens culinaris
NT2 macrotyloma geocarpum
NT2 macrotyloma uniflorum
NT2 peas
NT2 phaseolus acutifolius
NT2 phaseolus lunatus
NT2 phaseolus vulgaris
NT2 psophocarpus tetragonolobus
NT2 soyabeans
NT2 vicia faba
NT2 vigna aconitifolia
NT2 vigna angularis
NT2 vigna mungo
NT2 vigna radiata
NT2 vigna subterranea
NT2 vigna umbellata
NT2 vigna unguiculata
NT1 pseudocereals
NT2 amaranthus caudatus
NT2 amaranthus cruentus
NT2 amaranthus leucocarpus
NT2 buckwheat
NT2 chenopodium album
NT2 chenopodium nuttaliae
NT2 chenopodium quinoa
rt field crops
rt plants

GRAIN DRIERS
AF grain dryers
uf *driers, grain*
BT1 driers
BT2 farm machinery
BT3 machinery
NT1 floor driers
rt cross flow driers
rt deep bed driers
rt feed grains
rt food grains
rt grain drying
rt precleaners

GRAIN DRILLS
uf *drills, grain*
BT1 drills
BT2 farm machinery
BT3 machinery
rt feed grains
rt food grains

GRAIN DRYERS
BF grain driers
BT1 dryers

GRAIN DRYING
BT1 drying
BT2 dehydration
BT3 processing
NT1 drieration
rt feed grains
rt food grains
rt grain driers

GRAIN DUST
BT1 dust
rt feed grains
rt food grains

grain feed
USE **feed grains**

GRAIN LEGUMES
uf *pulses*
BT1 grain crops
BT1 legumes
NT1 cajanus cajan
NT1 canavalia ensiformis
NT1 cicer arietinum
NT1 cyamopsis tetragonoloba
NT1 groundnuts
NT1 lablab purpureus
NT1 lathyrus sativus
NT1 lens culinaris
NT1 macrotyloma geocarpum
NT1 macrotyloma uniflorum
NT1 peas
NT1 phaseolus acutifolius
NT1 phaseolus lunatus
NT1 phaseolus vulgaris
NT1 psophocarpus tetragonolobus
NT1 soyabeans
NT1 vicia faba
NT1 vigna aconitifolia
NT1 vigna angularis
NT1 vigna mungo
NT1 vigna radiata
NT1 vigna subterranea
NT1 vigna umbellata
NT1 vigna unguiculata
rt plants
rt vegetable legumes

GRAIN LOSS MONITORS
BT1 monitors
rt combine harvesters
rt feed grains
rt food grains
rt harvesting
rt losses

GRAIN MOTTLING
rt deterioration
rt feed grains
rt food grains

GRAIN SHRIVELLING
BT1 plant disorders
BT2 disorders

GRAIN SPROUTING
BT1 sprouting
BT2 plant development

GRAIN STORES
uf *stores, grain*
BT1 stores
NT1 maize cribs
rt feed grains
rt food grains
rt grain conservation

GRAIN TANKS
uf *tanks, grain*
BT1 combine harvesters
BT2 harvesters
BT3 farm machinery
BT4 machinery

gram
USE **black gram**
OR **green gram**

gram, black
USE **black gram**

gram, green
USE **green gram**

GRAM NEGATIVE BACTERIA
BT1 microbial flora
BT2 flora
rt bacteria
rt gracilicutes

GRAM POSITIVE BACTERIA
BT1 microbial flora
BT2 flora
rt bacteria
rt firmicutes

GRAMICIDIN
BT1 antibacterial agents
BT2 antiinfective agents
BT3 drugs
BT1 antibiotics

GRAMICIDIN S
BT1 antibacterial agents
BT2 antiinfective agents
BT3 drugs
BT1 antibiotics
BT1 cyclic peptides
BT2 oligopeptides
BT3 peptides
BT1 ionophores

GRAMINE
BT1 indole alkaloids
BT2 alkaloids
BT2 indoles
BT3 heterocyclic nitrogen compounds
BT4 organic nitrogen compounds

GRAMINEAE
uf *poaceae*
NT1 acroceras
NT2 acroceras macrum
NT1 aegilops
NT2 aegilops bicornis
NT2 aegilops caudata
NT2 aegilops columnaris
NT2 aegilops comosa
NT2 aegilops crassa
NT2 aegilops cylindrica
NT2 aegilops juvenalis
NT2 aegilops longissima
NT2 aegilops lorentii
NT2 aegilops mutica
NT2 aegilops ovata
NT2 aegilops speltoides
NT2 aegilops squarrosa
NT2 aegilops triaristata
NT2 aegilops triuncialis
NT2 aegilops umbellulata
NT2 aegilops uniaristata
NT2 aegilops variabilis
NT2 aegilops vavilovii
NT2 aegilops ventricosa
NT1 aeluropus
NT2 aeluropus lagopoides
NT2 aeluropus littoralis
NT1 agrohordeum
NT2 agrohordeum macounii
NT1 agropyron
NT2 agropyron cristatum
NT2 agropyron desertorum
NT2 agropyron fragile
NT2 agropyron imbricatum
NT2 agropyron scabrum
NT1 agrostis
NT2 agrostis alba
NT2 agrostis avenacea
NT2 agrostis borealis
NT2 agrostis canina
NT2 agrostis capillaris
NT2 agrostis castellana
NT2 agrostis exarata
NT2 agrostis gigantea
NT2 agrostis hiemalis
NT2 agrostis lazica
NT2 agrostis planifolia
NT2 agrostis setacea
NT2 agrostis stolonifera
NT2 agrostis stolonifera var. palustris
NT1 aira
NT2 aira caryophyllea
NT2 aira multiculmis
NT2 aira praecox
NT1 alopecurus
NT2 alopecurus aequalis
NT2 alopecurus aequalis var. amurensis
NT2 alopecurus brevifolius
NT2 alopecurus bulbosus
NT2 alopecurus geniculatus
NT2 alopecurus myosuroides
NT2 alopecurus pratensis
NT1 ammophila
NT2 ammophila arenaria

GRAMINEAE *cont.*
NT2 ammophila breviligulata
NT1 ampelodesmos
NT2 ampelodesmos mauritanica
NT1 andropogon
NT2 andropogon annulatus
NT2 andropogon bicornis
NT2 andropogon distachyos
NT2 andropogon divergens
NT2 andropogon filifolius
NT2 andropogon gayanus
NT2 andropogon gerardii
NT2 andropogon hallii
NT2 andropogon lateralis
NT2 andropogon paniculatus
NT2 andropogon perligulatus
NT2 andropogon schirensis
NT2 andropogon tectorum
NT2 andropogon virginicus
NT1 anthephora
NT2 anthephora pubescens
NT1 anthoxanthum
NT2 anthoxanthum alpinum
NT2 anthoxanthum odoratum
NT2 anthoxanthum puelii
NT1 apera
NT2 apera interrupta
NT2 apera spica-venti
NT1 apluda
NT2 apluda mutica
NT1 arctagrostis
NT2 arctagrostis latifolia
NT1 arctophila
NT2 arctophila fulva
NT1 aristida
NT2 aristida acutiflora
NT2 aristida adscensionis
NT2 aristida browniana
NT2 aristida caerulescens
NT2 aristida congesta
NT2 aristida contorta
NT2 aristida cyanantha
NT2 aristida dichotoma
NT2 aristida divaricata
NT2 aristida funiculata
NT2 aristida hamulosa
NT2 aristida jubata
NT2 aristida junciformis
NT2 aristida karelinii
NT2 aristida latifolia
NT2 aristida leptopoda
NT2 aristida longiflora
NT2 aristida longiseta
NT2 aristida meccana
NT2 aristida murina
NT2 aristida mutabilis
NT2 aristida oligantha
NT2 aristida pallens
NT2 aristida pungens
NT2 aristida purpurea
NT2 aristida ramosa
NT2 aristida rhiniochloa
NT2 aristida rufescens
NT2 aristida setifolia
NT2 aristida stipitata
NT2 aristida stricta
NT2 aristida transvaalensis
NT1 arrhenatherum
NT2 arrhenatherum elatius
NT2 arrhenatherum elatius subsp. bulbosum
NT1 arthraxon
NT2 arthraxon hispidus
NT1 arundinaria
NT2 arundinaria amabilis
NT2 arundinaria disticha
NT2 arundinaria pygmaea
NT1 arundinella
NT2 arundinella bengalensis
NT1 arundo
NT2 arundo donax
NT1 astrebla
NT2 astrebla elymoides
NT2 astrebla lappacea
NT2 astrebla pectinata
NT1 avena
NT2 avena abyssinica
NT2 avena barbata
NT2 avena byzantina
NT2 avena canariensis
NT2 avena clauda

GRAMINEAE *cont.*
NT2 avena fatua
NT2 avena hirtula
NT2 avena longiglumis
NT2 avena magna
NT2 avena maroccana
NT2 avena murphyi
NT2 avena nuda
NT2 avena persica
NT2 avena pilosa
NT2 avena sativa
NT2 avena sterilis
NT2 avena sterilis subsp. ludoviciana
NT2 avena sterilis subsp. sterilis
NT2 avena ventricosa
NT2 avena wiestii
NT1 avenula
NT2 avenula pratensis
NT2 avenula pubescens
NT1 axonopus
NT2 axonopus affinis
NT2 axonopus compressus
NT2 axonopus purpusii
NT1 bambusa
NT2 bambusa arundinacea
NT2 bambusa balcooa
NT2 bambusa blumeana
NT2 bambusa oldhami
NT2 bambusa tulda
NT2 bambusa vulgaris
NT1 beckmannia
NT2 beckmannia syzigachne
NT1 bellardiochloa
NT2 bellardiochloa violacea
NT1 bothriochloa
NT2 bothriochloa ambigua
NT2 bothriochloa barbinodis
NT2 bothriochloa bladhii
NT2 bothriochloa caucasica
NT2 bothriochloa insculpta
NT2 bothriochloa intermedia
NT2 bothriochloa ischaemum
NT2 bothriochloa macra
NT2 bothriochloa pertusa
NT1 bouteloua
NT2 bouteloua chasei
NT2 bouteloua curtipendula
NT2 bouteloua eriopoda
NT2 bouteloua gracilis
NT2 bouteloua hirsuta
NT2 bouteloua rothrockii
NT1 brachiaria
NT2 brachiaria brizantha
NT2 brachiaria decumbens
NT2 brachiaria deflexa
NT2 brachiaria dictyoneura
NT2 brachiaria distachya
NT2 brachiaria eruciformis
NT2 brachiaria hagerupii
NT2 brachiaria humidicola
NT2 brachiaria jubata
NT2 brachiaria miliiformis
NT2 brachiaria mutica
NT2 brachiaria plantaginea
NT2 brachiaria platyphylla
NT2 brachiaria pubigera
NT2 brachiaria radicans
NT2 brachiaria ramosa
NT2 brachiaria ruziziensis
NT2 brachiaria subquadripara
NT1 brachyelytrum
NT2 brachyelytrum erectum
NT1 brachypodium
NT2 brachypodium phoenicoides
NT2 brachypodium pinnatum
NT2 brachypodium ramosum
NT2 brachypodium sylvaticum
NT1 briza
NT2 briza maxima
NT2 briza media
NT2 briza minor
NT1 bromus
NT2 bromus benekenii
NT2 bromus biebersteinii
NT2 bromus brevis
NT2 bromus cappadocicus
NT2 bromus carinatus
NT2 bromus catharticus

GRAMINEAE *cont.*
NT2 bromus commutatus
NT2 bromus diandrus
NT2 bromus erectus
NT2 bromus hordeaceus
NT2 bromus inermis
NT2 bromus japonicus
NT2 bromus macrostachys
NT2 bromus madritensis
NT2 bromus marginatus
NT2 bromus molliformis
NT2 bromus oxyodon
NT2 bromus pumilio
NT2 bromus racemosus
NT2 bromus rigidus
NT2 bromus riparius
NT2 bromus rubens
NT2 bromus sarothrae
NT2 bromus scoparius
NT2 bromus secalinus
NT2 bromus sericeus
NT2 bromus sitchensis
NT2 bromus sterilis
NT2 bromus tectorum
NT2 bromus tomentellus
NT2 bromus variegatus
NT1 buchloe
NT2 buchloe dactyloides
NT1 calamagrostis
NT2 calamagrostis angustifolia
NT2 calamagrostis arctica
NT2 calamagrostis arundinacea
NT2 calamagrostis canadensis
NT2 calamagrostis canescens
NT2 calamagrostis deschampsiodes
NT2 calamagrostis epigejos
NT2 calamagrostis fauriei
NT2 calamagrostis gunniana
NT2 calamagrostis longiseta
NT2 calamagrostis montanensis
NT2 calamagrostis neglecta
NT2 calamagrostis purpurascens
NT2 calamagrostis purpurea
NT2 calamagrostis purpurea subsp. langsdorfii
NT2 calamagrostis rubescens
NT2 calamagrostis villosa
NT1 calamovilfa
NT2 calamovilfa longifolia
NT1 catabrosa
NT2 catabrosa aquatica
NT1 catapodium
NT1 cenchrus
NT2 cenchrus barbatus
NT2 cenchrus biflorus
NT2 cenchrus brownii
NT2 cenchrus ciliaris
NT2 cenchrus echinatus
NT2 cenchrus incertus
NT2 cenchrus longispinus
NT2 cenchrus prieurii
NT2 cenchrus setigerus
NT1 chasmopodium
NT2 chasmopodium caudatum
NT2 chasmopodium purpurascens
NT1 chimonobambusa
NT2 chimonobambusa jaunsarensis
NT1 chionachne
NT1 chionochloa
NT2 chionochloa antarctica
NT2 chionochloa crassiuscula
NT2 chionochloa flavescens
NT2 chionochloa juncea
NT2 chionochloa macra
NT2 chionochloa pallens
NT2 chionochloa rigida
NT2 chionochloa rubra
NT1 chloris
NT2 chloris barbata
NT2 chloris crinita
NT2 chloris gayana
NT2 chloris pilosa
NT2 chloris prieurii
NT2 chloris truncata
NT2 chloris virgata
NT1 chrysopogon
NT2 chrysopogon aucheri

GRAMINEAE *cont.*
NT2 chrysopogon echinulatus
NT2 chrysopogon fallax
NT2 chrysopogon fulvus
NT2 chrysopogon gryllus
NT2 chrysopogon serrulatus
NT1 chusquea
NT2 chusquea quila
NT1 coelorachis
NT1 coix
NT2 coix lacryma-jobi
NT1 cortaderia
NT2 cortaderia fulvida
NT2 cortaderia jubata
NT2 cortaderia selloana
NT1 corynephorus
NT2 corynephorus canescens
NT1 crypsis
NT2 crypsis schoenoides
NT1 cymbopogon
NT2 cymbopogon afronardus
NT2 cymbopogon caesius
NT2 cymbopogon citratus
NT2 cymbopogon commutatus
NT2 cymbopogon confertiflorus
NT2 cymbopogon distans
NT2 cymbopogon excavatus
NT2 cymbopogon flexuosus
NT2 cymbopogon jwarancusa
NT2 cymbopogon khasianus
NT2 cymbopogon martinii
NT2 cymbopogon nardus
NT2 cymbopogon nervatus
NT2 cymbopogon parkeri
NT2 cymbopogon pendulus
NT2 cymbopogon proximus
NT2 cymbopogon refractus
NT2 cymbopogon schoenanthus
NT2 cymbopogon winterianus
NT1 cynodon
NT2 cynodon aethiopicus
NT2 cynodon dactylon
NT2 cynodon magennisii
NT2 cynodon nlemfuensis
NT2 cynodon plectostachyus
NT1 cynosurus
NT2 cynosurus cristatus
NT2 cynosurus echinatus
NT1 cyrtococcum
NT2 cyrtococcum patens
NT1 dactylis
NT2 dactylis glomerata
NT1 dactyloctenium
NT2 dactyloctenium aegyptium
NT2 dactyloctenium ctenoides
NT2 dactyloctenium geminatum
NT2 dactyloctenium pilosum
NT2 dactyloctenium sindicum
NT1 danthonia
NT2 danthonia caespitosa
NT2 danthonia compressa
NT2 danthonia decumbens
NT2 danthonia linkii
NT2 danthonia penicillata
NT2 danthonia richardsonii
NT2 danthonia sericea
NT2 danthonia spicata
NT2 danthonia vestita
NT1 dasypyrum
NT2 dasypyrum villosum
NT1 dendrocalamus
NT2 dendrocalamus giganteus
NT2 dendrocalamus hamiltonii
NT2 dendrocalamus latiflorus
NT2 dendrocalamus strictus
NT1 deschampsia
NT2 deschampsia cespitosa
NT2 deschampsia flexuosa
NT2 deschampsia setacea
NT1 desmazeria
NT2 desmazeria marina
NT2 desmazeria rigida
NT1 desmostachya
NT2 desmostachya bipinnata
NT1 deyeuxia
NT2 deyeuxia youngii
NT1 diarrhena
NT1 dichanthium
NT2 dichanthium annulatum
NT2 dichanthium aristatum
NT2 dichanthium caricosum

GRAMINEAE *cont.*
NT2 dichanthium contortum
NT2 dichanthium sericeum
NT1 dichelachne
NT2 dichelachne sciurea
NT1 diectomis
NT2 diectomis fastigiata
NT1 digitaria
NT2 digitaria aegyptiaca
NT2 digitaria brownei
NT2 digitaria californica
NT2 digitaria ciliaris
NT2 digitaria cruciata
NT2 digitaria decumbens
NT2 digitaria didactyla
NT2 digitaria divaricatissima
NT2 digitaria exilis
NT2 digitaria filiformis
NT2 digitaria horizontalis
NT2 digitaria iburua
NT2 digitaria insularis
NT2 digitaria ischaemum
NT2 digitaria longiflora
NT2 digitaria macroblephara
NT2 digitaria macroglossa
NT2 digitaria marginata
NT2 digitaria milanjiana
NT2 digitaria monodactyla
NT2 digitaria pentzii
NT2 digitaria sanguinalis
NT2 digitaria scalarum
NT2 digitaria serotina
NT2 digitaria setivalva
NT2 digitaria smutsii
NT2 digitaria swazilandensis
NT2 digitaria tricholaenoides
NT2 digitaria velutina
NT2 digitaria violescens
NT1 diheteropogon
NT1 dinebra
NT2 dinebra retroflexa
NT1 dinochloa
NT2 dinochloa scandens
NT1 diplachne
NT2 diplachne fusca
NT1 distichlis
NT2 distichlis spicata
NT2 distichlis stricta
NT1 dupontia
NT2 dupontia fisheri
NT1 echinochloa
NT2 echinochloa colonum
NT2 echinochloa crus-galli
NT2 echinochloa crus-pavonis
NT2 echinochloa decompositum
NT2 echinochloa frumentacea
NT2 echinochloa glabrescens
NT2 echinochloa hispidula
NT2 echinochloa hostii
NT2 echinochloa muricata
NT2 echinochloa oryzoides
NT2 echinochloa polystachya
NT2 echinochloa pyramidalis
NT2 echinochloa spiralis
NT2 echinochloa stagnina
NT2 echinochloa turnerana
NT1 ehrharta
NT2 ehrharta calycina
NT1 eleusine
NT2 eleusine aegyptiaca
NT2 eleusine compressa
NT2 eleusine coracana
NT2 eleusine indica
NT2 eleusine jaegeri
NT2 eleusine kigeziensis
NT2 eleusine semisterilis
NT1 elionurus
NT2 elionurus argenteus
NT2 elionurus muticus
NT2 elionurus viridulus
NT1 elymus
NT2 elymus canadensis
NT2 elymus caninus
NT2 elymus dahuricus
NT2 elymus dentatus
NT2 elymus elongatus
NT2 elymus farctus
NT2 elymus fibrosus
NT2 elymus hispidus
NT2 elymus hispidus subsp. barbulatus

GRAMINEAE *cont.*
NT2 elymus kronokensis
NT2 elymus lanceolatus
NT2 elymus mutabilis
NT2 elymus pungens
NT2 elymus repens
NT2 elymus sibiricus
NT2 elymus smithii
NT2 elymus spicatus
NT2 elymus trachycaulus
NT1 enneapogon
NT2 enneapogon avenaceus
NT2 enneapogon cenchroides
NT2 enneapogon polyphyllus
NT1 enteropogon
NT1 entolasia
NT2 entolasia imbricata
NT1 eragrostis
NT2 eragrostis amabilis
NT2 eragrostis arida
NT2 eragrostis barrelieri
NT2 eragrostis bipinnata
NT2 eragrostis boehmii
NT2 eragrostis capensis
NT2 eragrostis chloromelas
NT2 eragrostis cilianensis
NT2 eragrostis ciliaris
NT2 eragrostis curvula
NT2 eragrostis decumbens
NT2 eragrostis dielsii
NT2 eragrostis elegantissima
NT2 eragrostis eriopoda
NT2 eragrostis exasperata
NT2 eragrostis falcata
NT2 eragrostis ferruginea
NT2 eragrostis heteromera
NT2 eragrostis lehmanniana
NT2 eragrostis lugens
NT2 eragrostis megastachya
NT2 eragrostis minor
NT2 eragrostis multicaulis
NT2 eragrostis oxylepis
NT2 eragrostis pallens
NT2 eragrostis pilosa
NT2 eragrostis plana
NT2 eragrostis racemosa
NT2 eragrostis setifolia
NT2 eragrostis subequiglumis
NT2 eragrostis superba
NT2 eragrostis tef
NT2 eragrostis tenella
NT2 eragrostis tremula
NT2 eragrostis trichodes
NT2 eragrostis unioloides
NT2 eragrostis viscosa
NT1 eremochloa
NT2 eremochloa ophiuroides
NT1 eriachne
NT2 eriachne mucronata
NT1 erianthus
NT1 eriochloa
NT2 eriochloa contracta
NT2 eriochloa gracilis
NT2 eriochloa polystachya
NT2 eriochloa procera
NT2 eriochloa villosa
NT1 erioneuron
NT2 erioneuron pulchellum
NT1 eustachys
NT1 festuca
NT2 festuca airoides
NT2 festuca altaica
NT2 festuca ampla
NT2 festuca arizonica
NT2 festuca arundinacea
NT2 festuca campestris
NT2 festuca filiformis
NT2 festuca gautieri
NT2 festuca gigantea
NT2 festuca glauca
NT2 festuca halleri
NT2 festuca hallii
NT2 festuca heterophylla
NT2 festuca idahoensis
NT2 festuca longifolia
NT2 festuca nigrescens
NT2 festuca novae-zelandiae
NT2 festuca occidentalis
NT2 festuca ovina
NT2 festuca paniculata
NT2 festuca pratensis

GRAMINEAE *cont.*
NT2 festuca pseudovina
NT2 festuca rubra
NT2 festuca rupicola
NT2 festuca scabrella
NT2 festuca trachyphylla
NT2 festuca valesiaca
NT2 festuca varia
NT2 festuca vivipara
NT1 gastridium
NT2 gastridium ventricosum
NT1 gigantochloa
NT2 gigantochloa apus
NT2 gigantochloa levis
NT1 glyceria
NT2 glyceria fluitans
NT2 glyceria maxima
NT1 guadua
NT2 guadua angustifolia
NT1 harpechloa
NT2 harpechloa falx
NT1 helictotrichon
NT2 helictotrichon sempervirens
NT1 hemarthria
NT2 hemarthria altissima
NT2 hemarthria sibirica
NT1 heteropogon
NT2 heteropogon contortus
NT1 hilaria
NT2 hilaria belangeri
NT2 hilaria mutica
NT2 hilaria rigida
NT1 holcus
NT2 holcus lanatus
NT2 holcus mollis
NT1 hordeum
NT2 hordeum agriocrithon
NT2 hordeum bulbosum
NT2 hordeum geniculatum
NT2 hordeum glaucum
NT2 hordeum irregulare
NT2 hordeum jubatum
NT2 hordeum marinum
NT2 hordeum murinum
NT2 hordeum murinum subsp. leporinum
NT2 hordeum pusillum
NT2 hordeum secalinum
NT2 hordeum spontaneum
NT2 hordeum vulgare
NT1 hymenachne
NT1 hyparrhenia
NT2 hyparrhenia filipendula
NT2 hyparrhenia hirta
NT2 hyparrhenia rufa
NT1 imperata
NT2 imperata cylindrica
NT1 isachne
NT2 isachne globosa
NT1 ischaemum
NT2 ischaemum afrum
NT2 ischaemum aristatum
NT2 ischaemum indicum
NT2 ischaemum rugosum
NT1 iseilema
NT2 iseilema laxum
NT1 ixophorus
NT2 ixophorus unisetus
NT1 kassella
NT1 koeleria
NT2 koeleria macrantha
NT1 lagurus (gramineae)
NT2 lagurus ovatus
NT1 lasiurus (gramineae)
NT2 lasiurus hirsutus
NT2 lasiurus scindicus
NT1 leersia
NT2 leersia hexandra
NT2 leersia japonica
NT2 leersia oryzoides
NT2 leersia sayanuki
NT1 leptochloa
NT2 leptochloa chinensis
NT2 leptochloa fascicularis
NT2 leptochloa filiformis
NT2 leptochloa panicea
NT2 leptochloa uninervia
NT1 leptothrium
NT1 leymus
NT2 leymus ajanensis
NT2 leymus angustus

GRAMINEAE *cont.*
NT2 leymus arenarius
NT2 leymus chinensis
NT2 leymus innovatus
NT2 leymus jacutensis
NT2 leymus ramosus
NT2 leymus secalinus
NT2 leymus triticoides
NT1 lolium
NT2 lolium multiflorum
NT2 lolium perenne
NT2 lolium remotum
NT2 lolium rigidum
NT2 lolium temulentum
NT1 lophochloa
NT1 loudetia
NT2 loudetia simplex
NT1 lycurus
NT2 lycurus phleoides
NT1 melanocenchris
NT2 melanocenchris jacquemontii
NT1 melica
NT2 melica nutans
NT1 melinis
NT2 melinis minutiflora
NT1 melocanna
NT2 melocanna baccifera
NT1 mibora
NT2 mibora minima
NT1 microchloa
NT1 microlaena
NT2 microlaena stipoides
NT1 micropogon (gramineae)
NT1 microstegium
NT2 microstegium vimineum
NT1 milium
NT1 miscanthus
NT2 miscanthus sacchariflorus
NT2 miscanthus sinensis
NT2 miscanthus transmorrisonensis
NT1 mnesithea
NT2 mnesithea laevis
NT1 molinia
NT2 molinia caerulea
NT1 monachather
NT2 monachather paradoxa
NT1 monocymbium
NT2 monocymbium ceresiiforme
NT1 muhlenbergia
NT2 muhlenbergia frondosa
NT2 muhlenbergia montana
NT2 muhlenbergia porteri
NT2 muhlenbergia richardsonis
NT2 muhlenbergia schreberi
NT1 nardus
NT2 nardus stricta
NT1 narenga
NT1 nassella
NT2 nassella trichotoma
NT1 neomolinia
NT1 notodanthonia
NT1 oplismenus
NT2 oplismenus compositus
NT1 oropetium
NT1 oryza
NT2 oryza barthii
NT2 oryza breviligulata
NT2 oryza glaberrima
NT2 oryza longistaminata
NT2 oryza nivara
NT2 oryza perennis
NT2 oryza punctata
NT2 oryza rufipogon
NT2 oryza sativa
NT2 oryza sativa var. fatua
NT1 oryzopsis
NT2 oryzopsis holciformis
NT2 oryzopsis hymenoides
NT2 oryzopsis miliacea
NT1 ottochloa
NT2 ottochloa nodosa
NT1 oxytenanthera
NT2 oxytenanthera abyssinica
NT1 panicum
NT2 panicum adspersum
NT2 panicum americanum
NT2 panicum antidotale
NT2 panicum bisulcatum
NT2 panicum brevifolium

GRAMINEAE *cont.*
NT2 panicum bulbosum
NT2 panicum capillare
NT2 panicum coloratum
NT3 panicum coloratum var. makarikariense
NT2 panicum dichotomiflorum
NT2 panicum fasciculatum
NT2 panicum glaucum
NT2 panicum laevifolium
NT2 panicum laxum
NT2 panicum maximum
NT3 panicum maximum var. trichoglume
NT2 panicum miliaceum
NT2 panicum miliare
NT2 panicum milioides
NT2 panicum nodosum
NT2 panicum oligosanthes
NT2 panicum repens
NT2 panicum schenckii
NT2 panicum spontaneum
NT2 panicum sumatrense
NT2 panicum texanum
NT2 panicum trichocladum
NT2 panicum turgidum
NT2 panicum virgatum
NT2 panicum zizanioides
NT1 paspalidium
NT2 paspalidium geminatum
NT1 paspalum
NT2 paspalum acuminatum
NT2 paspalum boscianum
NT2 paspalum conjugatum
NT2 paspalum digitaria
NT2 paspalum dilatatum
NT2 paspalum distachyon
NT2 paspalum distichum
NT2 paspalum fasciculatum
NT2 paspalum lividum
NT2 paspalum maritimum
NT2 paspalum millegrana
NT2 paspalum notatum
NT2 paspalum orbiculare
NT2 paspalum paniculatum
NT2 paspalum plicatulum
NT2 paspalum scrobiculatum
NT2 paspalum urvillei
NT2 paspalum vaginatum
NT2 paspalum virgatum
NT1 pennisetum
NT2 pennisetum alopecuroides
NT2 pennisetum americanum
NT2 pennisetum clandestinum
NT2 pennisetum macrourum
NT2 pennisetum pedicellatum
NT2 pennisetum polystachion
NT2 pennisetum purpureum
NT2 pennisetum schimperi
NT2 pennisetum setaceum
NT2 pennisetum setosum
NT2 pennisetum villosum
NT1 phalaris
NT2 phalaris aquatica
NT2 phalaris arundinacea
NT2 phalaris brachystachys
NT2 phalaris canariensis
NT2 phalaris minor
NT2 phalaris paradoxa
NT2 phalaris truncata
NT1 phippsia
NT1 phleum
NT2 phleum alpinum
NT2 phleum arenarium
NT2 phleum michelii
NT2 phleum pratense
NT2 phleum pratense subsp. bertolonii
NT1 phragmites
NT2 phragmites australis
NT2 phragmites karka
NT2 phragmites longivalvis
NT1 phyllostachys
NT2 phyllostachys bambusoides
NT2 phyllostachys dulcis
NT2 phyllostachys pubescens
NT2 phyllostachys purpurata
NT1 pleioblastus
NT2 pleioblastus chino
NT2 pleioblastus niitakayamensis

GRAMINEAE *cont.*
NT1 poa
NT2 poa alpina
NT2 poa ampla
NT2 poa angustifolia
NT2 poa annua
NT2 poa arctica
NT2 poa bulbosa
NT2 poa caespitosa
NT2 poa clivicola
NT2 poa compressa
NT2 poa labillardieri
NT2 poa nemoralis
NT2 poa palustris
NT2 poa pratensis
NT2 poa remota
NT2 poa sandbergii
NT2 poa secunda
NT2 poa sieberana
NT2 poa supina
NT2 poa trivialis
NT1 pogonarthria
NT2 pogonarthria squarrosa
NT1 polypogon
NT1 psathyrostachys
NT2 psathyrostachys juncea
NT1 pseudosasa
NT2 pseudosasa purpurascens
NT1 puccinellia
NT2 puccinellia capillaris
NT2 puccinellia distans
NT2 puccinellia palustris
NT1 rhynchelytrum
NT2 rhynchelytrum repens
NT1 rottboellia
NT2 rottboellia cochinchinensis
NT1 saccharum
NT2 saccharum barberi
NT2 saccharum edule
NT2 saccharum officinarum
NT2 saccharum sinense
NT2 saccharum spontaneum
NT1 sasa
NT2 sasa borealis
NT2 sasa nipponica
NT2 sasa palmata
NT2 sasa veitchii
NT1 sasaella
NT2 sasaella ramosa
NT1 schismus
NT2 schismus barbatus
NT1 schizachyrium
NT2 schizachyrium scoparium
NT2 schizachyrium stoloniferum
NT1 schoenefeldia
NT2 schoenefeldia gracilis
NT1 sclerostachya
NT1 secale
NT2 secale cereale
NT2 secale kuprijanovii
NT2 secale montanum
NT1 sehima
NT2 sehima nervosum
NT1 sesleria
NT2 sesleria caerulea
NT2 sesleria haynaldiana
NT1 setaria (gramineae)
NT2 setaria adhaerens
NT2 setaria argentina
NT2 setaria faberi
NT2 setaria geniculata
NT2 setaria italica
NT2 setaria leiantha
NT2 setaria macrostachya
NT2 setaria megaphylla
NT2 setaria palmifolia
NT2 setaria poiretiana
NT2 setaria pumila
NT2 setaria sphacelata
NT2 setaria sphacelata var. aurea
NT2 setaria sphacelata var. sericea
NT2 setaria sphacelata var. splendida
NT2 setaria sphacelata var. torta
NT2 setaria verticillata
NT2 setaria verticilliformis
NT2 setaria viridis
NT2 setaria viridis var. ma

GRAMINEAE *cont.*
NT2 setaria viridis var. ro
NT1 shibataea
NT1 sieglingia
NT1 sinarundinaria
NT2 sinarundinaria fangiana
NT1 sinocalamus
NT1 sitanion
NT2 sitanion hystrix
NT1 sorghastrum
NT2 sorghastrum nutans
NT1 sorghum
NT2 sorghum almum
NT2 sorghum arundinaceum
NT2 sorghum bicolor
NT2 sorghum bicolor x sorghum sudanense
NT2 sorghum dochna
NT2 sorghum durra
NT2 sorghum halepense
NT2 sorghum leiocladum
NT2 sorghum sudanense
NT2 sorghum verticilliflorum
NT1 spartina
NT2 spartina alterniflora
NT2 spartina anglica
NT2 spartina cynosuroides
NT2 spartina patens
NT2 spartina spartinae
NT2 spartina townsendii
NT1 sporobolus
NT2 sporobolus africanus
NT2 sporobolus airoides
NT2 sporobolus cryptandrus
NT2 sporobolus indicus
NT2 sporobolus poiretii
NT2 sporobolus pyramidalis
NT1 stapfiola
NT2 stapfiola bipinnata
NT1 stenotaphrum
NT2 stenotaphrum dimidiatum
NT2 stenotaphrum secundatum
NT1 stipa
NT2 stipa bigeniculata
NT2 stipa brachychaeta
NT2 stipa capensis
NT2 stipa capillata
NT2 stipa comata
NT2 stipa lessingiana
NT2 stipa leucotricha
NT2 stipa pennata
NT2 stipa sareptana
NT2 stipa tenacissima
NT2 stipa thurberiana
NT2 stipa trichotoma
NT2 stipa ukrainica
NT2 stipa variabilis
NT2 stipa viridula
NT1 stipagrostis
NT2 stipagrostis pennata
NT2 stipagrostis plumosa
NT1 taeniatherum
NT2 taeniatherum caput-medusae
NT1 themeda
NT2 themeda australis
NT2 themeda triandra
NT2 themeda villosa
NT1 thinopyrum
NT1 trachynia
NT2 trachynia distachya
NT1 trachypogon
NT2 trachypogon plumosus
NT2 trachypogon vestitus
NT1 tragus
NT1 trichachne
NT2 trichachne californica
NT2 trichachne insularis
NT1 tricholaena
NT2 tricholaena tenerrifae
NT1 triodia
NT1 tripsacum
NT2 tripsacum dactyloides
NT2 tripsacum laxum
NT1 trisetaria
NT1 trisetobromus
NT2 trisetobromus hirtus
NT1 trisetum
NT2 trisetum flavescens
NT2 trisetum spicatum
NT1 tristachya

GRAMINEAE *cont.*
NT2 tristachya hispida
NT1 triticum
NT2 triticum aestivum
NT2 triticum baeoticum
NT2 triticum dicoccoides
NT2 triticum dicoccon
NT2 triticum durum
NT2 triticum monococcum
NT2 triticum spelta
NT2 triticum turgidum
NT1 uniola
NT2 uniola paniculata
NT1 urochloa
NT2 urochloa mosambicensis
NT2 urochloa panicoides
NT1 vetiveria
NT2 vetiveria zizanioides
NT1 vossia
NT2 vossia cuspidata
NT1 vulpia
NT2 vulpia bromoides
NT2 vulpia fasciculata
NT2 vulpia megalura
NT2 vulpia myuros
NT1 zea
NT2 zea diploperennis
NT2 zea luxurians
NT2 zea mays
NT2 zea mexicana
NT2 zea perennis
NT1 zizania
NT2 zizania aquatica
NT2 zizania caduciflora
NT2 zizania palustris
NT1 zoysia
NT2 zoysia japonica
NT2 zoysia matrella
NT2 zoysia tenuifolia
rt awns
rt glumes
rt grasses
rt lawns and turf
rt mesocotyls
rt naked grain
rt scutellum

GRAMINELLA
BT1 cicadellidae
BT2 cicadelloidea
BT3 auchenorrhyncha
BT4 homoptera
NT1 graminella nigrifrons

GRAMINELLA NIGRIFRONS
BT1 graminella
BT2 cicadellidae
BT3 cicadelloidea
BT4 auchenorrhyncha
BT5 homoptera

GRAMMATOPHYLLUM
BT1 orchidaceae
NT1 grammatophyllum scriptum

GRAMMATOPHYLLUM SCRIPTUM
BT1 grammatophyllum
BT2 orchidaceae
BT1 ornamental orchids

GRANA CHEESE
BT1 cheeses
BT2 milk products
BT3 products

GRANADA
BT1 goat breeds
BT2 breeds

grand cayman
USE **cayman islands**

GRANDINIA
uf *tuberculina*
BT1 aphyllophorales
NT1 grandinia maxima

GRANDINIA MAXIMA
uf *tuberculina maxima*
BT1 grandinia
BT2 aphyllophorales

GRANDLURE
BT1 insect attractants

GRANDLURE *cont.*
BT2 attractants
BT1 sex pheromones
BT2 pheromones
BT3 semiochemicals
rt anthonomus grandis

GRANDPARENTS
BT1 ancestry
rt breeding
rt families
rt kinship

GRANGEA
BT1 compositae
NT1 grangea maderaspatana

GRANGEA MADERASPATANA
BT1 grangea
BT2 compositae

GRANITE
BT1 soil parent materials
rt granite soils

GRANITE SOILS
BT1 soil types (lithological)
rt granite

GRANODIORITE SOILS
BT1 soil types (lithological)

GRANTS
ufa *grants, research*
ufa *research grants*
BT1 support measures
NT1 educational grants
NT1 grubbing up grants
NT1 improvement grants
NT1 setting up grants
rt investment promotion
rt subsidies

grant's gazelle
USE **gazella granti**

grants, research
USE **grants**
AND **research support**

granular material
USE **granules**

GRANULATED HONEY
BT1 honey
BT2 hive products
BT3 animal products
BT4 products
rt creamed honey
rt extracted honey

GRANULATION
BT1 plant disorders
BT2 disorders
rt citrus fruits

GRANULES
uf *granular material*
BT1 particles
NT1 microsomes
NT1 starch granules
rt formulations
rt pellets
rt powders

GRANULOCYTES
BT1 leukocytes
BT2 blood cells
BT3 cells
NT1 basophils
NT1 eosinophils
NT1 neutrophils
rt bone marrow cells

GRANULOMA
BT1 tissue proliferation
NT1 hodgkin's disease

GRANULOSA CELLS
BT1 cells

GRANULOSIS VIRUSES
BT1 baculovirus
BT2 baculoviridae
BT3 insect viruses

GRANULOSIS VIRUSES *cont.*
BT4 entomopathogens
BT5 pathogens
BT3 viruses

GRAPE HARVESTERS
uf *harvesters, grape*
BT1 harvesters
BT2 farm machinery
BT3 machinery
rt grapes

grape hyacinth
USE **muscari**

GRAPE JUICE
BT1 fruit juices
BT2 fruit products
BT3 plant products
BT4 products
BT2 juices
BT3 liquids
NT1 grape must
rt grape marc
rt grapes
rt wine industry
rt wines

GRAPE MARC
BT1 winemaking residues
BT2 plant residues
BT3 residues
NT1 grape seeds
NT1 grape skins
rt grape juice
rt grape press cake
rt grapes
rt wine industry

GRAPE MUST
BT1 grape juice
BT2 fruit juices
BT3 fruit products
BT4 plant products
BT5 products
BT3 juices
BT4 liquids
rt grapes
rt wine industry
rt wines

GRAPE POMACE
BT1 pomace
BT2 fruit products
BT3 plant products
BT4 products
BT2 plant residues
BT3 residues
BT1 winemaking residues
BT2 plant residues
BT3 residues
rt grapes
rt wine industry

GRAPE PRESS CAKE
BT1 fruit products
BT2 plant products
BT3 products
BT1 winemaking residues
BT2 plant residues
BT3 residues
rt grape marc
rt grapes
rt wine industry
rt wines

GRAPE RESIDUES
BT1 winemaking residues
BT2 plant residues
BT3 residues
rt grapes
rt wine industry

GRAPE SEEDS
BT1 grape marc
BT2 winemaking residues
BT3 plant residues
BT4 residues
rt grapes
rt seeds

GRAPE SKINS
BT1 grape marc
BT2 winemaking residues

GRAPE SKINS *cont.*
BT3 plant residues
BT4 residues
rt grapes

GRAPEFRUIT JUICE
BT1 fruit juices
BT2 fruit products
BT3 plant products
BT4 products
BT2 juices
BT3 liquids

GRAPEFRUITS
BT1 citrus fruits
BT2 subtropical tree fruits
BT3 subtropical fruits
BT4 fruit crops
BT3 tree fruits
BT1 insecticidal plants
BT2 pesticidal plants
rt citrus paradisi

GRAPES
BT1 antiviral plants
BT1 essential oil plants
BT2 oil plants
BT1 fruit crops
BT1 oilseed plants
BT2 fatty oil plants
BT3 oil plants
rt coloure
rt dried fruit
rt grape harvesters
rt grape juice
rt grape marc
rt grape must
rt grape pomace
rt grape press cake
rt grape residues
rt grape seeds
rt grape skins
rt grapevine bulgarian latent virus
rt grapevine chrome mosaic nepovirus
rt grapevine fanleaf nepovirus
rt grapevine fleck virus
rt grapevine leaf roll virus
rt grapevine vein necrosis virus
rt grapevine yellow mosaic virus
rt millerandage
rt raisins
rt stalk necrosis
rt vineyards
rt viticulture
rt vitis labrusca
rt vitis rotundifolia
rt vitis vinifera
rt wine cultivars
rt wine industry
rt wines
rt woody plants

GRAPEVINE BULGARIAN LATENT VIRUS
BT1 miscellaneous plant viruses
BT2 plant viruses
BT3 plant pathogens
BT4 pathogens
rt grapes

GRAPEVINE CHROME MOSAIC NEPOVIRUS
HN from 1990
BT1 nepovirus group
BT2 plant viruses
BT3 plant pathogens
BT4 pathogens
rt grapes

GRAPEVINE CORKY BARK VIRUS
BT1 miscellaneous plant viruses
BT2 plant viruses
BT3 plant pathogens
BT4 pathogens

GRAPEVINE FANLEAF NEPOVIRUS
HN from 1990; previously "grapevine fanleaf virus"
uf *grapevine fanleaf virus*

GRAPEVINE FANLEAF NEPOVIRUS *cont.*
BT1 nepovirus group
BT2 plant viruses
BT3 plant pathogens
BT4 pathogens
rt grapes

grapevine fanleaf virus
USE **grapevine fanleaf nepovirus**

GRAPEVINE FLAVESCENCE DOREE VIRUS
BT1 miscellaneous plant viruses
BT2 plant viruses
BT3 plant pathogens
BT4 pathogens

GRAPEVINE FLECK VIRUS
BT1 miscellaneous plant viruses
BT2 plant viruses
BT3 plant pathogens
BT4 pathogens
rt grapes

GRAPEVINE LEAF ROLL VIRUS
BT1 miscellaneous plant viruses
BT2 plant viruses
BT3 plant pathogens
BT4 pathogens
rt grapes

GRAPEVINE VEIN NECROSIS VIRUS
BT1 miscellaneous plant viruses
BT2 plant viruses
BT3 plant pathogens
BT4 pathogens
rt grapes

GRAPEVINE VEINBANDING VIRUS
BT1 miscellaneous plant viruses
BT2 plant viruses
BT3 plant pathogens
BT4 pathogens

GRAPEVINE YELLOW MOSAIC VIRUS
BT1 miscellaneous plant viruses
BT2 plant viruses
BT3 plant pathogens
BT4 pathogens
rt grapes

GRAPEVINE YELLOW SPECKLE VIRUS
BT1 miscellaneous plant viruses
BT2 plant viruses
BT3 plant pathogens
BT4 pathogens

GRAPHIC ARTS
BT1 fine arts
BT2 arts

GRAPHIDIUM
BT1 trichostrongylidae
BT2 nematoda

GRAPHITE
BT1 nonclay minerals
BT2 minerals
rt lubricants

GRAPHOCEPHALA
BT1 cicadellidae
BT2 cicadelloidea
BT3 auchenorrhyncha
BT4 homoptera
NT1 graphocephala atropunctata

GRAPHOCEPHALA ATROPUNCTATA
BT1 graphocephala
BT2 cicadellidae
BT3 cicadelloidea
BT4 auchenorrhyncha
BT5 homoptera

GRAPHOGNATHUS
BT1 curculionidae
BT2 coleoptera
NT1 graphognathus leucoloma
NT1 graphognathus peregrinus

GRAPHOGNATHUS LEUCOLOMA
BT1 graphognathus
BT2 curculionidae
BT3 coleoptera

GRAPHOGNATHUS PEREGRINUS
BT1 graphognathus
BT2 curculionidae
BT3 coleoptera

grapholita
USE **cydia**

grapholita delineana
USE **cydia delineana**

grapholita funebrana
USE **cydia funebrana**

grapholita molesta
USE **cydia molesta**

GRAPHS
NT1 growth charts
NT1 nomograms
rt computer graphics
rt statistics

GRAPPLE METHODS
rt cables

GRAPTOPETALUM
BT1 crassulaceae
NT1 graptopetalum paraguayense

GRAPTOPETALUM PARAGUAYENSE
BT1 graptopetalum
BT2 crassulaceae
BT1 ornamental succulent plants
BT2 succulent plants

GRAPTOVERIA
BT1 crassulaceae
rt ornamental succulent plants

GRASS BRIQUETTES
BT1 briquettes

GRASS CLIPPINGS
BT1 mulches
rt grasses
rt mowing

GRASS JUICE
BT1 juices
BT2 liquids
rt grasses

GRASS MEAL
BT1 meal
rt grasses

GRASS PELLETS
BT1 feeds
BT1 pellets
rt grasses

GRASS SEEDS
uf caryopses
rt grasses
rt seeds

GRASS SICKNESS
BT1 digestive disorders
BT2 functional disorders
BT3 animal disorders
BT4 disorders
BT1 dysautonomia
BT2 nervous system diseases
BT3 organic diseases
BT4 diseases
rt horse diseases

GRASS SILAGE
BT1 silage
BT2 feeds
BT2 fermentation products
BT3 products
rt grasses

GRASS STRIPS
BT1 strip cropping
BT2 cropping systems
rt soil conservation

GRASS SWARD
rt grasses
rt sward destruction
rt sward renovation

GRASS TETANY
uf hypomagnesaemic tetany
uf tetany, hypomagnesaemic
BT1 hypomagnesaemia
BT2 mineral metabolism disorders
BT3 metabolic disorders
BT4 animal disorders
BT5 disorders
rt tetany

GRASS WATERWAYS
BT1 soil conservation
BT2 conservation
BT2 soil management
rt waterways

GRASSES
rt gramineae
rt grass clippings
rt grass juice
rt grass meal
rt grass pellets
rt grass seeds
rt grass silage
rt grass sward
rt grassland improvement
rt grasslands
rt herbage
rt herbage crops
rt plants
rt tillers

GRASSLAND IMPROVEMENT
BT1 grassland management
BT1 husbandry
BT1 improvement
rt grasses
rt grasslands
rt land improvement
rt sward renovation

GRASSLAND MANAGEMENT
uf management, grassland
uf pasture management
NT1 grassland improvement
NT1 stock piling
rt farm management
rt grasslands
rt grazing systems
rt management

GRASSLAND SOILS
uf pasture soils
BT1 soil types (cultural)
BT1 soil types (ecological)
rt pampas soils
rt prairie soils
rt steppe soils

grassland soils, semiarid
USE **semiarid soils**

GRASSLANDS
BT1 vegetation types
NT1 alpine grasslands
NT1 annual grasslands
NT1 campina
NT1 chalk grasslands
NT1 dehesa grasslands
NT1 dune grasslands
NT1 hill grasslands
NT1 leys
NT1 meadows
NT2 flood meadows
NT1 mountain grasslands
NT1 natural grasslands
NT1 pampas
NT1 pastures
NT2 irrigated pastures
NT2 mixed pastures
NT2 range pastures
NT1 permanent grasslands
NT1 prairies
NT1 riparian grasslands
NT1 savannas
NT1 sown grasslands
NT1 steppes

GRASSLANDS *cont.*
NT1 tropical grasslands
NT1 tussock grasslands
NT1 veld
NT1 woodland grasslands
rt foggage
rt grasses
rt grassland improvement
rt grassland management
rt land types

grasslands, alpine
USE **alpine grasslands**

grasslands, chalk
USE **chalk grasslands**

grasslands, dune
USE **dune grasslands**

grasslands, hill
USE **hill grasslands**

grasslands, mountain
USE **mountain grasslands**

grasslands, natural
USE **natural grasslands**

grasslands, sown
USE **sown grasslands**

grasslands, tussock
USE **tussock grasslands**

grasslands, woodland
USE **woodland grasslands**

GRASSOMYIA
HN from 1989
BT1 phlebotominae
BT2 psychodidae
BT3 diptera
NT1 grassomyia squamipleuris
rt phlebotomus
rt sergentomyia

GRASSOMYIA SQUAMIPLEURIS
HN from 1989; previously "sergentomyia squamipleuris"
uf phlebotomus squamipleuris
uf sergentomyia squamipleuris
BT1 grassomyia
BT2 phlebotominae
BT3 psychodidae
BT4 diptera

GRATED CHEESE
BT1 cheeses
BT2 milk products
BT3 products

GRATUITIES
uf tipping

GRAVEL
BT1 soil parent materials
rt gravel pits
rt gravel tunnel drains
rt gravelly soils
rt soil amendments

GRAVEL PITS
BT1 land types
rt gravel
rt mining

GRAVEL TUNNEL DRAINS
BT1 drainage
rt gravel
rt tunnels

GRAVELLY SOILS
BT1 soil types (textural)
rt gravel

GRAVIES (AGRICOLA)
BT1 sauces

GRAVITATIONAL WATER
BT1 soil water categories
BT2 soil water
BT3 water
rt gravity

GRAVITY
BT1 forces
NT1 zero gravity
rt centre of gravity
rt geotaxis
rt gravitational water
rt weight

grayia
USE **eremosemium**

grayling
USE **thymallus thymallus**

GRAZING
uf pasturing
NT1 grazing intensity
NT1 grazing systems
NT2 controlled grazing
NT2 creep grazing
NT2 mixed grazing
NT2 put and take
NT2 rotational grazing
NT2 selective grazing
NT2 set stocking
NT2 strip grazing
NT2 transhumance
NT2 zero grazing
NT1 grazing time
rt browse plants
rt feeding
rt foggage
rt grazing behaviour
rt grazing effects
rt grazing experiments
rt grazing tenancy
rt grazing trials
rt livestock farming
rt mixed pastures
rt pastures
rt rangelands
rt unrestricted feeding
rt weed palatability

GRAZING BEHAVIOR
BF grazing behaviour
BT1 feeding behavior
BT2 behavior

GRAZING BEHAVIOUR
AF grazing behavior
BT1 feeding behaviour
BT2 behaviour
NT1 overgrazing
rt grazing

grazing, controlled
USE **controlled grazing**

GRAZING EFFECTS
rt grazing

GRAZING EXPERIMENTS
BT1 experiments
NT1 grazing trials
rt grazing

GRAZING INTENSITY
BT1 grazing
rt controlled grazing
rt grazing time
rt stocking rate
rt sward destruction

grazing lands
USE **pastures**

grazing, mixed
USE **mixed grazing**

grazing, paddock
USE **controlled grazing**

grazing, rotational
USE **rotational grazing**

grazing, strip
USE **strip grazing**

GRAZING SYSTEMS
BT1 grazing
NT1 controlled grazing
NT1 creep grazing
NT1 mixed grazing
NT1 put and take

GRAZING SYSTEMS *cont.*
NT1 rotational grazing
NT1 selective grazing
NT1 set stocking
NT1 strip grazing
NT1 transhumance
NT1 zero grazing
rt animal husbandry
rt farming systems
rt grassland management
rt overgrazing
rt stock piling

GRAZING TENANCY
BT1 tenancy
BT2 tenure systems
rt grazing

GRAZING TIME
BT1 grazing
rt controlled grazing
rt grazing intensity

GRAZING TRIALS
BT1 grazing experiments
BT2 experiments
BT1 trials
BT2 research
rt grazing

GREASE CONTENT
BT1 composition
rt wool

GREAT BRITAIN
uf *gb*
BT1 uk
BT2 british isles
BT3 western europe
BT4 europe
NT1 england
NT2 east midlands of england
NT2 eastern england
NT2 northern england
NT2 south east england
NT2 south west england
NT2 west midlands of england
NT2 yorkshire and lancashire
NT1 scotland
NT2 eastern scotland
NT2 northern scotland
NT2 scottish highlands and islands
NT2 west scotland
NT1 wales

great comoro
USE **comoros**

GREBNECKIELLA
BT1 apicomplexa
BT2 protozoa
NT1 grebneckiella gracilis
NT1 grebneckiella pixellae

GREBNECKIELLA GRACILIS
BT1 grebneckiella
BT2 apicomplexa
BT3 protozoa

GREBNECKIELLA PIXELLAE
BT1 grebneckiella
BT2 apicomplexa
BT3 protozoa

GREECE
BT1 western europe
BT2 europe
rt european communities
rt mediterranean countries
rt oecd
rt threshold countries

GREEK
HN from 1990
BT1 goat breeds
BT2 breeds

GREEK ZACKEL
HN from 1990
BT1 sheep breeds
BT2 breeds

GREEN AND AMPT EQUATION
BT1 equations
rt soil water movement

green beans
USE **phaseolus vulgaris**

GREEN BELTS
BT1 open spaces
BT2 amenity and recreation areas
BT3 areas
rt land use
rt regional planning
rt urban areas
rt urban hinterland

GREEN CROP FRACTIONATION
HN from 1989
BT1 processing
rt fodder crops
rt fractionation
rt leaf protein concentrate
rt protein extraction

GREEN FEED
BT1 feeds
rt fodder plants

GREEN FODDERS
uf *fodders, green*
BT1 feeds
rt browse plants
rt fodder plants
rt pasture plants
rt silage plants

GREEN GRAM
uf *gram*
uf *gram, green*
rt vigna radiata

GREEN MANURES
BT1 manures
BT2 organic amendments
BT3 soil amendments
BT4 amendments
NT1 azolla pinnata
NT1 buckwheat
NT1 calopogonium mucunoides
NT1 canavalia campylocarpa
NT1 canavalia ensiformis
NT1 canavalia gladiata
NT1 cassia leschenaulthiana
NT1 centrosema plumieri
NT1 centrosema pubescens
NT1 crotalaria anagyroides
NT1 crotalaria juncea
NT1 desmodium tortuosum
NT1 lablab purpureus
NT1 leucaena leucocephala
NT1 lupinus albus
NT1 lupinus angustifolius
NT1 lupinus luteus
NT1 lupinus mutabilis
NT1 medicago lupulina
NT1 medicago orbicularis
NT1 medicago polymorpha
NT1 mucuna aterrima
NT1 mucuna deeringiana
NT1 najas flexilis
NT1 ornithopus sativus
NT1 phacelia tanacetifolia
NT1 secale cereale
NT1 tephrosia purpurea
NT1 trifolium alexandrinum
NT1 trifolium incarnatum
NT1 tripsacum laxum
NT1 vicia articulata
NT1 vicia benghalensis
NT1 vicia cracca
NT1 vicia narbonensis
NT1 vicia pannonica
NT1 vicia sativa
NT1 vicia villosa
NT1 vigna hosei
NT1 vigna unguiculata
NT1 vigna vexillata
rt cover crops
rt crops
rt plants

GREEN MONEY
BT1 currencies
rt european communities
rt european units of account
rt monetary policy

green panic
USE **panicum maximum var. trichoglume**

GREEN REVOLUTION
BT1 agricultural development
BT2 agricultural situation
rt high yielding varieties
rt improved varieties

GREEN SEAWEEDS
BT1 seaweeds
rt chlorophyta

green vegetables
USE **leafy vegetables**

GREENBACK
BT1 plant disorders
BT2 disorders
rt tomatoes

greengages
USE **plums**

GREENHOUSE CROPS
rt crops
rt greenhouses
rt horticultural crops
rt plants
rt protected cultivation

GREENHOUSE CULTURE
BT1 protected cultivation
BT2 cultural methods
rt greenhouse soils
rt greenhouses

GREENHOUSE SOILS
BT1 soil types (cultural)
rt greenhouse culture
rt greenhouses

GREENHOUSES
uf *glasshouses*
BT1 farm buildings
BT2 buildings
NT1 tower greenhouses
NT1 wide span greenhouses
rt cladding
rt double cladding
rt double glazing
rt frames
rt greenhouse crops
rt greenhouse culture
rt greenhouse soils
rt inflated roofs
rt polyethylene film
rt protected cultivation
rt soil heating
rt staging
rt thermal screens

greenhouses, wide span
USE **wide span greenhouses**

GREENING
(for plant disease use "greening disease")
BT1 plant physiology
BT2 physiology
rt chlorophyll
rt etiolation

GREENING DISEASE
HN from 1990
BT1 plant diseases
NT1 citrus greening

GREENLAND
BT1 north america
BT2 america
rt denmark

greenland halibut
USE **reinhardtius hippoglossoides**

GREGARINA
BT1 apicomplexa
BT2 protozoa
NT1 gregarina blaberae
NT1 gregarina coccinellae
NT1 gregarina cuneata
NT1 gregarina dimorpha
NT1 gregarina garnhami
NT1 gregarina hylobii
NT1 gregarina munieri
NT1 gregarina nigra
NT1 gregarina ovata
NT1 gregarina polymorpha
NT1 gregarina saenuridis

GREGARINA BLABERAE
BT1 gregarina
BT2 apicomplexa
BT3 protozoa

GREGARINA COCCINELLAE
BT1 gregarina
BT2 apicomplexa
BT3 protozoa

GREGARINA CUNEATA
BT1 gregarina
BT2 apicomplexa
BT3 protozoa

GREGARINA DIMORPHA
BT1 gregarina
BT2 apicomplexa
BT3 protozoa

GREGARINA GARNHAMI
BT1 gregarina
BT2 apicomplexa
BT3 protozoa

GREGARINA HYLOBII
BT1 gregarina
BT2 apicomplexa
BT3 protozoa

GREGARINA MUNIERI
BT1 gregarina
BT2 apicomplexa
BT3 protozoa

GREGARINA NIGRA
BT1 gregarina
BT2 apicomplexa
BT3 protozoa

GREGARINA OVATA
BT1 gregarina
BT2 apicomplexa
BT3 protozoa

GREGARINA POLYMORPHA
BT1 gregarina
BT2 apicomplexa
BT3 protozoa

GREGARINA SAENURIDIS
BT1 gregarina
BT2 apicomplexa
BT3 protozoa

GREGARINES
BT1 parasites
rt apicomplexa

GREGARIZATION PHEROMONES
BT1 pheromones
BT2 semiochemicals

GREGOPIMPLA
BT1 ichneumonidae
BT2 hymenoptera
rt ephialtes
rt scambus

GREMMENIELLA
uf *brunchorstia*
uf *scleroderris*
BT1 helotiales
NT1 gremmeniella abietina
rt ascocalyx
rt crumenula

GREMMENIELLA ABIETINA
uf *ascocalyx abietina*
uf *brunchorstia destruens*

GREMMENIELLA ABIETINA *cont.*
  uf *brunchorstia pinea*
  uf *crumenula abietina*
  uf *scleroderris lagerbergii*
  BT1 gremmeniella
   BT2 helotiales

GRENADA
  BT1 caribbean
   BT2 america
  rt acp
  rt caribbean community
  rt commonwealth of nations

grenadines
  USE **st. vincent and grenadines**

GREVILLEA
  BT1 proteaceae
  NT1 grevillea banksii
  NT1 grevillea chrysodendron
  NT1 grevillea laurifolia
  NT1 grevillea robusta
  NT1 grevillea rosmarinifolia
  NT1 grevillea striata

GREVILLEA BANKSII
  BT1 grevillea
   BT2 proteaceae
  BT1 ornamental woody plants

GREVILLEA CHRYSODENDRON
  BT1 grevillea
   BT2 proteaceae

GREVILLEA LAURIFOLIA
  BT1 grevillea
   BT2 proteaceae
  BT1 ornamental woody plants

GREVILLEA ROBUSTA
  BT1 antifungal plants
  BT1 forest trees
  BT1 grevillea
   BT2 proteaceae
  BT1 medicinal plants
  BT1 ornamental woody plants

GREVILLEA ROSMARINIFOLIA
  BT1 grevillea
   BT2 proteaceae
  BT1 ornamental woody plants

GREVILLEA STRIATA
  BT1 grevillea
   BT2 proteaceae

GREWIA
  BT1 tiliaceae
  NT1 grewia asiatica
  NT1 grewia hirsuta
  NT1 grewia mollis
  NT1 grewia subinaequalis
  rt forest trees

GREWIA ASIATICA
  BT1 grewia
   BT2 tiliaceae

GREWIA HIRSUTA
  BT1 grewia
   BT2 tiliaceae

GREWIA MOLLIS
  BT1 grewia
   BT2 tiliaceae

GREWIA SUBINAEQUALIS
  BT1 grewia
   BT2 tiliaceae

GREY ALPINE
  HN from 1990
  BT1 cattle breeds
   BT2 breeds

grey brown podzolic soils
  USE **parabraunerde**

GREY EARTHS
  BT1 luvisols
   BT2 soil types (genetic)

GREY FOREST SOILS
  BT1 greyzems

GREY FOREST SOILS *cont.*
   BT2 soil types (genetic)

GREY LITERATURE
  uf *non-conventional literature*
  BT1 publications
  rt literature

GREY LUVISOLS
  BT1 luvisols
   BT2 soil types (genetic)

grey mullets
  USE **mugilidae**

GREY SHIRAZI
  HN from 1990
  BT1 sheep breeds
   BT2 breeds

GREYHOUNDS
  BT1 racing animals
   BT2 working animals
    BT3 animals
  rt dogs

GREYZEMS
  BT1 soil types (genetic)
  NT1 grey forest soils
  NT1 pseudogleyed grey forest soils

GRID FLOORS
  BT1 floors
  BT1 grids
  rt permeable floors
  rt slatted floors

GRIDS
  NT1 electrocuting grids
  NT1 expanded metal
  NT1 grid floors

griffonia
  USE **bandeiraea**

griffonia simplicifolia
  USE **bandeiraea simplicifolia**

GRILLING (AGRICOLA)
  BT1 cooking methods (agricola)
   BT2 methodology

GRINDELIA
  BT1 compositae
  NT1 grindelia aphanactis
  NT1 grindelia integrifolia
  NT1 grindelia robusta
  NT1 grindelia squarrosa

GRINDELIA APHANACTIS
  BT1 grindelia
   BT2 compositae

grindelia humilis
  USE **grindelia squarrosa**

GRINDELIA INTEGRIFOLIA
  BT1 grindelia
   BT2 compositae

GRINDELIA ROBUSTA
  BT1 grindelia
   BT2 compositae

GRINDELIA SQUARROSA
  uf *grindelia humilis*
  BT1 grindelia
   BT2 compositae

GRINDERS
  BT1 farm machinery
   BT2 machinery
  rt crushers
  rt macerators
  rt mills

grinding
  USE **crushing**
  OR **milling**

GRISEIN
  uf *kormogrizein*
  BT1 antibiotics
  BT1 growth promoters
   BT2 growth regulators

GRISEIN *cont.*
   BT2 promoters

GRISELINIA
  BT1 griseliniaceae
  NT1 griselinia littoralis

GRISELINIA LITTORALIS
  BT1 griselinia
   BT2 griseliniaceae
  BT1 ornamental woody plants

GRISELINIACEAE
  NT1 griselinia
   NT2 griselinia littoralis

GRISEOFULVIN
  BT1 antibiotic fungicides
   BT2 antibiotics
   BT2 fungicides
    BT3 pesticides
  BT1 antifungal agents
   BT2 antiinfective agents
    BT3 drugs

GRIT
  BT1 particles
  NT1 shell grit

GROCERS (AGRICOLA)
  BT1 occupations

GROENLANDIA
  BT1 potamogetonaceae
  NT1 groenlandia densa

GROENLANDIA DENSA
  BT1 groenlandia
   BT2 potamogetonaceae

GROMPHADORHINA
  BT1 oxyhaloidae
   BT2 blattaria
    BT3 dictyoptera
  NT1 gromphadorhina portentosa

GROMPHADORHINA PORTENTOSA
  BT1 gromphadorhina
   BT2 oxyhaloidae
    BT3 blattaria
     BT4 dictyoptera

GRONINGEN
  uf *netherlands (groningen)*
  BT1 netherlands
   BT2 western europe
    BT3 europe

GROOMING
  BT1 animal behaviour
   BT2 behaviour

GROSS MARGINS
  BT1 farm results
   BT2 farm accounts
    BT3 accounts
  BT1 profitability
  rt economic analysis
  rt gross margins analysis
  rt variable costs

GROSS MARGINS ANALYSIS
  BT1 farm planning
   BT2 planning
  BT1 microeconomic analysis
   BT2 economic analysis
  rt gross margins
  rt management
  rt management by objectives

GROSS MOTOR DEVELOPMENT (AGRICOLA)
  BT1 motor development (agricola)

GROSS NATIONAL PRODUCT
  BT1 aggregate data
  NT1 national income
  rt national accounting

GROSSHEIMIA
  BT1 compositae
  NT1 grossheimia macrocephala

GROSSHEIMIA MACROCEPHALA
  BT1 grossheimia
   BT2 compositae

GROSSULARIACEAE
  NT1 ribes
   NT2 ribes alpinum
   NT2 ribes americanum
   NT2 ribes aureum
   NT2 ribes divaricatum
   NT2 ribes hirtellum
   NT2 ribes nigrum
   NT2 ribes petraeum
   NT2 ribes rubrum
   NT2 ribes sanguineum
   NT2 ribes uva-crispa

ground barley
  USE **barley meal**

GROUND BEEF (AGRICOLA)
  BT1 beef
   BT2 meat
    BT3 animal products
     BT4 products
    BT3 foods

ground clearance
  USE **clearance**

GROUND COVER
  rt ground cover plants
  rt leaf area index

GROUND COVER PLANTS
  rt cover crops
  rt ground cover
  rt ornamental plants
  rt plants

GROUND DRIVE
  BT1 components
  NT1 driven wheels
  rt drives
  rt tracks
  rt traction aids
  rt tractors
  rt vehicles
  rt wheels

ground oats
  USE **oatmeal**

GROUND PHOTOGRAMMETRY
  HN from 1990
  BT1 photogrammetry
   BT2 techniques

GROUND PRESSURE
  BT1 pressure
   BT2 physical properties
    BT3 properties
  rt inflation pressure
  rt tracks
  rt tyres

GROUND RENT
  BT1 rent
  rt land
  rt leases

ground squirrels
  USE **spermophilus**

GROUND SURFACE SPRAYING
  uf *spraying, ground surface*
  BT1 spraying
   BT2 application methods
    BT3 methodology

GROUND VEGETATION
  BT1 vegetation

GROUNDNUT BUTTER
  AF peanut butter
  BT1 nut products
   BT2 plant products
    BT3 products
  rt groundnut oil
  rt groundnuts

groundnut cake
  USE **groundnut oilmeal**

GROUNDNUT CHLOROTIC SPOT VIRUS
AF peanut chlorotic spot virus
BT1 miscellaneous plant viruses
BT2 plant viruses
BT3 plant pathogens
BT4 pathogens
rt arachis hypogaea

groundnut clump virus
USE **peanut clump furovirus**

GROUNDNUT FLOUR
AF peanut flour
BT1 flours
BT2 plant products
BT3 products
rt groundnuts

GROUNDNUT GREEN MOSAIC VIRUS
AF peanut green mosaic virus
BT1 miscellaneous plant viruses
BT2 plant viruses
BT3 plant pathogens
BT4 pathogens

GROUNDNUT HARVESTERS
AF peanut harvesters
uf *harvesters, groundnut*
BT1 harvesters
BT2 farm machinery
BT3 machinery
rt groundnuts

GROUNDNUT HAULM
AF peanut straw
BT1 straw
BT2 agricultural byproducts
BT3 byproducts
BT2 feeds
BT2 plant residues
BT3 residues

GROUNDNUT HUSKS
AF peanut husks
uf *groundnut shells*
BT1 husks
BT2 plant residues
BT3 residues
rt groundnuts

groundnut mottle virus
USE **peanut mottle potyvirus**

GROUNDNUT OIL
AF peanut oil
uf *arachis oil*
BT1 seed oils
BT2 plant oils
BT3 oils
BT3 plant products
BT4 products
rt groundnut butter
rt groundnuts

GROUNDNUT OILMEAL
AF peanut oilmeal
uf *groundnut cake*
BT1 oilmeals
BT2 feeds
BT2 meal
rt groundnuts

GROUNDNUT PROTEIN
AF peanut protein
BT1 legume protein
BT2 plant protein
BT3 protein
rt groundnuts

GROUNDNUT ROSETTE VIRUS
AF peanut rosette virus
BT1 miscellaneous plant viruses
BT2 plant viruses
BT3 plant pathogens
BT4 pathogens
rt arachis hypogaea

groundnut shells
USE **groundnut husks**

GROUNDNUT SILAGE
AF peanut silage

GROUNDNUT SILAGE *cont.*
BT1 silage
BT2 feeds
BT2 fermentation products
BT3 products
rt groundnuts

groundnut stunt virus
USE **peanut stunt cucumovirus**

GROUNDNUTS
AF peanuts
BT1 feeds
BT1 grain legumes
BT2 grain crops
BT2 legumes
BT1 insecticidal plants
BT2 pesticidal plants
BT1 nematicidal plants
BT2 pesticidal plants
BT1 nut crops
BT1 oilseed plants
BT2 fatty oil plants
BT3 oil plants
rt arachis hypogaea
rt groundnut butter
rt groundnut flour
rt groundnut harvesters
rt groundnut husks
rt groundnut oil
rt groundnut oilmeal
rt groundnut protein
rt groundnut silage
rt peanut clump furovirus
rt peanut mottle potyvirus
rt peanut stripe potyvirus
rt peanut stunt cucumovirus

GROUNDWATER
BT1 water
rt groundwater extraction
rt groundwater flow
rt groundwater recharge
rt irrigation water
rt salt water intrusion
rt soil water categories
rt water table
rt wells

GROUNDWATER EXTRACTION
rt groundwater

GROUNDWATER FLOW
BT1 flow
BT2 movement
rt groundwater
rt soil water movement

GROUNDWATER LEVEL
BT1 soil water regimes
NT1 water table
NT2 high water tables
rt groundwater

GROUNDWATER RECHARGE
BT1 soil water balance
BT2 water balance
rt groundwater
rt recharge

GROUP BEHAVIOR
BF group behaviour
uf *collective behavior*
BT1 social behavior
BT2 behavior
rt teamwork (agricola)

GROUP BEHAVIOUR
AF group behavior
uf *collective behaviour*
BT1 social behaviour
BT2 behaviour
NT1 group interaction
rt groups

GROUP BREEDING SCHEMES
HN from 1989
BT1 breeding programmes
BT2 projects

GROUP COUNSELING (AGRICOLA)
BT1 counseling (agricola)

GROUP EFFECT
BT1 animal behaviour
BT2 behaviour
rt honeybees

group farming
USE **cooperative farming**

GROUP FELLINGS
BT1 silvicultural systems
rt regeneration
rt shelterwood

GROUP INTERACTION
BT1 group behaviour
BT2 social behaviour
BT3 behaviour

GROUP PLANTING
BT1 planting
rt afforestation

GROUP SIZE
rt animal behaviour
rt groups
rt size

GROUP SPECIFIC ANTIGENS
BT1 antigens
BT2 immunological factors

GROUP THERAPY (AGRICOLA)
BT1 therapy

groupements agricoles d'exploitation en commun
USE **gaec**

GROUPERS
BT1 marine fishes
BT2 aquatic animals
BT3 animals
BT3 aquatic organisms
rt epinephelus
rt serranidae

GROUPS
NT1 age groups
NT2 adolescents
NT3 pregnant adolescents (agricola)
NT2 old age
NT2 youth
NT3 disadvantaged youth (agricola)
NT3 rural youth
NT1 buying groups
NT1 colonies
NT1 consortia
NT1 discussion groups
NT1 ethnic groups
NT2 american indians
NT2 asians (agricola)
NT2 blacks (agricola)
NT2 hispanics (agricola)
NT2 inuit
NT2 jews (agricola)
NT2 mexican-americans (agricola)
NT1 herds
NT2 beef herds
NT2 dairy herds
NT2 feral herds
NT2 herd structure
NT2 suckler herds
NT1 interest groups
NT2 beekeepers' associations
NT2 breeders' associations
NT2 clubs
NT3 4-h clubs (agricola)
NT3 health clubs
NT2 farmers' associations
NT2 pressure groups
NT2 trade associations
NT2 trade unions
NT3 agricultural trade unions
NT1 low income groups
NT1 target groups
rt collections
rt group behaviour
rt group size
rt membership
rt minorities
rt neighbourhoods

GROUPS *cont.*
rt social participation
rt teams

GROUSE
BT1 game birds
BT2 game animals
BT3 animals
rt lagopus lagopus

GROUSERS
BT1 tracks
BT2 components
rt lugs
rt track plates

GROVESINIA
HN from 1990
BT1 helotiales
NT1 grovesinia pyramidalis
rt cristulariella

GROVESINIA PYRAMIDALIS
HN from 1990
uf *cristulariella pyramidalis*
BT1 grovesinia
BT2 helotiales

GROWERS
BT1 farmers
BT2 occupations
rt horticulture

GROWING MEDIA
uf *media (propagation)*
uf *media, growing*
uf *potting composts*
uf *rooting media*
NT1 anthracite waste
NT1 bark
NT2 pine bark
NT1 coal
NT2 brown coal
NT1 hygromull
NT1 lapilli
NT1 leaf mould
NT1 limestone gravel
NT1 mineral wool
NT1 peat
NT1 perlite
NT1 pine litter
NT1 pumice
NT1 refuse compost
NT1 rockwool
NT1 sawdust
NT1 sewage sludge
NT2 activated sludge
NT1 urea formaldehyde foam
NT1 vermiculite
NT1 wood chips
NT2 whole tree chips
rt composts
rt plant residues
rt planting
rt plastic foam
rt polyethylene
rt potting
rt propagation

GROWING STOCK
HN from 1990
rt forest management
rt yield regulation

GROWTH
(biological growth only; in economics use "economic growth")
NT1 advance growth
NT1 cell growth
NT1 compensatory growth
NT1 fetal growth
NT1 growth rate
NT1 nutation
NT1 regrowth
NT1 seasonal growth
NT2 lammas growth
NT1 seedling growth
rt body measurements
rt body weight
rt bolting
rt branching
rt cell division

GROWTH *cont.*
rt development
rt developmental stages
rt differentiation
rt embryology
rt embryonic development
rt fattening performance
rt growth analysis
rt growth charts
rt growth curve
rt growth disorders
rt growth factors
rt growth models
rt growth period
rt growth promoters
rt growth retardation
rt growth rings
rt growth stages
rt growth studies
rt growth traits
rt growth yield relationship (agricola)
rt habit
rt hyperkeratosis
rt hypertrophy
rt increment
rt increment boring
rt increment tables
rt meristems
rt ontogeny
rt population growth
rt quantitative traits
rt regeneration
rt stem form
rt tropisms

GROWTH ANALYSIS
rt analysis
rt growth
rt leaf area index
rt net assimilation rate

GROWTH CHAMBERS
uf *phototrons*
uf *phytotrons*
BT1 equipment
rt environmental control

GROWTH CHARTS
BT1 graphs
rt growth
rt recording

GROWTH CURVE
rt growth
rt growth rate

GROWTH DISORDERS
BT1 animal disorders
BT2 disorders
NT1 dwarfism
NT1 gigantism
NT1 hypotrophy
NT1 metaplasia
NT1 runting
rt growth

growth, economic
USE **economic growth**

GROWTH EFFECTS
HN from 1990; previously "growth factors"
(properties of trees or timber related to conditions of growth)
BT1 effects
rt plant composition
rt wood anatomy
rt wood chemistry
rt wood density
rt wood properties

GROWTH FACTORS
BT1 hormones
NT1 epidermal growth factor
NT1 somatomedin
NT2 insulin-like growth factor
NT1 transforming growth factor
rt growth
rt growth promoters
rt growth rate

growth habit
USE **habit**

growth hormone
USE **somatotropin**

GROWTH INHIBITORS
BT1 inhibitors
BT1 plant growth regulators
BT2 growth regulators
NT1 abscisic acid
NT1 ancymidol
NT1 chlorphonium
NT1 chlorpropham
NT1 dikegulac
NT1 fluoridamid
NT1 germination inhibitors
NT1 glyphosine
NT1 isopyrimol
NT1 jasmonic acid
NT1 maleic hydrazide
NT1 mepiquat
NT1 morphactins
NT2 chlorflurenol
NT2 dichlorflurenol
NT2 flurenol
NT1 paclobutrazol
NT1 piproctanyl
NT1 propham
NT1 thidiazuron
NT1 tiba
NT1 triapenthenol
NT1 uniconazole
rt growth retardants
rt sprout inhibition

GROWTH MODELS
uf *models, growth*
BT1 models
rt growth

GROWTH PERIOD
NT1 earliness
rt developmental stages
rt growth
rt maturation period
rt vegetative period

growth phase
USE **developmental stages**

GROWTH PROMOTERS
uf *growth stimulants*
BT1 growth regulators
BT1 promoters
NT1 anabolic steroids
NT2 metandienone
NT2 methandriol
NT2 mibolerone
NT2 nandrolone
NT2 oxymesterone
NT2 trenbolone
NT1 arsanilic acid
NT1 avoparcin
NT1 bacitracin
NT1 carbadox
NT1 cyadox
NT1 diethylstilbestrol
NT1 grisein
NT1 lasalocid
NT1 monensin
NT1 nitrovin
NT1 nosiheptide
NT1 olaquindox
NT1 quindoxin
NT1 roxarsone
NT1 salinomycin
NT1 tiamulin
NT1 zeranol
rt antibiotics
rt feed additives
rt fertilizers
rt growth
rt growth factors

GROWTH RATE
(biological growth)
uf *biological growth rate*
BT1 growth
rt growth curve
rt growth factors

GROWTH REGULATORS
uf *growth substances*
NT1 growth promoters
NT2 anabolic steroids
NT3 metandienone
NT3 methandriol
NT3 mibolerone
NT3 nandrolone
NT3 oxymesterone
NT3 trenbolone
NT2 arsanilic acid
NT2 avoparcin
NT2 bacitracin
NT2 carbadox
NT2 cyadox
NT2 diethylstilbestrol
NT2 grisein
NT2 lasalocid
NT2 monensin
NT2 nitrovin
NT2 nosiheptide
NT2 olaquindox
NT2 quindoxin
NT2 roxarsone
NT2 salinomycin
NT2 tiamulin
NT2 zeranol
NT1 insect growth regulators
NT2 chitin synthesis inhibitors
NT3 buprofezin
NT3 chlorfluazuron
NT3 cyromazine
NT3 diflubenzuron
NT3 flufenoxuron
NT3 penfluron
NT3 teflubenzuron
NT3 triflumuron
NT2 juvenile hormone analogues
NT3 epofenonane
NT3 fenoxycarb
NT3 hydroprene
NT3 kinoprene
NT3 methoprene
NT3 triprene
NT2 precocenes
NT3 precocene i
NT3 precocene ii
NT3 precocene iii
NT1 mite growth regulators
NT2 clofentezine
NT2 flubenzimine
NT2 flufenoxuron
NT2 hexythiazox
NT1 plant growth regulators
NT2 p-coumaric acid
NT2 antiauxins
NT3 2,4,6-t
NT3 chlorophenoxyisobutyric acid
NT3 tiba
NT2 auxins
NT3 1-naphthol
NT3 2,4,5-t
NT3 2,4-d
NT3 2,4-db
NT3 2,4-dep
NT3 2-naphthoxyacetic acid
NT3 3,5-d
NT3 4-cpa
NT3 dicamba
NT3 dichlorprop
NT3 disul
NT3 fenoprop
NT3 iaa
NT3 iba
NT3 naa
NT3 naphthaleneacetamide
NT3 potassium naphthenate
NT3 sodium naphthenate
NT2 carbaryl
NT2 cytokinins
NT3 benzimidazole
NT3 benzyladenine
NT3 kinetin
NT3 zeatin
NT2 defoliants
NT3 s,s,s-tributyl phosphorotrithioate
NT3 calcium cyanamide
NT3 endothal

GROWTH REGULATORS *cont.*
NT3 ethephon
NT3 metoxuron
NT3 pentachlorophenol
NT3 thidiazuron
NT2 endogenous growth regulators
NT2 endothal
NT2 etacelasil
NT2 ethoxyquin
NT2 ethylene
NT2 ethylene releasers
NT3 acc
NT3 avg
NT3 ethephon
NT2 fenridazon
NT2 fusicoccin
NT2 gametocides
NT3 2,3-dichloroisobutyric acid
NT3 maleic hydrazide
NT2 gibberellins
NT3 gibberellic acid
NT2 glyoxime
NT2 growth inhibitors
NT3 abscisic acid
NT3 ancymidol
NT3 chlorphonium
NT3 chlorpropham
NT3 dikegulac
NT3 fluoridamid
NT3 germination inhibitors
NT3 glyphosine
NT3 isopyrimol
NT3 jasmonic acid
NT3 maleic hydrazide
NT3 mepiquat
NT3 morphactins
NT4 chlorflurenol
NT4 dichlorflurenol
NT4 flurenol
NT3 paclobutrazol
NT3 piproctanyl
NT3 propham
NT3 thidiazuron
NT3 tiba
NT3 triapenthenol
NT3 uniconazole
NT2 growth retardants
NT3 2,3-dichloroisobutyric acid
NT3 chlormequat
NT3 daminozide
NT3 flurprimidol
NT3 mefluidide
NT3 tetcyclacis
NT2 growth stimulators
NT3 brassinolide
NT3 folcysteine
NT3 succinic acid
NT3 triacontanol
NT2 nitrohumates

GROWTH RETARDANTS
BT1 plant growth regulators
BT2 growth regulators
BT1 retardants
NT1 2,3-dichloroisobutyric acid
NT1 chlormequat
NT1 daminozide
NT1 flurprimidol
NT1 mefluidide
NT1 tetcyclacis
rt dwarfing
rt growth inhibitors
rt growth retardation

GROWTH RETARDATION
rt growth
rt growth retardants

GROWTH RINGS
uf *annual rings*
uf *rings, growth*
uf *tree rings*
BT1 wood anatomy
BT2 plant anatomy
BT3 anatomy
BT4 biology
NT1 earlywood
NT1 latewood
rt age determination

GROWTH RINGS *cont.*
rt age of trees
rt dendrochronology
rt dendroclimatology
rt growth
rt increment
rt increment boring
rt seasonal growth

growth, seasonal
USE **seasonal growth**

GROWTH STAGES
rt crop growth stage
rt developmental stages
rt growth
rt maturity stage
rt plant development
rt preweaning period
rt youth

growth stimulants
USE **growth promoters**

GROWTH STIMULATORS
BT1 plant growth regulators
BT2 growth regulators
NT1 brassinolide
NT1 folcysteine
NT1 succinic acid
NT1 triacontanol

GROWTH STRESS
BT1 stresses
rt reaction wood

GROWTH STUDIES
rt growth

growth substances
USE **growth regulators**

GROWTH THEORY
BT1 economic theory
BT2 economics
rt economic growth

GROWTH TRAITS
BT1 traits
rt growth

GROWTH YIELD RELATIONSHIP (AGRICOLA)
HN from 1990
rt crop yield
rt growth
rt relationships
rt yields

GROZNY
BT1 sheep breeds
BT2 breeds

GRUBBING
NT1 stump removal
rt clear felling
rt felling
rt grubbing up grants
rt land clearance
rt stalk pullers
rt stump pullers
rt stumps

GRUBBING UP GRANTS
BT1 grants
BT2 support measures
rt grubbing

GRUIDAE
BT1 gruiformes
BT2 birds
NT1 grus
NT2 grus canadensis

GRUIFORMES
BT1 birds
NT1 gruidae
NT2 grus
NT3 grus canadensis
NT1 otidae
NT2 choriotis
NT2 otis
NT1 rallidae
NT2 fulica
NT3 fulica americana

GRUIFORMES *cont.*
NT3 fulica atra
NT2 gallinula
NT3 gallinula chloropus
NT2 rallus
NT3 rallus longirostris

grunts
USE **haemulidae**

GRUS
BT1 gruidae
BT2 gruiformes
BT3 birds
NT1 grus canadensis

GRUS CANADENSIS
BT1 grus
BT2 gruidae
BT3 gruiformes
BT4 birds

GRUYERE CHEESE
BT1 cheeses
BT2 milk products
BT3 products

GRYLLIDAE
uf *crickets*
BT1 orthoptera
NT1 acheta
NT2 acheta domesticus
NT1 euscyrtus
NT2 euscyrtus concinnus
NT1 gryllus
NT2 gryllus assimilis
NT2 gryllus bimaculatus
NT2 gryllus campestris
NT2 gryllus pennsylvanicus
NT1 oecanthus
NT2 oecanthus pellucens
NT1 teleogryllus
NT2 teleogryllus commodus
NT2 teleogryllus oceanicus

GRYLLOBLATTA
BT1 grylloblattidae
BT2 grylloblattodea

GRYLLOBLATTIDAE
BT1 grylloblattodea
NT1 grylloblatta

GRYLLOBLATTODEA
NT1 grylloblattidae
NT2 grylloblatta
rt insects

GRYLLOTALPA
BT1 gryllotalpidae
BT2 orthoptera
NT1 gryllotalpa africana
NT1 gryllotalpa gryllotalpa

GRYLLOTALPA AFRICANA
BT1 gryllotalpa
BT2 gryllotalpidae
BT3 orthoptera

GRYLLOTALPA GRYLLOTALPA
BT1 gryllotalpa
BT2 gryllotalpidae
BT3 orthoptera

GRYLLOTALPIDAE
BT1 orthoptera
NT1 gryllotalpa
NT2 gryllotalpa africana
NT2 gryllotalpa gryllotalpa
NT1 scapteriscus
NT2 scapteriscus abbreviatus
NT2 scapteriscus acletus
NT2 scapteriscus vicinus

GRYLLUS
BT1 gryllidae
BT2 orthoptera
NT1 gryllus assimilis
NT1 gryllus bimaculatus
NT1 gryllus campestris
NT1 gryllus pennsylvanicus
rt acheta

GRYLLUS ASSIMILIS
uf *acheta assimilis*

GRYLLUS ASSIMILIS *cont.*
BT1 gryllus
BT2 gryllidae
BT3 orthoptera

GRYLLUS BIMACULATUS
BT1 gryllus
BT2 gryllidae
BT3 orthoptera

GRYLLUS CAMPESTRIS
BT1 gryllus
BT2 gryllidae
BT3 orthoptera

gryllus domesticus
USE **acheta domesticus**

GRYLLUS PENNSYLVANICUS
uf *acheta pennsylvanicus*
BT1 gryllus
BT2 gryllidae
BT3 orthoptera

GRYON
BT1 scelionidae
BT2 hymenoptera

GUADELOUPE
uf *french west indies*
BT1 caribbean
BT2 america

GUADUA
BT1 gramineae
NT1 guadua angustifolia

GUADUA ANGUSTIFOLIA
BT1 guadua
BT2 gramineae

GUAIACOL
BT1 expectorants
BT2 antitussive agents
BT3 respiratory system agents
BT4 drugs
BT1 phenols
BT2 alcohols
BT2 phenolic compounds
BT3 aromatic compounds

GUAIANOLIDES
BT1 sesquiterpenoid lactones
BT2 lactones
BT3 heterocyclic oxygen compounds
BT3 ketones
BT2 sesquiterpenoids
BT3 terpenoids
BT4 isoprenoids
BT5 lipids

GUAIFENESIN
BT1 expectorants
BT2 antitussive agents
BT3 respiratory system agents
BT4 drugs
BT1 muscle relaxants
BT2 neurotropic drugs
BT3 drugs

GUAM
BT1 american oceania
BT2 oceania

guanaco
USE **lama guanicoe**

GUANGDONG
uf *china (kwantung)*
uf *kwantung*
BT1 china
BT2 east asia
BT3 asia

GUANGXI
uf *china (kwangsi)*
uf *kwangsi*
BT1 china
BT2 east asia
BT3 asia

GUANIDINE NITRATE
BT1 nitrate fertilizers
BT2 nitrogen fertilizers

GUANIDINE NITRATE *cont.*
BT3 fertilizers
BT1 nitrates (organic salts)
BT2 nitrates
BT2 organic salts
BT3 salts

GUANIDINES
BT1 organic nitrogen compounds
NT1 n-methyl-n-nitrosoguanidine
NT1 agmatine
NT1 cimetidine
NT1 creatine
NT1 dicyandiamide
NT1 dicyanodiamidine
NT1 phosphocreatine

GUANIDINOSUCCINIC ACID
BT1 dicarboxylic acids
BT2 carboxylic acids
BT3 organic acids
BT4 acids

GUANINE
BT1 hypoxanthines
BT2 purines
BT3 heterocyclic nitrogen compounds
BT4 organic nitrogen compounds

GUANINE DEAMINASE
(ec 3.5.4.3)
BT1 amidine hydrolases
BT2 hydrolases
BT3 enzymes

GUANO
BT1 manures
BT2 organic amendments
BT3 soil amendments
BT4 amendments
rt birds
rt faeces
rt phosphorus fertilizers

GUANOSINE
BT1 ribonucleosides
BT2 nucleosides
BT3 glycosides
BT4 carbohydrates
rt guanosine diphosphate
rt guanosine monophosphate
rt guanosine triphosphate

GUANOSINE DIPHOSPHATE
BT1 purine nucleotides
BT2 nucleotides
BT3 glycosides
BT4 carbohydrates
rt guanosine

GUANOSINE MONOPHOSPHATE
uf *gmp*
BT1 purine nucleotides
BT2 nucleotides
BT3 glycosides
BT4 carbohydrates
rt guanosine

GUANOSINE TRIPHOSPHATE
BT1 purine nucleotides
BT2 nucleotides
BT3 glycosides
BT4 carbohydrates
rt guanosine

GUANYLATE CYCLASE
(ec 4.6.1.2)
BT1 phosphorus-oxygen lyases
BT2 lyases
BT3 enzymes

GUAR
rt cyamopsis tetragonoloba

GUAR GUM
BT1 galactomannans
BT2 mannans
BT3 polysaccharides
BT4 carbohydrates
BT1 mucilages
BT2 polysaccharides
BT3 carbohydrates

GUAR GUM *cont.*
rt cyamopsis tetragonoloba

GUAR MEAL
BT1 meal
rt cyamopsis tetragonoloba

GUAR OIL
BT1 seed oils
BT2 plant oils
BT3 oils
BT3 plant products
BT4 products
rt cyamopsis tetragonoloba

GUARD CELLS
rt epidermis
rt stomata

GUARD DOGS
BT1 working animals
BT2 animals
rt dogs
rt guards

GUARD HAIRS
BT1 plant hairs
BT2 plant
rt epidermis
rt guards

GUARDS
NT1 tree guards
rt accident prevention
rt guard dogs
rt guard hairs
rt protection
rt safety devices

guards, tree
USE **tree guards**

GUAREA
BT1 meliaceae
NT1 guarea bijuga
NT1 guarea guidonia

GUAREA BIJUGA
BT1 guarea
BT2 meliaceae

GUAREA GUIDONIA
uf guarea trichilioides
BT1 guarea
BT2 meliaceae
BT1 medicinal plants

guarea trichilioides
USE **guarea guidonia**

GUATEMALA
BT1 central america
BT2 america
rt cacm
rt developing countries

guatemala grass
USE **tripsacum laxum**

GUATTERIA
BT1 annonaceae
NT1 guatteria elata
NT1 guatteria modesta

GUATTERIA ELATA
BT1 guatteria
BT2 annonaceae

GUATTERIA MODESTA
BT1 guatteria
BT2 annonaceae

GUAVAS
BT1 antibacterial plants
BT1 medicinal plants
BT1 tropical tree fruits
BT2 tree fruits
BT2 tropical fruits
BT3 fruit crops
rt psidium guajava

guayule
USE **parthenium argentatum**

GUAZATINE
BT1 aliphatic nitrogen fungicides

GUAZATINE *cont.*
BT2 fungicides
BT3 pesticides
BT1 antifeedants
BT2 inhibitors

GUAZUMA
BT1 sterculiaceae
NT1 guazuma tomentosa
NT1 guazuma ulmifolia

GUAZUMA TOMENTOSA
BT1 guazuma
BT2 sterculiaceae

GUAZUMA ULMIFOLIA
HN from 1990
BT1 forest trees
BT1 guazuma
BT2 sterculiaceae

GUBERNACULUM
BT1 ligaments
BT2 joints (animal)
BT3 musculoskeletal system
BT4 body parts
BT1 male genitalia
BT2 genitalia
BT3 urogenital system
BT4 body parts
BT1 teeth
BT2 jaws
BT3 bones
BT4 musculoskeletal system
BT5 body parts

GUERNSEY
BT1 cattle breeds
BT2 breeds

GUEST HOUSES
BT1 holiday accommodation
BT2 accommodation
rt bed and breakfast accommodation
rt hospitality industry

guests
USE **visitors**

GUIBOURTIA
BT1 leguminosae
NT1 guibourtia coleosperma

GUIBOURTIA COLEOSPERMA
BT1 guibourtia
BT2 leguminosae

GUIDANCE
NT1 steering
NT2 automatic guidance
NT2 automatic steering
NT2 power steering

GUIDE BOOKS
BT1 books
BT2 publications
NT1 buyers' guides
NT1 forest guides
rt handbooks
rt visitor interpretation

GUIDE DOGS
BT1 working animals
BT2 animals
rt dogs

GUIDED TOURS
BT1 tours
BT2 travel

GUIDELINES
HN from 1989

GUIERA
BT1 combretaceae
NT1 guiera senegalensis

GUIERA SENEGALENSIS
BT1 antibacterial plants
BT1 guiera
BT2 combretaceae

GUIGNARDIA
BT1 dothideales

GUIGNARDIA *cont.*
NT1 guignardia bidwellii
NT1 guignardia citricarpa
rt phoma

GUIGNARDIA BIDWELLII
BT1 guignardia
BT2 dothideales

GUIGNARDIA CITRICARPA
uf phoma citricarpa
BT1 guignardia
BT2 dothideales

guilielma
USE **bactris**

guilielma gasipaes
USE **bactris gasipaes**

guilielma speciosa
USE **bactris gasipaes**

guilielma utilis
USE **bactris gasipaes**

GUINEA
BT1 west africa
BT2 africa south of sahara
BT3 africa
rt acp
rt developing countries
rt francophone africa
rt least developed countries

GUINEA-BISSAU
BT1 west africa
BT2 africa south of sahara
BT3 africa
rt acp

guinea corn
USE **sorghum bicolor**

guinea, equatorial
USE **equatorial guinea**

guinea grass
USE **panicum maximum**

GUINEA GRASS MOSAIC POTYVIRUS
HN from 1990
BT1 potyvirus group
BT2 plant viruses
BT3 plant pathogens
BT4 pathogens
rt panicum maximum

GUINEA PIGS
BF guineapigs
uf cavia porcellus

GUINEAFOWL FATTENING
BT1 poultry fattening
BT2 fattening
BT3 animal feeding
BT4 feeding
rt guineafowls

GUINEAFOWL FEEDING
BT1 poultry feeding
BT2 livestock feeding
BT3 animal feeding
BT4 feeding
rt guineafowls

GUINEAFOWLS
uf numida meleagris
BT1 poultry
BT2 livestock
BT3 animals
rt galliformes
rt guineafowl fattening
rt guineafowl feeding
rt phasianidae

GUINEAPIGS
AF guinea pigs
uf cavia porcellus
BT1 laboratory mammals
BT2 laboratory animals
BT3 animals
BT1 meat animals
BT2 animals

GUINEAPIGS *cont.*
BT1 pets
BT2 animals
rt caviidae

GUIZHOU
uf china (kweichow)
uf kweichow
BT1 china
BT2 east asia
BT3 asia

GUIZOTIA
BT1 compositae
NT1 guizotia abyssinica

GUIZOTIA ABYSSINICA
uf niger (guizotia)
BT1 guizotia
BT2 compositae
BT1 oilseed plants
BT2 fatty oil plants
BT3 oil plants

GUJARAT
BT1 india
BT2 south asia
BT3 asia

GUJARATI
BT1 sheep breeds
BT2 breeds

GULF OF MEXICO
BT1 western central atlantic
BT2 atlantic ocean
BT3 marine areas

GULLIED LAND
HN from 1989
BT1 land types

gulls
USE **laridae**

GULLY EROSION
uf erosion, gully
BT1 erosion

GULO
BT1 mustelidae
BT2 fissipeda
BT3 carnivores
BT4 mammals
NT1 gulo gulo

GULO GULO
uf gulo luscus
uf wolverines
BT1 gulo
BT2 mustelidae
BT3 fissipeda
BT4 carnivores
BT5 mammals

gulo luscus
USE **gulo gulo**

L-GULONOLACTONE OXIDASE
(ec 1.1.3.8)
BT1 alcohol oxidoreductases
BT2 oxidoreductases
BT3 enzymes

GUM ARABIC
BT1 gums
BT2 polysaccharides
BT3 carbohydrates
rt acacia senegal

GUM PLANTS
NT1 acacia senegal
NT1 azadirachta indica
NT1 carobs
NT1 cashews
NT1 commiphora africana
NT1 kiwifruits
NT1 loxopterygium huasango
NT1 psophocarpus tetragonolobus
NT1 quinces
NT1 sterculia urens
rt gums
rt horticultural crops
rt industrial crops

GUM PLANTS *cont.*
rt plants

gum resins
USE **resins**

GUMMOSIS
BT1 plant diseases
BT1 plant disorders
BT2 disorders

GUMS
uf *gums, vegetable*
uf *vegetable gums*
BT1 polysaccharides
BT2 carbohydrates
NT1 dextran
NT1 dextrins
NT2 maltodextrins
NT1 gum arabic
NT1 xanthan
NT1 xylan
rt adhesives
rt degumming
rt gum plants
rt kinos
rt mucilages
rt non-food products
rt plant products
rt stabilizers

gums (mouth)
USE **gingiva**

gums, vegetable
USE **gums**

GUNFIRE AND BOMB DAMAGE
uf *bombs*
BT1 damage
rt war

GUNSHYNESS
HN from 1989
BT1 fearfulness
BT2 animal behaviour
BT3 behaviour

guppy
USE **poecilia reticulata**

GUR
BT1 sugars
BT2 carbohydrates
rt sugarcane

GUREZ
BT1 sheep breeds
BT2 breeds

GURLEYA
BT1 microspora
BT2 protozoa

gurnards
USE **triglidae**

gurnards, flying
USE **dactylopteridae**

GUSSETS
BT1 joints (timber)

GUSTAVIA
BT1 lecythidaceae

GUTIERREZIA
BT1 compositae
NT1 gutierrezia dracunculoides
NT1 gutierrezia lucida
NT1 gutierrezia sarothrae

GUTIERREZIA DRACUNCULOIDES
BT1 gutierrezia
BT2 compositae

GUTIERREZIA LUCIDA
BT1 gutierrezia
BT2 compositae

GUTIERREZIA SAROTHRAE
uf *xanthocephalum sarothrae*
BT1 gutierrezia
BT2 compositae
BT1 medicinal plants

GUTTATION
BT1 exudation
rt plant water relations
rt water

GUTTIFERAE
uf *clusiaceae*
uf *hypericaceae*
NT1 calophyllum
NT2 calophyllum antillanum
NT2 calophyllum brasiliense
NT2 calophyllum calaba
NT2 calophyllum elatum
NT2 calophyllum floribundum
NT2 calophyllum inophyllum
NT2 calophyllum mariae
NT1 garcinia
NT2 garcinia afzelii
NT2 garcinia cambogia
NT2 garcinia epunctata
NT2 garcinia hanburyi
NT2 garcinia kola
NT2 garcinia mangostana
NT2 garcinia mannii
NT2 garcinia subelliptica
NT2 garcinia xanthochymus
NT1 harungana
NT2 harungana madagascariensis
NT1 hypericum
NT2 hypericum androsaemum
NT2 hypericum annulatum
NT2 hypericum aucherii
NT2 hypericum calycinum
NT2 hypericum elegans
NT2 hypericum erectum
NT2 hypericum hirsutum
NT2 hypericum maculatum
NT2 hypericum montanum
NT2 hypericum olympicum
NT2 hypericum perforatum
NT2 hypericum polyphyllum
NT2 hypericum pulchrum
NT2 hypericum quadrangulum
NT1 kayea
NT2 kayea assamica
NT1 kielmeyera
NT2 kielmeyera coriacea
NT2 kielmeyera pinnata
NT1 mammea
NT2 mammea africana
NT2 mammea americana
NT2 mammea longifolia
NT1 mesua
NT2 mesua ferrea
NT1 pentadesma
NT2 pentadesma butyracea
NT1 psorospermum
NT2 psorospermum febrifugum
NT1 vismia
NT2 vismia baccifera

GUTTURAL POUCH
BT1 ears
BT2 sense organs
BT3 body parts

GUYANA
uf *british guiana*
BT1 south america
BT2 america
rt acp
rt caribbean community
rt commonwealth of nations
rt developing countries

guyana, netherlands
USE **surinam**

GUZERA
HN from 1990
BT1 cattle breeds
BT2 breeds

GUZMANIA
BT1 bromeliaceae
NT1 guzmania lingulata

GUZMANIA LINGULATA
uf *guzmania minor*
BT1 guzmania
BT2 bromeliaceae
BT1 ornamental bromeliads

guzmania minor
USE **guzmania lingulata**

GYMNASTICS
BT1 sport

GYMNEMA
BT1 asclepiadaceae
NT1 gymnema sylvestre

GYMNEMA SYLVESTRE
BT1 gymnema
BT2 asclepiadaceae
BT1 medicinal plants

GYMNOASCALES
NT1 ajellomyces
NT2 ajellomyces capsulatus
NT2 ajellomyces dermatitidis
NT1 arthroderma
NT2 arthroderma ajelloi
NT2 arthroderma benhamiae
NT2 arthroderma flavescens
NT2 arthroderma gertleri
NT2 arthroderma insingulare
NT2 arthroderma lenticularum
NT2 arthroderma quadrifidum
NT2 arthroderma simii
NT2 arthroderma tuberculatum
NT2 arthroderma uncinatum
NT2 arthroderma vanbreuseghemii
NT1 diehliomyces
NT2 diehliomyces microsporus
NT1 nannizzia
NT2 nannizzia borellii
NT2 nannizzia cajetani
NT2 nannizzia fulva
NT2 nannizzia grubyia
NT2 nannizzia gypsea
NT2 nannizzia incurvata
NT2 nannizzia obtusa
NT2 nannizzia otae
NT2 nannizzia persicolor
NT2 nannizzia racemosa
rt fungi

GYMNOCACTUS
BT1 cactaceae
rt thelocactus

gymnocactus viereckii
USE **thelocactus viereckii**

GYMNOCLADUS
BT1 leguminosae
NT1 gymnocladus dioica

GYMNOCLADUS DIOICA
BT1 gymnocladus
BT2 leguminosae

GYMNODINIUM
BT1 dinophyta
BT2 algae
BT1 sarcomastigophora
BT2 protozoa

GYMNOPHALLUS
BT1 microphallidae
BT2 digenea
BT3 trematoda
NT1 gymnophallus fossarum

GYMNOPHALLUS FOSSARUM
BT1 gymnophallus
BT2 microphallidae
BT3 digenea
BT4 trematoda

GYMNOPHYTON
BT1 hydrocotylaceae
NT1 gymnophyton isatidicarpum

GYMNOPHYTON ISATIDICARPUM
BT1 antibacterial plants
BT1 gymnophyton
BT2 hydrocotylaceae

GYMNOPODIUM
BT1 polygonaceae
NT1 gymnopodium antigonoides

GYMNOPODIUM ANTIGONOIDES
BT1 gymnopodium

GYMNOPODIUM ANTIGONOIDES *cont.*
BT2 polygonaceae

GYMNOSPERMS
rt coniferae
rt plants

GYMNOSPORANGIUM
BT1 uredinales
NT1 gymnosporangium fuscum
NT1 gymnosporangium juniperi-virginianae

GYMNOSPORANGIUM FUSCUM
uf *gymnosporangium sabinae*
BT1 gymnosporangium
BT2 uredinales

GYMNOSPORANGIUM JUNIPERI-VIRGINIANAE
BT1 gymnosporangium
BT2 uredinales

gymnosporangium sabinae
USE **gymnosporangium fuscum**

GYMNOSPORIA
BT1 celastraceae
NT1 gymnosporia emarginata
NT1 gymnosporia trilocularis
NT1 gymnosporia wallichiana

GYMNOSPORIA EMARGINATA
BT1 gymnosporia
BT2 celastraceae

gymnosporia montana
USE **maytenus senegalensis**

GYMNOSPORIA TRILOCULARIS
BT1 gymnosporia
BT2 celastraceae
BT1 medicinal plants

GYMNOSPORIA WALLICHIANA
BT1 gymnosporia
BT2 celastraceae

GYMNOTHORAX
BT1 muraenidae
BT2 anguilliformes
BT3 osteichthyes
BT4 fishes

GYNAIKOTHRIPS
BT1 phlaeothripidae
BT2 thysanoptera
NT1 gynaikothrips ficorum

GYNAIKOTHRIPS FICORUM
BT1 gynaikothrips
BT2 phlaeothripidae
BT3 thysanoptera

GYNOECIUM
uf *carpel*
uf *ovaries, plant*
uf *pistil*
uf *plant ovaries*
BT1 flowers
BT2 inflorescences
BT3 plant
NT1 ovules
NT1 stigma
NT1 styles
rt heterostyly
rt plant organs

GYNOGENESIS
BT1 parthenogenesis
BT2 reproduction

GYNURA
BT1 compositae
NT1 gynura crepidioides
NT1 gynura procumbens

GYNURA CREPIDIOIDES
BT1 gynura
BT2 compositae

GYNURA PROCUMBENS
uf *gynura sarmentosa*
BT1 gynura
BT2 compositae

GYNURA PROCUMBENS *cont.*
BT1 ornamental herbaceous plants

gynura sarmentosa
USE **gynura procumbens**

gypseous soils
USE **gypsiferous soils**

GYPSIFEROUS SOILS
uf *gypseous soils*
BT1 soil types (chemical)

GYPSONOMA
BT1 tortricidae
BT2 lepidoptera
NT1 gypsonoma aceriana
NT1 gypsonoma haimbachiana

GYPSONOMA ACERIANA
BT1 gypsonoma
BT2 tortricidae
BT3 lepidoptera

GYPSONOMA HAIMBACHIANA
BT1 gypsonoma
BT2 tortricidae
BT3 lepidoptera

GYPSOPHILA
BT1 caryophyllaceae
NT1 gypsophila elegans
NT1 gypsophila paniculata
NT1 gypsophila perfoliata
NT1 gypsophila trichotoma

GYPSOPHILA ELEGANS
BT1 gypsophila
BT2 caryophyllaceae

GYPSOPHILA PANICULATA
BT1 gypsophila
BT2 caryophyllaceae
BT1 medicinal plants
BT1 ornamental herbaceous plants

GYPSOPHILA PERFOLIATA
BT1 antibacterial plants
BT1 gypsophila
BT2 caryophyllaceae
BT1 medicinal plants

GYPSOPHILA TRICHOTOMA
BT1 gypsophila
BT2 caryophyllaceae

GYPSUM
BT1 calcium fertilizers
BT2 fertilizers
BT1 nonclay minerals
BT2 minerals
rt calcium sulfate
rt gypsum blocks
rt gypsum requirement
rt plaster
rt plaster of paris
rt soil amendments

GYPSUM BLOCKS
rt detectors
rt gypsum

GYPSUM REQUIREMENT
BT1 requirements
rt exchangeable sodium
rt gypsum
rt reclamation
rt sodic soils

GYRANUSOIDEA
HN from 1989
BT1 encyrtidae
BT2 hymenoptera
NT1 gyranusoidea tebygi

GYRANUSOIDEA TEBYGI
HN from 1989
BT1 gyranusoidea
BT2 encyrtidae
BT3 hymenoptera

GYRAULUS
BT1 planorbidae

GYRAULUS *cont.*
BT2 gastropoda
BT3 mollusca
NT1 gyraulus convexiusculus

GYRAULUS CONVEXIUSCULUS
BT1 gyraulus
BT2 planorbidae
BT3 gastropoda
BT4 mollusca

GYROCARPACEAE
NT1 gyrocarpus

GYROCARPUS
BT1 gyrocarpaceae

GYROCOTYLE
HN from 1990
BT1 cestodaria
BT2 cestoda

GYROCOTYLOIDES
HN from 1990
BT1 cestodaria
BT2 cestoda

GYRODACTYLIDAE
BT1 monogenea
NT1 gyrodactylus
NT2 gyrodactylus elegans
NT1 macrogyrodactylus

GYRODACTYLUS
BT1 gyrodactylidae
BT2 monogenea
NT1 gyrodactylus elegans

GYRODACTYLUS ELEGANS
BT1 gyrodactylus
BT2 gyrodactylidae
BT3 monogenea

GYROMETRA
HN from 1990
BT1 cestodaria
BT2 cestoda

GYROMITRA
BT1 pezizales
NT1 gyromitra esculenta

GYROMITRA ESCULENTA
BT1 gyromitra
BT2 pezizales
BT1 poisonous fungi
BT2 fungi
BT2 poisonous plants

GYROPIDAE
BT1 amblycera
BT2 mallophaga
BT3 phthiraptera
NT1 gliricola
NT2 gliricola porcelli
NT1 gyropus

GYROPUS
BT1 gyropidae
BT2 amblycera
BT3 mallophaga
BT4 phthiraptera
rt gliricola

gyropus gracilis
USE **gliricola porcelli**

GYROSTEMONACEAE

GYTTJA
BT1 subaqueous soils
BT2 soil types (genetic)

4-H CLUBS (AGRICOLA)
HN from 1989
BT1 clubs
BT2 interest groups
BT3 groups
BT3 organizations
BT2 recreational facilities

H-Y ANTIGEN
HN from 1989
BT1 antigens
BT2 immunological factors

HABENARIA
BT1 orchidaceae
NT1 habenaria medioflexa

HABENARIA MEDIOFLEXA
BT1 habenaria
BT2 orchidaceae
BT1 ornamental orchids

HABIT
(plants)
uf *growth habit*
uf *plant habit*
NT1 annual habit
NT1 determinate and indeterminate habit
NT1 everbearing habit
NT1 perennial habit
NT1 spring and winter habit
rt growth
rt plant development

HABITAT DESTRUCTION
BT1 destruction
rt environmental management
rt habitats
rt insect control
rt logging effects

HABITAT SELECTION
uf *site selection (by animals)*
BT1 selection
rt ecology
rt habitats

HABITATS
NT1 biotopes
NT1 breeding places
NT1 microhabitats
NT1 resting places
NT1 territory
NT1 tree holes
rt biota
rt ecology
rt ecotypes
rt environment
rt habitat destruction
rt habitat selection

HABITS
(animals and man)
NT1 feeding habits
NT2 browsing
NT2 coprophagy
NT3 caecotrophy
NT2 feeding frequency
NT2 feeding preferences
NT3 food preferences
NT4 food beliefs
NT4 salt preference
NT2 foraging
NT3 honey-getting capacity
NT2 haematophagy
NT2 nectar feeding
NT2 overeating
NT2 overfeeding
NT3 hyperalimentation
NT2 sugar feeding
NT1 tobacco smoking
rt behaviour

HABRANTHUS
BT1 amaryllidaceae
NT1 habranthus tubispathus

HABRANTHUS TUBISPATHUS
uf *zephyranthes robusta*
BT1 habranthus
BT2 amaryllidaceae
BT1 medicinal plants
BT1 ornamental bulbs

habrobracon
USE **bracon**

habrobracon hebetor
USE **bracon hebetor**

HABROLEPIS
BT1 encyrtidae
BT2 hymenoptera

HABRONEMA
BT1 habronematidae
BT2 nematoda

HABRONEMATIDAE
BT1 nematoda
NT1 draschia
NT1 habronema
rt animal parasitic nematodes

HABROPODA
BT1 apidae
BT2 hymenoptera

HACKNEY
BT1 horse breeds
BT2 breeds

HADDOCK
uf *melanogrammus aeglefinus*
BT1 marine fishes
BT2 aquatic animals
BT3 animals
BT3 aquatic organisms
rt gadidae

HADROBREGMUS
BT1 anobiidae
BT2 coleoptera
NT1 hadrobregmus pertinax

HADROBREGMUS PERTINAX
BT1 hadrobregmus
BT2 anobiidae
BT3 coleoptera

HAEM
AF heme
uf *protohaem*
BT1 porphyrins
BT2 heterocyclic nitrogen compounds
BT3 organic nitrogen compounds
rt haemadsorption reaction
rt haemagglutination
rt haemagglutination inhibition test
rt haemagglutination tests
rt haemagglutinins
rt haematology
rt haemoglobin

haem oxygenase (decyclizing)
USE **heme oxygenase (decyclizing)**

HAEMADIPSA
BT1 haemadipsidae
BT2 hirudinea
BT3 annelida

HAEMADIPSIDAE
BT1 hirudinea
BT2 annelida
NT1 haemadipsa

HAEMADSORPTION REACTION
AF hemadsorption reaction
rt adsorption
rt haem

HAEMAGGLUTINATION
AF hemagglutination
BT1 agglutination
NT1 passive haemagglutination
rt erythrocytes
rt haem
rt haemagglutination inhibition test
rt haemagglutination tests
rt haemagglutinins
rt immunological techniques

HAEMAGGLUTINATION INHIBITION TEST
AF hemagglutination inhibition test
BT1 haemagglutination tests
BT2 agglutination tests
BT3 immunological techniques
BT4 techniques
BT3 tests
rt haem
rt haemagglutination

HAEMAGGLUTINATION TESTS
AF hemagglutination tests
uf *passive haemagglutination test*
BT1 agglutination tests
BT2 immunological techniques
BT3 techniques
BT2 tests
NT1 antiglobulin test
NT1 coombs test
NT1 haemagglutination inhibition test
rt haem
rt haemagglutination

HAEMAGGLUTININS
AF hemagglutinins
BT1 agglutinins
BT2 antibodies
BT3 immunoglobulins
BT4 glycoproteins
BT5 proteins
BT6 peptides
BT4 immunological factors
NT1 viral haemagglutinins
rt haem
rt haemagglutination
rt phytohaemagglutinins

HAEMAGOGUS
BT1 culicidae
BT2 diptera
NT1 haemagogus capricornii
NT1 haemagogus celeste
NT1 haemagogus equinus
NT1 haemagogus janthinomys
NT1 haemagogus leucocelaenus
rt aedes

HAEMAGOGUS CAPRICORNII
BT1 haemagogus
BT2 culicidae
BT3 diptera

HAEMAGOGUS CELESTE
BT1 haemagogus
BT2 culicidae
BT3 diptera

HAEMAGOGUS EQUINUS
BT1 haemagogus
BT2 culicidae
BT3 diptera

HAEMAGOGUS JANTHINOMYS
BT1 haemagogus
BT2 culicidae
BT3 diptera

HAEMAGOGUS LEUCOCELAENUS
uf *aedes leucocelaenus*
BT1 haemagogus
BT2 culicidae
BT3 diptera

HAEMANTHUS
uf *scadoxus*
BT1 amaryllidaceae
NT1 haemanthus albiflos
NT1 haemanthus katherinae
NT1 haemanthus multiflorus

HAEMANTHUS ALBIFLOS
BT1 haemanthus
BT2 amaryllidaceae
BT1 ornamental bulbs

haemanthus kalbreyeri
USE **haemanthus multiflorus**

HAEMANTHUS KATHERINAE
BT1 haemanthus

HAEMANTHUS KATHERINAE *cont.*
BT2 amaryllidaceae
BT1 ornamental bulbs

HAEMANTHUS MULTIFLORUS
uf *haemanthus kalbreyeri*
BT1 haemanthus
BT2 amaryllidaceae
BT1 ornamental bulbs

HAEMAPHYSALIS
uf *alloceraea*
BT1 ixodidae
BT2 metastigmata
BT3 acari
NT1 haemaphysalis aciculifer
NT1 haemaphysalis bancrofti
NT1 haemaphysalis bispinosa
NT1 haemaphysalis concinna
NT1 haemaphysalis flava
NT1 haemaphysalis inermis
NT1 haemaphysalis intermedia
NT1 haemaphysalis japonica
NT1 haemaphysalis kinneari
NT1 haemaphysalis kyasanurensis
NT1 haemaphysalis leachii
NT1 haemaphysalis leporispalustris
NT1 haemaphysalis longicornis
NT1 haemaphysalis parva
NT1 haemaphysalis pospelovashtromae
NT1 haemaphysalis punctata
NT1 haemaphysalis silacea
NT1 haemaphysalis spinigera
NT1 haemaphysalis sulcata
NT1 haemaphysalis turturis
NT1 haemaphysalis verticalis

HAEMAPHYSALIS ACICULIFER
HN from 1990
BT1 haemaphysalis
BT2 ixodidae
BT3 metastigmata
BT4 acari

HAEMAPHYSALIS BANCROFTI
HN from 1989
BT1 haemaphysalis
BT2 ixodidae
BT3 metastigmata
BT4 acari

HAEMAPHYSALIS BISPINOSA
BT1 haemaphysalis
BT2 ixodidae
BT3 metastigmata
BT4 acari

HAEMAPHYSALIS CONCINNA
BT1 haemaphysalis
BT2 ixodidae
BT3 metastigmata
BT4 acari

haemaphysalis cretica
USE **haemaphysalis sulcata**

HAEMAPHYSALIS FLAVA
HN from 1989
BT1 haemaphysalis
BT2 ixodidae
BT3 metastigmata
BT4 acari

HAEMAPHYSALIS INERMIS
uf *alloceraea inermis*
BT1 haemaphysalis
BT2 ixodidae
BT3 metastigmata
BT4 acari

HAEMAPHYSALIS INTERMEDIA
BT1 haemaphysalis
BT2 ixodidae
BT3 metastigmata
BT4 acari

HAEMAPHYSALIS JAPONICA
BT1 haemaphysalis
BT2 ixodidae
BT3 metastigmata
BT4 acari

HAEMAPHYSALIS KINNEARI
HN from 1990
uf *haemaphysalis papuana kinneari*
BT1 haemaphysalis
BT2 ixodidae
BT3 metastigmata
BT4 acari

HAEMAPHYSALIS KYASANURENSIS
BT1 haemaphysalis
BT2 ixodidae
BT3 metastigmata
BT4 acari

HAEMAPHYSALIS LEACHII
BT1 haemaphysalis
BT2 ixodidae
BT3 metastigmata
BT4 acari

HAEMAPHYSALIS LEPORISPALUSTRIS
BT1 haemaphysalis
BT2 ixodidae
BT3 metastigmata
BT4 acari

HAEMAPHYSALIS LONGICORNIS
BT1 haemaphysalis
BT2 ixodidae
BT3 metastigmata
BT4 acari

haemaphysalis otophila
USE **haemaphysalis parva**

haemaphysalis papuana kinneari
USE **haemaphysalis kinneari**

HAEMAPHYSALIS PARVA
uf *haemaphysalis otophila*
BT1 haemaphysalis
BT2 ixodidae
BT3 metastigmata
BT4 acari

HAEMAPHYSALIS POSPELOVASHTROMAE
HN from 1990
BT1 haemaphysalis
BT2 ixodidae
BT3 metastigmata
BT4 acari

HAEMAPHYSALIS PUNCTATA
BT1 haemaphysalis
BT2 ixodidae
BT3 metastigmata
BT4 acari

HAEMAPHYSALIS SILACEA
HN from 1990
BT1 haemaphysalis
BT2 ixodidae
BT3 metastigmata
BT4 acari

HAEMAPHYSALIS SPINIGERA
BT1 haemaphysalis
BT2 ixodidae
BT3 metastigmata
BT4 acari

HAEMAPHYSALIS SULCATA
uf *haemaphysalis cretica*
BT1 haemaphysalis
BT2 ixodidae
BT3 metastigmata
BT4 acari

HAEMAPHYSALIS TURTURIS
BT1 haemaphysalis
BT2 ixodidae
BT3 metastigmata
BT4 acari

HAEMAPHYSALIS VERTICALIS
BT1 haemaphysalis
BT2 ixodidae
BT3 metastigmata
BT4 acari

haemaria
USE **ludisia**

HAEMATITE
AF hematite
BT1 nonclay minerals
BT2 minerals

HAEMATOBIA
uf *lyperosia*
BT1 muscidae
BT2 diptera
NT1 haematobia irritans
NT2 haematobia irritans exigua
NT2 haematobia irritans irritans
NT1 haematobia thirouxi
NT2 haematobia thirouxi potans
NT1 haematobia titillans
rt haematobosca
rt siphona

haematobia exigua
USE **haematobia irritans exigua**

HAEMATOBIA IRRITANS
uf *lyperosia irritans*
uf *siphona irritans*
BT1 haematobia
BT2 muscidae
BT3 diptera
NT1 haematobia irritans exigua
NT1 haematobia irritans irritans

HAEMATOBIA IRRITANS EXIGUA
HN from 1990
uf *haematobia exigua*
uf *lyperosia exigua*
BT1 haematobia irritans
BT2 haematobia
BT3 muscidae
BT4 diptera

HAEMATOBIA IRRITANS IRRITANS
HN from 1990
BT1 haematobia irritans
BT2 haematobia
BT3 muscidae
BT4 diptera

haematobia stimulans
USE **haematobosca stimulans**

HAEMATOBIA THIROUXI
BT1 haematobia
BT2 muscidae
BT3 diptera
NT1 haematobia thirouxi potans

HAEMATOBIA THIROUXI POTANS
HN from 1990
BT1 haematobia thirouxi
BT2 haematobia
BT3 muscidae
BT4 diptera

haematobia thirouxi titillans
USE **haematobia titillans**

HAEMATOBIA TITILLANS
HN from 1990
uf *haematobia thirouxi titillans*
uf *lyperosia titillans*
BT1 haematobia
BT2 muscidae
BT3 diptera

HAEMATOBOSCA
BT1 muscidae
BT2 diptera
NT1 haematobosca stimulans
rt haematobia

HAEMATOBOSCA STIMULANS
uf *haematobia stimulans*
BT1 haematobosca
BT2 muscidae
BT3 diptera

HAEMATOCRIT
AF hematocrit
uf *blood, packed cell volume*
BT1 instruments
rt blood

HAEMATODINIUM
BT1 sarcomastigophora
BT2 protozoa

HAEMATOLOGIC AGENTS
AF hematologic agents
BT1 drugs
NT1 anticoagulants
NT2 dicoumarol
NT2 edta
NT2 heparin
NT2 sodium citrate
NT2 warfarin
NT1 antilipaemics
NT2 d-thyroxine
NT2 3-hydroxy-3-methylglutaric acid
NT2 bezafibrate
NT2 clofibrate
NT2 colestipol
NT2 colestyramine
NT2 halofenate
NT2 niceritrol
NT2 ornithine
NT2 probucol
NT2 sucrose polyester
NT1 hypoglycaemic agents
NT2 buformin
NT2 chlorpropamide
NT2 glibenclamide
NT2 gliclazide
NT2 glipizide
NT2 glucagon
NT2 hypoglycine a
NT2 insulin
NT2 metformin
NT2 tolbutamide
NT1 hypolipaemic agents
NT2 orotic acid
NT1 plasma substitutes
NT2 polyvidone
NT1 prothrombin
NT1 thromboplastin
rt haematology

HAEMATOLOGY
AF hematology
rt blood
rt blood picture
rt haem
rt haematologic agents
rt platelets

HAEMATOMA
AF hematoma
BT1 haemorrhage
BT2 symptoms

HAEMATOPHAGOUS ARTHROPODS
AF hematophagous arthropods
uf *bloodsucking arthropods*
BT1 arthropod pests
BT2 pests
NT1 haematophagous insects
rt blood-meals
rt ectoparasites
rt gonotrophic cycles
rt haematophagy
rt host parasite relationships
rt host-seeking behaviour
rt parous rates

HAEMATOPHAGOUS INSECTS
AF hematophagous insects
BT1 haematophagous arthropods
BT2 arthropod pests
BT3 pests
BT1 insect pests
BT2 arthropod pests
BT3 pests
BT2 insects
BT3 arthropods
rt biting rates
rt insect bites

HAEMATOPHAGY
AF hematophagy
uf *blood feeding*
BT1 feeding habits
BT2 feeding behaviour
BT3 behaviour

HAEMATOPHAGY *cont.*
BT2 habits
rt blood-meals
rt haematophagous arthropods

HAEMATOPINIDAE
BT1 anoplura
BT2 phthiraptera
NT1 haematopinus
NT2 haematopinus asini
NT2 haematopinus eurysternus
NT2 haematopinus quadripertusus
NT2 haematopinus suis
NT2 haematopinus tuberculatus

HAEMATOPINUS
BT1 haematopinidae
BT2 anoplura
BT3 phthiraptera
NT1 haematopinus asini
NT1 haematopinus eurysternus
NT1 haematopinus quadripertusus
NT1 haematopinus suis
NT1 haematopinus tuberculatus

HAEMATOPINUS ASINI
BT1 haematopinus
BT2 haematopinidae
BT3 anoplura
BT4 phthiraptera

HAEMATOPINUS EURYSTERNUS
BT1 haematopinus
BT2 haematopinidae
BT3 anoplura
BT4 phthiraptera

HAEMATOPINUS QUADRIPERTUSUS
BT1 haematopinus
BT2 haematopinidae
BT3 anoplura
BT4 phthiraptera

HAEMATOPINUS SUIS
BT1 haematopinus
BT2 haematopinidae
BT3 anoplura
BT4 phthiraptera

HAEMATOPINUS TUBERCULATUS
BT1 haematopinus
BT2 haematopinidae
BT3 anoplura
BT4 phthiraptera

HAEMATOPOIESIS
AF hematopoiesis
uf *blood formation*
uf *haemopoiesis*
BT1 blood physiology
BT2 animal physiology
BT3 physiology
NT1 erythropoiesis
NT1 thrombocytopoiesis
rt blood
rt bone marrow
rt bone marrow cells
rt hydroxocobalamin

HAEMATOPOIETIC NECROSIS VIRUS
AF hematopoietic necrosis virus
uf *infectious haematopoietic necrosis virus*
BT1 fish rhabdovirus
BT2 vesiculovirus
BT3 rhabdoviridae
BT4 viruses

HAEMATOPOTA
BT1 tabanidae
BT2 diptera
NT1 haematopota crassicornis
NT1 haematopota italica
NT1 haematopota pluvialis
NT1 haematopota subcylindrica

HAEMATOPOTA CRASSICORNIS
BT1 haematopota
BT2 tabanidae

HAEMATOPOTA CRASSICORNIS *cont.*
BT3 diptera

HAEMATOPOTA ITALICA
HN from 1989
BT1 haematopota
BT2 tabanidae
BT3 diptera

HAEMATOPOTA PLUVIALIS
BT1 haematopota
BT2 tabanidae
BT3 diptera

HAEMATOPOTA SUBCYLINDRICA
BT1 haematopota
BT2 tabanidae
BT3 diptera

haematostereum
USE **stereum**

haematostereum sanguinolentum
USE **stereum sanguinolentum**

HAEMATOXENUS
BT1 apicomplexa
BT2 protozoa
NT1 haematoxenus separatus
NT1 haematoxenus veliferus

HAEMATOXENUS SEPARATUS
BT1 haematoxenus
BT2 apicomplexa
BT3 protozoa

HAEMATOXENUS VELIFERUS
BT1 haematoxenus
BT2 apicomplexa
BT3 protozoa

HAEMATOXYLUM
BT1 leguminosae
NT1 haematoxylum campechianum

HAEMATOXYLUM CAMPECHIANUM
BT1 haematoxylum
BT2 leguminosae
rt staining

HAEMATOZOA
BT1 protozoa

HAEMATRACTIDIUM
BT1 apicomplexa
BT2 protozoa

HAEMATURIA
AF hematuria
BT1 urinary tract diseases
BT2 organic diseases
BT3 diseases
rt blood
rt urine

HAEMENTERIA
BT1 glossiphoniidae
BT2 hirudinea
BT3 annelida

HAEMOBARTONELLA
BT1 anaplasmataceae
BT2 rickettsiales
BT3 bacteria
BT4 prokaryotes
NT1 haemobartonella bovis
NT1 haemobartonella canis
NT1 haemobartonella felis
NT1 haemobartonella muris

HAEMOBARTONELLA BOVIS
BT1 haemobartonella
BT2 anaplasmataceae
BT3 rickettsiales
BT4 bacteria
BT5 prokaryotes

HAEMOBARTONELLA CANIS
BT1 haemobartonella
BT2 anaplasmataceae
BT3 rickettsiales
BT4 bacteria

HAEMOBARTONELLA CANIS *cont.*
BT5 prokaryotes

HAEMOBARTONELLA FELIS
BT1 haemobartonella
BT2 anaplasmataceae
BT3 rickettsiales
BT4 bacteria
BT5 prokaryotes

HAEMOBARTONELLA MURIS
BT1 haemobartonella
BT2 anaplasmataceae
BT3 rickettsiales
BT4 bacteria
BT5 prokaryotes

HAEMOCHROMATOSIS
AF hemochromatosis
BT1 mineral metabolism disorders
BT2 metabolic disorders
BT3 animal disorders
BT4 disorders
BT1 pigmentation disorders
BT2 animal disorders
BT3 disorders
rt iron

HAEMOCYTES
HN from 1990 (invertebrate blood cells)
AF hemocytes
BT1 blood cells
BT2 cells

HAEMODIALYSIS
AF hemodialysis
BT1 dialysis
BT2 processing
BT2 separation
rt blood
rt extracorporeal circulation
rt kidney diseases

HAEMODORACEAE
NT1 anigozanthos
NT2 anigozanthos flavidus
NT2 anigozanthos fuliginosus
NT2 anigozanthos manglesii
NT1 lachnanthes
NT2 lachnanthes tinctorum
NT1 wachendorfia
NT2 wachendorfia paniculata

HAEMODYNAMICS
AF hemodynamics
BT1 blood circulation
BT2 physiological functions
NT1 blood pressure
NT1 blood volume
NT1 cardiac output
NT2 heart rate
NT1 vasoconstriction
NT1 vasodilation

HAEMOGAMASUS
BT1 laelapidae
BT2 mesostigmata
BT3 acari
NT1 haemogamasus nidi

HAEMOGAMASUS NIDI
BT1 haemogamasus
BT2 laelapidae
BT3 mesostigmata
BT4 acari

HAEMOGLOBIN
AF hemoglobin
BT1 blood proteins
BT2 animal proteins
BT3 proteins
BT4 peptides
BT1 metalloproteins
BT2 proteins
BT3 peptides
BT1 pigments
NT1 haemoglobin a1
NT1 haemoglobin a2
NT1 methaemoglobin
rt anaemia
rt blood picture
rt globins

HAEMOGLOBIN *cont.*
rt haem
rt haemoglobin value
rt iron

HAEMOGLOBIN A1
AF hemoglobin a1
BT1 haemoglobin
BT2 blood proteins
BT3 animal proteins
BT4 proteins
BT5 peptides
BT2 metalloproteins
BT3 proteins
BT4 peptides
BT2 pigments
rt blood sugar

HAEMOGLOBIN A2
AF hemoglobin a2
BT1 haemoglobin
BT2 blood proteins
BT3 animal proteins
BT4 proteins
BT5 peptides
BT2 metalloproteins
BT3 proteins
BT4 peptides
BT2 pigments

HAEMOGLOBIN VALUE
AF hemoglobin value
BT1 indexes
rt anaemia
rt blood composition
rt blood picture
rt haemoglobin

HAEMOGLOBINURIA
AF hemoglobinuria
BT1 anaemia
BT2 blood disorders
BT3 animal disorders
BT4 disorders
BT1 proteinuria
BT2 metabolic disorders
BT3 animal disorders
BT4 disorders
BT2 urinary tract diseases
BT3 organic diseases
BT4 diseases
rt urine

HAEMOGREGARINA
BT1 apicomplexa
BT2 protozoa
NT1 haemogregarina aegyptia
NT1 haemogregarina bigemina
NT1 haemogregarina boueti
NT1 haemogregarina crocodilinorum
NT1 haemogregarina cyprini
NT1 haemogregarina eremiae
NT1 haemogregarina gracilis
NT1 haemogregarina sachai
NT1 haemogregarina serpentinum
NT1 haemogregarina stepanowi

HAEMOGREGARINA AEGYPTIA
BT1 haemogregarina
BT2 apicomplexa
BT3 protozoa

HAEMOGREGARINA BIGEMINA
BT1 haemogregarina
BT2 apicomplexa
BT3 protozoa

HAEMOGREGARINA BOUETI
BT1 haemogregarina
BT2 apicomplexa
BT3 protozoa

HAEMOGREGARINA CROCODILINORUM
BT1 haemogregarina
BT2 apicomplexa
BT3 protozoa

HAEMOGREGARINA CYPRINI
BT1 haemogregarina
BT2 apicomplexa
BT3 protozoa

HAEMOGREGARINA EREMIAE
BT1 haemogregarina
BT2 apicomplexa
BT3 protozoa

HAEMOGREGARINA GRACILIS
BT1 haemogregarina
BT2 apicomplexa
BT3 protozoa

HAEMOGREGARINA SACHAI
BT1 haemogregarina
BT2 apicomplexa
BT3 protozoa

HAEMOGREGARINA SERPENTINUM
BT1 haemogregarina
BT2 apicomplexa
BT3 protozoa

HAEMOGREGARINA STEPANOWI
BT1 haemogregarina
BT2 apicomplexa
BT3 protozoa

haemolaelaps
USE **androlaelaps**

haemolaelaps glasgowi
USE **androlaelaps fahrenholzi**

HAEMOLYMPH
AF hemolymph
BT1 body fluids
BT2 fluids
rt blood
rt invertebrates
rt lymph

HAEMOLYMPH NODES
HN from 1990
AF hemolymph nodes
BT1 cardiovascular system
BT2 body parts
rt lymph nodes

HAEMOLYSINS
AF hemolysins
BT1 antibodies
BT2 immunoglobulins
BT3 glycoproteins
BT4 proteins
BT5 peptides
BT3 immunological factors
BT1 toxins
NT1 melittin
rt blood
rt complement

HAEMOLYSIS
AF hemolysis
BT1 blood disorders
BT2 animal disorders
BT3 disorders
BT1 lysis
rt anaemia
rt antigen antibody reactions
rt erythrocyte fragility
rt haemolytic anaemia
rt haemosiderosis
rt immune haemolysis

HAEMOLYTIC ANAEMIA
AF hemolytic anemia
uf *haemolytic disease*
BT1 anaemia
BT2 blood disorders
BT3 animal disorders
BT4 disorders
rt haemolysis
rt heinz bodies

haemolytic disease
USE **haemolytic anaemia**

HAEMONCHUS
BT1 trichostrongylidae
BT2 nematoda
NT1 haemonchus contortus
NT1 haemonchus longistipes
NT1 haemonchus similis

HAEMONCHUS CONTORTUS
BT1 haemonchus

HAEMONCHUS CONTORTUS *cont.*
BT2 trichostrongylidae
BT3 nematoda

HAEMONCHUS LONGISTIPES
BT1 haemonchus
BT2 trichostrongylidae
BT3 nematoda

HAEMONCHUS SIMILIS
BT1 haemonchus
BT2 trichostrongylidae
BT3 nematoda

HAEMOPEXIN
AF hemopexin
BT1 globulins
BT2 proteins
BT3 peptides
BT1 glycoproteins
BT2 proteins
BT3 peptides

HAEMOPHILIA
AF hemophilia
BT1 blood coagulation disorders
BT2 blood disorders
BT3 animal disorders
BT4 disorders
rt blood coagulation
rt clotting

HAEMOPHILUS
BT1 pasteurellaceae
BT2 gracilicutes
BT3 bacteria
BT4 prokaryotes
NT1 haemophilus equigenitalis
NT1 haemophilus paragallinarum
NT1 haemophilus somnus

HAEMOPHILUS EQUIGENITALIS
BT1 haemophilus
BT2 pasteurellaceae
BT3 gracilicutes
BT4 bacteria
BT5 prokaryotes

haemophilus gallinarum
USE **haemophilus paragallinarum**

HAEMOPHILUS PARAGALLINARUM
uf *haemophilus gallinarum*
BT1 haemophilus
BT2 pasteurellaceae
BT3 gracilicutes
BT4 bacteria
BT5 prokaryotes

haemophilus pleuropneumoniae
USE **actinobacillus pleuropneumoniae**

HAEMOPHILUS SOMNUS
uf *histophilus ovis*
BT1 haemophilus
BT2 pasteurellaceae
BT3 gracilicutes
BT4 bacteria
BT5 prokaryotes

haemopoiesis
USE **haematopoiesis**

HAEMOPROTEUS
BT1 apicomplexa
BT2 protozoa
NT1 haemoproteus borgesi
NT1 haemoproteus brodkorbi
NT1 haemoproteus canachites
NT1 haemoproteus columbae
NT1 haemoproteus crumenium
NT1 haemoproteus danilewskyi
NT1 haemoproteus fallisi
NT1 haemoproteus fringillae
NT1 haemoproteus handai
NT1 haemoproteus maccallumi
NT1 haemoproteus meleagridis
NT1 haemoproteus meleagris
NT1 haemoproteus multiparasitans
NT1 haemoproteus nettionis

HAEMOPROTEUS *cont.*
NT1 haemoproteus orizivorae
NT1 haemoproteus passeris
NT1 haemoproteus pelouroi
NT1 haemoproteus plataleae
NT1 haemoproteus sacharovi
NT1 haemoproteus velans
NT1 haemoproteus wenyoni

HAEMOPROTEUS BORGESI
BT1 haemoproteus
BT2 apicomplexa
BT3 protozoa

HAEMOPROTEUS BRODKORBI
BT1 haemoproteus
BT2 apicomplexa
BT3 protozoa

HAEMOPROTEUS CANACHITES
BT1 haemoproteus
BT2 apicomplexa
BT3 protozoa

HAEMOPROTEUS COLUMBAE
BT1 haemoproteus
BT2 apicomplexa
BT3 protozoa

HAEMOPROTEUS CRUMENIUM
BT1 haemoproteus
BT2 apicomplexa
BT3 protozoa

HAEMOPROTEUS DANILEWSKYI
BT1 haemoproteus
BT2 apicomplexa
BT3 protozoa

HAEMOPROTEUS FALLISI
BT1 haemoproteus
BT2 apicomplexa
BT3 protozoa

HAEMOPROTEUS FRINGILLAE
BT1 haemoproteus
BT2 apicomplexa
BT3 protozoa

HAEMOPROTEUS HANDAI
BT1 haemoproteus
BT2 apicomplexa
BT3 protozoa

HAEMOPROTEUS MACCALLUMI
BT1 haemoproteus
BT2 apicomplexa
BT3 protozoa

HAEMOPROTEUS MELEAGRIDIS
BT1 haemoproteus
BT2 apicomplexa
BT3 protozoa

HAEMOPROTEUS MELEAGRIS
BT1 haemoproteus
BT2 apicomplexa
BT3 protozoa

HAEMOPROTEUS MULTIPARASITANS
BT1 haemoproteus
BT2 apicomplexa
BT3 protozoa

HAEMOPROTEUS NETTIONIS
BT1 haemoproteus
BT2 apicomplexa
BT3 protozoa

HAEMOPROTEUS ORIZIVORAE
BT1 haemoproteus
BT2 apicomplexa
BT3 protozoa

HAEMOPROTEUS PASSERIS
BT1 haemoproteus
BT2 apicomplexa
BT3 protozoa

HAEMOPROTEUS PELOUROI
BT1 haemoproteus
BT2 apicomplexa
BT3 protozoa

HAEMOPROTEUS PLATALEAE
BT1 haemoproteus
BT2 apicomplexa
BT3 protozoa

HAEMOPROTEUS SACHAROVI
BT1 haemoproteus
BT2 apicomplexa
BT3 protozoa

HAEMOPROTEUS VELANS
BT1 haemoproteus
BT2 apicomplexa
BT3 protozoa

HAEMOPROTEUS WENYONI
BT1 haemoproteus
BT2 apicomplexa
BT3 protozoa

HAEMORRHAGE
AF hemorrhage
uf *bleeding*
BT1 symptoms
NT1 epistaxis
NT1 haematoma
rt circulatory disorders
rt fatty liver haemorrhagic syndrome
rt trauma

HAEMORRHAGIC DIATHESIS
AF hemorrhagic diathesis
uf *diathesis, haemorrhagic*
BT1 diatheses
rt constitution

HAEMORRHAGIC ENTERITIS
AF hemorrhagic enteritis
BT1 intestinal diseases
BT2 gastrointestinal diseases
BT3 digestive system diseases
BT4 organic diseases
BT5 diseases
BT1 viral diseases
BT2 infectious diseases
BT3 diseases
rt enteritis
rt haemorrhagic enteritis virus

HAEMORRHAGIC ENTERITIS VIRUS
AF hemorrhagic enteritis virus
BT1 aviadenovirus
BT2 adenoviridae
BT3 viruses
rt haemorrhagic enteritis

HAEMORRHAGIC SEPTICAEMIA
AF hemorrhagic septicemia
BT1 septicaemia
BT2 sepsis
BT3 infections
rt pasteurella multocida

HAEMORRHAGIC SEPTICAEMIA VIRUS
AF hemorrhagic septicemia virus
BT1 fish rhabdovirus
BT2 vesiculovirus
BT3 rhabdoviridae
BT4 viruses

HAEMORRHOIDS
AF hemorrhoids
BT1 vascular diseases
BT2 cardiovascular diseases
BT3 organic diseases
BT4 diseases
rt anus

HAEMOSIDERIN
AF hemosiderin
BT1 metalloproteins
BT2 proteins
BT3 peptides
rt haemosiderosis

HAEMOSIDEROSIS
AF hemosiderosis
rt haemolysis
rt haemosiderin
rt iron

HAEMOSIDEROSIS *cont.*
rt siderosis

HAEMOSTASIS
AF hemostasis
BT1 blood physiology
BT2 animal physiology
BT3 physiology

haemostereum
USE **stereum**

haemostereum sanguinolentum
USE **stereum sanguinolentum**

HAEMULIDAE
uf *grunts*
uf *pomadasyidae*
BT1 perciformes
BT2 osteichthyes
BT3 fishes
NT1 anisotremus
NT1 haemulon
NT2 haemulon sciurus
NT1 orthopristis
NT1 pomadasys
NT2 pomadasys jubelini
NT2 pomadasys maculatus

HAEMULON
uf *bathystoma*
BT1 haemulidae
BT2 perciformes
BT3 osteichthyes
BT4 fishes
NT1 haemulon sciurus

HAEMULON SCIURUS
BT1 haemulon
BT2 haemulidae
BT3 perciformes
BT4 osteichthyes
BT5 fishes

hafling
USE **haflinger**

HAFLINGER
HN from 1990; previouly "hafling"
uf *hafling*
BT1 horse breeds
BT2 breeds

HAFNIA
BT1 enterobacteriaceae
BT2 gracilicutes
BT3 bacteria
BT4 prokaryotes
NT1 hafnia alvei

HAFNIA ALVEI
HN from 1989
BT1 hafnia
BT2 enterobacteriaceae
BT3 gracilicutes
BT4 bacteria
BT5 prokaryotes

HAGENIA
BT1 rosaceae
NT1 hagenia abyssinica

HAGENIA ABYSSINICA
BT1 hagenia
BT2 rosaceae
BT1 medicinal plants

HAIL
BT1 precipitation
BT2 meteorological factors
BT3 climatic factors
rt hail damage
rt hail guns
rt stress factors

HAIL DAMAGE
BT1 damage
rt hail
rt hail insurance

HAIL GUNS
BT1 equipment
rt cloud seeding
rt hail

HAIL INSURANCE
BT1 agricultural insurance
BT2 insurance
rt hail damage

HAIMBACHIA
BT1 pyralidae
BT2 lepidoptera
NT1 haimbachia infusella
rt acigona

HAIMBACHIA INFUSELLA
HN from 1989; previously acigona infusellus
uf *acigona infusellus*
BT1 haimbachia
BT2 pyralidae
BT3 lepidoptera

HAIMEN
HN from 1990
BT1 goat breeds
BT2 breeds

HAINAN
HN from 1990
BT1 pig breeds
BT2 breeds

HAINAULT
uf *belgium (hainault)*
BT1 belgium
BT2 western europe
BT3 europe

HAIR
uf *hairs, animal*
BT1 integument
BT2 body parts
rt alopecia
rt bristles
rt fur
rt hair analysis (agricola)
rt hair follicles
rt hair meal
rt hypotrichosis
rt keratinization
rt moult
rt undercoat
rt wool

HAIR ANALYSIS (AGRICOLA)
BT1 diagnostic techniques
BT2 techniques
rt hair

hair balls
USE **bezoar**

HAIR FOLLICLES
BT1 follicles
rt hair

HAIR MEAL
BT1 meal
rt hair

hairs, animal
USE **hair**

hairs, plant
USE **plant hairs**

HAITI
BT1 caribbean
BT2 america
rt developing countries
rt least developed countries

HAKE
uf *merluccius merluccius*
BT1 marine fishes
BT2 aquatic animals
BT3 animals
BT3 aquatic organisms
rt gadidae

hake, pacific
USE **merluccius productus**

HAKEA
BT1 proteaceae

HALACRINATE
BT1 quinoline fungicides

HALACRINATE *cont.*
BT2 fungicides
BT3 pesticides
BT2 quinolines
BT3 heterocyclic nitrogen compounds
BT4 organic nitrogen compounds

HALARACHNIDAE
BT1 prostigmata
BT2 acari
NT1 pneumonyssoides
NT2 pneumonyssoides caninum
NT1 pneumonyssus
NT2 pneumonyssus simicola

HALCYON
BT1 alcedinidae
BT2 coraciiformes
BT3 birds
NT1 halcyon chloris
NT1 halcyon smyrnensis

HALCYON CHLORIS
BT1 halcyon
BT2 alcedinidae
BT3 coraciiformes
BT4 birds

HALCYON SMYRNENSIS
BT1 halcyon
BT2 alcedinidae
BT3 coraciiformes
BT4 birds

HALESIA
BT1 styracaceae

HALF LIFE
rt persistence
rt radionuclides

HALIBUT
uf *hippoglossus hippoglossus*
BT1 flatfishes
BT2 marine fishes
BT3 aquatic animals
BT4 animals
BT4 aquatic organisms

HALICTOPHAGIDAE
BT1 strepsiptera
NT1 halictophagus

HALICTOPHAGUS
BT1 halictophagidae
BT2 strepsiptera

HALICTUS
BT1 apidae
BT2 hymenoptera

HALIDES
BT1 inorganic salts
BT2 inorganic compounds
BT2 salts
NT1 bromides
NT2 potassium bromide
NT1 chlorides
NT2 ammonium chloride
NT2 calcium chloride
NT2 mercuric chloride
NT2 mercurous chloride
NT2 potassium chloride
NT2 sodium chloride
NT1 fluorides
NT2 ammonium fluoride
NT2 calcium fluoride
NT2 cryolite
NT2 sodium fluoride
NT1 iodides
NT2 potassium iodide

HALIOTIDAE
BT1 gastropoda
BT2 mollusca
NT1 haliotis
NT2 haliotis discus
NT2 haliotis rufescens

HALIOTIS
BT1 haliotidae
BT2 gastropoda

HALIOTIS *cont.*
BT3 mollusca
NT1 haliotis discus
NT1 haliotis rufescens
rt abalones

HALIOTIS DISCUS
BT1 haliotis
BT2 haliotidae
BT3 gastropoda
BT4 mollusca

HALIOTIS RUFESCENS
BT1 haliotis
BT2 haliotidae
BT3 gastropoda
BT4 mollusca

HALIOTREMA
BT1 dactylogyridae
BT2 monogenea

HALIPEGUS
BT1 hemiuridae
BT2 digenea
BT3 trematoda

HALITE
BT1 nonclay minerals
BT2 minerals
rt sylvinite

HALLIKAR
HN from 1990
BT1 cattle breeds
BT2 breeds

HALLOYSITE
BT1 clay minerals
BT2 minerals

HALLUCINOGENIC FUNGI
BT1 fungi
NT1 amanita muscaria
NT1 psilocybe caerulescens
rt hallucinogens

HALLUCINOGENS
BT1 psychotropic drugs
BT2 neurotropic drugs
BT3 drugs
NT1 psilocin
NT1 psilocybine
rt hallucinogenic fungi

HALOCNEMUM
BT1 chenopodiaceae
NT1 halocnemum strobilaceum

HALOCNEMUM STROBILACEUM
BT1 halocnemum
BT2 chenopodiaceae

HALOFANTRINE
BT1 antimalarials
BT2 antiprotozoal agents
BT3 antiparasitic agents
BT4 drugs

HALOFENATE
BT1 antilipaemics
BT2 haematologic agents
BT3 drugs

HALOFUGINONE
BT1 anthelmintics
BT2 antiparasitic agents
BT3 drugs
BT1 coccidiostats
BT2 antiprotozoal agents
BT3 antiparasitic agents
BT4 drugs

HALOGENATED ALIPHATIC HERBICIDES
BT1 herbicides
BT2 pesticides
NT1 dalapon
NT1 flupropanate
NT1 methyl bromide
NT1 tca

HALOGENATED HYDROCARBONS
BT1 organic halogen compounds
NT1 chlorinated hydrocarbons

HALOGENATED HYDROCARBONS *cont.*
NT2 carbon tetrachloride
NT2 chloroform
NT2 ethylene dichloride
NT2 hexachloroparaxylene
NT2 methylene chloride
NT2 polychlorinated biphenyls
NT2 polychlorinated terphenyls
NT1 ethylene dibromide
NT1 freons
NT1 halothane
NT1 methyl bromide
NT1 polybrominated biphenyls
rt halogens

HALOGENS
BT1 nonmetallic elements
BT2 elements
NT1 bromine
NT1 chlorine
NT1 fluorine
NT1 iodine
rt halogenated hydrocarbons

HALOGETON
BT1 chenopodiaceae
NT1 halogeton glomeratus

HALOGETON GLOMERATUS
BT1 halogeton
BT2 chenopodiaceae

HALOPERIDOL
BT1 ketones
BT1 neuroleptics
BT2 psychotropic drugs
BT3 neurotropic drugs
BT4 drugs

HALOPHILA
BT1 hydrocharitaceae
NT1 halophila ovalis

HALOPHILA OVALIS
BT1 halophila
BT2 hydrocharitaceae

HALOPHYTES
BT1 plant ecological groups
rt aeluropus
rt glycophytes
rt inorganic salts
rt soil salinity

HALORAGIDACEAE
NT1 myriophyllum
NT2 myriophyllum alterniflorum
NT2 myriophyllum aquaticum
NT2 myriophyllum exalbescens
NT2 myriophyllum heterophyllum
NT2 myriophyllum spicatum
NT2 myriophyllum verticillatum

HALOSTACHYS
BT1 chenopodiaceae
NT1 halostachys caspica

HALOSTACHYS CASPICA
BT1 halostachys
BT2 chenopodiaceae

HALOTHANE
BT1 halogenated hydrocarbons
BT2 organic halogen compounds
BT1 inhaled anaesthetics
BT2 anaesthetics
BT3 neurotropic drugs
BT4 drugs

HALOTYDEUS
BT1 eupodidae
BT2 prostigmata
BT3 acari
NT1 halotydeus destructor

HALOTYDEUS DESTRUCTOR
BT1 halotydeus
BT2 eupodidae
BT3 prostigmata
BT4 acari

HALOXON
BT1 anthelmintics
BT2 antiparasitic agents
BT3 drugs

HALOXYDINE
BT1 pyridine herbicides
BT2 herbicides
BT3 pesticides
BT2 pyridines
BT3 heterocyclic nitrogen compounds
BT4 organic nitrogen compounds

HALOXYFOP
BT1 aryloxyphenoxypropionic herbicides
BT2 phenoxypropionic herbicides
BT3 phenoxy herbicides
BT4 herbicides
BT5 pesticides

HALOXYLON
BT1 chenopodiaceae
NT1 haloxylon ammodendron
NT1 haloxylon aphyllum
NT1 haloxylon persicum

HALOXYLON AMMODENDRON
BT1 haloxylon
BT2 chenopodiaceae

HALOXYLON APHYLLUM
BT1 forest trees
BT1 haloxylon
BT2 chenopodiaceae

HALOXYLON PERSICUM
BT1 haloxylon
BT2 chenopodiaceae
rt sand stabilization

haltica
USE **altica**

HALTICOPTERA
BT1 pteromalidae
BT2 hymenoptera
NT1 halticoptera circulus

HALTICOPTERA CIRCULUS
BT1 halticoptera
BT2 pteromalidae
BT3 hymenoptera

HAM
BT1 pigmeat
BT2 meat
BT3 animal products
BT4 products
BT3 foods
rt bacon
rt pigs

HAMAMELIDACEAE
NT1 corylopsis
NT1 disanthus
NT1 distylium
NT2 distylium racemosum
NT1 fortunearia
NT1 fothergilla
NT2 fothergilla gardenii
NT2 fothergilla major
NT1 hamamelis
NT2 hamamelis intermedia
NT2 hamamelis japonica
NT2 hamamelis mollis
NT2 hamamelis virginiana
NT1 loropetalum
NT1 parrotia
NT1 parrotiopsis
NT1 sinowilsonia
NT1 sycopsis

HAMAMELIS
BT1 hamamelidaceae
NT1 hamamelis intermedia
NT1 hamamelis japonica
NT1 hamamelis mollis
NT1 hamamelis virginiana

HAMAMELIS INTERMEDIA
BT1 hamamelis
BT2 hamamelidaceae

HAMAMELIS JAPONICA
BT1 hamamelis
BT2 hamamelidaceae

HAMAMELIS MOLLIS
BT1 hamamelis
BT2 hamamelidaceae
BT1 ornamental woody plants

HAMAMELIS VIRGINIANA
BT1 algicidal plants
BT1 hamamelis
BT2 hamamelidaceae
BT1 medicinal plants
BT1 ornamental woody plants

HAMATOCACTUS
BT1 cactaceae
NT1 hamatocactus setispinus

HAMATOCACTUS SETISPINUS
BT1 hamatocactus
BT2 cactaceae
BT1 ornamental succulent plants
BT2 succulent plants

HAMBURGERS (AGRICOLA)
BT1 meat products
BT2 animal products
BT3 products

HAMELIA
BT1 rubiaceae
NT1 hamelia patens

HAMELIA PATENS
BT1 hamelia
BT2 rubiaceae
BT1 medicinal plants

HAMMER MILLS
uf *mills, hammer*
BT1 mills
BT2 machinery

HAMMER SEISMIC TIMING
BT1 surveying

HAMMERSCHMIDTIELLA
BT1 thelastomatidae
BT2 nematoda
NT1 hammerschmidtiella diesingi

HAMMERSCHMIDTIELLA DIESINGI
BT1 hammerschmidtiella
BT2 thelastomatidae
BT3 nematoda

HAMMONDIA
BT1 apicomplexa
BT2 protozoa
NT1 hammondia hammondi
NT1 hammondia heydorni

HAMMONDIA HAMMONDI
BT1 hammondia
BT2 apicomplexa
BT3 protozoa

HAMMONDIA HEYDORNI
BT1 hammondia
BT2 apicomplexa
BT3 protozoa

HAMPSHIRE
BT1 pig breeds
BT2 breeds

HAMPSHIRE DOWN
BT1 sheep breeds
BT2 breeds

hamster, chinese
USE **cricetulus barabensis**

HAMSTERS
BT1 laboratory mammals
BT2 laboratory animals
BT3 animals
BT1 pets
BT2 animals
NT1 golden hamsters

HAMULI
BT1 feathers
BT2 integument
BT3 body parts

HAN
HN from 1990
BT1 sheep breeds
BT2 breeds

HAND MILKING
BT1 milking
BT2 dairying

hand rearing
USE **artificial rearing**

HAND SAWS
HN from 1989
BT1 hand tools
BT2 tools
BT1 saws
BT2 forestry machinery
BT3 machinery
BT2 tools

HAND TOOLS
BT1 tools
NT1 forks
NT1 hand saws
NT1 spades
rt handles
rt manual operation

HANDBALL
BT1 ball games
BT2 games
BT2 sport

HANDBOOKS
uf *manuals*
BT1 books
BT2 publications
rt guide books
rt laboratory manuals (agricola)

HANDICAPPED CHILDREN (AGRICOLA)
BT1 children
BT2 people
BT1 handicapped persons
BT2 people

HANDICAPPED PERSONS
uf *disabled persons*
BT1 people
NT1 amputees (agricola)
NT1 disabled veterans (agricola)
NT1 handicapped children (agricola)
NT1 physically handicapped persons (agricola)
rt therapeutic recreation

HANDICRAFTS
NT1 macrame (agricola)
NT1 needlework
NT2 crochet (agricola)
NT2 embroidery (agricola)
NT2 knitting (agricola)
NT2 needlepoint (agricola)
NT2 sewing (agricola)
NT1 patchwork (agricola)
rt ancillary enterprises
rt crafts
rt hobbies
rt informal sector
rt rural industry
rt small businesses
rt souvenirs
rt spinning
rt woodworking

HANDLES
BT1 components
rt controls
rt hand tools

HANDLING
NT1 bulk handling
NT1 bunching
NT1 bundling
NT1 dehanding

HANDLING *cont.*
NT1 food handling (agricola)
NT1 loading
NT1 operational handling
NT1 packaging
NT2 aseptic packaging
NT2 bagging
NT2 baling
NT2 bottling
NT2 canning
NT2 flexible packaging (agricola)
NT2 food packaging (agricola)
NT2 thermoform (agricola)
NT2 vacuum packaging
NT2 zip top packaging (agricola)
NT1 packing
NT1 postharvest systems
NT1 postharvest treatment
NT1 stacking
NT1 unloading
NT1 wood handling
rt bruising
rt bundled wood
rt cultural methods
rt damage
rt fork lifts
rt grabs
rt handling machinery
rt harvesting
rt one man operation
rt pallet boxes
rt postharvest decay
rt postharvest losses
rt shafts
rt stackers
rt storage
rt straw trussers
rt transport
rt transporting quality

HANDLING MACHINERY
BT1 machinery
NT1 fillers
NT1 fork lifts
NT1 loaders
NT2 bale loaders
NT2 cutter loaders
NT2 front end loaders
NT2 rear loaders
NT1 palleting machines
NT1 stackers
rt handling

HANG GLIDING
BT1 gliding
BT2 aerosports
BT3 outdoor recreation
BT4 recreation
BT3 sport

HANG TAG (AGRICOLA)
rt clothing

HANGING BASKETS
BT1 containers
rt ornamental plants

HANSENIELLA
BT1 symphylida
BT2 arthropods
NT1 hanseniella ivorensis

HANSENIELLA IVORENSIS
BT1 hanseniella
BT2 symphylida
BT3 arthropods

HANSENULA
BT1 endomycetales

HANTAAN VIRUS
BT1 hantavirus
BT2 bunyaviridae
BT3 viruses

HANTAVIRUS
BT1 bunyaviridae
BT2 viruses
NT1 hantaan virus

HAPLAQUODS
BT1 spodosols

HAPLAQUODS *cont.*
BT2 podzols
BT3 soil types (genetic)

HAPLOBASIDION
BT1 deuteromycotina
NT1 haplobasidion musae

HAPLOBASIDION MUSAE
BT1 haplobasidion
BT2 deuteromycotina

HAPLODIPLOSIS
BT1 cecidomyiidae
BT2 diptera
NT1 haplodiplosis marginata

haplodiplosis equestris
USE **haplodiplosis marginata**

HAPLODIPLOSIS MARGINATA
uf *haplodiplosis equestris*
BT1 haplodiplosis
BT2 cecidomyiidae
BT3 diptera

HAPLOIDS
rt chromosome number
rt haploidy

HAPLOIDY
uf *monoploidy*
uf *polyhaploidy*
BT1 ploidy
rt androgenesis
rt anther culture
rt chromosome elimination
rt germ cells
rt haploids
rt ovule culture

HAPLOPAPPUS
BT1 compositae
NT1 haplopappus ciliatus
NT1 haplopappus helix
NT1 haplopappus pinifolius
NT1 haplopappus tenuisectus

HAPLOPAPPUS CILIATUS
BT1 haplopappus
BT2 compositae

HAPLOPAPPUS HELIX
BT1 haplopappus
BT2 compositae

HAPLOPAPPUS PINIFOLIUS
BT1 haplopappus
BT2 compositae

HAPLOPAPPUS TENUISECTUS
BT1 haplopappus
BT2 compositae

HAPLOPHRAGMA
BT1 bignoniaceae
NT1 haplophragma adenophyllum

HAPLOPHRAGMA ADENOPHYLLUM
BT1 haplophragma
BT2 bignoniaceae

HAPLOPHYLLUM
BT1 rutaceae
NT1 haplophyllum bungei
NT1 haplophyllum dubium
NT1 haplophyllum hispanicum
NT1 haplophyllum latifolium
NT1 haplophyllum obtusifolium
NT1 haplophyllum pedicellatum
NT1 haplophyllum perforatum
NT1 haplophyllum ramosissimum
NT1 haplophyllum schelkovnikovii
NT1 haplophyllum tuberculatum
NT1 haplophyllum versicolor

HAPLOPHYLLUM BUNGEI
BT1 haplophyllum
BT2 rutaceae

HAPLOPHYLLUM DUBIUM
BT1 haplophyllum

HAPLOPHYLLUM DUBIUM *cont.*
BT2 rutaceae

HAPLOPHYLLUM HISPANICUM
BT1 haplophyllum
BT2 rutaceae
BT1 medicinal plants

HAPLOPHYLLUM LATIFOLIUM
BT1 haplophyllum
BT2 rutaceae

HAPLOPHYLLUM OBTUSIFOLIUM
BT1 haplophyllum
BT2 rutaceae

HAPLOPHYLLUM PEDICELLATUM
BT1 haplophyllum
BT2 rutaceae

HAPLOPHYLLUM PERFORATUM
BT1 haplophyllum
BT2 rutaceae

HAPLOPHYLLUM RAMOSISSIMUM
BT1 haplophyllum
BT2 rutaceae

HAPLOPHYLLUM SCHELKOVNIKOVII
BT1 haplophyllum
BT2 rutaceae

HAPLOPHYLLUM TUBERCULATUM
BT1 antibacterial plants
BT1 haplophyllum
BT2 rutaceae

HAPLOPHYLLUM VERSICOLOR
BT1 haplophyllum
BT2 rutaceae

HAPLORCHIS
BT1 heterophyidae
BT2 digenea
BT3 trematoda
NT1 haplorchis pumilio

HAPLORCHIS PUMILIO
BT1 haplorchis
BT2 heterophyidae
BT3 digenea
BT4 trematoda

haplosporangium
USE **emmonsia**

haplosporangium parvum
USE **emmonsia parva**

HAPLOSPORIDIUM
BT1 ascetospora
BT2 protozoa
NT1 haplosporidium lusitanicum
NT1 haplosporidium nelsoni

HAPLOSPORIDIUM LUSITANICUM
BT1 haplosporidium
BT2 ascetospora
BT3 protozoa

HAPLOSPORIDIUM NELSONI
BT1 haplosporidium
BT2 ascetospora
BT3 protozoa

HAPLOTHRIPS
BT1 phlaeothripidae
BT2 thysanoptera
NT1 haplothrips aculeatus
NT1 haplothrips tritici

HAPLOTHRIPS ACULEATUS
BT1 haplothrips
BT2 phlaeothripidae
BT3 thysanoptera

HAPLOTHRIPS TRITICI
BT1 haplothrips
BT2 phlaeothripidae
BT3 thysanoptera

HAPLOTYPES
BT1 genotypes
BT1 species

HAPLOXEROLLS
BT1 kastanozems
BT2 soil types (genetic)

HAPLUDALFS
BT1 luvisols
BT2 soil types (genetic)

HAPLUDULTS
BT1 acrisols
BT2 soil types (genetic)

HAPTENS
HN from 1990
BT1 antigens
BT2 immunological factors

HAPTOGLOBINS
BT1 blood proteins
BT2 animal proteins
BT3 proteins
BT4 peptides
BT1 glycoproteins
BT2 proteins
BT3 peptides

HAPTOPHRYA
BT1 ciliophora
BT2 protozoa
NT1 haptophrya gigantica

HAPTOPHRYA GIGANTICA
BT1 haptophrya
BT2 ciliophora
BT3 protozoa

HARBIN WHITE
HN from 1990
BT1 pig breeds
BT2 breeds

HARBORS
BF harbours

HARBOURS
AF harbors
rt sea transport

HARD CLAMS
BT1 clams
BT2 seafoods
BT3 foods
BT2 shellfish
BT3 aquatic invertebrates
BT4 aquatic animals
BT5 animals
BT5 aquatic organisms

HARD FIBERS
BF hard fibres
BT1 plant fibers
BT2 fibers

HARD FIBRES
AF hard fibers
BT1 plant fibres
BT2 fibres

HARD SEEDS
uf *seed, hard*
rt dormancy
rt seeds

HARD SURFACE FLOORING (AGRICOLA)
uf *nonresilient flooring*
rt floors
rt resilient flooring (agricola)

HARD WHEAT
rt triticum durum
rt wheat

HARDBOARD
BT1 fibreboards
BT2 forest products
BT3 products
BT2 panels
BT3 building materials
BT4 materials

HARDENING
NT1 cold hardening
NT1 salt hardening
NT1 sclerosis

HARDENING *cont.*
NT1 sclerotization
NT1 seed hardening
NT1 surface hardening
NT2 case hardening
NT3 nitriding
rt caking
rt cold resistance
rt frost resistance
rt hardiness
rt tempering

HARDFACING
rt case hardening
rt surface hardening
rt welding

HARDINESS
NT1 winter hardiness
rt cold resistance
rt frost resistance
rt hardening

HARDNESS
rt firmness
rt hardness testing
rt tenderness
rt water hardness
rt wear

HARDNESS TESTING
uf *testing, hardness*
BT1 testing
rt hardness

HARDWOODS
HN from 1990
BT1 wood

HARES
BT1 meat animals
BT2 animals
BT1 small mammals
BT2 animals
rt leporidae
rt lepus

HARIANA
HN from 1990
BT1 cattle breeds
BT2 breeds

haricot beans
USE **phaseolus vulgaris**

HARMONIA
uf *leis*
BT1 coccinellidae
BT2 coleoptera
NT1 harmonia axyridis
NT1 harmonia octomaculata
rt coccinella

HARMONIA AXYRIDIS
uf *coccinella axyridis*
uf *leis axyridis*
BT1 harmonia
BT2 coccinellidae
BT3 coleoptera

HARMONIA OCTOMACULATA
BT1 harmonia
BT2 coccinellidae
BT3 coleoptera

HARNAI
HN from 1990
BT1 sheep breeds
BT2 breeds

HARNESS
rt riding animals

HARPAGOPHYTUM
BT1 pedaliaceae
NT1 harpagophytum procumbens
NT1 harpagophytum zeyheri

HARPAGOPHYTUM PROCUMBENS
BT1 harpagophytum
BT2 pedaliaceae
BT1 medicinal plants

HARPAGOPHYTUM ZEYHERI
BT1 harpagophytum

HARPAGOPHYTUM ZEYHERI *cont.*
BT2 pedaliaceae

HARPALUS
uf *ophonus*
BT1 carabidae
BT2 coleoptera
NT1 harpalus affinis
NT1 harpalus distinguendus
NT1 harpalus pennsylvanicus
NT1 harpalus rufipes

HARPALUS AFFINIS
BT1 harpalus
BT2 carabidae
BT3 coleoptera

HARPALUS DISTINGUENDUS
BT1 harpalus
BT2 carabidae
BT3 coleoptera

HARPALUS PENNSYLVANICUS
BT1 harpalus
BT2 carabidae
BT3 coleoptera

harpalus pubescens
USE **harpalus rufipes**

HARPALUS RUFIPES
uf *harpalus pubescens*
uf *ophonus pubescens*
uf *ophonus rufipes*
BT1 harpalus
BT2 carabidae
BT3 coleoptera

HARPECHLOA
BT1 gramineae
NT1 harpechloa falx

HARPECHLOA FALX
BT1 harpechloa
BT2 gramineae

HARPOSPORIUM
BT1 deuteromycotina
NT1 harposporium arcuatum

HARPOSPORIUM ARCUATUM
BT1 harposporium
BT2 deuteromycotina

HARRISINA
BT1 zygaenidae
BT2 lepidoptera
NT1 harrisina brillians

HARRISINA BRILLIANS
BT1 harrisina
BT2 zygaenidae
BT3 lepidoptera

HARROWING
BT1 tillage
BT2 cultivation
rt harrows

HARROWS
BT1 implements
NT1 disc harrows
NT1 reciprocating harrows
NT1 rotary harrows
NT1 spiked harrows
NT1 spring tine harrows
rt crumblers
rt harrowing
rt tines
rt weeders

harrows, disc
USE **disc harrows**

harrows, reciprocating
USE **reciprocating harrows**

harrows, rotary
USE **rotary harrows**

harrows, spiked
USE **spiked harrows**

harrows spring tine
USE **spring tine harrows**

HART PARK VIRUS
BT1 vesiculovirus
BT2 rhabdoviridae
BT3 viruses

hartebeest
USE **alcelaphus buselaphus**

HARTERTIA
BT1 hartertiidae
BT2 nematoda
NT1 hartertia gallinarum

HARTERTIA GALLINARUM
BT1 hartertia
BT2 hartertiidae
BT3 nematoda

HARTERTIIDAE
BT1 nematoda
NT1 hartertia
NT2 hartertia gallinarum
rt animal parasitic nematodes

HARTMANNELLA
BT1 sarcomastigophora
BT2 protozoa
NT1 hartmannella culbertsoni
NT1 hartmannella glebae
NT1 hartmannella leptocnemus
NT1 hartmannella rhysodes
NT1 hartmannella vermiformis

HARTMANNELLA CULBERTSONI
BT1 hartmannella
BT2 sarcomastigophora
BT3 protozoa

HARTMANNELLA GLEBAE
BT1 hartmannella
BT2 sarcomastigophora
BT3 protozoa

HARTMANNELLA LEPTOCNEMUS
BT1 hartmannella
BT2 sarcomastigophora
BT3 protozoa

HARTMANNELLA RHYSODES
BT1 hartmannella
BT2 sarcomastigophora
BT3 protozoa

HARTMANNELLA VERMIFORMIS
BT1 hartmannella
BT2 sarcomastigophora
BT3 protozoa

HARUNGANA
BT1 guttiferae
NT1 harungana madagascariensis

HARUNGANA MADAGASCARIENSIS
BT1 harungana
BT2 guttiferae
BT1 medicinal plants

harvest date
USE **harvesting date**

HARVEST INDEX
BT1 yield components
BT2 yields

HARVESTERS
BT1 farm machinery
BT2 machinery
NT1 aquatic plant harvesters
NT1 bean harvesters
NT1 binders
NT1 bulb harvesters
NT1 cabbage harvesters
NT1 catching frames
NT1 citrus harvesters
NT1 combine harvesters
NT2 axial flow combine harvesters
NT2 concaves
NT2 grain tanks
NT1 cotton pickers
NT1 crop lifters
NT1 cutter loaders
NT1 dividers

HARVESTERS *cont.*
NT1 flax pullers
NT1 forage harvesters
NT1 grape harvesters
NT1 groundnut harvesters
NT1 header harvesters
NT1 hemp harvesters
NT1 hop harvesters
NT1 lettuce harvesters
NT1 maize pickers
NT1 melon harvesters
NT1 nut harvesters
NT1 onion harvesters
NT1 pea viners
NT1 plot harvesters
NT1 root harvesters
NT2 beet harvesters
NT3 beet lifters
NT2 carrot harvesters
NT2 potato harvesters
NT3 potato diggers
NT4 shaker diggers
NT2 turnip harvesters
NT1 self propelled harvesters
NT1 soft fruit harvesters
NT2 black currant harvesters
NT2 raspberry harvesters
NT2 strawberry harvesters
NT1 sugarcane harvesters
NT1 tea harvesters
NT1 tobacco harvesters
NT1 tomato harvesters
NT1 vegetable harvesters
rt elevator diggers
rt elevators
rt harvesting
rt haulm strippers
rt stalk pullers
rt swath turners
rt toppers
rt tree shakers
rt windrowers

harvesters, aquatic plant
USE **aquatic plant harvesters**

harvesters, bean
USE **bean harvesters**

harvesters, beet
USE **beet harvesters**

harvesters, black currant
USE **black currant harvesters**

harvesters, bulb
USE **bulb harvesters**

harvesters, cabbage
USE **cabbage harvesters**

harvesters, carrot
USE **carrot harvesters**

harvesters, citrus
USE **citrus harvesters**

harvesters, combine
USE **combine harvesters**

harvesters, cotton
USE **cotton pickers**

harvesters, flax
USE **flax pullers**

harvesters, forage
USE **forage harvesters**

harvesters, fruit
USE **tree shakers**

harvesters, grain
USE **combine harvesters**

harvesters, grape
USE **grape harvesters**

harvesters, groundnut
USE **groundnut harvesters**

harvesters, header
USE **header harvesters**

harvesters, hemp
USE **hemp harvesters**

harvesters, hop
USE **hop harvesters**

harvesters, lettuce
USE **lettuce harvesters**

harvesters, maize
USE **maize pickers**

harvesters, melon
USE **melon harvesters**

harvesters, onion
USE **onion harvesters**

harvesters, potato
USE **potato harvesters**

harvesters, self propelled
USE **self propelled harvesters**

harvesters, soft fruit
USE **soft fruit harvesters**

harvesters, strawberry
USE **strawberry harvesters**

harvesters, sugarcane
USE **sugarcane harvesters**

harvesters, tobacco
USE **tobacco harvesters**

harvesters, turnip
USE **turnip harvesters**

harvesters, vegetable
USE **vegetable harvesters**

HARVESTING
NT1 combine harvesting
NT1 combing
NT1 haymaking
NT1 mechanical harvesting
NT1 once over harvesting
NT1 picking
NT1 plucking
NT1 stripping
NT1 swath harvesting
NT1 tapping
NT2 resin tapping
NT2 sap tapping (agricola)
NT1 topping
NT1 whole crop harvesting
rt biennial cropping
rt cultural methods
rt cutting
rt felling
rt forage conditioning
rt fruit picking aids
rt grain loss monitors
rt handling
rt harvesters
rt harvesting date
rt harvesting frequency
rt harvesting losses
rt lifting
rt loosening
rt picking platforms
rt postharvest systems
rt preharvest sprays
rt pulling
rt water harvesting
rt windrows
rt yields

harvesting, combine
USE **combine harvesting**

HARVESTING DATE
uf *harvest date*
NT1 cutting date
rt date
rt harvesting

HARVESTING FREQUENCY
BT1 frequency
NT1 cutting frequency
rt harvesting
rt once over harvesting

HARVESTING LOSSES
uf *haymaking losses*
BT1 losses
rt harvesting

harvesting, mechanical
USE **mechanical harvesting**

harvesting, once over
USE **once over harvesting**

HARVEYA
BT1 scrophulariaceae

HARYANA
BT1 india
BT2 south asia
BT3 asia

HARYANA ZEBU
BT1 zebu breeds
BT2 breeds

hashemite kingdom of jordan
USE **jordan**

HASHTNAGRI
HN from 1990
BT1 sheep breeds
BT2 breeds

HASSAN
HN from 1990
BT1 sheep breeds
BT2 breeds

HATCH
BT1 reproductive performance
BT2 performance

hatchability
USE **egg hatchability**

HATCHERIES
rt brooders
rt hatchery waste
rt hatching
rt poultry housing

HATCHERY WASTE
BT1 agricultural wastes
BT2 wastes
rt hatcheries

HATCHING
BT1 sexual reproduction
BT2 reproduction
NT1 hatching factors
NT1 hatching season
rt eggs
rt hatcheries
rt hatching date
rt hatching weight
rt incubation
rt preincubation period

HATCHING DATE
uf *hatching time*
rt date
rt hatching
rt hatching season
rt incubation

HATCHING FACTORS
BT1 hatching
BT2 sexual reproduction
BT3 reproduction

HATCHING SEASON
BT1 hatching
BT2 sexual reproduction
BT3 reproduction
rt hatching date
rt seasons

hatching time
USE **hatching date**

HATCHING WEIGHT
BT1 weight
rt chicks
rt hatching

HATIORA
BT1 cactaceae
NT1 hatiora salicornioides

HATIORA SALICORNIOIDES
BT1 hatiora
BT2 cactaceae
BT1 ornamental succulent plants

HATIORA SALICORNIOIDES *cont.*
BT2 succulent plants

HAULM DESTRUCTION
BT1 burning
BT1 destruction
rt haulms

HAULM STRIPPERS
BT1 farm machinery
BT2 machinery
rt harvesters
rt haulms
rt potato harvesters
rt stripping

HAULMS
rt haulm destruction
rt haulm strippers
rt stems

HAUSTORIA
HN from 1989
BT1 fungal morphology
BT2 morphology

HAWAII
BT1 pacific states of usa
BT2 western states of usa
BT3 usa
BT4 north america
BT5 america

HAWKS
BT1 predatory birds
BT2 predators
rt accipitridae

HAWORTHIA
BT1 liliaceae
NT1 haworthia altilinea
NT1 haworthia cooperi
NT1 haworthia cymbiformis
NT1 haworthia maughanii
NT1 haworthia setata
NT1 haworthia subfasciata
NT1 haworthia truncata
NT1 haworthia variegata

HAWORTHIA ALTILINEA
BT1 haworthia
BT2 liliaceae
BT1 ornamental succulent plants
BT2 succulent plants

HAWORTHIA COOPERI
uf *haworthia pilifera*
BT1 haworthia
BT2 liliaceae
BT1 ornamental succulent plants
BT2 succulent plants

HAWORTHIA CYMBIFORMIS
uf *haworthia planifolia*
BT1 haworthia
BT2 liliaceae
BT1 ornamental succulent plants
BT2 succulent plants

HAWORTHIA MAUGHANII
BT1 haworthia
BT2 liliaceae
BT1 ornamental succulent plants
BT2 succulent plants

haworthia pilifera
USE **haworthia cooperi**

haworthia planifolia
USE **haworthia cymbiformis**

HAWORTHIA SETATA
BT1 haworthia
BT2 liliaceae
BT1 ornamental succulent plants
BT2 succulent plants

HAWORTHIA SUBFASCIATA
BT1 haworthia
BT2 liliaceae
BT1 ornamental succulent plants
BT2 succulent plants

HAWORTHIA TRUNCATA
BT1 haworthia

HAWORTHIA TRUNCATA *cont.*
BT2 liliaceae
BT1 ornamental succulent plants
BT2 succulent plants

HAWORTHIA VARIEGATA
BT1 haworthia
BT2 liliaceae
BT1 ornamental succulent plants
BT2 succulent plants

hawthorn
USE **crataegus laevigata**

HAY
BT1 feeds
NT1 barley hay
NT1 clover hay
NT1 cowpea hay
NT1 lucerne hay
NT2 lucerne haylage
NT1 lupin hay
NT1 oat hay
NT1 ryegrass hay
NT1 sainfoin hay
NT1 sorghum hay
NT1 soya hay
rt farmer's lung
rt fodder crops
rt fodder plants
rt hay cubes
rt haylage
rt haymaking
rt mowers
rt roughage
rt stover
rt tedding
rt windrows

hay blowers
USE **forage blowers**

HAY CUBES
BT1 cubes
rt hay

HAYLAGE
BT1 feeds
BT1 silage
BT2 feeds
BT2 fermentation products
BT3 products
rt hay

HAYMAKING
uf *field curing*
BT1 harvesting
rt buckrakes
rt drying
rt feeds
rt forage
rt hay
rt swath aerators
rt swath turners
rt tedders
rt tedding
rt windrowers

haymaking losses
USE **harvesting losses**

haynaldia
USE **dasypyrum**

haynaldia villosa
USE **dasypyrum villosum**

HAZARAGIE
HN from 1990
BT1 sheep breeds
BT2 breeds

HAZARDS
NT1 explosive hazard
NT1 fire danger
NT1 health hazards
NT1 occupational hazards

HAZELNUTS
uf *cobnuts*
uf *filberts*
BT1 oilseed plants
BT2 fatty oil plants
BT3 oil plants

HAZELNUTS *cont.*
BT1 temperate tree nuts
BT2 nut crops
rt corylus avellana

HAZUNTA
BT1 apocynaceae
NT1 hazunta modesta

HAZUNTA MODESTA
BT1 hazunta
BT2 apocynaceae

hcb
USE **hexachlorobenzene**

HCG
uf *chorionic gonadotropin, human*
uf *gonadotropin, human chorionic*
uf *human chorionic gonadotropin*
uf *human gonadotropic hormone*
uf *urogonadotropin*
BT1 chorionic gonadotropin
BT2 gonadotropins
BT3 glycoproteins
BT4 proteins
BT5 peptides
BT3 sex hormones
BT4 hormones
BT2 placental hormones
BT3 hormones

HCH
uf *benzene hexachloride*
uf *bhc*
uf *hexachloran*
BT1 organochlorine insecticides
BT2 insecticides
BT3 pesticides
BT2 organochlorine pesticides
BT3 organochlorine compounds
BT4 organic halogen compounds
rt lindane

HEAD
BT1 body regions
NT1 beak
NT1 face
NT2 eyelids
NT2 lips
NT1 scalp
rt comb
rt decapitation
rt proboscis
rt skull

head circumference
USE **head dimensions (agricola)**

HEAD DIMENSIONS (AGRICOLA)
uf *head circumference*
rt body measurements

head fly
USE **hydrotaea irritans**

HEADACHES (AGRICOLA)
BT1 symptoms

HEADER HARVESTERS
uf *harvesters, header*
BT1 harvesters
BT2 farm machinery
BT3 machinery
rt maize pickers
rt stripping

HEADING
BT1 plant development
rt heading date

heading broccoli
USE **cauliflowers**

HEADING DATE
rt date
rt heading

HEADS OF FAMILIES
BT1 family structure

HEALING
uf *wound healing*
NT1 liver regeneration
NT1 tissue repair
rt hospitals
rt wounds

HEALTH
NT1 animal health
NT1 constitution
NT1 dental health (agricola)
NT2 nursing bottle syndrome (agricola)
NT1 fitness
NT1 mental health
NT1 physical fitness
NT2 aerobics (agricola)
NT1 public health
rt diseases
rt ergonomics
rt failure to thrive (agricola)
rt health centres
rt health clubs
rt health education
rt health hazards
rt health inspections (agricola)
rt health insurance (agricola)
rt health protection
rt health resorts
rt health services
rt health tourism
rt hospitals
rt illness (agricola)
rt morbidity
rt mortality
rt nudism
rt nutrition
rt physical education
rt sanitation
rt therapy
rt vigour
rt wellness (agricola)
rt who

HEALTH BELIEFS (AGRICOLA)
BT1 beliefs (agricola)

HEALTH CARE (AGRICOLA)
NT1 hospices (agricola)
NT1 patient care (agricola)
rt health care costs (agricola)
rt health maintenance organizations (agricola)
rt health services
rt home care (agricola)
rt home health aides (agricola)
rt intermediate care (agricola)
rt long term care (agricola)

HEALTH CARE COSTS (AGRICOLA)
BT1 costs
rt health care (agricola)

HEALTH CENTERS
BF health centres

HEALTH CENTRES
AF health centers
uf *clinics*
BT1 health services
BT2 social services
BT3 social welfare
NT1 health clinics
rt health
rt hospitals

HEALTH CLINICS
BT1 health centres
BT2 health services
BT3 social services
BT4 social welfare
rt health protection

HEALTH CLUBS
BT1 clubs
BT2 interest groups
BT3 groups
BT3 organizations
BT2 recreational facilities

HEALTH CLUBS *cont.*
rt health
rt physical fitness

HEALTH EDUCATION
BT1 education
NT1 prenatal education (agricola)
rt health
rt health programs (agricola)

HEALTH FOODS
BT1 foods

HEALTH HAZARDS
BT1 hazards
rt health
rt safety

HEALTH INSPECTIONS (AGRICOLA)
rt health
rt public health

HEALTH INSURANCE (AGRICOLA)
BT1 insurance
rt health

HEALTH MAINTENANCE ORGANIZATIONS (AGRICOLA)
BT1 organizations
rt health care (agricola)

HEALTH PROGRAMS (AGRICOLA)
BT1 programs (agricola)
rt health education
rt health services

HEALTH PROMOTION (AGRICOLA)
BT1 preventive medicine (agricola)
BT2 medicine
rt wellness (agricola)

HEALTH PROTECTION
BT1 protection
rt disease control
rt ergonomics
rt health
rt health clinics
rt health services
rt occupational disorders
rt operator comfort
rt protective clothing
rt public health

HEALTH RESORTS
uf *spas*
BT1 resorts
rt health
rt holiday accommodation

HEALTH SERVICES
uf *services, health*
BT1 social services
BT2 social welfare
NT1 community health services (agricola)
NT1 health centres
NT2 health clinics
NT1 maternity services
NT1 medical services
NT2 nursing homes
NT2 psychiatric services (agricola)
NT1 outpatient services (agricola)
NT1 school health services (agricola)
NT1 traditional health services
rt allied health occupations (agricola)
rt barefoot doctors
rt health
rt health care (agricola)
rt health programs (agricola)
rt health protection
rt hospitals
rt medical auxiliaries
rt public services
rt social security
rt tropical medicine

HEALTH TOURISM
BT1 tourism

HEALTH TOURISM *cont.*
rt health

health workers
USE **medical auxiliaries**

HEARD AND MCDONALD ISLANDS
BT1 australian oceania
BT2 oceania

HEARING
BT1 senses
NT1 auditory threshold
rt acoustics
rt deafness
rt ears
rt hearing impairment
rt hearing protectors
rt sounds

HEARING IMPAIRMENT
BT1 sensory disorders
BT2 functional disorders
BT3 animal disorders
BT4 disorders
BT2 nervous system diseases
BT3 organic diseases
BT4 diseases
NT1 deafness
rt ear diseases
rt hearing
rt noise

HEARING PROTECTORS
uf *ear muffs*
BT1 protective clothing
BT2 clothing
rt hearing
rt noise

HEARINGS (AGRICOLA)
rt committees (agricola)

HEART
BT1 cardiovascular system
BT2 body parts
NT1 endocardium
NT1 heart valves
NT1 ventricles
rt cardiac glycosides
rt cardiac output
rt cardiac rhythm
rt cardiovascular agents
rt heart and lung transplant
rt heart as food
rt heart diseases
rt heart girth
rt heart rate
rt heart sounds
rt heart transplant
rt myocardium
rt pericardium

HEART AND LUNG TRANSPLANT
HN from 1990
BT1 transplantation
BT2 surgical operations
rt heart
rt heart transplant
rt lungs

HEART AS FOOD
BT1 foods
BT1 offal
BT2 meat byproducts
BT3 agricultural byproducts
BT4 byproducts
rt heart

heart disease, ischaemic
USE **myocardial ischaemia**

HEART DISEASES
uf *coronary diseases*
uf *heart disorders*
BT1 cardiovascular diseases
BT2 organic diseases
BT3 diseases
NT1 arrhythmia
NT1 beriberi heart disease
NT1 cardiac insufficiency
NT1 cardiomegaly
NT1 cardiomyopathy

HEART DISEASES *cont.*
NT1 endocarditis
NT1 myocardial infarction
NT1 myocardial ischaemia
NT1 myocarditis
NT1 pericardial effusion
NT1 pericarditis
rt heart

heart disorders
USE **heart diseases**

heart disorders, ischaemic
USE **myocardial ischaemia**

HEART GIRTH
BT1 girth
BT2 dimensions
rt body measurements
rt heart

heart muscle
USE **myocardium**

heart output
USE **cardiac output**

HEART RATE
BT1 cardiac output
BT2 haemodynamics
BT3 blood circulation
BT4 physiological functions
rt ballistocardiography
rt heart
rt heart sounds
rt pulse rate

HEART SOUNDS
BT1 sounds
rt blood circulation
rt blood flow
rt heart
rt heart rate
rt pulsation

HEART TRANSPLANT
BT1 transplantation
BT2 surgical operations
rt heart
rt heart and lung transplant

HEART VALVES
BT1 heart
BT2 cardiovascular system
BT3 body parts
rt blood circulation

HEARTWATER
BT1 bacterial diseases
BT2 infectious diseases
BT3 diseases
rt cowdria ruminantium

HEARTWOOD
BT1 wood
NT1 abnormal heartwood
rt durability
rt sapwood

heartworm
USE **dirofilaria**

HEAT
rt burns
rt calories
rt calorific value
rt calorimetry
rt fires
rt fuel consumption
rt geothermal energy
rt heat conservation
rt heat consumption
rt heat exchangers
rt heat exhaustion
rt heat injury
rt heat lamps
rt heat processing
rt heat production
rt heat pumps
rt heat recovery
rt heat regulation
rt heat resistance
rt heat retention
rt heat stress

HEAT *cont.*
- rt heat sums
- rt heat tolerance
- rt heat treatment
- rt heaters
- rt heating
- rt inflammation
- rt infrared radiation
- rt nitriding
- rt shelter
- rt sweating
- rt temperature
- rt temperature resistance
- rt thermal degradation
- rt thermal properties
- rt thermal radiation
- rt thermal screens
- rt thermistors
- rt thermocouples
- rt thermodynamics
- rt thermoluminescence
- rt thermometers
- rt thermometric titrimetry
- rt thermostats

HEAT ADAPTATION
- *uf thermal adaptation*
- BT1 adaptation
- rt heat resistance
- rt heat tolerance
- rt thermoduric bacteria
- rt thermophilic bacteria
- rt thermophilic fungi

heat and drought resistance
- USE **drought resistance**
- OR **heat resistance**

HEAT BALANCE
- rt heat regulation
- rt heat stability
- rt heat transfer

heat capacity
- USE **specific heat**

HEAT CONSERVATION
- BT1 conservation
- NT1 heat retention
- NT2 waste heat utilization
- rt energy conservation
- rt heat
- rt heat loss
- rt heat recovery
- rt heat stability
- rt insulation

HEAT CONSUMPTION
- BT1 consumption
- rt heat
- rt heat loss
- rt heat transfer

HEAT EXCHANGE
- BT1 thermal properties
- BT2 physical properties
- BT3 properties
- rt heat exchangers
- rt heat flow

HEAT EXCHANGERS
- BT1 equipment
- rt energy conservation
- rt heat
- rt heat exchange
- rt heat pumps
- rt heat recovery
- rt waste heat utilization

HEAT EXHAUSTION
- *uf sunstroke*
- BT1 exhaustion
- rt heat
- rt heat resistance
- rt heat stress
- rt heat tolerance

HEAT FLOW
- *uf heat flux*
- BT1 flow
- BT2 movement
- rt convection
- rt heat exchange
- rt heat transfer

HEAT FLOW *cont.*
- rt thermal properties

heat flux
- USE **heat flow**

HEAT INJURY
- BT1 injuries
- rt heat

HEAT LAMPS
- BT1 heaters
- BT2 equipment
- BT1 lamps
- rt heat
- rt infrared heaters
- rt infrared radiation

HEAT LOSS
- BT1 losses
- NT1 body heat loss
- rt heat conservation
- rt heat consumption
- rt heat retention
- rt heat transfer
- rt thermal diffusion

HEAT OF SOLUTION
- HN from 1990
- BT1 thermochemical properties
- BT2 physicochemical properties
- BT3 properties
- rt dissolving
- rt solutes
- rt solutions

HEAT OF WETTING
- BT1 thermochemical properties
- BT2 physicochemical properties
- BT3 properties
- rt wetting

HEAT PROCESSING
- BT1 processing
- NT1 heat treatment
- NT2 hot air treatment
- NT2 hot water treatment
- NT2 parboiling
- NT2 scalding
- NT2 tempering
- NT2 toasting
- NT2 uht treatment
- rt heat
- rt sterilizing

HEAT PRODUCTION
- *uf calorigenesis*
- *uf thermogenesis*
- rt calorific value
- rt calorimeters
- rt calorimetry
- rt heat
- rt heaters
- rt waste heat utilization

HEAT PUMPS
- BT1 pumps
- BT2 machinery
- rt heat
- rt heat exchangers
- rt heaters

heat radiation
- USE **thermal radiation**

HEAT RECOVERY
- BT1 heat regulation
- BT1 recovery
- NT1 waste heat utilization
- rt heat
- rt heat conservation
- rt heat exchangers
- rt heat transfer

HEAT REGULATION
- NT1 clustering
- NT1 fanning
- NT1 heat recovery
- NT2 waste heat utilization
- NT1 heat stability
- NT1 sweating
- rt animal behaviour
- rt body temperature
- rt energy exchange

HEAT REGULATION *cont.*
- rt fans
- rt heat
- rt heat balance
- rt heat transfer
- rt thermal screens
- rt thermoregulation

HEAT RESISTANCE
- *uf heat and drought resistance*
- BT1 temperature resistance
- BT2 resistance
- rt drought resistance
- rt heat
- rt heat adaptation
- rt heat exhaustion
- rt heat stress
- rt heat tolerance
- rt susceptibility
- rt thermophilic bacteria
- rt thermophilic fungi

HEAT RETENTION
- BT1 heat conservation
- BT2 conservation
- NT1 waste heat utilization
- rt heat
- rt heat loss
- rt heat transfer

heat (sexual)
- USE **oestrus**

HEAT SHOCK
- BT1 shock
- rt heat shock proteins
- rt heat stress

HEAT SHOCK PROTEINS
- BT1 proteins
- BT2 peptides
- rt heat shock

HEAT STABILITY
- BT1 heat regulation
- BT1 thermal properties
- BT2 physical properties
- BT3 properties
- rt coagulation
- rt heat balance
- rt heat conservation
- rt heat transfer
- rt stability

HEAT STRESS
- BT1 stress
- NT1 hyperthermia
- rt ergonomics
- rt heat
- rt heat exhaustion
- rt heat resistance
- rt heat shock
- rt heat tolerance
- rt thermal screens

HEAT SUMS
- *uf accumulated temperature*
- *uf cumulative temperature*
- *uf day-degrees*
- *uf degree-days*
- *uf heat units*
- *uf temperature relations*
- *uf temperature sums*
- *uf thermal units*
- rt heat

HEAT TOLERANCE
- BT1 tolerance
- rt heat
- rt heat adaptation
- rt heat exhaustion
- rt heat resistance
- rt heat stress

HEAT TRANSFER
- *uf nusselt number*
- rt convection
- rt cooling
- rt environmental control
- rt heat balance
- rt heat consumption
- rt heat flow
- rt heat loss
- rt heat recovery

HEAT TRANSFER *cont.*
- rt heat regulation
- rt heat retention
- rt heat stability
- rt heating
- rt insulation
- rt waste heat utilization

HEAT TREATMENT
- BT1 heat processing
- BT2 processing
- NT1 hot air treatment
- NT1 hot water treatment
- NT1 parboiling
- NT1 scalding
- NT1 tempering
- NT1 toasting
- NT1 uht treatment
- rt cooking
- rt heat
- rt metallurgy
- rt sintered metals
- rt sterilizing
- rt treatment

heat units
- USE **heat sums**

HEATED FAT
- BT1 fat products
- BT2 products

HEATERS
- BT1 equipment
- NT1 air heaters
- NT1 boilers
- NT2 steam boilers
- NT1 burners
- NT1 electric heaters
- NT1 heat lamps
- NT1 infrared heaters
- rt heat
- rt heat production
- rt heat pumps
- rt heating systems
- rt radiators
- rt solar collectors

heaters, air
- USE **air heaters**

heaters, electric
- USE **electric heaters**

heaters, infrared
- USE **infrared heaters**

heather
- USE **calluna vulgaris**

HEATHLAND
- BT1 land types
- rt moorland

HEATHLAND SOILS
- BT1 soil types (ecological)

HEATING
- NT1 electric heating
- NT1 soil heating
- NT1 solar heating
- NT1 space heating
- NT1 spontaneous heating
- rt boiling
- rt combustion
- rt cooking
- rt drying
- rt environmental control
- rt heat
- rt heat transfer
- rt heating costs (agricola)
- rt heating systems
- rt melting
- rt pasteurization
- rt pyranometers
- rt radiators
- rt thawing
- rt toasting
- rt ventilation

HEATING COSTS (AGRICOLA)
- BT1 costs
- rt heating

HEATING SYSTEMS
BT1 systems
rt heaters
rt heating
rt radiators
rt solar collectors

HEAVY METALS
BT1 elements
BT1 metals

heavy soils
USE **clay soils**

HEBE
BT1 scrophulariaceae
NT1 hebe andersonii
NT1 hebe buxifolia
NT1 hebe elliptica

HEBE ANDERSONII
BT1 hebe
BT2 scrophulariaceae
BT1 ornamental woody plants

HEBE BUXIFOLIA
BT1 hebe
BT2 scrophulariaceae
BT1 ornamental woody plants

HEBE ELLIPTICA
BT1 hebe
BT2 scrophulariaceae
BT1 ornamental woody plants

HEBEI
uf *china (hopei)*
BT1 china
BT2 east asia
BT3 asia

HEBELOMA
BT1 agaricales
NT1 hebeloma crustuliniforme
NT1 hebeloma cylindrosporum

HEBELOMA CRUSTULINIFORME
BT1 hebeloma
BT2 agaricales
BT1 mycorrhizal fungi
BT2 fungi

HEBELOMA CYLINDROSPORUM
HN from 1990
BT1 hebeloma
BT2 agaricales

HECTORITE
BT1 clay minerals
BT2 minerals

HEDEOMA
BT1 labiatae
NT1 hedeoma oblongifolia
NT1 hedeoma pulegioides

HEDEOMA OBLONGIFOLIA
BT1 hedeoma
BT2 labiatae

HEDEOMA PULEGIOIDES
BT1 essential oil plants
BT2 oil plants
BT1 hedeoma
BT2 labiatae

HEDERA
BT1 araliaceae
NT1 hedera colchica
NT1 hedera helix
NT1 hedera helix subsp. canariensis
NT1 hedera rhombea
NT1 hedera taurica
rt ivy

hedera canariensis
USE **hedera helix subsp. canariensis**

HEDERA COLCHICA
BT1 hedera
BT2 araliaceae

HEDERA HELIX
BT1 antibacterial plants

HEDERA HELIX *cont.*
BT1 antifungal plants
BT1 hedera
BT2 araliaceae
BT1 insecticidal plants
BT2 pesticidal plants
BT1 medicinal plants
BT1 molluscicidal plants
BT2 pesticidal plants
BT1 ornamental woody plants

HEDERA HELIX SUBSP. CANARIENSIS
uf *hedera canariensis*
BT1 hedera
BT2 araliaceae
BT1 ornamental woody plants

HEDERA RHOMBEA
BT1 hedera
BT2 araliaceae
BT1 ornamental woody plants

HEDERA TAURICA
BT1 hedera
BT2 araliaceae

HEDGE CUTTERS
BT1 cutters
BT2 farm machinery
BT3 machinery
BT1 tools
rt hedges

hedgehogs
USE **erinaceidae**

hedgerow intercropping
USE **alley cropping**

HEDGEROW PLANTING
BT1 planting

HEDGEROW PLANTS
uf *hedging plants*
rt hedges
rt plants

HEDGES
rt agroforestry systems
rt fences
rt fencing
rt hedge cutters
rt hedgerow plants
rt live fences
rt shelterbelts
rt windbreaks

hedging
(financial)
USE **futures trading**

hedging plants
USE **hedgerow plants**

HEDYA
BT1 tortricidae
BT2 lepidoptera
NT1 hedya nubiferana
rt olethreutes

HEDYA NUBIFERANA
uf *olethreutes variegana*
BT1 hedya
BT2 tortricidae
BT3 lepidoptera

HEDYCARYA
BT1 monimiaceae
NT1 hedycarya arborea

HEDYCARYA ARBOREA
BT1 hedycarya
BT2 monimiaceae

HEDYCHIUM
BT1 zingiberaceae
NT1 hedychium coronarium
NT1 hedychium spicatum

HEDYCHIUM CORONARIUM
BT1 antifungal plants
BT1 hedychium
BT2 zingiberaceae

HEDYCHIUM SPICATUM
BT1 hedychium
BT2 zingiberaceae
BT1 medicinal plants

hedylepta
USE **omiodes**

hedylepta indicata
USE **omiodes indicata**

HEDYOTIS
BT1 rubiaceae
NT1 hedyotis acutangula
NT1 hedyotis auricularia
NT1 hedyotis corymbosa

HEDYOTIS ACUTANGULA
BT1 hedyotis
BT2 rubiaceae

HEDYOTIS AURICULARIA
BT1 hedyotis
BT2 rubiaceae

HEDYOTIS CORYMBOSA
BT1 hedyotis
BT2 rubiaceae

HEDYSARUM
BT1 leguminosae
NT1 hedysarum alpinum
NT1 hedysarum branthii
NT1 hedysarum coronarium
NT1 hedysarum dasycarpum
NT1 hedysarum flavescens
NT1 hedysarum hedysaroides
NT1 hedysarum neglectum
NT1 hedysarum sachalinense
NT1 hedysarum ussuriense

HEDYSARUM ALPINUM
BT1 hedysarum
BT2 leguminosae

HEDYSARUM BRANTHII
BT1 hedysarum
BT2 leguminosae

hedysarum caucasicum
USE **hedysarum hedysaroides**

HEDYSARUM CORONARIUM
uf *sulla*
BT1 fodder legumes
BT2 fodder plants
BT2 legumes
BT1 hedysarum
BT2 leguminosae

HEDYSARUM DASYCARPUM
BT1 hedysarum
BT2 leguminosae

HEDYSARUM FLAVESCENS
BT1 hedysarum
BT2 leguminosae

HEDYSARUM HEDYSAROIDES
uf *hedysarum caucasicum*
BT1 hedysarum
BT2 leguminosae

HEDYSARUM NEGLECTUM
BT1 hedysarum
BT2 leguminosae

HEDYSARUM SACHALINENSE
BT1 hedysarum
BT2 leguminosae

HEDYSARUM USSURIENSE
BT1 hedysarum
BT2 leguminosae

HEIDSCHNUCKE
HN from 1990; previously "german heath"
uf *german heath*
BT1 sheep breeds
BT2 breeds

HEIFERS
BT1 cows
BT2 female animals
BT3 animals

HEIFERS *cont.*
BT1 young animals
BT2 animals
NT1 bred heifers

HEIGHT
uf *elevation*
BT1 dimensions
NT1 plant height
rt altitude
rt biometry
rt body measurements
rt dwarfism
rt height-weight ratio (agricola)
rt high altitude
rt increment

HEIGHT CLASSES
HN from 1990
rt mensuration

HEIGHT-WEIGHT RATIO (AGRICOLA)
BT1 ratios
BT1 reference standards (agricola)
BT2 standards
rt height
rt height-weight tables (agricola)
rt weight

HEIGHT-WEIGHT TABLES (AGRICOLA)
rt body measurements
rt height-weight ratio (agricola)

HEILONGJIANG
uf *china (heilungkiang)*
BT1 china
BT2 east asia
BT3 asia

HEIMIA
BT1 lythraceae
NT1 heimia salicifolia

HEIMIA SALICIFOLIA
BT1 heimia
BT2 lythraceae

HEINZ BODIES
rt erythrocytes
rt haemolytic anaemia

HEJAZI
HN from 1990
BT1 sheep breeds
BT2 breeds

HELA CELLS
BT1 cell lines
BT2 cell cultures
BT3 cultures

HELARCTOS
BT1 ursidae
BT2 fissipeda
BT3 carnivores
BT4 mammals
NT1 helarctos malayanus

HELARCTOS MALAYANUS
BT1 helarctos
BT2 ursidae
BT3 fissipeda
BT4 carnivores
BT5 mammals

HELENALIN
BT1 phytotoxins
BT2 toxins
BT1 sesquiterpenoid lactones
BT2 lactones
BT3 heterocyclic oxygen compounds
BT3 ketones
BT2 sesquiterpenoids
BT3 terpenoids
BT4 isoprenoids
BT5 lipids

HELENIUM
uf *cephalophora*
BT1 compositae
NT1 helenium amarum
NT1 helenium aromaticum
NT1 helenium autumnale
NT1 helenium hoopesii
NT1 helenium microcephalum
NT1 helenium puberulum
rt helenium s carlavirus

HELENIUM AMARUM
BT1 helenium
BT2 compositae
BT1 medicinal plants

HELENIUM AROMATICUM
BT1 helenium
BT2 compositae
BT1 insecticidal plants
BT2 pesticidal plants

HELENIUM AUTUMNALE
BT1 helenium
BT2 compositae

HELENIUM HOOPESII
BT1 helenium
BT2 compositae
BT1 poisonous plants

HELENIUM MICROCEPHALUM
BT1 helenium
BT2 compositae
BT1 medicinal plants

HELENIUM PUBERULUM
BT1 helenium
BT2 compositae

HELENIUM S CARLAVIRUS
HN from 1990
BT1 carlavirus group
BT2 plant viruses
BT3 plant pathogens
BT4 pathogens
rt helenium

HELIABRAVOA
BT1 cactaceae
NT1 heliabravoa chende

HELIABRAVOA CHENDE
BT1 heliabravoa
BT2 cactaceae
BT1 ornamental succulent plants
BT2 succulent plants

HELIANTHEMUM
BT1 cistaceae
NT1 helianthemum ledifolium

HELIANTHEMUM LEDIFOLIUM
BT1 helianthemum
BT2 cistaceae

HELIANTHUS
BT1 compositae
NT1 helianthus annuus
NT1 helianthus annuus var. ruderalis
NT1 helianthus argophyllus
NT1 helianthus bolanderi
NT1 helianthus ciliaris
NT1 helianthus debilis
NT1 helianthus exilis
NT1 helianthus petiolaris
NT1 helianthus pumilus
NT1 helianthus scaberrimus
NT1 helianthus tuberosus

HELIANTHUS ANNUUS
BT1 fodder plants
BT1 helianthus
BT2 compositae
BT1 insecticidal plants
BT2 pesticidal plants
BT1 medicinal plants
BT1 ornamental herbaceous plants
rt sunflowers

HELIANTHUS ANNUUS VAR. RUDERALIS
BT1 helianthus

HELIANTHUS ANNUUS VAR. RUDERALIS *cont.*
BT2 compositae

HELIANTHUS ARGOPHYLLUS
BT1 helianthus
BT2 compositae

HELIANTHUS BOLANDERI
BT1 helianthus
BT2 compositae

HELIANTHUS CILIARIS
BT1 helianthus
BT2 compositae

HELIANTHUS DEBILIS
BT1 helianthus
BT2 compositae
BT1 ornamental herbaceous plants

HELIANTHUS EXILIS
BT1 helianthus
BT2 compositae

HELIANTHUS PETIOLARIS
BT1 helianthus
BT2 compositae

HELIANTHUS PUMILUS
BT1 helianthus
BT2 compositae

HELIANTHUS SCABERRIMUS
BT1 helianthus
BT2 compositae
BT1 ornamental herbaceous plants

HELIANTHUS TUBEROSUS
BT1 fodder plants
BT1 helianthus
BT2 compositae
rt jerusalem artichokes

HELICELLA
BT1 helicidae
BT2 gastropoda
BT3 mollusca
NT1 helicella candaharica
NT1 helicella itala
rt cernuella

HELICELLA CANDAHARICA
BT1 helicella
BT2 helicidae
BT3 gastropoda
BT4 mollusca

HELICELLA ITALA
HN from 1990
BT1 helicella
BT2 helicidae
BT3 gastropoda
BT4 mollusca

helicella virgata
USE **cernuella virgata**

HELICHRYSUM
BT1 compositae
NT1 helichrysum arenarium
NT1 helichrysum bracteatum
NT1 helichrysum italicum
NT1 helichrysum plicatum

HELICHRYSUM ARENARIUM
BT1 helichrysum
BT2 compositae

HELICHRYSUM BRACTEATUM
BT1 helichrysum
BT2 compositae
BT1 ornamental herbaceous plants

HELICHRYSUM ITALICUM
BT1 essential oil plants
BT2 oil plants
BT1 helichrysum
BT2 compositae

HELICHRYSUM PLICATUM
BT1 helichrysum
BT2 compositae

HELICIDAE
BT1 gastropoda
BT2 mollusca
NT1 cepaea
NT2 cepaea hortensis
NT2 cepaea nemoralis
NT1 cernuella
NT2 cernuella cespitum
NT2 cernuella virgata
NT1 cochlicella
NT2 cochlicella acuta
NT2 cochlicella ventricosa
NT1 helicella
NT2 helicella candaharica
NT2 helicella itala
NT1 helix
NT2 helix aspersa
NT2 helix pomatia
NT1 monacha
NT2 monacha cartusiana
NT1 theba
NT2 theba pisana

HELICOBASIDIUM
BT1 auriculariales
NT1 helicobasidium purpureum
rt rhizoctonia

HELICOBASIDIUM PURPUREUM
uf *rhizoctonia crocorum*
uf *rhizoctonia violacea*
BT1 helicobasidium
BT2 auriculariales

HELICONIA
BT1 heliconiaceae
NT1 heliconia bihai
NT1 heliconia collinsiana
NT1 heliconia irrasa

HELICONIA BIHAI
BT1 heliconia
BT2 heliconiaceae

HELICONIA COLLINSIANA
BT1 heliconia
BT2 heliconiaceae
rt ornamental foliage plants

HELICONIA IRRASA
BT1 heliconia
BT2 heliconiaceae
rt ornamental foliage plants

HELICONIACEAE
NT1 heliconia
NT2 heliconia bihai
NT2 heliconia collinsiana
NT2 heliconia irrasa

HELICOPHAGELLA
BT1 sarcophagidae
BT2 diptera
NT1 helicophagella melanura
rt bellieria
rt sarcophaga

HELICOPHAGELLA MELANURA
uf *bellieria melanura*
uf *sarcophaga melanura*
BT1 helicophagella
BT2 sarcophagidae
BT3 diptera

HELICOPTERS
BT1 aircraft
rt aerial surveys
rt logging

HELICOSPORIDIUM
BT1 myxozoa
BT2 protozoa
NT1 helicosporidium parasiticum

HELICOSPORIDIUM PARASITICUM
BT1 helicosporidium
BT2 myxozoa
BT3 protozoa

HELICOTYLENCHUS
BT1 hoplolaimidae
BT2 nematoda
NT1 helicotylenchus dihystera
NT1 helicotylenchus erythrinae

HELICOTYLENCHUS *cont.*
NT1 helicotylenchus multicinctus
NT1 helicotylenchus pseudorobustus

HELICOTYLENCHUS DIHYSTERA
BT1 helicotylenchus
BT2 hoplolaimidae
BT3 nematoda

HELICOTYLENCHUS ERYTHRINAE
BT1 helicotylenchus
BT2 hoplolaimidae
BT3 nematoda

HELICOTYLENCHUS MULTICINCTUS
BT1 helicotylenchus
BT2 hoplolaimidae
BT3 nematoda

HELICOTYLENCHUS PSEUDOROBUSTUS
BT1 helicotylenchus
BT2 hoplolaimidae
BT3 nematoda

HELICOVERPA
BT1 noctuidae
BT2 lepidoptera
NT1 helicoverpa armigera
NT1 helicoverpa assulta
NT1 helicoverpa punctigera
NT1 helicoverpa zea
rt heliothis

HELICOVERPA ARMIGERA
uf *heliothis armigera*
BT1 helicoverpa
BT2 noctuidae
BT3 lepidoptera

HELICOVERPA ASSULTA
uf *chloridea assulta*
uf *heliothis assulta*
BT1 helicoverpa
BT2 noctuidae
BT3 lepidoptera

HELICOVERPA PUNCTIGERA
uf *heliothis punctigera*
BT1 helicoverpa
BT2 noctuidae
BT3 lepidoptera

HELICOVERPA ZEA
uf *heliothis zea*
BT1 helicoverpa
BT2 noctuidae
BT3 lepidoptera

HELICTERES
BT1 sterculiaceae
NT1 helicteres isora

HELICTERES ISORA
BT1 helicteres
BT2 sterculiaceae
BT1 medicinal plants

HELICTOTRICHON
BT1 gramineae
NT1 helictotrichon sempervirens

helictotrichon pratensis
USE **avenula pratensis**

helictotrichon pubescens
USE **avenula pubescens**

HELICTOTRICHON SEMPERVIRENS
BT1 helictotrichon
BT2 gramineae

HELIETTA
BT1 rutaceae
NT1 helietta parviflora

HELIETTA PARVIFLORA
BT1 helietta
BT2 rutaceae

HELIGMONELLIDAE
BT1 nematoda
NT1 nippostrongylus

HELIGMONELLIDAE *cont.*
NT2 nippostrongylus brasiliensis
rt animal parasitic nematodes

HELIGMOSOMIDAE
BT1 nematoda
NT1 heligmosomoides
NT2 heligmosomoides polygyrus
NT1 heligmosomum
rt animal parasitic nematodes

HELIGMOSOMOIDES
uf *nematospiroides*
BT1 heligmosomidae
BT2 nematoda
NT1 heligmosomoides polygyrus

HELIGMOSOMOIDES POLYGYRUS
uf *nematospiroides dubius*
BT1 heligmosomoides
BT2 heligmosomidae
BT3 nematoda

HELIGMOSOMUM
BT1 heligmosomidae
BT2 nematoda

HELIOCHEILUS
BT1 noctuidae
BT2 lepidoptera
NT1 heliocheilus albipunctella
rt raghuva

HELIOCHEILUS ALBIPUNCTELLA
uf *raghuva albipunctella*
BT1 heliocheilus
BT2 noctuidae
BT3 lepidoptera

HELIOCIDARIS
BT1 echinoidea
BT2 echinodermata

HELIOMYCIN
BT1 antibiotics

HELIOPSIS
BT1 compositae
NT1 heliopsis helianthoides

HELIOPSIS HELIANTHOIDES
uf *heliopsis scabra*
BT1 heliopsis
BT2 compositae
BT1 ornamental herbaceous plants

heliopsis scabra
USE **heliopsis helianthoides**

HELIOTHIS
uf *chloridea*
BT1 noctuidae
BT2 lepidoptera
NT1 heliothis maritima
NT1 heliothis peltigera
NT1 heliothis subflexa
NT1 heliothis virescens
NT1 heliothis viriplaca
rt helicoverpa

heliothis armigera
USE **helicoverpa armigera**

heliothis assulta
USE **helicoverpa assulta**

heliothis dipsacea
USE **heliothis viriplaca**

HELIOTHIS MARITIMA
uf *chloridea maritima*
BT1 heliothis
BT2 noctuidae
BT3 lepidoptera

HELIOTHIS PELTIGERA
BT1 heliothis
BT2 noctuidae
BT3 lepidoptera

heliothis punctigera
USE **helicoverpa punctigera**

HELIOTHIS SUBFLEXA
BT1 heliothis
BT2 noctuidae
BT3 lepidoptera

HELIOTHIS VIRESCENS
BT1 heliothis
BT2 noctuidae
BT3 lepidoptera

HELIOTHIS VIRIPLACA
uf *chloridea dipsacea*
uf *chloridea viriplaca*
uf *heliothis dipsacea*
BT1 heliothis
BT2 noctuidae
BT3 lepidoptera

heliothis zea
USE **helicoverpa zea**

HELIOTHRIPS
BT1 thripidae
BT2 thysanoptera
NT1 heliothrips haemorrhoidalis

HELIOTHRIPS HAEMORRHOIDALIS
BT1 heliothrips
BT2 thripidae
BT3 thysanoptera

HELIOTROPISM
BT1 tropisms
BT2 movement
BT2 plant physiology
BT3 physiology
BT2 responses
rt phototropism
rt solar radiation

HELIOTROPIUM
BT1 boraginaceae
NT1 heliotropium arbainense
NT1 heliotropium arborescens
NT1 heliotropium curassavicum
NT1 heliotropium eichwaldii
NT1 heliotropium europaeum
NT1 heliotropium indicum
NT1 heliotropium maris-mortui
NT1 heliotropium rotundifolium

HELIOTROPIUM ARBAINENSE
BT1 heliotropium
BT2 boraginaceae

HELIOTROPIUM ARBORESCENS
uf *heliotropium peruvianum*
BT1 heliotropium
BT2 boraginaceae
BT1 ornamental herbaceous plants

HELIOTROPIUM CURASSAVICUM
BT1 heliotropium
BT2 boraginaceae

HELIOTROPIUM EICHWALDII
BT1 heliotropium
BT2 boraginaceae

HELIOTROPIUM EUROPAEUM
BT1 antibacterial plants
BT1 heliotropium
BT2 boraginaceae

HELIOTROPIUM INDICUM
BT1 heliotropium
BT2 boraginaceae

HELIOTROPIUM MARIS-MORTUI
BT1 heliotropium
BT2 boraginaceae

heliotropium peruvianum
USE **heliotropium arborescens**

HELIOTROPIUM ROTUNDIFOLIUM
BT1 heliotropium
BT2 boraginaceae

HELIPTERUM
BT1 compositae
rt ornamental herbaceous plants

HELISOMA
BT1 planorbidae
BT2 gastropoda
BT3 mollusca
NT1 helisoma duryi
NT1 helisoma trivolvis

HELISOMA DURYI
BT1 helisoma
BT2 planorbidae
BT3 gastropoda
BT4 mollusca

HELISOMA TRIVOLVIS
BT1 helisoma
BT2 planorbidae
BT3 gastropoda
BT4 mollusca

HELIUM
BT1 noble gases
BT2 inert gases
BT3 gases
BT2 nonmetallic elements
BT3 elements

HELIX
BT1 helicidae
BT2 gastropoda
BT3 mollusca
NT1 helix aspersa
NT1 helix pomatia
rt cepaea

HELIX ASPERSA
BT1 helix
BT2 helicidae
BT3 gastropoda
BT4 mollusca

helix hortensis
USE **cepaea hortensis**

helix nemoralis
USE **cepaea nemoralis**

HELIX POMATIA
BT1 helix
BT2 helicidae
BT3 gastropoda
BT4 mollusca

HELLEBORUS
BT1 ranunculaceae
NT1 helleborus abchasicus
NT1 helleborus cyclophyllus
NT1 helleborus dumetorum
NT1 helleborus foetidus
NT1 helleborus lividus
NT1 helleborus lividus subsp. corsicus
NT1 helleborus multifidus
NT1 helleborus niger
NT1 helleborus odorus
NT1 helleborus orientalis
NT1 helleborus purpurascens
NT1 helleborus viridis

HELLEBORUS ABCHASICUS
BT1 helleborus
BT2 ranunculaceae
BT1 ornamental herbaceous plants

helleborus caucasicus
USE **helleborus orientalis**

helleborus corsicus
USE **helleborus lividus subsp. corsicus**

HELLEBORUS CYCLOPHYLLUS
BT1 helleborus
BT2 ranunculaceae

HELLEBORUS DUMETORUM
BT1 helleborus
BT2 ranunculaceae

HELLEBORUS FOETIDUS
BT1 helleborus
BT2 ranunculaceae
BT1 ornamental herbaceous plants

HELLEBORUS LIVIDUS
BT1 helleborus
BT2 ranunculaceae
BT1 ornamental herbaceous plants

HELLEBORUS LIVIDUS SUBSP. CORSICUS
uf *helleborus corsicus*
BT1 helleborus
BT2 ranunculaceae

HELLEBORUS MULTIFIDUS
BT1 helleborus
BT2 ranunculaceae

HELLEBORUS NIGER
BT1 helleborus
BT2 ranunculaceae
BT1 ornamental herbaceous plants

HELLEBORUS ODORUS
BT1 helleborus
BT2 ranunculaceae

HELLEBORUS ORIENTALIS
uf *helleborus caucasicus*
BT1 helleborus
BT2 ranunculaceae
BT1 ornamental herbaceous plants

HELLEBORUS PURPURASCENS
BT1 helleborus
BT2 ranunculaceae
BT1 ornamental herbaceous plants

HELLEBORUS VIRIDIS
BT1 helleborus
BT2 ranunculaceae
BT1 ornamental herbaceous plants

HELLULA
BT1 pyralidae
BT2 lepidoptera
NT1 hellula undalis
rt oebia

HELLULA UNDALIS
uf *oebia undalis*
BT1 hellula
BT2 pyralidae
BT3 lepidoptera

HELMINTH INSECTICIDES
BT1 insecticides
BT2 pesticides
BT1 microbial pesticides
BT2 pesticides
NT1 neoaplectana carpocapsae
NT1 romanomermis culicivorax
rt entomophilic nematodes

HELMINTH LARVAE
BT1 helminths
BT2 parasites
BT1 larvae
BT2 developmental stages
NT1 acanthocephalan larvae
NT2 acanthellae
NT2 acanthors
NT2 cystacanths
NT1 cestode larvae
NT2 coracidia
NT2 oncospheres
NT1 digenean larvae
NT2 cercariae
NT2 diplostomula
NT2 metacercariae
NT2 miracidia
NT2 rediae
NT2 schistosomula
NT2 sporocysts
NT1 monogenean larvae
NT2 oncomiracidia
NT1 nematode larvae
NT2 microfilariae

HELMINTH OVA
BT1 helminths
BT2 parasites

HELMINTH OVA *cont.*
BT1 ova
BT2 gametes
BT2 germ cells
BT3 cells

HELMINTHIA
BT1 compositae

helminthia echioides
USE **picris echioides**

HELMINTHOLOGY
BT1 zoology
BT2 biology
NT1 medical helminthology
NT1 nematology
NT1 veterinary helminthology
rt agricultural sciences
rt helminths

helminthology, medical
USE **medical helminthology**

helminthology, veterinary
USE **veterinary helminthology**

HELMINTHOSES
BT1 parasitoses
BT2 diseases
NT1 cestode infections
NT2 cysticercosis
NT1 nematode infections
NT2 ascariasis
NT2 ascaridiosis
NT2 elephantiasis
NT2 filariasis
NT3 onchocerciasis
NT2 heterakidosis
NT2 larva migrans
NT3 visceral larva migrans
NT1 trematode infections
NT2 fascioliasis
NT2 schistosomiasis
rt helminths

HELMINTHOSPORIUM
BT1 deuteromycotina
NT1 helminthosporium solani
NT1 helminthosporium tucumense
rt bipolaris
rt cochliobolus
rt deightoniella
rt drechslera
rt magnaporthe
rt pleospora
rt pyrenophora
rt setosphaeria

helminthosporium atrovirens
USE **helminthosporium solani**

helminthosporium avenae
USE **pyrenophora avenae**

helminthosporium biseptatum
USE **drechslera biseptata**

helminthosporium bromi
USE **pyrenophora bromi**

helminthosporium carbonum
USE **cochliobolus carbonum**

helminthosporium cynodontis
USE **cochliobolus cynodontis**

helminthosporium dictyoides
USE **pyrenophora dictyoides**

helminthosporium dictyoides var. phlei
USE **drechslera phlei**

helminthosporium gossypii
USE **drechslera gossypii**

helminthosporium gramineum
USE **pyrenophora graminea**

helminthosporium halodes
USE **setosphaeria rostrata**

helminthosporium hawaiiense
USE **cochliobolus hawaiiensis**

helminthosporium heveae
USE **bipolaris heveae**

helminthosporium incurvatum
USE **bipolaris incurvata**

helminthosporium leucostylum
USE **cochliobolus nodulosus**

helminthosporium maydis
USE **cochliobolus heterostrophus**

helminthosporium monoceras
USE **setosphaeria monoceras**

helminthosporium nodulosum
USE **cochliobolus nodulosus**

helminthosporium oryzae
USE **cochliobolus miyabeanus**

helminthosporium papaveris
USE **pleospora papaveracea**

helminthosporium pedicellatum
USE **setosphaeria pedicellata**

helminthosporium portulacae
USE **drechslera portulacae**

helminthosporium rostratum
USE **setosphaeria rostrata**

helminthosporium sacchari
USE **bipolaris sacchari**

helminthosporium sativum
USE **cochliobolus sativus**

helminthosporium setariae
USE **cochliobolus setariae**

helminthosporium siccans
USE **pyrenophora lolii**

helminthosporium sigmoideum
USE **magnaporthe salvinii**

HELMINTHOSPORIUM SOLANI
uf *helminthosporium atrovirens*
uf *spondylocladium atrovirens*
BT1 helminthosporium
BT2 deuteromycotina

helminthosporium sorghicola
USE **bipolaris sorghicola**

helminthosporium sorokinianum
USE **cochliobolus sativus**

helminthosporium spiciferum
USE **cochliobolus spicifer**

helminthosporium stenospilum
USE **bipolaris stenospila**

helminthosporium teres
USE **pyrenophora teres**

helminthosporium tetramera
USE **cochliobolus spicifer**

helminthosporium torulosum
USE **deightoniella torulosa**

helminthosporium triseptatum
USE **drechslera triseptata**

helminthosporium tritici-repentis
USE **pyrenophora tritici-repentis**

helminthosporium tucumanensis
USE **glomerella tucumanensis**

HELMINTHOSPORIUM TUCUMENSE
BT1 helminthosporium
BT2 deuteromycotina

helminthosporium turcicum
USE **setosphaeria turcica**

helminthosporium vagans
USE **drechslera poae**

helminthosporium victoriae
USE **cochliobolus victoriae**

HELMINTHOSPOROSIDE
BT1 mycotoxins
BT2 toxins

HELMINTHS
uf *parasitic worms*
BT1 parasites
NT1 filariids
NT1 helminth larvae
NT2 acanthocephalan larvae
NT3 acanthellae
NT3 acanthors
NT3 cystacanths
NT2 cestode larvae
NT3 coracidia
NT3 oncospheres
NT2 digenean larvae
NT3 cercariae
NT3 diplostomula
NT3 metacercariae
NT3 miracidia
NT3 rediae
NT3 schistosomula
NT3 sporocysts
NT2 monogenean larvae
NT3 oncomiracidia
NT2 nematode larvae
NT3 microfilariae
NT1 helminth ova
NT1 hookworms
NT1 liver flukes
NT1 lungworms
rt acanthocephala
rt animal parasitic nematodes
rt eucestoda
rt helminthology
rt helminthoses
rt medical helminthology
rt monogenea
rt nematoda
rt nematomorpha
rt parasitism
rt platyhelminthes
rt trematoda
rt veterinary helminthology

HELOBDELLA
BT1 glossiphoniidae
BT2 hirudinea
BT3 annelida
NT1 helobdella stagnalis

HELOBDELLA STAGNALIS
BT1 helobdella
BT2 glossiphoniidae
BT3 hirudinea
BT4 annelida

HELOPELTIS
BT1 miridae
BT2 heteroptera
NT1 helopeltis antonii
NT1 helopeltis schoutedeni
NT1 helopeltis theivora

HELOPELTIS ANTONII
BT1 helopeltis
BT2 miridae
BT3 heteroptera

HELOPELTIS SCHOUTEDENI
BT1 helopeltis
BT2 miridae
BT3 heteroptera

HELOPELTIS THEIVORA
BT1 helopeltis
BT2 miridae
BT3 heteroptera

HELOTIALES
NT1 amorphotheca
NT2 amorphotheca resinae
NT1 ascocalyx
NT1 blumeriella
NT2 blumeriella jaapii
NT1 crumenula
NT1 crumenulopsis
NT2 crumenulopsis pinicola
NT2 crumenulopsis sororia
NT1 dasyscypha
NT1 diplocarpon
NT2 diplocarpon earlianum

HELOTIALES *cont.*
NT2 diplocarpon mespili
NT2 diplocarpon rosae
NT1 drepanopeziza
NT2 drepanopeziza populorum
NT2 drepanopeziza punctiformis
NT2 drepanopeziza ribis
NT1 fabraea
NT1 gremmeniella
NT2 gremmeniella abietina
NT1 grovesinia
NT2 grovesinia pyramidalis
NT1 lachnellula
NT1 leptotrochila
NT1 monilinia
NT2 monilinia fructicola
NT2 monilinia fructigena
NT2 monilinia laxa
NT2 monilinia linhartiana
NT1 ovulinia
NT2 ovulinia azaleae
NT1 pezicula
NT2 pezicula alba
NT2 pezicula corticola
NT2 pezicula malicorticis
NT2 pezicula populi
NT1 phacidium
NT2 phacidium infestans
NT1 pseudopeziza
NT2 pseudopeziza medicaginis
NT2 pseudopeziza trifolii
NT1 pyrenopeziza
NT2 pyrenopeziza brassicae
NT1 sclerotinia
NT2 sclerotinia borealis
NT2 sclerotinia bulborum
NT2 sclerotinia convoluta
NT2 sclerotinia draytonii
NT2 sclerotinia fuckeliana
NT2 sclerotinia homoeocarpa
NT2 sclerotinia minor
NT2 sclerotinia narcissicola
NT2 sclerotinia sclerotiorum
NT2 sclerotinia squamosa
NT2 sclerotinia trifoliorum
NT2 sclerotinia vaccinii-corymbosi
NT1 stromatinia
NT2 stromatinia gladioli
NT1 tapesia
NT1 trichoscyphella
NT2 trichoscyphella willkommii
rt fungi

HELVELLA
BT1 pezizales
NT1 helvella esculenta

HELVELLA ESCULENTA
BT1 edible fungi
BT2 fungi
BT2 vegetables
BT1 helvella
BT2 pezizales

HEMADSORPTION REACTION
BF haemadsorption reaction

HEMAGGLUTINATION
BF haemagglutination
NT1 passive hemagglutination
rt hemagglutination inhibition test
rt hemagglutination tests
rt hemagglutinins

HEMAGGLUTINATION INHIBITION TEST
BF haemagglutination inhibition test
BT1 hemagglutination tests
rt hemagglutination

HEMAGGLUTINATION TESTS
BF haemagglutination tests
NT1 hemagglutination inhibition test
rt hemagglutination

HEMAGGLUTININS
BF haemagglutinins
NT1 viral hemagglutinins
rt hemagglutination

HEMAGGLUTININS *cont.*
rt phytohemagglutinins

HEMARTHRIA
BT1 gramineae
NT1 hemarthria altissima
NT1 hemarthria sibirica

HEMARTHRIA ALTISSIMA
BT1 hemarthria
BT2 gramineae

HEMARTHRIA SIBIRICA
BT1 hemarthria
BT2 gramineae

HEMATITE
BF haematite

HEMATOCRIT
BF haematocrit

HEMATOLOGIC AGENTS
BF haematologic agents
NT1 hypolipemic agents

HEMATOLOGY
BF haematology

HEMATOMA
BF haematoma
BT1 hemorrhage

HEMATOPHAGOUS ARTHROPODS
BF haematophagous arthropods
NT1 hematophagous insects
rt hematophagy
rt host-seeking behavior

HEMATOPHAGOUS INSECTS
BF haematophagous insects
BT1 hematophagous arthropods
rt hematophagy

HEMATOPHAGY
BF haematophagy
rt hematophagous arthropods
rt hematophagous insects

HEMATOPOIESIS
BF haematopoiesis

HEMATOPOIETIC NECROSIS VIRUS
BF haematopoietic necrosis virus

HEMATURIA
BF haematuria

HEME
BF haem

HEME OXYGENASE (DECYCLIZING)
(ec 1.14.99.3)
uf *haem oxygenase (decyclizing)*
BT1 oxygenases
BT2 oxidoreductases
BT3 enzymes

HEMEL
BT1 chemosterilants
BT2 sterilants

HEMEROBIIDAE
BT1 neuroptera
NT1 hemerobius
NT1 micromus
NT2 micromus tasmaniae

HEMEROBIUS
BT1 hemerobiidae
BT2 neuroptera

HEMEROCALLIS
BT1 liliaceae
NT1 hemerocallis fulva
NT1 hemerocallis lilioasphodelus
NT1 hemerocallis minor

hemerocallis flava
USE **hemerocallis lilioasphodelus**

HEMEROCALLIS FULVA
BT1 hemerocallis
BT2 liliaceae
BT1 ornamental herbaceous plants

HEMEROCALLIS LILIOASPHODELUS
uf *hemerocallis flava*
BT1 hemerocallis
BT2 liliaceae
BT1 ornamental herbaceous plants

HEMEROCALLIS MINOR
BT1 hemerocallis
BT2 liliaceae
BT1 ornamental herbaceous plants

hemerocampa
USE **orgyia**

hemerocampa leucostigma
USE **orgyia leucostigma**

hemerocampa pseudotsugata
USE **orgyia pseudotsugata**

HEMIBERLESIA
BT1 diaspididae
BT2 coccoidea
BT3 sternorrhyncha
BT4 homoptera
NT1 hemiberlesia lataniae
NT1 hemiberlesia rapax

HEMIBERLESIA LATANIAE
BT1 hemiberlesia
BT2 diaspididae
BT3 coccoidea
BT4 sternorrhyncha
BT5 homoptera

HEMIBERLESIA RAPAX
BT1 hemiberlesia
BT2 diaspididae
BT3 coccoidea
BT4 sternorrhyncha
BT5 homoptera

HEMICELLULOSES
BT1 polysaccharides
BT2 carbohydrates
rt wood hemicellulose extract

HEMICHEYLETIA
BT1 cheyletidae
BT2 prostigmata
BT3 acari

HEMICRICONEMOIDES
BT1 criconematidae
BT2 nematoda
NT1 hemicriconemoides chitwoodi
NT1 hemicriconemoides cocophilus
NT1 hemicriconemoides mangiferae

HEMICRICONEMOIDES CHITWOODI
BT1 hemicriconemoides
BT2 criconematidae
BT3 nematoda

HEMICRICONEMOIDES COCOPHILUS
HN from 1990
BT1 hemicriconemoides
BT2 criconematidae
BT3 nematoda

HEMICRICONEMOIDES MANGIFERAE
BT1 hemicriconemoides
BT2 criconematidae
BT3 nematoda

HEMICYCLIOPHORA
BT1 criconematidae
BT2 nematoda
NT1 hemicycliophora arenaria

HEMICYCLIOPHORA ARENARIA
BT1 hemicycliophora
BT2 criconematidae
BT3 nematoda

HEMIDACTYLUS
BT1 gekkonidae
BT2 sauria
BT3 reptiles
NT1 hemidactylus flaviviridis

HEMIDACTYLUS FLAVIVIRIDIS
BT1 hemidactylus
BT2 gekkonidae
BT3 sauria
BT4 reptiles

HEMIDESMUS
BT1 periplocaceae
NT1 hemidesmus indicus

HEMIDESMUS INDICUS
BT1 antibacterial plants
BT1 hemidesmus
BT2 periplocaceae
BT1 medicinal plants

HEMIECHINUS
BT1 erinaceidae
BT2 insectivores
BT3 mammals
NT1 hemiechinus auritus

HEMIECHINUS AURITUS
BT1 hemiechinus
BT2 erinaceidae
BT3 insectivores
BT4 mammals

HEMILEIA
BT1 uredinales
NT1 hemileia vastatrix

HEMILEIA VASTATRIX
BT1 hemileia
BT2 uredinales

HEMILEUCA
BT1 saturniidae
BT2 lepidoptera
NT1 hemileuca oliviae

HEMILEUCA OLIVIAE
BT1 hemileuca
BT2 saturniidae
BT3 lepidoptera

HEMILUCILIA
BT1 calliphoridae
BT2 diptera
NT1 hemilucilia semidiaphana

hemilucilia flavifacies
USE **hemilucilia semidiaphana**

HEMILUCILIA SEMIDIAPHANA
uf *hemilucilia flavifacies*
BT1 hemilucilia
BT2 calliphoridae
BT3 diptera

HEMILUMINESCENCE
BT1 luminescence
BT2 radiation

HEMIONITIDACEAE
NT1 pityrogramma
NT2 pityrogramma austroamericana
NT2 pityrogramma calomelanos
NT2 pityrogramma chrysophylla
NT2 pityrogramma lehmannii

HEMIPTARSENUS
BT1 eulophidae
BT2 hymenoptera

HEMIPTERA
uf *bugs*
rt heteroptera
rt homoptera

HEMIRAMPHIDAE
BT1 cyprinodontiformes
BT2 osteichthyes
BT3 fishes

HEMIRAMPHIDAE *cont.*
NT1 hemiramphus
NT2 hemiramphus brachynopterus
NT1 hyporhamphus

HEMIRAMPHUS
BT1 hemiramphidae
BT2 cyprinodontiformes
BT3 osteichthyes
BT4 fishes
NT1 hemiramphus brachynopterus

HEMIRAMPHUS BRACHYNOPTERUS
BT1 hemiramphus
BT2 hemiramphidae
BT3 cyprinodontiformes
BT4 osteichthyes
BT5 fishes

hemisia
USE **centris**

HEMITARSONEMUS
BT1 tarsonemidae
BT2 prostigmata
BT3 acari
rt polyphagotarsonemus

hemitarsonemus latus
USE **polyphagotarsonemus latus**

HEMIURIDAE
BT1 digenea
BT2 trematoda
NT1 derogenes
NT2 derogenes ruber
NT1 dinurus
NT1 halipegus
NT1 lecithaster
NT1 lecithocladium
NT1 sterrhurus

HEMIZYGOSITY
BT1 gene dosage
BT2 genetics
BT3 biology
rt genes

HEMOCHROMATOSIS
BF haemochromatosis

HEMOCYTES
HN from 1990 (invertebrate blood cells)
BF haemocytes

HEMODIALYSIS
BF haemodialysis

HEMODYNAMICS
BF haemodynamics

HEMOGLOBIN
BF haemoglobin
NT1 hemoglobin a1
NT1 hemoglobin a2
rt hemoglobin value
rt hemoglobinuria

HEMOGLOBIN A1
BF haemoglobin a1
BT1 hemoglobin

HEMOGLOBIN A2
BF haemoglobin a2
BT1 hemoglobin

HEMOGLOBIN VALUE
BF haemoglobin value
rt hemoglobin

HEMOGLOBINURIA
BF haemoglobinuria
rt hemoglobin

HEMOLYMPH
BF haemolymph

HEMOLYMPH NODES
HN from 1990
BF haemolymph nodes

HEMOLYSINS
BF haemolysins
rt hemolysis

HEMOLYSIS
BF haemolysis
rt hemolysins
rt hemolytic anemia
rt immune hemolysis

HEMOLYTIC ANEMIA
BF haemolytic anaemia
BT1 anemia
rt hemolysis

HEMOPEXIN
BF haemopexin

HEMOPHILIA
BF haemophilia

HEMORRHAGE
BF haemorrhage
NT1 hematoma
rt fatty liver hemorrhagic syndrome
rt hemorrhagic diathesis
rt hemorrhagic enteritis
rt hemorrhagic septicemia

HEMORRHAGIC DIATHESIS
BF haemorrhagic diathesis
rt hemorrhage

HEMORRHAGIC ENTERITIS
BF haemorrhagic enteritis
rt hemorrhage
rt hemorrhagic enteritis virus

HEMORRHAGIC ENTERITIS VIRUS
BF haemorrhagic enteritis virus
rt hemorrhagic enteritis

HEMORRHAGIC SEPTICEMIA
BF haemorrhagic septicaemia
BT1 septicemia
rt hemorrhage
rt hemorrhagic septicemia virus

HEMORRHAGIC SEPTICEMIA VIRUS
BF haemorrhagic septicaemia virus
rt hemorrhagic septicemia

HEMORRHOIDS
BF haemorrhoids

HEMOSIDERIN
BF haemosiderin
rt hemosiderosis

HEMOSIDEROSIS
BF haemosiderosis
rt hemosiderin

HEMOSTASIS
BF haemostasis

HEMP
BT1 plant fibres
BT2 fibres
rt cannabis sativa
rt crotalaria juncea
rt furcraea
rt hemp harvesters
rt hibiscus cannabinus
rt musa textilis
rt phormium tenax
rt sansevieria
rt sida rhombifolia

HEMP HARVESTERS
uf *harvesters, hemp*
BT1 harvesters
BT2 farm machinery
BT3 machinery
rt hemp

hemp, manila
USE **musa textilis**

HEMPA
BT1 carcinogens
BT2 toxic substances

HEMPA *cont.*
BT1 chemosterilants
BT2 sterilants
BT1 phosphoric triamides
BT2 amides
BT3 organic nitrogen compounds
BT2 organophosphorus compounds
BT1 solvents

hen eggs
USE **eggs**

HEN FEEDING
BT1 poultry feeding
BT2 livestock feeding
BT3 animal feeding
BT4 feeding
rt hens
rt poultry farming
rt turkey hen feeding

HENAN
uf *honan*
BT1 china
BT2 east asia
BT3 asia

henbane
USE **hyoscyamus niger**

HENBANE MOSAIC POTYVIRUS
HN from 1990
BT1 potyvirus group
BT2 plant viruses
BT3 plant pathogens
BT4 pathogens
rt hyoscyamus niger

HENDERSONULA
BT1 deuteromycotina
rt nattrassia

hendersonula toruloidea
USE **nattrassia mangiferae**

HENEQUEN
rt agave fourcroydes

HENNEGUYA
BT1 myxozoa
BT2 protozoa
NT1 henneguya cerebralis
NT1 henneguya creplini
NT1 henneguya exilis
NT1 henneguya ophiocephali
NT1 henneguya oviperda
NT1 henneguya psorospermica
NT1 henneguya salminicola
NT1 henneguya waltairensis

HENNEGUYA CEREBRALIS
BT1 henneguya
BT2 myxozoa
BT3 protozoa

HENNEGUYA CREPLINI
BT1 henneguya
BT2 myxozoa
BT3 protozoa

HENNEGUYA EXILIS
BT1 henneguya
BT2 myxozoa
BT3 protozoa

HENNEGUYA OPHIOCEPHALI
BT1 henneguya
BT2 myxozoa
BT3 protozoa

HENNEGUYA OVIPERDA
BT1 henneguya
BT2 myxozoa
BT3 protozoa

HENNEGUYA PSOROSPERMICA
BT1 henneguya
BT2 myxozoa
BT3 protozoa

HENNEGUYA SALMINICOLA
BT1 henneguya
BT2 myxozoa

HENNEGUYA SALMINICOLA *cont.*
BT3 protozoa

HENNEGUYA WALTAIRENSIS
BT1 henneguya
BT2 myxozoa
BT3 protozoa

henosepilachna
USE **epilachna**

henosepilachna vigintioctopunctata
USE **epilachna vigintioctopunctata**

HENRIQUESIA
HN from 1990
BT1 rhytismatales
NT1 henriquesia coccifera
rt macroallantina

HENRIQUESIA COCCIFERA
HN from 1990
uf *macroallantina coccifera*
BT1 henriquesia
BT2 rhytismatales

HENS
uf *laying hens*
BT1 female animals
BT2 animals
rt fowls
rt hen feeding

HEPADNAVIRIDAE
BT1 viruses
NT1 hepatitis b virus

HEPARIN
uf *heparin sulfate*
uf *heparin sulphate*
BT1 acid mucopolysaccharides
BT2 mucopolysaccharides
BT3 polysaccharides
BT4 carbohydrates
BT1 anticoagulants
BT2 haematologic agents
BT3 drugs

heparin sulfate
USE **heparin**

heparin sulphate
USE **heparin**

HEPATECTOMY
uf *liver removal*
BT1 surgical operations
rt liver

HEPATICA
BT1 ranunculaceae

hepatics
USE **liverworts**

HEPATITIS
BT1 liver diseases
BT2 digestive system diseases
BT3 organic diseases
BT4 diseases
NT1 reye's syndrome
NT1 viral hepatitis
rt duck hepatitis virus

HEPATITIS A VIRUS
BT1 enterovirus
BT2 picornaviridae
BT3 viruses

HEPATITIS B VIRUS
BT1 hepadnaviridae
BT2 viruses

hepatitis, viral
USE **viral hepatitis**

HEPATOCYSTIS
BT1 apicomplexa
BT2 protozoa
NT1 hepatocystis brayi
NT1 hepatocystis kochi
NT1 hepatocystis malayensis
NT1 hepatocystis oriheli

HEPATOCYSTIS BRAYI
BT1 hepatocystis
BT2 apicomplexa
BT3 protozoa

HEPATOCYSTIS KOCHI
BT1 hepatocystis
BT2 apicomplexa
BT3 protozoa

HEPATOCYSTIS MALAYENSIS
BT1 hepatocystis
BT2 apicomplexa
BT3 protozoa

HEPATOCYSTIS ORIHELI
BT1 hepatocystis
BT2 apicomplexa
BT3 protozoa

hepatocytes
USE **liver cells**

HEPATOLENTICULAR DEGENERATION
uf *wilson's disease*
BT1 congenital abnormalities
BT2 abnormalities
BT1 degeneration
BT1 liver diseases
BT2 digestive system diseases
BT3 organic diseases
BT4 diseases
BT1 metabolic disorders
BT2 animal disorders
BT3 disorders
rt copper
rt nervous system diseases

HEPATOMA
BT1 liver diseases
BT2 digestive system diseases
BT3 organic diseases
BT4 diseases
BT1 neoplasms
BT2 diseases

HEPATOMEGALY
uf *liver enlargement*
BT1 liver diseases
BT2 digestive system diseases
BT3 organic diseases
BT4 diseases

HEPATOPANCREAS
BT1 glands (animal)
BT2 body parts
BT2 glands
rt liver
rt pancreas

HEPATOTOXINS
BT1 toxins
rt aflatoxins
rt liver

HEPATOZOON
BT1 apicomplexa
BT2 protozoa
NT1 hepatozoon canis
NT1 hepatozoon domerguei
NT1 hepatozoon erhardovae
NT1 hepatozoon griseisciuri
NT1 hepatozoon sylvatici
NT1 hepatozoon triatomae
NT1 hepatozoon tupinambis

HEPATOZOON CANIS
BT1 hepatozoon
BT2 apicomplexa
BT3 protozoa

HEPATOZOON DOMERGUEI
BT1 hepatozoon
BT2 apicomplexa
BT3 protozoa

HEPATOZOON ERHARDOVAE
BT1 hepatozoon
BT2 apicomplexa
BT3 protozoa

HEPATOZOON GRISEISCIURI
BT1 hepatozoon
BT2 apicomplexa

HEPATOZOON GRISEISCIURI *cont.*
BT3 protozoa

HEPATOZOON SYLVATICI
BT1 hepatozoon
BT2 apicomplexa
BT3 protozoa

HEPATOZOON TRIATOMAE
BT1 hepatozoon
BT2 apicomplexa
BT3 protozoa

HEPATOZOON TUPINAMBIS
BT1 hepatozoon
BT2 apicomplexa
BT3 protozoa

HEPIALIDAE
BT1 lepidoptera
NT1 dalaca
NT2 dalaca dimidiata
NT1 hepialus
NT2 hepialus lupulinus
NT1 wiseana
NT2 wiseana cervinata

HEPIALUS
BT1 hepialidae
BT2 lepidoptera
NT1 hepialus lupulinus
rt dalaca

hepialus dimidiatus
USE **dalaca dimidiata**

HEPIALUS LUPULINUS
BT1 hepialus
BT2 hepialidae
BT3 lepidoptera

HEPTACHLOR
BT1 cyclodiene insecticides
BT2 organochlorine insecticides
BT3 insecticides
BT4 pesticides
BT3 organochlorine pesticides
BT4 organochlorine compounds
BT5 organic halogen compounds

HEPTANE
BT1 alkanes
BT2 hydrocarbons

2-HEPTANONE
BT1 alarm pheromones
BT2 pheromones
BT3 semiochemicals
BT1 ketones
rt honeybees

HEPTAPTERA
uf colladonia
BT1 umbelliferae
NT1 heptaptera triquetra

HEPTAPTERA TRIQUETRA
uf colladonia triquetra
BT1 heptaptera
BT2 umbelliferae
BT1 medicinal plants

HEPTENOPHOS
BT1 organophosphate insecticides
BT2 organophosphorus insecticides
BT3 insecticides
BT4 pesticides
BT3 organophosphorus pesticides
BT4 organophosphorus compounds

HEQU
HN from 1990
BT1 horse breeds
BT2 breeds

HERACLEUM
BT1 umbelliferae
NT1 heracleum antasiaticum
NT1 heracleum candicans

HERACLEUM *cont.*
NT1 heracleum canescens
NT1 heracleum dissectum
NT1 heracleum grandiflorum
NT1 heracleum lanatum
NT1 heracleum lehmannianum
NT1 heracleum mantegazzianum
NT1 heracleum persicum
NT1 heracleum pinnatum
NT1 heracleum rapula
NT1 heracleum scabridum
NT1 heracleum sosnowskyi
NT1 heracleum sphondylium
NT1 heracleum stevenii
NT1 heracleum thomsoni
NT1 heracleum trachyloma
NT1 heracleum wallichii

HERACLEUM ANTASIATICUM
BT1 heracleum
BT2 umbelliferae

HERACLEUM CANDICANS
BT1 heracleum
BT2 umbelliferae

HERACLEUM CANESCENS
BT1 heracleum
BT2 umbelliferae

HERACLEUM DISSECTUM
BT1 heracleum
BT2 umbelliferae

HERACLEUM GRANDIFLORUM
BT1 heracleum
BT2 umbelliferae

heracleum laciniatum
USE **heracleum stevenii**

HERACLEUM LANATUM
BT1 heracleum
BT2 umbelliferae

HERACLEUM LEHMANNIANUM
BT1 heracleum
BT2 umbelliferae

HERACLEUM MANTEGAZZIANUM
BT1 heracleum
BT2 umbelliferae
BT1 ornamental herbaceous plants
BT1 poisonous plants

HERACLEUM PERSICUM
BT1 heracleum
BT2 umbelliferae
BT1 medicinal plants

HERACLEUM PINNATUM
BT1 heracleum
BT2 umbelliferae

HERACLEUM RAPULA
BT1 heracleum
BT2 umbelliferae

HERACLEUM SCABRIDUM
BT1 heracleum
BT2 umbelliferae

HERACLEUM SOSNOWSKYI
BT1 heracleum
BT2 umbelliferae

HERACLEUM SPHONDYLIUM
BT1 heracleum
BT2 umbelliferae
BT1 medicinal plants

HERACLEUM STEVENII
uf heracleum laciniatum
BT1 heracleum
BT2 umbelliferae

HERACLEUM THOMSONI
BT1 heracleum
BT2 umbelliferae

HERACLEUM TRACHYLOMA
BT1 heracleum
BT2 umbelliferae

HERACLEUM WALLICHII
BT1 heracleum
BT2 umbelliferae

HERBAGE
BT1 vegetation
rt browse plants
rt fodder plants
rt foggage
rt grasses
rt herbage crops
rt pasture plants
rt pastures
rt stock piling

HERBAGE CROPS
(species are listed under browse plants, fodder plants and pasture plants)
rt grasses
rt herbage

HERBAL TEAS (AGRICOLA)
BT1 beverages

HERBARIA
BT1 plant collections
BT2 collections

HERBICIDAL PROPERTIES
BT1 pesticidal properties
BT2 properties
NT1 algicidal properties
rt allelopathy
rt herbicides
rt phytotoxicity

herbicide antidotes
USE **herbicide safeners**

herbicide fertilizer mixtures
USE **fertilizer herbicide combinations**

HERBICIDE IMPURITIES
uf impurities, herbicide
BT1 adulterants
rt adulteration
rt herbicides

HERBICIDE MIXTURES
uf mixtures, herbicide
BT1 herbicides
BT2 pesticides
BT1 pesticide mixtures
BT2 mixtures
BT2 pesticides
NT1 fertilizer herbicide combinations

HERBICIDE RESIDUES
BT1 pesticide residues
BT2 residues
rt herbicides

HERBICIDE RESISTANCE
BT1 pesticide resistance
BT2 resistance
rt herbicide resistant weeds
rt herbicides
rt weed control

HERBICIDE RESISTANT WEEDS
rt herbicide resistance

HERBICIDE SAFENERS
uf antidotes, herbicide
uf herbicide antidotes
BT1 safeners
NT1 cyometrinil
NT1 dichlormid
NT1 dietholate
NT1 fenclorim
NT1 flurazole
NT1 oxabetrinil
rt herbicides

HERBICIDES
uf weedkillers
BT1 pesticides
NT1 algicides
NT2 fentin hydroxide
NT2 tannins
NT2 tributyltin oxide
NT1 amide herbicides

HERBICIDES *cont.*
NT2 allidochlor
NT2 anilide herbicides
NT3 arylalanine herbicides
NT4 benzoylprop-ethyl
NT4 flamprop
NT3 chloranocryl
NT3 chloroacetanilide herbicides
NT4 acetochlor
NT4 alachlor
NT4 butachlor
NT4 delachlor
NT4 diethatyl
NT4 dimethachlor
NT4 metazachlor
NT4 metolachlor
NT4 pretilachlor
NT4 propachlor
NT4 prynachlor
NT4 terbuchlor
NT3 clomeprop
NT3 cypromid
NT3 diflufenican
NT3 mefenacet
NT3 monalide
NT3 pentanochlor
NT3 perfluidone
NT3 propanil
NT2 benzadox
NT2 benzipram
NT2 bromobutide
NT2 cdea
NT2 chlorthiamid
NT2 cyprazole
NT2 diphenamid
NT2 fomesafen
NT2 isoxaben
NT2 napropamide
NT2 naptalam
NT2 propyzamide
NT2 tebutam
NT1 antibiotic herbicides
NT2 bilanafos
NT2 glufosinate
NT1 arboricides
NT2 cacodylic acid
NT1 aromatic acid herbicides
NT2 benzoic acid herbicides
NT3 2,3,6-tba
NT3 chloramben
NT3 dicamba
NT2 picolinic acid herbicides
NT3 clopyralid
NT3 picloram
NT2 quinolinecarboxylic acid herbicides
NT3 quinclorac
NT3 quinmerac
NT1 arsenical herbicides
NT2 cacodylic acid
NT2 cma
NT2 dsma
NT2 hexaflurate
NT2 mama
NT2 msma
NT1 benzofuranyl alkylsulfonate herbicides
NT2 benfuresate
NT2 ethofumesate
NT1 carbamate herbicides
NT2 asulam
NT2 dichlormate
NT2 karbutilate
NT2 terbucarb
NT1 carbanilate herbicides
NT2 barban
NT2 carbasulam
NT2 carbetamide
NT2 chlorbufam
NT2 chlorpropham
NT2 desmedipham
NT2 phenisopham
NT2 phenmedipham
NT2 phenmedipham-ethyl
NT2 propham
NT2 swep
NT1 cyclohexene oxime herbicides
NT2 alloxydim
NT2 cloproxydim

HERBICIDES *cont.*
NT2 cycloxydim
NT2 sethoxydim
NT2 tralkoxydim
NT1 dinitroaniline herbicides
NT2 benfluralin
NT2 butralin
NT2 dinitramine
NT2 ethalfluralin
NT2 fluchloralin
NT2 isopropalin
NT2 methalpropalin
NT2 nitralin
NT2 oryzalin
NT2 pendimethalin
NT2 prodiamine
NT2 profluralin
NT2 trifluralin
NT1 dinitrophenol herbicides
NT2 dinoseb
NT2 dinoterb
NT2 dnoc
NT2 medinoterb
NT1 halogenated aliphatic herbicides
NT2 dalapon
NT2 flupropanate
NT2 methyl bromide
NT2 tca
NT1 herbicide mixtures
NT2 fertilizer herbicide combinations
NT1 imidazolinone herbicides
NT2 imazamethabenz
NT2 imazapyr
NT2 imazaquin
NT2 imazethapyr
NT1 inorganic herbicides
NT2 ammonium sulfamate
NT2 borax
NT2 calcium chlorate
NT2 sodium chlorate
NT1 mycoherbicides
NT2 alternaria macrospora
NT2 cercospora rodmanii
NT2 gibberella baccata
NT2 glomerella cingulata f.sp. aeschynomene
NT2 phragmidium violaceum
NT2 puccinia chondrillina
NT1 nitrile herbicides
NT2 bromoxynil
NT2 dichlobenil
NT2 ioxynil
NT1 nitrophenyl ether herbicides
NT2 acifluorfen
NT2 aclonifen
NT2 bifenox
NT2 bromofenoxim
NT2 chlomethoxyfen
NT2 chlornitrofen
NT2 fluorodifen
NT2 fluoroglycofen
NT2 fluoronitrofen
NT2 furyloxyfen
NT2 nitrofen
NT2 nitrofluorfen
NT2 oxyfluorfen
NT1 organophosphorus herbicides
NT2 amiprofos-methyl
NT2 anilofos
NT2 bensulide
NT2 buminafos
NT2 butamifos
NT2 dmpa
NT2 fosamine
NT2 glyphosate
NT2 piperophos
NT1 phenoxy herbicides
NT2 2,4-dep
NT2 disul
NT2 erbon
NT2 etnipromid
NT2 fenteracol
NT2 phenoxyacetic herbicides
NT3 2,4,5-t
NT3 2,4,6-t
NT3 2,4-d
NT3 4-cpa
NT3 mcpa

HERBICIDES *cont.*
NT2 phenoxybutyric herbicides
NT3 2,4,5-tb
NT3 2,4-db
NT3 difenopenten
NT3 mcpb
NT2 phenoxypropionic herbicides
NT3 aryloxyphenoxypropionic herbicides
NT4 chlorazifop
NT4 clofop
NT4 diclofop
NT4 fenoxaprop
NT4 fenthiaprop
NT4 fluazifop
NT4 haloxyfop
NT4 propaquizafop
NT4 quizalofop
NT4 trifop
NT3 cloprop
NT3 dichlorprop
NT3 fenoprop
NT3 mecoprop
NT2 trifopsime
NT1 pyridazinone herbicides
NT2 chloridazon
NT2 dimidazon
NT2 metflurazon
NT2 norflurazon
NT2 pydanon
NT1 pyridine herbicides
NT2 cliodinate
NT2 fluroxypyr
NT2 haloxydine
NT2 triclopyr
NT1 quaternary ammonium herbicides
NT2 cyperquat
NT2 diethamquat
NT2 difenzoquat
NT2 diquat
NT2 morfamquat
NT2 paraquat
NT1 thiocarbamate herbicides
NT2 butylate
NT2 cycloate
NT2 di-allate
NT2 eptc
NT2 esprocarb
NT2 ethiolate
NT2 metham
NT2 methiobencarb
NT2 molinate
NT2 orbencarb
NT2 pebulate
NT2 prosulfocarb
NT2 sulfallate
NT2 thiobencarb
NT2 tiocarbazil
NT2 tri-allate
NT2 vernolate
NT1 thiocarbonate herbicides
NT2 dimexano
NT2 exd
NT1 triazine herbicides
NT2 ametryn
NT2 atraton
NT2 atrazine
NT2 aziprotryne
NT2 cyanatryn
NT2 cyanazine
NT2 cyprazine
NT2 desmetryn
NT2 dimethametryn
NT2 dipropetryn
NT2 methoprotryne
NT2 prometon
NT2 prometryn
NT2 propazine
NT2 secbumeton
NT2 simazine
NT2 simeton
NT2 simetryn
NT2 terbumeton
NT2 terbuthylazine
NT2 terbutryn
NT2 trietazine
NT1 triazinone herbicides
NT2 ametridione
NT2 hexazinone

HERBICIDES *cont.*
NT2 isomethiozin
NT2 metamitron
NT2 metribuzin
NT1 triazole herbicides
NT2 amitrole
NT2 epronaz
NT1 unclassified herbicides
NT2 acrolein
NT2 benazolin
NT2 bentazone
NT2 buthidazole
NT2 calcium cyanamide
NT2 cambendichlor
NT2 chlorfenac
NT2 chlorfenprop-methyl
NT2 chlorflurenol
NT2 chlorthal-dimethyl
NT2 cinmethylin
NT2 clomazone
NT2 dazomet
NT2 dimepiperate
NT2 endothal
NT2 ferrous sulfate
NT2 fluoromidine
NT2 fluridone
NT2 flurochloridone
NT2 flurtamone
NT2 methazole
NT2 methyl isothiocyanate
NT2 oxadiazon
NT2 pentachlorophenol
NT2 phenylmercury acetate
NT2 prosulfalin
NT2 pyrazolynate
NT2 pyridate
NT2 sulglycapin
NT2 tridiphane
NT2 trimeturon
NT2 tripropindan
NT1 uracil herbicides
NT2 bromacil
NT2 lenacil
NT2 terbacil
NT1 urea herbicides
NT2 benzthiazuron
NT2 buthiuron
NT2 buturon
NT2 chlorbromuron
NT2 chloreturon
NT2 chlorotoluron
NT2 chloroxuron
NT2 cycluron
NT2 dichloralurea
NT2 difenoxuron
NT2 dimefuron
NT2 diuron
NT2 ethidimuron
NT2 fenuron
NT2 fluometuron
NT2 fluothiuron
NT2 isocarbamid
NT2 isoproturon
NT2 isouron
NT2 linuron
NT2 methabenzthiazuron
NT2 metobromuron
NT2 metoxuron
NT2 monolinuron
NT2 monuron
NT2 neburon
NT2 noruron
NT2 phenobenzuron
NT2 siduron
NT2 sulfonylurea herbicides
NT3 bensulfuron
NT3 chlorimuron
NT3 chlorsulfuron
NT3 metsulfuron
NT3 pyrazosulfuron
NT3 sulfometuron
NT3 triasulfuron
NT2 tebuthiuron
NT2 tetrafluron
NT2 thiazafluron
rt algicidal plants
rt brush control
rt defoliants
rt desiccant herbicides
rt herbicidal properties
rt herbicide impurities

HERBICIDES *cont.*
rt herbicide residues
rt herbicide resistance
rt herbicide safeners
rt phytotoxicity
rt phytotoxins
rt scrub control
rt soil fumigants
rt toxic substances
rt weed control

herbigation
USE **irrigation**

HERBIVORES
NT1 detritivores
NT1 herbivorous fishes
rt ruminants

HERBIVOROUS FISHES
uf *fishes, herbivorous*
BT1 herbivores
rt fishes

herbs, culinary
USE **culinary herbs**

herbs, medicinal
USE **medicinal plants**

hercothrips
USE **caliothrips**

HERD IMPROVEMENT
rt animal breeding
rt animal husbandry
rt breeders' associations
rt herds

herd size
USE **livestock numbers**

HERD STRUCTURE
BT1 herds
BT2 groups
rt structure

HERDBOOKS
NT1 flockbooks
rt herds
rt recording
rt studbooks

HERDS
BT1 groups
NT1 beef herds
NT1 dairy herds
NT1 feral herds
NT1 herd structure
NT1 suckler herds
rt flocks
rt herd improvement
rt herdbooks
rt livestock
rt pastoralism

hereditary defects
USE **genetic defects**

HEREDITARY DISEASES
BT1 diseases
NT1 lesch-nyhan syndrome
rt congenital abnormalities
rt disease transmission
rt genetic defects
rt inheritance

heredity
USE **genetics**
OR **heritability**
OR **inheritance**

heredopathia atactica polyneuritiformis
USE **refsum's syndrome**

HEREFORD
BT1 cattle breeds
BT2 breeds
BT1 pig breeds
BT2 breeds

HERENS
BT1 cattle breeds
BT2 breeds

HERITABILITY
uf *heredity*
rt genetic variance
rt genetics
rt inheritance

HERITABLE LEASES
BT1 leases
BT2 tenancy
BT3 tenure systems
rt inheritance of property

HERITAGE AREAS
BT1 areas
NT1 heritage coasts
rt cultural heritage
rt historic sites
rt landscape conservation
rt nature conservation
rt nature conservation and reserves
rt nature reserves
rt parks
rt tourist attractions

HERITAGE COASTS
BT1 coastal areas
BT2 areas
BT1 heritage areas
BT2 areas
rt landscape
rt landscape conservation

HERITIERA
uf *tarrietia*
BT1 sterculiaceae
rt forest trees

HERMAPHRODITISM
HN from 1990
BT1 gonadal disorders
BT2 endocrine diseases
BT3 organic diseases
BT4 diseases
rt pseudohermaphroditism
rt sex

HERMETIA
BT1 stratiomyidae
BT2 diptera
NT1 hermetia illucens

HERMETIA ILLUCENS
BT1 hermetia
BT2 stratiomyidae
BT3 diptera

HERMETIC SEALING
rt preservation

HERNANDIA
BT1 hernandiaceae
NT1 hernandia ovigera

HERNANDIA OVIGERA
BT1 hernandia
BT2 hernandiaceae

HERNANDIACEAE
NT1 hernandia
NT2 hernandia ovigera

HERNIA
NT1 congenital hernia
NT2 spina bifida
NT1 hiatal hernia (agricola)
NT1 umbilical hernia
rt rupture

HERNIARIA
BT1 caryophyllaceae
NT1 herniaria glabra

HERNIARIA GLABRA
BT1 herniaria
BT2 caryophyllaceae

herons
USE **ardeidae**

HERPES SIMPLEX VIRUS
BT1 human herpesvirus
BT2 herpesviridae
BT3 viruses

HERPESTES
BT1 herpestidae
BT2 fissipeda
BT3 carnivores
BT4 mammals
NT1 herpestes auropunctatus
NT1 herpestes edwardsii

HERPESTES AUROPUNCTATUS
BT1 herpestes
BT2 herpestidae
BT3 fissipeda
BT4 carnivores
BT5 mammals

HERPESTES EDWARDSII
BT1 herpestes
BT2 herpestidae
BT3 fissipeda
BT4 carnivores
BT5 mammals

HERPESTIDAE
BT1 fissipeda
BT2 carnivores
BT3 mammals
NT1 herpestes
NT2 herpestes auropunctatus
NT2 herpestes edwardsii
rt mongooses

HERPESVIRIDAE
uf *herpetoviridae*
BT1 viruses
NT1 avian herpesvirus
NT2 avian laryngotracheitis virus
NT2 duck plague virus
NT2 marek's disease virus
NT2 pigeon herpesvirus
NT2 turkey herpesvirus
NT1 bovine herpesvirus
NT2 ibr ipv virus
NT2 malignant catarrhal fever virus
NT2 mammillitis herpesvirus
NT1 canine herpesvirus
NT1 channel catfish virus
NT1 cytomegalovirus
NT1 equine herpesvirus
NT2 equine rhinopneumonitis virus
NT1 feline herpesvirus
NT2 feline rhinotracheitis virus
NT1 human herpesvirus
NT2 epstein-barr virus
NT2 herpes simplex virus
NT2 varicella-zoster virus
NT1 porcine herpesvirus
NT2 aujeszky virus

HERPETOGRAMMA
BT1 pyralidae
BT2 lepidoptera
NT1 herpetogramma licarsisalis

HERPETOGRAMMA LICARSISALIS
BT1 herpetogramma
BT2 pyralidae
BT3 lepidoptera

HERPETOLOGY
BT1 zoology
BT2 biology
rt reptiles

HERPETOMONAS
BT1 sarcomastigophora
BT2 protozoa
NT1 herpetomonas ampelophilae
NT1 herpetomonas megaseliae
NT1 herpetomonas muscarum
NT1 herpetomonas samuelpessoai

HERPETOMONAS AMPELOPHILAE
BT1 herpetomonas
BT2 sarcomastigophora
BT3 protozoa

HERPETOMONAS MEGASELIAE
BT1 herpetomonas
BT2 sarcomastigophora
BT3 protozoa

HERPETOMONAS MUSCARUM
BT1 herpetomonas
BT2 sarcomastigophora
BT3 protozoa

HERPETOMONAS SAMUELPESSOAI
BT1 herpetomonas
BT2 sarcomastigophora
BT3 protozoa

herpetoviridae
USE **herpesviridae**

herpobdella
USE **erpobdella**

HERRANIA
BT1 sterculiaceae

HERRING OIL
BT1 fish oils
BT2 animal oils
BT3 fatty oils
BT4 oils
BT2 fish products
BT3 animal products
BT4 products
rt herrings

HERRINGS
uf *clupea harengus*
BT1 marine fishes
BT2 aquatic animals
BT3 animals
BT3 aquatic organisms
rt clupeidae
rt herring oil

HERTIA
BT1 compositae

HESPERALOE
BT1 agavaceae
rt fibre plants

HESPERENTOMON
BT1 protentomidae
BT2 protura
NT1 hesperentomon schusteri

HESPERENTOMON SCHUSTERI
BT1 hesperentomon
BT2 protentomidae
BT3 protura

HESPERETHUSA
BT1 rutaceae
NT1 hesperethusa crenulata

HESPERETHUSA CRENULATA
BT1 hesperethusa
BT2 rutaceae

HESPERIDIN
BT1 bioflavonoids
BT2 flavonoids
BT3 aromatic compounds
BT3 plant pigments
BT4 pigments
BT2 water-soluble vitamins
BT3 vitamins
BT1 glycoflavones
BT2 flavonoids
BT3 aromatic compounds
BT3 plant pigments
BT4 pigments
BT2 glycosides
BT3 carbohydrates

HESPERIIDAE
BT1 lepidoptera
NT1 calpodes
NT2 calpodes ethlius
NT1 erionota
NT2 erionota thrax
NT1 parnara
NT2 parnara guttatus
NT1 pelopidas
NT2 pelopidas mathias
NT1 thymelicus
NT2 thymelicus lineola
NT1 urbanus
NT2 urbanus proteus

HESPERIS
BT1 cruciferae
NT1 hesperis matronalis

HESPERIS MATRONALIS
BT1 hesperis
BT2 cruciferae

HESPEROMELES
BT1 rosaceae

HESPEROMYINAE
BT1 muridae
BT2 rodents
BT3 mammals
NT1 akodon
NT2 akodon longipilis
NT1 bolomys
NT2 bolomys lasiurus
NT1 calomys
NT2 calomys callosus
NT1 holochilus
NT2 holochilus brasiliensis
NT1 neotoma
NT2 neotoma albigula
NT2 neotoma cinerea
NT2 neotoma floridana
NT2 neotoma mexicana
NT1 onychomys
NT2 onychomys leucogaster
NT1 oryzomys
NT1 oxymycterus
NT1 peromyscus
NT2 peromyscus leucopus
NT2 peromyscus maniculatus
NT1 sigmodon
NT2 sigmodon hispidus
NT1 zygodontomys

HESSE
BT1 german federal republic
BT2 western europe
BT3 europe

HETERAKIDAE
BT1 nematoda
NT1 heterakis
NT2 heterakis gallinae

HETERAKIDOSIS
BT1 nematode infections
BT2 helminthoses
BT3 parasitoses
BT4 diseases
rt heterakis

HETERAKIS
BT1 heterakidae
BT2 nematoda
NT1 heterakis gallinae
rt heterakidosis

HETERAKIS GALLINAE
BT1 heterakis
BT2 heterakidae
BT3 nematoda

HETERANTHERA
BT1 pontederiaceae
NT1 heteranthera peduncularis

HETERANTHERA PEDUNCULARIS
BT1 heteranthera
BT2 pontederiaceae

HETERANTHIDIUM
BT1 apidae
BT2 hymenoptera

HETEROBASIDION
BT1 aphyllophorales
NT1 heterobasidion annosum
rt fomes
rt fomitopsis

HETEROBASIDION ANNOSUM
uf *fomes annosus*
uf *fomitopsis annosa*
BT1 heterobasidion
BT2 aphyllophorales

HETEROBILHARZIA
BT1 schistosomatidae
BT2 digenea
BT3 trematoda

HETEROBILHARZIA *cont.*
NT1 heterobilharzia americana

HETEROBILHARZIA AMERICANA
BT1 heterobilharzia
BT2 schistosomatidae
BT3 digenea
BT4 trematoda

HETEROCAMPA
BT1 notodontidae
BT2 lepidoptera
NT1 heterocampa guttivitta

HETEROCAMPA GUTTIVITTA
BT1 heterocampa
BT2 notodontidae
BT3 lepidoptera

HETEROCEPHALUS
BT1 bathyergidae
BT2 rodents
BT3 mammals
NT1 heterocephalus glaber

HETEROCEPHALUS GLABER
BT1 heterocephalus
BT2 bathyergidae
BT3 rodents
BT4 mammals

HETEROCHROMATIN
BT1 chromatin
BT2 nucleoproteins
BT3 proteins
BT4 peptides
rt chromocentres

HETEROCINETOPSIS
BT1 ciliophora
BT2 protozoa

HETEROCORDYLUS
BT1 miridae
BT2 heteroptera
NT1 heterocordylus malinus

HETEROCORDYLUS MALINUS
BT1 heterocordylus
BT2 miridae
BT3 heteroptera

HETEROCYCLIC NITROGEN COMPOUNDS
BT1 organic nitrogen compounds
NT1 acridines
NT2 acridine orange
NT2 ethacridine
NT2 quinacrine mustard
NT1 azines
NT2 piperazines
NT3 diethylcarbamazine
NT3 piperazine
NT2 pyrazines
NT1 azoles
NT2 conazole fungicides
NT3 diclobutrazol
NT3 etaconazole
NT3 imazalil
NT3 penconazole
NT3 prochloraz
NT3 propiconazole
NT3 triadimefon
NT3 triadimenol
NT2 imidazoles
NT3 allantoin
NT3 clotrimazole
NT3 creatinine
NT3 econazole
NT3 etomidate
NT3 fenticonazole
NT3 histamine
NT3 histidine
NT3 imidazole alkaloids
NT4 pilocarpine
NT3 imidazole fungicides
NT4 fenapanil
NT3 imidazolinone herbicides
NT4 imazamethabenz
NT4 imazapyr
NT4 imazaquin
NT4 imazethapyr
NT3 ketoconazole
NT3 metizoline

HETEROCYCLIC NITROGEN COMPOUNDS *cont.*
NT3 metomidate
NT3 miconazole
NT3 nitroimidazoles
NT4 dimetridazole
NT4 ipronidazole
NT4 metronidazole
NT4 ornidazole
NT4 ronidazole
NT4 secnidazole
NT4 tinidazole
NT3 urocanic acid
NT2 triazoles
NT3 fluconazole
NT3 triazole fungicides
NT4 bitertanol
NT4 fluotrimazole
NT4 triazbutil
NT3 triazole herbicides
NT4 amitrole
NT4 epronaz
NT1 benzimidazoles
NT2 albendazole
NT2 benzimidazole
NT2 cambendazole
NT2 ciclobendazole
NT2 fenbendazole
NT2 flubendazole
NT2 luxabendazole
NT2 mebendazole
NT2 oxfendazole
NT2 oxibendazole
NT2 parbendazole
NT1 benzodiazepines
NT2 chlordiazepoxide
NT2 diazepam
NT2 elfazepam
NT1 bisazir
NT1 carbazoles
NT1 dithiazanine iodide
NT1 ethyleneimine
NT1 indoles
NT2 5-hydroxyindoleacetic acid
NT2 5-methoxyindole-3-acetic acid
NT2 iaa
NT2 iba
NT2 indole alkaloids
NT3 ergot alkaloids
NT4 dihydroergocryptine
NT4 ergometrine
NT3 gramine
NT3 physostigmine
NT3 psilocin
NT3 psilocybine
NT3 reserpine
NT3 strychnine
NT3 vinblastine
NT3 yohimbine
NT2 indole-3-acetonitrile
NT2 indole-3-methanol
NT2 skatole
NT2 tryptamines
NT3 melatonin
NT3 serotonin
NT3 tryptamine
NT1 methenamine
NT1 oxazolidinethiones
NT2 goitrin
NT1 penicillins
NT2 amoxicillin
NT2 ampicillin
NT2 carbenicillin
NT2 cloxacillin
NT2 oxacillin
NT1 phenothiazines
NT2 chlorpromazine
NT2 methylene blue
NT2 phenothiazine
NT2 promazine
NT2 propiomazine
NT1 piperidines
NT2 cyproheptadine
NT2 pethidine
NT2 pipecolic acid
NT2 tibric acid
NT1 porphyrins
NT2 chlorophyll
NT2 chlorophyllides
NT2 cytochromes

HETEROCYCLIC NITROGEN COMPOUNDS *cont.*
NT3 cytochrome b
NT3 cytochrome c
NT3 cytochrome p-450
NT2 haem
NT2 protochlorophyll
NT2 protochlorophyllides
NT2 protoporphyrin
NT1 pteridines
NT2 aminopterin
NT2 biopterin
NT2 triamterene
NT1 purines
NT2 2-aminopurine
NT2 6-methylpurine
NT2 adenines
NT3 adenine
NT3 benzyladenine
NT3 isopentenyladenine
NT3 kinetin
NT3 zeatin
NT2 hypoxanthines
NT3 guanine
NT3 hypoxanthine
NT2 xanthines
NT3 uric acid
NT3 xanthine alkaloids
NT4 caffeine
NT4 theobromine
NT4 theophylline
NT1 pyridazines
NT2 maleic hydrazide
NT2 pyridazinone herbicides
NT3 chloridazon
NT3 dimidazon
NT3 metflurazon
NT3 norflurazon
NT3 pydanon
NT1 pyridines
NT2 4-aminopyridine
NT2 4-pyridoxic acid
NT2 clopidol
NT2 desmosine
NT2 disopyramide
NT2 metyrapone
NT2 metyridine
NT2 niceritrol
NT2 nicotinamide
NT2 nicotinic acid
NT2 picolinic acid
NT2 pyridine alkaloids
NT3 anabasine
NT3 arecoline
NT3 cathidine
NT3 mimosine
NT3 nicotine
NT3 nornicotine
NT3 trigonelline
NT2 pyridine fungicides
NT3 buthiobate
NT3 pyridinitril
NT2 pyridine herbicides
NT3 cliodinate
NT3 fluroxypyr
NT3 haloxydine
NT3 triclopyr
NT2 pyridoxal
NT2 pyridoxal phosphate
NT2 pyridoxamine
NT2 pyrithiamine
NT1 pyrimidines
NT2 allopurinol
NT2 alloxan
NT2 cytosine
NT2 flucytosine
NT2 pyrimethamine
NT2 pyrimidine fungicides
NT3 bupirimate
NT3 dimethirimol
NT3 ethirimol
NT3 fenarimol
NT3 nuarimol
NT3 triarimol
NT2 trimethoprim
NT2 uracil
NT2 uracil derivatives
NT3 5-aminouracil
NT3 5-bromouracil
NT3 fluorouracil
NT3 methylthiouracil

HETEROCYCLIC NITROGEN COMPOUNDS *cont.*
NT3 orotic acid
NT3 propylthiouracil
NT3 thiouracil
NT3 thymine
NT3 uracil herbicides
NT4 bromacil
NT4 lenacil
NT4 terbacil
NT1 quinolines
NT2 aminoquinolines
NT3 amodiaquine
NT3 chloroquine
NT3 primaquine
NT2 buquinolate
NT2 diiodohydroxyquinoline
NT2 hydroxyquinoline
NT2 quinidine
NT2 quinoline
NT2 quinoline alkaloids
NT3 quinine
NT2 quinoline fungicides
NT3 8-hydroxyquinoline sulfate
NT3 ethoxyquin
NT3 halacrinate
NT3 quinacetol sulfate
NT2 quinolinecarboxylic acid herbicides
NT3 quinclorac
NT3 quinmerac
NT2 xanthurenic acid
NT1 quinoxalines
NT2 quindoxin
NT2 quinoxaline acaricides
NT3 chinomethionat
NT3 thioquinox
NT2 quinoxaline fungicides
NT3 chinomethionat
NT3 chlorquinox
NT3 thioquinox
NT1 tetrazolium compounds
NT2 tetrazolium
NT2 tetrazolium dyes
NT3 2,3,5-triphenyltetrazolium chloride
NT3 nitroblue tetrazolium
NT1 toluidine blue
NT1 triazines
NT2 melamine
NT2 tretamine
NT2 triazine herbicides
NT3 ametryn
NT3 atraton
NT3 atrazine
NT3 aziprotryne
NT3 cyanatryn
NT3 cyanazine
NT3 cyprazine
NT3 desmetryn
NT3 dimethametryn
NT3 dipropetryn
NT3 methoprotryne
NT3 prometon
NT3 prometryn
NT3 propazine
NT3 secbumeton
NT3 simazine
NT3 simeton
NT3 simetryn
NT3 terbumeton
NT3 terbuthylazine
NT3 terbutryn
NT3 trietazine
NT2 triazinone herbicides
NT3 ametridione
NT3 hexazinone
NT3 isomethiozin
NT3 metamitron
NT3 metribuzin
rt alkaloids

HETEROCYCLIC OXYGEN COMPOUNDS
NT1 dioxane
NT1 ethylene oxide
NT1 furans
NT2 furfural
NT2 hmf
NT2 nitrofurans

HETEROCYCLIC OXYGEN COMPOUNDS *cont.*
NT3 furaltadone
NT3 furazolidone
NT3 nifuroxazide
NT3 nitrofural
NT3 nitrofurantoin
NT3 nitrovin
NT3 thiofuradene
NT1 lactones
NT2 bufadienolides
NT2 cardenolides
NT3 digitoxigenin
NT3 digoxigenin
NT2 coumarins
NT3 coumarin
NT3 coumarin rodenticides
NT4 brodifacoum
NT4 bromadiolone
NT4 coumachlor
NT4 coumatetralyl
NT4 difenacoum
NT4 flocoumafen
NT4 warfarin
NT3 coumoestrol
NT3 dicoumarol
NT2 limonin
NT2 macrolide antibiotics
NT3 clindamycin
NT3 erythromycin
NT3 lincomycin
NT3 oleandomycin
NT3 spiramycin
NT2 penicillic acid
NT2 propiolactone
NT2 resorcylic acid lactones
NT3 zearalenol
NT3 zearalenone
NT3 zeranol
NT2 sesquiterpenoid lactones
NT3 bisabolangelone
NT3 eupatoriopicrin
NT3 guaianolides
NT3 helenalin
NT3 qinghaosu
NT3 tenulin
NT2 spironolactone
NT2 sugar lactones
NT3 gluconolactone
NT1 phthalides
NT1 propylene oxide
NT1 pyrones
NT2 maltol
NT1 theaflavine
NT1 tutin

HETERODERA
BT1 heteroderidae
BT2 nematoda
NT1 heterodera avenae
NT1 heterodera cacti
NT1 heterodera carotae
NT1 heterodera cruciferae
NT1 heterodera glycines
NT1 heterodera goettingiana
NT1 heterodera humuli
NT1 heterodera oryzae
NT1 heterodera sacchari
NT1 heterodera schachtii
NT1 heterodera trifolii
rt globodera

HETERODERA AVENAE
BT1 heterodera
BT2 heteroderidae
BT3 nematoda

HETERODERA CACTI
BT1 heterodera
BT2 heteroderidae
BT3 nematoda

HETERODERA CAROTAE
BT1 heterodera
BT2 heteroderidae
BT3 nematoda

HETERODERA CRUCIFERAE
BT1 heterodera
BT2 heteroderidae
BT3 nematoda

HETERODERA GLYCINES
BT1 heterodera
BT2 heteroderidae
BT3 nematoda

HETERODERA GOETTINGIANA
BT1 heterodera
BT2 heteroderidae
BT3 nematoda

HETERODERA HUMULI
BT1 heterodera
BT2 heteroderidae
BT3 nematoda

HETERODERA ORYZAE
BT1 heterodera
BT2 heteroderidae
BT3 nematoda

heterodera pallida
USE **globodera pallida**

heterodera rostochiensis
USE **globodera rostochiensis**

HETERODERA SACCHARI
BT1 heterodera
BT2 heteroderidae
BT3 nematoda

HETERODERA SCHACHTII
BT1 heterodera
BT2 heteroderidae
BT3 nematoda

heterodera solanacearum
USE **globodera solanacearum**

HETERODERA TRIFOLII
BT1 heterodera
BT2 heteroderidae
BT3 nematoda

HETERODERIDAE
BT1 nematoda
NT1 atalodera
NT1 cactodera
NT1 dolichodera
NT1 globodera
NT2 globodera pallida
NT2 globodera rostochiensis
NT2 globodera solanacearum
NT1 heterodera
NT2 heterodera avenae
NT2 heterodera cacti
NT2 heterodera carotae
NT2 heterodera cruciferae
NT2 heterodera glycines
NT2 heterodera goettingiana
NT2 heterodera humuli
NT2 heterodera oryzae
NT2 heterodera sacchari
NT2 heterodera schachtii
NT2 heterodera trifolii
NT1 meloidodera
NT2 meloidodera floridensis
NT1 punctodera
NT2 punctodera punctata
NT1 sarisodera
NT1 thecavermiculatus
rt plant parasitic nematodes

HETERODOXUS
BT1 boopiidae
BT2 amblycera
BT3 mallophaga
BT4 phthiraptera
NT1 heterodoxus longitarsus
NT1 heterodoxus spiniger

HETERODOXUS LONGITARSUS
BT1 heterodoxus
BT2 boopiidae
BT3 amblycera
BT4 mallophaga
BT5 phthiraptera

HETERODOXUS SPINIGER
BT1 heterodoxus
BT2 boopiidae
BT3 amblycera
BT4 mallophaga
BT5 phthiraptera

HETEROGENEITY
BT1 genetic variation
BT2 genetic change
BT2 mutations
BT2 variation
rt genotypes

HETEROGONEMA
BT1 tetradonematidae
BT2 nematoda

HETEROHYRAX
BT1 procaviidae
BT2 hyracoidea
BT3 mammals
NT1 heterohyrax brucei

HETEROHYRAX BRUCEI
BT1 heterohyrax
BT2 procaviidae
BT3 hyracoidea
BT4 mammals

HETEROKARYOSIS
rt cells
rt cytology
rt nuclei

HETEROMELES
BT1 rosaceae
NT1 heteromeles arbutifolia

HETEROMELES ARBUTIFOLIA
uf *photinia arbutifolia*
BT1 heteromeles
BT2 rosaceae
BT1 ornamental woody plants

HETEROMETRUS
BT1 scorpionidae
BT2 scorpiones
BT3 arachnida
BT4 arthropods
NT1 heterometrus bengalensis
NT1 heterometrus fulvipes
NT1 heterometrus scaber

HETEROMETRUS BENGALENSIS
BT1 heterometrus
BT2 scorpionidae
BT3 scorpiones
BT4 arachnida
BT5 arthropods

HETEROMETRUS FULVIPES
BT1 heterometrus
BT2 scorpionidae
BT3 scorpiones
BT4 arachnida
BT5 arthropods

HETEROMETRUS SCABER
BT1 heterometrus
BT2 scorpionidae
BT3 scorpiones
BT4 arachnida
BT5 arthropods

HETEROMYIDAE
BT1 rodents
BT2 mammals
NT1 dipodomys
NT1 heteromys
NT1 perognathus

HETEROMYS
BT1 heteromyidae
BT2 rodents
BT3 mammals

HETERONYCHUS
BT1 scarabaeidae
BT2 coleoptera
NT1 heteronychus arator

HETERONYCHUS ARATOR
BT1 heteronychus
BT2 scarabaeidae
BT3 coleoptera

HETEROPAPPUS
BT1 compositae

HETEROPELMA
BT1 ichneumonidae

HETEROPELMA *cont.*
BT2 hymenoptera

HETEROPEZA
BT1 cecidomyiidae
BT2 diptera
NT1 heteropeza pygmaea

HETEROPEZA PYGMAEA
BT1 heteropeza
BT2 cecidomyiidae
BT3 diptera

HETEROPHOS
BT1 organothiophosphate insecticides
BT2 organophosphorus insecticides
BT3 insecticides
BT4 pesticides
BT3 organophosphorus pesticides
BT4 organophosphorus compounds
BT1 organothiophosphate nematicides
BT2 organophosphorus nematicides
BT3 nematicides
BT4 pesticides
BT3 organophosphorus pesticides
BT4 organophosphorus compounds

HETEROPHRAGMA
BT1 bignoniaceae
NT1 heterophragma quadriloculare

HETEROPHRAGMA QUADRILOCULARE
BT1 antifungal plants
BT1 climbers
BT1 heterophragma
BT2 bignoniaceae
BT1 medicinal plants

HETEROPHYES
BT1 heterophyidae
BT2 digenea
BT3 trematoda
NT1 heterophyes heterophyes

HETEROPHYES HETEROPHYES
BT1 heterophyes
BT2 heterophyidae
BT3 digenea
BT4 trematoda

HETEROPHYIDAE
BT1 digenea
BT2 trematoda
NT1 apophallus
NT1 cryptocotyle
NT2 cryptocotyle lingua
NT1 galactosomum
NT1 haplorchis
NT2 haplorchis pumilio
NT1 heterophyes
NT2 heterophyes heterophyes
NT1 metagonimus
NT2 metagonimus yokogawai
NT1 procerovum
NT2 procerovum calderoni

HETEROPLOIDY
NT1 aneuploidy
NT2 monosomy
NT2 trisomy
NT1 polyploidy
NT2 euploidy
NT2 tetraploidy
NT2 triploidy

HETEROPODA
HN from 1990
BT1 heteropodidae
BT2 araneae
BT3 arachnida
BT4 arthropods

HETEROPODIDAE
HN from 1990

HETEROPODIDAE *cont.*
BT1 araneae
BT2 arachnida
BT3 arthropods
NT1 heteropoda

HETEROPOGON
BT1 gramineae
NT1 heteropogon contortus

HETEROPOGON CONTORTUS
uf *andropogon contortus*
uf *spear grass*
BT1 heteropogon
BT2 gramineae

HETEROPSYLLA
HN from 1989
BT1 psyllidae
BT2 psylloidea
BT3 sternorrhyncha
BT4 homoptera
NT1 heteropsylla cubana

HETEROPSYLLA CUBANA
HN from 1989
uf *heteropsylla incisa*
BT1 heteropsylla
BT2 psyllidae
BT3 psylloidea
BT4 sternorrhyncha
BT5 homoptera

heteropsylla incisa
USE **heteropsylla cubana**

HETEROPTERA
NT1 anthocoridae
NT2 anthocoris
NT3 anthocoris nemoralis
NT3 anthocoris nemorum
NT2 orius
NT3 orius albidipennis
NT3 orius insidiosus
NT3 orius minutus
NT3 orius niger
NT3 orius tristicolor
NT3 orius vicinus
NT2 xylocoris
NT3 xylocoris flavipes
NT1 aradidae
NT2 aradus
NT3 aradus cinnamomeus
NT1 berytidae
NT2 jalysus
NT3 jalysus spinosus
NT1 cimicidae
NT2 cimex
NT3 cimex hemipterus
NT3 cimex lectularius
NT2 oeciacus
NT3 oeciacus hirundinis
NT1 coreidae
NT2 amblypelta
NT3 amblypelta cocophaga
NT3 amblypelta lutescens
NT3 amblypelta nitida
NT3 amblypelta theobromae
NT2 anoplocnemis
NT3 anoplocnemis curvipes
NT2 chelinidea
NT3 chelinidea vittiger
NT2 clavigralla
NT3 clavigralla gibbosa
NT3 clavigralla horrida
NT3 clavigralla tomentosicollis
NT2 cletus
NT3 cletus punctiger
NT2 gonocerus
NT3 gonocerus acuteangulatus
NT2 leptocorisa
NT3 leptocorisa acuta
NT3 leptocorisa chinensis
NT3 leptocorisa oratorius
NT2 leptoglossus
NT2 pseudotheraptus
NT3 pseudotheraptus devastans
NT2 riptortus
NT3 riptortus clavatus
NT3 riptortus dentipes
NT3 riptortus linearis
NT2 veneza

HETEROPTERA *cont.*
NT3 veneza corculus
NT3 veneza phyllopus
NT1 cydnidae
NT2 cyrtomenus
NT3 cyrtomenus bergi
NT1 lygaeidae
NT2 aphanus
NT2 blissus
NT3 blissus insularis
NT3 blissus leucopterus
NT2 cavelerius
NT3 cavelerius excavatus
NT3 cavelerius saccharivorus
NT2 elasmolomus
NT3 elasmolomus sordidus
NT2 geocoris
NT3 geocoris bullatus
NT3 geocoris pallens
NT3 geocoris punctipes
NT2 lygaeus
NT3 lygaeus equestris
NT2 nysius
NT3 nysius vinitor
NT2 oncopeltus
NT3 oncopeltus fasciatus
NT2 oxycarenus
NT3 oxycarenus hyalinipennis
NT2 spilostethus
NT3 spilostethus pandurus
NT1 miridae
NT2 adelphocoris
NT3 adelphocoris lineolatus
NT2 calocoris
NT3 calocoris angustatus
NT2 campylomma
NT3 campylomma verbasci
NT2 cyrtopeltis
NT3 cyrtopeltis tenuis
NT2 cyrtorhinus
NT3 cyrtorhinus lividipennis
NT2 deraeocoris
NT3 deraeocoris brevis
NT2 distantiella
NT3 distantiella theobroma
NT2 helopeltis
NT3 helopeltis antonii
NT3 helopeltis schoutedeni
NT3 helopeltis theivora
NT2 heterocordylus
NT3 heterocordylus malinus
NT2 lygidea
NT3 lygidea mendax
NT2 lygocoris
NT3 lygocoris communis
NT3 lygocoris pabulinus
NT2 lygus
NT3 lygus disponsi
NT3 lygus elisus
NT3 lygus hesperus
NT3 lygus lineolaris
NT3 lygus pratensis
NT3 lygus rugulipennis
NT2 phytocoris
NT2 platylygus
NT3 platylygus luridus
NT2 psallus
NT3 psallus seriatus
NT2 sahlbergella
NT3 sahlbergella singularis
NT2 sidnia
NT3 sidnia kinbergi
NT2 spanagonicus
NT3 spanagonicus albofasciatus
NT2 stenodema
NT3 stenodema laevigatum
NT2 taylorilygus
NT3 taylorilygus vosseleri
NT2 trigonotylus
NT3 trigonotylus coelestialium
NT2 tytthus
NT3 tytthus mundulus
NT1 nabidae
NT2 nabis
NT3 nabis alternatus
NT3 nabis americoferus
NT3 nabis kinbergii
NT3 nabis roseipennis
NT1 nepidae
NT2 nepa

HETEROPTERA *cont.*
NT3 nepa cinerea
NT1 notonectidae
NT2 notonecta
NT3 notonecta glauca
NT3 notonecta hoffmanni
NT1 pentatomidae
NT2 acrosternum
NT3 acrosternum hilare
NT2 aelia
NT3 aelia acuminata
NT3 aelia cognata
NT3 aelia germari
NT3 aelia rostrata
NT2 amyotea
NT3 amyotea malabarica
NT2 antestiopsis
NT3 antestiopsis intricata
NT3 antestiopsis orbitalis
NT2 arma
NT3 arma custos
NT2 axiagastus
NT3 axiagastus cambelli
NT2 bagrada
NT3 bagrada hilaris
NT2 bathycoelia
NT3 bathycoelia thalassina
NT2 chlorochroa
NT3 chlorochroa ligata
NT2 dolycoris
NT3 dolycoris baccarum
NT3 dolycoris indicus
NT2 eurygaster
NT3 eurygaster austriaca
NT3 eurygaster integriceps
NT3 eurygaster maura
NT2 euschistus
NT3 euschistus heros
NT3 euschistus servus
NT2 lincus
NT2 murgantia
NT3 murgantia histrionica
NT2 nezara
NT3 nezara antennata
NT3 nezara viridula
NT2 oebalus
NT3 oebalus poecilus
NT3 oebalus pugnax
NT2 perillus
NT3 perillus bioculatus
NT2 picromerus
NT3 picromerus bidens
NT2 piezodorus
NT3 piezodorus guildinii
NT2 plautia
NT3 plautia stali
NT2 podisus
NT3 podisus maculiventris
NT2 rhynchocoris
NT3 rhynchocoris humeralis
NT2 scotinophara
NT3 scotinophara coarctata
NT3 scotinophara lurida
NT2 tessaratoma
NT3 tessaratoma papillosa
NT2 tetyra
NT3 tetyra bipunctata
NT2 thyanta
NT3 thyanta perditor
NT2 zicrona
NT3 zicrona caerulea
NT1 piesmatidae
NT2 piesma
NT3 piesma quadratum
NT1 pyrrhocoridae
NT2 dysdercus
NT3 dysdercus cingulatus
NT3 dysdercus fasciatus
NT3 dysdercus intermedius
NT3 dysdercus koenigii
NT3 dysdercus superstitiosus
NT3 dysdercus voelkeri
NT2 probergrothius
NT2 pyrrhocoris
NT3 pyrrhocoris apterus
NT1 reduviidae
NT2 cavernicola
NT3 cavernicola pilosa
NT2 dipetalogaster
NT3 dipetalogaster maxima
NT2 panstrongylus

HETEROPTERA *cont.*
NT3 panstrongylus geniculatus
NT3 panstrongylus lignarius
NT3 panstrongylus megistus
NT3 panstrongylus rufotuberculatus
NT2 peregrinator
NT3 peregrinator biannulipes
NT2 psammolestes
NT3 psammolestes tertius
NT2 reduvius
NT3 reduvius personatus
NT2 rhodnius
NT3 rhodnius ecuadoriensis
NT3 rhodnius nasutus
NT3 rhodnius neglectus
NT3 rhodnius pallescens
NT3 rhodnius pictipes
NT3 rhodnius prolixus
NT3 rhodnius robustus
NT2 rhynocoris
NT2 triatoma
NT3 triatoma barberi
NT3 triatoma brasiliensis
NT3 triatoma dimidiata
NT3 triatoma dispar
NT3 triatoma gerstaeckeri
NT3 triatoma guasayana
NT3 triatoma infestans
NT3 triatoma lecticularia
NT3 triatoma maculata
NT3 triatoma pallidipennis
NT3 triatoma phyllosoma
NT3 triatoma protracta
NT3 triatoma pseudomaculata
NT3 triatoma rubida
NT3 triatoma rubrofasciata
NT3 triatoma rubrovaria
NT3 triatoma sordida
NT3 triatoma vitticeps
NT2 zelus
NT1 rhopalidae
NT2 leptocoris
NT1 tingidae
NT2 corythucha
NT3 corythucha ciliata
NT2 stephanitis
NT3 stephanitis pyri
NT3 stephanitis pyrioides
NT3 stephanitis typica
NT2 teleonemia
NT3 teleonemia scrupulosa
NT2 tingis
NT1 veliidae
NT2 microvelia
NT3 microvelia douglasi
NT4 microvelia douglasi atrolineata
rt hemiptera
rt insects

HETERORHABDITIDAE
BT1 nematoda
NT1 heterorhabditis
NT2 heterorhabditis bacteriophora
NT2 heterorhabditis heliothidis
rt entomophilic nematodes

HETERORHABDITIS
BT1 heterorhabditidae
BT2 nematoda
NT1 heterorhabditis bacteriophora
NT1 heterorhabditis heliothidis

HETERORHABDITIS BACTERIOPHORA
BT1 heterorhabditis
BT2 heterorhabditidae
BT3 nematoda

HETERORHABDITIS HELIOTHIDIS
BT1 heterorhabditis
BT2 heterorhabditidae
BT3 nematoda

heterosides
USE **glycosides**

HETEROSIS
uf *hybrid vigour*
BT1 genetic parameters

HETEROSIS *cont.*
rt combining ability
rt hybrid varieties
rt hybridization
rt overdominance
rt vigour

heterosporium
USE **cladosporium**

heterosporium phlei
USE **cladosporium phlei**

HETEROSTYLY
rt gynoecium
rt pollination
rt styles

HETEROTERMES
BT1 rhinotermitidae
BT2 isoptera
NT1 heterotermes indicola

HETEROTERMES INDICOLA
BT1 heterotermes
BT2 rhinotermitidae
BT3 isoptera

HETEROTHALLISM
rt differentiation
rt sexual reproduction

HETEROTHECA
BT1 compositae
NT1 heterotheca grandiflora
NT1 heterotheca ruthii
NT1 heterotheca subaxillaris

HETEROTHECA GRANDIFLORA
BT1 heterotheca
BT2 compositae

HETEROTHECA RUTHII
BT1 heterotheca
BT2 compositae
BT1 ornamental herbaceous plants

HETEROTHECA SUBAXILLARIS
BT1 heterotheca
BT2 compositae

HETEROTROPHIC MICROORGANISMS
uf *microorganisms, heterotrophic*
BT1 microorganisms
BT1 parasites
BT1 saprophytes

HETEROTYLENCHUS
BT1 allantonematidae
BT2 nematoda
NT1 heterotylenchus autumnalis

HETEROTYLENCHUS AUTUMNALIS
BT1 heterotylenchus
BT2 allantonematidae
BT3 nematoda

HETEROXYNEMATIDAE
BT1 nematoda
NT1 aspiculuris
rt animal parasitic nematodes

HETEROZYGOSITY
BT1 genetics
BT2 biology
rt alleles
rt genes
rt heterozygotes
rt homozygosity

HETEROZYGOTES
BT1 genotypes
NT1 balanced lethals
rt alleles
rt genes
rt genetic differences
rt heterozygosity
rt homozygotes

HEUCHERA
BT1 saxifragaceae

HEUCHERA *cont.*
NT1 heuchera sanguinea

HEUCHERA SANGUINEA
BT1 heuchera
BT2 saxifragaceae
BT1 ornamental herbaceous plants

HEVEA
BT1 euphorbiaceae
NT1 hevea brasiliensis
NT1 hevea guianensis
rt tapping

HEVEA BRASILIENSIS
uf *rubber (plants)*
BT1 forest trees
BT1 hevea
BT2 euphorbiaceae
BT1 oilseed plants
BT2 fatty oil plants
BT3 oil plants
BT1 rubber plants
rt rubber

HEVEA GUIANENSIS
BT1 hevea
BT2 euphorbiaceae

hexachloran
USE **hch**

HEXACHLOROBENZENE
uf *hcb*
BT1 aromatic fungicides
BT2 fungicides
BT3 pesticides

HEXACHLOROBUTADIENE
BT1 unclassified fungicides
BT2 fungicides
BT3 pesticides

HEXACHLOROETHANE
BT1 anthelmintics
BT2 antiparasitic agents
BT3 drugs
BT1 solvents

HEXACHLOROPARAXYLENE
uf *chloxyle*
BT1 anthelmintics
BT2 antiparasitic agents
BT3 drugs
BT1 chlorinated hydrocarbons
BT2 halogenated hydrocarbons
BT3 organic halogen compounds

HEXACHLOROPHENE
BT1 anthelmintics
BT2 antiparasitic agents
BT3 drugs

hexadecanoic acid
USE **palmitic acid**

1-HEXADECANOL
uf *cetyl alcohol*
BT1 antitranspirants
BT1 fatty alcohols
BT2 alcohols
BT2 lipids

HEXAFLURATE
BT1 arsenical herbicides
BT2 arsenicals
BT2 herbicides
BT3 pesticides

HEXALOBUS
BT1 annonaceae
NT1 hexalobus monopetalus

HEXALOBUS MONOPETALUS
BT1 hexalobus
BT2 annonaceae

HEXALURE
BT1 insect attractants
BT2 attractants

HEXAMASTIX
BT1 sarcomastigophora

HEXAMASTIX *cont.*
BT2 protozoa

HEXAMERMIS
BT1 mermithidae
BT2 nematoda
NT1 hexamermis albicans

HEXAMERMIS ALBICANS
BT1 hexamermis
BT2 mermithidae
BT3 nematoda

hexamethylenetetramine
USE **methenamine**

HEXAMITA
BT1 sarcomastigophora
BT2 protozoa
NT1 hexamita meleagridis
NT1 hexamita muris
NT1 hexamita salmonis

HEXAMITA MELEAGRIDIS
BT1 hexamita
BT2 sarcomastigophora
BT3 protozoa

HEXAMITA MURIS
BT1 hexamita
BT2 sarcomastigophora
BT3 protozoa

HEXAMITA SALMONIS
BT1 hexamita
BT2 sarcomastigophora
BT3 protozoa

HEXANCHIDAE
BT1 hexanchiformes
BT2 chondrichthyes
BT3 fishes
NT1 hexanchus

HEXANCHIFORMES
BT1 chondrichthyes
BT2 fishes
NT1 hexanchidae
NT2 hexanchus

HEXANCHUS
BT1 hexanchidae
BT2 hexanchiformes
BT3 chondrichthyes
BT4 fishes

HEXANE
BT1 alkanes
BT2 hydrocarbons
BT1 solvents

HEXANOIC ACID
uf *caproic acid*
BT1 saturated fatty acids
BT2 fatty acids
BT3 carboxylic acids
BT4 organic acids
BT5 acids
BT3 lipids
BT1 short chain fatty acids
BT2 fatty acids
BT3 carboxylic acids
BT4 organic acids
BT5 acids
BT3 lipids

1-HEXANOL
BT1 alcohols

HEXATHELIDAE
BT1 araneae
BT2 arachnida
BT3 arthropods
NT1 atrax
NT2 atrax robustus

HEXATYLUS
BT1 neotylenchidae
BT2 nematoda

HEXAZINONE
BT1 triazinone herbicides
BT2 herbicides
BT3 pesticides
BT2 triazines

HEXAZINONE *cont.*
BT3 heterocyclic nitrogen compounds
BT4 organic nitrogen compounds

HEXESTROL
uf *hexoestrol*
BT1 synthetic oestrogens
BT2 synthetic hormones

hexoestrol
USE **hexestrol**

HEXOKINASE
(ec 2.7.1.1)
BT1 kinases
BT2 transferases
BT3 enzymes

HEXOSAMINES
BT1 amino sugars
BT2 amino compounds
BT3 organic nitrogen compounds
BT2 sugars
BT3 carbohydrates
NT1 n-acetylglucosamine
NT1 galactosamine
NT1 glucosamine

hexosaminidase
USE **β-n-acetylhexosaminidase**

HEXOSES
BT1 aldoses
BT2 monosaccharides
BT3 carbohydrates
BT2 reducing sugars
BT3 sugars
BT4 carbohydrates
NT1 2-deoxy-d-glucose
NT1 fucose
NT1 galactose
NT1 glucose
NT1 mannose
NT1 rhamnose

HEXOSYLTRANSFERASES
(ec 2.4.1)
BT1 glycosyltransferases
BT2 transferases
BT3 enzymes
NT1 dextransucrase
NT1 glycogen (starch) synthase
NT1 lactose synthase
NT1 levansucrase
NT1 phosphorylase
NT2 glycogen phosphorylase
NT1 sucrose synthase

HEXULOSES
BT1 ketoses
BT2 monosaccharides
BT3 carbohydrates
BT2 nonreducing sugars
BT3 sugars
BT4 carbohydrates
NT1 fructose
NT1 psicose
NT1 sorbose

HEXYLRESORCINOL
BT1 anthelmintics
BT2 antiparasitic agents
BT3 drugs

HEXYLTHIOFOS
BT1 organophosphorus fungicides
BT2 fungicides
BT3 pesticides
BT2 organophosphorus pesticides
BT3 organophosphorus compounds

HEXYTHIAZOX
BT1 mite growth regulators
BT2 acaricides
BT3 pesticides
BT2 growth regulators

hfcs
USE **high fructose corn syrup**

HIATAL HERNIA (AGRICOLA)
BT1 hernia

HIBBERTIA
BT1 dilleniaceae

HIBERNATION
BT1 dormancy
rt diapause
rt winter

HIBISCUS
BT1 malvaceae
NT1 hibiscus asper
NT1 hibiscus cannabinus
NT1 hibiscus diversifolius
NT1 hibiscus elatus
NT1 hibiscus fuscus
NT1 hibiscus macrophyllus
NT1 hibiscus mutabilis
NT1 hibiscus rosa-sinensis
NT1 hibiscus sabdariffa
NT1 hibiscus schizopetalus
NT1 hibiscus squamosus
NT1 hibiscus surattensis
NT1 hibiscus syriacus
NT1 hibiscus ternatus
NT1 hibiscus tiliaceus
NT1 hibiscus trionum
NT1 hibiscus vitifolius
NT1 hibiscus waimeae
rt abelmoschus
rt hibiscus chlorotic ringspot carmovirus
rt hibiscus latent ringspot nepovirus

hibiscus abelmoschus
USE **abelmoschus moschatus**

HIBISCUS ASPER
BT1 hibiscus
BT2 malvaceae

HIBISCUS CANNABINUS
BT1 fibre plants
BT1 hibiscus
BT2 malvaceae
rt hemp
rt kenaf

HIBISCUS CHLOROTIC RINGSPOT CARMOVIRUS
HN from 1990
BT1 carmovirus group
BT2 plant viruses
BT3 plant pathogens
BT4 pathogens
rt hibiscus

HIBISCUS DIVERSIFOLIUS
BT1 hibiscus
BT2 malvaceae
BT1 ornamental woody plants

HIBISCUS ELATUS
BT1 hibiscus
BT2 malvaceae

hibiscus esculentus
USE **abelmoschus esculentus**

HIBISCUS FUSCUS
BT1 hibiscus
BT2 malvaceae
BT1 ornamental woody plants

HIBISCUS LATENT RINGSPOT NEPOVIRUS
HN from 1990
BT1 nepovirus group
BT2 plant viruses
BT3 plant pathogens
BT4 pathogens
rt hibiscus

HIBISCUS MACROPHYLLUS
BT1 hibiscus
BT2 malvaceae

HIBISCUS MUTABILIS
BT1 hibiscus

HIBISCUS MUTABILIS *cont.*
BT2 malvaceae
BT1 ornamental woody plants

HIBISCUS ROSA-SINENSIS
BT1 hibiscus
BT2 malvaceae
BT1 medicinal plants
BT1 ornamental woody plants

HIBISCUS SABDARIFFA
BT1 antibacterial plants
BT1 antifungal plants
BT1 fibre plants
BT1 hibiscus
BT2 malvaceae
BT1 medicinal plants
BT1 tropical small fruits
BT2 small fruits
BT2 tropical fruits
BT3 fruit crops
rt roselle

HIBISCUS SCHIZOPETALUS
BT1 hibiscus
BT2 malvaceae
BT1 ornamental woody plants

HIBISCUS SQUAMOSUS
BT1 hibiscus
BT2 malvaceae

HIBISCUS SURATTENSIS
BT1 fibre plants
BT1 hibiscus
BT2 malvaceae

HIBISCUS SYRIACUS
BT1 hibiscus
BT2 malvaceae
BT1 oilseed plants
BT2 fatty oil plants
BT3 oil plants
BT1 ornamental woody plants

HIBISCUS TERNATUS
BT1 hibiscus
BT2 malvaceae

HIBISCUS TILIACEUS
BT1 hibiscus
BT2 malvaceae

HIBISCUS TRIONUM
BT1 hibiscus
BT2 malvaceae

HIBISCUS VITIFOLIUS
BT1 fibre plants
BT1 hibiscus
BT2 malvaceae

HIBISCUS WAIMEAE
BT1 hibiscus
BT2 malvaceae
BT1 ornamental woody plants

hickory nuts
USE **pecans**

hicoria
USE **carya**

HIDE MEAL
BT1 meal
rt hides and skins

HIDE SCRAPINGS
uf *flesh side*
BT1 industrial wastes
BT2 wastes
rt hides and skins

hides
USE **hides and skins**

HIDES AND SKINS
uf *hides*
uf *skins*
BT1 animal products
BT2 products
rt furs
rt hide meal
rt hide scrapings
rt leather

HIDES AND SKINS *cont.*
rt leather industry
rt non-food products
rt parchment
rt skin producing animals
rt skinning

HIERACIUM
BT1 compositae
NT1 hieracium aurantiacum
NT1 hieracium florentinum
NT1 hieracium floribundum
NT1 hieracium murorum
NT1 hieracium pilosella
NT1 hieracium piloselloides
NT1 hieracium pratense

HIERACIUM AURANTIACUM
BT1 hieracium
BT2 compositae

HIERACIUM FLORENTINUM
BT1 hieracium
BT2 compositae

HIERACIUM FLORIBUNDUM
BT1 hieracium
BT2 compositae

HIERACIUM MURORUM
BT1 hieracium
BT2 compositae

HIERACIUM PILOSELLA
BT1 hieracium
BT2 compositae

HIERACIUM PILOSELLOIDES
BT1 hieracium
BT2 compositae

HIERACIUM PRATENSE
BT1 hieracium
BT2 compositae

HIEROGLYPHUS
BT1 acrididae
BT2 orthoptera
NT1 hieroglyphus banian
NT1 hieroglyphus nigrorepletus

HIEROGLYPHUS BANIAN
BT1 hieroglyphus
BT2 acrididae
BT3 orthoptera

HIEROGLYPHUS NIGROREPLETUS
BT1 hieroglyphus
BT2 acrididae
BT3 orthoptera

HIERONYMA
BT1 euphorbiaceae
NT1 hieronyma chocoensis

HIERONYMA CHOCOENSIS
BT1 hieronyma
BT2 euphorbiaceae

HIEROXESTIDAE
BT1 lepidoptera
NT1 opogona
NT2 opogona sacchari

higginsia
USE **blumeriella**

higginsia hiemalis
USE **blumeriella jaapii**

HIGH ALTITUDE
BT1 altitude
rt height

high blood pressure
USE **hypertension**

high calorie foods
USE **prepared foods**

HIGH CLEARANCE TRACTORS
BT1 tractors
BT2 cross country vehicles
BT3 vehicles

HIGH DENSITY BALERS
uf *balers, high density*
BT1 balers
BT2 farm machinery
BT3 machinery
rt high density bales

HIGH DENSITY BALES
HN from 1990
BT1 bales
BT2 packages
rt high density balers

HIGH DENSITY LIPOPROTEIN
uf *lipoprotein, high density*
BT1 lipoproteins
BT2 proteins
BT3 peptides

HIGH DENSITY PLANTING
BT1 planting
BT1 spacing
rt meadow orchards

HIGH FIBER DIETS (AGRICOLA)
BT1 diets

HIGH FREQUENCY DRYING
HN from 1989
BT1 drying
BT2 dehydration
BT3 processing

HIGH FRUCTOSE CORN SYRUP
uf *hfcs*
uf *isoglucose*
uf *isomerose*
uf *starch sugar*
BT1 sugar substitutes
BT2 substitutes
BT2 sweeteners
BT3 food additives
BT4 additives
BT1 syrups
BT2 liquids
rt fructose
rt fructose syrup
rt glucose
rt sugars

HIGH LIFT TRAILERS
BT1 trailers
BT2 vehicles
rt tipping trailers

high performance liquid chromatography
USE **hplc**

HIGH PLANE FEEDING
BT1 feeding

high pressure liquid chromatography
USE **hplc**

HIGH SCHOOL CURRICULUM (AGRICOLA)
BT1 curriculum
BT2 educational courses
rt high schools (agricola)

HIGH SCHOOL STUDENTS (AGRICOLA)
BT1 students
BT2 people
rt high schools (agricola)
rt junior high school students (agricola)

HIGH SCHOOLS (AGRICOLA)
BT1 schools
BT2 educational institutions
rt high school curriculum (agricola)
rt high school students (agricola)

HIGH SEASON
BT1 seasons

HIGH SPEED OPERATION
BT1 operation
rt tractors

HIGH SPEED PHOTOGRAPHY
BT1 photography
BT2 techniques

HIGH TEMPERATURE DRIERS
AF high temperature dryers
uf driers, high temperature
BT1 driers
BT2 farm machinery
BT3 machinery

HIGH TEMPERATURE DRYERS
BF high temperature driers
BT1 dryers

HIGH VOLUME SPRAYERS
uf sprayers, high volume
BT1 sprayers
BT2 spraying equipment
BT3 application equipment
BT4 equipment

HIGH VOLUME SPRAYING
uf spraying, high volume
BT1 spraying
BT2 application methods
BT3 methodology

HIGH WATER TABLES
BT1 water table
BT2 groundwater level
BT3 soil water regimes

HIGH YIELDING VARIETIES
uf hyv
BT1 varieties
NT1 elites
NT2 plus trees
rt green revolution
rt hybrid varieties
rt improved varieties

HIGHER EDUCATION
uf education, higher
BT1 education
NT1 graduate study (agricola)
NT1 veterinary schools
rt agricultural colleges
rt college programs (agricola)
rt colleges (agricola)
rt qualifications
rt theses
rt universities
rt vocational training

HIGHER NERVOUS ACTIVITY
BT1 nervous system
BT2 body parts

HIGHLAND
BT1 cattle breeds
BT2 breeds

HIGHLANDS
BT1 land types
rt hill land
rt mountain areas
rt mountains
rt plateaux
rt upland areas

highlands and islands of scotland
USE **scottish highlands and islands**

highways
USE **roads**

HIKING
BT1 walking
BT2 outdoor recreation
BT3 recreation
rt backpacking (agricola)

HILARIA
BT1 gramineae
NT1 hilaria belangeri
NT1 hilaria mutica
NT1 hilaria rigida

HILARIA BELANGERI
BT1 hilaria
BT2 gramineae

HILARIA MUTICA
BT1 hilaria
BT2 gramineae

HILARIA RIGIDA
BT1 hilaria
BT2 gramineae

HILDA
BT1 tettigometridae
BT2 fulgoroidea
BT3 auchenorrhyncha
BT4 homoptera
NT1 hilda patruelis

HILDA PATRUELIS
BT1 hilda
BT2 tettigometridae
BT3 fulgoroidea
BT4 auchenorrhyncha
BT5 homoptera

HILDEGARDIA
BT1 sterculiaceae
NT1 hildegardia barteri

HILDEGARDIA BARTERI
BT1 hildegardia
BT2 sterculiaceae
BT1 oilseed plants
BT2 fatty oil plants
BT3 oil plants

hill areas
USE **hill land**
OR **mountain areas**
OR **upland areas**

HILL GRASSLANDS
uf grasslands, hill
BT1 grasslands
BT2 vegetation types
rt alpine grasslands
rt hill land
rt mountain grasslands

HILL LAND
uf hill areas
BT1 land types
rt highlands
rt hill grasslands
rt less favoured areas
rt sloping land
rt upland areas

hill soils
USE **upland soils**

HILLING
BT1 cultivation

hills, missing
USE **missing hills**

hillside operations
USE **operation on slopes**

HILLSIDE TRACTORS
BT1 tractors
BT2 cross country vehicles
BT3 vehicles
rt operation on slopes

HILSA
BT1 clupeidae
BT2 clupeiformes
BT3 osteichthyes
BT4 fishes

HIMACHAL PRADESH
BT1 india
BT2 south asia
BT3 asia

HIMASTHLA
BT1 echinostomatidae
BT2 digenea
BT3 trematoda

HINDGUT
BT1 digestive system
BT2 body parts

HINDOLA
HN from 1990
BT1 machaerotidae

HINDOLA *cont.*
BT2 cercopoidea
BT3 auchenorrhyncha
BT4 homoptera
NT1 hindola fulva
NT1 hindola striata

HINDOLA FULVA
HN from 1990
BT1 hindola
BT2 machaerotidae
BT3 cercopoidea
BT4 auchenorrhyncha
BT5 homoptera

HINDOLA STRIATA
HN from 1990
BT1 hindola
BT2 machaerotidae
BT3 cercopoidea
BT4 auchenorrhyncha
BT5 homoptera

HINNIES
uf equus asinus x equus caballus
BT1 hybrids
BT1 working animals
BT2 animals
rt donkeys
rt equidae
rt horses
rt mules

HIP DYSPLASIA
BT1 congenital abnormalities
BT2 abnormalities
rt hips

HIPPEASTRUM
BT1 amaryllidaceae
NT1 hippeastrum puniceum
NT1 hippeastrum vittatum
rt hippeastrum mosaic potyvirus

hippeastrum equestre
USE **hippeastrum puniceum**

HIPPEASTRUM MOSAIC POTYVIRUS
HN from 1990; previously "hippeastrum mosaic virus"
uf hippeastrum mosaic virus
BT1 potyvirus group
BT2 plant viruses
BT3 plant pathogens
BT4 pathogens
rt hippeastrum

hippeastrum mosaic virus
USE **hippeastrum mosaic potyvirus**

HIPPEASTRUM PUNICEUM
uf hippeastrum equestre
BT1 hippeastrum
BT2 amaryllidaceae
BT1 ornamental bulbs

HIPPEASTRUM VITTATUM
uf amaryllis vittata
BT1 hippeastrum
BT2 amaryllidaceae

HIPPELATES
BT1 chloropidae
BT2 diptera
rt liohippelates

hippelates collusor
USE **liohippelates collusor**

hippelates pusio
USE **liohippelates pusio**

HIPPOBOSCA
uf keds
BT1 hippoboscidae
BT2 diptera
NT1 hippobosca camelina
NT1 hippobosca equina
NT1 hippobosca longipennis

HIPPOBOSCA CAMELINA
BT1 hippobosca
BT2 hippoboscidae
BT3 diptera

HIPPOBOSCA EQUINA
BT1 hippobosca
BT2 hippoboscidae
BT3 diptera

HIPPOBOSCA LONGIPENNIS
BT1 hippobosca
BT2 hippoboscidae
BT3 diptera

HIPPOBOSCIDAE
BT1 diptera
NT1 hippobosca
NT2 hippobosca camelina
NT2 hippobosca equina
NT2 hippobosca longipennis
NT1 lipoptena
NT2 lipoptena cervi
NT1 melophagus
NT2 melophagus ovinus
NT1 pseudolynchia
NT2 pseudolynchia canariensis
rt ectoparasites

HIPPOCAMPUS
uf brain, hippocampus
BT1 brain
BT2 central nervous system
BT3 nervous system
BT4 body parts

HIPPOCAMPUS (GENUS)
uf seahorses
BT1 syngnathidae
BT2 syngnathiformes
BT3 osteichthyes
BT4 fishes

HIPPOCASTANACEAE
NT1 aesculus
NT2 aesculus californica
NT2 aesculus carnea
NT2 aesculus glabra
NT2 aesculus hippocastanum
NT2 aesculus indica
NT2 aesculus parviflora
NT2 aesculus rubra

hippocrateaceae
USE **celastraceae**

HIPPODAMIA
uf adonia
uf semiadalia
BT1 coccinellidae
BT2 coleoptera
NT1 hippodamia convergens
NT1 hippodamia oculata
NT1 hippodamia parenthesis
NT1 hippodamia tredecimpunctata
NT1 hippodamia variegata

HIPPODAMIA CONVERGENS
BT1 hippodamia
BT2 coccinellidae
BT3 coleoptera

HIPPODAMIA OCULATA
uf adonia undecimnotata
uf semiadalia undecimnotata
BT1 hippodamia
BT2 coccinellidae
BT3 coleoptera

HIPPODAMIA PARENTHESIS
BT1 hippodamia
BT2 coccinellidae
BT3 coleoptera

HIPPODAMIA TREDECIMPUNCTATA
BT1 hippodamia
BT2 coccinellidae
BT3 coleoptera

HIPPODAMIA VARIEGATA
uf adonia variegata
BT1 hippodamia

HIPPODAMIA VARIEGATA *cont.*
BT2 coccinellidae
BT3 coleoptera

HIPPOGLOSSOIDES
BT1 pleuronectidae
BT2 pleuronectiformes
BT3 osteichthyes
BT4 fishes

HIPPOGLOSSUS
BT1 pleuronectidae
BT2 pleuronectiformes
BT3 osteichthyes
BT4 fishes

hippoglossus hippoglossus
USE **halibut**

HIPPOPHAE
BT1 elaeagnaceae
NT1 hippophae rhamnoides

HIPPOPHAE RHAMNOIDES
BT1 forest trees
BT1 hippophae
BT2 elaeagnaceae
BT1 medicinal plants
BT1 ornamental woody plants
BT1 temperate small fruits
BT2 small fruits
BT2 temperate fruits
BT3 fruit crops

HIPPOPOTAMIDAE
BT1 suiformes
BT2 artiodactyla
BT3 mammals
BT3 ungulates
NT1 hippopotamus
NT2 hippopotamus amphibius

HIPPOPOTAMUS
BT1 hippopotamidae
BT2 suiformes
BT3 artiodactyla
BT4 mammals
BT4 ungulates
NT1 hippopotamus amphibius

HIPPOPOTAMUS AMPHIBIUS
BT1 hippopotamus
BT2 hippopotamidae
BT3 suiformes
BT4 artiodactyla
BT5 mammals
BT5 ungulates

HIPPOSIDERIDAE
BT1 chiroptera
BT2 mammals
NT1 hipposideros

HIPPOSIDEROS
BT1 hipposideridae
BT2 chiroptera
BT3 mammals

HIPPOSPONGIA
BT1 parazoa

HIPPOTION
BT1 sphingidae
BT2 lepidoptera
NT1 hippotion celerio

HIPPOTION CELERIO
BT1 hippotion
BT2 sphingidae
BT3 lepidoptera

HIPPOTRAGUS
BT1 bovidae
BT2 ruminantia
BT3 artiodactyla
BT4 mammals
BT4 ungulates
NT1 hippotragus equinus
NT1 hippotragus niger

HIPPOTRAGUS EQUINUS
BT1 hippotragus
BT2 bovidae
BT3 ruminantia
BT4 artiodactyla

HIPPOTRAGUS EQUINUS *cont.*
BT5 mammals
BT5 ungulates

HIPPOTRAGUS NIGER
BT1 hippotragus
BT2 bovidae
BT3 ruminantia
BT4 artiodactyla
BT5 mammals
BT5 ungulates

HIPPURIC ACID
BT1 amides
BT2 organic nitrogen compounds
BT1 nonprotein amino acids
BT2 amino acids
BT3 carboxylic acids
BT4 organic acids
BT5 acids
BT3 organic nitrogen compounds

HIPPURIDACEAE
NT1 hippuris
NT2 hippuris vulgaris

HIPPURIS
BT1 hippuridaceae
NT1 hippuris vulgaris

HIPPURIS VULGARIS
BT1 hippuris
BT2 hippuridaceae

HIPS
BT1 limbs
BT2 body regions
rt hip dysplasia

hirame
USE **paralichthys olivaceus**

HIRED LABOR
BF hired labour
rt custom hiring (agricola)
rt labor

HIRED LABOUR
AF hired labor
BT1 labour

HIRING
BT1 capital leasing
NT1 boat hire
NT1 car hire
NT1 custom hiring (agricola)
rt contractors
rt rental costs (agricola)

HIRMOCYSTIS
BT1 apicomplexa
BT2 protozoa

HIROSIA
BT1 tabanidae
BT2 diptera
NT1 hirosia iyoensis
rt tabanus

HIROSIA IYOENSIS
uf *tabanus iyoensis*
BT1 hirosia
BT2 tabanidae
BT3 diptera

HIRSCHIOPORUS
BT1 aphyllophorales
rt trichaptum

hirschioporus abietinus
USE **trichaptum abietinum**

HIRSCHMANNIELLA
BT1 pratylenchidae
BT2 nematoda
NT1 hirschmanniella mucronata
NT1 hirschmanniella oryzae
NT1 hirschmanniella spinicaudata

HIRSCHMANNIELLA MUCRONATA
HN from 1990
BT1 hirschmanniella
BT2 pratylenchidae

HIRSCHMANNIELLA MUCRONATA *cont.*
BT3 nematoda

HIRSCHMANNIELLA ORYZAE
BT1 hirschmanniella
BT2 pratylenchidae
BT3 nematoda

HIRSCHMANNIELLA SPINICAUDATA
BT1 hirschmanniella
BT2 pratylenchidae
BT3 nematoda

HIRSTIA
HN from 1990
BT1 pyroglyphidae
BT2 astigmata
BT3 acari

HIRSTIONYSSUS
BT1 laelapidae
BT2 mesostigmata
BT3 acari
NT1 hirstionyssus isabellinus

HIRSTIONYSSUS ISABELLINUS
BT1 hirstionyssus
BT2 laelapidae
BT3 mesostigmata
BT4 acari

HIRSUTELLA
BT1 deuteromycotina
BT1 entomogenous fungi
BT2 entomopathogens
BT3 pathogens
BT2 fungi
NT1 hirsutella thompsonii

HIRSUTELLA THOMPSONII
BT1 fungal acaricides
BT2 acaricides
BT3 pesticides
BT2 microbial pesticides
BT3 pesticides
BT1 hirsutella
BT2 deuteromycotina
BT2 entomogenous fungi
BT3 entomopathogens
BT4 pathogens
BT3 fungi

HIRSUTIELLA
BT1 trombiculidae
BT2 prostigmata
BT3 acari
NT1 hirsutiella zachvatkini
rt neotrombicula

HIRSUTIELLA ZACHVATKINI
uf *neotrombicula zachvatkini*
BT1 hirsutiella
BT2 trombiculidae
BT3 prostigmata
BT4 acari

HIRUDIDAE
BT1 hirudinea
BT2 annelida
NT1 hirudo
NT2 hirudo medicinalis

HIRUDINEA
uf *leeches*
BT1 annelida
NT1 erpobdellidae
NT2 dina
NT3 dina anoculata
NT2 erpobdella
NT3 erpobdella octoculata
NT1 glossiphoniidae
NT2 glossiphonia
NT3 glossiphonia complanata
NT2 haementeria
NT2 helobdella
NT3 helobdella stagnalis
NT2 placobdella
NT2 theromyzon
NT3 theromyzon rude
NT1 haemadipsidae
NT2 haemadipsa
NT1 hirudidae

HIRUDINEA *cont.*
NT2 hirudo
NT3 hirudo medicinalis
NT1 piscicolidae
NT2 piscicola
NT3 piscicola geometra

HIRUDO
BT1 hirudidae
BT2 hirudinea
BT3 annelida
NT1 hirudo medicinalis

HIRUDO MEDICINALIS
BT1 hirudo
BT2 hirudidae
BT3 hirudinea
BT4 annelida

HIRUNDINIDAE
uf *swallows*
BT1 passeriformes
BT2 birds
NT1 delichon
NT2 delichon urbica
NT1 hirundo
NT2 hirundo rustica
NT1 petrochelidon
NT2 petrochelidon pyrrhonota
NT1 riparia
NT2 riparia riparia

HIRUNDO
BT1 hirundinidae
BT2 passeriformes
BT3 birds
NT1 hirundo rustica
rt petrochelidon

hirundo pyrrhonota
USE **petrochelidon pyrrhonota**

HIRUNDO RUSTICA
BT1 hirundo
BT2 hirundinidae
BT3 passeriformes
BT4 birds

HISHIMONUS
BT1 cicadellidae
BT2 cicadelloidea
BT3 auchenorrhyncha
BT4 homoptera
NT1 hishimonus phycitis
rt eutettix

HISHIMONUS PHYCITIS
uf *eutettix phycitis*
BT1 hishimonus
BT2 cicadellidae
BT3 cicadelloidea
BT4 auchenorrhyncha
BT5 homoptera

hispa
USE **dicladispa**

hispa armigera
USE **dicladispa armigera**

HISPANICS (AGRICOLA)
uf *puerto ricans*
BT1 ethnic groups
BT2 groups

HISSAR
HN from 1990
BT1 sheep breeds
BT2 breeds

HISTAMINE
BT1 biogenic amines
BT2 amines
BT3 amino compounds
BT4 organic nitrogen compounds
BT1 imidazoles
BT2 azoles
BT3 heterocyclic nitrogen compounds
BT4 organic nitrogen compounds
rt antihistaminics

HISTER
BT1 histeridae
BT2 coleoptera

HISTERIDAE
BT1 coleoptera
NT1 carcinops
NT2 carcinops pumilio
NT1 hister
NT1 teretriosoma
NT2 teretriosoma nigrescens

histidase
USE **histidine ammonia-lyase**

HISTIDINAEMIA
BT1 acidaemia
BT2 blood disorders
BT3 animal disorders
BT4 disorders
rt histidine
rt histidinemia (agricola)

HISTIDINE
BT1 essential amino acids
BT2 amino acids
BT3 carboxylic acids
BT4 organic acids
BT5 acids
BT3 organic nitrogen compounds
BT1 imidazoles
BT2 azoles
BT3 heterocyclic nitrogen compounds
BT4 organic nitrogen compounds
rt histidinaemia
rt methylhistidine

HISTIDINE AMMONIA-LYASE
(ec 4.3.1.3)
uf histidase
BT1 ammonia-lyases
BT2 lyases
BT3 enzymes

HISTIDINEMIA (AGRICOLA)
rt histidinaemia

HISTIOCYTES
BT1 cells

HISTIOCYTOSIS
BT1 blood disorders
BT2 animal disorders
BT3 disorders
rt blood cells
rt macrophages

HISTIOSTOMA
BT1 histiostomatidae
BT2 astigmata
BT3 acari

HISTIOSTOMATIDAE
uf anoetidae
BT1 astigmata
BT2 acari
NT1 histiostoma

HISTOCHEMISTRY
BT1 chemistry
BT1 histology
BT2 biology
NT1 immunohistochemistry

HISTOCOMPATIBILITY
BT1 compatibility
rt allografts
rt animal tissues
rt graft rejection
rt major histocompatibility complex
rt non-h-2 complex
rt non-rt1 complex

HISTOCOMPATIBILITY ANTIGENS
BT1 antigens
BT2 immunological factors
rt major histocompatibility complex

histocompatibility complex
USE **major histocompatibility complex**

HISTOENZYMOLOGY
uf enzyme histochemistry
BT1 enzymology
BT2 biochemistry
BT3 chemistry
BT1 histology
BT2 biology

HISTOLOGY
BT1 biology
NT1 histochemistry
NT2 immunohistochemistry
NT1 histoenzymology
NT1 plant histology
rt anatomy
rt histopathology
rt microscopy
rt sectioning
rt tissues

HISTOMONAS
BT1 sarcomastigophora
BT2 protozoa
NT1 histomonas meleagridis

HISTOMONAS MELEAGRIDIS
BT1 histomonas
BT2 sarcomastigophora
BT3 protozoa

histone kinase
USE **protamine kinase**

HISTONES
BT1 proteins
BT2 peptides
NT1 globins
rt nucleoproteins

HISTOPATHOLOGY
BT1 pathology
rt histology

HISTOPHILUS
BT1 pasteurellaceae
BT2 gracilicutes
BT3 bacteria
BT4 prokaryotes

histophilus ovis
USE **haemophilus somnus**

HISTOPLASMA
BT1 deuteromycotina
NT1 histoplasma capsulatum
NT1 histoplasma duboisii
NT1 histoplasma farciminosum
rt histoplasmosis

HISTOPLASMA CAPSULATUM
BT1 histoplasma
BT2 deuteromycotina
rt ajellomyces capsulatus
rt histoplasmin

HISTOPLASMA DUBOISII
BT1 histoplasma
BT2 deuteromycotina
rt african histoplasmosis

HISTOPLASMA FARCIMINOSUM
BT1 histoplasma
BT2 deuteromycotina
rt epizootic lymphangitis

HISTOPLASMIN
BT1 fungal antigens
BT2 antigens
BT3 immunological factors
rt histoplasma capsulatum

HISTOPLASMOSIS
BT1 mycoses
BT2 infectious diseases
BT3 diseases
NT1 african histoplasmosis
rt histoplasma

HISTORIC BUILDINGS
BT1 buildings
rt ancient monuments
rt cultural heritage
rt historic sites
rt history
rt monuments
rt museums

HISTORIC SITES
HN from 1989
BT1 site types
rt ancient monuments
rt heritage areas
rt historic buildings

HISTORICAL RECORDS
BT1 records
NT1 biographies
rt history

HISTORY
uf history and evolution
NT1 veterinary history
rt archaeological material
rt archaeology
rt historic buildings
rt historical records
rt life history
rt phylogeny

history and evolution
USE **evolution**
OR **history**

HISTOSOLS
BT1 soil types (genetic)
NT1 muck soils
rt bog soils
rt organic soils

HISTOTYLENCHUS
BT1 dolichodoridae
BT2 nematoda

HITCHES
BT1 components
NT1 automatic hitches
NT1 safety hitches
rt couplings
rt linkages
rt tractors
rt trailers

hitches, automatic
USE **automatic hitches**

hitches, safety
USE **safety hitches**

hiv
USE **human immunodeficiency virus**

HIVE ENTRANCE CLOSING DEVICES
BT1 hive parts
BT2 movable-comb hives
BT3 hives
rt hive entrance fittings

HIVE ENTRANCE FITTINGS
BT1 hive parts
BT2 movable-comb hives
BT3 hives
rt hive entrance closing devices

HIVE FLOORBOARDS
BT1 hive parts
BT2 movable-comb hives
BT3 hives

HIVE PARTS
BT1 movable-comb hives
BT2 hives
NT1 bee escapes
NT1 combs
NT2 cells (honeybees)
NT3 cappings
NT3 queen cells
NT2 comb starters
NT2 comb type
NT2 foundation
NT3 plastic foundation
NT2 framed combs
NT2 plastic combs
NT1 hive entrance closing devices
NT1 hive entrance fittings
NT1 hive floorboards
NT1 hive roofs
NT1 queen excluders
NT1 sections
NT1 super bodies
rt frames

HIVE PRODUCTS
BT1 animal products
BT2 products
NT1 bee-collected pollen
NT1 beeswax
NT1 honey
NT2 artificial honey
NT2 chunk honey
NT2 comb honey
NT2 creamed honey
NT2 dried honey
NT2 extracted honey
NT2 granulated honey
NT2 section honey
NT2 strained honey
NT2 stringy honey
NT1 honeybee venom
NT1 propolis
NT1 royal jelly
rt beekeeping
rt food products
rt hives
rt livestock products

HIVE RELOCATION
BT1 manipulations
BT2 beekeeping
rt hives

HIVE ROOFS
BT1 hive parts
BT2 movable-comb hives
BT3 hives

HIVES
NT1 compound hives
NT1 fixed-comb hives
NT2 skeps
NT1 mating hives
NT1 movable-comb hives
NT2 british standard hives
NT2 double-walled hives
NT2 hive parts
NT3 bee escapes
NT3 combs
NT4 cells (honeybees)
NT5 cappings
NT5 queen cells
NT4 comb starters
NT4 comb type
NT4 foundation
NT5 plastic foundation
NT4 framed combs
NT4 plastic combs
NT3 hive entrance closing devices
NT3 hive entrance fittings
NT3 hive floorboards
NT3 hive roofs
NT3 queen excluders
NT3 sections
NT3 super bodies
NT2 horizontal hives
NT2 langstroth hives
NT2 movable-comb frameless hives
NT2 nucleus hives
NT2 observation hives
NT2 plastic hives
NT2 scale hives
NT2 schenk hives
NT2 single-walled hives
NT2 top-opening hives
NT2 top-supering hives
NT2 warm-way hives
rt animal housing
rt beekeeping
rt hive products
rt hive relocation
rt hiving
rt manipulations

HIVING
BT1 manipulations
BT2 beekeeping
rt hives

HMF
uf *hydroxymethylfurfural*
BT1 aldehydes
BT1 furans
BT2 heterocyclic oxygen compounds
rt milk

HOBBIES
BT1 leisure activities
BT1 recreational activities
rt do it yourself activities
rt handicrafts
rt home based leisure
rt home economics

HOCKEY
BT1 ball games
BT2 games
BT2 sport

HOCKS
BT1 legs
BT2 limbs
BT3 body regions

HODGKIN'S DISEASE
(lymphadenosis or lymphogranuloma)
uf *lymphogranuloma*
BT1 granuloma
BT2 tissue proliferation
BT1 human diseases
BT2 diseases

HODOTERMES
BT1 hodotermitidae
BT2 isoptera
NT1 hodotermes mossambicus

HODOTERMES MOSSAMBICUS
BT1 hodotermes
BT2 hodotermitidae
BT3 isoptera

HODOTERMITIDAE
BT1 isoptera
NT1 anacanthotermes
NT2 anacanthotermes ahngerianus
NT2 anacanthotermes ochraceus
NT1 hodotermes
NT2 hodotermes mossambicus

HOEING
BT1 tillage
BT2 cultivation
rt manual weed control

HOES
uf *sweeps*
BT1 implements
NT1 rotary hoes
NT1 steerage hoes
rt thinners
rt weeders

hoes, rotary
USE **rotary hoes**

hoes, steerage
USE **steerage hoes**

HOFERELLUS
BT1 myxozoa
BT2 protozoa

hog cholera virus
USE **swine fever virus**

hogs
USE **pigs**

HOHENBERGIA
BT1 bromeliaceae

HOHERIA
BT1 malvaceae
NT1 hoheria angustifolia

HOHERIA ANGUSTIFOLIA
BT1 hoheria
BT2 malvaceae
BT1 ornamental woody plants

HOISTS
BT1 conveyors
rt cranes
rt elevators
rt loaders
rt power lifts

HOKKAIDO
uf *japan (hokkaido)*
BT1 japan
BT2 east asia
BT3 asia

holando-argentino
USE **argentine friesian**

HOLARRHENA
BT1 apocynaceae
NT1 holarrhena congolensis
NT1 holarrhena floribunda
NT1 holarrhena pubescens
NT1 holarrhena wulfsbergii

holarrhena antidysenterica
USE **holarrhena pubescens**

HOLARRHENA CONGOLENSIS
BT1 holarrhena
BT2 apocynaceae

holarrhena febrifuga
USE **holarrhena pubescens**

HOLARRHENA FLORIBUNDA
BT1 holarrhena
BT2 apocynaceae

HOLARRHENA PUBESCENS
uf *holarrhena antidysenterica*
uf *holarrhena febrifuga*
BT1 holarrhena
BT2 apocynaceae
BT1 medicinal plants

HOLARRHENA WULFSBERGII
BT1 holarrhena
BT2 apocynaceae

HOLCOCERA
BT1 blastobasidae
BT2 lepidoptera
rt pseudohypatopa

holcocera pulverea
USE **pseudohypatopa pulverea**

HOLCOPASITES
BT1 apidae
BT2 hymenoptera

HOLCOTHORAX
BT1 encyrtidae
BT2 hymenoptera
NT1 holcothorax testaceipes

HOLCOTHORAX TESTACEIPES
BT1 holcothorax
BT2 encyrtidae
BT3 hymenoptera

HOLCUS
BT1 gramineae
NT1 holcus lanatus
NT1 holcus mollis

HOLCUS LANATUS
BT1 holcus
BT2 gramineae
BT1 pasture plants

HOLCUS MOLLIS
BT1 holcus
BT2 gramineae
BT1 pasture plants

HOLIDAY ACCOMMODATION
AF vacation accommodation
BT1 accommodation
NT1 bed and breakfast accommodation
NT1 camp sites

HOLIDAY ACCOMMODATION *cont.*
NT1 caravan sites
NT1 farmhouse accommodation
NT1 guest houses
NT1 holiday camps
NT1 holiday chalets
NT1 holiday villages
NT1 hotels
NT2 budget hotels
NT2 economy hotels
NT2 luxury hotels
NT2 middle market hotels
NT2 reception
NT1 second homes
NT1 self catering accommodation
NT1 timesharing
rt health resorts
rt holidays
rt hospitality industry
rt resorts

HOLIDAY CAMPS
AF vacation camps
BT1 holiday accommodation
BT2 accommodation

HOLIDAY CHALETS
AF vacation chalets
BT1 holiday accommodation
BT2 accommodation
rt cabins

holiday resorts
USE **resorts**

HOLIDAY VILLAGES
AF vacation villages
BT1 holiday accommodation
BT2 accommodation

HOLIDAYS
AF vacations
BT1 tourism
NT1 activity holidays
NT1 camping
NT1 caravanning
NT1 cruises
NT1 farm holidays
NT1 package holidays
NT1 special interest holidays
rt destinations
rt holiday accommodation
rt leisure
rt resorts
rt tourist industry

holland, noord
USE **noord-holland**

holland, zuid
USE **zuid-holland**

HOLLOW HEART
BT1 plant disorders
BT2 disorders
rt celeriac
rt peas
rt potatoes

HOLLOW STEM
BT1 plant disorders
BT2 disorders
rt broccoli
rt cauliflowers

HOLLY
rt ilex aquifolium

hollyhocks
USE **alcea rosea**

HOLMSKIOLDIA
BT1 verbenaceae
NT1 holmskioldia sanguinea

HOLMSKIOLDIA SANGUINEA
BT1 holmskioldia
BT2 verbenaceae

HOLOCALYX
BT1 leguminosae
NT1 holocalyx balansae

HOLOCALYX BALANSAE
BT1 holocalyx
BT2 leguminosae

HOLOCARPHA
BT1 compositae

HOLOCENE SOILS
BT1 soil types (stratigraphic)

HOLOCHILUS
BT1 hesperomyinae
BT2 muridae
BT3 rodents
BT4 mammals
NT1 holochilus brasiliensis

HOLOCHILUS BRASILIENSIS
BT1 holochilus
BT2 hesperomyinae
BT3 muridae
BT4 rodents
BT5 mammals

HOLODISCUS
BT1 rosaceae
NT1 holodiscus discolor

HOLODISCUS DISCOLOR
BT1 holodiscus
BT2 rosaceae

HOLOGRAPHY
rt imagery
rt lasers
rt photography

HOLOMASTIGOTOIDES
BT1 sarcomastigophora
BT2 protozoa
NT1 holomastigotoides hartmanni

HOLOMASTIGOTOIDES HARTMANNI
BT1 holomastigotoides
BT2 sarcomastigophora
BT3 protozoa

HOLOPTELEA
BT1 ulmaceae
NT1 holoptelea integrifolia

HOLOPTELEA INTEGRIFOLIA
BT1 forest trees
BT1 holoptelea
BT2 ulmaceae

HOLOSTEUM
BT1 caryophyllaceae

HOLOTHUROIDEA
uf *sea cucumbers*
BT1 echinodermata
NT1 cucumaria
NT1 stichopus

holotrichia
USE **holotrichia (coleoptera)**
OR **holotrichia (protozoa)**

HOLOTRICHIA (COLEOPTERA)
uf *holotrichia*
uf *lachnosterna*
BT1 scarabaeidae
BT2 coleoptera
NT1 holotrichia consanguinea
NT1 holotrichia morosa
NT1 holotrichia serrata

HOLOTRICHIA CONSANGUINEA
uf *lachnosterna consanguinea*
BT1 holotrichia (coleoptera)
BT2 scarabaeidae
BT3 coleoptera

HOLOTRICHIA MOROSA
uf *lachnosterna morosa*
BT1 holotrichia (coleoptera)
BT2 scarabaeidae
BT3 coleoptera

HOLOTRICHIA (PROTOZOA)
uf *holotrichia*
BT1 ciliophora
BT2 protozoa

HOLOTRICHIA SERRATA
BT1 holotrichia (coleoptera)
BT2 scarabaeidae
BT3 coleoptera

HOLSTEIN
BT1 horse breeds
BT2 breeds

HOLSTEIN-FRIESIAN
BT1 cattle breeds
BT2 breeds

HOLTTUMARA
BT1 orchidaceae
rt ornamental orchids

holy see
USE **vatican**

HOMALANTHUS
BT1 euphorbiaceae
NT1 homalanthus populifolius

HOMALANTHUS POPULIFOLIUS
BT1 homalanthus
BT2 euphorbiaceae

HOMALICTUS
BT1 apidae
BT2 hymenoptera

HOMALOGASTER
BT1 paramphistomatidae
BT2 digenea
BT3 trematoda
NT1 homalogaster paloniae

HOMALOGASTER PALONIAE
BT1 homalogaster
BT2 paramphistomatidae
BT3 digenea
BT4 trematoda

HOMALOMENA
BT1 araceae
NT1 homalomena lindenii

HOMALOMENA LINDENII
uf *alocasia lindenii*
BT1 homalomena
BT2 araceae
rt ornamental foliage plants

HOMARUS
BT1 decapoda
BT2 malacostraca
BT3 crustacea
BT4 arthropods
NT1 homarus americanus
NT1 homarus gammarus
rt lobsters

HOMARUS AMERICANUS
BT1 homarus
BT2 decapoda
BT3 malacostraca
BT4 crustacea
BT5 arthropods

HOMARUS GAMMARUS
BT1 homarus
BT2 decapoda
BT3 malacostraca
BT4 crustacea
BT5 arthropods

HOME ACCIDENTS (AGRICOLA)
BT1 accidents
rt home safety (agricola)

HOME APPLIANCES (AGRICOLA)
BT1 appliances (agricola)
rt household equipment (agricola)

HOME-BASED BUSINESSES (AGRICOLA)
uf *home manufacture*
uf *home production*
BT1 businesses
rt small businesses

HOME BASED LEISURE
BT1 leisure activities
NT1 do it yourself activities

HOME BASED LEISURE *cont.*
NT1 gardening
rt hobbies

HOME BIRTH (AGRICOLA)
BT1 childbirth (agricola)

HOME CARE (AGRICOLA)
rt health care (agricola)
rt long term care (agricola)
rt outpatient services (agricola)

HOME DELIVERED MEALS (AGRICOLA)
uf *meals on wheels*
BT1 meals
rt food distribution programs (agricola)

HOME ECONOMICS
uf *domestic science*
NT1 interior decoration
rt cookery (agricola)
rt cooking
rt do it yourself activities
rt hobbies
rt home economics education (agricola)
rt home economics organizations (agricola)
rt home economists (agricola)
rt homemaking skills (agricola)
rt household consumption
rt household expenditure
rt housewives
rt housework
rt social sciences

HOME ECONOMICS EDUCATION (AGRICOLA)
BT1 professional education (agricola)
BT2 education
rt home economics

HOME ECONOMICS ORGANIZATIONS (AGRICOLA)
BT1 organizations
rt home economics

HOME ECONOMISTS (AGRICOLA)
BT1 occupations
rt home economics

home farming plots
USE **domestic gardens**
OR **private plots**

HOME FOOD PREPARATION (AGRICOLA)
BT1 food preparation (agricola)
rt blenders (agricola)

HOME FOOD PRESERVATION (AGRICOLA)
BT1 food preservation (agricola)
BT2 preservation
BT3 techniques

HOME GARDENS
(agroforestry systems on private land around houses with trees, annual and perennial crops and often small livestock)
(do not use for domestic gardens)
uf *homegardens*
uf *homestead gardens*
BT1 agrosilvopastoral systems
BT2 agroforestry systems
rt agrosilvicultural systems
rt domestic gardens
rt forest gardens
rt mixed gardens
rt tree gardens
rt village forest gardens

HOME HEALTH AIDES (AGRICOLA)
BT1 allied health occupations (agricola)
BT2 occupations
rt health care (agricola)

HOME MAINTENANCE (AGRICOLA)
BT1 maintenance
rt homes

HOME MANAGEMENT (AGRICOLA)
rt homemaking skills (agricola)
rt homes
rt management

home manufacture
USE **cottage industry**
OR **home-based businesses (agricola)**

home production
USE **cottage industry**
OR **home-based businesses (agricola)**

HOME SAFETY (AGRICOLA)
BT1 safety
rt home accidents (agricola)

homegardens
USE **home gardens**

homelands, south africa
USE **south african homelands**

HOMEMAKERS (AGRICOLA)
uf *househusbands*
NT1 displaced homemakers (agricola)
rt housewives
rt visiting homemakers (agricola)

HOMEMAKING SKILLS (AGRICOLA)
BT1 skills (agricola)
rt home economics
rt home management (agricola)

HOMEOPATHIC DRUGS
BT1 drugs
rt homeopathy

HOMEOPATHY
BT1 medicine
rt homeopathic drugs

HOMEOPRONEMATUS
BT1 tydeidae
BT2 prostigmata
BT3 acari
NT1 homeopronematus anconai

HOMEOPRONEMATUS ANCONAI
BT1 homeopronematus
BT2 tydeidae
BT3 prostigmata
BT4 acari

HOMEOSTASIS
BT1 regulation
rt equilibrium
rt stability

HOMEOWNERS (AGRICOLA)
rt homes

HOMEOWNERS' INSURANCE (AGRICOLA)
BT1 insurance
NT1 basic homeowners' insurance (agricola)
NT1 comprehensive homeowners' insurance (agricola)

HOMERIA
BT1 iridaceae

HOMES
BT1 housing
NT1 apartments (agricola)
NT1 boarding homes (agricola)
NT1 condominiums (agricola)
NT1 foster homes (agricola)
NT1 mobile homes (agricola)
NT1 retirement homes (agricola)
NT1 second homes

HOMES *cont.*
rt accommodation
rt home maintenance (agricola)
rt home management (agricola)
rt homeowners (agricola)
rt homesteading (agricola)

homestead gardens
USE **home gardens**

HOMESTEADING (AGRICOLA)
rt homes

HOMIDIUM
uf *ethidium*
BT1 quaternary ammonium compounds
BT2 ammonium compounds
BT2 organic nitrogen compounds
BT1 trypanocides
BT2 antiprotozoal agents
BT3 antiparasitic agents
BT4 drugs

HOMINIDAE
BT1 primates
BT2 mammals
NT1 homo
rt man

HOMO
BT1 hominidae
BT2 primates
BT3 mammals

homo sapiens
USE **man**

HOMOCYSTEINE
BT1 sulfur amino acids
BT2 amino acids
BT3 carboxylic acids
BT4 organic acids
BT5 acids
BT3 organic nitrogen compounds
BT2 organic sulfur compounds
rt adenosylhomocysteine
rt homocystinuria

HOMOCYSTINURIA
BT1 aminoaciduria
BT2 aciduria
BT3 metabolic disorders
BT4 animal disorders
BT5 disorders
BT1 brain disorders
BT2 nervous system diseases
BT3 organic diseases
BT4 diseases
rt homocysteine
rt mental retardation

HOMOEOSOMA
BT1 pyralidae
BT2 lepidoptera
NT1 homoeosoma electellum

HOMOEOSOMA ELECTELLUM
BT1 homoeosoma
BT2 pyralidae
BT3 lepidoptera

HOMOGENIZATION
BT1 milk processing
BT2 processing
rt cavitation
rt homogenized milk
rt mixing

HOMOGENIZED MILK
uf *milk, homogenized*
BT1 milk
BT2 animal products
BT3 products
rt homogenization
rt pasteurized milk

HOMOGENIZERS
BT1 dairy equipment
BT2 equipment

HOMOGLOSSUM
BT1 iridaceae
rt corms
rt ornamental bulbs

HOMOLOGOUS RECOMBINATION
HN from 1990
BT1 recombination
BT2 genetic change
rt targeted mutagenesis

HOMONA
BT1 tortricidae
BT2 lepidoptera
NT1 homona coffearia
NT1 homona magnanima

HOMONA COFFEARIA
BT1 homona
BT2 tortricidae
BT3 lepidoptera

HOMONA MAGNANIMA
BT1 homona
BT2 tortricidae
BT3 lepidoptera

HOMOPTERA
NT1 auchenorrhyncha
NT2 cercopoidea
NT3 aphrophoridae
NT4 aphrophora
NT5 aphrophora alni
NT4 philaenus
NT5 philaenus spumarius
NT3 cercopidae
NT4 aeneolamia
NT5 aeneolamia contigua
NT5 aeneolamia selecta
NT5 aeneolamia varia
NT4 deois
NT5 deois flavopicta
NT5 deois schach
NT4 mahanarva
NT5 mahanarva fimbriolata
NT5 mahanarva posticata
NT4 zulia
NT5 zulia colombiana
NT5 zulia entreriana
NT3 machaerotidae
NT4 hindola
NT5 hindola fulva
NT5 hindola striata
NT2 cicadelloidea
NT3 cicadellidae
NT4 agallia
NT5 agallia constricta
NT5 agallia laevis
NT4 alnetoidia
NT5 alnetoidia alneti
NT4 amplicephalus
NT4 amrasca
NT5 amrasca biguttula
NT5 amrasca devastans
NT4 anaceratagallia
NT4 chlorita
NT4 cicadella
NT5 cicadella viridis
NT4 cicadulina
NT5 cicadulina bipunctata
NT5 cicadulina chinai
NT5 cicadulina mbila
NT5 cicadulina parazeae
NT5 cicadulina storeyi
NT4 circulifer
NT5 circulifer tenellus
NT4 cofana
NT5 cofana spectra
NT4 colladonus
NT5 colladonus montanus
NT4 dalbulus
NT5 dalbulus elimatus
NT5 dalbulus gelbus
NT5 dalbulus maidis
NT4 empoasca
NT5 empoasca decipiens
NT5 empoasca dolichi
NT5 empoasca fabae
NT5 empoasca flavescens
NT5 empoasca kerri
NT5 empoasca kraemeri
NT4 empoascanara

HOMOPTERA *cont.*
NT5 empoascanara maculifrons
NT4 erythroneura
NT5 erythroneura elegantula
NT4 eupteryx
NT5 eupteryx atropunctata
NT4 euscelis
NT5 euscelis plebeja
NT4 eutettix
NT4 exitianus
NT5 exitianus exitiosus
NT4 fieberiella
NT5 fieberiella florii
NT4 graminella
NT5 graminella nigrifrons
NT4 graphocephala
NT5 graphocephala atropunctata
NT4 hishimonus
NT5 hishimonus phycitis
NT4 idiocerus
NT4 idioscopus
NT5 idioscopus clypealis
NT4 jacobiasca
NT5 jacobiasca lybica
NT4 jacobiella
NT5 jacobiella facialis
NT4 macrosteles
NT5 macrosteles fascifrons
NT5 macrosteles laevis
NT5 macrosteles sexnotatus
NT4 neoaliturus
NT4 nephotettix
NT5 nephotettix cincticeps
NT5 nephotettix malayanus
NT5 nephotettix nigropictus
NT5 nephotettix virescens
NT4 orosius
NT5 orosius argentatus
NT4 psammotettix
NT5 psammotettix striatus
NT4 recilia
NT5 recilia dorsalis
NT4 scaphoideus
NT5 scaphoideus titanus
NT4 scaphytopius
NT5 scaphytopius acutus
NT5 scaphytopius magdalensis
NT4 tettigoniella
NT4 thaia
NT5 thaia oryzivora
NT5 thaia subrufa
NT4 typhlocyba
NT4 zygina
NT4 zyginidia
NT3 membracidae
NT4 ceresa
NT5 ceresa bubalus
NT4 spissistilus
NT5 spissistilus festinus
NT4 stictocephala
NT5 stictocephala bisonia
NT2 cicadoidea
NT3 cicadidae
NT4 magicicada
NT5 magicicada cassinii
NT5 magicicada septendecim
NT5 magicicada septendecula
NT2 fulgoroidea
NT3 cixiidae
NT4 myndus
NT5 myndus crudus
NT3 delphacidae
NT4 delphacodes
NT4 javesella
NT5 javesella pellucida
NT4 laodelphax
NT5 laodelphax striatella
NT4 nilaparvata
NT5 nilaparvata bakeri
NT5 nilaparvata lugens
NT4 peregrinus
NT5 peregrinus maidis
NT4 perkinsiella
NT5 perkinsiella saccharicida
NT4 sogata

HOMOPTERA *cont.*
NT4 sogatella
NT5 sogatella furcifera
NT4 sogatodes
NT5 sogatodes cubanus
NT5 sogatodes orizicola
NT4 toya
NT5 toya propinqua
NT3 lophopidae
NT4 pyrilla
NT5 pyrilla perpusilla
NT3 tettigometridae
NT4 hilda
NT5 hilda patruelis
NT3 tropiduchidae
NT4 numicia
NT5 numicia viridis
NT1 sternorrhyncha
NT2 aleyrodoidea
NT3 aleyrodidae
NT4 aleurocanthus
NT5 aleurocanthus citriperdus
NT5 aleurocanthus spiniferus
NT5 aleurocanthus woglumi
NT4 aleurocybotus
NT5 aleurocybotus indicus
NT4 aleurodicus
NT5 aleurodicus cocois
NT5 aleurodicus dispersus
NT4 aleurolobus
NT5 aleurolobus barodensis
NT4 aleurothrixus
NT5 aleurothrixus floccosus
NT4 aleyrodes
NT5 aleyrodes brassicae
NT5 aleyrodes proletella
NT4 bemisia
NT5 bemisia giffardi
NT5 bemisia tabaci
NT4 dialeurodes
NT5 dialeurodes citri
NT5 dialeurodes citrifolii
NT4 parabemisia
NT5 parabemisia myricae
NT4 siphoninus
NT5 siphoninus phillyreae
NT4 trialeurodes
NT5 trialeurodes abutiloneus
NT5 trialeurodes vaporariorum
NT2 aphidoidea
NT3 adelgidae
NT4 adelges
NT5 adelges laricis
NT5 adelges tardus
NT4 cholodkovskya
NT5 cholodkovskya viridana
NT4 dreyfusia
NT5 dreyfusia nordmannianae
NT5 dreyfusia piceae
NT4 gilletteella
NT5 gilletteella cooleyi
NT4 pineus
NT5 pineus pini
NT4 sacchiphantes
NT5 sacchiphantes abietis
NT5 sacchiphantes viridis
NT3 aphididae
NT4 acyrthosiphon
NT5 acyrthosiphon assiniboinensis
NT5 acyrthosiphon caraganae
NT5 acyrthosiphon gossypii
NT5 acyrthosiphon kondoi
NT5 acyrthosiphon pisum
NT4 amphorophora
NT5 amphorophora agathonica
NT5 amphorophora rubi
NT4 anoecia
NT5 anoecia corni
NT4 anuraphis
NT5 anuraphis farfarae
NT4 aphis
NT5 aphis craccae
NT5 aphis craccivora

HOMOPTERA *cont.*
NT5 aphis euonymi
NT5 aphis fabae
NT6 aphis fabae solanella
NT5 aphis forbesi
NT5 aphis frangulae
NT5 aphis gossypii
NT5 aphis medicaginis
NT5 aphis middletonii
NT5 aphis nasturtii
NT5 aphis nerii
NT5 aphis pomi
NT5 aphis punicae
NT5 aphis spiraecola
NT4 aulacorthum
NT5 aulacorthum circumflexum
NT5 aulacorthum solani
NT4 brachycaudus
NT5 brachycaudus cardui
NT5 brachycaudus helichrysi
NT5 brachycaudus persicae
NT5 brachycaudus schwartzi
NT4 brachycolus
NT4 brachycorynella
NT5 brachycorynella asparagi
NT4 brevicoryne
NT5 brevicoryne brassicae
NT4 capitophorus
NT5 capitophorus elaeagni
NT5 capitophorus hippophaes
NT5 capitophorus horni
NT4 cavariella
NT5 cavariella aegopodii
NT4 cedrobium
NT5 cedrobium laportei
NT4 chaetosiphon
NT5 chaetosiphon fragaefolii
NT4 chromaphis
NT5 chromaphis juglandicola
NT4 cinara
NT5 cinara pinea
NT5 cinara pini
NT4 corylobium
NT5 corylobium avellanae
NT4 diuraphis
NT5 diuraphis noxia
NT4 drepanosiphum
NT5 drepanosiphum dixoni
NT5 drepanosiphum platanoidis
NT4 dysaphis
NT5 dysaphis crataegi
NT5 dysaphis devecta
NT5 dysaphis plantaginea
NT5 dysaphis pyri
NT5 dysaphis reaumuri
NT4 elatobium
NT5 elatobium abietinum
NT4 eriosoma
NT5 eriosoma lanigerum
NT5 eriosoma ulmi
NT4 eucallipterus
NT5 eucallipterus tiliae
NT4 eulachnus
NT5 eulachnus rileyi
NT4 eutrichosiphum
NT4 hyadaphis
NT5 hyadaphis coriandri
NT4 hyalopterus
NT5 hyalopterus amygdali
NT5 hyalopterus pruni
NT4 hyperomyzus
NT5 hyperomyzus lactucae
NT4 hysteroneura
NT5 hysteroneura setariae
NT4 illinoia
NT4 lachnus
NT4 lipaphis
NT5 lipaphis erysimi
NT4 macrosiphoniella
NT5 macrosiphoniella sanborni
NT4 macrosiphum
NT5 macrosiphum euphorbiae
NT5 macrosiphum rosae

HOMOPTERA *cont.*
NT4 megoura
NT5 megoura viciae
NT4 melanaphis
NT5 melanaphis sacchari
NT4 melanocallis
NT5 melanocallis caryaefoliae
NT4 metopolophium
NT5 metopolophium dirhodum
NT5 metopolophium festucae
NT4 microlophium
NT5 microlophium carnosum
NT4 monellia
NT5 monellia caryella
NT5 monellia nigropunctata
NT4 monelliopsis
NT5 monelliopsis pecanis
NT4 myzocallis
NT5 myzocallis castanicola
NT5 myzocallis coryli
NT4 myzus
NT5 myzus ascalonicus
NT5 myzus cerasi
NT5 myzus persicae
NT5 myzus varians
NT4 nasonovia
NT5 nasonovia ribisnigri
NT4 nearctaphis
NT5 nearctaphis bakeri
NT4 pachypappa
NT5 pachypappa tremulae
NT4 pemphigus
NT5 pemphigus bursarius
NT5 pemphigus fuscicornis
NT4 pentalonia
NT5 pentalonia nigronervosa
NT4 periphyllus
NT5 periphyllus acericola
NT4 phloeomyzus
NT5 phloeomyzus passerinii
NT4 phorodon
NT5 phorodon cannabis
NT5 phorodon humuli
NT4 rhodobium
NT5 rhodobium porosum
NT4 rhopalosiphoninus
NT5 rhopalosiphoninus latysiphon
NT4 rhopalosiphum
NT5 rhopalosiphum insertum
NT5 rhopalosiphum maidis
NT5 rhopalosiphum padi
NT5 rhopalosiphum rufiabdominalis
NT4 schizaphis
NT5 schizaphis graminum
NT4 schizolachnus
NT5 schizolachnus pineti
NT4 semiaphis
NT5 semiaphis heraclei
NT4 sipha
NT5 sipha elegans
NT5 sipha flava
NT5 sipha maydis
NT4 sitobion
NT5 sitobion avenae
NT5 sitobion fragariae
NT4 tetraneura
NT5 tetraneura nigriabdominalis
NT5 tetraneura ulmi
NT4 therioaphis
NT5 therioaphis riehmi
NT5 therioaphis trifolii
NT6 therioaphis trifolii form maculata
NT4 toxoptera
NT5 toxoptera aurantii
NT5 toxoptera citricidus
NT5 toxoptera odinae
NT4 uroleucon
NT5 uroleucon ambrosiae
NT5 uroleucon carthami
NT5 uroleucon compositae
NT5 uroleucon sonchi

HOMOPTERA *cont.*
NT3 mindaridae
NT4 mindarus
NT5 mindarus abietinus
NT3 phylloxeridae
NT4 phylloxera
NT4 viteus
NT5 viteus vitifoliae
NT3 thelaxidae
NT4 thelaxes
NT2 coccoidea
NT3 aclerdidae
NT4 aclerda
NT5 aclerda campinensis
NT3 asterolecaniidae
NT4 asterolecanium
NT5 asterolecanium pustulans
NT3 coccidae
NT4 anapulvinaria
NT5 anapulvinaria pistaciae
NT4 ceroplastes
NT5 ceroplastes destructor
NT5 ceroplastes floridensis
NT5 ceroplastes japonicus
NT5 ceroplastes rubens
NT5 ceroplastes rusci
NT4 chloropulvinaria
NT5 chloropulvinaria aurantii
NT5 chloropulvinaria floccifera
NT5 chloropulvinaria psidii
NT4 coccus
NT5 coccus hesperidum
NT5 coccus perlatus
NT5 coccus viridis
NT4 eulecanium
NT5 eulecanium tiliae
NT4 gascardia
NT4 kilifia
NT5 kilifia acuminata
NT4 palaeolecanium
NT5 palaeolecanium bituberculatum
NT4 parasaissetia
NT5 parasaissetia nigra
NT4 parthenolecanium
NT5 parthenolecanium corni
NT4 protopulvinaria
NT5 protopulvinaria pyriformis
NT4 pulvinaria
NT5 pulvinaria mesembryanthemi
NT5 pulvinaria regalis
NT4 pulvinariella
NT4 rhodococcus (homoptera)
NT5 rhodococcus turanicus
NT4 saissetia
NT5 saissetia coffeae
NT5 saissetia oleae
NT4 sphaerolecanium
NT5 sphaerolecanium prunastri
NT3 dactylopiidae
NT4 dactylopius
NT5 dactylopius ceylonicus
NT5 dactylopius opuntiae
NT3 diaspididae
NT4 abgrallaspis
NT5 abgrallaspis cyanophylli
NT4 aonidiella
NT5 aonidiella aurantii
NT5 aonidiella citrina
NT5 aonidiella orientalis
NT4 aonidomytilus
NT5 aonidomytilus albus
NT4 aspidiotus
NT5 aspidiotus destructor
NT5 aspidiotus nerii
NT4 aulacaspis
NT5 aulacaspis madiunensis
NT5 aulacaspis rosae
NT5 aulacaspis tegalensis
NT5 aulacaspis tubercularis
NT4 chionaspis
NT5 chionaspis pinifoliae
NT5 chionaspis salicis
NT4 chrysomphalus

HOMOPTERA *cont.*
NT5 chrysomphalus aonidum
NT5 chrysomphalus dictyospermi
NT4 diaspidiotus
NT4 diaspis
NT5 diaspis bromeliae
NT4 fiorinia
NT5 fiorinia theae
NT4 hemiberlesia
NT5 hemiberlesia lataniae
NT5 hemiberlesia rapax
NT4 insulaspis
NT4 lepidosaphes
NT5 lepidosaphes beckii
NT5 lepidosaphes gloverii
NT5 lepidosaphes ulmi
NT4 leucaspis
NT4 melanaspis
NT5 melanaspis glomerata
NT4 parlatoria
NT5 parlatoria blanchardii
NT5 parlatoria oleae
NT5 parlatoria pergandii
NT5 parlatoria ziziphi
NT4 pinnaspis
NT5 pinnaspis strachani
NT4 pseudaonidia
NT4 pseudaulacaspis
NT5 pseudaulacaspis pentagona
NT4 quadraspidiotus
NT5 quadraspidiotus ostreaeformis
NT5 quadraspidiotus perniciosus
NT4 selenaspidus
NT5 selenaspidus articulatus
NT4 unaspis
NT5 unaspis citri
NT5 unaspis euonymi
NT5 unaspis yanonensis
NT3 eriococcidae
NT4 cryptococcus (homoptera)
NT5 cryptococcus fagisuga
NT3 kermesidae
NT4 kermes
NT3 kerriidae
NT4 kerria (homoptera)
NT5 kerria lacca
NT3 margarodidae
NT4 icerya
NT5 icerya aegyptiaca
NT5 icerya purchasi
NT4 margarodes
NT4 matsucoccus
NT5 matsucoccus feytaudi
NT5 matsucoccus massonianae
NT5 matsucoccus matsumurae
NT5 matsucoccus pini
NT5 matsucoccus resinosae
NT4 porphyrophora
NT5 porphyrophora hamelii
NT3 pseudococcidae
NT4 antonina
NT5 antonina graminis
NT4 brevennia
NT5 brevennia rehi
NT4 dysmicoccus
NT5 dysmicoccus brevipes
NT4 eurycoccus
NT4 ferrisia
NT5 ferrisia virgata
NT4 hypogeococcus
NT4 maconellicoccus
NT5 maconellicoccus hirsutus
NT4 nipaecoccus
NT5 nipaecoccus viridis
NT4 phenacoccus
NT5 phenacoccus gossypii
NT5 phenacoccus herreni
NT5 phenacoccus manihoti
NT5 phenacoccus solani
NT4 planococcoides

HOMOPTERA *cont.*
NT5 planococcoides njalensis
NT4 planococcus
NT5 planococcus citri
NT5 planococcus ficus
NT4 pseudococcus
NT5 pseudococcus adonidum
NT5 pseudococcus affinis
NT5 pseudococcus calceolariae
NT5 pseudococcus comstocki
NT5 pseudococcus longispinus
NT5 pseudococcus maritimus
NT4 rastrococcus
NT5 rastrococcus iceryoides
NT5 rastrococcus invadens
NT4 rhizoecus
NT5 rhizoecus cacticans
NT4 saccharicoccus
NT5 saccharicoccus sacchari
NT4 trionymus
NT2 psylloidea
NT3 aphalaridae
NT4 agonoscena
NT5 agonoscena targionii
NT4 diaphorina
NT5 diaphorina citri
NT3 carsidaridae
NT4 mesohomotoma
NT5 mesohomotoma tessmanni
NT3 psyllidae
NT4 cacopsylla
NT5 cacopsylla mali
NT5 cacopsylla pyri
NT5 cacopsylla pyricola
NT5 cacopsylla pyrisuga
NT4 euphyllura
NT5 euphyllura olivina
NT4 heteropsylla
NT5 heteropsylla cubana
NT4 psylla
NT3 triozidae
NT4 trioza
NT5 trioza erytreae
rt hemiptera
rt insects

HOMOSERINE
BT1 nonprotein amino acids
BT2 amino acids
BT3 carboxylic acids
BT4 organic acids
BT5 acids
BT3 organic nitrogen compounds

homoserine dehydratase
USE **cystathionine γ-lyase**

HOMOSEXUALS
HN from 1989
rt acquired immune deficiency syndrome
rt immunocompromised hosts
rt opportunistic infections

HOMOVANILLIC ACID
BT1 benzenealkanoic acids
BT2 carboxylic acids
BT3 organic acids
BT4 acids

HOMOZYGOSITY
BT1 genetics
BT2 biology
rt genes
rt heterozygosity
rt inbreeding

HOMOZYGOTES
BT1 genotypes
rt genes
rt heterozygotes

honan
USE **henan**

HONDURAS
BT1 central america
BT2 america
rt cacm

honduras, british
USE **belize**

HONEY
BT1 hive products
BT2 animal products
BT3 products
NT1 artificial honey
NT1 chunk honey
NT1 comb honey
NT1 creamed honey
NT1 dried honey
NT1 extracted honey
NT1 granulated honey
NT1 section honey
NT1 strained honey
NT1 stringy honey
rt cappings
rt fermented honey
rt honey houses
rt honey hunting
rt honey sac
rt honey-getting capacity
rt nectar
rt poisonous honey
rt uncapping

HONEY-GETTING CAPACITY
BT1 foraging
BT2 feeding habits
BT3 feeding behaviour
BT4 behaviour
BT3 habits
rt capacity
rt honey
rt honeybee colonies
rt nectar

HONEY HOUSES
BT1 buildings
rt honey

HONEY HUNTING
BT1 wild honeybee colonies
BT2 honeybee colonies
BT3 honeybees
rt bee hunting
rt honey

HONEY SAC
BT1 digestive system
BT2 body parts
rt honey
rt honeybees
rt nectar

HONEYBEE BROOD
uf *broods*
BT1 honeybee colonies
BT2 honeybees
NT1 sealed brood
rt american foul brood
rt brood rearing
rt chalk brood
rt european foul brood
rt foul brood
rt larvae
rt prepupae
rt pupae
rt sac brood
rt stone brood

HONEYBEE COLONIES
uf *bee colonies*
BT1 honeybees
NT1 honeybee brood
NT2 sealed brood
NT1 multiple-queen colonies
NT1 nucleus honeybee colonies
NT1 queenlessness
NT1 queenrightness
NT1 swarms
NT2 casts
NT1 wild honeybee colonies
NT2 bee hunting
NT2 honey hunting
rt absconding
rt clustering

HONEYBEE COLONIES *cont.*
rt colony defence
rt drifting
rt eviction
rt fanning
rt fighting
rt foraging period
rt honey-getting capacity
rt robbing
rt seasonal cycle
rt supersedure
rt swarming
rt swarming impulse
rt swarming period
rt swarming preparations
rt swarms
rt winter cluster

HONEYBEE FORAGE
NT1 honeydew
NT2 honeydew flows
NT2 manna
NT1 nectar
NT1 pollen
NT1 propolis
rt forage
rt honeybees
rt seasonal cycle

HONEYBEE VENOM
BT1 hive products
BT2 animal products
BT3 products
BT1 venoms
rt apamin
rt honeybees
rt melittin
rt stinging
rt stings

HONEYBEES
uf *bees*
NT1 drone honeybees
NT2 drone congregation areas
NT1 honeybee colonies
NT2 honeybee brood
NT3 sealed brood
NT2 multiple-queen colonies
NT2 nucleus honeybee colonies
NT2 queenlessness
NT2 queenrightness
NT2 swarms
NT3 casts
NT2 wild honeybee colonies
NT3 bee hunting
NT3 honey hunting
NT1 package honeybees
NT1 queen honeybees
NT2 mated queen honeybees
NT2 virgin queen honeybees
NT1 worker honeybees
NT2 flying honeybees
NT2 house honeybees
NT2 laying worker honeybees
NT2 nurse honeybees
NT2 scout honeybees
rt 2-heptanone
rt apidae
rt apis
rt apis cerana
rt apis dorsata
rt apis florea
rt apis mellifera
rt bee diseases
rt bee viruses
rt beekeeping
rt beeswax
rt cells (honeybees)
rt fumagillin
rt group effect
rt honey sac
rt honeybee forage
rt honeybee venom
rt pollen dispensers
rt pollinators
rt polymorphism
rt stinging
rt subduing
rt swarming

HONEYCOMBING
BT1 wood defects

HONEYCOMBING *cont.*
BT2 defects

HONEYDEW
BT1 honeybee forage
BT1 secretions
NT1 honeydew flows
NT1 manna
rt insects

HONEYDEW FLOWS
BT1 honeydew
BT2 honeybee forage
BT2 secretions

HONEYSUCKLE LATENT CARLAVIRUS
HN from 1990
uf *lonicera latent carlavirus*
BT1 carlavirus group
BT2 plant viruses
BT3 plant pathogens
BT4 pathogens
rt lonicera

HONG KONG
BT1 east asia
BT2 asia
rt developing countries
rt threshold countries

HONSHU
uf *japan (honshu)*
BT1 japan
BT2 east asia
BT3 asia

hoof and claw
USE **claws**
OR **hooves**

hoof and claw diseases
USE **foot diseases**

HOOF AND HORN MEAL
BT1 manures
BT2 organic amendments
BT3 soil amendments
BT4 amendments
BT1 meal

HOOKWORMS
BT1 helminths
BT2 parasites
rt ancylostoma braziliense
rt ancylostoma caninum
rt ancylostoma ceylanicum
rt ancylostoma duodenale
rt ancylostoma tubaeforme
rt necator americanus
rt uncinaria stenocephala

HOOVES
uf *hoof and claw*
uf *hooves and claws*
BT1 integument
BT2 body parts
rt shoeing
rt ungulates

hooves and claws
USE **claws**
OR **hooves**

HOP GARDEN SOILS
BT1 soil types (cultural)
rt hop gardens

HOP GARDENS
BT1 plantations
rt hop garden soils
rt hops

HOP HARVESTERS
uf *harvesters, hop*
uf *hop pickers*
BT1 harvesters
BT2 farm machinery
BT3 machinery
rt hops

HOP LATENT CARLAVIRUS
HN from 1990; previously "hop latent virus"
uf *hop latent virus*

HOP LATENT CARLAVIRUS *cont.*
BT1 carlavirus group
BT2 plant viruses
BT3 plant pathogens
BT4 pathogens
rt hops
rt humulus lupulus

hop latent virus
USE **hop latent carlavirus**

HOP MOSAIC CARLAVIRUS
HN from 1990; previously "hop mosaic virus"
uf *hop mosaic virus*
BT1 carlavirus group
BT2 plant viruses
BT3 plant pathogens
BT4 pathogens
rt hops
rt humulus lupulus

hop mosaic virus
USE **hop mosaic carlavirus**

hop pickers
USE **hop harvesters**

HOP STUNT VIROID
BT1 viroids
BT2 plant pathogens
BT3 pathogens

HOP TREFOIL CRYPTIC 1 CRYPTOVIRUS
HN from 1990
BT1 cryptovirus group
BT2 plant viruses
BT3 plant pathogens
BT4 pathogens

HOP TREFOIL CRYPTIC 2 CRYPTOVIRUS
HN from 1990
BT1 cryptovirus group
BT2 plant viruses
BT3 plant pathogens
BT4 pathogens

HOPEA
BT1 dipterocarpaceae
rt forest trees

hopei
USE **hubei**

HOPLITIS
uf *formicapis*
uf *liosmia*
BT1 apidae
BT2 hymenoptera

HOPLOCAMPA
BT1 tenthredinidae
BT2 hymenoptera
NT1 hoplocampa flava
NT1 hoplocampa minuta
NT1 hoplocampa testudinea

HOPLOCAMPA FLAVA
BT1 hoplocampa
BT2 tenthredinidae
BT3 hymenoptera

hoplocampa fulvicornis
USE **hoplocampa minuta**

HOPLOCAMPA MINUTA
uf *hoplocampa fulvicornis*
BT1 hoplocampa
BT2 tenthredinidae
BT3 hymenoptera

HOPLOCAMPA TESTUDINEA
BT1 hoplocampa
BT2 tenthredinidae
BT3 hymenoptera

HOPLOCHELUS
BT1 scarabaeidae
BT2 coleoptera
NT1 hoplochelus marginalis

HOPLOCHELUS MARGINALIS
BT1 hoplochelus

HOPLOCHELUS MARGINALIS *cont.*
BT2 scarabaeidae
BT3 coleoptera

HOPLOLAIMIDAE
BT1 nematoda
NT1 acontylus
NT2 acontylus vipriensis
NT1 aphasmatylenchus
NT2 aphasmatylenchus straturatus
NT1 basirolaimus
NT1 helicotylenchus
NT2 helicotylenchus dihystera
NT2 helicotylenchus erythrinae
NT2 helicotylenchus multicinctus
NT2 helicotylenchus pseudorobustus
NT1 hoplolaimus
NT2 hoplolaimus columbus
NT2 hoplolaimus galeatus
NT2 hoplolaimus indicus
NT2 hoplolaimus pararobustus
NT2 hoplolaimus seinhorsti
NT1 pararotylenchus
NT1 peltamigratus
NT1 rotylenchulus
NT2 rotylenchulus parvus
NT2 rotylenchulus reniformis
NT1 rotylenchus
NT2 rotylenchus buxophilus
NT2 rotylenchus robustus
NT1 scutellonema
NT2 scutellonema brachyurum
NT2 scutellonema bradys
rt plant parasitic nematodes

HOPLOLAIMUS
BT1 hoplolaimidae
BT2 nematoda
NT1 hoplolaimus columbus
NT1 hoplolaimus galeatus
NT1 hoplolaimus indicus
NT1 hoplolaimus pararobustus
NT1 hoplolaimus seinhorsti
rt basirolaimus

HOPLOLAIMUS COLUMBUS
BT1 hoplolaimus
BT2 hoplolaimidae
BT3 nematoda

HOPLOLAIMUS GALEATUS
BT1 hoplolaimus
BT2 hoplolaimidae
BT3 nematoda

HOPLOLAIMUS INDICUS
BT1 hoplolaimus
BT2 hoplolaimidae
BT3 nematoda

HOPLOLAIMUS PARAROBUSTUS
BT1 hoplolaimus
BT2 hoplolaimidae
BT3 nematoda

HOPLOLAIMUS SEINHORSTI
BT1 hoplolaimus
BT2 hoplolaimidae
BT3 nematoda

HOPLOPLEURA
BT1 hoplopleuridae
BT2 anoplura
BT3 phthiraptera
NT1 hoplopleura acanthopus

HOPLOPLEURA ACANTHOPUS
BT1 hoplopleura
BT2 hoplopleuridae
BT3 anoplura
BT4 phthiraptera

HOPLOPLEURIDAE
BT1 anoplura
BT2 phthiraptera
NT1 hoplopleura
NT2 hoplopleura acanthopus

hoploprosopis
USE **hylaeus**

HOPLORHYNCHUS
BT1 apicomplexa
BT2 protozoa

HOPPEA
BT1 gentianaceae
NT1 hoppea dichotoma

HOPPEA DICHOTOMA
BT1 hoppea
BT2 gentianaceae
BT1 medicinal plants

HOPPERS
BT1 containers
rt bins
rt bunkers
rt loading
rt unloading

HOPPING QUALITY
uf *quality for hopping*
BT1 quality
rt brewing industry
rt brewing quality
rt hops
rt humulon
rt lupulon

HOPS
BT1 antifungal plants
BT1 industrial crops
BT1 medicinal plants
rt beers
rt brewing industry
rt cone withering
rt cones
rt hop gardens
rt hop harvesters
rt hop latent carlavirus
rt hop mosaic carlavirus
rt hopping quality
rt humulus lupulus
rt sets
rt spent hops
rt wort

hops, spent
USE **spent hops**

HORDEIN
BT1 prolamins
BT2 cereal proteins
BT3 plant proteins
BT4 proteins
BT5 peptides

HORDEIVIRUS GROUP
HN from 1990
BT1 plant viruses
BT2 plant pathogens
BT3 pathogens
NT1 barley stripe mosaic hordeivirus
NT1 lychnis ringspot hordeivirus
NT1 poa semilatent hordeivirus

HORDENINE
BT1 biogenic amines
BT2 amines
BT3 amino compounds
BT4 organic nitrogen compounds

HORDEUM
BT1 gramineae
NT1 hordeum agriocrithon
NT1 hordeum bulbosum
NT1 hordeum geniculatum
NT1 hordeum glaucum
NT1 hordeum irregulare
NT1 hordeum jubatum
NT1 hordeum marinum
NT1 hordeum murinum
NT1 hordeum murinum subsp. leporinum
NT1 hordeum pusillum
NT1 hordeum secalinum
NT1 hordeum spontaneum
NT1 hordeum vulgare

HORDEUM AGRIOCRITHON
BT1 hordeum
BT2 gramineae

HORDEUM BULBOSUM
BT1 hordeum
BT2 gramineae

hordeum distichum
USE **hordeum vulgare**

HORDEUM GENICULATUM
BT1 hordeum
BT2 gramineae

HORDEUM GLAUCUM
BT1 hordeum
BT2 gramineae

HORDEUM IRREGULARE
BT1 hordeum
BT2 gramineae

HORDEUM JUBATUM
BT1 hordeum
BT2 gramineae

hordeum leporinum
USE **hordeum murinum subsp. leporinum**

HORDEUM MARINUM
BT1 hordeum
BT2 gramineae

HORDEUM MURINUM
BT1 hordeum
BT2 gramineae

HORDEUM MURINUM SUBSP. LEPORINUM
uf *hordeum leporinum*
BT1 hordeum
BT2 gramineae

HORDEUM PUSILLUM
BT1 hordeum
BT2 gramineae

HORDEUM SECALINUM
BT1 hordeum
BT2 gramineae

HORDEUM SPONTANEUM
BT1 hordeum
BT2 gramineae

HORDEUM VULGARE
uf *hordeum distichum*
BT1 hordeum
BT2 gramineae
rt barley
rt barley stripe mosaic hordeivirus
rt barley yellow dwarf luteovirus
rt barley yellow mosaic virus
rt barley yellow striate mosaic rhabdovirus

HORIZONS
uf *soil horizons*
BT1 soil morphological features
NT1 a horizons
NT1 anthropogenic horizons
NT1 argillic horizons
NT1 b horizons
NT1 calcic horizons
NT1 cambic horizons
NT1 diagnostic horizons
NT1 humic horizons
NT1 humus horizons
NT1 indurated horizons
NT1 organic horizons
NT1 petrocalcic horizons
NT1 placic horizons
NT1 spodic horizons
NT1 vesicular horizons

HORIZONTAL FLOW
BT1 flow
BT2 movement
rt horizontal infiltration
rt soil water movement

HORIZONTAL HIVES
BT1 movable-comb hives
BT2 hives

HORIZONTAL INFILTRATION
BT1 soil water movement
BT2 movement
rt horizontal flow

HORIZONTAL INTEGRATION
uf *integration, horizontal*
uf *integration, lateral*
uf *lateral integration*
BT1 integration
BT2 concentration of production
BT3 socioeconomic organization

HORIZONTAL RESISTANCE
uf *resistance, horizontal*
BT1 resistance
rt water flow resistance

HORIZONTAL WELLS
BT1 wells
BT2 water supply
BT3 water systems
BT4 systems

HORMOCONIS
HN from 1990
BT1 deuteromycotina
rt amorphotheca

hormoconis resinae
USE **amorphotheca resinae**

HORMONAL CONTROL
uf *endocrine control*
BT1 controls
NT1 gonadotropin release
NT1 neurohormonal control
rt hormones

HORMONE ANTAGONISTS
BT1 antagonists
BT2 metabolic inhibitors
BT3 inhibitors
NT1 bromocriptine
NT1 juvenile hormone antagonists
NT2 precocenes
NT3 precocene i
NT3 precocene ii
NT3 precocene iii
NT1 saralasin
NT1 spironolactone
NT1 thyroid antagonists
NT2 goitrin
NT2 propylthiouracil
NT1 urogastrone
rt drugs
rt hormones

HORMONE RECEPTORS
BT1 receptors
rt hormones

HORMONE SECRETION
uf *endocrine function*
uf *endocrine secretion*
BT1 secretion
BT2 physiological functions
rt hormones
rt thyroid function

HORMONE SUPPLEMENTS
BT1 supplements

HORMONES
NT1 adrenal cortex hormones
NT2 glucocorticoids
NT3 corticosterone
NT3 cortisone
NT3 hydrocortisone
NT2 mineralocorticoids
NT3 aldosterone
NT3 corticosterone
NT3 cortisone
NT3 desoxycortone
NT3 hydrocortisone
NT1 adrenal medulla hormones
NT2 epinephrine
NT2 norepinephrine
NT1 arthropod hormones
NT2 adipokinetic hormones
NT2 juvenile hormones

HORMONES *cont.*
NT3 juvenile hormone i
NT3 juvenile hormone ii
NT3 juvenile hormone iii
NT2 moulting hormones
NT3 α-ecdysone
NT3 ecdysterone
NT2 prothoracicotropic hormones
NT1 cybernins
NT1 gastrointestinal hormones
NT2 gastrin
NT2 motilin
NT2 pancreozymin
NT2 secretin
NT2 substance p
NT2 urogastrone
NT2 vasoactive intestinal peptide
NT1 growth factors
NT2 epidermal growth factor
NT2 somatomedin
NT3 insulin-like growth factor
NT2 transforming growth factor
NT1 hypothalamic inhibiting hormones
NT2 prolactostatin
NT2 somatostatin
NT1 hypothalamic releasing hormones
NT2 corticoliberin
NT2 fshrh
NT2 gnrh
NT2 gonadorelin
NT2 lhrh
NT2 prolactoliberin
NT2 somatoliberin
NT2 thyrotropin releasing hormone
NT1 kinins
NT2 blastokinin
NT2 bradykinin
NT2 eledoisin
NT2 pancreozymin
NT2 substance p
NT1 melatonin
NT1 neurohormones
NT1 pancreatic hormones
NT2 glucagon
NT2 insulin
NT2 pancreatic polypeptide
NT1 parathyrin
NT1 pituitary hormones
NT2 adenohypophysis hormones
NT2 corticotropin
NT2 lipotropin
NT2 luteotropin
NT2 melanotropins
NT2 mesotocin
NT2 oxytocin
NT2 pituitary gonadotropins
NT3 fsh
NT3 lh
NT2 pro-opiomelanocortin
NT2 prolactin
NT2 somatotropin
NT2 thyrotropin
NT2 vasopressin
NT2 vasotocin
NT3 arginine vasotocin
NT1 placental hormones
NT2 choriomammotropin
NT2 chorionic gonadotropin
NT3 hcg
NT1 prostaglandins
NT2 prostacyclin
NT1 renal hormones
NT2 angiotensin
NT2 erythropoietin
NT2 vasopressin
NT1 sex hormones
NT2 androgens
NT3 androstenedione
NT3 androsterone
NT3 prasterone
NT3 testosterone
NT2 corpus luteum hormones
NT3 progesterone
NT3 relaxin
NT2 gonadotropins

HORMONES *cont.*
NT3 chorionic gonadotropin
NT4 hcg
NT3 human menopausal gonadotropin
NT3 pituitary gonadotropins
NT4 fsh
NT4 lh
NT3 pmsg
NT2 inhibin
NT2 oestrogens
NT3 catechol oestrogens
NT3 estradiol
NT3 estriol
NT3 estrone
NT3 plant oestrogens
NT4 coumoestrol
NT4 formononetin
NT4 zearalenone
NT2 progestogens
NT3 progesterone
NT1 steroid hormones
NT1 thymus hormones
NT2 thymopoietin
NT1 thyroid hormones
NT2 l-thyroxine
NT2 calcitonin
NT2 triiodothyronine
rt endocrine glands
rt endocrinology
rt hormonal control
rt hormone antagonists
rt hormone receptors
rt hormone secretion
rt hyperparathyroidism
rt neurohormonal control
rt synergism
rt synthetic hormones

hormones, plant
USE **plant growth regulators**

hornbeam
USE **carpinus betulus**

hornbills
USE **bucerotidae**

HORNS
BT1 integument
BT2 body parts
NT1 antlers
NT2 velvet
rt keratinization
rt moult
rt polled condition

horogenes
USE **diadegma**

horogenes fenestralis
USE **diadegma fenestralis**

horse
USE **horses**

HORSE ANTERIOR PITUITARY EXTRACT
HN from 1989
rt gonadotropins

horse beans
USE **faba beans**

HORSE BREEDING
BT1 animal breeding
BT2 breeding
rt horse breeds
rt horses
rt livestock farming

HORSE BREEDS
(only important and recognised breeds are listed)
BT1 breeds
NT1 akhal-teke
NT1 albanian
NT1 altai
NT1 american saddle horse
NT1 american trotter
NT1 anatolian native
NT1 andalusian
NT1 appaloosa
NT1 arab

HORSE BREEDS *cont.*
NT1 argentine criollo
NT1 auxois
NT1 azerbaijan
NT1 baluchi
NT1 barb
NT1 bashkir
NT1 belgian
NT1 bhotia pony
NT1 bosnian pony
NT1 boulonnais
NT1 breton
NT1 budyonny
NT1 byelorussian harness
NT1 campolino
NT1 canadian
NT1 chumysh
NT1 cleveland bay
NT1 clydesdale
NT1 comtois
NT1 connemara pony
NT1 crioulo
NT1 cukurova
NT1 dales pony
NT1 danube
NT1 dartmoor pony
NT1 don
NT1 dongola
NT1 east bulgarian
NT1 east friesian
NT1 edles warmblut
NT1 finnish
NT1 fjord
NT1 frederiksborg
NT1 french anglo-arab
NT1 french ardennais
NT1 french saddlebred
NT1 french trotter
NT1 gelderland (horse breed)
NT1 german riding horse
NT1 hackney
NT1 haflinger
NT1 hequ
NT1 holstein
NT1 hungarian draft
NT1 hutsul
NT1 iceland pony
NT1 jinzhou
NT1 karabair
NT1 kathiawari
NT1 kazakh
NT1 kirgiz
NT1 kushum
NT1 kustanai
NT1 lipitsa
NT1 lithuanian heavy draft
NT1 lokai
NT1 malopolski
NT1 mangalarga
NT1 manipuri pony
NT1 marwari
NT1 mingrelian
NT1 morgan
NT1 new kirgiz
NT1 nonius
NT1 noric
NT1 ob
NT1 oldenburg
NT1 orlov trotter
NT1 paint
NT1 palomino
NT1 pechora
NT1 percheron
NT1 pleven
NT1 poitou
NT1 polesian
NT1 quarter horse
NT1 romanian
NT1 rottal
NT1 russian heavy draft
NT1 russian trotter
NT1 sandalwood pony
NT1 schleswig
NT1 shan pony
NT1 shetland pony
NT1 shire
NT1 south german coldblood
NT1 soviet heavy draft
NT1 spiti pony
NT1 suffolk
NT1 swedish ardennes

HORSE BREEDS *cont.*
NT1 tavda
NT1 tennessee walking horse
NT1 tersk
NT1 thoroughbred
NT1 tibetan pony
NT1 tori
NT1 trakehner
NT1 tushin
NT1 ukrainian saddle horse
NT1 vladimir heavy draft
NT1 vyatka
NT1 waziri
NT1 welsh pony
NT1 western sudan pony
NT1 wielkopolski
NT1 wurttemberg
NT1 yakut
NT1 zaniskari pony
NT1 zemaitukai
NT1 zweibrucken
rt horse breeding
rt horses

horse chestnut
USE **aesculus hippocastanum**

HORSE DISEASES
BT1 animal diseases
BT2 diseases
NT1 african horse sickness
NT1 contagious equine metritis
NT1 dourine
NT1 equine infectious anaemia
NT1 glanders
NT1 sweet itch
rt foal diseases
rt grass sickness
rt horses
rt pulmonary emphysema
rt spavin

HORSE DUNG
BT1 faeces
BT2 excreta
BT3 animal wastes
BT4 wastes
rt horses

HORSE FEEDING
BT1 livestock feeding
BT2 animal feeding
BT3 feeding
NT1 mare feeding
rt horses

horse gram
USE **macrotyloma uniflorum**

horse mackerel
USE **trachurus trachurus**

HORSE MANURE
uf stable manure
BT1 animal manures
BT2 manures
BT3 organic amendments
BT4 soil amendments
BT5 amendments
rt horses

HORSE MEAT
BT1 meat
BT2 animal products
BT3 products
BT2 foods
rt horses

horse, przewalski's
USE **przewalski's horse**

HORSE RACING
BT1 animal sports
BT2 outdoor recreation
BT3 recreation
BT2 sport
rt gambling
rt horse riding

HORSE RIDING
BT1 animal sports
BT2 outdoor recreation
BT3 recreation
BT2 sport

HORSE RIDING *cont.*
NT1 pony trekking
NT1 show jumping
rt bridle paths
rt horse racing
rt horses
rt riding animals
rt saddle performance
rt saddles
rt three-day events

HORSERADISH
rt armoracia rusticana

HORSES
uf *equus caballus*
uf *horse*
uf *ponies*
BT1 livestock
BT2 animals
BT1 meat animals
BT2 animals
BT1 working animals
BT2 animals
rt colts
rt donkeys
rt equidae
rt foals
rt hinnies
rt horse breeding
rt horse breeds
rt horse diseases
rt horse dung
rt horse feeding
rt horse manure
rt horse meat
rt horse riding
rt mares
rt mules
rt przewalski's horse
rt racehorses
rt shoeing
rt show jumping
rt stables
rt stallions

horses, race
USE **racehorses**

HORTICULTURAL CROPS
rt algicidal plants
rt antibacterial plants
rt antifungal plants
rt antiviral plants
rt crops
rt culinary herbs
rt dye plants
rt essential oil plants
rt fatty oil plants
rt fibre plants
rt field crops
rt fruit crops
rt greenhouse crops
rt gum plants
rt horticulture
rt incense plants
rt industrial crops
rt medicinal plants
rt nut crops
rt ornamental plants
rt pesticidal plants
rt piscicidal plants
rt plantation crops
rt plants
rt rubber plants
rt spice plants
rt starch crops
rt stimulant plants
rt sugar crops
rt tan plants
rt vegetables

HORTICULTURAL SOILS
BT1 soil types (cultural)

HORTICULTURE
BT1 agricultural sciences
NT1 floriculture
NT1 fruit growing
NT1 vegetable growing
NT1 viticulture
rt agricultural production
rt agriculture

HORTICULTURE *cont.*
rt domestic gardens
rt gardening
rt growers
rt horticultural crops
rt landscape gardening
rt landscaping
rt market gardens
rt primary sector

HOSES
BT1 equipment
rt irrigation

HOSPICES (AGRICOLA)
BT1 health care (agricola)
rt death and dying (agricola)
rt hospitals

HOSPITAL CATERING
AF hospital food service
BT1 catering
rt hospital diets
rt hospitals
rt liquid diets
rt therapeutic diets

HOSPITAL DIETS
uf *diets in hospital*
BT1 diets
rt feeding
rt hospital catering

HOSPITAL FOOD SERVICE
BF hospital catering
BT1 food service

HOSPITALITY (AGRICOLA)
rt hospitality industry

HOSPITALITY INDUSTRY
BT1 industry
NT1 catering industry
rt guest houses
rt holiday accommodation
rt hospitality (agricola)
rt hotels
rt tourist industry

HOSPITALS
BT1 buildings
rt healing
rt health
rt health centres
rt health services
rt hospices (agricola)
rt hospital catering
rt medical services

hospitals, animal
USE **animal hospitals**

HOST GUEST RELATIONS
BT1 behaviour
rt relationships
rt rural urban relations
rt tourism
rt tourism impact

HOST PARASITE RELATIONSHIPS
uf *parasite host relationships*
NT1 cytoadherence
NT1 host preferences
NT1 host specificity
rt defence mechanisms
rt ectoparasites
rt haematophagous arthropods
rt intermediate hosts
rt parasites
rt parasitism
rt parasitology
rt relationships

HOST PLANTS
HN from 1989
(plant upon which an organism lives but does not feed)
BT1 hosts

HOST PREFERENCES
BT1 host parasite relationships
rt hosts

HOST RANGE
rt host specificity
rt hosts

host resistance
USE **pest resistance**

HOST-SEEKING BEHAVIOR
BF host-seeking behaviour
BT1 searching behavior
BT2 behavior
rt feeding behavior
rt hematophagous arthropods

HOST-SEEKING BEHAVIOUR
AF host-seeking behavior
BT1 searching behaviour
BT2 behaviour
rt feeding behaviour
rt haematophagous arthropods

HOST SPECIFICITY
BT1 host parasite relationships
rt host range

HOSTA
BT1 liliaceae
NT1 hosta fortunei
NT1 hosta ovata
NT1 hosta sieboldiana

HOSTA FORTUNEI
BT1 hosta
BT2 liliaceae
BT1 ornamental herbaceous plants

HOSTA OVATA
BT1 hosta
BT2 liliaceae
BT1 ornamental herbaceous plants

HOSTA SIEBOLDIANA
BT1 hosta
BT2 liliaceae
BT1 ornamental herbaceous plants

HOSTS
NT1 alternative hosts
NT1 food plants
NT1 host plants
NT1 hosts of plant diseases
NT2 weed hosts
NT1 hosts of plant pests
NT1 immunocompromised hosts
NT1 intermediate hosts
NT1 reservoir hosts
NT1 sentinel animals
rt host preferences
rt host range
rt new host records

HOSTS OF PLANT DISEASES
BT1 hosts
NT1 weed hosts

HOSTS OF PLANT PESTS
BT1 hosts
rt pests

HOT AIR TREATMENT
BT1 heat treatment
BT2 heat processing
BT3 processing
rt sterilizing
rt treatment

HOT BONING (AGRICOLA)
BT1 boning (agricola)
BT2 butchering (agricola)

HOT DOGS (AGRICOLA)
uf *frankfurters*
BT1 sausages
BT2 meat products
BT3 animal products
BT4 products

HOT WATER TREATMENT
BT1 heat treatment
BT2 heat processing
BT3 processing

HOT WATER TREATMENT *cont.*
rt sterilizing
rt treatment

HOTEL CATERING
AF hotel food service
BT1 catering
rt catering industry
rt hotels

HOTEL FOOD SERVICE
BF hotel catering
BT1 food service

HOTELS
BT1 holiday accommodation
BT2 accommodation
NT1 budget hotels
NT1 economy hotels
NT1 luxury hotels
NT1 middle market hotels
NT1 reception
rt catering industry
rt hospitality industry
rt hotel catering
rt room rates

HOUMIRIACEAE
NT1 humiriastrum
NT2 humiriastrum procera

hourly wages
USE **time wages**

HOUSE DUST
BT1 dust
rt house dust mites

HOUSE DUST MITES
BT1 mites
rt arthropod allergies
rt dermatophagoides
rt house dust

HOUSE HONEYBEES
BT1 worker honeybees
BT2 honeybees

HOUSE PLANTS
rt plants
rt pot plants

HOUSEHOLD BUDGETS (AGRICOLA)
BT1 budgets
rt family budgets
rt household income (agricola)
rt households

HOUSEHOLD CONSUMPTION
BT1 consumption
BT1 family budgets
BT2 budgets
rt consumer behaviour
rt consumer expenditure
rt consumer surveys
rt home economics
rt households

HOUSEHOLD EQUIPMENT (AGRICOLA)
BT1 equipment
NT1 can openers (agricola)
NT1 garbage disposals (agricola)
NT1 irons (agricola)
rt appliances (agricola)
rt cleaning equipment (agricola)
rt coffeemakers (agricola)
rt cooking utensils (agricola)
rt crystal (agricola)
rt dinnerware (agricola)
rt dishes (agricola)
rt dishwashers (agricola)
rt flatware (agricola)
rt home appliances (agricola)
rt households
rt mixers (kitchen appliance) (agricola)
rt ovens (agricola)
rt refrigerators (agricola)
rt sewing machines (agricola)
rt utensils (agricola)
rt washing machines (agricola)

HOUSEHOLD EXPENDITURE
uf *expenditure, household*
BT1 consumer expenditure
BT2 aggregate data
BT2 expenditure
BT1 family budgets
BT2 budgets
rt consumer surveys
rt home economics
rt household income (agricola)
rt households
rt living standards

HOUSEHOLD INCOME (AGRICOLA)
BT1 income
rt household budgets (agricola)
rt household expenditure
rt households

HOUSEHOLD SURVEYS (AGRICOLA)
BT1 surveys
rt households

HOUSEHOLDS
NT1 agricultural households
rt families
rt household budgets (agricola)
rt household consumption
rt household equipment (agricola)
rt household expenditure
rt household income (agricola)
rt household surveys (agricola)
rt housewives
rt housing

househusbands
USE **homemakers (agricola)**

HOUSEKEEPERS (AGRICOLA)
BT1 occupations

houses
USE **dwellings**

HOUSEWIVES
BT1 occupations
BT1 women
BT2 adults
rt home economics
rt homemakers (agricola)
rt households
rt marriage

HOUSEWORK
rt home economics

HOUSING
NT1 cooperative housing (agricola)
NT1 dwellings
NT1 homes
NT2 apartments (agricola)
NT2 boarding homes (agricola)
NT2 condominiums (agricola)
NT2 foster homes (agricola)
NT2 mobile homes (agricola)
NT2 retirement homes (agricola)
NT2 second homes
NT1 low-rent housing (agricola)
NT1 public housing (agricola)
NT1 rural housing
NT2 farm dwellings
NT3 tied cottages
NT1 single family housing (agricola)
rt animal housing
rt households
rt housing costs (agricola)
rt living conditions
rt living standards

HOUSING COSTS (AGRICOLA)
BT1 costs
rt housing

housing, rural
USE **rural housing**

HOUTTUYNIA
BT1 saururaceae
NT1 houttuynia cordata

HOUTTUYNIA CORDATA
BT1 houttuynia
BT2 saururaceae
BT1 ornamental herbaceous plants

HOVENIA
BT1 rhamnaceae
NT1 hovenia dulcis
NT1 hovenia tomentella

HOVENIA DULCIS
BT1 hovenia
BT2 rhamnaceae
BT1 medicinal plants

HOVENIA TOMENTELLA
BT1 hovenia
BT2 rhamnaceae

HOVERCRAFT
BT1 vehicles
rt aircraft

HOWARDULA
BT1 allantonematidae
BT2 nematoda

HOWEIA
BT1 palmae
NT1 howeia forsteriana

HOWEIA FORSTERIANA
BT1 howeia
BT2 palmae
BT1 ornamental palms

HOYA
BT1 asclepiadaceae
NT1 hoya australis
NT1 hoya bella
NT1 hoya carnosa

HOYA AUSTRALIS
BT1 hoya
BT2 asclepiadaceae
BT1 ornamental succulent plants
BT2 succulent plants

HOYA BELLA
BT1 hoya
BT2 asclepiadaceae

HOYA CARNOSA
BT1 hoya
BT2 asclepiadaceae
BT1 ornamental succulent plants
BT2 succulent plants

HPLC
HN from 1990
uf *high performance liquid chromatography*
uf *high pressure liquid chromatography*
BT1 liquid chromatography
BT2 chromatography
BT3 analytical methods
BT4 methodology

HT-2 TOXIN
BT1 trichothecenes
BT2 mycotoxins
BT3 toxins

HU
HN from 1990; previously "hu-yang"
uf *hu-yang*
BT1 sheep breeds
BT2 breeds

hu-yang
USE **hu**

HUAIPI
HN from 1990
BT1 goat breeds
BT2 breeds

HUANG-HUAI-HAI BLACK
HN from 1990

HUANG-HUAI-HAI BLACK *cont.*
BT1 pig breeds
BT2 breeds

HUBEI
uf *china (hupei)*
uf *hopei*
uf *hupei*
BT1 china
BT2 east asia
BT3 asia

HUBERODENDRON
BT1 bombacaceae
NT1 huberodendron patinoi

HUBERODENDRON PATINOI
BT1 huberodendron
BT2 bombacaceae

HUCHO
BT1 salmonidae
BT2 salmoniformes
BT3 osteichthyes
BT4 fishes
NT1 hucho hucho

HUCHO HUCHO
BT1 hucho
BT2 salmonidae
BT3 salmoniformes
BT4 osteichthyes
BT5 fishes

huckleberries
USE **gaylussacia**

HUGHES VIRUS
BT1 nairovirus
BT2 arboviruses
BT3 pathogens
BT2 bunyaviridae
BT3 viruses

HULLING
BT1 processing
rt decapping
rt decortication
rt fruit crops
rt husking
rt nut crops
rt peeling
rt shellers
rt shelling

HULLS
rt fruits
rt husks

HULTHEMIA
BT1 rosaceae
NT1 hulthemia persica

HULTHEMIA PERSICA
BT1 hulthemia
BT2 rosaceae
BT1 ornamental woody plants

HUMAN ACTIVITY
rt artefacts
rt man

HUMAN BEHAVIOR
HN from 1990
BF human behaviour
BT1 behavior
NT1 antisocial behavior (agricola)
NT2 child abuse
NT2 child neglect (agricola)
NT2 delinquent behavior
NT2 discipline problems (agricola)
NT2 elder abuse (agricola)
NT2 incest (agricola)
NT2 sexual harassment (agricola)
NT2 spouse abuse (agricola)
NT2 theft (agricola)
NT3 employee theft (agricola)
NT1 economic behavior
NT2 consumer behavior
NT1 leisure behavior
NT1 visitor behavior

HUMAN BEHAVIOUR
HN from 1990
AF human behavior
BT1 behaviour
NT1 economic behaviour
NT2 consumer behaviour
NT3 complaints
NT3 consumer preferences
NT3 purchasing habits
NT2 economic impact
NT1 leisure behaviour
NT1 visitor behaviour
NT2 visitor impact
rt man

human chorionic gonadotropin
USE **hcg**

HUMAN COLOSTRUM
HN from 1989
BT1 colostrum
BT2 body fluids
BT3 fluids
rt man

HUMAN CORONAVIRUS
BT1 coronavirus
BT2 coronaviridae
BT3 viruses

HUMAN DISEASES
BT1 diseases
NT1 acquired immune deficiency syndrome
NT1 alcoholism
NT1 alzheimer's disease
NT1 appendicitis (agricola)
NT1 cachexia
NT1 chagas' disease
NT1 childhood diseases (agricola)
NT2 tay-sachs disease (agricola)
NT1 cholera
NT1 common cold
NT1 dengue
NT2 dengue haemorrhagic fever
NT1 farmer's lung
NT1 favism
NT1 hodgkin's disease
NT1 infant disorders
NT1 lyme disease
NT1 malaria
NT2 airport malaria
NT2 blackwater fever
NT2 cerebral malaria
NT1 measles
NT1 psittacosis
NT1 q fever
NT1 schistosomiasis
NT1 sclerosis
NT1 sickle cell anaemia
NT1 sjogren's syndrome
NT1 typhoid
NT1 varicella
NT1 venereal diseases (agricola)
NT2 gonorrhea (agricola)
NT2 syphilis (agricola)
NT1 yaws
NT1 yellow fever
rt man
rt medical helminthology
rt medical mycology
rt medical parasitology
rt medical research
rt mycoses
rt organic diseases
rt pathology
rt systemic diseases
rt viral hepatitis
rt visceral larva migrans
rt zoonoses

HUMAN ECOLOGY
BT1 ecology
rt geography
rt man

human engineering
USE **ergonomics**

HUMAN EXPERIMENTATION (AGRICOLA)

HUMAN EXPERIMENTATION (AGRICOLA) *cont.*
BT1 methodology

HUMAN FAECES
AF human feces
BT1 faeces
BT2 excreta
BT3 animal wastes
BT4 wastes
rt man

HUMAN FECES
BF human faeces
BT1 feces

HUMAN FERTILITY
uf *fertility, human*
BT1 fertility
rt family planning
rt man
rt medical research

human gonadotropic hormone
USE **hcg**

HUMAN HERPESVIRUS
BT1 herpesviridae
BT2 viruses
NT1 epstein-barr virus
NT1 herpes simplex virus
NT1 varicella-zoster virus

HUMAN IMMUNODEFICIENCY VIRUS
uf *aids htlv-iii*
uf *hiv*
BT1 lentivirinae
BT2 retroviridae
BT3 viruses
rt acquired immune deficiency syndrome

HUMAN LACTATION
uf *lactation, human*
BT1 lactation
rt human milk

HUMAN MENOPAUSAL GONADOTROPIN
HN from 1989
BT1 gonadotropins
BT2 glycoproteins
BT3 proteins
BT4 peptides
BT2 sex hormones
BT3 hormones
rt man

HUMAN MILK
uf *breast milk*
uf *milk, breast*
uf *milk, human*
BT1 milks
BT2 body fluids
BT3 fluids
rt breast feeding
rt human lactation
rt human milk fat
rt humanized milk
rt mammary glands

HUMAN MILK FAT
uf *breast milk fat*
uf *milk fat, human*
BT1 milk fat
BT2 animal fat
BT3 fat
rt human milk

HUMAN NUTRITION RESEARCH (AGRICOLA)
BT1 nutrition research
BT2 research

HUMAN PARAMYXOVIRUS
BT1 paramyxovirus
BT2 paramyxoviridae
BT3 viruses
NT1 mumps virus
NT1 parainfluenza virus

HUMAN POPULATION
BT1 populations

HUMAN POPULATION *cont.*
rt agricultural population
rt man
rt population change
rt population density
rt population growth
rt population pressure
rt population structure
rt rural population
rt urban population
rt working population
rt world population

HUMAN POWER
BT1 power
rt animal power
rt appropriate technology
rt manual operation

HUMAN RELATIONS (AGRICOLA)
rt interpersonal relations
rt relationships

HUMAN RESOURCES
BT1 renewable resources
BT2 natural resources
BT3 resources
NT1 labor force (agricola)
rt economic resources
rt labour
rt man

HUMAN RIGHTS
NT1 civil rights
rt legal rights

HUMANIZED MILK
uf *milk, humanized*
BT1 milk products
BT2 products
rt human milk

humans
USE **man**

HUMATES
BT1 organic fertilizers
BT2 fertilizers
BT1 organic salts
BT2 salts
NT1 ammonium humate
NT1 nitrohumates
NT1 sodium humate
rt humic acids

HUMERUS
BT1 limb bones
BT2 bones
BT3 musculoskeletal system
BT4 body parts

HUMIC ACIDS
BT1 chelating agents
BT1 humus
BT2 soil organic matter
BT3 organic matter
BT3 soil chemistry
BT1 organic acids
BT2 acids
rt humates
rt melanins

HUMIC GLEYSOLS
BT1 gleysols
BT2 soil types (genetic)

HUMIC HORIZONS
uf *humose layers*
BT1 horizons
BT2 soil morphological features
rt humus
rt humus horizons

HUMICOLA
BT1 deuteromycotina
NT1 humicola fuscoatra
NT1 humicola lanuginosa

HUMICOLA FUSCOATRA
BT1 humicola
BT2 deuteromycotina

HUMICOLA LANUGINOSA
BT1 humicola
BT2 deuteromycotina

HUMID TROPICS
BT1 humid zones
BT2 climatic zones
BT1 tropics
BT2 climatic zones

HUMID ZONES
BT1 climatic zones
NT1 humid tropics
rt humidity

HUMIDIFIER DISEASE
BT1 allergies
BT2 immunological diseases
BT3 diseases
rt humidifiers

HUMIDIFIERS
BT1 equipment
rt air conditioners
rt environmental control
rt humidifier disease
rt humidity
rt microclimate
rt relative humidity

HUMIDITY
rt humid zones
rt humidifiers
rt humidity gauges
rt psychrometers
rt relative humidity

HUMIDITY GAUGES
BT1 gauges
BT2 instruments
rt humidity
rt hygrometers
rt psychrometers

HUMIFICATION
rt humus
rt soil formation

HUMIN
BT1 humus
BT2 soil organic matter
BT3 organic matter
BT3 soil chemistry

HUMIRIASTRUM
BT1 houmiriaceae
NT1 humiriastrum procera

HUMIRIASTRUM PROCERA
BT1 humiriastrum
BT2 houmiriaceae

HUMMINGBIRDS
BT1 pollinators
BT2 beneficial organisms
rt trochilidae

HUMMOCKS
BT1 physiographic features
BT1 soil morphological features
rt mounds

humofina
USE **bitumen emulsions**

HUMORAL IMMUNITY
BT1 immunity
rt antibodies
rt maternal antibodies

humose layers
USE **humic horizons**

HUMULON
uf *α-bitter acid*
BT1 bitter acids
BT1 food preservatives
BT2 preservatives
rt brewing quality
rt hopping quality
rt humulus lupulus
rt malting quality

HUMULUS
BT1 cannabidaceae
NT1 humulus japonica
NT1 humulus lupulus

HUMULUS JAPONICA
BT1 humulus
BT2 cannabidaceae

HUMULUS LUPULUS
BT1 humulus
BT2 cannabidaceae
rt hop latent carlavirus
rt hop mosaic carlavirus
rt hops
rt humulon
rt lupulon

HUMUS
BT1 soil organic matter
BT2 organic matter
BT2 soil chemistry
NT1 fulvic acids
NT1 humic acids
NT1 humin
NT1 humus forms
NT2 mor
NT2 mull
rt forest litter
rt humic horizons
rt humification
rt humus horizons
rt leaf mould
rt peat

HUMUS FORMS
BT1 humus
BT2 soil organic matter
BT3 organic matter
BT3 soil chemistry
NT1 mor
NT1 mull

HUMUS HORIZONS
BT1 horizons
BT2 soil morphological features
rt humic horizons
rt humus

HUNAN
uf *china (hunan)*
BT1 china
BT2 east asia
BT3 asia

hungarian combing wool merino
USE **hungarian merino**

HUNGARIAN DRAFT
HN from 1990
BT1 horse breeds
BT2 breeds

HUNGARIAN MERINO
HN from 1990; previously "hungarian combing wool merino"
uf *hungarian combing wool merino*
BT1 sheep breeds
BT2 breeds

HUNGARIAN PIED
BT1 cattle breeds
BT2 breeds

HUNGARIAN SIMMENTAL
HN from 1990
BT1 cattle breeds
BT2 breeds

HUNGARIAN WHITE
BT1 pig breeds
BT2 breeds

HUNGAROFRIES
HN from 1990
BT1 cattle breeds
BT2 breeds

HUNGARY
BT1 eastern europe
BT2 europe
rt cmea

HUNGER
NT1 hyperphagia
NT2 hyperalimentation
rt appetite
rt basic needs

HUNGER *cont.*
rt famine
rt fasting
rt malnutrition
rt poverty
rt starvation
rt underfeeding
rt undernutrition

HUNNEMANNIA
BT1 papaveraceae
NT1 hunnemannia fumariifolia

HUNNEMANNIA FUMARIIFOLIA
BT1 antibacterial plants
BT1 hunnemannia
BT2 papaveraceae

hunterellus
USE **ixodiphagus**

hunterellus hookeri
USE **ixodiphagus hookeri**

HUNTERIA
BT1 apocynaceae
NT1 hunteria congolana
NT1 hunteria elliottii

HUNTERIA CONGOLANA
BT1 hunteria
BT2 apocynaceae

HUNTERIA ELLIOTTII
BT1 hunteria
BT2 apocynaceae

HUNTEROIDES
HN from 1990
BT1 cestodaria
BT2 cestoda

HUNTING
BT1 animal sports
BT2 outdoor recreation
BT3 recreation
BT2 sport
rt forest recreation
rt game farming
rt game reserves
rt hunting dogs

HUNTING DOGS
BT1 working animals
BT2 animals
rt dogs
rt hunting

HUNTLEYA
BT1 orchidaceae
rt ornamental orchids

hupei
USE **hubei**

HURA
BT1 euphorbiaceae
NT1 hura crepitans

HURA CREPITANS
BT1 hura
BT2 euphorbiaceae
BT1 medicinal plants

HURRICANES
BT1 meteorological factors
BT2 climatic factors
rt storms
rt whirlwinds
rt wind

HUSBANDRY
NT1 animal husbandry
NT2 artificial rearing
NT2 barrier husbandry
NT2 battery husbandry
NT2 cattle husbandry
NT2 floor husbandry
NT2 free range husbandry
NT2 goat keeping
NT2 poultry farming
NT2 small animal rearing
NT1 crop husbandry
NT1 extensive husbandry
NT1 germfree husbandry

HUSBANDRY *cont.*
NT1 grassland improvement
NT1 intensive husbandry
NT1 large scale husbandry
NT1 spf husbandry
NT1 sward renovation
rt agriculture
rt farming

HUSKING
BT1 decortication
BT2 processing
rt hulling
rt husks
rt peeling
rt shellers
rt shelling

HUSKS
BT1 plant residues
BT2 residues
NT1 cocoa husks
NT1 cottonseed husks
NT1 groundnut husks
NT1 pecan shells
NT1 rice husks
NT1 soyabean husks
NT1 sunflower husks
rt hulls
rt husking
rt milling residues

HUSO
BT1 acipenseridae
BT2 acipenseriformes
BT3 osteichthyes
BT4 fishes
NT1 huso huso

HUSO HUSO
uf *beluga*
BT1 huso
BT2 acipenseridae
BT3 acipenseriformes
BT4 osteichthyes
BT5 fishes

HUTCHINSIA
BT1 cruciferae
NT1 hutchinsia alpina

HUTCHINSIA ALPINA
BT1 hutchinsia
BT2 cruciferae
BT1 ornamental herbaceous plants

HUTSUL
BT1 horse breeds
BT2 breeds

hyacinth beans
USE **lablab purpureus**

hyacinthaceae
USE **liliaceae**

HYACINTHOIDES
BT1 liliaceae
NT1 hyacinthoides hispanica
NT1 hyacinthoides non-scripta
rt endymion

HYACINTHOIDES HISPANICA
uf *endymion hispanicus*
uf *scilla campanulata*
BT1 hyacinthoides
BT2 liliaceae
BT1 ornamental bulbs

HYACINTHOIDES NON-SCRIPTA
uf *endymion non-scriptus*
uf *endymion nutans*
BT1 antibacterial plants
BT1 hyacinthoides
BT2 liliaceae
BT1 ornamental bulbs

HYACINTHS
BT1 essential oil plants
BT2 oil plants
BT1 ornamental bulbs
rt hyacinthus orientalis

HYACINTHUS
BT1 liliaceae
NT1 hyacinthus orientalis
NT1 hyacinthus transcaspicus

HYACINTHUS ORIENTALIS
BT1 hyacinthus
BT2 liliaceae
rt hyacinths

HYACINTHUS TRANSCASPICUS
BT1 hyacinthus
BT2 liliaceae
BT1 ornamental bulbs

HYADAPHIS
BT1 aphididae
BT2 aphidoidea
BT3 sternorrhyncha
BT4 homoptera
NT1 hyadaphis coriandri
rt lipaphis

HYADAPHIS CORIANDRI
BT1 hyadaphis
BT2 aphididae
BT3 aphidoidea
BT4 sternorrhyncha
BT5 homoptera

hyadaphis erysimi
USE **lipaphis erysimi**

hyadaphis pseudobrassicae
USE **lipaphis erysimi**

HYAENA
BT1 hyaenidae
BT2 fissipeda
BT3 carnivores
BT4 mammals

hyaenas
USE **hyaenidae**

HYAENIDAE
uf *hyaenas*
BT1 fissipeda
BT2 carnivores
BT3 mammals
NT1 crocuta
NT2 crocuta crocuta
NT1 hyaena

HYALINOCYSTA
BT1 microspora
BT2 protozoa

HYALOMMA
BT1 ixodidae
BT2 metastigmata
BT3 acari
NT1 hyalomma aegyptium
NT1 hyalomma anatolicum
NT2 hyalomma anatolicum anatolicum
NT2 hyalomma anatolicum excavatum
NT1 hyalomma arabica
NT1 hyalomma asiaticum
NT1 hyalomma brevipunctata
NT1 hyalomma detritum
NT1 hyalomma dromedarii
NT1 hyalomma hussaini
NT1 hyalomma impeltatum
NT1 hyalomma impressum
NT1 hyalomma lusitanicum
NT1 hyalomma marginatum
NT2 hyalomma marginatum isaaci
NT2 hyalomma marginatum marginatum
NT2 hyalomma marginatum rufipes
NT2 hyalomma marginatum turanicum
NT1 hyalomma nitidum
NT1 hyalomma truncatum

HYALOMMA AEGYPTIUM
BT1 hyalomma
BT2 ixodidae
BT3 metastigmata
BT4 acari

HYALOMMA ANATOLICUM
BT1 hyalomma
BT2 ixodidae
BT3 metastigmata
BT4 acari
NT1 hyalomma anatolicum anatolicum
NT1 hyalomma anatolicum excavatum

HYALOMMA ANATOLICUM ANATOLICUM
HN from 1990
BT1 hyalomma anatolicum
BT2 hyalomma
BT3 ixodidae
BT4 metastigmata
BT5 acari

HYALOMMA ANATOLICUM EXCAVATUM
HN from 1990
BT1 hyalomma anatolicum
BT2 hyalomma
BT3 ixodidae
BT4 metastigmata
BT5 acari

HYALOMMA ARABICA
HN from 1989
BT1 hyalomma
BT2 ixodidae
BT3 metastigmata
BT4 acari

HYALOMMA ASIATICUM
BT1 hyalomma
BT2 ixodidae
BT3 metastigmata
BT4 acari

HYALOMMA BREVIPUNCTATA
HN from 1989
BT1 hyalomma
BT2 ixodidae
BT3 metastigmata
BT4 acari

HYALOMMA DETRITUM
uf *hyalomma scupense*
BT1 hyalomma
BT2 ixodidae
BT3 metastigmata
BT4 acari

HYALOMMA DROMEDARII
BT1 hyalomma
BT2 ixodidae
BT3 metastigmata
BT4 acari

HYALOMMA HUSSAINI
BT1 hyalomma
BT2 ixodidae
BT3 metastigmata
BT4 acari

HYALOMMA IMPELTATUM
BT1 hyalomma
BT2 ixodidae
BT3 metastigmata
BT4 acari

HYALOMMA IMPRESSUM
BT1 hyalomma
BT2 ixodidae
BT3 metastigmata
BT4 acari

HYALOMMA LUSITANICUM
BT1 hyalomma
BT2 ixodidae
BT3 metastigmata
BT4 acari

HYALOMMA MARGINATUM
BT1 hyalomma
BT2 ixodidae
BT3 metastigmata
BT4 acari
NT1 hyalomma marginatum isaaci
NT1 hyalomma marginatum marginatum

HYALOMMA MARGINATUM *cont.*
NT1 hyalomma marginatum rufipes
NT1 hyalomma marginatum turanicum

HYALOMMA MARGINATUM ISAACI
HN from 1990
BT1 hyalomma marginatum
BT2 hyalomma
BT3 ixodidae
BT4 metastigmata
BT5 acari

HYALOMMA MARGINATUM MARGINATUM
HN from 1990
BT1 hyalomma marginatum
BT2 hyalomma
BT3 ixodidae
BT4 metastigmata
BT5 acari

HYALOMMA MARGINATUM RUFIPES
HN from 1990
BT1 hyalomma marginatum
BT2 hyalomma
BT3 ixodidae
BT4 metastigmata
BT5 acari

HYALOMMA MARGINATUM TURANICUM
HN from 1990
BT1 hyalomma marginatum
BT2 hyalomma
BT3 ixodidae
BT4 metastigmata
BT5 acari

HYALOMMA NITIDUM
HN from 1989
BT1 hyalomma
BT2 ixodidae
BT3 metastigmata
BT4 acari

hyalomma scupense
USE **hyalomma detritum**

HYALOMMA TRUNCATUM
BT1 hyalomma
BT2 ixodidae
BT3 metastigmata
BT4 acari

HYALOPHORA
uf *platysamia*
BT1 saturniidae
BT2 lepidoptera
NT1 hyalophora cecropia

HYALOPHORA CECROPIA
uf *platysamia cecropia*
BT1 hyalophora
BT2 saturniidae
BT3 lepidoptera

HYALOPHYSA
BT1 ciliophora
BT2 protozoa

HYALOPTERUS
BT1 aphididae
BT2 aphidoidea
BT3 sternorrhyncha
BT4 homoptera
NT1 hyalopterus amygdali
NT1 hyalopterus pruni

HYALOPTERUS AMYGDALI
BT1 hyalopterus
BT2 aphididae
BT3 aphidoidea
BT4 sternorrhyncha
BT5 homoptera

HYALOPTERUS PRUNI
BT1 hyalopterus
BT2 aphididae
BT3 aphidoidea
BT4 sternorrhyncha

HYALOPTERUS PRUNI *cont.*
BT5 homoptera

HYALURONIC ACID
BT1 acid mucopolysaccharides
BT2 mucopolysaccharides
BT3 polysaccharides
BT4 carbohydrates

HYALURONIDASE
(ec 3.2.1.35, 3.2.1.36)
BT1 o-glycoside hydrolases
BT2 glycosidases
BT3 hydrolases
BT4 enzymes
rt hyaluronoglucosaminidase

HYALURONOGLUCOSAMINIDASE
(ec 3.2.1.35)
uf *hyaluronoglucosidase*
BT1 o-glycoside hydrolases
BT2 glycosidases
BT3 hydrolases
BT4 enzymes
rt hyaluronidase

hyaluronoglucosidase
USE **hyaluronoglucosaminidase**

HYBANTHUS
BT1 violaceae
rt ornamental plants

HYBLAEA
BT1 hyblaeidae
BT2 lepidoptera
NT1 hyblaea puera

HYBLAEA PUERA
BT1 hyblaea
BT2 hyblaeidae
BT3 lepidoptera

HYBLAEIDAE
BT1 lepidoptera
NT1 hyblaea
NT2 hyblaea puera

HYBOMITRA
BT1 tabanidae
BT2 diptera
NT1 hybomitra arpadi
NT1 hybomitra bimaculata
NT1 hybomitra borealis
NT1 hybomitra caucasica
NT1 hybomitra lasiophthalma
NT1 hybomitra montana
NT1 hybomitra tarandina

HYBOMITRA ARPADI
BT1 hybomitra
BT2 tabanidae
BT3 diptera

HYBOMITRA BIMACULATA
BT1 hybomitra
BT2 tabanidae
BT3 diptera

HYBOMITRA BOREALIS
uf *hybomitra lapponica*
BT1 hybomitra
BT2 tabanidae
BT3 diptera

HYBOMITRA CAUCASICA
BT1 hybomitra
BT2 tabanidae
BT3 diptera

hybomitra lapponica
USE **hybomitra borealis**

HYBOMITRA LASIOPHTHALMA
BT1 hybomitra
BT2 tabanidae
BT3 diptera

HYBOMITRA MONTANA
BT1 hybomitra
BT2 tabanidae
BT3 diptera

HYBOMITRA TARANDINA
BT1 hybomitra

HYBOMITRA TARANDINA *cont.*
BT2 tabanidae
BT3 diptera

HYBRID CHLOROSIS
rt hybrid necrosis

HYBRID NECROSIS
BT1 necroses
BT2 plant disorders
BT3 disorders
rt hybrid chlorosis

HYBRID SEED PRODUCTION
BT1 seed production
BT2 seed industry
BT3 input industries
BT4 industry
rt hybrid varieties

HYBRID VARIETIES
BT1 hybrids
BT1 varieties
rt heterosis
rt high yielding varieties
rt hybrid seed production
rt synthetic varieties

hybrid vigour
USE **heterosis**

HYBRIDIZATION
uf *crossbreeding (plants)*
BT1 crossing
BT2 breeding
NT1 biparental mating
NT1 intergeneric hybridization
NT1 interspecific hybridization
NT1 somatic hybridization
NT1 wide hybridization
rt breeding
rt combining ability
rt crossing
rt dna hybridization
rt graft hybridization
rt heterosis
rt hybrids
rt introgression

hybridization, graft
USE **graft hybridization**

hybridization, intergeneric
USE **intergeneric hybridization**

hybridization, interspecific
USE **interspecific hybridization**

hybridization, vegetative
USE **vegetative hybridization**

hybridization, wide
USE **wide hybridization**

HYBRIDOMAS
BT1 cells

HYBRIDS
NT1 commercial hybrids
NT1 crosses
NT2 backcrosses
NT2 crossbreds
NT1 hinnies
NT1 hybrid varieties
NT1 mules
rt hybridization
rt mosaicism

HYCANTHONE
BT1 anthelmintics
BT2 antiparasitic agents
BT3 drugs

HYDATIDS
BT1 metacestodes
BT2 developmental stages
NT1 alveolar hydatids
NT1 unilocular hydatids
rt echinococcus

hydatids, alveolar
USE **alveolar hydatids**

hydatigera taeniaeformis
USE **taenia taeniaeformis**

HYDNOCARPUS
BT1 flacourtiaceae
NT1 hydnocarpus kurzii
NT1 hydnocarpus odorata
NT1 hydnocarpus wightiana

HYDNOCARPUS KURZII
BT1 hydnocarpus
BT2 flacourtiaceae

HYDNOCARPUS ODORATA
BT1 hydnocarpus
BT2 flacourtiaceae

HYDNOCARPUS WIGHTIANA
BT1 hydnocarpus
BT2 flacourtiaceae

HYDRA
BT1 coelenterata

HYDRACEAE
NT1 steccherinum

HYDRAECIA
BT1 noctuidae
BT2 lepidoptera
NT1 hydraecia micacea

HYDRAECIA MICACEA
BT1 hydraecia
BT2 noctuidae
BT3 lepidoptera

HYDRAMNIOS
BT1 pregnancy complications
BT2 reproductive disorders
BT3 functional disorders
BT4 animal disorders
BT5 disorders

HYDRANGEA
BT1 hydrangeaceae
NT1 hydrangea anomala
NT1 hydrangea arborescens
NT1 hydrangea aspera
NT1 hydrangea macrophylla
rt hydrangea ringspot potexvirus

HYDRANGEA ANOMALA
uf *hydrangea petiolaris*
BT1 hydrangea
BT2 hydrangeaceae
BT1 ornamental woody plants

HYDRANGEA ARBORESCENS
BT1 hydrangea
BT2 hydrangeaceae
BT1 ornamental woody plants

HYDRANGEA ASPERA
BT1 hydrangea
BT2 hydrangeaceae
BT1 ornamental woody plants

HYDRANGEA MACROPHYLLA
uf *hydrangea serrata*
BT1 hydrangea
BT2 hydrangeaceae
BT1 ornamental woody plants

hydrangea petiolaris
USE **hydrangea anomala**

HYDRANGEA RINGSPOT POTEXVIRUS
HN from 1990
BT1 potexvirus group
BT2 plant viruses
BT3 plant pathogens
BT4 pathogens
rt hydrangea

hydrangea serrata
USE **hydrangea macrophylla**

HYDRANGEACEAE
NT1 dichroa
NT2 dichroa febrifuga
NT1 hydrangea
NT2 hydrangea anomala
NT2 hydrangea arborescens
NT2 hydrangea aspera
NT2 hydrangea macrophylla

HYDRASTIDACEAE
NT1 hydrastis
NT2 hydrastis canadensis

HYDRASTIS
BT1 hydrastidaceae
NT1 hydrastis canadensis

HYDRASTIS CANADENSIS
BT1 hydrastis
BT2 hydrastidaceae

HYDRATION
BT1 processing
NT1 overhydration
rt wetting

HYDRAULIC BARKING
HN from 1989
BT1 barking
BT2 primary conversion
BT3 conversion

HYDRAULIC BRAKES
uf brakes, hydraulic
BT1 brakes
BT2 components
BT1 hydraulic equipment
BT2 equipment

HYDRAULIC CONDUCTIVITY
BT1 conductivity
BT2 physical properties
BT3 properties
BT1 soil water movement
BT2 movement
NT1 saturated hydraulic conductivity
NT1 unsaturated hydraulic conductivity
rt permeability

HYDRAULIC COUPLINGS
uf couplings, hydraulic
BT1 couplings
BT2 components
BT1 hydraulic equipment
BT2 equipment
rt automatic couplings
rt linkages

HYDRAULIC ENGINEERING
uf engineering, hydraulic
BT1 engineering
NT1 hydroelectric schemes
rt dams
rt drainage
rt hydraulic structures
rt hydraulics
rt reservoirs
rt sluices
rt turbines
rt water management

HYDRAULIC EQUIPMENT
BT1 equipment
NT1 hydraulic brakes
NT1 hydraulic couplings
NT1 hydraulic jacks
NT1 hydraulic motors
NT1 hydraulic rams
NT1 hydraulic transmissions
rt hydraulic power systems

HYDRAULIC JACKS
uf jacks, hydraulic
BT1 hydraulic equipment
BT2 equipment
BT1 jacks
BT2 tools

HYDRAULIC MOTORS
uf motors, hydraulic
BT1 hydraulic equipment
BT2 equipment
BT1 motors
BT2 components

HYDRAULIC POTENTIAL
BT1 potential energy
BT2 energy
BT1 soil water potential
BT2 water potential

HYDRAULIC POWER
uf power, hydraulic
BT1 power
rt pneumatic power
rt water power

HYDRAULIC POWER SYSTEMS
uf hydraulic systems
BT1 machinery
rt drives
rt hydraulic equipment
rt hydraulics
rt transmissions

HYDRAULIC RAMS
BT1 hydraulic equipment
BT2 equipment
BT1 pumps
BT2 machinery
BT1 rams (machinery)
BT2 components
rt hydraulics

HYDRAULIC RESISTANCE
BT1 resistance
rt hydraulics

HYDRAULIC STRUCTURES
BT1 structures
NT1 sluices
NT1 spillways
NT1 weirs
rt dams
rt flood control
rt hydraulic engineering
rt irrigation
rt reservoirs

hydraulic systems
USE **hydraulic power systems**

HYDRAULIC TRANSMISSIONS
BT1 hydraulic equipment
BT2 equipment
BT1 transmissions
BT2 components

HYDRAULICS
rt fluid mechanics
rt fluids
rt hydraulic engineering
rt hydraulic power systems
rt hydraulic rams
rt hydraulic resistance
rt hydrodynamics
rt liquids
rt water management

HYDRAZIDES
BT1 organic nitrogen compounds
NT1 daminozide
NT1 isoniazid
rt hydrazines

HYDRAZINE
BT1 hydrazines
BT2 organic nitrogen compounds
BT1 mutagens
BT1 reducing agents

HYDRAZINES
BT1 organic nitrogen compounds
NT1 1,2-dimethylhydrazine
NT1 hydrazine
rt hydrazides

HYDRELLIA
BT1 ephydridae
BT2 diptera
NT1 hydrellia griseola
NT1 hydrellia philippina

HYDRELLIA GRISEOLA
BT1 hydrellia
BT2 ephydridae
BT3 diptera

HYDRELLIA PHILIPPINA
BT1 hydrellia
BT2 ephydridae
BT3 diptera

HYDRIDES
BT1 inorganic compounds

HYDRIDES *cont.*
NT1 phosphine

HYDRILLA
BT1 hydrocharitaceae
NT1 hydrilla verticillata

HYDRILLA VERTICILLATA
BT1 hydrilla
BT2 hydrocharitaceae
BT1 weeds

HYDRO-LYASES
(ec 4.2.1)
uf dehydratases
BT1 lyases
BT2 enzymes
NT1 carbonate dehydratase
NT1 cystathionine β-synthase
NT1 porphobilinogen synthase
NT1 serine dehydratase
NT1 urocanate hydratase

HYDROBIA
BT1 hydrobiidae
BT2 gastropoda
BT3 mollusca
NT1 hydrobia ulvae

HYDROBIA ULVAE
BT1 hydrobia
BT2 hydrobiidae
BT3 gastropoda
BT4 mollusca

HYDROBIIDAE
BT1 gastropoda
BT2 mollusca
NT1 hydrobia
NT2 hydrobia ulvae

HYDROBIOLOGY
BT1 biology
BT1 hydrology
rt algae
rt aquatic animals
rt aquatic organisms
rt aquatic plants
rt fisheries

HYDROCARBONS
NT1 alkanes
NT2 biogas
NT2 decane
NT2 ethane
NT2 heptane
NT2 hexane
NT2 methane
NT2 nonane
NT2 octane
NT2 paraffin wax
NT2 pentane
NT2 petrolatum
NT2 propane
NT2 tricosane
NT1 alkenes
NT2 2-methyl-1-propene
NT2 allene
NT2 ethylene
NT2 propylene
NT2 squalene
NT1 alkynes
NT2 acetylene
NT2 polyacetylenes
NT1 aromatic hydrocarbons
NT2 azulene
NT2 benzene
NT2 benzopyrene
NT2 biphenyl
NT2 cymenes
NT3 p-cymene
NT2 naphthalene
NT2 phenanthrene
NT2 styrene
NT2 toluene
NT2 xylene
NT1 petroleum hydrocarbons
NT2 kerosene
NT1 polycyclic hydrocarbons

hydrocarbons, aromatic
USE **aromatic hydrocarbons**

HYDROCELE
BT1 male genital diseases
BT2 organic diseases
BT3 diseases

HYDROCEPHALUS
BT1 brain disorders
BT2 nervous system diseases
BT3 organic diseases
BT4 diseases
BT1 congenital oedema
BT2 oedema
BT3 water metabolism disorders
BT4 metabolic disorders
BT5 animal disorders
BT6 disorders

HYDROCHAERIDAE
BT1 rodents
BT2 mammals
NT1 hydrochaerus
rt capybaras

HYDROCHAERUS
BT1 hydrochaeridae
BT2 rodents
BT3 mammals

hydrochaerus hydrochaeris
USE **capybaras**

HYDROCHARITACEAE
NT1 damasonium
NT2 damasonium minus
NT1 elodea
NT2 elodea canadensis
NT2 elodea nodosus
NT2 elodea nuttallii
NT1 halophila
NT2 halophila ovalis
NT1 hydrilla
NT2 hydrilla verticillata
NT1 lagarosiphon
NT2 lagarosiphon major
NT1 limnobium
NT1 ottelia
NT2 ottelia alismoides
NT1 stratiotes
NT2 stratiotes aloides
NT1 vallisneria
NT2 vallisneria americana
NT2 vallisneria gigantea
NT2 vallisneria neotropicalis
NT2 vallisneria spiralis

HYDROCHLORIC ACID
BT1 digestants
BT2 gastrointestinal agents
BT3 drugs
BT1 inorganic acids
BT2 acids
BT2 inorganic compounds
BT1 silage additives
BT2 additives
rt gastric acid
rt hydrochloric acid secretion

HYDROCHLORIC ACID SECRETION
BT1 secretion
BT2 physiological functions
rt digestive system
rt gastric acid
rt hydrochloric acid
rt pepsinogen

HYDROCHLOROTHIAZIDE
BT1 diuretics
BT2 drugs

HYDROCLEYS
BT1 limnocharitaceae

HYDROCOOLERS
BT1 coolers

HYDROCORTISONE
uf cortisol
BT1 antiinflammatory agents
BT2 drugs
BT1 dermatological agents
BT2 drugs
BT1 glucocorticoids
BT2 adrenal cortex hormones

HYDROCORTISONE *cont.*
BT3 corticoids
BT3 hormones
BT1 mineralocorticoids
BT2 adrenal cortex hormones
BT3 corticoids
BT3 hormones
BT1 pregnanes
BT2 steroids
BT3 isoprenoids
BT4 lipids

HYDROCOTYLACEAE
NT1 centella
NT2 centella asiatica
NT1 gymnophyton
NT2 gymnophyton isatidicarpum
NT1 hydrocotyle
NT2 hydrocotyle bonariensis
NT2 hydrocotyle sibthorpioides
NT2 hydrocotyle vulgaris

HYDROCOTYLE
BT1 hydrocotylaceae
NT1 hydrocotyle bonariensis
NT1 hydrocotyle sibthorpioides
NT1 hydrocotyle vulgaris

HYDROCOTYLE BONARIENSIS
BT1 hydrocotyle
BT2 hydrocotylaceae
BT1 ornamental herbaceous plants

HYDROCOTYLE SIBTHORPIOIDES
BT1 hydrocotyle
BT2 hydrocotylaceae

HYDROCOTYLE VULGARIS
BT1 hydrocotyle
BT2 hydrocotylaceae

hydrocyanic acid
USE **hydrogen cyanide**

HYDRODICTYON
BT1 chlorophyta
BT2 algae
NT1 hydrodictyon reticulatum

HYDRODICTYON RETICULATUM
BT1 hydrodictyon
BT2 chlorophyta
BT3 algae

HYDRODYNAMIC DISPERSION
BT1 dispersion
BT1 transport processes

HYDRODYNAMIC DISPLACEMENT
BT1 displacement
BT1 transport processes

HYDRODYNAMICS
BT1 dynamics
BT2 mechanics
BT3 physics
rt hydraulics

HYDROELECTRIC SCHEMES
BT1 electrical engineering
BT2 engineering
BT1 hydraulic engineering
BT2 engineering
rt electricity generators
rt turbines

HYDROFLUORIC ACID
uf hydrogen fluoride
BT1 inorganic acids
BT2 acids
BT2 inorganic compounds

HYDROGEN
BT1 gases
BT1 nonmetallic elements
BT2 elements
NT1 deuterium
NT1 tritium
rt hydrogen bonding
rt hydrogen ions

HYDROGEN BONDING
HN from 1990

HYDROGEN BONDING *cont.*
rt hydrogen

HYDROGEN CYANIDE
uf hydrocyanic acid
uf prussic acid
BT1 fumigant insecticides
BT2 fumigants
BT3 pesticides
BT2 insecticides
BT3 pesticides
BT1 rodenticides
BT2 pesticides
rt cassava
rt cyanogenesis
rt cyanogenic glycosides

hydrogen fluoride
USE **hydrofluoric acid**

hydrogen ion concentration
USE **ph**

HYDROGEN IONS
BT1 cations
BT2 ions
rt hydrogen
rt ph

HYDROGEN PEROXIDE
BT1 oxidants
BT1 peroxides
BT2 inorganic compounds

HYDROGEN SULFIDE
uf hydrogen sulphide
BT1 gases
BT1 sulfides (inorganic)
BT2 inorganic compounds
BT2 sulfides

hydrogen sulphide
USE **hydrogen sulfide**

HYDROGENASE
(ec 1.18.99.1)
BT1 oxidoreductases
BT2 enzymes

HYDROGENATED FATS
BT1 fat products
BT2 products
rt hydrogenation

HYDROGENATED OILS
uf oils, hydrogenated
BT1 oils
rt hydrogenation

HYDROGENATION
BT1 processing
rt hydrogenated fats
rt hydrogenated oils
rt wood technology

HYDROGENIC SOILS
BT1 soil types (genetic)

HYDROL
HN from 1990
BT1 agroindustrial byproducts
BT2 byproducts
rt molasses

HYDROLAGUS
BT1 chimaeridae
BT2 chimaeriformes
BT3 chondrichthyes
BT4 fishes

HYDROLASES
(ec 3)
BT1 enzymes
NT1 acid anhydride hydrolases
NT2 adenosinetriphosphatase
NT2 pyrophosphatases
NT3 atp pyrophosphatase
NT3 inorganic pyrophosphatase
NT1 amide hydrolases
NT2 β-lactamase
NT2 amidase
NT2 asparaginase
NT2 glutaminase
NT2 urease

HYDROLASES *cont.*
NT1 amidine hydrolases
NT2 adenosine deaminase
NT2 amp deaminase
NT2 arginase
NT2 formiminoglutamase
NT2 guanine deaminase
NT1 epoxide hydrolase
NT1 esterases
NT2 carboxylic ester hydrolases
NT3 acetylcholinesterase
NT3 arylesterase
NT3 carboxylesterase
NT3 chlorophyllase
NT3 cholesterol esterase
NT3 cholinesterase
NT3 lipoprotein lipase
NT3 lysophospholipase
NT3 pectinesterase
NT3 phospholipase a
NT3 phospholipase a1
NT3 phospholipase a2
NT3 retinyl-palmitate esterase
NT3 tannase
NT3 triacylglycerol lipase
NT3 tropinesterase
NT2 nucleases
NT3 deoxyribonuclease i
NT3 ribonucleases
NT2 phosphoric diester hydrolases
NT3 phosphodiesterase i
NT3 phospholipase c
NT2 phosphoric monoester hydrolases
NT3 acid phosphatase
NT3 alkaline phosphatase
NT3 fructose-bisphosphatase
NT3 glucose-6-phosphatase
NT3 nucleotidase
NT3 phosphatidate phosphatase
NT3 phosphoprotein phosphatase
NT3 phosphorylase phosphatase
NT3 phytase
NT2 sulfuric ester hydrolases
NT3 arylsulfatase
NT2 thiolester hydrolases
NT3 palmitoyl-coa hydrolase
NT1 fumarylacetoacetase
NT1 glycosidases
NT2 n-glycoside hydrolases
NT3 n-acetyl-β-glucosaminidase
NT3 β-n-acetylhexosaminidase
NT3 nucleosidases
NT2 o-glycoside hydrolases
NT3 β-fructofuranosidase
NT3 β-glucanase
NT3 β-glucuronidase
NT3 amylases
NT4 α-amylase
NT4 β-amylase
NT3 cellulase
NT3 chitinase
NT3 dextranase
NT3 disaccharidases
NT3 galactosidases
NT4 α-galactosidase
NT4 β-galactosidase
NT3 glucosidases
NT4 α-glucosidase
NT4 β-glucosidase
NT4 glucan 1,4-α-glucosidase
NT4 oligo-1,6-glucosidase
NT4 sucrose α-glucosidase
NT3 hyaluronidase
NT3 hyaluronoglucosaminidase
NT3 inulinase
NT3 isoamylase
NT3 lichenase
NT3 lysozyme
NT3 mannosidases
NT4 α-mannosidase
NT4 β-mannosidase
NT3 polygalacturonase
NT3 pullulanase
NT3 sialidase

HYDROLASES *cont.*
NT3 trehalase
NT3 xylan 1,4-β-xylosidase
NT2 s-glycoside hydrolases
NT3 thioglucosidase
NT1 pancreatin
NT1 peptide hydrolases
NT2 peptidases
NT3 aminoacyl-histidine dipeptidase
NT3 aminopeptidases
NT4 aminopeptidase
NT4 cytosol aminopeptidase
NT4 microsomal aminopeptidase
NT3 carboxypeptidases
NT4 carboxypeptidase a
NT4 dipeptidyl carboxypeptidases
NT3 cathepsins
NT3 dipeptidase
NT3 proline dipeptidase
NT2 proteinases
NT3 γ-glutamyl hydrolase
NT3 acrosin
NT3 cathepsins
NT3 chymotrypsin
NT3 collagenase
NT3 elastase
NT3 endopeptidases
NT3 enteropeptidase
NT3 kallikrein
NT3 papain
NT3 pepsin
NT3 plasmin
NT3 plasminogen activator
NT3 renin
NT3 thrombin
NT3 trypsin
NT1 thiaminase

HYDROLOGICAL DATA
BT1 hydrology

HYDROLOGICAL FACTORS
BT1 hydrology
rt evapotranspiration
rt precipitation
rt soil water
rt water relations

HYDROLOGY
NT1 catchment hydrology
NT1 hydrobiology
NT1 hydrological data
NT1 hydrological factors
rt aquifers
rt physical geography
rt soil water
rt water
rt water resources

HYDROLYSATES
NT1 leather hydrolysate
NT1 protein hydrolysates
NT2 casein hydrolysate
NT2 fibrin hydrolysate
NT2 fish protein hydrolysate
NT2 keratin hydrolysate
rt hydrolysis

hydrolysed proteins
USE **protein hydrolysates**

HYDROLYSIS
HN from 1989
BT1 chemical reactions
rt hydrolysates
rt processing
rt proteolysis
rt saccharification
rt wood chemical industry

HYDROMECHANICAL TRANSMISSIONS
uf transmissions, hydromechanical
BT1 transmissions
BT2 components
rt automatic transmissions

HYDROMETERS
BT1 instruments

HYDROMETERS *cont.*
rt brix
rt specific gravity

HYDROMORPHIC SOILS
BT1 soil types (genetic)

HYDROPHILIC POLYMERS
uf polymers, hydrophilic
BT1 polymers

HYDROPHOBICITY
HN from 1990
BT1 physicochemical properties
BT2 properties

HYDROPHYLLACEAE
NT1 hydrophyllum
NT1 nemophila
NT1 phacelia
NT2 phacelia crenulata
NT2 phacelia purshii
NT2 phacelia tanacetifolia

HYDROPHYLLUM
BT1 hydrophyllaceae

HYDROPONICS
BT1 soilless culture
BT2 cultural methods
rt irrigation
rt nutrient film techniques
rt nutrient solutions

HYDROPRENE
BT1 juvenile hormone analogues
BT2 insect growth regulators
BT3 growth regulators
BT3 insecticides
BT4 pesticides

HYDROPS
BT1 water metabolism disorders
BT2 metabolic disorders
BT3 animal disorders
BT4 disorders

HYDROQUINONE
BT1 antioxidants
BT2 additives
BT1 phenols
BT2 alcohols
BT2 phenolic compounds
BT3 aromatic compounds

HYDROSEQUENCES
BT1 soil sequences

HYDROSTATIC TRANSMISSIONS
uf transmissions, hydrostatic
BT1 transmissions
BT2 components
rt automatic transmissions

HYDROSULFITES
HN from 1990
BT1 inorganic salts
BT2 inorganic compounds
BT2 salts
NT1 sodium hydrosulfite

hydrotachysterol
USE **dihydrotachysterol**

HYDROTAEA
uf ophyra
BT1 muscidae
BT2 diptera
NT1 hydrotaea aenescens
NT1 hydrotaea ignava
NT1 hydrotaea irritans
NT1 hydrotaea meteorica

HYDROTAEA AENESCENS
HN from 1990
uf ophyra aenescens
BT1 hydrotaea
BT2 muscidae
BT3 diptera

HYDROTAEA IGNAVA
uf ophyra leucostoma
BT1 hydrotaea
BT2 muscidae
BT3 diptera

HYDROTAEA IRRITANS
uf head fly
BT1 hydrotaea
BT2 muscidae
BT3 diptera

HYDROTAEA METEORICA
HN from 1989
BT1 hydrotaea
BT2 muscidae
BT3 diptera

HYDROTHERMAL SOILS
BT1 soil types (physiographic)

HYDROTHERMAL TREATMENT OF WOOD
rt treatment
rt wood technology

HYDROTHORAX
BT1 respiratory diseases
BT2 organic diseases
BT3 diseases

HYDROTROPISM
BT1 tropisms
BT2 movement
BT2 plant physiology
BT3 physiology
BT2 responses

HYDROXAMIC ACIDS
BT1 organic nitrogen compounds

HYDROXIDES
BT1 inorganic compounds
NT1 aluminium hydroxide
NT1 ammonium hydroxide
NT1 calcium hydroxide
NT1 copper hydroxide
NT1 iron hydroxides
NT2 ferric hydroxide
NT1 potassium hydroxide
NT1 sodium hydroxide

HYDROXOCOBALAMIN
uf aquocobalamin
BT1 vitamin b12
BT2 lipotropic factors
BT3 drugs
BT2 vitamin b complex
BT3 water-soluble vitamins
BT4 vitamins
rt haematopoiesis

(S)-2-HYDROXY-ACID OXIDASE
(ec 1.1.3.15)
uf α-hydroxyacid oxidase
uf glycolate oxidase
BT1 alcohol oxidoreductases
BT2 oxidoreductases
BT3 enzymes

HYDROXY FATTY ACIDS
BT1 fatty acids
BT2 carboxylic acids
BT3 organic acids
BT4 acids
BT2 lipids
NT1 3-hydroxybutyric acid
NT1 ricinoleic acid
NT1 trihydroxyoctadecenoic acid

α-hydroxyacid oxidase
USE **(s)-2-hydroxy-acid oxidase**

hydroxyamines
USE **amino alcohols**

hydroxyanisole, butylated
USE **butylated hydroxyanisole**

3-HYDROXYANTHRANILATE OXIDASE
(ec 1.10.3.5)
BT1 oxidoreductases
BT2 enzymes

HYDROXYANTHRANILIC ACID
BT1 aminobenzoic acids
BT2 amino compounds
BT3 organic nitrogen compounds

HYDROXYANTHRANILIC ACID *cont.*
BT2 benzoic acids
BT3 aromatic acids
BT4 aromatic compounds
BT4 organic acids
BT5 acids
BT1 phenolic acids
BT2 benzoic acids
BT3 aromatic acids
BT4 aromatic compounds
BT4 organic acids
BT5 acids
BT2 phenolic compounds
BT3 aromatic compounds

HYDROXYAPATITE
BT1 nonclay minerals
BT2 minerals

4-HYDROXYBENZOIC ACID
BT1 phenolic acids
BT2 benzoic acids
BT3 aromatic acids
BT4 aromatic compounds
BT4 organic acids
BT5 acids
BT2 phenolic compounds
BT3 aromatic compounds

hydroxybenzoic acids
USE **phenolic acids**

β-hydroxybutyrate
USE **3-hydroxybutyric acid**

3-HYDROXYBUTYRIC ACID
uf β-hydroxybutyrate
BT1 hydroxy fatty acids
BT2 fatty acids
BT3 carboxylic acids
BT4 organic acids
BT5 acids
BT3 lipids
BT1 ketone bodies
rt polyhydroxybutyrate

HYDROXYCARBAMIDE
uf hydroxyurea
BT1 amides
BT2 organic nitrogen compounds
BT1 antineoplastic agents
BT2 drugs

3α-hydroxycholanic acid
USE **lithocholic acid**

1α-HYDROXYCHOLECALCIFEROL
BT1 hydroxycholecalciferols
BT2 cholecalciferol derivatives
BT3 sterols
BT4 alcohols
BT4 steroids
BT5 isoprenoids
BT6 lipids
BT3 vitamin d
BT4 fat soluble vitamins
BT5 vitamins

25-hydroxycholecalciferol 1-hydroxylase
USE **calcidiol 1-monooxygenase**

25-hydroxycholecalciferol 1-monooxygenase
USE **calcidiol 1-monooxygenase**

HYDROXYCHOLECALCIFEROLS
BT1 cholecalciferol derivatives
BT2 sterols
BT3 alcohols
BT3 steroids
BT4 isoprenoids
BT5 lipids
BT2 vitamin d
BT3 fat soluble vitamins
BT4 vitamins
NT1 1α-hydroxycholecalciferol
NT1 24,25-dihydroxycholecalciferol
NT1 25,26-dihydroxycholecalciferol

HYDROXYCHOLECALCIFEROLS *cont.*
NT1 calcitriol

hydroxycinnamic acids
USE **coumaric acids**

20-hydroxyecdysone
USE **ecdysterone**

25-HYDROXYERGOCALCIFEROL
BT1 sterols
BT2 alcohols
BT2 steroids
BT3 isoprenoids
BT4 lipids
BT1 vitamin d
BT2 fat soluble vitamins
BT3 vitamins

5-HYDROXYINDOLEACETIC ACID
BT1 indoles
BT2 heterocyclic nitrogen compounds
BT3 organic nitrogen compounds

hydroxyisoxazole
USE **hymexazol**

HYDROXYLAMINE
BT1 mutagens

hydroxylases
USE **oxygenases**

HYDROXYLYSINE
BT1 nonessential amino acids
BT2 amino acids
BT3 carboxylic acids
BT4 organic acids
BT5 acids
BT3 organic nitrogen compounds

hydroxymethionine
USE **methionine hydroxy analogue**

hydroxymethylfurfural
USE **hmf**

3-HYDROXY-3-METHYLGLUTARIC ACID
BT1 antilipaemics
BT2 haematologic agents
BT3 drugs

HYDROXYMETHYLGLUTARYL-COA LYASE
(ec 4.1.3.4)
BT1 oxo-acid-lyases
BT2 lyases
BT3 enzymes

HYDROXYMETHYLGLUTARYL-COA REDUCTASE
(ec 1.1.1.34)
BT1 alcohol oxidoreductases
BT2 oxidoreductases
BT3 enzymes

2-hydroxy-4-methylthiobutyric acid
USE **methionine hydroxy analogue**

γ-HYDROXYORNITHINE
(for retrieval spell out "gamma")
BT1 amino acid derivatives
BT2 amino compounds
BT3 organic nitrogen compounds
rt ornithine

hydroxyphenylacetic acid
USE **mandelic acid**

HYDROXYPROLINE
uf oxyproline
BT1 nonessential amino acids
BT2 amino acids
BT3 carboxylic acids
BT4 organic acids
BT5 acids

HYDROXYPROLINE *cont.*
BT3 organic nitrogen compounds

HYDROXYQUINOLINE
uf *chinosol*
uf *oxine*
BT1 antitranspirants
BT1 chelating agents
BT1 disinfectants
BT1 quinolines
BT2 heterocyclic nitrogen compounds
BT3 organic nitrogen compounds

8-HYDROXYQUINOLINE CITRATE
BT1 cut flower preservatives
BT2 preservatives
BT1 disinfectants

8-HYDROXYQUINOLINE SULFATE
uf *8-hydroxyquinoline sulphate*
BT1 quinoline fungicides
BT2 fungicides
BT3 pesticides
BT2 quinolines
BT3 heterocyclic nitrogen compounds
BT4 organic nitrogen compounds

8-hydroxyquinoline sulphate
USE **8-hydroxyquinoline sulfate**

HYDROXYSTEROID DEHYDROGENASE
BT1 alcohol oxidoreductases
BT2 oxidoreductases
BT3 enzymes

hydroxytoluene, butylated
USE **butylated hydroxytoluene**

5-hydroxytryptamine
USE **serotonin**

hydroxyurea
USE **hydroxycarbamide**

HYDRURGA
BT1 phocidae
BT2 pinnipedia
BT3 carnivores
BT4 mammals
NT1 hydrurga leptonyx

HYDRURGA LEPTONYX
BT1 hydrurga
BT2 phocidae
BT3 pinnipedia
BT4 carnivores
BT5 mammals

HYGIENE
uf *cleanliness*
NT1 dairy hygiene
NT1 decontamination
NT1 food hygiene
NT2 meat hygiene
NT2 milk hygiene
rt cleaning
rt disinfection
rt public health
rt sanitation
rt sterilizing

HYGROMETERS
BT1 instruments
rt humidity gauges
rt psychrometers

HYGROMULL
BT1 growing media
BT1 soil conditioners
BT2 soil amendments
BT3 amendments
rt urea formaldehyde foam

HYGROMYCIN B
BT1 anthelmintics
BT2 antiparasitic agents
BT3 drugs
BT1 antibiotics

HYGROMYCIN B *cont.*
BT1 antiviral agents
BT2 antiinfective agents
BT3 drugs

HYGROPHILA
BT1 acanthaceae
NT1 hygrophila spinosa

HYGROPHILA SPINOSA
BT1 hygrophila
BT2 acanthaceae

HYGROSCOPIC MATERIALS
BT1 absorbents
rt hygroscopicity

HYGROSCOPICITY
BT1 chemical properties
BT2 properties
NT1 maximum hygroscopicity
rt absorbents
rt absorption
rt absorptivity
rt hygroscopic materials

HYLA
BT1 hylidae
BT2 anura
BT3 amphibia
NT1 hyla arborea
NT1 hyla fuscovaria

HYLA ARBOREA
BT1 hyla
BT2 hylidae
BT3 anura
BT4 amphibia

HYLA FUSCOVARIA
BT1 hyla
BT2 hylidae
BT3 anura
BT4 amphibia

HYLAEUS
uf *hoploprosopis*
uf *nesoprosopis*
uf *prosopis (hymenoptera)*
BT1 apidae
BT2 hymenoptera

HYLASTES
BT1 scolytidae
BT2 coleoptera
NT1 hylastes ater

HYLASTES ATER
BT1 hylastes
BT2 scolytidae
BT3 coleoptera

HYLECOETUS
BT1 lymexylidae
BT2 coleoptera
NT1 hylecoetus dermestoides

HYLECOETUS DERMESTOIDES
BT1 hylecoetus
BT2 lymexylidae
BT3 coleoptera

HYLEMYA
BT1 anthomyiidae
BT2 diptera
rt delia
rt phorbia
rt strobilomyia

hylemya antiqua
USE **delia antiqua**

hylemya brassicae
USE **delia radicum**

hylemya cilicrura
USE **delia platura**

hylemya coarctata
USE **delia coarctata**

hylemya floralis
USE **delia floralis**

hylemya florilega
USE **delia florilega**

hylemya laricicola
USE **strobilomyia laricicola**

hylemya liturata
USE **delia florilega**

hylemya platura
USE **delia platura**

hylemya securis
USE **phorbia securis**

HYLES
uf *celerio*
BT1 sphingidae
BT2 lepidoptera
NT1 hyles euphorbiae
NT1 hyles lineata

HYLES EUPHORBIAE
uf *celerio euphorbiae*
BT1 hyles
BT2 sphingidae
BT3 lepidoptera

HYLES LINEATA
uf *celerio lineata*
BT1 hyles
BT2 sphingidae
BT3 lepidoptera

HYLESIA
BT1 saturniidae
BT2 lepidoptera
NT1 hylesia urticans

HYLESIA URTICANS
BT1 hylesia
BT2 saturniidae
BT3 lepidoptera

HYLESINUS
uf *leperisinus*
BT1 scolytidae
BT2 coleoptera
NT1 hylesinus varius
rt acrantus

HYLESINUS VARIUS
uf *leperisinus varius*
BT1 hylesinus
BT2 scolytidae
BT3 coleoptera

hylesinus vestitus
USE **acrantus vestitus**

HYLIDAE
BT1 anura
BT2 amphibia
NT1 hyla
NT2 hyla arborea
NT2 hyla fuscovaria

HYLOBATES
BT1 hylobatidae
BT2 primates
BT3 mammals
NT1 hylobates lar

HYLOBATES LAR
uf *hylobates muelleri*
BT1 hylobates
BT2 hylobatidae
BT3 primates
BT4 mammals

hylobates muelleri
USE **hylobates lar**

HYLOBATIDAE
BT1 primates
BT2 mammals
NT1 hylobates
NT2 hylobates lar

hylobitelus
USE **hylobius**

hylobitelus abietis
USE **hylobius abietis**

HYLOBIUS
uf *hylobitelus*
BT1 curculionidae
BT2 coleoptera

HYLOBIUS *cont.*
NT1 hylobius abietis
NT1 hylobius pales

HYLOBIUS ABIETIS
uf *hylobitelus abietis*
BT1 hylobius
BT2 curculionidae
BT3 coleoptera

HYLOBIUS PALES
BT1 hylobius
BT2 curculionidae
BT3 coleoptera

HYLOCEREUS
BT1 cactaceae
NT1 hylocereus calcaratus
NT1 hylocereus trigonus
NT1 hylocereus undatus

HYLOCEREUS CALCARATUS
BT1 hylocereus
BT2 cactaceae
BT1 ornamental succulent plants
BT2 succulent plants

HYLOCEREUS TRIGONUS
BT1 hylocereus
BT2 cactaceae
BT1 ornamental succulent plants
BT2 succulent plants

HYLOCEREUS UNDATUS
uf *cereus triangularis*
BT1 hylocereus
BT2 cactaceae
BT1 ornamental succulent plants
BT2 succulent plants

HYLOCOMIUM
BT1 mosses
NT1 hylocomium splendens
NT1 hylocomium squarrosum

HYLOCOMIUM SPLENDENS
BT1 hylocomium
BT2 mosses

HYLOCOMIUM SQUARROSUM
BT1 hylocomium
BT2 mosses

hyloicus
USE **sphinx**

hyloicus pinastri
USE **sphinx pinastri**

HYLOMECON
BT1 papaveraceae
NT1 hylomecon vernalis

HYLOMECON VERNALIS
BT1 hylomecon
BT2 papaveraceae

HYLOTRUPES
BT1 cerambycidae
BT2 coleoptera
NT1 hylotrupes bajulus

HYLOTRUPES BAJULUS
BT1 hylotrupes
BT2 cerambycidae
BT3 coleoptera

HYLURGOPINUS
BT1 scolytidae
BT2 coleoptera
NT1 hylurgopinus rufipes

HYLURGOPINUS RUFIPES
BT1 hylurgopinus
BT2 scolytidae
BT3 coleoptera

HYLURGOPS
BT1 scolytidae
BT2 coleoptera
NT1 hylurgops palliatus

HYLURGOPS PALLIATUS
BT1 hylurgops
BT2 scolytidae
BT3 coleoptera

HYMENACHNE
BT1 gramineae
rt pasture plants

HYMENAEA
BT1 leguminosae
NT1 hymenaea courbaril

HYMENAEA COURBARIL
BT1 forest trees
BT1 hymenaea
BT2 leguminosae

HYMENIA
BT1 pyralidae
BT2 lepidoptera
NT1 hymenia recurvalis

HYMENIA RECURVALIS
BT1 hymenia
BT2 pyralidae
BT3 lepidoptera

HYMENOCALLIS
BT1 amaryllidaceae
NT1 hymenocallis festalis
NT1 hymenocallis littoralis
NT1 hymenocallis speciosa

HYMENOCALLIS FESTALIS
BT1 antifungal plants
BT1 hymenocallis
BT2 amaryllidaceae
BT1 ornamental bulbs

HYMENOCALLIS LITTORALIS
BT1 antifungal plants
BT1 antiviral plants
BT1 hymenocallis
BT2 amaryllidaceae
BT1 ornamental bulbs

HYMENOCALLIS SPECIOSA
uf *pancratium speciosum*
BT1 hymenocallis
BT2 amaryllidaceae

HYMENOGASTRALES
NT1 rhizopogon
NT2 rhizopogon luteolus
NT2 rhizopogon roseolus
rt fungi

HYMENOLEPIDIDAE
BT1 eucestoda
BT2 cestoda
NT1 aploparaksis
NT1 diorchis
NT1 fimbriaria
NT2 fimbriaria fasciolaris
NT1 hymenolepis
NT2 hymenolepis citelli
NT2 hymenolepis diminuta
NT2 hymenolepis microstoma
NT2 hymenolepis nana
NT1 microsomacanthus
NT1 retinometra
NT1 sobolevicanthus
NT2 sobolevicanthus gracilis
NT1 triodontolepis

HYMENOLEPIS
BT1 hymenolepididae
BT2 eucestoda
BT3 cestoda
NT1 hymenolepis citelli
NT1 hymenolepis diminuta
NT1 hymenolepis microstoma
NT1 hymenolepis nana

HYMENOLEPIS CITELLI
BT1 hymenolepis
BT2 hymenolepididae
BT3 eucestoda
BT4 cestoda

HYMENOLEPIS DIMINUTA
BT1 hymenolepis
BT2 hymenolepididae
BT3 eucestoda
BT4 cestoda

HYMENOLEPIS MICROSTOMA
BT1 hymenolepis
BT2 hymenolepididae

HYMENOLEPIS MICROSTOMA *cont.*
BT3 eucestoda
BT4 cestoda

HYMENOLEPIS NANA
BT1 hymenolepis
BT2 hymenolepididae
BT3 eucestoda
BT4 cestoda

HYMENOPTERA
NT1 aphelinidae
NT2 ablerus
NT3 ablerus clisiocampae
NT2 aphelinus
NT3 aphelinus abdominalis
NT3 aphelinus asychis
NT3 aphelinus mali
NT3 aphelinus semiflavus
NT3 aphelinus thomsoni
NT2 aphytis
NT3 aphytis africanus
NT3 aphytis chrysomphali
NT3 aphytis diaspidis
NT3 aphytis hispanicus
NT3 aphytis holoxanthus
NT3 aphytis lepidosaphes
NT3 aphytis lingnanensis
NT3 aphytis melinus
NT3 aphytis mytilaspidis
NT3 aphytis proclia
NT3 aphytis yanonensis
NT2 cales
NT3 cales noacki
NT2 coccobius
NT3 coccobius fulvus
NT2 coccophagus
NT3 coccophagus cowperi
NT3 coccophagus lycimnia
NT2 encarsia
NT3 encarsia berlesei
NT3 encarsia citrina
NT3 encarsia formosa
NT3 encarsia lahorensis
NT3 encarsia lutea
NT3 encarsia perniciosi
NT2 eretmocerus
NT3 eretmocerus haldemani
NT3 eretmocerus mundus
NT2 marietta
NT3 marietta javensis
NT2 protaphelinus
NT1 apidae
NT2 agapostemon
NT2 allodape
NT2 ancyloscelis
NT2 andrena
NT2 anthidiellum
NT2 anthidium
NT2 anthophora
NT2 apis
NT3 apis cerana
NT4 apis cerana indica
NT3 apis dorsata
NT3 apis florea
NT3 apis mellifera
NT4 apis mellifera adansonii
NT4 apis mellifera capensis
NT4 apis mellifera carnica
NT4 apis mellifera caucasica
NT4 apis mellifera cypria
NT4 apis mellifera lamarckii
NT4 apis mellifera ligustica
NT4 apis mellifera mellifera
NT4 apis mellifera scutellata
NT4 apis mellifera unicolor
NT2 ashmeadiella
NT2 augochlora
NT2 augochlorella
NT2 augochloropsis
NT2 bombus
NT2 braunsapis
NT2 callanthidium
NT2 calliopsis
NT2 centris
NT2 ceratina
NT2 chalicodoma
NT2 chelostoma
NT2 coelioxys
NT2 colletes
NT2 ctenoplectra
NT2 dasypoda

HYMENOPTERA *cont.*
NT2 diadasia
NT2 dialictus
NT2 dianthidium
NT2 dufourea
NT2 emphoropsis
NT2 epeolus
NT2 epicharis
NT2 euaspis
NT2 eucera
NT2 euglossa
NT2 eulaema
NT2 eulonchopria
NT2 eupetersia
NT2 euryglossa
NT2 exaerete
NT2 exomalopsis
NT2 exoneura
NT2 gaesischia
NT2 habropoda
NT2 halictus
NT2 heteranthidium
NT2 holcopasites
NT2 homalictus
NT2 hoplitis
NT2 hylaeus
NT2 hypotrigona
NT2 inquilina
NT2 lasioglossum
NT2 leioproctus
NT2 lestrimelitta
NT2 lithurge
NT2 megachile
NT3 megachile rotundata
NT2 melecta
NT2 melipona
NT2 melissodes
NT2 melitoma
NT2 melitta
NT2 melitturga
NT2 mesoplia
NT2 nomada
NT2 nomadopsis
NT2 nomia
NT3 nomia melanderi
NT2 nomioides
NT2 osmia
NT2 oxaea
NT2 palaeorhiza
NT2 panurginus
NT2 panurgus
NT2 paratetrapedia
NT2 perdita
NT2 pithitis
NT2 protandrena
NT2 proteriades
NT2 pseudagapostemon
NT2 psithyrus
NT2 ptiloglossa
NT2 rhathymus
NT2 rhophites
NT2 sphecodes
NT2 stelis
NT2 stenotritus
NT2 svastra
NT2 synhalonia
NT2 systropha
NT2 tetragonisca
NT2 tetralonia
NT2 tetrapedia
NT2 triepeolus
NT2 trigona
NT2 xenoglossa
NT2 xylocopa
NT1 argidae
NT2 arge
NT3 arge ochropus
NT3 arge pectoralis
NT3 arge pullata
NT1 bethylidae
NT2 cephalonomia
NT2 goniozus
NT3 goniozus nephantidis
NT1 braconidae
NT2 agathis (hymenoptera)
NT3 agathis cincta
NT3 agathis gibbosa
NT3 agathis pumila
NT2 aleiodes
NT2 allorhogas
NT2 apanteles

HYMENOPTERA *cont.*
NT3 apanteles diatraeae
NT3 apanteles fumiferanae
NT3 apanteles subandinus
NT2 aphaereta
NT3 aphaereta minuta
NT3 aphaereta pallipes
NT2 aphidius
NT3 aphidius colemani
NT3 aphidius ervi
NT3 aphidius gifuensis
NT3 aphidius matricariae
NT3 aphidius nigripes
NT3 aphidius picipes
NT3 aphidius rhopalosiphi
NT3 aphidius rosae
NT3 aphidius smithi
NT3 aphidius uzbekistanicus
NT2 ascogaster
NT3 ascogaster quadridentata
NT2 biosteres
NT3 biosteres arisanus
NT3 biosteres fullawayi
NT3 biosteres longicaudatus
NT2 bracon
NT3 bracon brevicornis
NT3 bracon gelechiae
NT3 bracon hebetor
NT3 bracon kirkpatricki
NT3 bracon mellitor
NT2 cardiochiles
NT3 cardiochiles nigriceps
NT2 chelonus
NT3 chelonus blackburni
NT3 chelonus insularis
NT2 coeloides
NT3 coeloides vancouverensis
NT2 cotesia
NT3 cotesia flavipes
NT3 cotesia glomerata
NT3 cotesia hyphantriae
NT3 cotesia kurdjumovi
NT3 cotesia marginiventris
NT3 cotesia melanoscelus
NT3 cotesia plutellae
NT3 cotesia rubecula
NT3 cotesia ruficrus
NT3 cotesia telengai
NT3 cotesia tibialis
NT2 dacnusa
NT3 dacnusa sibirica
NT2 dendrosoter
NT3 dendrosoter protuberans
NT2 diaeretiella
NT3 diaeretiella rapae
NT2 diaeretus
NT2 dinocampus
NT3 dinocampus coccinellae
NT2 dolichogenidea
NT3 dolichogenidea albipennis
NT3 dolichogenidea turionellae
NT2 ephedrus
NT3 ephedrus cerasicola
NT3 ephedrus plagiator
NT2 eubazus
NT3 eubazus atricornis
NT2 glabromicroplitis
NT3 glabromicroplitis croceipes
NT2 glyptapanteles
NT3 glyptapanteles africanus
NT3 glyptapanteles militaris
NT3 glyptapanteles pallipes
NT3 glyptapanteles porthetriae
NT2 illidops
NT3 illidops scutellaris
NT2 iphiaulax
NT2 leiophron
NT3 leiophron uniformis
NT2 lysiphlebia
NT3 lysiphlebia japonica
NT3 lysiphlebia mirzai
NT2 lysiphlebus
NT3 lysiphlebus confusus
NT3 lysiphlebus fabarum
NT3 lysiphlebus testaceipes
NT2 macrocentrus
NT3 macrocentrus ancylivorus
NT3 macrocentrus collaris
NT3 macrocentrus grandii
NT2 meteorus

HYMENOPTERA *cont.*
NT3 meteorus autographae
NT3 meteorus rubens
NT3 meteorus versicolor
NT2 microctonus
NT3 microctonus aethiopoides
NT2 microdus
NT3 microdus rufipes
NT2 microgaster
NT3 microgaster demolitor
NT3 microgaster mediator
NT3 microgaster rufiventris
NT2 monoctonus
NT3 monoctonus nervosus
NT2 nealiolus
NT3 nealiolus curculionis
NT2 opius
NT3 opius concolor
NT3 opius pallipes
NT2 orgilus
NT3 orgilus lepidus
NT3 orgilus obscurator
NT2 perilitus
NT2 peristenus
NT3 peristenus pallipes
NT3 peristenus stygicus
NT2 phanerotoma
NT3 phanerotoma flavitestacea
NT2 pholetesor
NT3 pholetesor bicolor
NT3 pholetesor circumscriptus
NT3 pholetesor ornigis
NT2 praon
NT3 praon dorsale
NT3 praon volucre
NT2 rogas
NT3 rogas aligharensi
NT3 rogas dimidiatus
NT2 stenobracon
NT3 stenobracon nicevillei
NT2 trioxys
NT3 trioxys complanatus
NT3 trioxys indicus
NT3 trioxys pallidus
NT2 xanthomicrogaster
NT3 xanthomicrogaster dignus
NT2 zele
NT1 cephidae
NT2 cephus
NT3 cephus cinctus
NT3 cephus pygmeus
NT2 trachelus
NT3 trachelus tabidus
NT1 ceraphronidae
NT2 aphanogmus
NT1 chalcididae
NT2 brachymeria
NT3 brachymeria intermedia
NT3 brachymeria lasus
NT3 brachymeria podagrica
NT2 chalcis
NT2 dirhinus
NT3 dirhinus giffardii
NT2 spilochalcis
NT3 spilochalcis albifrons
NT3 spilochalcis hirtifemora
NT1 charipidae
NT2 alloxysta
NT3 alloxysta victrix
NT1 cynipidae
NT2 andricus
NT2 dilyta
NT2 diplolepis
NT2 dryocosmus
NT3 dryocosmus kuriphilus
NT2 synergus
NT1 diapriidae
NT1 diprionidae
NT2 diprion
NT3 diprion pini
NT3 diprion similis
NT2 gilpinia
NT3 gilpinia frutetorum
NT3 gilpinia hercyniae
NT2 neodiprion
NT3 neodiprion abietis
NT3 neodiprion lecontei
NT3 neodiprion nanulus
NT3 neodiprion pratti
NT3 neodiprion sertifer

HYMENOPTERA *cont.*
NT3 neodiprion swainei
NT3 neodiprion taedae
NT3 neodiprion tsugae
NT2 nesodiprion
NT1 elasmidae
NT2 elasmus
NT1 encyrtidae
NT2 ageniaspis
NT3 ageniaspis fuscicollis
NT2 alamella
NT3 alamella kerrichi
NT2 anabrolepis
NT3 anabrolepis zetterstedtii
NT2 anagyrus
NT3 anagyrus fusciventris
NT3 anagyrus pseudococci
NT2 aphidencyrtus
NT3 aphidencyrtus africanus
NT3 aphidencyrtus aphidivorus
NT2 aphycus
NT2 blastothrix
NT3 blastothrix longipennis
NT2 cheiloneurus
NT3 cheiloneurus claviger
NT2 coccidoxenoides
NT3 coccidoxenoides peregrinus
NT2 comperiella
NT3 comperiella bifasciata
NT2 copidosoma
NT3 copidosoma koehleri
NT3 copidosoma truncatellum
NT2 encyrtus
NT2 epidinocarsis
NT3 epidinocarsis lopezi
NT2 gyranusoidea
NT3 gyranusoidea tebygi
NT2 habrolepis
NT2 holcothorax
NT3 holcothorax testaceipes
NT2 ixodiphagus
NT3 ixodiphagus hookeri
NT2 leptomastix
NT3 leptomastix dactylopii
NT2 litomastix
NT2 metaphycus
NT3 metaphycus bartletti
NT3 metaphycus flavus
NT3 metaphycus helvolus
NT3 metaphycus insidiosus
NT3 metaphycus lounsburyi
NT3 metaphycus punctipes
NT2 microterys
NT2 neodusmetia
NT3 neodusmetia sangwani
NT2 ooencyrtus
NT3 ooencyrtus clisiocampae
NT3 ooencyrtus ennomophagus
NT3 ooencyrtus kuvanae
NT2 pauridia
NT2 pseudaphycus
NT3 pseudaphycus malinus
NT2 psyllaephagus
NT2 syrphophagus
NT3 syrphophagus aeruginosus
NT2 trichomasthus
NT3 trichomasthus albimanus
NT1 eucoilidae
NT2 ganaspis
NT2 leptopilina
NT3 leptopilina boulardi
NT3 leptopilina heterotoma
NT2 trybliographa
NT3 trybliographa rapae
NT1 eulophidae
NT2 aceratoneuromyia
NT3 aceratoneuromyia indica
NT2 achrysocharoides
NT2 aprostocetus
NT3 aprostocetus diplosidis
NT3 aprostocetus galactopus
NT3 aprostocetus hagenowii
NT3 aprostocetus purpureus
NT3 aprostocetus venustus
NT2 chrysocharis
NT3 chrysocharis nitetis
NT3 chrysocharis parksi
NT2 chrysonotomyia

HYMENOPTERA *cont.*
NT3 chrysonotomyia formosa
NT2 cirrospilus
NT3 cirrospilus vittatus
NT2 dahlbominus
NT2 dicladocerus
NT3 dicladocerus westwoodii
NT2 diglyphus
NT3 diglyphus begini
NT3 diglyphus intermedius
NT3 diglyphus isaea
NT2 edovum
NT3 edovum puttleri
NT2 euplectrus
NT2 hemiptarsenus
NT2 minotetrastichus
NT3 minotetrastichus ecus
NT2 necremnus
NT2 pediobius
NT3 pediobius foveolatus
NT2 pnigalio
NT3 pnigalio agraules
NT3 pnigalio pectinicornis
NT2 sympiesis
NT3 sympiesis gordius
NT3 sympiesis marylandensis
NT3 sympiesis sericeicornis
NT2 tamarixia
NT3 tamarixia dryi
NT2 tetrastichus
NT3 tetrastichus blastophagi
NT3 tetrastichus brontispae
NT3 tetrastichus evonymellae
NT3 tetrastichus gallerucae
NT3 tetrastichus julis
NT3 tetrastichus pyrillae
NT3 tetrastichus rapo
NT3 tetrastichus schoenobii
NT3 tetrastichus servadeii
NT3 tetrastichus sokolowskii
NT2 trichospilus
NT3 trichospilus diatraeae
NT1 eupelmidae
NT2 anastatus
NT3 anastatus bifasciatus
NT3 anastatus gastropachae
NT3 anastatus japonicus
NT2 eupelmus
NT3 eupelmus australiensis
NT3 eupelmus tachardiae
NT3 eupelmus urozonus
NT2 neanastatus
NT3 neanastatus cinctiventris
NT1 eurytomidae
NT2 bruchophagus
NT3 bruchophagus roddi
NT2 eurytoma
NT3 eurytoma martellii
NT1 evaniidae
NT2 evania
NT3 evania appendigaster
NT2 prosevania
NT1 formicidae
NT2 acromyrmex
NT3 acromyrmex octospinosus
NT2 anoplolepis
NT3 anoplolepis custodiens
NT3 anoplolepis longipes
NT2 atta
NT3 atta cephalotes
NT3 atta sexdens
NT3 atta texana
NT3 atta vollenweideri
NT2 azteca
NT3 azteca chartifex
NT2 camponotus
NT3 camponotus acvapimensis
NT3 camponotus herculeanus
NT3 camponotus pennsylvanicus
NT3 camponotus rufipes
NT2 cataglyphis
NT3 cataglyphis aenescens
NT2 chalcoponera
NT2 crematogaster
NT3 crematogaster scutellaris
NT2 dorylus
NT2 formica
NT3 formica fusca
NT3 formica lugubris
NT3 formica nigricans

HYMENOPTERA *cont.*
NT3 formica polyctena
NT3 formica pratensis
NT3 formica rufa
NT3 formica sanguinea
NT3 formica yessensis
NT2 iridomyrmex
NT3 iridomyrmex humilis
NT3 iridomyrmex purpureus
NT2 lasius
NT3 lasius brunneus
NT3 lasius fuliginosus
NT3 lasius niger
NT2 messor
NT2 monomorium
NT3 monomorium destructor
NT3 monomorium minimum
NT3 monomorium pharaonis
NT2 myrmecia
NT3 myrmecia gulosa
NT3 myrmecia pilosula
NT2 myrmica
NT3 myrmica rubra
NT3 myrmica ruginodis
NT3 myrmica sabuleti
NT3 myrmica scabrinodis
NT3 myrmica sulcinodis
NT2 myrmicaria
NT3 myrmicaria striata
NT2 oecophylla
NT3 oecophylla longinoda
NT3 oecophylla smaragdina
NT2 pheidole
NT3 pheidole dentata
NT3 pheidole megacephala
NT2 pogonomyrmex
NT3 pogonomyrmex badius
NT3 pogonomyrmex occidentalis
NT3 pogonomyrmex rugosus
NT2 rhytidoponera
NT3 rhytidoponera metallica
NT2 solenopsis
NT3 solenopsis geminata
NT3 solenopsis invicta
NT3 solenopsis richteri
NT3 solenopsis saevissima
NT3 solenopsis xyloni
NT2 technomyrmex
NT3 technomyrmex albipes
NT2 tetramorium
NT3 tetramorium caespitum
NT2 veromessor
NT3 veromessor pergandei
NT1 ibaliidae
NT2 ibalia
NT3 ibalia leucospoides
NT1 ichneumonidae
NT2 agrothereutes
NT3 agrothereutes tunetanus
NT2 agrypon
NT3 agrypon flaveolatum
NT2 amblyteles
NT3 amblyteles castigator
NT3 amblyteles inspector
NT2 apechthis
NT3 apechthis quadridentatus
NT3 apechthis resinator
NT3 apechthis rufatus
NT2 bassus
NT2 bathyplectes
NT3 bathyplectes anurus
NT3 bathyplectes curculionis
NT2 campoletis
NT3 campoletis chlorideae
NT3 campoletis flavicincta
NT3 campoletis sonorensis
NT2 campoplex
NT2 charops
NT2 chorinaeus
NT2 cremastus
NT2 ctenichneumon
NT3 ctenichneumon panzeri
NT2 diadegma
NT3 diadegma armillata
NT3 diadegma eucerophaga
NT3 diadegma fenestralis
NT3 diadegma insularis
NT2 diadromus
NT3 diadromus pulchellus
NT2 diplazon

HYMENOPTERA *cont.*
NT3 diplazon laetatorius
NT2 dolichomitus
NT3 dolichomitus populneus
NT2 ephialtes
NT3 ephialtes ontario
NT2 exeristes
NT3 exeristes comstockii
NT3 exeristes roborator
NT2 glypta
NT3 glypta fumiferanae
NT2 gregopimpla
NT2 heteropelma
NT2 hyposoter
NT3 hyposoter exiguae
NT2 itoplectis
NT3 itoplectis conquisitor
NT3 itoplectis maculator
NT3 itoplectis naranyae
NT2 lemophagus
NT3 lemophagus curtus
NT2 liotryphon
NT3 liotryphon punctulatus
NT2 lissonota
NT2 mesochorus
NT3 mesochorus dimidiatus
NT2 mesoleius
NT3 mesoleius tenthredinis
NT2 olesicampe
NT3 olesicampe benefactor
NT2 ophion
NT3 ophion flavidus
NT2 phaeogenes
NT3 phaeogenes invisor
NT2 phobocampe
NT2 phygadeuon
NT3 phygadeuon trichops
NT2 phytodietus
NT2 pimpla
NT3 pimpla disparis
NT3 pimpla hesperus
NT3 pimpla hypochondriaca
NT3 pimpla turionellae
NT2 pimplopterus
NT3 pimplopterus dubius
NT2 pleolophus
NT3 pleolophus basizonus
NT2 pristomerus
NT3 pristomerus spinator
NT3 pristomerus vulnerator
NT2 rhyssa
NT3 rhyssa persuasoria
NT2 scambus
NT3 scambus brevicornis
NT3 scambus calobatus
NT3 scambus decorus
NT2 sinophorus
NT3 sinophorus xanthostomus
NT2 temelucha
NT3 temelucha interruptor
NT2 trichomma
NT3 trichomma enecator
NT2 venturia (hymenoptera)
NT3 venturia canescens
NT2 vulgichneumon
NT3 vulgichneumon leucaniae
NT2 xanthopimpla
NT3 xanthopimpla stemmator
NT1 leucospidae
NT2 leucospis
NT1 megaspilidae
NT2 dendrocerus
NT3 dendrocerus carpenteri
NT1 mymaridae
NT2 acmopolynema
NT3 acmopolynema hervali
NT2 anagrus
NT3 anagrus atomus
NT3 anagrus epos
NT2 anaphes
NT3 anaphes flavipes
NT3 anaphes fuscipennis
NT2 gonatocerus
NT2 polynema
NT1 pamphiliidae
NT2 acantholyda
NT3 acantholyda posticalis
NT2 cephalcia
NT3 cephalcia abietis
NT2 pamphilius
NT1 perilampidae

HYMENOPTERA *cont.*
NT2 perilampus
NT3 perilampus tristis
NT1 platygasteridae
NT2 amitus
NT3 amitus hesperidum
NT2 platygaster
NT3 platygaster matsutama
NT3 platygaster oryzae
NT1 pompilidae
NT1 pteromalidae
NT2 anisopteromalus
NT3 anisopteromalus calandrae
NT2 anogmus
NT3 anogmus laricis
NT2 asaphes
NT3 asaphes lucens
NT3 asaphes vulgaris
NT2 callitula
NT3 callitula bicolor
NT2 catolaccus
NT3 catolaccus aeneoviridis
NT2 cephaleta
NT3 cephaleta brunniventris
NT2 cyrtoptyx
NT2 dibrachys
NT3 dibrachys cavus
NT2 halticoptera
NT3 halticoptera circulus
NT2 mesopolobus
NT3 mesopolobus verditer
NT2 muscidifurax
NT3 muscidifurax raptor
NT3 muscidifurax raptorellus
NT3 muscidifurax uniraptor
NT3 muscidifurax zaraptor
NT2 nasonia
NT3 nasonia vitripennis
NT2 pachycrepoideus
NT3 pachycrepoideus vindemmiae
NT2 pachyneuron
NT3 pachyneuron aphidis
NT3 pachyneuron muscarum
NT3 pachyneuron siphonophorae
NT2 pteromalus
NT3 pteromalus puparum
NT2 roptrocerus
NT3 roptrocerus xylophagorum
NT2 scutellista
NT3 scutellista cyanea
NT2 spalangia
NT3 spalangia cameroni
NT3 spalangia endius
NT3 spalangia nigra
NT3 spalangia nigroaenea
NT2 stenomalina
NT2 theocolax
NT3 theocolax elegans
NT2 tomicobia
NT2 trichomalopsis
NT2 trichomalus
NT2 zatropis
NT1 scelionidae
NT2 gryon
NT2 scelio
NT2 telenomus
NT3 telenomus alsophilae
NT3 telenomus applanatus
NT3 telenomus beneficiens
NT3 telenomus californicus
NT3 telenomus chloropus
NT3 telenomus dendrolimi
NT3 telenomus fariai
NT3 telenomus gracilis
NT3 telenomus heliothidis
NT3 telenomus nitidulus
NT3 telenomus remus
NT3 telenomus rowani
NT3 telenomus tetratomus
NT2 trissolcus
NT3 trissolcus basalis
NT3 trissolcus grandis
NT3 trissolcus semistriatus
NT3 trissolcus simoni
NT1 signiphoridae
NT2 chartocerus
NT3 chartocerus subaeneus

HYMENOPTERA *cont.*
NT2 signiphora
NT2 thysanus
NT1 siricidae
NT2 sirex
NT3 sirex cyaneus
NT3 sirex juvencus
NT3 sirex noctilio
NT2 urocerus
NT3 urocerus gigas
NT2 xeris
NT3 xeris spectrum
NT1 sphecidae
NT2 philanthus
NT2 sphex
NT2 tachytes
NT1 tenthredinidae
NT2 ametastegia
NT3 ametastegia glabrata
NT2 ardis
NT3 ardis brunniventris
NT2 athalia
NT3 athalia lugens
NT3 athalia rosae
NT2 caliroa
NT3 caliroa annulipes
NT3 caliroa cerasi
NT2 fenusa
NT3 fenusa pusilla
NT2 hoplocampa
NT3 hoplocampa flava
NT3 hoplocampa minuta
NT3 hoplocampa testudinea
NT2 nematus
NT3 nematus ribesii
NT2 pachynematus
NT2 pikonema
NT3 pikonema alaskensis
NT2 pristiphora
NT3 pristiphora abietina
NT3 pristiphora erichsonii
NT1 torymidae
NT2 megastigmus
NT3 megastigmus pinus
NT3 megastigmus spermotrophus
NT2 monodontomerus
NT3 monodontomerus aereus
NT3 monodontomerus dentipes
NT2 torymus
NT3 torymus sinensis
NT1 trichogrammatidae
NT2 paracentrobia
NT2 trichogramma
NT3 trichogramma achaeae
NT3 trichogramma australicum
NT3 trichogramma brasiliense
NT3 trichogramma cacaeciae
NT3 trichogramma chilonis
NT3 trichogramma chilotraeae
NT3 trichogramma closterae
NT3 trichogramma cordubensis
NT3 trichogramma dendrolimi
NT3 trichogramma embryophagum
NT3 trichogramma evanescens
NT3 trichogramma exiguum
NT3 trichogramma fasciatum
NT3 trichogramma japonicum
NT3 trichogramma maidis
NT3 trichogramma minutum
NT3 trichogramma nubilale
NT3 trichogramma ostriniae
NT3 trichogramma pretiosum
NT3 trichogramma rhenanum
NT3 trichogramma semblidis
NT3 trichogramma semifumatum
NT2 trichogrammatoidea
NT3 trichogrammatoidea nana
NT1 vespidae
NT2 dolichovespula
NT3 dolichovespula arenaria
NT3 dolichovespula maculata
NT3 dolichovespula sylvestris
NT2 polistes
NT3 polistes annularis
NT3 polistes canadensis
NT3 polistes chinensis

HYMENOPTERA *cont.*
NT3 polistes erythrocephalus
NT3 polistes exclamans
NT3 polistes fuscatus
NT3 polistes gallicus
NT3 polistes jadwigae
NT2 polybia
NT3 polybia occidentalis
NT3 polybia paulista
NT2 vespa
NT3 vespa affinis
NT3 vespa crabro
NT3 vespa luctuosa
NT3 vespa mandarinia
NT3 vespa orientalis
NT3 vespa simillima
NT4 vespa simillima xanthoptera
NT3 vespa tropica
NT2 vespula
NT3 vespula atropilosa
NT3 vespula austriaca
NT3 vespula flavopilosa
NT3 vespula germanica
NT3 vespula maculifrons
NT3 vespula pensylvanica
NT3 vespula squamosa
NT3 vespula vulgaris
NT1 xiphydriidae
NT2 xiphydria
rt insects

HYMENOXYS
BT1 compositae
NT1 hymenoxys odorata

HYMENOXYS ODORATA
BT1 hymenoxys
BT2 compositae
BT1 poisonous plants

HYMENULA
BT1 deuteromycotina
NT1 hymenula cerealis
rt cephalosporium

HYMENULA CEREALIS
uf *cephalosporium gramineum*
BT1 hymenula
BT2 deuteromycotina

HYMEXAZOL
uf *hydroxyisoxazole*
BT1 oxazole fungicides
BT2 fungicides
BT3 pesticides

HYOBANCHE
BT1 scrophulariaceae
NT1 hyobanche sanguinea

HYOBANCHE SANGUINEA
BT1 hyobanche
BT2 scrophulariaceae

HYODEOXYCHOLIC ACID
BT1 bile acids

HYOSCYAMUS
BT1 solanaceae
NT1 hyoscyamus albus
NT1 hyoscyamus desertorum
NT1 hyoscyamus muticus
NT1 hyoscyamus niger
NT1 hyoscyamus pusillus

HYOSCYAMUS ALBUS
BT1 hyoscyamus
BT2 solanaceae

HYOSCYAMUS DESERTORUM
BT1 hyoscyamus
BT2 solanaceae

HYOSCYAMUS MUTICUS
BT1 hyoscyamus
BT2 solanaceae

HYOSCYAMUS NIGER
uf *henbane*
BT1 hyoscyamus
BT2 solanaceae
rt henbane mosaic potyvirus

HYOSCYAMUS PUSILLUS
BT1 hyoscyamus
BT2 solanaceae

HYOSTRONGYLUS
BT1 trichostrongylidae
BT2 nematoda
NT1 hyostrongylus rubidus

HYOSTRONGYLUS RUBIDUS
BT1 hyostrongylus
BT2 trichostrongylidae
BT3 nematoda

HYPARRHENIA
BT1 gramineae
NT1 hyparrhenia filipendula
NT1 hyparrhenia hirta
NT1 hyparrhenia rufa

HYPARRHENIA FILIPENDULA
BT1 hyparrhenia
BT2 gramineae
BT1 pasture plants

HYPARRHENIA HIRTA
BT1 hyparrhenia
BT2 gramineae

HYPARRHENIA RUFA
uf *jaragua grass*
BT1 hyparrhenia
BT2 gramineae
BT1 pasture plants

HYPERA
uf *phytonomus*
BT1 curculionidae
BT2 coleoptera
NT1 hypera meles
NT1 hypera nigrirostris
NT1 hypera postica

HYPERA MELES
BT1 hypera
BT2 curculionidae
BT3 coleoptera

HYPERA NIGRIROSTRIS
BT1 hypera
BT2 curculionidae
BT3 coleoptera

HYPERA POSTICA
uf *phytonomus variabilis*
BT1 hypera
BT2 curculionidae
BT3 coleoptera

HYPERACIDITY (AGRICOLA)
BT1 digestive disorders
BT2 functional disorders
BT3 animal disorders
BT4 disorders
rt acidity
rt gastric juices

HYPERACTIVITY
BT1 abnormal behaviour
BT2 behaviour

HYPERALIMENTATION
BT1 hyperphagia
BT2 hunger
BT1 overfeeding
BT2 feeding
BT2 feeding habits
BT3 feeding behaviour
BT4 behaviour
BT3 habits

HYPERAMINOACIDAEMIA
AF hyperaminoacidemia
BT1 amino acid disorders
BT2 metabolic disorders
BT3 animal disorders
BT4 disorders
NT1 hyperargininaemia
NT1 hyperglycinaemia
NT1 hypermethioninaemia
NT1 hyperphenylalaninaemia
rt amino acids
rt blood

HYPERAMINOACIDEMIA
BF hyperaminoacidaemia
NT1 hyperargininemia
NT1 hyperglycinemia
NT1 hypermethioninemia
NT1 hyperphenylalaninemia

HYPERAMINOACIDURIA
BT1 amino acid disorders
BT2 metabolic disorders
BT3 animal disorders
BT4 disorders
rt amino acids
rt urine

HYPERAMMONAEMIA
AF hyperammonemia
BT1 metabolic disorders
BT2 animal disorders
BT3 disorders
rt ammonia
rt blood

HYPERAMMONEMIA
BF hyperammonaemia

HYPERARGININAEMIA
AF hyperargininemia
BT1 hyperaminoacidaemia
BT2 amino acid disorders
BT3 metabolic disorders
BT4 animal disorders
BT5 disorders
rt blood

HYPERARGININEMIA
BF hyperargininaemia
BT1 hyperaminoacidemia

HYPERASPIS
BT1 coccinellidae
BT2 coleoptera

HYPERBILIRUBINAEMIA
AF hyperbilirubinemia
BT1 metabolic disorders
BT2 animal disorders
BT3 disorders
rt bilirubin
rt blood

HYPERBILIRUBINEMIA
BF hyperbilirubinaemia

HYPERCALCAEMIA
AF hypercalcemia
BT1 water-electrolyte imbalance
BT2 metabolic disorders
BT3 animal disorders
BT4 disorders
rt blood
rt calcium

HYPERCALCEMIA
BF hypercalcaemia

HYPERCALCIURIA
BT1 mineral metabolism disorders
BT2 metabolic disorders
BT3 animal disorders
BT4 disorders
rt calcium
rt urine

HYPERCAPNIA
BT1 respiratory disorders
BT2 functional disorders
BT3 animal disorders
BT4 disorders
BT2 respiratory diseases
BT3 organic diseases
BT4 diseases
rt blood
rt carbon dioxide

HYPERCAROTENAEMIA
AF hypercarotenemia
BT1 hyperlipaemia
BT2 lipid metabolism disorders
BT3 metabolic disorders
BT4 animal disorders
BT5 disorders
rt blood

HYPERCAROTENAEMIA *cont.*
rt retinol

HYPERCAROTENEMIA
BF hypercarotenaemia
BT1 hyperlipemia

HYPERCHOLESTEROLAEMIA
AF hypercholesterolemia
BT1 cholesterol metabolism disorders
BT2 lipid metabolism disorders
BT3 metabolic disorders
BT4 animal disorders
BT5 disorders
BT1 hyperlipaemia
BT2 lipid metabolism disorders
BT3 metabolic disorders
BT4 animal disorders
BT5 disorders
rt blood
rt cholesterol

HYPERCHOLESTEROLEMIA
BF hypercholesterolaemia
BT1 hyperlipemia
rt anticholesteremic agents (agricola)

HYPERCHYLOMICRONAEMIA
AF hyperchylomicronemia
BT1 hyperlipoproteinaemia
BT2 hyperlipaemia
BT3 lipid metabolism disorders
BT4 metabolic disorders
BT5 animal disorders
BT6 disorders
BT2 hyperproteinaemia
BT3 blood protein disorders
BT4 blood disorders
BT5 animal disorders
BT6 disorders
rt blood
rt chylomicron lipids

HYPERCHYLOMICRONEMIA
BF hyperchylomicronaemia
BT1 hyperlipoproteinemia
BT2 hyperlipemia
BT2 hyperproteinemia

HYPEREMESIS GRAVIDARUM
BT1 vomiting
BT2 digestive disorders
BT3 functional disorders
BT4 animal disorders
BT5 disorders
rt pregnancy

HYPERGLYCAEMIA
AF hyperglycemia
BT1 carbohydrate metabolism disorders
BT2 metabolic disorders
BT3 animal disorders
BT4 disorders
rt blood
rt blood sugar
rt diabetes
rt glucagon
rt obesity hyperglycaemia syndrome

HYPERGLYCEMIA
BF hyperglycaemia
rt obesity hyperglycemia syndrome

HYPERGLYCINAEMIA
AF hyperglycinemia
BT1 hyperaminoacidaemia
BT2 amino acid disorders
BT3 metabolic disorders
BT4 animal disorders
BT5 disorders
rt blood
rt glycine

HYPERGLYCINEMIA
BF hyperglycinaemia
BT1 hyperaminoacidemia

hypericaceae
USE **guttiferae**

HYPERICUM
BT1 guttiferae
NT1 hypericum androsaemum
NT1 hypericum annulatum
NT1 hypericum aucherii
NT1 hypericum calycinum
NT1 hypericum elegans
NT1 hypericum erectum
NT1 hypericum hirsutum
NT1 hypericum maculatum
NT1 hypericum montanum
NT1 hypericum olympicum
NT1 hypericum perforatum
NT1 hypericum polyphyllum
NT1 hypericum pulchrum
NT1 hypericum quadrangulum

HYPERICUM ANDROSAEMUM
BT1 hypericum
BT2 guttiferae

HYPERICUM ANNULATUM
uf *hypericum degenii*
BT1 hypericum
BT2 guttiferae

HYPERICUM AUCHERII
BT1 hypericum
BT2 guttiferae

HYPERICUM CALYCINUM
BT1 hypericum
BT2 guttiferae
BT1 ornamental woody plants

hypericum degenii
USE **hypericum annulatum**

HYPERICUM ELEGANS
BT1 hypericum
BT2 guttiferae
BT1 ornamental herbaceous plants

HYPERICUM ERECTUM
BT1 antiviral plants
BT1 hypericum
BT2 guttiferae
BT1 medicinal plants

HYPERICUM HIRSUTUM
BT1 hypericum
BT2 guttiferae

HYPERICUM MACULATUM
BT1 hypericum
BT2 guttiferae

HYPERICUM MONTANUM
BT1 hypericum
BT2 guttiferae

HYPERICUM OLYMPICUM
BT1 hypericum
BT2 guttiferae
BT1 ornamental herbaceous plants

HYPERICUM PERFORATUM
BT1 antibacterial plants
BT1 hypericum
BT2 guttiferae
BT1 medicinal plants

HYPERICUM POLYPHYLLUM
BT1 hypericum
BT2 guttiferae
BT1 ornamental herbaceous plants

HYPERICUM PULCHRUM
BT1 hypericum
BT2 guttiferae

HYPERICUM QUADRANGULUM
BT1 hypericum
BT2 guttiferae

hyperimmune serum
USE **immune serum**

HYPERIMMUNIZATION
BT1 immunization
BT2 immunostimulation
BT3 immunotherapy

HYPERIMMUNIZATION *cont.*
BT4 therapy

HYPERINFECTIONS
HN from 1989
BT1 infections

HYPERINSULINAEMIA
AF hyperinsulinemia
BT1 metabolic disorders
BT2 animal disorders
BT3 disorders
rt blood
rt insulin

HYPERINSULINEMIA
BF hyperinsulinaemia

HYPERINSULINISM
BT1 endocrine diseases
BT2 organic diseases
BT3 diseases
rt hypoglycaemia
rt insulin

hyperkalaemia
USE **hyperkaliaemia**

HYPERKALEMIA
BF hyperkaliaemia

HYPERKALIAEMIA
AF hyperkalemia
uf *hyperkalaemia*
BT1 water-electrolyte imbalance
BT2 metabolic disorders
BT3 animal disorders
BT4 disorders
rt blood
rt potassium

HYPERKERATOSIS
BT1 hypertrophy
BT2 abnormalities
BT1 skin diseases
BT2 organic diseases
BT3 diseases
rt eye diseases
rt growth
rt hyperkeratotic scabies

HYPERKERATOTIC SCABIES
HN from 1990
uf *crusted scabies*
uf *norwegian scabies*
BT1 scabies
BT2 ectoparasitoses
BT3 parasitoses
BT4 diseases
BT2 skin diseases
BT3 organic diseases
BT4 diseases
rt hyperkeratosis
rt immunosuppression

HYPERKETONAEMIA
AF hyperketonemia
BT1 metabolic disorders
BT2 animal disorders
BT3 disorders
rt blood
rt ketones
rt ketosis

HYPERKETONEMIA
BF hyperketonaemia

HYPERKINESIS
uf *overactivity*
BT1 physical activity
rt movement
rt muscular diseases

HYPERLIPAEMIA
AF hyperlipemia
BT1 lipid metabolism disorders
BT2 metabolic disorders
BT3 animal disorders
BT4 disorders
NT1 hypercarotenaemia
NT1 hypercholesterolaemia
NT1 hyperlipoproteinaemia
NT2 hyperchylomicronaemia
NT1 hypertriglyceridaemia

HYPERLIPAEMIA *cont.*
rt blood
rt blood lipids
rt cholesterol
rt lipaemia

HYPERLIPEMIA
BF hyperlipaemia
NT1 hypercarotenemia
NT1 hypercholesterolemia
NT1 hyperlipoproteinemia
NT2 hyperchylomicronemia
NT1 hypertriglyceridemia
rt antilipemics

HYPERLIPOPROTEINAEMIA
AF hyperlipoproteinemia
BT1 hyperlipaemia
BT2 lipid metabolism disorders
BT3 metabolic disorders
BT4 animal disorders
BT5 disorders
BT1 hyperproteinaemia
BT2 blood protein disorders
BT3 blood disorders
BT4 animal disorders
BT5 disorders
NT1 hyperchylomicronaemia
rt blood
rt lipoproteins

HYPERLIPOPROTEINEMIA
BF hyperlipoproteinaemia
BT1 hyperlipemia
BT1 hyperproteinemia
NT1 hyperchylomicronemia

HYPERMAGNESAEMIA
AF hypermagnesemia
BT1 mineral metabolism disorders
BT2 metabolic disorders
BT3 animal disorders
BT4 disorders
rt blood
rt magnesium

HYPERMAGNESEMIA
BF hypermagnesaemia

HYPERMARKETS
BT1 shops
BT2 retail marketing
BT3 marketing channels
BT4 marketing
rt markets
rt supermarkets

HYPERMETHIONINAEMIA
AF hypermethioninemia
BT1 hyperaminoacidaemia
BT2 amino acid disorders
BT3 metabolic disorders
BT4 animal disorders
BT5 disorders
rt blood
rt methionine

HYPERMETHIONINEMIA
BF hypermethioninaemia
BT1 hyperaminoacidemia

HYPERNATRAEMIA
AF hypernatremia
BT1 water-electrolyte imbalance
BT2 metabolic disorders
BT3 animal disorders
BT4 disorders
rt blood
rt sodium

HYPERNATREMIA
BF hypernatraemia

hyperodes
USE **listronotus**

hyperodes bonariensis
USE **listronotus bonariensis**

HYPEROMYZUS
BT1 aphididae
BT2 aphidoidea
BT3 sternorrhyncha

HYPEROMYZUS *cont.*
BT4 homoptera
NT1 hyperomyzus lactucae
rt amphorophora
rt nasonovia

HYPEROMYZUS LACTUCAE
uf *amphorophora lactucae*
uf *nasonovia lactucae*
BT1 hyperomyzus
BT2 aphididae
BT3 aphidoidea
BT4 sternorrhyncha
BT5 homoptera

HYPEROPLUS
BT1 ammodytidae
BT2 perciformes
BT3 osteichthyes
BT4 fishes

HYPEROSTOSIS
BT1 bone diseases
BT2 organic diseases
BT3 diseases

HYPEROXALURIA
BT1 metabolic disorders
BT2 animal disorders
BT3 disorders
rt oxalic acid
rt urine

HYPEROXIA
BT1 metabolic disorders
BT2 animal disorders
BT3 disorders
rt oxygen

HYPERPARASITISM
BT1 parasitism
rt parasites

HYPERPARASITOIDS
BT1 parasitoids
BT2 insects
BT3 arthropods
BT2 parasites

HYPERPARATHYROIDISM
BT1 parathyroid diseases
BT2 endocrine diseases
BT3 organic diseases
BT4 diseases
rt calcium
rt hormones
rt parathyrin

HYPERPHAGIA
BT1 hunger
NT1 hyperalimentation

HYPERPHENYLALANINAEMIA
AF hyperphenylalaninemia
BT1 hyperaminoacidaemia
BT2 amino acid disorders
BT3 metabolic disorders
BT4 animal disorders
BT5 disorders
rt blood
rt phenylalanine

HYPERPHENYLALANINEMIA
BF hyperphenylalaninaemia
BT1 hyperaminoacidemia

HYPERPHOSPHATAEMIA
AF hyperphosphatemia
BT1 mineral metabolism disorders
BT2 metabolic disorders
BT3 animal disorders
BT4 disorders
rt blood
rt phosphorus

hyperphosphate
USE **rock phosphate**

HYPERPHOSPHATEMIA
BF hyperphosphataemia

HYPERPHOSPHATURIA
BT1 mineral metabolism disorders

HYPERPHOSPHATURIA *cont.*
BT2 metabolic disorders
BT3 animal disorders
BT4 disorders
rt phosphorus
rt urine

HYPERPLASIA
BT1 congenital abnormalities
BT2 abnormalities
NT1 interdigital hyperplasia
NT1 mammary hyperplasia
NT1 megacolon

HYPERPROLACTINAEMIA
HN from 1989
AF hyperprolactinemia
BT1 hyperproteinaemia
BT2 blood protein disorders
BT3 blood disorders
BT4 animal disorders
BT5 disorders
rt prolactin

HYPERPROLACTINEMIA
HN from 1989
BF hyperprolactinaemia
BT1 hyperproteinemia

HYPERPROTEINAEMIA
AF hyperproteinemia
BT1 blood protein disorders
BT2 blood disorders
BT3 animal disorders
BT4 disorders
NT1 hyperlipoproteinaemia
NT2 hyperchylomicronaemia
NT1 hyperprolactinaemia

HYPERPROTEINEMIA
BF hyperproteinaemia
NT1 hyperlipoproteinemia
NT2 hyperchylomicronemia
NT1 hyperprolactinemia

HYPERSECRETION
BT1 secretion
BT2 physiological functions
rt functional disorders

HYPERSENSITIVITY
uf *allergic responses*
BT1 immune response
BT2 immunity
NT1 delayed type hypersensitivity
NT1 immediate hypersensitivity
NT2 allergic reactions
NT2 anaphylaxis
NT2 atopy
NT1 respiratory hypersensitivity
rt allergies
rt immunological diseases
rt resistance
rt susceptibility

hypersensitivity, drug
USE **drug allergies**

hypersensitivity, food
USE **food allergies**

HYPERTENSION
uf *blood pressure, high*
uf *high blood pressure*
BT1 vascular diseases
BT2 cardiovascular diseases
BT3 organic diseases
BT4 diseases
rt antihypertensive agents
rt blood pressure

HYPERTHERMIA
BT1 heat stress
BT2 stress
rt body temperature

HYPERTHYROIDISM
uf *thyrotoxicosis*
BT1 thyroid diseases
BT2 endocrine diseases
BT3 organic diseases
BT4 diseases

HYPERTRIGLYCERIDAEMIA
AF hypertriglyceridemia
BT1 hyperlipaemia
BT2 lipid metabolism disorders
BT3 metabolic disorders
BT4 animal disorders
BT5 disorders
rt blood
rt triacylglycerols

HYPERTRIGLYCERIDEMIA
BF hypertriglyceridaemia
BT1 hyperlipemia

HYPERTROPHY
BT1 abnormalities
NT1 hyperkeratosis
NT1 muscular hypertrophy
rt growth

HYPERURICAEMIA
AF hyperuricemia
BT1 metabolic disorders
BT2 animal disorders
BT3 disorders
rt blood
rt uric acid

HYPERURICEMIA
BF hyperuricaemia

hypervitaminosis a
USE **vitamin a excess**

HYPHAE
BT1 fungal morphology
BT2 morphology

HYPHAENE
BT1 palmae
NT1 hyphaene natalensis
NT1 hyphaene thebaica

HYPHAENE NATALENSIS
BT1 hyphaene
BT2 palmae

HYPHAENE THEBAICA
uf doum palm
BT1 hyphaene
BT2 palmae

HYPHANTRIA
BT1 arctiidae
BT2 lepidoptera
NT1 hyphantria cunea

HYPHANTRIA CUNEA
BT1 hyphantria
BT2 arctiidae
BT3 lepidoptera

hyphomyces destruens
USE **pythium destruens**

HYPOALBUMINAEMIA
AF hypoalbuminemia
BT1 hypoproteinaemia
BT2 blood protein disorders
BT3 blood disorders
BT4 animal disorders
BT5 disorders
rt albumins

HYPOALBUMINEMIA
BF hypoalbuminaemia
BT1 hypoproteinemia

HYPOASPIS
BT1 laelapidae
BT2 mesostigmata
BT3 acari
NT1 hypoaspis aculeifer

HYPOASPIS ACULEIFER
BT1 hypoaspis
BT2 laelapidae
BT3 mesostigmata
BT4 acari

HYPOBARIC STORAGE
BT1 storage
rt pressure

HYPOCALCAEMIA
AF hypocalcemia

HYPOCALCAEMIA *cont.*
BT1 water-electrolyte imbalance
BT2 metabolic disorders
BT3 animal disorders
BT4 disorders
NT1 tetany
rt blood
rt calcium
rt parturient paresis
rt phytic acid

HYPOCALCEMIA
BF hypocalcaemia

HYPOCALCIURIA
BT1 mineral metabolism disorders
BT2 metabolic disorders
BT3 animal disorders
BT4 disorders
rt calcium

HYPOCHLORITES
BT1 inorganic salts
BT2 inorganic compounds
BT2 salts
NT1 sodium hypochlorite

HYPOCHOERIS
BT1 compositae
NT1 hypochoeris glabra
NT1 hypochoeris radicata

HYPOCHOERIS GLABRA
BT1 hypochoeris
BT2 compositae

HYPOCHOERIS RADICATA
BT1 hypochoeris
BT2 compositae

HYPOCHOLESTEROLAEMIA
AF hypocholesterolemia
BT1 cholesterol metabolism disorders
BT2 lipid metabolism disorders
BT3 metabolic disorders
BT4 animal disorders
BT5 disorders
BT1 hypolipaemia
BT2 lipid metabolism disorders
BT3 metabolic disorders
BT4 animal disorders
BT5 disorders
rt blood
rt cholesterol

HYPOCHOLESTEROLEMIA
BF hypocholesterolaemia
BT1 hypolipemia

HYPOCHROMIC ANAEMIA
AF hypochromic anemia
BT1 anaemia
BT2 blood disorders
BT3 animal disorders
BT4 disorders
rt pigmentation
rt thalassaemia

HYPOCHROMIC ANEMIA
BF hypochromic anaemia
BT1 anemia

HYPOCOTYLS
BT1 seedlings
rt cotyledons
rt epicotyls

HYPOCREALES
NT1 calonectria
NT2 calonectria crotalariae
NT2 calonectria ilicicola
NT2 calonectria kyotensis
NT2 calonectria quinqueseptata
NT2 calonectria theae
NT1 gibberella
NT2 gibberella acuminata
NT2 gibberella avenacea
NT2 gibberella baccata
NT2 gibberella cyanogena
NT2 gibberella fujikuroi
NT3 gibberella fujikuroi var. subglutinans

HYPOCREALES *cont.*
NT2 gibberella gordonii
NT2 gibberella intricans
NT2 gibberella pulicaris
NT2 gibberella stilboides
NT2 gibberella zeae
NT1 nectria
NT2 nectria cinnabarina
NT2 nectria coccinea
NT2 nectria episphaeria
NT2 nectria flammea
NT2 nectria fuckeliana
NT2 nectria galligena
NT2 nectria haematococca
NT2 nectria radicicola
NT2 nectria rigidiuscula
NT1 neocosmospora
NT2 neocosmospora vasinfecta
NT1 sphaerostilbe
NT2 sphaerostilbe fuliginea
NT2 sphaerostilbe repens
rt fungi

HYPOCUPRAEMIA
AF hypocupremia
BT1 mineral metabolism disorders
BT2 metabolic disorders
BT3 animal disorders
BT4 disorders
rt blood
rt copper

HYPOCUPREMIA
BF hypocupraemia

HYPOCYRTA
BT1 gesneriaceae
NT1 hypocyrta glabra

HYPOCYRTA GLABRA
BT1 hypocyrta
BT2 gesneriaceae
BT1 ornamental woody plants

hypocyrta radicans
USE **nematanthus gregarius**

HYPODERMA
uf oedemagena
BT1 oestridae
BT2 diptera
NT1 hypoderma bovis
NT1 hypoderma diana
NT1 hypoderma lineatum
NT1 hypoderma tarandi

HYPODERMA BOVIS
BT1 hypoderma
BT2 oestridae
BT3 diptera

HYPODERMA DIANA
BT1 hypoderma
BT2 oestridae
BT3 diptera

HYPODERMA LINEATUM
BT1 hypoderma
BT2 oestridae
BT3 diptera

HYPODERMA TARANDI
uf oedemagena tarandi
uf reindeer warble fly
BT1 hypoderma
BT2 oestridae
BT3 diptera

HYPOESTES
BT1 acanthaceae
NT1 hypoestes aristata
NT1 hypoestes phyllostachya
NT1 hypoestes sanguinolenta

HYPOESTES ARISTATA
BT1 hypoestes
BT2 acanthaceae
rt ornamental foliage plants

HYPOESTES PHYLLOSTACHYA
BT1 hypoestes
BT2 acanthaceae
rt ornamental foliage plants

HYPOESTES SANGUINOLENTA
BT1 hypoestes
BT2 acanthaceae
rt ornamental foliage plants

HYPOGAMMAGLOBULINAEMIA
AF hypogammaglobulinemia
BT1 hypoproteinaemia
BT2 blood protein disorders
BT3 blood disorders
BT4 animal disorders
BT5 disorders
rt globulins

HYPOGAMMAGLOBULINEMIA
BF hypogammaglobulinaemia
BT1 hypoproteinemia

HYPOGASTRURA
BT1 hypogastruridae
BT2 collembola
NT1 hypogastrura tullbergi

HYPOGASTRURA TULLBERGI
BT1 hypogastrura
BT2 hypogastruridae
BT3 collembola

HYPOGASTRURIDAE
BT1 collembola
NT1 anurida
NT2 anurida granulata
NT1 brachystomella
NT1 hypogastrura
NT2 hypogastrura tullbergi

HYPOGEOCOCCUS
BT1 pseudococcidae
BT2 coccoidea
BT3 sternorrhyncha
BT4 homoptera

HYPOGEUSIA (AGRICOLA)
rt taste sensitivity

HYPOGLYCAEMIA
AF hypoglycemia
uf blood sugar, low
BT1 carbohydrate metabolism disorders
BT2 metabolic disorders
BT3 animal disorders
BT4 disorders
rt blood
rt blood sugar
rt hyperinsulinism
rt hypoglycaemic agents

HYPOGLYCAEMIC AGENTS
AF hypoglycemic agents
uf antidiabetics
BT1 haematologic agents
BT2 drugs
NT1 buformin
NT1 chlorpropamide
NT1 glibenclamide
NT1 gliclazide
NT1 glipizide
NT1 glucagon
NT1 hypoglycine a
NT1 insulin
NT1 metformin
NT1 tolbutamide
rt blood sugar
rt diabetes
rt hypoglycaemia

HYPOGLYCEMIA
BF hypoglycaemia
rt hypoglycemic agents

HYPOGLYCEMIC AGENTS
BF hypoglycaemic agents
rt hypoglycemia

HYPOGLYCINE A
BT1 cyclic amino acids
BT2 amino acids
BT3 carboxylic acids
BT4 organic acids
BT5 acids
BT3 organic nitrogen compounds
BT1 hypoglycaemic agents

HYPOGLYCINE A *cont.*
BT2 haematologic agents
BT3 drugs
rt blighia sapida

HYPOGONADISM
HN from 1990
BT1 gonadal disorders
BT2 endocrine diseases
BT3 organic diseases
BT4 diseases

HYPOHIDROSIS
BT1 skin diseases
BT2 organic diseases
BT3 diseases
rt sweating

hypokalaemia
USE **hypokaliaemia**

HYPOKALEMIA
BF hypokaliaemia

HYPOKALIAEMIA
AF hypokalemia
uf *hypokalaemia*
BT1 water-electrolyte imbalance
BT2 metabolic disorders
BT3 animal disorders
BT4 disorders
rt blood
rt potassium

HYPOLIPAEMIA
AF hypolipemia
BT1 lipid metabolism disorders
BT2 metabolic disorders
BT3 animal disorders
BT4 disorders
NT1 hypocholesterolaemia
NT1 hypolipoproteinaemia
NT2 abetalipoproteinaemia
rt blood
rt hypolipaemic agents
rt lipids

HYPOLIPAEMIC AGENTS
AF hypolipemic agents
BT1 haematologic agents
BT2 drugs
NT1 orotic acid
rt hypolipaemia

HYPOLIPEMIA
BF hypolipaemia
NT1 hypocholesterolemia
NT1 hypolipoproteinemia
NT2 abetalipoproteinemia

HYPOLIPEMIC AGENTS
BF hypolipaemic agents
BT1 hematologic agents

HYPOLIPOPROTEINAEMIA
AF hypolipoproteinemia
BT1 hypolipaemia
BT2 lipid metabolism disorders
BT3 metabolic disorders
BT4 animal disorders
BT5 disorders
BT1 hypoproteinaemia
BT2 blood protein disorders
BT3 blood disorders
BT4 animal disorders
BT5 disorders
NT1 abetalipoproteinaemia
rt lipoproteins

HYPOLIPOPROTEINEMIA
BF hypolipoproteinaemia
BT1 hypolipemia
BT1 hypoproteinemia
NT1 abetalipoproteinemia

HYPOMAGNESAEMIA
AF hypomagnesemia
BT1 mineral metabolism disorders
BT2 metabolic disorders
BT3 animal disorders
BT4 disorders
NT1 grass tetany
rt blood

HYPOMAGNESAEMIA *cont.*
rt magnesium

hypomagnesaemic tetany
USE **grass tetany**

HYPOMAGNESEMIA
BF hypomagnesaemia

HYPOMECIS
uf *boarmia*
BT1 geometridae
BT2 lepidoptera

HYPOMYCES
uf *dactylium*
BT1 clavicipitales
NT1 hypomyces rosellus

HYPOMYCES ROSELLUS
uf *dactylium dendroides*
BT1 hypomyces
BT2 clavicipitales

HYPONATRAEMIA
AF hyponatremia
BT1 water-electrolyte imbalance
BT2 metabolic disorders
BT3 animal disorders
BT4 disorders
rt blood
rt sodium

HYPONATREMIA
BF hyponatraemia

hyponomeuta
USE **yponomeuta**

hyponomeuta malinellus
USE **yponomeuta malinellus**

hyponomeuta padellus
USE **yponomeuta padellus**

HYPOPARATHYROIDISM
BT1 parathyroid diseases
BT2 endocrine diseases
BT3 organic diseases
BT4 diseases
rt thyroid hormones

HYPOPHARYNGEAL GLANDS
BT1 glands (animal)
BT2 body parts
BT2 glands

HYPOPHOSPHATAEMIA
AF hypophosphatemia
BT1 mineral metabolism disorders
BT2 metabolic disorders
BT3 animal disorders
BT4 disorders
rt bone diseases
rt hypophosphataemic rickets
rt phosphorus

HYPOPHOSPHATAEMIC RICKETS
AF hypophosphatemic rickets
uf *rickets, hypophosphataemic*
BT1 rickets
BT2 mineral metabolism disorders
BT3 metabolic disorders
BT4 animal disorders
BT5 disorders
rt bone diseases
rt hypophosphataemia
rt phosphorus

HYPOPHOSPHATASIA
BT1 enzyme deficiencies
BT2 deficiency
rt phosphoric monoester hydrolases

HYPOPHOSPHATEMIA
BF hypophosphataemia
rt hypophosphatemic rickets

HYPOPHOSPHATEMIC RICKETS
BF hypophosphataemic rickets
rt hypophosphatemia

HYPOPHYSATION
BT1 pituitary diseases
BT2 endocrine diseases
BT3 organic diseases
BT4 diseases
rt pituitary

HYPOPHYSECTOMY
uf *pituitary removal*
BT1 surgical operations
rt pituitary

hypophysis
USE **pituitary**

HYPOPLASIA
BT1 congenital abnormalities
BT2 abnormalities
NT1 hypotrichosis
NT1 microphthalmia

HYPOPROTEINAEMIA
AF hypoproteinemia
BT1 blood protein disorders
BT2 blood disorders
BT3 animal disorders
BT4 disorders
NT1 hypoalbuminaemia
NT1 hypogammaglobulinaemia
NT1 hypolipoproteinaemia
NT2 abetalipoproteinaemia
NT1 hypoprothrombinaemia

HYPOPROTEINEMIA
BF hypoproteinaemia
NT1 hypoalbuminemia
NT1 hypogammaglobulinemia
NT1 hypolipoproteinemia
NT2 abetalipoproteinemia
NT1 hypoprothrombinemia

HYPOPROTHROMBINAEMIA
AF hypoprothrombinemia
BT1 hypoproteinaemia
BT2 blood protein disorders
BT3 blood disorders
BT4 animal disorders
BT5 disorders
rt prothrombin

HYPOPROTHROMBINEMIA
BF hypoprothrombinaemia
BT1 hypoproteinemia

HYPORHAMPHUS
BT1 hemiramphidae
BT2 cyprinodontiformes
BT3 osteichthyes
BT4 fishes

hyposensitization
USE **immune desensitization**

HYPOSOTER
BT1 ichneumonidae
BT2 hymenoptera
NT1 hyposoter exiguae

HYPOSOTER EXIGUAE
BT1 hyposoter
BT2 ichneumonidae
BT3 hymenoptera

hypostasis
USE **epistasis**

HYPOTENSION
BT1 vascular diseases
BT2 cardiovascular diseases
BT3 organic diseases
BT4 diseases
rt blood pressure
rt rauvolfia serpentina

HYPOTHALAMIC INHIBITING HORMONES
BT1 hormones
NT1 prolactostatin
NT1 somatostatin
rt hypothalamus

HYPOTHALAMIC LESIONS
BT1 lesions
rt hypothalamus

HYPOTHALAMIC REGULATION
BT1 regulation
rt hypothalamus

HYPOTHALAMIC RELEASING HORMONES
uf *releasing factors*
uf *releasing hormones*
BT1 hormones
NT1 corticoliberin
NT1 fshrh
NT1 gnrh
NT1 gonadorelin
NT1 lhrh
NT1 prolactoliberin
NT1 somatoliberin
NT1 thyrotropin releasing hormone
rt hypothalamus

HYPOTHALAMUS
uf *brain, hypothalamus*
BT1 brain
BT2 central nervous system
BT3 nervous system
BT4 body parts
NT1 preoptic area
rt hypothalamic inhibiting hormones
rt hypothalamic lesions
rt hypothalamic regulation
rt hypothalamic releasing hormones

HYPOTHENEMUS
uf *stephanoderes*
BT1 scolytidae
BT2 coleoptera
NT1 hypothenemus hampei

HYPOTHENEMUS HAMPEI
uf *stephanoderes hampei*
BT1 hypothenemus
BT2 scolytidae
BT3 coleoptera

HYPOTHERMIA
BT1 cold stress
BT2 stress
rt body temperature
rt cold

HYPOTHYROIDISM
BT1 thyroid diseases
BT2 endocrine diseases
BT3 organic diseases
BT4 diseases

HYPOTRICHOMONAS
BT1 sarcomastigophora
BT2 protozoa

HYPOTRICHOSIS
BT1 hypoplasia
BT2 congenital abnormalities
BT3 abnormalities
rt alopecia
rt hair

HYPOTRIGONA
BT1 apidae
BT2 hymenoptera

HYPOTROPHY
BT1 growth disorders
BT2 animal disorders
BT3 disorders
rt abnormalities

HYPOVIRULENCE
BT1 virulence
BT2 pathogenicity

hypovitaminosis a
USE **vitamin a deficiency**

HYPOVOLAEMIA
AF hypovolemia
BT1 blood disorders
BT2 animal disorders
BT3 disorders

HYPOVOLEMIA
BF hypovolaemia

HYPOXANTHINE
BT1 hypoxanthines
BT2 purines
BT3 heterocyclic nitrogen compounds
BT4 organic nitrogen compounds

HYPOXANTHINES
BT1 purines
BT2 heterocyclic nitrogen compounds
BT3 organic nitrogen compounds
NT1 guanine
NT1 hypoxanthine

HYPOXIA
BT1 respiratory disorders
BT2 functional disorders
BT3 animal disorders
BT4 disorders
BT2 respiratory diseases
BT3 organic diseases
BT4 diseases
rt anoxia
rt oxygen

HYPOXIDACEAE
NT1 curculigo
NT2 curculigo orchioides
NT1 rhodohypoxis

HYPOXYLON
BT1 sphaeriales
NT1 hypoxylon mammatum
NT1 hypoxylon rubiginosum

HYPOXYLON MAMMATUM
uf *hypoxylon pruinatum*
BT1 hypoxylon
BT2 sphaeriales

hypoxylon pruinatum
USE **hypoxylon mammatum**

HYPOXYLON RUBIGINOSUM
BT1 hypoxylon
BT2 sphaeriales

HYPSIPYLA
BT1 pyralidae
BT2 lepidoptera
NT1 hypsipyla grandella

HYPSIPYLA GRANDELLA
BT1 hypsipyla
BT2 pyralidae
BT3 lepidoptera

HYPTIS
BT1 labiatae
NT1 hyptis emoryi
NT1 hyptis pectinata
NT1 hyptis spicigera
NT1 hyptis spicitigera
NT1 hyptis suaveolens
NT1 hyptis tomentosa

HYPTIS EMORYI
BT1 hyptis
BT2 labiatae

HYPTIS PECTINATA
BT1 hyptis
BT2 labiatae

HYPTIS SPICIGERA
BT1 hyptis
BT2 labiatae
BT1 insecticidal plants
BT2 pesticidal plants

HYPTIS SPICITIGERA
BT1 hyptis
BT2 labiatae

HYPTIS SUAVEOLENS
BT1 antifungal plants
BT1 hyptis
BT2 labiatae
BT1 medicinal plants

HYPTIS TOMENTOSA
BT1 hyptis

HYPTIS TOMENTOSA *cont.*
BT2 labiatae
BT1 medicinal plants

HYRACOIDEA
uf *hyraxes*
BT1 mammals
NT1 procaviidae
NT2 heterohyrax
NT3 heterohyrax brucei
NT2 procavia
NT3 procavia capensis

hyraxes
USE **hyracoidea**

HYSSOPUS
BT1 labiatae
NT1 hyssopus cuspidatus
NT1 hyssopus seravschanicus

HYSSOPUS CUSPIDATUS
BT1 hyssopus
BT2 labiatae

HYSSOPUS SERAVSCHANICUS
BT1 essential oil plants
BT2 oil plants
BT1 hyssopus
BT2 labiatae

HYSTERANGIUM
BT1 phallales
NT1 hysterangium crassum

HYSTERANGIUM CRASSUM
BT1 hysterangium
BT2 phallales

HYSTERECTOMY
BT1 surgical operations
rt uterus

HYSTERESIS
BT1 electrical properties
BT2 physical properties
BT3 properties
BT1 mechanical properties
BT2 properties
rt damping
rt soil water

hysteria
USE **neuroses**

HYSTERONEURA
BT1 aphididae
BT2 aphidoidea
BT3 sternorrhyncha
BT4 homoptera
NT1 hysteroneura setariae

HYSTERONEURA SETARIAE
BT1 hysteroneura
BT2 aphididae
BT3 aphidoidea
BT4 sternorrhyncha
BT5 homoptera

HYSTEROTOMY
BT1 surgical operations
rt uterus

HYSTRICHOPSYLLA
BT1 hystrichopsyllidae
BT2 siphonaptera
NT1 hystrichopsylla talpae

HYSTRICHOPSYLLA TALPAE
BT1 hystrichopsylla
BT2 hystrichopsyllidae
BT3 siphonaptera

HYSTRICHOPSYLLIDAE
BT1 siphonaptera
NT1 catallagia
NT1 ctenophthalmus
NT2 ctenophthalmus agyrtes
NT2 ctenophthalmus baeticus
NT2 ctenophthalmus dolichus
NT2 ctenophthalmus pseudagyrtes
NT2 ctenophthalmus wladimiri
NT1 hystrichopsylla
NT2 hystrichopsylla talpae

HYSTRICHOPSYLLIDAE *cont.*
NT1 neopsylla
NT2 neopsylla setosa
NT1 palaeopsylla
NT1 rhadinopsylla

HYSTRICIDAE
BT1 rodents
BT2 mammals
NT1 atherurus
NT2 atherurus africanus
NT1 hystrix
NT2 hystrix indica
rt porcupines

HYSTRIX
BT1 hystricidae
BT2 rodents
BT3 mammals
NT1 hystrix indica

HYSTRIX INDICA
BT1 hystrix
BT2 hystricidae
BT3 rodents
BT4 mammals

hyv
USE **high yielding varieties**

IAA
uf *indoleacetic acid*
uf *indolylacetic acid*
BT1 auxins
BT2 plant growth regulators
BT3 growth regulators
BT1 indoles
BT2 heterocyclic nitrogen compounds
BT3 organic nitrogen compounds

IAA OXIDASE
uf *indoleacetic acid oxidase*
BT1 oxidoreductases
BT2 enzymes

IAEA
(international atomic energy agen)
BT1 international organizations
BT2 organizations

IATROGENIC DISEASES
HN from 1990
BT1 diseases
rt accidental infection
rt adverse effects

IBA
uf *indolylbutyric acid*
BT1 auxins
BT2 plant growth regulators
BT3 growth regulators
BT1 indoles
BT2 heterocyclic nitrogen compounds
BT3 organic nitrogen compounds

IBALIA
BT1 ibaliidae
BT2 hymenoptera
NT1 ibalia leucospoides

IBALIA LEUCOSPOIDES
BT1 ibalia
BT2 ibaliidae
BT3 hymenoptera

IBALIIDAE
BT1 hymenoptera
NT1 ibalia
NT2 ibalia leucospoides

IBARAKI VIRUS
BT1 orbivirus
BT2 arboviruses
BT3 pathogens
BT2 reoviridae
BT3 viruses

IBDU
uf *diureidoisobutane*
uf *isobutylidene diurea*
BT1 slow release fertilizers
BT2 fertilizers
BT1 urea fertilizers
BT2 nitrogen fertilizers
BT3 fertilizers

IBERIS
BT1 cruciferae
NT1 iberis sempervirens

IBERIS SEMPERVIRENS
BT1 iberis
BT2 cruciferae
BT1 ornamental herbaceous plants

ibex
USE **capra ibex**

IBOZA
BT1 labiatae
NT1 iboza riparia

IBOZA RIPARIA
BT1 antibacterial plants
BT1 iboza
BT2 labiatae

IBR IPV VIRUS
uf *bovine rhinotracheitis virus*
BT1 bovine herpesvirus

IBR IPV VIRUS *cont.*
BT2 herpesviridae
BT3 viruses

ibrd
USE **world bank**

ICACINA
BT1 icacinaceae
NT1 icacina guesfeldtii

ICACINA GUESFELDTII
BT1 icacina
BT2 icacinaceae

ICACINACEAE
NT1 icacina
NT2 icacina guesfeldtii

ICARDA
(international center for agricultural research in dry areas)
BT1 cgiar
BT2 international organizations
BT3 organizations

ICE
BT1 water
rt freezing
rt frost
rt ice bank coolers
rt ice damage
rt ice-water interface
rt skating
rt snow
rt soil water categories

ICE BANK COOLERS
uf *coolers, ice bank*
BT1 coolers
rt ice
rt refrigeration

ICE CREAM
BT1 confectionery
BT1 milk products
BT2 products
NT1 water ices
rt ice cream cones
rt sandiness
rt wafers

ICE CREAM CONES
uf *cones, ice cream*
rt ice cream

ICE DAMAGE
uf *glaze*
BT1 damage
rt freezing
rt ice

ICE NUCLEATION
rt bacteria
rt freezing

ICE RINKS
BT1 recreational buildings
BT2 buildings

ICE-WATER INTERFACE
BT1 interface
rt ice
rt water

ICED TEA (AGRICOLA)
BT1 beverages
rt tea

ICELAND
BT1 scandinavia
BT2 europe
rt efta
rt oecd

ICELAND PONY
BT1 horse breeds
BT2 breeds

ICELANDIC
BT1 cattle breeds
BT2 breeds
BT1 sheep breeds
BT2 breeds

ICELINUS
BT1 cottidae
BT2 scorpaeniformes
BT3 osteichthyes
BT4 fishes

ICERYA
BT1 margarodidae
BT2 coccoidea
BT3 sternorrhyncha
BT4 homoptera
NT1 icerya aegyptiaca
NT1 icerya purchasi

ICERYA AEGYPTIACA
BT1 icerya
BT2 margarodidae
BT3 coccoidea
BT4 sternorrhyncha
BT5 homoptera

ICERYA PURCHASI
BT1 icerya
BT2 margarodidae
BT3 coccoidea
BT4 sternorrhyncha
BT5 homoptera

ICHNEUMONIDAE
BT1 hymenoptera
NT1 agrothereutes
NT2 agrothereutes tunetanus
NT1 agrypon
NT2 agrypon flaveolatum
NT1 amblyteles
NT2 amblyteles castigator
NT2 amblyteles inspector
NT1 apechthis
NT2 apechthis quadridentatus
NT2 apechthis resinator
NT2 apechthis rufatus
NT1 bassus
NT1 bathyplectes
NT2 bathyplectes anurus
NT2 bathyplectes curculionis
NT1 campoletis
NT2 campoletis chlorideae
NT2 campoletis flavicincta
NT2 campoletis sonorensis
NT1 campoplex
NT1 charops
NT1 chorinaeus
NT1 cremastus
NT1 ctenichneumon
NT2 ctenichneumon panzeri
NT1 diadegma
NT2 diadegma armillata
NT2 diadegma eucerophaga
NT2 diadegma fenestralis
NT2 diadegma insularis
NT1 diadromus
NT2 diadromus pulchellus
NT1 diplazon
NT2 diplazon laetatorius
NT1 dolichomitus
NT2 dolichomitus populneus
NT1 ephialtes
NT2 ephialtes ontario
NT1 exeristes
NT2 exeristes comstockii
NT2 exeristes roborator
NT1 glypta
NT2 glypta fumiferanae
NT1 gregopimpla
NT1 heteropelma
NT1 hyposoter
NT2 hyposoter exiguae
NT1 itoplectis
NT2 itoplectis conquisitor
NT2 itoplectis maculator
NT2 itoplectis naranyae
NT1 lemophagus
NT2 lemophagus curtus
NT1 liotryphon
NT2 liotryphon punctulatus
NT1 lissonota
NT1 mesochorus
NT2 mesochorus dimidiatus
NT1 mesoleius
NT2 mesoleius tenthredinis
NT1 olesicampe
NT2 olesicampe benefactor

ICHNEUMONIDAE *cont.*
NT1 ophion
NT2 ophion flavidus
NT1 phaeogenes
NT2 phaeogenes invisor
NT1 phobocampe
NT1 phygadeuon
NT2 phygadeuon trichops
NT1 phytodietus
NT1 pimpla
NT2 pimpla disparis
NT2 pimpla hesperus
NT2 pimpla hypochondriaca
NT2 pimpla turionellae
NT1 pimplopterus
NT2 pimplopterus dubius
NT1 pleolophus
NT2 pleolophus basizonus
NT1 pristomerus
NT2 pristomerus spinator
NT2 pristomerus vulnerator
NT1 rhyssa
NT2 rhyssa persuasoria
NT1 scambus
NT2 scambus brevicornis
NT2 scambus calobatus
NT2 scambus decorus
NT1 sinophorus
NT2 sinophorus xanthostomus
NT1 temelucha
NT2 temelucha interruptor
NT1 trichomma
NT2 trichomma enecator
NT1 venturia (hymenoptera)
NT2 venturia canescens
NT1 vulgichneumon
NT2 vulgichneumon leucaniae
NT1 xanthopimpla
NT2 xanthopimpla stemmator

ICHTHYOBODO
BT1 sarcomastigophora
BT2 protozoa
NT1 ichthyobodo necator

ICHTHYOBODO NECATOR
uf *costia necatrix*
BT1 ichthyobodo
BT2 sarcomastigophora
BT3 protozoa

ICHTHYOPHONUS
uf *ichthyosporidium*
BT1 entomophthorales
NT1 ichthyophonus hoferi

ICHTHYOPHONUS HOFERI
uf *ichthyosporidium hoferi*
BT1 ichthyophonus
BT2 entomophthorales

ICHTHYOPHTHIRIUS
BT1 ciliophora
BT2 protozoa
NT1 ichthyophthirius multifiliis

ICHTHYOPHTHIRIUS MULTIFILIIS
BT1 ichthyophthirius
BT2 ciliophora
BT3 protozoa

ichthyosporidium
USE **ichthyophonus**

ichthyosporidium hoferi
USE **ichthyophonus hoferi**

icing sugar
USE **powdered sugar**

icsh
USE **lh**

ICTALURIDAE
BT1 siluriformes
BT2 osteichthyes
BT3 fishes
NT1 ictalurus
NT2 ictalurus nebulosus
NT2 ictalurus punctatus
rt freshwater catfishes

ICTALURUS
BT1 ictaluridae

ICTALURUS *cont.*
BT2 siluriformes
BT3 osteichthyes
BT4 fishes
NT1 ictalurus nebulosus
NT1 ictalurus punctatus

ICTALURUS NEBULOSUS
BT1 ictalurus
BT2 ictaluridae
BT3 siluriformes
BT4 osteichthyes
BT5 fishes

ICTALURUS PUNCTATUS
uf *catfish, channel*
uf *channel catfish*
BT1 ictalurus
BT2 ictaluridae
BT3 siluriformes
BT4 osteichthyes
BT5 fishes
rt channel catfish virus

icterus
USE **jaundice**

ICUMSA
HN from 1990
(international commission for uniform methods of sugar analysis)
BT1 international organizations
BT2 organizations

IDAHO
BT1 mountain states of usa
BT2 western states of usa
BT3 usa
BT4 north america
BT5 america

IDENTIFICATION
uf *banding of animals*
NT1 branding
rt biological tags
rt characterization
rt cultivar identification
rt diagnosis
rt ear cropping
rt keys
rt marking
rt misidentification
rt pollen analysis
rt project identification
rt tattooing
rt taxonomy

IDENTIFICATION SERVICES
rt cab international
rt taxonomy

IDEOLOGY
BT1 value systems
rt attitudes
rt political systems
rt religion

IDEOTYPES
BT1 types
rt models

IDIOCERUS
BT1 cicadellidae
BT2 cicadelloidea
BT3 auchenorrhyncha
BT4 homoptera

idiogram
USE **chromosome morphology**

idiomelissodes
USE **svastra**

IDIOSCOPUS
BT1 cicadellidae
BT2 cicadelloidea
BT3 auchenorrhyncha
BT4 homoptera
NT1 idioscopus clypealis

IDIOSCOPUS CLYPEALIS
BT1 idioscopus
BT2 cicadellidae
BT3 cicadelloidea
BT4 auchenorrhyncha

IDIOSCOPUS CLYPEALIS *cont.*
BT5 homoptera

IDIOTYPES
BT1 immunoglobulins
BT2 glycoproteins
BT3 proteins
BT4 peptides
BT2 immunological factors

L-IDITOL DEHYDROGENASE
(ec 1.1.1.14)
uf *sorbitol dehydrogenase*
BT1 alcohol oxidoreductases
BT2 oxidoreductases
BT3 enzymes

idle time
USE **unproductive time**

IDOXURIDINE
uf *iododeoxyuridine*
BT1 antiviral agents
BT2 antiinfective agents
BT3 drugs
BT1 deoxyuridines
BT2 deoxyribonucleosides
BT3 nucleosides
BT4 glycosides
BT5 carbohydrates
BT1 metabolic inhibitors
BT2 inhibitors

IDRC
(international development research centre)
BT1 international organizations
BT2 organizations
rt canada
rt development agencies

IFAD
(international fund for agricultural development)
BT1 funds
BT1 international organizations
BT2 organizations
rt development agencies
rt development aid

IGA
BT1 immunoglobulins
BT2 glycoproteins
BT3 proteins
BT4 peptides
BT2 immunological factors

IGE
uf *reagin*
uf *reaginic antibodies*
BT1 immunoglobulins
BT2 glycoproteins
BT3 proteins
BT4 peptides
BT2 immunological factors

IGG
BT1 immunoglobulins
BT2 glycoproteins
BT3 proteins
BT4 peptides
BT2 immunological factors

IGM
HN from 1990
BT1 immunoglobulins
BT2 glycoproteins
BT3 proteins
BT4 peptides
BT2 immunological factors

IGNITION
NT1 spark ignition
NT1 spontaneous ignition
rt burning
rt combustion
rt explosions
rt internal combustion engines

ignition, spark
USE **spark ignition**

ignition, spontaneous
USE **spontaneous ignition**

IGUANA
BT1 iguanidae
BT2 sauria
BT3 reptiles

IGUANIDAE
BT1 sauria
BT2 reptiles
NT1 iguana

ILARVIRUS
NT1 asparagus 2 ilarvirus

ILARVIRUS GROUP
HN from 1990
BT1 plant viruses
BT2 plant pathogens
BT3 pathogens
NT1 apple mosaic ilarvirus
NT1 citrus leaf rugose ilarvirus
NT1 citrus variegation ilarvirus
NT1 elm mottle ilarvirus
NT1 lilac ring mottle ilarvirus
NT1 prune dwarf ilarvirus
NT1 prunus necrotic ringspot ilarvirus
NT1 spinach latent ilarvirus
NT1 tobacco streak ilarvirus
NT1 tulare apple mosaic ilarvirus

ilattia
USE **amyna**

ILE DE FRANCE
BT1 france
BT2 western europe
BT3 europe

ILE-DE-FRANCE
BT1 sheep breeds
BT2 breeds

ileitis
USE **enteritis**

ILEOSTOMY
BT1 surgical operations
rt ileum

ILEUM
BT1 small intestine
BT2 intestines
BT3 digestive system
BT4 body parts
rt ileostomy

ILEX
BT1 aquifoliaceae
NT1 ilex aquifolium
NT1 ilex attenuata
NT1 ilex cassine
NT1 ilex ciliospinosa
NT1 ilex colchica
NT1 ilex cornuta
NT1 ilex crenata
NT1 ilex decidua
NT1 ilex glabra
NT1 ilex integra
NT1 ilex latifolia
NT1 ilex opaca
NT1 ilex paraguariensis
NT1 ilex perado
NT1 ilex rotunda
NT1 ilex serrata
NT1 ilex spinigera
NT1 ilex verticillata
NT1 ilex vomitoria

ILEX AQUIFOLIUM
BT1 forest trees
BT1 ilex
BT2 aquifoliaceae
BT1 medicinal plants
BT1 ornamental woody plants
rt holly

ILEX ATTENUATA
BT1 ilex
BT2 aquifoliaceae
BT1 ornamental woody plants

ILEX CASSINE
BT1 ilex
BT2 aquifoliaceae

ILEX CILIOSPINOSA
BT1 ilex
BT2 aquifoliaceae
BT1 ornamental woody plants

ILEX COLCHICA
BT1 ilex
BT2 aquifoliaceae

ILEX CORNUTA
BT1 ilex
BT2 aquifoliaceae
BT1 medicinal plants
BT1 ornamental woody plants

ILEX CRENATA
BT1 ilex
BT2 aquifoliaceae
BT1 ornamental woody plants

ILEX DECIDUA
BT1 ilex
BT2 aquifoliaceae
BT1 ornamental woody plants

ILEX GLABRA
BT1 ilex
BT2 aquifoliaceae
BT1 ornamental woody plants

ILEX INTEGRA
BT1 ilex
BT2 aquifoliaceae
BT1 ornamental woody plants

ILEX LATIFOLIA
BT1 ilex
BT2 aquifoliaceae
BT1 ornamental woody plants

ILEX OPACA
BT1 ilex
BT2 aquifoliaceae
BT1 ornamental woody plants

ILEX PARAGUARIENSIS
BT1 ilex
BT2 aquifoliaceae
BT1 ornamental woody plants
BT1 stimulant plants
rt mate

ILEX PERADO
BT1 ilex
BT2 aquifoliaceae
BT1 ornamental woody plants

ILEX ROTUNDA
BT1 ilex
BT2 aquifoliaceae
BT1 ornamental woody plants

ILEX SERRATA
BT1 ilex
BT2 aquifoliaceae
BT1 ornamental woody plants

ILEX SPINIGERA
BT1 ilex
BT2 aquifoliaceae

ILEX VERTICILLATA
BT1 ilex
BT2 aquifoliaceae
BT1 ornamental woody plants

ILEX VOMITORIA
BT1 ilex
BT2 aquifoliaceae
BT1 ornamental woody plants

ilione
USE **elgiva**

ilione albiseta
USE **knutsonia albiseta**

ILLAWARRA
HN from 1990; previously "australian illawarra shorthorn"
uf *australian illawarra shorthorn*
BT1 cattle breeds
BT2 breeds

ILLEGITIMATE BIRTHS (AGRICOLA)
rt birth

ILLICIACEAE
NT1 illicium
NT2 illicium floridanum
NT2 illicium verum

ILLICIT FELLING
BT1 felling
BT2 forestry practices
BT3 forestry

ILLICIUM
BT1 illiciaceae
NT1 illicium floridanum
NT1 illicium verum

ILLICIUM FLORIDANUM
BT1 illicium
BT2 illiciaceae

ILLICIUM VERUM
BT1 essential oil plants
BT2 oil plants
BT1 illicium
BT2 illiciaceae
BT1 spice plants

ILLIDOPS
HN from 1990
BT1 braconidae
BT2 hymenoptera
NT1 illidops scutellaris
rt apanteles

ILLIDOPS SCUTELLARIS
HN from 1990; previously "apanteles scutellaris"
uf apanteles scutellaris
BT1 biological control agents
BT2 beneficial organisms
BT1 illidops
BT2 braconidae
BT3 hymenoptera

ILLINOIA
uf masonaphis
BT1 aphididae
BT2 aphidoidea
BT3 sternorrhyncha
BT4 homoptera

ILLINOIS
BT1 corn belt of usa
BT2 north central states of usa
BT3 usa
BT4 north america
BT5 america

ILLITE
BT1 clay minerals
BT2 minerals

ILLNESS (AGRICOLA)
rt diseases
rt health
rt wellness (agricola)

ILLUMINATION
rt artificial light
rt artificial lighting (agricola)
rt fluorescent light
rt intermittent light
rt lamps
rt light
rt light regime
rt lighting
rt luminescence
rt visibility

ILLUSTRATIONS
BT1 publications
rt descriptions
rt fashion illustration (agricola)
rt photographs

ILLUVIATION
BT1 soil formation
rt eluviation

ILMENITE
BT1 nonclay minerals
BT2 minerals

ILO
(international labour organization)
uf international labour organization
BT1 international organizations
BT2 organizations

IMAGE PROCESSORS
uf processors, image
BT1 equipment
rt imagery

IMAGERY
BT1 techniques
NT1 infrared imagery
NT2 infrared line scan imagery
NT2 thermal infrared imagery
NT1 multispectral imagery
NT1 satellite imagery
rt holography
rt image processors
rt photography
rt remote sensing

IMANIN
BT1 antibiotics
BT1 antiviral agents
BT2 antiinfective agents
BT3 drugs

IMAZALIL
BT1 conazole fungicides
BT2 azoles
BT3 heterocyclic nitrogen compounds
BT4 organic nitrogen compounds
BT2 fungicides
BT3 pesticides

IMAZAMETHABENZ
HN from 1990
BT1 imidazolinone herbicides
BT2 herbicides
BT3 pesticides
BT2 imidazoles
BT3 azoles
BT4 heterocyclic nitrogen compounds
BT5 organic nitrogen compounds

IMAZAPYR
BT1 imidazolinone herbicides
BT2 herbicides
BT3 pesticides
BT2 imidazoles
BT3 azoles
BT4 heterocyclic nitrogen compounds
BT5 organic nitrogen compounds

IMAZAQUIN
BT1 imidazolinone herbicides
BT2 herbicides
BT3 pesticides
BT2 imidazoles
BT3 azoles
BT4 heterocyclic nitrogen compounds
BT5 organic nitrogen compounds

IMAZETHAPYR
HN from 1990
BT1 imidazolinone herbicides
BT2 herbicides
BT3 pesticides
BT2 imidazoles
BT3 azoles
BT4 heterocyclic nitrogen compounds
BT5 organic nitrogen compounds

IMBALANCE
NT1 acid base imbalance (agricola)
rt relationships

IMBIBITION
BT1 uptake
rt absorption

IMBIBITION *cont.*
rt seeds
rt water uptake

IMBRASIA
uf gonimbrasia
uf nudaurelia
BT1 saturniidae
BT2 lepidoptera
NT1 imbrasia belina
NT1 imbrasia cytherea

IMBRASIA BELINA
uf gonimbrasia belina
uf nudaurelia belina
BT1 imbrasia
BT2 saturniidae
BT3 lepidoptera

IMBRASIA CYTHEREA
uf nudaurelia cytherea
BT1 imbrasia
BT2 saturniidae
BT3 lepidoptera

IMIDAZOLE ALKALOIDS
BT1 alkaloids
BT1 imidazoles
BT2 azoles
BT3 heterocyclic nitrogen compounds
BT4 organic nitrogen compounds
NT1 pilocarpine

IMIDAZOLE FUNGICIDES
BT1 fungicides
BT2 pesticides
BT1 imidazoles
BT2 azoles
BT3 heterocyclic nitrogen compounds
BT4 organic nitrogen compounds
NT1 fenapanil
rt conazole fungicides

IMIDAZOLES
BT1 azoles
BT2 heterocyclic nitrogen compounds
BT3 organic nitrogen compounds
NT1 allantoin
NT1 clotrimazole
NT1 creatinine
NT1 econazole
NT1 etomidate
NT1 fenticonazole
NT1 histamine
NT1 histidine
NT1 imidazole alkaloids
NT2 pilocarpine
NT1 imidazole fungicides
NT2 fenapanil
NT1 imidazolinone herbicides
NT2 imazamethabenz
NT2 imazapyr
NT2 imazaquin
NT2 imazethapyr
NT1 ketoconazole
NT1 metizoline
NT1 metomidate
NT1 miconazole
NT1 nitroimidazoles
NT2 dimetridazole
NT2 ipronidazole
NT2 metronidazole
NT2 ornidazole
NT2 ronidazole
NT2 secnidazole
NT2 tinidazole
NT1 urocanic acid

IMIDAZOLINONE HERBICIDES
BT1 herbicides
BT2 pesticides
BT1 imidazoles
BT2 azoles
BT3 heterocyclic nitrogen compounds
BT4 organic nitrogen compounds

IMIDAZOLINONE HERBICIDES *cont.*
NT1 imazamethabenz
NT1 imazapyr
NT1 imazaquin
NT1 imazethapyr

IMIDES
BT1 organic nitrogen compounds
NT1 cyanamide
NT1 phthalimide
NT1 thalidomide

IMIDOCARB
BT1 amides
BT2 organic nitrogen compounds
BT1 antiprotozoal agents
BT2 antiparasitic agents
BT3 drugs

IMITATION CREAM
uf cream substitutes
uf cream, imitation
BT1 imitation products
BT2 products
BT1 simulated foods
BT2 foods
rt cream

imitation foods
USE **simulated foods**

IMITATION MILK
uf milk, imitation
BT1 imitation products
BT2 products
BT1 simulated foods
BT2 foods
rt milk

IMITATION PRODUCTS
HN from 1989
BT1 products
NT1 imitation cream
NT1 imitation milk
rt milk products

IMMEDIATE HYPERSENSITIVITY
BT1 hypersensitivity
BT2 immune response
BT3 immunity
NT1 allergic reactions
NT1 anaphylaxis
NT1 atopy
rt allergens
rt asthma
rt immune desensitization
rt leukotrienes

immigrants
USE **immigration**

IMMIGRATION
uf immigrants
BT1 migration
rt migrant labour
rt seasonal labour
rt settlement

IMMISCIBLE DISPLACEMENT
BT1 transport processes
rt miscible displacement

IMMOBILIZATION
BT1 fixation
BT1 restraint
NT1 inactivation
rt binding site
rt mobilization

immobilizing agents
USE **muscle relaxants**
OR **neuroleptics**

IMMUNE COMPETENCE
uf competence, immunological
uf immunocompetence
uf immunological competence
BT1 immune response
BT2 immunity

IMMUNE COMPLEX DISEASES
HN from 1990

IMMUNE COMPLEX DISEASES *cont.*
(diseases resulting from deposition of antigen antibody complexes in tissues)
BT1 immunological diseases
BT2 diseases
rt immune complexes

IMMUNE COMPLEXES
uf *antigen antibody complexes*
BT1 immunological factors
rt immune complex diseases
rt immune response

immune deficiency
USE **immunological deficiency**

IMMUNE DESENSITIZATION
(administration of a graded series of doses of an allergen to subjects suffering from immediate hypersensitivity to that allergen, in order to reduce the likelihood of future reactions on casual contact with that allergen)
uf *desensitization, immunologic*
uf *hyposensitization*
BT1 specific immunosuppression
BT2 immunosuppression
BT3 immunotherapy
BT4 therapy
rt allergens
rt immediate hypersensitivity

immune globulins
USE **immunoglobulins**

IMMUNE HAEMOLYSIS
AF immune hemolysis
BT1 immune response
BT2 immunity
rt haemolysis

IMMUNE HEMOLYSIS
BF immune haemolysis
rt hemolysis

IMMUNE RESPONSE
uf *immunity reactions*
uf *immunological reactions*
BT1 immunity
NT1 antibody formation
NT1 antigen antibody reactions
NT2 cross reaction
NT2 rosette formation
NT2 virus neutralization
NT1 hypersensitivity
NT2 delayed type hypersensitivity
NT2 immediate hypersensitivity
NT3 allergic reactions
NT3 anaphylaxis
NT3 atopy
NT2 respiratory hypersensitivity
NT1 immune competence
NT1 immune haemolysis
NT1 mixed lymphocyte reaction
rt agglutination
rt allergies
rt antibodies
rt antigens
rt complement
rt immune complexes
rt immune serum
rt immunization
rt immunoglobulins
rt interferon
rt properdin
rt zymosan

immune sensitization
USE **immunization**

IMMUNE SERUM
uf *antiserum*
uf *hyperimmune serum*
BT1 serum
BT2 body fluids
BT3 fluids
rt antibodies
rt antitoxins
rt immune response

IMMUNE SERUM *cont.*
rt immunization
rt passive immunization

IMMUNE TOLERANCE
BT1 tolerance
rt immunity

IMMUNITY
uf *acquired immunity*
uf *active immunity*
uf *protective immunity*
uf *specific immunity*
NT1 autoimmunity
NT1 cell mediated immunity
NT2 cell mediated lympholysis
NT2 graft versus host reactions
NT2 lymphocyte transformation
NT1 cross immunity
NT1 humoral immunity
NT1 immune response
NT2 antibody formation
NT2 antigen antibody reactions
NT3 cross reaction
NT3 rosette formation
NT3 virus neutralization
NT2 hypersensitivity
NT3 delayed type hypersensitivity
NT3 immediate hypersensitivity
NT4 allergic reactions
NT4 anaphylaxis
NT4 atopy
NT3 respiratory hypersensitivity
NT2 immune competence
NT2 immune haemolysis
NT2 mixed lymphocyte reaction
NT1 local immunity
NT1 natural immunity
NT1 natural immunotolerance
NT1 naturally acquired immunity
NT1 passive immunity
NT2 adoptive immunity
NT2 maternal immunity
NT3 colostral immunity
NT1 premunition
rt allergies
rt antibodies
rt antitoxins
rt disease resistance
rt immune tolerance
rt immunization
rt immunocompetent cells
rt immunological factors
rt immunology
rt infectious diseases
rt resistance
rt serum

immunity reactions
USE **immune response**

IMMUNIZATION
(used for active immunization and for general studies)
uf *active immunization*
uf *immune sensitization*
uf *immunization, active*
uf *immunopotentiation, specific*
uf *immunostimulation, specific*
uf *inoculation*
uf *inoculation (immunization)*
uf *specific immunopotentiation*
uf *specific immunostimulation*
BT1 immunostimulation
BT2 immunotherapy
BT3 therapy
NT1 cross immunization
NT1 hyperimmunization
NT1 passive immunization
NT1 vaccination
NT2 oral vaccination
rt antigens
rt immune response
rt immune serum
rt immunity
rt immunology
rt vaccines
rt viral interference

immunization, active
USE **immunization**

IMMUNOASSAY
BT1 assays
BT1 immunological techniques
BT2 techniques
NT1 chemiluminescence immunoassays
NT1 enzyme immunoassay
NT2 elisa
NT1 radioimmunoassay
NT2 rast

immunoassays, chemiluminescent
USE **chemiluminescence immunoassays**

IMMUNOBLOTTING
HN from 1990
uf *blotting, immunological*
uf *western blotting*
uf *western immunoblotting*
BT1 immunological techniques
BT2 techniques

IMMUNOCHEMISTRY
BT1 immunology
NT1 immunocytochemistry
NT1 immunohistochemistry
rt antibodies
rt chemistry

immunocompetence
USE **immune competence**

IMMUNOCOMPETENT CELLS
BT1 cells
rt immunity

IMMUNOCOMPROMISED HOSTS
HN from 1989
BT1 hosts
rt acquired immune deficiency syndrome
rt homosexuals
rt intravenous drug users
rt opportunistic infections

IMMUNOCYTES
BT1 lymphocytes
BT2 leukocytes
BT3 blood cells
BT4 cells
rt immunology

IMMUNOCYTOCHEMISTRY
HN from 1990
BT1 immunochemistry
BT2 immunology

immunodeficiency
USE **immunological deficiency**

IMMUNODIAGNOSIS
uf *diagnosis, serological*
uf *serological diagnosis*
BT1 diagnosis
BT1 immunology
rt immunological techniques

IMMUNODIFFUSION

IMMUNODIFFUSION TESTS
HN from 1990; previously "gel precipitation tests"
uf *gel diffusion tests*
uf *gel precipitation tests*
BT1 immunoprecipitation tests
BT2 immunological techniques
BT3 techniques
BT2 tests

IMMUNOELECTROPHORESIS
BT1 electrophoresis
BT2 analytical methods
BT3 methodology
BT1 immunoprecipitation tests
BT2 immunological techniques
BT3 techniques
BT2 tests
NT1 counterimmunoelectrophoresis

IMMUNOENZYME TECHNIQUES
BT1 immunological techniques

IMMUNOENZYME TECHNIQUES *cont.*
BT2 techniques
NT1 enzyme immunoassay
NT2 elisa
NT1 immunoperoxidase technique

IMMUNOFLUORESCENCE
uf *fluorescence, immunological*
uf *fluorescent antibody technique*
uf *indirect fluorescent antibody technique*
BT1 immunological techniques
BT2 techniques
rt fluorescein
rt fluorescence

IMMUNOGENETICS
BT1 immunology
rt biochemical genetics
rt biochemical polymorphism
rt genetics
rt mixed lymphocyte reaction

immunogens
USE **antigens**

IMMUNOGLOBULIN STRUCTURAL GENES
BT1 genes
rt immunoglobulins
rt immunology

IMMUNOGLOBULINS
uf *γ-globulins*
uf *immune globulins*
BT1 glycoproteins
BT2 proteins
BT3 peptides
BT1 immunological factors
NT1 antibodies
NT2 agglutinins
NT3 haemagglutinins
NT4 viral haemagglutinins
NT3 lectins
NT4 phytohaemagglutinins
NT5 concanavalin a
NT5 limulins
NT5 ricin
NT2 antitoxins
NT2 autoantibodies
NT2 gliadin antibodies
NT2 haemolysins
NT3 melittin
NT2 local antibodies
NT2 maternal antibodies
NT2 natural antibodies
NT2 opsonins
NT2 precipitins
NT1 idiotypes
NT1 iga
NT1 ige
NT1 igg
NT1 igm
NT1 monoclonal antibodies
NT1 secretory component
rt allotypes
rt blood proteins
rt immune response
rt immunoglobulin structural genes
rt isotypes

IMMUNOHISTOCHEMISTRY
HN from 1989
BT1 histochemistry
BT2 chemistry
BT2 histology
BT3 biology
BT1 immunochemistry
BT2 immunology

immunological competence
USE **immune competence**

IMMUNOLOGICAL DEFICIENCY
(deficiency of humoral or cell mediated immunity)
uf *immune deficiency*
uf *immunodeficiency*
uf *immunomodulation*

IMMUNOLOGICAL DEFICIENCY *cont.*
uf *natural immunosuppression*
BT1 deficiency
BT1 immunological diseases
BT2 diseases
NT1 viral immunosuppression
NT2 acquired immune deficiency syndrome

IMMUNOLOGICAL DISEASES
BT1 diseases
NT1 allergic encephalomyelitis
NT1 allergies
NT2 arthropod allergies
NT2 drug allergies
NT2 farmer's lung
NT2 food allergies
NT3 milk allergy
NT2 humidifier disease
NT1 autoimmune diseases
NT2 autoimmune thyroiditis
NT1 immune complex diseases
NT1 immunological deficiency
NT2 viral immunosuppression
NT3 acquired immune deficiency syndrome
NT1 wasting disease
rt antibodies
rt chediak-higashi syndrome
rt hypersensitivity
rt immunology
rt immunosuppression

IMMUNOLOGICAL FACTORS
NT1 antigens
NT2 allergens
NT3 brucellin
NT2 autoantigens
NT2 bacterial antigens
NT3 tuberculin
NT2 blood group antigens
NT2 circulating antigens
NT2 exoantigens
NT2 fungal antigens
NT3 coccidioidin
NT3 histoplasmin
NT3 spherulin
NT2 group specific antigens
NT2 h-y antigen
NT2 haptens
NT2 histocompatibility antigens
NT2 lipopolysaccharides
NT2 lymphocyte antigens
NT2 neoplasm antigens
NT2 somatic antigens
NT2 surface antigens
NT2 toxoids
NT2 viral antigens
NT1 complement
NT1 immune complexes
NT1 immunoglobulins
NT2 antibodies
NT3 agglutinins
NT4 haemagglutinins
NT5 viral haemagglutinins
NT4 lectins
NT5 phytohaemagglutinins
NT6 concanavalin a
NT6 limulins
NT6 ricin
NT3 antitoxins
NT3 autoantibodies
NT3 gliadin antibodies
NT3 haemolysins
NT4 melittin
NT3 local antibodies
NT3 maternal antibodies
NT3 natural antibodies
NT3 opsonins
NT3 precipitins
NT2 idiotypes
NT2 iga
NT2 ige
NT2 igg
NT2 igm
NT2 monoclonal antibodies
NT2 secretory component
NT1 interferon
NT1 interleukins
NT2 interleukin 1
NT2 interleukin 2
NT1 lymphokines

IMMUNOLOGICAL FACTORS *cont.*
NT1 properdin
NT1 transfer factor
rt immunity
rt immunology

immunological reactions
USE **immune response**

IMMUNOLOGICAL TECHNIQUES
uf *serological techniques*
BT1 techniques
NT1 agglutination tests
NT2 haemagglutination tests
NT3 antiglobulin test
NT3 coombs test
NT3 haemagglutination inhibition test
NT2 immunosorbent agglutination assay
NT2 latex agglutination test
NT1 complement fixation tests
NT1 exoantigen tests
NT1 immunoassay
NT2 chemiluminescence immunoassays
NT2 enzyme immunoassay
NT3 elisa
NT2 radioimmunoassay
NT3 rast
NT1 immunoblotting
NT1 immunoenzyme techniques
NT2 enzyme immunoassay
NT3 elisa
NT2 immunoperoxidase technique
NT1 immunofluorescence
NT1 immunoprecipitation tests
NT2 immunodiffusion tests
NT2 immunoelectrophoresis
NT3 counterimmunoelectrophoresis
NT1 lymphocyte transformation tests
NT1 neutralization tests
NT1 rosette inhibition test
NT1 skin tests
NT2 passive cutaneous anaphylaxis test
rt antigen antibody reactions
rt haemagglutination
rt immunodiagnosis
rt immunology
rt serotypes

IMMUNOLOGY
NT1 immunochemistry
NT2 immunocytochemistry
NT2 immunohistochemistry
NT1 immunodiagnosis
NT1 immunogenetics
NT1 immunopathology
NT1 immunotaxonomy
rt antigens
rt biology
rt coombs test
rt immunity
rt immunization
rt immunocytes
rt immunoglobulin structural genes
rt immunological diseases
rt immunological factors
rt immunological techniques
rt immunotherapy
rt interferon
rt limulins
rt serology

immunomodulation
HN from 1989
(use "immunological deficiency" or one of its narrower terms for immunosuppression not resulting from human intervention; use "immunotherapy" or one of its narrower terms for immunosuppression or immunostimulation as a result of deliberate human intervention; use "nonspecific immunostimulation" for immunostimulation without human intervention)

IMMUNOMODULATION *cont.*
USE **immunological deficiency**
OR **immunotherapy**
OR **nonspecific immunostimulation**

IMMUNOPATHOLOGY
BT1 immunology
rt pathology

IMMUNOPEROXIDASE TECHNIQUE
uf *peroxidase-labelled antibody technique*
BT1 immunoenzyme techniques
BT2 immunological techniques
BT3 techniques

immunopotentiation, nonspecific
USE **nonspecific immunostimulation**

immunopotentiation, specific
USE **immunization**

IMMUNOPRECIPITATION TESTS
uf *flocculation tests*
uf *precipitation (immunological)*
uf *precipitation tests, immunological*
uf *precipitin tests*
BT1 immunological techniques
BT2 techniques
BT1 tests
NT1 immunodiffusion tests
NT1 immunoelectrophoresis
NT2 counterimmunoelectrophoresis
rt antigen antibody reactions

immunoradiometric assay
USE **radioimmunoassay**

IMMUNOSORBENT AGGLUTINATION ASSAY
HN from 1990
BT1 agglutination tests
BT2 immunological techniques
BT3 techniques
BT2 tests

IMMUNOSTIMULANTS
HN from 1990
rt adjuvants
rt drugs
rt immunostimulation
rt nonspecific immunostimulation

IMMUNOSTIMULATION
HN from 1990
(stimulation of the immune system by deliberate human intervention; for stimulation by other means use "nonspecific immunostimulation")
BT1 immunotherapy
BT2 therapy
NT1 immunization
NT2 cross immunization
NT2 hyperimmunization
NT2 passive immunization
NT2 vaccination
NT3 oral vaccination
rt immunostimulants
rt nonspecific immunostimulation

immunostimulation, nonspecific
USE **nonspecific immunostimulation**

immunostimulation, specific
USE **immunization**

immunosuppressants
USE **immunosuppressive agents**

IMMUNOSUPPRESSION
(deliberate, artificial inhibition of the immune response; for immunosuppression arising without human intervention, consider "immunological deficiency" or one of its narrower terms)
uf *chemical immunosuppression*
BT1 immunotherapy
BT2 therapy
NT1 specific immunosuppression
NT2 acquired immunotolerance
NT3 adoptive immunotolerance
NT2 immune desensitization
rt hyperkeratotic scabies
rt immunological diseases
rt immunosuppressive agents
rt irradiation
rt viral immunosuppression
rt wasting disease

immunosuppression, specific
USE **specific immunosuppression**

IMMUNOSUPPRESSIVE AGENTS
uf *immunosuppressants*
BT1 drugs
NT1 cyclophosphamide
rt immunosuppression

IMMUNOTAXONOMY
BT1 immunology
BT1 taxonomy
BT2 classification

IMMUNOTHERAPY
(treatment or prevention of disease, graft rejection or other pathological responses by deliberate enhancement or suppression of the immune response; use a more specific term when possible)
uf *immunomodulation*
BT1 therapy
NT1 immunostimulation
NT2 immunization
NT3 cross immunization
NT3 hyperimmunization
NT3 passive immunization
NT3 vaccination
NT4 oral vaccination
NT1 immunosuppression
NT2 specific immunosuppression
NT3 acquired immunotolerance
NT4 adoptive immunotolerance
NT3 immune desensitization
rt immunology
rt transfer factor

immunotolerance, acquired
USE **acquired immunotolerance**

immunotolerance, adoptive
USE **adoptive immunotolerance**

immunotolerance, artificial
USE **acquired immunotolerance**

immunotolerance, natural
USE **natural immunotolerance**

IMOGOLITE
BT1 clay minerals
BT2 minerals

IMPACT
rt impact loads
rt impact strength
rt impact tests
rt shock
rt shock waves

IMPACT LOADS
uf *loads, impact*

IMPACT LOADS *cont.*
BT1 loads
rt impact
rt impact strength
rt impact tests

IMPACT STRENGTH
uf *strength, impact*
BT1 strength
BT2 mechanical properties
BT3 properties
rt impact
rt impact loads
rt impact tests

IMPACT TESTS
BT1 tests
rt impact
rt impact loads
rt impact strength

impalas
USE **aepyceros melampus**

IMPATIENS
BT1 balsaminaceae
NT1 impatiens balsamina
NT1 impatiens capensis
NT1 impatiens glandulifera
NT1 impatiens walleriana

IMPATIENS BALSAMINA
BT1 impatiens
BT2 balsaminaceae
BT1 ornamental herbaceous plants

IMPATIENS CAPENSIS
BT1 impatiens
BT2 balsaminaceae

IMPATIENS GLANDULIFERA
BT1 impatiens
BT2 balsaminaceae

impatiens holstii
USE **impatiens walleriana**

impatiens sultani
USE **impatiens walleriana**

IMPATIENS WALLERIANA
uf *impatiens holstii*
uf *impatiens sultani*
BT1 impatiens
BT2 balsaminaceae
BT1 ornamental herbaceous plants

IMPEDANCE
BT1 acoustic properties
BT2 physical properties
BT3 properties
BT1 electrical properties
BT2 physical properties
BT3 properties
rt resistance

IMPEDED DRAINAGE
BT1 soil water regimes
rt drainage

IMPERATA
BT1 gramineae
NT1 imperata cylindrica

IMPERATA CYLINDRICA
BT1 imperata
BT2 gramineae
BT1 weeds

IMPERFECT COMPETITION
uf *restraint of trade*
uf *restrictive practices*
BT1 market competition
NT1 market segmentation
NT1 monopoly
NT2 cartels
NT2 oligopoly
NT1 trade discrimination
NT2 embargoes
rt market regulations
rt production controls

IMPERIALISM
BT1 political systems
BT2 politics
NT1 colonialism
rt colonies
rt economic systems

IMPLANTATION
BT1 surgical operations

implantation, embryo
USE **embryo implantation**

implantation, ovum
USE **embryo implantation**

IMPLEMENT CARRIERS
BT1 carriers
BT1 farm machinery
BT2 machinery
rt gantries
rt implement transporters
rt implements
rt tool carriers
rt tractors

implement draught
USE **draught**

implement trailers
USE **implement transporters**

IMPLEMENT TRANSPORTERS
uf *implement trailers*
uf *transporters, implement*
BT1 transporters
BT2 vehicles
rt implement carriers
rt implements
rt lorries
rt low loading trailers
rt trailers

implementation
USE **implementation of research**
OR **project implementation**

IMPLEMENTATION OF RESEARCH
HN from 1990
uf *implementation*
BT1 research policy
rt diffusion of research
rt feasibility studies
rt project implementation
rt research

IMPLEMENTS
NT1 bedders
NT1 crumblers
NT1 cultivators
NT2 disc cultivators
NT2 rippers
NT2 rotary cultivators
NT2 rotary diggers
NT2 seeder cultivators
NT2 tine cultivators
NT3 spring loaded tine cultivators
NT3 spring tine cultivators
NT1 furrow openers
NT1 furrow presses
NT1 harrows
NT2 disc harrows
NT2 reciprocating harrows
NT2 rotary harrows
NT2 spiked harrows
NT2 spring tine harrows
NT1 hoes
NT2 rotary hoes
NT2 steerage hoes
NT1 mounted implements
NT2 tool bars
NT1 ploughs
NT2 chisel ploughs
NT2 disc ploughs
NT2 drain ploughs
NT2 mole ploughs
NT2 multidepth ploughs
NT2 reversible ploughs
NT2 rotary ploughs
NT2 snow ploughs
NT2 stump jump ploughs
NT2 vineyard ploughs

IMPLEMENTS *cont.*
NT1 pruning implements
NT2 pruning saws
NT2 pruning shears
NT1 ridgers
NT2 disc ridgers
NT2 rotary ridgers
NT2 tie ridgers
NT1 rollers
NT2 cambridge rollers
NT2 crosskill rollers
NT2 spiked rollers
NT1 scarifiers
NT1 semimounted implements
NT1 subsoilers
NT1 subsoiling attachments
NT1 tool carriers
NT1 weeders
NT2 rod weeders
NT2 rotary weeders
rt blades
rt equipment
rt implement carriers
rt implement transporters
rt linkages
rt machinery
rt machinery cooperatives
rt machinery stocks
rt mechanical methods
rt mechanization
rt tines
rt tools

implements, mounted
USE **mounted implements**

implements, semimounted
USE **semimounted implements**

IMPORT CONTROLS
BT1 controls
BT1 trade barriers
BT2 trade protection
BT3 trade policy
BT4 economic policy
NT1 customs regulations
NT1 import levies
NT1 import quotas
NT1 non-tariff barriers to trade
NT2 tax agreements
NT1 tariffs
NT2 duty free allowances
NT2 preferential tariffs
rt imports
rt quarantine

IMPORT LEVIES
BT1 import controls
BT2 controls
BT2 trade barriers
BT3 trade protection
BT4 trade policy
BT5 economic policy
BT1 levies

IMPORT QUOTAS
BT1 import controls
BT2 controls
BT2 trade barriers
BT3 trade protection
BT4 trade policy
BT5 economic policy
BT1 quotas
BT2 quantity controls
BT3 production controls
BT4 production policy
BT5 economic policy
rt imports

IMPORT SUBSTITUTION
uf *substitution, import*
BT1 trade policy
BT2 economic policy
rt imports

IMPORTATION
rt introduced species
rt introduction

importations
USE **imported breeds**
OR **introduced species**

IMPORTED BREEDS
uf *importations*
BT1 breeds
NT1 exotics
rt introduction

IMPORTED INFECTIONS
HN from 1989
BT1 infections

IMPORTS
BT1 international trade
BT2 trade
rt exports
rt import controls
rt import quotas
rt import substitution
rt supply

IMPOTENCE
BT1 male infertility
BT2 infertility
BT2 reproductive disorders
BT3 functional disorders
BT4 animal disorders
BT5 disorders
BT1 sexual behaviour
BT2 behaviour

IMPREGNATED FABRICS
BT1 fabrics

IMPREGNATION
BT1 insemination
BT2 mating
BT3 sexual reproduction
BT4 reproduction
rt copulation
rt semen

IMPRINTING
HN from 1989
BT1 animal behaviour
BT2 behaviour

IMPROVED CONTEMPORARY COMPARISONS
BT1 contemporary comparisons
BT2 progeny testing
BT3 animal breeding methods
BT4 breeding methods
BT5 methodology
BT3 testing

IMPROVED FALLOW
BT1 fallow systems
BT2 cropping systems
rt fallow
rt shifting cultivation

IMPROVED SUMAVA
HN from 1990
BT1 sheep breeds
BT2 breeds

IMPROVED VALACHIAN
HN from 1990
BT1 sheep breeds
BT2 breeds

IMPROVED VARIETIES
BT1 varieties
rt green revolution
rt high yielding varieties

IMPROVED WOOD
BT1 wood
NT1 compressed wood
NT1 plasticized wood
NT1 wood plastic composites
rt bulking agents
rt chemical modification of wood

IMPROVEMENT
NT1 grassland improvement
NT1 improvement fellings
NT1 improvement planting
NT1 stand improvement
NT1 upgrading
rt improvement grants
rt land improvement
rt optimization

IMPROVEMENT FELLINGS
BT1 felling
BT2 forestry practices
BT3 forestry
BT1 improvement
rt thinning

IMPROVEMENT GRANTS
BT1 grants
BT2 support measures
rt farm development
rt improvement

IMPROVEMENT PLANTING
BT1 improvement
rt enrichment

impurities, herbicide
USE **herbicide impurities**

imputed costs
USE **estimated costs**

IN VITRO
HN from 1990
rt experiments

IN VITRO CULTURE
BT1 culture techniques
BT2 biological techniques
BT3 techniques
NT1 cell culture
NT1 somatic embryogenesis
NT1 tissue culture
NT2 anther culture
NT2 embryo culture
NT2 organ culture
NT2 ovule culture
NT2 shoot tip culture
rt in vitro selection
rt micropropagation
rt protoplast fusion

IN VITRO DIGESTIBILITY
uf digestibility in vitro
BT1 digestibility

IN VITRO SELECTION
BT1 artificial selection
BT2 selection
rt in vitro culture

INACTIVATED VACCINES
uf killed vaccines
BT1 vaccines

INACTIVATION
BT1 immobilization
BT2 fixation
BT2 restraint
BT1 inhibition

INAPPARENT INFECTIONS
BT1 infections

inappetence
USE **anorexia**

INARCHING
BT1 grafting
BT2 vegetative propagation
BT3 propagation

inazuma
USE **recilia**

inazuma dorsalis
USE **recilia dorsalis**

INBOUND TRAVEL
BT1 travel

INBRED LINES
uf pure lines
BT1 lines
rt inbreeding

INBRED STRAINS
HN from 1989
BT1 strains
rt inbreeding

INBREEDING
BT1 plant breeding methods
BT2 breeding methods
BT3 methodology

INBREEDING *cont.*
rt homozygosity
rt inbred lines
rt inbred strains
rt inbreeding depression
rt selfing

INBREEDING DEPRESSION
BT1 deterioration
rt inbreeding

INCAPRINA
BT1 protein foods
BT2 foods
rt plant protein

INCENSE PLANTS
NT1 amyris balsamifera
NT1 boswellia sacra
NT1 jurinea macrocephala
NT1 styrax tonkinensis
rt essential oil plants
rt horticultural crops
rt industrial crops
rt plants

INCENTIVE TOURISM
BT1 tourism
rt incentives

INCENTIVES
NT1 bonuses
NT1 tax incentives
rt disincentives
rt incentive tourism
rt motivation

INCEPTISOLS
BT1 soil types (genetic)

INCEST (AGRICOLA)
BT1 antisocial behavior (agricola)
BT2 human behavior
BT3 behavior

INCIDENCE
rt familial incidence
rt frequency
rt operating range

INCISING
BT1 wood preservation
BT2 preservation
BT3 techniques

inclusion bodies
USE **cytoplasmic inclusions**
OR **nuclear inclusions**

INCOME
NT1 annuities
NT1 earned income
NT2 wages
NT3 piece work wages
NT3 time wages
NT3 wages in kind
NT1 farmers' income
NT2 farm income
NT2 non-farm income
NT1 household income (agricola)
NT1 low income (agricola)
NT1 retirement income (agricola)
NT1 supplementary income (agricola)
rt allowances
rt cash flow
rt family budgets
rt fees
rt income distribution
rt income elasticities
rt income tax
rt income transfers
rt low income groups
rt national income
rt returns
rt social benefits

INCOME DISTRIBUTION
NT1 disparity
NT1 income transfers
NT1 parity
rt income
rt living standards
rt redistribution

INCOME ELASTICITIES
HN from 1990
BT1 elasticities
BT2 econometrics
rt income

income, farm
USE **farm income**

income, farmers'
USE **farmers' income**

income, national
USE **national income**

income, nonfarm
USE **non-farm income**

INCOME TAX
uf tax, income
BT1 direct taxation
BT2 taxes
BT3 fiscal policy
BT4 economic policy
BT4 public finance
rt income

INCOME TRANSFERS
BT1 income distribution
rt fiscal policy
rt income

INCOMPATIBILITY
uf sterility and fertility
NT1 antagonism
NT2 drug antagonism
NT1 graft rejection
NT1 self incompatibility
rt compatibility
rt infertility
rt sterility

INCOMPLETE VIRUSES
BT1 viruses

INCORPORATION
BT1 mixing
NT1 straw incorporation
rt incorporators

INCORPORATORS
BT1 farm machinery
BT2 machinery
rt application equipment
rt cultivators
rt incorporation

INCREMENT
rt basal area
rt diameter
rt forest management
rt girth
rt growth
rt growth rings
rt height
rt increment boring
rt increment tables
rt volume

INCREMENT BORING
rt growth
rt growth rings
rt increment

INCREMENT TABLES
BT1 yield tables
BT2 measurement tables
rt growth
rt increment

INCUBATION
NT1 egg turning
NT1 incubation duration
rt brooders
rt broodiness
rt hatching
rt hatching date
rt incubators
rt preincubation period

INCUBATION DURATION
BT1 incubation

INCUBATORS
BT1 poultry housing

INCUBATORS *cont.*
BT2 animal housing
rt brooders
rt incubation
rt poultry farming

INCURVARIIDAE
BT1 lepidoptera
NT1 lampronia

INDARBELA
BT1 metarbelidae
BT2 lepidoptera
NT1 indarbela quadrinotata

INDARBELA QUADRINOTATA
BT1 indarbela
BT2 metarbelidae
BT3 lepidoptera

indebtedness
USE **debt**

indemnification
USE **compensation**

INDENTED CYLINDER SEED CLEANERS
uf cleaners, indented cylinder seed
uf seed cleaners, indented cylinder
BT1 seed cleaners
BT2 cleaners
BT3 machinery

INDEPENDENT STUDY (AGRICOLA)
rt learning

INDEX OF NUTRITIONAL QUALITY (AGRICOLA)
BT1 indexes
rt food composition
rt nutritive value

INDEXES
NT1 bioclimatic indexes
NT1 gonadosomatic index
NT1 haemoglobin value
NT1 index of nutritional quality (agricola)
NT1 indexes of nutrient availability
NT2 activity ratios
NT2 e values
NT2 I values
NT2 q-i relationships
NT2 sorption isotherms
NT1 leaf area index
NT1 performance indexes
NT2 cow indexes
NT1 price indexes
NT1 refractive index
rt indexing
rt ratios

INDEXES OF NUTRIENT AVAILABILITY
BT1 indexes
NT1 activity ratios
NT1 e values
NT1 I values
NT1 q-i relationships
NT1 sorption isotherms
rt nutrient balance
rt nutrition

INDEXING
BT1 information processing
BT2 information
rt indexes
rt thesauri

INDIA
BT1 south asia
BT2 asia
NT1 andaman and nicobar islands
NT1 andhra pradesh
NT1 arunachal pradesh
NT1 assam
NT1 bihar
NT1 chandigarh

INDIA *cont.*
NT1 dadra and nagar haveli
NT1 delhi
NT1 goa, daman and diu
NT1 gujarat
NT1 haryana
NT1 himachal pradesh
NT1 indian punjab
NT1 jammu and kashmir
NT1 karnataka
NT1 kerala
NT1 laccadive, minicoy and amindivi is.
NT1 lakshadweep
NT1 madhya pradesh
NT1 maharashtra
NT1 manipur
NT1 meghalaya
NT1 mizoram
NT1 nagaland
NT1 orissa
NT1 pondicherry
NT1 rajasthan
NT1 sikkim
NT1 tamil nadu
NT1 tripura
NT1 uttar pradesh
NT1 west bengal
rt commonwealth of nations
rt least developed countries

INDIAN COOKERY (AGRICOLA)
BT1 cookery (agricola)

indian elephants
USE **elephas maximus**

indian jujube
USE **ziziphus mauritiana**

INDIAN MUSTARD
uf *mustard, indian*
uf *rai*
rt brassica juncea

INDIAN OCEAN
BT1 marine areas
NT1 eastern indian ocean
NT2 bay of bengal
NT1 western indian ocean
NT2 arabian sea
NT2 red sea

INDIAN PUNJAB
uf *punjab*
uf *punjab, indian*
BT1 india
BT2 south asia
BT3 asia

INDIANA
BT1 corn belt of usa
BT2 north central states of usa
BT3 usa
BT4 north america
BT5 america

INDICATING INSTRUMENTS
uf *instruments, indicating*
BT1 instruments
rt digital displays
rt displays
rt gauges

INDICATIVE PLANNING
uf *planning, indicative*
BT1 planning
NT1 working plans

INDICATOR PLANTS
(plants which, by their presence or vigour, indicate particular chemical or physical properties of a location)
uf *plant indicators*
BT1 indicator species
BT2 indicators
rt plant ecological groups
rt plants

INDICATOR SPECIES
BT1 indicators
NT1 indicator plants
NT1 virus indicators

INDICATORS
NT1 biological indicators
NT2 biological tags
NT1 economic indicators
NT1 indicator species
NT2 indicator plants
NT2 virus indicators

INDIGENOUS KNOWLEDGE
HN from 1989
BT1 knowledge (agricola)
rt traditional technology

indigestion
USE **dyspepsia**

INDIGOFERA
BT1 leguminosae
NT1 indigofera anil
NT1 indigofera arrecta
NT1 indigofera caroliniana
NT1 indigofera cordifolia
NT1 indigofera diphylla
NT1 indigofera glandulosa
NT1 indigofera hirsuta
NT1 indigofera obtusifolia
NT1 indigofera spicata
NT1 indigofera suffruticosa
NT1 indigofera tinctoria

INDIGOFERA ANIL
BT1 dye plants
BT1 indigofera
BT2 leguminosae
BT1 pasture legumes
BT2 legumes
BT2 pasture plants

INDIGOFERA ARRECTA
BT1 dye plants
BT1 indigofera
BT2 leguminosae
BT1 pasture legumes
BT2 legumes
BT2 pasture plants

INDIGOFERA CAROLINIANA
BT1 indigofera
BT2 leguminosae

INDIGOFERA CORDIFOLIA
BT1 indigofera
BT2 leguminosae

INDIGOFERA DIPHYLLA
BT1 indigofera
BT2 leguminosae

INDIGOFERA GLANDULOSA
BT1 indigofera
BT2 leguminosae

INDIGOFERA HIRSUTA
BT1 indigofera
BT2 leguminosae

INDIGOFERA OBTUSIFOLIA
BT1 indigofera
BT2 leguminosae

INDIGOFERA SPICATA
BT1 indigofera
BT2 leguminosae
BT1 pasture legumes
BT2 legumes
BT2 pasture plants

INDIGOFERA SUFFRUTICOSA
BT1 indigofera
BT2 leguminosae

INDIGOFERA TINCTORIA
BT1 dye plants
BT1 indigofera
BT2 leguminosae
BT1 medicinal plants
BT1 pasture legumes
BT2 legumes
BT2 pasture plants

indirect fluorescent antibody technique
USE **immunofluorescence**

INDIRECT SELECTION
HN from 1989
BT1 selection

INDIRECT TAXATION
uf *taxation, indirect*
BT1 taxes
BT2 fiscal policy
BT3 economic policy
BT3 public finance
NT1 stamp duty
NT1 value added tax
rt levies
rt tariffs

INDIUM
BT1 metallic elements
BT2 elements
BT2 metals

INDIVIDUAL CHARACTERISTICS (AGRICOLA)
BT1 characteristics

INDIVIDUAL COUNSELING (AGRICOLA)
BT1 counseling (agricola)
rt individuals

INDIVIDUAL FEEDING
BT1 feeding

individual producers
USE **private farms**
OR **private firms**

INDIVIDUAL QUARTERS
BT1 mammary glands
BT2 glands (animal)
BT3 body parts
BT3 glands
rt milking

INDIVIDUALIZED INSTRUCTION (AGRICOLA)
BT1 instruction (agricola)
rt teaching methods

INDIVIDUALS
rt individual counseling (agricola)
rt interpersonal relations
rt personal development

INDIVISIBLE ESTATES
BT1 estates
BT2 property
rt compensation
rt land ownership
rt succession

INDO-BRAZILIAN
BT1 cattle breeds
BT2 breeds

INDOCHINA
rt cambodia
rt lao
rt south east asia
rt vietnam

INDOLE ALKALOIDS
BT1 alkaloids
BT1 indoles
BT2 heterocyclic nitrogen compounds
BT3 organic nitrogen compounds
NT1 ergot alkaloids
NT2 dihydroergocryptine
NT2 ergometrine
NT1 gramine
NT1 physostigmine
NT1 psilocin
NT1 psilocybine
NT1 reserpine
NT1 strychnine
NT1 vinblastine
NT1 yohimbine

indoleacetic acid
USE **iaa**

indoleacetic acid oxidase
USE **iaa oxidase**

INDOLE-3-ACETONITRILE
BT1 indoles
BT2 heterocyclic nitrogen compounds
BT3 organic nitrogen compounds

indole-3-carbinol
USE **indole-3-methanol**

INDOLE-3-METHANOL
uf *indole-3-carbinol*
BT1 indoles
BT2 heterocyclic nitrogen compounds
BT3 organic nitrogen compounds

INDOLES
BT1 heterocyclic nitrogen compounds
BT2 organic nitrogen compounds
NT1 5-hydroxyindoleacetic acid
NT1 5-methoxyindole-3-acetic acid
NT1 iaa
NT1 iba
NT1 indole alkaloids
NT2 ergot alkaloids
NT3 dihydroergocryptine
NT3 ergometrine
NT2 gramine
NT2 physostigmine
NT2 psilocin
NT2 psilocybine
NT2 reserpine
NT2 strychnine
NT2 vinblastine
NT2 yohimbine
NT1 indole-3-acetonitrile
NT1 indole-3-methanol
NT1 skatole
NT1 tryptamines
NT2 melatonin
NT2 serotonin
NT2 tryptamine

indolylacetic acid
USE **iaa**

indolylbutyric acid
USE **iba**

INDOMETACIN
uf *indomethacin*
BT1 analgesics
BT2 neurotropic drugs
BT3 drugs
BT1 antiinflammatory agents
BT2 drugs

indomethacin
USE **indometacin**

INDONESIA
BT1 south east asia
BT2 asia
NT1 bali
NT1 irian jaya
NT1 java
NT1 kalimantan
NT1 lombok
NT1 loro sae
NT1 madura
NT1 maluku
NT1 nusa tenggara
NT1 sulawesi
NT1 sumatra
NT1 sunda islands
NT1 timur
rt asean
rt developing countries
rt opec

INDONESIAN FAT-TAILED
HN from 1990
BT1 sheep breeds
BT2 breeds

INDONESIAN SOYBEAN DWARF LUTEOVIRUS
HN from 1990
BT1 luteovirus group

INDONESIAN SOYBEAN DWARF LUTEOVIRUS *cont.*
BT2 plant viruses
BT3 plant pathogens
BT4 pathogens
rt glycine max
rt soyabeans

INDOOR ARENAS
HN from 1989
BT1 recreational buildings
BT2 buildings

INDOOR GAMES
BT1 games
BT1 indoor recreation
BT2 recreation
NT1 bingo
NT1 board games
NT1 card games
NT1 computer games
NT1 darts
rt ball games
rt children's games

INDOOR RECREATION
BT1 recreation
NT1 indoor games
NT2 bingo
NT2 board games
NT2 card games
NT2 computer games
NT2 darts
rt games
rt sport

INDOPLANORBIS
BT1 bulinidae
BT2 gastropoda
BT3 mollusca
NT1 indoplanorbis exustus

INDOPLANORBIS EXUSTUS
BT1 indoplanorbis
BT2 bulinidae
BT3 gastropoda
BT4 mollusca

INDRIIDAE
BT1 primates
BT2 mammals
NT1 avahi
NT2 avahi laniger
rt lemurs

INDUCED ABORTION
rt abortion

INDUCED INNOVATIONS
BT1 innovations
BT2 modernization
rt innovation adoption

INDUCED MUTATIONS
uf mutations, induced
BT1 mutations
rt induction

INDUCED RESISTANCE
BT1 disease resistance
BT2 resistance
rt induction

INDUCTION
rt induced mutations
rt induced resistance

INDURATED HORIZONS
uf cemented horizons
BT1 horizons
BT2 soil morphological features

INDUSTRIAL ACCIDENTS (AGRICOLA)
BT1 accidents
rt safety at work

INDUSTRIAL APPLICATIONS
BT1 applications
rt industry

INDUSTRIAL CATERING
AF industrial food service
BT1 catering
rt industrial methods

INDUSTRIAL COUNTRIES
BT1 developed countries
BT2 countries
rt industrialization

INDUSTRIAL CROPS
NT1 agave salmiana
NT1 agave tequilana
NT1 dioscoreophyllum cumminsii
NT1 euphorbia lathyris
NT1 hops
NT1 jatropha curcas
NT1 piper betle
NT1 quillaja saponaria
NT1 salsola kali
NT1 stevia rebaudiana
NT1 synsepalum dulcificum
NT1 thapsia garganica
NT1 thaumatococcus daniellii
rt algicidal plants
rt antibacterial plants
rt antifungal plants
rt antiviral plants
rt culinary herbs
rt dye plants
rt essential oil plants
rt fatty oil plants
rt fibre plants
rt field crops
rt fish poisons
rt fuel crops
rt gum plants
rt horticultural crops
rt incense plants
rt industrial processing quality
rt medicinal plants
rt oil plants
rt pesticidal plants
rt piscicidal plants
rt plants
rt rubber plants
rt spice plants
rt tan plants
rt wax plants
rt woody plants

INDUSTRIAL FOOD SERVICE
BF industrial catering
BT1 food service

INDUSTRIAL METHODS
BT1 industrialization
BT2 economic development
BT1 methodology
rt industrial catering
rt technical progress

INDUSTRIAL MICROBIOLOGY
BT1 microbiology
BT2 biology
rt industry

INDUSTRIAL PROCESSING QUALITY
uf quality for industrial processing
BT1 processing quality
BT2 quality
rt industrial crops
rt industry

INDUSTRIAL PRODUCTS
HN from 1989
BT1 products
rt industry

INDUSTRIAL RECREATION
BT1 recreation
rt work places

INDUSTRIAL SITES
BT1 site types

INDUSTRIAL SOCIETY
BT1 society
rt industrialization
rt industry
rt urban society

INDUSTRIAL WASTES
BT1 wastes
NT1 anthracite waste
NT1 bauxite residues
NT1 cannery wastes

INDUSTRIAL WASTES *cont.*
NT1 cotton gin trash
NT1 fluidized bed wastes
NT1 hide scrapings
NT1 leather waste
NT1 mine tailings
NT1 oil refinery wastes
NT1 oil shale wastes
NT1 paper mill sludge
NT1 radioactive wastes
NT1 slags
NT1 spoil
NT2 dredgings
NT2 mine spoil
NT3 coal mine spoil
NT2 spoil banks
NT1 sugar factory waste
NT1 sulfur factory wastes
NT1 tannery waste
NT2 tannery sludge
NT1 waste gases
NT2 factory fumes
NT1 waste liquors
NT2 sulfate liquor
NT2 sulfite liquor
NT1 waste water
NT1 waste wood
rt factory effluents
rt industry
rt soil amendments

INDUSTRIALIZATION
BT1 economic development
NT1 industrial methods
rt factory workers
rt industrial countries
rt industrial society
rt industry
rt mechanization
rt modernization
rt unido
rt urbanization

INDUSTRY
uf agroindustry
NT1 building industry
NT1 chemical industry
NT2 fertilizer industry
NT1 cottage industry
NT1 fish industry
NT1 food industry
NT2 bakery industry
NT2 beverage industry
NT3 brewing industry
NT3 coffee industry
NT3 distilling industry
NT3 tea industry
NT3 wine industry
NT2 canning industry
NT2 cocoa industry
NT2 confectionery industry
NT2 dairy industry
NT2 frozen foods industry
NT2 infant food industry (agricola)
NT2 oils and fats industry
NT2 sugar industry
NT1 forest products industries
NT2 wood chemical industry
NT1 hospitality industry
NT2 catering industry
NT1 input industries
NT2 agricultural machinery industry
NT2 feed industry
NT2 fertilizer industry
NT2 seed industry
NT3 seed certification
NT3 seed production
NT4 hybrid seed production
NT1 leisure industry
NT1 meat and livestock industry
NT1 milling industry
NT1 mining
NT2 bacterial leaching
NT1 non-food industries
NT2 leather industry
NT2 rubber industry
NT2 textile industry
NT3 cotton industry
NT4 cotton ginning
NT4 cotton system (agricola)

INDUSTRY *cont.*
NT3 sericulture
NT3 weaving
NT3 wool industry
NT4 woolen system (agricola)
NT4 worsted system (agricola)
NT2 tobacco industry
NT1 poultry industry
NT1 power industry
NT1 pulp and paper industry
NT1 rural industry
NT1 starch industry
NT1 tourist industry
rt factories
rt industrial applications
rt industrial microbiology
rt industrial processing quality
rt industrial products
rt industrial society
rt industrial wastes
rt industrialization
rt manufacture
rt secondary sector

industry and agriculture
USE **agroindustrial relations**

INERT GASES
uf gases, inert
BT1 gases
NT1 nitrogen
NT1 noble gases
NT2 argon
NT2 helium
NT2 radon
NT2 xenon

INFANT CAR SEATS (AGRICOLA)
BT1 seats
BT2 components
rt infants
rt traffic safety (agricola)

INFANT DEVELOPMENT (AGRICOLA)
rt child development (agricola)
rt development
rt early childhood development (agricola)
rt infants

INFANT DISORDERS
BT1 human diseases
BT2 diseases
rt childhood diseases (agricola)
rt failure to thrive (agricola)
rt infants

INFANT FEEDING
BT1 feeding
NT1 bottle feeding (agricola)
NT1 breast feeding
NT1 postweaning interval
rt child feeding
rt infant foods
rt infant nutrition (agricola)
rt infants
rt weaning

INFANT FOOD INDUSTRY (AGRICOLA)
BT1 food industry
BT2 industry
rt infant foods

INFANT FOODS
uf baby foods
BT1 foods
NT1 infant formulae
rt breast feeding
rt child feeding
rt infant feeding
rt infant food industry (agricola)
rt infant nutrition (agricola)
rt infants
rt maltodextrins
rt postweaning interval

INFANT FORMULAE
AF infant formulas
BT1 infant foods
BT2 foods

INFANT FORMULAS
BF infant formulae

INFANT MORTALITY
BT1 mortality
BT2 vital statistics
rt infants

INFANT NUTRITION (AGRICOLA)
BT1 nutrition
rt child nutrition (agricola)
rt infant feeding
rt infant foods
rt infants

INFANT STIMULATION CENTERS (AGRICOLA)
rt early childhood education (agricola)
rt infants

infant weaning
USE **weaning**

INFANTS
BT1 young animals
BT2 animals
NT1 low birth weight infants (agricola)
NT1 neonates
NT1 premature infants
rt children
rt cot death
rt infant car seats (agricola)
rt infant development (agricola)
rt infant disorders
rt infant feeding
rt infant foods
rt infant mortality
rt infant nutrition (agricola)
rt infant stimulation centers (agricola)
rt nursery schools (agricola)
rt postnatal development
rt postweaning interval
rt preschool education

infants, premature
USE **premature infants**

INFARCTION
BT1 necrosis

infarction, myocardial
USE **myocardial infarction**

INFECTION
(process of becoming infected)
BT1 disease transmission
BT2 transmission
NT1 accidental infection
NT1 airborne infection
NT1 cell invasion
NT2 erythrocyte invasion
NT1 congenital infection
NT1 cross infection
NT1 experimental infection
NT1 microbial contamination
NT1 reinfection
NT1 trickle infection
rt contamination
rt infectious diseases
rt infectivity
rt preincubation period
rt sanitation
rt virulence

INFECTIONS
(result of becoming infected)
NT1 disseminated infections
NT1 experimental infections
NT1 generalized infections
NT1 hyperinfections
NT1 imported infections
NT1 inapparent infections
NT1 latent infections
NT1 mixed infections
NT1 opportunistic infections

INFECTIONS *cont.*
NT1 sepsis
NT2 septicaemia
NT3 haemorrhagic septicaemia
rt antiinfective agents
rt disinfectants
rt infectious diseases
rt isolation techniques
rt seedborne fungi
rt seedborne viruses

INFECTIOUS BRONCHITIS VIRUS
uf *avian infectious bronchitis virus*
BT1 coronavirus
BT2 coronaviridae
BT3 viruses
rt bronchitis

infectious bursal disease
USE **avian infectious bursitis**

INFECTIOUS BURSAL DISEASE VIRUS
BT1 birnavirus
BT2 birnaviridae
BT3 viruses
rt avian infectious bursitis

INFECTIOUS DISEASES
BT1 diseases
NT1 algal diseases
NT2 protothecosis
NT1 bacterial diseases
NT2 actinomycosis
NT3 cervicofacial actinomycosis
NT2 anaplasmosis
NT2 anthrax
NT2 botulism
NT2 brucellosis
NT2 glanders
NT2 heartwater
NT2 leptospirosis
NT2 lyme disease
NT2 mycoplasmosis
NT2 pasteurellosis
NT2 psittacosis
NT2 salmonellosis
NT2 tetanus
NT2 tick pyaemia
NT2 tuberculosis
NT2 typhoid
NT1 mycoses
NT2 adiaspiromycosis
NT2 aspergillosis
NT3 allergic bronchopulmonary aspergillosis
NT3 aspergilloma
NT2 blastomycosis
NT2 candidosis
NT3 chronic mucocutaneous candidosis
NT2 chromoblastomycosis
NT2 chromomycosis
NT2 coccidioidomycosis
NT2 cryptococcosis
NT2 dermatomycoses
NT3 pityriasis versicolor
NT3 tinea nigra
NT2 epizootic lymphangitis
NT2 geotrichosis
NT2 histoplasmosis
NT3 african histoplasmosis
NT2 lobomycosis
NT2 mycetoma
NT2 mycotic abortion
NT2 mycotic keratitis
NT2 mycotic mastitis
NT2 oculomycosis
NT2 paracoccidioidomycosis
NT2 phycomycosis
NT3 zygomycosis
NT4 subcutaneous phycomycosis
NT2 piedra
NT3 black piedra
NT3 white piedra
NT2 rhinosporidiosis
NT2 sporotrichosis
NT1 viral diseases

INFECTIOUS DISEASES *cont.*
NT2 acquired immune deficiency syndrome
NT2 african horse sickness
NT2 african swine fever
NT2 aleutian disease
NT2 aujeszky's disease
NT2 avian infectious bursitis
NT2 avian reticuloendotheliosis
NT2 border disease
NT2 common cold
NT2 dengue
NT3 dengue haemorrhagic fever
NT2 foot and mouth disease
NT2 haemorrhagic enteritis
NT2 influenza
NT2 japanese encephalitis
NT2 malignant catarrhal fever
NT2 marek's disease
NT2 newcastle disease
NT2 puffinosis
NT2 rabies
NT2 rinderpest
NT2 sheep pox
NT2 swine fever
NT2 varicella
NT2 viral hepatitis
NT2 yellow fever
rt antiinfective agents
rt communicable diseases (agricola)
rt immunity
rt infection
rt infections
rt infectivity
rt protozoal infections

infectious haematopoietic necrosis virus
USE **haematopoietic necrosis virus**

INFECTIVITY
rt infection
rt infectious diseases

INFERTILITY
(animals and man; for plants use "sterility")
NT1 female infertility
NT2 pseudopregnancy
NT1 male infertility
NT2 impotence
NT2 spermiostasis
rt abortion
rt brucellosis
rt fertility
rt incompatibility
rt repeat breeders

INFESTATION
NT1 reinfestation
rt pests

INFILTRATION
rt infiltrometers
rt penetration
rt percolation
rt permeability

INFILTROMETERS
BT1 instruments
rt infiltration

INFINITE ALLELES MODEL
HN from 1990
rt models
rt neutral allele hypothesis

INFLAMMATION
NT1 serositis
rt abscesses
rt antiinflammatory agents
rt arthritis
rt cellulitis
rt cholecystitis
rt gastritis
rt gingivitis
rt heat
rt oedema
rt pain
rt phlebitis

INFLAMMATION *cont.*
rt sepsis
rt sinusitis
rt swelling
rt trauma

INFLATED ROOFS
uf *roofs, inflated*
BT1 roofs
rt greenhouses

INFLATED STRUCTURES
BT1 structures
rt building construction
rt buildings
rt inflation pressure

INFLATION
BT1 economic depression
BT2 economic crises
BT3 crises (agricola)
BT2 economic situation
BT1 monetary parity
BT2 monetary situation
rt deflation

INFLATION PRESSURE
BT1 pressure
BT2 physical properties
BT3 properties
rt ground pressure
rt inflated structures
rt tyres

INFLORESCENCES
uf *capitulums*
BT1 plant
NT1 flowers
NT2 androecium
NT3 stamens
NT4 anthers
NT5 pollen
NT2 calyx
NT2 corolla
NT2 gynoecium
NT3 ovules
NT3 stigma
NT3 styles
NT2 perianths
NT1 glumes
NT2 awns
NT1 spikelets
rt cones
rt curds
rt panicles
rt prolificacy
rt spikes
rt tassels

INFLUENZA
BT1 viral diseases
BT2 infectious diseases
BT3 diseases
rt influenzavirus

INFLUENZAVIRUS
BT1 orthomyxoviridae
BT2 viruses
NT1 avian influenzavirus
NT2 fowl plague virus
NT1 equine influenzavirus
NT1 swine influenzavirus
rt influenza

INFORMAL SECTOR
rt handicrafts
rt small businesses
rt subsistence farming

INFORMATION
NT1 consumer information
NT2 open dating (agricola)
NT1 information needs
NT1 information processing
NT2 abstracting
NT2 data processing
NT2 indexing
NT2 information retrieval
NT2 information storage
NT1 information science
NT1 nutrition information (agricola)
rt diffusion of information

INFORMATION *cont.*
- rt food data sources (agricola)
- rt information centres
- rt information science
- rt information services
- rt information systems
- rt market intelligence
- rt mass media
- rt misinformation (agricola)
- rt publications
- rt reviews
- rt visitor interpretation

INFORMATION CENTERS
- BF information centres
- rt resource centers (agricola)

INFORMATION CENTRES
- AF information centers
- BT1 information services
  - BT2 services
- NT1 advisory centres
  - NT2 demonstration farms
- NT1 visitor centres
- rt information
- rt libraries
- rt visitor interpretation

information dissemination
- USE **diffusion of information**

INFORMATION NEEDS
- BT1 information
- rt information services

INFORMATION PROCESSING
- *uf processing, information*
- BT1 information
- NT1 abstracting
- NT1 data processing
- NT1 indexing
- NT1 information retrieval
- NT1 information storage
- rt classification
- rt information science
- rt information systems
- rt processing

INFORMATION RETRIEVAL
- BT1 information processing
  - BT2 information
- rt information storage
- rt information systems

INFORMATION SCIENCE
- BT1 information
- rt communication theory
- rt information
- rt information processing
- rt information services
- rt information systems
- rt social sciences

INFORMATION SERVICES
- *uf information sources*
- BT1 services
- NT1 aglinet
- NT1 agricola
- NT1 agris
- NT1 card services
- NT1 caris
- NT1 diffusion of information
  - NT2 diffusion of research
- NT1 dispatcher systems
- NT1 information centres
  - NT2 advisory centres
    - NT3 demonstration farms
  - NT2 visitor centres
- NT1 microform
  - NT2 microfiche
- NT1 sdi services
- NT1 secondary journals
- rt cab international
- rt communication
- rt information
- rt information needs
- rt information science
- rt information systems
- rt libraries
- rt mass media
- rt public relations
- rt signboards and signposts
- rt technology transfer

INFORMATION SERVICES *cont.*
- rt telecommunications
- rt visitor interpretation

information sources
- USE **information services**

INFORMATION STORAGE
- *uf data storage*
- BT1 information processing
  - BT2 information
- rt databases
- rt information retrieval
- rt storage

INFORMATION SYSTEMS
- BT1 systems
- NT1 data banks
  - NT2 nutrient databanks (agricola)
- NT1 databases
- rt computers
- rt data collection
- rt information
- rt information processing
- rt information retrieval
- rt information science
- rt information services

INFRARED DRIERS
- AF infrared dryers
- *uf driers, infrared*
- BT1 driers
  - BT2 farm machinery
    - BT3 machinery
- rt infrared radiation

INFRARED DRYERS
- BF infrared driers
- BT1 dryers

INFRARED HEATERS
- *uf heaters, infrared*
- *uf lamps, infrared*
- BT1 heaters
  - BT2 equipment
- rt heat lamps
- rt infrared radiation

INFRARED IMAGERY
- BT1 imagery
  - BT2 techniques
- NT1 infrared line scan imagery
- NT1 thermal infrared imagery
- rt infrared photography
- rt remote sensing

INFRARED LINE SCAN IMAGERY
- BT1 infrared imagery
  - BT2 imagery
    - BT3 techniques
- rt remote sensing

INFRARED MOISTURE METERS
- *uf moisture meters, infrared*
- BT1 moisture meters
  - BT2 meters
    - BT3 instruments

INFRARED PHOTOGRAPHY
- BT1 photography
  - BT2 techniques
- rt infrared imagery
- rt mapping
- rt remote sensing
- rt surveying

INFRARED RADIATION
- BT1 electromagnetic radiation
  - BT2 radiation
- rt far red light
- rt heat
- rt heat lamps
- rt infrared driers
- rt infrared heaters
- rt microwave radiation
- rt thermal radiation

INFRARED SPECTROPHOTOMETRY
- BT1 spectrophotometry
  - BT2 analytical methods
    - BT3 methodology

INFRARED SPECTROSCOPY
- BT1 spectroscopy
  - BT2 analytical methods
    - BT3 methodology

INFRASTRUCTURE
- rt institution building
- rt planning
- rt public utilities
- rt services

INFUNDIBULORIUM
- BT1 ciliophora
  - BT2 protozoa

INFUNDIBULUM
- HN from 1989
- BT1 oviducts
  - BT2 female genitalia
    - BT3 genitalia
      - BT4 urogenital system
        - BT5 body parts

INFUSION
- HN from 1989
- BT1 techniques

INGA
- BT1 leguminosae
- NT1 inga brenesii
- NT1 inga jinicuil
- NT1 inga leptoloba
- NT1 inga punctata
- NT1 inga sapindoides
- rt forest trees

INGA BRENESII
- BT1 inga
  - BT2 leguminosae

INGA JINICUIL
- BT1 inga
  - BT2 leguminosae

INGA LEPTOLOBA
- BT1 inga
  - BT2 leguminosae

INGA PUNCTATA
- BT1 inga
  - BT2 leguminosae
- BT1 medicinal plants

INGA SAPINDOIDES
- BT1 inga
  - BT2 leguminosae

INGESTION
- BT1 food intake
  - BT2 intake
- rt eating

INGREDIENT ROOM (AGRICOLA)
- rt food preparation (agricola)
- rt ingredients (agricola)

INGREDIENTS (AGRICOLA)
- NT1 non-hygroscopic ingredients (agricola)
- rt food preparation (agricola)
- rt ingredient room (agricola)
- rt recipes (agricola)

INHALATION
- BT1 application methods
  - BT2 methodology

INHALED ANAESTHETICS
- AF inhaled anesthetics
- BT1 anaesthetics
  - BT2 neurotropic drugs
    - BT3 drugs
- NT1 ethyl ether
- NT1 halothane
- NT1 methoxyflurane
- NT1 nitrous oxide

INHALED ANESTHETICS
- BF inhaled anaesthetics
- BT1 anesthetics

INHERITANCE
- *uf heredity*
- NT1 cytoplasmic inheritance
- NT1 polygenic inheritance

INHERITANCE *cont.*
- NT1 xenia
- rt allelic exclusion
- rt ancestry
- rt animal breeding
- rt congenital abnormalities
- rt familial incidence
- rt genes
- rt genetic effects
- rt genetic regulation
- rt genetics
- rt germplasm
- rt hereditary diseases
- rt heritability
- rt linkage
- rt plant breeding
- rt sex limited characters
- rt threshold models

inheritance (economics)
- USE **inheritance of property**

inheritance of acquired characters
- USE **lamarckism**

INHERITANCE OF PROPERTY
- *uf inheritance (economics)*
- rt division of property (agricola)
- rt heritable leases
- rt inheritance tax
- rt wills (agricola)

INHERITANCE TAX
- *uf estate duty*
- *uf tax, inheritance*
- BT1 direct taxation
  - BT2 taxes
    - BT3 fiscal policy
      - BT4 economic policy
      - BT4 public finance
- rt inheritance of property

INHIBIN
- *uf folliculostatin*
- BT1 glycoproteins
  - BT2 proteins
    - BT3 peptides
- BT1 sex hormones
  - BT2 hormones

INHIBITION
- NT1 inactivation
- NT1 photoinhibition
- NT1 sprout inhibition
- rt cholinergic mechanisms
- rt gastric inhibitory polypeptides
- rt inhibitor genes
- rt resistance

INHIBITOR GENES
- BT1 genes
- rt gene interaction
- rt inhibition

INHIBITORS
- NT1 aggregation disrupters
- NT1 antifeedants
  - NT2 fentin acetate
  - NT2 fentin chloride
  - NT2 fentin hydroxide
  - NT2 guazatine
- NT1 growth inhibitors
  - NT2 abscisic acid
  - NT2 ancymidol
  - NT2 chlorphonium
  - NT2 chlorpropham
  - NT2 dikegulac
  - NT2 fluoridamid
  - NT2 germination inhibitors
  - NT2 glyphosine
  - NT2 isopyrimol
  - NT2 jasmonic acid
  - NT2 maleic hydrazide
  - NT2 mepiquat
  - NT2 morphactins
    - NT3 chlorflurenol
    - NT3 dichlorflurenol
    - NT3 flurenol
  - NT2 paclobutrazol
  - NT2 piproctanyl
  - NT2 propham

INHIBITORS *cont.*
NT2 thidiazuron
NT2 tiba
NT2 triapenthenol
NT2 uniconazole
NT1 mating disrupters
NT2 looplure
NT1 metabolic inhibitors
NT2 2,4-dinitrophenol
NT2 5-bromouracil
NT2 6-methylpurine
NT2 8-azaguanine
NT2 antagonists
NT3 amino acid antagonists
NT4 p-fluorophenylalanine
NT4 arginine antagonists
NT4 cycloleucine
NT4 methylmethionine
NT3 hormone antagonists
NT4 bromocriptine
NT4 juvenile hormone antagonists
NT5 precocenes
NT6 precocene i
NT6 precocene ii
NT6 precocene iii
NT4 saralasin
NT4 spironolactone
NT4 thyroid antagonists
NT5 goitrin
NT5 propylthiouracil
NT4 urogastrone
NT3 vitamin antagonists
NT4 vitamin a antagonists
NT4 vitamin b antagonists
NT5 4-deoxypyridoxine
NT5 benzimidazole
NT5 biotin antagonists
NT6 avidin
NT5 folate antagonists
NT6 aminopterin
NT6 methotrexate
NT5 picolinic acid
NT5 riboflavin antagonists
NT6 pyrithiamine
NT5 thiamin antagonists
NT4 vitamin c antagonists
NT5 dehydroascorbic acid
NT4 vitamin k antagonists
NT5 dicoumarol
NT5 warfarin
NT2 antimycin a
NT2 broxuridine
NT2 chitin synthesis inhibitors
NT3 buprofezin
NT3 chlorfluazuron
NT3 cyromazine
NT3 diflubenzuron
NT3 flufenoxuron
NT3 penfluron
NT3 teflubenzuron
NT3 triflumuron
NT2 cycloheximide
NT2 cycloserine
NT2 cytochalasin b
NT2 enzyme inhibitors
NT3 n-ethylmaleimide
NT3 acetazolamide
NT3 allopurinol
NT3 aminopterin
NT3 benfluorex
NT3 benzoquinone
NT3 cholinesterase inhibitors
NT4 neostigmine
NT4 physostigmine
NT3 glucaric acid
NT3 iodoacetic acid
NT3 nitrate reductase inhibitors
NT3 nordihydroguaiaretic acid
NT3 oligomycin
NT3 phaseolotoxin
NT3 proteinase inhibitors
NT4 chymotrypsin inhibitors
NT4 pepstatin
NT4 trypsin inhibitors
NT5 antitrypsin
NT3 urease inhibitors
NT4 ammonium thiosulfate
NT4 chloramben

INHIBITORS *cont.*
NT4 phenyl phosphorodiamidate
NT3 valinomycin
NT2 ethionine
NT2 fluorouracil
NT2 idoxuridine
NT2 malformin
NT2 methane inhibitors
NT2 mitomycin
NT2 monensin
NT2 nitrification inhibitors
NT3 ammonium thiosulfate
NT3 carbon disulfide
NT3 chloramphenicol
NT3 dicyandiamide
NT3 etridiazole
NT3 neem seed extract
NT3 nitrapyrin
NT3 potassium azide
NT3 potassium ethylxanthate
NT3 sulfathiazole
NT3 thiourea
NT2 protein synthesis inhibitors
NT3 chloramphenicol
NT3 puromycin
NT2 solanine
NT2 thiouracil
rt retardants

INITIATION
BT1 starting
rt organogenesis
rt plant development

INJECTABLE ANAESTHETICS
AF injectable anesthetics
BT1 anaesthetics
BT2 neurotropic drugs
BT3 drugs
NT1 chloral hydrate
NT1 etomidate
NT1 etorphine
NT1 fentanyl
NT1 ketamine
NT1 methadone
NT1 methitural
NT1 metomidate
NT1 pentobarbital
NT1 phencyclidine
NT1 phenobarbital
NT1 thiopental
NT1 urethane
rt barbiturates

INJECTABLE ANESTHETICS
BF injectable anaesthetics
BT1 anesthetics

INJECTION
BT1 application methods
BT2 methodology
NT1 intramuscular injection
NT1 intraperitoneal injection
NT1 intravenous injection
NT1 soil injection
NT1 subcutaneous injection
NT1 tree injection
rt injectors
rt parenteral administration

injection of trees
USE **tree injection**

INJECTORS
BT1 application equipment
BT2 equipment
NT1 soil injectors
NT1 tree injectors
rt injection

injectors, soil
USE **soil injectors**

injectors, tree
USE **tree injectors**

INJURIES
(plants; for animals and man use "trauma")
uf *traumas*
NT1 abiotic injuries
NT1 bruising

INJURIES *cont.*
NT1 cold injury
NT1 drought injury
NT1 fertilizer injury
NT1 frost injury
NT1 heat injury
NT1 salt injury
NT1 seed injury
rt abrasion
rt damage
rt injurious factors
rt wound periderm

INJURIOUS FACTORS
rt injuries

INLAND RESORTS
BT1 resorts

INLAND TRANSPORT
uf *transport, inland*
BT1 transport
rt inland waterway transport

INLAND WATERWAY TRANSPORT
uf *transport, inland waterway*
BT1 water transport
BT2 transport
rt inland transport

INLAND WATERWAYS
BT1 waterways
NT1 canals
rt boats
rt rivers
rt water transport

inner mongolia
USE **nei menggu**

INNERVATION
HN from 1990
BT1 neurons
BT2 nerve tissue
BT3 animal tissues
BT4 tissues
NT1 adrenergic innervation

INNOVATION ADOPTION
uf *adoption of innovations*
rt induced innovations
rt innovations
rt modernization
rt technology transfer

INNOVATIONS
BT1 modernization
NT1 induced innovations
rt educational innovation (agricola)
rt innovation adoption
rt new products
rt patents

INOCULANT CARRIERS
BT1 carriers
NT1 coal
NT2 brown coal
NT1 filter cake
NT1 peat
rt vaccines

inoculation
USE **immunization**
OR **seed inoculation**
OR **soil inoculation**

inoculation (immunization)
USE **immunization**

INOCULATION METHODS
HN from 1990
(introduction of nitrogen fixing bacteria, mycorrhizal fungi or bacterial fertilizers to plants in order to achieve nutritional or other benefits)
BT1 application methods
BT2 methodology
NT1 seed inoculation
NT1 soil inoculation
rt mycorrhizal fungi
rt nitrogen fixing bacteria

INOCULUM
rt inoculum density

INOCULUM DENSITY
rt density
rt inoculum

INONOTUS
BT1 aphyllophorales
NT1 inonotus hispidus
NT1 inonotus nidus-pici
NT1 inonotus radiatus
rt phellinus
rt polyporus
rt polystictus
rt poria

INONOTUS HISPIDUS
uf *polyporus hispidus*
BT1 inonotus
BT2 aphyllophorales

INONOTUS NIDUS-PICI
uf *polystictus nidus-pici*
uf *xanthochrous nidus-pici*
BT1 inonotus
BT2 aphyllophorales

INONOTUS RADIATUS
uf *polyporus radiatus*
BT1 inonotus
BT2 aphyllophorales

inonotus weirii
USE **phellinus weirii**

INOPUS
BT1 stratiomyidae
BT2 diptera
NT1 inopus rubriceps

INOPUS RUBRICEPS
BT1 inopus
BT2 stratiomyidae
BT3 diptera

INORGANIC ACIDS
uf *acids, inorganic*
BT1 acids
BT1 inorganic compounds
NT1 boric acid
NT1 gastric acid
NT1 hydrochloric acid
NT1 hydrofluoric acid
NT1 molybdic acid
NT1 nitric acid
NT1 phosphoric acid
NT1 polyphosphoric acid
NT2 superphosphoric acid
NT1 silicic acid
NT1 sulfuric acid
NT1 sulfurous acid

INORGANIC COMPOUNDS
NT1 ammonia
NT1 carbides
NT2 calcium carbide
NT1 hydrides
NT2 phosphine
NT1 hydroxides
NT2 aluminium hydroxide
NT2 ammonium hydroxide
NT2 calcium hydroxide
NT2 copper hydroxide
NT2 iron hydroxides
NT3 ferric hydroxide
NT2 potassium hydroxide
NT2 sodium hydroxide
NT1 inorganic acids
NT2 boric acid
NT2 gastric acid
NT2 hydrochloric acid
NT2 hydrofluoric acid
NT2 molybdic acid
NT2 nitric acid
NT2 phosphoric acid
NT2 polyphosphoric acid
NT3 superphosphoric acid
NT2 silicic acid
NT2 sulfuric acid
NT2 sulfurous acid
NT1 inorganic salts
NT2 arsenates
NT3 calcium arsenate

INORGANIC COMPOUNDS *cont.*
NT3 copper arsenate
NT3 copper chrome arsenate
NT3 lead arsenate
NT2 arsenites
NT3 sodium arsenite
NT2 bicarbonates
NT3 ammonium bicarbonate
NT3 carboxylin
NT3 sodium bicarbonate
NT2 bisulfites
NT3 sodium bisulfite
NT2 borates
NT3 borax
NT3 sodium borate
NT2 carbonates
NT3 calcium carbonate
NT3 copper carbonate
NT3 magnesium carbonate
NT3 potassium carbonate
NT3 sodium carbonate
NT2 chlorates
NT3 calcium chlorate
NT3 sodium chlorate
NT2 chlorites
NT2 cyanates
NT3 potassium cyanate
NT2 cyanides
NT3 potassium cyanide
NT2 ferrocyanides
NT2 halides
NT3 bromides
NT4 potassium bromide
NT3 chlorides
NT4 ammonium chloride
NT4 calcium chloride
NT4 mercuric chloride
NT4 mercurous chloride
NT4 potassium chloride
NT4 sodium chloride
NT3 fluorides
NT4 ammonium fluoride
NT4 calcium fluoride
NT4 cryolite
NT4 sodium fluoride
NT3 iodides
NT4 potassium iodide
NT2 hydrosulfites
NT3 sodium hydrosulfite
NT2 hypochlorites
NT3 sodium hypochlorite
NT2 metabisulfites
NT3 sodium metabisulfite
NT2 molybdates
NT3 sodium molybdate
NT3 thiomolybdates
NT2 nitrates (inorganic salts)
NT3 ammonium nitrate
NT3 calcium nitrate
NT3 magnesium nitrate
NT3 potassium nitrate
NT3 sodium nitrate
NT2 nitrites
NT3 sodium nitrite
NT2 perchlorates
NT3 ammonium perchlorate
NT2 permanganates
NT3 potassium permanganate
NT2 phosphates (salts)
NT3 aluminium phosphate
NT3 ammonium phosphates
NT4 ammonium metaphosphates
NT4 ammonium polyphosphates
NT5 ammonium polyphosphate sulfate
NT5 ammonium pyrophosphate
NT5 ammonium tripolyphosphate
NT5 diammonium pyrophosphate
NT5 tetraammonium pyrophosphate
NT5 triammonium pyrophosphate
NT5 urea ammonium polyphosphate
NT4 diammonium phosphate

INORGANIC COMPOUNDS *cont.*
NT4 magnesium ammonium phosphate
NT4 monoammonium phosphate
NT4 triammonium phosphate
NT4 urea ammonium phosphate
NT4 urea ammonium pyrophosphate
NT3 calcium phosphates
NT4 apatite
NT5 phosphorite
NT4 calcium ammonium trimetaphosphate
NT4 calcium phosphate
NT4 calcium polyphosphates
NT5 calcium pyrophosphate
NT4 dicalcium phosphate
NT4 monocalcium phosphate
NT4 octacalcium phosphate
NT4 rock phosphate
NT4 tricalcium phosphate
NT4 triple superphosphate
NT3 iron phosphates
NT4 ferric phosphate
NT3 metaphosphates
NT4 ammonium metaphosphates
NT4 potassium metaphosphate
NT4 trimetaphosphates
NT5 calcium ammonium trimetaphosphate
NT3 orthophosphates
NT3 potassium phosphates
NT4 dipotassium hydrogen phosphate
NT4 potassium dihydrogen phosphate
NT4 potassium metaphosphate
NT4 potassium polyphosphates
NT5 potassium dihydrogen triphosphate
NT5 potassium hydrogen tripolyphosphates
NT5 potassium pyrophosphate
NT5 urea potassium pyrophosphate
NT3 pyrophosphates
NT4 ammonium pyrophosphate
NT4 calcium pyrophosphate
NT4 diammonium pyrophosphate
NT4 potassium pyrophosphate
NT4 sodium pyrophosphate
NT4 tetraammonium pyrophosphate
NT4 triammonium pyrophosphate
NT4 urea ammonium pyrophosphate
NT4 urea potassium pyrophosphate
NT3 silicon phosphate
NT3 sodium phosphate
NT2 silicates
NT3 calcium silicate
NT3 magnesium silicate
NT3 mica
NT3 potassium silicates
NT4 potassium metasilicate
NT3 sodium silicate
NT3 talc
NT3 vermiculite
NT2 sulfamates
NT3 ammonium sulfamate
NT2 sulfates (inorganic salts)
NT3 aluminium sulfate
NT3 ammonium sulfate
NT3 barium sulfate
NT3 calcium sulfate
NT3 carboxylin
NT3 copper sulfate
NT3 ferric sulfate
NT3 ferrous sulfate

INORGANIC COMPOUNDS *cont.*
NT3 magnesium sulfate
NT4 epsom salts
NT3 manganous sulfate
NT3 potassium sulfate
NT3 sodium sulfate
NT3 thallium sulfate
NT3 zinc sulfate
NT2 sulfites (salts)
NT3 sodium sulfite
NT2 thiocyanates
NT3 ammonium thiocyanate
NT2 thiosulfates
NT3 ammonium thiosulfate
NT3 silver thiosulfate
NT1 iron oxyhydroxides
NT2 goethite
NT2 lepidocrocite
NT1 oxides
NT2 aluminium oxide
NT2 calcium oxide
NT2 carbon dioxide
NT2 carbon monoxide
NT2 chromic oxide
NT2 cuprous oxide
NT2 iron oxides
NT3 maghaemite
NT3 magnetite
NT2 lead oxides
NT3 red lead
NT2 magnesium oxide
NT2 manganese oxides
NT3 manganese dioxide
NT3 manganous oxide
NT2 mercuric oxide
NT2 nitrogen oxides
NT3 nitric oxide
NT3 nitrogen dioxide
NT3 nitrous oxide
NT2 phosphorus pentoxide
NT2 silica
NT2 sulfur dioxide
NT2 titanium dioxide
NT3 anatase
NT2 zinc oxide
NT1 peroxides
NT2 calcium peroxide
NT2 hydrogen peroxide
NT1 phosphides
NT2 zinc phosphide
NT1 sesquioxides
NT1 sulfides (inorganic)
NT2 hydrogen sulfide
NT2 pyrites
NT2 sodium sulfide

INORGANIC HERBICIDES
BT1 herbicides
BT2 pesticides
NT1 ammonium sulfamate
NT1 borax
NT1 calcium chlorate
NT1 sodium chlorate

INORGANIC MERCURY FUNGICIDES
BT1 mercury fungicides
BT2 fungicides
BT3 pesticides
NT1 mercuric chloride
NT1 mercuric oxide

INORGANIC PHOSPHORUS
uf *phosphorus, inorganic*
BT1 chemical composition
BT2 composition
rt phosphorus

INORGANIC PYROPHOSPHATASE
(ec 3.6.1.1)
BT1 pyrophosphatases
BT2 acid anhydride hydrolases
BT3 hydrolases
BT4 enzymes

INORGANIC SALTS
uf *salts, inorganic*
BT1 inorganic compounds
BT1 salts
NT1 arsenates
NT2 calcium arsenate
NT2 copper arsenate

INORGANIC SALTS *cont.*
NT2 copper chrome arsenate
NT2 lead arsenate
NT1 arsenites
NT2 sodium arsenite
NT1 bicarbonates
NT2 ammonium bicarbonate
NT2 carboxylin
NT2 sodium bicarbonate
NT1 bisulfites
NT2 sodium bisulfite
NT1 borates
NT2 borax
NT2 sodium borate
NT1 carbonates
NT2 calcium carbonate
NT2 copper carbonate
NT2 magnesium carbonate
NT2 potassium carbonate
NT2 sodium carbonate
NT1 chlorates
NT2 calcium chlorate
NT2 sodium chlorate
NT1 chlorites
NT1 cyanates
NT2 potassium cyanate
NT1 cyanides
NT2 potassium cyanide
NT1 ferrocyanides
NT1 halides
NT2 bromides
NT3 potassium bromide
NT2 chlorides
NT3 ammonium chloride
NT3 calcium chloride
NT3 mercuric chloride
NT3 mercurous chloride
NT3 potassium chloride
NT3 sodium chloride
NT2 fluorides
NT3 ammonium fluoride
NT3 calcium fluoride
NT3 cryolite
NT3 sodium fluoride
NT2 iodides
NT3 potassium iodide
NT1 hydrosulfites
NT2 sodium hydrosulfite
NT1 hypochlorites
NT2 sodium hypochlorite
NT1 metabisulfites
NT2 sodium metabisulfite
NT1 molybdates
NT2 sodium molybdate
NT2 thiomolybdates
NT1 nitrates (inorganic salts)
NT2 ammonium nitrate
NT2 calcium nitrate
NT2 magnesium nitrate
NT2 potassium nitrate
NT2 sodium nitrate
NT1 nitrites
NT2 sodium nitrite
NT1 perchlorates
NT2 ammonium perchlorate
NT1 permanganates
NT2 potassium permanganate
NT1 phosphates (salts)
NT2 aluminium phosphate
NT2 ammonium phosphates
NT3 ammonium metaphosphates
NT3 ammonium polyphosphates
NT4 ammonium polyphosphate sulfate
NT4 ammonium pyrophosphate
NT4 ammonium tripolyphosphate
NT4 diammonium pyrophosphate
NT4 tetraammonium pyrophosphate
NT4 triammonium pyrophosphate
NT4 urea ammonium polyphosphate
NT3 diammonium phosphate
NT3 magnesium ammonium phosphate

INORGANIC SALTS *cont.*
NT3 monoammonium phosphate
NT3 triammonium phosphate
NT3 urea ammonium phosphate
NT3 urea ammonium pyrophosphate
NT2 calcium phosphates
NT3 apatite
NT4 phosphorite
NT3 calcium ammonium trimetaphosphate
NT3 calcium phosphate
NT3 calcium polyphosphates
NT4 calcium pyrophosphate
NT3 dicalcium phosphate
NT3 monocalcium phosphate
NT3 octacalcium phosphate
NT3 rock phosphate
NT3 tricalcium phosphate
NT3 triple superphosphate
NT2 iron phosphates
NT3 ferric phosphate
NT2 metaphosphates
NT3 ammonium metaphosphates
NT3 potassium metaphosphate
NT3 trimetaphosphates
NT4 calcium ammonium trimetaphosphate
NT2 orthophosphates
NT2 potassium phosphates
NT3 dipotassium hydrogen phosphate
NT3 potassium dihydrogen phosphate
NT3 potassium metaphosphate
NT3 potassium polyphosphates
NT4 potassium dihydrogen triphosphate
NT4 potassium hydrogen tripolyphosphates
NT4 potassium pyrophosphate
NT4 urea potassium pyrophosphate
NT2 pyrophosphates
NT3 ammonium pyrophosphate
NT3 calcium pyrophosphate
NT3 diammonium pyrophosphate
NT3 potassium pyrophosphate
NT3 sodium pyrophosphate
NT3 tetraammonium pyrophosphate
NT3 triammonium pyrophosphate
NT3 urea ammonium pyrophosphate
NT3 urea potassium pyrophosphate
NT2 silicon phosphate
NT2 sodium phosphate
NT1 silicates
NT2 calcium silicate
NT2 magnesium silicate
NT2 mica
NT2 potassium silicates
NT3 potassium metasilicate
NT2 sodium silicate
NT2 talc
NT2 vermiculite
NT1 sulfamates
NT2 ammonium sulfamate
NT1 sulfates (inorganic salts)
NT2 aluminium sulfate
NT2 ammonium sulfate
NT2 barium sulfate
NT2 calcium sulfate
NT2 carboxylin
NT2 copper sulfate
NT2 ferric sulfate
NT2 ferrous sulfate
NT2 magnesium sulfate
NT3 epsom salts
NT2 manganous sulfate

INORGANIC SALTS *cont.*
NT2 potassium sulfate
NT2 sodium sulfate
NT2 thallium sulfate
NT2 zinc sulfate
NT1 sulfites (salts)
NT2 sodium sulfite
NT1 thiocyanates
NT2 ammonium thiocyanate
NT1 thiosulfates
NT2 ammonium thiosulfate
NT2 silver thiosulfate
rt desalinization
rt halophytes
rt salt sieving

INOSINE
BT1 ribonucleosides
BT2 nucleosides
BT3 glycosides
BT4 carbohydrates

inositol
USE **myo-inositol**

inositol hexaphosphate
USE **phytic acid**

INOSITOL PHOSPHATES
BT1 sugar phosphates
BT2 carbohydrates
BT2 phosphates (esters)
BT3 esters
BT3 phosphates
NT1 phytic acid

meso-inositol
USE **myo-inositol**

MYO-INOSITOL
uf *meso-inositol*
uf *inositol*
BT1 cyclitols
BT2 sugar alcohols
BT3 carbohydrates
BT3 polyols
BT4 alcohols
BT1 lipotropic factors
BT2 drugs
BT1 vitamin b complex
BT2 water-soluble vitamins
BT3 vitamins

INOUE-MELNICK VIRUS
BT1 unclassified viruses
BT2 viruses

INPUT INDUSTRIES
BT1 industry
NT1 agricultural machinery industry
NT1 feed industry
NT1 fertilizer industry
NT1 seed industry
NT2 seed certification
NT2 seed production
NT3 hybrid seed production
rt preagricultural sector

INPUT OUTPUT ANALYSIS
BT1 macroeconomic analysis
BT2 economic analysis
NT1 shift share analysis
rt national accounting
rt regional accounting

input prices
USE **farm inputs**
OR **prices**

INQUILINA
BT1 apidae
BT2 hymenoptera

insect allergies
USE **arthropod allergies**

INSECT ATTRACTANTS
uf *attractants, insect*
BT1 attractants
NT1 α-cubebene
NT1 cue-lure
NT1 disparlure
NT1 eugenol

INSECT ATTRACTANTS *cont.*
NT1 grandlure
NT1 hexalure
NT1 looplure
NT1 methyl eugenol
NT1 muscalure
NT1 oviposition attractants
NT1 sex attractants
NT1 trimedlure
rt insect control
rt insect traps
rt insects

INSECT BITES
(including stings)
BT1 bites
BT2 wounds
BT3 trauma
rt arthropod allergies
rt haematophagous insects

INSECT COMMUNITIES
BT1 arthropod communities
BT2 communities

INSECT CONTROL
BT1 pest control
BT2 control
NT1 aggregation disruption
NT1 mating disruption
NT1 mules' operation
NT1 sterile insect release
rt antifeedants
rt bed nets
rt controlled atmosphere storage
rt habitat destruction
rt insect attractants
rt insect pests
rt insect repellents
rt insect traps
rt insecticidal plants
rt insecticidal properties
rt insecticide resistance
rt insecticides
rt mating disrupters
rt plant protection
rt sex attractants
rt tsetse screens

INSECT GROWTH REGULATORS
BT1 growth regulators
BT1 insecticides
BT2 pesticides
NT1 chitin synthesis inhibitors
NT2 buprofezin
NT2 chlorfluazuron
NT2 cyromazine
NT2 diflubenzuron
NT2 flufenoxuron
NT2 penfluron
NT2 teflubenzuron
NT2 triflumuron
NT1 juvenile hormone analogues
NT2 epofenonane
NT2 fenoxycarb
NT2 hydroprene
NT2 kinoprene
NT2 methoprene
NT2 triprene
NT1 precocenes
NT2 precocene i
NT2 precocene ii
NT2 precocene iii
rt juvenile hormone antagonists
rt juvenile hormones
rt moulting hormones

insect larvae as food
USE **insects as food**

insect nematodes
USE **entomophilic nematodes**

INSECT PESTS
BT1 arthropod pests
BT2 pests
BT1 insects
BT2 arthropods
NT1 bark beetles
NT1 boring insects
NT2 stem borers

INSECT PESTS *cont.*
NT1 haematophagous insects
NT1 leaf miners
NT1 leafhoppers
NT1 locusts
NT1 planthoppers
rt insect control
rt insecticides
rt parasites of insect pests (agricola)
rt pest control
rt predators of insect pests (agricola)
rt stored products pests

INSECT REPELLENTS
BT1 repellents
NT1 butopyronoxyl
NT1 camphor
NT1 dibutyl phthalate
NT1 diethyltoluamide
NT1 dimethyl phthalate
NT1 ethohexadiol
NT1 oviposition deterrents
rt insect control
rt plant protection

INSECT TRAPS
BT1 traps
BT2 equipment
NT1 biconical traps
NT1 coloured sticky traps
NT1 electrocuting traps
NT1 funnel traps
NT1 light traps
NT2 cdc light traps
NT2 new jersey light traps
NT1 malaise traps
NT1 manitoba traps
NT1 oviposition traps
NT1 pheromone traps
NT1 pitfall traps
NT1 sex attractant traps
NT1 sound traps
NT1 sticky traps
NT1 suction traps
NT1 trap bands
NT1 trap crops
NT1 trap trees
NT1 visual traps
NT1 water traps
NT1 yellow sticky traps
NT1 yellow traps
rt insect attractants
rt insect control
rt insecticides
rt insects
rt plant protection

INSECT VIRUSES
BT1 entomopathogens
BT2 pathogens
NT1 ascovirus
NT1 baculoviridae
NT2 baculovirus
NT3 granulosis viruses
NT3 nuclear polyhedrosis viruses
NT4 baculovirus heliothis
NT1 bee viruses
NT2 arkansas bee virus
NT2 bee acute paralysis virus
NT2 bee chronic paralysis virus
NT2 bee chronic paralysis virus associate
NT2 black queen cell virus
NT2 kashmir bee virus
NT2 sacbrood virus
NT1 cytoplasmic polyhedrosis viruses
NT1 densovirus
NT2 densonucleosis viruses
NT1 entomopoxvirinae
NT2 entomopoxvirus
NT1 iridovirus
NT2 iridescent viruses
NT3 chilo iridescent virus
NT3 regular mosquito iridescent virus
NT3 turquoise mosquito iridescent virus
NT1 nodaviridae

INSECT VIRUSES *cont.*
NT2 black beetle virus
NT2 nodamura virus
NT1 polydnaviridae
NT2 polydnavirus
NT1 sigmavirus
rt astrovirus
rt biological control agents
rt parasites of insect pests (agricola)
rt viruses

insecta
USE **insects**

INSECTARIES
HN from 1990
rt insects
rt rearing techniques

INSECTICIDAL ACTION
rt insecticides

INSECTICIDAL PLANTS
BT1 pesticidal plants
NT1 achillea millefolium
NT1 acorus calamus
NT1 ageratum conyzoides
NT1 ajuga chamaepitys
NT1 ajuga iva
NT1 anabasis aphylla
NT1 angelica archangelica
NT1 angelica sylvestris
NT1 annona reticulata
NT1 annona squamosa
NT1 aristolochia bracteata
NT1 armoracia rusticana
NT1 artemisia abrotanum
NT1 artemisia absinthium
NT1 artemisia capillaris
NT1 artemisia monosperma
NT1 asclepias tuberosa
NT1 azadirachta indica
NT1 brassica nigra
NT1 callicarpa candicans
NT1 calotropis procea
NT1 calpurnia aurea
NT1 camptotheca acuminata
NT1 capsella bursa-pastoris
NT1 capsicum frutescens
NT1 cardamine hirsuta
NT1 cassia fistula
NT1 catalpa speciosa
NT1 catharanthus roseus
NT1 cestrum nocturnum
NT1 chamomilla recutita
NT1 chenopodium album
NT1 chenopodium ambrosioides
NT1 chrysanthemum coronarium
NT1 chrysanthemums
NT1 chrysothamnus nauseosus
NT1 citrus poonensis
NT1 coconuts
NT1 colchicum autumnale
NT1 croton tiglium
NT1 cuminum cyminum
NT1 curcuma longa
NT1 cymbopogon caesius
NT1 datura stramonium
NT1 delphinium staphisagria
NT1 derris elliptica
NT1 derris uliginosa
NT1 descurainia sophia
NT1 dioscorea rotundata
NT1 duranta repens
NT1 echinacea angustifolia
NT1 echinochloa crus-galli
NT1 elettaria cardamomum
NT1 erodium cicutarium
NT1 eruca vesicaria
NT1 eucalyptus deglupta
NT1 eucalyptus saligna
NT1 euonymus alatus
NT1 eupatorium japonicum
NT1 fennel
NT1 garlic
NT1 glycyrrhiza glabra
NT1 grapefruits
NT1 groundnuts
NT1 hedera helix
NT1 helenium aromaticum
NT1 helianthus annuus

INSECTICIDAL PLANTS *cont.*
NT1 hyptis spicigera
NT1 iris douglasiana
NT1 jatropha gossypiifolia
NT1 juniperus communis
NT1 juniperus virginiana
NT1 kalmia latifolia
NT1 lantana camara
NT1 leeks
NT1 lemons
NT1 leucanthemum vulgare
NT1 leuzea rhapontica
NT1 levisticum officinale
NT1 limes
NT1 linaria vulgaris
NT1 linum usitatissimum
NT1 litsea cubeba
NT1 lycopersicon hirsutum
NT1 maesa chisia
NT1 melia azedarach
NT1 melissa officinalis
NT1 mentha piperita
NT1 millettia auriculata
NT1 millettia pachycarpa
NT1 mundulea sericea
NT1 nepeta cataria
NT1 nicotiana rustica
NT1 nicotiana tabacum
NT1 nigella sativa
NT1 ocimum basilicum
NT1 ocimum sanctum
NT1 oil palms
NT1 olives
NT1 oranges
NT1 origanum majorana
NT1 otanthus maritimus
NT1 parsnips
NT1 parthenium hysterophorus
NT1 phytolacca dodecandra
NT1 pimpinella anisum
NT1 piper excelsum
NT1 piper futokadsura
NT1 piper guineense
NT1 piper nigrum
NT1 plumbago auriculata
NT1 podocarpus nagi
NT1 podocarpus neriifolius
NT1 podocarpus nivalis
NT1 poinsettias
NT1 polygonum hydropiper
NT1 pongamia pinnata
NT1 prunella vulgaris
NT1 quercus gambelii
NT1 rhaponticum carthamoides
NT1 rhaponticum integrifolium
NT1 ricinocarpodendron polystachyum
NT1 ricinus communis
NT1 ruta graveolens
NT1 ryania speciosa
NT1 sambucus racemosa
NT1 santalum album
NT1 saussurea lappa
NT1 schinus terebinthifolius
NT1 schoenocaulon officinale
NT1 serratula sogdiana
NT1 silene praemixta
NT1 simmondsia chinensis
NT1 stemona japonica
NT1 stevia rebaudiana
NT1 syzygium aromaticum
NT1 tagetes erecta
NT1 tagetes minuta
NT1 tagetes patula
NT1 tanacetum cinerariifolium
NT1 tanacetum coccineum
NT1 tanacetum parthenium
NT1 tanacetum vulgare
NT1 taraxacum officinale
NT1 tephrosia villosa
NT1 tephrosia vogelii
NT1 tetradium ruticarpum
NT1 tithonia diversifolia
NT1 tomatoes
NT1 tripterygium wilfordii
NT1 veratrum album
NT1 verbascum densiflorum
NT1 vernonia amygdalina
NT1 vitellaria paradoxa
rt aleurites
rt blumea

INSECTICIDAL PLANTS *cont.*
rt carnivorous plants
rt clerodendrum
rt diospyros
rt eucalyptus
rt insect control
rt insecticidal properties
rt insecticides
rt insectivorous plants
rt lavandula
rt lonchocarpus
rt plants
rt rhododendron

INSECTICIDAL PROPERTIES
BT1 pesticidal properties
BT2 properties
rt insect control
rt insecticidal plants
rt insecticide resistance
rt insecticides

INSECTICIDE RESIDUES
BT1 pesticide residues
BT2 residues

INSECTICIDE RESISTANCE
uf *resistance, insecticide*
BT1 pesticide resistance
BT2 resistance
rt behavioural resistance
rt cross resistance
rt insect control
rt insecticidal properties
rt insecticides

INSECTICIDES
BT1 pesticides
NT1 antibiotic insecticides
NT2 abamectin
NT2 ivermectin
NT2 thuringiensin
NT1 arsenical insecticides
NT2 calcium arsenate
NT2 copper acetoarsenite
NT2 copper arsenate
NT2 lead arsenate
NT2 sodium arsenite
NT1 bacterial insecticides
NT2 bacillus cereus
NT2 bacillus popilliae
NT2 bacillus sphaericus
NT2 bacillus thuringiensis subsp. dendrolimus
NT2 bacillus thuringiensis subsp. galleriae
NT2 bacillus thuringiensis subsp. israelensis
NT2 bacillus thuringiensis subsp. kurstaki
NT2 bacillus thuringiensis subsp. thuringiensis
NT1 botanical insecticides
NT2 anabasine
NT2 nicotine
NT2 pyrethrins
NT2 rotenone
NT2 sabadilla
NT1 carbamate insecticides
NT2 allyxycarb
NT2 aminocarb
NT2 bendiocarb
NT2 benfuracarb
NT2 bufencarb
NT2 butacarb
NT2 carbaryl
NT2 carbofuran
NT2 carbosulfan
NT2 cartap
NT2 cloethocarb
NT2 dimetilan
NT2 dioxacarb
NT2 ethiofencarb
NT2 fenobucarb
NT2 furathiocarb
NT2 isoprocarb
NT2 methiocarb
NT2 metolcarb
NT2 mexacarbate
NT2 oxime carbamate insecticides
NT3 aldicarb

INSECTICIDES *cont.*
NT3 aldoxycarb
NT3 butocarboxim
NT3 methomyl
NT3 oxamyl
NT3 thiodicarb
NT3 thiofanox
NT2 pirimicarb
NT2 promecarb
NT2 propoxur
NT2 tazimcarb
NT2 trimethacarb
NT1 dinitrophenol insecticides
NT2 dnoc
NT1 fluorine insecticides
NT2 cryolite
NT2 sodium hexafluorosilicate
NT1 formamidine insecticides
NT2 amitraz
NT2 chlordimeform
NT1 fumigant insecticides
NT2 para-dichlorobenzene
NT2 acetaldehyde
NT2 carbon disulfide
NT2 carbon tetrachloride
NT2 ethyl formate
NT2 ethylene dibromide
NT2 ethylene dichloride
NT2 hydrogen cyanide
NT2 methyl bromide
NT2 methylene chloride
NT2 phosphine
NT2 sulfuryl fluoride
NT1 fungal insecticides
NT2 beauveria bassiana
NT2 metarhizium anisopliae
NT2 verticillium lecanii
NT1 helminth insecticides
NT2 neoaplectana carpocapsae
NT2 romanomermis culicivorax
NT1 insect growth regulators
NT2 chitin synthesis inhibitors
NT3 buprofezin
NT3 chlorfluazuron
NT3 cyromazine
NT3 diflubenzuron
NT3 flufenoxuron
NT3 penfluron
NT3 teflubenzuron
NT3 triflumuron
NT2 juvenile hormone analogues
NT3 epofenonane
NT3 fenoxycarb
NT3 hydroprene
NT3 kinoprene
NT3 methoprene
NT3 triprene
NT2 precocenes
NT3 precocene i
NT3 precocene ii
NT3 precocene iii
NT1 organochlorine insecticides
NT2 camphechlor
NT2 cyclodiene insecticides
NT3 aldrin
NT3 chlordane
NT3 chlordecone
NT3 dieldrin
NT3 dilor
NT3 endosulfan
NT3 endrin
NT3 heptachlor
NT3 isobenzan
NT3 kelevan
NT3 mirex
NT2 ddt
NT2 ethyl-ddd
NT2 hch
NT2 lindane
NT2 methoxychlor
NT2 pentachlorophenol
NT1 organophosphorus insecticides
NT2 organophosphate insecticides
NT3 bromfenvinfos
NT3 chlorfenvinphos
NT3 crotoxyphos
NT3 dichlorvos
NT3 dicrotophos

INSECTICIDES *cont.*
NT3 heptenophos
NT3 mevinphos
NT3 monocrotophos
NT3 naled
NT3 phosphamidon
NT3 propaphos
NT3 tepp
NT3 tetrachlorvinphos
NT2 organothiophosphate insecticides
NT3 azamethiphos
NT3 azinphos-ethyl
NT3 azinphos-methyl
NT3 bromophos
NT3 bromophos-ethyl
NT3 carbophenothion
NT3 chlormephos
NT3 chlorphoxim
NT3 chlorpyrifos
NT3 chlorpyrifos-methyl
NT3 coumaphos
NT3 cyanophos
NT3 cythioate
NT3 demeton
NT3 demeton-o-methyl
NT3 demeton-s-methyl
NT3 demeton-s-methylsulphon
NT3 dialifos
NT3 diazinon
NT3 dichlofenthion
NT3 dimethoate
NT3 dioxabenzofos
NT3 dioxathion
NT3 disulfoton
NT3 ethoprophos
NT3 etrimfos
NT3 famphur
NT3 fenchlorphos
NT3 fenitrothion
NT3 fensulfothion
NT3 fenthion
NT3 formothion
NT3 fosmethilan
NT3 heterophos
NT3 isazofos
NT3 isoxathion
NT3 jodfenphos
NT3 malathion
NT3 mecarbam
NT3 menazon
NT3 methacrifos
NT3 methidathion
NT3 omethoate
NT3 oxydemeton-methyl
NT3 parathion
NT3 parathion-methyl
NT3 phenthoate
NT3 phorate
NT3 phosalone
NT3 phosmet
NT3 phoxim
NT3 pirimiphos-ethyl
NT3 pirimiphos-methyl
NT3 profenofos
NT3 prothiofos
NT3 pyrazophos
NT3 quinalphos
NT3 sulprofos
NT3 temephos
NT3 terbufos
NT3 thiometon
NT3 thionazin
NT3 triazophos
NT3 trichlormetaphos-3
NT3 trifenofos
NT2 phosphonate insecticides
NT3 butonate
NT3 trichlorfon
NT2 phosphonothioate insecticides
NT3 cyanofenphos
NT3 epn
NT3 fonofos
NT3 leptophos
NT3 trichloronat
NT2 phosphoramidate insecticides
NT3 crufomate
NT3 mephosfolan
NT3 phosfolan

INSECTICIDES *cont.*
NT2 phosphoramidothioate insecticides
NT3 acephate
NT3 isofenphos
NT3 methamidophos
NT3 propetamphos
NT1 pyrethroid insecticides
NT2 alpha-cypermethrin
NT2 lambda-cyhalothrin
NT2 allethrin
NT2 bifenthrin
NT2 bioallethrin
NT2 bioethanomethrin
NT2 biopermethrin
NT2 bioresmethrin
NT2 cismethrin
NT2 cyfluthrin
NT2 cyhalothrin
NT2 cypermethrin
NT2 deltamethrin
NT2 fenpropathrin
NT2 fenvalerate
NT2 flucythrinate
NT2 fluvalinate
NT2 permethrin
NT2 phenothrin
NT2 pyrethroid ether insecticides
NT3 etofenprox
NT2 resmethrin
NT2 tetramethrin
NT2 transpermethrin
NT1 unclassified insecticides
NT2 crotamiton
NT2 nifluridide
NT2 rafoxanide
NT2 thiocyclam
NT1 viral insecticides
NT2 baculovirus heliothis
rt bait traps
rt ectoparasiticides
rt flea collars
rt insect control
rt insect pests
rt insect traps
rt insecticidal action
rt insecticidal plants
rt insecticidal properties
rt insecticide resistance
rt insects
rt integrated control
rt mineral oils

insectivora
USE **insectivores**

INSECTIVORES
uf *insectivora*
BT1 mammals
NT1 erinaceidae
NT2 atelerix
NT3 atelerix albiventris
NT2 erinaceus
NT3 erinaceus europaeus
NT2 hemiechinus
NT3 hemiechinus auritus
NT1 soricidae
NT2 anourosorex
NT3 anourosorex squamipes
NT2 blarina
NT3 blarina brevicauda
NT2 crocidura
NT3 crocidura russula
NT3 crocidura suaveolens
NT2 neomys
NT3 neomys anomalus
NT3 neomys fodiens
NT2 sorex
NT3 sorex araneus
NT3 sorex caecutiens
NT2 suncus
NT3 suncus murinus
NT1 talpidae
NT2 talpa
NT3 talpa europaea
NT2 urotrichus

INSECTIVOROUS PLANTS
BT1 carnivorous plants
NT1 dionaea muscipula
NT1 pinguicula moranensis

INSECTIVOROUS PLANTS *cont.*
NT1 sarracenia flava
NT1 utricularia inflexa
rt insecticidal plants
rt insects
rt plants

INSECTS
(families, genera and species are listed under orders; orders are listed as related terms)
uf *insecta*
BT1 arthropods
NT1 aerial insects
NT1 aquatic insects
NT1 beneficial insects
NT2 dung beetles
NT2 silkworms
NT3 antheraea pernyi
NT3 bombyx mori
NT1 insect pests
NT2 bark beetles
NT2 boring insects
NT3 stem borers
NT2 haematophagous insects
NT2 leaf miners
NT2 leafhoppers
NT2 locusts
NT2 planthoppers
NT1 parasitoids
NT2 hyperparasitoids
NT1 predatory insects
NT1 social insects
NT1 soil insects
rt coleoptera
rt collembola
rt dermaptera
rt dictyoptera
rt diptera
rt embioptera
rt entomology
rt entomopathogens
rt ephemeroptera
rt grylloblattodea
rt heteroptera
rt homoptera
rt honeydew
rt hymenoptera
rt insect attractants
rt insect traps
rt insectaries
rt insecticides
rt insectivorous plants
rt insects as food
rt isoptera
rt lepidoptera
rt mecoptera
rt neuroptera
rt odonata
rt orthoptera
rt phasmida
rt phoresy
rt phthiraptera
rt plant pests
rt plecoptera
rt pollinators
rt protura
rt psocoptera
rt siphonaptera
rt strepsiptera
rt thysanoptera
rt thysanura
rt trichoptera

INSECTS AS FOOD
uf *edible insects*
uf *insect larvae as food*
BT1 foods
rt insects

INSEMINATION
BT1 mating
BT2 sexual reproduction
BT3 reproduction
NT1 double insemination
NT1 impregnation
rt artificial insemination
rt copulation
rt semen
rt service crates

INSERTIONAL MUTAGENESIS
HN from 1989
BT1 mutagenesis

INSERVICE TRAINING
BT1 vocational training
BT2 training
NT1 apprenticeship
NT1 on-farm training
rt continuing education
rt on-the-job training (agricola)
rt practical education

INSOLATION
BT1 meteorological factors
BT2 climatic factors
rt albedo
rt energy balance
rt shading
rt solar radiation
rt sunburn

INSPECTION
BT1 quality controls
BT2 consumer protection
BT3 protection
BT2 controls
NT1 food inspection
NT2 meat inspection
NT3 antemortem examinations (agricola)
NT3 carcass condemnation
rt sampling

INSTALLATION
rt drain laying

INSTALLATIONS
rt machinery

INSTALLMENT CREDIT (AGRICOLA)
BT1 credit
BT2 finance

INSTANT COFFEE
uf *coffee, instant*
BT1 convenience foods
BT2 foods
rt coffee

INSTANT FOODS
BT1 convenience foods
BT2 foods
rt solubilization

INSTANT MILK
uf *milk, instant*
BT1 convenience foods
BT2 foods
BT1 milk products
BT2 products

INSTANT SUGAR
HN from 1990
uf *transformed sugar*
BT1 sugar
BT2 plant products
BT3 products
rt amorphous sugar
rt instantizing process

INSTANTIZING PROCESS
BT1 processing
rt instant sugar
rt solubilization

INSTILLATION
BT1 application methods
BT2 methodology

INSTITUTION BUILDING
BT1 development planning
rt administration
rt infrastructure
rt social institutions

INSTITUTIONAL CATERING
AF institutional food service
BT1 catering
rt catering industry

INSTITUTIONAL FOOD SERVICE
BF institutional catering
BT1 food service

INSTITUTIONAL FOOD SERVICE cont.
rt institutions (agricola)

INSTITUTIONS (AGRICOLA)
NT1 correctional institutions
NT1 residential institutions
rt institutional food service
rt organizations

INSTRUCTION (AGRICOLA)
NT1 clothing instruction (agricola)
NT1 cooking instruction (agricola)
NT1 individualized instruction (agricola)
rt multimedia instruction (agricola)
rt teaching methods

instructional materials
USE **teaching materials**

instructional media
USE **audiovisual aids**

INSTRUMENTAL MUSIC
BT1 music
BT2 performing arts
BT3 arts
NT1 orchestras

INSTRUMENTATION
rt automatic control
rt automation
rt controls
rt data collection
rt data communication
rt experimental equipment
rt instruments
rt measurement
rt microprocessors
rt monitors

INSTRUMENTS
NT1 accelerometers
NT1 balances
NT1 callipers
NT1 cannulae
NT1 cautery
NT1 dendrometers
NT1 densitometers
NT1 dividers
NT1 dynamometers
NT1 ergometers
NT1 evaporimeters
NT1 gauges
NT2 humidity gauges
NT2 level gauges
NT2 pressure gauges
NT2 rain gauges
NT2 strain gauges
NT2 vacuum gauges
NT1 haematocrit
NT1 hydrometers
NT1 hygrometers
NT1 indicating instruments
NT1 infiltrometers
NT1 lysimeters
NT1 measuring orifices
NT1 meteorological instruments
NT2 anemometers
NT2 rain gauges
NT2 solarimeters
NT1 meters
NT2 fat meters
NT3 ultrasonic fat meters
NT2 flow meters
NT3 venturi tubes
NT2 milk meters
NT2 moisture meters
NT3 electrical moisture meters
NT3 infrared moisture meters
NT2 ohmeters
NT2 sound level meters
NT1 microscopes
NT2 electron microscopes
NT3 scanning electron microscopes
NT1 microsyringes
NT1 musical instruments
NT1 olfactometers

INSTRUMENTS *cont.*
NT1 optical instruments
NT1 penetrometers
NT1 photometers
NT2 spectrophotometers
NT1 piezometers
NT1 porometers
NT1 portable instruments
NT1 potentiometers
NT1 probes
NT1 profilometers
NT1 psychrometers
NT2 aspirated psychrometers
NT1 pyranometers
NT1 radiometers
NT1 recording instruments
NT2 counters
NT3 seed counters
NT2 tape recorders
NT2 video cameras
NT2 video recorders
NT1 spectrometers
NT2 mass spectrometers
NT1 speedometers
NT1 surgical instruments
NT1 surveying instruments
NT2 relascopes
NT2 wedge prisms
NT1 tachometers
NT1 tensiometers
NT1 testers
NT1 thermocouples
NT1 thermometers
NT2 temperature gauges
NT1 thermostats
NT1 timers
NT1 torquemeters
NT1 torsiometers
NT1 viscometers
NT1 weighers
NT2 cattle weighers
NT2 pig weighers
NT2 weighbridges
rt calibration
rt components
rt detectors
rt electronics
rt equipment
rt instrumentation
rt laboratory equipment
rt measurement
rt mirrors
rt monitors
rt sensors
rt transducers

instruments, indicating
USE **indicating instruments**

instruments, portable
USE **portable instruments**

instruments, recording
USE **recording instruments**

INSULASPIS
BT1 diaspididae
BT2 coccoidea
BT3 sternorrhyncha
BT4 homoptera
rt lepidosaphes

insulaspis gloverii
USE **lepidosaphes gloverii**

INSULATING MATERIALS
BT1 materials
NT1 asbestos
NT1 dielectrics
NT1 glassfibre
NT1 glasswool
NT1 polystyrenes
NT1 vermiculite
rt building materials
rt insulation

INSULATION
rt energy conservation
rt heat conservation
rt heat transfer
rt insulating materials
rt noise abatement
rt rockwool

INSULATION FINISHES (AGRICOLA)
BT1 textile finishes (agricola)
BT2 finishes

INSULIN
BT1 hypoglycaemic agents
BT2 haematologic agents
BT3 drugs
BT1 pancreatic hormones
BT2 hormones
BT1 polypeptides
BT2 peptides
rt c-peptide
rt diabetes
rt glucose tolerance
rt hyperinsulinaemia
rt hyperinsulinism
rt insulin secretion
rt pancreas
rt proinsulin

INSULIN-LIKE GROWTH FACTOR
HN from 1989
uf *somatomedin c*
BT1 somatomedin
BT2 growth factors
BT3 hormones
BT2 neuropeptides
BT3 peptides

INSULIN SECRETION
BT1 secretion
BT2 physiological functions
rt insulin
rt pancreas
rt pancreas islets

INSURANCE
NT1 agricultural insurance
NT2 animal insurance
NT2 crop insurance
NT2 hail insurance
NT1 automobile insurance (agricola)
NT2 collision insurance (agricola)
NT2 no fault automobile insurance (agricola)
NT1 basic hospital expense ihsurance (agricola)
NT1 cooperative insurance
NT1 credit insurance
NT2 export credits
NT1 disability insurance (agricola)
NT1 dread disease insurance (agricola)
NT1 health insurance (agricola)
NT1 homeowners' insurance (agricola)
NT2 basic homeowners' insurance (agricola)
NT2 comprehensive homeowners' insurance (agricola)
NT1 insurance premiums
NT1 liability insurance (agricola)
NT1 life insurance
NT2 adjustable life insurance (agricola)
NT2 universal life insurance (agricola)
NT2 variable life insurance (agricola)
NT2 whole life insurance (agricola)
NT1 major medical insurance (agricola)
NT1 medicare (agricola)
NT1 medigap insurance (agricola)
NT1 social insurance
NT2 accident benefits
NT2 old age benefits
NT2 sickness benefits
NT1 tenants' insurance (agricola)
NT1 term life insurance (agricola)
rt property protection
rt risk
rt social security
rt third party payments (agricola)

INSURANCE PREMIUMS
uf *premiums*
BT1 insurance

INTAKE
NT1 caloric intake (agricola)
NT1 energy intake
NT1 feed intake
NT2 plane of nutrition
NT1 fluid intake (agricola)
NT1 food intake
NT2 ingestion
NT1 nutrient intake (agricola)
NT2 recommended dietary intakes (agricola)
NT1 protein intake
NT1 voluntary intake
NT1 water intake

INTEGER PROGRAMMING
uf *discrete programming*
uf *programming, discrete*
uf *programming, integer*
BT1 programming
BT2 optimization methods
BT3 optimization
rt optimization methods

INTEGRATED CIRCUITS
BT1 circuits
rt electronics
rt microprocessors

INTEGRATED CONTROL
uf *integrated plant protection*
uf *plant protection, integrated*
BT1 pest control
BT2 control
rt biological control
rt insecticides
rt integrated pest management
rt plant protection
rt weed control

INTEGRATED PEST MANAGEMENT
uf *ipm*
BT1 pest management
BT2 pest control
BT3 control
rt integrated control

integrated plant protection
USE **integrated control**

integrated rural development
USE **rural development**

INTEGRATED SYSTEMS
BT1 systems

INTEGRATION
BT1 concentration of production
BT2 socioeconomic organization
NT1 horizontal integration
NT1 mergers
NT1 social integration
NT1 vertical integration
rt cartels
rt combines
rt contract legislation
rt cooperation
rt diversification
rt economic unions

integration, horizontal
USE **horizontal integration**

integration, lateral
USE **horizontal integration**

integration, vertical
USE **vertical integration**

INTEGUMENT
uf *tegument*
BT1 body parts
NT1 bristles
NT1 claws
NT1 comb
NT1 feathers
NT2 hamuli
NT1 hair

INTEGUMENT *cont.*
NT1 hooves
NT1 horns
NT2 antlers
NT3 velvet
NT1 nail
NT1 scales
NT1 shells
NT1 skin
NT2 dermis
NT2 skin folds
NT1 wattles
rt animal anatomy
rt cuticle

intelligence
USE **mental ability**

INTELLIGENCE TESTS (AGRICOLA)
BT1 tests
rt mental ability

INTENSIFICATION
rt farming systems
rt intensive production
rt labour intensity

INTENSIVE CROPPING
BT1 cropping systems
rt intensive crops
rt intensive farming
rt intensive production

INTENSIVE CROPS
rt crops
rt intensive cropping

INTENSIVE FARMING
BT1 farming
NT1 intensive livestock farming
NT2 factory farming
NT3 battery husbandry
rt intensive cropping
rt intensive husbandry
rt intensive production

intensive forestry
USE **intensive silviculture**

INTENSIVE HUSBANDRY
BT1 husbandry
rt animal husbandry
rt intensive farming

INTENSIVE LIVESTOCK FARMING
BT1 intensive farming
BT2 farming
BT1 livestock farming
BT2 farming
NT1 factory farming
NT2 battery husbandry
rt animal husbandry
rt feedlots

INTENSIVE PRODUCTION
uf production, intensive
BT1 agricultural production
BT2 production
rt intensification
rt intensive cropping
rt intensive farming
rt intensive silviculture
rt land use

INTENSIVE SILVICULTURE
uf intensive forestry
BT1 silviculture
BT2 forestry
rt intensive production

INTER-AMERICAN DEVELOPMENT BANK
BT1 development banks
BT2 banks
BT3 financial institutions
BT4 organizations
BT2 development agencies
BT3 organizations
BT1 international organizations
BT2 organizations
rt development policy

inter-farm enterprises
USE **cooperative farm enterprises**

INTERACTIONS
rt genotype environment interaction
rt genotype nutrition interaction
rt nutrient drug interactions (agricola)
rt nutrient nutrient interactions (agricola)
rt plant interaction
rt responses
rt surface interactions

INTERCELLULAR SPACES
HN from 1990
rt cells
rt wood anatomy

INTERCEPTION
rt canopy
rt evaporation
rt evapotranspiration
rt precipitation
rt stemflow
rt throughfall

INTERCEPTIONS
rt introduced species
rt quarantine

interchange
USE **chromosome translocation**

intercooperative enterprises
USE **cooperative farm enterprises**

INTERCROPPING
BT1 cropping systems
NT1 alley cropping
rt agroforestry
rt catch cropping
rt companion crops
rt crop mixtures
rt intercrops
rt interplanting
rt mixed cropping
rt oversowing

INTERCROPS
rt companion crops
rt crops
rt intercropping
rt interplanting

INTERDIGITAL DERMATITIS
BT1 dermatitis
BT2 skin diseases
BT3 organic diseases
BT4 diseases
rt foot diseases

INTERDIGITAL HYPERPLASIA
BT1 hyperplasia
BT2 congenital abnormalities
BT3 abnormalities
rt foot diseases

INTERDISCIPLINARY RESEARCH
uf research, interdisciplinary
BT1 research
rt organization of research

INTEREST GROUPS
BT1 groups
BT1 organizations
NT1 beekeepers' associations
NT1 breeders' associations
NT1 clubs
NT2 4-h clubs (agricola)
NT2 health clubs
NT1 farmers' associations
NT1 pressure groups
NT1 trade associations
NT1 trade unions
NT2 agricultural trade unions
rt occupations
rt target groups

INTEREST RATES
BT1 credit control
BT2 controls
NT1 preferential interest rates
rt interest repayment
rt loans

INTEREST REPAYMENT
BT1 repayment
rt interest rates

INTERFACE
NT1 ice-water interface
NT1 sediment water interface
rt contact angle
rt surface tension

INTERFERENCE
BT1 crossing over
rt chiasmata

INTERFEROMETRY
BT1 analytical methods
BT2 methodology

INTERFERON
BT1 antiviral agents
BT2 antiinfective agents
BT3 drugs
BT1 immunological factors
BT1 proteins
BT2 peptides
rt immune response
rt immunology
rt nonspecific immunostimulation
rt viral interference

INTERGENERIC HYBRIDIZATION
uf hybridization, intergeneric
BT1 hybridization
BT2 crossing
BT3 breeding
rt wide hybridization

INTERGRADE MINERALS
BT1 clay minerals
BT2 minerals
rt interstratified minerals

INTERIOR DECORATION
BT1 home economics
rt ornamental plants

INTERIOR DESIGN (AGRICOLA)
rt design

INTERLEUKIN 1
BT1 interleukins
BT2 immunological factors

INTERLEUKIN 2
BT1 interleukins
BT2 immunological factors

INTERLEUKINS
BT1 immunological factors
NT1 interleukin 1
NT1 interleukin 2

INTERMARRIAGE (AGRICOLA)
BT1 marriage
BT2 family structure

INTERMEDIATE CARE (AGRICOLA)
rt health care (agricola)

intermediate grades
USE **elementary education (agricola)**

INTERMEDIATE HOSTS
BT1 hosts
rt disease vectors
rt host parasite relationships
rt parasitism

intermediate technology
USE **appropriate technology**

INTERMITTENT DRYING
uf drying, intermittent
BT1 drying
BT2 dehydration
BT3 processing

INTERMITTENT LIGHT
uf light, intermittent
BT1 light
BT2 electromagnetic radiation
BT3 radiation
rt artificial light
rt illumination

INTERMITTENT SPRAYING
uf spraying, intermittent
BT1 spraying
BT2 application methods
BT3 methodology

INTERNAL BARK NECROSIS
BT1 necroses
BT2 plant disorders
BT3 disorders
rt apples

INTERNAL BREAKDOWN
BT1 storage disorders

INTERNAL BROWNING
BT1 plant disorders
BT2 disorders
rt pears

INTERNAL COMBUSTION ENGINES
uf engines, internal combustion
BT1 engines
BT2 machinery
NT1 spark ignition engines
rt distributors
rt fuel injection
rt ignition
rt spark ignition
rt sparking plugs
rt sparks
rt superchargers

INTERNAL DRAINAGE
BT1 soil water movement
BT2 movement
rt drainage

INTERNAL ELECTRIC POTENTIAL
BT1 electric potential
BT2 electricity
BT3 energy sources

INTERNAL PRESSURE
uf pressure, internal
BT1 pressure
BT2 physical properties
BT3 properties
rt wall pressure

INTERNATIONAL AGREEMENTS
uf commodity agreements
BT1 international cooperation
BT2 cooperation
BT3 socioeconomic organization
NT1 lome convention
NT1 monetary agreements
NT1 trade agreements
NT2 gatt
NT2 trade negotiations
NT2 trade preferences
NT1 treaty of rome
rt commodities
rt development aid
rt stabilization

INTERNATIONAL COMPARISONS
rt cross cultural studies

INTERNATIONAL COOPERATION
BT1 cooperation
BT2 socioeconomic organization
NT1 international agreements
NT2 lome convention
NT2 monetary agreements
NT2 trade agreements
NT3 gatt
NT3 trade negotiations
NT3 trade preferences
NT2 treaty of rome
rt development aid

INTERNATIONAL DAIRY FEDERATION
BT1 international organizations
BT2 organizations
rt dairy cooperatives
rt trade associations

international labour organization
USE **ilo**

INTERNATIONAL LOANS
BT1 loans
BT2 credit
BT3 finance

INTERNATIONAL MONETARY FUND
BT1 financial institutions
BT2 organizations
BT1 funds
BT1 international organizations
BT2 organizations
rt monetary policy

INTERNATIONAL ORGANIZATIONS
BT1 organizations
NT1 acp
NT1 aglinet
NT1 agrep
NT1 asean
NT1 benelux
NT1 cab international
NT1 cepfar
NT1 cgiar
NT2 cimmyt
NT2 icarda
NT1 cmea
NT1 colombo plan
NT1 common afro-mauritian organization
NT1 eaggf
NT1 efta
NT1 european communities
NT1 european farm accounting network
NT1 european parliament
NT1 european regional development fund
NT1 european social fund
NT1 european society for rural sociology
NT1 gatt
NT1 iaea
NT1 icumsa
NT1 idrc
NT1 ifad
NT1 ilo
NT1 inter-american development bank
NT1 international dairy federation
NT1 international monetary fund
NT1 iso
NT1 iufro
NT1 multinational corporations
NT1 nato
NT1 new international economic order
NT1 oecd
NT1 office international des epizooties
NT1 opec
NT1 seato
NT1 south pacific commission
NT1 un
NT2 food and agriculture organization
NT3 world food council
NT3 world food programme
NT2 unctad
NT2 undp
NT2 unep
NT2 unesco
NT2 unido
NT1 warsaw treaty organization
NT1 who
NT1 wmo
NT1 world bank
NT1 world tourism organization
rt commonwealth of nations

INTERNATIONAL TOURISM
BT1 tourism
rt international travel

INTERNATIONAL TRADE
uf trade, international
BT1 trade
NT1 exports
NT2 export diversification
NT1 imports
rt division of labour
rt new international economic order
rt trade agreements
rt trade barriers
rt trade diversion
rt trade liberalization
rt trade negotiations
rt trade policy
rt trade preferences
rt trade relations
rt transit trade
rt world markets

INTERNATIONAL TRANSPORT
uf transport, international
BT1 transport

INTERNATIONAL TRAVEL
BT1 travel
rt international tourism
rt passports

INTERNODES
BT1 nerve tissue
BT2 animal tissues
BT3 tissues
BT1 stems
BT2 plant

INTERPERSONAL RELATIONS
rt human relations (agricola)
rt individuals
rt relationships
rt social participation

INTERPLANTING
BT1 mixed cropping
BT2 cropping systems
BT1 planting
rt intercropping
rt intercrops
rt oversowing
rt underplanting
rt undersowing

INTERPRETATION
rt visitor interpretation

INTERRILL EROSION
uf erosion, interrill
BT1 water erosion
BT2 erosion
rt rill erosion

INTERROW CULTIVATION
BT1 cultivation
rt weed control

INTERSECTORAL PLANNING
uf intersectorial planning
uf planning, intersectoral
BT1 planning
rt economic sectors

intersectoral relations
USE **terms of trade**

intersectorial planning
USE **intersectoral planning**

INTERSEXUALITY
BT1 sex differentiation disorders
BT2 congenital abnormalities
BT3 abnormalities
BT2 reproductive disorders
BT3 functional disorders
BT4 animal disorders
BT5 disorders
NT1 freemartinism
NT1 pseudohermaphroditism

INTERSPECIFIC COMPETITION
BT1 biological competition
NT1 crop weed competition

INTERSPECIFIC HYBRIDIZATION
uf hybridization, interspecific
BT1 hybridization
BT2 crossing
BT3 breeding
rt wide hybridization

INTERSTITIAL FLUIDS
HN from 1989
BT1 body fluids
BT2 fluids

INTERSTOCKS
rt grafting
rt rootstock scion relationships
rt rootstocks
rt scions

INTERSTRATIFIED MINERALS
BT1 clay minerals
BT2 minerals
rt intergrade minerals

INTERVENTION
BT1 market regulations
BT2 regulations
rt marketing boards

INTERVERTEBRAL DISKS
BT1 spine
BT2 bones
BT3 musculoskeletal system
BT4 body parts

INTERVIEWS
BT1 data collection
BT2 collection

INTESTINAL ABSORPTION
BT1 digestive absorption
BT2 digestion
BT3 physiological functions
rt absorption

INTESTINAL DISEASES
uf enteropathy
uf gastroenteropathy
BT1 gastrointestinal diseases
BT2 digestive system diseases
BT3 organic diseases
BT4 diseases
NT1 appendicitis (agricola)
NT1 blind loop syndrome
NT1 coeliac syndrome
NT1 colitis
NT2 ulcerative colitis
NT1 crohn's disease
NT1 diverticulosis
NT1 dysentery
NT2 swine dysentery
NT1 enteritis
NT1 enterocolitis
NT1 gastroenteritis
NT1 haemorrhagic enteritis
NT1 irritable colon
NT1 short bowel syndrome
NT1 sprue
NT1 steatorrhoea
NT1 tropical sprue
NT1 typhlitis
rt enterotoxaemia
rt enterotoxins
rt intestines

INTESTINAL MICROORGANISMS
BT1 microbial flora
BT2 flora
BT1 microorganisms
rt intestines
rt rumen flora

INTESTINAL MOTILITY
BT1 digestive tract motility
BT2 motility
BT3 movement
rt intestines

INTESTINAL MUCOSA
uf intestine epithelium
BT1 digestive tract mucosa
BT2 mucosa
BT3 membranes
rt intestines

INTESTINAL OBSTRUCTION
uf obstruction, intestinal
BT1 obstruction
BT2 digestive disorders
BT3 functional disorders
BT4 animal disorders
BT5 disorders
NT1 duodenal obstruction
NT1 intussusception

INTESTINE BYPASS
BT1 surgical operations
rt intestines

intestine epithelium
USE **intestinal mucosa**

intestine, large
USE **large intestine**

INTESTINE RESECTION
BT1 surgical operations
rt intestines
rt obesity

intestine, small
USE **small intestine**

INTESTINES
BT1 digestive system
BT2 body parts
NT1 jejunum
NT1 large intestine
NT2 caecum
NT2 colon
NT1 midgut
NT1 rectum
NT1 small intestine
NT2 duodenum
NT2 ileum
NT2 villi
rt dysentery
rt endotoxins
rt enterotoxins
rt intestinal diseases
rt intestinal microorganisms
rt intestinal motility
rt intestinal mucosa
rt intestine bypass
rt intestine resection
rt peyer patches
rt trocarization

INTOLERANCE
NT1 food intolerance (agricola)
rt sucrose intolerance
rt susceptibility
rt tolerance

intracommunity markets
USE **intracommunity trade**

INTRACOMMUNITY TRADE
uf intracommunity markets
uf trade, intracommunity
BT1 trade
rt european communities

intradermal tests
USE **skin tests**

INTRAFARM TRANSPORT
uf transport, intrafarm
BT1 transport
rt farm roads
rt vehicles

INTRAGENIC RECOMBINATION
HN from 1989
BT1 recombination
BT2 genetic change

INTRALIPID
BT1 fat emulsions
BT2 emulsions
rt parenteral feeding

INTRAMUSCULAR INJECTION
BT1 injection
BT2 application methods
BT3 methodology
rt muscles

INTRAPERITONEAL INJECTION
BT1 injection

INTRAPERITONEAL INJECTION *cont.*
BT2 application methods
BT3 methodology
rt peritoneum

INTRASPECIFIC COMPETITION
BT1 biological competition
NT1 mating competitiveness

INTRAUTERINE DEVICES
BT1 contraceptives

INTRAUTERINE INSEMINATION
HN from 1989
BT1 artificial insemination
BT2 animal breeding methods
BT3 breeding methods
BT4 methodology

INTRAVENOUS DRUG USERS
HN from 1990
rt acquired immune deficiency syndrome
rt drug addiction
rt immunocompromised hosts
rt opportunistic infections
rt substance abuse (agricola)

INTRAVENOUS INJECTION
HN from 1990
BT1 injection
BT2 application methods
BT3 methodology

INTRINSIC FACTOR
BT1 mucoproteins
BT2 glycoproteins
BT3 proteins
BT4 peptides
rt vitamin b12

INTRODUCED SPECIES
uf *importations*
BT1 species
rt importation
rt interceptions
rt plant introduction

INTRODUCTION
NT1 plant introduction
rt biological control agents
rt importation
rt imported breeds

INTROGRESSION
rt hybridization

INTROMISSION
BT1 copulation
BT2 mating
BT3 sexual reproduction
BT4 reproduction
rt penis

INTRONS
HN from 1990
rt dna
rt exons
rt genes
rt transcription

INTSIA
BT1 leguminosae
NT1 intsia bijuga

INTSIA BIJUGA
BT1 intsia
BT2 leguminosae

INTUSSUSCEPTION
BT1 intestinal obstruction
BT2 obstruction
BT3 digestive disorders
BT4 functional disorders
BT5 animal disorders
BT6 disorders
rt colic

INUIT
HN from 1990; previously "eskimos"
uf *eskimos*
BT1 ethnic groups
BT2 groups
rt polar regions

INULA
BT1 compositae
NT1 inula bifrons
NT1 inula britannica
NT1 inula cappa
NT1 inula conyza
NT1 inula grandis
NT1 inula helenium
NT1 inula magnifica
NT1 inula obtusifolia
NT1 inula racemosa
NT1 inula royleana
NT1 inula salicina
NT1 inula spiraeifolia
NT1 inula viscosa

INULA BIFRONS
BT1 inula
BT2 compositae

INULA BRITANNICA
BT1 inula
BT2 compositae

INULA CAPPA
BT1 inula
BT2 compositae

INULA CONYZA
BT1 inula
BT2 compositae

INULA GRANDIS
BT1 inula
BT2 compositae

INULA HELENIUM
BT1 essential oil plants
BT2 oil plants
BT1 inula
BT2 compositae

INULA MAGNIFICA
BT1 inula
BT2 compositae

INULA OBTUSIFOLIA
BT1 inula
BT2 compositae

INULA RACEMOSA
BT1 antifungal plants
BT1 inula
BT2 compositae
BT1 medicinal plants

INULA ROYLEANA
BT1 inula
BT2 compositae

INULA SALICINA
BT1 inula
BT2 compositae

INULA SPIRAEIFOLIA
BT1 inula
BT2 compositae

INULA VISCOSA
BT1 inula
BT2 compositae
BT1 nematicidal plants
BT2 pesticidal plants

inulase
USE **inulinase**

INULIN
BT1 fructans
BT2 polysaccharides
BT3 carbohydrates
rt polymnia sonchifolia

inulin fructanohydrolase
USE **inulinase**

INULINASE
(ec 3.2.1.7)
uf *inulase*
uf *inulin fructanohydrolase*
BT1 o-glycoside hydrolases
BT2 glycosidases
BT3 hydrolases
BT4 enzymes

INVASION
HN from 1989
NT1 cell invasion
NT2 erythrocyte invasion
rt parasites
rt weeds

INVENTORIES
NT1 forest inventories
NT2 angle count
rt book-keeping
rt catalogues
rt data collection
rt enumeration
rt stocks

inventories, forest
USE **forest inventories**

INVERSION
rt chromosome translocation
rt inversion polymorphism
rt parturition complications
rt pericentric inversion
rt temperature inversion

INVERSION POLYMORPHISM
BT1 polymorphism
rt inversion

INVERT SUGAR
BT1 reducing sugars
BT2 sugars
BT3 carbohydrates
rt fructose
rt glucose
rt sucrose

invertase
USE **β-fructofuranosidase**

INVERTEBRATES
rt acanthocephala
rt animals
rt annelida
rt arthropods
rt brachiopoda
rt chaetognatha
rt coelenterata
rt echinodermata
rt echiuroidea
rt ectoprocta
rt endoprocta
rt haemolymph
rt mollusca
rt nematoda
rt nematomorpha
rt nemertea
rt parazoa
rt phoronida
rt platyhelminthes
rt pogonophora
rt protozoa
rt rotifera
rt sipunculoidea
rt urochordata

INVESTMENT
uf *capital outlay*
NT1 foreign investment
NT1 parental investment
NT1 private investment
NT1 public investment
NT1 reinvestment
rt amortization
rt capital
rt capital formation
rt development banks
rt finance
rt investment banks
rt investment planning
rt investment policy
rt investment requirements
rt risk

INVESTMENT BANKS
uf *banks, investment*
BT1 banks
BT2 financial institutions
BT3 organizations
rt development banks
rt investment
rt world bank

INVESTMENT PLANNING
BT1 planning
rt farm planning
rt investment
rt investment policy

INVESTMENT POLICY
uf *financial policy*
uf *policy, investment*
BT1 economic policy
NT1 investment promotion
NT1 investment requirements
rt investment
rt investment planning

INVESTMENT PROMOTION
BT1 investment policy
BT2 economic policy
rt funds
rt grants
rt preferential interest rates

INVESTMENT REQUIREMENTS
BT1 investment policy
BT2 economic policy
rt investment

investments
USE **assets**
OR **capital**

INVOLUTION
rt contraction
rt shrinkage
rt uterus

IODAMOEBA
BT1 sarcomastigophora
BT2 protozoa
NT1 iodamoeba buetschlii

IODAMOEBA BUETSCHLII
BT1 iodamoeba
BT2 sarcomastigophora
BT3 protozoa

IODIDE
BT1 anions
BT2 ions
rt iodides
rt iodine

IODIDES
BT1 halides
BT2 inorganic salts
BT3 inorganic compounds
BT3 salts
NT1 potassium iodide
rt iodide
rt iodine

iodinated casein
USE **thyroprotein**

IODINATED LIPIDS
BT1 lipids
rt iodination
rt iodine

IODINATED PROTEINS
uf *iodoprotein*
BT1 organoiodine compounds
BT2 organic halogen compounds
BT1 proteins
BT2 peptides
NT1 thyroglobulin
NT1 thyroprotein
rt iodination
rt iodine

IODINATION
BT1 processing
rt deiodination
rt iodinated lipids
rt iodinated proteins
rt iodine
rt iodized salt
rt thyroprotein

IODINE
BT1 antiseptics
BT2 antiinfective agents
BT3 drugs
BT1 disinfectants

IODINE *cont.*
BT1 halogens
BT2 nonmetallic elements
BT3 elements
BT1 trace elements
BT2 elements
rt iodide
rt iodides
rt iodinated lipids
rt iodinated proteins
rt iodination
rt iodized salt
rt iodophors
rt organoiodine compounds
rt thyroprotein

IODINE VALUE
rt fats

IODIZED SALT
uf salt, iodized
BT1 salt
BT2 flavour compounds
BT1 thyroactive substances
rt iodination
rt iodine

IODO AMINO ACIDS
uf amino acids, iodo
BT1 amino acids
BT2 carboxylic acids
BT3 organic acids
BT4 acids
BT2 organic nitrogen compounds
BT1 organoiodine compounds
BT2 organic halogen compounds
NT1 diiodothyronine
NT1 iodothyronine
NT1 thyroxine
NT2 d-thyroxine
NT2 l-thyroxine
NT1 triiodothyronine

iodoacetate
USE **iodoacetic acid**

IODOACETIC ACID
uf iodoacetate
BT1 enzyme inhibitors
BT2 metabolic inhibitors
BT3 inhibitors
BT1 monocarboxylic acids
BT2 carboxylic acids
BT3 organic acids
BT4 acids
BT1 organoiodine compounds
BT2 organic halogen compounds

iododeoxyuridine
USE **idoxuridine**

iodofenphos
USE **jodfenphos**

2-IODOPHENOL
BT1 organoiodine compounds
BT2 organic halogen compounds
BT1 phenols
BT2 alcohols
BT2 phenolic compounds
BT3 aromatic compounds

IODOPHORS
HN from 1989
BT1 disinfectants
rt iodine

iodoprotein
USE **iodinated proteins**

IODOTHYRONINE
BT1 iodo amino acids
BT2 amino acids
BT3 carboxylic acids
BT4 organic acids
BT5 acids
BT3 organic nitrogen compounds
BT2 organoiodine compounds

IODOTHYRONINE *cont.*
BT3 organic halogen compounds
BT1 thyroactive substances
rt thyroxine

ION ACTIVITY
HN from 1990
rt ion exchange
rt ions

ION BALANCE
uf cation-anion balance
rt ion exchange
rt ions

ION EXCHANGE
NT1 anion exchange
NT1 base saturation
NT1 cation exchange
NT1 charge characteristics
NT1 electrical double layer
NT1 exchange acidity
NT1 permanent charge
rt charge density
rt exchangeable cations
rt ion activity
rt ion balance
rt ion exchange capacity
rt ion exchange chromatography
rt ion exchange resins
rt ion exchange treatment
rt ions
rt sorption
rt variable charge

ION EXCHANGE CAPACITY
NT1 anion exchange capacity
NT1 cation exchange capacity
rt capacity
rt ion exchange
rt ions

ION EXCHANGE CHROMATOGRAPHY
BT1 chromatography
BT2 analytical methods
BT3 methodology
rt ion exchange

ION EXCHANGE RESINS
BT1 resins
NT1 anion exchange resins
NT2 colestipol
NT1 cation exchange resins
NT1 colestyramine
rt fertilizer carriers
rt ion exchange

ION EXCHANGE TREATMENT
BT1 processing
rt ion exchange
rt treatment

ION STRENGTH EFFECTS
rt ions
rt plant nutrition

ION TRANSPORT
rt active transport
rt electrolysis
rt ionophores
rt ions
rt transport

ION UPTAKE
BT1 uptake
rt ions

IONIZATION
NT1 air ionization
rt ionizing radiation

IONIZING RADIATION
uf radiation, ionizing
BT1 radiation
rt corona discharge
rt ionization

β-IONONE
(for retrieval spell out "beta")
BT1 ketones
rt retinol

IONOPHORES
NT1 gramicidin s
NT1 nigericin
NT1 polymyxin b
NT1 valinomycin
rt electrophoresis
rt ion transport
rt movement

IONS
NT1 anions
NT2 bromide
NT2 carbonate
NT2 chloride
NT2 dithionite
NT2 fluoride
NT2 iodide
NT2 nitrate
NT2 organic anions
NT2 sulfate
NT2 tungstate
NT1 cations
NT2 ammonium
NT2 exchangeable cations
NT3 exchangeable sodium
NT2 hydrogen ions
NT2 metal ions
NT3 calcium ions
NT3 ferric ions
NT3 ferrous ions
NT3 silver ions
rt electrolytes
rt ion activity
rt ion balance
rt ion exchange
rt ion exchange capacity
rt ion strength effects
rt ion transport
rt ion uptake
rt specific ion electrodes

IOTONCHUS
HN from 1990
BT1 mononchidae
BT2 nematoda

IOWA
BT1 corn belt of usa
BT2 north central states of usa
BT3 usa
BT4 north america
BT5 america

IOXYNIL
BT1 nitrile herbicides
BT2 herbicides
BT3 pesticides

IPHEION
BT1 liliaceae
NT1 ipheion uniflorum

IPHEION UNIFLORUM
uf brodiaea uniflora
uf triteleia uniflora
BT1 ipheion
BT2 liliaceae
BT1 ornamental bulbs

IPHIAULAX
BT1 braconidae
BT2 hymenoptera

IPHISEIUS
BT1 phytoseiidae
BT2 mesostigmata
BT3 acari

ipm
USE **integrated pest management**

IPOMOEA
uf morning glory
BT1 convolvulaceae
NT1 ipomoea aculeata
NT1 ipomoea aquatica
NT1 ipomoea arborescens
NT1 ipomoea aristolochiaefolia
NT1 ipomoea batatas
NT1 ipomoea cairica
NT1 ipomoea carnea
NT1 ipomoea congesta
NT1 ipomoea fastigiata

IPOMOEA *cont.*
NT1 ipomoea heptaphylla
NT1 ipomoea hirsutula
NT1 ipomoea lacunosa
NT1 ipomoea obscura
NT1 ipomoea operculata
NT1 ipomoea pandurata
NT1 ipomoea parasitica
NT1 ipomoea pentaphylla
NT1 ipomoea pes-caprae
NT1 ipomoea pes-tigridis
NT1 ipomoea plebeia
NT1 ipomoea repens
NT1 ipomoea rubra
NT1 ipomoea sepiaria
NT1 ipomoea stolonifera
NT1 ipomoea trichocarpa
NT1 ipomoea tricolor
NT1 ipomoea triloba
NT1 ipomoea turbinata
NT1 ipomoea wrightii
rt pharbitis

IPOMOEA ACULEATA
BT1 ipomoea
BT2 convolvulaceae

IPOMOEA AQUATICA
uf ipomoea reptans
BT1 ipomoea
BT2 convolvulaceae

IPOMOEA ARBORESCENS
BT1 ipomoea
BT2 convolvulaceae
BT1 ornamental woody plants

IPOMOEA ARISTOLOCHIAEFOLIA
BT1 ipomoea
BT2 convolvulaceae

IPOMOEA BATATAS
BT1 ipomoea
BT2 convolvulaceae
rt sweet potato chlorotic little leaf
rt sweet potato little leaf
rt sweet potato witches' broom
rt sweet potatoes

ipomoea biloba
USE **ipomoea pes-caprae**

IPOMOEA CAIRICA
uf ipomoea palmata
BT1 ipomoea
BT2 convolvulaceae

IPOMOEA CARNEA
uf ipomoea fistulosa
BT1 ipomoea
BT2 convolvulaceae
BT1 medicinal plants

ipomoea coccinea
USE **quamoclit coccinea**

IPOMOEA CONGESTA
BT1 ipomoea
BT2 convolvulaceae

IPOMOEA FASTIGIATA
BT1 ipomoea
BT2 convolvulaceae

ipomoea fistulosa
USE **ipomoea carnea**

ipomoea hederacea
USE **pharbitis hederacea**

ipomoea hederifolia
USE **quamoclit hederifolia**

IPOMOEA HEPTAPHYLLA
BT1 ipomoea
BT2 convolvulaceae

IPOMOEA HIRSUTULA
BT1 ipomoea
BT2 convolvulaceae

IPOMOEA LACUNOSA
BT1 ipomoea

IPOMOEA LACUNOSA *cont.*
BT2 convolvulaceae

ipomoea learii
USE **pharbitis learii**

ipomoea muricata
USE **calonyction muricatum**

ipomoea nil
USE **pharbitis nil**

IPOMOEA OBSCURA
BT1 ipomoea
BT2 convolvulaceae

IPOMOEA OPERCULATA
BT1 ipomoea
BT2 convolvulaceae

ipomoea palmata
USE **ipomoea cairica**

IPOMOEA PANDURATA
BT1 ipomoea
BT2 convolvulaceae

IPOMOEA PARASITICA
BT1 ipomoea
BT2 convolvulaceae

IPOMOEA PENTAPHYLLA
BT1 ipomoea
BT2 convolvulaceae

IPOMOEA PES-CAPRAE
uf *ipomoea biloba*
BT1 ipomoea
BT2 convolvulaceae
BT1 ornamental herbaceous plants

IPOMOEA PES-TIGRIDIS
BT1 ipomoea
BT2 convolvulaceae

IPOMOEA PLEBEIA
BT1 ipomoea
BT2 convolvulaceae

ipomoea purga
USE **exogonium purga**

ipomoea purpurea
USE **pharbitis purpurea**

ipomoea quamoclit
USE **quamoclit vulgaris**

IPOMOEA REPENS
BT1 ipomoea
BT2 convolvulaceae

ipomoea reptans
USE **ipomoea aquatica**

IPOMOEA RUBRA
BT1 ipomoea
BT2 convolvulaceae

IPOMOEA SEPIARIA
BT1 ipomoea
BT2 convolvulaceae

IPOMOEA STOLONIFERA
BT1 ipomoea
BT2 convolvulaceae
BT1 ornamental herbaceous plants

IPOMOEA TRICHOCARPA
BT1 ipomoea
BT2 convolvulaceae

IPOMOEA TRICOLOR
uf *ipomoea violacea*
BT1 ipomoea
BT2 convolvulaceae
BT1 ornamental herbaceous plants

IPOMOEA TRILOBA
BT1 ipomoea
BT2 convolvulaceae

ipomoea tuberosa
USE **merremia tuberosa**

IPOMOEA TURBINATA
BT1 ipomoea
BT2 convolvulaceae

ipomoea turpethum
USE **operculina turpethum**

ipomoea violacea
USE **ipomoea tricolor**

IPOMOEA WRIGHTII
BT1 ipomoea
BT2 convolvulaceae

IPOMOPSIS
BT1 polemoniaceae

IPPY VIRUS
BT1 unclassified viruses
BT2 viruses

IPROBENFOS
BT1 organophosphorus fungicides
BT2 fungicides
BT3 pesticides
BT2 organophosphorus pesticides
BT3 organophosphorus compounds

IPRODIONE
uf *glycophene*
BT1 dicarboximide fungicides
BT2 fungicides
BT3 pesticides

IPRONIDAZOLE
BT1 antiprotozoal agents
BT2 antiparasitic agents
BT3 drugs
BT1 nitroimidazoles
BT2 imidazoles
BT3 azoles
BT4 heterocyclic nitrogen compounds
BT5 organic nitrogen compounds

IPS
BT1 scolytidae
BT2 coleoptera
NT1 ips acuminatus
NT1 ips amitinus
NT1 ips avulsus
NT1 ips calligraphus
NT1 ips cembrae
NT1 ips grandicollis
NT1 ips paraconfusus
NT1 ips pini
NT1 ips sexdentatus
NT1 ips typographus
rt ipsdienol
rt ipsenol
rt orthotomicus
rt pityogenes
rt pityokteines

IPS ACUMINATUS
BT1 ips
BT2 scolytidae
BT3 coleoptera

IPS AMITINUS
BT1 ips
BT2 scolytidae
BT3 coleoptera

IPS AVULSUS
BT1 ips
BT2 scolytidae
BT3 coleoptera

IPS CALLIGRAPHUS
BT1 ips
BT2 scolytidae
BT3 coleoptera

IPS CEMBRAE
BT1 ips
BT2 scolytidae
BT3 coleoptera

ips chalcographus
USE **pityogenes chalcographus**

ips curvidens
USE **pityokteines curvidens**

ips erosus
USE **orthotomicus erosus**

IPS GRANDICOLLIS
BT1 ips
BT2 scolytidae
BT3 coleoptera

IPS PARACONFUSUS
BT1 ips
BT2 scolytidae
BT3 coleoptera

IPS PINI
BT1 ips
BT2 scolytidae
BT3 coleoptera

IPS SEXDENTATUS
BT1 ips
BT2 scolytidae
BT3 coleoptera

IPS TYPOGRAPHUS
BT1 ips
BT2 scolytidae
BT3 coleoptera

IPSDIENOL
BT1 aggregation pheromones
BT2 pheromones
BT3 semiochemicals
rt ips

IPSENOL
BT1 aggregation pheromones
BT2 pheromones
BT3 semiochemicals
rt ips

IRAN
BT1 west asia
BT2 asia
rt developing countries
rt middle east
rt opec
rt threshold countries

IRAQ
BT1 west asia
BT2 asia
rt arab countries
rt developing countries
rt middle east
rt opec
rt threshold countries

IRAQ KURDI
BT1 sheep breeds
BT2 breeds

IRAQI
HN from 1990
BT1 goat breeds
BT2 breeds

ireland
USE **irish republic**
OR **northern ireland**

ireland, northern
USE **northern ireland**

IRESINE
BT1 amaranthaceae
rt ornamental foliage plants

IRIAN JAYA
uf *irian, west*
uf *new guinea, west*
uf *west irian*
uf *west new guinea*
BT1 indonesia
BT2 south east asia
BT3 asia

irian, west
USE **irian jaya**

IRIDACEAE
NT1 acidanthera
NT2 acidanthera bicolor
NT1 antholyza

IRIDACEAE *cont.*
NT1 babiana
NT1 crocosmia
NT2 crocosmia crocosmiiflora
NT2 crocosmia crocosmiifolia
NT2 crocosmia masoniorum
NT1 crocus
NT2 crocus asumaniae
NT2 crocus boryi
NT2 crocus kotschyanus
NT2 crocus laevigatus
NT2 crocus olivieri
NT2 crocus pallasii
NT2 crocus sativus
NT2 crocus tommasinianus
NT2 crocus tournefortii
NT1 freesia
NT1 gladiolus
NT2 gladiolus atroviolaceus
NT2 gladiolus communis
NT2 gladiolus illyricus
NT2 gladiolus imbricatus
NT2 gladiolus italicus
NT2 gladiolus natalensis
NT2 gladiolus palustris
NT1 homeria
NT1 homoglossum
NT1 iris
NT2 iris albicans
NT2 iris camillai
NT2 iris cypriana
NT2 iris douglasiana
NT2 iris ensata
NT2 iris furcata
NT2 iris germanica
NT2 iris hollandica
NT2 iris hoogiana
NT2 iris iberica
NT2 iris kamaonensis
NT2 iris kashmiriana
NT2 iris longiscapa
NT2 iris mesopotamica
NT2 iris missouriensis
NT2 iris pallida
NT2 iris persica
NT2 iris planifolia
NT2 iris pseudacorus
NT2 iris ruthenica
NT2 iris sanguinea
NT2 iris schelkownikowii
NT2 iris setosa
NT2 iris sibirica
NT2 iris spuria
NT2 iris sulphurea
NT2 iris trojana
NT1 ixia
NT2 ixia polystachya
NT1 lapeirousia
NT2 lapeirousia laxa
NT1 libertia
NT1 melasphaerula
NT1 moraea
NT1 neomarica
NT2 neomarica coerulea
NT1 romulea
NT2 romulea rosea
NT1 schizostylis
NT1 sisyrinchium
NT2 sisyrinchium striatum
NT1 sparaxis
NT2 sparaxis grandiflora
NT2 sparaxis tricolor
NT1 tigridia
NT1 tritonia
NT2 tritonia crocata
NT1 watsonia

IRIDESCENT VIRUSES
BT1 iridovirus
BT2 insect viruses
BT3 entomopathogens
BT4 pathogens
BT2 iridoviridae
BT3 viruses
NT1 chilo iridescent virus
NT1 regular mosquito iridescent virus
NT1 turquoise mosquito iridescent virus

IRIDODIAL
BT1 aldehydes

IRIDODIAL *cont.*
BT1 iridoids
BT2 isoprenoids
BT3 lipids
rt iridomyrmex

IRIDOID GLYCOSIDES
BT1 glycosides
BT2 carbohydrates
BT1 iridoids
BT2 isoprenoids
BT3 lipids
NT1 aucubin
NT1 loganin

IRIDOIDS
BT1 isoprenoids
BT2 lipids
NT1 iridodial
NT1 iridoid glycosides
NT2 aucubin
NT2 loganin
NT1 secoiridoids
NT2 oleuropein
NT1 valepotriates
NT2 acevaltrate
NT2 valtrate

IRIDOMYRMEX
BT1 formicidae
BT2 hymenoptera
NT1 iridomyrmex humilis
NT1 iridomyrmex purpureus
rt iridodial

IRIDOMYRMEX HUMILIS
BT1 iridomyrmex
BT2 formicidae
BT3 hymenoptera

IRIDOMYRMEX PURPUREUS
BT1 iridomyrmex
BT2 formicidae
BT3 hymenoptera

IRIDOVIRIDAE
BT1 viruses
NT1 african swine fever virus
NT1 iridovirus
NT2 iridescent viruses
NT3 chilo iridescent virus
NT3 regular mosquito iridescent virus
NT3 turquoise mosquito iridescent virus
NT1 lymphocystis virus

IRIDOVIRUS
BT1 insect viruses
BT2 entomopathogens
BT3 pathogens
BT1 iridoviridae
BT2 viruses
NT1 iridescent viruses
NT2 chilo iridescent virus
NT2 regular mosquito iridescent virus
NT2 turquoise mosquito iridescent virus

IRIS
BT1 iridaceae
NT1 iris albicans
NT1 iris camillai
NT1 iris cypriana
NT1 iris douglasiana
NT1 iris ensata
NT1 iris furcata
NT1 iris germanica
NT1 iris hollandica
NT1 iris hoogiana
NT1 iris iberica
NT1 iris kamaonensis
NT1 iris kashmiriana
NT1 iris longiscapa
NT1 iris mesopotamica
NT1 iris missouriensis
NT1 iris pallida
NT1 iris persica
NT1 iris planifolia
NT1 iris pseudacorus
NT1 iris ruthenica
NT1 iris sanguinea

IRIS *cont.*
NT1 iris schelkownikowii
NT1 iris setosa
NT1 iris sibirica
NT1 iris spuria
NT1 iris sulphurea
NT1 iris trojana
rt iris mild mosaic potyvirus

iris alata
USE **iris planifolia**

IRIS ALBICANS
BT1 iris
BT2 iridaceae

IRIS CAMILLAI
BT1 iris
BT2 iridaceae

IRIS CYPRIANA
BT1 iris
BT2 iridaceae

IRIS DOUGLASIANA
BT1 insecticidal plants
BT2 pesticidal plants
BT1 iris
BT2 iridaceae

iris elegantissima
USE **iris iberica**

IRIS ENSATA
uf *iris kaempferi*
BT1 iris
BT2 iridaceae

iris florentina
USE **iris germanica**

IRIS FURCATA
BT1 iris
BT2 iridaceae

IRIS GERMANICA
uf *iris florentina*
BT1 essential oil plants
BT2 oil plants
BT1 iris
BT2 iridaceae
BT1 ornamental bulbs
rt rhizomes

IRIS HOLLANDICA
BT1 iris
BT2 iridaceae

IRIS HOOGIANA
BT1 iris
BT2 iridaceae

IRIS IBERICA
uf *iris elegantissima*
BT1 iris
BT2 iridaceae
BT1 ornamental bulbs
rt rhizomes

iris kaempferi
USE **iris ensata**

IRIS KAMAONENSIS
BT1 iris
BT2 iridaceae

IRIS KASHMIRIANA
BT1 iris
BT2 iridaceae

IRIS LONGISCAPA
BT1 iris
BT2 iridaceae

IRIS MESOPOTAMICA
BT1 iris
BT2 iridaceae

IRIS MILD MOSAIC POTYVIRUS
HN from 1990
uf *iris mosaic virus*
BT1 potyvirus group
BT2 plant viruses
BT3 plant pathogens
BT4 pathogens
rt iris

IRIS MISSOURIENSIS
BT1 iris
BT2 iridaceae
BT1 medicinal plants

iris mosaic virus
USE **iris mild mosaic potyvirus**

iris nertschinskia
USE **iris sanguinea**

IRIS PALLIDA
BT1 iris
BT2 iridaceae
BT1 ornamental bulbs
rt rhizomes

IRIS PERSICA
BT1 iris
BT2 iridaceae
BT1 ornamental bulbs

IRIS PLANIFOLIA
uf *iris alata*
BT1 iris
BT2 iridaceae
BT1 ornamental bulbs

IRIS PSEUDACORUS
BT1 dye plants
BT1 iris
BT2 iridaceae
BT1 tan plants

IRIS RUTHENICA
BT1 iris
BT2 iridaceae

IRIS SANGUINEA
uf *iris nertschinskia*
BT1 iris
BT2 iridaceae
BT1 ornamental bulbs
rt rhizomes

IRIS SCHELKOWNIKOWII
BT1 iris
BT2 iridaceae

IRIS SETOSA
BT1 iris
BT2 iridaceae

IRIS SIBIRICA
BT1 iris
BT2 iridaceae
BT1 ornamental bulbs
rt rhizomes

iris sogdiana
USE **iris spuria**

IRIS SPURIA
uf *iris sogdiana*
BT1 iris
BT2 iridaceae

IRIS SULPHUREA
BT1 iris
BT2 iridaceae

IRIS TROJANA
BT1 iris
BT2 iridaceae

IRISH REPUBLIC
uf *eire*
uf *ireland*
BT1 british isles
BT2 western europe
BT3 europe
NT1 connacht
NT1 leinster
NT1 munster
rt european communities
rt oecd

IRISH SEA
BT1 northeast atlantic
BT2 atlantic ocean
BT3 marine areas

IRON
BT1 trace elements
BT2 elements
BT1 transition elements

IRON *cont.*
BT2 metallic elements
BT3 elements
BT3 metals
rt deferoxamine
rt ferric ions
rt ferric sulfate
rt ferrous alloys
rt ferrous ions
rt ferrous sulfate
rt galvanized iron
rt galvanizing
rt haemochromatosis
rt haemoglobin
rt haemosiderosis
rt iron absorption
rt iron binding capacity
rt iron deficiency anaemia
rt iron fertilizers
rt iron hydroxides
rt iron oxides
rt iron oxyhydroxides
rt iron pans
rt iron phosphates
rt nutrients
rt pyrites
rt siderophilins
rt siderophores
rt siderosis
rt steel

IRON ABSORPTION
BT1 mineral absorption
BT2 absorption
BT3 sorption
rt iron

IRON BINDING CAPACITY
uf *iron binding protein*
rt capacity
rt chelation
rt ferritin
rt iron
rt lactoferrin

iron binding protein
USE **iron binding capacity**

IRON DEFICIENCY ANAEMIA
AF iron deficiency anemia
BT1 anaemia
BT2 blood disorders
BT3 animal disorders
BT4 disorders
BT1 deficiency diseases
BT2 diseases
BT2 nutritional disorders
BT3 animal disorders
BT4 disorders
rt iron

IRON DEFICIENCY ANEMIA
BF iron deficiency anaemia
BT1 anemia

IRON FERTILIZERS
BT1 trace element fertilizers
BT2 fertilizers
rt iron

iron, galvanized
USE **galvanized iron**

IRON HUMUS PODZOLS
BT1 podzols
BT2 soil types (genetic)

IRON HYDROXIDES
BT1 hydroxides
BT2 inorganic compounds
NT1 ferric hydroxide
rt iron

IRON OXIDES
BT1 nonclay minerals
BT2 minerals
BT1 oxides
BT2 inorganic compounds
BT1 soil conditioners
BT2 soil amendments
BT3 amendments
NT1 maghaemite
NT1 magnetite
rt iron

IRON OXIDIZING BACTERIA
HN from 1990
BT1 microbial flora
BT2 flora

IRON OXYHYDROXIDES
BT1 inorganic compounds
BT1 nonclay minerals
BT2 minerals
NT1 goethite
NT1 lepidocrocite
rt iron

IRON PANS
BT1 pans
BT2 soil morphological features
rt iron

IRON PHOSPHATES
BT1 phosphates (salts)
BT2 inorganic salts
BT3 inorganic compounds
BT3 salts
BT2 phosphates
BT1 phosphorus fertilizers
BT2 fertilizers
NT1 ferric phosphate
rt iron

iron pyrites
USE **pyrites**

iron reductase
USE **ferroxidase**

IRONING (AGRICOLA)
rt irons (agricola)
rt laundry (agricola)
rt pressing (clothing construction) (agricola)

IRONS (AGRICOLA)
BT1 appliances (agricola)
BT1 household equipment (agricola)
BT2 equipment
rt ironing (agricola)

IRPEX
HN from 1989
BT1 aphyllophorales
NT1 irpex lacteus

IRPEX LACTEUS
HN from 1989
BT1 irpex
BT2 aphyllophorales

IRRADIATED VACCINES
HN from 1990
BT1 live vaccines
BT2 vaccines

IRRADIATION
NT1 food irradiation
rt immunosuppression
rt processing
rt radapperization (agricola)
rt radiation
rt radiotherapy
rt treatment

IRREGULAR BEARING
uf *biennial bearing*
uf *fruiting, biennial*
uf *fruiting, irregular*
BT1 fruiting
BT2 plant development

IRRIGABILITY SURVEYS
BT1 surveys
rt irrigation

IRRIGATED CONDITIONS
BT1 soil water regimes
rt irrigation

IRRIGATED FARMING
BT1 farming
rt irrigation

IRRIGATED PASTURES
BT1 pastures
BT2 grasslands
BT3 vegetation types

IRRIGATED SITES
BT1 site types
rt irrigated stands
rt irrigation

IRRIGATED SOILS
BT1 soil types (cultural)
rt irrigation

IRRIGATED STANDS
rt irrigated sites
rt irrigation

IRRIGATION
uf *herbigation*
uf *watering*
NT1 basin irrigation
NT1 border irrigation
NT1 flood irrigation
NT1 furrow irrigation
NT1 mist irrigation
NT1 overhead irrigation
NT1 pulse irrigation
NT1 runoff irrigation
NT1 sprinkler irrigation
NT2 centre pivot irrigation
NT1 subsurface irrigation
NT1 surface irrigation
NT1 trickle irrigation
NT1 water spreading
rt cultural methods
rt fertigation
rt fogging
rt hoses
rt hydraulic structures
rt hydroponics
rt irrigability surveys
rt irrigated conditions
rt irrigated farming
rt irrigated sites
rt irrigated soils
rt irrigated stands
rt irrigation channels
rt irrigation equipment
rt irrigation requirements
rt irrigation scheduling
rt irrigation systems
rt irrigation water
rt plant water relations
rt soil management
rt water requirements

irrigation, basin
USE **basin irrigation**

irrigation, border
USE **border irrigation**

irrigation, centre pivot
USE **centre pivot irrigation**

IRRIGATION CHANNELS
BT1 channels
rt irrigation

irrigation, drip
USE **trickle irrigation**

IRRIGATION EQUIPMENT
BT1 equipment
NT1 emitters
NT1 plastic pipes
NT2 corrugated plastic pipes
rt irrigation
rt sprayers

irrigation, furrow
USE **furrow irrigation**

irrigation, mist
USE **mist irrigation**

irrigation, pulse
USE **pulse irrigation**

IRRIGATION REQUIREMENTS
BT1 water requirements
BT2 requirements
BT2 water relations
rt irrigation
rt soil water

irrigation, runoff
USE **runoff irrigation**

IRRIGATION SCHEDULING
rt irrigation

irrigation, sprinkler
USE **sprinkler irrigation**

irrigation, subsurface
USE **subsurface irrigation**

irrigation, surface
USE **surface irrigation**

IRRIGATION SYSTEMS
BT1 water systems
BT2 systems
NT1 automatic irrigation systems
NT1 mobile irrigation systems
NT1 self propelled irrigation systems
rt irrigation

irrigation systems, automatic
USE **automatic irrigation systems**

irrigation systems, self propelled
USE **self propelled irrigation systems**

irrigation, trickle
USE **trickle irrigation**

IRRIGATION WATER
uf *water, irrigation*
BT1 water
NT1 alkaline water
NT1 bicarbonate water
NT1 return flow
NT1 sodic water
rt brackish water
rt brewery effluent
rt groundwater
rt irrigation
rt river water
rt saline water

irritable bowel syndrome
USE **irritable colon**

IRRITABLE COLON
uf *irritable bowel syndrome*
BT1 intestinal diseases
BT2 gastrointestinal diseases
BT3 digestive system diseases
BT4 organic diseases
BT5 diseases
rt colon

IRRITANT PROPERTIES
HN from 1989
BT1 properties
rt wood properties

IRVINGIA
BT1 ixonanthaceae
NT1 irvingia gabonensis

IRVINGIA GABONENSIS
BT1 antifungal plants
BT1 irvingia
BT2 ixonanthaceae
BT1 oilseed plants
BT2 fatty oil plants
BT3 oil plants

IRYANTHERA
BT1 myristicaceae
NT1 iryanthera polyneura

IRYANTHERA POLYNEURA
BT1 iryanthera
BT2 myristicaceae
BT1 medicinal plants

ISACHNE
BT1 gramineae
NT1 isachne globosa

ISACHNE GLOBOSA
BT1 isachne
BT2 gramineae

ISARIA
BT1 deuteromycotina
NT1 isaria sinclairii
rt paecilomyces

isaria farinosa
USE **paecilomyces farinosus**

ISARIA SINCLAIRII
BT1 isaria
BT2 deuteromycotina

isariopsis
USE **phaeoisariopsis**

isariopsis griseola
USE **phaeoisariopsis griseola**

ISATIS
BT1 cruciferae
NT1 isatis tinctoria

ISATIS TINCTORIA
BT1 dye plants
BT1 isatis
BT2 cruciferae
BT1 medicinal plants

ISAZOFOS
BT1 organothiophosphate insecticides
BT2 organophosphorus insecticides
BT3 insecticides
BT4 pesticides
BT3 organophosphorus pesticides
BT4 organophosphorus compounds
BT1 organothiophosphate nematicides
BT2 organophosphorus nematicides
BT3 nematicides
BT4 pesticides
BT3 organophosphorus pesticides
BT4 organophosphorus compounds

ISCHAEMIA
AF ischemia
BT1 vascular diseases
BT2 cardiovascular diseases
BT3 organic diseases
BT4 diseases
rt vasoconstriction

ischaemic heart disease
USE **myocardial ischaemia**

ISCHAEMUM
BT1 gramineae
NT1 ischaemum afrum
NT1 ischaemum aristatum
NT1 ischaemum indicum
NT1 ischaemum rugosum

ISCHAEMUM AFRUM
BT1 ischaemum
BT2 gramineae

ISCHAEMUM ARISTATUM
BT1 ischaemum
BT2 gramineae

ISCHAEMUM INDICUM
BT1 ischaemum
BT2 gramineae

ISCHAEMUM RUGOSUM
BT1 ischaemum
BT2 gramineae

ISCHEMIA
BF ischaemia

ISCHIODON
BT1 syrphidae
BT2 diptera
NT1 ischiodon aegyptius
rt xanthogramma

ISCHIODON AEGYPTIUS
uf *xanthogramma aegyptium*
BT1 ischiodon
BT2 syrphidae
BT3 diptera

ISCHNOCERA
BT1 mallophaga
BT2 phthiraptera
NT1 goniodidae
NT2 campanulotes
NT3 campanulotes bidentatus
NT4 campanulotes bidentatus compar
NT2 goniocotes
NT3 goniocotes gallinae
NT2 goniodes
NT3 goniodes gigas
NT1 lipeuridae
NT2 lipeurus
NT3 lipeurus caponis
NT1 philopteridae
NT2 coloceras
NT2 columbicola
NT3 columbicola columbae
NT2 cuclotogaster
NT3 cuclotogaster heterographa
NT2 numidilipeurus
NT3 numidilipeurus lawrensis
NT4 numidilipeurus lawrensis tropicalis
NT1 trichodectidae
NT2 bovicola
NT3 bovicola bovis
NT3 bovicola caprae
NT3 bovicola crassipes
NT3 bovicola limbata
NT3 bovicola ovis
NT2 damalinia
NT2 trichodectes
NT3 trichodectes canis
NT2 werneckiella
NT3 werneckiella equi

ISCHNOPSYLLIDAE
BT1 siphonaptera
NT1 ischnopsyllus

ISCHNOPSYLLUS
BT1 ischnopsyllidae
BT2 siphonaptera

ISEILEMA
BT1 gramineae
NT1 iseilema laxum

ISEILEMA LAXUM
BT1 iseilema
BT2 gramineae
BT1 pasture plants

ISERTIA
BT1 leguminosae
NT1 isertia pittieri

ISERTIA PITTIERI
BT1 isertia
BT2 leguminosae

ISLAMABAD
BT1 pakistan
BT2 south asia
BT3 asia

ISLAMIC COUNTRIES
uf *muslim countries*
NT1 arab countries

ISLAND PRAMENKA
BT1 sheep breeds
BT2 breeds

ISLANDS
BT1 physiographic features
NT1 atolls

ISLE OF MAN
BT1 uk
BT2 british isles
BT3 western europe
BT4 europe

ISO
(international organization for standardization)
BT1 international organizations
BT2 organizations
rt standards

ISOAMYLASE
(ec 3.2.1.68)
BT1 o-glycoside hydrolases
BT2 glycosidases
BT3 hydrolases
BT4 enzymes

ISOASCORBIC ACID
uf *erythorbic acid*
BT1 antioxidants
BT2 additives
BT1 ascorbic acids
BT2 aldonic acids
BT3 sugar acids
BT4 carboxylic acids
BT5 organic acids
BT6 acids
BT4 monosaccharides
BT5 carbohydrates
BT1 food preservatives
BT2 preservatives

ISOBENZAN
BT1 cyclodiene insecticides
BT2 organochlorine insecticides
BT3 insecticides
BT4 pesticides
BT3 organochlorine pesticides
BT4 organochlorine compounds
BT5 organic halogen compounds

ISOBERLINIA
BT1 leguminosae
NT1 isoberlinia doka

ISOBERLINIA DOKA
BT1 isoberlinia
BT2 leguminosae

isobutylidene diurea
USE **ibdu**

ISOBUTYRIC ACID
BT1 volatile fatty acids
BT2 fatty acids
BT3 carboxylic acids
BT4 organic acids
BT5 acids
BT3 lipids
BT2 volatile compounds

ISOCARBAMID
BT1 urea herbicides
BT2 herbicides
BT3 pesticides

isocitrate
USE **isocitric acid**

ISOCITRATE DEHYDROGENASE
(ec 1.1.1.41, 42)
BT1 alcohol oxidoreductases
BT2 oxidoreductases
BT3 enzymes

ISOCITRATE LYASE
(ec 4.1.3.1)
BT1 oxo-acid-lyases
BT2 lyases
BT3 enzymes

ISOCITRIC ACID
uf *isocitrate*
BT1 tricarboxylic acids
BT2 carboxylic acids
BT3 organic acids
BT4 acids
rt citric acid

ISOCOMA
BT1 compositae
NT1 isocoma coronopifolia
NT1 isocoma drummondii
NT1 isocoma wrightii

ISOCOMA CORONOPIFOLIA
BT1 isocoma
BT2 compositae

ISOCOMA DRUMMONDII
BT1 isocoma
BT2 compositae

ISOCOMA WRIGHTII
BT1 isocoma
BT2 compositae

ISOELECTRIC FOCUSING
BT1 electrophoresis
BT2 analytical methods
BT3 methodology

ISOELECTRIC POINT
BT1 physicochemical properties
BT2 properties
rt colloidal properties
rt ph

ISOENZYMES
uf *isozymes*
BT1 enzymes
rt enzyme polymorphism

ISOETACEAE
NT1 isoetes
NT2 isoetes hystrix

ISOETES
BT1 isoetaceae
NT1 isoetes hystrix

ISOETES HYSTRIX
BT1 isoetes
BT2 isoetaceae

ISOFENPHOS
BT1 phosphoramidothioate insecticides
BT2 organophosphorus insecticides
BT3 insecticides
BT4 pesticides
BT3 organophosphorus pesticides
BT4 organophosphorus compounds

ISOFLAVANS
BT1 flavonoids
BT2 aromatic compounds
BT2 plant pigments
BT3 pigments

ISOFLAVONES
BT1 flavonoids
BT2 aromatic compounds
BT2 plant pigments
BT3 pigments
NT1 daidzein
NT1 dimethoxyisoflavone
NT1 formononetin
NT1 genistein
NT1 medicarpin
NT1 phaseollin
NT1 pisatin
NT1 rotenoids
NT2 rotenone

ISOGLOSSA
BT1 acanthaceae

isoglucose
USE **high fructose corn syrup**

ISOLATION
BT1 separation
rt extraction
rt isolation techniques

ISOLATION TECHNIQUES
BT1 techniques
rt infections
rt isolation

ISOLEUCINE
BT1 essential amino acids
BT2 amino acids
BT3 carboxylic acids
BT4 organic acids
BT5 acids
BT3 organic nitrogen compounds

ISOLONA
BT1 annonaceae
NT1 isolona campanulata

ISOLONA CAMPANULATA
BT1 isolona
BT2 annonaceae

ISOMALTOSE
BT1 disaccharides
BT2 oligosaccharides
BT3 carbohydrates

ISOMALTULOSE
HN from 1990
uf *palatinose*
BT1 disaccharides
BT2 oligosaccharides
BT3 carbohydrates

ISOMERASES
(ec 5)
BT1 enzymes
NT1 aldose 1-epimerase
NT1 chalcone isomerase
NT1 glucose-6-phosphate isomerase
NT1 mannose-6-phosphate isomerase
NT1 methylmalonyl-coa mutase
NT1 phosphotransferases
NT2 phosphoglucomutase
rt isomerization

ISOMERIZATION
HN from 1989
rt isomerases
rt isomers

ISOMERMIS
BT1 mermithidae
BT2 nematoda
NT1 isomermis lairdi

ISOMERMIS LAIRDI
BT1 isomermis
BT2 mermithidae
BT3 nematoda

isomerose
USE **high fructose corn syrup**

ISOMERS
HN from 1989
NT1 enantiomers
rt isomerization
rt molecular conformation

ISOMETAMIDIUM
BT1 quaternary ammonium compounds
BT2 ammonium compounds
BT2 organic nitrogen compounds
BT1 trypanocides
BT2 antiprotozoal agents
BT3 antiparasitic agents
BT4 drugs

ISOMETHIOZIN
BT1 triazinone herbicides
BT2 herbicides
BT3 pesticides
BT2 triazines
BT3 heterocyclic nitrogen compounds
BT4 organic nitrogen compounds

ISONIAZID
uf *isonicotinic acid hydrazide*
BT1 antibacterial agents
BT2 antiinfective agents
BT3 drugs
BT1 hydrazides
BT2 organic nitrogen compounds
rt tuberculosis

isonicotinic acid hydrazide
USE **isoniazid**

ISOODON
BT1 peramelidae
BT2 marsupials
BT3 mammals

ISOPARORCHIIDAE
BT1 digenea

ISOPARORCHIIDAE *cont.*
BT2 trematoda
NT1 isoparorchis

ISOPARORCHIS
BT1 isoparorchiidae
BT2 digenea
BT3 trematoda

ISOPENTENYLADENINE
BT1 adenines
BT2 purines
BT3 heterocyclic nitrogen compounds
BT4 organic nitrogen compounds

ISOPENTYL ACETATE
BT1 acetates (esters)
BT2 acetates
BT2 fatty acid esters
BT3 esters

ISOPODA
BT1 malacostraca
BT2 crustacea
BT3 arthropods
NT1 armadillidiidae
NT2 armadillidium
NT3 armadillidium vulgare
NT1 asellidae
NT2 asellus
NT3 asellus aquaticus
NT1 ligiidae
NT2 ligia
NT3 ligia oceanica
NT1 oniscidae
NT2 oniscus
NT3 oniscus asellus
NT1 philosciidae
NT2 philoscia
NT3 philoscia muscorum
NT1 porcellionidae
NT2 porcellio
NT3 porcellio scaber
NT1 trichoniscidae
NT2 trichoniscus
NT3 trichoniscus pusillus

ISOPOGON
BT1 proteaceae
rt ornamental woody plants

ISOPRENALINE
uf *isoproterenol*
BT1 amino alcohols
BT2 alcohols
BT2 amino compounds
BT3 organic nitrogen compounds
BT1 sympathomimetics
BT2 neurotropic drugs
BT3 drugs

ISOPRENOIDS
BT1 lipids
NT1 iridoids
NT2 iridodial
NT2 iridoid glycosides
NT3 aucubin
NT3 loganin
NT2 secoiridoids
NT3 oleuropein
NT2 valepotriates
NT3 acevaltrate
NT3 valtrate
NT1 polyprenols
NT2 dolichols
NT1 steroids
NT2 androstanes
NT3 androstenedione
NT3 androsterone
NT3 metandienone
NT3 methandriol
NT3 methyltestosterone
NT3 oxymesterone
NT3 prasterone
NT3 testosterone
NT2 bufadienolides
NT2 cardenolides
NT3 digitoxigenin
NT3 digoxigenin
NT2 cholanes

ISOPRENOIDS *cont.*
NT3 chenodeoxycholic acid
NT3 cholic acid
NT3 dehydrocholic acid
NT3 lithocholic acid
NT3 ursodeoxycholic acid
NT2 cholestanes
NT3 α-ecdysone
NT3 cholesterol
NT3 coprostanol
NT3 ecdysterone
NT2 ergostanes
NT3 campesterol
NT3 dihydrotachysterol
NT3 ergocalciferol
NT3 ergosterol
NT2 ketosteroids
NT3 androstenedione
NT3 androsterone
NT3 prasterone
NT2 lanostanes
NT3 lanosterol
NT2 oestranes
NT3 estradiol
NT3 estriol
NT3 estrone
NT3 mibolerone
NT3 nandrolone
NT3 trenbolone
NT2 oleananes
NT2 pregnanes
NT3 aldosterone
NT3 betamethasone
NT3 chlormadinone
NT3 corticosterone
NT3 cortisone
NT3 desoxycortone
NT3 dexamethasone
NT3 ethinylestradiol
NT3 fludrocortisone
NT3 flugestone
NT3 flumetasone
NT3 hydrocortisone
NT3 medroxyprogesterone
NT3 megestrol
NT3 melengestrol
NT3 mestranol
NT3 norethisterone
NT3 prednisolone
NT3 prednisone
NT3 progesterone
NT3 spironolactone
NT3 triamcinolone
NT2 solanidanes
NT3 solanidine
NT2 sterol esters
NT3 cholesteryl esters
NT2 sterols
NT3 25-hydroxyergocalciferol
NT3 cholecalciferol derivatives
NT4 hydroxycholecalciferols
NT5 1α-hydroxycholecalciferol
NT5 24,25-dihydroxycholecalciferol
NT5 25,26-dihydroxycholecalciferol
NT5 calcitriol
NT3 cholesterol
NT3 coprostanol
NT3 dihydrotachysterol
NT3 ergosterol
NT3 lanosterol
NT3 phytosterols
NT4 betulafolienetriol
NT4 brassinosteroids
NT5 brassinolide
NT4 campesterol
NT4 cucurbitacins
NT4 solanidine
NT4 stigmasterol
NT3 tachysterol
NT2 stigmastanes
NT3 stigmasterol
NT1 terpenoids
NT2 carotenoids
NT3 carotenes
NT4 α-carotene
NT4 β-carotene
NT4 lycopene
NT4 phytoene

ISOPRENOIDS *cont.*
NT4 phytofluene
NT3 retinoids
NT4 dehydroretinol
NT4 retinal
NT4 retinoic acid
NT4 retinol
NT4 retinyl esters
NT5 retinyl acetate
NT5 retinyl palmitate
NT3 xanthophylls
NT4 astaxanthin
NT4 canthaxanthin
NT4 capsanthin
NT4 violaxanthin
NT4 xanthophyll
NT4 zeaxanthin
NT2 diterpenoids
NT3 abietic acid
NT3 casbene
NT3 diterpenes
NT3 duvanes
NT3 gibberellins
NT4 gibberellic acid
NT3 kaurene
NT3 kaurenoic acid
NT3 phytol
NT3 pimaric acid
NT3 pyrethrins
NT3 steviol
NT2 monoterpenoids
NT3 borneol
NT3 camphor
NT3 cantharidin
NT3 carvone
NT3 chrysanthemic acid
NT3 citral
NT4 geranial
NT4 neral
NT3 dihydrocarvone
NT3 eucalyptol
NT3 eugenol
NT3 geraniol
NT3 linalool
NT3 menthol
NT3 monoterpenes
NT4 3-carene
NT4 α-pinene
NT4 β-pinene
NT4 camphene
NT4 limonene
NT4 myrcene
NT4 phellandrene
NT4 sabinene
NT3 ocimene
NT3 thymol
NT3 verbenol
NT3 verbenone
NT2 sesquiterpenoids
NT3 α-bisabolol
NT3 abscisic acid
NT3 capsidiol
NT3 dihydrophaseic acid
NT3 farnesol
NT3 juvenile hormone i
NT3 juvenile hormone ii
NT3 juvenile hormone iii
NT3 lubimin
NT3 phaseic acid
NT3 phytuberin
NT3 rishitin
NT3 sesquiterpenes
NT3 sesquiterpenoid lactones
NT4 bisabolangelone
NT4 eupatoriopicrin
NT4 guaianolides
NT4 helenalin
NT4 qinghaosu
NT4 tenulin
NT3 solavetivone
NT2 triterpenoids
NT3 β-amyrin
NT3 betulin
NT3 cucurbitacins
NT3 gossypol
NT3 limonoids
NT4 limonin
NT3 meliacins
NT4 azadirachtin
NT3 quassinoids
NT4 bruceantin

ISOPRENOIDS *cont.*
NT3 squalene
NT3 tocopherols
NT4 α-tocopherol
NT4 β-tocopherol
NT3 tocotrienols
NT3 triterpene acids
NT4 oleanolic acid
NT4 ursolic acid

ISOPROCARB
BT1 carbamate insecticides
BT2 carbamate pesticides
BT2 insecticides
BT3 pesticides

ISOPROPALIN
BT1 dinitroaniline herbicides
BT2 herbicides
BT3 pesticides

isopropanol
USE **isopropyl alcohol**

ISOPROPYL ALCOHOL
uf *2-propanol*
uf *isopropanol*
BT1 alcohols

ISOPROPYL METHANESULFONATE
uf *isopropyl methanesulphonate*
BT1 alkylating agents
BT1 mutagens
BT1 sulfonates
BT2 organic sulfur compounds

isopropyl methanesulphonate
USE **isopropyl methanesulfonate**

isoproterenol
USE **isoprenaline**

ISOPROTHIOLANE
BT1 unclassified fungicides
BT2 fungicides
BT3 pesticides

ISOPROTURON
BT1 urea herbicides
BT2 herbicides
BT3 pesticides

ISOPTERA
uf *termites*
NT1 hodotermitidae
NT2 anacanthotermes
NT3 anacanthotermes ahngerianus
NT3 anacanthotermes ochraceus
NT2 hodotermes
NT3 hodotermes mossambicus
NT1 kalotermitidae
NT2 cryptotermes
NT3 cryptotermes brevis
NT2 glyptotermes
NT3 glyptotermes dilatatus
NT2 kalotermes
NT3 kalotermes flavicollis
NT2 neotermes
NT1 rhinotermitidae
NT2 coptotermes
NT3 coptotermes acinaciformis
NT3 coptotermes formosanus
NT2 heterotermes
NT3 heterotermes indicola
NT2 reticulitermes
NT3 reticulitermes chinensis
NT3 reticulitermes flavipes
NT3 reticulitermes lucifugus
NT3 reticulitermes santonensis
NT1 termitidae
NT2 allodontermes
NT2 amitermes
NT3 amitermes evuncifer
NT3 amitermes meridionalis
NT2 cubitermes
NT2 macrotermes
NT3 macrotermes michaelseni
NT3 macrotermes subhyalinus

ISOPTERA *cont.*
NT2 microcerotermes
NT2 microtermes
NT3 microtermes obesi
NT2 nasutitermes
NT3 nasutitermes costalis
NT3 nasutitermes exitiosus
NT3 nasutitermes nigriceps
NT2 odontotermes
NT3 odontotermes distans
NT3 odontotermes feae
NT3 odontotermes formosanus
NT3 odontotermes obesus
NT3 odontotermes wallonensis
NT2 termes
NT2 trinervitermes
NT3 trinervitermes bettonianus
NT1 termopsidae
NT2 zootermopsis
NT3 zootermopsis angusticollis
rt insects
rt social insects
rt termitaria

ISOPYRIMOL
BT1 growth inhibitors
BT2 inhibitors
BT2 plant growth regulators
BT3 growth regulators

ISOPYRUM
BT1 ranunculaceae
NT1 isopyrum thalictroides

ISOPYRUM THALICTROIDES
BT1 isopyrum
BT2 ranunculaceae

ISOQUERCITRIN
BT1 glucosides
BT2 glycosides
BT3 carbohydrates
BT1 glycoflavones
BT2 flavonoids
BT3 aromatic compounds
BT3 plant pigments
BT4 pigments
BT2 glycosides
BT3 carbohydrates

ISOQUINOLINE ALKALOIDS
BT1 alkaloids
NT1 colchicine
NT1 dehydroemetine
NT1 demecolcine
NT1 emetine

ISORHAMNETIN
BT1 flavonols
BT2 alcohols
BT2 flavones
BT3 flavonoids
BT4 aromatic compounds
BT4 plant pigments
BT5 pigments

ISOSPORA
BT1 apicomplexa
BT2 protozoa
NT1 isospora arctopitheci
NT1 isospora belli
NT1 isospora bigemina
NT1 isospora buteonis
NT1 isospora canaria
NT1 isospora canis
NT1 isospora endocallimici
NT1 isospora felis
NT1 isospora heydorni
NT1 isospora hominis
NT1 isospora lacazei
NT1 isospora laidlawi
NT1 isospora lieberkuehni
NT1 isospora ohioensis
NT1 isospora rivolta
NT1 isospora schwetzi
NT1 isospora serini
NT1 isospora suis
NT1 isospora turdi
NT1 isospora vulpina
NT1 isospora wallacei

ISOSPORA ARCTOPITHECI
BT1 isospora
BT2 apicomplexa
BT3 protozoa

ISOSPORA BELLI
BT1 isospora
BT2 apicomplexa
BT3 protozoa

ISOSPORA BIGEMINA
BT1 isospora
BT2 apicomplexa
BT3 protozoa

ISOSPORA BUTEONIS
BT1 isospora
BT2 apicomplexa
BT3 protozoa

ISOSPORA CANARIA
BT1 isospora
BT2 apicomplexa
BT3 protozoa

ISOSPORA CANIS
BT1 isospora
BT2 apicomplexa
BT3 protozoa

ISOSPORA ENDOCALLIMICI
BT1 isospora
BT2 apicomplexa
BT3 protozoa

ISOSPORA FELIS
BT1 isospora
BT2 apicomplexa
BT3 protozoa

ISOSPORA HEYDORNI
BT1 isospora
BT2 apicomplexa
BT3 protozoa

ISOSPORA HOMINIS
BT1 isospora
BT2 apicomplexa
BT3 protozoa

ISOSPORA LACAZEI
BT1 isospora
BT2 apicomplexa
BT3 protozoa

ISOSPORA LAIDLAWI
BT1 isospora
BT2 apicomplexa
BT3 protozoa

ISOSPORA LIEBERKUEHNI
BT1 isospora
BT2 apicomplexa
BT3 protozoa

ISOSPORA OHIOENSIS
BT1 isospora
BT2 apicomplexa
BT3 protozoa

ISOSPORA RIVOLTA
BT1 isospora
BT2 apicomplexa
BT3 protozoa

ISOSPORA SCHWETZI
BT1 isospora
BT2 apicomplexa
BT3 protozoa

ISOSPORA SERINI
BT1 isospora
BT2 apicomplexa
BT3 protozoa

ISOSPORA SUIS
BT1 isospora
BT2 apicomplexa
BT3 protozoa

ISOSPORA TURDI
BT1 isospora
BT2 apicomplexa
BT3 protozoa

ISOSPORA VULPINA
BT1 isospora
BT2 apicomplexa
BT3 protozoa

ISOSPORA WALLACEI
BT1 isospora
BT2 apicomplexa
BT3 protozoa

ISOTHIOCYANATES
BT1 esters
BT1 organic sulfur compounds
NT1 allyl isothiocyanate
NT1 benzyl isothiocyanate
NT1 methyl isothiocyanate

ISOTOMA
BT1 isotomidae
BT2 collembola

ISOTOMIDAE
BT1 collembola
NT1 cryptopygus
NT2 cryptopygus antarcticus
NT1 folsomia
NT2 folsomia candida
NT1 folsomides
NT1 isotoma
NT1 parisotoma
NT1 proisotoma
NT2 proisotoma minuta

ISOTOPE DILUTION
BT1 dilution
rt isotopes

ISOTOPE LABELING (AGRICOLA)
BT1 labeling
rt isotopes

ISOTOPES
NT1 deuterium
NT1 radionuclides
NT2 tritium
NT1 stable isotopes (agricola)
rt isotope dilution
rt isotope labeling (agricola)

isotopes, radioactive
USE **radionuclides**

ISOTRIA
BT1 orchidaceae
rt ornamental orchids

ISOTRICHA
BT1 ciliophora
BT2 protozoa
NT1 isotricha intestinalis
NT1 isotricha prostoma

ISOTRICHA INTESTINALIS
BT1 isotricha
BT2 ciliophora
BT3 protozoa

ISOTRICHA PROSTOMA
BT1 isotricha
BT2 ciliophora
BT3 protozoa

ISOTYPE SWITCHING
HN from 1990
rt isotypes

ISOTYPES
HN from 1990
rt immunoglobulins
rt isotype switching

ISOURON
BT1 urea herbicides
BT2 herbicides
BT3 pesticides

ISOXABEN
uf *benzamizole*
BT1 amide herbicides
BT2 herbicides
BT3 pesticides

ISOXATHION
BT1 organothiophosphate insecticides

ISOXATHION *cont.*
BT2 organophosphorus insecticides
BT3 insecticides
BT4 pesticides
BT3 organophosphorus pesticides
BT4 organophosphorus compounds

ISOXSUPRINE
BT1 muscle relaxants
BT2 neurotropic drugs
BT3 drugs
BT1 vasodilator agents
BT2 cardiovascular agents
BT3 drugs

isozymes
USE **isoenzymes**

ISRAEL
BT1 west asia
BT2 asia
rt mediterranean countries
rt middle east
rt threshold countries

ISRAELI FRIESIAN
BT1 cattle breeds
BT2 breeds

ISRAELI SAANEN
HN from 1990
BT1 goat breeds
BT2 breeds

ISTIOPHORIDAE
BT1 perciformes
BT2 osteichthyes
BT3 fishes
NT1 istiophorus
NT2 istiophorus platypterus
NT1 makaira
NT1 tetrapturus
rt marlins

ISTIOPHORUS
BT1 istiophoridae
BT2 perciformes
BT3 osteichthyes
BT4 fishes
NT1 istiophorus platypterus

ISTIOPHORUS PLATYPTERUS
uf *sailfish*
BT1 istiophorus
BT2 istiophoridae
BT3 perciformes
BT4 osteichthyes
BT5 fishes

ISTOBEN
BT1 cattle breeds
BT2 breeds

ISTRIAN MILK
BT1 sheep breeds
BT2 breeds

ISURUS
BT1 lamnidae
BT2 lamniformes
BT3 chondrichthyes
BT4 fishes

ITALIAN
HN from 1990
BT1 buffalo breeds
BT2 breeds

ITALIAN BROWN
BT1 cattle breeds
BT2 breeds

ITALIAN CHEESE
BT1 cheeses
BT2 milk products
BT3 products

ITALIAN COOKERY (AGRICOLA)
BT1 cookery (agricola)

ITALIAN FRIESIAN
BT1 cattle breeds

ITALIAN FRIESIAN *cont.*
BT2 breeds

italian honeybees
USE **apis mellifera ligustica**

ITALIAN MARCHES
uf *marches (italy)*
BT1 italy
BT2 western europe
BT3 europe

ITALIAN RED PIED
HN from 1990; previously "red pied friuli"
uf *red pied friuli*
BT1 cattle breeds
BT2 breeds

italian ryegrass
USE **lolium multiflorum**

ITALY
BT1 western europe
BT2 europe
NT1 abruzzi
NT1 apulia
NT1 basilicata
NT1 calabria
NT1 campania
NT1 emilia romagna
NT1 friuli-venezia giulia
NT1 italian marches
NT1 latium
NT1 liguria
NT1 lombardy
NT1 molise
NT1 piedmont
NT1 sardinia
NT1 sicily
NT1 trentino-alto adige
NT1 tuscany
NT1 umbria
NT1 valle d'aosta
NT1 veneto
rt european communities
rt mediterranean countries
rt oecd
rt san marino
rt vatican

itchiness
USE **pruritus**

ITEA
BT1 iteaceae
NT1 itea virginica

ITEA VIRGINICA
BT1 itea
BT2 iteaceae
BT1 ornamental woody plants

ITEACEAE
NT1 itea
NT2 itea virginica

ITOPLECTIS
BT1 ichneumonidae
BT2 hymenoptera
NT1 itoplectis conquisitor
NT1 itoplectis maculator
NT1 itoplectis naranyae
rt pimpla

ITOPLECTIS CONQUISITOR
BT1 itoplectis
BT2 ichneumonidae
BT3 hymenoptera

ITOPLECTIS MACULATOR
BT1 itoplectis
BT2 ichneumonidae
BT3 hymenoptera

ITOPLECTIS NARANYAE
uf *pimpla naranyae*
BT1 itoplectis
BT2 ichneumonidae
BT3 hymenoptera

ITRACONAZOLE
HN from 1989
BT1 antifungal agents
BT2 antiinfective agents

ITRACONAZOLE *cont.*
BT3 drugs

IUFRO
(international union of forestry research organizations)
BT1 international organizations
BT2 organizations
rt forestry
rt research

IULIDAE
BT1 diplopoda
BT2 myriapoda
BT3 arthropods
NT1 cylindroiulus

IVA
BT1 compositae
NT1 iva axillaris
NT1 iva xanthiifolia

IVA AXILLARIS
BT1 iva
BT2 compositae

IVA XANTHIIFOLIA
BT1 iva
BT2 compositae

IVERMECTIN
BT1 anthelmintics
BT2 antiparasitic agents
BT3 drugs
BT1 antibiotic acaricides
BT2 acaricides
BT3 pesticides
BT2 antibiotics
BT1 antibiotic insecticides
BT2 antibiotics
BT2 insecticides
BT3 pesticides
BT1 avermectins
BT2 antibiotics
BT1 ectoparasiticides
BT2 antiparasitic agents
BT3 drugs

IVORY COAST
uf *cote d'ivoire*
BT1 west africa
BT2 africa south of sahara
BT3 africa
rt acp
rt developing countries
rt francophone africa

IVY
rt hedera

IXERBA
BT1 brexiaceae
NT1 ixerba brexioides

IXERBA BREXIOIDES
BT1 ixerba
BT2 brexiaceae

IXIA
BT1 iridaceae
NT1 ixia polystachya
rt ornamental plants

ixia flexuosa
USE **ixia polystachya**

IXIA POLYSTACHYA
uf *ixia flexuosa*
BT1 ixia
BT2 iridaceae
BT1 ornamental bulbs
rt corms

IXIANTHES
BT1 scrophulariaceae
NT1 ixianthes retzioides

IXIANTHES RETZIOIDES
BT1 ixianthes
BT2 scrophulariaceae

IXIOLIRION
BT1 amaryllidaceae
NT1 ixiolirion tataricum

ixiolirion montanum
USE **ixiolirion tataricum**

IXIOLIRION TATARICUM
uf *ixiolirion montanum*
BT1 ixiolirion
BT2 amaryllidaceae
BT1 ornamental bulbs

IXODES
uf *ceratixodes*
uf *pholeoixodes*
BT1 ixodidae
BT2 metastigmata
BT3 acari
NT1 ixodes apronophorus
NT1 ixodes arboricola
NT1 ixodes canisuga
NT1 ixodes cookei
NT1 ixodes crenulatus
NT1 ixodes dammini
NT1 ixodes dentatus
NT1 ixodes granulatus
NT1 ixodes hexagonus
NT1 ixodes holocyclus
NT1 ixodes kingi
NT1 ixodes lividus
NT1 ixodes nipponensis
NT1 ixodes ovatus
NT1 ixodes pacificus
NT1 ixodes pavlovskyi
NT1 ixodes persulcatus
NT1 ixodes redikorzevi
NT1 ixodes ricinus
NT1 ixodes rubicundus
NT1 ixodes scapularis
NT1 ixodes texanus
NT1 ixodes trianguliceps
NT1 ixodes uriae
NT1 ixodes ventalloi

IXODES APRONOPHORUS
BT1 ixodes
BT2 ixodidae
BT3 metastigmata
BT4 acari

IXODES ARBORICOLA
BT1 ixodes
BT2 ixodidae
BT3 metastigmata
BT4 acari

IXODES CANISUGA
uf *pholeoixodes canisuga*
BT1 ixodes
BT2 ixodidae
BT3 metastigmata
BT4 acari

IXODES COOKEI
BT1 ixodes
BT2 ixodidae
BT3 metastigmata
BT4 acari

IXODES CRENULATUS
HN from 1990
BT1 ixodes
BT2 ixodidae
BT3 metastigmata
BT4 acari

IXODES DAMMINI
BT1 ixodes
BT2 ixodidae
BT3 metastigmata
BT4 acari

IXODES DENTATUS
BT1 ixodes
BT2 ixodidae
BT3 metastigmata
BT4 acari

IXODES GRANULATUS
BT1 ixodes
BT2 ixodidae
BT3 metastigmata
BT4 acari

IXODES HEXAGONUS
uf *pholeoixodes hexagonus*
BT1 ixodes

IXODES HEXAGONUS *cont.*
BT2 ixodidae
BT3 metastigmata
BT4 acari

IXODES HOLOCYCLUS
BT1 ixodes
BT2 ixodidae
BT3 metastigmata
BT4 acari

IXODES KINGI
BT1 ixodes
BT2 ixodidae
BT3 metastigmata
BT4 acari

IXODES LIVIDUS
BT1 ixodes
BT2 ixodidae
BT3 metastigmata
BT4 acari

IXODES NIPPONENSIS
BT1 ixodes
BT2 ixodidae
BT3 metastigmata
BT4 acari

IXODES OVATUS
BT1 ixodes
BT2 ixodidae
BT3 metastigmata
BT4 acari

IXODES PACIFICUS
BT1 ixodes
BT2 ixodidae
BT3 metastigmata
BT4 acari

IXODES PAVLOVSKYI
BT1 ixodes
BT2 ixodidae
BT3 metastigmata
BT4 acari

IXODES PERSULCATUS
BT1 ixodes
BT2 ixodidae
BT3 metastigmata
BT4 acari

ixodes putus
USE **ixodes uriae**

IXODES REDIKORZEVI
BT1 ixodes
BT2 ixodidae
BT3 metastigmata
BT4 acari

IXODES RICINUS
BT1 ixodes
BT2 ixodidae
BT3 metastigmata
BT4 acari

IXODES RUBICUNDUS
BT1 ixodes
BT2 ixodidae
BT3 metastigmata
BT4 acari

IXODES SCAPULARIS
BT1 ixodes
BT2 ixodidae
BT3 metastigmata
BT4 acari

IXODES TEXANUS
BT1 ixodes
BT2 ixodidae
BT3 metastigmata
BT4 acari

IXODES TRIANGULICEPS
BT1 ixodes
BT2 ixodidae
BT3 metastigmata
BT4 acari

IXODES URIAE
uf *ceratixodes putus*
uf *ixodes putus*

IXODES URIAE *cont.*
BT1 ixodes
BT2 ixodidae
BT3 metastigmata
BT4 acari

IXODES VENTALLOI
BT1 ixodes
BT2 ixodidae
BT3 metastigmata
BT4 acari

ixodida
USE **metastigmata**

IXODIDAE
BT1 metastigmata
BT2 acari
NT1 amblyomma
NT2 amblyomma americanum
NT2 amblyomma brasiliense
NT2 amblyomma cajennense
NT2 amblyomma cohaerens
NT2 amblyomma cooperi
NT2 amblyomma cyprium
NT2 amblyomma dissimile
NT2 amblyomma gemma
NT2 amblyomma hebraeum
NT2 amblyomma inornatum
NT2 amblyomma integrum
NT2 amblyomma lepidum
NT2 amblyomma maculatum
NT2 amblyomma marmoreum
NT2 amblyomma neumanni
NT2 amblyomma oblongoguttatum
NT2 amblyomma ovale
NT2 amblyomma pomposum
NT2 amblyomma testudinarium
NT2 amblyomma triguttatum
NT2 amblyomma variegatum
NT1 anocentor
NT2 anocentor nitens
NT1 boophilus
NT2 boophilus annulatus
NT2 boophilus decoloratus
NT2 boophilus geigyi
NT2 boophilus kohlsi
NT2 boophilus microplus
NT1 dermacentor
NT2 dermacentor albipictus
NT2 dermacentor andersoni
NT2 dermacentor auratus
NT2 dermacentor daghestanicus
NT2 dermacentor marginatus
NT2 dermacentor nuttalli
NT2 dermacentor occidentalis
NT2 dermacentor parumapertus
NT2 dermacentor pictus
NT2 dermacentor reticulatus
NT2 dermacentor silvarum
NT2 dermacentor variabilis
NT1 haemaphysalis
NT2 haemaphysalis aciculifer
NT2 haemaphysalis bancrofti
NT2 haemaphysalis bispinosa
NT2 haemaphysalis concinna
NT2 haemaphysalis flava
NT2 haemaphysalis inermis
NT2 haemaphysalis intermedia
NT2 haemaphysalis japonica
NT2 haemaphysalis kinneari
NT2 haemaphysalis kyasanurensis
NT2 haemaphysalis leachii
NT2 haemaphysalis leporispalustris
NT2 haemaphysalis longicornis
NT2 haemaphysalis parva
NT2 haemaphysalis pospelovashtromae
NT2 haemaphysalis punctata
NT2 haemaphysalis silacea
NT2 haemaphysalis spinigera
NT2 haemaphysalis sulcata
NT2 haemaphysalis turturis
NT2 haemaphysalis verticalis
NT1 hyalomma
NT2 hyalomma aegyptium
NT2 hyalomma anatolicum

IXODIDAE *cont.*
NT3 hyalomma anatolicum anatolicum
NT3 hyalomma anatolicum excavatum
NT2 hyalomma arabica
NT2 hyalomma asiaticum
NT2 hyalomma brevipunctata
NT2 hyalomma detritum
NT2 hyalomma dromedarii
NT2 hyalomma hussaini
NT2 hyalomma impeltatum
NT2 hyalomma impressum
NT2 hyalomma lusitanicum
NT2 hyalomma marginatum
NT3 hyalomma marginatum isaaci
NT3 hyalomma marginatum marginatum
NT3 hyalomma marginatum rufipes
NT3 hyalomma marginatum turanicum
NT2 hyalomma nitidum
NT2 hyalomma truncatum
NT1 ixodes
NT2 ixodes apronophorus
NT2 ixodes arboricola
NT2 ixodes canisuga
NT2 ixodes cookei
NT2 ixodes crenulatus
NT2 ixodes dammini
NT2 ixodes dentatus
NT2 ixodes granulatus
NT2 ixodes hexagonus
NT2 ixodes holocyclus
NT2 ixodes kingi
NT2 ixodes lividus
NT2 ixodes nipponensis
NT2 ixodes ovatus
NT2 ixodes pacificus
NT2 ixodes pavlovskyi
NT2 ixodes persulcatus
NT2 ixodes redikorzevi
NT2 ixodes ricinus
NT2 ixodes rubicundus
NT2 ixodes scapularis
NT2 ixodes texanus
NT2 ixodes trianguliceps
NT2 ixodes uriae
NT2 ixodes ventalloi
NT1 margaropus
NT2 margaropus winthemi
NT1 nosomma
NT2 nosomma monstrosum
NT1 rhipicephalus
NT2 rhipicephalus appendiculatus
NT2 rhipicephalus bursa
NT2 rhipicephalus evertsi
NT3 rhipicephalus evertsi evertsi
NT3 rhipicephalus evertsi mimeticus
NT2 rhipicephalus glabroscutatum
NT2 rhipicephalus guilhoni
NT2 rhipicephalus haemaphysaloides
NT2 rhipicephalus longus
NT2 rhipicephalus lunulatus
NT2 rhipicephalus muhsamae
NT2 rhipicephalus pravus
NT2 rhipicephalus pulchellus
NT2 rhipicephalus pumilio
NT2 rhipicephalus pusillus
NT2 rhipicephalus rossicus
NT2 rhipicephalus sanguineus
NT2 rhipicephalus simus
NT2 rhipicephalus sulcatus
NT2 rhipicephalus turanicus
NT2 rhipicephalus zambeziensis

IXODIPHAGUS
uf *hunterellus*
BT1 encyrtidae
BT2 hymenoptera
NT1 ixodiphagus hookeri

IXODIPHAGUS HOOKERI
uf *hunterellus hookeri*
BT1 ixodiphagus

IXODIPHAGUS HOOKERI *cont.*
BT2 encyrtidae
BT3 hymenoptera

ixodoidea
USE **metastigmata**

IXONANTHACEAE
NT1 irvingia
NT2 irvingia gabonensis

IXOPHORUS
BT1 gramineae
NT1 ixophorus unisetus

IXOPHORUS UNISETUS
BT1 ixophorus
BT2 gramineae

IXORA
BT1 rubiaceae
NT1 ixora acuminata
NT1 ixora arborea
NT1 ixora banduca
NT1 ixora coccinea
NT1 ixora singaporensis

IXORA ACUMINATA
BT1 ixora
BT2 rubiaceae
BT1 ornamental woody plants

IXORA ARBOREA
BT1 ixora
BT2 rubiaceae
BT1 ornamental woody plants

IXORA BANDUCA
BT1 ixora
BT2 rubiaceae
BT1 ornamental woody plants

IXORA COCCINEA
BT1 ixora
BT2 rubiaceae
BT1 ornamental woody plants

IXORA SINGAPORENSIS
BT1 ixora
BT2 rubiaceae
BT1 ornamental woody plants